Equatorial Scale 1:80 000 000

THE WORLD : Physical

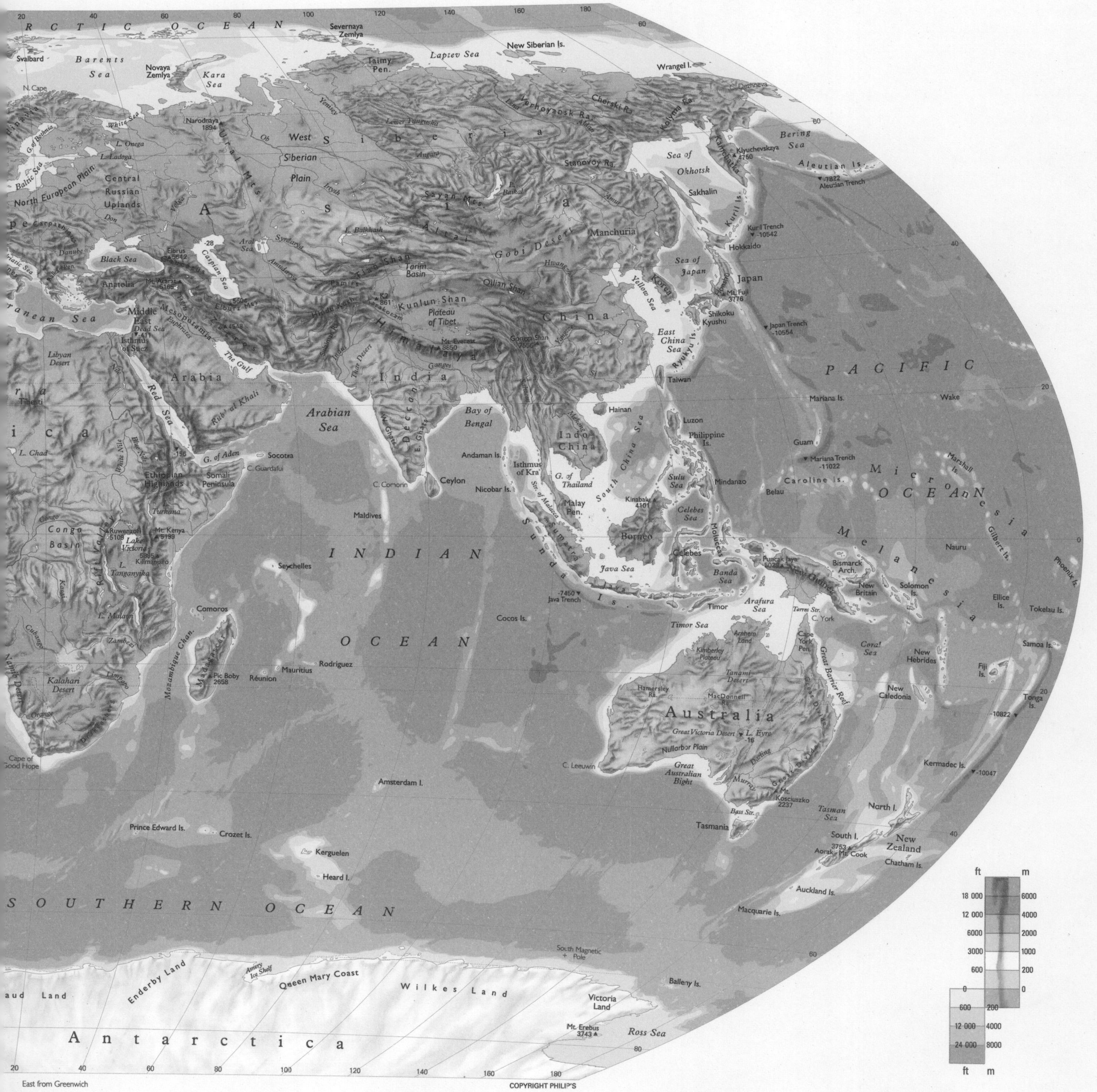

COPYRIGHT PHILIP'S

East from Greenwich

FIREFLY

GREAT WORLD ATLAS

FIREFLY
GREAT
WORLD
ATLAS

FIREFLY BOOKS

A FIREFLY BOOK

Published by Firefly Books Ltd. 2005

First printing

Publisher Cataloging-in-Publication Data (U.S.)

    Firefly great world atlas.
[304] p. : col. ill., photos. ; cm.
Includes index.
Summary: A reference atlas containing world topographical
maps; including introductory geographical information.
ISBN 1-55407-121-6
1. Atlases. I. Title.
912   dc22   G1021.F57 2005

Library and Archives Canada Cataloguing in Publication

    Firefly great world atlas.
Includes index.
ISBN 1-55407-121-6
    1. Atlases, Canadian. I. Title: Great world atlas.

G1021.F573 2005   912   C2005-902468-2

Published in the United States by
Firefly Books (U.S.) Inc.
P.O. Box 1338, Ellicott Station
Buffalo, New York 14205

Published in Canada by
Firefly Books Ltd.
66 Leek Crescent
Richmond Hill, Ontario L4B 1H1

**The editors are grateful to the following for acting as specialist geography
consultants on the "*Introduction to World Geography*" front section:**
Professor D. Brunsden, Kings College, University of London, U.K.
Dr C. Clarke, Oxford University, U.K.
Professor P. Haggett, University of Bristol, U.K.
Professor M-L. Hsu, University of Minnesota, U.S.
Professor K. McLachlan, Geopolitical and International Boundaries Research Centre,
School of Oriental and African Studies, University of London, U.K.
Professor M. Monmonier, Syracuse University, U.S.
Professor M. J. Tooley, University of St Andrews, U.K.
Dr T. Unwin, Royal Holloway, University of London, U.K.

The editors would also like to thank:
Keith Lye
Robin Scagell
Dr I. S. Evans, Durham University, U.K.
Dr Andrew Tatham, The Royal Geographical Society

Images of Earth (pages XVII–XXXII)
All satellite images in this section supplied by NPA Limited, Edenbridge, Kent, U.K.
(www.satmaps.com)

Introduction to World Geography
Picture Acknowledgements
Alamy /*Peter Bowater* 36
Corbis /*Jay Dickman* 47 (bottom left), /*Marc Garanger* 41, /*Royalty-Free* 27, 32, 35,
/*Vince Streano* 39, /*Liba Taylor* 42, /*David Turnley* 47 (bottom right)
NASA/GSFC 22 (bottom left and right), /*Cathy Clerbaux, NCAR Atmospheric Chemistry
Division* 21 (bottom right)
NOAO/AURA/NSF/Todd Boroson 2
NPA Limited 11, 13, 18, 48, /*Image provided by the USGS EROS Data Center
Satellite Systems Branch* 23
Science Photo Library /*Earth Satellite Corporation* 20

Star charts
Wil Tirion

Cartography by Philip's

Cover illustrations by Sideways Design

Printed in Spain

User Guide

The reference maps which form the main body of this atlas have been prepared in accordance with the highest standards of international cartography to provide an accurate and detailed representation of the Earth. The scales and projections used have been carefully chosen to give balanced coverage of the world, while emphasizing the most densely populated and economically significant regions. A hallmark of Philip's mapping is the use of hill shading and relief coloring to create a graphic impression of landforms: this makes the maps exceptionally easy to read. However, knowledge of the key features employed in the construction and presentation of the maps will enable the reader to derive the fullest benefit from the atlas.

Map Sequence

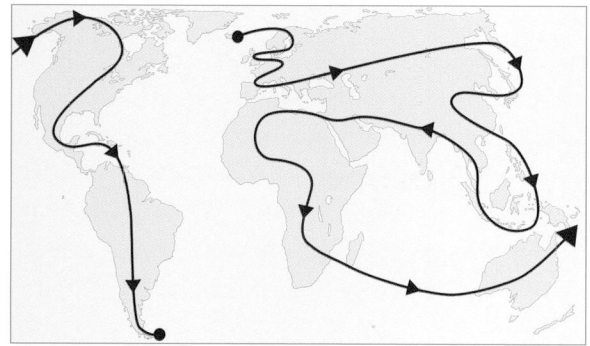

The atlas covers the Earth continent by continent: first Europe; then its land neighbor Asia (mapped north before south, in a clockwise sequence); then Africa, Australia and Oceania, North America, and South America. This is the classic arrangement adopted by most cartographers since the 16th century. For each continent, there are maps at a variety of scales. First, physical relief and political maps of the whole continent; then a series of larger-scale maps of the regions within the continent, each followed, where required, by still larger-scale maps of the most important or densely populated areas. The governing principle is that by turning the pages of the atlas, the reader moves steadily from north to south through each continent, with each map overlapping its neighbors.

Map Presentation

With very few exceptions (for example, for the Arctic and Antarctic), the maps are drawn with north at the top, regardless of whether they are presented upright or sideways on the page. In the borders will be found the map title; a locator diagram showing the area covered; continuation arrows showing the page numbers for maps of adjacent areas; the scale; the projection used; the degrees of latitude and longitude; and the letters and figures used in the index for locating place names and geographical features. Physical relief maps also have a height reference panel identifying the colors used for each layer of contouring.

Map Symbols

Each map contains a vast amount of detail which can only be conveyed clearly and accurately by the use of symbols. Points and circles of varying sizes locate and identify the relative importance of towns and cities; different styles of type are employed for administrative, geographical and regional place names to aid identification. A variety of pictorial symbols denote landforms such as glaciers, marshes, and coral reefs, and man-made structures including roads, railroads, airports, and canals. International borders are shown by red lines. Where neighboring countries are in dispute, for example in parts of the Middle East, the maps show the *de facto* boundary between nations, regardless of the legal or historical situation. The symbols are explained on the first page of the World Maps section of the atlas.

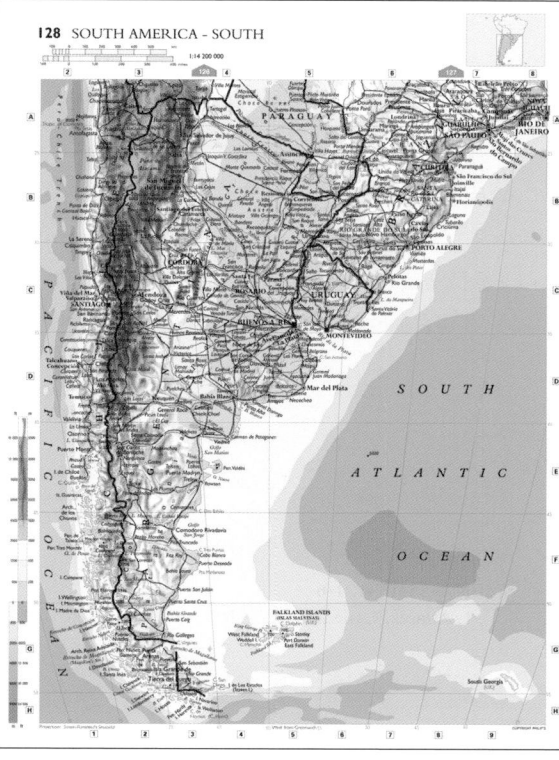

Map Scales

1:16 000 000
1 inch = 252 statute miles

The scale of each map is given in the numerical form known as the "representative fraction." The first figure is always one, signifying one unit of distance on the map; the second figure, usually in millions, is the number by which the map unit must be multiplied to give the equivalent distance on the Earth's surface. Calculations can easily be made in centimeters and kilometers, by dividing the Earth units figure by 100 000 (i.e. deleting the last five 0s). Thus 1:1 000 000 means 1 cm = 10 km. The calculation for inches and miles is more laborious, but 1 000 000 divided by 63 360 (the number of inches in a mile) shows that 1:1 000 000 means approximately 1 inch = 16 miles. The table below provides distance equivalents for scales down to 1:50 000 000.

LARGE SCALE		
1:1 000 000	1 cm = 10 km	1 inch = 16 miles
1:2 500 000	1 cm = 25 km	1 inch = 39.5 miles
1:5 000 000	1 cm = 50 km	1 inch = 79 miles
1:6 000 000	1 cm = 60 km	1 inch = 95 miles
1:8 000 000	1 cm = 80 km	1 inch = 126 miles
1:10 000 000	1 cm = 100 km	1 inch = 158 miles
1:15 000 000	1 cm = 150 km	1 inch = 237 miles
1:20 000 000	1 cm = 200 km	1 inch = 316 miles
1:50 000 000	1 cm = 500 km	1 inch = 790 miles
SMALL SCALE		

Measuring Distances

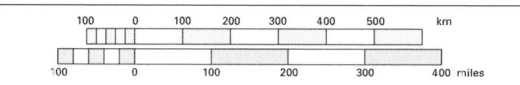

Although each map is accompanied by a scale bar, distances cannot always be measured with confidence because of the distortions involved in portraying the curved surface of the Earth on a flat page. As a general rule, the larger the map scale, the more accurate and reliable will be the distance measured. On small-scale maps, such as those of the world and of entire continents, measurement may only be accurate along the "standard parallels," or central axes, and should not be attempted without considering the map projection.

Map Projections

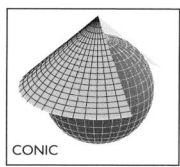

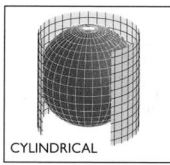

Unlike a globe, no flat map can give a true scale representation of the world in terms of area, shape and position of every region. Each of the numerous systems that have been devised for projecting the curved surface of the Earth on to a flat page involves the sacrifice of accuracy in one or more of these elements. The variations in shape and position of land masses such as Alaska, Greenland and Australia, for example, can be quite dramatic when different projections are compared.

For this atlas, the guiding principle has been to select projections that involve the least distortion of size and distance. The projection used for each map is noted in the border. Most fall into one of three categories – conic, azimuthal, or cylindrical – whose basic concepts are shown above. Each involves plotting the forms of the Earth's surface on a grid of latitude and longitude lines, which may be shown as parallels, curves, or radiating spokes.

Latitude and Longitude

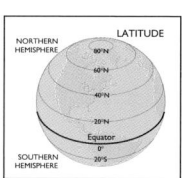
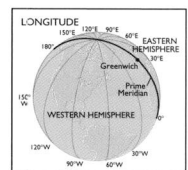
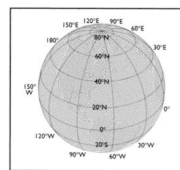

Accurate positioning of individual points on the Earth's surface is made possible by reference to the geometrical system of latitude and longitude. Latitude *parallels* are drawn west–east around the Earth and numbered by degrees north and south of the equator, which is designated 0° of latitude. Longitude *meridians* are drawn north–south and numbered by degrees east and west of the *prime meridian*, 0° of longitude, which passes through Greenwich in England. By referring to these coordinates and their subdivisions of minutes (1/60th of a degree) and seconds (1/60th of a minute), any place on Earth can be located to within a few hundred meters. Latitude and longitude are indicated by blue lines on the maps; they are straight or curved according to the projection employed. Reference to these lines is the easiest way of determining the relative positions of places on different maps, and for plotting compass directions.

Name Forms

For ease of reference, both English and local name forms appear in the atlas. Oceans, seas and countries are shown in English throughout the atlas; country names may be abbreviated to their commonly accepted form (for example, Germany, not The Federal Republic of Germany). Conventional English forms are also used for place names on the smaller-scale maps of the continents. However, local name forms are used on all large-scale and regional maps, with the English form given in brackets only for important cities – the large-scale map of Russia and Central Asia thus shows Moskva (Moscow). For countries which do not use a Roman script, place names have been transcribed according to the systems adopted by the British and US Geographic Names Authorities. For China, the Pin Yin system has been used, with some more widely known forms appearing in brackets, as with Beijing (Peking). Both the English and local names appear in the index, the English form being cross-referenced to the local form.

Contents

World Statistics

Countries	X
Cities	XI
Distances	XII
Climate	XIII
Physical Dimensions	XIV–XV
Regions in the News	XVI

Images of Earth

San Francisco, USA	XVII
Grand Canyon, USA	XVIII
Chicago, USA	XIX
Niagara Falls, USA/Canada	XX
New York, USA	XXI
Washington, DC, USA	XXII
Miami, USA	XXIII
River Amazon, Brazil	XXIV
Buenos Aires, Argentina	XXV
London, UK	XXVI
IJsselmeer, Netherlands	XXVII
Cairo, Egypt	XXVIII
Western Cape, South Africa	XXIX
Shanghai, China	XXX
Tokyo, Japan	XXXI
Sydney, Australia	XXXII

Introduction to World Geography

The Universe	2–3
The Solar System	4–5
Time and Motion	6–7
Geology of the Earth	8–9
Landforms	10–11
Oceans	12–13
The Atmosphere	14–15
Climate	16–17
Water and Vegetation	18–19
The Natural Environment	20–21
People and the Environment	22–23
Population	24–25
Cities	26–27
The Human Family	28–29
Conflict and Cooperation	30–31
Agriculture	32–33
Energy	34–35
Minerals	36–37
Manufacturing	38–39
Trade	40–41
Health	42–43
Wealth	44–45
Standards of Living	46–47

World Maps

Map Symbols	1
The World: Political 1:80 000 000	2–3
Arctic Ocean 1:29 400 000	4
Antarctica 1:29 400 000	5

Europe

Europe: Physical 1:16 800 000	6
Europe: Political 1:16 800 000	7
Scandinavia 1:4 200 000 Iceland 1: 4 200 000 Færoe Islands 1: 4 200 000	8–9

Denmark and Southern Sweden 1:2 100 000	10–11

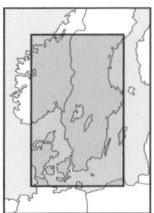

Ireland 1:1 700 000	12

Scotland 1:1 700 000	13

Asia

Asia: Physical   **50**
1:42 000 000

Asia: Political   **51**
1:42 000 000

Russia and Central Asia   **52–53**
1:16 800 000

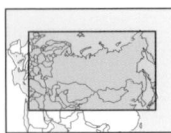

Japan   **54–55**
1:4 200 000

Northern China and Korea   **56–57**
1:5 000 000

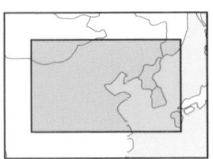

Southern China   **58–59**
1:5 000 000

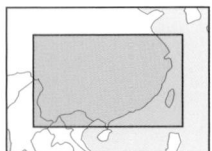

China   **60**
1:16 800 000

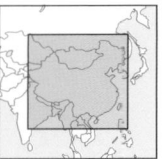

The Philippines   **61**
1:6 300 000

Indonesia and the Philippines   **62–63**
1:10 500 000
Java and Madura 1:6 300 000
Bali 1:1 700 000

Mainland Southeast Asia   **64–65**
1:5 000 000
Ko Phuket 1:840 000
Ko Samui 1:840 000
Pinang 1:840 000
Singapore 1:840 000

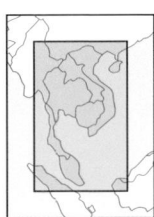

South Asia   **66–67**
1:8 400 000

Northern India and Nepal   **68–69**
1:5 000 000
Jammu and Kashmir 1:5 000 000

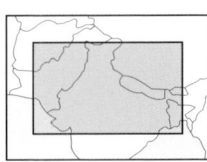

The Middle East   **70–71**
1:5 900 000

Turkey and Transcaucasia   **72–73**
1:4 200 000

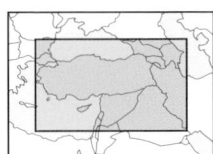

The Near East   **74**
1:2 100 000

Arabia and the Horn of Africa   **75**
1:12 600 000

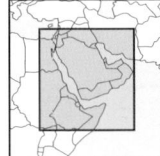

Africa

Africa: Physical   **76**
1:35 300 000

Africa: Political   **77**
1:35 300 000

Northern Africa   **78–79**
1:12 600 000

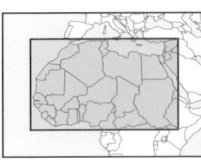

The Nile Valley   **80–81**
1:6 700 000
The Nile Delta 1:3 400 000

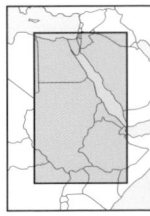

West Africa   **82–83**
1:6 700 000

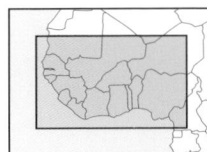

**Central and Southern
 Africa**   **84–85**
1:12 600 000

East Africa   **86–87**
1:6 700 000

Southern Africa   **88–89**
1:6 700 000

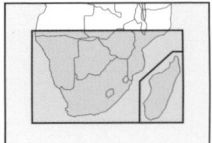

Australia and Oceania

**Australia and Oceania:
  Physical and Political**   **90**
1:42 000 000

New Zealand   **91**
1:5 000 000
Samoan Islands 1:10 100 000
Fiji and Tonga 1:10 100 000

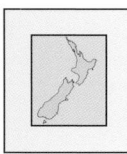

Western Australia   **92–93**
1:6 700 000

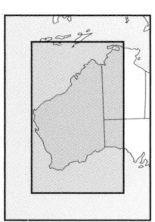

Eastern Australia   **94–95**
1:6 700 000
Whitsunday Islands 1:2 100 000
Tasmania 1:6 700 000

Pacific Ocean   **96–97**
1:45 400 000

North America

North America: Physical   **98**
1:29 400 000

North America: Political   **99**
1:29 400 000

Canada   **100–101**
1:12 600 000
Alaska 1:25 200 000

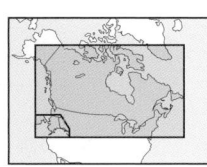

Western Canada   **102–103**
1:5 900 000

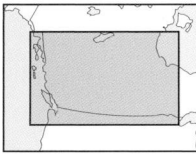

Eastern Canada   **104–105**
1:5 900 000

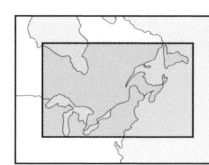

United States   **106–107**
1:10 100 000
Hawaii 1:8 400 000

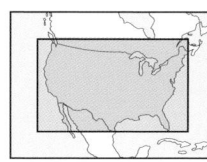

Western United States   **108–109**
1:5 000 000

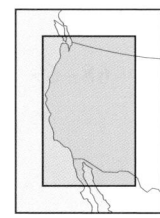

**Central and Southern
California and
Western Washington**   **110–111**
1:2 100 000

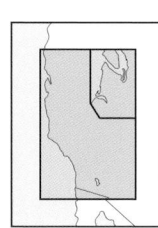

Middle United States   **112–113**
1:5 000 000

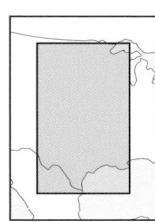

Eastern United States   **114–115**
1:5 000 000

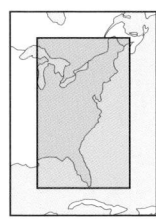

**Northeastern United
States**   **116–117**
1:2 100 000

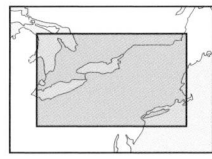

Mexico   **118–119**
1:6 700 000

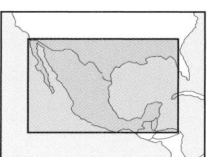

**Central America and
  the West Indies**   **120–121**
1:6 700 000
Jamaica 1:2 500 000
Guadeloupe 1:1 700 000
Martinique 1:1 700 000
Puerto Rico 1:2 500 000
Virgin Islands 1:1 700 000
St Lucia 1:840 000
Barbados 1:840 000

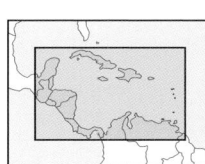

South America

South America: Physical   **122**
1:29 400 000

South America: Political   **123**
1:29 400 000

South America – North   **124–125**
1:13 400 000
Trinidad and Tobago 1:2 100 000

Central South America   **126–127**
1:6 700 000

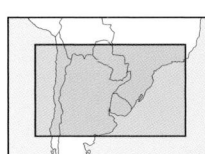

South America – South   **128**
1:13 400 000

Index to
World Maps   **129–224**

World Statistics: Countries

This alphabetical list includes the principal countries and territories of the world. If a territory is not completely independent, the country it is associated with is named. The area figures give the total area of land, inland water, and ice. The population figures are 2004 estimates where available. The annual income is the Gross Domestic Product per capita[†] in US dollars. The figures are the latest available, usually 2002 estimates.

Country/Territory	Area km² Thousands	Area miles² Thousands	Population Thousands	Capital	Annual Income US $
Afghanistan	652	252	28,514	Kabul	700
Albania	28.7	11.1	3,545	Tirana	4,400
Algeria	2,382	920	32,129	Algiers	5,400
American Samoa (US)	0.20	0.08	58	Pago Pago	8,000
Andorra	0.47	0.18	70	Andorra La Vella	19,000
Angola	1,247	481	10,979	Luanda	1,700
Anguilla (UK)	0.10	0.04	13	The Valley	8,600
Antigua & Barbuda	0.44	0.17	68	St John's	11,000
Argentina	2,780	1,074	39,145	Buenos Aires	10,500
Armenia	29.8	11.5	2,991	Yerevan	3,600
Aruba (Netherlands)	0.19	0.07	71	Oranjestad	28,000
Australia	7,741	2,989	19,913	Canberra	26,900
Austria	83.9	32.4	8,175	Vienna	27,900
Azerbaijan	86.6	33.4	7,868	Baku	3,700
Azores (Portugal)	2.2	0.86	236	Ponta Delgada	15,000
Bahamas	13.9	5.4	300	Nassau	15,300
Bahrain	0.69	0.27	678	Manama	15,100
Bangladesh	144	55.6	141,340	Dhaka	1,800
Barbados	0.43	0.17	278	Bridgetown	15,000
Belarus	208	80.2	10,311	Minsk	8,700
Belgium	30.5	11.8	10,348	Brussels	29,200
Belize	23.0	8.9	273	Belmopan	4,900
Benin	113	43.5	7,250	Porto-Novo	1,100
Bermuda (UK)	0.05	0.02	65	Hamilton	35,200
Bhutan	47.0	18.1	2,186	Thimphu	1,300
Bolivia	1,099	424	8,724	La Paz/Sucre	2,500
Bosnia-Herzegovina	51.2	19.8	4,008	Sarajevo	1,900
Botswana	582	225	1,562	Gaborone	8,500
Brazil	8,514	3,287	184,101	Brasília	7,600
Brunei	5.8	2.2	365	Bandar Seri Begawan	18,600
Bulgaria	111	42.8	7,518	Sofia	6,500
Burkina Faso	274	106	13,575	Ouagadougou	1,100
Burma (= Myanmar)	677	261	42,720	Rangoon	1,700
Burundi	27.8	10.7	6,231	Bujumbura	500
Cambodia	181	69.9	13,363	Phnom Penh	1,600
Cameroon	475	184	16,064	Yaoundé	1,700
Canada	9,971	3,850	32,508	Ottawa	29,300
Canary Is. (Spain)	7.2	2.8	1,682	Las Palmas/Santa Cruz	19,900
Cape Verde Is.	4.0	1.6	415	Praia	1,400
Cayman Is. (UK)	0.26	0.10	43	George Town	35,000
Central African Republic	623	241	3,742	Bangui	1,200
Chad	1,284	496	9,539	Ndjaména	1,000
Chile	757	292	15,824	Santiago	10,100
China	9,597	3,705	1,298,848	Beijing	4,700
Colombia	1,139	440	42,311	Bogotá	6,100
Comoros	2.2	0.86	652	Moroni	700
Congo	342	132	2,998	Brazzaville	900
Congo (Dem. Rep. of the)	2,345	905	58,318	Kinshasa	600
Cook Is. (NZ)	0.24	0.09	21	Avarua	5,000
Costa Rica	51.1	19.7	3,957	San José	8,300
Croatia	56.5	21.8	4,497	Zagreb	9,800
Cuba	111	42.8	11,309	Havana	2,700
Cyprus	9.3	3.6	776	Nicosia	13,200
Czech Republic	78.9	30.5	10,246	Prague	15,300
Denmark	43.1	16.6	5,413	Copenhagen	28,900
Djibouti	23.2	9.0	467	Djibouti	1,300
Dominica	0.75	0.29	69	Roseau	5,400
Dominican Republic	48.5	18.7	8,834	Santo Domingo	6,300
East Timor	14.9	5.7	1,019	Dili	500
Ecuador	284	109	13,213	Quito	3,200
Egypt	1,001	387	76,117	Cairo	4,000
El Salvador	21.0	8.1	6,588	San Salvador	4,600
Equatorial Guinea	28.1	10.8	523	Malabo	2,700
Eritrea	118	45.4	4,447	Asmara	700
Estonia	45.1	17.4	1,342	Tallinn	11,000
Ethiopia	1,104	426	67,851	Addis Ababa	700
Faroe Is. (Denmark)	1.4	0.54	47	Tórshavn	22,000
Fiji	18.3	7.1	881	Suva	5,600
Finland	338	131	5,215	Helsinki	25,800
France	552	213	60,424	Paris	26,000
French Guiana (France)	90.0	34.7	191	Cayenne	14,400
French Polynesia (France)	4.0	1.5	266	Papeete	5,000
Gabon	268	103	1,355	Libreville	6,500
Gambia, The	11.3	4.4	1,547	Banjul	1,800
Gaza Strip (OPT)*	0.36	0.14	1,325	–	600
Georgia	69.7	26.9	4,694	Tbilisi	3,200
Germany	357	138	82,425	Berlin	26,200
Ghana	239	92.1	20,757	Accra	2,000
Gibraltar (UK)	0.006	0.002	28	Gibraltar Town	17,500
Greece	132	50.9	10,648	Athens	19,100
Greenland (Denmark)	2,176	840	56	Nuuk (Godthåb)	20,000
Grenada	0.34	0.13	89	St George's	5,000
Guadeloupe (France)	1.7	0.66	445	Basse-Terre	9,000
Guam (US)	0.55	0.21	166	Agana	21,000
Guatemala	109	42.0	14,281	Guatemala City	3,900
Guinea	246	94.9	9,246	Conakry	2,100
Guinea-Bissau	36.1	13.9	1,388	Bissau	700
Guyana	215	83.0	706	Georgetown	3,800
Haiti	27.8	10.7	7,656	Port-au-Prince	1,400
Honduras	112	43.3	6,824	Tegucigalpa	2,500
Hong Kong (China)	1.1	0.42	6,855	–	27,200
Hungary	93.0	35.9	10,032	Budapest	13,300
Iceland	103	39.8	294	Reykjavik	30,200
India	3,287	1,269	1,065,071	New Delhi	2,600
Indonesia	1,905	735	238,453	Jakarta	3,100
Iran	1,648	636	69,019	Tehran	6,800
Iraq	438	169	25,375	Baghdad	2,400
Ireland	70.3	27.1	3,970	Dublin	29,300
Israel	20.6	8.0	6,199	Jerusalem	19,500
Italy	301	116	58,057	Rome	25,100
Ivory Coast (= Côte d'Ivoire)	322	125	17,328	Yamoussoukro	1,400
Jamaica	11.0	4.2	2,713	Kingston	3,800
Japan	378	146	127,333	Tokyo	28,700
Jordan	89.3	34.5	5,611	Amman	4,300
Kazakhstan	2,725	1,052	15,144	Astana	7,200
Kenya	580	224	32,022	Nairobi	1,100
Kiribati	0.73	0.28	101	Tarawa	800
Korea, North	121	46.5	22,698	Pyŏngyang	1,000
Korea, South	99.3	38.3	48,598	Seoul	19,600
Kuwait	17.8	6.9	2,258	Kuwait City	17,500
Kyrgyzstan	200	77.2	5,081	Bishkek	2,900
Laos	237	91.4	6,068	Vientiane	1,800
Latvia	64.6	24.9	2,306	Riga	8,900
Lebanon	10.4	4.0	3,777	Beirut	4,800
Lesotho	30.4	11.7	1,865	Maseru	2,700
Liberia	111	43.0	3,391	Monrovia	1,000
Libya	1,760	679	5,632	Tripoli	6,200
Liechtenstein	0.16	0.06	33	Vaduz	25,000
Lithuania	65.2	25.2	3,608	Vilnius	8,400
Luxembourg	2.6	1.0	463	Luxembourg	48,900
Macau (China)	0.02	0.007	445	–	18,500
Macedonia (FYROM)	25.7	9.9	2,071	Skopje	5,100
Madagascar	587	227	17,502	Antananarivo	800
Madeira (Portugal)	0.78	0.30	241	Funchal	22,700
Malawi	118	45.7	11,907	Lilongwe	600
Malaysia	330	127	23,522	Kuala Lumpur/Putrajaya	8,800
Maldives	0.30	0.12	339	Malé	3,900
Mali	1,240	479	11,957	Bamako	900
Malta	0.32	0.12	397	Valletta	17,200
Marshall Is.	0.18	0.07	58	Majuro	1,600
Martinique (France)	1.1	0.43	430	Fort-de-France	10,700
Mauritania	1,026	396	2,999	Nouakchott	1,700
Mauritius	2.0	0.79	1,220	Port Louis	10,100
Mayotte (France)	0.37	0.14	186	Mamoundzou	600
Mexico	1,958	756	104,960	Mexico City	8,900
Micronesia, Fed. States of	0.70	0.27	108	Palikir	2,000
Moldova	33.9	13.1	4,446	Chişinău	2,600
Monaco	0.001	0.0004	32	Monaco	27,000
Mongolia	1,567	605	2,751	Ulan Bator	1,900
Montserrat (UK)	0.10	0.04	9	Plymouth	3,400
Morocco	447	172	32,209	Rabat	3,900
Mozambique	802	309	18,812	Maputo	1,100
Namibia	824	318	1,954	Windhoek	6,900
Nauru	0.02	0.008	13	Yaren District	5,000
Nepal	147	56.8	27,071	Katmandu	1,400
Netherlands	41.5	16.0	16,318	Amsterdam/The Hague	27,200
Netherlands Antilles (Neths)	0.80	0.31	218	Willemstad	11,400
New Caledonia (France)	18.6	7.2	214	Nouméa	14,000
New Zealand	271	104	3,994	Wellington	20,100
Nicaragua	130	50.2	5,360	Managua	2,200
Niger	1,267	489	11,361	Niamey	800
Nigeria	924	357	137,253	Abuja	900
Northern Mariana Is. (US)	0.46	0.18	78	Saipan	12,500
Norway	324	125	4,575	Oslo	33,000
Oman	310	119	2,903	Muscat	8,300
Pakistan	796	307	159,196	Islamabad	2,000
Palau	0.46	0.18	20	Koror	9,000
Panama	75.5	29.2	3,000	Panamá	6,200
Papua New Guinea	463	179	5,420	Port Moresby	2,100
Paraguay	407	157	6,191	Asunción	4,300
Peru	1,285	496	27,544	Lima	5,000
Philippines	300	116	86,242	Manila	4,600
Poland	323	125	38,626	Warsaw	9,700
Portugal	88.8	34.3	10,524	Lisbon	19,400
Puerto Rico (US)	8.9	3.4	3,898	San Juan	11,100
Qatar	11.0	4.2	840	Doha	20,100
Réunion (France)	2.5	0.97	766	St-Denis	5,600
Romania	238	92.0	22,356	Bucharest	7,600
Russia	17,075	6,593	143,782	Moscow	9,700
Rwanda	26.3	10.2	7,954	Kigali	1,200
St Kitts & Nevis	0.26	0.10	39	Basseterre	8,800
St Lucia	0.54	0.21	164	Castries	5,400
St Vincent & Grenadines	0.39	0.15	117	Kingstown	2,900
Samoa	2.8	1.1	178	Apia	5,600
San Marino	0.06	0.02	29	San Marino	34,600
São Tomé & Príncipe	0.96	0.37	182	São Tomé	1,200
Saudi Arabia	2,150	830	25,796	Riyadh	11,400
Senegal	197	76.0	10,852	Dakar	1,500
Serbia & Montenegro	102	39.4	10,826	Belgrade	2,200
Seychelles	0.46	0.18	81	Victoria	7,800
Sierra Leone	71.7	27.7	5,884	Freetown	500
Singapore	0.68	0.26	4,354	Singapore City	25,200
Slovak Republic	49.0	18.9	5,424	Bratislava	12,400
Slovenia	20.3	7.8	2,011	Ljubljana	19,200
Solomon Is.	28.9	11.2	524	Honiara	1,700
Somalia	638	246	8,305	Mogadishu	600
South Africa	1,221	471	42,719	C. Town/Pretoria/Bloem.	10,000
Spain	498	192	40,281	Madrid	21,200
Sri Lanka	65.6	25.3	19,905	Colombo	3,700
Sudan	2,506	967	39,148	Khartoum	1,400
Suriname	163	63.0	437	Paramaribo	3,400
Swaziland	17.4	6.7	1,169	Mbabane	4,800
Sweden	450	174	8,986	Stockholm	26,000
Switzerland	41.3	15.9	7,451	Bern	32,000
Syria	185	71.5	18,017	Damascus	3,700
Taiwan	36.0	13.9	22,750	Taipei	18,000
Tajikistan	143	55.3	7,012	Dushanbe	1,300
Tanzania	945	365	36,588	Dodoma	600
Thailand	513	198	64,866	Bangkok	7,000
Togo	56.8	21.9	5,557	Lomé	1,400
Tonga	0.65	0.25	110	Nuku'alofa	2,200
Trinidad & Tobago	5.1	2.0	1,097	Port of Spain	10,000
Tunisia	164	63.2	9,975	Tunis	6,800
Turkey	775	299	68,894	Ankara	7,300
Turkmenistan	488	188	4,863	Ashkhabad	6,700
Turks & Caicos Is. (UK)	0.43	0.17	20	Cockburn Town	9,600
Tuvalu	0.03	0.01	11	Fongafale	1,100
Uganda	241	93.1	26,405	Kampala	1,200
Ukraine	604	233	47,732	Kiev	4,500
United Arab Emirates	83.6	32.3	2,524	Abu Dhabi	22,100
United Kingdom	242	93.4	60,271	London	25,500
United States of America	9,629	3,718	293,028	Washington, DC	36,300
Uruguay	175	67.6	3,399	Montevideo	7,900
Uzbekistan	447	173	26,410	Tashkent	2,600
Vanuatu	12.2	4.7	203	Port-Vila	2,900
Vatican City	0.0004	0.0002	1	Vatican City	N/A
Venezuela	912	352	25,017	Caracas	5,400
Vietnam	332	128	82,690	Hanoi	2,300
Virgin Is. (UK)	0.15	0.06	22	Road Town	16,000
Virgin Is. (US)	0.35	0.13	109	Charlotte Amalie	19,000
Wallis & Futuna Is. (France)	0.20	0.08	16	Mata-Utu	2,000
West Bank (OPT)*	5.9	2.3	2,311	–	800
Western Sahara	266	103	267	El Aaiún	N/A
Yemen	528	204	20,025	Sana'	800
Zambia	753	291	10,462	Lusaka	800
Zimbabwe	391	151	12,672	Harare	2,100

*OPT = Occupied Palestinian Territory   N/A = Not Available

[†] Gross Domestic Product per capita has been measured using the purchasing power parity method. This enables comparisons to be made between countries through their purchasing power (in US dollars), showing real price levels of goods and services rather than using currency exchange rates.

World Statistics: Cities

This list shows the principal cities with more than 750,000 inhabitants. The figures are taken from the most recent census or estimate available, usually 2000, and as far as possible are the population of the metropolitan area or urban agglomeration (for example, greater New York, Mexico, or Paris). All the figures are in thousands. Local name forms have been used for the smaller cities (for example, Thessaloniki).

AFGHANISTAN
Kabul — 2,602
ALGERIA
Algiers — 1,722
ANGOLA
Luanda — 2,697
ARGENTINA
Buenos Aires — 12,024
Córdoba — 1,368
Rosario — 1,279
Mendoza — 934
San Miguel de Tucumán — 792
ARMENIA
Yerevan — 1,407
AUSTRALIA
Sydney — 4,086
Melbourne — 3,466
Brisbane — 1,627
Perth — 1,381
Adelaide — 1,096
AUSTRIA
Vienna — 1,807
AZERBAIJAN
Baku — 1,792
BANGLADESH
Dhaka — 12,519
Chittagong — 3,651
Khulna — 1,442
Rajshahi — 1,035
BELARUS
Minsk — 1,717
BELGIUM
Brussels — 964
BOLIVIA
La Paz — 1,487
Santa Cruz — 1,035
Cochabamba — 797
BRAZIL
São Paulo — 17,962
Rio de Janeiro — 10,652
Belo Horizonte — 4,224
Pôrto Alegre — 3,757
Recife — 3,346
Salvador — 3,238
Fortaleza — 3,066
Curitiba — 2,562
Brasília — 2,051
Belém — 1,658
Manaus — 1,467
Campinas — 1,434
Santos — 1,270
Goiânia — 1,117
São José dos Campos — 972
São Luís — 968
Maceió — 886
Teresina — 848
Campo Grande — 821
Natal — 806
BULGARIA
Sofia — 1,187
BURKINA FASO
Ouagadougou — 831
BURMA (MYANMAR)
Rangoon — 4,393
Mandalay — 770
CAMBODIA
Phnom Penh — 1,070
CAMEROON
Douala — 1,642
Yaoundé — 1,420
CANADA
Toronto — 4,881
Montréal — 3,511
Vancouver — 2,079
Ottawa — 1,107
Calgary — 972
Edmonton — 957
CHILE
Santiago — 5,467
CHINA
Shanghai — 12,887
Beijing — 10,839
Tianjin — 9,156
Hong Kong — 6,860
Wuhan — 5,169
Chongqing — 4,900
Shenyang — 4,828
Guangzhou — 3,893
Chengdu — 3,294
Xi'an — 3,123
Changchun — 3,093
Harbin — 2,928
Nanjing — 2,740
Zibo — 2,675
Dalian — 2,628
Jinan — 2,568
Guiyang — 2,533
Linyi — 2,498
Taiyuan — 2,415
Qingdao — 2,316
Zhengzhou — 2,070
Zaozhuang — 2,048
Liupanshui — 2,023
Handan — 1,996
Jinxi — 1,821
Lu'an — 1,818
Hangzhou — 1,780
Tianmen — 1,779
Changsha — 1,775
Wanxian — 1,759
Lanzhou — 1,730
Nanchang — 1,722
Kunming — 1,701
Yantai — 1,681
Tangshan — 1,671
Xuzhou — 1,636
Xiantao — 1,614
Shijiazhuang — 1,603
Heze — 1,600
Yancheng — 1,562
Yulin — 1,558
Xinghua — 1,556
Tai'an — 1,503
Pingxiang — 1,502
Anshan — 1,453
Luoyang — 1,451
Jilin — 1,435
Qiqihar — 1,435
Suining, Sichuan — 1,428
Ürümqi — 1,415
Fushun — 1,413
Fuzhou — 1,397
Neijiang — 1,393
Changde — 1,374
Zhanjiang — 1,368
Huainan — 1,354
Yiyang — 1,343
Xintai — 1,325
Baotou — 1,319
Dongguan — 1,319
Nanning — 1,311
Weifang — 1,287
Wenzhou — 1,269
Hefei — 1,242
Huaian — 1,232
Yueyang — 1,213
Suqian — 1,189
Tianshui — 1,187
Suzhou — 1,183
Shantou — 1,176
Ningbo — 1,173
Yuzhou — 1,173
Datong — 1,165
Jingmen — 1,153
Leshan — 1,137
Shenzhen — 1,131
Wuxi — 1,127
Xiaoshan — 1,124
Zaoyang — 1,121
Yixing — 1,108
Yongzhou — 1,097
Chifeng — 1,087
Huzhou — 1,077
Daqing — 1,076
Zigong — 1,072
Mianyang — 1,065
Nanchong — 1,055
Fuyu — 1,025
Jining, Shandong — 1,019
Hohhot — 978
Xinyi, Guangdong — 973
Benxi — 957
Jixi — 949
Liuzhou — 928
Xiangxiang — 908
Yichun, Heilongjiang — 904
Xianyang — 896
Linqing — 891
Changzhou — 886
Zhangjiagang — 886
Zhangjiakou — 880
Jiamusi — 874
Yichun, Jiangxi — 871
Zhaotong — 851
Yuyao — 848
Jinzhou — 834
Xuanzhou — 823
Huaibei — 814
Xinyu — 808
Mudanjiang — 801
Hengyang — 799
Jiaxing — 791
Anshun — 789
Fuxin — 785
Tongliao — 785
Hunjiang — 772
Kaifeng — 769
COLOMBIA
Bogotá — 6,771
Medellín — 2,866
Cali — 2,233
Barranquilla — 1,683
Bucaramanga — 937
Cartagena — 845
Cúcuta — 772
CONGO
Brazzaville — 1,306
CONGO (DEM. REP.)
Kinshasa — 5,054
Lubumbashi — 965
Mbuji-Mayi — 806
COSTA RICA
San José — 961
CROATIA
Zagreb — 1,067
CUBA
Havana — 2,256
CZECH REPUBLIC
Prague — 1,203
DENMARK
Copenhagen — 1,332
DOMINICAN REPUBLIC
Santo Domingo — 2,563
Santiago de los Caballeros — 804
ECUADOR
Guayaquil — 2,118
Quito — 1,616
EGYPT
Cairo — 9,462
Alexandria — 3,506
Shubrâ el Kheima — 937
EL SALVADOR
San Salvador — 1,341
ETHIOPIA
Addis Ababa — 2,645
FINLAND
Helsinki — 937
FRANCE
Paris — 9,630
Lyons — 1,353
Marseilles — 1,290
Lille — 991
Nice — 889
Toulouse — 761
Bordeaux — 754
GEORGIA
Tbilisi — 1,406
GERMANY
Berlin — 3,387
Hamburg — 1,705
Munich — 1,195
Cologne — 963
GHANA
Accra — 1,868
GREECE
Athens — 3,116
Thessaloniki — 789
GUATEMALA
Guatemala — 3,242
GUINEA
Conakry — 1,232
HAITI
Port-au-Prince — 1,769
HONDURAS
Tegucigalpa — 949
HUNGARY
Budapest — 1,819
INDIA
Mumbai — 16,086
Kolkata — 13,058
Delhi — 12,441
Chennai — 6,353
Bangalore — 5,567
Hyderabad — 5,445
Ahmedabad — 4,427
Pune — 3,655
Surat — 2,699
Kanpur — 2,641
Jaipur — 2,259
Lucknow — 2,221
Nagpur — 2,089
Patna — 1,658
Indore — 1,597
Vadodara — 1,465
Bhopal — 1,425
Coimbatore — 1,420
Ludhiana — 1,368
Cochin — 1,340
Visakhapatnam — 1,309
Agra — 1,293
Varanasi — 1,199
Madurai — 1,187
Meerut — 1,143
Nashik — 1,117
Jabalpur — 1,100
Jamshedpur — 1,081
Asansol — 1,065
Bhilainagar-Durg — 1,049
Dhanbad — 1,046
Allahabad — 1,035
Faridabad — 1,018
Vijayawada — 999
Rajkot — 974
Amritsar — 955
Srinagar — 954
Ghaziabad — 928
Trivandrum — 885
Calicut — 875
Aurangabad — 868
Gwalior — 855
Solapur — 853
Ranchi — 844
Tiruchchirapalli — 837
Jodhpur — 833
Guwahati — 797
Chandigarh — 791
Hubli-Dharwad — 776
Mysore — 776
INDONESIA
Jakarta — 11,018
Bandung — 3,409
Surabaya — 2,461
Medan — 1,879
Palembang — 1,422
Ujung Pandang — 1,051
Bandar Lampung — 915
Malang — 787
Semarang — 787
Tegal — 762
Bogor — 761
IRAN
Tehran — 6,979
Mashhad — 1,990
Esfahan — 1,381
Tabriz — 1,274
Karaj — 1,200
Shiraz — 1,124
Qom — 888
Ahvaz — 871
Bakhtaran — 771
IRAQ
Baghdad — 4,865
Basra — 1,338
Mosul — 1,131
Irbil — 840
IRELAND
Dublin — 985
ISRAEL
Tel Aviv-Yafo — 2,001
ITALY
Rome — 2,649
Milan — 1,183
Naples — 993
Turin — 857
JAPAN
Tokyo — 12,064
Yokohama — 6,427
Osaka — 2,599
Nagoya — 2,172
Sapporo — 1,922
Kobe — 1,493
Kyoto — 1,468
Fukuoka — 1,341
Kawasaki — 1,250
Hiroshima — 1,126
Kitakyushu — 1,011
Sendai — 1,008
Chiba — 887
Sakai — 792
JORDAN
Amman — 1,148
KAZAKHSTAN
Almaty — 1,130
KENYA
Nairobi — 2,233
KOREA, NORTH
Pyöngyang — 3,124
Hamhung — 821
KOREA, SOUTH
Seoul — 9,888
Pusan — 3,830
Inch'on — 2,884
Taegu — 2,675
Taejön — 1,522
Kwangju — 1,379
Söngnam — 1,353
Ulsan — 1,340
Ansan — 984
Puch'on — 900
Suwön — 876
P'ohang — 790
KUWAIT
Kuwait — 879
LATVIA
Riga — 811
LEBANON
Beirut — 2,070
LIBYA
Tripoli — 1,733
Benghazi — 829
MADAGASCAR
Antananarivo — 1,603
MALAYSIA
Kuala Lumpur — 1,379
MALI
Bamako — 1,114
MEXICO
Mexico City — 18,066
Guadalajara — 3,697
Monterrey — 3,267
Puebla — 1,888
Toluca — 1,455
Tijuana — 1,297
León — 1,293
Ciudad Juárez — 1,239
Torreón — 1,012
San Luis Potosí — 857
Mérida — 849
Querétaro — 798
Mexicali — 771
Culiacán — 750
MONGOLIA
Ulan Bator — 764
MOROCCO
Casablanca — 3,357
Rabat — 1,616
Fès — 907
Marrakesh — 822
MOZAMBIQUE
Maputo — 1,094
NEPAL
Katmandu — 1,176
NETHERLANDS
Amsterdam — 1,105
Rotterdam — 1,078
NEW ZEALAND
Auckland — 1,102
NICARAGUA
Managua — 1,009
NIGER
Niamey — 775
NIGERIA
Lagos — 8,665
Ibadan — 1,549
Ogbomosho — 809
NORWAY
Oslo — 779
PAKISTAN
Karachi — 10,032
Lahore — 5,452
Faisalabad — 2,142
Rawalpindi — 1,521
Gujranwala — 1,325
Multan — 1,263
Hyderabad — 1,221
Peshawar — 1,066
Islamabad — 791
PANAMA
Panamá — 1,173
PARAGUAY
Asunción — 1,262
PERU
Lima — 7,443
PHILIPPINES
Manila — 9,950
Davao — 1,146
POLAND
Warsaw — 1,626
Lódz — 815
PORTUGAL
Lisbon — 3,861
Porto — 1,940
PUERTO RICO
San Juan — 2,217
ROMANIA
Bucharest — 2,001
RUSSIA
Moscow — 8,367
Saint Petersburg — 4,635
Nizhniy Novgorod — 1,332
Novosibirsk — 1,321
Yekaterinburg — 1,218
Omsk — 1,174
Samara — 1,132
Ufa — 1,102
Kazan — 1,063
Chelyabinsk — 1,045
Perm — 1,014
Rostov — 1,012
Volgograd — 1,000
Voronezh — 918
Saratov — 881
Simbirsk — 864
Krasnoyarsk — 840
Togliatti — 771
SAUDI ARABIA
Riyadh — 3,180
Jedda — 1,490
Mecca — 770
SENEGAL
Dakar — 2,078
SERBIA AND MONTENEGRO
Belgrade — 1,673
SIERRA LEONE
Freetown — 822
SINGAPORE
Singapore — 4,131
SOMALIA
Mogadishu — 1,162
SOUTH AFRICA
Johannesburg — 2,950
Cape Town — 2,930
Durban / eThekwini — 2,391
Pretoria / Tshwane — 1,590
Port Elizabeth — 1,006
SPAIN
Madrid — 3,017
Barcelona — 1,527
SUDAN
Khartoum — 2,742
SWEDEN
Stockholm — 1,612
Gothenburg — 778
SWITZERLAND
Zürich — 939
SYRIA
Aleppo — 2,229
Damascus — 2,144
Homs — 811
TAIWAN
Taipei — 2,550
Kaohsiung — 1,463
T'aichung — 950
TANZANIA
Dar es Salaam — 2,115
THAILAND
Bangkok — 7,372
TUNISIA
Tunis — 1,892
TURKEY
Istanbul — 8,953
Ankara — 3,203
Izmir — 2,250
Bursa — 1,184
Adana — 1,133
Gaziantep — 862
Konya — 761
UGANDA
Kampala — 1,213
UKRAINE
Kiev — 2,621
Kharkov — 1,521
Dnepropetrovsk — 1,122
Donetsk — 1,065
Odessa — 1,027
Zaporozhye — 863
Lvov — 794
UNITED ARAB EMIRATES
Abu Dhabi — 928
Dubai — 886
UNITED KINGDOM
London — 8,089
Birmingham — 2,373
Manchester — 2,353
Liverpool — 852
Glasgow — 832
UNITED STATES OF AMERICA
New York — 17,800
Los Angeles — 11,789
Chicago — 8,308
Philadelphia — 5,149
Miami — 4,919
Dallas–Fort Worth — 4,146
Boston — 4,032
Washington — 3,934
Detroit — 3,903
Houston — 3,823
Atlanta — 3,500
San Francisco — 3,229
Phoenix — 2,907
Seattle — 2,712
San Diego — 2,674
Minneapolis–St Paul — 2,389
St Louis — 2,078
Baltimore — 2,076
Tampa–St Petersburg — 2,062
Denver — 1,985
Cleveland — 1,787
Pittsburgh — 1,753
Portland — 1,583
San Jose — 1,538
San Bernardino — 1,507
Cincinnati — 1,503
Norfolk–Virginia Beach — 1,394
Sacramento — 1,393
Kansas City — 1,362
San Antonio — 1,328
Las Vegas — 1,314
Milwaukee — 1,309
Indianapolis — 1,219
Providence — 1,175
Orlando — 1,157
Columbus — 1,133
New Orleans — 1,009
Buffalo — 977
Memphis — 972
Austin — 902
Stamford — 889
Salt Lake City — 888
Jacksonville — 882
Louisville — 864
Hartford — 852
Richmond — 819
Charlotte — 759
URUGUAY
Montevideo — 1,324
UZBEKISTAN
Tashkent — 2,148
VENEZUELA
Caracas — 3,153
Maracaibo — 1,901
Valencia — 1,893
Maracay — 1,100
Ciudad Guayana — 966
Barquisimeto — 923
VIETNAM
Ho Chi Minh City — 4,619
Hanoi — 3,751
Haiphong — 1,676
YEMEN
Sana' — 1,327
ZAMBIA
Lusaka — 1,653
ZIMBABWE
Harare — 1,791
Bulawayo — 824

World Statistics: Distances

The table shows air distances in miles and kilometers between 30 major cities. Known as "Great Circle" distances, these measure the shortest routes between the cities, which aircraft use wherever possible. The maps show the world centered on six cities, and illustrate, for example, why direct flights from Japan to northern America and Europe are across the Arctic regions. The maps have been constructed on an Azimuthal Equidistant projection, on which all distances measured through the center point are true to scale. The red lines are drawn at 5,000, 10,000, and 15,000 km from the central city.

Distance table — values above the diagonal are in **kilometers (km)**; values below the diagonal are in **miles**.

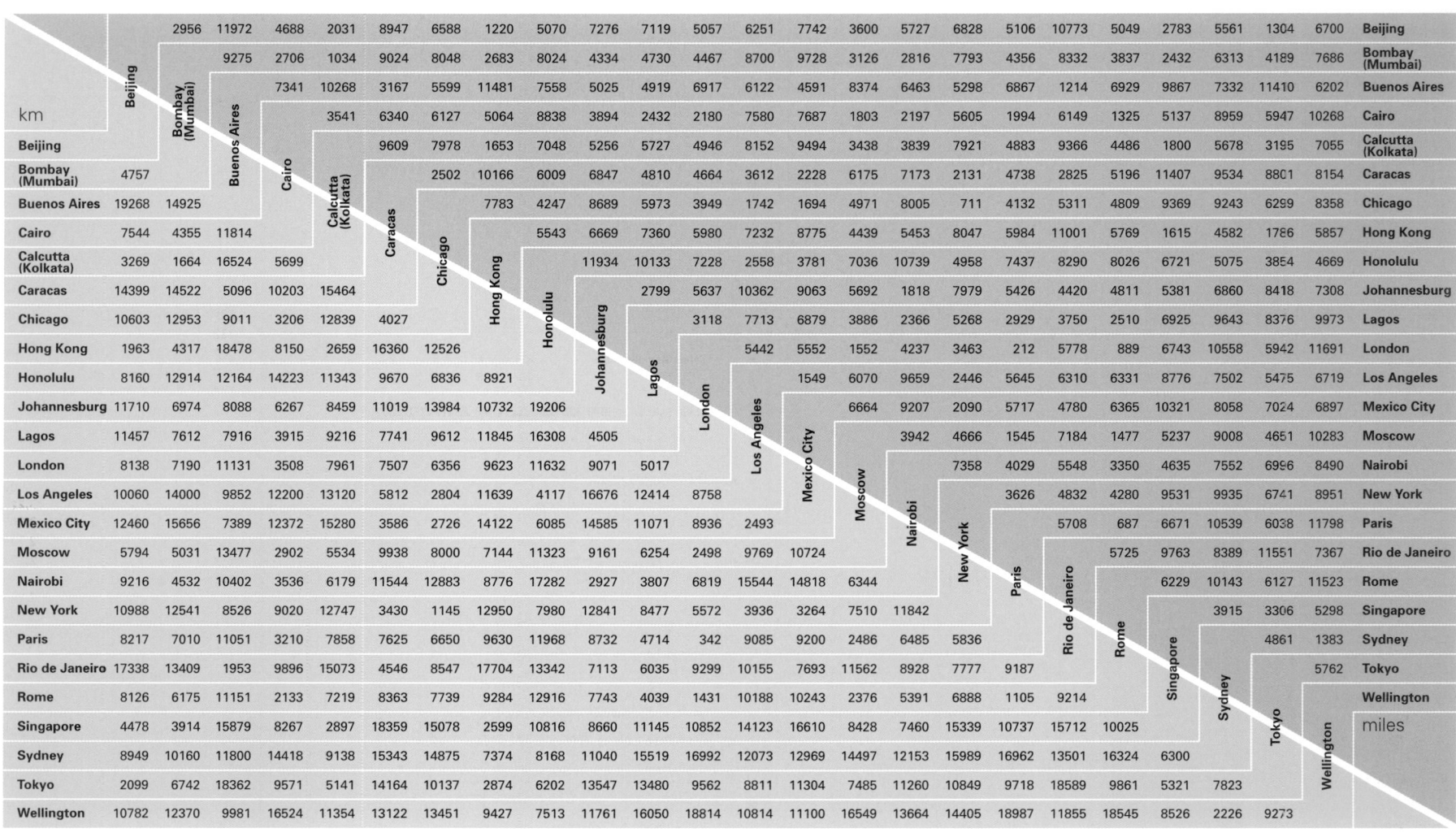

	Beijing	Bombay (Mumbai)	Buenos Aires	Cairo	Calcutta (Kolkata)	Caracas	Chicago	Hong Kong	Honolulu	Johannesburg	Lagos	London	Los Angeles	Mexico City	Moscow	Nairobi	New York	Paris	Rio de Janeiro	Rome	Singapore	Sydney	Tokyo	Wellington
Beijing		2956	11972	4688	2031	8947	6588	1220	5070	7276	7119	5057	6251	7742	3600	5727	6828	5106	10773	5049	2783	5561	1304	6700
Bombay (Mumbai)	4757		9275	2706	1034	9024	8048	2683	8024	4334	4730	4467	8700	9728	3126	2816	7793	4356	8332	3837	2432	6313	4189	7686
Buenos Aires	19268	14925		7341	10268	3167	5599	11481	7558	5025	4919	6917	6122	4591	8374	6463	5298	6867	1214	6929	9867	7332	11410	6202
Cairo	7544	4355	11814		3541	6340	6127	5064	8838	3894	2432	2180	7580	7687	1803	2197	5605	1994	6149	1325	5137	8959	5947	10268
Calcutta (Kolkata)	3269	1664	16524	5699		9609	7978	1653	7048	5256	5727	4946	8152	9494	3438	3839	7921	4883	9366	4486	1800	5678	3195	7055
Caracas	14399	14522	5096	10203	15464		2502	10166	6009	6847	4810	4664	3612	2228	6175	7173	2131	4738	2825	5196	11407	9534	8801	8154
Chicago	10603	12953	9011	3206	12839	4027		7783	4247	8689	5973	3949	1742	1694	4971	8005	711	4132	5311	4809	9369	9243	6299	8358
Hong Kong	1963	4317	18478	8150	2659	16360	12526		5543	6669	7360	5980	7232	8775	4439	5453	8047	5984	11001	5769	1615	4582	1786	5857
Honolulu	8160	12914	12164	14223	11343	9670	6836	8921		11934	10133	7228	2558	3781	7036	10739	4958	7437	8290	8026	6721	5075	3854	4669
Johannesburg	11710	6974	8088	6267	8459	11019	13984	10732	19206		2799	5637	10362	9063	5692	1818	7979	5426	4420	4811	5381	6860	8418	7308
Lagos	11457	7612	7916	3915	9216	7741	9612	11845	16308	4505		3118	7713	6879	3886	2366	5268	2929	3750	2510	6925	9643	8376	9973
London	8138	7190	11131	3508	7961	7507	6356	9623	11632	9071	5017		5442	5552	1552	4237	3463	212	5778	889	6743	10558	5942	11691
Los Angeles	10060	14000	9852	12200	13120	5812	2804	11639	4117	16676	12414	8758		1549	6070	9659	2446	5645	6310	6331	8776	7502	5475	6719
Mexico City	12460	15656	7389	12372	15280	3586	2726	14122	6085	14585	11071	8936	2493		6664	9207	2090	5717	4780	6365	10321	8058	7024	6897
Moscow	5794	5031	13477	2902	5534	9938	8000	7144	11323	9161	6254	2498	9769	10724		3942	4666	1545	7184	1477	5237	9008	4651	10283
Nairobi	9216	4532	10402	3536	6179	11544	12883	8776	17282	2927	3807	6819	15544	14818	6344		7358	4029	5548	3350	4635	7552	6996	8490
New York	10988	12541	8526	9020	12747	3430	1145	12950	7980	12841	8477	5572	3936	3264	7510	11842		3626	4832	4280	9531	9935	6741	8951
Paris	8217	7010	11051	3210	7858	7625	6650	9630	11968	8732	4714	342	9085	9200	2486	6485	5836		5708	687	6671	10539	6038	11798
Rio de Janeiro	17338	13409	1953	9896	15073	4546	8547	17704	13342	7113	6035	9299	10155	7693	11562	8928	7777	9187		5725	9763	8389	11551	7367
Rome	8126	6175	11151	2133	7219	8363	7739	9284	12916	7743	4039	1431	10188	10243	2376	5391	6888	1105	9214		6229	10143	6127	11523
Singapore	4478	3914	15879	8267	2897	18359	15078	2599	10816	8660	11145	10852	14123	16610	8428	7460	15339	10737	15712	10025		3915	3306	5298
Sydney	8949	10160	11800	14418	9138	15343	14875	7374	8168	11040	15519	16992	12073	12969	14497	12153	15989	16962	13501	16324	6300		4861	1383
Tokyo	2099	6742	18362	9571	5141	14164	10137	2874	6202	13547	13480	9562	8811	11304	7485	11260	10849	9718	18589	9861	5321	7823		5762
Wellington	10782	12370	9981	16524	11354	13122	13451	9427	7513	11761	16050	18814	10814	11100	16549	13664	14405	18987	11855	18545	8526	2226	9273	

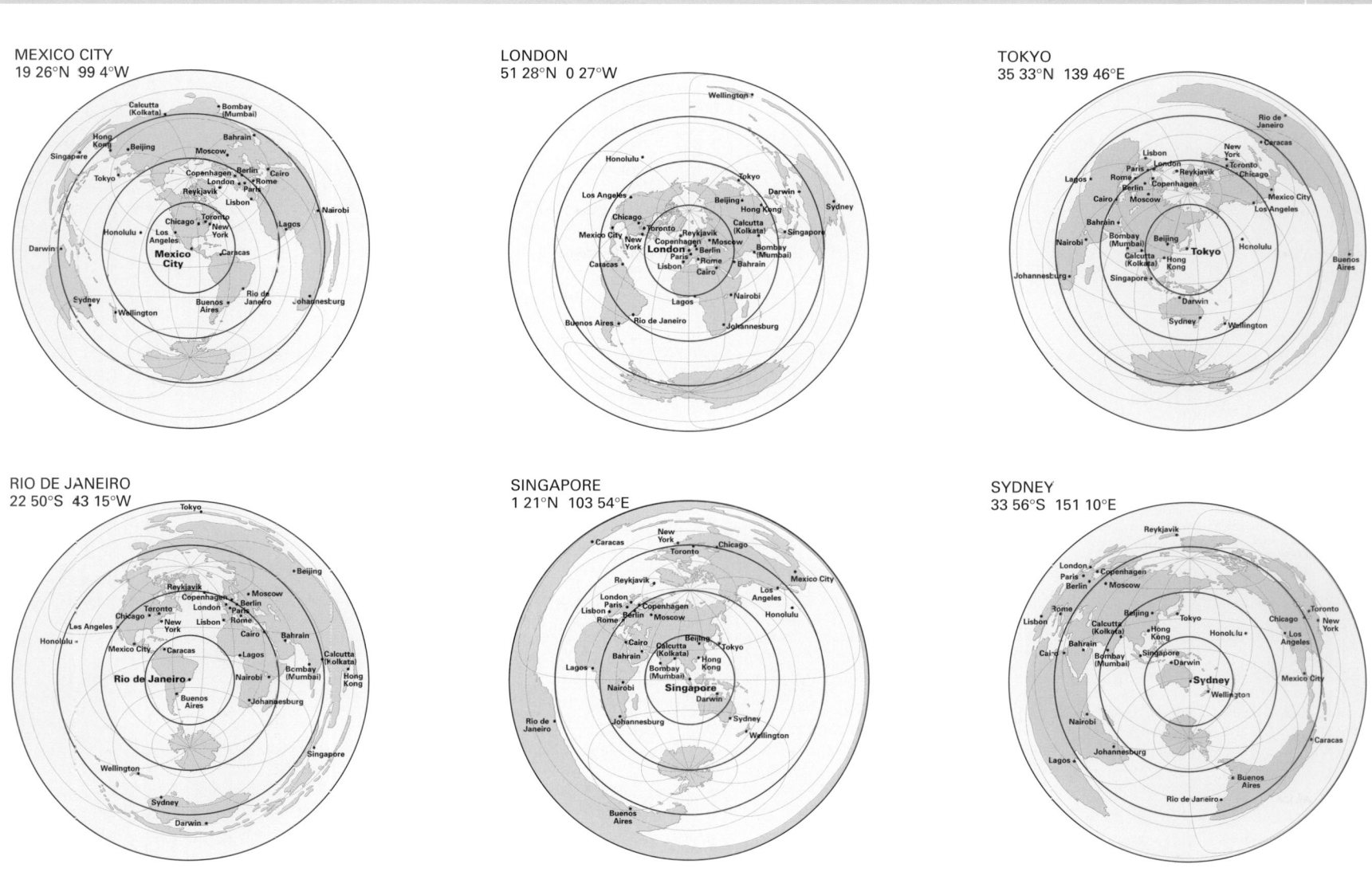

MEXICO CITY
19 26°N 99 4°W

LONDON
51 28°N 0 27°W

TOKYO
35 33°N 139 46°E

RIO DE JANEIRO
22 50°S 43 15°W

SINGAPORE
1 21°N 103 54°E

SYDNEY
33 56°S 151 10°E

World Statistics: Climate

Rainfall and temperature figures are provided for more than 70 cities around the world. As climate is affected by altitude, the height of each city is shown in meters beneath its name. For each location, the top row of figures shows the total rainfall or snow in millimeters, and the bottom row the average temperature in degrees Celsius; the total annual rainfall and average annual temperature are at the end of the rows.

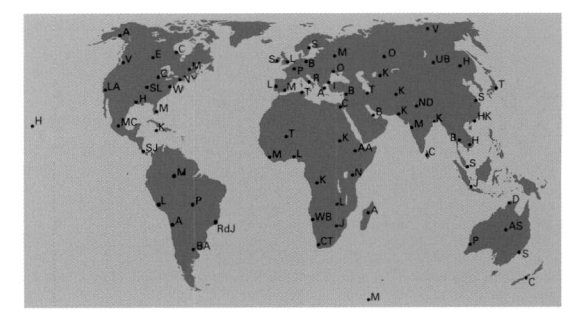

EUROPE

	Jan.	Feb.	Mar.	Apr.	May	June	July	Aug.	Sept.	Oct.	Nov.	Dec.	Year
Athens, Greece 107 m	62	37	37	23	23	14	6	7	15	51	56	71	402
	10	10	12	16	20	25	28	28	24	20	15	11	18
Berlin, Germany 55 m	46	40	33	42	49	65	73	69	48	49	46	43	603
	-1	0	4	9	14	17	19	18	15	9	5	1	9
Istanbul, Turkey 14 m	109	92	72	46	38	34	34	30	58	81	103	119	816
	5	6	7	11	16	20	23	23	20	16	12	8	14
Lisbon, Portugal 77 m	111	76	109	54	44	16	3	4	33	62	93	103	708
	11	12	14	16	17	20	22	23	21	18	14	12	17
London, UK 5 m	54	40	37	37	46	45	57	59	49	57	64	48	593
	4	5	7	9	12	16	18	17	15	11	8	5	11
Málaga, Spain 33 m	61	51	62	46	26	5	1	3	29	64	64	62	474
	12	13	16	17	19	29	25	26	23	20	16	13	18
Moscow, Russia 156 m	39	38	36	37	53	58	88	71	58	45	47	54	624
	-13	-10	-4	6	13	16	18	17	12	6	-1	-7	4
Odesa, Ukraine 64 m	57	62	30	21	34	34	42	37	37	13	35	71	473
	-3	-1	2	9	15	20	22	22	18	12	9	1	10
Paris, France 75 m	56	46	35	42	57	54	59	64	55	50	51	50	619
	3	4	8	11	15	18	20	19	17	12	7	4	12
Rome, Italy 17 m	71	62	57	51	46	37	15	21	63	99	129	93	744
	8	9	11	14	18	22	25	25	22	17	13	10	16
Shannon, Irish Republic 2 m	94	67	56	53	61	57	77	79	86	86	96	117	929
	5	5	7	9	12	14	16	16	14	11	8	6	10
Stockholm, Sweden 44 m	43	30	25	31	34	45	61	76	60	48	53	48	554
	-3	-3	-1	5	10	15	18	17	12	7	3	0	7

ASIA

	Jan.	Feb.	Mar.	Apr.	May	June	July	Aug.	Sept.	Oct.	Nov.	Dec.	Year
Bahrain 5 m	8	18	13	8	<3	0	0	0	0	0	18	18	81
	17	18	21	25	29	32	33	34	31	28	24	19	26
Bangkok, Thailand 2 m	8	20	36	58	198	160	160	175	305	206	66	5	1,397
	26	28	29	30	29	29	28	28	28	28	26	25	28
Beirut, Lebanon 34 m	191	158	94	53	18	3	<3	<3	5	51	132	185	892
	14	14	16	18	22	24	27	28	26	24	19	16	21
Colombo, Sri Lanka 7 m	89	69	147	231	371	224	135	109	160	348	315	147	2,365
	26	26	27	28	28	27	27	27	27	27	26	26	27
Harbin, China 160 m	6	5	10	23	43	94	112	104	46	33	8	5	488
	-18	-15	-5	6	13	19	22	21	14	4	-6	-16	3
Ho Chi Minh, Vietnam 9 m	15	3	13	43	221	330	315	269	335	269	114	56	1,984
	26	27	29	30	29	28	28	28	27	27	27	26	28
Hong Kong, China 33 m	33	46	74	137	292	394	381	361	257	114	43	31	2,162
	16	15	18	22	26	28	28	28	27	25	21	18	23
Jakarta, Indonesia 8 m	300	300	211	147	114	97	64	43	66	112	142	203	1,798
	26	26	27	27	27	27	27	27	27	27	27	26	27
Kabul, Afghanistan 1,815 m	31	36	94	102	20	5	3	3	<3	15	20	10	338
	-3	-1	6	13	18	22	25	24	20	14	7	3	12
Karachi, Pakistan 4 m	13	10	8	3	3	18	81	41	13	<3	3	5	196
	19	20	24	28	30	31	30	29	28	28	24	20	26
Kazalinsk, Kazakhstan 63 m	10	10	13	15	15	5	5	8	5	8	10	15	125
	-12	-11	-3	6	18	23	25	23	16	8	-1	-7	7
Kolkata (Calcutta), India 6 m	10	31	36	43	140	297	325	328	252	114	20	5	1,600
	20	22	27	30	30	30	29	29	29	28	23	19	26
Mumbai (Bombay), India 11 m	3	3	3	<3	18	485	617	340	264	64	13	3	1,809
	24	24	26	28	30	29	27	27	27	28	27	26	27
New Delhi, India 218 m	23	18	13	8	13	74	180	172	117	10	3	10	640
	14	17	23	28	33	34	31	30	29	26	20	15	25
Omsk, Russia 85 m	15	8	8	13	31	51	51	51	28	25	18	20	318
	-22	-19	-12	-1	10	16	18	16	10	1	-11	-18	-1
Shanghai, China 7 m	48	58	84	94	94	180	147	142	130	71	51	36	1,135
	4	5	9	14	20	24	28	28	23	19	12	7	16
Singapore 10 m	252	173	193	188	173	173	170	196	178	208	254	257	2,413
	26	27	28	28	28	28	28	27	27	27	27	27	27
Tehran, Iran 1,220 m	46	38	46	36	13	3	3	3	3	8	20	31	246
	2	5	9	16	21	26	30	29	25	18	12	6	17
Tokyo, Japan 6 m	48	74	107	135	147	165	142	152	234	208	97	56	1,565
	3	4	7	13	17	21	25	26	23	17	11	6	14
Ulan Bator, Mongolia 1,325 m	<3	<3	3	5	10	28	76	51	23	5	5	3	208
	-26	-21	-13	-1	6	14	16	14	8	-1	-13	-22	-3
Verkhoyansk, Russia 100 m	5	5	3	5	5	8	23	28	13	8	8	5	134
	-50	-45	-32	-15	0	12	14	9	2	-15	-38	-48	-17

AFRICA

	Jan.	Feb.	Mar.	Apr.	May	June	July	Aug.	Sept.	Oct.	Nov.	Dec.	Year
Addis Ababa, Ethiopia 2,450 m	<3	3	25	135	213	201	206	239	102	28	<3	0	1,151
	19	20	20	20	19	18	18	19	21	22	21	20	20
Antananarivo, Madagas. 1,372 m	300	279	178	53	18	8	8	10	18	61	135	287	1,356
	21	21	21	19	18	15	15	17	19	21	21	19	
Cairo, Egypt 116 m	5	5	5	3	3	<3	0	0	<3	<3	3	5	28
	13	15	18	21	25	28	28	28	26	24	20	15	22
Cape Town, S. Africa 17 m	15	8	18	48	79	84	89	66	43	31	18	10	508
	21	21	20	17	14	13	12	13	14	16	18	19	17
Johannesburg, S. Africa 1,665 m	114	109	89	38	25	8	8	8	23	56	107	125	709
	20	20	18	16	13	10	11	13	16	18	19	20	16

	Jan.	Feb.	Mar.	Apr.	May	June	July	Aug.	Sept.	Oct.	Nov.	Dec.	Year
Khartoum, Sudan 390 m	<3	<3	<3	<3	3	8	53	71	18	5	<3	0	158
	24	25	28	31	33	34	32	31	32	32	28	25	29
Kinshasa, Congo (D.R.) 325 m	135	145	196	196	158	8	3	3	31	119	221	142	1,354
	26	26	27	27	26	24	23	24	25	26	26	26	25
Lagos, Nigeria 3 m	28	46	102	150	269	460	279	64	140	206	69	25	1,836
	27	28	29	28	28	26	26	25	26	26	28	28	27
Lusaka, Zambia 1,277 m	231	191	142	18	3	<3	<3	0	<3	10	91	150	836
	21	22	21	21	19	16	16	18	22	24	23	22	21
Monrovia, Liberia 23 m	31	56	97	216	516	973	996	373	744	772	236	130	5,138
	26	26	27	27	26	25	24	25	25	25	26	26	26
Nairobi, Kenya 1,820 m	38	64	125	211	158	46	15	23	31	53	109	86	958
	19	19	19	19	18	16	16	16	18	19	18	18	18
Timbuktu, Mali 301 m	<3	<3	3	<3	5	23	79	81	38	3	<3	<3	231
	22	24	28	32	34	35	32	30	32	31	28	23	29
Tunis, Tunisia 66 m	64	51	41	36	18	8	3	8	33	51	48	61	419
	10	11	13	16	19	23	26	27	25	20	16	11	18
Walvis Bay, Namibia 7 m	<3	5	8	3	3	<3	<3	<3	<3	<3	<3	<3	23
	19	19	19	18	17	16	15	14	14	15	17	18	18

AUSTRALIA, NEW ZEALAND AND ANTARCTICA

	Jan.	Feb.	Mar.	Apr.	May	June	July	Aug.	Sept.	Oct.	Nov.	Dec.	Year
Alice Springs, Australia 579 m	43	33	28	10	15	13	8	8	8	18	31	38	252
	29	28	25	20	15	12	12	14	18	23	26	28	21
Christchurch, N. Zealand 10 m	56	43	48	48	66	66	69	48	46	43	48	56	638
	16	16	14	12	9	6	6	7	9	12	14	16	11
Darwin, Australia 30 m	386	312	254	97	15	3	<3	3	13	51	119	239	1,491
	29	29	29	29	28	26	25	26	28	29	30	29	28
Mawson, Antarctica 14 m	11	30	20	10	44	180	4	40	3	20	0	0	362
	0	-5	-10	-14	-15	-16	-18	-18	-19	-13	-5	-1	-11
Perth, Australia 60 m	8	10	20	43	130	180	170	149	86	56	20	13	881
	23	23	22	19	16	14	13	13	15	16	19	22	18
Sydney, Australia 42 m	89	102	127	135	127	117	117	76	73	71	73	73	1,181
	22	22	21	18	15	13	12	13	15	18	19	21	17

NORTH AMERICA

	Jan.	Feb.	Mar.	Apr.	May	June	July	Aug.	Sept.	Oct.	Nov.	Dec.	Year
Anchorage, Alaska, USA 40 m	20	18	15	10	13	18	41	66	66	56	25	23	371
	-11	-8	-5	2	7	12	14	13	9	2	-5	-11	2
Chicago, Illinois, USA 251 m	51	51	66	71	86	89	84	81	79	66	61	51	836
	-4	-3	2	9	14	20	23	22	19	12	5	-1	10
Churchill, Man., Canada 13 m	15	13	18	23	32	44	46	58	51	43	39	21	402
	-28	-26	-20	-10	-2	6	12	11	5	-2	-12	-22	-7
Edmonton, Alta., Canada 676 m	25	19	19	22	43	77	89	78	39	17	16	25	466
	-15	-10	-5	4	11	15	17	16	11	6	-4	-10	3
Honolulu, Hawaii, USA 12 m	104	66	79	48	25	18	23	28	36	48	64	104	643
	23	18	19	20	22	24	25	26	26	24	22	19	22
Houston, Texas, USA 12 m	89	76	84	91	119	117	99	99	104	94	89	109	1,171
	12	13	17	21	24	27	28	29	26	22	16	12	21
Kingston, Jamaica 34 m	23	15	23	31	102	89	38	91	99	180	74	36	800
	25	25	25	26	26	28	28	28	27	27	26	26	26
Los Angeles, Calif., USA 95 m	79	76	71	25	10	3	<3	<3	5	15	31	66	381
	13	14	14	16	17	19	21	22	21	18	16	14	17
Mexico City, Mexico 2,309 m	13	5	10	20	53	119	170	152	130	51	18	8	747
	12	13	16	18	19	19	17	18	18	16	14	13	16
Miami, Florida, USA 8 m	71	53	64	81	173	178	155	160	203	234	71	51	1,516
	20	20	22	23	25	27	28	28	27	25	22	21	24
Montréal, Que., Canada 57 m	72	65	74	74	66	82	90	92	88	76	81	87	946
	-10	-9	-3	-6	13	18	21	20	15	9	2	-7	6
New York City, NY, USA 96 m	94	97	91	81	81	84	107	109	86	89	76	91	1,092
	-1	-1	3	10	16	20	23	23	21	15	7	1	11
St Louis, Mo., USA 173 m	58	64	89	97	114	114	89	86	81	74	71	64	1,001
	0	2	7	13	19	24	26	26	22	15	8	2	14
San José, Costa Rica 1,146 m	15	5	20	46	229	241	211	241	305	300	145	41	1,798
	19	19	21	21	22	21	21	21	21	20	20	19	20
Vancouver, BC, Canada 14 m	154	115	101	60	52	45	32	41	67	114	150	182	1,113
	3	5	6	9	12	15	17	17	14	10	6	4	10
Washington, DC, USA 22 m	86	76	91	84	94	99	112	109	94	74	66	79	1,064
	1	2	7	12	18	23	25	24	20	14	8	3	13

SOUTH AMERICA

	Jan.	Feb.	Mar.	Apr.	May	June	July	Aug.	Sept.	Oct.	Nov.	Dec.	Year
Antofagasta, Chile 94 m	0	0	0	<3	<3	<3	5	3	<3	3	<3	0	13
	21	21	20	18	16	15	14	14	15	16	18	19	17
Buenos Aires, Argentina 27 m	79	71	109	89	76	61	56	61	79	86	84	99	950
	23	23	21	17	13	9	10	11	13	15	19	22	16
Lima, Peru 120 m	3	<3	<3	<3	5	5	8	8	8	3	3	<3	41
	23	24	24	22	19	17	16	17	17	18	19	21	20
Manaus, Brazil 44 m	249	231	262	221	170	84	58	38	46	107	142	203	1,811
	28	28	28	27	28	28	28	29	29	29	29	28	28
Paraná, Brazil 260 m	287	236	239	102	15	<3	<3	5	28	127	231	310	1,582
	23	23	23	23	23	21	21	22	24	24	24	23	23
Rio de Janeiro, Brazil 61 m	125	122	130	107	79	53	41	43	66	79	104	137	1,082
	26	26	25	24	22	21	21	21	22	23	25	25	23

World Statistics: Physical Dimensions

Each topic list is divided into continents and within a continent the items are listed in order of size. The order of the continents is the same as in the atlas, beginning with Europe and ending with South America. The bottom part of many of the lists is selective in order to give examples from as many different countries as possible. The world top ten are shown in square brackets; in the case of mountains this has not been done because the world top 30 are all in Asia. The figures are rounded as appropriate.

WORLD, CONTINENTS, OCEANS

THE WORLD	km²	miles²	%
The World	509,450,000	196,672,000	–
Land	149,450,000	57,688,000	29.3
Water	360,000,000	138,984,000	70.7
Asia	44,500,000	17,177,000	29.8
Africa	30,302,000	11,697,000	20.3
North America	24,241,000	9,357,000	16.2
South America	17,793,000	6,868,000	11.9
Antarctica	14,100,000	5,443,000	9.4
Europe	9,957,000	3,843,000	6.7
Australia and Oceania	8,557,000	3,303,000	5.7
Pacific Ocean	179,679,000	69,356,000	49.9
Atlantic Ocean	92,373,000	35,657,000	25.7
Indian Ocean	73,917,000	28,532,000	20.5
Arctic Ocean	14,090,000	5,439,000	3.9

SEAS

PACIFIC	km²	miles²
South China Sea	2,974,600	1,148,500
Bering Sea	2,268,000	875,000
Sea of Okhotsk	1,528,000	590,000
East China and Yellow	1,249,000	482,000
Sea of Japan	1,008,000	389,000
Gulf of California	162,000	62,500
Bass Strait	75,000	29,000

ATLANTIC	km²	miles²
Caribbean Sea	2,766,000	1,068,000
Mediterranean Sea	2,516,000	971,000
Gulf of Mexico	1,543,000	596,000
Hudson Bay	1,232,000	476,000
North Sea	575,000	223,000
Black Sea	462,000	178,000
Baltic Sea	422,170	163,000
Gulf of St Lawrence	238,000	92,000

INDIAN	km²	miles²
Red Sea	438,000	169,000
Persian Gulf	239,000	92,000

MOUNTAINS

EUROPE		m	ft
Elbrus	Russia	5,642	18,510
Mont Blanc	France/Italy	4,807	15,771
Monte Rosa	Italy/Switzerland	4,634	15,203
Dom	Switzerland	4,545	14,911
Liskamm	Switzerland	4,527	14,852
Weisshorn	Switzerland	4,505	14,780
Taschorn	Switzerland	4,490	14,730
Matterhorn/Cervino	Italy/Switz.	4,478	14,691
Mont Maudit	France/Italy	4,465	14,649
Dent Blanche	Switzerland	4,356	14,291
Nadelhorn	Switzerland	4,327	14,196
Grandes Jorasses	France/Italy	4,208	13,806
Jungfrau	Switzerland	4,158	13,642
Barre des Ecrins	France	4,103	13,461
Gran Paradiso	Italy	4,061	13,323
Piz Bernina	Italy/Switzerland	4,049	13,284
Eiger	Switzerland	3,970	13,025
Monte Viso	Italy	3,841	12,602
Grossglockner	Austria	3,797	12,457
Wildspitze	Austria	3,772	12,382
Monte Disgrazia	Italy	3,678	12,066
Mulhacén	Spain	3,478	11,411
Pico de Aneto	Spain	3,404	11,168
Marmolada	Italy	3,342	10,964
Etna	Italy	3,340	10,958
Punta del'Argentera	Italy	3,297	10,817
Zugspitze	Germany	2,962	9,718
Musala	Bulgaria	2,925	9,596
Olympus	Greece	2,917	9,570
Triglav	Slovenia	2,863	9,393
Monte Cinto	France (Corsica)	2,710	8,891
Gerlachovsky	Slovak Republic	2,655	8,711
Torre de Cerrado	Spain	2,648	8,688
Galdhøpiggen	Norway	2,469	8,100
Hvannadalshnúkur	Iceland	2,119	6,952
Kebnekaise	Sweden	2,117	6,946
Ben Nevis	UK	1,342	4,403

ASIA		m	ft
Everest	China/Nepal	8,850	29,035
K2 (Godwin Austen)	China/Kashmir	8,611	28,251
Kanchenjunga	India/Nepal	8,598	28,208
Lhotse	China/Nepal	8,516	27,939
Makalu	China/Nepal	8,481	27,824
Cho Oyu	China/Nepal	8,201	26,906
Dhaulagiri	Nepal	8,172	26,811
Manaslu	Nepal	8,156	26,758
Nanga Parbat	Kashmir	8,126	26,660
Annapurna	Nepal	8,078	26,502
Gasherbrum	China/Kashmir	8,068	26,469
Broad Peak	China/Kashmir	8,051	26,414
Xixabangma	China	8,012	26,286
Kangbachen	India/Nepal	7,902	25,925
Jannu	India/Nepal	7,902	25,925
Gayachung Kang	Nepal	7,897	25,909
Himalchuli	Nepal	7,893	25,896
Disteghil Sar	Kashmir	7,885	25,869
Nuptse	Nepal	7,879	25,849
Khunyang Chhish	Kashmir	7,852	25,761
Masherbrum	Kashmir	7,821	25,659
Nanda Devi	India	7,817	25,646
Rakaposhi	Kashmir	7,788	25,551
Batura	Kashmir	7,785	25,541
Namche Barwa	China	7,756	25,446
Kamet	India	7,756	25,446
Soltoro Kangri	Kashmir	7,742	25,400
Gurla Mandhata	China	7,728	25,354
Trivor	Pakistan	7,720	25,328
Kongur Shan	China	7,719	25,324
Tirich Mir	Pakistan	7,690	25,229
K'ula Shan	Bhutan/China	7,543	24,747
Pik Kommunizma	Tajikistan	7,495	24,590
Demavend	Iran	5,604	18,386
Ararat	Turkey	5,165	16,945
Gunong Kinabalu	Malaysia (Borneo)	4,101	13,455
Yu Shan	Taiwan	3,997	13,113
Fuji-San	Japan	3,776	12,388

AFRICA		m	ft
Kilimanjaro	Tanzania	5,895	19,340
Mt Kenya	Kenya	5,199	17,057
Ruwenzori			
(Margherita)	Uganda/Congo (D.R.)	5,109	16,762
Ras Dashen	Ethiopia	4,620	15,157
Meru	Tanzania	4,565	14,977
Karisimbi	Rwanda/Congo (D.R.)	4,507	14,787
Mt Elgon	Kenya/Uganda	4,321	14,176
Batu	Ethiopia	4,307	14,130
Guna	Ethiopia	4,231	13,882
Toubkal	Morocco	4,165	13,665
Irhil Mgoun	Morocco	4,071	13,356
Mt Cameroun	Cameroon	4,070	13,353
Amba Ferit	Ethiopia	3,875	13,042
Pico del Teide	Spain (Tenerife)	3,718	12,198
Thabana Ntlenyana	Lesotho	3,482	11,424
Emi Koussi	Chad	3,415	11,204
Mt aux Sources	Lesotho/S. Africa	3,282	10,768
Mt Piton	Réunion	3,069	10,069

OCEANIA		m	ft
Puncak Jaya	Indonesia	5,029	16,499
Puncak Trikora	Indonesia	4,730	15,518
Puncak Mandala	Indonesia	4,702	15,427
Mt Wilhelm	Papua NG	4,508	14,790
Mauna Kea	USA (Hawaii)	4,205	13,796
Mauna Loa	USA (Hawaii)	4,169	13,681
Aoraki Mt Cook	New Zealand	3,753	12,313
Mt Balbi	Solomon Is.	2,439	8,002
Orohena	Tahiti	2,241	7,352
Mt Kosciuszko	Australia	2,230	7,316

NORTH AMERICA		m	ft
Mt McKinley (Denali)	USA (Alaska)	6,194	20,321
Mt Logan	Canada	5,959	19,551
Pico de Orizaba	Mexico	5,610	18,405
Mt St Elias	USA/Canada	5,489	18,008
Popocatépetl	Mexico	5,452	17,887
Mt Foraker	USA (Alaska)	5,304	17,401
Iztaccihuatl	Mexico	5,286	17,343
Lucania	Canada	5,226	17,146
Mt Steele	Canada	5,073	16,644
Mt Bona	USA (Alaska)	5,005	16,420
Mt Blackburn	USA (Alaska)	4,996	16,391
Mt Sanford	USA (Alaska)	4,940	16,207
Mt Wood	Canada	4,848	15,905
Nevado de Toluca	Mexico	4,670	15,321

NORTH AMERICA (continued)		m	ft
Mt Fairweather	USA (Alaska)	4,663	15,298
Mt Hunter	USA (Alaska)	4,442	14,573
Mt Whitney	USA	4,418	14,495
Mt Elbert	USA	4,399	14,432
Mt Harvard	USA	4,395	14,419
Mt Rainier	USA	4,392	14,409
Blanca Peak	USA	4,372	14,344
Longs Peak	USA	4,345	14,255
Tajumulco	Guatemala	4,220	13,845
Grand Teton	USA	4,197	13,770
Mt Waddington	Canada	3,994	13,104
Mt Robson	Canada	3,954	12,972
Chirripó Grande	Costa Rica	3,837	12,589
Pico Duarte	Dominican Rep.	3,175	10,417

SOUTH AMERICA		m	ft
Aconcagua	Argentina	6,962	22,841
Bonete	Argentina	6,872	22,546
Ojos del Salado	Argentina/Chile	6,863	22,516
Pissis	Argentina	6,779	22,241
Mercedario	Argentina/Chile	6,770	22,211
Huascarán	Peru	6,768	22,204
Llullaillaco	Argentina/Chile	6,723	22,057
Nudo de Cachi	Argentina	6,720	22,047
Yerupaja	Peru	6,632	21,758
N. de Tres Cruces	Argentina/Chile	6,620	21,719
Incahuasi	Argentina/Chile	6,601	21,654
Cerro Galan	Argentina	6,600	21,654
Tupungato	Argentina/Chile	6,570	21,555
Sajama	Bolivia	6,520	21,391
Illimani	Bolivia	6,485	21,276
Coropuna	Peru	6,425	21,079
Ausangate	Peru	6,384	20,945
Cerro del Toro	Argentina	6,380	20,932
Siula Grande	Peru	6,356	20,853
Chimborazo	Ecuador	6,267	20,561
Alpamayo	Peru	5,947	19,511
Cotapaxi	Ecuador	5,896	19,344
Pico Cristóbal Colón	Colombia	5,800	19,029
Pico Bolivar	Venezuela	5,007	16,427

ANTARCTICA		m	ft
Vinson Massif		4,897	16,066
Mt Kirkpatrick		4,528	14,855
Mt Markham		4,349	14,268

OCEAN DEPTHS

ATLANTIC OCEAN	m	ft	
Puerto Rico (Milwaukee) Deep	9,220	30,249	[7]
Cayman Trench	7,680	25,197	[10]
Gulf of Mexico	5,203	17,070	
Mediterranean Sea	5,121	16,801	
Black Sea	2,211	7,254	
North Sea	660	2,165	
Baltic Sea	463	1,519	
Hudson Bay	258	846	

INDIAN OCEAN	m	ft
Java Trench	7,450	24,442
Red Sea	2,635	8,454
Persian Gulf	73	239

PACIFIC OCEAN	m	ft	
Mariana Trench	11,022	36,161	[1]
Tonga Trench	10,882	35,702	[2]
Japan Trench	10,554	34,626	[3]
Kuril Trench	10,542	34,587	[4]
Mindanao Trench	10,497	34,439	[5]
Kermadec Trench	10,047	32,962	[6]
Peru–Chile Trench	8,050	26,410	[8]
Aleutian Trench	7,822	25,662	[9]

ARCTIC OCEAN	m	ft
Molloy Deep	5,608	18,399

LAND LOWS

THE WORLD		m	ft
Caspian Sea	Europe	−28	−92
Dead Sea	Asia	−411	−1,348
Lake Assal	Africa	−156	−512
Lake Eyre North	Oceania	−16	−52
Death Valley	N. America	−86	−282
Valdés Peninsula	S. America	−40	−131

RIVERS

EUROPE

		km	miles	
Volga	Caspian Sea	3,700	2,300	
Danube	Black Sea	2,850	1,770	
Ural	Caspian Sea	2,535	1,575	
Dnepr (Dnipro)	Black Sea	2,285	1,420	
Kama	Volga	2,030	1,260	
Don	Black Sea	1,990	1,240	
Petchora	Arctic Ocean	1,790	1,110	
Oka	Volga	1,480	920	
Belaya	Kama	1,420	880	
Dnister (Dniester)	Black Sea	1,400	870	
Vyatka	Kama	1,370	850	
Rhine	North Sea	1,320	820	
N. Dvina	Arctic Ocean	1,290	800	
Desna	Dnepr (Dnipro)	1,190	740	
Elbe	North Sea	1,145	710	
Wisla	Baltic Sea	1,090	675	
Loire	Atlantic Ocean	1,020	635	

ASIA

		km	miles	
Yangtze	Pacific Ocean	6,380	3,960	[3]
Yenisey–Angara	Arctic Ocean	5,550	3,445	[5]
Huang He	Pacific Ocean	5,464	3,395	[6]
Ob–Irtysh	Arctic Ocean	5,410	3,360	[7]
Mekong	Pacific Ocean	4,500	2,795	[9]
Amur	Pacific Ocean	4,400	2,730	[10]
Lena	Arctic Ocean	4,400	2,730	
Irtysh	Ob	4,250	2,640	
Yenisey	Arctic Ocean	4,090	2,540	
Ob	Arctic Ocean	3,680	2,285	
Indus	Indian Ocean	3,100	1,925	
Brahmaputra	Indian Ocean	2,900	1,800	
Syrdarya	Aral Sea	2,860	1,775	
Salween	Indian Ocean	2,800	1,740	
Euphrates	Indian Ocean	2,700	1,675	
Vilyuy	Lena	2,650	1,645	
Kolyma	Arctic Ocean	2,600	1,615	
Amudarya	Aral Sea	2,540	1,575	
Ural	Caspian Sea	2,535	1,575	
Ganges	Indian Ocean	2,510	1,560	
Si Kiang	Pacific Ocean	2,100	1,305	
Irrawaddy	Indian Ocean	2,010	1,250	
Tarim–Yarkand	Lop Nor	2,000	1,240	
Tigris	Indian Ocean	1,900	1,180	

AFRICA

		km	miles	
Nile	Mediterranean	6,670	4,140	[1]
Congo	Atlantic Ocean	4,670	2,900	[8]
Niger	Atlantic Ocean	4,180	2,595	
Zambezi	Indian Ocean	3,540	2,200	
Oubangi/Uele	Congo (D.R.)	2,250	1,400	
Kasai	Congo (D.R.)	1,950	1,210	
Shaballe	Indian Ocean	1,930	1,200	
Orange	Atlantic Ocean	1,860	1,155	
Cubango	Okavango Delta	1,800	1,120	
Limpopo	Indian Ocean	1,600	995	
Senegal	Atlantic Ocean	1,600	995	
Volta	Atlantic Ocean	1,500	930	

AUSTRALIA

		km	miles	
Murray–Darling	Indian Ocean	3,750	2,330	
Darling	Murray	3,070	1,905	
Murray	Indian Ocean	2,575	1,600	
Murrumbidgee	Murray	1,690	1,050	

NORTH AMERICA

		km	miles	
Mississippi–Missouri	Gulf of Mexico	6,020	3,740	[4]
Mackenzie	Arctic Ocean	4,240	2,630	
Mississippi	Gulf of Mexico	4,120	2,560	
Missouri	Mississippi	3,780	2,350	
Yukon	Pacific Ocean	3,185	1,980	
Rio Grande	Gulf of Mexico	3,030	1,880	
Arkansas	Mississippi	2,340	1,450	
Colorado	Pacific Ocean	2,330	1,445	
Red	Mississippi	2,040	1,270	
Columbia	Pacific Ocean	1,950	1,210	
Saskatchewan	Lake Winnipeg	1,940	1,205	
Snake	Columbia	1,670	1,040	
Churchill	Hudson Bay	1,600	990	
Ohio	Mississippi	1,580	980	
Brazos	Gulf of Mexico	1,400	870	
St Lawrence	Atlantic Ocean	1,170	730	

SOUTH AMERICA

		km	miles	
Amazon	Atlantic Ocean	6,450	4,010	[2]
Paraná–Plate	Atlantic Ocean	4,500	2,800	
Purus	Amazon	3,350	2,080	
Madeira	Amazon	3,200	1,990	
São Francisco	Atlantic Ocean	2,900	1,800	
Paraná	Plate	2,800	1,740	

SOUTH AMERICA (continued)

		km	miles
Tocantins	Atlantic Ocean	2,750	1,710
Paraguay	Paraná	2,550	1,580
Orinoco	Atlantic Ocean	2,500	1,550
Pilcomayo	Paraná	2,500	1,550
Araguaia	Tocantins	2,250	1,400
Juruá	Amazon	2,000	1,240
Xingu	Amazon	1,980	1,230
Ucayali	Amazon	1,900	1,180
Maranón	Amazon	1,600	990
Uruguay	Plate	1,600	990

LAKES

EUROPE

		km²	miles²
Lake Ladoga	Russia	17,700	6,800
Lake Onega	Russia	9,700	3,700
Saimaa system	Finland	8,000	3,100
Vänern	Sweden	5,500	2,100
Rybinskoye Res.	Russia	4,700	1,800

ASIA

		km²	miles²	
Caspian Sea	Asia	371,800	143,550	[1]
Lake Baykal	Russia	30,500	11,780	[8]
Aral Sea	Kazakh./Uzbekistan	28,687	11,086	[10]
Tonlé Sap	Cambodia	20,000	7,700	
Lake Balqash	Kazakhstan	18,500	7,100	
Lake Dongting	China	12,000	4,600	
Lake Ysyk	Kyrgyzstan	6,200	2,400	
Lake Orumiyeh	Iran	5,900	2,300	
Lake Koko	China	5,700	2,200	
Lake Poyang	China	5,000	1,900	
Lake Khanka	China/Russia	4,400	1,700	
Lake Van	Turkey	3,500	1,400	

AFRICA

		km²	miles²	
Lake Victoria	E. Africa	68,000	26,000	[3]
Lake Tanganyika	C. Africa	33,000	13,000	[6]
Lake Malawi/Nyasa	E. Africa	29,600	11,430	[9]
Lake Chad	C. Africa	25,000	9,700	
Lake Turkana	Ethiopia/Kenya	8,500	3,300	
Lake Volta	Ghana	8,500	3,300	
Lake Bangweulu	Zambia	8,000	3,100	
Lake Rukwa	Tanzania	7,000	2,700	
Lake Mai-Ndombe	Congo (D.R.)	6,500	2,500	
Lake Kariba	Zam./Zimbabwe	5,300	2,000	
Lake Albert	Ug./Congo (D.R.)	5,300	2,000	
Lake Nasser	Egypt/Sudan	5,200	2,000	
Lake Mweru	Zam./Congo (D.R.)	4,900	1,900	
Lake Cabora Bassa	Mozambique	4,500	1,700	
Lake Kyoga	Uganda	4,400	1,700	
Lake Tana	Ethiopia	3,630	1,400	

AUSTRALIA

		km²	miles²
Lake Eyre	Australia	8,900	3,400
Lake Torrens	Australia	5,800	2,200
Lake Gairdner	Australia	4,800	1,900

NORTH AMERICA

		km²	miles²	
Lake Superior	Canada/USA	82,350	31,800	[2]
Lake Huron	Canada/USA	59,600	23,010	[4]
Lake Michigan	USA	58,000	22,400	[5]
Great Bear Lake	Canada	31,800	12,280	[7]
Great Slave Lake	Canada	28,500	11,000	
Lake Erie	Canada/USA	25,700	9,900	
Lake Winnipeg	Canada	24,400	9,400	
Lake Ontario	Canada/USA	19,500	7,500	
Lake Nicaragua	Nicaragua	8,200	3,200	
Lake Athabasca	Canada	8,100	3,100	
Smallwood Reservoir	Canada	6,530	2,520	
Reindeer Lake	Canada	6,400	2,500	
Nettilling Lake	Canada	5,500	2,100	
Lake Winnipegosis	Canada	5,400	2,100	

SOUTH AMERICA

		km²	miles²
Lake Titicaca	Bolivia/Peru	8,300	3,200
Lake Poopo	Bolivia	2,800	1,100

ISLANDS

EUROPE

		km²	miles²	
Great Britain	UK	229,880	88,700	[8]
Iceland	Atlantic Ocean	103,000	39,800	
Ireland	Ireland/UK	84,400	32,600	
Novaya Zemlya (N.)	Russia	48,200	18,600	
W. Spitzbergen	Norway	39,000	15,100	
Novaya Zemlya (S.)	Russia	33,200	12,800	
Sicily	Italy	25,500	9,800	
Sardinia	Italy	24,000	9,300	
N. E. Spitzbergen	Norway	15,000	5,600	

EUROPE (continued)

		km²	miles²
Corsica	France	8,700	3,400
Crete	Greece	8,350	3,200
Zealand	Denmark	6,850	2,600

ASIA

		km²	miles²	
Borneo	S. E. Asia	744,360	287,400	[3]
Sumatra	Indonesia	473,600	182,860	[6]
Honshu	Japan	230,500	88,980	[7]
Sulawesi (Celebes)	Indonesia	189,000	73,000	
Java	Indonesia	126,700	48,900	
Luzon	Philippines	104,700	40,400	
Mindanao	Philippines	101,500	39,200	
Hokkaido	Japan	78,400	30,300	
Sakhalin	Russia	74,060	28,600	
Sri Lanka	Indian Ocean	65,600	25,300	
Taiwan	Pacific Ocean	36,000	13,900	
Kyushu	Japan	35,700	13,800	
Hainan	China	34,000	13,100	
Timor	Indonesia	33,600	13,000	
Shikoku	Japan	18,800	7,300	
Halmahera	Indonesia	18,000	6,900	
Ceram	Indonesia	17,150	6,600	
Sumbawa	Indonesia	15,450	6,000	
Flores	Indonesia	15,200	5,900	
Samar	Philippines	13,100	5,100	
Negros	Philippines	12,700	4,900	
Bangka	Indonesia	12,000	4,600	
Palawan	Philippines	12,000	4,600	
Panay	Philippines	11,500	4,400	
Sumba	Indonesia	11,100	4,300	
Mindoro	Philippines	9,750	3,800	

AFRICA

		km²	miles²	
Madagascar	Indian Ocean	587,040	226,660	[4]
Socotra	Indian Ocean	3,600	1,400	
Réunion	Indian Ocean	2,500	965	
Tenerife	Atlantic Ocean	2,350	900	
Mauritius	Indian Ocean	1,865	720	

OCEANIA

		km²	miles²	
New Guinea	Indon./Papua NG	821,030	317,000	[2]
New Zealand (S.)	Pacific Ocean	150,500	58,100	
New Zealand (N.)	Pacific Ocean	114,700	44,300	
Tasmania	Australia	67,800	26,200	
New Britain	Papua NG	37,800	14,600	
New Caledonia	Pacific Ocean	19,100	7,400	
Viti Levu	Fiji	10,500	4,100	
Hawaii	Pacific Ocean	10,450	4,000	
Bougainville	Papua NG	9,600	3,700	
Guadalcanal	Solomon Is.	6,500	2,500	
Vanua Levu	Fiji	5,550	2,100	
New Ireland	Papua NG	3,200	1,200	

NORTH AMERICA

		km²	miles²	
Greenland	Atlantic Ocean	2,175,600	839,800	[1]
Baffin Is.	Canada	508,000	196,100	[5]
Victoria Is.	Canada	212,200	81,900	[9]
Ellesmere Is.	Canada	212,000	81,800	[10]
Cuba	Caribbean Sea	110,860	42,800	
Newfoundland	Canada	110,680	42,700	
Hispaniola	Dom. Rep./Haiti	76,200	29,400	
Banks Is.	Canada	67,000	25,900	
Devon Is.	Canada	54,500	21,000	
Melville Is.	Canada	42,400	16,400	
Vancouver Is.	Canada	32,150	12,400	
Somerset Is.	Canada	24,300	9,400	
Jamaica	Caribbean Sea	11,400	4,400	
Puerto Rico	Atlantic Ocean	8,900	3,400	
Cape Breton Is.	Canada	4,000	1,500	

SOUTH AMERICA

		km²	miles²
Tierra del Fuego	Arg./Chile	47,000	18,100
Falkland Is. (East)	Atlantic Ocean	6,800	2,600
South Georgia	Atlantic Ocean	4,200	1,600
Galapagos (Isabela)	Pacific Ocean	2,250	870

World: Regions in the News

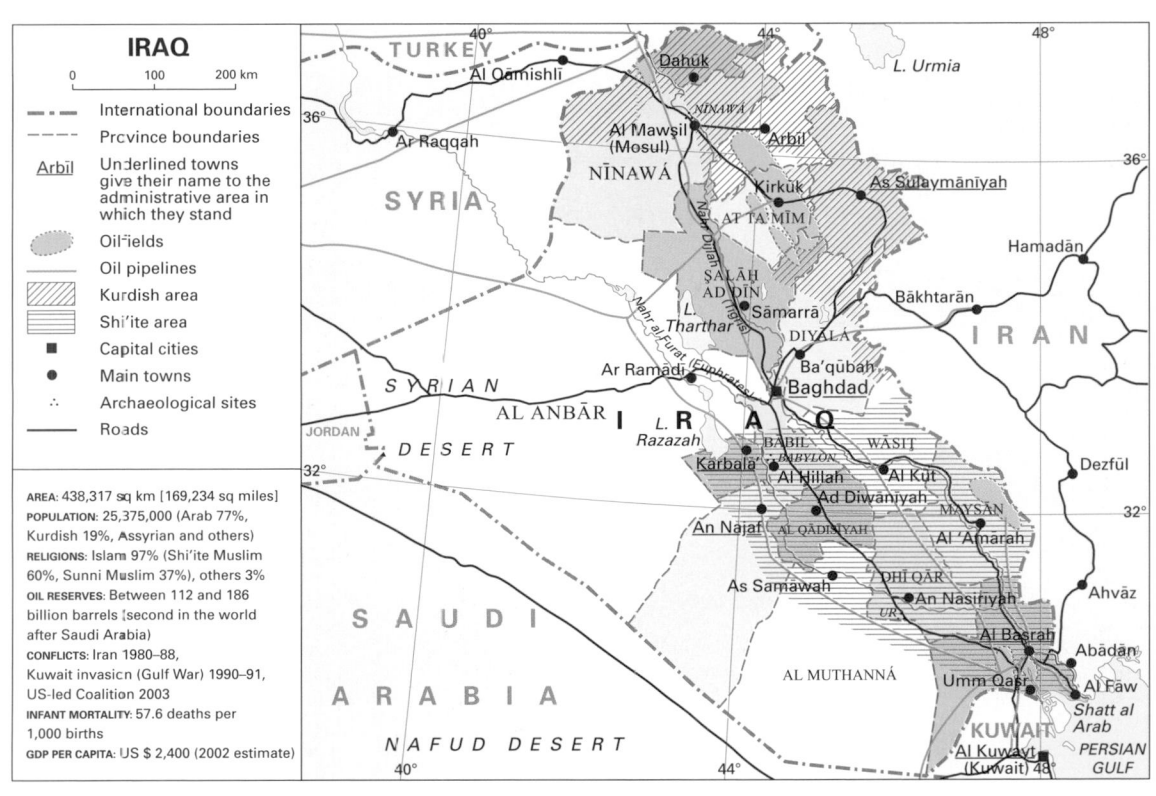

IRAQ

0	100	200 km

- –··–··– International boundaries
- – – – Province boundaries
- <u>Arbil</u> Underlined towns give their name to the administrative area in which they stand
- Oilfields
- Oil pipelines
- Kurdish area
- Shi'ite area
- ■ Capital cities
- ● Main towns
- ∴ Archaeological sites
- —— Roads

AREA: 438,317 sq km (169,234 sq miles)
POPULATION: 25,375,000 (Arab 77%, Kurdish 19%, Assyrian and others)
RELIGIONS: Islam 97% (Shi'ite Muslim 60%, Sunni Muslim 37%), others 3%
OIL RESERVES: Between 112 and 186 billion barrels (second in the world after Saudi Arabia)
CONFLICTS: Iran 1980–88, Kuwait invasion (Gulf War) 1990–91, US-led Coalition 2003
INFANT MORTALITY: 57.6 deaths per 1,000 births
GDP PER CAPITA: US $ 2,400 (2002 estimate)

INDIAN OCEAN TSUNAMI

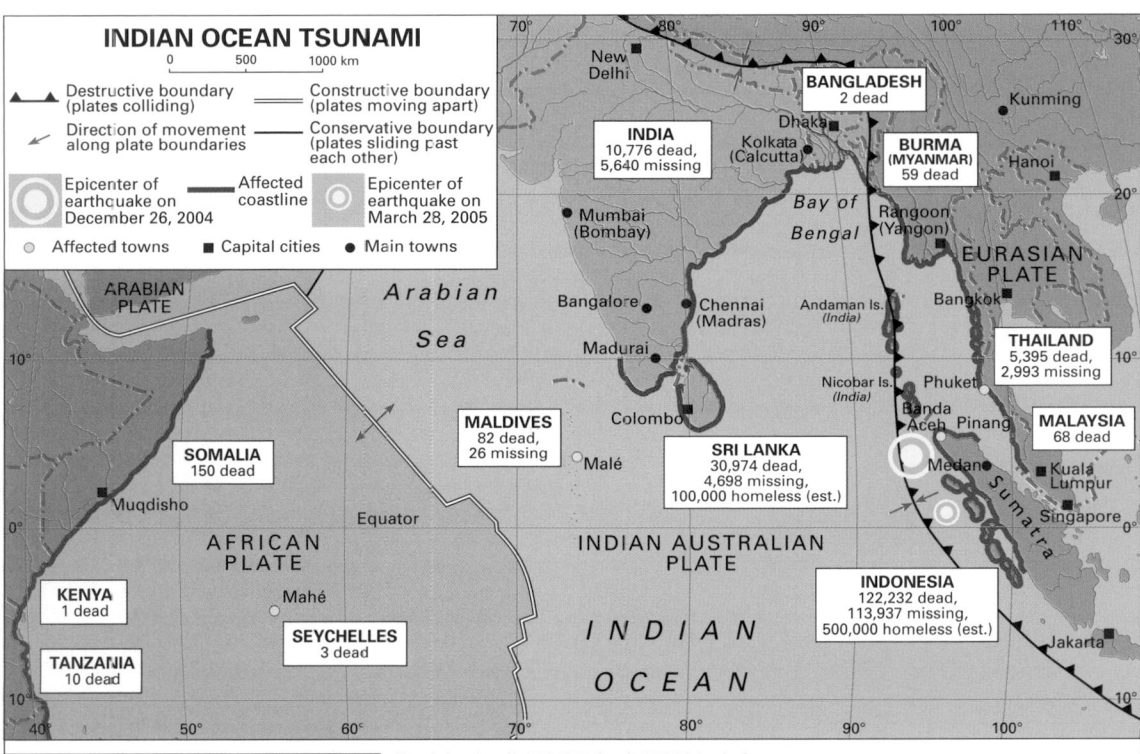

0	500	1000 km

- ▲ Destructive boundary (plates colliding)
- ↙ Direction of movement along plate boundaries
- —— Constructive boundary (plates moving apart)
- —— Conservative boundary (plates sliding past each other)
- ◎ Epicenter of earthquake on December 26, 2004
- —— Affected coastline
- ◎ Epicenter of earthquake on March 28, 2005
- ○ Affected towns
- ■ Capital cities
- ● Main towns

BANGLADESH 2 dead
INDIA 10,776 dead, 5,640 missing
BURMA (MYANMAR) 59 dead
THAILAND 5,395 dead, 2,993 missing
MALAYSIA 68 dead
MALDIVES 82 dead, 26 missing
SRI LANKA 30,974 dead, 4,698 missing, 100,000 homeless (est.)
INDONESIA 122,232 dead, 113,937 missing, 500,000 homeless (est.)
SOMALIA 150 dead
KENYA 1 dead
SEYCHELLES 3 dead
TANZANIA 10 dead

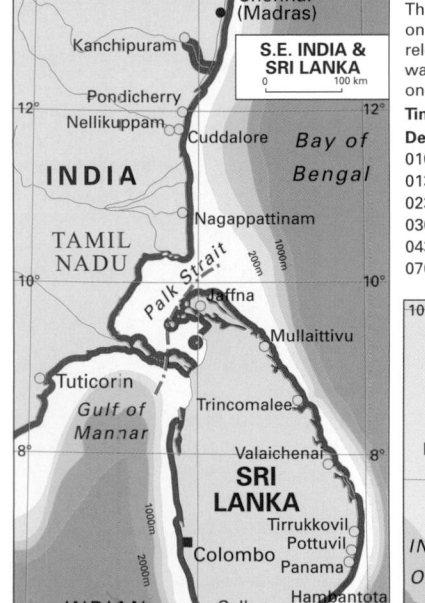

S.E. INDIA & SRI LANKA
0	100 km

Total death toll: 169,752 dead, 127,294 missing

The December 26, 2004, earthquake measured 9.3 on the Richter Scale, whereas the earthquake on March 28, 2005, measured 8.7. The Richter Scale is a logarithmic scale, so in terms of energy released, the earthquake on December 26 was five times larger than the one on March 28 and was the second largest in recorded history. The December earthquake generated waves that, once they reached the land, were up to 20 m (65 ft) in height.

Timeline:

December 26, 2004	
0100 GMT	Earthquake occurs
0130 GMT	Tsunami hits Sumatra
0230 GMT	Thailand hit
0300 GMT	Sri Lanka and India hit
0430 GMT	Maldives hit
0700 GMT	East Africa hit

Aid Recipients:

Recipient	Pledges	Donations received (at March 22, 2005)
Indonesia	US $929 million	US $220.8 million
Sri Lanka	US $413.5 million	US $249 million
India	US $57.9 million	US $56.7 million
Thailand	US $13.3 million	US $7.5 million
Somalia	US $9.4 million	US $5 million

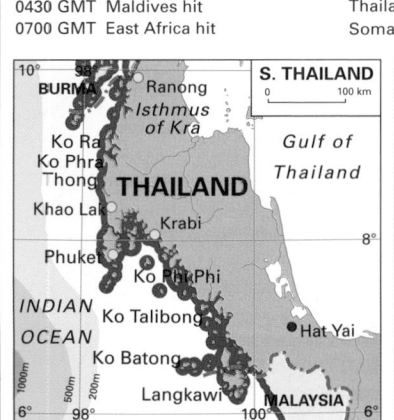

S. THAILAND
0	100 km

THAILAND

W. INDONESIA
0	100 km

INDONESIA

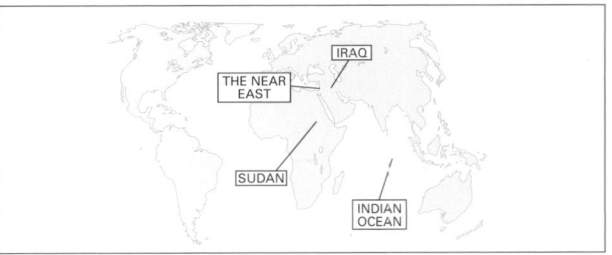

THE NEAR EAST

0	25	50 km

- – – – 1949 Armistice Line
- —— 1950 Armistice Line
- – – – 1974 Cease-fire Line
- ☐ Palestinian control
- ▨ Joint Israeli/Palestinian control
- *Efrata* Main Jewish settlements
- *Halhul* Main Palestinian Arab towns
- —— Israeli security fence completed
- —— Israeli security fence under construction or planned

ISRAEL
POPULATION: 6,199,000 (inc. Israeli settlers in West Bank, Gaza Strip, and Golan Heights)
INFANT MORTALITY: 6.2 deaths per 1,000 births
GDP PER CAPITA: US $19,500 (2002 estimate)

West Bank
POPULATION: 2,311,000 (Muslim 75%, Jewish 17%)
INFANT MORTALITY: 21.2 deaths per 1,000 births
GDP PER CAPITA: US $800 (2002 estimate)

Gaza Strip
POPULATION: 1,325,000 (Muslim 98.7%, Christian 0.7%, Jewish 0.6%)
INFANT MORTALITY: 24.8 deaths per 1,000 births
GDP PER CAPITA: US $600 (2002 estimate)

JORDAN
POPULATION: 5,611,000 (Palestinian Arab 50%)

LEBANON
POPULATION: 3,777,000 (Palestinian Arab 11%)

SUDAN

0	500	1000 km

- – – – Regional boundaries
- ■ Capital cities
- ● Main towns

AREA: 2,505,813 sq km (967,494 sq miles)
POPULATION: 39,148,000 (Black 52%, Arab 39%, Beja 6%, others)
RELIGIONS: Islam 70% (mainly Sunni Muslim), traditional beliefs 25%, Christianity 5%
BIRTH RATE: 35.79 births per 1,000 population
DEATH RATE: 9.37 deaths per 1,000 population
INFANT MORTALITY: 64.05 deaths per 1,000 births
GDP PER CAPITA: US $1,400 (2002 estimate)

Sudan has more internally displaced people than any other country (4.4 million in 2004). Up to 1.6 million people have left their homes and 70,000 are estimated to have been killed since conflict began in the Darfur region in early 2003.

The largest country in Africa, Sudan is one quarter the size of the USA, or 10 times the size of the UK. The country's inhabitants are divided into three main groups: those in the north, consisting of Muslim Arab and Nubian peoples; those in the south, consisting of traditional Nilotic and Bantu peoples; and those in the west, most of whom immigrated from western Africa in the 20th century.

IMAGES
OF EARTH

– GRAND CANYON, ARIZONA, USA –
The River Colorado has cut through a sedimentary rock
plateau to form this feature, the eastern part of which
is shown. The canyon is almost 1 mile (1.6 km) deep and
12 miles (19 km) wide from rim to rim, at its widest point.

– CHICAGO, ILLINOIS, USA –

This image shows the entire urban area of greater Chicago, which is situated on the southwestern shore of Lake Michigan. The runway pattern of the second busiest airport in the world, O'Hare International, can be clearly seen toward the top of the image.

– NIAGARA FALLS, USA/CANADA –

Lake Erie can be seen at the bottom of this image, with
Lake Ontario at the top. Flowing northward between them
is the Niagara River; just to the north of Grand Island,
the river dissects the Niagara escarpment and has formed the
Horseshoe (Canadian) and American Falls, 182 ft (55 m)
and 173 ft (53 m) high, respectively. Toronto is at
the far north of the image.

– WASHINGTON DC, USA –

The large body of water to the right of the image is
Chesapeake Bay, a flooded river valley with an average depth
of only 20 ft (6 m) that still supports a fishing industry
Around this has evolved the Washington-Baltimore
metropolitan area, with a population in excess of 6 million
people. Washington is the southernmost of the two large
urban areas on the Potomac River, on the left. Pollution
control and monitoring is vital to protect the Bay.

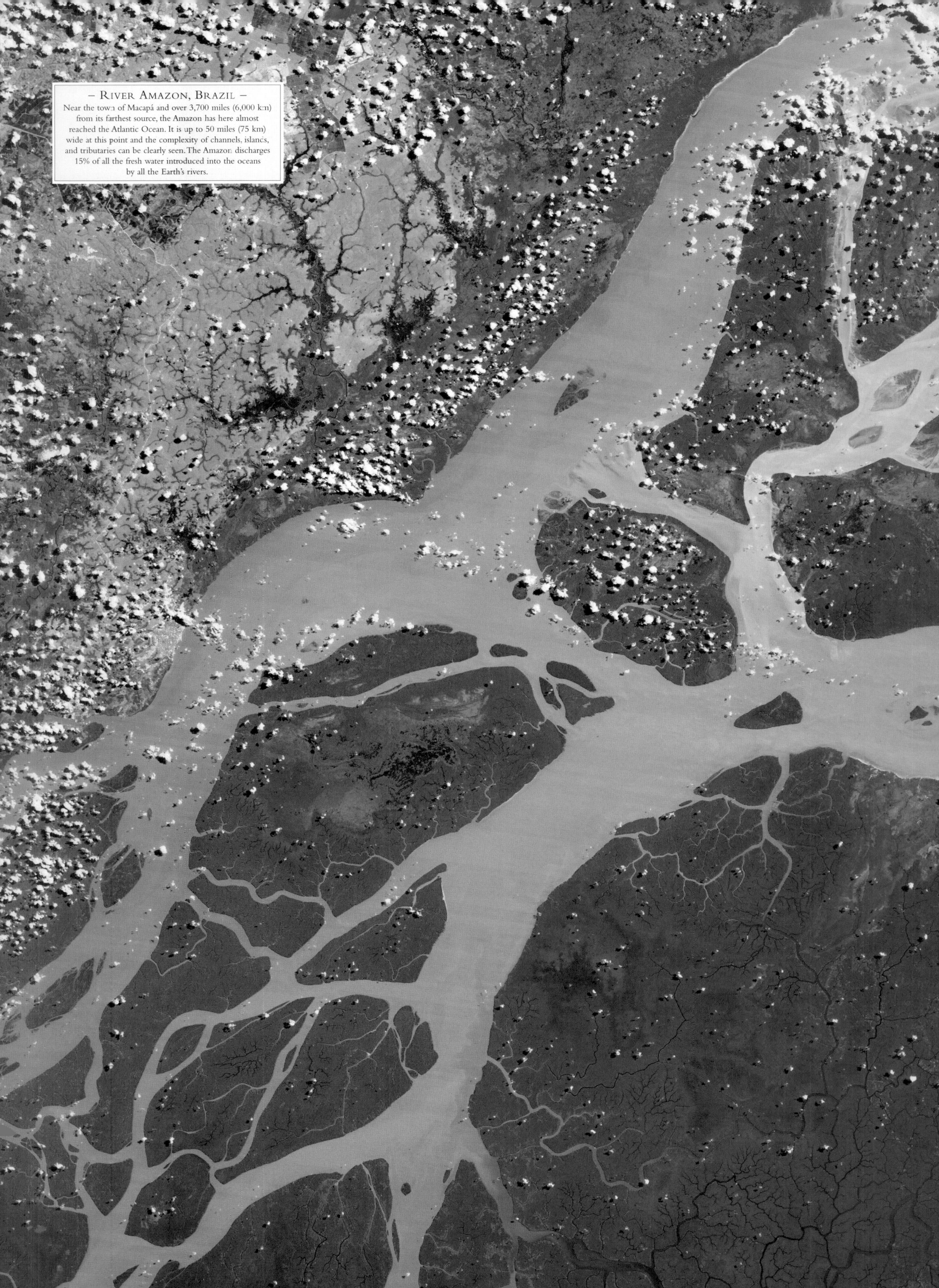

— RIVER AMAZON, BRAZIL —

Near the town of Macapá and over 3,700 miles (6,000 km)
from its farthest source, the Amazon has here almost
reached the Atlantic Ocean. It is up to 50 miles (75 km)
wide at this point and the complexity of channels, islands,
and tributaries can be clearly seen. The Amazon discharges
15% of all the fresh water introduced into the oceans
by all the Earth's rivers.

— IJSSELMEER, NETHERLANDS —

This unique feature was created in the 13th century when
the sea breached a protective sand bar, flooding all the
low-lying land. The remnants of the bar can still be seen
as the chain of Frisian Islands at the top of the image.
Large-scale reclamation started in 1932 with the
completion of the causeway in the north. Since then,
four "polders" have been drained and reclaimed. The city
of Amsterdam can be seen at bottom left.

– CAIRO, EGYPT –

The largest city in Africa with almost 10 million inhabitants,
Cairo evolved on the eastern bank of the River Nile, near
its delta. This image clearly shows the differences between the
arid desert areas to the southeast and southwest, the fertile
lands of the Nile flood plain, and the urban area itself.
The shadows of the Pyramids on the Giza Plateau can
be seen on the left-hand edge of the cultivated area.
below where the road crosses it.

— WESTERN CAPE, SOUTH AFRICA —

Cape Town sits to the bottom left of this image, with
the Cape Peninsula running southeast to the Cape of
Good Hope. Inland from the fertile coastal plain, where
most of South Africa's wine is produced, is the rugged
interior of the Great Karoo where parallel mountain
ranges are dissected by river valleys.

INTRODUCTION TO WORLD GEOGRAPHY

THE UNIVERSE	2	WATER AND VEGETATION	18	AGRICULTURE	32
THE SOLAR SYSTEM	4	THE NATURAL ENVIRONMENT	20	ENERGY	34
TIME AND MOTION	6	PEOPLE AND THE ENVIRONMENT	22	MINERALS	36
GEOLOGY OF THE EARTH	8			MANUFACTURING	38
LANDFORMS	10	POPULATION	24	TRADE	40
OCEANS	12	CITIES	26	HEALTH	42
THE ATMOSPHERE	14	THE HUMAN FAMILY	28	WEALTH	44
CLIMATE	16	CONFLICT AND COOPERATION	30	STANDARDS OF LIVING	46

THE UNIVERSE

For more information:
4 Orbits of the planets
  Planetary data

About 13.7 billion years ago, time and space began with the most colossal explosion in cosmic history: the so-called Big Bang that is believed to have initiated the Universe. According to current theory, in the first millionth of a second of its existence it expanded from a dimensionless point of infinite mass and density into a fireball about 19 billion miles across – and it has been expanding ever since.

It took about 300,000 years for the primal fireball to cool enough for atoms to form. They were mostly hydrogen, which is still the most abundant material in the Universe. But the new matter was not evenly distributed around the young Universe, and by another billion years or so, atoms in relatively dense regions had begun to cling together under the influence of gravity, forming distinct masses of gas separated by vast expanses of empty space. To begin with, these first proto-galaxies were dark places: the Universe had cooled. But gravitational attraction continued, condensing matter into coherent lumps inside the galactic gas clouds. By about 3 billion years later, some of these masses had contracted so much that their internal pressure created the high temperatures necessary to bring about nuclear fusion: the first stars were born.

There were several generations of stars, each feeding on the wreckage of its extinct predecessors as well as the original galactic gas swirls. With each new generation, progressively larger atoms were forged in stellar furnaces, and the galaxy's range of elements, once restricted to hydrogen and helium, grew larger. About 9 billion years after the Big Bang, a star formed on the outskirts of our galaxy with enough matter left over to create a retinue of planets. Nearly 5 billion years after that, human beings evolved.

The Sun is one of more than 100 billion stars in the home galaxy alone. Our galaxy, in turn, forms part of a local group consisting of approximately 30 similar structures, mostly small "dwarf" galaxies but a few large ones, and one – the Andromeda Galaxy – larger than our own. There are at least 100 billion galaxies in the Universe, many of which are members of huge galaxy clusters.

LIFE OF A STAR

For most of its existence, a star produces energy by the nuclear fusion of hydrogen into helium at its core. The duration of this hydrogen-burning period – known as the *main sequence* – depends on the star's mass; the greater the mass, the higher the core temperatures and the sooner the star's supply of hydrogen is exhausted. Dim, dwarf stars consume their hydrogen slowly, eking it out over billions of years. The Sun, like other stars of its mass, should spend about 10 billion years on the main sequence; since it was formed less than 5 billion years ago, it still has half its life left.

Once all of a star's core hydrogen has been fused into helium, nuclear activity moves outward into layers of unconsumed hydrogen. For a time, energy production sharply increases: the star grows hotter and expands enormously, turning into a so-called red giant. Its energy output will increase a thousandfold, and it will swell to a hundred times its former diameter.

After a few hundred million years, helium in the core will become sufficiently compressed to initiate a new cycle of nuclear fusion: from helium to carbon. The star will contract somewhat, before beginning its last expansion, in the Sun's case engulfing the Earth and perhaps Mars. In this bloated condition, the Sun's outer layers will break off into space, leaving a tiny inner core, mainly of carbon, that shrinks progressively under its own gravity. The white dwarf star thus formed can attain a density more than 10,000 times that of normal matter, with crushing surface gravity to match. Gradually, the nuclear fires will die down, and the Sun will reach its terminal stage: a black dwarf, emitting insignificant amounts of energy.

Black holes

However, stars more massive than the Sun may undergo a different transformation. The additional mass allows gravitational collapse to continue indefinitely: eventually, all the star's remaining matter shrinks to a point, and its density approaches infinity – a state that will not permit even subatomic structures to survive.

The star has become a *black hole*: an anomalous "singularity" in the fabric of space and time. Although vast coruscations of radiation will be emitted by any matter falling into its grasp, the singularity itself has an escape velocity that exceeds the speed of light, and nothing can ever be released from it. Within the boundaries of the black hole, the laws of physics are suspended.

GALACTIC STRUCTURES

Many of the Universe's 100 billion galaxies show clear structural patterns, originally classified by the American astronomer Edwin Hubble in 1925. Spiral galaxies like our own have a central, almost spherical bulge and a surrounding disk composed of spiral arms. Barred spirals have a central bar of stars across the nucleus, with spiral arms trailing from the ends of the bar. Elliptical galaxies have a more uniform appearance, ranging from a flattened disk to a near sphere.

▲ M51, the Whirlpool Nebula, comprises the large spiral galaxy NGC 5194 and its smaller, barred companion NGC 5195. M51 was the first astronomical object in which a spiral structure was identified, in 1845. Although smaller and less massive than our own Galaxy, M51 is much brighter, due to recent star formation.

Most galaxies, however, have no obvious structure at all. Galaxies also vary enormously in size, from dwarf galaxies only 2,000 light-years across to great assemblies of stars 80 or more times larger.

THE NEAREST STARS

The 22 nearest stars, excluding the Sun, with their distance from Earth in light-years*

Proxima Centauri	4.2	UV Ceti A	8.7	61 Cygni A	11.4
Alpha Centauri A	4.4	UV Ceti B	8.7	Procyon A	11.4
Alpha Centauri B	4.4	Ross 154	9.7	Procyon B	11.4
Barnard's Star	5.9	Ross 248	10.3	61 Cygni B	11.4
Wolf 359	7.8	Epsilon Eridani	10.5	HD 173740	11.5
Lalande 21185	8.3	HD 217387	10.7	HD 173739	11.7
Sirius A	8.6	Ross 128	10.9	* A light-year is about 5,900	
Sirius B	8.6	L789-6	11.2	billion miles [9,500 billion km]	

THE HOME GALAXY

The Sun and its planets are located in one of the spiral arms of the Galaxy, about 26,000 light-years from the galactic center and orbiting around it in a period of about 220 million years. The center is invisible from the Earth, masked by vast, light-absorbing clouds of interstellar dust.

The Galaxy is probably around 12 billion years old and, like other spiral galaxies, has three distinct regions. The central bulge is about 30,000 light-years in diameter. The disk in which the Sun is located is not much more than 1,000 light-years thick, but approximately 100,000 light-years from end to end. Around the Galaxy is the halo, a spherical zone 300,000 light-years across, studded with globular star clusters and sprinkled with individual suns.

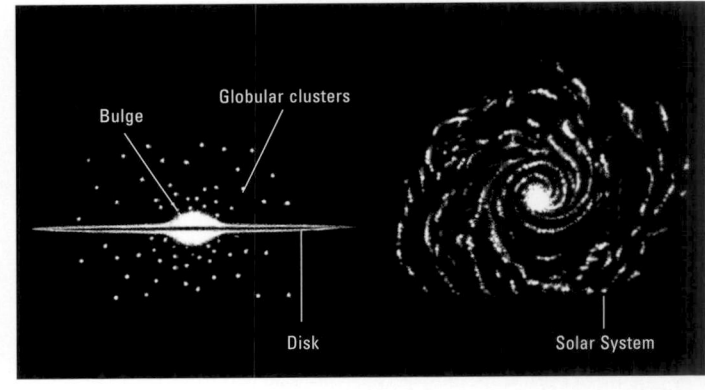

THE END OF THE UNIVERSE

The likely fate of the Universe is disputed. According to one theory (*top of diagram, below*), the expansion begun at the time of the Big Bang will continue "indefinitely," with aging galaxies moving further and further apart in an immense, dark graveyard.

Alternatively, gravity may overcome the expansion (*bottom of diagram*). Galaxies will fall back together until everything is again concentrated at a single point, followed by a new Big Bang and a new expansion, in an endlessly repeated cycle.

The first theory is supported by the amount of visible matter in the Universe; the second theory assumes that there is enough dark material in the Universe to bring about the gravitational collapse.

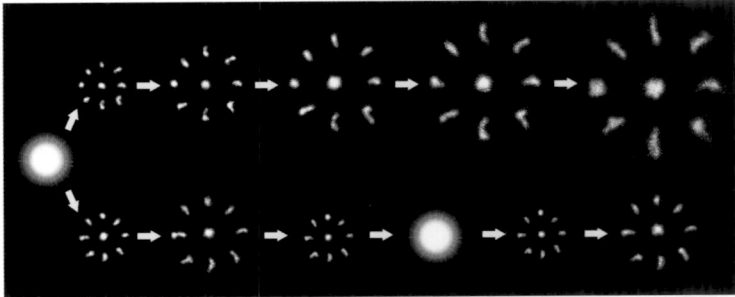

Many of the nearest stars, like Alpha Centauri A and B, are double stars, orbiting about their common center of gravity and to all intents and purposes equidistant from Earth. Many of them are dim objects, with no name other than the designation given to them by the astronomers who first investigated them.

However, they include Sirius, the brightest star in the sky, and Procyon, the seventh brightest. Both are larger than the Sun; of the nearest stars, only Epsilon Eridani is similar in size and luminosity. Most of the other bright stars in the sky are within 500 light-years of the Sun – a small fraction of the diameter of our Galaxy.

STAR CHARTS

NORTHERN HEMISPHERE SKY

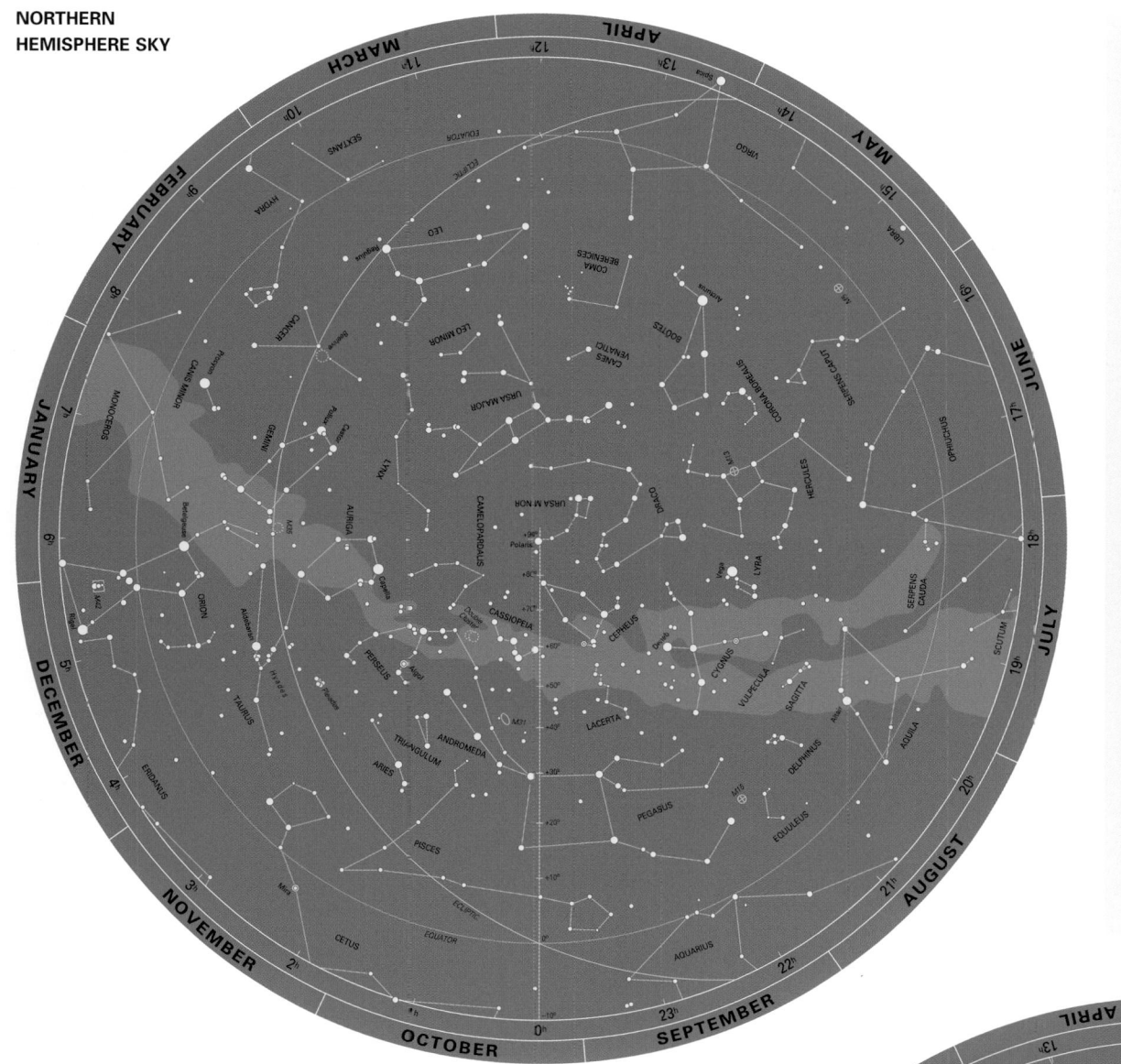

THE CONSTELLATIONS
The constellations and their English names

Andromeda	Andromeda	Lacerta	Lizard
Antlia	Air Pump	Leo	Lion
Apus	Bird of Paradise	Leo Minor	Little Lion
Aquarius	Water Carrier	Lepus	Hare
Aquila	Eagle	Libra	Scales
Ara	Altar	Lupus	Wolf
Aries	Ram	Lynx	Lynx
Auriga	Charioteer	Lyra	Lyre
Boötes	Herdsman	Mensa	Table Mountain
Caelum	Chisel	Microscopium	Microscope
Camelopardalis	Giraffe	Monoceros	Unicorn
Cancer	Crab	Musca	Fly
Canes Venatici	Hunting Dogs	Norma	Level
Canis Major	Great Dog	Octans	Octant
Canis Minor	Little Dog	Ophiuchus	Serpent Bearer
Capricornus	Sea Goat	Orion	Orion
Carina	Ship's Keel	Pavo	Peacock
Cassiopeia	Cassiopeia	Pegasus	Winged Horse
Centaurus	Centaur	Perseus	Perseus
Cepheus	Cepheus	Phoenix	Phoenix
Cetus	Whale	Pictor	Easel
Chamaeleon	Chameleon	Pisces	Fishes
Circinus	Compasses	Piscis Austrinus	Southern Fish
Columba	Dove	Puppis	Ship's Stern
Coma Berenices	Berenice's Hair	Pyxis	Mariner's Compass
Corona Australis	Southern Crown	Reticulum	Net
Corona Borealis	Northern Crown	Sagitta	Arrow
Corvus	Crow	Sagittarius	Archer
Crater	Cup	Scorpius	Scorpion
Crux	Southern Cross	Sculptor	Sculptor
Cygnus	Swan	Scutum	Shield
Delphinus	Dolphin	Serpens	Serpent
Dorado	Swordfish	Sextans	Sextant
Draco	Dragon	Taurus	Bull
Equuleus	Little Horse	Telescopium	Telescope
Eridanus	Eridanus	Triangulum	Triangle
Fornax	Furnace	Triangulum Australe	Southern Triangle
Gemini	Twins	Tucana	Toucan
Grus	Crane	Ursa Major	Great Bear
Hercules	Hercules	Ursa Minor	Little Bear
Horologium	Clock	Vela	Ship's Sails
Hydra	Water Snake	Virgo	Virgin
Hydrus	Sea Serpent	Volans	Flying Fish
Indus	Indian	Vulpecula	Fox

SOUTHERN HEMISPHERE SKY

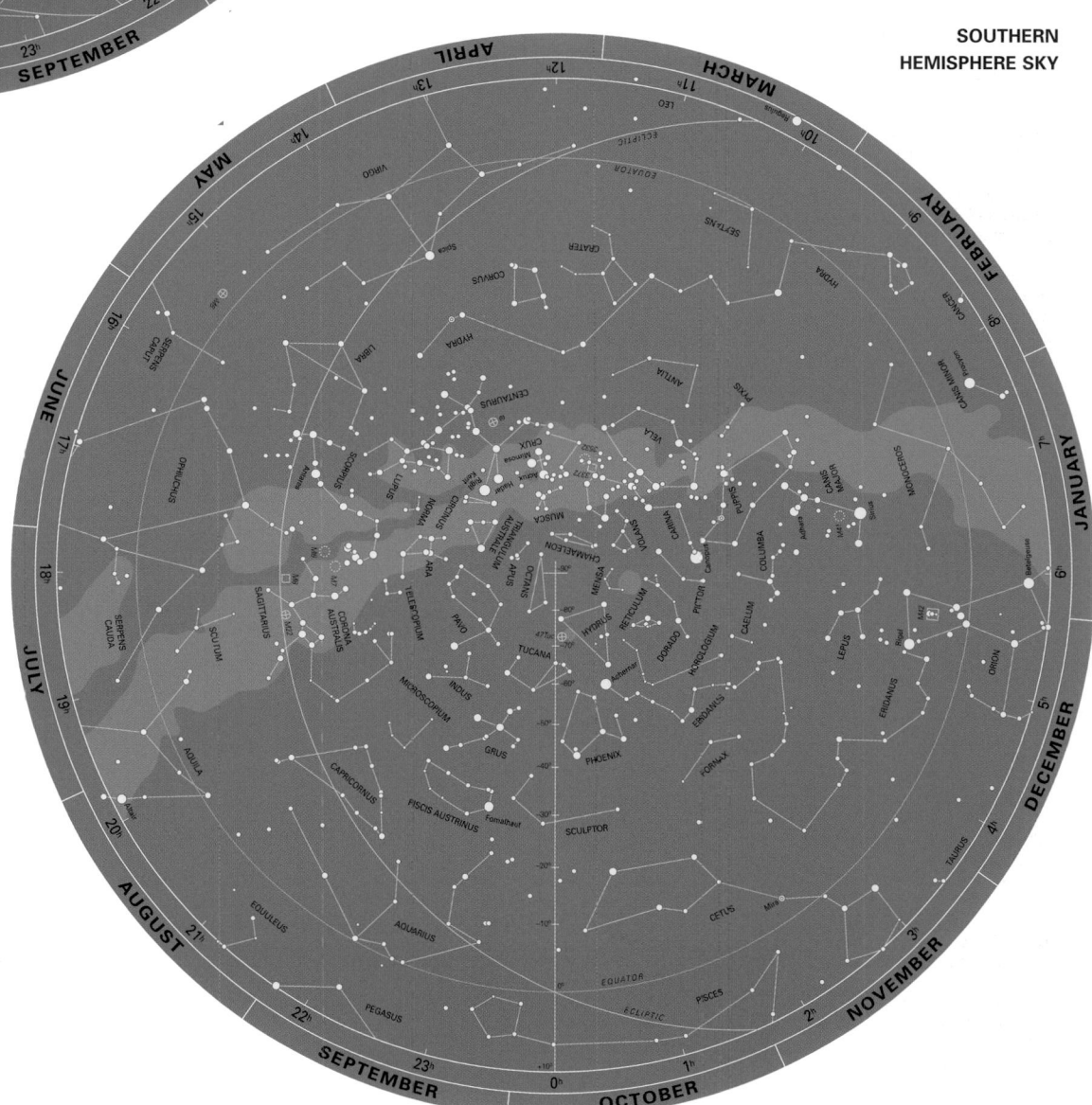

The charts on this page show the entire heavens divided into northern and southern hemispheres, with 10° of overlap between them around the perimeter of each one. However, the view from any particular location on Earth will be different, and will change both hourly as the Earth turns, and throughout the year as the Earth goes around the Sun.

The Sun's annual path through the heavens is known as the "ecliptic," and is shown here by an orange line. When the Sun is in the sky its light drowns out our view of the stars, so only that part of the heavens opposite the Sun is visible at a particular time. The sky's equivalent of longitude is known as "right ascension." As the stars appear to rotate around the Earth once every 24 hours, right ascension is measured eastward in hours and minutes and is marked around the edge of the maps. The equivalent of latitude is "declination," measured in degrees north or south of the celestial equator, and shown by the vertical line on each chart.

Using the charts
At any place and time you can see half of the whole sky, assuming a flat horizon. If you were at one of the poles your view would be shown as a circle centered on the middle of the map for the appropriate hemisphere, with the horizon marked by the celestial equator. From all other locations the center of your view (your overhead point) will be at some other point on the map whose location changes with time. The closer you are to Earth's equator, the closer the center will be to the edge of the map and more stars in the opposite hemisphere will be visible.

So first choose the appropriate chart for your hemisphere and hold it with the month at the bottom. At 11 p.m., not allowing for daylight saving time (Summer Time), your overhead point will be at the same declination as your geographical latitude and stars lower on the map will be due south (or north in the southern hemisphere). From latitude 50° in mid August, for example, your overhead point will be close to the star Deneb in the constellation of Cygnus. Stars on the opposite side of the map will be below your northern horizon, while stars below Deneb will be due south.

STAR MAGNITUDES
Apparent visual magnitudes

The magnitude scale of star brightnesses is developed from the system used by the Ancient Greeks in which the brightest stars were first magnitude and the faintest visible to the naked eye were sixth. Today the scale has a mathematical basis and extends, at the brightest end, through to negative magnitudes.

The Milky Way is shown in light blue on these charts.

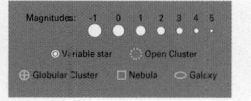

THE SOLAR SYSTEM

For more information:

2 The Home Galaxy

6 The seasons

   Day and night

7 The Moon

Lying about halfway from the center of one of billions of galaxies that populate the observable Universe, our Solar System contains nine planets and their moons, innumerable asteroids and comets, and a miscellany of dust and gas, all tethered by the immense gravitational field of the Sun, the middling-sized star whose thermonuclear furnaces provide them all with heat and light.

The Solar System was formed about 5 billion years ago, when a spinning cloud of gas, mostly hydrogen but seeded with other heavier elements, condensed enough to ignite a nuclear reaction and create a star. The Sun still accounts for almost 99.9% of the system's total mass.

By composition as well as distance, the planetary array divides quite neatly in two: an inner system of four small, solid planets, including the Earth, and an outer system, from Jupiter to Neptune, of four much larger planets composed of lighter materials, such as gas, liquid, and ice. Lying mostly between the two groups is a scattering of rocky asteroids, numbering perhaps a million or more. They may be debris left over from the formation of the inner Solar System. The outermost planet, Pluto, may simply be the largest member of the Kuiper Belt of rock–ice bodies orbiting beyond Neptune, left over from the formation of the outer Solar System.

Much of the early history of science is the story of people trying to make sense of the wandering points of light that were all they knew of the planets. Now, men have themselves stood on the Earth's Moon, space probes have landed on Mars and Venus, and distant landscapes have been mapped with astonishing accuracy, transforming our knowledge of our celestial environment.

In the 1980s, the Voyager space probes skimmed all four major planets of the outer Solar System, bringing new revelations with each close approach. The Magellan (Venus), Galileo (Jupiter), and Cassini–Huygens (Saturn) missions have transformed our knowledge of those planets and the giants' moons, and a host of orbiters and landers have shown us Mars in a new light. There are even plans to visit distant Pluto.

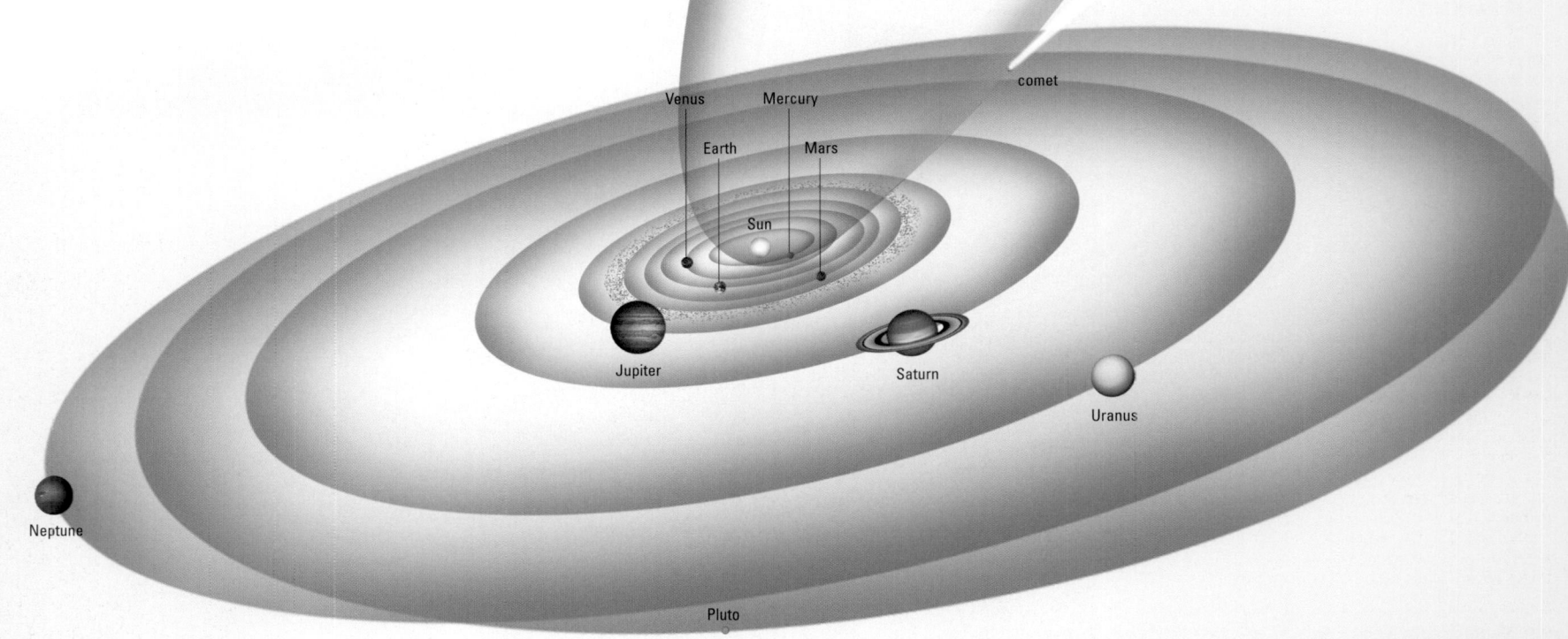

Diagram not drawn to scale

ORBITS OF THE PLANETS

The diagram above shows the Solar System as it might appear to an observer a few light-hours away in the direction of the constellation Hercules. Seen from such a position, above the plane of the ecliptic, all the planets revolve about the Sun in a counterclockwise direction. The perspective view exaggerates the elliptical form of all the planetary orbits: only Pluto and Mercury follow paths that deviate noticeably from circularity.

Near perihelion – its closest approach to the Sun – Pluto actually passes inside the orbit of Neptune, an event that last occurred in 1979. Pluto did not regain its station as the Sun's outermost planet until February 1999. The diagram also shows the main swarm of asteroids between Mars and Jupiter, and the orbit of a comet. Comets reside in a vast spherical halo beyond the Solar System, and are occasionally diverted toward the Sun on highly elliptical orbits.

PLANETARY DATA

	Mean distance from Sun (million miles)	Mass (Earth = 1)	Period of orbit (Earth days/years)	Period of rotation (Earth days)	Equatorial diameter (miles)	Average density (water = 1)	Surface gravity (Earth = 1)	Number of known satellites*
Sun	–	332,946	–	25.38	865,000	1.41	27.9	–
Mercury	36.0	0.06	87.97d	58.65	3,032	5.43	0.38	0
Venus	67.2	0.82	224.7d	243.02	7,521	5.24	0.91	0
Earth	93.0	1.00	365.3d	1.00	7,926	5.52	1.00	1
Mars	141.6	0.11	687.0d	1.029	4,220	3.94	0.38	2
Jupiter	483.7	317.8	11.86y	0.411	88,848	1.33	2.36	63
Saturn	886.6	95.2	29.50y	0.428	74,900	0.69	0.91	46
Uranus	1,784.0	14.5	84.02y	0.720	31,764	1.27	0.89	27
Neptune	2,795.2	17.2	164.8y	0.673	30,776	1.64	1.13	13
Pluto	3,670.2	0.002	247.9y	6.39	1,485	1.8	0.07	1

Planetary days are given in sidereal time – that is, with respect to the stars rather than the Sun. Most of the information in the table was confirmed by spacecraft and often obtained from photographs and other data transmitted back to the Earth. In the case of Pluto, however, only Earthbound observations have been made, and no spacecraft will encounter it until well into the 21st century. Given the planet's small size and great distance, figures for its diameter and rotation period have only recently been confirmed. Pluto is not massive enough to account for the perturbations in the orbits of Uranus and Neptune that led to its discovery in 1930, but it is now widely believed that these perturbations can be explained away as observational errors made by the earlier observers.

* At the start of 2005

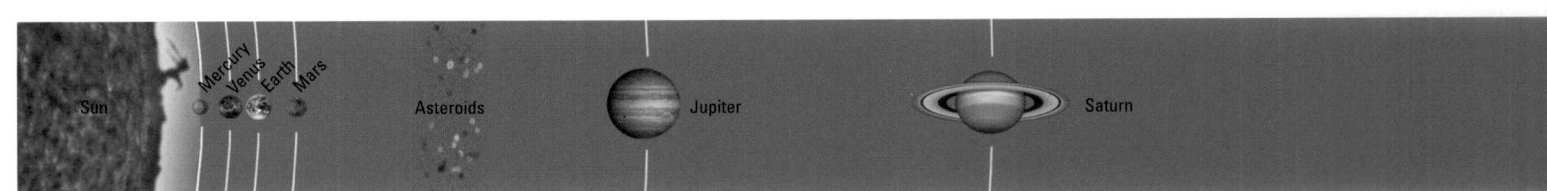

THE PLANETS

Mercury is the closest planet to the Sun and hence the fastest-moving. It is very hot, with a cratered, wrinkled surface very similar to that of Earth's Moon. It is small and has low gravity, so there is no significant atmosphere.

Venus has much the same physical dimensions as Earth. Its dense atmosphere is composed of 97% carbon dioxide resulting in a runaway greenhouse effect that makes the surface, at 890°F, the hottest of all the planets in the Solar System. Radar mapping revealed a terrain consisting of highland regions and vast, rolling plains crossed by volcanic flows and dotted with craters. Discharges from volcanic regions could explain the sulfuric-acid rain detected by spacecraft. Soft-landers last less than an hour in Venus's fierce climate.

Earth seen from space is easily the most beautiful of the inner planets; it is also, and more objectively, the largest, as well as the only known home of life. Living things are the main reason why the Earth is able to retain a substantial proportion of reactive oxygen in its atmosphere; the oxygen in turn supports the life that constantly regenerates it. The Earth's natural satellite, the Moon, is believed to have been created when an asteroid struck our planet in its infancy.

Mars, smaller and cooler than the Earth, is nevertheless the most likely planet other than Earth where life may have formed. The planet was until recently (in astronomical terms) a geologically active world with water on its surface: rivers, lakes, and even an ocean. Liquid water may well exist today, but trapped beneath its dusty, boulder-strewn surface. The Martian landscape features huge extinct volcanoes, a giant canyon system, craters, and sand dunes. Its thin atmosphere is mostly carbon dioxide, and its polar caps are of frozen carbon dioxide and water ice. It has two tiny moons, probably captured asteroids.

Jupiter has about three times the mass of all the other planets combined. The planet is mostly gas, under intense pressure in the lower atmosphere above a core of fiercely compressed hydrogen and helium. The upper layers form strikingly colored rotating belts, the outward sign of the intense storms created by Jupiter's rapid rotation. The Great Red Spot is a storm feature that has persisted for at least 170 years. Jupiter has at least 63 moons. Most are very small, but the four largest – Io, Europa, Ganymede, and Callisto – are fascinating worlds in their own right. Io is the most volcanically active world known, and Europa possesses an ocean deep below its icy surface. The planet also has a system of rings, though nowhere near as prominent as Saturn's.

Saturn is structurally similar to Jupiter, rotating fast enough to produce an obvious bulge at its equator. It is composed of 89% hydrogen and 11% helium, and has wind velocities in the outer atmosphere of 1,600 ft/sec. Ever since the invention of the telescope, Saturn's rings have been the feature that has most attracted observers. The rings consist of thousands of individual ringlets, composed of icy particles ranging in size from 30 feet down to microscopic. Titan, the largest of Saturn's 46 known moons, has a dense atmosphere.

Uranus was unknown to the ancients. Although it is faintly visible to the naked eye, it was not established as a planet until 1781. In its interior is probably a rocky core surrounded by frozen methane, water, and ammonia; the atmosphere is of hydrogen, helium, and some methane, which gives the planet its greenish-blue color. There is a system of thin, dark rings and a retinue of 27 moons, all but five of which are small.

Neptune is always more than 2.5 billion miles from Earth, and despite its diameter of nearly 31,000 miles, it can only be seen by telescope. Its discovery in 1846 was the result of mathematical predictions by astronomers seeking to explain irregularities in the orbit of Uranus. Like Uranus, it has a ring system; recent observations have revealed a total of 13 moons.

Pluto is the most mysterious of the solar planets, if only because even the most powerful telescopes can scarcely resolve it from a point of light to a disk. It was discovered as recently as 1930, as the result of a search based on analysing irregularities in the orbits of Uranus and Neptune. Its lone moon, Charon, is the largest in the Solar System with respect to its parent planet. Pluto is the only planet yet to be visited by spacecraft.

Mean distance from the Sun in millions of miles

Mercury	36.0 Mercury
Venus	67.2 Venus
Earth	93.0 Earth
Mars	141.6 Mars
Jupiter	483.7 Jupiter
Saturn	886.6 Saturn
Uranus	1,784.0 Uranus
Neptune	2,795.2 Neptune
Pluto	3,670.2 Pluto

Diagrams not drawn to scale

Uranus   Neptune   Pluto

Time and Motion

For more information:

4 Orbits of the planets

13 Ocean currents

14 Circulation of the air

16 Climate

The basic units of time measurement are the day and the year. The day is one rotation of the Earth on its axis. Our present calendar is based on the solar year of 365.24 days, the time taken by the Earth to orbit the Sun. Calendars based on the movements of the Sun and Moon have been used since ancient times. The length of the year, reckoned by the Julian Calendar introduced by Julius Caesar, was about 11 minutes too long. The cumulative error was rectified in 1582 by the Gregorian Calendar, when Pope Gregory XIII decreed that the day following October 4 was October 15, and that century years did not count as leap years unless they were divisible by 400. England finally adopted the reformed calendar in 1752, when it was 11 days behind the European mainland.

The rotation of the Earth on its axis causes day and night. The Earth rotates through 360° every 24 hours, and the world is divided into 24 time zones centered on lines of longitude at 15° intervals.

The tilt of the Earth's axis, which is also called the "obliquity of the ecliptic," accounts for the seasons which are so familiar in the middle latitudes. However, geological evidence shows that, over long periods of time, climates change, and the advances and retreats of the ice during the Pleistocene Ice Age may have been caused by regular variations in the Earth's tilt, its orbit around the Sun, and changes in the season when it is closest to the Sun (perihelion).

THE SEASONS

Seasons occur because the Earth's axis is tilted at an angle of approximately 23½°. When the northern hemisphere is tilted to a maximum extent toward the Sun, on June 21, the Sun is overhead at the Tropic of Cancer (latitude 23½° North). This is midsummer, or the summer solstice, in the northern hemisphere.

On September 22 or 23, the Sun is overhead at the equator, and day and night are of equal length throughout the world. This is the autumnal equinox in the northern hemisphere.

On December 21 or 22, the Sun is overhead at the Tropic of Capricorn (23½° South), the winter solstice in the northern hemisphere. The overhead Sun then tracks north until, on March 21, it is overhead at the equator. This is the spring (vernal) equinox in the northern hemisphere.

In the southern hemisphere, the seasons are the reverse of those in the north.

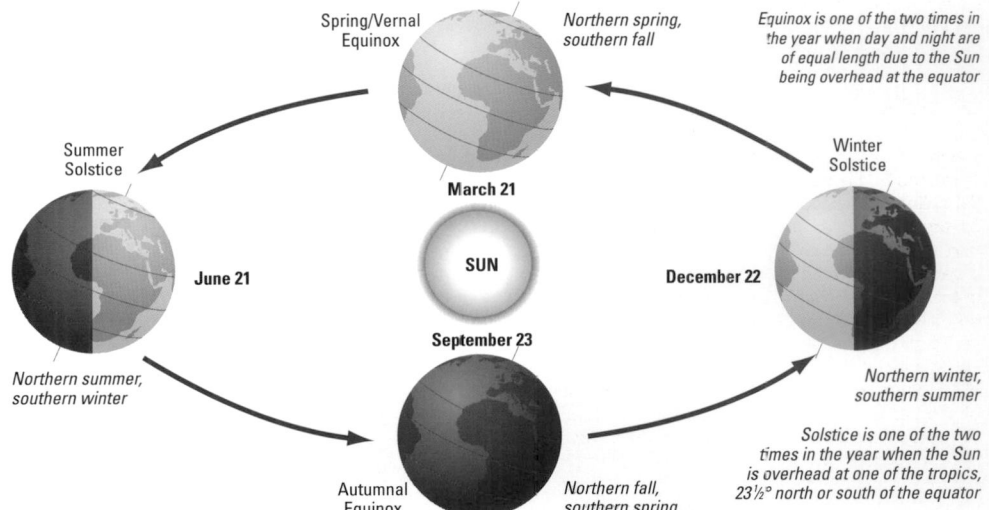

DAY AND NIGHT

The Sun appears to rise in the east, reach its highest point at noon, and then set in the west, to be followed by night. In reality, it is not the Sun that is moving but the Earth rotating from west to east. The moment when the Sun's upper limb first appears above the horizon is termed sunrise; the moment when the Sun's upper limb disappears below the horizon is sunset.

At the summer solstice in the northern hemisphere (June 21), the Arctic has total daylight and the Antarctic total darkness. The opposite occurs at the winter solstice (December 21 or 22). At the equator, the length of day and night are almost equal all year.

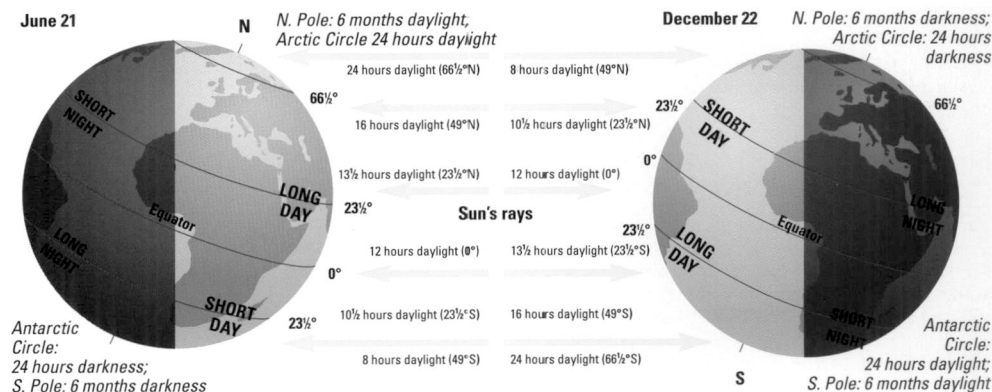

EARTH DATA

Maximum distance from Sun (aphelion):	94,508,166 miles	**Length of year:**	365 days, 5 hours, 48 minutes, 46 seconds of mean solar time	**Polar circumference:**	24,860 miles
Minimum distance from Sun (perihelion):	91,403,477 miles			**Equatorial diameter:**	7,926 miles
		Superficial area:	197,000,000 sq miles	**Polar diameter:**	7,900 miles
Angle of tilt (obliquity of the ecliptic):	23° 27' 08"	**Land surface:**	57,500,000 sq miles (29.2%)	**Equatorial radius:**	3,963 miles
				Polar radius:	3,950 miles
Length of year – solar tropical (equinox to equinox):	365.24 days	**Water surface:**	139,500,000 sq miles (70.8%)	**Volume of the Earth:**	$259,880 \times 10^{6}$ cu miles
		Equatorial circumference:	24,901 miles	**Mass of the Earth:**	5.97×10^{24} kg

SUNRISE AND SUNSET

The term "equinox" comes from the Latin for "equal night." At the spring and autumnal equinoxes, the Sun is vertically overhead at midday at the equator and all places on Earth have 12 hours of darkness and 12 hours of daylight. The graphs of sunrise and sunset show that these occasions occur on March 21 and on September 22 or 23. The graphs also show that, because the Sun remains high in the sky at the equator throughout the year, the length of day and night there remains roughly the same throughout the year, with sunrise around 6 a.m. and sunset around 6 p.m.

The further north or south one travels, the greater the difference between the number of hours of daylight and darkness. For example, the graph (*right*) shows that at latitude 60°N sunrise varies from just after 9 a.m. in midwinter (on December 22 or 23) to about 2.30 a.m. in midsummer (around the summer solstice on June 21). By contrast, the second graph (*far right*) shows that sunset at latitude 60°N occurs at about 2.45 p.m. in midwinter and 9.20 p.m. in midsummer.

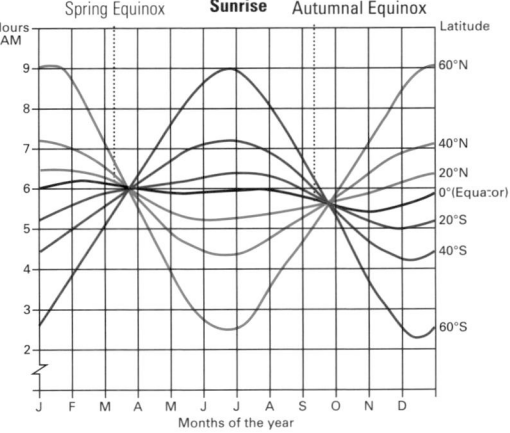

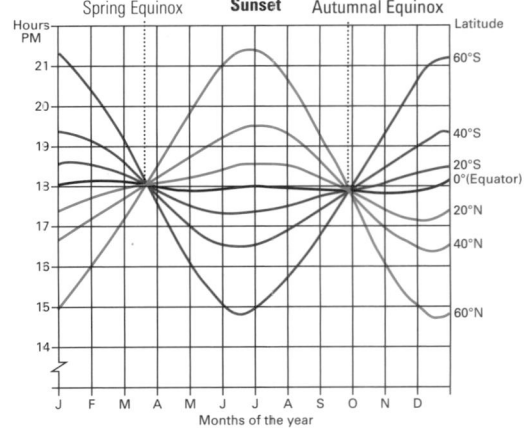

THE MOON

The Moon rotates more slowly than the Earth, taking just over 27 days to make one complete rotation on its axis. Since this corresponds to the Moon's orbital period around the Earth, the Moon always presents the same hemisphere toward us, and we never see the far side. The interval between one New Moon and the next is 29½ days – this is called a lunation, or lunar month. The Moon shines only by reflected sunlight, and emits no light of its own. During each lunation the Moon displays a complete cycle of phases, caused by the changing angle of illumination from the Sun.

PHASES OF THE MOON

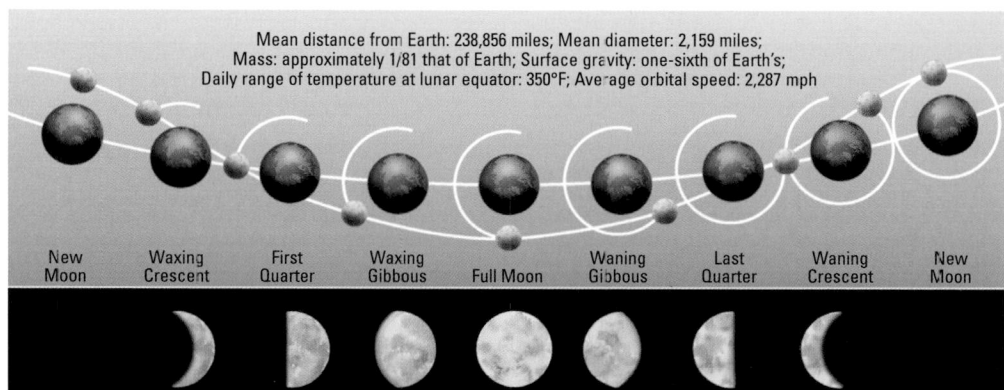

Mean distance from Earth: 238,856 miles; Mean diameter: 2,159 miles; Mass: approximately 1/81 that of Earth; Surface gravity: one-sixth of Earth's; Daily range of temperature at lunar equator: 350°F; Average orbital speed: 2,287 mph

New Moon | Waxing Crescent | First Quarter | Waxing Gibbous | Full Moon | Waning Gibbous | Last Quarter | Waning Crescent | New Moon

MOON DATA

Distance from Earth
The Moon orbits at a mean distance of 238,856 miles, at an average speed of 2,287 mph in relation to the Earth.

Size and mass
The average diameter of the Moon is 2,159 miles. It is 400 times smaller than the Sun but is about 400 times closer to the Earth, so we see them as the same size. The Moon has a mass of 7.35×10^{22} kg, with a density 3.344 times that of water.

Visibility
Only 59% of the Moon's surface is visible from the Earth over time. Sunlight reflected from the Moon takes 1.3 seconds to reach the Earth (the Sun itself is around 8½ light-minutes away).

Temperature
With the Sun overhead, the temperature on the lunar equator can reach 243°F [117.2°C]. At night it can sink to −261°F [−162.7°C].

ECLIPSES

When the Moon passes between the Sun and the Earth, the Sun becomes partially eclipsed (1). A partial eclipse can become a total eclipse if the Moon covers the Sun completely (2) and the dark central part of the lunar shadow touches the Earth. The broad geographical zone covered by the Moon's outer shadow (P) has only a very small central area (often less than 62 miles wide) that experiences totality. Totality can never last for more than 7½ minutes, and it is usually briefer than this. Lunar eclipses take place when the Moon moves through the shadow of the Earth, and can also be partial or total. Any single location on Earth can experience a maximum of four solar and three lunar eclipses in any single year, while a total solar eclipse occurs an average of once every 360 years for any given location.

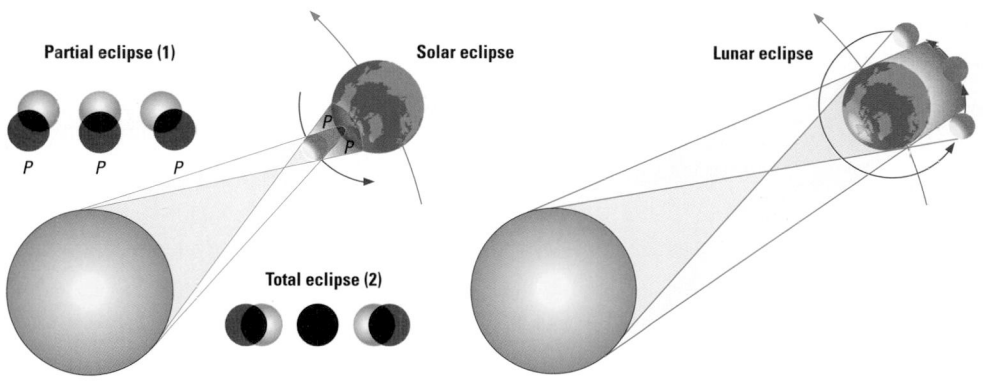

Partial eclipse (1)
P P P

Solar eclipse
P
P

Lunar eclipse

Total eclipse (2)

TIDES

The daily rise and fall of the ocean's tides are the result of the gravitational pull of the Moon and that of the Sun, though the effect of the latter is not as strong as that of the Moon. This effect is greatest on the hemisphere facing the Moon and causes a tidal "bulge." When the Sun, Earth, and Moon are in line, spring tides occur: high tide reaches the highest values, and low tide falls to low levels. When lunar and solar forces are least coincidental with the Sun and Moon at an angle (near the Moon's first and third quarters), neap tides occur, which have a small tidal range.

Spring tide
Neap tide
Spring tide
Last quarter
New Moon
Full Moon
Neap tide
Gravitational pull by the Sun
First quarter

TIME ZONES

The Earth rotates through 360° in 24 hours, and so moves 15° every hour. The world is divided into 24 standard time zones, each centered on lines of longitude at 15° intervals. At the center of the first zone is the Prime meridian or Greenwich meridian. All places to the west of Greenwich are one hour behind for every 15° of longitude; places to the east are ahead by one hour for every 15°.

International Date Line
When it is 12 noon on the Greenwich meridian, 180° east it is midnight of the same day – while 180° west the day is just beginning. To overcome this, the International Date Line was established, approximately following the 180° meridian. Thus, if you were to travel eastward from Japan (140°E) to Samoa (170°W), you would pass from Sunday night into Sunday morning.

10 — Hours slow or fast of UT or Coordinated Universal Time

Zones using UT (GMT)

Zones behind UT (GMT)

International boundaries

Zones ahead of UT (GMT)

Half-hour zones

Time zone boundaries

International Date Line

Actual solar time when time at Greenwich is 12:00 (noon)

Note: Some of the above time zones are affected by the incidence of daylight saving time in countries where it is adopted.

Projection: Mercator

GEOLOGY OF THE EARTH

For more information:

10 Types of rock
   Mountain building
11 Surface processes
21 The carbon cycle
36 Minerals

Every year, earthquakes and volcanic eruptions cause much destruction throughout the world. Such phenomena were once thought to be unconnected, but since the late 1960s, scientists have understood that these events are surface manifestations of the tremendous forces operating in the Earth's interior that are slowly but constantly changing the face of our planet.

The Earth is divided into three zones. The crust, a brittle, low-density zone, overlies the dense mantle. Separating the crust from the mantle is a distinct boundary called the Mohorovičić (or Moho) discontinuity. Enclosed by the mantle is the Earth's core, which consists mainly of iron and nickel.

Temperatures inside the Earth range from about 1,600°F in the upper mantle to perhaps 9,000°F in the core. Heat creates convection currents in a semimolten part of the mantle called the asthenosphere. Above the asthenosphere is the lithosphere, a solid layer about 40 miles thick, consisting of the crust and part of the mantle. The lithosphere is divided into rigid plates, moved around by the currents in the asthenosphere, a process named plate tectonics.

The Earth was formed around 4.6 billion years ago. Lighter elements floated toward the surface, where they formed crustal rocks. The oldest rocks so far discovered are about 4 billion years old, while the oldest fossils occur in rocks formed around 3.5 billion years ago. An explosion of life occurred at the start of the Cambrian period, 570 million years ago. The fossil record since the start of the Cambrian has enabled scientists to piece together the story of life on Earth.

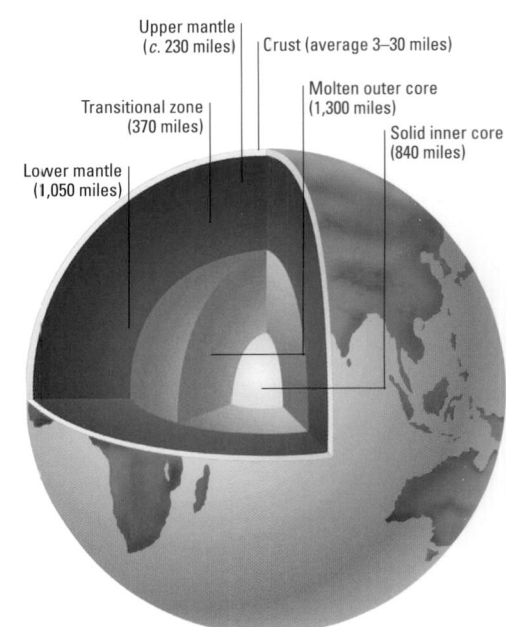

Upper mantle (c. 230 miles) | Crust (average 3–30 miles)
Transitional zone (370 miles) | Molten outer core (1,300 miles)
Lower mantle (1,050 miles) | Solid inner core (840 miles)

CONTINENTAL DRIFT

— Trench
— Rift
▒ New ocean floor
— Zones of slippage

In 1915, Alfred Wegener produced a series of world maps proposing that, around 200 million years ago, the continents had been joined together in a supercontinent that he called Pangaea. This land mass started to break up about 180 million years ago and the parts drifted to their present positions. In the 1950s and 1960s, evidence from studies of the ocean floor suggested that the low-density continents rest on huge slow-moving plates. The arrows on the present-day world map (*below*) show that the continents are still on the move.

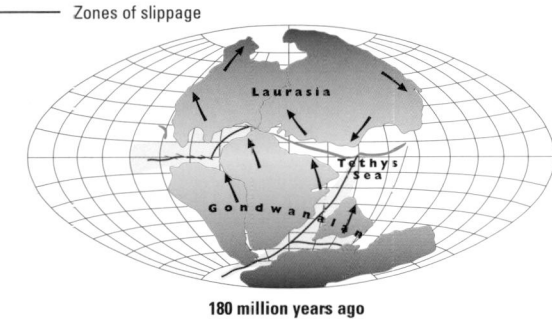

180 million years ago

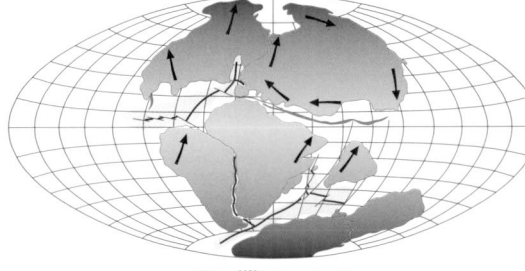

135 million years ago

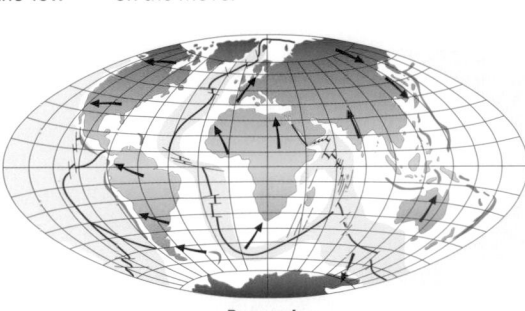

Present day

DISTRIBUTION OF VOLCANOES

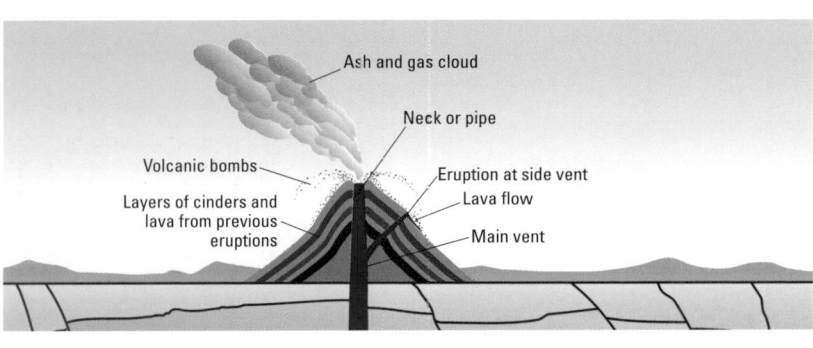

Ash and gas cloud
Neck or pipe
Volcanic bombs
Eruption at side vent
Lava flow
Layers of cinders and lava from previous eruptions
Main vent

Volcanoes occur when hot liquefied rock beneath the Earth's crust is pushed up by pressure to the surface as molten lava. There are some 550 known active volcanoes, around 20 of which are erupting at any one time.

● Submarine volcanoes
▲ Land volcanoes active since 1700
— Boundaries of tectonic plates

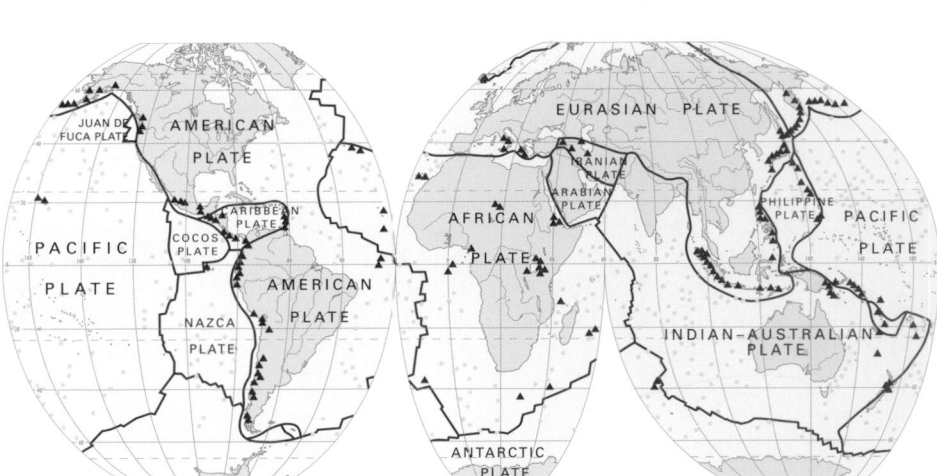

PLATE TECTONICS

The huge ridges that run through the oceans represent boundaries between plates. Here plates are diverging and molten magma from the mantle rises along a central rift valley to form new crustal rock. These ocean ridges, which are active zones where earthquakes and volcanic eruptions are common, are called constructive plate margins. Destructive plate margins, which occur when two plates converge, are marked by deep-ocean trenches as one plate is forced under the other. The descending plate is melted to produce the magma that fuels volcanoes alongside the trenches. Movements of descending plates are often sudden, triggering earthquakes in overlying continental areas.

Sea-floor spreading in the Atlantic Ocean and plate collision

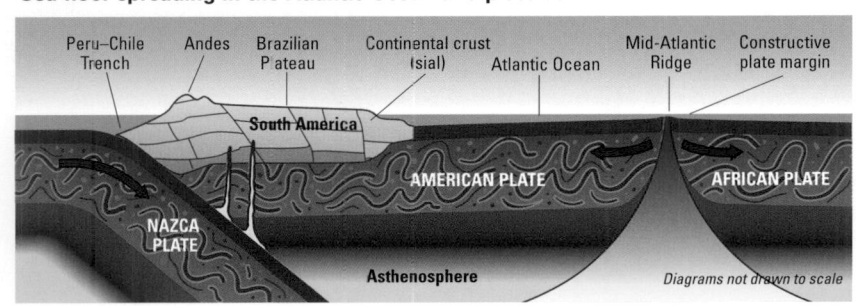

Sea-floor spreading in the Indian Ocean and continental plate collision

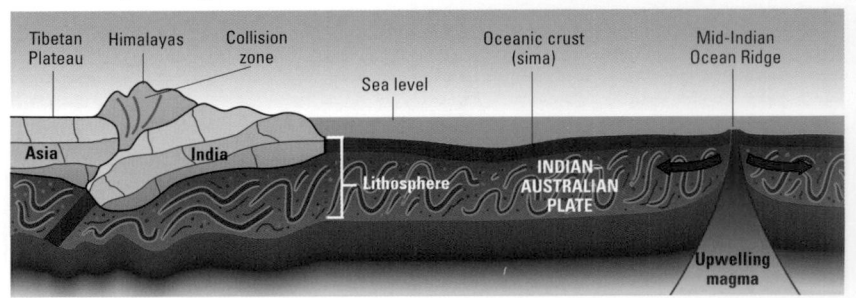

GEOLOGICAL TIME

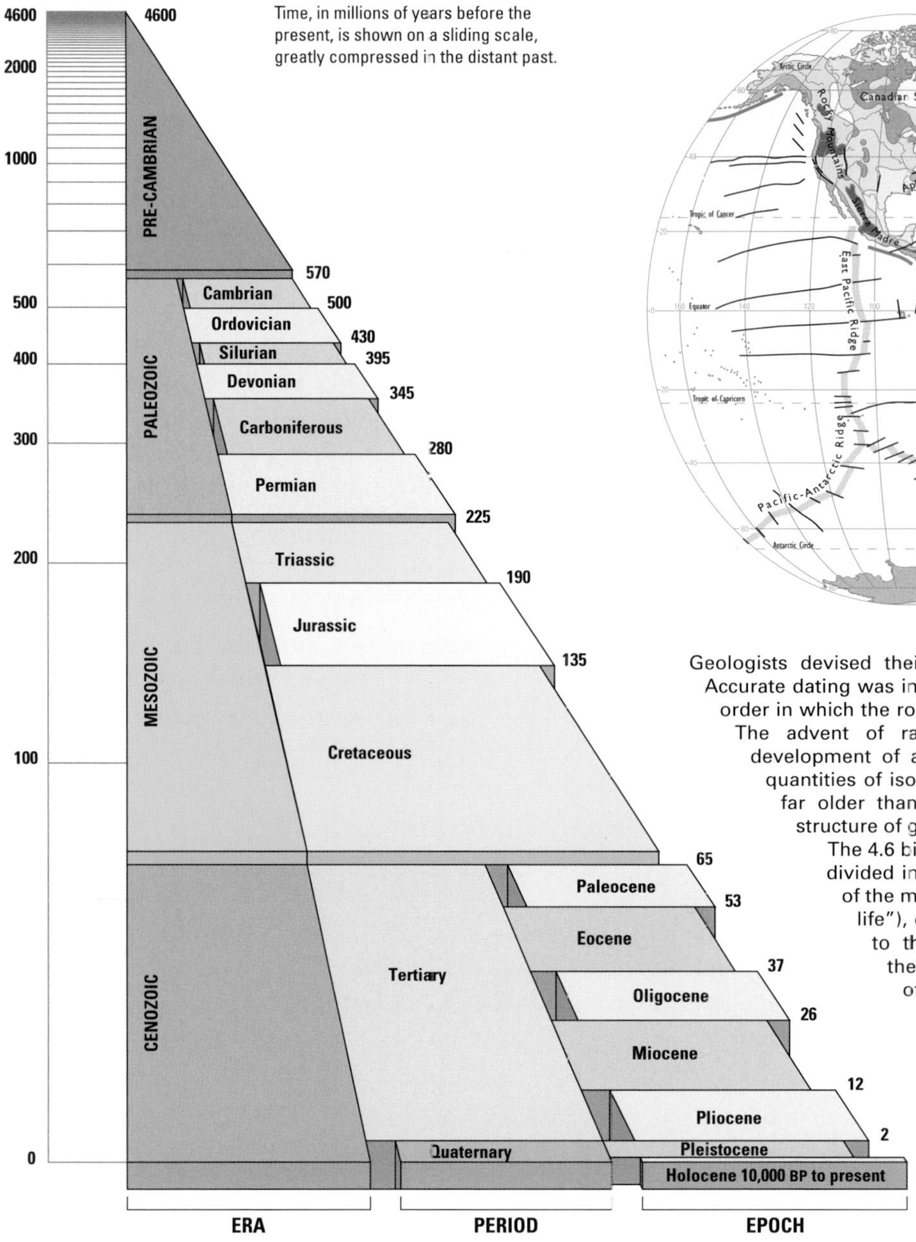

Time, in millions of years before the present, is shown on a sliding scale, greatly compressed in the distant past.

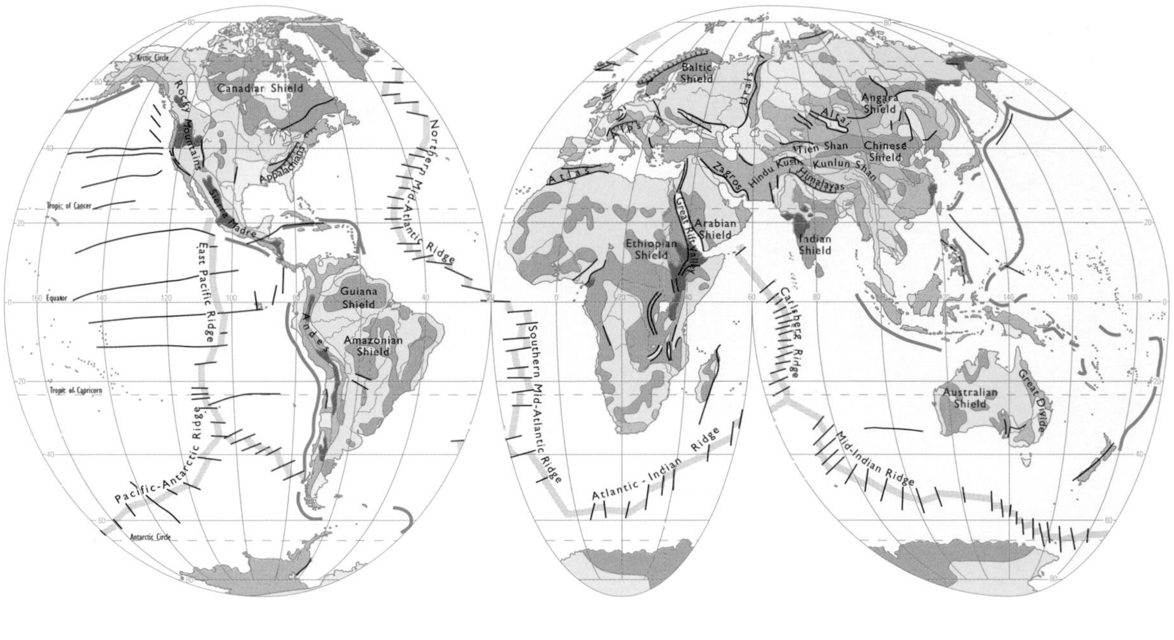

4600

PRE-CAMBRIAN	4600
Cambrian	570
Ordovician	500
Silurian	430
Devonian	395
Carboniferous	345
Permian	280
Triassic	225
Jurassic	190
Cretaceous	135
Paleocene	65
Eocene	53
Oligocene	37
Miocene	26
Pliocene	12
Pleistocene	2
Holocene 10,000 BP to present	

ERA — PERIOD — EPOCH

Geologists devised their timescale on the basis of relative, not calendar, ages. Accurate dating was impossible and estimates were often bitterly disputed, but the order in which the rocks were formed could be deduced from careful observation. The advent of radioactive dating – culminating in the 1950s with the development of a mass spectrometer capable of accurately measuring tiny quantities of isotopes – appears to have settled the arguments. The Earth is far older than geologists first imagined, but their painstakingly-created structure of geological time has withstood the advent of high technology.

The 4.6 billion (4,600 million) years since the formation of the Earth are divided into four great eras, further split into periods and, in the case of the most recent era, epochs. The present era is the Cenozoic ("new life"), extending backward through "middle life" and "ancient life" to the Pre-Cambrian, named after the Latin word for Wales, the location of some of the earliest known fossils. Most of the Earth's geological history is encompassed by the Pre-Cambrian: though traces of ancient life have since been found, it was largely the proliferation of fossils from the beginning of the Paleozoic era onward, some 570 million years ago, which first allowed precise subdivisions to be made.

Like the Cambrian, most are named after regions exemplifying a period's geology. Others – such as the Carboniferous ("coal-bearing") or the Cretaceous ("chalk-bearing") – are more directly descriptive.

- Pre-Cambrian shields
- Sedimentary cover on Pre-Cambrian shields
- Paleozoic (Caledonian and Hercynian) folding
- Sedimentary cover on Paleozoic folding
- Mesozoic folding
- Sedimentary cover on Mesozoic folding
- Cenozoic (Alpine) folding
- Sedimentary cover on Cenozoic folding
- Intensive Mesozoic and Cenozoic vulcanism
- Principal faults
- Oceanic marginal troughs
- Midoceanic ridges
- Overthrust faults

EARTHQUAKES

Earthquake magnitude is usually rated according to either the Richter or the Modified Mercalli scale, both devised by seismologists in the 1930s. The Richter scale measures absolute earthquake power with mathematical precision: each step upward represents a tenfold increase in the amplitude of the shockwave. Theoretically, there is no upper limit, but most of the largest earthquakes measured have been rated at between 8.8 and 8.9. The 12-point Mercalli scale, based on observed effects, is often more meaningful, ranging from I (earthquakes noticed only by seismographs) to XII (total destruction); intermediate points include V (people awakened at night; unstable objects overturned), VII (collapse of ordinary buildings; chimneys and monuments fall), and IX (conspicuous cracks in ground; serious damage to reservoirs).

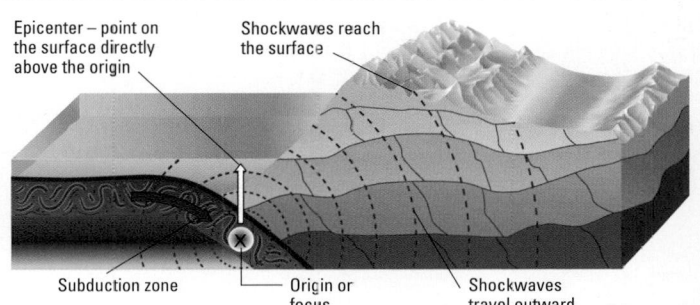

Epicenter – point on the surface directly above the origin

Shockwaves reach the surface

Subduction zone

Origin or focus

Shockwaves travel outward

Notable Earthquakes Since 1900

Year	Location	Mag.	Deaths
1906	San Francisco, USA	8.3	3,000
1906	Valparaiso, Chile	8.6	22,000
1908	Messina, Italy	7.5	83,000
1915	Avezzano, Italy	7.5	30,000
1920	Gansu (Kansu), China	8.6	180,000
1923	Yokohama, Japan	8.3	143,000
1927	Nan Shan, China	8.3	200,000
1932	Gansu (Kansu), China	7.6	70,000
1933	Sanriku, Japan	8.9	2,990
1934	Bihar, India/Nepal	8.4	10,700
1935	Quetta, India*	7.5	60,000
1939	Chillan, Chile	8.3	28,000
1939	Erzincan, Turkey	7.9	30,000
1960	S.W. Chile	9.5	2,200
1960	Agadir, Morocco	5.8	12,000
1962	Khorasan, Iran	7.1	12,230
1964	Anchorage, USA	9.2	125
1968	N. E. Iran	7.4	12,000
1970	N. Peru	7.8	70,000
1972	Managua, Nicaragua	6.2	5,000
1974	N. Pakistan	6.3	5,200
1976	Guatemala	7.5	22,500
1976	Tangshan, China	8.2	255,000
1978	Tabas, Iran	7.7	25,000
1980	El Asnam, Algeria	7.3	20,000
1980	S. Italy	7.2	4,800
1985	Mexico City, Mexico	8.1	4,200
1988	N.W. Armenia	6.8	55,000
1990	N. Iran	7.7	36,000
1992	Flores, Indonesia	6.8	1,895
1993	Maharashtra, India	6.4	30,000
1994	Los Angeles, USA	6.6	51
1995	Kobe, Japan	7.2	5,000
1995	Sakhalin Is., Russia	7.5	2,000
1996	Yunnan, China	7.0	240
1997	N. E. Iran	7.1	2,400
1998	Takhar, Afghanistan	6.1	4,200
1998	Rostaq, Afghanistan	7.0	5,000
1999	Izmit, Turkey	7.4	15,000
1999	Taipei, Taiwan	7.6	1,700
2001	Gujarat, India	7.7	14,000
2002	Afyon, Turkey	6.5	44
2002	Baghlan, Afghanistan	6.1	1,000
2003	Boumerdes, Algeria	6.8	2,200
2003	Bam, Iran	6.6	30,000
2004	Sumatra, Indonesia	9.0	250,000

An earthquake off the coast of Sumatra on December 26, 2004, triggered a deadly tsunami that swept across the Indian Ocean, causing devastation in many countries, in particular Sri Lanka, India, Thailand, and Indonesia, where the loss of life was greatest.

* now Pakistan

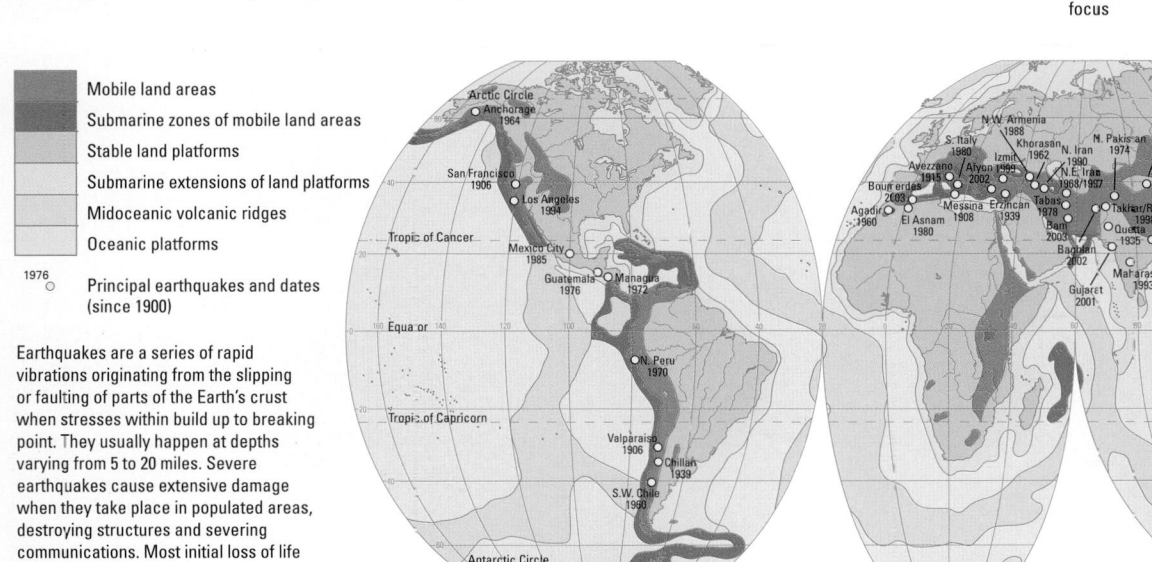

- Mobile land areas
- Submarine zones of mobile land areas
- Stable land platforms
- Submarine extensions of land platforms
- Midoceanic volcanic ridges
- Oceanic platforms

1976 ○ Principal earthquakes and dates (since 1900)

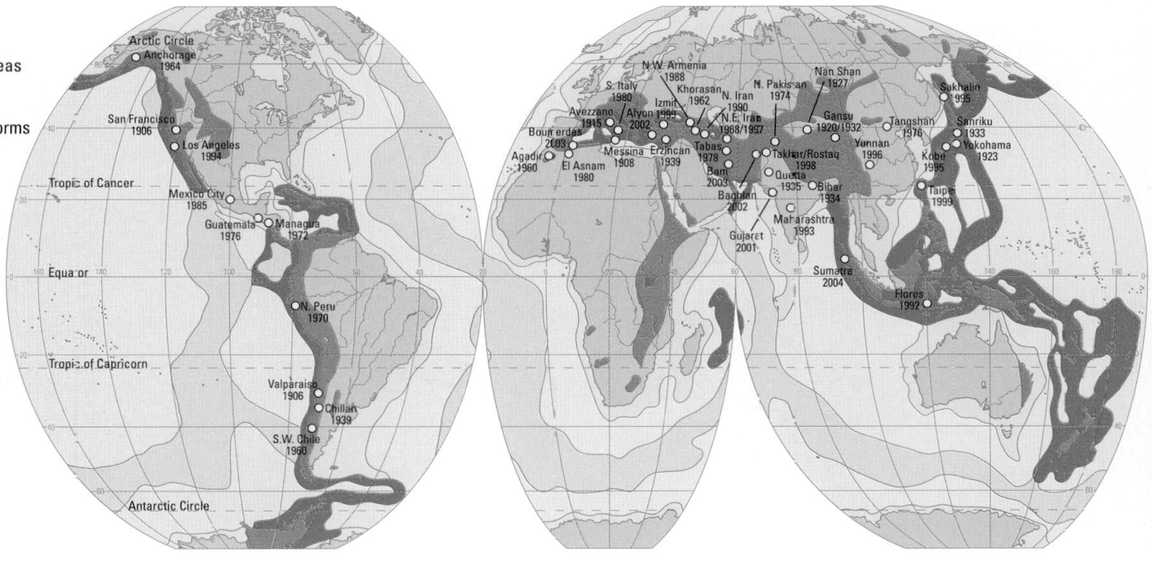

Earthquakes are a series of rapid vibrations originating from the slipping or faulting of parts of the Earth's crust when stresses within build up to breaking point. They usually happen at depths varying from 5 to 20 miles. Severe earthquakes cause extensive damage when they take place in populated areas, destroying structures and severing communications. Most initial loss of life occurs due to secondary causes such as falling masonry, fires, and flooding.

LANDFORMS

For more information:
8 The Earth's structure
   Plate tectonics
   Volcanoes
9 Geological time
12 Oceans
18 Hydrological cycle
37 Structural regions

The theory of plate tectonics has offered new insights into how the Earth works, elucidating mysteries concerning continental drift, volcanic eruptions, and earthquakes. It has also contributed to our understanding of how collisions between plates can squeeze up layers of sediments on seabeds, forming fold mountain ranges, such as the Himalayas.

Yet even as mountains rise, natural forces are wearing them away. In hot, dry climates, mechanical weathering (a result of rapid temperature changes) causes the outer layers of rocks to peel away, while, in cold mountain regions, boulders are prised apart when water freezes in cracks in rocks. Chemical weathering is responsible for hollowing out limestone caves and decomposing granites.

Climatic conditions have a great bearing on the principal agent of erosion in any particular area. Running water is most important in moist temperate regions. In cold regions, ice is the major agent of erosion, and in many mountain ranges, U-shaped valleys are evidence of the erosive power of valley glaciers.

Ice sheets molded much of the Earth's surface during the Ice Ages, the most recent of which, in the northern hemisphere, ended only 10,000 years ago. Polar climates also shape the scenery of the periglacial areas that border bodies of ice. Such areas are subject to constant freeze-thaw action, which creates such features as pingos (domed mounds).

Climatic change has also affected many of the landforms in hot deserts, which were shaped by running water at a time when the deserts enjoyed much wetter climates. However, the major agent of erosion in deserts today is wind-blown sand, which erodes rock strata to form mushroom-shaped rocks and caves.

The surface of the Earth is under constant assault from tectonic processes and the agents of erosion. The products of erosion, fragments of rock such as sand, are deposited to form sedimentary rocks. Metamorphic rocks are created when igneous or sedimentary rocks are buried and metamorphosed by heat and pressure. Eventually the rocks are recycled to form magma, which rises upward to start the rock cycle all over again.

THE ROCK CYCLE

James Hutton first proposed the rock cycle in the late 1700s after he observed the slow but steady effects of erosion.

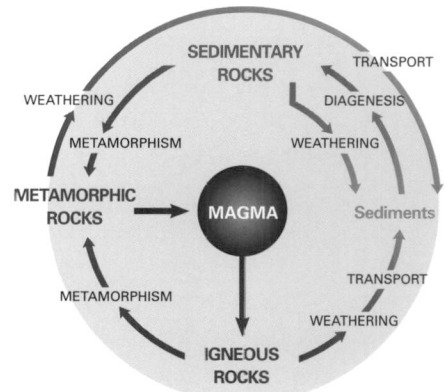

Rocks are divided into three types, according to the way in which they are formed:

Igneous rocks, including granite and basalt, are formed when magma cools inside the Earth's crust or on the surface.

Metamorphic rocks, such as slate, marble, and quartzite, are formed below the Earth's surface by the compression or baking of existing rocks.

Sedimentary rocks, like sandstone and limestone, are formed on the surface of the Earth from the remains of living organisms and eroded fragments of older rocks.

MOUNTAIN BUILDING

Mountains are formed when pressures on the Earth's crust caused by continental drift become so intense that the surface buckles or cracks. This happens where oceanic crust is subducted by continental crust or, more dramatically, where two tectonic plates collide: the Rockies, Andes, Alps, Urals, and Himalayas resulted from such impacts. These are known as fold mountains because they were formed by the compression of the rocks. The Himalayas were formed from the folded former sediments of the Tethys Sea, which was trapped in the collision zone between the Indian–Australian and Eurasian plates.

The other main mountain-building processes occur when the crust fractures to create faults, allowing rock to be forced upward in large blocks, or when the pressure of magma within the crust forces the surface to bulge into a dome, or erupts to form a volcano.

Large mountain ranges may reveal a combination of these features. The Alps, for example, have been compressed so violently that the folds are fragmented by numerous faults and intrusions of molten igneous rock.

Over millions of years, even the greatest mountain ranges can be reduced by the agents of erosion (especially rivers) to a low, rugged landscape known as a peneplain.

Types of faults: Faults occur where the crust is being stretched or compressed so violently that the rock strata break in a horizontal or vertical movement. They are classified by the direction in which the blocks of rock have moved. A normal fault results when a vertical movement causes the surface to break apart; compression causes a reverse fault. Horizontal movement causes shearing, known as a strike-slip fault. When the rock breaks in two places, the central block may be pushed up in a horst fault, or sink (creating a rift valley) in a graben fault.

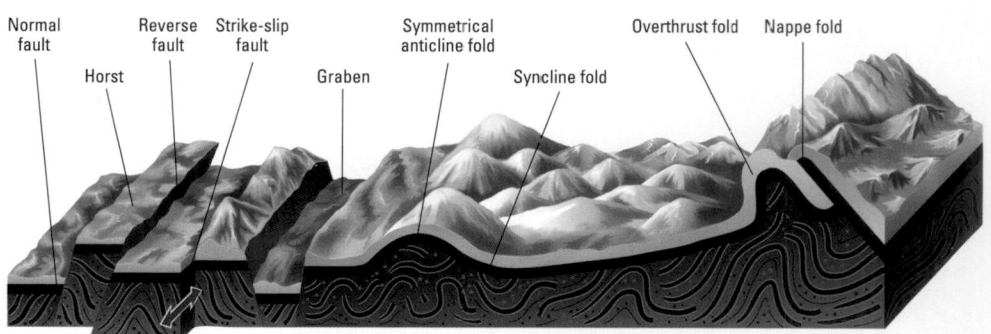

Normal fault | Reverse fault | Strike-slip fault | Horst | Graben | Symmetrical anticline fold | Syncline fold | Overthrust fold | Nappe fold

Types of fold: Folds occur when rock strata are squeezed and compressed. They are common, therefore, at destructive plate margins and where plates have collided, forcing the rocks to buckle into mountain ranges. Geographers give different names to the degrees of fold that result from continuing pressure on the rock. A simple fold may be symmetric, with even slopes on either side, but as the pressure builds up, one slope becomes steeper and the fold becomes asymmetric. Later, the ridge or "anticline" at the top of the fold may slide over the lower ground or "syncline" to form a recumbent fold. Eventually, the rock strata may break under the pressure to form an overthrust and finally a nappe fold.

CONTINENTAL GLACIATION

Many landforms in the northern hemisphere were shaped by ice sheets and meltwater during the Pleistocene Ice Age, which began about 2 million years ago. During the Ice Age, the ice sheets periodically advanced and retreated. The first map (*below left*) shows the ice cover at its greatest extent about 200,000 years BP (before the present), when it covered about 30% of the land surface, as compared with 10% today. About 18,000 years BP, the ice covered most of Canada and extended as far south as the Bristol Channel in England. Around the ice sheets, land areas experienced periglacial conditions.

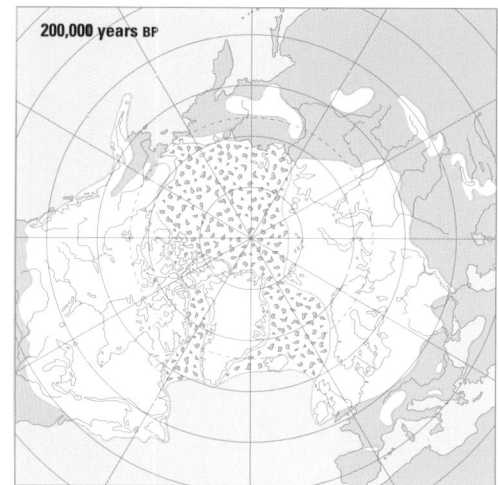

200,000 years BP

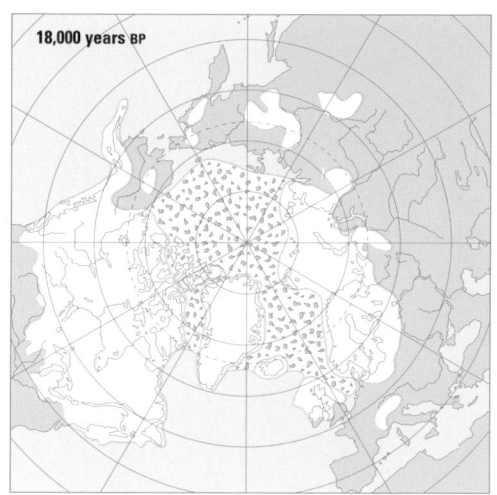

18,000 years BP

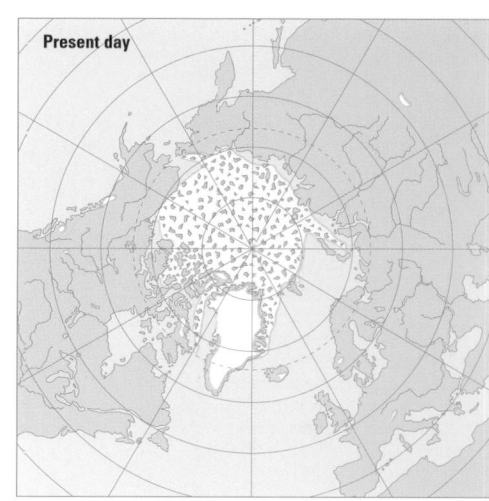

Present day

NATURAL LANDFORMS

Natural landforms reflect the influence of plate tectonics, through mountain-building and the generation of new rocks from the Earth's interior, together with the agents of erosion – running water, ice, winds, and coastal waves. Over millions of years, mountains are gradually eroded, with the eroded material redistributed, usually at lower levels. The resultant landforms reflect the major forces that have been at work, as well as the underlying geology, the climatic conditions, which often vary over time, and the vegetation cover. The study of these processes and the landforms they create is called geomorphology. The stylized diagram (*below*) shows some major natural landforms found in the mid-latitudes.

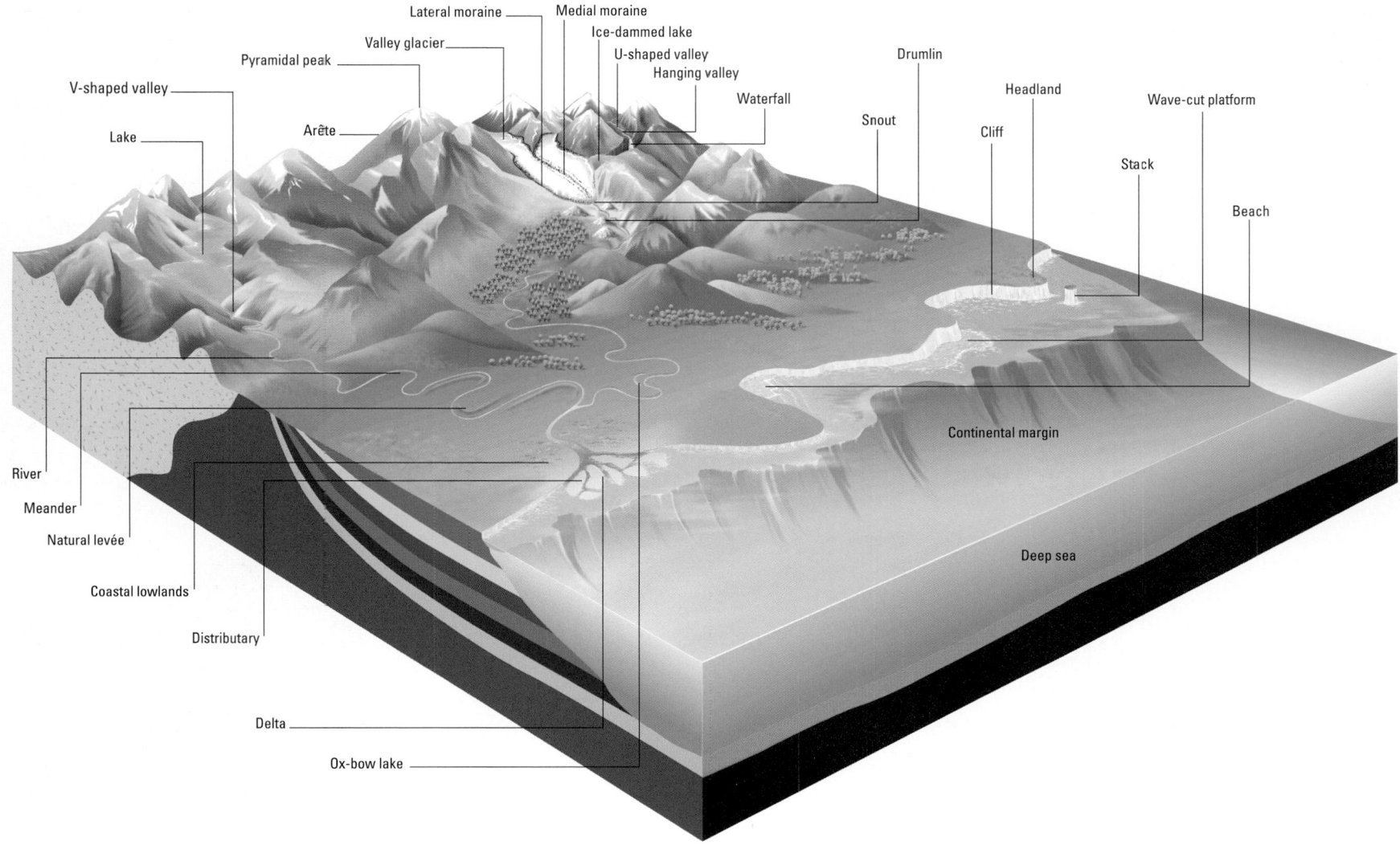

Lateral moraine
Medial moraine
Valley glacier
Ice-dammed lake
Pyramidal peak
U-shaped valley
Drumlin
V-shaped valley
Hanging valley
Headland
Waterfall
Wave-cut platform
Lake
Snout
Cliff
Stack
Arête
Beach

River
Meander
Natural levée
Coastal lowlands
Distributary
Continental margin
Deep sea
Delta
Ox-bow lake

SURFACE PROCESSES

Catastrophic changes to landforms are caused periodically by such phenomena as avalanches, landslides, and volcanic eruptions, but most of the processes that shape the Earth's surface operate extremely slowly in human terms.

Chemical weathering is at its greatest in warm, humid regions, while mechanical weathering (the physical breakup of rocks) predominates in cold mountain or hot desert regions. The most familiar type of chemical weathering is caused by the reaction of rainwater containing dissolved carbon dioxide on limestone; this leads to the creation of labyrinthine cave networks dissolved by groundwater. Mechanical weathering includes frost action, while in hot deserts, rapid temperature changes cause the outer layers of rocks to expand and contract until they crack and peel away, a process called exfoliation.

Running water is probably the world's leading agent of erosion and transportation. The energy of a river depends on several factors, including its velocity and volume, and its erosive power is at its peak when it is in full flood, sweeping soil, pebbles and even boulders along its course, cutting downward into the bedrock or widening its valley.

Sea waves also exert tremendous erosive power during storms, when they hurl pebbles and large rocks against the shore, undercutting cliffs and hollowing out caves. Headlands are often attacked on both sides, forming caves, then a natural arch and eventually an isolated stack.

Glacier ice forms in mountain hollows, called cirques, and spills out to form valley glaciers, which transport rocks shattered by frost action. As a glacier moves, rocks embedded in the base and sides scrape away bedrock, eroding steep-sided, flat-bottomed, U-shaped valleys. Evidence of past glaciation in mountain regions includes cirques, knife-edged ridges, or arêtes, and pyramidal peaks, or horns.

DESERT LANDFORMS

Deserts are defined as places with an average annual precipitation of 10 inches [250 mm] per year, though places with a higher rainfall and a high evaporation rate may also qualify as deserts.

The three types of desert landforms are known by their Arabic names, a reflection of the fact that the Sahara in North Africa is the world's largest desert. Sand desert, called *erg*, covers about one-fifth of the world's deserts. The rest is divided between *hammada* (areas of bare rock) and *reg* (broad plains covered by loose gravel or pebbles).

The shapes of dunes in sand deserts reflect the character of local winds. Where winds are constant in direction, the sand often piles up in crescent-shaped dunes, called *barchans*. Barchans are constantly on the move and their forward march, unless halted by vegetation, may overwhelm settlements at oases. *Seif* dunes, named after the Arabic word for "sword," are long ridges of sand that lie parallel to the direction of the wind, but where winds are variable, the sand sheets are often featureless.

Wind-blown sand is an effective agent of erosion, but because of the weight of sand grains, this type of erosion is confined to within approximately 7 feet [2 meters] of the land surface, creating caves and mushroom-shaped rocks.

In assessing desert landforms, it is important to remember that other processes were at work in the past when the climate was very different from today. For example, cave paintings suggest that the Sahara had a much wetter climate after the end of the Ice Age and only began to dry up after about 5000 BC. However, human action, including overgrazing and the cutting down of trees for firewood, can turn a grassland region into desert – a process known as desertification.

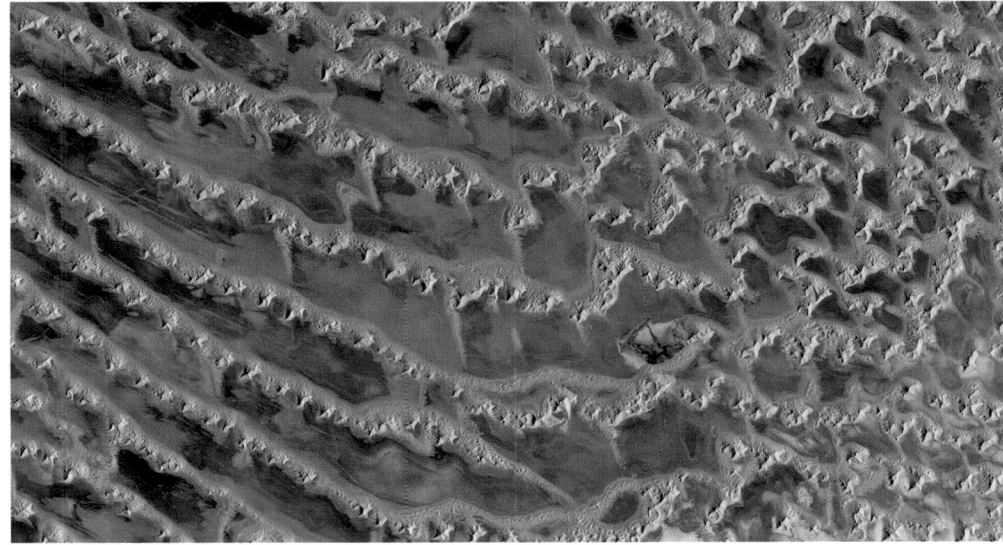

◀ This false-color satellite image of part of the Rub' al Khali, or "Empty Quarter," in Saudi Arabia shows part of the world's largest sand sea (*erg*), which covers almost 232,000 sq miles [600,000 sq km]. Showing many different types of sand dune, the image enhances the difference in color between the dune sand and the interdune areas, which have a higher clay composition. The blue "eye" is a partially flooded clay basin (*playa*).

OCEANS

For more information:

7 Tides
8 Plate tectonics
14 Atmosphere
18 Hydrological cycle
   Water distribution
19 Watersheds
23 Water pollution
41 World shipping

The last 40 years have been described as the "Space Age," but another exciting and perhaps even more important area of discovery, proceeding at the same time, has been the exploration of the oceans which cover more than 70% of our planet. Studies of the ocean floor and oceanic islands have revealed features that help to explain how continents move, and how the movements are related to earthquakes and volcanic activity.

Manned submersibles have established that life exists even in the deepest trenches, where the pressure reaches 1,000 atmospheres, the equivalent of the force of six and a half tons bearing down on every square inch. Further exploration in the pitch-black environment of the ocean ridges has revealed strange forms of marine life around scalding hot vents. The creatures include giant tubeworms, blind shrimps, and bacteria, some of which are genetically very different from any other known life forms. In 1996, an analysis of one microorganism revealed that at least half of its 1,700 or so genes were hitherto unknown. This environment, which is based on chemicals, not sunlight, may resemble the places where life on Earth first began.

Another vital area of contemporary research concerns the interactions between the oceans and the atmosphere, as exemplified in the El Niño–Southern Oscillation (ENSO) cycle, and the bearing that these have on climatic change (*see below*).

Most geographers divide the world's ocean waters into four areas: the Pacific, Atlantic, Indian, and Arctic oceans. The most active zone in the oceans is the sunlit upper layer, where the water is moved around by wind-blown currents. It is the home of most sea life and acts as a membrane through which the ocean breathes,

LIFE IN THE OCEANS

An imaginary profile of the typical coastal and oceanic zones is shown, with a selection of the life forms that might occur in the waters off the Pacific Coast of Central America. The animals illustrated are not drawn to scale as the range of sizes is too great. Most marine life is confined to the first 650 feet, the upper sunlit (photic) zone, where sunlight can still penetrate. Plant and animal plankton, the basis of life in the oceans, occur in great quantities in all zones.

In the pelagic environment (open sea), vertical gradients, including those of light, temperature, and salinity, determine the distribution of organisms. From the tidal zone at the coastline, the continental shelf, geologically still part of the continental land mass, drops gently to about 650 feet – the sunlit zone. At the end of the shelf, the seabed falls away in the steeper angle of the continental slope. The subsequent descent to the deep-ocean floor, known as the continental rise, is more gentle, with gradients between 1 in 100 and 1 in 700 until the abyssal plains and hills between 8,000 and 19,500 feet below the surface.

The deep-sea floor contains seamounts, some of which are capped by coral reefs, ocean ridges – the longest mountain chains on Earth – and deep-ocean trenches, especially in the Pacific Ocean where six trenches reach depths of more than 33,000 feet, including the Mariana Trench at 36,161 feet deep.

Each of these zones contains a distinctive community of species adapted to the different conditions of salinity, temperature, and light intensity. Indeed, a few organisms have been found even in the abyssal darkness of the great ocean trenches.

absorbing great quantities of carbon dioxide and partly exchanging it for oxygen.

As the depth increases, so light fades and temperatures fall until just before 3,000 feet where there is a marked temperature change at the thermocline, the boundary between the warm surface zone and the cold deep zone. Below the thermocline, slow currents are caused by density differences between bodies of water with varying temperatures and salinity.

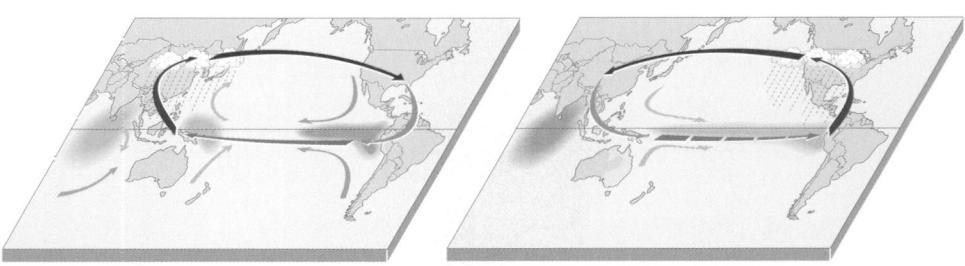

Normal year – Walker Circulation Cell

El Niño event

ATOLL BUILDING

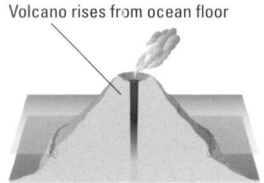

Volcano rises from ocean floor

Fringing reef

Extinct, eroding volcanic island

After subsidence, reef covers buried volcanic island

Lagoon

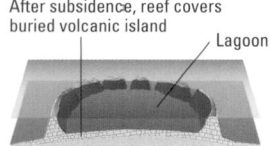

A coral atoll usually begins existence as a bare volcanic peak, thrusting above the surface of the ocean. A colony of coral – organisms with calcium carbonate skeletons – forms itself in the shallow water around the peak. The volcano is eroded and slowly sinks, leaving the coral forming a ring of hard limestone around its remnant. In time, the barrier reef of an atoll is all that remains.

EL NIÑO PHENOMENON

The importance of the ocean–atmosphere interaction is nowhere more dramatically demonstrated than in the El Niño phenomenon of the southern Pacific Ocean. Under normal conditions, called La Niña, cold, nutrient-rich water rises to the surface and spreads westward. In the western Pacific, sea surface temperatures reach 82°F or more and warm air rises, creating a low-pressure air system and causing heavy rains. The rising air spreads out and some of it descends over South America and the eastern Pacific, creating a high-pressure air system from which winds blow westward. This rotating system is called a Walker Circulation Cell.

An El Niño event is characterized by a reversal of currents. The upwelling of cold water off South America is greatly reduced and surface water temperatures rise, causing a drastic reduction in fish life. The heaviest rainfall is over the eastern Pacific, while Southeast Asia is drier than usual.

During an intense El Niño, the effects of the current and wind reversals affect the weather around the world. In 1982–3, the monsoon rainfall was reduced in Australia and Southeast Asia, while in 1983–4 a severe drought occurred in the Sahel, south of the Sahara, and also in southern Africa. The southeast coast of the United States suffered storms and heavy rainfall, and even Europe experienced changes in weather patterns, possibly as a result of consequent changes in the course of the jet stream.

Scientists have found evidence that the frequency of the El Niño event, which normally occurs every three to seven years, and lasts between 12–18 months, may have increased in recent years. Another intense El Niño occurred in 1997–8, with resultant freak weather conditions across the entire Pacific region.

We do not fully understand the causes of the El Niño event, though some researchers are investigating possible connections between major volcanic eruptions in the tropical Pacific region, the ENSO cycle, and atmospheric circulation.

Crab
Seaweed
SEA LEVEL
Jellyfish
Anchovy
Green turtle
Dolphin

SUNLIT ZONE
650 feet

Marlin
Snake eel
Bonito
Blue Whale

TWILIGHT ZONE
3,000 feet

Phytoplankton and zooplankton
Lantern fish
Ray
Sperm whale

DARK ZONE
19,500 feet

Deep-sea squid

Anglerfish
Halosaur
Sea cucumber
Sponge

TRENCH ZONE
33,000 feet

Isopod

OCEAN CURRENTS

JANUARY CURRENTS AND TEMPERATURES
(Northern Hemisphere: winter)

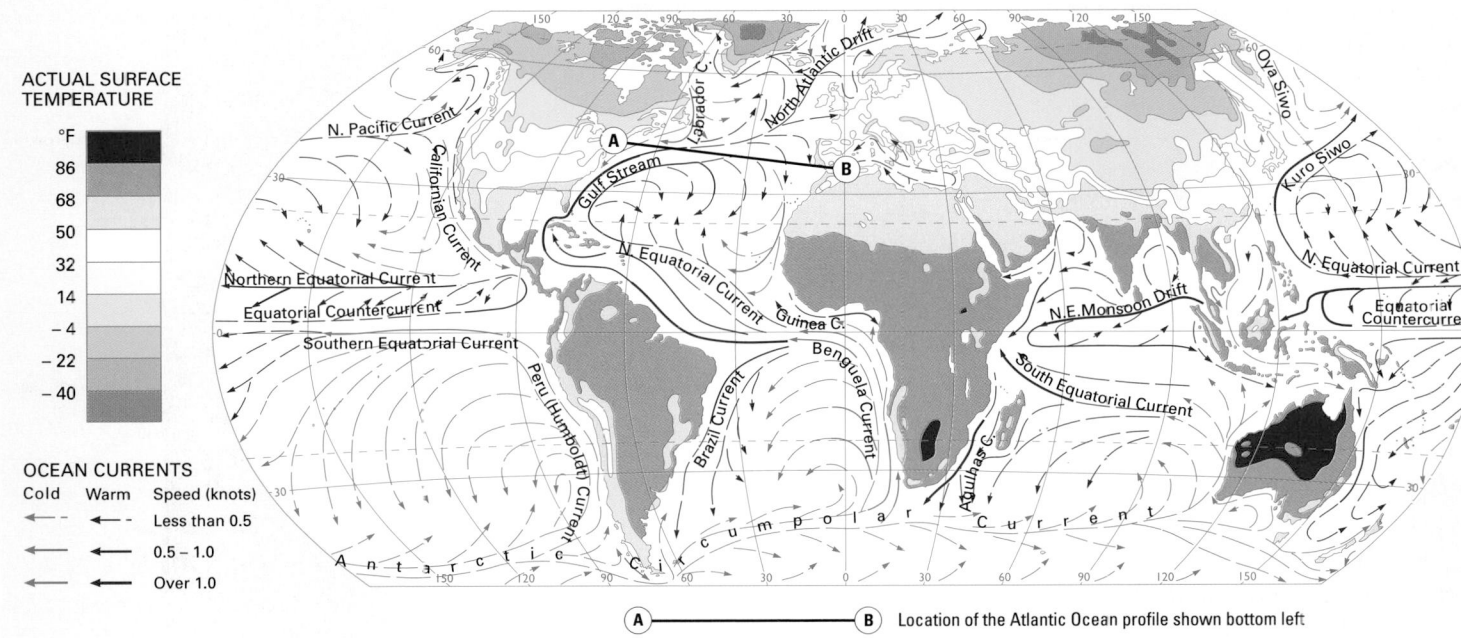

ACTUAL SURFACE
TEMPERATURE

°F

86	
68	
50	
32	
14	
- 4	
- 22	
- 40	

OCEAN CURRENTS

Cold	Warm	Speed (knots)
← – –	← – –	Less than 0.5
←	←	0.5 – 1.0
←	←	Over 1.0

(A) ———————————— (B) Location of the Atlantic Ocean profile shown bottom left

JULY CURRENTS AND TEMPERATURES
(Northern Hemisphere: summer)

ACTUAL SURFACE
TEMPERATURE

°F

86	
68	
50	
32	
14	

OCEAN CURRENTS

Cold	Warm	Speed (knots)
← – –	← – –	Less than 0.5
←	←	0.5 – 1.0
←	←	Over 1.0

Moving immense quantities of energy as well as billions of tons of water every hour, the ocean currents are a vital part of the great heat engine that drives the Earth's climate. They themselves are produced by a twofold mechanism. At the surface, winds push huge masses of water before them; in the deep ocean, below an abrupt temperature gradient that separates the churning surface waters from the still depths, density variations cause slow vertical movements.

Coriolis effect
The pattern of circulation of the great surface currents is determined by the displacement known as the *Coriolis effect*. As the Earth turns, the vast mass of ocean water is deflected to one side. The deflection is most obvious near the equator, where the Earth's surface is spinning eastward at 1,000 mph; currents moving poleward are curved clockwise in the northern hemisphere and counterclockwise in the southern hemisphere.

Ocean currents
The result is a system of spinning circles known as "gyres." Warm currents move constantly from the equator toward the poles, while cold water moves in the reverse direction. In this way, ocean currents act like a thermostat, helping to regulate temperatures around the world.
Depending on the annual movements of the prevailing wind belts, some currents on or near the equator may reverse their direction in the course of the year, a variation on which Asia's monsoon rains depend and whose occasional failure has brought disaster to millions of people.

TOPOGRAPHY OF THE OCEAN FLOOR

Profile of the Atlantic Ocean

The deep-ocean floor was once believed to be flat, but sonar readings have shown that it is no more uniform than the surface of the continents. The profile (*below*) shows some of the features on the Atlantic Ocean floor between Massachusetts in North America and Gibraltar (*for location of profile, see maps above*).

Around the continents are shallow continental shelves composed of rocks that are less dense than the underlying oceanic crust. The continents end at the top of the steep continental slope, which descends to the abyss via the continental rise, made up of sediments washed down from the continental shelves.

The abyss contains large plains overlain by oozes but broken by volcanic seamounts and guyots (flat-topped seamounts), a few of which reach the surface as islands. The Mid-Atlantic Ridge contains a rift valley where new crustal rock is being formed as the plates on either side move apart.

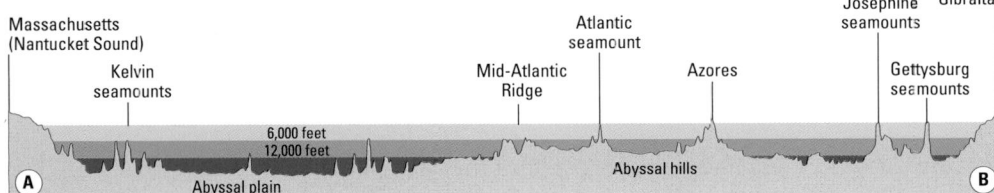

Topography of the ocean floor around Australia

In the image on the right, land areas are shown in gray, with shaded relief. The colors represent sea depths, with red representing the shallowest areas, through yellow and green to dark blue (the deepest). The data for the sea topography are from the Seasat radar satellite. The deep blue area in the upper left is the Java Trench, which forms the boundary between the Indian–Australian plate and the Eurasian plate. In the top right, the New Guinea trench, which has a maximum depth of 29,865 feet, forms the border of the Indian–Australian and Pacific plates. Alongside the trenches are volcanic islands formed from magma, created as the edge of the Indian–Australian plate is subducted and melted.

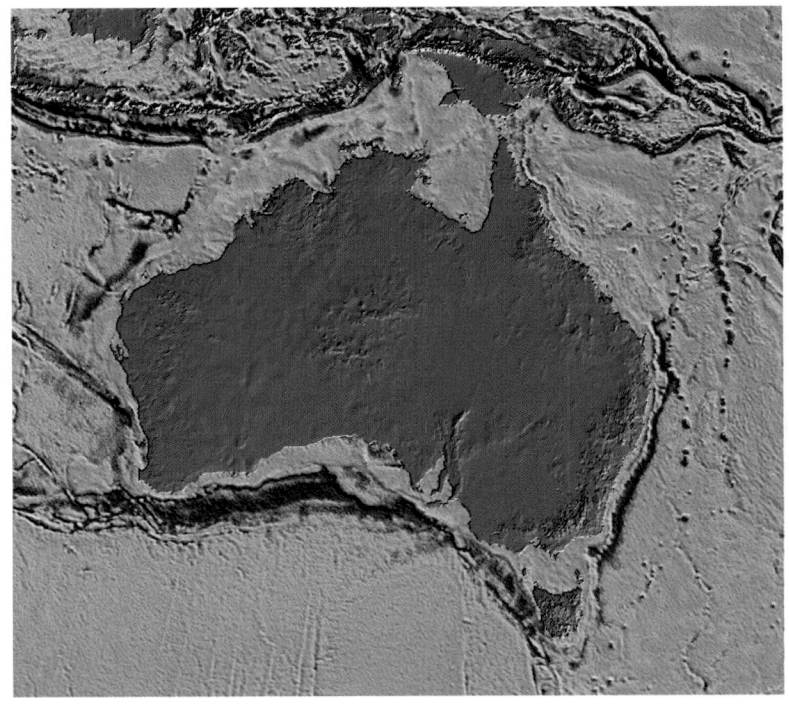

THE ATMOSPHERE

For more information:
13 Ocean currents
17 Beaufort wind scale
   Climate change
   Monsoon
21 Solar energy
   Greenhouse effect
22 Greenhouse power
23 Acid rain

The atmosphere is a meteor shield, a radiation deflector, a thermal blanket, and a source of chemical energy for the Earth's diverse life forms. Five-sixths of its mass is in the lowest layer, the troposphere, which ranges in thickness from 11–6 miles between the equator and the poles. Powered by the Sun, the air is always on the move, flowing generally from high- to low-pressure areas. The troposphere is the layer where virtually all weather phenomena, including clouds, precipitation and winds, occur. Above the troposphere is the stratosphere, which contains the important ozone layer and extends to about 30 miles above the Earth's surface. Beyond 60 miles, atmospheric density is lower than most laboratory vacuums.

STRUCTURE OF THE ATMOSPHERE

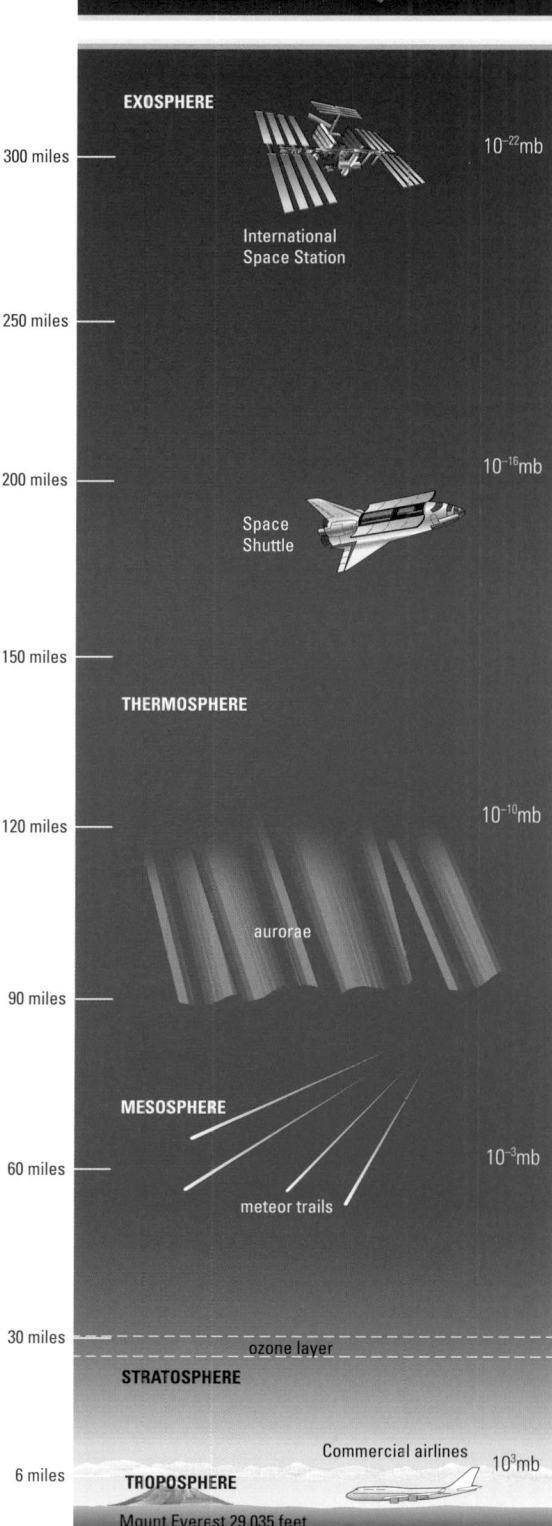

400 miles — Hubble Space Telescope — pressure 10⁻³⁵mb

EXOSPHERE

300 miles — 10⁻²²mb

International Space Station

250 miles

200 miles — Space Shuttle — 10⁻¹⁶mb

150 miles

THERMOSPHERE

120 miles — 10⁻¹⁰mb

aurorae

90 miles

MESOSPHERE

60 miles — 10⁻³mb

meteor trails

30 miles — ozone layer

STRATOSPHERE

6 miles — Commercial airlines — 10³mb

TROPOSPHERE

Mount Everest 29,035 feet

CIRCULATION OF THE AIR

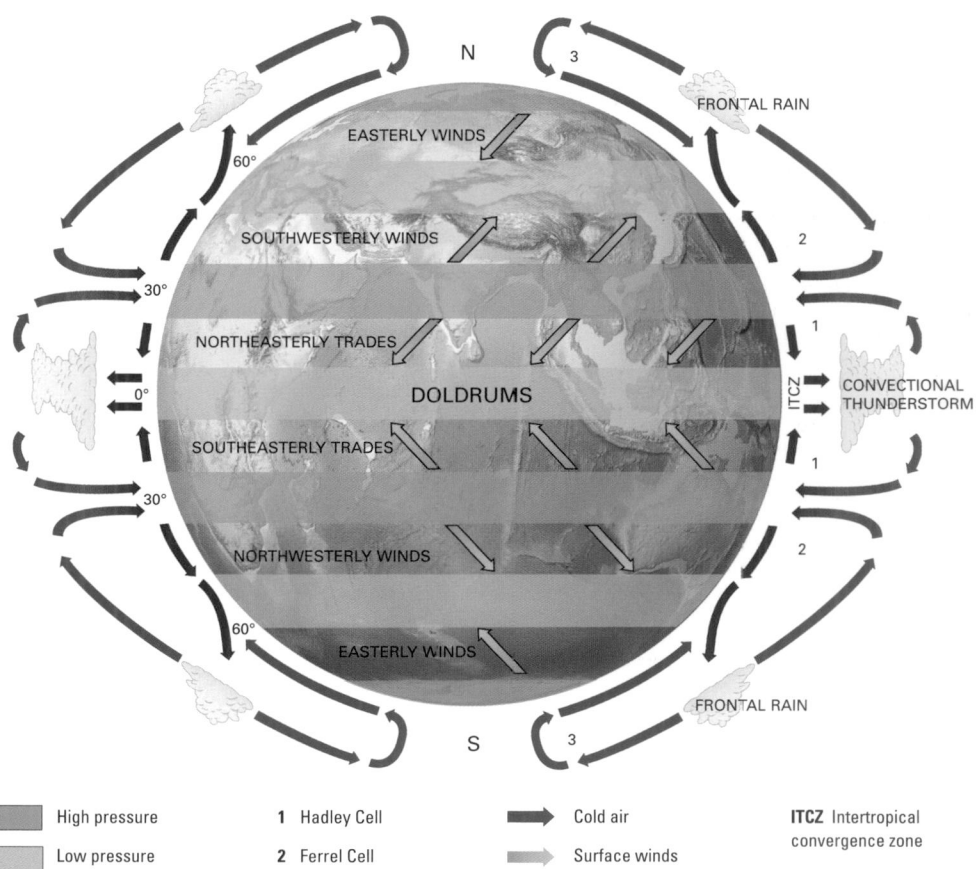

N
3
FRONTAL RAIN
EASTERLY WINDS
60°
SOUTHWESTERLY WINDS
2
30°
NORTHEASTERLY TRADES
1
ITCZ
0° DOLDRUMS — CONVECTIONAL THUNDERSTORM
SOUTHEASTERLY TRADES
1
30°
NORTHWESTERLY WINDS
2
60°
EASTERLY WINDS
FRONTAL RAIN
S
3

High pressure	1 Hadley Cell	Cold air →	ITCZ Intertropical convergence zone
Low pressure	2 Ferrel Cell	Surface winds →	
Warm air →	3 Polar Cell	Clouds	

FRONTAL SYSTEMS

Depressions, or cyclones, form along the polar front where dense polar easterlies meet warm subtropical westerlies. Depressions occur when warm air flows into waves in the polar front, while cold air flows in behind it, creating rotating air systems that bring changeable weather.

Along the warm front (the boundary on the ground between the warm and cold air), the warm air flows upward over the cold air, producing a sequence of clouds that help forecasters to predict a depression's advance. Along the cold front, the advancing cold air forces warm air to rise steeply. Towering cumulonimbus clouds form in the rising air.

When the cold front overtakes the warm front, the warm air is pushed above ground level to form an occluded front. Cloud and rain persist along occlusions until temperatures equalize, the air mixes, and the depression dies out.

Depressions with these distinctive features are known as "frontal." The diagram below shows a cross-section through a depression and the associated cloud types and weather conditions that may be experienced.

CHEMICAL COMPOSITION

Gaseous composition of the principal atmospheric layers

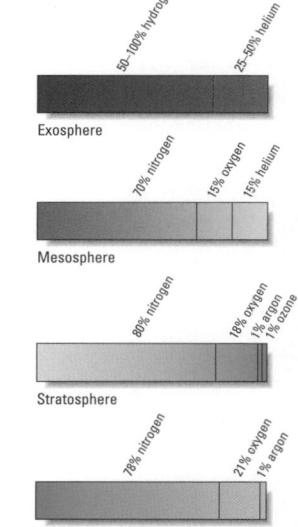

50–100% hydrogen | 25–50% helium
Exosphere

Helium vanishes with increasing altitude. Above 1,500 miles the exosphere is almost entirely composed of hydrogen.

70% nitrogen | 15% oxygen | 15% helium
Mesosphere

The high energy of mesospheric gas gives it a notional temperature of more than 3,600°F, although its density is negligible.

80% nitrogen | 18% oxygen | 1% argon | 1% ozone
Stratosphere

Stratospheric air contains enough ozone to make it poisonous, although it is in any case too rarified to breathe.

78% nitrogen | 21% oxygen | 1% argon
Troposphere

The narrowest of all the layers, this thin region contains about 85% of the atmosphere's total mass and almost all of its water vapor. It is also the realm of the Earth's weather.

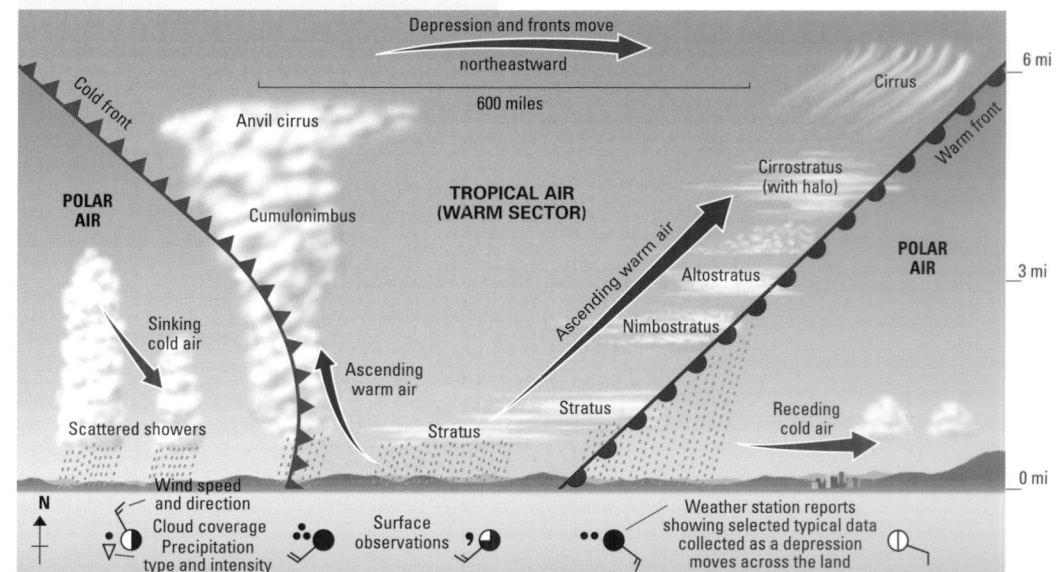

Depression and fronts move northeastward
600 miles
Cold front
Anvil cirrus
Cirrus
Warm front
POLAR AIR
Cumulonimbus
TROPICAL AIR (WARM SECTOR)
Cirrostratus (with halo)
Ascending warm air
Altostratus
POLAR AIR
Sinking cold air
Ascending warm air
Nimbostratus
Stratus
Scattered showers
Stratus
Receding cold air
6 mi
3 mi
0 mi
N
Wind speed and direction
Cloud coverage
Precipitation type and intensity
Surface observations
Weather station reports showing selected typical data collected as a depression moves across the land

AIR MASSES

Air masses are bodies of air whose characteristics are broadly the same over a large area. Around the equator, where the Sun's heat creates relatively high surface temperatures, warm air rises to create a zone of low pressure called the doldrums. The air cools and finally spreads out toward the poles. Around latitudes 30° north and south, the air sinks back to the surface, becoming warmer as it descends and creating zones of high pressure called the horse latitudes.

The high- and low-pressure zones are both areas of comparative calm, but between them lie the prevailing trade wind belts. Air also flows north and south from the high-pressure horse latitudes and these airflows meet up with cold, dense air flowing from the poles along the polar front.

This basic circulatory system is complicated by the Coriolis effect, brought about by the spinning Earth. Because of the Coriolis effect, the prevailing winds do not flow directly north–south but are deflected to the right in the northern hemisphere and to the left in the southern. Along the polar front, depressions form where the polar easterlies meet the westerlies.

The first classification of clouds was developed by a London chemist, Luke Howard, in 1803, and it was later modified by the World Meteorological Organization. The main types are divided into three groups according to their altitude, and into sub-groups according to their shape, which vary from hairlike filaments (cirrus), heaps or piles (cumulus), and layers (stratus). Each cloud carries some kind of message, though not always a clear one, to weather forecasters.

CLASSIFICATION OF CLOUDS

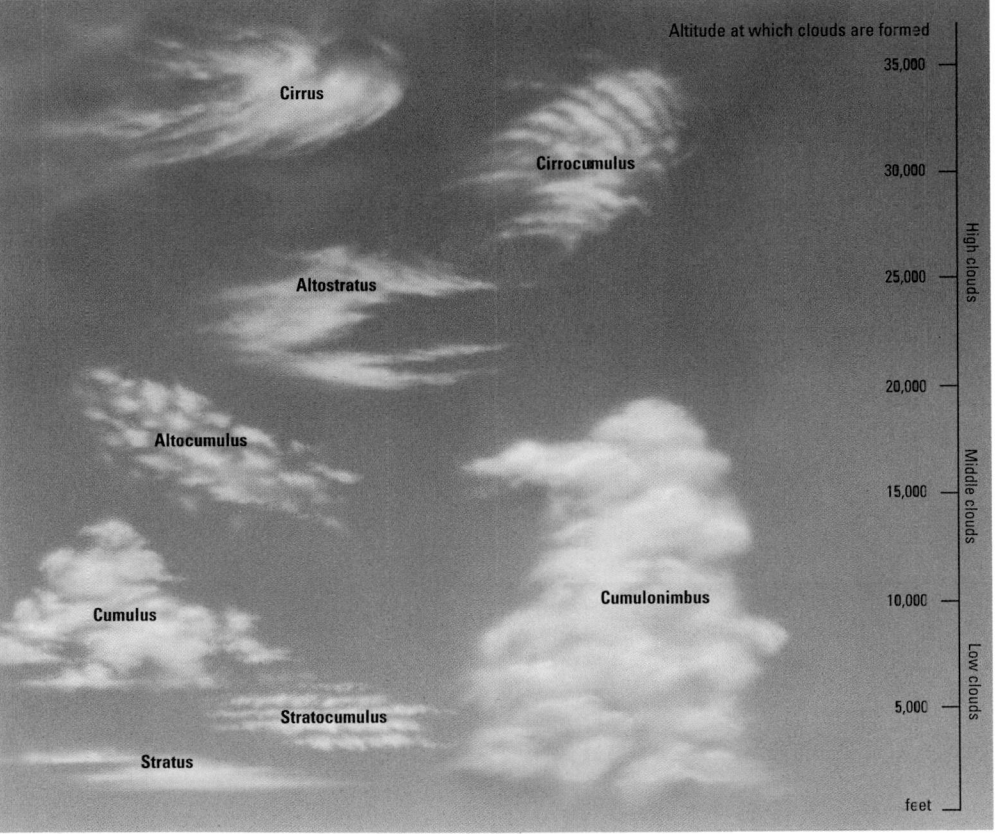

Clouds form when damp, usually rising, air is cooled. Thus they form when a wind rises to cross hills or mountains; when a mass of air rises over, or is pushed up by, another mass of denser air; or when local heating of the ground causes convection currents.

The types of clouds are classified according to altitude as high, middle, or low. The high ones, composed of ice crystals, are cirrus, cirrostratus, and cirrocumulus.

The middle clouds are altostratus – a gray or bluish striated, fibrous or uniform sheet producing light drizzle – and altocumulus, a thicker and fluffier version of cirrocumulus.

Low clouds include nimbo-stratus, a dark gray layer that brings rain or snow; cumulus, a detached heap, dark at the base; stratus, which forms dull, overcast skies at low levels; and stratocumulus, which consists of fluffy grayish-white layers.

Cumulonimbus, associated with storms and rains, heavy and dense with a flat base and a high, fluffy outline, can be tall enough to occupy middle as well as low altitudes.

PRESSURE AND SURFACE WINDS

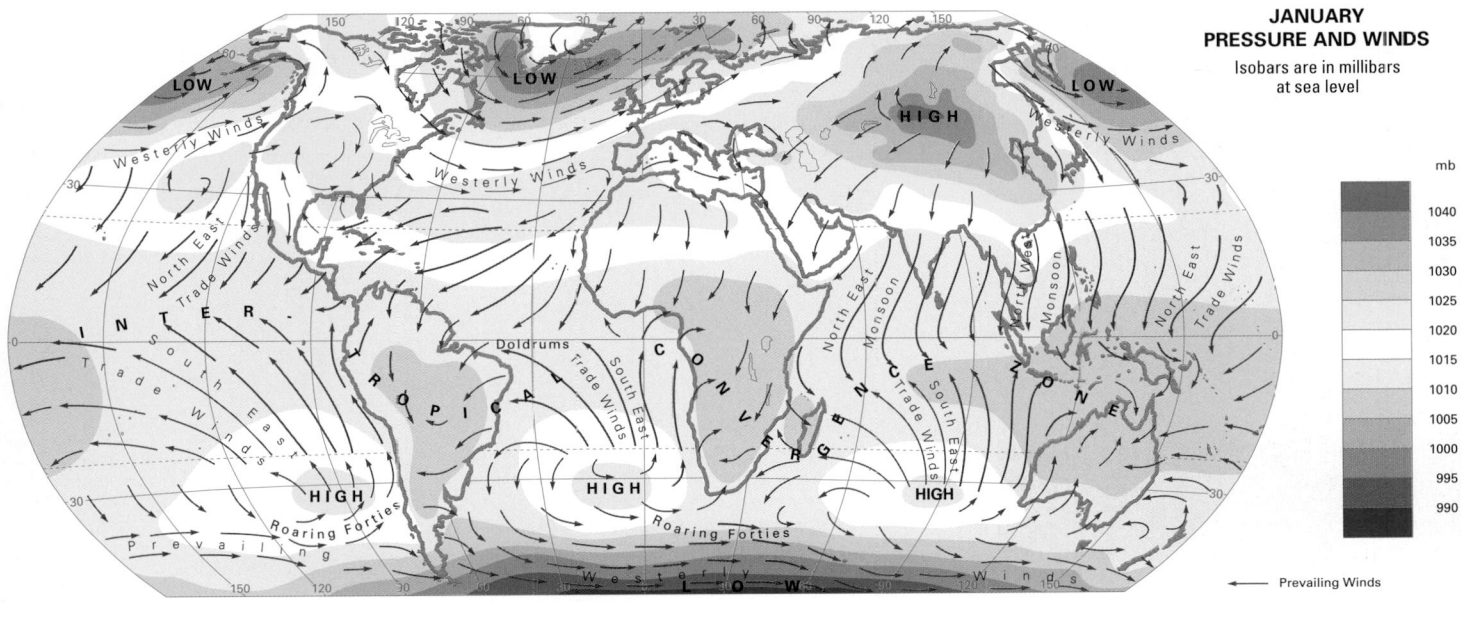

JANUARY PRESSURE AND WINDS
Isobars are in millibars at sea level

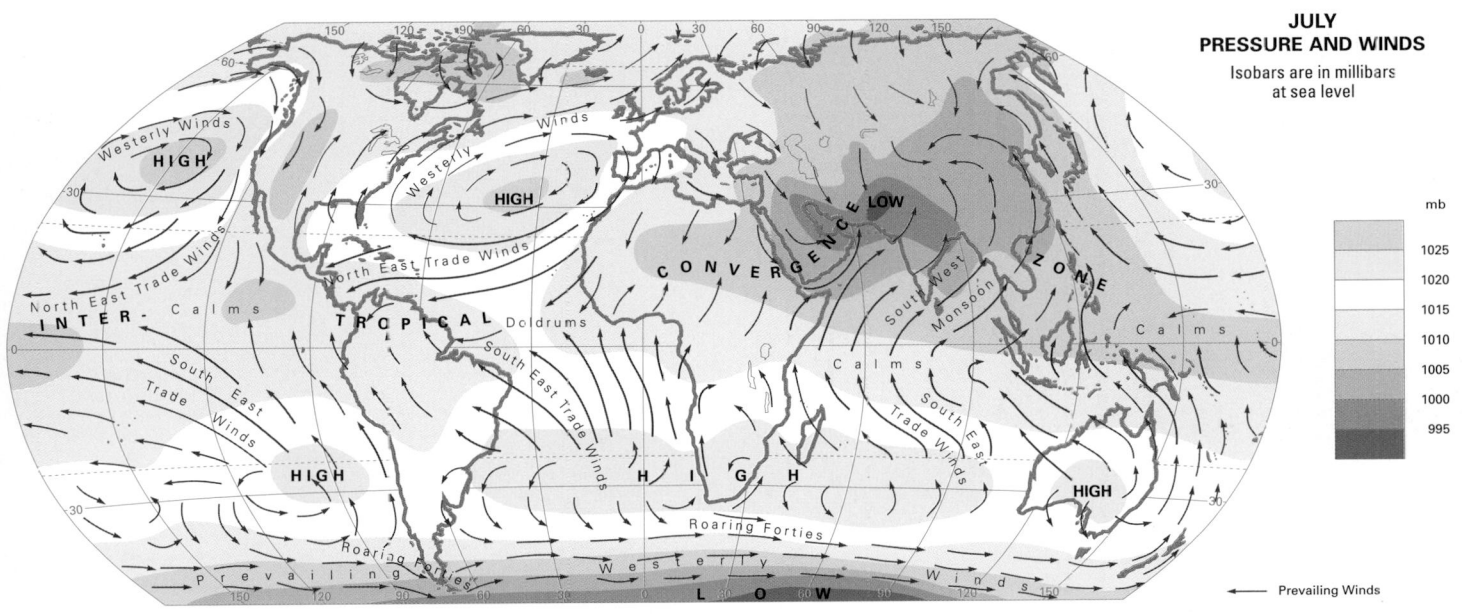

JULY PRESSURE AND WINDS
Isobars are in millibars at sea level

CLIMATE RECORDS

Pressure and winds

Highest barometric pressure:
Agata, Siberia, 1,083.8 mb at altitude 862 ft [262 m], December 31, 1968.

Lowest barometric pressure:
Typhoon Tip, 300 mi [480 km] west of Guam, Pacific Ocean, 870 mb, October 12, 1979.

Highest recorded wind speed:
Mt Washington, New Hampshire, USA, 231 mph [371 km/h], April 12, 1934. This is three times as strong as hurricane force on the Beaufort Scale.

Windiest place:
Commonwealth Bay, George V Coast, Antarctica, where gales frequently reach over 200 mph [320 km/h].

Worst recorded storm:
Bangladesh (then East Pakistan) cyclone*, November 13, 1970 – over 300,000 dead or missing. The 1991 cyclone, Bangladesh's and the world's second worst in terms of loss of life, killed an estimated 138,000 people.

Worst recorded tornado:
Missouri/Illinois/Indiana, USA, March 18, 1925 – 792 deaths. The tornado was only 300 yds [275 m] wide.

* Tropical cyclones are known as hurricanes in Central and North America, as typhoons in the Far East, and as willy-willies in northern Australia.

CLIMATE

For more information:
13 Ocean currents
14 Circulation of the air
15 Classification of clouds
   Pressure and winds
18 Hydrological cycle
19 Natural vegetation
21 Greenhouse effect
22 Global warming

Weather is the day-to-day or hour-to-hour condition of the air, while climate is weather in the long term – the seasonal pattern of hot and cold, wet and dry, averaged over a long period.

Most classifications of climate are based on a system developed in the early 19th century by Vladimir Köppen, a Russian meteorologist. Using a code based on letters and a classification centered on two main features, temperature and precipitation, he identified five main climatic types: tropical (A), dry (B), warm temperate (C), cold temperate (D), and polar (E). A highland mountain climate (H) was added later to account for the variety of altitudinal climatic zones on high mountains. Each

of these main regions was then further subdivided.

Latitude is a major factor in determining climate, but other factors add to the complexity. These include the differential heating of land and sea, the distance from the sea, the effect of mountains on winds, and the influence of ocean currents. For example, New York City, Naples, and the Gobi Desert share almost the same latitude, but their climates are very different.

During the last Ice Age, the Earth underwent alternating cold periods, called glacials, separated by warm interglacials. The Milankovich theory suggests such cycles may be caused by variations in the Earth's path around the Sun, changing

from almost circular to elliptical every 95,000 years, and variations in the Earth's tilt from 21.5° to 24.5° every 42,000 years. Another factor is that the Earth is now closest to the Sun in the middle of winter in the northern hemisphere and furthest away in summer. But 12,000 years ago, at the height of the last glacial period, the northern winter fell with the Sun at its most distant.

Studies of these cycles suggest that we are now in an interglacial with a new glacial period on the way. However, scientists believe that global warming, largely a result of burning fossil fuels and deforestation, may be occurring much faster than the great, slow cycles of the Solar System.

Tropical rainy climates
All mean monthly temperatures above 64°F.

Af	Rain forest climate
Am	Monsoon climate
Aw	Savanna climate

Dry climates
Low rainfall combined with a wide range of temperatures

| BS | Steppe climate |
| BW | Desert climate |

Warm temperate rainy climates
The mean temperature is below 64°F but above 26°F and that of the warmest month is over 50°F.

Cw	Dry winter climate
Cs	Dry summer climate
Cf	Climate with no dry season

Cold temperate rainy climates
The mean temperature of the coldest month is below 26°F but that of the warmest month is still over 50°F.

| Dw | Dry winter climate |
| Df | Climate with no dry season |

Polar climates
The mean temperature of the warmest month is below 50°F, giving permanently frozen subsoil.

| ET | Tundra climate |

The mean temperature of the warmest month is below 32°F, giving permanent ice and snow.

| EF | Polar climate |

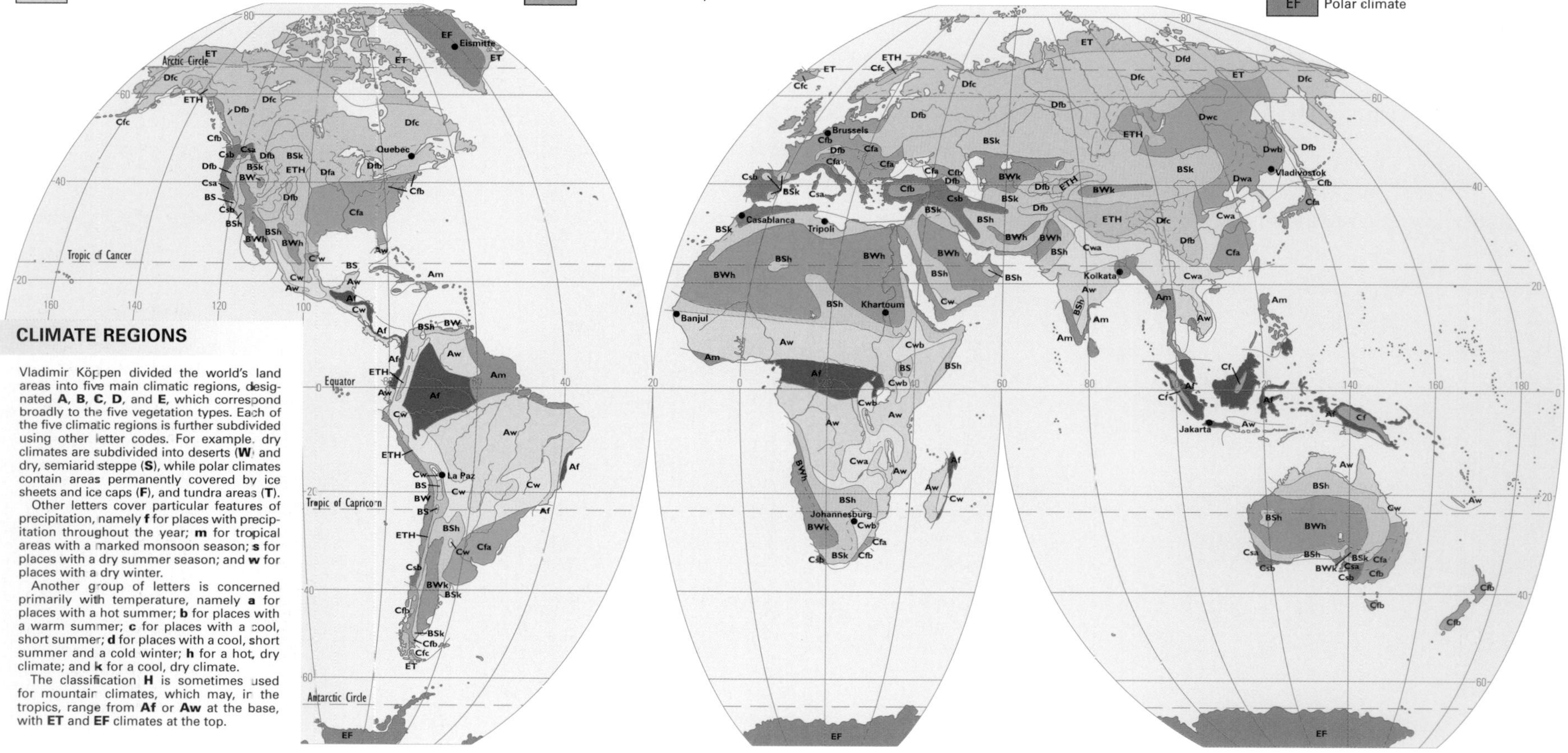

CLIMATE REGIONS

Vladimir Köppen divided the world's land areas into five main climatic regions, designated **A**, **B**, **C**, **D**, and **E**, which correspond broadly to the five vegetation types. Each of the five climatic regions is further subdivided using other letter codes. For example, dry climates are subdivided into deserts (**W**) and dry, semiarid steppe (**S**), while polar climates contain areas permanently covered by ice sheets and ice caps (**F**), and tundra areas (**T**).

Other letters cover particular features of precipitation, namely **f** for places with precipitation throughout the year; **m** for tropical areas with a marked monsoon season; **s** for places with a dry summer season; and **w** for places with a dry winter.

Another group of letters is concerned primarily with temperature, namely **a** for places with a hot summer; **b** for places with a warm summer; **c** for places with a cool, short summer; **d** for places with a cool, short summer and a cold winter; **h** for a hot, dry climate; and **k** for a cool, dry climate.

The classification **H** is sometimes used for mountain climates, which may, in the tropics, range from **Af** or **Aw** at the base, with **ET** and **EF** climates at the top.

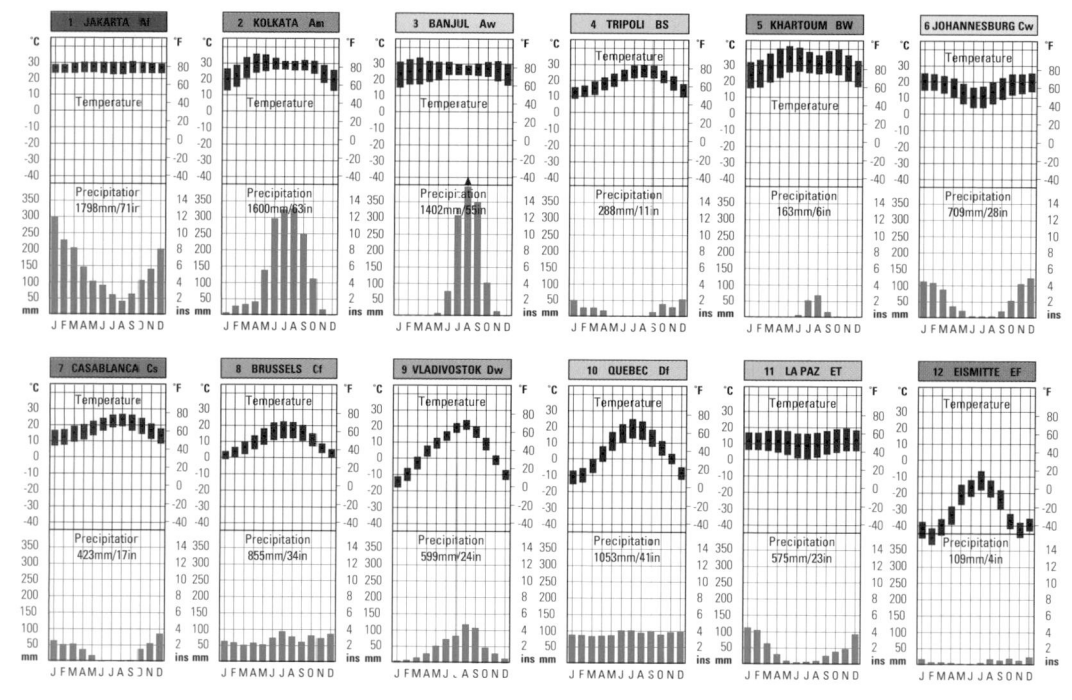

CLIMATE AND WEATHER TERMS

Anticyclone: area of high pressure with light winds and generally quiet weather.

Absolute humidity: amount of water vapor contained in a given volume of air.

Cloud cover: amount of cloud in the sky; measured in oktas (from 1–8), with 0 clear, and 8 total cover.

Condensation: the conversion of water vapor, or moisture in the air, into liquid.

Cyclone: violent storm resulting from counterclockwise rotation of winds in the northern hemisphere and clockwise in the southern: called hurricane in North America, typhoon in the Far East.

Depression: area of low pressure. The pressure gradient is toward the center.

Dew: water droplets condensed out of the air after the ground has cooled at night.

Dew point: temperature at which air becomes saturated (reaches a relative humidity of 100%) at a constant pressure.

Drizzle: precipitation where drops are less than 0.02 inches [0.5 mm] in diameter.

Evaporation: conversion of water from liquid into vapor or moisture in the air.

Front: the dividing line between two air masses.

Frost: dew that has frozen when the air temperature falls below freezing point.

Hail: frozen rain; small balls of ice, often falling during thunderstorms.

Hoar frost: formed on objects when the dew point is below freezing point.

Humidity: amount of moisture in the air.

Isobar: cartographic line connecting places of equal atmospheric pressure.

Isotherm: cartographic line connecting places of equal temperature.

Lightning: massive electrical discharge released in thunderstorm from cloud to cloud or cloud to ground, the result of the top becoming positively charged and the bottom negatively charged.

Precipitation: measurable rain, snow, sleet, or hail.

Prevailing wind: most common direction of wind at a given location.

Rain: precipitation of liquid particles with diameter larger than 0.02 inches [0.5 mm].

Relative humidity: amount of water vapor contained in a given volume of air at a given temperature.

Snow: formed when water vapor condenses below freezing point.

Thunder: sound produced by the rapid expansion of air heated by lightning.

Tornado: severe funnel-shaped storm that twists as hot air spins vertically (waterspout at sea).

Whirlwind: rapidly rotating column of air, only a few feet across, made visible by dust.

CLIMATE CHANGE

Human factors, such as the emission of greenhouse gases through the burning of fossil fuels and deforestation, have contributed to global warming. The histogram (*below*) shows in blue the average global temperatures from 1860 to 1996. The red line is a 10-year running average. Overall, there is an upward trend, particularly so since the 1970s, when global warming became a matter of concern in scientific circles. The large year-to-year changes indicate the Earth's natural climatic variability and the influence of such factors as major volcanic eruptions.

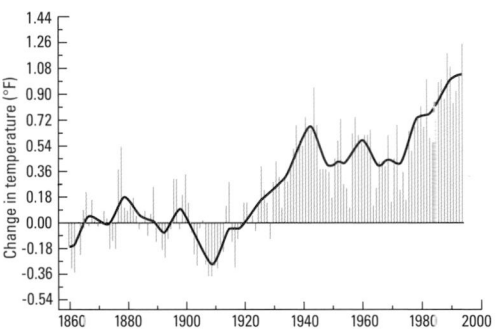

Data from the Hadley Center for Climate Research and Prediction

BEAUFORT WIND SCALE

Named after Admiral Sir Francis Beaufort, the 19th-century British naval officer who devised it, the Beaufort Scale assesses wind speed according to its effects. It was originally designed as an aid for sailors, but has since been adapted for use on the land. It is used internationally.

Scale	Wind speed mph	km/h	Effect
0	0–1	0–1	**Calm** Smoke rises vertically
1	1–3	1–5	**Light air** Wind direction shown only by smoke drift
2	4–7	6–11	**Light breeze** Wind felt on face; leaves rustle; vanes moved by wind
3	8–12	12–19	**Gentle breeze** Leaves and small twigs in constant motion; wind extends small flag
4	13–18	20–28	**Moderate** Raises dust and loose paper; small branches move
5	19–24	29–38	**Fresh** Small trees in leaf sway; crested wavelets on inland waters
6	25–31	39–49	**Strong** Large branches move; difficult to use umbrellas; overhead wires whistle
7	32–38	50–61	**Near gale** Whole trees in motion; difficult to walk against wind
8	39–46	62–74	**Gale** Twigs break from trees; walking very difficult
9	47–54	75–88	**Strong gale** Slight structural damage
10	55–63	89–102	**Storm** Trees uprooted; serious structural damage
11	64–72	103–117	**Violent storm** Widespread damage
12	73+	118+	**Hurricane**

THE MONSOON

Monsoon is the term given to the seasonal reversal of wind direction, most noticeably in Southeast Asia. It results from a combination of factors: the extreme heating and cooling of large land masses in relation to the less marked changes in temperature of the adjacent seas; the northward movement of the Intertropical Convergence Zone (ITCZ); and the effect of the Himalayas on the circulation of the air.

In March, winds blow outward from the mainland. But as the Sun and the ITCZ move northward, the land is intensely heated, and a low-pressure system develops. The southeast trade winds change direction and are sucked into the interior to become southwesterlies, bringing heavy rain. By November, the Sun and the ITCZ have again moved south and the wind directions are again reversed. Cool winds blow from the Asian interior to the sea, losing any moisture on the Himalayas before descending to the coast.

TEMPERATURE

Average temperature in January

Average temperature

86°F
68°F
50°F
32°F
14°F
−4°F
−22°F
−40°F

Average temperature in July

Average temperature

86°F
68°F
50°F
32°F
14°F

PRECIPITATION (RAINFALL AND SNOW)

Average annual precipitation

120 inches
80 inches
40 inches
20 inches
10 inches

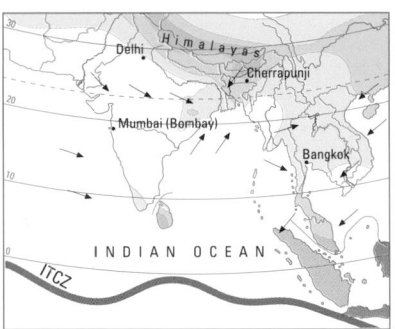

March – Start of the hot, dry season. The ITCZ is over the southern Indian Ocean.

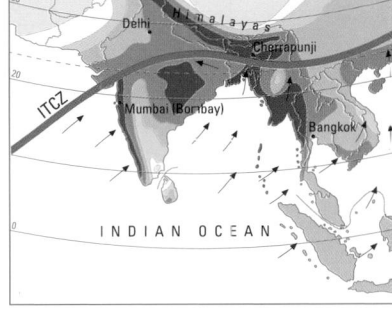

July – The rainy season. The ITCZ has migrated northward; winds blow onshore.

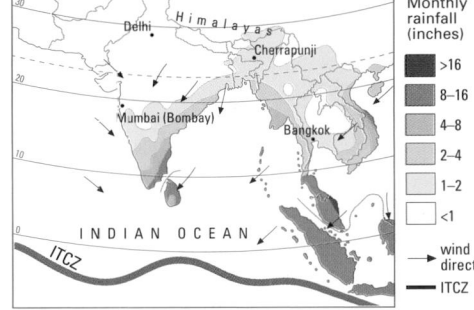

November – The ITCZ has returned south. The offshore winds are cool and dry.

Monthly rainfall (inches)

>16
8–16
4–8
2–4
1–2
<1

→ wind direction
— ITCZ

CLIMATE RECORDS

TEMPERATURE

Highest recorded temperature:
Al Aziziyah, Libya, 136.4°F [58°C], September 13, 1922.

Highest mean annual temperature:
Dallol, Ethiopia, 94°F [34.4°C], 1960–6.

Longest heatwave:
Marble Bar, W. Australia, 162 days over 100°F [38°C], October 23, 1923, to April 7, 1924.

Lowest recorded temperature (outside poles):
Verkhoyansk, Siberia, −90°F [−68°C], February 6, 1933. Verkhoyansk also registered the greatest annual range of temperature: −90°F to 98°F [−68°C to 37°C].

Lowest mean annual temperature:
Polus Nedostupnosti, Pole of Cold, Antarctica, −72°F [−57.8°C].

PRECIPITATION

Driest place:
Calama, N. Chile: no recorded rainfall in 400 years to 1971.

Wettest place (average):
Tututendo, Colombia: mean annual rainfall 463.4 inches [11,770 mm].

Wettest place (12 months):
Cherrapunji, Meghalaya, N.E. India, 1,040 inches [26,470 mm], August 1860 to August 1861. Cherrapunji also holds the record for rainfall in one month: 115 inches [2,930 mm], July 1861. (*See maps below.*)

Wettest place (24 hours):
Cilaos, Réunion, Indian Ocean, 73.6 inches [1,870 mm], March 15–16, 1952.

Heaviest hailstones:
Gopalganj, Bangladesh, up to 2.25 lb [1.02 kg], April 14, 1986 (killed 92 people).

Heaviest snowfall (continuous):
Bessans, Savoie, France, 68 inches [1,730 mm] in 19 hours, April 5–6, 1969.

Heaviest snowfall (season/year):
Paradise Ranger Station, Mt Rainier, Washington, USA, 1,224.5 inches [31,102 mm], February 19, 1971, to February 18, 1972.

WATER AND VEGETATION

For more information:
16 Climate regions
17 Precipitation
20 Biodiversity
23 Water pollution
    Deforestation

Without the hydrological cycle, by which water is constantly recycled between the oceans, the atmosphere and the land, the continents would be barren. Precipitation enables plants to grow and soils to form, creating the world's natural vegetation regions and the ecosystems that support animal life.

Running water also plays a major role in shaping landforms. Yet in many parts of the world, people do not have safe water to drink and suffer from diseases caused by water-borne organisms and pollution. In 2002, an estimated 1 billion people lacked access to safe water and 2.6 billion people lacked basic sanitation.

Experts argue that world demand for water is increasing at about twice the rate of population growth. It is predicted that, by 2025, half the world's population will face water shortages. This could lead to conflict and even boundary wars – 300 major rivers cross national frontiers and access to their water is likely to be disputed.

THE HYDROLOGICAL CYCLE

The world's water balance is regulated by the constant recycling of water between the oceans, the atmosphere and the land. The movement of water between these three reservoirs is known as the *hydrological cycle*. The oceans play a vital role in the hydrological cycle: 74% of the total precipitation falls over the oceans and 84% of the total evaporation comes from the oceans. Water vapor in the atmosphere circulates around the planet, transporting energy as well as the water itself. When the vapor cools, it falls as rain or snow. The whole cycle is driven by the Sun.

WATER DISTRIBUTION

The distribution of planetary water, by percentage. Oceans and ice caps together account for more than 99% of the total; the breakdown of the remainder is estimated.

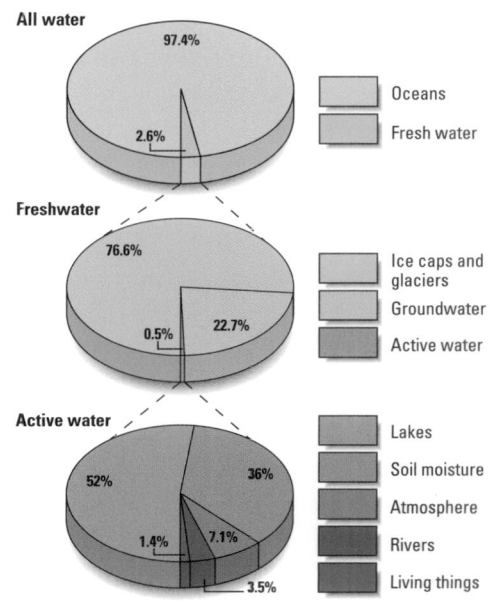

All water
97.4% — Oceans
2.6% — Fresh water

Freshwater
76.6% — Ice caps and glaciers
0.5% — Groundwater
22.7% — Active water

Active water
52% — Lakes
36% — Soil moisture
1.4% — Atmosphere
7.1% — Rivers
3.5% — Living things

Almost all the world's water is 3,000 million years old, and all of it cycles endlessly through the hydrosphere, though at different rates. Water vapor circulates over days, even hours; deep-ocean water circulates over millennia; and ice-cap water remains solid for millions of years.

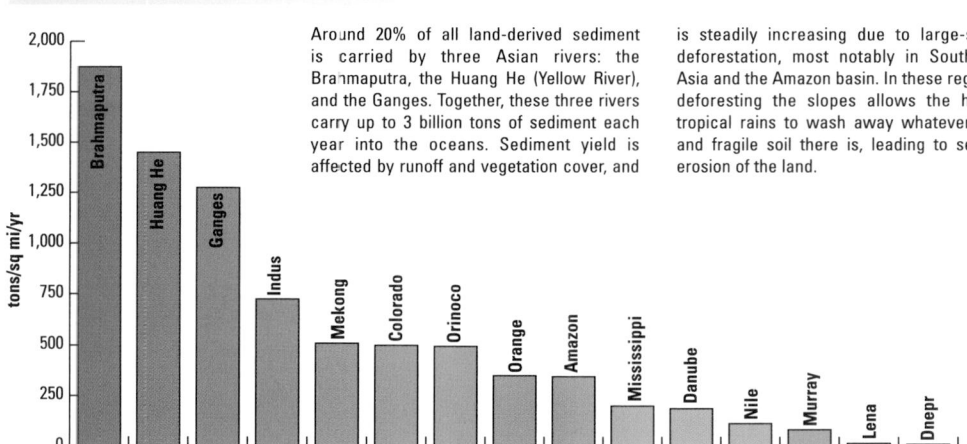

Transfer of water vapor
10% of the balance of precipitation/
evaporation over oceans

Evaporation from oceans
84% of total
evaporation

Evapotranspiration
16% of total evaporation

Precipitation
26% of total
precipitation

Precipitation
74% of total
precipitation

Runoff
10% of the balance of
precipitation/evaporation
over land

Surface runoff

Surface
storage

Infiltration

Groundwater flow

ANNUAL SEDIMENT YIELD

Around 20% of all land-derived sediment is carried by three Asian rivers: the Brahmaputra, the Huang He (Yellow River), and the Ganges. Together, these three rivers carry up to 3 billion tons of sediment each year into the oceans. Sediment yield is affected by runoff and vegetation cover, and is steadily increasing due to large-scale deforestation, most notably in Southeast Asia and the Amazon basin. In these regions, deforesting the slopes allows the heavy tropical rains to wash away whatever thin and fragile soil there is, leading to severe erosion of the land.

tons/sq mi/yr

Brahmaputra, Huang He, Ganges, Indus, Mekong, Colorado, Orinoco, Orange, Amazon, Mississippi, Danube, Nile, Murray, Lena, Dnepr

WATER RUNOFF

Annual freshwater runoff by continent in cubic miles

3,167
2,492
472
747
1,014
1,430

Asia
North America
South America
Australasia
Europe
Africa

► The River Amazon is the world's second-longest river (after the River Nile), draining the vast rain forest basin of northern South America. The Amazon carries by far the greatest volume of water of any river in the world: the average rate of discharge is approximately 3,355,000 cu ft [95,000 cu m] per second, nearly three times as much as its nearest rival, the Congo. The flow is so great that its silt discolors the water up to 125 miles [200 km] into the Atlantic. At approximately 2.7 million sq miles [7 million sq km], the Amazon basin comprises nearly 40% of the whole of South America.

18

WATERSHEDS

The map below shows the world's major rivers, with the ranking of the 20 longest rivers shown in square brackets after their name, led by the Nile [1] and the Amazon [2].

The map shows the direction of freshwater flow on a continental scale, whereas the water runoff chart on the facing page indicates the quantities involved annually.

The rate of runoff varies seasonally and is affected by the surface vegetation and climate. Most of the world's major rivers discharge into the Atlantic Ocean.

Where the rivers run

Pacific Ocean

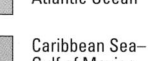
Indian Ocean

Arctic Ocean

Atlantic Ocean

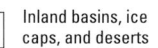
Caribbean Sea–Gulf of Mexico

Mediterranean Sea

Inland basins, ice caps, and deserts

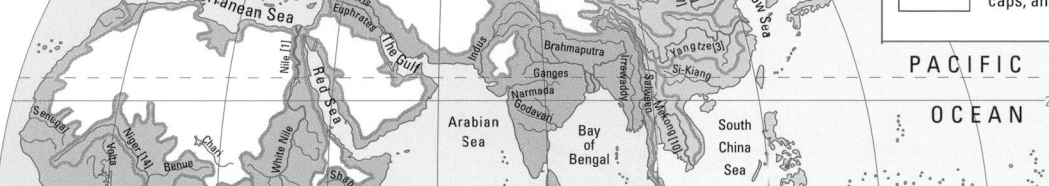

NATURAL VEGETATION

The map below illustrates the natural "climax vegetation" of a region, as dictated by its climate and topography. In most cases, human agricultural activity has drastically altered the pattern of the vegetation. Western Europe, for example, lost most of its broadleaf forests many centuries ago, while elsewhere irrigation has turned some natural semideserts into productive land. The various vegetation regions support different kinds of animals and wildlife, and, in an undisturbed state, they are highly developed biological communities, or "biomes."

The blue line on the map represents the northern limit of tree growth, and the red lines indicate the northern and southern limits of palm growth.

Tropical rain forest

Subtropical and temperate rain forest

Monsoon woodland and open jungle

Subtropical and temperate woodland, scrub, and bush

Tropical savanna, with low trees and bush

Tropical savanna and grasslands

Dry semidesert, with shrub and grass

Desert shrub

Desert

Dry steppe and shrub

Temperate grasslands, prairie, and steppe

Mediterranean hardwood forest and scrub

Temperate deciduous forest and meadow

Temperate deciduous and coniferous forest

Northern coniferous forest (taïga)

Mountainous forest, mainly coniferous

High plateau steppe and tundra

Arctic tundra

Polar and mountainous ice desert

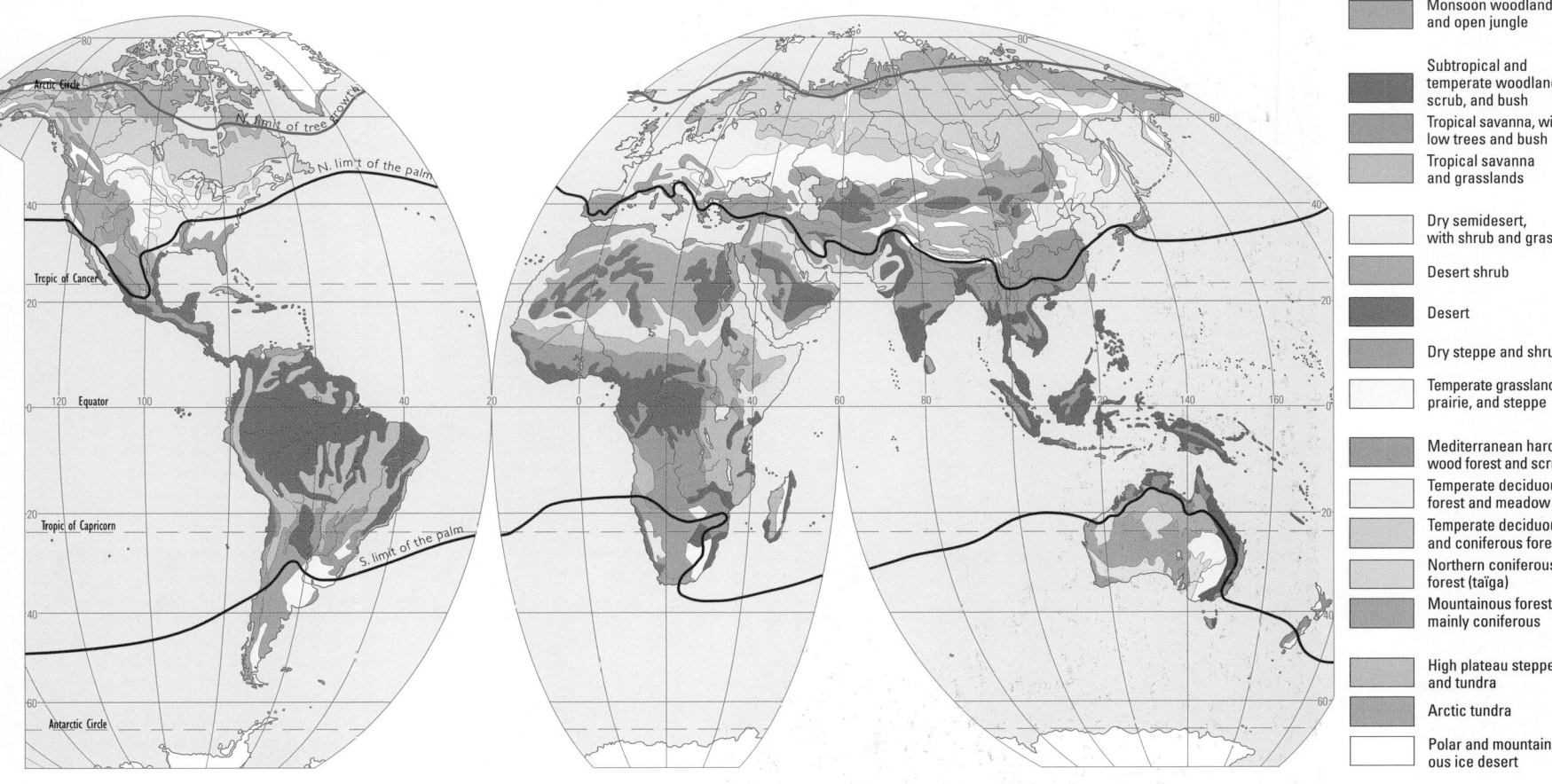

THE NATURAL ENVIRONMENT

For more information:

12 Oceans
14 Atmosphere
19 Natural vegetation
22 Carbon dioxide
   Greenhouse power
   Global warming
23 Acid rain
   Desertification
   Deforestation
   Water pollution

Recent discoveries of life forms in some of the world's most hostile environments, such as around the black smokers along the ocean ridges, prepared the way for the announcement by NASA scientists in 1996 that they had found microfossils in a Martian meteorite. But other scientists were sceptical, believing them to be natural mineral structures and not evidence of extraterrestrial life.

Until further evidence is available, the Earth remains the only planet where we know for sure that life exists. According to the fossil record, life on Earth appeared at least 3,500 million years ago. Since then, it has evolved from its primitive beginnings to its modern biodiversity, including millions of plants, animals and micro-organisms. Living organisms have not only adapted to the environ-

ment, but they have also changed their environment to suit themselves. For example, the Earth's early atmosphere contained little oxygen, but the emergence of multicelled, oxygen-producing algae, around 2,000 million years ago, led to the creation of an oxygen-rich atmosphere. This enabled land animals to populate the ancient continents.

The amount of the greenhouse-gas carbon dioxide in the atmosphere would steadily increase from its present 0.03% were it not for plants. Without them, the Earth's atmosphere would, in a few million years, be similar to that of Venus, where surface temperatures reach 890°F. The Earth has evolved into a complex control system, sensing and reacting to changes and tending always to maintain the balance it has achieved.

Much discussion has centered on how that balance changes. Only recently, scientists were suggesting that we may be living in an interglacial stage of the Pleistocene Ice Age. Since the 1980s, however, predictions of future climate patterns have concentrated more on global warming, caused by pollution that has led to an increase in greenhouse gases in the atmosphere. Interference in the natural cycles that control the environment may have consequences that are hard to predict.

Furthermore, we are currently experiencing a period of mass extinction of species, causing a rapid reduction in our planet's biodiversity. In 2002, a report by the International Union for the Conservation of Nature listed 11,167 organisms facing extinction. This was 121 more than in 2000.

THREATENED MAMMALS

The map shows the percentage of mammal species classified as threatened in 2002. Many scientists believe we are currently experiencing a period of mass extinction of species, rivaling five other periods in the past half a billion years. Among the most threatened mammals today are elephants, primates, and rhinoceroses.

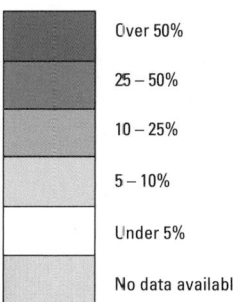

Over 50%

25 – 50%

10 – 25%

5 – 10%

Under 5%

No data available

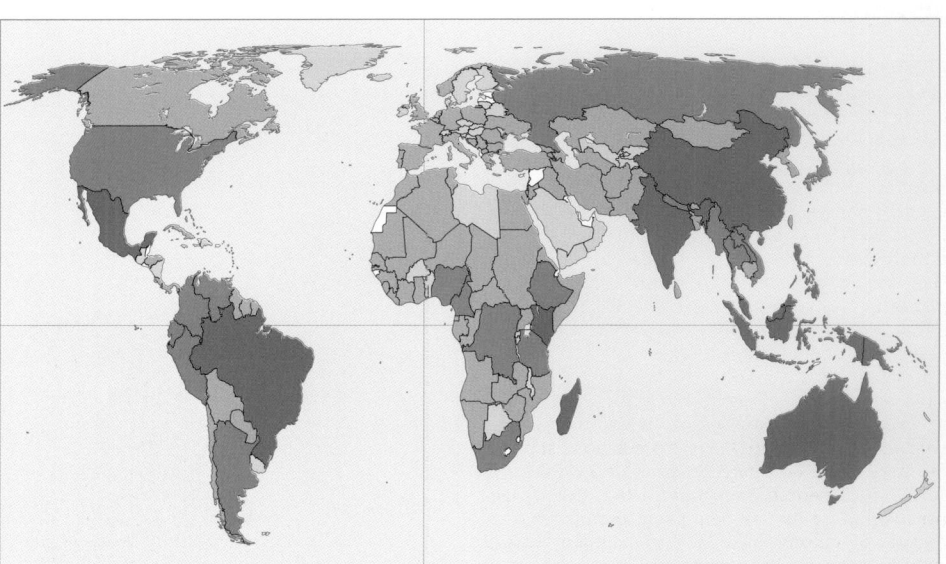

BIODIVERSITY IN CALIFORNIA, USA

This false-color satellite image of central California shows San Francisco lying just below the entrance to San Francisco Bay, with Oakland on the far side and San Jose to the southeast. California, nicknamed the Golden State, is the third largest state in the United States and the most populous.

Due to its varied terrain and climate, California has a wide range of diverse habitats within a relatively small area. East of the forested Coast Ranges (the gray and red areas just inland from the bay) lies the fertile Central Valley, which appears as a red-and-blue checkerboard. In the northwest and southwest of the state (*not shown here*) lie parts of the Basin and Range region, much of which is desert. It includes Death Valley, which contains the country's lowest point on land, at 282 feet below sea level.

Natural vegetation

Forests cover about 40% of California and they include bristlecone pines, thought to be the oldest living things on Earth, together with coastal redwoods, the world's tallest trees. Wildlife is still abundant, though some species, such as the rare California condor, are on the endangered list.

The state has achieved much to protect its biodiversity. It contains eight of the 56 national parks in the United States. Two of them, Death Valley and Joshua Tree, were designated national parks as recently as 1994, as part of a conservation measure, including the protection of large areas of wilderness in the deserts.

California has vast resources and, were it a separate nation, it would rank among the world's ten most productive in terms of the total value of its goods and services. This means that, like the United States as a whole, it has resources, which many developing countries lack, to finance conservation measures. For example, the World Conservation Union reported in 1996 that 8% of mammals were threatened in the United States, as compared with 32% in the Philippines and 44% in Madagascar, two countries where habitat destruction has been proceeding on a large scale.

THE EARTH'S ENERGY BALANCE

Apart from a modest quantity of internal heat from its molten core, the Earth receives all of its energy from the Sun. If the planet is to remain at a constant temperature, it must reradiate exactly as much energy as it receives. Even a minute surplus would lead to a warmer Earth, a deficit to a cooler one. The temperature at which thermal equilibrium is reached depends on many factors, including the relative brightness of the Earth (its index of reflectivity, called the "albedo") and the heat-trapping capacity of the atmosphere (the "greenhouse effect").

Most of the Sun's energy arrives in the form of short-wave radiation. Some of the energy is reflected straight back into space, while some is absorbed by the atmosphere or by the Earth itself. Absorbed energy heats the Earth and its atmosphere alike, but since its temperature is much lower than that of the Sun, the outgoing energy is emitted at longer infrared wavelengths.

The diagram (*right*) shows short-wave radiation in yellow, with long-wave radiation in orange.

THE GREENHOUSE EFFECT

Constituting less than 1% of the atmosphere, the natural greenhouse gases (water vapor, carbon dioxide, methane, nitrous oxide, and ozone) have a disproportionate effect on the Earth's climate, and even its habitability. Like the glass panes in a greenhouse, the gases are transparent to most incoming short-wave radiation, which passes freely to heat the planet beneath. But when the warmed Earth retransmits that energy, in the form of longer-wave infrared radiation, the gases function as an opaque shield, preventing some of it from escaping, so that the planetary surface (like the interior of a greenhouse) stays relatively hot.

Over the last 150 years, there has been a gradual increase in the levels of greenhouse gases (with the exception of water vapor, which remains a constant in the system). Current predictions suggest that there could be a further rise of 2.5–8°F by the year 2100. A serious reduction in the greenhouse gases would be just as damaging, though. A total absence of carbon dioxide, for example, would leave the planet with a temperature roughly 60°F colder than it is at present.

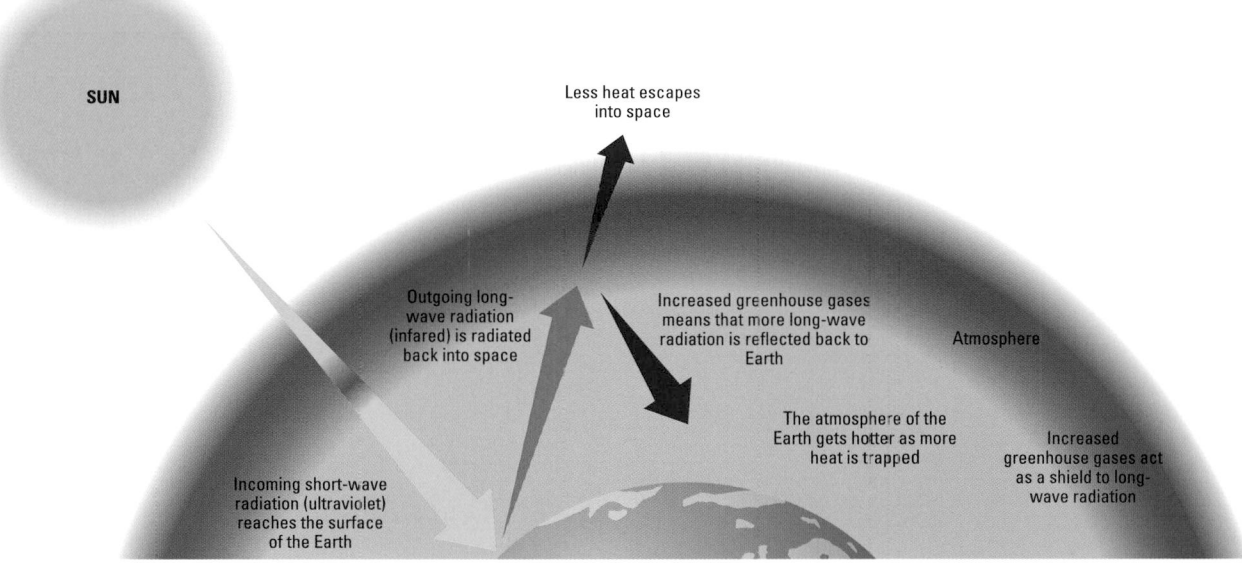

23% reflected by the cloud layer

25% absorbed by the atmosphere

21% diffuse radiation, some scattered back into space

3% absorbed by the clouds

24% reaches the Earth's surface

Atmosphere

Clouds

4% reflected from Earth's surface

SUN

Less heat escapes into space

Outgoing long-wave radiation (infared) is radiated back into space

Increased greenhouse gases means that more long-wave radiation is reflected back to Earth

Atmosphere

The atmosphere of the Earth gets hotter as more heat is trapped

Increased greenhouse gases act as a shield to long-wave radiation

Incoming short-wave radiation (ultraviolet) reaches the surface of the Earth

THE CARBON CYCLE

The Earth has a huge supply of carbon, only a small quantity of which is in the form of carbon dioxide. Of that, around 98% is dissolved in the sea; the fraction circulating in the air amounts to only 340 parts per million of the atmosphere, where its capacity as a greenhouse gas is the key regulator of the planetary temperature.

Living things, however, circulate carbon. Plants absorb carbon dioxide from the atmosphere and the carbon is then returned to circul-ation when the plants die, or is passed up the food chain to the herbivores, and then to the carnivores that feed on them. As organisms at each of these trophic levels die, they decay, releasing the carbon, which then combines once more with the oxygen released during life. However, a small proportion of carbon is removed almost permanently, buried beneath mud on land or at sea, sinking as dead matter to the ocean floor. In time, it is slowly compressed into sedimentary rocks, such as limestone and chalk.

The carbon cycle has continued for a very long time. However, human beings have found a way to release fixed carbon at a faster rate than existing global systems can re-circulate it. It has taken only a few human generations to deplete the fossil fuels that represent many millions of years of carbon accumulation.

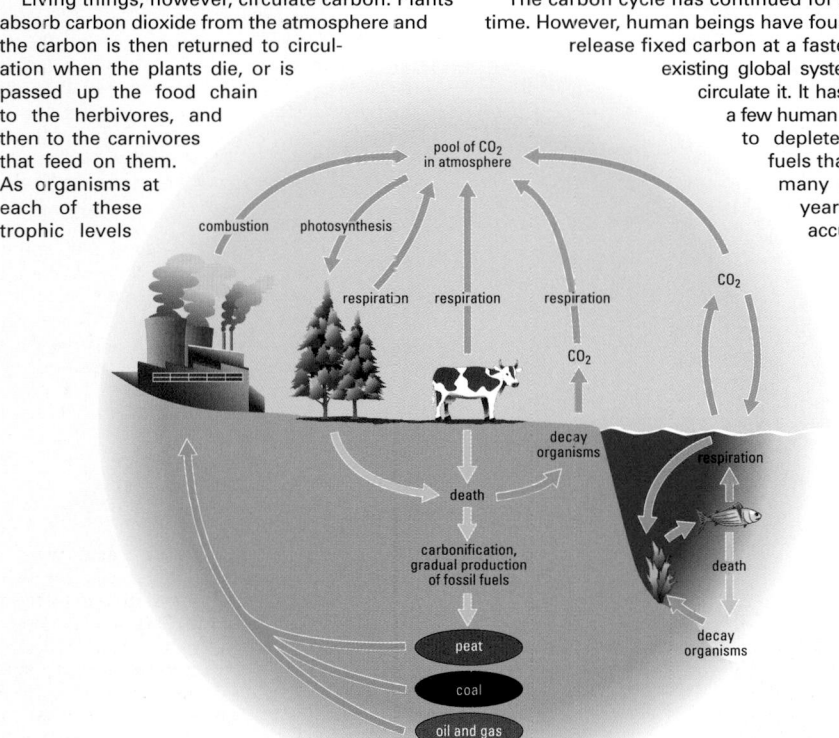

pool of CO₂ in atmosphere

combustion photosynthesis

respiration respiration respiration

CO₂

CO₂

decay organisms

respiration

death

carbonification, gradual production of fossil fuels

death

decay organisms

peat

coal

oil and gas

CARBON MONOXIDE CONCENTRATION

A colorless, odorless and poisonous gas, carbon monoxide (CO) is formed during the incomplete combustion of fossil fuels, occurring, for example, in coal gas and the exhaust fumes of cars. It is a major air pollutant and is now regulated by many world nations. The images below show the seasonal amounts and geographical sources of atmospheric carbon monoxide in the spring and summer months. Progressively higher levels of carbon monoxide are shown in green, yellow, orange, and red, while the blue areas have little or no atmospheric carbon monoxide.

Carbon monoxide can remain in the atmosphere for up to several months and can affect air quality in regions that are a long way from the original source of the pollution emissions.

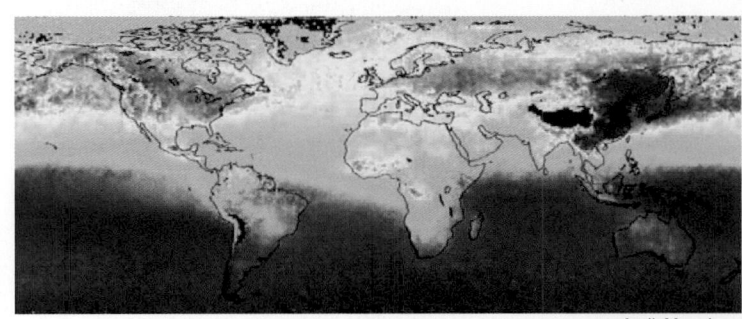

April, May, June

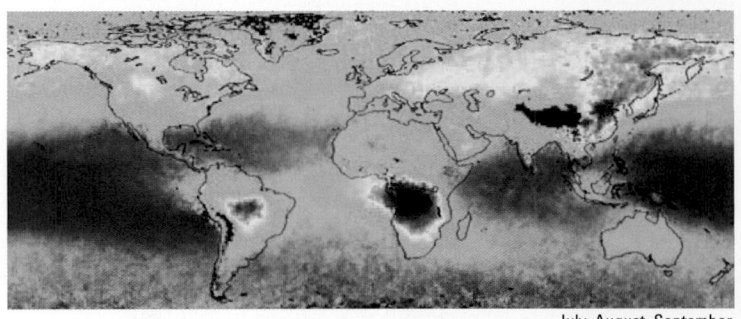

July, August, September

Carbon monoxide concentration (parts per billion by volume)

0   50   100   150   200   >250   no data

21

PEOPLE AND THE ENVIRONMENT

For more information:
12 Oceans
14 Atmosphere
16 Climate
21 Greenhouse effect
26 Urban pollution

In 1996, the Intergovernmental Panel on Climate Change issued a report stating that "The balance of evidence suggests a discernible human influence on global climate through emissions of carbon dioxide and other greenhouse gases." The report acknowledged that average global temperatures had risen by about 0.9°F since the mid-19th century, though there were still reasons for caution on attributing this entirely to actions taken by humans.

Human interference with nature is nothing new, at least since people turned from hunting and gathering to agriculture more than 10,000 years ago. At first, human actions seemed to have no ill effects because the systems that regulate the global environment were able to absorb damage. But from the late 18th century, the Industrial Revolution and the population explosion have caused massive pollution that threatens to overwhelm the Earth's ability to cope.

The 20th century experienced many disasters, including the dumping of industrial wastes in rivers and seas, accidents at nuclear power stations, and the creation of acid rain through the release of sulfur dioxides and nitrous oxides by the burning of fossil fuels. The release of greenhouse gases are held to be the main reason for global warming, while CFCs (chlorofluorocarbons) have damaged the ozone layer in the stratosphere, the planet's screen against ultraviolet radiation.

In December 1998, an international conference in Kyoto, Japan, reached an agreement to reduce the emission of greenhouse gases by 5.2% by 2012. But, in the early 21st century, the United States, which produces about a third of all emissions, opposed the Kyoto protocol.

Global warming will lead to melting ice sheets and the flooding of fertile coastal plains. Computer models suggest that it might affect ocean currents so that northwestern Europe, which owes its mild climate to the Gulf Stream, could expect bitterly cold winters. Some models have also suggested that cloud cover could increase, reflecting more solar energy back into space and thus start a new Ice Age.

In many tropical areas, deforestation is making productive land barren, while in the dry grasslands bordering deserts, the removal of plant cover is causing desertification. But human ingenuity can respond to this crisis in planet management.

GLOBAL WARMING

High atmospheric concentrations of heat-absorbing gases appear to be causing a rise in average temperatures worldwide – up to 3°F [1.5°C] by the year 2020, according to some estimates. Global warming is likely to bring about a rise in sea levels that may flood some of the world's densely populated coastal areas.

Evidence of global warming is attributed mainly to the "greenhouse effect," caused by the emission of certain gases, notably carbon dioxide, into the atmosphere (*see page 21*). Despite international action to control emissions of some greenhouse gases, carbon dioxide levels are still rising.

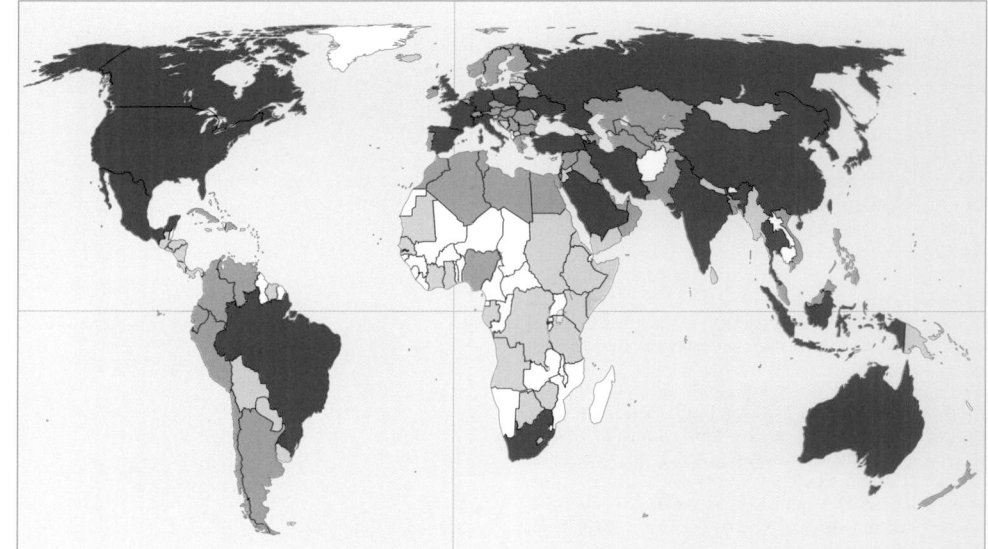

Carbon dioxide emissions in tons (latest available year)
- Over 50 million
- 5 – 50 million
- 0.5 – 5 million
- Under 0.5 million
- No data available

GREENHOUSE POWER

Relative contributions to the "greenhouse effect" by the major heat-absorbing gases in the atmosphere
The chart combines greenhouse potency and volume. Carbon dioxide has a greenhouse potential of only 1, but its concentration of 350 parts per million makes it predominate. CFC 12, with 25,000 times the absorption capacity of CO_2, is present only as 0.00044 ppm.

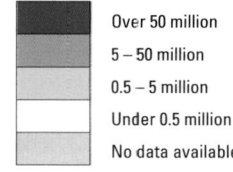

- Carbon dioxide (CO_2)
- Ozone
- Methane
- Nitrous oxide
- CFC 12
- CFC 11

CARBON DIOXIDE
Estimated percentage share of total world CO_2 emissions (2000)

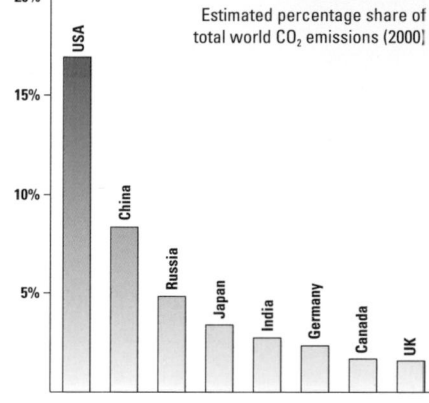

USA, China, Russia, Japan, India, Germany, Canada, UK

TEMPERATURE RISE
The rise in average temperatures caused by carbon dioxide and other greenhouse gases, assuming present trends continue (1960–2020)

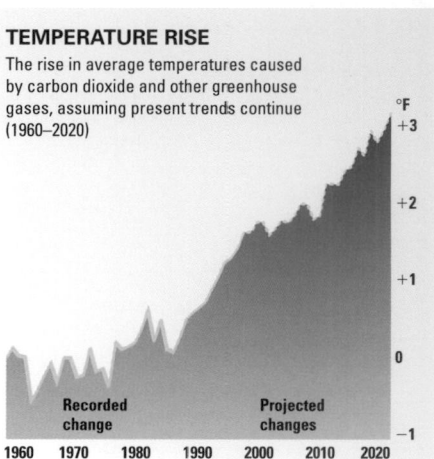

Recorded change — Projected changes
1960 1970 1980 1990 2000 2010 2020

THE THINNING OZONE LAYER

Total atmospheric ozone concentration in the southern and northern hemispheres (Dobson Units, 2000)
In 1985, scientists working in Antarctica discovered a thinning of the ozone layer, commonly known as an "ozone hole." This caused immediate alarm because the ozone layer absorbs most of the Sun's dangerous ultraviolet radiation, which is believed to cause an increase in skin cancer, cataracts, and damage to the immune system.

Since 1985, ozone depletion has increased and, by 2002, the ozone hole over the South Pole was estimated to be three times as large as the USA. The false-color images (*right*) show the total atmospheric ozone concentration in the southern hemisphere (in September 2000) and the northern hemisphere (in March 2000) with the ozone hole clearly identifiable at the center. The data is from the Tiros weather satellite. The colors represent the ozone concentration in Dobson Units (DU).

Scientists agree that ozone depletion is caused by CFCs, a group of manufactured chemicals used in air-conditioning systems and refrigerators. In a 1987 treaty most industrial nations agreed to phase out CFCs and a complete ban on most CFCs was agreed after the end of 1995. However, scientists believe that the chemicals will remain in the atmosphere for 50 to 100 years. As a result, ozone depletion will continue for many years.

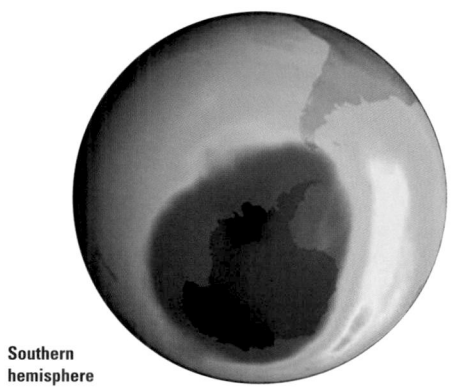

Southern hemisphere

Northern hemisphere

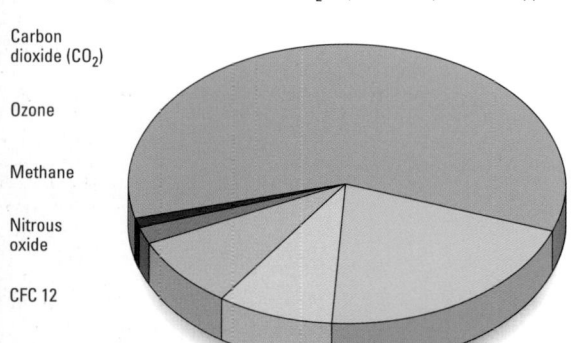

WORLD POLLUTION

Acid rain and sources of acidic emissions (latest available year)
Acid rain is caused by high levels of sulfur and nitrogen in the atmosphere. They combine with water vapor and oxygen to form acids (H_2SO_4 and HNO_3) which fall as precipitation.

 Regions where sulfur and nitrogen oxides are released in high concentrations, mainly from fossil fuel combustion

• Major cities with high levels of air pollution (including nitrogen and sulfur emissions)

Areas of heavy acid deposition
pH numbers indicate acidity, decreasing from a neutral 7. Normal rain, slightly acid from dissolved carbon dioxide, never exceeds a pH of 5.6.

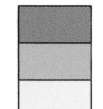
pH less than 4.0 (most acidic)
pH 4.0 to 4.5
pH 4.5 to 5.0

- - - - Areas where acid rain is a potential problem

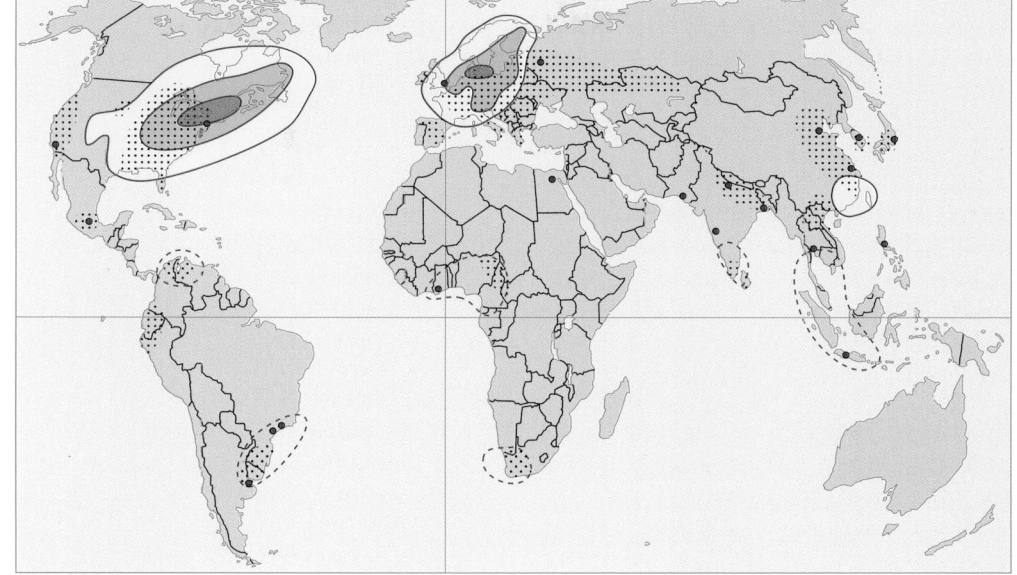

WATER POLLUTION

 Severely polluted sea areas and lakes

 Polluted sea areas and lakes

 Areas of frequent oil pollution by shipping

 Major oil tanker spills

▲ Major oil rig blow-outs

▼ Offshore dumpsites for industrial and municipal waste

——— Severely polluted rivers and estuaries

In December 2002, oil slicks from the 77,000-ton *Prestige* tanker, which broke up off Spain, caused environmental damage to the north coast of Spain and, in 2003, to the southwest coast of France. This was a small incident by comparison with some earlier events, such as the collision between the *Atlantic Empress* and the *Aegean Captain* in July 1979. This was the worst tanker incident ever, polluting the Caribbean with 1,890,000 barrels of crude oil.

Oil spills, however, declined in the 1980s, from a peak of 750,000 tons in 1979 to less than 50,000 tons in 1990. The most notorious spill of that period – when the *Exxon Valdez* ran aground in Prince William Sound, Alaska, in March 1989 – released only 267,000 barrels, a relatively small amount when compared with the 2,500,000 barrels spilled during the Gulf War of 1991. Oil spillage, poisoned rivers, and domestic sewage have in recent years badly contaminated parts of the oceans.

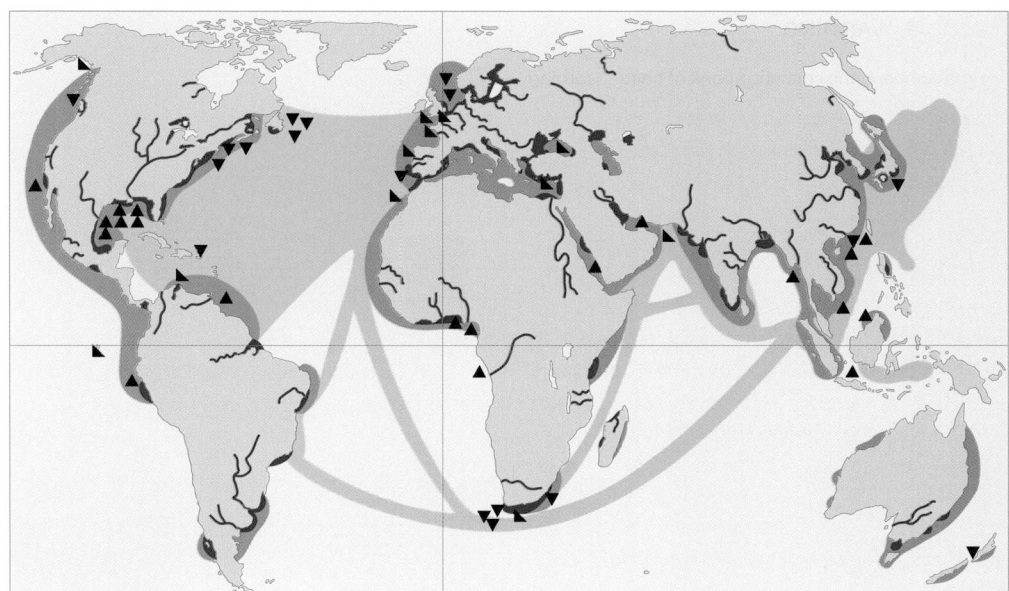

DESERTIFICATION

 Existing deserts

 Areas with a high risk of desertification

 Areas with a moderate risk of desertification

 Former areas of rain forest

 Existing rain forest

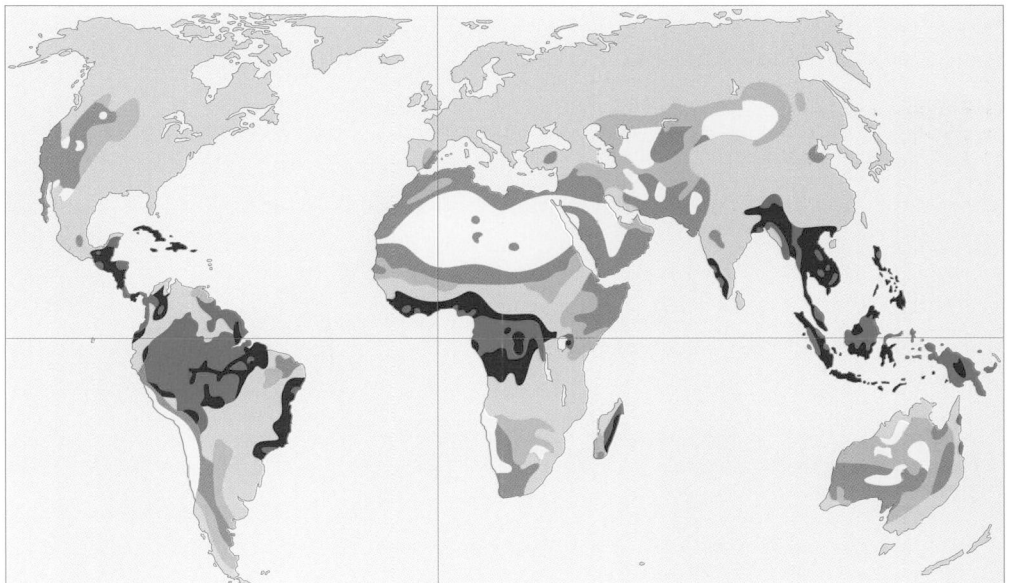

DEFORESTATION

Bolivia has over 100,000 sq miles [250,000 sq km] of dry tropical forest, home to animals such as jaguars and ocelots. It is, however, being cleared at a rate of over 2% per annum. This false-color image shows an area that has been almost completely cleared. The darkest areas are remnants of the original forest, some retained as wind breaks between newly created arable fields, growing such crops as soybeans.

Where deforestation occurs, there is an immediate danger that the vital topsoil will be eroded by wind or by rain. Proposals to clear large regions of the Amazonian rain forests, which play a key role in maintaining the Earth's oxygen balance, could cause an environmental catastrophe.

ANTARCTICA

The vast Antarctic ice sheet, containing some 70% of the Earth's fresh water, plays a crucial role in the circulation of the atmosphere and oceans, and hence the Earth's climate. The frozen southern continent is also the last remaining wilderness – the largest area to remain free from human colonization.

Various countries have pressed territorial claims over sections of Antarctica, spurred in recent years by its known and suspected mineral wealth: enough iron ore to supply the world at present levels for 200 years, large oil reserves and, probably, the biggest coal deposits on Earth.

The 1961 Antarctic Treaty set aside the area for peaceful uses only, guaranteeing freedom of scientific investigation, banning waste disposal and nuclear testing, and suspending the issue of territorial rights. By 1990, the original 12 signatories had grown to 25; a further 15 nations were granted observer status in subsequent deliberations.

In July 1991, a new accord banned all mineral exploration for a further 50 years. The ban can only be rescinded if all the present signatories, plus a majority of any future adherents, agree.

While the treaty has always lacked a formal mechanism for enforcement, it is firmly underwritten by public concern generated by the efforts of environmental pressure groups such as Greenpeace, which have campaigned vigorously to have Antarctica declared a "World Park."

However, from the mid-1990s, the continent appeared to be under threat from global warming, which some scientists believe was the cause of the breakup of ice shelves along the Antarctic peninsula. Rising temperatures have also disturbed the breeding patterns of Adelie penguins.

POPULATION

For more information:

26 Urbanization of
the Earth

Urban population

27 Largest cities

33 Food and
population

44 Wealth and
population

In 8000 BC, following the development of agriculture, the world had an estimated population of 8 million and by AD 1000 it was about 300 million. The onset of the Industrial Revolution in the late 18th century led to a population explosion. The 1,000 million mark was passed by 1850, it doubled by the 1920s, and doubled again to 4,000 million by 1975.

In the 1990s, demographers estimated that the world's population, which passed the 6 billion mark in 1999, would reach 8.9 billion by 2050 and only level out in 2200, at a peak of around 11 billion. However, in the early 21st century, after the rate of population growth had shown signs of decline, the Institute for Applied Systems Analysis suggested that the world's population might peak at about 9 billion in 2070. Whatever the global projections, everyone agreed that the greatest population growth would be in the developing countries.

The developing world includes what the World Bank (2001) describes as low-income economies (average per capita GNP of US $420), lower-middle-income economies (average per capita GNP of US $1,200) and upper-middle-income economies (average per capita GNP of US $4,870). Most developing countries are in Africa, Asia, and Latin America. The developed world, made up of high-income, industrialized economies (average per capita GNP of US $26,440), contains Australasia, most of Europe and North America, and Japan.

In developing countries, a high proportion of the population is young and so these countries face high expenditure on health and education. In developed countries, the population pyramids are becoming top-heavy, with increasingly aging populations.

LARGEST NATIONS

The world's most populous nations, in millions (2004 est.)

1.	China	1,299
2.	India	1,065
3.	USA	293
4.	Indonesia	238
5.	Brazil	184
6.	Pakistan	159
7.	Russia	144
8.	Bangladesh	141
9.	Nigeria	137
10.	Japan	127
11.	Mexico	105
12.	Philippines	86
13.	Vietnam	83
14.	Germany	82
15.	Egypt	76
16.	Iran	69
17.	Turkey	69
18.	Ethiopia	68
19.	Thailand	65
20.	France	60
21.	UK	60
22.	Congo (Dem.Rep.)	58
23.	Italy	58
24.	South Korea	49
25.	Ukraine	48

MOST CROWDED NATIONS

Population per square mile (2004 est.)

1.	Monaco	80,000
2.	Singapore	16,746
3.	Vatican City	5,000
4.	Malta	3,308
5.	Maldives	2,825
6.	Bangladesh	2,542
7.	Bahrain	2,530
8.	Taiwan	1,637
9.	Barbados	1,635
10.	Nauru	1,625

LEAST CROWDED NATIONS

Population per square mile (2004 est.)

1.	Mongolia	4.5
2.	Namibia	6.1
3.	Australia	6.7
4.	Suriname	6.9
5.	Botswana	6.9
6.	Iceland	7.4
7.	Mauritania	7.6
8.	Libya	8.3
9.	Canada	8.4
10.	Guyana	8.5

POPULATION CHANGE 1990–2000

The population change for the years 1990–2000

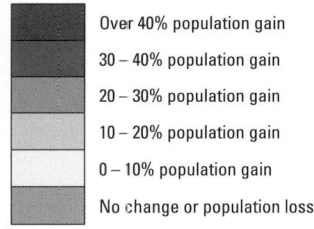

- Over 40% population gain
- 30 – 40% population gain
- 20 – 30% population gain
- 10 – 20% population gain
- 0 – 10% population gain
- No change or population loss

Top 5 countries		Bottom 5 countries	
Kuwait	+75.9%	Belgium	–0.1%
Namibia	+62.5%	Hungary	–0.2%
Afghanistan	+60.1%	Grenada	–2.4%
Mali	+55.5%	Germany	–3.2%
Tanzania	+54.6%	Tonga	–3.2%

POPULATION DENSITY

The places marked on the map reflect the size of the urban agglomerations and conurbations, rather than the actual city limits. San Francisco itself, for example, has an official population of less than a million people.

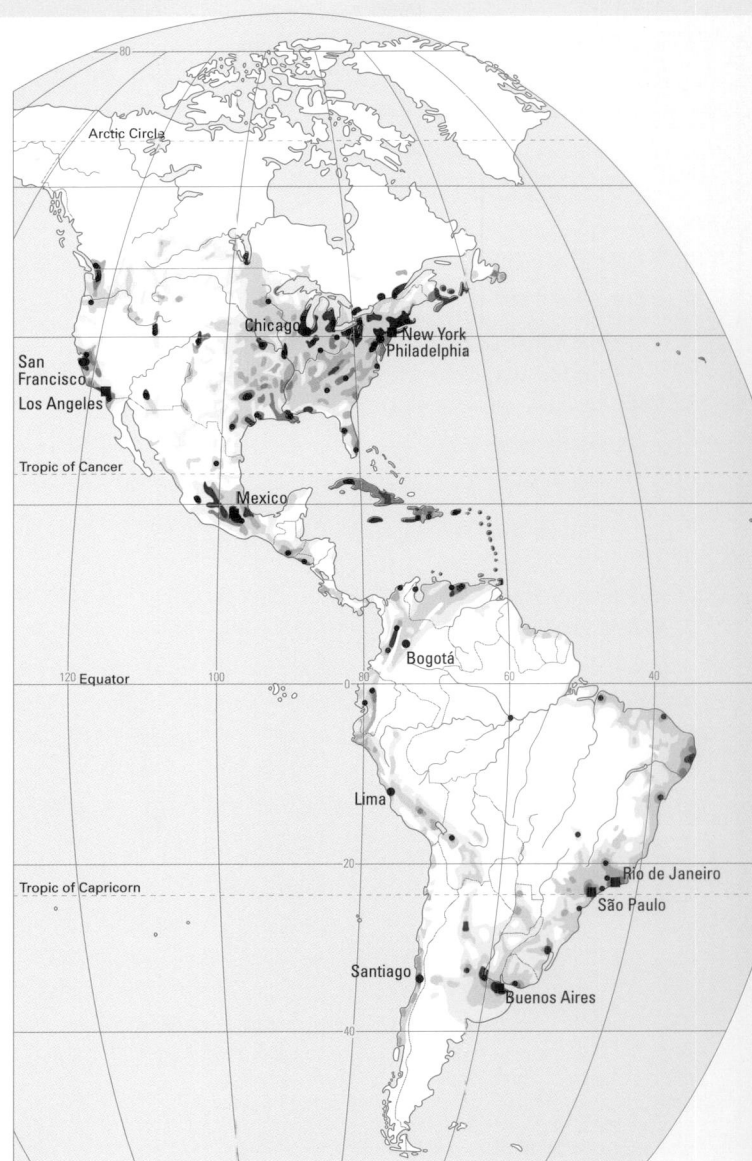

Inhabitants per square mile

- Over 500
- 250 – 500
- 125 – 250
- 65 – 125
- 15 – 65
- 8 – 15
- 3 – 8
- Under 3

Urban population

- ■ Over 10,000,000
- ● 5,000,000 – 10,000,000
- • 1,000,000 – 5,000,000

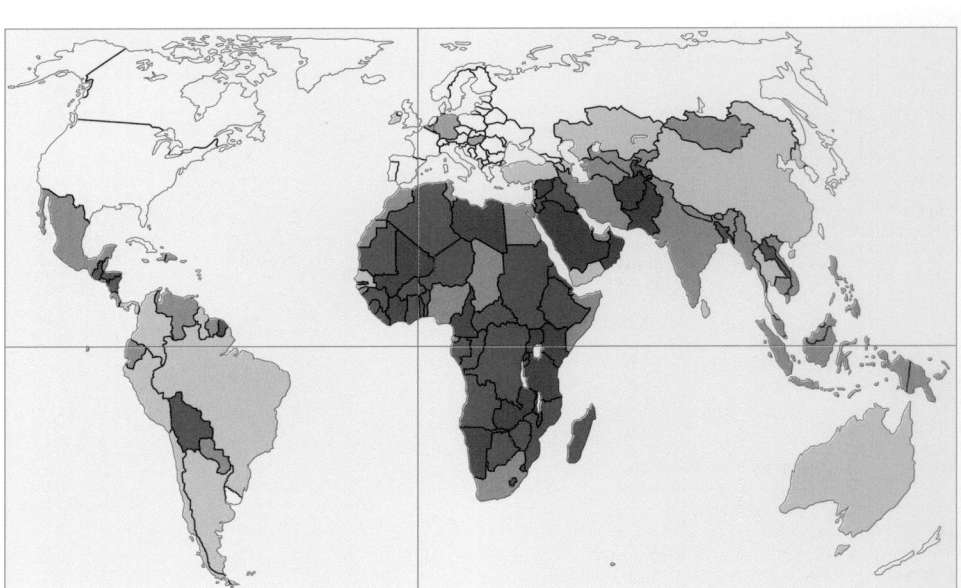

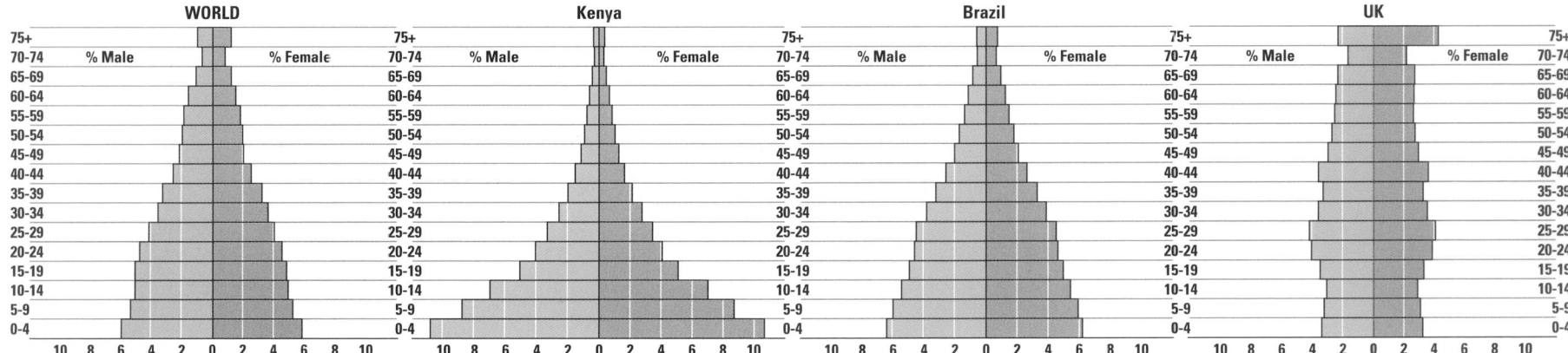

COPYRIGHT PHILIP'S

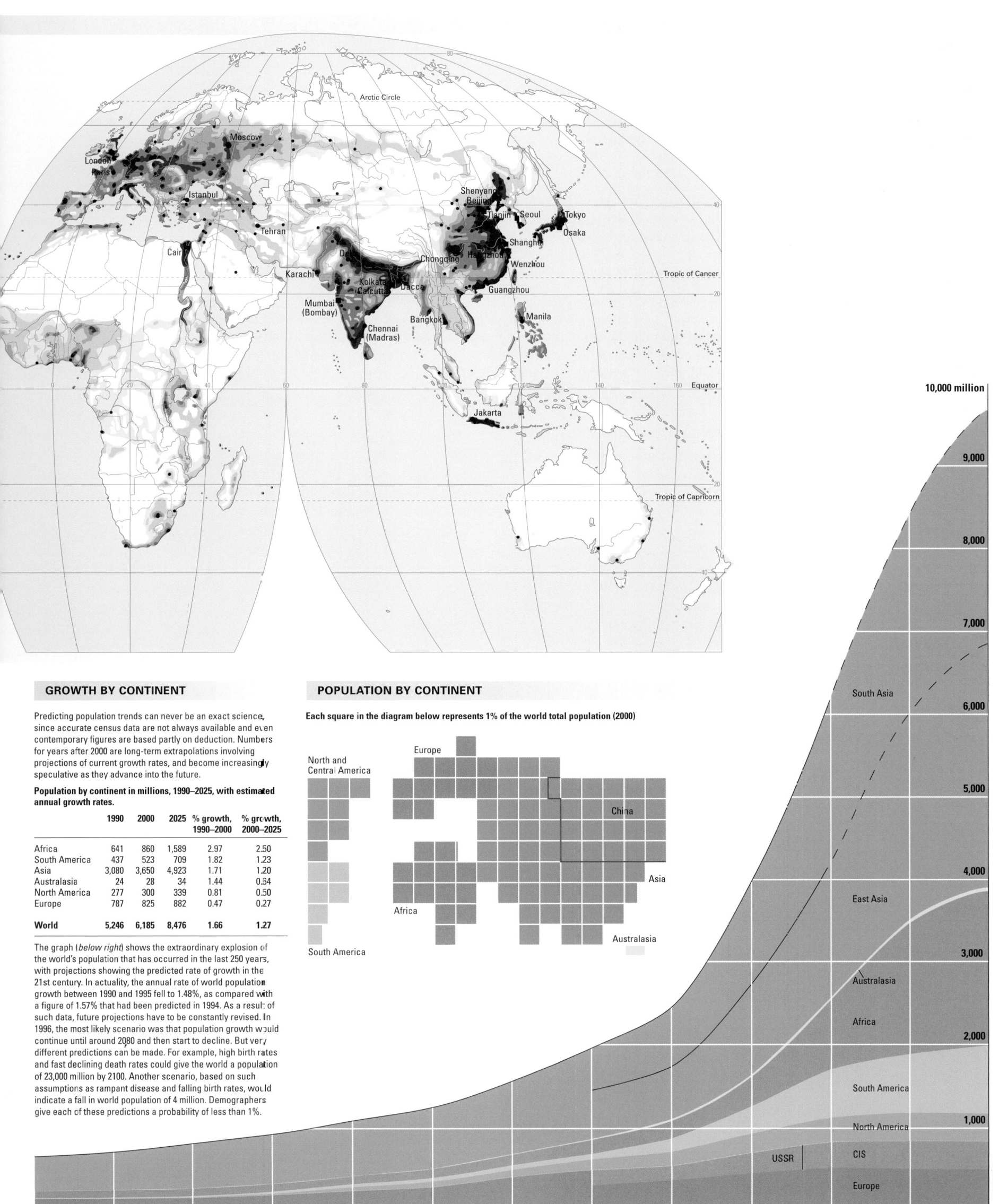

Arctic Circle

Moscow

London
Paris

Istanbul

Tehran

Cairo

Karachi

Delhi

Shenyang
Beijing
Tianjin Seoul Tokyo
                Ōsaka
Shanghai
Chongqing Hangzhou
                Wenzhou
Kolkata
(Calcutta) Dacca
                Guangzhou
Mumbai
(Bombay) Bangkok
                        Manila
Chennai
(Madras)

Tropic of Cancer

Equator

Jakarta

Tropic of Capricorn

GROWTH BY CONTINENT

Predicting population trends can never be an exact science, since accurate census data are not always available and even contemporary figures are based partly on deduction. Numbers for years after 2000 are long-term extrapolations involving projections of current growth rates, and become increasingly speculative as they advance into the future.

Population by continent in millions, 1990–2025, with estimated annual growth rates.

	1990	2000	2025	% growth, 1990–2000	% growth, 2000–2025
Africa	641	860	1,589	2.97	2.50
South America	437	523	709	1.82	1.23
Asia	3,080	3,650	4,923	1.71	1.20
Australasia	24	28	34	1.44	0.64
North America	277	300	339	0.81	0.50
Europe	787	825	882	0.47	0.27
World	**5,246**	**6,185**	**8,476**	**1.66**	**1.27**

The graph (*below right*) shows the extraordinary explosion of the world's population that has occurred in the last 250 years, with projections showing the predicted rate of growth in the 21st century. In actuality, the annual rate of world population growth between 1990 and 1995 fell to 1.48%, as compared with a figure of 1.57% that had been predicted in 1994. As a result of such data, future projections have to be constantly revised. In 1996, the most likely scenario was that population growth would continue until around 2080 and then start to decline. But very different predictions can be made. For example, high birth rates and fast declining death rates could give the world a population of 23,000 million by 2100. Another scenario, based on such assumptions as rampant disease and falling birth rates, would indicate a fall in world population of 4 million. Demographers give each of these predictions a probability of less than 1%.

POPULATION BY CONTINENT

Each square in the diagram below represents 1% of the world total population (2000)

North and Central America

Europe

China

Asia

Africa

Australasia

South America

10,000 million

9,000

8,000

7,000

South Asia

6,000

5,000

East Asia

4,000

Australasia

Africa

3,000

South America

2,000

North America

1,000

USSR CIS

Europe

1750 1775 1800 1825 1850 1875 1900 1925 1950 1975 2000 2025 2050

CITIES

For more information:
18 Water distribution
24 Population density
41 The great ports

Following the development of agriculture more than 10,000 years ago, people began to live in farming villages. Around 5,500 years ago, the world's first cities appeared in the lower Tigris and Euphrates valleys in Mesopotamia. Cities were founded in Ancient Egypt around 5,000 years ago and in China around 3,600 years ago. By contrast with the villages, most people in the early cities were not engaged in farming. Instead, they worked in craft industries, in government services, in religion, and in trade. The cities became centers of early civilizations and, through trade, their influence spread far and wide. However, they were dependent on the surrounding farming communities for their food and other materials.

In 1750, prior to the start of the Industrial Revolution, barely 3% of the world's population lived in urban areas. By 1850, London and Paris had more than a million people, and, by 1900, 14% of the world's population lived in cities. By 1950, the world had 83 cities with more than a million people, and by 1996 there were 280; by 2015, experts predict there will be more than 500. New York City was the only city with a population in excess of 10 million in 1950; by 2015, experts predict there will be 27 such cities worldwide, the majority located in the developing world.

However, predictions have to be constantly revised in light of new data. For example, in the late 1990s, demographers calculated that urban areas then accounted for 50% of the world's population. But after much lower census figures emerged for many cities in the early 21st century, the estimated date by which half of the world's population would be living in cities was pushed back to 2007.

Urbanization is greatest in industrialized countries. For example, in 2000, 77.2% of the people in the United States lived in urban areas. However, in low-income countries, which contained nearly 60% of the world's population in the late 1990s, only 28% lived in urban areas.

The rapid rate of urbanization has created many social problems, especially in cities that have been unable to provide enough jobs and services for the new arrivals. Many of the new city dwellers come from rural areas and take time to adjust to urban life and employment possibilities.

A typical city in a developing country contains millions of people living, often illegally, in shanty towns (or "informal settlements"), while thousands live on the streets. Yet many of these shanty towns are healthier than the industrial cities of 19th-century Europe and North America. Indeed, surveys have shown that migrants to cities in developing countries are less likely to face poverty than they are in rural areas, while benefiting from greater access to healthcare services and education.

Modern cities face many problems today, including pollution, crime, and unemployment. Yet, given competent central and local government, they are capable of generating the wealth they need to solve them, as well as making a major contribution to the nation's economy.

URBAN POPULATION

Percentage of total population living in towns and cities (2000)

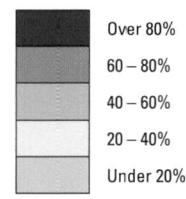

- Over 80%
- 60 – 80%
- 40 – 60%
- 20 – 40%
- Under 20%

Most urbanized		Least urbanized	
Belgium	97%	Rwanda	6%
W. Sahara	96%	Bhutan	7%
Singapore	93%	East Timor	7%
UAE	93%	Burundi	9%
Iceland	93%	Nepal	11%

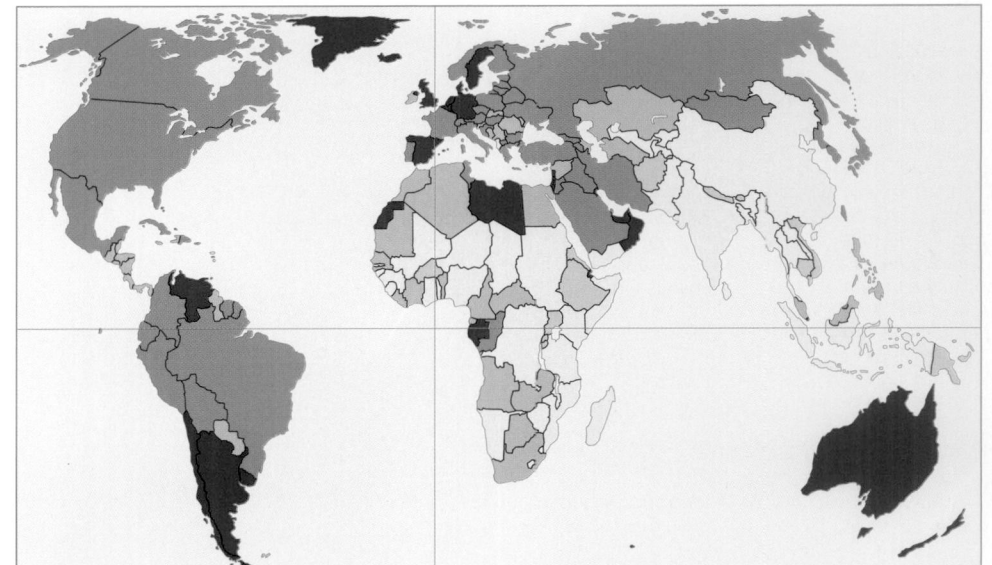

THE URBANIZATION OF THE EARTH

City-building, 1850–2000; each white spot represents a city of at least 1 million inhabitants

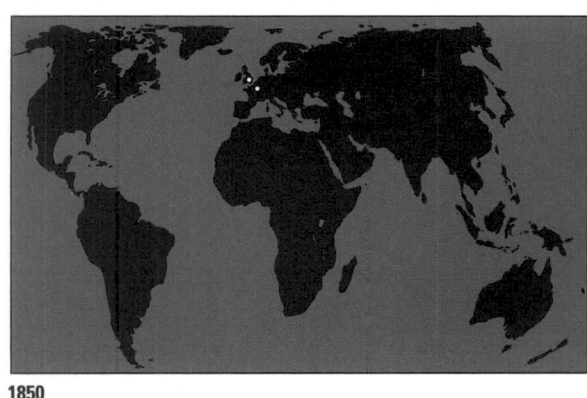

1850

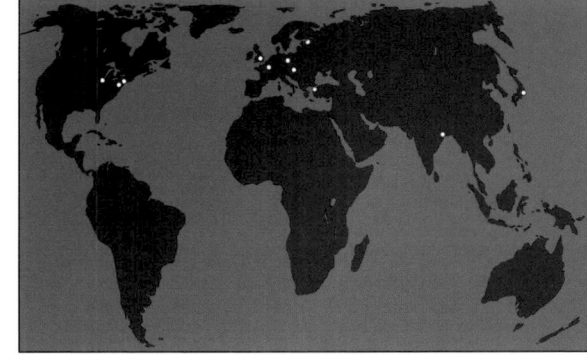

1900

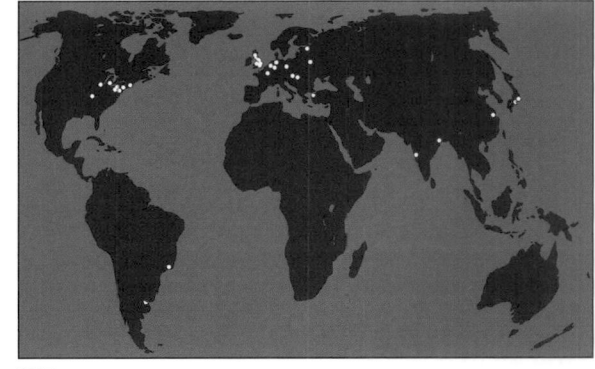

1925

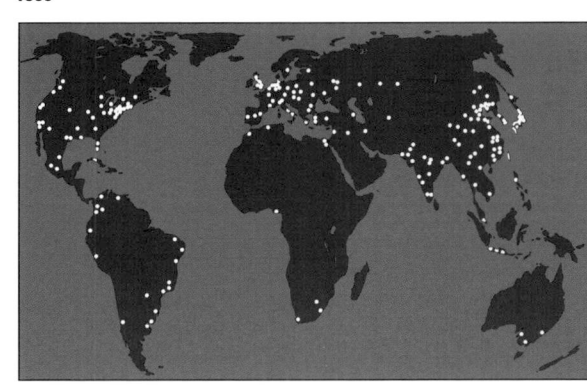

1950

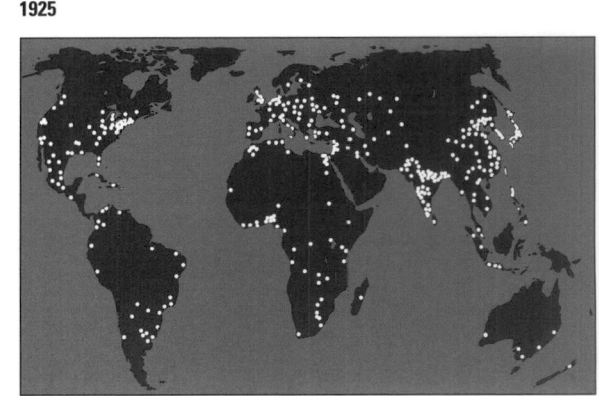

1975

2000

EXPANDING CITIES

These graphs show the projected growth of some of the world's megacities between 1950 and 2015. New York City, the world's largest city in 1950, reached a peak in 1970, but it has since experienced periods of negative growth. London's population also declined between 1970 and 1985, before resuming a modest rate of increase.

In both cases, the divergence from world trends is explained in part by counting methods. Each lies at the center of a great agglomeration, and definitions of the "city limits" may vary over time. Also, in developing countries, many areas around the megacities, which are counted as urban, are in fact rural in character.

The rates of city population growth in developing countries have also often been over-estimated. For example, it was once predicted that Kolkata (Calcutta) would have a population of 40 million by the late 1990s. The reason why many estimates have proven incorrect is partly explained by a new trend, namely that rapid urban growth is now greatest, in some regions, in the smaller cities. For example, the main expansion in West Bengal is no longer in Kolkata (Calcutta), but in a rash of small cities across the state.

The growth of some of the world's largest cities in millions, 1950–2015
Comparisons of city populations over time are problematic due to changes in the definition of the city limits. These figures attempt to take such changes into consideration. The figure for London is the metropolitan region.

■ 1950   ■ 2015

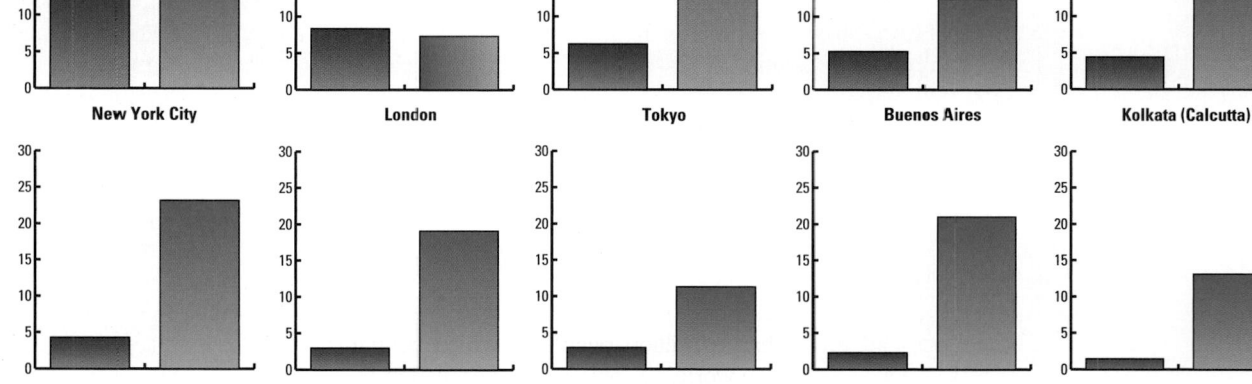

New York City · London · Tokyo · Buenos Aires · Kolkata (Calcutta) · Shanghai · Mexico City · Rio de Janeiro · São Paulo · Seoul

CITIES IN DANGER

In mid-2002, a "brown haze," stretching 2 miles [3 km] high, covered much of southern Asia. Caused mainly by the burning of coal and biomass, it caused respiratory diseases and many deaths. Alarm concerning urban air pollution had been expressed much earlier, but controls since the 1980s had proved difficult to enforce and expensive to introduce.

Those cities taking part in the United Nation's Global Environment Monitoring System frequently show dangerous levels of pollutants, ranging from soot to sulfur dioxide and photochemical smog. Air in the majority of cities without such sampling equipment is likely to be at least as bad. Traffic, a major source of air pollution worldwide, loses Thailand's work force 44 working days each year.

URBAN HOUSING NEEDS

Urbanization in most developing countries has been proceeding so rapidly that local governments have been unable to provide the necessary services and housing to meet demand.

In some cities, many people make their homes in squatter settlements, which are frequently without power, water, and sanitation. Yet these communities are often a dynamic part of the city's economy, while their inhabitants sometimes take the initiative in setting up their own local government and self-help associations.

Some of the world's richest cities also have a homeless underclass, although calculating the numbers of people involved is problematic. Yet it is the case that homelessness and unemployment are currently affecting an increasing number of people in the developed world.

LARGEST CITIES

◀ The business district of Hong Kong City is located on the northern shore of Hong Kong Island. The cluster of modern high-rise buildings reflects the financial success of this tiny region, which has one of the strongest economies in Asia.

Early in the 21st century for the first time in history, the majority of the world's population will live in cities. Below is a list of all the cities with more than 10 million inhabitants, based on estimates for the year 2015.

1.	Tokyo–Yokohama	28.7
2.	Mumbai (Bombay)	27.4
3.	Lagos	24.1
4.	Shanghai	23.2
5.	Jakarta	21.5
6.	São Paulo	21.0
7.	Karachi	20.6
8.	Beijing	19.6
9.	Dhaka	19.2
10.	Mexico City	19.1
11.	Kolkata (Calcutta)	17.6
12.	Delhi	17.5
13.	New York City	17.4
14.	Tianjin	17.1
15.	Manila	14.9
16.	Cairo	14.7
17.	Los Angeles	14.5
18.	Seoul	13.1
19.	Buenos Aires	12.5
20.	Istanbul	12.1
21.	Rio de Janeiro	11.3
22.	Lahore	10.9
23.	Hyderabad	10.6
24.	Bangkok	10.4
25.	Osaka	10.2
26.	Lima	10.1
27.	Tehran	10.0

The city populations above are based on urban agglomerations rather than legal city limits. In some cases, where two adjacent cities have merged into one concentration, such as Tokyo–Yokohama, they have been regarded as a single unit.

URBAN ADVANTAGES

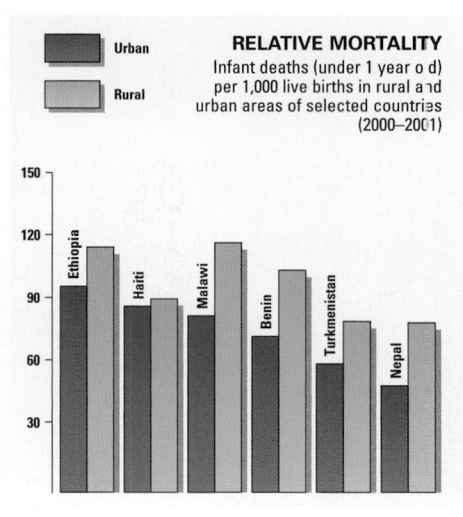

■ Urban ■ Rural
RELATIVE MORTALITY
Infant deaths (under 1 year old) per 1,000 live births in rural and urban areas of selected countries (2000–2001)

Ethiopia · Haiti · Malawi · Benin · Turkmenistan · Nepal

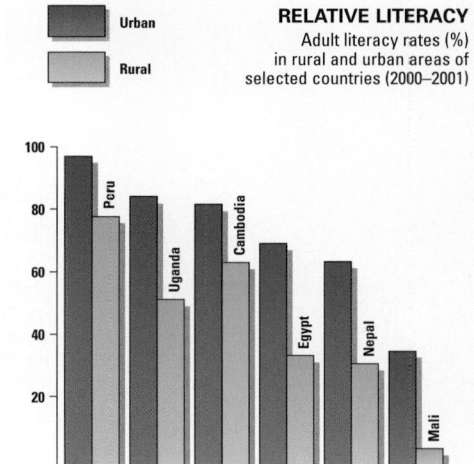

■ Urban ■ Rural
RELATIVE LITERACY
Adult literacy rates (%) in rural and urban areas of selected countries (2000–2001)

Peru · Uganda · Cambodia · Egypt · Nepal · Mali

Despite overcrowding and poor housing, living standards in the developing world's cities are almost invariably better than in the surrounding countryside. Resources – financial, material, and administrative – are concentrated in the towns, which are usually also the centers of political activity and pressure. Governments – frequently unstable, and rarely established on a solid democratic base – are usually more responsive to urban discontent than to rural misery.

In many developing countries, especially in Africa, food prices are kept artificially low, thus appeasing the underemployed urban masses at the expense of agricultural development.

This imbalance encourages further cityward migration, helping to account for the astonishing rate of post-1950 urbanization and putting great strain on the ability of many nations to provide even modest improvements for their people.

THE HUMAN FAMILY

For more information:
24 Population density
30 The world's refugees
   War since 1945
31 United Nations
   International
   organizations

Racial, language, and religious differences have led to appalling acts of inhumanity throughout history. Yet, strictly speaking, all human beings belong to one species, *Homo sapiens*, which has no subspecies. The differences between the three racial types which most people identify – Caucasoid, Mongoloid, and Negroid – reflect not so much evolutionary differences as long periods of separation.

Migration has recently mingled the various groups to an unprecedented extent, and most nations now have some degree of racial mixing. For example, the USA has often been called a melting pot, because of the large numbers of people from various geographical locations which make up the population. The country has no official language but, until recently, English was spoken by the vast majority of the people. But in recent years, some of the immigrants from Mexico, Cuba, and other parts of Latin America have not learned English and speak only Spanish. This development disturbs those Americans who believe that the use of English binds the nation together, and several states have passed laws stating that English is their only official language.

Language is fundamental to human culture. Because definitions of languages vary, estimates of the total number range from 3,000 to 6,000, although most are spoken by only a few people. Chinese is spoken by more people as a first language than any other, while English ranks second, but English is the leading international language, because so many people speak it as their second tongue.

Like language, religion encourages cohesion in single human groups and it satisfies a deep human need by assigning people a place in a divinely ordered world. Religion is a way in which a culture can express its individuality. For example, the rise of Islamic fundamentalism in the late 20th century was partly an expression of resentment that secular Western values were being imposed on Muslims.

WORLD MIGRATION

The greatest voluntary migration was the colonization of North America by 30–35 million European settlers during the 19th century. The greatest forced migration involved 9–11 million Africans taken as slaves to America between 1550 and 1830. The migrations shown on the map below are mostly international, as population movements within borders are not usually recorded. Many of the statistics are necessarily estimates as so many refugees and migrant workers enter countries illegally and unrecorded. Emigrants may have a variety of motives for leaving, thus making it difficult to distinguish between voluntary and involuntary migrations.

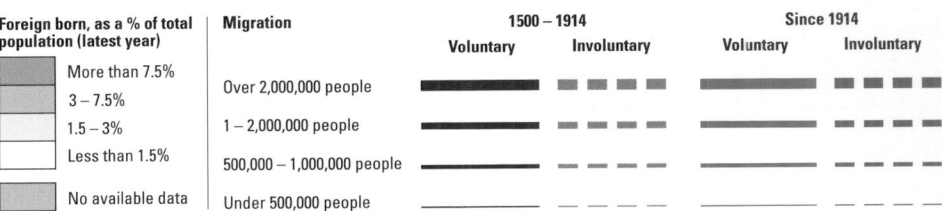

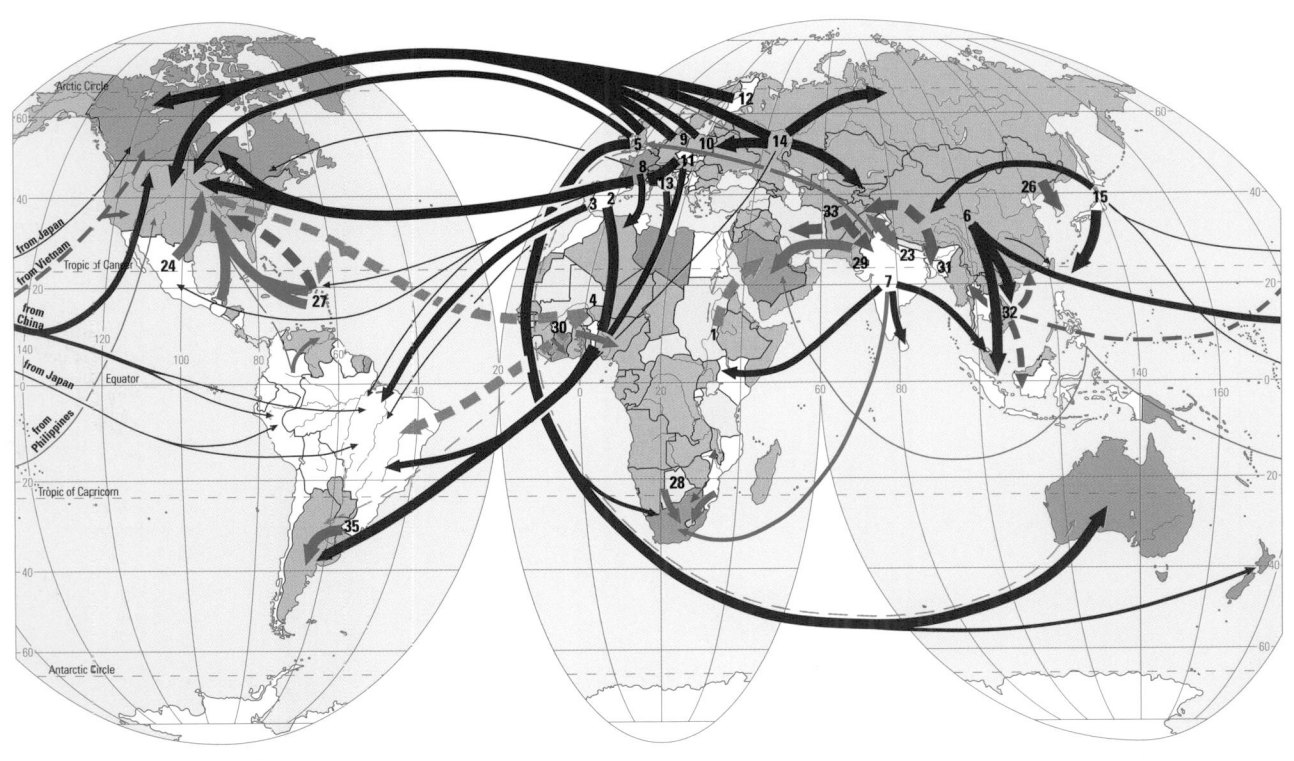

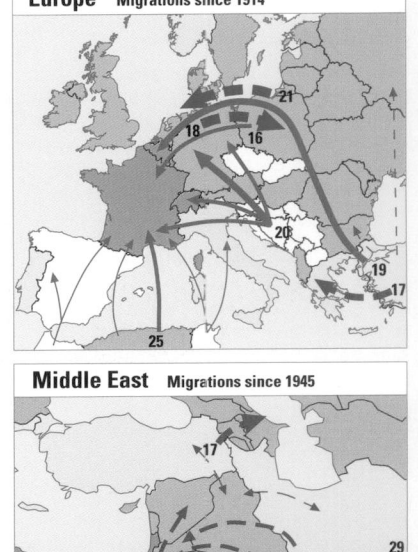

Major world migrations since 1500 (over 1 million people)

1. North and East African slaves to Arabia (4.3m)	1500–1900
2. Spanish to South and Central America (2.3m)	1530–1914
3. Portuguese to Brazil (1.4m)	1530–1914
4. West African slaves to South America (4.6m)	1550–1860
to Caribbean (4m)	1580–1860
to North/Central America (1m)	1650–1820
5. British and Irish to North America (13.5m)	1620–1914
to Australasia and South Africa (3m)	1790–1914
6. Chinese to Southeast Asia (22m)	1820–1914
to North America (1m)	1880–1914
7. Indian migrant workers (3m)	1850–1914
8. French to North Africa (1.5m)	1850–1914
9. Germans to North America (5m)	1850–1914
10. Poles to North America (3.6m)	1850–1914
11. Austro-Hungarians to North America (3.2m)	1850–1914
to Western Europe (3.4m)	1850–1914
to South America (1.8m)	1850–1914

12. Scandinavians to North America (2.7m)	1850–1914
13. Italians to North America (5m)	1860–1914
to South America (3.7m)	1860–1914
14. Russians to North America (2.2m)	1880–1914
to Western Europe (2.2m)	1880–1914
to Siberia (6m)	1880–1914
to Central Asia (4m)	1880–1914
15. Japanese to Eastern Asia, Southeast Asia and America (8m)	1900–1914
16. Poles to Western Europe (1m)	1920–1940
17. Greeks and Armenians from Turkey (1.6m)	1922–1923
18. European Jews to extermination camps (5m)	1940–1944
19. Turks to Western Europe (1.9m)	1940–
20. Yugoslavs to Western Europe (2m)	1940–
21. Germans to Western Europe (9.8m)	1945–1947
22. Palestinian refugees (2m)	1947–
23. Indian and Pakistani refugees (15m)	1947
24. Mexicans to North America (9m)	1950–

25. North Africans to Western Europe (1.1m)	1950–
26. Korean refugees (5m)	1950–1954
27. Latin Americans and West Indians to North America (4.7m)	1960–
28. Migrant workers to South Africa (1.5m)	1960–
29. Indians and Pakistanis to the Persian Gulf (2.4m)	1970–
30. Migrant workers to Nigeria and Ivory Coast (3m)	1970–
31. Bangladeshi and Pakistani refugees (2m)	1972
32. Vietnamese and Cambodian refugees (1.5m)	1975–
33. Afghan refugees (6.1m)	1979–
34. Egyptians to the Persian Gulf and Libya (2.9m)	1980–
35. Migrant workers to Argentina (2m)	1980–
36. Mozambique refugees (1.7m)	1985–
37. Yugoslav/Balkan refugees (1.7m)	1992–
38. Rwanda/Burundi refugees (2.6m)	1994–

BUILDING THE USA

US Immigration, 1920 and 2000

For decades the USA was the magnet that attracted millions of immigrants, notably from Central and Eastern Europe, the flow peaking in the early years of the 20th century. By the mid-1990s the proportion of immigrants had increased again to pre-World War II rates, reaching almost 10% by 2000. However, the balance of origin had swung from Europe to Latin America and Asia, as the graphs indicate.

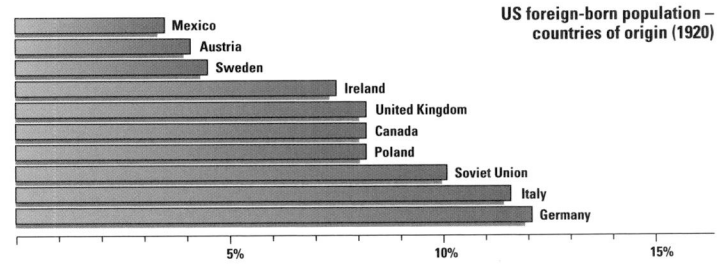

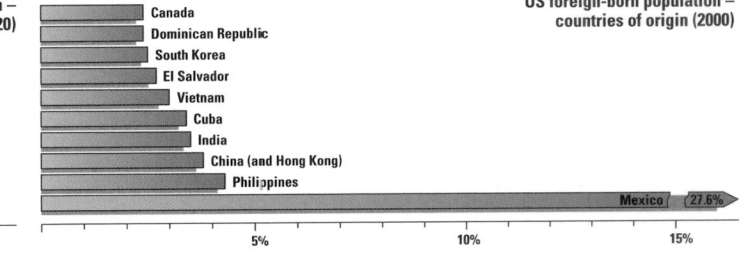

PREDOMINANT LANGUAGES

INDO-EUROPEAN FAMILY

1	Balto-Slavic group (incl. Russian, Ukrainian)
2	Germanic group (incl. English, German)
3	Celtic group
4	Greek
5	Albanian
6	Iranian group
7	Armenian
8	Romance group (incl. Spanish, Portuguese, French, Italian)
9	Indo-Aryan group (incl. Hindi, Bengali, Urdu, Punjabi, Marathi)
10	**CAUCASIAN FAMILY**

AFRO-ASIATIC FAMILY

11	Semitic group (incl. Arabic)
12	Kushitic group
13	Berber group
14	**KHOISAN FAMILY**
15	**NIGER-CONGO FAMILY**
16	**NILO-SAHARAN FAMILY**
17	**URALIC FAMILY**

ALTAIC FAMILY

18	Turkic group (incl. Turkish)
19	Mongolian group
20	Tungus-Manchu group
21	Japanese and Korean

SINO-TIBETAN FAMILY

22	Sinitic (Chinese) languages (incl. Mandarin, Wu, Yue)
23	Tibetic-Burmic languages
24	**TAI FAMILY**

AUSTRO-ASIATIC FAMILY

25	Mon-Khmer group
26	Munda group
27	Vietnamese
28	**DRAVIDIAN FAMILY** (incl. Telugu, Tamil)
29	**AUSTRONESIAN FAMILY** (incl. Malay-Indonesian, Javanese)
30	**OTHER LANGUAGES**

First-language speakers, in millions (1999)

Mandarin Chinese	885m
Spanish	332m
English	322m
Bengali	189m
Hindi	182m
Portuguese	170m
Russian	170m
Japanese	125m
German	98m
Wu Chinese	77m
Javanese	76m
Korean	75m
French	72m
Vietnamese	68m
Yue Chinese	66m
Marathi	65m
Tamil	63m
Turkish	59m
Urdu	58m

Languages form a kind of tree of development, splitting from a few ancient proto-tongues into branches that have grown apart and further divided with the passage of time. English and Hindi, for example, both belong to the great Indo-European family, although the relationship is only apparent after much analysis and comparison with non-Indo-European languages such as Chinese or Arabic. Hindi is part of the Indo-Aryan subgroup, whereas English is a member of Indo-European's Germanic branch. French, another Indo-European tongue, traces its descent through the Latin, or Romance, branch. A few languages – Basque is one example – have no apparent links with any other, living or dead. Most modern languages, of course, have acquired enormous quantities of vocabulary from each other.

DISTRIBUTION OF LIVING LANGUAGES

The figures refer to the number of languages currently in use in the regions shown

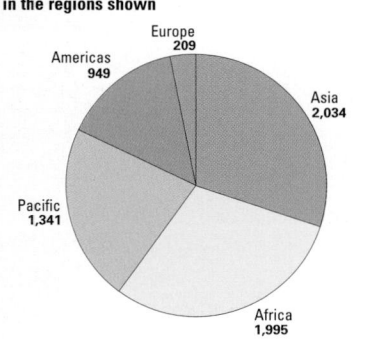

Europe **209**
Americas **949**
Asia **2,034**
Pacific **1,341**
Africa **1,995**

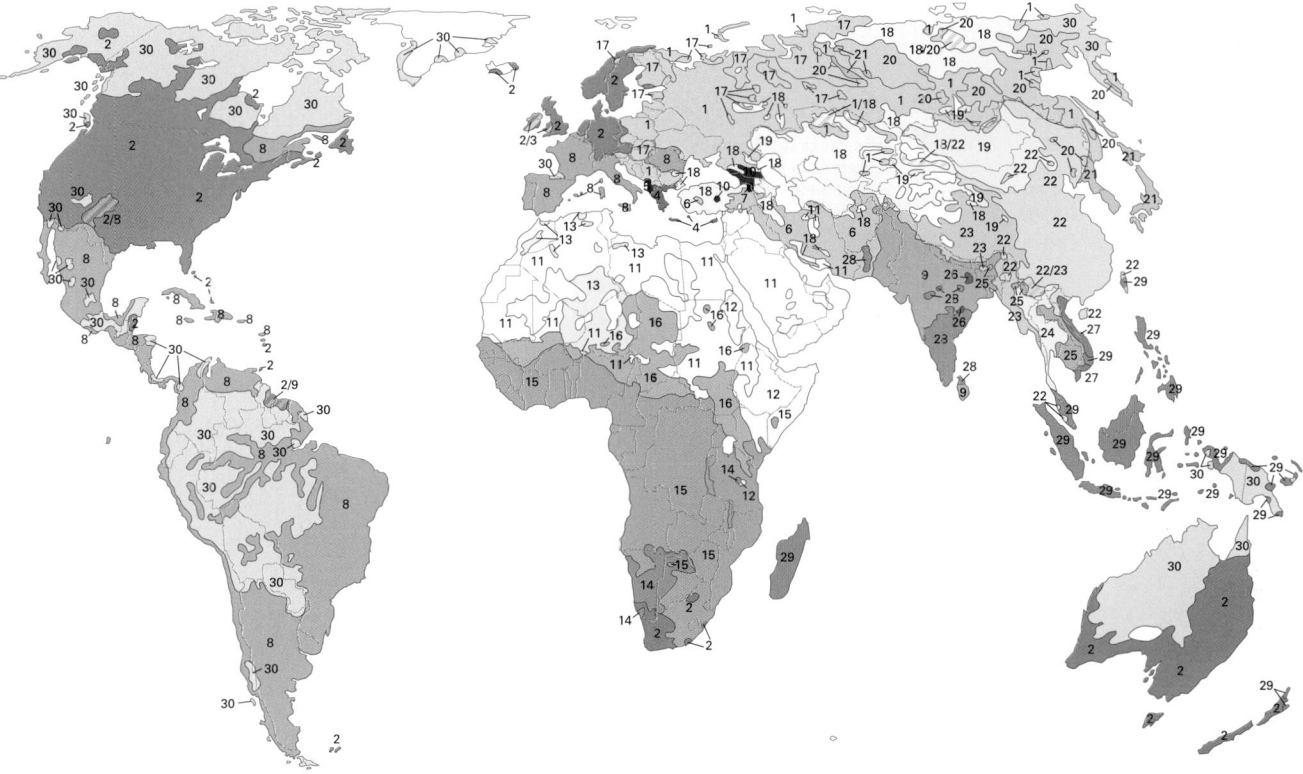

PREDOMINANT RELIGIONS

▲	Roman Catholicism
	Orthodox and other Eastern Churches
●	Protestantism
	Sunni Islam
	Shia Islam
	Buddhism
	Hinduism
	Confucianism
★	Judaism
	Shintoism
	Tribal Religions

Religions are not as easily mapped as the physical contours of the land. Divisions are often blurred and frequently overlapping: most nations include people of many different faiths – or no faith at all. Some religions, like Islam and Christianity, have proselytes worldwide; others, like Hinduism and Confucianism, are restricted to a particular area, though modern migrations have taken some Indians and Chinese very far from their cultural origins. It is also difficult to show the degree to which religion controls daily life: Christian Western Europe, for example, is now far less dominated by its religion than are the Islamic nations of the Middle East. Similarly, figures for the major faiths' adherents make no distinction between nominal believers enrolled at birth and those for whom religion is a vital part of their existence.

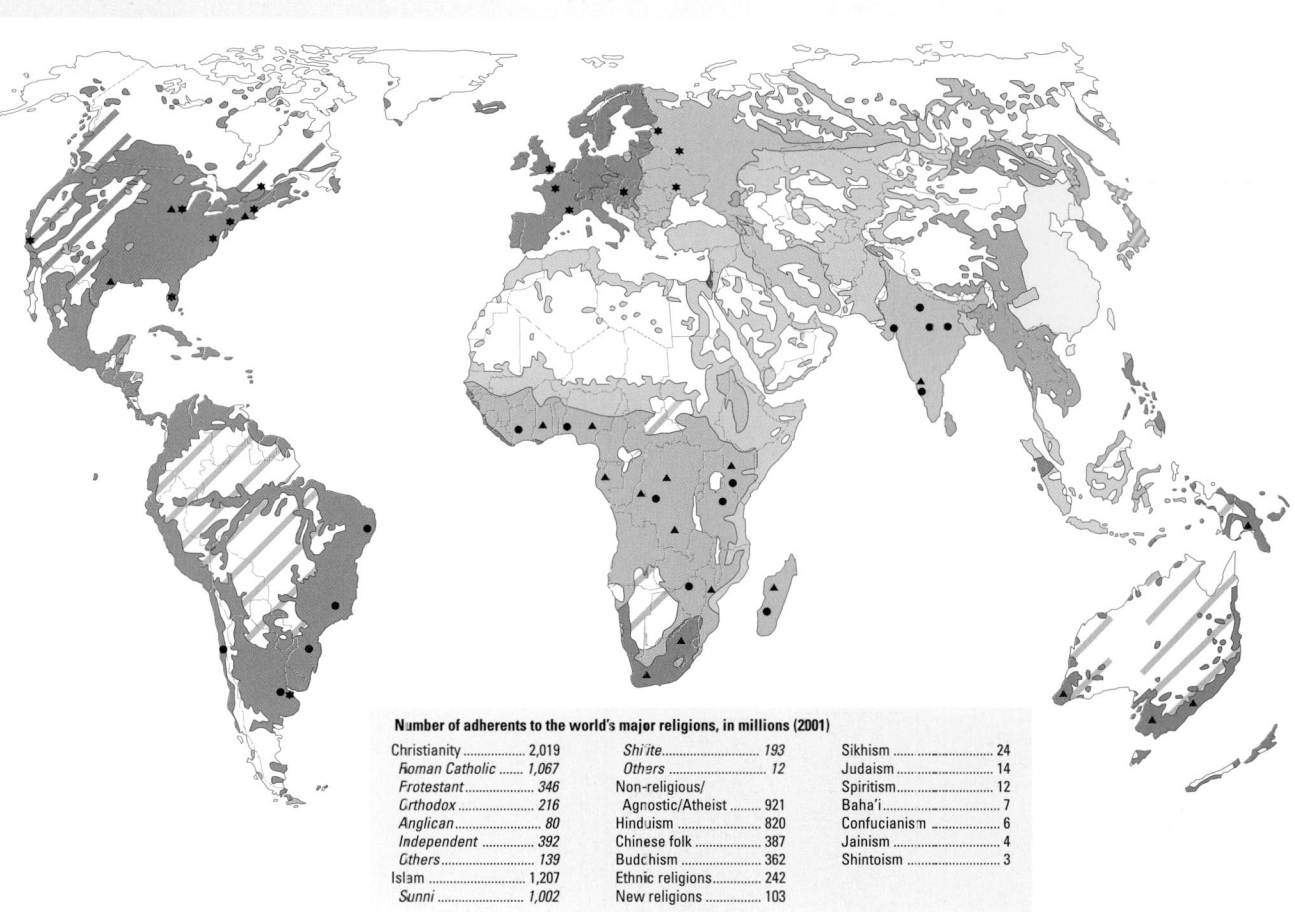

Number of adherents to the world's major religions, in millions (2001)

Christianity	2,019	Shi'ite	193	Sikhism	24
Roman Catholic	1,067	Others	12	Judaism	14
Protestant	346	Non-religious/		Spiritism	12
Orthodox	216	Agnostic/Atheist	921	Baha'i	7
Anglican	80	Hinduism	820	Confucianism	6
Independent	392	Chinese folk	387	Jainism	4
Others	139	Buddhism	362	Shintoism	3
Islam	1,207	Ethnic religions	242		
Sunni	1,002	New religions	103		

CONFLICT AND COOPERATION

For more information:
28 Migration
29 Religion

The 20th century witnessed two world wars, followed by a Cold War which several times threatened to erupt into a third world war, fought with nuclear weapons. The Cold War was marked by a great number of conflicts. Some were colonial wars, as the empires of the first half of the century fell apart, some were border wars, and some were civil wars. All the wars have caused great suffering among civilians, many of whom were forced to join the ranks of the world's refugees.

In the late 1980s, many people hoped that the end of the Cold War, following the collapse of Communist regimes in the former Soviet Union and Eastern Europe, would herald a new era of international stability. Instead, old ethnic and religious antagonisms surfaced in many areas, leading to civil war in such places as Chechenia, in Russia, and the former Yugoslavia. Nationalist rivalries, suppressed under Communist rule, replaced ideological factors as the major cause of conflict.

War is a very human activity, with no real equivalent in any other species. Yet humans also function well when they cooperate. Evolution has made this so. Hunter-gatherers in cooperative bands were far more effective than animals that prowled. Agriculture, urbanization, and industrialization all depend on the ability of humans to cooperate.

The creation of the United Nations in 1945 held out hope that the world's nations, tired of war, would have the means to control humanity's aggressive instincts. Although the UN lacks the power to halt conflicts, it has often helped to achieve negotiation. Economic pressures have led to another kind of cooperation, resulting in the creation of common markets and economic unions, such as ASEAN in Southeast Asia, the European Union, and NAFTA in North America.

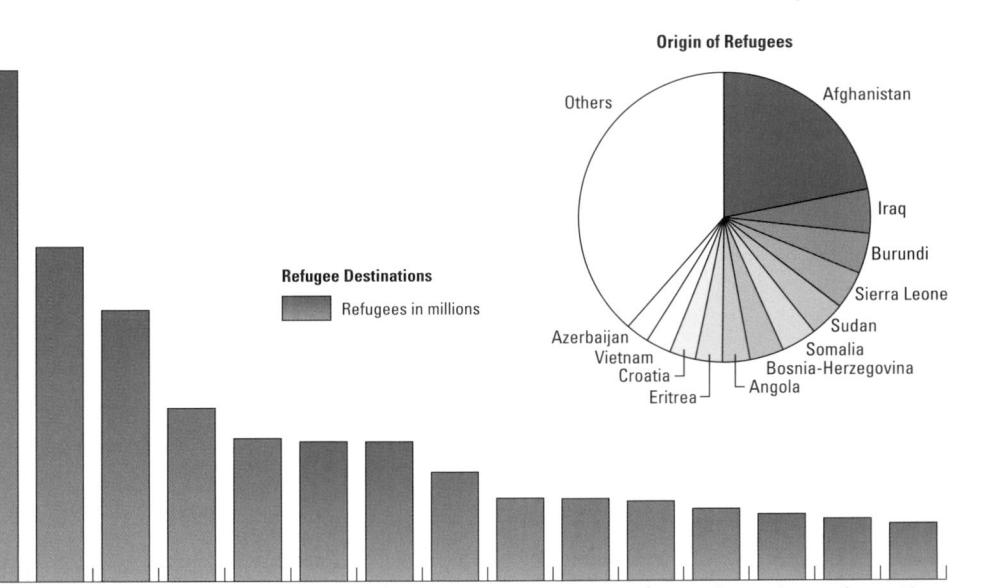

Origin of Refugees

Refugee Destinations
Refugees in millions

THE WORLD'S REFUGEES

Refugees by host nation (bar chart, left) and by nation of origin (pie chart, left) (2000). The source is the United Nations High Commission for Refugees (UNHCR). The 3.2 million Palestinian refugees living in Jordan, Syria, Lebanon, Gaza, and the West Bank fall under the mandate of United Nations Relief and Works Agency (UNRWA) and are not included on the graphs.

The pie chart shows the origins of the world's refugees, while the bar chart below shows their destinations. According to the United Nations High Commission for Refugees (UNHCR) in 2000 there were 12.1 million refugees. However, the UNHCR definition of a refugee, "a person who has left or remains outside their own country because they have a well-founded fear of persecution, or because their safety is threatened by events seriously disturbing public order," does not include people who are in a refugee-like situation but who have not been formally recognized. In 2000, there were a further 5.3 million people who were internally displaced, and a total "population of concern" 21.1 million people, worldwide.

All but a few who cross international boundaries seek asylum in neighboring countries, which are often the least equipped to deal with them. Lacking any rights or power, they frequently become an unwelcome burden to their hosts. Usually, the best any refugee can hope for is rudimentary food and shelter in temporary camps. Many Palestinians have been forced to live in camps since 1948.

WAR SINCE 1945

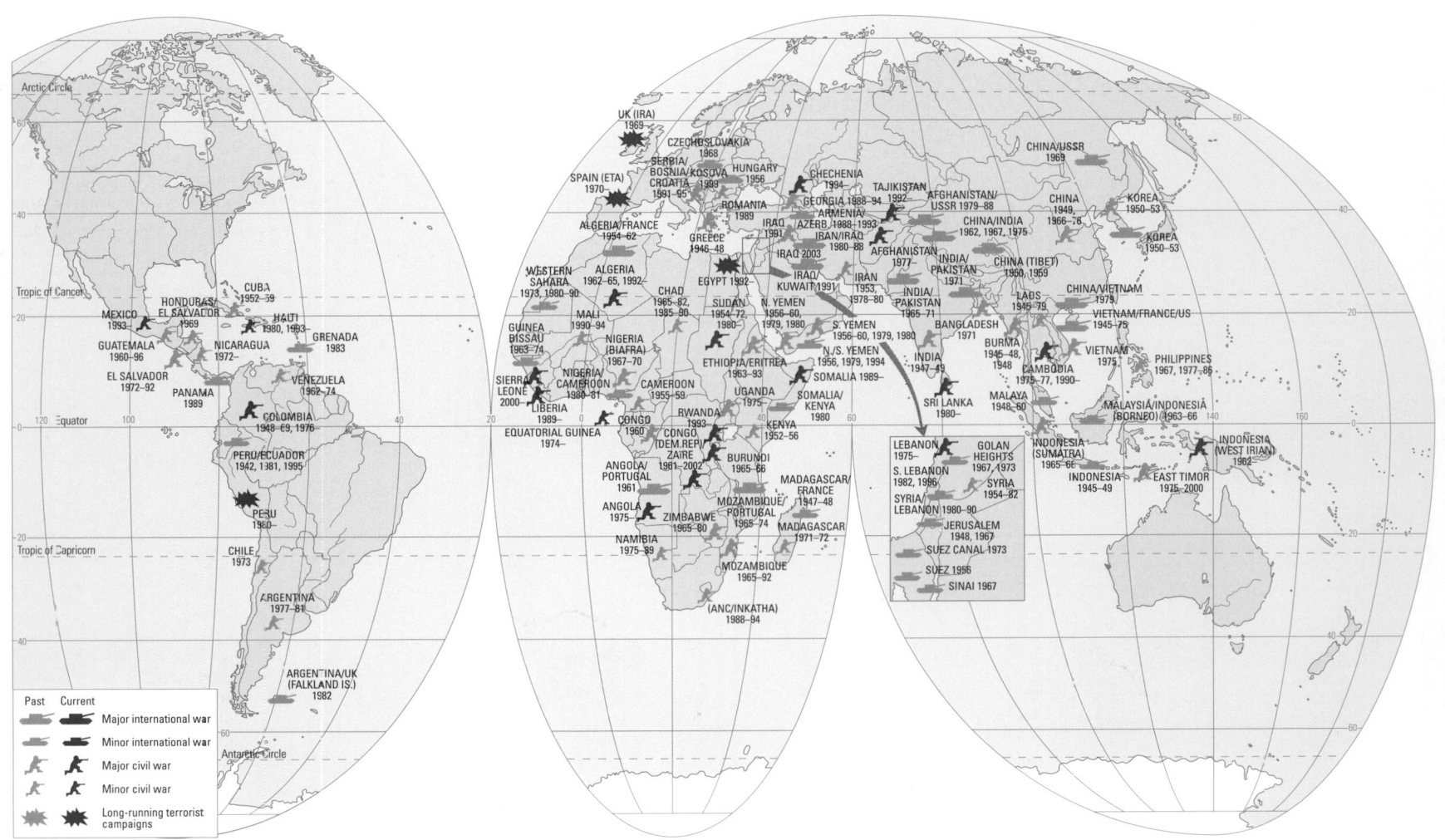

INTERNATIONAL ORGANIZATIONS

OAS Organization of American States (formed in 1948). It aims to promote social and economic cooperation between countries in the developed North America and developing Latin America.
EFTA European Free Trade Organization (founded 1960). Since Austria, Finland, Portugal and Sweden left to join the EU, it has four members: Iceland, Liechtenstein, Norway, and Switzerland.
EU European Union (evolved from the European Community in 1993). Cyprus, the Czech Republic, Estonia, Hungary, Latvia, Lithuania, Malta, Poland, the Slovak Republic, and Slovenia joined the EU in May 2004. The other 15 members of the EU are Austria, Belgium, Denmark, Finland, France, Germany, Greece, Ireland, Italy, Luxembourg, Netherlands, Portugal, Spain, Sweden, and the UK – together they aim to integrate economies, coordinate social developments and bring about political union. Bulgaria and Romania are expected to join in 2007.
AU The African Union was set up in 2002, taking over from the Organization of African Unity (1963). It has 53 members. Working languages are Arabic, English, French, and Portuguese.
COLOMBO PLAN (formed in 1951) Its 25 members aim to promote economic and social development in Asia and the Pacific.

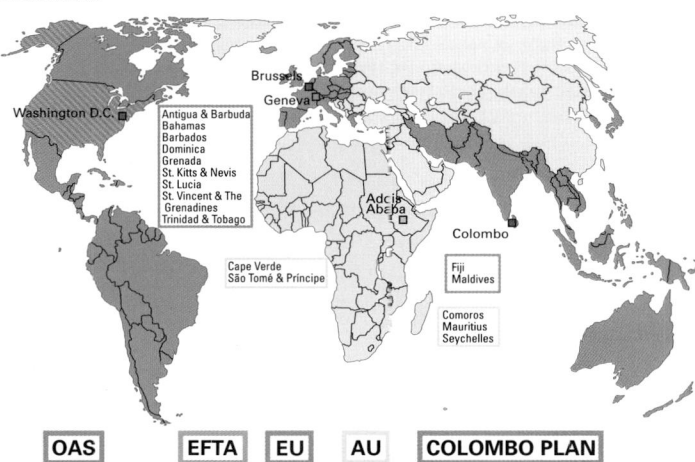

| OAS | EFTA | EU | AU | COLOMBO PLAN |

G8 Group of eight leading industrialized nations, comprising Canada, France, Germany, Italy, Japan, Russia, the UK, and the USA. Periodic meetings are held to discuss major world issues, such as world recessions.
OECD Organization for Economic Cooperation and Development (formed in 1961). It comprises 30 major free-market economies. The "G8" is its "inner group" of leading industrial nations, comprising Canada, France, Germany, Italy, Japan, Russia, the UK, and the USA.
ACP African-Caribbean-Pacific (formed in 1963). Members enjoy economic ties with the EU.
OPEC Organization of Petroleum Exporting Countries (formed in 1960). It controls about three-quarters of the world's oil supply. Gabon formally withdrew from OPEC in August 1996.
CIS The Commonwealth of Independent States (formed in 1991) comprises the countries of the former Soviet Union except for Estonia, Latvia, and Lithuania.

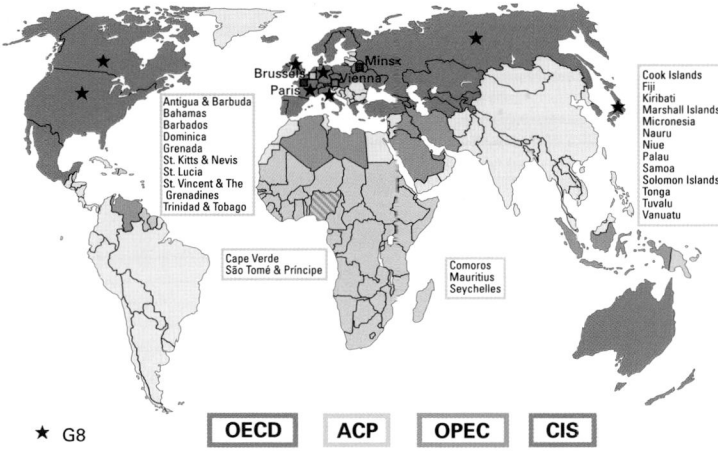

★ G8 | OECD | ACP | OPEC | CIS |

NATO North Atlantic Treaty Organization (formed in 1949). It continues despite the winding up of the Warsaw Pact in 1991. Bulgaria, Estonia, Latvia, Lithuania, Romania, the Slovak Republic, and Slovenia became members in 2004.
LAIA The Latin American Integration Association (formed in 1980) superceded the Latin American Free Trade Association formed in 1961. Its aim is to promote freer regional trade.
ARAB LEAGUE (1945) Aims to promote economic, social, political, and military cooperation. There are 22 member nations.
COMMONWEALTH The Commonwealth of Nations evolved from the British Empire. Pakistan was suspended in 1999, but reinstated in 2004. Zimbabwe was suspended in 2002 and, in response to its continued suspension, Zimbabwe left the Commonwealth in December 2003. It now comprises 16 Queen's realms, 31 republics, and 6 indigenous monarchies, giving a total of 53 member states.
ASEAN Association of Southeast Asian Nations (formed in 1967). Cambodia joined in 1999.

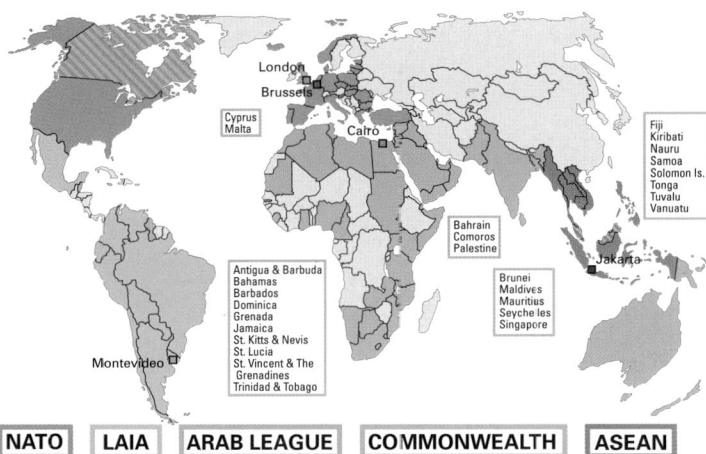

| NATO | LAIA | ARAB LEAGUE | COMMONWEALTH | ASEAN |

UNITED NATIONS

The United Nations Organization was born as World War II drew to its conclusion. Six years of strife had strengthened the world's desire for peace, but an effective international organization was needed to help achieve it. That body would replace the League of Nations which, since its inception in 1920, had failed to curb the aggression of at least some of its member nations. At the United Nations Conference on International Organization held in San Francisco, the United Nations Charter was drawn up. Ratified by the Security Council and signed by the 51 original members, it came into effect on October 24, 1945.

The Charter set out the aims of the organization: to maintain peace and security, and develop friendly relations between nations; to achieve international cooperation in solving economic, social, cultural, and humanitarian problems; to promote respect for human rights and fundamental freedoms; and to harmonize the activities of nations in order to achieve these common goals.

The United Nations has five principal organs:

The General Assembly The forum at which member nations discuss moral and political issues affecting world development, peace and security meets annually in September, under a newly-elected President whose tenure lasts one year. Any member can bring business to the agenda, and each member nation has one vote.

The Security Council A legislative and executive body, the Security Council is the primary instrument for establishing and maintaining international peace by attempting to settle disputes between nations. It has the power to dispatch UN forces, and member nations undertake to provide armed forces, assistance and facilities. The Security Council has ten temporary members elected by the General Assembly for two-year terms, and five permanent members – China, France, Russia, the UK, and the USA.

The Economic and Social Council By far the largest United Nations executive, the Council operates as a conduit between the General Assembly and the many United Nations agencies it instructs to implement Assembly decisions, and whose work it coordinates. The Council also commissions studies on economic conditions, collects data and makes recommendations to the Assembly.

The Secretariat This is the staff of the United Nations, and its task is to administer the policies and programs of the UN and its organs, and assist and advise the Head of the Secretariat, the Secretary-General – a full-time, non-political appointment made by the General Assembly.

The Trusteeship Council This no longer administers any of the original 11 trust territories as they are all now independent.

The International Court of Justice (the World Court) The World Court is the judicial organ of the United Nations. It deals only with United Nations disputes and all members are subject to its jurisdiction. There are 15 judges, elected for nine-year terms by the General Assembly and the Security Council.

The social and humanitarian operations of the UN include:

United Nations Development Program (UNDP) Plans and funds projects to help developing countries make better use of their resources.
United Nations International Childrens' Fund (UNICEF) Created at the General Assembly's first session in 1945 to help children in the aftermath of World War II, it now provides basic health care and aid worldwide.
Food and Agriculture Organization (FAO) Aims to raise living standards and nutrition levels in rural areas by improving food production and distribution.
United Nations Educational, Scientific and Cultural Organization (UNESCO) Promotes international cooperation through broader and better education.
World Health Organization (WHO) Promotes and provides for better health care, public and environmental health, and medical research.

United Nations agencies are involved in many aspects of international trade, safety and security:

International Maritime Organization (IMO) Promotes unity amongst merchant shipping, especially in regard to safety, marine pollution, and standardization.
International Labor Organization (ILO) Seeks to improve labor conditions and promote productive employment to raise living standards.
World Meteorological Organization (WMO) Promotes cooperation in weather observation, reporting and forecasting.
World Trade Organization (WTO) On January 1, 1995, the WTO replaced GATT. It advocates a common code of conduct and its aim is the liberalization of world trade.
Disarmament Commission Considers and makes recommendations to the General Assembly on disarmament issues.
International Atomic Energy Agency (IAEA) Fosters development of peaceful uses for nuclear energy and establishes safety standards.

The World Bank comprises three United Nations agencies:

International Monetary Fund (IMF) Cultivates international monetary cooperation and the expansion of trade.
International Bank for Reconstruction and Development (IBRD) Provides funds and technical assistance to developing countries.
International Finance Corporation (IFC) Encourages the growth of productive private enterprise in less developed countries.

Membership There are two independent states which are not members of the UN – Taiwan and Vatican City. Official languages are Chinese, English, French, Russian, Spanish, and Arabic.

Funding The UN regular budget for 2002 was US $1.3 billion. Contributions are assessed by the members' ability to pay, with the maximum 22% of the total (USA's share), the minimum 0.01%. The EU pays over 37% of the budget.

Peacekeeping The UN has been involved in 54 peacekeeping operations worldwide since 1948.

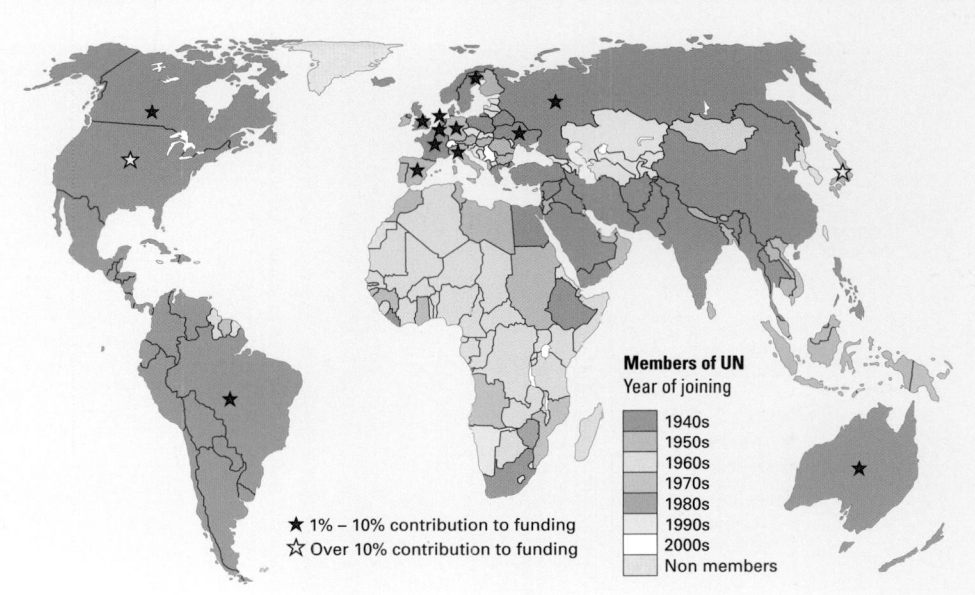

Members of UN
Year of joining

1940s
1950s
1960s
1970s
1980s
1990s
2000s
Non members

★ 1% – 10% contribution to funding
☆ Over 10% contribution to funding

AGRICULTURE

For more information:

16 Climate regions

17 Temperature and precipitation

18 Water distribution

19 Natural vegetation

38 Division of employment

When harvests are bad and world grain reserves fall, an old debate is revived, namely whether the population explosion will cause major food crises in the 21st century. Experts estimate that 3 billion tons of cereals will be needed to feed the world's population in 25 years' time, as compared with 1.9 billion tons at present. To expand food production to this extent, some argue, will place great strain on the environment.

Other experts, however, argue that there should be no food crises. World grain production tripled between 1950 and 1990, largely as a result of the Green Revolution, during which genetically improved, high-yield varieties of maize, rice, and wheat, the world's three leading staple crops, were developed.

These new varieties have helped many developing countries achieve food surpluses and prevent widespread starvation. Some people, however, oppose the use of genet-ically modified crops. In 2002, with severe droughts causing widespread starvation, Zambia and Zimbabwe both refused large maize donations from the USA because they might be genetically modified.

The only region of the world which seems likely to suffer food shortages in the 21st century is sub-Saharan Africa, where in the late 1990s the average daily calorie intake was 6% less than what was needed and where the population is expected to double in 20 years. Improved land management and a huge increase in global trade, especially in food distribution, is necessary if sub-Saharan Africans are not to go hungry.

The development of agriculture more than 10,000 years ago transformed human existence more than any other major advance. By supporting larger populations, it led to the growth of early civilizations and later it sustained people in the industrial cities that sprang up in the 19th century.

Today, agricultural production varies a great deal between the developed world, where it is highly mechanized and employs few people, such as 2% of the work force in the United States, and the developing world, such as sub-Saharan Africa, where it employs 66% of the work force. Many Africans are engaged in subsistence farming, providing the basic needs of their families but not con-tributing to the national economy. Much of Africa also suffers from economic misman-agement, as well as civil war and corruption.

Political problems have also affected food production in other parts of the world. The former USSR had much excellent farmland, but the failure of the collectives and state farms to maintain sufficiently high levels of production helped to bring about the collapse of Communism.

Farmers are under pressure not only to maintain high levels of production but also to increase them. However, the cultivation of marginal areas is one of the prime causes of soil erosion and desertification.

▶ The wheat harvest – photographed in Oregon, USA. Wheat, corn, rye, oats, and barley are grown in temperate regions, whereas rice, millet, sorghum, and maize require more tropical climates. Cereal cultivation was the basis of early civilizations, and, with the development of high-yielding strains, remains the world's most important food source today.

LAND USE

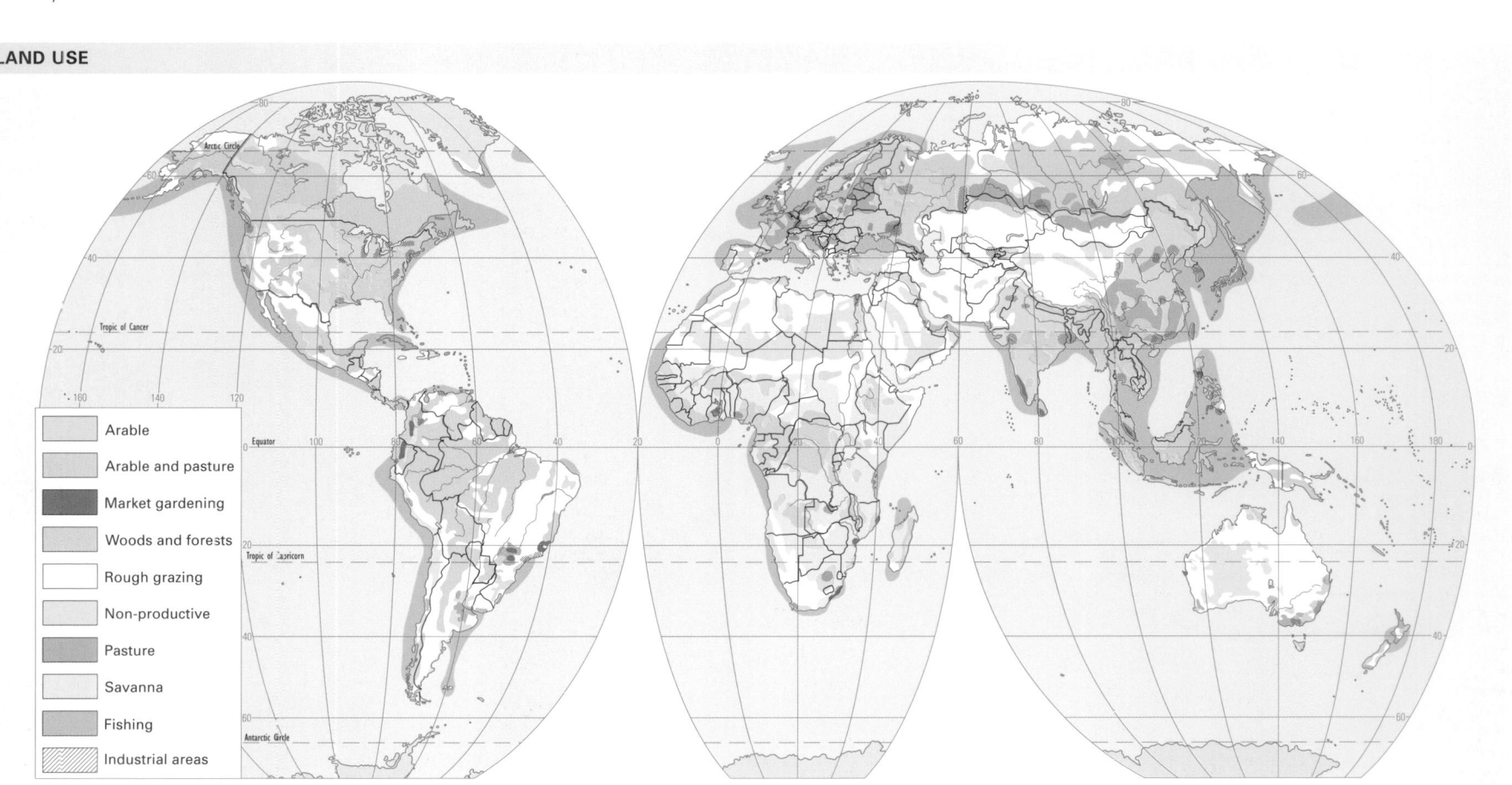

- Arable
- Arable and pasture
- Market gardening
- Woods and forests
- Rough grazing
- Non-productive
- Pasture
- Savanna
- Fishing
- Industrial areas

STAPLE CROPS

Wheat: Grown in a range of climates, with most varieties – including the highest-quality bread wheats – requiring temperate conditions. Mainly used in baking, it is also used for pasta and breakfast cereals.

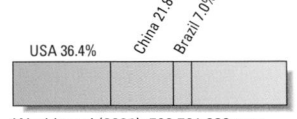

China 18.9% | India 12.2% | USA 11.0% | France 5.7% | Russia 5.5% | Canada 4.6%

World total (2000): 576,317,000 tons

Maize: Originating in the New World and still an important human food in Africa and Latin America, in the developed world it is processed into breakfast cereals, oil, starches, and adhesives. It is also used for animal feed.

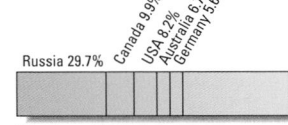

USA 36.4% | China 21.8% | Brazil 7.0%

World total (2000): 590,791,000 tons

Oats: Most widely used to feed livestock, but eaten by humans as oatmeal or porridge. Oats have a beneficial effect on the cardiovascular system, and human consumption is likely to increase.

Russia 29.7% | Canada 9.9% | USA 8.2% | Australia 6.7% | Germany 5.6%

World total (2000): 25,953,000 tons

Millet: The name covers a number of small-grained cereals, members of the grass family with a short growing season. Used to produce flour, meal, and animal feed, and fermented to make beer, especially in Africa.

India 33.2% | Nigeria 18.3% | China 16.1% | Niger 6.4%

World total (2000): 27,255,000 tons

SUGARS

Sugarcane: Confined to tropical regions, cane sugar accounts for the bulk of international trade in sugar. Most is produced as a foodstuff, but some countries, notably Brazil and South Africa, distil sugarcane to make motor fuels.

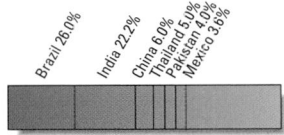

Brazil 26.0% | India 22.2% | China 6.0% | Thailand 5.0% | Pakistan 4.0% | Mexico 3.8%

World total (2000): 1,278,093,000 tons

CEREALS & TUBERS

Cereals: These are grasses with starchy, edible seeds; every important civilization has depended on them as a source of food. The major cereal grains contain about 10% protein and 75% carbohydrate. Grain contributes more than any other group of foods to the energy and protein content of the human diet.

Starchy tuber crops or root crops: Second in importance after cereals as staple foods; easily cultivated, they provide high yields for little effort.

Rice: Thrives on the high humidity and temperatures of the Far East, where it is the traditional staple food of half the human race. Usually grown standing in water, rice responds well to continuous cultivation, with three or four crops annually.

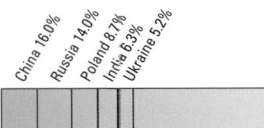

China 34.0% | India 21.7% | Indonesia 9.0% | Bangladesh 4.8% | Vietnam 4.4% | Thailand 3.8%

World total (2000): 598,852,000 tons

Potatoes: The most important of the edible tubers, potatoes grow in well-watered, temperate areas. Though weight for weight less nutritious than grain, they are a human staple as well as an important animal feed.

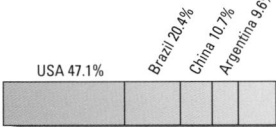

China 16.0% | Russia 14.0% | Poland 8.7% | India 6.9% | Ukraine 5.2%

World total (2000): 311,288,000 tons

Soya: Beans from soya bushes (soybeans) are very high (30–40%) in protein. Most are processed into oil and proprietary protein foods. Consumption since 1950 has tripled, mainly due to the health-conscious developed world.

USA 47.1% | Brazil 20.4% | China 10.7% | Argentina 9.6%

World total (2000): 161,993,000 tons

Cassava: A tropical shrub that needs high rainfall (over 1,000 mm annually) and a 10–30 month growing season to produce its large, edible tubers. Used as flour by humans, as cattle feed and in industrial starches.

Nigeria 19.2% | Brazil 15.6% | Thailand 11.1% | Congo (D.R.) 10.7% | Indonesia 9.4% | Ghana 4.2%

World total (2000): 172,737,000 tons

Sugar beet: Closely related to the beetroot, sugar beet's yield after processing is indistinguishable from cane sugar. It is replacing sugarcane imports in Europe, to the detriment of the developing countries that rely on it as a major cash crop.

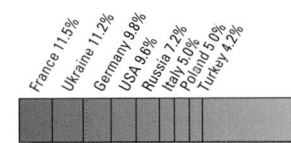

France 11.5% | Ukraine 11.2% | Germany 9.6% | USA 8.6% | Russia 7.2% | Italy 5.0% | Poland 5.0% | Turkey 4.2%

World total (2000): 244,780,000 tons

FOOD & POPULATION

Comparison of food production and population by continent

The left column indicates the % of world food production and the right shows population in proportion.

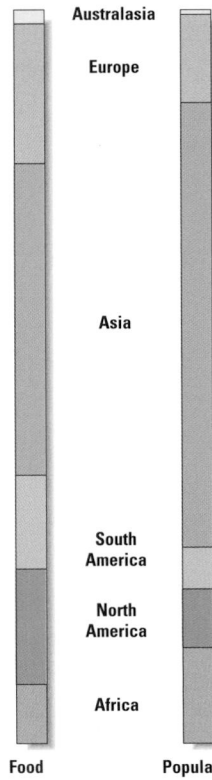

Australasia | Europe | Asia | South America | North America | Africa

Food | Population

AGRICULTURAL POPULATION

Percentage of the total population dependent on agriculture for their livelihood (2000)

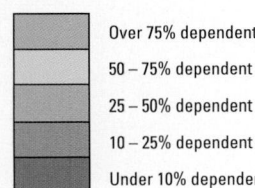

- Over 75% dependent
- 50 – 75% dependent
- 25 – 50% dependent
- 10 – 25% dependent
- Under 10% dependent

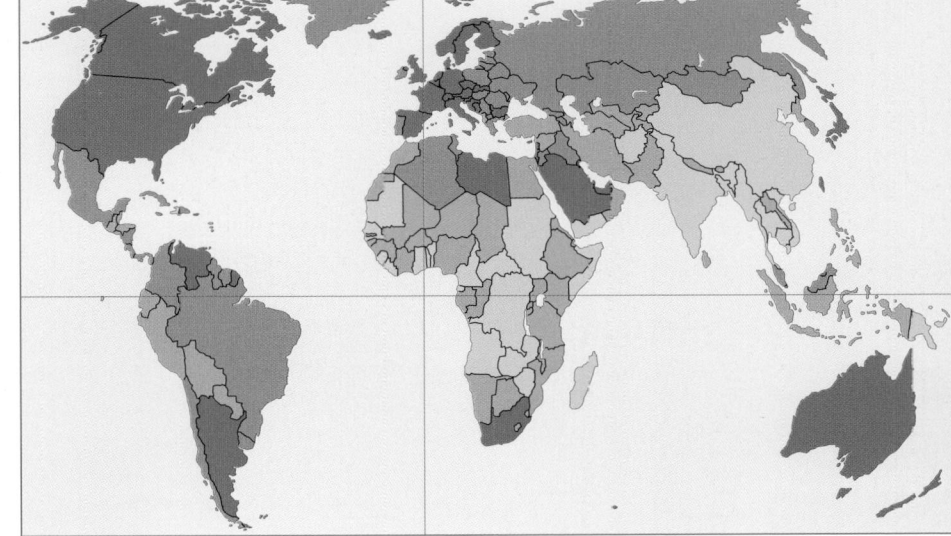

Top 5 countries		Bottom 5 countries	
Bhutan	93.7%	Singapore	0.1%
Nepal	93.0%	Brunei	0.7%
Burkina Faso	92.3%	Bahrain	1.0%
Burundi	90.4%	Kuwait	1.1%
Rwanda	90.3%	Qatar	1.3%

ANIMAL PRODUCTS

Traditionally, food animals subsisted on land unsuitable for cultivation, supporting agricultural production with their fertilizing dung. But free-ranging animals grow slowly and yield less meat than those more intensively reared; the demands of urban markets in the developed world have encouraged the growth of factory-like production methods.

A large proportion of staple crops, especially cereals, are fed to animals – an inefficient way to produce protein, but one likely to continue as long as people value meat and dairy products in their diet.

Cheese: Least perishable of all dairy products, cheese is milk fermented with selected bacterial strains to produce a foodstuff with a potentially immense range of flavors and textures. The vast majority of cheeses are made from cow's milk, although sheep and goat cheeses are highly prized.

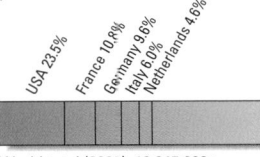

USA 23.5% | France 10.8% | Germany 9.6% | Italy 6.0% | Netherlands 4.6%

World total (2000): 16,045,000 tons

Beef and Veal: Most beef and veal is reared for home markets, and the top five producers are also the biggest consumers. The United States produces nearly a quarter of the world's beef and eats even more.

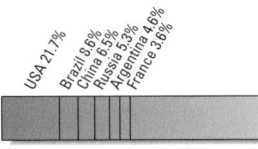

USA 21.7% | Brazil 5.6% | China 6.5% | Russia 5.3% | Argentina 4.6% | France 3.6%

World total (2000): 57,170,000 tons

Milk: Many human groups, including most Asians, find raw milk indigestible after infancy, and it is often only the starting point for other dairy products such as butter, cheese, and yoghurt. Most world production comes from cows, but sheep's milk and goats' milk are also important.

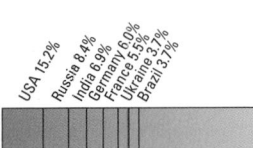

USA 15.2% | Russia 8.4% | India 6.9% | Germany 6.0% | France 5.5% | Brazil 3.7%

World total (2000): 2,504,000 tons

Butter: A traditional source of vitamin A as well as calories, butter has lost much popularity in the developed world for health reasons, although it remains a valuable food. Most butter from India, the world's largest producer, is clarified into ghee, which has religious as well as nutritional importance.

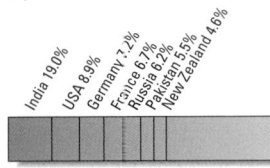

India 19.0% | USA 8.9% | Germany 7.2% | France 6.7% | Russia 5.7% | Pakistan 5.2% | New Zealand 4.6%

World total (2000): 7,049,000 tons

Pork: Although pork is forbidden to many millions, notably Muslims, on religious grounds, more is produced than any other meat in the world, mainly because it is the cheapest. It accounts for about 90% of China's meat output, although the per capita meat consumption is relatively low.

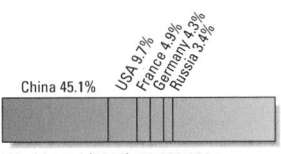

China 45.1% | USA 9.7% | France 4.9% | Germany 4.3% | Russia 3.4%

World total (2000): 90,909,000 tons

CRISIS IN AFRICA

Each year 40 million people, almost half of whom are children, die from starvation and related diseases. In 2000, 600 million people worldwide were estimated to be suffering from malnutrition. Africa suffers from more natural disasters than any other continent; pests such as locusts destroy crops, and tropical storms and floods ruin harvests. Famines periodically affect parts of Africa causing widespread hardship, even though enough food is produced worldwide to feed everyone.

A major phenomenon that affects the weather over tropical and subtropical regions areas around the world is called El Niño (see page 12). It occurs when there is unusual warming in the tropical eastern Pacific Ocean, causing changes in the wind and pressure systems. Normal years are called La Niña. El Niño years included 1973–4, 1982–3, 1986–7, 1992, 1997–8, and 2002.

| Ocean areas affected by El Niño and La Niña temperature fluctuations |
| Countries affected by 4 years of continuous drought, 1996–2000 |
| Areas liable to flood |

Crop Failure
| Areas liable to periodic crop failure |
| Areas where crop failures are rare |
| Desert |

Desert Locusts
| Areas liable to invasions by desert locusts |
| Areas affected by 1993 swarm of desert locusts |
| Major famines since 1900 (with dates) |

ENERGY

For more information:

21 The carbon cycle
22 Global warming
   Carbon dioxide
   Greenhouse power
23 Water pollution
36 Minerals
41 World shipping

Every year, the world's energy consumption is about the equivalent of what would come from burning 9 billion tons of oil (9,000 MtOe) – a 20-fold increase since 1850. Two-fifths of this total actually comes from burning oil and most of the rest comes from coal and natural gas.

The oil crises in the 1970s precipitated concern over dependence on finite fossil fuels as the primary source of energy, and growing environmental awareness has added impetus to the search for alternative energy resources. Fossil fuel combustion damages the environment through the release of gases and particulate matter, but two other major sources of energy, hydro-electricity and nuclear power, are also controversial. Hydroelectricity production involves flooding large areas to create reservoirs, while nuclear power stations generate dangerous radioactive wastes and can cause major disasters. Significantly, by 2002, five European countries – Belgium, Germany, the Netherlands, Spain, and Sweden – had plans to phase out the use of nuclear energy.

Alternative energy resources may soon provide a much larger proportion of the world's energy consumption. Solar and wind energy may become important in such countries as China and India, while tidal, wave and geothermal energy all have potential in appropriate areas. Experts calculate that solar power could, in theory, supply between five and ten times the present electricity supply of developing countries.

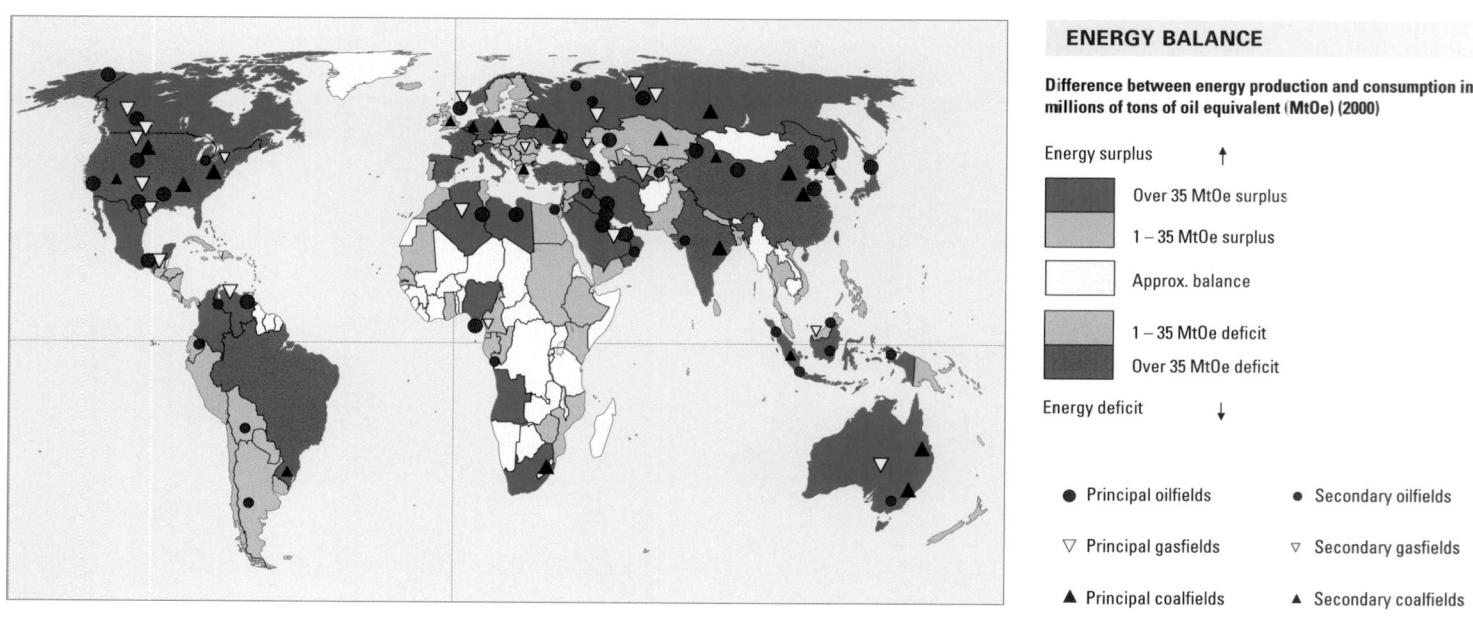

ENERGY BALANCE

Difference between energy production and consumption in millions of tons of oil equivalent (MtOe) (2000)

Energy surplus ↑

Over 35 MtOe surplus

1 – 35 MtOe surplus

Approx. balance

1 – 35 MtOe deficit

Over 35 MtOe deficit

Energy deficit ↓

● Principal oilfields ● Secondary oilfields

▽ Principal gasfields ▽ Secondary gasfields

▲ Principal coalfields ▲ Secondary coalfields

ENERGY CONSUMPTION

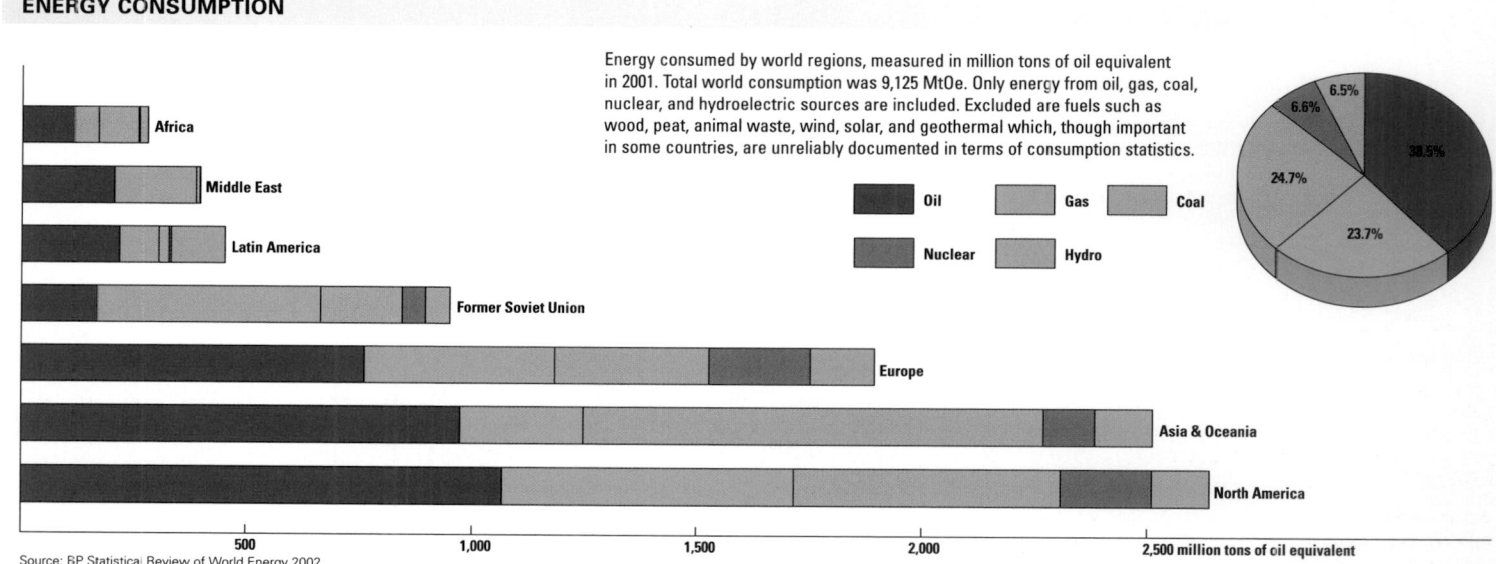

Energy consumed by world regions, measured in million tons of oil equivalent in 2001. Total world consumption was 9,125 MtOe. Only energy from oil, gas, coal, nuclear, and hydroelectric sources are included. Excluded are fuels such as wood, peat, animal waste, wind, solar, and geothermal which, though important in some countries, are unreliably documented in terms of consumption statistics.

■ Oil   ■ Gas   ■ Coal

■ Nuclear   ■ Hydro

Source: BP Statistical Review of World Energy 2002

ENERGY PRODUCTION

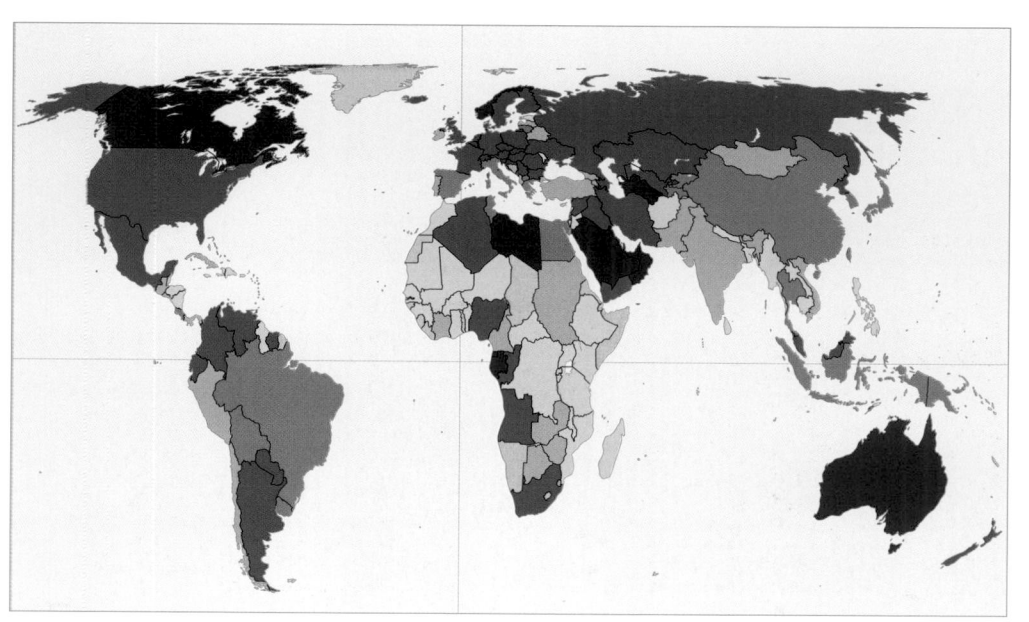

Energy production in tons of oil equivalent per capita (2000)

Over 10

1 – 10

0.5 – 1

0.1 – 0.5

Under 0.1

No data available

In developing countries traditional fuels are still very important. These so-called biomass fuels include wood, charcoal, and dried dung. The pie chart (*right*) highlights the importance of biomass in terms of energy consumption in Nigeria. Collecting fuelwood can be a time-consuming task, sometimes taking all day.

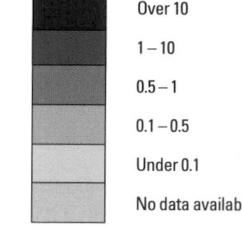

Nigeria

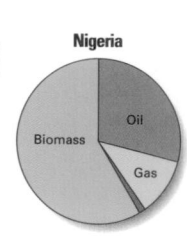

OIL MOVEMENTS

Major world movements of oil in millions of tons (2001)

1.	Middle East to Asia (not China or Japan)	316.7
2.	Middle East to Japan	208.8
3.	Former Soviet Union to Europe	181.2
4.	Middle East to Europe	176.2
5.	Middle East to USA	138.0
6.	South and Central America to USA	126.3
7.	North Africa to Europe	96.9
8.	Canada to USA	88.0
9.	Mexico to USA	70.8
10.	West Africa to USA	68.1
11.	Europe to USA	46.2
12.	Middle East to Africa	41.0
13.	West Africa to Asia (not China or Japan)	36.9
14.	West Africa to Europe	34.9
15.	Middle East to China	34.2
16.	Asia (not China) to Japan	34.2
Total world imports		**2,159,300,000 tons**

◄ With many of the world's onshore oilfields reaching their maturity, exploration and production in ever-deeper ocean waters is taking place to try to satisfy demand. The current deepest production well is in 6,004 ft [1,829 m] of water, offshore of Brazil. However, exploration wells off the coasts of Angola and Nigeria are already being drilled in water 8,000 ft [2,438 m] deep, and it is believed that wells in 10,000 ft [3,048 m] of water will soon be developed.

ENERGY RESERVES

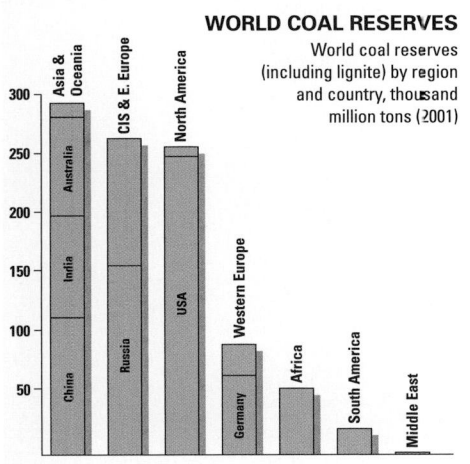

WORLD COAL RESERVES
World coal reserves (including lignite) by region and country, thousand million tons (2001)

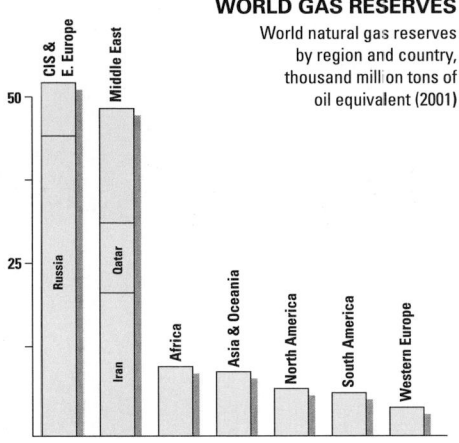

WORLD GAS RESERVES
World natural gas reserves by region and country, thousand million tons of oil equivalent (2001)

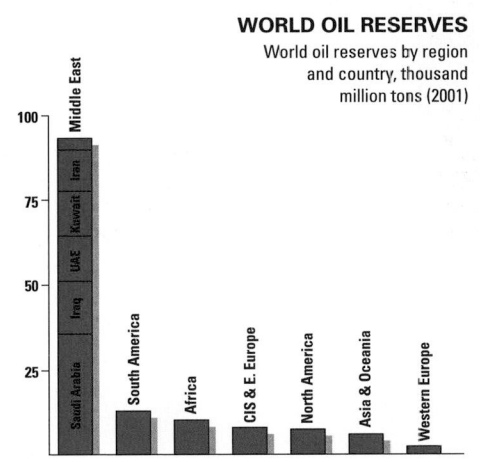

WORLD OIL RESERVES
World oil reserves by region and country, thousand million tons (2001)

NUCLEAR POWER

Major producers by percentage of world total (2000) and by percentage of domestic electricity generation (1999)

Country	% of world total production	Country	% of nuclear as proportion of domestic electricity
1. USA	30.5%	1. Lithuania	76.1%
2. France	15.7%	2. France	75.1%
3. Japan	12.6%	3. Belgium	58.2%
4. Germany	6.7%	4. Slovak Rep.	47.5%
5. Russia	4.6%	5. Sweden	44.2%
6. South Korea	4.1%	6. Ukraine	41.6%
7. UK	3.8%	7. Bulgaria	41.4%
8. Canada	2.9%	8. South Korea	39.1%
9. Ukraine	2.8%	9. Hungary	38.1%
= Sweden	2.8%	10. Slovenia	35.9%

Although the 1980s were a bad time for the nuclear power industry (major projects ran over budget and fears of long-term environmental damage were heavily reinforced by the 1986 disaster at Chernobyl), the industry picked up in the early 1990s. Whilst the number of reactors is still increasing, however, orders for new plants have shrunk. In 1997, the Swedish government began to decommission the country's 12 nuclear power plants.

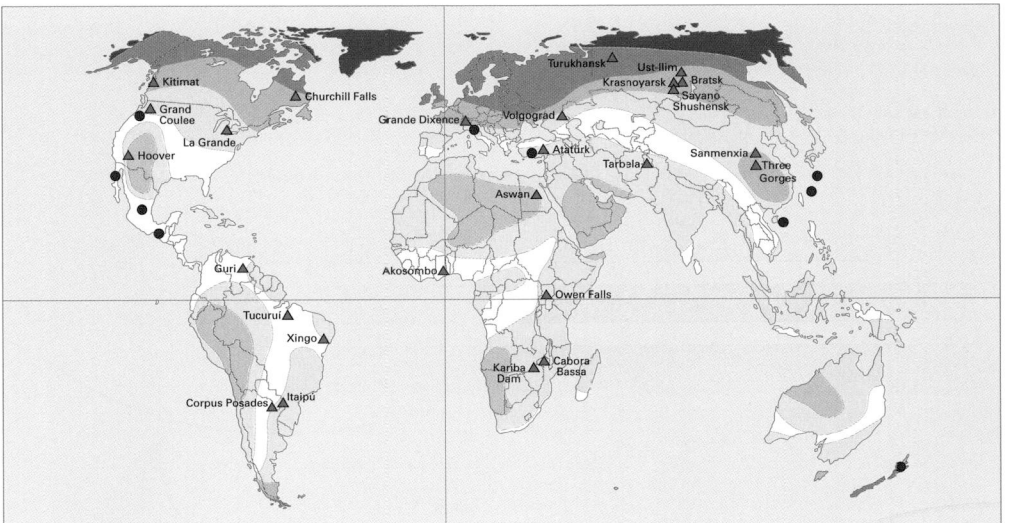

RENEWABLE ENERGY

Average annual solar irradiance in kWh/m², with selected major hydroelectric and geothermal power stations

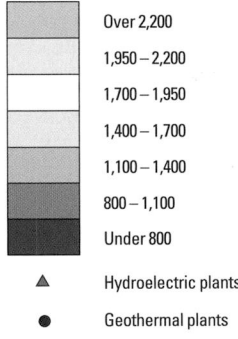

- Over 2,200
- 1,950 – 2,200
- 1,700 – 1,950
- 1,400 – 1,700
- 1,100 – 1,400
- 800 – 1,100
- Under 800

▲ Hydroelectric plants

● Geothermal plants

HYDROELECTRICITY

Major producers by percentage of world total (2000) and by percentage of domestic electricity generation (1999)

Country	% of world total production	Country	% of hydroelectric as proportion of domestic electricity
1. Canada	13.1%	1. Bhutan	99.9%
2. USA	12.0%	2. Paraguay	99.8%
3. Brazil	11.1%	= Zambia	99.8%
4. China	8.5%	4. Norway	99.1%
5. Russia	6.1%	5. Ethiopia	98.1%
6. Norway	4.6%	6. Congo (Rep. Dem.)	97.9%
7. Japan	3.3%	7. Tajikistan	97.8%
8. India	3.1%	8. Cameroon	97.3%
9. France	2.8%	9. Albania	97.2%
10. Sweden	2.7%	= Laos	97.2%

Countries heavily reliant on hydroelectricity are usually small and non-industrial: a high proportion of hydroelectric power more often reflects a modest energy budget than vast hydroelectric resources. The USA, for instance, produces only 8.5% of its power requirements from hydroelectricity; yet that 8.5% amounts to more than three times the hydropower generated by most of Africa.

ALTERNATIVE ENERGY RESOURCES

Solar: Each year the Sun bestows upon the Earth almost a million times as much energy as is locked up in all the planet's oil reserves, but only an insignificant fraction is trapped and used commercially. In a few installations around the world, mirrors focus the Sun's rays on to boilers, whose steam generates electricity by spinning turbines.

Wind: Caused by uneven heating of the Earth, winds are themselves a form of solar energy. Windmills have been long used for wind power; recent models, often arranged in banks on wind-swept high ground or off coastlines, usually generate electricity. Wind-power figures are given in the table (right) – it is the world's fastest growing energy source. In 2002, Germany, the USA, Spain, and Denmark produced nearly 16,000 MW.

Tidal: The energy from tides is potentially enormous, although only a few installations have so far been built to exploit it. In theory at least, waves and currents could also provide almost unimaginable power, and the thermal differences in the ocean depths are another huge well

of potential energy. But work on extracting it is still at the experimental stage.

Geothermal: The Earth's temperature rises by 1°F for every 50 feet descent, with much steeper temperature gradients in geologically active areas. El Salvador, for example, produces 39% of its electricity from geothermal power stations, whilst the USA is the world's leading producer. Some of the oldest and most successful applications are in Iceland, where 86% of all households are heated by geothermal energy.

Biomass: The oldest of human fuels ranges from animal dung, still burned in cooking fires in much of North Africa and elsewhere, to sugarcane plantations feeding high-technology distilleries to produce ethanol for motor-vehicle engines. In Brazil and South Africa, plant ethanol provides up to 25% of motor fuel. Throughout the developing world, most biomass energy comes from firewood: although accurate figures are impossible to obtain, it may yield as much as 10% of the world's total energy consumption.

WIND POWER

World wind energy generating capacity, in megawatts

1980	10
1982	90
1984	600
1986	1,270
1988	1,580
1989	1,730
1990	1,930
1991	2,170
1992	2,510
1993	3,050
1994	3,710
1995	4,820
1996	6,115
1997	7,630
1998	9,600

Wind power is the fastest growing source of energy. Between 1998 and 2002, world production more than doubled.

MINERALS

For more information:

8 Geology
39 Patterns of production
41 World shipping

The use of metals played a vital part in the evolving technologies of early peoples. Copper first came into use around 10,000 years ago, bronze about 5,000 years ago, and iron 3,300 years ago. In the early stages of the Industrial Revolution, the location of coal, iron ore, and water power usually determined the location of new industries. But due to continuing improvements in transport, including oil pipelines, industries can now be located almost anywhere.

Minerals are distributed unevenly and some industrial countries, lacking their own mineral resources, import most of the raw materials they need. Some imports come from mineral-rich countries, such as Australia, but others come from developing countries, especially in Africa and South America. Most developing countries export unprocessed ores, losing out on the higher revenues gained from exporting metals.

Most minerals come from land deposits, because undersea deposits, with the exception of oil reserves under the continental shelves, have been inaccessible. But shortages of terrestrial minerals may one day encourage exploitation of the ocean floor.

▶ An aerial view of gold mine excavations in Zimbabwe, for extraction both above and below ground. Once a major producer of gold, Zimbabwe's gold mining industry has greatly declined in recent years as a result of political and social unrest.

URANIUM

Uranium was first discovered by the German chemist Martin Klaproth in 1789. In its pure state, uranium is an immensely heavy, white metal. But although spent uranium is employed as a projectile in anti-missile cannons, where its mass ensures a lethal punch, its main use is as a fuel in nuclear reactors, and in nuclear weaponry.

Uranium is very scarce: the main source is the rare ore pitchblende, which itself contains only 0.2% uranium oxide. This blackish, lustrous ore occurs in quartz veins. Only a minute fraction of that is the radioactive U^{235} isotope, though so-called breeder reactors can transmute the more common U^{238} into highly radioactive plutonium.

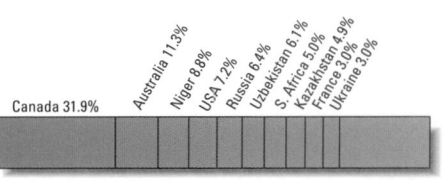

Canada 31.9% | Australia 11.3% | Niger 8.8% | USA 7.2% | Russia 6.4% | Uzbekistan 6.1% | S. Africa 5.0% | Kazakhstan 4.9% | France 3.0% | Ukraine 3.0%

World total (2000): 34,746 tons

DIAMOND

Most of the world's diamond is found in kimberlite, or "blue ground," a basic peridotite rock; erosion may wash the diamond from its kimberlite matrix and deposit it with sand or gravel on river beds. Only a small proportion of the world's diamond, the most flawless, is cut into gemstones – "diamonds"; most are used in industry, where the material's remarkable hardness and abrasion resistance finds a use in cutting tools, drills, and dies. Australia produced 31.6% of the world's total in 2000. The other main producers are the Democratic Republic of the Congo (24.7%), Russia (20%), South Africa (10.5%), and Botswana (3.5%). Natural diamonds now account for less than 10% of all industrial diamond output. Synthetic diamond production in centers such as Ireland, Japan, Russia, and the USA far exceeds it.

METALS

* Figures for aluminum are for refined metal; all other figures refer to ore production

The world's leading producers of aluminum ore (bauxite) in 2000 were as follows:

1. Australia 38.6%
2. Guinea 11.8%
3. Brazil 10.4%
4. Jamaica 8.8%
5. China 6.3%
6. India 4.9%
7. Venezuela 3.5%
8. Suriname 3.1%
9. Russia 3.1%
10. Guyana 2.6%

The figures shown above are in stark contrast to the figures showing aluminum production (*see above right*). Australia, for example, produces 38.6% of the world's bauxite but only 5.9% of aluminum. Guinea and Jamaica account for over 20% of the bauxite mined but have no smelters and export virtually all of it to countries like the USA and Canada.

Aluminum: Produced mainly from its oxide, bauxite, which yields 25% of its weight in aluminum. The cost of refining and production is often too high for producer-countries to bear, so bauxite is largely exported. Lightweight and corrosion resistant, aluminum alloys are widely used in aircraft, vehicles, cans, and packaging.

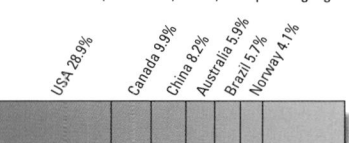

USA 28.9% | Canada 9.9% | China 8.2% | Australia 5.9% | Brazil 5.7% | Norway 4.1%

World total (2000): 23,900,000 tons *

Lead: A soft metal, obtained mainly from galena (lead sulfide), which occurs in veins associated with iron, zinc and silver sulfides. Its use in vehicle batteries accounts for the USA's prime consumer status; lead is also made into sheeting and piping. Its use as an additive to paints and petrol is decreasing.

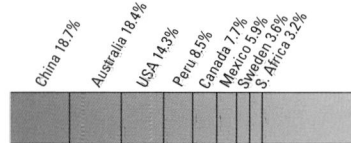

China 18.7% | Australia 18.4% | USA 14.3% | Peru 8.5% | Canada 7.7% | Mexico 5.9% | Sweden 3.6% | S. Africa 3.2%

World total (2000): 2,980,000 tons *

Tin: Soft, pliable and non-toxic, used to coat "tin" (tin-plated steel) cans, in the manufacture of foils and in alloys. The principal tin-bearing mineral is cassiterite (SnO_2), found in ore formed from molten rock. Producers and refiners were hit by a price collapse in 1991.

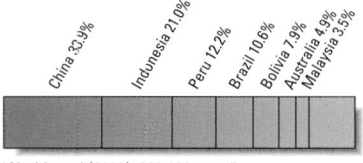

China 33.9% | Indonesia 21.0% | Peru 12.2% | Brazil 10.6% | Bolivia 7.9% | Malaysia 3.5%

World total (2000): 200,000 tons *

Gold: Regarded for centuries as the most valuable metal in the world and used to make coins, gold is still recognized as the monetary standard. A soft metal, it is alloyed to make jewelry; the electronics industry values its corrosion resistance and conductivity.

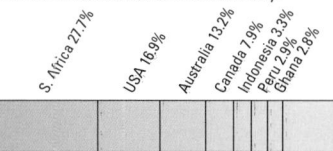

S. Africa 27.1% | USA 16.9% | Australia 13.2% | Canada 7.9% | Indonesia 3.3% | Peru 2.9% | Ghana 2.8%

World total (2000): 2,445 tons *

Copper: Derived from low-yielding sulfide ores, copper is an important export for several developing countries. An excellent conductor of heat and electricity, it forms part of most electrical items, and is used in the manufacture of brass and bronze. Major importers include Japan and Germany.

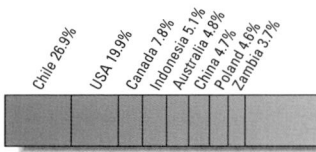

Chile 26.9% | USA 19.9% | Canada 7.8% | Indonesia 5.1% | Australia 4.6% | China 4.1% | Poland 4.5% | Zambia 3.7%

World total (2000): 12,900,000 tons *

Mercury: The only metal that is liquid at normal temperatures, most is derived from its sulfide, cinnabar, found only in small quantities in volcanic areas. Apart from its value in thermometers and other instruments, most mercury production is used in anti-fungal and anti-fouling preparations, and to make detonators.

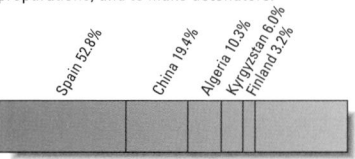

Spain 52.8% | China 19.4% | Algeria 10.3% | Kyrgyzstan 6.0% | Finland 3.2%

World total (2000): 1,800 tons *

Zinc: Often found in association with lead ores, zinc is highly resistant to corrosion, and about 40% of the refined metal is used to plate sheet steel, particularly vehicle bodies – a process known as galvanizing. Zinc is also used in dry batteries, paints, and dyes.

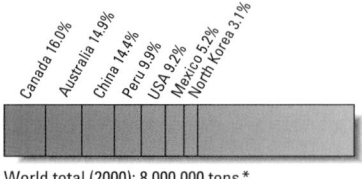

Canada 16.0% | Australia 14.9% | China 14.4% | Peru 9.9% | USA 9.2% | Mexico 5.2% | North Korea 3.1%

World total (2000): 8,000,000 tons *

Silver: Most silver comes from ores mined and processed for other metals (including lead and copper). Pure or alloyed with harder metals, it is used for jewelry and ornaments. Industrial use includes dentistry, electronics, photography, and as a chemical catalyst.

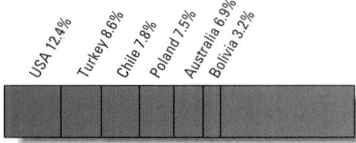

USA 12.4% | Turkey 8.6% | Chile 7.8% | Poland 7.5% | Australia 6.9% | Bolivia 3.2%

World total (2000): 17,900 tons *

DISTRIBUTION OF MINERALS

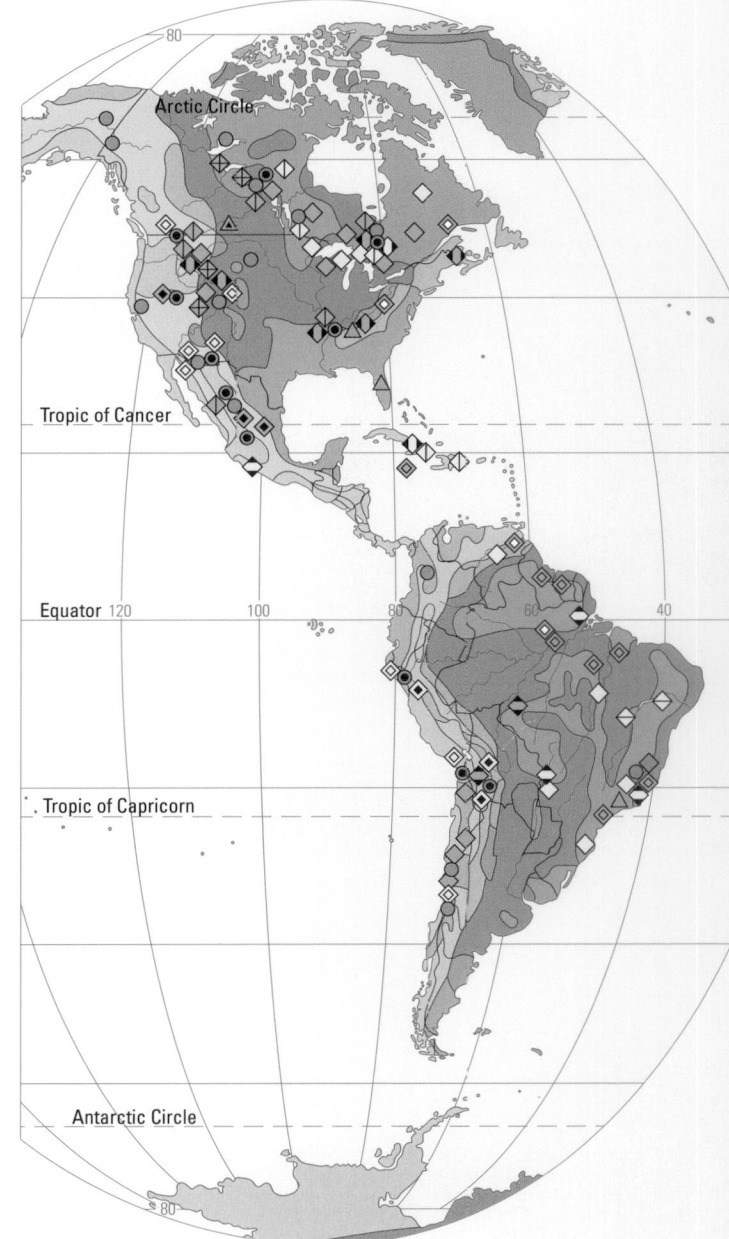

Arctic Circle

Tropic of Cancer

Equator

Tropic of Capricorn

Antarctic Circle

IRON ORE

Ever since the art of high-temperature smelting was discovered, some time in the second millennium BC, iron has been by far the most important metal known to man. The earliest iron plows transformed primitive agriculture and led to the first human population explosion, while iron weapons – or the lack of them – ensured the rise or fall of entire cultures.

Widely distributed around the world, iron ores usually contain 25–60% iron; blast furnaces process the raw product into pig-iron, which is then alloyed with carbon and other minerals to produce steels of various qualities. From the time of the Industrial Revolution, steel has been almost literally the backbone of modern civilization, the prime structural material on which all else is built.

Iron smelting usually developed close to the sources of ore and, later, to the coalfields that fueled the furnaces. Today, most ore comes from a few richly-endowed locations where large-scale mining is possible.

Iron and steel plants are generally built at coastal sites so that giant ore carriers, which account for a sizable proportion of the world's merchant fleet, can easily discharge their cargoes.

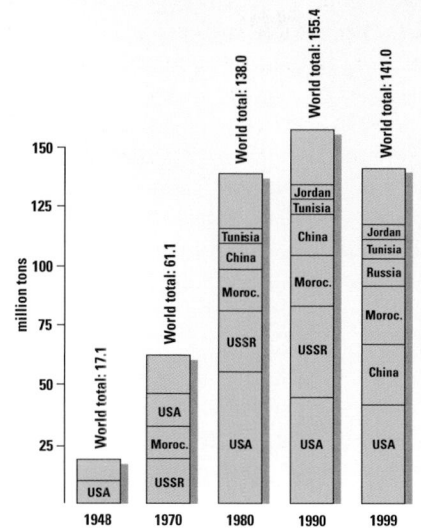

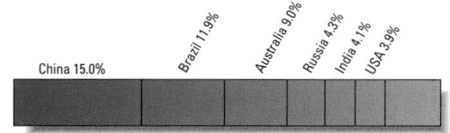

World total production of iron ore (2000): 1,010,000,000 tons

China 15.0% | Brazil 11.9% | Australia 9.0% | Russia 4.3% | India 4.1% | USA 3.9%

World production of phosphates in millions of tons (1999): Phosphate production is vital to the economies of several small countries. Nauru, for example, is heavily dependent on phosphate exports – the island has one of the world's richest deposits. In 1999, 500,000 tons were mined, employing 1,000 people. In Togo, earnings from phosphate exports have superseded all agricultural exports.

Percentage of total world phosphate production (1999)

1. USA	28.8%	7. Brazil	2.9%
2. China	17.8%	8. Israel	2.9%
3. Morocco	17.0%	9. South Africa	2.1%
4. Russia	7.9%	10. Syria	1.5%
5. Tunisia	5.7%	11. Senegal	1.3%
6. Jordan	4.3%	12. India	1.2%

World production of pig-iron (2000): All countries with an annual output of more than 1 million tons are shown

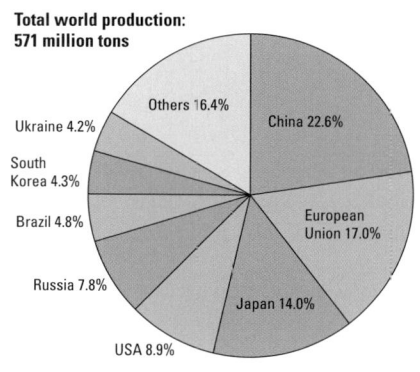

Total world production: 571 million tons

China 22.6% · European Union 17.0% · Japan 14.0% · USA 8.9% · Russia 7.8% · Brazil 4.8% · South Korea 4.3% · Ukraine 4.2% · Others 16.4%

Manganese: In its pure state, manganese is a hard, brittle metal. Alloyed with chrome, iron, and nickel, it produces abrasion-resistant steels; manganese-aluminum alloys are light but tough. Found in batteries and inks, manganese is also used in glass production. Manganese ores are frequently found in the same location as sedimentary iron ores. Pyrolusite (MnO_2) and psilomelane are the main economically-exploitable sources.

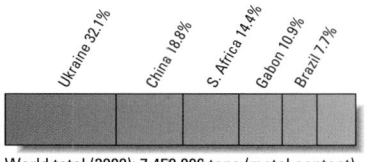

Ukraine 32.1% | China 18.8% | S. Africa 14.4% | Gabon 10.9% | Brazil 7.7%

World total (2000): 7,450,000 tons (metal content)

Chromium: Most of the world's chromium production is alloyed with iron and other metals to produce steels with various different properties. Combined with iron, nickel, cobalt, and tungsten, chromium produces an exceptionally hard steel, resistant to heat; chrome steels are used for many household items where utility must be matched with appearance – cutlery, for example. Chromium is also used in the production of refractory bricks, and its salts for tanning and dyeing leather and cloth.

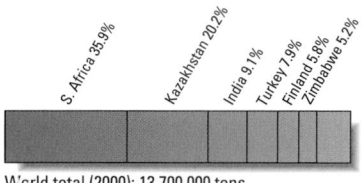

S. Africa 35.9% | Kazakhstan 20.2% | India 9.1% | Turkey 7.9% | Finland 5.6% | Zimbabwe 5.2%

World total (2000): 13,700,000 tons

Nickel: Combined with chrome and iron, nickel produces stainless and high-strength steels; similar alloys go to make magnets and electrical heating elements. Nickel combined with copper is widely used to make coins; cupro-nickel alloy is very resistant to corrosion. Its ores yield only modest quantities of nickel – 0.5% to 3% – but also contain copper, iron, and small amounts of precious metals. Japan, USA, UK, Germany, and France are the principal importers.

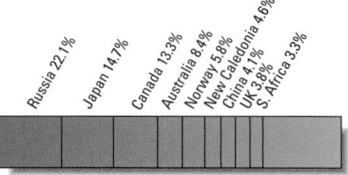

Russia 22.1% | Japan 14.7% | Canada 13.3% | Australia 8.4% | Norway 5.8% | New Caledonia 4.6% | China 4.1% | UK 3.9% | S. Africa 3.3%

World total (2000): 1,230,000 tons

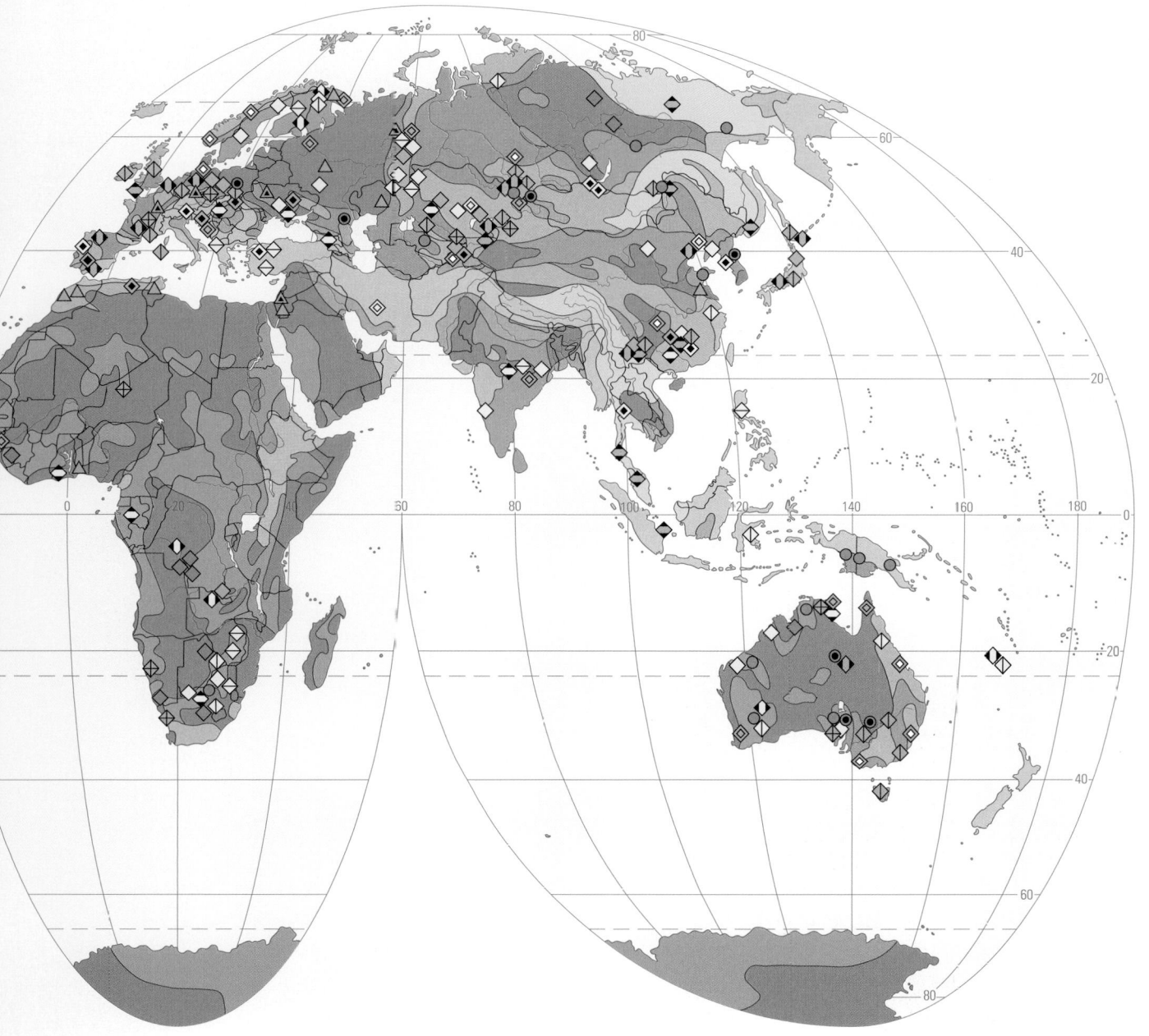

STRUCTURAL REGIONS

- Pre-Cambrian shields
- Sedimentary cover on Pre-Cambrian shields
- Paleozoic (Caledonian and Hercynian) folding
- Sedimentary cover on Paleozoic folding
- Mesozoic folding
- Sedimentary cover on Mesozoic folding
- Cenozoic (Alpine) folding
- Sedimentary cover on Cenozoic folding
- Intensive Mesozoic and Cenozoic vulcanism

DISTRIBUTION

Iron and ferroalloys

- Chrome
- Cobalt
- Iron ore
- Manganese
- Molybdenum
- Nickel ore
- Tungsten

Non-ferrous metals

- Bauxite (Aluminum)
- Copper
- Lead
- Mercury
- Tin
- Zinc
- Uranium

Precious metals and stones

- Diamonds
- Gold
- Silver

Fertilizers

- Phosphates
- Potash

MANUFACTURING

For more information:

18 Water distribution
32 Land use
36 Minerals
37 Iron and ferroalloys
40 Major exports
   Traded products

The Industrial Revolution which began in Britain in the late 18th century, represented a major technological advance in the evolution of human society. It enabled a group of countries to become prosperous by replacing expensive human labor with increasingly sophisticated machinery. In economic terms, manufacturing is the transformation of raw materials, energy, labor, and machines into finished goods, which have a higher value than the various elements used in production.

The economies of countries can be compared by reference to their per capita Gross National Products (or per capita GNPs), namely, the total value of goods and services produced in a country in a year, divided by the population.

The industrialized, or developed, countries accounted for 15% of the world's population in 2000 with an average per capita GNP of more than US $25,000. On the other hand, low-income developing countries, with small industrial sectors, accounted for 34% of the world's population. Their per capita GNPs are less than $755, with some as low as $200.

Kenya, with its low-income economy, had a per capita GNP in 2000 of US $350. Agriculture employs 19% of the people, industry 18%, and services 64%. The main industries are the processing of agricultural imports and import substitution (making such necessities as cement, footwear, and textiles). Heavy industry plays only a small part. By contrast, Germany had a per capita GNP in 2000 of $25,120. Agriculture employs only 2% of the population, with 30% in industry and 68% in services. Germany's industrial sector differs greatly from Kenya's, with its emphasis on vehicles, machinery, chemicals, and electronics.

Since the 1970s, some former developing countries in eastern Asia achieved rapid economic growth through industrialization. Despite setbacks in the late 1990s, they demonstrated that a developing industrial sector can transform an economy, which starts off with certain advantages, such as low labor costs. But economic success also depends on such factors as education to provide skills, and regulations that attract foreign investors. China, whose economy grew by more than 9% per year between 1989 and 2002, satisfies many of these criteria, though its record on human rights leaves much to be desired.

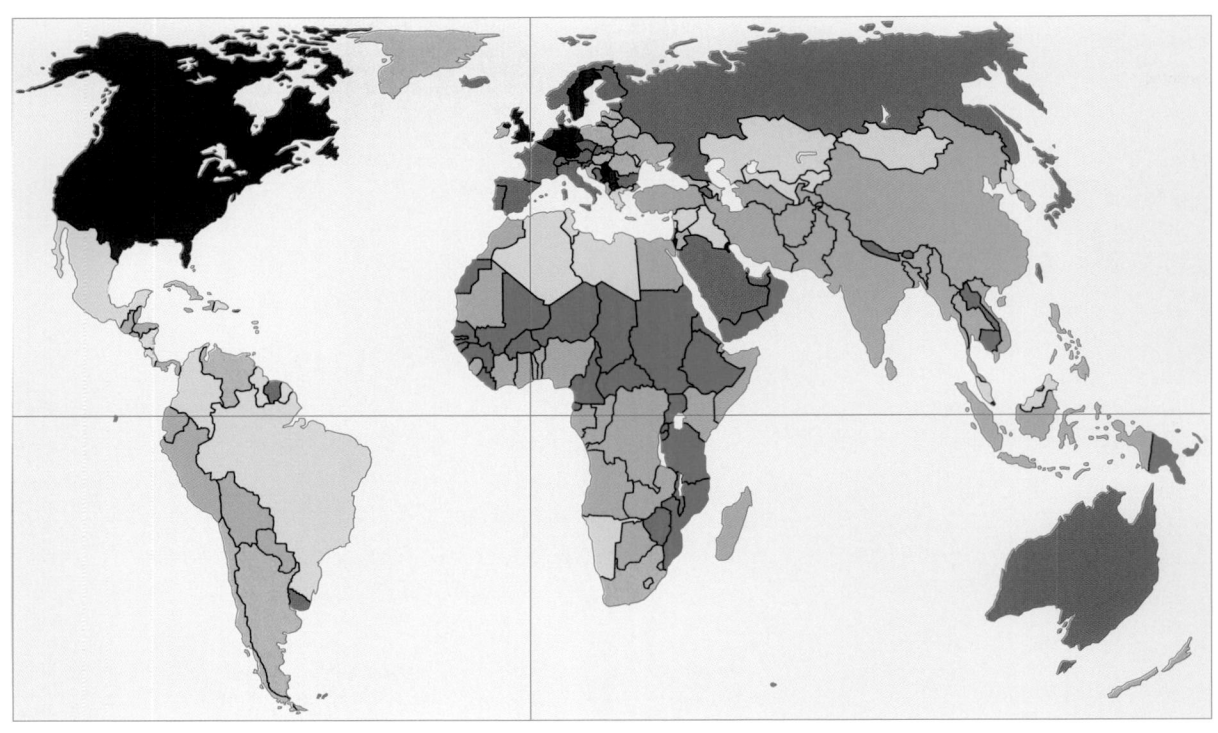

EMPLOYMENT

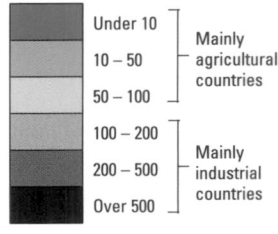

The number of workers employed in manufacturing for every 100 workers engaged in agriculture (latest available year)

Under 10	Mainly agricultural countries
10 – 50	
50 – 100	
100 – 200	Mainly industrial countries
200 – 500	
Over 500	

Selected countries (latest available year)

Singapore	8,860
UK	1,270
Belgium	820
Germany	800
Kuwait	767
Bahrain	660
USA	657
Israel	633

DIVISION OF EMPLOYMENT

Distribution of workers between agriculture, industry and services, selected countries (latest available year)

The six countries selected illustrate the usual stages of economic development, from dependence on agriculture through industrial growth to the expansion of the service sector.

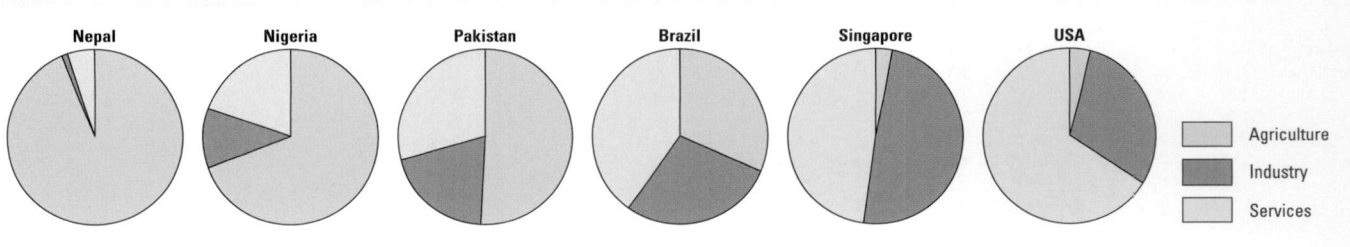

Nepal   Nigeria   Pakistan   Brazil   Singapore   USA

- Agriculture
- Industry
- Services

THE WORK FORCE

Percentages of men and women between 15 and 64 in employment, selected countries (latest available year)

The figures include employees and the self-employed, who in developing countries are often subsistence farmers. People in full-time education are excluded. Because of the population age structure in developing countries, the employed population has to support a far larger number of non-workers than its industrial equivalent. For example, more than 52% of Kenya's people are under 15, an age group that makes up less than a tenth of the UK population.

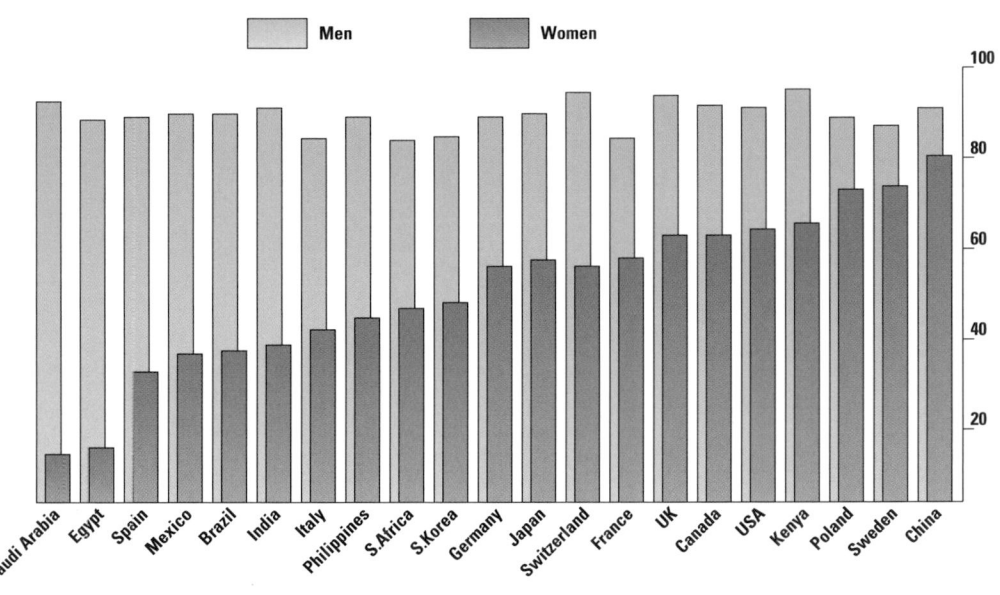

Men   Women

Saudi Arabia, Egypt, Spain, Mexico, Brazil, India, Italy, Philippines, S.Africa, S.Korea, Germany, Japan, Switzerland, France, UK, Canada, USA, Kenya, Poland, Sweden, China

WEALTH CREATION

The Gross National Income (GNI) of the world's largest economies, US $ million (2001)

1. USA	9,900,724	21. Austria	194,463
2. Japan	4,574,164	22. Hong Kong	176,157
3. Germany	1,947,951	23. Turkey	168,335
4. UK	1,451,442	24. Denmark	166,345
5. France	1,377,389	25. Poland	163,907
6. China	1,130,984	26. Norway	160,577
7. Italy	1,123,478	27. Saudi Arabia	149,932
8. Canada	661,881	28. Indonesia	144,731
9. Spain	586,874	29. South Africa	125,486
10. Mexico	550,456	30. Greece	124,553
11. Brazil	528,503	31. Finland	124,171
12. India	474,323	32. Thailand	120,871
13. South Korea	447,698	33. Venezuela	117,169
14. Netherlands	385,401	34. Iran	112,855
15. Australia	383,291	35. Portugal	109,156
16. Switzerland	266,503	36. Israel	104,128
17. Argentina	260,994	37. Egypt	99,406
18. Russia	253,413	38. Singapore	99,404
19. Belgium	239,779	39. Ireland	88,385
20. Sweden	225,894	40. Malaysia	86,510

INDUSTRIAL OUTPUT

Industrial output (mining, manufacturing, construction, energy and water production), US $ billion (latest available year)

1.	Japan	1,941	21.	Sweden	73
2.	USA	1,808	22.	Saudi Arabia	67
3.	Germany	780	=	Thailand	67
4.	France	415	24.	Mexico	65
5.	UK	354	25.	Turkey	51
6.	Italy	337	26.	Denmark	50
7.	China	335	27.	Finland	46
8.	Brazil	255	=	Poland	46
9.	South Korea	196	29.	Norway	44
10.	Spain	187	30.	Malaysia	37
11.	Canada	174	=	Portugal	37
12.	Russia	131	32.	Ukraine	34
13.	Netherlands	107	33.	Greece	33
14.	Australia	98	34.	Singapore	30
15.	Switzerland	96	35.	Venezuela	29
16.	India	94	=	Israel	29
17.	Argentina	87	37.	Chile	24
18.	Belgium	83	=	Colombia	24
=	Indonesia	83	=	Hong Kong	24
20.	Austria	79	=	Philippines	24

INDUSTRY AND TRADE

Manufactured goods (including machinery and transport) as a percentage of total exports (1999)

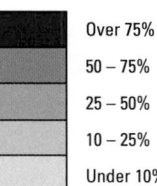

- Over 75%
- 50 – 75%
- 25 – 50%
- 10 – 25%
- Under 10%

Countries most dependent on the export of manufactured goods

Malta	91%
Bangladesh	90%
China	90%
Japan	88%
South Korea	83%
Luxembourg	83%
Pakistan	83%

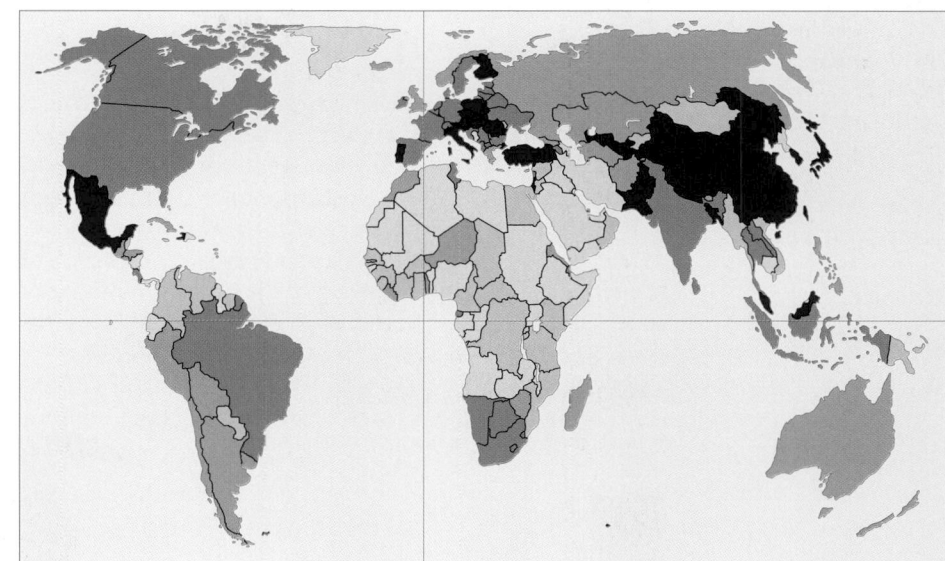

PATTERNS OF PRODUCTION

Breakdown of industrial output by value, selected countries (latest available year)

	Food & agric. products	Textiles & clothing	Machinery & transport	Chemicals	Other
Algeria	26%	20%	11%	1%	41%
Argentina	24%	10%	16%	12%	37%
Australia	18%	7%	21%	8%	45%
Austria	17%	8%	25%	6%	43%
Belgium	19%	8%	23%	13%	36%
Brazil	15%	12%	24%	9%	40%
Burkina Faso	62%	18%	2%	1%	17%
Canada	15%	7%	25%	9%	44%
Denmark	22%	6%	23%	10%	39%
Egypt	20%	27%	13%	10%	31%
Finland	13%	6%	24%	7%	50%
France	18%	7%	33%	9%	33%
Germany	12%	5%	38%	10%	36%
Greece	20%	22%	14%	7%	38%
Hungary	6%	11%	37%	11%	35%
India	11%	16%	26%	15%	32%
Indonesia	23%	11%	10%	10%	47%
Iran	13%	22%	22%	7%	36%
Ireland	28%	7%	20%	15%	28%
Israel	13%	10%	28%	8%	42%
Italy	7%	13%	32%	10%	38%
Japan	10%	6%	38%	10%	37%
Kenya	35%	12%	14%	9%	29%
Malaysia	21%	5%	23%	14%	37%
Mexico	24%	12%	14%	12%	39%
Netherlands	19%	4%	28%	11%	38%
New Zealand	26%	10%	16%	6%	43%
Norway	21%	3%	26%	7%	44%
Pakistan	34%	21%	8%	12%	25%
Philippines	40%	7%	7%	10%	35%
Poland	15%	16%	30%	6%	33%
Portugal	17%	22%	16%	8%	38%
Singapore	6%	5%	46%	8%	36%
South Africa	14%	8%	17%	11%	49%
South Korea	15%	17%	24%	9%	35%
Spain	17%	9%	22%	9%	43%
Sweden	10%	2%	35%	8%	44%
Thailand	30%	17%	14%	6%	33%
Turkey	20%	14%	15%	8%	43%
UK	14%	6%	32%	11%	36%
USA	12%	5%	35%	10%	38%
Venezuela	23%	8%	9%	11%	49%

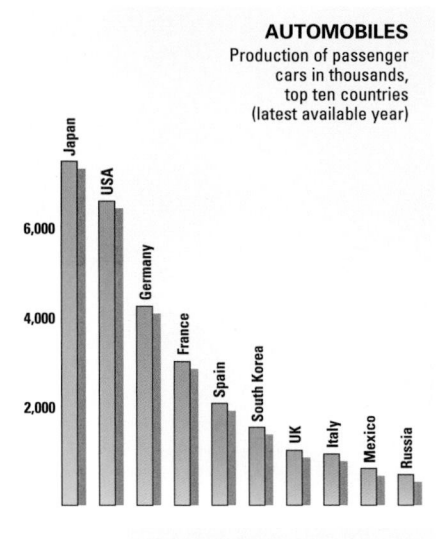

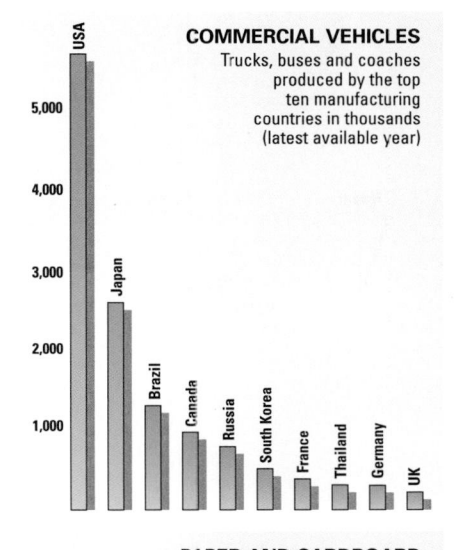

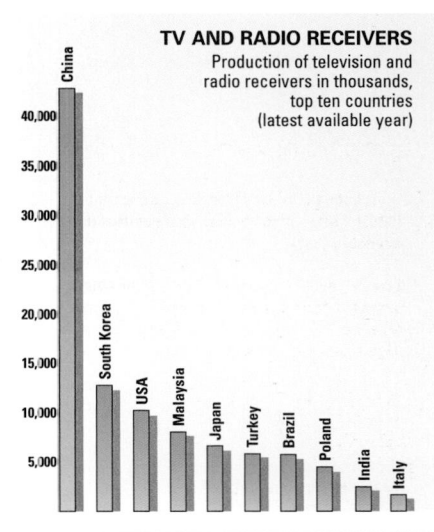

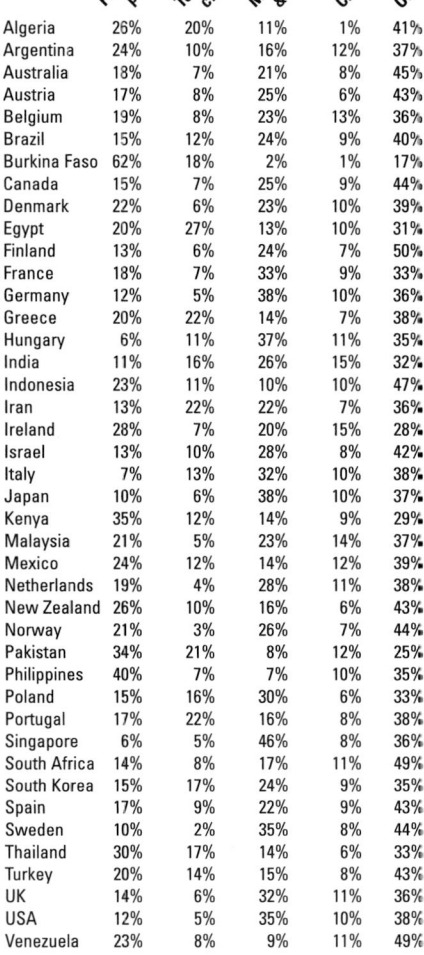

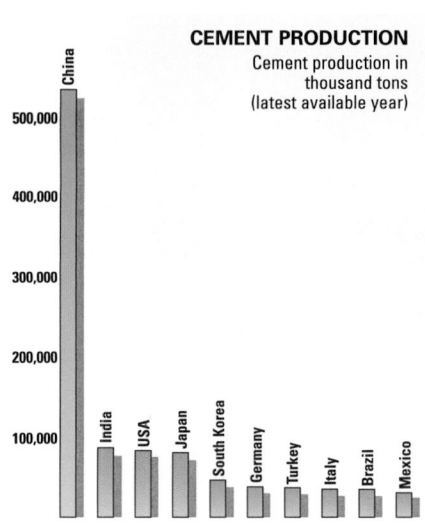

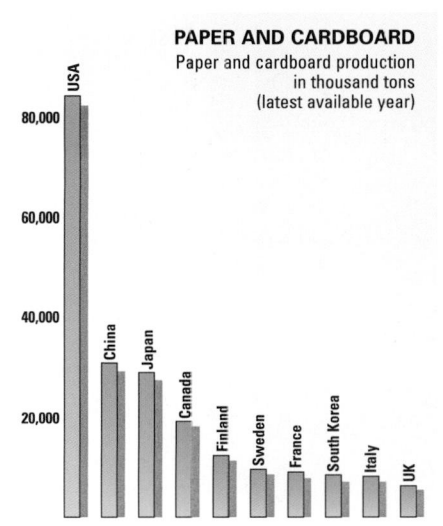

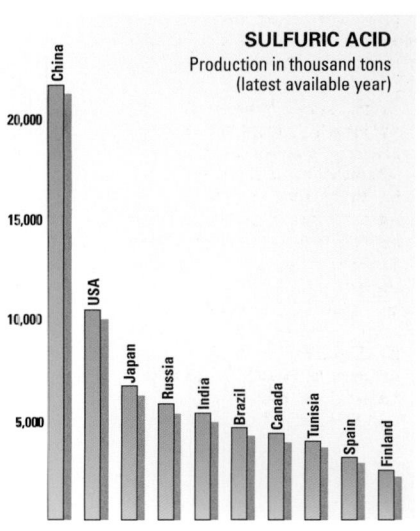

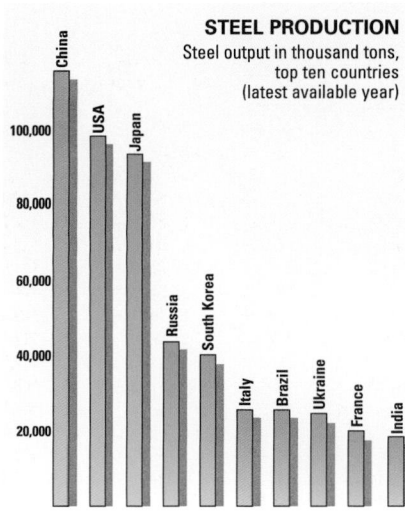

◄ This photograph shows a cement-manufacturing plant in Riverside, California, USA. Cement production figures are often an indicator of the relative prosperity of a country, since they show the construction of roads, dams and other infrastructure projects (*see the graph below*).

AUTOMOBILES
Production of passenger cars in thousands, top ten countries (latest available year)

COMMERCIAL VEHICLES
Trucks, buses and coaches produced by the top ten manufacturing countries in thousands (latest available year)

TV AND RADIO RECEIVERS
Production of television and radio receivers in thousands, top ten countries (latest available year)

STEEL PRODUCTION
Steel output in thousand tons, top ten countries (latest available year)

CEMENT PRODUCTION
Cement production in thousand tons (latest available year)

PAPER AND CARDBOARD
Paper and cardboard production in thousand tons (latest available year)

SULFURIC ACID
Production in thousand tons (latest available year)

TRADE

For more information:

31 International organizations

35 Movements of oil

36 Minerals

38 Wealth creation

39 Industry and trade

45 Air travel and tourism

Inflation

Trade played a vital role in the growth of early civilizations and it was later a spur to European exploration and colonization. The colonial powers grew rich by exporting cheap manufactures, such as clothing and footwear, while obtaining primary products from their colonies.

From the late 19th century to the early 1950s, as transport technology improved, primary products, especially oil in the later stages of this period, dominated world trade. However, since that time, manufactures have become the chief commodities in world trade, which is dominated by the industrialized countries. Nearly half of all world trade flows between the developed market economies of the European Union, the United States, and Japan, although a number of Asian economies, notably China, Malaysia, Singapore, South Korea, Taiwan, and Thailand, increased their share in the 1990s.

China's remarkable economic growth meant that, by 2002, it had overtaken Japan to become the fourth biggest exporter to the United States. China's low production costs, especially its cheap labor, was estimated to be one-twentieth of those of Japan, making its high-quality exports highly competitive in price. Growth in world trade is regarded as a sign of economic health, as is a favorable balance of trade (or trade surplus) in any country.

WORLD TRADE

Percentage share of total world exports by value (2000)

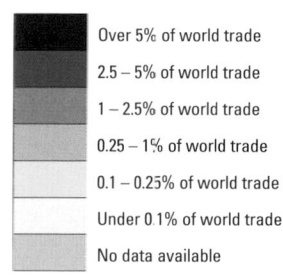

- Over 5% of world trade
- 2.5 – 5% of world trade
- 1 – 2.5% of world trade
- 0.25 – 1% of world trade
- 0.1 – 0.25% of world trade
- Under 0.1% of world trade
- No data available

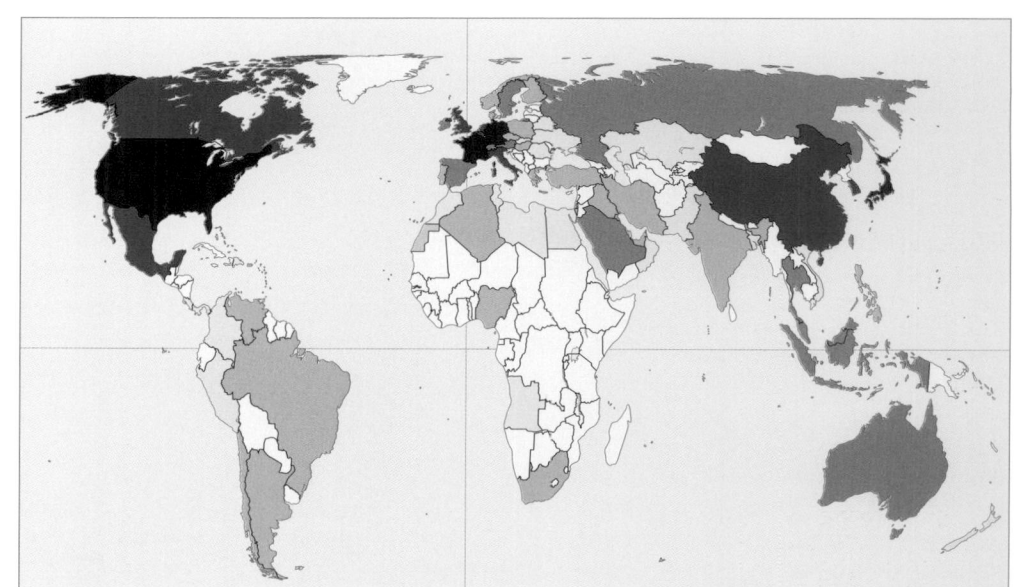

International trade is dominated by a handful of powerful maritime nations. The members of "G8" (Canada, France, Germany, Italy, Japan, Russia, the United Kingdom, and the United States) account for more than half the total. The majority of nations contribute less than a quarter of 1% to the worldwide total of exports. The countries of the European Union account for 35%, whereas the Pacific Rim nations account for over 50%.

DEPENDENCE ON TRADE

Exports as a percentage of GDP (2001)

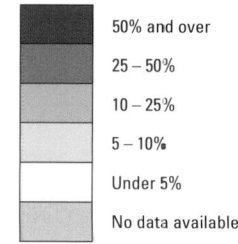

- 50% and over
- 25 – 50%
- 10 – 25%
- 5 – 10%
- Under 5%
- No data available

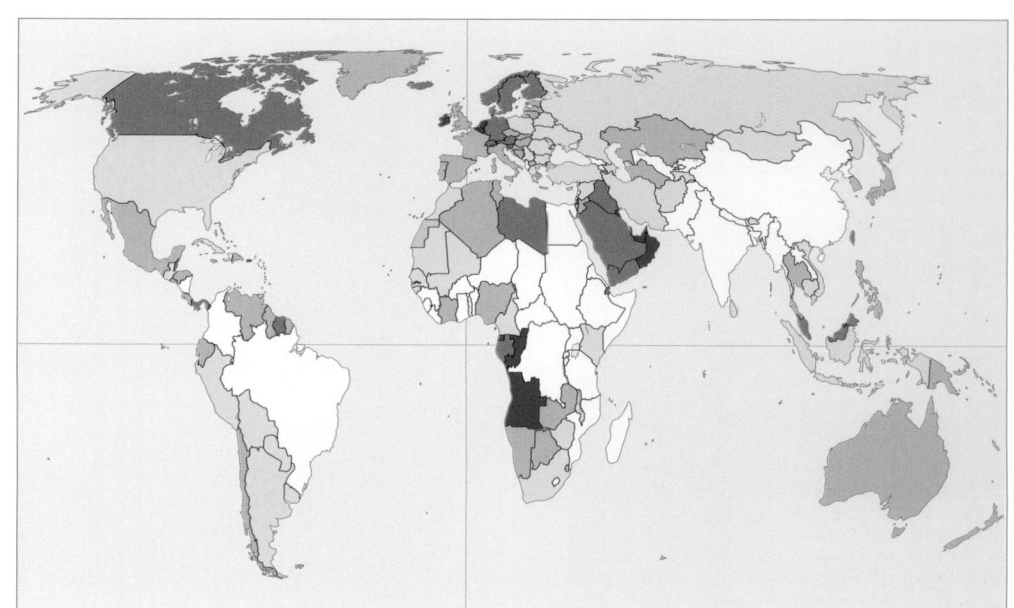

The character of world trade has changed a great deal in the last 50 years or so. While many developing countries still remain heavily dependent on exporting mineral ores, fossil fuels or farm products, such as coffee or cocoa, world trade is now dominated by manufactured goods. Since the 1980s, high-tech products, such as computer equipment, telecommunications gear, and transistors, have become increasingly important.

TRADED PRODUCTS

Major manufactures traded by value, in millions of US $ (2000)

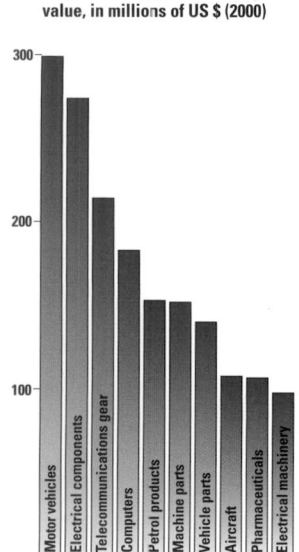

MAJOR EXPORTS

Leading manufactured items and their exporters (2000)

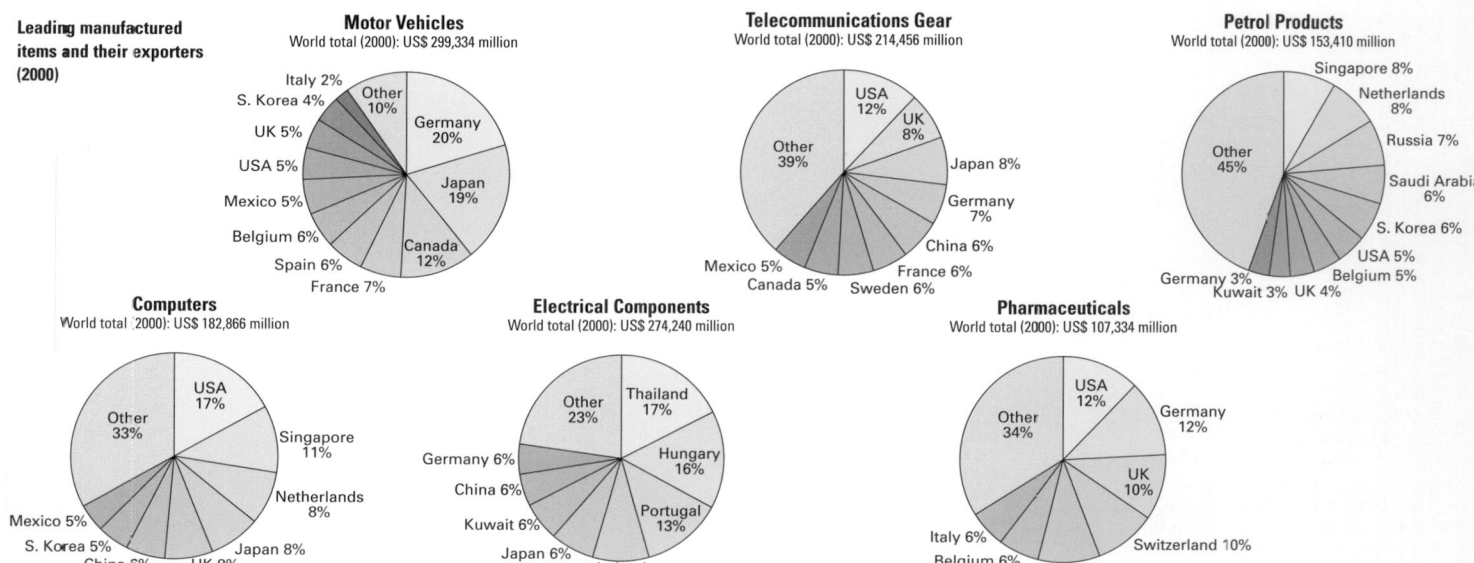

WORLD SHIPPING

While ocean passenger traffic is relatively modest nowadays, sea transport still carries most of the world's trade. Oil and bulk carriers make up the majority of the world fleet, although the general cargo category is the fastest growing. Two innovations have revolutionized sea transport. The first is the development of the roll-on/roll-off (Ro-Ro) method where trucks or even trains loaded with freight are driven straight on to the ship, thus saving time. The second is containerization in which goods are packed into containers (the dimensions of which are fixed) at the factory, driven to the port, and loaded on board by specialist machinery.

Almost 30% of world shipping today sails under a "flag of convenience," whereby owners take advantage of low taxes by registering their vessels in a foreign country the ships will never see, notably Panama and Liberia.

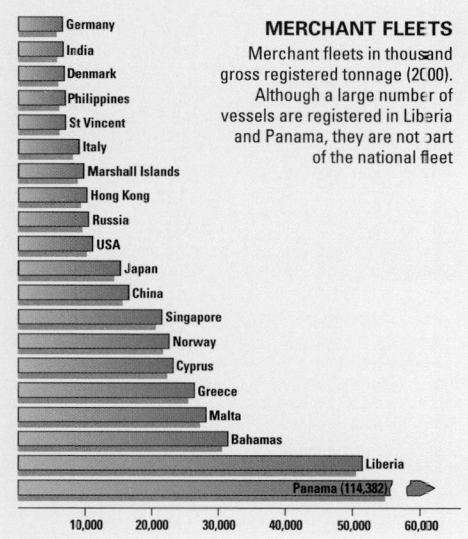

MERCHANT FLEETS
Merchant fleets in thousand gross registered tonnage (2000). Although a large number of vessels are registered in Liberia and Panama, they are not part of the national fleet

THE GREAT PORTS
Total cargo traffic, in million tons (2000)

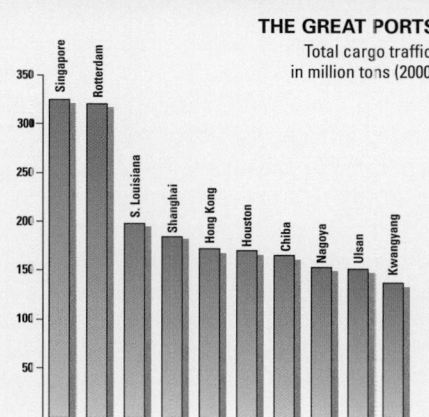

TYPES OF VESSELS
World merchant fleet by type of vessel and deadweight tonnage (2000)

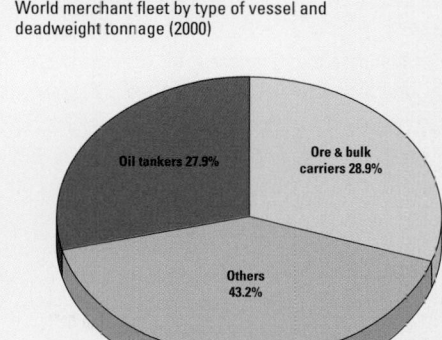

▲ Shanghai is the largest port in China, lying on the Yangtze River, which is navigable for over 600 miles [1,000 km]. In this image more modern shipping can be seen alongside smaller traditional craft, which are used to trans-ship cargoes to smaller ports.

TRADE IN PRIMARY PRODUCTS

Primary products (excluding fuels, metals, and minerals) as a percentage of total export value (2000)

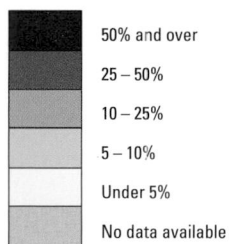

- 50% and over
- 25 – 50%
- 10 – 25%
- 5 – 10%
- Under 5%
- No data available

Primary products are raw materials or partly processed products that form the basis for manufacturing. They are the necessary requirements of industries and include agricultural products, minerals and timber, as well as many semimanufactured goods such as cotton, which has been spun but not woven, wood pulp or flour. Many developed countries have few natural resources and rely on imports for the majority of their primary products. The countries of Southeast Asia export hardwoods to the rest of the world, while many South American countries are heavily dependent on coffee exports.

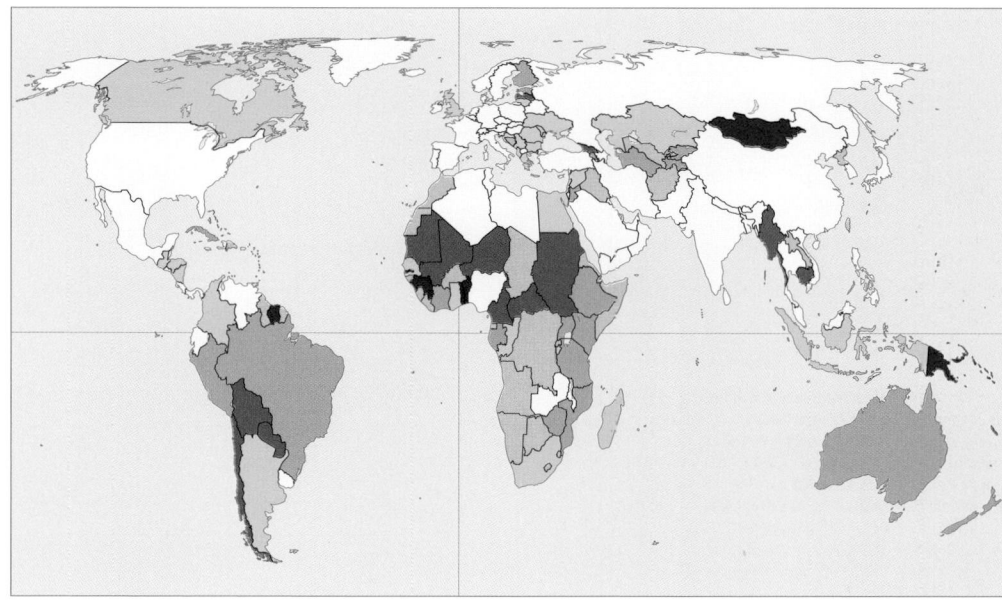

BALANCE OF TRADE

Value of exports in proportion to the value of imports (2000)

Imports exceed exports by:
- More than 40%
- 10 – 40%
- 10% either side
- 10 – 40%
- More than 40%%
Exports exceed imports by:

- No data available

The total world trade balance should amount to zero, since exports must equal imports on a global scale. In practice, though, at least US $100 billion in exports go unrecorded, leaving the world with an apparent deficit and many countries in a better position than public accounting reveals. However, a favorable trade balance is not necessarily a sign of prosperity: many poorer countries must maintain a high surplus in order to service debts, and do so by restricting imports below the levels needed to sustain successful economies.

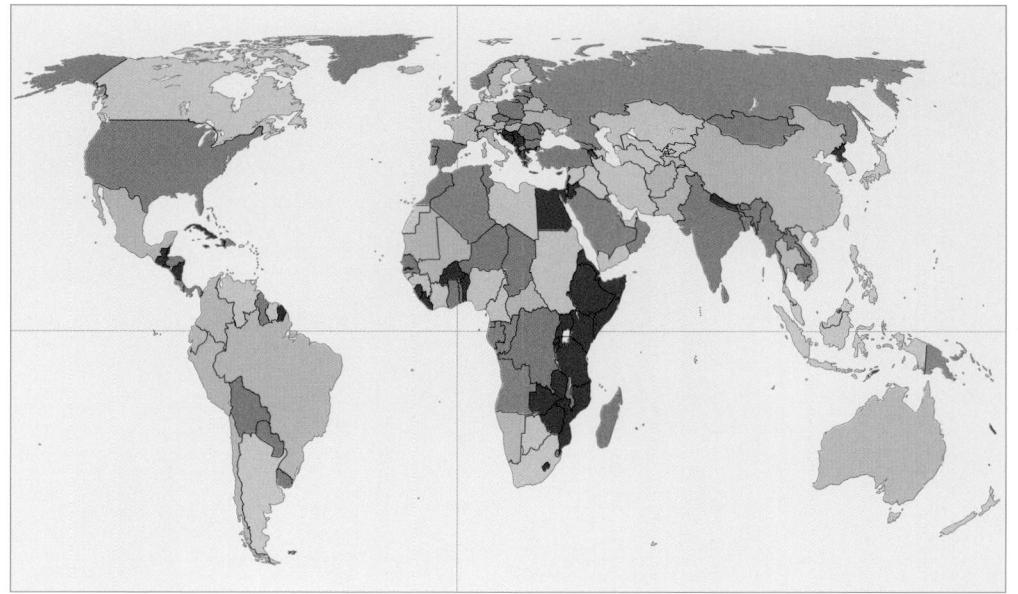

HEALTH

For more information:
18 Water distribution
27 Urban pollution
   Urban advantages
33 Crisis in Africa
   Food and population
47 Distribution of
   spending

Until the late 1990s, when the full extent of the AIDS crisis emerged, average life expectancies at birth were rising almost everywhere. By 2000, they ranged from 78 years in high income economies to 47 in sub-Saharan Africa. These figures represented an enormous advance on the situation in 1880, when citizens of Berlin had an estimated life expectancy of 30 years.

The ravages of AIDS have been greatest in southern Africa. One of the worst affected countries is Botswana, where nearly 40% of the adult population were thought to be infected by 2002. In Botswana, life expectancies were expected to fall to 27 years in 2010 instead of an original estimate of 74 years. However, in much of the world, average life expectancies are still increasing. The rises are attributed to improvements in agriculture and, hence, nutrition, as well as health education, improved sanitation and the quality of drinking water, together with advances in medicine.

Besides AIDS, the people of the developing world are subject to another affliction – malnutrition. The map below shows that in most of Africa, Asia and Latin America, the average daily calorie supply per person is so low as to cause malnutrition. Malnutrition is a serious condition – among pregnant women it causes high rates of child mortality.

Deficiency diseases occur when people do not have a balanced diet. Protein deficiency causes stunting and kwashiorkor, which can be fatal, especially among young children, while vitamin deficiencies cause such illnesses as beri beri, pellagra, scurvy, and rickets. Iron deficiency causes anaemia, while a lack of iodine causes mental retardation.

Infectious diseases, in association with deficient diets, continue to affect people in developing countries. Around the turn of the century, a WHO report stated that infectious diseases cause over 16 million deaths a year. Most of the victims are young and otherwise fit people in developing countries. The major killers are AIDS, cholera, dysentery, malaria, measles, pneumonia, respiratory infections, tuberculosis, and typhoid.

Infectious diseases are much less important as causes of death in developed countries, where cancer and circulatory diseases, such as atherosclerosis and hypertension, which cause strokes and heart attacks, are the most common causes of fatality. Because these diseases tend to kill older people, they are relatively less important in the developing countries where people have shorter lifespans.

Harmful habits are also generally practiced more by the rich than the poor. For example, smoking is an important cause of death in developed countries, while high alcohol consumption has bad effects on health.

▲ Almost 17% of the world's population does not have access to safe water (the diagram at the bottom left-hand corner of this page shows how this breaks down by continent). This places a huge strain on the millions of mainly women and children who have to walk, collect and carry drinkable water in order to survive. UNICEF is dedicated to help improve this situation and to react swiftly in the case of emergencies such as civil war, as with the case of this man in Liberia.

FOOD CONSUMPTION

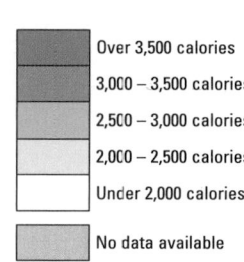

Average daily food intake in calories per person (2000)

- Over 3,500 calories
- 3,000 – 3,500 calories
- 2,500 – 3,000 calories
- 2,000 – 2,500 calories
- Under 2,000 calories
- No data available

The daily food intake rated adequate by the World Health Organization is between 2,300 and 2,500 calories per day. Approximately 6 million children under the age of 5 years die of starvation each year, the vast majority in Africa. In 2000, the FAO estimated that 840 million people were undernourished, contrasting sharply with the overconsumption of food in some Western cultures.

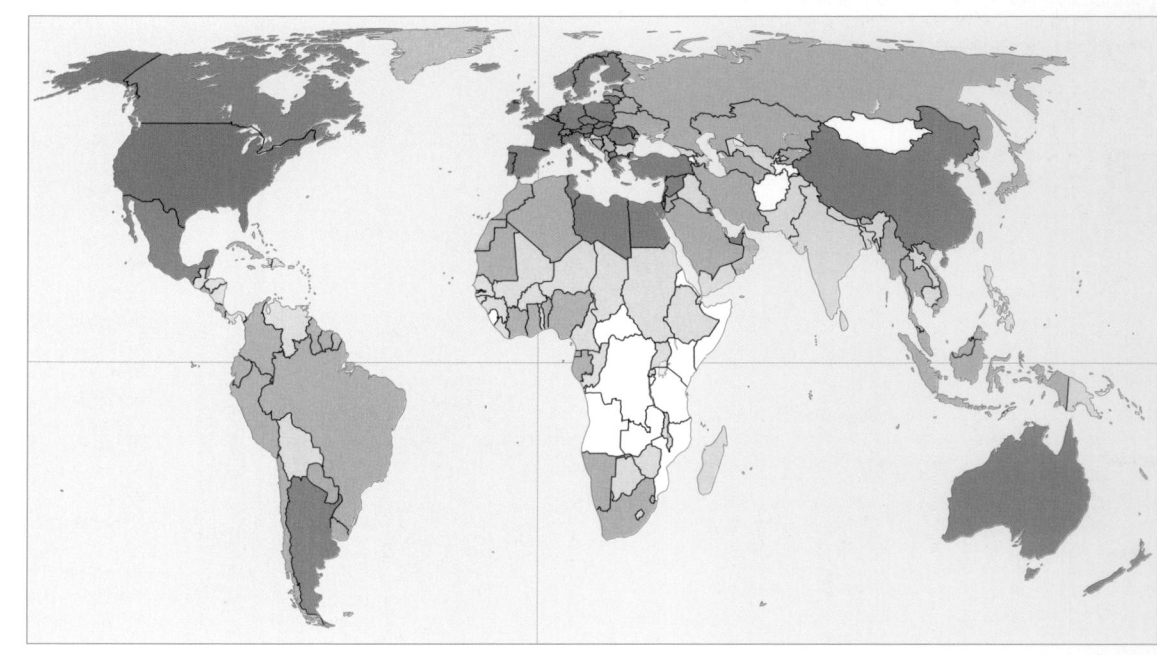

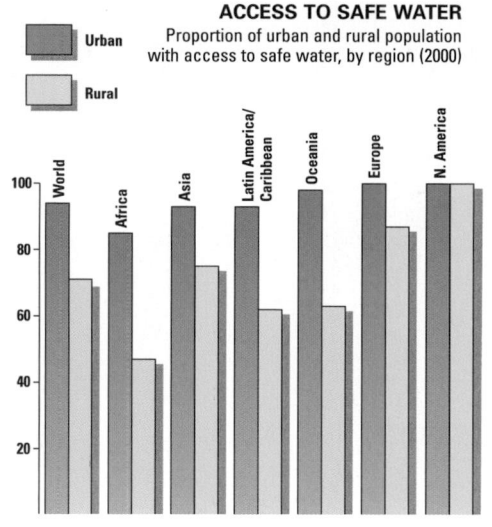

ACCESS TO SAFE WATER

- Urban
- Rural

Proportion of urban and rural population with access to safe water, by region (2000)

Regions: World, Africa, Asia, Latin America/Caribbean, Oceania, Europe, N. America

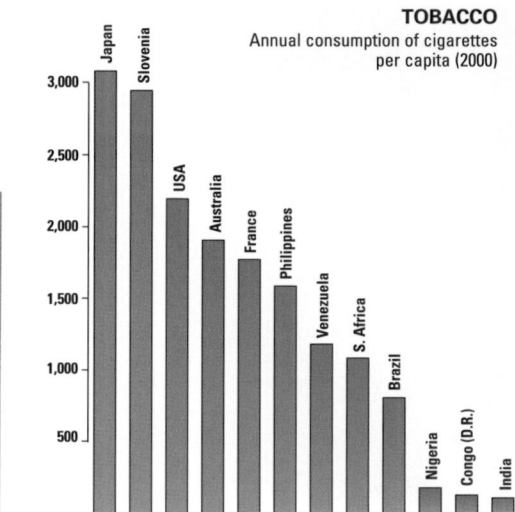

TOBACCO
Annual consumption of cigarettes per capita (2000)

Countries: Japan, Slovenia, USA, Australia, France, Philippines, Venezuela, S. Africa, Brazil, Nigeria, Congo (D.R.), India

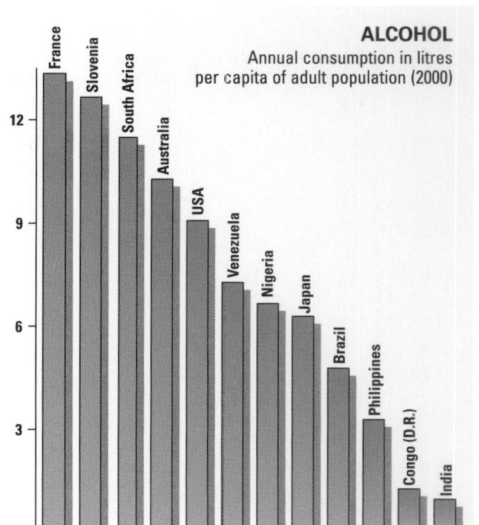

ALCOHOL
Annual consumption in litres per capita of adult population (2000)

Countries: France, Slovenia, South Africa, Australia, USA, Venezuela, Nigeria, Japan, Brazil, Philippines, Congo (D.R.), India

INFANT MORTALITY

Number of babies who died under the age of one, per 1,000 births (2000)

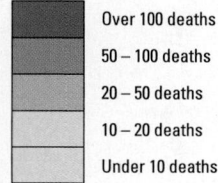

- Over 100 deaths
- 50 – 100 deaths
- 20 – 50 deaths
- 10 – 20 deaths
- Under 10 deaths

Highest infant mortality

Afghanistan ....137 deaths
Western Sahara ....134 deaths
Malawi ....131 deaths

Lowest infant mortality

Iceland ....5 deaths
Finland ....4 deaths
Japan ....4 deaths

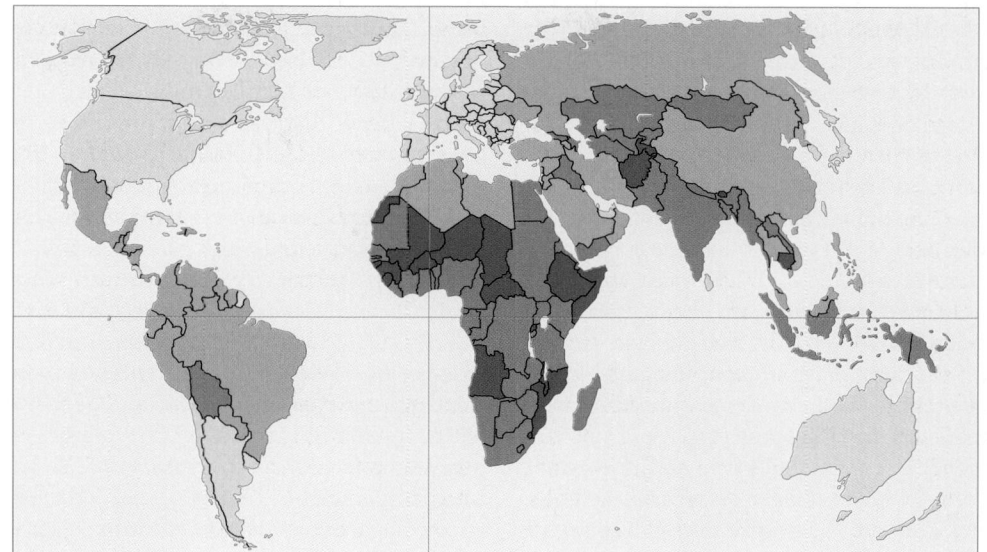

THE AIDS CRISIS

The Acquired Immune Deficiency Syndrome (AIDS) was first identified in 1981 when American doctors found otherwise healthy young men succumbing to rare infections. By 1984 the cause had been traced to the Human Immunodeficiency Virus (HIV), which can remain dormant for many years and perhaps indefinitely: only half of those known to carry the virus in 1981 had developed AIDS ten years later.

In Western countries in the 1990s, most AIDS deaths were among male homosexuals or needle-sharing drug-users. However, the disease is spreading fastest among heterosexual men and women, which is its usual vector in the developing world where most of its victims live.

In 2002, 25 million people had already died of AIDS and another 42 million were infected with the HIV virus. Around 30 million of them live in Africa. In some southern African countries, more than a third of the population carries the virus. In South Africa, which has the largest number of HIV infections, about 6 million people were expected to die of the disease between 2002 and 2012.

AIDS also has other serious consequences. A report by UNAIDS and UNICEF stated that the number of children orphaned by AIDS rose threefold between 1996 and 2002, reaching an all-time high of 13.4 million.

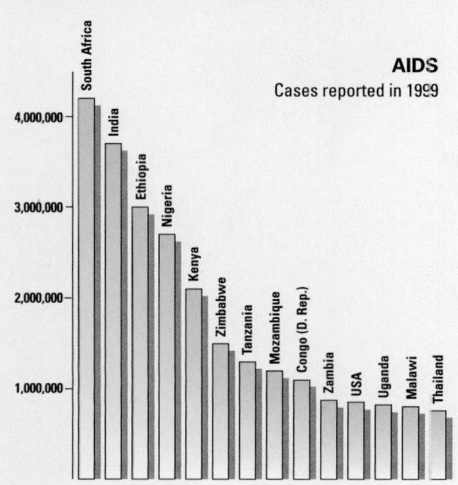

AIDS
Cases reported in 1999

MEDICAL PROVISION

Doctors per 100,000 population, selected countries (2000)

Although the ratio of people to doctors gives a good approximation of a country's health provision, it is not an absolute indicator. Raw numbers may mask inefficiency and other weaknesses: the high proportion of physicians in Hungary, for example, has not prevented infant mortality rates more than twice as high as in the United Kingdom.

The definition of a doctor also varies from nation to nation. As well as registered medical practitioners, it may include trained medical assistants – an especially important category in developing countries, where they provide many of the same services as fully qualified physicians, including simple operations.

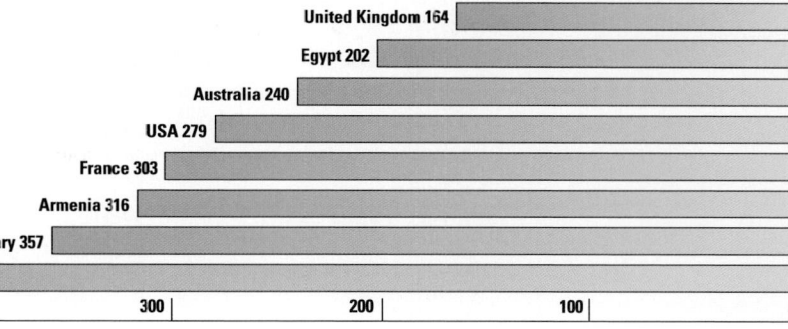

CAUSES OF DEATH

- Accidents, poisoning, and violence
- Respiratory and digestive diseases
- Nervous and circulatory diseases
- Metabolic disorders
- Cancers
- Infectious and parasitic diseases

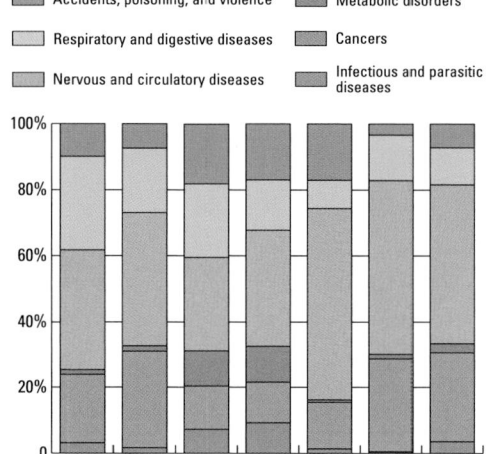

EXPENDITURE ON HEALTH

Public health expenditure per capita, in US $ (latest available year)

Countries with the highest spending		Countries with the lowest spending	
USA	$4,271	Mozambique	$8
Switzerland	$3,857	Tanzania	$8
Norway	$3,182	Sierra Leone	$8
Denmark	$2,785	Indonesia	$8
Luxembourg	$2,731	Chad	$7
Iceland	$2,701	Laos	$6
Germany	$2,697	Niger	$5
France	$2,288	Madagascar	$5
Japan	$2,243	Burundi	$5
Netherlands	$2,173	Ethiopia	$4

The allocation of limited funds for health care in developing countries is rarely evenly spread – the quality of treatment can vary enormously from place to place within the same country. Urban dwellers tend to have much better access to health provisions than those living in rural areas.

SANITATION

Percentage of population with access to sanitation services, selected countries (latest available year)

- Urban
- Rural

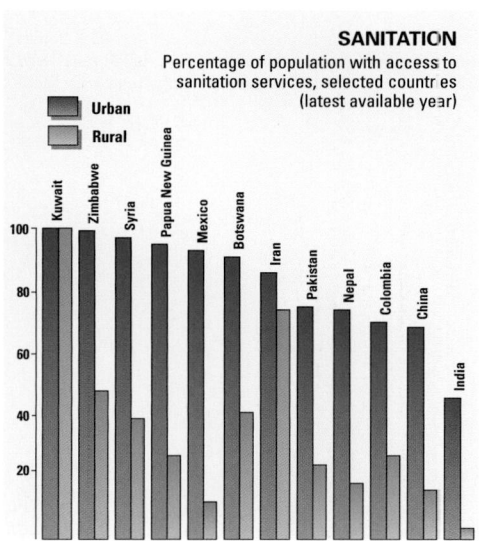

MALARIA

Cases of malaria per 100,000 people exposed to malaria-infected environments, selected countries* (latest available year)

*data not available for Africa where 80% of malaria cases occur

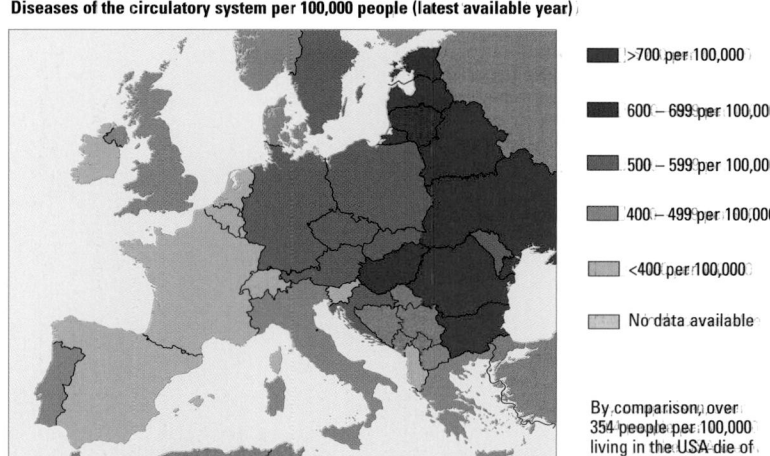

CIRCULATORY DISEASE IN EUROPE

Diseases of the circulatory system per 100,000 people (latest available year)

- >700 per 100,000
- 600 – 699 per 100,000
- 500 – 599 per 100,000
- 400 – 499 per 100,000
- <400 per 100,000
- No data available

By comparison, over 354 people per 100,000 living in the USA die of heart disease.

WEALTH

For more information:

38 Wealth creation
39 Industrial output
40 World trade
   Major exports
41 Balance of trade
47 Distribution of
   spending

Perhaps the most glaring differences in the world today are those between the rich and the poor. The World Bank divides countries into three main groups based on average economic production expressed in terms of per capita GNP (Gross National Product). They are the low-income economies, including most African countries and much of Asia; the middle-income economies, including most of Latin America and most of the former USSR; and the high-income economies of Canada, the United States, Western Europe, Japan, and Australia.

Per capita GNPs are a measure of the total goods and services produced by a country divided by the population, and then converted into US dollars at official exchange rates. They are useful indicators of a country's prosperity, though, like all statistics, they must be treated with care. For example, the prices for goods and services in China are far cheaper than they are in the United States. China's per capita GNP in 2000 was $840 (as compared with $34,100 in the USA), but the PPP (Purchasing Power Parity) estimate of China's per capita GNP was considerably higher at $3,920. Another problem with per capita GNPs is that they are averages, which often conceal wide internal variations.

The pattern of poverty varies from region to region. In Latin America, much progress has been made through industrialization, though startling inequalities still exist between rich and poor. China and other countries in eastern Asia, including South Korea and Taiwan, have followed Japan's example in pursuing export-led industrial policies. The success of China's Special Economic Zones, where foreign investment is encouraged, has led to a huge rise in China's per capita GNP.

Solutions to poverty in Africa are much harder to find because of its high population growth, civil wars, natural disasters, and high inflation rates. Although Africa receives more aid than any other continent, aid is only a partial solution. Much aid has been wasted on overambitious projects, in the servicing of huge national debts, or lost by inexperienced or corrupt governments. One initiative in some African countries has been to improve the infrastructure and develop tourism, creating employment and providing much-needed foreign currency. But tourism alone cannot solve the problems of under-development.

The International Monetary Fund and the World Bank argue that real economic progress in Africa will be achieved only when African countries create market-friendly economies that encourage trade through export-led manufacturing, while at the same time strictly controlling public spending on welfare, the civil service, and other areas.

CONTINENTAL SHARES

Shares of population and of wealth (GNP) by continent

These generalized continental figures show the startling difference between rich and poor, but mask the successes or failures of individual countries. Japan, for example, with less than 4% of Asia's population, produces almost 70% of the continent's output. Within countries, the difference between rich and poor can also be startling. In Brazil, for example, the richest 20% of the population own 60% of the wealth.

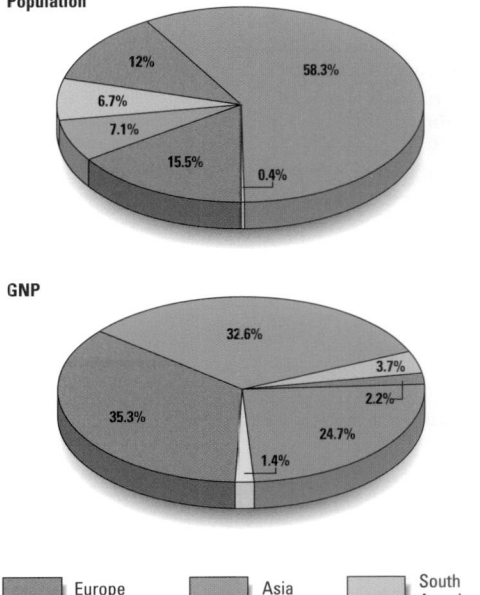

Population

GNP

Europe | Asia | South America
Australia | Africa | North America

LEVELS OF INCOME

Gross National Income per capita: the value of total production divided by the population (2000)

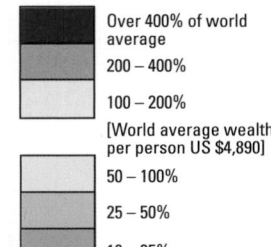

Over 400% of world average
200 – 400%
100 – 200%
[World average wealth per person US $4,890]
50 – 100%
25 – 50%
10 – 25%
Under 10%

Top 5 countries
Luxembourg $42,060
Switzerland $38,140
Japan $35,620
Norway $34,530
Bermuda $34,470

Bottom 5 countries
Ethiopia................................ $100
Burundi $110
Sierra Leone $130
Eritrea $170
Malawi $170

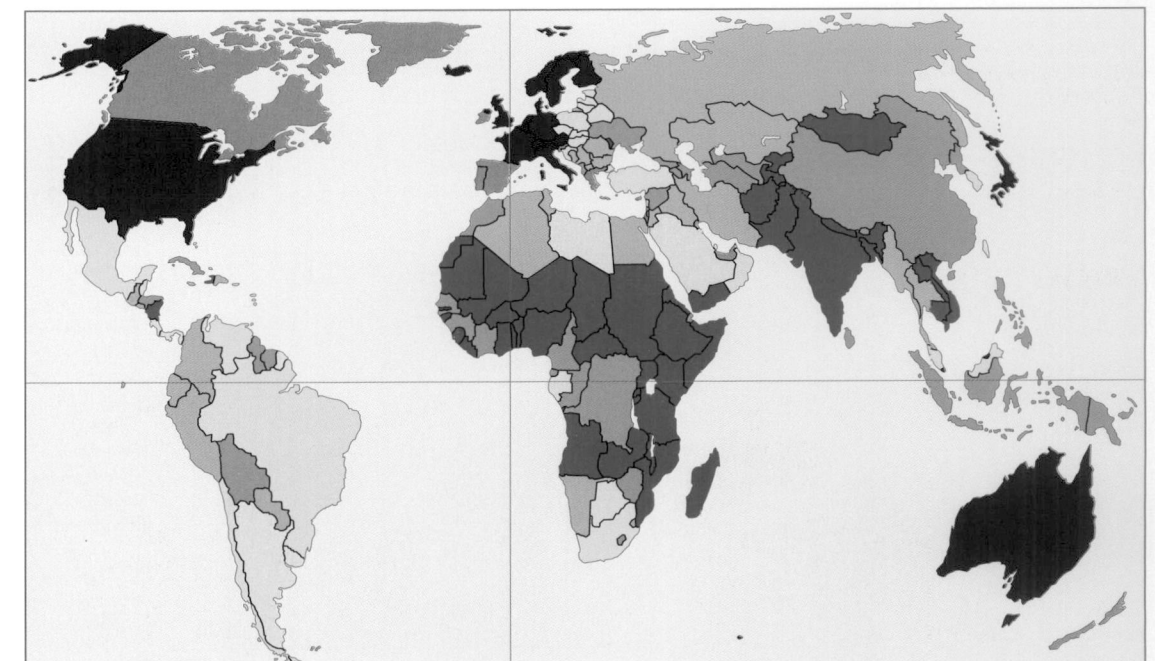

INDICATORS

The gap between the world's rich and poor is now so great that it is difficult to illustrate on a single graph. Within each income group (as defined by the World Bank), however, comparisons have some meaning. The wealth gap in many developing countries, though, is wide, with a small, rich class and a large, impoverished majority, while many high-income countries contain an underclass of unemployed and homeless people.

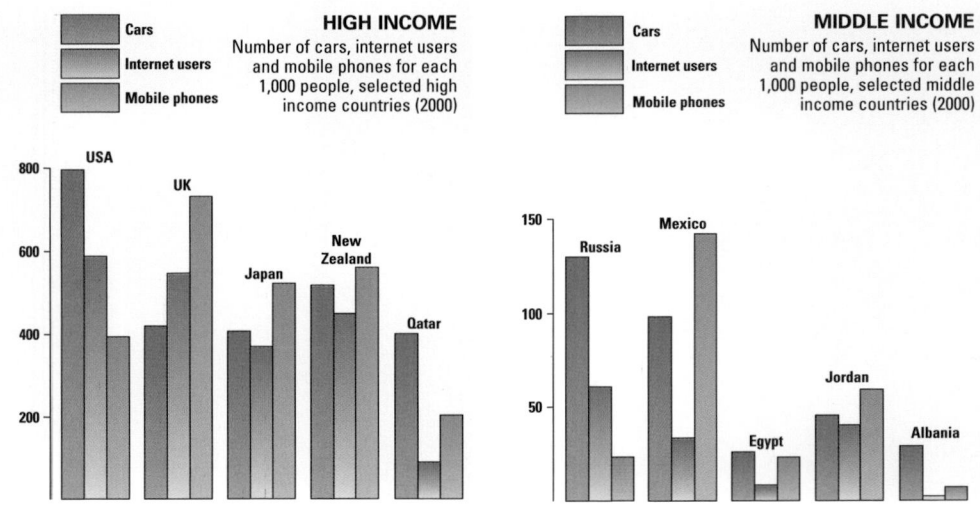

Cars
Internet users
Mobile phones

HIGH INCOME
Number of cars, internet users and mobile phones for each 1,000 people, selected high income countries (2000)

MIDDLE INCOME
Number of cars, internet users and mobile phones for each 1,000 people, selected middle income countries (2000)

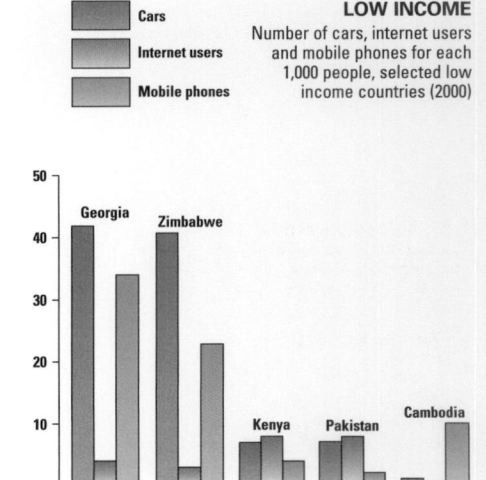

Cars
Internet users
Mobile phones

LOW INCOME
Number of cars, internet users and mobile phones for each 1,000 people, selected low income countries (2000)

STATE FINANCE

Inflation rates (*shown on the map, right*) are an indication of a country's financial stability and, usually, of its prosperity. Annual inflation rates above 20% are usually marked by slow or even negative growth of the GNP. Above 50%, it becomes hyperinflation and an economy is left reeling.

In the late 1980s and early 1990s, many high-income countries had to contend with annual inflation rates of 10% or more, while Japan, the growth leader, had an average inflation rate of just 1.3% between 1985 and 1994.

Market-friendly policies, including low taxes and state spending, liberal trade policies and a warm welcome for foreign investors, are major factors in countries that have enjoyed rapid economic growth in the decades since 1980. For example, the setting up of Special Economic Zones in eastern China has led to a spectacular rise in that country's per capita GNP.

Other successful countries include South Korea and Singapore, although an Asian market crash in 1997 temporarily halted the dramatic economic expansion of these countries.

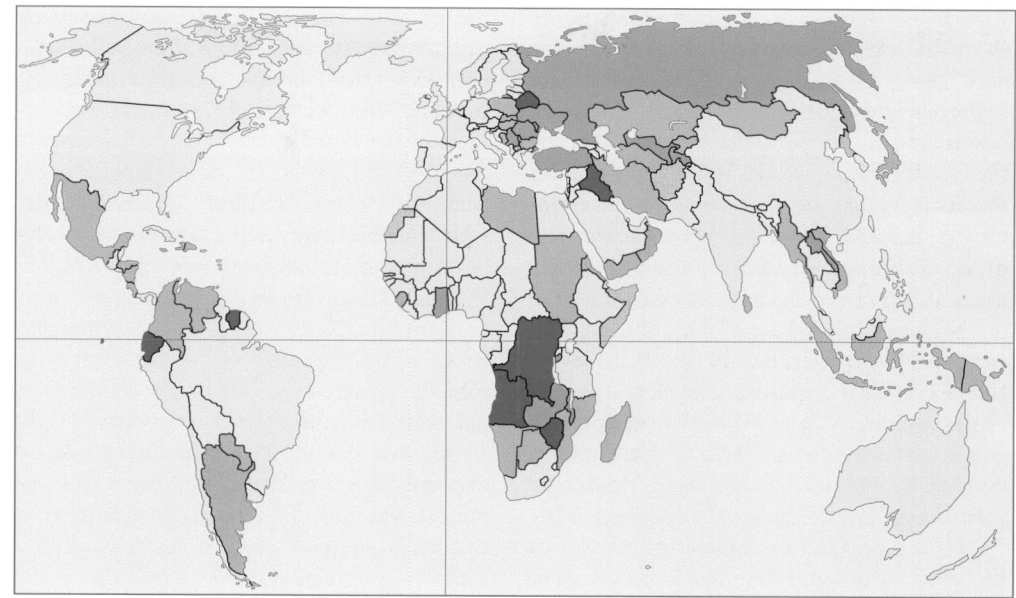

INFLATION

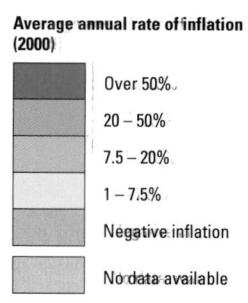

Average annual rate of inflation (2000)

- Over 50%
- 20 – 50%
- 7.5 – 20%
- 1 – 7.5%
- Negative inflation
- No data available

Highest average inflation
Congo (Dem. Rep.)	1,423%
Angola	740%
Turkmenistan	407%

Lowest average inflation
Antigua and Barbuda	–11.5%
Argentina*	–3.1%
Bahrain	–0.1%

* During 2002, Argentina experienced a sharp rise in inflation which is not reflected on this map.

GROWTH IN GNI

GNI per capita annual growth rate (1998–9)

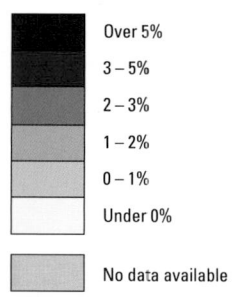

- Over 5%
- 3 – 5%
- 2 – 3%
- 1 – 2%
- 0 – 1%
- Under 0%
- No data available

Countries with highest growth rates
Equatorial Guinea	15.0%
Mozambique	10.0%
Palau	10.0%
South Korea	10.0%
Guinea-Bissau	9.5%

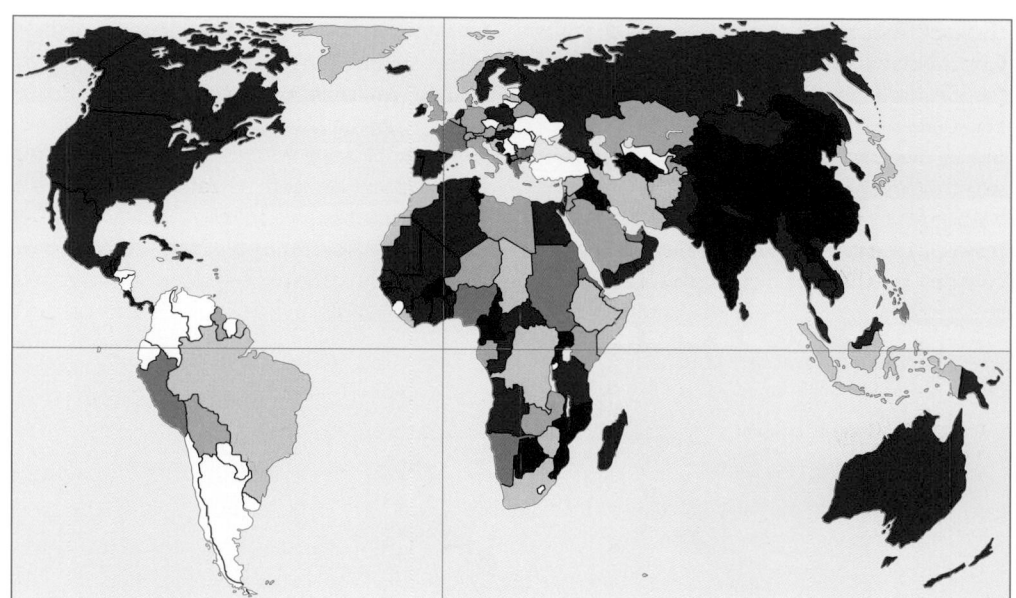

WORLD AIR TRAVEL

Leisure and tourism is the world's second largest industry in terms of revenue generated. Small economies in attractive areas are often completely dominated by tourism: in some Caribbean islands, tourist spending provides over 90% of the total income and is the biggest foreign exchange earner. In cash terms, the USA is the world leader: its 2000 earnings exceeded US $82 billion, though that sum amounted to approximately 0.9% of its total GDP. Of the 51 million visitors to the USA, 29% came from Canada and 20% from Mexico. Germany spends the most on overseas tourism; this amounts to over US $50,000 million. The next biggest spenders are the USA, Japan, and the UK.

The world's busiest airport in terms of total number of passengers is Atlanta (76.9 million passengers in 2002); the busiest international airport is London's Heathrow.

Traffic in passenger miles
Passengers carried (international and local) multiplied by distance flown from airport of origin (1998)

- 30,000 million and over
- 6,000 – 30,000 million
- 600 – 6,000 million
- Under 600 million

Major airports
Number of passengers (international and domestic) per year

- ● Over 25 million
- ● 15 – 25 million
- · 10 – 15 million

Major air routes
Number of international flights per year

- ➜ Over 50 million
- ➜ 10 – 50 million
- ➜ 5 – 10 million

WORLD'S BUSIEST AIRPORTS
Total passengers in millions (2002)
1.	Atlanta Hartsfield Intl. (ATL)	76.9
2.	Chicago O'Hare Intl. (ORD)	66.6
3.	London Heathrow (LHR)	63.3
4.	Tokyo Haneda (HND)	61.1
5.	Los Angeles Intl. (LAX)	56.2
6.	Dallas/Fort Worth Intl. (DFW)	52.8
7.	Frankfurt Intl. (FRA)	48.5
8.	Paris Charles de Gaulle (CDG)	48.4
9.	Amsterdam Schiphol (AMS)	40.7
10.	Denver Intl. (DEN)	35.7

STANDARDS OF LIVING

For more information:
18 Water supply
24 Population density
26 Urban population
27 Urban advantages
30 World's refugees
   War since 1945
38 Employment
   The work force
43 Infant mortality
44 Wealth

Wealth is a basic factor in determining standards of living. Everywhere, the rich have more of everything, including higher average life expectancies, while the poor have to spend most of their income on basic human needs, such as food and clothing. Yet poverty and wealth are relative terms: slum dwellers living on social security in an industrial society feel their poverty acutely, but have far more resources than an average African living in a rural area.

In 1990 the United Nations Development Program published its first Human Development Index (HDI), an attempt to construct a comparative scale by which a simplified form of well-being might be measured. The HDI, expressed as a value between 0 and 0.999, combines figures for life expectancy and literacy with a wealth scale, based on Purchasing Power Parity.

The world's countries are divided into three groups, those with a high HDI (0.800 and above); those with a medium HDI (0.500 to 0.799); and those with a low HDI (below 0.500). In 2002, Norway was top in the world rankings and Sierra Leone was bottom. In fact, of the 36 countries with a low HDI, 29 were from Africa, six from Asia, plus Haiti from the Caribbean. Besides having low per capita GNPs, the

average life expectancy in these countries was 59 years, while the adult literacy rate was 58%. By comparison, the average life expectancy at birth in countries in the high HDI group was 78 years, while the literacy rate was 98%.

Comparisons between countries with similar per capita GNPs reveal the effects of government actions. For example, the World Bank classifies both India and China as low-income economies, but India's HDI at 0.577 is much lower than that of China, at 0.726. This reflects not only China's economic progress in the 1980s and 1990s, but also differences in average life expectancies (63 years in India and 70 years in China), and adult literacy rates (52% in India and 82% in China).

Disparities in standards of living exist not only between countries but also between individuals, groups and regions within countries. For example, income distribution figures for 1995 show that, in the United States, the poorest 20% of households received less than 4% of the income.

Other contrasts exist in developing countries between rural communities, where incomes are low and basic services are often in short supply, and urban areas, where even those living in slums are

generally better off than their rural neighbors. Other striking differences exist between men and women. For example, while adult literacy rates for men and women living in developed countries are more or less the same, large differences exist in many developing countries. In 2001, in countries in the lowest HDI category, only 64% of women were literate, as compared with 73% of men.

Female education is a factor in population control, especially as women's fertility rates appear to fall in direct proportion to the amount of secondary education they receive. This point was acknowledged in 1994 by the UN Population Fund, which defined four main objectives relating to women and population control: the reduction of maternal, infant, and child mortality; better education, especially for girls; universal access to reproductive health services; and gender equality.

Statistical analysis presents many problems of interpretation, especially when trying to define such intangible factors as a sense of well-being. For example, education helps create wealth; but are rich countries wealthy because their people are well educated, or are they well educated because they are rich?

HUMAN DEVELOPMENT INDEX

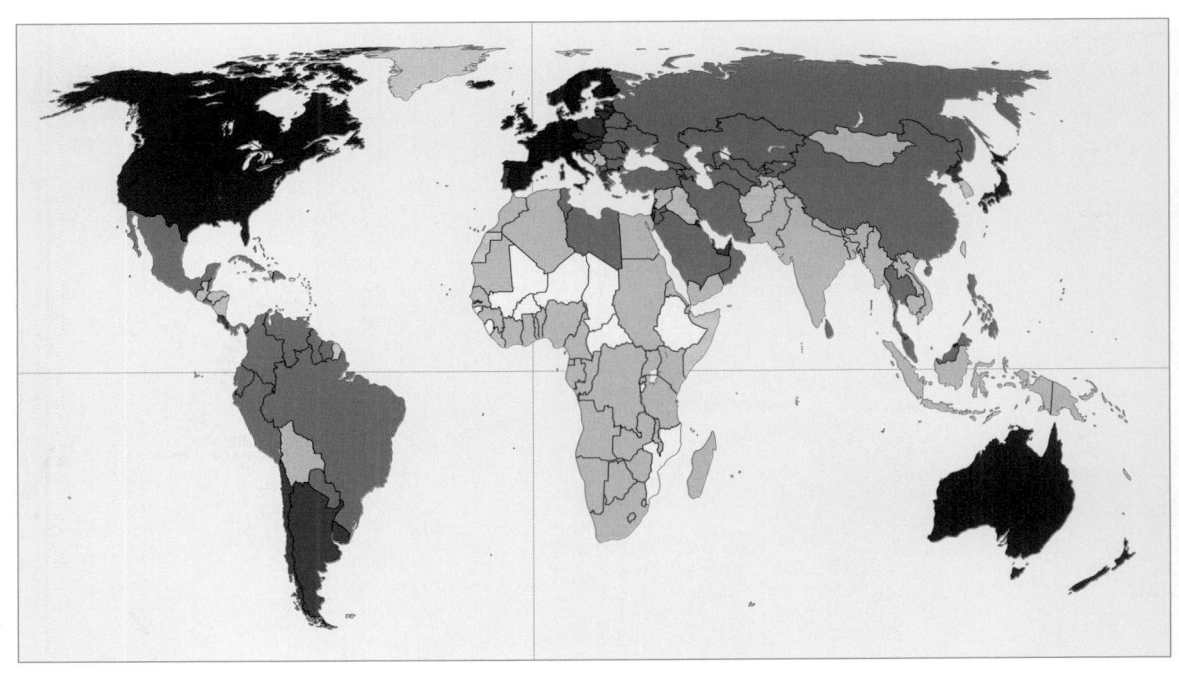

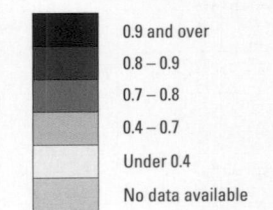

The Human Development Index (HDI), calculated by the UN Development Program (UNDP), gives a value to countries using indicators of life expectancy, education and standards of living in 2000. Higher values show more developed countries.

- 0.9 and over
- 0.8 – 0.9
- 0.7 – 0.8
- 0.4 – 0.7
- Under 0.4
- No data available

Highest values
Norway	0.942
Sweden	0.941
Canada	0.940
USA	0.939
Belgium	0.939

Lowest values
Sierra Leone	0.275
Niger	0.277
Burundi	0.313
Mozambique	0.322
Burkina Faso	0.325

EDUCATION

The developing countries made great efforts in the 1970s and 1980s to bring at least a basic education to their people. In all but the poorest nations, primary school enrolments rose above 60%. However, figures often include teenagers or young adults, and there are still 300 million children worldwide who receive no schooling at all. A lack of resources has restricted the development of secondary and higher education. Most primary school education is free in the poorer countries, but fees are often paid for secondary and higher education, thus heightening the differences between rich and poor.

PRIMARY
Percentage of age group in primary school, selected countries (2000)

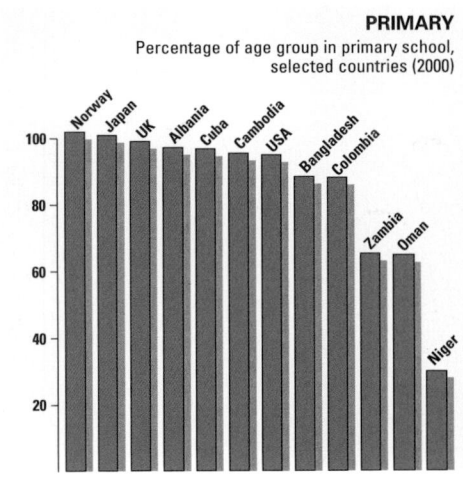

SECONDARY
Percentage of age group in secondary school, selected countries (2000)

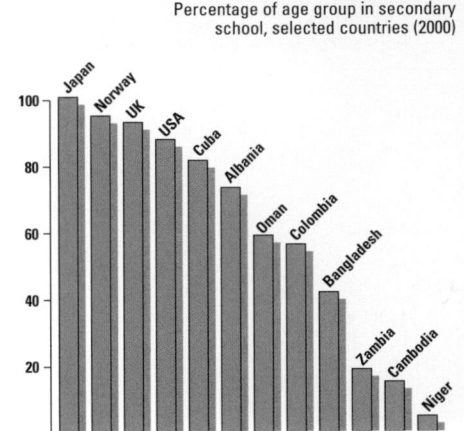

HIGHER
Percentage of age group in higher education, selected countries (2000)

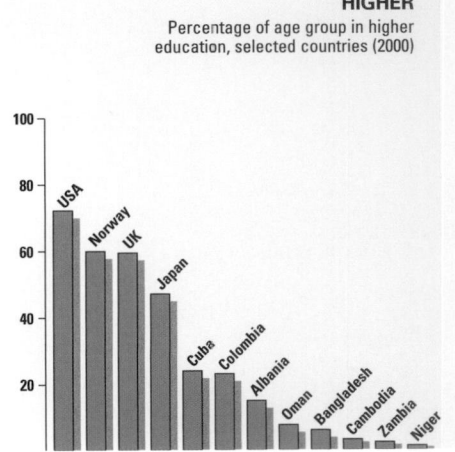

DISTRIBUTION OF SPENDING

Percentage share of household spending (latest available year)

A high proportion of the average income of house-holds in developing nations is spent on basic needs such as food and clothing. In most Western countries food and clothing account for less than 25% of expenditure.

Legend:
- Food
- Medicine & Education
- Clothing
- Transport
- Energy & Housing
- Other

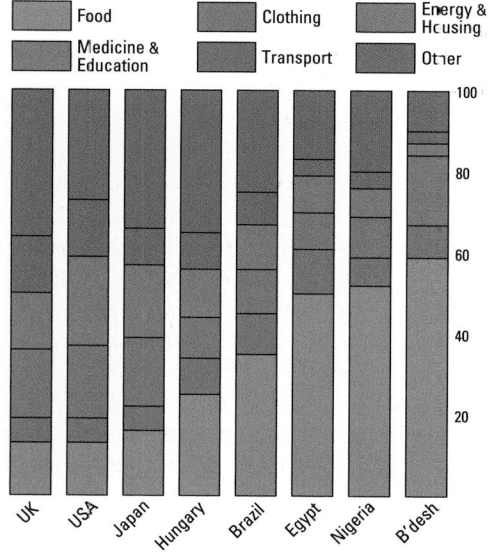

(Chart countries: UK, USA, Japan, Hungary, Brazil, Egypt, Nigeria, B'desh)

STANDARDS OF LIVING IN THE USA BY RACE, AGE AND RELIGION

A comparison of measures of income and education, by selected characteristics (2001–2)

Median income per household (US $), by age and region

15–24 years	28,196
25–34 years	45,086
35–44 years	53,320
45–54 years	58,045
55–64 years	45,864
65 years and over	23,118
Northeast	45,716
Midwest	43,834
South	38,904
West	45,637

Per capita income (US $), by race and Hispanic origin of householder

ALL RACES	22,851
White	24,127
Black	14,953
Asian and Pacific Is.	24,277
Hispanic (any race)	13,003

The poorest 20% of households received just 3.6% of the income, whereas the richest 20% received 48.2%.

Percentage of persons aged 25 and over who have completed High School, by race or origin

ALL RACES	1975	62.5
	2001	84.1
White	1975	64.5
	2001	84.4
Black	1975	42.5
	2001	78.7
Hispanic	1975	37.9
	2001	57.0

FERTILITY AND EDUCATION

Fertility rates compared with female education, selected countries (1995–2000)

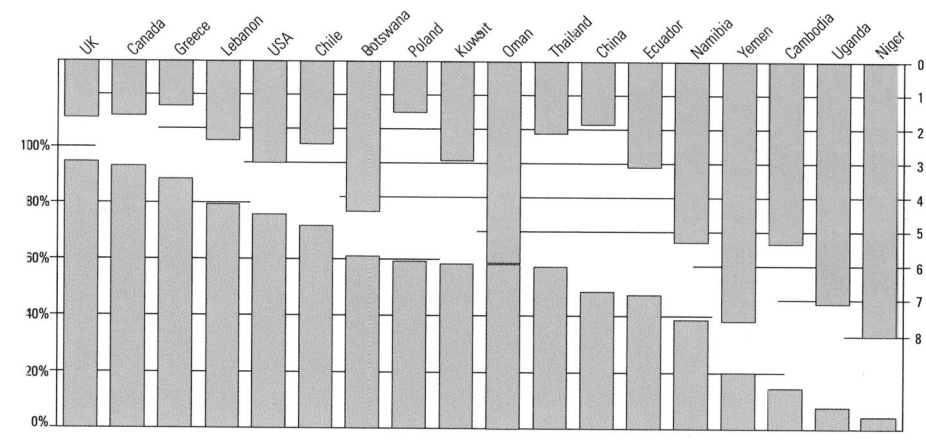

(Chart countries: UK, Canada, Greece, Lebanon, USA, Chile, Botswana, Poland, Kuwait, Oman, Thailand, China, Ecuador, Namibia, Yemen, Cambodia, Uganda, Niger)

Legend:
- Fertility rate: average number of children borne per woman
- Percentage of females aged 12–17 in secondary education

Access to secondary education is closely linked to low fertility rates in developed countries. By contrast, in many developing countries, women's lives are dominated by agriculture, or they lack access to secondary and higher education for cultural reasons, as in Muslim countries. Such disparities are reflected in women's parliamentary representation which is only one-seventh that of men, despite the emergence of such figures as Mrs Indira Gandhi, India's former prime minister. Female wages are also, on average, only two-thirds of those of men.

GENDER DEVELOPMENT INDEX

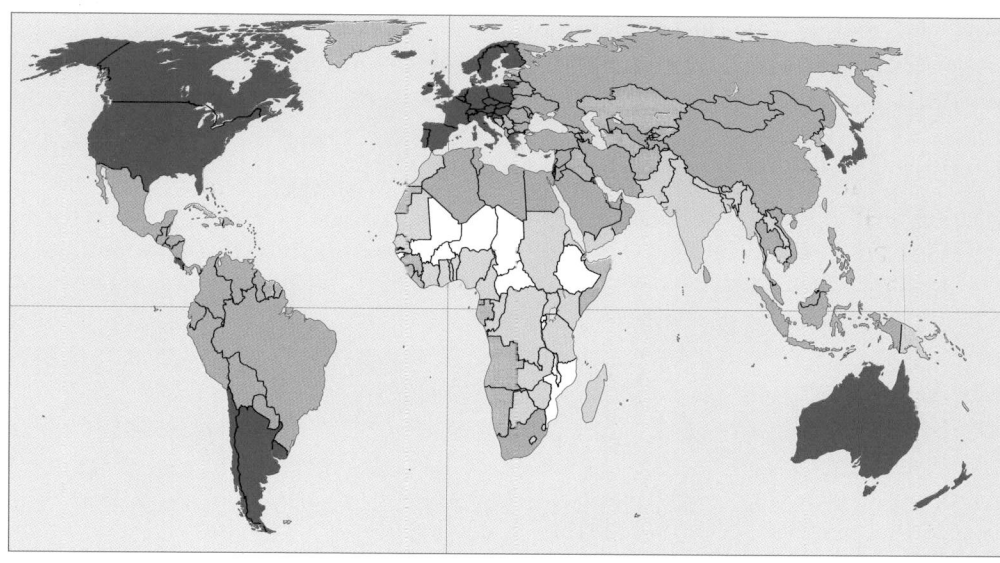

The Gender Development Index (GDI) shows economic and social differences between men and women by using various UNDP indicators (2002). Countries with higher values of GDI have more equality between men and women.

- 0.8 and over
- 0.6 – 0.8
- 0.4 – 0.6
- Under 0.4
- No data available

Highest values

Norway	0.941
Australia	0.938
Canada	0.938
USA	0.937

Lowest values

Niger	0.263
Burundi	0.306
Mozambique	0.307
Burkina Faso	0.312

REGIONAL INEQUALITY IN ITALY

The southern part of Italy, known as the *Mezzogiorno*, has been described as one of the poorest parts of the European Union. It is identifiable on the map (*right*) as all the regions with a GDP per capita of less than US $12,000 (including the two islands of Sicily and Sardinia), plus Abruzzi whose capital is L'Aquila.

The *Mezzogiorno* region suffers from a lack of energy resources, minerals, industry, commerce, services, and skilled labor. As a result, standards of living in the region are well below the rest of Italy. Employment is predominantly agricultural and small-scale.

The north of Italy accounts for 60% of the population but 80% of the GDP, whereas the *Mezzogiorno* accounts for 40% of the population and only 20% of the GDP. Manpower surpluses in the south led to emigration to other parts of Europe and the Americas.

It has also led, especially in the last 50 years, to inter-regional migration from the islands and the southern mainland to the north. The main regions attracting migrants are the northwest (the prosperous Liguria–Piedmont–Lombardy triangle, with its great industrial cities of Genoa, Milan, and Turin) and the Venetia region in the northeast.

As a result, the north has experienced much higher population growth rates than the rest of Italy.

Gross Domestic Product (GDP) per capita in Italy, by region (1999)

- Over US $20,000
- $16,000 – $19,999
- $12,000 – $15,999
- $8,000 – $11,999
- Under $8,000

The average GNI (Gross National Income) per capita for Italy was US $20,170. By comparison, the GNI for the UK was $23,590; for the USA $31,910; and for the EU $22,250.

The number of inhabitants per doctor, another social indicator, varies from less than 500 in the northwest of Italy to over 800 in the far south (the *Mezzogiorno*), with a national average of 607.

◄ These two images illustrate the reality of suburban life for people at either end of the economic scale. On the far left is part of a huge area of "tract housing" in California, where large houses of a similar design are laid out by a developer, complete with gardens, drives, and swimming pools. On the right is a much more haphazard arrangement of home-built, rudimentary shelters, many without sanitation and most with no electricity in Crossroads Township, outside Cape Town in South Africa.

— MT EVEREST, CHINA/NEPAL —

Part of the Himalaya range, Mt Everest – the highest
mountain in the world at 29,035 ft (8,850 m) – lies just
north of center in this image. The two arms of the Rongbuk
glacier flow away from the triangular shaded north wall, with
the Kangshung glacier due east. The international boundary
between China and Nepal bisects the peak, which was
first climbed on May 28, 1953.

WORLD MAPS

SETTLEMENTS

▣ **PARIS**   ◉ **Rotterdam**   ◉ **Livorno**   ◉ **Brugge**   ◎ Exeter   ◦ *Torremolinos*   ◦ *Oberammergau*   ◦*Thira*

Settlement symbols and type styles vary according to the scale of each map and indicate the importance
of towns on the map rather than specific population figures

• *Vaduz*   Capital cities have red infills

⬠   Urban agglomerations

∴   Ruins or archaeological sites

˅   Wells in desert

ADMINISTRATION

——————   International boundaries

---- - - -·   International boundaries
(undefined or disputed)

·············   Internal boundaries

⬠   National parks

PERU   Country names

KENT   Administrative
area names

International boundaries show the *de facto* situation where there are rival claims to territory

COMMUNICATIONS

═══════   Motorways, freeways
and expressways

———————   Principal roads

⌒⌒⌒   Other roads

→ ┈ ┄   Road tunnels

————   Principal railways

- - ⌐ - -   Railways
under construction

⌒⌒⌒   Other railways

→ ┈ ┄   Railway tunnels

ᴸᴴᴿ ✈   Principal airports

⊕   Other airports

············   Principal canals

⋈   Passes

PHYSICAL FEATURES

⌇⌇   Perennial streams

- - - -   Intermittent streams

⬯   Perennial lakes

⬭   Intermittent lakes

🝫   Swamps and marshes

❄   Permanent ice
and glaciers

▲ 8850   Elevations in metres

▼ 8500   Sea depths in metres

1134   Height of lake surface
above sea level in metres

ELEVATION AND DEPTH TINTS

Height of land above sea level

Land below sea level

Depth of sea

in metres	6000	4000	3000	2000	1500	1000	400	200	0							in feet
in feet	18 000	12 000	9000	6000	4500	3000	1200	600		6000	12 000	15 000	18 000	24 000		in metres
									0	200	2000	4000	5000	6000	8000

Some of the maps have different contours to highlight and clarify the principal relief features

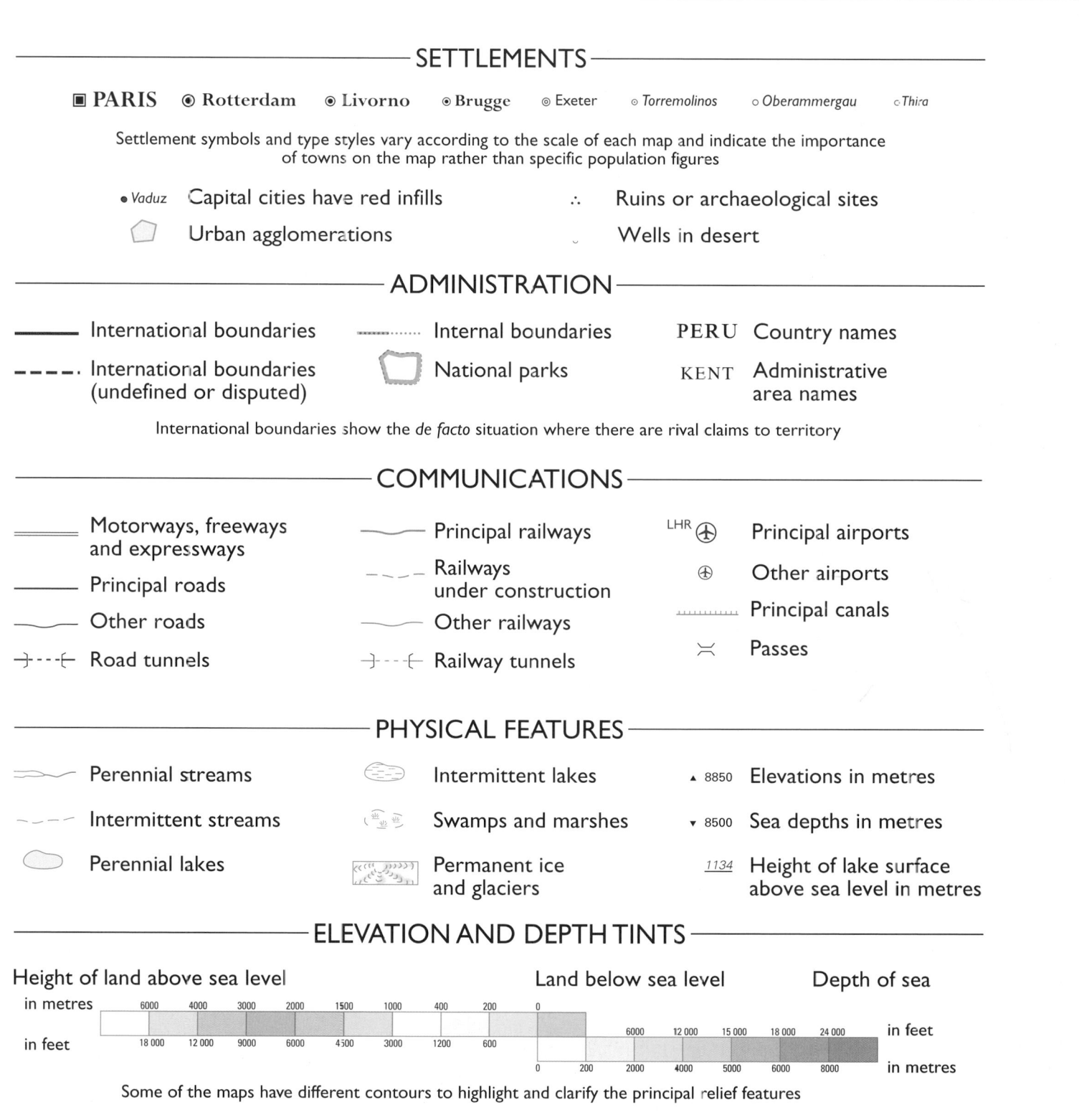

Projection: Hammer Equal Area

Hanoi ● Capital Cities

COPYRIGHT PHILIP'S

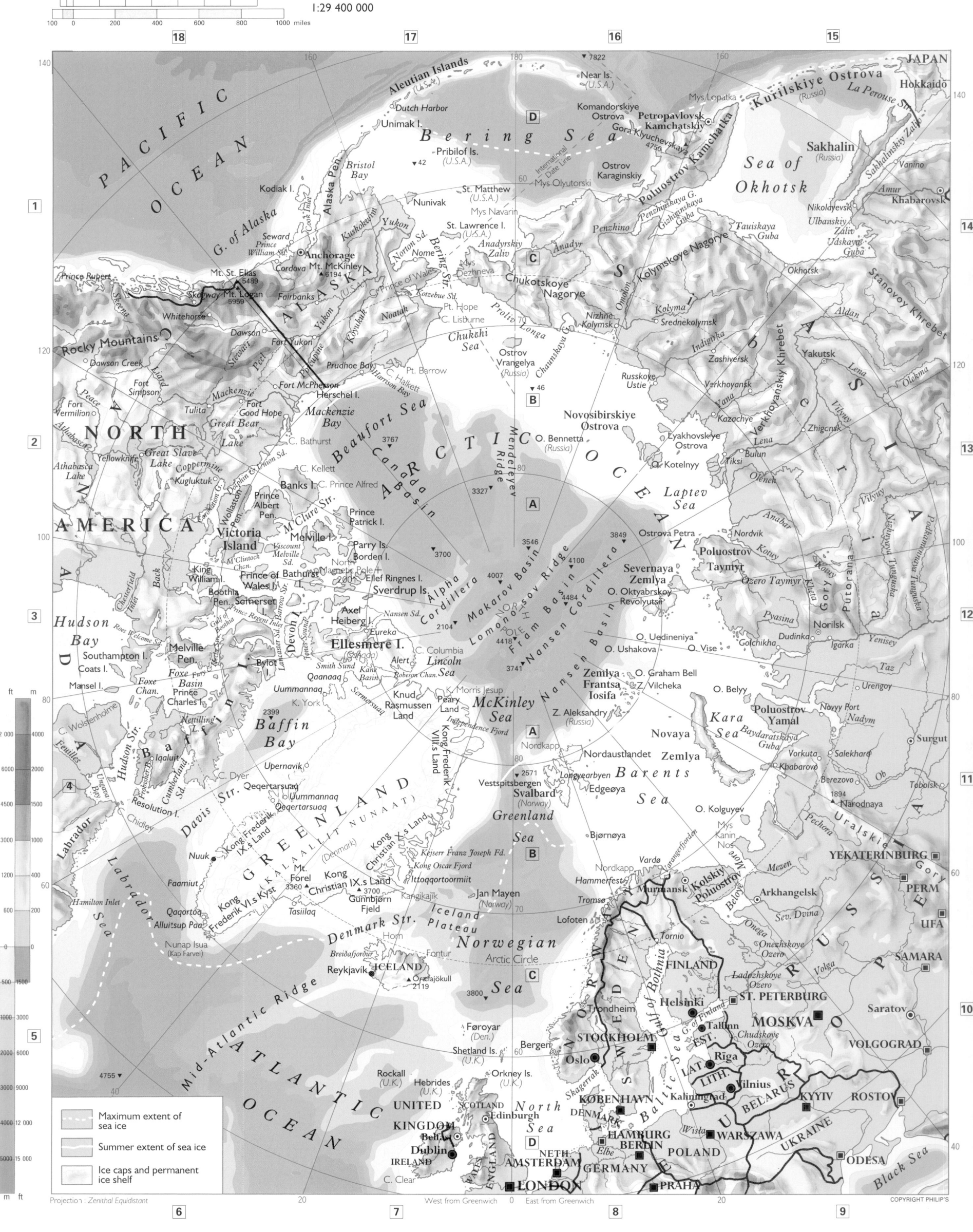

1:29 400 000

Maximum extent of sea ice

Summer extent of sea ice

Ice caps and permanent ice shelf

Projection : Zenithal Equidistant

West from Greenwich   East from Greenwich

COPYRIGHT PHILIP'S

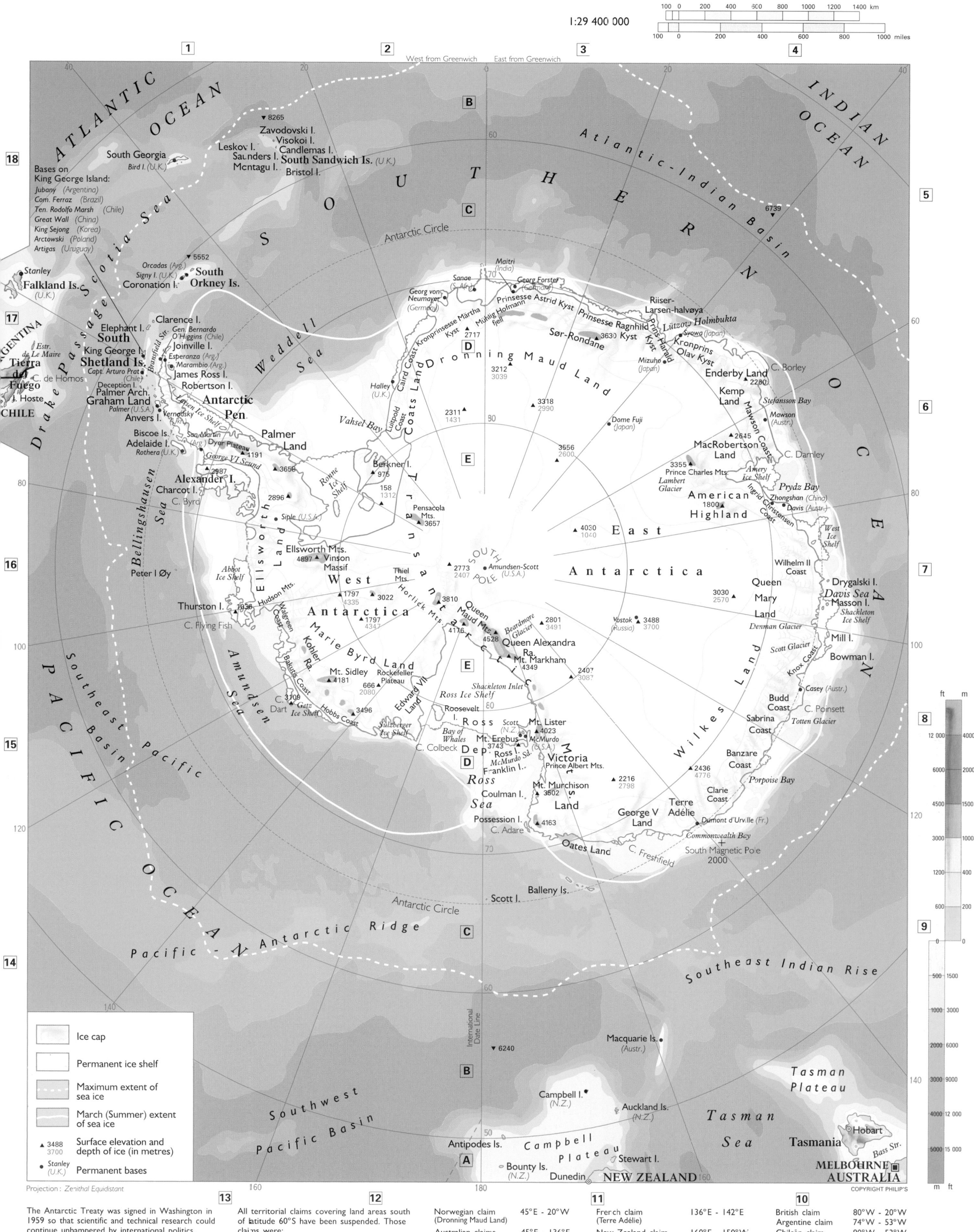

ANTARCTICA 5

1:29 400 000

100 0 200 400 600 800 1000 1200 1400 km
100 0 200 400 600 800 1000 miles

1 **2** West from Greenwich | East from Greenwich **3** **4**

ATLANTIC OCEAN

INDIAN OCEAN

S O U T H E R N

Atlantic-Indian Basin

▼8265

Zavodovski I.
Leskov I. Visokoi I.
Saunders I. Candlemas I.
Montagu I. **South Sandwich Is.** (U.K.)
Bristol I.

South Georgia
Bird I. (U.K.)

18

Bases on
King George Island:
Jubany (Argentina)
Com. Ferraz (Brazil)
Ten. Rodolfo Marsh (Chile)
Great Wall (China)
King Sejong (Korea)
Arctowski (Poland)
Artigas (Uruguay)

5

▼6739

C Antarctic Circle

Maitri (India)
Sanae
Georg von Neumayer (Germany)
Georg Forster (Germany)
Prinsesse Astrid Kyst
Riiser-Larsen-halvøya

Orcadas (Arg.) ▼5552
Signy I. (U.K.) **South Orkney Is.**
Coronation I.

17 Falkland Is. Stanley (U.K.)

Weddell Sea

Scotia Sea

Drake Passage

Prinsesse Ragnhild Kyst
Prins Harald Kyst
Lützow Holmbukta
Syowa (Japan)

D Dronning Maud Land
2717
Sør-Rondane
3630

Kronprins Olav Kyst
Mizuho (Japan)
Enderby Land
Kemp Land
2280

6
C. Borley

Argentina
Tierra del Fuego
CHILE

Clarence I.
Elephant I.
Gen. Bernardo O'Higgins (Chile)
South Shetland Is. King George I.
Joinville I.
Esperanza (Arg.)
Marambio (Arg.)
James Ross I.
Capt. Arturo Prat (Chile)
Robertson I.
Deception I.
Palmer Arch.
Graham Land
Palmer (U.S.A.)
Vernadsky

Halley (U.K.)

Caird Coast
Coats Land
Luitpold Coast
Vahsel Bay

3212
3039

3318
2990

Dome Fuji (Japan)

3556
2600

Stefansson Bay
Mawson (Austr.)
2645
C. Darnley

Anvers I.
Biscoe Is.
Adelaide I.
Rothera (U.K.)
San Martín (Arg.)

Antarctic Pen.
Dyer Plateau
Palmer Land

2311
1431

3355
Prince Charles Mts.
Lambert Glacier
Amery Ice Shelf
Ingrid Christensen Coast
Zhongshan (China)
Davis (Austr.)
Prydz Bay

MacRobertson Land

80
Alexander I.
2987
Charcot I.
C. Byrd
4191
George VI Sound
3656

2896
Siple (U.S.A.)
Pensacola Mts.
3657

Berkner I.
975
158 1312

Ronne Ice Shelf
Filchner Ice Shelf

American Highland
1800

4030
1040

East Antarctica

West Ice Shelf
Wilhelm II Coast

Bellingshausen Sea

16

Peter I Øy

Ellsworth Land

Ellsworth Mts.
4897
Vinson Massif

Thiel Mts.
2773 2407

S O U T H   P O L E
Amundsen-Scott (U.S.A.)

3030 2570

Queen Mary Land

Drygalski I.
Davis Sea
Masson I.
Shackleton Ice Shelf

7

Thurston I.
1936
C. Flying Fish

Hudson Mts.
Walgreen Coast

West Antarctica
1797 4335
3022

Horlick Mts.
3810
4176

Queen Maud Mts.
Beardmore Glacier
2801 3491

Vostok (Russia) 3488 3700

Denman Glacier
Scott Glacier
Mill I.
Knox Coast
Bowman I.

100
1797 4343
4528
Queen Alexandra Ra.
Mt. Markham 4349

2407 3087

Wilkes Land

Budd Coast
Casey (Austr.)
C. Poinsett
Totten Glacier
Sabrina Coast

C. Flying Fish
Kohler Ra.
Bakutis Coast
Mt. Sidley 4181
Rockefeller Plateau
666 2080

Marie Byrd Land

Edward VII Land
Shackleton Inlet
Ross Ice Shelf
Roosevelt I.

PACIFIC OCEAN
Southeast Pacific Basin

Amundsen Sea

C. Dart 3109
Getz Ice Shelf
Hobbs Coast
3496
Salzberger Ice Shelf

Bay of Whales
C. Colbeck

Ross Dep.
Scott (N.Z.)
McMurdo (U.S.A.)
Mt. Lister 4023
Mt. Erebus 3743
Ross I.
McMurdo Sd.
Franklin I.

15
Banzare Coast
2436 4776
Porpoise Bay

Victoria Land
Prince Albert Mts.

Clarie Coast
Terre Adélie
George V Land
2216 2798
3602

Dumont d'Urville (Fr.)

120
Ross Sea
Coulman I.
Mt. Murchison
Possession I. 4163
C. Adare

Commonwealth Bay
South Magnetic Pole 2000

Oates Land
C. Freshfield

Pacific-Antarctic Ridge
C Antarctic Circle
Scott I.
Balleny Is.

Southeast Indian Rise

14

International Date Line

▼6240

Macquarie Is. (Austr.)

Tasman Plateau

B

Southwest Pacific Basin

Campbell I. (N.Z.)
Auckland Is. (N.Z.)

Tasman Sea

Tasmania
Hobart
Bass Str.

A
Antipodes Is.
Bounty Is. (N.Z.)
Campbell Plateau
Stewart I.
Dunedin
NEW ZEALAND

MELBOURNE
AUSTRALIA

COPYRIGHT PHILIP'S

Projection: Zenithal Equidistant

13 **12** **11** **10**

Legend

	Ice cap
	Permanent ice shelf
	Maximum extent of sea ice
	March (Summer) extent of sea ice
▲ 3488 / 3700	Surface elevation and depth of ice (in metres)
● Stanley (U.K.)	Permanent bases

ft | m
12 000 | 4000
9000 | 3000
6000 | 2000
4500 | 1500
3000 | 1000
1200 | 400
600 | 200
0 | 0
500 | 1500
2000 | 6000
3000 | 9000
5000 | 15 000

The Antarctic Treaty was signed in Washington in 1959 so that scientific and technical research could continue unhampered by international politics.

All territorial claims covering land areas south of latitude 60°S have been suspended. Those claims were:

Norwegian claim (Dronning Maud Land)	45°E – 20°W
Australian claims	45°E – 136°E / 142°E – 160°E
French claim (Terre Adélie)	136°E – 142°E
New Zealand claim (Ross Dependency)	160°E – 150°W
British claim	80°W – 20°W
Argentine claim	74°W – 53°W
Chilean claim	90°W – 53°W

1:16 800 000

1:16 800 000

100   0   100   200   300   400   500   600   700   800 km
100   0   100   200   300   400   500 miles

OCEAN
ATLANTIC

Norwegian Sea

ICELAND
Reykjavik

Arctic Circle

Faroe Is. (Den.)
Shetland Is.
Orkney Is.

UNITED KINGDOM
SCOTLAND
Aberdeen
Dundee
Glasgow
Edinburgh
Newcastle-upon-Tyne
IRELAND
Belfast
Dublin
Cork
ENGLAND
WALES
Isle of Man
Liverpool
Manchester
Leeds
Sheffield
Birmingham
Cardiff
Bristol
Southampton
Plymouth
LONDON
Channel Is.
English Channel

NORWAY
Tromsø
Narvik
Bodø
Trondheim
Bergen
Stavanger
Oslo
Kristiansand

SWEDEN
Kiruna
Luleå
Skellefteå
Umeå
Sundsvall
Gävle
Uppsala
Stockholm
Örebro
Norrköping
Jönköping
Gothenburg
Malmö

FINLAND
Vaasa
Tampere
Turku
Helsinki

DENMARK
Ålborg
Århus
Odense
Copenhagen

Gulf of Bothnia
Baltic Sea
North Sea
Kattegat

White Sea
L. Onega
L. Ladoga

RUSSIA
Murmansk
Arkhangelsk
St. Petersburg
Moscow
Smolensk
Tula
Orel
Kursk
Voronezh
Tambov
Penza
Saratov
Samara
Kazan
Nizhniy Novgorod
Yaroslavl
Vologda
Kostroma
Kirov
Perm
Ufa
Orenburg

ESTONIA
Tallinn
LATVIA
Riga
LITHUANIA
Vilnius
Kaunas
Kaliningrad

BELARUS
Minsk
Vitebsk
Mahilyow
Homel

POLAND
Warsaw
Gdańsk
Szczecin
Bydgoszcz
Poznań
Łódź
Wrocław
Katowice
Kraków
Lublin
Białystok

UKRAINE
Kiev
Kharkov
Lvov
Donetsk
Dnepropetrovsk
Zaporozhye
Krivoy Rog
Odessa
Nikolayev
Kherson

GERMANY
Berlin
Hamburg
Bremen
Hannover
Magdeburg
Dortmund
Essen
Cologne
Frankfurt am Main
Leipzig
Dresden
Chemnitz
Nuremberg
Stuttgart
Munich

NETHERLANDS
Amsterdam
The Hague
Rotterdam
BELGIUM
Brussels
Antwerp
LUXEMBOURG

FRANCE
PARIS
Lille
Le Havre
Rouen
Rennes
Nantes
Brest
Bordeaux
Toulouse
Marseilles
Nice
Lyons
St-Étienne
Dijon
Strasbourg
Limoges

CZECH REP.
Prague
SLOVAK REP.
Bratislava
AUSTRIA
Vienna
Linz
Salzburg
Innsbruck
Graz
SWITZERLAND
Bern
Zurich
Geneva
Basel
HUNGARY
Budapest
Debrecen
Miskolc
SLOVENIA
Ljubljana
CROATIA
Zagreb
BOSNIA-HERZ.
Sarajevo
SERBIA & MONTENEGRO
Belgrade
Niš

ROMANIA
Bucharest
Cluj-Napoca
Timişoara
Galaţi
Constanţa
Braşov
Ploieşti
MOLDOVA
Kishinev

BULGARIA
Sofia
Plovdiv
Varna
MACEDONIA
Skopje
ALBANIA
Tirana

ITALY
Rome
Milan
Turin
Genoa
Venice
Bologna
Florence
Naples
Bari
Táranto
Palermo
Messina
Catania
Sardinia
Sicily
Corsica
SAN MARINO
MONACO

Adriatic Sea
Ionian Sea
Tyrrhenian Sea
Aegean Sea

GREECE
Athens
Thessaloníki
Patras
Crete

Black Sea
Mediterranean Sea

SPAIN
Madrid
Barcelona
Valencia
Seville
Málaga
Zaragoza
Bilbao
Córdoba
Murcia
Granada
Cádiz
La Coruña
Valladolid
Balearic Is.
Palma
Majorca
Minorca
Ibiza

PORTUGAL
Lisbon
Porto

ANDORRA
ANDORRA-la-Vella

Bay of Biscay

KAZAKHSTAN
Uralsk
Atyrau

Caspian Sea
Astrakhan
Makhachkala

GEORGIA
Tbilisi
ARMENIA
Yerevan
AZERBAIJAN
Baku

TURKEY
Ankara
Istanbul
Izmir
Bursa
Konya
Antalya
Adana
Kayseri

IRAN
Tabriz
IRAQ
Baghdad
SYRIA
Aleppo
CYPRUS
Nicosia

MOROCCO
ALGERIA
Algiers
Constantine
Annaba
Oran
TUNISIA
Tunis
MALTA
Valletta

AFRICA

West from Greenwich   East from Greenwich
Projection: Bonne

■ LONDON Capital Cities

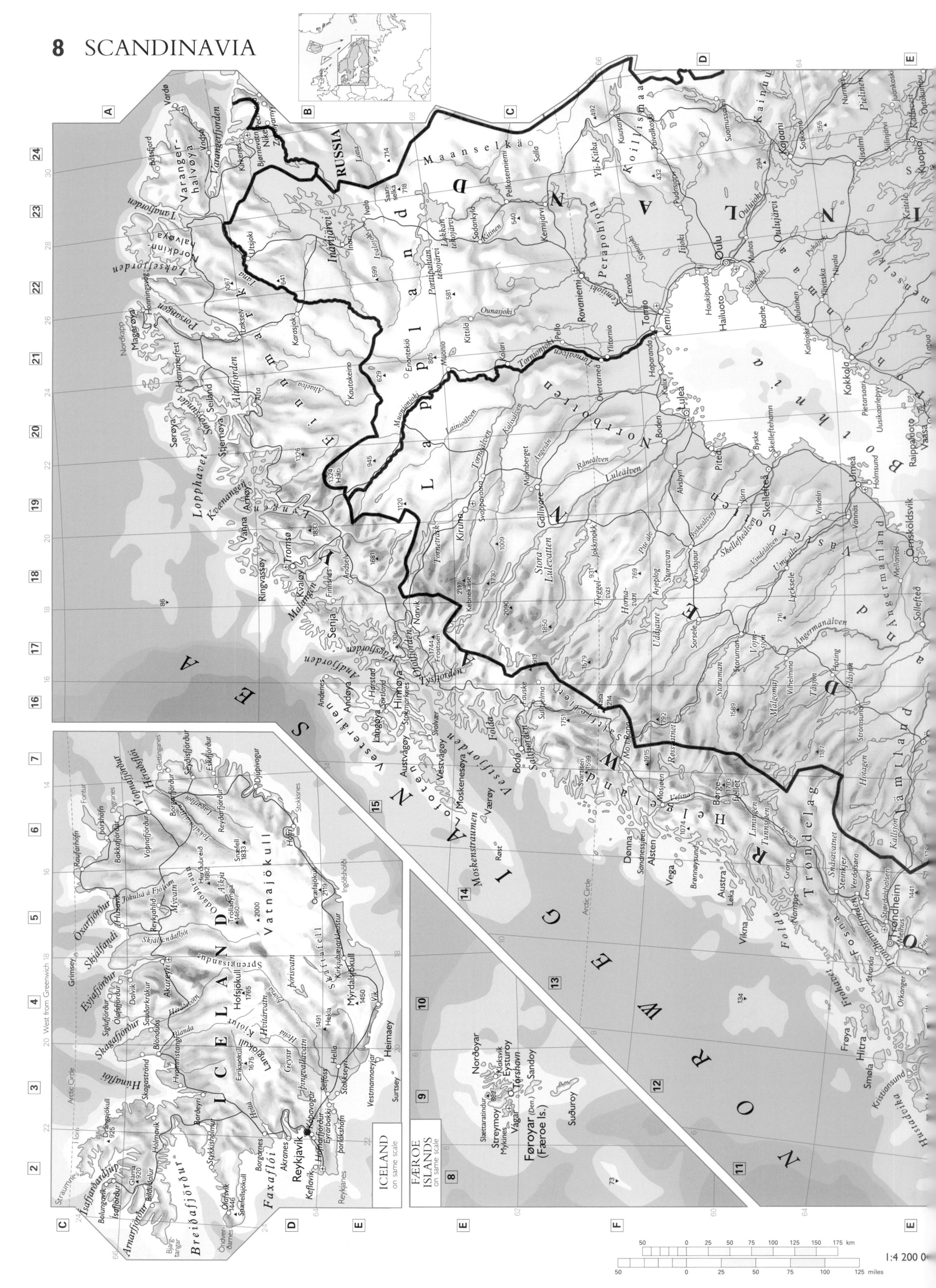

ICELAND
on same scale

FAROE
ISLANDS
on same scale

1:4 200 000

East from Greenwich

Projection: Conical with two standard parallels

1:2 100 000

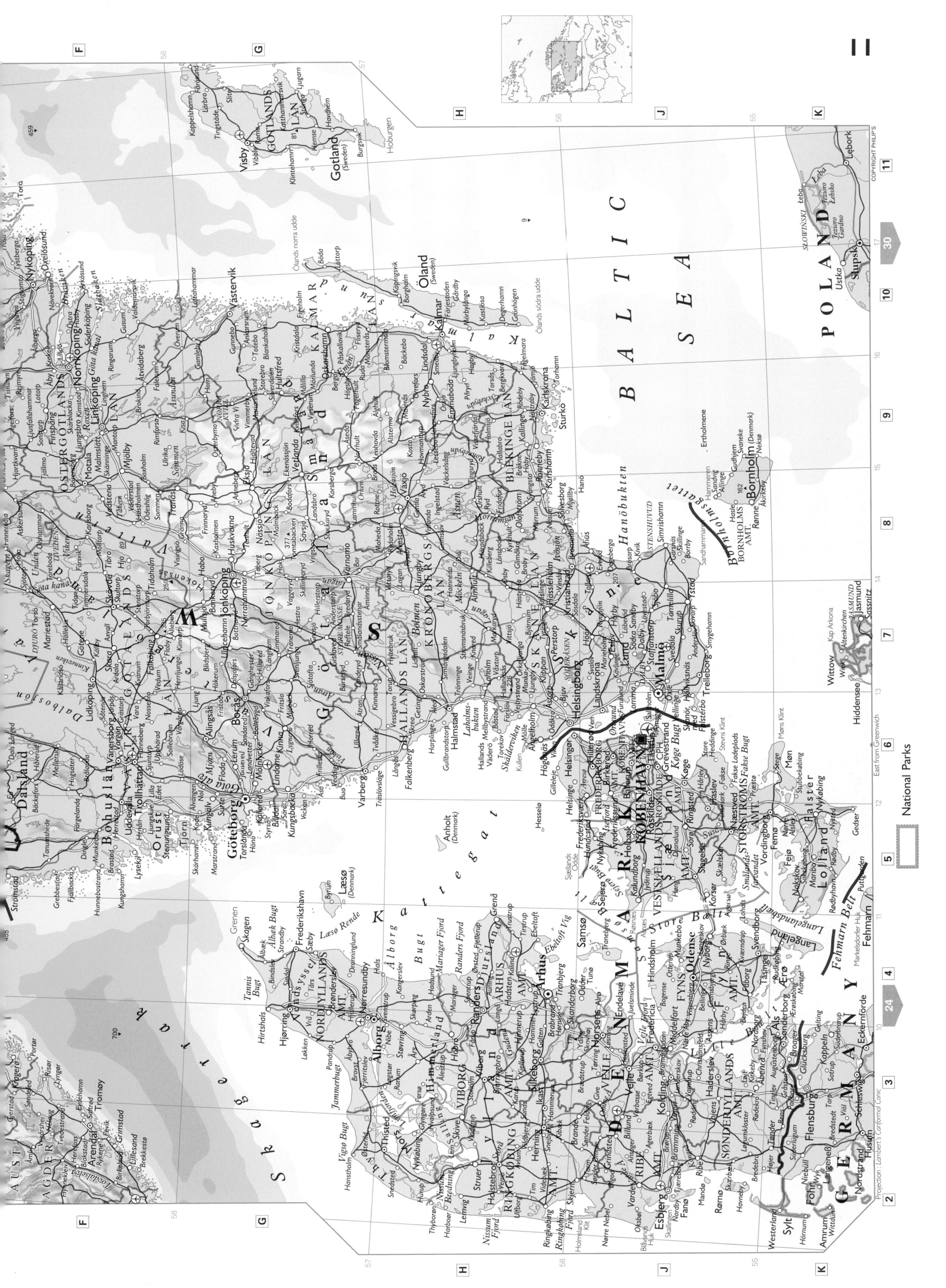

1:1 700 000

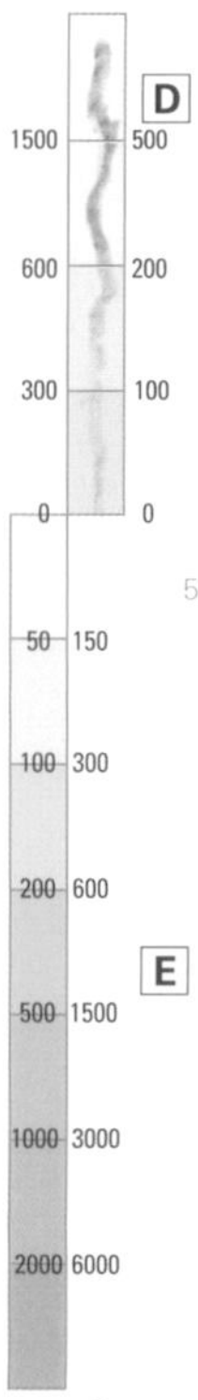

Projection: Lambert's Conformal Conic

West from Greenwich

COPYRIGHT PHILIP'S

National Parks

SCOTLAND

NORTHERN IRELAND

IRELAND

Ulster — Connacht — Leinster — Munster

ATLANTIC OCEAN

IRISH SEA

CELTIC SEA

St. George's Channel

North Channel

WALES

Dublin · Belfast · Londonderry · Cork · Limerick · Galway · Waterford · Sligo · Dundalk · Drogheda

1:1 700 000

10   0   10   20   30   40   50   60   70   80 km
10   0   10   20   30   40   50 miles

Key to Scottish unitary authorities on map
1 CITY OF ABERDEEN   8 EAST RENFREWSHIRE
2 DUNDEE CITY   9 NORTH LANARKSHIRE
3 WEST DUNBARTONSHIRE   10 FALKIRK
4 EAST DUNBARTONSHIRE   11 CLACKMANNANSHIRE
5 CITY OF GLASGOW   12 WEST LOTHIAN
6 INVERCLYDE   13 CITY OF EDINBURGH
7 RENFREWSHIRE   14 MIDLOTHIAN

ORKNEY IS. on same scale

ORKNEY

SHETLAND IS. on same scale

SHETLAND

Projection : Lambert's Conformal Conic

West from Greenwich

COPYRIGHT PHILIP'S

Forest Parks in Scotland

ATLANTIC OCEAN

NORTH SEA

NORTH CHANNEL

SCOTLAND

ENGLAND

NORTHERN IRELAND

1:1 700 000

10   0   10   20   30   40   50   60   70   80 km
10   0   10   20   30   40   50 miles

A   B   C   D

Key to English unitary
authorities on map

25 HARTLEPOOL
26 DARLINGTON
27 STOCKTON-ON-TEES
28 MIDDLESBROUGH
29 REDCAR AND CLEVELAND
30 BLACKPOOL
31 BLACKBURN WITH DARWEN
32 HALTON
33 WARRINGTON
34 KINGSTON UPON HULL
35 NORTH EAST LINCOLNSHIRE
36 STOKE-ON-TRENT
37 TELFORD AND WREKIN
38 DERBY CITY
39 CITY OF NOTTINGHAM
40 LEICESTER CITY
41 RUTLAND
42 PETERBOROUGH
43 MILTON KEYNES
44 LUTON
45 NORTH SOMERSET
46 CITY OF BRISTOL
47 BATH AND NORTH EAST SOMERSET
48 SWINDON
49 READING
50 WOKINGHAM
51 WINDSOR AND MAIDENHEAD
52 SLOUGH
53 BRACKNELL FOREST
54 THURROCK
55 SOUTHEND-ON-SEA
56 MEDWAY
57 PLYMOUTH
58 TORBAY
59 POOLE
60 BOURNEMOUTH
61 SOUTHAMPTON
62 PORTSMOUTH
63 BRIGHTON AND HOVE

Key to Welsh unitary
authorities on map

15 SWANSEA
16 NEATH PORT TALBOT
17 BRIDGEND
18 RHONDDA CYNON TAFF
19 MERTHYR TYDFIL
20 CAERPHILLY
21 BLAENAU GWENT
22 TORFAEN
23 CARDIFF
24 NEWPORT

NORTH SEA

IRISH SEA

North Channel

NORTHERN IRELAND

SCOTLAND

ENGLAND

WALES

ISLE OF MAN

Newcastle-upon-Tyne
Sunderland
Middlesbrough
Hartlepool
Kingston upon Hull
Leeds
Bradford
Sheffield
Manchester
Liverpool
Stoke-on-Trent
Derby
Nottingham
Lincoln
Blackpool
Preston
Chester
Carlisle
York
Scarborough
Edinburgh
Glasgow
Belfast

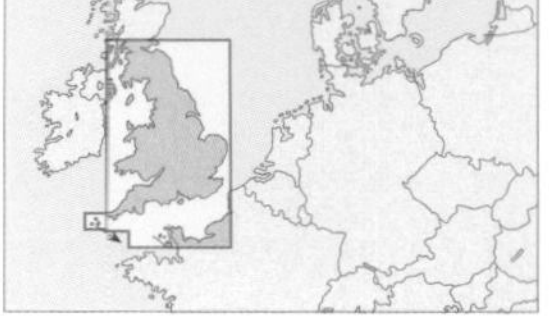

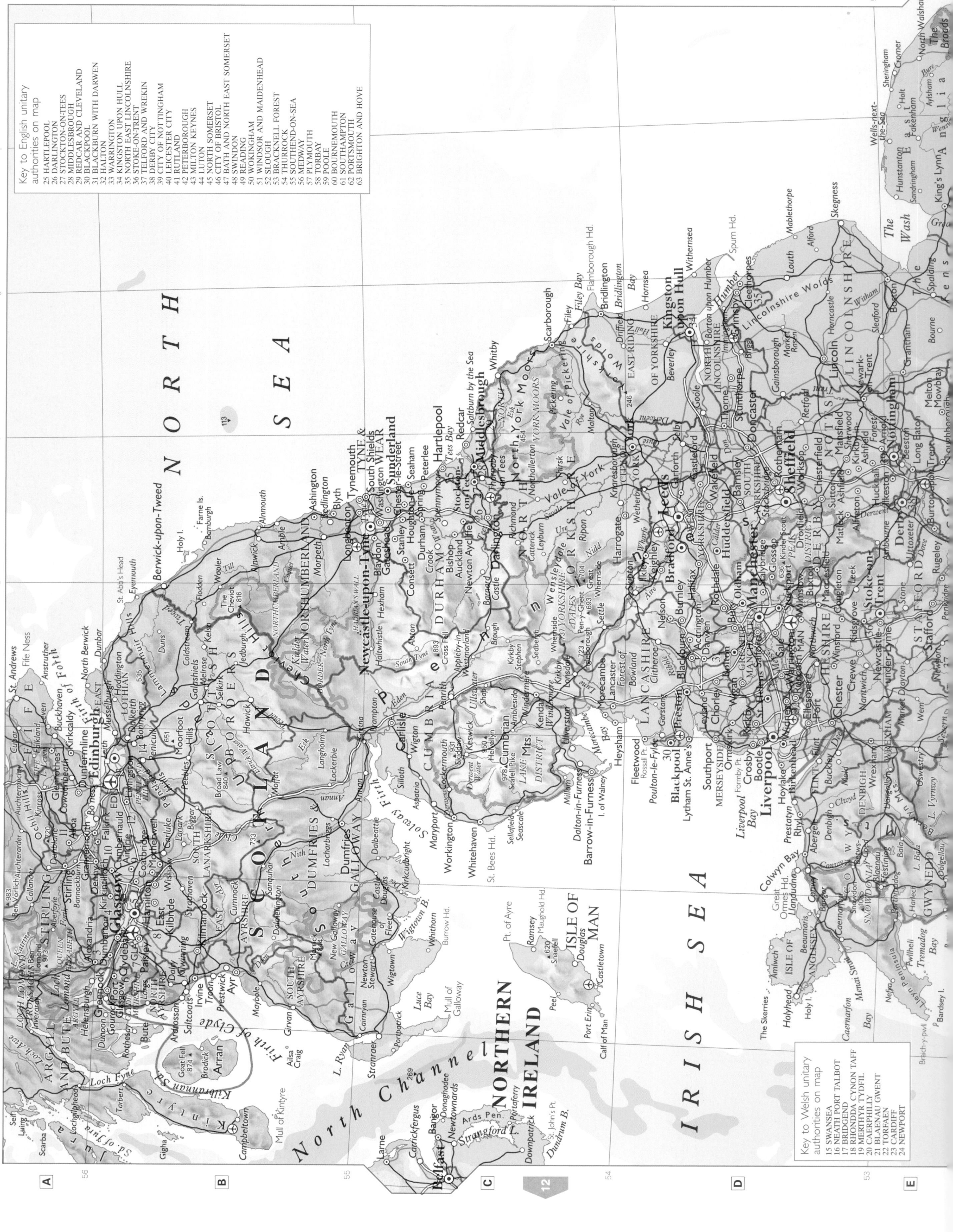

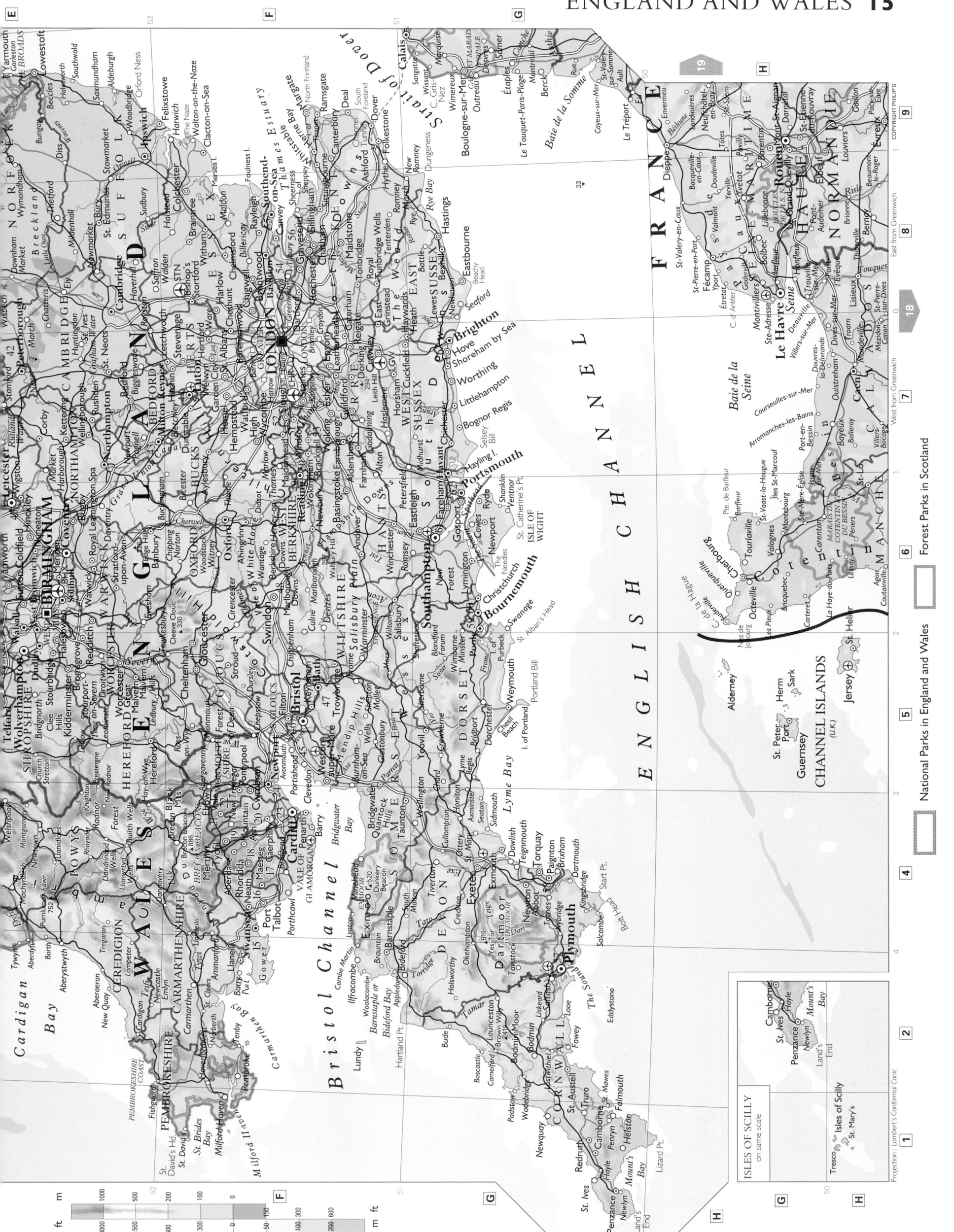

National Parks in England and Wales

Forest Parks in Scotland

ISLES OF SCILLY
on same scale

Projection: Lambert's Conformal Conic

1:4 200 000

Projection: Conical with two standard parallels

East from Greenwich COPYRIGHT PHILIP'S

West from Greenwich

1:2 100 000

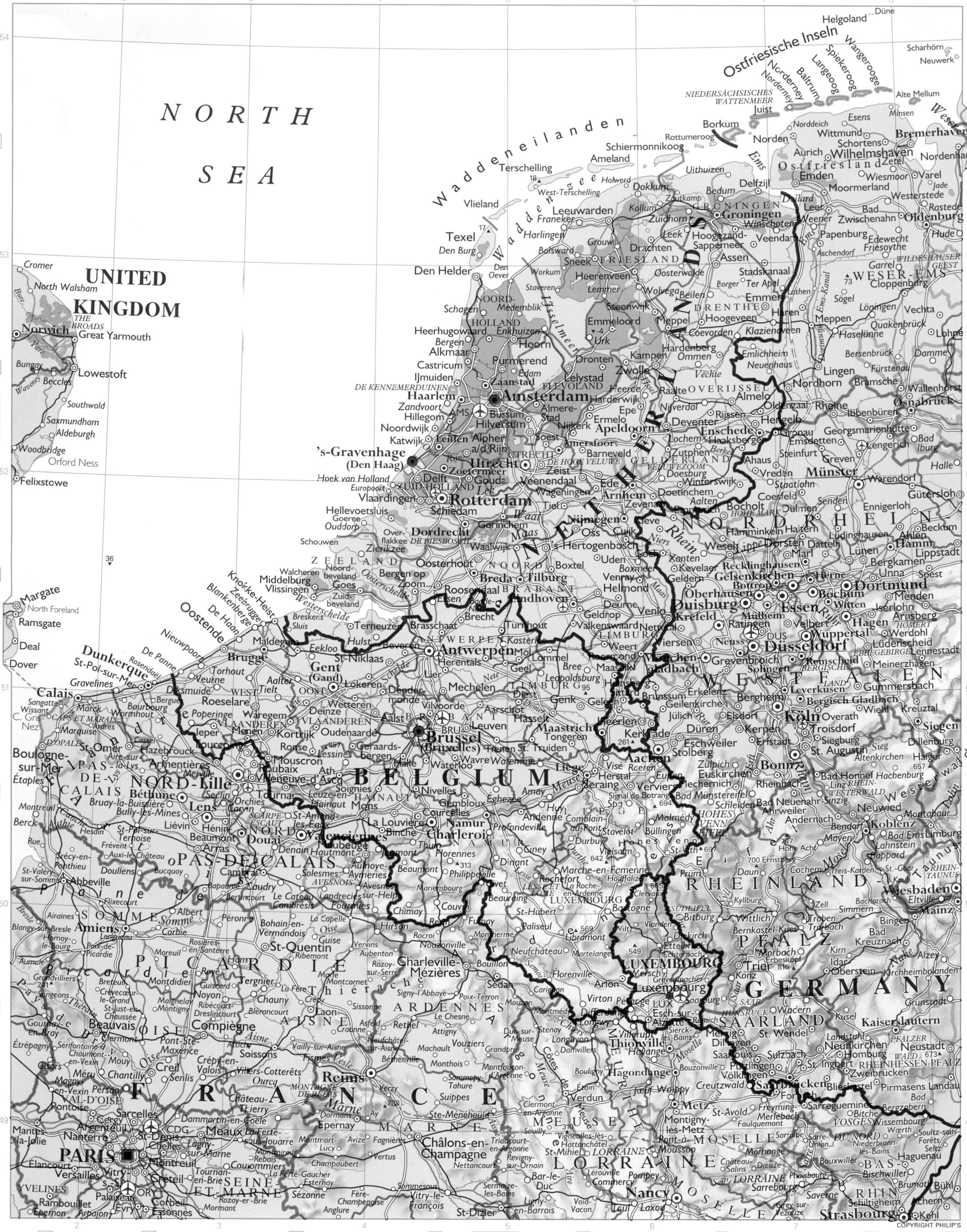

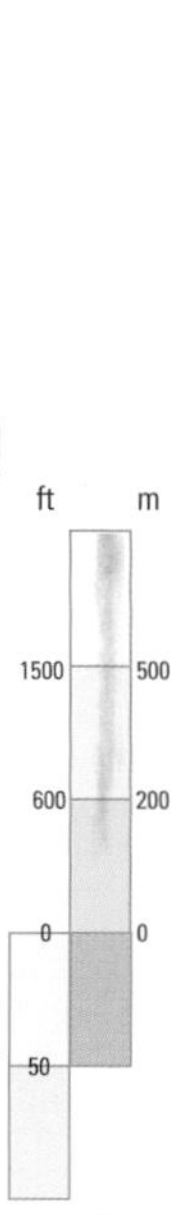

10 20 30 40 50 60 70 80 90 km
10 0 10 20 30 40 50 60 miles

NORTH SEA

UNITED KINGDOM

NETHERLANDS

BELGIUM

LUXEMBOURG

GERMANY

FRANCE

Amsterdam · 's-Gravenhage (Den Haag) · Rotterdam · Utrecht · Groningen · Leeuwarden · Den Helder · Haarlem · Zwolle · Arnhem · Nijmegen · Eindhoven · Tilburg · Breda · Middelburg · Vlissingen

Brussel (Bruxelles) · Antwerpen · Gent (Gand) · Brugge · Namur · Charleroi · Liège · Mons · Hasselt · Maastricht · Aachen

Luxembourg · Esch-sur-Alzette · Diekirch

Köln · Düsseldorf · Bonn · Dortmund · Essen · Duisburg · Bochum · Wuppertal · Münster · Osnabrück · Oldenburg · Bremerhaven · Wilhelmshaven · Emden · Saarbrücken · Trier · Koblenz · Wiesbaden · Mainz

Lille · Calais · Dunkerque · Boulogne-sur-Mer · Valenciennes · Reims · Paris · Amiens · Nancy · Metz · Strasbourg

NORTH SEA · WADDENEILANDEN · Ostfriesische Inseln · Helgoland

ZEELAND · BRABANT · FRIESLAND · DRENTHE · OVERIJSSEL · GELDERLAND · LIMBURG · FLEVOLAND · HOLLAND

VLAANDEREN · HAINAUT · NORD-PAS-DE-CALAIS · PICARDIE · SOMME · OISE · AISNE · MARNE · ARDENNES · LORRAINE · MEUSE · MOSELLE · SEINE-ET-MARNE

NORDRHEIN-WESTFALEN · RHEINLAND-PFALZ · SAARLAND · WESER-EMS

National Parks

Underlined towns give their name to the administrative area in which they stand.

ft m
1500 500
600 200
0 0
50

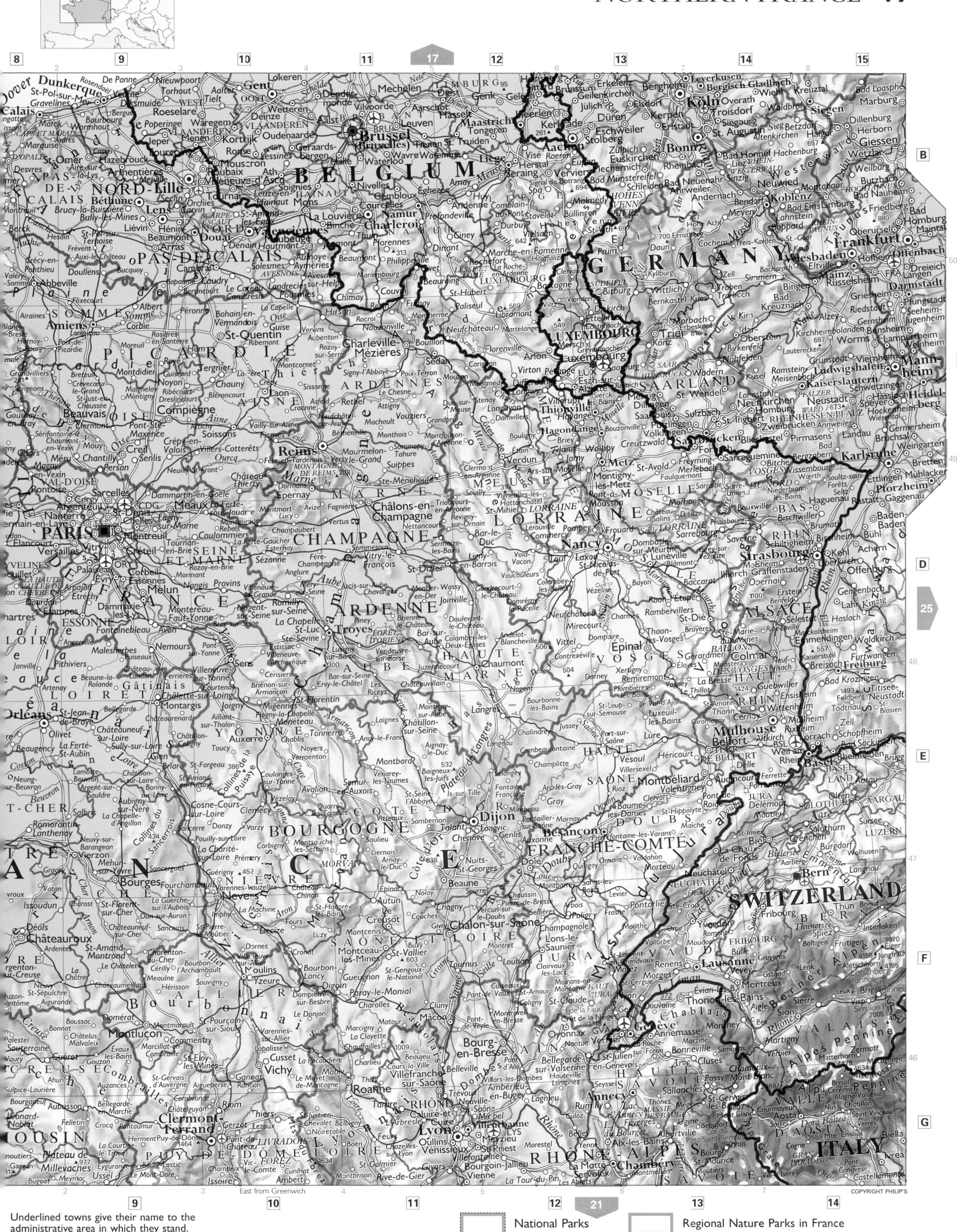

Underlined towns give their name to the
administrative area in which they stand.

National Parks   Regional Nature Parks in France

East from Greenwich

COPYRIGHT PHILIP'S

National Parks   Regional Nature Parks in France

COPYRIGHT PHILIP'S

1:4 200 000

50 0 25 50 75 100 125 150 175 km
50 0 25 50 75 100 125 miles

Projection: Conical with two standard parallels

NORTH SEA

BALTIC SEA

ADRIATIC SEA

DENMARK

UNITED KINGDOM

NETHERLANDS

BELGIUM

LUXEMBOURG

GERMANY

FRANCE

SWITZERLAND

LIECHTENSTEIN

AUSTRIA

ITALY

CZECH

SLOVENIA

Golfo di Génova

ft m
12000 4000
9000 3000
6000 2000
4500 1500
1500 500
600 200
0 0
150 50
300 100
600 200
1500 500
3000 1000
6000 2000
m ft

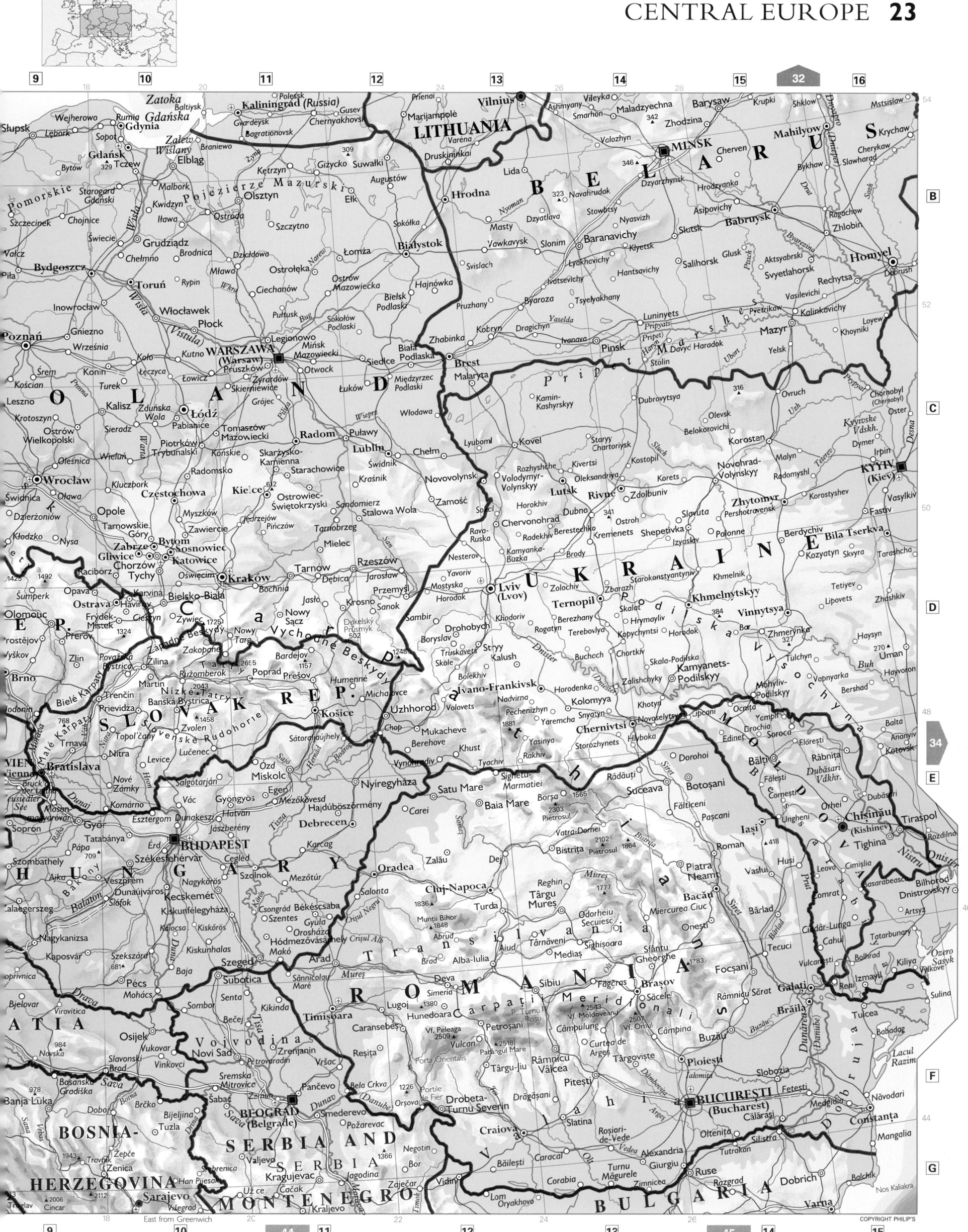

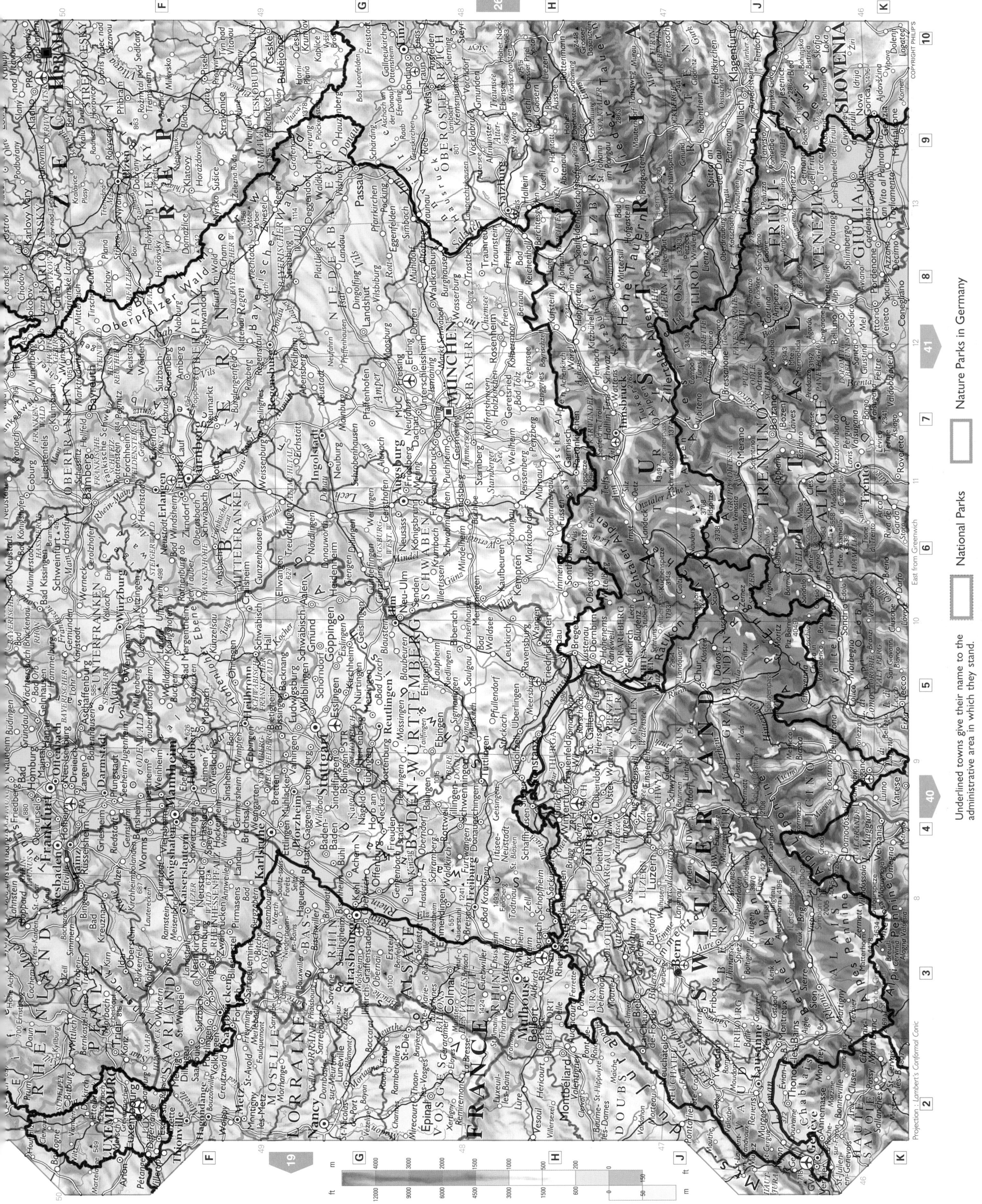

Nature Parks in Germany

National Parks

Underlined towns give their name to the administrative area in which they stand.

Projection : Lambert's Conformal Conic

COPYRIGHT PHILIP'S

East from Greenwich

National Parks

Underlined towns give their name to the
administrative area in which they stand.

COPYRIGHT PHILIP'S

1:2 100 000

Administrative divisions in Croatia:
1 Brodsko-Posavska   5 Osječko-Baranjska   9 Vukovarsko-Srijemska
2 Koprivničko-Križevačka 6 Požeško-Slavonska
4 Medimurska   8 Virovitičko-Podravska

East from Greenwich

Inter-entity boundaries as agreed
at the 1995 Dayton Peace Agreement

National Parks

Underlined towns give their name to the
administrative area in which they stand.

COPYRIGHT PHILIP'S

1:2 100 000

10 0 10 20 30 40 50 60 70 80 90 km
10 0 10 20 30 40 50 60 miles

Underlined towns give their name to the administrative area in which they stand.

National Parks

East from Greenwich

Projection: Lambert's Conformal Conic

COPYRIGHT PHILIP'S

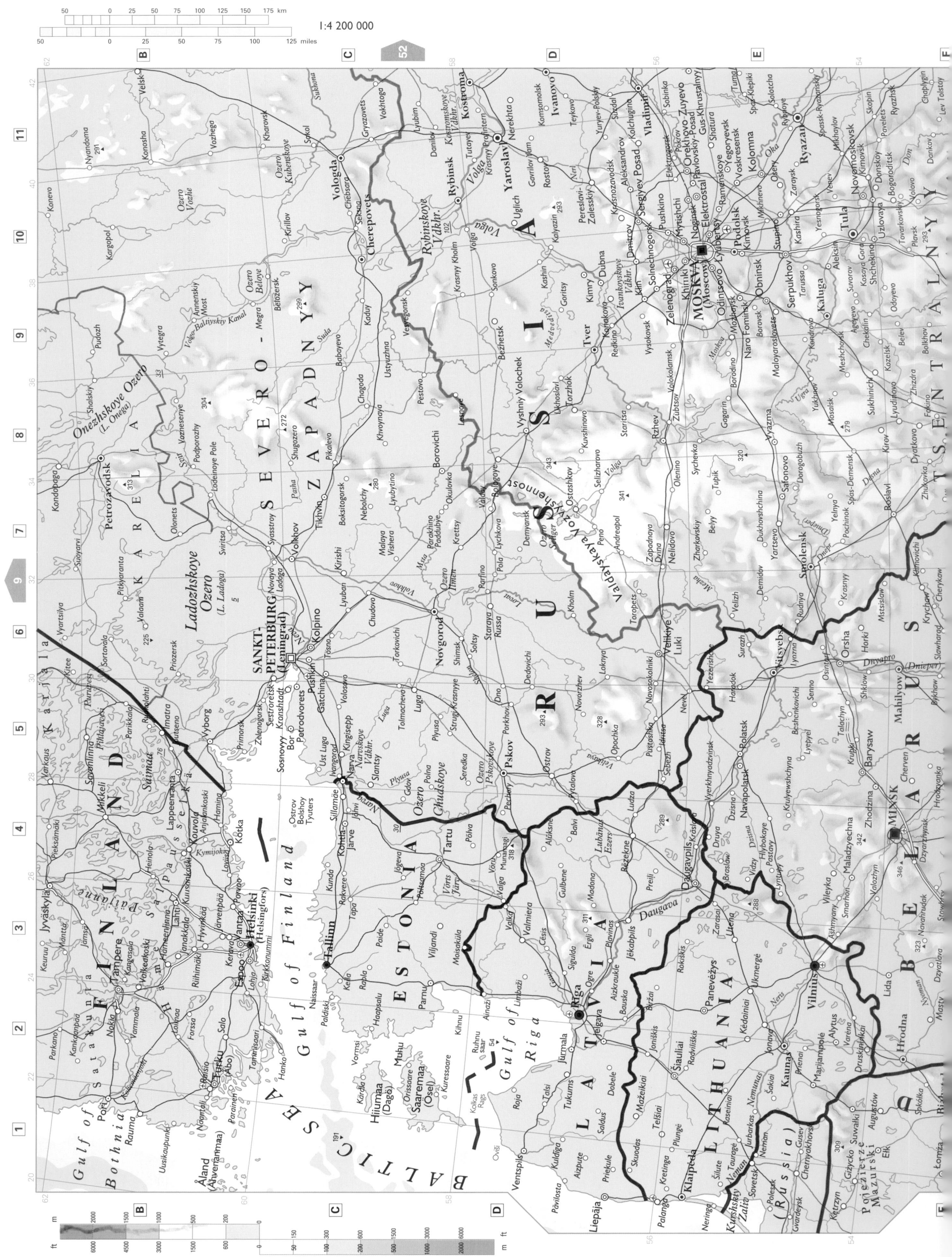

1:4 200 000

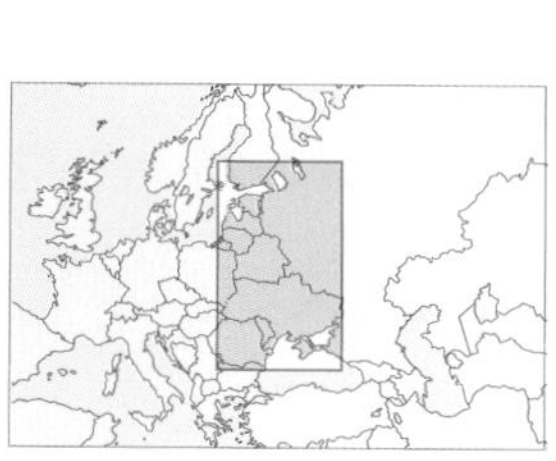

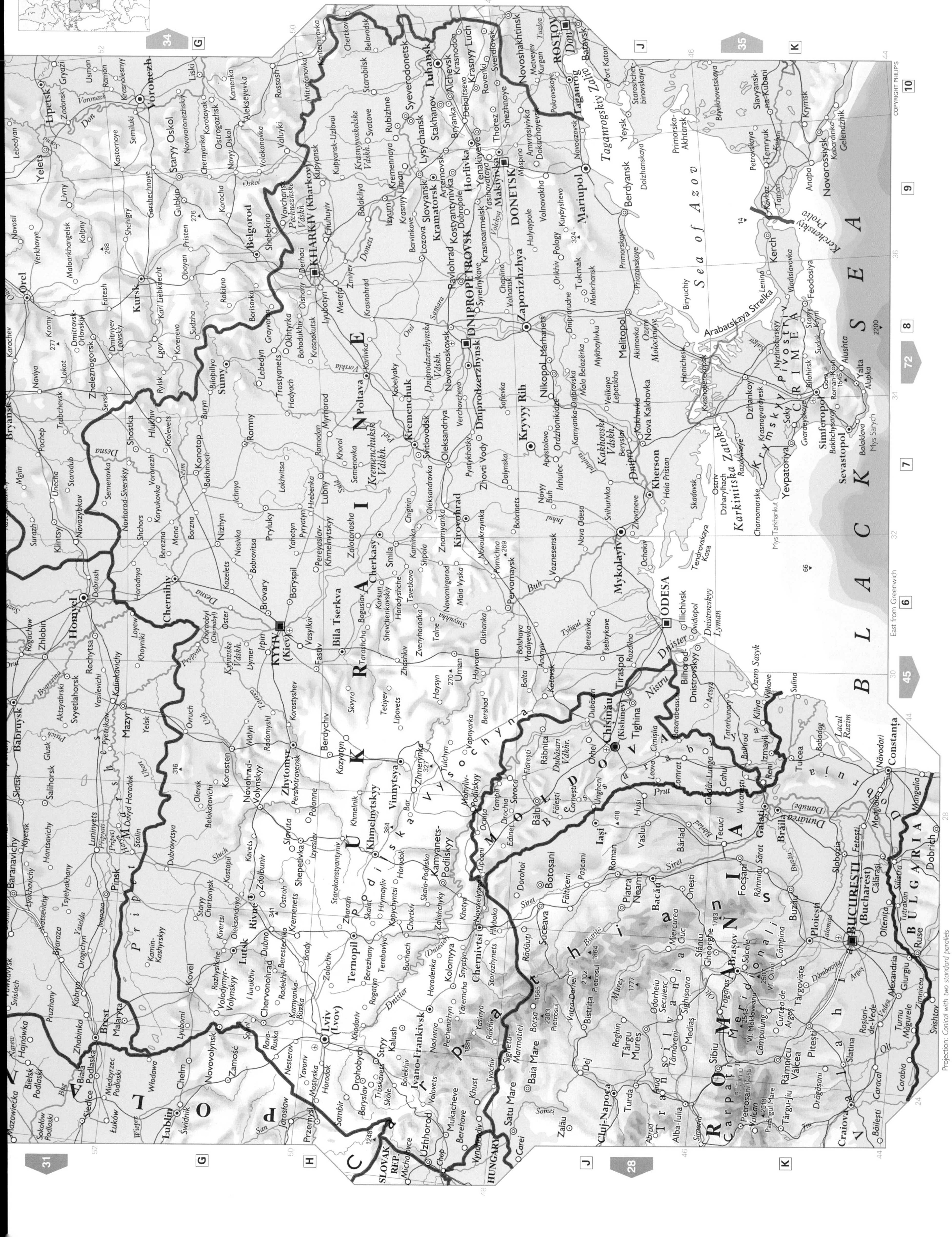

UKRAINE
ROMANIA
MOLDOVA
BULGARIA
BLACK SEA
Sea of Azov
CRIMEA
KYIV (Kiev)
KHARKIV (Kharkov)
DNIPROPETROVSK
DONETSK
ODESA
CHIŞINĂU (Kishinev)
BUCUREŞTI (Bucharest)
ROSTOV
Voronezh
Kursk
Belgorod
Zaporizhzhya
Kryvyy Rih
Mykolayiv
Kherson
Simferopol
Sevastopol
Lviv (Lvov)
Chernivtsi
Homyel
Brest
Pinsk
Lublin
Cluj-Napoca
Iaşi
Galaţi
Constanţa
Mariupol
Luhansk
Poltava
Cherkasy
Vinnytsya
Zhytomyr
Rivne
Lutsk
Ternopil
Chernihiv
Sumy
Kirovohrad
Kremenchuk
SLOVAK REP.
HUNGARY
Projection: Conical with two standard parallels
East from Greenwich
COPYRIGHT PHILIP'S

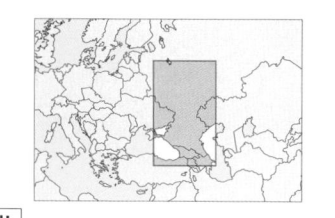

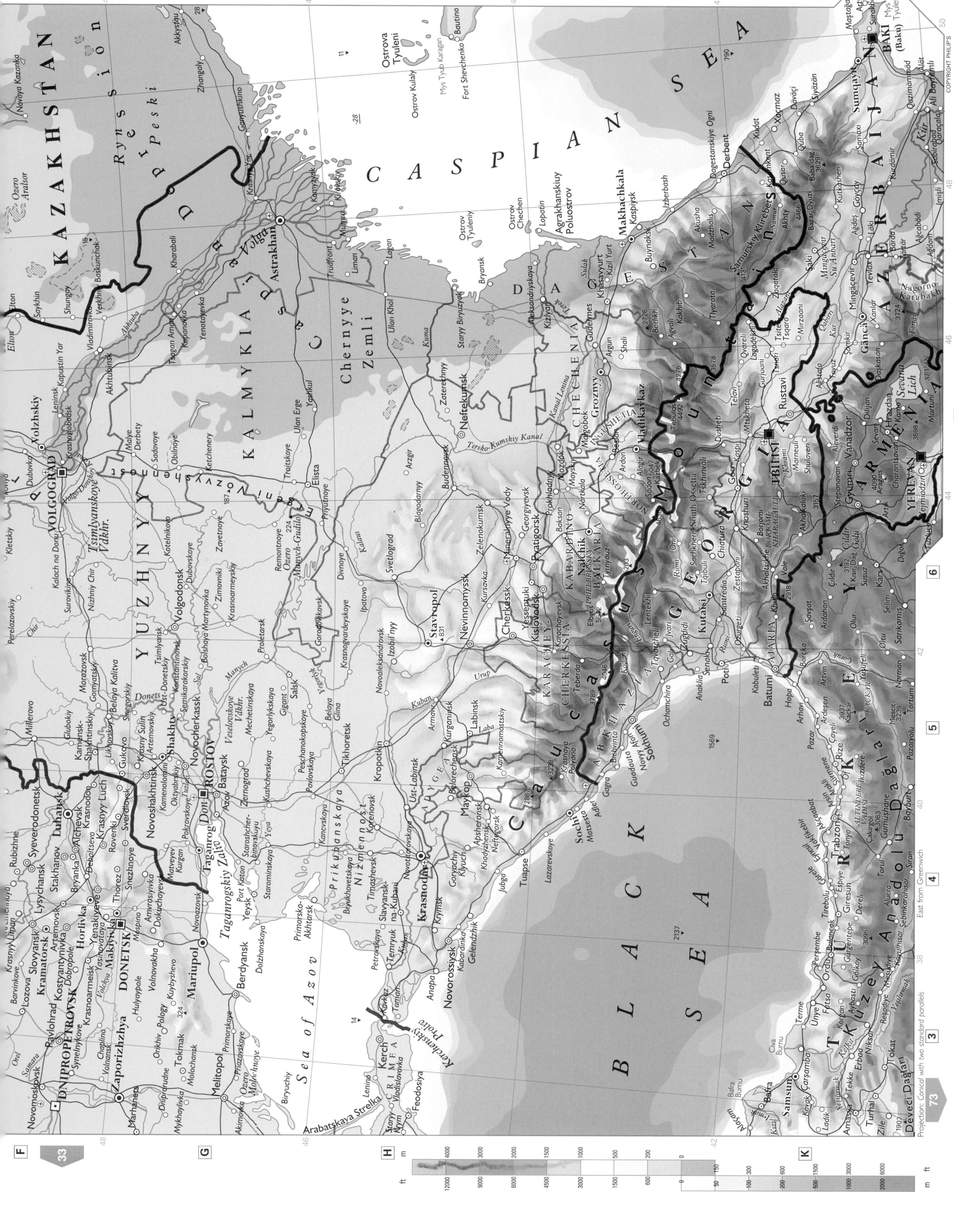

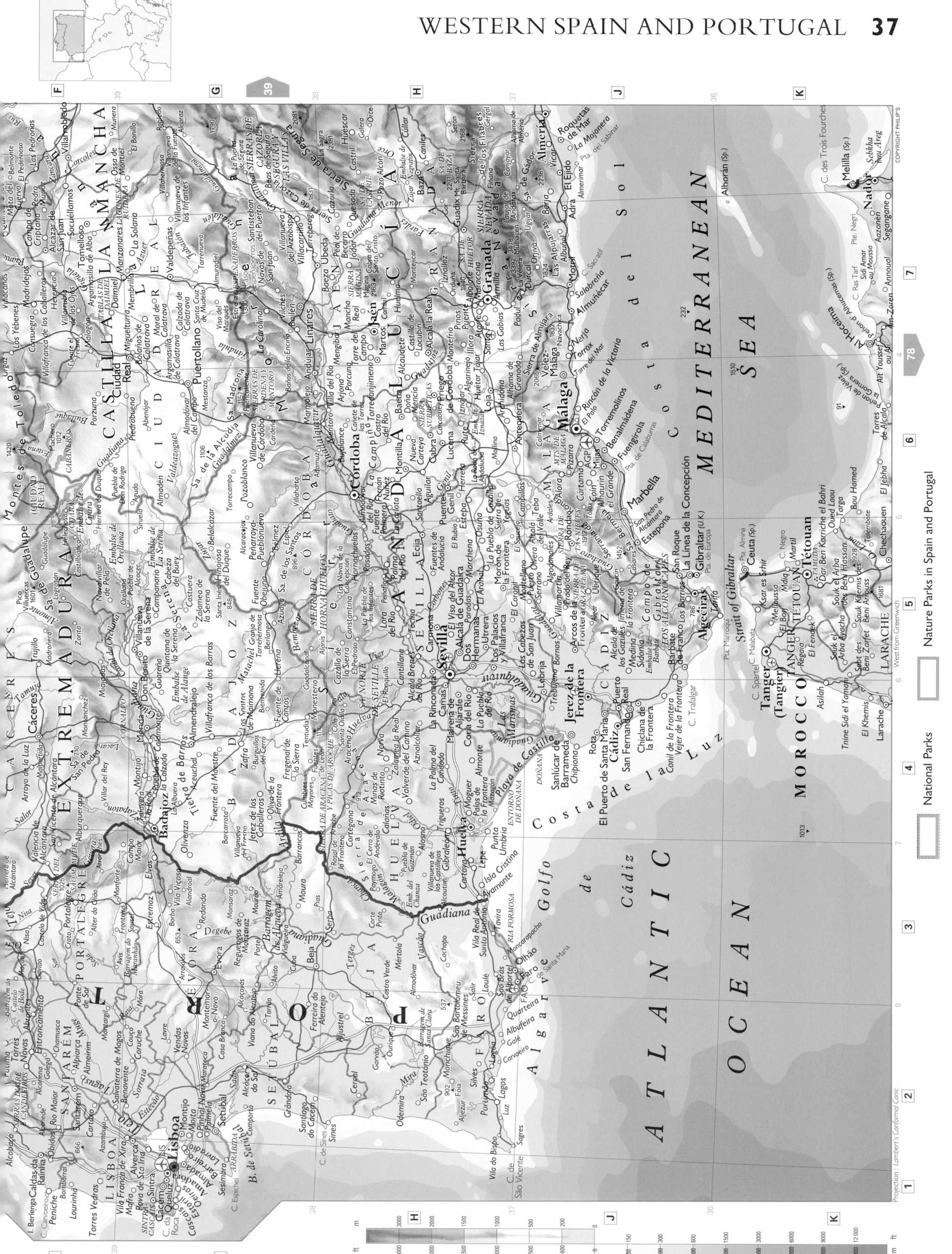

MEDITERRANEAN SEA

ATLANTIC OCEAN

MOROCCO

Nature Parks in Spain and Portugal

National Parks

1:2 100 000

National Parks

Nature Parks in Spain

National Parks

Underlined towns give their name to t
administrative area in which they stand

Projection : Lambert's Conformal Conic

Administrative divisions in Croatia:

Brodsko-Posavska	4 Medimurska	8 Virovitičko-Fodravska
Koprivničko-Križevačka	6 Poželko-Slavonska	10 Zagreba čka
Krapinsko-Zagorska	7 Varaždinska	

☐ Nature Parks in Italy

- - - Inter-entity boundaries as agreed
at the 1995 Dayton Peace Agreement

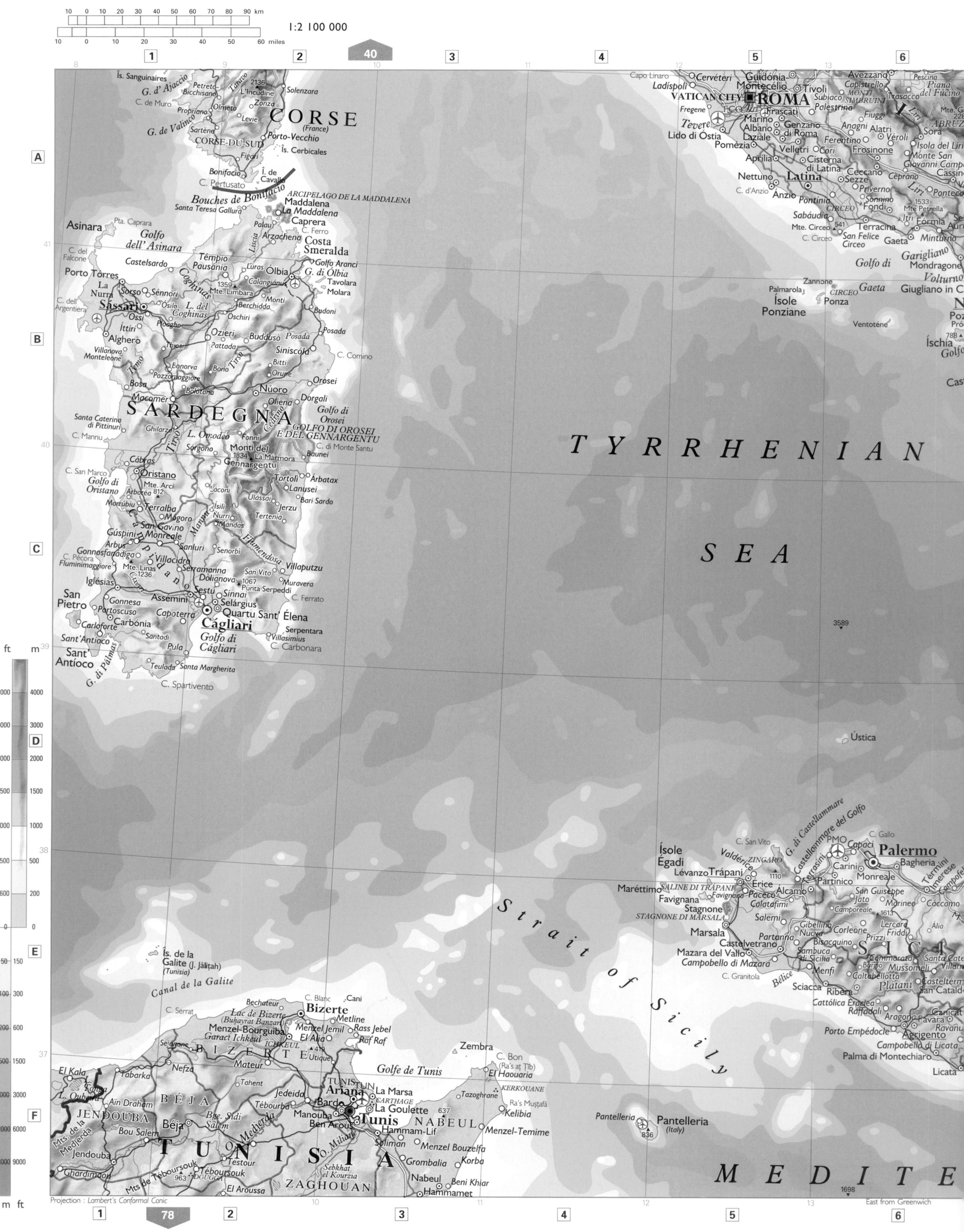

1:2 100 000

Projection : Lambert's Conformal Conic

East from Greenwich

Nature Parks in Italy   National Parks

Underlined towns give their name to the administrative area in which they stand.

1:2 100 000

Projection : Lambert's Conformal Conic

- - - - Inter-entity boundaries as agreed
at the 1995 Dayton Peace Agreement

ROMANIA

WALLACHIA
OLT
VÂLCEA
ARGEŞ
DÂMBOVIŢA
PRAHOVA
BUZĂU
BRĂILA
IALOMIŢA
GIURGIU
CĂLĂRAŞI
TELEORMAN
CONSTANŢA
TULCEA
DELTA DUNĂREA

Râmnicu Vâlcea · Piteşti · Târgovişte · Ploieşti · Câmpulung · Sinaia · Comârnic · Câmpina · Buzău · Brăila · Galaţi · Tulcea · Mangalia · Constanţa · Năvodari · Ovidiu · Medgidia · Cernavodă · Feteşti · Slobozia · Urziceni · BUCUREŞTI (Bucharest) · Giurgiu · Alexandria · Caracal · Slatina

BULGARIA

Ruse · Pleven · Lovech · Gabrovo · Veliko Tŭrnovo · Sevlievo · Troyan · Botev 2376 · Kazanlŭk · Stara Zagora · Sliven · Yambol · Nova Zagora · Plovdiv · Pazardzhik · Asenovgrad · Haskovo · Kŭrdzhali · Smolyan · Dimitrovgrad · Shumen · Razgrad · Dobrich · Varna · Burgas · Burgaski Zaliv · Nesebŭr · Sozopol · Balchik · Kavarna · Silistra · Tŭrgovishte · Popovo

DOBRICH · VARNA · BURGAS · PLOVDIV · KHASKOVO · SLIVEN · LOVECH · RUSE

Iztochni Rodopi · Zapaden Rodopi · Stara Planina · Sredna Gora · Balkan · Kotlenska Planina · Preslavska Planina · Aytoska Planina · Udvoy Balkan · Strandzha

TURKEY

İstanbul · Üsküdar · Kartal · Pendik · Gebze · Kocaeli (İzmit) · Bursa · Çanakkale · Gelibolu (Gallipoli) · Edirne · Kırklareli · Lüleburgaz · Tekirdağ · Çorlu · Bandırma · İnegöl · Gönen · Biga · Yalova · Gölcük · Karacabey

EDİRNE · KIRKLARELİ · TEKİRDAĞ · KOCAELİ

Thrace · Marmara Denizi (Sea of Marmara) · Çanakkale Boğazı (Dardanelles) · İstanbul Boğazı (Bosporus) · Saros Körfezi · Gelibolu Yarımadası · Uludağ 2543

GREECE

ANATOLIKÍ MAKEDHONÍA · THRAKI · Kaválla · Xánthi · Komotiní · Alexandroúpolis · Orestiás · Dhidhimótikhon · Évros · Thásos · Samothráki · Límnos · Thrakikón Pélagos

EVROS · RODHOPI

BLACK SEA

Nos Kaliakra · Nos Emine · Maslen Nos · Cape labels

Dunărea (Danube) / Dunav · Dunărea Delta · Ostrov Sfântu Gheorghe · Braţul Chilia · Braţul Sulina · Braţul Sfântu Gheorghe · Lacul Razim · Lacul Sinoie

National Parks

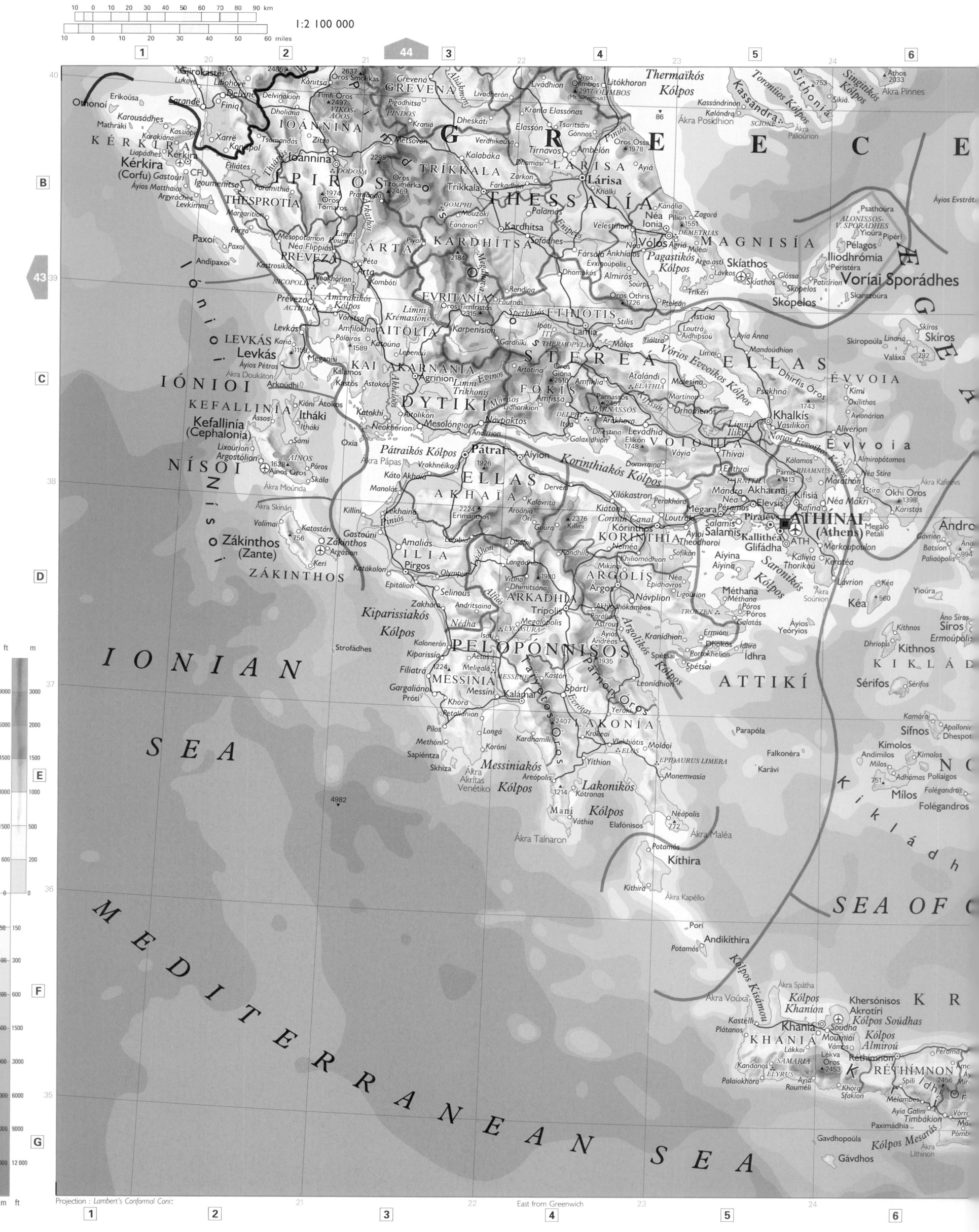

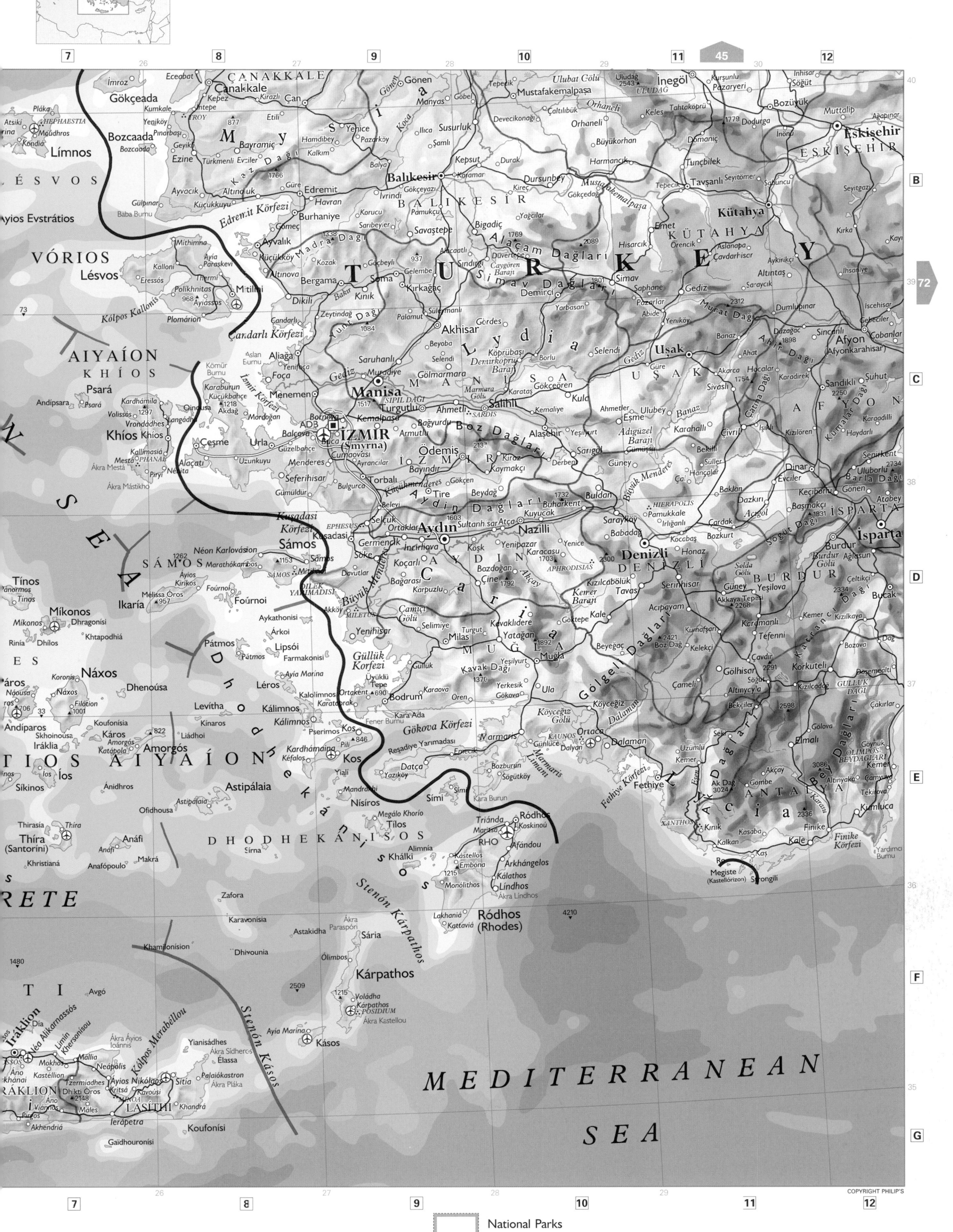

National Parks

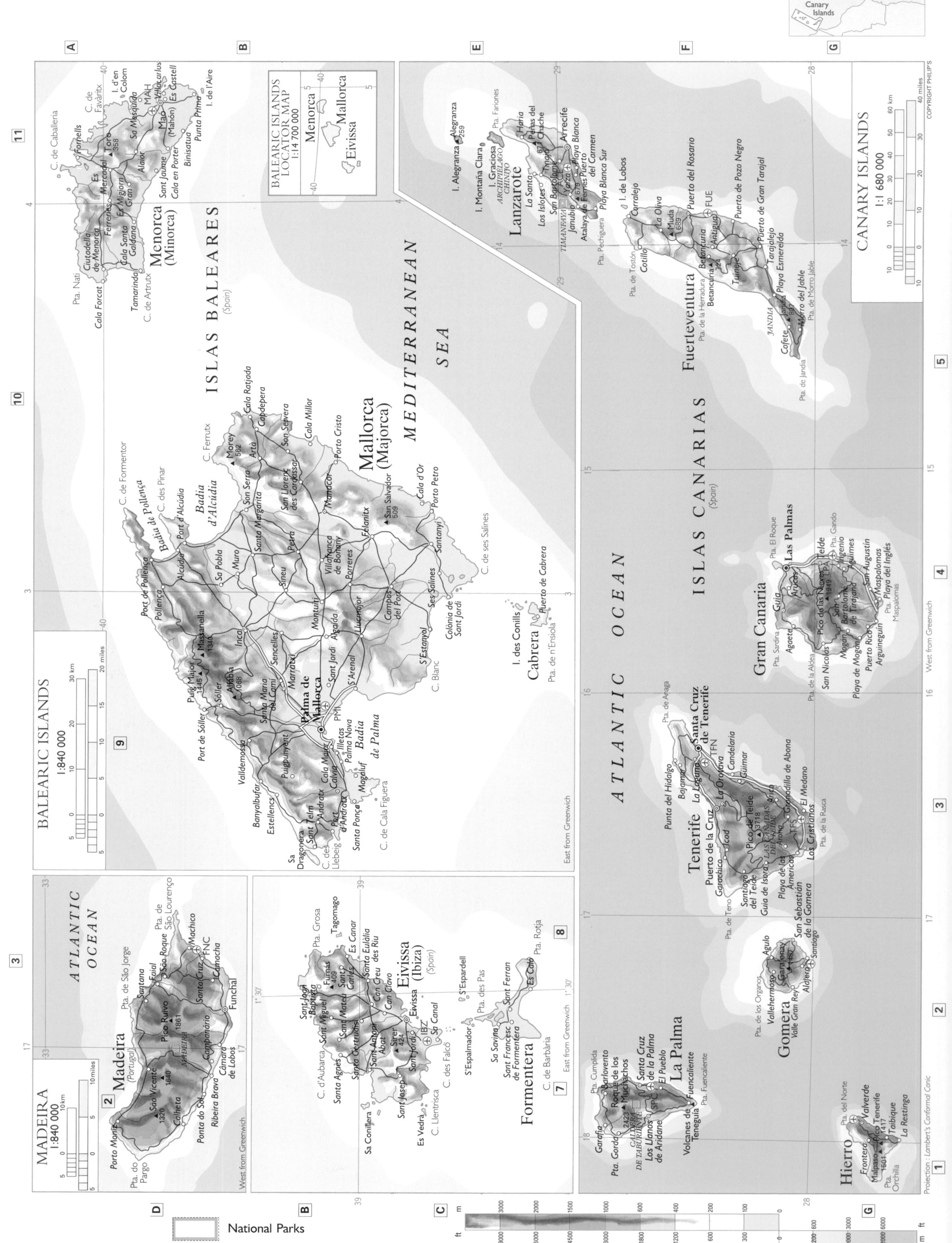

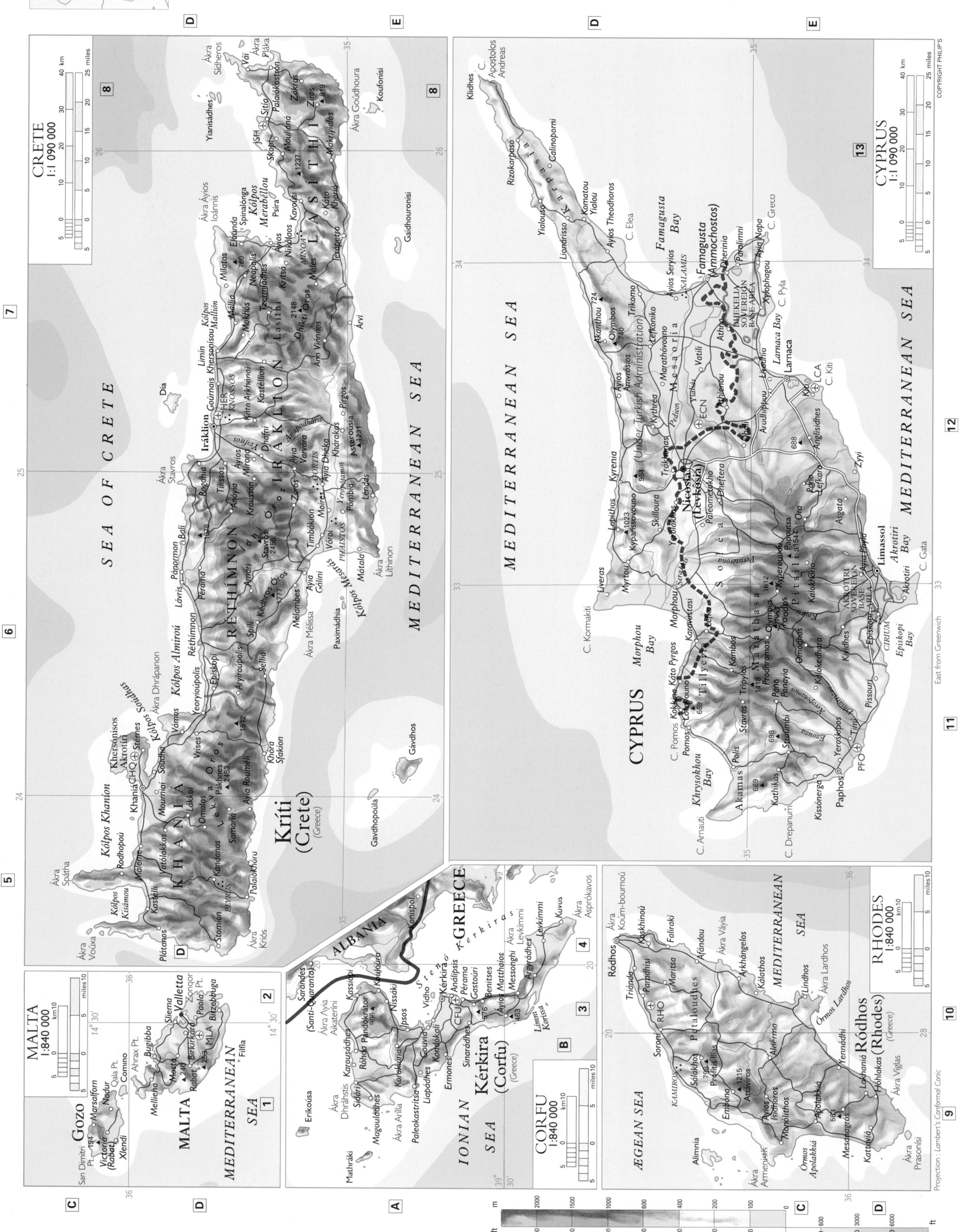

CRETE
1:1 090 000

SEA OF CRETE

MEDITERRANEAN SEA

Kríti
(Crete)
(Greece)

MEDITERRANEAN SEA

MEDITERRANEAN SEA

CYPRUS

CYPRUS
1:1 090 000

Morphou Bay

Famagusta Bay

Larnaca Bay

East from Greenwich

MALTA
1:840 000

GOZO

MEDITERRANEAN SEA

CORFU
1:840 000

GREECE

ALBANIA

Kérkira (Corfu)
(Greece)

IONIAN SEA

AEGEAN SEA

RHODES
1:840 000

Ródhos (Rhodes)
(Greece)

MEDITERRANEAN SEA

Projection: Lambert's Conformal Conic

COPYRIGHT PHILIP'S

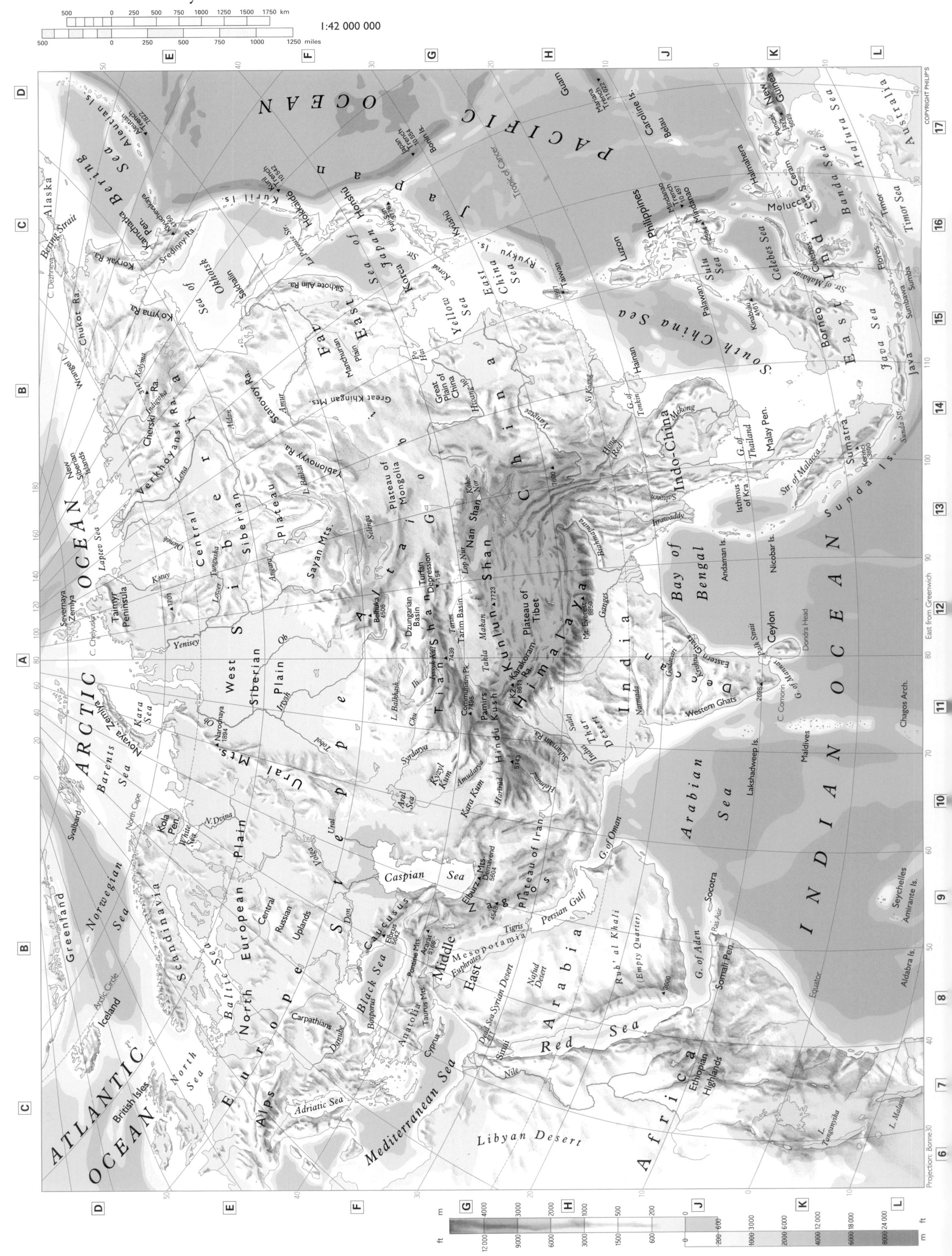

1:42 000 000

500 250 0 250 500 750 1000 1250 1500 1750 km
500 0 250 500 750 1000 1250 miles

COPYRIGHT PHILIP'S

Projection: Bonne-30

m 4000 3000 2000 1000 500 200 0 200 600 m
ft 12 000 9000 6000 3000 1500 600 0 600 3000 6000 12 000 18 000 24 000 ft

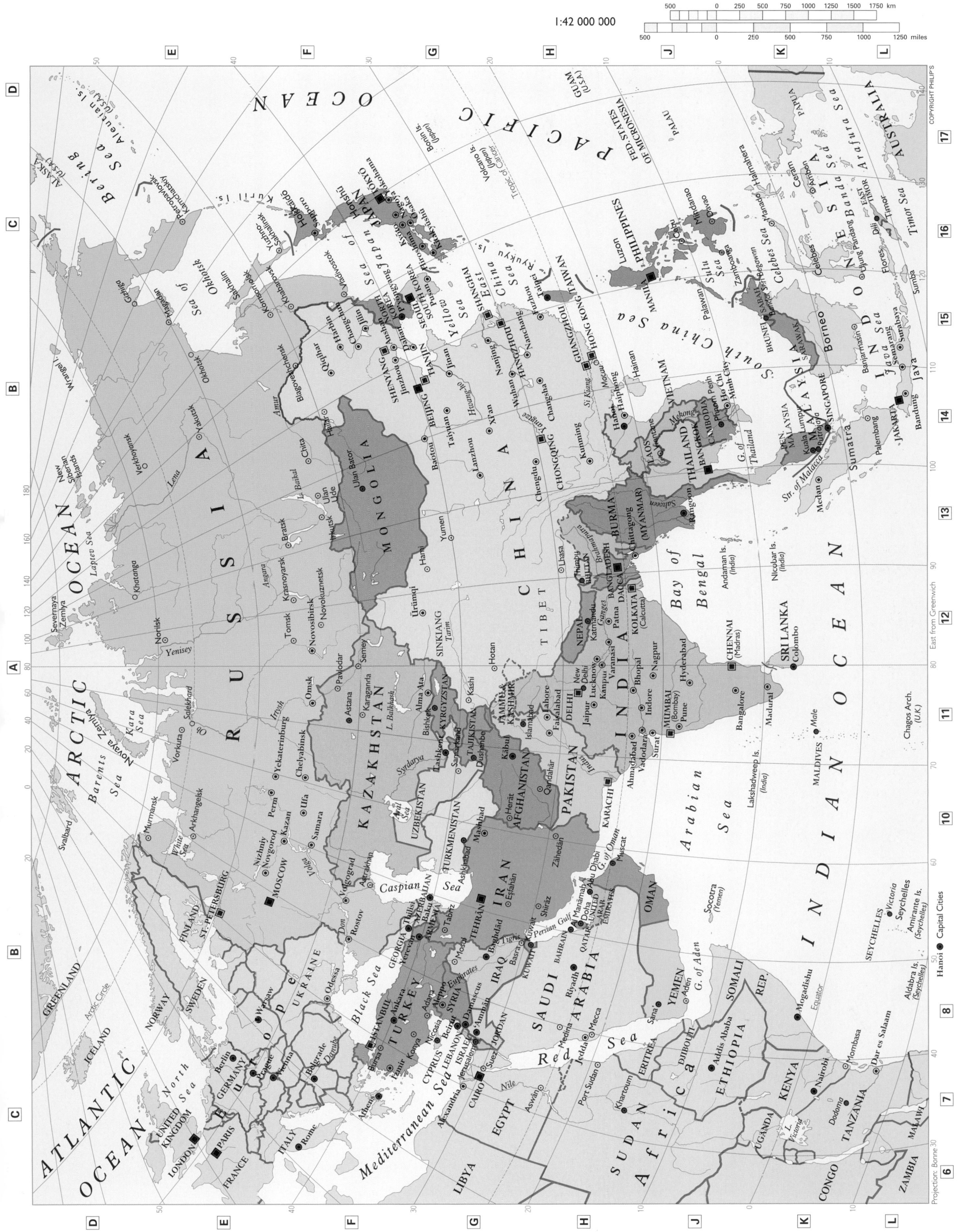

1:42 000 000

500   0   250   500   750   1000   1250   1500   1750 km

500   0   250   500   750   1000   1250 miles

COPYRIGHT PHILIP'S

Projection: Bonne 30

1:16 800 000

Projection: Conical Orthomorphic with two standard parallels

1:4 200 000

50 0 25 50 75 100 125 150 175 km
50 0 25 50 75 100 125 miles

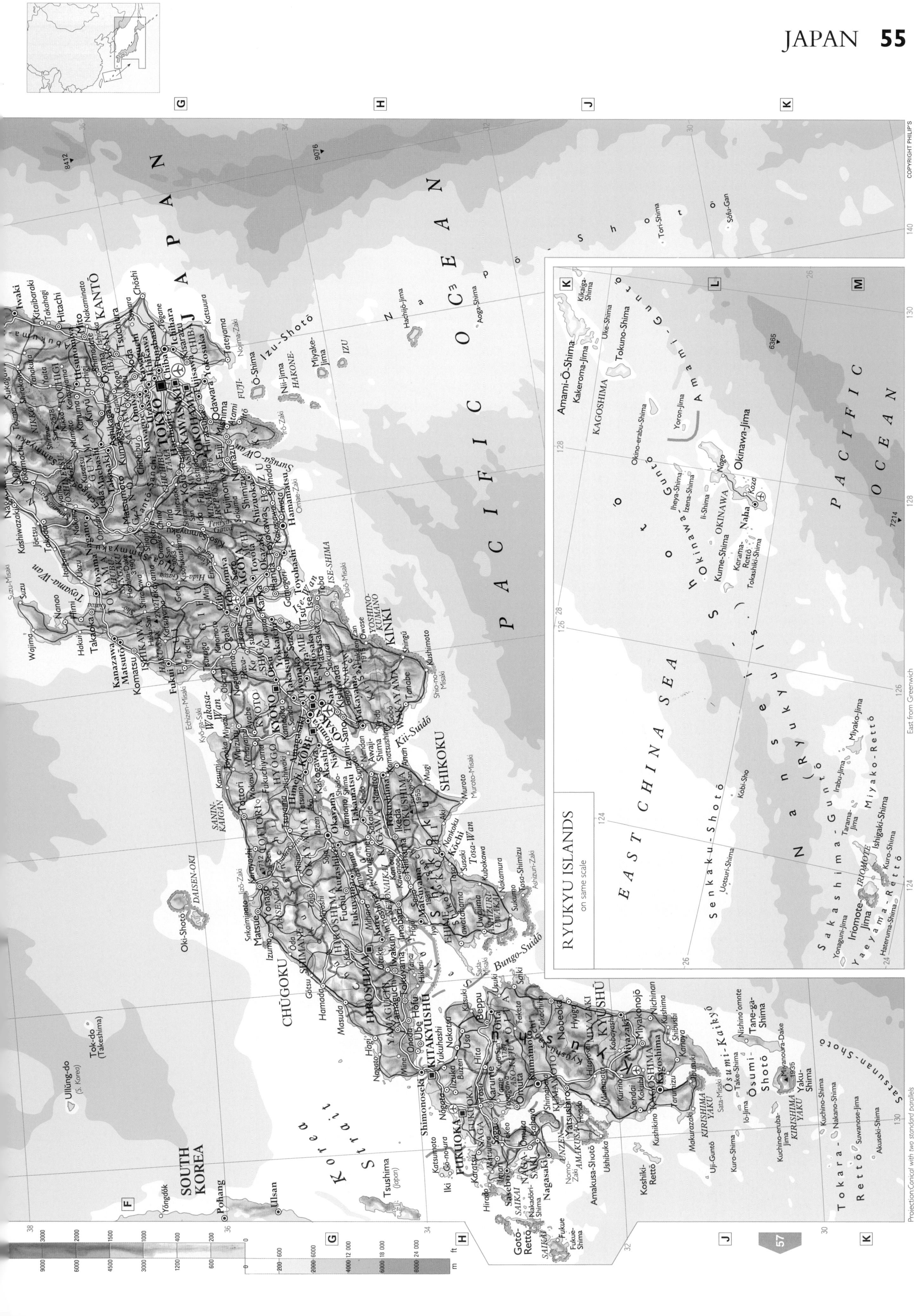

RYUKYU ISLANDS
on same scale

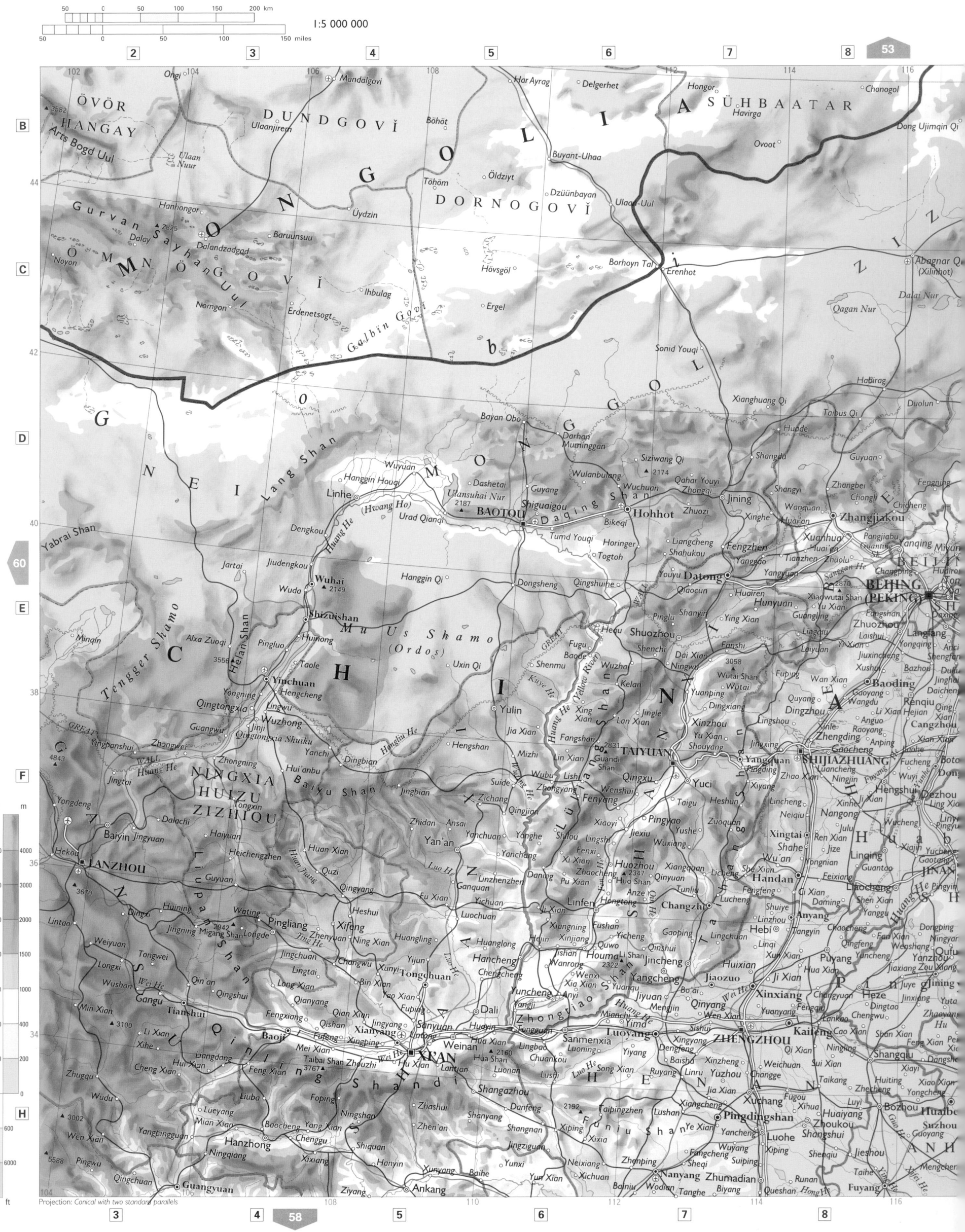

SEA OF JAPAN (EAST SEA)

YELLOW SEA

(Huang Hai)

NORTH KOREA

SOUTH KOREA

JAPAN

Bo Hai

Projection: Conical with two standard parallels

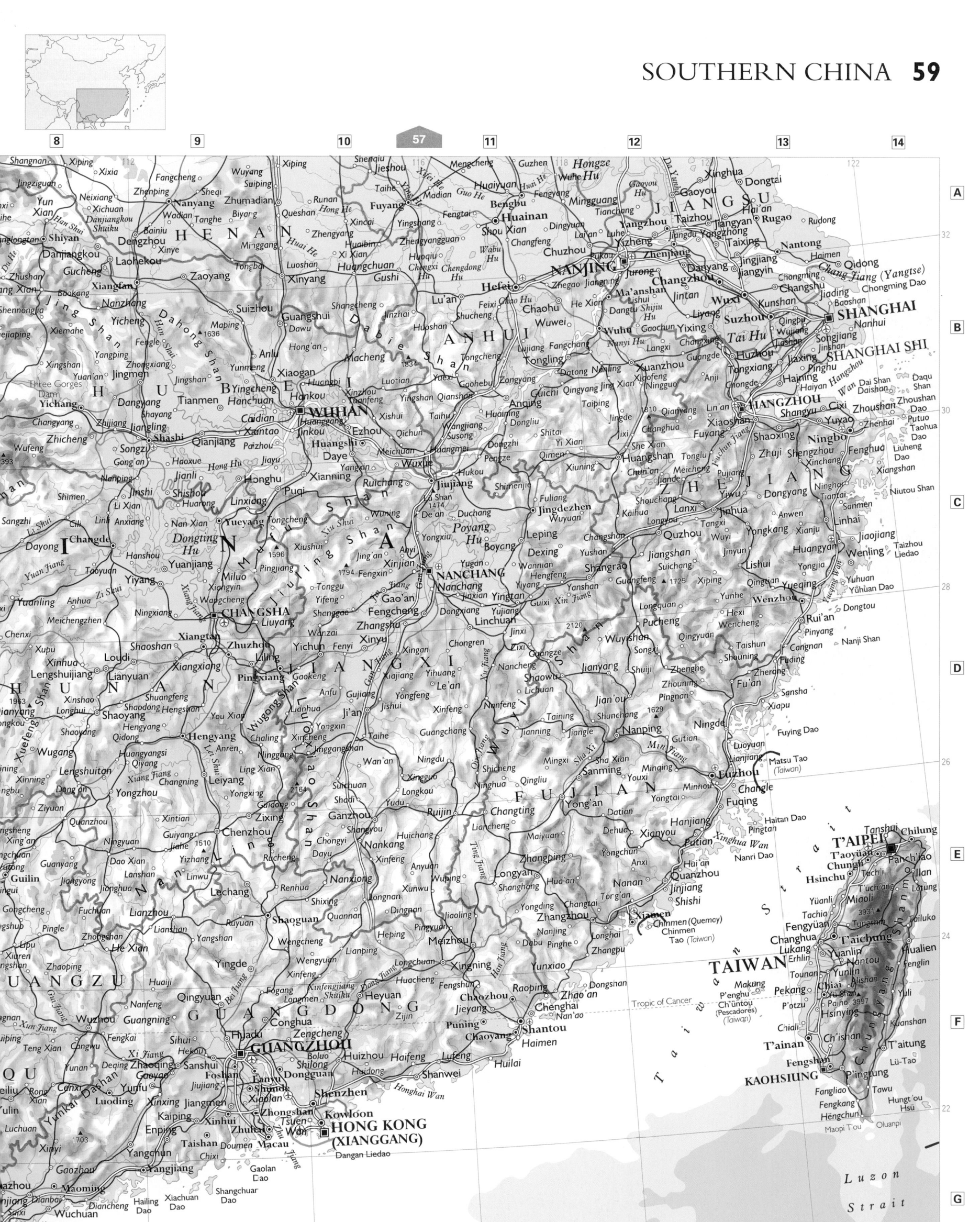

1:16 800 000

100 0 100 200 300 400 500 600 700 800 km
100 0 100 200 300 400 500 miles

COPYRIGHT PHILIP'S

Projection: Bonne

East from Greenwich

Tropic of Cancer

RUSSIA

KAZAKHSTAN

KYRGYZSTAN

MONGOLIA

Ulaanbaatar

NEI MONGGOL (INNER MONGOLIA)

HEILONGJIANG

HARBIN

JILIN

CHANGCHUN

LIAONING

SHENYANG

NORTH KOREA

PYONGYANG

SOUTH KOREA

SEOUL

JAPAN

FUKUOKA

BEIJING (PEKING)

TIANJIN

HEBEI

SHANXI

TAIYUAN

SHANDONG

QINGDAO

JINAN

SHIJIAZHUANG

HENAN

ZHENGZHOU

JIANGSU

NANJING

SHANGHAI

ANHUI

HEFEI

HUBEI

WUHAN

ZHEJIANG

HANGZHOU

NINGBO

JIANGXI

NANCHANG

HUNAN

CHANGSHA

FUJIAN

FUZHOU

TAIWAN (FORMOSA)

T'AIPEI

KAOHSIUNG

GUANGDONG

GUANGZHOU (CANTON)

HONG KONG

Macau

Hainan Dao

HAINAN

HAIKOU

GUANGXI ZIZHIQU

NANNING

GUIZHOU

GUIYANG

YUNNAN

KUNMING

SICHUAN

CHENGDU

CHONGQING

SHAANXI

XI'AN

GANSU

LANZHOU

NINGXIA HUIZU ZIZHIQU

QINGHAI

XINING

XIZANG ZIZHIQU (TIBET)

Lhasa

XINJIANG UYGUR ZIZHIQU (SINKIANG)

ÜRÜMQI

Tarim Pendi

Taklamakan Shamo

Junggar Pendi

Qaidam Pendi

JAMMU & KASHMIR

NEPAL

KATMANDU

BHUTAN

BANGLADESH

DHAKA

INDIA

KOLKATA (CALCUTTA)

BURMA (MYANMAR)

VIETNAM

HANOI

HAIPHONG

THAILAND (SIAM)

EAST CHINA SEA

YELLOW SEA

SOUTH CHINA SEA

BAY OF BENGAL

PHILIPPINES

RYUKYU-RETTO

Bo Hai

Huang He

Chang Jiang

Mt. Everest 8848

K2 8611

GREAT WALL

GOBI DESERT

Altun Shan

Kunlun Shan

Himalaya

Tian Shan

Bayan Har Shan

Qilian Shan

Da Hinggan Ling (GREATER KHINGAN)

Daxue Shan

Khabarovsk

Vladivostok

Irkutsk

Oz. Baykal

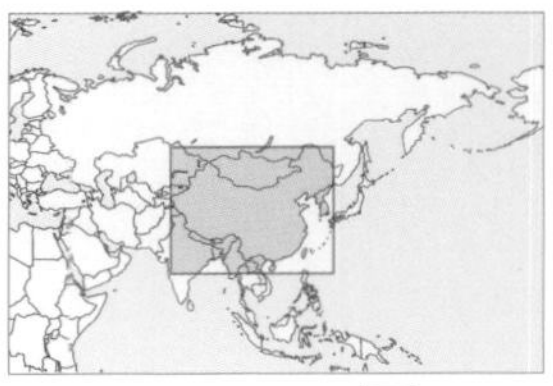

1:6 300 000

50 0   100   150   200   250   300 km
50   0   50   100   150   200 miles

PACIFIC

OCEAN

Dongsha Dao
(China)

Itbayat I.
Batan Is.
Batan I.

Balintang Channel

Calayan I.   Babuyan I.
Dalupiri I.   Babuyan
  Islands   Camiguin I.
Mayraira Pt.   Fuga I.
        Babuyan Channel
Bacarra   Bangui   Claveria   Santa Ana
San Nicolas Batac   Aparri   Gonzaga
Cabugao   ▲2360   Kabugao   Gattaran
Vigan   Bangued   Tuao   Tuguegarao
Santa   ▲ Mt. Cresta
Maria   Lubuagan   ▲1685
Condon   Bontoc   Ilagan
Tcgudin   San Mateo   Palanan Pt.
Balaoan   Santiago   Palanan
San Fernando Mt. Pulog   Cordon
Lingayen   ▲2928   Luzon
Bolinao   HUNDRED   Bayombong
ISLANDS   Baguio   Mt. Anacuao
Alaminos   Rosario   ▲1852
Lingayen   Dagupan   C. San Ildefonso
  Gulf
San Carlos   PHILIPPINE
Bayambang San Manuel
Camiling   San Jose   Baler Bay   SEA
Santa Cruz   Noncada   Baler
Masinloc   Victoria   AURORA MEMORIAL
Iba   ▲2037   Cabanatuan   Dingalan
Concepcion   La   Gapan
▲1780   Paz   Angeles   PHILIPPINES
Mt. Pinatubo   San Fernando   Polillo Is.
San Antonio   Malabon   Fatnanongan I.
Olongapo   Orani   Caloocan   Jomalig I.
Bataan   Manila   Quezon City
Mariveles   Bay   MANILA   Lamon Bay
Cavite   Pasay   Santa Cruz   Paracale
Dasmariñas   Lucban   Alabat I.   Pandan
Nasugbu   San   Atimonan   Viga   Catanduanes
Tagaytay   Pablo   QUEZON   Daet   San Andres
Balayan   Lemery   Lipa   Calauag   BICOL   Calabanga
Batangas   Lucena   Lopez   Naga   ▲1976   Virac
Lubang   Lobo   Catanauan   Mt. Isarog   Rapu Rapu I.
Is.   Verde I. Pass   Tayabas Bay   ▲2421   Tebaco
C. Calavite   Boac   Marin-   Nabua   Mayon Vol.
Calapan   Victoria   duque   Ligao   Legazpi
Mamburao   LAKE   Pinamalayan   Burias I.   Sorsogon
Mindoro   NAUJAN   SIBUYAN   Donsol   Gubat
Sablayan   Mt. Baco   Magallanes   San Bernardino Str.
  ▲2487   Romblon   Bulan   Irosin   Allen
Bongabong   Tablas I.   Sibuyan I.   Ticao I.   Laoang
APO REEF   Roxas   Odiongan   SEA   Catarman   Mondragon
Busuanga I.   San Jose   Masbate   Gamay
Culion I.   Ilin I.   Mandaon   Masbate   Calbayog   Arteche
Calamian   Semirara Is.   Mikagros   Oras
Group   Placer   Catbalogan   Taft   Samar
Linapacan Str.   Pandan   Kalibo   Bilinan I.   Pardnos   Borongan
Linapacan I.   Dao   Roxas   VISAYAN   Calbiran   Santa
Cuyo West Pass   Cuyo Is.   Pilar   Bantayan   SEA   Rita   Llorente
Taytay   Cuyo   Tibiao   ▲2117   Sara   Carigara   Basey   General MacArthur
Cuyo East Pass   Bugasong   Panay   Ajuy   Passi   Palompon   Leyte   Guiuan
San Jose   Pototan   Cadiz   Tacloban   Homonhon I.
Dumaran I.   Iloilo   Silay   Sagay   Tuburan   Dulag   Leyte Gulf
Palawan   Guimaras   Bacolod   Victorias   Camotes Is.   Abuyog
ST PAUL   Jordan   San Carlos   Camotes   Baybay
▲1593   Hinigaran   La   Danao   CENTRAL CEBU   Sogod   Dinagat I.
Irahuan   Honda Bay   Binalbagan   Carlota   ▲2450   Mandaue   Sea Bato   San Juan
Puerto Princesa   Hinamaylan   Cebu   Maasin   Surigao Str.
Cayagan Is.   Kabankalan   Guihulngan   Carcar   Panaon I.   Siargao I.
Sipalay   Argao   Bohol I.   Maasin   Dinagat
Mt. Mantalingajan   Bais   Tanjay   Oslob   RAJAH   Siquijor I.   Placer   Bucas Grande I.
▲2085   Hinoba-an   Dumaguete   SIKATUNA   Tagbilaran   Surigao   Carrasca I.
Negros   Siaton   Zamboanguita   BOHOL   Cabadbaran   Lanuza
C. Buliluyan   Bayawan   Camiguin I.   ▲2012   Tandag
Bugsuk I.   SULU   Talisayan   Mainit   Tcgo   Marihatag
Balabac I.   TUBBATAHA   SEA   Nasipit   Butuan   Lianga
Balabangan   REEFS   Dipolog   Balingasag   Esperanza   Bayugar   Hinatuan
Langkon   SEA   Dapitan   Iligan   Dpol   Talacogan   Bislig
Kudat   Manukan   Oroquieta   Bay   Cagayan de Oro
Tenghilan   Senaja   Sindangan   MT. OZAMIZ   Iligan   ▲2938   Malaybalay
G. Kinabulu   Jembongan   Labason   MALINDANG   Marawi City   Bunawan
▲4101   Suba Talan   Loay   Tubod   ▲2815   Panabo   Cateel
Kota   Telok   Turtle Is.   Siocon   Kabasalan   Pagadian   L. Lanao   Baganga
Belud   Labuk   Caga-yan Sulu I.   Margosatubig   Malabang   Midsayap   Tagum
Papar   Sandakan   Pikit   Panabo   Pantukan
Keningau   Margosatubig   Illana   Cotabato   Manay
MALAYSIA   Panguturan   Bay   Datu Piang   Mt. Apo   Mati
Banjaran   SABAH   Group   Parang   Talayan   ▲2954   Davao
Crocker   Pilas   Basilan   Lebak   Digos   Davao Gulf
Borneo   Group   Isabela   Kalamansig   San Isidro
Melalap   Pata I.   Basilan I.   Palimbang   Koronadal   Malita
Kuamat   Samales   ▲2083   General
Silam   Group   Santos
Teluk Darvel   Jolo   Kiamba
Tg. Libian   Jolo Group   Sarangani Bay   C. San Agustin
Sibutu   Talipao   Tinaca Pt.
Group   Pata I.
Semporna   Siasi I.   CELEBES
Tawi-tawi   Tapul   Sarangani Is.
  Group   SEA
Sulu Archipelago

SOUTH

CHINA

SEA

Mindanao

Trench

▼ 10 497

Luzon

Mindoro

Panay

Leyte

Samar

Negros

Bohol

Cebu

Palawan

Mindanao

SULU

SEA

Moro Gulf

Singuay
Bay

Pangalan
Bay

INDONESIA   Kep. Talaud

Projection: Lambert's Conformal Conic

East from Greenwich

COPYRIGHT PHILIP'S

m ft

ft   m
9000   3000
6000   2000
4500   1500
3000   1000
1200   400
600   200
0
200   600
4000   12 000
8000   24 000

National Parks

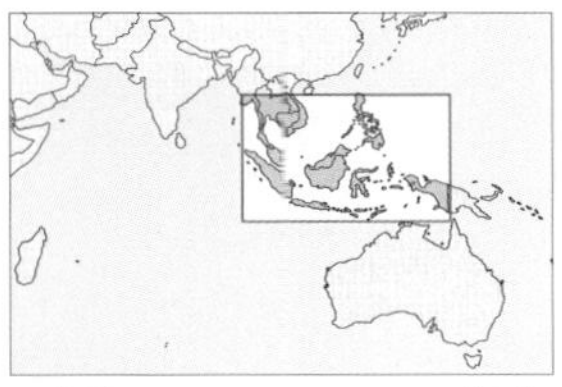

JAVA AND MADURA
1:6 300 000

50 0 50 100 150 200 250 300 km
50 0 50 100 150 200 miles

BALI
1:1 700 000

10 0 10 20 30 km
10 0 10 20 miles

PHILIPPINE SEA

Luzon

MANILA
Quezon City

JAKARTA
BANTEN
BANDUNG
TENGAH
SEMARANG
SURABAYA
Madura
SURAKARTA
YOGYAKARTA
Malang
Bali

SULU SEA

Mindanao
Zamboanga
Davao
General Santos

CELEBES SEA

BANDA SEA

Jawa
Bali
Denpasar
Kuta
Lombok
Mataram
Nusa Penida

INDIAN OCEAN

PACIFIC OCEAN

Manado
GORONTALO
UTARA
Halmahera
UTARA
Ternate
Tidore

Sulawesi
(Celebes)
TENGAH
TENGGARA
SELATAN

Buru
Seram (Ceram)
Ambon
MALUKU

Equator

PAPUA NEW GUINEA
Pegunungan Maoke
Jayapura

ARAFURA SEA

FLORES SEA

Flores
Sumba
Sawu Sea
NUSA TENGGARA TIMUR
EAST TIMOR
Dili
Kupang

SAVU SEA

94

1:5 000 000

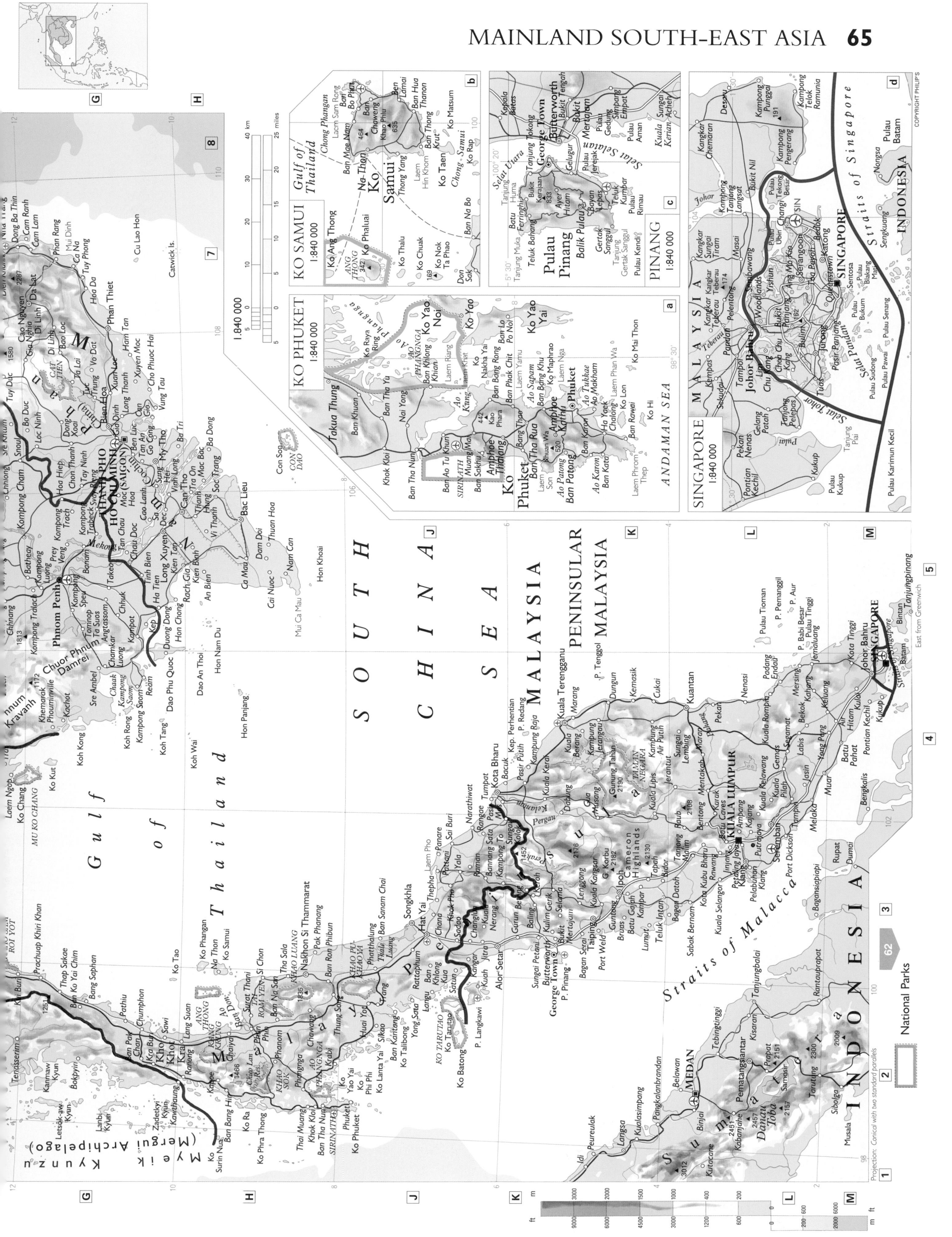

COPYRIGHT PHILIP'S

KO SAMUI
1:840 000

Gulf of Thailand

Ko
Samui

KO PHUKET
1:840 000

ANDAMAN SEA

Ko
Phuket

**Pulau
Pinang**

PINANG
1:840 000

George Town

Butterworth

SINGAPORE
1:840 000

MALAYSIA

Johor Baharu

SINGAPORE

Straits of Singapore

INDONESIA

SOUTH

CHINA

SEA

M U O N G

A N N A M

HO CHI MINH
(SAIGON)

Phnom Penh

Mekong

Gulf

of

Thailand

MU KO CHANG

ROI YOT

M y e i k

(Mergui Archipelago)

K y u n z u

M A L A Y S I A

PENINSULAR
MALAYSIA

KUALA LUMPUR

George Town

Butterworth

P. Pinang

Straits of Malacca

I N D O N E S I A

MEDAN

SINGAPORE

Johor Baharu

East from Greenwich

Projection: Conical with two standard parallels

National Parks

62

ft   m

1:8 400 000

50   0   100   200   300   400 km
50   0   50   100   150   200   250 miles

Projection: Conical with two standard parallels

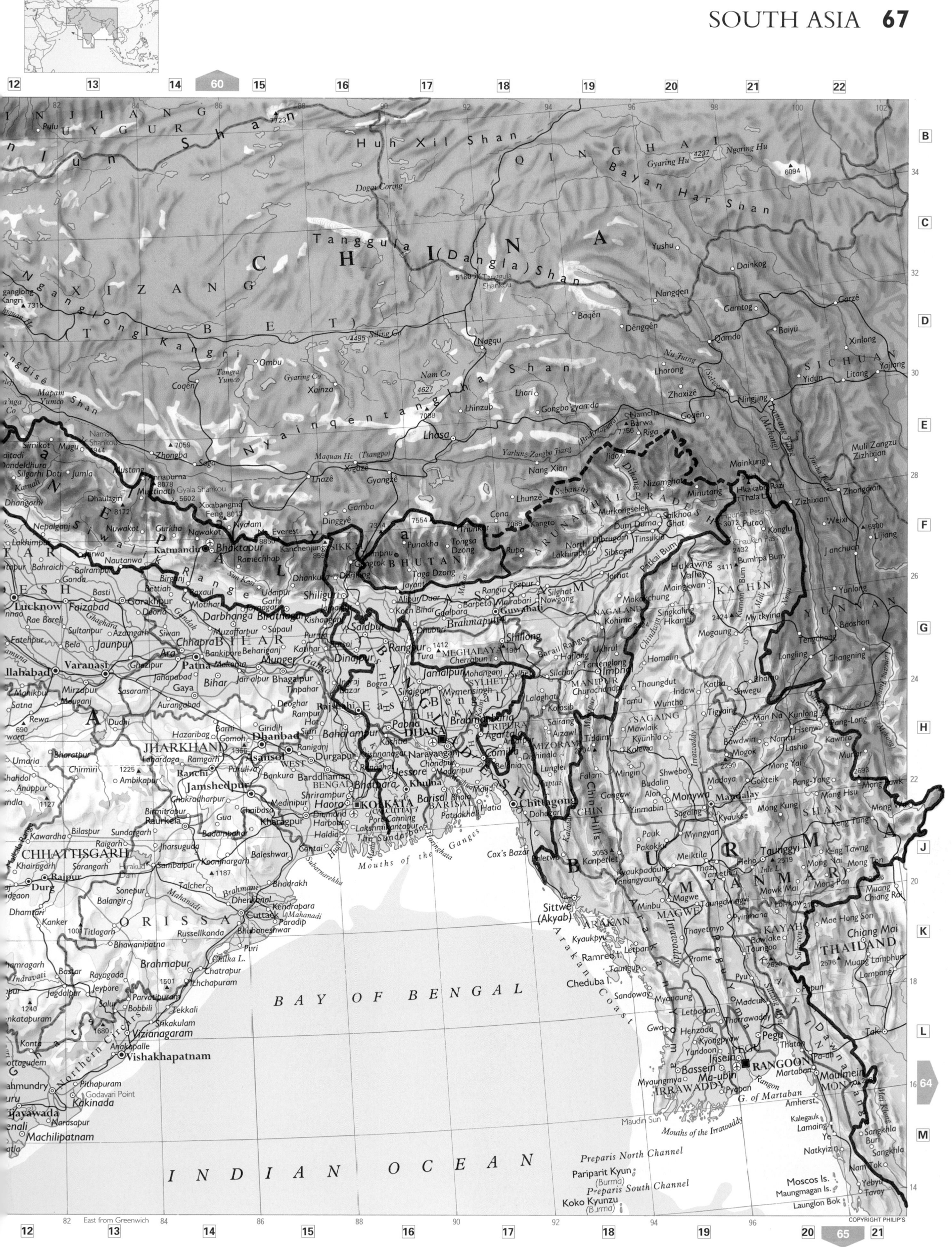

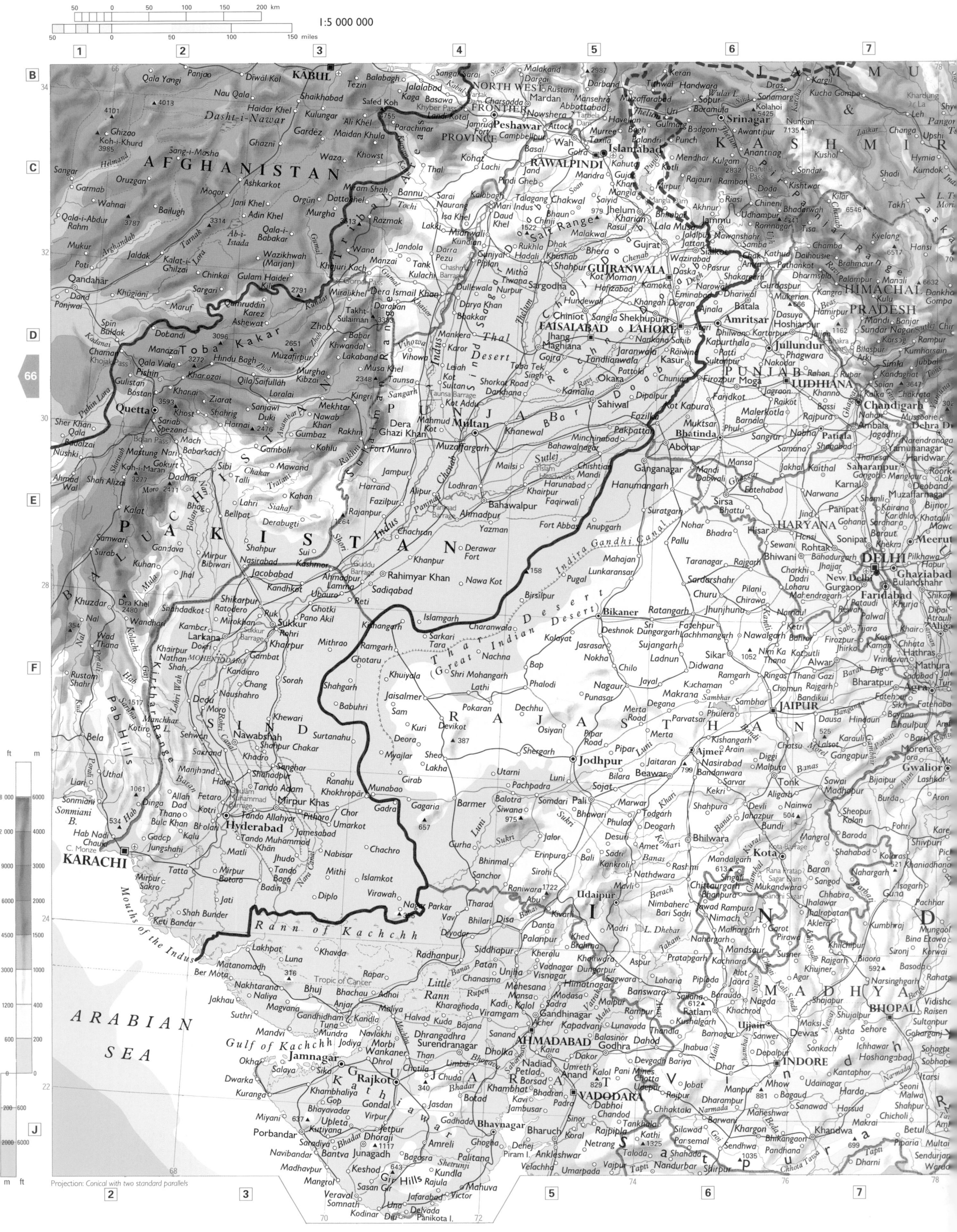

JAMMU AND KASHMIR
on same scale
AFGHANISTAN
CHINA
NORTH WEST FRONTIER
Northern Areas
Azad Kashmir
JAMMU & KASHMIR
PUNJAB
ISLAMABAD
RAWALPINDI
Srinagar
HIMACHAL PRADESH
Karakoram Range
Ladakh Range
Zaskar Mountains
Kunlun Shan
Aksai Chin
Soda Plains
Deosai Mts.
Siachen Glacier
XIZANG ZIZHIQU (TIBET)
Gangdisê Shan
Nganglong Kangri
Yarlung Zangbo Jiang (Brahmaputra)
Mt. Everest (Chomolungma or Sagarmatha)
NEPAL
Katmandu
Himalaya
Mahabharat Lekh
Siwalik Range
UTTARANCHAL
UTTAR PRADESH
LUCKNOW
KANPUR
Allahabad
VARANASI
BIHAR
PATNA
SIKKIM
Darjeeling (Darjeeling)
Gangtok
BHUTAN
Thimphu
ASSAM
BANGLADESH
DHAKA
RAJSHAHI
KHULNA
JHARKHAND
Ranchi
Jamshedpur
Dhanbad
WEST BENGAL
KOLKATA
Haora
MADHYA PRADESH
Jabalpur
CHHATTISGARH
Kaimur Hills
Maikala Range
Rajmahal Hills
Garo Hills
Mouths of the Ganges
The Sandheads
East from Greenwich
COPYRIGHT PHILIP'S

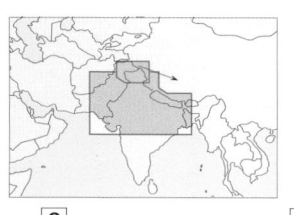

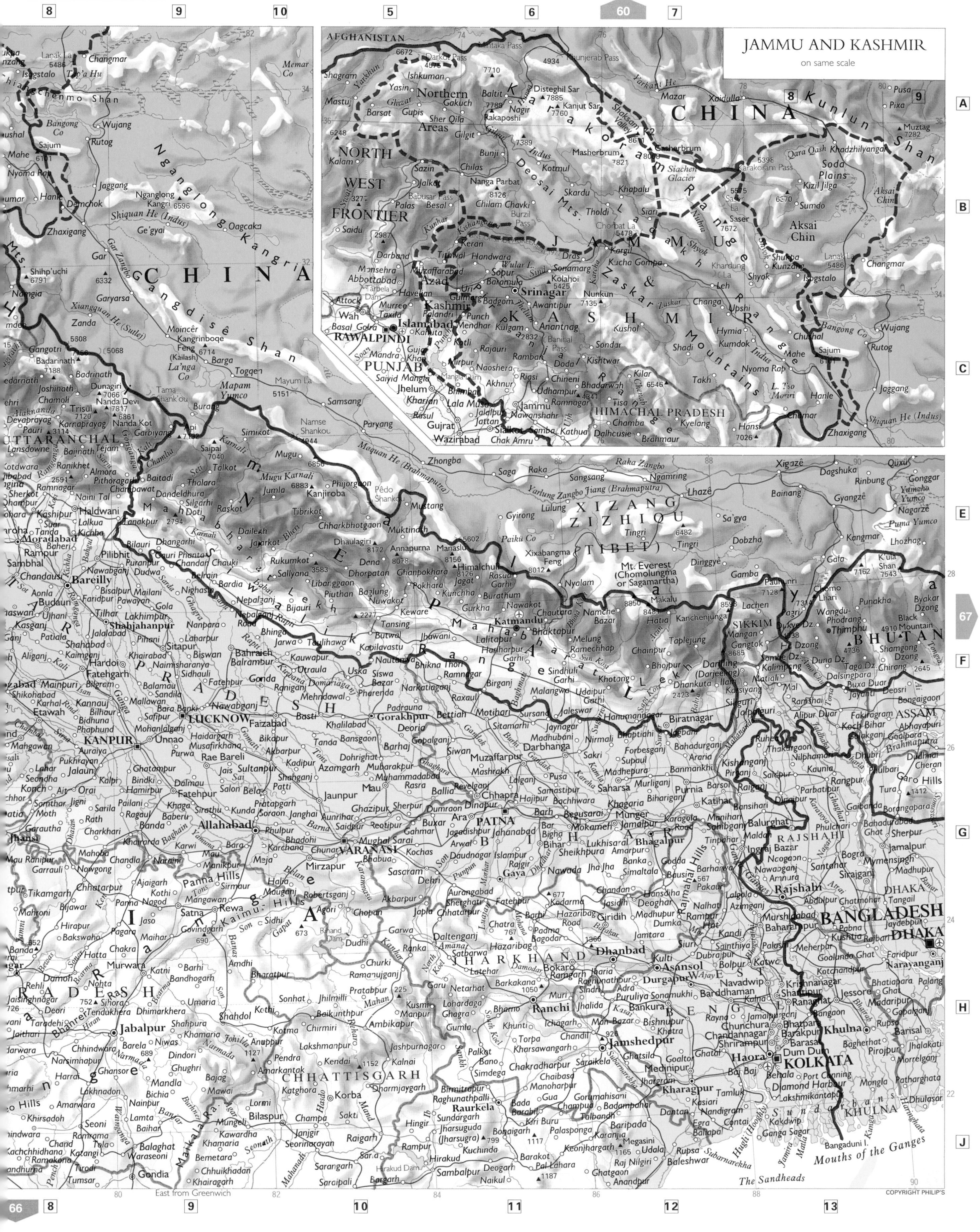

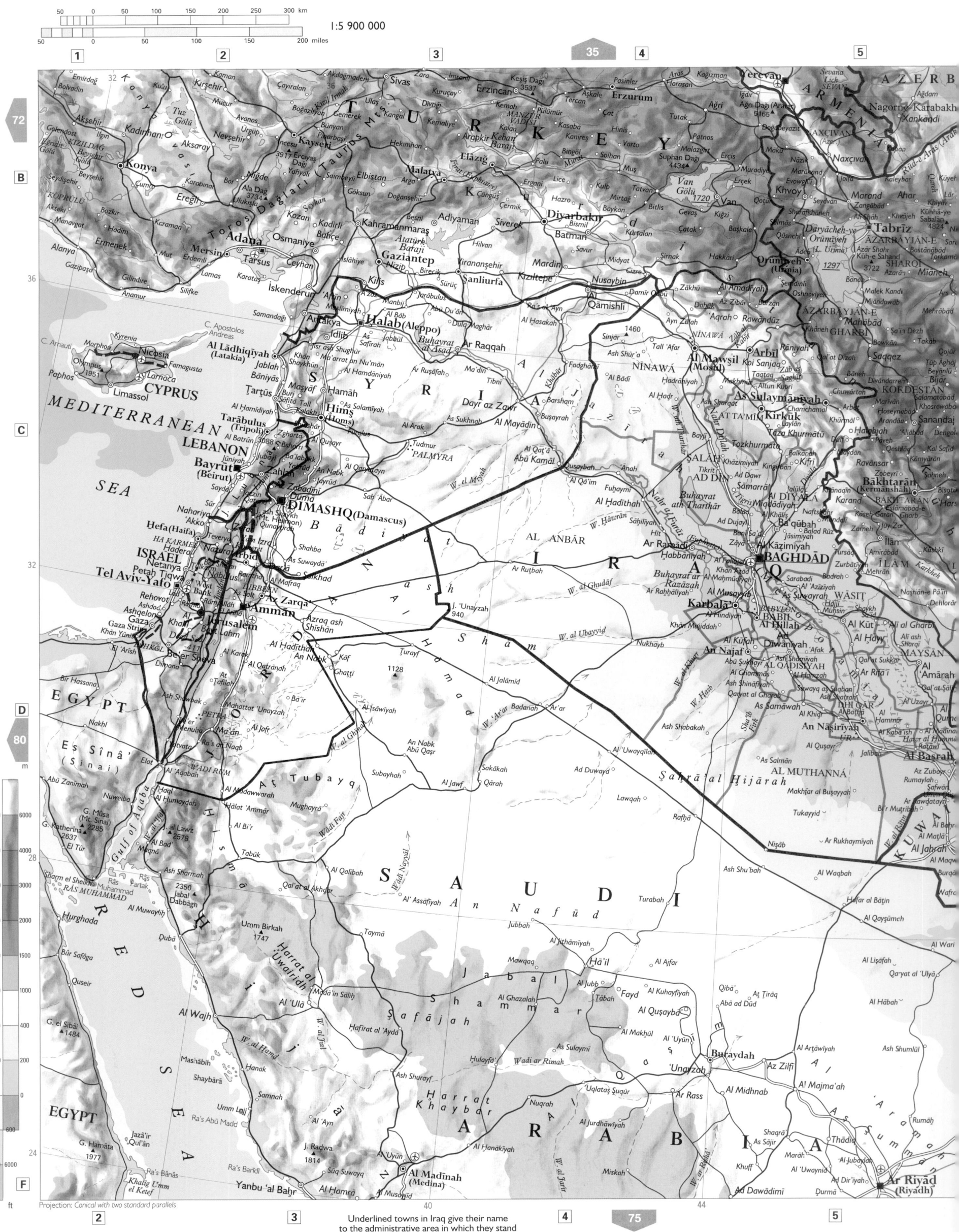

1:5 900 000

Underlined towns in Iraq give their name
to the administrative area in which they stand

6
7
8
9
10
B
C
D
E
F
66
TURKMENISTAN
Kara Kum
Kopet Dagh
CASPIAN SEA
BAKI (Baku)
Türkmenbashi
Ashgabat
Mary
Chärjew
Amudarya
Mashhad
Neyshābūr
Sabzevār
Gorgān
Rasht
Qazvīn
Karaj
TEHRĀN
Tajrish
Damāvand
5604
Semnān
Reshteh-ye Kūhhā-ye Alborz
Qom
Kāshān
Dasht-e Kavīr
Dasht-e Lūt
IRAN
Eşfahān
Yazd
Kermān
Shīrāz
Hamadān
Arāk
Khorramābād
Ahvāz
Ābādān
Khorramshahr
Dezfūl
Būshehr
Bandar-e Abbās
Zāhedān
Bīrjand
Herāt
AFGHANISTAN
PAKISTAN
Farāh
Zābol
Hāmūn-e Jaz Mūrīān
SĪSTĀN VA BALŪCHESTĀN
KHORĀSĀN
KERMĀN
FĀRS
HORMOZGĀN
PERSIAN GULF
Gulf of Oman
Str. of Hormuz
Al Kuwayt (Kuwait)
Ad Dammām
Al Manāmah
BAHRAIN
Ad Dawḩah (Doha)
QATAR
Dubayy (Dubai)
Abū Z̧aby (Abu Dhabi)
Ash Shāriqah (Sharjah)
Al Fujayrah
UNITED ARAB EMIRATES
OMAN
Tropic of Cancer
East from Greenwich
COPYRIGHT PHILIP'S

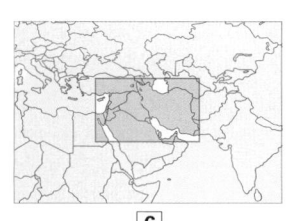

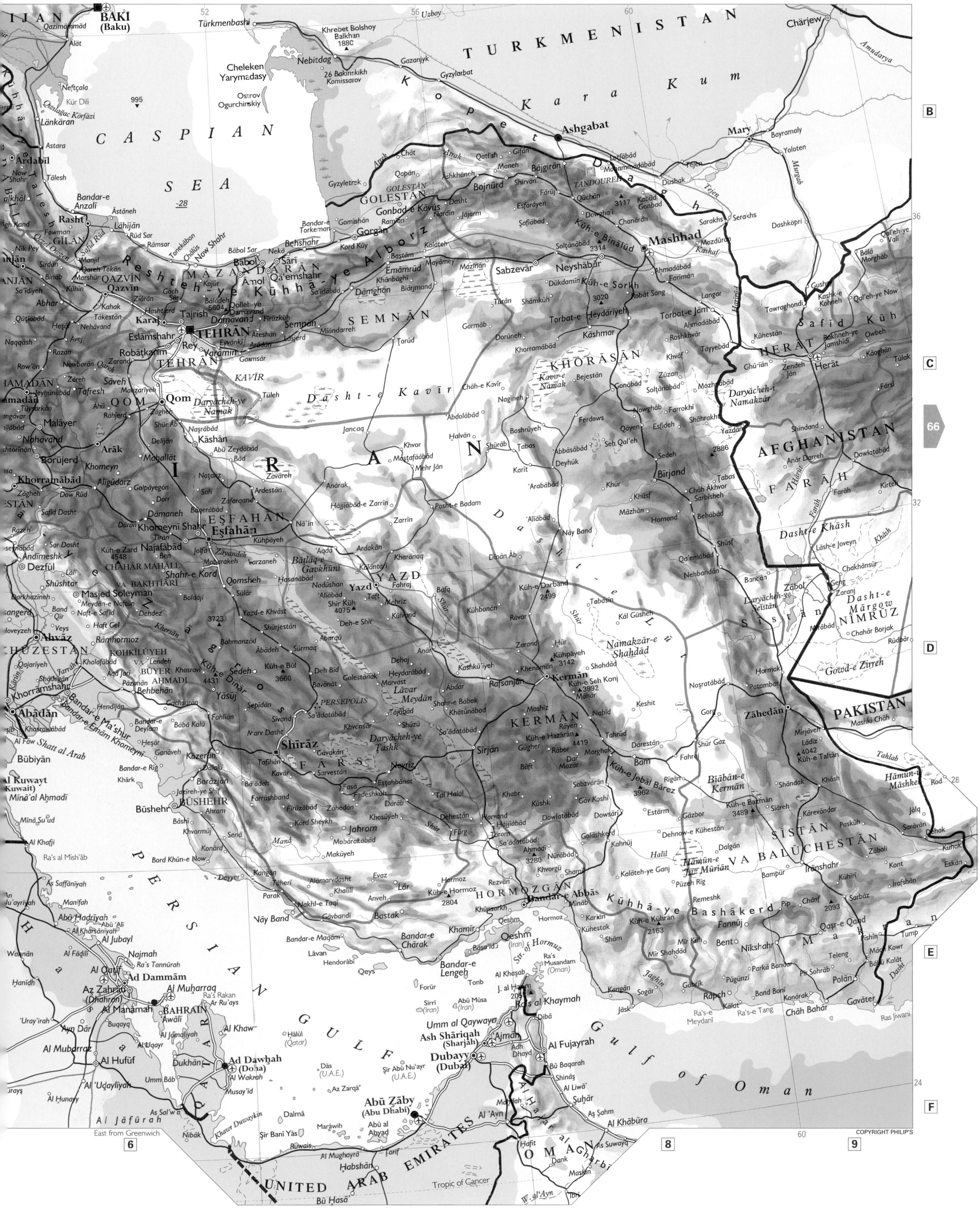

1: 4 200 000

50 0 25 50 75 100 125 150 175 km
50 0 25 50 75 100 125 miles

| 1 | 2 | 3 | 4 | 33 | 5 | 6 | 7 |

A

BULGARIA

B L A C K   S E A

Stara Zagora
Yambol
Aytos
Burgas
Nos Emine
Michurin
1830
2206

45

Elkhovo
Arda
Kırklareli
1018
Edirne
İğneada Burnu
Pınarhisar
Demirköy
Kerempe Burnu
İnce Burun
Sinop
Hayrabolu
Uzunköprü
Lüleburgaz
Babaeski
Vize
Çerkezköy
Zonguldak
Kilimli
İnebolu
Abana
Çatalzeytin
Gerze
Bafra Burnu
Civa Burnu

B

Évros
Murath
Çorlu
İstanbul Boğazı
(Bosporus)
Kandıra
Karasu
Akçakoca
Devrek
Ereğli
Kozlu
Karabük
Safranbolu
Daday
Araç
Kastamonu
Küre
Devrekâni
Ayancık
Samsun
Terme
Ünye
Fatsa
Ord

İpsala
Keşan
Malkara
Tekirdağ
Büyükçekmece
İSTANBUL
Kartal
Kocaeli (İzmit)
Sakarya (Adapazarı)
Hendek
Düzce
Bolu
Gerede
Çerkeş
İlgaz Dağları
2565
Tosya
Osmancık
İskilip
Çankırı
1784
Çorum
Mecitözü
Amasya
Tekke
Erbaa
Niksar
Kuze

Saros Körfezi
Şarköy
Marmara Denizi (Sea of Marmara)
Gebze
Darıca
Gölcük
Orhangazi
Gemlik
İznik Gölü
Geyve
Göynük
Mudurnu
Seben
2378
Kızılcahamam
Çubuk
Kızılırmak
Delice
Sungurlu
Ortaköy
Alaca
1907
Zile
Reşadiye
Turhal
Yeşilırmak
Çırçır

1600
Eceabat
Çanakkale (Dardanelles)
Biga
Gönen
Bandırma
Karacabey
Bursa
Uludağ 2543
İnegöl
Bilecik
Söğüt
Bozüyük
Eskişehir
Alpu
Mihalıççık
Ayaş
Sincan
ANKARA
Elmadağ
Gölbaşı
Kırıkkale
Keskin
Yozgat
Sorgun
Akdağmadeni
Yıldızeli
Hafik
SIVAS
2802

C

Gökçeada
Boz-caada
Ezine
Ayvacık
Bayramiç 1766
Edremit
Balya
Balıkesir
Susurluk
Mustafakemalpaşa
Orhaneli
Domaniç
Tavşanlı
Kütahya
Emet
Gediz
Simav
Seyitgazi
Kırka
Çifteler
Sakarya
Haymana
Bâlâ
Kaman
Kırşehir
Boğazlıyan
Çayıralan
Gemerek
2235
Ak Dağları
Sarıkışla
Şarkışla
Kangal
Tecer Dağ

Babo Burnu
Edremit Körfezi
Bergama
Soma
Demirci
Alaçam Dağları
2089
Uşak
Banaz
Afyon (Afyonkarahisar)
2610
Emirdağ
Yunak
Sülüklü
Kulu
Mucur
Hacıbektaş
Gülşehir
Nevşehir
GÖREME
3370
Tomarza
Gürün
Darende
Hekimhan

38

Khíos
Foça
Karaburun
Manisa
Menemen
Turgutlu
İZMİR (Smyrna)
Boz Dağları
Salihli
Alaşehir
Eşme
Ulubey
Çivril
Sandıklı
Şuhut
Akşehir Gölü
Akşehir
Sarayönü
Kadınhanı
Obruk
Ereğli
KAYSERİ
Talas
Pınarbaşı
Develi
Yeşilhisar
Bünyan
Tohma

T U R K E Y

D

Khíos
1297
Çeşme
Urla
Torbalı
Bayındır
Ödemiş
Tire
Nazilli
Aydın
Söke
Büyük Menderes
Karacasu
Denizli
Sarayköy
Çardak
Dinar
Çal
Uluborlu
Eğridir Gölü
Gelendost
Isparta
Beyşehir Gölü
Beyşehir
Konya
Cumra
Karapınar
3734
Niğde
Bor
Aksaray
Derinkuyu
Gölcük
Yahyalı
Bakırdağı
Göksun
Afşin
3075
Elbistan
Doğanşehir

Sámos
Ikaría
Kuşadası
1153
EPHESUS
MILETUS
Milas
Yatağan
Muğla
Göl Gölü
Köyceğiz
Acıgöl
Burdur
Ağlasun
Sütçüler
Bucak
2980
116
Beyşehir
Seydişehir
Suğla Gölü
Bozkır
Karaman
Ayrancı
3430
Karapınar
Ulukışla
Pozantı
3488
Kozan
Kadirli
İmamoğlu
Ceyhan
KAHRAMANMARAŞ
Gölbaşı
Pazarcık
Besni
Araban

47

Kálymnos
Kos
Bodrum
Gökova Körfezi
Datça
Marmaris
Ortaca
Dalaman
Köyceğiz
2598
Fethiye
3024
Aykırıkçı
Elmalı
3070
Korkuteli
Antalya
Kemer
Manavgat
Side
Alanya
Hadim
Toros Dağları
Ermenek
Mut
2464
2339
Gülnar
Anamur
Silifke
2339
İncekum Burnu
Mersin (İçel)
Tarsus
Adana
Karataş
Yumurtalık
İskenderun Körfezi
İskenderun
Gaziantep
Nizip
Kilis
A'zâz
Al Bâb

GREECE
Ródhos (Rhodes)
1215
Kalkan
Kaş
Finike
Yardımcı Burnu
Gazipaşa
Anamur Burnu
Antakya
Harbiye
İdlib
HALAB (Aleppo)
As Sufīrah

E

Kárpathos
1215
Kásos
4210
Megísti

Antalya Körfezi
Pamphylia
Cilicia

Rizokarpaso
C. Apostolos Andreas
Al Lādhiqīyah (Latakia)
Jablah
Ma'arrat an Nu'mān
Khān Shaykhūn

Morphou
Kyrenia
Famagusta
Nicosia
Olympus 1951
Troodos
Larnaca
Polis
Paphos
Episkopi
Limassol
Bāniyās
1385
Hamāh
S Y

34

Tartūs
Maşyāf
Burj Şāfīta
As Salamīyah
Tall
Hims (Homs)
3088
Al Hamīdīyah

CYPRUS

Tarābulus (Tripoli)
Al Batrūn
Zgharta
Shinshar
Furqlus
Al Qataynah

F

M E D I T E R R A N E A N

S E A

2775

LEBANON
Bsharri
Jubayl
Juniyah
An Nabk
BAYRŪT (Beirut)
Zahlah
Yabrūd
Saydā
Dūmā
B
DIMASHQ (Damascus)
Jaramānah
2814
Şūr
Qatanā
Qiryat Shemona
Naharriyya
'Akko
Zefat
Teverya
Qunaytirah
As Suwaydā'
1800
Shahba
Salkhad

G

ISRAEL
Hadera
Netanya
Tel Aviv-Yafo
West Bank
Rehovot
Ashdod
Ashqelon
JERUSALEM
El Arīha
Ramla
Nazerat
Nāblus
As Salt
Az Zarqā
Irbid
Dar'ā
1247
Busrā ash Shām
Al Mafraq
AMMĀN
JORDA

| 80 | 3 | 4 | 5 | 74 | 6 | 7 |

Projection: Conical with two standard parallels

– – – – Division between Greeks and Turks in Cyprus; Turks to the North.

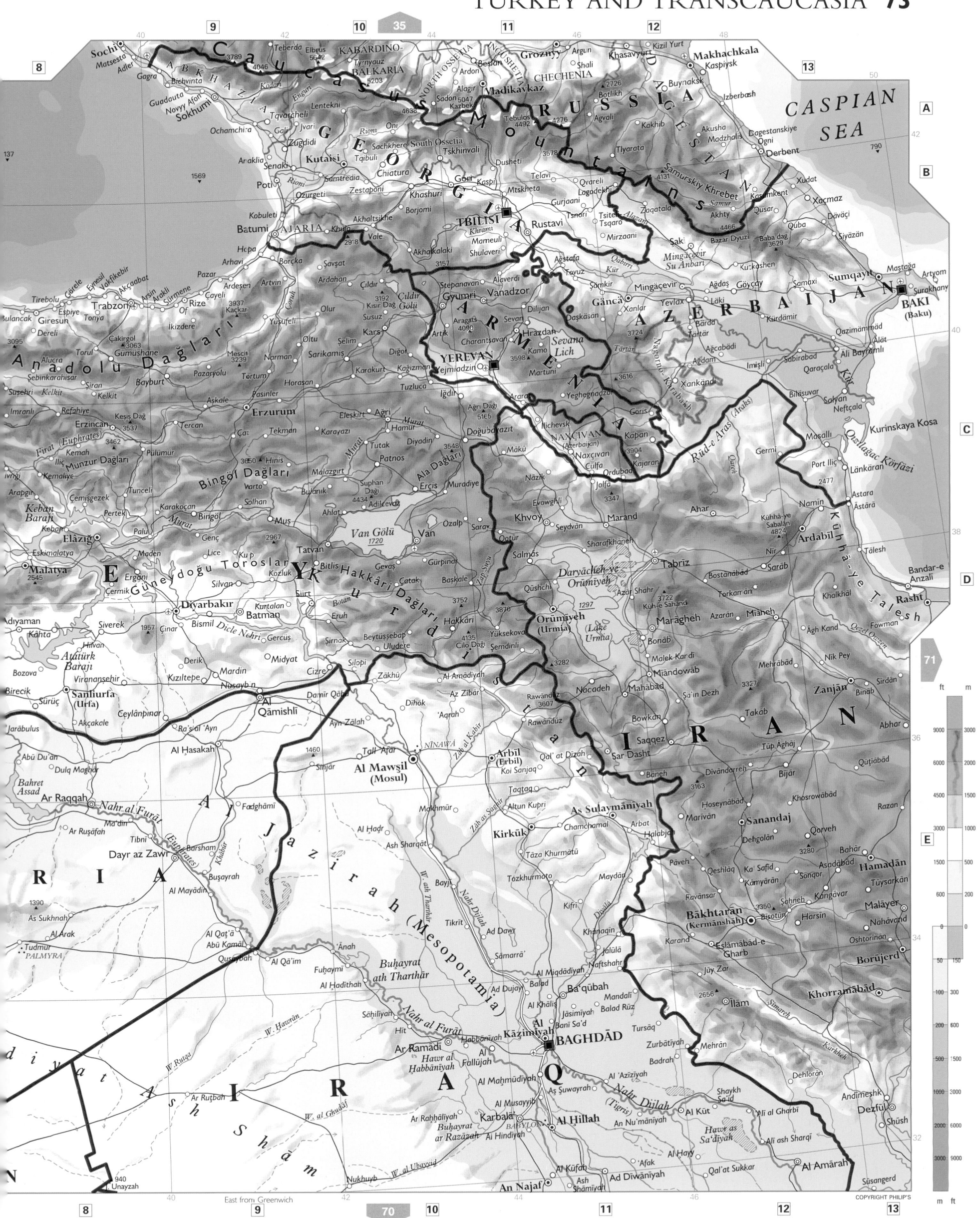

1:2 100 000

10 0 10 20 30 40 50 60 70 80 100 km
10 0 10 20 30 40 50 60 miles

1 | **2** | **3** | **4** | **72** **5** | **6**

CYPRUS
Paphos
Episkopi
Limassol
Akrotiri Bay
Episkopi Bay
C. Gata

Al Ḥamīdīyah
Ḥimṣ (Ḥoms)
Tell Kalakh
Shinshār
Furqlus
Ḥalbā
ASH SHAMĀL
Al Ḥirmil
Al Qusayr
Tarābulus (Tripoli)
Zgharta
Qurnat as Sawdā'
3088
Al Batrūn
Bsharri
Al Labwah
2464
Al Qaryatayn
Jubayl
Qartabā
Ibrāhīm
2616
An Nabk
Bi'r Ghadīr

MEDITERRANEAN

SEA

2628
J. Sannīn
Jūniyah
Bikfayyā
Ba'labakk
Yabrūd
BAYRŪT (Beirut)
Ash Shuwayfāt
'Alayh
Zaḥlah
Sirghāyā
Khān Abū Shāmat
Ad Dāmūr
JABAL LUBNĀN
Ḥawsh
Mussá
Al Qutayfah
Dumayr
LEBANON
1942
J. al Bārūk
Az Zabadānī
DIMASHQ (Damascus)
SYRIA

Saydā (Sidon)
Qatanā
Al Kiswah
Al Ḥājānah
Jazzīn
Jabal ash Shaykh (Mt Hermon)
2814
Marj 'Uyūn
DIMASHQ
An Nabaṭīyah at Taḥtā
Al Khiyām
AL JANŪB
Sūr (Tyre)
Qiryat Shemona
Mas'ada
As Sanamayn
Golan Heights
1197
Al Qunayṭirah
Burāq

Nahariyya
Me'ona
Ar Rafid
Zefat
DAR'Ā
Izra'
Shahbā
'Akko (Acre)
HAGALIL
Qiryat Karmi'el
Yamā
Fiq
Shaykh Miskīn
JABAL AD DURŪZ
Mifraz Hefa
Qiryat Yam
HAZAFON
Teverya (Tibenas)
-210
Sahm al Jawlān
AS SUWAYDĀ
Hefa (Haifa)
Qiryat Ata
Nazerat (Nazareth)
Dar'ā
As Suwaydā
1800
Dāliyat el Karmel
HEFA KARMEL
Afula
Yarmūk
 IRBID
Al Ramthā
Salah
TEL MEGIDDO
Ṭayiba
Buṣrá ash Shām
Salkhad
CAESAREA
Umm el Faḥm
Bet She'an
Malaḥ
Hadera
SHŌMRŌN
Jenin
'AJLŪN
Al Mafraq
ISRAEL
Pardes Hanna-Karkur
Ṭūbās
Ajlūn
Umm ad Dana
Umm al Qittayn
HAMERKAZ
Tulkarm
SAMARIA
1247
Jarash
AL MAFRAQ
Netanya
Nābulus
JARASH
Herzliyya
W. al Fār'a
N. az Zarqā
Benē Beraq
SHILO
As Salṭ
Kefar Sava
AL BALQĀ
Az Zarqā
Petah Tiqwa
Wādī as Sīr
AMMĀN
Tel Aviv-Yafo
Ramat Gan
-219
Karama
Bat Yam
WEST BANK
Azraq ash Shīshān
Rishon le Ziyyon
Rām Allāh
Na'ūr
AMM
Yavne
Rehovot
El Arīḥā (Jericho)
At Tunayb
'AMMĀN
Lod
Ramla
AZ ZARQĀ
Ashdod
Bet Shemesh
Jerusalem (Yerushalayim) (Al Quds)
Ma'ān
Qiryat Mal'akhi
Qiryat Gat
Bayt Laḥm (Bethlehem)
MA'DĀBĀ
Ashqelon
Qiryat
Al Khalīl (Hebron)
Mā'daba
Gaza
N. Shiqma
Dhībān
Sederot
Az Zāhirīyah
W. al Ḥaydān
Gaza Strip
-411
Khān Yūnis
ESHKOL
Arad
Rafaḥ
Be'er Sheva (Beersheba)
Bor Mashash
W. al Ḥasā
Sedom
1305
Al Karak
El 'Arīsh
Dimona
AL KARAK
Al Mazar
Bûr Sa'îd (Port Said)
Bûr Fu'ad
Ras Burun
Sabkhet el Bardawîl
El Daheir
HADAROM
Bîr el 'Abd
Bîr el Garârât
Bîr Lahfân
Ramâni
Qezi'ot
Sedé Boqér
At Tafila
Khalig el Tina
Bîr Qatia
Bîr Kaseiba
-335
AT TAFILAH
El Qantara
Bîr el Duweidar
JORDAN
El Suweis (Suez)
SHAMÂL SÎNÎ
Muweilih
W. al Ḥasā
Wâhid
Bîr Madkûr
Bîr el Jafir
Birein
Ismâ'îliya
El Quseima
-121
An Naqb
1072
Talâta
892
Mizpe Ramon
Nijil
ash Shawmari
ISMÂ'ILIYA
Bîr el Mâlhi
Hanegev
Mahattat 'Unayzah
Khamsa
Bîr Hasana
G.Yi 'Allaq
Rujm Talat al Jamāsh
El Buheirat el Murrat el Kubra (Bitter Lakes)
1094
N. Paran
1736
PETRA
Gineifa
Bîr el Thamâda
W. el Bruk
N. Hiyyon
El 'Agrûd
Wadi Mūsa
Ma'ān
EGYPT
Mamar Mitlâ
Bîr Gebeil Hisn
W. el Mahasham
El Qurâya
Mā'ÁN
Bîr al Mārī
EL SUWEIS
SÎNÂ (Sinai)
N. Paran
948
W. al Jirâfi
El 'Agrûd
Bi'r al Māri
G. el Kabrît
Ra's an Naqb
El Wabeira
En 'Evrona
Bir al Butayyihât
Bi'r al Qattār
1435
Gebel el Tih
El Thamad
'Ên Yahav
Yatvata
Mahattat ash Shidiyah
Ghubbet el Bûs
El Kuntilla
SAUDI
JANÛB SÎNÎ
Nakhl
Bîr Abu Muhammad
1592
WADI RUM
Batn al Ghûl
Abu Sandûg
1272
Bîr el Biarât
1754
Rum
ARABIA
Bîr el Thamâda
Elat
At Tubayq
W. Abu Ga'da
Al 'Aqabah
Bîr Wuseit
Bîr el Heim
1165
Gulf of Aqaba
W. an Niraba
Haql
Al Mudawwarah

Projection: Polyconic
East from Greenwich
COPYRIGHT PHILIP'S

1 | **2** **80** | **3** | **4** | **5** | **6**

≡≡≡ 1974 Cease Fire Lines | ☐ National Parks

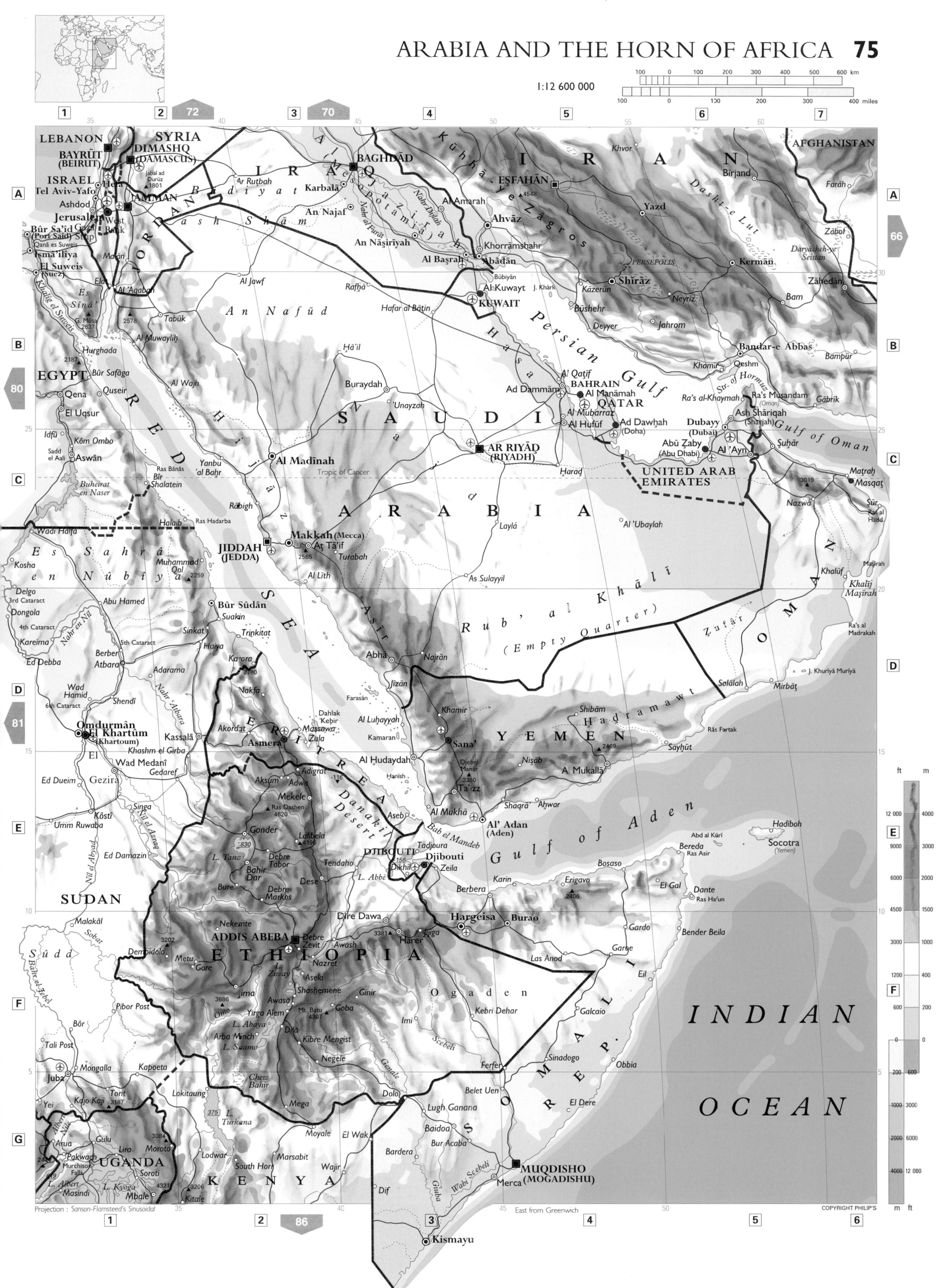

1:12 600 000

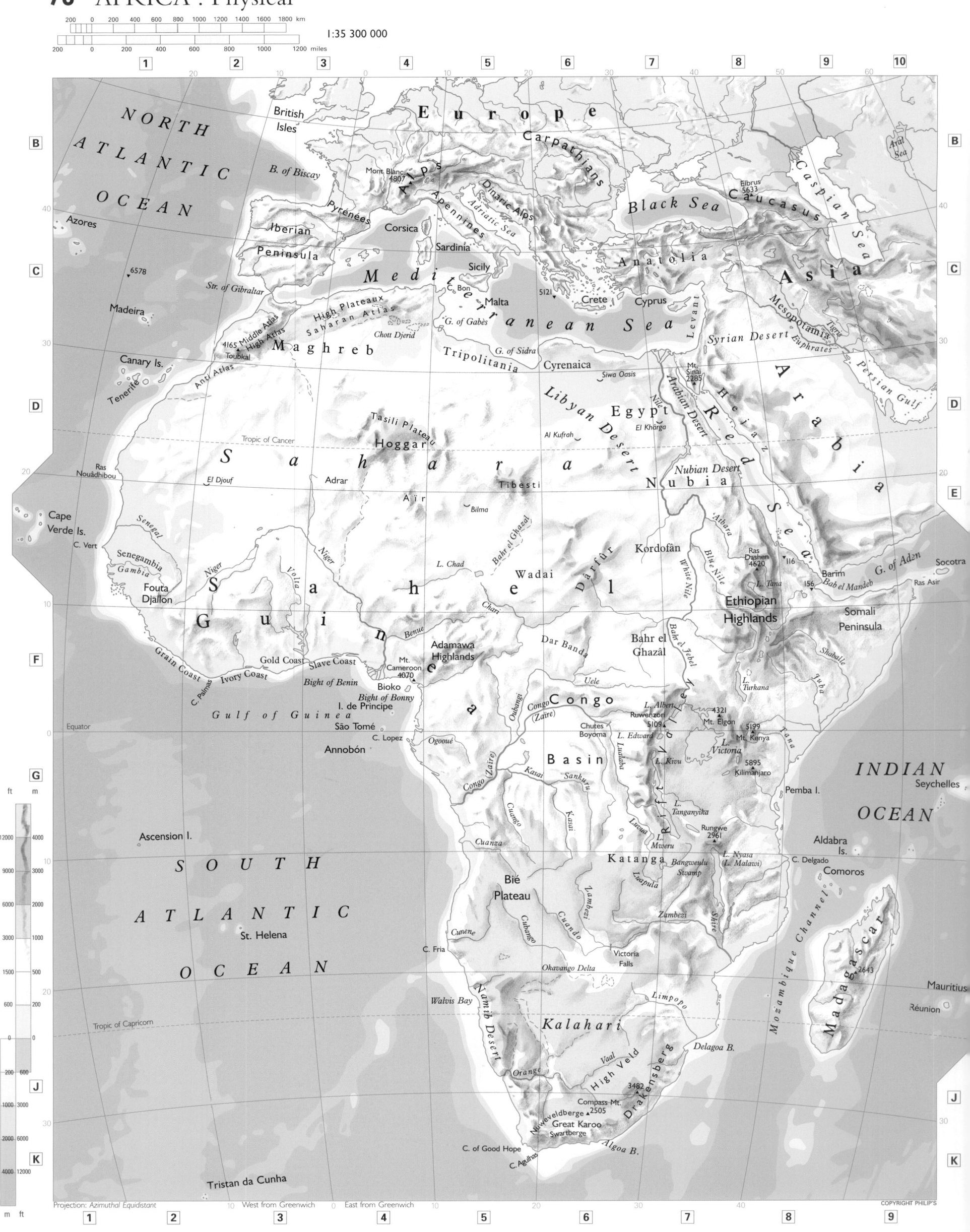

1:35 300 000

Projection: Azimuthal Equidistant

West from Greenwich   East from Greenwich

COPYRIGHT PHILIP'S

1:35 300 000

200 0 200 400 600 800 1000 1200 1400 1600 1800 km
200 0 200 400 600 800 1000 1200 miles

Projection: Azimuthal Equidistant

West from Greenwich   East from Greenwich

COPYRIGHT PHILIP'S

● Dakar Capital Cities

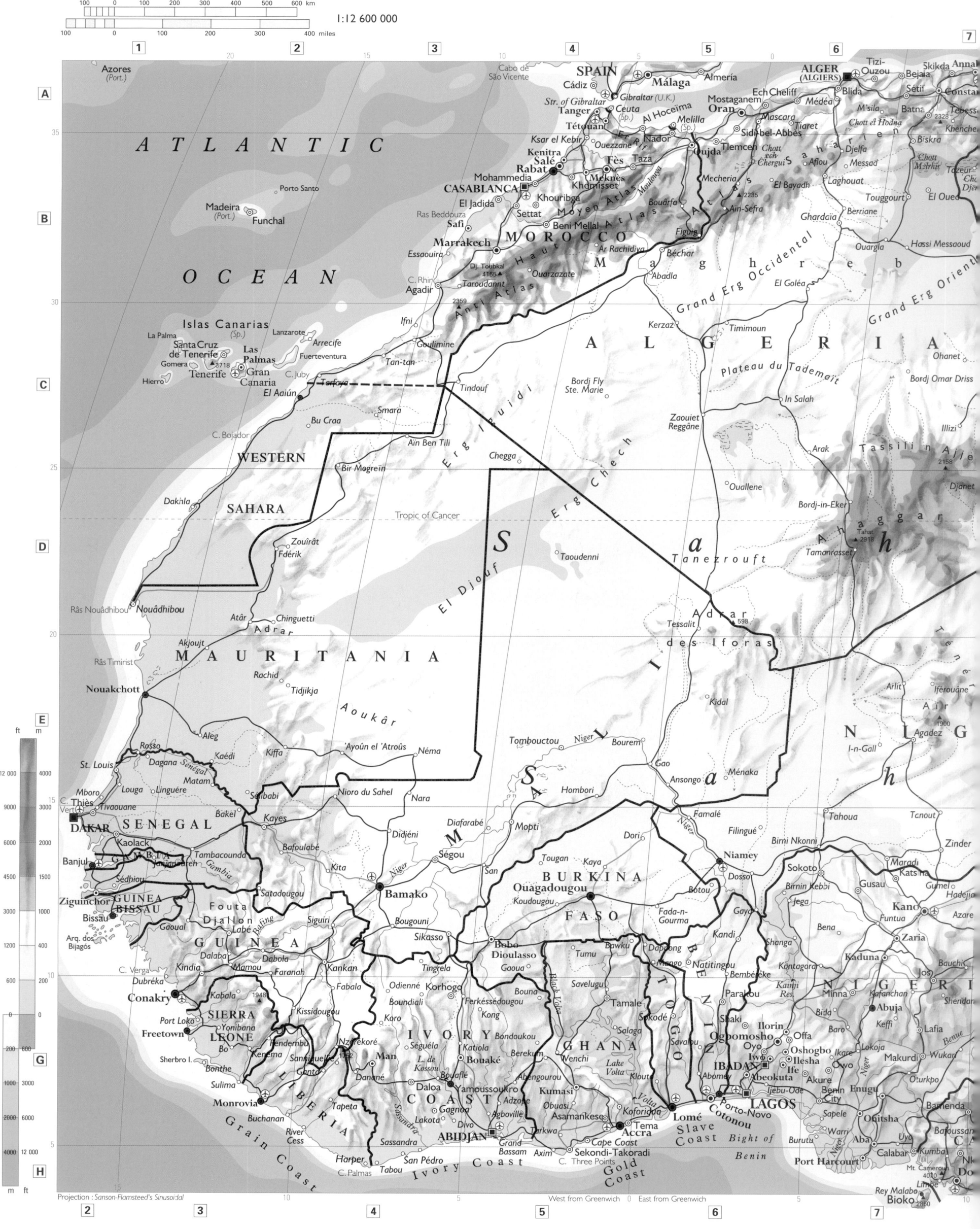

1:12 600 000

Projection : Sanson-Flamsteed's Sinusoidal

West from Greenwich   East from Greenwich

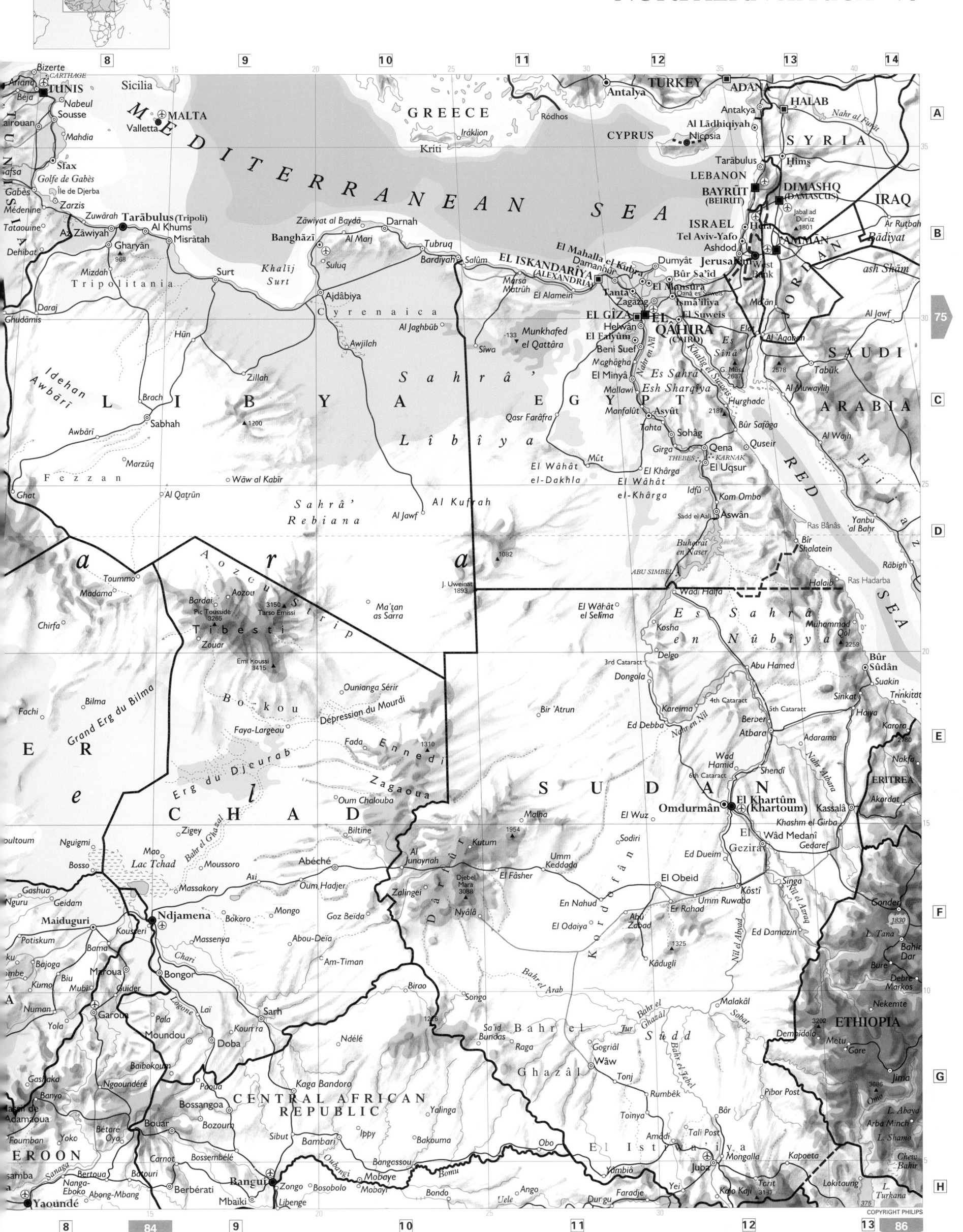

1:6 700 000

THE NILE DELTA
1:3 400 000

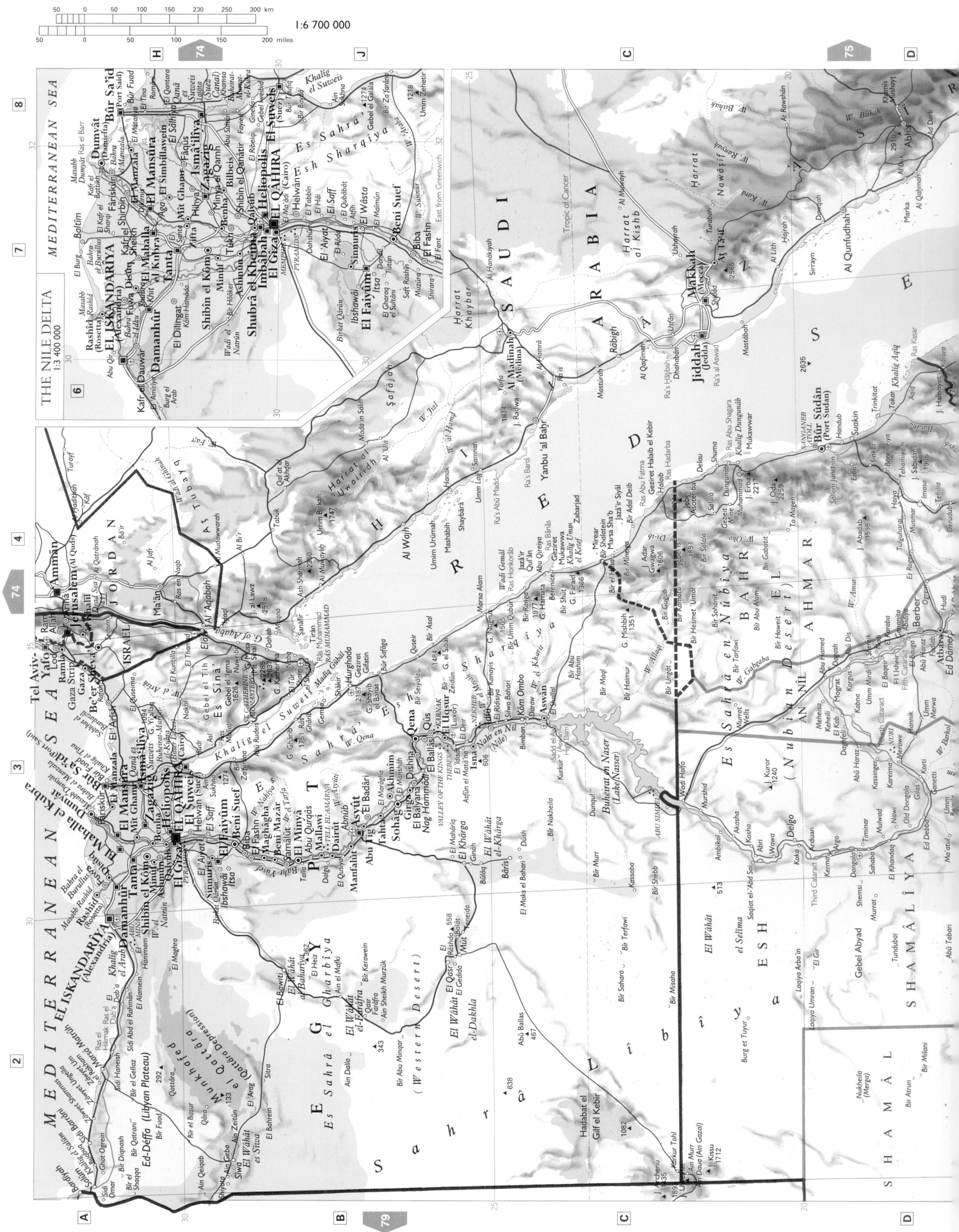

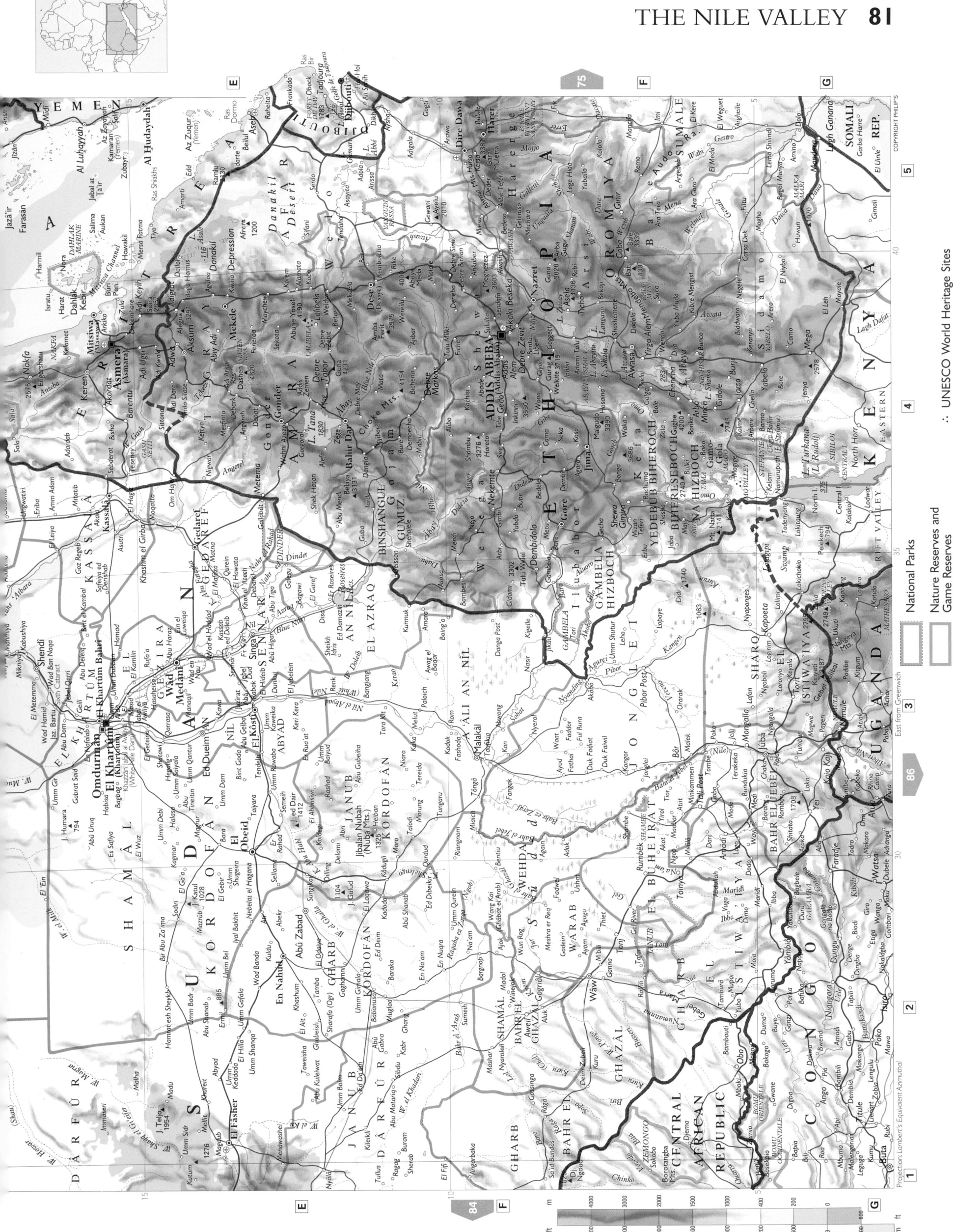

National Parks

Nature Reserves and
Game Reserves

∴ UNESCO World Heritage Sites

A T L A N T I C

O C E A N

G U L F

Projection : Lambert's Equivalent Azimuthal

West from Greenw

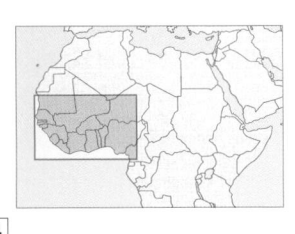

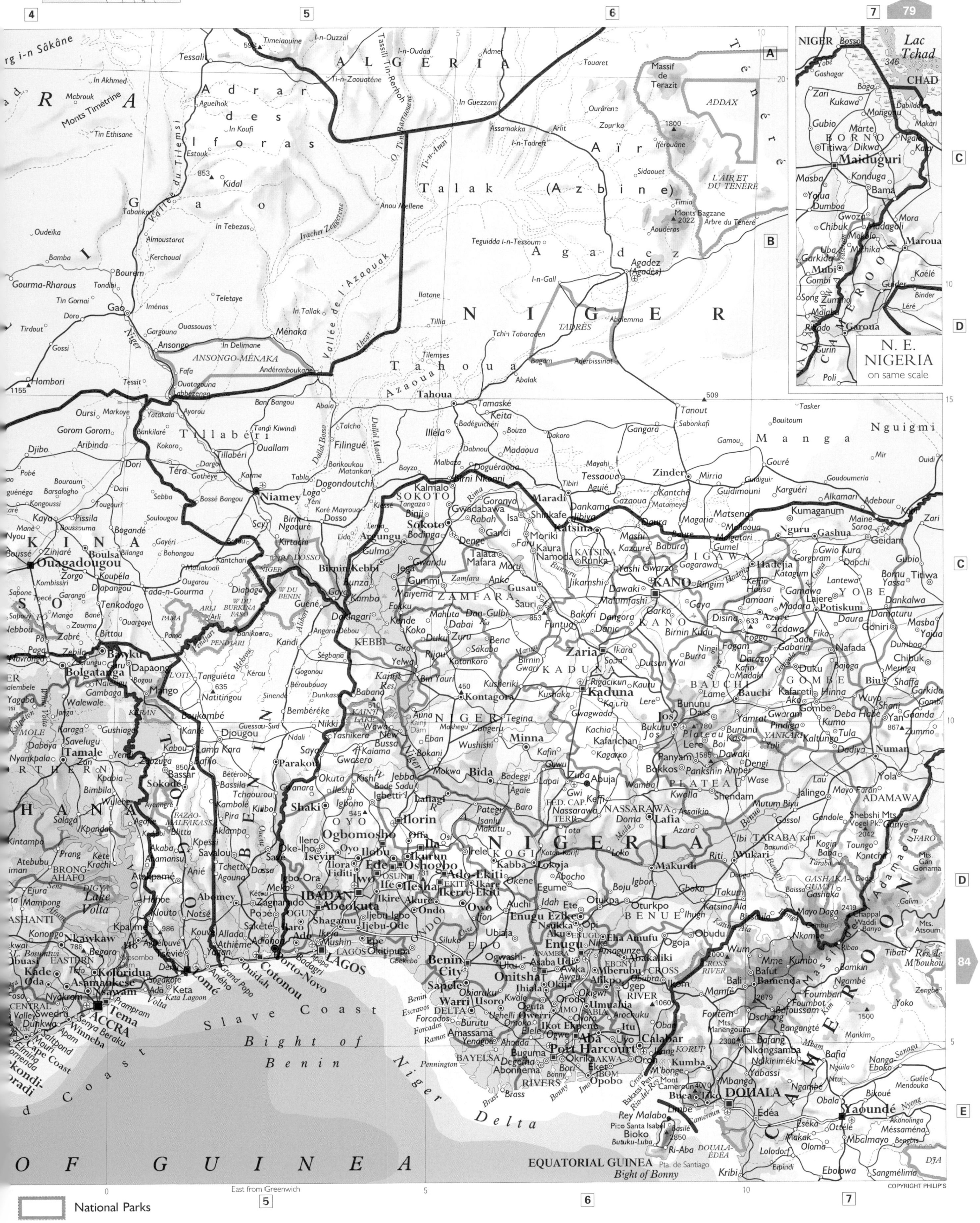

N. E. NIGERIA
on same scale

National Parks

Nature Reserves and
Game Reserves

∴ UNESCO World Heritage Sites

East from Greenwich

COPYRIGHT PHILIP'S

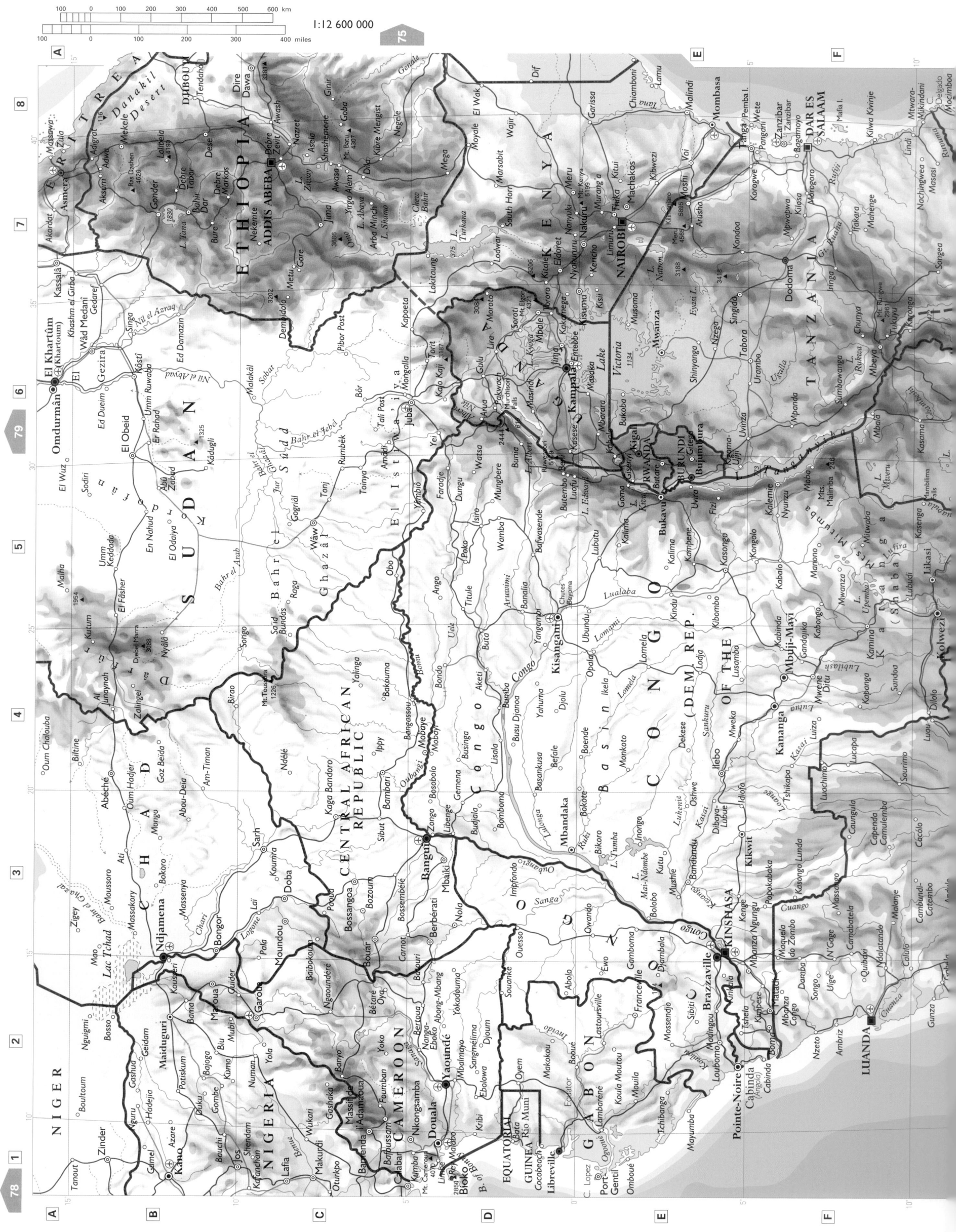

ATLANTIC OCEAN
INDIAN OCEAN
Skeleton Coast
Namib Desert
Kalahari
ZAMBIA
ZIMBABWE
MOZAMBIQUE
BOTSWANA
NAMIBIA
SOUTH AFRICA
LESOTHO
SWAZILAND
MALAWI
Lusaka
HARARE
PRETORIA
JOHANNESBURG
MAPUTO
Maseru
Windhoek
Gaborone
Bulawayo
Beira
DURBAN
CAPE TOWN
Port Elizabeth
East London
Bloemfontein
Kimberley
Livingstone
Caprivi Strip
Tropic of Capricorn
MADAGASCAR
on same scale
Antananarivo
Toamasina
Mahajanga
Fianarantsoa
Toliara
Taolanaro
Projection : Sanson-Flamsteed's Sinusoidal
COPYRIGHT PHILIPS
East from Greenwich

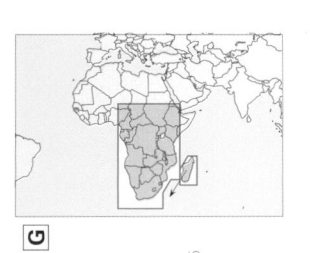

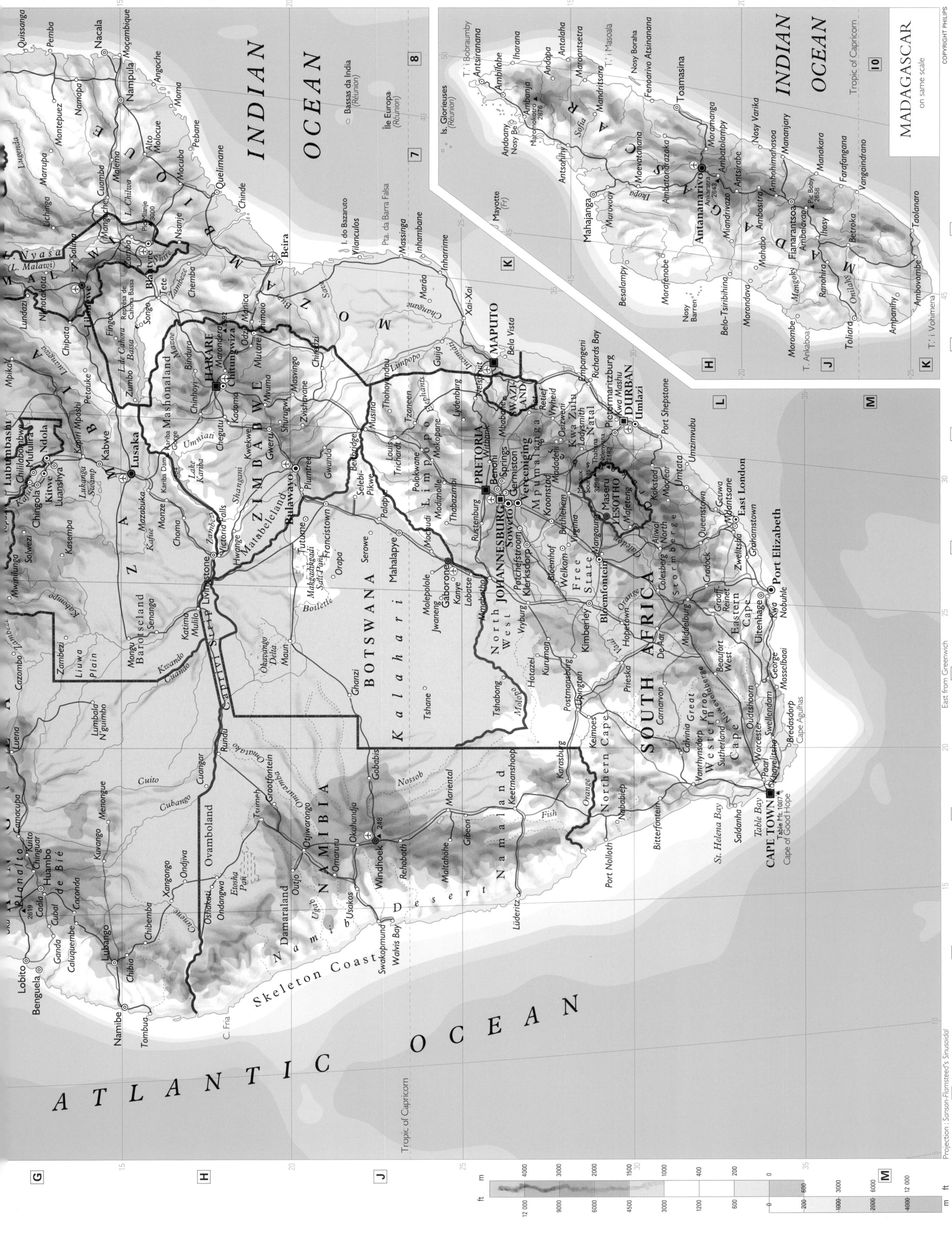

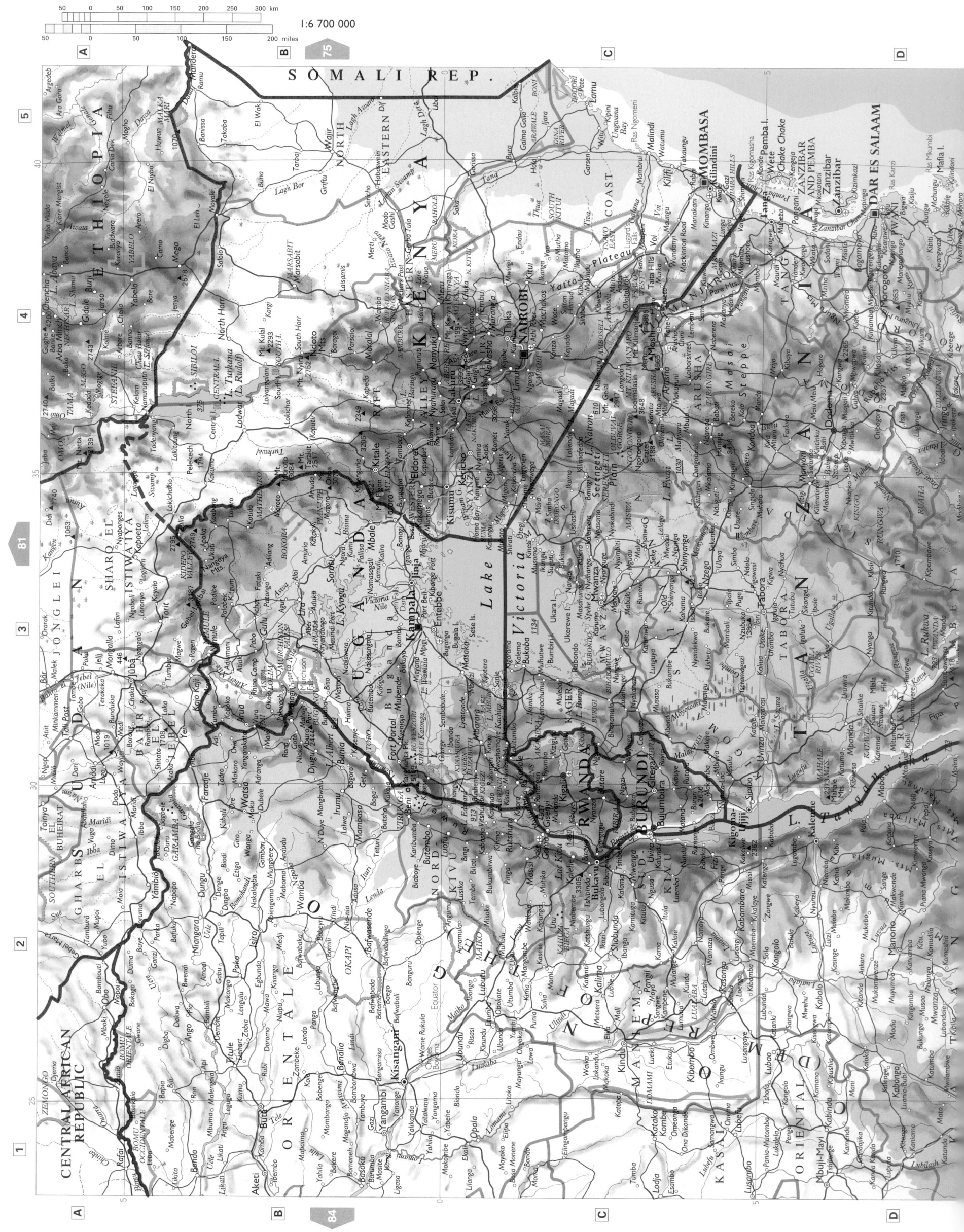

1:6 700 000

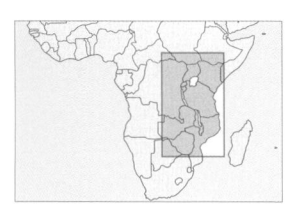

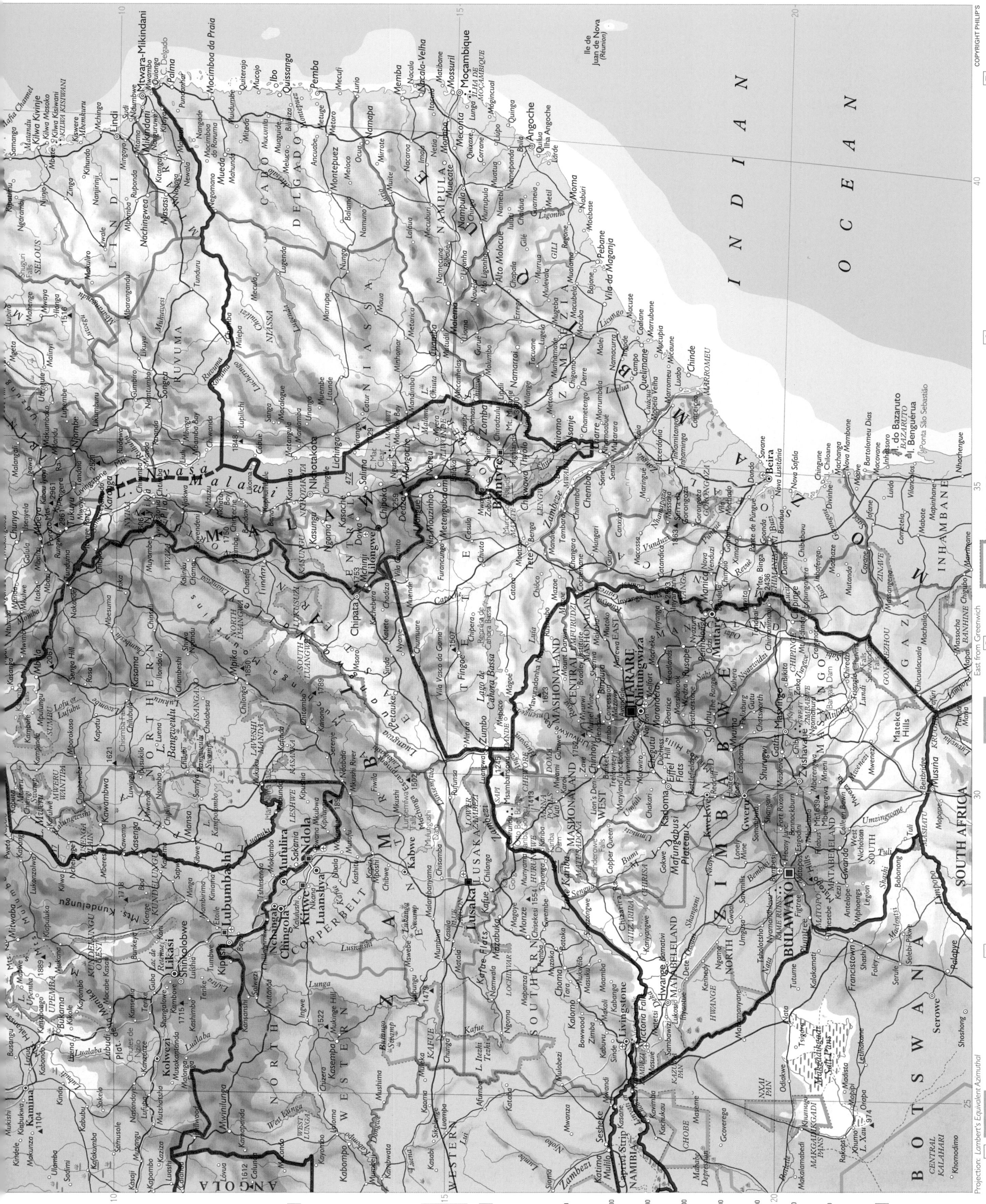

National Parks

Nature Reserves and
Game Reserves

∴ UNESCO World Heritage Sites

COPYRIGHT PHILIP'S

Projection: Lambert's Equivalent Azimuthal

East from Greenwich

1:6 700 000

Projection: Lambert's Equivalent Azimuthal

MOZAMBIQUE CHANNEL

ZIMBABWE

ZAMBEZIA

MALAWI

MOZAMBIQUE

MADAGASCAR

LIMPOPO

PRETORIA

JOHANNESBURG

Vereeniging

SWAZILAND

Maputo

DURBAN

INDIAN OCEAN

ANTANANARIVO

Toamasina

FIANARANTSOA

Mahajanga

Toliara

Taolanaro

Tropic of Capricorn

INDIAN OCEAN

MADAGASCAR
on same scale

National Parks

Nature Reserves and
Game Reserves

∴ UNESCO World Heritage Sites

East from Greenwich

COPYRIGHT PHILIP'S

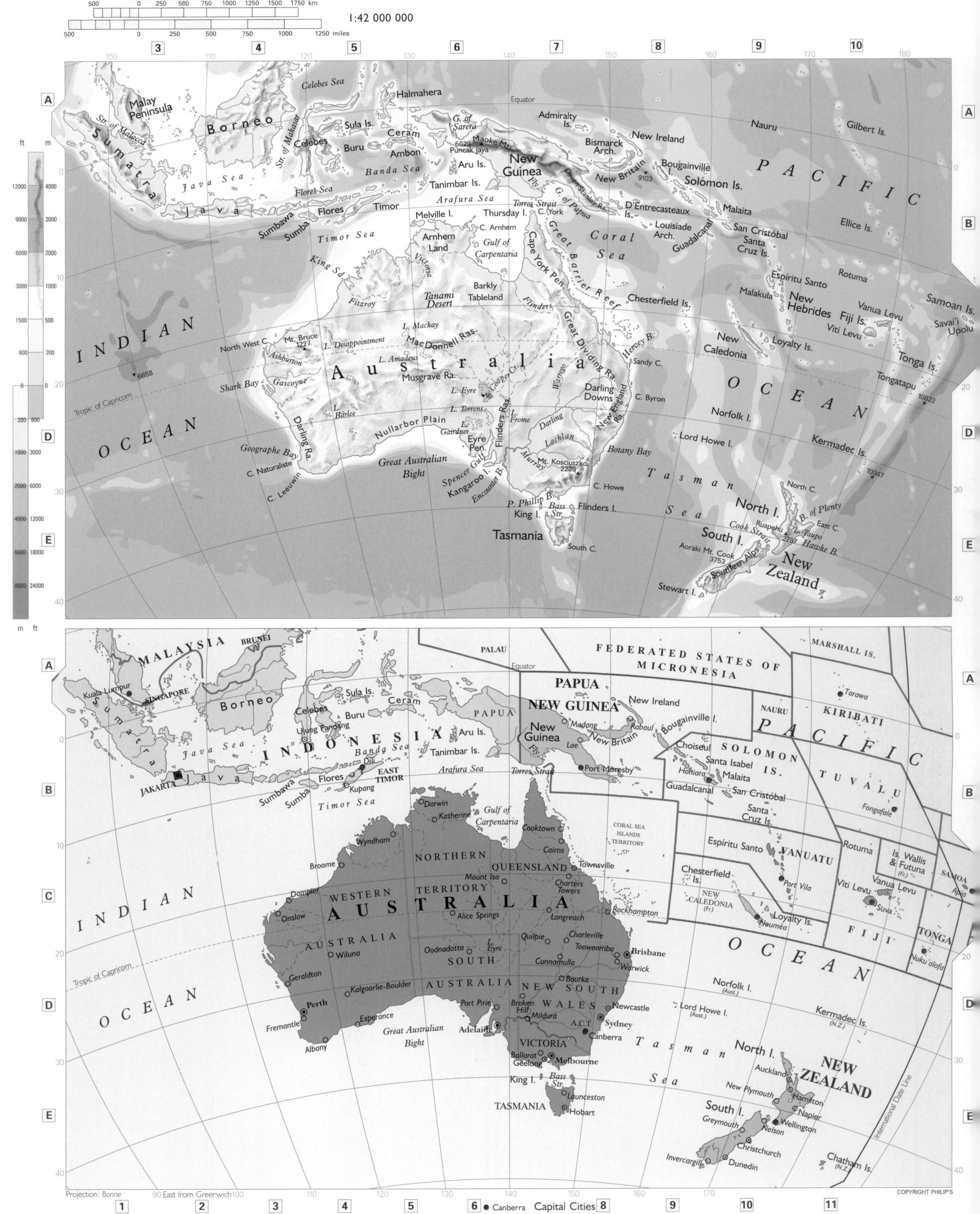

1:5 000 000

50 0 50 100 150 200 km
50 0 50 100 150 miles

| 1 | 2 | 3 | 4 | 96 | 5 | 6 | 7 |

North Island

C. Reinga
C. Maria van Diemen
North C.
Rangaunu B.
Houhora Heads
Doubtless B.
Mongonui
Whangaroa Harb.
Ahipara B.
Kaitaia
Okaihau
Waitangi
Otaua
Tauroa Pt.
Rawene
Kaikohe
Hikurangi
B. of Islands
C. Brett
Hokianga Harbour
Waipoua Forest
Whangarei
Whangarei Harb.
Bream Hd.
Bream B.
Waipu
Little Barrier I.
Dargaville
Warkworth
Great Barrier I.
C. Rodney
C. Colville
Cuvier I.
Kaipara Harbour
Helensville
Hauraki Gulf
Coromandel
Whitianga
Takapuna
AUCKLAND
Manukau
Papakura
Pukekohe
Thames
Whangamata
Waiuku
Mercer
Waihi
Mayor I.
Waikato
Huntly
Te Aroha
Paeroa
Tauranga Harb.
Mount Maunganui
Whakaari (White I.)
Raglan
Morrinsville
Cambridge
Te Puke
C. Runaway
Hamilton
Tauranga
Whakatane
Opotiki
Bay of Plenty
East C.
Kawhia
Te Awamutu
Putaruru
Rotorua
Kawerau
Taneatua
Raukumara Ra.
Hikurangi 1753
Kawhia Harbour
Otorohanga
L. Rotorua
Murupara
UREWERA
Motu
Waitomo Caves
Tokoroa
Te Kuiti
Kinleith
Mokai
Waipiro
Mokau
Wairakel
Taupo
Waikaremoana
Tolaga Bay
North Taranaki Bight
Moawa
Ongarue
L. Taupo
Rangitaiki
Nuhaka
Ormond
Gisborne
Waitara
WHANGANUI
Turangi
Kaimanawa Mts.
Tarawera
Wairoa
Waikokopu
Poverty Bay
New Plymouth
Inglewood
Whangamomona
Ruapehu 2797
Targwera
Mahia Pen.
Mt. Taranaki or Mt. Egmont 2518
EGMONT
Stratford
Ohakune
TONGARIRO
Bay View
Hawke Bay
Opunake
Kaponga
Eltham
Raetihi
Waiouru
Napier
Hawera
Patea
Waverley
Taihape
Ruahine Ra.
Hastings
C. Kidnappers
South Taranaki Bight
Mangaweka
Wanganui
Hunterville
Waipawa
Marton
Halcombe
Feilding
Danevirke
Waipukurau
Bulls
Palmerston North
Woodville
Pahiatua
Foxton
Shannon
C. Turnagain
Levin
Eketahuna
Otaki
Paraparaumu
Masterton
Kapiti I.
Carterton
Greytown
Upper Hutt
Featherston
Martinborough
Pelorus Sd.
Petone
Lower Hutt
L. Wairarapa
Wellington
Eastbourne
Cook Strait

South Island

C. Farewell
Golden B.
D'Urville I.
ABEL TASMAN
Collingwood
KAHURANGI
Takaka
Tasman Mts.
Tasman B.
Motueka
Karamea
Karamea Bight
Nelson
Havelock
Picton
Tadmor
Richmond
Wakefield
Seddonville
Granity
Wairau
Anakoa
Westport
Lyell
Murchison
NELSON LAKES
Tapuae-o-Uenuku 2885
Ward
Inangahua
L. Rotoroa
PAPAROA
Mt. Travers 2338
Seddon
Punakaiki
Reefton
Spenser Mts.
Lewis
Clarence
Blackball
Grey
Runanga
Stillwater
Hanmer Springs
Kaikoura
Greymouth
L. Brunner
ARTHUR'S PASS
Waiau
Kumara
Jacksons
Waiau
Hokitika
Arthur's Pass
Culverden
Ross
Waikari
Hurunui
Waipara
Amberley
Oxford
Pegasus Bay
WESTLAND
Coleridge
Rangiora
Abut Hd.
Aoraki
Mt. Cook 3753
Springfield
Kaiapoi
Christchurch
Methven
Whitecliffs
Riccarton
New Brighton
Jackson B.
MT. COOK
Mount Cook
Tiritiri o te Moana
Staveley
Lincoln
Lyttelton
Haast
Rakaia
Banks Pen.
Akaroa
Olau
Southbridge
Little River
Canterbury Plains
Fairlie
Rakaia
MOUNT ASPIRING
Mt. Aspiring 3027
Tekapo
Ellesmere
Southern Alps
Ashburton
Pukaki
Geraldine
Ashburton Bight
Milford Sd.
Earnslaw 2818
Mt. Earnslaw
L. Wanaka
Haast Pass
Ohau
Timaru
Sutherland Falls
Bligh Sound
George Sound
Milford Sound
Wanaka
Kurow
St. Andrews
Secretary I.
Arrowtown
Dunstan Mts.
Tokarahi
Waimate
Doubtful Sd.
L. Anau
Kingston
Cromwell
Maheno
FIORDLAND
Queenstown
Clyde
Naseby
Oamaru
Breaksea Sd.
L. Manapouri
Alexandra
Hampden
Dusky Sd.
Mossburn
Eyre Mts.
Roxburgh
Danback
Palmerston
Resolution I.
Manapouri
Lumsden
Garvie Mts.
Waikouaiti
Port Chalmers
Otago Harbour
Chalky Inlet
Clifden
Otago
Waikaia
Umbrella Mts.
Lawrence
Milton
C. Saunders
Tuatapere
Edievale
Kelso
Dunedin
Te Waewae B.
Orepuki
Hedgehope
Winton
Clinton
Mataura
Balclutha
Preservation Inlet
Nightcaps
Gore
Kaitangata
Owaka
Solander I.
Riverton
Tapanui
Wyndham
Nugget Pt.
Invercargill
Bluff
Ruapuke I.
Takahopa
Foveaux Str.
Halfmoon Bay
Stewart I. (Rakiura)
RAKIURA
Port Pegasus
South West C.

TASMAN SEA

PACIFIC OCEAN

Westland Bight

SAMOAN ISLANDS
1:10 100 000

SAMOA
AMERICAN SAMOA
Savai'i
Apia
Upolu
Pago Pago
Tutuila
West from Greenwich

FIJI AND TONGA
1:10 100 000

Wallis & Futuna (Fr.)
Futuna
Niuafo'ou (Tonga)
Thikombia
Labasa
Vanua Levu
Yasawa Group
Taveuni
Vanua Balavu
Koro
FIJI
Lautoka 1323
Levuka
Lau Group
Nandi
Viti Levu
Ovalau
Lakeba
Suva
Gau
Koro Sea
PACIFIC OCEAN
Vava'u
Moala
Kandavu
Vatoa
Tofua
TONGA (Friendly Is.)
Nuku'alofa
Tongatapu
East from Greenwich
West from Greenwich

50 0 50 100 150 200 km
50 0 50 100 150 miles

Projection: Conical with two standard parallels

National Parks

ft   m
9000   3000
6000   2000
3000   1000
1200   400
600   200
0   0
200   600
2000   6000
4000   12 000
6000   18 000
m   ft

COPYRIGHT PHILIP'S

1:6 700 000

INDIAN

OCEAN

SOUTHERN

OCEAN

WESTERN AUSTRALIA

SOUTH

AUSTRALIA

Great Victoria Desert

Nullarbor Plain

Hampton Tableland

Great Australian Bight

PERTH

Fremantle
Rockingham
Mandurah
Bunbury
Busselton

Geraldton

Kalgoorlie-
Boulder

Esperance

Albany

COPYRIGHT PHILIP'S

East from Greenwich

Projection: Bonne

National Parks

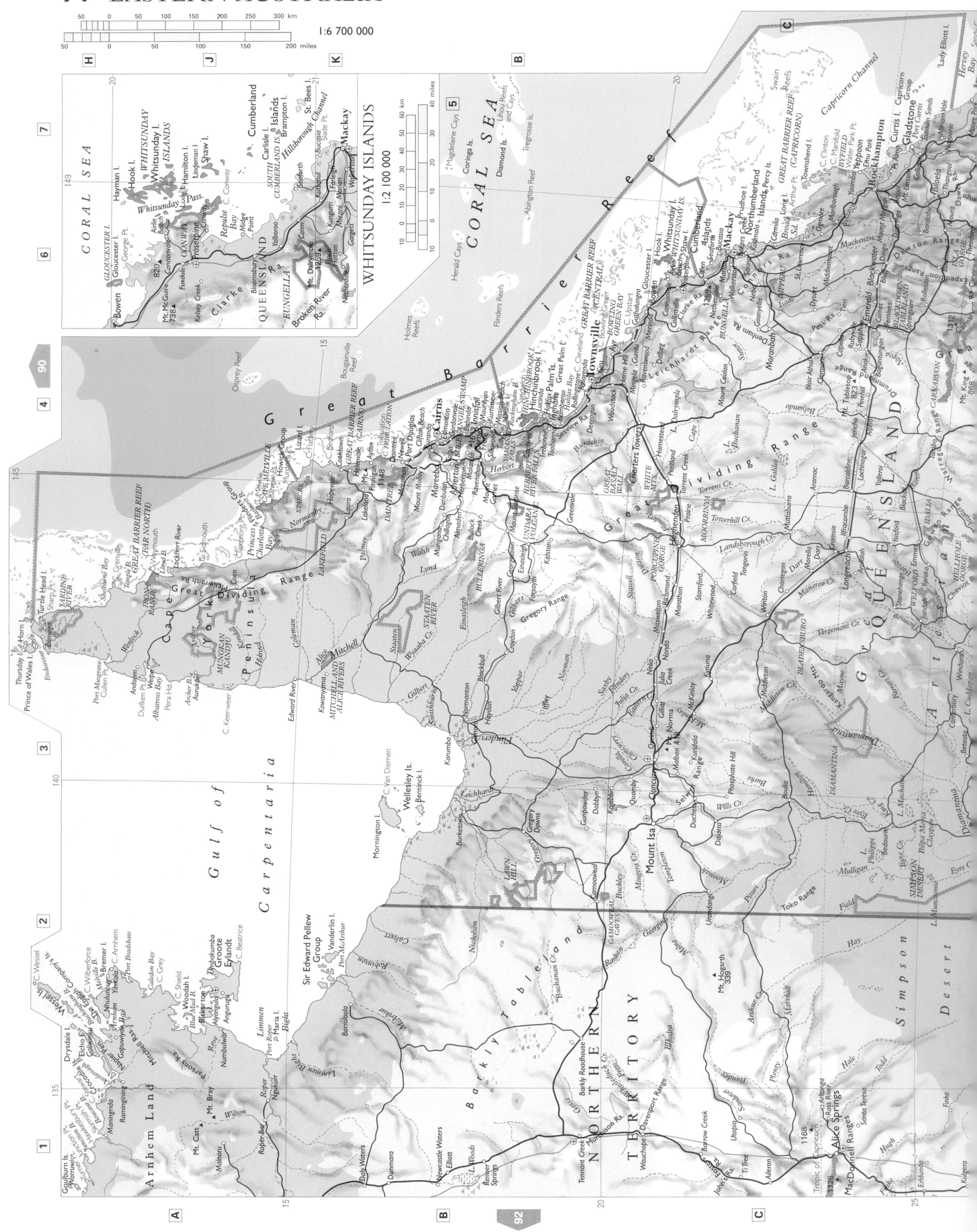

1:6 700 000

WHITSUNDAY ISLANDS

1:2 100 000

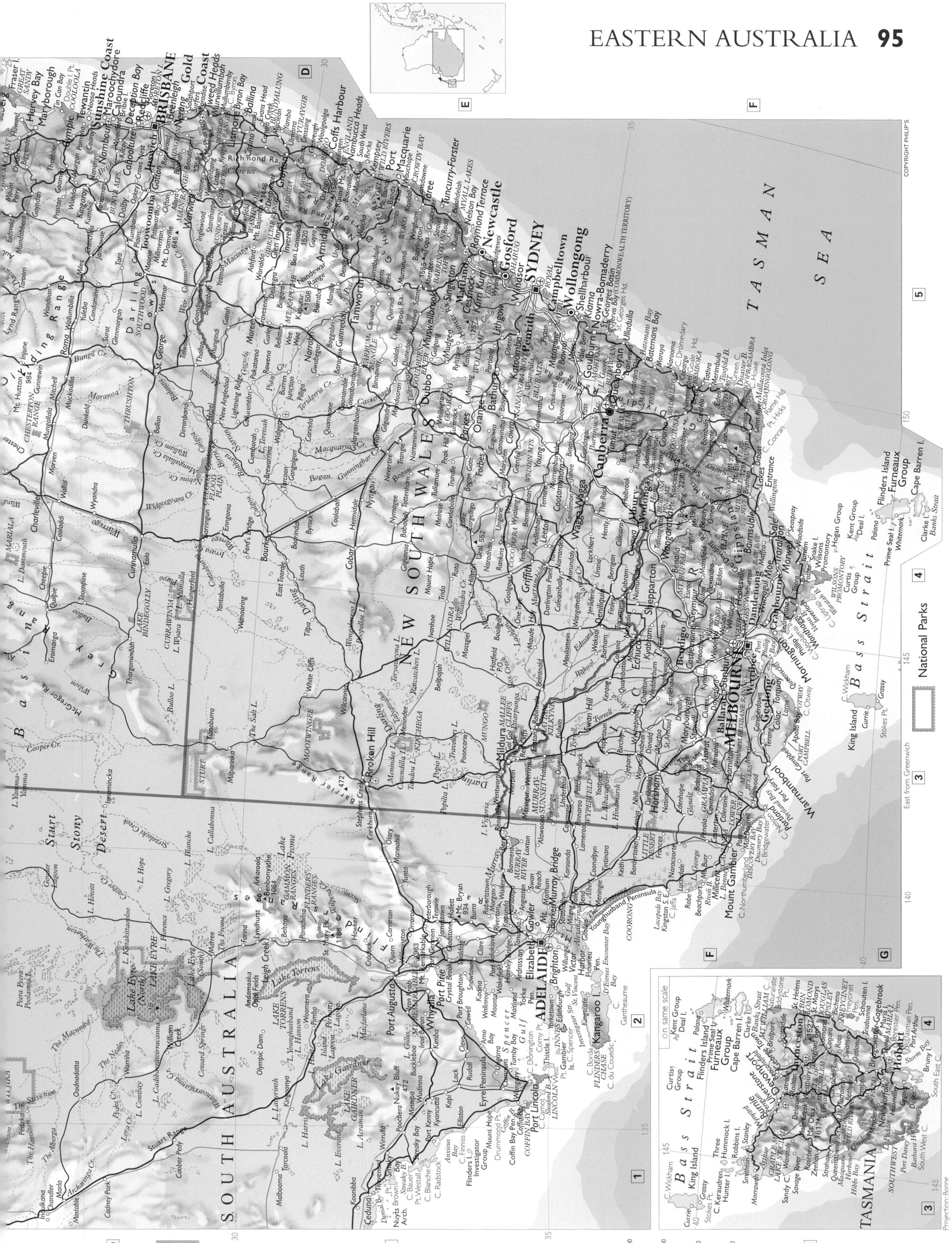

COPYRIGHT PHILIP'S

TASMAN SEA

Major cities and towns

BRISBANE, Gold Coast, Sunshine Coast, Ipswich, Caboolture, Redcliffe, Maroochydore, Caloundra, Beenleigh, Nerang, Maryborough, Harvey Bay, Gympie, Nambour, Tewantin, Warwick, Toowoomba, Dalby, Roma, Charleville, Cunnamulla

SYDNEY, Newcastle, Gosford, Wollongong, Shellharbour, Kiama, Nowra-Bomaderry, Campbelltown, Penrith, Windsor, Katoomba, Lithgow, Bathurst, Orange, Dubbo, Parkes, Forbes, Young, Cowra, Goulburn, Queanbeyan, **Canberra**, Tamworth, Armidale, Inverell, Moree, Narrabri, Gunnedah, Coffs Harbour, Grafton, Lismore, Ballina, Tweed Heads, Port Macquarie, Taree, Tuncurry-Forster, Kempsey, Nambucca Heads, Broken Hill, Wagga Wagga, Albury, Wodonga, Griffith, Leeton, Deniliquin

MELBOURNE, Geelong, Ballarat, Bendigo, Shepparton, Echuca, Wangaratta, Benalla, Horsham, Mount Gambier, Warrnambool, Hamilton, Portland, Sale, Traralgon, Morwell, Bairnsdale, Dandenong, Frankston, Cranbourne, Mornington, Werribee

ADELAIDE, Elizabeth, Gawler, Murray Bridge, Victor Harbor, Port Augusta, Port Pirie, Whyalla, Port Lincoln, Kadina, Clare

NEW SOUTH WALES
SOUTH AUSTRALIA
TASMANIA

Hobart, Launceston, Devonport, Burnie, Ulverstone, New Norfolk

Bass Strait, Flinders Island, Furneaux Group, Cape Barren I., King Island, Kent Group, Deal I.

Great Dividing Range, Darling Downs, Liverpool Ra., Warrumbungle Ra., Blue Mts., Snowy Mts., Mt. Kosciuszko 2228, Gippsland, Wilsons Promontory, Murray R., Darling R., Lachlan R., Murrumbidgee R., Lake Eyre, Lake Torrens, Lake Gairdner, Lake Frome, Lake Blanche, Flinders Ranges, Gammon Ranges, Gawler Ranges, Sturt Stony Desert, Cooper Cr., Strzelecki Cr.

Spencer Gulf, Gulf St. Vincent, Kangaroo I., Yorke Peninsula, Eyre Peninsula, Investigator Strait, Encounter Bay, Coorong Peninsula

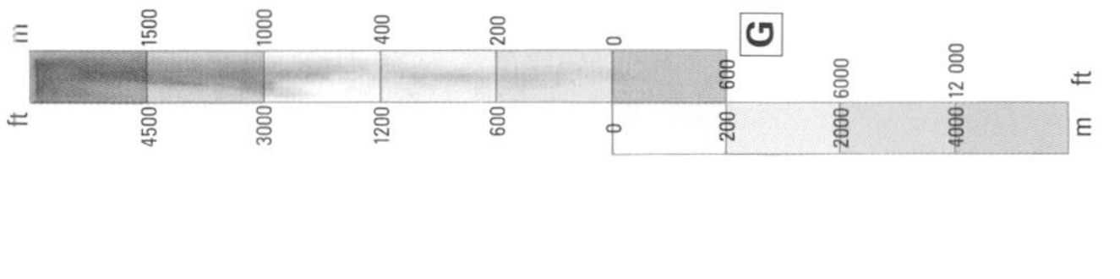

National Parks

East from Greenwich

on same scale

Projection: Bonne

93

Oceans/Seas:
Bering Sea
Sea of Okhotsk
Sea of Japan
Yellow Sea
East China Sea
South China Sea
Bay of Bengal
Philippine Sea
Sulu Sea
Celebes Sea
Banda Sea
Flores Sea
Java Sea
Arafura Sea
Coral Sea
Tasman Sea
INDIAN OCEAN
PACIFIC OCEAN

Countries/Regions:
RUSSIA
KAZAKHSTAN
MONGOLIA
CHINA
XIZANG
NEPAL
INDIA
BANGLADESH
BURMA
THAILAND
LAOS
CAMBODIA
VIETNAM
MALAYSIA
INDONESIA
PHILIPPINES
JAPAN
NORTH KOREA
SOUTH KOREA
TAIWAN
AFGHANISTAN
PAKISTAN
TAJIKISTAN
KYRGYZSTAN
SRI LANKA
BRUNEI
SARAWAK
SABAH
PEN. MALAYSIA
PAPUA NEW GUINEA
AUSTRALIA
NEW ZEALAND
NORTHERN MARIANAS (U.S.A.)
GUAM (U.S.A.)
MARSHALL IS.
FEDERATED STATES OF MICRONESIA
PALAU
NAURU
SOLOMON IS.
TUVALU
VANUATU
FIJI
TONGA
SAMOA
KIRIBATI
NEW CALEDONIA (Fr.)
EAST TIMOR

Cities/Places:
Yekaterinburg
MOSKVA
Tomsk
Novosibirsk
Irkutsk
Chita
Astana (Aqmola)
Semey
Ulaanbaatar
Changchun
Harbin
Blagoveshchensk
Khabarovsk
Okhotsk
Sakhalin
Petropavlovsk-Kamchatskiy
Poluostrov Kamchatka
Komandorskiye Ostrova (Russia)
Near Is. (U.S.A.)
Andreanof Is. (U.S.A.)
Almaty
ÜRÜMQI
Toshkent
Kabul
Srinagar
Lahore
DELHI
Kanpur
Hyderabad
CHENNAI (Madras)
Colombo
BEIJING
TIANJIN
Taiyuan
SHENYANG
Dalian
SOUL
Qingdao
Nagoya
Kyoto
Osaka
Kitakyūshū
Shikoku
Kyūshū
TOKYO
Yokohama
Sendai
Sapporo
Hakodate
Vladivostok
Lanzhou
Xi'an
Nanjing
Wuhan
CHONGQING
Changsha
Lhasa
Kunming
Fuzhou
HANGZHOU
SHANGHAI
GUANGZHOU
HONG KONG
Macau
Taipei
KOLKATA (Calcutta)
DHAKA
Mandalay
Hanoi
Hainan
Rangoon
BANGKOK
Phnom Penh
Thanh Pho Ho Chi Minh
Kuala Lumpur
SINGAPORE
Palembang
JAKARTA
Surabaya
Ujung Pandang
Luzon
Mindoro
MANILA
Samar
Palawan
Mindanao
Koror
PALAU
Yap
Truk
Pohnpei
Palikir
Saipan
Enewetak Atoll
Bikini Atoll
Dalap-Uliga-Darrit
Jaluit I.
Tarawa
Banaba
Butaritari
Honiara
Guadalcanal
Rabaul
Bougainville
Port Moresby
Lae
Fongafale
Funafuti
Espíritu Santo
Port Vila
Vanua Levu
Viti Levu
Suva
Nuku'alofa
Nouméa
Apia
Rotuma
Darwin
C. Arnhem
Gulf of Carpentaria
Cairns
Townsville
Mount Isa
Alice Springs
Brisbane
Broome
North West C.
Geraldton
Perth
Albany
Adelaide
Sydney
Canberra
Melbourne
Hobart
Tasmania
Auckland
Wellington
Christchurch
Dunedin
Invercargill

Physical features:
Volga
Aral Sea
Belqash Köl
Atai
Ob
Lena
Oz. Baykal
Amur
Huang He
Chang J.
Yangtze
Ganga
Brahmaputra
Irrawaddy
Salween
Mekong
Himalaya
Kunlun Shan
Mt. Everest 8850
Fuji-San 3776
Japan Trench 10,554
Kuril Trench 10,542
La Perouse Str.
Kurilskiye Ostrova (Russia)
Emperor Seamount Chain
Aleutian Trench 7822
South Honshū Ridge
Ogasawara Gunto (Japan)
Kazan-Rettō (Japan)
Minami-Tori-Shima (Japan)
Ryūkyū-rettō (Japan)
Wake I. (U.S.A.)
Midway Is. (U.S.A.)
Lisianski I. (U.S.A.)
Necker Ridge
International Dateline
Mariana Trench 11,022
Marcus Necker Ridge
Caroline Is.
C. Engano
Paracel Is.
Andaman Is. (India)
Nicobar Is. (India)
G. of Thailand
Borneo
Sulawesi
Buru
Seram
Halmahera
Maluku
Flores
Bali
Sumbawa
Sumba
Timor
Torres Strait
C. York
Puncak Jaya 5029
Admiralty Is.
New Ireland
Bismarck Arch.
New Britain
Louisiade Arch.
Santa Cruz I. 9165
Is. Chesterfield
Is. Loyauté
Vanua Levu
Phoenix Is.
Abariringa Enderbury
Howland I. / Baker I. (U.S.)
Gilbert Is.
Tokelau (N.Z.)
Is. Wallis & Futuna (Fr.)
Norfolk I. (Austral.)
Lord Howe I. (Austral.)
Kermadec Is. (N.Z.)
Kermadec Trench 10,047
Tonga Trench 10,822
Chatham Is. (N.Z.)
Bounty Is. (N.Z.)
Antipodes Is. (N.Z.)
Auckland Is. (N.Z.)
Macquarie Is. (Austral.)
Campbell I. (N.Z.)
Cook Strait
Aoraki Mt. Cook 3753
Great Dividing Ra.
Great Barrier Reef
Great Australian Bight
Murray
Darling
L. Eyre
Mt. Kosciuszko 2230
Bass Str.
Rockhampton
Lord Howe Rise
Christmas I. (Austral.)
Cocos Is. (Austral.)
Sunda Islands
Selat Sunda
Sumatera
Java Trench
Mid-Indian Ridge
Nouvelle Amsterdam (Fr.)
I. St. Paul (Fr.)
Is. Crozet (Fr.)
Kerguelen (Fr.)
Heard I. (Austral.)
Micronesia
Melanesia
Polynesia

Scale bar:
ft / m
12 000 / 4000
9000 / 3000
6000 / 2000
3000 / 1000
1500 / 500
600 / 200
0 / 0
600 / 200
3000 / 1000
6000 / 2000
12 000 / 4000
18 000 / 6000
24 000 / 8000
m / ft

Projection: Mollweide's Homolographic
East from Greenwich

11 **12** **13** **14**

Arctic Circle

15

ALASKA
(U.S.A.)
Anchorage

5959

16 **17** **18** **19** **20**

Bristol Bay

Gulf of Alaska

Juneau

Prince of Wales I.
(U.S.A.) *Prince Rupert*
Queen Charlotte Is.
(Canada)

Edmonton

Calgary

Winnipeg

L. Winnipeg

C A N A D A

Newfoundland

N O R T H

B

Vancouver
Vancouver I.
Victoria
Seattle
Portland

Boise

Regina

Minneapolis

Winnipeg

L. Superior

Toronto
Detroit
CHICAGO

Québec
Ottawa
L. Ontario
L. Erie
Buffalo

Montréal
St. Lawrence

Boston

St. John's

50

C

Salt Lake
City
Sacramento
SAN FRANCISCO

Denver
Colorado

Kansas City

St. Louis
Cincinnati
Pittsburgh

NEW YORK
PHILADELPHIA
Baltimore
Washington D.C.

40

ATLANTIC

D

6741

4418

UNITED STATES

LOS ANGELES
San Diego

Phoenix

Oklahoma City

Memphis

Atlanta

C. Hatteras

Bermuda
(U.K.)

Sargasso Sea

Dallas

Houston
San Antonio

Mississippi

Jacksonville

30

Guadalupe
(Mex.)

Ciudad
Juárez

Gulf of Mexico

New
Orleans

Miami

BAHAMAS

OCEAN

E

Tropic of Cancer

Honolulu

Oahu
4205
HAWAIIAN IS.
(U.S.A.)
Hawaii

C. San Lucas

Monterrey

La Habana

CUBA

West Indies

Johnston I.
(U.S.A.)

Guadalajara

Is. Revilla Gigedo
(Mex.)

MEXICO
5610
Puebla

Mérida

7680

HAITI

9230

DOMINICAN REP.

JAMAICA

Kingston

PUERTO
RICO
(U.S.A.)

Leeward
Is.

20

F

C I F I C

Acapulco

I. Clipperton
(Fr.)

GUATEMALA
Guatemala
San Salvador
EL SALVADOR

BELIZE

HONDURAS
Managua

Caribbean Sea

Nicaragua

Barranquilla
San José

Maracaibo

BARBADOS
Windward Is.

Caracas

10

Palmyra Is.
(U.S.A.)

Teraina

Tabuaeran
Kiritimati

North West Christmas Ridge

Equator

COSTA
RICA

Colón
PANAMA

Panamá

I. del Coco
(Costa Rica)

Medellín

Bogotá

VENEZUELA

Orinoco

G

Jarvis I.
(U.S.A.)

Malden I.

Starbuck I.

Galápagos
(Ecuador)

I. de Malpelo
(Colombia)

Quito
ECUADOR

Cali

COLOMBIA

0

B A T I

L I N E

Line Is.

Equator

Guayaquil

Iquitos

Amazonas

BRAZIL

H

Tongareva

Pukapuka
Manihiki

Suwarrow Is.

Vostok I.

Flint I.

Caroline I.
(Millennium I.)

Is. Marquises

Is. de la
Société
Papeete
Tahiti

Is. Tuamotu

C. Pariñas

Trujillo

6369

PERU

10

J

Rarotonga

Cook Is.
(N.Z.)

FRENCH POLYNESIA

Mururoa

Is. Tubuai

Tuamotu

Austral Seamount Chain

LIMA

Cuzco

L. Titicaca

Arequipa

6866

Nevada Ancohuma
6550

La Paz
BOLIVIA

Peru

Arica

K

East Pacific Ridge

Tropic of Capricorn

Ducie I.

Pitcairn I.
(U.K.)

Rapa

Sala-y-Gómez
(Chile)

I. de Pascua
(Chile)

San Félix
(Chile)

San Ambrosio
(Chile)

Iquique
Chile

Antofagasta

8050
Trench

Paraguay

San Miguel
de Tucumán

Asunción
PARAGUAY

Porto
Alegre

30

L

Arch. de
Juan Fernández
(Chile)

Valparaíso

Córdoba
Aconcagua
6962
Rosario

SANTIAGO
Concepción

BUENOS
AIRES

Rio de la Plata

URUGUAY
Montevideo

ARGENTINA

40

M

Chile Rise

SOUTH

ATLANTIC

Pacific Antarctic Ridge

Patagonia

6212

OCEAN

50

N

Punta Arenas

Tierra del Fuego
Est. de Magallanes

Falkland Is.
(U.K.)

South Georgia
(U.K.)

C. de Hornos

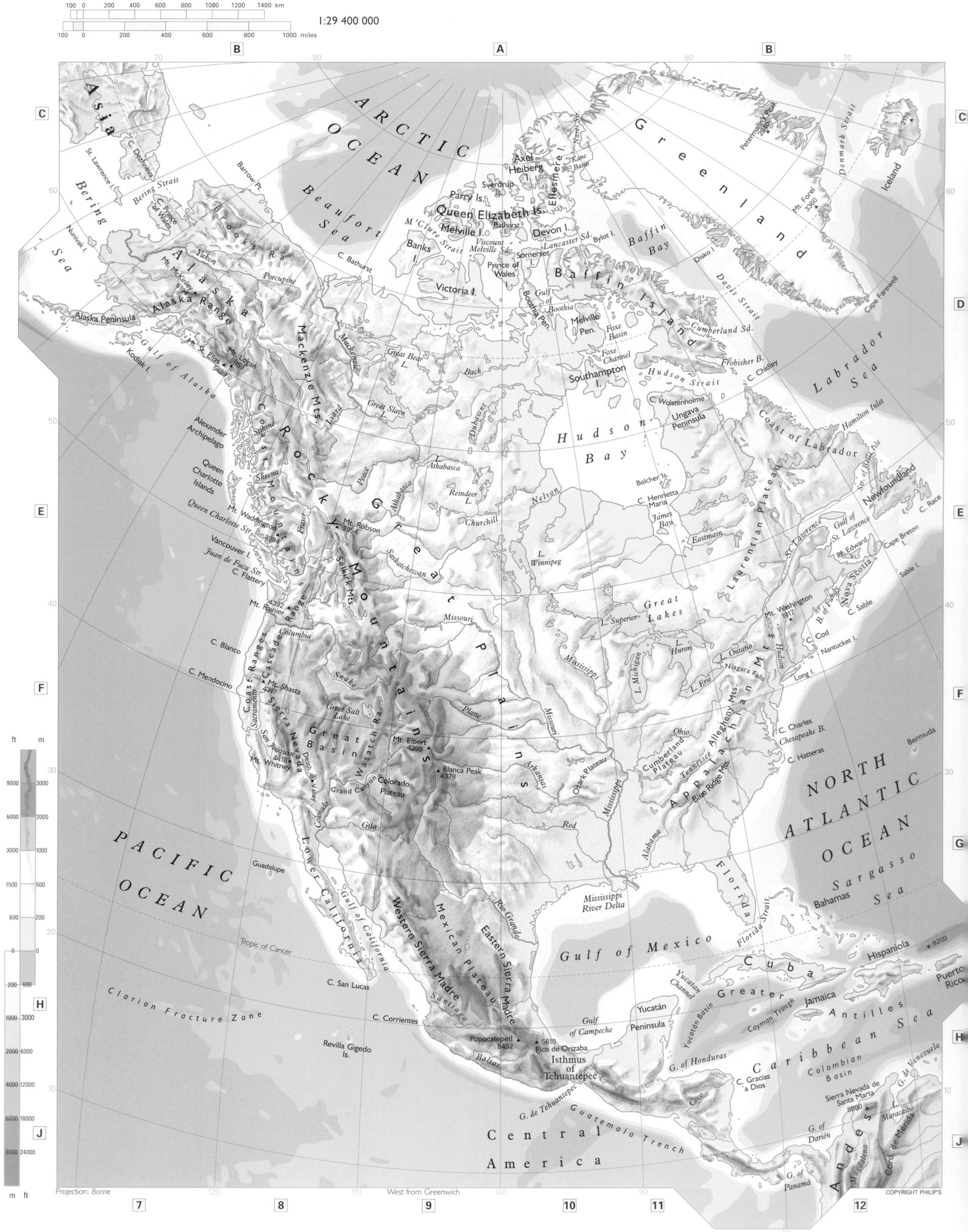

100 0 200 400 600 800 1000 1200 1400 km

100 0 200 400 600 800 1000 miles

1:29 400 000

Projection: Bonne

West from Greenwich

COPYRIGHT PHILIP'S

1:29 400 000

100 0 100 200 300 400 500 600 km
100 0 100 200 300 400 miles

1:12 600 000

Projection : Bonne

ALASKA
1:25 200 000

100 0 100 200 300 400 500 600 km
100 0 100 200 300 400 miles

West from Greenwich

West from Greenwich

COPYRIGHT PHILIP'S

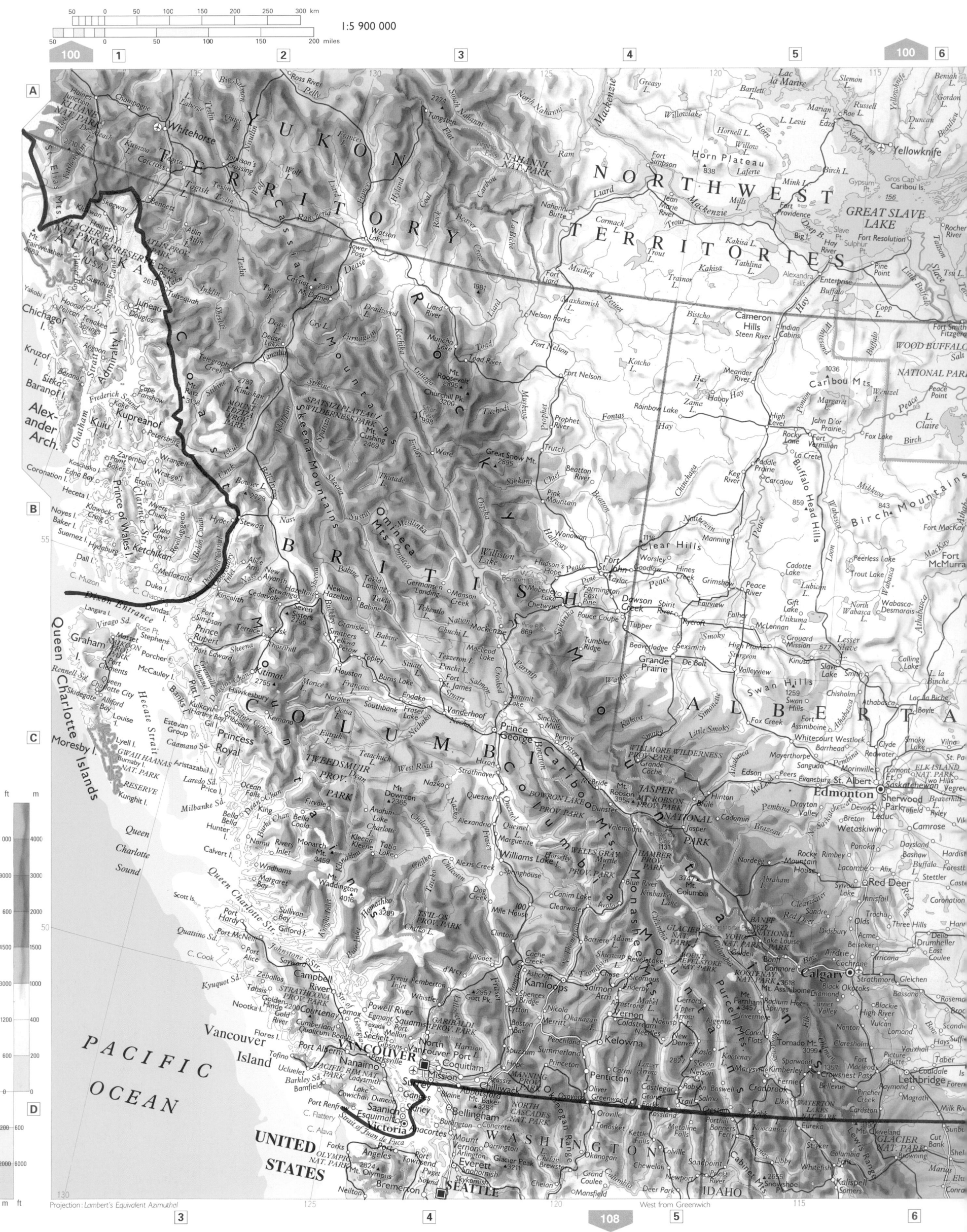

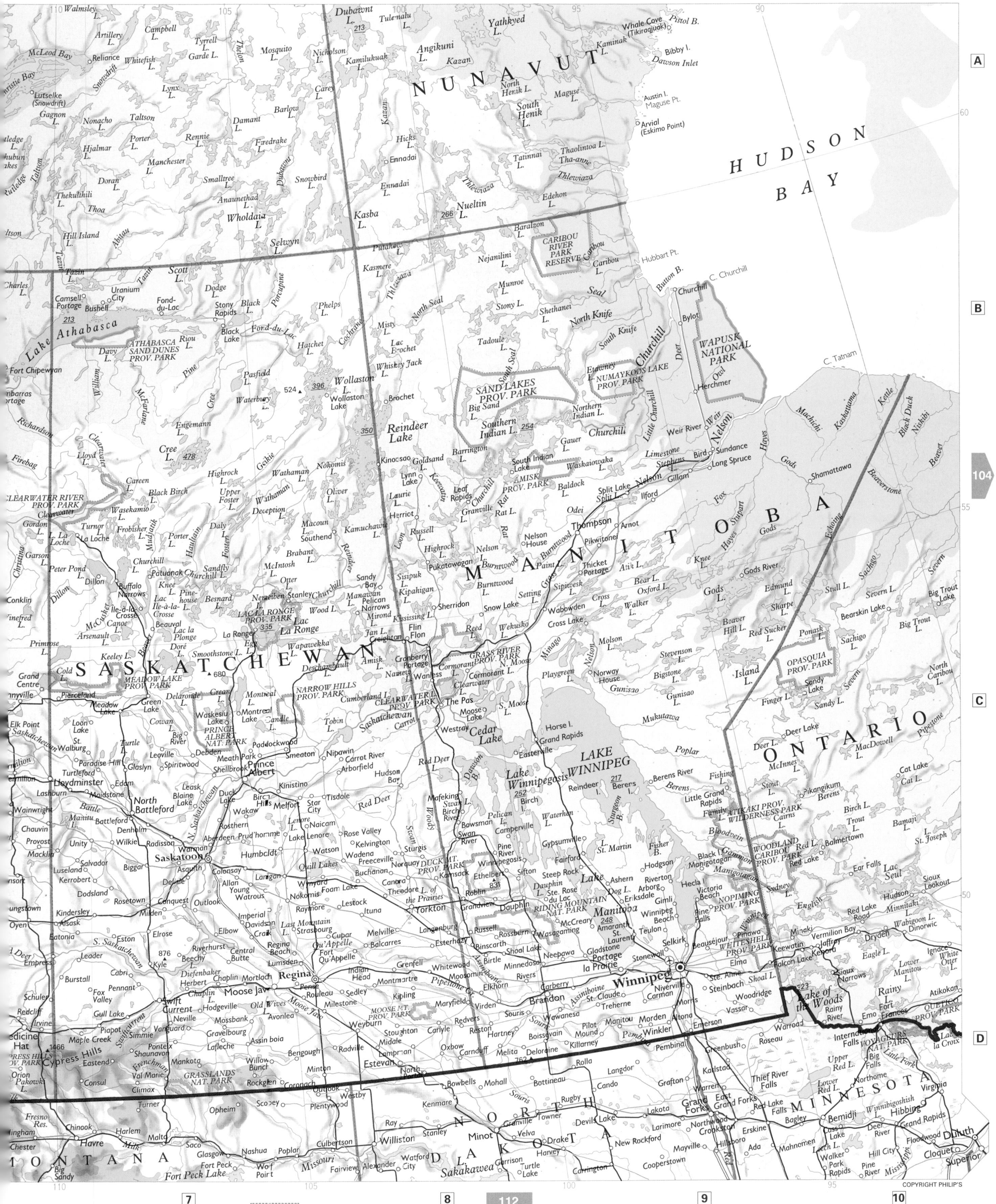

National Parks

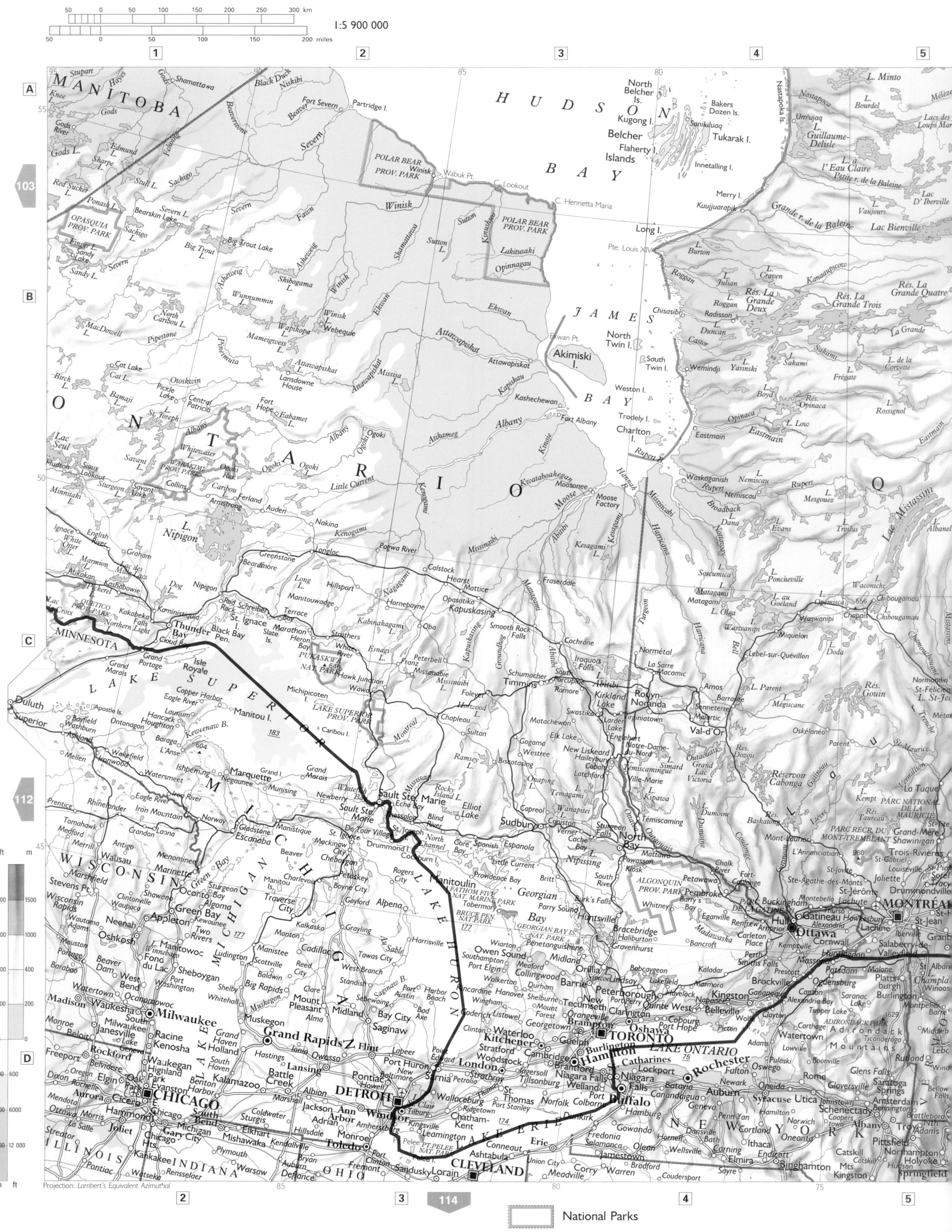

1:5 900 000

National Parks

Projection: Lambert's Equivalent Azimuthal

LABRADOR SEA

NEWFOUNDLAND & LABRADOR

Labrador

Smallwood Reservoir

Churchill Falls

Happy Valley-Goose Bay

L'Anse aux Meadows

St. Anthony

LABRADOR

Newfoundland

GROS MORNE NAT. PARK

Corner Brook

Grand Falls Windsor

Gander

TERRA NOVA NAT. PARK

St. John's

Mt. Pearl

GULF OF ST. LAWRENCE

Î. d'Anticosti

Dét. d'Honguedo

Sept-Îles

Baie-Comeau

Pén. de la Gaspésie

Mts. Chic-Chocs

PARC DE LA GASPÉSIE

Îs. de la Madeleine (Québec)

Cabot Strait

ST-PIERRE et MIQUELON (France)

CAPE BRETON HIGHLANDS NAT. PARK

Cape Breton Island

PRINCE EDWARD ISLAND

Charlottetown

Sydney

Glace Bay

NEW BRUNSWICK

Fredericton

Moncton

KOUCHIBOUGUAC NAT. PARK

Saint John

FUNDY NAT. PARK

NOVA SCOTIA

Truro

Dartmouth

Halifax

Sable I. (Nova Scotia)

ATLANTIC OCEAN

MAINE

Bangor

Augusta

Portland

NEW HAMPSHIRE

Concord

Manchester

UNITED STATES

BOSTON

Québec

Lévis

Chicoutimi

Jonquière

Rimouski

Rivière-du-Loup

Edmundston

Presque Isle

1:10 100 000

Projection: Albers' Equal Area with two standard parallels

West from Greenwich

HAWAII 1:8 400 000

8 9 10 11 12 101 13

119 8 9 10 11 120 12

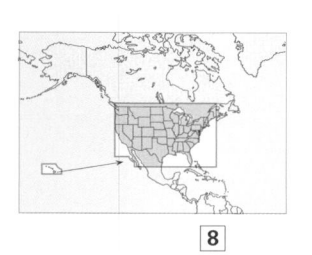

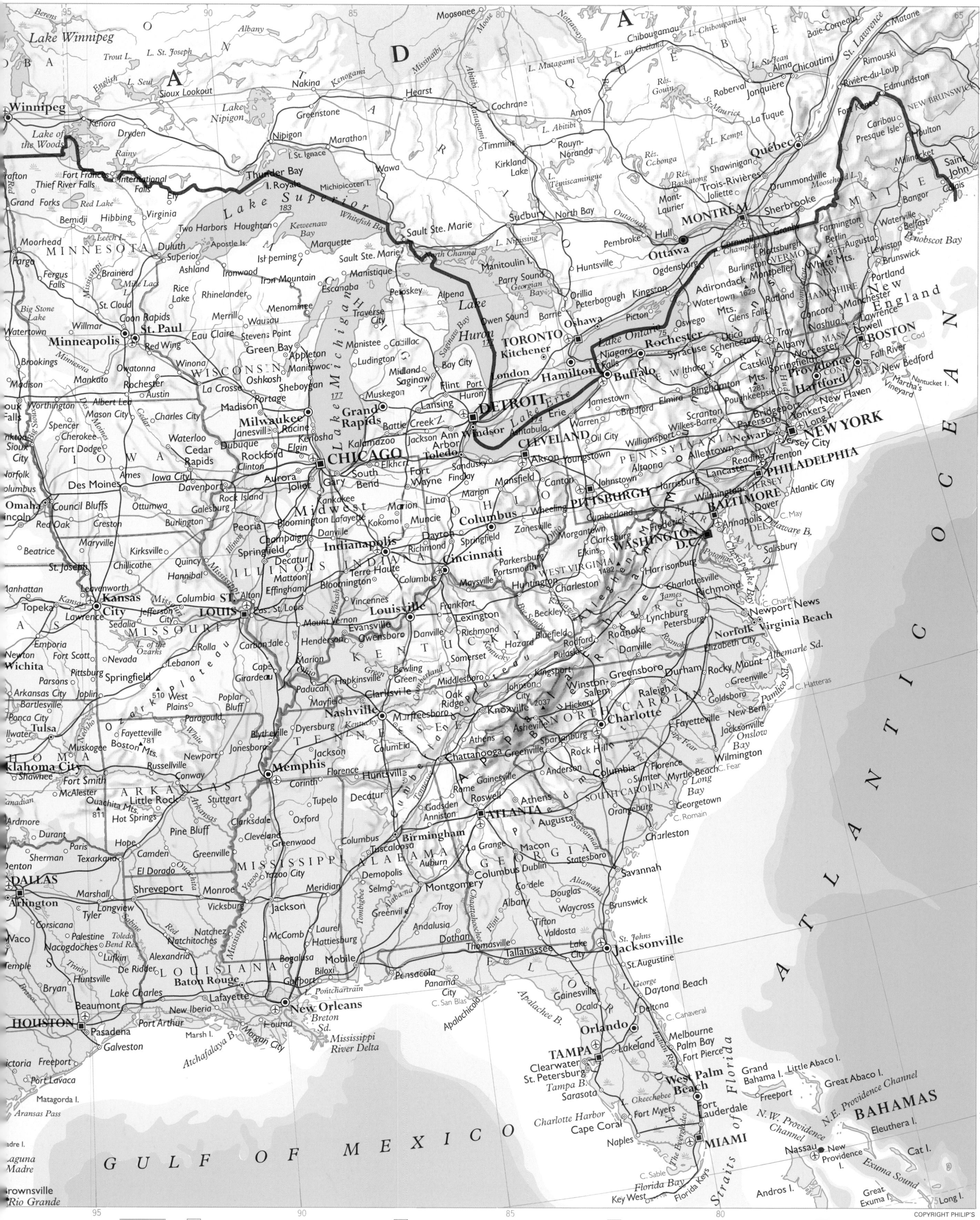

National Parks

National Parks

West from Greenwich

Projection: Bonne

1:5 000 000

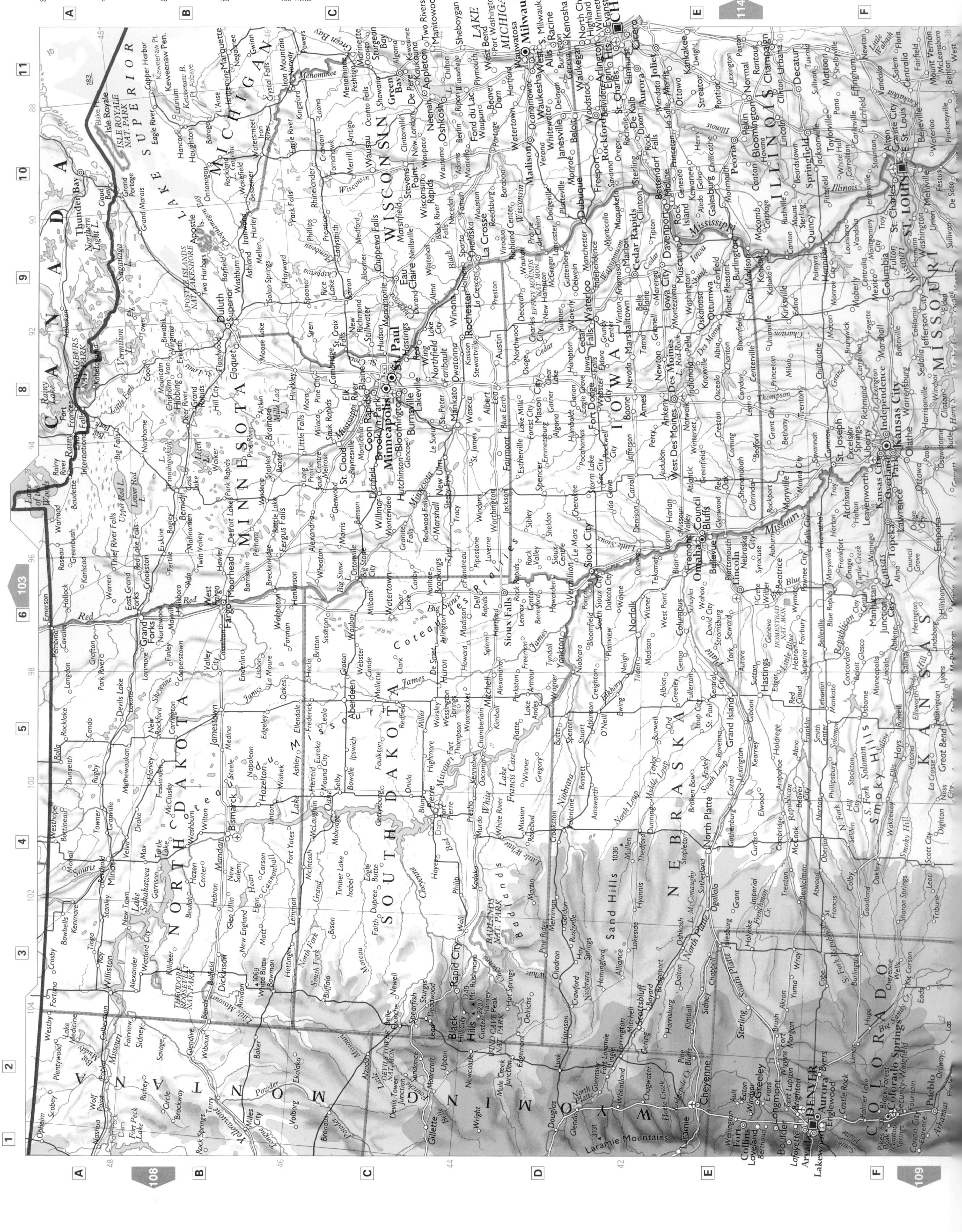

CANADA

LAKE SUPERIOR

MICHIGAN

WISCONSIN

MINNESOTA

NORTH DAKOTA

SOUTH DAKOTA

NEBRASKA

IOWA

ILLINOIS

MISSOURI

KANSAS

WYOMING

COLORADO

CHICAGO

Milwaukee

Minneapolis

St. Paul

Duluth

Des Moines

Sioux Falls

Omaha

Lincoln

Kansas City

St. Louis

Denver

Colorado Springs

Pueblo

Bismarck

Rapid City

Black Hills

Sand Hills

Badlands

Missouri

Mississippi

LAKE MICHIGAN

ISLE ROYALE NAT. PARK

THEODORE ROOSEVELT NAT. PARK

WIND CAVE NAT. PARK

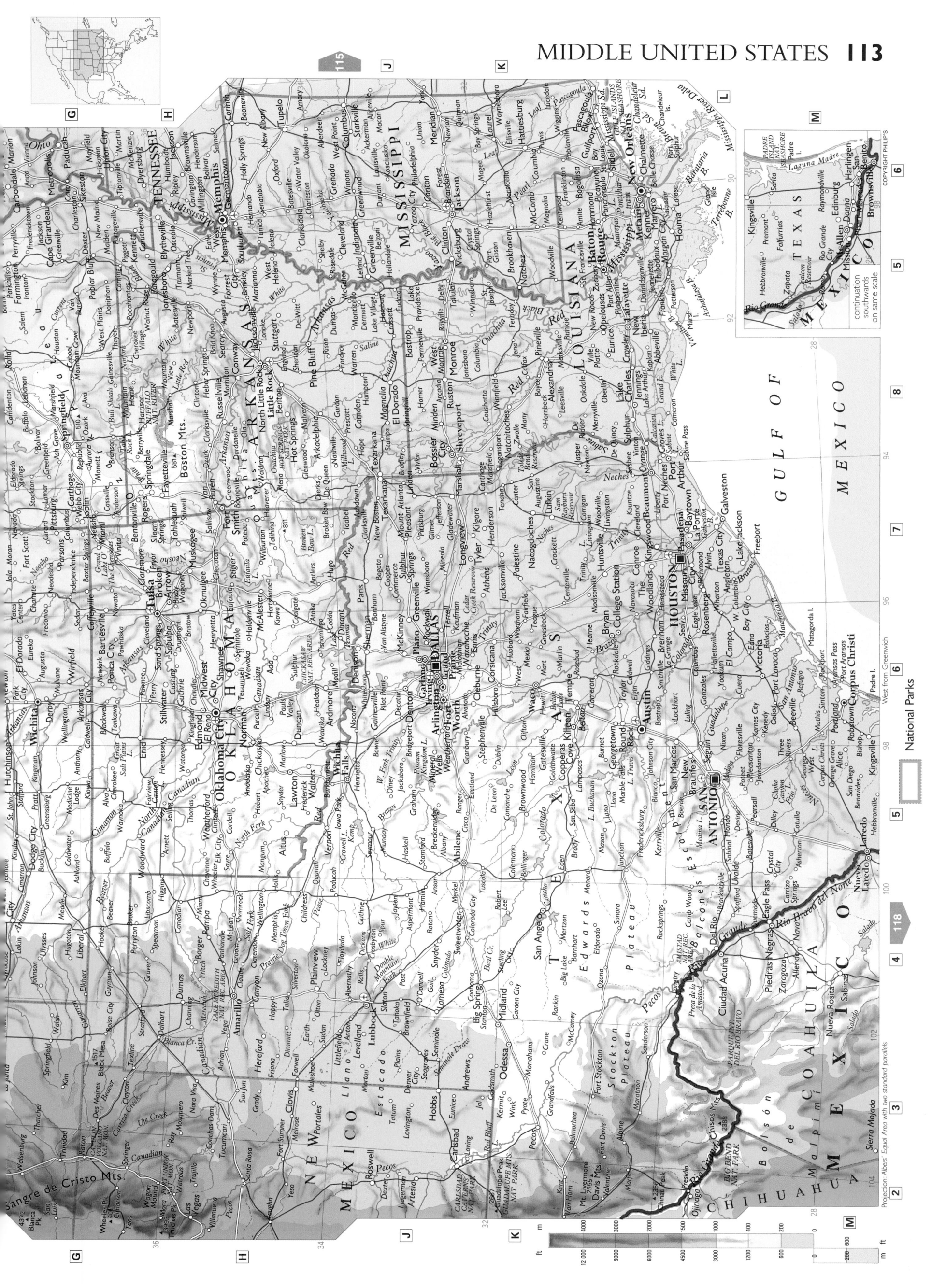

National Parks

Projection: Albers' Equal Area with two standard parallels

COPYRIGHT PHILIP'S

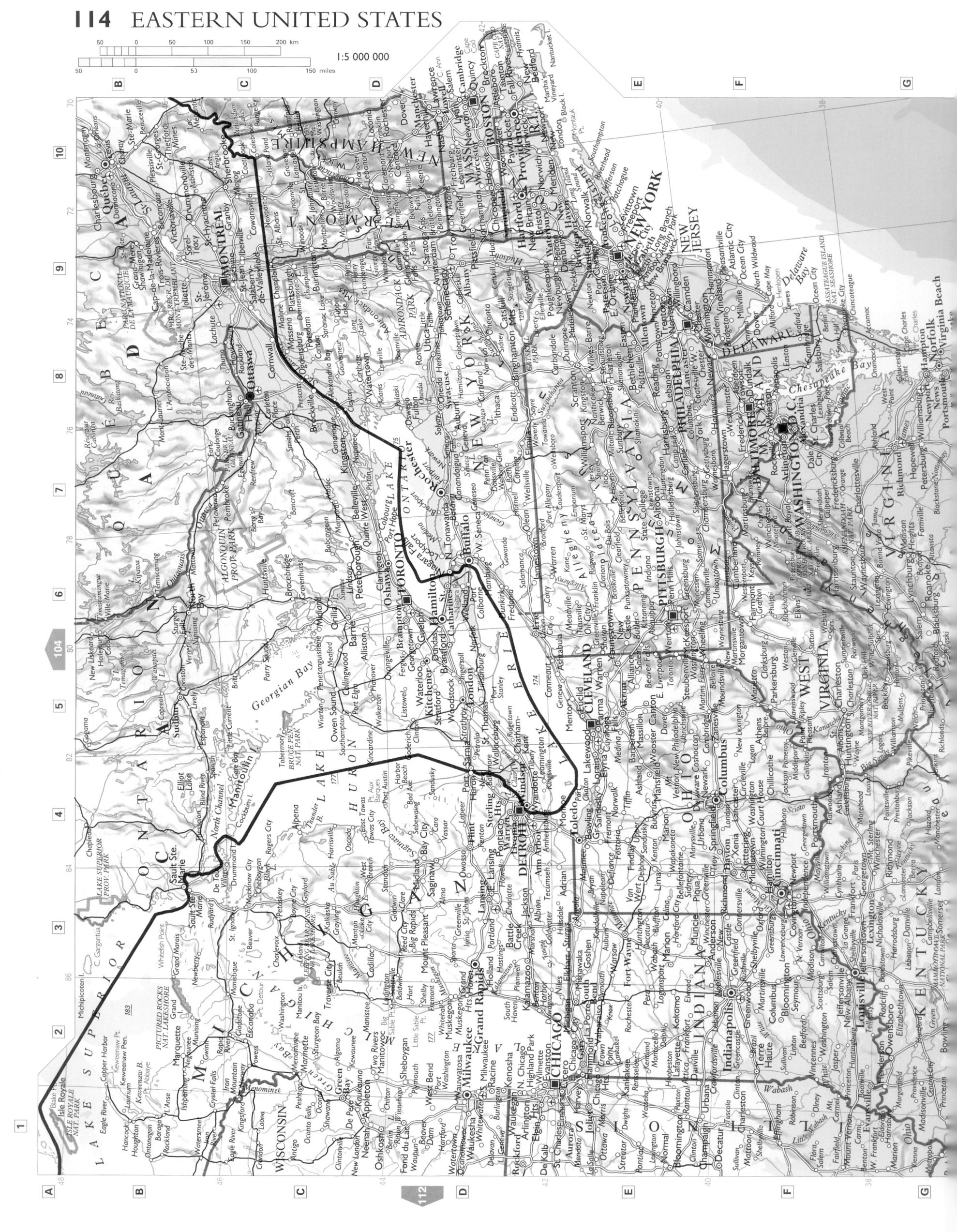

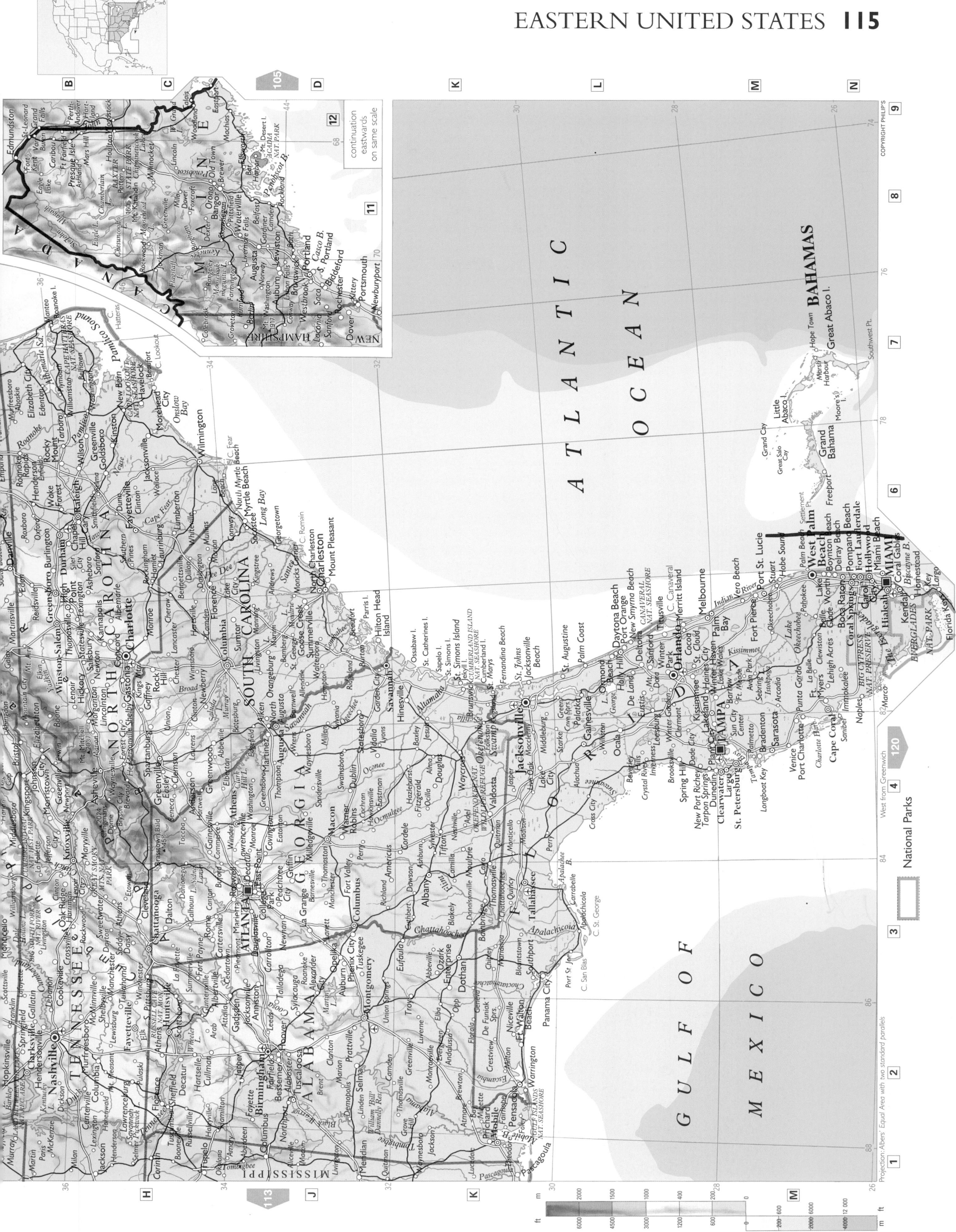

continuation eastwards on same scale

ATLANTIC

OCEAN

BAHAMAS

GULF OF

MEXICO

A T L A N T I C

National Parks

Projection: Albers' Equal Area with two standard parallels

West from Greenwich

1:2 100 000

National Parks

Projection: Bonne

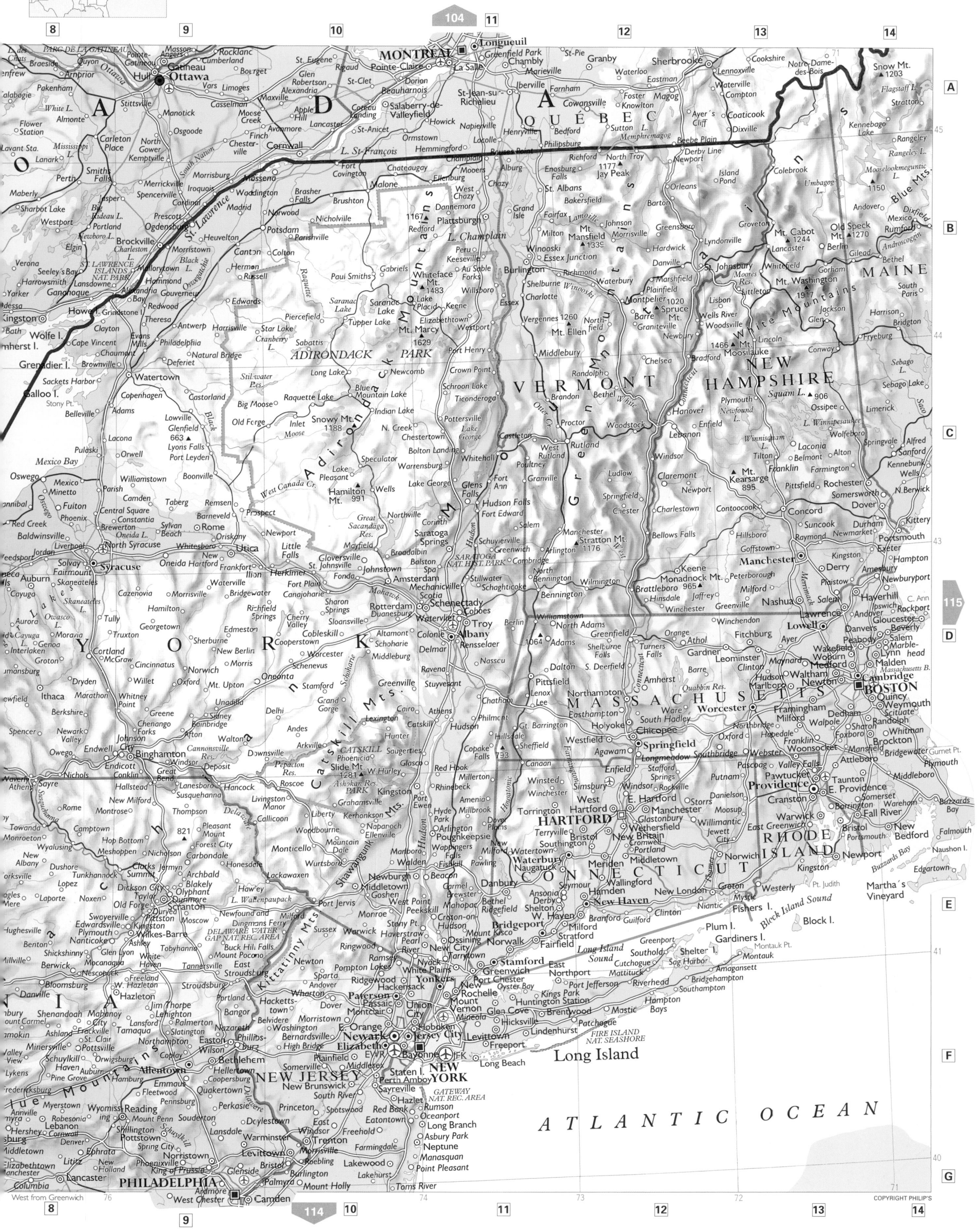

50 0 50 100 150 200 250 300 km

1:6 700 000

50 0 50 100 150 200 miles

Projection: Bi-polar oblique Conical Orthomorphic

West from Greenwich

National Parks

State names in Central Mexico

1 DISTRITO FEDERAL   5 MÉXICO
2 AGUASCALIENTES   6 MORELOS
3 GUANAJUATO   7 QUERÉTARO
4 HIDALGO   8 TLAXCALA

1:6 700 000

50 0 50 100 150 200 250 300 km
50 0 50 100 150 200 miles

JAMAICA
1:2 500 000

10 0 10 20 50 km
10 0 10 20 30 miles

GUADELOUPE AND MARTINIQUE
1:1 700 000

10 0 10 20 30 40 50 60 km
10 0 10 20 30 40 miles

GUADELOUPE
(Fr.)

MARTINIQUE
(Fr.)

Projection: Bi-polar oblique Conical Orthomorphic

ATLANTIC OCEAN

PUERTO RICO
1:2 500 000 | d
10 0 10 20 30 40 50 km
10 0 10 20 30 miles

PUERTO RICO (U.S.A.)

Pta. Aguijereada
Isabela
Aguadilla
Arecibo
Barceloneta
Manati
Vega Baja
Bayamón
San Juan SJU
Rio Grande
Carolina
Mayagüez
San Sebastián
Utuado
Cordillera Central
Caguas
Fajardo
Pta. Puerca
Dewey
Culebra
Adjuntas
1338 Cerro de Punta
Cayey
Humacao
Naguabo
Vieques
Esperanza
San German
Yauco
Coamo
Yabucoa
Ponce
Pta. Aguila
Guanica
Guayama
I. Caja de Muertos

VIRGIN ISLANDS
1:1 700 000 | e
10 0 10 20 30 km
10 0 10 20 miles

Rufling Pt.
The Settlement
Anegada
East Pt.
Virgin Islands (U.K.)
Jost Van Dyke I.
Great Camanoe
Guana I.
521 Beef I.
Virgin Gorda
Spanish Town
Virgin Is. (U.S.A.)
Hans Lollik I.
Tortola
Road Town
Peter I.
Charlotte Amalie
St. John I.
St. Thomas I.

ST. LUCIA
1:840 000 | f
5 0 10 km
5 0 5 10 miles

Cap Point
Pte. Hardy
Esperance Bay
Gros Islet
Marquis
Castries
L'Anse la Raye
Millet
Dennery
Canaries
Mt. Gimie 950
Soufrière
750 Petit Piton
Trou Gras Pt.
Soufrière Bay
795 Gros Piton
Micoud
Gros Piton Pt.
Vierge Pt.
Choiseul
ST. LUCIA
Laborie
Vieux Fort
C. Moule à Chique

ATLANTIC OCEAN
Crabhill
North Point
Spring Hall
Fustic
Portland
Boscobelle
Speightstown
245 Belleplaine
Westmoreland
Bathsheba
BARBADOS
Holetown
Mt. Hillaby 340
Hillcrest
Martin's Bay
Jackson
Bridgefield
Massiah Street
Ragged Pt.
Black Rock
Ellerton
Six Cross Roads
Bridgetown
Ivy
Edey
The Crane
St. Martins
Carlisle Bay
Oistins
Worthing
Oistins Bay
Chancery Lane
South Point

BARBADOS
1:840 000 | g
5 0 10 km
5 0 5 10 miles

AMAS

ATLANTIC OCEAN

Arthur's Town
The Bight
Cat I.
San Salvador I.
Conception I.
Rum Cay
Tropic of Cancer
Long I.
Clarence Town
Samana Cay
Crooked I. Passage
Crooked I.
Plana Cays
Albert Town
Snug Corner
Mayaguana I.
Acklins I.
Mira por vos Cay
Hogsty Reef
Caicos Passage
Turks & Caicos (U.K.)
Little Inagua I.
Caicos Is.
Cockburn Town
INAGUA
Turks Island Passage
Lake Rose
Great Inagua I.
Turks Is.
Matthew Town

Moa
Baracoa
Pta. de Maisi
Maisi
Î. de la Tortue
Monte Cristi
LA ISABELA
Santiago de los Cabelleros
Puerto Rico Trench
GUANTANAMO
Paso de los Vientos (Windward Passage)
Cap-Haïtien
Port-de-Paix
Milwaukee Deep 9200
GUANTANAMO (U.S.A.)
Jean Rabel
Cap-à-Foux
Puerto Plata
San Francisco de Macorís
Nagua
Samana
Fort Liberté
Gonaïves
La Vega
Sanchez
Sabana de la Mar
Mayari
St-Marc
Hinche
Central
3175
Pico Duarte HAITISES
Bayamón
SAN JUAN
Anegada
Virgin Gorda
Virgin Is. (U.K.)
Sombrero (U.K.)
Jérémie
Î. de la Gonâve
PORT-AU-PRINCE
L. Enriquillo
San Juan
Higüey
Hato Mayor
C. Engaño
Arecibo
Carolina
St. Thomas
Tortola
Road Town
Anguilla (U.K.)
ravassa I. (U.S.A.)
Dame
Petit Goâve
2280
SANTO DOMINGO
San Pedro de Macorís
La Romana
Aguadilla
1338
Fajardo
Charlotte Amalie
St-Martin (Fr.)
Marie
Les Cayes
Aquin
Jacmel
SIERRA DE BAORUCO
San Cristóbal
B. de Yuma
Mayagüez
Ponce
Caguas
Virgin Is. (U.S.A.)
St. Maarten (Neth.)
St-Barthélemy (Fr.)
Carcasse
Î. à Vache
Pedernales
Barahona
Isla de Compostela
I. Saona
Guayama
Christiansted
Saba (Neth.)
Barbuda
Pointe-à-Gravois
Hispaniola
I. Beata
C. Beata
Isla Mona (U.S.A.)
PUERTO RICO (U.S.A.)
Frederiksted
St. Croix
St. Eustatius (Neth.)
ST. KITTS & NEVIS
ANTIGUA & BARBUDA
Antilles
Nevis
Redonda
St. John's
Antigua
Montserrat (U.K.)
Ste-Rose
Moule
La Désirade
1467
GUADELOUPE (Fr.)
Pointe-à-Pitre
Basse-Terre
Marie-Galante (Fr.)
Grand-Bourg
I. des Saintes (Fr.)
Dominica Passage
I. de Aves (Venezuela)
Portsmouth
1447
DOMINICA
Roseau
MORNE TROIS PITONS
Martinique Passage
Mt. Pelée 1397
Ste-Marie
Le François
Fort-de-France
Rivière-Pilote
MARTINIQUE (Fr.)
St. Lucia Channel
Castries
ST. LUCIA
Soufrière
St. Vincent Passage
Soufrière 1234
St. Vincent
Kingstown
Speightstown
BARBADOS
Bridgetown
ST. VINCENT & THE GRENADINES
Hillsborough
Grenadines
St. George's
GRENADA

BEAN **SEA**

CARIBBEAN SEA

Lesser Antilles

Leeward Islands
Windward Islands

Pta. Gallinas
Oranjestad
Aruba (Neth.)
Curaçao
Bonaire
C. San Román
NETH. ANTILLES
I. Blanquilla (Ven.)
Tobago
MACURIA
Pen. de la Guajira
Pen. de Paraguaná
Willemstad
Is. Las Aves (Ven.)
ARC. LOS ROQUES
I. Orchila (Ven.)
I. Los Hermanos (Ven.)
Scarborough
Port of Spain
Punto Fijo
Is. Los Roques (Ven.)
Is. Los Testigos (Ven.)
COLOMBIA
Ríohacha
Uribia
Golfo de Venezuela
Punta Cardón
NUEVA ESPARTA
I. de Margarita (Ven.)
Tobago
Santa Marta
GUAJIRA
Pta. Espada
MÉDANOS DE CORO
Puerto Cumarebo
Cerro El Copey
Porlamar
Port of Spain
TAYRONA
ISLA DE SALAMANCA
Pen. de la Guajira
La Vela de Coro
Cerro El Copey
La Asunción
Río Caribe
Pen. de Paria
Trinidad
Ciénaga
Sierra Nevada de Sta. Marta
CUEVA DE LA QUEBRADA DEL TORO
FALCÓN
Tucacas
Maiquetía
La Guaira
I. La Tortuga (Ven.)
Cumaná
Carúpano
Güiria
Arima
QUILLA
Baranoa
San Rafael
Mene de Mauroa
Tocuyo
Puerto Cabello
CARACAS
VARGAS
Higuerote
Río Chico
LAGUNA DE LA RESTINGA
Cariaco
TURÉPANO
Río Claro
TRINIDAD & TOBAGO
LÁNTICO
Soledad
La Concepción
Santa Rita
Cabimas
San Felipe
Maracay
MIRANDA
Puerto La Cruz
Los Teques
Carúpano
San Fernando
Fundación
Calamar
Agustín Codazzi
Ciudad Ojeda
Carora
CARABOBO
Barcelona
Caicara
MAGDALENA
MARACAIBO
LARA
Valencia
Villa de Cura
Ocumare del Tuy
MONAGAS
Carmen
Machiques
Lago de Maracaibo
BARQUISIMETO
YARACUY
San Juan de los Morros
Maturín
MARIUSA
César
ZULIA
Mene Grande
TEREMINA
El Tocuyo
Aragua de Barcelona
Anaco
DELTA
Zambrano
PERIJA
TRUJILLO
CHIVACOA
El Guache
GUÁRICO
El Tigre
Tucupita
Mompos
CIÉNAGAS DEL CATATUMBO
Betijoque
COJEDES
El Sombrero
AMACURO
Sincé
Magangué
Valera
PORTUGUESA
Valle de la Pascua
Los Barrancos
Corozal
El Banco
Trujillo
Guanare
Portuguesa
Cantaura
Ayapel
Entrerríos
San Carlos del Zulia
MÉRIDA
Acarigua
Calabozo
Pariaguán
Ciudad Guayana
NORTE DE SANTANDER
TÁCHIRA
Barinas
El Baúl
Santa María de Ipire
Soledad
Sierra Imataca
Carmen
Ocaña
Libertad
BARINAS
GUÁRICO
ANZOÁTEGUI
El Pao
Marcos Planeta
Cord. de Mérida
Bolivia
Puerto de Nutrias
Uñare
Ciudad Bolívar
Rica
SANTANDER
Cúcuta
VENEZUELA
San Fernando de Apure
Manapire
Mapire
BA
Caucasia
Simití
Barbara
Bruzual
Apure
Embalse de Guri
El Callao
Orinoco
Guasipati
Cúcuta
Calcara
Upata
Tumeremo

West from Greenwich

COPYRIGHT PHILIP'S

4000 3000 2000 1500 1000 400 200 0
12 000 9000 6000 4500 3000 1200 600 0 ft
600 6000 12 000 18 000 24 000 ft
200 2000 4000 6000 8000 m

National Parks

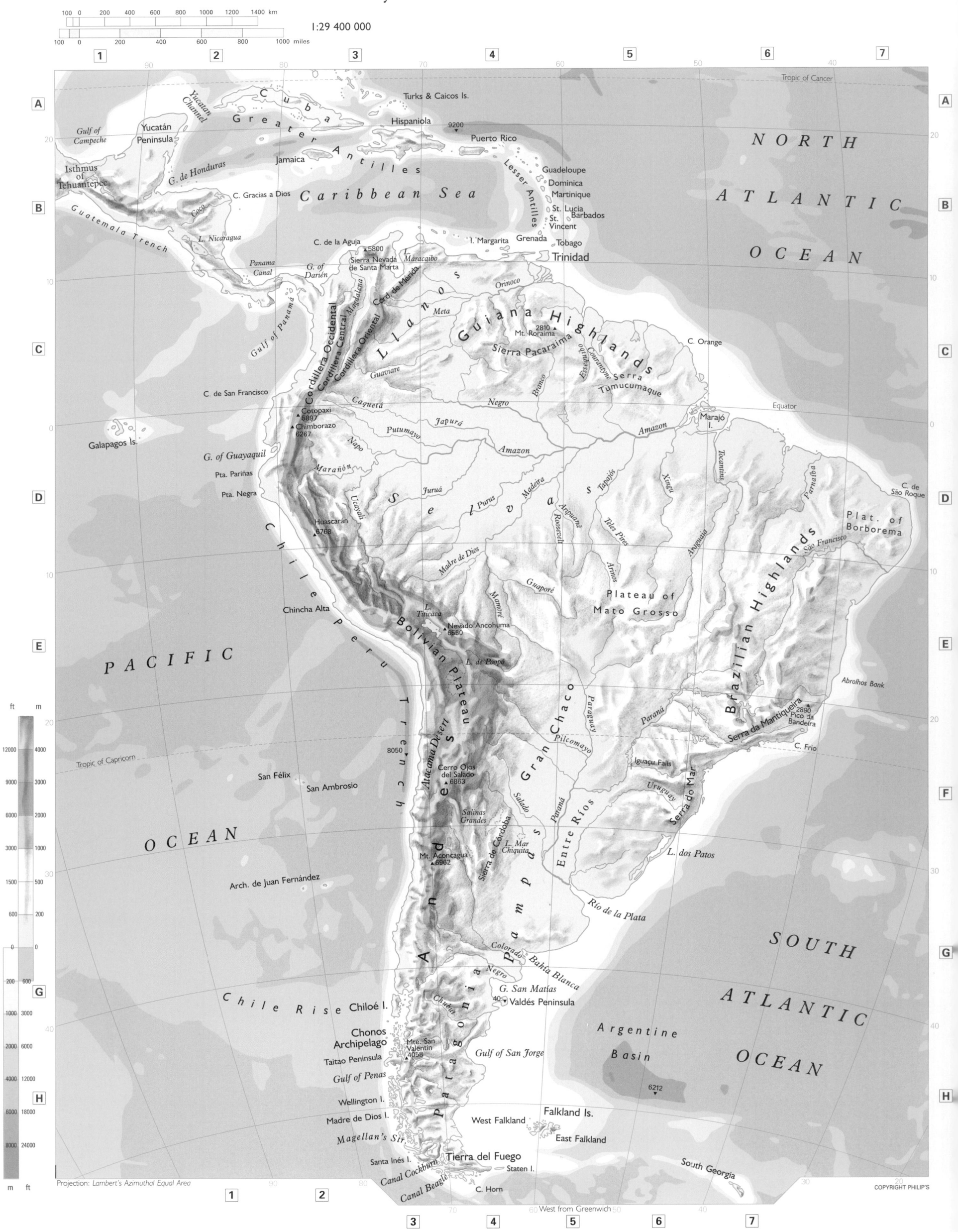

1:29 400 000

Projection: Lambert's Azimuthal Equal Area

COPYRIGHT PHILIP'S

1:29 400 000

Projection: Lambert's Azimuthal Equal Area

COPYRIGHT PHILIP'S

■ LIMA Capital Cities

1:13 400 000

ATLANTIC

OCEAN

TRINIDAD AND TOBAGO
1:2 100 000

Tobago

Trinidad

ATLANTIC OCEAN

Golfo de Paria

Port of Spain

Serpent's Mouth

VENEZUELA

West from Greenwich

AMAPÁ

A M A Z O N

P A R Á

MARANHÃO

PIAUÍ

CEARÁ

RIO GRANDE DO NORTE

PARAÍBA

PERNAMBUCO

FORTALEZA

Natal

RECIFE

João Pessoa

TERESINA

SÃO LUÍS

BELÉM

ALAGOAS

SERGIPE

BAHIA

Aracaju

SALVADOR

TOCANTINS

B R A Z I L

BRASÍLIA

GOIÁS

Goiânia

MINAS GERAIS

BELO HORIZONTE

MATO GROSSO

MATO GROSSO DO SUL

Campo Grande

SÃO PAULO

RIO DE JANEIRO

Vitória

COPYRIGHT PHILIP'S

1:6 700 000

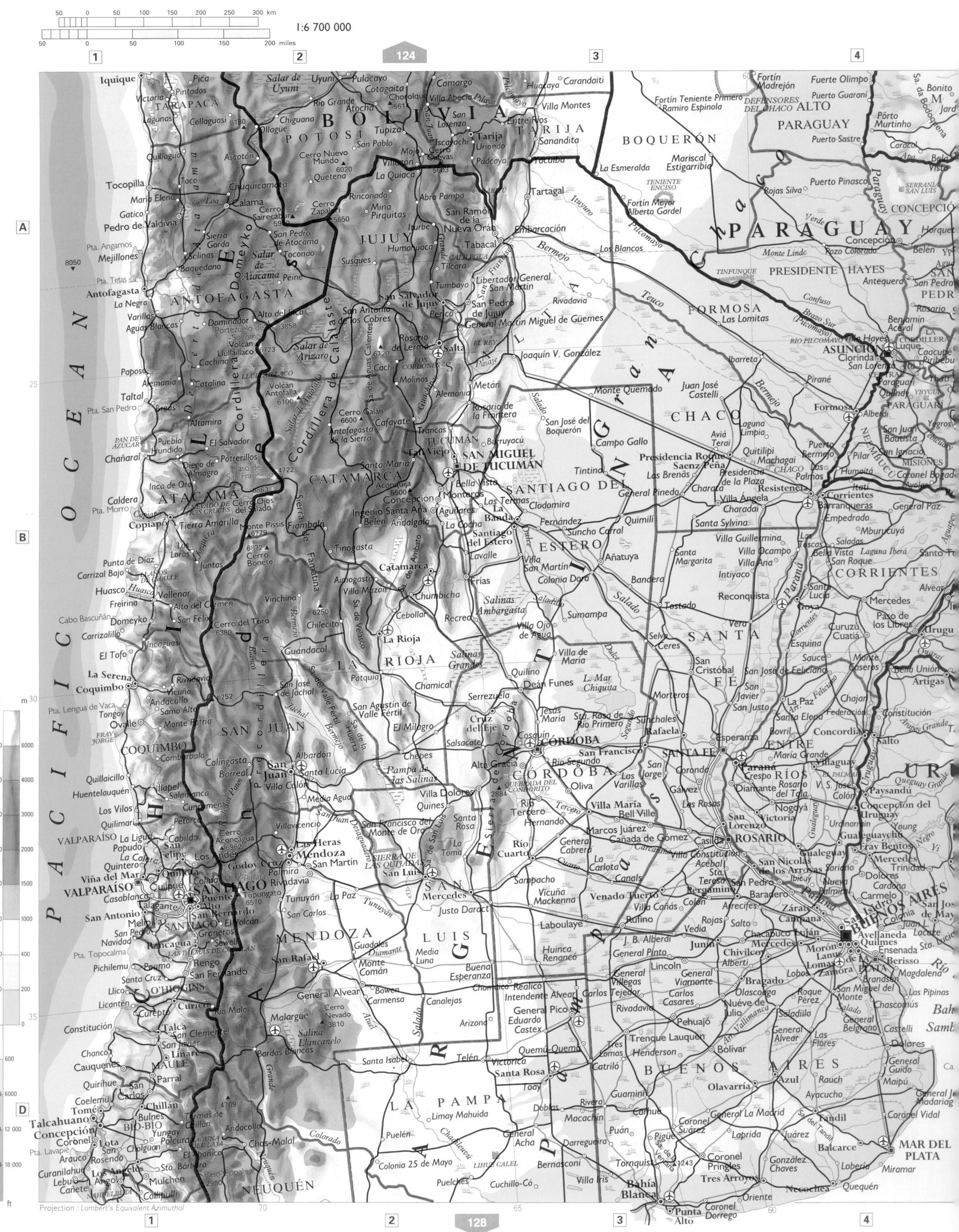

ATLANTIC

OCEAN

National Parks

1:13 400 000

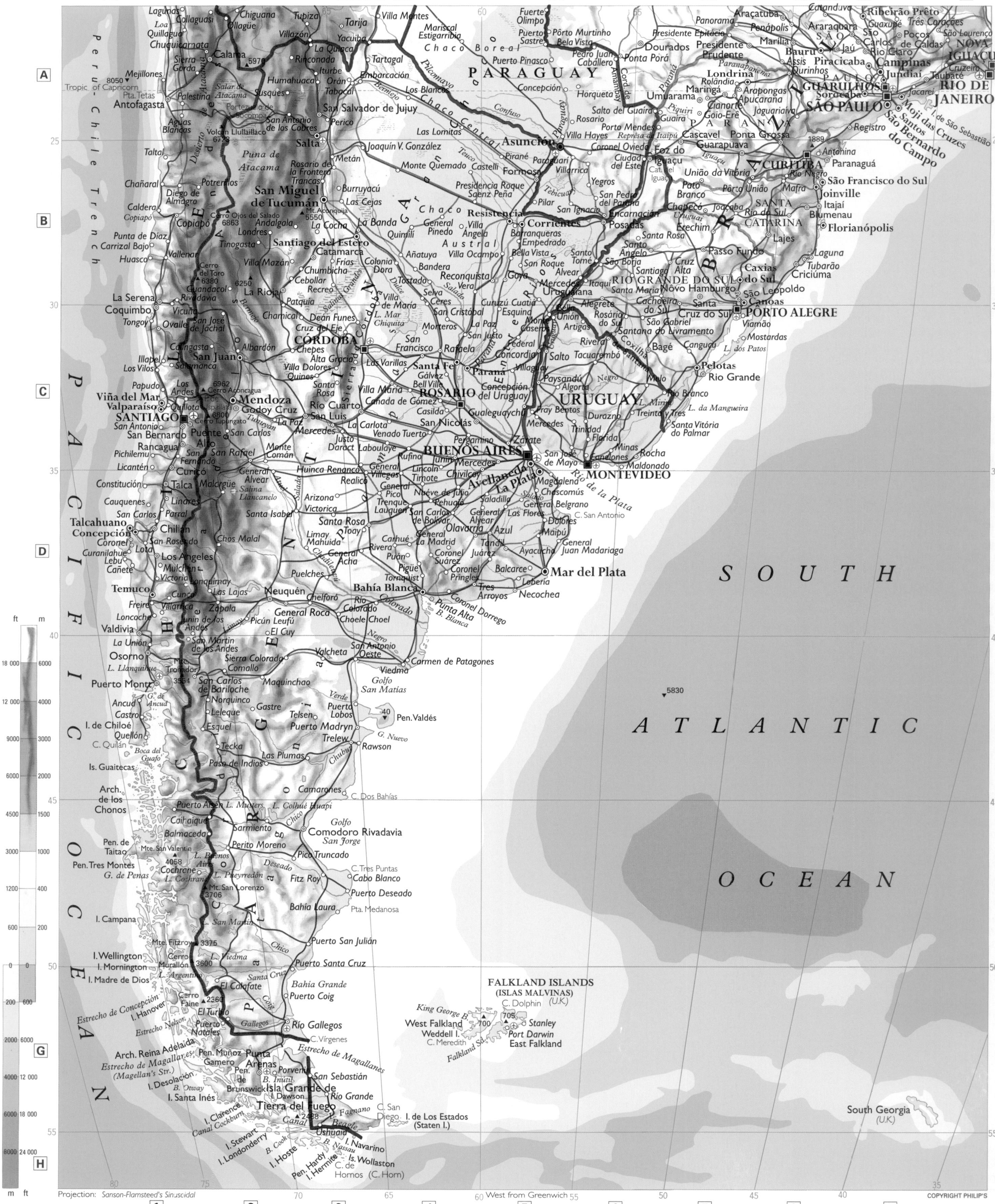

Projection: Sanson-Flamsteed's Sinusoidal

West from Greenwich

COPYRIGHT PHILIP'S

PARAGUAY

URUGUAY

SÃO PAULO

RIO DE JANEIRO

CURITIBA

PORTO ALEGRE

RIO GRANDE DO SUL

SANTA CATARINA

PARANÁ

ASUNCIÓN

CÓRDOBA

ROSARIO

BUENOS AIRES

MONTEVIDEO

SANTIAGO

MENDOZA

Mar del Plata

Bahía Blanca

Neuquén

Valdivia

Puerto Montt

Comodoro Rivadavia

Río Gallegos

Punta Arenas

Ushuaia

Tierra del Fuego

Isla Grande de Tierra del Fuego

C. de Hornos (C. Horn)

Estrecho de Magallanes (Magellan's Str.)

Pen. Valdés

Golfo San Matías

Golfo San Jorge

FALKLAND ISLANDS (ISLAS MALVINAS) (U.K.)

West Falkland

East Falkland

Stanley

Port Darwin

South Georgia (U.K.)

SOUTH ATLANTIC OCEAN

PACIFIC OCEAN

Peru–Chile Trench

Tropic of Capricorn

Chaco Boreal

Puna de Atacama

Desierto de Atacama

INDEX TO WORLD MAPS

How to use the index

The index contains the names of all the principal places and features shown on the World Maps. Each name is followed by an additional entry in italics giving the country or region within which it is located. The alphabetical order of names composed of two or more words is governed primarily by the first word and then by the second. This is an example of the rule:

Mīr Kūh, *Iran*	**71 E8**	26 22N 58 55 E
Mīr Shahdād, *Iran*	**71 E8**	26 15N 58 29 E
Mira, *Italy*	**41 C9**	45 26N 12 8 E
Mira por vos Cay, *Bahamas* .	**121 B5**	22 9N 74 30W
Miraj, *India*	**66 L9**	16 50N 74 45 E

Physical features composed of a proper name (Erie) and a description (Lake) are positioned alphabetically by the proper name. The description is positioned after the proper name and is usually abbreviated:

Erie, L., *N. Amer.* **116 D4** 42 15N 81 0W

Where a description forms part of a settlement or administrative name however, it is always written in full and put in its true alphabetic position:

Mount Isa, *Australia* .... **94 C2** 20 42 S 139 26 E

Names beginning with M' and Mc are indexed as if they were spelled Mac. Names beginning St. are alphabetized under Saint, but Sankt, Sint, Sant' Santa and San are all spelt in full and are alphabetized accordingly. If the same place name occurs two or more times in the index and all are in the same country, each is followed by the name of the administrative subdivision in which it is located.

The number in bold type which follows each name in the index refers to the number of the map page where that feature or place will be found. This is usually the largest scale at which the place or feature appears.

The letter and figure which are in bold type immediately after the page number give the grid square on the map page, within which the feature is situated. The letter represents the latitude and the figure the longitude. A lower case letter immediately after the page number refers to an inset map on that page.

In some cases the feature itself may fall within the specified square, while the name is outside. This is usually the case only with features which are larger than a grid square.

The geographical co-ordinates which follow the letter-figure references give the latitude and longitude of each place. The first co-ordinate indicates latitude – the distance north or south of the Equator. The second co-ordinate indicates longitude – the distance east or west of the Greenwich Meridian. Both latitude and longitude are measured in degrees and minutes (there are 60 minutes in a degree).

The latitude is followed by N(orth) or S(outh) and the longitude by E(ast) or W(est).

Rivers are indexed to their mouths or confluences, and carry the symbol ➔ after their names. The following symbols are also used in the index: ■ country, ☑ overseas territory or dependency, ☐ first order administrative area, △ national park, ⌒ other park (provincial park, nature reserve or game reserve), ✈ (LHR) principal airport (and location identifier).

How to pronounce place names

English-speaking people usually have no difficulty in reading and pronouncing correctly English place names. However, foreign place name pronunciations may present many problems. Such problems can be minimised by following some simple rules. However, these rules cannot be applied to all situations, and there will be many exceptions.

1. In general, stress each syllable equally, unless your experience suggests otherwise.
2. Pronounce the letter 'a' as a broad 'a' as in 'arm'.
3. Pronounce the letter 'e' as a short 'e' as in 'elm'.
4. Pronounce the letter 'i' as a cross between a short 'i' and long 'e', as the two 'i's in 'California'.
5. Pronounce the letter 'o' as an intermediate 'o' as in 'soft'.
6. Pronounce the letter 'u' as an intermediate 'u' as in 'sure'.
7. Pronounce consonants hard, except in the Romance-language areas where 'g's are likely to be pronounced softly like 'j' in 'jam'; 'j' itself may be pronounced as 'y'; and 'x's may be pronounced as 'h'.
8. For names in mainland China, pronounce 'q' like the 'ch' in 'chin', 'x' like the 'sh' in 'she', 'zh' like the 'j' in 'jam', and 'z' as if it were spelled 'dz'. In general pronounce 'a' as in 'father', 'e' as in 'but', 'i' as in 'keep', 'o' as in 'or', and 'u' as in 'rule'.

Moreover, English has no diacritical marks (accent and pronunciation signs), although some languages do. The following is a brief and general guide to the pronunciation of those most frequently used in the principal Western European languages.

		Pronunciation as in
French	é	day and shows that the e is to be pronounced; e.g. Orléans.
	è	mare
	î	used over any vowel and does not affect pronunciation; shows contraction of the name, usually omission of s' following a vowel.
	ç	's' before 'a', 'o' and 'u'.
	ë, ï, ü	over 'e', 'i' and 'u' when they are used with another vowel and shows that each is to be pronounced.
German	ä	fate
	ö	fur
	ü	no English equivalent; like French 'tu'
Italian	à, é	over vowels and indicates stress.
Portuguese	ã, õ	vowels pronounced nasally.
	ç	boss
	á	shows stress
	ô	shows that a vowel has an 'i' or 'u' sound combined with it.
Spanish	ñ	canyon
	ü	pronounced as w and separately from adjoining vowels.
	á	usually indicates that this is a stressed vowel.

Abbreviations

A.C.T. – Australian Capital Territory
A.R. – Autonomous Region
Afghan. – Afghanistan
Afr. – Africa
Ala. – Alabama
Alta. – Alberta
Amer. – America(n)
Arch. – Archipelago
Ariz. – Arizona
Ark. – Arkansas
Atl. Oc. – Atlantic Ocean
B. – Baie, Bahía, Bay, Bucht, Bugt
B.C. – British Columbia
Bangla. – Bangladesh
Barr. – Barrage
Bos.-H. – Bosnia-Herzegovina
C. – Cabo, Cap, Cape, Coast
C.A.R. – Central African Republic
C. Prov. – Cape Province
Calif. – California
Cat. – Catarata
Cent. – Central
Chan. – Channel
Colo. – Colorado
Conn. – Connecticut
Cord. – Cordillera
Cr. – Creek
Czech. – Czech Republic
D.C. – District of Columbia
Del. – Delaware
Dem. – Democratic
Dep. – Dependency
Des. – Desert
Dét. – Détroit
Dist. – District
Dj. – Djebel
Domin. – Dominica
Dom. Rep. – Dominican Republic

E. – East
E. Salv. – El Salvador
Eq. Guin – Equatorial Guinea
Est. – Estrecho
Falk. Is. – Falkland Is.
Fd. – Fjord
Fla. – Florida
Fr. – French
G. – Golfe, Golfo, Gulf, Guba, Gebel
Ga. – Georgia
Gt. – Great, Greater
Guinea-Biss. – Guinea-Bissau
H.K. – Hong Kong
H.P. – Himachal Pradesh
Hants. – Hampshire
Harb. – Harbor, Harbour
Hd. – Head
Hts. – Heights
I.(s). – Île, Ilha, Insel, Isla, Island, Isle
Ill. – Illinois
Ind. – Indiana
Ind. Oc. – Indian Ocean
Ivory C. – Ivory Coast
J. – Jabal, Jebel
Jaz. – Jazīrah
Junc. – Junction
K. – Kap, Kapp
Kans. – Kansas
Kep. – Kepulauan
Ky. – Kentucky
L. – Lac, Lacul, Lago, Lagoa, Lake, Limni, Loch, Lough
La. – Louisiana
Ld. – Land
Liech. – Liechtenstein
Lux. – Luxembourg
Mad. P. – Madhya Pradesh

Madag. – Madagascar
Man. – Manitoba
Mass. – Massachusetts
Md. – Maryland
Me. – Maine
Medit. S. – Mediterranean Sea
Mich. – Michigan
Minn. – Minnesota
Miss. – Mississippi
Mo. – Missouri
Mont. – Montana
Mozam. – Mozambique
Mt.(s) – Mont, Montaña, Mountain
Mte. – Monte
Mti. – Monti
N. – Nord, Norte, North, Northern, Nouveau
N.B. – New Brunswick
N.C. – North Carolina
N. Cal. – New Caledonia
N. Dak. – North Dakota
N.H. – New Hampshire
N.I. – North Island
N.J. – New Jersey
N. Mex. – New Mexico
N.S. – Nova Scotia
N.S.W. – New South Wales
N.W.T. – North West Territory
N.Y. – New York
N.Z. – New Zealand
Nac. – Nacional
Nat. – National
Nebr. – Nebraska
Neths. – Netherlands
Nev. – Nevada
Nfld. – Newfoundland
Nic. – Nicaragua
O. – Oued, Ouadi
Occ. – Occidentale

Okla. – Oklahoma
Ont. – Ontario
Or. – Orientale
Oreg. – Oregon
Os. – Ostrov
Oz. – Ozero
P. – Pass, Passo, Pasul, Pulau
P.E.I. – Prince Edward Island
Pa. – Pennsylvania
Pac. Oc. – Pacific Ocean
Papua N.G. – Papua New Guinea
Pass. – Passage
Peg. – Pegunungan
Pen. – Peninsula, Péninsule
Phil. – Philippines
Pk. – Peak
Plat. – Plateau
Prov. – Province, Provincial
Pt. – Point
Pta. – Ponta, Punta
Pte. – Pointe
Qué. – Québec
Queens. – Queensland
R. – Rio, River
R.I. – Rhode Island
Ra. – Range
Raj. – Rajasthan
Recr. – Recreational, Récréatif
Reg. – Region
Rep. – Republic
Res. – Reserve, Reservoir
Rhid-Pfz. – Rheinland-Pfalz
S. – South, Southern, Sur
Si. Arabia – Saudi Arabia
S.C. – South Carolina
S. Dak. – South Dakota
S.I. – South Island
S. Leone – Sierra Leone
Sa. – Serra, Sierra

Sask. – Saskatchewan
Scot. – Scotland
Sd. – Sound
Serbia & M. – Serbia & Montenegro
Sev. – Severnaya
Sib. – Siberia
Sprs. – Springs
St. – Saint
Sta. – Santa
Ste. – Sainte
Sto. – Santo
Str. – Strait, Stretto
Switz. – Switzerland
Tas. – Tasmania
Tenn. – Tennessee
Terr. – Territory, Territoire
Tex. – Texas
Tg. – Tanjung
Trin. & Tob. – Trinidad & Tobago
U.A.E. – United Arab Emirates
U.K. – United Kingdom
U.S.A. – United States of America
Ut. P. – Uttar Pradesh
Va. – Virginia
Vdkhr. – Vodokhranilishche
Vdskh. – Vodoskhovyshche
Vf. – Vîrful
Vic. – Victoria
Vol. – Volcano
Vt. – Vermont
W. – Wadi, West
W. Va. – West Virginia
Wall. & F. Is. – Wallis and Futuna Is.
Wash. – Washington
Wis. – Wisconsin
Wlkp. – Wielkopolski
Wyo. – Wyoming
Yorks. – Yorkshire

A

A 'Âli an Nîl □, Sudan 81 F3 9 30N 33 0 E
A Baña, Spain 36 C2 42 58N 8 46W
A Cañiza, Spain 36 C2 42 13N 8 16W
A Coruña, Spain 36 B2 43 20N 8 25W
A Estrada, Spain 36 C2 42 43N 8 27W
A Fonsagrada, Spain 36 B3 43 8N 7 4W
A Guarda, Spain 36 D2 41 56N 8 52W
A Gudiña, Spain 36 C3 42 4N 7 8W
A Rúa, Spain 36 C3 42 24N 7 6W
Aachen, Germany 24 E2 50 45N 6 6 E
Aalborg = Ålborg, Denmark 11 G3 57 2N 9 54 E
Aalen, Germany 25 G6 48 51N 10 6 E
Aalst, Belgium 17 D4 50 56N 4 2 E
Aalten, Neths. 17 C6 51 56N 6 35 E
Aalter, Belgium 17 C3 51 5N 3 28 E
Äänekoski, Finland 9 E21 62 36N 25 44 E
Aarau, Switz. 25 H4 47 23N 8 4 E
Aarberg, Switz. 25 H3 47 2N 7 16 E
Aare →, Switz. 25 H4 47 33N 8 14 E
Aargau □, Switz. 25 H4 47 26N 8 10 E
Aarhus = Århus, Denmark 11 H4 56 8N 10 11 E
Aarschot, Belgium 17 D4 50 59N 4 49 E
Aba, China 58 A3 32 59N 101 42 E
Aba, Dem. Rep. of the Congo 86 B3 3 58N 30 17 E
Aba, Nigeria 83 D6 5 10N 7 19 E
Âbâ, Jazîrat, Sudan 81 E3 13 30N 32 31 E
Abaco I., Bahamas 120 A4 26 25N 77 10W
Abadab, J., Sudan 80 D4 18 54N 35 56 E
Ābādān, Iran 71 D6 30 22N 48 20 E
Abade, Ethiopia 81 F4 9 22N 38 3 E
Ābādeh, Iran 71 D7 31 8N 52 40 E
Abadin, Spain 36 B3 43 21N 7 29W
Abadla, Algeria 78 B5 31 2N 2 45W
Abaetetuba, Brazil 125 D9 1 40 S 48 50W
Abagnar Qi, China 56 C9 43 52N 116 2 E
Abah, Tanjung, Indonesia 63 K18 8 46 S 115 38 E
Abai, Paraguay 127 B4 25 58 S 55 54W
Abak, Nigeria 83 E6 4 58N 7 50 E
Abakaliki, Nigeria 83 D6 6 22N 8 2 E
Abakan, Russia 53 D10 53 40N 91 10 E
Abala, Niger 83 C5 14 56N 3 22 E
Abalak, Niger 83 B6 15 22N 6 21 E
Abalemma, Niger 83 B6 16 12N 7 50 E
Abana, Turkey 72 B6 41 59N 34 1 E
Abancay, Peru 124 F4 13 35 S 72 55W
Abano Terme, Italy 41 C8 45 22N 11 46 E
Abarán, Spain 39 G3 38 12N 1 23W
Abariringa, Kiribati 96 H10 2 50 S 171 40W
Abarqū, Iran 71 D7 31 10N 53 20 E
Abashiri, Japan 54 B12 44 0N 144 15 E
Abashiri-Wan, Japan 54 C12 44 0N 144 30 E
Abaújszántó, Hungary 28 B6 48 16N 21 12 E
Abava →, Latvia 30 A8 57 6N 21 54 E
Ābay = Nîl el Azraq →, Sudan 81 D3 15 38N 32 31 E
Abay, Kazakhstan 52 E8 49 38N 72 53 E
Abaya, L., Ethiopia 81 F4 6 30N 37 50 E
Abayita-Shala Lakes △, Ethiopia 81 F4 7 40N 38 37 E
Abaza, Russia 52 D9 52 39N 90 6 E
Abbadia di Fiastra ⌂, Italy 41 E10 43 12N 13 24 E
Abbadia San Salvatore, Italy 41 F8 42 53N 11 41 E
'Abbāsābād, Iran 71 C8 33 34N 58 23 E
Abbay = Nîl el Azraq →, Sudan 81 D3 15 38N 32 31 E
Abbaye, Pt., U.S.A. 114 B1 46 58N 88 8W
Abbé, L., Ethiopia 81 E5 11 8N 41 47 E
Abbeville, France 19 B8 50 6N 1 49 E
Abbeville, Ala., U.S.A. 115 K3 31 34N 85 15W
Abbeville, La., U.S.A. 113 L8 29 58N 92 8W
Abbeville, S.C., U.S.A. 115 H4 34 11N 82 23W
Abbiategrasso, Italy 40 C5 45 24N 8 54 E
Abbot Ice Shelf, Antarctica 5 D16 73 0 S 92 0W
Abbottabad, Pakistan 68 B5 34 10N 73 15 E
Abd al Kūrī, Yemen 75 E5 12 5N 52 20 E
Ābdar, Iran 71 D7 30 16N 55 19 E
'Abdolābād, Iran 71 C8 34 12N 56 30 E
Abdulpur, Bangla. 69 G13 24 15N 88 59 E
Abéché, Chad 79 F10 13 50N 20 35 E
Abejar, Spain 38 D2 41 48N 2 47W
Abekr, Sudan 81 E2 12 45N 28 50 E
Abel Tasman △, N.Z. 91 J4 40 59 S 173 3 E
Abengourou, Ivory C. 82 D4 6 42N 3 27W
Abenójar, Spain 37 G6 38 53N 4 21W
Åbenrå, Denmark 11 J3 55 3N 9 25 E
Abensberg, Germany 25 G7 48 48N 11 51 E
Abeokuta, Nigeria 83 D5 7 3N 3 19 E
Aber, Uganda 86 B3 2 12N 32 25 E
Aberaeron, U.K. 15 E3 52 15N 4 15W
Aberayron = Aberaeron, U.K. 15 E3 52 15N 4 15W
Aberchirder, U.K. 13 D6 57 34N 2 37W
Abercorn, Australia 95 D5 25 12 S 151 5 E
Aberdare, U.K. 15 F4 51 43N 3 27W
Aberdare △, Kenya 86 C4 0 22 S 36 44 E
Aberdare Ra., Kenya 86 C4 0 15 S 36 50 E
Aberdeen, Australia 95 E5 32 9 S 150 56 E
Aberdeen, Canada 103 C7 52 20N 106 8W
Aberdeen, S. Africa 88 E3 32 28 S 24 2 E
Aberdeen, U.K. 13 D6 57 9N 2 5W
Aberdeen, Ala., U.S.A. 115 J1 33 49N 88 33W
Aberdeen, Idaho, U.S.A. 108 E7 42 57N 112 50W
Aberdeen, Md., U.S.A. 114 F7 39 31N 76 10W
Aberdeen, S. Dak., U.S.A. 112 C5 45 28N 98 29W
Aberdeen, Wash., U.S.A. 110 D3 46 59N 123 50W
Aberdeen, City of □, U.K. 13 D6 57 10N 2 10W
Aberdeenshire □, U.K. 13 D6 57 17N 2 36W
Aberdovey = Aberdyfi, U.K. 15 E3 52 33N 4 3W
Aberdyfi, U.K. 15 E3 52 33N 4 3W
Aberfeldy, U.K. 13 E5 56 37N 3 51W
Aberfoyle, U.K. 13 E4 56 11N 4 23W
Abergavenny, U.K. 15 F4 51 49N 3 1W
Abergele, U.K. 14 D4 53 17N 3 35W
Abernathy, U.S.A. 113 J4 33 50N 101 51W
Abert, L., U.S.A. 108 E3 42 38N 120 14W
Aberystwyth, U.K. 15 E3 52 25N 4 5W
Abhā, Si. Arabia 75 D3 18 0N 42 34 E
Abhar, Iran 71 B6 36 9N 49 13 E
Abhayapuri, India 69 F14 26 24N 90 38 E
Abia □, Nigeria 83 D6 5 30N 7 35 E
Abide, Turkey 47 C11 38 55N 29 20 E
Abidiya, Sudan 80 D3 18 18N 34 3 E
Abidjan, Ivory C. 82 D4 5 26N 3 58W
Abilene, Kans., U.S.A. 112 F6 38 55N 97 13W
Abilene, Tex., U.S.A. 113 J5 32 28N 99 43W
Abingdon, U.K. 15 F6 51 40N 1 17W
Abingdon, U.S.A. 115 G5 36 43N 81 59W
Abington Reef, Australia 94 B4 18 0 S 149 35 E
Abitau →, Canada 103 B7 59 53N 109 3W
Abitibi →, Canada 104 B3 51 3N 80 55W
Abitibi, L., Canada 104 C4 48 40N 79 40W
Abiy Adi, Ethiopia 81 E4 13 39N 39 3 E
Abkhaz Republic = Abkhazia □, Georgia 35 J5 43 12N 41 5 E
Abkhazia □, Georgia 35 J5 43 12N 41 5 E
Abminga, Australia 95 D1 26 8 S 134 51 E
Abnûb, Egypt 80 B3 27 18N 31 4 E
Åbo = Turku, Finland 9 F20 60 30N 22 19 E
Abocho, Nigeria 83 D6 7 35N 6 56 E
Abohar, India 68 D6 30 10N 74 10 E
Aboisso, Ivory C. 82 D4 5 30N 3 5W
Abomey, Benin 83 D5 7 10N 2 5 E
Abong-Mbang, Cameroon 84 D2 4 0N 13 8 E
Abonnema, Nigeria 83 E6 4 41N 6 49 E
Abony, Hungary 28 C5 47 12N 20 3 E
Aboso, Ghana 82 D4 5 23N 1 57W
Abou-Deïa, Chad 79 F9 11 20N 19 20 E
Aboyne, U.K. 13 D6 57 4N 2 47W
Abra Pampa, Argentina 126 A2 22 43 S 65 42W
Abraham L., Canada 102 C5 52 15N 116 35W
Abrantes, Portugal 37 F2 39 24N 8 7W
Abreojos, Pta., Mexico 118 B2 26 50N 113 40W
Abri, Esh Shamâliya, Sudan 80 C3 20 50N 30 27 E
Abri, Janub Kordofân, Sudan 81 E3 11 40N 30 21 E
Abrolhos, Banka, Brazil 122 E7 18 0 S 38 0W
Abrud, Romania 28 D8 46 19N 23 5 E
Abruzzo □, Italy 41 F10 42 15N 14 0 E
Absaroka Range, U.S.A. 108 D9 44 45N 109 50W
Abtenau, Austria 26 D6 47 33N 13 21 E
Abu, India 68 G5 24 41N 72 50 E
Abū al Abyad, U.A.E. 71 E7 24 11N 53 50 E
Abū al Khaşīb, Iraq 71 D6 30 25N 48 0 E
Abū 'Alī, Si. Arabia 71 E6 27 20N 49 27 E
Abū 'Alī →, Lebanon 74 A4 34 25N 35 50 E
Abu Ballas, Egypt 80 C2 24 26N 27 36 E
Abu Deleiq, Sudan 81 D3 15 57N 33 48 E
Abu Dhabi = Abū Ẓāby, U.A.E. 71 E7 24 28N 54 22 E
Abu Dis, Sudan 80 D3 19 12N 33 38 E
Abu Dom, Sudan 81 D3 16 18N 32 25 E
Abū Du'ān, Syria 70 B3 36 25N 38 15 E
Abu el Gairi, W. →, Egypt 74 F2 29 35N 33 30 E
Abu Fatma, Ras, Sudan 80 C4 22 25N 36 25 E
Abu Gabra, Sudan 81 E2 11 2N 26 50 E
Abu Ga'da, W. →, Egypt 74 F1 29 15N 32 53 E
Abu Gelba, Sudan 81 E3 13 11N 31 52 E
Abu Gubeiha, Sudan 81 E3 11 30N 31 15 E
Abu Habl, Khawr →, Sudan 81 E3 12 37N 31 0 E
Abū Ḩadrīyah, Si. Arabia 71 E6 27 20N 48 58 E
Abu Hamed, Sudan 80 D3 19 32N 33 13 E
Abu Haraz, An Nîl el Azraq, Sudan 80 D3 18 1N 33 58 E
Abu Haraz, El Gezira, Sudan 81 E3 14 35N 33 30 E
Abu Haraz, Esh Shamâliya, Sudan 80 D3 19 8N 32 18 E
Abu Higar, Sudan 81 E3 12 50N 33 59 E
Abū Kamāl, Syria 70 C4 34 30N 41 0 E
Abu Kuleiwat, Sudan 81 E2 12 20N 26 0 E
Abū Madd, Ra's, Si. Arabia 70 E3 24 50N 37 7 E
Abu Matariq, Sudan 81 E2 10 59N 26 9 E
Abu Mendi, Ethiopia 81 E4 11 48N 35 42 E
Abū Mūsā, U.A.E. 71 E7 25 52N 55 3 E
Abū Qaşr, Si. Arabia 70 D3 30 21N 38 34 E
Abu Qir, Egypt 80 H7 31 18N 30 0 E
Abu Qireiya, Egypt 80 C4 24 5N 35 28 E
Abu Qurqâs, Egypt 80 B3 28 1N 30 44 E
Abu Shagara, Ras, Sudan 80 C4 21 4N 37 19 E
Abu Shanab, Sudan 81 E2 13 58N 27 49 E
Abu Simbel, Egypt 80 C3 22 18N 31 40 E
Abū Şukhayr, Iraq 70 D5 31 54N 44 30 E
Abu Sultân, Egypt 80 H8 30 24N 32 21 E
Abu Tabari, Sudan 80 D2 17 32N 28 32 E
Abu Tig, Egypt 80 B3 27 4N 31 15 E
Abu Tiga, Sudan 81 E3 12 47N 34 12 E
Abu Tineitin, Sudan 81 E3 14 24N 31 1 E
Abu Uruq, Sudan 81 D3 15 52N 30 25 E
Abu Zabad, Sudan 81 E2 12 25N 29 10 E
Abū Ẓāby, U.A.E. 71 E7 24 28N 54 22 E
Abū Zeydābād, Iran 71 C6 33 54N 51 45 E
Abuja, Nigeria 83 D6 9 5N 7 32 E
Abukuma-Gawa →, Japan 54 E10 38 6N 140 52 E
Abukuma-Sammyaku, Japan 54 F10 37 30N 140 45 E
Abunã, Brazil 124 E5 9 40 S 65 20W
Abunã →, Brazil 124 E5 9 41 S 65 20W
Abune Yosef, Ethiopia 81 E4 12 5N 39 12 E
Aburo, Dem. Rep. of the Congo 86 B3 2 4N 30 53 E
Abut Hd., N.Z. 91 K3 43 7 S 170 15 E
Abuye Meda, Ethiopia 81 E4 10 30N 39 49 E
Abwong, Sudan 81 F3 9 2N 32 14 E
Åby, Sweden 11 F10 58 40N 16 10 E
Aby, Lagune, Ivory C. 82 D4 5 15N 3 14W
Abyad, Sudan 81 E2 13 47N 26 24 E
Åbybro, Denmark 11 G3 57 10N 9 44 E
Acadia △, U.S.A. 115 C11 44 20N 68 13W
Açailândia, Brazil 125 D9 4 57 S 47 0W
Acajutla, El Salv. 120 D2 13 36N 89 50W
Acámbaro, Mexico 118 D4 20 0N 100 40W
Acanthus, Greece 44 F7 40 27N 23 47 E
Acaponeta, Mexico 118 C3 22 30N 105 20W
Acapulco, Mexico 119 D5 16 51N 99 56W
Acarai, Serra, Brazil 124 C7 1 50N 57 50W
Acarigua, Venezuela 124 B5 9 33N 69 12W
Acatlán, Mexico 119 D5 18 10N 98 3W
Acayucan, Mexico 119 D6 17 59N 94 58W
Accéglio, Italy 40 D4 44 28N 7 0 E
Accomac, U.S.A. 114 G8 37 43N 75 40W
Accous, France 20 E3 43 0N 0 36W
Accra, Ghana 83 D4 5 35N 0 6W
Accrington, U.K. 14 D5 53 45N 2 22W
Acebal, Argentina 126 C3 33 20 S 60 50W
Aceh □, Indonesia 62 D1 4 15N 97 30 E
Acerra, Italy 43 B7 40 57N 14 22 E
Aceuchal, Spain 37 G4 38 39N 6 30W
Achalpur, India 66 J10 21 22N 77 32 E
Acheng, China 57 B14 45 30N 126 58 E
Achenkirch, Austria 26 D4 47 32N 11 45 E
Achensee, Austria 26 D4 47 26N 11 45 E
Acher, India 68 H5 23 10N 72 32 E
Achern, Germany 25 G4 48 37N 8 4 E
Achill Hd., Ireland 12 C1 53 58N 10 15W
Achill I., Ireland 12 C1 53 58N 10 1W
Achim, Germany 24 B5 53 1N 9 3 E
Achinsk, Russia 53 D10 56 20N 90 20 E
Acıgöl, Turkey 47 D11 37 50N 29 50 E
Acıpayam, Turkey 47 D11 37 26N 29 22 E
Acireale, Italy 43 E8 37 37N 15 10 E
Ackerman, U.S.A. 113 J10 33 19N 89 11W
Acklins I., Bahamas 121 B5 22 30N 74 0W
Acme, Canada 102 C6 51 33N 113 30W
Acme, U.S.A. 116 F5 40 8N 79 26W
Aconcagua, Cerro, Argentina 126 C2 32 39 S 70 0W
Aconquija, Mt., Argentina 126 B2 27 0 S 66 0W
Açores, Is. dos, Atl. Oc. 78 A1 38 0N 27 0W
Acornhoek, S. Africa 89 C5 24 37 S 31 2 E
Acquapendente, Italy 41 F8 42 44N 11 52 E
Acquasanta Terme, Italy 41 F10 42 46N 13 24 E
Acquasparta, Italy 41 F9 42 41N 12 33 E
Acquaviva delle Fonti, Italy 43 B9 40 54N 16 50 E
Ácqui Terme, Italy 40 D5 44 41N 8 28 E
Acraman, L., Australia 95 E2 32 2 S 135 23 E
Acre = 'Akko, Israel 74 C4 32 55N 35 4 E
Acre □, Brazil 124 E4 9 1 S 71 0W
Acre →, Brazil 124 E5 8 45 S 67 22W
Acri, Italy 43 C9 39 29N 16 23 E
Acs, Hungary 28 C3 47 42N 18 2 E
Actium, Greece 46 C2 38 57N 20 45 E
Acton, Canada 116 C4 43 38N 80 3W
Acuña, Mexico 118 B4 29 18N 100 55W
Ad Dammām, Si. Arabia 71 E6 26 20N 50 5 E
Ad Dāmūr, Lebanon 74 B4 33 44N 35 27 E
Ad Dawādimī, Si. Arabia 70 E5 24 35N 44 15 E
Ad Dawḩah, Qatar 71 E6 25 15N 51 35 E
Ad Dawr, Iraq 70 C4 34 27N 43 47 E
Ad Dir'īyah, Si. Arabia 70 E5 24 44N 46 35 E
Ad Dīwānīyah, Iraq 70 D5 32 0N 45 0 E
Ad Dujayl, Iraq 70 C5 33 51N 44 14 E
Ad Duwayd, Si. Arabia 70 D4 30 15N 42 17 E
Ada, Ghana 83 D5 5 44N 0 40 E
Ada, Serbia & M. 28 E5 45 49N 20 9 E
Ada, Minn., U.S.A. 112 B6 47 18N 96 31W
Ada, Okla., U.S.A. 113 H6 34 46N 96 41W
Adabiya, Egypt 74 F1 29 53N 32 28 E
Adair, C., Canada 101 A12 71 30N 71 34W
Adaja →, Spain 36 D6 41 32N 4 52W
Adak I., U.S.A. 100 C2 51 45N 176 45W
Adamaoua, Massif de l', Cameroon 83 D7 7 20N 12 20 E
Adamawa □, Nigeria 83 D7 9 20N 12 30 E
Adamawa Highlands = Adamaoua, Massif de l', Cameroon 83 D7 7 20N 12 20 E
Adamello ⌂, Italy 40 B7 46 4N 10 28 E
Adamello, Mte., Italy 40 B7 46 9N 10 30 E
Adami Tulu, Ethiopia 81 F4 7 53N 38 41 E
Adaminaby, Australia 95 F4 36 0 S 148 45 E
Adams, Mass., U.S.A. 117 D11 42 38N 73 7W
Adams, N.Y., U.S.A. 117 C8 43 49N 76 1W
Adams, Wis., U.S.A. 112 D10 43 57N 89 49W
Adams, Mt., U.S.A. 110 D5 46 12N 121 30W
Adam's Bridge, Sri Lanka 66 Q11 9 15N 79 40 E
Adams L., Canada 102 C5 51 10N 119 40W
Adam's Peak, Sri Lanka 66 R12 6 48N 80 30 E
Adamuz, Spain 37 G6 38 2N 4 32W
Adana, Turkey 70 B2 37 0N 35 16 E
Adanero, Spain 36 E6 40 56N 4 36W
Adapazarı = Sakarya, Turkey 72 B4 40 48N 30 25 E
Adar Gwagwa, J., Sudan 80 C4 22 15N 35 20 E
Adarama, Sudan 81 D3 17 10N 34 52 E
Adare, C., Antarctica 5 D11 71 0 S 171 0 E
Adarte, Eritrea 81 E5 13 18N 42 8 E
Adaut, Indonesia 63 F8 8 8 S 131 7 E
Adavale, Australia 95 D3 25 52 S 144 32 E
Adda →, Italy 40 C6 45 8N 9 53 E
Addis Ababa = Addis Abeba, Ethiopia 81 F4 9 2N 38 42 E
Addis Abeba, Ethiopia 81 F4 9 2N 38 42 E
Addis Alem, Ethiopia 81 F4 9 0N 38 17 E
Addis Zemen, Ethiopia 81 E4 12 7N 37 47 E
Addison, U.S.A. 116 D7 42 1N 77 14W
Addo, S. Africa 88 E4 33 32 S 25 45 E
Addo △, S. Africa 88 E4 33 30 S 25 50 E
Adebour, Niger 83 C7 13 17N 11 50 E
Ādeh, Iran 70 B5 37 42N 45 11 E
Adel, U.S.A. 115 K4 31 8N 83 25W
Adelaide, Australia 95 E2 34 52 S 138 30 E
Adelaide, S. Africa 88 E4 32 42 S 26 20 E
Adelaide I., Antarctica 5 C17 67 15 S 68 30W
Adelaide Pen., Canada 100 B10 68 15N 97 30W
Adelaide River, Australia 92 B5 13 15 S 131 7 E
Adelaide Village, Bahamas 120 A4 25 0N 77 31W
Adelanto, U.S.A. 111 L9 34 35N 117 22W
Adele I., Australia 92 C3 15 32 S 123 9 E
Adélie, Terre, Antarctica 5 C10 68 0 S 140 0 E
Adelie Land = Adélie, Terre, Antarctica 5 C10 68 0 S 140 0 E
Adelsk, Belarus 30 E10 53 24N 23 47 E
Ademuz, Spain 38 E3 40 5N 1 13W
Aden = Al 'Adan, Yemen 75 E4 12 45N 45 0 E
Aden, G. of, Asia 75 E4 12 30N 47 30 E
Adendorp, S. Africa 88 E3 32 15 S 24 30 E
Aderbissinat, Niger 83 B6 15 34N 7 54 E
Adh Dhayd, U.A.E. 71 E7 25 17N 55 53 E
Adhoi, India 68 H4 23 26N 70 32 E
Adi, Indonesia 63 E8 4 15 S 133 30 E
Adi Arkai, Ethiopia 81 E4 13 35N 37 57 E
Adi Daro, Ethiopia 81 E4 14 20N 38 14 E
Adi Keyih, Eritrea 81 E4 14 51N 39 22 E
Adi Kwala, Eritrea 81 E4 14 38N 38 48 E
Adi Ugri, Eritrea 81 E4 14 58N 38 48 E
Adieu, C., Australia 93 F5 32 0 S 132 10 E
Adieu Pt., Australia 92 C3 15 14 S 124 35 E
Adigala, Ethiopia 81 E5 10 24N 42 15 E
Adige →, Italy 41 C9 45 9N 12 20 E
Adigrat, Ethiopia 81 E4 14 20N 39 26 E
Adıgüzel Barajı, Turkey 47 C11 38 13N 29 14 E
Adilabad, India 66 K11 19 33N 78 20 E
Adilcevaz, Turkey 73 C10 38 47N 42 43 E
Adirondack ⌂, U.S.A. 117 C10 44 0N 74 20W
Adirondack Mts., U.S.A. 117 C10 44 0N 74 0W
Adis Abeba = Addis Abeba, Ethiopia 81 F4 9 2N 38 42 E
Adıyaman, Turkey 73 D8 37 45N 38 16 E
Adjohon, Benin 83 D5 6 41N 2 32 E
Adjud, Romania 29 D12 46 7N 27 10 E
Adjumani, Uganda 86 B3 3 20N 31 50 E
Adjuntas, Puerto Rico 121 d 18 10N 66 43W
Adlavik Is., Canada 105 B8 55 0N 58 40W
Adler, Russia 35 J4 43 28N 39 52 E
Admer, Algeria 83 A6 20 21N 5 27 E
Admiralty G., Australia 92 B4 14 20 S 125 55 E
Admiralty I., U.S.A. 102 B2 57 30N 134 30W
Admiralty Is., Papua N. G. 96 H6 2 0 S 147 0 E
Adnan Menderes, İzmir ✈ (ADB), Turkey 47 C9 38 23N 27 6 E
Ado, Nigeria 83 D5 6 36N 2 56 E
Ado-Ekiti, Nigeria 83 D6 7 38N 5 12 E
Adok, Sudan 81 F3 8 10N 30 20 E
Adola, Ethiopia 81 E5 11 14N 41 44 E
Adonara, Indonesia 63 F6 8 15 S 123 5 E
Adoni, India 66 M10 15 33N 77 18 E
Adony, Hungary 28 C3 47 6N 18 52 E
Adour →, France 20 E2 43 32N 1 32W
Adra, India 69 H12 23 30N 86 42 E
Adra, Spain 37 J7 36 43N 3 3W
Adrano, Italy 43 E7 37 40N 14 50 E
Adrar, Mauritania 78 D3 20 30N 7 30 E
Adrar des Iforas, Algeria 78 C5 27 51N 0 11 E
Ádria, Italy 41 C9 45 3N 12 3 E
Adrian, Mich., U.S.A. 114 E3 41 54N 84 2W
Adrian, Tex., U.S.A. 113 H3 35 16N 102 40W
Adriatic Sea, Medit. S. 6 G9 43 0N 16 0 E
Adua, Indonesia 63 E7 1 45 S 129 50 E
Adwa, Ethiopia 81 E4 14 15N 38 52 E
Adygea □, Russia 35 H5 45 0N 40 0 E
Adzhar Republic = Ajaria □, Georgia 35 K6 41 30N 42 0 E
Adzopé, Ivory C. 82 D4 6 7N 3 49W
Ægean Sea, Medit. S. 47 C7 38 30N 25 0 E
Aerhtai Shan, Mongolia 60 B4 46 40N 92 45 E
Ærø, Denmark 11 K4 54 52N 10 25 E
Ærøskøbing, Denmark 11 K4 54 53N 10 24 E
Aëtós, Greece 46 D3 37 15N 21 50 E
'Afak, Iraq 70 C5 32 4N 45 15 E
Afándou, Greece 49 C10 36 18N 28 12 E
Afar □, Ethiopia 81 E5 12 0N 41 0 E
Afghanistan ■, Asia 66 C4 33 0N 65 0 E
Afikpo, Nigeria 83 D6 5 53N 7 54 E
Aflou, Algeria 78 B6 34 7N 2 3 E
Afragóla, Italy 43 B7 40 55N 14 18 E
Afram →, Ghana 83 D4 7 0N 0 52W
Afrera, Ethiopia 81 E5 13 16N 41 5 E
Africa 76 E6 10 0N 20 0 E
'Afrīn, Syria 70 B3 36 32N 36 50 E
Afşin, Turkey 72 C7 38 14N 36 55 E
Afton, N.Y., U.S.A. 117 D9 42 14N 75 32W
Afton, Wyo., U.S.A. 108 E8 42 44N 110 56W
Afuá, Brazil 125 D8 0 15 S 50 20W
'Afula, Israel 74 C4 32 37N 35 17 E
Afyon, Turkey 47 C12 38 45N 30 33 E
Afyon □, Turkey 47 C12 38 25N 30 30 E
Afyonkarahisar = Afyon, Turkey 47 C12 38 45N 30 33 E
Aga, Egypt 80 H7 30 55N 31 10 E
Agadès = Agadez, Niger 83 B6 16 58N 7 59 E
Agadez, Niger 83 B6 16 58N 7 59 E
Agadir, Morocco 78 B4 30 28N 9 55W
Agaete, Canary Is. 48 F4 28 6N 15 43W
Agaie, Nigeria 83 D6 9 1N 6 18 E
Again, Sudan 81 F2 8 28N 29 55 E
Agalega Is., Mauritius 3 E12 11 0 S 57 0 E
Ağapınar, Turkey 47 B12 39 48N 30 47 E
Agar, India 68 H7 23 40N 76 2 E
Agaro, Ethiopia 81 F4 7 50N 36 38 E
Agartala, India 67 H17 23 50N 91 23 E
Agăş, Romania 29 D11 46 28N 26 15 E
Agassiz, Canada 102 D4 49 14N 121 46W
Agats, Indonesia 63 F9 5 33 S 138 0 E
Agawam, U.S.A. 117 D12 42 5N 72 37W
Agbélouvé, Togo 83 D5 6 35N 1 14 E
Agboville, Ivory C. 82 D4 5 55N 4 15W
Ağcabädi, Azerbaijan 35 K8 40 5N 47 27 E
Ağdam, Azerbaijan 35 L8 40 0N 46 58 E
Ağdaş, Azerbaijan 35 K8 40 44N 47 22 E
Agde, France 20 E7 43 19N 3 28 E
Agde, C. d', France 20 E7 43 16N 3 28 E
Agdzhabedi = Ağcabädi, Azerbaijan 35 K8 40 5N 47 27 E
Agen, France 20 D4 44 12N 0 38 E
Agerbæk, Denmark 11 J2 55 36N 8 48 E
Agersø, Denmark 11 J5 55 13N 11 12 E
Ageyevo, Russia 32 E9 54 10N 36 27 E
Aggteleki △, Hungary 28 B5 48 27N 20 36 E
Āgh Kand, Iran 71 B6 37 15N 48 4 E
Aghireşu, Romania 29 D8 46 53N 23 15 E
Aginskoye, Russia 53 D12 51 6N 114 32 E
Ağlasun, Turkey 47 D12 37 39N 30 31 E
Agly →, France 20 F7 42 46N 3 3 E
Agnew, Australia 93 E3 28 1 S 120 31 E
Agnibilékrou, Ivory C. 82 D4 7 10N 3 11W
Agnita, Romania 29 E9 45 59N 24 40 E
Agnone, Italy 41 G11 41 48N 14 22 E
Agofie, Ghana 83 D5 8 27N 0 15 E
Agogna →, Italy 40 C5 45 4N 8 54 E
Agogo, Sudan 81 F2 7 50N 28 45 E
Agön, Sweden 10 C11 61 34N 17 23 E
Agon Coutainville, France 18 C5 49 2N 1 34W
Ágordo, Italy 41 B9 46 18N 12 2 E
Agori, India 69 G10 24 33N 82 57 E
Agouna, Benin 83 D5 7 39N 1 47 E
Agout →, France 20 E5 43 47N 1 41 E
Agra, India 68 F7 27 17N 77 58 E
Agrakhanskiuy Poluostrov, Russia 35 J8 43 42N 47 36 E
Agramunt, Spain 38 D6 41 48N 1 6 E
Agreda, Spain 38 D3 41 51N 1 55W
Ağri, Turkey 73 C10 39 44N 43 3 E
Agri →, Italy 43 B9 40 13N 16 44 E
Ağrı Dağı, Turkey 70 B5 39 50N 44 15 E
Ağri Karakose = Ağri, Turkey 73 C10 39 44N 43 3 E
Agriá, Greece 46 B5 39 20N 23 1 E
Agrigento, Italy 42 E6 37 19N 13 34 E
Agrínion, Greece 46 C3 38 37N 21 27 E
Agrópoli, Italy 43 B7 40 21N 14 59 E
Ağstafa, Azerbaijan 35 K7 41 7N 45 27 E
Agua Caliente, Baja Calif., Mexico 111 N10 32 29N 116 59W
Agua Caliente, Sinaloa, Mexico 118 B3 26 30N 108 20W
Agua Caliente Springs, U.S.A. 111 N10 32 56N 116 19W
Água Clara, Brazil 125 H8 20 25 S 52 45W
Agua Fria ⌂, U.S.A. 109 J8 34 14N 112 0W
Agua Hechicero, Mexico 111 N10 32 26N 116 14W
Agua Prieta, Mexico 118 A3 31 20N 109 32W
Aguadilla, Puerto Rico 121 d 18 26N 67 10W
Aguadulce, Panama 120 E3 8 15N 80 32W
Aguanga, U.S.A. 111 M10 33 27N 116 51W
Aguanish, Canada 105 B7 50 14N 62 2W
Aguanus →, Canada 105 B7 50 13N 62 5W
Aguapey →, Argentina 126 B4 29 7 S 56 36W
Aguaray Guazú →, Paraguay 126 A4 24 47 S 57 19W
Aguarico →, Ecuador 124 D3 0 59 S 75 11W
Aguaro-Guariquito △, Venezuela 121 E6 8 20N 66 35W
Aguas →, Spain 38 D4 41 20N 0 30W
Aguas Blancas, Chile 126 A2 24 15 S 69 55W
Aguas Calientes, Sierra de, Argentina 126 B2 25 26 S 66 40W
Aguascalientes, Mexico 118 C4 21 53N 102 12W
Aguascalientes □, Mexico 118 C4 22 0N 102 20W
Agudo, Spain 37 G6 38 59N 4 52W
Águeda, Portugal 36 E2 40 34N 8 27W
Agueda →, Spain 36 D4 41 2N 6 56W
Aguelhok, Mali 83 B5 19 29N 0 52 E
Aguié, Niger 83 C6 13 31N 7 46 E
Aguila, Punta, Puerto Rico 121 d 17 57N 67 13W
Aguilafuente, Spain 36 D6 41 13N 4 7W
Aguilar, Spain 37 H6 37 31N 4 40W
Aguilar de Campóo, Spain 36 C6 42 47N 4 15W
Aguilares, Argentina 126 B2 27 26 S 65 35W
Aguilas, Spain 39 H3 37 23N 1 35W
Agüimes, Canary Is. 48 G4 27 58N 15 27W
Aguja, C. de la, Colombia 122 B3 11 18N 74 12W
Agujereada, Pta., Puerto Rico 121 d 18 30N 67 8W
Agulaa, Ethiopia 81 E4 13 40N 39 40 E
Agulhas, C., S. Africa 88 E3 34 52 S 20 0 E
Agulo, Canary Is. 48 F2 28 11N 17 12W
Agung, Gunung, Indonesia 63 J18 8 20 S 115 28 E
Agur, Uganda 86 B3 2 28N 32 55 E
Agusan →, Phil. 61 G6 9 0N 125 30 E
Ağva, Turkey 45 E13 41 8N 29 51 E
Agvali, Russia 35 J8 42 36N 46 8 E
Aha Mts., Botswana 88 B3 19 45 S 21 0 E
Ahaggar, Algeria 78 D7 23 0N 6 30 E
Ahamansu, Ghana 83 D5 7 38N 0 35 E
Ahar, Iran 70 B5 38 35N 47 0 E
Ahat, Turkey 47 C11 38 39N 29 47 E
Ahaus, Germany 24 C2 52 4N 7 0 E
Ahipara B., N.Z. 91 F4 35 5 S 173 5 E
Ahir Dağı, Turkey 47 C12 38 45N 30 10 E
Ahiri, India 66 K12 19 30N 80 0 E
Ahlat, Turkey 73 C10 38 45N 42 29 E
Ahlen, Germany 24 D3 51 45N 7 53 E
Ahmad Wal, Pakistan 68 E1 29 18N 65 58 E
Ahmadabad, India 68 H5 23 0N 72 40 E
Aḩmadābād, Khorāsān, Iran 71 C9 35 3N 60 50 E
Aḩmadābād, Khorāsān, Iran 71 C8 35 49N 59 42 E
Aḩmadī, Iran 71 E8 27 56N 56 42 E
Ahmadnagar, India 66 K9 19 7N 74 46 E
Ahmadpur, Pakistan 68 E4 29 12N 71 10 E
Ahmadpur Lamma, Pakistan 68 E4 28 19N 70 3 E
Ahmar, Ethiopia 81 F5 9 20N 41 15 E
Ahmedabad = Ahmadabad, India 68 H5 23 0N 72 40 E
Ahmednagar = Ahmadnagar, India 66 K9 19 7N 74 46 E
Ahmetbey, Turkey 45 E11 41 26N 27 34 E
Ahmetler, Turkey 47 C11 38 28N 29 5 E
Ahmetli, Turkey 47 C9 38 32N 27 57 E
Ahoada, Nigeria 83 D6 5 8N 6 36 E
Ahome, Mexico 118 B3 25 55N 109 11W
Ahoskie, U.S.A. 115 G7 36 17N 76 59W
Ahr →, Germany 24 E3 50 32N 7 16 E
Ahram, Iran 71 D6 28 52N 51 16 E
Ahrax Pt., Malta 49 D1 36 0N 14 22 E
Ahrensbök, Germany 24 A6 54 2N 10 35 E
Ahrensburg, Germany 24 B6 53 40N 10 13 E
Āhū, Iran 71 C6 34 33N 50 2 E
Ahuachapán, El Salv. 120 D2 13 54N 89 52W
Ahun, France 19 F9 46 4N 2 5 E
Åhus, Sweden 11 J8 55 56N 14 18 E
Ahvāz, Iran 71 D6 31 20N 48 40 E
Ahvenanmaa, Finland 9 F19 60 15N 20 0 E
Aḩwar, Yemen 75 E4 13 30N 46 40 E
Ahzar →, Mali 83 B5 15 30N 3 20 E
Ai →, India 69 F14 26 26N 90 44 E
Ai-Ais, Namibia 88 D2 27 54 S 17 59 E
Ai-Ais and Fish River Canyon △, Namibia 88 C2 24 45 S 17 15 E
Aichach, Germany 25 G7 48 27N 11 8 E
Aichi □, Japan 55 G8 35 0N 137 15 E
Aigle, Switz. 25 J2 46 18N 6 58 E
Aignay-le-Duc, France 19 E11 47 40N 4 43 E
Aigoual, Mt., France 20 D7 44 8N 3 35 E
Aigre, France 20 C4 45 54N 0 1 E
Aigua, Uruguay 127 C5 34 13 S 54 46W
Aigueperse, France 19 F10 46 3N 3 13 E
Aigues →, France 21 D8 44 7N 4 43 E
Aigues-Mortes, France 21 E8 43 35N 4 12 E
Aigues-Mortes, G. d', France 21 E8 43 31N 4 3 E
Aigües Tortes y Lago San Mauricio △, Spain 38 C4 42 38N 0 31W
Aiguilles, France 21 D10 44 47N 6 51 E
Aiguillon, France 20 D4 44 18N 0 21 E
Aigurande, France 19 F8 46 27N 1 49 E
Aihui, China 60 A7 50 10N 127 30 E
Aija, Peru 124 E3 9 50 S 77 45W
Aikawa, Japan 54 E9 38 2N 138 15 E
Aiken, U.S.A. 115 J5 33 34N 81 43W
Ailao Shan, China 58 F3 24 0N 101 20 E
Aileron, Australia 94 C1 22 39 S 133 20 E
Aillant-sur-Tholon, France 19 E10 47 52N 3 20 E
Aillik, Canada 105 A8 55 11N 59 18W
Ailsa Craig, U.K. 13 F3 55 15N 5 6W
Aim, Russia 53 D14 59 0N 133 55 E
Aimere, Indonesia 63 F6 8 45 S 121 3 E
Aimogasta, Argentina 126 B2 28 33 S 66 50W
Ain □, France 19 F12 46 5N 5 20 E
Ain →, France 21 C9 45 45N 5 11 E
Aïn Ben Tili, Mauritania 78 C4 25 59N 9 27W
Ain Dalla, Egypt 80 B2 27 20N 27 23 E
Ain el Mafki, Egypt 80 B2 27 30N 28 15 E
Ain Girba, Egypt 80 B2 29 20N 25 14 E
Ain Murr, Sudan 80 C2 21 50N 25 9 E
Ain Qeiqab, Egypt 80 B1 29 42N 24 55 E
Aïn Sefra, Algeria 78 B5 32 47N 0 37W
Ain Sheikh Murzûk, Egypt 80 B2 26 47N 27 45 E
Ain Sudr, Egypt 74 F2 29 50N 33 6 E
Ain Sukhna, Egypt 80 J8 29 32N 32 20 E
Ain Zeitûn, Egypt 80 B2 29 10N 25 48 E
Ainaži, Latvia 9 H21 57 50N 24 24 E

Aínos Óros, Greece ... 46 C2 38 9N 20 40 E
Ainsworth, U.S.A. ... 112 D5 42 33N 99 52W
Aiquile, Bolivia ... 124 G5 18 10 S 65 10W
Aïr, Niger ... 83 B6 18 30N 8 0 E
Air Force I., Canada ... 101 B12 67 58N 74 5W
Air Hitam, Malaysia ... 65 M4 1 55N 103 11 E
Airaines, France ... 19 C8 49 58N 1 55 E
Airdrie, Canada ... 102 C6 51 18N 114 2W
Airdrie, U.K. ... 13 F5 55 52N 3 57W
Aire →, France ... 19 C11 49 18N 4 49 E
Aire →, U.K. ... 14 D7 53 43N 0 55W
Aire, I. de l', Spain ... 48 B11 39 48N 4 16 E
Aire-sur-la-Lys, France ... 19 B9 50 37N 2 22 E
Aire-sur-l'Adour, France ... 20 E3 43 42N 0 15W
Airlie Beach, Australia ... 94 J6 20 16 S 148 43 E
Airvault, France ... 18 F6 46 50N 0 8W
Aisch →, Germany ... 25 F6 49 46N 10 58 E
Aisne □, France ... 19 C10 49 42N 3 40 E
Aisne →, France ... 19 C9 49 26N 2 50 E
Ait, India ... 69 G8 25 54N 79 14 E
Aitana, Sierra de, Spain ... 39 G4 38 35N 0 24W
Aitkin, U.S.A. ... 112 B8 46 32N 93 42W
Aitolía kai Akarnanía □, Greece ... 46 C3 38 45N 21 18 E
Aitolikón, Greece ... 46 C3 38 26N 21 21 E
Aiud, Romania ... 29 D8 46 19N 23 44 E
Aix-en-Provence, France ... 21 E9 43 32N 5 27 E
Aix-la-Chapelle = Aachen, Germany ... 24 E2 50 45N 6 6 E
Aix-les-Bains, France ... 21 C9 45 41N 5 53 E
Aixe-sur-Vienne, France ... 20 C5 45 47N 1 9 E
Aíyina, Greece ... 46 D5 37 45N 23 26 E
Aiyínion, Greece ... 44 F6 40 28N 22 28 E
Aíyion, Greece ... 46 C4 38 15N 22 5 E
Aizawl, India ... 67 H18 23 40N 92 44 E
Aizenay, France ... 18 F5 46 44N 1 38W
Aizkraukle, Latvia ... 9 H21 56 36N 25 11 E
Aizpute, Latvia ... 9 H19 56 43N 21 40 E
Aizuwakamatsu, Japan ... 54 F9 37 30N 139 56 E
Ajaccio, France ... 21 G12 41 55N 8 40 E
Ajaccio, G. d', France ... 21 G12 41 52N 8 40 E
Ajai →, Uganda ... 86 B3 2 52N 31 16 E
Ajaigarh, India ... 69 G9 24 52N 80 16 E
Ajalpan, Mexico ... 119 D5 18 22N 97 15W
Ajanta Ra., India ... 66 J9 20 28N 75 50 E
Ajari Rep. = Ajaria □, Georgia ... 35 K6 41 30N 42 0 E
Ajaria □, Georgia ... 35 K6 41 30N 42 0 E
Ajax, Canada ... 116 C5 43 50N 79 1W
Ajdâbiyâ, Libya ... 79 B10 30 54N 20 4 E
Ajdovščina, Slovenia ... 41 C10 45 54N 13 54 E
Ajibar, Ethiopia ... 81 E4 10 35N 38 36 E
Ajka, Hungary ... 28 C2 47 4N 17 31 E
'Ajlûn, Jordan ... 74 C4 32 18N 35 47 E
'Ajlûn □, Jordan ... 74 C4 32 18N 35 47 E
'Ajmân, U.A.E. ... 71 E7 25 25N 55 30 E
Ajmer, India ... 68 F6 26 28N 74 37 E
Ajnala, India ... 68 D6 31 50N 74 48 E
Ajo, U.S.A. ... 109 K7 32 22N 112 52W
Ajo, C. de, Spain ... 36 B7 43 31N 3 35W
Ajok, Sudan ... 81 F2 9 15N 28 28 E
Ajuy, Phil. ... 61 F5 11 10N 123 1 E
Ak Dağ, Turkey ... 47 E11 36 30N 29 32 E
Ak Dağları, Muğla, Turkey ... 47 E11 36 30N 29 30 E
Ak Dağları, Sivas, Turkey ... 72 C7 39 32N 36 12 E
Akaba, Togo ... 83 D5 8 10N 1 2 E
Akabira, Japan ... 54 C11 43 33N 142 5 E
Akagera △, Rwanda ... 86 C3 1 31 S 30 33 E
Akaki Beseka, Ethiopia ... 81 F4 8 55N 38 45 E
Akala, Sudan ... 81 D4 15 39N 36 13 E
Akamas, Cyprus ... 49 D11 35 3N 32 18 E
Akan △, Japan ... 54 C12 43 20N 144 20 E
Akanthou, Cyprus ... 49 D12 35 22N 33 45 E
Akarca, Turkey ... 47 C11 38 35N 29 35 E
Akaroa, N.Z. ... 91 K4 43 49 S 172 59 E
Akasha, Sudan ... 80 C3 21 10N 30 32 E
Akashi, Japan ... 55 G7 34 45N 134 58 E
Akbarpur, Bihar, India ... 69 G10 24 39N 83 58 E
Akbarpur, Ut. P., India ... 69 F10 26 25N 82 32 E
Akçaabat, Turkey ... 73 B8 41 1N 39 34 E
Akçadağ, Turkey ... 72 C7 38 27N 37 43 E
Akçakale, Turkey ... 73 D8 36 41N 38 56 E
Akçakoca, Turkey ... 72 B4 41 5N 31 8 E
Akçaova, Turkey ... 45 E13 41 3N 29 57 E
Akçay, Turkey ... 47 E11 36 36N 29 45 E
Akçay →, Turkey ... 47 D10 37 50N 28 15 E
Akdağ, Turkey ... 47 C8 38 30N 26 30 E
Akdağmadeni, Turkey ... 72 C6 39 35N 35 54 E
Akelamo, Indonesia ... 63 D7 1 35N 129 40 E
Åkers styckebruk, Sweden ... 10 E11 59 15N 17 5 E
Åkersberga, Sweden ... 10 E12 59 29N 18 18 E
Aketi, Dem. Rep. of the Congo ... 84 D4 2 38N 23 47 E
Akhaïa □, Greece ... 46 C3 38 5N 21 45 E
Akhalkalaki, Georgia ... 35 K6 41 27N 43 25 E
Akhaltsikhe, Georgia ... 35 K6 41 40N 43 0 E
Akharnaí, Greece ... 46 C5 38 5N 23 44 E
Akhelóös →, Greece ... 46 C3 38 19N 21 7 E
Akhendría, Greece ... 47 G7 34 59N 25 13 E
Akhisar, Turkey ... 47 C9 38 56N 27 48 E
Akhladhókambos, Greece ... 46 D4 37 31N 22 35 E
Akhmím, Egypt ... 80 B3 26 31N 31 47 E
Akhnur, India ... 69 C6 32 52N 74 45 E
Akhtopol, Bulgaria ... 45 D11 42 6N 27 56 E
Akhtuba →, Russia ... 35 G8 47 41N 46 55 E
Akhtubinsk, Russia ... 35 F8 48 13N 46 7 E
Akhty, Russia ... 35 K8 41 30N 47 45 E
Akhtyrka = Okhtyrka, Ukraine ... 33 G8 50 25N 35 0 E
Aki, Japan ... 55 H6 33 30N 133 54 E
Akimiski I., Canada ... 104 B3 52 50N 81 30W
Akimovka, Ukraine ... 33 J8 46 44N 35 0 E
Åkirkeby, Denmark ... 11 J8 55 4N 14 55 E
Akita, Japan ... 54 E10 39 45N 140 7 E
Akita □, Japan ... 54 E10 39 40N 140 30 E
Akjoujt, Mauritania ... 82 B2 19 45N 14 15W
Akka, Mali ... 83 B4 15 24N 4 11W
Akkaya Tepesi, Turkey ... 47 D11 37 25N 29 38 E
Akkeshi, Japan ... 54 C12 43 2N 144 51 E
'Akko, Israel ... 74 C4 32 55N 35 4 E
Akköy, Turkey ... 47 D9 37 29N 27 15 E
Aklampa, Benin ... 83 D5 8 15N 2 10 E
Aklavik, Canada ... 100 B6 68 12N 135 0W
Aklera, India ... 68 G7 24 26N 76 32 E
Akmenė, Lithuania ... 30 B9 56 15N 22 45 E
Akmenrags, Latvia ... 30 B8 56 50N 21 4 E
Akmonte = Almonte, Spain ... 37 H4 37 13N 6 38W
Akô, Japan ... 55 G7 34 45N 134 24 E
Ako, Nigeria ... 83 C7 10 19N 10 48 E
Akôbô, Sudan ... 81 F3 7 47N 33 1 E
Akobo →, Ethiopia ... 81 F3 7 48N 33 3 E
Akola, India ... 66 J10 20 42N 77 2 E

Akonolinga, Cameroon ... 83 E7 3 50N 12 18 E
Akor, Mali ... 82 C3 14 59N 6 58W
Akordat, Eritrea ... 83 D5 6 20N 0 5 E
Akosombo Dam, Ghana ... 83 D5 6 20N 0 5 E
Akot, Sudan ... 81 F3 6 31N 30 9 E
Akoupé, Ivory C. ... 82 D4 6 23N 3 54W
Akpatok I., Canada ... 101 B13 60 25N 68 8W
Ákrahamn, Norway ... 9 G11 59 15N 5 10 E
Akranes, Iceland ... 8 D2 64 19N 22 5W
Akreïjit, Mauritania ... 82 B3 18 19N 9 11W
Akrítas Venétiko, Ákra, Greece ... 46 E3 36 43N 21 54 E
Akron, Colo., U.S.A. ... 112 E3 40 10N 103 13W
Akron, Ohio, U.S.A. ... 116 E3 41 5N 81 31W
Akrotíri, Cyprus ... 49 E11 34 36N 32 57 E
Akrotíri, Ákra, Greece ... 45 F9 40 26N 25 27 E
Akrotíri Bay, Cyprus ... 49 E12 34 35N 33 10 E
Aksai Chin, China ... 69 B8 35 15N 79 55 E
Aksaray, Turkey ... 70 B2 38 25N 34 2 E
Aksay, Kazakhstan ... 52 D6 51 11N 53 0 E
Akşehir, Turkey ... 70 B1 38 18N 31 30 E
Akşehir Gölü, Turkey ... 72 C4 38 30N 31 25 E
Akstafa = Ağstafa, Azerbaijan ... 35 K7 41 7N 45 27 E
Aksu, China ... 60 B3 41 5N 80 10 E
Aksu →, Turkey ... 72 D4 36 52N 30 57 E
Aksum, Ethiopia ... 81 E4 14 5N 38 40 E
Aktash, Russia ... 34 C11 55 2N 52 3 E
Aktogay, Kazakhstan ... 52 E8 46 57N 79 40 E
Aktsyabrski, Belarus ... 33 F5 52 38N 28 53 E
Aktyubinsk = Aqtöbe, Kazakhstan ... 52 D6 50 17N 57 10 E
Aku, Nigeria ... 83 D6 6 40N 7 18 E
Akure, Nigeria ... 83 D6 7 15N 5 5 E
Akureyri, Iceland ... 8 D4 65 40N 18 6W
Akuseki-Shima, Japan ... 55 K4 29 27N 129 37 E
Akusha, Russia ... 35 J8 42 18N 47 30 E
Akwa-Ibom □, Nigeria ... 83 E6 4 30N 7 30 E
Akyab = Sittwe, Burma ... 67 J18 20 18N 92 45 E
Akyazı, Turkey ... 72 B4 40 40N 30 38 E
Al 'Adan, Yemen ... 75 E4 12 45N 45 0 E
Al Aḥsā = Hasa □, Si. Arabia ... 71 E6 25 50N 49 0 E
Al Ajfar, Si. Arabia ... 70 E4 27 26N 43 0 E
Al Amādīyah, Iraq ... 70 B4 37 5N 43 30 E
Al 'Amārah, Iraq ... 70 D5 31 55N 47 15 E
Al Aqabah, Jordan ... 74 F4 29 31N 35 0 E
Al 'Aqabah □, Jordan ... 74 F4 29 30N 35 0 E
Al Arak, Syria ... 70 C3 34 38N 38 35 E
Al 'Aramah, Si. Arabia ... 70 E5 25 30N 46 0 E
Al 'Arṭāwīyah, Si. Arabia ... 70 E5 26 31N 45 20 E
Al 'Āṣimah = 'Ammān □, Jordan ... 74 D5 31 40N 36 30 E
Al 'Assāfīyah, Si. Arabia ... 70 D3 28 17N 38 59 E
Al 'Ayn, Si. Arabia ... 70 E3 24 15N 38 6 E
Al 'Ayn, U.A.E. ... 71 E7 24 15N 55 45 E
Al 'Azīzīyah, Iraq ... 70 C5 32 54N 45 4 E
Al Bāb, Syria ... 70 B3 36 23N 37 29 E
Al Bad', Si. Arabia ... 70 D2 28 28N 35 1 E
Al Bādī, Iraq ... 70 C4 35 56N 41 32 E
Al Baḥrah, Kuwait ... 70 D5 29 40N 47 52 E
Al Baḥral Mayyit = Dead Sea, Asia ... 74 D4 31 30N 35 30 E
Al Balqā' □, Jordan ... 74 C4 32 5N 35 45 E
Al Bārūk, J., Lebanon ... 74 B4 33 39N 35 40 E
Al Baṣrah, Iraq ... 70 D5 30 30N 47 50 E
Al Batḥā, Iraq ... 70 D5 31 6N 45 53 E
Al Batrūn, Lebanon ... 74 A4 34 15N 35 40 E
Al Bayḍā, Libya ... 79 B10 32 50N 21 44 E
Al Biqā, Lebanon ... 74 A5 34 10N 36 10 E
Al Bi'r, Si. Arabia ... 70 D3 28 51N 36 16 E
Al Burayj, Syria ... 74 A5 34 15N 36 46 E
Al Fadilī, Si. Arabia ... 71 E6 26 58N 49 10 E
Al Fallūjah, Iraq ... 70 C4 33 20N 43 55 E
Al Fāw, Iraq ... 71 D6 30 0N 48 30 E
Al Fujayrah, U.A.E. ... 71 E8 25 7N 56 18 E
Al Ghadaf, W. →, Jordan ... 74 D5 31 26N 36 43 E
Al Ghammās, Iraq ... 70 D5 31 45N 44 37 E
Al Ghazālah, Si. Arabia ... 70 E4 26 48N 41 19 E
Al Ḥadīthah, Iraq ... 70 C4 34 0N 41 13 E
Al Ḥadīthah, Si. Arabia ... 70 D3 31 28N 37 8 E
Al Ḥaḍr, Iraq ... 70 C4 35 35N 42 44 E
Al Ḥājānah, Syria ... 74 B5 33 20N 36 33 E
Al Ḥajar al Gharbī, Oman ... 71 E8 24 10N 56 15 E
Al Ḥāmad, Si. Arabia ... 70 D3 31 30N 39 30 E
Al Ḥamdāniyah, Syria ... 70 C3 35 25N 36 50 E
Al Ḥamīdīyah, Syria ... 74 A4 34 42N 35 57 E
Al Ḥammār, Iraq ... 70 D5 30 57N 46 51 E
Al Ḥamrā', Si. Arabia ... 70 E3 24 2N 38 55 E
Al Ḥamzah, Iraq ... 70 D5 31 43N 44 58 E
Al Ḥanākīyah, Si. Arabia ... 70 E4 24 51N 40 31 E
Al Ḥarīr, W. →, Syria ... 74 C4 32 44N 35 59 E
Al Ḥasakah, Syria ... 70 B4 36 35N 40 45 E
Al Ḥaydān, W. →, Jordan ... 74 D4 31 29N 35 34 E
Al Ḥayy, Iraq ... 70 C5 32 5N 46 5 E
Al Ḥijarah, Asia ... 70 D4 30 0N 44 0 E
Al Ḥillah, Iraq ... 70 C5 32 30N 44 25 E
Al Ḥillah, Si. Arabia ... 75 B4 23 35N 46 50 E
Al Hindīyah, Iraq ... 70 C4 32 30N 44 10 E
Al Hirmil, Lebanon ... 74 A5 34 26N 36 24 E
Al Hoceïma, Morocco ... 78 A5 35 8N 3 58W
Al Ḥudaydah, Yemen ... 75 E3 14 50N 43 0 E
Al Hufūf, Si. Arabia ... 71 E6 25 25N 49 45 E
Al Ḥumaydah, Si. Arabia ... 70 D2 29 14N 34 56 E
Al Ḥunayy, Si. Arabia ... 71 E6 25 58N 48 45 E
Al Isāwīyah, Si. Arabia ... 70 D3 30 43N 37 59 E
Al Jafr, Jordan ... 74 E5 30 18N 36 14 E
Al Jāfūrah, Si. Arabia ... 71 E7 25 0N 50 15 E
Al Jaghbūb, Libya ... 79 C10 29 42N 24 38 E
Al Jahrah, Kuwait ... 70 D5 29 25N 47 40 E
Al Jalāmīd, Si. Arabia ... 70 D3 31 20N 40 6 E
Al Jamalīyah, Qatar ... 71 E6 25 37N 51 5 E
Al Janūb □, Lebanon ... 74 B4 33 20N 35 20 E
Al Jawf, Libya ... 79 D10 24 10N 23 24 E
Al Jawf, Si. Arabia ... 70 D3 29 55N 39 40 E
Al Jazirah, Iraq ... 70 C5 33 30N 44 0 E
Al Jithāmīyah, Si. Arabia ... 70 E4 27 41N 41 43 E
Al Jubayl, Si. Arabia ... 71 E6 27 0N 49 50 E
Al Jubaylah, Si. Arabia ... 70 E5 24 55N 46 25 E
Al Jubb, Si. Arabia ... 70 E4 27 11N 42 17 E
Al Junaynah, Sudan ... 79 F10 13 27N 22 45 E
Al Kaba'ish, Iraq ... 70 D5 30 58N 47 0 E
Al Karak, Jordan ... 74 D4 31 11N 35 42 E
Al Karak □, Jordan ... 74 D5 31 22N 36 5 E
Al Kāẓimīyah, Iraq ... 70 C5 33 22N 44 18 E
Al Khābūra, Oman ... 71 F8 23 57N 57 5 E
Al Khafji, Si. Arabia ... 71 E6 28 24N 48 29 E
Al Khalīl, West Bank ... 74 D4 31 32N 35 6 E
Al Khāliṣ, Iraq ... 70 C5 33 49N 44 32 E

Al Kharsānīyah, Si. Arabia ... 71 E6 27 13N 49 18 E
Al Khaṣab, Oman ... 71 E8 26 14N 56 15 E
Al Khawr, Qatar ... 71 E6 25 41N 51 30 E
Al Khiḍr, Iraq ... 70 D5 31 12N 45 33 E
Al Khiyām, Lebanon ... 74 B4 33 20N 35 36 E
Al Khums, Libya ... 79 B8 32 40N 14 17 E
Al Kiswah, Syria ... 74 B5 33 23N 36 14 E
Al Kūfah, Iraq ... 70 C5 32 2N 44 24 E
Al Kufrah, Libya ... 79 D10 24 17N 23 15 E
Al Kuhayfiyah, Si. Arabia ... 70 E4 27 12N 43 3 E
Al Kūt, Iraq ... 70 C5 32 30N 46 0 E
Al Kuwayt, Kuwait ... 70 D5 29 30N 48 0 E
Al Labwah, Lebanon ... 74 A5 34 11N 36 20 E
Al Lādhiqīyah, Syria ... 70 C2 35 30N 35 45 E
Al Līth, Si. Arabia ... 75 C3 20 9N 40 15 E
Al Liwā', Oman ... 71 E8 24 31N 56 36 E
Al Luḥayyah, Yemen ... 75 D3 15 45N 42 40 E
Al Madīnah, Iraq ... 70 D5 30 57N 47 16 E
Al Madīnah, Si. Arabia ... 70 E3 24 35N 39 52 E
Al Mafraq, Jordan ... 74 C5 32 17N 36 14 E
Al Mafraq □, Jordan ... 74 C5 32 17N 36 15 E
Al Maḥmūdīyah, Iraq ... 70 C5 33 3N 44 21 E
Al Majma'ah, Si. Arabia ... 70 E5 25 57N 45 22 E
Al Makhruq, W. →, Jordan ... 74 D6 31 28N 37 0 E
Al Makhūl, Si. Arabia ... 70 E4 26 37N 42 39 E
Al Manāmah, Bahrain ... 71 E6 26 10N 50 30 E
Al Maqwa', Kuwait ... 70 D5 29 10N 47 59 E
Al Marj, Libya ... 79 B10 32 25N 20 30 E
Al Maṭlā, Kuwait ... 70 D5 29 24N 47 40 E
Al Mawjib, W. →, Jordan ... 74 D4 31 28N 35 36 E
Al Mawṣil, Iraq ... 70 B4 36 15N 43 5 E
Al Mayādin, Syria ... 70 C4 35 1N 40 27 E
Al Mazār, Jordan ... 74 D4 31 4N 35 41 E
Al Midhnab, Si. Arabia ... 70 E5 25 50N 44 18 E
Al Mīnā', Lebanon ... 74 A4 34 24N 35 49 E
Al Miqdādīyah, Iraq ... 70 C5 34 0N 45 0 E
Al Mubarraz, Si. Arabia ... 71 E6 25 30N 49 40 E
Al Mudawwarah, Jordan ... 74 F5 29 19N 36 0 E
Al Mughayrā', U.A.E. ... 71 E7 24 5N 53 32 E
Al Muḥarraq, Bahrain ... 71 E6 26 15N 50 40 E
Al Mukallā, Yemen ... 75 E4 14 33N 49 2 E
Al Mukhā, Yemen ... 75 E3 13 18N 43 15 E
Al Musayjīd, Si. Arabia ... 70 E3 24 5N 39 5 E
Al Musayyib, Iraq ... 70 C5 32 49N 44 20 E
Al Muthanná □, Iraq ... 70 D5 30 30N 45 15 E
Al Muwayh, Si. Arabia ... 80 C5 22 41N 41 37 E
Al Muwayliḥ, Si. Arabia ... 70 E2 27 40N 35 30 E
Al Owuho = Otukpa, Nigeria ... 83 D6 7 9N 7 41 E
Al Qādisīyah □, Iraq ... 70 D5 32 0N 45 0 E
Al Qā'im, Iraq ... 70 C4 34 21N 41 7 E
Al Qalībah, Si. Arabia ... 70 D3 28 24N 37 42 E
Al Qāmishlī, Syria ... 70 B4 37 2N 41 14 E
Al Qaryatayn, Syria ... 74 A6 34 12N 37 13 E
Al Qaşīm, Si. Arabia ... 70 E4 26 0N 43 0 E
Al Qaṭ'ā, Syria ... 70 C4 34 40N 40 48 E
Al Qaṭīf, Si. Arabia ... 71 E6 26 35N 50 0 E
Al Qaṭrānah, Jordan ... 74 D5 31 12N 36 6 E
Al Qaṭrūn, Libya ... 79 D9 24 56N 15 3 E
Al Qayṣūmah, Si. Arabia ... 70 D5 28 20N 46 7 E
Al Quds = Jerusalem, Israel ... 74 D4 31 47N 35 10 E
Al Qunayṭirah, Syria ... 74 C4 32 55N 35 45 E
Al Qunfudhah, Si. Arabia ... 80 D5 19 3N 41 4 E
Al Qurnah, Iraq ... 70 D5 31 1N 47 25 E
Al Quşayr, Iraq ... 70 D5 30 39N 45 50 E
Al Quşayr, Syria ... 74 A5 34 31N 36 34 E
Al Qutayfah, Syria ... 74 B5 33 44N 36 36 E
Al 'Ubaylah, Si. Arabia ... 75 C5 21 59N 50 57 E
Al 'Udayliyah, Si. Arabia ... 71 E6 25 8N 49 18 E
Al 'Ulā, Si. Arabia ... 70 E3 26 35N 38 0 E
Al 'Uqayr, Si. Arabia ... 71 E6 25 40N 50 15 E
Al 'Uwaynid, Si. Arabia ... 70 E5 24 50N 46 0 E
Al 'Uwayqīlah, Si. Arabia ... 70 D4 30 30N 42 10 E
Al 'Uyūn, Ḥijāz, Si. Arabia ... 70 E3 24 33N 39 35 E
Al 'Uyūn, Najd, Si. Arabia ... 70 E4 26 30N 43 50 E
Al 'Uzayr, Iraq ... 70 D5 31 19N 47 25 E
Al Wajh, Si. Arabia ... 70 E3 26 10N 36 30 E
Al Wakrah, Qatar ... 71 E6 25 10N 51 40 E
Al Waqbah, Si. Arabia ... 70 D5 28 48N 45 33 E
Al Wari'ah, Si. Arabia ... 70 E5 27 51N 47 25 E
Ala, Italy ... 40 C8 45 45N 11 0 E
Ala Dağ, Turkey ... 70 B2 37 44N 35 9 E
Ala Dağları, Turkey ... 73 C10 39 15N 43 33 E
Alabama □, U.S.A. ... 115 J2 33 0N 87 0W
Alabama →, U.S.A. ... 115 K2 31 8N 87 57W
Alabaster, U.S.A. ... 115 J2 33 15N 86 49W
Alaca, Turkey ... 72 B6 40 10N 34 51 E
Alaçam, Turkey ... 72 B6 41 36N 35 36 E
Alaçam Dağları, Turkey ... 47 B10 39 18N 28 49 E
Alacant = Alicante, Spain ... 39 G4 38 23N 0 30W
Alaçatı, Turkey ... 47 C9 38 16N 26 23 E
Alachua, U.S.A. ... 115 L4 29 47N 82 30W
Alaejos, Spain ... 36 D5 41 18N 5 13W
Alagna, Greece ... 49 C9 36 9N 27 57 E
Alagir, Russia ... 35 J7 43 3N 44 14 E
Alagna Valsésia, Italy ... 40 C4 45 51N 7 56 E
Alagoa Grande, Brazil ... 125 E11 7 3 S 35 35W
Alagoas □, Brazil ... 125 E11 9 0 S 36 0W
Alagoinhas, Brazil ... 125 F11 12 7 S 38 20W
Alagón, Spain ... 38 D3 41 46N 1 12W
Alagón →, Spain ... 36 F4 39 44N 6 53W
Alaior, Spain ... 48 B11 39 57N 4 8 E
Alajero, Canary Is. ... 48 F2 28 3N 17 13W
Alajuela, Costa Rica ... 120 D3 10 2N 84 8W
Alakamisy, Madag. ... 89 C8 21 19N 47 14 E
Alaknanda →, India ... 69 D8 30 8N 78 36 E
Alakol, Ozero, Kazakhstan ... 60 B3 46 0N 81 5 E
Alamarvdasht, Iran ... 71 E7 27 37N 52 59 E
Alamata, Ethiopia ... 81 E4 12 25N 39 33 E
Alameda, Calif., U.S.A. ... 110 H4 37 46N 122 15W
Alameda, N. Mex., U.S.A. ... 109 J10 35 11N 106 37W
Alaminos, Phil. ... 61 C3 16 10N 119 59 E
Alamo, U.S.A. ... 111 J11 37 22N 115 10W
Alamo Crossing, U.S.A. ... 111 L13 34 16N 113 33W
Álamos, Mexico ... 118 B3 27 0N 109 0W
Alamosa, U.S.A. ... 109 H11 37 28N 105 52W
Åland = Ahvenanmaa, Finland ... 9 F19 60 15N 20 0 E
Alandroal, Portugal ... 37 G3 38 41N 7 24W
Ålands hav, Europe ... 9 F18 60 0N 19 30 E
Alange, Embalse d', Spain ... 37 G4 38 45N 6 18W

Alania = North Ossetia □, Russia ... 35 J7 43 30N 44 30 E
Alanís, Spain ... 37 G5 38 3N 5 43W
Alanya, Turkey ... 70 B1 36 38N 32 0 E
Alaotra, Farihin', Madag. ... 89 B8 17 30 S 48 30 E
Alapayevsk, Russia ... 52 D7 57 52N 61 42 E
Alappuzha = Alleppey, India ... 66 Q10 9 30N 76 28 E
Alar del Rey, Spain ... 36 C6 42 38N 4 20W
Alaraz, Spain ... 36 E5 40 45N 5 17W
Alarcón, Embalse de, Spain ... 38 F2 39 36N 2 10W
Alarobia-Vohiposa, Madag. ... 89 C8 20 59 S 47 9 E
Alaşehir, Turkey ... 47 C10 38 23N 28 30 E
Alaska □, U.S.A. ... 100 B5 64 0N 154 0W
Alaska, G. of, Pac. Oc. ... 100 C5 58 0N 145 0W
Alaska Peninsula, U.S.A. ... 100 C4 56 0N 159 0W
Alaska Range, U.S.A. ... 100 B4 62 50N 151 0W
Alássio, Italy ... 40 E5 44 0N 8 10 E
Ālāt, Azerbaijan ... 35 L9 39 58N 49 25 E
Alatri, Italy ... 41 G10 41 43N 13 21 E
Alatyr, Russia ... 34 C8 54 55N 46 35 E
Alatyr →, Russia ... 34 C8 54 52N 46 36 E
Alausi, Ecuador ... 124 D3 2 0 S 78 50W
Álava □, Spain ... 38 C2 42 48N 2 28 E
Alava, C., U.S.A. ... 108 B1 48 10N 124 44W
Alaverdi, Armenia ... 35 K7 41 15N 44 37 E
Alavo = Alavus, Finland ... 9 E20 62 35N 23 36 E
Alavus, Finland ... 9 E20 62 35N 23 36 E
Alawoona, Australia ... 95 E3 34 45 S 140 30 E
'Alayh, Lebanon ... 74 B4 33 46N 35 33 E
Alazani →, Azerbaijan ... 35 K8 41 5N 46 40 E
Alba, Italy ... 40 D5 44 42N 8 2 E
Alba □, Romania ... 29 D8 46 10N 23 30 E
Alba Adriática, Italy ... 41 F10 42 50N 13 56 E
Alba-Iulia, Romania ... 29 D8 46 8N 23 39 E
Albac, Romania ... 28 D7 46 28N 22 58 E
Albacete, Spain ... 39 F3 39 0N 1 50W
Albacete □, Spain ... 39 G3 38 50N 2 0W
Albacutya, L., Australia ... 95 F3 35 45 S 141 58 E
Ålbæk, Denmark ... 11 G4 57 36N 10 25 E
Ålbæk Bugt, Denmark ... 11 G4 57 35N 10 40 E
Albaida, Spain ... 39 G4 38 51N 0 31W
Albalate de las Nogueras, Spain ... 38 E2 40 22N 2 18W
Albalate del Arzobispo, Spain ... 38 D4 41 6N 0 31W
Albanel, L., Canada ... 104 B5 50 55N 73 12W
Albania ■, Europe ... 44 E4 41 0N 20 0 E
Albano Laziale, Italy ... 41 G9 41 44N 12 39 E
Albany, Australia ... 93 G2 35 1 S 117 58 E
Albany, Ga., U.S.A. ... 115 K3 31 35N 84 10W
Albany, N.Y., U.S.A. ... 117 D11 42 39N 73 45W
Albany, Oreg., U.S.A. ... 108 D2 44 38N 123 6W
Albany, Tex., U.S.A. ... 113 J5 32 44N 99 18W
Albany →, Canada ... 104 B3 52 17N 81 31W
Albardón, Argentina ... 126 C2 31 20 S 68 30W
Albarracín, Spain ... 38 E3 40 25N 1 26W
Albarracín, Sierra de, Spain ... 38 E3 40 30N 1 30W
Albatera, Spain ... 39 G4 38 11N 0 52W
Albatross B., Australia ... 94 A3 12 45 S 141 30 E
Albegna →, Italy ... 41 F8 42 30N 11 11 E
Albemarle, U.S.A. ... 115 H5 35 21N 80 11W
Albemarle Sd., U.S.A. ... 115 H7 36 5N 76 0W
Albenga, Italy ... 40 D5 44 3N 8 13 E
Alberche →, Spain ... 36 F6 39 58N 4 46W
Alberdi, Paraguay ... 126 B4 26 14 S 58 20W
Alberès, Mts., France ... 20 F7 42 28N 2 56 E
Alberga →, Australia ... 95 D2 27 6 S 135 33 E
Albersdorf, Germany ... 24 A5 54 8N 9 17 E
Albert, France ... 19 C9 50 0N 2 38 E
Albert, L., Africa ... 86 B3 1 30N 31 0 E
Albert, L., Australia ... 95 F2 35 30 S 139 10 E
Albert Edward Ra., Australia ... 92 C4 18 17 S 127 57 E
Albert Lea, U.S.A. ... 112 D8 43 39N 93 22W
Albert Nile →, Uganda ... 86 B3 3 36N 32 2 E
Albert Town, Bahamas ... 121 B5 22 37N 74 33W
Alberta □, Canada ... 102 C6 54 40N 115 0W
Alberti, Argentina ... 126 D3 35 1 S 60 16W
Albertinia, S. Africa ... 88 E3 34 11 S 21 34 E
Albertirsa, Hungary ... 28 C4 47 14N 19 37 E
Alberton, Canada ... 105 C7 46 50N 64 0W
Albertville, France ... 21 C10 45 40N 6 22 E
Albertville, U.S.A. ... 115 H2 34 16N 86 13W
Albi, France ... 20 E6 43 56N 2 9 E
Albia, U.S.A. ... 112 E8 41 2N 92 48W
Albina, Suriname ... 125 B8 5 37N 54 15W
Albina, Ponta, Angola ... 88 B1 15 52 S 11 44 E
Albino, Italy ... 40 C6 45 47N 9 48 E
Albion, Mich., U.S.A. ... 114 D3 42 15N 84 45W
Albion, Nebr., U.S.A. ... 112 E5 41 42N 98 0W
Albion, Pa., U.S.A. ... 116 E4 41 53N 80 22W
Albocácer, Spain ... 38 E5 40 21N 0 1 E
Alborán, Medit. S. ... 37 K7 35 57N 3 0W
Alborea, Spain ... 39 F3 39 17N 1 24W
Ålborg, Denmark ... 11 G3 57 2N 9 54 E
Ålborg Bugt, Denmark ... 11 H4 56 50N 10 35 E
Alborz, Reshteh-ye Kūhhā-ye, Iran ... 71 C7 36 0N 52 0 E
Albox, Spain ... 39 H2 37 23N 2 8W
Albufeira, Portugal ... 37 H2 37 5N 8 15W
Albula →, Switz. ... 25 J5 46 38N 9 28 E
Albuñol, Spain ... 37 J7 36 48N 3 11W
Albuquerque, U.S.A. ... 109 J10 35 5N 106 39W
Albuquerque, Cayos de, Caribbean ... 120 D3 12 10N 81 50W
Alburg, U.S.A. ... 117 B11 44 59N 73 18W
Alburquerque, Spain ... 37 F4 39 15N 6 59W
Albury = Albury-Wodonga, Australia ... 95 F4 36 3 S 146 56 E
Albury-Wodonga, Australia ... 95 F4 36 3 S 146 56 E
Alcácer do Sal, Portugal ... 37 G2 38 22N 8 30W
Alcáçovas, Portugal ... 37 G2 38 23N 8 9W
Alcalá de Chivert, Spain ... 38 E5 40 19N 0 13 E
Alcalá de Guadaira, Spain ... 37 H5 37 20N 5 50W
Alcalá de Henares, Spain ... 36 E7 40 28N 3 22W
Alcalá de los Gazules, Spain ... 37 J5 36 29N 5 43W
Alcalá del Júcar, Spain ... 39 F3 39 12N 1 26W
Alcalá del Río, Spain ... 37 H5 37 31N 5 59W
Alcalá del Valle, Spain ... 37 J5 36 54N 5 10W
Alcalá la Real, Spain ... 37 H7 37 27N 3 57W
Álcamo, Italy ... 42 E5 37 59N 12 55 E
Alcanadre →, Spain ... 38 C2 41 43N 0 12W

Alcanadre →, Spain ... 38 D4 41 43N 0 12W
Alcanar, Spain ... 38 E5 40 33N 0 28 E
Alcanede, Portugal ... 37 F2 39 25N 8 49W
Alcanena, Portugal ... 37 F2 39 27N 8 40W
Alcañices, Spain ... 36 D4 41 41N 6 21W
Alcañiz, Spain ... 38 D4 41 2N 0 8W
Alcântara, Brazil ... 125 D10 2 20 S 44 30W
Alcántara, Spain ... 36 F4 39 44N 6 57W
Alcántara, Embalse de, Spain ... 36 F4 39 44N 6 50W
Alcantarilla, Spain ... 39 H3 37 59N 1 12W
Alcaracejos, Spain ... 37 G6 38 24N 4 58W
Alcaraz, Spain ... 39 G2 38 40N 2 29W
Alcaraz, Sierra de, Spain ... 39 G2 38 40N 2 20W
Alcaudete, Spain ... 37 H6 37 35N 4 5W
Alcázar de San Juan, Spain ... 37 F7 39 24N 3 12W
Alchevsk, Ukraine ... 33 H10 48 30N 38 45 E
Alcira = Alzira, Spain ... 39 F4 39 9N 0 30W
Alcoba, Portugal ... 37 F2 39 32N 8 58W
Alcobendas, Spain ... 36 E7 40 32N 3 38W
Alcolea del Pinar, Spain ... 38 D2 41 2N 2 28W
Alcora, Spain ... 38 E4 40 5N 0 14W
Alcorcón, Spain ... 36 E7 40 20N 3 50W
Alcoutim, Portugal ... 37 H3 37 25N 7 28W
Alcova, U.S.A. ... 108 E10 42 34N 106 43W
Alcoy, Spain ... 39 G4 38 43N 0 30W
Alcubierre, Sierra de, Spain ... 38 D4 41 45N 0 22W
Alcublas, Spain ... 38 F4 39 48N 0 43W
Alcúdia, Spain ... 48 B10 39 51N 3 7 E
Alcúdia, B. d', Spain ... 48 B10 39 47N 3 15 E
Alcúdia, Sierra de la, Spain ... 37 G6 38 34N 4 30W
Aldabra Is., Seychelles ... 77 G8 9 22 S 46 28 E
Aldama, Mexico ... 119 C5 23 0N 98 4W
Aldan, Russia ... 53 D13 58 40N 125 30 E
Aldan →, Russia ... 53 C13 63 28N 129 35 E
Aldea, Pta. de la, Canary Is. ... 48 G4 28 0N 15 50W
Aldeburgh, U.K. ... 15 E9 52 10N 1 37 E
Alder Pk., U.S.A. ... 110 K5 35 53N 121 22W
Alderney, U.K. ... 15 H5 49 42N 2 11W
Aldershot, U.K. ... 15 F7 51 15N 0 44W
Åled, Sweden ... 11 H6 56 44N 12 57 E
Aledo, U.S.A. ... 112 E9 41 12N 90 45W
Alefa, Ethiopia ... 81 E4 11 55N 36 55 E
Aleg, Mauritania ... 82 B2 17 3N 13 55W
Alegranza, Canary Is. ... 48 E6 29 23N 13 32W
Alegranza, I., Canary Is. ... 48 E6 29 23N 13 32W
Alegre, Brazil ... 127 A7 20 50 S 41 30W
Alegrete, Brazil ... 127 B4 29 40 S 56 0W
Aleisk, Russia ... 52 D9 52 40N 83 0 E
Aleksandriya = Oleksandriya, Kirovohrad, Ukraine ... 33 H7 48 42N 33 3 E
Aleksandriya = Oleksandriya, Rivne, Ukraine ... 33 G4 50 37N 26 19 E
Aleksandriyskaya, Russia ... 35 J8 43 58N 47 14 E
Aleksandrov, Russia ... 32 D10 56 23N 38 44 E
Aleksandrov Gay, Russia ... 34 E9 50 9N 48 34 E
Aleksandrovac, Serbia & M. ... 44 C5 43 28N 21 3 E
Aleksandrovac, Serbia & M. ... 44 B5 44 28N 21 13 E
Aleksandrovka = Oleksandrovka, Ukraine ... 33 H7 48 55N 32 20 E
Aleksandrovo, Bulgaria ... 45 C8 43 14N 24 51 E
Aleksandrovsk-Sakhalinskiy, Russia ... 53 D15 50 50N 142 20 E
Aleksandrów Kujawski, Poland ... 31 F5 52 53N 18 43 E
Aleksandrów Łódzki, Poland ... 31 G6 51 49N 19 17 E
Aleksandry, Z., Russia ... 4 A10 80 25N 48 0 E
Alekseyevka, Samara, Russia ... 34 D10 52 35N 51 17 E
Alekseyevka, Voronezh, Russia ... 33 G10 50 43N 38 40 E
Aleksin, Russia ... 32 E9 54 31N 37 9 E
Aleksinac, Serbia & M. ... 44 C5 43 31N 21 42 E
Além Paraíba, Brazil ... 127 A7 21 52 S 42 41W
Alemania, Argentina ... 126 B2 25 40 S 65 30W
Alemania, Chile ... 126 B2 25 10 S 69 55W
Alençon, France ... 18 D7 48 27N 0 4 E
Alenquer, Brazil ... 125 D8 1 56 S 54 46W
Alenuihaha Channel, U.S.A. ... 106 H17 20 30N 156 0W
Alépé, Ivory C. ... 82 D4 5 30N 3 40W
Aleppo = Ḥalab, Syria ... 70 B3 36 10N 37 15 E
Aléria, France ... 21 F13 42 5N 9 26 E
Alert, Canada ... 4 A4 83 2N 60 0W
Alès, France ... 21 D8 44 9N 4 5 E
Aleşd, Romania ... 28 C7 47 3N 22 22 E
Alessándria, Italy ... 40 D5 44 54N 8 37 E
Ålestrup, Denmark ... 11 H3 56 42N 9 29 E
Ålesund, Norway ... 9 E12 62 28N 6 12 E
Alet-les-Bains, France ... 20 F6 42 59N 2 14 E
Aletschhorn, Switz. ... 25 J4 46 28N 8 0 E
Aleutian Is., Pac. Oc. ... 100 C2 52 0N 175 0W
Aleutian Trench, Pac. Oc. ... 96 C10 48 0N 180 0 E
Alexander, U.S.A. ... 112 B3 47 51N 103 39W
Alexander, Mt., Australia ... 93 E3 28 58 S 120 16 E
Alexander Arch., U.S.A. ... 100 C6 56 0N 136 0W
Alexander City, U.S.A. ... 115 J3 32 56N 85 58W
Alexander I., Antarctica ... 5 C17 69 0 S 70 0W
Alexandra, Australia ... 95 F4 37 8 S 145 40 E
Alexandra, N.Z. ... 91 L2 45 14 S 169 25 E
Alexandra Falls, Canada ... 102 A5 60 29N 116 18W
Alexandria = El Iskandarîya, Egypt ... 80 H7 31 13N 29 58 E
Alexandria, B.C., Canada ... 102 C4 52 35N 122 27W
Alexandria, Ont., Canada ... 117 A10 45 19N 74 38W
Alexandria, Romania ... 29 G10 43 57N 25 24 E
Alexandria, S. Africa ... 88 E4 33 38 S 26 28 E
Alexandria, U.K. ... 13 F4 55 59N 4 35W
Alexandria, La., U.S.A. ... 113 K8 31 18N 92 27W
Alexandria, Minn., U.S.A. ... 112 C7 45 53N 95 22W
Alexandria, S. Dak., U.S.A. ... 112 D6 43 39N 97 47W
Alexandria, Va., U.S.A. ... 114 F7 38 48N 77 3W
Alexandria Bay, U.S.A. ... 117 B9 44 20N 75 55W
Alexandrina, L., Australia ... 95 F2 35 25 S 139 10 E
Alexandroúpolis, Greece ... 45 F9 40 50N 25 54 E
Alexis →, Canada ... 105 B8 52 33N 56 8W
Alexis Creek, Canada ... 102 C4 52 10N 123 20W

Alfabia, Spain 48 B9 39 44N 2 44 E
Alfambra, Spain 38 E3 40 33N 1 5W
Alfândega da Fé, Portugal 36 D4 41 20N 6 59W
Alfaro, Spain 38 C3 42 10N 1 50W
Alfatar, Bulgaria 45 C11 43 59N 27 13 E
Alfaz del Pi, Spain 39 G4 38 35N 0 5W
Alfeld, Germany 24 D5 51 59N 9 50 E
Alfenas, Brazil 127 A6 21 20 S 46 10W
Alfiós →, Greece 46 D3 37 40N 21 33 E
Alföld, Hungary 28 D5 46 30N 20 0 E
Alfonsine, Italy 41 D9 44 30N 12 3 E
Alford, Aberds., U.K. 13 D6 57 14N 2 41W
Alford, Lincs., U.K. 14 D8 53 15N 0 10 E
Alfred, Maine, U.S.A. 117 C14 43 29N 70 43W
Alfred, N.Y., U.S.A. 116 D7 42 16N 77 48W
Alfreton, U.K. 14 D6 53 6N 1 24W
Alfta, Sweden 10 C10 61 21N 16 4 E
Alga, Kazakhstan 52 E6 49 53N 57 20 E
Algaida, Spain 48 B9 39 33N 2 53 E
Algar, Spain 37 J5 36 40N 5 39W
Ålgård, Norway 9 G11 58 46N 5 53 E
Algarinejo, Spain 37 H6 37 19N 4 9W
Algarve, Portugal 37 J2 36 58N 8 20W
Algeciras, Spain 37 J5 36 9N 5 28W
Algemesí, Spain 39 F4 39 11N 0 27W
Alger, Algeria 78 A6 36 42N 3 8 E
Alger ✈ (ALG), Algeria 39 J8 36 39N 3 13 E
Algeria ■, Africa 78 C6 28 30N 2 0 E
Alghero, Italy 42 B1 40 33N 8 19 E
Älghult, Sweden 11 G9 57 0N 15 35 E
Algiers = Alger, Algeria 78 A6 36 42N 3 8 E
Algoa B., S. Africa 88 E4 33 50 S 25 45 E
Algodonales, Spain 37 J5 36 54N 5 24W
Algodor →, Spain 36 F7 39 55N 3 53W
Algoma, U.S.A. 114 C2 44 36N 87 26W
Algona, U.S.A. 112 D7 43 4N 94 14W
Algonac, U.S.A. 116 D2 42 37N 82 32W
Algonquin △, Canada 104 C4 45 50N 78 30W
Algorta, Uruguay 128 C5 32 25 S 57 23W
Alhama de Almería, Spain 37 J8 36 57N 2 34W
Alhama de Aragón, Spain 38 D3 41 18N 1 54W
Alhama de Granada, Spain 37 H7 37 0N 3 59W
Alhama de Murcia, Spain 39 H3 37 51N 1 25W
Alhambra, U.S.A. 111 L8 34 8N 118 6W
Alhaurín el Grande, Spain 37 J6 36 39N 4 41W
Alhucemas = Al Hoceïma, Morocco 78 A5 35 8N 3 58W
'Alī al Gharbī, Iraq 70 C5 32 30N 46 45 E
'Alī ash Sharqī, Iraq 70 C5 32 7N 46 44 E
Āli Bayramlı, Azerbaijan 35 L9 39 59N 48 52 E
'Alī Khēl, Afghan. 68 C3 33 57N 69 43 E
Ali Sahîh, Djibouti 81 E5 11 10N 42 44 E
Alī Shāh, Iran 70 B5 38 9N 45 50 E
Ália, Italy 42 E6 37 47N 13 43 E
'Alīābād, Khorāsān, Iran 71 C8 32 30N 57 30 E
'Alīābād, Kordestān, Iran 70 C5 35 4N 46 58 E
'Alīābād, Yazd, Iran 71 D7 31 41N 53 49 E
Aliaga, Spain 38 E4 40 40N 0 42W
Aliağa, Turkey 47 C8 38 47N 26 59 E
Aliákmon →, Greece 44 F6 40 30N 22 36 E
Alibo, Ethiopia 81 F4 9 52N 37 5 E
Alibori →, Benin 83 C5 11 56N 3 17 E
Alibunar, Serbia & M. 28 E5 45 5N 20 57 E
Alicante, Spain 39 G4 38 23N 0 30W
Alicante □, Spain 39 G4 38 30N 0 37W
Alicante ✈ (ALC), Spain 39 G4 38 14N 0 36W
Alice, S. Africa 88 E4 32 48 S 26 55 E
Alice, U.S.A. 113 M5 27 45N 98 5W
Alice →, Queens., Australia 94 C3 24 2 S 144 50 E
Alice →, Queens., Australia 94 B3 15 35 S 142 20 E
Alice, Punta, Italy 43 C10 39 24N 17 9 E
Alice Arm, Canada 102 B3 55 29N 129 31W
Alice Springs, Australia 94 C1 23 40 S 133 50 E
Alicedale, S. Africa 88 E4 33 15 S 26 4 E
Aliceville, U.S.A. 115 J1 33 8N 88 9W
Alicudi, Italy 43 D7 38 33N 14 20 E
Aliganj, India 69 F8 27 30N 79 10 E
Aligarh, Raj., India 68 G7 25 55N 76 15 E
Aligarh, Ut. P., India 68 F8 27 55N 78 10 E
Alīgūdarz, Iran 71 C6 33 25N 49 45 E
Alijó, Portugal 36 D3 41 16N 7 27W
Alimnía, Greece 49 C9 36 16N 27 43 E
Alingsås, Sweden 11 G6 57 56N 12 31 E
Alipur, Pakistan 68 E4 29 25N 70 55 E
Alipur Duar, India 67 F16 26 30N 89 35 E
Aliquippa, U.S.A. 116 F4 40 37N 80 15W
Alishan, Taiwan 59 F13 23 31N 120 48 E
Aliste →, Spain 36 D5 41 34N 5 58W
Alitus = Alytus, Lithuania 9 J21 54 24N 24 3 E
Alivérion, Greece 46 C6 38 24N 24 2 E
Aliwal North, S. Africa 88 E4 30 45 S 26 45 E
Alix, Canada 102 C6 52 24N 113 11W
Aljezur, Portugal 37 H2 37 18N 8 49W
Aljustrel, Portugal 37 H2 37 55N 8 10W
Alkamari, Niger 83 C7 13 27N 11 10 E
Alkmaar, Neths. 17 B4 52 37N 4 45 E
All American Canal, U.S.A. 109 K6 32 45N 115 15W
Allada, Benin 83 D5 6 41N 2 9 E
Allagash →, U.S.A. 115 B11 47 5N 69 3W
Allah Dad, Pakistan 68 G2 25 38N 67 34 E
Allahabad, India 69 G9 25 25N 81 58 E
Allan, Canada 103 C7 51 53N 106 4W
Allanche, France 20 C6 45 14N 2 57 E
Allanridge, S. Africa 88 D4 27 45 S 26 40 E
Allaqi, Wadi →, Egypt 80 C3 23 7N 32 47 E
Allariz, Spain 36 C3 42 11N 7 50W
Allassac, France 20 C5 45 15N 1 29 E
Älleberg, Sweden 11 F7 58 8N 13 36 E
Allegany, U.S.A. 116 D6 42 6N 78 30W
Allegheny →, U.S.A. 116 F5 40 27N 80 1W
Allegheny Mts., U.S.A. 114 G6 38 15N 80 10W
Allegheny Reservoir, U.S.A. 116 E6 41 50N 79 0W
Allègre, France 20 C7 45 12N 3 41 E
Allègre, Pte., Guadeloupe 120 b 16 22N 61 46W
Allen, Bog of, Ireland 12 C5 53 15N 7 0W
Allen, L., Ireland 12 B3 54 8N 8 4W
Allendale, U.S.A. 115 J5 33 1N 81 18W
Allende, Mexico 118 B4 28 20N 100 50W
Allentown, U.S.A. 117 F9 40 37N 75 29W
Allentsteig, Austria 26 C8 48 41N 15 20 E
Alleppey, India 66 Q10 9 30N 76 28 E
Allepuz, Spain 38 E4 40 29N 0 44W
Aller →, Germany 24 C5 52 56N 9 12 E
Alleynes B., Barbados 121 g 13 13N 59 39W
Alliance, Nebr., U.S.A. 112 D3 42 6N 102 52W
Alliance, Ohio, U.S.A. 116 F3 40 55N 81 6W
Allier □, France 19 F9 46 25N 2 40 E
Allier →, France 19 F10 46 57N 3 4 E
Alliford Bay, Canada 102 C2 53 12N 131 58W
Alligator Pond, Jamaica 120 a 17 52N 77 34W
Allinge, Denmark 11 J8 55 17N 14 50 E
Alliston = New Tecumseth, Canada 116 B5 44 9N 79 52W
Alloa, U.K. 13 E5 56 7N 3 47W
Allones, France 18 D8 48 20N 1 40 E
Allora, Australia 95 D5 28 2 S 152 0 E
Allos, France 21 D10 44 15N 6 38 E
Alluitsup Paa, Greenland 101 B15 60 30N 45 35W
Alma, Canada 105 C5 48 35N 71 40W
Alma, Ga., U.S.A. 115 K4 31 33N 82 28W
Alma, Kans., U.S.A. 112 F6 39 1N 96 17W
Alma, Mich., U.S.A. 114 D3 43 23N 84 39W
Alma, Nebr., U.S.A. 112 E5 40 6N 99 22W
Alma Ata = Almaty, Kazakhstan 52 E8 43 15N 76 57 E
Almacelles, Spain 38 D5 41 43N 0 27 E
Almada, Portugal 37 G1 38 40N 9 9W
Almaden, Australia 94 B3 17 22 S 144 40 E
Almadén, Spain 37 G6 38 49N 4 52W
Almanor, L., U.S.A. 108 F3 40 14N 121 9W
Almansa, Spain 39 G3 38 51N 1 5W
Almanza, Spain 36 C5 42 39N 5 3W
Almanzor, Pico, Spain 36 E5 40 15N 5 18W
Almanzora →, Spain 39 H3 37 14N 1 46W
Almaş, Munţii, Romania 28 F7 44 49N 22 12 E
Almassora, Spain 38 F4 39 57N 0 3W
Almaty, Kazakhstan 52 E8 43 15N 76 57 E
Almazán, Spain 38 D2 41 30N 2 30W
Almeirim, Brazil 125 D8 1 30 S 52 34W
Almeirim, Portugal 37 F2 39 12N 8 37W
Almelo, Neths. 17 B6 52 22N 6 42 E
Almenar de Soria, Spain 38 D2 41 43N 2 12W
Almenara, Spain 38 F4 39 46N 0 14W
Almenara, Sierra de la, Spain 39 H3 37 34N 1 32W
Almendra, Embalse de, Spain 36 D4 41 10N 6 5W
Almendralejo, Spain 37 G4 38 41N 6 26W
Almere-Stad, Neths. 17 B5 52 20N 5 15 E
Almería, Spain 37 J8 36 52N 2 27W
Almería □, Spain 39 H2 37 20N 2 20W
Almería, G. de, Spain 39 J2 36 41N 2 28W
Almetyevsk, Russia 34 C11 54 53N 52 20 E
Älmhult, Sweden 11 H8 56 33N 14 8 E
Almirante, Panama 120 E3 9 10N 82 30W
Almiropótamos, Greece 46 C6 38 16N 24 11 E
Almirós, Greece 46 B4 39 11N 22 45 E
Almiroú, Kólpos, Greece 49 D6 35 23N 24 20 E
Almodôvar, Portugal 37 H2 37 31N 8 2W
Almodóvar del Campo, Spain 37 G6 38 43N 4 10W
Almodóvar del Río, Spain 37 H5 37 48N 5 1W
Almond, U.S.A. 116 D7 42 19N 77 44W
Almont, U.S.A. 116 D1 42 55N 83 3W
Almonte, Canada 117 A8 45 14N 76 12W
Almonte, Spain 37 H4 37 13N 6 38W
Almora, India 69 E8 29 38N 79 40 E
Almoradí, Spain 39 G4 38 7N 0 46W
Almorox, Spain 36 E6 40 14N 4 24W
Almoustarat, Mali 83 B5 17 35N 0 8 E
Älmsta, Sweden 10 E12 59 58N 18 50 E
Almudévar, Spain 38 C4 42 3N 0 35W
Almuñécar, Spain 37 J7 36 43N 3 41W
Almunge, Sweden 10 E12 59 53N 18 3 E
Almuradiel, Spain 37 G7 38 32N 3 28W
Alness, U.K. 13 D4 57 41N 4 16W
Alnmouth, U.K. 14 B6 55 24N 1 37W
Alnwick, U.K. 14 B6 55 24N 1 42W
Aloi, Uganda 86 B3 2 16N 33 10 E
Alon, Burma 67 H19 22 12N 95 5 E
Alonissos-Vorίai Sporades △, Greece 46 B6 39 15N 24 5 E
Alor, Indonesia 63 F6 8 15 S 124 30 E
Alor Setar, Malaysia 65 J3 6 7N 100 22 E
Álora, Spain 37 J6 36 49N 4 46W
Alosno, Spain 37 H3 37 33N 7 7W
Alot, India 68 H6 23 56N 75 40 E
Aloysius, Mt., Australia 93 E4 26 0 S 128 38 E
Alpaugh, U.S.A. 110 K7 35 53N 119 29W
Alpe Apuane △, Italy 40 D7 44 4N 10 15 E
Alpedrinha, Portugal 36 E3 40 6N 7 27W
Alpena, U.S.A. 114 C4 45 4N 83 27W
Alpes-de-Haute-Provence □, France 21 D10 44 8N 6 10 E
Alpes-Maritimes □, France 21 E11 43 55N 7 10 E
Alpha, Australia 94 C4 23 39 S 146 37 E
Alpha Cordillera, Arctic 4 A2 84 0N 118 0W
Alphen aan den Rijn, Neths. 17 B4 52 7N 4 40 E
Alpiarça, Portugal 37 F2 39 15N 8 35W
Alpine, Ariz., U.S.A. 109 K9 33 51N 109 9W
Alpine, Calif., U.S.A. 111 N10 32 50N 116 46W
Alpine, Tex., U.S.A. 113 K3 30 22N 103 40W
Alps, Europe 6 F7 46 30N 9 30 E
Alpu, Turkey 72 C4 39 46N 30 58 E
Alqueta, Barragem do, Portugal 37 G3 38 20N 7 25W
Alrø, Denmark 11 J4 55 52N 10 5 E
Als, Denmark 11 K3 54 59N 9 55 E
Alsace □, France 19 D14 48 15N 7 25 E
Alsask, Canada 103 C7 51 21N 109 59W
Alsasua, Spain 38 C2 42 54N 2 10W
Alsek →, U.S.A. 102 B1 59 10N 138 12W
Alsfeld, Germany 24 E5 50 44N 9 16 E
Alsten, Norway 8 D15 65 58N 12 40 E
Alstermo, Sweden 11 H9 56 58N 15 38 E
Alston, U.K. 14 C5 54 49N 2 25W
Alta, Norway 8 B20 69 57N 23 10 E
Alta, Sierra, Spain 38 E3 40 31N 1 30W
Alta Gracia, Argentina 126 C3 31 40 S 64 30W
Alta Sierra, U.S.A. 111 K8 35 42N 118 33W
Altaelva →, Norway 8 B20 69 54N 23 17 E
Altafjorden, Norway 8 A20 70 5N 23 5 E
Altai = Aerhtai Shan, Mongolia 60 B4 46 40N 92 45 E
Altamaha →, U.S.A. 115 K5 31 20N 81 20W
Altamira, Brazil 125 D8 3 12 S 52 10W
Altamira, Chile 126 B2 25 47 S 69 51W
Altamira, Mexico 119 C5 22 24N 97 55W
Altamira, Cuevas de, Spain 36 B6 43 20N 4 5W
Altamont, U.S.A. 117 D10 42 43N 74 3W
Altamura, Italy 43 B9 40 49N 16 33 E
Altanbulag, Mongolia 60 A5 50 16N 106 30 E
Altar, Mexico 118 A2 30 40N 111 50W
Altar, Desierto de, Mexico 118 B2 30 10N 112 0W
Altata, Mexico 118 C3 24 30N 108 0W
Altavista, U.S.A. 114 G6 37 6N 79 17W
Altay, China 60 B3 47 48N 88 10 E
Altdorf, Switz. 25 J4 46 52N 8 36 E
Alte Mellum, Germany 24 B4 53 43N 8 10 E
Altea, Spain 39 G4 38 38N 0 2W
Altenberg, Germany 24 E9 50 45N 13 45 E
Altenbruch, Germany 24 B4 53 49N 8 46 E
Altenburg, Germany 24 E8 50 59N 12 25 E
Altenkirchen, Mecklenburg-Vorpommern, Germany 24 A9 54 38N 13 22 E
Altenkirchen, Rhld-Pfz., Germany 24 E3 50 41N 7 39 E
Altenmarkt, Austria 26 D7 47 43N 14 39 E
Alter do Chão, Portugal 37 F3 39 12N 7 40W
Altınoluk, Turkey 47 B8 39 34N 26 45 E
Altınova, Turkey 47 B8 39 12N 26 47 E
Altıntaş, Turkey 47 B12 39 4N 30 7 E
Altınyaka, Turkey 47 E12 36 33N 30 20 E
Altınyayla, Turkey 47 D11 37 0N 29 33 E
Altiplano, Bolivia 122 E4 17 0 S 68 0W
Altkirch, France 19 E14 47 37N 7 15 E
Altmark, Germany 24 C7 52 45N 11 30 E
Altmühl →, Germany 25 G7 48 54N 11 52 E
Altmühltal △, Germany 25 G7 48 55N 11 15 E
Altmunster, Austria 26 D6 47 54N 13 45 E
Alto Adige = Trentino-Alto Adige □, Italy 41 B8 46 30N 11 20 E
Alto Araguaia, Brazil 125 G8 17 15 S 53 20W
Alto Cuchumatanes = Cuchumatanes, Sierra de los, Guatemala 120 C1 15 35N 91 25W
Alto del Carmen, Chile 126 B1 28 46 S 70 30W
Alto del Inca, Chile 126 A2 24 10 S 68 10W
Alto Garda Bresciano △, Italy 40 C7 45 42N 10 38 E
Alto Ligonha, Mozam. 87 F4 15 30 S 38 11 E
Alto Molocue, Mozam. 87 F4 15 50 S 37 35 E
Alto Paraguay □, Paraguay 126 A4 21 0 S 58 30W
Alto Paraná □, Paraguay 127 B5 25 30 S 54 50W
Alton, Canada 116 C4 43 54N 80 5W
Alton, U.K. 15 F7 51 9N 0 59W
Alton, Ill., U.S.A. 112 F9 38 53N 90 11W
Alton, N.H., U.S.A. 117 C13 43 27N 71 13W
Altona, Canada 103 D9 49 6N 97 33W
Altoona, U.S.A. 116 F6 40 31N 78 24W
Altötting, Germany 25 G8 48 12N 12 39 E
Altstätten, Switz. 25 H5 47 22N 9 33 E
Altun Kupri, Iraq 70 C5 35 45N 44 9 E
Altun Shan, China 60 C3 38 30N 88 0 E
Alturas, U.S.A. 108 F3 41 29N 120 32W
Altus, U.S.A. 113 H5 34 38N 99 20W
Alubijid, Phil. 61 G6 8 35N 124 29 E
Alucra, Turkey 73 B8 40 22N 38 47 E
Aluk, Sudan 81 F2 8 25N 27 30 E
Alūksne, Latvia 9 H22 57 24N 27 3 E
Alunda, Sweden 10 D12 60 4N 18 5 E
Alunite, U.S.A. 111 K12 35 59N 114 55W
Aluoro →, Ethiopia 81 F3 8 26N 33 24 E
Alupka, Ukraine 33 K8 44 23N 34 2 E
Alushta, Ukraine 33 K8 44 40N 34 25 E
Alusi, Indonesia 63 F8 7 35 S 131 40 E
Alustante, Spain 38 E3 40 36N 1 40W
Alva, U.S.A. 113 G5 36 48N 98 40W
Alvaiázere, Portugal 36 F2 39 49N 8 23W
Älvängen, Sweden 11 G6 57 58N 12 8 E
Alvão △, Portugal 36 D3 41 22N 7 48W
Alvarado, Mexico 119 D5 18 40N 95 50W
Alvarado, U.S.A. 113 J6 32 24N 97 13W
Alvaro Obregón, Presa, Mexico 118 B3 27 55N 109 52W
Älvdalen, Sweden 10 C8 61 13N 14 4 E
Alvear, Argentina 126 B4 29 5 S 56 30W
Alverca, Portugal 37 G1 38 56N 9 1W
Alvesta, Sweden 11 H8 56 54N 14 35 E
Alvin, U.S.A. 113 L7 29 26N 95 15W
Alvinston, Canada 116 D3 42 49N 81 52W
Alvito, Portugal 37 G3 38 15N 7 58W
Älvkarleby, Sweden 10 D11 60 34N 17 26 E
Alvord Desert, U.S.A. 108 E4 42 30N 118 25W
Älvros, Sweden 10 B8 62 3N 14 38 E
Älvsbyn, Sweden 8 D19 65 40N 21 0 E
Alwar, India 68 F7 27 38N 76 34 E
Alxa Zuoqi, China 56 E3 38 50N 105 40 E
Alyangula, Australia 94 A2 13 55 S 136 30 E
Alyata = Älät, Azerbaijan 35 L9 39 58N 49 25 E
Alyth, U.K. 13 E5 56 38N 3 13W
Alytus, Lithuania 9 J21 54 24N 24 3 E
Alzada, U.S.A. 112 C2 45 2N 104 25W
Alzey, Germany 25 F4 49 45N 8 7 E
Alzira, Spain 39 F4 39 9N 0 30W
Am Timan, Chad 79 F10 11 0N 20 10 E
Amadeus, L., Australia 93 D5 24 54 S 131 0 E
Amadi, Dem. Rep. of the Congo 86 B2 3 40N 26 40 E
Amâdi, Sudan 81 F3 5 29N 30 25 E
Amadjuak L., Canada 101 B12 65 0N 71 8W
Amadora, Portugal 37 G1 38 45N 9 13W
Amagansett, U.S.A. 117 F12 40 59N 72 9W
Amagasaki, Japan 55 G7 34 42N 135 20 E
Amager, Denmark 11 J6 55 37N 12 35 E
Amagunze, Nigeria 83 D6 6 20N 7 40 E
Amahai, Indonesia 63 E7 3 20 S 128 55 E
Amakusa-Shotō, Japan 55 H5 32 15N 130 10 E
Åmål, Sweden 10 E6 59 3N 12 42 E
Amalfi, Italy 43 B7 40 38N 14 36 E
Amaliás, Greece 46 D3 37 47N 21 22 E
Amalner, India 66 J9 21 5N 75 5 E
Amamapare, Indonesia 63 E9 4 53 S 136 38 E
Amambaí, Brazil 127 A4 23 5 S 55 13W
Amambaí →, Brazil 127 A5 23 22 S 53 56W
Amambay □, Paraguay 127 A4 23 0 S 56 0W
Amambay, Cordillera de, S. Amer. 127 A4 23 0 S 55 45W
Amami-Guntō, Japan 55 L4 27 16N 129 21 E
Amami-Ō-Shima, Japan 55 L4 28 0N 129 0 E
Aman, Pulau, Malaysia 65 c 5 16N 100 24 E
Amaná, L., Brazil 124 D6 2 35 S 64 40W
Amanat →, India 69 G11 24 7N 84 4 E
Amanda Park, U.S.A. 110 C3 47 28N 123 55W
Amangeldy, Kazakhstan 52 D7 50 10N 65 10 E
Amantea, Italy 43 C9 39 8N 16 4 E
Amapá, Brazil 125 C8 2 5N 50 50W
Amapá □, Brazil 125 C8 1 40N 52 0W
Amara, Sudan 81 E3 10 25N 34 10 E
Amara □, Ethiopia 81 E4 12 30N 37 30 E
Amarante, Brazil 125 E10 6 14 S 42 50W
Amarante, Portugal 36 D2 41 16N 8 5W
Amaranth, Canada 103 C9 50 36N 98 43W
Amareleja, Portugal 37 G3 38 12N 7 13W
Amargosa →, U.S.A. 111 J10 36 14N 116 51W
Amargosa Range, U.S.A. 111 J10 36 20N 116 45W
Amári, Greece 49 D6 35 13N 24 40 E
Amarillo, U.S.A. 113 H4 35 13N 101 50W
Amarkantak, India 69 H9 22 40N 81 45 E
Amârna, Tell el', Sudan 80 B3 27 38N 30 52 E
Amaro, Mte., Italy 41 F11 42 5N 14 5 E
Amarpur, India 69 G12 25 5N 87 0 E
Amarti, Eritrea 81 E5 14 17N 41 6 E
Amarwara, India 69 H8 22 18N 79 10 E
Amasra, Turkey 72 B5 41 45N 32 23 E
Amassama, Nigeria 83 D6 5 1N 6 2 E
Amasya, Turkey 72 B6 40 40N 35 50 E
Amata, Australia 93 E5 26 9 S 131 9 E
Amatikulu, S. Africa 89 D5 29 3 S 31 33 E
Amatitlán, Guatemala 120 D1 14 29N 90 38W
Amatrice, Italy 41 F10 42 38N 13 17 E
Amay, Belgium 17 D5 50 33N 5 19 E
Amazon = Amazonas →, S. Amer. 125 D9 0 5 S 50 0W
Amazonas □, Brazil 124 E6 5 0 S 65 0W
Amazonas →, S. Amer. 125 D9 0 5 S 50 0W
Amba Ferit, Ethiopia 81 E4 10 55N 38 50 E
Ambah, India 68 F8 26 43N 78 13 E
Ambahakily, Madag. 89 C7 21 36 S 43 41 E
Ambahita, Madag. 89 C8 24 1 S 45 16 E
Ambala, India 68 D7 30 23N 76 56 E
Ambalavao, Madag. 89 C8 21 50 S 46 56 E
Ambanja, Madag. 89 A8 13 40 S 48 27 E
Ambararata, Madag. 89 B8 15 3 S 48 33 E
Ambarchik, Russia 53 C17 69 40N 162 20 E
Ambarijeby, Madag. 89 A8 14 56 S 47 41 E
Ambaro, Helodranon', Madag. 89 A8 13 23 S 48 38 E
Ambato, Ecuador 124 D3 1 5 S 78 42W
Ambato, Madag. 89 A8 13 24 S 48 29 E
Ambato, Sierra de, Argentina 126 B2 28 25 S 66 10W
Ambato Boeny, Madag. 89 B8 16 28 S 46 43 E
Ambatofinandrahana, Madag. 89 C8 20 33 S 46 48 E
Ambatolampy, Madag. 89 B8 19 20 S 47 35 E
Ambatomainty, Madag. 89 B8 17 41 S 45 40 E
Ambatomanoina, Madag. 89 B8 18 18 S 47 37 E
Ambatondrazaka, Madag. 89 B8 17 55 S 48 28 E
Ambatosoratra, Madag. 89 B8 17 37 S 48 31 E
Ambelón, Greece 46 B4 39 45N 22 22 E
Ambenja, Madag. 89 B8 15 17 S 46 58 E
Amberg, Germany 25 F7 49 26N 11 52 E
Ambergris Cay, Belize 119 D7 18 0N 87 55W
Ambérieu-en-Bugey, France 21 C9 45 57N 5 20 E
Amberley, N.Z. 91 K4 43 9 S 172 44 E
Ambert, France 20 C7 45 33N 3 44 E
Ambidédi, Mali 82 C2 14 35N 11 47W
Ambikapur, India 69 H10 23 15N 83 15 E
Ambikol, Sudan 80 C3 21 20N 30 50 E
Ambilobé, Madag. 89 A8 13 10 S 49 3 E
Ambinanindrano, Madag. 89 C8 20 5 S 48 23 E
Ambinanitelo, Madag. 89 B8 15 21 S 49 35 E
Ambinda, Madag. 89 B8 16 25 S 45 52 E
Amble, U.K. 14 B6 55 20N 1 36W
Ambleside, U.K. 14 C5 54 26N 2 58W
Ambo, Peru 124 F3 10 5 S 76 10W
Amboahangy, Madag. 89 C8 24 15 S 46 22 E
Ambodifototra, Madag. 89 B8 16 59 S 49 52 E
Ambodilazana, Madag. 89 B8 18 6 S 49 10 E
Ambodiriana, Madag. 89 B8 17 55 S 49 18 E
Ambohidratrimo, Madag. 89 B8 18 50 S 47 26 E
Ambohidray, Madag. 89 B8 18 36 S 48 18 E
Ambohimahamasina, Madag. 89 C8 21 56 S 47 11 E
Ambohimahasoa, Madag. 89 C8 21 7 S 47 13 E
Ambohimanga, Madag. 89 C8 20 52 S 47 36 E
Ambohimitombo, Madag. 89 C8 20 43 S 47 26 E
Ambohitra, Madag. 89 A8 12 30 S 49 10 E
Amboise, France 18 E8 47 24N 1 2 E
Ambon, Indonesia 63 E7 3 43 S 128 12 E
Ambondro, Madag. 89 D8 25 13 S 45 44 E
Amboseli △, Kenya 86 C4 2 37 S 37 13 E
Amboseli, L., Kenya 86 C4 2 40 S 37 10 E
Ambositra, Madag. 89 C8 20 31 S 47 25 E
Ambovombe, Madag. 89 D8 25 11 S 46 5 E
Amboy, U.S.A. 111 L11 34 33N 115 45W
Amboyna Cay, S. China Sea 62 C4 7 50N 112 50 E
Ambridge, U.S.A. 116 F4 40 36N 80 14W
Ambriz, Angola 84 F2 7 48 S 13 8 E
Amchitka I., U.S.A. 100 C1 51 32N 179 0 E
Amderma, Russia 52 C7 69 45N 61 30 E
Amdhi, India 69 H9 23 51N 81 27 E
Ameca, Mexico 118 C4 20 30N 104 0W
Ameca →, Mexico 118 C3 20 40N 105 15W
Amecameca, Mexico 119 D5 19 7N 98 46W
Ameland, Neths. 17 A5 53 27N 5 45 E
Amélia, Italy 41 F9 42 33N 12 25 E
Amendolara, Italy 43 C9 39 57N 16 35 E
Amenia, U.S.A. 117 E11 41 51N 73 33W
American Falls, U.S.A. 108 E7 42 47N 112 51W
American Falls Reservoir, U.S.A. 108 E7 42 47N 112 52W
American Fork, U.S.A. 108 F8 40 23N 111 48W
American Highland, Antarctica 5 D6 73 0 S 75 0 E
American Samoa ☑, Pac. Oc. 91 B13 14 20 S 170 40W
Americana, Brazil 127 A6 22 45 S 47 20W
Americus, U.S.A. 115 K3 32 4N 84 14W
Amerigo Vespucci, Firenze ✈ (FLR), Italy 40 E8 43 49N 11 13 E
Amersfoort, Neths. 17 B5 52 9N 5 23 E
Amersfoort, S. Africa 89 D4 26 59 S 29 53 E
Amery Ice Shelf, Antarctica 5 C6 69 30 S 72 0 E
Ames, Spain 36 C2 42 54N 8 38W
Ames, U.S.A. 112 E8 42 2N 93 37W
Amesbury, U.S.A. 117 D14 42 51N 70 56W
Amet, India 68 G5 25 18N 73 56 E
Amfíklia, Greece 46 C4 38 38N 22 35 E
Amfilokhía, Greece 46 C3 38 52N 21 9 E
Amfípolis, Greece 44 F7 40 48N 23 52 E
Ámfissa, Greece 46 C4 38 32N 22 22 E
Amga, Russia 53 C14 60 50N 132 0 E
Amga →, Russia 53 C14 62 38N 134 32 E
Amgu, Russia 53 E14 45 45N 137 15 E
Amgun →, Russia 53 D14 52 56N 139 38 E
Amherst, Canada 105 C7 45 48N 64 8W
Amherst, Mass., U.S.A. 117 D12 42 23N 72 31W
Amherst, N.Y., U.S.A. 116 D6 42 59N 78 48W
Amherst, Ohio, U.S.A. 116 E2 41 24N 82 14W
Amherst I., Canada 117 B8 44 8N 76 43W
Amherstburg, Canada 104 D3 42 6N 83 6W
Amiata, Mte., Italy 41 F8 42 53N 11 37 E
Amidon, U.S.A. 112 B3 46 29N 103 19W
Amiens, France 19 C9 49 54N 2 16 E
Amindaion, Greece 44 F5 40 42N 21 42 E
Åminne, Sweden 11 G7 57 7N 14 0 E
Amino, Ethiopia 81 G5 4 25N 41 52 E
Aminuis, Namibia 88 C2 23 43 S 19 21 E
Amīrābād, Iran 70 C5 33 20N 46 16 E
Amirante Is., Seychelles 50 K9 6 0 S 53 0 E
Amisk △, Canada 103 B9 56 43N 98 0W
Amisk L., Canada 103 C8 54 35N 102 15W
Amistad △, U.S.A. 113 L4 29 32N 101 12W
Amistad, Presa de la, Mexico 118 B4 29 24N 101 0W
Amite, U.S.A. 113 K9 30 44N 90 30W
Amla, India 68 J8 21 56N 78 7 E
Amlapura = Karangasem, Indonesia 63 J18 8 27 S 115 37 E
Amlia I., U.S.A. 100 C2 52 4N 173 30W
Amlwch, U.K. 14 D3 53 24N 4 20W
Amm Adam, Sudan 81 D4 16 20N 36 1 E
'Ammān, Jordan 74 D4 31 57N 35 52 E
'Ammān □, Jordan 74 D5 31 40N 36 30 E
'Ammān ✈ (AMM), Jordan 74 D5 31 45N 36 2 E
Ammanford, U.K. 15 F4 51 48N 3 59W
Ammassalik = Tasiilaq, Greenland 4 C6 65 40N 37 20W
Ammerån →, Sweden 10 A10 63 9N 16 13 E
Ammersee, Germany 25 G7 48 0N 11 7 E
Ammochostos = Famagusta, Cyprus 49 D12 35 8N 33 55 E
Ammon, U.S.A. 108 E8 43 28N 111 58W
Amnat Charoen, Thailand 64 E5 15 51N 104 38 E
Amnura, Bangla. 69 G13 24 37N 88 25 E
Amo Jiang →, China 58 F3 23 0N 101 50 E
Āmol, Iran 71 B7 36 23N 52 20 E
Amorgós, Greece 47 E7 36 50N 25 57 E
Amory, U.S.A. 115 J1 33 59N 88 29W
Amos, Canada 104 C4 48 35N 78 5W
Åmot, Norway 9 G13 59 57N 9 54 E
Åmotfors, Sweden 10 E6 59 47N 12 22 E
Amoy = Xiamen, China 59 E12 24 25N 118 4 E
Ampanavoana, Madag. 89 B9 15 41 S 50 22 E
Ampang, Malaysia 65 L3 3 8N 101 45 E
Ampangalana, Lakandranon', Madag. 89 C8 22 48 S 47 50 E
Ampanihy, Madag. 89 C7 24 40 S 44 45 E
Amparafaravola, Madag. 89 B8 17 35 S 48 13 E
Ampasinambo, Madag. 89 C8 20 31 S 48 0 E
Ampasindava, Helodranon', Madag. 89 A8 13 40 S 48 15 E
Ampasindava, Saikanosy, Madag. 89 A8 13 42 S 47 55 E
Ampenan, Indonesia 63 K18 8 34 S 116 4 E
Amper, Nigeria 83 D6 9 25N 9 40 E
Amper →, Germany 25 G7 48 29N 11 55 E
Ampezzo, Italy 41 B9 46 25N 12 48 E
Amphoe Kathu, Thailand 65 a 7 55N 98 21 E
Amphoe Thalang, Thailand 65 a 8 1N 98 20 E
Ampitsikinana, Réunion 89 A8 12 57 S 49 49 E
Ampombiantambo, Madag. 89 A8 12 42 S 48 57 E
Amposta, Spain 38 E5 40 43N 0 34 E
Ampotaka, Madag. 89 D7 25 3 S 44 41 E
Ampoza, Madag. 89 C7 22 20 S 44 44 E
Amqui, Canada 105 C6 48 28N 67 27W
Amravati, India 66 J10 20 55N 77 45 E
Amreli, India 68 J4 21 35N 71 17 E
Amritsar, India 68 D6 31 35N 74 57 E
Amroha, India 69 E8 28 53N 78 30 E
Amrum, Germany 24 A4 54 38N 8 22 E
Amsterdam, Neths. 17 B4 52 23N 4 54 E
Amsterdam, U.S.A. 117 D10 42 56N 74 11W
Amsterdam ✈ (AMS), Neths. 17 B4 52 18N 4 45 E
Amsterdam, I. = Nouvelle-Amsterdam, Î., Ind. Oc. 3 F13 38 30 S 77 30 E
Amstetten, Austria 26 C7 48 7N 14 51 E
Amudarya →, Uzbekistan 52 E6 43 58N 59 34 E
Amundsen Gulf, Canada 100 A7 71 0N 124 0W
Amundsen-Scott, Antarctica 5 E 90 0 S 166 0 E
Amundsen Sea, Antarctica 5 D15 72 0 S 115 0W
Amungen, Sweden 10 C9 61 10N 15 40 E
Amuntai, Indonesia 62 E5 2 28 S 115 25 E
Amur →, Russia 53 D15 52 56N 141 10 E
Amur, W. →, Sudan 80 D3 18 56N 33 34 E
Amurang, Indonesia 63 D6 1 5N 124 40 E
Amurrio, Spain 38 B1 43 3N 3 0W
Amursk, Russia 53 D14 50 14N 136 54 E
Amusco, Spain 36 C6 42 10N 4 28W
Amvrakikós Kólpos, Greece 46 C2 39 0N 20 55 E
Amvrosiyivka, Ukraine 33 J10 47 43N 38 30 E
Amyderya = Amudarya →, Uzbekistan 52 E6 43 58N 59 34 E
An Anbār □, Iraq 70 C4 33 25N 42 0 E
An Bien, Vietnam 65 H5 9 45N 105 0 E
An Hoa, Vietnam 64 E7 15 40N 108 5 E
An Nabatīyah at Tahta, Lebanon 74 B4 33 23N 35 27 E
An Nabk, Si. Arabia 70 D3 31 20N 37 20 E
An Nabk, Syria 74 A5 34 2N 36 44 E
An Nafūd, Si. Arabia 70 D4 28 15N 41 0 E
An Najaf, Iraq 70 C5 32 3N 44 15 E
An Nāşirīyah, Iraq 70 D5 31 0N 46 15 E
An Nhon, Vietnam 64 F7 13 55N 109 7 E
An Nil □, Sudan 80 D3 19 30N 33 0 E
An Nil el Abyad □, Sudan 81 E3 14 0N 32 15 E
An Nil el Azraq □, Sudan 81 E3 11 30N 34 30 E
An Nu'ayrīyah, Si. Arabia 71 E6 27 30N 48 30 E
An Nu'mānīyah, Iraq 73 F11 32 32N 45 25 E
An Nuwayb'ī, W. →, Si. Arabia 74 F3 29 18N 34 57 E
An Thoi, Dao, Vietnam 65 H4 9 58N 104 0 E
An Uaimh, Ireland 12 C5 53 39N 6 41W
Anabar →, Russia 53 B12 73 8N 113 36 E
'Anabtā, West Bank 74 C4 32 19N 35 7 E
Anaconda, U.S.A. 108 C7 46 8N 112 57W
Anacortes, U.S.A. 110 B4 48 30N 122 37W
Anacuao, Mt., Phil. 61 C4 16 16N 121 53 E
Anadarko, U.S.A. 113 H5 35 4N 98 15W
Anadia, Portugal 36 E2 40 26N 8 27W

Anadolu, Turkey ..... **72 C5** 39 0N 30 0 E
Anadyr, Russia ..... **53 C18** 64 35N 177 20 E
Anadyr →, Russia ... **53 C18** 64 55N 176 5 E
Anadyrskiy Zaliv, Russia ..... **53 C19** 64 0N 180 0 E
Anáfi, Greece ..... **47 E7** 36 22N 25 48 E
Anafópoulo, Greece ... **47 E7** 36 17N 25 50 E
Anaga, Pta. de, Canary Is. **48 F3** 28 34N 16 9W
Anagni, Italy ..... **41 G10** 41 44N 13 9 E
'Anah, Iraq ..... **70 C4** 34 25N 42 0 E
Anaheim, U.S.A. **111 M9** 33 50N 117 55W
Anahim Lake, Canada . **102 C3** 52 28N 125 18W
Anáhuac, Mexico **118 B4** 27 14N 100 9W
Anakapalle, India ..... **67 L13** 17 42N 83 6 E
Anakie, Australia ..... **94 C4** 23 32 S 147 45 E
Anaklia, Georgia ..... **35 J5** 42 22N 41 35 E
Analalava, Madag. ..... **89 A8** 14 35 S 48 0 E
Analavoka, Madag. .... **89 C8** 22 23 S 46 30 E
Análipsis, Greece ..... **49 A3** 39 36N 19 55 E
Anambar →, Pakistan . **68 D3** 30 15N 68 50 E
Anambas, Kepulauan, Indonesia ..... **62 D3** 3 20N 106 30 E
Anambas Is. = Anambas, Kepulauan, Indonesia ..... **62 D3** 3 20N 106 30 E
Anambra □, Nigeria ... **83 D6** 6 20N 7 0 E
Anamosa, U.S.A. **112 D9** 42 7N 91 17W
Anamur, Turkey ..... **70 B2** 36 8N 32 58 E
Anamur Burnu, Turkey . **72 D5** 36 2N 32 47 E
Anan, Japan ..... **55 H7** 33 54N 134 40 E
Anand, India ..... **68 H5** 22 32N 72 59 E
Anánes, Greece ..... **46 E6** 36 33N 24 9 E
Anantapur, India ..... **66 M10** 14 39N 77 42 E
Anantnag, India ..... **69 C6** 33 45N 75 10 E
Ananyiv, Ukraine ..... **29 C14** 47 44N 29 58 E
Anapa, Russia ..... **33 K9** 44 55N 37 25 E
Anapodháris →, Greece **49 E7** 34 59N 25 20 E
Anápolis, Brazil ..... **125 G9** 16 15 S 48 50W
Anapu →, Brazil ..... **125 D8** 1 53 S 50 53W
Anár, Iran ..... **71 D7** 30 55N 55 13 E
Anārak, Iran ..... **71 C7** 33 25N 53 40 E
Anas →, India ..... **68 H5** 23 26N 74 0 E
Anatolia = Anadolu, Turkey ..... **72 C5** 39 0N 30 0 E
Anatsogno, Madag. .... **89 C7** 23 33 S 43 46 E
Añatuya, Argentina ... **126 B3** 28 20 S 62 50W
Anaunethad L., Canada . **103 A8** 60 55N 104 25W
Anbyŏn, N. Korea ..... **57 E14** 39 1N 127 35 E
Ancares, Spain **36 C4** 42 50N 6 40W
Ancares, Sierra de, Spain **36 C4** 42 51N 6 52W
Ancaster, Canada **116 C5** 43 13N 79 59W
Ancenis, France **18 E5** 47 21N 1 10W
Anchor Bay, U.S.A. ... **110 G3** 38 48N 123 34W
Anchorage, U.S.A. **100 B5** 61 13N 149 54W
Anci, China ..... **56 E9** 39 20N 116 40 E
Ancohuma, Nevado, Bolivia ..... **124 G5** 16 0 S 68 50W
Ancón, Peru ..... **124 F3** 11 50 S 77 10W
Ancona, Italy ..... **41 E10** 43 38N 13 30 E
Ancud, Chile ..... **128 E2** 42 0 S 73 50W
Ancud, G. de, Chile ... **128 E2** 42 0 S 73 0W
Ancy-le-Franc, France . **19 E11** 47 46N 4 10 E
Andacollo, Argentina .. **126 D1** 37 10 S 70 42W
Andacollo, Chile ..... **126 C1** 30 14 S 71 6W
Andaingo, Madag. ..... **89 B8** 18 12 S 48 17 E
Andalgalá, Argentina .. **126 B2** 27 40 S 66 30W
Åndalsnes, Norway .... **9 E12** 62 35N 7 43 E
Andalucía □, Spain **37 H6** 37 35N 5 0W
Andalusia = Andalucía □, Spain **37 H6** 37 35N 5 0W
Andalusia, U.S.A. **115 K2** 31 18N 86 29W
Andaman Is., Ind. Oc. . **50 H13** 12 30N 92 45 E
Andaman Sea, Ind. Oc. . **62 B1** 13 0N 96 0 E
Andamooka Opal Fields, Australia ... **95 E2** 30 27 S 137 9 E
Andapa, Madag. ..... **89 A8** 14 39 S 49 39 E
Andara, Namibia ..... **88 B3** 18 2 S 21 9 E
Andelot-Blancheville, France ..... **19 D12** 48 15N 5 18 E
Andenes, Norway ..... **8 B17** 69 19N 16 18 E
Andenne, Belgium ..... **17 D5** 50 28N 5 5 E
Andéranboukane, Mali . **83 B5** 15 26N 3 2 E
Andermatt, Switz. .... **25 J4** 46 38N 8 35 E
Andernach, Germany ... **24 E3** 50 26N 7 24 E
Andernos-les-Bains, France **20 D2** 44 44N 1 6W
Anderslöv, Sweden .... **11 J7** 55 26N 13 19 E
Anderson, Alaska, U.S.A. **100 B5** 64 25N 149 15W
Anderson, Calif., U.S.A. **108 F2** 40 27N 122 18W
Anderson, Ind., U.S.A. . **114 E3** 40 10N 85 41W
Anderson, Mo., U.S.A. . **113 G7** 36 39N 94 27W
Anderson, S.C., U.S.A. . **115 H4** 34 31N 82 39W
Anderson →, Canada .. **100 B7** 69 42N 129 0W
Anderstorp, Sweden ... **11 G7** 57 19N 13 39 E
Andes, U.S.A. **117 D10** 42 12N 74 47W
Andes, Cord. de los, S. Amer. ..... **124 H5** 20 0 S 68 0W
Andfjorden, Norway .. **8 B17** 69 10N 16 20 E
Andhra Pradesh □, India ..... **66 L11** 18 0N 79 0 E
Andijon, Uzbekistan ... **52 E8** 41 10N 72 15 E
Andikíthira, Greece ... **46 F5** 35 52N 23 15 E
Andilamena, Madag. ... **89 B8** 17 1 S 48 35 E
Andímeshk, Iran ..... **71 C6** 32 27N 48 21 E
Andímilos, Greece ..... **46 E6** 36 47N 24 12 E
Andíparos, Greece ..... **47 D7** 37 0N 25 3 E
Andípaxoi, Greece ..... **49 B2** 39 9N 20 13 E
Andípsara, Greece ..... **47 C7** 38 30N 25 29 E
Andírrion, Greece ..... **46 C3** 38 20N 21 46 E
Andizhan = Andijon, Uzbekistan ..... **52 E8** 41 10N 72 15 E
Andoain, Spain **38 B2** 43 13N 2 1W
Andoany, Madag. ..... **89 A8** 13 25 S 48 16 E
Andohahela △, Madag. . **89 C8** 24 35 S 46 44 E
Andong, S. Korea ..... **57 F15** 36 40N 128 43 E
Andongwei, China ..... **57 G10** 35 14N 119 20 E
Andoom, Australia .... **94 A3** 12 25 S 141 53 E
Andorra, Spain **38 E4** 40 59N 0 28W
Andorra ■, Europe .... **20 F5** 42 30N 1 30 E
Andorra La Vella, Andorra ..... **20 F5** 42 31N 1 32 E
Andover, U.K. **15 F6** 51 12N 1 29W
Andover, Maine, U.S.A. **117 B14** 44 38N 70 45W
Andover, Mass., U.S.A. **117 D13** 42 40N 71 8W
Andover, N.J., U.S.A. .. **117 F10** 40 59N 74 45W
Andover, N.Y., U.S.A. . **116 D7** 42 10N 77 48W
Andover, Ohio, U.S.A. . **116 E4** 41 36N 80 34W
Andøya, Norway ..... **8 B16** 69 10N 15 50 E
Andradina, Brazil ..... **125 H8** 20 54 S 51 23W
Andramasina, Madag. .. **89 B8** 19 11 S 47 35 E
Andranopasy, Madag. .. **89 C7** 21 17 S 43 44 E
Andranovory, Madag. .. **89 C7** 23 8 S 44 10 E

Andratx, Spain ..... **48 B9** 39 39N 2 25 E
Andreanof Is., U.S.A. .. **100 C2** 51 30N 176 0W
Andreapol, Russia ..... **32 D7** 56 40N 32 17 E
Andrews, S.C., U.S.A. . **115 J6** 33 27N 79 34W
Andrews, Tex., U.S.A. . **113 J3** 32 19N 102 33W
Andreyevka, Russia ... **34 D10** 52 19N 51 55 E
Ándria, Italy ..... **43 A9** 41 13N 16 17 E
Andriamena, Madag. .. **89 B8** 17 26 S 47 30 E
Andriandampy, Madag. **89 C8** 22 45 S 45 41 E
Andriba, Madag. ..... **89 B8** 17 30 S 46 58 E
Andrijevica, Serbia & M. **44 D3** 42 45N 19 48 E
Andringitra △, Madag. . **89 C8** 22 13 S 46 5 E
Andrítsaina, Greece ... **46 D3** 37 29N 21 52 E
Androka, Madag. ..... **89 C7** 24 58 S 44 2 E
Ándros, Greece ..... **46 D6** 37 50N 24 57 E
Andros I., Bahamas ... **120 B4** 24 30N 78 0W
Andros Town, Bahamas **120 B4** 24 43N 77 47W
Androscoggin →, U.S.A. **117 C14** 43 58N 70 0W
Andrychów, Poland ... **31 J6** 49 51N 19 18 E
Andselv, Norway ..... **8 B18** 69 4N 18 34 E
Andújar, Spain **37 G6** 38 3N 4 5W
Andulo, Angola ..... **84 G3** 11 25 S 16 45 E
Aneby, Sweden ..... **11 G8** 57 48N 14 49 E
Anegada, Br Virgin Is. . **121 e** 18 45N 64 20W
Anegada Passage, W. Indies **121 C7** 18 15N 63 45W
Aného, Togo ..... **83 D5** 6 12N 1 34 E
Anenni-Noi, Moldova .. **29 D14** 46 53N 29 15 E
Aneto, Pico de, Spain . **38 C5** 42 37N 0 40 E
Anfu, China ..... **59 D10** 27 21N 114 40 E
Ang Mo Kio, Singapore **65 d** 1 23N 103 50 E
Ang Thong, Thailand .. **64 E3** 14 35N 100 31 E
Ang Thong △, Thailand **65 H2** 9 40N 99 43 E
Ang Thong, Ko, Thailand ..... **65 b** 9 37N 99 41 E
Angamos, Punta, Chile . **126 A1** 23 1 S 70 32W
Angara →, Russia ..... **53 D10** 58 5N 94 20 E
Angara-Débou, Benin . **83 C5** 11 9N 3 3 E
Angarsk, Russia ..... **53 D11** 52 30N 104 0 E
Angas Hills, Australia . **92 D4** 23 0 S 127 50 E
Angaston, Australia ... **95 E2** 34 30 S 139 8 E
Ånge, Sweden ..... **10 B9** 62 31N 15 35 E
Angel, Salto = Angel Falls, Venezuela ... **124 B6** 5 57N 62 30W
Ángel de la Guarda, I., Mexico **118 B2** 29 30N 113 30W
Angel Falls, Venezuela . **124 B6** 5 57N 62 30W
Angeles, Phil. ..... **61 D4** 15 9N 120 33 E
Ängelholm, Sweden ... **11 H6** 56 15N 12 58 E
Angels Camp, U.S.A. .. **110 G6** 38 4N 120 32W
Ängelsberg, Sweden ... **10 E10** 59 58N 16 0 E
Anger →, Ethiopia .... **81 F4** 9 37N 36 6 E
Angereb →, Ethiopia .. **81 E4** 13 45N 36 40 E
Ångermanälven →, Sweden ..... **10 B11** 62 40N 18 0 E
Ångermanland □, Sweden ..... **8 E18** 63 36N 17 45 E
Angermünde, Germany . **24 B9** 53 1N 14 0 E
Angers, Canada **117 A9** 45 31N 75 29W
Angers, France **18 E6** 47 30N 0 35W
Angerville, France .... **19 D9** 48 19N 2 0 E
Ängesån →, Sweden ... **8 C20** 66 16N 22 47 E
Angikuni L., Canada ... **103 A9** 62 12N 99 59W
Angkor, Cambodia .... **64 F4** 13 22N 103 50 E
Anglès, Spain ..... **38 D7** 41 57N 2 38 E
Anglesey, Isle of □, U.K. **14 D3** 53 16N 4 18W
Anglet, France **20 E2** 43 29N 1 31W
Angleton, U.S.A. **113 L7** 29 10N 95 26W
Anglin →, France ..... **20 B4** 46 42N 0 52 E
Anglisidhes, Cyprus ... **49 E12** 34 51N 33 27 E
Anglure, France ..... **19 D10** 48 35N 3 50 E
Angmagssalik = Tasiilaq, Greenland . **4 C6** 65 40N 37 20W
Ango, Dem. Rep. of the Congo ..... **86 B2** 4 10N 26 5 E
Angoche, Mozam. ..... **87 F4** 16 8 S 39 55 E
Angoche, I., Mozam. ... **87 F4** 16 20 S 39 50 E
Angol, Chile ..... **126 D1** 37 56 S 72 45W
Angola, Ind., U.S.A. ... **114 E3** 41 38N 85 0W
Angola, N.Y., U.S.A. .. **116 D5** 42 38N 79 2W
Angola ■, Africa ..... **85 G3** 12 0 S 18 0 E
Angoulême, France .... **20 C4** 45 39N 0 10 E
Angoumois, France .... **20 C4** 45 50N 0 25 E
Angra dos Reis, Brazil . **127 A7** 23 0 S 44 10W
Angrapa →, Russia .... **30 D8** 54 37N 21 54 E
Angren, Uzbekistan ... **52 E8** 41 1N 70 12 E
Angtassom, Cambodia . **65 G5** 11 1N 104 41 E
Angu, Dem. Rep. of the Congo ..... **86 B1** 3 23N 24 30 E
Anguang, China ..... **57 B12** 45 15N 123 45 E
Anguilla ■, W. Indies . **121 C7** 18 14N 63 5W
Anguo, China ..... **56 E8** 38 28N 115 15 E
Angurugu, Australia ... **94 A2** 14 0 S 136 25 E
Angus □, U.K. **13 E6** 56 46N 2 56W
Angwa →, Zimbabwe .. **89 B5** 16 0 S 30 23 E
Anhanduí →, Brazil ... **127 A5** 21 46 S 52 9W
Anholt, Denmark ..... **11 H5** 56 42N 11 33 E
Anhua, China ..... **59 C8** 28 23N 111 12 E
Anhui □, China ..... **59 B11** 32 0N 117 0 E
Anhwei = Anhui □, China ..... **59 B11** 32 0N 117 0 E
Anichab, Namibia ..... **88 C1** 21 0 S 14 46 E
Ánidhros, Greece ..... **47 E7** 36 38N 25 43 E
Anié, Togo ..... **83 D5** 7 42N 1 8 E
Animas →, U.S.A. **109 H9** 36 43N 108 13W
Anina, Romania ..... **28 E6** 45 6N 21 51 E
Aninoasa, Romania .... **29 F9** 44 47N 24 10 E
Anivorano, Madag. .... **89 B8** 18 44 S 48 58 E
Anjalankoski, Finland . **9 F22** 60 45N 26 51 E
Anjar, India ..... **68 H4** 23 6N 70 10 E
Anji, China ..... **59 B12** 30 46N 119 40 E
Anjou, France **18 E6** 47 20N 0 15W
Anjozorobe, Madag. ... **89 B8** 18 22 S 47 52 E
Anju, N. Korea ..... **57 E13** 39 36N 125 40 E
Anka, Nigeria ..... **83 C6** 12 13N 5 58 E
Ankaboa, Tanjona, Madag. ..... **89 C7** 21 58 S 43 20 E
Ankang, China ..... **56 H5** 32 40N 109 1 E
Ankara, Turkey ..... **72 C5** 39 57N 32 54 E
Ankarafantsika △, Madag. ..... **89 B8** 16 8 S 47 5 E
Ankaramena, Madag. .. **89 C8** 21 57 S 46 39 E
Ankaratra, Madag. .... **85 H9** 19 25 S 47 12 E
Ankarsrum, Sweden ... **11 G10** 57 41N 16 20 E
Ankasakasa, Madag. ... **89 B7** 16 21 S 44 52 E
Ankazoabo, Madag. ... **89 C7** 22 18 S 44 31 E
Ankazobe, Madag. .... **89 B8** 18 20 S 47 10 E
Ankeny, U.S.A. **112 E8** 41 44N 93 36W
Ankililoaka, Madag. ... **89 C7** 22 45 S 43 45 E
Ankisabe, Madag. ..... **89 B8** 19 17 S 46 29 E
Anklam, Germany ..... **24 B9** 53 51N 13 41 E
Ankoro, Dem. Rep. of the Congo ..... **86 D2** 6 45 S 26 55 E

Ankororoka, Madag. .. **89 D8** 25 30 S 45 11 E
Anlong, China ..... **58 E5** 25 2N 105 27 E
Anlu, China ..... **59 B9** 31 15N 113 45 E
Anmyŏn-do, S. Korea . **57 F14** 36 25N 126 25 E
Ånn, Sweden ..... **10 A6** 63 19N 12 34 E
Ann, C., U.S.A. **117 D14** 42 38N 70 35W
Ann Arbor, U.S.A. **114 D4** 42 17N 83 45W
Anna, Russia ..... **34 E5** 51 28N 40 23 E
Anna, U.S.A. **113 G10** 37 28N 89 15W
Annaba, Algeria ..... **78 A7** 36 50N 7 46 E
Annaberg-Buchholz, Germany ..... **24 E9** 50 34N 13 0 E
Annalee →, Ireland ... **12 B4** 54 2N 7 24W
Annam, Vietnam ..... **64 E7** 16 0N 108 0 E
Annamitique, Chaîne, Asia ..... **64 D6** 17 0N 106 0 E
Annan, U.K. **13 G5** 54 59N 3 16W
Annan →, U.K. **13 G5** 54 58N 3 16W
Annapolis, U.S.A. **114 F7** 38 59N 76 30W
Annapolis Royal, Canada **105 D6** 44 44N 65 32W
Annapurna, Nepal .... **69 E10** 28 34N 83 50 E
Annean, L., Australia .. **93 E2** 26 54 S 118 14 E
Anneberg, Sweden .... **11 G8** 57 44N 14 49 E
Annecy, France ..... **21 C10** 45 55N 6 8 E
Annecy, Lac d', France . **21 C10** 45 52N 6 10 E
Annemasse, France ... **19 F13** 46 12N 6 16 E
Annenskiy Most, Russia **32 B9** 60 45N 37 10 E
Anning, China ..... **58 E4** 24 55N 102 26 E
Anniston, U.S.A. **115 J3** 33 39N 85 50W
Annobón, Atl. Oc. .... **77 G4** 1 25 S 5 36 E
Annonay, France ..... **21 C8** 45 15N 4 40 E
Annot, France ..... **21 E10** 43 58N 6 38 E
Annotto B., Jamaica ... **120 a** 18 17N 76 45W
Ånnsjön, Sweden ..... **10 A6** 63 19N 12 34 E
Annville, U.S.A. **117 F8** 40 20N 76 31W
Annweiler, Germany .. **25 F3** 49 12N 7 57 E
Áno Arkhánai, Greece . **49 D7** 35 16N 25 11 E
Áno Porróia, Greece .. **44 E7** 41 17N 23 2 E
Áno Síros, Greece ..... **46 D6** 37 29N 24 56 E
Áno Viánnos, Greece .. **49 D7** 35 2N 25 21 E
Anorotsangana, Madag. **89 A8** 13 56 S 47 55 E
Anosibe, Madag. ..... **89 B8** 19 26 S 48 13 E
Anou Mellene, Mali ... **83 B5** 17 29N 0 33 E
Anoumaba, Ivory C. ... **82 D4** 6 23N 4 38W
Anóyia, Greece ..... **49 D6** 35 16N 24 52 E
Anping, Hebei, China .. **56 E8** 38 15N 115 30 E
Anping, Liaoning, China **57 D12** 41 5N 123 30 E
Anpu Gang, China .... **58 G7** 21 25N 109 50 E
Anqing, China ..... **59 B11** 30 30N 117 3 E
Anqiu, China ..... **57 F10** 36 25N 119 10 E
Anren, China ..... **59 D9** 26 43N 113 18 E
Ansager, Denmark .... **11 J2** 55 43N 8 45 E
Ansai, China ..... **56 F5** 36 50N 109 20 E
Ansbach, Germany .... **25 F6** 49 28N 10 34 E
Anse la Raye, St. Lucia **121 f** 13 55N 61 3W
Anseba →, Eritrea .... **81 D4** 16 0N 38 30 E
Ansfelden, Austria .... **26 C7** 48 12N 14 17 E
Anshan, China ..... **57 D12** 41 5N 122 58 E
Anshun, China ..... **58 D5** 26 18N 105 57 E
Ansião, Portugal **36 F2** 39 56N 8 27W
Ansley, U.S.A. **112 E5** 41 18N 99 23W
Ansó, Spain **38 C4** 42 51N 0 48W
Ansoain, Spain **38 C3** 42 50N 1 38W
Anson, U.S.A. **113 J5** 32 45N 99 54W
Anson B., Australia ... **92 B5** 13 20 S 130 6 E
Ansongo, Mali ..... **83 B5** 15 25N 0 35 E
Ansongo-Ménaka △, Mali ..... **83 B5** 15 3N 1 37 E
Ansonia, U.S.A. **117 E11** 41 21N 73 5W
Anstruther, U.K. **13 E6** 56 14N 2 41W
Ansudu, Indonesia .... **63 E9** 2 11 S 139 22 E
Antabamba, Peru ..... **124 F4** 14 40 S 73 0W
Antakya, Turkey ..... **70 B3** 36 14N 36 10 E
Antalaha, Madag. ..... **89 A9** 14 57 S 50 20 E
Antalya, Turkey ..... **72 D4** 36 52N 30 45 E
Antalya □, Turkey .... **47 E12** 36 30N 30 0 E
Antalya Körfezi, Turkey **72 D4** 36 15N 31 30 E
Antambohobe, Madag. . **89 C8** 22 20 S 46 47 E
Antanambao-Manampotsy, Madag. **89 B8** 19 29 S 48 34 E
Antanambe, Madag. ... **89 B8** 16 26 S 49 52 E
Antananarivo, Madag. . **89 B8** 18 55 S 47 31 E
Antananarivo □, Madag. **89 B8** 19 0 S 47 0 E
Antanifotsy, Madag. ... **89 B8** 19 39 S 47 19 E
Antanimbaribe, Madag. **89 C7** 21 30 S 44 48 E
Antanimora, Madag. .. **89 C8** 24 49 S 45 40 E
Antarctic Pen., Antarctica ..... **5 C18** 67 0 S 60 0W
Antarctica ..... **5 E3** 90 0 S 0 0W
Antelope, Zimbabwe .. **87 G2** 21 2 S 28 31 E
Antequera, Paraguay .. **126 A4** 24 8 S 57 7W
Antequera, Spain **37 H6** 37 5N 4 33W
Antero, Mt., U.S.A. ... **109 G10** 38 41N 106 15W
Antevamena, Madag. .. **89 C7** 21 2 S 44 8 E
Anthemous, Greece ... **44 F7** 40 31N 23 15 E
Anthony, Kans., U.S.A. **113 G5** 37 9N 98 2W
Anthony, N. Mex., U.S.A. **109 K10** 32 0N 106 36W
Anti Atlas, Morocco ... **78 C4** 30 0N 8 30W
Anti-Lebanon = Ash Sharqi, Al Jabal, Lebanon ..... **74 B5** 33 40N 36 10 E
Antibes, France ..... **21 E11** 43 34N 7 6 E
Antibes, C. d', France . **21 E11** 43 31N 7 7 E
Anticosti, Î. d', Canada **105 C7** 49 30N 63 0W
Antifer, C. d', France .. **18 C7** 49 41N 0 10 E
Antigo, U.S.A. **112 C10** 45 9N 89 9W
Antigonish, Canada ... **105 C7** 45 38N 61 58W
Antigua, Canary Is. ... **48 F5** 28 24N 14 1W
Antigua, Guatemala ... **120 D1** 14 34N 90 41W
Antigua, W. Indies **121 C7** 17 0N 61 50W
Antigua & Barbuda ■, W. Indies **121 C7** 17 20N 61 48W
Antilla, Cuba **120 B4** 20 40N 75 50W
Antilles = West Indies, Cent. Amer. **121 D7** 15 0N 65 0W
Antioch, U.S.A. **110 G5** 38 1N 121 48W
Antioche, Pertuis d', France **20 B2** 46 6N 1 20W
Antioquia, Colombia .. **124 B3** 6 40N 75 55W
Antipodes Is., Pac. Oc. . **96 M9** 49 45 S 178 40 E
Antlers, U.S.A. **113 H7** 34 14N 95 37W
Antoetra, Madag. ..... **89 C8** 20 46 S 47 20 E
Antofagasta, Chile .... **126 A1** 23 50 S 70 30W
Antofagasta □, Chile .. **126 A2** 24 0 S 69 0W
Antofagasta de la Sierra, Argentina ..... **126 B2** 26 5 S 67 20W
Antofalla, Argentina .. **126 B2** 25 30 S 68 5W
Antofalla, Salar de, Argentina ..... **126 B2** 25 40 S 67 45W
Anton, U.S.A. **113 J3** 33 49N 102 10W
Antongila, Helodrano, Madag. ..... **89 B8** 15 30 S 49 50 E
Antonibé, Madag. ..... **89 B8** 15 7 S 47 24 E
Antonibé, Presqu'île d', Madag. ..... **89 A8** 14 55 S 47 20 E

Antonina, Brazil ..... **127 B6** 25 26 S 48 42W
Antrain, France **18 D5** 48 28N 1 30W
Antrim, U.K. **12 B5** 54 43N 6 14W
Antrim, U.S.A. **116 F3** 40 7N 81 21W
Antrim □, U.K. **12 B5** 54 56N 6 25W
Antrim, Mts. of, U.K. .. **12 A5** 55 3N 6 14W
Antrim Plateau, Australia ..... **92 C4** 18 8 S 128 20 E
Antrodoco, Italy ..... **41 F10** 42 25N 13 5 E
Antropovo, Russia .... **34 A6** 58 24N 43 6 E
Antsakabary, Madag. .. **89 B8** 15 3 S 48 56 E
Antsalova, Madag. .... **89 B7** 18 40 S 44 37 E
Antsenavolo, Madag. .. **89 C8** 21 24 S 48 3 E
Antsiafabositra, Madag. **89 B8** 17 18 S 46 57 E
Antsirabe, Antananarivo, Madag. **89 B8** 19 55 S 47 2 E
Antsirabe, Antsiranana, Madag. ..... **89 A8** 14 0 S 49 59 E
Antsirabe, Mahajanga, Madag. ..... **89 B8** 15 57 S 48 58 E
Antsiranana, Madag. .. **89 A8** 12 25 S 49 20 E
Antsohihy, Madag. .... **89 A8** 14 50 S 47 59 E
Antsohimbondrona Seranana, Madag. .. **89 A8** 13 7 S 48 48 E
Antu, China ..... **57 C15** 42 30N 128 20 E
Antwerp = Antwerpen, Belgium ..... **17 C4** 51 13N 4 25 E
Antwerp, U.S.A. **117 B9** 44 12N 75 37W
Antwerpen, Belgium ... **17 C4** 51 13N 4 25 E
Antwerpen □, Belgium **17 C4** 51 15N 4 40 E
Anupgarh, India ..... **68 E5** 29 10N 73 10 E
Anuppur, India ..... **69 H9** 23 6N 81 41 E
Anuradhapura, Sri Lanka ..... **66 Q12** 8 22N 80 28 E
Anveh, Iran ..... **71 E7** 27 23N 54 11 E
Anvers = Antwerpen, Belgium ..... **17 C4** 51 13N 4 25 E
Anvers I., Antarctica .. **5 C17** 64 30 S 63 40W
Anwen, China ..... **59 C13** 29 4N 120 16 E
Anxi, Fujian, China ... **59 E12** 25 2N 118 12 E
Anxi, Gansu, China ... **60 B4** 40 30N 95 43 E
Anxian, China ..... **58 B5** 31 40N 104 25 E
Anxiang, China ..... **59 C9** 29 27N 112 11 E
Anxious B., Australia .. **95 E1** 33 24 S 134 45 E
Anyama, Ivory C. **82 D4** 5 30N 4 3W
Anyang, China ..... **56 F8** 36 5N 114 21 E
Anyer-Kidul, Indonesia **63 G11** 6 4 S 105 53 E
Anyi, Jiangxi, China ... **59 C10** 28 49N 115 25 E
Anyi, Shanxi, China ... **56 G6** 35 2N 111 2 E
Anyuan, China ..... **59 E10** 25 9N 115 21 E
Anyue, China ..... **58 B5** 30 9N 105 50 E
Anze, China ..... **56 F7** 36 10N 112 12 E
Anzhero-Sudzhensk, Russia ..... **52 D9** 56 10N 86 0 E
Ánzio, Italy ..... **42 A5** 41 27N 12 37 E
Ao Makham, Thailand . **65 a** 7 50N 98 24 E
Ao Phangnga △, Thailand ..... **65 a** 8 10N 98 32 E
Aoga-Shima, Japan ... **55 H9** 32 28N 139 46 E
Aoiz, Spain **38 C3** 42 46N 1 22W
Aomen = Macau, China **59 F9** 22 12N 113 33 E
Aomori, Japan ..... **54 D10** 40 45N 140 45 E
Aomori □, Japan ..... **54 D10** 40 45N 140 40 E
Aonla, India ..... **69 E8** 28 16N 79 11 E
Aoraki Mount Cook, N.Z. ..... **91 K3** 43 36 S 170 9 E
Aosta, Italy ..... **40 C4** 45 45N 7 20 E
Aotearoa = New Zealand ■, Oceania . **91 J6** 40 0 S 176 0 E
Aoudéras, Niger ..... **83 B6** 17 45N 8 20 E
Aoukâr, Mauritania ... **82 B3** 17 40N 10 0W
Aozou, Couloir d', Chad **79 D2** 22 0N 19 0 E
Apa →, S. Amer. ..... **126 A4** 22 6 S 58 2W
Apache, U.S.A. **113 H5** 34 54N 98 22W
Apache Junction, U.S.A. **109 K8** 33 25N 111 33W
Apalachee B., U.S.A. .. **115 L4** 30 0N 84 0W
Apalachicola, U.S.A. .. **115 L3** 29 43N 84 59W
Apalachicola →, U.S.A. **115 L3** 29 43N 84 58W
Apam, Ghana **83 D4** 5 19N 0 42W
Apaporis →, Colombia **124 D5** 1 23 S 69 25W
Aparados da Serra △, Brazil ..... **127 B5** 29 10 S 50 8W
Aparri, Phil. ..... **61 B4** 18 22N 121 38 E
Apateu, Romania ..... **28 D6** 46 36N 21 47 E
Apatin, Serbia & M. ... **28 E4** 45 40N 19 0 E
Apatity, Russia ..... **52 C4** 67 34N 33 22 E
Apatzingán, Mexico ... **118 D4** 19 0N 102 20W
Apeldoorn, Neths. .... **17 B5** 52 13N 5 57 E
Apen, Germany ..... **24 B3** 53 13N 7 48 E
Apennines = Appennini, Italy ..... **40 D7** 44 0N 10 0 E
Aphrodisias, Turkey .. **47 D10** 37 42N 28 46 E
Apia, Samoa ..... **91 A13** 13 50 S 171 50W
Apiacás, Serra dos, Brazil ..... **124 E7** 9 50 S 57 0W
Apiaú →, S. Africa .... **89 D4** 25 15 S 28 8 E
Apizaco, Mexico **119 D5** 19 26N 98 9W
Aplao, Peru ..... **124 G4** 16 0 S 72 40W
Apo, Mt., Phil. ..... **63 C7** 6 53N 125 14 E
Apolakkiá, Greece .... **49 C9** 36 5N 27 48 E
Apolakkiá, Órmos, Greece ..... **49 C9** 36 5N 27 45 E
Apolda, Germany ..... **24 D7** 51 1N 11 32 E
Apollonia, Greece ..... **46 E6** 36 58N 24 43 E
Apolo, Bolivia ..... **124 F5** 14 30 S 68 30W
Aporé →, Brazil ..... **125 G8** 19 27 S 50 57W
Apostle Is., U.S.A. **112 B9** 47 0N 90 40W
Apostle Islands △, U.S.A. **112 B9** 46 57N 90 53W
Apóstoles, Argentina .. **127 B4** 28 0 S 56 0W
Apostolos Andreas, C., Cyprus ..... **49 D13** 35 42N 34 35 E
Apostolovo, Ukraine .. **33 J7** 47 39N 33 24 E
Apoteri, Guyana **124 C7** 4 2N 58 32W
Appalachian Mts., U.S.A. **114 G6** 38 0N 80 0W
Appelbo, Sweden ..... **10 D8** 60 29N 14 1 E
Appennini, Italy ..... **40 D7** 44 0N 10 0 E
Appennino Ligure, Italy **40 D6** 44 30N 9 0 E
Appenzell-Ausser Rhoden □, Switz. ... **25 H5** 47 23N 9 23 E
Appenzell-Inner Rhoden □, Switz. ... **25 H5** 47 20N 9 25 E
Appiano, Italy ..... **41 B8** 46 38N 11 15 E
Apple Hill, Canada **117 A10** 45 13N 74 46W
Apple Valley, U.S.A. .. **111 L9** 34 32N 117 14W
Appleby-in-Westmorland, U.K. .. **14 C5** 54 35N 2 29W
Appledore, U.K. **15 F3** 51 3N 4 13W
Appleton, U.S.A. **114 C1** 44 16N 88 25W
Approuague →, Fr. Guiana **125 C8** 4 30N 51 57W
Aprícena, Italy ..... **41 G12** 41 47N 15 27 E
Apríla, Italy ..... **42 A5** 41 36N 12 39 E

Apsheronsk, Russia ... **35 H4** 44 28N 39 42 E
Apsley, Canada **116 B6** 44 45N 78 6W
Apt, France ..... **21 E9** 43 53N 5 24 E
Apuane, Alpi, Italy .... **40 D7** 44 7N 10 14 E
Apucarana, Brazil ..... **127 A5** 23 55 S 51 33W
Apulia = Púglia □, Italy **43 A9** 41 15N 16 15 E
Apure →, Venezuela .. **124 B5** 7 37N 66 25W
Apurímac →, Peru .... **124 F4** 12 17 S 73 56W
Apuseni, Munții, Romania ..... **28 D7** 46 30N 22 45 E
Āq Jārī, Iran ..... **71 D6** 30 42N 49 50 E
Aqaba = Al 'Aqabah, Jordan ..... **74 F4** 29 31N 35 0 E
Aqaba, G. of, Red Sea . **70 D2** 28 15N 33 20 E
'Aqabah, Khalīj al = Aqaba, G. of, Red Sea **70 D2** 28 15N 33 20 E
Aqdā, Iran ..... **71 C7** 32 26N 53 37 E
Aqiq, Sudan ..... **80 D4** 18 14N 38 12 E
Aqiq, Khalīg, Sudan ... **80 D4** 18 20N 38 10 E
'Aqrah, Iraq ..... **70 B4** 36 46N 43 45 E
Aqtaū, Kazakhstan .... **52 E6** 43 39N 51 12 E
Aqtöbe, Kazakhstan ... **52 D6** 50 17N 57 10 E
Aquidauana, Brazil ... **125 H7** 20 30 S 55 50W
Aquiles Serdán, Mexico **118 B3** 28 37N 105 54W
Aquin, Haiti **121 C5** 18 16N 73 24W
Aquitain □, France **20 D3** 44 25N 0 30W
Ar Rachidiya = Er Rachidia, Morocco . **78 B5** 31 58N 4 20W
Ar Rafid, Syria ..... **74 C4** 32 57N 35 52 E
Ar Raḥḥālīyah, Iraq ... **70 C4** 32 44N 43 23 E
Ar Ramādī, Iraq ..... **70 C4** 33 25N 43 20 E
Ar Ramthā, Jordan .... **74 C5** 32 34N 36 0 E
Ar Raqqah, Syria ..... **70 C3** 35 59N 39 8 E
Ar Rass, Si. Arabia .... **70 E4** 25 50N 43 40 E
Ar Rawshān, Si. Arabia **80 C5** 20 2N 42 36 E
Ar Rifā'ī, Iraq ..... **70 D5** 31 50N 46 10 E
Ar Riyāḍ, Si. Arabia ... **70 E5** 24 41N 46 42 E
Ar Ru'ays, Qatar ..... **71 E6** 26 8N 51 12 E
Ar Rukhaymīyah, Iraq **70 D5** 29 22N 45 38 E
Ar Ruṣāfah, Syria ..... **70 C3** 35 45N 38 49 E
Ar Ruṭbah, Iraq ..... **70 C4** 33 0N 40 15 E
Ara, India ..... **69 G11** 25 35N 84 32 E
Ara Goro, Ethiopia .... **81 F5** 5 48N 41 18 E
Ara Tera, Ethiopia .... **81 F5** 4 36N 41 3 E
'Arab, Bahr el →, Sudan ..... **81 F2** 9 0N 29 30 E
Arab, Khalig el, Egypt . **80 A2** 30 55N 29 0 E
Arab, Shatt al →, Asia **71 D6** 30 0N 48 31 E
'Araba, W. →, Egypt .. **80 J8** 28 19N 33 31 E
'Arabābād, Iran ..... **71 C8** 33 2N 57 41 E
Araban, Turkey ..... **72 D7** 37 28N 37 44 E
Arabatskaya Strelka, Ukraine ..... **33 K8** 45 40N 35 0 E
Arabba, Italy ..... **41 B8** 46 30N 11 52 E
Arabia, Asia ..... **50 G8** 25 0N 45 0 E
Arabian Desert = Es Sahrâ' Esh Sharqîya, Egypt ..... **80 B3** 27 30N 32 30 E
Arabian Gulf = Persian Gulf, Asia ..... **71 E6** 27 0N 50 0 E
Arabian Sea, Ind. Oc. . **50 H10** 16 0N 65 0 E
Araç, Turkey ..... **72 B5** 41 15N 33 21 E
Aracaju, Brazil ..... **125 F11** 10 55 S 37 4W
Aracati, Brazil ..... **125 D11** 4 30 S 37 44W
Araçatuba, Brazil ..... **127 A5** 21 10 S 50 30W
Aracena, Spain **37 H4** 37 53N 6 38W
Aracena, Sierra de, Spain **37 H4** 37 50N 6 50W
Aračinovo, Macedonia . **44 D5** 42 1N 21 34 E
Araçuaí, Brazil ..... **125 G10** 16 52 S 42 4W
'Arad, Israel ..... **74 D4** 31 15N 35 12 E
Arad, Romania ..... **28 D6** 46 10N 21 20 E
Arad □, Romania ..... **28 D6** 46 20N 22 0 E
Arādān, Iran ..... **71 C7** 35 21N 52 30 E
Aradhippou, Cyprus .. **49 E12** 34 57N 33 36 E
Arafura Sea, E. Indies . **96 H5** 9 0 S 135 0 E
Aragats, Armenia ..... **35 K7** 40 30N 44 15 E
Aragón □, Spain **38 D4** 41 25N 0 40W
Aragón →, Spain **38 C3** 42 13N 1 44W
Aragona, Italy ..... **42 E6** 37 24N 13 37 E
Araguacema, Brazil ... **125 E9** 8 50 S 49 20W
Araguaia →, Brazil ... **125 E9** 5 21 S 48 41W
Araguaína, Brazil ..... **125 E9** 7 12 S 48 12W
Araguari, Brazil ..... **125 G9** 18 38 S 48 11W
Araguari →, Brazil **125 C9** 1 15N 49 55W
Arain, India ..... **68 F6** 26 27N 75 2 E
Arak, Algeria ..... **78 C6** 25 20N 3 45 E
Arāk, Iran ..... **71 C6** 34 0N 49 40 E
Araka, Sudan ..... **81 G3** 4 20N 30 23 E
Arakan Coast, Burma . **67 K19** 19 0N 94 0 E
Arakan Yoma, Burma . **67 K19** 20 0N 94 40 E
Arákhova, Greece ..... **46 C4** 38 28N 22 35 E
Arakli, Turkey ..... **73 B8** 41 6N 40 2 E
Araks = Aras, Rūd-e →, Asia ..... **35 K9** 40 5N 48 29 E
Aral, Kazakhstan ..... **52 E7** 46 41N 61 45 E
Aral Sea, Asia ..... **52 E7** 44 30N 60 0 E
Aral Tengizi = Aral Sea, Asia ..... **52 E7** 44 30N 60 0 E
Aralsk = Aral, Kazakhstan ..... **52 E7** 46 41N 61 45 E
Aralskoye More = Aral Sea, Asia ..... **52 E7** 44 30N 60 0 E
Aralsor, Ozero, Kazakhstan ..... **35 F9** 49 5N 48 12 E
Aramac, Australia ..... **94 C4** 22 58 S 145 14 E
Aran I., Ireland **12 A3** 55 0N 8 30W
Aran Is., Ireland **12 C2** 53 6N 9 38W
Aranda de Duero, Spain **36 D7** 41 39N 3 42W
Arandān, Iran ..... **70 C5** 35 23N 46 55 E
Arandjelovac, Serbia & M. ..... **44 B4** 44 18N 20 34 E
Aranjuez, Spain **36 E7** 40 1N 3 40W
Aranos, Namibia ..... **88 C2** 24 9 S 19 7 E
Aransas Pass, U.S.A. .. **113 M6** 27 55N 97 9W
Aranyaprathet, Thailand **64 F4** 13 41N 102 30 E
Araouane, Mali **82 B4** 18 55N 3 30W
Arapahoe, U.S.A. **112 E5** 40 18N 99 54W
Arapey Grande →, Uruguay ..... **126 C4** 30 55 S 57 49W
Arapgir, Turkey ..... **70 B3** 39 5N 38 30 E
Arapiraca, Brazil ..... **125 E11** 9 45 S 36 39W
Arapongas, Brazil ..... **127 A5** 23 29 S 51 28W
Ar'ar, Si. Arabia ..... **70 D4** 30 59N 41 2 E
Araranguá, Brazil ..... **127 B6** 29 0 S 49 30W
Araraquara, Brazil .... **125 H9** 21 50 S 48 0W
Ararás, Serra das, Brazil **127 B5** 25 0 S 53 10W
Ararat, Armenia ..... **73 C11** 39 50N 44 15 E
Ararat, Australia ..... **95 F3** 37 16 S 143 0 E
Ararat, Mt. = Ağrı Dağı, Turkey ..... **70 B5** 39 50N 44 15 E
Araria, India ..... **69 F12** 26 9N 87 33 E
Araripe, Chapada do, Brazil ..... **125 E11** 7 20 S 40 0W
Araruama, L. de, Brazil **127 A7** 22 53 S 42 12W
Aras, Rūd-e →, Asia .. **35 K9** 40 5N 48 29 E

Aratãne, Mauritania 82 B3 18 24N 8 32W
Arauca, Colombia 124 B4 7 0N 70 40W
Arauca →, Venezuela 124 B5 7 24N 66 35W
Arauco, Chile 126 D1 37 16 S 73 25W
Arawa, Ethiopia 81 F5 9 57N 41 58 E
Arawale ⌓, Kenya 86 C5 1 24 S 40 9 E
Araxá, Brazil 125 G9 19 35 S 46 55W
Araya, Pen. de, Venezuela 124 A6 10 40N 64 0W
Arba Gugu, Ethiopia 81 F5 8 40N 40 15 E
Arba Minch, Ethiopia 81 F4 6 0N 37 30 E
Arbat, Iraq 70 C5 35 25N 45 35 E
Árbatax, Italy 42 C2 39 56N 9 42 E
Arbi, Ethiopia 81 F4 9 4N 35 7 E
Arbīl, Iraq 70 B5 36 15N 44 5 E
Arboga, Sweden 10 E9 59 24N 15 52 E
Arbois, France 19 F12 46 55N 5 46 E
Arbore, Ethiopia 81 F4 5 3N 36 50 E
Arboréa, Italy 42 C1 39 46N 8 35 E
Arborfield, Canada 103 C8 53 6N 103 39W
Arborg, Canada 103 C9 50 54N 97 13W
Arbre du Ténéré, Niger 83 B7 17 50N 10 4 E
Arbroath, U.K. 13 E6 56 34N 2 35W
Arbuckle, U.S.A. 110 F4 39 1N 122 3W
Arbus, Italy 42 C1 39 30N 8 33 E
Arc →, France 21 C10 45 34N 6 12 E
Arc-lès-Gray, France 19 E12 47 28N 5 34 E
Arcachon, France 20 D2 44 40N 1 10W
Arcachon, Bassin d', France 20 D2 44 42N 1 10W
Arcade, Calif., U.S.A. 111 L8 34 2N 118 15W
Arcade, N.Y., U.S.A. 116 D6 42 32N 78 25W
Arcadia, Fla., U.S.A. 115 M5 27 13N 81 52W
Arcadia, La., U.S.A. 113 J8 32 33N 92 55W
Arcadia, Pa., U.S.A. 116 F6 40 47N 78 51W
Arcata, U.S.A. 108 F1 40 52N 124 5W
Arcévia, Italy 41 E9 43 30N 12 56 E
Archangel = Arkhangelsk, Russia 52 C5 64 38N 40 36 E
Archar, Bulgaria 44 C6 43 50N 22 54 E
Archbald, U.S.A. 117 E9 41 30N 75 32W
Archena, Spain 39 G3 38 9N 1 16W
Archer →, Australia 94 A3 13 28 S 141 41 E
Archer B., Australia 94 A3 13 20 S 141 30 E
Archer Bend = Mungkan Kandju △, Australia 94 A3 13 35 S 142 52 E
Archers Post, Kenya 86 B4 0 35N 37 35 E
Arches △, U.S.A. 109 G9 38 45N 109 25W
Archidona, Spain 37 H6 37 6N 4 22W
Archipel-de-Mingan △, Canada 105 B7 50 13N 63 10W
Archipiélago Chinijo △, Canary Is. 48 E6 29 20N 13 30W
Archipiélago Los Roques △, Venezuela 121 D6 11 50N 66 44W
Arci, Mte., Italy 42 C1 39 47N 8 45 E
Arcidosso, Italy 41 F8 42 52N 11 33 E
Arcipelago de la Maddalena △, Italy 42 A2 41 14N 9 24 E
Arcipelago Toscano △, Italy 40 F7 42 45N 10 15 E
Arcis-sur-Aube, France 19 D11 48 32N 4 10 E
Arckaringa Cr. →, Australia 95 D2 28 10 S 135 22 E
Arco, Italy 40 C7 45 55N 10 53 E
Arco, U.S.A. 108 E7 43 38N 113 18W
Arcos de Jalón, Spain 38 D2 41 12N 2 16W
Arcos de la Frontera, Spain 37 J5 36 45N 5 49W
Arcos de Valdevez, Portugal 36 D2 41 55N 8 22W
Arcot, India 66 N11 12 53N 79 20 E
Arcozelo, Portugal 36 E3 40 32N 7 47W
Arctic Bay, Canada 101 A11 73 1N 85 7W
Arctic Ocean, Arctic 4 B18 78 0N 160 0W
Arctic Red River = Tsiigehtchic, Canada 100 B6 67 15N 134 0W
Arctowski, Antarctica 5 C18 62 30 S 58 0W
Arda →, Bulgaria 45 E10 41 40N 26 30 E
Arda →, Italy 40 C7 45 2N 10 2 E
Ardabīl, Iran 71 B6 38 15N 48 18 E
Ardabīl □, Iran 71 B6 38 15N 48 20 E
Ardahan, Turkey 73 B10 41 7N 42 41 E
Ardakān = Sepīdān, Iran 71 D7 30 20N 52 5 E
Ardakān, Iran 71 C7 32 19N 53 59 E
Ardala, Sweden 11 F7 58 22N 13 19 E
Ardales, Spain 37 J6 36 53N 4 51W
Ardèche □, France 21 D8 44 42N 4 16 E
Ardèche →, France 21 D8 44 16N 4 39 E
Ardee, Ireland 12 C5 53 52N 6 33W
Arden, Canada 116 B8 44 43N 76 56W
Arden, Denmark 11 H3 56 46N 9 52 E
Arden, Calif., U.S.A. 110 G5 38 36N 121 33W
Arden, Nev., U.S.A. 111 J11 36 1N 115 14W
Ardenne, Belgium 17 E5 49 50N 5 5 E
Ardennes = Ardenne, Belgium 17 E5 49 50N 5 5 E
Ardennes □, France 19 C11 49 35N 4 40 E
Ardentes, France 19 F8 46 45N 1 50 E
Arderin, Ireland 12 C4 53 2N 7 39W
Ardeşen, Turkey 73 B9 41 12N 41 2 E
Ardestān, Iran 71 C7 33 20N 52 25 E
Árdhas →, Greece 45 E10 41 40N 26 30 E
Ardhéa, Greece 44 F6 40 58N 22 3 E
Ardila →, Portugal 37 G3 38 12N 7 28W
Ardino, Bulgaria 45 E9 41 34N 25 9 E
Ardivachar Pt., U.K. 13 D1 57 23N 7 26W
Ardlethan, Australia 95 E4 34 22 S 146 53 E
Ardmore, Okla., U.S.A. 113 H6 34 10N 97 8W
Ardmore, Pa., U.S.A. 117 G9 39 58N 75 18W
Ardnamurchan, Pt. of, U.K. 13 E2 56 43N 6 14W
Ardnave Pt., U.K. 13 F2 55 53N 6 20W
Ardon, Russia 35 J7 43 10N 44 18 E
Ardore, Italy 43 D9 38 11N 16 10 E
Ardres, France 19 B8 50 50N 1 59 E
Ardrossan, Australia 95 E2 34 26 S 137 53 E
Ardrossan, U.K. 13 F4 55 39N 4 49W
Ards Pen., U.K. 12 B6 54 33N 5 34W
Arduan, Sudan 80 D3 19 54N 30 20 E
Ardud, Romania 28 C7 47 37N 22 52 E
Åre, Sweden 10 A7 63 22N 13 15 E
Arecibo, Puerto Rico 121 d 18 29N 66 43W
Areia Branca, Brazil 125 E11 5 0 S 37 0W
Arena, Pt., U.S.A. 110 G3 38 57N 123 44W
Arenal, Honduras 120 C2 15 21N 86 50W
Arenas = Las Arenas, Spain 36 B6 43 17N 4 50W
Arenas de San Pedro, Spain 36 E5 40 12N 5 5W
Arendal, Norway 9 G13 58 28N 8 46 E
Arendsee, Germany 24 C7 52 52N 11 27 E
Arenys de Mar, Spain 38 D7 41 35N 2 33 E
Arenzano, Italy 40 D5 44 24N 8 41 E
Areópolis, Greece 46 E4 36 40N 22 22 E
Arequipa, Peru 124 G4 16 20 S 71 30W
Arero, Ethiopia 81 G4 4 41N 38 50 E
Arès, France 20 D2 44 47N 1 8W
Arévalo, Spain 36 D6 41 3N 4 43W
Arezzo, Italy 41 E8 43 25N 11 53 E
Arga, Turkey 70 B3 38 21N 37 59 E
Arga →, Spain 38 C3 42 18N 1 47W
Argalastí, Greece 46 B5 39 13N 23 13 E
Argamasilla de Alba, Spain 37 F7 39 8N 3 5W
Argamasilla de Calatrava, Spain 37 G6 38 44N 4 4W
Arganda, Spain 36 E7 40 19N 3 26W
Arganil, Portugal 36 E2 40 13N 8 3W
Argedeb, Ethiopia 81 F5 6 11N 41 13 E
Argelès-Gazost, France 20 E3 43 0N 0 6W
Argelès-sur-Mer, France 20 F7 42 34N 3 1 E
Argens →, France 21 E10 43 24N 6 44 E
Argent-sur-Sauldre, France 19 E9 47 33N 2 25 E
Argenta, Canada 102 C5 50 11N 116 56W
Argenta, Italy 41 D8 44 37N 11 50 E
Argentan, France 18 D6 48 45N 0 1W
Argentário, Mte., Italy 41 F8 42 24N 11 9 E
Argentat, France 20 C5 45 6N 1 56 E
Argentera, Italy 40 D4 44 12N 7 5 E
Argenteuil, France 19 D9 48 57N 2 14 E
Argentia, Canada 105 C9 47 18N 53 58W
Argentiera, C. dell', Italy 42 B1 40 44N 8 8 E
Argentina ■, S. Amer. 128 D3 35 0 S 66 0W
Argentine Basin, S. Amer. 122 H5 45 0 S 58 0W
Argentino, L., Argentina 128 G2 50 10 S 73 0W
Argenton-Château, France 18 F6 46 59N 0 27W
Argenton-sur-Creuse, France 19 F8 46 36N 1 30 E
Argeş □, Romania 29 F9 45 0N 24 45 E
Argeş →, Romania 29 F11 44 5N 26 38 E
Arghandab →, Afghan. 68 D1 31 30N 64 15 E
Argheile, Ethiopia 81 F5 5 19N 42 4 E
Argo, Sudan 80 D3 19 28N 30 30 E
Argolikós Kólpos, Greece 46 D4 37 20N 22 52 E
Argolís □, Greece 46 D4 37 38N 22 50 E
Argonne, France 19 C12 49 10N 5 0 E
Árgos, Greece 46 D4 37 40N 22 43 E
Árgos Orestikón, Greece 44 F5 40 27N 21 18 E
Argostólion, Greece 46 C2 38 11N 20 29 E
Arguedas, Spain 38 C3 42 11N 1 36W
Arguello, Pt., U.S.A. 111 L6 34 35N 120 39W
Arguineguín, Canary Is. 48 G4 27 46N 15 41W
Argun, Russia 35 J7 43 18N 45 52 E
Argun →, Russia 53 D13 53 20N 121 28 E
Argungu, Nigeria 83 C5 12 40N 4 31 E
Argus Pk., U.S.A. 111 K9 35 52N 117 26W
Argyle, L., Australia 92 C4 16 20 S 128 40 E
Argyll ⌓, U.K. 13 E4 56 6N 5 0W
Argyll & Bute □, U.K. 13 E3 56 13N 5 28W
Arhavi, Turkey 73 B9 41 21N 41 18 E
Århus, Denmark 11 H4 56 8N 10 11 E
Århus Amtskommune □, Denmark 11 H4 56 15N 10 15 E
Ariadnoye, Russia 54 B7 45 8N 134 25 E
Ariamsvlei, Namibia 88 D2 28 9 S 19 51 E
Ariano Irpino, Italy 43 A8 41 9N 15 5 E
Aribinda, Burkina Faso 83 C4 14 17N 0 52W
Arica, Chile 124 G4 18 32 S 70 20W
Arica, Colombia 124 D4 2 0 S 71 50W
Arico, Canary Is. 48 F3 28 9N 16 29W
Arid, C., Australia 93 F3 34 1 S 123 10 E
Arida, Japan 55 G7 34 5N 135 8 E
Ariège □, France 20 F5 42 56N 1 30 E
Ariège →, France 20 E5 43 30N 1 25 E
Arieş →, Romania 29 D8 46 24N 23 20 E
Arihā, Israel 80 A4 31 51N 35 27 E
Arilje, Serbia & M. 44 C4 43 44N 20 7 E
Arílla, Ákra, Greece 49 A3 39 43N 19 39 E
Arima, Trin. & Tob. 121 D7 10 38N 61 17W
Arinos →, Brazil 124 F7 10 25 S 58 20W
Ario de Rosales, Mexico 118 D4 19 12N 102 0W
Ariogala, Lithuania 30 C10 55 16N 23 28 E
Aripo, Mt., Trin. & Tob. 125 K15 10 45N 61 15W
Aripuanã, Brazil 124 E6 9 25 S 60 30W
Aripuanã →, Brazil 124 E6 5 7 S 60 25W
Ariquemes, Brazil 124 E6 9 55 S 63 6W
Arisaig, U.K. 13 E3 56 55N 5 51W
Arîsh, W. el →, Egypt 80 A3 31 9N 33 49 E
Arissa, Ethiopia 81 E5 11 10N 41 35 E
Aristazabal I., Canada 102 C3 52 40N 129 10W
Arivonimamo, Madag. 89 B8 19 1 S 47 11 E
Ariza, Spain 38 D2 41 19N 2 3W
Arizaro, Salar de, Argentina 126 A2 24 40 S 67 50W
Arizona, Argentina 126 D2 35 45 S 65 25W
Arizona □, U.S.A. 109 J8 34 0N 112 0W
Arizpe, Mexico 118 A2 30 20N 110 11W
Årjäng, Sweden 10 E6 59 24N 12 8 E
Arjeplog, Sweden 8 D18 66 3N 17 54 E
Arjepluovve = Arjeplog, Sweden 8 D18 66 3N 17 54 E
Arjona, Colombia 124 A3 10 14N 75 22W
Arjona, Spain 37 H6 37 56N 4 4W
Arjuna, Indonesia 63 G15 7 49 S 112 34 E
Arka, Russia 53 C15 60 15N 142 0 E
Arkadak, Russia 34 E6 51 58N 43 30 E
Arkadelphia, U.S.A. 113 H8 34 7N 93 4W
Arkadhía □, Greece 46 D4 37 30N 22 20 E
Arkaig, L., U.K. 13 E3 56 59N 5 10W
Arkalyk = Arqalyk, Kazakhstan 52 D7 50 13N 66 50 E
Arkansas □, U.S.A. 113 H8 35 0N 92 30W
Arkansas →, U.S.A. 113 J9 33 47N 91 4W
Arkansas City, U.S.A. 113 G6 37 4N 97 2W
Arkaroola, Australia 95 E2 30 20 S 139 22 E
Árkathos →, Greece 46 B3 39 20N 21 4 E
Arkhángelos, Greece 49 C10 36 13N 28 7 E
Arkhangelsk, Russia 52 C5 64 38N 40 36 E
Arkhangelskoye, Russia 34 E5 51 32N 40 58 E
Arki, India 68 D7 31 9N 76 58 E
Arkiko, Eritrea 81 D4 15 33N 39 30 E
Arklow, Ireland 12 D5 52 48N 6 10W
Árkoi, Greece 47 D8 37 24N 26 44 E
Arkona, Kap, Germany 24 A9 54 42N 13 26 E
Arkösund, Sweden 11 F10 58 29N 16 56 E
Arkoúdhi Nisís, Greece 46 C2 38 33N 20 43 E
Arkport, U.S.A. 116 D7 42 24N 77 42W
Arkticheskiy, Mys, Russia 53 A10 81 10N 95 0 E
Arkul, Russia 34 B10 57 17N 50 3 E
Arkville, U.S.A. 117 D10 42 9N 74 37W
Årla, Sweden 10 E10 59 17N 16 40 E
Arlanda, Stockholm ✈ (ARN), Sweden 10 E11 59 41N 17 56 E
Arlanza →, Spain 36 C6 42 6N 4 9W
Arlanzón →, Spain 36 C6 42 3N 4 17W
Arlbergpass, Austria 26 D3 47 9N 10 12 E
Arles, France 21 E8 43 41N 4 40 E
Arli, Burkina Faso 83 C5 11 35N 1 28 E
Arli △, Burkina Faso 83 C5 11 35N 1 28 E
Arlington, S. Africa 89 D4 28 1 S 27 53 E
Arlington, N.Y., U.S.A. 117 E11 41 42N 73 54W
Arlington, Oreg., U.S.A. 108 D3 45 43N 120 12W
Arlington, S. Dak., U.S.A. 112 C6 44 22N 97 8W
Arlington, Tex., U.S.A. 113 J6 32 44N 97 7W
Arlington, Va., U.S.A. 114 F7 38 53N 77 7W
Arlington, Vt., U.S.A. 117 C11 43 5N 73 9W
Arlington, Wash., U.S.A. 110 B4 48 12N 122 8W
Arlington Heights, U.S.A. 114 D2 42 5N 87 59W
Arlit, Niger 78 E7 19 0N 7 38 E
Arlon, Belgium 17 E5 49 42N 5 49 E
Arltunga, Australia 94 C1 23 26 S 134 41 E
Armagh, U.K. 12 B5 54 21N 6 39W
Armagh □, U.K. 12 B5 54 18N 6 37W
Armagnac, France 20 E4 43 50N 0 10 E
Armançon →, France 19 E10 47 59N 3 30 E
Armando Bermudez △, Dom. Rep. 121 C5 19 3N 71 0W
Armavir, Russia 35 H5 45 2N 41 7 E
Armenia, Colombia 124 C3 4 35N 75 45W
Armenia ■, Asia 35 K7 40 20N 45 0 E
Armeniş, Romania 28 E7 45 13N 22 17 E
Armenistís, Ákra, Greece 49 C9 36 8N 27 42 E
Armentières, France 19 B9 50 40N 2 50 E
Armidale, Australia 95 E5 30 30 S 151 40 E
Armilla, Spain 37 H7 37 9N 3 37W
Armorique ⌓, France 18 D3 48 22N 3 50W
Armour, U.S.A. 112 D5 43 19N 98 21W
Armstrong, B.C., Canada 102 C5 50 25N 119 10W
Armstrong, Ont., Canada 104 B2 50 18N 89 4W
Armutlu, Bursa, Turkey 45 F12 40 31N 28 50 E
Armutlu, İzmir, Turkey 47 C9 38 24N 27 34 E
Arnaía, Greece 44 F7 40 30N 23 38 E
Arnarfjörður, Iceland 8 D2 65 48N 23 40W
Arnaud →, Canada 101 B12 59 59N 69 46W
Arnauti, C., Cyprus 49 D11 35 6N 32 17 E
Arnay-le-Duc, France 19 E11 47 10N 4 27 E
Arnedillo, Spain 38 C2 42 13N 2 14W
Arnedo, Spain 38 C2 42 12N 2 5W
Arnett, U.S.A. 113 G5 36 8N 99 46W
Arnhem, Neths. 17 C5 51 58N 5 55 E
Arnhem, C., Australia 94 A2 12 20 S 137 30 E
Arnhem B., Australia 94 A2 12 20 S 136 10 E
Arnhem Land, Australia 94 A1 13 10 S 134 30 E
Árnissa, Greece 44 F5 40 47N 21 49 E
Arno →, Italy 40 E7 43 41N 10 17 E
Arno Bay, Australia 95 E2 33 54 S 136 34 E
Arnold, U.K. 14 D6 53 1N 1 7W
Arnold, U.S.A. 110 G6 38 15N 120 20W
Arnoldstein, Austria 26 E6 46 33N 13 43 E
Arnon →, France 19 E9 47 13N 2 1 E
Arnot, Canada 103 B9 55 56N 96 41W
Arnøy, Norway 8 A19 70 9N 20 40 E
Arnprior, Canada 117 A8 45 26N 76 21W
Arnsberg, Germany 24 D4 51 24N 8 5 E
Arnsberger Wald ⌓, Germany 24 D4 51 25N 8 20 E
Arnstadt, Germany 24 E6 50 50N 10 56 E
Aroab, Namibia 88 D2 26 41 S 19 39 E
Aroánia Óri, Greece 46 D4 37 56N 22 12 E
Aroche, Spain 37 H4 37 56N 6 57W
Arochuku, Nigeria 83 D6 5 21N 7 54 E
Arolsen, Germany 24 D5 51 23N 9 2 E
Aron, India 68 G6 25 57N 77 56 E
Aron →, France 19 F10 46 50N 3 28 E
Arona, Canary Is. 48 F3 28 6N 16 40W
Arona, Italy 40 C5 45 46N 8 34 E
Aroroy, Phil. 61 E5 12 31N 123 24 E
Arosa, Ría de, Spain 36 C2 42 28N 8 57W
Arpajon, France 19 D9 48 36N 2 15 E
Arpajon-sur-Cère, France 20 D6 44 53N 2 28 E
Arpaşu de Jos, Romania 29 E9 45 47N 24 37 E
Arqalyk, Kazakhstan 52 D7 50 13N 66 50 E
Arrah = Ara, India 69 G11 25 35N 84 32 E
Arrah, Ivory C. 82 D4 6 40N 3 58W
Arraiolos, Portugal 37 G3 38 44N 7 59W
Arran, U.K. 13 F3 55 34N 5 12W
Arras, France 19 B9 50 17N 2 46 E
Arrasate, Spain 38 B2 43 4N 2 30W
Arrats →, France 20 D4 44 6N 0 52 E
Arreau, France 20 F4 42 54N 0 22 E
Arrecife, Canary Is. 48 F6 28 57N 13 37W
Arrecifes, Argentina 126 C3 34 6 S 60 9W
Arrée, Mts. d', France 18 D3 48 26N 3 55W
Arresø, Denmark 11 J6 55 58N 12 6 E
Arriaga, Chiapas, Mexico 119 D6 16 15N 93 52W
Arriaga, San Luis Potosí, Mexico 118 C4 21 55N 101 23W
Arribes del Duero ⌓, Spain 36 D4 41 11N 6 39W
Arrilalah, Australia 94 C3 23 43 S 143 54 E
Arrino, Australia 93 E2 29 30 S 115 40 E
Arriondas, Spain 36 B5 43 23N 5 11W
Arromanches-les-Bains, France 18 C6 49 20N 0 38W
Arronches, Portugal 37 F3 39 8N 7 16W
Arros →, France 20 E3 43 40N 0 2W
Arrow, L., Ireland 12 B3 54 3N 8 19W
Arrowhead, L., U.S.A. 111 L9 34 16N 117 10W
Arrowtown, N.Z. 91 L2 44 57 S 168 50 E
Arroyo de la Luz, Spain 37 F4 39 30N 6 38W
Arroyo Grande, U.S.A. 111 K6 35 7N 120 35W
Års, Denmark 11 H3 56 48N 9 30 E
Ars, Iran 70 B5 37 9N 47 46 E
Ars-sur-Moselle, France 19 C13 49 5N 6 4 E
Arsenault L., Canada 103 B7 55 6N 108 32W
Arsenev, Russia 54 B6 44 10N 133 15 E
Arsi, Ethiopia 81 F4 7 45N 39 0 E
Arsiero, Italy 41 C8 45 48N 11 21 E
Arsin, Turkey 73 B8 41 8N 39 55 E
Arsk, Russia 34 B9 56 10N 49 50 E
Årsunda, Sweden 10 D10 60 31N 16 45 E
Árta, Greece 46 B3 39 8N 21 2 E
Artà, Spain 48 B10 39 41N 3 21 E
Árta □, Greece 46 B3 39 15N 21 5 E
Arteaga, Mexico 118 D4 18 50N 102 20W
Arteche, Phil. 61 E6 12 17N 125 22 E
Arteijo = Arteixo, Spain 36 B2 43 19N 8 29W
Arteixo, Spain 36 B2 43 19N 8 29W
Artem = Artyom, Azerbaijan 35 K10 40 28N 50 20 E
Artem, Russia 54 C6 43 22N 132 13 E
Artemovsk, Russia 53 D10 54 45N 93 35 E
Artemovsk, Ukraine 33 H9 48 35N 38 0 E
Artemovskiy, Russia 35 G5 47 45N 40 16 E
Artenay, France 19 D8 48 5N 1 50 E
Artern, Germany 24 D7 51 22N 11 18 E
Artesa de Segre, Spain 38 D6 41 54N 1 3 E
Artesia = Mosomane, Botswana 88 C4 24 2 S 26 19 E
Artesia, U.S.A. 113 J2 32 51N 104 24W
Arthington, Liberia 82 D2 6 35N 10 45W
Arthur, Canada 116 C4 43 50N 80 32W
Arthur →, Australia 95 G3 41 2 S 144 40 E
Arthur Cr. →, Australia 94 C2 22 30 S 136 25 E
Arthur Pt., Australia 94 C5 22 7 S 150 3 E
Arthur River, Australia 93 F2 33 20 S 117 2 E
Arthur's Pass, N.Z. 91 K3 42 54 S 171 35 E
Arthur's Pass △, N.Z. 91 K3 42 53 S 171 42 E
Arthur's Town, Bahamas 121 B4 24 38N 75 42W
Artigas, Antarctica 5 C18 62 30 S 58 0W
Artigas, Uruguay 126 C4 30 20 S 56 30W
Artik, Armenia 35 K6 40 38N 43 58 E
Artillery L., Canada 103 A7 63 9N 107 52W
Artois, France 19 B9 50 20N 2 30 E
Artotína, Greece 46 C4 38 42N 22 2 E
Artrutx, C. de, Spain 48 B10 39 55N 3 49 E
Artsyz, Ukraine 29 D14 46 4N 29 26 E
Artvin, Turkey 73 B9 41 14N 41 44 E
Artyom, Azerbaijan 35 K10 40 28N 50 20 E
Aru, Kepulauan, Indonesia 63 F8 6 0 S 134 30 E
Aru Is. = Aru, Kepulauan, Indonesia 63 F8 6 0 S 134 30 E
Arua, Uganda 86 B3 3 1N 30 58 E
Aruanã, Brazil 125 F8 14 54 S 51 10W
Aruba ☑, W. Indies 121 D6 12 30N 70 0W
Arucas, Canary Is. 48 F4 28 7N 15 32W
Arudy, France 20 E3 43 7N 0 28W
Arun →, Nepal 69 F12 26 55N 87 10 E
Arun →, U.K. 15 G7 50 49N 0 33W
Arunachal Pradesh □, India 67 F19 28 0N 95 0 E
Arusha, Tanzania 86 C4 3 20 S 36 40 E
Arusha □, Tanzania 86 C4 4 0 S 36 30 E
Arusha △, Tanzania 86 C4 3 16 S 36 47 E
Arusha Chini, Tanzania 86 C4 3 32 S 37 20 E
Aruwimi →, Dem. Rep. of the Congo 86 B1 1 13N 23 36 E
Arvada, Colo., U.S.A. 112 F2 39 48N 105 5W
Arvada, Wyo., U.S.A. 108 D10 44 39N 106 8W
Arve →, France 19 F13 46 11N 6 8 E
Árvi, Greece 49 E7 34 59N 25 28 E
Arviat, Canada 103 A10 61 6N 93 59W
Arvidsjaur, Sweden 8 D18 65 35N 19 10 E
Arvika, Sweden 10 E6 59 40N 12 36 E
Arvin, U.S.A. 111 K8 35 12N 118 50W
Arwal, India 69 G11 25 15N 84 41 E
Arxan, China 60 B6 47 11N 119 57 E
Åryd, Sweden 11 H8 56 49N 14 59 E
Aryirádhes, Greece 49 B3 39 27N 19 58 E
Aryiroúpolis, Greece 49 D6 35 17N 24 20 E
Arys, Kazakhstan 52 E7 42 26N 68 48 E
Arzachena, Italy 42 A2 41 5N 9 23 E
Arzamas, Russia 34 C6 55 27N 43 55 E
Arzgir, Russia 35 H7 45 18N 44 23 E
Arzignano, Italy 41 C8 45 31N 11 20 E
Arzúa, Spain 36 C2 42 56N 8 9W
Aš, Czech Rep. 26 A5 50 13N 12 12 E
Ås, Sweden 10 A8 63 15N 14 34 E
As Pontes de García Rodríguez, Spain 36 B3 43 27N 7 50W
Aş Şafā, Syria 74 B6 33 10N 37 0 E
As Saffānīyah, Si. Arabia 71 E6 27 55N 48 50 E
As Safīrah, Syria 70 B3 36 5N 37 21 E
Aş Şahm, Oman 71 E8 24 10N 56 53 E
As Sājir, Si. Arabia 70 E5 25 11N 44 36 E
As Salamīyah, Syria 70 C3 35 1N 37 2 E
As Salmān, Iraq 70 D5 30 30N 44 32 E
As Salţ, Jordan 74 C4 32 2N 35 43 E
As Sal'w'a, Qatar 71 E6 24 23N 50 50 E
As Samāwah, Iraq 70 D5 31 15N 45 15 E
As Sanamayn, Syria 74 B5 33 3N 36 10 E
As Sohar = Şuḩār, Oman 71 E8 24 20N 56 40 E
As Sukhnah, Syria 70 C3 34 52N 38 52 E
As Sulaymānīyah, Iraq 70 C5 35 35N 45 29 E
As Sulaymī, Si. Arabia 70 E4 26 17N 41 21 E
As Sulayyil, Si. Arabia 75 C4 20 27N 45 34 E
As Summān, Si. Arabia 70 E5 25 0N 47 0 E
As Suwaydā', Syria 74 C5 32 40N 36 30 E
As Suwaydā' □, Syria 74 C5 32 45N 36 45 E
As Suwayq, Oman 71 F8 23 51N 57 26 E
Aş Şuwayrah, Iraq 70 C5 32 55N 45 0 E
Åsa, Sweden 11 G6 57 21N 12 8 E
Asab, Namibia 88 D2 25 30 S 18 0 E
Asaba, Nigeria 83 D6 6 12N 6 38 E
Asad, Buḩayrat al, Syria 70 C3 36 0N 38 15 E
Asadābād, Iran 73 E13 34 47N 48 7 E
Asafo, Ghana 82 D4 6 20N 2 40W
Asahi-Gawa →, Japan 55 G6 34 36N 133 58 E
Asahigawa, Japan 54 C11 43 46N 142 22 E
Asale, L., Ethiopia 81 E5 14 0N 40 20 E
Asamankese, Ghana 83 D4 5 50N 0 40W
Asan →, India 69 F8 26 37N 78 24 E
Asansol, India 69 H12 23 40N 87 1 E
Åsarna, Sweden 10 B8 62 39N 14 22 E
Asayita, Ethiopia 81 E5 11 35N 41 23 E
Asbe Teferi, Ethiopia 81 F5 9 4N 40 49 E
Asbesberge, S. Africa 88 D3 29 0 S 23 0 E
Asbestos, Canada 105 C5 45 47N 71 58W
Asbury Park, U.S.A. 117 F10 40 13N 74 1W
Ascea, Italy 43 B8 40 8N 15 11 E
Ascensión, Mexico 118 A3 31 6N 107 59W
Ascensión, B. de la, Mexico 119 D7 19 50N 87 20W
Ascension I., Atl. Oc. 77 G2 7 57 S 14 23W
Aschach an der Donau, Austria 26 C7 48 22N 14 2 E
Aschaffenburg, Germany 25 F5 49 58N 9 6 E
Aschendorf, Germany 24 B3 53 3N 7 19 E
Aschersleben, Germany 24 D7 51 45N 11 29 E
Asciano, Italy 41 E8 43 14N 11 33 E
Áscoli Piceno, Italy 41 F10 42 51N 13 34 E
Áscoli Satriano, Italy 43 A8 41 11N 15 32 E
Ascope, Peru 124 E3 7 46 S 79 8W
Ascotán, Chile 126 A2 21 45 S 68 17W
Aseb, Eritrea 81 E5 13 0N 42 40 E
Åseda, Sweden 11 G9 57 10N 15 20 E
Asela, Ethiopia 81 F4 8 0N 39 0 E
Åsen, Sweden 10 C7 61 17N 13 50 E
Asenovgrad, Bulgaria 45 D8 42 1N 24 51 E
Aserradero, Mexico 118 C3 23 40N 105 43W
Asfeld, France 19 C11 49 27N 4 5 E
Asfûn el Matâ'na, Egypt 80 B3 25 26N 32 30 E
Asgata, Cyprus 49 E12 34 46N 33 15 E
Ash Fork, U.S.A. 109 J7 35 13N 112 29W
Ash Grove, U.S.A. 113 G8 37 19N 93 35W
Ash Shabakah, Iraq 70 D4 30 49N 43 39 E
Ash Shamāl □, Lebanon 74 A5 34 25N 36 0 E
Ash Shāmīyah, Iraq 70 D5 31 55N 44 35 E
Ash Shāriqah, U.A.E. 71 E7 25 23N 55 26 E
Ash Sharmah, Si. Arabia 70 D2 28 1N 35 16 E
Ash Sharqāt, Iraq 70 C4 35 27N 43 16 E
Ash Sharqi, Al Jabal, Lebanon 74 B5 33 40N 36 10 E
Ash Shaţrah, Iraq 70 D5 31 30N 46 10 E
Ash Shawbak, Jordan 70 D2 30 32N 35 34 E
Ash Shawmari, J., Jordan 74 E5 30 35N 36 35 E
Ash Shināfīyah, Iraq 70 D5 31 35N 44 39 E
Ash Shu'bah, Si. Arabia 70 D5 28 54N 44 44 E
Ash Shumlūl, Si. Arabia 70 E5 26 31N 47 20 E
Ash Shūr'a, Iraq 70 C4 35 58N 43 13 E
Ash Shurayf, Si. Arabia 70 E3 25 43N 39 14 E
Ash Shuwayfāt, Lebanon 74 B4 33 45N 35 30 E
Ashanti □, Ghana 83 D4 7 30N 1 30W
Ashau, Vietnam 64 D6 16 6N 107 22 E
Ashbourne, U.K. 14 D6 53 2N 1 43W
Ashburn, U.S.A. 115 K4 31 43N 83 39W
Ashburton, N.Z. 91 K3 43 53 S 171 48 E
Ashburton →, Australia 92 D1 21 40 S 114 56 E
Ashcroft, Canada 102 C4 50 40N 121 20W
Ashdod, Israel 74 D3 31 49N 34 35 E
Ashdown, U.S.A. 113 J7 33 40N 94 8W
Asheboro, U.S.A. 115 H6 35 43N 79 49W
Ashern, Canada 103 C9 51 11N 98 21W
Asherton, U.S.A. 113 L5 28 27N 99 46W
Asheville, U.S.A. 115 H4 35 36N 82 33W
Ashewat, Pakistan 68 D3 31 22N 68 32 E
Asheweig →, Canada 104 B2 54 17N 87 12W
Ashford, Australia 95 D5 29 15 S 151 3 E
Ashford, U.K. 15 F8 51 8N 0 53 E
Ashgabat, Turkmenistan 52 F6 38 0N 57 50 E
Ashibetsu, Japan 54 C11 43 31N 142 11 E
Ashikaga, Japan 55 F9 36 28N 139 29 E
Ashington, U.K. 14 B6 55 11N 1 33W
Ashizuri-Uwakai △, Japan 55 H6 32 56N 132 32 E
Ashizuri-Zaki, Japan 55 H6 32 44N 133 0 E
Ashkarkot, Afghan. 68 C2 33 3N 67 58 E
Ashkhabad = Ashgabat, Turkmenistan 52 F6 38 0N 57 50 E
Āshkhāneh, Iran 71 B8 37 26N 56 55 E
Ashland, Kans., U.S.A. 113 G5 37 11N 99 46W
Ashland, Ky., U.S.A. 114 F4 38 28N 82 38W
Ashland, Mont., U.S.A. 108 D10 45 36N 106 16W
Ashland, Ohio, U.S.A. 116 F2 40 52N 82 19W
Ashland, Oreg., U.S.A. 108 E2 42 12N 122 43W
Ashland, Pa., U.S.A. 117 F8 40 45N 76 22W
Ashland, Va., U.S.A. 114 G7 37 46N 77 29W
Ashland, Wis., U.S.A. 112 B9 46 35N 90 53W
Ashley, N. Dak., U.S.A. 112 B5 46 2N 99 22W
Ashley, Pa., U.S.A. 117 E9 41 12N 75 55W
Ashmore and Cartier Is., Ind. Oc. 92 B3 12 15 S 123 0 E
Ashmore Reef, Australia 92 B3 12 14 S 123 5 E
Ashmûn, Egypt 80 H7 30 18N 30 55 E
Ashmyany, Belarus 9 J21 54 26N 25 52 E
Ashokan Reservoir, U.S.A. 117 E10 41 56N 74 13W
Ashqelon, Israel 74 D3 31 42N 34 35 E
Ashta, India 68 H7 23 1N 76 43 E
Ashtabula, U.S.A. 116 E4 41 52N 80 47W
Ashton, S. Africa 88 E3 33 50 S 20 5 E
Ashton, U.S.A. 108 D8 44 4N 111 27W
Ashuanipi, L., Canada 105 B6 52 45N 66 15W
Ashuapmushuan →, Canada 104 C5 48 37N 72 20W
Ashville, U.S.A. 116 F6 40 34N 78 33W
'Āşī →, Asia 72 D6 36 1N 35 59 E
Asia 50 E11 45 0N 75 0 E
Asia, Kepulauan, Indonesia 63 D8 1 0N 131 13 E
Asiago, Italy 41 C8 45 52N 11 30 E
Asifabad, India 66 K11 19 20N 79 24 E
Asinara, Italy 42 A1 41 4N 8 16 E
Asinara, G. dell', Italy 42 A1 41 0N 8 30 E
Asino, Russia 52 D9 57 0N 86 0 E
Asipovichy, Belarus 32 F5 53 19N 28 33 E
'Asīr □, Si. Arabia 75 D3 18 40N 42 30 E
Asir, Ras, Somali Rep. 75 E5 11 55N 51 10 E
Aşkale, Turkey 73 C9 39 55N 40 41 E
Askersund, Sweden 11 F8 58 53N 14 55 E
Askham, S. Africa 88 D3 26 59 S 20 47 E
Askim, Norway 9 G14 59 35N 11 10 E
Askja, Iceland 8 D5 65 3N 16 48W
Askøy, Norway 9 F11 60 29N 5 10 E
Asl, Egypt 80 B3 29 33N 32 44 E
Aslan Burnu, Turkey 47 C8 38 44N 26 45 E
Aslanapa, Turkey 47 B11 39 13N 29 52 E
Asmara = Asmera, Eritrea 81 D4 15 19N 38 55 E
Asmera, Eritrea 81 D4 15 19N 38 55 E
Asnæs, Denmark 11 J4 55 40N 11 0 E
Åsnen, Sweden 11 H8 56 37N 14 45 E
Aso Kuju △, Japan 55 H5 32 53N 131 6 E
Ásola, Italy 40 C7 45 13N 10 24 E
Asosa, Ethiopia 81 E3 10 3N 34 32 E
Asoteriba, Jebel, Sudan 80 C4 21 51N 36 30 E
Aspatria, U.K. 14 C4 54 47N 3 19W
Aspe, Spain 39 G4 38 20N 0 40W
Aspen, U.S.A. 109 G10 39 11N 106 49W
Aspendos, Turkey 72 D4 36 54N 31 7 E
Aspermont, U.S.A. 113 J4 33 8N 100 14W
Aspet, France 20 E4 43 1N 0 48 E
Aspiring, Mt., N.Z. 91 L2 44 23 S 168 46 E
Aspres-sur-Buëch, France 21 D9 44 32N 5 44 E
Asprókavos, Ákra, Greece 49 B4 39 21N 20 6 E
Aspromonte △, Italy 43 D8 38 9N 15 58 E
Aspur, India 68 H6 23 58N 74 7 E
Asquith, Canada 103 C7 52 8N 107 13W
Assab = Aseb, Eritrea 81 E5 13 0N 42 40 E
Assâba, Massif de l', Mauritania 82 B2 16 10N 11 45W
Assagny △, Ivory C. 82 D4 5 10N 4 48W
Assaikio, Nigeria 83 D6 8 34N 8 55 E
Assal, L., Djibouti 81 E5 11 40N 42 26 E
Assam □, India 67 G18 26 0N 93 0 E
Assamakka, Niger 83 B6 19 21N 5 38 E
Assateague Island ⌓, U.S.A. 114 F8 38 15N 75 10W
Asse, Belgium 17 D4 50 24N 4 10 E
Assémini, Italy 42 C1 39 17N 9 0 E
Assen, Neths. 17 A6 53 0N 6 35 E
Assens, Denmark 11 J3 55 16N 9 55 E
Assini, Ivory C. 82 D4 5 9N 3 17W
Assiniboia, Canada 103 D7 49 40N 105 59W
Assiniboine →, Canada 103 D9 49 53N 97 8W
Assiniboine, Mt., Canada 102 C5 50 52N 115 39W
Assis, Brazil 127 A5 22 40 S 50 20W
Assisi, Italy 41 E9 43 4N 12 37 E
Ássos, Greece 46 C2 38 22N 20 33 E

Assynt, L., U.K. ... 13 C3 58 10N 5 3W
Astaffort, France ... 20 D4 44 4N 0 40 E
Astakídha, Greece ... 47 F8 35 53N 26 50 E
Astakós, Greece ... 46 C3 38 32N 21 5 E
Astana, Kazakhstan ... 52 D8 51 10N 71 30 E
Ästäneh, Iran ... 71 B6 37 17N 49 59 E
Astara, Azerbaijan ... 71 B6 38 30N 48 50 E
Ästärä, Iran ... 73 C13 38 20N 48 52 E
Asteroúsia, Greece ... 49 E7 34 59N 25 3 E
Asti, Italy ... 40 D5 44 54N 8 12 E
Astipálaia, Greece ... 47 E8 36 32N 26 22 E
Astorga, Spain ... 36 C4 42 29N 6 8W
Astoria, U.S.A. ... 110 D3 46 11N 123 50W
Åstorp, Sweden ... 11 H6 56 6N 12 55 E
Astrakhan, Russia ... 35 G9 46 25N 48 5 E
Astudillo, Spain ... 36 C6 42 12N 4 22W
Asturias □, Spain ... 36 B5 43 15N 6 0W
Asturias ✈ (OVD), Spain ... 36 B4 43 33N 6 3 E
Asunción, Paraguay ... 126 B4 25 10 S 57 30W
Asunción Nochixtlán, Mexico ... 119 D5 17 28N 97 14W
Åsunden, Sweden ... 11 F9 58 0N 15 51 E
Asutri, Sudan ... 81 D4 15 25N 35 45 E
Aswa →, Uganda ... 86 B3 3 43N 31 55 E
Aswa-Lolim □, Uganda ... 86 B3 2 43N 31 35 E
Aswad, Ra's al, Si. Arabia ... 80 C4 21 20N 39 0 E
Aswân, Egypt ... 80 C3 24 4N 32 57 E
Aswan Dam = Sadd el Aali, Egypt ... 80 C3 23 54N 32 54 E
Asyût, Egypt ... 80 B3 27 11N 31 4 E
Asyûti, Wadi →, Egypt ... 80 B3 27 11N 31 16 E
Aszód, Hungary ... 28 C4 47 39N 19 28 E
At Ţafilah, Jordan ... 74 E4 30 45N 35 30 E
At Ţafilah □, Jordan ... 74 E4 30 45N 35 30 E
Aţ Ţā'if, Si. Arabia ... 75 C3 21 5N 40 27 E
At Ta'mīm □, Iraq ... 70 C5 35 30N 44 20 E
Aţ Ţirāq, Si. Arabia ... 70 E5 27 19N 44 33 E
Aţ Ţubayq, Si. Arabia ... 70 D3 29 30N 37 0 E
Atabey, Turkey ... 47 D12 37 57N 30 39 E
Atacama □, Chile ... 126 B2 27 30 S 70 0W
Atacama, Desierto de, Chile ... 126 A2 24 0 S 69 20W
Atacama, Salar de, Chile ... 126 A2 23 30 S 68 20W
Atakpamé, Togo ... 83 D5 7 31N 1 13 E
Atalaya, Peru ... 124 F4 10 45 S 73 50W
Atalaya de Femes, Canary Is. ... 48 F6 28 56N 13 47W
Atami, Japan ... 55 G9 35 5N 139 4 E
Atapupu, E. Timor ... 63 F7 9 0 S 124 51 E
Atâr, Mauritania ... 78 D3 20 30N 13 5W
Atarfe, Spain ... 37 H7 37 13N 3 40W
Atari, Pakistan ... 68 D6 30 56N 74 2 E
Atascadero, U.S.A. ... 110 K6 35 29N 120 40W
Atasu, Kazakhstan ... 52 E8 48 30N 71 0 E
Ataturk, Istanbul ✈ (IST), Turkey ... 45 F12 40 59N 28 49 E
Atatürk Baraji, Turkey ... 73 D8 37 28N 38 30 E
Atauro, E. Timor ... 63 F7 8 10 S 125 30 E
'Atbara, Sudan ... 80 D3 17 42N 33 59 E
'Atbara →, Sudan ... 80 D3 17 40N 33 56 E
Atbasar, Kazakhstan ... 52 D7 51 48N 68 20 E
Atça, Turkey ... 47 D10 37 53N 28 13 E
Atchafalaya B., U.S.A. ... 113 L9 29 25N 91 25W
Atchison, U.S.A. ... 112 F7 39 34N 95 7W
Atebubu, Ghana ... 83 D4 7 47N 1 0W
Ateca, Spain ... 38 D3 41 20N 1 49W
Aterno →, Italy ... 41 F10 42 11N 13 51 E
Äteshān, Iran ... 71 C7 35 35N 52 37 E
Atesine, Alpi, Italy ... 41 B8 46 55N 11 30 E
Atessa, Italy ... 41 F11 42 4N 14 27 E
Atfih, Egypt ... 80 J7 29 25N 31 15 E
Ath, Belgium ... 17 D3 50 38N 3 47 E
Athabasca, Canada ... 102 C6 54 45N 113 20W
Athabasca →, Canada ... 103 B6 58 40N 110 50W
Athabasca, L., Canada ... 103 B7 59 15N 109 15W
Athabasca Sand Dunes □, Canada ... 103 B7 59 4N 108 43W
Athboy, Ireland ... 12 C5 53 37N 6 56W
Athenry, Ireland ... 12 C3 53 18N 8 44W
Athens = Athínai, Greece ... 46 D5 37 58N 23 46 E
Athens, Ala., U.S.A. ... 115 H2 34 48N 86 58W
Athens, Ga., U.S.A. ... 115 J4 33 57N 83 23W
Athens, N.Y., U.S.A. ... 117 D11 42 16N 73 49W
Athens, Ohio, U.S.A. ... 114 F4 39 20N 82 6W
Athens, Pa., U.S.A. ... 117 E8 41 57N 76 31W
Athens, Tenn., U.S.A. ... 115 H3 35 27N 84 36W
Athens, Tex., U.S.A. ... 113 J7 32 12N 95 51W
Atherley, Canada ... 116 B5 44 37N 79 20W
Atherton, Australia ... 94 B4 17 17 S 145 30 E
Athiéme, Benin ... 83 D5 6 37N 1 40 E
Athienou, Cyprus ... 49 D12 35 3N 33 32 E
Athínai, Greece ... 46 D5 37 58N 23 46 E
Athínai ✈ (ATH), Greece ... 46 D5 37 52N 23 55 E
Athlone, Ireland ... 12 C4 53 25N 7 56W
Athna, Cyprus ... 49 D12 35 3N 33 47 E
Athol, U.S.A. ... 117 D12 42 36N 72 14W
Atholl, Forest of, U.K. ... 13 E5 56 51N 3 50W
Atholville, Canada ... 105 C6 47 59N 66 43W
Áthos, Greece ... 45 F8 40 9N 24 22 E
Athy, Ireland ... 12 C5 53 0N 7 0W
Ati, Chad ... 79 F9 13 13N 18 20 E
Ati, Sudan ... 81 E2 13 5N 29 2 E
Atiak, Uganda ... 86 B3 3 12N 32 2 E
Atienza, Spain ... 38 D2 41 12N 2 52W
Atiit, Sudan ... 81 F3 6 10N 30 35 E
Atik, L., Canada ... 103 B9 55 15N 96 0W
Atikaki □, Canada ... 103 C9 51 30N 95 31W
Atikameg →, Canada ... 104 B3 52 30N 82 46W
Atikokan, Canada ... 104 C1 48 45N 91 37W
Atikonak L., Canada ... 105 B7 52 40N 64 32W
Atimonan, Phil. ... 61 E4 14 0N 121 55 E
Atitlán □, Cent. Amer. ... 119 E6 14 38N 91 10W
Atka, Russia ... 53 C16 60 50N 151 48 E
Atka I., U.S.A. ... 100 C2 52 7N 174 30W
Atkarsk, Russia ... 34 E7 51 55N 45 2 E
Atkinson, U.S.A. ... 112 D5 42 32N 98 59W
Atlanta, Ga., U.S.A. ... 115 J3 33 45N 84 23W
Atlanta, Tex., U.S.A. ... 113 J7 33 7N 94 10W
Atlantic, U.S.A. ... 112 E7 41 24N 95 1W
Atlantic City, U.S.A. ... 114 F8 39 21N 74 27W
Atlantic-Indian Basin, Antarctica ... 5 B4 60 0 S 30 0 E
Atlantic-Indian Ridge, S. Ocean ... 5 B3 53 0 S 5 0W
Atlantic Ocean ... 2 E9 0 0 20 0W
Atlas Mts. = Haut Atlas, Morocco ... 78 B4 32 30N 5 0W
Atlin, Canada ... 102 B2 59 31N 133 41W
Atlin □, Canada ... 102 B2 59 10N 134 30W
Atlin L., Canada ... 102 B2 59 26N 133 45W
Atmore, U.S.A. ... 115 K2 31 2N 87 29W
Atoka, U.S.A. ... 113 H6 34 23N 96 8W

Átokos Nísis, Greece ... 46 C2 38 28N 20 49 E
Atolia, U.S.A. ... 111 K9 35 19N 117 37W
Atrai →, Bangla. ... 69 G13 24 7N 89 22 E
Atrak →, Turkmenistan ... 71 B8 37 35N 53 58 E
Ätran, Sweden ... 11 G6 57 7N 12 57 E
Ätran →, Sweden ... 11 H6 56 53N 12 30 E
Atrauli, India ... 68 E8 28 2N 78 20 E
Atri, Italy ... 41 F10 42 35N 13 58 E
Atsikí, Greece ... 47 B7 39 56N 25 13 E
Atsoum, Mts., Cameroon ... 83 D7 6 41N 12 57 E
Atsuta, Japan ... 54 C10 43 24N 141 26 E
Attalla, U.S.A. ... 115 H2 34 1N 86 6W
Attapu, Laos ... 64 E6 14 48N 106 50 E
Attáviros, Greece ... 49 C9 36 12N 27 50 E
Attawapiskat, Canada ... 104 B3 52 56N 82 24W
Attawapiskat →, Canada ... 104 B3 52 57N 82 18W
Attawapiskat L., Canada ... 104 B2 52 18N 87 54W
Attersee, Austria ... 26 D6 47 55N 13 32 E
Attica, Ind., U.S.A. ... 114 E2 40 18N 87 15W
Attica, Ohio, U.S.A. ... 116 E2 41 4N 82 53W
Attichy, France ... 19 C10 49 25N 3 3 E
Attigny, France ... 19 C11 49 28N 4 35 E
Attika = Attikí □, Greece ... 46 D5 37 10N 23 40 E
Attikamager L., Canada ... 105 B6 55 0N 66 30W
Attikí □, Greece ... 46 D5 37 10N 23 40 E
Attleboro, U.S.A. ... 117 E13 41 57N 71 17W
Attock, Pakistan ... 68 C5 33 52N 72 20 E
Attopeu = Attapu, Laos ... 64 E6 14 48N 106 50 E
Attu I., U.S.A. ... 100 C1 52 55N 172 55 E
Attur, India ... 66 P11 11 35N 78 30 E
Atuel →, Argentina ... 126 D2 36 17 S 66 50W
Åtvidaberg, Sweden ... 11 F10 58 12N 16 0 E
Atwater, U.S.A. ... 110 H6 37 21N 120 37W
Atwood, Canada ... 116 C3 43 40N 81 1W
Atwood, U.S.A. ... 112 F4 39 48N 101 3W
Atyraū, Kazakhstan ... 52 E6 47 5N 52 0 E
Au Sable, U.S.A. ... 116 B1 44 25N 83 20W
Au Sable →, U.S.A. ... 114 C4 44 25N 83 20W
Au Sable Forks, U.S.A. ... 117 B11 44 27N 73 41W
Au Sable Pt., U.S.A. ... 116 B1 44 20N 83 20W
Aubagne, France ... 21 E9 43 17N 5 37 E
Aubarca, C. d', Spain ... 48 B7 39 4N 1 22 E
Aube □, France ... 19 D11 48 15N 4 10 E
Aube →, France ... 19 D10 48 34N 3 43 E
Aubenas, France ... 21 D8 44 37N 4 24 E
Aubenton, France ... 19 C11 49 50N 4 12 E
Auberry, U.S.A. ... 110 H7 37 7N 119 29W
Aubigny-sur-Nère, France ... 19 E9 47 30N 2 24 E
Aubin, France ... 20 D6 44 33N 2 15 E
Aubrac, Mts. d', France ... 20 D7 44 40N 3 2 E
Auburn, Ala., U.S.A. ... 115 J3 32 36N 85 29W
Auburn, Calif., U.S.A. ... 110 G5 38 54N 121 4W
Auburn, Ind., U.S.A. ... 114 E3 41 22N 85 4W
Auburn, Maine, U.S.A. ... 115 C10 44 6N 70 14W
Auburn, N.Y., U.S.A. ... 117 D8 42 56N 76 34W
Auburn, Nebr., U.S.A. ... 112 E7 40 23N 95 51W
Auburn, Pa., U.S.A. ... 117 F8 40 36N 76 6W
Auburn, Wash., U.S.A. ... 110 C4 47 18N 122 14W
Auburn Ra., Australia ... 95 D5 25 15 S 150 30 E
Auburndale, U.S.A. ... 115 L5 28 4N 81 48W
Aubusson, France ... 20 C6 45 57N 2 11 E
Auce, Latvia ... 30 B9 56 28N 22 53 E
Auch, France ... 20 E4 43 39N 0 36 E
Auchi, Nigeria ... 83 D6 7 6N 6 13 E
Auchterarder, U.K. ... 13 E5 56 18N 3 41W
Auchtermuchty, U.K. ... 13 E5 56 18N 3 13W
Auckland, N.Z. ... 91 G5 36 52 S 174 46 E
Auckland Is., Pac. Oc. ... 96 N8 50 40 S 166 5 E
Aude □, France ... 20 E7 43 8N 2 28 E
Aude →, France ... 20 E7 43 13N 3 14 E
Auden, Canada ... 104 B2 50 14N 87 53W
Auderville, France ... 18 C5 49 43N 1 57W
Audierne, France ... 18 D2 48 1N 4 34W
Audincourt, France ... 19 E13 47 30N 6 50 E
Audo Ra., Ethiopia ... 81 F5 6 20N 41 50 E
Audubon, U.S.A. ... 112 E7 41 43N 94 56W
Aue, Germany ... 24 E8 50 35N 12 41 E
Auerbach, Germany ... 24 E8 50 30N 12 24 E
Augathella, Australia ... 95 D4 25 48 S 146 35 E
Aughnacloy, U.K. ... 12 B5 54 25N 6 59W
Augrabies Falls, S. Africa ... 88 D3 28 35 S 20 20 E
Augrabies Falls △, S. Africa ... 88 D3 28 40 S 20 22 E
Augsburg, Germany ... 25 G6 48 25N 10 52 E
Augsburg-Westliche Wälder △, Germany ... 25 G6 48 22N 10 40 E
Augusta, Australia ... 93 F2 34 19 S 115 9 E
Augusta, Italy ... 43 E8 37 13N 15 13 E
Augusta, Ark., U.S.A. ... 113 H9 35 17N 91 22W
Augusta, Ga., U.S.A. ... 115 J5 33 28N 81 58W
Augusta, Kans., U.S.A. ... 113 G6 37 41N 96 59W
Augusta, Maine, U.S.A. ... 101 D13 44 19N 69 47W
Augusta, Mont., U.S.A. ... 108 C7 47 30N 112 24W
Augustenborg, Denmark ... 11 K3 54 57N 9 53 E
Augustów, Poland ... 30 E9 53 51N 23 0 E
Augustus, Mt., Australia ... 93 D2 24 20 S 116 50 E
Augustus I., Australia ... 92 C3 15 20 S 124 30 E
Aukan, Eritrea ... 81 D5 15 29N 40 50 E
Aukrug △, Germany ... 24 A5 54 5N 9 45 E
Aukum, U.S.A. ... 110 G6 38 34N 120 43W
Auld, L., Australia ... 92 D3 22 25 S 123 50 E
Aulla, Italy ... 40 D6 44 12N 9 58 E
Aulnay, France ... 20 B3 46 2N 0 22W
Aulnoye-Aymeries, France ... 19 B10 50 12N 3 50 E
Ault, France ... 18 B8 50 8N 1 26 E
Aulus-les-Bains, France ... 20 F5 42 49N 1 19 E
Aumale, France ... 19 C8 49 46N 1 46 E
Aumont-Aubrac, France ... 20 D7 44 43N 3 17 E
Auna, Nigeria ... 83 C5 10 9N 4 42 E
Auning, Denmark ... 11 H4 56 26N 10 22 E
Aunis, France ... 20 B3 46 5N 0 50W
Auponhia, Indonesia ... 63 E7 1 58 S 125 27 E
Aups, France ... 21 E10 43 37N 6 15 E
Aur, Pulau, Malaysia ... 65 L5 2 35N 104 10 E
Auraiya, India ... 69 F8 26 28N 79 33 E
Aurangabad, Bihar, India ... 69 G11 24 45N 84 18 E
Aurangabad, Maharashtra, India ... 66 K9 19 50N 75 23 E
Auray, France ... 18 E4 47 40N 2 59W
Aurich, Germany ... 24 B3 53 28N 7 28 E
Aurillac, France ... 20 D6 44 55N 2 26 E
Auronzo di Cadore, Italy ... 41 B9 46 33N 12 26 E
Aurora, Canada ... 116 C5 44 0N 79 28W
Aurora, S. Africa ... 88 E2 32 40 S 18 29 E
Aurora, Colo., U.S.A. ... 112 F2 39 44N 104 52W
Aurora, Ill., U.S.A. ... 114 E1 41 45N 88 19W

Aurora, Mo., U.S.A. ... 113 G8 36 58N 93 43W
Aurora, N.Y., U.S.A. ... 117 D8 42 45N 76 42W
Aurora, Nebr., U.S.A. ... 112 E6 40 52N 98 0W
Aurora, Ohio, U.S.A. ... 116 E3 41 21N 81 20W
Aurukun, Australia ... 94 A3 13 20 S 141 45 E
Aus, Namibia ... 88 D2 26 35 S 16 12 E
Ausable →, Canada ... 116 C3 43 19N 81 46W
Auschwitz = Oświęcim, Poland ... 31 H6 50 2N 19 11 E
Austerlitz = Slavkov u Brna, Czech Rep. ... 27 B9 49 10N 16 52 E
Austin, Minn., U.S.A. ... 112 D8 43 40N 92 58W
Austin, Nev., U.S.A. ... 108 G5 39 30N 117 4W
Austin, Pa., U.S.A. ... 116 E6 41 38N 78 6W
Austin, Tex., U.S.A. ... 113 K6 30 17N 97 45W
Austin, L., Australia ... 93 E2 27 40 S 118 0 E
Austin I., Canada ... 103 A10 61 10N 94 0W
Austra, Norway ... 8 D14 65 8N 11 55 E
Austral Is. = Tubuai Is., French Polynesia ... 97 K13 25 0 S 150 0W
Austral Seamount Chain, Pac. Oc. ... 97 K13 24 0 S 150 0W
Australia ■, Oceania ... 96 K5 23 0 S 135 0 E
Australian Capital Territory □, Australia ... 95 F4 35 30 S 149 0 E
Australind, Australia ... 93 F2 33 17 S 115 42 E
Austria ■, Europe ... 26 E7 47 0N 14 0 E
Austvågøy, Norway ... 8 B16 68 20N 14 40 E
Auterive, France ... 20 E5 43 21N 1 29 E
Authie →, France ... 19 B8 50 22N 1 38 E
Authon-du-Perche, France ... 18 D7 48 12N 0 54 E
Autlán, Mexico ... 118 D4 19 40N 104 30W
Autun, France ... 19 F11 46 58N 4 17 E
Auvergne □, France ... 20 C7 45 20N 3 15 E
Auvergne, Mts. d', France ... 20 C6 45 20N 2 55 E
Auvézère →, France ... 20 C4 45 12N 0 50 E
Auxerre, France ... 19 E10 47 48N 3 32 E
Auxi-le-Château, France ... 19 B9 50 15N 2 8 E
Auxonne, France ... 19 E12 47 10N 5 20 E
Auzances, France ... 19 F9 46 2N 2 30 E
Ava, U.S.A. ... 113 G8 36 57N 92 40W
Avallon, France ... 19 E10 47 30N 3 53 E
Avalon, U.S.A. ... 111 M8 33 21N 118 20W
Avalon Pen., Canada ... 105 C9 47 30N 53 20W
Avaré, Brazil ... 127 A6 23 4 S 48 58W
Ávas, Greece ... 45 F9 40 57N 25 56 E
Avawatz Mts., U.S.A. ... 111 K10 35 40N 116 30W
Aveiro, Brazil ... 125 D7 3 10 S 55 5W
Aveiro, Portugal ... 36 E2 40 37N 8 38W
Aveiro □, Portugal ... 36 E2 40 40N 8 35W
Avej, Iran ... 71 C6 35 40N 49 15 E
Avellaneda, Argentina ... 126 C4 34 50 S 58 10W
Avellino, Italy ... 43 B7 40 54N 14 47 E
Avenal, U.S.A. ... 110 K6 36 0N 120 8W
Aversa, Italy ... 43 B7 40 58N 14 12 E
Avery, U.S.A. ... 108 C6 47 15N 115 49W
Aves, I. de, W. Indies ... 121 C7 15 45N 63 55W
Aves, Is. las, Venezuela ... 121 D6 12 0N 67 30W
Avesnes-sur-Helpe, France ... 19 B10 50 8N 3 55 E
Avesnois, France ... 19 B10 50 10N 3 45 E
Avesta, Sweden ... 10 D10 60 9N 16 10 E
Aveyron □, France ... 20 D6 44 22N 2 45 E
Aveyron →, France ... 20 D5 44 5N 1 16 E
Avezzano, Italy ... 41 F10 42 2N 13 25 E
Avgó, Greece ... 47 F7 35 33N 25 37 E
Aviá Terai, Argentina ... 126 B3 26 45 S 60 50W
Aviano, Italy ... 41 B9 46 3N 12 35 E
Aviemore, U.K. ... 13 D5 57 12N 3 50W
Avigliana, Italy ... 40 C4 45 5N 7 23 E
Avigliano, Italy ... 43 B8 40 44N 15 43 E
Avignon, France ... 21 E8 43 57N 4 50 E
Ávila, Spain ... 36 E6 40 39N 4 43W
Ávila □, Spain ... 36 E6 40 30N 5 0W
Ávila, Sierra de, Spain ... 36 E5 40 40N 5 15W
Avila Beach, U.S.A. ... 111 K6 35 11N 120 44W
Avilés, Spain ... 36 B5 43 35N 5 57W
Avintes, Portugal ... 36 D2 41 7N 8 33W
Avionárion, Greece ... 46 C6 38 31N 24 8 E
Avis, Portugal ... 37 F3 39 4N 7 53W
Avis, U.S.A. ... 116 E7 41 11N 77 19W
Avísio →, Italy ... 40 B8 46 7N 11 5 E
Avize, France ... 19 D11 48 59N 4 1 E
Avlum, Denmark ... 11 H2 56 16N 8 47 E
Avoca →, Australia ... 95 F3 35 40 S 143 43 E
Avoca →, Ireland ... 12 D5 52 48N 6 10W
Avoca, Canada ... 102 C5 51 45N 119 19W
Avola, Italy ... 43 F8 36 56N 15 7 E
Avon, U.S.A. ... 116 D7 42 55N 77 45W
Avon →, Australia ... 93 F2 31 40 S 116 7 E
Avon →, Bristol, U.K. ... 15 F5 51 29N 2 41W
Avon →, Dorset, U.K. ... 15 G6 50 44N 1 46W
Avon →, Warks., U.K. ... 15 E5 52 0N 2 8W
Avon Park, U.S.A. ... 115 M5 27 36N 81 31W
Avondale, Zimbabwe ... 87 F3 17 43 S 30 58 E
Avonlea, Canada ... 103 D8 50 0N 105 0W
Avonmore, Canada ... 117 A10 45 10N 74 58W
Avonmouth, U.K. ... 15 F5 51 30N 2 42W
Avramov, Bulgaria ... 45 D10 42 45N 26 38 E
Avranches, France ... 18 D5 48 40N 1 20W
Avre →, France ... 18 D8 48 47N 1 22 E
Avrig, Romania ... 29 E9 45 43N 24 21 E
Avrillé, France ... 18 E6 47 30N 0 35W
Avtovac, Bos.-H. ... 44 C2 43 9N 18 35 E
Awag el Baqar, Sudan ... 81 E3 10 10N 33 10 E
A'waj →, Syria ... 74 B5 33 23N 36 20 E
Awaji-Shima, Japan ... 55 G7 34 30N 134 50 E
'Awālī, Bahrain ... 71 E6 26 0N 50 30 E
Awantipur, India ... 69 C6 33 55N 75 3 E
Awasa, Ethiopia ... 81 F4 7 2N 38 28 E
Awasa □, Ethiopia ... 81 F4 7 0N 38 30 E
Awash, Ethiopia ... 81 F5 9 1N 40 10 E
Awash →, Ethiopia ... 81 E5 11 45N 41 5 E
Awaso, Ghana ... 82 D4 6 15N 2 22W
Awatere →, N.Z. ... 91 J5 41 37 S 174 10 E
Awbārī, Libya ... 79 C8 26 46N 12 57 E
Awbārī, Idehan, Libya ... 79 C8 27 10N 11 30 E
Awe, L., U.K. ... 13 E3 56 17N 5 16W
Awjilah, Libya ... 79 C10 29 8N 21 7 E
Awka, Nigeria ... 83 D6 6 12N 7 6 E
Axat, France ... 20 F6 42 48N 2 13 E
Axe →, U.K. ... 15 F5 50 42N 3 4W
Axel Heiberg I., Canada ... 98 A10 80 0N 90 0W
Axim, Ghana ... 82 E4 4 51N 2 15W
Axintele, Romania ... 29 F11 44 37N 26 49 E
Axiós →, Greece ... 44 F6 40 57N 22 35 E
Axminster, U.K. ... 15 G4 50 46N 3 0W

Axvall, Sweden ... 11 F7 58 23N 13 34 E
Ay, France ... 19 C11 49 3N 4 1 E
Ayabaca, Peru ... 124 D3 4 40 S 79 53W
Ayabe, Japan ... 55 G7 35 20N 135 20 E
Ayacucho, Argentina ... 126 D4 37 5 S 58 20W
Ayacucho, Peru ... 124 F4 13 0 S 74 0W
Ayamé, Ivory C. ... 82 D4 5 35N 3 9W
Ayamonte, Spain ... 37 H3 37 12N 7 24W
Ayan, Russia ... 53 D14 56 30N 138 16 E
Ayancık, Turkey ... 72 B6 41 57N 34 35 E
Ayas, Turkey ... 72 B5 40 2N 32 21 E
Ayaviri, Peru ... 124 F4 14 50 S 70 35W
Aybastı, Turkey ... 72 B7 40 41N 37 23 E
Aydın, Turkey ... 72 D2 37 51N 27 51 E
Aydın □, Turkey ... 47 D9 37 50N 28 0 E
Aydın Dağları, Turkey ... 47 D10 38 0N 28 0 E
Ayelu, Ethiopia ... 81 E5 10 5N 40 42 E
Ayenngré, Togo ... 83 D5 8 40N 1 12 E
Ayer, U.S.A. ... 117 D13 42 34N 71 35W
Ayer Hitam, Malaysia ... 65 e 5 24N 100 16 E
Ayerbe, Spain ... 38 C4 42 17N 0 41W
Ayer's Cliff, Canada ... 117 A12 45 10N 72 3W
Ayers Rock, Australia ... 93 E5 25 23 S 131 5 E
Ayiá, Greece ... 46 B4 39 43N 22 45 E
Ayía Aikateríni, Ákra, Greece ... 49 A3 39 50N 19 50 E
Ayía Ánna, Greece ... 46 C5 38 52N 23 24 E
Ayía Dhéka, Greece ... 49 D6 35 3N 24 58 E
Ayía Gálini, Greece ... 49 D6 35 6N 24 41 E
Ayía Marína, Kásos, Greece ... 47 F8 35 27N 26 53 E
Ayía Marína, Léros, Greece ... 47 D8 37 11N 26 48 E
Ayía Napa, Cyprus ... 49 E13 34 59N 34 0 E
Ayía Paraskeví, Greece ... 47 B8 39 14N 26 21 E
Ayía Phyla, Cyprus ... 49 E12 34 43N 33 1 E
Ayía Rouméli, Greece ... 46 F5 35 14N 23 58 E
Ayía Varvára, Greece ... 49 D7 35 8N 25 1 E
Ayiássos, Greece ... 47 B8 39 5N 26 23 E
Ayíoi Theódhoroi, Greece ... 46 D5 37 55N 23 9 E
Ayion Óros □, Greece ... 45 F8 40 25N 24 6 E
Áyios Amvrósios, Cyprus ... 49 D12 35 20N 33 35 E
Áyios Andréas, Greece ... 46 D4 37 21N 22 45 E
Áyios Evstrátios, Greece ... 45 B6 39 34N 24 58 E
Áyios Ioánnis, Ákra, Greece ... 49 D7 35 20N 25 40 E
Áyios Isidhoros, Greece ... 49 C9 36 9N 27 51 E
Áyios Kírikos, Greece ... 47 D8 37 34N 26 17 E
Áyios Matthaíos, Greece ... 49 B3 39 30N 19 47 E
Áyios Mírono, Greece ... 47 F7 35 15N 25 1 E
Áyios Nikólaos, Greece ... 49 D7 35 11N 25 41 E
Áyios Pétros, Greece ... 46 C2 38 40N 20 36 E
Áyios Seryios, Cyprus ... 49 D12 35 12N 33 53 E
Áyios Theódhoros, Cyprus ... 49 D13 35 22N 34 1 E
Áyios Yeóryios, Greece ... 46 D5 37 28N 23 57 E
Aykathonísi, Greece ... 47 D8 37 27N 27 0 E
Aykırıkçi, Turkey ... 47 B12 39 8N 30 9 E
Aylmer, Canada ... 116 D4 42 46N 80 59W
Aylmer, L., Canada ... 100 B8 64 0N 110 8W
'Ayn, Wādī al, Oman ... 71 F7 22 15N 55 28 E
Ayn Dār, Si. Arabia ... 71 E7 25 55N 49 10 E
Ayn Zālah, Iraq ... 70 B4 36 45N 42 35 E
Ayna, Spain ... 39 G2 38 34N 2 3W
Ayod, Sudan ... 81 F3 8 7N 31 26 E
Ayolas, Paraguay ... 126 B4 27 10 S 56 59W
Ayom, Sudan ... 81 F2 7 49N 28 23 E
Ayon, Ostrov, Russia ... 53 C17 69 50N 169 0 E
Ayora, Spain ... 39 F3 39 3N 1 3W
Ayorou, Niger ... 83 C5 14 53N 1 0 E
'Ayoûn el 'Atroûs, Mauritania ... 82 B3 16 38N 9 37W
Ayr, Australia ... 94 B4 19 35 S 147 25 E
Ayr, Canada ... 116 C4 43 17N 80 27W
Ayr, U.K. ... 13 F4 55 28N 4 38W
Ayr →, U.K. ... 13 F4 55 28N 4 38W
Ayranci, Turkey ... 72 D5 37 21N 33 41 E
Ayrancılar, Turkey ... 47 C9 38 15N 27 18 E
Ayre, Pt. of, I. of Man ... 14 C3 54 25N 4 21W
Aysha, Ethiopia ... 81 E5 10 50N 42 23 E
Ayton, Australia ... 94 B4 15 56 S 145 22 E
Aytos, Bulgaria ... 45 D11 42 42N 27 16 E
Aytoska Planina, Bulgaria ... 45 D11 42 45N 27 30 E
Ayu, Kepulauan, Indonesia ... 63 D8 0 35N 131 5 E
Ayutla, Guatemala ... 120 D1 14 40N 92 10W
Ayutla, Mexico ... 119 D5 16 58N 99 17W
Ayvacık, Turkey ... 72 C2 39 36N 26 24 E
Ayvalık, Turkey ... 47 B8 39 20N 26 46 E
Az Zabadānī, Syria ... 74 B5 33 43N 36 5 E
Az Zāhīriyah, West Bank ... 74 D3 31 25N 34 58 E
Az Zahrān, Si. Arabia ... 71 E6 26 10N 50 7 E
Az Zarqā, Jordan ... 74 C5 32 5N 36 4 E
Az Zarqā, U.A.E. ... 71 E7 24 53N 53 4 E
Az Zarqā □, Jordan ... 74 C5 32 5N 36 4 E
Az Zāwiyah, Libya ... 79 B8 32 52N 12 56 E
Az Zibār, Iraq ... 70 B5 36 52N 44 4 E
Az Zilfī, Si. Arabia ... 70 E5 26 12N 44 52 E
Az Zubayr, Iraq ... 70 D5 30 26N 47 40 E
Az Zuqar, Yemen ... 81 E5 14 0N 42 45 E
Azad Kashmir □, Pakistan ... 69 C5 33 50N 73 50 E
Azambuja, Portugal ... 37 F2 39 4N 8 51W
Azamgarh, India ... 69 F10 26 5N 83 13 E
Azángaro, Peru ... 124 F4 14 55 S 70 13W
Azaouad, Mali ... 82 B4 19 0N 3 0W
Azaouak, Vallée de l', Mali ... 83 B5 15 50N 4 0 E
Azār Shahr, Iran ... 70 B5 37 45N 45 59 E
Azara, Nigeria ... 83 D6 8 22N 9 12 E
Azarān, Iran ... 70 B5 37 25N 47 16 E
Azārbāyjān = Azerbaijan ■, Asia ... 35 K9 40 20N 48 0 E
Azārbāyjān-e Gharbī □, Iran ... 70 B5 37 0N 44 30 E
Azārbāyjān-e Sharqī □, Iran ... 70 B5 37 0N 47 0 E
Azare, Nigeria ... 83 C7 11 55N 10 10 E
Azay-le-Rideau, France ... 18 E7 47 16N 0 30 E
Azbine = Aïr, Niger ... 83 B6 18 30N 8 0 E
A'zāz, Syria ... 70 B3 36 36N 37 4 E
Azerbaijan ■, Asia ... 35 K9 40 20N 48 0 E
Azerbaijchan = Azerbaijan ■, Asia ... 35 K9 40 20N 48 0 E
Azezo, Ethiopia ... 81 E4 12 28N 37 15 E
Azimganj, India ... 69 G13 24 14N 88 16 E
Aznalcóllar, Spain ... 37 H4 37 32N 6 17W
Azogues, Ecuador ... 124 D3 2 35 S 78 0W
Azores = Açores, Is. dos, Atl. Oc. ... 78 A1 38 0N 27 0W

Azov, Russia ... 35 G4 47 3N 39 25 E
Azov, Sea of, Europe ... 33 J9 46 0N 36 30 E
Azovskoye More = Azov, Sea of, Europe ... 33 J9 46 0N 36 30 E
Azpeitia, Spain ... 38 B2 43 12N 2 19W
Azraq ash Shīshān, Jordan ... 74 D5 31 50N 36 49 E
Aztec, U.S.A. ... 109 H10 36 49N 107 59W
Azúa de Compostela, Dom. Rep. ... 121 C5 18 25N 70 44W
Azuaga, Spain ... 37 G5 38 16N 5 39W
Azuara, Spain ... 38 D4 41 15N 0 53W
Azuer →, Spain ... 37 F7 39 8N 3 36W
Azuero, Pen. de, Panama ... 120 E3 7 30N 80 30W
Azuga, Romania ... 29 E10 45 27N 25 33 E
Azul, Argentina ... 126 D4 36 42 S 59 43W
Azusa, U.S.A. ... 111 L9 34 8N 117 52W
Azzano Décimo, Italy ... 41 C9 45 52N 12 56 E

B

Ba Be △, Vietnam ... 64 A5 22 25N 105 37 E
Ba Don, Vietnam ... 64 D6 17 45N 106 26 E
Ba Dong, Vietnam ... 65 H6 9 40N 106 33 E
Ba Ngoi = Cam Lam, Vietnam ... 65 G7 11 54N 109 10 E
Ba Tri, Vietnam ... 65 G6 10 2N 106 36 E
Ba Vì △, Vietnam ... 64 B5 21 1N 105 22 E
Ba Xian = Bazhou, China ... 56 E9 39 8N 116 22 E
Baa, Indonesia ... 63 F6 10 50 S 123 0 E
Baamonde, Spain ... 36 B3 43 7N 7 44W
Baardheere = Bardera, Somali Rep. ... 75 G3 2 20N 42 27 E
Baarle-Nassau, Belgium ... 17 C4 51 27N 4 56 E
Bab el Mandeb, Red Sea ... 75 E3 12 35N 43 25 E
Bābā, Koh-i-, Afghan. ... 66 B5 34 30N 67 0 E
Baba Burnu, Turkey ... 47 B8 39 29N 26 2 E
Baba dag, Azerbaijan ... 35 K9 41 0N 48 19 E
Babadag, Romania ... 29 F13 44 53N 28 44 E
Babadağ, Turkey ... 47 D10 37 49N 28 52 E
Babaeski, Turkey ... 45 E11 41 26N 27 6 E
Babahoyo, Ecuador ... 124 D3 1 40 S 79 30W
Babai = Sarju →, India ... 69 F9 27 21N 81 23 E
Babana, Nigeria ... 83 C5 10 31N 3 46 E
Babanusa, Sudan ... 81 E2 11 20N 27 48 E
Babar, Indonesia ... 63 F7 8 0 S 129 30 E
Babar, Pakistan ... 68 D3 31 7N 69 32 E
Babarkach, Pakistan ... 68 E3 29 45N 68 0 E
Babayevo, Russia ... 32 C8 59 24N 35 55 E
Babb, U.S.A. ... 108 B7 48 51N 113 27W
Babenhausen, Germany ... 25 F4 49 57N 8 57 E
Băbeni, Romania ... 29 F9 44 59N 24 11 E
Baberu, India ... 69 G9 25 33N 80 43 E
Babi Besar, Pulau, Malaysia ... 65 L4 2 25N 103 59 E
Babia Gora, Europe ... 31 J6 49 38N 19 38 E
Babian Jiang →, China ... 58 F3 22 55N 101 47 E
Bābil □, Iraq ... 70 C5 32 30N 44 30 E
Babile, Ethiopia ... 81 F5 9 16N 42 11 E
Babimost, Poland ... 31 F2 52 10N 15 49 E
Babinda, Australia ... 94 B4 17 20 S 145 56 E
Babine, Canada ... 102 B3 55 22N 126 37W
Babine →, Canada ... 102 B3 55 45N 127 44W
Babine L., Canada ... 102 C3 54 48N 126 0W
Babiogórski △, Poland ... 31 J6 49 38N 19 39 E
Babo, Indonesia ... 63 E8 2 30 S 133 30 E
Babócsa, Hungary ... 28 D2 46 2N 17 21 E
Bābol, Iran ... 71 B7 36 40N 52 50 E
Bābol Sar, Iran ... 71 B7 36 45N 52 45 E
Baborów, Poland ... 31 H5 50 7N 18 1 E
Babruysk, Belarus ... 33 F5 53 10N 29 15 E
Babuhri, India ... 68 F3 26 49N 69 43 E
Babuna, Macedonia ... 44 E5 41 30N 21 40 E
Babura, Nigeria ... 83 C6 12 51N 8 59 E
Babushkin, Russia ... 53 D11 51 40N 105 30 E
Babuyan Chan., Phil. ... 61 B4 18 40N 121 30 E
Babylon, Iraq ... 70 C5 32 34N 44 22 E
Bač, Serbia & M. ... 28 E4 45 29N 19 17 E
Bac, Moldova ... 29 D14 46 55N 29 26 E
Bac Giang, Vietnam ... 58 G6 21 16N 106 11 E
Bac Lieu, Vietnam ... 65 H5 9 17N 105 43 E
Bac Ninh, Vietnam ... 58 G6 21 13N 106 4 E
Bac Phan, Vietnam ... 64 B5 22 0N 105 0 E
Bac Quang, Vietnam ... 58 F5 22 30N 104 48 E
Bacabal, Brazil ... 125 D10 4 15 S 44 45W
Bacalar, Mexico ... 119 D7 18 50N 87 27W
Bacan, Kepulauan, Indonesia ... 63 E7 0 35 S 127 30 E
Bacarra, Phil. ... 61 B4 18 15N 120 37 E
Bacău, Romania ... 29 D11 46 35N 26 55 E
Bacău □, Romania ... 29 D11 46 30N 26 45 E
Baccarat, France ... 19 D13 48 28N 6 42 E
Bacerac, Mexico ... 118 A3 30 18N 108 50W
Băcești, Romania ... 29 D12 46 50N 27 11 E
Bach Long Vi, Dao, Vietnam ... 64 B6 20 10N 107 40 E
Bach Ma △, Vietnam ... 64 D6 16 11N 107 49 E
Bacharach, Germany ... 25 E3 50 3N 7 46 E
Bachhwara, India ... 69 G11 25 35N 85 54 E
Bachuma, Ethiopia ... 81 F4 6 48N 35 53 E
Backa, Serbia & M. ... 44 C5 43 42N 21 23 E
Back →, Canada ... 100 B9 65 10N 104 0W
Bačka, Serbia & M. ... 28 E4 45 17N 19 27 E
Bačka Topola, Serbia & M. ... 28 E4 45 49N 19 39 E
Bäckebo, Sweden ... 11 H10 56 53N 16 4 E
Bäckefors, Sweden ... 11 F6 58 48N 12 9 E
Bäckhammar, Sweden ... 10 E8 59 10N 14 11 E
Bački Petrovac, Serbia & M. ... 28 E4 45 29N 19 32 E
Backnang, Germany ... 25 G5 48 56N 9 26 E
Baco, Mt., Phil. ... 61 E4 12 49N 121 10 E
Bacolod, Phil. ... 61 F5 10 40N 122 57 E
Bacqueville-en-Caux, France ... 18 C8 49 47N 1 0 E
Bács-Kiskun □, Hungary ... 28 D4 46 43N 19 30 E
Bácsalmás, Hungary ... 28 D4 46 8N 19 17 E
Bacuag = Placer, Phil. ... 61 G6 9 36N 125 36 E
Bacuk, Malaysia ... 65 J4 6 4N 102 25 E
Bād, Iran ... 71 C7 33 41N 52 1 E
Bad →, U.S.A. ... 112 C4 44 21N 100 22W
Bad Aussee, Austria ... 26 D6 47 43N 13 45 E
Bad Axe, U.S.A. ... 114 C2 43 48N 83 0W
Bad Bergzabern, Germany ... 25 F3 49 6N 7 59 E
Bad Berleburg, Germany ... 24 D4 51 2N 8 26 E

Bad Bevensen, Germany . 24 B6 53 5N 10 35 E
Bad Bramstedt,
  Germany .... 24 B5 53 55N 9 53 E
Bad Brückenau,
  Germany .... 25 E5 50 18N 9 47 E
Bad Doberan, Germany . 24 A7 54 6N 11 53 E
Bad Driburg, Germany . 24 D5 51 43N 9 1 E
Bad Ems, Germany .... 25 E3 50 20N 7 43 E
Bad Frankenhausen,
  Germany .... 24 D7 51 21N 11 5 E
Bad Freienwalde,
  Germany .... 24 C10 52 46N 14 1 E
Bad Goisern, Austria .. 26 D6 47 38N 13 38 E
Bad Harzburg, Germany 24 D6 51 52N 10 34 E
Bad Hersfeld, Germany . 24 E5 50 52N 9 42 E
Bad Hofgastein, Austria 26 D6 47 17N 13 6 E
Bad Homburg, Germany . 25 E4 50 13N 8 38 E
Bad Honnef, Germany .. 24 E3 50 38N 7 13 E
Bad Iburg, Germany .... 24 C4 52 10N 8 3 E
Bad Ischl, Austria .... 26 D6 47 44N 13 38 E
Bad Kissingen, Germany 25 E6 50 11N 10 4 E
Bad Königshofen,
  Germany .... 25 E6 50 17N 10 28 E
Bad Kreuznach,
  Germany .... 25 F3 49 50N 7 51 E
Bad Krozingen,
  Germany .... 25 H3 47 54N 7 42 E
Bad Laasphe, Germany . 24 E4 50 56N 8 25 E
Bad Lands, U.S.A. 112 D3 43 40N 102 10W
Bad Langensalza,
  Germany .... 24 D6 51 5N 10 38 E
Bad Lauterberg,
  Germany .... 24 D6 51 38N 10 28 E
Bad Leonfelden, Austria 26 C7 48 31N 14 18 E
Bad Liebenwerda,
  Germany .... 24 D9 51 31N 13 24 E
Bad Mergentheim,
  Germany .... 25 F5 49 28N 9 42 E
Bad Münstereifel,
  Germany .... 24 E2 50 33N 6 46 E
Bad Nauheim, Germany . 25 E4 50 21N 8 43 E
Bad Neuenahr-
  Ahrweiler, Germany . 24 E3 50 32N 7 5 E
Bad Neustadt, Germany . 25 E6 50 18N 10 13 E
Bad Oeynhausen,
  Germany .... 24 C4 52 12N 8 46 E
Bad Oldesloe, Germany . 24 B6 53 48N 10 22 E
Bad Orb, Germany .... 25 E5 50 12N 9 22 E
Bad Pyrmont, Germany . 24 D5 51 59N 9 16 E
Bad Reichenhall,
  Germany .... 25 H8 47 43N 12 54 E
Bad Säckingen,
  Germany .... 25 H3 47 33N 7 56 E
Bad Salzuflen, Germany 24 C4 52 5N 8 45 E
Bad Salzungen,
  Germany .... 24 E6 50 48N 10 14 E
Bad Schwartau,
  Germany .... 24 B6 53 55N 10 41 E
Bad Segeberg, Germany 24 B6 53 56N 10 17 E
Bad St. Leonhard,
  Austria .... 26 E7 46 58N 14 47 E
Bad Tölz, Germany .... 25 H7 47 45N 11 34 E
Bad Urach, Germany ... 25 G5 48 29N 9 23 E
Bad Vöslau, Austria ... 27 D9 47 58N 16 13 E
Bad Waldsee, Germany . 25 H5 47 55N 9 45 E
Bad Wildungen,
  Germany .... 24 D5 51 6N 9 7 E
Bad Wimpfen, Germany 25 F5 49 13N 9 11 E
Bad Windsheim,
  Germany .... 25 F6 49 36N 10 25 E
Bad Zwischenahn,
  Germany .... 24 B4 53 12N 8 1 E
Bada Barabil, India .. 69 H11 22 7N 85 24 E
Badagara, India ..... 66 P9 11 35N 75 40 E
Badagri, Nigeria ..... 83 D5 6 25N 2 55 E
Badajós, L., Brazil ... 124 D6 3 15 S 62 50W
Badajoz, Spain 37 G4 38 50N 6 59W
Badajoz □, Spain 37 G4 38 40N 6 30W
Badakhshān □, Afghan. 66 A7 36 30N 71 0 E
Badalona, Spain ...... 38 D7 41 26N 2 15 E
Badalzai, Afghan. .... 68 E1 29 50N 65 35 E
Badampahar, India ... 67 H15 22 10N 86 10 E
Badanah, Si. Arabia .. 70 D4 30 58N 41 30 E
Badarinath, India .... 69 D8 30 45N 79 30 E
Badas, Kepulauan,
  Indonesia .... 62 D3 0 45N 107 5 E
Baddo →, Pakistan ... 66 F4 28 0N 64 20 E
Bade, Indonesia ...... 63 F9 7 10 S 139 35 E
Badeggi, Nigeria ..... 83 D6 9 3N 6 9 E
Badéguichéri, Niger .. 83 C6 14 30N 5 22 E
Baden, Austria ...... 27 C9 48 1N 16 13 E
Baden, Switz. .... 25 H4 47 28N 8 18 E
Baden, U.S.A. 116 F4 40 38N 80 14W
Baden-Baden, Germany 25 G4 48 44N 8 13 E
Baden-Württemberg □,
  Germany .... 25 G4 48 20N 8 40 E
Badgastein, Austria ... 26 D6 47 7N 13 9 E
Badger, Canada 105 C8 49 0N 56 4W
Badger, U.S.A. 110 J7 36 38N 119 1W
Bādghīs □, Afghan. .. 66 B3 35 0N 63 0 E
Badgingarra △,
  Australia .... 93 F2 30 23 S 115 22 E
Badgom, India ...... 69 B6 34 1N 74 45 E
Badia Polésine, Italy . 41 C8 45 5N 11 29 E
Badiar △, Guinea 82 C2 13 37N 13 11W
Badin, Pakistan ..... 68 G3 24 38N 68 54 E
Badinka △, Mali 82 C3 13 31N 9 28W
Badlands, U.S.A. 112 D3 43 38N 102 56W
Badogo, Mali 82 C3 11 2N 8 13W
Badoumbé, Mali 82 C2 13 42N 10 15W
Badrah, Iraq .... 70 C5 33 6N 45 58 E
Badrinath, India .... 69 D8 30 45N 79 29 E
Badulla, Sri Lanka .. 66 R12 7 1N 81 7 E
Badung, Selat, Indonesia 63 K18 8 40 S 115 22 E
Baena, Spain 37 H6 37 37N 4 20W
Baeza, Spain 37 H7 37 57N 3 25W
Bafang, Cameroon ... 83 D7 5 9N 10 11 E
Bafatá, Guinea-Biss. . 82 C2 12 8N 14 40W
Baffin B., Canada ... 101 A13 72 0N 64 0W
Baffin I., Canada 101 B12 68 0N 75 0W
Bafia, Cameroon .... 83 E7 4 40N 11 10 E
Bafilo, Togo .... 83 D5 9 22N 1 22 E
Bafing △, Mali 82 C2 12 38N 10 28W
Bafing →, Mali 82 C2 13 49N 10 50W
Bafliyūn, Syria ..... 70 B3 36 37N 36 59 E
Bafoulabé, Mali 82 C2 13 50N 10 55W
Bafoussam, Cameroon . 83 D7 5 28N 10 25 E
Bāfq, Iran .... 71 D7 31 40N 55 25 E
Bafra, Turkey ...... 72 B6 41 34N 35 54 E
Bafra Burnu, Turkey . 72 B7 41 45N 36 2 E
Bāft, Iran .... 71 D8 29 15N 56 38 E
Bafut, Cameroon ... 83 D7 6 6N 10 2 E
Bafwasende, Dem. Rep.
  of the Congo ...... 86 B2 1 3N 27 5 E
Bagam, Niger ...... 83 B6 15 43N 6 35 E
Bagamoyo, Tanzania . 86 D4 6 28 S 38 55 E
Bagan Datoh, Malaysia 65 L3 3 59N 100 47 E

Bagan Serai, Malaysia . 65 K3 5 1N 100 32 E
Baganga, Phil. ...... 61 H7 7 34N 126 33 E
Bagani, Namibia .... 88 B3 18 7S 21 41 E
Bagansiapiapi, Indonesia 62 D2 2 12N 100 50 E
Bagasra, India ...... 68 J4 21 30N 71 0 E
Bagaud, India ...... 68 H6 22 19N 75 53 E
Bagawi, Sudan ...... 81 E3 12 20N 34 18 E
Bagbag, Sudan ...... 81 D3 15 23N 31 30 E
Bagdad, U.S.A. 111 L11 34 35N 115 53W
Bagdarin, Russia .... 53 D12 54 26N 113 36 E
Bagé, Brazil .... 127 C5 31 20 S 54 15W
Bagenalstown = Muine
  Bheag, Ireland 12 D5 52 42N 6 58W
Baggs, U.S.A. 108 F10 41 2N 107 39W
Bagh, Pakistan ..... 69 C5 33 59N 73 45 E
Baghain →, India .... 69 G9 25 32N 81 1 E
Baghdād, Iraq ...... 70 C5 33 20N 44 30 E
Bagheria, Italy ..... 42 D6 38 5N 13 30 E
Baghlān, Afghan. ... 66 A6 32 12N 68 46 E
Baghlān □, Afghan. .. 66 B6 36 0N 68 30 E
Bagley, U.S.A. 112 B7 47 32N 95 24W
Bagnara Cálabra, Italy . 43 D8 38 17N 15 48 E
Bagnasco, Italy ..... 40 D5 44 18N 8 2 E
Bagnères-de-Bigorre,
  France .... 20 E4 43 5N 0 9 E
Bagnères-de-Luchon,
  France .... 20 F4 42 47N 0 38 E
Bagni di Lucca, Italy .. 40 D7 44 1N 10 35 E
Bagno di Romagna, Italy 41 E8 43 50N 11 57 E
Bagnoles-de-l'Orne,
  France 18 D6 48 32N 0 25W
Bagnols-sur-Cèze,
  France .... 21 D8 44 10N 4 36 E
Bagnorégio, Italy .... 41 F9 42 37N 12 5 E
Bago = Pegu, Burma . 67 L20 17 20N 96 29 E
Bagodar, India ...... 69 G11 24 5N 85 52 E
Bagrationovsk, Russia . 9 J19 54 23N 20 39 E
Bagrdan, Serbia & M. . 44 B5 44 5N 21 11 E
Baguio, Phil. .... 61 C4 16 26N 120 34 E
Bağyurdu, Turkey ... 47 C9 38 25N 27 41 E
Bagzane, Monts, Niger . 83 B6 17 43N 8 45 E
Bah, India .... 69 F8 26 53N 78 36 E
Bahabón de Esgueva,
  Spain 36 D7 41 52N 3 43W
Bahadurganj, India .. 69 F12 26 16N 87 49 E
Bahadurgarh, India .. 68 E7 28 40N 76 57 E
Bahama, Canal Viejo de,
  W. Indies 120 B4 22 10N 77 30W
Bahamas ■, N. Amer. . 121 B5 24 0N 75 0W
Bahār, Iran .... 73 E13 34 54N 48 26 E
Baharampur, India .. 69 G13 24 2N 88 27 E
Bahariya, El Wâhât al,
  Egypt .... 80 B2 28 0N 28 50 E
Baharu Pandan =
  Pandan, Malaysia ... 65 d 1 32N 103 46 E
Bahawalnagar, Pakistan 68 E5 30 0N 73 15 E
Bahawalpur, Pakistan . 68 E4 29 24N 71 40 E
Bahçe, Turkey ...... 72 D7 37 13N 36 34 E
Bahçecik, Turkey .... 45 F13 40 41N 29 44 E
Baheri, India .... 69 E8 28 45N 79 34 E
Bahgul →, India .... 69 F8 27 45N 79 36 E
Bahi, Tanzania ...... 86 D4 5 58 S 35 21 E
Bahi Swamp, Tanzania 86 D4 6 10 S 35 0 E
Bahía □, Brazil ..... 125 F11 12 0 S 42 0W
Bahía, Is. de la,
  Honduras 120 C2 16 45N 86 15W
Bahía Blanca, Argentina 126 D3 38 35 S 62 13W
Bahía de Caráquez,
  Ecuador .... 124 D2 0 40 S 80 27W
Bahía Honda, Cuba .. 120 B3 22 54N 83 10W
Bahía Laura, Argentina 128 F3 48 10 S 66 30W
Bahía Negra, Paraguay 124 H7 20 5 S 58 5W
Bahir Dar, Ethiopia .. 81 E4 11 37N 37 10 E
Bahmanzād, Iran .... 71 D6 31 15N 51 47 E
Bahr el Ahmar □, Sudan 80 D4 20 0N 35 0 E
Bahr el Ghazâl □, Sudan 81 F2 7 0N 28 0 E
Bahr el Jabal □, Sudan 81 G3 6 0N 31 0 E
Bahraich, India ..... 69 F9 27 38N 81 37 E
Bahrain ■, Asia .... 71 E6 26 0N 50 35 E
Bahror, India .... 68 F7 27 51N 76 20 E
Ba'labakk, Lebanon .. 74 B5 34 0N 36 10 E
Balabalangan,
  Kepulauan, Indonesia 62 E5 2 20 S 117 30 E
Bălăcița, Romania ... 29 F8 44 23N 23 8 E
Balad, Iraq .... 70 C5 34 1N 44 9 E
Balad Rūz, Iraq ..... 70 C5 33 42N 45 5 E
Bālādeh, Fārs, Iran ... 71 D6 29 17N 51 56 E
Bālādeh, Māzandaran,
  Iran .... 71 B6 36 12N 51 48 E
Balaghat, India ..... 66 J12 21 49N 80 12 E
Balaghat Ra., India .. 66 K10 18 50N 76 30 E
Balaguer, Spain ..... 38 D5 41 50N 0 50 E
Balakhna, Russia ... 34 B6 56 25N 43 32 E
Balaklava, Ukraine .. 33 K7 44 30N 33 30 E
Balakliya, Ukraine ... 33 H9 49 28N 36 55 E
Balakovo, Russia .... 34 D8 52 4N 47 55 E
Balamau, India ..... 69 F9 27 10N 80 21 E
Bālān, Romania .... 29 D10 46 39N 25 49 E
Balancán, Mexico ... 119 D6 17 48N 91 32W
Balanivka, Ukraine .. 29 B14 48 29N 29 24 E
Balashov, Russia .... 34 E6 51 30N 43 10 E
Balasinor, India .... 68 H5 22 57N 73 15 E
Balasore = Baleshwar,
  India .... 67 J15 21 35N 87 3 E
Balassagyarmat,
  Hungary .... 28 B4 48 4N 19 15 E
Balât, Egypt .... 80 B2 25 36N 29 19 E
Balaton, Hungary ... 28 D2 46 50N 17 40 E
Balaton-Felvidéki △,
  Hungary .... 28 D2 46 50N 17 30 E
Balatonboglár, Hungary 28 D2 46 46N 17 40 E
Balatonfüred, Hungary 28 D2 46 58N 17 54 E
Balatonszentgyörgy,
  Hungary .... 28 D2 46 41N 17 19 E
Balayan, Phil. ...... 61 E4 13 57N 120 44 E
Balazote, Spain 39 G2 38 54N 2 9W
Balbieriškis, Lithuania . 30 D10 54 32N 23 53 E
Balbigny, France .... 21 C8 45 49N 4 11 E
Balbina, Reprêsa de,
  Brazil .... 124 D7 2 0 S 59 30W
Balboa, Panama 120 E4 8 57N 79 34W
Balbriggan, Ireland .. 12 C5 53 37N 6 11W
Balcarce, Argentina .. 126 D4 38 0 S 58 10W
Balcarres, Canada ... 103 C8 50 50N 103 35W
Bălcești, Romania ... 29 F8 44 37N 23 57 E
Balchik, Bulgaria ... 45 C12 43 28N 28 11 E
Balclutha, N.Z. ..... 91 M2 46 15 S 169 45 E
Balcones Escarpment,
  U.S.A. 113 L5 29 30N 99 15W
Balçova, Turkey .... 47 C9 38 23N 27 3 E
Bald Hd., Australia .. 93 G2 35 6 S 118 1 E
Bald I., Australia .... 93 F2 34 57 S 118 27 E
Bald Knob, U.S.A. .. 113 H9 35 19N 91 34W
Baldock L., Canada .. 103 B9 56 33N 97 57W
Baldwin, Mich., U.S.A. 114 D3 43 54N 85 51W
Baldwin, Pa., U.S.A. . 116 F5 40 23N 79 59W
Baldwinsville, U.S.A. . 117 C8 43 10N 76 20W
Baldy Mt., U.S.A. ... 108 B9 48 9N 109 39W
Baldy Peak, U.S.A. .. 109 K9 33 54N 109 34W
Bale, Croatia .... 41 C10 45 4N 13 46 E

Baixa Limia-Sierra do
  Xurés △, Spain 36 D2 41 59N 8 2W
Baiyin, China ...... 56 F3 36 45N 104 14 E
Baiyü, China .... 58 B2 31 16N 98 50 E
Baiyu Shan, China ... 56 F4 37 15N 107 30 E
Baiyuda, Sudan ..... 80 D3 17 35N 32 7 E
Baj Baj, India ...... 69 H13 22 30N 88 5 E
Baja, Hungary ...... 28 D3 46 12N 18 59 E
Baja, Pta., Mexico ... 118 B1 29 50N 116 0W
Baja California, Mexico 118 A1 31 10N 115 12W
Baja California □,
  Mexico 118 B2 30 0N 115 0W
Baja California Sur □,
  Mexico 118 B2 25 50N 111 50W
Bajag, India .... 69 H9 22 40N 81 21 E
Bajamar, Canary Is. .. 48 F3 28 33N 16 20W
Bajana, India ...... 68 H4 23 7N 71 49 E
Bajatej, Indonesia ... 63 J17 8 29 S 114 19 E
Bajera, Indonesia ... 63 J18 8 31 S 115 2 E
Bägirän, Iran ...... 71 B8 37 36N 58 24 E
Bajimba, Mt., Australia 95 D5 29 17 S 152 6 E
Bajina Bašta,
  Serbia & M. .... 44 C3 43 58N 19 35 E
Bajmok, Serbia & M. . 28 E4 45 57N 19 24 E
Bajo Nuevo, Caribbean 120 C4 15 40N 78 50W
Bajoga, Nigeria ..... 83 C7 10 57N 11 20 E
Bajool, Australia .... 94 C5 23 40 S 150 35 E
Bak, Hungary ...... 28 D1 46 43N 16 51 E
Bakar, Croatia ...... 41 C11 45 18N 14 32 E
Bakasi Pen., Cameroon 83 E6 4 42N 8 20 E
Bakel, Senegal 82 C2 14 56N 12 20W
Baker, Calif., U.S.A. . 111 K10 35 16N 116 4W
Baker, Mont., U.S.A. . 112 B2 46 22N 104 17W
Baker, L., Canada ... 100 B10 64 0N 96 0W
Baker, Mt., U.S.A. .. 108 B3 48 50N 121 49W
Baker I., Pac. Oc. 96 G10 0 10N 176 35W
Baker I., U.S.A. 102 B2 55 20N 133 40W
Baker L., Australia .. 93 E4 26 54 S 126 5 E
Baker Lake, Canada . 100 B10 64 20N 96 3W
Bakers Creek, Australia 94 C4 21 13 S 149 7 E
Bakers Dozen Is.,
  Canada 104 A4 56 45N 78 45W
Bakersfield, Calif.,
  U.S.A. 111 K8 35 23N 119 1W
Bakersfield, Vt., U.S.A. 117 B12 44 45N 72 48W
Bakhchysaray, Ukraine 33 K7 44 40N 33 45 E
Bakhmach, Ukraine .. 33 G7 51 10N 32 45 E
Bākhtarān, Iran .... 70 C5 34 23N 47 0 E
Bākhtarān □, Iran ... 70 C5 34 0N 46 30 E
Bakı, Azerbaijan .... 35 K9 40 29N 49 56 E
Bakır →, Turkey .... 47 C9 38 55N 27 0 E
Bakırdaği, Turkey ... 72 C6 38 13N 35 46 E
Bakkafjörður, Iceland . 8 C6 66 2N 14 48W
Baklan, Turkey ..... 47 C11 38 0N 29 36 E
Bako, Ethiopia ..... 81 F4 5 51N 36 23 E
Bako, Ivory C. 82 D3 9 9N 7 40W
Bakony, Hungary ... 28 C2 47 10N 17 30 E
Bakony Forest =
  Bakony, Hungary ... 28 C2 47 10N 17 30 E
Bakori, Nigeria ..... 83 C6 11 34N 7 25 E
Bakouma, C.A.R. .... 84 C4 5 40N 22 56 E
Bakswaho, India .... 69 G8 24 15N 79 18 E
Bakundi, Nigeria .... 83 D7 8 10N 10 45 E
Bakutis Coast,
  Antarctica .... 5 D15 74 0 S 120 0W
Baky = Bakı, Azerbaijan 35 K9 40 29N 49 56 E
Bala, Canada 116 A5 45 1N 79 37W
Bala, Senegal 82 C2 14 1N 13 8W
Bâlâ, Turkey .... 72 C5 39 32N 33 6 E
Bala, U.K. 14 E4 52 54N 3 36W
Bala, L., U.K. 14 E4 52 53N 3 37W
Balabac I., Phil. .... 62 C5 8 0N 117 0 E
Balabac Str., E. Indies 62 C5 7 53N 117 5 E
Balabagh, Afghan. ... 68 B4 34 25N 70 12 E

Bale, Ethiopia ...... 81 F5 6 57N 40 8 E
Bale, Ethiopia ...... 81 F5 6 20N 41 30 E
Bale Mts. △, Ethiopia 81 F4 6 59N 39 52 E
Baleares, Is., Spain .. 48 B10 39 30N 3 0 E
Balearic Is. = Baleares,
  Is., Spain .... 48 B10 39 30N 3 0 E
Baleine = Whale →,
  Canada 105 A6 58 15N 67 40W
Baleine, Petite R. de
  la →, Canada 104 A4 56 0N 76 45W
Băleni, Romania .... 29 E12 45 48N 27 51 E
Baler, Phil. .... 61 D4 15 46N 121 34 E
Baler Bay, Phil. ..... 61 D4 15 50N 121 35 E
Baleshare, U.K. 13 D1 57 31N 7 22W
Baleshwar, India .... 67 J15 21 35N 87 3 E
Balezino, Russia .... 34 B11 58 2N 53 6 E
Balfate, Honduras ... 120 C2 15 48N 86 25W
Bali, Cameroon ..... 83 D7 5 54N 10 0 E
Balí, Greece .... 49 D6 35 25N 24 47 E
Bali, India .... 68 G5 25 11N 73 17 E
Bali, Indonesia ..... 63 J18 8 20 S 115 0 E
Bali □, Indonesia ... 63 J18 8 20 S 115 0 E
Bali, Selat, Indonesia . 63 J17 8 18 S 114 25 E
Bali Sea, Indonesia .. 63 J17 8 0 S 115 0 E
Balia, S. Leone 82 D2 9 22N 11 1W
Baliapal, India ..... 69 J12 21 40N 87 17 E
Baligród, Poland .... 31 J9 49 20N 22 17 E
Balik Pulau, Malaysia . 65 c 5 21N 100 14 E
Balikeşir, Turkey .... 47 B9 39 39N 27 53 E
Balikeşir □, Turkey .. 47 B9 39 45N 28 0 E
Balıkliçeşme, Turkey . 45 F11 40 18N 27 5 E
Balikpapan, Indonesia 62 E5 1 10 S 116 55 E
Balimbing, Phil. .... 63 C5 5 10N 119 58 E
Baling, Malaysia .... 65 K3 5 41N 100 55 E
Balingen, Germany .. 25 G4 48 16N 8 51 E
Balintang Channel, Phil. 61 B4 19 49N 121 40 E
Balipara, India ..... 67 F18 26 50N 92 45 E
Baliza, Brazil ...... 125 G8 16 0 S 52 20W
Balk, Afghan. ...... 66 B5 36 44N 66 47 E
Balkan Mts. = Stara
  Planina, Bulgaria ... 44 C7 43 15N 23 0 E
Balkhash = Balqash,
  Kazakhstan .... 52 E8 46 50N 74 50 E
Balkhash, Ozero =
  Balqash Köl,
  Kazakhstan .... 52 E8 46 0N 74 50 E
Balla, Bangla. ...... 67 G17 24 10N 91 35 E
Balladonia, Australia . 93 F3 32 27 S 123 51 E
Ballaghaderreen, Ireland 12 C3 53 55N 8 34W
Ballarat, Australia ... 95 F3 37 33 S 143 50 E
Ballard, L., Australia . 93 E3 29 20 S 120 40 E
Ballater, U.K. 13 D5 57 3N 3 3W
Ballé, Mali 82 B3 15 18N 8 33W
Ballena Gris = Ojo de
  Liebre △, Mexico .. 118 B2 27 50N 114 0W
Ballenas, Canal de,
  Mexico 118 B2 29 10N 113 45W
Balleny Is., Antarctica . 5 C11 66 30 S 163 0 E
Balleroy, France 18 C6 49 11N 0 50W
Ballerup, Denmark .. 11 J6 55 44N 12 21 E
Ballı, Turkey .... 45 F11 40 56N 27 3 E
Ballia, India .... 69 G11 25 46N 84 12 E
Ballina, Australia ... 95 D5 28 50 S 153 31 E
Ballina, Ireland 12 B2 54 7N 9 9W
Ballinasloe, Ireland .. 12 C3 53 20N 8 13W
Ballinger, U.S.A. 113 K5 31 45N 99 57W
Ballinrobe, Ireland .. 12 C2 53 38N 9 13W
Ballinskelligs B., Ireland 12 E1 51 48N 10 13W
Ballon, France ..... 18 D7 48 10N 0 14 E
Ballons des Vosges △,
  France .... 19 E14 48 0N 7 0 E
Ballsh, Albania ..... 44 F3 40 36N 19 44 E
Ballston Spa, U.S.A. . 117 D11 43 0N 73 51W
Ballybunion, Ireland . 12 D2 52 31N 9 40W
Ballycastle, Ireland .. 12 A5 55 12N 6 15W
Ballyclare, U.K. 12 B5 54 46N 6 0W
Ballyhaunis, Ireland .. 12 C3 53 46N 8 46W
Ballymena, U.K. 12 B5 54 52N 6 17W
Ballymoney, U.K. ... 12 A5 55 5N 6 31W
Ballymote, Ireland .. 12 B3 54 5N 8 31W
Ballynahinch, U.K. .. 12 B6 54 24N 5 54W
Ballyquintin Pt., U.K. 12 B6 54 20N 5 30W
Ballyshannon, Ireland . 12 B3 54 30N 8 11W
Balmaceda, Chile .... 128 F2 46 0 S 71 50W
Balmaseda, Spain ... 38 B1 43 11N 3 12W
Balmertown, Canada . 103 C10 51 4N 93 41W
Balmoral, Australia .. 95 F3 37 15 S 141 48 E
Balmorhea, U.S.A. .. 113 K3 30 59N 103 45W
Balochistan =
  Baluchistan □,
  Pakistan .... 66 F4 27 30N 65 0 E
Balonne →, Australia . 95 D4 28 47 S 147 56 E
Balotra, India ...... 68 G5 25 50N 72 14 E
Balqash, Kazakhstan . 52 E8 46 50N 74 50 E
Balqash Köl,
  Kazakhstan .... 52 E8 46 0N 74 50 E
Balrampur, India .... 69 F10 27 30N 82 20 E
Balranald, Australia .. 95 E3 34 38 S 143 33 E
Balş, Romania ...... 29 F9 44 22N 24 5 E
Balsas →, Brazil .... 125 E9 7 15 S 44 35W
Balsas →, Mexico ... 118 D4 17 55N 102 10W
Bålsta, Sweden ..... 10 E11 59 35N 17 30 E
Balston Spa, U.S.A. . 117 D11 43 0N 73 52W
Balta, Romania ..... 28 F7 44 54N 22 38 E
Balta, Ukraine ...... 29 B14 48 2N 29 45 E
Baltanás, Spain 36 D6 41 56N 4 15W
Bălți, Moldova ...... 29 C12 47 48N 27 58 E
Baltic Sea, Europe ... 9 H18 57 0N 19 0 E
Baltım, Egypt ...... 80 H7 31 35N 31 10 E
Baltimore, Ireland ... 12 E2 51 29N 9 22W
Baltimore, Md., U.S.A. 114 F7 39 17N 76 37W
Baltimore, Ohio, U.S.A. 116 G2 39 51N 82 36W
Baltistan, Pakistan ... 69 A6 36 15N 74 40 E
Baltiysk, Russia .... 9 J18 54 41N 19 58 E
Baltra, Germany .... 24 B3 53 43N 7 24 E
Baluchistan □, Pakistan 66 F4 27 30N 65 0 E
Balurghat, India .... 69 G13 25 15N 88 44 E
Balvi, Latvia .... 9 H22 57 8N 27 15 E
Balya, Turkey ...... 47 B9 39 44N 27 35 E
Bam, Iran .... 71 D8 29 7N 58 14 E
Bama, China .... 58 E6 24 8N 107 12 E
Bama, Nigeria ...... 83 C7 11 33N 13 41 E
Bamaga, Australia ... 94 A3 10 50 S 142 25 E
Bamaji L., Canada .. 104 B1 51 9N 91 25W
Bamako, Mali 82 C3 12 34N 7 55W
Bamba, Mali 83 B4 17 5N 1 24W
Bamba Maoundé,
  Mali 82 B4 13 26N 4 3W
Bambari, C.A.R. .... 84 C4 5 40N 20 35 E
Bambaroo, Australia . 94 B4 18 50 S 146 10 E
Bambaya, Guinea ... 82 D2 10 55N 10 54 E
Bamberg, Germany .. 25 F6 49 54N 10 54 E
Bamberg, U.S.A. 115 J5 33 18N 81 2W
Bambesi, Ethiopia ... 81 F3 9 45N 34 40 E
Bambey, Senegal 82 C1 14 42N 16 28W

Bambili, Dem. Rep. of
  the Congo .... 86 B2 3 40N 26 0 E
Bamboi, Ghana 82 D4 8 13N 2 1W
Bamburgh, U.K. 14 B6 55 37N 1 43W
Bamenda, Cameroon . 83 D7 5 57N 10 11 E
Bamfield, Canada ... 102 D3 48 45N 125 10W
Bāmīān □, Afghan. .. 66 B5 35 0N 67 0 E
Bamiancheng, China . 57 C13 43 15N 124 2 E
Bamkin, Cameroon .. 83 D7 6 3N 11 27 E
Bampūr, Iran .... 71 E9 27 15N 60 21 E
Ban, Burkina Faso ... 82 C4 14 5N 2 27W
Ban Ao Tu Khun,
  Thailand .... 65 a 8 9N 98 20 E
Ban Ban, Laos ...... 64 C4 19 31N 103 30 E
Ban Bang Hin, Thailand 65 H2 9 32N 98 35 E
Ban Bang Khu, Thailand 65 a 7 57N 98 23 E
Ban Bang Rong,
  Thailand .... 65 a 8 3N 98 25 E
Ban Bo Phut, Thailand 65 b 9 33N 100 2 E
Ban Chaweng, Thailand 65 b 9 32N 100 3 E
Ban Chiang Klang,
  Thailand .... 64 C3 19 25N 100 55 E
Ban Chik, Laos ..... 64 D4 17 15N 102 22 E
Ban Choho, Thailand . 64 E4 15 2N 102 9 E
Ban Dan Lan Hoi,
  Thailand .... 64 D2 17 0N 99 35 E
Ban Don = Surat Thani,
  Thailand .... 65 H2 9 6N 99 20 E
Ban Don, Vietnam ... 64 F6 12 53N 107 48 E
Ban Don, Ao →,
  Thailand .... 65 H2 9 20N 99 25 E
Ban Dong, Thailand . 64 C3 19 30N 100 59 E
Ban Hong, Thailand . 64 C2 18 18N 98 50 E
Ban Hua Thanon,
  Thailand .... 65 b 9 26N 100 1 E
Ban Kaeng, Thailand . 64 D3 17 29N 100 7 E
Ban Kantang, Thailand 65 J2 7 25N 99 31 E
Ban Karon, Thailand . 65 a 7 51N 98 18 E
Ban Kata, Thailand .. 65 a 7 50N 98 18 E
Ban Keun, Laos ..... 64 C4 18 22N 102 35 E
Ban Khai, Thailand .. 64 F3 12 46N 101 18 E
Ban Kheua, Laos .... 64 B3 20 13N 101 7 E
Ban Khlong Khian,
  Thailand .... 65 a 8 10N 98 26 E
Ban Khlong Kua,
  Thailand .... 65 J3 6 57N 100 8 E
Ban Khuan, Thailand . 65 a 8 20N 98 25 E
Ban Khun Mao,
  Thailand .... 65 J2 7 50N 99 37 E
Ban Ko Yai Chim,
  Thailand .... 65 G2 11 17N 99 26 E
Ban Kok, Thailand .. 64 D4 16 40N 103 40 E
Ban Laem, Thailand . 64 F2 13 13N 99 59 E
Ban Lamai, Thailand . 65 b 9 28N 100 3 E
Ban Lao Ngam, Laos . 64 E6 15 28N 106 10 E
Ban Le Kathe, Thailand 64 E2 15 49N 98 53 E
Ban Lo Po Noi,
  Thailand .... 65 a 8 1N 98 34 E
Ban Mae Chedi,
  Thailand .... 64 C2 19 11N 99 31 E
Ban Mae Laeng,
  Thailand .... 64 B2 20 1N 99 17 E
Ban Mae Nam, Thailand 65 b 9 34N 100 0 E
Ban Mae Sariang,
  Thailand .... 64 C1 18 10N 97 56 E
Ban Mê Thuôt = Buon
  Ma Thuột, Vietnam . 64 F7 12 40N 108 3 E
Ban Mi, Thailand ... 64 E3 15 3N 100 32 E
Ban Muong Mo, Laos . 64 C4 19 4N 103 58 E
Ban Na Bo, Thailand . 65 b 9 19N 99 41 E
Ban Na Mo, Laos ... 64 D5 17 7N 105 40 E
Ban Na San, Thailand . 65 H2 8 53N 99 52 E
Ban Na Tong, Laos .. 64 B3 20 56N 101 47 E
Ban Nam Bac, Laos .. 64 B4 20 38N 102 20 E
Ban Nam Ma, Laos .. 64 A3 22 2N 101 37 E
Ban Nong Bok, Laos . 64 D5 17 5N 104 48 E
Ban Nong Boua, Laos . 64 E6 15 40N 106 33 E
Ban Nong Pling,
  Thailand .... 64 E3 15 40N 100 10 E
Ban Pak Chan, Thailand 65 G2 10 32N 98 51 E
Ban Patong, Thailand . 65 a 7 54N 98 18 E
Ban Phai, Thailand .. 64 D4 16 4N 102 44 E
Ban Phak Chit, Thailand 65 a 8 9N 98 24 E
Ban Pong, Thailand .. 64 F2 13 50N 99 55 E
Ban Rawai, Thailand . 65 a 7 47N 98 20 E
Ban Ron Phibun,
  Thailand .... 65 H2 8 9N 99 51 E
Ban Sakhu, Thailand . 65 a 8 4N 98 18 E
Ban Sanam Chai,
  Thailand .... 65 J3 7 33N 100 25 E
Ban Sangkha, Thailand 64 E4 14 37N 103 52 E
Ban Tak, Thailand .. 64 D2 17 2N 99 4 E
Ban Tako, Thailand .. 64 E4 14 5N 102 40 E
Ban Tha Dua, Thailand 64 D2 17 59N 98 39 E
Ban Tha Li, Thailand . 64 D3 17 37N 101 25 E
Ban Tha Nun, Thailand 65 a 8 12N 98 18 E
Ban Thahine, Laos ... 64 E5 14 12N 105 33 E
Ban Thong Krut,
  Thailand .... 65 b 9 25N 99 57 E
Ban Xien Kok, Laos .. 64 B3 20 54N 100 39 E
Ban Yen Nhan, Vietnam 64 B6 20 57N 106 2 E
Banaba, Kiribati .... 96 H8 0 45 S 169 50 E
Banalia, Dem. Rep. of
  the Congo .... 86 B2 1 32N 25 5 E
Banam, Cambodia ... 65 G5 11 20N 105 17 E
Banamba, Mali 82 C3 13 29N 7 22W
Banana Is., S. Leone . 82 D2 8 7N 13 15W
Bananal, I. do, Brazil . 125 F8 11 30 S 50 30W
Banaras = Varanasi,
  India .... 69 G10 25 22N 83 0 E
Banas →, Gujarat, India 68 H4 23 45N 71 25 E
Banas →, Mad. P., India 69 G9 24 15N 81 30 E
Bânâs, Ras, Egypt ... 80 C4 23 57N 35 59 E
Banaz, Turkey ...... 47 C11 38 44N 29 46 E
Banaz →, Turkey ... 47 C11 38 46N 29 40 E
Banbridge, U.K. 12 B5 54 22N 6 16W
Banbury, U.K. 15 E6 52 4N 1 20W
Banchory, U.K. 13 D6 57 3N 2 29W
Banco, Ethiopia .... 81 G2 5 9N 37 6 E
Bancroft, Canada ... 116 A7 45 3N 77 51W
Band, Romania ..... 29 D9 46 30N 24 25 E
Band Boni, Iran .... 71 E8 25 30N 59 33 E
Band Qīr, Iran ...... 71 D6 31 39N 48 53 E
Banda, Ut. P., India . 69 G9 25 30N 80 26 E
Banda, Kepulauan,
  Indonesia .... 63 E7 4 37 S 129 50 E
Banda Aceh, Indonesia 62 C1 5 35N 95 20 E
Banda Banda, Mt.,
  Australia .... 95 E5 31 10 S 152 28 E
Banda Elat, Indonesia . 63 F8 5 40 S 133 5 E
Banda Is. = Banda,
  Kepulauan, Indonesia 63 E7 4 37 S 129 50 E
Banda Sea, Indonesia . 63 F7 6 0 S 130 0 E

Bandai-Asahi △, *Japan* **54 F10** 37 38N 140 5 E
Bandai-San, *Japan* **54 F10** 37 36N 140 4 E
Bandama ➤, *Ivory C.* **82 D3** 6 32N 4 30W
Bandama Blanc ➤,
  Ivory C. **82 D3** 6 55N 5 30W
Bandama Rouge ➤,
  Ivory C. **82 D4** 6 55N 5 30W
Bandān, *Iran* **71 D9** 31 23N 60 44 E
Bandanaira, *Indonesia* **63 E7** 4 32 S 129 54 E
Bandanwara, *India* **68 F6** 26 9N 74 38 E
Bandar =
  Machilipatnam, *India* **67 L12** 16 12N 81 8 E
Bandar-e Abbās, *Iran* **71 E8** 27 15N 56 15 E
Bandar-e Anzalī, *Iran* **71 B6** 37 30N 49 30 E
Bandar-e Emām
  Khomeynī, *Iran* **71 D6** 30 30N 49 5 E
Bandar-e Lengeh, *Iran* **71 E7** 26 35N 54 58 E
Bandar-e Maqām, *Iran* **71 E7** 26 45N 54 20 E
Bandar-e Ma'shur, *Iran* **71 D6** 30 35N 49 10 E
Bandar-e Rīg, *Iran* **71 D6** 29 29N 50 38 E
Bandar-e Torkeman,
  Iran **71 B7** 37 0N 54 10 E
Bandar Lampung =
  Tanjungkarang
  Telukbetung,
  Indonesia **62 F3** 5 20 S 105 10 E
Bandar Maharani =
  Muar, *Malaysia* **65 L4** 2 3N 102 34 E
Bandar Penggaram =
  Batu Pahat, *Malaysia* **65 M4** 1 50N 102 56 E
Bandar Seri Begawan,
  Brunei **62 C4** 4 52N 115 0 E
Bandar Sri Aman,
  Malaysia **62 D4** 1 15N 111 32 E
Bandawe, *Malawi* **87 E3** 11 58 S 34 5 E
Bande, *Spain* **36 C3** 42 3N 7 58W
Bandeira, Pico da, *Brazil* **127 A7** 20 26 S 41 47W
Bandera, *Argentina* **126 B3** 28 55 S 62 20W
Banderas, B. de, *Mexico* **118 C3** 20 40N 105 30W
Bandhogarh, *India* **69 H9** 23 40N 81 2 E
Bandi ➤, *India* **68 F6** 26 12N 75 47 E
Bandiagara, *Mali* **82 C4** 14 12N 3 29W
Bandikui, *India* **68 F7** 27 3N 76 34 E
Bandırma, *Turkey* **45 F11** 40 20N 28 0 E
Bandjarmasin =
  Banjarmasin,
  Indonesia **62 E4** 3 20 S 114 35 E
Bandol, *France* **21 E9** 43 8N 5 46 E
Bandon, *Ireland* **12 E3** 51 44N 8 44W
Bandon ➤, *Ireland* **12 E3** 51 43N 8 37W
Bandula, *Mozam.* **87 F3** 19 0 S 33 7 E
Bandundu, *Dem. Rep. of
  the Congo* **84 E3** 3 15 S 17 22 E
Bandung, *Indonesia* **63 G12** 6 54 S 107 36 E
Bané, *Burkina Faso* **83 C4** 11 42N 0 5W
Băneasa, *Romania* **29 E12** 45 56N 27 55 E
Băneh, *Iran* **70 C5** 35 59N 45 53 E
Bañeres, *Spain* **39 G4** 38 44N 0 38W
Banes, *Cuba* **121 B4** 21 0N 75 42W
Banff, *Canada* **102 C5** 51 10N 115 34W
Banff, *U.K.* **13 D6** 57 40N 2 33W
Banff △, *Canada* **102 C5** 51 30N 116 15W
Banfora, *Burkina Faso* **82 C4** 10 40N 4 40W
Bang Fai ➤, *Laos* **64 D5** 16 57N 104 45 E
Bang Hieng ➤, *Laos* **64 D5** 16 10N 105 10 E
Bang Krathum, *Thailand* **64 D3** 16 34N 100 18 E
Bang Lamung, *Thailand* **64 F3** 13 3N 100 56 E
Bang Mun Nak,
  Thailand **64 D3** 16 2N 100 23 E
Bang Pa In, *Thailand* **64 E3** 14 14N 100 35 E
Bang Rakam, *Thailand* **64 D3** 16 45N 100 7 E
Bang Saphan, *Thailand* **65 G2** 11 14N 99 28 E
Bang Thao, *Thailand* **65 a** 7 59N 98 18 E
Bangaduni I., *India* **69 J13** 21 34N 88 52 E
Bangala Dam,
  Zimbabwe **87 G3** 21 7 S 31 25 E
Bangalore, *India* **66 N10** 12 59N 77 40 E
Banganga ➤, *India* **68 F6** 27 6N 77 25 E
Bangangté, *Cameroon* **83 D7** 5 8N 10 32 E
Bangaon, *India* **69 H13** 23 0N 88 47 E
Bangassou, *C.A.R.* **84 D4** 4 55N 23 7 E
Banggai, *Indonesia* **63 E6** 1 34 S 123 30 E
Banggai, Kepulauan,
  Indonesia **63 E6** 1 40 S 123 30 E
Banggai Arch. =
  Banggai, Kepulauan,
  Indonesia **63 E6** 1 40 S 123 30 E
Banggi, *Malaysia* **62 C5** 7 17N 117 12 E
Banghāzī, *Libya* **79 B10** 32 11N 20 3 E
Bangjang, *Sudan* **81 E3** 11 23N 32 41 E
Bangka, *Sulawesi,
  Indonesia* **63 D7** 1 50N 125 5 E
Bangka, *Sumatera,
  Indonesia* **62 E3** 2 0 S 105 50 E
Bangka, Selat, *Indonesia* **62 E3** 2 30 S 105 30 E
Bangka-Belitung □,
  Indonesia **62 E3** 2 30 S 107 0 E
Bangkalan, *Indonesia* **63 G15** 7 2 S 112 46 E
Bangkinang, *Indonesia* **62 D2** 0 18N 101 5 E
Bangko, *Indonesia* **62 E2** 2 5 S 102 9 E
Bangkok, *Thailand* **64 F3** 13 45N 100 35 E
Bangladesh ■, *Asia* **67 H17** 24 0N 90 0 E
Bangli, *Indonesia* **63 J18** 8 27 S 115 21 E
Bangolo, *Ivory C.* **82 D3** 7 1N 7 29W
Bangong Co, *India* **69 B8** 35 50N 79 20 E
Bangor, *Down, U.K.* **12 B6** 54 40N 5 40W
Bangor, *Gwynedd, U.K.* **14 D3** 53 14N 4 8W
Bangor, *Maine, U.S.A.* **101 D13** 44 48N 68 46W
Bangor, *Pa., U.S.A.* **117 F9** 40 52N 75 13W
Bangued, *Phil.* **61 C4** 17 40N 120 37 E
Bangui, *C.A.R.* **84 D3** 4 23N 18 35 E
Bangui, *Phil.* **61 B4** 18 32N 120 46 E
Banguru, *Dem. Rep. of
  the Congo* **86 B2** 0 30N 27 10 E
Bangweulu, L., *Zambia* **87 E3** 11 0 S 30 0 E
Bangweulu Swamp,
  Zambia **87 E3** 11 20 S 30 15 E
Banhine △, *Mozam.* **89 C5** 22 49 S 32 55 E
Baní, *Dom. Rep.* **121 C5** 18 16N 70 22W
Bani ➤, *Mali* **82 C4** 14 30N 4 12W
Bani Bangou, *Niger* **83 B5** 15 3N 2 42 E
Banī Sa'd, *Iraq* **70 C5** 33 34N 44 32 E
Bania, *Ivory C.* **82 D4** 9 4N 3 6W
Banihal Pass, *India* **69 C6** 33 30N 75 12 E
Banikoara, *Benin* **83 C5** 11 18N 2 26 E
Bāniyās, *Syria* **70 C3** 35 10N 36 0 E
Banja Luka, *Bos.-H.* **28 B7** 44 49N 17 11 E
Banjar, *India* **68 D7** 31 38N 77 21 E
Banjar, *Indonesia* **63 G13** 7 24 S 108 30 E
Banjarmasin, *Indonesia* **62 E4** 3 20 S 114 35 E
Banjul, *Gambia* **82 C1** 13 28N 16 40W
Banka, *India* **69 G12** 24 53N 86 55 E
Bankas, *Mali* **82 C4** 14 4N 3 31W

Bankeryd, *Sweden* **11 G8** 57 53N 14 6 E
Bankilaré, *Niger* **83 C5** 14 35N 0 44 E
Bankipore, *India* **83 C5** 14 35N 0 44 E
Banks I., *B.C., Canada* **102 C3** 53 20N 130 0W
Banks I., *N.W.T.,
  Canada* **100 A7** 73 15N 121 30W
Banks Pen., *N.Z.* **91 K4** 43 45 S 173 15 E
Banks Str., *Australia* **95 G4** 40 40 S 148 10 E
Bankura, *India* **69 H12** 23 11N 87 18 E
Bankya, *Bulgaria* **44 D7** 42 43N 23 8 E
Banmankhi, *India* **69 G12** 25 53N 87 11 E
Bann ➤, *Arm., U.K.* **12 B5** 54 30N 6 31W
Bann ➤, *L'derry., U.K.* **12 A5** 55 8N 6 41W
Bannalec, *France* **18 E3** 47 57N 3 42W
Bannang Sata, *Thailand* **65 J3** 6 16N 101 16 E
Banning, *U.S.A.* **111 M10** 33 56N 116 53W
Bannockburn, *Canada* **116 B7** 44 39N 77 33W
Bannockburn, *U.K.* **13 E5** 56 5N 3 55W
Bannockburn,
  Zimbabwe **87 G2** 20 17 S 29 48 E
Bannu, *Pakistan* **66 C7** 33 0N 70 18 E
Bano, *India* **69 H11** 22 40N 84 55 E
Bañolas = Banyoles,
  Spain **38 C7** 42 16N 2 44 E
Banon, *France* **21 D9** 44 2N 5 38 E
Baños de la Encina,
  Spain **37 G7** 38 10N 3 46W
Baños de Molgas, *Spain* **36 C3** 42 15N 7 40W
Bánovce nad Bebravou,
  Slovak Rep. **27 C11** 48 44N 18 16 E
Banovići, *Bos.-H.* **28 B3** 44 25N 18 32 E
Bansgaon, *India* **69 F10** 26 33N 83 21 E
Banská Bystrica,
  Slovak Rep. **27 C12** 48 46N 19 14 E
Banská Štiavnica,
  Slovak Rep. **27 C11** 48 25N 18 55 E
Bansko, *Bulgaria* **44 E7** 41 52N 23 28 E
Banswara, *India* **68 H6** 23 32N 74 24 E
Bantaeng, *Indonesia* **63 F5** 5 32 S 119 56 E
Bantaji, *Nigeria* **83 D7** 8 6N 10 5 E
Bantayan, *Phil.* **61 F5** 11 10N 123 43 E
Banten □, *Indonesia* **63 G13** 6 30 S 106 0 E
Bantry, *Ireland* **12 E2** 51 41N 9 27W
Bantry B., *Ireland* **12 E2** 51 37N 9 44W
Bantul, *Indonesia* **63 G14** 7 55 S 110 19 E
Bantva, *India* **68 J4** 21 29N 70 12 E
Banya, *Bulgaria* **45 D8** 42 33N 24 50 E
Banyak, Kepulauan,
  Indonesia **62 D1** 2 10N 97 10 E
Banyalbufar, *Spain* **48 B9** 39 42N 2 31 E
Banyo, *Cameroon* **83 D7** 6 52N 11 45 E
Banyoles, *Spain* **38 C7** 42 16N 2 44 E
Banyuls-sur-Mer, *France* **20 F7** 42 28N 3 8 E
Banyumas, *Indonesia* **63 G13** 7 32 S 109 18 E
Banyuwangi, *Indonesia* **63 J17** 8 13 S 114 21 E
Banzare Coast,
  Antarctica **5 C9** 68 0 S 125 0 E
Bao Ha, *Vietnam* **58 F5** 22 11N 104 21 E
Bao Lac, *Vietnam* **64 A5** 22 57N 105 40 E
Bao Loc, *Vietnam* **65 G6** 11 32N 107 48 E
Bao'an = Shenzhen,
  China **59 F10** 22 32N 114 5 E
Baocheng, *China* **56 H4** 33 12N 106 56 E
Baode, *China* **56 E6** 39 1N 111 5 E
Baoding, *China* **56 E8** 38 50N 115 28 E
Baoji, *China* **56 G4** 34 20N 107 5 E
Baojing, *China* **58 C7** 28 45N 109 41 E
Baokang, *China* **59 B8** 31 54N 111 12 E
Baoshan, *Shanghai,
  China* **59 B13** 31 27N 121 26 E
Baoshan, *Yunnan, China* **58 E2** 25 10N 99 5 E
Baotou, *China* **56 D6** 40 32N 110 2 E
Baoxing, *China* **58 B4** 30 24N 102 50 E
Baoying, *China* **57 H10** 33 17N 119 20 E
Bap, *India* **68 F5** 27 23N 72 18 E
Bapatla, *India* **67 M12** 15 55N 80 30 E
Bapaume, *France* **19 B9** 50 7N 2 50 E
Bāqerābād, *Iran* **70 C5** 33 45N 44 50 E
Ba'qūbah, *Iraq* **70 C5** 33 45N 44 50 E
Baquedano, *Chile* **126 A2** 23 20 S 69 52W
Bar, *Serbia & M.* **44 D3** 42 8N 19 6 E
Bar, *Ukraine* **33 H4** 49 4N 27 40 E
Bar Bigha, *India* **69 G11** 25 21N 85 47 E
Bar Harbor, *U.S.A.* **115 C11** 44 23N 68 13W
Bar-le-Duc, *France* **19 D12** 48 47N 5 10 E
Bar-sur-Aube, *France* **19 D11** 48 14N 4 40 E
Bar-sur-Seine, *France* **19 D11** 48 7N 4 20 E
Bara, *India* **69 G9** 25 16N 81 43 E
Bâra, *Romania* **29 C12** 47 2N 27 3 E
Bara Banki, *India* **69 F9** 26 55N 81 12 E
Barabai, *Indonesia* **62 E5** 2 32 S 115 34 E
Baraboo, *U.S.A.* **112 D10** 43 28N 89 45W
Baracoa, *Cuba* **121 B5** 20 20N 74 30W
Baradero, *Argentina* **126 C4** 33 52 S 59 29W
Baraga, *U.S.A.* **112 B10** 46 47N 88 30W
Bărăganul, *Romania* **29 F12** 44 49N 27 31 E
Barah ➤, *India* **68 F6** 27 42N 77 5 E
Barahona, *Dom. Rep.* **121 C5** 18 13N 71 7W
Barahona, *Spain* **38 D2** 41 17N 2 39W
Barail Range, *India* **67 G18** 25 15N 93 20 E
Barajas, Madrid ✈
  (MAD), *Spain* **36 E7** 40 26N 3 34W
Baraka, *Sudan* **81 E2** 10 59N 27 59 E
Baraka ➤, *Sudan* **80 D4** 18 13N 37 35 E
Barakaldo, *Spain* **38 B2** 43 18N 2 59W
Barakar ➤, *India* **69 G12** 24 7N 86 14 E
Barakhola, *India* **67 G18** 25 0N 92 45 E
Barakot, *India* **69 J11** 21 33N 84 59 E
Barakpur, *India* **69 H13** 22 44N 88 30 E
Baralaba, *Australia* **94 C4** 24 13 S 149 50 E
Baralla, *Spain* **36 C3** 42 53N 7 15W
Baralzon L., *Canada* **103 B9** 60 0N 98 3W
Barameiya, *Sudan* **80 D4** 18 32N 36 38 E
Baramula, *India* **69 B6** 34 15N 74 20 E
Baran, *India* **68 G7** 25 9N 76 40 E
Baran ➤, *Pakistan* **68 G3** 25 13N 68 17 E
Barañain, *Spain* **38 C3** 42 48N 1 40W
Baranavichy, *Belarus* **33 F4** 53 10N 26 0 E
Barani, *Burkina Faso* **82 C4** 13 9N 3 51W
Baranof, *U.S.A.* **102 C2** 57 5N 135 0W
Baranof I., *U.S.A.* **100 C6** 57 0N 135 0W
Baranów Sandomierski,
  Poland **31 H8** 50 29N 21 30 E
Baranya □, *Hungary* **28 E3** 46 0N 18 15 E
Baraolt, *Romania* **29 D10** 46 5N 25 34 E
Barapasi, *Indonesia* **63 E9** 2 15 S 137 5 E
Barasat, *India* **69 H13** 22 46N 88 31 E
Barat Daya, Kepulauan,
  Indonesia **63 F7** 7 30 S 128 0 E
Barataria B., *U.S.A.* **113 L10** 29 20N 89 55W
Barauda, *India* **68 H6** 23 33N 75 15 E

Baraut, *India* **68 E7** 29 13N 77 7 E
Barbacena, *Brazil* **127 A7** 21 15 S 43 56W
Barbados ■, *W. Indies* **121 g** 13 10N 59 30W
Barban, *Croatia* **41 C11** 45 5N 14 4 E
Barbària, C. de, *Spain* **48 C7** 38 39N 1 24 E
Barbaros, *Turkey* **45 F11** 40 54N 27 27 E
Barbastro, *Spain* **38 C5** 42 2N 0 5 E
Barbate de Franco,
  Spain **37 J5** 36 13N 5 56W
Barberino di Mugello,
  Italy **41 E8** 44 0N 11 15 E
Barberton, *S. Africa* **89 D5** 25 42 S 31 2 E
Barberton, *U.S.A.* **116 E3** 41 0N 81 39W
Barbezieux-St-Hilaire,
  France **20 C3** 45 28N 0 9W
Barbosa, *Colombia* **124 B4** 5 57N 73 37W
Barbourville, *U.S.A.* **115 G4** 36 52N 83 53W
Barbuda, *W. Indies* **121 C7** 17 30N 61 40W
Barca, *Romania* **29 G8** 43 59N 23 36 E
Barcaldine, *Australia* **94 C4** 23 43 S 145 6 E
Barcarrota, *Spain* **37 G4** 38 31N 6 51W
Barcellona Pozzo di
  Gotto, *Italy* **43 D8** 38 9N 15 13 E
Barcelona, *Spain* **38 D7** 41 21N 2 10 E
Barcelona, *Venezuela* **124 A6** 10 10N 64 40W
Barcelona □, *Spain* **38 D7** 41 30N 2 0 E
Barceloneta,
  Puerto Rico **121 d** 18 27N 66 32W
Barcelonnette, *France* **21 D10** 44 23N 6 40 E
Barcelos, *Brazil* **124 D6** 1 0 S 63 0W
Barcin, *Poland* **31 F4** 52 52N 17 55 E
Barclayville, *Liberia* **82 E3** 4 48N 8 10W
Barcoo ➤, *Australia* **94 D3** 25 30 S 142 50 E
Barcs, *Hungary* **28 E2** 45 58N 17 28 E
Barczewo, *Poland* **30 E7** 53 50N 20 42 E
Bärdä, *Azerbaijan* **35 K8** 40 25N 47 10 E
Bardaï, *Chad* **79 D9** 21 25N 17 0 E
Bardas Blancas,
  Argentina **126 D2** 35 49 S 69 45W
Barddhaman, *India* **69 H12** 23 14N 87 39 E
Bardejov, *Slovak Rep.* **27 B14** 49 18N 21 15 E
Bardera, *Somali Rep.* **75 G3** 2 20N 42 27 E
Bardi, *Italy* **40 D6** 44 38N 9 44 E
Bardīyah, *Libya* **79 B10** 31 45N 25 5 E
Bardolino, *Italy* **40 C7** 45 33N 10 43 E
Bardonécchia, *Italy* **40 C3** 45 5N 6 42 E
Bardsey I., *U.K.* **14 E3** 52 45N 4 47W
Bardstown, *U.S.A.* **114 G3** 37 49N 85 28W
Bareilly, *India* **69 E8** 28 22N 79 27 E
Barela, *India* **69 H9** 23 6N 80 3 E
Barentin, *France* **18 C7** 49 33N 0 58 E
Barenton, *France* **18 D6** 48 38N 0 50W
Barents Sea, *Arctic* **50 B7** 73 0N 39 0 E
Barentu, *Eritrea* **81 D4** 15 2N 37 35 E
Barfleur, *France* **18 C5** 49 40N 1 17W
Barfleur, Pte. de, *France* **18 C5** 49 42N 1 16W
Barga, *Italy* **40 D7** 44 4N 10 29 E
Bargara, *Australia* **94 C5** 24 50 S 152 25 E
Bargas, *Spain* **36 F6** 39 56N 4 3W
Bârgăului Bistriţa,
  Romania **29 C9** 47 13N 24 38 E
Barge, *Italy* **40 D4** 44 43N 7 20 E
Bargnop, *Sudan* **81 F2** 9 32N 28 25 E
Bargteheide, *Germany* **24 B6** 53 44N 10 14 E
Barguzin, *Russia* **53 D11** 53 37N 109 37 E
Barh, *India* **69 G11** 25 29N 85 46 E
Barhaj, *India* **69 F10** 26 18N 83 44 E
Barharwa, *India* **69 G12** 24 52N 87 47 E
Barhi, *India* **69 G11** 24 15N 85 25 E
Bari, *India* **68 F7** 26 39N 77 39 E
Bari, *Italy* **43 A9** 41 8N 16 51 E
Bari Doab, *Pakistan* **68 D5** 30 20N 73 0 E
Bari Sadri, *India* **68 G6** 24 28N 74 30 E
Bari Sardo, *Italy* **42 C2** 39 50N 9 38 E
Barīdī, Ra's, *Si. Arabia* **70 E3** 24 17N 37 31 E
Barīm, *Yemen* **76 E8** 12 39N 43 25 E
Barinas, *Venezuela* **124 B4** 8 36N 70 15W
Baring, C., *Canada* **100 B8** 70 0N 117 30W
Baringo, L., *Kenya* **86 B4** 0 47N 36 16 E
Bârîs, *Egypt* **80 C3** 24 42N 30 31 E
Barisal, *Bangla.* **67 H17** 22 45N 90 20 E
Barisal □, *Bangla.* **67 H17** 22 40N 90 20 E
Barisan, Bukit,
  Indonesia **62 E2** 3 30 S 102 15 E
Barito ➤, *Indonesia* **62 E4** 4 0 S 114 50 E
Baritú △, *Argentina* **126 A3** 22 43 S 64 40W
Barjac, *France* **21 D8** 44 20N 4 22 E
Barjols, *France* **21 E10** 43 34N 6 2 E
Bark L., *Canada* **116 A7** 45 27N 77 51W
Barka = Baraka ➤,
  Sudan **80 D4** 18 13N 37 35 E
Barkakana, *India* **69 H11** 23 37N 85 29 E
Barkam, *China* **58 B4** 31 51N 102 28 E
Barker, *U.S.A.* **116 C6** 43 20N 78 33W
Barkley, L., *U.S.A.* **115 G2** 37 1N 88 14W
Barkley Sound, *Canada* **102 D3** 48 50N 125 10W
Barkly East, *S. Africa* **88 E4** 30 58 S 27 33 E
Barkly Roadhouse,
  Australia **94 B2** 19 52 S 135 50 E
Barkly Tableland,
  Australia **94 B2** 17 50 S 136 40 E
Barkly West, *S. Africa* **88 D3** 28 5 S 24 31 E
Barkol, Wadi ➤, *Sudan* **80 D3** 17 40N 32 0 E
Barla Dağı, *Turkey* **47 C12** 38 5N 30 40 E
Bârlad, *Romania* **29 D12** 46 15N 27 38 E
Bârlad ➤, *Romania* **29 E12** 45 38N 27 32 E
Barlee, L., *Australia* **93 E2** 29 15 S 119 30 E
Barlee, Mt., *Australia* **93 D4** 24 38 S 128 13 E
Barletta, *Italy* **43 A9** 41 19N 16 17 E
Barlinek, *Poland* **30 E1** 53 0N 15 15 E
Barlovento, *Canary Is.* **48 F2** 28 48N 17 48W
Barlow L., *Canada* **103 A8** 62 0N 103 0W
Barmedman, *Australia* **95 E4** 34 9 S 147 21 E
Barmer, *India* **68 G4** 25 45N 71 20 E
Barmera, *Australia* **95 E3** 34 15 S 140 28 E
Barmouth, *U.K.* **14 E3** 52 44N 4 4W
Barmstedt, *Germany* **24 B5** 53 47N 9 46 E
Barna ➤, *India* **69 G10** 25 21N 83 3 E
Barnala, *India* **68 D6** 30 23N 75 33 E
Barnard Castle, *U.K.* **14 C6** 54 33N 1 55W
Barnaul, *Russia* **52 D9** 53 20N 83 40 E
Barnesville, *U.S.A.* **115 J3** 33 3N 84 9W
Barnet □, *U.K.* **15 F7** 51 38N 0 9W
Barneveld, *Neths.* **17 B5** 52 7N 5 36 E
Barneveld, *U.S.A.* **117 C9** 43 16N 75 14W
Barneville-Carteret,
  France **18 C5** 49 23N 1 46W
Barnhart, *U.S.A.* **113 K4** 31 8N 101 10W
Barnsley, *U.K.* **14 D6** 53 34N 1 27W
Barnstaple, *U.K.* **15 F3** 51 5N 4 4W
Barnstaple Bay =
  Bideford Bay, *U.K.* **15 F3** 51 5N 4 20W

Barnsville, *U.S.A.* **112 B6** 46 43N 96 28W
Barnwell, *U.S.A.* **115 J5** 33 15N 81 23W
Baro, *Nigeria* **83 D6** 8 35N 6 18 E
Baro ➤, *Ethiopia* **81 F3** 8 26N 33 13 E
Baroda = Vadodara,
  India **68 H5** 22 20N 73 10 E
Baroda, *India* **68 G7** 25 29N 76 35 E
Baroe, *S. Africa* **88 E3** 33 13 S 24 33 E
Baron Ra., *Australia* **92 D4** 23 30 S 127 45 E
Barong, *China* **58 B2** 31 3N 99 20 E
Barotseland, *Zambia* **85 H4** 15 0 S 24 0 E
Barouéli, *Mali* **82 C3** 13 4N 6 50W
Barpeta, *India* **67 F17** 26 20N 91 10 E
Barques, Pt. Aux, *U.S.A.* **116 B2** 44 4N 82 58W
Barquísimeto, *Venezuela* **124 A5** 10 4N 69 19W
Barr, Ras el, *Egypt* **80 H7** 31 32N 31 5E E
Barr Smith Range,
  Australia **93 E3** 27 4 S 120 20 E
Barra, *Brazil* **125 F10** 11 5 S 43 10W
Barra, *U.K.* **13 E1** 57 0N 7 29W
Barra, Sd. of, *U.K.* **13 D1** 57 4N 7 25W
Barra de Navidad,
  Mexico **118 D4** 19 12N 104 41W
Barra do Corda, *Brazil* **125 E9** 5 30 S 45 10W
Barra do Piraí, *Brazil* **127 A7** 22 30 S 43 50W
Barra Falsa, Pta. da,
  Mozam. **89 C6** 22 58 S 35 37 E
Barra Hd., *U.K.* **13 E1** 56 47N 7 40W
Barra Mansa, *Brazil* **127 A7** 22 35 S 44 12W
Barraba, *Australia* **95 E5** 30 21 S 150 35 E
Barrackpur = Barakpur,
  India **69 H13** 22 44N 88 30 E
Barradale Roadhouse,
  Australia **92 D1** 22 42 S 114 58 E
Barrafranca, *Italy* **43 E7** 37 22N 14 12 E
Barraigh = Barra, *U.K.* **13 E1** 57 0N 7 29W
Barranca, *Lima, Peru* **124 F3** 10 45 S 77 50W
Barranca, *Loreto, Peru* **124 D3** 4 50 S 76 50W
Barranca del Cobre △,
  Mexico **118 B3** 27 18N 107 40W
Barrancabermeja,
  Colombia **124 B4** 7 0N 73 50W
Barrancas, *Venezuela* **124 B6** 8 55N 62 5W
Barrancos, *Portugal* **37 G4** 38 10N 6 58W
Barranqueras, *Argentina* **126 B4** 27 30 S 59 0W
Barranquilla, *Colombia* **124 A4** 11 0N 74 50W
Barraute, *Canada* **104 C4** 48 26N 77 38W
Barre, *Mass., U.S.A.* **117 D12** 42 25N 72 6W
Barre, *Vt., U.S.A.* **117 B12** 44 12N 72 30W
Barreal, *Argentina* **126 C2** 31 33 S 69 28W
Barreiras, *Brazil* **125 F10** 12 8 S 45 0W
Barreirinhas, *Brazil* **125 D10** 2 30 S 42 50W
Barreiro, *Portugal* **37 G1** 38 40N 9 6W
Barrême, *France* **21 E10** 43 57N 6 23 E
Barren, Nosy, *Madag.* **89 B7** 18 25 S 43 40 E
Barretos, *Brazil* **125 H9** 20 30 S 48 35W
Barrhead, *Canada* **102 C6** 54 10N 114 24W
Barrie, *Canada* **116 B5** 44 24N 79 40W
Barrier Ra., *Australia* **95 E3** 31 0 S 141 30 E
Barrière, *Canada* **102 C4** 51 12N 120 7W
Barrington, *U.S.A.* **117 E13** 41 44N 71 18W
Barrington L., *Canada* **103 B8** 56 55N 100 15W
Barrington Tops,
  Australia **95 E5** 32 6 S 151 28 E
Barringun, *Australia* **95 D4** 29 1 S 145 41 E
Barro do Garças, *Brazil* **125 G8** 15 54 S 52 16W
Barron, *U.S.A.* **112 C9** 45 24N 91 51W
Barrow, *U.S.A.* **100 A4** 71 18N 156 47W
Barrow ➤, *Ireland* **12 D5** 52 25N 6 58W
Barrow Creek, *Australia* **94 C1** 21 30 S 133 55 E
Barrow I., *Australia* **92 D2** 20 45 S 115 20 E
Barrow-in-Furness, *U.K.* **14 C4** 54 7N 3 14W
Barrow Pt., *Australia* **94 A3** 14 20 S 144 40 E
Barrow Pt., *U.S.A.* **98 B4** 71 10N 156 20W
Barrow Ra., *Australia* **93 E4** 26 0 S 127 40 E
Barrow Str., *Canada* **4 B3** 74 20N 95 0W
Barrueco Pardo, *Spain* **36 D4** 41 4N 6 40W
Barruelo de Santullán,
  Spain **36 C6** 42 54N 4 17W
Barry, *U.K.* **15 F4** 51 24N 3 16W
Barry's Bay, *Canada* **116 A7** 45 29N 77 41W
Barsalogho,
  Burkina Faso **83 C4** 13 25N 1 3W
Barsat, *Pakistan* **69 A5** 36 10N 72 45 E
Barsham, *Syria* **70 C4** 35 21N 40 33 E
Barsi, *India* **66 K9** 18 10N 75 50 E
Barsinghausen,
  Germany **24 C5** 52 18N 9 28 E
Barsoi, *India* **67 G15** 25 48N 87 57 E
Barstow, *U.S.A.* **111 L9** 34 54N 117 1W
Barth, *Germany* **24 A8** 54 22N 12 42 E
Barthélemy, Col,
  Vietnam **64 C5** 19 26N 104 6 E
Bartin, *Turkey* **72 B5** 41 38N 32 21 E
Bartle Frere, *Australia* **94 B4** 17 27 S 145 50 E
Bartlesville, *U.S.A.* **113 G7** 36 45N 95 59W
Bartlett, *U.S.A.* **110 J8** 36 29N 118 2W
Bartlett, L., *Canada* **102 A5** 63 5N 118 20W
Bartolomeu Dias,
  Mozam. **87 G4** 21 10 S 35 8 E
Barton, *U.S.A.* **117 B12** 44 45N 72 11W
Barton upon Humber,
  U.K. **14 D7** 53 41N 0 25W
Bartoszyce, *Poland* **30 D7** 54 15N 20 55 E
Bartow, *U.S.A.* **115 M5** 27 54N 81 50W
Barú, Volcan, *Panama* **120 E3** 8 55N 82 35W
Barumba, *Dem. Rep. of
  the Congo* **86 B1** 1 3N 23 37 E
Baruth, *Germany* **24 C9** 52 4N 13 30 E
Baruunsuu, *Mongolia* **56 C3** 43 43N 105 35 E
Barvinkove, *Ukraine* **33 H9** 48 57N 37 0 E
Barwani, *India* **68 H6** 22 2N 74 57 E
Barwice, *Poland* **30 E3** 53 44N 16 11 E
Barycz ➤, *Poland* **31 G3** 51 42N 16 15 E
Barysaw, *Belarus* **32 E5** 54 17N 28 28 E
Barysh, *Russia* **34 D8** 53 39N 47 8 E
Barzán, *Iraq* **70 B5** 36 55N 44 3 E
Bârzava, *Romania* **28 D6** 46 7N 21 59 E
Bas-Rhin □, *France* **19 D14** 48 40N 7 30 E
Bašaïd, *Serbia & M.* **28 E5** 45 38N 20 25 E
Bāsa'idū, *Iran* **71 E7** 26 35N 55 20 E
Bāsa'idū, *Iran* **71 E7** 26 35N 55 20 E
Basal, *Pakistan* **68 C5** 33 33N 72 13 E
Basankusu, *Dem. Rep. of
  the Congo* **84 D3** 1 5N 19 50 E
Basarabeasca, *Moldova* **29 D13** 46 21N 28 58 E
Basarabi, *Romania* **29 F13** 44 10N 28 26 E
Basawa, *Afghan.* **68 B4** 34 15N 70 50 E
Bascuñán, C., *Chile* **126 B1** 28 52 S 71 35W
Basel, *Switz.* **25 H3** 47 35N 7 35 E
Basel, Euroairport ✈
  (BSL), *Europe* **19 E14** 47 36N 7 33 E
Basel-Landschaft □,
  Switz. **25 H3** 47 26N 7 45 E

Basento ➤, *Italy* **43 B9** 40 20N 16 49 E
Bashäkerd, Kühhä-ye,
  Iran **71 E8** 26 42N 58 35 E
Bashaw, *Canada* **102 C6** 52 35N 112 58W
Bāshī, *Iran* **71 D6** 28 41N 51 4 E
Bashkir Republic =
  Bashkortostan □,
  Russia **52 D6** 54 0N 57 0 E
Bashkortostan □, *Russia* **52 D6** 54 0N 57 0 E
Bashtanivka, *Ukraine* **29 E14** 45 46N 29 29 E
Basibasy, *Madag.* **89 C7** 22 10 S 43 40 E
Basilan I., *Phil.* **61 H5** 6 35N 122 0 E
Basilan Str., *Phil.* **61 H5** 6 50N 122 0 E
Basildon, *U.K.* **15 F8** 51 34N 0 28 E
Basile, Eq. Guin.* **83 E6** 3 42N 8 48 E
Basilicata □, *Italy* **43 B9** 40 30N 16 30 E
Basim = Washim, *India* **66 J10** 20 3N 77 0 E
Basin, *U.S.A.* **108 D9** 44 23N 108 2W
Basingstoke, *U.K.* **15 F6** 51 15N 1 5W
Baška, *Croatia* **41 D11** 44 58N 14 45 E
Başkale, *Turkey* **73 C10** 38 2N 43 59 E
Baskatong, Rés., *Canada* **104 C4** 46 46N 75 50W
Basle = Basel, *Switz.* **25 H3** 47 35N 7 35 E
Başmakçı, *Turkey* **47 D12** 37 54N 30 1 E
Basoda, *India* **68 H7** 23 52N 77 54 E
Basodino, *Dem. Rep. of
  the Congo* **86 B1** 1 16N 23 40 E
Basque, Pays, *France* **20 E2** 43 15N 1 20W
Basque Provinces = País
  Vasco □, *Spain* **38 C2** 42 50N 2 45W
Basra = Al Başrah, *Iraq* **70 D5** 30 30N 47 50 E
Bass Str., *Australia* **95 F4** 39 15 S 146 30 E
Bassano, *Canada* **102 C6** 50 48N 112 20W
Bassano del Grappa,
  Italy **41 C8** 45 46N 11 44 E
Bassar, *Togo* **83 D5** 9 19N 0 57 E
Bassas da India, *Ind. Oc.* **85 J7** 22 0 S 39 0 E
Basse-Normandie □,
  France **18 D6** 48 45N 0 30W
Basse-Pointe,
  Martinique **120 c** 14 52N 61 8W
Basse Santa-Su, *Gambia* **82 C2** 13 13N 14 15W
Basse-Terre,
  Guadeloupe **120 b** 16 0N 61 44W
Basse Terre,
  Trin. & Tob. **125 K15** 10 7N 61 19W
Bassein, *Burma* **67 L19** 16 45N 94 30 E
Basses, Pte. des,
  Guadeloupe **120 b** 15 52N 61 17W
Basseterre,
  St. Kitts & Nevis **121 C7** 17 17N 62 43W
Bassett, *U.S.A.* **112 D5** 42 35N 99 32W
Bassigny, *France* **19 E12** 48 0N 5 30 E
Bassikounou, *Mauritania* **82 B3** 15 55N 6 1W
Bassila, *Benin* **83 D5** 9 1N 1 46 E
Bassum, *Germany* **24 C4** 52 50N 8 42 E
Båstad, *Sweden* **11 H6** 56 25N 12 51 E
Bastak, *Iran* **71 E7** 27 15N 54 25 E
Baştām, *Iran* **71 B7** 36 29N 55 4 E
Bastar, *India* **67 K12** 19 15N 81 40 E
Bastelica, *France* **21 F13** 42 1N 9 3 E
Basti, *India* **69 F10** 26 52N 82 55 E
Bastia, *France* **21 F13** 42 40N 9 30 E
Bastogne, *Belgium* **17 D5** 50 1N 5 43 E
Bastrop, La., U.S.A.* **113 J9** 32 47N 91 55W
Bastrop, Tex., U.S.A.* **113 K6** 30 7N 97 19W
Bat Yam, *Israel* **74 C3** 32 2N 34 44 E
Bata, *Eq. Guin.* **84 D1** 1 57N 9 50 E
Bata, *Romania* **28 D7** 46 1N 22 4 E
Bataan □, *Phil.* **61 D4** 14 40N 120 25 E
Batabanó, *Cuba* **120 B3** 22 41N 82 18W
Batabanó, G. de, *Cuba* **120 B3** 22 30N 82 30W
Batac, *Phil.* **61 B4** 18 3N 120 34 E
Batagai, *Russia* **53 C14** 67 38N 134 38 E
Batajnica, *Serbia & M.* **44 B4** 44 54N 20 17 E
Batak, *Bulgaria* **45 E8** 41 57N 24 12 E
Batala, *India* **68 D6** 31 48N 75 12 E
Batalha, *Portugal* **36 F2** 39 40N 8 50W
Batama, *Dem. Rep. of
  the Congo* **86 B2** 0 58N 26 33 E
Batamay, *Russia* **53 C13** 63 30N 129 15 E
Batang, *China* **58 B2** 30 1N 99 0 E
Batang, *Indonesia* **63 G13** 6 55 S 109 45 E
Batangas, *Phil.* **61 E4** 13 35N 121 10 E
Batanta, *Indonesia* **63 E8** 0 55 S 130 40 E
Batatais, *Brazil* **127 A6** 20 54 S 47 37W
Batavia, *U.S.A.* **116 D6** 43 0N 78 11W
Bataysk, *Russia* **35 J10** 47 3N 39 45 E
Batchelor, *Australia* **92 B5** 13 4 S 131 1 E
Batdambang, *Cambodia* **64 F4** 13 7N 103 12 E
Batemans B., *Australia* **95 F5** 35 40 S 150 12 E
Batemans Bay, *Australia* **95 F5** 35 44 S 150 11 E
Bates Ra., *Australia* **93 E3** 27 27 S 121 5 E
Batesburg-Leesville,
  U.S.A. **115 J5** 33 54N 81 33W
Batesville, Ark., U.S.A.* **113 H9** 35 46N 91 39W
Batesville, Miss., U.S.A.* **113 H10** 34 19N 89 57W
Batesville, Tex., U.S.A.* **113 L5** 28 58N 99 37W
Bath, *Canada* **117 B8** 44 11N 76 47W
Bath, *U.K.* **15 F5** 51 23N 2 22W
Bath, *Maine, U.S.A.* **115 D11** 43 55N 69 49W
Bath, *N.Y., U.S.A.* **116 D7** 42 20N 77 19W
Bath & North East
  Somerset □, *U.K.* **15 F5** 51 21N 2 27W
Batheay, *Cambodia* **65 G5** 11 59N 104 57 E
Bathsheba, *Barbados* **121 g** 13 13N 59 32W
Bathurst, *Australia* **95 E4** 33 25 S 149 31 E
Bathurst, *Canada* **105 C6** 47 37N 65 43W
Bathurst, *S. Africa* **88 E4** 33 30 S 26 50 E
Bathurst, C., *Canada* **100 A7** 70 34N 128 0W
Bathurst B., *Australia* **94 A3** 14 16 S 144 25 E
Bathurst Harb.,
  Australia **95 G4** 43 15 S 146 10 E
Bathurst I., *Australia* **92 B5** 11 30 S 130 10 E
Bathurst I., *Canada* **98 B9** 76 0N 100 30W
Bathurst Inlet, *Canada* **100 B9** 66 50N 108 1W
Bati, *Ethiopia* **81 E5** 11 10N 40 0 E
Batie, *Burkina Faso* **82 D4** 9 53N 2 53W
Batlow, *Australia* **95 F4** 35 31 S 148 9 E
Batman, *Turkey* **70 B4** 37 55N 41 5 E
Batn al Ghūl, *Jordan* **74 F4** 29 36N 35 56 E
Batna, *Algeria* **78 A7** 35 34N 6 15 E
Batobato = San Isidro,
  Phil. **61 H7** 6 50N 126 5 E
Batočina, Serbia & M.* **44 B5** 44 7N 21 5 E
Batoka, *Zambia* **87 F2** 16 45 S 27 15 E
Baton Rouge, *U.S.A.* **113 K9** 30 27N 91 11W
Batong, Ko, *Thailand* **65 J2** 6 32N 99 12 E
Bátonyterenye, *Hungary* **28 C4** 47 59N 19 50 E
Batopilas, *Mexico* **118 B3** 27 0N 107 45W
Batouri, *Cameroon* **84 D2** 4 30N 14 27 E
Båtsfjord, *Norway* **8 A23** 70 38N 29 39 E
Battambang =
  Batdambang,
  Cambodia **64 F4** 13 7N 103 12 E
Batticaloa, *Sri Lanka* **66 R12** 7 43N 81 45 E

Battipáglia, *Italy* ...... 43 B7 40 37N 14 58 E
Battle, *U.K.* .... 15 G8 50 55N 0 30 E
Battle →, *Canada* 103 C7 52 43N 108 15W
Battle Creek, *U.S.A.* .. 114 D3 42 19N 85 11W
Battle Ground, *U.S.A.* . 110 E4 45 47N 122 22W
Battle Harbour, *Canada* 105 B8 52 16N 55 35W
Battle Lake, *U.S.A.* ... 112 B7 46 17N 95 43W
Battle Mountain, *U.S.A.* 108 F5 40 38N 116 56W
Battlefields, *Zimbabwe* 87 F2 18 37 S 29 47 E
Battleford, *Canada* ... 103 C7 52 45N 108 15W
Battonya, *Hungary* .... 28 D6 46 16N 21 3 E
Batu, *Ethiopia* ...... 81 F4 6 55N 39 45 E
Batu, Kepulauan,
  Indonesia .... 62 E1 0 30 S 98 25 E
Batu Caves, *Malaysia* . 65 L3 3 15N 101 40 E
Batu Ferringhi, *Malaysia* 65 c 5 28N 100 15 E
Batu Gajah, *Malaysia* . 65 K3 4 28N 101 3 E
Batu Is. = Batu,
  Kepulauan, *Indonesia* 62 E1 0 30 S 98 25 E
Batu Pahat, *Malaysia* . 65 M4 1 50N 102 56 E
Batuata, *Indonesia* ... 63 F6 6 12 S 122 42 E
Batugondang, Tanjung,
  Indonesia .... 63 J17 8 6 S 114 29 E
Batukau, Gunung,
  Indonesia .... 63 J18 8 20 S 115 5 E
Batumi, *Georgia* ...... 35 K5 41 39N 41 44 E
Batur, *Indonesia* ..... 63 J18 8 15 S 115 20 E
Batur, Gunung,
  Indonesia .... 63 J18 8 14 S 115 23 E
Baturaja, *Indonesia* .. 62 E2 4 11 S 104 15 E
Baturité, *Brazil* ...... 125 D11 4 28 S 38 45W
Baturiti, *Indonesia* ... 63 J18 8 19 S 115 11 E
Bau, *Malaysia* .... 62 D4 1 25N 110 9 E
Baubau, *Indonesia* ... 63 F6 5 25 S 122 38 E
Baucau, *E. Timor* .... 63 F7 8 27 S 126 27 E
Bauchi, *Nigeria* ...... 83 C6 10 22N 9 48 E
Bauchi □, *Nigeria* .... 83 C7 10 30N 10 0 E
Baud, *France* 18 E3 47 52N 3 1W
Baudette, *U.S.A.* 112 A7 48 43N 94 36W
Bauer, C., *Australia* .. 95 E1 32 44 S 134 4 E
Bauhinia, *Australia* .. 94 C4 24 35 S 149 18 E
Baukau = Baucau,
  E. Timor .... 63 F7 8 27 S 126 27 E
Bauld, C., *Canada* 101 C14 51 38N 55 26W
Baume-les-Dames,
  France .... 19 E13 47 22N 6 22 E
Baunatal, *Germany* ... 24 D5 51 14N 9 24 E
Baunei, *Italy* .... 42 B2 40 2N 9 40 E
Baure, *Nigeria* .... 83 C6 12 52N 8 50 E
Bauru, *Brazil* .... 127 A6 22 10 S 49 0W
Bausi, *India* .... 69 G12 24 48N 24 15 E
Bautino, *Kazakhstan* . 35 H10 44 35N 50 14 E
Bautzen, *Germany* ... 24 D10 51 10N 14 26 E
Bauya, *S. Leone* 82 D2 8 12N 12 38W
Bavānāt, *Iran* .... 71 D7 30 28N 53 27 E
Bavanište, *Serbia & M.* 28 F5 44 49N 20 55 E
Bavaria = Bayern □,
  Germany .... 25 G7 48 50N 12 0 E
Båven, *Sweden* ...... 10 E10 59 0N 16 56 E
Bavispe →, *Mexico* ... 118 B3 29 30N 109 11W
Bawdwin, *Burma* ..... 67 H20 23 5N 97 20 E
Bawean, *Indonesia* ... 62 F4 5 46 S 112 35 E
Bawku, *Ghana* 83 C4 11 3N 0 19W
Bawlake, *Burma* ..... 67 K20 19 11N 97 21 E
Bawolung, *China* .... 58 C3 28 50N 101 16 E
Baxley, *U.S.A.* 115 K4 31 47N 82 21W
Baxoi, *China* .... 58 B1 30 1N 96 50 E
Baxter, *U.S.A.* 112 B7 46 21N 94 17W
Baxter Springs, *U.S.A.* 113 G7 37 2N 94 44W
Baxter State △, *U.S.A.* 115 B11 46 5N 68 57W
Bay, L. de, *Phil.* ..... 61 D4 14 20N 121 11 E
Bay City, *Mich., U.S.A.* 114 D4 43 36N 83 54W
Bay City, *Tex., U.S.A.* 113 L7 28 59N 95 58W
Bay Minette, *U.S.A.* .. 115 K2 30 53N 87 46W
Bay Roberts, *Canada* . 105 C9 47 36N 53 16W
Bay St. Louis, *U.S.A.* . 113 K10 30 19N 89 20W
Bay Springs, *U.S.A.* .. 113 K10 31 59N 89 17W
Bay View, *N.Z.* ...... 91 H6 39 25 S 176 50 E
Baya, *Dem. Rep. of
  the Congo* .... 87 E2 11 53 S 27 25 E
Bayamo, *Cuba* 120 B4 20 20N 76 40W
Bayamón, *Puerto Rico* 121 d 18 24N 66 9W
Bayan Har Shan, *China* 60 C4 34 0N 98 0 E
Bayan Hot = Alxa
  Zuoqi, *China* ...... 56 E3 38 50N 105 40 E
Bayan Lepas, *Malaysia* 65 c 5 17N 100 16 E
Bayan Obo, *China* ... 56 D5 41 52N 109 59 E
Bayan-Ovoo =
  Erdenetsogt,
  Mongolia .... 56 C4 42 55N 106 5 E
Bayana, *India* .... 68 F7 26 55N 77 18 E
Bayanaüyl, *Kazakhstan* 52 D8 50 45N 75 45 E
Bayandalay, *Mongolia* 56 C3 43 30N 103 29 E
Bayanhongor, *Mongolia* 60 B5 46 8N 102 43 E
Bayard, *N. Mex., U.S.A.* 109 K9 32 46N 108 8W
Bayard, *Nebr., U.S.A.* . 112 E3 41 45N 103 20W
Bayawan, *Phil.* ...... 61 G5 9 46N 122 45 E
Baybay, *Phil.* .... 61 F6 10 40N 124 55 E
Bayburt, *Turkey* ..... 73 B9 40 15N 40 20 E
Baydhabo = Baidoa,
  Somali Rep. .... 75 G3 3 8N 43 30 E
Bayelsa □, *Nigeria* ... 83 E6 4 30N 6 0 E
Bayerische Alpen,
  Germany .... 25 H7 47 35N 11 30 E
Bayerische Rhön △,
  Germany .... 25 E6 50 15N 10 5 E
Bayerischer Spessart △,
  Germany .... 25 F6 49 58N 10 15 E
Bayerischer Wald,
  Germany .... 25 G8 48 56N 12 50 E
Bayern □, *Germany* .. 25 G7 48 50N 12 0 E
Bayeux, *France* 18 C6 49 17N 0 42W
Bayfield, *Canada* 116 C3 43 34N 81 42W
Bayfield, *U.S.A.* 112 B9 46 49N 90 49W
Bayındır, *Turkey* .... 47 C9 38 13N 27 39 E
Bayjī, *Iraq* .... 70 C4 35 0N 43 30 E
Baykal, Oz., *Russia* .. 53 D11 53 0N 108 0 E
Baykan, *Turkey* ...... 70 B4 38 7N 41 44 E
Baykonur = Bayqongyr,
  Kazakhstan .... 52 E7 47 48N 65 50 E
Baynes Mts., *Namibia* . 88 B1 17 15 S 13 0 E
Bayombong, *Phil.* .... 61 C4 16 30N 121 10 E
Bayon, *France* .... 19 D13 48 30N 6 20 E
Bayona = Baiona, *Spain* 36 C2 42 6N 8 52W
Bayonne, *France* 20 E2 43 30N 1 28W
Bayonne, *U.S.A.* 117 F10 40 40N 74 7W
Bayovar, *Peru* .... 124 E2 5 50 S 81 0W
Bayqongyr, *Kazakhstan* 52 E7 47 48N 65 50 E
Bayram-Ali =
  Bayramaly,
  Turkmenistan ...... 52 F7 37 37N 62 10 E
Bayramaly,
  Turkmenistan ...... 52 F7 37 37N 62 10 E
Bayramiç, *Turkey* .... 47 B8 39 48N 26 36 E
Bayreuth, *Germany* .. 25 F7 49 56N 11 35 E
Bayrischzell, *Germany* . 25 H8 47 41N 12 0 E

Bayrūt, *Lebanon* ...... 74 B4 33 53N 35 31 E
Bays, L. of, *Canada* ... 116 A5 45 15N 79 4 E
Baysville, *Canada* 116 A5 45 9N 79 7W
Bayt Lahm, *West Bank* 74 D4 31 43N 35 12 E
Baytown, *U.S.A.* 113 L7 29 43N 94 59W
Bayzo, *Niger* .... 83 C5 13 52N 4 35 E
Baza, *Spain* 37 H8 37 30N 2 47W
Bazar Dyuzi, *Russia* .. 35 K8 41 12N 47 50 E
Bazardüzü = Bazar
  Dyuzi, *Russia* ...... 35 K8 41 12N 47 50 E
Bazarny Karabulak,
  Russia .... 34 D8 52 20N 46 29 E
Bazarnyy Syzgan, *Russia* 34 D8 53 45N 46 40 E
Bazaruto △, *Mozam.* .. 89 C6 21 42 S 35 26 E
Bazaruto, I. do, *Mozam.* 89 C6 21 40 S 35 28 E
Bazas, *France* 20 D3 44 27N 0 13W
Bazhong, *China* ...... 58 B6 31 52N 106 46 E
Bazhou, *China* .... 56 E9 39 8N 116 22 E
Bazmān, Kūh-e, *Iran* . 71 D9 28 4N 60 1 E
Beach, *U.S.A.* 112 B3 46 58N 104 0W
Beach City, *U.S.A.* ... 116 F3 40 39N 81 35W
Beachport, *Australia* . 95 F3 37 29 S 140 0 E
Beachy Hd., *U.K.* .... 15 G8 50 44N 0 15 E
Beacon, *Australia* .... 93 F2 30 26 S 117 52 E
Beacon, *U.S.A.* 117 E11 41 30N 73 58W
Beaconsfield, *Australia* 95 G4 41 11 S 146 48 E
Beagle, Canal, *S. Amer.* 128 H3 55 0 S 68 30W
Beagle Bay, *Australia* . 92 C3 16 58 S 122 40 E
Bealanana, *Madag.* .. 89 A8 14 33 S 48 44 E
Beals Cr. →, *U.S.A.* .. 113 J4 32 10N 100 51W
Beamsville, *Canada* .. 116 C5 43 12N 79 28W
Bear →, *Calif., U.S.A.* 110 G5 38 56N 121 36W
Bear →, *Utah, U.S.A.* 106 B4 41 30N 112 8W
Béar, C., *France* ..... 20 F7 42 31N 3 8 E
Bear I., *Ireland* 12 E2 51 38N 9 50W
Bear L., *Canada* 103 B9 55 8N 96 0W
Bear L., *U.S.A.* 108 F8 41 59N 111 21W
Beardmore, *Canada* .. 104 C2 49 36N 87 57W
Beardmore Glacier,
  Antarctica .... 5 E11 84 30 S 170 0 E
Beardstown, *U.S.A.* .. 112 F9 40 1N 90 26W
Bearma →, *India* ..... 69 G8 24 20N 79 51 E
Béarn, *France* 20 E3 43 20N 0 30W
Bearpaw Mts., *U.S.A.* 108 B9 48 12N 109 30W
Bearskin Lake, *Canada* 104 B1 53 58N 91 2W
Beas →, *India* .... 68 D6 31 10N 74 59 E
Beas de Segura, *Spain* 37 G8 38 15N 2 53W
Beasain, *Spain* 38 B2 43 3N 2 11W
Beata, C., *Dom. Rep.* . 121 C5 17 40N 71 30W
Beata, I., *Dom. Rep.* .. 121 C5 17 34N 71 31W
Beatrice, *U.S.A.* 112 E6 40 16N 96 45W
Beatrice, *Zimbabwe* .. 87 F3 18 15 S 30 55 E
Beatrice, C., *Australia* 94 A2 14 20 S 136 55 E
Beatton →, *Canada* .. 102 B4 56 15N 120 45W
Beatton River, *Canada* 102 B4 57 26N 121 20W
Beatty, *U.S.A.* 110 J10 36 54N 116 46W
Beaucaire, *France* ... 21 E8 43 48N 4 39 E
Beauce, Plaine de la,
  France .... 19 D8 48 10N 1 45 E
Beauceville, *Canada* .. 105 C5 46 13N 70 46W
Beaudesert, *Australia* . 95 D5 27 59 S 153 0 E
Beaufort, *Malaysia* .. 62 C5 5 30N 115 40 E
Beaufort, *N.C., U.S.A.* 115 H7 34 43N 76 40W
Beaufort, *S.C., U.S.A.* 115 J5 32 26N 80 40W
Beaufort Sea, *Arctic* . 98 B5 72 0N 140 0W
Beaufort West, *S. Africa* 88 E3 32 18 S 22 36 E
Beaugency, *France* ... 19 E8 47 47N 1 38 E
Beauharnois, *Canada* . 117 A11 45 20N 73 52W
Beaujeu, *France* ..... 19 F11 46 10N 4 35 E
Beaujolais, *France* ... 19 F11 46 0N 4 22 E
Beaulieu →, *Canada* . 102 A6 62 3N 113 11W
Beaulieu-sur-Dordogne,
  France .... 20 D5 44 58N 1 50 E
Beaulieu-sur-Mer,
  France .... 21 E11 43 42N 7 20 E
Beauly, *U.K.* 13 D4 57 30N 4 28W
Beauly →, *U.K.* 13 D4 57 29N 4 27W
Beaumaris, *U.K.* 14 D3 53 16N 4 6W
Beaumont, *Belgium* .. 17 D4 50 15N 4 14 E
Beaumont, *France* ... 20 D4 44 45N 0 46 E
Beaumont, *U.S.A.* ... 113 K7 30 5N 94 6W
Beaumont-de-Lomagne,
  France .... 20 E5 43 53N 1 0 E
Beaumont-le-Roger,
  France .... 18 C7 49 4N 0 47 E
Beaumont-sur-Sarthe,
  France .... 18 D7 48 13N 0 8 E
Beaune, *France* ...... 19 E11 47 2N 4 50 E
Beaune-la-Rolande,
  France .... 19 D9 48 4N 2 25 E
Beaupré, *Canada* 105 C5 47 3N 70 54W
Beaupréau, *France* ... 18 E6 47 12N 1 0W
Beauraing, *Belgium* .. 17 D4 50 7N 4 57 E
Beaurepaire, *France* . 21 C9 45 22N 5 1 E
Beausejour, *Canada* .. 103 C9 50 5N 96 35W
Beauvais, *France* .... 19 C9 49 25N 2 8 E
Beauval, *Canada* 103 B7 55 9N 107 37W
Beauvoir-sur-Mer,
  France 18 F4 46 55N 2 2W
Beauvoir-sur-Niort,
  France 20 B3 46 12N 0 30W
Beaver, *Okla., U.S.A.* . 113 G4 36 49N 100 31W
Beaver, *Pa., U.S.A.* .. 116 F4 40 42N 80 19W
Beaver, *Utah, U.S.A.* . 109 G7 38 17N 112 38W
Beaver →, *B.C., Canada* 102 B4 59 52N 124 20W
Beaver →, *Ont., Canada* 104 A2 55 55N 87 48W
Beaver →, *Sask.,
  Canada* 103 B7 55 26N 107 45W
Beaver →, *U.S.A.* 113 G5 36 35N 99 30W
Beaver City, *U.S.A.* .. 112 E5 40 8N 99 50W
Beaver Creek, *Canada* 100 B5 63 0N 141 0W
Beaver Dam, *U.S.A.* . 112 D10 43 28N 88 50W
Beaver Falls, *U.S.A.* . 116 F4 40 46N 80 20W
Beaver Hill L., *Canada* 103 C10 54 5N 94 50W
Beaver I., *U.S.A.* 114 C3 45 40N 85 33W
Beaverhill L., *Canada* 102 C6 53 27N 112 32W
Beaverlodge, *Canada* . 102 B5 55 11N 119 29W
Beaverstone →, *Canada* 104 B2 54 59N 89 25W
Beaverton, *Canada* ... 116 B5 44 26N 79 9W
Beaverton, *U.S.A.* ... 110 E4 45 29N 122 48W
Beawar, *India* .... 68 F6 26 3N 74 18 E
Bebedouro, *Brazil* ... 127 A6 21 0 S 48 25W
Bebra, Tanjung,
  Indonesia .... 63 K18 8 44 S 115 51 E
Beboa, *Madag.* ...... 89 B7 17 22 S 44 33 E
Bebra, *Germany* ..... 24 E5 50 58N 9 48 E
Becan, *Mexico* 119 D7 18 31N 89 28W
Beccles, *U.K.* .... 15 E9 52 27N 1 35 E
Bečej, *Serbia & M.* ... 28 E5 45 36N 20 3 E
Beceni, *Romania* .... 29 E11 45 23N 26 48 E
Becerreá, *Spain* 36 C3 42 51N 7 10W
Béchar, *Algeria* 78 B5 31 38N 2 18W
Bechyně, *Czech Rep.* . 26 B7 49 17N 14 29 E
Beckley, *U.S.A.* 114 G5 37 47N 81 11W
Beckum, *Germany* ... 24 D4 51 45N 8 2 E

Beclean, *Romania* .... 29 C9 47 11N 24 11 E
Bečov nad Teplou,
  Czech Rep. .... 26 A5 50 5N 12 49 E
Bečva →, *Czech Rep.* 27 B10 49 31N 17 20 E
Bédar, *Spain* 39 H3 37 11N 1 59W
Bédarieux, *France* ... 20 E7 43 37N 3 10 E
Beddouza, Ras,
  Morocco 78 B4 32 33N 9 9W
Bedele, *Ethiopia* ..... 81 F4 8 31N 36 23 E
Bederkesa, *Germany* . 24 B4 53 37N 8 50 E
Bedeso, *Ethiopia* .... 81 F5 9 58N 40 52 E
Bedford, *Canada* 117 A12 45 7N 72 59W
Bedford, *S. Africa* ... 88 E4 32 40 S 26 10 E
Bedford, *U.K.* 15 E7 52 8N 0 28W
Bedford, *Ind., U.S.A.* . 114 F2 38 52N 86 29W
Bedford, *Iowa, U.S.A.* 112 E7 40 40N 94 44W
Bedford, *Ohio, U.S.A.* 116 E3 41 23N 81 32W
Bedford, *Pa., U.S.A.* . 116 F6 40 1N 78 30W
Bedford, *Va., U.S.A.* . 114 G6 37 20N 79 31W
Bedford, C., *Australia* 94 B4 15 14 S 145 21 E
Bedfordshire □, *U.K.* . 15 E7 52 4N 0 28W
Będków, *Poland* ..... 31 G6 51 36N 19 44 E
Bednja →, *Croatia* ... 41 B13 46 12N 16 52 E
Bednodemyanovsk,
  Russia .... 34 D6 53 55N 43 15 E
Bedok, *Singapore* .... 65 d 1 19N 103 56 E
Bedónia, *Italy* .... 40 D6 44 30N 9 38 E
Bedourie, *Australia* .. 94 C2 24 30 S 139 30 E
Bedum, *Neths.* ...... 17 A6 53 18N 6 36 E
Będzin, *Poland* ...... 31 H6 50 19N 19 7 E
Beebe Plain, *Canada* . 117 A12 45 1N 72 9W
Beech Creek, *U.S.A.* . 116 E7 41 5N 77 36W
Beef I., *Br. Virgin Is.* . 121 e 18 26N 64 30W
Beelitz, *Germany* .... 24 C8 52 14N 12 58 E
Beenleigh, *Australia* . 95 D5 27 43 S 153 10 E
Be'er Menuha, *Israel* . 70 D2 30 19N 35 8 E
Be'er Sheva →, *Israel* 74 D3 31 15N 34 48 E
Beersheba = Be'er
  Sheva, *Israel* ...... 74 D3 31 15N 34 48 E
Beeskow, *Germany* .. 24 C10 52 10N 14 15 E
Beestekraal, *S. Africa* . 89 D4 25 23 S 27 38 E
Beeston, *U.K.* 14 E6 52 56N 1 14W
Beeville, *U.S.A.* 113 L6 28 24N 97 45W
Befale, *Dem. Rep. of
  the Congo* .... 84 D4 0 25N 20 45 E
Befandriana,
  Mahajanga, Madag. 89 B8 15 16 S 48 32 E
Befandriana, *Toliara,
  Madag.* .... 89 C7 21 55 S 44 0 E
Befasy, *Madag.* ...... 89 C7 20 33 S 44 23 E
Befotaka, *Antsiranana,
  Madag.* .... 89 A8 13 15 S 48 16 E
Befotaka, *Fianarantsoa,
  Madag.* .... 89 C8 23 49 S 47 0 E
Bega, *Australia* ...... 95 F4 36 41 S 149 51 E
Bega, Canalul, *Romania* 28 E5 45 37N 20 46 E
Bégard, *France* 18 D3 48 38N 3 18W
Beğendik, *Turkey* .... 45 F10 40 55N 26 34 E
Begoro, *Ghana* 83 D4 6 23N 0 23W
Begusarai, *India* ..... 69 G12 25 24N 86 9 E
Behābād, *Iran* .... 71 C8 32 24N 59 47 E
Behala, *India* .... 69 H13 22 30N 88 20 E
Behara, *Madag.* ..... 89 C8 24 55 S 46 20 E
Behbehān, *Iran* ...... 71 D6 30 30N 50 15 E
Behm Canal, *U.S.A.* . 102 B2 55 10N 131 0W
Behshahr, *Iran* ...... 71 B7 36 45N 53 35 E
Bei Jiang →, *China* .. 59 F9 23 2N 112 58 E
Bei'an, *China* .... 60 B7 48 10N 126 20 E
Beibei, *China* .... 58 C6 29 47N 106 22 E
Beichuan, *China* ..... 58 B5 31 55N 104 39 E
Beihai, *China* .... 58 G7 21 28N 109 6 E
Beijing, *China* .... 56 E9 39 55N 116 20 E
Beijing □, *China* ..... 56 E9 39 55N 116 20 E
Beilen, *Neths.* ...... 17 B6 52 52N 6 27 E
Beiliu, *China* .... 59 F8 22 41N 110 21 E
Beilngries, *Germany* . 25 F7 49 1N 11 28 E
Beilpajah, *Australia* .. 95 E3 32 54 S 143 52 E
Beilul, *Eritrea* .... 81 E5 13 15N 42 24 E
Beinn na Faoghla =
  Benbecula, *U.K.* 13 D1 57 26N 7 21W
Beipan Jiang →, *China* 58 E5 25 7N 106 1 E
Beipiao, *China* ...... 57 D11 41 52N 120 32 E
Beira, *Mozam.* ...... 87 F3 19 50 S 34 52 E
Beirut = Bayrūt,
  Lebanon .... 74 B4 33 53N 35 31 E
Beiseker, *Canada* 102 C6 51 23N 113 32W
Beitaolaizhao, *China* . 57 B13 44 58N 125 58 E
Beitbridge, *Zimbabwe* 87 G3 22 12 S 30 0 E
Beiuș, *Romania* ...... 28 D7 46 40N 22 21 E
Beizhen = Binzhou,
  China .... 57 F10 37 20N 118 2 E
Beizhen, *China* ...... 57 D11 41 38N 121 54 E
Beizhengzhen, *China* . 57 B12 44 31N 123 30 E
Beja, *Portugal* 37 G3 38 2N 7 53W
Beja □, *Portugal* 37 H3 37 55N 7 55W
Béja, *Tunisia* .... 79 A7 36 43N 9 12 E
Bejaïa, *Algeria* ...... 78 A7 36 42N 5 2 E
Béjar, *Spain* 36 E5 40 23N 5 46W
Bejestān, *Iran* .... 71 C8 34 30N 58 5 E
Bekaa Valley = Al Biqā,
  Lebanon .... 74 A5 34 10N 36 10 E
Bekçiler, *Turkey* ..... 47 E11 36 56N 29 44 E
Békés, *Hungary* ..... 28 D6 46 47N 21 9 E
Békés □, *Hungary* ... 28 D6 46 45N 21 5 E
Békéscsaba, *Hungary* 28 D6 46 40N 21 5 E
Bekilli, *Turkey* ...... 47 C11 38 17N 29 27 E
Bekily, *Madag.* ...... 89 C8 24 13 S 45 19 E
Bekisopa, *Madag.* ... 89 C8 21 40 S 45 54 E
Bekitro, *Madag.* ..... 89 C8 24 33 S 45 18 E
Bekodoka, *Madag.* .. 89 B8 16 58 S 45 7 E
Bekoji, *Ethiopia* ..... 81 F4 7 40N 39 17 E
Bekok, *Malaysia* ..... 65 L4 2 20N 103 7 E
Bekopaka, *Madag.* .. 89 B7 19 9 S 44 48 E
Bekuli, *Indonesia* .... 63 J18 8 23 S 114 13 E
Bekwai, *Ghana* 83 D4 6 30N 1 34W
Bela, *India* .... 69 G10 25 50N 83 0 E
Bela, *Pakistan* ...... 68 F2 26 12N 66 20 E
Bela Bela, *S. Africa* .. 89 C4 24 51 S 28 19 E
Bela Crkva, *Serbia & M.* 28 F6 44 55N 21 27 E
Bela Palanka,
  Serbia & M. .... 44 C6 43 13N 22 17 E
Bela Vista, *Brazil* .... 126 A4 22 12 S 56 20W
Bela Vista, *Mozam.* .. 89 D5 26 10 S 32 44 E
Belábre, *France* ...... 20 B5 46 34N 1 8 E
Belalcázar, *Spain* 37 G5 38 35N 5 10W
Belan →, *India* ...... 69 G9 24 2N 81 45 E
Belanovica, *Serbia & M.* 44 B4 44 15N 20 23 E
Belarus ■, *Europe* ... 32 F4 53 30N 27 0 E
Belau = Palau ■,
  Pac. Oc. .... 96 G5 7 30N 134 30 E
Belavenona, *Madag.* . 89 C8 24 50 S 47 4 E
Belawan, *Indonesia* .. 62 D1 3 33N 98 32 E
Belaya, *Ethiopia* ..... 81 E4 11 25N 36 8 E
Belaya →, *Russia* .... 34 C9 54 40N 56 0 E
Belaya Glina, *Russia* . 35 G5 46 5N 40 48 E
Belaya Kalitva, *Russia* 35 F5 48 13N 40 50 E
Belaya Tserkov = Bila
  Tserkva, *Ukraine* ... 33 H6 49 45N 30 10 E

Belceşti, *Romania* .... 29 C12 47 19N 27 7 E
Bełchatów, *Poland* ... 31 G6 51 21N 19 22 E
Belcher Is., *Canada* .. 104 A3 56 15N 78 45W
Belchite, *Spain* 38 D4 41 18N 0 43W
Belden, *U.S.A.* 110 E5 40 2N 121 17W
Beled Weyne = Belet
  Uen, *Somali Rep.* ... 75 G4 4 30N 45 5 E
Belén, *Argentina* .... 126 B2 27 40 S 67 5W
Belén, *Paraguay* ..... 126 A4 23 30 S 57 6W
Belen, *U.S.A.* 109 J10 34 40N 106 46W
Belene, *Bulgaria* ..... 45 C9 43 39N 25 10 E
Beleni, *Turkey* ...... 72 D7 36 31N 36 10 E
Belet Uen, *Somali Rep.* 75 G4 4 30N 45 5 E
Belev, *Russia* .... 32 F9 53 50N 36 5 E
Belevi, *Turkey* ...... 47 C9 38 0N 27 28 E
Belfair, *U.S.A.* 110 C4 47 27N 122 50W
Belfast, *S. Africa* .... 89 D5 25 42 S 30 2 E
Belfast, *U.K.* 12 B6 54 37N 5 56W
Belfast, *Maine, U.S.A.* 115 C11 44 26N 69 1W
Belfast, *N.Y., U.S.A.* . 116 D6 42 21N 78 7W
Belfast L., *U.K.* 12 B6 54 40N 5 50W
Belfield, *U.S.A.* 112 B3 46 53N 103 12W
Belfort, *France* ...... 19 E13 47 38N 6 50 E
Belfort, Territoire de □,
  France .... 19 E13 47 40N 6 55 E
Belfry, *U.S.A.* 108 D9 45 9N 109 1W
Belgaum, *India* ...... 66 M9 15 55N 74 35 E
Belgioioso, *Italy* ..... 40 C6 45 10N 9 19 E
Belgium ■, *Europe* .. 17 D4 50 30N 5 0 E
Belgodère, *France* ... 21 F13 42 35N 9 1 E
Belgorod, *Russia* .... 33 G9 50 35N 36 35 E
Belgorod-
  Dnestrovskiy =
  Bilhorod-
  Dnistrovskyy, *Ukraine* 33 J6 46 11N 30 23 E
Belgrade = Beograd,
  Serbia & M. .... 44 B4 44 50N 20 37 E
Belgrade, *U.S.A.* 108 D8 45 47N 111 11W
Belhaven, *U.S.A.* 115 H7 35 33N 76 37W
Beli Drim →, *Europe* 44 D4 42 6N 20 25 E
Beli Manastir, *Croatia* 28 E3 45 45N 18 36 E
Beli Timok →,
  Serbia & M. .... 44 C6 43 53N 22 14 E
Bélice →, *Italy* ...... 42 E5 37 35N 12 55 E
Belimbing, *Indonesia* 63 J18 8 24 S 115 2 E
Belinskiy, *Russia* .... 34 D6 53 0N 43 25 E
Belinyu, *Indonesia* .. 62 E3 1 35 S 105 50 E
Beliton Is. = Belitung,
  Indonesia .... 62 E3 3 10 S 107 50 E
Belitung, *Indonesia* .. 62 E3 3 10 S 107 50 E
Beliu, *Romania* ...... 28 D6 46 30N 22 0 E
Belize ■, *Cent. Amer.* 119 D7 17 0N 88 30W
Belize City, *Belize* ... 119 D7 17 25N 88 10W
Beljakovci, *Macedonia* 44 D5 42 6N 21 59 E
Beljanica, *Serbia & M.* 44 B5 44 8N 21 43 E
Belkovskiy, Ostrov,
  Russia .... 53 B14 75 32N 135 44 E
Bell →, *Canada* 104 C4 49 48N 77 38W
Bell I., *Canada* 105 B8 50 46N 55 35W
Bell-Irving →, *Canada* 102 B3 56 12N 129 5W
Bell Peninsula, *Canada* 101 B11 63 50N 82 0W
Bell Ville, *Argentina* .. 126 C3 32 40 S 62 40W
Bella, *Italy* .... 43 B8 40 45N 15 32 E
Bella Bella, *Canada* .. 102 C3 52 10N 128 10W
Bella Coola, *Canada* . 102 C3 52 25N 126 40W
Bella Unión, *Uruguay* 126 C4 30 15 S 57 40W
Bella Vista, *Corrientes,
  Argentina* .... 126 B4 28 33 S 59 0W
Bella Vista, *Tucuman,
  Argentina* .... 126 B2 27 10 S 65 25W
Bellac, *France* .... 20 B5 46 7N 1 3 E
Bellágio, *Italy* .... 40 C6 45 59N 9 15 E
Bellaire, *U.S.A.* 116 F4 40 1N 80 45W
Bellária, *Italy* .... 41 D9 44 9N 12 28 E
Bellary, *India* .... 66 M10 15 10N 76 56 E
Bellata, *Australia* .... 95 D4 29 53 S 149 46 E
Belle-Chasse, *U.S.A.* . 113 L10 29 51N 89 59W
Belle Fourche, *U.S.A.* 112 C3 44 40N 103 51W
Belle Fourche →,
  U.S.A. 112 C3 44 26N 102 18W
Belle Glade, *U.S.A.* .. 115 M5 26 41N 80 40W
Belle-Île, *France* 18 E3 47 20N 3 10W
Belle Isle, *Canada* ... 105 B8 51 57N 55 25W
Belle Isle, Str. of,
  Canada 105 B8 51 30N 56 30W
Belle Plaine, *U.S.A.* .. 112 E8 41 54N 92 17W
Belle Yella, *Liberia* .. 82 D3 7 24N 10 0W
Belledonne, *France* .. 21 C10 45 11N 6 0 E
Bellefontaine, *U.S.A.* 114 E4 40 22N 83 46W
Bellefonte, *U.S.A.* ... 116 F7 40 55N 77 47W
Bellegarde, *France* ... 19 E9 47 59N 2 26 E
Bellegarde-en-Marche,
  France .... 20 C6 45 59N 2 18 E
Bellegarde-sur-
  Valserine, *France* .. 19 F12 46 4N 5 50 E
Bellême, *France* ..... 18 D7 48 22N 0 34 E
Belleoram, *Canada* .. 105 C8 47 31N 55 25W
Belleplaine, *Barbados* 121 g 13 15N 59 34W
Belleville, *Canada* ... 116 B7 44 10N 77 23W
Belleville, *U.S.A.* .... 19 F11 46 7N 4 45 E
Belleville, *Ill., U.S.A.* . 112 F10 38 31N 89 59W
Belleville, *Kans., U.S.A.* 112 F6 39 50N 97 38W
Belleville, *N.Y., U.S.A.* 117 C8 43 46N 76 10W
Belleville-sur-Vie,
  France 18 F5 46 46N 1 25W
Bellevue, *Canada* 102 D6 49 35N 114 22W
Bellevue, *Idaho, U.S.A.* 108 E6 43 28N 114 16W
Bellevue, *Nebr., U.S.A.* 112 E7 41 8N 95 53W
Bellevue, *Ohio, U.S.A.* 116 E2 41 17N 82 51W
Bellevue, *Wash., U.S.A.* 110 C4 47 37N 122 12W
Belley, *France* .... 21 C9 45 46N 5 41 E
Bellin = Kangirsuk,
  Canada 101 B13 60 0N 70 0W
Bellingen, *Australia* .. 95 E5 30 25 S 152 50 E
Bellingham, *U.S.A.* .. 110 B4 48 46N 122 29W
Bellinghausen Sea,
  Antarctica .... 5 C17 66 0 S 80 0W
Bellinzona, *Switz.* ... 25 J5 46 11N 9 1 E
Bello, *Colombia* 124 B3 6 20N 75 33W
Bellows Falls, *U.S.A.* . 117 C12 43 8N 72 27W
Bellpat, *Pakistan* .... 68 E3 29 0N 68 5 E
Bellpuig d'Urgell, *Spain* 38 D6 41 37N 1 1 E
Belluno, *Italy* .... 41 B9 46 9N 12 13 E
Bellwood, *U.S.A.* 116 F6 40 36N 78 20W
Bélmez, *Spain* 37 G5 38 17N 5 17W
Belmont, *Canada* 116 D3 42 53N 81 5W
Belmont, *S. Africa* ... 88 D3 29 28 S 24 22 E
Belmont, *U.S.A.* 116 D6 42 14N 78 2W
Belmonte, *Brazil* ..... 125 G11 16 0 S 39 0W
Belmonte, *Portugal* .. 36 E3 40 21N 7 20W
Belmonte, *Spain* 38 F2 39 34N 2 43W
Belmopan, *Belize* ... 119 D7 17 18N 88 30W
Belmullet, *Ireland* ... 12 B2 54 14N 9 58W
Belo Horizonte, *Brazil* 125 G10 19 55 S 43 56W

Belo-sur-Mer, *Madag.* 89 C7 20 42 S 44 0 E
Belo-Tsiribihina, *Madag.* 89 B7 19 40 S 44 30 E
Belogorsk = Bilohirsk,
  Ukraine .... 33 K8 45 3N 34 35 E
Belogorsk, *Russia* ... 53 D13 51 0N 128 20 E
Belogradchik, *Bulgaria* 44 C6 43 53N 22 42 E
Belogradets, *Bulgaria* 45 C11 43 22N 27 18 E
Beloha, *Madag.* ..... 89 D8 25 10 S 45 3 E
Beloit, *Kans., U.S.A.* . 112 F5 39 28N 98 6W
Beloit, *Wis., U.S.A.* .. 112 D10 42 31N 89 2W
Belokorovichi, *Ukraine* 33 G5 51 7N 28 2 E
Belomorsk, *Russia* ... 52 C4 64 35N 34 54 E
Belonia, *India* .... 67 H17 23 15N 91 30 E
Belopolye = Bilopillya,
  Ukraine .... 33 G8 51 14N 34 20 E
Belorechensk, *Russia* 35 H4 44 46N 39 52 E
Belorussia = Belarus ■,
  Europe .... 32 F4 53 30N 27 0 E
Beloslav, *Bulgaria* ... 45 C11 43 11N 27 42 E
Belovo, *Bulgaria* ..... 45 D8 42 13N 24 1 E
Belovo, *Russia* ...... 52 D9 54 30N 86 0 E
Belovodsk, *Ukraine* .. 33 H10 49 13N 39 36 E
Beloye, Ozero, *Russia* 32 B9 60 11N 37 35 E
Beloye More, *Russia* . 52 C4 66 30N 38 0 E
Belozem, *Bulgaria* ... 45 D9 42 12N 25 2 E
Belozersk, *Russia* ... 32 B9 60 1N 37 45 E
Belpasso, *Italy* ...... 43 E7 37 35N 14 58 E
Belpre, *U.S.A.* 114 F5 39 17N 81 34W
Belrain, *India* .... 69 E9 28 23N 80 55 E
Belt, *U.S.A.* 108 C8 47 23N 110 55W
Beltana, *Australia* ... 95 E2 30 48 S 138 25 E
Belterra, *Brazil* ..... 125 D8 2 45 S 55 0W
Beltinci, *Slovenia* .... 41 B13 46 37N 16 20 E
Belton, *U.S.A.* 113 K6 31 3N 97 28W
Belton L., *U.S.A.* 113 K6 31 8N 97 32W
Beltsy = Bălţi, *Moldova* 29 C12 47 48N 27 58 E
Belturbet, *Ireland* ... 12 B4 54 6N 7 26W
Belukha, *Russia* ..... 52 E9 49 50N 86 50 E
Beluran, *Malaysia* ... 62 C5 5 48N 117 35 E
Belušić, *Serbia & M.* . 44 C5 43 50N 21 10 E
Belvedere Maríttimo,
  Italy .... 43 C8 39 37N 15 52 E
Belvès, *France* ...... 20 D5 44 46N 1 0 E
Belvidere, *Ill., U.S.A.* . 112 D10 42 15N 88 50W
Belvidere, *N.J., U.S.A.* 117 F9 40 50N 75 5W
Belvis de la Jara, *Spain* 36 F6 39 45N 4 57W
Belyando →, *Australia* 94 C4 21 38 S 146 50 E
Belyy, *Russia* .... 32 E7 55 49N 33 3 E
Belyy, Ostrov, *Russia* 52 B8 73 30N 71 0 E
Belyy Yar, *Russia* ... 52 D9 58 26N 84 39 E
Belz, *Ukraine* .... 31 H11 50 23N 24 1 E
Bełzec, *Poland* ...... 31 H10 50 23N 23 26 E
Belzig, *Germany* ..... 24 C8 52 8N 12 35 E
Belzoni, *U.S.A.* 113 J9 33 11N 90 29W
Bełżyce, *Poland* ..... 31 G9 51 11N 22 17 E
Bemaraha,
  Lembalemban' i,
  Madag. .... 89 B7 18 40 S 44 45 E
Bemarivo, *Madag.* ... 89 C7 21 45 S 44 45 E
Bemarivo →,
  Antsiranana, Madag. 89 A9 14 9 S 50 9 E
Bemarivo →,
  Mahajanga, Madag. 89 B8 15 27 S 47 40 E
Bemavo, *Madag.* .... 89 C8 21 33 S 45 25 E
Bembéréke, *Benin* ... 83 C5 10 11N 2 43 E
Bembesi, *Zimbabwe* . 87 G2 20 0 S 28 58 E
Bembesi →, *Zimbabwe* 87 F2 18 57 S 27 47 E
Bembézar →, *Spain* .. 37 H5 37 45N 5 13W
Bembibre, *Spain* 36 C4 42 41N 6 25W
Bemetara, *India* ..... 69 J9 21 42N 81 32 E
Bemidji, *U.S.A.* 112 B7 47 28N 94 53W
Bemolanga, *Madag.* . 89 B8 17 44 S 45 6 E
Ben, *Iran* .... 71 C6 32 32N 50 45 E
Ben Cruachan, *U.K.* . 13 E3 56 26N 5 8W
Ben Dearg, *U.K.* 13 D4 57 47N 4 56W
Ben En △, *Vietnam* .. 64 C5 19 37N 105 30 E
Ben Hope, *U.K.* 13 C4 58 25N 4 36W
Ben Lawers, *U.K.* 13 E4 56 32N 4 14W
Ben Lomond, *N.S.W.,
  Australia* .... 95 E5 30 1 S 151 43 E
Ben Lomond, *Tas.,
  Australia* .... 95 G4 41 38 S 147 42 E
Ben Lomond, *U.K.* ... 13 E4 56 11N 4 38W
Ben Lomond △,
  Australia .... 95 G4 41 33 S 147 39 E
Ben Luc, *Vietnam* ... 65 G6 10 39N 106 29 E
Ben Macdhui, *U.K.* .. 13 D5 57 4N 3 40W
Ben Mhor, *U.K.* 13 D1 57 15N 7 18W
Ben More, *Arg. & Bute,
  U.K.* 13 E2 56 26N 6 1W
Ben More, *Stirl., U.K.* 13 E4 56 23N 4 32W
Ben More Assynt, *U.K.* 13 C4 58 8N 4 52W
Ben Nevis, *U.K.* 13 E3 56 48N 5 1W
Ben Quang, *Vietnam* 64 D6 17 3N 106 55 E
Ben Vorlich, *U.K.* 13 E4 56 21N 4 14W
Ben Wyvis, *U.K.* 13 D4 57 40N 4 35W
Bena, *Nigeria* .... 83 C6 11 20N 5 50 E
Benalla, *Australia* ... 95 F4 36 30 S 146 0 E
Benalmádena, *Spain* . 37 J6 36 36N 4 34W
Benares = Varanasi,
  India .... 69 G10 25 22N 83 0 E
Bénat, C., *France* .... 21 E10 43 5N 6 22 E
Benavente, *Portugal* . 37 G2 38 59N 8 49W
Benavente, *Spain* 36 C5 42 2N 5 43W
Benavides, *U.S.A.* ... 113 M5 27 36N 98 25W
Benavides de Órbigo,
  Spain 36 C5 42 30N 5 54W
Benbecula, *U.K.* 13 D1 57 26N 7 21W
Benbonyathe, *Australia* 95 E2 30 25 S 139 11 E
Bend, *U.S.A.* 108 D3 44 4N 121 19W
Bender Beila,
  Somali Rep. .... 75 F5 9 30N 50 48 E
Bendery = Tighina,
  Moldova .... 29 D14 46 50N 29 30 E
Bendorf, *Germany* ... 24 E3 50 25N 7 35 E
Bene Beraq, *Israel* ... 74 C3 32 6N 34 51 E
Bénéna, *Mali* 82 C4 13 9N 4 17W
Benenitra, *Madag.* ... 89 C8 23 27 S 45 5 E
Benešov, *Czech Rep.* 26 B7 49 46N 14 41 E
Benevento, *Italy* ..... 43 A7 41 8N 14 45 E
Benfeld, *France* ..... 19 D14 48 22N 7 34 E
Benga, *Mozam.* ..... 87 F3 16 11 S 33 40 E
Bengal, Bay of, *Ind. Oc.* 67 M17 15 0N 90 0 E
Bengaluru = Bangalore,
  India .... 66 N10 12 59N 77 40 E
Bengbis, *Cameroon* .. 83 E7 3 27N 12 36 E
Bengbu, *China* ...... 57 H9 32 58N 117 20 E
Benghazi = Banghāzī,
  Libya .... 79 B10 32 11N 20 3 E
Bengkalis, *Indonesia* 62 D2 1 30N 102 10 E
Bengkulu, *Indonesia* 62 E2 3 50 S 102 12 E
Bengkulu □, *Indonesia* 62 E2 3 48 S 102 16 E
Bengough, *Canada* .. 103 D7 49 25N 105 10W
Bengtsfors, *Sweden* . 10 E6 59 2N 12 6 E
Benguela, *Angola* ... 85 G2 12 37 S 13 25 E

Benguérua, I., Mozam. 89 C6 21 58 S 35 28 E
Benha, Egypt 80 H7 30 26N 31 8 E
Beni, Dem. Rep. of
the Congo 86 B2 0 30N 29 27 E
Beni →, Bolivia 124 F5 10 23 S 65 24W
Beni Mazâr, Egypt 80 B3 28 32N 30 44 E
Beni Mellal, Morocco 78 B4 32 21N 6 21W
Beni Suef, Egypt 80 J7 29 5N 31 6 E
Beniah L., Canada 102 A6 63 23N 112 17W
Benicarló, Spain 38 E5 40 23N 0 23 E
Benicàssim, Spain 38 E5 40 3N 0 4 E
Benicia, U.S.A. 110 G4 38 3N 122 9W
Benidorm, Spain 39 G4 38 33N 0 9W
Benin ■, Africa 83 D5 10 0N 2 0 E
Benin →, Nigeria 83 D6 5 45N 5 4 E
Benin, Bight of, W. Afr. 83 E5 5 0N 3 0 E
Benin City, Nigeria 83 D6 6 20N 5 31 E
Benisa, Spain 39 G5 38 43N 0 3 E
Benitses, Greece 49 A3 39 32N 19 55 E
Benjamin Aceval,
Paraguay 126 A4 24 58 S 57 34W
Benjamin Constant,
Brazil 124 D4 4 40 S 70 15W
Benjamin Hill, Mexico 118 A2 30 10N 111 10W
Benkelman, U.S.A. 112 E4 40 3N 101 32W
Benkovac, Croatia 41 D12 44 2N 15 37 E
Bennett, Canada 102 B2 59 56N 134 53W
Bennett, L., Australia 92 D5 22 50 S 131 2 E
Bennetta, Ostrov, Russia 53 B15 76 21N 148 56 E
Bennettsville, U.S.A. 115 H6 34 37N 79 41W
Bennichchâb,
Mauritania 82 B1 19 32N 15 12W
Bennington, N.H.,
U.S.A. 117 D11 43 0N 71 55W
Bennington, Vt., U.S.A. 117 D11 42 53N 73 12W
Bénodet, France 18 E2 47 53N 4 7W
Benoni, S. Africa 89 D4 26 11 S 28 18 E
Benque Viejo del
Carmen, Belize 119 D7 17 5N 89 8W
Bensheim, Germany 25 F4 49 40N 8 38 E
Benson, Ariz., U.S.A. 109 L8 31 58N 110 18W
Benson, Minn., U.S.A. 112 C7 45 19N 95 36W
Bent, Iran 71 E8 26 20N 59 31 E
Benteng, Indonesia 63 F6 6 10 S 120 30 E
Bentinck I., Australia 94 B2 17 3 S 139 35 E
Bentiu, Sudan 81 F2 9 10N 29 55 E
Bento Gonçalves, Brazil 127 B5 29 10 S 51 31W
Benton, Ark., U.S.A. 113 H8 34 34N 92 35W
Benton, Calif., U.S.A. 110 H8 37 48N 118 32W
Benton, Ill., U.S.A. 112 G10 38 0N 88 55W
Benton, Pa., U.S.A. 117 E8 41 12N 76 23W
Benton Harbor, U.S.A. 114 D2 42 6N 86 27W
Bentong, Malaysia 65 L3 3 31N 101 55 E
Bentonville, U.S.A. 113 G7 36 22N 94 13W
Bentu Liben, Ethiopia 81 F4 8 32N 38 21 E
Benue □, Nigeria 83 D6 7 20N 8 45 E
Benue →, Nigeria 83 D6 7 48N 6 46 E
Benxi, China 57 D12 41 20N 123 48 E
Beo, Indonesia 63 D7 4 25N 126 50 E
Beograd, Serbia & M. 44 B4 44 50N 20 37 E
Beograd ✈ (BEG),
Serbia & M. 44 C4 43 49N 20 17 E
Beoumi, Ivory C. 82 D3 7 45N 5 23W
Bepan Jiang →, China 58 E6 24 55N 106 5 E
Beppu, Japan 55 H5 33 15N 131 30 E
Beqaa Valley = Al Biqâ,
Lebanon 74 A5 34 10N 36 10 E
Ber Mota, India 68 H3 23 27N 68 34 E
Berach →, India 68 G6 25 15N 75 2 E
Beraketa, Madag. 89 C7 23 7 S 44 25 E
Berane, Serbia & M. 44 D3 42 51N 19 52 E
Berat, Albania 44 D3 40 43N 19 59 E
Berau, Teluk, Indonesia 63 E8 2 30 S 132 30 E
Beravina, Madag. 89 B8 18 16 S 44 51 E
Berber, Sudan 80 D3 18 0N 34 0 E
Berbera, Somali Rep. 75 E4 10 30N 45 2 E
Berbérati, C.A.R. 84 D3 4 15N 15 40 E
Berbice →, Guyana 124 B7 6 20N 57 32W
Berceto, Italy 40 D6 44 31N 9 51 E
Berchidda, Italy 42 B2 40 47N 9 10 E
Berchtesgaden,
Germany 25 H8 47 38N 13 0 E
Berchtesgaden △,
Germany 25 H8 47 34N 12 55 E
Berck, France 19 B8 50 25N 1 36 E
Berdichev = Berdychiv,
Ukraine 33 H5 49 57N 28 30 E
Berdsk, Russia 52 D9 54 47N 83 2 E
Berdyansk, Ukraine 33 J9 46 45N 36 50 E
Berdychiv, Ukraine 33 H5 49 57N 28 30 E
Berea, U.S.A. 114 G3 37 34N 84 17W
Berebere, Indonesia 63 D7 2 25N 128 45 E
Bereda, Somali Rep. 75 E5 11 45N 51 0 E
Berehomet, Ukraine 29 B10 48 10N 25 19 E
Berehove, Ukraine 28 B7 48 15N 22 35 E
Berekum, Ghana 82 D4 7 29N 2 34W
Berenice, Egypt 80 C4 24 2N 35 25 E
Berens →, Canada 103 C9 52 25N 97 2W
Berens I., Canada 103 C9 52 18N 97 18W
Berens River, Canada 103 C9 52 25N 97 0W
Beresford, U.S.A. 112 D6 43 5N 96 47W
Berestechko, Ukraine 33 G3 50 22N 25 5 E
Bereşti, Romania 29 D12 46 6N 27 50 E
Beretău →, Romania 28 C6 47 2N 21 50 E
Berettyó →, Hungary 28 D6 46 59N 21 7 E
Berettyóújfalu, Hungary 28 C6 47 13N 21 33 E
Berevo, Mahajanga,
Madag. 89 B7 17 14 S 44 17 E
Berevo, Toliara, Madag. 89 B7 19 44 S 44 58 E
Bereza = Byaroza,
Belarus 33 F3 52 31N 24 51 E
Berezhany, Ukraine 33 H3 49 26N 24 58 E
Berezina =
Byarezina →, Belarus 33 F6 52 33N 30 14 E
Berezivka, Ukraine 33 J6 47 14N 30 55 E
Berezna, Ukraine 33 G6 51 35N 31 46 E
Berezniki, Russia 52 C5 52 51N 42 40 E
Berezniki, Russia 52 C6 59 24N 56 46 E
Berezovo, Russia 52 C7 64 0N 65 0 E
Berezyne, Ukraine 29 D14 46 14N 29 12 E
Berga, Spain 38 C6 42 6N 1 48 E
Berga, Sweden 11 G10 57 14N 16 3 E
Bérgamo, Italy 40 C6 45 41N 9 43 E
Bergara, Spain 38 B2 43 9N 2 28W
Bergby, Sweden 10 D11 60 57N 17 2 E
Bergedorf, Germany 24 B6 53 28N 10 6 E
Bergeforsen, Sweden 10 B11 62 32N 17 23 E
Bergen,
Mecklenburg-Vorpommern,
Germany 24 A9 54 25N 13 25 E
Bergen, Niedersachsen,
Germany 24 C5 52 49N 9 57 E
Bergen, Neths. 17 B4 52 40N 4 43 E
Bergen, Norway 9 F11 60 20N 5 20 E
Bergen op Zoom, Neths. 17 C4 51 28N 4 18 E

Bergerac, France 20 D4 44 51N 0 30 E
Bergheim, Germany 24 E2 50 57N 6 38 E
Bergholz, U.S.A. 116 F4 40 31N 80 53W
Bergisch Gladbach,
Germany 17 D7 50 59N 7 8 E
Bergisches Land □,
Germany 24 E3 51 0N 7 30 E
Bergkamen, Germany 24 D3 51 37N 7 38 E
Bergkvara, Sweden 11 H10 56 23N 16 5 E
Bergshamra, Sweden 10 E12 59 38N 18 37 E
Bergsjö, Sweden 10 C11 61 59N 17 3 E
Bergstrasse-
Odenwald □,
Germany 25 F1 49 45N 5 55 E
Bergues, France 19 B9 50 58N 2 24 E
Bergviken, Sweden 10 C10 61 15N 16 40 E
Bergville, S. Africa 89 D4 28 52 S 29 18 E
Berhala, Selat, Indonesia 62 E2 1 0 S 104 15 E
Berhampore =
Baharampur, India 69 G13 24 2N 88 27 E
Berhampur =
Brahmapur, India 67 K14 19 15N 84 54 E
Berheci →, Romania 29 E12 45 58N 27 28 E
Bering Sea, Pac. Oc. 100 C1 58 0N 171 0 E
Bering Strait, Pac. Oc. 100 B3 65 30N 169 0W
Beringovskiy, Russia 53 C18 63 3N 179 19 E
Berisso, Argentina 126 C4 34 56 S 57 50W
Berja, Spain 37 J8 36 50N 2 56W
Berkeley, U.S.A. 110 H4 37 52N 122 16W
Berkner I., Antarctica 5 D18 79 30 S 50 0W
Berkovitsa, Bulgaria 44 C7 43 16N 23 8 E
Berkshire, U.S.A. 117 D8 42 19N 76 11W
Berkshire Downs, U.K. 15 F6 51 33N 1 29W
Berlanga, Spain 37 G5 38 17N 5 50W
Berlenga, I., Portugal 37 F1 39 25N 9 30W
Berlin, Germany 24 C9 52 30N 13 25 E
Berlin, Md., U.S.A. 114 F8 38 20N 75 13W
Berlin, N.H. U.S.A. 117 B13 44 28N 71 11W
Berlin, N.Y., U.S.A. 117 D11 42 42N 73 23W
Berlin, Wis., U.S.A. 114 D1 43 58N 88 57W
Berlin □, Germany 24 C9 52 30N 13 20 E
Berlin Tegel ✈ (TXL),
Germany 24 C9 52 35N 13 14 E
Bermeja, Sierra, Spain 37 J5 36 30N 5 11W
Bermejo → Formosa,
Argentina 126 B4 26 51 S 58 23W
Bermejo → San Juan,
Argentina 126 C2 32 30 S 67 30W
Bermen, L., Canada 105 B6 53 35N 68 55 E
Bermeo, Spain 38 B2 43 25N 2 47W
Bermillo de Sayago,
Spain 36 D4 41 22N 6 8W
Bermuda ☑, Atl. Oc. 98 F13 32 45N 65 0W
Bern, Switz. 25 J3 46 57N 7 28 E
Bern □, Switz. 25 J3 46 45N 7 40 E
Bernalda, Italy 43 B9 40 24N 16 41 E
Bernalillo, U.S.A. 109 J10 35 18N 106 33W
Bernardo de Irigoyen,
Argentina 127 B5 26 15 S 53 40W
Bernardo O'Higgins □,
Chile 126 C1 34 15 S 70 45W
Bernardsville, U.S.A. 117 F10 40 43N 74 34W
Bernasconi, Argentina 126 D3 37 55 S 63 44W
Bernau, Bayern,
Germany 25 H8 47 47N 12 22 E
Bernau, Brandenburg,
Germany 24 C9 52 40N 13 35 E
Bernay, France 18 C7 49 5N 0 35 E
Bernburg, Germany 24 D7 51 47N 11 44 E
Berndorf, Austria 26 D9 47 59N 16 1 E
Berne = Bern, Switz. 25 J3 46 57N 7 28 E
Berne □ = Bern □, Switz. 25 J3 46 45N 7 40 E
Berner Alpen, Switz. 25 J3 46 27N 7 35 E
Berneray, U.K. 13 D1 57 43N 7 11W
Bernier I., Australia 93 D1 24 50 S 113 12 E
Bernina, Piz, Switz. 25 J5 46 20N 9 54 E
Bernkastel-Kues,
Germany 25 F3 49 55N 7 4 E
Beroroha, Madag. 89 C8 21 40 S 45 10 E
Bérounouay Benin 83 C5 10 34N 2 46 E
Beroun, Czech Rep. 26 B7 49 57N 14 5 E
Berounka →,
Czech Rep. 26 B7 50 0N 14 22 E
Berovo, Macedonia 44 E6 41 38N 22 51 E
Berre, Étang de, France 21 E9 43 27N 5 5 E
Berre-l'Étang, France 21 E9 43 27N 5 10 E
Berri, Australia 95 E3 34 14 S 140 35 E
Berriane, Algeria 78 B6 32 50N 3 46 E
Berry, Australia 95 E5 34 46 S 150 43 E
Berry, France 19 F8 46 50N 2 0 E
Berry Is., Bahamas 120 A4 25 40N 77 50W
Berryessa L., U.S.A. 110 G4 38 31N 122 6W
Berryville, U.S.A. 113 G8 36 22N 93 34W
Berseba, Namibia 88 D2 26 0 S 17 46 E
Bersenbrück, Germany 24 C3 52 34N 7 56 E
Bershad, Ukraine 29 B14 48 22N 29 31 E
Berthold, U.S.A. 112 A4 48 19N 101 44W
Berthoud, U.S.A. 112 E2 40 19N 105 5W
Bertincourt, France 19 B9 50 5N 2 58 E
Bertoua, Cameroon 84 D2 4 30N 13 45 E
Bertraghboy B., Ireland 12 C2 53 22N 9 54W
Berwick, U.S.A. 117 E8 41 3N 76 14W
Berwick-upon-Tweed,
U.K. 14 B6 55 46N 2 0W
Berwyn Mts., U.K. 14 E4 52 54N 3 26W
Beryslav, Ukraine 33 J7 46 50N 33 30 E
Berzasca, Romania 28 F6 44 39N 21 58 E
Berzence, Hungary 28 D2 46 12N 17 11 E
Besal, Pakistan 69 B5 35 4N 73 56 E
Besalampy, Madag. 89 B7 16 43 S 44 29 E
Besançon, France 19 E13 47 15N 6 2 E
Besar, Indonesia 62 E5 2 40 S 116 0 E
Beshenkovichi, Belarus 32 E5 55 2N 29 29 E
Beška, Serbia & M. 28 E5 45 8N 20 6 E
Besna Kobila,
Serbia & M. 44 D6 42 31N 22 10 E
Besnard L., Canada 103 B7 55 25N 106 0W
Besni, Turkey 70 B3 37 41N 37 52 E
Besor, N. →, Egypt 74 D3 31 28N 34 22 E
Bessarabiya, Moldova 33 J5 47 0N 28 10 E
Bessarabka =
Basarabeasca,
Moldova 29 D13 46 21N 28 58 E
Bessèges, France 21 D8 44 18N 4 8 E
Bessemer, Ala., U.S.A. 115 J2 33 24N 86 58W
Bessemer, Mich., U.S.A. 112 B9 46 29N 90 3W
Bessemer, Pa., U.S.A. 116 F4 40 59N 80 30W
Bessin, France 18 C6 49 18N 1 0W
Bessines-sur-Gartempe,
France 20 B5 46 6N 1 22 E
Beswick, Australia 92 B5 14 34 S 132 53 E
Bet She'an, Israel 74 C4 32 30N 35 30 E
Bet Shemesh, Israel 74 D4 31 44N 35 0 E
Betafo, Madag. 89 B8 19 50 S 46 51 E
Betancuria, Canary Is. 48 F5 28 25N 14 3W

Betanzos, Spain 36 B2 43 15N 8 12W
Bétaré Oya, Cameroon 84 C2 5 40N 14 5 E
Betatao, Madag. 89 B8 18 11 S 47 52 E
Betera, Spain 39 F4 39 35N 0 28W
Bétérou, Benin 83 D5 9 12N 2 16 E
Bethal, S. Africa 89 D4 26 27 S 29 28 E
Bethanien, Namibia 88 D2 26 31 S 17 8 E
Bethany, Canada 116 B6 44 11N 78 34W
Bethany, U.S.A. 112 E7 40 16N 94 2W
Bethel, Alaska, U.S.A. 100 B3 60 48N 161 45W
Bethel, Conn., U.S.A. 117 E11 41 22N 73 25W
Bethel, Maine, U.S.A. 117 B14 44 25N 70 47W
Bethel, Vt., U.S.A. 117 C12 43 50N 72 38W
Bethel Park, U.S.A. 116 F4 40 20N 80 1W
Béthenville, France 19 C11 49 18N 4 23 E
Bethlehem = Bayt
Lahm, West Bank 74 D4 31 43N 35 12 E
Bethlehem, S. Africa 89 D4 28 14 S 28 18 E
Bethlehem, U.S.A. 117 F9 40 37N 75 23W
Bethulie, S. Africa 88 E4 30 30 S 25 59 E
Béthune, France 19 B9 50 30N 2 38 E
Béthune →, France 18 C8 49 53N 1 4 E
Betioky, Madag. 89 C7 23 48 S 44 20 E
Betong, Thailand 65 K3 5 45N 101 5 E
Betoota, Australia 94 D3 25 45 S 140 42 E
Betor, Ethiopia 81 E4 11 37N 39 2 E
Betroka, Madag. 89 C8 23 16 S 46 0 E
Betsiamites, Canada 105 C6 48 56N 68 40W
Betsiamites →, Canada 105 C6 48 56N 68 38W
Betsiboka →, Madag. 89 B8 16 3 S 46 36 E
Bettendorf, U.S.A. 112 E9 41 32N 90 30W
Bettiah, India 69 F11 26 48N 84 33 E
Bettna, Sweden 11 F10 58 55N 16 38 E
Béttola, Italy 40 D6 44 47N 9 36 E
Betul, India 66 J10 21 58N 77 59 E
Betung, Malaysia 62 D4 1 24N 111 31 E
Betws-y-Coed, U.K. 14 D4 53 5N 3 48W
Betxi, Spain 38 F4 39 56N 0 12W
Betzdorf, Germany 24 E3 50 46N 7 52 E
Beulah, Mich., U.S.A. 114 C2 44 38N 86 6W
Beulah, N. Dak., U.S.A. 112 B4 47 16N 101 47W
Beuvron →, France 18 E8 47 29N 1 15 E
Beveren, Belgium 17 C4 51 12N 4 16 E
Beverley, Australia 93 F2 32 9 S 116 56 E
Beverley, U.K. 14 D7 53 51N 0 26W
Beverly, U.S.A. 117 D14 42 33N 70 53W
Beverly Hills, U.S.A. 111 L8 34 4N 118 25W
Beverungen, Germany 24 D5 51 39N 9 22 E
Bevoalavo, Madag. 89 D7 25 13 S 45 26 E
Bewas →, India 69 H8 23 59N 79 21 E
Bex, Switz. 25 J3 46 15N 7 1 E
Bexhill, U.K. 15 G8 50 51N 0 29 E
Bey Dağları, Turkey 47 E12 36 38N 30 29 E
Beyânlu, Iran 70 C5 36 0N 47 51 E
Beyazköy, Turkey 45 E11 41 21N 27 42 E
Beyçayırı, Turkey 45 F10 40 25N 26 55 E
Beydağ, Turkey 47 D10 38 5N 28 13 E
Beyeğaç, Turkey 47 D10 37 14N 28 53 E
Beyin, Ghana 82 D4 5 1N 2 41W
Beykoz, Turkey 45 E13 41 8N 29 7 E
Beyla, Guinea 82 D3 8 30N 8 38W
Beynat, France 20 C5 45 8N 1 44 E
Beyneu, Kazakhstan 52 E6 45 18N 55 9 E
Beyoba, Turkey 47 C9 38 48N 27 47 E
Beyoğlu, Turkey 45 E12 41 2N 29 0 E
Beypazarı, Turkey 72 B4 40 10N 31 56 E
Beyşehir, Turkey 72 D4 37 41N 31 43 E
Beyşehir Gölü, Turkey 70 B1 37 41N 31 33 E
Beytüşşebap, Turkey 73 D10 37 35N 43 10 E
Bezdan, Serbia & M. 28 E3 45 50N 18 57 E
Bezhetsk, Russia 32 D9 57 47N 36 39 E
Béziers, France 20 E7 43 20N 3 12 E
Bezwada = Vijayawada,
India 67 L12 16 31N 80 39 E
Bhabua, India 69 G10 25 3N 83 37 E
Bhachau, India 66 H7 23 20N 70 16 E
Bhadar →, Gujarat,
India 68 H5 22 17N 72 20 E
Bhadar →, Gujarat,
India 68 J3 21 27N 69 47 E
Bhadarwah, India 69 C6 32 58N 75 46 E
Bhadgaon = Bhaktapur,
Nepal 69 F11 27 38N 85 24 E
Bhadohi, India 69 G10 25 25N 82 34 E
Bhadra, India 68 E6 29 8N 75 14 E
Bhadrakh, India 67 J15 21 10N 86 30 E
Bhadran, India 68 H5 22 19N 72 6 E
Bhadravati, India 66 N9 13 49N 75 40 E
Bhag, Pakistan 68 E2 29 2N 67 49 E
Bhagalpur, India 69 G12 25 10N 87 0 E
Bhagirathi →,
Uttaranchal, India 69 D8 30 8N 78 35 E
Bhagirathi →,
W. Bengal, India 69 H13 23 25N 88 23 E
Bhakkar, Pakistan 68 D4 31 40N 71 5 E
Bhakra Dam, India 68 D7 31 30N 76 45 E
Bhaktapur, Nepal 69 F11 27 38N 85 24 E
Bhamo, Burma 67 G20 24 15N 97 15 E
Bhandara, India 66 J11 21 5N 79 42 E
Bhanpura, India 68 G6 24 31N 75 44 E
Bhanrer Ra., India 69 H8 23 40N 79 45 E
Bhaptiahi, India 69 F12 26 19N 86 44 E
Bharat = India ■, Asia 66 K11 20 0N 78 0 E
Bharatpur, Chhattisgarh,
India 69 H9 23 44N 81 46 E
Bharatpur, Raj., India 68 F7 27 15N 77 30 E
Bharno, India 69 H11 23 14N 84 53 E
Bharuch, India 66 J8 21 47N 73 0 E
Bhatinda, India 68 D6 30 15N 74 57 E
Bhatpara, India 69 H13 22 50N 88 25 E
Bhattu, India 68 E6 29 36N 75 19 E
Bhaun, Pakistan 68 C5 32 55N 72 40 E
Bhaunagar = Bhavnagar,
India 66 J8 21 45N 72 10 E
Bhawari, India 68 G5 25 42N 73 4 E
Bhera, Pakistan 68 C5 32 29N 72 57 E
Bhikangaon, India 68 J6 21 52N 75 57 E
Bhilsa = Vidisha, India 68 H7 23 28N 77 53 E
Bhilwara, India 68 G6 25 25N 74 38 E
Bhima →, India 66 L10 16 25N 77 17 E
Bhimbar, Pakistan 69 C6 32 59N 74 3 E
Bhind, India 69 F8 26 30N 78 46 E
Bhinga, India 69 F9 27 43N 81 56 E
Bhinmal, India 68 G5 25 0N 72 15 E
Bhiwandi, India 66 K8 19 20N 73 0 E
Bhiwani, India 68 E7 28 50N 76 9 E
Bhogava →, India 68 H5 22 26N 72 20 E
Bhola, Bangla. 67 H17 22 45N 90 35 E
Bholari, Pakistan 68 G3 25 19N 68 13 E
Bhopal, India 68 H7 23 20N 77 30 E
Bhubaneshwar, India 67 J14 20 15N 85 50 E
Bhuj, India 68 H3 23 15N 69 49 E

Bhusawal, India 66 J9 21 3N 75 46 E
Bhutan ■, Asia 67 F17 27 25N 90 30 E
Biafra, B. of = Bonny,
Bight of, Africa 83 E6 3 30N 9 20 E
Biak, Indonesia 63 E9 1 10 S 136 6 E
Biała, Poland 31 H4 50 24N 17 40 E
Biała →, Poland 31 H7 50 3N 20 55 E
Biała Piska, Poland 30 E9 53 37N 22 5 E
Biała Podlaska, Poland 31 F10 52 4N 23 6 E
Biała Rawska, Poland 31 G7 51 48N 20 29 E
Białobrzegi, Poland 31 G7 51 39N 20 54 E
Białogard, Poland 30 D2 54 2N 15 58 E
Białowieski △, Poland 31 F10 52 43N 23 50 E
Białowieża, Poland 31 F10 52 41N 23 49 E
Biały Bór, Poland 30 E3 53 53N 16 51 E
Białystok, Poland 31 E10 53 10N 23 10 E
Biancavilla, Italy 43 E7 37 38N 14 52 E
Bianco, Italy 43 D9 38 5N 16 9 E
Biankouma, Ivory C. 82 D3 7 50N 7 40W
Biaro, Indonesia 63 D7 2 5N 125 26 E
Biarritz, France 20 E2 43 29N 1 33W
Bias, Indonesia 63 J18 8 24 S 115 36 E
Biasca, Switz. 25 J4 46 22N 8 58 E
Biba, Egypt 80 J7 28 55N 31 0 E
Bibai, Japan 54 C10 43 19N 141 52 E
Bibbiena, Italy 41 E8 43 42N 11 49 E
Bibby I., Canada 103 A10 61 55N 93 0W
Bibel →, Spain 36 C3 42 24N 7 13W
Biberach, Germany 25 G5 48 5N 9 47 E
Bibiani, Ghana 82 D4 6 30N 2 8W
Biboohra, Australia 94 B4 16 56 S 145 25 E
Bibungwa, Dem. Rep. of
the Congo 86 C2 2 40 S 28 15 E
Bic, Canada 44 E4 41 58N 20 25 E
Bicaz, Romania 29 D11 46 53N 26 5 E
Bicaz Ardelean,
Romania 29 D10 46 51N 25 56 E
Bíccari, Italy 43 A8 41 23N 15 12 E
Bicester, U.K. 15 F6 51 54N 1 9W
Bichena, Ethiopia 81 E4 10 28N 38 10 E
Bicheno, Australia 95 G4 41 52 S 148 18 E
Bichia, India 69 H9 22 27N 80 42 E
Bichvinta, Georgia 35 J5 43 9N 40 21 E
Bickerton I., Australia 94 A2 13 45 S 136 10 E
Biçki, Hungary 28 C3 47 29N 18 38 E
Bida, Nigeria 83 D6 9 3N 5 58 E
Bidar, India 66 L10 17 55N 77 35 E
Biddeford, U.S.A. 115 D10 43 30N 70 28W
Biddwara, Ethiopia 81 F4 5 11N 38 34 E
Bideford, U.K. 15 F3 51 1N 4 13W
Bideford Bay, U.K. 15 F3 51 5N 4 20W
Bidhuna, India 69 F8 26 49N 79 31 E
Bidor, Malaysia 65 K3 4 6N 101 15 E
Bie, Sweden 10 E10 59 5N 16 12 E
Bié, Planalto de, Angola 85 G3 12 0 S 16 0 E
Bieber, U.S.A. 108 F3 41 7N 121 8W
Biebrza →, Poland 31 E9 53 13N 22 25 E
Biebrzański △, Poland 30 E9 53 36N 22 42 E
Biecz, Poland 31 J8 49 44N 21 15 E
Biel, Switz. 25 H3 47 8N 7 14 E
Bielawa, Poland 31 H3 50 43N 16 37 E
Bielefeld, Germany 24 C4 52 1N 8 33 E
Bielersee, Switz. 25 H3 47 6N 7 5 E
Biella, Italy 40 C5 45 34N 8 3 E
Bielsk Podlaski, Poland 31 F10 52 47N 23 12 E
Bielsko-Biała, Poland 31 J6 49 50N 19 2 E
Bien Hoa, Vietnam 65 G6 10 57N 106 49 E
Bienne = Biel, Switz. 25 H3 47 8N 7 14 E
Bienvenida, Spain 37 G4 38 18N 6 12W
Bienville, L., Canada 104 A5 55 5N 72 40W
Bierné, France 18 E6 47 48N 0 33W
Bierun, Poland 31 H6 50 6N 19 6 E
Bierutów, Poland 31 G4 51 7N 17 32 E
Biescas, Spain 38 C4 42 37N 0 20W
Biese →, Germany 24 C7 52 53N 11 46 E
Biesiesfontein, S. Africa 88 E2 30 57 S 17 58 E
Bieszczadzki △, Poland 31 J9 49 5N 22 43 E
Bietigheim-Bissingen,
Germany 25 G5 48 58N 9 8 E
Bievre, Belgium 17 E5 49 57N 5 1 E
Biferno →, Italy 41 G12 41 59N 15 2 E
Big →, Canada 105 B8 54 50N 58 55W
Big B., Canada 105 A7 55 43N 60 35W
Big Bear City, U.S.A. 111 L10 34 16N 116 51W
Big Bear Lake, U.S.A. 111 L10 34 15N 116 56W
Big Belt Mts., U.S.A. 108 C8 46 30N 111 25W
Big Bend, Swaziland 89 D5 26 50 S 31 58 E
Big Bend △, U.S.A. 113 L3 29 20N 103 5W
Big Black →, U.S.A. 113 K9 32 3N 91 4W
Big Blue →, U.S.A. 112 F6 39 35N 96 34W
Big Creek, U.S.A. 110 H7 37 11N 119 14W
Big Cypress △, U.S.A. 115 M5 26 0N 81 10W
Big Cypress Swamp,
U.S.A. 115 M5 26 15N 81 30W
Big Falls, U.S.A. 112 A8 48 12N 93 48W
Big Fork →, U.S.A. 112 A8 48 31N 93 43W
Big Horn Mts. =
Bighorn Mts., U.S.A. 108 D10 44 30N 107 30W
Big I., Canada 102 A5 61 7N 116 45W
Big Lake, U.S.A. 113 K4 31 12N 101 28W
Big Moose, U.S.A. 117 C10 43 49N 74 58W
Big Muddy Cr. →,
U.S.A. 112 A2 48 8N 104 36W
Big Pine, U.S.A. 110 H8 37 10N 118 17W
Big Piney, U.S.A. 108 E8 42 32N 110 7W
Big Rapids, U.S.A. 114 D3 43 42N 85 29W
Big Rideau L., Canada 117 B8 44 40N 76 15W
Big River, Canada 103 C7 53 50N 107 0W
Big Run, U.S.A. 116 F6 40 57N 78 55W
Big Sable Pt., U.S.A. 114 C2 44 3N 86 1W
Big Salmon →, Canada 102 A2 61 52N 134 55W
Big Sand L., Canada 103 B9 57 45N 99 45W
Big Sandy, U.S.A. 108 B8 48 11N 110 7W
Big Sandy →, U.S.A. 114 F4 38 25N 82 36W
Big Sandy Cr. →, U.S.A. 112 F3 38 7N 102 29W
Big Sioux →, U.S.A. 112 D6 42 29N 96 27W
Big South Fork △,
U.S.A. 115 G3 36 27N 84 47W
Big Spring, U.S.A. 113 J4 32 15N 101 28W
Big Stone City, U.S.A. 112 C6 45 18N 96 28W
Big Stone Gap, U.S.A. 115 G4 36 52N 82 47W
Big Stone L., U.S.A. 112 C6 45 30N 96 35W
Big Sur, U.S.A. 110 J5 36 15N 121 48W
Big Timber, U.S.A. 108 D9 45 50N 109 57W
Big Trout L., Canada 104 B2 53 40N 90 0W
Big Trout Lake, Canada 104 B2 53 45N 90 0W
Biga, Turkey 45 F11 40 13N 27 14 E
Bigadiç, Turkey 47 B10 39 22N 28 7 E
Biganos, France 20 D3 44 39N 0 59W
Biggar, Canada 103 C7 52 4N 108 0W
Biggar, U.K. 13 F5 55 38N 3 32W
Bigge I., Australia 92 B4 14 35 S 125 10 E
Biggenden, Australia 95 D5 25 31 S 152 4 E
Biggleswade, U.K. 15 E7 52 5N 0 14W
Biggs, U.S.A. 110 F5 39 25N 121 43W

Bighorn, U.S.A. 108 C10 46 10N 107 27W
Bighorn →, U.S.A. 108 C10 46 10N 107 28W
Bighorn Canyon △,
U.S.A. 108 D9 45 10N 108 0W
Bighorn L., U.S.A. 108 D9 44 55N 108 15W
Bighorn Mts., U.S.A. 108 D10 44 30N 107 30W
Bignona, Senegal 82 C1 12 52N 16 14W
Bigorre, France 20 E4 43 10N 0 5 E
Bigstone L., Canada 103 C9 53 42N 95 44W
Biguglia, Étang de,
France 21 F13 42 36N 9 23 E
Bigwa, Tanzania 86 D4 7 10 S 39 10 E
Bihać, Bos.-H. 41 D12 44 49N 15 57 E
Bihar, India 69 G11 25 5N 85 40 E
Bihar □, India 69 G12 25 0N 86 0 E
Biharamulo, Tanzania 86 C3 2 25 S 31 25 E
Biharamulo □, Tanzania 86 C3 2 24 S 31 26 E
Biharganj, India 69 G12 25 44N 86 59 E
Biharkeresztes, Hungary 28 C6 47 8N 21 44 E
Bihor □, Romania 28 C7 47 0N 22 10 E
Bihor, Munţii, Romania 28 D7 46 29N 22 47 E
Bijagós, Arquipélago
dos, Guinea-Biss. 82 C1 11 15N 16 10W
Bijaipur, India 68 F7 26 2N 77 20 E
Bijapur, Chhattisgarh,
India 67 K12 18 50N 80 50 E
Bijapur, Karnataka,
India 66 L9 16 50N 75 55 E
Bijär, Iran 70 C5 35 52N 47 35 E
Bijawar, India 69 G8 24 38N 79 30 E
Bijeljina, Bos.-H. 28 F4 44 46N 19 14 E
Bijelo Polje, Serbia & M. 44 C3 43 1N 19 45 E
Bijie, China 58 D5 27 20N 105 16 E
Bijnor, India 68 E8 29 27N 78 11 E
Bikaner, India 68 E5 28 2N 73 18 E
Bikapur, India 69 F10 26 30N 82 7 E
Bikeqi, China 56 D6 40 43N 111 20 E
Bikfayyâ, Lebanon 74 B4 33 55N 35 41 E
Bikin, Russia 54 A7 46 51N 134 2 E
Bikin →, Russia 54 A7 46 51N 134 2 E
Bikini Atoll, Marshall Is. 96 F8 12 0N 167 30 E
Bikita, Zimbabwe 89 C5 20 6 S 31 41 E
Bikoué, Cameroon 83 E7 3 55N 11 50 E
Bila Tserkva, Ukraine 33 H6 49 45N 30 10 E
Bilanga, Burkina Faso 83 C4 12 40N 0 1W
Bilara, India 68 F5 26 14N 73 53 E
Bilaspur, Chhattisgarh,
India 69 H10 22 2N 82 15 E
Bilaspur, Punjab, India 68 D7 31 19N 76 50 E
Biläsuvar, Azerbaijan 73 C13 39 27N 48 32 E
Bilauk Taungdan,
Thailand 64 F2 13 0N 99 0 E
Bilbao, Spain 38 B2 43 16N 2 56W
Bilbao ✈ (BIO), Spain 36 B8 43 18N 2 57W
Bilbeis, Egypt 80 H7 30 25N 31 34 E
Bilbor, Romania 29 C10 47 6N 25 30 E
Bilce-Zolote, Ukraine 29 B10 48 47N 25 53 E
Bilciuresti, Romania 29 F10 44 44N 25 48 E
Bîldudalur, Iceland 8 D2 65 41N 23 36W
Bílé Karpaty, Europe 27 B11 49 5N 18 0 E
Bileća, Bos.-H. 44 D2 42 53N 18 27 E
Bilecik, Turkey 72 B4 40 5N 30 5 E
Biłgoraj, Poland 31 H9 50 33N 22 42 E
Bilgram, India 69 F9 27 11N 80 2 E
Bilhaur, India 69 F9 26 51N 80 5 E
Bilhorod-Dnistrovskyy,
Ukraine 33 J6 46 11N 30 23 E
Bilibino, Russia 53 C17 68 3N 166 20 E
Bilibiza, Mozam. 87 E5 12 30 S 40 20 E
Bilisht, Albania 44 F5 40 37N 21 2 E
Billabong Roadhouse,
Australia 93 E2 27 25 S 115 49 E
Billdal, Sweden 11 G5 57 35N 11 57 E
Billiluna, Australia 92 C4 19 37 S 127 41 E
Billings, U.S.A. 108 D9 45 47N 108 30W
Billiton Is. = Belitung,
Indonesia 62 E3 3 10 S 107 50 E
Billsta, Sweden 10 A12 63 20N 18 28 E
Billund, Denmark 11 J3 55 44N 9 6 E
Bilma, Niger 79 E8 18 50N 13 30 E
Bilo Gora, Croatia 28 E2 45 53N 17 15 E
Biloela, Australia 94 C5 24 24 S 150 31 E
Bilohirsk, Ukraine 33 K8 45 3N 34 3 E
Bilopillya, Ukraine 33 G8 51 14N 34 20 E
Biloxi, U.S.A. 113 K10 30 24N 88 53W
Bilpa Morea Claypan,
Australia 94 D3 25 0 S 140 0 E
Biltine, Chad 79 F10 14 40N 20 50 E
Bilyarsk, Russia 34 C10 54 58N 50 22 E
Bima, Indonesia 63 F5 8 22 S 118 49 E
Bimban, Egypt 80 C3 24 24N 32 54 E
Bimbila, Ghana 83 D5 8 54N 0 5 E
Bimini Is., Bahamas 120 A4 25 42N 79 25W
Bin Xian, Heilongjiang,
China 57 B14 45 42N 127 32 E
Bin Xian, Shaanxi,
China 56 G5 35 2N 108 4 E
Bin Yauri, Nigeria 83 C5 10 46N 4 45 E
Bina-Etawah, India 68 G8 24 13N 78 14 E
Bināb, Iran 71 B6 36 35N 48 41 E
Binalbagan, Phil. 61 F5 10 12N 122 50 E
Binalong, Australia 95 E4 34 40 S 148 39 E
Binalud, Kūh-e, Iran 71 B8 36 30N 58 30 E
Binatang = Bintangor,
Malaysia 62 D4 2 10N 111 40 E
Binche, Belgium 17 D4 50 26N 4 10 E
Binchuan, China 58 E3 25 42N 100 38 E
Binder, Chad 83 D7 9 56N 14 27 E
Bindki, India 69 F9 26 2N 80 36 E
Bindslev, Denmark 11 G4 57 33N 10 11 E
Bindura, Zimbabwe 87 F3 17 18 S 31 18 E
Binefar, Spain 38 D5 41 51N 0 18 E
Bingara, Australia 95 D5 29 52 S 150 36 E
Bingen, Germany 25 F3 49 57N 7 55 E
Bingerville, Ivory C. 82 D4 5 18N 3 49W
Bingham, U.S.A. 115 C11 45 3N 69 53W
Binghamton, U.S.A. 117 D9 42 6N 75 55W
Bingöl, Turkey 70 B4 38 53N 40 29 E
Bingöl Dağları, Turkey 73 C9 39 16N 41 9 E
Binh Dinh = An Nhon,
Vietnam 64 F7 13 55N 109 7 E
Binh Khe, Vietnam 64 F7 13 57N 108 51 E
Binh Son, Vietnam 64 E7 15 20N 108 40 E
Binhai, China 57 G10 34 2N 119 49 E
Binic, France 18 D4 48 36N 2 49W
Binisatua, Spain 48 B11 39 50N 4 11 E
Binjai, Indonesia 62 D3 3 20N 98 30 E
Binji, Nigeria 83 C5 13 10N 4 55 E
Binnaway, Australia 95 E4 31 28 S 149 24 E
Binongko, Indonesia 63 F6 5 55 S 123 55 E
Binscarth, Canada 103 C8 50 37N 101 17W
Binshangul Gumuz □,
Ethiopia 81 E4 11 0N 35 30 E
Bint Goda, Sudan 81 E3 13 17N 31 33 E
Bintan, Indonesia 62 D2 1 0N 104 0 E

Bintangor, *Malaysia* .... **62 D4** 2 10N 111 40 E
Bintulu, *Malaysia* .... **62 D4** 3 10N 113 0 E
Bintuni, *Indonesia* .... **63 E8** 2 7S 133 32 E
Binyang, *China* .... **58 F7** 23 12N 108 47 E
Binz, *Germany* .... **24 A9** 54 24N 13 35 E
Binzert = Bizerte,
  Tunisia .... **79 A7** 37 15N 9 50 E
Binzhou, *China* .... **57 F10** 37 20N 118 2 E
Bío Bío □, *Chile* .... **126 D1** 37 35 S 72 0 W
Biograd na Moru,
  Croatia .... **41 E12** 43 56N 15 29 E
Biogradska Gora △,
  Serbia & M. .... **44 D3** 42 55N 19 40 E
Bioko, *Eq. Guin.* .... **83 E6** 3 30N 8 40 E
Biokovo, *Croatia* .... **41 E14** 43 23N 17 0 E
Bipindi, *Cameroon* .... **83 E7** 3 6N 10 50 E
Bir, *India* .... **66 K9** 19 4N 75 46 E
Bir, Ras, *Djibouti* .... **81 E5** 12 0N 43 20 E
Bîr Abu Hashim, *Egypt* .... **80 C3** 23 42N 34 6 E
Bîr Abu Minqar, *Egypt* .... **80 B2** 26 33N 27 33 E
Bîr Abu Muḥammad,
  Egypt .... **74 F3** 29 44N 34 14 E
Bi'r ad Dabbāghāt,
  Jordan .... **74 E4** 30 26N 35 32 E
Bîr Adal Deib, *Sudan* .... **80 C4** 22 35N 36 10 E
Bi'r al Butayyihāt,
  Jordan .... **74 F4** 29 47N 35 20 E
Bi'r al Mārī, *Jordan* .... **74 E4** 30 4N 35 33 E
Bi'r al Qaṭṭār, *Jordan* .... **74 F4** 29 47N 35 32 E
Bîr 'Asal, *Egypt* .... **80 B3** 25 55N 34 20 E
Bîr Atrun, *Sudan* .... **80 D2** 18 15N 26 40 E
Bîr Beïda, *Egypt* .... **74 E3** 30 25N 34 29 E
Bîr Diqnash, *Egypt* .... **80 A2** 31 3N 25 23 E
Bîr el 'Abd, *Egypt* .... **74 D2** 31 2N 33 0 E
Bîr el Basur, *Egypt* .... **80 B2** 29 51N 25 49 E
Bîr el Biarât, *Egypt* .... **74 F3** 29 30N 34 43 E
Bîr el Duweidar, *Egypt* .... **74 E1** 30 56N 32 32 E
Bîr el Garârât, *Egypt* .... **74 D2** 31 3N 33 34 E
Bîr el Gellaz, *Egypt* .... **80 A2** 30 50N 26 40 E
Bîr el Heisi, *Egypt* .... **74 F4** 29 22N 34 36 E
Bîr el Jafir, *Egypt* .... **74 E1** 30 50N 32 41 E
Bîr el Mâlhi, *Egypt* .... **74 E2** 30 38N 33 19 E
Bîr el Shaqqa, *Egypt* .... **80 A2** 30 54N 25 1 E
Bîr el Thamâda, *Egypt* .... **74 E2** 30 12N 33 27 E
Bîr Fuad, *Egypt* .... **80 A2** 30 35N 26 28 E
Bîr Gebeil Ḥiṣn, *Egypt* .... **74 E2** 30 2N 33 18 E
Bi'r Ghadîr, *Syria* .... **74 A6** 34 6N 37 3 E
Bîr Haimur, *Egypt* .... **80 C3** 22 45N 33 40 E
Bîr Ḥaṣana, *Egypt* .... **74 E2** 30 29N 33 46 E
Bîr Hōōker, *Egypt* .... **80 H7** 30 22N 30 21 E
Bîr Kanayis, *Egypt* .... **80 C3** 24 59N 33 15 E
Bîr Kaseiba, *Egypt* .... **74 E2** 31 0N 33 17 E
Bîr Kerawein, *Egypt* .... **80 B2** 27 10N 28 25 E
Bîr Lahfân, *Egypt* .... **74 E1** 30 44N 32 33 E
Bîr Madkûr, *Egypt* .... **74 D1** 30 2N 32 36 E
Bîr Maql, *Egypt* .... **80 C3** 23 7N 33 40 E
Bîr Mîneiga, *Sudan* .... **80 C4** 22 47N 35 12 E
Bîr Misaha, *Egypt* .... **80 C2** 22 13N 27 59 E
Bîr Mogreïn, *Mauritania* .... **78 C3** 25 10N 11 25 W
Bîr Murr, *Egypt* .... **80 C3** 23 28N 30 10 E
Bi'r Muṭribah, *Kuwait* .... **70 D5** 29 54N 47 17 E
Bîr Nakheila, *Egypt* .... **80 C3** 24 1N 30 50 E
Bîr Qaţia, *Egypt* .... **74 E1** 30 58N 32 45 E
Bîr Qatrani, *Egypt* .... **80 A2** 30 55N 26 10 E
Bîr Ranga, *Egypt* .... **80 C4** 24 25N 35 15 E
Bîr Sahara, *Egypt* .... **80 C2** 22 54N 28 40 E
Bîr Seiyâla, *Egypt* .... **80 B3** 26 10N 33 50 E
Bîr Shalatein, *Egypt* .... **80 C4** 23 5N 35 25 E
Bîr Shebb, *Egypt* .... **80 C2** 22 25N 29 40 E
Bîr Shût, *Egypt* .... **80 C2** 23 50N 35 15 E
Bîr Terfawi, *Egypt* .... **80 C2** 22 57N 28 55 E
Bîr Umm Qubûr, *Egypt* .... **80 C3** 24 35N 34 2 E
Bîr Ungât, *Egypt* .... **80 C3** 22 8N 33 48 E
Bîr Za'farâna, *Egypt* .... **80 J8** 29 10N 32 40 E
Bîr Zeidûn, *Egypt* .... **80 B3** 25 45N 33 40 E
Biramféro, *Guinea* .... **82 C3** 11 40N 9 10 W
Biratnagar, *Nepal* .... **69 F12** 26 27N 87 17 E
Birawa, *Dem. Rep. of
the Congo* .... **86 C2** 2 20 S 28 48 E
Birch →, *Canada* .... **102 B6** 58 28N 112 17 W
Birch Hills, *Canada* .... **103 C7** 52 59N 105 25 W
Birch I., *Canada* .... **103 C9** 52 26N 99 54 W
Birch L., *N.W.T.*,
  Canada .... **102 A5** 62 4N 116 33 W
Birch L., *Ont.*, *Canada* .... **104 B1** 51 23N 92 18 W
Birch Mts., *Canada* .... **102 B6** 57 30N 113 10 W
Birch River, *Canada* .... **103 C8** 52 24N 101 6 W
Birchip, *Australia* .... **95 F3** 35 56 S 142 55 E
Birchiş, *Romania* .... **28 E7** 45 58N 22 9 E
Bird, *Canada* .... **103 B10** 56 30N 94 13 W
Bird I. = Aves, I. de,
  W. Indies .... **121 C7** 15 45N 63 55 W
Bird I., *Antarctica* .... **5 B1** 54 0 S 38 0 W
Birdsville, *Australia* .... **94 D2** 25 51 S 139 20 E
Birdum Cr. →, *Australia* .... **92 C5** 15 14 S 133 0 E
Birecik, *Turkey* .... **70 B3** 37 2N 38 0 E
Birein, *Israel* .... **74 E3** 30 50N 34 28 E
Bireuen, *Indonesia* .... **62 C1** 5 14N 96 39 E
Biri →, *Sudan* .... **81 F2** 7 56N 26 32 E
Birifo, *Gambia* .... **82 C2** 13 30N 14 0 W
Birigui, *Brazil* .... **127 A5** 21 18 S 50 16 W
Bîrjand, *Iran* .... **71 C8** 32 53N 59 13 E
Birkenfeld, *Germany* .... **25 F3** 49 38N 7 9 E
Birkenhead, *U.K.* .... **14 D4** 53 23N 3 2 W
Birkerød, *Denmark* .... **11 J6** 55 50N 12 26 E
Birket Qârûn, *Egypt* .... **80 J7** 29 30N 30 40 E
Birkfeld, *Austria* .... **26 D8** 47 21N 15 45 E
Bîrlad = Bârlad,
  Romania .... **29 D12** 46 15N 27 38 E
Birmingham, *U.K.* .... **13 E6** 52 29N 1 52 W
Birmingham, *U.S.A.* .... **115 J2** 33 31N 86 48 W
Birmingham
  International ✈
  (BHX), *U.K.* .... **15 E6** 52 26N 1 45 W
Birmitrapur, *India* .... **67 H14** 22 24N 84 46 E
Birni Ngaouré, *Niger* .... **83 C5** 13 5N 2 51 E
Birni Nkonni, *Niger* .... **83 C6** 13 55N 5 15 E
Birnin Gwari, *Nigeria* .... **83 C6** 11 0N 6 45 E
Birnin Kebbi, *Nigeria* .... **83 C5** 12 32N 4 12 E
Birnin Kudu, *Nigeria* .... **83 C6** 11 30N 9 29 E
Birobidzhan, *Russia* .... **53 E14** 48 50N 132 50 E
Birr, *Ireland* .... **12 C4** 53 6N 7 54 W
Birrie →, *Australia* .... **95 D4** 29 43 S 146 37 E
Birsilpur, *India* .... **68 E5** 28 11N 72 15 E
Birsk, *Russia* .... **52 D6** 55 25N 55 30 E
Birštonas, *Lithuania* .... **30 D11** 54 37N 24 2 E
Birtle, *Canada* .... **103 C8** 50 30N 101 5 W
Birur, *India* .... **66 N9** 13 30N 75 55 E
Biryuchiy, *Ukraine* .... **33 J8** 46 10N 35 0 E
Biržai, *Lithuania* .... **9 H21** 56 11N 24 45 E
Birzebbugia, *Malta* .... **49 D2** 35 50N 14 32 E
Bisa, *Indonesia* .... **63 E7** 1 15 S 127 28 E
Bisáccia, *Italy* .... **43 A8** 41 1N 15 22 E
Bisalpur, *India* .... **69 E8** 28 14N 79 48 E
Bisbee, *U.S.A.* .... **109 L9** 31 27N 109 55 W
Biscarrosse, *France* .... **20 D2** 44 22N 1 20 W

Biscarrosse et de
  Parentis, Étang de,
  France .... **20 D2** 44 21N 1 10 W
Biscay, B. of, *Atl. Oc.* .... **6 F5** 45 0N 2 0 W
Biscayne B., *U.S.A.* .... **115 N5** 25 40N 80 12 W
Biscéglie, *Italy* .... **43 A9** 41 14N 16 30 E
Bischheim, *France* .... **19 D14** 48 37N 7 46 E
Bischofshofen, *Austria* .... **26 D6** 47 26N 13 14 E
Bischofswerda, *Germany* .... **24 D10** 51 7N 14 10 E
Bischwiller, *France* .... **19 D14** 48 46N 7 50 E
Biscoe Is., *Antarctica* .... **5 C17** 66 0 S 67 0 W
Biscotasing, *Canada* .... **104 C3** 47 18N 82 9 W
Bíševo, *Croatia* .... **41 F13** 42 57N 16 3 E
Bisha, *Eritrea* .... **81 D4** 15 30N 37 31 E
Bishah, W. →,
  Si. Arabia .... **80 C5** 21 24N 43 26 E
Bishan, *China* .... **58 C6** 29 33N 106 12 E
Bishkek, *Kyrgyzstan* .... **52 E8** 42 54N 74 46 E
Bishnupur, *India* .... **69 H12** 23 8N 87 20 E
Bisho, *S. Africa* .... **89 E4** 32 50 S 27 23 E
Bishop, *Calif.*, *U.S.A.* .... **110 H8** 37 22N 118 24 W
Bishop, *Tex.*, *U.S.A.* .... **113 M6** 27 35N 97 48 W
Bishop Auckland, *U.K.* .... **14 C6** 54 39N 1 40 W
Bishop's Falls, *Canada* .... **105 C8** 49 2N 55 30 W
Bishop's Stortford, *U.K.* .... **15 F8** 51 52N 0 10 E
Bisignano, *Italy* .... **43 C9** 39 31N 16 17 E
Bisina, L., *Uganda* .... **86 B3** 1 38N 33 56 E
Biskra, *Algeria* .... **78 B7** 34 50N 5 44 E
Biskupiec, *Poland* .... **30 E7** 53 53N 20 58 E
Bismarck, *U.S.A.* .... **112 B4** 46 48N 100 47 W
Bismarck Arch.,
  Papua N. G. .... **96 H7** 2 30 S 150 0 E
Bismarck, *Germany* .... **24 C7** 52 40N 11 33 E
Bismil, *Turkey* .... **73 D9** 37 51N 40 40 E
Biso, *Uganda* .... **86 B3** 1 44N 31 26 E
Bison, *U.S.A.* .... **112 C3** 45 31N 102 28 W
Bisotūn, *Iran* .... **70 C5** 34 23N 47 26 E
Bispgården, *Sweden* .... **10 A10** 63 2N 16 40 E
Bissagos = Bijagós,
  Arquipélago dos,
  Guinea-Biss. .... **82 C1** 11 15N 16 10 W
Bissau, *Guinea-Biss.* .... **82 C1** 11 45N 15 45 W
Bissaula, *Nigeria* .... **83 D7** 7 0N 10 27 E
Bissikrima, *Guinea* .... **82 C2** 10 50N 10 58 W
Bissorã, *Guinea-Biss.* .... **82 C1** 12 16N 15 35 W
Bistcho L., *Canada* .... **102 B5** 59 45N 118 50 W
Bistreţ, *Romania* .... **29 G8** 43 54N 23 23 E
Bistrica = Ilirska-
  Bistrica, *Slovenia* .... **41 C11** 45 34N 14 14 E
Bistriţa, *Romania* .... **29 C9** 47 9N 24 35 E
Bistriţa →, *Romania* .... **29 D11** 46 30N 26 57 E
Bistriţa Năsăud □,
  Romania .... **29 C9** 47 15N 24 30 E
Bistriţei, Munţii,
  Romania .... **29 C10** 47 15N 25 40 E
Biswan, *India* .... **69 F9** 27 29N 81 2 E
Bisztynek, *Poland* .... **30 D7** 54 8N 20 53 E
Bitburg, *Germany* .... **25 F2** 49 58N 6 31 E
Bitche, *France* .... **19 C14** 49 2N 7 25 E
Bithynia, *Turkey* .... **72 B4** 40 40N 31 0 E
Bitlis, *Turkey* .... **70 B4** 38 20N 42 3 E
Bitola, *Macedonia* .... **44 E5** 41 1N 21 20 E
Bitolj = Bitola,
  Macedonia .... **44 E5** 41 1N 21 20 E
Bitonto, *Italy* .... **43 A9** 41 6N 16 41 E
Bitter Creek, *U.S.A.* .... **108 F9** 41 33N 108 33 W
Bitter L. = Buheirat-
  Murrat-el-Kubra,
  Egypt .... **80 H8** 30 18N 32 26 E
Bitterfeld, *Germany* .... **24 D8** 51 37N 12 20 E
Bitterfontein, *S. Africa* .... **88 E2** 31 1 S 18 32 E
Bitterroot →, *U.S.A.* .... **108 C6** 46 52N 114 7 W
Bitterroot Range, *U.S.A.* .... **108 D6** 46 0N 114 20 W
Bitterwater, *U.S.A.* .... **110 J6** 36 23N 121 0 W
Bitti, *Italy* .... **42 B2** 40 29N 9 23 E
Bittou, *Burkina Faso* .... **83 C4** 11 17N 0 18 W
Biu, *Nigeria* .... **83 C7** 10 40N 12 3 E
Bivolari, *Romania* .... **29 C12** 47 31N 27 27 E
Bivolu, Vf., *Romania* .... **29 C10** 47 16N 25 58 E
Biwa-Ko, *Japan* .... **55 G8** 35 15N 136 10 E
Biwabik, *U.S.A.* .... **112 B8** 47 32N 92 21 W
Bixad, *Romania* .... **29 C8** 47 56N 23 28 E
Bixby, *U.S.A.* .... **113 H7** 35 57N 95 53 W
Biyang, *China* .... **56 H7** 32 38N 113 21 E
Biysk, *Russia* .... **52 D9** 52 40N 85 0 E
Bizana, *S. Africa* .... **89 E4** 30 50 S 29 52 E
Bizen, *Japan* .... **55 G7** 34 43N 134 8 E
Bizerte, *Tunisia* .... **79 A7** 37 15N 9 50 E
Bjargtangar, *Iceland* .... **8 D1** 65 30N 24 30 W
Bjärnum, *Sweden* .... **11 H7** 56 17N 13 43 E
Bjästa, *Sweden* .... **10 A12** 63 12N 18 29 E
Bjelasica, *Serbia & M.* .... **44 D3** 42 50N 19 40 E
Bjelašnica, *Bos.-H.* .... **28 G3** 43 43N 18 9 E
Bjelovar, *Croatia* .... **41 C13** 45 56N 16 49 E
Bjerringbro, *Denmark* .... **11 H3** 56 23N 9 39 E
Bjørbo, *Sweden* .... **10 D8** 60 27N 14 44 E
Björklinge, *Sweden* .... **10 D11** 60 2N 17 33 E
Björneborg = Pori,
  Finland .... **9 F19** 61 29N 21 48 E
Björneborg, *Sweden* .... **10 E8** 59 14N 14 16 E
Bjørnevatn, *Norway* .... **8 B23** 69 40N 30 0 E
Bjørnøya, *Arctic* .... **4 B8** 74 30N 19 0 E
Bjursås, *Sweden* .... **10 D9** 60 44N 15 25 E
Bjuv, *Sweden* .... **11 H6** 56 5N 12 55 E
Bla, *Mali* .... **82 C3** 12 56N 5 47 W
Blace, *Serbia & M.* .... **44 C5** 43 18N 21 17 E
Blachownia, *Poland* .... **31 H5** 50 49N 18 56 E
Black = Da →, *Vietnam* .... **58 G5** 21 15N 105 20 E
Black →, *Canada* .... **116 B5** 44 42N 79 19 W
Black →, *Ariz.*, *U.S.A.* .... **109 K8** 33 44N 110 13 W
Black →, *Ark.*, *U.S.A.* .... **113 H9** 35 38N 91 20 W
Black →, *Mich.*, *U.S.A.* .... **116 D2** 42 59N 82 27 W
Black →, *N.Y.*, *U.S.A.* .... **117 C8** 43 59N 76 4 W
Black →, *Wis.*, *U.S.A.* .... **112 D9** 43 57N 91 22 W
Black Bay Pen., *Canada* .... **104 C2** 48 38N 88 21 W
Black Birch L., *Canada* .... **103 B7** 56 53N 107 45 W
Black Canyon of the
  Gunnison △, *U.S.A.* .... **109 G10** 38 40N 107 35 W
Black Diamond, *Canada* .... **102 C6** 50 45N 114 14 W
Black Duck →, *Canada* .... **104 A2** 56 51N 89 2 W
Black Forest =
  Schwarzwald,
  Germany .... **25 G4** 48 30N 8 20 E
Black Forest, *U.S.A.* .... **112 F2** 39 0N 104 43 W
Black Hd., *Ireland* .... **12 C2** 53 9N 9 16 W
Black Hills, *U.S.A.* .... **112 D3** 44 0N 103 45 W
Black I., *Canada* .... **103 C9** 51 12N 96 30 W
Black L., *Canada* .... **103 B7** 59 12N 105 15 W
Black L., *Mich.*, *U.S.A.* .... **114 C3** 45 28N 84 16 W
Black L., *N.Y.*, *U.S.A.* .... **117 B9** 44 31N 75 36 W
Black Lake, *Canada* .... **103 B7** 59 11N 105 20 W
Black Mesa, *U.S.A.* .... **113 G3** 36 58N 102 58 W
Black Mt. = Mynydd Du,
  U.K. .... **15 F4** 51 52N 3 50 W
Black Mts., *U.K.* .... **15 F4** 51 55N 3 7 W
Black Range, *U.S.A.* .... **109 K10** 33 15N 107 50 W
Black River, *Jamaica* .... **120 a** 18 0N 77 50 W

Black River Falls, *U.S.A.* .... **112 C9** 44 18N 90 51 W
Black Rock, *Barbados* .... **121 g** 13 7N 59 37 W
Black Sea, *Eurasia* .... **6 G12** 43 30N 35 0 E
Black Tickle, *Canada* .... **105 B8** 53 28N 55 45 W
Black Volta →, *Africa* .... **82 D4** 8 41N 1 33 W
Black Warrior →,
  U.S.A. .... **115 J2** 32 32N 87 51 W
Blackall, *Australia* .... **94 C4** 24 25 S 145 45 E
Blackball, *N.Z.* .... **91 K3** 42 22 S 171 26 E
Blackbull, *Australia* .... **94 B3** 17 55 S 141 45 E
Blackburn, *U.K.* .... **14 D5** 53 45N 2 29 W
Blackburn with
  Darwen □, *U.K.* .... **14 D5** 53 45N 2 29 W
Blackdown Tableland △,
  Australia .... **94 C4** 23 52 S 149 8 E
Blackfoot →, *U.S.A.* .... **108 E7** 43 11N 112 21 W
Blackfoot →, *U.S.A.* .... **108 C7** 46 52N 113 53 W
Blackfoot River
  Reservoir →, *U.S.A.* .... **108 E8** 43 0N 111 43 W
Blackpool, *U.K.* .... **14 D4** 53 49N 3 3 W
Blackpool □, *U.K.* .... **14 D4** 53 49N 3 3 W
Blackriver, *U.S.A.* .... **116 B1** 44 46N 83 17 W
Blacks Harbour, *Canada* .... **105 C6** 45 3N 66 49 W
Blacksburg, *U.S.A.* .... **114 G5** 37 14N 80 25 W
Blacksod B., *Ireland* .... **12 B1** 54 6N 10 0 W
Blackstone, *U.S.A.* .... **114 G7** 37 4N 78 0 W
Blackstone Ra.,
  Australia .... **93 E4** 26 0 S 128 30 E
Blackwater = West
  Road →, *Canada* .... **102 C4** 53 18N 122 53 W
Blackwater, *Australia* .... **94 C4** 23 35 S 148 53 E
Blackwater →, *Meath,
  Ireland* .... **12 C4** 53 39N 6 41 W
Blackwater →,
  Waterford, Ireland .... **12 D4** 52 4N 7 52 W
Blackwater →, *U.K.* .... **12 B5** 54 31N 6 35 W
Blackwell, *U.S.A.* .... **113 G6** 36 48N 97 17 W
Blackwells Corner,
  U.S.A. .... **111 K7** 35 37N 119 47 W
Bladensburg △,
  Australia .... **94 C3** 22 30 S 142 59 E
Blaenau Ffestiniog, *U.K.* .... **14 E4** 53 0N 3 56 W
Blaenau Gwent □, *U.K.* .... **15 F4** 51 48N 3 12 W
Blagaj, *Bos.-H.* .... **44 C1** 43 16N 17 55 E
Blagnac, *France* .... **20 E5** 43 37N 1 23 E
Blagnac, Toulouse ✈
  (TLS), *France* .... **20 E5** 43 37N 1 22 E
Blagodarnoye =
  Blagodarnyy, *Russia* .... **35 H6** 45 7N 43 37 E
Blagodarnyy, *Russia* .... **35 H6** 45 7N 43 37 E
Blagoevgrad, *Bulgaria* .... **44 D7** 42 2N 23 5 E
Blagoveshchensk, *Russia* .... **53 D13** 50 20N 127 30 E
Blahkiuh, *Indonesia* .... **63 J18** 8 31 S 115 12 E
Blain, *France* .... **18 E5** 47 29N 1 45 W
Blain, *U.S.A.* .... **116 F7** 40 20N 77 31 W
Blaine, *Minn.*, *U.S.A.* .... **112 C8** 45 10N 93 13 W
Blaine, *Wash.*, *U.S.A.* .... **110 B4** 48 59N 122 45 W
Blaine Lake, *Canada* .... **103 C7** 52 51N 106 52 W
Blair, *U.S.A.* .... **112 E6** 41 33N 96 8 W
Blair Athol, *Australia* .... **94 C4** 22 42 S 147 31 E
Blair Atholl, *U.K.* .... **13 E5** 56 46N 3 50 W
Blairgowrie, *U.K.* .... **13 E5** 56 35N 3 21 W
Blairsden, *U.S.A.* .... **110 F6** 39 47N 120 37 W
Blairsville, *U.S.A.* .... **116 F5** 40 26N 79 16 W
Blaj, *Romania* .... **29 D8** 46 10N 23 57 E
Blakang Mati, Pulau,
  Singapore .... **65 d** 1 15N 103 50 E
Blake Pt., *U.S.A.* .... **112 A10** 48 11N 88 25 W
Blakely, *Ga.*, *U.S.A.* .... **115 K3** 31 23N 84 56 W
Blakely, *Pa.*, *U.S.A.* .... **117 E9** 41 28N 75 37 W
Blâmont, *France* .... **19 D13** 48 35N 6 50 E
Blanc, *C.*, *Spain* .... **48 B9** 39 21N 2 51 E
Blanc, Mont, *Europe* .... **21 C10** 45 48N 6 50 E
Blanc-Sablon, *Canada* .... **105 B8** 51 24N 57 12 W
Blanca, B., *Argentina* .... **128 D4** 39 10 S 61 30 W
Blanca Peak, *U.S.A.* .... **109 H11** 37 35N 105 29 W
Blanche, C., *Australia* .... **95 E1** 33 1 S 134 9 E
Blanche, L., *S. Austral.*,
  Australia .... **95 D2** 29 15 S 139 40 E
Blanche, L., *W. Austral.*,
  Australia .... **92 D3** 22 25 S 123 17 E
Blanchisseuse,
  Trin. & Tob. .... **125 K15** 10 48N 61 18 W
Blanco, *S. Africa* .... **88 E3** 33 55 S 22 23 E
Blanco, *U.S.A.* .... **113 K5** 30 6N 98 25 W
Blanco →, *Argentina* .... **126 C2** 30 20 S 68 42 W
Blanco, C., *Costa Rica* .... **120 E2** 9 34N 85 8 W
Blanco, C., *U.S.A.* .... **108 E1** 42 51N 124 34 W
Blanda →, *Iceland* .... **8 D3** 65 37N 20 9 W
Blandford Forum, *U.K.* .... **15 G5** 50 51N 2 9 W
Blanding, *U.S.A.* .... **109 H9** 37 37N 109 29 W
Blanes, *Spain* .... **38 D7** 41 40N 2 48 E
Blangy-sur-Bresle,
  France .... **19 C8** 49 55N 1 37 E
Blanice →, *Czech Rep.* .... **26 B7** 49 10N 14 5 E
Blankenhom, *Sweden* .... **11 G10** 57 36N 16 31 E
Blankenberge, *Belgium* .... **17 C3** 51 20N 3 9 E
Blankenburg, *Germany* .... **24 D6** 51 47N 10 57 E
Blanquefort, *France* .... **20 D3** 44 55N 0 38 W
Blanquillo, *Uruguay* .... **127 C4** 32 53 S 55 37 W
Blansko, *Czech Rep.* .... **27 B9** 49 22N 16 40 E
Blantyre, *Malawi* .... **87 F4** 15 45 S 35 0 E
Blarney, *Ireland* .... **12 E3** 51 56N 8 33 W
Blasdell, *U.S.A.* .... **116 D6** 42 48N 78 50 W
Błaszki, *Poland* .... **31 G5** 51 38N 18 30 E
Blatná, *Czech Rep.* .... **26 B6** 49 25N 13 52 E
Blato, *Croatia* .... **41 F13** 42 56N 16 48 E
Blaubeuren, *Germany* .... **25 G5** 48 24N 9 46 E
Blaustein, *Germany* .... **25 G5** 48 25N 9 53 E
Blåvands Huk, *Denmark* .... **11 J2** 55 33N 8 4 E
Blaydon, *U.K.* .... **14 C6** 54 58N 1 42 W
Blaye, *France* .... **20 C3** 45 8N 0 40 W
Blaye-les-Mines, *France* .... **20 D6** 44 1N 2 8 E
Blayney, *Australia* .... **95 E4** 33 32 S 149 14 E
Blaze, Pt., *Australia* .... **92 B5** 12 56 S 130 11 E
Błażowa, *Poland* .... **31 J9** 49 53N 22 7 E
Bleckede, *Germany* .... **24 B6** 53 17N 10 43 E
Bled, *Slovenia* .... **41 B11** 46 27N 14 7 E
Bleiburg, *Austria* .... **26 E7** 46 35N 14 49 E
Blejeşti, *Romania* .... **29 F10** 44 19N 25 27 E
Blekinge □, *Sweden* .... **11 H9** 56 20N 15 20 E
Blekinge län □, *Sweden* .... **11 H9** 56 20N 15 20 E
Blenheim, *Canada* .... **116 D3** 42 20N 82 0 W
Blenheim, *N.Z.* .... **91 J4** 41 38 S 173 57 E
Bléone →, *France* .... **21 D10** 44 5N 6 0 E
Blérancourt, *France* .... **19 C10** 49 30N 3 9 E
Bletchley, *U.K.* .... **15 F7** 51 59N 0 44 W
Blida, *Algeria* .... **78 A6** 36 30N 2 49 E
Blidö, *Sweden* .... **10 E12** 59 37N 18 53 E
Blidsberg, *Sweden* .... **11 G7** 57 56N 13 30 E
Blieskastel, *Germany* .... **25 F3** 49 14N 7 12 E
Bligh Sound, *N.Z.* .... **91 L1** 44 47 S 167 32 E
Blind River, *Canada* .... **104 C3** 46 10N 82 58 W
Blinishti, *Albania* .... **44 E3** 41 52N 19 59 E
Bliss, *U.S.A.* .... **108 E6** 42 56N 114 57 W
Bliss, *N.Y.*, *U.S.A.* .... **116 D6** 42 34N 78 15 W
Blissfield, *U.S.A.* .... **116 F3** 41 50N 83 51 W

Blitar, *Indonesia* .... **63 H15** 8 5 S 112 11 E
Blitta, *Togo* .... **83 D5** 8 23N 1 6 E
Block I., *U.S.A.* .... **117 E13** 41 11N 71 35 W
Block Island Sd., *U.S.A.* .... **117 E13** 41 15N 71 40 W
Bloemfontein, *S. Africa* .... **88 D4** 29 6 S 26 7 E
Bloemhof, *S. Africa* .... **88 D4** 27 38 S 25 32 E
Blois, *France* .... **18 E8** 47 35N 1 20 E
Blomskog, *Sweden* .... **10 E6** 59 16N 12 2 E
Blomstermåla, *Sweden* .... **11 H10** 56 59N 16 21 E
Blönduós, *Iceland* .... **8 D3** 65 40N 20 12 W
Blongas, *Indonesia* .... **63 K19** 8 53 S 116 2 E
Błonie, *Poland* .... **31 F7** 52 12N 20 37 E
Bloodvein →, *Canada* .... **103 C9** 51 47N 96 43 W
Bloody Foreland,
  Ireland .... **12 A3** 55 10N 8 17 W
Bloomer, *U.S.A.* .... **112 C9** 45 6N 91 29 W
Bloomfield, *Canada* .... **116 C7** 43 59N 77 14 W
Bloomfield,
  Iowa, U.S.A. .... **112 E8** 40 45N 92 25 W
Bloomfield, *N. Mex.*,
  U.S.A. .... **109 H10** 36 43N 107 59 W
Bloomfield, *Nebr.*,
  U.S.A. .... **112 D6** 42 36N 97 39 W
Bloomington, *Ill.*, *U.S.A.* .... **112 E10** 40 28N 89 0 W
Bloomington, *Ind.*,
  U.S.A. .... **114 F2** 39 10N 86 32 W
Bloomington, *Minn.*,
  U.S.A. .... **112 C8** 44 50N 93 17 W
Bloomsburg, *U.S.A.* .... **117 F8** 41 0N 76 27 W
Bloomsbury, *Australia* .... **94 J6** 20 48 S 148 38 E
Blora, *Indonesia* .... **63 G14** 6 57 S 111 25 E
Blossburg, *U.S.A.* .... **116 E7** 41 41N 77 4 W
Blouberg, *S. Africa* .... **89 C4** 23 8 S 28 59 E
Blountstown, *U.S.A.* .... **115 K3** 30 27N 85 3 W
Bludenz, *Austria* .... **26 D2** 47 10N 9 50 E
Blue Earth, *U.S.A.* .... **112 D8** 43 38N 94 6 W
Blue Hole △, *Belize* .... **120 C2** 17 8N 88 30 W
Blue Lagoon △, *Zambia* .... **87 F2** 15 28 S 27 26 E
Blue Mesa Reservoir,
  U.S.A. .... **109 G10** 38 28N 107 20 W
Blue Mountain Lake,
  U.S.A. .... **117 C10** 43 52N 74 30 W
Blue Mountain Pk.,
  Jamaica .... **120 a** 18 3N 76 36 W
Blue Mts., *Jamaica* .... **120 a** 18 3N 76 36 W
Blue Mts., *Maine*, *U.S.A.* .... **117 B14** 44 50N 70 35 W
Blue Mts., *Oreg.*, *U.S.A.* .... **108 D4** 45 15N 119 0 W
Blue Mts., *Pa.*, *U.S.A.* .... **117 F7** 40 30N 76 30 W
Blue Mud B., *Australia* .... **94 A2** 13 30 S 136 0 E
Blue Nile = Nîl el
  Azraq →, *Sudan* .... **81 D3** 15 38N 32 31 E
Blue Rapids, *U.S.A.* .... **112 F6** 39 41N 96 39 W
Blue Ridge Mts., *U.S.A.* .... **115 G5** 36 30N 80 15 W
Blue River, *Canada* .... **102 C5** 52 6N 119 18 W
Bluefield, *U.S.A.* .... **114 G5** 37 15N 81 17 W
Bluefields, *Nic.* .... **120 D3** 12 20N 83 50 W
Bluff, *Australia* .... **94 C4** 23 35 S 149 4 E
Bluff, *N.Z.* .... **91 M2** 46 37 S 168 20 E
Bluff, *U.S.A.* .... **109 H9** 37 17N 109 33 W
Bluff Knoll, *Australia* .... **93 F2** 34 24 S 118 15 E
Bluff Pt., *Australia* .... **93 E1** 27 50 S 114 5 E
Bluffton, *U.S.A.* .... **114 E3** 40 44N 85 11 W
Blumenau, *Brazil* .... **127 B6** 27 0 S 49 0 W
Blunt, *U.S.A.* .... **112 C5** 44 31N 99 59 W
Bly, *U.S.A.* .... **108 E3** 42 24N 121 3 W
Blyde River Canyon △,
  S. Africa .... **89 C5** 24 37 S 31 2 E
Blyth, *Canada* .... **116 C3** 43 44N 81 26 W
Blyth, *U.K.* .... **14 B6** 55 8N 1 31 W
Blythe, *U.S.A.* .... **111 M12** 33 37N 114 36 W
Blytheville, *U.S.A.* .... **113 H10** 35 56N 89 55 W
Bo, *S. Leone* .... **82 D2** 7 55N 11 50 W
Bo Duc, *Vietnam* .... **65 G6** 11 58N 106 50 E
Bo Hai, *China* .... **57 E10** 39 0N 119 0 E
Bo Xian = Bozhou,
  China .... **56 H8** 33 55N 115 41 E
Boa Vista, *Brazil* .... **124 C6** 2 48N 60 30 W
Boac, *Phil.* .... **61 E4** 13 27N 121 50 E
Boaco, *Nic.* .... **120 D2** 12 29N 85 35 W
Bo'ai, *China* .... **56 G7** 35 10N 113 3 E
Boal, *Spain* .... **36 B4** 43 25N 6 49 W
Boalsburg, *U.S.A.* .... **116 F7** 40 46N 77 47 W
Boane, *Mozam.* .... **89 D5** 26 6 S 32 19 E
Boardman, *U.S.A.* .... **116 E4** 41 2N 80 40 W
Bobadah, *Australia* .... **95 E4** 32 19 S 146 41 E
Bobai, *China* .... **58 F7** 22 17N 109 59 E
Bobbili, *India* .... **67 K13** 18 35N 83 30 E
Bóbbio, *Italy* .... **40 D6** 44 46N 9 23 E
Bobcaygeon, *Canada* .... **114 B6** 44 33N 78 33 W
Böblingen, *Germany* .... **25 G5** 48 40N 9 1 E
Bobo-Dioulasso,
  Burkina Faso .... **82 C4** 11 8N 4 13 W
Bobolice, *Poland* .... **30 E3** 53 58N 16 37 E
Boboshevo, *Bulgaria* .... **44 D7** 42 20N 23 0 E
Bobov Dol, *Bulgaria* .... **44 D6** 42 20N 23 0 E
Bóbr →, *Poland* .... **31 F2** 52 4N 15 4 E
Bobraomby, Tanjon' i,
  Madag. .... **89 A8** 12 40 S 49 10 E
Bobrinets, *Ukraine* .... **33 H7** 48 4N 32 5 E
Bobrov, *Russia* .... **34 E5** 51 5N 40 2 E
Bobrovitsa, *Ukraine* .... **33 G6** 50 45N 31 23 E
Bobruysk = Babruysk,
  Belarus .... **33 F5** 53 10N 29 15 E
Boby, Pic, *Madag.* .... **85 J9** 22 12 S 46 55 E
Boca do Acre, *Brazil* .... **124 E5** 8 50 S 67 27 W
Boca Raton, *U.S.A.* .... **115 M5** 26 21N 80 5 W
Bocanda, *Ivory C.* .... **82 D4** 7 5N 4 31 W
Bocas del Toro, *Panama* .... **120 E3** 9 15N 82 20 W
Boceguillas, *Spain* .... **36 D7** 41 20N 3 39 W
Bochnia, *Poland* .... **31 J7** 49 58N 20 27 E
Bocholt, *Germany* .... **24 D2** 51 50N 6 36 E
Bochum, *Germany* .... **24 C6** 52 1N 10 8 E
Bockenem, *Germany* .... **24 C6** 52 1N 10 8 E
Bočki, *Poland* .... **31 F10** 52 39N 23 3 E
Bocognano, *France* .... **21 F13** 42 5N 9 4 E
Bocoyna, *Mexico* .... **118 B3** 27 52N 107 35 W
Bôcşa, *Romania* .... **28 E6** 45 21N 21 47 E
Boda, *Dalarna, Sweden* .... **10 C9** 61 1N 15 13 E
Böda, *Sweden* .... **11 G11** 57 15N 17 3 E
Boda, *Västernorrland,
  Sweden* .... **11 B10** 62 53N 16 39 E
Bodafors, *Sweden* .... **11 G8** 57 48N 14 23 E
Bodaybo, *Russia* .... **53 D7** 59 56N 118 0 E
Boddam, *U.K.* .... **13 B7** 59 56N 1 17 W
Boddington, *Australia* .... **93 F2** 32 50 S 116 30 E
Bode Sadu, *Nigeria* .... **83 D5** 9 3N 4 48 E
Bodega Bay, *U.S.A.* .... **110 G3** 38 20N 123 3 W
Boden, *Sweden* .... **8 D19** 65 50N 21 42 E
Bodensee, *Europe* .... **25 H5** 47 35N 9 25 E
Bodenteich, *Germany* .... **24 C6** 52 49N 10 41 E
Bodhan, *India* .... **66 K10** 18 40N 77 44 E
Bodinayakkanur, *India* .... **66 P10** 10 2N 77 17 E
Bodmin, *U.K.* .... **15 G3** 50 28N 4 43 W
Bodmin Moor, *U.K.* .... **15 G3** 50 33N 4 36 W

Bodø, *Norway* .... **8 C16** 67 17N 14 24 E
Bodrog →, *Hungary* .... **28 B6** 48 11N 21 22 E
Bodrum, *Turkey* .... **47 D9** 37 3N 27 30 E
Bódva →, *Hungary* .... **28 B5** 48 19N 20 45 E
Boën, *France* .... **21 C8** 45 44N 4 1 E
Boende, *Dem. Rep. of
the Congo* .... **84 E4** 0 24 S 21 12 E
Boerne, *U.S.A.* .... **113 L5** 29 47N 98 44 W
Boesmans →, *S. Africa* .... **88 E4** 33 42 S 26 39 E
Boffa, *Guinea* .... **82 C2** 10 16N 14 3 W
Bogalusa, *U.S.A.* .... **113 K10** 30 47N 89 52 W
Bogan →, *Australia* .... **95 D4** 30 20 S 146 55 E
Bogan Gate, *Australia* .... **95 E4** 33 7 S 147 49 E
Bogandé, *Burkina Faso* .... **83 C4** 13 2N 0 8 W
Bogantungan, *Australia* .... **94 C4** 23 41 S 147 17 E
Bogata, *U.S.A.* .... **113 J7** 33 28N 95 13 W
Bogatić, *Serbia & M.* .... **44 B3** 44 51N 19 30 E
Boğazkale, *Turkey* .... **72 B6** 40 2N 34 36 E
Boğazlıyan, *Turkey* .... **72 C6** 39 11N 35 14 E
Bogen, *Sweden* .... **10 D6** 60 4N 12 33 E
Bogen, *Indonesia* .... **63 G12** 6 36 S 106 48 E
Bogerodsk, *Russia* .... **32 F10** 53 47N 38 8 E
Bogorodsk, *Russia* .... **34 B6** 56 4N 43 30 E
Bogoso, *Ghana* .... **82 D4** 5 38N 2 3 W
Bogotá, *Colombia* .... **124 C4** 4 34N 74 0 W
Bogotol, *Russia* .... **52 D9** 56 15N 89 50 E
Bogou, *Togo* .... **83 C5** 10 40N 0 12 E
Bogra, *Bangla.* .... **67 G16** 24 51N 89 22 E
Boguchany, *Russia* .... **53 D10** 58 40N 97 30 E
Boguchar, *Russia* .... **34 F5** 49 55N 40 32 E
Bogué, *Mauritania* .... **82 B2** 16 45N 14 10 W
Boguslav, *Ukraine* .... **33 H6** 49 47N 30 56 E
Boguszów-Gorce,
  Poland .... **31 H3** 50 45N 16 12 E
Bohain-en-Vermandois,
  France .... **19 C10** 49 59N 3 28 E
Bohdan, *Ukraine* .... **29 B9** 48 2N 24 22 E
Bohemian Forest =
  Böhmerwald,
  Germany .... **25 F9** 49 8N 13 14 E
Bohinjska Bistrica,
  Slovenia .... **41 B11** 46 17N 14 1 E
Böhmerwald, *Germany* .... **25 F9** 49 8N 13 14 E
Bohmte, *Germany* .... **24 C4** 52 22N 8 19 E
Bohodukhiv, *Ukraine* .... **33 G8** 50 9N 35 33 E
Bohol □, *Phil.* .... **61 G6** 9 50N 124 10 E
Bohol Sea, *Phil.* .... **61 G6** 9 0N 124 0 E
Bohonong,
  Burkina Faso .... **83 C5** 12 30N 0 40 E
Böhönye, *Hungary* .... **28 D2** 46 25N 17 28 E
Bohorodchany, *Ukraine* .... **29 B9** 48 48N 24 32 E
Bohuslän, *Sweden* .... **11 F5** 58 25N 12 0 E
Boi, *Nigeria* .... **83 D6** 9 35N 9 27 E
Boi, Pta. de, *Brazil* .... **127 A6** 23 55 S 45 15 W
Boiaçu, *Brazil* .... **124 D6** 0 27 S 61 46 W
Boileau, C., *Australia* .... **92 C3** 17 40 S 122 7 E
Boing'o, *Sudan* .... **81 F3** 9 58N 33 44 E
Boiro, *Spain* .... **36 C2** 42 39N 8 54 W
Boise, *U.S.A.* .... **108 E5** 43 37N 116 13 W
Boise City, *U.S.A.* .... **113 G3** 36 44N 102 31 W
Boissevain, *Canada* .... **103 D8** 49 15N 100 5 W
Bóite →, *Italy* .... **41 B9** 46 5N 12 5 E
Boitzenburg, *Germany* .... **24 B9** 53 16N 13 35 E
Boizenburg, *Germany* .... **24 B6** 53 23N 10 43 E
Bojador, C., *W. Sahara* .... **78 C3** 26 0N 14 30 W
Bojana →, *Albania* .... **44 E3** 41 52N 19 22 E
Bojano, *Italy* .... **43 A7** 41 29N 14 29 E
Bojanowo, *Poland* .... **31 G3** 51 43N 16 42 E
Bojnik, *Serbia & M.* .... **44 C5** 43 0N 21 45 E
Bojnūrd, *Iran* .... **71 B8** 37 30N 57 20 E
Bojonegoro, *Indonesia* .... **63 G14** 7 11 S 111 54 E
Boju, *Nigeria* .... **83 D6** 7 22N 7 55 E
Boka, *Serbia & M.* .... **28 E5** 45 22N 20 52 E
Boka Kotorska,
  Serbia & M. .... **44 D2** 42 23N 18 32 E
Bokala, *Ivory C.* .... **82 D4** 8 31N 4 33 W
Bokani, *Nigeria* .... **83 D6** 9 27N 5 13 E
Bokaro, *India* .... **69 H11** 23 46N 85 55 E
Boké, *Guinea* .... **82 C2** 10 56N 14 17 W
Bokhara →, *Australia* .... **95 D4** 29 55 S 146 42 E
Bokkos, *Nigeria* .... **83 D6** 9 17N 9 1 E
Boknafjorden, *Norway* .... **9 G11** 59 14N 5 40 E
Bokora △, *Uganda* .... **86 B3** 2 12N 34 32 E
Bokoro, *Chad* .... **79 F9** 12 25N 17 14 E
Bokpyin, *Burma* .... **65 G2** 11 18N 98 42 E
Boksitogorsk, *Russia* .... **32 C7** 59 32N 33 56 E
Bol, *Croatia* .... **41 E13** 43 18N 16 38 E
Bolama, *Guinea-Biss.* .... **82 C1** 11 30N 15 30 W
Bolan →, *Pakistan* .... **68 E2** 28 38N 67 42 E
Bolan Pass, *Pakistan* .... **68 E2** 29 50N 67 20 E
Bolaños →, *Mexico* .... **118 C4** 21 14N 104 8 W
Bolaños de Calatrava,
  Spain .... **37 G7** 38 54N 3 40 W
Bolayır, *Turkey* .... **45 F10** 40 31N 26 45 E
Bolbec, *France* .... **18 C7** 49 30N 0 30 E
Boldeşti-Scăeni,
  Romania .... **29 E11** 45 3N 26 2 E
Bolders →, *Ukraine* .... **33 H7** 48 3N 33 10 E
Boldu, *Romania* .... **60 B3** 15 11N 81 37 E
Boldājī, *Iran* .... **71 D6** 31 56N 51 3 E
Bole, *China* .... **60 B3** 45 11N 81 37 E
Bole, *Ethiopia* .... **81 F4** 6 36N 37 20 E
Bolekhiv, *Ukraine* .... **33 H2** 49 0N 23 57 E
Bolesławiec, *Poland* .... **31 G2** 51 17N 15 37 E
Bolgatanga, *Ghana* .... **83 C4** 10 44N 0 53 W
Bolgrad = Bolhrad,
  Ukraine .... **29 E13** 45 40N 28 32 E
Bolhrad, *Ukraine* .... **29 E13** 45 40N 28 32 E
Bolinao, *Phil.* .... **61 C3** 16 23N 119 54 E
Bolintin-Vale, *Romania* .... **29 F10** 44 27N 25 46 E
Bolívar, *Argentina* .... **126 D3** 36 15 S 60 53 W
Bolívar, *Mo.*, *U.S.A.* .... **113 G8** 37 37N 93 25 W
Bolívar, *N.Y.*, *U.S.A.* .... **116 D6** 42 4N 78 10 W
Bolívar, *Tenn.*, *U.S.A.* .... **113 H10** 35 12N 89 0 W
Bolivia ■, *S. Amer.* .... **124 G6** 17 6 S 64 0 W
Bolivian Plateau =
  Altiplano, *Bolivia* .... **122 E4** 17 0 S 68 0 W
Boljevac, *Serbia & M.* .... **44 C5** 43 51N 21 58 E
Bolków, *Poland* .... **31 H3** 50 55N 16 6 E
Bollène, *France* .... **21 D8** 44 18N 4 45 E
Bollnäs, *Sweden* .... **10 C10** 61 21N 16 24 E
Bollon, *Australia* .... **95 D4** 28 2 S 147 29 E
Bollstabruk, *Sweden* .... **10 B11** 62 59N 17 40 E
Bolmen, *Sweden* .... **11 H7** 56 55N 13 40 E

Bolobo, *Dem. Rep. of the Congo* .... 84 E3 2 6 S 16 20 E
Bologna, *Italy* .... 41 D8 44 29N 11 20 E
Bologna ✈ (BLQ), *Italy* 41 D8 44 34N 11 16 E
Bologoye, *Russia* .... 32 D8 57 55N 34 5 E
Bolon, Ozero, *Russia* .. 60 B8 49 50N 133 0 E
Bolonchenticul, *Mexico* 119 D7 20 0N 89 49W
Bolótana, *Italy* .... 42 B1 40 20N 8 52 E
Boloven, Cao Nguyen, *Laos* .... 64 E6 15 10N 106 30 E
Bolpur, *India* .... 69 H12 23 40N 87 45 E
Bolsena, *Italy* .... 41 F8 42 39N 11 59 E
Bolsena, L. di, *Italy* .. 41 F8 42 36N 11 56 E
Bolshakovo, *Russia* .. 30 D8 54 53N 21 40 E
Bolshaya Chernigovka, *Russia* .... 34 D10 52 6N 50 52 E
Bolshaya Glushitsa, *Russia* .... 34 D10 52 28N 50 30 E
Bolshaya Martynovka, *Russia* .... 35 G5 47 19N 41 37 E
Bolshaya Vradiyevka, *Ukraine* .... 33 J6 47 50N 30 40 E
Bolshevik, Ostrov, *Russia* .... 53 B11 78 30N 102 0 E
Bolshoy Anyuy ➤, *Russia* .... 53 C17 68 30N 160 49 E
Bolshoy Begichev, Ostrov, *Russia* ..... 53 B12 74 20N 112 30 E
Bolshoy Kavkas = Caucasus Mountains, *Eurasia* .... 35 J7 42 50N 44 0 E
Bolshoy Lyakhovskiy, Ostrov, *Russia* ... 53 B15 73 35N 142 0 E
Bolshoy Tyuters, Ostrov, *Russia* .... 9 G22 59 51N 27 13 E
Bolsward, *Neths.* ..... 17 A5 53 3N 5 32 E
Bolt Head, *U.K.* 15 G4 50 12N 3 48W
Boltaña, *Spain* ...... 38 C5 42 28N 0 4 E
Boltigen, *Switz.* ..... 25 J3 46 38N 7 24 E
Bolton, *Canada* 116 C5 43 54N 79 45W
Bolton, *U.K.* 14 D5 53 35N 2 26W
Bolton Landing, *U.S.A.* 117 C11 43 32N 73 35W
Bolu, *Turkey* .... 72 B4 40 45N 31 35 E
Bolungavík, *Iceland* .. 8 C2 66 9N 23 15W
Boluo, *China* .... 59 F10 23 3N 114 21 E
Bolvadin, *Turkey* .... 70 B1 38 45N 31 4 E
Bolzano, *Italy* ...... 41 B8 46 31N 11 22 E
Bom Jesus da Lapa, *Brazil* .... 125 F10 13 15 S 43 25W
Boma, *Dem. Rep. of the Congo* .... 84 F2 5 50 S 13 4 E
Bombala, *Australia* ... 95 F4 36 56 S 149 15 E
Bombarral, *Portugal* .. 37 F1 39 15N 9 9W
Bombay = Mumbai, *India* .... 66 K8 18 55N 72 50 E
Bombedor, Pta., *Venezuela* 125 L15 9 53N 61 37W
Bomboma, *Dem. Rep. of the Congo* .... 84 D3 2 25N 18 55 E
Bombombwa, *Dem. Rep. of the Congo* .... 86 B2 1 40N 25 40 E
Bomi Hills, *Liberia* ... 82 D2 7 1N 10 38W
Bomili, *Dem. Rep. of the Congo* .... 86 B2 1 45N 27 5 E
Bømlo, *Norway* ..... 9 G11 59 37N 5 13 E
Bomokandi ➤, *Dem. Rep. of the Congo* .... 86 B2 3 39N 26 8 E
Bomu ➤, *C.A.R.* .... 84 D4 4 40N 22 30 E
Bon, C., *Tunisia* .... 76 C5 37 1N 11 2 E
Bon Sar Pa, *Vietnam* . 64 F6 12 24N 107 35 E
Bonāb, *Iran* .... 73 D12 37 20N 46 4 E
Bonaigarh, *India* .... 69 J11 21 50N 84 57 E
Bonaire, *Neth. Ant.* .. 121 D6 12 10N 68 15W
Bonampak, *Mexico* .. 119 D6 16 44N 91 5W
Bonang, *Australia* ... 95 F4 37 11 S 148 41 E
Bonanza, *Nic.* 120 D3 13 54N 84 35W
Bonaparte Arch., *Australia* .... 92 B3 14 0 S 124 30 E
Boñar, *Spain* 36 C5 42 52N 5 19W
Bonar Bridge, *U.K.* .. 13 D4 57 54N 4 20W
Bonasse, *Trin. & Tob.* . 125 K15 10 5N 61 54W
Bonaventure, *Canada* . 105 C6 48 5N 65 32W
Bonavista, *Canada* ... 105 C9 48 40N 53 5W
Bonavista, C., *Canada* . 105 C9 48 42N 53 5W
Bonavista B., *Canada* . 105 C9 48 45N 53 25W
Bondeno, *Italy* ...... 41 D8 44 53N 11 25 E
Bondo, *Dem. Rep. of the Congo* .... 86 B1 3 55N 23 53 E
Bondoukou, *Ivory C.* . 82 D4 8 2N 2 47W
Bondowoso, *Indonesia* . 63 G15 7 55 S 113 49 E
Bonerate, *Indonesia* .. 63 F6 7 25 S 121 5 E
Bonerate, Kepulauan, *Indonesia* .... 63 F6 6 30 S 121 10 E
Bo'ness, *U.K.* 13 E5 56 1N 3 37W
Bonete, Cerro, *Argentina* .... 126 B2 27 55 S 68 40W
Bong Son = Hoai Nhon, *Vietnam* .... 64 E7 14 28N 109 1 E
Bonga, *Ethiopia* ..... 81 F4 7 15N 36 14 E
Bongabong, *Phil.* .... 61 E4 12 45N 121 29 E
Bongor, *Chad* ...... 79 F9 10 35N 15 20 E
Bongouanou, *Ivory C.* . 82 D4 6 42N 4 15W
Bonham, *U.S.A.* 113 J6 33 35N 96 11W
Boni, *Mali* 82 B4 15 3N 2 10W
Boni △, *Kenya* ...... 86 C5 1 35 S 41 18 E
Bonifacio, *France* .... 21 G13 41 24N 9 10 E
Bonifacio, Bouches de, *Medit. S.* .... 42 A2 41 12N 9 15 E
Bonin Is. = Ogasawara Gunto, *Pac. Oc.* .. 96 E6 27 0N 142 0 E
Bonke, *Ethiopia* ..... 81 F4 6 5N 37 16 E
Bonkoukou, *Niger* ... 83 C5 14 0N 3 15 E
Bonn, *Germany* ..... 24 E3 50 46N 7 6 E
Bonnat, *France* ..... 19 F8 46 20N 1 54 E
Bonne Terre, *U.S.A.* . 112 G9 37 55N 90 33W
Bonners Ferry, *U.S.A.* 108 B5 48 42N 116 19W
Bonnétable, *France* .. 18 D7 48 11N 0 25 E
Bonneval, *France* .... 21 C11 45 22N 7 3 E
Bonneval-sur-Arc, *France* .... 18 D8 48 11N 1 24 E
Bonneville, *France* ... 19 F13 46 4N 6 24 E
Bonney, L., *Australia* . 95 F3 37 50 S 140 20 E
Bonnie Rock, *Australia* 93 F2 30 29 S 118 22 E
Bonny, *Nigeria* ...... 83 E6 4 25N 7 13 E
Bonny ➤, *Nigeria* ... 83 E6 4 20N 7 10 E
Bonny, Bight of, *Africa* 83 E6 3 30N 9 20 E
Bonny-sur-Loire, *France* 19 E9 47 33N 2 50 E
Bonnyrigg, *U.K.* 13 F5 55 53N 3 6W
Bonnyville, *Canada* .. 103 C6 54 20N 110 45W
Bono, *Italy* .... 42 B2 40 25N 9 2 E
Bonoi, *Indonesia* .... 63 E9 1 45 S 137 41 E
Bonorva, *Italy* ...... 42 B1 40 25N 8 46 E
Bonsall, *U.S.A.* 111 M9 33 16N 117 14W
Bontang, *Indonesia* .. 62 D5 0 10N 117 30 E

Bontebok △, *S. Africa* 88 E3 34 5 S 20 28 E
Bonthe, *S. Leone* 82 D2 7 30N 12 33W
Bontoc, *Phil.* .... 61 C4 17 7N 120 58 E
Bonyeri, *Ghana* 82 D4 5 1N 2 46W
Bonyhád, *Hungary* .. 28 D3 46 18N 18 32 E
Bonython Ra., *Australia* 92 D4 23 40 S 128 45 E
Bookabie, *Australia* .. 93 F5 31 50 S 132 41 E
Booker, *U.S.A.* 113 G4 36 27N 100 32W
Boola, *Guinea* ...... 82 D3 8 22N 8 41 E
Booligal, *Australia* ... 95 E3 33 58 S 144 53 E
Boonah, *Australia* ... 95 D5 27 58 S 152 41 E
Boone, Iowa, *U.S.A.* . 112 D8 42 4N 93 53W
Boone, N.C., *U.S.A.* . 115 G5 36 13N 81 41W
Booneville, *Ark., U.S.A.* 113 H8 35 8N 93 55W
Booneville, *Miss., U.S.A.* 113 H1 34 39N 88 34W
Boonville, *Calif., U.S.A.* 110 F3 39 1N 123 22W
Boonville, *Ind., U.S.A.* 114 F2 38 3N 87 16W
Boonville, *Mo., U.S.A.* 112 F8 38 58N 92 44W
Boonville, *N.Y., U.S.A.* 117 C9 43 29N 75 20W
Boorabbin △, *Australia* 93 F4 31 30 S 129 57 E
Boorindal, *Australia* . 95 E4 30 22 S 146 11 E
Boorowa, *Australia* .. 95 E4 34 28 S 148 44 E
Boosaaso = Bosaso, *Somali Rep.* ...... 75 E4 11 12N 49 18 E
Boothia, Gulf of, *Canada* 101 A11 71 0N 90 0W
Boothia Pen., *Canada* . 100 A10 71 0N 94 0W
Bootle, *U.K.* 14 D4 53 28N 3 1W
Booué, *Gabon* ...... 84 E2 0 5 S 11 55 E
Boppard, *Germany* .. 25 E3 50 13N 7 35 E
Boquete, *Panama* ... 120 E3 8 46N 82 27W
Boquilla, Presa de la, *Mexico* 118 B3 27 40N 105 30W
Boquillas del Carmen, *Mexico* 118 B4 29 17N 102 53W
Bor, *Czech Rep.* .... 26 B5 49 41N 12 45 E
Bor, *Russia* .... 34 B7 56 28N 43 59 E
Bor, *Serbia & M.* .... 44 B6 44 5N 22 7 E
Bôr, *Sudan* .... 81 F3 6 10N 31 40 E
Bor, *Sweden* .... 11 G8 57 9N 14 10 E
Bor, *Turkey* .... 72 D6 37 54N 34 32 E
Bor Mashash, *Israel* . 74 D3 31 7N 34 50 E
Borah Peak, *U.S.A.* .. 108 D7 44 8N 113 47W
Borang, *Sudan* ...... 81 G3 4 50N 30 59 E
Borås, *Sweden* ...... 11 G6 57 43N 12 56 E
Borāzjān, *Iran* ...... 71 D6 29 22N 51 10 E
Borba, *Brazil* .... 124 D7 4 12 S 59 34W
Borba, *Portugal* 37 G3 38 50N 7 26W
Borborema, Planalto da, *Brazil* .... 122 D7 7 0 S 37 0W
Borcea, *Romania* .... 29 F12 44 20N 27 45 E
Borça, *Turkey* ...... 73 B9 41 25N 41 41 E
Bord Khûn-e Now, *Iran* 71 D6 31 31N 51 28 E
Borda, C., *Australia* .. 95 F2 35 45 S 136 34 E
Bordeaux, *France* 20 D3 44 50N 0 36W
Bordeaux ✈ (BOD), *France* 20 D3 44 50N 0 36W
Borden, *Australia* .... 93 F2 34 3 S 118 12 E
Borden-Carleton, *Canada* 105 C7 46 18N 63 47W
Borden I., *Canada* ... 4 B2 78 30N 111 30W
Borden Pen., *Canada* . 101 A11 73 0N 83 0W
Border Ranges △, *Australia* .... 95 D5 28 24 S 152 56 E
Borders = Scottish Borders □, *U.K.* ... 13 F6 55 35N 2 50W
Bordertown, *Australia* . 95 F3 36 19 S 140 45 E
Borðeyri, *Iceland* 8 D3 65 12N 21 6W
Bordighera, *Italy* .... 40 E4 43 46N 7 39 E
Bordj Fly Ste. Marie, *Algeria* 78 C5 27 19N 2 32W
Bordj-in-Eker, *Algeria* 78 D7 24 9N 5 3 E
Bordj Omar Driss, *Algeria* .... 78 C7 28 10N 6 40 E
Bore, *Ethiopia* ...... 81 G4 4 39N 37 39 E
Borehamwood, *U.K.* . 15 F7 51 40N 0 15W
Borek Wielkopolski, *Poland* .... 31 G4 51 54N 17 11 E
Borensberg, *Sweden* . 11 F9 58 34N 15 17 E
Borgà = Porvoo, *Finland* 9 F21 60 24N 25 40 E
Borgarfjörður, *Iceland* . 8 D7 65 31N 13 49W
Borgarnes, *Iceland* ... 8 D3 64 32N 21 55W
Børgefjellet, *Norway* . 8 D15 65 20N 13 45 E
Borger, *Neths.* ...... 17 B6 52 54N 6 44 E
Borger, *U.S.A.* 113 H4 35 39N 101 24W
Borgholm, *Sweden* .. 11 H10 56 52N 16 39 E
Bórgia, *Italy* .... 43 D9 38 49N 16 30 E
Borgo San Dalmazzo, *Italy* .... 40 D4 44 20N 7 30 E
Borgo San Lorenzo, *Italy* .... 41 E8 43 57N 11 23 E
Borgo Val di Taro, *Italy* 40 D6 44 29N 9 46 E
Borgomanero, *Italy* .. 40 C5 45 42N 8 28 E
Borgorose, *Italy* ..... 41 F10 42 11N 13 13 E
Borgosésia, *Italy* .... 40 C5 45 43N 8 16 E
Borhoyn Tal, *Mongolia* 56 C6 43 50N 111 58 E
Bori, *Nigeria* .... 83 E6 4 42N 7 21 E
Borikhane, *Laos* .... 64 C4 18 33N 103 43 E
Borisoglebsk, *Russia* . 34 E6 51 27N 42 5 E
Borisov = Barysaw, *Belarus* .... 32 E5 54 17N 28 28 E
Borisovka, *Russia* ... 33 G9 50 36N 36 1 E
Borja, *Peru* .... 124 D3 4 20 S 77 40W
Borja, *Spain* 38 D3 41 48N 1 34W
Borjas Blancas = Les Borges Blanques, *Spain* .... 38 D5 41 31N 0 52 E
Borjomi, *Georgia* .... 35 K6 41 48N 43 28 E
Børkop, *Denmark* ... 11 J3 55 39N 9 39 E
Borkou, *Chad* .... 79 E9 18 15N 18 50 E
Borkum, *Germany* ... 24 B2 53 34N 6 40 E
Borlänge, *Sweden* ... 10 D9 60 29N 15 26 E
Borley, C., *Antarctica* . 5 C5 66 15 S 52 30 E
Borlu, *Turkey* ...... 47 C10 38 44N 28 27 E
Bormida ➤, *Italy* ... 40 D5 44 23N 8 13 E
Bórmio, *Italy* .... 40 B7 46 28N 10 22 E
Borna, *Germany* ..... 24 D8 51 7N 12 31 E
Borne Sulinowo, *Poland* 30 E3 53 32N 16 36 E
Borneo, *E. Indies* ... 62 D5 1 0N 115 0 E
Bornholm, *Denmark* . 11 J8 55 10N 15 0 E
Bornholms Amtskommune □, *Denmark* .... 11 J8 55 5N 15 0 E
Bornholmsgattet, *Europe* .... 11 J8 55 15N 14 20 E
Borno □, *Nigeria* ... 83 C7 11 30N 13 0 E
Bornos, *Spain* 37 J5 36 48N 5 42W
Bornova, *Turkey* .... 47 C9 38 27N 27 14 E
Bornu Yassa, *Nigeria* . 83 C7 12 14N 12 25 E
Boro ➤, *Sudan* ..... 81 F2 8 52N 26 11 E
Borobudur, *Indonesia* . 63 G13 7 54 S 110 26 E
Borodino, *Russia* .... 32 E8 55 31N 35 40 E
Borodyanka, *Ukraine* . 29 D14 46 18N 29 15 E
Borogontsy, *Russia* .. 53 C14 62 42N 131 8 E
Boromo, *Burkina Faso* 82 C4 11 45N 2 58W
Borongan, *Phil.* ..... 61 F6 11 37N 125 26 E

Borotangba Mts., *C.A.R.* 81 F2 6 30N 25 0 E
Borotou, *Ivory C.* 82 D3 8 46N 7 30W
Borovan, *Bulgaria* ... 44 C7 43 27N 23 45 E
Borovichi, *Russia* .... 32 C7 58 25N 33 55 E
Borovsk, *Russia* ..... 32 E9 55 12N 36 24 E
Borrby, *Sweden* ..... 11 J8 55 27N 14 10 E
Borrego Springs, *U.S.A.* 111 M10 33 15N 116 23W
Borriol, *Spain* 38 E4 40 4N 0 4W
Borroloola, *Australia* . 94 B2 16 4 S 136 17 E
Borşa, *Cluj, Romania* . 29 D8 46 56N 23 40 E
Borşa, *Maramureş, Romania* .... 29 C9 47 41N 24 50 E
Borsad, *India* .... 68 H5 22 25N 72 54 E
Borsec, *Romania* .... 29 D10 46 57N 25 34 E
Borshchiv, *Ukraine* .. 29 B11 48 48N 26 3 E
Borsod-Abaúj-Zemplén □, *Hungary* . 28 B6 48 20N 21 0 E
Bort-les-Orgues, *France* 20 C6 45 24N 2 29 E
Borth, *U.K.* 15 E3 52 29N 4 2W
Börtnan, *Sweden* .... 10 B7 62 45N 14 0 E
Borūjerd, *Iran* ...... 71 C6 33 55N 48 50 E
Borynya, *Ukraine* .... 31 J10 49 4N 23 0 E
Boryslav, *Ukraine* ... 31 J10 49 18N 23 28 E
Boryspil, *Ukraine* ... 33 G6 50 21N 30 59 E
Borzhomi = Borjomi, *Georgia* .... 35 K6 41 48N 43 28 E
Borzna, *Ukraine* .... 33 G7 51 18N 32 26 E
Borzya, *Russia* ...... 53 D12 50 24N 116 31 E
Bosa, *Italy* .... 42 B1 40 18N 8 30 E
Bosanska Dubica, *Bos.-H.* .... 41 C13 45 10N 16 50 E
Bosanska Gradiška, *Bos.-H.* .... 28 E2 45 10N 17 15 E
Bosanska Kostajnica, *Bos.-H.* .... 41 C13 45 11N 16 33 E
Bosanska Krupa, *Bos.-H.* .... 41 D13 44 53N 16 10 E
Bosanski Brod, *Bos.-H.* 28 E2 45 10N 18 0 E
Bosanski Novi, *Bos.-H.* 41 C13 45 2N 16 22 E
Bosanski Petrovac, *Bos.-H.* .... 41 D13 44 35N 16 21 E
Bosanski Šamac, *Bos.-H.* 28 E3 45 3N 18 29 E
Bosansko Grahovo, *Bos.-H.* .... 41 D13 44 12N 16 26 E
Bosaso, *Somali Rep.* . 75 E4 11 12N 49 18 E
Boscastle, *U.K.* 15 G3 50 41N 4 42W
Boscobelle, *Barbados* . 121 g 13 17N 59 35W
Bose, *China* .... 58 F6 23 53N 106 35 E
Boshan, *China* ...... 57 F9 36 28N 117 49 E
Boshof, *S. Africa* .... 88 D4 28 31 S 25 13 E
Boshrūyeh, *Iran* ..... 71 C8 33 50N 57 30 E
Bosilegrad, *Serbia & M.* 44 D6 42 30N 22 27 E
Boskovice, *Czech Rep.* 27 B9 49 29N 16 40 E
Bosna ➤, *Bos.-H.* ... 28 E3 45 4N 18 29 E
Bosna i Hercegovina = Bosnia-Herzegovina ■, *Europe* .... 28 G2 44 0N 18 0 E
Bosnia-Herzegovina ■, *Europe* .... 28 G2 44 0N 18 0 E
Bosnik, *Indonesia* ... 63 E9 1 5 S 136 10 E
Bosobolo, *Dem. Rep. of the Congo* .... 84 D3 4 15N 19 50 E
Bosporus = İstanbul Boğazı, *Turkey* ... 45 E13 41 10N 29 10 E
Bosque Farms, *U.S.A.* 109 J10 34 53N 106 40W
Bossangoa, *C.A.R.* ... 84 C3 6 35N 17 30 E
Bossé Bangou, *Niger* . 83 C5 13 17N 1 15 E
Bossier City, *U.S.A.* .. 113 J8 32 31N 93 44W
Bosso, *Niger* .... 83 C7 13 43N 13 19 E
Bosso, Dallol ➤, *Niger* 83 C5 12 25N 2 50 E
Bostan, *Pakistan* .... 68 D2 30 26N 67 2 E
Bostānābād, *Iran* .... 70 B5 37 50N 46 50 E
Bosten Hu, *China* ... 60 B3 41 55N 87 40 E
Boston, *U.K.* 14 E7 52 59N 0 2W
Boston, *U.S.A.* 117 D13 42 22N 71 4W
Boston Bar, *Canada* .. 102 D4 49 52N 121 30W
Boston Mts., *U.S.A.* .. 113 H8 35 42N 93 15W
Bosutmwi, L., *Ghana* . 83 D4 6 30N 1 25W
Bosut ➤, *Croatia* .... 28 E3 45 20N 18 45 E
Boswell, *Canada* 102 D5 49 28N 116 45W
Boswell, *U.S.A.* 116 F5 40 10N 79 2W
Botad, *India* .... 68 H4 22 15N 71 40 E
Botan ➤, *Turkey* ... 73 D10 37 57N 42 2 E
Botene, *Laos* .... 64 D3 17 35N 101 12 E
Botev, *Bulgaria* ..... 45 D8 42 44N 24 52 E
Botevgrad, *Bulgaria* . 44 D7 42 55N 23 47 E
Bothaville, *S. Africa* .. 88 D4 27 23 S 26 34 E
Bothnia, G. of, *Europe* 8 E19 62 0N 20 0 E
Bothwell, *Australia* ... 95 G4 42 20 S 147 1 E
Bothwell, *Canada* 116 D3 42 38N 81 52W
Boticas, *Portugal* 36 D3 41 41N 7 40W
Botletle ➤, *Botswana* 88 C3 20 10 S 23 15 E
Botlikh, *Russia* ..... 35 J8 42 39N 46 7 E
Botna ➤, *Moldova* .. 29 D14 46 45N 29 34 E
Botoroaga, *Romania* . 29 F10 44 8N 25 32 E
Botoșani, *Romania* ... 29 C11 47 42N 26 41 E
Botoșani □, *Romania* . 29 C11 47 50N 26 50 E
Botou, *Burkina Faso* . 83 C5 12 40N 2 3 E
Botricello, *Italy* ..... 43 D9 38 56N 16 51 E
Botro, *Ivory C.* 82 D3 7 51N 5 19W
Botswana ■, *Africa* .. 88 C3 22 0 S 24 0 E
Bottineau, *U.S.A.* ... 112 A4 48 50N 100 27W
Bottnaryd, *Sweden* .. 11 G7 57 47N 13 50 E
Bottrop, *Germany* ... 17 C6 51 31N 6 58 E
Botucatu, *Brazil* ..... 127 A6 22 55 S 48 30W
Botwood, *Canada* 105 C8 49 6N 55 23W
Bou Djébéha, *Mali* .. 82 B4 18 25N 2 45W
Bou Izakarn, *Morocco* 78 C4 29 12N 9 46W
Bou Rjeïmât, *Mauritania* 82 B1 19 4N 15 9W
Bouaflé, *Ivory C.* 82 D3 7 1N 5 47W
Bouaké, *Ivory C.* 82 D3 7 40N 5 2W
Bouar, *C.A.R.* ...... 84 C3 6 0N 15 40 E
Bouârfa, *Morocco* ... 78 B5 32 32N 1 58W
Boucaut B., *Australia* . 94 A1 12 0 S 134 25 E
Bouches-du-Rhône □, *France* .... 21 E9 43 37N 5 2 E
Boucle de Baoulé △, *Mali* 82 C3 13 53N 9 0W
Boucles de la Seine Normande △, *France* 18 C7 49 30N 0 47 E
Bouctouche, *Canada* . 105 C7 46 30N 64 45W
Bougainville, C., *Australia* .... 92 B4 13 57 S 126 4 E
Bougainville I., *Papua N. G.* ...... 96 H7 6 0 S 155 0 E
Bougainville Reef, *Australia* .... 94 B4 15 30 S 147 5 E
Bougie = Bejaïa, *Algeria* 78 A7 36 42N 5 2 E
Bougouni, *Mali* 82 C3 11 30N 7 20W
Bouillon, *Belgium* ... 17 E5 49 44N 5 3 E
Bouïnan, *Algeria* .... 48 H5 36 25N 3 0 E
Boukombé, *Benin* ... 83 C5 10 13N 1 9 E
Boulal, *Mali* 82 B3 16 8N 8 21W
Boulazac, *France* .... 20 C4 45 10N 0 47 E
Boulder, Colo., *U.S.A.* 108 E2 40 1N 105 17W
Boulder, Mont., *U.S.A.* 108 C7 46 14N 112 7W
Boulder City, *U.S.A.* . 111 K12 35 59N 114 50W
Boulder Creek, *U.S.A.* 110 H4 37 7N 122 7W

Boulder Dam = Hoover Dam, *U.S.A.* 111 K12 36 1N 114 44W
Bouli, *Mauritania* 82 B2 15 17N 12 18W
Boulia, *Australia* .... 94 C2 22 52 S 139 51 E
Bouligny, *France* .... 19 C12 49 17N 5 45 E
Boulogne ➤, *France* . 18 E5 47 12N 1 47W
Boulogne-sur-Gesse, *France* .... 20 E4 43 18N 0 38 E
Boulogne-sur-Mer, *France* .... 19 B8 50 42N 1 36 E
Bouloire, *France* ..... 18 E7 47 59N 0 45 E
Boulouli, *Mali* 82 B3 15 30N 9 25W
Boulsa, *Burkina Faso* . 83 C4 12 39N 0 34W
Boultoum, *Niger* .... 83 C7 14 45N 10 25 E
Boûmdeïd, *Mauritania* 82 B2 17 25N 9 50W
Boun Neua, *Laos* .... 64 B3 21 38N 101 54 E
Boun Tai, *Laos* ..... 64 B3 21 30N 101 58 E
Bouna, *Ivory C.* 82 D4 9 10N 3 0W
Boundary Peak, *U.S.A.* 110 H8 37 51N 118 21W
Boundiali, *Ivory C.* ... 82 D3 9 30N 6 20W
Bountiful, *U.S.A.* 108 F8 40 53N 111 53W
Bounty Is., *Pac. Oc.* . 96 M9 48 0 S 178 30 E
Boura, *Mali* 82 C4 12 25N 4 33W
Bourbon-Lancy, *France* 19 F10 46 37N 3 45 E
Bourbon-l'Archambault, *France* .... 19 F10 46 36N 3 4 E
Bourbonnais, *France* . 19 F10 46 28N 3 0 E
Bourbonne-les-Bains, *France* .... 19 E12 47 54N 5 45 E
Bourbourg, *France* ... 19 B9 50 56N 2 12 E
Bourdel L., *Canada* .. 104 A5 56 43N 74 10W
Bourem, *Mali* 83 B4 17 0N 0 24W
Bourg, *France* 20 C3 45 3N 0 34W
Bourg-Argental, *France* 21 C8 45 18N 4 32 E
Bourg-de-Péage, *France* 21 C9 45 2N 5 3 E
Bourg-en-Bresse, *France* 19 F12 46 13N 5 12 E
Bourg-Lastic, *France* . 20 C6 45 39N 2 35 E
Bourg-Madame, *France* 20 F5 42 26N 1 55 E
Bourg-St-Andéol, *France* .... 21 D8 44 23N 4 39 E
Bourg-St-Maurice, *France* .... 21 C10 45 35N 6 46 E
Bourganeuf, *France* .. 20 C5 45 57N 1 45 E
Bourges, *France* ..... 19 E9 47 9N 2 25 E
Bourget, *Canada* 117 A9 45 26N 75 9W
Bourgneuf, B. de, *France* 18 E4 47 3N 2 10W
Bourgneuf-en-Retz, *France* 18 E5 47 2N 1 58W
Bourgogne □, *France* 19 F11 47 0N 4 50 E
Bourgoin-Jallieu, *France* 21 C9 45 36N 5 17 E
Bourgueil, *France* .... 18 E7 47 17N 0 10 E
Bourke, *Australia* .... 95 E4 30 8 S 145 55 E
Bourne, *U.K.* 14 E7 52 47N 0 22W
Bournemouth, *U.K.* .. 15 G6 50 43N 1 52W
Bournemouth □, *U.K.* 15 G6 50 43N 1 52W
Bouroum, *Burkina Faso* 83 C4 13 37N 0 39W
Bouse, *U.S.A.* 111 M13 33 55N 114 0W
Boussac, *France* ..... 19 F9 46 22N 2 13 E
Boussé, *Burkina Faso* 83 C4 12 39N 1 15W
Boussouma, *Burkina Faso* 83 C4 12 52N 1 13W
Boutilimit, *Mauritania* 82 B2 17 45N 14 40W
Boutonne ➤, *France* . 20 C3 45 54N 0 50W
Bouvet I. = Bouvetøya, *Antarctica* .... 3 G10 54 25 S 3 24 E
Bouvetøya, *Antarctica* 3 G10 54 25 S 3 24 E
Bouxwiller, *France* ... 19 D14 48 49N 7 27 E
Bouza, *Niger* .... 83 C6 14 29N 6 2 E
Bouzonville, *France* .. 19 C13 49 17N 6 32 E
Bova Marina, *Italy* ... 43 E8 37 58N 15 55 E
Bovalino Marina, *Italy* 43 D9 38 10N 16 10 E
Bovec, *Slovenia* ..... 41 B10 46 20N 13 33 E
Bovill, *U.S.A.* 108 C5 46 51N 116 24W
Bovino, *Italy* .... 43 A8 41 15N 15 20 E
Bovril, *Argentina* .... 126 C4 31 21 S 59 26W
Bow ➤, *Canada* 102 C6 49 57N 111 41W
Bow Island, *Canada* . 102 D6 49 50N 111 23W
Bowbells, *U.S.A.* 112 A3 48 48N 102 15W
Bowdle, *U.S.A.* 112 C5 45 27N 99 39W
Bowelling, *Australia* .. 93 F2 33 25 S 116 30 E
Bowen, *Argentina* ... 126 D2 35 0 S 67 31W
Bowen, *Australia* .... 94 J6 20 0 S 148 16 E
Bowen Mts., *Australia* 95 F4 37 0 S 147 50 E
Bowie, *Ariz., U.S.A.* . 109 K9 32 19N 109 29W
Bowie, *Tex., U.S.A.* .. 113 J6 33 34N 97 51W
Bowkān, *Iran* .... 70 B5 36 31N 46 12 E
Bowland, Forest of, *U.K.* 14 D5 54 0N 2 30W
Bowling Green, Ky., *U.S.A.* 114 G2 36 59N 86 27W
Bowling Green, Ohio, *U.S.A.* 114 E4 41 23N 83 39W
Bowling Green, C., *Australia* .... 94 B4 19 19 S 147 25 E
Bowling Green Bay △, *Australia* .... 94 B4 19 25 S 146 57 E
Bowman, *U.S.A.* 112 B3 46 11N 103 24W
Bowman I., *Antarctica* 5 C8 65 0 S 104 0 E
Bowmanville = Clarington, *Canada* 116 C6 43 55N 78 41W
Bowmore, *U.K.* 13 F2 55 45N 6 17W
Bowral, *Australia* .... 95 E5 34 26 S 150 27 E
Bowraville, *Australia* . 95 E5 30 37 S 152 52 E
Bowron ➤, *Canada* . 102 C4 54 3N 121 50W
Bowron Lake △, *Canada* 102 C4 53 10N 121 5W
Bowser L., *Canada* .. 102 B3 56 30N 129 30W
Bowsman, *Canada* ... 103 C8 52 14N 101 12W
Bowwood, *Zambia* .. 87 F2 17 5 S 26 20 E
Box Cr. ➤, *Australia* . 95 E3 34 10 S 143 50 E
Boxholm, *Sweden* ... 11 F9 58 12N 15 3 E
Boxmeer, *Neths.* .... 17 C5 51 38N 5 56 E
Boxtel, *Neths.* ...... 17 C5 51 36N 5 20 E
Boyabat, *Turkey* .... 72 B6 41 28N 34 47 E
Boyalıca, *Turkey* .... 47 F13 40 23N 29 8 E
Boyang, *China* ...... 59 C11 29 0N 116 38 E
Boyanup, *Ukraine* ... 33 G6 50 0N 33 0 E
Boyce, *U.S.A.* 113 K8 31 23N 92 40W
Boyd L., *Canada* 104 B4 52 46N 76 42W
Boyle, *Canada* 102 C6 54 35N 112 49W
Boyle, *Ireland* 12 C3 53 59N 8 18W
Boyne ➤, *Ireland* ... 12 C5 53 43N 6 15W
Boyne City, *U.S.A.* .. 114 C3 45 13N 85 1W
Boynitsa, *Bulgaria* ... 44 C6 43 58N 22 32 E
Boynton Beach, *U.S.A.* 115 M5 26 32N 80 4W
Boyoma, Chutes, *Dem. Rep. of the Congo* .... 86 B2 0 35N 25 23 E
Boysen Reservoir, *U.S.A.* 108 E9 43 25N 108 11W
Boyuibe, *Bolivia* ..... 124 G6 20 25 S 63 17W
Boyup Brook, *Australia* 93 F2 33 50 S 116 23 E
Boz Burun, *Turkey* .. 45 F12 40 32N 28 46 E
Boz Dağ, *Turkey* .... 47 D10 38 20N 28 0 E
Boz Dağları, *Turkey* . 47 C10 38 20N 28 0 E
Bozaada, *Turkey* .... 47 E10 39 49N 26 3 E
Bozburun, *Turkey* ... 47 E10 36 49N 28 5 E
Bozcaada, *Turkey* ... 72 C2 39 49N 26 3 E

Bozdoğan, *Turkey* ... 47 D10 37 40N 28 17 E
Bozeman, *U.S.A.* 108 D8 45 41N 111 2W
Bozen = Bolzano, *Italy* 41 B8 46 31N 11 22 E
Boževac, *Serbia & M.* 44 B5 44 32N 21 24 E
Bozhou, *China* ...... 56 H8 33 55N 115 41 E
Bozkır, *Turkey* ...... 72 D5 37 11N 32 14 E
Bozkurt, *Turkey* ..... 47 D11 37 50N 29 37 E
Bozouls, *France* ..... 20 D6 44 28N 2 43 E
Bozoum, *C.A.R.* ..... 84 C3 6 25N 16 35 E
Bozova, *Antalya, Turkey* 47 D12 37 13N 30 18 E
Bozova, *Sanlıurfa, Turkey* .... 73 D8 37 21N 38 32 E
Bozovici, *Romania* ... 28 F7 44 56N 22 0 E
Bozüyük, *Turkey* .... 47 B12 39 54N 30 3 E
Bra, *Italy* .... 40 D4 44 42N 7 51 E
Braås, *Sweden* ...... 11 G9 57 4N 15 3 E
Brabant □, *Belgium* .. 17 D4 50 46N 4 30 E
Brabant L., *Canada* .. 103 B8 55 58N 103 43W
Brabrand, *Denmark* .. 11 H4 56 9N 10 9 E
Brač, *Croatia* .... 41 E13 43 20N 16 40 E
Bracadale, L., *U.K.* .. 13 D2 57 20N 6 30W
Bracciano, *Italy* ..... 41 F9 42 6N 12 10 E
Bracciano, L. di, *Italy* . 41 F9 42 7N 12 14 E
Bracebridge, *Canada* . 116 A5 45 2N 79 19W
Brach, *Libya* .... 79 C8 27 31N 14 20 E
Bracieux, *France* .... 18 E8 47 30N 1 30 E
Bräcke, *Sweden* ..... 10 B9 62 45N 15 26 E
Brackettville, *U.S.A.* . 113 L4 29 19N 100 25W
Brački Kanal, *Croatia* 41 E13 43 24N 16 40 E
Bracknell, *U.K.* 15 F7 51 25N 0 43W
Bracknell Forest □, *U.K.* 15 F7 51 25N 0 44W
Brad, *Romania* ...... 28 D7 46 10N 22 50 E
Brádano ➤, *Italy* .... 43 B9 40 23N 16 51 E
Bradenton, *U.S.A.* ... 115 M4 27 30N 82 34W
Bradford, *Canada* ... 116 B5 44 7N 79 34W
Bradford, *U.K.* 14 D6 53 47N 1 45W
Bradford, Pa., *U.S.A.* 116 E6 41 58N 78 38W
Bradford, Vt., *U.S.A.* 117 C12 43 59N 72 9W
Bradley, Ark., *U.S.A.* . 113 J8 33 6N 93 39W
Bradley, Calif., *U.S.A.* 110 K6 35 52N 120 48W
Bradley Institute, *Zimbabwe* .... 87 F3 17 7 S 31 25 E
Brady, *U.S.A.* 113 K5 31 9N 99 20W
Brædstrup, *Denmark* 11 J3 55 58N 9 37 E
Braeside, *Canada* 117 A8 45 28N 76 24W
Braga, *Portugal* 36 D2 41 35N 8 25W
Braga □, *Portugal* ... 36 D2 41 30N 8 30W
Bragadiru, *Romania* . 29 G10 43 46N 25 31 E
Bragado, *Argentina* .. 126 D3 35 2 S 60 27W
Bragança, *Brazil* ..... 125 D9 1 0 S 47 2W
Bragança, *Portugal* .. 36 D4 41 48N 6 50W
Bragança □, *Portugal* . 36 D4 41 30N 6 45W
Bragança Paulista, *Brazil* .... 127 A6 22 55 S 46 32W
Brahestad = Raahe, *Finland* .... 8 D21 64 40N 24 28 E
Brahmanbaria, *Bangla.* 67 H17 23 58N 91 15 E
Brahmani ➤, *India* ... 67 J15 20 39N 86 46 E
Brahmapur, *India* .... 67 K14 19 15N 84 54 E
Brahmaputra ➤, *Asia* 69 H13 23 40N 90 35 E
Braich-y-pwll, *U.K.* .. 14 E3 52 47N 4 46W
Braidwood, *Australia* . 95 F4 35 27 S 149 49 E
Brăila, *Romania* ..... 29 E12 45 19N 27 59 E
Brăila □, *Romania* ... 29 E12 45 5 S 27 30 E
Brainerd, *U.S.A.* 112 B7 46 22N 94 12W
Braintree, *U.K.* ..... 15 F8 51 53N 0 34 E
Braintree, *U.S.A.* 117 D14 42 13N 71 0W
Brak ➤, *S. Africa* ... 88 D3 29 35 S 22 55 E
Brake, *Germany* ..... 24 B4 53 20N 8 28 E
Brakel, *Germany* .... 24 D5 51 43N 9 11 E
Bräkne-Hoby, *Sweden* 11 H9 56 14N 15 6 E
Brakwater, *Namibia* . 88 C2 22 28 S 17 3 E
Brålanda, *Sweden* ... 11 F6 58 34N 12 21 E
Bramberg, *Germany* . 25 E6 50 6N 10 40 E
Bramdrupdam, *Denmark* .... 11 J3 55 31N 9 28 E
Bramming, *Denmark* . 11 J2 55 28N 8 42 E
Brämön, *Sweden* .... 10 B11 62 14N 17 40 E
Brampton, *Canada* .. 116 C5 43 45N 79 45W
Brampton, *U.K.* 14 C5 54 57N 2 44W
Bramsche, *Germany* . 24 C3 52 24N 7 59 E
Bramton I., *Australia* . 94 J7 20 50 S 149 17 E
Branco ➤, *Brazil* .... 124 D6 1 20 S 61 50W
Brandberg, *Namibia* . 88 C1 21 10 S 14 33 E
Brandberg A., *Namibia* 88 C1 21 10 S 14 30 E
Brande, *Denmark* .... 11 J3 55 57N 9 8 E
Brandenburg = Neubrandenburg, *Germany* .... 24 B9 53 33N 13 15 E
Brandenburg, *Germany* 24 C8 52 25N 12 33 E
Brandenburg □, *Germany* .... 24 C9 52 50N 13 0 E
Brandfort, *S. Africa* .. 88 D4 28 40 S 26 30 E
Brandon, *France* .... 21 F13 42 47N 9 27 E
Brandon, *Canada* ... 103 D9 49 50N 99 57W
Brandon, *U.S.A.* 117 C11 43 48N 73 4W
Brandon B., *Ireland* .. 12 D1 52 17N 10 8W
Brandon Mt., *Ireland* . 12 D1 52 15N 10 15W
Brandsen, *Argentina* . 126 D4 35 10 S 58 15W
Brandvlei, *S. Africa* .. 88 E3 30 25 S 20 30 E
Brandýs nad Labem, *Czech Rep.* ...... 26 A7 50 10N 14 40 E
Brăneşti, *Romania* ... 29 F11 44 27N 26 20 E
Branford, *U.S.A.* 117 E12 41 17N 72 49W
Braniewo, *Poland* ... 30 D6 54 25N 19 50 E
Bransfield Str., *Antarctica* .... 5 C18 63 0 S 59 0W
Brańsk, *Poland* ..... 31 F9 52 45N 22 50 E
Branson, *U.S.A.* 113 G8 36 39N 93 13W
Brantford, *Canada* .. 116 C4 43 10N 80 15W
Brantôme, *France* ... 20 C4 45 22N 0 39 E
Branxi, *Italy* .... 40 C6 45 16N 9 46 E
Bras d'Or L., *Canada* . 105 C7 45 50N 60 50W
Brasher Falls, *U.S.A.* . 117 B10 44 49N 74 47W
Brasil, Planalto, *Brazil* 122 E6 18 0 S 46 30W
Brasiléia, *Brazil* ..... 124 F5 11 0 S 68 45W
Brasília, *Brazil* ...... 125 G9 15 47 S 47 55W
Brasília Legal, *Brazil* . 125 D7 3 49 S 55 36W
Braslaw, *Belarus* .... 9 J22 55 38N 27 0 E
Braslovče, *Slovenia* .. 41 B12 46 21N 15 3 E
Braşov, *Romania* .... 29 E10 45 40N 25 15 E
Brass, *Nigeria* ...... 83 E6 4 35N 6 13 E
Brass ➤, *Nigeria* .... 83 E6 4 15N 6 13 E
Brassac-les-Mines, *France* .... 20 C7 45 24N 3 20 E
Brasschaat, *Belgium* . 17 C4 51 19N 4 27 E
Brassey, Banjaran, *Malaysia* .... 62 D5 5 0N 117 15 E
Brassey Ra., *Australia* 93 E3 25 8 S 122 15 E
Brasstown Bald, *U.S.A.* 115 H4 34 53N 83 49W
Brastad, *Sweden* .... 11 F5 58 23N 11 30 E
Bratan = Morozov, *Bulgaria* .... 45 D9 42 30N 25 10 E
Brateş, *Romania* .... 29 E11 45 58N 27 7 E
Bratislava, *Slovak Rep.* 27 C10 48 10N 17 7 E

Bratislava M.R.
  Stefanik ✈ (BTS),
  Slovak Rep. .... 27 C10 48 11N 17 9 E
Bratislavský □,
  Slovak Rep. ...... 27 C10 48 15N 17 20 E
Bratsigovo, Bulgaria .. 45 D8 42 1N 24 22 E
Bratsk, Russia .... 53 D11 56 10N 101 30 E
Brattleboro, U.S.A. ... 117 D12 42 51N 72 34W
Bratunac, Bos.-H. .... 28 F4 44 13N 19 21 E
Braunau, Austria ..... 26 C6 48 15N 13 3 E
Braunschweig, Germany 24 C6 52 15N 10 31 E
Brauntorr, U.K. 15 F3 51 7N 4 10W
Bravicea, Moldova .... 29 C13 47 22N 28 27 E
Bråviken, Sweden .... 11 F10 58 38N 16 32 E
Bravo del Norte, Rio =
  Grande, Rio →,
  U.S.A. 113 N6 25 58N 97 9W
Brawley, U.S.A. 111 N11 32 59N 115 31W
Bray, Ireland 12 C5 53 13N 6 7W
Bray, Mt., Australia ... 94 A1 14 0 S 134 30 E
Bray-sur-Seine, France 19 D10 48 25N 3 14 E
Brazeau →, Canada ... 102 C5 52 55N 115 14W
Brazil, U.S.A. 114 F2 39 32N 87 8W
Brazil ■, S. Amer. .... 125 F9 12 0 S 50 0W
Brazilian Highlands =
  Brasil, Planalto, Brazil 122 E6 18 0 S 46 30W
Brazo Sur →, S. Amer. 126 B4 25 21 S 57 42W
Brazos →, U.S.A. 113 L7 28 53N 95 23W
Brazzaville, Congo .... 84 E3 4 9 S 15 12 E
Brčko, Bos.-H. ...... 28 F3 44 54N 18 46 E
Brda →, Poland ..... 31 E5 53 8N 18 8 E
Brdy, Czech Rep. .... 26 B6 49 43N 13 55 E
Breaden L., Australia .. 93 E4 25 51 S 125 28 E
Breaksea Sd., N.Z. ... 91 L1 45 35 S 166 35 E
Bream B., N.Z. ...... 91 F5 35 56 S 174 28 E
Bream Hd., N.Z. ..... 91 F5 35 51 S 174 36 E
Breas, Chile .... 126 B1 25 29 S 70 24W
Breaza, Romania ..... 29 E10 45 11N 25 40 E
Brebes, Indonesia .... 63 G13 6 52 S 109 3 E
Brechin, Canada 116 B5 44 32N 79 10W
Brechin, U.K. 13 E6 56 44N 2 39W
Brecht, Belgium ..... 17 C4 51 21N 4 38 E
Breckenridge, Colo.,
  U.S.A. 108 G10 39 29N 106 3W
Breckenridge, Minn.,
  U.S.A. 112 B6 46 16N 96 35W
Breckenridge, Tex.,
  U.S.A. 113 J5 32 45N 98 54W
Breckland, U.K. ..... 15 E8 52 30N 0 40 E
Břeclav, Czech Rep. .. 27 C9 48 46N 16 53 E
Brecon, U.K. 15 F4 51 57N 3 23W
Brecon Beacons, U.K. . 15 F4 51 53N 3 26W
Brecon Beacons △, U.K. 15 F4 51 50N 3 30W
Breda, Neths. .... 17 C4 51 35N 4 45 E
Bredaryd, Sweden .... 11 G7 57 10N 13 45 E
Bredasdorp, S. Africa . 88 E3 34 33 S 20 2 E
Bredbro, Denmark .... 11 J2 55 4N 8 50 E
Bredstedt, Germany ... 24 A4 54 37N 8 55 E
Bree, Belgium .... 17 C5 51 8N 5 35 E
Bregalnica →,
  Macedonia .... 44 E6 41 43N 22 9 E
Bregenz, Austria ..... 26 D2 47 30N 9 45 E
Bregovo, Bulgaria .... 44 B6 44 9N 22 39 E
Bréhal, France 18 D5 48 53N 1 30W
Bréhat, Î. de, France . 18 D4 48 51N 3 0W
Breiðafjörður, Iceland . 8 D2 65 15N 23 15W
Breil-sur-Roya, France 21 E11 43 56N 7 31 E
Breisach, Germany .... 25 G3 48 1N 7 36 E
Brejo, Brazil .... 125 D10 3 41 S 42 47W
Bremen, Germany .... 24 B4 53 4N 8 47 E
Bremen □, Germany .. 24 B4 53 4N 8 50 E
Bremer Bay, Australia . 93 F2 34 21 S 119 20 E
Bremer I., Australia ... 94 A2 12 5 S 136 45 E
Bremerhaven, Germany 24 B4 53 33N 8 36 E
Bremerton, U.S.A. ... 110 C4 47 34N 122 38W
Bremervörde, Germany 24 B5 53 29N 9 8 E
Brenes, Spain 37 H5 37 32N 5 54W
Brenham, U.S.A. 113 K6 30 10N 96 24W
Brenne, France ...... 20 B5 46 44N 1 14 E
Brenne △, France .... 20 B5 46 40N 1 15 E
Brennerpass, Austria .. 26 D4 47 2N 11 30 E
Breno, Italy .... 40 C7 45 57N 10 18 E
Brent, U.S.A. 115 J2 32 56N 87 10W
Brenta →, Italy ..... 41 C9 45 11N 12 18 E
Brentwood, U.K. ..... 15 F8 51 37N 0 19 E
Brentwood, Calif.,
  U.S.A. 110 H5 37 56N 121 42W
Brentwood, N.Y., U.S.A. 117 F11 40 47N 73 15W
Bréscia, Italy .... 40 C7 45 33N 10 15 E
Breskens, Neths. ..... 17 C3 51 23N 3 33 E
Breslau = Wrocław,
  Poland .... 31 G4 51 5N 17 5 E
Bresle →, France .... 18 B8 50 4N 1 22 E
Bressanone, Italy .... 41 B8 46 43N 11 39 E
Bressay, U.K. 13 A7 60 9N 1 6W
Bresse, France ...... 19 F12 46 50N 5 10 E
Bressuire, France 18 F6 46 51N 0 30W
Brest, Belarus ...... 33 F2 52 10N 23 40 E
Brest, France 18 D2 48 24N 4 31W
Brest-Litovsk = Brest,
  Belarus .... 33 F2 52 10N 23 40 E
Bretagne □, France .. 18 D3 48 10N 3 0W
Breţcu, Romania ..... 29 D11 46 7N 26 18 E
Bretenoux, France .... 20 D5 44 54N 1 51 E
Breteuil, Eure, France . 18 D7 48 50N 0 57 E
Breteuil, Oise, France . 19 C9 49 38N 2 18 E
Breton, Canada 102 C6 53 7N 114 28W
Breton, Pertuis, France 20 B2 46 17N 1 25W
Breton Sd., U.S.A. ... 113 L10 29 35N 89 15W
Brett, C., N.Z. ...... 91 F5 35 10 S 174 20 E
Bretten, Germany .... 25 F4 49 2N 8 42 E
Breuil-Cervínia, Italy .. 40 C4 45 56N 7 38 E
Brevard, U.S.A. 115 H4 35 14N 82 44W
Breves, Brazil .... 125 D8 1 40 S 50 29W
Brewarrina, Australia . 95 E4 30 0 S 146 51 E
Brewer, U.S.A. 113 C11 44 48N 68 46W
Brewer, Mt., U.S.A. .. 110 J8 36 44N 118 28W
Brewerville, Liberia ... 82 D2 6 26N 10 47W
Brewster, N.Y., U.S.A. 117 E11 41 23N 73 37W
Brewster, Ohio, U.S.A. 116 F3 40 43N 81 36W
Brewster, Wash., U.S.A. 108 B4 48 6N 119 47W
Brewster, Kap =
  Kangikajik, Greenland 4 B6 70 7N 22 0W
Brewton, U.S.A. 115 K2 31 7N 87 4W
Breyten, S. Africa .... 89 D5 26 16 S 30 0 E
Breza, Bos.-H. ...... 28 F3 44 2N 18 16 E
Březice, Slovenia .... 41 C12 45 54N 15 35 E
Breznik, Bulgaria .... 44 D6 42 44N 22 50 E
Brezno, Slovak Rep. .. 27 C12 48 50N 19 40 E
Brezoi, Romania ..... 29 E9 45 21N 24 15 E
Brezovica, Serbia & M. 44 D5 42 15N 21 3 E
Brezovo, Bulgaria .... 45 D9 42 21N 25 5 E
Briançon, France .... 21 D10 44 54N 6 39 E
Briare, France ...... 19 E9 47 38N 2 44 E
Briático, Italy ...... 43 D9 38 43N 16 2 E
Bribie I., Australia ... 95 D5 27 0 S 153 10 E

Bribri, Costa Rica 120 E3 9 38N 82 50W
Briceni, Moldova ..... 29 B12 48 22N 27 6 E
Bricquebec, France ... 18 C5 49 28N 1 38W
Bridgefield, Barbados . 121 g 13 9N 59 36W
Bridgehampton, U.S.A. 117 F12 40 56N 72 19W
Bridgend, U.K. 15 F4 51 30N 3 34W
Bridgend □, U.K. 15 F4 51 36N 3 36W
Bridgeport, Calif.,
  U.S.A. 110 G7 38 15N 119 14W
Bridgeport, Conn.,
  U.S.A. 117 E11 41 11N 73 12W
Bridgeport, Nebr.,
  U.S.A. 112 E3 41 40N 103 6W
Bridgeport, Tex., U.S.A. 113 J6 33 13N 97 45W
Bridgeton, U.S.A. 114 F8 39 26N 75 14W
Bridgetown, Australia . 93 F2 33 58 S 116 7 E
Bridgetown, Barbados . 121 g 13 6N 59 37W
Bridgetown, Canada .. 105 D6 44 55N 65 18W
Bridgewater, Canada .. 105 D7 44 25N 64 31W
Bridgewater, Mass.,
  U.S.A. 117 E14 41 59N 70 58W
Bridgewater, N.Y. 117 D9 42 53N 75 15W
Bridgewater, C.,
  Australia .... 95 F3 38 23 S 141 23 E
Bridgewater-
  Gagebrook, Australia 95 G4 42 44 S 147 14 E
Bridgnorth, U.K. 15 E5 52 32N 2 25W
Bridgton, U.S.A. 117 B14 44 3N 70 42W
Bridgwater, U.K. 15 F5 51 8N 2 59W
Bridgwater B., U.K. ... 15 F4 51 15N 3 15W
Bridlington, U.K. 14 C7 54 5N 0 12W
Bridlington B., U.K. ... 14 C7 54 4N 0 10W
Bridport, Australia ... 95 G4 40 59 S 147 23 E
Bridport, U.K. 15 G5 50 44N 2 45W
Briec, France 18 D2 48 6N 4 0W
Brienne-le-Château,
  France .... 19 D11 48 24N 4 30 E
Brienon-sur-Armançon,
  France .... 19 E10 47 59N 3 38 E
Brienz, Switz. .... 25 J4 46 46N 8 2 E
Brienzersee, Switz. ... 25 J3 46 44N 7 53 E
Brière △, France 18 E4 47 22N 2 13W
Brig, Switz. .... 25 J3 46 18N 7 59 E
Brigg, U.K. 14 D7 53 34N 0 28W
Brigham City, U.S.A. . 108 F7 41 31N 112 1W
Bright, Australia ..... 95 F4 36 42 S 146 56 E
Brighton, Australia ... 95 F2 35 5 S 138 30 E
Brighton, Canada 116 B7 44 2N 77 44W
Brighton, Trin. & Tob. . 125 K15 10 13N 61 39W
Brighton, U.K. 15 G7 50 49N 0 7W
Brighton, Colo., U.S.A. 112 F2 39 59N 104 49W
Brighton, N.Y., U.S.A. 116 C7 43 8N 77 34W
Brignogan-Plage, France 18 D2 48 40N 4 20W
Brignoles, France .... 21 E10 43 25N 6 5 E
Brihuega, Spain 38 E2 40 45N 2 52W
Brikama, Gambia 82 C1 13 15N 16 45W
Brilliant, U.S.A. 116 F4 40 15N 80 39W
Brilon, Germany ..... 24 D4 51 23N 8 35 E
Bríndisi, Italy .... 43 B10 40 39N 17 55 E
Brinje, Croatia ...... 41 D12 44 59N 15 9 E
Brinkley, U.S.A. 113 H9 34 53N 91 12W
Brinnon, U.S.A. 110 C4 47 41N 122 54W
Brion, Î., Canada 105 C7 47 46N 61 26W
Brionne, France ..... 18 C7 49 11N 0 43 E
Brionski, Croatia .... 41 D10 44 55N 13 45 E
Brioude, France ..... 20 C7 45 18N 3 24 E
Briouze, France 18 D6 48 42N 0 23W
Brisbane, Australia ... 95 D5 27 25 S 153 2 E
Brisbane →, Australia . 95 D5 27 24 S 153 9 E
Brisighella, Italy ..... 41 D8 44 13N 11 46 E
Bristol, U.K. 15 F5 51 26N 2 35W
Bristol, Conn., U.S.A. . 117 E12 41 40N 72 57W
Bristol, Pa., U.S.A. ... 117 F10 40 6N 74 51W
Bristol, R.I., U.S.A. ... 117 E13 41 40N 71 16W
Bristol, Tenn., U.S.A. . 115 G4 36 36N 82 11W
Bristol, City of □, U.K. 15 F5 51 27N 2 36W
Bristol B., U.S.A. 100 C4 58 0N 160 0W
Bristol Channel, U.K. . 15 F3 51 18N 4 30W
Bristol I., Antarctica .. 5 B1 58 45 S 28 0W
Bristol L., U.S.A. 109 J5 34 23N 116 50W
Bristow, U.S.A. 113 H6 35 50N 96 23W
Britain = Great Britain,
  Europe 6 E5 54 0N 2 15W
British Columbia □,
  Canada 102 C3 55 0N 125 15W
British Indian Ocean
  Terr. = Chagos
  Arch. ☑, Ind. Oc. .. 50 K11 6 0 S 72 0 E
British Isles, Europe ... 6 D4 54 0N 4 0W
British Virgin Is. ☑,
  W. Indies .... 121 e 18 30N 64 30W
Brits, S. Africa ...... 89 D4 25 37 S 27 48 E
Britstown, S. Africa ... 88 E3 30 37 S 23 30 E
Britt, Canada 104 C3 45 46N 80 34W
Brittany = Bretagne □,
  France 18 D3 48 10N 3 0W
Britton, U.S.A. 112 C6 45 48N 97 45W
Brive-la-Gaillarde,
  France .... 20 C5 45 10N 1 32 E
Briviesca, Spain 36 C7 42 32N 3 19W
Brixen = Bressanone,
  Italy .... 41 B8 46 43N 11 39 E
Brixham, U.K. 15 G4 50 23N 3 31W
Brnaze, Croatia ...... 41 E13 43 41N 16 40 E
Brnenský □, Czech Rep. 27 B9 49 10N 16 40 E
Brno, Czech Rep. .... 27 B9 49 10N 16 35 E
Broach = Bharuch, India 66 J8 21 47N 73 0 E
Broad →, U.S.A. 115 J5 34 1N 81 4W
Broad Arrow, Australia 93 F3 30 23 S 121 15 E
Broad B., U.K. 13 C2 58 14N 6 18W
Broad Haven, Ireland . 12 B2 54 20N 9 55W
Broad Law, U.K. 13 F5 55 30N 3 21W
Broad Sd., Australia .. 94 C4 22 0 S 149 45 E
Broadalbin, U.S.A. ... 117 C10 43 4N 74 12W
Broadback →, Canada 104 B4 51 21N 78 52W
Broadhurst Ra.,
  Australia .... 92 D3 22 30 S 122 30 E
Broads, U.K. .... 15 E9 52 45N 1 30 E
Broads, The, U.K. .... 14 E9 52 45N 1 30 E
Broadus, U.S.A. 112 C2 45 27N 105 25W
Broager, Denmark .... 11 K3 54 53N 9 40 E
Broby, Sweden ...... 11 H8 56 15N 14 4 E
Broceni, Latvia ...... 30 B9 56 42N 22 32 E
Brochet, Canada 103 B8 57 53N 101 40W
Brochet, L., Canada .. 103 B8 58 36N 101 35W
Brocken, Germany .... 24 D6 51 47N 10 37 E
Brockport, U.S.A. 116 C7 43 13N 77 56W
Brockton, U.S.A. 117 D13 42 5N 71 1W
Brockville, Canada ... 117 B9 44 35N 75 41W
Brockway, Mont., U.S.A. 112 B2 47 18N 105 45W
Brockway, Pa., U.S.A. . 116 E6 41 15N 78 47W
Brocton, U.S.A. 116 D5 42 23N 79 26W
Brod, Macedonia ..... 44 E5 41 32N 21 17 E
Brodarevo, Serbia & M. 44 C3 43 14N 19 44 E
Brodeur Pen., Canada 101 A11 72 30N 88 10W

Brodhead, Mt., U.S.A. 116 E7 41 39N 77 47W
Brodick, U.K. 13 F3 55 35N 5 9W
Brodnica, Poland .... 31 E6 53 15N 19 25 E
Brody, Ukraine ...... 33 G3 50 5N 25 10 E
Brogan, U.S.A. 108 D5 44 15N 117 31W
Broglie, France ...... 18 C7 49 2N 0 30 E
Brok, Poland .... 31 F8 52 43N 21 52 E
Broken Arrow, U.S.A. . 113 G7 36 3N 95 48W
Broken Bow, Nebr.,
  U.S.A. 112 E5 41 24N 99 38W
Broken Bow, Okla.,
  U.S.A. 113 H7 34 2N 94 44W
Broken Bow Lake,
  U.S.A. 113 H7 34 9N 94 40W
Broken Hill, Australia . 95 E3 31 58 S 141 29 E
Broken River Ra.,
  Australia .... 94 K6 21 0 S 148 22 E
Brokind, Sweden .... 11 F9 58 13N 15 42 E
Bromley □, U.K. .... 15 F8 51 24N 0 2 E
Bromo, Indonesia .... 63 G15 7 55 S 112 55 E
Bromölla, Sweden .... 11 H8 56 5N 14 28 E
Bromsgrove, U.K. 15 E5 52 21N 2 2W
Brønderslev, Denmark 11 G3 57 16N 9 57 E
Brong-Ahafo □, Ghana 82 D4 7 50N 2 0W
Bronkhorstspruit,
  S. Africa .... 89 D4 25 46 S 28 45 E
Brønnøysund, Norway . 8 D15 65 28N 12 14 E
Bronte, Italy .... 43 E7 37 47N 14 50 E
Brook Park, U.S.A. ... 116 E4 41 24N 81 51W
Brookhaven, U.S.A. .. 113 K9 31 35N 90 26W
Brookings, Oreg., U.S.A. 108 E1 42 3N 124 17W
Brookings, S. Dak.,
  U.S.A. 112 C6 44 19N 96 48W
Brooklin, Canada 116 C6 43 55N 78 55W
Brooklyn Park, U.S.A. 112 C8 45 6N 93 23W
Brooks, Canada 102 C6 50 35N 111 55W
Brooks Range, U.S.A. . 100 B5 68 0N 152 0W
Brooksville, U.S.A. ... 115 L4 28 33N 82 23W
Brookton, Australia ... 93 F2 32 22 S 117 0 E
Brookville, U.S.A. ... 116 E5 41 10N 79 5W
Broom, L., U.K. 13 D3 57 55N 5 15W
Broome, Australia .... 92 C3 18 0 S 122 15 E
Broons, France 18 D4 48 20N 2 16W
Brora, U.K. 13 C5 58 0N 3 52W
Brora →, U.K. 13 C5 58 0N 3 51W
Brørup, Denmark .... 11 J2 55 29N 9 1 E
Brösarp, Sweden .... 11 J8 55 43N 14 6 E
Brosna →, Ireland ... 12 C4 53 14N 7 58W
Broșteni, Mehedinți,
  Romania .... 28 F7 44 45N 22 59 E
Broșteni, Suceava,
  Romania .... 29 C10 47 14N 25 43 E
Brothers, U.S.A. 108 E3 43 49N 120 36W
Brou, France .... 18 D8 48 13N 1 11 E
Brouage, France 20 C2 45 52N 1 4W
Brough, U.K. 14 C5 54 32N 2 18W
Brough Hd., U.K. 13 B5 59 8N 3 20W
Broughton Island =
  Qikiqtarjuaq, Canada 101 B13 67 33N 63 0W
Broumov, Czech Rep. . 27 A9 50 35N 16 20 E
Brovary, Ukraine .... 33 G6 50 34N 30 48 E
Brovst, Denmark .... 11 G3 57 6N 9 31 E
Brown, L., Australia .. 93 F2 31 5 S 118 15 E
Brown, Pt., Australia . 95 E1 32 32 S 133 50 E
Brown City, U.S.A. ... 116 C2 43 13N 82 59W
Brown Willy, U.K. ... 15 G3 50 35N 4 37W
Brownfield, U.S.A. ... 113 J3 33 11N 102 17W
Browning, U.S.A. 108 B7 48 34N 113 1W
Brownsville, Oreg.,
  U.S.A. 108 D2 44 24N 122 59W
Brownsville, Pa., U.S.A. 116 F5 40 1N 79 53W
Brownsville, Tenn.,
  U.S.A. 113 H10 35 36N 89 16W
Brownsville, Tex., U.S.A. 113 N6 25 54N 97 30W
Brownwood, U.S.A. .. 113 K5 31 43N 98 59W
Browse I., Australia .. 92 B3 14 7 S 123 33 E
Bruas, Malaysia ..... 65 K3 4 30N 100 47 E
Bruay-la-Buissière,
  France .... 19 B9 50 29N 2 33 E
Bruce, Mt., Australia . 92 D2 22 37 S 118 8 E
Bruce Pen., Canada .. 116 B3 45 0N 81 30W
Bruce Peninsula △,
  Canada 116 A3 45 14N 81 36W
Bruce Rock, Australia . 93 F2 31 52 S 118 8 E
Bruche →, France ... 19 D14 48 34N 7 43 E
Bruchsal, Germany ... 25 F4 49 7N 8 35 E
Bruck an der Leitha,
  Austria .... 27 C9 48 1N 16 47 E
Bruck an der Mur,
  Austria .... 26 D8 47 24N 15 16 E
Brue →, U.K. 15 F5 51 13N 2 59W
Bruges = Brugge,
  Belgium .... 17 C3 51 13N 3 13 E
Brugg, Switz. .... 25 H4 47 29N 8 11 E
Brugge, Belgium ..... 17 C3 51 13N 3 13 E
Bruin, U.S.A. 116 E5 41 3N 79 43W
Brûlé, Canada 102 C5 53 15N 117 58W
Brûlon, France 18 E6 47 58N 0 15W
Brumado, Brazil ..... 125 F10 14 14 S 41 40W
Brumath, France ..... 19 D14 48 43N 7 40 E
Brumunddal, Norway . 9 F14 60 53N 10 56 E
Bruneau, U.S.A. 108 E6 42 53N 115 48W
Bruneau →, U.S.A. .. 108 E6 42 56N 115 57W
Bruneck = Brunico, Italy 41 B8 46 48N 11 56 E
Brunei = Bandar Seri
  Begawan, Brunei ... 62 C4 4 52N 115 0 E
Brunei ■, Asia ...... 62 D4 4 50N 115 0 E
Brunflo, Sweden ..... 10 A8 63 5N 14 50 E
Brunico, Italy .... 41 B8 46 48N 11 56 E
Brunna, Sweden ..... 10 E11 59 52N 17 25 E
Brunnen, Switz. ..... 25 J4 46 59N 8 37 E
Brunner, L., N.Z. .... 91 K3 42 37 S 171 27 E
Brunsbüttel, Germany . 24 B5 53 53N 9 6 E
Brunssum, Neths. .... 17 D5 50 57N 5 59 E
Brunswick =
  Braunschweig,
  Germany .... 24 C6 52 15N 10 31 E
Brunswick, Maine,
  U.S.A. 115 D11 43 55N 69 58W
Brunswick, Md., U.S.A. 114 F7 39 19N 77 38W
Brunswick, Mo., U.S.A. 112 F8 39 26N 93 8W
Brunswick, Ohio, U.S.A. 116 E3 41 14N 81 51W
Brunswick, Pen. de,
  Chile .... 128 G2 53 30 S 71 30W
Brunswick B., Australia 92 C3 15 15 S 124 50 E
Brunswick Junction,
  Australia .... 93 F2 33 15 S 115 50 E
Bruntál, Czech Rep. .. 27 B10 49 57N 17 27 E
Bruny I., Australia .... 95 G4 43 20 S 147 15 E
Brus Laguna, Honduras 120 C3 15 47N 84 35W
Brusartsi, Bulgaria ... 44 C7 43 40N 23 5 E
Brush, U.S.A. 112 E3 40 15N 103 37W
Brushton, U.S.A. 117 B10 44 50N 74 31W
Brusio, Switz. ...... 25 J6 46 14N 10 8 E

Brusque, Brazil ...... 127 B6 27 5 S 49 0W
Brussel, Belgium ..... 17 D4 50 51N 4 21 E
Brussel ✈ (BRU),
  Belgium .... 17 D5 50 54N 5 41 E
Brussels = Brussel,
  Belgium .... 17 D4 50 51N 4 21 E
Brussels, Canada 116 C3 43 44N 81 15W
Brusy, Poland .... 30 E4 53 53N 17 43 E
Bruthen, Australia ... 95 F4 37 42 S 147 50 E
Bruxelles = Brussel,
  Belgium .... 17 D4 50 51N 4 21 E
Bruyères, France .... 19 D13 48 10N 6 40 E
Bruz, France 18 D5 48 1N 1 46W
Brwinów, Poland .... 31 F7 52 9N 20 40 E
Bryagovo, Bulgaria ... 45 E9 41 58N 25 8 E
Bryan, Ohio, U.S.A. .. 114 E3 41 28N 84 33W
Bryan, Mt., Australia . 95 E2 33 30 S 139 0 E
Bryan, Tex., U.S.A. ... 113 K6 30 40N 96 22W
Bryansk, Bryansk,
  Russia .... 33 F8 53 13N 34 25 E
Bryansk, Dagestan,
  Russia .... 35 H8 44 20N 47 10 E
Bryanskoye = Bryansk,
  Russia .... 35 H8 44 20N 47 10 E
Bryce Canyon △, U.S.A. 109 H7 37 30N 112 10W
Bryne, Norway ...... 9 G11 58 44N 5 38 E
Bryson City, U.S.A. .. 115 H4 35 26N 83 27W
Bryukhovetskaya,
  Russia .... 33 K10 45 48N 39 0 E
Brza Palanka,
  Serbia & M. .... 44 B6 44 28N 22 27 E
Brzeg, Poland .... 31 H4 50 52N 17 30 E
Brzeg Dolny, Poland .. 31 G3 51 16N 16 41 E
Brześć Kujawski, Poland 31 F5 52 36N 18 55 E
Brzesko, Poland ..... 31 J7 49 59N 20 34 E
Brzeziny, Poland .... 31 G6 51 49N 19 42 E
Brzozów, Poland .... 31 J9 49 41N 22 3 E
Bsharri, Lebanon .... 74 A5 34 15N 36 0 E
Bū Baqarah, U.A.E. .. 71 E8 25 35N 56 25 E
Bu Craa, W. Sahara .. 78 C3 26 45N 12 50W
Bū Ḥasā, U.A.E. .... 71 F7 23 30N 53 20 E
Bua, Sweden .... 11 G6 57 14N 12 7 E
Bua Yai, Thailand .... 64 E4 15 33N 102 26 E
Buapinang, Indonesia . 63 E6 4 40 S 121 30 E
Buba, Guinea-Biss. ... 82 C1 11 40N 14 59W
Bubanza, Burundi .... 86 C2 3 6 S 29 23 E
Bubaque, Guinea-Biss. 82 C1 11 16N 15 51W
Bube, Ethiopia ...... 81 F4 8 46N 35 48 E
Bübiyān, Kuwait ..... 71 D6 29 45N 48 15 E
Buca, Turkey .... 47 C9 38 22N 27 11 E
Bucak, Turkey ...... 47 D12 37 28N 30 36 E
Bucaramanga, Colombia 124 B4 7 0N 73 0W
Bucas Grande I., Phil. . 61 G6 9 40N 125 57 E
Bucasia, Australia .... 94 K7 21 2 S 149 10 E
Buccaneer Arch.,
  Australia .... 92 C3 16 7 S 123 20 E
Buccino, Italy .... 43 B8 40 38N 15 22 E
Buccoo Reef,
  Trin. & Tob. 125 J16 11 10N 60 51W
Bucecea, Romania ... 29 C11 47 47N 26 28 E
Bucegi △, Romania .. 29 E10 45 25N 25 28 E
Buchach, Ukraine .... 33 H3 49 5N 25 25 E
Buchan, U.K. 13 D6 57 32N 2 21W
Buchan Ness, U.K. ... 13 D7 57 29N 1 46W
Buchanan, Canada ... 103 C8 51 40N 102 45W
Buchanan, Liberia ... 82 D2 5 57N 10 2W
Buchanan, L., Queens.,
  Australia .... 94 C4 21 35 S 145 52 E
Buchanan, L.,
  W. Austral., Australia 93 E3 25 33 S 123 2 E
Buchanan, L., U.S.A. . 113 K5 30 45N 98 25W
Buchanan Cr. →,
  Australia .... 94 B2 19 13 S 136 33 E
Buchans, Canada 105 C8 48 50N 56 52W
Bucharest = București,
  Romania .... 29 F11 44 27N 26 10 E
Buchen, Germany .... 25 F5 49 32N 9 20 E
Buchholz, Germany .. 24 B5 53 19N 9 52 E
Buchloe, Germany ... 25 G6 48 1N 10 44 E
Buchon, Pt., U.S.A. .. 110 K6 35 15N 120 54W
Buciumi, Romania ... 28 C8 47 3N 23 1 E
Buck Hill Falls, U.S.A. 117 E9 41 11N 75 16W
Buckeburg, Germany . 24 C5 52 16N 9 7 E
Buckeye, U.S.A. 109 K7 33 22N 112 35W
Buckeye Lake, U.S.A. . 116 G2 39 55N 82 29W
Buckhannon, U.S.A. .. 114 F5 39 0N 80 8W
Buckhaven, U.K. 13 E5 56 11N 3 3W
Buckhorn L., Canada . 116 B6 44 29N 78 23W
Buckie, U.K. 13 D6 57 41N 2 58W
Buckingham, Canada . 104 C4 45 37N 75 24W
Buckingham, U.K. 15 E7 51 59N 0 57W
Buckingham B.,
  Australia .... 94 A2 12 10 S 135 40 E
Buckinghamshire □,
  U.K. 15 F7 51 53N 0 55W
Buckle Hd., Australia . 92 B4 14 26 S 127 52 E
Buckleboo, Australia . 95 E2 32 54 S 136 12 E
Buckley →, Australia . 94 C2 20 10 S 138 49 E
Buckley, U.K. 14 D4 53 10N 3 5W
Bucklin, U.S.A. 113 G5 37 33N 99 38W
Bucks L., U.S.A. 110 F5 39 54N 121 12W
Bucquoy, France .... 19 B9 50 9N 2 43 E
București, Romania ... 29 F11 44 27N 26 10 E
Bucyrus, U.S.A. 114 E4 40 48N 82 59W
Budacu, Vf., Romania . 29 C10 47 7N 25 41 E
Budalin, Burma ..... 67 H19 22 20N 95 10 E
Budaörs, Hungary .... 28 C3 47 8N 18 58 E
Budapest, Hungary ... 28 C4 47 29N 19 5 E
Budapest □, Hungary 28 C4 47 29N 19 5 E
Budapest ✈ (BUD),
  Hungary .... 28 C4 47 25N 19 12 E
Budaun, India ...... 69 E8 28 5N 79 10 E
Budd Coast, Antarctica 5 C8 68 0 S 112 0 E
Buddusò, Italy ...... 42 B2 40 35N 9 15 E
Bude, U.K. 15 G3 50 49N 4 34W
Budennovsk, Russia .. 35 H7 44 50N 44 10 E
Budeşti, Romania .... 29 F11 44 13N 26 30 E
Budeyi, Ukraine ..... 29 B14 48 3N 29 16 E
Budge Budge = Baj Baj,
  India .... 69 H13 22 30N 88 5 E
Budgewoi, Australia .. 95 E5 33 13 S 151 34 E
Budia, Spain 38 E2 40 38N 2 46W
Büdingen, Germany .. 25 E5 50 16N 9 7 E
Budjala, Dem. Rep. of
  the Congo .... 84 D3 2 50N 19 40 E
Budoni, Italy .... 42 B2 40 34N 9 43 E
Búdrio, Italy .... 41 D8 44 32N 11 32 E
Budva, Serbia & M. .. 44 D3 42 17N 18 50 E
Budzyń, Poland ..... 31 F3 52 54N 16 59 E
Buea, Cameroon ..... 83 E6 4 10N 9 9 E
Buellton, U.S.A. 111 L6 34 37N 120 12W
Buena Esperanza,
  Argentina .... 126 C2 34 45 S 65 15W
Buena Park, U.S.A. .. 111 M9 33 52N 117 59W

Buena Vista, Colo.,
  U.S.A. 109 G10 38 51N 106 8W
Buena Vista, Va., U.S.A. 114 G6 37 44N 79 21W
Buena Vista Lake Bed,
  U.S.A. 111 K7 35 12N 119 18W
Buenaventura,
  Colombia 124 C3 3 53N 77 4W
Buenaventura, Mexico . 118 B3 29 50N 107 30W
Buendía, Embalse de,
  Spain 38 E2 40 25N 2 43W
Buenos Aires, Argentina 126 C4 34 30 S 58 20W
Buenos Aires,
  Costa Rica 120 E3 9 10N 83 20W
Buenos Aires □,
  Argentina .... 126 D4 36 30 S 60 0W
Buenos Aires, L., Chile 128 F2 46 35 S 72 30W
Buffalo, Mo., U.S.A. .. 113 G8 37 39N 93 6W
Buffalo, N.Y., U.S.A. . 116 D6 42 53N 78 53W
Buffalo, Okla., U.S.A. . 113 G5 36 50N 99 38W
Buffalo, S. Dak., U.S.A. 112 C3 45 35N 103 33W
Buffalo, Wyo., U.S.A. . 108 D10 44 21N 106 42W
Buffalo →, Canada .. 102 A5 60 5N 115 5W
Buffalo →, S. Africa . 89 D5 28 43 S 30 37 E
Buffalo Head Hills,
  Canada 102 B5 57 25N 115 55W
Buffalo L., Alta., Canada 102 C6 52 27N 112 54W
Buffalo L., N.W.T.,
  Canada 102 A5 60 12N 115 25W
Buffalo Narrows,
  Canada 103 B7 55 51N 108 29W
Buffalo Springs △,
  Kenya .... 86 B4 0 32N 37 35 E
Buffels →, S. Africa .. 88 D2 29 36 S 17 3 E
Buford, U.S.A. 115 H4 34 10N 84 0W
Bug = Buh →, Ukraine 33 J6 46 59N 31 58 E
Bug = Buh →, Poland 31 F8 52 31N 21 5 E
Buga, Colombia 124 C3 4 0N 76 15W
Bugala I., Uganda .... 86 C3 0 40 S 32 20 E
Buganda, Uganda .... 86 C3 0 0 31 30 E
Buganga, Uganda .... 86 C3 0 3 S 32 0 E
Bugasong, Phil. ..... 61 F5 11 3N 122 4 E
Bugel, Tanjung,
  Indonesia .... 63 G14 6 26 S 111 3 E
Bugibba, Malta ...... 49 D1 35 57N 14 25 E
Bugsuk, Phil. .... 61 G1 8 15N 117 15 E
Buguma, Nigeria ..... 83 E6 4 42N 6 55 E
Bugun Shara, Mongolia 60 B5 49 0N 104 0 E
Bugungu □, Uganda .. 86 B3 2 17N 31 50 E
Buguruslan, Russia ... 52 D6 53 39N 52 26 E
Buh →, Ukraine .... 33 J6 46 59N 31 58 E
Buhakarent, Turkey .. 47 D10 37 58N 28 44 E
Buheirat-Murrat-el-
  Kubra, Egypt ...... 80 H8 30 18N 32 26 E
Buhera, Zimbabwe ... 89 B5 19 18 S 31 29 E
Bühl, Germany ...... 25 G4 48 40N 8 8 E
Buhl, U.S.A. 108 E6 42 36N 114 46W
Buhuşi, Romania .... 29 D11 46 41N 26 45 E
Bui □, Ghana 82 D4 8 21N 2 21W
Builth Wells, U.K. ... 15 E4 52 9N 3 25W
Buinsk, Russia ...... 34 C9 55 0N 48 18 E
Buir Nur, Mongolia ... 60 B6 47 50N 117 42 E
Buis-les-Baronnies,
  France .... 21 D9 44 17N 5 16 E
Buitrago del Lozoya,
  Spain 36 E7 40 58N 3 38W
Bujalance, Spain 37 H6 37 54N 4 23W
Bujanovac, Serbia & M. 44 D5 42 28N 21 44 E
Bujaraloz, Spain 38 D4 41 29N 0 10W
Buje, Croatia .... 41 C10 45 24N 13 39 E
Bujumbura, Burundi .. 86 C2 3 16 S 29 18 E
Bük, Hungary .... 28 C1 47 22N 16 45 E
Buk, Poland .... 31 F3 52 21N 16 30 E
Bukachacha, Russia .. 53 D12 52 55N 116 50 E
Bukama, Dem. Rep. of
  the Congo .... 87 D2 9 10 S 25 50 E
Bukavu, Dem. Rep. of
  the Congo .... 86 C2 2 20 S 28 52 E
Bukene, Tanzania .... 86 C3 4 15 S 32 48 E
Bukhara = Bukhoro,
  Uzbekistan .... 52 F7 39 48N 64 25 E
Bukhoro, Uzbekistan . 52 F7 39 48N 64 25 E
Bukima, Tanzania .... 86 C3 1 50 S 33 25 E
Bukit Badung, Indonesia 63 K18 8 49 S 115 10 E
Bukit Kerajaan,
  Malaysie .... 65 c 5 25N 100 15 E
Bukit Mertajam,
  Malaysia .... 65 c 5 22N 100 28 E
Bukit Ni, Malaysia ... 65 d 1 22N 104 12 E
Bukit Panjang,
  Singapore .... 65 d 1 23N 103 46 E
Bukit Tengah, Malaysia 65 c 5 22N 100 28 E
Bukittinggi, Indonesia . 62 E2 0 20 S 100 20 E
Bükk, Hungary ...... 28 B5 48 0N 20 30 E
Bükki △, Hungary ... 28 B5 48 3N 20 30 E
Bukoba, Tanzania .... 86 C3 1 20 S 31 49 E
Bukum, Pulau,
  Singapore .... 65 d 1 14N 103 46 E
Bukuru, Nigeria ..... 83 D6 9 42N 8 48 E
Bukuya, Uganda ..... 86 B3 0 40N 31 52 E
Bül, Kuh-e, Iran ..... 71 D7 30 48N 52 45 E
Bula, Guinea-Biss. ... 82 C1 12 7N 15 43W
Bula, Indonesia ..... 63 E8 3 6 S 130 30 E
Bülach, Switz. ...... 25 H4 47 31N 8 32 E
Bulahdelah, Australia . 95 E5 32 23 S 152 13 E
Bulan, Phil. .... 61 E5 12 40N 123 52 E
Bulancak, Turkey .... 73 B8 40 56N 38 14 E
Bulandshahr, India ... 68 E7 28 28N 77 51 E
Bulanik, Turkey ..... 73 C10 39 4N 42 14 E
Bûlâq, Egypt .... 80 B3 25 10N 30 38 E
Bulawayo, Zimbabwe . 87 G2 20 7 S 28 32 E
Buldan, Turkey ..... 47 C10 38 2N 28 50 E
Buldana, India ...... 66 J10 20 30N 76 18 E
Bulgan, Mongolia .... 60 B5 48 45N 103 34 E
Bulgaria ■, Europe .. 45 D8 42 35N 25 30 E
Bulgheria, Monte, Italy 43 B8 40 4N 15 26 E
Bulgurca, Turkey .... 47 D9 38 3N 27 4 E
Buli, Teluk, Indonesia . 63 D7 0 48N 128 25 E
Buliluyan, C., Phil. ... 61 G2 8 20N 117 15 E
Bulim, Singapore .... 65 d 1 22N 103 43 E
Bulki, Ethiopia ...... 81 F4 6 11N 36 31 E
Bulkley →, Canada .. 102 B3 55 15N 127 40W
Bull Shoals L., U.S.A. . 113 G8 36 22N 92 35W
Bullaque →, Spain ... 37 G6 38 59N 4 17W
Bullas, Spain 39 G3 38 2N 1 40W
Bulle, Switz. .... 25 J3 46 37N 7 3 E
Bullhead City, U.S.A. . 111 K12 35 8N 114 32W
Buller →, N.Z. ..... 91 J5 41 44 S 171 31 E
Bullhead Creek, U.S.A. 116 E4 41 1N 81 38W
Bulloo →, Australia .. 95 D3 28 43 S 142 30 E
Bulloo L., Australia .. 95 D3 28 43 S 142 25 E
Bulls, N.Z. .... 91 J5 40 10 S 175 24 E
Bully-les-Mines, France 19 B9 50 27N 2 44 E
Bulnes, Chile .... 126 D1 36 42 S 72 19W

Bulsar = Valsad, *India* . **66 J8** 20 40N 72 58 E
Bultfontein, *S. Africa* . **88 D4** 28 18 S 26 10 E
Bulukumba, *Indonesia* . **63 F6** 5 33 S 120 11 E
Bulun, *Russia* .... **53 B13** 70 37N 127 30 E
Bumba, *Dem. Rep. of
the Congo* .... **84 D4** 2 13N 22 30 E
Bumbeşti-Jiu, *Romania* . **29 E8** 45 10N 23 24 E
Bumbiri I., *Tanzania* .. **86 C3** 1 40 S 31 55 E
Bumbuna, *S. Leone* ... **82 D2** 9 2N 11 49W
Bumhpa Bum, *Burma* .. **67 F20** 26 51N 97 14 E
Bumi →, *Zimbabwe* .. **87 F2** 17 0 S 28 20 E
Buna, *Kenya* .... **86 B4** 2 58N 39 30 E
Bunawan, *Phil.* ...... **61 G6** 8 12N 125 57 E
Bunbury, *Australia* ... **93 F2** 33 20 S 115 35 E
Bunclody, *Ireland* **12 D5** 52 39N 6 40W
Buncrana, *Ireland* **12 A4** 55 8N 7 27W
Bundaberg, *Australia* .. **95 C5** 24 54 S 152 22 E
Bünde, *Germany* ..... **24 C4** 52 11N 8 35 E
Bundey →, *Australia* .. **94 C2** 21 46 S 135 37 E
Bundi, *India* .... **68 G6** 25 30N 75 35 E
Bundjalung △, *Australia* **95 D5** 29 16 S 153 21 E
Bundoran, *Ireland* **12 B3** 54 28N 8 16W
Bundukia, *Sudan* .... **81 F3** 5 14N 30 55 E
Bung Kan, *Thailand* .. **64 C4** 18 23N 103 37 E
Bunga →, *Nigeria* ... **83 C6** 11 23N 9 56 E
Bungay, *U.K.* .... **15 E9** 52 27N 1 28 E
Bungil Cr. →, *Australia* **95 D4** 27 5 S 149 5 E
Bungle Bungle =
Purnululu △, *Australia* **92 C4** 17 20 S 128 20 E
Bungo-Suidō, *Japan* .. **55 H6** 33 0N 132 15 E
Bungoma, *Kenya* .... **86 B3** 0 34N 34 34 E
Bungotakada, *Japan* .. **55 H5** 33 35N 131 25 E
Bungu, *Tanzania* .... **86 D4** 7 35 S 39 0 E
Bunia, *Dem. Rep. of
the Congo* .... **86 B3** 1 35N 30 20 E
Bunji, *Pakistan* ..... **69 B6** 35 45N 74 40 E
Bunkie, *U.S.A.* **113 K8** 30 57N 92 11W
Bunnell, *U.S.A.* **115 L5** 29 28N 81 16W
Buñol, *Spain* **39 F4** 39 25N 0 47W
Bunsuru, *Nigeria* .... **83 C5** 13 0N 5 8 E
Buntok, *Indonesia* ... **62 E4** 1 40 S 114 58 E
Bununu Dass, *Nigeria* . **83 C6** 10 5N 9 31 E
Bununu Kasa, *Nigeria* . **83 D6** 9 51N 9 32 E
Bunya Mts., *Australia* . **95 D5** 26 51 S 151 34 E
Bünyan, *Turkey* ..... **72 C6** 38 51N 35 51 E
Bunyu, *Indonesia* .... **62 D5** 3 35N 117 50 E
Bunza, *Nigeria* ..... **83 C5** 12 8N 4 0 E
Buol, *Indonesia* ..... **63 D6** 1 15N 121 32 E
Buon Brieng, *Vietnam* . **64 F7** 13 9N 108 12 E
Buon Ma Thuot,
Vietnam .... **64 F7** 12 40N 108 3 E
Buong Long, *Cambodia* . **64 F6** 13 44N 106 59 E
Buorkhaya, Mys, *Russia* **53 B14** 71 50N 132 40 E
Buqayq, *Si. Arabia* ... **71 E6** 26 0N 49 45 E
Buqbuq, *Egypt* ..... **80 A2** 31 29N 25 29 E
Bur Acaba, *Somali Rep.* **75 G3** 3 12N 44 20 E
Bûr Fuad, *Egypt* .... **80 H8** 31 15N 32 20 E
Bûr Safâga, *Egypt* ... **70 E2** 26 43N 33 57 E
Bûr Sa'îd, *Egypt* .... **80 H8** 31 16N 32 18 E
Bûr Sûdân, *Sudan* ... **80 D4** 19 32N 37 9 E
Bûr Taufiq, *Egypt* ... **80 J8** 29 54N 32 32 E
Bura, *Kenya* .... **86 C4** 1 4 S 39 58 E
Burakin, *Australia* ... **93 F2** 30 31 S 117 10 E
Buram, *Sudan* ...... **81 E2** 10 51N 25 9 E
Burao, *Somali Rep.* ... **75 F4** 9 32N 45 32 E
Burāq, *Syria* .... **74 B5** 33 11N 36 29 E
Buraydah, *Si. Arabia* .. **70 E4** 26 20N 43 59 E
Burbank, *U.S.A.* **111 L8** 34 11N 118 19W
Burda, *India* .... **68 G6** 25 50N 77 35 E
Burdekin →, *Australia* . **94 B4** 19 38 S 147 25 E
Burdur, *Turkey* ..... **47 D12** 37 45N 30 17 E
Burdur □, *Turkey* ... **47 D12** 37 45N 30 0 E
Burdur Gölü, *Turkey* .. **47 D12** 37 44N 30 10 E
Burdwan =
Barddhaman, *India* . **69 H12** 23 14N 87 39 E
Bure, *Gojam, Ethiopia* . **81 E4** 10 40N 37 4 E
Bure, *Ilubabor, Ethiopia* **81 F4** 8 19N 35 8 E
Bure →, *U.K.* ...... **14 E9** 52 38N 1 43 E
Büren, *Germany* ..... **24 D4** 51 33N 8 35 E
Bureya →, *Russia* ... **53 E13** 49 27N 129 30 E
Burford, *Canada* **116 C4** 43 7N 80 27W
Burg, *Germany* ..... **24 C7** 52 16N 11 51 E
Burg auf Fehmarn,
Germany .... **24 A7** 54 28N 11 9 E
Burg el Arab, *Egypt* .. **80 H6** 30 54N 29 32 E
Burg et Tuyur, *Sudan* . **80 C2** 20 55N 27 56 E
Burg Stargard, *Germany* **24 B9** 53 29N 13 18 E
Burgas, *Bulgaria* .... **45 D11** 42 33N 27 29 E
Burgas □, *Bulgaria* .. **45 D10** 42 30N 26 50 E
Burgaski Zaliv, *Bulgaria* **45 D11** 42 30N 27 39 E
Burgdorf, *Germany* ... **24 C6** 52 27N 10 1 E
Burgdorf, *Switz.* .... **25 H3** 47 3N 7 37 E
Burgenland □, *Austria* . **27 D9** 47 20N 16 20 E
Burgeo, *Canada* **105 C8** 47 37N 57 38W
Burgersdorp, *S. Africa* . **88 E4** 31 0 S 26 20 E
Burges, Mt., *Australia* . **93 F3** 30 50 S 121 5 E
Burghausen, *Germany* . **25 G8** 48 9N 12 49 E
Burghead, *U.K.* **13 D5** 57 43N 3 30W
Bûrgio, *Italy* ...... **42 E6** 37 36N 13 17 E
Burglengenfeld,
Germany .... **25 F8** 49 12N 12 2 E
Burgohondo, *Spain* .. **36 E6** 40 26N 4 47W
Burgos, *Spain* **36 C7** 42 21N 3 41W
Burgos □, *Spain* **36 C7** 42 21N 3 42W
Burgstädt, *Germany* .. **24 E8** 50 54N 12 49 E
Burgsvik, *Sweden* ... **11 G12** 57 3N 18 19 E
Burguillos del Cerro,
Spain **37 G4** 38 23N 6 35W
Burgundy =
Bourgogne □, *France* **19 F11** 47 0N 4 50 E
Burhaniye, *Turkey* ... **47 B8** 39 30N 26 58 E
Burhanpur, *India* ... **66 J10** 21 18N 76 14 E
Burhi Gandak →, *India* **69 H9** 22 43N 80 31 E
Burhner →, *India* ... **69 H9** 22 43N 80 31 E
Buri Pen., *Eritrea* ... **81 E4** 15 25N 39 55 E
Burias I., *Phil.* ..... **61 E5** 12 55N 123 5 E
Burica, Pta., *Costa Rica* **120 E3** 8 3N 82 51W
Burien, *U.S.A.* **110 C4** 47 28N 122 21W
Burigi △, *Tanzania* .. **86 C3** 2 20 S 31 6 E
Burigi, L., *Tanzania* .. **86 C3** 2 2 S 31 22 E
Burin, *Canada* **105 C8** 47 1N 55 14W
Buriram, *Thailand* ... **64 E4** 15 0N 103 0 E
Burj Şāfīṭā, *Syria* ... **70 C3** 34 48N 36 7 E
Burji, *Ethiopia* ..... **81 F4** 5 29N 37 51 E
Burkburnett, *U.S.A.* .. **113 H5** 34 6N 98 34W
Burke →, *Australia* .. **94 C2** 23 12 S 139 33 E
Burke Chan., *Canada* . **102 C3** 52 10N 127 30W
Burketown, *Australia* . **94 B2** 17 45 S 139 33 E
Burkina Faso ■, *Africa* **82 C4** 12 0N 1 0W
Burk's Falls, *Canada* .. **104 C4** 45 37N 79 24W
Burlada, *Spain* **38 C3** 42 49N 1 36W
Burleigh Falls, *Canada* . **116 B6** 44 33N 78 12W
Burley, *U.S.A.* **108 E7** 42 32N 113 48W
Burligame, *U.S.A.* ... **110 H4** 37 35N 122 21W
Burlington, *Canada* .. **116 C5** 43 18N 79 45W
Burlington, Colo.,
U.S.A. **112 F3** 39 18N 102 16W

Burlington, *Iowa, U.S.A.* **112 E9** 40 49N 91 14W
Burlington, *Kans.,
U.S.A.* **112 F7** 38 12N 95 45W
Burlington, *N.C., U.S.A.* **115 G6** 36 6N 79 26W
Burlington, *N.J., U.S.A.* **117 F10** 40 4N 74 51W
Burlington, *Vt., U.S.A.* . **117 B11** 44 29N 73 12W
Burlington, *Wash.,
U.S.A.* **110 B4** 48 28N 122 20W
Burlington, *Wis., U.S.A.* **114 D1** 42 41N 88 17W
Burlyu-Tyube,
Kazakhstan ...... **52 E8** 46 30N 79 10 E
Burma ■, *Asia* ..... **67 J20** 21 0N 96 30 E
Burnaby I., *Canada* .. **102 C2** 52 25N 131 19W
Burnet, *U.S.A.* **113 K5** 30 45N 98 14W
Burney, *U.S.A.* **108 F3** 40 53N 121 40W
Burnham, *U.S.A.* **116 F7** 40 38N 77 34W
Burnham-on-Sea, *U.K.* **15 F5** 51 14N 3 0W
Burnie, *Australia* .... **95 G4** 41 4 S 145 56 E
Burnley, *U.K.* **14 D5** 53 47N 2 14W
Burns, *U.S.A.* **108 E4** 43 35N 119 3W
Burns Lake, *Canada* .. **102 C3** 54 20N 125 45W
Burnside →, *Canada* . **100 B9** 66 51N 108 4W
Burnside, L., *Australia* . **93 E3** 25 22 S 123 0 E
Burnt L., *Canada* **105 B7** 53 35N 64 4W
Burnt River, *Canada* .. **116 B6** 44 41N 78 42W
Burntwood →, *Canada* **103 B9** 56 8N 96 34W
Burntwood L., *Canada* . **103 B8** 55 22N 100 26W
Burqān, *Kuwait* .... **70 D5** 29 0N 47 57 E
Burra, *Australia* ..... **95 E2** 33 40 S 138 55 E
Burra, *Nigeria* ..... **83 C6** 11 0N 8 56 E
Burray, *U.K.* **13 C6** 58 51N 2 54W
Burrel, *Albania* ..... **44 E4** 41 36N 20 1 E
Burren △, *Ireland* ... **12 C3** 53 1N 8 58W
Burren Junction,
Australia .... **95 E4** 30 7 S 148 59 E
Burriana, *Spain* **38 F4** 39 50N 0 4W
Burrinjuck Res.,
Australia .... **95 F4** 35 0 S 148 36 E
Burro, Serranías del,
Mexico **118 B4** 29 0N 102 0W
Burrow Hd., *U.K.* ... **13 G4** 54 41N 4 24W
Burrum Coast △,
Australia .... **95 D5** 25 13 S 152 36 E
Burruyacú, *Argentina* . **126 B3** 26 30 S 64 40W
Burry Port, *U.K.* **15 F3** 51 41N 4 15W
Bursa, *Turkey* ...... **45 F13** 40 15N 29 5 E
Burseryd, *Sweden* ... **11 G7** 57 12N 13 17 E
Burstall, *Canada* **103 C7** 50 39N 109 54W
Burton, *Ohio, U.S.A.* . **116 E3** 41 28N 81 8W
Burton, *S.C., U.S.A.* .. **115 J5** 32 25N 80 45W
Burton, L., *Canada* .. **104 B4** 54 45N 78 20W
Burton upon Trent, *U.K.* **14 E6** 52 48N 1 38W
Buru, *Indonesia* ..... **63 E7** 3 30 S 126 30 E
Burullus, Bahra el,
Egypt .... **80 H7** 31 25N 31 0 E
Burūn, Râs, *Egypt* ... **74 D2** 31 14N 33 7 E
Burundi ■, *Africa* ... **86 C3** 3 15 S 30 0 E
Bururi, *Burundi* ..... **86 C2** 3 57 S 29 37 E
Burutu, *Nigeria* ..... **83 D6** 5 20N 5 29 E
Burwell, *U.S.A.* **112 E5** 41 47N 99 8W
Burwick, *U.K.* **13 C5** 58 45N 2 58W
Bury, *U.K.* **14 D5** 53 35N 2 17W
Bury St. Edmunds, *U.K.* **15 E8** 52 15N 0 43 E
Buryatia □, *Russia* .. **53 D11** 53 0N 110 0 E
Buryn, *Ukraine* ..... **33 G7** 51 13N 33 50 E
Burzenin, *Poland* .... **31 G5** 51 28N 18 47 E
Busalla, *Italy* ...... **40 D5** 44 34N 8 57 E
Busan = Pusan, *S. Korea* **57 G15** 35 5N 129 0 E
Busango Swamp,
Zambia .... **87 E2** 14 15 S 25 45 E
Buşayrah, *Syria* ..... **70 C4** 35 9N 40 26 E
Busca, *Italy* .... **40 D4** 44 31N 7 29 E
Bushat, *Albania* ..... **44 E3** 41 58N 19 34 E
Büshehr, *Iran* ...... **71 D6** 28 55N 50 55 E
Büshehr □, *Iran* .... **71 D6** 28 20N 51 45 E
Bushell, *Canada* **103 B7** 59 31N 108 45W
Bushenyi, *Uganda* ... **86 C3** 0 35N 30 10 E
Bushire = Büshehr, *Iran* **71 D6** 28 55N 50 55 E
Bushtyna, *Ukraine* .. **29 B8** 48 3N 23 28 E
Busie, *Ghana* **82 C4** 10 29N 2 22W
Businga, *Dem. Rep. of
the Congo* ...... **84 D4** 3 16N 20 59 E
Busko-Zdrój, *Poland* . **31 H7** 50 28N 20 42 E
Busovača, *Bos.-H.* ... **42 G2** 44 6N 17 53 E
Buşra ash Shām, *Syria* **74 C5** 32 30N 36 25 E
Busselton, *Australia* .. **93 F2** 33 42 S 115 15 E
Busseri →, *Sudan* ... **81 F2** 7 41N 28 3 E
Busseto, *Italy* ...... **40 D7** 44 59N 10 2 E
Bussière-Badil, *France* . **20 C4** 45 39N 0 36 E
Bussum, *Neths.* ..... **17 B5** 52 16N 5 10 E
Buşteni, *Romania* ... **29 E10** 45 24N 25 32 E
Busto, C., *Spain* **36 B4** 43 34N 6 28W
Busto Arsízio, *Italy* .. **40 C5** 45 37N 8 51 E
Busu Djanoa, *Dem. Rep.
of the Congo* ..... **84 D4** 1 43N 21 23 E
Busuanga I., *Phil.* ... **61 E3** 12 10N 120 0 E
Büsum, *Germany* .... **24 A4** 54 7N 8 51 E
Busungbiu, *Indonesia* . **63 J17** 8 16 S 114 58 E
Buta, *Dem. Rep. of
the Congo* ...... **86 B1** 2 50N 24 53 E
Butare, *Rwanda* .... **86 C2** 2 31 S 29 52 E
Butaritari, *Kiribati* ... **96 G9** 3 30N 174 0 E
Bute, *U.K.* **13 F3** 55 48N 5 2W
Bute Inlet, *Canada* .. **102 C4** 50 40N 124 53W
Butemba, *Uganda* ... **86 B3** 1 9N 31 37 E
Butembo, *Dem. Rep. of
the Congo* ...... **86 B2** 0 9N 29 18 E
Buteni, *Romania* .... **28 D7** 46 19N 22 7 E
Butera, *Italy* .... **43 E7** 37 11N 14 11 E
Butha Qi, *China* .... **60 B7** 48 0N 122 32 E
Butiaba, *Uganda* .... **86 B3** 1 50N 31 20 E
Butler, *Mo., U.S.A.* .. **112 F7** 38 16N 94 20W
Butler, *Pa., U.S.A.* ... **116 F5** 40 52N 79 54W
Buton, *Indonesia* .... **63 E6** 5 0 S 122 45 E
Butte, *Mont., U.S.A.* .. **108 C7** 46 0N 112 32W
Butte, *Nebr., U.S.A.* .. **112 D5** 42 58N 98 51W
Butte Creek →, *U.S.A.* **110 F5** 39 12N 121 56W
Butterworth = Gcuwa,
S. Africa .... **89 E4** 32 20 S 28 11 E
Butterworth, *Malaysia* . **65 c** 5 24N 100 23 E
Buttevant, *Ireland* ... **12 D3** 52 14N 8 40W
Buttfield, Mt., *Australia* **93 D4** 24 45 S 128 9 E
Button B., *Canada* ... **103 B10** 58 45N 94 23W
Buttonwillow, *U.S.A.* . **111 K7** 35 24N 119 28W
Butty Hd., *Australia* .. **93 F3** 33 54 S 121 39 E
Butuan, *Phil.* ...... **61 G6** 8 57N 125 33 E
Butuku-Luba, *Eq. Guin.* **83 E6** 3 29N 8 33 E
Butung = Buton,
Indonesia ...... **63 E6** 5 0 S 122 45 E
Buturlinovka, *Russia* . **34 E5** 50 50N 40 35 E
Butzbach, *Germany* .. **24 E4** 50 25N 8 40 E
Bützow, *Germany* ... **24 B7** 53 50N 11 58 E
Buur Hakaba = Bur
Acaba, *Somali Rep.* . **75 G3** 3 12N 44 20 E
Buxa Duar, *India* .... **69 F13** 27 45N 89 35 E

Buxar, *India* .... **69 G10** 25 34N 83 58 E
Buxtehude, *Germany* . **24 B5** 53 28N 9 39 E
Buxton, *U.K.* **14 D6** 53 16N 1 54W
Buxy, *France* ...... **19 F11** 46 44N 4 40 E
Buy, *Russia* .... **34 A5** 58 28N 41 28 E
Buynaksk, *Russia* ... **35 J8** 42 48N 47 7 E
Buyo, *Ivory C.* **82 D3** 6 21N 7 1W
Buyo, L. de, *Ivory C.* . **82 D3** 6 16N 7 10W
Büyük Menderes →,
Turkey .... **47 D9** 37 28N 27 11 E
Büyükçekmece, *Turkey* **45 E12** 41 2N 28 35 E
Büyükkarıştıran, *Turkey* **45 E11** 41 18N 27 33 E
Büyükkemikli Burnu,
Turkey .... **45 F10** 40 18N 26 14 E
Büyükorhan, *Turkey* .. **45 F10** 39 46N 28 56 E
Büyükyoncalı, *Turkey* . **45 E11** 41 20N 27 55 E
Buzançais, *France* ... **18 F8** 46 54N 1 25 E
Buzău, *Romania* .... **29 E11** 45 10N 26 50 E
Buzău □, *Romania* .. **29 E11** 45 20N 26 30 E
Buzău →, *Romania* .. **29 E12** 45 26N 27 44 E
Buzău, Pasul, *Romania* **29 E11** 45 35N 26 12 E
Buzen, *Japan* ...... **55 H5** 33 35N 131 5 E
Buzet, *Croatia* ..... **41 C10** 45 24N 13 58 E
Buzi →, *Mozam.* .... **87 F3** 19 50 S 34 43 E
Buziaş, *Romania* .... **28 E6** 45 38N 21 36 E
Buzuluk, *Russia* .... **52 D6** 52 48N 52 12 E
Buzuluk →, *Russia* .. **34 E6** 50 15N 42 7 E
Buzzards Bay, *U.S.A.* . **117 E14** 41 44N 70 37W
Buzzards Bay, *U.S.A.* . **117 E14** 41 44N 70 37W
Bwana Mkubwe,
*Dem. Rep. of
the Congo* ...... **87 E2** 13 8 S 28 38 E
Bwindi △, *Uganda* .. **86 C2** 1 2 S 29 42 E
Byala, *Ruse, Bulgaria* . **45 C9** 43 28N 25 44 E
Byala, *Varna, Bulgaria* . **45 C11** 42 53N 27 55 E
Byala Slatina, *Bulgaria* **44 C7** 43 26N 23 58 E
Byarezina →, *Belarus* . **33 F6** 52 33N 30 14 E
Byaroza, *Belarus* .... **33 F3** 52 31N 24 51 E
Bychawa, *Poland* .... **31 G9** 51 1N 22 36 E
Byczyna, *Poland* .... **31 G5** 51 7N 18 12 E
Bydgoszcz, *Poland* .. **31 E5** 53 10N 18 0 E
Byelarus = Belarus ■,
Europe .... **32 F4** 53 30N 27 0 E
Byelorussia = Belarus ■,
Europe .... **32 F4** 53 30N 27 0 E
Byers, *U.S.A.* **112 F2** 39 43N 104 14W
Byesville, *U.S.A.* **116 G3** 39 58N 81 32W
Byfield △, *Australia* .. **94 C5** 22 52 S 150 45 E
Byford, *Australia* .... **93 F2** 32 15 S 116 0 E
Bykhaw, *Belarus* .... **32 F6** 53 31N 30 14 E
Bykhov = Bykhaw,
Belarus .... **32 F6** 53 31N 30 14 E
Bykovo, *Russia* ..... **34 F7** 49 50N 45 25 E
Bylas, *U.S.A.* **109 K8** 33 8N 110 7W
Bylot, *Canada* **103 B10** 58 25N 94 8W
Bylot I., *Canada* **101 A12** 73 13N 78 34W
Byrd, C., *Antarctica* .. **5 C17** 69 38 S 76 7W
Byrock, *Australia* .... **95 E4** 30 40 S 146 27 E
Byron, C., *Australia* .. **95 D5** 28 43 S 153 38 E
Byron, C., *Australia* .. **95 D5** 28 43 S 153 37 E
Byron Bay, *Australia* . **95 D5** 28 43 S 153 37 E
Byrranga, Gory, *Russia* **53 B11** 75 0N 100 0 E
Byrranga Mts. =
Byrranga, Gory,
Russia .... **53 B11** 75 0N 100 0 E
Byrum, *Denmark* .... **11 G5** 57 16N 11 0 E
Byske, *Sweden* ..... **8 D19** 64 57N 21 11 E
Byskeälven →, *Sweden* **8 D19** 64 57N 21 13 E
Bystrytsya, *Ukraine* .. **29 B9** 48 27N 24 14 E
Bystrzyca →,
Dolnośląskie, Poland **31 G3** 51 12N 16 55 E
Bystrzyca →, *Lubelskie,
Poland* .... **31 G9** 51 21N 22 46 E
Bystrzyca Kłodzka,
Poland .... **31 H3** 50 19N 16 39 E
Bytča, *Slovak Rep.* ... **27 B11** 49 13N 18 34 E
Bytkiv, *Ukraine* ..... **29 B9** 48 38N 24 28 E
Bytom, *Poland* ..... **31 H5** 50 25N 18 54 E
Bytom Odrzański,
Poland .... **31 G2** 51 44N 15 48 E
Bytów, *Poland* ..... **30 D4** 54 10N 17 30 E
Byumba, *Rwanda* ... **86 C3** 1 35 S 30 4 E
Bzenec, *Czech Rep.* .. **27 C10** 48 58N 17 18 E
Bzura →, *Poland* ... **31 F7** 52 25N 20 15 E

C

Ca →, *Vietnam* ..... **64 C5** 18 45N 105 45 E
Ca Mau, *Vietnam* ... **65 H5** 9 7N 105 8 E
Ca Mau, Mui, *Vietnam* **65 H5** 8 38N 104 44 E
Ca Na, *Vietnam* .... **65 G7** 11 20N 108 54 E
Caacupé, *Paraguay* .. **126 B4** 25 23 S 57 5W
Caaguazú □, *Paraguay* **126 B4** 26 5 S 55 31W
Caála, *Angola* ...... **85 G3** 12 46 S 15 30 E
Caamaño Sd., *Canada* **102 C3** 52 55N 129 25W
Caazapá, *Paraguay* .. **126 B4** 26 8 S 56 19W
Caazapá □, *Paraguay* . **127 B4** 26 10 S 56 0W
Cabadbaran, *Phil.* ... **61 G6** 9 10N 125 38 E
Cabalian = San Juan,
Phil. .... **61 F6** 10 16N 125 10 E
Caballería, C. de, *Spain* **48 A11** 40 5N 4 5 E
Cabana, *Spain* ...... **48 B11** 40 5N 4 5 E
Cabanatuan, *Phil.* ... **61 D4** 15 30N 120 58 E
Cabañeros △, *Spain* .. **37 F6** 39 18N 4 35W
Cabanes, *Spain* ..... **38 E5** 40 9N 0 2 E
Cabano, *Canada* **105 C6** 47 40N 68 56W
Çabar, *Croatia* ..... **41 C11** 45 36N 14 39 E
Cabazon, *U.S.A.* **111 M10** 33 55N 116 47W
Cabedelo, *Brazil* .... **125 E12** 7 0 S 34 50W
Cabeza del Buey, *Spain* **37 G5** 38 44N 5 13W
Cabezón de la Sal, *Spain* **36 B6** 43 18N 4 12W
Cabildo, *Chile* ...... **126 C1** 32 30 S 71 5W
Cabimas, *Venezuela* .. **124 A4** 10 23N 71 25W
Cabinda, *Angola* .... **84 F2** 5 33 S 12 11 E
Cabinda □, *Angola* .. **84 F2** 5 0 S 12 30 E
Cabinet Mts., *U.S.A.* . **108 C6** 48 0N 115 30W
Cabo Blanco, *Argentina* **128 F3** 47 15 S 65 47W
Cabo de Gata-Níjar △,
Spain **39 J2** 36 51N 2 6W
Cabo Frio, *Brazil* .... **127 A7** 22 51 S 42 3W
Cabo Pantoja, *Peru* .. **124 D3** 1 0 S 75 10W
Cabonga, Réservoir,
Canada **104 C4** 47 20N 76 40W
Cabool, *U.S.A.* **113 G8** 37 7N 92 6W
Caboolture, *Australia* . **95 D5** 27 5 S 152 58 E
Cabora Bassa Dam =
Cahora Bassa,
Reprêsa de, *Mozam.* **87 F3** 15 20 S 32 50 E
Caborca, *Mexico* **118 A2** 30 40N 112 10W
Cabot, Mt., *U.S.A.* ... **117 B13** 44 30N 71 25W
Cabot Hd., *Canada* .. **116 A3** 45 14N 81 17W
Cabot Str., *Canada* .. **105 C8** 47 15N 59 40W
Cabra, *Spain* **37 H6** 37 30N 4 28W
Cabra del Santo Cristo,
Spain **37 H7** 37 42N 3 16W

Cábras, *Italy* .... **42 C1** 39 56N 8 32 E
Cabrera, *Spain* ..... **48 B9** 39 8N 2 57 E
Cabrera △, *Spain* ... **39 F7** 39 13N 2 53 E
Cabrera, Sierra, *Spain* . **36 C4** 42 12N 6 40W
Cabri, *Canada* **103 C7** 50 35N 108 25W
Cabriel →, *Spain* ... **39 F3** 39 14N 1 3W
Cabugao, *Phil.* ..... **61 C4** 17 48N 120 27 E
Cacabelos, *Spain* **36 C4** 42 36N 6 44W
Caçador, *Brazil* ..... **127 B5** 26 47 S 51 0W
Čačak, *Serbia & M.* .. **44 C4** 43 54N 20 20 E
Caçapava do Sul, *Brazil* **127 C5** 30 30 S 53 30W
Cáccamo, *Italy* ..... **42 E6** 37 56N 13 40 E
Cacém, *Portugal* **37 G1** 38 46N 9 23W
Cáceres, *Brazil* ..... **124 G7** 16 5 S 57 40W
Cáceres, *Spain* **37 F4** 39 26N 6 23W
Cáceres □, *Spain* ... **36 F5** 39 45N 6 0W
Cache Bay, *Canada* .. **104 C4** 46 22N 80 0W
Cache Cr. →, *U.S.A.* . **110 G5** 38 42N 121 42W
Cache Creek, *Canada* . **102 C4** 50 48N 121 19W
Cacheu, *Guinea-Biss.* . **82 C1** 12 14N 16 8W
Cachi, *Argentina* .... **126 B2** 25 5 S 66 10W
Cachimbo, Serra do,
Brazil .... **125 E7** 9 30 S 55 30W
Cachinal de la Sierra,
Chile .... **126 A2** 24 58 S 69 32W
Cachoeira, *Brazil* .... **125 F11** 12 30 S 39 0W
Cachoeira do Sul, *Brazil* **127 C5** 30 3 S 52 53W
Cachoeiro de
Itapemirim, *Brazil* . **127 A7** 20 51 S 41 7W
Cachopo, *Portugal* ... **37 H3** 37 20N 7 49W
Cacine, *Guinea-Biss.* . **82 C1** 11 18N 14 57W
Cacoal, *Brazil* ...... **124 F6** 11 32 S 61 18W
Cacólo, *Angola* ..... **84 G3** 10 9 S 19 21 E
Caconda, *Angola* .... **85 G3** 13 48 S 15 8 E
Cacongo, *Angola* .... **84 F2** 5 11 S 12 5 E
Čačinci, *Croatia* .... **42 E2** 45 37N 17 53 E
Čadca, *Slovak Rep.* .. **27 B11** 49 26N 18 45 E
Caddo, *U.S.A.* **113 H6** 34 7N 96 16W
Cader Idris, *U.K.* **15 E4** 52 42N 3 53W
Cadereyta, *Mexico* ... **118 B5** 25 36N 100 0W
Cadí, Sierra del, *Spain* **38 C6** 42 17N 1 42 E
Cadí-Moixeró △, *Spain* **38 C3** 42 17N 1 44 E
Cadibarrawirracanna, L.,
Australia .... **95 D2** 28 52 S 135 27 E
Cadillac, *France* **20 D3** 44 38N 0 20W
Cadillac, *U.S.A.* **114 C3** 44 15N 85 24W
Cadiz, *Phil.* .... **61 F5** 10 57N 123 15 E
Cádiz, *Spain* **37 J4** 36 30N 6 20W
Cadiz, *Calif., U.S.A.* .. **111 L11** 34 30N 115 28W
Cadiz, *Ohio, U.S.A.* .. **116 F4** 40 22N 81 0W
Cádiz □, *Spain* **37 J5** 36 35N 5 45W
Cádiz, G. de, *Spain* .. **37 J5** 36 40N 7 0W
Cadiz L., *U.S.A.* **109 J6** 34 18N 115 24W
Cadney Park, *Australia* **95 D1** 27 55 S 134 3 E
Cadomin, *Canada* ... **102 C5** 53 2N 117 20W
Cadotte Lake, *Canada* **102 B5** 56 26N 116 23W
Cadours, *France* ..... **20 E5** 43 44N 1 2 E
Cadoux, *Australia* ... **93 F2** 30 46 S 117 7 E
Caen, *France* **18 C6** 49 10N 0 22W
Caernarfon, *U.K.* **14 D3** 53 8N 4 16W
Caernarfon B., *U.K.* .. **14 D3** 53 4N 4 40W
Caernarvon =
Caernarfon, *U.K.* .. **14 D3** 53 8N 4 16W
Caerphilly, *U.K.* **15 F4** 51 35N 3 13W
Caerphilly □, *U.K.* ... **15 F4** 51 37N 3 12W
Caesarea, *Israel* ..... **74 C3** 32 30N 34 53 E
Cāetité, *Brazil* ...... **125 F10** 13 50 S 42 32W
Cafayate, *Argentina* .. **126 B2** 26 2 S 66 0W
Cafu, *Angola* ...... **88 B2** 16 30 S 15 8 E
Cagayan →, *Phil.* ... **61 B4** 18 25N 121 42 E
Cagayan de Oro, *Phil.* . **61 G6** 8 30N 124 40 E
Cagayan Is., *Phil.* ... **61 G4** 9 40N 121 16 E
Cagayan Sulu I., *Phil.* . **61 H3** 7 1N 118 30 E
Cagli, *Italy* .... **41 E9** 43 33N 12 39 E
Cágliari, *Italy* ...... **42 C2** 39 13N 9 7 E
Cágliari, G. di, *Italy* .. **42 C2** 39 8N 9 11 E
Cagnano Varano, *Italy* **41 G12** 41 49N 15 47 E
Cagnes-sur-Mer, *France* **21 E11** 43 40N 7 9 E
Caguán →, *Colombia* . **124 D4** 0 8 S 74 18W
Caguas, *Puerto Rico* .. **121 d** 18 14N 66 2W
Caha Mts., *Ireland* .. **12 E2** 51 45N 9 40W
Cahama, *Angola* .... **88 B1** 16 17 S 14 19 E
Caher, *Ireland* **12 D4** 52 22N 7 56W
Caherciveen, *Ireland* . **12 E1** 51 56N 10 14W
Cahora Bassa, L. de,
Mozam. .... **87 F3** 15 35 S 32 0 E
Cahora Bassa, Reprêsa
de, *Mozam.* ..... **87 F3** 15 20 S 32 50 E
Cahore Pt., *Ireland* .. **12 D5** 52 33N 6 12W
Cahors, *France* ..... **20 D5** 44 27N 1 27 E
Cahul, *Moldova* ..... **29 E13** 45 50N 28 15 E
Cai Bau, Dao, *Vietnam* **58 G6** 21 10N 107 27 E
Cai Nuoc, *Vietnam* .. **65 H5** 8 56N 105 1 E
Caia, *Mozam.* ...... **87 F4** 17 51 S 35 24 E
Caianda, *Angola* .... **87 E1** 11 2 S 23 31 E
Caibarién, *Cuba* **120 B4** 22 30N 79 30W
Caibiran, *Phil.* ..... **61 F6** 11 34N 124 35 E
Caicara, *Venezuela* ... **124 B5** 7 38N 66 10W
Caicó, *Brazil* .... **125 E11** 6 20 S 37 0W
Caicos Is.,
Turks & Caicos ... **121 B5** 21 40N 71 40W
Caicos Passage,
W. Indies **121 B5** 22 45N 72 45W
Caidian, *China* ..... **59 B10** 30 35N 114 2 E
Căinari, *Moldova* .... **29 D14** 46 41N 29 3 E
Caird Coast, *Antarctica* **5 D1** 75 0 S 25 0W
Cairn Gorm, *U.K.* ... **13 D5** 57 7N 3 39W
Cairngorm Mts., *U.K.* . **13 D5** 57 6N 3 42W
Cairnryan, *U.K.* **13 G3** 54 59N 5 1W
Cairns, *Australia* .... **94 B4** 16 57 S 145 45 E
Cairns L., *Canada* ... **103 C10** 51 42N 94 30W
Cairo = El Qâhira,
Egypt .... **80 H7** 30 1N 31 14 E
Cairo, *Ga., U.S.A.* ... **115 K3** 30 52N 84 13W
Cairo, *Ill., U.S.A.* **113 G10** 37 0N 89 11W
Cairo, *N.Y., U.S.A.* ... **117 D11** 42 18N 74 0W
Cairo Montenotte, *Italy* **40 D5** 44 23N 8 16 E
Caithness, *U.K.* **13 C5** 58 25N 3 35W
Caithness, Ord of, *U.K.* **13 C5** 58 8N 3 36W
Caja de Muertos, I.,
Puerto Rico ..... **121 d** 17 54N 66 32W
Cajamarca, *Peru* .... **124 E3** 7 5 S 78 28W
Cajarc, *France* ..... **20 D5** 44 29N 1 50 E
Cajàzeiras, *Brazil* .... **125 E11** 6 52 S 38 30W
Çajetina, *Serbia & M.* . **44 C3** 43 47N 19 42 E
Çakirgol, *Turkey* .... **73 B8** 40 33N 39 40 E
Çakirlar, *Turkey* .... **47 E12** 36 50N 30 33 E
Čakovec, *Croatia* .... **41 B13** 46 23N 16 26 E
Çal, *Turkey* .... **47 C11** 38 4N 29 23 E
Cala →, *Spain* **37 H4** 37 59N 6 21W
Cala →, *Spain* **37 H4** 37 6N 5 7W
Cala Cadolar, Punta
de = Rotja, Pta., *Spain* **48 C7** 38 38N 1 35 E
Cala d'Or, *Spain* .... **48 B10** 39 23N 3 14 E
Cala en Porter, *Spain* . **48 B11** 39 52N 4 8 E
Cala Figuera, C. de,
Spain .... **48 B9** 39 27N 2 31 E
Cala Forcat, *Spain* ... **48 B10** 40 0N 3 47 E

Cala Major, *Spain* .... **48 B9** 39 33N 2 37 E
Cala Mezquida = Sa
Mesquida, *Spain* .. **48 B11** 39 55N 4 16 E
Cala Millor, *Spain* ... **48 B10** 39 35N 3 22 E
Cala Ratjada, *Spain* .. **48 B10** 39 43N 3 27 E
Cala Santa Galdana,
Spain .... **48 B10** 39 56N 3 58 E
Calabanga, *Phil.* .... **61 E5** 13 42N 123 17 E
Calabar, *Nigeria* .... **83 E6** 4 57N 8 20 E
Calabogie, *Canada* .. **117 A8** 45 18N 76 43W
Calabozo, *Venezuela* . **124 B5** 9 0N 67 28W
Calábria □, *Italy* .... **43 C9** 39 0N 16 30 E
Calábria □, *Italy* .... **43 C9** 39 0N 16 35 E
Calaburras, Pta. de,
Spain **37 J6** 36 30N 4 38W
Calaceite, *Spain* ..... **38 D5** 41 1N 0 11 E
Calacuccia, *France* ... **21 F13** 42 21N 9 1 E
Calafat, *Romania* .... **28 G7** 43 58N 22 59 E
Calafate, *Argentina* .. **128 G2** 50 19 S 72 15W
Calafell, *Spain* ...... **38 D6** 41 13N 1 34 E
Calahorra, *Spain* **38 C3** 42 18N 1 59W
Calais, *France* ...... **19 B8** 50 57N 1 56 E
Calais, *U.S.A.* **115 C12** 45 11N 67 17W
Calakmul, *Mexico* ... **119 D7** 18 14N 89 48W
Calalaste, Cord. de,
Argentina ...... **126 B2** 25 0 S 67 0W
Calama, *Brazil* ...... **124 E6** 8 0 S 62 50W
Calama, *Chile* ...... **126 A2** 22 30 S 68 55W
Calamar, *Colombia* .. **124 A4** 10 15N 74 55W
Calamian Group, *Phil.* **61 F3** 11 50N 119 55 E
Calamocha, *Spain* ... **38 E3** 40 50N 1 17W
Calamonte, *Spain* ... **37 G4** 38 53N 6 23W
Călan, *Romania* .... **28 E7** 45 44N 22 59 E
Calañas, *Spain* **37 H4** 37 40N 6 53W
Calanda, *Spain* **38 E4** 40 56N 0 15W
Calang, *Indonesia* ... **62 D1** 4 37N 95 37 E
Calangiánus, *Italy* ... **42 B2** 40 56N 9 1 E
Calapan, *Phil.* ..... **61 E4** 13 25N 121 7 E
Călărasi, *Moldova* ... **29 C13** 47 16N 28 19 E
Călăraşi, *Romania* ... **29 F12** 44 12N 27 20 E
Călăraşi □, *Romania* . **29 F12** 44 12N 27 20 E
Calasparra, *Spain* ... **39 G3** 38 14N 1 41W
Calatafimi, *Italy* ..... **42 E5** 37 55N 12 52 E
Calatayud, *Spain* **38 D3** 41 20N 1 40W
Călăţele, *Romania* ... **28 D8** 46 46N 23 1 E
Calato = Kálathos,
Greece .... **47 E10** 36 9N 28 8 E
Calauag, *Phil.* ...... **61 E5** 13 55N 122 15 E
Calavà, C., *Italy* ..... **43 D7** 38 11N 14 55 E
Calavite, C., *Phil.* .... **61 E4** 13 26N 120 20 E
Calayan, *Phil.* ...... **61 B4** 19 16N 121 28 E
Calbayog, *Phil.* ..... **61 E6** 12 4N 124 38 E
Calca, *Peru* .... **124 F4** 13 22 S 72 0W
Calcasieu L., *U.S.A.* .. **113 L8** 29 55N 93 18W
Calcutta = Kolkata,
India .... **69 H13** 22 36N 88 24 E
Calcutta, *U.S.A.* **116 F4** 40 40N 80 34W
Caldaro, *Italy* ...... **41 B8** 46 25N 11 14 E
Caldas da Rainha,
Portugal **37 F1** 39 24N 9 8W
Caldas de Reis, *Spain* . **36 C2** 42 36N 8 39W
Calder →, *U.K.* **14 D6** 53 44N 1 22W
Caldera, *Chile* ...... **126 B1** 27 5 S 70 55W
Caldera de
Taburiente △,
Canary Is. **48 F2** 28 43N 17 52W
Caldwell, *Idaho, U.S.A.* **108 E5** 43 40N 116 41W
Caldwell, *Kans., U.S.A.* **113 G6** 37 2N 97 37W
Caldwell, *Tex., U.S.A.* . **113 K6** 30 32N 96 42W
Caledon, *S. Africa* ... **88 E2** 34 14 S 19 26 E
Caledon →, *S. Africa* . **88 E4** 30 31 S 26 5 E
Caledon B., *Australia* . **94 A2** 12 45 S 137 0 E
Caledonia, *Canada* .. **116 C5** 43 7N 79 58W
Caledonia, *U.S.A.* ... **116 D7** 42 58N 77 51W
Calella, *Spain* ...... **38 D7** 41 37N 2 40 E
Calemba, *Angola* .... **88 B2** 16 0 S 15 44 E
Calen, *Australia* .... **94 J6** 20 56 S 148 48 E
Calenzana, *France* ... **21 F12** 42 31N 8 51 E
Caletones, *Chile* .... **126 C1** 34 6 S 70 27W
Calexico, *U.S.A.* **111 N11** 32 40N 115 30W
Calf of Man, *I. of Man* **14 C3** 54 3N 4 48W
Calgary, *Canada* **102 C6** 51 0N 114 10W
Calheta, *Madeira* **48 D2** 32 44N 17 11W
Calhoun, *U.S.A.* **115 H3** 34 30N 84 57W
Cali, *Colombia* **124 C3** 3 25N 76 35W
Calicut, *India* ...... **66 P9** 11 15N 75 43 E
Caliente, *U.S.A.* **109 H6** 37 37N 114 31W
California, *U.S.A.* **112 F8** 38 38N 92 34W
California, *Pa., U.S.A.* . **116 F5** 40 4N 79 54W
California □, *U.S.A.* .. **110 H7** 37 30N 119 30W
California, Baja, *Mexico* **118 A1** 32 10N 115 12W
California, Baja, T.N. =
Baja California □,
Mexico **118 B2** 30 0N 115 0W
California, Baja, T.S. =
Baja California Sur □,
Mexico **118 B2** 25 50N 111 50W
California, G. de,
Mexico **118 B2** 27 0N 111 0W
California City, *U.S.A.* . **111 K9** 35 10N 117 55W
California Hot Springs,
U.S.A. **111 K8** 35 51N 118 41W
Calilegua △, *Argentina* **126 A2** 23 36 S 64 50W
Călimăneşti, *Romania* . **29 E9** 45 14N 24 20 E
Călimani, Munţii,
Romania .... **29 C10** 47 12N 25 0 E
Calingasta, *Argentina* . **126 C2** 31 15 S 69 30W
Calipatria, *U.S.A.* ... **111 M11** 33 8N 115 31W
Calistoga, *U.S.A.* **110 G4** 38 35N 122 35W
Calitri, *Italy* .... **43 B8** 40 54N 15 26 E
Calitzdorp, *S. Africa* .. **88 E3** 33 33 S 21 42 E
Callabonna, L., *Australia* **95 D3** 29 40 S 140 5 E
Callac, *France* **18 D3** 48 25N 3 27W
Callan, *Ireland* **12 D4** 52 32N 7 24W
Callander, *U.K.* **13 E4** 56 15N 4 13W
Callao, *Peru* .... **124 F3** 12 0 S 77 0W
Calles, *Mexico* **119 C5** 23 2N 98 42W
Callicoon, *U.S.A.* **117 E9** 41 46N 75 3W
Calling Lake, *Canada* . **102 B6** 55 15N 113 12W
Calliope, *Australia* ... **94 C5** 24 0 S 151 16 E
Callosa de Ensarriá,
Spain **39 G4** 38 40N 0 8W
Callosa de Segura, *Spain* **39 G4** 38 7N 0 53W
Calne, *U.K.* **15 F6** 51 26N 2 0W
Calola, *Angola* ..... **88 B2** 16 25 S 17 48 E
Calolbon = San Andres,
Phil. .... **61 E6** 13 36N 124 6 E
Calonge, *Spain* ..... **38 D8** 41 52N 3 5 E
Caloocan, *Phil.* ..... **61 D4** 14 39N 120 58 E
Calore →, *Italy* ..... **43 A7** 41 11N 14 28 E
Caloundra, *Australia* . **95 D5** 26 45 S 153 10 E
Calpe, *Spain* .... **39 G5** 38 39N 0 3 E
Calpella, *U.S.A.* **110 F3** 39 14N 123 12W
Calpine, *U.S.A.* **110 F6** 39 40N 120 27W
Calstock, *Canada* ... **104 C3** 49 47N 84 9W
Caltabellotta, *Italy* ... **42 E6** 37 34N 13 13 E
Caltagirone, *Italy* .... **43 E7** 37 14N 14 31 E

Caltanissetta, Italy ..... **43 E7** 37 29N 14 4 E
Çaltılbük, Turkey .... **45 G12** 39 57N 28 36 E
Caluire-et-Cuire, France **19 G11** 45 48N 4 52 E
Calulo, Angola .... **84 G2** 10 1S 14 56 E
Caluso, Italy .... **40 C4** 45 18N 7 53 E
Calvados □, France ... **18 C6** 49 5N 0 15W
Calvert →, Australia .. **94 B2** 16 17S 137 44 E
Calvert Ra., Australia .. **92 D3** 24 0S 122 30 E
Calvert I., Canada **102 C3** 51 30N 128 0W
Calvi, France .... **21 F12** 42 34N 8 45 E
Calviá, Spain .... **39 F7** 39 34N 2 31 E
Calvillo, Mexico **118 C4** 21 51N 102 43W
Calvinia, S. Africa .... **88 E2** 31 28S 19 45 E
Calvo, Mte., Italy ..... **41 G12** 41 44N 15 46 E
Calwa, U.S.A. **110 J7** 36 42N 119 46W
Calzada Almuradiel =
  Almuradiel, Spain .. **37 G7** 38 32N 3 28W
Calzada de Calatrava,
  Spain **37 G7** 38 42N 3 46W
Cam →, U.K. .... **15 E8** 52 21N 0 16 E
Cam Lam, Vietnam ... **65 G7** 11 54N 109 10 E
Cam Pha, Vietnam .... **58 G6** 21 7N 107 18 E
Cam Ranh, Vietnam ... **65 G7** 11 54N 109 12 E
Cam Xuyen, Vietnam .. **64 C6** 18 15N 106 0 E
Camabatela, Angola .. **84 F3** 8 20S 15 26 E
Camacha, Madeira **48 D3** 32 41N 16 49W
Camacho, Mexico **118 C4** 24 25N 102 18W
Camacupa, Angola .... **85 G3** 11 58S 17 22 E
Camagüey, Cuba **120 B4** 21 20N 77 55W
Camaiore, Italy ...... **40 E7** 43 56N 1C 18 E
Camaná, Peru **124 G4** 16 30S 72 50W
Camanche Reservoir,
  U.S.A. **110 G6** 38 14N 121 1W
Camaquã, Brazil **127 C5** 30 51S 51 49W
Camaquã →, Brazil ... **127 C5** 31 17S 51 47W
Câmara de Lobos,
  Madeira **48 D3** 32 39N 16 59W
Camarat, C., France ... **21 E10** 43 12N 6 41 E
Camarès, France ..... **20 E6** 43 49N 2 53 E
Camaret-sur-Mer,
  France **18 D2** 48 16N 4 37W
Camargo, Mexico **119 B5** 26 19N 98 50W
Camargue, France .... **21 E8** 43 34N 4 34 E
Camargue △, France .. **21 E8** 43 30N 4 40 E
Camarillo, U.S.A. **111 L7** 34 13N 119 2W
Camariñas, Spain **36 B1** 43 8N 9 12W
Camarón, C., Honduras **120 C2** 16 0N 85 5W
Camarones, Argentina . **128 E3** 44 50S 65 40W
Camas, Spain **37 H4** 37 24N 6 2W
Camas, U.S.A. **110 E4** 45 35N 122 24W
Camas Valley, U.S.A. .. **108 E2** 43 2N 123 40W
Camballin, Australia .. **92 C3** 17 59S 124 12 E
Cambará, Brazil **127 A5** 23 2S 50 5W
Cambay = Khambhat,
  India .... **68 H5** 22 23N 72 33 E
Cambay, G. of =
  Khambhat, G. of,
  India .... **66 J8** 20 45N 72 30 E
Cambil, Spain **37 H7** 37 40N 3 33W
Cambo-les-Bains, France **20 E2** 43 22N 1 23W
Cambodia ■, Asia .... **64 F5** 12 15N 105 0 E
Camborne, U.K. **15 G2** 50 12N 5 19W
Cambrai, France ..... **19 B10** 50 11N 3 14 E
Cambre, Spain **36 B2** 43 17N 8 18W
Cambria, U.S.A. **110 K5** 35 34N 121 5W
Cambrian Mts., U.K. .. **15 E4** 52 3N 3 57W
Cambridge, Canada ... **116 C4** 43 23N 80 15W
Cambridge, Jamaica .. **120 a** 18 18N 77 54W
Cambridge, N.Z. ..... **91 G5** 37 54S 175 29 E
Cambridge, U.K. ..... **15 E8** 52 12N 0 8 E
Cambridge, Mass.,
  U.S.A. **117 D13** 42 22N 71 6W
Cambridge, Minn.,
  U.S.A. **112 C8** 45 34N 93 13W
Cambridge, N.Y., U.S.A. **117 C11** 43 2N 73 22W
Cambridge, Nebr.,
  U.S.A. **112 E4** 40 17N 100 10W
Cambridge, Ohio,
  U.S.A. **116 F3** 40 2N 81 35W
Cambridge Bay =
  Ikaluktutiak, Canada **100 B9** 69 10N 105 0W
Cambridge G., Australia **92 B4** 14 55S 128 15 E
Cambridge Springs,
  U.S.A. **116 E4** 41 48N 80 4W
Cambridgeshire □, U.K. **15 E7** 52 25N 0 7W
Cambrils, Spain ...... **38 D6** 41 8N 1 3 E
Cambuci, Brazil **127 A7** 21 35S 41 55W
Cambundi-Catembo,
  Angola .... **84 G3** 10 10S 17 35 E
Camden, Ala., U.S.A. .. **115 K2** 31 59N 87 17W
Camden, Ark., U.S.A. .. **113 J8** 33 35N 92 50W
Camden, Maine, U.S.A. **115 C11** 44 13N 69 4W
Camden, N.J., U.S.A. .. **117 G9** 39 56N 75 7W
Camden, N.Y., U.S.A. .. **117 C9** 43 20N 75 45W
Camden, S.C., U.S.A. .. **115 H5** 34 16N 80 36W
Camden Sd., Australia . **92 C3** 15 27S 124 25 E
Camdenton, U.S.A. ... **113 F8** 38 1N 92 45W
Camelford, U.K. **15 G3** 50 37N 4 42W
Çameli, Turkey ...... **47 D11** 37 5N 29 24 E
Camenca, Moldova ... **29 B13** 48 3N 28 42 E
Camerino, Italy ...... **41 E10** 43 8N 13 4 E
Cameron, Ariz., U.S.A. **109 J8** 35 53N 111 25W
Cameron, La., U.S.A. .. **113 L8** 29 48N 93 20W
Cameron, Mo., U.S.A. . **112 F7** 39 44N 94 14W
Cameron, Tex., U.S.A. . **113 K6** 30 51N 96 59W
Cameron Highlands,
  Malaysia .... **65 K3** 4 27N 101 22 E
Cameron Hills, Canada **102 B5** 59 48N 118 0W
Cameroon ■, Africa .. **79 G7** 6 0N 12 30 E
Camerota, Italy ...... **43 B8** 40 2N 15 22 E
Cameroun →,
  Cameroon .... **83 E6** 4 0N 9 35 E
Cameroun, Mt.,
  Cameroon .... **83 E6** 4 13N 9 10 E
Cametá, Brazil **125 D9** 2 12S 49 30W
Çamiçi Gölü, Turkey .. **47 D9** 37 29N 27 28 E
Camiguin □, Phil. .... **61 G6** 9 11N 124 42 E
Camiguin I., Phil. .... **61 B4** 18 56N 121 55 E
Camiling, Phil. ...... **61 D4** 15 42N 120 24 E
Camilla, U.S.A. **115 K3** 31 14N 84 12W
Caminha, Portugal ... **36 D2** 41 50N 8 50W
Camira Creek, Australia **95 D5** 29 15S 152 58 E
Cammal, U.S.A. **116 E7** 41 24N 77 28W
Cammarata, Italy ..... **42 E6** 37 38N 13 39 E
Camocim, Brazil **125 D10** 2 55S 40 50W
Camooweal, Australia . **94 B2** 19 56S 138 7 E
Camooweal Caves △,
  Australia .... **94 C2** 20 1S 138 11 E
Camopi, Fr. Guiana .. **125 C8** 3 12N 52 17W
Camotes Is., Phil. .... **61 F6** 10 40N 124 24 E
Camotes Sea, Phil. ... **61 F6** 10 30N 124 15 E
Camp Borden, Canada **116 B5** 44 18N 79 56W
Camp Hill, U.S.A. **116 F8** 40 14N 76 55W
Camp Nelson, U.S.A. . **111 J8** 36 8N 118 39W
Camp Pendleton, U.S.A. **111 M9** 33 16N 117 23W
Camp Verde, U.S.A. .. **109 J8** 34 34N 111 51W

Camp Wood, U.S.A. .. **113 L5** 29 40N 100 1W
Campagna, Italy ..... **43 B8** 40 40N 15 6 E
Campana, Argentina .. **126 C4** 34 10S 58 55W
Campana, I., Chile **128 F1** 48 20S 75 20W
Campanário, Madeira . **48 D2** 32 39N 17 2W
Campanario, Spain ... **37 G5** 38 52N 5 36W
Campánia □, Italy .... **43 B7** 41 0N 14 30 E
Campbell, S. Africa ... **88 D3** 28 48S 23 44 E
Campbell, Calif., U.S.A. **110 H5** 37 17N 121 57W
Campbell, Ohio, U.S.A. **116 E4** 41 5N 80 37W
Campbell I., Pac. Oc. .. **96 N8** 52 30S 169 0 E
Campbell L., Canada .. **103 A7** 63 14N 106 55W
Campbell River, Canada **102 C3** 50 5N 125 20W
Campbell Town,
  Australia .... **95 G4** 41 52S 147 30 E
Campbellford, Canada . **116 B7** 44 18N 77 48W
Campbellpur, Pakistan **68 C5** 33 46N 72 26 E
Campbellsville, U.S.A. **114 G3** 37 21N 85 20W
Campbellton, Canada . **105 C6** 47 57N 66 43W
Campbelltown, Australia **95 E5** 34 4S 150 49 E
Campbeltown, U.K. ... **13 F3** 55 26N 5 36W
Campeche, Mexico ... **119 D6** 19 50N 90 32W
Campeche □, Mexico . **119 D6** 19 50N 90 32W
Campeche, Golfo de,
  Mexico **119 D6** 19 30N 93 0W
Campello, Spain **39 G4** 38 26N 0 24W
Câmpeni, Romania ... **28 D8** 46 22N 23 3 E
Camperdown, Australia **95 F3** 38 14S 143 9 E
Camperville, Canada .. **103 C8** 51 59N 100 9W
Campi Salentina, Italy . **43 B11** 40 24N 18 1 E
Câmpia Turzii, Romania **29 D8** 46 34N 23 53 E
Campidano, Italy ..... **42 C1** 39 30N 8 47 E
Campíglia Maríttima,
  Italy .... **40 E7** 43 4N 10 37 E
Campillo de Altobuey,
  Spain **39 F3** 39 36N 1 49W
Campillos, Spain **37 H6** 37 4N 4 51W
Câmpina, Romania ... **29 E10** 45 10N 25 45 E
Campina Grande, Brazil **125 E11** 7 20S 35 47W
Campinas, Brazil **127 A6** 22 50S 47 0W
Campli, Italy .... **41 F10** 42 43N 13 41 E
Campo, Spain .... **38 C5** 42 25N 0 24 E
Campo de Criptana,
  Spain **37 F7** 39 24N 3 7W
Campo de Gibraltar,
  Spain **37 J5** 36 15N 5 25W
Campo Grande, Brazil **125 H8** 20 25S 54 40W
Campo Maior, Brazil .. **125 D10** 4 50S 42 12W
Campo Maior, Portugal **37 F3** 39 2N 7 7W
Campo Mourão, Brazil **127 A5** 24 3S 52 22W
Campo Túres, Italy ... **41 B8** 46 53N 11 55 E
Campobasso, Italy .... **43 A7** 41 34N 14 39 E
Campobello di Licata,
  Italy .... **42 E6** 37 15N 13 55 E
Campobello di Mazara,
  Italy .... **42 E5** 37 38N 12 45 E
Campofelice di Roccella,
  Italy .... **42 E6** 37 59N 13 53 E
Campomarino, Italy ... **41 G12** 41 57N 15 2 E
Camporeale, Italy .... **42 E6** 37 54N 13 6 E
Camporrobles, Spain . **38 F3** 39 39N 1 24W
Campos, Brazil **127 A7** 21 50S 41 20W
Campos Belos, Brazil . **125 F9** 13 10S 47 3W
Campos del Port, Spain **48 B10** 39 26N 3 1 E
Campos Novos, Brazil . **127 B5** 27 21S 51 50W
Camprodón, Spain ... **38 C7** 42 19N 2 23 E
Camptonville, U.S.A. . **110 F5** 39 27N 121 3W
Camptown, U.S.A. ... **117 E8** 41 44N 76 14W
Câmpulung, Argeş,
  Romania .... **29 E10** 45 17N 25 3 E
Câmpulung, Suceava,
  Romania .... **29 C10** 47 32N 25 30 E
Câmpuri, Romania ... **29 D11** 46 0N 26 50 E
Camrose, Canada **102 C6** 53 0N 112 50W
Camsell Portage,
  Canada **103 B7** 59 37N 109 15W
Çamyuva, Turkey .... **47 E12** 36 30N 30 30 E
Çan, Turkey .... **45 F11** 40 2N 27 3 E
Can Clavo, Spain .... **48 C7** 38 57N 1 27 E
Can Creu, Spain ..... **48 C7** 38 58N 1 28 E
Can Gio, Vietnam .... **65 G6** 10 25N 106 58 E
Can Tho, Vietnam .... **65 G5** 10 2N 105 46 E
Canada ■, N. Amer. .. **100 C10** 60 0N 100 0W
Canada Basin, Arctic . **4 B18** 80 0N 145 0W
Cañada de Gómez,
  Argentina **126 C3** 32 40S 61 30W
Canadian, U.S.A. **113 H4** 35 55N 100 23W
Canadian →, U.S.A. .. **113 H7** 35 28N 95 3W
Canajoharie, U.S.A. .. **117 D10** 42 54N 74 35W
Çanakkale, Turkey ... **45 F10** 40 8N 26 24 E
Çanakkale □, Turkey . **45 F10** 40 10N 26 25 E
Çanakkale Boğazı,
  Turkey .... **45 F10** 40 17N 26 32 E
Canal Flats, Canada .. **102 C5** 50 10N 115 48W
Canalejas, Argentina . **126 D2** 35 15S 66 34W
Canals, Argentina **126 C3** 33 35S 62 53W
Canals, Spain **39 G4** 38 58N 0 35W
Canandaigua, U.S.A. . **116 D7** 42 54N 77 17W
Canandaigua L., U.S.A. **116 D7** 42 47N 77 19W
Cananea, Mexico **118 A2** 31 0N 110 20W
Canarias, Is., Atl. Oc. . **48 F4** 28 30N 16 0W
Canaries, St. Lucia ... **121 f** 13 55N 61 4W
Canarreos, Arch. de los,
  Cuba **120 B3** 21 35N 81 40W
Canary Is. = Canarias,
  Is., Atl. Oc. **48 F4** 28 30N 16 0W
Canaseraga, U.S.A. .. **116 D7** 42 27N 77 45W
Canatlán, Mexico **118 C4** 24 31N 104 47W
Canaveral △, U.S.A. .. **115 L5** 28 28N 80 34W
Canaveral, C., U.S.A. . **115 L5** 28 27N 80 32W
Cañavrruelas, Spain .. **38 E2** 40 24N 2 38W
Canavieiras, Brazil ... **125 G11** 15 39S 39 0W
Canberra, Australia .. **95 F4** 35 15S 149 8 E
Canby, Calif., U.S.A. . **108 F3** 41 27N 120 52W
Canby, Minn., U.S.A. . **112 C6** 44 43N 96 16W
Canby, Oreg., U.S.A. . **110 E4** 45 16N 122 42W
Cancale, France **18 D5** 48 40N 1 50W
Canche →, France .... **19 B8** 50 31N 1 39 E
Cancún, Mexico **119 C7** 21 8N 86 44W
Candanchu, Spain ... **38 C4** 42 47N 0 32W
Candela, Italy .... **47 C8** 38 56N 26 56 E
Candé, France **18 E5** 47 34N 1 0W
Candela, Italy .... **43 A8** 41 8N 15 31 E
Candelaria, Argentina **127 B4** 27 29S 55 44W
Candelaria, Canary Is. **48 F3** 28 22N 16 22W
Candelario □, Spain .. **36 E5** 40 10N 5 46W
Candeleda, Spain **36 E5** 40 10N 5 14W
Candelo, Australia ... **95 F4** 36 47S 149 43 E
Candi Dasa, Indonesia **63 J18** 8 30S 115 34 E
Candia = Iráklion,
  Greece .... **49 D7** 35 20N 25 12 E
Candia, Sea of = Crete,
  Sea of, Greece .... **47 E7** 36 0N 25 0 E
Candle L., Canada ... **103 C7** 53 50N 105 18W

Candlemas I., Antarctica **5 B1** 57 3S 26 40W
Cando, U.S.A. **112 A5** 48 32N 99 12W
Candon, Phil. .... **61 C4** 17 12N 120 27 E
Canea = Khaniá, Greece **49 D5** 35 30N 24 4 E
Canelli, Italy .... **40 D5** 44 43N 8 17 E
Canelones, Uruguay .. **127 C4** 34 32S 56 17W
Canet-Plage, France .. **20 F7** 42 41N 3 2 E
Cañete, Chile **126 D1** 37 50S 73 30W
Cañete, Peru **124 F3** 13 8S 76 30W
Cañete, Spain **38 E3** 40 3N 1 54W
Cañete de las Torres,
  Spain **37 H6** 37 53N 4 19W
Cangas, Spain **36 C2** 42 16N 8 47W
Cangas de Narcea, Spain **36 B4** 43 10N 6 32W
Cangas de Onís, Spain **36 B5** 43 21N 5 8W
Cangnan, China ..... **59 D13** 27 30N 120 23 E
Canguaretama, Brazil **125 E11** 6 20S 35 5W
Canguçu, Brazil **127 C5** 31 22S 52 43W
Canguçu, Serra do,
  Brazil **127 C5** 31 20S 52 40W
Cangwu, China ...... **59 F8** 23 25N 111 17 E
Cangxi, China .... **58 B5** 31 47N 105 59 E
Cangyuan, China .... **58 F2** 23 12N 99 14 E
Cangzhou, China .... **56 E9** 38 19N 116 52 E
Caniapiscau →, Canada **105 A6** 56 40N 69 30W
Caniapiscau, L. de,
  Canada **105 B6** 54 10N 69 55W
Canicattì, Italy ...... **42 E6** 37 21N 13 51 E
Canicattini Bagni, Italy **43 E8** 37 2N 15 4 E
Caniles, Spain **37 H8** 37 26N 2 43W
Canim Lake, Canada .. **102 C4** 51 47N 120 54W
Canindeyú □, Paraguay **127 A5** 24 10S 55 0W
Canino, Italy .... **41 F8** 42 28N 11 45 E
Canisteo, U.S.A. **116 D7** 42 16N 77 36W
Canisteo →, U.S.A. ... **116 D7** 42 7N 77 8W
Cañitas, Mexico **118 C4** 23 36N 102 43W
Cañizal, Spain **36 D5** 41 12N 5 22W
Canjáyar, Spain **37 H8** 37 1N 2 44W
Çankırı, Turkey ...... **72 B5** 40 40N 33 37 E
Cankuzo, Burundi ... **86 C3** 3 10S 30 31 E
Canmore, Canada **102 C5** 51 7N 115 18W
Cann River, Australia . **95 F4** 37 35S 149 7 E
Canna, U.K. **13 D2** 57 3N 6 33W
Cannanore, India .... **66 P9** 11 53N 75 27 E
Cannes, France ...... **21 E11** 43 32N 7 1 E
Canning Town = Port
  Canning, India .... **69 H13** 22 23N 88 40 E
Cannington, Canada .. **116 B5** 44 20N 79 2W
Cannóbio, Italy ...... **40 B5** 46 4N 8 42 E
Cannock, U.K. **15 E5** 52 41N 2 1W
Cannon Ball →, U.S.A. **112 B4** 46 20N 100 38W
Cannondale Mt.,
  Australia .... **94 D4** 25 13S 148 57 E
Cannonsville Reservoir,
  U.S.A. **117 D9** 42 4N 75 22W
Cannonvale, Australia . **94 J6** 20 17S 148 43 E
Canoas, Brazil **127 B5** 29 56S 51 11W
Canoe L., Canada **103 B7** 55 10N 108 15W
Canon City, U.S.A. ... **112 F2** 38 27N 105 14W
Cañón de Rio Blanco △,
  Mexico **119 D5** 18 43N 97 15W
Cañón del Río Lobos △,
  Spain **36 D7** 41 46N 3 28W
Cañón del Sumidero △,
  Mexico **119 D5** 19 22N 96 24W
Canora, Canada **103 C8** 51 40N 102 30W
Canosa di Púglia, Italy **43 A9** 41 13N 16 4 E
Canowindra, Australia **95 E4** 33 35S 148 38 E
Canso, Canada **105 C7** 45 20N 61 0W
Cantabria □, Spain ... **36 B7** 43 10N 4 0W
Cantabria, Sierra de,
  Spain **38 C2** 42 40N 2 30W
Cantabrian Mts. =
  Cantábrica,
  Cordillera, Spain .. **36 C5** 43 0N 5 10W
Cantábrica, Cordillera,
  Spain **36 C5** 43 0N 5 10W
Cantal □, France ..... **20 C6** 45 5N 2 45 E
Cantal, Plomb du,
  France .... **20 C6** 45 3N 2 45 E
Cantanhede, Portugal **36 E2** 40 20N 8 36W
Cantavieja, Spain **38 E4** 40 31N 0 25W
Čantavir, Serbia & M. . **28 E4** 45 55N 19 46 E
Cantemir, Moldova .. **29 D13** 46 17N 28 14 E
Canterbury, Australia . **94 D3** 25 23S 141 53 E
Canterbury, U.K. .... **15 F9** 51 16N 1 6 E
Canterbury Bight, N.Z. **91 L3** 44 16S 171 55 E
Canterbury Plains, N.Z. **91 K3** 43 55S 171 22 E
Cantil, U.S.A. **111 K9** 35 18N 117 58W
Cantillana, Spain **37 H5** 37 36N 5 50W
Canton = Guangzhou,
  China .... **59 F9** 23 5N 113 10 E
Canton, Ga., U.S.A. .. **115 H3** 34 14N 84 29W
Canton, Ill., U.S.A. ... **112 E9** 40 33N 90 2W
Canton, Miss., U.S.A. . **113 J9** 32 37N 90 2W
Canton, Mo., U.S.A. .. **112 E9** 40 8N 91 32W
Canton, N.Y., U.S.A. .. **117 B9** 44 36N 75 10W
Canton, Ohio, U.S.A. . **116 F3** 40 48N 81 23W
Canton, Pa., U.S.A. .. **116 E8** 41 39N 76 51W
Canton, S. Dak., U.S.A. **112 D6** 43 18N 96 35W
Canton L., U.S.A. **113 G5** 36 6N 98 35W
Cantù, Italy .... **40 C6** 45 44N 9 8 E
Canudos, Brazil **124 E7** 7 13S 58 5W
Canumã →, Brazil ... **124 D7** 3 55S 59 10W
Canutama, Brazil **124 E6** 6 30S 64 20W
Canutillo, U.S.A. **109 L10** 31 55N 106 36W
Canvey, U.K. .... **15 F8** 51 31N 0 37 E
Canyon, U.S.A. **113 H4** 34 59N 101 55W
Canyon De Chelly △,
  U.S.A. **109 H9** 36 10N 109 20W
Canyon of the
  Ancients △, U.S.A. . **109 H9** 37 30N 108 50W
Canyonlands △, U.S.A. **109 G9** 38 15N 110 0W
Canyonville, U.S.A. .. **108 E2** 42 56N 123 17W
Cao Bang, Vietnam .. **58 F6** 22 40N 106 15 E
Cao He →, China .... **57 D13** 40 10N 124 32 E
Cao Lanh, Vietnam .. **65 G5** 10 27N 105 38 E
Cao Xian, China .... **56 G8** 34 50N 115 35 E
Cáorle, Italy .... **41 C9** 45 36N 12 53 E
Cap-aux-Meules,
  Canada **105 C7** 47 23N 61 52W
Cap-Chat, Canada ... **105 C6** 49 6N 66 40W
Cap-de-la-Madeleine,
  Canada **104 C5** 46 22N 72 31W
Cap-Haïtien, Haiti ... **121 C5** 19 40N 72 20W
Cap Pt., St. Lucia .... **121 f** 14 7N 60 57W
Capac, U.S.A. **116 C2** 43 1N 82 56W
Capáccio, Italy ...... **43 B8** 40 25N 15 5 E
Capaci, Italy .... **42 D6** 38 10N 13 14 E
Capanaparo →,
  Venezuela **124 B5** 7 1N 67 7W
Capánnori, Italy ..... **40 E7** 43 50N 10 35 E
Capbreton, France ... **20 E2** 43 39N 1 26W
Capdenac, France .... **20 D6** 44 34N 2 5 E
Capdepera, Spain .... **38 F8** 39 42N 3 26 E
Cape →, Australia .... **94 C4** 20 59S 146 51 E
Cape Arid △, Australia **93 F3** 33 58S 123 13 E

Cape Barren I.,
  Australia .... **95 G4** 40 25S 148 15 E
Cape Breton
  Highlands △, Canada **105 C7** 46 50N 60 40W
Cape Breton I., Canada **105 C7** 46 0N 60 30W
Cape Charles, U.S.A. . **114 G8** 37 16N 76 1W
Cape Coast, Ghana ... **83 D4** 5 5N 1 15W
Cape Coral, U.S.A. .. **115 H4** 41 56N 70 6W
Cape Dorset, Canada . **101 B12** 64 14N 76 32W
Cape Fear →, U.S.A. . **115 H6** 33 53N 78 1W
Cape Girardeau, U.S.A. **113 G10** 37 19N 89 32W
Cape Hatteras △, U.S.A. **115 H8** 35 45N 76 25W
Cape Lee △, Australia . **93 F3** 33 54S 122 26 E
Cape Lookout △, U.S.A. **115 H7** 35 45N 76 25W
Cape May, U.S.A. **114 F8** 38 56N 74 56W
Cape May Point, U.S.A. **114 F8** 38 56N 74 58W
Cape Melville △,
  Australia .... **94 A3** 14 23S 144 18 E
Cape Mount →, Liberia **82 D2** 6 44N 11 24W
Cape Peninsula △,
  S. Africa .... **88 E2** 34 20S 18 28 E
Cape Range △, Australia **92 D1** 22 3S 111 0 E
Cape Tormentine,
  Canada **105 C7** 46 8N 63 47W
Cape Town, S. Africa . **88 E2** 33 55S 18 22 E
Cape Tribulation △,
  Australia .... **94 B4** 16 5S 145 25 E
Cape Verde Is. ■,
  Atl. Oc. **77 E1** 16 0N 24 0W
Cape Vincent, U.S.A. . **117 B8** 44 8N 76 20W
Cape York Peninsula,
  Australia .... **94 A3** 12 0S 142 30 E
Capela, Brazil **125 F11** 10 30S 37 0W
Capella, Australia .... **94 C4** 23 2S 148 1 E
Capendu, France .... **20 E6** 43 11N 2 31 E
Capestang, France ... **20 E7** 43 20N 3 2 E
Capesterre-Belle-Eau,
  Guadeloupe ...... **120 b** 16 4N 61 36W
Capesterre-de-Marie-
  Galante, Guadeloupe **120 b** 15 53N 61 14W
Capim →, Brazil **125 D9** 1 40S 47 47W
Capistrello, Italy ..... **41 G10** 41 57N 13 21 E
Capitan, U.S.A. **109 K11** 33 35N 105 35W
Capitán Arturo Prat,
  Antarctica **5 C17** 63 0S 61 0W
Capitol Reef △, U.S.A. **109 G8** 38 15N 111 10W
Capitola, U.S.A. **110 J5** 36 59N 121 57W
Capizzi, Italy .... **43 E7** 37 51N 14 29 E
Capodichino, Nápoli ✈
  (NAP), Italy ...... **43 B7** 40 53N 14 16 E
Capoterra, Italy ..... **42 C1** 39 11N 8 58 E
Cappadocia, Turkey . **72 C6** 39 0N 35 0 E
Capraia, Italy .... **40 E6** 43 2N 9 50 E
Caprara, Pta., Italy ... **42 A1** 41 7N 8 19 E
Caprarola, Italy ..... **41 F9** 42 19N 12 14 E
Capreol, Canada **104 C3** 46 43N 80 56W
Caprera, Italy .... **42 A2** 41 12N 9 28 E
Capri, Italy .... **43 B7** 40 33N 14 14 E
Capricorn Group,
  Australia .... **94 C5** 23 30S 151 55 E
Capricorn Ra., Australia **92 D2** 23 20S 116 50 E
Caprino Veronese, Italy **40 C7** 45 36N 10 47 E
Caprivi Game △,
  Namibia .... **88 B3** 17 55S 22 37 E
Caprivi Strip, Namibia **88 B3** 18 0S 23 0 E
Caps et Marais
  d'Opale △, France . **19 B9** 50 40N 2 0 E
Captain's Flat, Australia **95 F4** 35 35S 149 27 E
Captieux, France **20 D3** 44 18N 0 16W
Capulin Volcano △,
  U.S.A. **113 G3** 36 47N 103 58W
Caquetá →, Colombia **124 D5** 1 15S 69 15W
Caracal, Romania .... **29 F9** 44 8N 24 22 E
Caracas, Venezuela .. **124 A5** 10 30N 66 55W
Caracol,
  Mato Grosso do Sul,
  Brazil **126 A4** 22 18S 57 1W
Caracol, Piauí, Brazil . **125 E10** 9 15S 43 22W
Carácio, Italy .... **40 D4** 44 25N 7 26 E
Carajas, Brazil **125 E8** 6 5S 50 23W
Carajás, Serra dos,
  Brazil **125 E8** 6 0S 51 30W
Carangola, Brazil **127 A7** 20 44S 42 5W
Caransebeş, Romania **28 E7** 45 28N 22 18 E
Carantec, France **18 D3** 48 40N 3 55W
Caraquet, Canada ... **105 C6** 47 48N 64 57W
Caras →, Peru **124 E3** 9 3S 77 47W
Caraş Severin □,
  Romania .... **28 E7** 45 10N 22 10 E
Caraşova, Romania .. **28 E6** 45 11N 21 51 E
Caratasca, L., Honduras **120 C3** 15 20N 83 40W
Caratinga, Brazil **125 G10** 19 50S 42 10W
Caraúbas, Brazil **125 E11** 5 43S 37 33W
Caravaca de la Cruz,
  Spain **39 G3** 38 8N 1 52W
Caravággio, Italy .... **40 C6** 45 30N 9 38 E
Caravela, Guinea-Biss. **82 C1** 11 30N 16 30W
Caravelas, Brazil **125 G11** 17 45S 39 15W
Caraveli, Peru **124 G4** 15 45S 73 25W
Caravelle, Presqu'île de
  la, Martinique .... **120 c** 14 46N 60 48W
Caràzinho, Brazil **127 B5** 28 16S 52 46W
Carballeda = O
  Carballiño, Spain .. **36 C2** 42 26N 8 5W
Carballino, Spain **36 B2** 43 13N 8 41W
Carballo, Spain **103 D9** 49 50N 99 25W
Carberry, Canada ... **103 D9** 49 50N 99 25W
Carbó, Mexico **118 B2** 29 42N 110 58W
Carbonara, C., Italy .. **42 C2** 39 6N 9 31 E
Carbondale, Colo.,
  U.S.A. **108 G10** 39 24N 107 13W
Carbondale, Ill., U.S.A. **113 G10** 37 44N 89 13W
Carbondale, Pa., U.S.A. **117 E9** 41 35N 75 30W
Carbonear, Canada .. **105 C9** 47 42N 53 13W
Carboneras, Spain ... **39 J3** 36 59N 1 53W
Carboneras de
  Guadazón, Spain .. **38 F3** 39 54N 1 50W
Carbónia, Italy ...... **42 C1** 39 10N 8 30 E
Carcabuey, Spain ... **37 H6** 37 27N 4 17W
Carcagente =
  Carcaixent, Spain . **39 F4** 39 8N 0 28W
Carcaixent, Spain ... **39 F4** 39 8N 0 28W
Carcajou, Canada ... **102 B5** 57 47N 117 6W
Carcar, Phil. .... **61 F5** 10 8N 123 38 E
Carcarana →, Argentina **126 C3** 32 27S 60 48W
Carcasse, C., Haiti ... **121 C5** 18 30N 74 28W
Carcassonne, France . **20 E6** 43 13N 2 20 E
Carcross, Canada ... **102 A2** 60 13N 134 45W
Çardak, Çanakkale,
  Turkey .... **45 F10** 40 22N 26 43 E
Çardak, Denizli, Turkey **47 D11** 37 49N 29 34 E
Cardamon Hills, India **66 Q10** 9 30N 77 15 E
Cardeña, Spain **37 G6** 38 16N 4 20W
Cárdenas,
  San Luis Potosí,
  Mexico **119 C5** 22 0N 99 41W

Cárdenas, Tabasco,
  Mexico **119 D6** 17 59N 93 21W
Cardenete, Spain **38 F3** 39 46N 1 41W
Cardiff, U.K. **15 F4** 51 29N 3 10W
Cardiff □, U.K. **15 F4** 51 31N 3 12W
Cardiff-by-the-Sea,
  U.S.A. **111 M9** 33 1N 117 17W
Cardigan, U.K. **15 E3** 52 5N 4 40W
Cardigan B., U.K. **15 E3** 52 30N 4 30W
Cardinal, Canada **117 B9** 44 47N 75 23W
Cardona, Spain ..... **38 D6** 41 56N 1 35 E
Cardona, Uruguay ... **126 C4** 33 53S 57 18W
Cardoner →, Spain .. **38 D6** 41 41N 1 51 E
Cardoso, Ilha do, Brazil **127 B5** 25 8S 47 58W
Cardston, Canada ... **102 D6** 49 15N 113 20W
Cardwell, Australia .. **94 B4** 18 14S 146 2 E
Careen L., Canada ... **103 B7** 57 0N 108 11W
Carei, Romania ...... **28 C7** 47 40N 22 29 E
Careme = Ciremay,
  Indonesia .... **63 G13** 6 55S 108 27 E
Carentan, France **18 C5** 49 19N 1 15W
Carey, U.S.A. **108 E7** 43 19N 113 57W
Carey, L., Australia .. **93 E3** 29 0S 122 15 E
Carey L., Canada **103 A8** 62 12N 102 55W
Careysburg, Liberia .. **82 D2** 6 34N 10 30W
Cargèse, France ..... **21 F12** 42 7N 8 35 E
Carhaix-Plouguer,
  France **18 D3** 48 18N 3 36W
Carhué, Argentina ... **126 D3** 37 10S 62 50W
Caria, Turkey .... **47 D10** 37 30N 28 10 E
Cariacica, Brazil **125 H10** 20 16S 40 25W
Cariati, Italy .... **43 C9** 39 30N 16 57 E
Caribbean Sea,
  W. Indies **121 D5** 15 0N 75 0W
Cariboo Mts., Canada **102 C4** 53 0N 121 0W
Caribou →, Man.,
  Canada **115 B12** 46 52N 68 1W
Caribou →, N.W.T.,
  Canada **102 A3** 61 27N 125 45W
Caribou L., Canada .. **104 C2** 47 22N 85 49W
Caribou Is., Canada .. **102 A6** 61 55N 113 15W
Caribou L., Man.,
  Canada **103 B9** 59 21N 96 10W
Caribou L., Ont.,
  Canada **104 B2** 50 25N 89 5W
Caribou Mts., Canada **102 B5** 59 12N 115 40W
Caribou River △,
  Canada **103 B9** 59 35N 96 35W
Caribrod =
  Dimitrovgrad,
  Serbia & M. ...... **44 C6** 43 2N 22 48 E
Carichic, Mexico **118 B3** 27 56N 107 3W
Carigara, Phil. ...... **61 F6** 11 18N 124 41 E
Carignan, France .... **19 C12** 49 38N 5 10 E
Carignano, Italy ..... **40 D4** 44 55N 7 40 E
Carillo, Mexico **118 B4** 26 50N 103 55W
Carinda, Australia ... **95 E4** 30 28S 147 41 E
Cariñena, Spain **38 D3** 41 20N 1 13W
Carinhanha, Brazil .. **125 F10** 14 15S 44 46W
Carinhanha →, Brazil **125 F10** 14 20S 43 47W
Carini, Italy .... **42 D6** 38 8N 13 11 E
Cariño, Spain **36 B3** 43 45N 7 52W
Carínola, Italy ...... **42 A6** 41 11N 13 58 E
Carinthia = Kärnten □,
  Austria .... **26 E6** 46 52N 13 30 E
Caripito, Venezuela .. **124 A6** 10 8N 63 6W
Carlet, Spain **39 F4** 39 14N 0 31W
Carleton, Mt., Canada **105 C6** 47 23N 66 53W
Carleton Place, Canada **117 A8** 45 8N 76 9W
Carletonville, S. Africa **88 D4** 26 23S 27 22 E
Cârlibaba, Romania .. **29 C10** 47 33N 25 8 E
Carlin, U.S.A. **108 F5** 40 43N 116 7W
Carlingford L., U.K. .. **12 B5** 54 3N 6 9W
Carlinville, U.S.A. ... **112 F10** 39 17N 89 53W
Carlisle, U.K. **14 C5** 54 54N 2 56W
Carlisle, U.S.A. **116 F7** 40 12N 77 12W
Carlisle B., Barbados . **121 g** 13 5N 59 37W
Carlisle I., Australia .. **94 J7** 20 49S 149 18 E
Carlit, Pic, France ... **20 F5** 42 35N 1 55 E
Carloforte, Italy ..... **42 C1** 39 8N 8 18 E
Carlos Casares,
  Argentina **126 D3** 35 32S 61 20W
Carlos Tejedor,
  Argentina **126 D3** 35 25S 62 25W
Carlow, Ireland **12 D5** 52 50N 6 56W
Carlow □, Ireland ... **12 D5** 52 43N 6 50W
Carlsbad, Calif., U.S.A. **111 M9** 33 10N 117 21W
Carlsbad, N. Mex.,
  U.S.A. **113 J2** 32 25N 104 14W
Carlsbad Caverns △,
  U.S.A. **113 J2** 32 10N 104 35W
Carluke, U.K. **13 F5** 55 45N 3 50W
Carlyle, Canada **103 D8** 49 40N 102 20W
Carmacks, Canada ... **100 B6** 62 5N 136 16W
Carmagnola, Italy ... **40 D4** 44 51N 7 43 E
Carman, Canada **103 D9** 49 30N 98 0W
Carmarthen, U.K. ... **15 F3** 51 52N 4 19W
Carmarthen B., U.K. . **15 F3** 51 40N 4 30W
Carmarthenshire □,
  U.K. **15 F3** 51 55N 4 13W
Carmaux, France .... **20 D6** 44 3N 2 10 E
Carmel, U.S.A. **117 E11** 41 26N 73 41W
Carmel-by-the-Sea,
  U.S.A. **110 J5** 36 33N 121 55W
Carmel Valley, U.S.A. **110 J5** 36 29N 121 43W
Carmelo, Uruguay ... **126 C4** 34 0S 58 20W
Carmen, Colombia ... **124 B3** 9 43N 75 8W
Carmen, Paraguay ... **127 B4** 27 13S 56 12W
Carmen →, Mexico .. **118 A3** 30 42N 106 29W
Carmen, I., Mexico .. **118 B2** 26 0N 111 20W
Carmen de Patagones,
  Argentina **128 E4** 40 50S 63 0W
Cármenes, Spain **36 C5** 42 58N 5 34W
Carmensa, Argentina **126 D2** 35 15S 67 40W
Carmi, Canada **102 D5** 49 36N 119 8W
Carmi, U.S.A. **114 F1** 38 5N 88 10W
Carmichael, U.S.A. .. **110 G5** 38 38N 121 19W
Carmila, Australia ... **94 C4** 21 55S 149 24 E
Carmona, Costa Rica . **120 E2** 10 0N 85 15W
Carmona, Spain **37 H5** 37 28N 5 42W
Carn Ban, U.K. **13 D5** 57 7N 4 15W
Carn Eige, U.K. **13 D3** 57 17N 5 8W
Carnamah, Australia . **93 E2** 29 41S 115 53 E
Carnarvon, Australia . **93 D1** 24 51S 113 42 E
Carnarvon, S. Africa . **88 E3** 30 56S 22 8 E
Carnarvon △, Australia **94 C4** 24 54S 148 2 E
Carnarvon Ra., Queens.,
  Australia .... **94 D4** 25 15S 148 30 E
Carnarvon Ra.,
  W. Austral., Australia **93 E3** 25 20S 120 45 E
Carnation, U.S.A. ... **110 C5** 47 39N 121 55W
Carndonagh, Ireland **12 A4** 55 16N 7 15W
Carnduff, Canada ... **103 D8** 49 10N 101 50W
Carnegie, U.S.A. **116 F4** 40 24N 80 5W
Carnegie, L., Australia **93 E3** 26 5S 122 30 E
Carnic Alps = Karnische
  Alpen, Europe .... **26 E6** 46 36N 13 0 E

Carniche Alpi = Karnische Alpen, Europe ... 26 E6 46 36N 13 0 E
Carnot, C.A.R. ... 84 D3 4 59N 15 56 E
Carnot, C., Australia ... 95 E2 34 57 S 135 38 E
Carnot B., Australia ... 92 C3 17 20 S 122 15 E
Carnoustie, U.K. ... 13 E6 56 30N 2 42W
Carnsore Pt., Ireland ... 12 D5 52 10N 6 22W
Caro, U.S.A. ... 114 D4 43 29N 83 24W
Carol City, U.S.A. ... 115 N5 25 56N 80 16W
Carolina, Brazil ... 125 E9 7 10 S 47 30W
Carolina, Puerto Rico ... 121 d 18 23N 65 58W
Carolina, S. Africa ... 89 D5 26 5 S 30 6 E
Caroline Is., Micronesia ... 96 G7 8 0N 150 0 E
Caroni, Trin. & Tob. ... 125 K15 10 34N 61 23W
Caroní →, Venezuela ... 124 B6 8 21N 62 43W
Caronie = Nébrodi, Monti, Italy ... 43 E7 37 54N 14 35 E
Caroona, Australia ... 95 E5 31 24 S 150 26 E
Carpathians, Europe ... 6 F10 49 30N 21 0 E
Carpaţii Meridionali, Romania ... 29 E9 45 30N 25 0 E
Carpentaria, G. of, Australia ... 94 A2 14 0 S 139 0 E
Carpentras, France ... 21 D9 44 3N 5 2 E
Carpi, Italy ... 40 D7 44 47N 10 53 E
Cărpineni, Moldova ... 29 D13 46 56N 28 22 E
Carpinteria, U.S.A. ... 111 L7 34 24N 119 31W
Carpio, Spain ... 36 D5 41 13N 5 7W
Carr Boyd Ra., Australia ... 92 C4 16 15 S 128 35 E
Carrabelle, U.S.A. ... 115 L3 29 51N 84 40W
Carral, Spain ... 36 B2 43 14N 8 21W
Carranza, Presa V., Mexico ... 118 B4 27 20N 100 50W
Carrara, Italy ... 40 D7 44 5N 10 6 E
Carrascal, Phil. ... 61 G6 9 22N 125 56 E
Carrascosa del Campo, Spain ... 38 E2 40 2N 2 45W
Carrauntoohill, Ireland ... 12 D2 52 0N 9 45W
Carrick-on-Shannon, Ireland ... 12 C3 53 57N 8 5W
Carrick-on-Suir, Ireland ... 12 D4 52 21N 7 24W
Carrickfergus, U.K. ... 12 B6 54 43N 5 49W
Carrickmacross, Ireland ... 12 C5 53 59N 6 43W
Carrieton, Australia ... 95 E2 32 25 S 138 31 E
Carrington, U.S.A. ... 112 B5 47 27N 99 8W
Carrión →, Spain ... 36 D6 41 53N 4 32W
Carrión de los Condes, Spain ... 36 C6 42 20N 4 37W
Carrizal Bajo, Chile ... 126 B1 28 5 S 71 20W
Carrizalillo, Chile ... 126 B1 29 5 S 71 30W
Carrizo Cr. →, U.S.A. ... 113 G3 36 55N 103 55W
Carrizo Plain △, U.S.A. ... 110 K7 35 12N 119 48W
Carrizo Springs, U.S.A. ... 113 L5 28 31N 99 52W
Carrizozo, U.S.A. ... 109 K11 33 38N 105 53W
Carroll, U.S.A. ... 112 D7 42 4N 94 52W
Carrollton, Ga., U.S.A. ... 115 J3 33 35N 85 5W
Carrollton, Ill., U.S.A. ... 112 F9 39 18N 90 24W
Carrollton, Ky., U.S.A. ... 114 F3 38 41N 85 11W
Carrollton, Mo., U.S.A. ... 112 F8 39 22N 93 30W
Carrollton, Ohio, U.S.A. ... 116 F3 40 34N 81 5W
Carron →, U.K. ... 13 D4 57 53N 4 22W
Carron, L., U.K. ... 13 D3 57 22N 5 35W
Carrot →, Canada ... 103 C8 53 50N 101 17W
Carrot River, Canada ... 103 C8 53 17N 103 35W
Carrouges, France ... 18 D6 48 34N 0 10W
Carrù, Italy ... 40 D4 44 29N 7 52 E
Carruthers, Canada ... 103 C7 52 52N 109 16W
Carsa Det, Ethiopia ... 81 F4 5 13N 39 54 E
Çarşamba, Turkey ... 72 B7 41 11N 36 44 E
Carsòli, Italy ... 41 F10 42 6N 13 5 E
Carson, Calif., U.S.A. ... 111 M8 33 48N 118 17W
Carson, N. Dak., U.S.A. ... 112 B4 46 25N 101 34W
Carson →, U.S.A. ... 110 F8 39 45N 118 40W
Carson City, U.S.A. ... 110 F7 39 10N 119 46W
Carson Sink, U.S.A. ... 108 G4 39 50N 118 25W
Cartagena, Colombia ... 124 A3 10 25N 75 33W
Cartagena, Spain ... 39 H4 37 38N 0 59W
Cartago, Colombia ... 124 C3 4 45N 75 55W
Cartago, Costa Rica ... 120 E3 9 50N 83 55W
Cártama, Spain ... 37 J6 36 43N 4 39W
Cartaxo, Portugal ... 37 F2 39 10N 8 47W
Cartaya, Spain ... 37 H3 37 16N 7 9W
Cartersville, U.S.A. ... 115 H3 34 10N 84 48W
Carterton, N.Z. ... 91 J5 41 2 S 175 31 E
Carthage, Tunisia ... 42 F3 36 50N 10 21 E
Carthage, Ill., U.S.A. ... 112 E9 40 25N 91 8W
Carthage, Mo., U.S.A. ... 113 G7 37 11N 94 19W
Carthage, N.Y., U.S.A. ... 114 D8 43 59N 75 37W
Carthage, Tex., U.S.A. ... 113 J7 32 9N 94 20W
Cartier I., Australia ... 92 B3 12 31 S 123 29 E
Cartwright, Canada ... 105 B8 53 41N 56 58W
Caruaru, Brazil ... 125 E11 8 15 S 35 55W
Carúpano, Venezuela ... 124 A6 10 39N 63 15W
Caruthersville, U.S.A. ... 113 G10 36 11N 89 39W
Carvin, France ... 19 B9 50 30N 2 57 E
Carvoeiro, Brazil ... 124 D6 1 30 S 61 59W
Carvoeiro, C., Portugal ... 37 F1 39 21N 9 24W
Cary, U.S.A. ... 115 H6 35 47N 78 46W
Casa, Pas de la = Envalira, Port d', Europe ... 38 C6 42 33N 1 43 E
Casa Branca, Portugal ... 37 G2 38 29N 8 12W
Casa Grande, U.S.A. ... 109 K8 32 53N 111 45W
Casablanca, Chile ... 126 C1 33 20 S 71 25W
Casablanca, Morocco ... 78 B4 33 36N 7 36W
Casacalenda, Italy ... 41 G11 41 44N 14 51 E
Casalbordino, Italy ... 41 F11 42 10N 14 35 E
Casale Monferrato, Italy ... 40 C5 45 8N 8 27 E
Casalmaggiore, Italy ... 40 D7 44 59N 10 26 E
Casalpusterlengo, Italy ... 40 C6 45 11N 9 40 E
Casamance →, Senegal ... 82 C1 12 33N 16 46W
Casares, Spain ... 37 J5 36 27N 5 16W
Casas Ibáñez, Spain ... 39 F3 39 17N 1 30W
Casasimarro, Spain ... 39 F2 39 22N 2 3W
Casatejada, Spain ... 36 F5 39 54N 5 40W
Casavieja, Spain ... 36 E6 40 17N 4 46W
Cascada de Basaseachic △, Mexico ... 118 B3 28 9N 108 15W
Cascade, Idaho, U.S.A. ... 108 D5 44 31N 116 2W
Cascade, Mont., U.S.A. ... 108 C8 47 16N 111 42W
Cascade Locks, U.S.A. ... 110 E5 45 40N 121 54W
Cascade Ra., U.S.A. ... 110 D5 47 0N 121 30W
Cascade Reservoir, U.S.A. ... 108 D5 44 32N 116 3W
Cascais, Portugal ... 37 G1 38 41N 9 25W
Cascavel, Brazil ... 127 A5 24 57 S 53 28W
Cáscina, Italy ... 40 E7 43 41N 10 33 E
Casco B., U.S.A. ... 115 D10 43 45N 70 0W
Caselle Torinese, Italy ... 40 C4 45 10N 7 39 E
Casey, Antarctica ... 5 C8 66 0 S 76 0 E
Caseyr, Raas = Asir, Ras, Somali Rep. ... 75 E5 11 55N 51 10 E

Cashel, Ireland ... 12 D4 52 30N 7 53W
Casiguran, Phil. ... 61 C5 16 22N 122 7 E
Casilda, Argentina ... 126 C3 33 10 S 61 10W
Casimcea, Romania ... 29 F13 44 45N 28 23 E
Casino, Australia ... 95 D5 28 52 S 153 3 E
Casiquiare →, Venezuela ... 124 C5 2 1N 67 7W
Čáslav, Czech Rep. ... 26 B8 49 54N 15 22 E
Casma, Peru ... 124 E3 9 30 S 78 20W
Casmalia, U.S.A. ... 111 L6 34 50N 120 32W
Cásola Valsénio, Italy ... 41 D8 44 12N 11 40 E
Cásoli, Italy ... 41 F11 42 7N 14 18 E
Caspe, Spain ... 38 D4 41 14N 0 1W
Casper, U.S.A. ... 108 E10 42 51N 106 19W
Caspian Depression, Eurasia ... 35 G9 47 0N 48 0 E
Caspian Sea, Eurasia ... 52 E6 43 0N 50 0 E
Cass Lake, U.S.A. ... 112 B7 47 23N 94 37W
Cassà de la Selva, Spain ... 38 D7 41 53N 2 52 E
Cassadaga, U.S.A. ... 116 D5 42 20N 79 19W
Cassano allo Iónio, Italy ... 43 C9 39 47N 16 20 E
Cassel, France ... 19 B9 50 48N 2 29 E
Casselman, Canada ... 117 A9 45 19N 75 5W
Casselton, U.S.A. ... 112 B6 46 54N 97 13W
Cassiar, Canada ... 102 B3 59 16N 129 40W
Cassiar Mts., Canada ... 102 B2 59 30N 130 30W
Cassino, Italy ... 42 A6 41 30N 13 49 E
Cassis, France ... 21 E9 43 14N 5 32 E
Cassville, U.S.A. ... 113 G8 36 41N 93 52W
Castagneto Carducci, Italy ... 40 E7 43 9N 10 36 E
Castaic, U.S.A. ... 111 L8 34 30N 118 38W
Castalia, U.S.A. ... 116 E2 41 24N 82 49W
Castanhal, Brazil ... 125 D9 1 18 S 47 55W
Castara, Trin. & Tob. ... 125 J16 11 17N 60 42W
Castéggio, Italy ... 40 C6 45 0N 9 7 E
Castejón de Monegros, Spain ... 38 D4 41 37N 0 15W
Castèl di Sangro, Italy ... 41 G11 41 47N 14 6 E
Castèl San Giovanni, Italy ... 40 C6 45 4N 9 26 E
Castèl San Pietro Terme, Italy ... 41 D8 44 24N 11 35 E
Castelbuono, Italy ... 43 E7 37 56N 14 5 E
Castelfidardo, Italy ... 41 E10 43 28N 13 33 E
Castelfiorentino, Italy ... 40 E7 43 36N 10 58 E
Castelfranco Emília, Italy ... 40 D8 44 37N 11 3 E
Castelfranco Véneto, Italy ... 41 C8 45 40N 11 55 E
Casteljaloux, France ... 20 D4 44 19N 0 6 E
Castellabate, Italy ... 43 B7 40 17N 14 57 E
Castellammare, G. di, Italy ... 42 D5 38 8N 12 54 E
Castellammare del Golfo, Italy ... 42 D5 38 1N 12 53 E
Castellammare di Stábia, Italy ... 43 B7 40 42N 14 29 E
Castellamonte, Italy ... 40 C4 45 23N 7 42 E
Castellane, France ... 21 E10 43 50N 6 31 E
Castellaneta, Italy ... 43 B9 40 38N 16 56 E
Castelli, Argentina ... 126 D4 36 7 S 57 47W
Castelló de la Plana, Spain ... 38 F4 39 58N 0 3W
Castellón de la Plana □, Spain ... 38 E4 40 15N 0 5W
Castellote, Spain ... 38 E4 40 48N 0 15W
Castelmáuro, Italy ... 41 G11 41 50N 14 43 E
Castelnau-de-Médoc, France ... 20 C3 45 2N 0 48W
Castelnau-Magnoac, France ... 20 E4 43 17N 0 31 E
Castelnaudary France ... 20 E5 43 20N 1 58 E
Castelnovo ne' Monti, Italy ... 40 D7 44 26N 10 24 E
Castelnuovo di Cécina, Italy ... 40 E7 43 12N 10 59 E
Castelo, Brazil ... 127 A7 20 33 S 41 14W
Castelo Branco, Portugal ... 36 F3 39 50N 7 31W
Castelo Branco □, Portugal ... 36 F3 39 52N 7 45W
Castelo de Paiva, Portugal ... 36 D2 41 2N 8 16W
Castelo de Vide, Portugal ... 37 F3 39 25N 7 27W
Castelsardo, Italy ... 42 B1 40 55N 8 43 E
Castelsarrasin, France ... 20 D5 44 2N 1 7 E
Casteltérmini, Italy ... 42 E6 37 32N 13 39 E
Castelvetrano, Italy ... 42 E5 37 41N 12 47 E
Casterton, Australia ... 95 F3 37 30 S 141 30 E
Castets, France ... 20 E2 43 52N 1 6W
Castiglion Fiorentino, Italy ... 41 E8 43 20N 11 55 E
Castiglione del Lago, Italy ... 41 E9 43 7N 12 3 E
Castiglione della Pescáia, Italy ... 40 F7 42 46N 10 53 E
Castiglione delle Stiviere, Italy ... 40 C7 45 23N 10 29 E
Castilblanco, Spain ... 37 F5 39 17N 5 5W
Castilla, Playa de, Spain ... 37 J4 37 0N 6 33W
Castilla-La Mancha □, Spain ... 6 H5 39 30N 3 30W
Castilla y León □, Spain ... 36 D6 42 0N 5 0W
Castillo de Locubín, Spain ... 37 H7 37 32N 3 56W
Castillon-en-Couserans, France ... 20 F5 42 56N 1 1 E
Castillonès, France ... 20 D4 44 39N 0 37 E
Castillos, Uruguay ... 127 C5 34 12 S 53 52W
Castle Dale, U.S.A. ... 108 G8 39 13N 111 1W
Castle Douglas, U.K. ... 13 G5 54 56N 3 56W
Castle Rock, Colo., U.S.A. ... 112 F2 39 22N 104 51W
Castle Rock, Wash., U.S.A. ... 110 D4 46 17N 122 54W
Castlebar, Ireland ... 12 C2 53 52N 9 18W
Castlebay, U.K. ... 13 E1 56 57N 7 31W
Castleblayney, Ireland ... 12 B5 54 7N 6 44W
Castlederg, U.K. ... 12 B4 54 42N 7 35W
Castleford, U.K. ... 14 D6 53 43N 1 21W
Castlegar, Canada ... 102 D5 49 20N 117 40W
Castlemaine, Australia ... 95 F3 37 2 S 144 12 E
Castlepollard, Ireland ... 12 C4 53 41N 7 19W
Castlerea, Ireland ... 12 C3 53 46N 8 29W
Castlereagh →, Australia ... 95 E4 30 12 S 147 32 E
Castlereagh B., Australia ... 94 A2 12 10 S 135 10 E
Castleton, U.S.A. ... 117 C11 43 37N 73 11W
Castletown, I. of Man ... 14 C3 54 5N 4 38W
Castletown Bearhaven, Ireland ... 12 E2 51 39N 9 55W
Castor, Canada ... 102 C6 52 15N 111 50W
Castor →, Canada ... 104 B4 53 24N 78 58W
Castorland, U.S.A. ... 117 C9 43 53N 75 31W

Castres, France ... 20 E6 43 37N 2 13 E
Castricum, Neths. ... 17 B4 52 33N 4 40 E
Castries, St. Lucia ... 121 f 14 2N 60 58W
Castril, Spain ... 37 H8 37 48N 2 46W
Castro, Brazil ... 127 A6 24 45 S 50 0W
Castro, Chile ... 128 E2 42 30 S 73 50W
Castro Alves, Brazil ... 125 F11 12 46 S 39 33W
Castro del Río, Spain ... 37 H6 37 41N 4 29W
Castro-Urdiales, Spain ... 36 B7 43 23N 3 11W
Castro Verde, Portugal ... 37 H2 37 41N 8 4W
Castrojeriz, Spain ... 36 C6 42 17N 4 9W
Castropol, Spain ... 36 B3 43 32N 7 0W
Castroreale, Italy ... 43 D8 38 6N 15 12 E
Castrovillari, Italy ... 43 C9 39 49N 16 12 E
Castroville, U.S.A. ... 110 J5 36 46N 121 45W
Castuera, Spain ... 37 G5 38 43N 5 37W
Çat, Turkey ... 73 C9 39 40N 41 3 E
Cat Ba △, Vietnam ... 64 B6 20 50N 107 0 E
Cat Ba, Dao, Vietnam ... 64 B6 20 50N 107 0 E
Cat I., Bahamas ... 121 B4 24 30N 75 30W
Cat L., Canada ... 104 B1 51 40N 91 50W
Cat Lake, Canada ... 104 B1 51 40N 91 50W
Cat Tien △, Vietnam ... 65 G6 11 25N 107 17 E
Čata, Slovak Rep. ... 27 D11 47 58N 18 38 E
Catacamas, Honduras ... 120 D2 14 54N 85 56W
Cataguases, Brazil ... 127 A7 21 23 S 42 39W
Çatak, Turkey ... 73 C10 38 1N 43 8 E
Catalão, Brazil ... 125 G9 18 10 S 47 57W
Çatalca, Turkey ... 45 E12 41 8N 28 27 E
Catalina, Canada ... 105 C9 48 31N 53 4W
Catalina, Chile ... 126 B2 25 13 S 69 43W
Catalina, U.S.A. ... 109 K8 32 30N 110 50W
Catalonia = Cataluña □, Spain ... 38 D6 41 40N 1 15 E
Cataluña □, Spain ... 38 D6 41 40N 1 15 E
Çatalzeytin, Turkey ... 72 B6 41 57N 34 12 E
Catamarca, Argentina ... 126 B2 28 30 S 65 50W
Catamarca □, Argentina ... 126 B2 27 0 S 65 50W
Catanauan, Phil. ... 61 E5 13 36N 122 19 E
Catanduanes □, Phil. ... 61 E6 13 50N 124 20 E
Catanduva, Brazil ... 127 A6 21 5 S 48 58W
Catánia, Italy ... 43 E8 37 30N 15 6 E
Catánia, G. di, Italy ... 43 E8 37 24N 15 9 E
Catanzaro, Italy ... 43 D9 38 54N 16 35 E
Catarman, Phil. ... 61 E6 12 28N 124 35 E
Catatumbo-Barí △, Colombia ... 121 E5 9 3N 73 12W
Catbalogan, Phil. ... 61 F6 11 46N 124 53 E
Cateel, Phil. ... 61 H7 7 47N 126 24 E
Catembe, Mozam. ... 89 D5 26 0 S 32 33 E
Caterham, U.K. ... 15 F7 51 15N 0 4W
Cathcart, S. Africa ... 88 E4 32 18 S 27 10 E
Cathlamet, U.S.A. ... 110 D3 46 12N 123 23W
Catio, Guinea-Biss. ... 82 C1 11 17N 15 15W
Catlettsburg, U.S.A. ... 114 F4 38 25N 82 36W
Çatma Dağı, Turkey ... 47 C11 38 25N 29 50 E
Catoche, C., Mexico ... 119 C7 21 40N 87 8W
Cátria, Mte., Italy ... 41 E9 43 28N 12 42 E
Catril, Argentina ... 126 D3 36 26 S 63 24W
Catrimani, Brazil ... 124 C6 0 27N 61 41W
Catrimani →, Brazil ... 124 C6 0 28N 61 44W
Catskill, U.S.A. ... 117 D11 42 14N 73 52W
Catskill Mts., U.S.A. ... 117 D10 42 10N 74 25W
Catt, Mt., Australia ... 94 A1 13 49 S 134 23 E
Cattaraugus, U.S.A. ... 116 D6 42 22N 78 52W
Catterick, U.K. ... 14 C6 54 23N 1 37W
Cáttolica, Italy ... 43 D7 38 2N 12 44 E
Cáttolica Eraclea, Italy ... 42 E6 37 26N 13 24 E
Catuala, Angola ... 88 B2 16 25 S 19 2 E
Catuane, Mozam. ... 89 D5 26 48 S 32 18 E
Catur, Mozam. ... 87 E4 13 45 S 35 30 E
Catwick Is., Vietnam ... 65 G7 10 0N 109 0 E
Cauca →, Colombia ... 124 B4 8 54N 74 28W
Caucaia, Brazil ... 125 D11 3 40 S 38 35W
Caucasus Mountains, Eurasia ... 35 J7 42 50N 44 0 E
Caudete, Spain ... 39 G3 38 42N 1 2W
Caudry, France ... 19 B10 50 7N 3 22 E
Caulnes, France ... 18 D4 48 18N 2 10W
Caulónia, Italy ... 43 D9 38 23N 16 24 E
Caungula, Angola ... 84 F3 8 26 S 18 38 E
Cauquenes, Chile ... 126 D1 36 0 S 72 22W
Caura →, Venezuela ... 124 B6 7 38N 64 53W
Cauresi →, Mozam. ... 87 F3 17 8 S 33 0 E
Căuşani, Moldova ... 29 D14 46 38N 29 25 E
Causapscal, Canada ... 105 C6 48 19N 67 12W
Caussade, France ... 20 D5 44 10N 1 33 E
Causse-Méjean, France ... 20 D7 44 18N 3 42 E
Causses du Quercy △, France ... 20 D5 44 35N 1 35 E
Cauterets, France ... 20 F3 42 52N 0 8W
Cauvery →, India ... 66 P11 11 9N 78 52 E
Caux, Pays de, France ... 18 C7 49 38N 0 35 E
Cava de' Tirreni, Italy ... 43 B7 40 42N 14 42 E
Cávado →, Portugal ... 36 D2 41 32N 8 48W
Cavagrande del Cassibile △, Italy ... 43 F8 36 58N 15 6 E
Cavaillon, France ... 21 E9 43 50N 5 2 E
Cavalaire-sur-Mer, France ... 21 E10 43 10N 6 33 E
Cavalese, Italy ... 41 B8 46 17N 11 27 E
Cavalier, U.S.A. ... 112 A6 48 48N 97 37W
Cavalla = Cavally →, Africa ... 82 E3 4 22N 7 32W
Cavallo, Î. de, France ... 21 G13 41 22N 9 16 E
Cavally →, Africa ... 82 E3 4 22N 7 32W
Cavan, Ireland ... 12 B4 54 0N 7 22W
Cavan □, Ireland ... 12 C4 54 1N 7 16W
Cavárzere, Italy ... 41 C9 45 8N 12 5 E
Çavdarhisar, Turkey ... 47 B11 39 12N 29 37 E
Çavdır, Turkey ... 47 D11 37 10N 29 42 E
Cave Creek, U.S.A. ... 109 K7 33 50N 111 57W
Cavenagh Ra., Australia ... 93 E4 26 12 S 122 55 E
Cavendish, Australia ... 95 F3 37 31 S 142 2 E
Caviana, I., Brazil ... 125 C8 0 10N 50 10W
Cavite, Phil. ... 61 D4 14 29N 120 55 E
Cavnic, Romania ... 29 C8 47 40N 23 52 E
Cavour, Italy ... 40 D4 44 47N 7 22 E
Cavtat, Croatia ... 44 D2 42 35N 18 13 E
Cawndilla L., Australia ... 95 E3 32 30 S 142 15 E
Cawnpore = Kanpur, India ... 69 F9 26 28N 80 20 E
Caxias, Brazil ... 125 D10 4 55 S 43 20W
Caxias do Sul, Brazil ... 127 B5 29 10 S 51 10W
Çay, Turkey ... 72 C4 38 35N 31 1 E
Cay Sal Bank, Bahamas ... 120 B4 23 45N 80 0W
Cayambe, Ecuador ... 124 C3 0 3N 78 8W
Çaycuma, Turkey ... 72 B5 41 5N 32 2 E
Çayeli, Turkey ... 73 B9 41 5N 40 45 E
Cayenne, Fr. Guiana ... 125 B8 5 5N 52 18W
Cayey, Puerto Rico ... 121 d 18 7N 66 10W
Caygören Baraji, Turkey ... 47 B10 39 15N 28 12 E
Çayıralan, Turkey ... 72 C6 39 18N 35 40 E
Caylus, France ... 20 D5 44 15N 1 47 E
Cayman Brac, Cayman Is. ... 120 C4 19 43N 79 49W

Cayman Is. ☑, W. Indies ... 120 C3 19 40N 80 30W
Cayman Trough, Caribbean ... 98 H11 19 0N 81 0W
Cayres, France ... 20 D7 44 55N 3 48 E
Cayuga, U.S.A. ... 117 D8 42 54N 76 44W
Cayuga L., U.S.A. ... 117 D8 42 41N 76 41W
Cazalla de la Sierra, Spain ... 37 H5 37 56N 5 45W
Căzăneşti, Romania ... 29 F12 44 36N 27 3 E
Cazaubon, France ... 20 E3 43 55N 0 3W
Cazaux et de Sanguinet, Étang de, France ... 20 D2 44 29N 1 10W
Cazenovia, U.S.A. ... 117 D9 42 55N 75 51W
Cazères, France ... 20 E5 43 13N 1 5 E
Cazin, Bos.-H. ... 41 D12 44 57N 15 57 E
Čazma, Croatia ... 41 C13 45 45N 16 39 E
Cazombo, Angola ... 85 G4 11 54 S 22 56 E
Cazorla, Spain ... 37 H8 37 55N 3 2W
Cazorla, Sierra de, Spain ... 37 G8 38 5N 2 55W
Cea →, Spain ... 36 C5 42 0N 5 36W
Ceamurlia de Jos, Romania ... 29 F13 44 43N 28 47 E
Ceanannus Mor, Ireland ... 12 C5 53 44N 6 53W
Ceará = Fortaleza, Brazil ... 125 D11 3 45 S 38 35W
Ceará □, Brazil ... 125 E11 5 0 S 40 0W
Ceará Mirim, Brazil ... 125 E11 5 38 S 35 25W
Ceauru, L., Romania ... 29 F8 44 58N 23 11 E
Cebaco, I. de, Panama ... 120 E3 7 33N 81 9W
Cebollar, Argentina ... 126 B2 29 10 S 66 35W
Cebollera, Sierra de, Spain ... 38 D2 42 0N 2 30W
Cebreros, Spain ... 36 E6 40 27N 4 28W
Cebu, Phil. ... 61 F5 10 18N 123 54 E
Čečava, Bos.-H. ... 28 F2 44 43N 17 44 E
Ceccano, Italy ... 42 A6 41 34N 13 20 E
Cece, Hungary ... 28 D3 46 46N 18 39 E
Cechi, Ivory C. ... 82 D4 6 15N 4 25W
Cecil Plains, Australia ... 95 D5 27 30 S 151 11 E
Cécina, Italy ... 40 E7 43 18N 10 31 E
Cécina →, Italy ... 40 E7 43 18N 10 29 E
Ceclavín, Spain ... 36 F4 39 50N 6 45W
Cedar →, U.S.A. ... 112 E9 41 17N 91 21W
Cedar City, U.S.A. ... 109 H7 37 41N 113 4W
Cedar Creek Reservoir, U.S.A. ... 113 J6 32 11N 96 4W
Cedar Falls, Iowa, U.S.A. ... 112 D8 42 32N 92 27W
Cedar Falls, Wash., U.S.A. ... 110 C5 47 25N 121 45W
Cedar Key, U.S.A. ... 115 L4 29 8N 83 2W
Cedar L., Canada ... 103 C9 53 10N 100 0W
Cedar Rapids, U.S.A. ... 112 E9 41 59N 91 40W
Cedartown, U.S.A. ... 115 H3 34 1N 85 15W
Cedarvale, Canada ... 102 B3 55 1N 128 22W
Cedarville, S. Africa ... 89 E4 30 23 S 29 3 E
Cedeira, Spain ... 36 B2 43 39N 8 2W
Cedral, Mexico ... 118 C4 23 50N 100 42W
Cedrino →, Italy ... 42 B2 40 11N 9 24 E
Cedro, Brazil ... 125 E11 6 34 S 39 3W
Cedros, I. de, Mexico ... 118 B1 28 10N 115 20W
Cedros B., Trin. & Tob. ... 125 K15 10 16N 61 54W
Ceduna, Australia ... 95 E1 32 7 S 133 46 E
Cedynia, Poland ... 31 F1 52 53N 14 12 E
Cée, Spain ... 36 C1 42 57N 9 10W
Cefalù, Italy ... 43 D7 38 2N 14 1 E
Cega →, Spain ... 36 D6 41 33N 4 46W
Cegléd, Hungary ... 28 C4 47 11N 19 47 E
Céglie Messápico, Italy ... 43 B10 40 39N 17 31 E
Cehegín, Spain ... 39 G3 38 6N 1 48W
Ceheng, China ... 58 E5 24 58N 105 48 E
Cehu-Silvaniei, Romania ... 29 C8 47 24N 23 9 E
Ceica, Romania ... 28 D7 46 53N 22 10 E
Ceira →, Portugal ... 36 E2 40 13N 8 16W
Cekik, Indonesia ... 63 J17 8 12 S 114 27 E
Čelákovice, Czech Rep. ... 26 A7 50 10N 14 46 E
Celano, Italy ... 41 F10 42 5N 13 33 E
Celanova, Spain ... 36 C3 42 9N 7 58W
Celaque △, Honduras ... 120 D2 14 28N 88 43W
Celaya, Mexico ... 118 C4 20 31N 100 37W
Celebes = Sulawesi, Indonesia ... 63 E6 2 0 S 120 0 E
Celebes Sea, Indonesia ... 63 D6 3 0N 123 0 E
Čelić, Bos.-H. ... 28 E3 44 43N 18 49 E
Celina, U.S.A. ... 114 E3 40 33N 84 35W
Celinac, Bos.-H. ... 28 F2 44 44N 17 22 E
Celje, Slovenia ... 41 B12 46 16N 15 18 E
Celldömölk, Hungary ... 28 C2 47 16N 17 10 E
Celle, Germany ... 24 C6 52 37N 10 4 E
Celorico da Beira, Portugal ... 36 E3 40 38N 7 24W
Celtic Sea, Atl. Oc. ... 9 F9 50 9N 9 34W
Çeltikçi, Turkey ... 47 D12 37 32N 30 29 E
Çemişgezek, Turkey ... 73 C8 39 3N 38 56 E
Cenderwasih, Teluk, Indonesia ... 63 E9 3 0 S 135 20 E
Cengong, China ... 58 D7 27 13N 108 44 E
Ceno →, Italy ... 40 D7 44 43N 10 5 E
Cenrallo, Italy ... 40 D4 44 23N 7 35 E
Centelles, Spain ... 38 D7 41 50N 2 14 E
Center, N. Dak., U.S.A. ... 112 B4 47 7N 101 18W
Center, Tex., U.S.A. ... 113 K7 31 48N 94 11W
Centerburg, U.S.A. ... 116 F2 40 18N 82 42W
Centerville, Calif., U.S.A. ... 110 J7 36 44N 119 30W
Centerville, Iowa, U.S.A. ... 112 E8 40 44N 92 52W
Centerville, Pa., U.S.A. ... 116 F5 40 3N 79 59W
Centerville, Tenn., U.S.A. ... 115 H2 35 47N 87 28W
Centerville, Tex., U.S.A. ... 113 K7 31 16N 95 59W
Central = Tsentralnyy □, Russia ... 34 D4 52 0N 40 0 E
Central □, Ghana ... 83 D4 5 30N 1 0W
Central □, Kenya ... 86 C4 0 30 S 37 30 E
Central □, Malawi ... 87 E3 13 30 S 33 30 E
Central □, Zambia ... 87 E2 14 25 S 28 50 E
Central, Cordillera, Colombia ... 124 C4 5 0N 75 0W
Central, Cordillera, Costa Rica ... 120 D3 10 10N 84 5W
Central, Cordillera, Dom. Rep. ... 121 C5 19 15N 71 0W
Central, Cordillera, Phil. ... 61 C4 17 20N 120 57 E
Central, Cordillera, Puerto Rico ... 121 d 18 8N 66 35W
Central African Rep. ■, Africa ... 79 G9 7 0N 20 0 E
Central America, America ... 98 H11 12 0N 85 0W
Central Butte, Canada ... 103 C7 50 48N 106 31W
Central City, Colo., U.S.A. ... 108 G11 39 48N 105 31W
Central City, Ky., U.S.A. ... 114 G2 37 18N 87 7W
Central City, Nebr., U.S.A. ... 112 E6 41 7N 98 0W

Central I., Kenya ... 86 B4 3 30N 36 0 E
Central Island △, Kenya ... 86 B4 2 33N 36 1 E
Central Kalahari △, Botswana ... 88 C3 22 36 S 23 58 E
Central Makran Range, Pakistan ... 66 F4 26 30N 64 15 E
Central Patricia, Canada ... 104 B1 51 30N 90 9W
Central Point, U.S.A. ... 108 E2 42 23N 122 55W
Central Russian Uplands, Europe ... 6 E13 54 0N 36 0 E
Central Siberian Plateau, Russia ... 50 C14 65 0N 105 0 E
Central Square, U.S.A. ... 117 C8 43 17N 76 9W
Centralia, Ill., U.S.A. ... 112 F10 38 32N 89 8W
Centralia, Mo., U.S.A. ... 112 F8 39 13N 92 8W
Centralia, Wash., U.S.A. ... 110 D4 46 43N 122 58W
Cenxi, China ... 59 F8 22 57N 110 57 E
Čeotina →, Bos. ... 44 C2 43 36N 18 50 E
Cephalonia = Kefalliniá, Greece ... 46 C2 38 15N 20 30 E
Čepin, Croatia ... 28 E3 45 32N 18 34 E
Ceprano, Italy ... 42 A6 41 33N 13 31 E
Ceptura, Romania ... 29 E11 45 1N 26 21 E
Cepu, Indonesia ... 63 G14 7 9 S 111 35 E
Ceram = Seram, Indonesia ... 63 E7 3 10 S 129 0 E
Ceram Sea = Seram Sea, Indonesia ... 63 E7 2 30 S 128 30 E
Cerbère, France ... 20 F7 42 26N 3 10 E
Cercal, Portugal ... 37 H2 37 48N 8 40W
Cerdaña, Spain ... 38 C6 42 22N 1 35 E
Cère →, France ... 20 D5 44 55N 1 49 E
Cerea, Italy ... 41 C8 45 12N 11 13 E
Ceredigion □, U.K. ... 15 E3 52 16N 4 15W
Ceres, Argentina ... 126 B3 29 55 S 61 55W
Ceres, S. Africa ... 88 E2 33 21 S 19 18 E
Ceres, U.S.A. ... 110 H6 37 35N 120 57W
Céret, France ... 20 F6 42 30N 2 42 E
Cergy, France ... 19 C9 49 2N 2 4 E
Cerignola, Italy ... 43 A8 41 17N 15 53 E
Cerigo = Kíthira, Greece ... 46 E5 36 8N 23 0 E
Cérilly, France ... 19 F9 46 37N 2 50 E
Cerisiers, France ... 19 D10 48 8N 3 30 E
Cerizay, France ... 18 F6 46 50N 0 40W
Çerkeş, Turkey ... 72 B5 40 49N 32 52 E
Çerkezköy, Turkey ... 45 E12 41 17N 28 0 E
Cerknica, Slovenia ... 41 C11 45 48N 14 21 E
Cerkovica, Bulgaria ... 45 C8 43 41N 24 50 E
Cermei, Romania ... 28 D6 46 33N 21 15 E
Cermerno, Serbia & M. ... 44 C4 43 35N 20 25 E
Çermik, Turkey ... 73 C8 38 8N 39 26 E
Cerna, Romania ... 29 E13 45 4N 28 17 E
Cerna →, Romania ... 29 F8 44 38N 23 58 E
Cernavodă, Romania ... 29 F13 44 22N 28 3 E
Cernay, France ... 19 E14 47 44N 7 10 E
Cernik, Croatia ... 28 E2 45 17N 17 22 E
Cerralvo, I., Mexico ... 118 C3 24 20N 109 45W
Cërrik, Albania ... 44 E3 41 2N 19 58 E
Cerritos, Mexico ... 118 C4 22 27N 100 20W
Cerro Corá, Uruguay ... 127 C4 33 6 S 55 8W
Cerro Cord △, Paraguay ... 127 A4 22 35 S 56 2W
Cerro el Copey △, Venezuela ... 121 D7 10 59N 63 53W
Cerro Hoya △, Panama ... 120 E3 7 17N 80 45W
Cerro Saroche △, Venezuela ... 121 D6 10 8N 69 38W
Certaldo, Italy ... 40 E8 43 33N 11 2 E
Cervaro →, Italy ... 43 A8 41 30N 15 52 E
Cervati, Monte, Italy ... 43 B8 40 17N 15 29 E
Cervera, Spain ... 38 D6 41 40N 1 16 E
Cervera de Pisuerga, Spain ... 36 C6 42 51N 4 30W
Cervera del Río Alhama, Spain ... 38 C3 42 2N 1 58W
Cervéteri, Italy ... 41 F9 42 0N 12 6 E
Cérvia, Italy ... 41 D9 44 15N 12 22 E
Cervignano del Friuli, Italy ... 41 C10 45 49N 13 20 E
Cervinara, Italy ... 43 A7 41 1N 14 37 E
Cervione, France ... 21 F13 42 20N 9 29 E
Cervo, Spain ... 36 B3 43 40N 7 24W
Cesaró, Italy ... 43 E7 37 50N 14 38 E
Cesena, Italy ... 41 D9 44 12N 12 15 E
Cesenático, Italy ... 41 D9 44 12N 12 24 E
Cēsis, Latvia ... 9 H21 57 18N 25 15 E
Česká Lípa, Czech Rep. ... 26 A7 50 45N 14 30 E
Česká Třebová, Czech Rep. ... 27 B9 49 54N 16 27 E
České Budějovice, Czech Rep. ... 26 C7 48 55N 14 25 E
České Velenice, Czech Rep. ... 26 C7 48 45N 14 57 E
Českobudějovický □, Czech Rep. ... 26 C7 49 0N 14 30 E
Českomoravská Vrchovina, Czech Rep. ... 26 B8 49 30N 15 40 E
Český Brod, Czech Rep. ... 26 A7 50 4N 14 52 E
Český Krumlov, Czech Rep. ... 26 C7 48 43N 14 21 E
Český Těšín, Czech Rep. ... 27 B11 49 45N 18 39 E
Cesma →, Croatia ... 41 C13 45 35N 16 29 E
Çeşme, Turkey ... 47 C8 38 20N 26 23 E
Cessnock, Australia ... 95 E5 32 50 S 151 21 E
Cesson-Sévigné, France ... 18 D5 48 7N 1 23W
Cestas, France ... 20 D3 44 44N 0 41W
Cestos →, Liberia ... 82 D3 5 40N 9 10W
Cestos Sehnkwehn △, Liberia ... 82 D3 5 40N 9 10W
Cetate, Romania ... 29 F8 44 7N 23 2 E
Cetin Grad, Croatia ... 41 C12 45 9N 15 45 E
Cetina →, Croatia ... 41 E13 43 26N 16 42 E
Cetinje, Serbia & M. ... 44 D2 42 23N 18 59 E
Cetraro, Italy ... 43 C8 39 31N 15 55 E
Ceuta, N. Afr. ... 37 J5 35 52N 5 18W
Ceva, Italy ... 40 D5 44 23N 8 2 E
Cévennes, France ... 20 D7 44 10N 3 50 E
Ceyhan, Turkey ... 70 B2 37 4N 35 47 E
Ceyhan →, Turkey ... 72 D6 36 38N 35 40 E
Ceylânpınar, Turkey ... 73 D9 36 50N 40 2 E
Ceylon = Sri Lanka ■, Asia ... 66 R12 7 30N 80 50 E
Cha-am, Thailand ... 64 F2 12 48N 99 58 E
Cha Pa, Vietnam ... 64 A4 22 20N 103 47 E
Chabanais, France ... 20 C4 45 52N 0 48 E
Chabeuil, France ... 21 D9 44 54N 5 3 E
Chablais, France ... 19 E13 46 20N 6 36 E
Chablis, France ... 19 E10 47 47N 3 48 E
Chachapoyas, Peru ... 124 E3 6 15 S 77 50W
Chachoengsao, Thailand ... 64 F3 13 42N 101 5 E
Chachran, Pakistan ... 68 E4 28 55N 70 30 E
Chachro, Pakistan ... 68 G4 25 5N 70 15 E
Chaco □, Argentina ... 126 B4 27 0 S 59 30W

Chaco □, Argentina ... 126 B3 26 30 S 61 0W
Chaco □, Paraguay .. 126 B4 26 0 S 60 0W
Chaco →, U.S.A. 109 H9 36 46N 108 39W
Chaco Austral, S. Amer. 128 B4 27 0 S 61 30W
Chaco Boreal, S. Amer. 124 H6 22 0 S 60 0W
Chaco Central, S. Amer. 128 A4 24 0 S 61 0W
Chaco Culture △, U.S.A. 109 J10 36 3N 107 58W
Chacon, C., U.S.A. ... 102 C2 54 42N 132 0W
Chad ■, Africa ...... 79 F8 15 0N 17 15 E
Chad, L. = Tchad, L.,
 Chad .... 79 F8 13 30N 14 30 E
Chadan, Russia ...... 53 D10 51 17N 91 35 E
Chadileuvú →,
 Argentina .... 126 D2 37 46 S 66 0W
Chadiza, Zambia ..... 87 E3 14 45 S 32 27 E
Chadron, U.S.A. 112 D3 42 50N 103 0W
Chadyr-Lunga = Ciadâr-
 Lunga, Moldova .. 29 D13 46 3N 28 51 E
Chae Hom, Thailand .. 64 C2 18 43N 99 35 E
Chae Son △, Thailand . 64 C2 18 42N 99 20 E
Chaem →, Thailand .. 64 C2 18 11N 98 38 E
Chaeryŏng, N. Korea . 57 E13 38 24N 125 36 E
Chagai Hills = Chāh Gay
 Hills, Afghan. ..... 66 E3 29 30N 64 0 E
Chagda, Russia ...... 53 D14 58 45N 130 38 E
Chaghcharān, Afghan. . 66 B4 34 31N 65 15 E
Chagny, France ...... 19 F11 46 57N 4 45 E
Chagoda, Russia ..... 32 C8 59 10N 35 15 E
Chagos Arch. ☒,
 Ind. Oc. .... 50 K11 6 0 S 72 0 E
Chagres →, Panama .. 120 E4 9 33N 79 37W
Chagrin Falls, U.S.A. . 116 E3 41 26N 81 24W
Chaguanas, Trin. & Tob. 125 K15 10 30N 61 26W
Chāh Akhvor, Iran ... 71 C8 32 41N 59 40 E
Chāh Bahar, Iran .... 71 E9 25 20N 60 40 E
Chāh-e Kavīr, Iran ... 71 C8 34 29N 56 52 E
Chāh Gay Hills, Afghan. 66 E3 29 30N 64 0 E
Chahar Burjak, Afghan. 66 D3 30 15N 62 0 E
Chahār Mahāll va
 Bakhtīarī □, Iran .. 71 C6 32 0N 49 0 E
Chaibasa, India ...... 67 H14 22 42N 85 49 E
Chaillé-les-Marais,
 France 20 B2 46 25N 1 2W
Chainat, Thailand .... 64 E3 15 11N 100 8 E
Chaiya, Thailand ..... 65 H2 9 23N 99 14 E
Chaiyaphum, Thailand 64 E4 15 48N 102 2 E
Chaj Doab, Pakistan .. 68 C5 32 15N 73 0 E
Chajari, Argentina ... 126 C4 30 42 S 58 0W
Chak Amru, Pakistan . 68 C6 32 22N 75 11 E
Chaka, Sudan .... 81 G3 4 49N 31 14 E
Chakar →, Pakistan .. 68 E3 29 29N 68 2 E
Chakari, Zimbabwe ... 89 B4 18 5 S 29 51 E
Chake Chake, Tanzania 86 D4 5 15 S 39 45 E
Chakhānsūr, Afghan. .. 66 D3 31 10N 62 0 E
Chakonipau, L., Canada 105 A6 56 18N 68 30W
Chakradharpur, India . 69 H11 22 45N 85 40 E
Chakrata, India ...... 68 D7 30 42N 77 51 E
Chakwal, Pakistan ... 68 C5 32 56N 72 53 E
Chala, Peru .... 124 G4 15 48 S 74 20W
Chalais, France ...... 20 C4 45 16N 0 3 E
Chalchihuites, Mexico . 118 C4 23 29N 103 53W
Chalcis = Khalkís,
 Greece .... 46 C5 38 27N 23 42 E
Châlette-sur-Loing,
 France .... 19 D9 48 1N 2 44 E
Chaleur B., Canada ... 105 C6 47 55N 65 30W
Chalfant, U.S.A. 110 H8 37 32N 118 21W
Chalhuanca, Peru .... 124 F4 14 15 S 73 15W
Chalindrey, France ... 19 E12 47 43N 5 26 E
Chaling, China ...... 59 D9 26 58N 113 30 E
Chalisgaon, India .... 66 J9 20 30N 75 10 E
Chalk River, Canada .. 104 C4 46 1N 77 27W
Chalky Inlet, N.Z. .... 91 M1 46 3 S 166 31 E
Challans, France 18 F5 46 50N 1 52W
Challapata, Bolivia ... 124 G5 18 53 S 66 50W
Challis, U.S.A. 108 D6 44 30N 114 14W
Chalmette, U.S.A. 113 L10 29 56N 89 58W
Chalon-sur-Saône,
 France .... 19 F11 46 48N 4 50 E
Chalonnes-sur-Loire,
 France 18 E6 47 20N 0 45W
Châlons-en-Champagne,
 France .... 19 D11 48 58N 4 20 E
Châlus, France ...... 20 C4 45 39N 0 58 E
Chālūs, Iran .... 71 B6 36 38N 51 26 E
Cham, Germany ...... 25 F8 49 13N 12 39 E
Cham, Cu Lao, Vietnam 64 E7 15 57N 108 30 E
Chama, U.S.A. 109 H10 36 54N 106 35W
Chamaicó, Argentina . 126 D3 35 3 S 64 58W
Chaman, Pakistan .... 66 D5 30 58N 66 25 E
Chamba, India .... 68 C7 32 35N 76 10 E
Chamba, Tanzania .... 87 E4 11 37 S 37 0 E
Chambal →, India ... 69 F8 26 29N 79 15 E
Chamberlain, U.S.A. .. 112 D5 43 49N 99 20W
Chamberlain →,
 Australia .... 92 C4 15 30 S 127 54 E
Chamberlain L., U.S.A. 115 B11 46 14N 69 19W
Chambers, U.S.A. 109 J9 35 11N 109 26W
Chambersburg, U.S.A. 114 F7 39 56N 77 40W
Chambéry, France ... 21 C9 45 34N 5 55 E
Chambeshi →, Zambia 84 G6 11 53 S 29 48 E
Chambly, Canada 117 A11 45 27N 73 17W
Chambord, Canada ... 105 C5 48 25N 72 6W
Chamboulive, France . 20 C5 45 26N 1 42 E
Chamchamal, Iraq ... 70 C5 35 32N 44 50 E
Chamela, Mexico 118 D3 19 32N 105 5W
Chamical, Argentina .. 126 C2 30 22 S 66 27W
Chamkar Luong,
 Cambodia .... 65 G4 11 0N 103 45 E
Chamoli, India ...... 69 D8 30 24N 79 21 E
Chamonix-Mont Blanc,
 France .... 21 C10 45 55N 6 51 E
Champa, India .... 69 H10 22 2N 82 43 E
Champagne, Canada .. 102 A1 60 49N 136 30W
Champagne, France .. 19 D11 48 40N 4 20 E
Champagnole, France . 19 F12 46 45N 5 55 E
Champaign, U.S.A. ... 114 E1 40 7N 88 15W
Champassak, Laos .... 64 E5 14 53N 105 52 E
Champaubert, France . 19 D10 48 50N 3 45 E
Champawat, India .... 69 E9 29 20N 80 6 E
Champdeniers-St-Denis,
 France 20 B3 46 29N 0 25W
Champdôré, L., Canada 105 A6 55 55N 65 49W
Champeix, France .... 20 C7 45 37N 3 8 E
Champion, U.S.A. 116 E4 41 19N 80 51W
Champlain, U.S.A. ... 117 B11 44 59N 73 27W
Champlain, L., U.S.A. . 117 B11 44 40N 73 20W
Champotón, Mexico .. 119 D6 19 20N 90 50W
Champua, India ...... 69 H11 22 5N 85 40 E
Chamusca, Portugal .. 37 F2 39 21N 8 29W
Chana, Thailand ..... 65 J3 6 55N 100 44 E
Chañaral, Chile ...... 126 B1 26 23 S 70 40W
Chanārān, Iran ...... 71 B8 36 39N 59 6 E
Chanasma, India ..... 68 H5 23 44N 72 5 E
Chancery Lane,
 Barbados .... 121 g 13 3N 59 30W

Chanco, Chile .... 126 D1 35 44 S 72 32W
Chand, India .... 69 J8 21 57N 79 7 E
Chandan, India ...... 69 G12 24 38N 86 40 E
Chandan Chauki, India 69 E9 28 33N 80 47 E
Chandannagar, India . 69 H13 22 52N 88 24 E
Chandausi, India ..... 69 E8 28 27N 78 49 E
Chandeleur Is., U.S.A. . 113 L10 29 55N 88 57W
Chandeleur Sd., U.S.A. 113 L10 29 55N 89 0W
Chandigarh, India .... 68 D7 30 43N 76 47 E
Chandil, India .... 69 H12 22 58N 86 3 E
Chandler, Australia ... 95 D1 27 0 S 133 19 E
Chandler, Canada 105 C7 48 18N 64 46W
Chandler, Ariz., U.S.A. 109 K8 33 18N 111 50W
Chandler, Okla., U.S.A. 113 H6 35 42N 96 53W
Chandod, India ...... 68 J5 21 59N 73 28 E
Chandpur, India ..... 69 E8 29 8N 78 19 E
Chandpur, Bangla. ... 67 H17 23 8N 90 45 E
Chandrapur, India ... 66 K11 19 57N 79 25 E
Changane →, Mozam. 89 C5 24 30 S 33 30 E
Changbai, China ..... 57 D15 41 25N 128 5 E
Changbai Shan, China . 57 C15 42 20N 129 0 E
Changchiak'ou =
 Zhangjiakou, China . 56 D8 40 48N 114 55 E
Ch'angchun =
 Changchun, China .. 57 B13 43 57N 125 17 E
Changchun, China ... 57 B13 43 57N 125 17 E
Changchunling, China 57 B13 45 15N 125 19 E
Changde, China ...... 59 C8 29 4N 111 35 E
Changdo-ri, N. Korea . 57 E14 38 30N 127 40 E
Changfeng, China .... 59 A11 32 28N 117 10 E
Changhai = Shanghai,
 China .... 59 B13 31 15N 121 26 E
Changhua, China .... 59 B12 30 12N 119 12 E
Changhua, Taiwan ... 59 E13 24 2N 120 30 E
Changhŭng, S. Korea . 57 G14 34 41N 126 52 E
Changhŭngni, N. Korea 57 D15 40 24N 128 19 E
Changi, Singapore ... 65 d 1 23N 103 59 E
Changi, Singapore ✈
 (SIN), Singapore ... 65 M4 1 23N 103 59 E
Changjiang, China ... 64 C7 19 20N 108 55 E
Changjin, N. Korea ... 57 D14 40 23N 127 15 E
Changjin-chŏsuji,
 N. Korea .... 57 D14 40 30N 127 15 E
Changle, China ...... 59 E12 25 59N 119 27 E
Changli, China ...... 57 E10 39 40N 119 13 E
Changling, China .... 57 B12 44 20N 123 58 E
Changlun, Malaysia .. 65 J3 6 25N 100 26 E
Changning, Hunan,
 China .... 59 D9 26 28N 112 22 E
Changning, Sichuan,
 China .... 58 C5 28 40N 104 56 E
Changning, Yunnan,
 China .... 58 E2 24 45N 99 30 E
Changping, China .... 56 D9 40 14N 116 12 E
Changsha, China .... 59 C9 28 12N 113 0 E
Changshan, China ... 59 C12 28 55N 118 27 E
Changshu, China .... 59 B13 31 33N 120 43 E
Changshun, China ... 58 D6 26 3N 106 25 E
Changtai, China ..... 59 E11 24 35N 117 42 E
Changting, China .... 59 E11 25 50N 116 22 E
Changwu, China ..... 56 G4 35 10N 107 45 E
Changxing, China .... 59 B12 31 0N 119 55 E
Changyang, China ... 59 B8 30 30N 111 10 E
Changyi, China ...... 57 F10 36 40N 119 30 E
Changyŏn, N. Korea . 57 E13 38 15N 125 6 E
Changyuan, China ... 56 G8 35 15N 114 42 E
Changzhi, China ..... 56 F7 36 10N 113 6 E
Changzhou, China ... 59 B12 31 47N 119 58 E
Chanhanga, Angola .. 88 B1 16 0 S 14 8 E
Chania = Khaniá, Greece 49 D6 35 30N 24 4 E
Chanlar = Xanlar,
 Azerbaijan .... 35 K8 40 37N 46 12 E
Channapatna, India .. 66 N10 12 40N 77 15 E
Channel Is., U.K. 15 H5 49 19N 2 24W
Channel Is., U.S.A. ... 111 M7 33 40N 119 15W
Channel Islands △,
 U.S.A. 111 L7 34 0N 119 24W
Channel-Port aux
 Basques, Canada .. 105 C8 47 30N 59 9W
Channel Tunnel, Europe 15 F9 51 0N 1 30 E
Channing, U.S.A. 113 H3 35 41N 102 20W
Chantada, Spain 36 C3 42 36N 7 46W
Chanthaburi, Thailand 64 F4 12 38N 102 12 E
Chantilly, France .... 19 C9 49 12N 2 29 E
Chantonnay, France . 18 F5 46 40N 1 3W
Chantrey Inlet, Canada 100 B10 67 48N 96 20W
Chanute, U.S.A. 113 G7 37 41N 95 27W
Chanza →, Spain 37 H3 37 32N 7 30W
Chao Hu, China ..... 59 B11 31 30N 117 30 E
Chao Phraya →,
 Thailand .... 64 F3 13 32N 100 36 E
Chao Phraya Lowlands,
 Thailand .... 64 E3 15 30N 100 0 E
Chaocheng, China ... 56 F8 36 4N 115 37 E
Chaohu, China ...... 59 B11 31 38N 117 50 E
Chaoyang, Guangdong,
 China .... 59 F11 23 17N 116 30 E
Chaoyang, Liaoning,
 China .... 57 D11 41 35N 120 22 E
Chaozhou, China .... 59 F11 23 42N 116 32 E
Chapais, Canada 104 C5 49 47N 74 51W
Chapala, Mozam. .... 87 F4 15 50 S 37 35 E
Chapala, L. de, Mexico 118 C4 20 10N 103 20W
Chapayev, Kazakhstan 34 E10 50 25N 51 10 E
Chapayevsk, Russia .. 34 D9 53 0N 49 40 E
Chapecó, Brazil ..... 127 B5 27 14 S 52 41W
Chapel Hill, U.S.A. ... 115 H6 35 55N 79 4W
Chapleau, Canada ... 104 C3 47 50N 83 24W
Chaplin, Canada 103 C7 50 28N 106 40W
Chaplin L., Canada .. 103 C7 50 22N 106 36W
Chaplino, Ukraine ... 33 H9 48 8N 36 15 E
Chaplygin, Russia ... 32 F11 53 15N 40 0 E
Chappell, U.S.A. 112 E3 41 6N 102 28W
Chapra = Chhapra, India 69 G11 25 48N 84 44 E
Chara, Russia .... 53 D12 56 54N 118 20 E
Charadai, Argentina . 126 B4 27 35 S 59 55W
Charagua, Bolivia ... 124 G6 19 45 S 63 10W
Charambirá, Punta,
 Colombia 124 C3 4 16N 77 32W
Charaña, Bolivia .... 124 G5 17 30 S 69 25W
Charantsavan, Armenia 35 K7 40 35N 44 41 E
Charanwala, India ... 68 F5 27 51N 72 10 E
Charata, Argentina .. 126 B3 27 13 S 61 14W
Charcas, Mexico 118 C4 23 10N 101 20W
Charcot I., Antarctica . 5 C17 70 0 S 70 0W
Chard, U.K. 15 G5 50 52N 2 58W
Chardon, U.S.A. 116 E3 41 35N 81 12W
Chardzhou = Chärjew,
 Turkmenistan ..... 52 F7 39 6N 63 34 E
Charente □, France .. 20 C4 45 50N 0 16 E

Charente →, France .. 20 C2 45 57N 1 5W
Charente-Maritime □,
 France 20 C3 45 45N 0 45W
Chari →, Chad ...... 79 F8 12 58N 14 31 E
Chārīkār, Afghan. ... 66 B6 35 0N 69 10 E
Chariton →, U.S.A. .. 112 F8 39 19N 92 58W
Chärjew, Turkmenistan 52 F7 39 6N 63 34 E
Charkhari, India ..... 69 G8 25 24N 79 45 E
Charkhi Dadri, India . 68 E7 28 37N 76 17 E
Charleroi, Belgium ... 17 D4 50 24N 4 27 E
Charleroi, U.S.A. 116 F5 40 9N 79 57W
Charles, C., U.S.A. ... 114 G8 37 7N 75 58W
Charles City, U.S.A. .. 112 D8 43 4N 92 41W
Charles de Gaulle,
 Paris ✈ (CDG),
 France .... 19 D9 49 0N 2 32 E
Charles L., Canada ... 103 B6 59 50N 110 33W
Charles Town, U.S.A. . 114 F7 39 17N 77 52W
Charleston, Ill., U.S.A. 114 F1 39 30N 88 10W
Charleston, Miss., U.S.A. 113 H9 34 1N 90 4W
Charleston, Mo., U.S.A. 113 G10 36 55N 89 21W
Charleston, W. Va.,
 U.S.A. 114 F5 38 21N 81 38W
Charleston L., Canada . 117 B9 44 32N 76 0W
Charleston Peak, U.S.A. 111 J11 36 16N 115 42W
Charlestown, Ireland .. 12 C3 53 58N 8 48W
Charlestown, S. Africa . 89 D4 27 26 S 29 53 E
Charlestown, Ind.,
 U.S.A. 114 F3 38 27N 85 40W
Charlestown, N.H.,
 U.S.A. 117 C12 43 14N 72 25W
Charlestown of
 Aberlour, U.K. 13 D5 57 28N 3 14W
Charleville = Rath Luirc,
 Ireland 12 D3 52 21N 8 40W
Charleville, Australia .. 95 D4 26 24 S 146 15 E
Charleville-Mézières,
 France .... 19 C11 49 44N 4 40 E
Charlevoix, U.S.A. ... 114 C3 45 19N 85 16W
Charlieu, France ..... 19 F11 46 10N 4 10 E
Charlotte, Mich., U.S.A. 114 D3 42 34N 84 50W
Charlotte, N.C., U.S.A. 115 H5 35 13N 80 51W
Charlotte, Vt., U.S.A. . 117 B11 44 19N 73 14W
Charlotte Amalie,
 U.S. Virgin Is. ..... 121 e 18 21N 64 56W
Charlotte Harbor,
 U.S.A. 115 M4 26 50N 82 10W
Charlotte L., Canada .. 102 C3 52 12N 125 19W
Charlottenberg, Sweden 10 E6 59 54N 12 17 E
Charlottesville, U.S.A. 114 F6 38 2N 78 30W
Charlottetown,
 Nfld. & L., Canada . 105 B8 52 46N 56 7W
Charlottetown, P.E.I.,
 Canada 105 C7 46 14N 63 8W
Charlotteville,
 Trin. & Tob. 125 J16 11 20N 60 33W
Charlton, Australia ... 95 F3 36 16 S 143 24 E
Charlton, U.S.A. 112 E8 40 59N 93 20W
Charlton I., Canada .. 104 B4 52 0N 79 20W
Charmes, France ..... 19 D13 48 22N 6 17 E
Charny, Canada 105 C5 46 43N 71 15W
Charnany, Belarus ... 31 G11 51 59N 24 12 E
Charolles, France .... 19 F11 46 27N 4 16 E
Charost, France ...... 19 F9 47 0N 2 7 E
Charre, Mozam. ..... 87 F4 17 13 S 35 10 E
Charroux, France .... 20 B4 46 9N 0 25 E
Charsadda, Pakistan . 68 B4 34 7N 71 45 E
Charters Towers,
 Australia .... 94 C4 20 5 S 146 13 E
Chartres, France ..... 18 D8 48 29N 1 30 E
Chartreuse △, France . 21 C9 45 22N 5 42 E
Chascomús, Argentina 126 D4 35 30 S 58 0W
Chasefu, Zambia ..... 87 E3 11 55 S 33 8 E
Chashma Barrage,
 Pakistan .... 68 C4 32 27N 71 20 E
Chashniki, Belarus ... 32 E5 54 51N 29 10 E
Chasseneuil-sur-
 Bonnieure, France . 20 C4 45 52N 0 29 E
Chāt, Iran .... 71 B7 37 59N 55 16 E
Chatal Balkan = Udvoy
 Balkan, Bulgaria ... 45 D10 42 50N 26 50 E
Château-Arnoux-St-
 Auban, France .... 21 D10 44 6N 6 0 E
Château-Chinon, France 19 E10 47 4N 3 56 E
Château-d'Olonne,
 France 20 B2 46 30N 1 44W
Château-du-Loir, France 18 E7 47 40N 0 25 E
Château-Gontier, France 18 E6 47 50N 0 48W
Château-la-Vallière,
 France .... 18 E7 47 30N 0 20 E
Château-Landon, France 19 D9 48 8N 2 40 E
Château-Renard, France 19 E9 47 56N 2 55 E
Château-Renault,
 France .... 18 E7 47 36N 0 56 E
Château-Salins, France 19 D13 48 50N 6 30 E
Château-Thierry, France 19 C10 49 3N 3 20 E
Châteaubourg, France . 18 D5 48 7N 1 25W
Châteaubriant, France . 18 E5 47 43N 1 23W
Châteaudun, France .. 18 D8 48 3N 1 20 E
Châteaugay, U.S.A. .. 117 B10 44 56N 74 5W
Châteauguay, L.,
 Canada 105 A5 56 26N 70 3W
Châteaulin, France ... 18 D2 48 11N 4 8W
Châteaumeillant, France 19 F9 46 35N 2 12 E
Châteauneuf-du-Faou,
 France 18 D3 48 11N 3 50W
Châteauneuf-sur-
 Charente, France .. 20 C3 45 36N 0 3W
Châteauneuf-sur-Cher,
 France .... 19 F9 46 52N 2 18 E
Châteauneuf-sur-Loire,
 France .... 19 E9 47 52N 2 13 E
Châteauroux, France . 21 E8 43 53N 4 51 E
Châteauroux, France . 19 F8 46 50N 1 40 E
Châteaux, Pte. des,
 Guadeloupe ...... 120 b 16 15N 61 10W
Châtelaillon-Plage,
 France 20 B2 46 5N 1 5W
Châtelguyon, France . 20 C7 45 55N 3 4 E
Châtellerault, France . 18 F7 46 50N 0 30 E
Châtelus-Malvaleix,
 France .... 19 F9 46 18N 2 1 E
Chatham = Chatham-
 Kent, Canada 116 D2 42 24N 82 11W
Chatham = Miramichi,
 Canada 105 C6 47 2N 65 28W
Chatham, U.K. ...... 15 F8 51 22N 0 32 E
Chatham, U.S.A. 117 D11 42 21N 73 36W
Chatham, Is., Pac. Oc. 96 M10 44 0 S 176 40W
Chatham-Kent, Canada 116 D2 42 24N 82 11W
Châtillon, Italy ...... 40 C4 45 45N 7 37 E
Châtillon-Coligny,
 France .... 19 E9 47 50N 2 51 E

Châtillon-en-Diois,
 France .... 21 D9 44 41N 5 29 E
Châtillon-sur-Indre,
 France .... 18 F8 46 59N 1 10 E
Châtillon-sur-Loire,
 France .... 19 E9 47 35N 2 44 E
Châtillon-sur-Seine,
 France .... 19 E11 47 50N 4 33 E
Chatmohar, Bangla. .. 69 G13 24 15N 89 15 E
Chatra, India .... 69 G11 24 12N 84 56 E
Chatrapur, India .... 67 K14 19 22N 85 2 E
Chats, L. des, Canada . 117 A8 45 30N 76 20W
Chatsu, India .... 68 F6 26 36N 75 57 E
Chatsworth, Canada . 116 B4 44 27N 80 54W
Chatsworth, Zimbabwe 87 F3 19 38 S 31 13 E
Chattahoochee, U.S.A. 115 K3 30 42N 84 51W
Chattahoochee →,
 U.S.A. 115 K3 30 54N 84 57W
Chattanooga, U.S.A. . 115 H3 35 3N 85 19W
Chatteris, U.K. ...... 15 E8 52 28N 0 2 E
Chaturat, Thailand ... 64 E3 15 40N 101 51 E
Chau Doc, Vietnam .. 65 G5 10 42N 105 7 E
Chaudes-Aigues, France 20 D7 44 51N 3 1 E
Chauffailles, France .. 19 F11 46 13N 4 20 E
Chaukan Pass, Burma . 67 F20 27 0N 97 15 E
Chaumont, France ... 19 D12 48 7N 5 8 E
Chaumont, U.S.A. ... 117 B8 44 4N 76 8W
Chaumont-en-Vexin,
 France .... 19 C8 49 16N 1 53 E
Chaumont-sur-Loire,
 France .... 18 E8 47 29N 1 11 E
Chaunay, France .... 20 B4 46 13N 0 9 E
Chaunskaya G., Russia 4 C16 69 0N 169 0 E
Chauny, France ...... 19 C10 49 37N 3 12 E
Chausey, Îs., France .. 18 D5 48 52N 1 49W
Chaussin, France .... 19 F12 46 59N 5 22 E
Chautauqua L., U.S.A. 116 D5 42 10N 79 24W
Chauvigny, France ... 18 F7 46 34N 0 39 E
Chaves, Brazil ...... 125 D9 0 15 S 49 55W
Chaves, Portugal 36 D3 41 45N 7 32W
Chawang, Thailand .. 65 H2 8 25N 99 30 E
Chazelles-sur-Lyon,
 France .... 21 C8 45 39N 4 22 E
Chazy, U.S.A. 117 B11 44 53N 73 26W
Cheb, Czech Rep. .... 26 A5 50 9N 12 28 E
Cheboksarskoye Vdkhr.,
 Russia .... 34 B8 56 13N 46 58 E
Cheboksary, Russia .. 34 B8 56 8N 47 12 E
Cheboygan, U.S.A. .. 114 C3 45 39N 84 29W
Chebsara, Russia .... 32 C10 59 10N 38 59 E
Chech, Erg, Africa ... 78 D5 25 0N 2 15W
Chechania □, Russia . 35 J7 43 30N 45 29 E
Chechen, Ostrov, Russia 35 H8 43 59N 47 40 E
Chechenia = Chechnya =
 Chechenia □, Russia 35 J7 43 30N 45 29 E
Checheno-Ingush
 Republic =
 Chechenia □, Russia 35 J7 43 30N 45 29 E
Chechnya =
 Chechenia □, Russia 35 J7 43 30N 45 29 E
Chechon, S. Korea ... 57 F15 37 8N 128 12 E
Chęciny, Poland ..... 31 H7 50 46N 20 28 E
Checotah, U.S.A. 113 H7 35 28N 95 31W
Chedabucto B., Canada 105 C7 45 25N 61 8W
Cheduba I., Burma ... 67 K18 18 45N 93 40 E
Cheepie, Australia ... 95 D4 26 33 S 145 1 E
Chef-Boutonne, France 20 B3 46 7N 0 4W
Chegdomyn, Russia .. 53 D14 51 7N 133 1 E
Chegga, Mauritania .. 78 C4 25 27N 5 40W
Chegutu, Zimbabwe .. 87 F3 18 10 S 30 14 E
Chehalis, U.S.A. 110 D4 46 40N 122 58W
Chehalis →, U.S.A. .. 110 D3 46 57N 123 50W
Cheile Nerei-
 Beusnita △, Romania 28 F6 44 56N 21 52 E
Cheiron, Mt., France . 21 E10 43 49N 6 58 E
Cheju, do, S. Korea .. 57 H14 33 29N 126 34 E
Chekalin, Russia ..... 32 E9 54 10N 36 10 E
Chekhov, Russia ..... 30 D7 54 33N 20 43 E
Chekiang = Zhejiang □,
 China .... 59 C13 29 0N 120 0 E
Chel = Kuru, Bahr el →,
 Sudan .... 81 F2 8 10N 26 50 E
Chela, Sa. da, Angola . 88 B1 16 20 S 13 20 E
Chelan, U.S.A. 108 C4 47 51N 120 1W
Chelan, L., U.S.A. ... 108 B3 48 11N 120 30W
Cheleken, Turkmenistan 52 F6 39 34N 53 16 E
Cheleken Yarymadasy,
 Turkmenistan ..... 71 B7 39 30N 53 15 E
Chelforó, Argentina .. 128 D3 39 0 S 66 33W
Chelkar = Shalqar,
 Kazakhstan .... 52 E6 47 48N 59 39 E
Chelkar Tengiz,
 Solonchak,
 Kazakhstan .... 52 E7 48 5N 63 7 E
Chella, Ethiopia ..... 81 F4 5 0N 37 26 E
Chelles, France ...... 19 D9 48 52N 2 33 E
Chełm, Poland ...... 31 G10 51 8N 23 30 E
Chełmno, Poland .... 31 E5 53 20N 18 30 E
Chelmsford, U.K. .... 15 F8 51 44N 0 29 E
Chełmża, Poland .... 31 E5 53 10N 18 39 E
Chelsea, U.S.A. 117 C12 43 59N 72 27W
Cheltenham, U.K. ... 15 F5 51 54N 2 4W
Chelva, Spain 38 F4 39 45N 1 0W
Chelyabinsk, Russia .. 52 D7 55 10N 61 24 E
Chelyuskin, C. =
 Chelyuskin, Mys,
 Russia .... 53 B11 77 30N 103 0 E
Chelyuskin, Mys, Russia 53 B11 77 30N 103 0 E
Chemainus, Canada .. 102 D4 48 55N 123 42W
Chemba, Mozam. .... 85 H6 17 9 S 34 53 E
Chembar = Belinskiy,
 Russia .... 34 D6 53 0N 43 25 E
Chemillé, France 18 E6 47 14N 0 45W
Chemnitz, Germany .. 24 E8 50 51N 12 54 E
Chemult, U.S.A. 108 E3 43 14N 121 47W
Chen, Gora, Russia .. 53 C15 65 16N 141 50 E
Chenab →, Pakistan . 68 D4 30 23N 71 2 E
Chenango Forks, U.S.A. 117 D9 42 15N 75 51W
Chencha, Ethiopia ... 81 F4 6 15N 37 32 E
Chenchiang =
 Zhenjiang, China .. 59 A12 32 11N 119 26 E
Cheng Xian, China ... 56 H3 33 43N 105 42 E
Chengbu, China ..... 59 D8 26 18N 110 16 E
Chengcheng, China .. 56 G5 35 8N 109 56 E
Chengchou =
 Zhengzhou, China . 56 G7 34 45N 113 34 E
Chengde, China ..... 57 D9 40 59N 117 58 E
Chengdong Hu, China 59 A11 32 15N 116 50 E
Chengdu, China ..... 58 B5 30 38N 104 2 E
Chenggong, China ... 58 E4 24 55N 102 50 E
Chenggu, China ..... 56 H4 33 10N 107 21 E
Chenghai, China ..... 59 F11 23 30N 116 42 E
Chengjiang, China ... 58 E4 24 39N 103 0 E

Chengkou, China .... 58 B7 31 54N 108 31 E
Ch'engmai, China ... 64 C7 19 50N 109 58 E
Ch'engtu = Chengdu,
 China .... 58 B5 30 38N 104 2 E
Chengwu, China ..... 56 G8 34 58N 115 50 E
Chengxi Hu, China ... 59 A11 32 15N 116 10 E
Chengyang, China ... 57 F11 36 18N 120 21 E
Chenjiagang, China .. 57 G10 34 23N 119 47 E
Chenkán, Mexico 119 D6 19 8N 90 58W
Chennai, India ...... 66 N12 13 8N 80 19 E
Chenôve, France .... 19 E12 47 16N 5 1 E
Chenxi, China .... 59 C8 28 2N 110 12 E
Chenzhou, China .... 59 E9 25 47N 113 1 E
Cheo Reo, Vietnam .. 62 B3 13 25N 108 28 E
Cheom Ksan, Cambodia 64 E5 14 13N 104 56 E
Chepelare, Bulgaria .. 45 E8 41 44N 24 40 E
Chepén, Peru .... 124 E3 7 15 S 79 23W
Chepes, Argentina ... 126 C2 31 20 S 66 35W
Chepo, Panama 120 E4 9 10N 79 6W
Chepstow, U.K. 15 F5 51 38N 2 41W
Chequamegon B.,
 U.S.A. 112 B9 46 40N 90 30W
Cher □, France ...... 19 E9 47 10N 2 30 E
Cher →, France ..... 18 E7 47 21N 0 29 E
Chéradi, Italy .... 43 B10 40 27N 17 10 E
Cherasco, Italy ...... 40 D4 44 39N 7 51 E
Cheraw, U.S.A. 115 H6 34 42N 79 53W
Cherbourg, France ... 18 C5 49 39N 1 40W
Cherdakly, Russia ... 34 C9 54 25N 48 50 E
Cherdyn, Russia ..... 52 C6 60 24N 56 29 E
Cheremkhovo, Russia 53 D11 53 8N 103 1 E
Cherepanovo, Russia . 52 D9 54 15N 83 30 E
Cherepovets, Russia .. 32 C9 59 5N 37 55 E
Chergui, Chott ech,
 Algeria .... 78 B6 34 21N 0 25 E
Cherikov = Cherykaw,
 Belarus .... 32 F6 53 32N 31 20 E
Cherkasy, Ukraine ... 33 H7 49 27N 32 4 E
Cherkessk, Russia ... 35 H6 44 15N 42 5 E
Cherlak, Russia ..... 52 D8 54 15N 74 55 E
Chernaya, Russia .... 53 B9 70 30N 89 10 E
Chernelytsya, Ukraine 29 B10 48 49N 25 16 E
Cherni, Bulgaria ..... 44 D7 42 35N 23 18 E
Chernigov = Chernihiv,
 Ukraine .... 33 G6 51 28N 31 20 E
Chernihiv, Ukraine ... 33 G6 51 28N 31 20 E
Cherniveska □, Ukraine 29 B10 48 20N 26 0 E
Chernivtsi, Ukraine .. 29 B13 48 32N 28 9 E
Chernivtsi, Ukraine .. 29 B10 48 15N 25 52 E
Chernobyl = Chornobyl,
 Ukraine .... 33 G6 51 20N 30 15 E
Chernogorsk, Russia . 53 D10 53 49N 91 18 E
Chernomorskoye =
 Chornomorske,
 Ukraine .... 33 K7 45 31N 32 40 E
Chernovtsy = Chernivtsi,
 Ukraine .... 29 B10 48 15N 25 52 E
Chernyakhovsk, Russia 9 J19 54 36N 21 48 E
Chernyanka, Russia .. 33 G9 50 56N 37 49 E
Chernysheskiy, Russia 53 C12 63 0N 112 30 E
Chernyye Zemli, Russia 35 H8 46 10N 46 0 E
Cherokee, Iowa, U.S.A. 112 D7 42 45N 95 33W
Cherokee, Okla., U.S.A. 113 G5 36 45N 98 21W
Cherokee Village,
 U.S.A. 113 G9 36 17N 91 30W
Cherokees, Grand Lake
 O' The, U.S.A. 113 G7 36 28N 95 2W
Cherrapunji, India ... 67 G17 25 17N 91 47 E
Cherry Valley, Calif.,
 U.S.A. 111 M10 33 59N 116 57W
Cherry Valley, N.Y.,
 U.S.A. 117 D10 42 48N 74 45W
Cherskiy, Russia ..... 53 C17 68 45N 161 18 E
Cherskogo Khrebet,
 Russia .... 53 C15 65 0N 143 0 E
Chertkovo, Russia ... 35 H11 49 25N 40 19 E
Cherven, Belarus .... 32 F5 53 45N 28 28 E
Cherven-Bryag, Bulgaria 45 C8 43 17N 24 7 E
Chervonoarmiyske,
 Ukraine .... 29 E13 45 47N 28 44 E
Cherwell →, U.K. ... 15 F6 51 44N 1 14W
Cherykaw, Belarus ... 32 F6 53 32N 31 20 E
Chesapeake, U.S.A. .. 114 G7 36 50N 76 17W
Chesapeake B., U.S.A. 114 G7 38 0N 76 10W
Cheshire □, U.K. 14 D5 53 14N 2 30W
Cheshskaya Guba,
 Russia .... 52 C5 67 20N 47 0 E
Cheshunt, U.K. 15 F7 51 43N 0 1W
Chesil Beach, U.K. ... 15 G5 50 37N 2 33W
Chesley, Canada 116 B3 44 17N 81 5W
Cheste, Spain 39 F4 39 30N 0 41W
Chester, U.K. 14 D5 53 12N 2 53W
Chester, Calif., U.S.A. 108 F3 40 19N 121 14W
Chester, Ill., U.S.A. .. 113 G10 37 55N 89 49W
Chester, Mont., U.S.A. 108 B8 48 31N 110 58W
Chester, Pa., U.S.A. . 114 F8 39 51N 75 22W
Chester, S.C., U.S.A. . 115 H5 34 43N 81 12W
Chester, Vt., U.S.A. .. 117 C12 43 16N 72 36W
Chester, W. Va., U.S.A. 116 F4 40 37N 80 34W
Chester-le-Street, U.K. 14 C6 54 51N 1 34W
Chesterfield, U.K. 14 D6 53 15N 1 25W
Chesterfield, Is., N. Cal. 96 J7 19 52 S 158 15 E
Chesterfield Inlet,
 Canada 100 B10 63 30N 90 45W
Chesterton Ra. △,
 Australia .... 95 D4 25 30 S 147 27 E
Chestertown, U.S.A. . 117 C11 43 40N 73 48W
Chesterville, Canada . 117 A9 45 6N 75 14W
Chestnut Ridge, U.S.A. 116 F5 40 20N 79 10W
Chesuncook L., U.S.A. 115 C11 46 0N 69 21W
Chéticamp, Canada .. 105 C7 46 37N 60 59W
Chetrosu, Moldova .. 29 B12 48 7N 27 14 E
Chetumal, Mexico ... 119 D7 18 30N 88 20W
Chetumal, B. de, Mexico 119 D7 18 40N 88 0W
Chetwynd, Canada .. 102 B4 55 45N 121 36W
Chevanceaux, France 20 C3 45 18N 0 14W
Cheviot, The, U.K. ... 14 B5 55 29N 2 9W
Cheviot Hills, U.K. ... 14 B5 55 20N 2 30W
Cheviot Ra., Australia 94 D3 25 20 S 143 45 E
Chew Bahir, Ethiopia . 81 G4 4 40N 36 50 E
Chewelah, U.S.A. ... 108 B5 48 17N 117 43W
Chewore △, Zimbabwe 87 F2 16 0 S 29 52 E
Cheyenne, Okla., U.S.A. 113 H5 35 37N 99 40W
Cheyenne, Wyo., U.S.A. 112 E2 41 8N 104 49W
Cheyenne →, U.S.A. 112 C4 44 41N 101 18W
Cheyenne Wells, U.S.A. 112 F3 38 49N 102 21W
Cheyne B., Australia . 93 F2 34 35 S 118 50 E
Chhabra, India ...... 68 G7 24 40N 76 54 E
Chhaktala, India ..... 68 H6 22 34N 74 11 E
Chhapra, India ...... 69 G11 25 48N 84 44 E
Chhata, India .... 68 F7 27 42N 77 30 E
Chhatarpur, Jharkhand,
 India .... 69 G11 24 23N 84 11 E
Chhatarpur, Mad. P.,
 India .... 69 G8 24 55N 79 35 E

Chhattisgarh □, *India* . **69 J10** 22 0N 82 0 E
Chhep, *Cambodia* ..... **64 F5** 13 45N 105 24 E
Chhindwara, *Mad. P.,*
  India .... **69 H8** 23 3N 79 29 E
Chhindwara, *Mad. P.,*
  India .... **69 H8** 22 2N 78 59 E
Chhlong, *Cambodia* ... **65 F5** 12 15N 105 58 E
Chhota Tawa ➤, *India* **68 H7** 22 14N 76 36 E
Chhoti Kali Sindh ➤,
  India .... **68 G6** 24 2N 75 31 E
Chhukhadan, *India* ... **69 J9** 21 32N 80 59 E
Chhuk, *Cambodia* ..... **65 G5** 10 46N 104 28 E
Chi ➤, *Thailand* ...... **64 E5** 15 11N 104 43 E
Chiai, *Taiwan* .... **59 F13** 23 29N 120 25 E
Chiali, *Taiwan* .... **59 F13** 23 10N 120 11 E
Chiamboni, *Somali Rep.* **84 E8** 1 39 S 41 35 E
Chianciano Terme, *Italy* **41 E8** 43 2N 11 49 E
Chiang Dao, *Thailand* . **64 C2** 19 22N 98 58 E
Chiang Kham, *Thailand* **64 C3** 19 32N 100 18 E
Chiang Khan, *Thailand* **64 D3** 17 52N 101 36 E
Chiang Khong, *Thailand* **58 G3** 20 17N 100 24 E
Chiang Mai, *Thailand* . **64 C2** 18 47N 98 59 E
Chiang Rai, *Thailand* . **58 H2** 19 52N 99 50 E
Chiang Saen, *Thailand* . **58 G3** 20 16N 100 5 E
Chianti, *Italy* .... **41 E8** 43 32N 11 25 E
Chiapa ➤, *Mexico* **119 D6** 16 42N 93 0W
Chiapa de Corzo,
  Mexico **119 D6** 16 42N 93 0W
Chiapas □, *Mexico* **119 D6** 17 0N 92 45W
Chiaramonte Gulfi, *Italy* **43 E7** 37 2N 14 42 E
Chiaravalle, *Italy* .... **41 E10** 43 36N 13 19 E
Chiaravalle Centrale,
  Italy .... **43 D9** 38 41N 16 25 E
Chiari, *Italy* .... **40 C6** 45 32N 9 56 E
Chiatura, *Georgia* .... **35 J6** 42 15N 43 17 E
Chiautla, *Mexico* **119 D5** 18 18N 98 34W
Chiávari, *Italy* ...... **40 D6** 44 19N 9 19 E
Chiavenna, *Italy* ..... **40 B6** 46 19N 9 24 E
Chiba, *Japan* .... **55 G10** 35 30N 140 7 E
Chiba □, *Japan* ...... **55 G10** 35 30N 140 20 E
Chibabava, *Mozam.* ... **89 C5** 20 17 S 33 35 E
Chibemba, *Cunene,*
  Angola .... **85 H2** 15 48 S 14 8 E
Chibemba, *Huila,*
  Angola .... **88 B2** 16 20 S 15 20 E
Chibi, *Zimbabwe* ..... **89 C5** 20 18 S 30 25 E
Chibia, *Angola* .... **85 H2** 15 10 S 13 42 E
Chibougamau, *Canada* **104 C5** 49 56N 74 24W
Chibougamau, L.,
  Canada **104 C5** 49 50N 74 20W
Chibuk, *Nigeria* ...... **83 C7** 10 52N 12 50 E
Chibuto, *Mozam.* ..... **89 C5** 24 40 S 33 33 E
Chic-Chocs, Mts.,
  Canada **105 C6** 48 55N 66 0W
Chicacole = Srikakulam,
  India .... **67 K13** 18 14N 83 58 E
Chicago, *U.S.A.* **114 E2** 41 53N 87 38W
Chicago Heights, *U.S.A.* **114 E2** 41 30N 87 38W
Chicagof I., *U.S.A.* ... **100 C6** 57 30N 135 30W
Chichén-Itzá, *Mexico* .. **119 C7** 20 40N 88 36W
Chicheng, *China* ..... **56 D8** 40 55N 115 55 E
Chichester, *U.K.* **15 G7** 50 50N 0 47W
Chichester Ra., *Australia* **92 D2** 22 12 S 119 15 E
Chichibu, *Japan* ..... **55 F9** 35 59N 139 10 E
Chichibu-Tama △,
  Japan .... **55 G9** 35 52N 138 42 E
Ch'ich'ihaerh = Qiqihar,
  China .... **53 E13** 47 26N 124 0 E
Chicholi, *India* ...... **68 H8** 22 1N 77 40 E
Chickasaw △, *U.S.A.* . **113 H6** 34 26N 97 0W
Chickasha, *U.S.A.* **113 H6** 35 3N 97 58W
Chiclana de la Frontera,
  Spain **37 J4** 36 26N 6 9W
Chiclayo, *Peru* .... **124 E3** 6 42 S 79 50W
Chico, *U.S.A.* **110 F5** 39 44N 121 50W
Chico ➤, *Chubut,*
  Argentina .... **128 E3** 44 0 S 67 0W
Chico ➤, *Santa Cruz,*
  Argentina .... **128 G3** 50 0 S 68 30W
Chicomo, *Mozam.* .... **89 C5** 24 31 S 34 6 E
Chicomostoc, *Mexico* .. **118 C4** 22 28N 102 49W
Chicontepec, *Mexico* .. **119 C5** 20 58N 98 10W
Chicopee, *U.S.A.* **117 D12** 42 9N 72 37W
Chicoutimi, *Canada* ... **105 C5** 48 28N 71 5W
Chicualacuala, *Mozam.* **89 C5** 22 6 S 31 42 E
Chidambaram, *India* .. **66 P11** 11 20N 79 45 E
Chidenguele, *Mozam.* . **89 C5** 24 55 S 34 11 E
Chidley, C., *Canada* .. **101 B13** 60 23N 64 26W
Chiducuane, *Mozam.* .. **89 C5** 24 35 S 34 25 E
Chiede, *Angola* ...... **88 B2** 17 15 S 16 22 E
Chiefs Pt., *Canada* ... **116 B3** 44 41N 81 18W
Chiem Hoa, *Vietnam* .. **64 A5** 22 12N 105 17 E
Chiemsee, *Germany* ... **25 H8** 47 53N 12 28 E
Chiengi, *Zambia* ..... **87 D2** 8 45 S 29 10 E
Chiengmai = Chiang
  Mai, *Thailand* ..... **64 C2** 18 47N 98 59 E
Chienti ➤, *Italy* ..... **41 E10** 43 18N 13 45 E
Chieri, *Italy* .... **40 C4** 45 1N 7 49 E
Chiers ➤, *France* ..... **19 C11** 49 39N 4 59 E
Chiesa in Valmalenco,
  Italy .... **40 B6** 46 16N 9 51 E
Chiese ➤, *Italy* ...... **40 C7** 45 8N 10 25 E
Chieti, *Italy* .... **41 F11** 42 21N 14 10 E
Chifeng, *China* ...... **57 C10** 42 18N 118 58 E
Chigirin, *Ukraine* .... **33 H7** 49 4N 32 38 E
Chignecto B., *Canada* . **105 C7** 45 30N 64 40W
Chiguana, *Bolivia* .... **126 A2** 21 0 S 67 58W
Chigwell, *U.K.* ...... **15 F8** 51 37N 0 5 E
Chiha-ri, *N. Korea* ... **57 E14** 38 40N 126 30 E
Chihli, G. of = Bo Hai,
  China .... **57 E10** 39 0N 119 0 E
Chihuahua, *Mexico* ... **118 B3** 28 40N 106 3W
Chihuahua □, *Mexico* . **118 B3** 28 40N 106 3W
Chiili = Shïeli,
  Kazakhstan .... **52 E7** 44 20N 66 15 E
Chik Bollapur, *India* .. **66 N10** 13 25N 77 45 E
Chikmagalur, *India* ... **66 N9** 13 15N 75 45 E
Chikwawa, *Malawi* ... **87 F3** 16 2 S 34 50 E
Chilac, *Mexico* **119 D5** 18 20N 97 24W
Chilam Chavki, *Pakistan* **69 B6** 35 5N 75 5 E
Chilanga, *Zambia* .... **87 F2** 15 33 S 28 16 E
Chilapa, *Mexico* **119 D5** 17 40N 99 11W
Chilas, *Pakistan* ..... **69 B6** 35 25N 74 5 E
Chilaw, *Sri Lanka* .... **66 R11** 7 30N 79 50 E
Chilcotin ➤, *Canada* .. **102 C4** 51 44N 122 23W
Childers, *Australia* .... **95 D5** 25 15 S 152 17 E
Childress, *U.S.A.* **113 H4** 34 25N 100 13W
Chile ■, *S. Amer.* ..... **128 D2** 35 0 S 72 0W
Chile Rise, *Pac. Oc.* .. **97 L18** 38 0 S 92 0W
Chilecito, *Argentina* ... **126 B2** 29 10 S 67 30W
Chilete, *Peru* .... **124 E3** 7 10 S 78 50W
Chilia, Bra**ț**ul ➤,
  Romania .... **29 E14** 45 14N 29 42 E
Chililabombwe, *Zambia* **87 E2** 12 18 S 27 43 E
Chilin = Jilin, *China* .. **57 C14** 43 44N 126 30 E
Chilka L., *India* ...... **67 K14** 19 40N 85 25 E
Chilko ➤, *Canada* **102 C4** 52 0N 123 40W

Chilko L., *Canada* **102 C4** 51 20N 124 10W
Chillagoe, *Australia* ... **94 B3** 17 7 S 144 33 E
Chillán, *Chile* .... **126 D1** 36 40 S 72 10W
Chillicothe, *Ill., U.S.A.* . **112 E10** 40 55N 89 29W
Chillicothe, *Mo., U.S.A.* **112 F8** 39 48N 93 33W
Chillicothe, *Ohio, U.S.A.* **114 F4** 39 20N 82 59W
Chilliwack, *Canada* ... **102 D4** 49 10N 121 54W
Chilo, *India* .... **68 F5** 27 25N 73 32 E
Chiloane, I., *Mozam.* .. **89 C5** 20 40 S 34 55 E
Chiloé, I. de, *Chile* ... **128 E2** 42 30 S 73 50W
Chilpancingo, *Mexico* . **119 D5** 17 30N 99 30W
Chiltern Hills, *U.K.* .. **15 F7** 51 40N 0 53W
Chilton, *U.S.A.* **114 C1** 44 2N 88 10W
Chilubi, *Zambia* ..... **87 E2** 11 5 S 29 58 E
Chilubula, *Zambia* .... **87 E3** 10 14 S 30 51 E
Chilumba, *Malawi* .... **87 E3** 10 28 S 34 12 E
Chilung, *Taiwan* ..... **59 E13** 25 3N 121 45 E
Chilwa, L., *Malawi* ... **87 F4** 15 15 S 35 40 E
Chimaltitán, *Mexico* .. **118 C4** 21 46N 103 50W
Chimán, *Panama* **120 E4** 8 45N 78 40W
Chimanimani,
  Zimbabwe .... **89 B5** 19 48 S 32 52 E
Chimanimani △,
  Zimbabwe .... **87 F3** 19 48 S 33 0 E
Chimay, *Belgium* ..... **17 D4** 50 3N 4 20 E
Chimayo, *U.S.A.* **109 H11** 36 0N 105 56W
Chimbay, *Uzbekistan* . **52 E6** 42 57N 59 47 E
Chimborazo, *Ecuador* . **124 D3** 1 29 S 78 55W
Chimbote, *Peru* ...... **124 E3** 9 0 S 78 35W
Chimkent = Shymkent,
  Kazakhstan .... **52 E7** 42 18N 69 36 E
Chimoio, *Mozam.* ..... **87 F3** 19 4 S 33 30 E
Chimpembe, *Zambia* .. **87 D2** 9 31 S 29 33 E
Chin □, *Burma* ...... **67 J18** 22 0N 93 0 E
Chin Ling Shan =
  Qinling Shandi, *China* **56 H5** 33 50N 108 10 E
China, *Mexico* **119 B5** 25 40N 99 20W
China ■, *Asia* .... **60 D6** 30 0N 110 0 E
China, Great Plain of,
  Asia .... **50 F15** 35 0N 115 0 E
China Lake, *U.S.A.* ... **111 K9** 35 44N 117 37W
Chinan = Jinan, *China* . **56 F9** 36 38N 117 1 E
Chinandega, *Nic.* **120 D2** 12 35N 87 12W
Chinati Peak, *U.S.A.* .. **113 L2** 29 57N 104 29W
Chincha Alta, *Peru* ... **124 F3** 13 25 S 76 7W
Chinchaga ➤, *Canada* . **102 B5** 58 53N 118 20W
Chinchilla, *Australia* ... **95 D5** 26 45 S 150 38 E
Chinchilla de Monte
  Aragón, *Spain* **39 G3** 38 53N 1 40W
Chinchorro, Banco,
  Mexico **119 D7** 18 35N 87 20W
Chinchou = Jinzhou,
  China .... **57 D11** 41 5N 121 3 E
Chincoteague, *U.S.A.* . **114 G8** 37 56N 75 23W
Chinde, *Mozam.* ...... **87 F4** 18 35 S 36 30 E
Chindo, *S. Korea* ..... **57 G14** 34 28N 126 15 E
Chindwin ➤, *Burma* .. **67 J19** 21 26N 95 15 E
Chineni, *India* .... **69 C6** 33 2N 75 15 E
Chinga, *Mozam.* ..... **87 F4** 15 13 S 38 35 E
Chingola, *Zambia* .... **87 E2** 12 31 S 27 53 E
Chingole, *Malawi* .... **87 E3** 13 4 S 34 17 E
Ch'ingtao = Qingdao,
  China .... **57 F11** 36 5N 120 20 E
Chinguetti, *Mauritania* . **78 D3** 20 25N 12 24W
Chingune, *Mozam.* .... **89 C5** 20 33 S 34 58 E
Chinhae, *S. Korea* .... **57 G15** 35 9N 128 47 E
Chinhanguanine,
  Mozam. .... **89 D5** 25 21 S 32 30 E
Chinhoyi, *Zimbabwe* .. **87 F3** 17 20 S 30 8 E
Chini, *India* .... **68 D8** 31 32N 78 15 E
Chiniot, *Pakistan* ..... **68 D5** 31 45N 73 0 E
Chínipas, *Mexico* **118 B3** 27 22N 108 32W
Chinji, *Pakistan* ...... **68 C5** 32 42N 72 22 E
Chinju, *S. Korea* ..... **57 G15** 35 12N 128 2 E
Chinle, *U.S.A.* **109 H9** 36 9N 109 33W
Chinmen, *Taiwan* ..... **59 E13** 24 26N 118 19 E
Chinmen Tao, *Taiwan* . **59 E12** 24 27N 118 23 E
Chinnampo = Namp'o,
  N. Korea .... **57 E13** 38 52N 125 10 E
Chino, *Japan* .... **55 G9** 35 59N 138 9 E
Chino, *U.S.A.* **111 M9** 34 1N 117 41W
Chino Valley, *U.S.A.* .. **109 J7** 34 45N 112 27W
Chinon, *France* ...... **18 E7** 47 10N 0 15 E
Chinook, *U.S.A.* **108 B9** 48 35N 109 14W
Chinsali, *Zambia* ..... **87 E3** 10 30 S 32 2 E
Chióggia, *Italy* .... **41 C9** 45 13N 12 17 E
Chíos = Khíos, *Greece* . **47 C8** 38 27N 26 9 E
Chipata, *Zambia* ..... **87 E3** 13 38 S 32 28 E
Chiperceni, *Moldova* .. **29 C13** 47 31N 28 50 E
Chipinge, *Zimbabwe* .. **87 G3** 20 13 S 32 28 E
Chipinge △, *Zimbabwe* **87 G3** 20 14 S 33 0 E
Chipiona, *Spain* **37 J4** 36 44N 6 26W
Chipley, *U.S.A.* **115 K3** 30 47N 85 32W
Chipman, *Canada* **105 C6** 46 6N 65 53W
Chipoka, *Malawi* ..... **87 E3** 13 57 S 34 28 E
Chippenham, *U.K.* ... **15 F5** 51 27N 2 6W
Chippewa ➤, *U.S.A.* .. **112 C8** 44 25N 92 5W
Chippewa Falls, *U.S.A.* **112 C9** 44 56N 91 24W
Chipping Norton, *U.K.* **15 F6** 51 56N 1 32W
Chiprovtsi, *Bulgaria* ... **44 C6** 43 24N 22 52 E
Chiputneticook Lakes,
  U.S.A. **115 C11** 45 35N 67 35W
Chiquián, *Peru* ...... **124 F3** 10 10 S 77 0W
Chiquibul △, *Belize* ... **120 C2** 16 49N 88 52W
Chiquimula, *Guatemala* **120 D2** 14 51N 89 37W
Chiquinquira, *Colombia* **124 B4** 5 37N 73 50W
Chir ➤, *Russia* .... **35 F6** 48 30N 43 0 E
Chirala, *India* .... **66 M12** 15 50N 80 26 E
Chiramba, *Mozam.* .... **87 F3** 16 55 S 34 39 E
Chiredzi, *Zimbabwe* .. **89 C5** 21 0 S 31 38 E
Chiricahua △, *U.S.A.* . **109 L9** 32 1N 109 21W
Chiricahua Peak, *U.S.A.* **109 L9** 31 51N 109 18W
Chiriquí, G. de, *Panama* **120 E3** 8 0N 82 10W
Chiriquí, L. de, *Panama* **120 E3** 9 10N 82 0W
Chirivira Falls,
  Zimbabwe .... **87 F2** 17 53 S 28 15 E
Chirmiri, *India* ...... **67 H13** 23 15N 82 20 E
Chirnogi, *Romania* ... **29 F11** 44 7N 26 32 E
Chirpan, *Bulgaria* .... **45 D9** 42 10N 25 19 E
Chirripó Grande, Cerro,
  Costa Rica **120 E3** 9 29N 83 29W
Chirundu, *Zimbabwe* .. **89 B4** 16 3 S 28 50 E
Chisamba, *Zambia* .... **87 E2** 14 55 S 28 20 E
Chisapani Garhi, *Nepal* **67 F14** 27 30N 84 2 E
Chisasibi, *Canada* **104 B4** 53 50N 79 0W
Ch'ishan, *Taiwan* ..... **59 F13** 22 44N 120 31 E
Chisholm, *Canada* **102 C6** 54 55N 114 10W
Chisholm, *U.S.A.* **112 B8** 47 29N 92 53W
Chishtian Mandi,
  Pakistan .... **68 E5** 29 50N 72 55 E
Chishui, *China* .... **58 C5** 28 30N 105 42 E
Chishui He ➤, *China* .. **58 C5** 28 49N 105 50 E
Chisimaio, *Somali Rep.* **77 G8** 0 22 S 42 32 E
Chisimba Falls, *Zambia* **87 E3** 10 12 S 30 56 E

Chișinău, *Moldova* ... **29 C13** 47 2N 28 50 E
Chișinău ✠ (KIV),
  Moldova .... **29 C13** 47 3N 28 46 E
Chișineu Criș, *Romania* **28 D6** 46 32N 21 37 E
Chisone ➤, *Italy* ..... **40 D4** 44 49N 7 25 E
Chisos Mts., *U.S.A.* ... **113 L3** 29 5N 103 15W
Chistopol, *Russia* .... **34 C10** 55 25N 50 38 E
Chita, *Russia* .... **53 D12** 52 0N 113 35 E
Chitipa, *Malawi* ..... **87 D3** 9 41 S 33 19 E
Chitose, *Japan* ...... **54 C10** 42 49N 141 39 E
Chitral, *Pakistan* ..... **66 B7** 35 50N 71 56 E
Chitré, *Panama* **120 E3** 7 59N 80 27W
Chittagong, *Bangla.* ... **67 H17** 22 19N 91 48 E
Chittagong □, *Bangla.* . **67 G17** 24 5N 91 0 E
Chittaurgarh, *India* ... **68 G6** 24 52N 74 38 E
Chittoor, *India* ...... **66 N11** 13 15N 79 5 E
Chitungwiza, *Zimbabwe* **87 F3** 18 0 S 31 6 E
Chiusi, *Italy* .... **41 E8** 43 1N 11 57 E
Chiva, *Spain* **39 F4** 39 27N 0 41W
Chivasso, *Italy* ...... **40 C4** 45 11N 7 53 E
Chivhu, *Zimbabwe* ... **87 F3** 19 2 S 30 52 E
Chivilcoy, *Argentina* .. **126 C4** 34 55 S 60 0W
Chiwanda, *Tanzania* .. **87 E3** 11 23 S 34 55 E
Chixi, *China* .... **59 G9** 22 0N 112 58 E
Chizarira, *Zimbabwe* .. **87 F2** 17 36 S 27 45 E
Chizarira △, *Zimbabwe* **87 F2** 17 44 S 27 52 E
Chizera, *Zambia* ..... **87 E2** 13 10 S 25 0 E
Chkalov = Orenburg,
  Russia .... **52 D6** 51 45N 55 6 E
Chkolovsk, *Russia* .... **34 B6** 56 50N 43 10 E
Chloride, *U.S.A.* **111 K12** 35 25N 114 12W
Chlumec nad Cidlinou,
  Czech Rep. .... **26 A8** 50 9N 15 29 E
Chmielnik, *Poland* .... **31 H7** 50 37N 20 43 E
Cho Bo, *Vietnam* ..... **58 G5** 20 46N 105 10 E
Cho-do, *N. Korea* ..... **57 E13** 38 30N 124 40 E
Cho Phuoc Hai, *Vietnam* **65 G6** 10 26N 107 18 E
Choa Chu Kang,
  Singapore .... **65 d** 1 22N 103 41 E
Choba, *Kenya* .... **86 B4** 2 30N 38 5 E
Chobe △, *Botswana* ... **88 B4** 18 37 S 24 23 E
Ch'och'iwŏn, *S. Korea* . **57 F14** 36 37N 127 18 E
Chociano, *Poland* ..... **31 G2** 51 27N 15 55 E
Chociwel, *Poland* ..... **30 E2** 53 29N 15 21 E
Chocolate Mts., *U.S.A.* **111 M11** 33 15N 115 15W
Choctawhatchee ➤,
  U.S.A. **115 K3** 30 25N 86 8W
Chodecz, *Poland* ..... **31 F6** 52 24N 19 2 E
Chodov, *Czech Rep.* ... **26 A5** 50 15N 12 45 E
Chodziez, *Poland* ..... **31 F3** 52 58N 16 58 E
Choele Choel, *Argentina* **128 D3** 39 11 S 65 40W
Choiseul, *St. Lucia* .... **121 f** 13 47N 61 3W
Choix, *Mexico* **118 B3** 26 40N 108 23W
Chojna, *Poland* .... **31 F1** 52 58N 14 25 E
Chojnice, *Poland* ..... **31 B5** 53 42N 17 32 E
Chojnów, *Poland* ..... **31 G2** 51 18N 15 58 E
Chōkai-San, *Japan* .... **54 E10** 39 6N 140 3 E
Choke Canyon L.,
  U.S.A. **113 L5** 28 30N 98 20W
Choke Mts., *Ethiopia* .. **81 E4** 11 18N 37 15 E
Chokurdakh, *Russia* ... **53 B15** 70 38N 147 55 E
Cholame, *U.S.A.* **110 K6** 35 44N 120 18W
Cholet, *France* **18 E6** 47 4N 0 52W
Choluguan, *Chile* ..... **126 D1** 37 10 S 72 3W
Choluteca, *Honduras* .. **120 D2** 13 20N 87 14W
Choluteca ➤, *Honduras* **120 D2** 13 0N 87 20W
Chom Bung, *Thailand* . **64 F2** 13 37N 99 36 E
Chom Thong, *Thailand* **64 C2** 18 25N 98 41 E
Choma, *Zambia* ...... **87 F2** 16 48 S 26 59 E
Chomolungma =
  Everest, Mt., *Nepal* . **69 E12** 28 5N 86 58 E
Chomun, *India* ...... **68 F6** 27 15N 75 40 E
Chomutov, *Czech Rep.* . **26 A6** 50 28N 13 23 E
Chon Buri, *Thailand* .. **64 F3** 13 21N 101 1 E
Chon Thanh, *Vietnam* . **65 G6** 11 24N 106 36 E
Ch'onan, *S. Korea* .... **57 F14** 36 48N 127 9 E
Chone, *Ecuador* ...... **124 D3** 0 40 S 80 0W
Chong Kal, *Cambodia* . **64 F4** 13 57N 103 35 E
Chong Mek, *Thailand* . **64 E5** 15 10N 105 27 E
Chong Phangan,
  Thailand .... **65 b** 9 39N 100 0 E
Chong Samui, *Thailand* **65 b** 9 21N 99 50 E
Chongde, *China* ...... **59 B13** 30 32N 120 26 E
Chongdo, *S. Korea* .... **57 G15** 35 38N 128 42 E
Chongha, *S. Korea* .... **57 F15** 36 12N 129 21 E
Chongjin, *N. Korea* ... **57 D15** 41 47N 129 50 E
Chongju, *N. Korea* .... **57 E13** 39 40N 125 5 E
Chŏngju, *S. Korea* .... **57 F14** 36 39N 127 27 E
Chongli, *China* .... **56 D8** 40 58N 115 15 E
Chongming Dao, *China* **59 B13** 31 40N 121 30 E
Chongqing, *Chongqing,*
  China .... **58 C6** 29 35N 106 25 E
Chongqing, *Sichuan,*
  China .... **58 B4** 30 38N 103 40 E
Chongqing Shi □, *China* **58 C6** 30 0N 108 0 E
Chongren, *China* ..... **59 D11** 27 46N 116 3 E
Chonguene, *Mozam.* .. **89 C5** 25 3 S 33 49 E
Chŏngŭp, *S. Korea* ... **57 G14** 35 35N 126 50 E
Chongyi, *China* ...... **59 E10** 25 45N 114 29 E
Chongzuo, *China* ..... **58 F6** 22 23N 107 20 E
Chŏnju, *S. Korea* ..... **57 G14** 35 50N 127 4 E
Chonos, Arch. de los,
  Chile .... **128 F2** 45 0 S 75 0W
Chop, *Ukraine* .... **28 B7** 48 26N 22 12 E
Chopim ➤, *Brazil* ..... **127 B5** 25 35 S 53 5W
Chor, *Pakistan* .... **68 G3** 25 31N 69 46 E
Chorbat La, *India* ..... **69 B7** 34 42N 76 37 E
Chorley, *U.K.* **14 D5** 53 39N 2 38W
Chorna, *Ukraine* ..... **29 C14** 47 36N 29 20 E
Chornobyl, *Ukraine* ... **33 G6** 51 20N 30 15 E
Chornomorske, *Ukraine* **33 K7** 45 31N 32 40 E
Choroque, Cerro,
  Bolivia .... **126 A2** 20 59 S 66 5W
Choroszcz, *Poland* .... **31 E9** 53 10N 22 59 E
Chorregon, *Australia* .. **94 C3** 22 40 S 143 32 E
Chorro el Indio △,
  Venezuela **121 E5** 7 43N 72 9W
Chortkiv, *Ukraine* .... **33 H3** 49 2N 25 46 E
Ch'orwon, *S. Korea* ... **57 E14** 38 15N 127 10 E
Chorzele, *Poland* ..... **31 E7** 53 15N 20 50 E
Chorzów, *Poland* ..... **31 H5** 50 18N 18 57 E
Chos-Malal, *Argentina* . **126 D1** 37 20 S 70 15W
Ch'osan, *N. Korea* .... **57 D13** 40 50N 125 47 E
Choszczno, *Poland* .... **31 E2** 53 7N 15 25 E
Choteau, *U.S.A.* **108 C7** 47 49N 112 11W
Chot**ě**bo**ř**, *Czech Rep.* . **26 B8** 49 43N 15 40 E
Chotila, *India* .... **68 H4** 22 23N 71 15 E
Chotta Udepur, *India* . **68 H6** 22 19N 74 1 E
Chowchilla, *U.S.A.* ... **110 H6** 37 7N 120 16W
Choybalsan, *Mongolia* . **60 B6** 48 4N 114 30 E
Christchurch, *N.Z.* .... **91 K4** 43 33 S 172 47 E
Christchurch, *U.K.* **15 G6** 50 44N 1 47W
Christian I., *Canada* ... **116 B4** 44 50N 80 12W
Christiana, *S. Africa* ... **88 D4** 27 52 S 25 8 E
Christiansfeld, *Denmark* **11 J3** 55 21N 9 29 E
Christiansted,
  U.S. Virgin Is. **121 C7** 17 45N 64 42W

Christie B., *Canada* ... **103 A6** 62 32N 111 10W
Christina ➤, *Canada* .. **103 B6** 56 40N 111 3W
Christmas Cr. ➤,
  Australia .... **92 C4** 18 29 S 125 23 E
Christmas I. =
  Kiritimati, *Kiribati* . **97 G12** 1 58N 157 27W
Christmas I., *Ind. Oc.* . **96 J2** 10 30 S 105 40 E
Christopher L., *Australia* **93 D4** 24 49 S 127 42 E
Chrudim, *Czech Rep.* .. **26 B8** 49 58N 15 43 E
Chrzanów, *Poland* .... **31 H6** 50 10N 19 21 E
Chtimba, *Malawi* ..... **87 E3** 10 35 S 34 13 E
Chū = Shū, *Kazakhstan* **52 E8** 43 36N 73 42 E
Chū = Shū ➤,
  Kazakhstan .... **50 E10** 45 0N 67 44 E
Chu ➤, *Vietnam* ...... **64 C5** 19 53N 105 45 E
Chu Lai, *Vietnam* ..... **64 E7** 15 28N 108 45 E
Chuak, Ko, *Thailand* .. **65 b** 9 28N 99 41 E
Ch'uanchou =
  Quanzhou, *China* ... **59 E12** 24 55N 118 34 E
Chuankou, *China* ..... **56 G6** 34 20N 110 59 E
Chubbuck, *U.S.A.* **108 E7** 42 55N 112 28W
Chūbu □, *Japan* ...... **55 F8** 36 45N 137 30 E
Chūbu-Sangaku △,
  Japan .... **55 F8** 36 30N 137 40 E
Chubut ➤, *Argentina* .. **128 E3** 43 20 S 65 5W
Chuchi L., *Canada* **102 B4** 55 12N 124 30W
Chuda, *India* .... **68 H4** 22 29N 71 41 E
Chudovo, *Russia* ..... **32 C6** 59 10N 31 41 E
Chudskoye, Ozero,
  Russia .... **9 G22** 58 13N 27 30 E
Chūgoku □, *Japan* .... **55 G6** 35 0N 133 0 E
Chūgoku-Sanchi, *Japan* **55 G6** 35 0N 133 0 E
Chuguyev = Chuhuyiv,
  Ukraine .... **33 H9** 49 55N 36 45 E
Chugwater, *U.S.A.* ... **112 E2** 41 46N 104 50W
Chuhuyiv, *Ukraine* ... **33 H9** 49 55N 36 45 E
Chukchi Sea, *Russia* .. **53 C19** 68 0N 175 0W
Chukotskoye Nagorye,
  Russia .... **53 C18** 68 0N 175 0 E
Chula Vista, *U.S.A.* ... **111 N9** 32 39N 117 5W
Chulucanas, *Peru* .... **124 E2** 5 8 S 80 10W
Chulym ➤, *Russia* .... **52 D9** 57 43N 83 51 E
Chum Phae, *Thailand* . **64 D4** 16 40N 102 6 E
Chum Saeng, *Thailand* **64 E3** 15 55N 100 15 E
Chumar, *India* .... **69 C8** 32 40N 78 35 E
Chumbicha, *Argentina* . **126 B2** 29 0 S 66 10W
Chumerna, *Bulgaria* ... **45 D9** 42 45N 25 55 E
Chumikan, *Russia* .... **53 D14** 54 40N 135 10 E
Chumphon, *Thailand* .. **65 G2** 10 35N 99 14 E
Chumuare, *Mozam.* ... **87 E3** 14 31 S 31 50 E
Chumunjin, *S. Korea* .. **57 F15** 37 55N 128 54 E
Chuna ➤, *Russia* ..... **53 D10** 57 47N 94 37 E
Chun'an, *China* ...... **59 C12** 29 35N 119 3 E
Ch'unch'ŏn, *S. Korea* .. **57 F14** 37 58N 127 44 E
Chunchura, *India* ..... **69 H13** 22 53N 88 27 E
Chunga, *Zambia* ..... **87 F2** 15 0 S 26 2 E
Chunggang-ŭp, *N. Korea* **57 D14** 41 48N 126 48 E
Chunghwa, *N. Korea* .. **57 E13** 38 52N 125 47 E
Ch'ungju, *S. Korea* ... **57 F14** 36 58N 127 58 E
Chungking =
  Chongqing, *China* .. **58 C6** 29 35N 106 25 E
Chungli, *Taiwan* ..... **59 E13** 24 57N 121 13 E
Ch'ungmu, *S. Korea* .. **57 G15** 34 50N 128 20 E
Chungt'iaoshan =
  Zhongtiao Shan,
  China .... **56 G6** 35 0N 111 10 E
Chungyang Shanmo,
  Taiwan .... **59 F13** 23 10N 121 0 E
Chunian, *Pakistan* .... **68 D6** 30 57N 74 0 E
Chunya, *Tanzania* .... **87 D3** 8 30 S 33 27 E
Chunyang, *China* ..... **57 C15** 43 38N 129 23 E
Chupara Pt.,
  Trin. & Tob. **125 K15** 10 49N 61 22W
Chuquibamba, *Peru* ... **124 G4** 15 47 S 72 44W
Chuquicamata, *Chile* .. **126 A2** 22 15 S 69 0W
Chur, *Switz.* .... **25 J5** 46 52N 9 32 E
Churachandpur, *India* . **67 G18** 24 20N 93 40 E
Church Stretton, *U.K.* . **15 E5** 52 32N 2 48W
Churchill ➤, *Man.,*
  Canada **103 B10** 58 47N 94 11W
Churchill ➤, *Nfld. & L.,*
  Canada **105 B7** 53 19N 60 10W
Churchill, C., *Canada* . **103 B10** 58 47N 94 12W
Churchill Falls, *Canada* **105 B7** 53 36N 64 19W
Churchill L., *Canada* .. **103 B7** 55 55N 108 20W
Churchill Pk., *Canada* . **102 B3** 58 10N 125 10W
Churu, *India* .... **68 E6** 28 20N 74 50 E
Churún Merú = Angel
  Falls, *Venezuela* ... **124 B6** 5 57N 62 30W
Chushal, *India* .... **69 C8** 33 40N 78 40 E
Chuska Mts., *U.S.A.* .. **109 H9** 36 15N 108 50W
Chusovoy, *Russia* ..... **52 D6** 58 22N 57 50 E
Chute-aux-Outardes,
  Canada **105 C6** 49 7N 68 24W
Chuuronjang, *N. Korea* **57 D15** 41 35N 129 40 E
Chuvash Republic =
  Chuvashia □, *Russia* **34 C8** 55 30N 47 0 E
Chuvashia □, *Russia* .. **34 C8** 55 30N 47 0 E
Chuwārtah, *Iraq* ..... **70 C5** 35 43N 45 34 E
Chuxiong, *China* ..... **58 E3** 25 2N 101 28 E
Chuy, *Uruguay* .... **127 C5** 33 41 S 53 27W
Chuzhou, *China* ...... **59 A12** 32 19N 118 20 E
Chyhyryn, *Ukraine* ... **28 B7** 48 29N 22 50 E
Ci Xian, *China* .... **56 F8** 36 20N 114 25 E
Ciacova, *Romania* .... **28 E6** 45 35N 21 10 E
Ciadâr-Lunga, *Moldova* **29 D13** 46 3N 28 51 E
Ciamis, *Indonesia* .... **63 G13** 7 20 S 108 21 E
Cianjur, *Indonesia* .... **63 G12** 6 49 S 107 8 E
Cianorte, *Brazil* ...... **127 A5** 23 37 S 52 37W
Cibola, *U.S.A.* **111 M12** 33 17N 114 42W
Cicero, *U.S.A.* **114 E2** 41 51N 87 45W
Cidacos ➤, *Spain* **38 C3** 42 21N 1 38W
Cide, *Turkey* .... **72 B5** 41 53N 33 1 E
Ciechanów, *Poland* .... **31 F7** 52 52N 20 38 E
Ciechanowiec, *Poland* . **31 F9** 52 41N 22 31 E
Ciechocinek, *Poland* .. **31 F5** 52 53N 18 45 E
Ciego de Ávila, *Cuba* .. **120 B4** 21 50N 78 50W
Ciénaga, *Colombia* ... **124 A4** 11 1N 74 15W
Cienfuegos, *Cuba* **120 B3** 22 10N 80 30W
Cieplice Śląskie Zdrój,
  Poland .... **31 H2** 50 50N 15 40 E
Cíes, Is., *Spain* **36 C2** 42 12N 8 55W
Cieszanów, *Poland* .... **31 H10** 50 14N 23 8 E
Cieszyn, *Poland* ...... **31 J5** 49 45N 18 35 E
Cieza, *Spain* **39 G3** 38 17N 1 23W
Cifsuentes, *Spain* **38 E2** 40 47N 2 37W
Çifteler, *Turkey* ...... **72 C4** 39 22N 31 2 E
Cihanbeyli, *Turkey* ... **72 C5** 38 40N 32 55 E
Cihuatlán, *Mexico* **118 D4** 19 14N 104 35W
Cijara, Embalse de,
  Spain **37 F6** 39 18N 4 52W
Cijara ➤, *Spain* **37 F6** 39 18N 4 35W
Cijulang, *Indonesia* ... **63 G13** 7 42 S 108 27 E

Cilacap, *Indonesia* .... **63 G13** 7 43 S 109 0 E
Çıldır, *Turkey* .... **73 B10** 41 7N 43 8 E
Çıldır Gölü, *Turkey* ... **73 B10** 41 5N 43 15 E
Cilento e Vallo di
  Diano △, *Italy* ..... **43 B8** 40 15N 15 20 E
Cili, *China* .... **59 C8** 29 30N 111 8 E
Cilibia, *Romania* ..... **29 E12** 45 4N 27 4 E
Cilicia, *Turkey* ...... **72 D5** 36 30N 33 40 E
Cill Chainnigh =
  Kilkenny, *Ireland* ... **12 D4** 52 39N 7 15W
Cilo Dağı, *Turkey* .... **73 D10** 37 28N 43 55 E
Cima, *U.S.A.* **111 K11** 35 14N 115 30W
Cimarron, Kans., U.S.A. **113 G4** 37 48N 100 21W
Cimarron, N. Mex.,
  U.S.A. **113 G2** 36 31N 104 55W
Cimarron ➤, *U.S.A.* ... **113 G6** 36 10N 96 17W
Cimișlia, *Moldova* .... **29 D13** 46 34N 28 44 E
Cimone, Mte., *Italy* ... **40 D7** 44 12N 10 42 E
Çınar, *Turkey* .... **73 D9** 37 46N 40 19 E
Çınarcık, *Turkey* ..... **45 F13** 40 38N 29 10 E
Cinca ➤, *Spain* ...... **38 D5** 41 26N 0 21 E
Cincar, Bos.-H. .... **42 G2** 43 55N 17 5 E
Cincinnati, *U.S.A.* **114 F3** 39 6N 84 31W
Cincinnatus, *U.S.A.* ... **117 D9** 42 33N 75 54W
Çine, *Turkey* .... **47 D10** 37 37N 28 2 E
Ciney, *Belgium* ...... **17 D5** 50 18N 5 5 E
Cíngoli, *Italy* .... **41 E10** 43 23N 13 10 E
Cinigiano, *Italy* ...... **41 F8** 42 53N 11 24 E
Cinto, Mte., *France* ... **21 F12** 42 24N 8 54 E
Cintruénigo, *Spain* ... **38 C3** 42 5N 1 49W
Ciocile, *Romania* ..... **29 F12** 44 49N 27 14 E
Ciolănești din Deal,
  Romania .... **29 F10** 44 19N 25 5 E
Ciorani, *Romania* .... **29 F11** 44 45N 26 25 E
Ciovo, *Croatia* .... **41 E13** 43 30N 16 17 E
Circeo, Mte., *Italy* .... **42 A6** 41 14N 13 3 E
Çirçir, *Turkey* .... **72 C7** 40 50N 37 19 E
Cisco, *U.S.A.* **113 J5** 32 23N 98 59W
Cislău, *Romania* ..... **29 E11** 45 14N 26 20 E
Cisna, *Poland* .... **31 J9** 49 12N 22 20 E
Cisnădie, *Romania* ... **29 E9** 45 42N 24 9 E
Cisterna di Latina, *Italy* **42 A5** 41 35N 12 49 E
Cisternino, *Italy* ..... **43 B10** 40 44N 17 25 E
Cistierna, *Spain* **36 C5** 42 48N 5 7W
Citeli-Ckaro = Tsiteli-
  Tsqaro, *Georgia* .... **35 K8** 41 33N 46 0 E
Citlaltépetl = Orizaba,
  Pico de, *Mexico* **119 D5** 19 0N 97 20W
Citrus Heights, *U.S.A.* . **110 G5** 38 42N 121 17W
Citrusdal, S. Africa .... **88 E2** 32 35 S 19 0 E
Città della Pieve, *Italy* . **41 F9** 42 57N 12 1 E
Città di Castello, *Italy* . **41 E9** 43 27N 12 14 E
Città Sant'Angelo, *Italy* **41 F11** 42 32N 14 5 E
Cittadella, *Italy* ...... **41 C8** 45 39N 11 47 E
Cittaducale, *Italy* ..... **41 F9** 42 23N 12 57 E
Cittanova, *Italy* ...... **43 D9** 38 21N 16 5 E
Ciuc, Munții, *Romania* . **29 E11** 46 25N 26 5 E
Ciucaș, Vf., *Romania* .. **29 E10** 45 31N 25 56 E
Ciucea, *Romania* ..... **28 D7** 46 57N 22 49 E
Ciuciulea, *Moldova* ... **29 C12** 47 40N 27 29 E
Ciuciuleni, *Moldova* .. **29 C13** 47 2N 28 25 E
Ciudad Altamirano,
  Mexico **118 D4** 18 20N 100 40W
Ciudad Bolívar,
  Venezuela **124 B6** 8 5N 63 36W
Ciudad Camargo,
  Mexico **118 B3** 27 41N 105 10W
Ciudad de Valles,
  Mexico **119 C5** 22 0N 99 0W
Ciudad del Carmen,
  Mexico **119 D6** 18 38N 91 50W
Ciudad del Este,
  Paraguay .... **127 B5** 25 30 S 54 50W
Ciudad Delicias =
  Delicias, *Mexico* ... **118 B3** 28 10N 105 30W
Ciudad Guayana,
  Venezuela **124 B6** 8 0N 62 30W
Ciudad Guerrero,
  Mexico **118 B3** 28 33N 107 28W
Ciudad Guzmán, *Mexico* **118 D4** 19 40N 103 30W
Ciudad Juárez, *Mexico* **118 A3** 31 40N 106 28W
Ciudad Madero, *Mexico* **119 C5** 22 19N 97 50W
Ciudad Mante, *Mexico* **119 C5** 22 50N 99 0W
Ciudad Obregón,
  Mexico **118 B3** 27 28N 109 59W
Ciudad Real, *Spain* ... **37 G7** 38 59N 3 55W
Ciudad Real □, *Spain* . **37 G7** 38 50N 4 0W
Ciudad Rodrigo, *Spain* **36 E4** 40 35N 6 32W
Ciudad Victoria, *Mexico* **119 C5** 23 41N 99 9W
Ciudadela, *Spain* ..... **48 B10** 40 0N 3 50 E
Ciulnița, *Romania* .... **29 F12** 44 26N 27 22 E
Ciumeghiu, *Romania* . **28 D6** 46 44N 21 35 E
Ciuperceni, *Romania* .. **29 G8** 43 45N 23 4 E
Civa Burnu, *Turkey* ... **72 B7** 41 21N 36 38 E
Cividale del Friuli, *Italy* **41 B10** 46 6N 13 25 E
Civita Castellana, *Italy* . **41 F9** 42 18N 12 24 E
Civitanova Marche, *Italy* **41 E10** 43 18N 13 44 E
Civitavécchia, *Italy* .... **41 F8** 42 6N 11 48 E
Civray, *France* .... **20 B4** 46 10N 0 17 E
Çivril, *Turkey* .... **47 C11** 38 20N 29 43 E
Cixerri ➤, *Italy* ...... **42 C1** 39 17N 8 59 E
Cixi, *China* .... **59 B13** 30 17N 121 9 E
Cizur Mayor, *Spain* ... **38 C3** 42 47N 1 41W
Clackmannanshire □,
  U.K. **13 E5** 56 10N 3 43W
Clacton-on-Sea, *U.K.* . **15 F9** 51 47N 1 11 E
Clain ➤, *France* ...... **18 F7** 46 47N 0 33 E
Claire, L., *Canada* **102 B6** 58 35N 112 5W
Claire, *U.S.A.* **95 F5** 40 18N 79 53W
Clairton, *U.S.A.* **116 F5** 40 18N 79 53W
Clairvaux-les-Lacs,
  France .... **19 F12** 46 35N 5 45 E
Claise ➤, *France* ..... **20 B5** 46 56N 0 42 E
Clallam Bay, *U.S.A.* ... **110 B2** 48 15N 124 16W
Clamecy, *France* ..... **19 E10** 47 28N 3 30 E
Clanton, *U.S.A.* **115 J2** 32 51N 86 38W
Clanwilliam, *S. Africa* . **88 E2** 32 11 S 18 52 E
Clara, *Ireland* **12 C4** 53 21N 7 37W
Claraville, *U.S.A.* **111 K8** 35 24N 118 20W
Clare, *Australia* ...... **95 E2** 33 50 S 138 37 E
Clare, *U.S.A.* **114 D3** 43 49N 84 46W
Clare □, *Ireland* **12 D3** 52 45N 9 0W
Clare ➤, *Ireland* **12 C2** 53 20N 9 2W

Clare I., *Ireland* **12 C1** 53 49N 10 0W
Claremont, *Calif., U.S.A.* **111 L9** 34 6N 117 43W
Claremont, *N.H., U.S.A.* **117 C12** 43 23N 72 20W
Claremont Pt., *Australia* **94 A3** 14 1S 143 41 E
Claremore, *U.S.A.* **113 G7** 36 19N 95 36W
Claremorris, *Ireland* **12 C3** 53 45N 9 0W
Clarence →, *Australia* . **95 D5** 29 25 S 153 22 E
Clarence →, *N.Z.* ...... **91 K4** 42 10 S 173 56 E
Clarence, I., *Chile* ..... **128 G2** 54 0 S 72 0W
Clarence I., *Antarctica* . **5 C18** 61 10 S 54 0W
Clarence Str., *Australia* **92 B5** 12 0 S 131 0 E
Clarence Town,
  Bahamas **121 B5** 23 6N 74 59W
Clarendon, *Pa., U.S.A.* . **116 E5** 41 47N 79 6W
Clarendon, *Tex., U.S.A.* **113 H4** 34 56N 100 53W
Clarenville-Shoal
  Harbour, *Canada* ... **105 C9** 48 10N 54 1W
Claresholm, *Canada* ... **102 D6** 50 2N 113 33W
Clarie Coast, *Antarctica* **5 C9** 68 0 S 135 0 E
Clarinda, *U.S.A.* **112 E7** 40 44N 95 2W
Clarington, *Canada* **114 C5** 43 55N 78 41W
Clarion, *Iowa, U.S.A.* . **112 D8** 42 44N 93 44W
Clarion, *Pa., U.S.A.* ... **116 E5** 41 13N 79 23W
Clarion →, *U.S.A.* **116 E5** 41 7N 79 41W
Clarion Fracture Zone,
  Pac. Oc. **98 H7** 20 0N 120 0W
Clark, *U.S.A.* **112 C6** 44 53N 97 44W
Clark, Pt., *Canada* **116 B3** 44 4N 81 45W
Clark Fork, *U.S.A.* **108 B5** 48 9N 116 11W
Clark Fork →, *U.S.A.* . **108 B5** 48 9N 116 15W
Clarkdale, *U.S.A.* **109 J7** 34 46N 112 3W
Clarke City, *Canada* ... **105 B6** 50 12N 66 38W
Clarke I., *Australia* .... **95 G4** 40 32 S 148 10 E
Clarke Ra., *Australia* .. **94 J6** 20 40 S 148 30 E
Clark's Fork →, *U.S.A.* **108 D9** 45 39N 108 43W
Clark's Harbour,
  Canada **105 D6** 43 25N 65 38W
Clarks Hill L., *U.S.A.* . **115 J4** 33 40N 82 12W
Clarks Summit, *U.S.A.* **117 E9** 41 30N 75 42W
Clarksburg, *U.S.A.* **114 F5** 39 17N 80 30W
Clarksdale, *U.S.A.* **113 H9** 34 12N 90 35W
Clarksville, *Ark., U.S.A.* **113 H8** 35 28N 93 28W
Clarksville, *Tenn.,*
  U.S.A. **115 G2** 36 32N 87 21W
Clarksville, *Tex., U.S.A.* **113 J7** 33 37N 95 3W
Clatskanie, *U.S.A.* **110 D3** 46 6N 123 12W
Claude, *U.S.A.* **113 H4** 35 7N 101 22W
Claveria, *Phil.* .... **61 B4** 18 37N 121 4 E
Clay, *U.S.A.* **110 G5** 38 17N 121 10W
Clay Center, *U.S.A.* ... **112 F6** 39 23N 97 8W
Claypool, *U.S.A.* **109 K8** 33 25N 110 51W
Claysburg, *U.S.A.* **116 F6** 40 17N 78 27W
Claysville, *U.S.A.* **116 F4** 40 7N 80 25W
Clayton, *N. Mex., U.S.A.* **113 G3** 36 27N 103 11W
Clayton, *N.Y., U.S.A.* . **117 B8** 44 14N 76 5W
Clear, C., *Ireland* **12 E2** 51 25N 9 32W
Clear, L., *Canada* **116 A7** 45 26N 77 12W
Clear Hills, *Canada* ... **102 B5** 56 40N 119 30W
Clear I., *Ireland* **12 E2** 51 26N 9 30W
Clear L., *U.S.A.* **110 F4** 39 2N 122 47W
Clear Lake, *Iowa, U.S.A.* **112 D8** 43 8N 93 23W
Clear Lake, *S. Dak.,*
  U.S.A. **112 C6** 44 45N 96 41W
Clear Lake Reservoir,
  U.S.A. **108 F3** 41 56N 121 5W
Clearfield, *Pa., U.S.A.* . **116 E6** 41 2N 78 27W
Clearfield, *Utah, U.S.A.* **108 F8** 41 7N 112 2W
Clearlake, *U.S.A.* **108 G2** 38 57N 122 38W
Clearlake Highlands,
  U.S.A. **110 G4** 38 57N 122 38W
Clearwater, *Canada* ... **102 C4** 51 38N 120 2W
Clearwater, *U.S.A.* **115 M4** 27 58N 82 48W
Clearwater →, *Alta.,*
  Canada **102 C6** 52 22N 114 57W
Clearwater →, *Alta.,*
  Canada **103 B6** 56 44N 111 23W
Clearwater →, *U.S.A.* . **103 C9** 53 34N 99 49W
Clearwater L. ○,
  Canada **103 C8** 54 0N 101 0W
Clearwater Mts., *U.S.A.* **108 C6** 46 5N 115 20W
Clearwater River ○,
  Canada **103 B7** 56 55N 109 10W
Cleburne, *U.S.A.* **113 J6** 32 21N 97 23W
Clee Hills, *U.K.* **15 E5** 52 26N 2 35W
Cleethorpes, *U.K.* **14 D7** 53 33N 0 3W
Cleeve Cloud, *U.K.* **15 F6** 51 56N 2 0W
Clelles, *France* .... **21 D9** 44 50N 5 38 E
Clemson, *U.S.A.* **115 H4** 34 41N 82 50W
Clerke Reef, *Australia* . **92 C2** 17 22 S 1.9 20 E
Clermont, *Australia* ... **94 C4** 22 49 S 147 39 E
Clermont, *France* ..... **19 C9** 49 23N 2 24 E
Clermont, *U.S.A.* **115 L5** 28 33N 81 46W
Clermont-en-Argonne,
  France .... **19 C12** 49 5N 5 4 E
Clermont-Ferrand,
  France .... **20 C7** 45 46N 3 4 E
Clermont-l'Hérault,
  France .... **20 E7** 43 38N 3 26 E
Clerval, *France* .... **19 E13** 47 25N 6 30 E
Clervaux, *Lux.* .... **17 D6** 50 4N 6 2 E
Cles, *Italy* .... **40 B8** 46 22N 11 2 E
Clevedon, *U.K.* **15 F5** 51 26N 2 52W
Cleveland, *Miss., U.S.A.* **113 J9** 33 45N 90 43W
Cleveland, *Ohio, U.S.A.* **116 E3** 41 30N 81 42W
Cleveland, *Okla., U.S.A.* **113 G6** 36 19N 96 28W
Cleveland, *Tenn., U.S.A.* **115 H3** 35 10N 84 53W
Cleveland, *Tex., U.S.A.* **113 K7** 30 21N 95 5W
Cleveland, C., *Australia* **94 B4** 19 11 S 147 1 E
Cleveland, Mt., *U.S.A.* **108 B7** 48 56N 113 51W
Cleveland Heights,
  U.S.A. **116 E3** 41 30N 81 34W
Clevelândia, *Brazil* .... **127 B5** 26 24 S 52 23W
Clew B., *Ireland* **12 C2** 53 50N 9 49W
Clewiston, *U.S.A.* **115 M5** 26 45N 80 56W
Clifden, *Ireland* **12 C1** 53 29N 10 1W
Clifden, *N.Z.* .... **91 M1** 46 1 S 167 42 E
Cliffdell, *U.S.A.* **110 D5** 46 56N 121 5W
Cliffy Hd., *Australia* ... **93 G2** 35 1 S 116 29 E
Clifton, *Australia* ..... **95 D5** 27 59 S 151 53 E
Clifton, *Ariz., U.S.A.* . **109 K9** 33 3N 109 18W
Clifton, *Colo., U.S.A.* . **109 G9** 39 7N 108 25W
Clifton, *Tex., U.S.A.* .. **113 K6** 31 47N 97 35W
Clifton Beach, *Australia* **94 B4** 16 46 S 145 39 E
Climax, *Canada* **103 D7** 49 10N 108 20W
Clinch →, *U.S.A.* ..... **115 H3** -35 53N 84 29W
Clingmans Dome,
  U.S.A. **115 H4** 35 34N 83 30W
Clint, *U.S.A.* **109 L10** 31 35N 106 14W
Clinton, *B.C., Canada* . **102 C4** 51 6N 121 35W
Clinton, *Ont., Canada* . **116 C3** 43 37N 81 32W
Clinton, *N.Z.* .... **91 M2** 46 12 S 169 23 E
Clinton, *Ark., U.S.A.* . **113 H8** 35 36N 92 28W
Clinton, *Conn., U.S.A.* . **117 E12** 41 17N 72 32W
Clinton, *Ill., U.S.A.* ... **112 E10** 40 9N 88 57W
Clinton, *Ind., U.S.A.* .. **114 F2** 39 40N 87 24W
Clinton, *Iowa, U.S.A.* . **112 E9** 41 51N 90 12W
Clinton, *Mass., U.S.A.* **117 D13** 42 25N 71 41W

Clinton, *Miss., U.S.A.* . **113 J9** 32 20N 90 20W
Clinton, *Mo., U.S.A.* .. **112 F8** 38 22N 93 46W
Clinton, *N.C., U.S.A.* . **115 H6** 35 0N 78 22W
Clinton, *Okla., U.S.A.* . **113 H5** 35 31N 98 58W
Clinton, *S.C., U.S.A.* .. **115 H5** 34 29N 81 53W
Clinton, *Tenn., U.S.A.* . **115 G3** 36 6N 84 8W
Clinton, *Wash., U.S.A.* **110 C4** 47 59N 122 21W
Clinton C., *Australia* ... **94 C5** 22 30 S 150 45 E
Clinton Colden L.,
  Canada **100 B9** 63 58N 107 27W
Clintonville, *U.S.A.* ... **112 C10** 44 37N 88 46W
Clipperton, I., *Pac. Oc.* **97 F17** 10 18N 109 13W
Clisham, *U.K.* **13 D2** 57 57N 6 49W
Clisson, *France* **18 E5** 47 5N 1 16W
Clitheroe, *U.K.* **14 D5** 53 53N 2 22W
Clo-oose, *Canada* **110 B2** 48 39N 124 49W
Cloates, Pt., *Australia* . **92 D1** 22 43 S 113 40 E
Clocolan, *S. Africa* .... **89 D4** 28 55 S 27 34 E
Clodomira, *Argentina* . **126 B3** 27 35 S 64 14W
Clogher Hd., *Ireland* .. **12 C5** 53 48N 6 14W
Clonakilty, *Ireland* **12 E3** 51 37N 8 53W
Clonakilty B., *Ireland* . **12 E3** 51 35N 8 51W
Cloncurry, *Australia* ... **94 C3** 20 40 S 140 28 E
Cloncurry →, *Australia* **94 B3** 18 37 S 140 40 E
Clondalkin, *Ireland* ... **12 C5** 53 19N 6 25W
Clones, *Ireland* **12 B4** 54 11N 7 15W
Clonmel, *Ireland* **12 D4** 52 21N 7 42W
Cloppenburg, *Germany* **24 C4** 52 51N 8 1 E
Cloud Bay, *Canada* **104 C2** 48 5N 89 26W
Cloud Peak, *U.S.A.* ... **108 D10** 44 23N 107 11W
Cloudcroft, *U.S.A.* **109 K11** 32 58N 105 45W
Cloverdale, *U.S.A.* **110 G4** 38 48N 123 1W
Clovis, *Calif., U.S.A.* .. **110 J7** 36 49N 119 42W
Clovis, *N. Mex., U.S.A.* **113 H3** 34 24N 103 12W
Cloyes-sur-le-Loir,
  France .... **18 E8** 48 0N 1 14 E
Cloyne, *Canada* **116 B7** 44 49N 77 11W
Cluj □, *Romania* ...... **29 D8** 46 45N 23 30 E
Cluj-Napoca, *Romania* **29 D8** 46 47N 23 38 E
Clunes, *Australia* ..... **95 F3** 37 20 S 143 45 E
Cluny, *France* .... **19 F11** 46 26N 4 38 E
Cluses, *France* .... **19 F13** 46 5N 6 35 E
Clusone, *Italy* .... **40 C6** 45 53N 9 57 E
Clutha →, *N.Z.* .... **91 M2** 46 20 S 169 49 E
Clwyd □, *U.K.* **14 D5** 53 19N 3 31W
Clwyd →, *U.K.* **14 D4** 53 20N 3 30W
Clyde, *Canada* **102 C6** 54 9N 113 39W
Clyde, *N.Z.* .... **91 L2** 45 12 S 169 20 E
Clyde, *U.S.A.* **116 C8** 43 5N 76 52W
Clyde →, *U.K.* **13 F4** 55 55N 4 30W
Clyde, Firth of, *U.K.* .. **13 F3** 55 22N 5 1W
Clyde Muirshiel ○, *U.K.* **13 F3** 55 50N 4 40W
Clyde River, *Canada* .. **101 A13** 70 30N 68 30W
Clydebank, *U.K.* **13 F4** 55 54N 4 23W
Clymer, *N.Y., U.S.A.* .. **116 D5** 42 1N 79 37W
Clymer, *Pa., U.S.A.* ... **116 D5** 40 40N 79 1W
Čmielów, *Poland* ...... **31 H8** 50 53N 21 31 E
Côa →, *Portugal* **36 D3** 41 5N 7 6W
Coachella, *U.S.A.* **111 M10** 33 41N 116 10W
Coachella Canal, *U.S.A.* **111 N12** 32 43N 114 57W
Coahoma, *U.S.A.* **113 J4** 32 18N 101 18W
Coahuayana →, *Mexico* **118 D4** 18 41N 103 45W
Coahuila □, *Mexico* ... **118 B4** 27 0N 103 0W
Coal →, *Canada* **102 B3** 59 39N 126 57W
Coalane, *Mozam.* ..... **87 F4** 17 48 S 37 2 E
Coalcomán, *Mexico* ... **118 D4** 18 40N 103 10W
Coaldale, *Canada* **102 D6** 49 45N 112 35W
Coalgate, *U.S.A.* **113 H6** 34 32N 96 13W
Coalinga, *U.S.A.* **110 J6** 36 9N 120 21W
Coalisland, *U.K.* ...... **12 B5** 54 33 S 6 42W
Coalville, *U.K.* **14 E6** 52 44N 1 23W
Coalville, *U.S.A.* **108 F8** 40 55N 111 24W
Coamo, *Puerto Rico* .. **121 d** 18 5N 66 22W
Coari, *Brazil* .... **124 D6** 4 8 S 63 7W
Coast □, *Kenya* .... **86 C4** 2 40 S 39 45 E
Coast Mts., *Canada* ... **102 C3** 55 0N 129 20W
Coast Ranges, *U.S.A.* . **110 G4** 39 0N 123 0W
Coatbridge, *U.K.* **13 F4** 55 52N 4 6W
Coatepec, *Mexico* **119 D5** 19 27N 96 58W
Coatepeque, *Guatemala* **120 D1** 14 46N 91 55W
Coatesville, *U.S.A.* **114 F8** 39 59N 75 50W
Coaticook, *Canada* **117 A13** 45 10N 71 46W
Coats I., *Canada* **101 B11** 62 30N 83 0W
Coats Land, *Antarctica* **5 D1** 77 0 S 25 0W
Coatzacoalcos, *Mexico* **119 D6** 18 7N 94 25W
Coba, *Mexico* **119 C7** 20 31N 87 39W
Cobadin, *Romania* .... **29 F13** 44 5N 28 13 E
Cobalt, *Canada* **104 C4** 47 25N 79 42W
Cobán, *Guatemala* **120 C1** 15 30N 90 21W
Çobanlar, *Turkey* ..... **47 C12** 38 41N 30 47 E
Cobar, *Australia* ...... **95 E4** 31 27 S 145 48 E
Cóbh, *Ireland* **12 E3** 51 51N 8 17W
Cobija, *Bolivia* .... **124 F5** 11 0 S 68 50W
Cobleskill, *U.S.A.* **117 D10** 42 41N 74 29W
Coboconk, *Canada* **116 B6** 44 39N 78 48W
Cobourg, *Canada* **116 C6** 43 58N 78 10W
Cobourg △, *Australia* . **92 B5** 11 26 S 131 58 E
Cobourg Pen., *Australia* **92 B5** 11 20 S 132 15 E
Cobram, *Australia* .... **95 F4** 35 54 S 145 40 E
Cóbué, *Mozam.* .... **87 E3** 12 0 S 34 58 E
Coburg, *Germany* ..... **25 E6** 50 15N 10 58 E
Coca, *Spain* **36 D6** 41 13N 4 32W
Cocanada = Kakinada,
  India .... **67 L13** 16 57N 82 11 E
Cocentaina, *Spain* **39 G4** 38 45N 0 27W
Cochabamba, *Bolivia* . **124 G5** 17 26 S 66 10W
Cochem, *Germany* .... **25 E3** 50 9N 7 9 E
Cochemane, *Mozam.* .. **87 F3** 17 0 S 32 54 E
Cochin, *India* .... **66 Q10** 9 58N 76 20 E
Cochin China = Nam-
  Phan, *Vietnam* .... **65 G6** 10 30N 106 0 E
Cochran, *U.S.A.* **115 J4** 32 23N 83 21W
Cochrane, *Alta., Canada* **102 C6** 51 11N 114 30W
Cochrane, *Ont., Canada* **104 C3** 49 0N 81 0W
Cochrane, *Chile* ...... **128 F2** 47 15 S 72 33W
Cochrane →, *Canada* . **103 B8** 59 0N 103 40W
Cochrane, L., *Chile* ... **128 F2** 47 10 S 72 0W
Cochranton, *U.S.A.* ... **116 E4** 41 31N 80 3W
Cockburn, *Australia* ... **95 E3** 32 5 S 141 0 E
Cockburn, Canal, *Chile* **128 G2** 54 30 S 72 0W
Cockburn I., *Canada* .. **104 C3** 45 55N 83 22W
Cockburn Ra., *Australia* **92 C4** 15 46 S 128 0 E
Cockermouth, *U.K.* ... **14 C4** 54 40N 3 22W
Cocklebiddy, *Australia* **93 F4** 32 0 S 126 3 E
Cockpit Country, The,
  Jamaica .... **120 a** 18 15N 77 45W
Coco →, *Cent. Amer.* . **120 D3** 15 0N 83 8W
Coco, I. del, *Pac. Oc.* . **97 G19** 5 25N 87 55W
Cocoa, *U.S.A.* **115 L5** 28 21N 80 44W
Cocobeach, *Gabon* .... **84 D1** 0 59N 9 34 E
Cocora, *Romania* ..... **29 F12** 44 45N 27 3 E
Cocos B., *Trin. & Tob.* . **125 K15** 10 25N 61 2W
Cocos Is., *Ind. Oc.* ... **96 J1** 12 10 S 96 55 E
Cod, C., *U.S.A.* **114 D10** 42 5N 70 10W
Codajás, *Brazil* .... **124 D6** 3 55 S 62 0W
Codigoro, *Italy* .... **41 D9** 44 49N 12 8 E

Codlea, *Romania* ..... **29 E10** 45 42N 25 27 E
Codó, *Brazil* .... **125 D10** 4 30 S 43 55W
Codogno, *Italy* .... **40 C6** 45 9N 9 42 E
Codróipo, *Italy* .... **41 C10** 45 58N 13 0 E
Codru, Munții, *Romania* **28 D7** 46 30N 22 15 E
Cody, *U.S.A.* **108 D9** 44 32N 109 3W
Coe Hill, *Canada* **116 B7** 44 52N 77 50W
Coelemu, *Chile* .... **126 D1** 36 30 S 72 48W
Coen, *Australia* .... **94 A3** 13 52 S 143 12 E
Coesfeld, *Germany* .... **24 D3** 51 56N 7 10 E
Cœur d'Alene, *U.S.A.* . **108 C5** 47 45N 116 51W
Cœur d'Alene L., *U.S.A.* **108 C5** 47 32N 116 48W
Coevorden, *Neths.* .... **17 B6** 52 40N 6 44 E
Cofete, *Canary Is.* **48 F5** 28 6N 14 23W
Coffeyville, *U.S.A.* **113 G7** 37 2N 95 37W
Coffin B., *Australia* ... **95 E2** 34 38 S 135 28 E
Coffin Bay, *Australia* .. **95 E2** 34 37 S 135 29 E
Coffin Bay Peninsula,
  Australia .... **95 E2** 34 32 S 135 15 E
Coffs Harbour, *Australia* **95 E5** 30 16 S 153 5 E
Cofre de Perote △,
  Mexico **119 D5** 19 29N 97 8W
Cofrentes, *Spain* **39 F3** 39 13N 1 5W
Cogalnic →, *Moldova* . **29 E14** 45 49N 29 40 E
Cogealac, *Romania* ... **29 F13** 44 36N 28 36 E
Coghinas →, *Italy* .... **42 B1** 40 55N 8 48 E
Coghinas, L. del, *Italy* . **42 B2** 40 46N 9 3 E
Cognac, *France* **20 C3** 45 41N 0 20W
Cogne, *Italy* .... **40 C4** 45 37N 7 21 E
Cogolin, *France* .... **21 E10** 43 15N 6 32 E
Cogolludo, *Spain* **38 E1** 40 59N 3 10W
Cohocton, *U.S.A.* **116 D7** 42 30N 77 30W
Cohocton →, *U.S.A.* .. **116 D7** 42 9N 77 6W
Cohoes, *U.S.A.* **117 D11** 42 46N 73 42W
Cohuna, *Australia* .... **95 F3** 35 45 S 144 15 E
Coiba, I., *Panama* **120 E3** 7 30N 81 40W
Coig →, *Argentina* ... **128 G3** 51 0 S 69 10W
Coigeach, Rubha, *U.K.* **13 C3** 58 6N 5 26W
Coihaique, *Chile* ...... **128 F2** 45 30 S 71 45W
Coimbatore, *India* .... **66 P10** 11 2N 76 59 E
Coimbra, *Brazil* ...... **124 G7** 19 55 S 57 48W
Coimbra, *Portugal* **36 E2** 40 15N 8 27W
Coimbra □, *Portugal* .. **36 E2** 40 12N 8 25W
Coín, *Spain* **37 J6** 36 40N 4 48W
Coipasa, Salar de,
  Bolivia .... **124 G5** 19 26 S 68 9W
Cojimies, *Ecuador* **124 C3** 0 20N 80 0W
Cojocna, *Romania* .... **29 D8** 46 45N 23 50 E
Cojutepequé, *El Salv.* . **120 D2** 13 41N 88 54W
Čoka, *Serbia & M.* .... **28 E5** 45 57N 20 12 E
Cokeville, *U.S.A.* **108 E8** 42 5N 110 57W
Colac, *Australia* ...... **95 F3** 38 21 S 143 35 E
Colatina, *Brazil* ...... **125 G10** 19 32 S 40 37W
Colbeck, C., *Antarctica* **5 D13** 77 6 S 157 48W
Colborne, *Canada* **116 C7** 44 0N 77 53W
Colby, *U.S.A.* **112 F4** 39 24N 101 3W
Colchester, *U.K.* ...... **15 F8** 51 54N 0 55 E
Cold L., *Canada* **103 C7** 54 33N 110 5W
Coldstream, *Canada* .. **102 C5** 50 13N 119 11W
Coldstream, *U.K.* **13 F6** 55 39N 2 15W
Coldwater, *Canada* ... **116 B5** 44 42N 79 40W
Coldwater, *Kans., U.S.A.* **113 G5** 37 16N 99 20W
Coldwater, *Mich., U.S.A.* **114 E3** 41 57N 85 0W
Colebrook, *U.S.A.* **117 B13** 44 54N 71 30W
Coleman, *U.S.A.* **113 K5** 31 50N 99 26W
Coleman →, *Australia* **94 B3** 15 6 S 141 38 E
Colenso, *S. Africa* .... **89 D4** 28 44 S 29 50 E
Coleraine, *Australia* .. **95 F3** 37 36 S 141 40 E
Coleraine, *U.K.* **12 A5** 55 8N 6 41W
Coleridge, L., *N.Z.* .... **91 K3** 43 17 S 171 30 E
Colesberg, *S. Africa* ... **88 E4** 30 45 S 25 5 E
Coleville, *U.S.A.* **110 G7** 38 34N 119 30W
Colfax, *Calif., U.S.A.* . **110 F6** 39 6N 120 57W
Colfax, *La., U.S.A.* **113 K8** 31 31N 92 42W
Colfax, *Wash., U.S.A.* . **108 C5** 46 53N 117 22W
Colhué Huapi, L.,
  Argentina .... **128 F3** 45 30 S 69 0W
Colibași, *Moldova* .... **29 E13** 45 43N 28 11 E
Colibași, *Romania* .... **29 F9** 44 56N 24 54 E
Cólico, *Italy* .... **40 B6** 46 8N 9 22 E
Coligny, *France* .... **19 F12** 46 23N 5 21 E
Coligny, *S. Africa* ..... **89 D4** 26 17 S 26 15 E
Colima, *Mexico* **118 D4** 19 14N 103 43W
Colima □, *Mexico* **118 D4** 19 10N 103 40W
Colima, Nevado de,
  Mexico **118 D4** 19 35N 103 45W
Colina, *Chile* .... **126 C1** 33 13 S 70 45W
Colina do Norte,
  Guinea-Biss. **82 C2** 12 28N 15 0W
Colinas, *Brazil* .... **125 E10** 6 0 S 44 10W
Colindres, *Spain* **36 B7** 43 24N 3 27W
Coll, *U.K.* **13 E2** 56 39N 6 34W
Collaguasi, *Chile* ..... **126 A2** 21 5 S 68 45W
Collarada, Peña, *Spain* . **38 C4** 42 43N 0 29W
Collarenebri, *Australia* **95 D4** 29 33 S 148 34 E
Colle di Val d'Elsa, *Italy* **40 E8** 43 25N 11 7 E
Collécchio, *Italy* ...... **40 D7** 44 45N 10 13 E
Colleen Bawn,
  Zimbabwe .... **87 G2** 21 0 S 29 12 E
College Park, *U.S.A.* .. **115 J3** 33 40N 84 27W
College Station, *U.S.A.* **113 K6** 30 37N 96 21W
Collesalvetti, *Italy* .... **40 E7** 43 34N 10 27 E
Colli Euganei △, *Italy* . **41 C8** 45 18N 11 43 E
Collie, *Australia* ...... **93 F2** 33 22 S 116 8 E
Collier B., *Australia* ... **92 C3** 16 10 S 124 15 E
Collier Ra., *Australia* .. **93 D2** 24 45 S 119 10 E
Collier Range △,
  Australia .... **93 D2** 24 39 S 119 7 E
Collina, Passo di, *Italy* . **40 D7** 44 2N 10 56 E
Collingwood, *Canada* . **116 B4** 44 29N 80 13W
Collingwood, *N.Z.* .... **91 J4** 40 41 S 172 40 E
Collins, *Canada* **104 B2** 50 17N 89 27W
Collinsville, *Australia* .. **94 C4** 20 30 S 147 56 E
Collipulli, *Chile* ...... **126 D1** 37 55 S 72 30W
Collooney, *Ireland* **12 B3** 54 11N 8 29W
Colmar, *France* .... **19 D14** 48 5N 7 20 E
Colmars, *France* ...... **21 D10** 44 11N 6 39 E
Colmenar de Oreja,
  Spain **36 E7** 40 6N 3 23W
Colmenar Viejo, *Spain* **36 E7** 40 39N 3 47W
Colo →, *Australia* .... **95 E5** 33 25 S 150 52 E
Cologne = Köln,
  Germany .... **24 E2** 50 56N 6 57 E
Colom, I. d'en, *Spain* . **48 B11** 39 58N 4 16 E
Coloma, *U.S.A.* **110 G6** 38 48N 120 53W
Colomb-Béchar =
  Béchar, *Algeria* **78 B5** 31 38N 2 18W
Colombey-les-Belles,
  France .... **19 D12** 48 32N 5 54 E
Colombey-les-Deux-
  Églises, *France* .... **19 D11** 48 13N 4 50 E
Colombia ■, *S. Amer.* . **124 C4** 3 45N 73 0W
Colombian Basin,
  S. Amer. **98 H12** 14 0N 76 0W
Colombo, *Sri Lanka* ... **66 R11** 6 56N 79 58 E

Colomiers, *France* .... **20 E5** 43 36N 1 21 E
Colón, *Buenos Aires,*
  Argentina .... **126 C3** 33 53 S 61 7W
Colón, *Entre Ríos,*
  Argentina .... **126 C4** 32 12 S 58 10W
Colón, *Cuba* **120 B3** 22 42N 80 54W
Colón, *Panama* **120 E4** 9 20N 79 54W
Colón, Arch. de,
  Ecuador **97 H18** 0 0 91 0W
Colònia de Sant Jordi,
  Spain .... **48 B9** 39 19N 2 59 E
Colonia del Sacramento,
  Uruguay .... **126 C4** 34 25 S 57 50W
Colonia Dora, *Argentina* **126 B3** 28 34 S 62 59W
Colonial Beach, *U.S.A.* **114 F7** 38 15N 76 58W
Colonie, *U.S.A.* **117 D11** 42 43N 73 50W
Colonna, C., *Italy* ..... **43 C10** 39 2N 17 12 E
Colonsay, *Canada* **103 C7** 51 59N 105 52W
Colonsay, *U.K.* **13 E2** 56 5N 6 12W
Colorado □, *U.S.A.* ... **109 G10** 39 30N 105 30W
Colorado →, *Argentina* **128 D4** 39 50 S 62 8W
Colorado →, *N. Amer.* **109 L6** 31 45N 114 40W
Colorado →, *U.S.A.* .. **113 L7** 28 36N 95 59W
Colorado City, *U.S.A.* . **113 J4** 32 24N 100 52W
Colorado Plateau,
  U.S.A. **109 H8** 37 0N 111 0W
Colorado River
  Aqueduct, *U.S.A.* .. **111 L12** 34 17N 114 10W
Colorado Springs,
  U.S.A. **112 F2** 38 50N 104 49W
Colorno, *Italy* .... **40 D7** 44 56N 10 22 E
Colotlán, *Mexico* **118 C4** 22 6N 103 16W
Colstrip, *U.S.A.* **108 D10** 45 53N 106 38W
Colton, *U.S.A.* **117 B10** 44 33N 74 56W
Columbia, *Ky., U.S.A.* **114 G3** 37 6N 85 18W
Columbia, *La., U.S.A.* . **113 J8** 32 6N 92 5W
Columbia, *Miss., U.S.A.* **113 K10** 31 15N 89 50W
Columbia, *Mo., U.S.A.* **112 F8** 38 57N 92 20W
Columbia, *Pa., U.S.A.* . **117 F8** 40 2N 76 30W
Columbia, *S.C., U.S.A.* **115 J5** 34 0N 81 2W
Columbia, *Tenn., U.S.A.* **115 H2** 35 37N 87 2W
Columbia →, *N. Amer.* **110 D2** 46 15N 124 5W
Columbia, C., *Canada* . **4 A4** 83 6N 69 57W
Columbia, District of □,
  U.S.A. **114 F7** 38 55N 77 0W
Columbia, Mt., *Canada* **102 C5** 52 8N 117 20W
Columbia Basin, *U.S.A.* **108 C4** 46 45N 119 5W
Columbia Falls, *U.S.A.* **108 B6** 48 23N 114 11W
Columbia Plateau,
  U.S.A. **108 D5** 44 0N 117 30W
Columbiana, *U.S.A.* ... **116 F4** 40 53N 80 42W
Columbretes, Is., *Spain* **38 F5** 39 50N 0 50 E
Columbus, *Ga., U.S.A.* **115 J3** 32 28N 84 59W
Columbus, *Ind., U.S.A.* **114 F3** 39 13N 85 55W
Columbus, *Kans., U.S.A.* **113 G7** 37 10N 94 50W
Columbus, *Miss., U.S.A.* **115 J1** 33 30N 88 25W
Columbus, *Mont., U.S.A.* **108 D9** 45 38N 109 15W
Columbus, *N. Mex.,*
  U.S.A. **109 L10** 31 50N 107 38W
Columbus, *Nebr., U.S.A.* **112 E6** 41 26N 97 22W
Columbus, *Ohio, U.S.A.* **114 F4** 39 58N 83 0W
Columbus, *Tex., U.S.A.* **113 L6** 29 42N 96 33W
Colunga, *Spain* **36 B5** 43 29N 5 16W
Colusa, *U.S.A.* **110 F4** 39 13N 122 1W
Colville, *U.S.A.* **108 B5** 48 33N 117 54W
Colville →, *U.S.A.* **100 A4** 70 25N 150 30W
Colville, C., *N.Z.* ...... **91 G5** 36 29 S 175 21 E
Colwood, *Canada* **110 B3** 48 26N 123 29W
Colwyn Bay, *U.K.* **14 D4** 53 18N 3 44W
Coma, *Ethiopia* ...... **81 F4** 8 29N 36 53 E
Comácchio, *Italy* ..... **41 D9** 44 42N 12 11 E
Comalcalco, *Mexico* .. **119 D6** 18 16N 93 13W
Comallo, *Argentina* ... **128 E2** 41 0 S 70 5W
Comana, *Romania* .... **29 F11** 44 10N 26 10 E
Comanche, *U.S.A.* **113 K5** 31 54N 98 36W
Comandante Ferraz,
  Antarctica .... **5 C18** 62 30 S 58 0W
Comănești, *Romania* .. **29 D11** 46 25N 26 26 E
Comarnic, *Romania* ... **29 E10** 45 15N 25 38 E
Comayagua, *Honduras* **120 D2** 14 25N 87 37W
Combahee →, *U.S.A.* . **115 J5** 32 30N 80 31W
Combarbalá, *Chile* .... **126 C1** 31 11 S 71 2W
Combe Martin, *U.K.* .. **15 F3** 51 12N 4 3W
Combeaufontaine,
  France .... **19 E12** 47 38N 5 54 E
Comber, *Canada* **116 D2** 42 14N 82 33W
Comber, *U.K.* **12 B6** 54 33N 5 45W
Combermere, *Canada* . **116 A7** 45 22N 77 37W
Comblain-au-Pont,
  Belgium .... **17 D5** 50 29N 5 35 E
Combourg, *France* **18 D5** 48 25N 1 46W
Combrailles, *France* .. **19 F9** 46 8N 2 8 E
Combronde, *France* ... **20 C7** 45 58N 3 5 E
Comeragh Mts., *Ireland* **12 D4** 52 18N 7 34W
Comet, *Australia* ..... **94 C4** 23 36 S 148 38 E
Comilla, *Bangla.* ..... **67 H17** 23 28N 91 10 E
Comino, *Malta* .... **49 C1** 36 1N 14 20 E
Comino, C., *Italy* ..... **42 B2** 40 32N 9 49 E
Cómiso, *Italy* .... **43 F7** 36 59N 14 36 E
Comitán, *Mexico* **119 D6** 16 18N 92 9W
Commentry, *France* ... **19 F9** 46 20N 2 46 E
Commerce, *Ga., U.S.A.* **115 H4** 34 12N 83 28W
Commerce, *Tex., U.S.A.* **113 J7** 33 15N 95 54W
Commercy, *France* .... **19 D12** 48 43N 5 34 E
Committee B., *Canada* **101 B11** 68 30N 86 30W
Commonwealth B.,
  Antarctica .... **5 C10** 67 0 S 144 0 E
Commoron Cr. →,
  Australia .... **95 D5** 28 22 S 150 8 E
Communism Pk. =
  Kommunizma, Pik,
  Tajikistan .... **52 F8** 39 0N 72 2 E
Como, *Italy* .... **40 C6** 45 47N 9 5 E
Como, Lago di, *Italy* .. **40 B6** 46 0N 9 11 E
Comodoro Rivadavia,
  Argentina .... **128 F3** 45 50 S 67 40W
Comoé △, *Ivory C.* **82 D4** 9 0N 3 35W
Comorâște, *Romania* .. **28 E6** 45 10N 21 35 E
Comorin, C., *India* .... **66 Q10** 8 3N 77 40 E
Comoros =
  Comoros ■, *Ind. Oc.* **77 H8** 12 10 S 44 15 E
Comoros ■, *Ind. Oc.* . **77 H8** 12 10 S 44 15 E
Comox, *Canada* **102 D4** 49 42N 124 55W
Compiègne, *France* ... **19 C9** 49 24N 2 50 E
Comporta, *Portugal* .. **37 G2** 38 22N 8 46W
Compostela, *Mexico* .. **118 C4** 21 15N 104 53W
Comprida, I., *Brazil* ... **127 A6** 24 50 S 47 42W
Compton, *Canada* **117 A13** 45 14N 71 49W
Compton, *U.S.A.* **111 M8** 33 54N 118 13W
Comrat, *Moldova* .... **29 D13** 46 18N 28 40 E
Comrie, *U.K.* **13 E5** 56 22N 4 0W
Con Cuong, *Vietnam* . **64 C5** 19 2N 104 54 E
Con Dao △, *Vietnam* . **65 H6** 8 42N 106 35 E
Con Son, *Vietnam* .... **65 H6** 8 41N 106 37 E
Conakry, *Guinea* **82 D2** 9 29N 13 49W
Conara, *Australia* ..... **95 G4** 41 50 S 147 26 E
Concarneau, *France* .. **18 E3** 47 52N 3 56W

Conceição, *Mozam.* ... **87 F4** 18 47 S 36 7 E
Conceição da Barra,
  Brazil .... **125 G11** 18 35 S 39 45W
Conceição do Araguaia,
  Brazil .... **125 E9** 8 0 S 49 2W
Concepción, *Argentina* **126 B2** 27 20 S 65 35W
Concepción, *Bolivia* .. **124 G6** 16 15 S 62 8W
Concepción, *Chile* .... **126 D1** 36 50 S 73 0W
Concepción, *Mexico* .. **119 D6** 18 15N 90 5W
Concepción, *Paraguay* **126 A4** 23 22 S 57 26W
Concepción □, *Chile* .. **126 D1** 37 0 S 72 30W
Concepción →, *Mexico* **118 A2** 30 32N 113 2W
Concepción, Est. de,
  Chile .... **128 G2** 50 30 S 74 55W
Concepción, L., *Bolivia* **124 G6** 17 20 S 61 20W
Concepción, Punta,
  Mexico **118 B2** 26 55N 111 59W
Concepción del Oro,
  Mexico **118 C4** 24 40N 101 30W
Concepción del
  Uruguay, *Argentina* **126 C4** 32 35 S 58 20W
Conception, Pt., *U.S.A.* **111 L6** 34 27N 120 28W
Conception B., *Canada* **105 C9** 47 45N 53 0W
Conception B., *Namibia* **88 C1** 23 55 S 14 22 E
Conception I., *Bahamas* **121 B4** 23 52N 75 9W
Concession, *Zimbabwe* **87 F3** 17 27 S 30 56 E
Conchas Dam, *U.S.A.* . **113 H2** 35 22N 104 11W
Conches-en-Ouche,
  France .... **18 D7** 48 58N 0 56 E
Concho, *U.S.A.* **109 J9** 34 28N 109 36W
Concho →, *U.S.A.* **113 K5** 31 34N 99 43W
Conchos →, *Chihuahua,*
  Mexico **118 B4** 29 32N 105 0W
Conchos →,
  Tamaulipas, Mexico **119 B5** 25 9N 98 35W
Concord, *Calif., U.S.A.* **110 H4** 37 59N 122 2W
Concord, *N.C., U.S.A.* **115 H5** 35 25N 80 35W
Concord, *N.H., U.S.A.* **117 C13** 43 12N 71 32W
Concordia, *Argentina* . **126 C4** 31 20 S 58 2W
Concórdia, *Brazil* ..... **124 D5** 4 36 S 66 36W
Concordia, *Mexico* ... **118 C3** 23 18N 106 2W
Concordia, *U.S.A.* **112 F6** 39 34N 97 40W
Concrete, *U.S.A.* **108 B3** 48 32N 121 45W
Condamine, *Australia* . **95 D5** 26 56 S 150 9 E
Condat, *France* .... **20 C6** 45 21N 2 46 E
Conde, *U.S.A.* **112 C5** 45 9N 98 6W
Condé-sur-Noireau,
  France **18 D6** 48 51N 0 33W
Condeúba, *Brazil* ..... **125 F10** 14 52 S 42 0W
Condoboin, *Australia* . **95 E4** 33 4 S 147 6 E
Condom, *France* ...... **20 E4** 43 57N 0 22 E
Condon, *U.S.A.* **108 D3** 45 14N 120 11W
Conegliano, *Italy* ..... **41 C9** 45 53N 12 18 E
Conejera I. = Conills, I.
  des, *Spain* .... **48 B9** 39 11N 2 58 E
Conejos, *Mexico* **118 B4** 26 14N 103 53W
Conemaugh →, *U.S.A.* **116 F5** 40 28N 79 19W
Conero △, *Italy* .... **41 E10** 43 32N 13 35 E
Confolens, *France* .... **20 B4** 46 2N 0 40 E
Confuso →, *Paraguay* . **126 B4** 25 9 S 57 34W
Congaz, *Moldova* ..... **29 D13** 46 7N 28 36 E
Conghua, *China* ...... **59 F9** 23 36N 113 31 E
Congjiang, *China* ..... **58 E7** 25 43N 108 52 E
Congleton, *U.K.* **14 D5** 53 10N 2 13W
Congo (Kinshasa) =
  Congo, Dem. Rep. of
  the ■, *Africa* ...... **84 E4** 3 0 S 23 0 E
Congo ■, *Africa* ...... **84 E3** 1 0 S 16 0 E
Congo →, *Africa* ..... **84 F2** 6 4 S 12 24 E
Congo, Dem. Rep. of
  the ■, *Africa* ...... **84 E4** 3 0 S 23 0 E
Congo Basin, *Africa* .. **84 E4** 0 10 S 24 30 E
Congonhas, *Brazil* .... **127 A7** 20 30 S 43 52W
Congress, *U.S.A.* **109 J7** 34 9N 112 51W
Conil de la Frontera,
  Spain **37 J4** 36 17N 6 10W
Conills, I. des, *Spain* .. **48 B9** 39 11N 2 58 E
Coniston, *Canada* **104 C3** 46 29N 80 51W
Conjeeveram =
  Kanchipuram, *India* . **66 N11** 12 52N 79 45 E
Conklin, *Canada* **103 B6** 55 38N 111 5W
Conklin, *U.S.A.* **117 D9** 42 2N 75 49W
Conn, L., *Ireland* **12 B2** 54 3N 9 15W
Connacht □, *Ireland* .. **12 C2** 53 43N 9 12W
Conneaut, *U.S.A.* **116 E4** 41 57N 80 34W
Connecticut □, *U.S.A.* **117 E12** 41 30N 72 45W
Connecticut →, *U.S.A.* **117 E12** 41 16N 72 20W
Connell, *U.S.A.* **108 C4** 46 40N 118 52W
Connellsville, *U.S.A.* .. **116 F5** 40 1N 79 35W
Connemara, *Ireland* .. **12 C2** 53 29N 9 45W
Connemara △, *Ireland* **12 C2** 53 32N 9 52W
Connerré, *France* ..... **18 D7** 48 3N 0 30 E
Connersville, *U.S.A.* .. **114 F3** 39 39N 85 8W
Connors Ra., *Australia* **94 C4** 21 40 S 149 10 E
Conquest, *Canada* **103 C7** 51 32N 107 14W
Conrad, *U.S.A.* **108 B8** 48 10N 111 57W
Conran, C., *Australia* . **95 F4** 37 49 S 148 44 E
Conroe, *U.S.A.* **113 K7** 30 19N 95 27W
Consecon, *Canada* **116 C7** 44 0N 77 31W
Conselheiro Lafaiete,
  Brazil .... **127 A7** 20 40 S 43 48W
Conselve, *Italy* .... **41 C8** 45 14N 11 52 E
Consett, *U.K.* **14 C6** 54 51N 1 50W
Consort, *Canada* **103 C6** 52 1N 110 46W
Constance = Konstanz,
  Germany .... **25 H5** 47 40N 9 10 E
Constance, L. =
  Bodensee, *Europe* .. **25 H5** 47 35N 9 25 E
Constanța, *Romania* .. **29 F13** 44 14N 28 38 E
Constanța □, *Romania* **29 F13** 44 15N 28 15 E
Constantia, *U.S.A.* ... **117 C8** 43 15N 76 1W
Constantina, *Spain* ... **37 H5** 37 51N 5 40W
Constantine, *Algeria* .. **78 A7** 36 25N 6 42 E
Constitución, *Chile* ... **126 D1** 35 20 S 72 30W
Constitución, *Uruguay* **126 C4** 31 0 S 57 50W
Constitución de 1857 △,
  Mexico **118 A1** 32 4N 115 55W
Consuegra, *Spain* **37 F7** 39 28N 3 43W
Consul, *Canada* **103 D7** 49 20N 109 30W
Contact, *U.S.A.* **108 F6** 41 46N 114 45W
Contai, *India* .... **69 J12** 21 54N 87 46 E
Contamana, *Peru* ..... **124 E4** 7 19 S 74 55W
Contarina, *Italy* ...... **41 C9** 45 2N 12 13 E
Contas →, *Brazil* ..... **125 F11** 14 17 S 39 1W
Contes, *France* .... **21 E11** 43 49N 7 19 E
Contoocook, *U.S.A.* .. **117 C13** 43 13N 71 45W
Contra Costa, *Mozam.* **89 D5** 25 9 S 33 30 E
Contres, *France* ...... **18 E8** 47 24N 1 26 E
Contrexéville, *France* . **19 D12** 48 10N 5 53 E
Contwoyto L., *Canada* **100 B8** 65 42N 110 50W
Conversano, *Italy* ... **43 B10** 40 58N 17 2 E
Conway = Conwy, *U.K.* **14 D4** 53 17N 3 50W
Conway = Conwy →,
  U.K. **14 D4** 53 17N 3 50W
Conway, *Australia* .... **94 J6** 20 24 S 148 41 E
Conway, *Ark., U.S.A.* . **113 H8** 35 5N 92 26W

Conway, N.H., U.S.A. . **117 C13** 43 59N 71 7W
Conway, S.C., U.S.A. . **115 J6** 33 51N 79 3W
Conway, C., Australia . **94 J6** 20 34 S 148 46 E
Conway, L., Australia . **95 D2** 28 17 S 135 35 E
Conwy □, U.K. **14 D4** 53 17N 3 50W
Conwy, U.K. **14 D4** 53 10N 3 44W
Conwy →, U.K. **14 D4** 53 17N 3 50W
Coober Pedy, Australia **95 D1** 29 1 S 134 43 E
Cooch Behar = Koch
Bihar, India . . . . . **67 F16** 26 22N 89 29 E
Cooinda, Australia . . **92 B5** 13 15 S 130 5 E
Cook, Australia . . . . . **93 F5** 30 37 S 130 25 E
Cook, U.S.A. **112 B8** 47 49N 92 39W
Cook, B., Chile . . . . . **128 H3** 55 10 S 70 0W
Cook, C., Canada . . . **102 C3** 50 8N 127 55W
Cook, Mt. = Aoraki
Mount Cook, N.Z. . . **91 K3** 43 36 S 170 9 E
Cook Inlet, U.S.A. . . . **100 C4** 60 0N 152 0W
Cook Is., Pac. Oc. . . . **97 J12** 17 0 S 160 0W
Cook Strait, N.Z. . . . **91 J5** 41 15 S 174 29 E
Cookeville, U.S.A. . . . **115 G3** 36 10N 85 30W
Cookhouse, S. Africa . **88 E4** 32 44 S 25 47 E
Cookshire, Canada . . **117 A13** 45 25N 71 38W
Cookstown, U.K. . . . **12 B5** 54 39N 6 45W
Cooksville, Canada . . **116 C5** 43 36N 79 35W
Cooktown, Australia . **94 B4** 15 30 S 145 16 E
Coolabah, Australia . **95 E4** 31 1 S 146 43 E
Cooladdi, Australia . . **95 D4** 26 37 S 145 23 E
Coolah, Australia . . . **95 E4** 31 48 S 149 41 E
Coolamon, Australia . **95 E4** 34 46 S 147 8 E
Coolgardie, Australia **93 F3** 30 55 S 121 8 E
Coolidge, U.S.A. **109 K8** 32 59N 111 31W
Coolidge Dam, U.S.A. **109 K8** 33 0N 110 20W
Cooloola △, Australia **95 D5** 26 13 S 153 2 E
Cooma, Australia . . . **95 F4** 36 12 S 149 8 E
Coon Rapids, U.S.A. . **112 C8** 45 9N 93 19W
Coonabarabran,
Australia . . . . **95 E4** 31 14 S 149 18 E
Coonamble, Australia **95 E4** 30 56 S 148 27 E
Coonana, Australia . . **93 F3** 31 0 S 123 0 E
Coondapoor, India . . **66 N9** 13 42N 74 40 E
Cooninie, L., Australia **95 D2** 26 4 S 139 59 E
Cooper, U.S.A. **113 J7** 33 23N 95 42W
Cooper Cr. →, Australia **95 D2** 28 29 S 137 46 E
Cooperstown, N. Dak.,
U.S.A. **112 B5** 47 27N 98 8W
Cooperstown, N.Y.,
U.S.A. **117 D10** 42 42N 74 56W
Coorabie, Australia . . **93 F5** 31 54 S 132 18 E
Coorong, The, Australia **95 F2** 35 50 S 139 20 E
Coorow, Australia . . . **93 E2** 29 53 S 116 2 E
Cooroy, Australia . . . **95 D5** 26 22 S 152 54 E
Coos Bay, U.S.A. . . . **108 E1** 43 22N 124 13W
Coosa →, U.S.A. . . . **115 J2** 32 30N 86 16W
Cootamundra, Australia **95 E4** 34 36 S 148 1 E
Cootehill, Ireland . . . **12 B4** 54 4N 7 5W
Copahue Paso,
Argentina . . . . . . **126 D1** 37 49 S 71 8W
Copainalá, Mexico . . **119 D6** 17 8N 93 11W
Copake Falls, U.S.A. . **117 D11** 42 7N 73 31W
Copalnic Mănăştur,
Romania . . . . **29 C8** 47 30N 23 41 E
Copán, Honduras . . . **120 D2** 14 50N 89 9W
Cope, U.S.A. **112 F3** 39 40N 102 51W
Cope, C., Spain **39 H3** 37 26N 1 28W
Copenhagen =
København, Denmark **11 J6** 55 41N 12 34 E
Copenhagen, U.S.A. . . **117 C9** 43 54N 75 41W
Copertino, Italy . . . . **43 B11** 40 16N 18 2 E
Copiapó, Chile . . . . . **126 B1** 27 30 S 70 20W
Copiapó →, Chile . . . **126 B1** 27 19 S 70 56W
Coplay, U.S.A. **117 F9** 40 44N 75 29W
Copp L., Canada . . . **102 A6** 60 14N 114 40W
Copparo, Italy . . . . . **41 D8** 44 54N 11 49 E
Coppename →,
Suriname **125 B7** 5 48N 55 55W
Copper Harbor, U.S.A. **114 B2** 47 28N 87 53W
Copper Queen,
Zimbabwe . . . . . . **87 F2** 17 29 S 29 18 E
Copperas Cove, U.S.A. **113 K6** 31 8N 97 54W
Copperbelt □, Zambia **87 E2** 13 15 S 27 30 E
Coppermine =
Kugluktuk, Canada **100 B8** 67 50N 115 5W
Coppermine →, Canada **100 B8** 67 49N 116 4W
Copperopolis, U.S.A. . **110 H6** 37 58N 120 38W
Copşa Mică, Romania . **29 D9** 46 7N 24 15 E
Coquet →, U.K. **14 B6** 55 20N 1 32W
Coquille, U.S.A. **108 E1** 43 11N 124 11W
Coquimbo, Chile . . . **126 C1** 30 0 S 71 20W
Coquimbo □, Chile . . **126 C1** 31 0 S 71 0W
Corabia, Romania . . . **29 G9** 43 48N 24 30 E
Coracora, Peru . . . . . **124 G4** 15 5 S 73 45W
Coraki, Australia . . . **95 D5** 28 59 S 153 17 E
Coral, U.S.A. **116 F5** 40 29N 79 10W
Coral Gables, U.S.A. . **115 N5** 25 45N 80 16W
Coral Harbour, Canada **101 B11** 64 8N 83 10W
Coral Sea, Pac. Oc. . . **96 J7** 15 0 S 150 0 E
Coral Springs, U.S.A. **115 M5** 26 16N 80 13W
Coraopolis, U.S.A. . . **116 F4** 40 31N 80 10W
Corato, Italy . . . . . . **43 A9** 41 9N 16 25 E
Corbeil-Essonnes,
France . . . . **19 D9** 48 36N 2 26 E
Corbie, France . . . . . **19 C9** 49 54N 2 30 E
Corbières, France . . . **20 F6** 42 55N 2 35 E
Corbigny, France . . . **19 E10** 47 16N 3 40 E
Corbin, U.S.A. **114 G3** 36 57N 84 6W
Corbones →, Spain . . **37 H5** 37 36N 5 39W
Corby, Romania . . . . **29 F13** 44 25N 28 0 E
Corby, U.K. **15 E7** 52 30N 0 41W
Corcaigh = Cork, Ireland **12 E3** 51 54N 8 29W
Corcoran, U.S.A. . . . **110 J7** 36 6N 119 33W
Corcovado △,
Costa Rica **120 E3** 8 33N 83 35W
Cordele, U.S.A. **115 K4** 31 58N 83 47W
Cordell, U.S.A. **113 H5** 35 17N 98 59W
Cordenòns, Italy . . . **41 C9** 45 59N 12 42 E
Cordes-sur-Ciel, France **20 D5** 44 5N 1 57 E
Córdoba, Argentina . . **126 C3** 31 20 S 64 10W
Córdoba, Mexico . . . **119 D5** 18 50N 97 0W
Córdoba, Spain **37 H6** 37 50N 4 50W
Córdoba □, Argentina **126 C3** 31 22 S 64 15W
Córdoba □, Spain . . . **37 G6** 38 5N 5 0W
Córdoba, Sierra de,
Argentina . . . . . . **126 C3** 31 10 S 64 25W
Cordon, Phil. . . . . . . **61 C4** 16 42N 121 32 E
Cordova, U.S.A. **100 B5** 60 33N 145 45W
Corella, Spain **38 C3** 42 7N 1 48W
Corella →, Australia . **94 B3** 19 34 S 140 47 E
Corfield, Australia . . **94 C3** 21 40 S 143 21 E
Corfu = Kérkira, Greece **49 A3** 39 38N 19 50 E
Corfu ✈ (CFU), Greece **46 B1** 39 35N 19 54 E
Corfu, Str. of, Greece . **49 A4** 39 34N 20 0 E
Corgo = O Corgo, Spain **36 C3** 42 56N 7 25W
Cori, Italy . . . . **42 A5** 41 39N 12 55 E
Coria, Spain **36 F4** 39 58N 6 33W
Coria del Río, Spain . **37 H4** 37 16N 6 3W
Corigliano Cálabro, Italy **43 C9** 39 36N 16 31 E

Coringa Is., Australia . . **94 B4** 16 58 S 149 58 E
Corinth = Kórinthos,
Greece . . . . **46 D4** 37 56N 22 55 E
Corinth, Miss., U.S.A. **115 H1** 34 56N 88 31W
Corinth, N.Y., U.S.A. . **117 C11** 43 15N 73 49W
Corinth, G. of =
Korinthiakòs Kólpos,
Greece . . . . **46 C4** 38 16N 22 30 E
Corinth Canal, Greece **46 D4** 37 58N 23 0 E
Corinto, Brazil . . . . . **125 G10** 18 20 S 44 30W
Corinto, Nic. **120 D2** 12 30N 87 10W
Cork, Ireland **12 E3** 51 54N 8 29W
Cork □, Ireland **12 E3** 51 57N 8 40W
Cork Harbour, Ireland **12 E3** 51 47N 8 16W
Corlay, France **18 D3** 48 20N 3 5W
Corleone, Italy . . . . . **42 E6** 37 49N 13 18 E
Corleto Perticara, Italy **43 B9** 40 23N 16 2 E
Çorlu, Turkey . . . . . **45 E11** 41 11N 27 49 E
Cormack L., Canada . **102 A4** 60 56N 121 37W
Cormòns, Italy . . . . . **41 C10** 45 58N 13 28 E
Cormorant, Canada . . **103 C8** 54 14N 100 35W
Cormorant L., Canada **103 C8** 54 15N 100 50W
Corn Is. = Maíz, Is. del,
Nic. **120 D3** 12 15N 83 4W
Cornalvo △, Spain . . **37 F4** 39 1N 6 13W
Cornélio Procópio,
Brazil . . . . **127 A5** 23 7 S 50 40W
Corner Brook, Canada **105 C8** 48 57N 57 58W
Corneşti, Moldova . . **29 C13** 47 21N 28 1 E
Corníglio, Italy . . . . **40 D7** 44 29N 10 5 E
Corning, Ark., U.S.A. . **113 G9** 36 25N 90 35W
Corning, Calif., U.S.A. **108 G2** 39 56N 122 11W
Corning, Iowa, U.S.A. **112 E7** 40 59N 94 44W
Corning, N.Y., U.S.A. **116 D7** 42 9N 77 3W
Corno Grande, Italy . **41 F10** 42 28N 13 34 E
Cornwall, Canada . . . **117 A10** 45 2N 74 44W
Cornwall, U.S.A. **117 F8** 40 17N 76 25W
Cornwall □, U.K. **15 G3** 50 26N 4 40W
Corny Pt., Australia . . **95 E2** 34 55 S 137 0 E
Coro, Venezuela **124 A5** 11 25N 69 41W
Coroatá, Brazil . . . . . **125 D10** 4 8 S 44 0W
Corocoro, Bolivia . . . **124 G5** 17 15 S 68 28W
Coroico, Bolivia . . . . **124 G5** 16 0 S 67 50W
Coromandel, N.Z. . . . **91 G5** 36 45 S 175 31 E
Coromandel Coast,
India . . . . **66 N12** 12 30N 81 0 E
Corona, Calif. U.S.A. . **111 M9** 33 53N 117 34W
Corona, N. Mex., U.S.A. **109 J11** 34 15N 105 36W
Coronach, Canada . . **103 D7** 49 7N 105 31W
Coronado, U.S.A. . . . **111 N9** 32 41N 117 11W
Coronado, B. de,
Costa Rica **120 E3** 9 0N 83 40W
Coronados, Is. los,
U.S.A. **111 N9** 32 25N 117 15W
Coronation, Canada . **102 C6** 52 5N 111 27W
Coronation Gulf,
Canada **100 B8** 68 25N 110 0W
Coronation I., Antarctica **5 C18** 60 45 S 46 0W
Coronation Is., Australia **92 B3** 14 57 S 124 55 E
Coronda, Argentina . . **126 C3** 31 58 S 60 56W
Coronel, Chile . . . . . **126 D1** 37 0 S 73 10W
Coronel Bogado,
Paraguay . . . . **126 B4** 27 11 S 56 18W
Coronel Dorrego,
Argentina . . . . . . **126 D3** 38 40 S 61 10W
Coronel Oviedo,
Paraguay . . . . **126 B4** 25 24 S 56 30W
Coronel Pringles,
Argentina . . . . . . **126 D3** 38 0 S 61 30W
Coronel Suárez,
Argentina . . . . . . **126 D3** 37 30 S 61 52W
Coronel Vidal,
Argentina . . . . . . **126 D4** 37 28 S 57 45W
Coropuna, Nevado, Peru **124 G4** 15 30 S 72 41W
Corowa, Australia . . . **95 F4** 35 58 S 146 21 E
Corozal, Belize **119 D7** 18 23N 88 23W
Corozal Pt., Trin. & Tob. **125 K15** 10 45N 61 37W
Corps, France . . . . . . **21 D9** 44 50N 5 56 E
Corpus, Argentina . . **127 B4** 27 10 S 55 30W
Corpus Christi, U.S.A. **113 M6** 27 47N 97 24W
Corpus Christi, L.,
U.S.A. **113 L6** 28 2N 97 52W
Corral de Almaguer,
Spain **36 F7** 39 45N 3 10W
Corralejo, Canary Is. . **48 F6** 28 43N 13 53W
Corraun Pen., Ireland **12 C2** 53 54N 9 54W
Corréggio, Italy . . . . **40 D7** 44 46N 10 47 E
Correntes, C. das,
Mozam. . . . . **89 C6** 24 6 S 35 34 E
Corrèze □, France . . . **20 C5** 45 20N 1 45 E
Corrèze →, France . . **20 C5** 45 10N 1 28 E
Corrib, L., Ireland . . . **12 C2** 53 27N 9 16W
Corridónia, Italy . . . **41 E10** 43 15N 13 30 E
Corrientes, Argentina **126 B4** 27 30 S 58 45W
Corrientes □, Argentina **126 B4** 28 0 S 57 0W
Corrientes →, Argentina **126 C4** 30 42 S 59 38W
Corrientes →, Peru . . **124 D4** 3 43 S 74 35W
Corrientes, C., Colombia **124 B3** 5 30N 77 34W
Corrientes, C., Cuba . **120 B3** 21 43N 84 30W
Corrientes, C., Mexico **118 C3** 20 25N 105 42W
Corrigan, U.S.A. **113 K7** 31 0N 94 52W
Corrigin, Australia . . **93 F2** 32 20 S 117 53 E
Corry, U.S.A. **116 E5** 41 55N 79 39W
Corse, France . . . . . . **21 F13** 42 14N 9 10 E
Corse □, France . . . . **21 G13** 42 0N 9 0 E
Corse, C., France . . . **21 E13** 43 1N 9 25 E
Corse-du-Sud □, France **21 G13** 41 45N 9 0 E
Corsica = Corse □,
France . . . . **21 G13** 42 0N 9 0 E
Corsicana, U.S.A. . . . **113 J6** 32 6N 96 28W
Corte, France . . . . . . **21 F13** 42 19N 9 11 E
Corte Pinto, Portugal **37 H3** 37 42N 7 29W
Cortegana, Spain . . . **37 H4** 37 52N 6 49W
Cortés, Mar de =
California, G. de,
Mexico **118 B2** 27 0N 111 0W
Cortez, U.S.A. **109 H9** 37 21N 108 35W
Cortina d'Ampezzo,
Italy . . . . **41 B9** 46 32N 12 8 E
Cortland, N.Y., U.S.A. **117 D8** 42 36N 76 11W
Cortland, Ohio, U.S.A. **116 E4** 41 20N 80 44W
Cortona, Italy . . . . . **41 E8** 43 16N 11 59 E
Corubal →,
Guinea-Biss. **82 C2** 11 57N 15 5W
Coruche, Portugal . . . **37 G2** 38 57N 8 30W
Çoruh →, Turkey . . . **35 K5** 41 38N 41 38 E
Çorum, Turkey . . . . **72 B6** 40 30N 34 57 E
Corumbá, Brazil . . . . **124 G7** 19 0 S 57 30W
Corund, Romania . . . **29 D10** 46 30N 25 13 E
Corunna = A Coruña,
Spain **36 B2** 43 20N 8 25W
Corvallis, U.S.A. . . . **108 D2** 44 34N 123 16W
Corvette, L. de la,
Canada **104 B5** 53 25N 74 3W
Corydon, U.S.A. **112 E8** 40 46N 93 19W

Cosamaloapan, Mexico **119 D5** 18 23N 95 50W
Cosenza, Italy . . . . . **43 C9** 39 18N 16 15 E
Coşereni, Romania . . **29 F11** 44 38N 26 35 E
Coshocton, U.S.A. . . . **116 F3** 40 16N 81 51W
Cosmo Newberry,
Australia . . . . **93 E3** 28 0 S 122 54 E
Cosne-Cours-sur-Loire,
France . . . . **19 E9** 47 24N 2 54 E
Coso Junction, U.S.A. **111 J9** 36 13N 117 44W
Coso Pk., U.S.A. **111 J9** 36 13N 117 44W
Cospeito, Spain **36 B3** 43 12N 7 34W
Cosquín, Argentina . . **126 C3** 31 15 S 64 30W
Cossato, Italy . . . . . **40 C5** 45 34N 8 10 E
Cossé-le-Vivien, France **18 E6** 47 57N 0 54W
Cosson →, France . . . **18 E8** 47 30N 1 15 E
Costa Blanca, Spain . **39 G4** 38 25N 0 10W
Costa Brava, Spain . . **38 D8** 41 30N 3 0 E
Costa del Sol, Spain . **37 J6** 36 30N 4 30W
Costa Dorada, Spain . **38 D6** 41 12N 1 15 E
Costa Mesa, U.S.A. . . **111 M9** 33 38N 117 55W
Costa Rica ■,
Cent. Amer. **120 E3** 10 0N 84 0W
Costa Smeralda, Italy **42 A2** 41 5N 9 35 E
Costeşti, Romania . . . **29 F9** 44 40N 24 53 E
Costigliole d'Asti, Italy **40 D5** 44 47N 8 11 E
Cosumnes →, U.S.A. **110 G5** 38 16N 121 26W
Coswig, Sachsen,
Germany . . . . **24 D9** 51 7N 13 34 E
Coswig, Sachsen-Anhalt,
Germany . . . . **24 D8** 51 53N 12 27 E
Cotabato, Phil. . . . . . **61 H6** 7 14N 124 15 E
Cotagaita, Bolivia . . **126 A2** 20 45 S 65 40W
Côte-d'Azur, France . **21 E11** 43 25N 7 10 E
Côte-d'Ivoire = Ivory
Coast ■, Africa . . . **82 D4** 7 30N 5 0W
Côte-d'Or □, France . **19 E11** 47 10N 4 50 E
Côte d'Or, France . . . **19 E11** 47 30N 4 50 E
Coteau des Prairies,
U.S.A. **112 C6** 45 20N 97 50W
Coteau du Missouri,
U.S.A. **112 B4** 47 0N 100 0W
Cotentin, France **18 C5** 49 15N 1 30W
Côtes-d'Armor □,
France **18 D4** 48 25N 2 40W
Côtes-de-Meuse, France **19 C12** 49 15N 5 22 E
Côtes-du-Nord = Côtes-
d'Armor □, France . **18 D4** 48 25N 2 40W
Cotiella, Spain . . . . . **38 C5** 42 31N 0 19 E
Cotillo, Canary Is. . . **48 F5** 28 41N 14 1W
Cotiujeni, Moldova . . **29 C13** 47 51N 28 33 E
Cotonou, Benin . . . . **83 D5** 6 20N 2 25 E
Cotopaxi, Ecuador . . **124 D3** 0 40 S 78 30W
Cotronei, Italy . . . . . **43 C9** 39 9N 16 47 E
Cotswold Hills, U.K. . **15 F5** 51 42N 2 10W
Cottage Grove, U.S.A. **108 E2** 43 48N 123 3W
Cottbus, Germany . . . **24 D10** 51 45N 14 20 E
Cottonwood, U.S.A. . **109 J7** 34 45N 112 1W
Cotulla, U.S.A. **113 L5** 28 26N 99 14W
Coubre, Pte. de la,
France **20 C2** 45 42N 1 15W
Couches, France . . . . **19 F11** 46 53N 4 30 E
Couço, Portugal **37 G2** 38 59N 8 17W
Coudersport, U.S.A. . **116 E6** 41 46N 78 1W
Couedic, C. du, Australia **95 F2** 36 5 S 136 40 E
Couéron, France **18 E5** 47 13N 1 44W
Couesnon →, France . **18 D5** 48 38N 1 32W
Couhé, France . . . . . **20 B4** 46 17N 0 11 E
Coulanges-sur-Yonne,
France . . . . **19 E10** 47 31N 3 33 E
Coulee City, U.S.A. . . **108 C4** 47 37N 119 17W
Coulman I., Antarctica **5 D11** 73 35 S 170 0 E
Coulommiers, France **19 D10** 48 50N 3 3 E
Coulon →, France . . . **21 E9** 43 51N 5 6 E
Coulonge →, Canada **104 C4** 45 52N 76 46W
Coulonges-sur-l'Autize,
France **20 B3** 46 29N 0 36W
Coulouieix-Chamiers,
France . . . . **20 C4** 45 11N 0 42 E
Coulterville, U.S.A. . . **110 H6** 37 43N 120 12W
Council, U.S.A. **108 D5** 44 44N 116 26W
Council Bluffs, U.S.A. **112 E7** 41 16N 95 52W
Council Grove, U.S.A. **112 F6** 38 40N 96 29W
Coupeville, U.S.A. . . **108 B4** 48 13N 122 41W
Courantyne →, S. Amer. **124 B7** 5 55N 57 5W
Courcelles, Belgium . **17 D4** 50 28N 4 22 E
Courchevel, France . . **21 C10** 45 25N 6 36 E
Courçon, France **20 B3** 46 15N 0 50W
Courmayeur, Italy . . **40 C3** 45 47N 6 58 E
Couronne, C., France **21 E9** 43 19N 5 3 E
Cours-la-Ville, France **19 F11** 46 7N 4 19 E
Coursan, France . . . . **20 E7** 43 14N 3 4 E
Courseulles-sur-Mer,
France **18 C6** 49 20N 0 29W
Courtenay, Canada . . **102 D4** 49 45N 125 0W
Courtenay, France . . . **19 D10** 48 2N 3 3 E
Courtland, U.S.A. . . . **110 G5** 38 20N 121 34W
Courtrai = Kortrijk,
Belgium . . . . **17 D3** 50 50N 3 17 E
Coushatta, U.S.A. . . . **113 J8** 32 1N 93 21W
Coutances, France . . **18 C5** 49 3N 1 28W
Couto de Magalhães,
Brazil . . . . **125 C9** ...
Coutras, France **20 C3** 45 3N 0 8W
Couts Crossing,
Australia . . . . **95 D5** 29 49 S 152 55 E
Couva, Trin. & Tob. . . **125 K15** 10 25N 61 27W
Couzin, Belgium . . . **17 D4** 50 3N 4 29 E
Covarrubias, Spain . . **36 C7** 42 4N 3 31W
Covasna, Romania . . **29 E11** 45 50N 26 10 E
Covasna □, Romania . **29 E11** 45 50N 26 0 E
Cove I., Canada **116 A3** 45 17N 81 44W
Coventry, U.K. **15 E6** 52 25N 1 28W
Covilhã, Portugal . . . **36 E3** 40 17N 7 31W
Covington, Ga., U.S.A. **115 J4** 33 36N 83 51W
Covington, Ky., U.S.A. **114 F3** 39 5N 84 31W
Covington, Okla., U.S.A. **113 G6** 36 18N 97 35W
Covington, Tenn., U.S.A. **113 H10** 35 34N 89 39W
Covington, Va., U.S.A. **114 G5** 37 47N 79 59W
Cowal, L., Australia . . **95 E4** 33 40 S 147 25 E
Cowan, L., Australia . **93 F3** 31 45 S 121 45 E
Cowan, L., Canada . . **103 C7** 54 0N 107 15W
Cowangie, Australia . **95 F3** 35 12 S 141 26 E
Cowansville, Canada . **117 A12** 45 14N 72 46W
Coward Springs,
Australia . . . . **95 D2** 29 24 S 136 49 E
Cowcowing Lakes,
Australia . . . . **93 F2** 30 55 S 117 20 E
Cowdenbeath, U.K. . . **13 E5** 56 7N 3 21W
Cowell, Australia . . . **95 E2** 33 39 S 136 56 E
Cowes, U.K. **15 G6** 50 45N 1 18W
Cowichan L., Canada . **110 B2** 48 53N 124 17W
Cowlitz →, U.S.A. . . . **110 D4** 46 5N 122 54W
Cowra, Australia . . . . **95 E4** 33 49 S 148 42 E
Cox, Australia . . . . . . **94 A3** 14 30 S 135 8 E
Coxilha Grande, Brazil **127 B5** 28 18 S 51 30W
Coxim, Brazil . . . . . . **125 G8** 18 30 S 54 55W
Cox's Bazar, Bangla. . **67 J17** 21 26N 91 59 E
Coyote Wells, U.S.A. . **111 N11** 32 44N 115 58W

Coyuca de Benítez,
Mexico **119 D4** 17 1N 100 8W
Coyuca de Catalan,
Mexico **118 D4** 18 18N 100 41W
Cozad, U.S.A. **112 E5** 40 52N 99 59W
Cozes, France **20 C3** 45 34N 0 49W
Cozumel, Mexico . . . **119 C7** 20 31N 86 55W
Cozumel, Isla, Mexico **119 C7** 20 30N 86 40W
Crab Hill, Barbados . . **121 g** 13 19N 59 38W
Cracow = Kraków,
Poland . . . . **31 H6** 50 4N 19 57 E
Cracow, Australia . . . **95 D5** 25 17 S 150 17 E
Cradle Mt.-Lake St.
Clair △, Australia . . **95 G4** 41 49 S 147 56 E
Cradock, Australia . . **95 E2** 32 6 S 138 31 E
Cradock, S. Africa . . **88 E4** 32 8 S 25 36 E
Craig, U.S.A. **108 F10** 40 31N 107 33W
Craigavon, U.K. **12 B5** 54 27N 6 23W
Craigmore, Zimbabwe **87 G3** 20 28 S 32 50 E
Craik, Canada **103 C7** 51 3N 105 49W
Crailsheim, Germany . **25 F6** 49 8N 10 5 E
Craiova, Romania . . . **29 F8** 44 21N 23 48 E
Cramsie, Australia . . **94 C3** 23 20 S 144 15 E
Cranberry L., U.S.A. . **117 B10** 44 11N 74 50W
Cranberry Portage,
Canada **103 C8** 54 35N 101 23W
Cranbrook, Australia . **93 F2** 34 18 S 117 33 E
Cranbrook, Canada . . **102 D5** 49 30N 115 46W
Crandon, U.S.A. **112 C10** 45 34N 88 54W
Crane, Oreg., U.S.A. . **108 E4** 43 25N 118 35W
Crane, Tex., U.S.A. . . **113 K3** 31 24N 102 21W
Cranston, U.S.A. **117 E13** 41 47N 71 26W
Craon, France **18 E6** 47 50N 0 58W
Craonne, France . . . . **19 C10** 49 27N 3 46 E
Craponne-sur-Arzon,
France . . . . **20 C7** 45 19N 3 51 E
Crasna, Romania . . . **29 D12** 46 32N 27 51 E
Crasna →, Romania . **28 C7** 47 44N 22 35 E
Crasnei, Munţii,
Romania . . . . **29 C8** 47 0N 23 20 E
Crater L., U.S.A. **108 E2** 42 56N 122 6W
Crater Lake △, U.S.A. **108 E2** 42 55N 122 10W
Craters of the Moon △,
U.S.A. **108 E7** 43 25N 113 30W
Cratéus, Brazil . . . . . **125 E10** 5 10 S 40 39W
Crati →, Italy . . . . . . **43 C9** 39 43N 16 31 E
Crato, Brazil . . . . . . **125 E11** 7 10 S 39 25W
Crato, Portugal **37 F3** 39 16N 7 39W
Craven, L., Canada . . **104 B4** 54 20N 76 56W
Crawford, U.S.A. . . . **112 D3** 42 41N 103 25W
Crawfordsville, U.S.A. **114 E2** 40 2N 86 54W
Crawley, U.K. **15 F7** 51 7N 0 11W
Crazy Mts., U.S.A. . . . **108 C8** 46 12N 110 20W
Crean L., Canada . . . **103 C7** 54 5N 106 9W
Crécy-en-Ponthieu,
France . . . . **19 B8** 50 15N 1 53 E
Crediton, Canada . . . **116 C3** 43 17N 81 33W
Crediton, U.K. **15 G4** 50 47N 3 40W
Cree →, Canada **103 B7** 58 57N 105 47W
Cree →, U.K. **13 G4** 54 55N 4 25W
Cree L., Canada **103 B7** 57 30N 106 30W
Creede, U.S.A. **109 H10** 37 51N 106 56W
Creekside, U.S.A. . . . **116 F5** 40 40N 79 11W
Creel, Mexico **118 B3** 27 45N 107 38W
Creemore, Canada . . **116 B4** 44 19N 80 6W
Creighton, Canada . . **103 C8** 54 45N 101 54W
Creighton, U.S.A. . . . **112 D6** 42 28N 97 54W
Creil, France . . . . . . **19 C9** 49 15N 2 29 E
Crema, Italy . . . . **40 C6** 45 22N 9 41 E
Cremona, Italy . . . . . **40 C7** 45 7N 10 2 E
Crepaja, Serbia & M. . **28 E5** 45 1N 20 38 E
Crépy, France . . . . . . **19 C10** 49 37N 3 32 E
Crépy-en-Valois, France **19 C9** 49 14N 2 54 E
Cres, Croatia . . . . . . **41 D11** 44 58N 14 25 E
Crescent City, U.S.A. . **108 F1** 41 45N 124 12W
Crescentino, Italy . . . **40 C5** 45 11N 8 6 E
Crespino, Argentina . . **126 C3** 32 2 S 60 19W
Cresson, U.S.A. **116 F6** 40 28N 78 36W
Crest, France . . . . . . **21 D9** 44 44N 5 2 E
Cresta, Mt., Phil. . . . . **61 C5** 17 17N 122 6 E
Crestline, Calif., U.S.A. **111 L9** 34 14N 117 18W
Crestline, Ohio, U.S.A. **116 F2** 40 47N 82 44W
Creston, Canada **102 D5** 49 10N 116 31W
Creston, Calif., U.S.A. **110 K6** 35 32N 120 33W
Creston, Iowa, U.S.A. **112 E7** 41 4N 94 22W
Crestview, Calif., U.S.A. **110 H8** 37 46N 118 58W
Crestview, Fla., U.S.A. **115 K2** 30 46N 86 34W
Crêt de la Neige, France **19 F12** 46 16N 5 58 E
Crete = Kríti, Greece . **49 D7** 35 15N 25 0 E
Crete, U.S.A. **112 E6** 40 38N 96 58W
Crete, Sea of, Greece . **47 E7** 36 0N 25 0 E
Créteil, France . . . . . **19 D9** 48 47N 2 28 E
Creus, C. de, Spain . . **38 C8** 42 20N 3 19 E
Creuse □, France . . . **19 F9** 46 10N 2 0 E
Creuse →, France . . . **20 B4** 47 0N 0 34 E
Creutzwald, France . . **19 C13** 49 12N 6 42 E
Creuzburg, Germany . **24 D6** 51 3N 10 14 E
Crèvecœur-le-Grand,
France . . . . **19 C9** 49 37N 2 5 E
Crevillente, Spain . . . **39 G4** 38 12N 0 48W
Crewe, U.K. **14 D5** 53 6N 2 26W
Crewkerne, U.K. **15 G5** 50 53N 2 48W
Crianlarich, U.K. . . . **13 E4** 56 24N 4 37W
Criciúma, Brazil . . . . **127 B6** 28 40 S 49 23W
Cricova, Moldova . . . **29 C13** 47 8N 28 52 E
Crieff, U.K. **13 E5** 56 22N 3 50W
Crikvenica, Croatia . . **41 C11** 45 11N 14 40 E
Crimea □, Ukraine . . **33 K8** 45 30N 33 10 E
Crimean Pen. =
Krymskyy Pivostriv,
Ukraine . . . . **33 K8** 45 0N 34 0 E
Crimmitschau, Germany **24 E8** 50 48N 12 24 E
Cristuru Secuiesc,
Romania . . . . **29 D10** 46 17N 25 2 E
Crişul Alb →, Romania **28 D6** 46 42N 21 17 E
Crişul Negru →,
Romania . . . . **28 D6** 46 42N 21 16 E
Crişul Repede →,
Romania . . . . **28 D5** 46 55N 20 59 E
Criuleni, Moldova . . **29 C13** 47 8N 28 19 E
Crivitz, Germany . . . **24 B7** 53 34N 11 39 E
Crna →, Macedonia . **44 E5** 41 33N 21 59 E
Crna Gora =
Montenegro □,
Serbia & M. . . . . . **44 D3** 42 40N 19 20 E
Crna Gora, Macedonia **44 D5** 42 10N 21 30 E
Crna Reka = Crna →,
Macedonia . . . . . . **44 E5** 41 33N 21 59 E
Crna Trava, Serbia & M. **44 D6** 42 49N 22 19 E
Crni Drim →,
Macedonia . . . . . . **44 E4** 41 17N 20 40 E
Crni Timok →,
Serbia & M. . . . . . **44 C6** 43 53N 22 15 E
Crnoljeva Planina,
Serbia & M. . . . . . **44 D5** 42 20N 21 0 E
Črnomelj, Slovenia . . **41 C12** 45 33N 15 10 E
Croagh Patrick, Ireland **12 C2** 53 46N 9 40W

Croatia ■, Europe . . . **41 C13** 45 20N 16 0 E
Crocker, Banjaran,
Malaysia . . . . **62 C5** 5 40N 116 30 E
Crockett, U.S.A. **113 K7** 31 19N 95 27W
Crocodile =
Krokodil →, Mozam. **89 D5** 25 14 S 32 18 E
Crocodile Is., Australia **94 A1** 12 3 S 134 58 E
Crocq, France . . . . . . **20 C6** 45 52N 2 21 E
Crodo, Italy . . . . **40 B5** 46 13N 8 19 E
Crohy Hd., Ireland . . **12 B3** 54 55N 8 26W
Croisette, C., France . **21 E9** 43 14N 5 22 E
Croisic, Pte. du, France **18 E4** 47 19N 2 31W
Croix, L. La, Canada . **104 C1** 48 20N 92 15W
Croker, C., Australia . **92 B5** 10 58 S 132 35 E
Croker, C., Canada . . **116 B4** 44 58N 80 59W
Croker I., Australia . . **92 B5** 11 12 S 132 32 E
Cromarty, U.K. **13 D4** 57 40N 4 2W
Cromer, U.K. . . . . . . **14 E9** 52 56N 1 17 E
Cromwell, N.Z. . . . . . **91 L2** 45 3 S 169 14 E
Cromwell, U.S.A. . . . **117 E12** 41 36N 72 39W
Cronat, France . . . . . **19 F10** 46 43N 3 40 E
Crook, U.K. **14 C6** 54 43N 1 45W
Crooked →, Canada . **102 C4** 54 50N 122 54W
Crooked →, U.S.A. . . **108 D3** 44 32N 121 16W
Crooked I., Bahamas . **121 B5** 22 50N 74 10W
Crooked Island Passage,
Bahamas **121 B5** 22 55N 74 35W
Crookston, Minn.,
U.S.A. **112 B6** 47 47N 96 37W
Crookston, Nebr., U.S.A. **112 D4** 42 56N 100 45W
Crookwell, Australia . **95 E4** 34 28 S 149 24 E
Cropane-Micone △,
Italy . . . . **43 D9** 38 31N 16 18 E
Crosby, U.K. **14 D4** 53 30N 3 3W
Crosby, N. Dak., U.S.A. **112 A3** 48 55N 103 18W
Crosby, Pa., U.S.A. . . **116 E6** 41 45N 78 23W
Crosbyton, U.S.A. . . . **113 J4** 33 40N 101 14W
Crosía, Italy . . . . **43 C9** 39 35N 16 45 E
Cross →, Nigeria . . . **83 E6** 4 42N 8 21 E
Cross City, U.S.A. . . . **115 L4** 29 38N 83 7W
Cross Fell, U.K. **14 C5** 54 43N 2 28W
Cross L., Canada **103 C9** 54 45N 97 30W
Cross Lake, Canada . . **103 C9** 54 37N 97 47W
Cross River □, Nigeria **83 D6** 6 0N 8 0 E
Cross River △, Nigeria **83 D6** 5 50N 9 50 E
Cross Sound, U.S.A. . **100 C6** 58 0N 135 0W
Crossett, U.S.A. **113 J9** 33 8N 91 58W
Crosshaven, Ireland . **12 E3** 51 47N 8 17W
Crossville, U.S.A. . . . **115 G3** 35 57N 85 2W
Croswell, U.S.A. **116 C2** 43 16N 82 37W
Croton-on-Hudson,
U.S.A. **117 E11** 41 12N 73 55W
Crotone, Italy . . . . . . **43 C10** 39 5N 17 8 E
Crow →, Canada . . . **102 B4** 59 41N 124 20W
Crow Agency, U.S.A. . **108 D10** 45 36N 107 28W
Crow Hd., Ireland . . . **12 E1** 51 35N 10 9W
Crowell, U.S.A. **113 J5** 33 59N 99 43W
Crowley, U.S.A. **113 K8** 30 13N 92 22W
Crowley, L., U.S.A. . . **110 H8** 37 35N 118 42W
Crown Point, Ind.,
U.S.A. **114 E2** 41 25N 87 22W
Crown Point, N.Y.,
U.S.A. **117 C11** 43 57N 73 26W
Crown Pt., Trin. & Tob. **125 J16** 11 18N 60 51W
Crownpoint, U.S.A. . . **109 J9** 35 41N 108 9W
Crows Landing, U.S.A. **110 H5** 37 23N 121 6W
Crows Nest, Australia **95 D5** 27 16 S 152 4 E
Crowsnest Pass, Canada **102 D6** 49 40N 114 40W
Croydon, Australia . . **94 B3** 18 13 S 142 14 E
Croydon □, U.K. . . . **15 F7** 51 22N 0 5W
Crozet, Is., Ind. Oc. . . **3 G12** 46 27 S 52 0 E
Crozon, France **18 D2** 48 15N 4 18W
Cruz, C., Cuba **120 C4** 19 50N 77 50W
Cruz Alta, Brazil . . . . **127 B5** 28 45 S 53 40W
Cruz Bay, U.S. Virgin Is. **121 e** 18 20N 64 48W
Cruz de Incio, Spain . **36 C3** 42 37N 7 21W
Cruz del Eje, Argentina **126 C3** 30 45 S 64 50W
Cruzeiro, Brazil . . . . **127 A7** 22 33 S 45 0W
Cruzeiro do Oeste,
Brazil . . . . **127 A5** 23 46 S 53 4W
Cruzeiro do Sul, Brazil **124 E4** 7 35 S 72 35W
Cry L., Canada **102 B3** 58 45N 129 0W
Crystal Bay, U.S.A. . . **110 F7** 39 15N 120 0W
Crystal Brook, Australia **95 E2** 33 21 S 138 12 E
Crystal City, U.S.A. . . **113 L5** 28 41N 99 50W
Crystal Falls, U.S.A. . **114 B1** 46 5N 88 20W
Crystal River, U.S.A. . **115 L4** 28 54N 82 35W
Crystal Springs, U.S.A. **113 K9** 31 59N 90 21W
Csenger, Hungary . . . **28 C7** 47 50N 22 41 E
Csongrád, Hungary . . **28 D5** 46 43N 20 12 E
Csongrád □, Hungary **28 D5** 46 32N 20 15 E
Csorna, Hungary . . . **28 C3** 47 38N 17 18 E
Csurgo, Hungary . . . **28 D2** 46 16N 17 9 E
Cu Lao Hon, Vietnam **65 G7** 10 54N 108 18 E
Cua Rao, Vietnam . . . **64 C5** 19 16N 104 27 E
Cuácua →, Mozam. . **87 F4** 17 54 S 37 0 E
Cuamato, Angola . . . **88 B2** 17 2 S 15 7 E
Cuamba, Mozam. . . . **87 E4** 14 45 S 36 22 E
Cuando →, Angola . . **85 H4** 17 30 S 23 15 E
Cuando Cubango □,
Angola . . . . **88 B3** 16 25 S 20 0 E
Cuangar, Angola . . . **88 B2** 17 36 S 18 39 E
Cuango = Kwango →,
Dem. Rep. of
the Congo . . . . . . **84 E3** 3 14 S 17 22 E
Cuanza →, Angola . . **84 F2** 9 21 S 13 9 E
Cuarto →, Argentina **126 C3** 33 25 S 63 2W
Cuatrociénegas, Mexico **118 B4** 26 59N 102 5W
Cuauhtémoc, Mexico . **118 B3** 28 25N 106 52W
Cuba, Portugal **37 G3** 38 10N 7 54W
Cuba, N. Mex., U.S.A. **109 J10** 36 1N 107 4W
Cuba, N.Y., U.S.A. . . **116 D6** 42 13N 78 17W
Cuba ■, W. Indies . . **120 B4** 22 0N 79 0W
Cubango →, Africa . . **88 B3** 18 50 S 22 25 E
Çubuk, Turkey . . . . . **72 B5** 40 14N 33 0 E
Cuc Phuong △, Vietnam **64 B5** 20 17N 105 38 E
Cuchumatanes, Sierra de
los, Guatemala . . . **120 C1** 15 35N 91 25W
Cuckfield, U.K. **15 F7** 51 1N 0 8W
Cucú, Brazil **124 C5** 1 12N 66 50W
Cucurpe, Mexico . . . **118 A2** 30 20N 110 43W
Cúcuta, Colombia . . . **124 B4** 7 54N 72 31W
Cudalbi, Romania . . . **29 E12** 45 46N 27 41 E
Cuddalore, India . . . **66 P11** 11 46N 79 45 E
Cuddapah, India . . . . **66 M11** 14 30N 78 47 E
Cuddapan, L., Australia **94 D3** 25 45 S 141 26 E
Cudillero, Spain **36 B4** 43 33N 6 9W
Cue, Australia . . . . . **93 E2** 27 25 S 117 54 E
Cuéllar, Spain **36 D6** 41 23N 4 21W
Cuenca, Ecuador . . . **124 D3** 2 50 S 79 9W
Cuenca, Spain **38 E2** 40 5N 2 10W
Cuenca □, Spain **38 F3** 40 0N 2 0W
Cuenca, Serranía de,
Spain **38 F3** 39 55N 1 50W
Cuenca Alta del
Manzanares △, Spain **36 E7** 40 40N 3 55W
Cuerdo del Pozo,
Embalse de la, Spain **38 D2** 41 51N 2 44W

Cuernavaca, Mexico ... 119 D5 18 55N 99 15W
Cuero, U.S.A. 113 L6 29 6N 97 17W
Cuers, France .... 21 E10 43 14N 6 5 E
Cueva de la Quebrada
del Toro △, Venezuela 121 D6 10 46N 69 3W
Cuevas del Almanzora,
Spain 39 H3 37 18N 1 58W
Cuevo, Bolivia .... 124 H6 20 15 S 63 30W
Cugir, Romania ...... 29 E8 45 48N 23 25 E
Cugnaux, France ..... 20 E5 43 32N 1 20 E
Cuhai-Bakony →,
Hungary .... 28 C2 47 35N 17 54 E
Cuiabá, Brazil .... 125 G7 15 30 S 56 0W
Cuiabá →, Brazil ..... 125 G7 17 5 S 56 36W
Cuijk, Neths. .... 17 C5 51 44N 5 50 E
Cuilco, Guatemala ... 120 C1 15 24N 91 58W
Cuillin Hills, U.K. ... 13 D2 57 13N 6 15W
Cuillin Sd., U.K. 13 D2 57 4N 6 20W
Cuiseaux, France ..... 19 F12 46 30N 5 22 E
Cuito →, Angola ..... 88 B3 18 1 S 20 48 E
Cuitzeo, L. de, Mexico . 118 D4 19 55N 101 5W
Cujmir, Romania ..... 28 F7 44 13N 22 57 E
Cukai, Malaysia ..... 65 K4 4 13N 103 25 E
Culbertson, U.S.A. ... 112 A2 48 9N 104 31W
Culcairn, Australia ... 95 F4 35 41 S 147 3 E
Culebra, Isla de,
Puerto Rico .... 121 d 18 19N 65 18W
Culebra, Sierra de la,
Spain 36 D4 41 55N 6 20W
Culfa, Azerbaijan .... 73 C11 38 57N 45 38 E
Culgoa →, Australia .. 95 D4 29 56 S 146 20 E
Culgoa Flood Plain △,
Australia .... 95 D4 28 58 S 147 5 E
Culiacán, Mexico 118 C3 24 50N 107 23W
Culiacán →, Mexico .. 118 C3 24 30N 107 42W
Culik, Indonesia ..... 63 J18 8 21 S 115 37 E
Culion, Phil. .... 61 F4 11 54N 119 58 E
Cúllar, Spain 37 H8 37 35N 2 34W
Cullarin Ra., Australia . 95 E4 34 30 S 149 30 E
Cullen, U.K. 13 D6 57 42N 2 49W
Cullen Pt., Australia .. 94 A3 11 57 S 141 54 E
Cullera, Spain 39 F4 39 9N 0 17W
Cullman, U.S.A. 115 H2 34 11N 86 51W
Cullompton, U.K. 15 G4 50 51N 3 24W
Culoz, France .... 21 C9 45 47N 5 46 E
Culpeper, U.S.A. 114 F7 38 30N 78 0W
Culuene →, Brazil ... 125 F8 12 56 S 52 51W
Culver, Pt., Australia . 93 F3 32 54 S 124 43 E
Culverden, N.Z. ..... 91 K4 42 47 S 172 49 E
Cumaná, Venezuela .. 124 A6 10 30N 64 5W
Cumaovası, Turkey ... 47 C9 38 15N 27 9 E
Cumberland, B.C.,
Canada 102 D4 49 40N 125 0W
Cumberland, Ont.,
Canada 117 A9 45 29N 75 24W
Cumberland, U.S.A. .. 114 F6 39 39N 78 46W
Cumberland →, U.S.A. 115 G2 36 15N 87 0W
Cumberland, L., U.S.A. 115 G3 36 57N 84 55W
Cumberland Gap △,
U.S.A. 115 G4 36 36N 83 40W
Cumberland Is.,
Australia .... 94 J7 20 35 S 149 10 E
Cumberland Island △,
U.S.A. 115 K5 30 12N 81 24W
Cumberland L., Canada 103 C8 54 3N 102 18W
Cumberland Pen.,
Canada 101 B13 67 0N 64 0W
Cumberland Plateau,
U.S.A. 115 H3 36 0N 85 0W
Cumberland Sd., Canada 101 B13 65 30N 66 0W
Cumbernauld, U.K. ... 13 F5 55 57N 3 58W
Cumborah, Australia . 95 D4 29 40 S 147 45 E
Cumbres de Majalca △,
Mexico 118 B3 28 52N 106 24W
Cumbres de
Monterrey △, Mexico 118 B4 25 40N 100 35W
Cumbres Mayores,
Spain 37 G4 38 4N 6 39W
Cumbria □, U.K. 14 C5 54 42N 2 52W
Cumbrian Mts., U.K. . 14 C5 54 30N 3 0W
Cumbum, India ...... 66 M11 15 40N 79 10 E
Cuminá →, Brazil .... 125 D7 1 30 S 56 0W
Cummings Mt., U.S.A. . 111 K8 35 2N 118 34W
Cummins, Australia .. 95 E2 34 16 S 135 43 E
Cumnock, Australia .. 95 E4 32 59 S 148 46 E
Cumnock, U.K. 13 F4 55 28N 4 17W
Cumpas, Mexico 118 B3 30 0N 109 48W
Cumplida, Pta.,
Canary Is. 48 F2 28 50N 17 48W
Çumra, Turkey ...... 72 D5 37 34N 32 45 E
Cunco, Chile .... 128 D2 38 55 S 72 2W
Cumcumén, Chile .... 126 C1 31 53 S 70 38W
Cunderdin, Australia . 93 F2 31 37 S 117 12 E
Cunene →, Angola ... 88 B1 17 20 S 11 50 E
Cúneo, Italy .... 40 D4 44 23N 7 32 E
Çüngüş, Turkey ..... 70 B3 38 13N 39 17 E
Cunillera, I. = Sa
Conillera, Spain .... 48 C7 38 59N 1 13 E
Cunlhat, France ..... 20 C7 45 38N 3 32 E
Cunnamulla, Australia . 95 D4 28 2 S 145 38 E
Cuorgnè, Italy ...... 40 C4 45 23N 7 39 E
Cupar, Canada 103 C8 50 57N 104 10W
Cupar, U.K. 13 E5 56 19N 3 1W
Cupcini, Moldova .... 29 B12 48 6N 27 23 E
Cupica, G. de, Colombia 124 B3 6 25N 77 30W
Čuprija, Serbia & M. .. 44 C5 43 57N 21 26 E
Curaçao, Neth. Ant. .. 121 D6 12 10N 69 0W
Curanilahue, Chile ... 126 D1 37 29 S 73 28W
Curaray →, Peru .... 124 D4 2 20 S 74 5W
Cure →, France ..... 19 E10 47 40N 3 41 E
Curepto, Chile ...... 126 D1 35 8 S 72 1W
Curiapo, Venezuela .. 124 B6 8 33N 61 5W
Curicó, Chile .... 126 C1 34 55 S 71 20W
Curinga, Italy .... 43 D9 38 49N 16 19 E
Curitiba, Brazil ..... 127 B6 25 20 S 49 10W
Curitibanos, Brazil ... 127 B5 27 18 S 50 36W
Currabubula, Australia . 95 E5 31 16 S 150 44 E
Currais Novos, Brazil . 125 E11 6 13 S 36 30W
Curralinho, Brazil ... 125 D9 1 45 S 49 46W
Currant, U.S.A. 108 G6 38 51N 115 32W
Currawinya △, Australia 95 D3 28 55 S 144 27 E
Current →, U.S.A. ... 113 G9 36 15N 90 55W
Currie, Australia ..... 95 F3 39 56 S 143 53 E
Currie, U.S.A. 108 F6 40 16N 114 45W
Curtea de Argeş,
Romania .... 29 E9 45 12N 24 42 E
Curtici, Romania .... 28 D6 46 21N 21 18 E
Curtis, U.S.A. 112 E4 40 38N 100 31W
Curtis Group, Australia 94 F4 39 30 S 146 37 E
Curtis I., Australia ... 94 C5 23 35 S 151 10 E
Curuá →, Brazil ..... 125 D7 1 30 S 56 0W
Curuápanema →, Brazil 125 D7 2 25 S 55 2W
Curuçá, Brazil ...... 125 D9 0 43 S 47 50W
Uruguaty, Paraguay .. 127 A4 24 31 S 55 42W
Curup, Indonesia .... 62 E2 4 26 S 102 13 E
Curuçú, Brazil ...... 125 D10 1 50 S 44 50W
Curuzú Cuatiá,
Argentina .... 126 B4 29 50 S 58 5W

Curvelo, Brazil ...... 125 G10 18 45 S 44 27W
Cushing, U.S.A. 113 H6 35 59N 96 46W
Cushing, Mt., Canada . 102 B3 57 35N 126 57W
Cusihuiriáchic, Mexico 118 B3 28 10N 106 50W
Cusna, Mte., Italy ... 40 D7 44 17N 10 23 E
Cusset, France ...... 19 F10 46 8N 3 28 E
Custer, U.S.A. 112 D3 43 46N 103 36W
Cut Bank, U.S.A. 108 B7 48 38N 112 20W
Cutchogue, U.S.A. ... 117 E12 41 1N 72 30W
Cuthbert, U.S.A. 115 K3 31 46N 84 48W
Cutler, U.S.A. 110 J7 36 31N 119 17W
Cutro, Italy .... 43 C9 39 2N 16 59 E
Cuttaburra →, Australia 95 D3 29 43 S 144 22 E
Cuttack, India ...... 67 J14 20 25N 85 57 E
Cuvier, C., Australia .. 93 D1 23 14 S 113 22 E
Cuvier I., N.Z. ...... 91 G5 36 27 S 175 50 E
Cuxhaven, Germany .. 24 B4 53 51N 8 41 E
Cuyahoga Falls, U.S.A. 116 E3 41 8N 81 29W
Cuyahoga Valley △,
U.S.A. 116 E3 41 15N 81 33W
Cuyapo, Phil. .... 61 D4 15 46N 120 40 E
Cuyo, Phil. .... 61 F4 10 50N 121 5 E
Cuyo East Pass, Phil. . 61 F4 11 0N 121 28 E
Cuyo West Pass, Phil. 61 F4 11 0N 120 55 E
Cuyuni →, Guyana ... 124 B7 6 23N 58 41W
Cuzco, Bolivia ...... 124 H5 20 0 S 66 50W
Cuzco, Peru .... 124 F4 13 32 S 72 0W
Čvrsnica, Bos.-H. ... 28 G2 43 36N 17 35 E
Cwmbran, U.K. 15 F4 51 39N 3 2W
Cyangugu, Rwanda .. 86 C2 2 29 S 28 54 E
Cybinka, Poland ..... 31 F1 52 12N 14 46 E
Cyclades = Kikládhes,
Greece .... 46 E6 37 0N 24 30 E
Cygnet, Australia .... 95 G4 43 8 S 147 1 E
Cynthiana, U.S.A. ... 114 F3 38 23N 84 18W
Cypress Hills, Canada 103 D7 49 40N 109 30W
Cypress Hills △, Canada 103 D7 49 40N 109 30W
Cyprus ■, Asia ...... 49 E12 35 0N 33 0 E
Cyrenaica, Libya .... 79 C10 27 0N 23 0 E
Czaplinek, Poland ... 30 E3 53 34N 16 14 E
Czar, Canada 103 C6 52 27N 110 50W
Czarna →, Łódzkie,
Poland .... 31 G6 51 18N 19 55 E
Czarna →,
Świętokrzyskie,
Poland .... 31 H8 50 28N 21 21 E
Czarna Białostocka,
Poland .... 31 E10 53 18N 23 17 E
Czarna Woda, Poland . 30 E5 53 51N 18 6 E
Czarne, Poland ...... 30 E3 53 42N 16 58 E
Czarnków, Poland ... 31 F3 52 55N 16 38 E
Czech Rep. ■, Europe 26 B8 50 0N 15 0 E
Czechowice-Dziedzice,
Poland .... 31 J5 49 54N 18 59 E
Czempiń, Poland .... 31 F3 52 9N 16 43 E
Czeremcha, Poland .. 31 F10 52 31N 23 21 E
Czerniejewo, Poland . 31 F4 52 26N 17 30 E
Czersk, Poland ...... 30 E4 53 46N 17 58 E
Czerwieńsk, Poland .. 31 F2 52 1N 15 23 E
Czerwionka-Leszczyny,
Poland .... 31 H5 50 7N 18 37 E
Częstochowa, Poland . 31 H6 50 49N 19 7 E
Człopa, Poland ...... 31 E3 53 6N 16 6 E
Człuchów, Poland ... 30 E4 53 41N 17 22 E
Czyżew-Osada, Poland 31 F9 52 48N 22 19 E

D

Da →, Vietnam ...... 58 G5 21 15N 105 20 E
Da Hinggan Ling, China 60 B7 48 0N 121 0 E
Da Lat, Vietnam ..... 65 G7 11 56N 108 25 E
Da Nang, Vietnam ... 64 D7 16 4N 108 13 E
Da Qaidam, China ... 60 C4 37 50N 95 15 E
Da Yunhe →, China .. 57 G11 34 25N 120 5 E
Da'an, China .... 57 B13 45 30N 124 7 E
Daan Viljoen △,
Namibia .... 88 C2 22 2 S 16 45 E
Dab'a, Ras el, Egypt .. 80 H6 31 3N 28 31 E
Daba Shan, China ... 58 B7 32 0N 109 0 E
Dabai, Nigeria ...... 83 C6 11 25N 5 15 E
Dabakala, Ivory C. ... 82 D4 8 15N 4 20W
Dabas, Hungary ..... 28 C4 47 11N 19 19 E
Dabat, Ethiopia ..... 81 E4 12 58N 37 41 E
Dabbagh, Jabal,
Si. Arabia .... 70 E2 27 52N 35 45 E
Dabhoi, India .... 68 H5 22 10N 73 20 E
Dąbie, Poland .... 31 F5 52 5N 18 50 E
Dabie Shan, China ... 59 B10 31 20N 115 20 E
Dabilda, Cameroon .. 83 C7 12 45N 14 35 E
Dabnou, Niger ...... 83 C6 14 10N 5 22 E
Dabo = Pasirkuning,
Indonesia .... 62 E2 0 30 S 104 33 E
Dabola, Guinea 82 C2 10 50N 11 5W
Dabou, Ivory C. 82 D4 5 20N 4 23W
Daboya, Ghana 83 D4 9 30N 1 20W
Dabravolya, Belarus . 31 F10 52 55N 23 59 E
Dąbrowa Białostocka,
Poland .... 30 E10 53 40N 23 21 E
Dąbrowa Górnicza,
Poland .... 31 H6 50 15N 19 10 E
Dąbrowa Tarnowska,
Poland .... 31 H7 50 10N 20 59 E
Dabu, China .... 59 E11 24 22N 116 41 E
Dabung, Malaysia ... 65 K4 5 23N 102 1 E
Dabus →, Ethiopia .. 81 E4 10 48N 35 10 E
Dacato →, Ethiopia .. 81 F5 7 25N 42 40 E
Dacca = Dhaka, Bangla. 69 H14 23 43N 90 26 E
Dacca = Dhaka □,
Bangla. .... 69 G14 24 25N 90 25 E
Dachau, Germany ... 25 G7 48 15N 11 26 E
Dachstein, Hoher,
Austria .... 26 D6 47 28N 13 35 E
Dačice, Czech Rep. .. 26 B8 49 5N 15 26 E
Dadanawa, Guyana .. 124 C7 2 50N 59 30W
Daday, Turkey ...... 72 B5 41 28N 33 27 E
Dade City, U.S.A. 115 L4 28 22N 82 11W
Dadhar, Pakistan .... 68 E2 29 28N 67 39 E
Dadiya, Nigeria ..... 83 D7 9 35N 11 24 E
Dadra & Nagar
Haveli □, India .... 66 J8 20 5N 73 0 E
Dadri = Charkhi Dadri,
India .... 68 E7 28 37N 76 17 E
Dadu, Pakistan ...... 68 F2 26 45N 67 45 E
Dadu He →, China ... 58 C5 29 31N 103 46 E
Daet, Phil. .... 61 D5 14 2N 122 55 E
Dafang, China ...... 58 D5 27 9N 105 39 E
Dağ, Turkey .... 47 D12 37 12N 30 31 E
Dagana, Senegal 82 B1 16 30N 15 35W
Dagash, Sudan ...... 80 D3 19 19N 33 25 E
Dagestan □, Russia .. 35 J8 42 30N 47 0 E
Dagestanskiye Ogni,
Russia .... 35 J9 42 6N 48 12 E
Daggett, U.S.A. 111 L10 34 52N 116 52W
Daghestan Republic =
Dagestan □, Russia . 35 J8 42 30N 47 0 E

Daghfeli, Sudan ..... 80 D3 19 18N 32 40 E
Dağlıq Qarabağ =
Nagorno-Karabakh □,
Azerbaijan .... 70 B5 39 55N 46 45 E
Dago = Hiiumaa,
Estonia .... 9 G20 58 50N 22 45 E
Dagu, China .... 57 E9 38 59N 117 40 E
Dagupan, Phil. ...... 61 C4 16 3N 120 20 E
Daguragu, Australia .. 92 C5 17 33 S 130 30 E
Dahab, Egypt .... 80 B3 28 31N 34 31 E
Dahlak △, Eritrea .... 81 D5 15 35N 40 1 E
Dahlak Kebir, Eritrea . 81 D5 15 50N 40 10 E
Dahlenburg, Germany 24 B6 53 11N 10 44 E
Dahlonega, U.S.A. ... 115 H4 34 32N 83 59W
Dahme, Germany .... 24 D9 51 52N 13 25 E
Dahod, India .... 68 H6 22 50N 74 15 E
Dahong Shan, China . 59 B9 31 25N 113 0 E
Dahra, Senegal 82 B1 15 22N 15 30W
Dahshûr, Egypt ..... 80 J7 29 55N 31 14 E
Dahûk, Iraq .... 70 B3 36 50N 43 1 E
Dai Hao, Vietnam ... 64 C6 18 1N 106 25 E
Dai-Sen, Japan ...... 55 G6 35 22N 133 32 E
Dai Shan, China ..... 59 B14 30 25N 122 10 E
Dai Xian, China ..... 56 E7 39 4N 112 58 E
Daicheng, China .... 56 E9 38 42N 116 38 E
Daimiel, Spain 37 F7 39 5N 3 35W
Daingean, Ireland ... 12 C4 53 18N 7 17W
Dainkog, China ..... 58 A1 32 30N 97 58 E
Daintree, Australia .. 94 B4 16 20 S 145 20 E
Daintree △, Australia . 94 B4 16 8 S 145 2 E
Daiō-Misaki, Japan .. 55 G8 34 15N 136 45 E
Dair, J. ed, Sudan ... 81 E3 12 27N 30 42 E
Dairût, Egypt .... 80 B3 27 34N 30 43 E
Daisen-Oki △, Japan . 55 G6 35 20N 133 34 E
Daisetsu-Zan, Japan . 54 C11 43 30N 142 57 E
Daisetsu-Zan △, Japan 54 C11 43 30N 142 55 E
Dajarra, Australia ... 94 C2 21 42 S 139 30 E
Dajin Chuan →, China 58 B3 31 16N 101 59 E
Dak Dam, Cambodia . 64 F6 12 20N 107 21 E
Dak Nhe, Vietnam ... 64 E6 15 28N 107 48 E
Dak Pek, Vietnam ... 64 E6 15 4N 107 44 E
Dak Song, Vietnam .. 65 F6 12 19N 107 35 E
Dak Sui, Vietnam .... 64 E6 14 55N 107 43 E
Dakar, Senegal 82 C1 14 34N 17 29W
Dakhla, W. Sahara ... 78 D2 23 50N 15 53W
Dakhla, El Wâhât el-,
Egypt .... 80 B2 25 30N 28 50 E
Dakingari, Nigeria ... 83 C5 11 37N 4 1 E
Dakor, India .... 68 H5 22 45N 73 11 E
Dakoro, Niger ...... 83 C6 14 31N 6 46 E
Dakota City, U.S.A. .. 112 D6 42 25N 96 25W
Đakovica, Serbia & M. 44 D4 42 22N 20 26 E
Đakovo, Croatia ..... 28 E3 45 19N 18 24 E
Dalaba, Guinea 82 C2 10 47N 12 12W
Dalachi, China ...... 56 F3 36 48N 105 0 E
Dalai Nur, China .... 56 C9 43 20N 116 45 E
Dālakī, Iran .... 71 D6 29 26N 51 17 E
Dalälven →, Sweden . 10 D10 60 12N 16 43 E
Dalaman, Turkey .... 47 E10 36 48N 28 47 E
Dalaman →, Turkey . 47 E10 36 41N 28 43 E
Dalandzadgad,
Mongolia .... 56 C3 43 27N 104 30 E
Dalap-Uliga-Darrit,
Marshall Is. .... 96 G9 7 7N 171 24 E
Dalarna, Sweden .... 10 D8 61 0N 14 0 E
Dalarnas län □, Sweden 10 D8 61 0N 14 15 E
Dālbandīn, Pakistan . 66 E4 29 0N 64 23 E
Dalbeattie, U.K. 13 G5 54 56N 3 50W
Dalbeg, Australia .... 94 C4 20 16 S 147 18 E
Dalbosjön, Sweden .. 11 F6 58 40N 12 45 E
Dalby, Australia ..... 95 D5 27 10 S 151 17 E
Dalby, Sweden ...... 11 J7 55 40N 13 22 E
Dalby Söderskog △,
Sweden .... 11 J7 55 41N 13 21 E
Dale City, U.S.A. 114 F7 38 38N 77 18W
Dale Hollow L., U.S.A. 115 G3 36 32N 85 27W
Dalga, Egypt .... 80 B3 27 39N 30 41 E
Dalgán, Iran .... 71 E8 27 31N 59 19 E
Dalhart, U.S.A. 113 G3 36 4N 102 31W
Dalhousie, Canada ... 105 C6 48 5N 66 26W
Dalhousie, India .... 68 C6 32 38N 75 58 E
Dali, Shaanxi, China . 56 G5 34 48N 109 58 E
Dali, Yunnan, China . 58 E3 25 40N 100 10 E
Dalian, China .... 57 E11 38 50N 121 40 E
Daliang Shan, China . 58 D4 28 0N 102 45 E
Daling He →, China . 57 D11 40 55N 121 40 E
Dāliyat el Karmel, Israel 74 C4 32 43N 35 2 E
Dalj, Croatia .... 28 E3 45 29N 18 59 E
Dalkeith, U.K. 13 F5 55 54N 3 4W
Dallas, Oreg., U.S.A. . 108 D2 44 55N 123 19W
Dallas, Tex., U.S.A. .. 113 J6 32 47N 96 49W
Dalli, Ethiopia ...... 81 E5 14 14N 40 17 E
Dalmā, U.A.E. ...... 71 E7 24 30N 52 20 E
Dalmacija, Croatia .. 41 E13 43 20N 17 0 E
Dalmas, L., Canada .. 105 B5 53 30N 71 50W
Dalmatia = Dalmacija,
Croatia .... 41 E13 43 20N 17 0 E
Dalmau, India ...... 69 F9 26 4N 81 2 E
Dalmellington, U.K. .. 13 F4 55 19N 4 23W
Dalnegorsk, Russia .. 53 E14 44 32N 135 33 E
Dalnerechensk, Russia 53 E14 45 50N 133 40 E
Dalnevostochnyy □,
Russia .... 53 C14 67 0N 140 0 E
Daloa, Ivory C. 82 D3 7 0N 6 30W
Dalou Shan, China .. 58 C6 28 15N 107 0 E
Dalry, U.K. 13 F4 55 42N 4 43W
Dalrymple, L., Australia 94 C4 20 40 S 147 0 E
Dalrymple, Mt.,
Australia .... 94 K6 21 1 S 148 39 E
Dals Långed, Sweden . 11 F6 58 52N 12 19 E
Dalsjöfors, Sweden .. 11 G7 57 46N 13 5 E
Dalsland, Sweden ... 11 F6 58 50N 12 15 E
Daltenganj, India .... 69 H11 24 0N 84 4 E
Dalton, Ga., U.S.A. .. 115 H3 34 46N 84 58W
Dalton, Mass., U.S.A. 117 D11 42 28N 73 11W
Dalton, Nebr., U.S.A. 112 E3 41 25N 102 58W
Dalton-in-Furness, U.K. 14 C4 54 10N 3 11W
Dalupiri I., Phil. ..... 61 B4 19 5N 121 12 E
Dalvík, Iceland 8 D4 65 58N 18 32W
Dálvvadis = Jokkmokk,
Sweden .... 8 C18 66 35N 19 50 E
Dalwallinu, Australia . 93 F2 30 17 S 116 40 E
Daly →, Australia ... 92 B5 13 35 S 130 19 E
Daly City, U.S.A. 110 H4 37 42N 122 28W
Daly L., Canada 103 B7 56 32N 105 39W
Daly River, Australia . 92 B5 13 46 S 130 42 E
Daly Waters, Australia 94 B1 16 15 S 133 24 E
Dalyan, Turkey ..... 47 E10 36 48N 28 39 E
Dam Doi, Vietnam ... 65 H5 8 50N 105 12 E
Dam Ha, Vietnam ... 64 B6 21 21N 107 36 E
Damachova, Belarus . 31 G10 51 45N 23 36 E
Daman, India .... 66 J8 20 25N 72 57 E
Dámaneh, Iran ...... 71 C6 33 1N 50 29 E
Damanhûr, Egypt ... 80 H7 31 0N 30 30 E
Damant L., Canada .. 103 A7 61 45N 105 5W
Damanzhuang, China 56 E9 38 5N 116 35 E

Damar, Indonesia .... 63 F7 7 7 S 128 40 E
Damaraland, Namibia 88 C2 20 0 S 15 0 E
Damascus = Dimashq,
Syria .... 74 B5 33 30N 36 18 E
Damaturu, Nigeria ... 83 C7 11 45N 11 55 E
Dāmāvand, Iran ..... 71 C7 35 47N 52 0 E
Dāmāvand, Qolleh-ye,
Iran .... 71 C7 35 56N 52 10 E
Damba, Angola ...... 84 F3 6 44 S 15 20 E
Dâmbovița □, Romania 29 F10 45 0N 25 30 E
Dâmbovița →, Romania 29 F11 44 12N 26 26 E
Dâmbovnic →,
Romania .... 29 F9 44 28N 25 18 E
Dame Marie, Haiti ... 121 C5 18 36N 74 26W
Dâmghān, Iran ...... 71 B7 36 10N 54 17 E
Dămienesti, Romania 29 D11 46 44N 26 59 E
Damietta = Dumyât,
Egypt .... 80 H7 31 24N 31 48 E
Daming, China ...... 56 F8 36 15N 115 6 E
Damīr Qābū, Syria ... 70 B4 36 58N 41 51 E
Dammam = Ad
Dammām, Si. Arabia 71 E6 26 20N 50 5 E
Dammarie-les-Lys,
France .... 19 D9 48 31N 2 39 E
Dammartin-en-Goële,
France .... 19 C9 49 3N 2 41 E
Damme, Germany ... 24 C4 52 32N 8 11 E
Damodar →, India ... 69 H12 23 17N 87 35 E
Damoh, India .... 69 H8 23 50N 79 28 E
Dampier, Australia .. 92 D2 20 41 S 116 42 E
Dampier, Selat,
Indonesia .... 63 E8 0 40 S 131 0 E
Dampier Arch.,
Australia .... 92 D2 20 38 S 116 32 E
Damrei, Chuor Phnum,
Cambodia .... 65 G4 11 30N 103 0 E
Damville, France .... 18 D8 48 51N 1 5 E
Damvillers, France .. 19 C12 49 20N 5 21 E
Dan Xian, China .... 64 C7 19 31N 109 33 E
Dana, Indonesia ..... 63 F6 11 0 S 122 52 E
Dana, L., Canada 104 B4 50 53N 77 20W
Dana, Mt., U.S.A. ... 110 H7 37 54N 119 12W
Danakil Desert,
Ethiopia .... 81 E5 12 45N 41 0 E
Danané, Ivory C. 82 D3 7 16N 8 9W
Danao, Phil. .... 61 F6 10 31N 124 1 E
Danau Poso, Indonesia 63 E6 1 52 S 120 35 E
Danba, China .... 58 B3 30 54N 101 48 E
Danbury, U.S.A. 117 E11 41 24N 73 28W
Danby L., U.S.A. 109 J6 34 13N 115 5W
Dand, Afghan. ...... 68 D1 31 28N 65 32 E
Dande →, Ethiopia .. 81 F4 6 39N 38 31 E
Dandeldhura, Nepal . 69 E9 29 20N 80 35 E
Dandeli, India ...... 66 M9 15 5N 74 30 E
Dandenong, Australia 95 F4 38 0 S 145 15 E
Dandîl, Egypt ...... 80 J7 29 10N 31 2 E
Dandong, China .... 57 D13 40 10N 124 20 E
Danfeng, China ..... 56 H6 33 45N 110 25 E
Dangan Liedao, China 59 F10 22 15N 114 25 E
Dangé-St-Romain,
France .... 20 B4 46 56N 0 36 E
Dângeni, Romania .. 29 C11 47 51N 26 58 E
Danger Is. = Pukapuka,
Cook Is. .... 97 J11 10 53 S 165 49W
Danger Pt., S. Africa . 88 E2 34 40 S 19 17 E
Danginpuri, Indonesia 63 K18 8 40 S 115 13 E
Dangla, Ethiopia .... 81 E4 11 18N 36 56 E
Dangla Shan = Tanggula
Shan, China .... 60 C4 32 40N 92 10 E
Dangora, Nigeria .... 83 C6 11 30N 8 7 E
Dangrek, Phnom,
Thailand .... 64 E5 14 15N 105 0 E
Dangriga, Belize 119 D7 17 0N 88 13W
Dangshan, China .... 56 G9 34 27N 116 22 E
Dangtu, China ...... 59 B12 31 32N 118 25 E
Dangyang, China .... 59 B8 30 52N 111 44 E
Dani, Burkina Faso .. 83 C4 13 43N 0 10W
Daniel, U.S.A. 108 E8 42 52N 110 4W
Daniel's Harbour,
Canada 105 B8 50 13N 57 35W
Danielskuil, S. Africa . 88 D3 28 11 S 23 33 E
Danielson, U.S.A. ... 117 E13 41 48N 71 53W
Danilov, Russia ..... 32 C11 58 16N 40 13 E
Danilovgrad,
Serbia & M. .... 44 D3 42 38N 19 4 E
Danilovka, Russia ... 34 E7 50 25N 44 12 E
Daning, China ...... 56 F6 36 28N 110 45 E
Danja, Nigeria ...... 83 C6 11 21N 7 30 E
Danjiangkou, China .. 59 A8 32 31N 111 30 E
Danjiangkou Shuiku,
China .... 59 A8 32 33N 111 30 E
Dank, Oman .... 71 F8 23 33N 56 16 E
Dankalwa, Nigeria ... 83 C7 11 52N 12 12 E
Dankama, Nigeria ... 83 C6 13 20N 7 44 E
Dankhar Gompa, India 66 C11 32 10N 78 10 E
Dankov, Russia ..... 32 F10 53 20N 39 5 E
Danleng, China ..... 58 B4 30 1N 103 31 E
Danlí, Honduras 120 D2 14 4N 86 35W
Dannemora, U.S.A. .. 117 B11 44 43N 73 44W
Dannenberg, Germany 24 B7 53 6N 11 5 E
Dannevirke, N.Z. .... 91 J6 40 12 S 176 8 E
Dannhauser, S. Africa 89 D5 28 0 S 30 3 E
Dansville, U.S.A. 116 D7 42 34N 77 42W
Danta, India .... 68 G5 24 11N 72 46 E
Dantan, India .... 69 J12 21 57N 87 20 E
Danube = Dunărea →,
Europe .... 29 E14 45 20N 29 40 E
Danvers, U.S.A. 117 D14 42 34N 70 56W
Danville, Ill., U.S.A. . 114 E2 40 8N 87 37W
Danville, Ky., U.S.A. . 114 G3 37 39N 84 46W
Danville, Pa., U.S.A. . 117 F8 40 58N 76 37W
Danville, Va., U.S.A. . 115 G6 36 36N 79 23W
Danville, Vt., U.S.A. . 117 B12 44 25N 72 9W
Danyang, China ..... 59 B12 32 0N 119 31 E
Danzhai, China ..... 58 D6 26 11N 107 48 E
Danzig = Gdańsk,
Poland .... 30 D5 54 22N 18 40 E
Dão →, Portugal 36 E2 40 20N 8 11W
Dao Xian, China .... 59 E8 25 36N 111 31 E
Daokro, Ivory C. 82 D4 7 10N 3 58W
Daora, Togo .... 83 D5 9 35N 1 16 E
Dapchi, Nigeria ..... 83 C7 12 30N 11 31 E
Dapitan, Phil. .... 61 G5 8 39N 123 25 E
Daqing Shan, China .. 56 D6 40 40N 111 0 E
Daqu Shan, China ... 59 B14 30 25N 122 20 E
Dar Banda, Africa ... 76 F6 8 0N 23 0 E
Dar el Beida =
Casablanca, Morocco 78 B4 33 36N 7 36W
Dar es Salaam, Tanzania 86 D4 6 50 S 39 12 E
Dar Mazār, Iran ..... 71 D8 29 14N 57 20 E
Dar'ā, Syria .... 74 C5 32 36N 36 7 E
Dar'ā □, Syria ...... 74 C5 32 55N 36 10 E
Dārāb, Iran .... 71 D7 28 50N 54 30 E
Daraban, Pakistan ... 68 D4 31 44N 70 20 E

Darabani, Romania .. 29 B11 48 10N 26 39 E
Daraina, Madag. .... 89 A8 13 12 S 49 40 E
Daraj, Libya .... 79 B8 30 10N 10 28 E
Dārān, Iran .... 71 C6 32 59N 50 24 E
Daravica, Serbia & M. 44 D4 42 32N 20 8 E
Daraw, Egypt .... 80 C3 24 22N 32 51 E
Dārayyā, Syria ...... 74 B5 33 28N 36 15 E
Darazo, Nigeria ..... 83 C7 11 1N 10 24 E
Darband, Pakistan ... 68 B5 34 20N 72 50 E
Darband, Kūh-e, Iran 71 D8 31 34N 57 8 E
Darbhanga, India ... 69 F11 26 15N 85 55 E
D'Arcy, Canada 102 C4 50 27N 122 35W
Darda, Croatia ...... 28 E3 45 40N 18 41 E
Dardanelle, Ark., U.S.A. 113 H8 35 13N 93 9W
Dardanelle, Calif.,
U.S.A. 110 G7 38 20N 119 50W
Dardanelles =
Çanakkale Boğazı,
Turkey .... 45 F10 40 17N 26 32 E
Dare →, Ethiopia ... 81 F5 7 20N 42 11 E
Darende, Turkey .... 72 C7 38 31N 37 30 E
Dārestān, Iran ...... 71 D8 29 9N 58 42 E
Darfo, Italy .... 40 C7 45 53N 10 11 E
Dârfûr, Sudan ...... 79 F10 13 40N 24 0 E
Dargai, Pakistan .... 68 B4 34 25N 71 55 E
Dargan Ata,
Turkmenistan ..... 52 E7 40 29N 62 10 E
Dargaville, N.Z. ..... 91 F4 35 57 S 173 52 E
Darhan, Mongolia ... 60 B5 49 37N 106 21 E
Darhan Muminggan
Lianheqi, China .... 56 D6 41 40N 110 28 E
Dari, Sudan .... 81 F3 5 48N 30 26 E
Darica, Turkey ...... 45 F13 40 45N 29 23 E
Darién △, Panama ... 120 E4 7 36N 77 57W
Darién, G. del,
Colombia 124 B3 9 0N 77 0W
Dariganga = Ovoot,
Mongolia .... 56 B7 45 21N 113 45 E
Darinskoye, Kazakhstan 34 E10 51 20N 51 44 E
Darjeeling = Darjiling,
India .... 69 F13 27 3N 88 18 E
Darjiling, India ...... 69 F13 27 3N 88 18 E
Darkan, Australia ... 93 F2 33 20 S 116 43 E
Darkhana, Pakistan . 68 D5 30 39N 72 11 E
Darkhazīneh, Iran ... 71 D6 31 54N 48 39 E
Darkot Pass, Pakistan 69 A5 36 45N 73 26 E
Darling →, Australia . 95 E3 34 4 S 141 54 E
Darling Downs,
Australia .... 95 D5 27 30 S 150 30 E
Darling Ra., Australia . 93 F2 32 30 S 116 0 E
Darlington, U.K. 14 C6 54 32N 1 33W
Darlington, U.S.A. .. 115 H6 34 18N 79 52W
Darlington, L., S. Africa 88 E4 33 10 S 25 9 E
Darlot, L., Australia . 93 E3 27 48 S 121 35 E
Darłowo, Poland .... 30 D3 54 25N 16 25 E
Dărmănești, Bacău,
Romania .... 29 D11 46 21N 26 33 E
Dărmănești, Suceava,
Romania .... 29 C11 47 44N 26 9 E
Darmstadt, Germany 25 F4 49 51N 8 39 E
Darnah, Libya ...... 79 B10 32 45N 22 45 E
Darnall, S. Africa ... 89 D5 29 23 S 31 18 E
Darney, France ..... 19 D13 48 5N 6 2 E
Darnley, C., Antarctica 5 C6 68 0 S 69 0 E
Darnley B., Canada .. 100 B7 69 30N 123 30W
Daroca, Spain 38 D3 41 9N 1 25W
Darou-Mousti, Senegal 82 B1 15 3N 16 3W
Darr →, Australia ... 94 C3 23 39 S 143 50 E
Darra Pezu, Pakistan 68 C4 32 19N 70 44 E
Darrequeira, Argentina 126 D3 37 42 S 63 10W
Darrington, U.S.A. .. 108 B3 48 15N 121 36W
Darsser Ort, Germany 24 A8 54 28N 12 32 E
Dart →, U.K. 15 G4 50 24N 3 39W
Dart, C., Antarctica .. 5 D14 73 6 S 126 0W
Dartford, U.K. ...... 15 F8 51 26N 0 13 E
Dartmoor, U.K. 15 G4 50 38N 3 57W
Dartmoor △, U.K. ... 15 G4 50 37N 3 59W
Dartmouth, Canada . 105 D7 44 40N 63 30W
Dartmouth, U.K. 15 G4 50 21N 3 36W
Dartmouth Res.,
Australia .... 95 D4 26 4 S 145 18 E
Dartuch, C. = Artrutx,
C. de, Spain .... 48 B10 39 55N 3 49 E
Daruvar, Croatia .... 28 E2 45 35N 17 14 E
Darvaza, Turkmenistan 52 E6 40 11N 58 24 E
Darvel, Teluk = Lahad
Datu, Teluk, Malaysia 63 D5 4 50N 118 20 E
Darwen, U.K. 14 D5 53 42N 2 29W
Darwendale, Zimbabwe 89 B5 17 41 S 30 33 E
Darwha, India ...... 66 J10 20 15N 77 45 E
Darwin, Australia ... 92 B5 12 25 S 130 51 E
Darwin, U.S.A. 111 J9 36 15N 117 35W
Darya Khan, Pakistan 68 D4 31 48N 71 6 E
Daryoi Amu =
Amudarya →,
Uzbekistan .... 52 E6 43 58N 59 34 E
Dås, U.A.E. .... 71 E7 25 20N 53 30 E
Dashen, Ras, Ethiopia 81 E4 13 8N 38 26 E
Dashetai, China ..... 56 D5 41 0N 109 5 E
Dashhowuz,
Turkmenistan ..... 52 E6 41 49N 59 58 E
Dashkesan = Daşkäsän,
Azerbaijan .... 35 K7 40 25N 46 0 E
Dashköpri,
Turkmenistan ..... 71 B9 36 16N 62 8 E
Dasht, Iran .... 71 B8 37 17N 56 7 E
Dasht →, Pakistan .. 66 G2 25 10N 61 40 E
Daska, Pakistan ..... 68 C6 32 20N 74 20 E
Daşkäsän, Azerbaijan 35 K7 40 25N 46 0 E
Dassa, Benin .... 83 D5 7 46N 2 14 E
Dassuya, India ...... 68 D6 31 49N 75 40 E
Datça, Turkey ...... 47 E9 36 46N 27 40 E
Datia, India .... 69 G8 25 39N 78 27 E
Datian, China ...... 59 E11 25 40N 117 50 E
Datong, Anhui, China 59 B11 30 48N 117 44 E
Datong, Shanxi, China 56 D7 40 6N 113 18 E
Dattakhel, Pakistan . 68 C3 32 54N 69 46 E
Datu, Tanjung,
Indonesia .... 62 D3 2 5N 109 39 E
Datu Piang, Phil. .... 61 H6 7 2N 124 30 E
Datu, Tanjong = Datu,
Tanjung, Indonesia . 62 D3 2 5N 109 39 E
Daua = Dawa →, Africa 81 G5 4 11N 42 6 E
Daud Khel, Pakistan . 68 C4 32 53N 71 34 E
Daudnagar, India ... 69 G11 25 2N 84 24 E
Daulpur, India ...... 68 F7 26 45N 77 59 E
Daun, Germany ..... 25 E2 50 11N 6 49 E
Daung Kyun, Burma . 103 C8 51 9N 100 5W
Dauphin, U.S.A. 116 F8 40 22N 76 56W
Dauphiné, France ... 21 C9 45 15N 5 25 E
Daura, Borno, Nigeria 83 C7 11 31N 11 24 E

Daura, *Katsina, Nigeria* **83 C6** 13 2N 8 21 E
Dausa, *India* **68 F7** 26 52N 76 20 E
Dāvāçi, *Azerbaijan* **35 K9** 41 15N 48 57 E
Davangere, *India* **66 M9** 14 25N 75 55 E
Davao, *Phil.* **61 H6** 7 0N 125 40 E
Davao G., *Phil.* **61 H6** 6 30N 125 48 E
Dāvar Panāh = Sarāvān, *Iran* **71 E9** 27 25N 62 15 E
Davenport, *Calif., U.S.A.* **110 H4** 37 1N 122 12W
Davenport, *Iowa, U.S.A.* **112 E9** 41 32N 90 35W
Davenport, *Wash., U.S.A.* **108 C4** 47 39N 118 9W
Davenport Ra., *Australia* **94 C1** 20 28 S 134 0 E
Daventry, *U.K.* **15 E6** 52 16N 1 10W
David, *Panama* **120 E3** 8 30N 82 30W
David City, *U.S.A.* **112 E6** 41 15N 97 8W
David Gorodok = Davyd Haradok, *Belarus* **33 F4** 52 4N 27 8 E
Davidson, *Canada* **103 C7** 51 16N 105 59W
Davis, *Antarctica* **5 C6** 68 34 S 77 55 E
Davis, *U.S.A.* **110 G5** 38 33N 121 44W
Davis Dam, *U.S.A.* **111 K12** 35 11N 114 34W
Davis Inlet, *Canada* **105 A7** 55 50N 60 59W
Davis Mts., *U.S.A.* **113 K2** 30 50N 103 55W
Davis Sea, *Antarctica* **5 C7** 66 0 S 92 0 E
Davis Str., *N. Amer.* **101 B14** 65 0N 58 0W
Davo →, *Ivory C.* **82 D3** 5 0N 6 10W
Davos, *Switz.* **25 J5** 46 48N 9 49 E
Davutlar, *Turkey* **47 D9** 37 43N 27 17 E
Davy L., *Canada* **103 B7** 58 53N 108 18W
Davyd Haradok, *Belarus* **33 F4** 52 4N 27 8 E
Dawa →, *Africa* **81 G5** 4 11N 42 6 E
Dawaki, *Bauchi, Nigeria* **83 D6** 9 25N 9 33 E
Dawaki, *Kano, Nigeria* **83 C6** 12 5N 8 23 E
Dawei = Tavoy, *Burma* **64 E2** 14 2N 98 12 E
Dawes Ra., *Australia* **94 C5** 24 40 S 150 40 E
Dawlish, *U.K.* **15 G4** 50 35N 3 28W
Dawna Ra., *Burma* **64 D2** 16 30N 98 30 E
Dawros Hd., *Ireland* **12 B3** 54 50N 8 33W
Dawson, *Canada* **100 B6** 64 10N 139 30W
Dawson, *U.S.A.* **115 K3** 31 46N 84 27W
Dawson, I., *Chile* **128 G2** 53 50 S 70 50W
Dawson B., *Canada* **103 C8** 52 53N 100 49W
Dawson Creek, *Canada* **102 B4** 55 45N 120 15W
Dawson Inlet, *Canada* **103 A10** 61 50N 93 25W
Dawson Ra., *Australia* **94 C4** 24 30 S 149 48 E
Dawu, *Hubei, China* **59 B9** 31 34N 114 7 E
Dawu, *Sichuan, China* **58 B3** 30 55N 101 10 E
Dax, *France* **20 E2** 43 44N 1 3W
Daxian, *China* **58 B6** 31 15N 107 23 E
Daxin, *China* **58 F6** 22 50N 107 11 E
Daxindian, *China* **57 F11** 37 30N 120 50 E
Daxinggou, *China* **57 C15** 43 25N 129 40 E
Daxue Shan, *Sichuan, China* **58 B3** 30 30N 101 30 E
Daxue Shan, *Yunnan, China* **58 F2** 23 42N 99 48 E
Dayao, *China* **58 E3** 25 43N 101 20 E
Daye, *China* **59 B10** 30 6N 114 58 E
Dayet en Naharat, *Mali* **82 B4** 17 39N 3 10W
Dayi, *China* **58 B4** 30 41N 103 29 E
Daylesford, *Australia* **95 F3** 37 21 S 144 9 E
Dayong, *China* **59 C8** 29 11N 110 30 E
Dayr az Zawr, *Syria* **70 C4** 35 20N 40 5 E
Daysland, *Canada* **102 C6** 52 50N 112 20W
Dayton, *Nev., U.S.A.* **110 F7** 39 14N 119 36W
Dayton, *Ohio, U.S.A.* **114 F3** 39 45N 84 12W
Dayton, *Pa., U.S.A.* **116 F5** 40 53N 79 15W
Dayton, *Tenn., U.S.A.* **115 H3** 35 30N 85 1W
Dayton, *Wash., U.S.A.* **108 C4** 46 19N 117 59W
Dayton, *Wyo., U.S.A.* **108 D10** 44 53N 107 16W
Daytona Beach, *U.S.A.* **115 L5** 29 13N 81 1W
Dayu, *China* **59 E10** 25 24N 114 22 E
Dayville, *U.S.A.* **108 D4** 44 28N 119 32W
Dazhu, *China* **58 B6** 30 41N 107 15 E
Dazkırı, *Turkey* **47 D11** 37 57N 29 52 E
Dazu, *China* **58 C5** 29 40N 105 42 E
De Aar, *S. Africa* **88 E3** 30 39 S 24 0 E
De Biesbosch Δ, *Neths.* **17 C4** 51 45N 4 48 E
De Funiak Springs, *U.S.A.* **115 K2** 30 43N 86 7W
De Grey →, *Australia* **92 D2** 20 12 S 119 13 E
De Haan, *Belgium* **17 C3** 51 16N 3 2 E
De Hoge Veluwe Δ, *Neths.* **17 B5** 52 5N 5 46 E
De Hoop Δ, *S. Africa* **88 E3** 34 30 S 20 28 E
De Kalb, *U.S.A.* **112 E10** 41 56N 88 46W
De Kennemerduinen Δ, *Neths.* **17 B4** 52 27N 4 33 E
De Land, *U.S.A.* **115 L5** 29 2N 81 18W
De Leon, *U.S.A.* **113 J5** 32 7N 98 32W
De Panne, *Belgium* **17 C2** 51 6N 2 34 E
De Pere, *U.S.A.* **114 C1** 44 27N 88 4W
De Queen, *U.S.A.* **113 H7** 34 2N 94 21W
De Quincy, *U.S.A.* **113 K8** 30 27N 93 26W
De Ridder, *U.S.A.* **113 K8** 30 51N 93 17W
De Smet, *U.S.A.* **112 C6** 44 23N 97 33W
De Soto, *U.S.A.* **112 F9** 38 8N 90 34W
De Tour Village, *U.S.A.* **114 C4** 46 0N 83 56W
De Witt, *U.S.A.* **113 H9** 34 18N 91 20W
Dead Sea, *Asia* **74 D4** 31 30N 35 30 E
Deadwood, *U.S.A.* **112 C3** 44 23N 103 44W
Deadwood L., *Canada* **102 B3** 59 10N 128 30W
Deal, *U.K.* **15 F9** 51 13N 1 25 E
Deal I., *Australia* **95 F4** 39 30 S 147 20 E
Dealesville, *S. Africa* **88 D4** 28 41 S 25 44 E
De'an, *China* **59 C10** 29 21N 115 46 E
Dean →, *Canada* **102 C3** 52 49N 126 58W
Dean, Forest of, *U.K.* **15 F5** 51 45N 2 33W
Dean Chan., *Canada* **102 C3** 52 30N 127 15W
Deán Funes, *Argentina* **126 C3** 30 20 S 64 20W
Dease →, *Canada* **102 B3** 59 56N 128 32W
Dease Lake, *Canada* **102 B2** 58 25N 130 6W
Death Valley, *U.S.A.* **111 J10** 36 15N 116 50W
Death Valley Junction, *U.S.A.* **111 J10** 36 20N 116 25W
Deauville, *France* **18 C7** 49 23N 0 2 E
Deba, *Spain* **38 B2** 43 18N 2 21W
Deba Habe, *Nigeria* **83 C7** 10 14N 11 20 E
Debaltsevo, *Ukraine* **33 H10** 48 22N 38 26 E
Debao, *China* **58 F6** 23 21N 106 46 E
Debar, *Macedonia* **44 E4** 41 31N 20 30 E
Debark, *Ethiopia* **81 E4** 13 1N 37 48 E
Debden, *Canada* **103 C7** 53 30N 106 50W
Dębica, *Poland* **31 H8** 50 2N 21 25 E
Dęblin, *Poland* **31 G8** 51 34N 21 50 E
Dębno, *Poland* **31 F1** 52 44N 14 41 E
Débo, L., *Mali* **82 B4** 15 14N 4 15W
DeBolt, *Canada* **102 B5** 55 12N 118 1W
Deborah East, L., *Australia* **93 F2** 30 45 S 119 0 E
Deborah West, L., *Australia* **93 F2** 30 45 S 118 50 E

Debre, *Serbia & M.* **44 B3** 44 38N 19 53 E
Debre Birhan, *Ethiopia* **81 F4** 9 41N 39 31 E
Debre Markos, *Ethiopia* **81 E4** 10 20N 37 40 E
Debre May, *Ethiopia* **81 E4** 11 20N 37 25 E
Debre Sina, *Ethiopia* **81 F4** 9 51N 39 50 E
Debre Tabor, *Ethiopia* **81 E4** 11 50N 38 26 E
Debre Zebit, *Ethiopia* **81 E4** 11 48N 38 30 E
Debre Zeyit, *Ethiopia* **81 F4** 8 50N 39 0 E
Debrecen, *Hungary* **28 C6** 47 33N 21 42 E
Debrzno, *Poland* **30 E4** 53 31N 17 14 E
Dečani, *Serbia & M.* **44 D4** 42 30N 20 18 E
Decatur, *Ala., U.S.A.* **115 H2** 34 36N 86 59W
Decatur, *Ga., U.S.A.* **115 J3** 33 47N 84 18W
Decatur, *Ill., U.S.A.* **112 F10** 39 51N 88 57W
Decatur, *Ind., U.S.A.* **114 E3** 40 50N 84 56W
Decatur, *Tex., U.S.A.* **113 J6** 33 14N 97 35W
Decazeville, *France* **20 D6** 44 34N 2 15 E
Deccan, *India* **66 L11** 18 0N 79 0 E
Deception Bay, *Australia* **95 D5** 27 10 S 153 5 E
Deception I., *Antarctica* **5 C17** 63 0 S 60 15W
Deception L., *Canada* **103 B8** 56 33N 104 13W
Dechang, *China* **58 D4** 27 25N 102 11 E
Dechhu, *India* **68 F5** 26 46N 72 20 E
Děčín, *Czech Rep.* **26 A7** 50 47N 14 12 E
Decize, *France* **19 F10** 46 50N 3 28 E
Deckerville, *U.S.A.* **116 C2** 43 32N 82 44W
Decollatura, *Italy* **43 C9** 39 3N 16 21 E
Decorah, *U.S.A.* **112 D9** 43 18N 91 48W
Deda, *Romania* **29 D9** 46 56N 24 50 E
Dédéagach = Alexandroúpolis, *Greece* **45 F9** 40 50N 25 54 E
Deder, *Ethiopia* **81 F5** 9 19N 41 27 E
Dedham, *U.S.A.* **117 D13** 42 15N 71 10W
Dédougou, *Burkina Faso* **82 C4** 12 30N 3 25W
Dedovichi, *Russia* **32 D5** 57 32N 29 56 E
Dedza, *Malawi* **87 E3** 14 20N 34 20 E
Dee →, *Aberds., U.K.* **13 D6** 57 9N 2 5W
Dee →, *Dumf. & Gall., U.K.* **13 G4** 54 51N 4 3W
Dee →, *Wales, U.K.* **14 D4** 53 22N 3 17W
Deep B., *Canada* **102 A5** 61 15N 116 35W
Deepwater, *Australia* **95 D5** 29 25 S 151 51 E
Deer →, *Canada* **103 B10** 58 23N 94 13W
Deer L., *Canada* **103 C10** 52 40N 94 20W
Deer Lake, *Nfld. & L., Canada* **105 C8** 49 11N 57 27W
Deer Lake, *Ont., Canada* **103 C10** 52 36N 94 20W
Deer Lodge, *U.S.A.* **108 C7** 46 24N 112 44W
Deer Park, *U.S.A.* **108 C5** 47 57N 117 28W
Deer River, *U.S.A.* **112 B8** 47 20N 93 48W
Deeragun, *Australia* **94 B4** 19 16 S 146 33 E
Deerdepoort, *S. Africa* **88 C4** 24 37 S 26 27 E
Deferiet, *U.S.A.* **117 B9** 44 2N 75 41W
Defiance, *U.S.A.* **114 E3** 41 17N 84 22W
Degana, *India* **68 F6** 26 50N 74 20 E
Dêgê, *China* **58 B2** 31 44N 98 39 E
Degebe →, *Portugal* **37 G3** 38 13N 7 29W
Degeberga, *Sweden* **11 J8** 55 51N 14 5 E
Dégelis, *Canada* **105 C6** 47 30N 68 35W
Degema, *Nigeria* **83 E6** 4 50N 6 48 E
Degerfors, *Sweden* **10 E8** 59 15N 14 27 E
Degerhamn, *Sweden* **11 H10** 56 20N 16 24 E
Deggendorf, *Germany* **25 G8** 48 50N 12 57 E
Degh →, *Pakistan* **68 D5** 31 3N 73 21 E
Değirmendere, *Turkey* **45 F13** 40 42N 29 47 E
Deh Bīd, *Iran* **71 D7** 30 39N 53 11 E
Dehaj, *Iran* **71 D7** 30 42N 54 53 E
Dehak, *Iran* **71 E9** 27 11N 62 37 E
Dehdez, *Iran* **71 D6** 31 43N 50 17 E
Dehej, *India* **68 J5** 21 44N 72 40 E
Dehestān, *Iran* **71 D7** 28 30N 55 35 E
Dehgolān, *Iran* **70 C5** 35 17N 47 25 E
Dehibat, *Tunisia* **79 B8** 32 0N 10 47 E
Dehlorān, *Iran* **70 C5** 32 41N 47 16 E
Dehnow-e Kūhestān, *Iran* **71 E8** 27 58N 58 32 E
Dehra Dun, *India* **68 D8** 30 20N 78 4 E
Dehri, *India* **69 G11** 24 50N 84 15 E
Dehua, *China* **59 E12** 25 26N 118 14 E
Dehui, *China* **57 B13** 44 30N 125 40 E
Deim Zubeir, *Sudan* **81 F2** 7 49N 26 16 E
Deinze, *Belgium* **17 D3** 50 59N 3 32 E
Dej, *Romania* **29 C8** 47 10N 23 52 E
Deje, *Sweden* **10 E7** 59 35N 13 29 E
Deka →, *Zimbabwe* **88 B4** 18 4 S 26 42 E
Dekemhare, *Eritrea* **81 D4** 15 6N 39 0 E
Dekese, *Dem. Rep. of the Congo* **84 E4** 3 24 S 21 24 E
Del Mar, *U.S.A.* **111 N9** 32 58N 117 16W
Del Norte, *U.S.A.* **109 H10** 37 41N 106 21W
Del Rio, *U.S.A.* **113 L4** 29 22N 100 54W
Delai, *Sudan* **80 D4** 17 21N 36 6 E
Delambre I., *Australia* **92 D2** 20 26 S 117 5 E
Delami, *Sudan* **81 E3** 11 38N 30 32 E
Delano, *U.S.A.* **111 K7** 35 46N 119 15W
Delano Peak, *U.S.A.* **109 G7** 38 22N 112 22W
Delareyville, *S. Africa* **88 D4** 26 41 S 25 26 E
Delaronde L., *Canada* **103 C7** 54 31N 107 3W
Delavan, *U.S.A.* **112 D10** 42 38N 88 39W
Delaware, *U.S.A.* **114 E4** 40 18N 83 4W
Delaware □, *U.S.A.* **114 F8** 39 0N 75 20W
Delaware →, *U.S.A.* **117 G9** 39 15N 75 20W
Delaware B., *U.S.A.* **114 F8** 39 0N 75 10W
Delaware Water Gap Δ, *U.S.A.* **117 E10** 41 10N 74 55W
Delay →, *Canada* **105 A5** 56 56N 71 28W
Delbrück, *Germany* **24 D4** 51 46N 8 34 E
Delčevo, *Macedonia* **44 E6** 41 58N 22 46 E
Delegate, *Australia* **95 F4** 37 4 S 148 56 E
Delémont, *Switz.* **25 H3** 47 22N 7 20 E
Delft, *Neths.* **17 B4** 52 1N 4 22 E
Delfzijl, *Neths.* **17 A6** 53 20N 6 55 E
Delgado, *Spain* **87 E5** 10 45 S 40 40 E
Delgerhet, *Mongolia* **56 B6** 45 50N 110 30 E
Delgo, *Sudan* **80 C3** 20 6N 30 40 E
Delhi, *Canada* **116 D4** 42 51N 80 30W
Delhi, *India* **68 E7** 28 38N 77 17 E
Delhi, *La., U.S.A.* **113 J9** 32 28N 91 30W
Delhi, *N.Y., U.S.A.* **117 D10** 42 17N 74 55W
Deli Jovan, *Serbia & M.* **44 B6** 44 13N 22 9 E
Delia, *Canada* **102 C6** 51 38N 112 23W
Delice, *Turkey* **72 C6** 39 54N 34 2 E
Delicias, *Mexico* **118 B3** 28 10N 105 30W
Delijān, *Iran* **71 C6** 33 59N 50 40 E
Déline, *Canada* **100 B7** 65 11N 123 25W
Delisle, *Canada* **103 C7** 51 55N 107 8W
Delitzsch, *Germany* **24 D7** 51 31N 12 20 E
Dell City, *U.S.A.* **109 L11** 31 56N 105 12W
Dell Rapids, *U.S.A.* **112 D6** 43 50N 96 43W
Delle, *France* **19 E14** 47 30N 7 2 E

Delmar, *U.S.A.* **117 D11** 42 37N 73 47W
Delmenhorst, *Germany* **24 B4** 53 3N 8 37 E
Delnice, *Croatia* **41 C11** 45 23N 14 50 E
Delonga, Ostrova, *Russia* **53 B15** 76 40N 149 20 E
Deloraine, *Australia* **95 G4** 41 30 S 146 40 E
Deloraine, *Canada* **103 D8** 49 15N 100 29W
Delphi, *Greece* **46 C4** 38 28N 22 30 E
Delphi, *U.S.A.* **114 E2** 40 36N 86 41W
Delphos, *U.S.A.* **114 E3** 40 51N 84 21W
Delportshoop, *S. Africa* **88 D3** 28 22 S 24 20 E
Delray Beach, *U.S.A.* **115 M5** 26 28N 80 4W
Delsbo, *Sweden* **10 C10** 61 48N 16 32 E
Delta, *Colo., U.S.A.* **109 G9** 38 44N 108 4W
Delta, *Utah, U.S.A.* **108 G7** 39 21N 112 35W
Delta □, *Nigeria* **83 D6** 5 30N 6 0 E
Delta del Ebro □, *Spain* **38 E5** 40 43N 0 40 E
Delta del Po □, *Italy* **41 D9** 44 50N 12 15 E
Delta du Saloum Δ, *Senegal* **82 C1** 13 42N 16 43W
Delta Dunărea □, *Romania* **29 E14** 45 15N 29 25 E
Delta Junction, *U.S.A.* **100 B5** 64 2N 145 44W
Deltona, *U.S.A.* **115 L5** 28 54N 81 16W
Delungra, *Australia* **95 D5** 29 39 S 150 51 E
Delvada, *India* **68 J4** 20 46N 71 2 E
Delvinákion, *Greece* **46 B2** 39 57N 20 32 E
Delvinë, *Albania* **44 G4** 39 59N 20 6 E
Demak, *Indonesia* **63 G14** 6 53 S 110 38 E
Demanda, Sierra de la, *Spain* **38 C2** 42 15N 3 0W
Demavend = Damāvand, Qolleh-ye, *Iran* **71 C7** 35 56N 52 10 E
Dembecha, *Ethiopia* **81 E4** 10 32N 37 30 E
Dembi, *Ethiopia* **81 F4** 8 5N 36 25 E
Dembia, *Dem. Rep. of the Congo* **86 B2** 3 33N 25 48 E
Dembidolo, *Ethiopia* **81 F3** 8 34N 34 50 E
Demchok, *India* **69 C8** 32 42N 79 29 E
Demer →, *Belgium* **17 D4** 50 57N 4 42 E
Demetrias, *Greece* **46 B4** 39 22N 23 1 E
Demidov, *Russia* **32 E6** 55 16N 31 30 E
Deming, *N. Mex., U.S.A.* **109 K10** 32 16N 107 46W
Deming, *Wash., U.S.A.* **110 B4** 48 50N 122 13W
Demini →, *Brazil* **124 D6** 0 46 S 62 56W
Demirci, *Turkey* **47 B10** 39 2N 28 38 E
Demirköprü Baraji, *Turkey* **47 C10** 38 42N 28 25 E
Demirköy, *Turkey* **45 E11** 41 49N 27 45 E
Demmin, *Germany* **24 B9** 53 54N 13 2 E
Demonte, *Italy* **40 D4** 44 19N 7 17 E
Demopolis, *U.S.A.* **115 J2** 32 31N 87 50W
Dempo, *Indonesia* **62 E2** 4 2 S 103 15 E
Demyansk, *Russia* **32 D7** 57 40N 32 27 E
Den Burg, *Neths.* **17 A4** 53 3N 4 47 E
Den Chai, *Thailand* **64 D3** 17 59N 100 4 E
Den Haag = 's-Gravenhage, *Neths.* **17 B4** 52 7N 4 17 E
Den Helder, *Neths.* **17 B4** 52 57N 4 45 E
Den Oever, *Neths.* **17 B5** 52 56N 5 2 E
Denain, *France* **19 B10** 50 20N 3 22 E
Denair, *U.S.A.* **110 H6** 37 32N 120 48W
Denau, *Uzbekistan* **52 F7** 38 16N 67 54 E
Denbigh, *Canada* **116 A7** 45 8N 77 15W
Denbigh, *U.K.* **14 D4** 53 12N 3 25W
Denbighshire □, *U.K.* **14 D4** 53 8N 3 22W
Dendang, *Indonesia* **62 E3** 3 7 S 107 56 E
Dendermonde, *Belgium* **17 C4** 51 2N 4 5 E
Deneba, *Ethiopia* **81 F4** 9 47N 39 10 E
Dengchuan, *China* **58 E3** 25 59N 100 3 E
Denge, *Nigeria* **83 C6** 12 52N 5 21 E
Dengfeng, *China* **56 G7** 34 25N 113 2 E
Dengi, *Nigeria* **83 D6** 9 25N 9 55 E
Dengkou, *China* **56 D4** 40 18N 106 55 E
Dengzhou, *China* **59 A9** 32 34N 112 4 E
Denham, *Australia* **93 E1** 25 56 S 113 31 E
Denham, Mt., *Jamaica* **120 a** 18 13N 77 32W
Denham Ra., *Australia* **94 C4** 21 55 S 147 46 E
Denham Sd., *Australia* **93 E1** 25 45 S 113 15 E
Denholm, *Canada* **103 C7** 52 39N 108 1W
Denia, *Spain* **39 G5** 38 49N 0 8 E
Denial B., *Australia* **95 E1** 32 14 S 133 32 E
Deniliquin, *Australia* **95 F3** 35 30 S 144 58 E
Denison, *Iowa, U.S.A.* **112 E7** 42 1N 95 21W
Denison, *Tex., U.S.A.* **113 J6** 33 45N 96 33W
Denison Plains, *Australia* **92 C4** 18 35 S 128 0 E
Denizli, *Turkey* **47 D11** 37 42N 29 2 E
Denizli □, *Turkey* **47 D11** 37 45N 29 5 E
Denman Glacier, *Antarctica* **5 C7** 66 45 S 99 25 E
Denmark, *Australia* **93 F2** 34 59 S 117 25 E
Denmark ■, *Europe* **11 J3** 55 45N 10 0 E
Denmark Str., *Atl. Oc.* **4 C6** 66 0N 30 0W
Dennery, *St. Lucia* **121 f** 13 55N 60 54W
Dennison, *U.S.A.* **116 F3** 40 24N 81 19W
Denpasar, *Indonesia* **63 K18** 8 44 S 115 10 E
Denpasar ✈ (DPS), *Indonesia* **63 K18** 8 44 S 115 10 E
Denton, *Mont., U.S.A.* **108 C9** 47 19N 109 57W
Denton, *Tex., U.S.A.* **113 J6** 33 13N 97 8W
D'Entrecasteaux Δ, *Australia* **93 F2** 34 20 S 115 33 E
D'Entrecasteaux, Pt., *Australia* **93 F2** 34 50 S 115 33 E
Denu, *Ghana* **83 D5** 6 4N 1 8 E
Denver, *Colo., U.S.A.* **112 F2** 39 44N 104 59W
Denver, *U.S.A.* **112 E8** 42 40N 92 20W
Denver City, *U.S.A.* **113 J3** 32 58N 102 50W
Deoband, *India* **68 E7** 29 42N 77 43 E
Deogarh, *India* **68 G5** 25 32N 73 54 E
Deoghar, *India* **69 G12** 24 30N 86 42 E
Deolali, *India* **66 K8** 19 58N 73 50 E
Deoli, *India* **68 G6** 25 50N 75 20 E
Deoli = Devli, *India* **69 J9** 21 54N 79 22 E
Deori, *India* **69 H8** 23 24N 79 1 E
Deoria, *India* **69 F10** 26 31N 83 48 E
Deosai Mts., *Pakistan* **69 B6** 35 40N 75 0 E
Depalpur, *India* **68 H6** 22 51N 75 33 E
Deping, *China* **57 F9** 37 25N 116 58 E
Deputatskiy, *Russia* **53 C14** 69 18N 139 54 E
Dêqên, *China* **58 C2** 28 34N 98 51 E
Deqing, *China* **59 F8** 23 8N 111 42 E
Dera Ghazi Khan, *Pakistan* **68 D4** 30 5N 70 43 E
Dera Ismail Khan, *Pakistan* **68 D4** 31 50N 70 50 E
Derabugti, *Pakistan* **68 E3** 29 2N 69 9 E
Derawar Fort, *Pakistan* **68 E4** 28 46N 71 20 E
Derbent, *Russia* **35 J9** 42 5N 48 15 E

Derbent, *Turkey* **47 C10** 38 11N 28 33 E
Derby, *Australia* **92 C3** 17 18 S 123 38 E
Derby, *U.K.* **14 E6** 52 56N 1 28W
Derby, *Conn., U.S.A.* **117 E11** 41 19N 73 5W
Derby, *Kans., U.S.A.* **113 G6** 37 33N 97 16W
Derby, *N.Y., U.S.A.* **116 D6** 42 41N 78 58W
Derby City □, *U.K.* **14 E6** 52 56N 1 28W
Derby Line, *U.S.A.* **117 B12** 45 0N 72 6W
Derbyshire □, *U.K.* **14 D6** 53 11N 1 38W
Đerdap △, *Serbia & M.* **44 B6** 44 40N 22 23 E
Derdepoort, *S. Africa* **88 C4** 24 38 S 26 24 E
Dereham, *U.K.* **15 E8** 52 41N 0 57 E
Derecske, *Hungary* **28 C6** 47 20N 21 33 E
Dereköy, *Turkey* **45 E11** 41 55N 27 21 E
Dereli, *Turkey* **73 B8** 40 44N 38 26 E
Derg →, *U.K.* **12 B4** 54 44N 7 26W
Derg, L., *Ireland* **12 D3** 53 0N 8 20W
Dergachi = Derhaci, *Ukraine* **33 G9** 50 9N 36 11 E
Dergaon, *India* **67 F19** 26 45N 94 0 E
Derhaci, *Ukraine* **33 G9** 50 9N 36 11 E
Derik, *Turkey* **73 D9** 37 21N 40 18 E
Derinkuyu, *Turkey* **72 C6** 38 22N 34 45 E
Dermantsi, *Bulgaria* **45 C8** 43 24N 24 17 E
Dermott, *U.S.A.* **113 J9** 33 32N 91 26W
Dêrong, *China* **58 C2** 28 44N 99 9 E
Derry = Londonderry, *U.K.* **12 B4** 55 0N 7 20W
Derry = Londonderry □, *U.K.* **12 B4** 55 0N 7 20W
Derry, *N.H., U.S.A.* **117 D13** 42 53N 71 19W
Derry, *Pa., U.S.A.* **116 F5** 40 20N 79 18W
Derryveagh Mts., *Ireland* **12 B3** 54 56N 8 11W
Derudub, *Sudan* **80 D4** 17 31N 36 7 E
Derval, *France* **18 E5** 47 40N 1 41W
Derveni, *Greece* **46 C4** 38 8N 22 25 E
Derventa, *Bos.-H.* **28 F2** 44 59N 17 55 E
Derwent →, *Cumb., U.K.* **14 C4** 54 39N 3 33W
Derwent →, *Derby, U.K.* **14 E6** 52 57N 1 28W
Derwent →, *N. Yorks., U.K.* **14 D7** 53 45N 0 58W
Derwent Water, *U.K.* **14 C4** 54 35N 3 9W
Des Moines, *Iowa, U.S.A.* **112 E8** 41 35N 93 37W
Des Moines, *N. Mex., U.S.A.* **113 G3** 36 46N 103 50W
Des Moines →, *U.S.A.* **112 E9** 40 23N 91 25W
Desa, *Romania* **28 G8** 43 52N 23 2 E
Desaguadero →, *Argentina* **126 C2** 34 30 S 66 46W
Desaguadero →, *Bolivia* **124 G5** 16 35 S 69 5W
Desantne, *Ukraine* **29 E14** 45 34N 29 32 E
Desar, *Malaysia* **65 d** 1 31N 104 17 E
Descanso, Pta., *Mexico* **111 N9** 32 21N 117 3W
Descartes, *France* **20 B4** 46 59N 0 42 E
Deschaillons-sur-St-Laurent, *Canada* **105 C5** 46 32N 72 7W
Deschambault L., *Canada* **103 C8** 54 50N 103 30W
Deschutes →, *U.S.A.* **108 D3** 45 38N 120 55W
Dese, *Ethiopia* **81 E4** 11 5N 39 40 E
Deseado →, *Argentina* **128 F3** 47 45 S 65 54W
Desenzano del Garda, *Italy* **40 C7** 45 28N 10 32 E
Desert Center, *U.S.A.* **111 M11** 33 43N 115 24W
Desert Hot Springs, *U.S.A.* **111 M10** 33 58N 116 30W
Deshnok, *India* **68 F5** 27 48N 73 21 E
Desierto Central de Baja California △, *Mexico* **118 B2** 29 40N 114 43W
Desna →, *Ukraine* **33 G6** 50 33N 30 32 E
Desnăţui →, *Romania* **29 G8** 43 53N 23 35 E
Desolación, I., *Chile* **128 G2** 53 0 S 74 0W
Despeñaperros △, *Spain* **37 G7** 38 25N 3 31 E
Despeñaperros, Paso, *Spain* **37 G7** 38 24N 3 30W
Despotovac, *Serbia & M.* **44 B5** 44 6N 21 30 E
Dessau, *Germany* **24 D8** 51 51N 12 14 E
Dessye = Dese, *Ethiopia* **81 E4** 11 5N 39 40 E
D'Estrees B., *Australia* **95 F2** 35 55 S 137 45 E
Desuri, *India* **68 G5** 25 18N 73 35 E
Desvres, *France* **19 B8** 50 40N 1 48 E
Det Udom, *Thailand* **64 E5** 14 54N 105 5 E
Deta, *Romania* **28 E6** 45 24N 21 13 E
Dete, *Zimbabwe* **88 B4** 18 38 S 26 50 E
Đetinja →, *Serbia & M.* **44 C4** 43 51N 20 5 E
Detmold, *Germany* **24 D4** 51 56N 8 52 E
Detour, Pt., *U.S.A.* **114 C2** 45 40N 86 40W
Detroit, *U.S.A.* **116 D1** 42 20N 83 3W
Detroit Lakes, *U.S.A.* **112 B7** 46 49N 95 51W
Detva, *Slovak Rep.* **27 C12** 48 34N 19 25 E
Deurne, *Neths.* **17 C5** 51 27N 5 49 E
Deutsch-Luxemburgischer △, *Germany* **25 F2** 49 58N 6 12 E
Deutsche Bucht, *Germany* **24 A4** 54 15N 8 0 E
Deutschlandsberg, *Austria* **26 E8** 46 49N 15 14 E
Deux-Sèvres □, *France* **18 F6** 46 35N 0 20W
Deva, *Romania* **28 E7** 45 53N 22 55 E
Devakottai, *India* **66 Q11** 9 55N 78 45 E
Devaprayag, *India* **69 D8** 30 13N 78 58 E
Dévaványa, *Hungary* **28 C5** 47 2N 20 58 E
Deveci Dağları, *Turkey* **72 B7** 40 6N 36 15 E
Devecikonağı, *Turkey* **45 G12** 39 55N 28 34 E
Devecser, *Hungary* **28 C2** 47 6N 17 26 E
Develi, *Turkey* **72 C6** 38 23N 35 29 E
Deventer, *Neths.* **17 B6** 52 15N 6 10 E
Deveron →, *U.K.* **13 D6** 57 41N 2 32W
Devesel, *Romania* **28 F7** 44 28N 22 41 E
Devgadh Bariya, *India* **68 H5** 22 40N 73 55 E
Devikot, *India* **68 F4** 26 42N 71 12 E
Devil's Den, *U.S.A.* **110 K7** 35 46N 119 58W
Devils Lake, *U.S.A.* **112 A5** 48 7N 98 52W
Devils Paw, *Canada* **102 B2** 58 47N 134 0W
Devils Postpile △, *U.S.A.* **110 H7** 37 37N 119 5W
Devils Tower △, *U.S.A.* **112 C2** 44 35N 104 43W
Devils Tower Junction, *U.S.A.* **112 C2** 44 31N 104 57W
Devin, *Bulgaria* **45 E8** 41 44N 24 24 E
Devine, *U.S.A.* **113 L5** 29 8N 98 54W
Devizes, *U.K.* **15 F6** 51 22N 1 58W
Devli, *India* **68 G6** 25 50N 75 20 E
Devnya, *Bulgaria* **45 C11** 43 13N 27 33 E
Devoll →, *Albania* **44 F4** 40 57N 20 15 E
Devon, *Canada* **102 C6** 53 24N 113 44W
Devon □, *U.K.* **15 G4** 50 50N 3 40W
Devon I., *Canada* **98 B11** 75 10N 85 0W
Devonport, *Australia* **94 G4** 41 10 S 146 22 E
Devonport, *N.Z.* **91 G5** 36 49 S 174 49 E
Devrek, *Turkey* **72 B5** 41 13N 31 57 E

Devrekâni, *Turkey* **72 B5** 41 36N 33 50 E
Devrez →, *Turkey* **72 B6** 41 6N 34 25 E
Dewas, *India* **68 H7** 22 59N 76 3 E
Dewetsdorp, *S. Africa* **88 D4** 29 33 S 26 39 E
Dewey, *Puerto Rico* **121 d** 18 18N 65 18W
Dexing, *China* **59 C11** 28 46N 117 30 E
Dexter, *Maine, U.S.A.* **115 C11** 45 1N 69 18W
Dexter, *Mo., U.S.A.* **113 G10** 36 48N 89 57W
Dexter, *N. Mex., U.S.A.* **113 J2** 33 12N 104 22W
Dey-Dey, L., *Australia* **93 E5** 29 12 S 131 4 E
Deyang, *China* **58 B5** 31 3N 104 27 E
Deyhūk, *Iran* **71 C8** 33 15N 57 30 E
Deyyer, *Iran* **71 E6** 27 55N 51 55 E
Dezadeash L., *Canada* **102 A1** 60 28N 136 58W
Dezfūl, *Iran* **71 C6** 32 20N 48 30 E
Dezhneva, Mys, *Russia* **53 C19** 66 5N 169 40W
Dezhou, *China* **56 F9** 37 26N 116 18 E
Dhadhar →, *India* **69 G11** 25 36N 85 24 E
Dháfni, *Kríti, Greece* **49 D7** 35 13N 25 3 E
Dháfni, *Pelopónnisos, Greece* **46 D4** 37 48N 22 1 E
Dhahaban, *Si. Arabia* **80 C4** 21 58N 39 3 E
Dhahiriya = Aẓ Ẓāhiriyah, *West Bank* **74 D3** 31 25N 34 58 E
Dhahran = Aẓ Ẓahrān, *Si. Arabia* **71 E6** 26 10N 50 7 E
Dhak, *Pakistan* **68 C5** 32 25N 72 33 E
Dhaka, *Bangla.* **69 H14** 23 43N 90 26 E
Dhaka □, *Bangla.* **69 G14** 24 25N 90 25 E
Dhali, *Cyprus* **49 D12** 35 1N 33 25 E
Dhamási, *Greece* **46 B4** 39 43N 22 11 E
Dhampur, *India* **69 E8** 29 19N 78 33 E
Dhamtari, *India* **67 J12** 20 42N 81 35 E
Dhanbad, *India* **69 H12** 23 50N 86 30 E
Dhangarhi, *Nepal* **67 E12** 28 55N 80 40 E
Dhankuta, *Nepal* **69 F12** 26 55N 87 40 E
Dhar, *India* **68 H6** 22 35N 75 26 E
Dharampur, *India* **68 H6** 22 13N 75 18 E
Dharamsala = Dharmsala, *India* **68 C7** 32 16N 76 23 E
Dhariwal, *India* **68 D6** 31 57N 75 19 E
Dharla →, *Bangla.* **69 G13** 25 46N 89 42 E
Dharmapuri, *India* **66 N11** 12 10N 78 10 E
Dharmjaygarh, *India* **69 H10** 22 28N 83 13 E
Dharmsala, *India* **68 C7** 32 16N 76 23 E
Dharni, *India* **68 J7** 21 33N 76 53 E
Dharwad, *India* **66 M9** 15 30N 75 4 E
Dhasan →, *India* **69 G8** 25 48N 79 24 E
Dhaulagiri, *Nepal* **69 E10** 28 39N 83 28 E
Dhebar, L., *India* **68 G6** 24 10N 74 0 E
Dheftera, *Cyprus* **49 D12** 35 5N 33 16 E
Dhenkanal, *India* **67 J14** 20 45N 85 35 E
Dhenoúsa, *Greece* **47 D7** 37 8N 25 48 E
Dherinia, *Cyprus* **49 D12** 35 3N 33 57 E
Dheskáti, *Greece* **44 G5** 39 55N 21 49 E
Dhespotikó, *Greece* **46 E6** 36 57N 24 58 E
Dhestina, *Greece* **46 C4** 38 25N 22 31 E
Dhī Qār □, *Iraq* **70 D5** 31 0N 46 15 E
Dhiarrizos →, *Cyprus* **49 E11** 34 41N 32 34 E
Dhībān, *Jordan* **74 D4** 31 30N 35 46 E
Dhidhimótikhon, *Greece* **45 E10** 41 22N 26 29 E
Dhikti Óros, *Greece* **49 D7** 35 8N 25 30 E
Dhilianáta, *Greece* **46 C2** 38 13N 20 45 E
Dhílos, *Greece* **47 D7** 37 23N 25 15 E
Dhilwan, *India* **68 D6** 31 31N 75 21 E
Dhimarkhera, *India* **69 H9** 23 28N 80 22 E
Dhimitsána, *Greece* **46 D4** 37 36N 22 3 E
Dhírfis Óros, *Greece* **46 C5** 38 40N 23 54 E
Dhodhekánisos, *Greece* **47 E8** 36 35N 27 0 E
Dhodhekánisos □, *Greece* **47 E8** 36 35N 27 0 E
Dhokós, *Greece* **46 D5** 37 20N 23 20 E
Dholiana, *Greece* **46 B2** 39 54N 20 32 E
Dholka, *India* **68 H5** 22 44N 72 29 E
Dhomokós, *Greece* **46 B4** 39 10N 22 18 E
Dhoraji, *India* **68 J4** 21 45N 70 37 E
Dhoxáton, *Greece* **45 E8** 41 9N 24 16 E
Dhragónisi, *Greece* **47 D7** 37 27N 25 29 E
Dhráhstis, Ákra, *Greece* **49 A3** 39 48N 19 40 E
Dhrangadhra, *India* **68 H4** 22 59N 71 31 E
Dhrápanon, Ákra, *Greece* **49 D6** 35 28N 24 14 E
Dhrol, *India* **68 H4** 22 33N 70 25 E
Dhuburi, *India* **67 F16** 26 2N 89 59 E
Dhule, *India* **66 J9** 20 58N 74 50 E
Di-ib, W. →, *Sudan* **80 C4** 22 8N 36 6 E
Di Linh, *Vietnam* **65 G7** 11 35N 108 4 E
Di Linh, Cao Nguyen, *Vietnam* **65 G7** 11 30N 108 0 E
Día, *Greece* **49 D7** 35 28N 25 14 E
Diabakania, *Guinea* **82 C2** 10 38N 10 58W
Diablo, *U.S.A.* **110 H5** 37 53N 121 56W
Diablo Range, *U.S.A.* **110 J5** 37 20N 121 25W
Diafarabé, *Mali* **82 C4** 14 9N 4 57W
Diala, *Mali* **82 C3** 14 10N 9 58W
Dialakoro, *Mali* **82 C3** 12 18N 7 54W
Dialakoto, *Senegal* **82 C2** 13 21N 13 19W
Diallassagou, *Mali* **82 C4** 13 47N 3 41W
Diamante, *Argentina* **126 C3** 32 5 S 60 40W
Diamante →, *Argentina* **126 C2** 34 30 S 66 46W
Diamantina, *Brazil* **125 G10** 18 17 S 43 40W
Diamantina △, *Australia* **94 C3** 23 33 S 141 23 E
Diamantina →, *Australia* **95 D2** 26 45 S 139 10 E
Diamantino, *Brazil* **125 F7** 14 30 S 56 30W
Diamond Bar, *U.S.A.* **111 L9** 34 1N 117 48W
Diamond Harbour, *India* **69 H13** 22 11N 88 14 E
Diamond Is., *Australia* **94 B5** 17 25 S 151 5 E
Diamond Mts., *U.S.A.* **108 G6** 39 50N 115 30W
Diamond Springs, *U.S.A.* **110 G6** 38 42N 120 49W
Dian Chi, *China* **58 E4** 24 40N 102 43 E
Dianalund, *Denmark* **11 J5** 55 32N 11 30 E
Dianbai, *China* **59 G8** 21 30N 111 20 E
Diancheng, *China* **59 G8** 21 30N 111 20 E
Dianjiang, *China* **58 B6** 30 5N 107 20 E
Diano Marina, *Italy* **40 E5** 43 54N 8 5 E
Dianra, *Ivory C.* **82 D3** 8 45N 6 14W
Diapangou, *Burkina Faso* **83 C5** 12 5N 1 46 E
Diariguila, *Guinea* **82 C2** 10 35N 10 2W
Dibâ, *U.A.E.* **71 E8** 25 45N 56 16 E
Dibai, *India* **68 E8** 28 13N 78 15 E
Dibaya-Lubue, *Dem. Rep. of the Congo* **84 E3** 4 12 S 19 54 E
Dibbeen △, *Jordan* **74 C4** 32 20N 35 45 E
Dibete, *Botswana* **88 C4** 23 45 S 26 32 E
Dibrugarh, *India* **67 F19** 27 29N 94 55 E
Dickens, *U.S.A.* **113 J4** 33 37N 100 50W
Dickinson, *U.S.A.* **112 B3** 46 53N 102 47W
Dickson, *U.S.A.* **115 G2** 36 5N 87 23W
Dickson City, *U.S.A.* **117 E9** 41 29N 75 40W

Dicle Nehri →, Turkey 73 D9 37 44N 41 10 E
Dicomano, Italy 41 E8 43 53N 11 31 E
Didesa, W. →, Ethiopia 81 F4 10 2N 35 32 E
Didi, Sudan 81 F3 6 18N 34 29 E
Didsbury, Canada 102 C6 51 35N 114 10W
Didwana, India 68 F6 27 23N 74 36 E
Die, France 21 D9 44 47N 5 22 E
Diébougou,
 Burkina Faso 82 C4 11 0N 3 15W
Diecke, Guinea 82 D3 7 27N 8 54W
Diefenbaker, L., Canada 103 C7 51 0N 106 55W
Diego de Almagro, Chile 126 B1 26 22 S 70 3W
Diego Garcia, Ind. Oc. 3 E13 7 50 S 72 50 E
Diekirch, Lux. 17 E6 49 52N 6 10 E
Diéma, Mali 82 C3 14 32N 9 12W
Diembéring, Senegal 82 C1 12 29N 16 47W
Diemelsee ○, Germany 24 D4 51 20N 8 40 E
Dien Ban, Vietnam 64 E7 15 53N 108 16 E
Dien Bien, Vietnam 58 G4 21 20N 103 0 E
Dien Khanh, Vietnam 65 F7 12 15N 109 6 E
Diepholz, Germany 24 C4 52 37N 8 22 E
Dieppe, France 18 C8 49 54N 1 4 E
Dierks, U.S.A. 113 H8 34 7N 94 1W
Diest, Belgium 17 D5 50 58N 5 4 E
Dietikon, Switz. 25 H4 47 24N 8 24 E
Dieulefit, France 21 D9 44 32N 5 4 E
Dieuze, France 19 D13 48 49N 6 43 E
Dif, Somali Rep. 75 G3 0 59N 40 58 E
Differdange, Lux. 17 E5 49 31N 5 54 E
Dig, India 68 F7 27 28N 77 20 E
Digba, Dem. Rep. of
 the Congo 86 B2 4 25N 25 48 E
Digby, Canada 105 D6 44 38N 65 50W
Diggi, India 68 F6 26 22N 75 26 E
Dighinala, Bangla. 67 H18 23 15N 92 5 E
Dighton, U.S.A. 112 F4 38 29N 100 28W
Digna, Mali 82 C3 14 48N 8 10W
Digne-les-Bains, France 21 D10 44 5N 6 12 E
Digoin, France 19 F11 46 29N 4 1 E
Digor, Turkey 73 B10 40 22N 43 25 E
Digos, Phil. 61 H6 6 45N 125 20 E
Digranes, Iceland 8 C6 66 4N 14 44W
Digul →, Indonesia 63 F9 7 7 S 138 42 E
Digya △, Ghana 83 D5 7 15N 0 5 E
Dihang =
 Brahmaputra →, Asia 69 H13 23 40N 90 35 E
Dijlah, Nahr →, Asia 70 D5 31 0N 47 25 E
Dijon, France 19 E12 47 20N 5 3 E
Dikhil, Djibouti 81 E5 11 8N 42 20 E
Dikili, Turkey 47 B8 39 4N 26 53 E
Dikirnis, Egypt 80 H7 31 6N 31 35 E
Dikkil = Dikhil, Djibouti 81 E5 11 8N 42 20 E
Dikodougou, Ivory C. 82 D3 9 4N 5 45W
Diksmuide, Belgium 17 C2 51 2N 2 52 E
Dikson, Russia 52 B9 73 40N 80 5 E
Dikwa, Nigeria 83 C7 12 4N 13 30 E
Dila, Ethiopia 81 F4 6 21N 38 22 E
Dilek Yarimadisi △,
 Turkey 47 D9 37 40N 27 10 E
Dili, E. Timor 63 F7 8 39 S 125 34 E
Dilijan, Armenia 35 K7 40 46N 44 57 E
Dilizhan = Dilijan,
 Armenia 35 K7 40 46N 44 57 E
Dilj, Croatia 28 E3 45 29N 18 1 E
Dillenburg, Germany 24 E4 50 43N 8 17 E
Dilley, U.S.A. 113 L5 28 40N 99 10W
Dilli = Delhi, India 68 E7 28 38N 77 17 E
Dilling, Sudan 81 E2 12 3N 29 35 E
Dillingen, Bayern,
 Germany 25 G6 48 36N 10 30 E
Dillingen, Saarland,
 Germany 25 F2 49 22N 6 43 E
Dillingham, U.S.A. 100 C4 59 3N 158 28W
Dillon, Canada 103 B7 55 56N 108 35W
Dillon, Mont., U.S.A. 108 D7 45 13N 112 38W
Dillon, S.C., U.S.A. 115 H6 34 25N 79 22W
Dillon →, Canada 103 B7 55 56N 108 56W
Dillsburg, U.S.A. 116 F7 40 7N 77 2W
Dilly, Mali 82 C3 15 1N 7 40W
Dilolo, Dem. Rep. of
 the Congo 84 G4 10 28 S 22 18 E
Dilove, Ukraine 29 C9 47 56N 24 11 E
Dimas, Mexico 118 C3 23 43N 106 47W
Dimashq, Syria 74 B5 33 30N 36 18 E
Dimashq □, Syria 74 B5 33 30N 36 30 E
Dimbaza, S. Africa 89 E4 32 50 S 27 14 E
Dimbokro, Ivory C. 82 D4 6 45N 4 46W
Dimboola, Australia 95 F3 36 28 S 142 7 E
Dîmbovita =
 Dâmbovita →,
 Romania 29 F11 44 12N 26 26 E
Dimbulah, Australia 94 B4 17 8 S 145 4 E
Dimitrovgrad, Bulgaria 45 D9 42 5N 25 35 E
Dimitrovgrad, Russia 34 C9 54 14N 49 39 E
Dimitrovgrad,
 Serbia & M. 44 C6 43 2N 22 48 E
Dimitrovo = Pernik,
 Bulgaria 44 D7 42 35N 23 2 E
Dimmitt, U.S.A. 113 H3 34 33N 102 19W
Dimo, Sudan 81 F2 5 19N 29 10 E
Dimona, Israel 74 D4 31 2N 35 1 E
Dimovo, Bulgaria 44 C6 43 43N 22 50 E
Dinagat, Phil. 61 F6 10 10N 125 40 E
Dinajpur, Bangla. 67 G16 25 33N 88 43 E
Dinan, France 18 D4 48 28N 2 2W
Dīnān Āb, Iran 71 C8 32 4N 56 49 E
Dinant, Belgium 17 D4 50 16N 4 55 E
Dinapur, India 69 G11 25 38N 85 5 E
Dinar, Turkey 47 C12 38 5N 30 10 E
Dīnār, Kūh-e, Iran 71 D6 30 42N 51 46 E
Dinara Planina, Croatia 41 D13 44 0N 16 30 E
Dinard, France 18 D4 48 38N 2 6W
Dinaric Alps = Dinara
 Planina, Croatia 41 D13 44 0N 16 30 E
Dindanko, Mali 82 C3 14 8N 9 30W
Dinder →, Sudan 81 E3 14 6N 33 40 E
Dinder, Nahr ed →,
 Sudan 81 E3 14 6N 33 40 E
Dindigul, India 66 P11 10 25N 78 0 E
Dindori, India 69 H9 22 57N 81 5 E
Ding Xian = Dingzhou,
 China 56 E8 38 30N 114 59 E
Dinga, Pakistan 68 G2 25 26N 67 10 E
Dingalan, Phil. 61 D4 15 18N 121 25 E
Dingbian, China 56 F4 37 35N 107 32 E
Dingelstädt, Germany 24 D6 51 18N 10 19 E
Dingle, Ireland 12 D1 52 9N 10 17W
Dingle, Sweden 11 F5 58 32N 11 35 E
Dingle B., Ireland 12 D1 52 3N 10 20W
Dingmans Ferry, U.S.A. 117 E10 41 13N 74 55W
Dingnan, China 59 E10 24 45N 115 0 E
Dingo, Australia 94 C4 23 38 S 149 19 E
Dingolfing, Germany 25 G8 48 37N 12 30 E
Dinguira, Mali 82 C2 13 5N 10 50W
Dinguiraye, Guinea 82 C2 11 18N 10 49W

Dingwall, U.K. 13 D4 57 36N 4 26W
Dingxi, China 56 G3 35 30N 104 33 E
Dingxiang, China 56 E7 38 30N 112 58 E
Dingyuan, China 59 A11 32 32N 117 41 E
Dinh, Mui, Vietnam 65 G7 11 22N 109 1 E
Dinh Lap, Vietnam 58 G6 21 33N 107 6 E
Dinira △, Venezuela 121 E6 9 57N 70 6W
Dinokwe, Botswana 88 C4 23 29 S 26 37 E
Dinorwic, Canada 103 D10 49 41N 92 30W
Dinosaur △, Canada 102 C6 50 47N 111 30W
Dinosaur △, U.S.A. 108 F9 40 30N 108 45W
Dinuba, U.S.A. 110 J7 36 32N 119 23W
Diö, Sweden 11 H8 56 37N 14 15 E
Dioïla, Mali 82 C3 12 23N 6 50W
Dioka, Mali 82 C2 14 57N 10 4W
Diongoï, Mali 82 C3 14 38N 8 34W
Diósgyör, Hungary 28 B5 48 7N 20 43 E
Diosig, Romania 28 C7 47 18N 22 2 E
Diougani, Mali 82 C4 14 19N 2 44W
Diouloulou, Senegal 82 C1 13 5N 16 38W
Dioura, Mali 82 C3 14 59N 5 12W
Diourbel, Senegal 82 C1 14 39N 16 12W
Dipalpur, Pakistan 68 D5 30 40N 73 39 E
Diplo, Pakistan 68 G3 24 35N 69 35 E
Dipolog, Phil. 61 G5 8 36N 123 20 E
Dipperu △, Australia 94 C4 21 56 S 148 42 E
Dir, Pakistan 66 B7 35 8N 71 59 E
Diré, Mali 82 B4 16 20N 3 25W
Dire Dawa, Ethiopia 81 F5 9 35N 41 45 E
Diriamba, Nic. 120 D2 11 51N 86 19W
Dirk Hartog I., Australia 93 E1 25 50 S 113 5 E
Dirranbandi, Australia 95 D4 28 33 S 148 17 E
Disa, India 68 G5 24 18N 72 10 E
Disa, Sudan 81 E3 12 5N 34 15 E
Disappointment, C.,
 U.S.A. 108 C2 46 18N 124 5W
Disappointment, L.,
 Australia 92 D3 23 20 S 122 40 E
Disaster B., Australia 95 F4 37 15 S 149 58 E
Discovery B., Australia 95 F3 38 10 S 140 40 E
Disentis Muster, Switz. 25 J4 46 42N 8 50 E
Dishna, Egypt 80 B3 26 9N 32 32 E
Disina, Nigeria 83 C6 11 35N 9 50 E
Disko = Qeqertarsuaq,
 Greenland 101 B5 69 45N 53 30W
Disna = Dzisna →,
 Belarus 32 E5 55 34N 28 12 E
Diss, U.K. 15 E9 52 23N 1 7 E
Disteghil Sar, Pakistan 69 A6 36 20N 75 12 E
Distrito Federal □,
 Brazil 125 G9 15 45 S 47 45W
Distrito Federal □,
 Mexico 119 D5 19 15N 99 10W
Disûq, Egypt 80 H7 31 8N 30 35 E
Diu, India 68 J4 20 45N 70 58 E
Dīvāndarreh, Iran 70 C5 35 55N 47 2 E
Dives →, France 18 C6 49 18N 0 7W
Dives-sur-Mer, France 18 C6 49 18N 0 8W
Divichi =
 Dəvəçi, Azerbaijan 35 K9 41 15N 48 57 E
Divide, U.S.A. 108 D7 45 45N 112 45W
Dividing Ra., Australia 93 E2 27 45 S 116 0 E
Divinópolis, Brazil 125 H10 20 10 S 44 54W
Divjake, Albania 44 F3 41 0N 19 32 E
Divnoye, Russia 35 H6 45 55N 43 21 E
Divo, Ivory C. 82 D3 5 48N 5 15W
Divriği, Turkey 73 C8 39 22N 38 7 E
Diwal Kol, Afghan. 68 B2 34 23N 67 52 E
Dixie Mt., U.S.A. 110 F6 39 55N 120 16W
Dixon, Calif., U.S.A. 110 G5 38 27N 121 49W
Dixon, Ill., U.S.A. 112 E10 41 50N 89 29W
Dixon Entrance, U.S.A. 100 C6 54 30N 132 0W
Dixville, Canada 117 A13 45 4N 71 46W
Diyadin, Turkey 73 C10 39 33N 43 40 E
Diyālá □, Iraq 70 C5 33 45N 44 50 E
Diyālá →, Iraq 70 C5 33 14N 44 31 E
Diyarbakır, Turkey 70 B4 37 55N 40 18 E
Diyodar, India 68 G4 24 8N 71 50 E
Djakarta = Jakarta,
 Indonesia 63 G12 6 9 S 106 49 E
Djamba, Angola 88 B1 16 45 S 13 58 E
Djambala, Congo 84 E2 2 32 S 14 30 E
Djanet, Algeria 78 D7 24 35N 9 32 E
Djawa = Jawa, Indonesia 62 F3 7 0 S 110 0 E
Djelfa, Algeria 78 B6 34 40N 3 15 E
Djema, C.A.R. 86 A2 6 3N 25 15 E
Djenné, Mali 82 C4 14 0N 4 30W
Djerba, I. de, Tunisia 79 B8 33 50N 10 48 E
Djerid, Chott, Tunisia 78 B7 33 42N 8 30 E
Djibo, Burkina Faso 83 C4 14 9N 1 35W
Djibouti, Djibouti 81 E5 11 30N 43 5 E
Djibouti ■, Africa 81 E5 12 0N 43 0 E
Djolu, Dem. Rep. of
 the Congo 84 D4 0 35N 22 5 E
Djougou, Benin 83 D5 9 40N 1 45 E
Djoum, Cameroon 84 D2 2 41N 12 35 E
Djourab, Erg du, Chad 79 E9 16 40N 18 50 E
Djugu, Dem. Rep. of
 the Congo 86 B3 1 55N 30 35 E
Djúpivogur, Iceland 8 D6 64 39N 14 17W
Djurås, Sweden 10 D9 60 34N 15 8 E
Djurö △, Sweden 11 F7 58 52N 13 28 E
Djursland, Denmark 11 H4 56 27N 10 45 E
Dmitriya Lapteva,
 Proliv, Russia 53 B15 73 0N 140 0 E
Dmitriyev Lgovskiy,
 Russia 33 F8 52 10N 35 0 E
Dmitrov, Russia 32 D9 56 25N 37 32 E
Dmitrovsk-Orlovskiy,
 Russia 33 F8 52 29N 35 10 E
Dnepr = Dnipro →,
 Ukraine 33 J7 46 30N 32 18 E
Dneprodzerzhinsk =
 Dniprodzerzhynsk,
 Ukraine 33 H8 48 32N 34 37 E
Dneprodzerzhinskoye
 Vdkhr. =
 Dniprodzerzhynske
 Vdskh., Ukraine 33 H8 48 49N 34 18 E
Dnepropetrovsk =
 Dnipropetrovsk,
 Ukraine 33 H8 48 30N 35 0 E
Dneprorudnoye =
 Dniprorudne, Ukraine 33 J8 47 21N 34 58 E
Dnestr = Dnister →,
 Europe 33 J6 46 18N 30 17 E
Dnieper = Dnipro →,
 Ukraine 33 J7 46 30N 32 18 E
Dniester = Dnister →,
 Europe 33 J6 46 18N 30 17 E
Dnipro →, Ukraine 33 J7 46 30N 32 18 E
Dniprodzerzhynsk,
 Ukraine 33 H8 48 32N 34 37 E
Dniprodzerzhynske
 Vdskh., Ukraine 33 H8 48 49N 34 18 E
Dnipropetrovsk,
 Ukraine 33 H8 48 30N 35 0 E
Dniprorudne, Ukraine 33 J8 47 21N 34 58 E

Dnister →, Europe 33 J6 46 18N 30 17 E
Dnistrovskyy Lyman,
 Ukraine 33 J6 46 15N 30 17 E
Dno, Russia 32 D5 57 50N 29 58 E
Dnyapro = Dnipro →,
 Ukraine 33 J7 46 30N 32 18 E
Doaktown, Canada 105 C6 46 33N 66 8W
Doan Hung, Vietnam 58 G5 21 30N 105 10 E
Doany, Madag. 89 A8 14 21 S 49 30 E
Doba, Chad 79 G9 8 40N 16 50 E
Dobandi, Pakistan 68 D2 31 13N 66 50 E
Dobbiaco, Italy 41 B9 46 44N 12 14 E
Dobbyn, Australia 94 B3 19 44 S 140 2 E
Dobczyce, Poland 31 J7 49 52N 20 25 E
Dobele, Latvia 9 H20 56 37N 23 16 E
Döbeln, Germany 24 D9 51 6N 13 7 E
Doberai, Jazirah,
 Indonesia 63 E8 1 25 S 133 0 E
Dobiegniew, Poland 31 F2 52 59N 15 45 E
Doblas, Argentina 126 D3 37 5 S 64 0W
Dobo, Indonesia 63 F8 5 45 S 134 15 E
Doboj, Bos.-H. 28 F3 44 46N 18 4 E
Dobra, Wielkopolskie,
 Poland 31 G5 51 55N 18 37 E
Dobra,
 Zachodnio-Pomorskie,
 Poland 30 E2 53 34N 15 20 E
Dobra, Dâmbovita,
 Romania 29 F10 44 52N 25 40 E
Dobra, Hunedoara,
 Romania 28 E7 45 54N 22 36 E
Dobre Miasto, Poland 30 E7 53 58N 20 26 E
Dobrešti, Romania 28 D7 46 51N 22 36 E
Dobrich, Bulgaria 45 C11 43 37N 27 49 E
Dobrinishta, Bulgaria 44 E7 41 49N 23 34 E
Dobříš, Czech Rep. 26 B7 49 46N 14 10 E
Dobron, Ukraine 28 B7 48 25N 22 23 E
Dobropole, Ukraine 33 H9 48 25N 37 2 E
Dobrovolsk, Russia 30 D9 54 46N 22 31 E
Dobruja, Europe 29 F13 44 30N 28 15 E
Dobrush, Belarus 33 F6 52 25N 31 22 E
Dobrzany, Poland 30 E2 53 22N 15 25 E
Dobrzyń nad Wisłą,
 Poland 31 F6 52 39N 19 22 E
Doc, Mui, Vietnam 64 D6 17 58N 106 30 E
Docker River, Australia 93 E4 24 52 S 129 5 E
Docksta, Sweden 10 A12 63 3N 18 18 E
Doctor Arroyo, Mexico 118 C4 23 40N 100 11W
Doda, India 69 C6 33 10N 75 34 E
Doda, L., Canada 104 C4 49 25N 75 13W
Dodecanese =
 Dhodhekánisos,
 Greece 47 E8 36 35N 27 0 E
Dodge City, U.S.A. 113 G5 37 45N 100 1W
Dodge L., Canada 103 B7 59 50N 105 36W
Dodgeville, U.S.A. 112 D9 42 58N 90 8W
Dodo, Cameroon 83 D7 7 30N 12 3 E
Dodo, Sudan 81 F2 5 10N 29 57 E
Dodola, Ethiopia 81 F4 6 59N 39 11 E
Dodoma, Tanzania 86 D4 6 8 S 35 45 E
Dodoma □, Tanzania 86 D4 6 0 S 36 0 E
Dodona, Greece 46 B2 39 40N 20 46 E
Dodori △, Kenya 86 C5 1 55 S 41 7 E
Dodsland, Canada 103 C7 51 50N 108 45W
Dodson, U.S.A. 108 B9 48 24N 108 15W
Dodurga, Turkey 47 B11 39 49N 29 57 E
Doesburg, Neths. 17 B6 52 1N 6 9 E
Doetinchem, Neths. 17 C6 51 59N 6 18 E
Dog Creek, Canada 102 C4 51 35N 122 14W
Dog L., Man., Canada 103 C9 51 2N 98 31W
Dog L., Ont., Canada 104 C2 48 48N 89 30W
Doğanşehir, Turkey 72 C7 38 5N 37 53 E
Dogliani, Italy 40 D4 44 32N 7 56 E
Dogondoutchi, Niger 83 C5 13 38N 4 2 E
Dogran, Pakistan 68 D5 31 48N 73 35 E
Doğubayazıt, Turkey 70 B5 39 31N 44 5 E
Doguéraoua, Niger 83 C6 14 0N 5 31 E
Doha = Ad Dawḥah,
 Qatar 71 E6 25 15N 51 35 E
Dohazari, Bangla. 67 H18 22 10N 92 5 E
Dohrighat, India 69 F10 26 16N 83 31 E
Doi, Indonesia 63 D7 2 14N 127 49 E
Doi Inthanon △,
 Thailand 64 C2 18 33N 98 34 E
Doi Khuntan △,
 Thailand 64 C2 18 33N 99 14 E
Doi Luang, Thailand 64 C3 18 30N 101 0 E
Doi Luang △, Thailand 64 C2 19 22N 99 35 E
Doi Saket, Thailand 64 C2 18 52N 99 9 E
Doi Suthep △, Thailand 64 C2 18 49N 98 53 E
Dois Irmãos, Sa., Brazil 125 E10 9 0 S 42 30W
Dojransko Jezero,
 Macedonia 44 E6 41 13N 22 44 E
Dokkum, Neths. 17 A5 53 20N 5 59 E
Dokri, Pakistan 68 F3 27 25N 68 7 E
Dokuchayevsk, Ukraine 33 J9 47 44N 37 40 E
Dol-de-Bretagne, France 18 D5 48 34N 1 47W
Dolac, Serbia & M. 44 D4 42 50N 20 38 E
Dolak, Pulau, Indonesia 63 F9 8 0 S 138 30 E
Dolbeau-Mistassini,
 Canada 105 C5 48 53N 72 14W
Dole, France 19 E12 47 7N 5 31 E
Doleib, Wadi →, Sudan 81 E3 12 10N 33 15 E
Dolenji Logatec,
 Slovenia 41 C11 45 56N 14 15 E
Dolgellau, U.K. 14 E4 52 45N 3 53W
Dolgelley = Dolgellau,
 U.K. 14 E4 52 45N 3 53W
Dolhasca, Romania 29 C11 47 26N 26 36 E
Dolianova, Italy 42 C2 39 22N 9 10 E
Dolinskaya = Dolynska,
 Ukraine 33 H7 48 6N 32 46 E
Dolj □, Romania 29 F8 44 10N 23 30 E
Dollard, Neths. 17 A7 53 20N 7 10 E
Dolna Banya, Bulgaria 45 D8 42 18N 23 44 E
Dolní Dúbník, Bulgaria 45 C8 43 24N 24 26 E
Dolnoślaskie □, Poland 31 G3 51 0N 16 30 E
Dolný Kubín,
 Slovak Rep. 27 B12 49 12N 19 18 E
Dolo, Ethiopia 81 G5 4 11N 42 3 E
Dolo, Italy 41 C9 45 25N 12 5 E
Dolomites = Dolomiti,
 Italy 41 B8 46 23N 11 51 E
Dolomiti, Italy 41 B8 46 23N 11 51 E
Dolomiti Bellunesi △,
 Italy 41 B9 46 10N 12 5 E
Dolores, Argentina 126 D4 36 20 S 57 40W
Dolores, Uruguay 126 C4 33 34 S 58 15W
Dolores, U.S.A. 109 H9 37 28N 108 30W
Dolores →, U.S.A. 109 G9 38 49N 108 17W
Dolovo, Serbia & M. 28 F5 44 55N 20 52 E

Dolphin and Union Str.,
 Canada 100 B8 69 5N 114 45W
Dolsk, Poland 31 G4 51 59N 17 3 E
Dolyna, Ukraine 29 B9 48 58N 24 1 E
Dolynska, Ukraine 33 H7 48 6N 32 46 E
Dolynske, Ukraine 29 C14 47 32N 29 58 E
Dolzhanskaya, Russia 33 J9 46 37N 37 48 E
Dom Pedrito, Brazil 127 C5 31 0 S 54 40W
Doma, Nigeria 83 D6 8 25N 8 18 E
Doma = Zimbabwe 87 F3 16 28 S 30 12 E
Domaniç, Turkey 47 B11 39 48N 29 36 E
Domariaganj →, India 69 F10 26 17N 83 44 E
Domasi, Malawi 87 F4 15 15 S 35 22 E
Domažlice, Czech Rep. 26 B5 49 28N 12 58 E
Dombås, Norway 9 E13 62 4N 9 8 E
Dombasle-sur-Meurthe,
 France 19 D13 48 38N 6 21 E
Dombes, France 21 C9 45 58N 5 0 E
Dombóvár, Hungary 28 D3 46 21N 18 9 E
Dombrád, Hungary 28 B6 48 13N 21 54 E
Dome Fuji, Antarctica 5 D5 77 20 S 39 45 E
Domel I. = Letsôk-aw
 Kyun, Burma 65 G2 11 30N 98 25 E
Domérat, France 19 F9 46 21N 2 32 E
Domeyko, Chile 126 B1 29 0 S 71 0W
Domeyko, Cordillera,
 Chile 126 A2 24 30 S 69 0W
Domfront, France 18 D6 48 37N 0 40W
Dominador, Chile 126 A2 24 21 S 69 20W
Dominica ■, W. Indies 121 C7 15 20N 61 20W
Dominica Passage,
 W. Indies 121 C7 15 10N 61 20W
Dominican Rep. ■,
 W. Indies 121 C5 19 0N 70 30W
Dömitz, Germany 24 B7 53 8N 11 15 E
Domme, France 20 D5 44 48N 1 12 E
Domnești, Romania 29 E9 45 12N 24 50 E
Domodóssola, Italy 40 B5 46 7N 8 17 E
Domogled-Valea
 Cernei △, Romania 28 F7 44 52N 22 27 E
Dompaire, France 19 D13 48 14N 6 14 E
Dompierre-sur-Besbre,
 France 19 F10 46 31N 3 41 E
Dompim, Ghana 82 D4 5 10N 2 5W
Domrémy-la-Pucelle,
 France 19 D12 48 26N 5 40 E
Domville, Mt., Australia 95 D5 28 1 S 151 15 E
Domvraína, Greece 46 C4 38 15N 22 59 E
Domžale, Slovenia 41 B11 46 9N 14 35 E
Don →, Russia 33 J10 47 4N 39 18 E
Don →, Aberds., U.K. 13 D6 57 11N 2 5W
Don →, S. Yorks., U.K. 14 D7 53 41N 0 52W
Don, C., Australia 92 B5 11 18 S 131 46 E
Don Benito, Spain 37 G5 38 53N 5 51W
Don Figueredo Mts.,
 Jamaica 120 a 18 5N 77 36W
Don Sak, Thailand 65 b 9 18N 99 41 E
Dona Ana =
 Nhamaabué, Mozam. 87 F4 17 25 S 35 5 E
Doña Mencía, Spain 37 H6 37 33N 4 21W
Donaghadee, U.K. 12 B6 54 39N 5 33W
Donald, Australia 95 F3 36 23 S 143 0 E
Donaldsonville, U.S.A. 113 K9 30 6N 90 59W
Donalsonville, U.S.A. 115 K3 31 3N 84 53W
Doñana △, Spain 37 J4 36 59N 6 23W
Donau = Dunărea →,
 Europe 29 E14 45 20N 29 40 E
Donau →, Austria 27 C10 48 10N 17 0 E
Donau Auen △, Austria 27 C9 48 8N 16 44 E
Donaueschingen,
 Germany 25 H4 47 56N 8 29 E
Donauwörth, Germany 25 G6 48 43N 10 47 E
Doncaster, U.K. 14 D6 53 32N 1 6W
Dondo, Mozam. 87 F3 19 33 S 34 46 E
Dondo, Teluk, Indonesia 63 D6 0 50N 120 30 E
Dondra Head, Sri Lanka 66 S12 5 55N 80 40 E
Dondușeni, Moldova 29 B12 48 14N 27 36 E
Donegal, Ireland 12 B3 54 39N 8 5W
Donegal □, Ireland 12 B4 54 53N 8 0W
Donegal B., Ireland 12 B3 54 31N 8 49W
Donets →, Russia 35 G5 47 33N 40 55 E
Donets Basin, Ukraine 6 F13 49 0N 38 0 E
Donetsk, Ukraine 33 J9 48 0N 37 45 E
Dong Ba Thin, Vietnam 65 F7 12 8N 109 13 E
Dong Dang, Vietnam 58 G6 21 54N 106 42 E
Dong Giam, Vietnam 64 C5 19 25N 105 31 E
Dong Ha, Vietnam 64 D6 16 40N 107 8 E
Dong Hene, Laos 64 D5 16 40N 105 31 E
Dong Hoi, Vietnam 64 D6 17 29N 106 36 E
Dong Jiang →, China 59 F10 23 6N 114 0 E
Dong Khe, Vietnam 58 F6 22 26N 106 27 E
Dong Ujimqin Qi, China 56 B9 43 52N 116 55 E
Dong Van, Vietnam 58 F5 23 16N 105 22 E
Dong Xoai, Vietnam 65 G6 11 32N 106 55 E
Donga, Nigeria 83 D7 7 45N 10 2 E
Donga →, Nigeria 83 D7 8 20N 9 58 E
Dong'an, China 59 D8 26 6N 111 0 E
Dongara, Australia 93 E1 29 14 S 114 57 E
Dongbei, China 57 D13 45 0N 125 0 E
Dongchuan, China 58 D4 26 8N 103 1 E
Donges, France 18 E4 47 18N 2 4W
Dongfang, China 64 C7 18 50N 108 33 E
Dongfeng, China 57 C13 42 52N 125 34 E
Donggala, Indonesia 63 E5 0 30 S 119 40 E
Donggan, China 58 E7 24 22N 110 18 E
Donggou, China 57 E13 39 52N 124 10 E
Dongguan, China 59 F9 22 58N 113 44 E
Dongguang, China 56 F9 37 50N 116 30 E
Donghai Dao, China 59 G8 20 0N 110 15 E
Dongjingcheng, China 57 B15 44 5N 129 10 E
Dongkou, China 59 D8 27 6N 110 2 E
Donglan, China 58 E6 24 30N 107 21 E
Dongliu, China 59 B11 30 13N 116 55 E
Dongmen, China 58 F6 22 20N 107 48 E
Dongning, China 57 B16 44 2N 131 5 E
Dongnyi, China 58 C3 29 50N 101 37 E
Dongola, Sudan 80 D3 19 9N 30 22 E
Dongping, China 56 G9 35 55N 116 20 E
Dongshan, China 59 F11 23 43N 117 30 E
Dongsheng, China 56 E6 39 50N 110 0 E
Dongtai, China 57 H11 32 51N 120 21 E
Dongting Hu, China 59 C9 29 18N 112 45 E
Dongtou, China 59 D13 27 50N 121 5 E
Dongxiang, China 59 C11 28 14N 116 38 E
Dongxing, China 58 G7 21 34N 108 0 E
Dongzhi, China 59 B11 30 3N 117 13 E
Donington, C., Australia 95 E2 34 45 S 136 0 E
Doniphan, U.S.A. 113 G9 36 37N 90 50W
Donja Stubica, Croatia 41 C12 45 59N 15 59 E
Donji Dušnik,
 Serbia & M. 44 C6 43 12N 22 5 E
Donji Miholjac, Croatia 28 E3 45 45N 18 10 E
Donji Milanovac,
 Serbia & M. 44 B6 44 28N 22 6 E

Donji Vakuf, Bos.-H. 28 F2 44 8N 17 24 E
Dønna, Norway 8 C15 66 6N 12 30 E
Donnaconna, Canada 105 C5 46 41N 71 41W
Donnelly's Crossing,
 N.Z. 91 F4 35 42 S 173 38 E
Donnybrook, Australia 93 F2 33 34 S 115 48 E
Donnybrook, S. Africa 89 D4 29 59 S 29 48 E
Donora, U.S.A. 116 F5 40 11N 79 52W
Donostia = Donostia-
 San Sebastián, Spain 38 B3 43 17N 1 58W
Donostia-San Sebastián,
 Spain 38 B3 43 17N 1 58W
Donskoy, Russia 32 F10 53 55N 38 15 E
Donsol, Phil. 61 E5 12 54N 123 36 E
Donzère, France 21 D8 44 28N 4 43 E
Donzy, France 19 E10 47 20N 3 6 E
Doon →, U.K. 13 F4 55 27N 4 39W
Dora, L., Australia 92 D3 22 0 S 123 0 E
Dora Báltea →, Italy 40 C5 45 11N 8 3 E
Dora Ripária →, Italy 40 C4 45 5N 7 44 E
Doran L., Canada 103 A7 61 13N 108 6W
Dorchester, U.K. 15 G5 50 42N 2 27W
Dorchester, C., Canada 101 B12 65 27N 77 27W
Dordabis, Namibia 88 C2 22 52 S 17 38 E
Dordogne □, France 20 C4 45 5N 0 40 E
Dordogne →, France 20 C3 45 2N 0 36W
Dordrecht, Neths. 17 C4 51 48N 4 39 E
Dordrecht, S. Africa 88 E4 31 20 S 27 3 E
Dore →, France 20 C6 45 50N 3 35 E
Dore, Mts., France 20 C6 45 32N 2 50 E
Doré L., Canada 103 C7 54 46N 107 17W
Doré Lake, Canada 103 C7 54 38N 107 36W
Dorfen, Germany 25 G8 48 16N 12 10 E
Dorgali, Italy 42 B2 40 17N 9 35 E
Dori, Burkina Faso 83 C4 14 3N 0 2W
Doring →, S. Africa 88 E2 31 54 S 18 39 E
Doringbos, S. Africa 88 E2 31 59 S 19 16 E
Dorking, U.K. 15 F7 51 14N 0 19W
Dormaa-Ahenkro,
 Ghana 82 D4 7 15N 2 52W
Dormans, France 19 C10 49 4N 3 38 E
Dormo, Ras, Eritrea 81 E5 13 14N 42 35 E
Dornbirn, Austria 26 D2 47 25N 9 45 E
Dornes, France 19 F10 46 48N 3 18 E
Dornești, Romania 29 C11 47 52N 26 1 E
Dornie, U.K. 13 D3 57 17N 5 31W
Dornoch, U.K. 13 D4 57 53N 4 2W
Dornoch Firth, U.K. 13 D4 57 51N 4 4W
Dornogovĭ □, Mongolia 56 C6 44 0N 110 0 E
Doro, Mali 83 B4 16 9N 0 51W
Dorog, Hungary 28 C3 47 42N 18 45 E
Dorogobuzh, Russia 32 E7 54 50N 33 18 E
Dorohoi, Romania 29 C11 47 56N 26 23 E
Döröö Nuur, Mongolia 60 B4 48 0N 93 0 E
Dorr, Iran 71 C6 33 17N 57 0 E
Dorre I., Australia 93 E1 25 13 S 113 12 E
Dorrigo, Australia 95 E5 30 20 S 152 44 E
Dorris, U.S.A. 108 F3 41 58N 121 55W
Dorset, Canada 116 A6 45 14N 78 54W
Dorset □, U.K. 15 G5 50 45N 2 26W
Dorset, C., Canada 101 B11 64 2N 76 30W
Dorsten, Germany 24 D2 51 40N 6 58 E
Dortmund, Germany 24 D3 51 30N 7 28 E
Dortmund-Ems-
 Kanal →, Germany 24 D3 51 50N 7 26 E
Dörtyol, Turkey 72 D7 36 50N 36 13 E
Dorum, Germany 24 B4 53 41N 8 34 E
Doruma, Dem. Rep. of
 the Congo 86 B2 4 42N 27 33 E
Dorūneh, Iran 71 C8 35 10N 57 18 E
Dos Bahías, C.,
 Argentina 128 E3 44 58 S 65 32W
Dos Hermanas, Spain 37 H5 37 16N 5 55W
Dos Palos, U.S.A. 110 J6 36 59N 120 37W
Dösemealtı, Turkey 47 D12 37 4N 30 36 E
Dosso, Niger 83 C5 13 0N 3 13 E
Dosso △, Niger 83 C5 12 36N 2 36 E
Dothan, U.S.A. 115 K3 31 13N 85 24W
Doty, U.S.A. 110 D3 46 38N 123 17W
Douai, France 19 B10 50 21N 3 4 E
Douako, Guinea 82 D2 9 45N 10 8W
Douala, Cameroon 83 E6 4 0N 9 45 E
Douarnenez, France 18 D2 48 6N 4 21W
Doubabougou, Mali 82 C3 14 13N 7 59W
Double Island Pt.,
 Australia 95 D5 25 56 S 153 11 E
Double Mountain
 Fork →, U.S.A. 113 J4 33 16N 100 0W
Doubrava →,
 Czech Rep. 26 A8 50 2N 15 20 E
Doubs □, France 19 E13 47 10N 6 20 E
Doubs →, France 19 F12 46 53N 5 1 E
Doubtful Sd., N.Z. 91 L1 45 20 S 166 49 E
Doubtless B., N.Z. 91 F4 34 55 S 173 26 E
Doudeville, France 18 C7 49 43N 0 47 E
Doué-la-Fontaine,
 France 18 E6 47 11N 0 16W
Douentza, Mali 82 C4 14 58N 2 48W
Douglas, I. of Man 14 C3 54 10N 4 28W
Douglas, S. Africa 88 D3 29 4 S 23 46 E
Douglas, Ariz., U.S.A. 109 L9 31 21N 109 33W
Douglas, Ga., U.S.A. 115 K4 31 31N 82 51W
Douglas, Wyo., U.S.A. 112 D2 42 45N 105 24W
Douglas Apsley △,
 Australia 95 G4 41 45 S 148 11 E
Douglas Chan., Canada 102 C3 53 40N 129 20W
Douglas Pt., Canada 116 B3 44 19N 81 37W
Douglasville, U.S.A. 115 J3 33 45N 84 45W
Doukáton, Ákra, Greece 46 C2 38 34N 20 33 E
Doulevant-le-Château,
 France 19 D11 48 23N 4 55 E
Doullens, France 19 B9 50 10N 2 20 E
Doumé, Mali 83 B4 13 35N 6 4W
Dounreay, U.K. 13 C5 58 35N 3 44W
Dourada, Serra, Brazil 125 F9 13 10 S 48 45W
Dourados, Brazil 127 A5 22 9 S 54 50W
Dourados →, Brazil 127 A5 21 58 S 54 18W
Dourados, Serra dos,
 Brazil 127 A5 23 30 S 53 30W
Dourdan, France 19 D9 48 30N 2 1 E
Douro →, Europe 36 D2 41 8N 8 40W
Douvaine, France 19 F13 46 19N 6 16 E
Douvres-la-Délivrande,
 France 18 C6 49 17N 0 23W
Douze →, France 20 E3 43 54N 0 30W
Dove →, U.K. 14 E6 52 51N 1 36W
Dove Creek, U.S.A. 109 H9 37 46N 108 54W
Dover, Australia 95 G4 43 18 S 147 2 E
Dover, U.K. 15 F9 51 7N 1 19 E
Dover, Del., U.S.A. 114 F8 39 10N 75 32W
Dover, N.H., U.S.A. 117 C14 43 12N 70 56W
Dover, N.J., U.S.A. 117 F10 40 53N 74 34W
Dover, Ohio, U.S.A. 114 F3 40 32N 81 29W
Dover, Pt., Australia 93 F4 32 32 S 125 32 E
Dover, Str. of, Europe 15 G9 51 0N 1 30 E

Dover-Foxcroft, U.S.A. 115 C11 45 11N 69 13W
Dover Plains, U.S.A. 117 E11 41 43N 73 35W
Dovey = Dyfi →, U.K. 15 E3 52 32N 4 3W
Dovhe, Ukraine 29 B8 48 22N 23 17 E
Dovrefjell, Norway 9 E13 62 15N 9 33 E
Dow Rūd, Iran 71 C6 33 28N 49 4 E
Dowa, Malawi 87 E3 13 38 S 33 58 E
Dowagiac, U.S.A. 114 E2 41 59N 86 6W
Dowerin, Australia 93 F2 31 12 S 117 2 E
Dowgha'i, Iran 71 B8 36 54N 58 32 E
Dowlatābād, Iran 71 D8 28 20N 56 40 E
Down □, U.K. 12 B5 54 23N 6 2W
Downey, Calif. U.S.A. 111 M8 33 56N 118 7W
Downey, Idaho, U.S.A. 108 E7 42 26N 112 7W
Downham Market, U.K. 15 E8 52 37N 0 23 E
Downieville, U.S.A. 110 F6 39 34N 120 50W
Downpatrick, U.K. 12 B6 54 20N 5 43W
Downpatrick Hd., Ireland 12 B2 54 20N 9 21W
Downsville, U.S.A. 117 D10 42 5N 74 50W
Downton, Mt., Canada 102 C4 52 42N 124 52W
Dowsāri, Iran 71 D8 28 25N 57 59 E
Doyle, U.S.A. 110 E6 40 2N 120 6W
Doylestown, U.S.A. 117 F9 40 21N 75 10W
Dozois, Rés., Canada 104 C4 47 30N 77 5W
Dra Khel, Pakistan 68 F2 27 58N 66 45 E
Drac →, France 21 C9 45 13N 5 42 E
Dračevo, Macedonia 44 E5 41 56N 21 31 E
Drachten, Neths. 17 A6 53 7N 6 5 E
Drăgănești, Moldova 29 C13 47 43N 28 15 E
Drăgănești-Olt, Romania 29 F9 44 9N 24 32 E
Drăgănești-Vlașca, Romania 29 F10 44 5N 25 33 E
Dragaš, Serbia & M. 44 D4 42 5N 20 41 E
Drăgășani, Romania 29 F9 44 39N 24 17 E
Dragichyn, Belarus 33 F3 52 15N 25 8 E
Dragocvet, Serbia & M. 44 C5 43 58N 21 15 E
Dragon's Mouth = Boca de Drago, Venezuela 125 K15 11 0N 61 50W
Dragovishtitsa, Bulgaria 44 D6 42 22N 22 39 E
Draguignan, France 21 E10 43 32N 6 27 E
Drahove, Ukraine 29 B8 48 14N 23 33 E
Drain, U.S.A. 108 E2 43 40N 123 19W
Drake, U.S.A. 112 B4 47 55N 100 23W
Drake Passage, S. Ocean 5 B17 58 0 S 68 0W
Drakensberg, S. Africa 89 D4 31 0 S 28 0 E
Dráma, Greece 45 E8 41 9N 24 10 E
Dráma □, Greece 45 E8 41 20N 24 0 E
Drammen, Norway 9 G14 59 42N 10 12 E
Drangajökull, Iceland 8 C2 66 9N 22 15W
Dranov, Ostrov, Romania 29 F14 44 55N 29 30 E
Dras, India 69 B6 34 25N 75 48 E
Drau = Drava →, Croatia 28 E3 45 33N 18 55 E
Drava →, Croatia 28 E3 45 33N 18 55 E
Dravograd, Slovenia 41 B12 46 36N 15 5 E
Drawa →, Poland 31 E2 52 52N 15 59 E
Drawieński △, Poland 31 E2 52 56N 15 58 E
Drawno, Poland 31 E2 53 13N 15 46 E
Drawsko Pomorskie, Poland 30 E2 53 35N 15 50 E
Drayton Valley, Canada 102 C6 53 12N 114 58W
Dreieich, Germany 25 E4 50 1N 8 41 E
Dren, Serbia & M. 44 C4 43 8N 20 46 E
Drenthe □, Neths. 17 B6 52 52N 6 40 E
Drepanum, C., Cyprus 49 E11 34 54N 32 19 E
Dresden, Canada 116 D2 42 35N 82 11W
Dresden, Germany 24 D9 51 3N 13 44 E
Dreux, France 18 D8 48 44N 1 23 E
Drezdenko, Poland 31 F2 52 50N 15 49 E
Driffield, U.K. 14 C7 54 0N 0 26W
Driftwood, U.S.A. 116 E6 41 20N 78 8W
Driggs, U.S.A. 108 E8 43 44N 111 6W
Drin →, Albania 44 D3 42 1N 19 38 E
Drin i Zi →, Albania 44 D4 41 37N 20 28 E
Drina →, Bos.-H. 44 B3 44 53N 19 21 E
Drincea →, Romania 28 F7 44 20N 22 55 E
Drinjača →, Bos.-H. 28 F4 44 15N 19 8 E
Drissa = Vyerkhnyadzvinsk, Belarus 32 E4 55 45N 27 58 E
Drniš, Croatia 41 E13 43 51N 16 10 E
Drøbak, Norway 9 G14 59 39N 10 39 E
Drobeta-Turnu Severin, Romania 28 F7 44 39N 22 41 E
Drobin, Poland 31 F6 52 42N 19 58 E
Drochia, Moldova 29 B12 48 2N 27 48 E
Drogheda, Ireland 12 C5 53 43N 6 22W
Drogichin = Dragichyn, Belarus 33 F3 52 15N 25 8 E
Drogobych = Drohobych, Ukraine 31 J10 49 20N 23 30 E
Drohiczyn, Poland 31 F9 52 24N 22 39 E
Drohobych, Ukraine 31 J10 49 20N 23 30 E
Droichead Atha = Drogheda, Ireland 12 C5 53 43N 6 22W
Droichead Nua, Ireland 12 C5 53 11N 6 48W
Droitwich, U.K. 15 E5 52 16N 2 8W
Drôme □, France 21 D9 44 38N 5 15 E
Drôme →, France 21 D8 44 46N 4 46 E
Dromedary, C., Australia 95 F5 36 17 S 150 10 E
Drömling △, Germany 24 C7 52 29N 11 5 E
Dromore □, U.K. 12 B4 54 31N 7 28W
Dromore West, Ireland 12 B3 54 15N 8 52W
Dronero, Italy 40 D4 44 28N 7 22 E
Dronfield, U.K. 14 D6 53 19N 1 27W
Dronne →, France 20 C3 45 2N 0 9W
Dronning Maud Land, Antarctica 5 D3 72 30 S 12 0 E
Dronninglund, Denmark 11 G4 57 10N 10 19 E
Dronten, Neths. 17 B5 52 32N 5 43 E
Dropt →, France 20 D3 44 35N 0 6W
Drosendorf, Austria 26 C8 48 52N 15 37 E
Droué, France 18 D8 48 2N 1 5 E
Drumbo, Canada 116 C4 43 16N 80 35W
Drumheller, Canada 102 C6 51 25N 112 40W
Drummond, U.S.A. 108 C7 46 40N 113 9W
Drummond I., U.S.A. 114 C4 46 1N 83 39W
Drummond Pt., Australia 95 E2 34 9 S 135 16 E
Drummond Ra., Australia 94 C4 23 45 S 147 10 E
Drummondville, Canada 104 C5 45 55N 72 25W
Drumright, U.S.A. 113 H6 35 59N 96 36W
Druskininkai, Lithuania 9 J20 54 3N 23 58 E
Drut →, Belarus 33 F6 53 8N 30 5 E
Druya, Belarus 32 E4 55 45N 27 28 E
Družba, Bulgaria 45 C13 43 15N 28 1 E
Druzhina, Russia 53 C15 68 14N 145 18 E
Drvar, Bos.-H. 41 D13 44 21N 16 23 E
Drvenik, Croatia 41 E13 43 27N 16 3 E
Drwęca →, Poland 31 E5 53 0N 18 42 E
Dry Harbour Mts., Jamaica 120 a 18 19N 77 24W
Dry Tortugas, U.S.A. 120 B3 24 38N 82 55W

Dryanovo, Bulgaria 45 D9 42 59N 25 28 E
Dryden, Canada 103 D10 49 47N 92 50W
Dryden, U.S.A. 117 D8 42 30N 76 18W
Drygalski I., Antarctica 5 C7 66 0 S 92 0 E
Drygalski →, Australia 13 E3 53 59 S 126 51 E
Drysdale I., Australia 94 A2 11 41 S 136 0 E
Drysdale River △, Australia 92 B4 14 56 S 127 2 E
Drzewica, Poland 31 G7 51 27N 20 29 E
Drzewiczka →, Poland 31 G7 51 36N 20 36 E
Dschang, Cameroon 83 D7 5 32N 10 3 E
Du Bois, U.S.A. 116 E6 41 8N 78 46W
Du Gué →, Canada 104 A5 57 21N 70 45W
Du He, China 59 A8 32 48N 110 40 E
Du Quoin, U.S.A. 112 G10 38 1N 89 14W
Du'an, China 58 F7 23 59N 108 3 E
Duanesburg, U.S.A. 117 D10 42 45N 74 11W
Duaringa, Australia 94 C4 23 42 S 149 42 E
Duarte, Pico, Dom. Rep. 121 D5 19 2N 70 59W
Dubā, Si. Arabia 70 E2 27 10N 35 40 E
Dubai = Dubayy, U.A.E. 71 E7 25 18N 55 20 E
Dubāsari, Moldova 29 C14 47 15N 29 10 E
Dubāsari Vdkhr., Moldova 29 C13 47 30N 29 0 E
Dubawnt →, Canada 103 A8 64 33N 100 6W
Dubawnt L., Canada 103 A8 63 8N 101 28W
Dubayy, U.A.E. 71 E7 25 18N 55 20 E
Dubbo, Australia 95 E4 32 11 S 148 35 E
Dubele, Dem. Rep. of the Congo 86 B2 2 56N 29 35 E
Dübendorf, Switz. 25 H4 47 24N 8 37 E
Dubica, Croatia 41 C13 45 11N 16 48 E
Dublin, Ireland 12 C5 53 21N 6 15W
Dublin, Ga. U.S.A. 115 J4 32 32N 82 54W
Dublin, Tex., U.S.A. 113 J5 32 5N 98 21W
Dublin □, Ireland 12 C5 53 24N 6 20W
Dublin ✈ (DUB), Ireland 12 C5 53 26N 6 15W
Dubna, Russia 32 D9 56 44N 37 10 E
Dubnica nad Váhom, Slovak Rep. 27 C11 48 58N 18 11 E
Dubno, Ukraine 33 G3 50 25N 25 45 E
Dubois, U.S.A. 108 D7 44 10N 112 14W
Dubossary = Dubāsari, Moldova 29 C14 47 15N 29 10 E
Dubossary Vdkhr. = Dubāsari Vdkhr., Moldova 29 C13 47 30N 29 0 E
Dubove, Ukraine 29 B8 48 10N 23 53 E
Dubovka, Russia 35 F7 49 5N 44 50 E
Dubovskoye, Russia 35 G6 47 28N 42 46 E
Dubrajpur, India 69 H12 23 48N 87 25 E
Dubréka, Guinea 82 D2 9 46N 13 31W
Dubrovitsa = Dubrovytsya, Ukraine 33 G4 51 31N 26 35 E
Dubrovnik, Croatia 44 D2 42 39N 18 6 E
Dubrovytsya, Ukraine 33 G4 51 31N 26 35 E
Dubuque, U.S.A. 112 D9 42 30N 90 41W
Duchang, China 59 C11 29 18N 116 12 E
Duchesne, U.S.A. 108 F8 40 10N 110 24W
Duchess, Australia 94 C2 21 20 S 139 52 E
Ducie I., Pac. Oc. 97 K15 24 40 S 124 48W
Duck →, U.S.A. 115 G2 36 2N 87 52W
Duck Cr. →, Australia 92 D2 22 37 S 116 53 E
Duck Lake, Canada 103 C7 52 50N 106 16W
Duck Mountain △, Canada 103 C8 51 45N 101 0W
Duckwall, Mt., U.S.A. 110 H6 37 58N 120 7W
Duderstadt, Germany 24 D6 51 30N 10 15 E
Dudhi, India 67 G13 24 15N 83 10 E
Dudley, U.K. 15 E5 52 31N 2 5W
Dudwa, India 69 E9 28 30N 80 41 E
Duékoué, Ivory C. 82 D3 6 40N 7 15W
Dueñas, Spain 36 D6 41 52N 4 33W
Duero = Douro →, Europe 36 D2 41 8N 8 40W
Dufftown, U.K. 13 D5 57 27N 3 8W
Dufourspitz, Switz. 25 K3 45 5N 7 52 E
Dŭgĭ Kalā, Afghan. 66 C3 32 20N 62 50 E
Dugi Otok, Croatia 41 D11 44 0N 15 3 E
Dugo Selo, Croatia 41 C13 45 51N 16 18 E
Duifken Pt., Australia 94 A3 12 33 S 141 38 E
Duisburg, Germany 24 D2 51 26N 6 45 E
Duiwelskloof, S. Africa 89 C5 23 42 S 30 10 E
Dujiangyan, China 58 B4 31 2N 103 38 E
Duk Fadiat, Sudan 81 F3 7 45N 31 25 E
Duk Faiwil, Sudan 81 F3 7 30N 31 29 E
Dukat, Albania 44 F3 40 16N 19 32 E
Dūkdamin, Iran 71 C8 35 59N 57 43 E
Dukelský Průsmyk, Slovak Rep. 27 B14 49 25N 21 42 E
Dukhān, Qatar 71 E6 25 25N 50 50 E
Dukhovshchina, Russia 32 E7 55 15N 32 27 E
Duki, Pakistan 66 D6 30 14N 68 25 E
Dukla, Poland 31 J8 49 30N 21 35 E
Duku, Bauchi, Nigeria 83 C7 10 43N 10 43 E
Duku, Sokoto, Nigeria 83 C5 11 11N 4 55 E
Dulag, Phil. 61 F6 10 57N 125 2 E
Dulce, U.S.A. 109 H10 36 56N 107 0W
Dulce →, Argentina 126 C3 30 32 S 62 33W
Dulce, G., Costa Rica 120 E3 8 40N 83 20W
Dulf, Iraq 70 C5 35 7N 45 51 E
Dŭlgopol, Bulgaria 45 C11 43 3N 27 22 E
Dulit, Banjaran, Malaysia 62 D4 3 15N 114 30 E
Duliu, China 56 E9 39 2N 116 55 E
Dullewala, Pakistan 68 D4 31 50N 71 25 E
Dullstroom, S. Africa 89 D5 25 27 S 30 7 E
Dülmen, Germany 24 D3 51 49N 7 17 E
Dulovo, Bulgaria 45 C11 43 48N 27 9 E
Dulq Maghār, Syria 70 B3 36 22N 38 39 E
Duluth, U.S.A. 112 B8 46 47N 92 6W
Dum Dum, India 69 H13 22 39N 88 33 E
Dumaguete, Phil. 61 G5 9 17N 123 15 E
Dumai, Indonesia 62 D2 1 35N 101 28 E
Dumaran, Phil. 61 F3 10 33N 119 50 E
Dumas, Ark., U.S.A. 113 J9 33 53N 91 29W
Dumas, Tex., U.S.A. 113 H4 35 52N 101 58W
Dŭmayr, Syria 74 B5 33 34N 36 24 E
Dumbarton, U.K. 13 F4 55 57N 4 33W
Dumbier, Slovak Rep. 27 C12 48 56N 19 58 E
Dumbleyung, Australia 93 F2 33 17 S 117 42 E
Dumboa, Nigeria 83 C7 11 15N 12 5 E
Dumbrăveni, Romania 29 D9 46 14N 24 34 E
Dumfries, U.K. 13 F5 55 4N 3 37W
Dumfries & Galloway □, U.K. 13 F5 55 9N 3 58W
Dumitrești, Romania 29 E11 45 31N 26 55 E
Dumka, India 69 G12 24 12N 87 15 E
Dumlupinar, Turkey 47 C12 39 7N 29 58 E
Dümmer, Germany 24 C4 52 31N 8 20 E
Dumoine →, Canada 104 C4 46 13N 77 51W
Dumoine, L., Canada 104 C4 46 55N 77 55W

Dumont d'Urville, Antarctica 5 C10 67 0 S 110 0 E
Dun Dealgan = Dundalk, Ireland 12 B5 54 1N 6 24W
Dún Laoghaire, Ireland 12 C5 53 17N 6 8W
Dun-le-Palestel, France 19 F8 46 18N 1 39 E
Dun-sur-Auron, France 19 F9 46 53N 2 33 E
Dun-sur-Meuse, France 19 C12 49 23N 5 11 E
Duna = Dunărea →, Europe 29 E14 45 20N 29 40 E
Duna →, Hungary 28 E3 45 51N 18 48 E
Duna-Drava △, Hungary 28 D3 46 15N 18 50 E
Duna-völgyi-főcsatorna, Hungary 28 D4 46 40N 19 14 E
Dunaföldvár, Hungary 28 D3 46 50N 18 57 E
Dunagiri, India 69 D8 30 31N 79 52 E
Dunaj = Dunărea →, Europe 29 E14 45 20N 29 40 E
Dunaj →, Slovak Rep. 27 D11 47 50N 18 50 E
Dunajec →, Poland 31 H7 50 15N 20 44 E
Dunajská Streda, Slovak Rep. 27 C10 48 0N 17 37 E
Dunakeszi, Hungary 28 C4 47 37N 19 8 E
Dunapataj, Hungary 28 D4 46 39N 19 4 E
Dunărea →, Europe 29 E14 45 20N 29 40 E
Dunaszekcső, Hungary 28 D3 46 6N 18 45 E
Dunaújváros, Hungary 28 D3 46 58N 18 57 E
Dunav = Dunărea →, Europe 29 E14 45 20N 29 40 E
Dunavățu de Jos, Romania 29 F14 44 59N 29 13 E
Dunavtsi, Bulgaria 44 C6 43 57N 22 53 E
Dunay, Russia 54 C6 42 52N 132 22 E
Dunayivtsi, Ukraine 29 B11 48 54N 26 50 E
Dunback, N.Z. 91 L3 45 23 S 170 36 E
Dunblane, U.K. 13 E5 56 11N 3 58W
Duncan, Canada 102 D4 48 45N 123 40W
Duncan, Ariz., U.S.A. 109 K9 32 43N 109 6W
Duncan, Okla., U.S.A. 113 H6 34 30N 97 57W
Duncan L., Canada 104 B4 53 29N 77 58W
Duncan L., Canada 102 A6 62 51N 113 58W
Duncan Town, Bahamas 120 B4 22 15N 75 45W
Duncannon, U.S.A. 116 F7 40 23N 77 2W
Duncansby Head, U.K. 13 C5 58 38N 3 1W
Duncansville, U.S.A. 116 F6 40 25N 78 26W
Dundaga, Latvia 30 A9 57 31N 22 21 E
Dundalk, Canada 116 B4 44 10N 80 24W
Dundalk, Ireland 12 B5 54 1N 6 24W
Dundalk Bay, Ireland 12 C5 53 55N 6 15W
Dundas = Uummannaq, Greenland 4 B4 77 0N 69 0W
Dundas = Uummannaq, Greenland 4 B5 70 58N 52 0W
Dundas, Canada 116 C5 43 17N 79 59W
Dundas, L., Australia 93 F3 32 35 S 121 50 E
Dundas I., Canada 102 C2 54 30N 130 50W
Dundas Str., Australia 92 B5 11 15 S 131 35 E
Dundee, S. Africa 89 D5 28 11 S 30 15 E
Dundee, U.K. 13 E6 56 28N 2 59W
Dundee, U.S.A. 116 D8 42 32N 76 59W
Dundee City □, U.K. 13 E6 56 30N 2 58W
Dundgovĭ □, Mongolia 56 B4 45 10N 106 0 E
Dundrum, U.K. 12 B6 54 16N 5 52W
Dundrum B., U.K. 12 B6 54 13N 5 47W
Dunedin, N.Z. 91 L3 45 50 S 170 33 E
Dunedin, U.S.A. 115 L4 28 1N 82 47W
Dunfermline, U.K. 13 E5 56 5N 3 27W
Dungannon, Canada 116 C3 43 51N 81 36W
Dungannon, U.K. 12 B5 54 31N 6 46W
Dungarpur, India 68 H5 23 52N 73 45 E
Dungarvan, Ireland 12 D4 52 5N 7 37W
Dungarvan Harbour, Ireland 12 D4 52 4N 7 35W
Dungeness, U.K. 15 G8 50 54N 0 59 E
Dungo, L. do, Angola 88 B2 17 15 S 19 0 E
Dungog, Australia 95 E5 32 22 S 151 46 E
Dungu, Dem. Rep. of the Congo 86 B2 3 40N 28 32 E
Dungun, Malaysia 65 K4 4 45N 103 25 E
Dungunāb, Sudan 80 C4 21 10N 37 9 E
Dungunāb, Khalig, Sudan 80 C4 21 5N 37 10 E
Dunhua, China 57 C15 43 20N 128 14 E
Dunhuang, China 60 B4 40 8N 94 36 E
Dunk I., Australia 94 B4 17 59 S 146 29 E
Dunkassa, Benin 83 C5 10 23N 3 10 E
Dunkeld, Australia 95 E4 33 25 S 149 29 E
Dunkeld, U.K. 13 E5 56 34N 3 35W
Dunkerque, France 19 A9 51 2N 2 20 E
Dunkery Beacon, U.K. 15 F4 51 9N 3 36W
Dunkirk = Dunkerque, France 19 A9 51 2N 2 20 E
Dunkirk, U.S.A. 116 D5 42 29N 79 20W
Dunkuj, Sudan 81 E3 12 50N 32 49 E
Dunkwa, Central, Ghana 82 D4 6 0N 1 47W
Dunkwa, Central, Ghana 83 D4 5 30N 1 0W
Dúnleary = Dún Laoghaire, Ireland 12 C5 53 17N 6 8W
Dunleer, Ireland 12 C5 53 50N 6 24W
Dunmanus B., Ireland 12 E2 51 31N 9 50W
Dunmanway, Ireland 12 E2 51 43N 9 6W
Dunmara, Australia 94 B1 16 42 S 133 25 E
Dunmore, U.S.A. 117 E9 41 25N 75 38W
Dunmore Hd., Ireland 12 D1 52 10N 10 35W
Dunmore Town, Bahamas 120 A4 25 30N 76 39W
Dunn, U.S.A. 115 H6 35 19N 78 37W
Dunnellon, U.S.A. 115 L4 29 3N 82 28W
Dunnet Hd., U.K. 13 C5 58 40N 3 21W
Dunning, U.S.A. 112 E4 41 50N 100 6W
Dunnville, Canada 116 D5 42 54N 79 36W
Dunolly, Australia 95 F3 36 51 S 143 44 E
Dunoon, U.K. 13 F4 55 57N 4 56W
Dunphy, U.S.A. 108 F5 40 42N 116 31W
Dunqul, Egypt 80 C3 23 26N 31 37 E
Duns, U.K. 13 F6 55 47N 2 20W
Dunseith, U.S.A. 112 A4 48 50N 100 3W
Dunsmuir, U.S.A. 108 F2 41 13N 122 16W
Dunstable, U.K. 15 F7 51 53N 0 32W
Dunstan Mts., N.Z. 91 L2 44 53 S 169 35 E
Dunster, Canada 102 C5 53 8N 119 50W
Dunvegan L., Canada 103 A7 60 8N 107 10W
Duolun, China 56 C9 42 12N 116 28 E
Duong Dong, Vietnam 65 G4 10 13N 103 58 E
Dupree, U.S.A. 112 C4 45 4N 101 35W
Dupuyer, U.S.A. 108 B7 48 13N 112 30W
Duque de Caxias, Brazil 127 A7 22 45 S 43 19W
Durack →, Australia 92 C4 15 33 S 127 52 E
Durack Ra., Australia 92 C4 16 50 S 127 40 E
Durağan, Turkey 72 B6 41 35N 35 5 E
Durak, Turkey 47 B10 39 42N 28 17 E

Đurakovac, Serbia & M. 44 D4 42 43N 20 29 E
Durance →, France 21 E8 43 55N 4 45 E
Durand, U.S.A. 112 C9 44 38N 91 58W
Durango, Mexico 118 C4 24 3N 104 39W
Durango, U.S.A. 109 H10 37 16N 107 53W
Durango □, Mexico 118 C4 25 0N 105 0W
Durant, Miss., U.S.A. 113 J10 33 4N 89 51W
Durant, Okla., U.S.A. 113 J6 33 59N 96 25W
Duratón →, Spain 36 D6 41 37N 4 7W
Durazno, Uruguay 126 C4 33 25 S 56 31W
Durazzo = Durrës, Albania 44 E3 41 19N 19 28 E
Durban, France 20 F6 42 59N 2 49 E
Durban, S. Africa 89 D5 29 49 S 31 1 E
Durbuy, Belgium 17 D5 50 21N 5 28 E
Dúrcal, Spain 37 H7 37 9N 3 34W
Đurđevac, Croatia 28 D2 46 2N 17 3 E
Düren, Germany 24 E2 50 48N 6 29 E
Durg, India 67 J12 21 15N 81 22 E
Durgapur, India 69 H12 23 30N 87 20 E
Durham, Canada 116 B4 44 10N 80 49W
Durham, U.K. 14 C6 54 47N 1 34W
Durham, Calif., U.S.A. 110 F5 39 39N 121 48W
Durham, N.C., U.S.A. 115 H6 35 59N 78 54W
Durham, N.H., U.S.A. 117 C14 43 8N 70 56W
Durham □, U.K. 14 C6 54 42N 1 45W
Durlești, Moldova 29 C13 47 1N 28 46 E
Durmā, Si. Arabia 70 E5 24 37N 46 8 E
Durmitor, Serbia & M. 44 C2 43 10N 19 0 E
Durmitor △, Serbia & M. 44 C3 43 15N 19 5 E
Durness, U.K. 13 C4 58 34N 4 45W
Durrës, Albania 44 E3 41 19N 19 28 E
Durrow, Ireland 12 D4 52 51N 7 24W
Dursey I., Ireland 12 E1 51 36N 10 12W
Dursley, U.K. 15 F5 51 40N 2 21W
Dursunbey, Turkey 47 B10 39 35N 28 37 E
Durtal, France 18 E6 47 40N 0 18W
Duru, Dem. Rep. of the Congo 86 B2 4 14N 28 50 E
Duru Gölü, Turkey 45 E12 41 20N 28 35 E
Durusu, Turkey 45 E12 41 17N 28 41 E
Durūz, Jabal ad, Jordan 74 C5 32 35N 36 40 E
D'Urville, Tanjung, Indonesia 63 E9 1 28 S 137 54 E
D'Urville I., N.Z. 91 J4 40 50 S 173 55 E
Duryea, U.S.A. 117 E9 41 20N 75 45W
Dūsh, Egypt 80 C3 24 35N 30 41 E
Dushak, Turkmenistan 52 F7 37 13N 60 1 E
Dushan, China 58 E6 25 48N 107 30 E
Dushanbe, Tajikistan 52 F7 38 33N 68 48 E
Dusheti, Georgia 35 J7 42 10N 44 42 E
Dushore, U.S.A. 117 E8 41 31N 76 24W
Dusky Sd., N.Z. 91 L1 45 47 S 166 30 E
Dussejour, C., Australia 92 B4 14 45 S 128 13 E
Düsseldorf, Germany 24 D2 51 14N 6 47 E
Düsseldorf Rhein-Ruhr ✈ (DUS), Germany 24 D2 51 17N 6 46 E
Duszniki-Zdrój, Poland 31 H3 50 24N 16 24 E
Dutch Harbor, U.S.A. 100 C3 53 53N 166 32W
Dutlwe, Botswana 88 C3 23 58 S 23 46 E
Dutton, Canada 116 D3 42 39N 81 30W
Dutton →, Australia 94 C3 20 44 S 143 10 E
Duved, Sweden 10 A6 63 23N 12 51 E
Duyun, China 58 D6 26 18N 107 29 E
Düzağac, Turkey 47 C12 38 48N 30 10 E
Düzce, Turkey 72 B4 40 50N 31 10 E
Dve Mogili, Bulgaria 45 C9 43 35N 25 55 E
Dvina, Severnaya →, Russia 52 C5 64 32N 40 30 E
Dvinsk = Daugavpils, Latvia 9 J22 55 53N 26 32 E
Dvor, Croatia 41 C13 45 4N 16 22 E
Dvůr Králové nad Labem, Czech Rep. 26 A8 50 27N 15 50 E
Dwarka, India 68 H3 22 18N 69 8 E
Dwellingup, Australia 93 F2 32 43 S 116 4 E
Dwight, Canada 116 A5 45 20N 79 1W
Dwight, U.S.A. 114 E1 41 5N 88 26W
Dyakova, Ukraine 28 B7 48 1N 23 0 E
Dyatkovo, Russia 32 F8 53 40N 34 27 E
Dyatlovo = Dzyatlava, Belarus 32 F3 53 28N 25 28 E
Dyce, U.K. 13 D6 57 13N 2 12W
Dyer, C., Canada 101 B13 66 37N 61 16W
Dyer Bay, Canada 116 A3 45 10N 81 20W
Dyer Plateau, Antarctica 5 D17 70 45 S 65 30W
Dyersburg, U.S.A. 113 G10 36 3N 89 23W
Dyfi →, U.K. 15 E3 52 32N 4 3W
Dyje →, Czech Rep. 27 C9 48 37N 16 56 E
Dymer, Ukraine 33 G6 50 47N 30 18 E
Dynów, Poland 31 J9 49 50N 22 11 E
Dysart, Australia 94 C4 22 32 S 148 23 E
Dyviziya, Ukraine 29 E14 45 55N 29 59 E
Dzerzhinsk, Russia 34 B6 56 14N 43 30 E
Dzhalinda, Russia 53 D13 53 26N 124 0 E
Dzhambul = Taraz, Kazakhstan 52 E8 42 54N 71 22 E
Dzhankoy, Ukraine 33 K8 45 40N 34 20 E
Dzhanybek, Kazakhstan 34 F8 49 5N 46 50 E
Dzharylhach, Ostriv, Ukraine 33 J7 46 2N 32 55 E
Dzhezkazgan = Zhezqazghan, Kazakhstan 52 E7 47 44N 67 40 E
Dzhizak = Jizzakh, Uzbekistan 52 E7 40 6N 67 50 E
Dzhugdzur, Khrebet, Russia 53 D14 57 30N 138 0 E
Dzhvari, Georgia 35 J6 42 42N 42 4 E
Działdowo, Poland 31 E7 53 15N 20 15 E
Działoszyce, Poland 31 H7 50 22N 20 20 E
Działoszyn, Poland 31 G5 51 6N 18 50 E
Dzibilchaltún, Mexico 119 C7 21 5N 89 36W
Dzierzgoń, Poland 30 E6 53 58N 19 26 E
Dzierżoniów, Poland 31 H3 50 45N 16 39 E
Dzilam de Bravo, Mexico 119 C7 21 24N 88 53W
Dzisna, Belarus 32 E5 55 14N 28 11 E
Dzisna →, Belarus 32 E5 55 34N 28 12 E
Dziwnów, Poland 30 D1 54 2N 14 45 E
Dzungaria = Junggar Pendi, China 60 B3 44 30N 86 0 E
Dzungarian Basin = Junggar Pendi, China 60 B3 44 30N 86 0 E
Dzungarian Gate, Asia 60 B5 45 0N 82 0 E
Dzuumod, Mongolia 60 B5 47 45N 106 58 E
Dzyarzhynsk, Belarus 32 F4 53 40N 27 1 E
Dzyatlava, Belarus 32 F3 53 28N 25 4 E

E

E.C. Manning △, Canada 102 D4 49 5N 120 45W
Eabamet L., Canada 104 B2 51 30N 87 46W
Eads, U.S.A. 112 F3 38 29N 102 47W
Eagar, U.S.A. 109 J9 34 6N 109 17W
Eagle, Alaska, U.S.A. 100 B5 64 47N 141 12W
Eagle, Colo., U.S.A. 108 G10 39 39N 106 50W
Eagle →, Canada 105 B8 53 36N 57 26W
Eagle Butte, U.S.A. 112 C4 45 0N 101 10W
Eagle Grove, U.S.A. 112 D8 42 40N 93 54W
Eagle L., Canada 103 D10 49 42N 93 13W
Eagle L., Calif., U.S.A. 108 F3 40 39N 120 45W
Eagle L., Maine, U.S.A. 115 B11 46 20N 69 22W
Eagle Lake, Canada 116 A6 45 8N 78 29W
Eagle Lake, Maine, U.S.A. 115 B11 47 3N 68 36W
Eagle Lake, Tex., U.S.A. 113 L6 29 35N 96 20W
Eagle Mountain, U.S.A. 111 M11 33 49N 115 27W
Eagle Nest, U.S.A. 109 H11 36 33N 105 16W
Eagle Pass, U.S.A. 113 L4 28 43N 100 30W
Eagle Pk., U.S.A. 110 G7 38 10N 119 25W
Eagle Pt., Australia 92 C3 16 11 S 124 23 E
Eagle River, Mich., U.S.A. 114 B1 47 24N 88 18W
Eagle River, Wis., U.S.A. 112 C10 45 55N 89 15W
Eaglehawk, Australia 95 F3 36 44 S 144 15 E
Eagles Mere, U.S.A. 117 E8 41 25N 76 33W
Ealing □, U.K. 15 F7 51 31N 0 20W
Ear Falls, Canada 103 C10 50 38N 93 13W
Earle, U.S.A. 113 H9 35 16N 90 28W
Earlimart, U.S.A. 111 K7 35 53N 119 16W
Earn →, U.K. 13 E5 56 21N 3 18W
Earn, L., U.K. 13 E4 56 23N 4 13W
Earnslaw, Mt., N.Z. 91 L2 44 32 S 168 27 E
Earth, U.S.A. 113 H3 34 14N 102 24W
Easley, U.S.A. 115 H4 34 50N 82 36W
East Angus, Canada 105 C5 45 30N 71 40W
East Antarctica, Antarctica 5 D7 80 0 S 90 0 E
East Aurora, U.S.A. 116 D6 42 46N 78 37W
East Ayrshire □, U.K. 13 F4 55 26N 4 11W
East Bengal, Bangla. 67 H17 24 0N 90 0 E
East Beskids = Vychodné Beskydy, Europe 27 B15 49 20N 22 0 E
East Brady, U.S.A. 116 F5 40 59N 79 36W
East C., N.Z. 91 G7 37 42 S 178 35 E
East Chicago, U.S.A. 114 E2 41 38N 87 27W
East China Sea, Asia 60 C7 30 0N 126 0 E
East Coulee, Canada 102 C6 51 23N 112 27W
East Dereham = Dereham, U.K. 15 E8 52 41N 0 57 E
East Dunbartonshire □, U.K. 13 F4 55 57N 4 13W
East Falkland, Falk. Is. 128 G5 51 30 S 58 30W
East Grand Forks, U.S.A. 112 B6 47 56N 97 1W
East Greenwich, U.S.A. 117 E13 41 40N 71 27W
East Grinstead, U.K. 15 F8 51 7N 0 0W
East Hartford, U.S.A. 117 E12 41 46N 72 39W
East Helena, U.S.A. 108 C8 46 35N 111 56W
East Indies, Asia 50 K15 0 0 120 0 E
East Kilbride, U.K. 13 F4 55 47N 4 11W
East Lansing, U.S.A. 114 D3 42 44N 84 29W
East Liverpool, U.S.A. 116 F4 40 37N 80 35W
East London, S. Africa 89 E4 33 0 S 27 55 E
East Lothian □, U.K. 13 F6 55 58N 2 44W
East Main = Eastmain, Canada 104 B4 52 10N 78 30W
East Northport, U.S.A. 117 F11 40 53N 73 20W
East Orange, U.S.A. 117 F10 40 46N 74 13W
East Pacific Ridge, Pac. Oc. 97 J17 15 0 S 110 0W
East Palestine, U.S.A. 116 F4 40 50N 80 33W
East Pine, Canada 102 B4 55 48N 120 12W
East Point, U.S.A. 115 J3 33 41N 84 27W
East Providence, U.S.A. 117 E13 41 49N 71 23W
East Pt., Br. Virgin Is. 121 e 18 40N 64 18W
East Pt., Canada 105 C7 46 27N 61 58W
East Renfrewshire □, U.K. 13 F4 55 46N 4 21W
East Retford = Retford, U.K. 14 D7 53 19N 0 56W
East Riding of Yorkshire □, U.K. 14 D7 53 55N 0 30W
East Rochester, U.S.A. 116 C7 43 7N 77 29W
East St. Louis, U.S.A. 112 F9 38 37N 90 9W
East Schelde = Oosterschelde →, Neths. 17 C4 51 33N 4 0 E
East Sea = Japan, Sea of, Asia 54 E7 40 0N 135 0 E
East Siberian Sea, Russia 53 B17 73 0N 160 0 E
East Stroudsburg, U.S.A. 117 E9 41 1N 75 11W
East Sussex □, U.K. 15 G8 50 56N 0 19 E
East Tawas, U.S.A. 114 C4 44 17N 83 29W
East Timor ■, Asia 63 F7 8 50 S 126 0 E
East Toorale, Australia 95 E4 30 27 S 145 28 E
East Walker →, U.S.A. 110 G7 38 52N 119 10W
East Windsor, U.S.A. 117 F10 40 17N 74 34W
Eastbourne, N.Z. 91 J5 41 19 S 174 55 E
Eastbourne, U.K. 15 G8 50 46N 0 18 E
Eastend, Canada 103 D7 49 32N 108 50W
Easter I. = Pascua, I. de, Chile 97 K17 27 7 S 109 23W
Eastern □, Ghana 83 D4 6 30N 0 30W
Eastern □, Kenya 86 C4 0 0 38 30 E
Eastern □, S. Leone 82 D2 8 15N 11 0W
Eastern Cape □, S. Africa 88 E4 32 0 S 26 0 E
Eastern Ghats, India 66 N11 14 0N 78 50 E
Eastern Group = Lau Group, Fiji 91 C9 17 0 S 178 30W
Eastern Group, Australia 93 F3 33 30 S 124 30 E
Eastern Transvaal = Mpumalanga □, S. Africa 89 D5 26 0 S 30 0 E
Easterville, Canada 103 C9 53 8N 99 49W
Easthampton, U.S.A. 117 D12 42 16N 72 40W
Eastlake, U.S.A. 116 E3 41 40N 81 26W
Eastland, U.S.A. 113 J5 32 24N 98 49W
Eastleigh, U.K. 15 G6 50 58N 1 21W
Eastmain, Canada 104 B4 52 10N 78 30W
Eastmain →, Canada 104 B4 52 27N 78 26W
Eastman, Canada 117 A12 45 18N 72 19W
Eastman, U.S.A. 115 J4 32 12N 83 11W
Easton, Md., U.S.A. 114 F7 38 47N 76 5W
Easton, Pa., U.S.A. 117 F9 40 41N 75 13W
Easton, Wash., U.S.A. 110 C5 47 14N 121 11W

Eastpointe, *U.S.A.* **116 D2** 42 27N 82 56W
Eastport, *U.S.A.* **115 C12** 44 56N 67 0W
Eastsound, *U.S.A.* **110 B4** 48 42N 122 55W
Eaton, *U.S.A.* **112 E2** 40 32N 104 42W
Eatonia, *Canada* **103 C7** 51 13N 109 25W
Eatonton, *U.S.A.* **115 J4** 33 20N 83 23W
Eatontown, *U.S.A.* **117 F10** 40 19N 74 4W
Eatonville, *U.S.A.* **110 D4** 46 52N 122 16W
Eau Claire, *U.S.A.* **112 C9** 44 49N 91 30W
Eau Claire, L. à l',
  Canada **104 A5** 56 10N 74 0W
Eauze, *France* .... **20 E4** 43 53N 0 7 E
Eban, *Nigeria* .... **83 D5** 9 40N 4 50 E
Ebbegebirge △,
  Germany .... **24 D3** 51 10N 7 55 E
Ebbw Vale, *U.K.* **15 F4** 51 46N 3 12W
Ebeltoft, *Denmark* .... **11 H4** 56 12N 10 41 E
Ebeltoft Vig, *Denmark* **11 H4** 56 10N 10 35 E
Ebensburg, *U.S.A.* **116 F6** 40 29N 78 44W
Ebensee, *Austria* ...... **26 D6** 47 48N 13 46 E
Eber Gölü, *Turkey* .... **72 C4** 38 38N 31 11 E
Eberbach, *Germany* .... **25 F4** 49 28N 8 59 E
Eberswalde-Finow,
  Germany .... **24 C9** 52 50N 13 49 E
Ebetsu, *Japan* .... **54 C10** 43 7N 141 34 E
Ebey's Landing △,
  U.S.A. **110 B4** 48 13N 122 41W
Ebian, *China* .... **58 C4** 29 11N 103 13 E
Ebingen, *Germany* ..... **25 G5** 48 13N 9 1 E
Éboli, *Italy* .... **43 B8** 40 39N 15 2 E
Ebolowa, *Cameroon* .... **83 E7** 2 55N 11 10 E
Ebonyi □, *Nigeria* ..... **83 D6** 6 20N 8 0 E
Ebrach, *Germany* ...... **25 F6** 49 51N 10 29 E
Ébrié, Lagune, *Ivory C.* **82 D4** 5 12N 4 26W
Ebro →, *Spain* .... **38 E5** 40 43N 0 54 E
Ebro, Embalse del,
  Spain **36 C7** 43 0N 3 58W
Ebstorf, *Germany* ..... **24 B6** 53 2N 10 24 E
Eceabat, *Turkey* ...... **45 F10** 40 11N 26 21 E
Ech Chélif, *Algeria* .... **78 A6** 36 10N 1 20 E
Echigo-Sammyaku,
  Japan .... **55 F9** 36 50N 139 50 E
Échirolles, *France* ..... **21 C9** 45 8N 5 44 E
Echizen-Misaki, *Japan* . **55 G7** 35 59N 135 57 E
Echmiadzin =
  Yejmiadzin, *Armenia* **35 K7** 40 12N 44 19 E
Echo Bay, *N.W.T.,*
  Canada **100 B8** 66 5N 117 55W
Echo Bay, *Ont., Canada* **104 C3** 46 29N 84 4W
Echoing →, *Canada* **104 B1** 55 51N 92 5W
Echternach, *Lux.* ...... **17 E6** 49 49N 6 25 E
Echuca, *Australia* ..... **95 F3** 36 10N 144 45 E
Ecija, *Spain* **37 H5** 37 30N 5 10W
Eckental, *Germany* .... **25 F7** 49 35N 11 12 E
Eckernförde, *Germany* . **24 A5** 54 28N 9 50 E
Eclipse I., *Australia* ... **93 G2** 35 5S 117 58 E
Eclipse Is., *Australia* ... **92 B4** 13 54 S 126 19 E
Eclipse Sd., *Canada* **101 A11** 72 38N 79 0W
Écommoy, *France* ...... **18 E7** 47 50N 0 17 E
Écouché, *France* **18 D6** 48 42N 0 10W
Ecrins △, *France* ...... **21 D10** 44 54N 6 18 E
Ecuador ■, *S. Amer.* ... **124 D3** 2 0S 78 0W
Écueillé, *France* .... **18 E8** 47 5N 1 19 E
Ed, *Sweden* .... **11 F5** 58 55N 11 55 E
Ed Damazin, *Sudan* .... **80 D3** 17 40N 34 15 E
Ed Da'ein, *Sudan* ...... **81 E2** 11 26N 26 9 E
Ed Damazin, *Sudan* .... **79 F12** 11 46N 34 21 E
Ed Dâmer, *Sudan* ...... **80 D3** 17 27N 34 0 E
Ed Dar el Beida =
  Casablanca, *Morocco* **78 B4** 33 36N 7 36W
Ed Debba, *Sudan* ...... **80 D3** 18 0N 30 51 E
Ed-Déffa, *Egypt* .... **80 A2** 30 40N 26 30 E
Ed Deim, *Sudan* .... **81 E2** 10 10N 28 20 E
Ed Dueim, *Sudan* ...... **81 E3** 14 0N 32 10 E
Edam, *Canada* **103 C7** 53 11N 108 46W
Edam, *Neths.* .... **17 B5** 52 31N 5 3 E
Edane, *Sweden* .... **10 E6** 59 38N 12 49 E
Eday, *U.K.* **13 B6** 59 11N 2 47W
Edd, *Eritrea* .... **81 E5** 14 0N 41 38 E
Eddrachillis B., *U.K.* ... **13 C3** 58 17N 5 14W
Eddystone, *U.K.* **15 G3** 50 11N 4 16W
Eddystone Pt., *Australia* **95 G4** 40 59 S 148 20 E
Ede, *Neths.* .... **17 B5** 52 4N 5 40 E
Ede, *Nigeria* .... **83 D5** 7 45N 4 29 E
Édéa, *Cameroon* .... **83 E7** 3 51N 10 9 E
Edebäck, *Sweden* ...... **10 D7** 60 4N 13 32 E
Edehon L., *Canada* **103 A9** 60 25N 97 15W
Edelény, *Hungary* ..... **28 B5** 48 18N 20 44 E
Eden, *Australia* .... **95 F4** 37 3 S 149 55 E
Eden, *N.C., U.S.A.* **115 G6** 36 29N 79 53W
Eden, *N.Y., U.S.A.* **116 D6** 42 39N 78 55W
Eden, *Tex., U.S.A.* **113 K5** 31 13N 99 51W
Eden →, *U.K.* **14 C4** 54 57N 3 1W
Edenburg, *S. Africa* ... **88 D4** 29 43 S 25 58 E
Edendale, *S. Africa* .... **89 D5** 29 39 S 30 18 E
Edenderry, *Ireland* **12 C4** 53 21N 7 4W
Edenton, *U.S.A.* **115 G7** 36 4N 76 39W
Edenville, *S. Africa* .... **89 D4** 27 37 S 27 34 E
Eder →, *Germany* ...... **24 D5** 51 12N 9 28 E
Eder-Stausee, *Germany* **24 D4** 51 10N 8 57 E
Edewecht, *Germany* .... **24 B3** 53 8N 7 58 E
Edgar, *U.S.A.* **112 E6** 40 22N 97 58W
Edgartown, *U.S.A.* **117 E14** 41 23N 70 31W
Edge Hill, *U.K.* **15 E6** 52 8N 1 26W
Edgefield, *U.S.A.* **115 J5** 33 47N 81 56W
Edgeley, *U.S.A.* **112 B5** 46 22N 98 43W
Edgemont, *U.S.A.* **112 D3** 43 18N 103 50W
Edgeøya, *Svalbard* ..... **4 B9** 77 45N 22 30 E
Édhessa, *Greece* .... **44 F6** 40 48N 22 5 E
Edievale, *N.Z.* .... **91 L2** 45 49 S 169 22 E
Edina, *Liberia* **82 D2** 6 0N 10 10W
Edina, *U.S.A.* **112 E8** 40 10N 92 11W
Edinboro, *U.S.A.* **116 E4** 41 52N 80 8W
Edinburg, *U.S.A.* **113 M5** 26 18N 98 10W
Edinburgh, *U.K.* **13 F5** 55 57N 3 13W
Edinburgh ✈ (EDI),
  U.K. **13 F5** 55 54N 3 22W
Edinburgh, City of □,
  U.K. **13 F5** 55 57N 3 17W
Edineț, *Moldova* ...... **29 B11** 48 9N 27 18 E
Edirne, *Turkey* .... **45 E10** 41 40N 26 34 E
Edirne □, *Turkey* ...... **45 E10** 41 12N 26 30 E
Edison, *U.S.A.* **110 B4** 48 33N 122 27W
Edithburgh, *Australia* . **95 F2** 35 5 S 137 43 E
Edmeston, *U.S.A.* **117 D9** 42 42N 75 15W
Edmond, *U.S.A.* **113 H6** 35 39N 97 29W
Edmonds, *U.S.A.* **110 C4** 47 49N 122 23W
Edmonton, *Australia* .. **94 B4** 17 2 S 145 46 E
Edmonton, *Canada* **102 C6** 53 30N 113 30W
Edmund L., *Canada* **104 B1** 54 45N 93 17W
Edmundston, *Canada* .. **105 C6** 47 23N 68 20W
Edna, *U.S.A.* **113 L6** 28 59N 96 39W
Edo □, *Nigeria* .... **83 D6** 6 30N 6 0 E
Edolo, *Italy* .... **40 B7** 46 10N 10 21 E

Edremit, *Turkey* ...... **47 B9** 39 34N 27 0 E
Edremit Körfezi, *Turkey* **47 B8** 39 30N 26 45 E
Edsbro, *Sweden* .... **10 E12** 59 54N 18 29 E
Edsbyn, *Sweden* .... **10 C9** 61 23N 15 49 E
Edson, *Canada* **102 C5** 53 35N 116 28W
Eduardo Castex,
  Argentina .... **126 D3** 35 50 S 64 18W
Edward →, *Australia* .. **95 F3** 35 5 S 143 30 E
Edward, L., *Africa* ..... **86 C2** 0 25 S 29 40 E
Edward River, *Australia* **94 A3** 14 59 S 141 26 E
Edward VII Land,
  Antarctica .... **5 E13** 80 0 S 150 0W
Edwards, *Calif., U.S.A.* **111 L9** 34 55N 117 51W
Edwards, *N.Y., U.S.A.* . **117 B9** 44 20N 75 15W
Edwards Air Force
  Base, *U.S.A.* **111 L9** 34 50N 117 40W
Edwards Plateau, *U.S.A.* **113 K4** 30 45N 101 20W
Edwardsville, *U.S.A.* ... **117 E9** 41 15N 75 56W
Edxná, *Mexico* **119 D6** 19 35N 90 15W
Edzo, *Canada* **102 A5** 62 49N 116 4W
Eeklo, *Belgium* .... **17 C3** 51 11N 3 33 E
Eferding, *Austria* ...... **26 C7** 48 18N 14 1 E
Effigy Mounds △,
  U.S.A. **112 D9** 43 5N 91 11W
Effingham, *U.S.A.* **114 F1** 39 7N 88 33W
Eforie, *Romania* .... **29 F13** 44 1N 28 37 E
Ega →, *Spain* **38 C3** 42 19N 1 55W
Égadi, Ísole, *Italy* ..... **42 E5** 37 55N 12 16 E
Egan Range, *U.S.A.* ... **108 G6** 39 35N 114 55W
Eganville, *Canada* **116 A7** 45 32N 77 5W
Eger = Cheb,
  Czech Rep. .... **26 A5** 50 9N 12 28 E
Eger, *Hungary* .... **28 C5** 47 53N 20 27 E
Eger →, *Hungary* ..... **28 C5** 47 38N 20 50 E
Egersund, *Norway* .... **9 G12** 58 26N 6 1 E
Egg L., *Canada* **103 B7** 55 5N 105 30W
Eggegebirge Südlicher
  Teutoburger Wald △,
  Germany .... **24 D4** 51 40N 8 59 E
Eggenburg, *Austria* .... **26 C8** 48 38N 15 50 E
Eggenfelden, *Germany* . **25 G8** 48 23N 12 46 E
Éghezée, *Belgium* ...... **17 D4** 50 35N 4 55 E
Égletons, *France* ...... **20 C6** 45 24N 2 3 E
Egmont, *Canada* **102 D4** 49 45N 123 56W
Egmont △, *N.Z.* .... **91 H5** 39 17 S 174 5 E
Egmont, C., *N.Z.* ..... **91 H4** 39 16 S 173 45 E
Egmont, Mt. = Taranaki,
  Mt., *N.Z.* .... **91 H5** 39 17 S 174 5 E
Egra, *India* .... **69 J12** 21 54N 87 32 E
Eğridir, *Turkey* .... **72 D4** 37 52N 30 51 E
Eğridir Gölü, *Turkey* .. **70 B1** 37 53N 30 50 E
Egtved, *Denmark* ...... **11 J3** 55 38N 9 18 E
Egume, *Nigeria* .... **83 D6** 7 30N 7 14 E
Éguzon-Chantôme,
  France .... **19 F8** 46 27N 1 33 E
Egvekinot, *Russia* **53 C19** 66 19N 179 50W
Egyek, *Hungary* .... **28 C5** 47 39N 20 52 E
Egypt ■, *Africa* .... **80 B3** 28 0N 31 0 E
Eha Amufu, *Nigeria* ... **83 D6** 6 30N 7 46 E
Ehime □, *Japan* .... **55 H6** 33 30N 132 40 E
Ehingen, *Germany* ..... **25 G5** 48 16N 9 43 E
Ehrenberg, *U.S.A.* **111 M12** 33 36N 114 31W
Ehrwald, *Austria* ...... **26 D3** 47 24N 10 56 E
Eibar, *Spain* **38 B2** 43 11N 2 28W
Eichstätt, *Germany* .... **25 G7** 48 54N 11 11 E
Eider →, *Germany* .... **24 A4** 54 19N 8 57 E
Eidsvold, *Australia* .... **95 D5** 25 25 S 151 12 E
Eidsvoll, *Norway* ...... **9 F14** 60 19N 11 14 E
Eifel, *Germany* .... **24 E2** 50 15N 6 50 E
Eiffel Flats, *Zimbabwe* . **87 F3** 18 20 S 30 0 E
Eiger, *Switz.* .... **40 B5** 46 34N 8 1 E
Eigg, *U.K.* **13 E2** 56 54N 6 10W
Eighty Mile Beach,
  Australia .... **92 C3** 19 30 S 120 40 E
Eil, *Somali Rep.* .... **75 F4** 8 0N 49 50 E
Eil, L., *U.K.* **13 E3** 56 51N 5 16W
Eildon, *Australia* ...... **95 F4** 37 10 S 146 0 E
Eildon, L., *Australia* ... **95 F4** 37 10 S 146 0 E
Ein el Luweiqa, *Sudan* . **81 E3** 14 5N 33 50 E
Einasleigh, *Australia* ... **94 B3** 18 32 S 144 5 E
Einasleigh →, *Australia* **94 B3** 17 30 S 142 17 E
Einbeck, *Germany* ..... **24 D5** 51 49N 9 53 E
Eindhoven, *Neths.* ..... **17 C5** 51 26N 5 28 E
Einsiedeln, *Switz.* ..... **25 H4** 47 7N 8 46 E
Eire = Ireland ■,
  Europe **12 C4** 53 50N 7 52W
Eiríksjökull, *Iceland* ... **8 D3** 64 46N 20 24W
Eirunepé, *Brazil* ...... **124 E5** 6 35 S 69 53W
Eiseb →, *Namibia* ..... **88 C2** 20 33 S 20 59 E
Eisenach, *Germany* .... **24 E6** 50 58N 10 19 E
Eisenberg, *Germany* ... **24 E7** 50 58N 11 54 E
Eisenerz, *Austria* ...... **26 D7** 47 32N 14 54 E
Eisenhüttenstadt,
  Germany .... **24 C10** 52 9N 14 38 E
Eisenkappel, *Austria* ... **26 E7** 46 29N 14 36 E
Eisenstadt, *Austria* .... **27 D9** 47 51N 16 31 E
Eisfeld, *Germany* ...... **25 E6** 50 25N 10 54 E
Eisleben, *Germany* ..... **24 D7** 51 32N 11 32 E
Eivissa, *Spain* .... **48 C7** 38 54N 1 26 E
Eixe, Serra do, *Spain* .. **36 C4** 42 24N 6 54W
Ejea de los Caballeros,
  Spain **38 C3** 42 7N 1 9W
Ejeda, *Madag.* .... **89 C7** 24 20 S 44 31 E
Ejura, *Ghana* **83 D4** 7 23N 1 15W
Ejutla, *Mexico* **119 D5** 16 34N 96 44W
Ekalaka, *U.S.A.* **112 C2** 45 53N 104 33W
Ekenäs = Tammisaari,
  Finland .... **9 F20** 60 0N 23 26 E
Ekenässjön, *Sweden* ... **11 G9** 57 28N 15 1 E
Ekerö, *Sweden* .... **10 E11** 59 16N 17 45 E
Eket, *Nigeria* .... **83 E6** 4 38N 7 56 E
Eketahuna, *N.Z.* ...... **91 J5** 40 38 S 175 43 E
Ekhínos, *Greece* ...... **45 E9** 41 16N 25 1 E
Ekibastuz, *Kazakhstan* **52 D8** 51 50N 75 10 E
Ekiti □, *Nigeria* .... **83 D6** 7 25N 5 20 E
Ekoli, *Dem. Rep. of
  the Congo* .... **86 C1** 0 23 S 24 13 E
Ekoln, *Sweden* .... **10 E11** 59 45N 17 37 E
Ekshärad, *Sweden* ..... **10 D7** 60 10N 13 30 E
Ekuma →, *Namibia* ... **88 B2** 18 40 S 16 2 E
Ekwan →, *Canada* **104 B3** 53 12N 82 15W
Ekwan Pt., *Canada* **104 B3** 53 16N 82 7W
El Aaiún, *W. Sahara* ... **78 C3** 27 9N 13 12W
El Abanico, *Chile* ...... **126 D1** 37 20 S 71 31W
El Abbasiya, *Sudan* .... **81 E3** 12 10N 31 18 E
El 'Agrūd, *Egypt* ...... **74 E3** 30 14N 34 24 E
El Ait, *Sudan* .... **81 E2** 12 22N 27 27 E
El 'Aiyat, *Egypt* ...... **80 J7** 29 36N 31 15 E
El 'Alamein, *Egypt* .... **80 A2** 30 48N 28 58 E
El 'Aqaba, W. →, *Egypt* **74 E2** 30 7N 33 54 E
El 'Arag, *Egypt* .... **80 B2** 28 40N 26 20 E
El Arahal, *Spain* **37 H5** 37 15N 5 33W
El Ariḥā, *West Bank* ... **74 D4** 31 52N 35 27 E
El 'Arîsh, *Egypt* ...... **74 D2** 31 8N 33 50 E
El 'Arîsh, W. →, *Egypt* **74 D2** 31 8N 33 47 E

El Asnam = Ech Chéliff,
  Algeria .... **78 A6** 36 10N 1 20 E
El Astillero, *Spain* **36 B7** 43 24N 3 49W
El Badâri, *Egypt* ...... **80 B3** 27 4N 31 25 E
El Ballâs, *Egypt* .... **80 B3** 26 2N 32 43 E
El Balyana, *Egypt* ..... **80 B3** 26 10N 32 3 E
El Baqeir, *Sudan* ...... **80 D3** 18 40N 33 40 E
El Barco de Ávila, *Spain* **36 E5** 40 21N 5 31W
El Barco de
  Valdeorras = O Barco,
  Spain **36 C4** 42 23N 6 58W
El Bauga, *Sudan* ...... **80 D3** 18 18N 33 52 E
El Bawiti, *Egypt* .... **80 B2** 28 25N 28 45 E
El Bayadh, *Algeria* ..... **78 B6** 33 40N 1 1 E
El Bierzo, *Spain* **36 C4** 42 45N 6 30W
El Bonillo, *Spain* **39 G2** 38 57N 2 35W
El Brûk, W. →, *Egypt* . **74 E2** 30 15N 33 50 E
El Buheirat □, *Sudan* .. **81 F3** 7 0N 30 0 E
El Burgo de Osma,
  Spain **38 D1** 41 35N 3 4W
El Cajon, *U.S.A.* **111 N10** 32 48N 116 58W
El Campo, *U.S.A.* **113 L6** 29 12N 96 16W
El Centro, *U.S.A.* **111 N11** 32 48N 115 34W
El Cerro, *Bolivia* ...... **124 G6** 17 30 S 61 40W
El Cerro de Andévalo,
  Spain **37 H4** 37 45N 6 57W
El Compadre, *Mexico* .. **111 N10** 32 20N 116 14W
El Coronil, *Spain* **37 H5** 37 5N 5 38W
El Cuy, *Argentina* ..... **128 D3** 39 55 S 68 25W
El Cuyo, *Mexico* **119 C7** 21 30N 87 40W
El Dab'a, *Egypt* .... **80 H6** 31 0N 28 27 E
El Daheir, *Egypt* ...... **74 D3** 31 13N 34 10 E
El Dátil, *Mexico* **118 B2** 30 7N 112 15W
El Deir, *Egypt* .... **80 B3** 25 25N 32 20 E
El Dere, *Somali Rep.* ... **75 G4** 3 50N 47 8 E
El Descanso, *Mexico* ... **111 N10** 32 12N 116 58W
El Desemboque, *Mexico* **118 A2** 30 30N 112 57W
El Dilingat, *Egypt* ..... **80 H7** 30 50N 30 31 E
El Diviso, *Colombia* **124 C3** 1 22N 78 14W
El Djouf, *Mauritania* ... **78 D4** 20 0N 9 0W
El Dorado, *Ark., U.S.A.* **113 J8** 33 12N 92 40W
El Dorado, *Kans.,
  U.S.A.* **113 G6** 37 49N 96 52W
El Dorado, *Venezuela* .. **124 B6** 6 55N 61 37W
El 'Ein, *Sudan* .... **81 D2** 16 55N 29 22 E
El Ejido, *Spain* **37 J8** 36 47N 2 49W
El Escorial, *Spain* **36 E6** 40 35N 4 7W
El Espinar, *Spain* **36 E6** 41 43N 4 15W
El Faiyûm, *Egypt* ...... **80 J7** 29 19N 30 50 E
El Fâsher, *Sudan* ...... **81 E2** 13 33N 25 26 E
El Fashn, *Egypt* .... **80 J7** 28 50N 30 54 E
El Ferrol = Ferrol, *Spain* **36 B2** 43 29N 8 15W
El Fifi, *Sudan* .... **81 E2** 10 4N 25 0 E
El Fuerte, *Mexico* **118 B3** 26 30N 108 40W
El Ga'a, *Sudan* .... **81 E2** 14 16N 29 59 E
El Gal, *Somali Rep.* .... **75 E5** 10 58N 50 20 E
El Garef, *Sudan* .... **81 E3** 12 3N 34 19 E
El Gebir, *Egypt* .... **81 E2** 13 40N 29 40 E
El Gedida, *Egypt* ...... **80 B2** 25 40N 28 30 E
El Geneina = Al
  Junaynah, *Sudan* ... **79 F10** 13 27N 22 45 E
El Geteina, *Sudan* ..... **81 E3** 14 50N 32 27 E
El Gezira □, *Sudan* .... **81 E3** 15 0N 33 0 E
El Gîr, *Egypt* .... **80 D2** 19 56N 28 18 E
El Gîza, *Egypt* .... **80 J7** 30 0N 31 10 E
El Gogorrón △, *Mexico* **118 C4** 21 50N 100 50W
El Goléa, *Algeria* ...... **78 B6** 30 30N 2 50 E
El Grau, *Spain* **39 G4** 39 0N 0 7W
El Guácharo △,
  Venezuela **121 D7** 10 8N 63 21W
El Guache △, *Venezuela* **121 E6** 9 45N 69 30W
El Hagiz, *Sudan* .... **81 D4** 15 15N 35 50 E
El Hâi, *Egypt* .... **80 J7** 29 39N 31 18 E
El Hammam, *Egypt* .... **80 A2** 30 52N 29 25 E
El Hawata, *Sudan* ..... **81 E3** 13 25N 34 42 E
El Heiz, *Egypt* .... **80 B2** 27 50N 28 40 E
El Hideib, *Sudan* ...... **81 E3** 13 0N 32 50 E
El Hilla, *Sudan* .... **81 E2** 13 24N 27 2 E
El 'Idisât, *Egypt* .... **80 B3** 25 30N 32 35 E
El Iskandarîya, *Egypt* .. **80 H7** 31 13N 29 58 E
El Istiwa'iya, *Sudan* ... **79 G11** 5 0N 28 0 E
El Jadida, *Morocco* **78 B4** 33 11N 8 17W
El Jardal, *Honduras* **120 D2** 14 54N 88 50W
El Jebelein, *Sudan* ..... **81 E3** 12 40N 32 55 E
El Kab, *Sudan* .... **80 D3** 19 27N 32 46 E
El Kabrît, G., *Egypt* ... **74 E2** 29 42N 33 16 E
El Kafr el Sharqi, *Egypt* **80 H7** 31 16N 31 10 E
El Kamlin, *Sudan* ...... **81 D3** 15 3N 33 11 E
El Karaba, *Sudan* ...... **80 D3** 18 32N 33 41 E
El Kere, *Ethiopia* ...... **81 F5** 5 50N 42 5 E
El Khandaq, *Sudan* .... **80 D3** 18 30N 30 33 E
El Khârga, *Egypt* ...... **80 B3** 25 30N 30 33 E
El Khartûm ■, *Sudan* . **81 D3** 15 31N 32 35 E
El Khartûm Bahrî,
  Sudan .... **81 D3** 15 40N 32 31 E
El Kuntilla, *Egypt* ..... **74 E3** 30 1N 34 45 E
El Laqâwa, *Sudan* ..... **81 E2** 11 25N 29 1 E
El Leh, *Ethiopia* .... **81 G4** 3 45N 39 13 E
El Leiya, *Sudan* .... **81 D4** 16 15N 35 28 E
El Maestrazgo, *Spain* .. **38 E4** 40 30N 0 25W
El Mafâza, *Sudan* ..... **81 E3** 13 38N 34 30 E
El Maghra, *Egypt* ...... **80 A2** 30 15N 28 55 E
El Mahalla el Kubra,
  Egypt .... **80 H7** 31 0N 31 0 E
El Mahârîq, *Egypt* ..... **80 B3** 25 35N 30 35 E
El Maïmûn, *Egypt* ..... **80 J7** 29 14N 31 12 E
El Maks el Bahari,
  Egypt .... **80 C3** 24 30N 30 40 E
El Malpais △, *U.S.A.* .. **109 J10** 34 53N 108 0W
El Manshâh, *Egypt* .... **80 B3** 26 26N 31 50 E
El Mansûra, *Egypt* ..... **80 H7** 31 0N 31 19 E
El Manzala, *Egypt* ..... **80 H8** 31 10N 31 50 E
El Marâgha, *Egypt* ..... **80 B3** 26 35N 31 10 E
El Masid, *Sudan* ...... **81 D3** 15 15N 33 0 E
El Masnou, *Spain* ...... **38 D7** 41 28N 2 20 E
El Matariya, *Egypt* ..... **80 H8** 31 15N 32 0 E
El Meda, *Ethiopia* ..... **81 F5** 5 39N 46 47 E
El Medano, *Canary Is.* . **48 F3** 28 3N 16 32W
El Metemma, *Sudan* ... **81 D3** 16 50N 33 10 E
El Milagro, *Argentina* .. **126 C2** 30 59 S 65 59W
El Minyâ, *Egypt* .... **80 B3** 28 7N 30 33 E
El Monte, *U.S.A.* **111 L8** 34 4N 118 1W
El Montseny, *Spain* .... **38 D7** 41 55N 2 25 E
El Mreyyé, *Mauritania* . **82 B3** 18 30N 7 0W
El Niybo, *Ethiopia* ..... **81 G4** 4 40N 39 55 E
El Obeid, *Sudan* .... **81 E3** 13 8N 30 10 E
El Odaiya, *Sudan* ...... **81 E2** 12 8N 28 12 E
El Oro, *Mexico* **119 D4** 19 48N 100 8W
El Oued, *Algeria* .... **78 B7** 33 20N 6 58 E
El Palmar, *Argentina* .. **126 C4** 32 10 S 58 31W
El Palmito, Presa,
  Mexico **118 B3** 25 40N 105 30W
El Paso, *U.S.A.* **109 L10** 31 45N 106 29W
El Paso Robles, *U.S.A.* . **110 K6** 35 38N 120 41W

El Pedernoso, *Spain* **39 F2** 39 29N 2 45W
El Pedroso, *Spain* **37 H5** 37 51N 5 45W
El Pinacate y Gran
  Desierto de Altar =
  Gran Desierto del
  Pinacate △, *Mexico* . **118 A2** 31 51N 113 32W
El Pobo de Dueñas,
  Spain **38 E3** 40 46N 1 39W
El Portal, *U.S.A.* **110 H7** 37 41N 119 47W
El Porvenir, *Mexico* **118 A3** 31 15N 105 51W
El Prat de Llobregat,
  Spain .... **38 D7** 41 18N 2 3 E
El Progreso, *Honduras* . **120 C2** 15 26N 87 51W
El Pueblito, *Mexico* **118 B3** 29 3N 105 4W
El Pueblo, *Canary Is.* .. **48 F2** 28 36N 17 47W
El Puente del
  Arzobispo, *Spain* ... **36 F5** 39 48N 5 10W
El Puerto de Santa
  María, *Spain* **37 J4** 36 36N 6 13W
El Qâhira, *Egypt* ...... **80 H7** 30 1N 31 14 E
El Qantara, *Egypt* ..... **74 E1** 30 51N 32 20 E
El Qasr, *Egypt* .... **80 B2** 25 44N 28 42 E
El Qubâbât, *Egypt* ..... **80 J7** 29 28N 31 16 E
El Quesima, *Egypt* ..... **74 E3** 30 40N 34 15 E
El Qusîya, *Egypt* ...... **80 B3** 27 29N 30 44 E
El Râshda, *Egypt* ...... **80 B2** 25 36N 28 57 E
El Real, *Panama* **124 B3** 8 0N 77 40W
El Reno, *U.S.A.* **113 H6** 35 32N 97 57W
El Rey △, *Argentina* ... **126 A3** 24 40 S 64 34W
El Ridisiya, *Egypt* ...... **80 C3** 24 56N 32 51 E
El Rio, *U.S.A.* **111 L7** 34 14N 119 10W
El Ronquillo, *Spain* **37 H4** 37 44N 6 10W
El Roque, Pta.,
  Canary Is. **48 F4** 28 10N 15 25W
El Rosarito, *Mexico* **118 B2** 28 38N 114 4W
El Rubio, *Spain* **37 H5** 37 22N 5 0W
El Saff, *Egypt* .... **80 J7** 29 34N 31 16 E
El Saheira, W. →, *Egypt* **74 E2** 30 5N 33 25 E
El Salto, *Mexico* **118 C3** 23 47N 105 22W
El Salvador ■,
  Cent. Amer. **120 D2** 13 50N 89 0W
El Sauce, *Nic.* **120 D2** 12 53N 86 40W
El Saucejo, *Spain* **37 H5** 37 4N 5 6W
El Shallal, *Egypt* ...... **80 C3** 24 0N 32 53 E
El Simbillawein, *Egypt* . **80 H7** 30 48N 31 13 E
El Sueco, *Mexico* **118 B3** 29 54N 106 24W
El Suweis, *Egypt* ...... **80 J8** 29 58N 32 31 E
El Tabbin, *Egypt* ...... **80 J7** 29 47N 31 18 E
El Tamarâni, W. →,
  Egypt .... **74 E3** 30 7N 34 43 E
El Thamad, *Egypt* ..... **74 F3** 29 40N 34 28 E
El Tigre, *Venezuela* **124 B6** 8 44N 64 15W
El Tîh, Gebal, *Egypt* ... **74 F2** 29 40N 33 50 E
El Tîna, *Egypt* .... **80 H8** 31 3N 32 22 E
El Tîna, Khalîg, *Egypt* . **74 D1** 31 10N 32 40 E
El Tofo, *Chile* .... **126 B1** 29 22 S 71 18W
El Tránsito, *Chile* ..... **126 B1** 28 52 S 70 17W
El Tûr, *Egypt* .... **70 D2** 28 14N 33 36 E
El Turbio, *Argentina* ... **128 G2** 51 45 S 72 5W
El Uqsur, *Egypt* .... **80 B3** 25 41N 32 38 E
El Valle □, *Spain* **39 H3** 37 56N 1 6W
El Venado, *Mexico* **118 C4** 22 56N 101 10W
El Vendrell, *Spain* ..... **38 D6** 41 10N 1 30 E
El Vergel, *Mexico* **118 B3** 26 28N 106 22W
El Vigía, *Venezuela* **124 B4** 8 38N 71 39W
El Viso del Alcor, *Spain* **37 H5** 37 23N 5 43W
El Wabeira, *Egypt* ..... **74 F2** 29 34N 33 6 E
El Wak, *Kenya* .... **86 B5** 2 49N 40 56 E
El Waqf, *Egypt* .... **80 B3** 25 45N 32 15 E
El Weguet, *Ethiopia* .... **81 F5** 5 28N 42 17 E
El Wuz, *Sudan* .... **81 D3** 15 5N 30 7 E
Elafónisos, *Greece* ..... **46 E4** 36 29N 22 56 E
Élancourt, *France* ...... **19 D8** 48 47N 1 58 E
Élassa, *Greece* .... **47 F8** 35 18N 26 21 E
Elassón, *Greece* .... **46 B4** 39 53N 22 12 E
Elat, *Israel* .... **74 F3** 29 30N 34 56 E
Eláthia, *Greece* .... **46 C4** 38 37N 22 46 E
Elâzığ, *Turkey* .... **73 C8** 38 37N 39 14 E
Elba, *Italy* .... **40 F7** 42 46N 10 17 E
Elba, *U.S.A.* **115 K2** 31 25N 86 4W
Elbasan, *Albania* ...... **44 E4** 41 9N 20 9 E
Elbe, *U.S.A.* **110 D4** 46 45N 122 10W
Elbe →, *Europe* .... **24 B4** 53 50N 9 0 E
Elbe-Seitenkanal,
  Germany .... **24 C6** 52 45N 10 32 E
Elbert, Mt., *U.S.A.* **109 G10** 39 7N 106 27W
Elberton, *U.S.A.* **115 H4** 34 7N 82 52W
Elbeuf, *France* .... **18 C8** 49 17N 1 2 E
Elbidtan, *Turkey* ...... **70 B3** 38 13N 37 12 E
Elbistan, *Turkey* ...... **72 C7** 38 13N 37 15 E
Elblag, *Poland* .... **30 D6** 54 10N 19 25 E
Elbow, *Canada* **103 C7** 51 7N 106 35W
Elbrus, *Asia* .... **35 J6** 43 21N 42 30 E
Elbufer-Drawehn △,
  Germany .... **24 B6** 53 8N 10 58 E
Elburz Mts. = Alborz,
  Reshteh-ye Kûhhā-ye,
  Iran .... **71 C7** 36 0N 52 0 E
Elche, *Spain* **39 G4** 38 15N 0 42W
Elche de la Sierra, *Spain* **39 G2** 38 27N 2 3W
Elcho I., *Australia* ..... **94 A2** 11 55 S 135 45 E
Elda, *Spain* **39 G4** 38 29N 0 47W
Elde →, *Germany* ...... **24 B7** 53 7N 11 15 E
Eldon, *Mo., U.S.A.* **112 F8** 38 21N 92 35W
Eldon, *Wash., U.S.A.* ... **110 C3** 47 33N 123 3W
Eldora, *U.S.A.* **112 D8** 42 22N 93 5W
Eldorado, *Argentina* ... **127 B5** 26 28 S 54 43W
Eldorado, *Canada* **103 B7** 59 35N 108 30W
Eldorado, *Mexico* **118 C3** 24 20N 107 22W
Eldorado, *Ill., U.S.A.* ... **114 G1** 37 49N 88 26W
Eldorado, *Tex., U.S.A.* . **113 K4** 30 52N 100 36W
Eldorado Springs,
  U.S.A. **113 G8** 37 52N 94 1W
Eldoret, *Kenya* .... **86 B4** 0 30N 35 17 E
Eldred, *U.S.A.* **116 E6** 41 58N 78 23W
Elea, C., *Cyprus* ...... **49 D13** 35 19N 34 4 E
Eleanora, Pk., *U.S.A.* ... **93 F3** 32 57 S 121 9 E
Elefantes →, *Africa* .... **89 C5** 24 10 S 32 40 E
Elektrogorsk, *Russia* ... **32 E10** 55 41N 38 32 E
Elektrostal, *Russia* .... **32 E10** 55 41N 38 32 E
Elele, *Nigeria* .... **83 D6** 5 5N 6 50 E
Elena, *Bulgaria* .... **45 C10** 42 55N 25 53 E
Elephant Butte
  Reservoir △, *U.S.A.* . **109 K10** 33 9N 107 11W
Elephant I., *Antarctica* . **5 C18** 61 0 S 55 0W
Eleshnitsa, *Bulgaria* ... **44 E8** 41 52N 23 45 E
Eleşkirt, *Turkey* ...... **73 C10** 39 50N 42 50 E
Eleuthera, *Bahamas* ... **120 B4** 25 0N 76 20W
Elevsís, *Greece* .... **46 C5** 38 4N 23 26 E
Elevtheroúpolis, *Greece* **45 F8** 40 52N 24 20 E
Elgin, *Canada* **117 B8** 44 36N 76 13W
Elgin, *U.K.* **13 D5** 57 39N 3 19W
Elgin, *Ill., U.S.A.* **114 D1** 42 2N 88 17W
Elgin, *N. Dak., U.S.A.* . **112 B4** 46 24N 101 51W
Elgin, *Oreg., U.S.A.* **108 D5** 45 34N 117 55W
Elgin, *Tex., U.S.A.* **113 K6** 30 21N 97 22W

Elgoibar, *Spain* **38 B2** 43 13N 2 24W
Elgon, Mt., *Africa* ..... **86 B3** 1 10N 34 30 E
Eliase, *Indonesia* ...... **63 F8** 8 21 S 130 48 E
Elikón, *Greece* .... **46 C4** 38 18N 22 45 E
Elim, *Namibia* .... **88 B2** 17 48 S 15 31 E
Elim, *S. Africa* .... **88 E2** 34 35 S 19 45 E
Elin Pelin, *Bulgaria* .... **44 D7** 42 40N 23 36 E
Elista, *Russia* .... **35 G7** 46 16N 44 14 E
Elizabeth, *Australia* ... **95 E2** 34 42 S 138 41 E
Elizabeth, *U.S.A.* **117 F10** 40 40N 74 13W
Elizabeth City, *U.S.A.* .. **115 G7** 36 18N 76 14W
Elizabethton, *U.S.A.* ... **115 G4** 36 21N 82 13W
Elizabethtown, *Ky.,
  U.S.A.* **114 G3** 37 42N 85 52W
Elizabethtown, *N.Y.,
  U.S.A.* **117 B11** 44 13N 73 36W
Elizabethtown, *Pa.,
  U.S.A.* **117 F8** 40 9N 76 36W
Elizondo, *Spain* **38 B3** 43 12N 1 30W
Ełk, *Poland* .... **30 E9** 53 50N 22 21 E
Elk →, *Canada* **102 C5** 49 11N 115 14W
Elk →, *Poland* .... **30 E9** 53 41N 22 28 E
Elk →, *U.S.A.* **115 H2** 34 46N 87 16W
Elk City, *U.S.A.* **113 H5** 35 25N 99 25W
Elk Creek, *U.S.A.* **110 F4** 39 36N 122 32W
Elk Grove, *U.S.A.* **110 G5** 38 25N 121 22W
Elk Island △, *Canada* .. **102 C6** 53 35N 112 59W
Elk Lake, *Canada* **104 C3** 47 40N 80 25W
Elk Point, *Canada* **103 C6** 53 54N 110 55W
Elk River, *Idaho, U.S.A.* **108 C5** 46 47N 116 11W
Elk River, *Minn., U.S.A.* **112 C8** 45 18N 93 35W
Elkedra →, *Australia* .. **94 C2** 21 8 S 136 22 E
Elkhart, *Ind., U.S.A.* ... **114 E3** 41 41N 85 58W
Elkhart, *Kans., U.S.A.* . **113 G4** 37 0N 101 54W
Elkhorn, *Canada* **103 D8** 49 59N 101 14W
Elkhorn →, *U.S.A.* **112 E6** 41 8N 96 19W
Elkhovo, *Bulgaria* ..... **45 D10** 42 10N 26 35 E
Elkin, *U.S.A.* **115 G5** 36 15N 80 51W
Elkins, *U.S.A.* **114 F6** 38 55N 79 51W
Elkland, *U.S.A.* **116 E7** 41 59N 77 19W
Elko, *Canada* **102 D5** 49 20N 115 10W
Elko, *U.S.A.* **108 F6** 40 50N 115 46W
Elkton, *U.S.A.* **116 C1** 43 49N 83 11W
Ell, L., *Australia* ...... **93 E4** 29 13 S 127 46 E
Ellef Ringnes I., *Canada* **4 B2** 78 30N 102 2W
Ellen, Mt., *U.S.A.* **117 B12** 44 9N 72 56W
Ellenburg, *U.S.A.* **117 B11** 44 54N 73 48W
Ellendale, *U.S.A.* **112 B5** 46 0N 98 32W
Ellensburg, *U.S.A.* **108 C3** 46 59N 120 34W
Ellenville, *U.S.A.* **117 E10** 41 43N 74 24W
Ellerton, *Barbados* ..... **121 g** 13 7N 59 33W
Ellery, Mt., *Australia* ... **95 F4** 37 28 S 148 47 E
Ellesmere, L., *N.Z.* ..... **91 M4** 43 47 S 172 28 E
Ellesmere I., *Canada* ... **98 B11** 79 30N 80 0W
Ellesmere Port, *U.K.* ... **14 D5** 53 17N 2 54W
Ellice Is. = Tuvalu ■,
  Pac. Oc. .... **96 H9** 8 0 S 178 0 E
Ellicottville, *U.S.A.* **116 D6** 42 17N 78 40W
Ellinikón, Athínai, ✈
  (ATH), *Greece* ..... **46 D5** 37 52N 23 55 E
Elliot, *Australia* .... **94 B1** 17 33 S 133 32 E
Elliot, *S. Africa* .... **89 E4** 31 22 S 27 48 E
Elliot Lake, *Canada* **104 C3** 46 25N 82 35W
Elliotdale = Xhora,
  S. Africa .... **89 E4** 31 55 S 28 38 E
Ellis, *U.S.A.* **112 F5** 38 56N 99 34W
Elliston, *Australia* ..... **95 E1** 33 39 S 134 53 E
Ellisville, *U.S.A.* **113 K10** 31 36N 89 12W
Ellon, *U.K.* **13 D6** 57 22N 2 4W
Ellore = Eluru, *India* ... **67 L12** 16 48N 81 8 E
Ellsworth, *Kans., U.S.A.* **112 F5** 38 44N 98 14W
Ellsworth, *Maine, U.S.A.* **115 C11** 44 33N 68 25W
Ellsworth Land,
  Antarctica .... **5 D16** 76 0 S 89 0W
Ellsworth Mts.,
  Antarctica .... **5 D16** 78 30 S 85 0W
Ellwangen, *Germany* ... **25 G6** 48 57N 10 8 E
Ellwood City, *U.S.A.* ... **116 F4** 40 52N 80 17W
Elm, *Switz.* .... **25 J5** 46 54N 9 10 E
Elm-Lappwald △,
  Germany .... **24 C6** 52 15N 10 50 E
Elma, *Canada* **103 D9** 49 52N 95 55W
Elma, *U.S.A.* **110 D3** 47 0N 123 25W
Elmadağ, *Turkey* ...... **72 C5** 39 55N 33 14 E
Elmalı, *Turkey* .... **47 E11** 36 44N 29 56 E
Elmhurst, *U.S.A.* **114 E2** 41 53N 87 56W
Elmina, *Ghana* **83 D4** 5 5N 1 21W
Elmira, *Canada* **116 C4** 43 36N 80 33W
Elmira, *U.S.A.* **116 D8** 42 6N 76 48W
Elmira Heights, *U.S.A.* . **116 D8** 42 8N 76 50W
Elmore, *Australia* ..... **95 F3** 36 30 S 144 37 E
Elmore, *U.S.A.* **111 M11** 33 7N 115 49W
Elmshorn, *Germany* .... **24 B5** 53 43N 9 40 E
Elmvale, *Canada* **116 B5** 44 35N 79 52W
Elne, *France* .... **20 F6** 42 36N 2 58 E
Elora, *Greece* .... **46 E4** 36 46N 22 43 E
Eloúnda, *Greece* ...... **49 D7** 35 16 S 25 42 E
Eloy, *U.S.A.* **109 K8** 32 45N 111 33W
Éloyes, *France* .... **19 D13** 48 6N 6 36 E
Elrose, *Canada* **103 C7** 51 12N 108 0W
Elsdorf, *Germany* ...... **24 E2** 50 55N 6 34 E
Elsie, *U.S.A.* **116 C3** 43 5N 84 23W
Elsinore = Helsingør,
  Denmark .... **11 H6** 56 2N 12 35 E
Elster →, *Germany* ..... **24 D7** 51 25N 11 57 E
Elsterwerda, *Germany* . **24 D9** 51 27N 13 31 E
Eltham, *N.Z.* .... **91 H5** 39 26 S 174 19 E
Elton, *Russia* .... **35 F8** 49 5N 46 52 E
Elton, Ozero, *Russia* ... **35 F8** 49 5N 46 42 E
Eltville, *Germany* ...... **25 E4** 50 1N 8 6 E
Eluru, *India* .... **67 L12** 16 48N 81 8 E
Elvas, *Portugal* **37 G3** 38 50N 7 10W
Elven, *France* **18 E4** 47 44N 2 36W
Elverum, *Norway* ..... **9 F14** 60 53N 11 34 E
Elvire →, *Australia* .... **92 C4** 17 51 S 128 11 E
Elvire, Mt., *Australia* ... **93 E2** 29 22 S 119 36 E
Elvo →, *Italy* .... **40 C5** 45 23N 8 21 E
Elwell, L., *U.S.A.* **108 B8** 48 22N 111 17W
Elwood, *Ind., U.S.A.* ... **114 E3** 40 17N 85 50W
Elwood, *Nebr., U.S.A.* . **112 E5** 40 36N 99 52W
Elx = Elche, *Spain* **39 G4** 38 15N 0 42W
Ely, *U.K.* .... **15 E8** 52 24N 0 16 E
Ely, *Minn., U.S.A.* **112 B9** 47 55N 91 51W
Ely, *Nev., U.S.A.* **108 G6** 39 15N 114 54W
Elyria, *U.S.A.* **116 E2** 41 22N 82 7W
Elyrus, *Greece* .... **49 D5** 35 15 S 23 45 E
Elz →, *Germany* ...... **25 G3** 48 18N 7 44 E
Emådalen, *Sweden* ..... **10 C8** 61 20N 14 44 E
Emämrūd, *Iran* .... **71 B7** 36 30N 55 0 E
Emån →, *Sweden* ..... **11 G10** 57 3N 16 30 E
Emba, *Kazakhstan* ..... **52 E6** 48 50N 58 8 E
Emba →, *Kazakhstan* .. **52 E6** 48 50N 58 8 E
Embarcación, *Argentina* **126 A3** 23 10 S 64 0W
Embarras Portage,
  Canada **103 B6** 58 27N 111 28W
Embetsu, *Japan* .... **54 B10** 44 44N 141 47 E

Embi = Emba, Kazakhstan ... 52 E6 48 50N 58 8 E
Embi = Emba ➤, Kazakhstan ... 52 E6 46 55N 53 28 E
Embóna, Greece ... 49 C9 36 13N 27 51 E
Embrun, France ... 21 D10 44 34N 6 30 E
Embu, Kenya ... 86 C4 0 32 S 37 38 E
Emden, Germany ... 24 B3 53 21N 7 12 E
Emecik, Turkey ... 47 E9 36 46N 27 49 E
Emerald, Australia ... 94 C4 23 32 S 148 10 E
Emerson, Canada ... 103 D9 49 0N 97 10W
Emet, Turkey ... 47 B11 39 20N 29 15 E
Emi Koussi, Chad ... 79 E9 19 45N 18 55 E
Emília-Romagna □, Italy ... 40 D8 44 45N 11 0 E
Emilius, Mte., Italy ... 40 C4 45 45N 7 20 E
Eminabad, Pakistan ... 68 C6 32 2N 74 8 E
Emine, Nos, Bulgaria ... 45 D11 42 40N 27 56 E
Emirdağ, Turkey ... 72 C4 39 2N 31 8 E
Emissi, Tarso, Chad ... 79 D9 21 27N 18 36 E
Emlenton, U.S.A. ... 116 E5 41 11N 79 43W
Emlichheim, Germany ... 24 C2 52 37N 6 51 E
Emmaboda, Sweden ... 11 H9 56 37N 15 32 E
Emmaus, S. Africa ... 88 D4 29 2 S 25 15 E
Emmaus, U.S.A. ... 117 F9 40 32N 75 30W
Emme ➤, Switz. ... 25 H3 47 14N 7 32 E
Emmeloord, Neths. ... 17 B5 52 44N 5 46 E
Emmen, Neths. ... 17 B6 52 48N 6 57 E
Emmen, Switz. ... 25 H4 47 5N 8 18 E
Emmendingen, Germany ... 25 G3 48 6N 7 51 E
Emmental, Switz. ... 25 J3 46 55N 7 40 E
Emmerich, Germany ... 24 D2 51 50N 6 15 E
Emmet, Australia ... 94 C3 24 45 S 144 30 E
Emmetsburg, U.S.A. ... 112 D7 43 7N 94 41W
Emmett, Idaho, U.S.A. ... 108 E5 43 52N 116 30W
Emmett, Mich., U.S.A. ... 116 D2 42 59N 82 46W
Emmonak, U.S.A. ... 100 B3 62 46N 164 30W
Emo, Canada ... 103 D10 48 38N 93 50W
Emőd, Hungary ... 28 C5 47 57N 20 47 E
Empalme, Mexico ... 118 B2 28 1N 110 49W
Empangeni, S. Africa ... 89 D5 28 50 S 31 52 E
Empedrado, Argentina ... 126 B4 28 0 S 58 46W
Emperor Seamount Chain, Pac. Oc. ... 96 D9 40 0N 170 0 E
Empoli, Italy ... 40 E7 43 43N 10 57 E
Emporia, Kans., U.S.A. ... 112 F6 38 25N 96 11W
Emporia, Va., U.S.A. ... 115 G7 36 42N 77 32W
Emporium, U.S.A. ... 116 E6 41 31N 78 14W
Empress, Canada ... 103 C7 50 57N 110 0W
Empty Quarter = Rub' al Khālī, Si. Arabia ... 75 D4 19 0N 48 0 E
Ems ➤, Germany ... 24 B3 53 20N 7 12 E
Emsdale, Canada ... 116 A5 45 32N 79 19W
Emsdetten, Germany ... 24 C3 52 10N 7 32 E
Emu, China ... 57 C15 43 40N 128 6 E
Emu Park, Australia ... 94 C5 23 13 S 150 50 E
'En 'Avrona, Israel ... 74 F4 29 43N 35 0 E
En Nahud, Sudan ... 81 E2 12 45N 28 25 E
En Nofalab, Sudan ... 81 D3 15 52N 32 32 E
Ena, Japan ... 55 G8 35 25N 137 25 E
Enana, Namibia ... 88 B2 17 30 S 16 23 E
Enånger, Sweden ... 10 C11 61 30N 17 9 E
Enard B., U.K. ... 13 C3 58 5N 5 20W
Enare = Inarijärvi, Finland ... 8 B22 69 0N 28 0 E
Enarotali, Indonesia ... 63 E9 3 55 S 136 21 E
Encampment, U.S.A. ... 108 F10 41 12N 106 47W
Encantadas, Serra, Brazil ... 127 C5 30 40 S 53 0W
Encarnación, Paraguay ... 127 B4 27 15 S 55 50W
Encarnación de Diaz, Mexico ... 118 C4 21 30N 102 13W
Enchi, Ghana ... 82 D4 5 53N 2 48W
Encinitas, U.S.A. ... 111 M9 33 3N 117 17W
Encino, U.S.A. ... 109 J11 34 39N 105 28W
Encounter B., Australia ... 95 F2 35 45 S 138 45 E
Encs, Hungary ... 28 B6 48 20N 21 8 E
Endako, Canada ... 102 C3 54 6N 125 2W
Ende, Indonesia ... 63 F6 8 45 S 121 40 E
Endeavour Str., Australia ... 94 A3 10 45 S 142 0 E
Endelave, Denmark ... 11 J4 55 46N 10 18 E
Enderbury I., Kiribati ... 96 H10 3 8 S 171 5W
Enderby, Canada ... 102 C5 50 35N 119 10W
Enderby I., Australia ... 92 D2 20 35 S 116 30 E
Enderby Land, Antarctica ... 5 C5 66 0 S 53 0 E
Enderlin, U.S.A. ... 112 B6 46 38N 97 36W
Endicott, U.S.A. ... 117 D8 42 6N 76 4W
Endwell, U.S.A. ... 117 D8 42 6N 76 2W
Endyalgout I., Australia ... 92 B5 11 40 S 132 35 E
Eneabba, Australia ... 93 E2 29 49 S 115 16 E
Enewetak Atoll, Marshall Is. ... 96 F8 11 30N 162 15 E
Enez, Turkey ... 45 F10 40 45N 26 5 E
Enfer, Pte. d', Martinique ... 120 c 14 22N 60 54W
Enfield, Canada ... 105 D7 44 56N 63 32W
Enfield, Conn., U.S.A. ... 117 E12 41 58N 72 36W
Enfield, N.H., U.S.A. ... 117 C12 43 39N 72 9W
Engadin, Switz. ... 25 J6 46 45N 10 10 E
Engaño, C., Dom. Rep. ... 121 C6 18 30N 68 20W
Engaño, C., Phil. ... 63 A6 18 35N 122 23 E
Engaru, Japan ... 54 B11 44 3N 143 31 E
Engcobo, S. Africa ... 89 E4 31 37 S 28 0 E
Engelberg, Switz. ... 25 J4 46 48N 8 26 E
Engels, Russia ... 34 E8 51 28N 46 6 E
Engemann L., Canada ... 103 B7 58 0N 106 55W
Engershatu, Eritrea ... 81 D4 16 7N 38 34 E
Enggano, Indonesia ... 62 F2 5 20 S 102 40 E
England, U.S.A. ... 113 H9 34 33N 91 58W
England □, U.K. ... 15 E5 53 0N 2 0W
Englee, Canada ... 105 B8 50 45N 56 5W
Englehart, Canada ... 104 C4 47 49N 79 52W
Englewood, U.S.A. ... 112 F2 39 39N 104 59W
English ➤, Canada ... 103 C10 49 12N 91 5W
English Bazar = Ingraj Bazar, India ... 69 G13 24 58N 88 10 E
English Channel, Europe ... 15 G6 50 0N 2 0W
English Company's Is., The, Australia ... 94 A2 11 50 S 136 32 E
English River, Canada ... 104 C1 49 14N 91 0W
Engures ezers, Latvia ... 30 A10 57 16N 23 6 E
Enguri ➤, Georgia ... 35 J5 42 37N 41 38 E
Enid, U.S.A. ... 113 G6 36 24N 97 53W
Enipévs ➤, Greece ... 46 B4 39 22N 22 17 E
Enkhuizen, Neths. ... 17 B5 52 42N 5 17 E
Enköping, Sweden ... 10 E11 59 37N 17 4 E
Enle, China ... 58 F3 24 0N 101 9 E
Enna, Italy ... 43 E7 37 34N 14 16 E
Ennadai, Canada ... 103 A8 61 8N 100 53W
Ennadai L., Canada ... 103 A8 60 58N 101 20W
Ennedi, Chad ... 79 E10 17 15N 22 0 E
Enngonia, Australia ... 95 D4 29 21 S 145 50 E

Ennigerloh, Germany ... 24 D4 51 50N 8 2 E
Ennis, Ireland ... 12 D3 52 51N 8 59W
Ennis, Mont., U.S.A. ... 108 D8 45 21N 111 44W
Ennis, Tex., U.S.A. ... 113 J6 32 20N 96 38W
Enniscorthy, Ireland ... 12 D5 52 30N 6 34W
Enniskillen, U.K. ... 12 B4 54 21N 7 39W
Ennistimon, Ireland ... 12 D2 52 57N 9 17W
Enns, Austria ... 26 C7 48 12N 14 28 E
Enns ➤, Austria ... 26 C7 48 14N 14 32 E
Enontekiö, Finland ... 8 B20 68 23N 23 37 E
Enosburg Falls, U.S.A. ... 117 B12 44 55N 72 48W
Enping, China ... 59 F9 22 16N 112 21 E
Enriquillo, L., Dom. Rep. ... 121 C5 18 20N 72 5W
Enschede, Neths. ... 17 B6 52 13N 6 53 E
Ensenada, Argentina ... 126 C4 34 55 S 57 55W
Ensenada, Mexico ... 118 A1 31 50N 116 50W
Ensenada de los Muertos, Mexico ... 118 C2 23 59N 109 50W
Enshi, China ... 58 B7 30 18N 109 29 E
Ensiola, Pta. de n', Spain ... 48 B9 39 7N 2 55 E
Ensisheim, France ... 19 E14 47 50N 7 20 E
Entebbe, Uganda ... 86 B3 0 4N 32 28 E
Enterprise, Canada ... 102 A5 60 47N 115 45W
Enterprise, Ala., U.S.A. ... 115 K3 31 19N 85 51W
Enterprise, Oreg., U.S.A. ... 108 D5 45 25N 117 17W
Entorno de Doñana △, Spain ... 37 J4 37 0N 6 26W
Entraygues-sur-Truyère, France ... 20 D6 44 38N 2 35 E
Entre Ríos, Bolivia ... 126 A3 21 30 S 64 25W
Entre Ríos □, Argentina ... 126 C4 30 30 S 58 30W
Entrepeñas, Embalse de, Spain ... 38 E2 40 34N 2 42W
Entroncamento, Portugal ... 37 F2 39 28N 8 28W
Enugu, Nigeria ... 83 D6 6 30N 7 30 E
Enugu □, Nigeria ... 83 D6 6 30N 7 45 E
Enugu Ezike, Nigeria ... 83 D6 7 0N 7 29 E
Enumclaw, U.S.A. ... 110 C5 47 12N 121 59W
Envalira, Port d', Europe ... 38 C6 42 33N 1 43 E
Envermeu, France ... 18 C8 49 53N 1 15 E
Enviken, Sweden ... 10 D9 60 49N 15 46 E
Enying, Hungary ... 28 D3 46 56N 18 15 E
Enza ➤, Italy ... 40 D7 44 54N 10 31 E
Eólie, Ís., Italy ... 43 D7 38 30N 14 57 E
Epanomí, Greece ... 44 F6 40 25N 22 59 E
Epe, Neths. ... 17 B5 52 21N 5 59 E
Epe, Nigeria ... 83 D5 6 36N 3 59 E
Épernay, France ... 19 C10 49 3N 3 56 E
Épernon, France ... 19 D8 48 35N 1 40 E
Ephesus, Turkey ... 47 D9 37 55N 27 22 E
Ephraim, U.S.A. ... 108 G8 39 22N 111 35W
Ephrata, Pa., U.S.A. ... 117 F8 40 11N 76 11W
Ephrata, Wash., U.S.A. ... 108 C4 47 19N 119 33W
Epidaurus Limera, Greece ... 46 E5 36 46N 23 0 E
Épila, Spain ... 38 D3 41 36N 1 17W
Épinac, France ... 19 F11 46 59N 4 31 E
Épinal, France ... 19 D13 48 10N 6 27 E
Episkopi, Cyprus ... 49 E11 34 40N 32 54 E
Episkopí, Greece ... 49 D6 35 20N 24 20 E
Episkopi Bay, Cyprus ... 49 E11 34 35N 32 50 E
Epitálion, Greece ... 46 D3 37 37N 21 30 E
Eppan = Appiano, Italy ... 40 B8 46 28N 11 15 E
Eppingen, Germany ... 25 F4 49 8N 8 53 E
Epsom, U.K. ... 15 F7 51 19N 0 16W
Epukiro, Namibia ... 88 C2 21 40 S 19 9 E
Equatoria = Istiwa'iya, Sudan ... 79 G11 5 0N 28 0 E
Equatorial Guinea ■, Africa ... 84 D1 2 0N 8 0 E
Er Hai, China ... 58 E3 25 48N 100 11 E
Er Rachidia, Morocco ... 78 B5 31 58N 4 20W
Er Rahad, Sudan ... 81 E3 12 45N 30 32 E
Er Rif, Morocco ... 78 A5 35 1N 4 1W
Er Rogel, Sudan ... 80 D4 18 10N 35 25 E
Er Roseires, Sudan ... 81 E3 11 55N 34 30 E
Er Rua'at, Sudan ... 81 E3 12 21N 32 17 E
Eraclea, Italy ... 41 C9 45 35N 12 40 E
Erāwadī Myit = Irrawaddy ➤, Burma ... 67 M19 15 50N 95 6 E
Erāwadī Myitwanya = Irrawaddy, Mouths of the, Burma ... 67 M19 15 30N 95 0 E
Erba, Italy ... 40 C6 45 48N 9 15 E
Erba, Sudan ... 80 D4 19 5N 36 51 E
Erba, J., Sudan ... 80 C4 20 48N 36 47 E
Erbaa, Turkey ... 72 B7 40 42N 36 36 E
Erbeskopf, Germany ... 25 F3 49 44N 7 2 E
Erbil = Arbil, Iraq ... 70 B5 36 15N 44 5 E
Erbu, Ethiopia ... 81 E3 6 44N 34 53 E
Erçek, Turkey ... 70 B4 38 39N 43 36 E
Erçiş, Turkey ... 73 C10 39 2N 43 21 E
Erciyaş Dağı, Turkey ... 70 B3 38 30N 35 30 E
Érd, Hungary ... 28 C3 47 22N 18 56 E
Erdao Jiang ➤, China ... 57 C14 43 0N 127 0 E
Erdek, Turkey ... 45 F11 40 23N 27 47 E
Erdemli, Turkey ... 72 D6 36 36N 34 19 E
Erdene = Ulaan-Uul, Mongolia ... 56 B6 44 13N 111 10 E
Erdenetsogt, Mongolia ... 56 C4 42 55N 106 5 E
Erding, Germany ... 25 G7 48 18N 11 54 E
Erdre ➤, France ... 18 E5 47 13N 1 32W
Erebus, Mt., Antarctica ... 5 D11 77 35 S 167 0 E
Erechim, Brazil ... 127 B5 27 35 S 52 15W
Ereğli, Konya, Turkey ... 70 B2 37 31N 34 4 E
Ereğli, Zonguldak, Turkey ... 72 B4 41 15N 31 24 E
Erei, Monti, Italy ... 43 E7 37 20N 14 20 E
Erenhot, China ... 56 C7 43 48N 112 2 E
Eresma ➤, Spain ... 36 D6 41 26N 4 45W
Eressós, Greece ... 47 B7 39 11N 25 57 E
Erfenisdam, S. Africa ... 88 D4 28 30 S 26 50 E
Erftstadt, Germany ... 24 E2 50 49N 6 47 E
Erfurt, Germany ... 24 E7 50 58N 11 2 E
Ergani, Turkey ... 70 B3 38 17N 39 49 E
Ergel, Mongolia ... 56 C5 43 8N 109 5 E
Ergene ➤, Turkey ... 45 E10 41 1N 26 22 E
Ergeni Vozvyshennost, Russia ... 35 G7 47 0N 44 0 E
Ērgļi, Latvia ... 9 H21 56 54N 25 38 E
Erhlin, Taiwan ... 59 F13 23 54N 120 22 E
Eria ➤, Spain ... 36 C5 42 3N 5 44W
Eriba, Sudan ... 81 D4 16 40N 36 10 E
Eribol, U.K. ... 13 C4 58 30N 4 42W
Érice, Italy ... 42 D5 38 2N 12 35 E
Erie, U.S.A. ... 116 D4 42 8N 80 5W
Erie, L., N. Amer. ... 116 D4 42 15N 81 0W
Erie Canal, U.S.A. ... 116 C7 43 5N 78 43W
Erieau, Canada ... 116 D3 42 16N 81 57W
Erigavo = Ceerigaabo, Somali Rep. ... 75 E4 10 35N 47 20 E
Erikoúsa, Greece ... 49 A3 39 53N 19 34 E
Eriksdale, Canada ... 103 C9 50 52N 98 7W
Erímanthos, Greece ... 46 D3 37 57N 21 50 E

Erimo-misaki, Japan ... 54 D11 41 50N 143 15 E
Erin Pt., Trin. & Tob. ... 125 K15 10 3N 61 39W
Erinpura, India ... 68 G5 25 9N 73 3 E
Eritrea ■, Africa ... 81 E4 14 0N 38 30 E
Erjas ➤, Portugal ... 36 F3 39 40N 7 1W
Erkelenz, Germany ... 24 D2 51 4N 6 19 E
Erkner, Germany ... 24 C9 52 25N 13 44 E
Erlangen, Germany ... 25 F6 49 36N 11 0 E
Erldunda, Australia ... 94 D1 25 14 S 133 12 E
Ermelo, Neths. ... 17 B5 52 18N 5 35 E
Ermelo, S. Africa ... 89 D4 26 31 S 29 59 E
Ermenek, Turkey ... 70 B2 36 38N 33 0 E
Ermil, Sudan ... 81 E2 13 35N 27 40 E
Ermióni, Greece ... 46 D5 37 23N 23 15 E
Ermoúpolis, Greece ... 49 A3 37 37N 19 46 E
Ernakulam, India ... 66 Q10 9 59N 76 22 E
Erne ➤, Ireland ... 12 B3 54 30N 8 16W
Erne, Lower L., U.K. ... 12 B4 54 28N 7 47W
Erne, Upper L., U.K. ... 12 B4 54 14N 7 32W
Ernée, France ... 18 D6 48 18N 0 56W
Ernest Giles Ra., Australia ... 93 E3 27 0 S 123 45 E
Ernstberg, Germany ... 25 E2 50 13N 6 47 E
Erode, India ... 66 P10 11 24N 77 45 E
Eromanga, Australia ... 95 D3 26 40 S 143 11 E
Erongo, Namibia ... 88 C2 21 39 S 15 58 E
Erquy, France ... 18 D4 48 38N 2 29W
Erramala Hills, India ... 66 M11 15 30N 78 15 E
Errer ➤, Ethiopia ... 81 F5 7 32N 42 35 E
Errigal, Ireland ... 12 A3 55 2N 8 6W
Erris Hd., Ireland ... 12 B1 54 19N 10 0W
Erseke, Albania ... 44 F4 40 22N 20 40 E
Erskine, U.S.A. ... 112 B7 47 40N 96 0W
Erstein, France ... 19 D14 48 25N 7 38 E
Ertholmene, Denmark ... 11 J9 55 19N 15 11 E
Ertil, Russia ... 34 E5 51 55N 40 50 E
Ertis = Irtysh ➤, Russia ... 52 C7 61 4N 68 52 E
Eruh, Turkey ... 73 D10 37 46N 42 13 E
Eruwa, Nigeria ... 83 D5 7 33N 3 26 E
Ervy-le-Châtel, France ... 19 D10 48 2N 3 55 E
Erwin, U.S.A. ... 115 G4 36 9N 82 25W
Eryuan, China ... 58 D2 26 7N 99 57 E
Erzgebirge, Germany ... 24 E8 50 27N 12 55 E
Erzin, Russia ... 53 D10 50 15N 95 10 E
Erzincan, Turkey ... 70 B3 39 46N 39 30 E
Erzurum, Turkey ... 70 B4 39 57N 41 15 E
Es Caló, Spain ... 48 C8 38 40N 1 30 E
Es Canar, Spain ... 48 B8 39 2N 1 36 E
Es Mercadal, Spain ... 48 B11 39 59N 4 5 E
Es Migjorn Gran, Spain ... 48 B11 39 57N 4 3 E
Es Safiya, Sudan ... 81 D3 15 31N 30 7 E
Es Sînâ', Egypt ... 80 B3 27 30N 34 0 E
Es Sûkî, Sudan ... 81 E3 13 20N 33 58 E
Es Vedrà, Spain ... 48 C7 38 52N 1 12 E
Esambo, Dem. Rep. of the Congo ... 86 C1 3 48 S 23 30 E
Esan-Misaki, Japan ... 54 D10 41 40N 141 10 E
Esashi, Hokkaidō, Japan ... 54 B11 44 56N 142 35 E
Esashi, Hokkaidō, Japan ... 54 D10 41 52N 140 7 E
Esbjerg, Denmark ... 11 J2 55 29N 8 29 E
Esbo = Espoo, Finland ... 9 F21 60 12N 24 40 E
Escalante, U.S.A. ... 109 H8 37 47N 111 36W
Escalante ➤, U.S.A. ... 109 H8 37 24N 110 57W
Escalón, Mexico ... 118 B4 26 46N 104 20W
Escambia ➤, U.S.A. ... 115 K2 30 32N 87 11W
Escanaba, U.S.A. ... 114 C2 45 45N 87 4W
Esch-sur-Alzette, Lux. ... 17 E6 49 32N 6 0 E
Eschede, Germany ... 24 C6 52 44N 10 14 E
Eschwege, Germany ... 24 D6 51 11N 10 2 E
Eschweiler, Germany ... 24 E2 50 49N 6 15 E
Escondido, U.S.A. ... 111 M9 33 7N 117 5W
Escravos ➤, Nigeria ... 83 D6 5 35N 5 10 E
Escuinapa, Mexico ... 118 C3 22 50N 105 50W
Escuintla, Guatemala ... 120 D1 14 20N 90 48W
Eséka, Cameroon ... 83 E7 3 41N 10 44 E
Esenguly, Turkmenistan ... 52 F6 37 37N 53 59 E
Esens, Germany ... 24 B3 53 38N 7 36 E
Esenyurt, Turkey ... 45 E12 41 3N 28 48 E
Esera ➤, Spain ... 38 C5 42 6N 0 15 E
Eşfahān, Iran ... 71 C6 32 39N 51 43 E
Eşfahān □, Iran ... 71 C6 32 50N 51 50 E
Esfarāyen, Iran ... 71 B8 37 4N 57 30 E
Esfideh, Iran ... 71 C8 33 39N 59 46 E
Esgueva ➤, Spain ... 36 D6 41 40N 4 43W
Esh Sham = Dimashq, Syria ... 74 B5 33 30N 36 18 E
Esh Shamâlîya □, Sudan ... 80 D2 19 0N 29 0 E
Esha Ness, U.K. ... 13 A7 60 29N 1 38W
Eshan, China ... 58 E4 24 11N 102 24 E
Esher, U.K. ... 15 F7 51 21N 0 20W
Eshkol ➤, Israel ... 74 D3 31 20N 34 30 E
Eshowe, S. Africa ... 89 D5 28 50 S 31 30 E
Esiama, Ghana ... 82 E4 4 56N 2 25W
Esigodini, Zimbabwe ... 89 C4 20 18 S 28 56 E
Esil = Ishim ➤, Russia ... 52 D8 57 45N 71 10 E
Esino ➤, Italy ... 41 E10 43 39N 13 22 E
Esira, Madag. ... 89 C8 24 20 S 46 42 E
Esk ➤, Cumb., U.K. ... 13 G5 54 58N 3 4W
Esk ➤, N. Yorks., U.K. ... 14 C7 54 30N 0 37W
Eskān, Iran ... 71 E9 26 48N 63 9 E
Esker, Canada ... 105 B6 53 53N 66 25W
Eskifjörður, Iceland ... 8 D7 65 3N 13 55W
Eskilstuna, Sweden ... 11 F7 59 22N 16 32 E
Eskimalatya, Turkey ... 70 B3 38 23N 38 50 E
Eskimo Point = Arviat, Canada ... 103 A10 61 6N 93 59W
Eskişehir, Turkey ... 47 B12 39 50N 30 30 E
Eskişehir □, Turkey ... 47 B12 39 40N 31 0 E
Esla ➤, Spain ... 36 D4 41 29N 6 3W
Eslāmābād-e Gharb, Iran ... 70 C5 34 10N 46 30 E
Eslāmshahr, Iran ... 71 C6 35 40N 51 10 E
Eslöv, Sweden ... 11 J7 55 50N 13 20 E
Eşme, Turkey ... 47 C10 38 23N 28 58 E
Esmeraldas, Ecuador ... 124 C3 1 0N 79 40W
Esnagi L., Canada ... 104 C3 48 36N 84 33W
Espalion, France ... 20 D6 44 32N 2 47 E
Espanola, Canada ... 104 C3 46 15N 81 46W
Española, U.S.A. ... 109 H10 35 59N 106 5W
Esparreguera, Spain ... 38 D6 41 33N 1 52 E
Esparta, Costa Rica ... 120 E3 9 59N 84 40W
Esparza, Costa Rica ... 120 E3 9 59N 84 40W
Esperance, Australia ... 93 F3 33 45 S 121 55 E
Esperance B., Australia ... 93 F3 33 48 S 121 55 E
Esperance Harbour, St. Lucia ... 121 f 14 4N 60 55W
Esperanza, Antarctica ... 5 C18 65 0 S 55 0W
Esperanza, Argentina ... 126 C3 31 29 S 61 3W
Esperanza, Phil. ... 61 G6 8 43N 125 36 E
Esperanza, Puerto Rico ... 121 d 18 6N 65 28W
Espéraza, France ... 20 F6 42 56N 2 14 E

Espichel, C., Portugal ... 37 G1 38 22N 9 16W
Espiel, Spain ... 37 G5 38 11N 5 1W
Espigão, Serra do, Brazil ... 127 B5 26 35 S 50 30W
Espinazo, Sierra del = Espinhaço, Serra do, Brazil ... 125 G10 17 30 S 43 30W
Espinhaço, Serra do, Brazil ... 125 G10 17 30 S 43 30W
Espinho, Portugal ... 36 D2 41 1N 8 38W
Espinilho, Serra do, Brazil ... 127 B5 28 30 S 55 0W
Espinosa de los Monteros, Spain ... 36 B7 43 5N 3 34W
Espírito Santo □, Brazil ... 125 H10 20 0 S 40 45W
Espíritu Santo, Vanuatu ... 96 J8 15 15 S 166 50 E
Espíritu Santo, B. del, Mexico ... 119 D7 19 15N 87 0W
Espíritu Santo, I., Mexico ... 118 C2 24 30N 110 23W
Espita, Mexico ... 119 C7 21 1N 88 19W
Espiye, Turkey ... 73 B8 40 56N 38 43 E
Espluga de Francolí, Spain ... 38 D6 41 24N 1 7 E
Espoo, Finland ... 9 F21 60 12N 24 40 E
Espuña, Sierra de, Spain ... 39 H3 37 51N 1 35W
Espungabera, Mozam. ... 89 C5 20 29 S 32 45 E
Esquel, Argentina ... 128 E2 42 55 S 71 20W
Esquimalt, Canada ... 102 D4 48 26N 123 25W
Esquina, Argentina ... 126 C4 30 0 S 59 30W
Essaouira, Morocco ... 78 B4 31 32N 9 42W
Essebie, Dem. Rep. of the Congo ... 86 B3 2 58N 30 40 E
Essen, Belgium ... 17 C4 51 28N 4 28 E
Essen, Germany ... 24 D3 51 28N 7 2 E
Essendon, Mt., Australia ... 93 E3 25 0 S 120 29 E
Essequibo ➤, Guyana ... 124 B7 6 50N 58 30W
Essex, Canada ... 116 D2 42 10N 82 49W
Essex, Calif., U.S.A. ... 111 L11 34 44N 115 15W
Essex, N.Y., U.S.A. ... 117 B11 44 19N 73 21W
Essex □, U.K. ... 15 F8 51 54N 0 27 E
Essex Junction, U.S.A. ... 117 B11 44 29N 73 7W
Esslingen, Germany ... 25 G5 48 44N 9 18 E
Essonne □, France ... 19 D9 48 30N 2 20 E
Estaca de Bares, C. de, Spain ... 36 B3 43 46N 7 42W
Estadilla, Spain ... 38 C5 42 4N 0 16 E
Estados, I. de Los, Argentina ... 128 G4 54 40 S 64 30W
Estagel, France ... 20 F6 42 47N 2 40 E
Eştahbānāt, Iran ... 71 D7 29 8N 54 4 E
Estância, Brazil ... 125 F11 11 16 S 37 26W
Estancia, U.S.A. ... 109 J10 34 46N 106 4W
Eştārm, Iran ... 71 D8 28 21N 58 21 E
Estarreja, Portugal ... 36 E2 40 45N 8 35W
Estats, Pic d', Spain ... 38 C6 42 40N 1 24 E
Estcourt, S. Africa ... 89 D4 29 0 S 29 53 E
Este, Italy ... 41 C8 45 14N 11 39 E
Esteban, Dom. Rep. ... 121 C6 18 14N 68 42W
Estelí, Nic. ... 120 D2 13 9N 86 22W
Estella, Spain ... 38 C2 42 40N 2 2W
Estena ➤, Spain ... 37 F6 39 23N 4 44W
Estepa, Spain ... 37 H6 37 17N 4 52W
Estepona, Spain ... 37 J5 36 24N 5 7W
Esterhazy, Canada ... 103 C8 50 37N 102 5W
Esternay, France ... 19 D10 48 44N 3 33 E
Esterri d'Aneu, Spain ... 38 C6 42 38N 1 5 E
Estevan, Canada ... 103 D8 49 10N 102 59W
Estevan Group, Canada ... 102 C3 53 3N 129 38W
Estherville, U.S.A. ... 112 D7 43 24N 94 50W
Estissac, France ... 19 D10 48 16N 3 48 E
Eston, Canada ... 103 C7 51 8N 108 40W
Estonia ■, Europe ... 9 G21 58 30N 25 30 E
Estoril, Portugal ... 37 G1 38 42N 9 23W
Estouk, Mali ... 83 B5 18 14N 1 2 E
Estreito, Brazil ... 125 E9 6 32 S 47 25W
Estrela, Serra da, Portugal ... 36 E3 40 10N 7 45W
Estrella, Spain ... 37 G7 38 25N 3 35W
Estremoz, Portugal ... 37 G3 38 51N 7 39W
Estrondo, Serra do, Brazil ... 125 E9 7 20 S 48 0W
Esztergom, Hungary ... 28 C3 47 47N 18 44 E
Et Tîdra, Mauritania ... 82 B1 19 45N 16 20W
Etah, India ... 69 F8 27 35N 78 40 E
Étain, France ... 19 C12 49 13N 5 38 E
Étampes, France ... 19 D9 48 26N 2 10 E
Etanga, Namibia ... 88 B1 17 55 S 13 0 E
Étaples, France ... 19 B8 50 30N 1 39 E
Etawah, India ... 69 F8 26 48N 79 6 E
Etawney L., Canada ... 103 B9 57 50N 96 50W
Ete, Nigeria ... 83 D6 7 2N 7 28 E
Ethel, U.S.A. ... 110 D4 46 32N 122 46W
Ethelbert, Canada ... 103 C8 51 32N 100 25W
Ethiopia ■, Africa ... 75 F3 8 0N 40 0 E
Ethiopian Highlands, Ethiopia ... 50 J7 10 0N 37 0 E
Etili, Turkey ... 45 G10 39 59N 26 54 E
Etive, L., U.K. ... 13 E3 56 29N 5 10W
Etna, Italy ... 43 E7 37 50N 14 55 E
Etoile, Dem. Rep. of the Congo ... 87 E2 11 33 S 27 30 E
Etosha ➤, Namibia ... 88 B2 19 0 S 16 0 E
Etosha Pan, Namibia ... 88 B2 18 40 S 16 30 E
Etowah, U.S.A. ... 115 H3 35 20N 84 32W
Étréchy, France ... 19 D9 48 30N 2 12 E
Étrépagny, France ... 19 C8 49 18N 1 36 E
Étretat, France ... 18 C7 49 42N 0 12 E
Etropole, Bulgaria ... 45 D8 42 50N 24 0 E
Ettelbruck, Lux. ... 17 E6 49 51N 6 5 E
Ettrick Water ➤, U.K. ... 13 F6 55 31N 2 55W
Etuku, Dem. Rep. of the Congo ... 86 C2 3 42 S 25 45 E
Etzatlán, Mexico ... 118 C4 20 48N 104 5W
Etzná-Tixmucuy = Edzná, Mexico ... 119 D6 19 35N 90 15W
Eu, France ... 18 B8 50 3N 1 26 E
Eubenangee Swamp △, Australia ... 94 B4 16 25 S 146 1 E
Euboea = Évvoia, Greece ... 46 C6 38 30N 24 0 E
Eucla, Australia ... 93 F4 31 41 S 128 52 E
Euclid, U.S.A. ... 116 E3 41 34N 81 32W
Eucumbene, L., Australia ... 95 F4 36 2 S 148 40 E
Eudora, U.S.A. ... 113 J9 33 7N 91 16W
Eufaula, Ala., U.S.A. ... 115 K3 31 54N 85 9W
Eufaula, Okla., U.S.A. ... 113 H7 35 17N 95 35W
Eufaula L., U.S.A. ... 113 H7 35 18N 95 21W
Eugene, U.S.A. ... 108 E2 44 5N 123 4W
Eugowra, Australia ... 95 E4 33 22 S 148 24 E
Eulo, Australia ... 95 D4 28 10 S 145 3 E
Eungella △, Australia ... 94 C4 20 57 S 148 40 E
Eunice, La., U.S.A. ... 113 K8 30 30N 92 25W

Eunice, N. Mex., U.S.A. ... 113 J3 32 26N 103 10W
Eupen, Belgium ... 17 D6 50 37N 6 3 E
Euphrates = Furāt, Nahr al ➤, Asia ... 70 D5 31 0N 47 25 E
Eure □, France ... 18 C8 49 10N 1 0 E
Eure ➤, France ... 18 C8 49 18N 1 12 E
Eure-et-Loir □, France ... 18 D8 48 22N 1 30 E
Eureka, Canada ... 4 B3 80 0N 85 56W
Eureka, Calif., U.S.A. ... 108 F1 40 47N 124 9W
Eureka, Kans., U.S.A. ... 113 G6 37 49N 96 17W
Eureka, Mont., U.S.A. ... 108 B6 48 53N 115 3W
Eureka, Nev., U.S.A. ... 108 G5 39 31N 115 58W
Eureka, S. Dak., U.S.A. ... 112 C5 45 46N 99 38W
Eureka, Mt., Australia ... 93 E3 26 35 S 121 35 E
Euroa, Australia ... 95 F4 36 44 S 145 35 E
Europa, Île, Ind. Oc. ... 85 J8 22 20 S 40 22 E
Europa, Picos de, Spain ... 36 B6 43 10N 4 49W
Europa, Pta. de, Gib. ... 37 J5 36 3N 5 21W
Europe ... 6 E10 50 0N 20 0 E
Europoort, Neths. ... 17 C4 51 57N 4 10 E
Euskirchen, Germany ... 24 E2 50 39N 6 48 E
Eustis, U.S.A. ... 115 L5 28 51N 81 41W
Eutsuk L., Canada ... 102 C3 53 20N 126 45W
Evale, Angola ... 88 B2 16 33 S 15 44 E
Evans, U.S.A. ... 112 E2 40 23N 104 41W
Evans, L., Canada ... 104 B4 50 50N 77 0W
Evans City, U.S.A. ... 116 F4 40 46N 80 4W
Evans Head, Australia ... 95 D5 29 7 S 153 27 E
Evans Mills, U.S.A. ... 117 B9 44 6N 75 48W
Evansburg, Canada ... 102 C5 53 36N 114 59W
Evanston, Ill., U.S.A. ... 114 E2 42 3N 87 41W
Evanston, Wyo., U.S.A. ... 108 F8 41 16N 110 58W
Evansville, U.S.A. ... 114 G2 37 58N 87 35W
Évaux-les-Bains, France ... 19 F9 46 12N 2 29 E
Evaz, Iran ... 71 E7 27 46N 53 59 E
Evciler, Afyon, Turkey ... 47 C11 38 4N 29 54 E
Evciler, Çanakkale, Turkey ... 47 B8 39 47N 26 44 E
Eveleth, U.S.A. ... 112 B8 47 28N 92 32W
Evensk, Russia ... 53 C16 62 12N 159 30 E
Everard, L., Australia ... 95 E2 31 30 S 135 0 E
Everard Ranges, Australia ... 93 E5 27 5 S 132 28 E
Everest, Mt., Nepal ... 69 E12 28 5N 86 58 E
Everett, Pa., U.S.A. ... 116 F6 40 1N 78 23W
Everett, Wash., U.S.A. ... 110 C4 47 59N 122 12W
Everglades, U.S.A. ... 115 N5 25 50N 81 0W
Everglades, The, U.S.A. ... 115 N5 25 50N 81 0W
Everglades City, U.S.A. ... 115 N5 25 52N 81 23W
Evergreen, Ala., U.S.A. ... 115 K2 31 26N 86 57W
Evergreen, Mont., U.S.A. ... 108 B6 48 9N 114 13W
Everöd, Sweden ... 11 J8 55 53N 14 5 E
Evertsberg, Sweden ... 10 C7 61 8N 13 58 E
Evesham, U.K. ... 15 E6 52 6N 1 56W
Évian-les-Bains, France ... 19 F13 46 24N 6 35 E
Évinos ➤, Greece ... 46 C3 38 27N 21 40 E
Évisa, France ... 21 F12 42 15N 8 48 E
Evje, Norway ... 9 G12 58 36N 7 51 E
Évora, Portugal ... 37 G3 38 33N 7 57W
Évora □, Portugal ... 37 G3 38 33N 7 50W
Evowghlī, Iran ... 70 B5 38 43N 45 13 E
Évreux, France ... 18 C8 49 3N 1 8 E
Evritanía □, Greece ... 46 B3 39 5N 21 30 E
Évron, France ... 18 D6 48 10N 0 24W
Évros □, Greece ... 45 E10 41 10N 26 0 E
Évros ➤, Greece ... 72 B2 41 40N 26 34 E
Evrótas ➤, Greece ... 46 E4 36 50N 22 40 E
Évry, France ... 19 D9 48 38N 2 27 E
Évvoia, Greece ... 46 C6 38 30N 24 0 E
Évvoia □, Greece ... 46 C5 38 30N 24 0 E
Evxinoúpolis, Greece ... 46 B4 39 12N 22 42 E
Ewe, L., U.K. ... 13 D3 57 49N 5 38W
Ewing, U.S.A. ... 112 D5 42 16N 98 21W
Ewo, Congo ... 84 E2 0 48 S 14 45 E
Exaltación, Bolivia ... 124 F5 13 10 S 65 20W
Excelsior Springs, U.S.A. ... 112 F7 39 20N 94 13W
Excideuil, France ... 20 C5 45 20N 1 4 E
Exe ➤, U.K. ... 15 G4 50 41N 3 29W
Exeter, Canada ... 116 C3 43 21N 81 29W
Exeter, U.K. ... 15 G4 50 43N 3 31W
Exeter, Calif., U.S.A. ... 110 J7 36 18N 119 9W
Exeter, N.H., U.S.A. ... 117 D14 42 59N 70 57W
Exmoor, U.K. ... 15 F4 51 12N 3 45W
Exmoor △, U.K. ... 15 F4 51 8N 3 42W
Exmouth, Australia ... 92 D1 21 54 S 114 10 E
Exmouth, U.K. ... 15 G4 50 37N 3 25W
Exmouth G., Australia ... 92 D1 22 15 S 114 15 E
Expedition △, Australia ... 95 D4 25 41 S 149 7 E
Expedition Ra., Australia ... 94 C4 24 30 S 149 12 E
Extremadura □, Spain ... 37 F4 39 30N 6 5W
Exuma Sound, Bahamas ... 120 B4 24 30N 76 20W
Eyasi, L., Tanzania ... 86 C4 3 30 S 35 0 E
Eye Pen., U.K. ... 13 C2 58 13N 6 10W
Eyemouth, U.K. ... 13 F6 55 52N 2 5W
Eygues = Aigues ➤, France ... 21 D8 44 7N 4 43 E
Eygurande, France ... 19 G9 45 40N 2 26 E
Eyjafjörður, Iceland ... 8 C4 66 15N 18 30W
Eymet, France ... 20 D4 44 40N 0 25 E
Eymoutiers, France ... 20 C5 45 40N 1 45 E
Eynesil, Turkey ... 73 B8 41 4N 39 9 E
Eyre (North), L., Australia ... 95 D2 28 30 S 137 20 E
Eyre (South), L., Australia ... 95 D2 29 18 S 137 25 E
Eyre Mts., N.Z. ... 91 L2 45 25 S 168 25 E
Eyre Pen., Australia ... 95 E2 33 30 S 136 17 E
Eysturoy, Færoe Is. ... 8 E9 62 13N 6 54W
Eyvānkī, Iran ... 71 C6 35 24N 51 56 E
Ez Zeidab, Sudan ... 80 D3 17 25N 33 55 E
Ezcaray, Spain ... 38 C1 42 19N 3 0W
Ežerėlis, Lithuania ... 30 D10 54 53N 23 37 E
Ezhou, China ... 59 B10 30 23N 114 55 E
Ezine, Turkey ... 47 B8 39 48N 26 20 E
Ezouza ➤, Cyprus ... 49 E11 34 44N 32 27 E

F

F.Y.R.O.M. = Macedonia ■, Europe ... 44 E5 41 53N 21 40 E
Fabala, Guinea ... 82 D3 9 44N 9 5W
Fabens, U.S.A. ... 109 L10 31 30N 106 10W
Fabero, Spain ... 36 C4 42 46N 6 37W
Fabriano, Italy ... 41 E9 43 20N 12 54 E
Fǎcǎeni, Romania ... 29 F12 44 32N 27 53 E
Fachi, Niger ... 79 E8 18 6N 11 34 E
Fada, Chad ... 79 E10 17 13N 21 34 E
Fada-n-Gourma, Burkina Faso ... 83 C5 12 10N 0 30 E
Fadd, Hungary ... 28 D3 46 28N 18 49 E
Faddeyevskiy, Ostrov, Russia ... 53 B15 76 0N 144 0 E

Faddor, Sudan .... **81 F3** 8 7N 32 17 E
Fadghāmī, Syria ..... **70 C4** 35 53N 40 52 E
Fadlab, Sudan .... **80 D3** 17 42N 34 2 E
Faenza, Italy .... **41 D8** 44 17N 11 53 E
Færoe Is. = Føroyar,
  Atl. Oc. **8 F9** 62 0N 7 0W
Fafa, Mali .... **83 B5** 15 22N 0 48 E
Fafe, Portugal **36 D2** 41 27N 8 11W
Fagam, Nigeria ...... **83 C7** 11 1N 10 1 E
Făgăras, Romania .... **29 E9** 45 48N 24 58 E
Făgăras, Munţii,
  Romania .... **29 E9** 45 40N 24 40 E
Fågelmara, Sweden ... **11 H9** 56 16N 15 58 E
Fagerhult, Sweden ... **11 G9** 57 8N 15 40 E
Fagersta, Sweden .... **10 D9** 60 1N 15 46 E
Fåget, Romania ...... **29 D9** 45 52N 22 10 E
Făget, Munţii, Romania **29 C8** 47 40N 23 10 E
Fagnano, L., Argentina **128 G3** 54 30 S 68 0W
Fagnières, France .... **19 D11** 48 58N 4 20 E
Faguibine, L., Mali ... **82 B4** 16 45N 4 0W
Fahliān, Iran .... **71 D6** 30 11N 51 28 E
Fahraj, Kermān, Iran . **71 D8** 29 0N 59 0 E
Fahraj, Yazd, Iran ... **71 D7** 31 46N 54 36 E
Fai Tsi Long, Vietnam . **58 G6** 21 0N 107 30 E
Faial, Madeira **48 D3** 32 47N 16 53W
Fair Haven, U.S.A. ... **114 D9** 43 36N 73 16W
Fair Hd., U.K. **12 A5** 55 14N 6 9W
Fair Oaks, U.S.A. ... **110 G5** 38 39N 121 16W
Fairbanks, U.S.A. ... **100 B5** 64 51N 147 43W
Fairbury, U.S.A. **112 E6** 40 8N 97 11W
Fairfax, U.S.A. **117 B11** 44 40N 73 1W
Fairfield, Ala., U.S.A. . **115 J2** 33 29N 86 55W
Fairfield, Calif., U.S.A. **114 G4** 38 15N 122 3W
Fairfield, Conn., U.S.A. **117 E11** 41 9N 73 16W
Fairfield, Idaho, U.S.A. **108 E6** 43 21N 114 44W
Fairfield, Ill., U.S.A. .. **114 F1** 38 23N 88 22W
Fairfield, Iowa, U.S.A. . **112 E9** 40 56N 91 57W
Fairfield, Tex., U.S.A. . **113 K7** 31 44N 96 10W
Fairhope, U.S.A. **115 K2** 30 31N 87 54W
Fairlie, N.Z. .... **91 L3** 44 5 S 170 49 E
Fairmead, U.S.A. **110 H6** 37 5N 120 10W
Fairmont, Minn., U.S.A. **112 D7** 43 39N 94 28W
Fairmont, W. Va., U.S.A. **114 F5** 39 29N 80 9W
Fairmount, Calif., U.S.A. **111 L8** 34 45N 118 26W
Fairmount, N.Y., U.S.A. **117 C8** 43 5N 76 12W
Fairplay, U.S.A. **109 G11** 39 15N 106 2W
Fairport, U.S.A. **116 C7** 43 6N 77 27W
Fairport Harbor, U.S.A. **116 E3** 41 45N 81 17W
Fairview, Canada **102 B5** 56 5N 118 25W
Fairview, Mont., U.S.A. **112 B2** 47 51N 104 3W
Fairview, Okla., U.S.A. **113 G5** 36 16N 98 29W
Fairweather, Mt., U.S.A. **100 C6** 58 55N 137 32W
Faisalabad, Pakistan . **68 D5** 31 30N 73 5 E
Faith, U.S.A. **112 C3** 45 2N 102 2W
Faizabad, India ..... **69 F10** 26 45N 82 10 E
Fajardo, Puerto Rico . **121 d** 18 20N 65 39W
Fajr, W. →, Si. Arabia **70 D3** 29 10N 38 10 E
Fakenham, U.K. ..... **14 E8** 52 51N 0 51 E
Fåker, Sweden ...... **10 A8** 63 0N 14 34 E
Fakfak, Indonesia ... **63 E8** 2 55 S 132 18 E
Fakiya, Bulgaria .... **45 D11** 42 10N 27 6 E
Fakobli, Ivory C. **82 D3** 7 23N 7 23W
Fakse, Denmark .... **11 J6** 55 15N 12 8 E
Fakse Bugt, Denmark . **11 J6** 55 11N 12 15 E
Fakse Ladeplads,
  Denmark .... **11 J6** 55 11N 12 9 E
Faku, China .... **57 C12** 42 32N 123 21 E
Falaba, S. Leone **82 D2** 9 54N 11 22W
Falaise, France **18 D6** 48 54N 0 12W
Falaise, Mui, Vietnam . **64 C5** 19 6N 105 45 E
Falakrón Óros, Greece . **44 E7** 41 15N 23 58 E
Falam, Burma ...... **67 H18** 23 0N 93 45 E
Falces, Spain **38 C3** 42 24N 1 48W
Fălciu, Romania .... **29 D13** 46 17N 28 7 E
Falcó, C. des, Spain .. **48 C7** 38 50N 1 23 E
Falcón, Presa, Mexico **119 B5** 26 35N 99 10W
Falcon Lake, Canada . **103 D9** 49 42N 95 15W
Falcon Reservoir, U.S.A. **113 M5** 26 34N 99 10W
Falconara Maríttima,
  Italy .... **41 E10** 43 37N 13 24 E
Falcone, C. del, Italy . **42 B1** 40 58N 8 12 E
Falconer, U.S.A. **116 D5** 42 7N 79 13W
Faléa, Mali **82 C2** 12 16N 11 17W
Falémé →, Senegal . **82 C2** 14 46N 12 14W
Falerum, Sweden ... **11 F10** 58 8N 16 13 E
Faleshty = Fălești,
  Moldova .... **29 C12** 47 32N 27 44 E
Fălești, Moldova .... **29 C12** 47 32N 27 44 E
Falfurrias, U.S.A. ... **113 M5** 27 14N 98 9W
Falher, Canada **102 B5** 55 44N 117 15W
Falirakí, Greece .... **49 C10** 36 22N 28 12 E
Falkenberg, Germany . **24 D9** 51 35N 13 14 E
Falkenberg, Sweden . **11 H6** 56 54N 12 30 E
Falkensee, Germany . **24 C9** 52 34N 13 4 E
Falkirk, U.K. **13 F5** 56 0N 3 47W
Falkirk □, U.K. **13 F5** 55 58N 3 49W
Falkland, U.K. **13 E5** 56 16N 3 12W
Falkland Is. ☑, Atl. Oc. **128 G5** 51 30 S 59 0W
Falkland Sd., Falk. Is. . **128 G5** 52 0 S 60 0W
Falkonéra, Greece ... **46 E5** 36 50N 23 52 E
Falköping, Sweden .. **11 F7** 58 12N 13 33 E
Fall River, U.S.A. ... **117 E13** 41 43N 71 10W
Fallbrook, U.S.A. ... **111 M9** 33 23N 117 15W
Fallon, U.S.A. **108 G4** 39 28N 118 47W
Falls City, U.S.A. ... **112 E7** 40 3N 95 36W
Falls Creek, U.S.A. .. **116 E6** 41 9N 78 48W
Falmouth, Jamaica .. **120 a** 18 30N 77 40W
Falmouth, U.K. **15 G2** 50 9N 5 5W
Falmouth, U.S.A. ... **117 E14** 41 33N 70 37W
Falsa, Pta., Mexico .. **118 B1** 27 51N 115 3W
False B., S. Africa ... **88 E2** 34 15 S 18 40 E
False, C. Honduras .. **120 C3** 15 12N 83 21W
Falset, Denmark .... **11 K5** 54 45N 11 55 E
Falsterbo, Sweden .. **9 J15** 55 23N 12 50 E
Fălticeni, Romania .. **29 C11** 47 21N 26 20 E
Falun, Sweden ...... **10 D9** 60 37N 15 37 E
Famagusta, Cyprus .. **49 D12** 35 8N 33 55 E
Famagusta Bay, Cyprus **49 D13** 35 15N 34 0 E
Famalé, Niger ...... **78 F6** 14 33N 1 5 E
Famatina, Sierra de,
  Argentina .... **126 B2** 27 30 S 68 0W
Family L., Canada ... **103 C9** 51 54N 95 27W
Famoso, U.S.A. **111 K7** 35 37N 119 12W
Fan Xian, China .... **56 G8** 35 55N 115 38 E
Fana, Mali **82 C3** 13 0N 6 56W
Fanad Hd., Ireland .. **12 A4** 55 17N 7 38W
Fanárion, Greece ... **46 B3** 39 24N 21 47 E
Fandriana, Madag. .. **89 C8** 20 14 S 47 21 E
Fánes-Sénnes e
  Braies △, Italy .... **41 B9** 46 38N 12 4 E
Fang, Thailand ..... **58 H2** 19 55N 99 13 E
Fang Xian, China ... **59 A8** 32 3N 110 40 E
Fangaga, Sudan .... **80 D3** 17 40N 30 53 E
Fangak, Sudan ..... **81 F3** 9 4N 30 53 E
Fangchang, China ... **59 B12** 31 5N 118 4 E
Fangcheng, China ... **56 H7** 33 18N 112 59 E

Fangchenggang, China . **58 G7** 21 42N 108 21 E
Fangliao, Taiwan .... **59 F13** 22 22N 120 38 E
Fangshan, China .... **56 E6** 38 3N 111 25 E
Fangzi, China ...... **57 F10** 36 33N 119 10 E
Fani i Madh →, Albania **44 E4** 41 56N 20 16 E
Fanjakana, Madag. .. **89 C8** 21 10 S 46 53 E
Fanjiatun, China .... **57 C13** 43 40N 125 15 E
Fannich, L., U.K. ... **13 D4** 57 38N 4 59W
Fannūj, Iran .... **71 E8** 26 35N 59 38 E
Fanø, Denmark ..... **11 J2** 55 25N 8 25 E
Fanshi, China ...... **56 E7** 39 12N 113 20 E
Fao = Al Fāw, Iraq .. **71 D6** 30 0N 48 30 E
Faqirwali, Pakistan .. **68 E5** 29 27N 73 0 E
Fāqūs, Egypt .... **80 H7** 30 44N 31 47 E
Far East =
  Dalnevostochnyy □,
  Russia .... **53 C14** 67 0N 140 0 E
Far East, Asia ...... **50 E16** 40 0N 130 0 E
Fara in Sabina, Italy .. **41 F9** 42 12N 12 43 E
Faradje, Dem. Rep. of
  the Congo .... **86 B2** 3 50N 29 45 E
Farafangana, Madag. . **89 C8** 22 49 S 47 50 E
Farāfra, El Wâhât el-,
  Egypt .... **80 B2** 27 15N 28 20 E
Farāh, Afghan. ...... **66 C3** 32 20N 62 7 E
Farāh □, Afghan. .... **66 C3** 32 25N 62 10 E
Farahalana, Madag. . **89 A9** 14 26 S 50 10 E
Faraid, Gebel, Egypt . **80 C4** 23 33N 35 19 E
Farako, Ivory C. **82 D4** 10 45N 6 50W
Faramana, Burkina Faso **82 C4** 11 56N 4 45W
Faranah, Guinea **82 C2** 10 3N 10 45W
Farasān, Jazā'ir,
  Si. Arabia .... **75 D3** 16 45N 41 55 E
Farasan Is. = Farasān,
  Jazā'ir, Si. Arabia .. **75 D3** 16 45N 41 55 E
Faratsiho, Madag. ... **89 B8** 19 24 S 46 57 E
Fardes →, Spain **37 H7** 37 35N 3 0W
Fareham, U.K. **15 G6** 50 51N 1 11W
Farewell, L., Canada . **91 J4** 40 29 S 172 43 E
Farewell C. = Nunap
  Isua, Greenland **101 C15** 59 48N 43 55W
Färgelanda, Sweden . **11 F5** 58 34N 12 0 E
Farghona, Uzbekistan . **52 E8** 40 23N 71 19 E
Fargo, U.S.A. **112 B6** 46 53N 96 48W
Fār'iah, W. al →,
  West Bank .... **74 C4** 32 12N 35 27 E
Faribault, U.S.A. **112 C8** 44 18N 93 16W
Faridabad, India .... **68 E6** 28 26N 77 19 E
Faridkot, India ..... **68 D6** 30 44N 74 45 E
Faridpur, Bangla. .... **69 H13** 23 15N 89 55 E
Faridpur, India ..... **69 E8** 28 13N 79 33 E
Fårila, Sweden ..... **10 C9** 61 48N 15 50 E
Farim, Guinea-Biss. .. **82 C1** 12 27N 15 9W
Farīmān, Iran ...... **71 C8** 35 40N 59 49 E
Farina, Australia .... **95 E2** 30 3 S 138 15 E
Fariones, Pta.,
  Canary Is. **48 E6** 29 13N 13 28W
Fâriskûr, Egypt ..... **80 H7** 31 20N 31 43 E
Färjestaden, Sweden . **11 H10** 56 39N 16 27 E
Farkadhón, Greece .. **46 B4** 39 36N 22 4 E
Farleigh, Australia ... **94 K7** 21 4 S 149 8 E
Farmakonisi, Greece . **47 D9** 37 17N 27 5 E
Farmerville, U.S.A. .. **113 J8** 32 47N 92 24W
Farmingdale, U.S.A. . **117 F10** 40 12N 74 10W
Farmington, Canada . **102 B4** 55 54N 120 30W
Farmington, Calif.,
  U.S.A. **110 H6** 37 55N 120 59W
Farmington, Maine,
  U.S.A. **115 C10** 44 40N 70 9W
Farmington, Mo., U.S.A. **113 G9** 37 47N 90 25W
Farmington, N.H.,
  U.S.A. **117 C13** 43 24N 71 4W
Farmington, N. Mex.,
  U.S.A. **109 H9** 36 44N 108 12W
Farmington, Utah,
  U.S.A. **108 F8** 41 0N 111 12W
Farmington →, U.S.A. **117 E12** 41 51N 72 38W
Farmville, U.S.A. **114 G6** 37 18N 78 24W
Färnäs, Sweden .... **10 D8** 61 0N 14 39 E
Farne Is., U.K. **14 B6** 55 38N 1 37W
Färnebofjärden △,
  Sweden .... **10 D10** 60 10N 16 48 E
Farnham, Canada ... **117 A12** 45 17N 72 59W
Farnham, Mt., Canada **102 C5** 50 29N 116 30W
Faro, Brazil .... **125 D7** 2 10 S 56 39W
Faro, Canada **100 B6** 62 11N 133 22W
Faro, Portugal **37 H3** 37 2N 7 55W
Fårö, Sweden .... **9 H18** 57 55N 19 5 E
Faro □, Portugal **37 H2** 37 12N 8 10W
Faro ✈ (FAO), Portugal **37 H3** 37 1N 7 57W
Fårösund, Sweden ... **11 G13** 57 52N 19 2 E
Farquhar, C., Australia **93 D1** 23 50 S 113 36 E
Farrars Cr. →, Australia **94 D3** 25 35 S 140 43 E
Farrāshband, Iran ... **71 D7** 28 57N 52 5 E
Farrell, U.S.A. **116 E4** 41 13N 80 30W
Farrokhi, Iran ...... **71 C8** 33 50N 59 31 E
Farruch, C. = Ferrutx,
  C., Spain .... **48 B10** 39 47N 3 21 E
Fārs □, Iran .... **71 D7** 29 30N 55 0 E
Fársala, Greece ..... **46 B4** 39 17N 22 23 E
Farsø, Denmark ..... **11 H3** 56 46N 9 19 E
Farson, U.S.A. **108 E9** 42 6N 109 27W
Farsund, Norway ... **9 G12** 58 5N 6 55 E
Fartak, Râs, Si. Arabia **70 D2** 28 5N 34 34 E
Fartak, Ra's, Yemen .. **75 D5** 15 38N 52 15 E
Fărţăneşti, Romania . **29 E12** 45 49N 27 59 E
Fartura, Serra da, Brazil **127 B5** 26 21 S 52 52W
Faru, Nigeria .... **83 C6** 12 48N 6 12 E
Fārūj, Iran .... **71 B8** 37 14N 58 14 E
Fårup, Denmark .... **11 H3** 56 33N 9 51 E
Farvel, Kap = Nunap
  Isua, Greenland **101 C15** 59 48N 43 55W
Farwell, U.S.A. **113 H3** 34 23N 103 2W
Faryāb □, Afghan. ... **66 B4** 36 0N 65 0 E
Fasā, Iran .... **71 D7** 29 0N 53 39 E
Fasano, Italy .... **43 B10** 40 50N 17 22 E
Fashoda, Sudan .... **81 F3** 9 50N 32 2 E
Fasa, Mali .... **82 B4** 14 18N 0 15 E
Fastiv, Ukraine ..... **33 G5** 50 7N 29 57 E
Fastnet Rock, Ireland . **12 E2** 51 22N 9 37W
Fastov = Fastiv, Ukraine **33 G5** 50 7N 29 57 E
Fatagar, Tanjung,
  Indonesia .... **63 E8** 2 46 S 131 57 E
Fatehabad, Haryana,
  India .... **68 E6** 29 31N 75 27 E
Fatehabad, Ut. P., India **68 F8** 27 1N 78 19 E
Fatehgarh, India .... **69 F8** 27 25N 79 35 E
Fatehpur, Bihar, India **69 G11** 24 38N 85 14 E
Fatehpur, Raj., India . **68 F6** 28 0N 74 40 E
Fatehpur, Ut. P., India **69 G9** 25 56N 81 13 E
Fatehpur, Ut. P., India **69 F9** 27 10N 81 13 E
Fatehpur Sikri, India . **68 F6** 27 6N 77 40 E
Fathai, Sudan ...... **81 F3** 8 5N 32 38 E
Fathom Five △, Canada **116 A3** 45 17N 81 40W
Fatick, Senegal **82 C1** 14 19N 16 27W

Fatima, Canada **105 C7** 47 24N 61 53W
Fátima, Portugal **37 F2** 39 37N 8 39W
Fatoya, Guinea **82 C3** 11 37N 9 10W
Fatsa, Turkey ...... **72 B7** 41 2N 37 31 E
Faucille, Col de la,
  France .... **19 F13** 46 22N 6 2 E
Faulkton, U.S.A. **112 C5** 45 2N 99 8W
Faulquemont, France . **19 C13** 49 3N 6 36 E
Faure I., Australia ... **93 E1** 25 52 S 113 50 E
Fâurei, Romania .... **29 E12** 45 6N 27 19 E
Fauresmith, S. Africa . **88 D4** 29 44 S 25 17 E
Fauske, Norway .... **8 C16** 67 17N 15 25 E
Favara, Italy .... **42 E6** 37 19N 13 39 E
Favāritx, C. de, Spain . **48 B11** 40 0N 4 15 E
Faverges, France .... **21 C10** 45 45N 6 17 E
Favignana, Italy .... **42 E5** 37 56N 12 19 E
Favignana, I., Italy ... **42 E5** 37 56N 12 19 E
Fawcett, Pt., Australia **92 B5** 11 46 S 130 2 E
Fawn →, Canada ... **104 A2** 55 20N 87 35W
Fawnskin, U.S.A. **111 L10** 34 16N 116 56W
Faxaflói, Iceland **8 D2** 64 29N 23 0W
Faxälven →, Sweden **10 A10** 63 13N 17 13 E
Faya-Largeau, Chad . **79 E9** 17 58N 19 6 E
Fayd, Si. Arabia .... **70 E4** 27 1N 42 52 E
Fayence, France .... **21 E10** 43 38N 6 42 E
Fayette, Ala., U.S.A. . **115 J2** 33 41N 87 50W
Fayette, Mo., U.S.A. . **112 F8** 39 9N 92 41W
Fayetteville, Ark.,
  U.S.A. **113 G7** 36 4N 94 10W
Fayetteville, N.C.,
  U.S.A. **115 H6** 35 3N 78 53W
Fayetteville, Tenn.,
  U.S.A. **115 H2** 35 9N 86 34W
Fayied, Egypt ...... **80 H8** 30 18N 32 16 E
Fayón, Spain .... **38 D5** 41 15N 0 20 E
Fazao-Malfakassa △,
  Togo .... **83 D5** 8 45N 0 50 E
Fazilka, India .... **68 D6** 30 27N 74 2 E
Fazilpur, Pakistan ... **68 E4** 29 18N 70 29 E
Fdérik, Mauritania .. **78 D3** 22 40N 12 45W
Feale →, Ireland ... **12 D2** 52 27N 9 37W
Fear, C., U.S.A. **115 J7** 33 50N 77 58W
Feather →, U.S.A. .. **108 G3** 38 47N 121 36W
Feather Falls, U.S.A. . **110 F5** 39 36N 121 16W
Featherston, N.Z. ... **91 J5** 41 6 S 175 20 E
Featherstone, Zimbabwe **87 F3** 18 42 S 30 55 E
Fécamp, France ..... **18 C7** 49 45N 0 22 E
Fedala = Mohammedia,
  Morocco **78 B4** 33 44N 7 21W
Federación, Argentina **126 C4** 31 0 S 57 55W
Féderal, Argentina .. **128 C5** 30 57 S 58 48W
Federal Capital Terr. □,
  Nigeria .... **83 D6** 9 0N 7 10 E
Federal Way, U.S.A. . **110 C4** 47 18N 122 19W
Fedeshküh, Iran .... **71 D7** 28 49N 53 50 E
Fehérgyarmat, Hungary **28 C7** 47 58N 22 30 E
Fehmarn, Germany .. **24 A7** 54 27N 11 7 E
Fehmarn Bælt, Europe **11 K5** 54 35N 11 20 E
Fehmarn Belt =
  Fehmarn Bælt,
  Europe .... **11 K5** 54 35N 11 20 E
Fei Xian, China ..... **57 G9** 35 18N 117 59 E
Feijó, Brazil .... **124 E4** 8 9 S 70 21W
Feilding, N.Z. ...... **91 J5** 40 13 S 175 35 E
Feira de Santana, Brazil **125 F11** 12 15 S 38 57W
Feixi, China .... **59 B11** 31 43N 117 59 E
Feixiang, China ..... **56 F8** 36 30N 114 45 E
Fejér □, Hungary ... **28 C3** 47 9N 18 30 E
Fejø, Denmark ..... **11 K5** 54 55N 11 30 E
Feke, Turkey .... **72 D6** 37 48N 35 56 E
Fekete →, Hungary . **28 E3** 45 47N 18 15 E
Felanitx, Spain ..... **48 B10** 39 28N 3 9 E
Feldbach, Austria ... **26 E8** 46 57N 15 52 E
Feldberg, Baden-W.,
  Germany .... **25 H3** 47 52N 8 0 E
Feldberg,
  Mecklenburg-Vorpommern,
  Germany .... **24 B9** 53 20N 13 26 E
Feldkirch, Austria ... **26 D2** 47 15N 9 37 E
Feldkirchen, Austria . **26 E7** 46 44N 14 6 E
Felipe Carrillo Puerto,
  Mexico **119 D7** 19 38N 88 3W
Felixburg, Zimbabwe . **89 B5** 19 29 S 30 51 E
Felixstowe, U.K. .... **15 F9** 51 58N 1 23 E
Felletin, France ..... **20 C6** 45 53N 2 11 E
Fellingsbro, Sweden . **10 E9** 59 26N 15 37 E
Felton, U.S.A. **110 H4** 37 3N 122 4W
Feltre, Italy .... **41 B8** 46 1N 11 54 E
Femer Bælt = Fehmarn
  Bælt, Europe ...... **11 K5** 54 35N 11 20 E
Femø, Denmark ..... **11 K5** 54 58N 11 35 E
Femunden, Norway . **9 E14** 62 10N 11 53 E
Fen He →, China ... **56 G6** 35 36N 110 42 E
Fene, Spain **36 B2** 43 27N 8 9W
Fenelon Falls, Canada **116 B6** 44 32N 78 45W
Fener Burnu, Turkey . **47 E9** 36 58N 27 18 E
Feneroa, Ethiopia ... **81 E4** 13 5N 39 3 E
Feng Xian, Jiangsu,
  China .... **56 G9** 34 43N 116 35 E
Feng Xian, Shaanxi,
  China .... **56 H4** 33 54N 106 40 E
Fengári, Greece ..... **45 F9** 40 25N 25 32 E
Fengcheng, Jiangxi,
  China .... **59 C10** 28 12N 115 48 E
Fengcheng, Liaoning,
  China .... **57 D13** 40 28N 124 5 E
Fengfeng, China .... **56 F8** 36 28N 114 8 E
Fenggang, China .... **58 D6** 27 57N 107 47 E
Fenghua, China ..... **59 C13** 29 40N 121 25 E
Fenghuang, China ... **58 D7** 27 57N 109 29 E
Fengkai, China ..... **59 F8** 23 24N 111 30 E
Fengkang, Taiwan ... **59 F13** 22 12N 120 41 E
Fengle, China ...... **59 B9** 31 29N 112 29 E
Fengling, Taiwan .... **59 F13** 23 45N 121 26 E
Fengning, China .... **56 D9** 41 10N 116 33 E
Fengqing, China .... **58 E2** 24 38N 99 55 E
Fengqiu, China ..... **56 G8** 35 2N 114 25 E
Fengrun, China ..... **57 E10** 39 48N 118 8 E
Fengshan,
  Guangxi Zhuangzu,
  China .... **58 E7** 24 39N 109 15 E
Fengshan,
  Guangxi Zhuangzu,
  China .... **58 E6** 24 31N 107 3 E
Fengshan, Taiwan ... **59 F13** 22 38N 120 21 E
Fengshun, China .... **59 F11** 23 48N 116 10 E
Fengtai, Anhui, China **59 A11** 32 50N 116 40 E
Fengtai, Beijing, China **56 E9** 39 50N 116 20 E
Fengxian, China .... **59 B13** 30 55N 121 26 E
Fengxin, China ..... **59 C10** 28 41N 115 18 E
Fengyang, China .... **57 H9** 32 51N 117 29 E
Fengyi, China ...... **58 E3** 25 59N 100 20 E
Fengzhen, China .... **56 D7** 40 25N 113 2 E
Feno, C. de, France .. **21 G12** 41 58N 8 33 E
Fenoarivo, Fianarantsoa,
  Madag. .... **89 C8** 21 43 S 46 24 E

Fenoarivo, Fianarantsoa,
  Madag. .... **89 C8** 20 52 S 46 53 E
Fenoarivo Afovoany,
  Madag. .... **89 B8** 18 26 S 46 34 E
Fenoarivo Atsinanana,
  Madag. .... **89 B8** 17 22 S 49 25 E
Fens, The, U.K. **14 E7** 52 38N 0 2W
Fensmark, Denmark . **11 J5** 55 17N 11 48 E
Fenton, U.S.A. **114 D4** 42 48N 83 42W
Fenxi, China .... **56 F6** 36 40N 111 31 E
Fenyang, China ..... **56 F6** 37 18N 111 48 E
Fenyi, China .... **59 D10** 27 45N 114 47 E
Feodosiya, Ukraine .. **33 K8** 45 2N 35 16 E
Ferdows, Iran ...... **71 C8** 33 58N 58 2 E
Fère-Champenoise,
  France .... **19 D10** 48 45N 3 59 E
Fère-en-Tardenois,
  France .... **19 C10** 49 10N 3 30 E
Ferentino, Italy ..... **41 G10** 41 42N 13 15 E
Ferfer, Somali Rep. .. **75 F4** 5 4N 45 9 E
Fergana = Farghona,
  Uzbekistan .... **52 E8** 40 23N 71 19 E
Fergus, Canada **116 C4** 43 43N 80 24W
Fergus Falls, U.S.A. . **112 B6** 46 17N 96 4W
Feričanci, Croatia ... **28 E2** 45 32N 18 0 E
Ferihegy, Budapest ✈
  (BUD), Hungary ... **28 C4** 47 25N 19 12 E
Ferkéssédougou,
  Ivory C. **82 D3** 9 35N 5 6W
Ferlach, Austria ..... **26 E7** 46 32N 14 18 E
Ferland, Canada **104 B2** 50 19N 88 27W
Ferlo, Vallée du, Senegal **82 B2** 15 15N 14 15W
Ferlo-Nord □, Senegal **82 B2** 15 43N 14 0W
Ferlo-Sud □, Senegal . **82 B2** 15 43N 14 0W
Fermanagh □, U.K. . **12 B4** 54 21N 7 40W
Fermo, Italy .... **41 E10** 43 9N 13 43 E
Fermont, Canada ... **105 B6** 52 47N 67 5W
Fermoselle, Spain ... **36 D4** 41 19N 6 27W
Fermoy, Ireland **12 D3** 52 9N 8 16W
Fernán Núñez, Spain . **37 H6** 37 40N 4 44W
Fernández, Argentina **126 B3** 27 55 S 63 50W
Fernandina Beach,
  U.S.A. **115 K5** 30 40N 81 27W
Fernando de Noronha,
  Brazil .... **125 D12** 4 0 S 33 10W
Fernando Póo = Bioko,
  Eq. Guin. .... **83 E6** 3 30N 8 40 E
Ferndale, U.S.A. **110 B4** 40 35N 124 16W
Fernie, Canada **102 D5** 49 30N 115 5W
Fernlees, Australia .. **94 C4** 23 51 S 148 7 E
Fernley, U.S.A. **108 G4** 39 36N 119 15W
Ferozepore = Firozpur,
  India .... **68 D6** 30 55N 74 40 E
Férrai, Greece ...... **45 F10** 40 53N 26 10 E
Ferrandina, Italy .... **43 B9** 40 29N 16 27 E
Ferrara, Italy .... **41 D8** 44 50N 11 35 E
Ferrato, C., Italy .... **42 C2** 39 18N 9 38 E
Ferreira do Alentejo,
  Portugal **37 G2** 38 4N 8 6W
Ferreñafe, Peru ..... **124 E3** 6 42 S 79 50W
Ferrerías, Spain .... **48 B11** 39 59N 4 1 E
Ferret, C., France ... **20 D2** 44 38N 1 15W
Ferriday, U.S.A. **113 K9** 31 38N 91 33W
Ferrière, Italy ...... **40 D6** 44 40N 9 30 E
Ferrières, France .... **19 D9** 48 5N 2 48 E
Ferro, Capo, Italy ... **42 A2** 41 9N 9 31 E
Ferrol, Spain **36 B2** 43 29N 8 15W
Ferron, U.S.A. **109 G8** 39 5N 111 8W
Ferrutx, C., Spain ... **48 B10** 39 47N 3 21 E
Ferryland, Canada .. **105 C9** 47 2N 52 53W
Fertile, U.S.A. **112 B6** 47 32N 96 17W
Fertőszentmiklós,
  Hungary .... **28 C1** 47 35N 16 53 E
Fertőtavi △, Hungary **28 C1** 47 25N 16 50 E
Fès, Morocco **78 B5** 34 0N 5 0W
Fessenden, U.S.A. .. **112 B5** 47 39N 99 38W
Festus, U.S.A. **112 F9** 38 13N 90 24W
Fetà Bowé, Senegal . **82 C2** 14 56N 13 30W
Fetești, Romania ... **29 F12** 44 22N 27 51 E
Fethiye, Turkey ..... **47 E11** 36 36N 29 6 E
Fethiye Körfezi, Turkey **47 E10** 36 40N 28 50 E
Fetlar, U.K. **13 A8** 60 36N 0 52W
Feuilles →, Canada . **101 C12** 58 47N 70 4W
Feurs, France .... **21 C8** 45 45N 4 13 E
Fez = Fès, Morocco .. **79 C8** 27 0N 13 0 E
Fezzan, Libya ...... **79 C8** 27 0N 13 0 E
Fiambalá, Argentina . **126 B2** 27 45 S 67 37W
Fianarantsoa, Madag. **89 C8** 21 26 S 47 5 E
Fianarantsoa □, Madag. **89 B8** 19 30 S 47 0 E
Fiche, Ethiopia ..... **81 F4** 9 50N 38 46 E
Fichtelgebirge, Germany **25 E7** 50 10N 11 55 E
Fichtelgebirge △,
  Germany .... **25 E8** 50 8N 12 0 E
Ficksburg, S. Africa . **89 D4** 28 51 S 27 53 E
Fidenza, Italy ...... **40 D7** 44 52N 10 3 E
Fiditi, Nigeria ...... **83 D5** 7 45N 3 53 E
Field →, Australia .. **94 C2** 23 48 S 138 0 E
Field I., Australia ... **92 B5** 12 5 S 132 23 E
Fieni, Romania ..... **29 E10** 45 8N 25 25 E
Fier, Albania .... **44 F3** 40 43N 19 33 E
Fierzë, Albania ..... **44 D4** 42 15N 20 1 E
Fife □, U.K. **13 E5** 56 5N 3 1W
Fife Ness, U.K. **13 E6** 56 17N 2 35W
Fifth Cataract, Sudan . **80 D3** 18 22N 33 50 E
Figari, France ...... **21 G13** 41 29N 9 7 E
Figeac, France ...... **20 D6** 44 37N 2 2 E
Figeholm, Sweden .. **11 G10** 57 22N 16 33 E
Figline Valdarno, Italy **41 E8** 43 37N 11 29 E
Figtree, Zimbabwe .. **87 G2** 20 22 S 28 20 E
Figueira Castelo
  Rodrigo, Portugal . **36 E4** 40 57N 6 58W
Figueira da Foz,
  Portugal **36 E2** 40 7N 8 54W
Figueira dos Vinhos,
  Portugal **36 F2** 39 55N 8 16W
Figueres, Spain ..... **38 C7** 42 18N 2 58 E
Figuig, Morocco **78 B5** 32 5N 1 11W
Fihaonana, Madag. . **89 B8** 18 36 S 47 12 E
Fiherenana →, Madag. **89 C7** 23 19 S 43 37 E
Fiji ■, Pac. Oc. ..... **91 C8** 17 20 S 179 0 E
Fik, Ethiopia .... **81 F5** 8 10N 42 19 E
Fika, Nigeria .... **83 C7** 11 15N 11 13 E
Filabres, Sierra de los,
  Spain **37 H8** 37 13N 2 20W
Filabusi, Zimbabwe . **89 C4** 20 34 S 29 20 E
Filadélfia, Italy ..... **43 D9** 38 47N 16 17 E
Fiľakovo, Slovak Rep. **27 C12** 48 17N 19 50 E
Filey, U.K. **14 C7** 54 12N 0 18W
Filey B., U.K. **14 C7** 54 12N 0 15W
Filfla, Malta .... **49 D1** 35 47N 14 24 E
Filiaşi, Romania .... **29 F8** 44 32N 23 31 E
Filiátes, Greece .... **46 B2** 39 38N 20 16 E
Filiatrá, Greece ..... **46 D3** 37 9N 21 35 E
Filicudi, Italy .... **43 D7** 38 35N 14 33 E

Filingué, Niger ..... **83 C5** 14 21N 3 22 E
Filiouri →, Greece .. **45 E9** 41 15N 25 40 E
Filipstad, Sweden ... **10 E8** 59 43N 14 9 E
Filisur, Switz. ...... **25 J5** 46 41N 9 41 E
Fillmore, Calif., U.S.A. **111 L8** 34 24N 118 55W
Fillmore, Utah, U.S.A. **109 G7** 38 58N 112 20W
Filótion, Greece ..... **47 D7** 37 3N 25 30 E
Filottrano, Italy ..... **41 E10** 43 26N 13 21 E
Filtu, Ethiopia ...... **81 F5** 5 8N 40 35 E
Fina, Mali **82 C3** 13 15N 8 46W
Finale Emília, Italy ... **41 D8** 44 50N 11 18 E
Finale Lígure, Italy .. **40 D5** 44 10N 8 20 E
Fiñana, Spain **37 H8** 37 10N 2 50W
Finch, Canada **117 A9** 45 11N 75 7W
Finch Hatton, Australia **94 K6** 20 25 S 148 39 E
Findhorn →, U.K. .. **13 D5** 57 38N 3 38W
Findlay, U.S.A. **114 E4** 41 2N 83 39W
Finger L., Canada ... **104 B1** 53 33N 124 18W
Finger Lakes, U.S.A. . **117 D8** 42 40N 76 30W
Fíngoè, Mozam. .... **87 E3** 14 55 S 31 50 E
Finike, Turkey ...... **47 E12** 36 21N 30 10 E
Finike Körfezi, Turkey **47 E12** 36 7N 30 16 E
Finiq, Albania ...... **44 G4** 39 54N 20 3 E
Finistère □, France .. **18 D3** 48 20N 4 0W
Finisterre = Fisterra,
  Spain **36 C1** 42 54N 9 16W
Finisterre, C. = Fisterra,
  C., Spain **36 C1** 42 50N 9 19W
Finke, Australia ..... **94 D1** 25 34 S 134 35 E
Finke Gorge △,
  Australia .... **92 D5** 24 8 S 132 49 E
Finland ■, Europe .. **8 E22** 63 0N 27 0 E
Finland, G. of, Europe **9 G21** 60 0N 26 0 E
Finlay →, Canada .. **102 B3** 57 0N 125 10W
Finley, Australia .... **95 F4** 35 38 S 145 35 E
Finley, U.S.A. **112 B6** 47 31N 97 50W
Finn →, Ireland ... **12 B4** 54 51N 7 28W
Finnerödja, Sweden . **11 F8** 58 57N 14 24 E
Finnigan, Mt., Australia **94 B4** 15 49 S 145 17 E
Finniss, C., Australia . **95 E1** 33 8 S 134 51 E
Finnmark, Norway .. **8 B20** 69 37N 23 57 E
Finnsnes, Norway .. **8 B18** 69 14N 18 0 E
Finspång, Sweden .. **11 F9** 58 43N 15 47 E
Finsteraarhorn, Switz. **25 J4** 46 31N 8 10 E
Finsterwalde, Germany **24 D9** 51 37N 13 42 E
Fiora →, Italy ...... **41 F8** 42 20N 11 34 E
Fiordland △, N.Z. .. **91 L1** 45 46 S 167 0 E
Fiorenzuola d'Arda,
  Italy .... **40 D6** 44 56N 9 55 E
Fiq, Syria .... **74 C4** 32 46N 35 41 E
Firat = Furāt, Nahr
  al →, Asia .... **70 D5** 31 0N 47 25 E
Fire Island △, U.S.A. **117 F11** 40 38N 73 8W
Firebag →, Canada . **103 B6** 57 45N 111 21W
Firebaugh, U.S.A. .. **110 J6** 36 52N 120 27W
Firedrake L., Canada **103 A8** 61 25N 104 30W
Firenze, Italy ...... **41 E8** 43 46N 11 15 E
Firenze Amerigo
  Vespucci ✈ (FLR),
  Italy .... **40 E8** 43 49N 11 13 E
Firenze Pisa ✈ (PSA),
  Italy .... **40 E7** 43 40N 10 22 E
Firenzuola, Italy .... **41 D8** 44 7N 11 23 E
Firk, Sha'ib →, Iraq . **70 D5** 30 59N 44 34 E
Firmi, France .... **20 D6** 44 32N 2 19 E
Firminy, France ..... **21 C8** 45 23N 4 18 E
Firozabad, India .... **69 F8** 27 10N 78 25 E
Firozpur, India ..... **68 D6** 30 55N 74 40 E
Firozpur-Jhirka, India **68 F7** 27 48N 76 57 E
Fīrūzābād, Iran ..... **71 D7** 28 52N 52 50 E
Fīrūzkūh, Iran ...... **71 C7** 35 50N 52 50 E
Firvale, Canada **102 C3** 52 27N 126 13W
Fish →, Namibia ... **88 D2** 28 7 S 17 10 E
Fish →, S. Africa ... **88 E3** 31 30 S 20 16 E
Fish River Canyon,
  Namibia .... **88 D2** 27 40 S 17 35 E
Fisher, Australia .... **93 F5** 30 30 S 131 0 E
Fisher B., Canada ... **103 C9** 51 35N 97 13W
Fisher Branch, Canada **117 E13** 41 15N 72 0W
Fishguard, U.K. **15 E3** 52 0N 4 58W
Fishing L., Canada .. **103 C9** 52 10N 95 24W
Fishkill, U.S.A. **117 E11** 41 32N 73 53W
Fismes, France ..... **19 C10** 49 20N 3 40 E
Fisterra, Spain **36 C1** 42 50N 9 19W
Fisterra, C., Spain .. **36 C1** 42 50N 9 19W
Fitchburg, U.S.A. ... **117 D13** 42 35N 71 48W
Fitz Roy, Argentina . **128 F3** 47 0 S 67 0W
Fitzgerald, Canada .. **102 B6** 59 51N 111 36W
Fitzgerald, U.S.A. .. **115 K4** 31 43N 83 15W
Fitzgerald River △,
  Australia .... **93 F3** 33 53 S 120 3 E
Fitzmaurice →,
  Australia .... **92 B5** 14 45 S 130 5 E
Fitzroy →, Queens.,
  Australia .... **94 C5** 23 32 S 150 52 E
Fitzroy →, W. Austral.,
  Australia .... **92 C3** 17 31 S 123 35 E
Fitzroy, Mte., Argentina **128 F2** 49 17 S 73 5W
Fitzroy Crossing,
  Australia .... **92 C4** 18 9 S 125 38 E
Fitzwilliam I., Canada **116 A3** 45 30N 81 45W
Fiuggi, Italy .... **41 G10** 41 48N 13 13 E
Fiume = Rijeka, Croatia **41 C11** 45 20N 14 21 E
Fiumicino, Roma ✈
  (FCO), Italy .... **41 G9** 41 48N 12 15 E
Five Points, U.S.A. .. **110 J6** 36 26N 120 6W
Fivizzano, Italy ..... **40 D7** 44 14N 10 8 E
Fizi, Dem. Rep. of
  the Congo .... **86 C2** 4 17 S 28 55 E
Fjällbacka, Sweden . **11 F5** 58 36N 11 17 E
Fjärdhundra, Sweden **10 E10** 59 47N 16 56 E
Fjellerup, Denmark . **11 H4** 56 29N 10 34 E
Fjerritslev, Denmark . **11 G3** 57 5N 9 15 E
Fjugesta, Sweden ... **10 E8** 59 10N 15 0 E
Flagstaff, U.S.A. **109 J8** 35 12N 111 39W
Flagstaff L., U.S.A. . **115 C10** 45 7N 70 37W
Flaherty I., Canada . **104 A4** 56 15N 79 15W
Flåm, Norway ...... **9 F12** 60 50N 7 7 E
Flambeau →, U.S.A. **112 C9** 45 18N 91 14W
Flamborough Hd., U.K. **14 C7** 54 7N 0 5W
Fláming, Germany ... **24 C8** 52 6N 12 23 E
Flaming Gorge △,
  U.S.A. **108 F9** 41 10N 109 25W
Flaming Gorge
  Reservoir, U.S.A. .. **108 F9** 41 10N 109 25W
Flamingo, Teluk,
  Indonesia .... **63 F9** 5 30 S 138 0 E
Flanders = Flandre,
  Europe .... **19 B9** 50 50N 2 30 E
Flandre, Europe .... **19 B9** 50 50N 2 30 E
Flandre-Occidentale =
  West-Vlaanderen □,
  Belgium .... **17 D2** 51 0N 3 0 E
Flandre-Orientale =
  Oost-Vlaanderen □,
  Belgium .... **17 C3** 51 5N 3 50 E
Flandreau, U.S.A. ... **112 C6** 44 3N 96 36W

Flanigan, U.S.A. 110 E7 40 10N 119 53W
Flannan Is., U.K. 13 C1 58 9N 7 52W
Flåsjön, Sweden ...... 8 D16 64 5N 18 42 E
Flat →, Canada 102 A3 61 33N 125 18W
Flathead L., U.S.A. 108 C7 47 51N 114 8E
Flattery, C., Australia .. 94 A4 14 58 S 145 21 E
Flattery, C., U.S.A. .. 110 B2 48 23N 124 29W
Flatwoods, U.S.A. 114 F4 38 31N 82 43W
Fleetwood, U.S.A. 14 D4 53 55N 3 1W
Fleetwood, U.S.A. 117 F9 40 27N 75 49W
Flekkefjord, Norway .... 9 G12 58 18N 6 39 E
Flemington, U.S.A. .. 116 E7 41 7N 77 28W
Flen, Sweden ...... 10 E10 59 4N 16 35 E
Flensburg, Germany .. 24 A5 54 47N 9 27 E
Flers, France 18 D6 48 47N 0 33W
Flesherton, Canada .. 116 B4 44 16N 80 33W
Flesko, Tanjung,
   Indonesia ...... 63 D6 0 29N 124 30 E
Fleurance, France .... 20 E4 43 52N 0 40 E
Fleurier, Switz. ...... 25 J2 46 54N 6 35 E
Fleurieu Pen., Australia 95 F2 35 40 S 138 5 E
Flevoland □, Neths. .. 17 B5 52 30N 5 30 E
Flin Flon, Canada .. 103 C8 54 46N 101 53W
Flinders →, Australia .. 94 B3 17 36 S 140 36 E
Flinders B., Australia .. 93 F2 34 19 S 115 19 E
Flinders Group,
   Australia ...... 94 A3 14 11 S 144 15 E
Flinders I., S. Austral.,
   Australia ...... 95 E1 33 44 S 134 41 E
Flinders I., Tas.,
   Australia ...... 95 G4 40 0 S 148 0 E
Flinders Ranges,
   Australia ...... 95 E2 31 30 S 138 30 E
Flinders Reefs, Australia 94 B4 17 37 S 148 31 E
Flint, U.K. 14 D4 53 15N 3 8W
Flint, U.S.A. 114 D4 43 1N 83 41W
Flint →, U.S.A. 115 K3 30 57N 84 34W
Flint I., Kiribati ...... 97 J12 11 26 S 151 48W
Flintshire □, U.K. 14 D4 53 17N 3 17W
Fliseryd, Sweden .... 11 G10 57 6N 16 15 E
Flix, Spain ...... 38 D5 41 14N 0 32 E
Flixecourt, France .... 19 B9 50 1N 2 5 E
Floby, Sweden ...... 11 F7 58 8N 13 20 E
Floda, Sweden ...... 11 G6 57 49N 12 22 E
Flodden, U.K. 14 B5 55 37N 2 8W
Flogny-la-Chapelle,
   France ...... 19 E10 47 57N 3 57 E
Floodwood, U.S.A. .. 112 B8 46 55N 92 55W
Flora, U.S.A. 114 F1 38 40N 88 29W
Florala, U.S.A. 115 K2 31 0N 86 20W
Florac, France ...... 20 D7 44 20N 3 37 E
Florala, U.S.A. 115 K2 31 0N 86 20W
Florence = Firenze, Italy 41 E8 43 46N 11 15 E
Florence, Ala., U.S.A. .. 115 H2 34 48N 87 41W
Florence, Ariz., U.S.A. .. 109 K8 33 2N 111 23W
Florence, Colo., U.S.A. .. 108 G2 38 23N 105 8W
Florence, Oreg., U.S.A. .. 108 E1 43 58N 124 7W
Florence, S.C., U.S.A. .. 115 H6 34 12N 79 46W
Florence, L., Australia .. 95 D2 28 53 S 138 9 E
Florencia, Colombia .. 124 C3 1 36N 75 36W
Florennes, Belgium .. 17 D4 50 15N 4 35 E
Florenville, Belgium .. 17 E5 49 40N 5 19 E
Flores, Guatemala .. 120 C2 16 59N 89 50W
Flores, Indonesia ...... 63 F6 8 35 S 121 0 E
Flores I., Canada 102 D3 49 20N 126 10W
Flores Sea, Indonesia .. 63 F6 6 30 S 120 0 E
Floresti, Moldova .. 29 C13 47 53N 28 17 E
Floresville, U.S.A. .. 113 L5 29 8N 98 10W
Floriano, Brazil ...... 125 E10 6 50 S 43 0W
Florianópolis, Brazil .. 127 B6 27 30 S 48 30W
Florida, Cuba 120 B4 21 32N 78 14W
Florida, Uruguay .... 127 C4 34 7 S 56 10W
Florida □, U.S.A. 115 L5 28 0N 82 0W
Florida, Straits of,
   U.S.A. 120 B4 25 0N 80 0W
Florida B., U.S.A. 120 B3 25 0N 80 45W
Florida Keys, U.S.A. .. 115 N5 24 40N 81 0W
Floridia, Italy ...... 43 E8 37 5N 15 9 E
Flórina, Greece ...... 44 F5 40 48N 21 26 E
Flórina □, Greece .... 44 F5 40 45N 21 20 E
Florø, Norway ...... 9 F11 61 35N 5 1 E
Flower Station, Canada 117 A8 45 10N 76 41W
Flowerpot I., Canada .. 116 A3 45 18N 81 38W
Floydada, U.S.A. 113 J4 33 59N 101 20W
Fluk, Indonesia ...... 63 E7 1 42 S 127 44 E
Flúmen →, Spain 38 D4 41 43N 0 9W
Flumendosa →, Italy .. 42 C2 39 26N 9 37 E
Fluminimaggiore, Italy .. 42 C1 39 26N 8 30 E
Flushing = Vlissingen,
   Neths. ...... 17 C3 51 26N 3 34 E
Fluvià →, Spain ...... 38 C8 42 12N 3 7 E
Flying Fish, C.,
   Antarctica ...... 5 D15 72 6 S 102 29W
Foam Lake, Canada .. 103 C8 51 40N 103 32W
Foča, Bos.-H. ...... 44 C2 43 31N 18 47 E
Foça, Turkey ...... 47 C8 38 39N 26 46 E
Fochabers, U.K. 13 D5 57 37N 3 6W
Focșani, Romania .. 29 E12 45 41N 27 15 E
Fodécontéa, Guinea .. 82 C2 10 50N 14 22W
Fogang, China ...... 59 F9 23 52N 113 30 E
Fóggia, Italy ...... 43 A8 41 27N 15 34 E
Foggo, Nigeria ...... 83 C6 11 21N 9 57 E
Foglia →, Italy ...... 41 E9 43 55N 12 54 E
Fogo, Canada 105 C9 49 43N 54 17W
Fogo I., Canada 105 C9 49 40N 54 5W
Fohnsdorf, Austria .. 26 D7 47 12N 14 40 E
Föhr, Germany ...... 24 A4 54 43N 8 30 E
Foia, Portugal 37 H2 37 19N 8 37W
Foix, France ...... 20 E5 42 58N 1 38 E
Fojnica, Bos.-H. ...... 28 G2 43 59N 17 51 E
Fokino, Russia ...... 32 F8 53 30N 34 22 E
Fokís □, Greece ...... 46 C4 38 30N 22 15 E
Fokku, Nigeria ...... 83 C5 11 36N 4 32 E
Folda, Nord-Trøndelag,
   Norway ...... 8 D14 64 32N 10 30 E
Folda, Nordland,
   Norway ...... 8 C16 67 38N 14 50 E
Földeák, Hungary .... 28 D5 46 19N 20 30 E
Folégandros, Greece .. 46 E6 36 40N 24 55 E
Foley, Botswana ...... 88 C4 21 34 S 27 21 E
Foley, U.S.A. 115 K2 30 24N 87 41W
Foleyet, Canada 104 C3 48 15N 82 25W
Folgefonni, Norway .. 9 F12 60 3N 6 23 E
Foligno, Italy ...... 41 F9 42 57N 12 42 E
Folkestone, U.K. ...... 15 F9 51 5N 1 12 E
Follansbee, U.S.A. .. 116 F4 40 19N 80 35W
Follett, U.S.A. 113 G4 36 26N 100 8W
Follónica, Italy ...... 40 F7 42 55N 10 45 E
Follónica, G. di, Italy .. 40 F7 42 54N 10 43 E
Folsom L., U.S.A. 110 G5 38 42N 121 9W
Foltești, Romania .. 29 E13 45 45N 28 3 E
Fond du Lac, Canada .. 103 B7 59 17N 107 12W
Fond du Lac, U.S.A. .. 112 D10 43 47N 88 27W
Fond-du-Lac →,
   Canada 103 B7 59 17N 106 0W
Fonda, U.S.A. 117 D10 42 57N 74 22W
Fondi, Italy ...... 42 A6 41 21N 13 25 E

Fonfría, Spain 36 D4 41 37N 6 9W
Fongafale, Tuvalu .... 96 H9 8 31 S 179 13 E
Fonni, Italy ...... 42 B2 40 7N 9 15 E
Fonsagrada = A
   Fonsagrada, Spain .. 36 B3 43 8N 7 4W
Fonseca, G. de,
   Cent. Amer. 120 D2 13 10N 87 40W
Font-Romeu-Odeillo-
   Via, France ...... 20 F5 42 31N 2 3 E
Fontaine-Française,
   France ...... 19 E12 47 32N 5 21 E
Fontainebleau, France .. 19 D9 48 24N 2 40 E
Fontana, U.S.A. 111 L9 34 6N 117 26W
Fontas →, Canada .. 102 B4 58 14N 121 48W
Fonte Boa, Brazil .... 124 D5 2 33 S 66 0W
Fontem, Cameroon .... 83 D6 5 32N 9 52 E
Fontenay-le-Comte,
   France 18 F5 46 28N 0 48W
Fontenelle Reservoir,
   U.S.A. 108 E8 42 1N 110 3W
Fontur, Iceland 8 C6 66 23N 14 32W
Fonyód, Hungary .... 28 D2 46 44N 17 33 E
Foochow = Fuzhou,
   China ...... 59 D12 26 5N 119 16 E
Foping, China ...... 56 H5 33 41N 108 0 E
Forbach, France .... 19 C13 49 10N 6 52 E
Forbes, Australia .... 95 E4 33 22 S 148 0 E
Forbesganj, India .... 69 F12 26 17N 87 18 E
Forcados, Nigeria .... 83 D6 5 26N 5 26 E
Forcados →, Nigeria .. 83 D6 5 25N 5 19 E
Forcalquier, France .. 21 E9 43 58N 5 47 E
Forchheim, Germany .. 25 F7 49 43N 11 2 E
Ford City, Calif., U.S.A. .. 111 K7 35 9N 119 27W
Ford City, Pa., U.S.A. .. 116 F5 40 46N 79 32W
Førde, Norway ...... 9 F11 61 27N 5 53 E
Ford's Bridge, Australia 95 D4 29 41 S 145 29 E
Fordyce, U.S.A. 113 J8 33 49N 92 25W
Forécariah, Guinea .. 82 D2 9 28N 13 10W
Forel, Mt., Greenland .. 98 C16 66 52N 36 55W
Foremost, Canada .. 102 D6 49 26N 111 34W
Forest, Canada 116 C3 43 6N 82 0W
Forest, U.S.A. 113 J10 32 22N 89 29W
Forest City, Iowa, U.S.A. 112 D8 43 16N 93 39W
Forest City, N.C., U.S.A. 115 H5 35 20N 81 52W
Forest City, Pa., U.S.A. 117 E9 41 39N 75 28W
Forest Grove, U.S.A. .. 110 E3 45 31N 123 7W
Forestburg, Canada .. 102 C6 52 35N 112 1W
Foreste Casentinesi-
   Monte Falterona-
   Campigna △, Italy .. 41 E8 43 50N 11 48 E
Foresthill, U.S.A. 110 G6 39 1N 120 49W
Forestier Pen., Australia 95 G4 43 0 S 148 0 E
Forestville, Canada .. 105 C6 48 48N 69 2W
Forestville, Calif., U.S.A. 110 G4 38 28N 122 54W
Forestville, N.Y., U.S.A. 116 D5 42 28N 79 10W
Forêt d'Orient △, France 19 D11 48 16N 4 25 E
Forez, Mts. du, France .. 20 C7 45 40N 3 50 E
Forfar, U.K. 13 E6 56 39N 2 53W
Forillon △, Canada .. 105 C7 48 46N 64 12W
Forks, U.S.A. 110 C2 47 57N 124 23W
Forksville, U.S.A. 117 E8 41 29N 76 35W
Forlì, Italy ...... 41 D9 44 13N 12 3 E
Forman, U.S.A. 112 B6 46 7N 97 38W
Formazza, Italy ...... 40 B5 46 23N 8 26 E
Formby Pt., U.K. 14 D4 53 33N 3 6W
Formentera, Spain .. 48 C7 38 43N 1 27 E
Formentor, C. de, Spain 48 B10 39 58N 3 13 E
Former Yugoslav
   Republic of
   Macedonia =
   Macedonia ■, Europe 44 E5 41 53N 21 40 E
Fórmia, Italy ...... 42 A6 41 15N 13 37 E
Formígine, Italy ...... 40 D7 44 37N 10 51 E
Formosa = Taiwan ■,
   Asia ...... 59 F13 23 30N 121 0 E
Formosa, Argentina .. 126 B4 26 15 S 58 10W
Formosa, Brazil ...... 125 G9 15 32 S 47 20W
Formosa □, Argentina .. 126 B4 25 0 S 60 0W
Formosa, Serra, Brazil .. 125 F8 12 0 S 55 0W
Formosa B. = Ungwana
   B., Kenya ...... 86 C5 2 40 S 40 20 E
Fornells, Spain ...... 48 A11 40 3N 4 7 E
Fornos de Algodres,
   Portugal 36 E3 40 38N 7 32W
Fornovo di Taro, Italy .. 40 D7 44 42N 10 6 E
Føroyar, Atl. Oc. 8 F9 62 0N 7 0W
Forres, U.K. 13 D5 57 37N 3 37W
Forrest, Australia .... 93 F4 30 51 S 128 6 E
Forrest, Mt., Australia .. 93 D4 24 48 S 127 45 E
Forrest City, U.S.A. .. 113 H9 35 1N 90 47W
Forsayth, Australia .. 94 B3 18 33 S 143 34 E
Forshaga, Sweden .... 10 E7 59 33N 13 29 E
Förslöv, Sweden ...... 11 H6 56 21N 12 48 E
Forsmo, Sweden ...... 10 A11 63 16N 17 11 E
Forssa, Finland ...... 9 F20 60 49N 23 38 E
Forst, Germany ...... 24 D10 51 45N 14 37 E
Forsvik, Sweden ...... 11 F8 58 35N 14 26 E
Forsyth, U.S.A. 108 C10 46 16N 106 41W
Fort Abbas, Pakistan .. 68 E5 29 12N 72 52 E
Fort Albany, Canada .. 104 B3 52 15N 81 35W
Fort Ann, U.S.A. 117 C11 43 25N 73 30W
Fort Assiniboine,
   Canada 102 C6 54 20N 114 45W
Fort Augustus, U.K. .. 13 D4 57 9N 4 42W
Fort Beaufort, S. Africa 88 E4 32 46 S 26 40 E
Fort Benton, U.S.A. .. 108 C8 47 49N 110 40W
Fort Bragg, U.S.A. .. 108 G2 39 26N 123 48W
Fort Bridger, U.S.A. .. 108 F8 41 19N 110 23W
Fort Chipewyan, Canada 103 B6 58 42N 111 8W
Fort Clatsop, U.S.A. .. 110 D3 46 8N 123 53W
Fort Collins, U.S.A. .. 108 E2 40 35N 105 5W
Fort-Coulonge, Canada 104 C4 45 50N 76 45W
Fort Covington, U.S.A. 117 B10 44 59N 74 29W
Fort Davis, U.S.A. .. 113 K3 30 35N 103 54W
Fort-de-France,
   Martinique ...... 120 c 14 36N 61 2W
Fort Defiance, U.S.A. .. 109 J9 35 45N 109 5W
Fort Dodge, U.S.A. .. 112 D7 42 30N 94 11W
Fort Edward, U.S.A. .. 117 C11 43 16N 73 35W
Fort Erie, Canada 116 D6 42 54N 78 56W
Fort Fairfield, U.S.A. .. 115 B12 46 46N 67 50W
Fort Frances, Canada .. 103 D10 48 36N 93 24W
Fort Franklin = Déline,
   Canada 100 B7 65 11N 123 25W
Fort Garland, U.S.A. .. 109 H11 37 26N 105 26W
Fort George = Chisasibi,
   Canada 104 B4 53 50N 79 0W
Fort Good Hope,
   Canada 100 B7 66 14N 128 40W
Fort Hancock, U.S.A. .. 109 L11 31 18N 105 51W
Fort Hope, Canada .. 104 B2 51 30N 88 0W
Fort Irwin, U.S.A. .. 111 K10 35 16N 116 34W
Fort Kent, U.S.A. .. 115 B11 47 15N 68 36W
Fort Klamath, U.S.A. .. 108 E3 42 42N 122 0W
Fort Laramie, U.S.A. .. 108 E2 42 13N 104 31W
Fort Lauderdale, U.S.A. 115 M5 26 7N 80 8W

Fort Liard, Canada .. 102 A4 60 14N 123 30W
Fort Liberté, Haiti .. 121 C5 19 42N 71 51W
Fort Lupton, U.S.A. .. 112 E2 40 5N 104 49W
Fort MacKay, Canada .. 102 B6 57 12N 111 41W
Fort Macleod, Canada .. 102 D6 49 45N 113 30W
Fort McMurray, Canada 102 B6 56 44N 111 7W
Fort McPherson,
   Canada 100 B6 67 30N 134 55W
Fort Madison, U.S.A. .. 112 E9 40 38N 91 27W
Fort Meade, U.S.A. .. 115 M5 27 45N 81 48W
Fort Morgan, U.S.A. .. 112 E3 40 15N 103 48W
Fort Myers, U.S.A. .. 115 M5 26 39N 81 52W
Fort Nelson, Canada .. 102 B4 58 50N 122 44W
Fort Nelson →,
   Canada 102 B4 59 32N 124 0W
Fort Norman = Tulita,
   Canada 100 B7 64 57N 125 30W
Fort Payne, U.S.A. .. 115 H3 34 26N 85 43W
Fort Peck, U.S.A. .. 108 B10 48 1N 106 27W
Fort Peck Dam, U.S.A. 108 C10 48 0N 106 26W
Fort Peck L., U.S.A. .. 108 C10 48 0N 106 26W
Fort Pierce, U.S.A. .. 115 M5 27 27N 80 20W
Fort Pierre, U.S.A. .. 112 C4 44 21N 100 22W
Fort Plain, U.S.A. .. 117 D10 42 56N 74 37W
Fort Portal, Uganda .. 86 B3 0 40N 30 20 E
Fort Providence, Canada 102 A5 61 3N 117 40W
Fort Qu'Appelle,
   Canada 103 C8 50 45N 103 50W
Fort Resolution, Canada 102 A6 61 10N 113 40W
Fort Rixon, Zimbabwe .. 87 G2 20 2 S 29 17 E
Fort Ross, U.S.A. .. 110 G3 38 32N 123 13W
Fort Rupert =
   Waskaganish, Canada 104 B4 51 30N 78 40W
Fort St. James, Canada 102 C4 54 30N 124 10W
Fort St. John, Canada .. 102 B4 56 15N 120 50W
Fort Saskatchewan,
   Canada 102 C6 53 40N 113 15W
Fort Scott, U.S.A. .. 113 G7 37 50N 94 42W
Fort Severn, Canada .. 104 A2 56 0N 87 40W
Fort Shevchenko,
   Kazakhstan ...... 35 H10 44 35N 50 23 E
Fort Simpson, Canada .. 102 A4 61 45N 121 15W
Fort Smith, Canada .. 102 B6 60 0N 111 51W
Fort Smith, U.S.A. .. 113 H7 35 23N 94 25W
Fort Stockton, U.S.A. .. 113 K3 30 53N 102 53W
Fort Sumner, U.S.A. .. 113 H2 34 28N 104 15W
Fort Thompson, U.S.A. 112 C5 44 3N 99 26W
Fort Union △, U.S.A. .. 113 H2 35 54N 105 1W
Fort Valley, U.S.A. .. 115 J4 32 33N 83 53W
Fort Vermilion, Canada 102 B5 58 24N 116 0W
Fort Walton Beach,
   U.S.A. 115 K2 30 25N 86 36W
Fort Wayne, U.S.A. .. 114 E3 41 4N 85 9W
Fort William, U.K. .. 13 E3 56 49N 5 7W
Fort Worth, U.S.A. .. 113 J6 32 45N 97 18W
Fort Yates, U.S.A. .. 112 B4 46 5N 100 38W
Fort Yukon, U.S.A. .. 100 B5 66 34N 145 16W
Fortaleza, Brazil .... 125 D11 3 45 S 38 35W
Forteau, Canada 105 B8 51 28N 56 58W
Fortescue →, Australia 92 D2 21 0 S 116 4 E
Forth →, U.K. 13 E5 56 9N 3 50W
Forth, Firth of, U.K. .. 13 E6 56 5N 2 55W
Fortore →, Italy ...... 41 G12 41 55N 15 17 E
Fortrose, U.K. 13 D4 57 35N 4 9W
Fortuna, Spain 39 G3 38 11N 1 7W
Fortuna, Calif., U.S.A. .. 108 F1 40 36N 124 9W
Fortuna, N. Dak., U.S.A. 112 A3 48 55N 103 47W
Fortune, Canada 105 C8 47 4N 55 50W
Fortune B., Canada .. 105 C8 47 30N 55 22W
Forūr, Iran ...... 71 E7 26 17N 54 32 E
Fos-sur-Mer, France .. 21 E8 43 26N 4 56 E
Foshan, China ...... 59 F9 23 4N 113 5 E
Fosna, Norway ...... 8 E14 63 50N 10 20 E
Fosnavåg, Norway .... 9 E11 62 22N 5 38 E
Foso, Ghana 83 D4 5 43N 1 15W
Fossano, Italy ...... 40 D4 44 33N 7 43 E
Fossil, U.S.A. 108 D3 45 0N 120 9W
Fossil Butte △, U.S.A. .. 108 F8 41 50N 110 27W
Fossombrone, Italy .. 41 E9 43 41N 12 48 E
Foster, Canada 117 A12 45 17N 72 30W
Foster →, Canada 103 B7 55 47N 105 49W
Fosters Ra., Australia .. 94 C1 21 35 S 133 48 E
Fostoria, U.S.A. 114 E4 41 10N 83 25W
Fotadrevo, Madag. .... 89 C8 24 3 S 45 1 E
Fougamou, France 18 D5 48 21N 1 14W
Foul Pt., Sri Lanka .. 66 Q12 8 35N 81 18 E
Foula, U.K. 13 A6 60 10N 2 5W
Foulalaba, Mali 82 C3 10 40N 7 20W
Foulness I., U.K. .... 15 F8 51 36N 0 55 E
Foulpointe, Madag. .. 89 B8 17 41 S 49 31 E
Foulweather, C., U.S.A. 106 B2 44 50N 124 5W
Fouman, Cameroon .. 83 D7 5 45N 10 50 E
Foumbot, Cameroon .. 83 D7 5 30N 10 28 E
Foundiougne, Senegal .. 82 C1 14 5N 16 32W
Fountain, U.S.A. 112 F2 38 41N 104 42W
Fountain Springs, U.S.A. 111 K8 35 54N 118 51W
Fourchambault, France 19 E10 47 1N 3 3 E
Fouriesburg, S. Africa .. 88 D4 28 38 S 28 14 E
Fourmies, France .... 19 B11 50 1N 4 2 E
Fournás, Greece ...... 46 B3 39 3N 21 52 E
Foúrnoi, Greece ...... 47 D8 37 36N 26 32 E
Fours, France ...... 19 F10 46 50N 3 42 E
Fourth Cataract, Sudan 80 D3 18 47N 32 3 E
Fouta Djallon, Guinea .. 82 C2 11 20N 12 10W
Foux, Cap-à-, Haiti .. 121 C5 19 43N 73 27W
Foveaux Str., N.Z. .. 91 M2 46 42 S 168 10 E
Fowey, U.K. 15 G3 50 20N 4 39W
Fowler, Calif., U.S.A. .. 110 J7 36 38N 119 41W
Fowler, Colo., U.S.A. .. 112 F3 38 8N 104 2W
Fowlers B., Australia .. 93 F5 31 59 S 132 34 E
Fowman, Iran ...... 71 B6 37 13N 49 19 E
Fox →, Canada 103 B10 56 3N 93 18W
Fox Creek, Canada .. 102 C5 54 24N 116 48W
Fox Lake, Canada .. 102 B6 58 28N 114 31W
Fox Valley, Canada .. 103 C7 50 30N 109 25W
Foxboro, U.S.A. 117 D13 42 4N 71 16W
Foxdale, Australia .. 94 J6 20 22 S 148 35 E
Foxe Basin, Canada .. 101 B11 66 0N 77 0W
Foxe Chan., Canada .. 101 B11 65 0N 80 0W
Foxe Pen., Canada .. 101 B12 65 0N 76 0W
Foxton, N.Z. ...... 91 J5 40 29 S 175 18 E
Foyle, Lough, U.K. .. 12 A4 55 7N 7 4W
Foynes, Ireland 12 D2 52 37N 9 7W
Foz do Cunene, Angola 88 B1 17 15 S 11 48 E
Foz do Iguaçu, Brazil .. 127 B5 25 30 S 54 30W
Frackville, U.S.A. 117 F8 40 47N 76 14W
Fraga, Spain ...... 38 D5 41 32N 0 21 E
Fraile Muerto, Uruguay 127 C5 32 31 S 54 32W
Fram Basin, Arctic .... 4 A 87 30N 80 0 E
Framingham, U.S.A. .. 117 D13 42 17N 71 25W
Frampol, Poland ...... 31 H9 50 41N 22 40 E
Franca, Brazil ...... 125 H9 20 33 S 47 30W
Francavilla al Mare, Italy 41 F11 42 25N 14 17 E
Francavilla Fontana,
   Italy ...... 43 B10 40 32N 17 35 E

France ■, Europe .... 7 F6 47 0N 3 0 E
Frances, Australia .... 95 F3 36 41 S 140 55 E
Frances →, Canada .. 102 A3 60 16N 129 10W
Frances L., Canada .. 102 A3 61 23N 129 30W
Franceville, Gabon .... 84 E2 1 40 S 13 32 E
Franche-Comté □,
   France ...... 19 F12 46 50N 5 55 E
Francis Case, L., U.S.A. 112 D5 43 4N 98 34W
Francisco Beltrão, Brazil 127 B5 26 5 S 53 4W
Francisco I. Madero,
   Coahuila, Mexico .. 118 B4 25 48N 103 18W
Francisco I. Madero,
   Durango, Mexico .. 118 C4 24 32N 104 22W
Francistown, Botswana 89 C4 21 7 S 27 33 E
Francofonte, Italy .. 43 E7 37 14N 14 53 E
François, Canada 105 C8 47 35N 56 45W
François L., Canada .. 102 C3 54 0N 125 30W
François Peron △,
   Australia ...... 93 E1 25 42 S 113 33 E
Franeker, Neths. .... 17 A5 53 12N 5 33 E
Frank Hann △, Australia 93 F3 32 52 S 120 19 E
Frankado, Djibouti .. 81 E5 12 30N 43 12 E
Frankenberg, Germany 24 D4 51 3N 8 48 E
Frankenberg, Germany 24 D4 51 3N 8 48 E
Frankenhöhe △,
   Germany ...... 25 F6 49 20N 10 25 E
Frankenwald, Germany 25 E7 50 20N 11 30 E
Frankenwald △,
   Germany ...... 25 E7 50 15N 11 30 E
Frankford, Canada .. 116 B7 44 12N 77 36W
Frankfort, Ind., U.S.A. .. 114 E2 40 17N 86 31W
Frankfort, Kans., U.S.A. 112 F6 39 42N 96 25W
Frankfort, Ky., U.S.A. .. 114 F3 38 12N 84 52W
Frankfort, N.Y., U.S.A. 117 C9 43 2N 75 4W
Frankfurt, Brandenburg,
   Germany ...... 24 C10 52 20N 14 32 E
Frankfurt, Hessen,
   Germany ...... 25 E4 50 7N 8 41 E
Frankfurt × (FRA),
   Germany ...... 25 E4 50 1N 8 34 E
Fränkische Alb,
   Germany ...... 25 F7 49 10N 11 23 E
Fränkische Rezat →,
   Germany ...... 25 F7 49 11N 11 1 E
Fränkische Saale →,
   Germany ...... 25 E5 50 3N 9 42 E
Fränkische Schweiz,
   Germany ...... 25 F7 49 50N 11 16 E
Fränkische Schweiz-
   Veldensteiner
   Forst △, Germany .. 25 F7 49 45N 11 22 E
Frankland →, Australia 93 G2 35 0 S 116 48 E
Franklin, Ky., U.S.A. .. 115 G2 36 43N 86 35W
Franklin, La., U.S.A. .. 113 L9 29 48N 91 30W
Franklin, Mass., U.S.A. 117 D13 42 5N 71 24W
Franklin, N.H., U.S.A. .. 117 C13 43 27N 71 39W
Franklin, Nebr., U.S.A. 112 E5 40 6N 98 57W
Franklin, Pa., U.S.A. .. 116 E5 41 24N 79 50W
Franklin, Va., U.S.A. .. 115 G7 36 41N 76 56W
Franklin, W. Va., U.S.A. 114 F6 38 39N 79 20W
Franklin B., Canada .. 100 B7 69 45N 126 0W
Franklin D. Roosevelt
   L., U.S.A. 108 B4 48 18N 118 9W
Franklin-Gordon Wild
   Rivers △, Australia .. 95 G4 42 19 S 145 51 E
Franklin I., Antarctica .. 5 D11 76 10 S 168 30 E
Franklin L., U.S.A. .. 108 F6 40 25N 115 22W
Franklin Mts., Canada .. 100 B7 65 0N 125 0W
Franklin Str., Canada .. 100 A10 72 0N 96 0W
Franklinton, U.S.A. .. 113 K9 30 51N 90 9W
Franklinville, U.S.A. .. 116 D6 42 20N 78 27W
Frankston, Australia .. 95 F4 38 8 S 145 8 E
Frånö, Sweden ...... 10 B11 62 55N 17 50 E
Fransfontein, Namibia .. 88 C2 20 12 S 15 1 E
Fränsta, Sweden ...... 10 B10 62 30N 16 11 E
Frantsa Iosifa, Zemlya,
   Russia ...... 52 A6 82 0N 55 0 E
Franz, Canada 104 C3 48 25N 84 30W
Franz Josef Land =
   Frantsa Iosifa,
   Zemlya, Russia .... 52 A6 82 0N 55 0 E
Franz Josef Strauss,
   München × (MUC),
   Germany ...... 25 G7 48 20N 11 50 E
Franzburg, Germany .. 24 A8 54 11N 12 51 E
Frascati, Italy ...... 41 G9 41 48N 12 41 E
Fraser, U.S.A. 116 D2 42 32N 82 57W
Fraser →, B.C., Canada 102 D4 49 7N 123 11W
Fraser →, Nfld. & L.,
   Canada 105 A7 56 39N 62 10W
Fraser, Mt., Australia .. 93 E2 25 35 S 118 20 E
Fraser I., Australia .. 95 D5 25 15 S 153 10 E
Fraser Lake, Canada .. 102 C4 54 0N 124 50W
Fraserburg, S. Africa .. 88 E3 31 55 S 21 30 E
Fraserburgh, U.K. 13 D6 57 42N 2 1W
Fraserdale, Canada .. 104 C3 49 55N 81 37W
Frashër, Albania ...... 44 F4 40 23N 20 30 E
Fraser, U.S.A. 112 E5 40 9N 98 57W
Frătești, Romania .. 29 G10 43 58N 25 58 E
Fray Bentos, Uruguay .. 126 C4 33 10 S 58 15W
Fray Jorge △, Chile .. 126 C1 30 42 S 71 40W
Frechilla, Spain 36 C6 42 8N 4 50W
Fredericia, Denmark .. 11 J3 55 34N 9 45 E
Frederick, Md., U.S.A. .. 114 F7 39 25N 77 25W
Frederick, Okla., U.S.A. 113 H5 34 23N 99 1W
Frederick, S. Dak.,
   U.S.A. 112 C5 45 50N 98 31W
Fredericksburg, Pa.,
   U.S.A. 117 F8 40 27N 76 26W
Fredericksburg, Tex.,
   U.S.A. 113 K5 30 16N 98 52W
Fredericksburg, Va.,
   U.S.A. 114 F7 38 18N 77 28W
Fredericktown, Mo.,
   U.S.A. 113 G9 37 34N 90 18W
Fredericktown, Ohio,
   U.S.A. 116 F2 40 29N 82 33W
Frederico I. Madero,
   Presa, Mexico 118 B3 28 7N 105 40W
Frederico Westphalen,
   Brazil ...... 127 B5 27 22 S 53 24W
Fredericton, Canada .. 105 C6 45 57N 66 40W
Fredericton Junction,
   Canada 105 C6 45 41N 66 40W
Frederiksberg
   Amtskommune □,
   Denmark ...... 11 J6 55 50N 12 10 E
Frederikshåb = Paamiut,
   Greenland 101 B15 62 0N 49 43W
Frederikshamn =
   Hamina, Finland .. 9 F22 60 34N 27 12 E
Frederikshavn, Denmark 11 G4 57 28N 10 31 E
Frederikssund, Denmark 11 J6 55 50N 12 3 E
Frederiksted,
   U.S. Virgin Is. 121 C7 17 43N 64 53W

Frederiksværk, Denmark 11 J6 55 58N 12 4 E
Fredonia, Ariz., U.S.A. .. 109 H7 36 57N 112 32W
Fredonia, Kans., U.S.A. 113 G7 37 32N 95 49W
Fredonia, N.Y., U.S.A. .. 116 D5 42 26N 79 20W
Fredriksberg, Sweden .. 10 D8 60 8N 14 23 E
Fredrikstad, Norway .. 9 G14 59 13N 10 57 E
Free State □, S. Africa .. 88 D4 28 30 S 27 0 E
Freehold, U.S.A. 117 F10 40 16N 74 17W
Freel Peak, U.S.A. .. 110 G7 38 52N 119 54W
Freeland, U.S.A. 117 E9 41 1N 75 54W
Freeman, Calif., U.S.A. 111 K9 35 35N 117 53W
Freeman, S. Dak.,
   U.S.A. 112 D6 43 21N 97 26W
Freeport, Bahamas .. 120 A4 26 30N 78 47W
Freeport, Ill., U.S.A. .. 112 D10 42 17N 89 36W
Freeport, N.Y., U.S.A. 117 F11 40 39N 73 35W
Freeport, Ohio, U.S.A. 116 F3 40 12N 81 15W
Freeport, Pa., U.S.A. .. 116 F5 40 41N 79 41W
Freeport, Tex., U.S.A. .. 113 L7 28 57N 95 21W
Freetown, S. Leone .. 82 D2 8 30N 13 17W
Frégate, L. de la,
   Canada 104 B5 53 15N 74 45W
Fregenal de la Sierra,
   Spain 37 G4 38 10N 6 39W
Fregene, Italy ...... 41 G9 41 51N 12 12 E
Fréhel, C., France .. 18 D4 48 40N 2 20W
Freiberg, Germany .. 24 E9 50 55N 13 20 E
Freibourg = Fribourg,
   Switz. ...... 25 J3 46 49N 7 9 E
Freiburg, Baden-W.,
   Germany ...... 25 H3 47 59N 7 51 E
Freiburg, Niedersachsen,
   Germany ...... 24 B5 53 49N 9 16 E
Freilassing, Germany .. 25 H8 47 50N 12 58 E
Freire, Chile ...... 128 D2 38 54 S 72 38W
Freising, Germany .. 25 G7 48 24N 11 45 E
Freistadt, Austria .. 26 C7 48 30N 14 30 E
Freital, Germany .. 24 D9 51 1N 13 39 E
Fréjus, France ...... 21 E10 43 25N 6 44 E
Fremantle, Australia .. 93 F2 32 7 S 115 47 E
Fremont, Calif., U.S.A. 110 H4 37 32N 121 57W
Fremont, Mich., U.S.A. 114 D3 43 28N 85 57W
Fremont, Nebr., U.S.A. 112 E6 41 26N 96 30W
Fremont, Ohio, U.S.A. .. 114 E4 41 21N 83 7W
Fremont →, U.S.A. .. 109 G8 38 24N 110 42W
French Camp, U.S.A. .. 110 H5 37 53N 121 16W
French Cays = Plana
   Cays, Bahamas 121 B5 22 38N 73 30W
French Creek →, U.S.A. 116 E5 41 24N 79 50W
French Guiana ☐,
   S. Amer. 125 C8 4 0N 53 0W
French Polynesia ☐,
   Pac. Oc. ...... 97 K13 20 0 S 145 0W
Frenchman Cr. →,
   N. Amer. 108 B10 48 31N 107 10W
Frenchman Cr. →,
   U.S.A. 112 E4 40 14N 100 50W
Frenštát pod
   Radhoštěm,
   Czech Rep. ...... 27 B11 49 33N 18 13 E
Fresco, Ivory C. 82 D3 5 3N 5 31W
Fresco →, Brazil .... 125 E8 7 15 S 51 30W
Freshfield, C., Antarctica 5 C10 68 25 S 151 10 E
Fresnay-sur-Sarthe,
   France ...... 18 D7 48 17N 0 1 E
Fresnillo, Mexico .. 118 C4 23 10N 103 0W
Fresno, U.S.A. 110 J7 36 44N 119 47W
Fresno Alhandiga, Spain 36 E5 40 42N 5 37W
Fresno Reservoir, U.S.A. 108 B9 48 36N 109 57W
Freudenstadt, Germany 25 G4 48 27N 8 24 E
Frévent, France ...... 19 B9 50 15N 2 17 E
Frew →, Australia .. 94 C2 20 0 S 135 38 E
Frewsburg, U.S.A. .. 116 D5 42 3N 79 10W
Freycinet △, Australia .. 95 G4 42 11 S 148 19 E
Freycinet Pen., Australia 95 G4 42 10 S 148 25 E
Freyming-Merlebach,
   France ...... 19 C13 49 9N 6 48 E
Freyung, Germany .. 25 G9 48 48N 13 31 E
Fria, Guinea 82 C2 10 27N 13 38W
Fria, C., Namibia .. 88 B1 18 0 S 12 0 E
Friant, U.S.A. 110 J7 36 59N 119 43W
Frías, Argentina .. 126 B2 28 40 S 65 5W
Fribourg, Switz. ...... 25 J3 46 49N 7 9 E
Fribourg □, Switz. .. 25 J3 46 40N 7 0 E
Fridafors, Sweden .. 11 H8 56 25N 14 39 E
Friday Harbor, U.S.A. .. 110 B3 48 32N 123 1W
Friedberg, Bayern,
   Germany ...... 25 G6 48 21N 10 59 E
Friedberg, Hessen,
   Germany ...... 25 E4 50 19N 8 45 E
Friedens, U.S.A. 116 F6 40 3N 78 59W
Friedland, Germany .. 24 B9 53 40N 13 33 E
Friedrichshafen,
   Germany ...... 25 H5 47 39N 9 30 E
Friedrichskoog,
   Germany ...... 24 A4 54 1N 8 53 E
Friedrichstadt, Germany 24 A5 54 23N 9 6 E
Friendship, U.S.A. .. 116 D6 42 12N 78 8W
Friesack, Germany .. 24 C8 52 44N 12 34 E
Friesland □, Neths. .. 17 A5 53 5N 5 50 E
Friesoythe, Germany .. 24 B3 53 1N 7 51 E
Friggesund, Sweden .. 10 C10 61 54N 16 33 E
Frillesås, Sweden .. 11 G6 57 20N 12 12 E
Frinnaryd, Sweden .. 11 G8 57 58N 14 58 E
Frio →, U.S.A. 113 L5 28 26N 98 11W
Frio, C., Brazil ...... 122 F6 22 50 S 41 50W
Friol, Spain 36 B3 43 1N 7 55W
Friona, U.S.A. 113 H3 34 38N 102 43W
Fristad, Sweden ...... 11 G6 57 50N 13 1 E
Fritch, U.S.A. 113 H4 35 38N 101 36W
Fritsla, Sweden ...... 11 G6 57 33N 12 47 E
Fritzlar, Germany .. 24 D5 51 7N 9 16 E
Friuli-Venézia Giúlia □,
   Italy ...... 41 B9 46 0N 13 0 E
Frobisher B., Canada .. 101 B13 62 30N 66 0W
Frobisher Bay = Iqaluit,
   Canada 101 B13 63 44N 68 31W
Frobisher L., Canada .. 103 B7 56 20N 108 15W
Frohavet, Norway .. 8 E13 64 0N 9 30 E
Frohnleiten, Austria .. 26 D8 47 16N 15 19 E
Frolovo, Russia ...... 34 F6 49 45N 43 40 E
Frombork, Poland .. 30 D6 54 21N 19 41 E
Frome, U.K. 15 F5 51 14N 2 19W
Frome →, U.K. 15 G5 50 41N 2 6W
Frome, L., Australia .. 95 E2 30 45 S 139 45 E
Frome, The →,
   Australia ...... 95 D2 19 8 S 137 54 E
Frómista, Spain 36 C6 42 16N 4 25W
Front Range, U.S.A. .. 106 C5 40 25N 105 45W
Front Royal, U.S.A. .. 114 F6 38 55N 78 12W
Fronteira, Portugal .. 37 F3 39 3N 7 39W
Frontera, Canary Is. .. 48 G2 27 47N 17 59W
Frontera, Mexico .. 119 D6 18 30N 92 40W
Fronteras, Mexico .. 118 A3 30 56N 109 31W

158 Frontignan INDEX TO WORLD MAPS

Frontignan, *France* .... **20 E7** 43 27N 3 45 E
Frosinone, *Italy* .... **42 A6** 41 38N 13 19 E
Frostburg, *U.S.A.* **114 F6** 39 39N 78 56W
Frostisen, *Norway* .... **8 B17** 68 14N 17 10 E
Frouard, *France* ...... **19 D13** 48 47N 6 8 E
Frövi, *Sweden* .... **10 E9** 59 28N 15 24 E
Frøya, *Norway* .... **8 E13** 63 43N 8 40 E
Frumoasa, *Romania* ... **29 D10** 46 28N 25 48 E
Frunze = Bishkek, *Kyrgyzstan* .... **52 E8** 42 54N 74 46 E
Frunzivka, *Ukraine* .... **29 C14** 47 20N 29 45 E
Fruška Gora, *Serbia & M.* .... **28 E4** 45 7N 19 30 E
Fruška Gora △, *Serbia & M.* .... **44 A3** 45 8N 19 40 E
Frutal, *Brazil* .... **125 H9** 20 0 S 49 0W
Frutigen, *Switz.* .... **25 J3** 46 35N 7 38 E
Frýdek-Místek, *Czech Rep.* .... **27 B11** 49 40N 18 20 E
Frýdlant, *Czech Rep.* .. **26 A8** 50 56N 15 9 E
Fryeburg, *U.S.A.* **117 B14** 44 1N 70 59W
Fryvaldov = Jeseník, *Czech Rep.* .... **27 A10** 50 14N 17 8 E
Fthiótis □, *Greece* .... **46 C4** 38 50N 22 25 E
Fu Jiang →, *China* .... **58 C6** 30 0N 106 16 E
Fu Xian = Wafangdian, *China* .... **57 E11** 39 38N 121 58 E
Fu Xian, *China* .... **56 G5** 36 0N 109 20 E
Fu'an, *China* .... **59 D12** 27 11N 119 36 E
Fubian, *China* .... **58 B4** 31 17N 102 22 E
Fucécchio, *Italy* .... **40 E7** 43 44N 10 48 E
Fucheng, *China* .... **56 F9** 37 50N 116 10 E
Fuchou = Fuzhou, *China* **59 D12** 26 5N 119 16 E
Fuchū, *Japan* .... **55 G6** 34 34N 133 14 E
Fuchuan, *China* .... **59 E8** 24 50N 111 5 E
Fuchun Jiang →, *China* **59 B13** 30 5N 120 5 E
Fúcino, Piana del, *Italy* **41 F10** 42 1N 13 31 E
Fuding, *China* .... **59 D13** 27 20N 120 12 E
Fuencaliente, *Canary Is.* **48 F2** 28 28N 17 50W
Fuencaliente, *Spain* ... **37 G6** 38 25N 4 18W
Fuencaliente, Pta., *Canary Is.* **48 F2** 28 27N 17 51W
Fuengirola, *Spain* **37 J6** 36 32N 4 41W
Fuenlabrada, *Spain* **36 E7** 40 17N 3 48W
Fuensalida, *Spain* **36 E6** 40 3N 4 12W
Fuente-Álamo, *Spain* .. **39 G3** 38 44N 1 24W
Fuente-Álamo de Murcia, *Spain* **39 H3** 37 42N 1 6W
Fuente de Cantos, *Spain* **37 G4** 38 15N 6 18W
Fuente del Maestre, *Spain* **37 G4** 38 31N 6 28W
Fuente el Fresno, *Spain* **37 F7** 39 14N 3 46W
Fuente Obejuna, *Spain* **37 G5** 38 15N 5 25W
Fuente Palmera, *Spain* . **37 H5** 37 42N 5 6W
Fuentes de Andalucía, *Spain* **37 H5** 37 28N 5 20W
Fuentes de Ebro, *Spain* **38 D4** 41 31N 0 38W
Fuentes de León, *Spain* **37 G4** 38 5N 6 32W
Fuentes de Oñoro, *Spain* **36 E4** 40 33N 6 52W
Fuentesaúco, *Spain* ... **36 D5** 41 15N 5 30W
Fuerte →, *Mexico* **118 B3** 25 50N 109 25W
Fuerte Olimpo, *Paraguay* .... **126 A4** 21 0 S 57 51W
Fuerteventura, *Canary Is.* **48 F6** 28 30N 14 0W
Fuerteventura ✈ (FUE), *Canary Is.* **48 F6** 28 24N 13 52W
Fufeng, *China* .... **56 G5** 34 22N 108 0 E
Fuga I., *Phil.* .... **61 B4** 18 52N 121 20 E
Fugong, *China* .... **58 D2** 27 5N 98 47 E
Fugou, *China* .... **56 G8** 34 3N 114 25 E
Fugu, *China* .... **56 E6** 39 2N 111 3 E
Fuhai, *China* .... **60 B3** 47 2N 87 25 E
Fuḩaymī, *Iraq* .... **70 C4** 34 16N 42 10 E
Fuhlsbüttel, Hamburg ✈ (HAM), *Germany* .. **24 B5** 53 35N 9 59 E
Fuji, *Japan* .... **55 G9** 35 9N 138 39 E
Fuji-Hakone-Izu △, *Japan* .... **55 G9** 35 15N 138 45 E
Fuji-San, *Japan* .... **55 G9** 35 22N 138 44 E
Fuji-Yoshida, *Japan* ... **55 G9** 35 30N 138 46 E
Fujian □, *China* .... **59 E12** 26 0N 118 0 E
Fujinomiya, *Japan* .... **55 G9** 35 10N 138 40 E
Fujisawa, *Japan* .... **55 G9** 35 22N 139 29 E
Fujiyama, Mt. = Fuji-San, *Japan* .... **55 G9** 35 22N 138 44 E
Fukagawa, *Japan* ...... **54 C11** 43 43N 142 2 E
Fukien = Fujian □, *China* .... **59 E12** 26 0N 118 0 E
Fukuchiyama, *Japan* ... **55 G7** 35 19N 135 9 E
Fukue-Shima, *Japan* ... **55 H4** 32 40N 128 45 E
Fukui, *Japan* .... **55 F8** 36 5N 136 10 E
Fukui □, *Japan* .... **55 G8** 36 0N 136 12 E
Fukuoka, *Japan* .... **55 H5** 33 39N 130 21 E
Fukuoka □, *Japan* ..... **55 H5** 33 30N 131 0 E
Fukushima, *Japan* ..... **54 F10** 37 44N 140 28 E
Fukushima □, *Japan* .. **54 F10** 37 30N 140 15 E
Fukuyama, *Japan* ..... **55 G6** 34 35N 133 20 E
Fulacunda, *Guinea-Biss.* **82 C1** 11 44N 15 3W
Fulda, *Germany* ...... **24 E5** 50 32N 9 40 E
Fulda →, *Germany* ... **24 D5** 51 25N 9 39 E
Fulford Harbour, *Canada* **110 B3** 48 47N 123 27W
Fuliang, *China* .... **59 C11** 29 23N 117 14 E
Fullerton, *Calif., U.S.A.* **111 M9** 33 53N 117 56W
Fullerton, *Nebr., U.S.A.* **112 E6** 41 22N 97 58W
Fulongquan, *China* .... **57 B13** 44 20N 124 42 E
Fülöpszállás, *Hungary* . **28 D4** 46 49N 19 15 E
Fulton, *Mo., U.S.A.* ... **112 F9** 38 52N 91 57W
Fulton, *N.Y., U.S.A.* ... **117 C8** 43 19N 76 25W
Fuluälven →, *Sweden* . **10 C7** 61 18N 13 4 E
Fulufjället, *Sweden* .... **10 C6** 61 32N 12 41 E
Fumay, *France* .... **19 C11** 49 58N 4 40 E
Fumel, *France* .... **20 D4** 44 30N 0 58 E
Fumin, *China* .... **58 E4** 25 10N 102 20 E
Funabashi, *Japan* ..... **55 G10** 35 45N 140 0 E
Funafuti = Fongafale, *Tuvalu* .... **96 H9** 8 31 S 179 13 E
Funäsdalen, *Sweden* ... **10 B6** 62 33N 12 32 E
Funchal, *Madeira* **48 D3** 32 38N 16 54W
Funchal ✈ (FNC), *Madeira* **48 D3** 32 42N 16 45W
Fundación, *Colombia* .. **124 A4** 10 31N 74 11W
Fundão, *Portugal* **36 E3** 40 8N 7 30W
Fundu Moldovei, *Romania* .... **29 C10** 47 32N 25 24 E
Fundulea, *Romania* ... **29 F11** 44 28N 26 31 E
Fundy △, *Canada* **105 C6** 45 35N 65 10W
Fundy, B. of, *Canada* .. **105 D6** 45 0N 66 0W
Funhalouro, *Mozam.* .. **89 C5** 23 3 S 34 25 E
Funing, *Hebei, China* .. **57 E10** 39 53N 119 12 E
Funing, *Jiangsu, China* . **57 H10** 33 45N 119 50 E
Funing, *Yunnan, China* **58 F5** 23 35N 105 45 E
Funiu Shan, *China* .... **56 H7** 33 30N 112 20 E
Funsi, *Ghana* **82 C4** 10 21N 1 54W
Funtua, *Nigeria* .... **83 C6** 11 30N 7 18 E
Fuping, *Hebei, China* .. **56 E8** 38 48N 114 12 E
Fuping, *Shaanxi, China* **56 G5** 34 42N 109 10 E
Fuqing, *China* .... **59 E12** 25 41N 119 21 E
Fuquan, *China* .... **58 D6** 26 40N 107 27 E
Furano, *Japan* .... **54 C11** 43 21N 142 23 E
Furāt, Nahr al →, *Asia* **70 D5** 31 0N 47 25 E
Fūrg, *Iran* .... **71 D7** 28 18N 55 13 E
Furmanov, *Russia* ..... **34 B5** 57 10N 41 9 E
Furmanovo, *Kazakhstan* **34 F9** 49 42N 49 25 E
Furnás, *Spain* .... **48 B8** 39 3N 1 32 E
Furnas, Represa de, *Brazil* .... **127 A6** 20 50 S 45 30W
Furneaux Group, *Australia* .... **95 G4** 40 10 S 147 50 E
Furqlus, *Syria* .... **74 A6** 34 36N 37 8 E
Fürstenau, *Germany* .. **24 C3** 52 31N 7 40 E
Fürstenberg, *Germany* . **24 B9** 53 10N 13 8 E
Fürstenfeld, *Austria* .. **26 D9** 47 3N 16 3 E
Fürstenfeldbruck, *Germany* .... **25 G7** 48 11N 11 15 E
Fürstenwalde, *Germany* **24 C10** 52 22N 14 3 E
Fürth, *Germany* ...... **25 F6** 49 28N 10 59 E
Furth im Wald, *Germany* .... **25 F8** 49 18N 12 50 E
Furtwangen, *Germany* . **25 G4** 48 2N 8 12 E
Furudal, *Sweden* ..... **10 C9** 61 10N 15 11 E
Furukawa, *Japan* ..... **54 E10** 38 34N 140 58 E
Furulund, *Sweden* .... **11 J7** 55 46N 13 6 E
Fury and Hecla Str., *Canada* **101 B11** 69 56N 84 0W
Fusagasuga, *Colombia* . **124 C4** 4 21N 74 22W
Fuscaldo, *Italy* .... **43 C9** 39 25N 16 2 E
Fushan, *Shandong, China* .... **57 F11** 37 30N 121 15 E
Fushan, *Shanxi, China* . **56 G6** 35 58N 111 51 E
Fushë Arrëz, *Albania* .. **44 D4** 42 4N 20 2 E
Fushë Krujë, *Albania* .. **44 E3** 41 29N 19 43 E
Fushun, *Liaoning, China* **57 D12** 41 50N 123 56 E
Fushun, *Sichuan, China* **58 C5** 29 13N 104 52 E
Fusong, *China* .... **57 C14** 42 20N 127 15 E
Füssen, *Germany* ..... **25 H6** 47 34N 10 42 E
Fustic, *Barbados* ..... **121 g** 13 16N 59 38W
Fusui, *China* .... **58 F6** 22 40N 107 56 E
Futog, *Serbia & M.* .... **28 E4** 45 15N 19 42 E
Futuna, *Wall. & F. Is.* .. **91 B8** 14 25 S 178 20W
Fuwa, *Egypt* .... **80 H7** 31 12N 30 33 E
Fuxian Hu, *China* .... **58 E4** 24 30N 102 53 E
Fuxin, *China* .... **57 C11** 42 5N 121 48 E
Fuyang, *Anhui, China* . **56 H8** 33 0N 115 48 E
Fuyang, *Zhejiang, China* **59 B12** 30 5N 119 57 E
Fuyang He →, *China* .. **56 E9** 38 12N 117 0 E
Fuying Dao, *China* ... **59 D13** 26 34N 120 9 E
Fuyu, *China* .... **57 B13** 45 12N 124 43 E
Fuyuan, *China* .... **58 E5** 25 40N 104 16 E
Füzesgyarmat, *Hungary* **28 C6** 47 6N 21 14 E
Fuzhou, *China* .... **59 D12** 26 5N 119 16 E
Fylde, *U.K.* **14 D5** 53 50N 2 58W
Fyn, *Denmark* .... **11 J4** 55 20N 10 30 E
Fyne, L., *U.K.* **13 F3** 55 59N 5 23W
Fyns Amtskommune □, *Denmark* .... **11 J4** 55 15N 10 30 E
Fynshav, *Denmark* ... **11 K3** 54 59N 9 59 E

G

Ga, *Ghana* **82 D4** 9 47N 2 30W
Gaanda, *Nigeria* ..... **83 C7** 10 10N 12 27 E
Gabarin, *Nigeria* .... **83 C7** 11 8N 10 27 E
Gabas →, *France* **20 E3** 43 46N 0 42W
Gabela, *Angola* ...... **84 G2** 11 0 S 14 24 E
Gabès, *Tunisia* ...... **79 B8** 33 53N 10 2 E
Gabès, G. de, *Tunisia* .. **79 B8** 34 0N 10 30 E
Gabgaba, W. →, *Egypt* **80 C3** 22 10N 33 5 E
Gąbin, *Poland* ...... **31 F6** 52 23N 19 41 E
Gabon ■, *Africa* ..... **84 E2** 0 10 S 10 0 E
Gaborone, *Botswana* .. **88 C4** 24 45 S 25 57 E
Gabriels, *U.S.A.* **117 B10** 44 26N 74 12W
Gābrīk, *Iran* .... **71 E8** 25 44N 58 28 E
Gabrovo, *Bulgaria* ... **45 D9** 42 52N 25 19 E
Gacé, *France* .... **18 D7** 48 49N 0 20 E
Gāch Sār, *Iran* ...... **71 B6** 36 7N 51 19 E
Gachsārān, *Iran* ..... **71 D6** 30 15N 50 45 E
Gacko, *Bos.-H.* ...... **44 C2** 43 10N 18 33 E
Gadag, *India* .... **66 M9** 15 30N 75 45 E
Gadamai, *Sudan* .... **81 D4** 17 11N 36 10 E
Gadap, *Pakistan* .... **68 G2** 25 5N 67 28 E
Gadarwara, *India* ... **69 H8** 22 50N 78 50 E
Gadebusch, *Germany* . **24 B7** 53 42N 11 7 E
Gadein, *Sudan* ..... **81 F2** 8 10N 28 45 E
Gadhada, *India* .... **68 J4** 22 0N 71 35 E
Gádor, Sierra de, *Spain* **37 J8** 36 57N 2 45W
Gadra, *Pakistan* .... **68 G4** 25 40N 70 38 E
Gadsden, *U.S.A.* **115 H3** 34 1N 86 1W
Gadwal, *India* ...... **66 L10** 16 10N 77 50 E
Gadyach = Hadyach, *Ukraine* .... **33 G8** 50 21N 34 0 E
Găeşti, *Romania* .... **29 F10** 44 48N 25 19 E
Gaeta, *Italy* .... **42 A6** 41 12N 13 35 E
Gaeta, G. di, *Italy* ... **42 A6** 41 6N 13 30 E
Gaffney, *U.S.A.* **115 H5** 35 5N 81 39W
Gafsa, *Tunisia* ...... **78 B7** 34 24N 8 43 E
Gagarawa, *Nigeria* .. **83 C6** 12 25N 9 32 E
Gagaria, *India* ..... **68 G4** 25 43N 70 46 E
Gagarin, *Russia* .... **32 E8** 55 38N 35 0 E
Găgăuzia □, *Moldova* . **29 D13** 46 10N 28 40 E
Gaggenau, *Germany* .. **25 G4** 48 48N 8 18 E
Gaghamni, *Sudan* ... **81 E2** 11 41N 28 19 E
Gagino, *Russia* ..... **34 C7** 55 15N 45 1 E
Gagliano del Capo, *Italy* **43 C11** 39 50N 18 22 E
Gagnef, *Sweden* .... **10 D9** 60 36N 15 5 E
Gagnoa, *Ivory C.* ... **82 D3** 6 56N 5 16W
Gagnon, *Canada* **105 B6** 51 50N 68 5W
Gagnon, L., *Canada* . **103 A6** 62 3N 110 27W
Gagra, *Georgia* .... **35 J5** 43 20N 40 10 E
Gahini, *Rwanda* .... **86 C3** 1 50 S 30 30 E
Gahmar, *India* ..... **69 G10** 25 27N 83 49 E
Gai Xian = Gaizhou, *China* .... **57 D12** 40 22N 122 20 E
Gaïdhouronísi, *Greece* . **49 E7** 34 53N 25 41 E
Gail, *U.S.A.* **113 J4** 32 46N 101 27W
Gail →, *Austria* .... **26 E6** 46 36N 13 53 E
Gaillac, *France* .... **20 E5** 43 54N 1 54 E
Gaillimh = Galway, *Ireland* **12 C2** 53 17N 9 3W
Gaillon, *France* .... **18 C8** 49 10N 1 20 E
Gaines, *U.S.A.* **116 E7** 41 46N 77 35W
Gainesville, *Fla., U.S.A.* **115 L4** 29 40N 82 20W
Gainesville, *Ga., U.S.A.* **115 H4** 34 18N 83 50W
Gainesville, *Mo., U.S.A.* **113 G8** 36 36N 92 26W
Gainesville, *Tex., U.S.A.* **113 J6** 33 38N 97 8W
Gainsborough, *U.K.* .. **14 D7** 53 24N 0 46W
Gairdner, L., *Australia* . **95 E2** 31 30 S 136 0 E
Gairloch, *U.K.* **13 D3** 57 43N 5 41W
Gairloch, L., *U.K.* ... **13 D3** 57 43N 5 45W
Gaizhou, *China* .... **57 D12** 40 22N 122 20 E
Gaj, *Croatia* .... **28 E2** 45 28N 17 3 E
Gaj →, *Pakistan* .... **68 F2** 26 26N 67 21 E
Gakuch, *Pakistan* ... **69 A5** 36 7N 73 45 E
Galala, Gebel el, *Egypt* **80 J8** 29 21N 32 22 E
Galán, Cerro, *Argentina* **126 B2** 25 55 S 66 52W
Galana →, *Kenya* .... **86 C5** 3 9 S 40 8 E
Galanta, *Slovak Rep.* .. **27 C10** 48 11N 17 45 E
Galapagar, *Spain* **36 E7** 40 36N 3 58W
Galápagos = Colón, Arch. de, *Ecuador* .. **97 H18** 0 0 91 0W
Galashiels, *U.K.* **13 F6** 55 37N 2 49W
Galatás, *Greece* .... **46 D5** 37 30N 23 26 E
Galaţi, *Romania* ... **29 E13** 45 27N 28 2 E
Galaţi □, *Romania* .. **29 E12** 45 45N 27 30 E
Galatia, *Turkey* .... **72 C5** 39 30N 33 0 E
Galatina, *Italy* ..... **43 B11** 40 10N 18 10 E
Galátone, *Italy* .... **43 B11** 40 9N 18 4 E
Galax, *U.S.A.* **115 G5** 36 40N 80 56W
Galaxídhion, *Greece* .. **46 C4** 38 22N 22 23 E
Galcaio, *Somali Rep.* .. **75 F4** 6 30N 47 30 E
Galdhøpiggen, *Norway* **9 F12** 61 38N 8 18 E
Galeana, *Chihuahua, Mexico* **118 A3** 30 7N 107 38W
Galeana, *Nuevo León, Mexico* **118 A3** 24 50N 100 4W
Galegu, *Sudan* ..... **81 E4** 12 36N 35 2 E
Galela, *Indonesia* ... **63 D7** 1 50N 127 49 E
Galena, *U.S.A.* **100 B4** 64 44N 156 56W
Galeota Pt., *Trin. & Tob.* **125 K16** 10 8N 60 59W
Galera, *Spain* **39 H2** 37 45N 2 33W
Galera Pt., *Trin. & Tob.* **121 D7** 10 49N 60 54W
Galesburg, *U.S.A.* .. **112 E9** 40 57N 90 22W
Galeton, *U.S.A.* **116 E7** 41 44N 77 39W
Galga, *Ethiopia* .... **81 F4** 6 39N 37 47 E
Gali, *Georgia* ...... **35 J5** 42 37N 41 46 E
Galicea Mare, *Romania* **29 F8** 44 4N 23 19 E
Galich, *Russia* ..... **34 A6** 58 22N 42 24 E
Galiche, *Bulgaria* ... **44 C7** 43 34N 23 53 E
Galicia □, *Spain* **36 C3** 42 43N 7 45W
Galičica △, *Macedonia* **44 E4** 41 2N 20 55 E
Galilee = Hagalil, *Israel* **74 C4** 32 53N 35 18 E
Galilee, L., *Australia* .. **94 C4** 22 20 S 145 50 E
Galilee, Sea of = Yam Kinneret, *Israel* ..... **74 C4** 32 45N 35 35 E
Galim, *Cameroon* .... **83 D7** 7 6N 12 25 E
Galina Pt., *Jamaica* .. **120 a** 18 24N 76 58W
Galinoporni, *Cyprus* .. **49 D13** 35 31N 34 18 E
Galion, *U.S.A.* **116 F2** 40 44N 82 47W
Galiuro Mts., *U.S.A.* .. **109 K8** 32 30N 110 20W
Galiwinku, *Australia* .. **94 A2** 12 2 S 135 34 E
Gallabat, *Sudan* .... **81 E4** 12 58N 36 11 E
Gallan Hd., *U.K.* ... **13 C1** 58 15N 7 2W
Gallarate, *Italy* .... **40 C5** 45 40N 8 48 E
Gallatin, *U.S.A.* ... **115 G2** 36 24N 86 27W
Galle, *Sri Lanka* .... **66 R12** 6 5N 80 10 E
Gállego →, *Spain* ... **38 D4** 41 39N 0 51W
Gallegos →, *Argentina* **128 G3** 51 35 S 69 0W
Galletti →, *Ethiopia* .. **81 F5** 8 46N 41 10 E
Galley Hd., *Ireland* .. **12 E3** 51 32N 8 55W
Galliate, *Italy* ...... **40 C5** 45 29N 8 42 E
Gallinas, Pta., *Colombia* **124 A4** 12 28N 71 40W
Gallipoli = Gelibolu, *Turkey* .... **45 F10** 40 28N 26 43 E
Gallípoli, *Italy* ..... **43 B10** 40 3N 17 58 E
Gallipolis, *U.S.A.* ... **114 F4** 38 49N 82 12W
Gällivare, *Sweden* ... **8 C19** 67 9N 20 40 E
Gallneukirchen, *Austria* **26 C7** 48 21N 14 25 E
Gällö, *Sweden* ..... **10 B9** 62 55N 15 13 E
Gallo, C., *Italy* .... **42 D6** 38 13N 13 19 E
Gallocanta, L. de, *Spain* **38 E3** 40 58N 1 30W
Galloo I., *U.S.A.* ... **117 C8** 43 55N 76 25W
Galloway, *U.K.* **13 F4** 55 1N 4 29W
Galloway ⌓, *U.K.* ... **13 F4** 55 3N 4 20W
Galloway, Mull of, *U.K.* **13 G4** 54 39N 4 52W
Gallup, *U.S.A.* **109 J9** 35 32N 108 45W
Gallur, *Spain* **38 D3** 41 52N 1 19W
Galoya, *Sri Lanka* ... **66 Q12** 8 10N 80 55 E
Galt, *U.S.A.* **110 G5** 38 15N 121 18W
Galten, *Denmark* ... **11 H3** 56 9N 9 54 E
Galtür, *Austria* .... **26 E3** 46 58N 10 11 E
Galty Mts., *Ireland* .. **12 D3** 52 22N 8 10W
Galtymore, *Ireland* .. **12 D3** 52 21N 8 11W
Galva, *U.S.A.* **112 E9** 41 10N 90 3W
Galve de Sorbe, *Spain* . **38 D1** 41 13N 3 10W
Galveston, *U.S.A.* .. **113 L7** 29 18N 94 48W
Galveston B., *U.S.A.* . **113 L7** 29 36N 94 50W
Gálvez, *Argentina* ... **126 C3** 32 0 S 61 14W
Galway, *Ireland* **12 C2** 53 17N 9 3W
Galway □, *Ireland* .. **12 C2** 53 22N 9 1W
Galway B., *Ireland* .. **12 C2** 53 13N 9 10W
Gam →, *Vietnam* ... **64 B5** 21 55N 105 12 E
Gamagōri, *Japan* ... **55 G8** 34 50N 137 14 E
Gamari, L., *Ethiopia* .. **81 E5** 11 32N 41 40 E
Gamawa, *Nigeria* ... **83 C7** 12 10N 10 31 E
Gamay, *Phil.* .... **61 E6** 12 23N 125 18 E
Gambaga, *Ghana* ... **83 C4** 10 30N 0 28W
Gambat, *Pakistan* ... **68 F3** 27 17N 68 26 E
Gambela, *Ethiopia* ... **81 F3** 8 14N 34 38 E
Gambela △, *Ethiopia* .. **81 F3** 8 0N 34 0 E
Gambela-Hizboch □, *Ethiopia* .... **81 F3** 8 0N 34 0 E
Gambhir →, *India* ... **68 F6** 26 58N 77 27 E
Gambia ■, *W. Afr.* ... **82 C1** 13 25N 16 0W
Gambia →, *W. Afr.* ... **82 C1** 13 28N 16 34W
Gambier, *U.S.A.* **116 F2** 40 22N 82 23W
Gambier, C., *Australia* . **92 B5** 11 56 S 130 57 E
Gambier Is., *Australia* . **95 F2** 35 3 S 136 30 E
Gambo, *Canada* **105 C9** 48 47N 54 13W
Gamboli, *Pakistan* .. **68 E3** 29 53N 68 24 E
Gamboma, *Congo* ... **84 E3** 1 55 S 15 52 E
Gamka →, *S. Africa* .. **88 E3** 33 18 S 21 39 E
Gamkab →, *Namibia* . **88 D2** 28 4 S 17 54 E
Gamla Uppsala, *Sweden* **10 E11** 59 54N 17 40 E
Gamlakarleby = Kokkola, *Finland* .. **8 E20** 63 50N 23 8 E
Gamleby, *Sweden* ... **11 G10** 57 54N 16 24 E
Gammon →, *Canada* .. **103 C9** 51 24N 95 44W
Gammon Ranges △, *Australia* .... **95 E2** 30 38 S 139 8 E
Gamo-Gofa, *Ethiopia* . **81 F4** 5 40N 36 40 E
Gamou, *Niger* ..... **83 C6** 14 20N 9 55 E
Gamtoos →, *S. Africa* . **88 E4** 33 58 S 25 1 E
Gan, *France* **20 E3** 43 12N 0 27W
Gan Goriama, Mts., *Cameroon* .... **83 D7** 7 44N 12 45 E
Gan Jiang →, *China* .. **59 C11** 29 15N 116 0 E
Ganado, *U.S.A.* **109 J9** 35 43N 109 33W
Gananita, *Sudan* ... **80 D3** 18 22N 33 50 E
Gananoque, *Canada* .. **117 B8** 44 20N 76 10W
Ganāveh, *Iran* ..... **71 D6** 29 35N 50 35 E
Gäncä, *Azerbaijan* .. **35 K8** 40 45N 46 20 E
Gancheng, *China* ... **64 C7** 18 51N 108 37 E
Gand = Gent, *Belgium* . **17 C3** 51 2N 3 42 E
Ganda, *Angola* .... **85 G2** 13 3 S 14 35 E
Gandajika, *Dem. Rep. of the Congo* .... **84 F4** 6 45 S 23 57 E
Gandak →, *India* ... **69 G11** 25 39N 85 13 E
Gandava, *Pakistan* .... **68 E2** 28 32N 67 32 E
Gander, *Canada* **105 C9** 48 58N 54 35W
Gander L., *Canada* **105 C9** 48 58N 54 35W
Ganderkesee, *Germany* **24 B4** 53 2N 8 32 E
Ganderowe Falls, *Zimbabwe* .... **87 F2** 17 20 S 29 10 E
Gandesa, *Spain* ...... **38 D5** 41 3N 0 26 E
Gandhi Sagar, *India* ... **68 G6** 24 40N 75 40 E
Gandhinagar, *India* ... **68 H5** 23 15N 72 45 E
Gandi, *Nigeria* ...... **83 C6** 12 55N 5 49 E
Gandía, *Spain* **39 G4** 38 58N 0 9W
Gandino, *Italy* .... **40 C6** 45 49N 9 54 E
Gando, Pta., *Canary Is.* **48 G4** 27 55N 15 22W
Gandole, *Nigeria* .... **83 D7** 8 28N 11 35 E
Gâneb, *Mauritania* ... **82 B2** 18 29N 10 8W
Ganedidalem = Gani, *Indonesia* .... **63 E7** 0 48 S 128 14 E
Ganetti, *Sudan* ...... **80 D3** 18 0N 31 10 E
Ganga →, *India* ..... **69 H14** 23 20N 90 30 E
Ganga Sagar, *India* ... **69 J13** 21 38N 88 5 E
Gangafani, *Mali* **82 C4** 14 20N 2 20W
Gangan →, *India* .... **69 E8** 28 38N 78 58 E
Ganganagar, *India* ... **68 E5** 29 56N 73 56 E
Gangapur, *India* ..... **68 F7** 26 32N 76 49 E
Gangara, *Niger* ...... **83 C6** 14 35N 8 29 E
Gangaw, *Burma* ..... **67 H19** 22 5N 94 5 E
Gangdisê Shan, *China* . **67 D12** 31 20N 81 0 E
Ganges = Ganga →, *India* .... **69 H14** 23 20N 90 30 E
Ganges, *Canada* **102 D4** 48 51N 123 31W
Ganges, *France* ..... **20 E7** 43 56N 3 42 E
Ganges, Mouths of the, *India* .... **69 J14** 21 30N 90 0 E
Gånghester, *Sweden* .. **11 G7** 57 42N 13 1 E
Gangi, *Italy* .... **43 E7** 37 48N 14 12 E
Gângiova, *Romania* ... **29 G8** 43 54N 23 50 E
Gangoh, *India* ...... **68 E7** 29 46N 77 18 E
Gangotri, *India* ..... **69 D8** 30 50N 79 10 E
Gangtok, *India* ..... **67 F16** 27 20N 88 37 E
Gangu, *China* .... **56 G3** 34 40N 105 15 E
Gangyao, *China* ..... **57 B14** 44 12N 126 37 E
Gani, *Indonesia* ..... **63 E7** 0 48 S 128 14 E
Ganj, *India* .... **69 F8** 27 45N 78 57 E
Ganluc, *China* ...... **58 C4** 28 58N 102 59 E
Gannat, *France* ..... **19 F10** 46 7N 3 11 E
Gannett Peak, *U.S.A.* .. **108 E9** 43 11N 109 39W
Ganquan, *China* ..... **56 F5** 36 20N 109 20 E
Gänserdorf, *Austria* .. **27 C9** 48 20N 16 43 E
Ganshui, *China* ..... **58 C6** 28 40N 106 40 E
Gansu □, *China* ..... **56 G3** 36 0N 104 0 E
Ganta, *Liberia* **82 D3** 7 15N 8 59W
Gantheaume, C., *Australia* .... **95 F2** 36 4 S 137 32 E
Gantheaume B., *Australia* .... **93 E1** 27 40 S 114 10 E
Gantsevichi = Hantsavichy, *Belarus* **33 F4** 52 49N 26 30 E
Ganye, *Nigeria* ..... **83 D7** 8 25N 12 4 E
Ganyem = Genyem, *Indonesia* .... **63 E10** 2 46 S 140 12 E
Ganyu, *China* ...... **57 G10** 34 50N 119 8 E
Ganyushkino, *Kazakhstan* .... **35 G9** 46 35N 49 20 E
Ganzhou, *China* .... **59 E10** 25 51N 114 56 E
Gao, *Mali* **83 B4** 16 15N 0 5W
Gao Xian, *China* .... **58 C5** 28 21N 104 32 E
Gao'an, *China* ..... **59 C10** 28 26N 115 17 E
Gaochun, *China* .... **59 B12** 31 20N 118 49 E
Gaohe, *China* ...... **59 F9** 22 46N 112 57 E
Gaohebu, *China* .... **59 B11** 30 43N 116 49 E
Gaokeng, *China* .... **59 D9** 27 40N 113 58 E
Gaolan Dao, *China* ... **59 G9** 21 55N 113 10 E
Gaoligong Shan, *China* **58 E2** 24 45N 98 45 E
Gaomi, *China* ...... **57 F10** 36 20N 119 42 E
Gaoming, *China* .... **59 F9** 36 9N 113 1 E
Gaoping, *China* .... **56 G7** 35 45N 112 55 E
Gaotang, *China* .... **56 F9** 36 50N 116 15 E
Gaoua, *Burkina Faso* .. **82 C4** 10 20N 3 8W
Gaoual, *Guinea* **82 C2** 11 45N 13 25W
Gaoxiong = Kaohsiung, *Taiwan* .... **59 F13** 22 35N 120 16 E
Gaoyang, *China* .... **56 E8** 38 40N 115 45 E
Gaoyao, *China* .... **59 F9** 23 3N 112 27 E
Gaoyou, *China* .... **59 A12** 32 47N 119 26 E
Gaoyou Hu, *China* ... **57 H10** 32 45N 119 20 E
Gaoyuan, *China* .... **57 F9** 37 8N 117 58 E
Gaozhou, *China* .... **59 G8** 21 58N 110 50 E
Gap, *France* .... **21 D10** 44 33N 6 5 E
Gapan, *Phil.* .... **61 D4** 15 19N 120 57 E
Gapat →, *India* .... **69 G10** 24 30N 82 28 E
Gapuwiyak, *Australia* . **94 A2** 12 25 S 135 43 E
Gar, *China* .... **60 C2** 32 10N 79 58 E
Garabogazköl Aylagy, *Turkmenistan* .... **52 E6** 41 0N 53 30 E
Garachico, *Canary Is.* . **48 F3** 28 22N 16 46W
Garachiné, *Panama* .. **120 E4** 8 0N 78 12W
Garafia, *Canary Is.* ... **48 F2** 28 48N 17 57W
Garah, *Australia* .... **95 D4** 29 5 S 149 38 E
Garajonay, *Canary Is.* . **48 F2** 28 7N 17 14W
Garamba △, *Dem. Rep. of the Congo* .... **86 B2** 4 10N 29 40 E
Garango, *Burkina Faso* **83 C4** 11 48N 0 34W
Garanhuns, *Brazil* ... **125 E11** 8 50 S 36 30W
Garautha, *India* .... **69 G8** 25 34N 79 18 E
Garawe, *Liberia* **82 E3** 4 35N 8 0W
Garba Tula, *Kenya* ... **86 B4** 0 30N 38 32 E
Garberville, *U.S.A.* .. **108 F2** 40 6N 123 48W
Garbiyang, *India* ... **69 D9** 30 8N 80 54 E
Garbsen, *Germany* ... **24 C5** 52 26N 9 31 E
Gard □, *France* .... **21 D8** 44 2N 4 10 E
Gard →, *France* .... **21 E8** 43 51N 4 37 E
Garda, L. di, *Italy* ... **40 C7** 45 40N 10 41 E
Gardanne, *France* ... **21 E9** 43 27N 5 27 E
Gårdby, *Sweden* .... **11 H10** 56 36N 16 38 E
Garde L., *Canada* ... **103 A7** 62 50N 106 13W
Gardelegen, *Germany* . **24 C7** 52 32N 11 24 E
Garden City, *Ga., U.S.A.* **115 J5** 32 6N 81 9W
Garden City, *Kans., U.S.A.* **113 G4** 37 58N 100 53W
Garden City, *Tex., U.S.A.* **113 K4** 31 52N 101 29W
Garden Grove, *U.S.A.* . **111 M9** 33 47N 117 55W
Gardēz, *Afghan.* .... **68 C3** 33 37N 69 9 E
Gardhíki, *Greece* ... **46 C3** 38 50N 21 55 E
Gardiner, *Maine, U.S.A.* **115 C11** 44 14N 69 47W
Gardiner, *Mont., U.S.A.* **108 D8** 45 2N 110 22W
Gardiners I., *U.S.A.* .. **117 E12** 41 6N 72 6W
Gardner, *U.S.A.* **117 D13** 42 34N 71 59W
Gardner Canal, *Canada* **102 C3** 53 27N 128 8W
Gardnerville, *U.S.A.* .. **110 G7** 38 56N 119 45W
Gardno, Jezioro, *Poland* **30 D4** 54 40N 17 7 E
Gardo, *Somali Rep.* ... **75 F4** 9 30N 49 6 E
Gardone Val Trómpia, *Italy* .... **40 C7** 45 41N 10 11 E
Gárdony, *Hungary* ... **28 C3** 47 12N 18 39 E
Garešnica, *Croatia* ... **41 C13** 45 36N 16 56 E
Garéssio, *Italy* ..... **40 D5** 44 12N 8 2 E
Garey, *U.S.A.* **111 L6** 34 53N 120 19W
Garfield, *U.S.A.* **108 C5** 47 1N 117 9W
Garforth, *U.K.* **14 D6** 53 47N 1 24W
Gargaliánoi, *Greece* ... **46 D3** 37 4N 21 38 E
Gargan, Mt., *France* ... **20 C5** 45 37N 1 39 E
Gargano △, *Italy* ...... **41 G12** 41 43N 15 52 E
Gargett, *Australia* ..... **94 K6** 21 9 S 148 46 E
Gargouna, *Mali* .... **83 B5** 15 56N 0 13 E
Gargždai, *Lithuania* ... **30 C8** 55 43N 21 24 E
Garibaldi ⌓, *Canada* .. **102 D4** 49 50N 122 40W
Gariep, L., *S. Africa* ... **88 E4** 30 40 S 25 40 E
Garies, *S. Africa* ...... **88 E2** 30 32 S 17 59 E
Garigliano →, *Italy* ... **42 A6** 41 13N 13 45 E
Garissa, *Kenya* .... **86 C4** 0 25 S 39 40 E
Garkida, *Nigeria* ..... **83 C7** 10 27N 12 36 E
Garko, *Nigeria* ...... **83 C6** 11 45N 8 35 E
Garland, *Tex., U.S.A.* . **113 J6** 32 55N 96 38W
Garland, *Utah, U.S.A.* . **108 F7** 41 47N 112 10W
Garlasco, *Italy* ...... **40 C5** 45 12N 8 55 E
Garliava, *Lithuania* ... **30 D10** 54 49N 23 52 E
Garlin, *France* **20 E3** 43 33N 0 16W
Garm, *Tajikistan* ..... **52 F8** 39 0N 70 20 E
Garmāb, *Iran* .... **71 C8** 35 25N 56 45 E
Garmisch-Partenkirchen, *Germany* .... **25 H7** 47 30N 11 6 E
Garmo, Qullai = Kommunizma, Pik, *Tajikistan* .... **52 F8** 39 0N 72 2 E
Garmsār, *Iran* .... **71 C7** 35 20N 52 25 E
Garner, *U.S.A.* **112 D8** 43 6N 93 36W
Garnett, *U.S.A.* **112 F7** 38 17N 95 14W
Garo Hills, *India* .... **69 G14** 25 30N 90 30 E
Garoe, *Somali Rep.* ... **75 F4** 8 25N 48 33 E
Garonne →, *France* ... **20 C3** 45 2N 0 36W
Garonne, Canal Latéral à la, *France* .... **20 D4** 44 15N 0 18 E
Garoowe = Garoe, *Somali Rep.* .... **75 F4** 8 25N 48 33 E
Garot, *India* .... **68 G6** 24 19N 75 41 E
Garoua, *Cameroon* ... **83 D7** 9 19N 13 21 E
Garpenberg, *Sweden* .. **10 D10** 60 19N 16 12 E
Garphyttan, *Sweden* .. **10 E8** 59 18N 14 56 E
Garrauli, *India* ...... **69 G8** 25 5N 79 22 E
Garrel, *Germany* ..... **24 C4** 52 57N 8 1 E
Garrigues, *France* .... **20 E7** 43 40N 3 55 E
Garrison, *Mont., U.S.A.* **108 C7** 46 31N 112 49W
Garrison, *N. Dak., U.S.A.* **112 B4** 47 40N 101 25W
Garrison Res. = Sakakawea, L., *U.S.A.* **112 B4** 47 30N 101 25W
Garron Pt., *U.K.* **12 A6** 55 3N 5 59W
Garrovillas, *Spain* **37 F4** 39 40N 6 33W
Garrucha, *Spain* **39 H3** 37 11N 1 49W
Garry →, *U.K.* **13 E5** 56 44N 3 47W
Garry, L., *Canada* **100 B9** 65 58N 100 18W
Garsen, *Kenya* .... **86 C5** 2 20 S 40 5 E
Gärsnäs, *Sweden* ..... **11 J8** 55 32N 14 10 E
Garson L., *Canada* ... **103 B6** 56 19N 110 2W
Garstang, *U.K.* **14 D5** 53 55N 2 46W
Gartempe →, *France* .. **20 B4** 46 47N 0 49 E
Gartz, *Germany* ..... **24 B10** 53 13N 14 22 E
Garu, *Ghana* **83 C4** 10 55N 0 11W
Garu, *India* .... **69 H11** 23 40N 84 14 E
Garub, *Namibia* ..... **88 D2** 26 37 S 16 0 E
Garut, *Indonesia* .... **63 G12** 7 14 S 107 53 E
Garvão, *Portugal* **37 H2** 37 42N 8 21W
Garvie Mts., *N.Z.* .... **91 L2** 45 30 S 168 50 E
Garwa = Garoua, *Cameroon* .... **83 D7** 9 19N 13 21 E
Garwa, *India* .... **69 G10** 24 11N 83 47 E
Garwolin, *Poland* .... **31 G8** 51 55N 21 38 E
Gary, *U.S.A.* **114 E2** 41 36N 87 20W
Garz, *Germany* ...... **24 A9** 54 19N 13 20 E
Garzê, *China* .... **58 B3** 31 38N 100 1 E
Garzón, *Colombia* **124 C3** 2 10N 75 40W
Gas-San, *Japan* ...... **54 E10** 38 32N 140 1 E
Gasan Kuli = Esenguly, *Turkmenistan* .... **52 F6** 37 37N 53 59 E
Gascogne, *France* .... **20 E4** 43 45N 0 20 E
Gascogne, G. de, *Europe* **20 E2** 44 0N 2 0W
Gascony = Gascogne, *France* .... **20 E4** 43 45N 0 20 E
Gascoyne →, *Australia* **93 D1** 24 52 S 113 37 E
Gascoyne Junction, *Australia* .... **93 E2** 25 2 S 115 17 E
Gascueña, *Spain* **38 E2** 40 18N 2 31W
Gash, Wadi →, *Ethiopia* **81 D4** 16 48N 35 51 E
Gash-Setit ⌓, *Eritrea* .. **81 D4** 15 12N 36 58 E
Gashagar, *Nigeria* ... **83 C7** 13 22N 12 47 E
Gashaka, *Nigeria* .... **83 D7** 7 20N 11 29 E
Gashaka-Gumti △, *Nigeria* .... **83 D7** 7 23N 11 34 E
Gasherbrum, *Pakistan* . **69 B7** 35 40N 76 40 E
Gashua, *Nigeria* ..... **83 C7** 12 54N 11 0 E
Gasparillo, *Trin. & Tob.* **125 K15** 10 18N 61 26W
Gaspé, *Canada* **105 C7** 48 52N 64 30W
Gaspé, C., *Canada* ... **105 C7** 48 48N 64 7W
Gaspé Pen. = Gaspésie, Pén. de la, *Canada* .. **105 C6** 48 45N 65 40W
Gaspésie ⌓, *Canada* .. **105 C6** 48 55N 66 10W
Gaspésie, Pén. de la, *Canada* **105 C6** 48 45N 65 40W
Gassan, *Burkina Faso* . **82 C4** 12 49N 3 12W
Gassol, *Nigeria* ..... **83 D7** 8 34N 10 25 E
Gasteiz = Vitoria-Gasteiz, *Spain* **38 C2** 42 50N 2 41W
Gastonia, *U.S.A.* **115 H5** 35 16N 81 11W
Gastoúni, *Greece* .... **46 D3** 37 51N 21 15 E
Gastoúri, *Greece* .... **46 B1** 39 34N 19 54 E
Gastre, *Argentina* ... **128 E3** 42 20 S 69 15W
Gästrikland, *Sweden* .. **10 D10** 60 45N 16 40 E
Gata, C., *Cyprus* .... **49 E12** 34 34N 33 2 E
Gata, C. de, *Spain* ... **39 J2** 36 41N 2 13W
Gata, Sierra de, *Spain* . **36 E4** 40 20N 6 45W
Gataga →, *Canada* ... **102 B3** 58 35N 126 59W
Gătaia, *Romania* .... **28 E6** 45 26N 21 30 E
Gatchina, *Russia* .... **32 C6** 59 35N 30 9 E
Gatehouse of Fleet, *U.K.* **13 G4** 54 53N 4 12W
Gates, *U.S.A.* **116 C7** 43 9N 77 42W
Gateshead, *U.K.* **14 C6** 54 57N 1 35W
Gatesville, *U.S.A.* ... **113 K6** 31 26N 97 45W
Gateway ⌓, *U.S.A.* ... **117 F11** 40 26N 73 59W
Gaths, *Zimbabwe* .... **87 G3** 20 2 S 30 32 E
Gatico, *Chile* .... **126 A1** 22 29 S 70 20W
Gâtinais, *France* .... **19 D9** 48 5N 2 40 E
Gâtine, Hauteurs de, *France* **20 B3** 46 35N 0 45W
Gatineau, *Canada* ... **117 A9** 45 29N 75 38W
Gatineau ⌓, *Canada* .. **104 C4** 45 40N 76 0W
Gatineau →, *Canada* . **104 C4** 45 27N 75 42W
Gattaran, *Phil.* ...... **61 B4** 18 4N 121 38 E
Gattinara, *Italy* ..... **40 C5** 45 37N 8 22 E
Gatton, *Australia* .... **95 D5** 27 32 S 152 17 E
Gatun, L., *Panama* ... **120 E4** 9 7N 79 56W
Gatwick, London ✈ (LGW), *U.K.* **15 F7** 51 10N 0 11W

Gatyana, *S. Africa* .... **89 E4** 32 16 S 28 31 E
Gau, *Fiji* .... **91 D8** 18 2 S 179 18 E
Gaucín, *Spain* **37 J5** 36 31N 5 19W
Gauer L., *Canada* **103 B9** 57 0N 97 50W
Gauhati = Guwahati,
  India .... **67 F17** 26 10N 91 45 E
Gauja →, *Latvia* .... **9 H21** 57 10N 24 16 E
Gaula →, *Norway* .... **8 E14** 63 21N 10 14 E
Gauri Phanta, *India* .... **69 E9** 28 41N 80 36 E
Gausta, *Norway* .... **9 G13** 59 48N 8 40 E
Gauteng □, *S. Africa* .. **89 D4** 26 0 S 28 0 E
Gāv Koshī, *Iran* .... **71 D8** 28 38N 57 12 E
Gāvakān, *Iran* .... **71 D7** 29 37N 53 10 E
Gavallaí △, *Liberia* .. **82 D3** 5 8N 7 20W
Gavarnie, *France* **20 F3** 42 44N 0 1W
Gāväter, *Iran* .... **71 E9** 25 10N 61 31 E
Gāvbandī, *Iran* .... **71 E7** 27 12N 53 4 E
Gavdhopoúla, *Greece* .. **49 E6** 34 56N 24 0 E
Gávdhos, *Greece* .... **49 E6** 34 50N 24 5 E
Gavi, *Italy* .... **40 D5** 44 41N 8 49 E
Gavião, *Portugal* **37 F3** 39 28N 7 56W
Gaviota, *U.S.A.* **111 L6** 34 29N 120 13W
Gävle, *Sweden* .... **10 D11** 60 40N 17 9 E
Gävleborgs län □,
  Sweden ...... **10 C10** 61 30N 16 15 E
Gävlebukten, *Sweden* . **10 D11** 60 40N 17 20 E
Gavorrano, *Italy* .... **40 F7** 42 55N 10 54 E
Gavray, *France* **18 D5** 48 55N 1 20W
Gavrilov Yam, *Russia* . **32 D10** 57 18N 39 49 E
Gávrion, *Greece* .... **46 D6** 37 54N 24 44 E
Gawachab, *Namibia* .. **88 D2** 27 4 S 17 55 E
Gawilgarh Hills, *India* .. **66 J10** 21 15N 76 45 E
Gawler, *Australia* .... **95 E2** 34 30 S 138 42 E
Gawu, *Nigeria* .... **83 D6** 9 14N 6 52 E
Gaxun Nur, *China* .... **60 B5** 42 22N 100 30 E
Gaya, *India* .... **69 G11** 24 47N 85 4 E
Gaya, *Niger* .... **83 C5** 11 52N 3 28 E
Gaya, *Nigeria* .... **83 C6** 11 57N 9 0 E
Gayéri, *Burkina Faso* . **83 C5** 12 39N 0 29 E
Gaylord, *U.S.A.* **114 C3** 45 2N 84 41W
Gayndah, *Australia* .. **95 D5** 25 35 S 151 32 E
Gaysin = Haysyn,
  Ukraine ...... **29 B14** 48 57N 29 25 E
Gayvoron = Hayvoron,
  Ukraine ...... **29 B14** 48 22N 29 52 E
Gaza, *Gaza Strip* .... **74 D3** 31 30N 34 28 E
Gaza □, *Mozam.* .... **89 C5** 23 10 S 32 45 E
Gaza Strip □, *Asia* .. **74 D3** 31 29N 34 25 E
Gazanjyk, *Turkmenistan* **71 B7** 39 16N 55 32 E
Gāzbor, *Iran* ...... **71 D8** 28 5N 58 51 E
Gazi, *Dem. Rep. of*
  the Congo ...... **86 B1** 1 3N 24 30 E
Gaziantep, *Turkey* .. **70 B3** 37 6N 37 23 E
Gazimağosa =
  Famagusta, *Cyprus* . **49 D12** 35 8N 33 55 E
Gazipaşa, *Turkey* .. **72 D5** 36 16N 32 18 E
Gbarnga, *Liberia* **82 D3** 7 19N 9 13W
Gbekebo, *Nigeria* .... **83 D5** 6 20N 4 56 E
Gboko, *Nigeria* .... **83 D6** 7 17N 9 4 E
Gbongan, *Nigeria* .. **83 D5** 7 28N 4 20 E
Gcoverega, *Botswana* .. **88 B3** 19 8 S 24 18 E
Gcuwa, *S. Africa* .... **89 E4** 32 20 S 28 11 E
Gdańsk, *Poland* .... **30 D5** 54 22N 18 40 E
Gdansk ✈ (GDN),
  Poland .... **30 D5** 54 22N 18 30 E
Gdańska, Zatoka,
  Poland .... **30 D6** 54 30N 19 20 E
Gdov, *Russia* ...... **9 G22** 58 48N 27 55 E
Gdynia, *Poland* .... **30 D5** 54 35N 18 33 E
Geba →, *Guinea-Biss.* . **82 C1** 11 46N 15 36W
Gebe, *Indonesia* .... **63 D7** 0 5N 129 25 E
Gebeciler, *Turkey* .... **47 C12** 38 46N 30 46 E
Gebeit Mine, *Sudan* .. **80 C4** 21 3N 36 29 E
Gebel Abyad, *Sudan* .. **80 D3** 16 0N 28 0 E
Gebel Iweibid, *Egypt* .. **80 H8** 30 8N 32 13 E
Gebze, *Turkey* .... **45 F13** 40 47N 29 25 E
Gecha, *Ethiopia* .... **81 F4** 7 30N 35 18 E
Gedaref, *Sudan* .... **81 E4** 14 2N 35 28 E
Gedaref □, *Sudan* .. **81 E4** 14 0N 35 0 E
Gediz, *Turkey* ...... **47 B11** 39 1N 29 24 E
Gediz →, *Turkey* .... **47 C8** 38 35N 26 48 E
Gedo, *Ethiopia* .... **81 F4** 9 2N 37 25 E
Gèdre, *France* ...... **20 F4** 42 47N 0 2 E
Gedser, *Denmark* .... **11 K5** 54 35N 11 55 E
Gedung, Pulau, *Malaysia* **65 c** 5 17N 100 23 E
Geegully Cr. →,
  Australia ...... **92 C3** 18 32 S 123 41 E
Geel, *Belgium* ...... **17 C4** 51 10N 4 59 E
Geelong, *Australia* .. **95 F3** 38 10 S 144 22 E
Geelvink B. =
  Cenderwasih, Teluk,
  Indonesia ...... **63 E9** 3 0 S 135 20 E
Geelvink Chan.,
  Australia ...... **93 E1** 28 30 S 114 0 E
Geesthacht, *Germany* . **24 B6** 53 26N 10 22 E
Geidam, *Nigeria* .... **83 C7** 12 57N 11 57 E
Geikie →, *Canada* .. **103 B8** 57 45N 103 52W
Geikie Gorge △,
  Australia ...... **92 C4** 18 3 S 125 41 E
Geilenkirchen, *Germany* **24 E2** 50 58N 6 8 E
Geili, *Sudan* ...... **81 D3** 16 1N 32 37 E
Geisingen, *Germany* .. **25 H4** 47 55N 8 38 E
Geislingen, *Germany* . **25 G5** 48 37N 9 50 E
Geistown, *U.S.A.* **116 F6** 40 18N 78 52W
Geita, *Tanzania* .... **86 C3** 2 48 S 32 12 E
Gejiu, *China* ...... **58 F4** 23 20N 103 10 E
Gel →, *Sudan* ...... **81 F2** 7 5N 29 10 E
Gel, Meydān-e, *Iran* . **71 D7** 29 4N 54 50 E
Gel River, *Sudan* .... **81 F2** 7 5N 29 10 E
Gela, *Italy* .... **43 E7** 37 4N 14 15 E
Gela, G. di, *Italy* .... **43 F7** 37 0N 14 20 E
Gelahun, *Liberia* **82 D2** 7 55N 10 28W
Gelang Patah, *Malaysia* **65 d** 1 27N 103 35 E
Gelderland □, *Neths.* . **17 B6** 52 5N 6 10 E
Geldern, *Germany* .... **24 D2** 51 31N 6 20 E
Geldrop, *Neths.* .... **17 D5** 50 57N 5 49 E
Geleen, *Neths.* ...... **17 D5** 50 57N 5 49 E
Gelehun, *S. Leone* **82 D2** 8 20N 11 40W
Gelembe, *Turkey* .... **47 B9** 39 10N 27 50 E
Gelemso, *Ethiopia* .. **81 F5** 8 49N 40 31 E
Gelendost, *Turkey* .. **72 C4** 38 7N 31 1 E
Gelendzhik, *Russia* .. **33 K10** 44 33N 38 10 E
Gelibolu, *Turkey* .... **45 F10** 40 28N 26 43 E
Gelibolu Yarımadası,
  Turkey .... **45 F10** 40 20N 26 30 E
Gelidonya Burnu,
  Turkey .... **72 D4** 36 12N 30 24 E
Gelnhausen, *Germany* . **25 E5** 50 11N 9 11 E
Gelnica, *Slovak Rep.* . **27 C13** 48 51N 20 55 E
Gelsenkirchen, *Germany* **24 D3** 51 32N 7 6 E
Gelugur, *Malaysia* .. **65 c** 5 22N 100 18 E
Gemas, *Malaysia* .... **65 L4** 2 37N 102 36 E
Gembloux, *Belgium* .. **17 D4** 50 34N 4 43 E
Gembu, *Nigeria* .... **83 D7** 6 42N 11 10 E

Gemena, *Dem. Rep. of*
  the Congo ...... **84 D3** 3 13N 19 48 E
Gemerek, *Turkey* .... **70 B3** 39 15N 36 10 E
Gemla, *Sweden* .... **11 H8** 56 52N 14 39 E
Gemlik, *Turkey* .... **45 F13** 40 26N 29 9 E
Gemlik Körfezi, *Turkey* **45 F12** 40 25N 28 55 E
Gemona del Friuli, *Italy* **41 B10** 46 16N 13 9 E
Gemsa, *Egypt* ...... **80 B3** 27 39N 33 35 E
Gemsbok △, *Botswana* **88 D3** 25 5 S 21 1 E
Gemünden, *Germany* .. **25 E5** 50 3N 9 42 E
Genale →, *Ethiopia* .. **81 F4** 6 2N 39 1 E
Genç, *Turkey* ...... **73 C9** 38 44N 40 34 E
Gençay, *France* .... **20 B4** 46 23N 0 23 E
Geneina, Gebel, *Egypt* **80 B3** 29 2N 33 55 E
General Acha,
  Argentina ...... **126 D3** 37 20 S 64 38W
General Alvear,
  Buenos Aires,
  Argentina ...... **126 D4** 36 0 S 60 0W
General Alvear,
  Mendoza, *Argentina* . **126 D2** 35 0 S 67 40W
General Artigas,
  Paraguay ...... **126 B4** 26 52 S 56 16W
General Belgrano,
  Argentina ...... **126 D4** 36 35 S 58 47W
General Bernardo
  O'Higgins *Antarctica* **5 C18** 63 0 S 58 3W
General Cabrera,
  Argentina ...... **126 C3** 32 53 S 63 52W
General Cepeda, *Mexico* **118 B4** 25 23N 101 27W
General Guido,
  Argentina ...... **126 D4** 36 40 S 57 50W
General Juan
  Madariaga, *Argentina* **126 D4** 37 0 S 57 0W
General La Madrid,
  Argentina ...... **126 D3** 37 17 S 61 20W
General MacArthur,
  Phil. .... **61 F6** 11 18N 125 28 E
General Martín Miguel
  de Güemes, *Argentina* **126 A3** 24 50 S 65 0W
General Paz, *Argentina* **126 B4** 27 45 S 57 36W
General Pico, *Argentina* **126 D3** 35 45 S 63 50W
General Pinedo,
  Argentina ...... **126 B3** 27 15 S 61 20W
General Pinto,
  Argentina ...... **126 C3** 34 45 S 61 50W
General Roca, *Argentina* **128 D3** 39 2 S 67 35W
General Santos, *Phil.* . **61 H6** 6 5N 125 14 E
General Toshevo,
  Bulgaria ...... **45 C12** 43 42N 28 6 E
General Trevino,
  Mexico **119 B5** 26 14N 99 29W
General Trías, *Mexico* . **118 B3** 28 21N 106 22W
General Viamonte,
  Argentina ...... **126 D3** 35 1 S 61 3W
General Villegas,
  Argentina ...... **126 D3** 35 5 S 63 0W
Genesee, *Idaho, U.S.A.* **108 C5** 46 33N 116 56W
Genesee, *Pa. U.S.A.* .. **116 E7** 41 59N 77 54W
Genesee →, *U.S.A.* .. **116 C7** 43 16N 77 36W
Geneseo, *Ill., U.S.A.* . **112 E9** 41 27N 90 9W
Geneseo, *N.Y., U.S.A.* **116 D7** 42 48N 77 49W
Geneva = Genève,
  Switz. .... **25 J2** 46 12N 6 9 E
Geneva, *Ala. U.S.A.* .. **115 K3** 31 2N 85 52W
Geneva, *N.Y., U.S.A.* . **116 D8** 42 52N 76 59W
Geneva, *Nebr., U.S.A.* **112 E6** 40 32N 97 36W
Geneva, *Ohio, U.S.A.* . **116 E4** 41 48N 80 57W
Geneva, L. = Léman, L.,
  Europe .... **19 F13** 46 26N 6 30 E
Geneva, L., *U.S.A.* .. **114 D1** 42 38N 88 30W
Genève, *Switz.* ...... **25 J2** 46 12N 6 9 E
Gengenbach, *Germany* **25 G4** 48 24N 8 1 E
Gengma, *China* .... **58 F2** 23 32N 99 20 E
Genichesk = Henichesk,
  Ukraine ...... **33 J8** 46 12N 34 50 E
Genil →, *Spain* **37 H5** 37 42N 5 19W
Genk, *Belgium* ...... **17 D5** 50 58N 5 32 E
Genlis, *France* ...... **19 E12** 47 11N 5 12 E
Gennargentu, Mti. del,
  Italy .... **42 B2** 40 1N 9 19 E
Gennes, *France* **18 E6** 47 20N 0 17W
Genoa = Génova, *Italy* **40 D5** 44 25N 8 57 E
Genoa, *Australia* .... **95 F4** 37 29 S 149 35 E
Genoa, *N.Y., U.S.A.* .. **117 D8** 42 40N 76 32W
Genoa, *Nebr. U.S.A.* . **112 E6** 41 27N 97 44W
Genoa, *Nev., U.S.A.* . **110 F7** 39 2N 119 50W
Génova, *Italy* ...... **40 D5** 44 25N 8 57 E
Génova ✈ (GOA), *Italy* **40 D5** 44 25N 8 56 E
Génova, G. d., *Italy* . **40 E6** 44 0N 9 0 E
Genriyetty, Ostrov,
  Russia .... **53 B16** 77 6N 156 30 E
Gent, *Belgium* ...... **17 C3** 51 2N 3 42 E
Genteng, Bal., *Indonesia* **63 J17** 8 22 S 114 9 E
Genteng, Jawa,
  Indonesia ...... **63 G12** 7 22 S 106 24 E
Genthin, *Germany* .... **24 C8** 52 25N 12 9 E
Genyem, *Indonesia* .. **63 E10** 2 46 S 140 12 E
Genzano di Lucánia,
  Italy .... **43 B9** 40 51N 16 2 E
Genzano di Roma, *Italy* **41 G9** 41 42N 12 41 E
Geoagiu, *Romania* .... **29 E8** 45 55N 23 12 E
Geographe B., *Australia* **93 F2** 33 30 S 115 15 E
Geographe Chan.,
  Australia ...... **93 D1** 24 30 S 113 0 E
Geokchay = Göyçay,
  Azerbaijan ...... **35 K8** 40 42N 47 43 E
Georg Forster,
  Antarctica ...... **5 D3** 71 0 S 12 0 E
Georg von Neumayer,
  Antarctica ...... **5 D17** 71 0 S 68 30W
Georga, Zemlya, *Russia* **52 A5** 80 30N 49 0 E
George, *S. Africa* .... **88 E3** 33 58 S 22 29 E
George →, *Canada* .. **105 A6** 58 49N 66 10W
George, L., *N.S.W.,*
  Australia ...... **95 F4** 35 10 S 149 25 E
George, L., *S. Austral.,*
  Australia ...... **95 F3** 37 25 S 140 0 E
George, L., *W. Austral.,*
  Australia ...... **92 D3** 22 45 S 123 40 E
George, L., *Uganda* .. **86 B3** 0 5N 30 10 E
George, L., *Fla., U.S.A.* **115 L5** 29 17N 81 36W
George, L., *N.Y., U.S.A.* **117 C11** 43 37N 73 33W
George Gill Ra.,
  Australia ...... **92 D5** 24 22 S 131 45 E
George Pt., *Australia* . **94 J6** 20 6 S 148 36 E
George River =
  Kangiqsualujjuaq,
  Canada **101 C13** 58 30N 65 59W
George Sound, *N.Z.* .. **91 L1** 44 52 S 167 25 E
George Town, *Bahamas* **120 B4** 23 33N 75 47W
George Town,
  Cayman Is. **120 C3** 19 20N 81 24W
George Town, *Malaysia* **65 c** 5 25N 100 20 E
George V Land,
  Antarctica ...... **5 C10** 69 0 S 148 0 E

George VI Sound,
  Antarctica ...... **5 D17** 71 0 S 68 0W
George West, *U.S.A.* . **113 L5** 28 20N 98 7W
Georgetown =
  Janjanbureh, *Gambia* **82 C2** 13 30N 14 47W
Georgetown, *Australia* **94 B3** 18 17 S 143 33 E
Georgetown, *Ont.,*
  Canada **116 C5** 43 40N 79 56W
Georgetown, *P.E.I.,*
  Canada **105 C7** 46 13N 62 24W
Georgetown, *Guyana* . **124 B7** 6 50N 58 12W
Georgetown, *Calif.,*
  U.S.A. **110 G6** 38 54N 120 50W
Georgetown, *Colo.,*
  U.S.A. **108 G11** 39 42N 105 42W
Georgetown, *Ky., U.S.A.* **114 F3** 38 13N 84 33W
Georgetown, *N.Y.,*
  U.S.A. **117 D9** 42 46N 75 44W
Georgetown, *Ohio,*
  U.S.A. **114 F4** 38 52N 83 54W
Georgetown, *S.C.,*
  U.S.A. **115 J6** 33 23N 79 17W
Georgetown, *Tex.,*
  U.S.A. **113 K6** 30 38N 97 41W
Georgia □, *U.S.A.* .. **115 K5** 32 50N 83 15W
Georgia ■, *Asia* .... **35 J6** 42 0N 43 0 E
Georgia, Str. of, *Canada* **102 D4** 49 25N 124 0W
Georgian B., *Canada* .. **116 A4** 45 15N 81 0W
Georgina →, *Australia* **94 C2** 23 30 S 139 47 E
Georgina I., *Canada* .. **116 B5** 44 22N 79 17W
Georgiyevsk, *Russia* .. **35 H6** 44 12N 43 28 E
Georgsmarienhütte,
  Germany .... **24 C4** 52 13N 8 1 E
Gera, *Germany* ...... **24 E8** 50 53N 12 4 E
Geraardsbergen,
  Belgium .... **17 D3** 50 45N 3 53 E
Geral, Serra, *Brazil* .. **127 B6** 26 25 S 50 0W
Geral de Goiás, Serra,
  Brazil .... **125 F9** 12 0 S 46 0W
Geraldine, *U.S.A.* **108 C8** 47 36N 110 16W
Geraldton, *Australia* .. **93 E1** 28 48 S 114 32 E
Geraldton, *Canada* .. **104 C2** 49 44N 86 59W
Gérardmer, *France* .. **19 D13** 48 3N 6 50 E
Gerçüş, *Turkey* .... **73 D9** 37 34N 41 23 E
Gerede, *Turkey* .... **72 B5** 40 47N 32 10 E
Gerês, Sierra do,
  Portugal **36 D3** 41 48N 8 0W
Gereshk, *Afghan.* .... **66 D4** 31 47N 64 35 E
Geretsried, *Germany* .. **25 H7** 47 51N 11 28 E
Gérgal, *Spain* **39 H2** 37 7N 2 31W
Gerik, *Malaysia* .... **65 K3** 5 50N 101 15 E
Gering, *U.S.A.* **112 E3** 41 50N 103 40W
Gerlach, *U.S.A.* **108 F4** 40 39N 119 21W
Gerlachovský štít,
  Slovak Rep. ...... **27 B13** 49 11N 20 7 E
German Planina,
  Macedonia ...... **44 D6** 42 20N 22 0 E
Germansen Landing,
  Canada **102 B4** 55 43N 124 40W
Germantown, *U.S.A.* . **113 M10** 35 5N 89 49W
Germany ■, *Europe* .. **24 E6** 51 0N 10 0 E
Germencik, *Turkey* .. **47 D9** 37 52N 27 37 E
Germering, *Germany* .. **25 G7** 48 8N 11 22 E
Germersheim, *Germany* **25 F4** 49 12N 8 22 E
Germí, *Iran* .... **71 B6** 39 1N 48 3 E
Germiston, *S. Africa* . **89 D4** 26 15 S 28 10 E
Gernika-Lumo, *Spain* . **38 B2** 43 19N 2 40W
Gernsheim, *Germany* .. **25 F4** 49 45N 8 30 E
Gero, *Japan* .... **55 G8** 35 48N 137 14 E
Gerokgak, *Indonesia* .. **63 J17** 8 11 S 114 27 E
Gerolzhofen, *Germany* **25 F6** 49 54N 10 21 E
Gerona = Girona, *Spain* **38 D7** 41 58N 2 46 E
Gerrard, *Canada* **102 C5** 50 30N 117 17W
Gers □, *France* .... **20 E4** 43 35N 0 30 E
Gers →, *France* .... **20 D4** 44 9N 0 39 E
Gersfeld, *Germany* .. **24 E5** 50 27N 9 56 E
Gersthofen, *Germany* . **25 G6** 48 25N 10 53 E
Gertak Sanggul,
  Malaysia ...... **65 c** 5 17N 100 12 E
Gertak Sanggul,
  Tanjung, *Malaysia* .. **65 c** 5 16N 100 11 E
Gerung, *Indonesia* .. **63 K19** 8 43 S 116 7 E
Gerzat, *France* .... **20 C7** 45 48N 3 8 E
Gerze, *Turkey* ...... **72 B6** 41 48N 35 12 E
Geseke, *Germany* .... **24 D4** 51 38N 8 31 E
Geser, *Indonesia* .... **63 E8** 3 50 S 130 54 E
Gesso →, *Italy* .... **40 D4** 44 24N 7 33 E
Gestro, Wabi →,
  Ethiopia .... **81 G5** 4 12N 42 2 E
Getafe, *Spain* **36 E7** 40 18N 3 44W
Getinge, *Sweden* .... **11 H6** 56 49N 12 44 E
Gettysburg, *Pa., U.S.A.* **114 F7** 39 50N 77 14W
Gettysburg, *S. Dak.,*
  U.S.A. **112 C5** 45 1N 99 57W
Getxo, *Spain* **38 B2** 43 21N 2 59W
Getz Ice Shelf,
  Antarctica ...... **5 D14** 75 0 S 130 0W
Gevaş, *Turkey* ...... **73 C10** 38 15N 43 6 E
Gévaudan, *France* .. **20 D7** 44 40N 3 40 E
Gevgelija, *Macedonia* . **44 E6** 41 9N 22 30 E
Gévora →, *Spain* .. **37 G4** 38 53N 6 57W
Gewani, *Ethiopia* .... **81 E5** 10 12N 40 40 E
Gex, *France* .... **19 F13** 46 21N 6 3 E
Geyikli, *Turkey* .... **47 B8** 39 48N 26 12 E
Geyser, *U.S.A.* **108 C8** 47 16N 110 30W
Geyserville, *U.S.A.* .. **110 G4** 38 42N 122 54W
Geyve, *Turkey* ...... **72 B4** 40 30N 30 18 E
Ghâbat el Arab = Wang
  Kai, *Sudan* ...... **81 F2** 9 3N 29 23 E
Ghabeish, *Sudan* .... **81 E2** 12 9N 27 21 E
Ghaggar →, *India* .. **68 E6** 29 30N 74 53 E
Ghaghara →, *India* .. **69 G11** 25 45N 84 40 E
Ghaghat →, *India* .. **69 G13** 25 19N 89 38 E
Ghagra, *India* ...... **69 H11** 23 17N 84 33 E
Ghagra →, *India* .. **69 F9** 27 29N 81 9 E
Ghalla, Wadi el →,
  Sudan .... **81 E2** 10 25N 27 32 E
Ghana ■, *W. Afr.* .. **83 D4** 8 0N 1 0W
Ghansor, *India* ...... **69 H9** 22 39N 80 1 E
Ghanzi, *Botswana* .. **88 C3** 21 50 S 21 34 E
Gharb el Istiwa'iya □,
  Sudan .... **81 G3** 5 0N 30 0 E
Gharb Kordofân □,
  Sudan .... **81 E2** 12 0N 28 0 E
Gharbîya, Es Sahrâ el,
  Egypt .... **80 B2** 27 40N 26 30 E
Ghardaïa, *Algeria* .... **78 B6** 32 20N 3 37 E
Ghârib, *Sudan* ...... **81 E3** 13 0N 33 58 E
Ghârib, Mt., *Egypt* .. **80 B3** 28 6N 32 54 E
Gharyân, *Libya* .... **79 B8** 32 10N 13 0 E
Ghat, *Libya* .... **79 D8** 24 59N 10 11 E
Ghatal, *India* ...... **69 H12** 22 40N 87 46 E
Ghatampur, *India* .. **69 F9** 26 8N 80 13 E
Ghats, Eastern, *India* . **66 N11** 14 0N 78 50 E
Ghats, Western, *India* **66 N9** 14 0N 75 0 E

Ghatsila, *India* ...... **69 H12** 22 36N 86 29 E
Ghaṭṭī, *Si. Arabia* .. **70 D3** 31 16N 37 31 E
Ghawdex = Gozo, *Malta* **49 C1** 36 3N 14 15 E
Ghazal, Bahr el →,
  Chad .... **79 F9** 13 0N 15 47 E
Ghazâl, Bahr el →,
  Sudan .... **81 F3** 9 31N 30 25 E
Ghaziabad, *India* .... **68 E7** 28 42N 77 26 E
Ghazipur, *India* .... **69 G10** 25 38N 83 35 E
Ghazni, *Afghan.* .... **68 C3** 33 30N 68 28 E
Ghazni □, *Afghan.* .. **66 C3** 33 0N 68 0 E
Ghedi, *Italy* .... **40 C7** 45 24N 10 16 E
Ghelari, *Romania* .... **28 E7** 45 38N 22 45 E
Ghent = Gent, *Belgium* **17 C3** 51 2N 3 42 E
Gheorghe Gheorghiu-
  Dej = Onești,
  Romania ...... **29 D11** 46 17N 26 47 E
Gheorgheni, *Romania* . **29 D10** 46 43N 25 41 E
Gherla, *Romania* .... **29 C8** 47 2N 23 57 E
Ghidigeni, *Romania* .. **29 D12** 46 3N 27 30 E
Ghilarza, *Italy* ...... **42 B1** 40 7N 8 50 E
Ghimeş-Făget, *Romania* **29 D11** 46 35N 26 2 E
Ghinah, Wādī al →,
  Si. Arabia ...... **70 D3** 30 27N 38 14 E
Ghisonaccia, *France* .. **21 F13** 42 1N 9 26 E
Ghisoni, *France* .... **21 F13** 42 7N 9 12 E
Ghizao, *Afghan.* .... **68 C1** 33 20N 65 44 E
Ghizar →, *Pakistan* .. **69 A5** 36 15N 73 43 E
Ghot Ogrein, *Egypt* .. **80 A2** 31 10N 25 20 E
Ghotaru, *India* ...... **68 F4** 27 20N 70 1 E
Ghotki, *Pakistan* .... **68 E3** 28 5N 69 21 E
Ghowr □, *Afghan.* .. **66 C4** 34 0N 64 20 E
Ghudāf, W. al →, *Iraq* **70 C4** 32 56N 43 30 E
Ghudāmis, *Libya* .... **77 C4** 30 11N 9 29 E
Ghūghāmis □, *Libya* .. **79 B8** 30 25N 10 25 E
Ghughri, *India* ...... **69 H9** 22 39N 80 41 E
Ghugus, *India* ...... **66 K11** 19 58N 79 12 E
Ghulam Mohammad
  Barrage, *Pakistan* .. **68 G3** 25 30N 68 20 E
Ghūrīān, *Afghan.* .... **66 B2** 34 17N 61 25 E
Gia Dinh, *Vietnam* .. **65 G6** 10 49N 106 42 E
Gia Lai = Plei Ku,
  Vietnam ...... **64 F7** 13 57N 108 0 E
Gia Nghia, *Vietnam* .. **65 G6** 11 58N 107 42 E
Gia Ngoc, *Vietnam* .. **64 E7** 14 50N 108 58 E
Gia Vuc, *Vietnam* .. **64 E7** 14 42N 108 34 E
Giannutri, *Italy* .... **40 F8** 42 15N 11 6 E
Giant Forest, *U.S.A.* . **110 J8** 36 36N 118 43W
Giant Mts. = Krkonoše,
  Czech Rep. ...... **26 A8** 50 50N 15 35 E
Giant Sequoia □, *U.S.A.* **110 K8** 36 0N 118 32W
Giants Causeway, *U.K.* **12 A5** 55 16N 6 29W
Gianyar, *Indonesia* .. **63 K18** 8 32 S 115 20 E
Giarabub = Al Jaghbūb,
  Libya .... **79 C10** 29 42N 24 38 E
Giarre, *Italy* .... **43 E8** 37 43N 15 11 E
Giaveno, *Italy* ...... **40 C4** 45 3N 7 20 E
Gibara, *Cuba* **120 B4** 21 9N 76 11W
Gibb River, *Australia* . **92 C4** 16 26 S 126 26 E
Gibbon, *U.S.A.* **112 E5** 40 45N 98 51W
Gibe →, *Ethiopia* .. **81 F4** 7 20N 37 36 E
Gibellina Nuova, *Italy* . **42 E5** 37 47N 12 58 E
Gibeon, *Namibia* .... **88 D2** 25 9 S 17 43 E
Gibraléon, *Spain* **37 H4** 37 23N 6 58W
Gibraltar ☑, *Europe* . **37 J5** 36 7N 5 22W
Gibraltar, Str. of,
  Medit. S. **37 K5** 35 55N 5 40W
Gibraltar Range △,
  Australia ...... **95 D5** 29 31 S 152 19 E
Gibson Desert, *Australia* **92 D4** 24 0 S 126 0 E
Gibsons, *Canada* **102 D4** 49 24N 123 32W
Gibsonville, *U.S.A.* .. **110 F6** 39 46N 120 54W
Giddings, *U.S.A.* **113 K6** 30 11N 96 56W
Gidole, *Ethiopia* .... **81 F4** 5 40N 37 25 E
Giebnegáisi =
  Kebnekaise, *Sweden* . **8 C18** 67 53N 18 33 E
Gien, *France* ...... **19 E9** 47 40N 2 36 E
Giengen, *Germany* .. **25 G6** 48 37N 10 14 E
Giessen, *Germany* .. **24 E4** 50 34N 8 41 E
Gīfan, *Iran* .... **71 B8** 37 54N 57 28 E
Gifatin, Geziret, *Egypt* **80 B3** 27 10N 33 50 E
Gifhorn, *Germany* .... **24 C6** 52 30N 10 33 E
Gift Lake, *Canada* .. **102 B5** 55 53N 115 49W
Gifu, *Japan* ...... **55 G8** 35 30N 136 45 E
Gifu □, *Japan* ...... **55 G8** 35 40N 137 0 E
Gigant, *Russia* ...... **35 G5** 46 28N 41 20 E
Giganta, Sa. de la,
  Mexico **118 B2** 25 30N 111 30W
Gigen, *Bulgaria* .... **45 C8** 43 40N 24 28 E
Gigha, *U.K.* **13 F3** 55 42N 5 44W
Giglio, *Italy* .... **40 F7** 42 20N 10 52 E
Gignac, *France* .... **20 E7** 43 39N 3 32 E
Giguela →, *Spain* .. **37 F7** 39 8N 3 44W
Gijón, *Spain* **36 B5** 43 32N 5 42W
Gila →, *U.S.A.* **109 K6** 32 43N 114 33W
Gila Bend, *U.S.A.* .. **109 K7** 32 57N 112 43W
Gila Bend Mts., *U.S.A.* **109 K7** 33 10N 113 0W
Gila Cliff Dwellings △,
  U.S.A. **109 K9** 33 12N 108 16W
Gīlān □, *Iran* ...... **71 B6** 37 0N 50 0 E
Gilău, *Romania* .... **29 D8** 46 45N 23 23 E
Gilbert →, *Australia* . **94 B3** 16 35 S 141 15 E
Gilbert Is., *Kiribati* .. **96 G9** 1 0N 172 0 E
Gilbert River, *Australia* **94 B3** 18 9 S 142 52 E
Gilead, *U.S.A.* **117 B14** 44 24N 70 59W
Gilf el Kebîr, Hadabat
  el, *Egypt* ...... **80 C2** 23 50N 25 50 E
Gilford I., *Canada* .. **102 C3** 50 40N 126 30W
Gilgandra, *Australia* . **95 E4** 31 43 S 148 39 E
Gilgil, *Kenya* ...... **86 C4** 0 30 S 36 20 E
Gilgit, *India* ...... **69 B6** 35 50N 74 15 E
Gilgit →, *Pakistan* .. **69 B6** 35 44N 74 37 E
Gili △, *Mozam.* .... **87 F4** 16 39 S 38 27 E
Gilimanuk, *Indonesia* . **63 J17** 8 10 S 114 26 E
Giljeva Planina,
  Serbia & M. ...... **44 C3** 43 9N 20 0 E
Gillam, *Canada* **103 B10** 56 20N 94 40W
Gilleleje, *Denmark* .. **11 H6** 56 8N 12 19 E
Gillen, L., *Australia* .. **93 E3** 26 11 S 124 38 E
Gilles, L., *Australia* .. **95 E2** 32 50 S 136 45 E
Gillette, *U.S.A.* **112 C2** 44 18N 105 30W
Gilliat, *Australia* .... **94 C3** 20 40 S 141 28 E
Gillingham, *U.K.* .... **15 F8** 51 23N 0 33 E
Gilmer, *U.S.A.* **113 J7** 32 44N 94 57W
Gilmore, *Australia* .. **93 F3** 32 29 S 121 37 E
Gilmore, L., *Australia* **93 F3** 32 29 S 121 37 E
Gilo →, *Ethiopia* .. **81 F3** 8 10N 33 15 E
Gilort →, *Romania* .. **29 F8** 44 38N 23 32 E
Gilroy, *U.S.A.* **110 H5** 37 1N 121 34W
Gimbi, *Ethiopia* .... **81 F4** 9 3N 35 42 E
Gimie, Mt, *St. Lucia* . **121 f** 13 54N 61 0W
Gimli, *Canada* **103 C9** 50 40N 97 0W
Gimone →, *France* .. **20 E5** 44 0N 1 6 E
Gimont, *France* .... **20 E4** 43 38N 0 52 E
Gin Gin, *Australia* .. **95 D5** 25 0 S 151 58 E
Ginâh, *Egypt* ...... **80 B3** 25 21N 30 30 E

Gineifa, *Egypt* ...... **80 H8** 30 12N 32 25 E
Gingin, *Australia* .... **93 F2** 31 22 S 115 54 E
Gingindlovu, *S. Africa* **89 D5** 29 2 S 31 30 E
Ginir, *Ethiopia* ...... **81 F5** 7 6N 40 40 E
Ginosa, *Italy* ...... **43 B9** 40 35N 16 45 E
Ginzo de Limia = Xinzo
  de Limia, *Spain* .. **36 C3** 42 3N 7 47W
Gióia, G. di, *Italy* .. **43 D8** 38 30N 15 45 E
Gióia del Colle, *Italy* . **43 B9** 40 48N 16 55 E
Gióia Táuro, *Italy* .. **43 D8** 38 25N 15 54 E
Gioiosa Iónica, *Italy* . **43 D9** 38 20N 16 18 E
Gioiosa Marea, *Italy* . **43 D7** 38 10N 14 54 E
Gióna, Óros, *Greece* .. **46 C4** 38 38N 22 14 E
Giovi, Passo dei, *Italy* **40 D5** 44 33N 8 57 E
Giovinazzo, *Italy* .... **43 A9** 41 11N 16 40 E
Gir Hills, *India* ...... **68 J4** 21 0N 71 0 E
Girab, *India* .... **68 F4** 26 2N 70 38 E
Girâfi, W. →, *Egypt* . **74 F3** 29 58N 34 39 E
Giraltovce, *Slovak Rep.* **27 B14** 49 7N 21 32 E
Girard, *Kans., U.S.A.* . **113 G7** 37 31N 94 51W
Girard, *Ohio, U.S.A.* . **116 E4** 41 9N 80 42W
Girard, *Pa., U.S.A.* .. **116 E4** 42 0N 80 19W
Girdle Ness, *U.K.* .. **13 D6** 57 9N 2 3W
Giresun, *Turkey* .... **73 B8** 40 55N 38 30 E
Girga, *Egypt* ...... **80 B3** 26 17N 31 55 E
Giri →, *India* ...... **68 D7** 30 28N 77 41 E
Giridih, *India* ...... **69 G12** 24 10N 86 21 E
Girifalco, *Italy* ...... **43 D9** 38 49N 16 25 E
Girne = Kyrenia, *Cyprus* **49 D12** 35 20N 33 20 E
Giro, *Nigeria* ...... **83 C5** 11 7N 4 42 E
Giromagny, *France* .. **19 E13** 47 45N 6 50 E
Giron = Kiruna, *Sweden* **8 C19** 67 52N 20 15 E
Girona, *Spain* ...... **38 D7** 41 58N 2 46 E
Girona □, *Spain* .... **38 C7** 42 11N 2 30 E
Gironde □, *France* .. **20 D3** 44 45N 0 30W
Gironde →, *France* .. **20 C2** 45 32N 1 7W
Gironella, *Spain* .... **38 C6** 42 2N 1 53 E
Girraween △, *Australia* **95 D5** 28 46 S 151 54 E
Giru, *Australia* ...... **94 B4** 19 30 S 147 5 E
Girvan, *U.K.* **13 F4** 55 14N 4 51W
Gisborne, *N.Z.* ...... **91 H7** 38 39 S 178 5 E
Gisenyi, *Rwanda* .... **86 C2** 1 41 S 29 15 E
Gislaved, *Sweden* .... **11 G7** 57 19N 13 32 E
Gisors, *France* ...... **19 C8** 49 15N 1 47 E
Gitega, *Burundi* .... **86 C2** 3 26 S 29 56 E
Giuba →, *Somali Rep.* **75 G3** 1 30N 42 35 E
Giugliano in Campania,
  Italy .... **43 B7** 40 55N 14 12 E
Giuliano, *Italy* ...... **41 F10** 42 45N 13 57 E
Giurgeni, *Romania* .. **29 F12** 44 45N 27 48 E
Giurgiu, *Romania* .... **29 G10** 43 52N 25 57 E
Giurgiu □, *Romania* .. **29 F10** 44 20N 26 0 E
Giurgiulești, *Moldova* . **29 E13** 45 29N 28 12 E
Give, *Denmark* ...... **11 J3** 55 51N 9 13 E
Givet, *France* ...... **19 B11** 50 8N 4 49 E
Givors, *France* ...... **21 C8** 45 35N 4 45 E
Givry, *France* ...... **19 F11** 46 41N 4 46 E
Giyon, *Ethiopia* .... **81 F4** 8 33N 38 1 E
Giza = El Gîza, *Egypt* **80 J7** 30 0N 31 10 E
Gizhiga, *Russia* .... **53 C17** 62 3N 160 30 E
Gizhiginskaya Guba,
  Russia .... **53 C16** 61 0N 158 0 E
Giżycko, *Poland* .... **30 D8** 54 2N 21 48 E
Gizzeria, *Italy* ...... **43 D9** 38 59N 16 12 E
Gjalicë e Lumës, Mal.,
  Albania ...... **44 D4** 42 2N 20 25 E
Gjegjan, *Albania* .... **44 E4** 41 58N 20 3 E
Gjirokastër, *Albania* . **44 F4** 40 7N 20 10 E
Gjoa Haven, *Canada* . **100 B10** 68 38N 95 53W
Gjøvik, *Norway* .... **9 F14** 60 47N 10 43 E
Gjuhës, Kep i, *Albania* **44 F3** 40 28N 19 15 E
Glace Bay, *Canada* .. **105 C8** 46 11N 59 58W
Glacier △, *Canada* .. **102 C5** 51 15N 117 30W
Glacier △, *U.S.A.* .. **108 B7** 48 30N 113 18W
Glacier Bay △, *U.S.A.* **102 B1** 58 45N 136 30W
Glacier Bay △, *U.S.A.* **108 B3** 48 7N 121 7W
Gladewater, *U.S.A.* .. **113 J7** 32 33N 94 56W
Gladstone, Queens.,
  Australia ...... **94 C5** 23 52 S 151 16 E
Gladstone, *S. Austral.,*
  Australia ...... **95 E2** 33 15 S 138 22 E
Gladstone, *Canada* .. **103 C9** 50 13N 98 57W
Gladstone, *U.S.A.* .. **114 C2** 45 51N 87 1W
Gladwin, *U.S.A.* **114 D3** 43 59N 84 29W
Glafsfjorden, *Sweden* . **10 E6** 59 30N 12 18 E
Glagah, *Indonesia* .. **63 J17** 8 13 S 114 18 E
Głagów Małopolski,
  Poland .... **31 H8** 50 10N 21 56 E
Glåma = Glomma →,
  Norway ...... **9 G14** 59 12N 10 57 E
Gláma, *Iceland* **8 D2** 65 48N 23 0W
Glamis, *U.S.A.* **111 N11** 32 55N 115 5W
Glamoč, *Bos.-H.* .... **41 D13** 44 3N 16 51 E
Glamorgan, Vale of □,
  U.K. **15 F4** 51 28N 3 25W
Glamsbjerg, *Denmark* . **11 J4** 55 17N 10 6 E
Glarus, *Switz.* ...... **25 H5** 47 3N 9 4 E
Glarus □, *Switz.* .... **25 J5** 47 0N 9 5 E
Glasco, *Kans., U.S.A.* **112 F6** 39 22N 97 50W
Glasco, *N.Y., U.S.A.* . **117 D11** 42 3N 73 57W
Glasgow, *U.K.* **13 F4** 55 51N 4 15W
Glasgow, *Ky., U.S.A.* . **114 G3** 37 0N 85 55W
Glasgow, *Mont., U.S.A.* **108 B10** 48 12N 106 38W
Glasgow, City of □, *U.K.* **13 F4** 55 51N 4 12W
Glasgow International ✈
  (GLA), *U.K.* **13 F4** 55 51N 4 21W
Glaslyn, *Canada* **103 C7** 53 22N 108 21W
Glastonbury, *U.K.* .. **15 F5** 51 9N 2 43W
Glastonbury, *U.S.A.* . **117 E12** 41 43N 72 37W
Glauchau, *Germany* .. **24 E8** 50 49N 12 31 E
Glava, *Sweden* ...... **10 E6** 59 33N 12 18 E
Glavice, *Croatia* .... **41 E13** 43 43N 16 41 E
Glazov, *Russia* ...... **34 A11** 58 9N 52 40 E
Gleichen, *Canada* .. **102 C6** 50 52N 113 3W
Gleisdorf, *Austria* .. **26 D8** 47 6N 15 44 E
Gleiwitz = Gliwice,
  Poland .... **31 H5** 50 22N 18 41 E
Glen, *U.S.A.* **117 B13** 44 7N 71 11W
Glen Affric, *U.K.* **13 D3** 57 17N 5 1W
Glen Canyon, *U.S.A.* . **109 H8** 37 15N 111 0W
Glen Canyon △, *U.S.A.* **109 H8** 37 15N 111 0W
Glen Canyon Dam,
  U.S.A. **109 H8** 36 57N 111 29W
Glen Coe, *U.K.* **13 E3** 56 40N 5 0W
Glen Cove, *U.S.A.* .. **117 F11** 40 52N 73 38W
Glen Garry, *U.K.* **13 D3** 57 3N 5 7W
Glen Innes, *Australia* **95 D5** 29 44 S 151 44 E
Glen Lyon, *U.S.A.* .. **117 E8** 41 10N 76 5W
Glen Mor, *U.K.* **13 D4** 57 9N 4 37W
Glen More △, *U.K.* .. **13 D5** 57 8N 3 40W
Glen Moriston, *U.K.* . **13 D4** 57 11N 4 52W
Glen Robertson, *Canada* **117 A10** 45 22N 74 30W
Glen Spean, *U.K.* **13 E4** 56 53N 4 40W
Glen Ullin, *U.S.A.* .. **112 B4** 46 49N 101 50W
Glénan, Îs. de, *France* **18 E3** 47 42N 4 0W
Glenarm △, *Ireland* .. **12 A5** 55 2N 6 10W
Glencoe, *Canada* .. **116 D3** 42 45N 81 43W

Glencoe, S. Africa .... 89 D5 28 11 S 30 11 E
Glencoe, U.S.A. 112 C7 44 46N 94 9W
Glendale, Ariz., U.S.A. 109 K7 33 32N 112 11W
Glendale, Calif., U.S.A. 111 L8 34 9N 118 15W
Glendale, Zimbabwe .. 87 F3 17 22 S 31 5 E
Glendive, U.S.A. 112 B2 47 7N 104 43W
Glendo, U.S.A. 112 D2 42 30N 105 2W
Glenelg →, Australia .. 95 F3 38 4 S 140 59 E
Glenfield, U.S.A. 117 C9 43 43N 75 24W
Glengarriff, Ireland .. 12 E2 51 45N 9 34W
Glenmont, U.S.A. 116 F2 40 31N 82 6W
Glenmorgan, Australia 95 D4 27 14 S 149 42 E
Glenn, U.S.A. 114 F4 39 31N 122 1W
Glennallen, U.S.A. ... 100 B5 62 7N 145 33W
Glennamaddy, Ireland . 12 C3 53 37N 8 33W
Glenns Ferry, U.S.A. . 108 E6 42 57N 115 18W
Glenore, Australia .... 94 B3 17 50 S 141 12 E
Glenreagh, Australia .. 95 E5 30 2 S 153 1 E
Glenrock, U.S.A. 108 E11 42 52N 105 52W
Glenrothes, U.K. 13 E5 56 12N 3 10W
Glens Falls, U.S.A. ... 117 C11 43 19N 73 39W
Glenside, U.S.A. 117 F9 40 6N 75 9W
Glenties, Ireland 12 B3 54 49N 8 16W
Glenveagh △, Ireland . 12 A3 55 3N 8 1W
Glenville, U.S.A. 114 F5 38 56N 80 50W
Glenwood, Canada 105 C9 49 0N 54 58W
Glenwood, Ark., U.S.A. 113 H8 34 20N 93 33W
Glenwood, Iowa, U.S.A. 112 E7 41 3N 95 45W
Glenwood, Minn.,
 U.S.A. 112 C7 45 39N 95 23W
Glenwood, Wash.,
 U.S.A. 110 D5 46 1N 121 17W
Glenwood Springs,
 U.S.A. 108 G10 39 33N 107 19W
Glettinganes, Iceland .. 8 D7 65 30N 13 37W
Glifádha, Greece ..... 46 D5 37 52N 23 45 E
Glímåkra, Sweden .... 11 H8 56 19N 14 7 E
Glina, Croatia .... 41 C13 45 20N 16 6 E
Glinojeck, Poland .... 31 F7 52 49N 20 21 E
Gliwice, Poland ...... 31 H5 50 22N 18 41 E
Globe, U.S.A. 109 K8 33 24N 110 47W
Glodeanu Siliştea,
 Romania .... 29 F11 44 50N 26 48 E
Glodeni, Moldova .... 29 C12 47 45N 27 31 E
Glödnitz, Austria ..... 26 E7 46 53N 14 7 E
Gloggnitz, Austria .... 26 D8 47 41N 15 56 E
Głogów, Poland ...... 31 G3 51 37N 16 5 E
Głogówek, Poland .... 31 H4 50 21N 17 53 E
Glomma →, Norway .. 9 G14 59 12N 10 57 E
Glorieuses, Is., Ind. Oc. 89 A8 11 30 S 47 20 E
Glóssa, Greece ...... 46 B5 39 10N 23 45 E
Glossop, U.K. 14 D6 53 27N 1 56W
Gloucester, Australia .. 95 E5 32 0 S 151 59 E
Gloucester, U.K. 15 F5 51 53N 2 15W
Gloucester, U.S.A. ... 117 D14 42 37N 70 40W
Gloucester I., Australia 94 J6 20 0 S 148 30 E
Gloucester Island △,
 Australia .... 94 J6 20 2 S 148 30 E
Gloucester Point, U.S.A. 114 G7 37 15N 76 29W
Gloucestershire □, U.K. 15 F5 51 46N 2 15W
Gloversville, U.S.A. ... 117 C10 43 3N 74 21W
Glovertown, Canada .. 105 C9 48 40N 54 3W
Głowno, Poland ...... 31 G6 51 59N 19 42 E
Głubczyce, Poland .... 31 H4 50 13N 17 52 E
Glubokiy, Russia ..... 35 F5 48 35N 40 25 E
Glubokoye =
 Hlybokaye, Belarus . 32 E4 55 10N 27 45 E
Głuchołazy, Poland ... 31 H4 50 19N 17 24 E
Glücksburg, Germany . 24 A5 54 50N 9 33 E
Glückstadt, Germany . 24 B5 53 45N 9 25 E
Glukhov = Hlukhiv,
 Ukraine .... 33 G7 51 40N 33 58 E
Glusk, Belarus .... 33 F5 52 53N 28 41 E
Głuszyca, Poland ..... 31 H3 50 41N 16 23 E
Glyngøre, Denmark ... 11 H2 56 46N 8 52 E
Gmünd, Kärnten,
 Austria .... 26 E6 46 54N 13 31 E
Gmünd,
 Niederösterreich,
 Austria .... 26 C8 48 45N 15 0 E
Gmunden, Austria .... 26 D6 47 55N 13 48 E
Gnarp, Sweden ...... 10 B11 62 3N 17 16 E
Gnesta, Sweden ...... 10 E11 59 3N 17 17 E
Gniew, Poland .... 30 E5 53 50N 18 50 E
Gniewkowo, Poland ... 31 F5 52 54N 18 25 E
Gniezno, Poland ..... 31 F4 52 30N 17 35 E
Gnjilane, Serbia & M. . 44 D5 42 28N 21 29 E
Gnoien, Germany ..... 24 B8 53 58N 12 41 E
Gnosjö, Sweden ...... 11 G7 57 22N 13 43 E
Gnowangerup, Australia 93 F2 33 58 S 117 59 E
Go Cong, Vietnam .... 65 G6 10 22N 106 40 E
Gō-no-ura, Japan .... 55 H4 33 44N 129 40 E
Goa, India .... 66 M8 15 33N 73 59 E
Goa □, India .... 66 M8 15 33N 73 59 E
Goalen Hd., Australia . 95 F5 36 33 S 150 4 E
Goalpara, India ...... 67 F17 26 10N 90 40 E
Goaltor, India .... 69 H12 22 43N 87 10 E
Goalundo Ghat, Bangla. 69 H13 23 50N 89 47 E
Goaso, Ghana 82 D4 6 48N 2 30W
Goat Fell, U.K. 13 F3 55 38N 5 11W
Goba, Ethiopia ...... 81 F4 7 1N 39 59 E
Goba, Mozam. .... 89 D5 26 15 S 32 13 E
Gobabis, Namibia .... 88 C2 22 30 S 19 0 E
Göbel, Turkey .... 45 F12 40 0N 28 9 E
Gobi, Asia .... 56 C6 44 0N 110 0 E
Gobō, Japan .... 55 H7 33 53N 135 10 E
Gobo, Sudan .... 81 F3 5 40N 31 10 E
Göçbeyli, Turkey ..... 47 B9 39 13N 27 25 E
Goch, Germany ...... 24 D2 51 41N 6 9 E
Gochas, Namibia ..... 88 C2 24 59 S 18 55 E
Godalming, U.K. 15 F7 51 11N 0 36W
Godavari →, India .... 67 L13 16 25N 82 18 E
Godavari Pt., India ... 67 L13 17 0N 82 20 E
Godbout, Canada 105 C6 49 20N 67 38W
Godda, India .... 69 G12 24 50N 87 13 E
Goderich, Canada 116 C3 43 45N 81 41W
Goderville, France ... 18 C7 49 38N 0 22 E
Godfrey Ra., Australia . 93 D2 24 0 S 117 0 E
Godhavn =
 Qeqertarsuaq,
 Greenland 101 B14 69 15N 53 38W
Godhra, India .... 68 H5 22 49N 73 40 E
Gödöllő, Hungary .... 28 C4 47 38N 19 25 E
Godoy Cruz, Argentina 126 C2 32 56 S 68 52W
Gods →, Canada 104 A1 56 22N 92 51W
Gods L., Canada 104 B1 54 40N 94 15W
Gods River, Canada ... 103 C10 54 50N 94 5W
Godthåb = Nuuk,
 Greenland 101 B14 64 10N 51 35W
Goeie Hoop, Kaap die =
 Good Hope, C. of,
 S. Africa .... 88 E2 34 24 S 18 30 E
Goéland, L. au, Canada 104 C4 49 50N 76 48W
Goélands, L. aux,
 Canada 105 A7 55 27N 64 17W
Goeree, Neths. ...... 17 C3 51 50N 4 0 E

Goes, Neths. .... 17 C3 51 30N 3 55 E
Goffstown, U.S.A. 117 C13 43 1N 71 36W
Gogama, Canada 104 C3 47 35N 81 43W
Gogebic, L., U.S.A. ... 112 B10 46 30N 89 35W
Gogolin, Poland ...... 31 H5 50 30N 18 0 E
Gogonou, Benin ..... 83 C5 10 50N 2 50 E
Gogra = Ghaghara →,
 India .... 69 G11 25 45N 84 40 E
Gogriâl, Sudan ...... 81 F2 8 30N 28 8 E
Gogti, Ethiopia ...... 81 E5 10 7N 42 51 E
Gohana, India .... 68 E7 29 8N 76 42 E
Goharganj, India ..... 68 H7 23 1N 77 41 E
Goi →, India .... 68 H6 22 4N 74 46 E
Goiânia, Brazil ...... 125 G9 16 43 S 49 20W
Goiás, Brazil .... 125 F8 15 55 S 50 10W
Goiás □, Brazil ...... 125 F9 12 10 S 48 0W
Goio-Erê, Brazil ..... 127 A5 24 12 S 53 1W
Góis, Portugal 36 E2 40 10N 8 6W
Gojam, Ethiopia ..... 81 E4 10 55N 36 30 E
Gojeb, Wabi →,
 Ethiopia .... 81 F4 7 12N 36 40 E
Gojō, Japan .... 55 G7 34 21N 135 42 E
Gojra, Pakistan ..... 68 D5 31 10N 72 40 E
Gökçeada, Turkey .... 45 F9 40 10N 25 50 E
Gökçedağ, Turkey .... 47 B10 39 33N 28 56 E
Gökçen, Turkey ...... 47 C9 38 7N 27 56 E
Gökçeören, Turkey ... 47 C10 38 37N 28 35 E
Gökçeyazı, Turkey ... 47 B9 39 40N 27 40 E
Gökırmak →, Turkey . 72 B6 41 25N 35 8 E
Gökova, Turkey ...... 47 D10 37 1N 28 17 E
Gökova Körfezi, Turkey 47 E9 36 55N 27 50 E
Göksu →, Turkey .... 72 D6 36 15N 34 5 E
Göksun, Turkey ...... 72 C7 38 2N 36 30 E
Göktepe, Turkey ..... 47 D10 37 25N 28 34 E
Gokurt, Pakistan .... 68 E2 29 40N 67 26 E
Gokwe, Zimbabwe .... 89 B4 18 7 S 28 58 E
Gola, India .... 69 E9 28 3N 80 32 E
Golakganj, India ..... 69 F13 26 8N 89 52 E
Golan Heights =
 Hagolan, Syria .... 74 C4 33 0N 35 45 E
Gołańcz, Poland ..... 31 F4 52 57N 17 18 E
Goläshkerd, Iran ..... 71 E8 27 59N 57 16 E
Golaya Pristen = Hola
 Pristan, Ukraine ... 33 J7 46 29N 32 32 E
Gölbaşı, Adıyaman,
 Turkey .... 72 D7 37 43N 37 25 E
Gölbaşı, Ankara, Turkey 72 C5 39 47N 32 49 E
Golchikha, Russia .... 4 B12 71 45N 83 30 E
Golconda, U.S.A. 108 F5 40 58N 117 30W
Gölcük, Kocaeli, Turkey 45 F13 40 42N 29 48 E
Gölcük, Niğde, Turkey 72 C6 38 14N 34 47 E
Gold, U.S.A. 116 E7 41 52N 77 50W
Gold Beach, U.S.A. ... 108 E1 42 25N 124 25W
Gold Coast, W. Afr. .. 83 E4 4 0N 1 40W
Gold Hill, U.S.A. 108 E2 42 26N 123 3W
Gold River, Canada .. 102 D3 49 46N 126 3W
Goldap, Poland ...... 30 D9 54 19N 22 18 E
Goldberg, Germany .. 24 B8 53 35N 12 4 E
Golden, Canada 102 C5 51 20N 116 59W
Golden B., N.Z. ..... 91 J4 40 40 S 172 50 E
Golden Gate, U.S.A. .. 108 H2 37 54N 122 30W
Golden Gate
 Highlands △, S. Africa 89 D4 28 40 S 28 40 E
Golden Hinde, Canada 102 D3 49 40N 125 44W
Golden Lake, Canada . 116 A7 45 34N 77 21W
Golden Spike △, U.S.A. 108 F7 41 37N 112 33W
Golden Vale, Ireland .. 12 D3 52 33N 8 17W
Goldendale, U.S.A. ... 108 D3 45 49N 120 50W
Goldfield, U.S.A. 109 H5 37 42N 117 14W
Goldsand L., Canada . 103 B8 57 2N 101 8W
Goldsboro, U.S.A. 115 H7 35 23N 77 59W
Goldsmith, U.S.A. ... 113 K3 31 59N 102 37W
Goldsworthy, Australia 92 D2 20 21 S 119 30 E
Goldthwaite, U.S.A. .. 113 K5 31 27N 98 34W
Golegã, Portugal 37 F2 39 24N 8 29W
Goleniów, Poland .... 30 E1 53 35N 14 50 E
Golestān □, Iran .... 71 B7 37 20N 55 25 E
Golestānak, Iran ..... 71 D7 30 36N 54 14 E
Goleta, U.S.A. 111 L7 34 27N 119 50W
Golfito, Costa Rica ... 120 E3 8 41N 83 5W
Golfo Aranci, Italy .... 42 B2 40 59N 9 38 E
Golfo di Orosei e del
 Gennargentu △, Italy 42 B2 40 5N 9 15 E
Gölgeli Dağları, Turkey 47 D10 37 10N 28 55 E
Gölhisar, Turkey ..... 47 D11 37 8N 29 32 E
Goliad, U.S.A. 113 L6 28 40N 97 23W
Golija, Serbia & M. ... 44 C2 43 5N 18 45 E
Golija, Serbia & M. ... 44 C4 43 22N 20 15 E
Golina, Poland ...... 31 F5 52 15N 18 4 E
Gölköy, Turkey ...... 72 B7 40 41N 37 37 E
Göllersdorf, Austria .. 26 C9 48 29N 16 7 E
Gölmarmara, Turkey . 47 C9 38 42N 27 55 E
Golo →, France ..... 21 F13 42 31N 9 32 E
Gölova, Turkey ...... 47 E12 36 48N 30 5 E
Golpāyegān, Iran .... 71 C6 33 27N 50 18 E
Gölpazarı, Turkey ... 72 B4 40 16N 30 18 E
Golra, Pakistan ..... 68 C5 33 37N 72 56 E
Golspie, U.K. 13 D5 57 58N 3 59W
Golub-Dobrzyń, Poland 31 E6 53 7N 19 2 E
Golubac, Serbia & M. . 44 B5 44 38N 21 38 E
Golyam Perelik,
 Bulgaria .... 45 E8 41 36N 24 33 E
Golyama Kamchiya →,
 Bulgaria .... 45 C11 43 10N 27 55 E
Goma, Dem. Rep. of
 the Congo .... 86 C2 1 37 S 29 10 E
Gomal Pass, Pakistan . 68 D3 31 56N 69 50 E
Gomati →, India ..... 69 G10 25 32N 83 11 E
Gombari, Dem. Rep. of
 the Congo .... 86 B2 2 45N 29 3 E
Gombe, Nigeria ...... 83 C7 10 19N 11 2 E
Gombe →, Tanzania . 86 C3 4 38 S 31 40 E
Gombe □, Nigeria .... 83 C7 10 15N 11 30 E
Gombi, Nigeria ...... 83 C7 10 12N 12 30 E
Gomel = Homyel,
 Belarus .... 33 F6 52 28N 31 0 E
Gómez Palacio, Mexico 118 B4 25 40N 104 0W
Gomīshān, Iran ..... 71 B7 37 4N 54 6 E
Gommern, Germany .. 24 C7 52 4N 11 50 E
Gomogomo, Indonesia 63 F8 6 39 S 134 43 E
Gomoh, India .... 67 H15 23 52N 86 10 E
Gomotartsi, Bulgaria . 44 B6 44 6N 22 57 E
Gompa = Ganta, Liberia 82 D3 7 15N 8 59W
Gomphi, Greece ..... 46 B3 39 26N 21 36 E
Gonābād, Iran ...... 71 C8 34 15N 58 45 E
Gonaïves, Haiti 121 C5 19 20N 72 42W
Gonarezhou △,
 Zimbabwe .... 87 G3 21 32 S 31 55 E
Gonâve, G. de la, Haiti 121 C5 19 29N 72 42W
Gonâve, Île de la, Haiti 121 C5 18 51N 73 3W
Gonbad-e Kāvūs, Iran 71 B7 37 20N 55 25 E
Gönc, Hungary ...... 28 B6 48 28N 21 14 E
Gonda, India .... 69 F9 27 9N 81 58 E

Gondal, India .... 68 J4 21 58N 70 52 E
Gonder, Ethiopia .... 81 E4 12 39N 37 30 E
Gondia, India .... 66 J12 21 23N 80 10 E
Gondola, Mozam. .... 87 F3 19 10 S 33 37 E
Gondomar, Portugal . 36 D2 41 10N 8 35W
Gondrecourt-le-
 Château, France ... 19 D12 48 31N 5 30 E
Gönen, Balıkesir,
 Turkey .... 45 F11 40 6N 27 39 E
Gönen, Isparta, Turkey 47 D12 37 57N 30 31 E
Gönen →, Turkey .... 45 F11 40 6N 27 39 E
Gong Xian, China .... 58 C5 28 23N 104 47 E
Gong'an, China ...... 59 B9 30 7N 112 12 E
Gongcheng, China .... 59 E8 24 50N 110 49 E
Gongga Shan, China .. 58 C3 29 40N 101 55 E
Gongguan, China .... 58 G7 21 48N 109 36 E
Gonghe, China .... 60 C5 36 18N 100 32 E
Gongola →, Nigeria .. 83 D7 9 30N 12 4 E
Gongolgon, Australia . 95 E4 30 21 S 146 54 E
Gongshan, China .... 58 D2 27 43N 98 29 E
Gongtan, China ...... 58 C7 28 55N 108 20 E
Gongzhuling, China .. 57 C13 43 30N 124 40 E
Goni, Greece .... 46 B4 39 52N 22 29 E
Goniadz, Poland ..... 30 E9 53 30N 22 44 E
Goniri, Nigeria ...... 83 C7 11 30N 12 15 E
Gonjo, China .... 58 B2 30 52N 98 17 E
Gonnesa, Italy ...... 42 C1 39 16N 8 28 E
Gónnos, Greece ...... 46 B4 39 52N 22 29 E
Gonnosfanádiga, Italy . 42 C1 39 30N 8 39 E
Gonzaga, Phil. ...... 61 B5 18 16N 122 6 E
Gonzales, Calif., U.S.A. 110 J5 36 30N 121 26W
Gonzales, Tex., U.S.A. 113 L6 29 30N 97 27W
González Chaves,
 Argentina .... 126 D3 38 2 S 60 5W
Good Hope, C. of,
 S. Africa .... 88 E2 34 24 S 18 30 E
Gooderham, Canada .. 116 B6 44 54N 78 21W
Goodhouse, S. Africa . 88 D2 28 57 S 18 13 E
Gooding, U.S.A. 108 E6 42 56N 114 43W
Goodland, U.S.A. 112 F4 39 21N 101 43W
Goodlow, Canada 102 B4 56 20N 120 8W
Goodooga, Australia .. 95 D4 29 3 S 147 28 E
Goodsprings, U.S.A. .. 111 K11 35 49N 115 27W
Goole, U.K. 14 D7 53 42N 0 53W
Goolgowi, Australia .. 95 E4 33 58 S 145 41 E
Goomalling, Australia . 93 F2 31 15 S 116 49 E
Goomeri, Australia ... 95 D5 26 12 S 152 6 E
Goonda, Mozam. .... 87 F3 19 48 S 33 57 E
Goondiwindi, Australia 95 D5 28 30 S 150 21 E
Goongarrie, Australia . 93 F3 30 7 S 121 30 E
Goongarrie, L.,
 Australia .... 93 F3 30 3 S 121 9 E
Goonyella, Australia .. 94 C4 21 47 S 147 58 E
Goose →, Canada 105 B7 53 20N 60 35W
Goose Creek, U.S.A. .. 115 J5 32 59N 80 2W
Goose L., U.S.A. 108 F3 41 56N 120 26W
Gop, India .... 66 H6 22 5N 69 50 E
Gopalganj, India ..... 69 F11 26 28N 84 30 E
Göppingen, Germany . 25 G5 48 42N 9 39 E
Gor, Spain 37 H8 37 23N 2 58W
Góra, Dolnośląskie,
 Poland .... 31 G3 51 40N 16 31 E
Góra, Mazowieckie,
 Poland .... 31 F7 52 39N 20 6 E
Góra Kalwaria, Poland 31 G8 51 59N 21 14 E
Gorakhpur, India .... 69 F10 26 47N 83 23 E
Goražde, Bos.-H. .... 28 G3 43 38N 18 58 E
Gorbatov, Russia .... 34 B6 56 12N 43 2 E
Gorbea, Peña, Spain .. 38 B2 43 1N 2 50W
Gorczański △, Poland . 31 J7 49 30N 20 10 E
Gorda, U.S.A. 110 K5 35 53N 121 26W
Gorda, Pta., Canary Is. 48 F2 28 45N 18 0W
Gorda, Pta., Nic. 120 D3 14 20N 83 10W
Gordan B., Australia .. 92 B5 11 35 S 130 10 E
Gördes, Turkey ...... 47 C10 38 54N 28 2 E
Gordon, U.S.A. 112 D3 42 48N 102 12W
Gordon →, Australia . 95 G4 42 27 S 145 30 E
Gordon L., Alta.,
 Canada 103 B6 56 30N 110 25W
Gordon L., N.W.T.,
 Canada 102 A6 63 5N 113 11W
Gordonvale, Australia . 94 B4 17 5 S 145 50 E
Gore, Ethiopia ...... 81 F4 8 12N 35 32 E
Gore, N.Z. .... 91 M2 46 5 S 168 58 E
Gore Bay, Canada 104 C3 45 57N 82 28W
Görele, Turkey ...... 73 B8 41 2N 39 0 E
Goreme, Turkey ..... 72 C6 38 35N 34 52 E
Gorey, Ireland 12 D5 52 41N 6 18W
Gorg, Iran .... 71 D8 29 29N 59 43 E
Gorgān, Iran .... 71 B7 36 55N 54 30 E
Gorgona, Italy ...... 40 E6 43 26N 9 54 E
Gorgona, I., Colombia 124 C3 3 0N 78 10W
Gorgora, Ethiopia ... 81 E4 12 15N 37 17 E
Gorgoram, Nigeria ... 83 C7 12 40N 10 45 E
Gorham, U.S.A. 117 B13 44 23N 71 10W
Gori, Georgia .... 35 J7 42 0N 44 7 E
Goriganga →, India .. 69 E9 29 45N 80 23 E
Gorinchem, Neths. ... 17 C4 51 50N 4 59 E
Goris, Armenia ...... 73 C12 39 31N 46 22 E
Goritsy, Russia ...... 32 D9 57 4N 36 43 E
Gorízia, Italy .... 41 C10 45 56N 13 37 E
Gorj □, Romania .... 29 E8 45 5N 23 15 E
Gorki = Horki, Belarus 32 E6 54 17N 30 59 E
Gorki = Nizhniy
 Novgorod, Russia .. 34 B7 56 20N 44 0 E
Gorkiy = Nizhniy
 Novgorod, Russia .. 34 B7 56 20N 44 0 E
Gorkovskoye Vdkhr.,
 Russia .... 34 B6 57 2N 43 4 E
Gorleston, U.K. ..... 15 E9 52 35N 1 44 E
Gorlice, Poland ...... 31 J8 49 35N 21 11 E
Görlitz, Germany .... 24 D10 51 9N 14 58 E
Gorlovka = Horlivka,
 Ukraine .... 33 H10 48 19N 38 5 E
Gorman, U.S.A. 111 L8 34 47N 118 51W
Gorna Dzhumaya =
 Blagoevgrad, Bulgaria 44 D7 42 2N 23 5 E
Gorna Oryakhovitsa,
 Bulgaria .... 45 C9 43 7N 25 40 E
Gornja Radgona,
 Slovenia .... 41 B13 46 40N 16 2 E
Gornja Tuzla, Bos.-H. . 28 F3 44 35N 18 46 E
Gornji Grad, Slovenia . 41 B11 46 20N 14 52 E
Gornji Milanovac,
 Serbia & M. .... 44 B4 44 0N 20 29 E
Gornji Vakuf, Bos.-H. . 28 G2 43 57N 17 34 E
Gorno Ablanovo,
 Bulgaria .... 45 C9 43 37N 25 43 E
Gorno-Altay □, Russia 52 D9 51 0N 86 0 E
Gorno-Altaysk, Russia 52 D9 51 50N 86 5 E
Gornyatskiy, Russia .. 35 F5 48 30N 48 56 E
Gornyi, Saratov, Russia 34 E8 51 50N 48 30 E
Gornyy, Sib., Russia .. 54 B6 44 57N 133 59 E
Gorodenka =
 Horodenka, Ukraine 29 B10 48 41N 25 29 E
Gorodets, Russia .... 34 B6 56 38N 43 28 E
Gorodishche =
 Horodyshche, Ukraine 33 H6 49 17N 31 27 E

Gorodishche, Russia .. 34 D7 53 13N 45 40 E
Gorodnya = Horodnya,
 Ukraine .... 33 G6 51 55N 31 33 E
Gorodok = Haradok,
 Belarus .... 32 E6 55 30N 30 3 E
Gorodok = Horodok,
 Ukraine .... 33 H2 49 46N 23 32 E
Gorodovikovsk, Russia 35 G5 46 8N 41 58 E
Gorokhov = Horokhiv,
 Ukraine .... 33 G3 50 30N 24 45 E
Gorokhovets, Russia .. 34 B6 56 13N 42 39 E
Gorom Gorom,
 Burkina Faso 83 C4 14 26N 0 14W
Goromonzi, Zimbabwe 87 F3 17 52 S 31 22 E
Gorong, Kepulauan,
 Indonesia .... 63 E8 3 59 S 131 25 E
Gorongosa →, Mozam. 89 B5 18 50 S 34 29 E
Gorongose →, Mozam. 89 C5 20 30 S 34 40 E
Gorongoza, Mozam. .. 87 F3 18 44 S 34 2 E
Gorongoza, Sa. da,
 Mozam. .... 87 F3 18 27 S 34 2 E
Gorontalo, Indonesia . 63 D6 0 35N 123 5 E
Gorontalo □, Indonesia 63 D6 0 50N 122 20 E
Goronyo, Nigeria .... 83 C6 13 29N 5 39 E
Górowo Iławeckie,
 Poland .... 30 D7 54 17N 20 30 E
Gorron, France 18 D6 48 25N 0 50W
Gorshechnoye, Russia 33 G10 51 31N 38 2 E
Gort, Ireland 12 C3 53 3N 8 49W
Gortis, Greece ...... 49 D6 35 4N 24 58 E
Góry Bystrzyckie,
 Poland .... 31 H3 50 16N 16 33 E
Goryachiy Klyuch,
 Russia .... 35 H4 44 38N 39 8 E
Gorzkowice, Poland .. 31 G6 51 13N 19 36 E
Górzno, Poland ...... 31 E6 53 12N 19 38 E
Gorzów Śląski, Poland 31 G5 51 3N 18 22 E
Gorzów Wielkopolski,
 Poland .... 31 F2 52 43N 15 15 E
Goshen, Calif., U.S.A. 110 J7 36 21N 119 25W
Goshen, Ind., U.S.A. . 114 E3 41 35N 85 50W
Goshen, N.Y., U.S.A. . 117 E10 41 24N 74 20W
Goshogawara, Japan .. 54 D10 40 48N 140 27 E
Goslar, Germany .... 24 D6 51 54N 10 25 E
Gospič, Croatia ..... 41 D12 44 35N 15 23 E
Gosport, U.K. 15 G6 50 48N 1 9W
Gossas, Senegal 82 C1 14 28N 16 9W
Gosse →, Australia .. 94 B1 19 32 S 134 37 E
Gossi, Mali 83 B4 15 48N 1 20W
Gossinga, Sudan ..... 81 F2 8 36N 25 59 E
Gostivar, Macedonia . 44 E4 41 48N 20 57 E
Gostyń, Poland ...... 31 G4 51 50N 17 3 E
Gostynin, Poland .... 31 F6 52 26N 19 29 E
Göta älv →, Sweden .. 11 G5 57 42N 11 54 E
Göta kanal, Sweden .. 11 F9 58 30N 15 58 E
Götaland, Sweden ... 11 G8 57 30N 14 30 E
Göteborg, Sweden ... 11 G5 57 43N 11 59 E
Götene, Sweden ..... 11 F7 58 32N 13 30 E
Goteşti, Moldova .... 29 D13 46 9N 28 10 E
Gotha, Germany ..... 24 E6 50 56N 10 42 E
Gothenburg =
 Göteborg, Sweden .. 11 G5 57 43N 11 59 E
Gothenburg, U.S.A. .. 112 E4 40 56N 100 10W
Gothèye, Niger ...... 83 C5 13 52N 1 34 E
Gotland, Sweden .... 11 G8 57 30N 18 33 E
Gotlands län □, Sweden 11 G12 57 30N 18 33 E
Gotō-Rettō, Japan ... 55 H4 32 55N 129 5 E
Gotse Delchev, Bulgaria 44 E7 41 36N 23 46 E
Gotska Sandön, Sweden 9 G18 58 24N 19 15 E
Götsu, Japan .... 55 G6 35 0N 132 14 E
Gott Pk., Canada 102 C4 50 18N 122 16W
Gottwald = Zmiyev,
 Ukraine .... 33 H9 49 39N 36 27 E
Gottwaldov = Zlín,
 Czech Rep. .... 27 B10 49 14N 17 40 E
Goubangzi, China .... 57 D11 41 20N 121 52 E
Gouda, Neths. ...... 17 B4 52 1N 4 42 E
Goúdhoura, Ákra,
 Greece .... 49 E8 34 59N 26 6 E
Goudiry, Senegal 82 C2 14 15N 12 45W
Goudoumaria, Niger . 83 C7 13 40N 11 10 E
Gouéké, Guinea 82 D3 8 2N 8 43W
Gough I., Atl. Oc. .... 2 G9 40 10 S 9 45W
Gouin, Rés., Canada . 104 C5 48 35N 74 40W
Goukou →, China .... 57 E9 39 10N 117 10 E
Goulburn, Australia .. 95 E4 34 44 S 149 44 E
Goulburn →, Australia 95 F4 36 10 S 144 55 E
Goulburn Is., Australia 94 A1 11 40 S 133 20 E
Goulia, Ivory C. 82 D3 10 1N 7 11W
Goulimine, Morocco . 78 C3 28 56N 10 0W
Goumbou, Mali 82 B3 15 25N 7 28W
Goundam, Mali 82 B4 16 27N 3 40W
Goûra, Greece ...... 46 D4 37 56N 22 20 E
Gouménissa, Greece .. 44 F6 40 56N 22 37 E
Gournbassi, Mali 82 C2 13 24N 11 38W
Gournay-en-Bray,
 France .... 19 C8 49 29N 1 44 E
Gourock, U.K. 13 F4 55 57N 4 49W
Goursi, Burkina Faso . 82 C4 12 42N 2 37W
Gouverneur, U.S.A. .. 117 B9 44 20N 75 28W
Gouviá, Greece ...... 49 A3 39 39N 19 50 E
Gouzon, France ..... 19 F9 46 12N 2 14 E
Governador Valadares,
 Brazil .... 125 G10 18 15 S 41 57W
Governor's Harbour,
 Bahamas 120 A4 25 10N 76 14W
Govindgarh, India ... 69 G9 24 23N 81 18 E
Gowan Ra., Australia . 94 D4 25 0 S 145 0 E
Gowanda, U.S.A. 116 D6 42 28N 78 56W
Gower, U.K. 15 F3 51 35N 4 10W
Gowna, L., Ireland ... 12 C4 53 51N 7 34W
Goya, Argentina .... 126 B4 29 10 S 59 10W
Göyçay, Azerbaijan ... 35 K8 40 42N 47 43 E
Goyder Lagoon,
 Australia .... 95 D2 27 3 S 138 58 E
Goyllarisquisga, Peru . 124 F3 10 31 S 76 24W
Göynük, Antalya,
 Turkey .... 47 E12 36 41N 30 33 E
Göynük, Bolu, Turkey 72 B4 40 24N 30 48 E
Goz Beîda, Chad .... 79 F10 12 10N 21 20 E
Goz Regeb, Sudan ... 81 D4 16 3N 35 33 E
Gozo, Malta .... 49 C1 36 3N 14 15 E
Graaff-Reinet, S. Africa 88 E3 32 13 S 24 32 E
Grabo, Ivory C. 82 E3 4 57N 7 40W
Grabow, Germany ... 24 B7 53 17N 11 34 E
Grabów nad Prosną,
 Poland .... 31 G5 51 31N 18 7 E
Gračac, Croatia ..... 41 D12 44 18N 15 57 E

Gračanica, Bos.-H. .... 28 F3 44 43N 18 18 E
Graçay, France ...... 19 E8 47 10N 1 50 E
Gracias a Dios, C.,
 Honduras 120 D3 15 0N 83 10W
Graciosa, I., Canary Is. 48 E6 29 15N 13 32W
Grad Sofiya □, Bulgaria 44 D7 42 45N 23 20 E
Gradac, Serbia & M. .. 44 C3 43 23N 19 9 E
Gradačac, Bos.-H. .... 28 F3 44 52N 18 26 E
Gradeška Planina,
 Macedonia .... 44 E6 41 30N 22 15 E
Gradets, Bulgaria .... 45 D10 42 46N 26 30 E
Gradišče, Slovenia ... 41 B12 46 37N 15 50 E
Grădiştea de Munte,
 Romania .... 29 E8 45 37N 23 13 E
Grado, Italy .... 41 C10 45 40N 13 23 E
Grado, Spain 36 B4 43 23N 6 4W
Grady, U.S.A. 113 H3 34 49N 103 19W
Graeca, Lacul, Romania 29 F11 44 5N 26 10 E
Grafenau, Germany .. 25 G9 48 51N 13 24 E
Grafham Water, U.K. . 15 E7 52 19N 0 18W
Grafton, Australia ... 95 D5 29 38 S 152 58 E
Grafton, N. Dak., U.S.A. 112 A6 48 25N 97 25W
Grafton, W. Va., U.S.A. 114 F5 39 21N 80 2W
Graham, Canada 104 C1 49 20N 90 30W
Graham, U.S.A. 113 J5 33 6N 98 35W
Graham, Mt., U.S.A. . 109 K9 32 42N 109 52W
Graham Bell, Ostrov =
 Greem-Bell, Ostrov,
 Russia .... 52 A7 81 0N 62 0 E
Graham I., Canada ... 102 C2 53 40N 132 30W
Graham Land,
 Antarctica .... 5 C17 65 0 S 64 0W
Grahamstown, S. Africa 89 E4 33 19 S 26 31 E
Grahamsville, U.S.A. . 117 E10 41 51N 74 33W
Grahovo, Serbia & M. . 44 D2 42 40N 18 40 E
Graie, Alpi, Europe .. 21 C11 45 30N 7 10 E
Grain Coast, W. Afr. . 82 E3 4 20N 10 0W
Grajagan, Indonesia . 63 K17 8 35 S 114 13 E
Grajagan, Teluk,
 Indonesia .... 63 K17 8 40 S 114 18 E
Grajaú, Brazil ...... 125 E9 5 50 S 46 4W
Grajaú →, Brazil .... 125 D10 3 41 S 44 48W
Grajewo, Poland .... 30 E9 53 39N 22 30 E
Gramada, Bulgaria ... 44 C6 43 49N 22 39 E
Gramat, France ..... 20 D5 44 48N 1 43 E
Grammichele, Italy .. 43 E7 37 13N 14 38 E
Grámmos, Óros, Greece 44 F4 40 18N 20 47 E
Grampian, U.S.A. ... 116 F6 40 58N 78 37W
Grampian Highlands =
 Grampian Mts., U.K. 13 E5 56 50N 4 0W
Grampian Mts., U.K. . 13 E5 56 50N 4 0W
Grampians, The,
 Australia .... 95 F3 37 0 S 142 20 E
Gramsh, Albania .... 44 F4 40 52N 20 12 E
Gran Canaria,
 Canary Is. 48 G4 27 55N 15 35W
Gran Chaco, S. Amer. 126 B3 25 0 S 61 0W
Gran Desierto del
 Pinacate △, Mexico 118 A2 31 51N 113 32W
Gran Paradiso, Italy .. 40 C4 45 33N 7 17 E
Gran Sasso d'Itália, Italy 41 F10 42 27N 13 42 E
Gran Sasso e Monti
 Della Laga △, Italy .. 41 F10 42 32N 13 22 E
Granada, Nic. 120 D2 11 58N 86 0W
Granada, Spain 37 H7 37 10N 3 35W
Granada, U.S.A. 113 F3 38 4N 102 19W
Granada □, Spain 37 H7 37 18N 3 0W
Granadilla de Abona,
 Canary Is. 48 F3 28 7N 16 33W
Granard, Ireland 12 C4 53 47N 7 30W
Granbury, U.S.A. 113 J6 32 27N 97 47W
Granby, Canada 117 A12 45 25N 72 45W
Granby, U.S.A. 108 F11 40 5N 105 56W
Grand →, Mo., U.S.A. 112 F8 39 23N 93 7W
Grand →, S. Dak.,
 U.S.A. 112 C4 45 40N 100 45W
Grand Bahama I.,
 Bahamas 120 A4 26 40N 78 30W
Grand Bank, Canada . 105 C8 47 6N 55 48W
Grand Bassam, Ivory C. 82 D4 5 10N 3 49W
Grand Béréby, Ivory C. 82 E3 4 38N 6 55W
Grand-Bourg,
 Guadeloupe .... 120 b 15 53N 61 19W
Grand Canal = Yun
 Ho →, China ...... 57 E9 39 10N 117 10 E
Grand Canyon, U.S.A. 109 H7 36 3N 112 9W
Grand Canyon △,
 U.S.A. 109 H7 36 15N 112 30W
Grand Canyon-
 Parashant △, U.S.A. 109 H7 36 30N 113 20W
Grand Cayman,
 Cayman Is. 120 C3 19 20N 81 20W
Grand Centre, Canada 103 C6 54 25N 110 13W
Grand Cess, Liberia .. 82 E3 4 40N 8 12W
Grand Coulee, U.S.A. 108 C4 47 57N 119 0W
Grand Coulee Dam,
 U.S.A. 108 C4 47 57N 118 59W
Grand Falls, Canada .. 105 C6 47 3N 67 44W
Grand Falls-Windsor,
 Canada 105 C8 48 56N 55 40W
Grand Forks, Canada . 102 D5 49 0N 118 30W
Grand Forks, U.S.A. .. 112 B6 47 55N 97 3W
Grand Gorge, U.S.A. . 117 D10 42 21N 74 29W
Grand Haven, U.S.A. . 114 D2 43 4N 86 13W
Grand I., Mich., U.S.A. 114 B2 46 31N 86 40W
Grand I., N.Y., U.S.A. 116 D6 43 0N 78 58W
Grand Island, U.S.A. . 112 E5 40 55N 98 21W
Grand Isle, La., U.S.A. 113 L9 29 14N 90 0W
Grand Isle, Vt., U.S.A. 117 B11 44 43N 73 18W
Grand Junction, U.S.A. 109 G9 39 4N 108 33W
Grand L., N.B., Canada 105 C6 45 57N 66 7W
Grand L., Nfld. & L.,
 Canada 105 C8 49 0N 57 30W
Grand L., Nfld. & L.,
 Canada 105 B7 53 40N 60 30W
Grand L., U.S.A. 113 L8 29 55N 92 47W
Grand Lahou, Ivory C. 82 D3 5 10N 5 0W
Grand Lake, U.S.A. .. 108 F11 40 15N 105 49W
Grand-Lieu, L. de,
 France 18 E5 47 6N 1 40W
Grand Manan I., Canada 105 D6 44 45N 66 52W
Grand Marais, Canada 112 B9 47 45N 90 25W
Grand Marais, U.S.A. 114 B3 46 40N 85 59W
Grand-Mère, Canada . 104 C5 46 36N 72 40W
Grand Popo, Benin .. 83 D5 6 15N 1 57 E
Grand Portage, U.S.A. 112 B10 47 58N 89 41W
Grand Prairie, U.S.A. 113 J6 32 47N 97 0W
Grand Rapids, Canada 103 C9 53 12N 99 19W
Grand Rapids, Mich.,
 U.S.A. 114 D2 42 58N 85 40W
Grand Rapids, Minn.,
 U.S.A. 112 B8 47 14N 93 31W
Grand St-Bernard, Col
 du, Europe .... 25 K3 45 50N 7 10 E
Grand Staircase-
 Escalante △, U.S.A. 109 H8 37 5N 112 0W

Grand Teton, U.S.A. . . **108 E8** 43 54N 111 50W
Grand Teton △, U.S.A. **108 D8** 43 50N 110 50W
Grand Union Canal,
U.K. **15 E7** 52 7N 0 53W
Grand-Vigie, Pte. de la,
Guadeloupe . . . . **120 b** 16 32N 61 27W
Grandas de Salime,
Spain **36 B4** 43 13N 6 53W
Grande, Jujuy,
Argentina . . . . **126 A2** 24 20 S 65 2W
Grande, Mendoza,
Argentina . . . . **126 D2** 36 52 S 69 45W
Grande →, Bolivia . . **124 G6** 15 51 S 64 39W
Grande →, Bahia,
Brazil . . . . **125 F10** 11 30 S 44 30W
Grande →,
Minas Gerais, Brazil **125 H8** 20 6 S 51 4W
Grande, B., Argentina . **128 G3** 50 30 S 68 20W
Grande, Rio →, U.S.A. **113 N6** 25 58N 97 9W
Grande Baleine, R. de
la →, Canada **104 A4** 55 16N 77 47W
Grande Cache, Canada **102 C5** 53 53N 119 8W
Grande Casse, Pte. de la,
France . . . . **21 C10** 45 24N 6 49 E
Grande-Entrée, Canada **105 C7** 47 30N 61 40W
Grande Prairie, Canada **102 B5** 55 10N 118 50W
Grande-Rivière, Canada **105 C7** 48 26N 64 30W
Grande-Terre,
Guadeloupe . . . . . **120 b** 16 20N 61 25W
Grande-Vallée, Canada **105 C6** 49 14N 65 8W
Grandfalls, U.S.A. . . . **113 K3** 31 20N 102 51W
Grândola, Portugal . . **37 G2** 38 12N 8 35W
Grandpré, France . . . **19 C11** 49 20N 4 50 E
Grands Causses △,
France . . . . **20 D6** 44 5N 2 58 E
Grands-Jardins △,
Canada **105 C5** 47 41N 70 51W
Grandview, Canada . . **103 C8** 51 10N 100 42W
Grandview, U.S.A. . . . **108 C4** 46 15N 119 54W
Grandvilliers, France . **19 C8** 49 40N 1 57 E
Graneros, Chile . . . . **126 C1** 34 5 S 70 45W
Grangemouth, U.K. . . **13 E5** 56 1N 3 42W
Granger, U.S.A. **108 F9** 41 35N 109 58W
Grängesberg, Sweden . **10 D9** 60 6N 15 1 E
Grangeville, U.S.A. . . **108 D5** 45 56N 116 7W
Granisle, Canada . . . **102 C3** 54 53N 126 13W
Granite City, U.S.A. . . **112 F9** 38 42N 90 9W
Granite Falls, U.S.A. . **112 C7** 44 49N 95 33W
Granite L., Canada . . **105 C8** 48 8N 57 5W
Granite Mt., U.S.A. . . **111 M10** 33 5N 116 28W
Granite Pk., U.S.A. . . **108 D9** 45 10N 109 48W
Graniteville, U.S.A. . . **117 B12** 44 8N 72 29W
Granitola, C., Italy . . **42 E5** 37 34N 12 33 E
Granity, N.Z. . . . . . . **91 J3** 41 39 S 171 51 E
Granja, Brazil . . . . . **125 D10** 3 7 S 40 50W
Granja de Moreruela,
Spain **36 D5** 41 48N 5 44W
Granja de
Torrehermosa, Spain **37 G5** 38 19N 5 35W
Gränna, Sweden . . . . **11 F8** 58 1N 14 28 E
Granollers, Spain . . . **38 D7** 41 39N 2 18 E
Gransee, Germany . . . **24 B9** 53 1N 13 10 E
Grant, U.S.A. **112 E4** 40 53N 101 42W
Grant, Mt., U.S.A. . . . **108 G4** 38 34N 118 48W
Grant City, U.S.A. . . . **112 E7** 40 29N 94 25W
Grant I., Australia . . . **92 B5** 11 10 S 132 52 E
Grant Range, U.S.A. . **109 G6** 38 30N 115 25W
Grantham, U.K. **14 E7** 52 55N 0 38W
Grantown-on-Spey, U.K. **13 D5** 57 20N 3 36W
Grants, U.S.A. **109 J10** 35 9N 107 52W
Grants Pass, U.S.A. . . **108 E2** 42 26N 123 19W
Grantsville, U.S.A. . . **108 F7** 40 36N 112 28W
Granville, France . . . **18 D5** 48 50N 1 35W
Granville, N. Dak.,
U.S.A. **112 A4** 48 16N 100 47W
Granville, N.Y., U.S.A. **117 C11** 43 24N 73 16W
Granville, Ohio, U.S.A. **116 F2** 40 4N 82 31W
Granville L., Canada . **103 B8** 56 18N 100 30W
Graskop, S. Africa . . **89 C5** 24 56 S 30 49 E
Gräsö, Sweden . . . . **10 D12** 60 28N 18 35 E
Grass →, Canada . . . **103 B9** 56 3N 96 33W
Grass Range, U.S.A. . **108 C9** 47 0N 109 0W
Grass River △, Canada **103 C8** 54 40N 100 50W
Grass Valley, Calif.,
U.S.A. **110 F6** 39 13N 121 4W
Grass Valley, Oreg.,
U.S.A. **108 D3** 45 22N 120 47W
Grassano, Italy . . . . **43 B9** 40 38N 16 17 E
Grasse, France . . . . **21 E10** 43 38N 6 56 E
Grassflat, U.S.A. . . . **116 F6** 41 0N 78 6W
Grasslands △, Canada **103 D7** 49 11N 107 38W
Grassy, Australia . . . **95 G3** 40 3 S 144 5 E
Gråsten, Denmark . . **11 K3** 54 55N 9 35 E
Grästorp, Sweden . . . **11 F6** 58 20N 12 40 E
Gratkorn, Austria . . . **26 D8** 47 8N 15 21 E
Graubünden □, Switz. **25 J5** 46 45N 9 30 E
Graulhet, France . . . **20 E5** 43 45N 1 59 E
Graus, Spain . . . . . . **38 C5** 42 11N 0 20 E
Grave, Pte. de, France **20 C2** 45 34N 1 4W
Gravelbourg, Canada . **103 D7** 49 50N 106 35W
Gravelines, France . . **19 A9** 51 1N 2 10 E
's-Gravenhage, Neths. **17 B4** 52 7N 4 17 E
Gravenhurst, Canada . **116 B5** 44 52N 79 20W
Gravesend, Australia . **95 D5** 29 35 S 150 20 E
Gravesend, U.K. . . . . **15 F8** 51 26N 0 22 E
Gravina in Púglia, Italy **43 B9** 40 49N 16 25 E
Gravois, Pointe-à-, Haiti **121 C5** 16 15N 73 56W
Gravone →, France . . **21 G12** 41 58N 8 45 E
Gray, France . . . . . . **19 E12** 47 22N 5 35 E
Grayling, U.S.A. **114 C3** 44 40N 84 43W
Grays, U.K. . . . . **15 F8** 51 28N 0 21 E
Grays Harbor, U.S.A. . **108 C1** 46 59N 124 1W
Grays L., U.S.A. **108 E8** 43 4N 111 26W
Grays River, U.S.A. . . **110 D3** 46 21N 123 37W
Grayvoron, Russia . . **33 G8** 50 29N 35 41 E
Graz, Austria . . . . . **26 D8** 47 4N 15 27 E
Grdelica, Serbia & M. . **44 D6** 42 55N 22 3 E
Greasy L., Canada . . **102 A4** 62 55N 122 12W
Great Abaco I. = Abaco
I., Bahamas **120 A4** 26 25N 77 10W
Great Artesian Basin,
Australia . . . . **94 C3** 23 0 S 144 0 E
Great Australian Bight,
Australia . . . . **93 F5** 33 30 S 130 0 E
Great Bahama Bank,
Bahamas **120 B4** 23 15N 78 0W
Great Barrier I., N.Z. . **91 G5** 36 11 S 175 25 E
Great Barrier Reef,
Australia . . . . **94 B4** 18 0 S 146 50 E
Great Barrier Reef △,
Australia . . . . **94 B4** 20 0 S 150 0 E
Great Barrington,
U.S.A. **117 D11** 42 12N 73 22W
Great Basalt Wall △,
Australia . . . . **94 B4** 19 52 S 145 43 E
Great Basin, U.S.A. . . **108 G5** 40 0N 117 0W
Great Basin △, U.S.A. **108 G6** 38 55N 114 14W

Great Bear →, Canada **100 B7** 65 0N 124 0W
Great Bear L., Canada **100 B7** 65 30N 120 0W
Great Belt = Store Bælt,
Denmark . . . . **11 J4** 55 20N 11 0 E
Great Bend, Kans.,
U.S.A. **112 F5** 38 22N 98 46W
Great Bend, Pa., U.S.A. **117 E9** 41 58N 75 45W
Great Blasket I., Ireland **12 D1** 52 6N 10 32W
Great Britain, Europe . **6 E5** 54 0N 2 15W
Great Camaror,
Br. Virgin Is. . . . . **121 e** 18 30N 64 35W
Great Codroy, Canada **105 C8** 47 51N 59 16W
Great Dividing Ra.,
Australia . . . . **94 C4** 23 0 S 146 0 E
Great Driffield =
Driffield, U.K. . . . **14 C7** 54 0N 0 26W
Great Exuma I.,
Bahamas **120 B4** 23 30N 75 50W
Great Falls, U.S.A. . . **108 C8** 47 30N 111 17W
Great Fish →, Groot
Vis →, S. Africa . . **88 E4** 33 28 S 27 5 E
Great Guana Cay,
Bahamas **120 B4** 24 0N 76 20W
Great Inagua I.,
Bahamas **121 B5** 21 0N 73 20W
Great Indian Desert =
Thar Desert, India . **68 F5** 28 0N 72 0 E
Great Karoo, S. Africa **88 E3** 31 55 S 21 0 E
Great Khingan Mts. =
Da Hinggan Ling,
China . . . . **60 B7** 48 0N 121 0 E
Great Lake, Australia . **95 G4** 41 50 S 146 40 E
Great Lakes, N. Amer. **98 E11** 46 0N 84 0W
Great Malvern, U.K. . **15 E5** 52 7N 2 18W
Great Miami →, U.S.A. **114 F3** 39 20N 84 40W
Great Ormes Head,
U.K. **14 D4** 53 20N 3 52W
Great Ouse →, U.K. . **14 E8** 52 48N 0 21 E
Great Palm I. Australia **94 B4** 18 45 S 146 40 E
Great Pedro Bluff,
Jamaica . . . . **120 a** 17 51N 77 44W
Great Plains, N. Amer. **98 E4** 47 0N 105 0W
Great Ruaha →,
Tanzania . . . . **86 D4** 7 56 S 37 52 E
Great Sacandaga L.,
U.S.A. **117 C10** 43 6N 74 16W
Great Saint Bernard
Pass = Grand St-
Bernard, Col du,
Europe . . . . **25 K3** 45 50N 7 10 E
Great Salt L., U.S.A. . **108 F7** 41 15N 112 40W
Great Salt Lake Desert,
U.S.A. **108 F7** 40 50N 113 30W
Great Salt Plains L.,
U.S.A. **113 G5** 36 45N 98 8W
Great Sand Dunes △,
U.S.A. **109 H11** 37 48N 105 45W
Great Sandy △,
Australia . . . . **95 D5** 26 13 S 153 2 E
Great Sandy Desert,
Australia . . . . **92 D3** 21 0 S 124 0 E
Great Sangi = Sangihe,
Pulau, Indonesia . . **63 D7** 3 35N 125 30 E
Great Scarcies →,
S. Leone **82 D2** 9 0N 13 0W
Great Skellig, Ireland . **12 E1** 51 47N 10 33W
Great Slave L., Canada **102 A5** 61 23N 115 38W
Great Smoky Mts. △,
U.S.A. **115 H4** 35 40N 83 40W
Great Snow Mt., Canada **102 B4** 57 26N 124 0W
Great Stour = Stour →,
U.K. . . . . **15 F9** 51 18N 1 22 E
Great Victoria Desert,
Australia . . . . **93 E4** 29 30 S 126 30 E
Great Wall, Antarctica **5 C18** 62 30 S 58 0W
Great Wall, China . . **56 E5** 38 30N 109 30 E
Great Wherns de, U.K. **14 C6** 54 10N 1 58W
Great Yarmouth, U.K. **15 E9** 52 37N 1 44 E
Great Zab →, Záb al
Kabīr →, Iraq . . . **70 C4** 36 1N 43 24 E
Great Zimbabwe,
Zimbabwe . . . . . . **87 G3** 20 16 S 30 54 E
Greater Antilles,
W. Indies **121 C5** 17 40N 74 0W
Greater London □, U.K. **15 F7** 51 31N 0 6W
Greater Manchester □,
U.K. **14 D5** 53 30N 2 15W
Greater St. Lucia
Wetlands △, S. Africa **89 D5** 28 6 S 32 27 E
Greater Sudbury =
Sudbury, Canada . . **104 C3** 46 30N 81 0W
Greater Sunda Is.,
Indonesia . . . . . . **62 F4** 7 0 S 112 0 E
Grebbestad, Sweden . **11 F5** 58 42N 11 15 E
Grebenka = Hrebenka,
Ukraine . . . . **33 G7** 50 9N 32 22 E
Greco, C., Cyprus . . . **49 E13** 34 57N 34 5 E
Greco, Mte., Italy . . . **41 G10** 41 48N 13 58 E
Gredos, Sierra de, Spain **36 E6** 40 20N 5 0W
Greece, U.S.A. **116 C7** 43 13N 77 41W
Greece ■, Europe . . . **46 B3** 40 0N 23 0 E
Greeley, Colo., U.S.A. **112 E2** 40 25N 104 42W
Greeley, Nebr., U.S.A. **112 E5** 41 33N 98 32W
Greem-Bell, Ostrov,
Russia . . . . **52 A7** 81 0N 62 0 E
Green, U.S.A. **108 E2** 43 7N 123 22W
Green →, Ky., U.S.A. **114 G2** 37 54N 87 30W
Green →, Utah, U.S.A. **109 G9** 38 11N 109 53W
Green B., U.S.A. **114 C2** 45 0N 87 30W
Green Bay, U.S.A. . . . **114 C2** 44 31N 88 0W
Green C., Australia . . **95 F5** 37 13 S 150 1 E
Green Cove Springs,
U.S.A. **115 L5** 29 59N 81 42W
Green Lake, Canada . **103 C7** 54 17N 107 47W
Green Mts., U.S.A. . . **117 C12** 43 45N 72 45W
Green River, Utah,
U.S.A. **109 G8** 38 59N 110 10W
Green River, Wyo.,
U.S.A. **108 F9** 41 32N 109 28W
Green Valley, U.S.A. . **109 L8** 31 52N 110 56W
Greenbank, U.S.A. . . **110 B4** 48 6N 122 34W
Greenbush, Mich.,
U.S.A. **116 B1** 44 35N 83 19W
Greenbush, Minn.,
U.S.A. **112 A6** 48 42N 96 11W
Greencastle, U.S.A. . . **114 F2** 39 38N 86 52W
Greene, U.S.A. **117 D9** 42 20N 75 46W
Greenfield, Calif.,
U.S.A. **110 J5** 36 19N 121 15W
Greenfield, Calif.,
U.S.A. **111 K8** 35 15N 119 0W
Greenfield, Ind., U.S.A. **114 F3** 39 47N 85 46W
Greenfield, Iowa, U.S.A. **112 E7** 41 18N 94 28W
Greenfield, Mass.,
U.S.A. **117 D12** 42 35N 72 36W
Greenfield, Mo., U.S.A. **113 G8** 37 25N 93 51W
Greenfield Park, Canada **117 A11** 45 29N 73 29W

Greenland ☑, N. Amer. **4 C5** 66 0N 45 0W
Greenland Sea, Arctic . **4 B7** 73 0N 10 0W
Greenock, U.K. **13 F4** 55 57N 4 46W
Greenore, Ireland . . . **12 B5** 54 2N 6 8W
Greenore Pt., Ireland . **12 D5** 52 14N 6 19W
Greenough, Australia . **93 E1** 28 58 S 114 43 E
Greenough →, Australia **93 E1** 28 51 S 114 38 E
Greenport, U.S.A. . . . **117 E12** 41 6N 72 22W
Greensboro, Ga., U.S.A. **115 J4** 33 35N 83 11W
Greensboro, N.C.,
U.S.A. **115 G6** 36 4N 79 48W
Greensboro, Vt., U.S.A. **117 B12** 44 36N 72 18W
Greensburg, Ind., U.S.A. **114 F3** 39 20N 85 29W
Greensburg, Kans.,
U.S.A. **113 G5** 37 36N 99 18W
Greensburg, Pa., U.S.A. **116 F5** 40 18N 79 33W
Greenstone Pt., U.K. . **13 D3** 57 55N 5 37W
Greenvale, Australia . **94 B4** 18 59 S 145 7 E
Greenville, Liberia . . **82 D3** 5 1N 9 6W
Greenville, Ala., U.S.A. **115 K2** 31 50N 86 38W
Greenville, Calif., U.S.A. **110 E6** 40 8N 120 57W
Greenville, Maine,
U.S.A. **115 C11** 45 28N 69 35W
Greenville, Mich.,
U.S.A. **114 D3** 43 11N 85 15W
Greenville, Miss., U.S.A. **113 J9** 33 24N 91 4W
Greenville, Mo., U.S.A. **113 G9** 37 8N 90 27W
Greenville, N.C., U.S.A. **115 H7** 35 37N 77 23W
Greenville, N.H., U.S.A. **117 D13** 42 46N 71 49W
Greenville, N.Y., U.S.A. **117 D10** 42 25N 74 1W
Greenville, Ohio, U.S.A. **114 E3** 40 6N 84 38W
Greenville, Pa., U.S.A. **116 E4** 41 24N 80 23W
Greenville, S.C., U.S.A. **115 H4** 34 51N 82 24W
Greenville, Tenn.,
U.S.A. **115 G4** 36 13N 82 51W
Greenville, Tex., U.S.A. **113 J6** 33 8N 96 7W
Greenwater Lake △,
Canada **103 C8** 52 32N 103 30W
Greenwich, Conn.,
U.S.A. **117 E11** 41 2N 73 38W
Greenwich, N.Y., U.S.A. **117 C11** 43 5N 73 30W
Greenwich, Ohio, U.S.A. **116 E2** 41 2N 82 31W
Greenwich □, U.K. . . **15 F8** 51 29N 0 1 E
Greenwood, Canada . **102 D5** 49 10N 118 40W
Greenwood, Ark.,
U.S.A. **113 H7** 35 13N 94 16W
Greenwood, Ind., U.S.A. **114 F2** 39 37N 86 7W
Greenwood, Miss.,
U.S.A. **113 J9** 33 31N 90 11W
Greenwood, Mt.,
Australia . . . . **92 B5** 13 48 S 130 4 E
Gregbe, Ivory C. . . . **82 D3** 6 48N 6 43W
Gregory, U.S.A. **112 D5** 43 14N 99 20W
Gregory →, Australia . **94 B2** 17 53 S 139 17 E
Gregory △, Australia . **92 C5** 15 38 S 131 15 E
Gregory, L., S. Austral.,
Australia . . . . **95 D2** 28 55 S 139 0 E
Gregory, L., W. Austral.,
Australia . . . . **93 E2** 25 38 S 119 58 E
Gregory Downs,
Australia . . . . **94 B2** 18 35 S 138 45 E
Gregory L., Australia . **92 D4** 20 0 S 127 40 E
Gregory Ra., Queens.,
Australia . . . . **94 B3** 19 30 S 143 40 E
Gregory Ra.,
W. Austral., Australia **92 D3** 21 20 S 121 12 E
Greiffenberg, Germany **24 B9** 53 5N 13 57 E
Greifswald, Germany . **24 A9** 54 5N 13 23 E
Greifswalder Bodden,
Germany . . . . **24 A9** 54 12N 13 35 E
Grein, Austria . . . . . **26 C7** 48 14N 14 51 E
Greiz, Germany . . . . **24 E8** 50 39N 12 10 E
Gremikha, Russia . . . **52 C4** 67 59N 39 47 E
Grená, Denmark . . . . **11 H4** 56 25N 10 53 E
Grenada, U.S.A. **113 J10** 33 47N 89 49W
Grenada ■, W. Indies . **121 D7** 12 10N 61 40W
Grenade, France . . . . **20 E5** 43 47N 1 17 E
Grenadier I., U.S.A. . . **117 B8** 44 3N 76 22W
Grenadines, The,
St. Vincent **121 D7** 12 40N 61 20W
Grenchen, Switz. . . . **25 H3** 47 12N 7 24 E
Grenen, Denmark . . . **11 G4** 57 44N 10 40 E
Grenfell, Australia . . **95 E4** 33 52 S 148 8 E
Grenfell, Canada . . . **103 C8** 50 30N 102 56W
Grenoble, France . . . **21 C9** 45 12N 5 42 E
Grenville, C., Australia **94 A3** 12 0 S 143 13 E
Grenville Chan., Canada **102 C3** 53 40N 129 46W
Gréoux-les-Bains,
France . . . . **21 E9** 43 45N 5 52 E
Gresham, U.S.A. **110 E4** 45 30N 122 26W
Gresik, Indonesia . . . **63 G15** 7 13 S 112 38 E
Gretna, U.K. **13 F5** 55 0N 3 3W
Greven, Germany . . . **24 C3** 52 6N 7 37 E
Grevená, Greece . . . . **44 F5** 40 4N 21 25 E
Grevená □, Greece . . **44 F5** 40 2N 21 25 E
Grevenbroich, Germany **24 D2** 51 5N 6 35 E
Grevenmacher, Lux. . **17 E6** 49 41N 6 26 E
Grevesmühlen,
Germany . . . . **24 B7** 53 52N 11 12 E
Grevestrand, Denmark **11 J6** 55 36N 12 19 E
Grey →, Canada **105 C8** 47 34N 57 6W
Grey →, N.Z. . . . . . . **91 K3** 42 27 S 171 12 E
Grey, C., Australia . . **94 A2** 13 0 S 136 35 E
Grey Ra., Australia . . **95 D3** 27 0 S 143 30 E
Greybull, U.S.A. **108 D9** 44 30N 108 3W
Greymouth, N.Z. . . . **91 K3** 42 29 S 171 13 E
Greystones, Ireland . . **12 C5** 53 9N 6 5W
Greytown, N.Z. . . . . **91 J5** 41 5 S 175 29 E
Greytown, S. Africa . . **89 D5** 29 1 S 30 36 E
Gribanovskiy, Russia . **34 E5** 51 28N 41 50 E
Gribbell I., Canada . . **102 C3** 53 23N 129 0W
Gribës, Mali i, Albania **44 F4** 40 17N 19 45 E
Gridley, U.S.A. **110 F5** 39 22N 121 42W
Griekwastad, S. Africa **88 D3** 28 49 S 23 15 E
Griesheim, Germany . **25 F4** 49 51N 8 33 E
Grieskirchen, Austria . **26 C6** 48 16N 13 48 E
Griffin, U.S.A. **115 J3** 33 15N 84 16W
Griffith, Australia . . . **95 E4** 34 18 S 146 2 E
Griffith, Canada **116 A7** 45 15N 77 10W
Griffith I., Canada . . **116 B4** 44 50N 80 55W
Grignols, France . . . **20 D3** 44 23N 0 3 E
Grigoriopol, Moldova . **29 C14** 47 9N 29 18 E
Grimailov = Hrymayliv,
Ukraine . . . . **33 H4** 49 20N 26 5 E
Grimari, C.A.R. . . . . **84 G4** 5 43N 20 6 E
Grimaylov = Hrymayliv,
Ukraine . . . . **33 H4** 49 20N 26 5 E
Grimes, U.S.A. **110 F5** 39 4N 121 54W
Grimma, Germany . . **24 D8** 51 14N 12 43 E
Grimmen, Germany . . **24 A9** 54 7N 13 3 E
Grimsay, U.K. **13 D1** 57 29N 7 14W
Grimsby, Canada . . . **116 C5** 43 12N 79 34W
Grimsby, U.K. **14 D7** 53 34N 0 5W
Grímsey, Iceland . . . **8 C5** 66 33N 17 58W
Grimshaw, Canada . . **102 B5** 56 10N 117 40W
Grimslöv, Sweden . . **11 H8** 56 44N 14 34 E
Grimstad, Norway . . **9 G13** 58 20N 8 35 E
Grindelwald, Switz. . . **25 J4** 46 38N 8 2 E

Grindsted, Denmark . . **11 J2** 55 46N 8 55 E
Grindstone I., Canada . **117 B8** 44 43N 76 14W
Grindu, Romania . . . **29 F11** 44 44N 26 50 E
Grinnell, U.S.A. **112 E8** 41 45N 92 43W
Gríntavec, Slovenia . . **41 B11** 46 22N 14 32 E
Grisolles, France . . . **20 E5** 43 49N 1 19 E
Grisons =
Graubünden □, Switz. **25 J5** 46 45N 9 30 E
Grisslehamn, Sweden . **10 D12** 60 5N 18 49 E
Grmeč Planina, Bos.-H. **41 D13** 44 43N 16 16 E
Groais I., Canada . . . **105 B8** 50 55N 55 35W
Grobiņa, Latvia . . . . **30 B8** 56 33N 21 10 E
Groblersdal, S. Africa **89 D4** 25 15 S 29 25 E
Groblershoop, S. Africa **88 D3** 28 54 S 18 0 E
Grocka, Serbia & M. . **44 B5** 44 40N 20 42 E
Gródek, Poland . . . . **31 H4** 50 43N 17 21 E
Grodno = Hrodna,
Belarus . . . . **30 E10** 53 42N 23 52 E
Grodzisk Mazowiecki,
Poland . . . . **31 F7** 52 7N 20 37 E
Grodzisk Wielkopolski,
Poland . . . . **31 F3** 52 15N 16 22 E
Grodzyanka =
Hrodzyanka, Belarus **32 F5** 53 31N 28 42 E
Groesbeck, U.S.A. . . **113 K6** 30 48N 96 31W
Groix, France **18 E3** 47 38N 3 29W
Groix, Î. de, France . . **18 E3** 47 38N 3 28W
Grójec, Poland . . . . . **31 G7** 51 50N 20 58 E
Gronau, Niedersachsen,
Germany . . . . **24 C5** 52 5N 9 47 E
Gronau,
Nordrhein-Westfalen,
Germany . . . . **24 C3** 52 12N 7 2 E
Grong, Norway . . . . **8 D15** 64 25N 12 8 E
Grönhögen, Sweden . **11 H10** 56 16N 16 24 E
Groningen, Neths. . . **17 A6** 53 15N 6 35 E
Groningen □, Neths. . **17 A6** 53 16N 6 40 E
Groom, U.S.A. **113 H4** 35 12N 101 6W
Groot →, S. Africa . . **88 E3** 33 45 S 24 36 E
Groot Berg →, S. Africa **88 E2** 32 47 S 18 8 E
Groot Vis →, S. Africa **88 E4** 33 28 S 27 5 E
Groot-Brakrivier,
S. Africa . . . . **88 E3** 34 2 S 22 18 E
Groot Karasberge,
Namibia . . . . **88 D2** 27 20 S 18 40 E
Groot-Kei →, S. Africa **89 E4** 32 41 S 28 22 E
Groot Vis →, S. Africa **88 E4** 33 28 S 27 5 E
Grootdrink, S. Africa . **88 D3** 28 33 S 21 42 E
Groote Eylandt,
Australia . . . . **94 A2** 14 0 S 136 40 E
Grootfontein, Namibia **88 B2** 19 31 S 18 6 E
Grootlaagte →, Africa **88 C3** 20 55 S 21 27 E
Grootvloer →, S. Africa **88 E3** 30 0 S 20 40 E
Gros C., Canada **102 A6** 61 59N 113 32W
Gros Islet, St. Lucia . **121 f** 14 5N 60 58W
Gros Morne △, Canada **105 C8** 49 40N 57 50W
Gros Piton, St. Lucia . **121 f** 13 49N 61 5W
Gros Piton Pt., St. Lucia **121 f** 13 49N 61 5W
Grósio, Italy . . . . . . **40 B7** 46 18N 10 16 E
Grosne →, France . . . **19 F11** 46 44N 4 56 E
Grossa, Pta., Spain . . **48 B8** 39 6N 1 36 E
Grossenbrode, Germany **24 A7** 54 21N 11 4 E
Grossenhain, Germany **24 D9** 51 17N 13 32 E
Grosser Arber,
Germany . . . . **25 F9** 49 6N 13 8 E
Grosser Plöner See,
Germany . . . . **24 A6** 54 10N 10 22 E
Grosseto, Italy . . . . . **41 F8** 42 46N 11 8 E
Grossgerungs, Austria **26 C7** 48 34N 14 57 E
Grossglockner, Austria **26 D5** 47 5N 12 40 E
Groswater B., Canada **105 B8** 54 20N 57 40W
Groton, Conn., U.S.A. **117 E12** 41 21N 72 5W
Groton, N.Y., U.S.A. . **117 D8** 42 36N 76 22W
Groton, S. Dak., U.S.A. **112 C5** 45 27N 98 6W
Grottáglie, Italy . . . . **43 B10** 40 32N 17 26 E
Grottaminarda, Italy . **43 A8** 41 4N 15 2 E
Grottammare, Italy . . **41 F10** 42 59N 13 52 E
Grouard Mission,
Canada **102 B5** 55 33N 116 9W
Grouin, Pte. du, France **18 D5** 48 43N 1 51W
Groundhog →, Canada **104 C3** 48 45N 82 58W
Grouw, Neths. . . . . . **17 A5** 53 5N 5 51 E
Grove City, U.S.A. . . **116 E4** 41 10N 80 5W
Grove Hill, U.S.A. . . . **115 K2** 31 42N 87 47W
Groveland, U.S.A. . . . **110 H6** 37 50N 120 14W
Grover City, U.S.A. . . **111 K6** 35 7N 120 37W
Groves, U.S.A. **113 L8** 29 57N 93 54W
Groveton, U.S.A. . . . **117 B13** 44 36N 71 31W
Grožnjan, Croatia . . . **41 C10** 45 22N 13 43 E
Groznyy, Russia . . . . **35 J7** 43 20N 45 45 E
Grubišno Polje, Croatia **28 E2** 45 44N 17 12 E
Grudovo, Bulgaria . . **45 D11** 42 21N 27 10 E
Grudusk, Poland . . . . **31 E7** 53 30N 20 38 E
Grudziądz, Poland . . **30 E5** 53 30N 18 47 E
Gruinard B., U.K. . . . **13 D3** 57 56N 5 35W
Gruissan, France . . . **20 E7** 43 8N 3 7 E
Grumo Áppula, Italy . **43 A9** 41 1N 16 42 E
Grums, Sweden . . . . **10 E7** 59 22N 13 5 E
Grünberg, Germany . . **24 E4** 50 35N 8 58 E
Gründau, Germany . . **25 E5** 50 10N 9 9 E
Grundy Center, U.S.A. **112 D8** 42 22N 92 47W
Grünstadt, Germany . **25 F4** 49 34N 8 9 E
Gruppo di Tessa △, Italy **40 B8** 46 47N 11 0 E
Gruvberget, Sweden . **10 C10** 61 18N 16 10 E
Gruver, U.S.A. **113 G4** 36 16N 101 24W
Gruyères, Switz. . . . **25 J3** 46 35N 7 4 E
Gruža, Serbia & M. . . **44 C5** 43 54N 20 46 E
Gryazovets, Russia . . **34 B5** 58 50N 40 10 E
Gryazi, Russia . . . . . **33 F10** 52 30N 39 58 E
Gryfice, Poland . . . . **30 E2** 53 55N 15 13 E
Gryfino, Poland . . . . **31 E1** 53 16N 14 29 E
Gryfów Śląski, Poland **31 G2** 51 2N 15 24 E
Gryhyttan, Sweden . . **10 E8** 59 41N 14 32 E
Gstaad, Switz. . . . . . **25 J3** 46 28N 7 18 E
Gua, India . . . . **67 H14** 22 18N 85 20 E
Gua Musang, Malaysia **65 K3** 4 53N 101 58 E
Guacanayabo, G. de,
Cuba **120 B4** 20 40N 77 20W
Guachípas →, Argentina **126 B2** 25 40 S 65 30W
Guadajoz →, Spain . . **37 H6** 37 50N 4 51W
Guadalajara, Mexico . **118 C4** 20 40N 103 20W
Guadalajara, Spain . . **38 E1** 40 37N 3 12W
Guadalajara □, Spain . **38 E2** 40 47N 2 30W
Guadalcanal,
Solomon Is. . . . . . **96 H8** 9 32 S 160 12 E
Guadalcanal, Spain . . **37 G5** 38 5N 5 52W
Guadales, Argentina . **126 C2** 34 30 S 67 55W
Guadalete →, Spain . . **37 J4** 36 35N 6 13W
Guadalhorce →, Spain **37 J6** 36 41N 4 27W
Guadalimar →, Spain . **37 G7** 38 5N 3 28W
Guadalmena →, Spain **37 G2** 38 19N 2 56W
Guadalmez →, Spain . **37 G5** 38 46N 5 4W
Guadalope →, Spain . **38 D4** 41 15N 0 3W
Guadalquivir →, Spain **37 J4** 36 47N 6 22W

Grindsted, Denmark
Guadalupe =
Guadeloupe ☑,
W. Indies . . . . . . **120 b** 16 20N 61 40W
Guadalupe, Mexico . . **111 N10** 32 4N 116 32W
Guadalupe, Spain . . . **37 F5** 39 27N 5 17W
Guadalupe, U.S.A. . . **111 L6** 34 59N 120 33W
Guadalupe →, Mexico **111 N10** 32 6N 116 51W
Guadalupe →, U.S.A. **113 L6** 28 27N 96 47W
Guadalupe, Sierra de,
Spain **37 F5** 39 28N 5 30W
Guadalupe Bravos,
Mexico **118 A3** 31 20N 106 10W
Guadalupe I., Pac. Oc. **98 G8** 29 0N 118 50W
Guadalupe Mts. △,
U.S.A. **113 K2** 31 40N 104 30W
Guadalupe Peak, U.S.A. **113 K2** 31 50N 104 52W
Guadalupe y Calvo,
Mexico **118 B3** 26 6N 106 58W
Guadarrama, Sierra de,
Spain **36 E7** 41 0N 4 0W
Guadauta, Georgia . . **35 J5** 43 7N 40 32 E
Guadeloupe △,
Guadeloupe . . . . . **120 b** 16 10N 61 40W
Guadeloupe ☑,
W. Indies . . . . . . **120 b** 16 20N 61 40W
Guadeloupe Passage,
W. Indies **121 C7** 16 50N 62 15W
Guadiamar →, Spain . **37 J4** 36 55N 6 24W
Guadiana →, Portugal **37 H3** 37 14N 7 22W
Guadiana Menor →,
Spain **37 H7** 37 56N 3 15W
Guadiaro →, Spain . . **37 J5** 36 17N 5 17W
Guadiato →, Spain . . **37 H5** 37 48N 5 5W
Guadiela →, Spain . . **38 E2** 40 22N 2 49W
Guadix, Spain **37 H7** 37 18N 3 11W
Guafo, Boca del, Chile **128 E2** 43 35 S 74 0W
Guaico, Trin. & Tob. . **125 K15** 10 35N 61 9W
Guainía →, Colombia **124 C5** 2 1N 67 7W
Guaíra, Brazil . . . . . **127 A5** 24 5 S 54 10W
Guaíra □, Paraguay . . **126 B4** 25 45 S 56 30W
Guaitecas, Is., Chile . **128 E2** 44 0 S 74 30W
Guajará-Mirim, Brazil **124 F5** 10 50 S 65 20W
Guajira, Pen. de la,
Colombia **124 A4** 12 0N 72 0W
Gualán, Guatemala . . **120 C2** 15 8N 89 22W
Gualdo Tadino, Italy . **41 E9** 43 14N 12 47 E
Gualeguay, Argentina **126 C4** 33 10 S 59 14W
Gualeguay →,
Argentina . . . . . . **126 C4** 33 3 S 59 31W
Gualeguaychú,
Argentina . . . . . . **126 C4** 33 3 S 58 31W
Guam ☑, Pac. Oc. . . **96 F6** 13 27N 144 45 E
Guamini, Argentina . . **126 D3** 37 1 S 62 28W
Guamúchil, Mexico . . **118 B3** 25 25N 108 3W
Guana I., Br. Virgin Is. **121 e** 18 30N 64 30W
Guanabacoa, Cuba . . **120 B3** 23 8N 82 18W
Guanacaste △,
Costa Rica **120 D2** 10 57N 85 30W
Guanacaste, Cordillera
del, Costa Rica . . . **120 D2** 10 40N 85 4W
Guanaceví, Mexico . . **118 B3** 25 40N 106 0W
Guanahani = San
Salvador I., Bahamas **121 B5** 24 0N 74 40W
Guanajay, Cuba **120 B3** 22 56N 82 42W
Guanajuato, Mexico . **118 C4** 21 0N 101 20W
Guanajuato □, Mexico **118 C4** 20 40N 101 20W
Guandacol, Argentina **126 B2** 29 30 S 68 40W
Guane, Cuba **120 B3** 22 10N 84 7W
Guang'an, China . . . **58 B6** 30 28N 106 35 E
Guangchang, China . . **59 D11** 26 50N 116 21 E
Guangde, China . . . . **59 B12** 30 54N 119 25 E
Guangdong □, China . **59 F9** 23 0N 113 0 E
Guangfeng, China . . . **59 C12** 28 10N 118 15 E
Guanghan, China . . . **58 B5** 30 58N 104 17 E
Guanghua, China . . . **59 A8** 32 22N 111 38 E
Guangling, China . . . **56 E8** 39 47N 114 22 E
Guangnan, China . . . **58 E5** 24 5N 105 4 E
Guangning, China . . . **59 F9** 23 40N 112 22 E
Guangrao, China . . . **57 F10** 37 5N 118 25 E
Guangshui, China . . . **59 B9** 31 37N 114 0 E
Guangshun, China . . **58 D6** 26 8N 106 21 E
Guangwu, China . . . **56 F3** 37 48N 105 57 E
Guangxi Zhuangzu
Zizhiqu □, China . . **58 F7** 24 0N 109 0 E
Guangyuan, China . . **58 A5** 32 26N 105 51 E
Guangze, China . . . . **59 D11** 27 30N 117 12 E
Guangzhou, China . . **59 F9** 23 5N 113 10 E
Guanipa →, Venezuela **124 B6** 9 56N 62 26W
Guanling, China . . . . **58 E5** 25 56N 105 35 E
Guannan, China . . . . **57 G10** 34 8N 119 21 E
Guantánamo, Cuba . . **121 B4** 20 10N 75 14W
Guantánamo B., Cuba **121 C4** 19 59N 75 10W
Guantao, China . . . . **56 F8** 36 42N 115 25 E
Guanyang, China . . . **59 E8** 25 30N 111 8 E
Guanyun, China . . . . **57 G10** 34 20N 119 18 E
Guápiles, Costa Rica . **120 D3** 10 10N 83 46W
Guapo B., Trin. & Tob. **125 K15** 10 12N 61 41W
Guaporé, Brazil . . . . **127 B5** 28 51 S 51 54W
Guaporé →, Brazil . . **124 F5** 11 55 S 65 4W
Guaqui, Bolivia . . . . **124 G5** 16 41 S 68 54W
Guara, Sierra de, Spain **38 C4** 42 19N 0 15W
Guaramacal △,
Venezuela **121 E5** 9 13N 70 12W
Guaraparí, Brazil . . . **127 A7** 20 40 S 40 30W
Guarapuava, Brazil . . **127 B5** 25 20 S 51 30W
Guaratinguetá, Brazil **127 A6** 22 49 S 45 9W
Guaratuba, Brazil . . . **127 B6** 25 53 S 48 38W
Guarda, Portugal . . . **36 E3** 40 32N 7 20W
Guarda □, Portugal . . **36 E3** 40 40N 7 20W
Guardafui, C. = Asir,
Ras, Somali Rep. . . **75 E5** 11 55N 51 10 E
Guardamar del Segura,
Spain **39 G4** 38 5N 0 39W
Guardavalle, Italy . . . **43 D9** 38 30N 16 30 E
Guárdia Sanframondi,
Italy . . . . **43 A7** 41 15N 14 36 E
Guardo, Spain **36 C6** 42 47N 4 50W
Guareña, Spain **37 G4** 38 51N 6 6W
Guareña →, Spain . . **36 D5** 41 29N 5 23W
Guárico □, Venezuela **124 B5** 8 40N 66 35W
Guarujá, Brazil . . . . **127 A6** 24 2 S 46 25W
Guarulhos, Brazil . . . **127 A6** 23 29 S 46 33W
Guarus, Brazil . . . . . **127 A7** 21 44 S 41 20W
Guasave, Mexico . . . **118 B3** 25 34N 108 27W
Guasdualito, Venezuela **124 B4** 7 15N 70 44W
Guastalla, Italy . . . . **40 D7** 44 55N 10 39 E
Guatemala ■,
Cent. Amer. **120 D1** 14 40N 90 22W
Guatemala □, Guatemala **120 D1** 14 40N 90 22W
Guatemala Trench,
Pac. Oc. **98 H10** 15 0N 95 0W
Guatopo △, Venezuela **121 D6** 10 5N 66 30W
Guatuaro Pt.,
Trin. & Tob. **125 K16** 10 19N 60 59W
Guaviare →, Colombia **124 C5** 4 3N 67 44W
Guaxupé, Brazil . . . . **127 A6** 21 10 S 47 5W

Guayaguayare,
  Trin. & Tob. **125 K15** 10 8N 61 2W
Guayama, Puerto Rico . **121 d** 17 59N 66 7W
Guayaquil, Ecuador .. **124 D3** 2 15 S 79 52W
Guayaquil, G. de,
  Ecuador .... **124 D2** 3 10 S 81 0W
Guaymas, Mexico **118 B2** 27 59N 110 54W
Guba, Dem. Rep. of
  the Congo .... **87 E2** 10 38 S 26 27 E
Guba, Ethiopia ...... **81 E4** 11 17N 35 20 E
Gûbâl, Madiq, Egypt .. **80 B3** 27 30N 34 0 E
Gubat, Phil. .... **61 E6** 12 55N 124 7 E
Gubbio, Italy .... **41 E9** 43 21N 12 35 E
Guben, Germany .... **24 D10** 51 57N 14 42 E
Gubin, Poland ...... **31 G1** 51 57N 14 43 E
Gubio, Nigeria ...... **83 C7** 12 30N 12 42 E
Gubkin, Russia ..... **33 G9** 51 17N 37 32 E
Guča, Serbia & M. ... **44 C4** 43 46N 20 15 E
Gucheng, China ..... **59 A8** 32 20N 111 30 E
Gudata = Guadauta,
  Georgia .... **35 J5** 43 7N 40 32 E
Gudbrandsdalen,
  Norway .... **9 F14** 61 33N 10 10 E
Guddu Barrage,
  Pakistan .... **66 E6** 28 30N 69 50 E
Gudenå ➤, Denmark . **11 H4** 56 29N 10 13 E
Gudermes, Russia .... **35 J8** 43 24N 46 5 E
Gudhjem, Denmark .. **11 J8** 55 12N 14 58 E
Gudur, India .... **66 M11** 14 12N 79 55 E
Guebwiller, France .. **19 E14** 47 55N 7 12 E
Guecho = Getxo, Spain **38 B2** 43 21N 2 59W
Guékédou, Guinea ... **82 D2** 8 40N 10 5W
Guéle Mendouka,
  Cameroon .... **83 E7** 4 23N 12 55 E
Guelmine = Goulimine,
  Morocco **78 C3** 28 56N 10 0W
Guelph, Canada **116 C4** 43 35N 80 20W
Guémené-Penfao,
  France **18 E5** 47 38N 1 50W
Guémené-sur-Scorff,
  France **18 D3** 48 4N 3 13W
Guéné, Benin .... **83 C5** 11 44N 3 16 E
Guer, France **18 E4** 47 54N 2 8W
Guérande, France ... **18 E4** 47 20N 2 26W
Guéret, France ..... **19 F8** 46 11N 1 51 E
Guérigny, France .... **19 E10** 47 6N 3 10 E
Guerneville, U.S.A. .. **110 G4** 38 30N 123 0W
Guernica = Gernika-
  Lumo, Spain **38 B2** 43 19N 2 40W
Guernsey, U.K. **15 H5** 49 26N 2 35W
Guernsey, U.S.A. **112 D2** 42 19N 104 45W
Guerrero □, Mexico .. **119 D5** 17 30N 100 0W
Guessou-Sud, Benin .. **83 C5** 10 3N 2 38 E
Gueugnon, France ... **19 F11** 46 36N 4 4 E
Guéyo, Ivory C. **82 D3** 5 25N 6 5W
Gughe, Ethiopia .... **81 F4** 6 12N 37 30 E
Gûgher, Iran .... **71 D8** 29 28N 56 27 E
Guglionesi, Italy .... **41 G11** 41 55N 14 55 E
Guhakolak, Tanjung,
  Indonesia .... **63 G11** 6 50 S 105 14 E
Gui Jiang ➤, China .. **59 F8** 23 30N 111 15 E
Guia, Canary Is. **48 F4** 28 8N 15 38W
Guia de Isora, Canary Is. **48 F3** 28 12N 16 46W
Guia Lopes da Laguna,
  Brazil .... **127 A4** 21 26 S 56 7W
Guiana Highlands,
  S. Amer. **122 C4** 5 10N 60 40W
Guibéroua, Ivory C. .. **82 D3** 6 14N 6 10W
Guichi, China ...... **59 B11** 30 39N 117 27 E
Guider, Cameroon ... **83 D7** 9 56N 13 57 E
Guidiguir, Niger .... **83 C6** 13 40N 9 50 E
Guidimouni, Niger ... **83 C6** 13 42N 9 31 E
Guiding, China ..... **58 D6** 26 34N 107 11 E
Guidong, China ..... **59 D9** 26 7N 113 57 E
Guidónia-Montecélio,
  Italy .... **41 F9** 42 1N 12 45 E
Guiers, L. de, Senegal . **82 B1** 16 10N 15 50W
Guigang, China ..... **58 F7** 23 8N 109 35 E
Guiglo, Ivory C. **82 D3** 6 45N 7 30W
Guihulñgan, Phil. ... **61 F5** 10 7N 123 16 E
Guiyá, Mozam. ..... **89 C5** 24 27 S 33 0 E
Guijuelo, Spain **36 E5** 40 33N 5 40W
Guildford, U.K. **15 F7** 51 14N 0 34W
Guilford, U.S.A. **117 E12** 41 17N 72 41W
Guilin, China ...... **59 E8** 25 18N 110 15 E
Guillaume-Delisle, L.,
  Canada **104 A4** 56 15N 76 17W
Guillaumes, France .. **21 D10** 44 5N 6 52 E
Guillestre, France ... **21 D10** 44 39N 6 40 E
Guilvinec, France ... **18 E2** 47 48N 4 17W
Güimar, Canary Is. .. **48 F3** 28 18N 16 24W
Guimarães, Portugal . **36 D2** 41 28N 8 24W
Guimaras □, Phil. ... **61 F5** 10 35N 122 37 E
Guinda, U.S.A. **110 G4** 38 50N 122 12W
Guinea, Africa ...... **76 F4** 8 0N 8 0 E
Guinea ■, W. Afr. ... **82 C2** 10 20N 11 30W
Guinea, Gulf of, Atl. Oc. **83 E5** 3 0N 2 30 E
Guinea-Bissau ■, Africa **82 C2** 12 0N 15 0W
Güines, Cuba **120 B3** 22 50N 82 0W
Guingamp, France ... **18 D3** 48 34N 3 10W
Guinguinéo, Senegal . **82 C1** 14 20N 15 57W
Guipavas, France **18 D2** 48 26N 4 29W
Guiping, China ..... **59 F8** 23 21N 110 2 E
Guipúzcoa □, Spain . **38 B2** 43 12N 2 15W
Guir, Mali **82 B4** 18 52N 2 52W
Guirel, Mauritania .. **82 B3** 15 30N 7 3W
Güiria, Venezuela ... **124 A6** 10 32N 62 18W
Guiscard, France .... **19 C10** 49 40N 3 1 E
Guise, France ...... **19 C10** 49 52N 3 35 E
Guitiríz, Spain **36 B3** 43 11N 7 50W
Guitri, Ivory C. **82 D3** 5 30N 5 14W
Guiuan, Phil. ...... **61 F6** 11 5N 125 55 E
Guixi, China ...... **59 C11** 28 16N 117 15 E
Guiyang, Guizhou,
  China .... **58 D6** 26 32N 106 40 E
Guiyang, Hunan, China **59 E9** 25 46N 112 42 E
Guizhou □, China ... **58 D6** 27 0N 107 0 E
Gujan-Mestras, France **20 D2** 44 38N 1 4W
Gujar Khan, Pakistan . **68 C5** 33 16N 73 19 E
Gujarat □, India .... **68 H4** 23 20N 71 0 E
Gujiang, China ..... **59 D10** 27 11N 114 47 E
Gujranwala, Pakistan . **68 C6** 32 10N 74 12 E
Gujrat, Pakistan .... **68 C6** 32 40N 74 2 E
Gukovo, Russia ..... **35 F5** 48 1N 39 58 E
Gulbarga, India .... **66 L10** 17 20N 76 50 E
Gulbene, Latvia .... **9 H22** 57 8N 26 52 E
Gulf, The = Persian
  Gulf, Asia .... **71 E7** 27 0N 50 0 E
Gulf Islands □, U.S.A. **115 E2** 30 15N 87 50W
Gulfport, U.S.A. **113 K10** 30 22N 89 6W
Gulgong, Australia .. **95 E4** 32 20 S 149 49 E
Gulin, China ...... **58 C5** 28 10N 105 50 E
Gulistan, Pakistan .. **68 D2** 30 30N 66 35 E
Gull Lake, Canada .. **103 C7** 50 10N 108 29W
Gullbrandstorp, Sweden **11 H6** 56 42N 12 43 E
Gullspång, Sweden .. **11 F8** 58 59N 14 6 E
Güllük, Turkey ..... **47 D9** 37 14N 27 35 E

Güllük Daği △, Turkey **47 E12** 37 0N 30 30 E
Güllük Korfezi, Turkey **47 D9** 37 12N 27 30 E
Gulma, Nigeria ..... **83 C5** 12 40N 4 23 E
Gulmarg, India ..... **69 B6** 34 3N 74 25 E
Gülnar, Turkey ..... **72 D5** 36 19N 33 24 E
Gülpınar, Turkey ... **47 B8** 39 32N 26 7 E
Gülşehir, Turkey .... **72 C6** 38 44N 34 37 E
Gulshad, Kazakhstan . **52 E8** 46 45N 74 25 E
Gulu, Uganda ...... **86 B3** 2 48N 32 17 E
Gülübovo, Bulgaria .. **45 D9** 42 8N 25 55 E
Gulud, J., Sudan .... **81 E2** 11 41N 29 31 E
Gulwe, Tanzania .... **86 D4** 6 30 S 36 25 E
Gulyaypole =
  Hulyaypole, Ukraine **33 J9** 47 45N 36 21 E
Gumal ➤, Pakistan .. **68 D4** 31 40N 71 50 E
Gumbaz, Pakistan ... **68 D3** 30 2N 69 0 E
Gumel, Nigeria ..... **83 C6** 12 39N 9 22 E
Gumiel de Hizán, Spain **36 D7** 41 46N 3 41W
Gumla, India ...... **69 H11** 23 3N 84 33 E
Gumlu, Australia ... **94 B4** 19 53 S 147 41 E
Gumma □, Japan ... **55 F9** 36 30N 138 20 E
Gummersbach,
  Germany .... **24 D3** 51 1N 7 34 E
Gummi, Nigeria .... **83 C6** 12 4N 5 9 E
Gümüldür, Turkey .. **47 C9** 38 6N 27 0 E
Gümüşçay, Turkey .. **45 F11** 40 16N 27 17 E
Gümüşhacıköy, Turkey **72 B6** 40 50N 35 18 E
Gümüşhane, Turkey . **73 B8** 40 30N 39 30 E
Gümüşsu, Turkey ... **47 C11** 38 14N 29 43 E
Gumzai, Indonesia .. **63 F8** 5 28 S 134 42 E
Guna, Ethiopia ..... **81 F4** 8 18N 39 52 E
Guna, India .... **68 G7** 24 40N 77 19 E
Gundelfingen, Germany **25 G6** 48 34N 10 22 E
Güney, Burdur, Turkey **47 D11** 37 29N 29 34 E
Güney, Denizli, Turkey **47 C11** 38 10N 29 4 E
Güneydoğu Toroslar,
  Turkey .... **73 C9** 38 20N 40 30 E
Gunisao ➤, Canada . **103 C9** 53 56N 97 53W
Gunisao L., Canada .. **103 C9** 53 33N 96 15W
Gunjyal, Pakistan ... **68 C4** 32 20N 71 55 E
Günlüce, Turkey .... **47 E10** 36 50N 28 20 E
Gunnarskog, Sweden . **10 E6** 59 45N 12 34 E
Gunnbjørn Fjeld,
  Greenland **4 C6** 68 55N 29 47W
Gunnebo, Sweden .. **11 G10** 57 44N 16 32 E
Gunnedah, Australia . **95 E5** 30 59 S 150 15 E
Gunnewin, Australia . **95 D4** 25 59 S 148 33 E
Gunningbar Cr. ➤,
  Australia .... **95 E4** 31 14 S 147 6 E
Gunnison, Colo., U.S.A. **109 G10** 38 33N 106 56W
Gunnison, Utah, U.S.A. **108 G8** 39 9N 111 49W
Gunnison ➤, U.S.A. . **109 G9** 39 4N 108 35W
Gunpowder, Australia **94 B2** 19 42 S 139 22 E
Guntakal, India .... **66 M10** 15 11N 77 27 E
Guntersville, U.S.A. . **115 H2** 34 21N 86 18W
Guntong, Malaysia .. **65 K3** 4 36N 101 3 E
Guntur, India ...... **67 L12** 16 23N 80 30 E
Gunungapi, Indonesia **63 F7** 6 45 S 126 30 E
Gunungsitoli, Indonesia **62 D1** 1 15N 97 30 E
Günz ➤, Germany .. **25 G6** 48 27N 10 16 E
Gunza, Angola ..... **84 G2** 10 50 S 13 50 E
Günzburg, Germany . **25 G6** 48 26N 10 17 E
Gunzenhausen,
  Germany .... **25 F6** 49 7N 10 44 E
Guo He ➤, China ... **57 H9** 32 59N 117 10 E
Guoyang, China .... **56 H9** 33 32N 116 12 E
Gupis, Pakistan .... **69 A5** 36 15N 73 20 E
Gura Humorului,
  Romania .... **29 C10** 47 35N 25 53 E
Gura-Teghii, Romania **29 E11** 45 30N 26 25 E
Gurag, Ethiopia .... **81 F4** 8 20N 38 20 E
Gurahonţ, Romania . **28 D7** 46 16N 22 21 E
Gurdaspur, India ... **68 C6** 32 5N 75 31 E
Gurdon, U.S.A. **113 J8** 33 55N 93 9W
Güre, Balıkesir, Turkey **47 B8** 39 36N 26 54 E
Güre, Uşak, Turkey .. **47 C11** 38 39N 29 10 E
Gurgaon, India ..... **68 E7** 28 27N 77 1 E
Gürgentepe, Turkey . **72 B7** 40 51N 37 50 E
Gurghiu, Munţii,
  Romania .... **29 D10** 46 41N 25 15 E
Gurgueia ➤, Brazil .. **125 E10** 6 50 S 43 24W
Gurha, India ...... **68 G4** 25 12N 71 39 E
Guri, Embalse de,
  Venezuela **124 B6** 7 50N 62 52W
Gurig △, Australia ... **92 B5** 11 36 S 132 7 E
Gurin, Nigeria ..... **83 D7** 9 5N 12 54 E
Gurjaani, Georgia ... **35 K7** 41 43N 45 52 E
Gurk ➤, Austria .... **26 E7** 46 35N 14 31 E
Gurkha, Nepal ..... **69 E11** 28 5N 84 40 E
Gurley, Australia ... **95 D4** 29 45 S 149 48 E
Gurnet Point, U.S.A. **117 D14** 42 1N 70 34W
Guro, Mozam. ..... **87 F3** 17 26 S 32 30 E
Gürpınar, İst., Turkey **45 F12** 40 59N 28 37 E
Gürpınar, Van, Turkey **73 C10** 38 18N 43 25 E
Gürsu, Turkey ..... **45 F13** 40 13N 29 11 E
Gurué, Mozam. ..... **87 F4** 15 25 S 36 58 E
Gurun, Malaysia ... **65 K3** 5 49N 100 27 E
Gürün, Turkey ..... **72 C7** 38 43N 37 15 E
Gurupá, Brazil ..... **125 D8** 1 25 S 51 35W
Gurupá, I. Grande de,
  Brazil .... **125 D8** 1 25 S 51 45W
Gurupi, Brazil ..... **125 F9** 11 43 S 49 4W
Gurupi ➤, Brazil ... **125 D9** 1 13 S 46 6W
Guruwe, Zimbabwe . **89 B5** 16 40 S 30 42 E
Guryev = Atyraū,
  Kazakhstan .... **52 E6** 47 5N 52 0 E
Guryevsk, Russia ... **30 D7** 54 47N 20 38 E
Gus-Khrustalnyy, Russia **34 C5** 55 42N 40 44 E
Gusau, Nigeria ..... **83 C6** 12 12N 6 40 E
Gusev, Russia ...... **9 J20** 54 35N 22 10 E
Gushan, China ..... **57 E12** 39 50N 123 35 E
Gushgy, Turkmenistan **52 F7** 35 20N 62 18 E
Gushi, China ...... **59 A10** 32 11N 115 41 E
Gushiago, Ghana ... **83 D4** 9 55N 0 15W
Gusinje, Serbia & M. . **44 D3** 42 35N 19 50 E
Gusinoozersk, Russia . **53 D11** 51 16N 106 27 E
Gúspini, Italy ...... **42 C1** 39 32N 8 37 E
Güssing, Austria .... **27 D9** 47 3N 16 20 E
Gustavsberg, Sweden **10 E12** 59 19N 18 23 E
Gustavus, U.S.A. **102 B1** 58 25N 135 44W
Gustine, U.S.A. **110 H6** 37 16N 121 0W
Güstrow, Germany .. **24 B8** 53 47N 12 10 E
Gusum, Sweden .... **11 F10** 58 16N 16 30 E
Guta = Kolárovo,
  Slovak Rep. .... **27 D10** 47 54N 18 0 E
Güterslon, Germany . **24 D4** 51 54N 8 24 E
Gutha, Australia .... **93 E2** 28 58 S 115 55 E
Guthalungra, Australia **94 B4** 19 52 S 147 50 E
Guthrie, Okla., U.S.A. **113 H6** 35 53N 97 25W
Guthrie, Tex., U.S.A. **113 J4** 33 37N 100 19W
Gutian, China ..... **59 D12** 26 32N 118 43 E
Guttenberg, U.S.A. . **112 D9** 42 47N 91 6W
Gutu, Zimbabwe ... **89 B5** 19 41 S 31 9 E
Guwahati, India .... **67 F17** 26 10N 91 45 E
Guy Fawkes River △,
  Australia .... **95 D5** 30 0 S 152 20 E
Guyana ■, S. Amer. . **124 C7** 5 0N 59 0W

Guyane française =
  French Guiana ☑,
  S. Amer. **125 C8** 4 0N 53 0W
Guyenne, France ... **20 D4** 44 30N 0 40 E
Guymon, U.S.A. **113 G4** 36 41N 101 29W
Guyra, Australia .... **95 E5** 30 15 S 151 40 E
Guyuan, Hebei, China **56 D8** 41 37N 115 40 E
Guyuan, Ningxia Huizu,
  China .... **56 G4** 36 0N 106 20 E
Güzelbahçe, Turkey . **47 C8** 38 21N 26 54 E
Güzelyurt = Morphou,
  Cyprus .... **49 D11** 35 12N 32 59 E
Guzhang, China .... **58 C7** 28 42N 109 58 E
Guzhen, China ..... **57 H9** 33 22N 117 18 E
Guzmán, L. de, Mexico **118 A3** 31 25N 107 25W
Gvardeysk, Russia ... **9 J19** 54 39N 21 5 E
Gvardeyskoye, Ukraine **33 K8** 45 7N 34 1 E
Gwa, Burma .... **67 L19** 17 36N 94 34 E
Gwaai, Zimbabwe ... **87 F2** 19 15 S 27 45 E
Gwaai ➤, Zimbabwe . **87 F2** 17 59 S 26 52 E
Gwabegar, Australia . **95 E4** 30 31 S 149 0 E
Gwädar, Pakistan ... **66 G3** 25 10N 62 18 E
Gwagwada, Nigeria . **83 C6** 10 15N 7 15 E
Gwaii Haanas △,
  Canada **102 C2** 52 21N 131 26W
Gwalior, India ..... **68 F8** 26 12N 78 10 E
Gwanara, Nigeria ... **83 D5** 8 55N 3 9 E
Gwanda, Zimbabwe . **87 G2** 20 55 S 29 0 E
Gwandu, Nigeria ... **83 C5** 12 30N 4 41 E
Gwane, Dem. Rep. of
  the Congo .... **86 B2** 4 45N 25 48 E
Gwaram, Nigeria ... **83 C7** 10 15N 10 25 E
Gwarzo, Nigeria .... **83 C6** 12 20N 8 55 E
Gwasero, Nigeria ... **83 D5** 9 29N 3 30 E
Gwda ➤, Poland ... **31 E3** 53 3N 16 44 E
Gweebarra B., Ireland **12 B3** 54 51N 8 23W
Gweedore, Ireland .. **12 A3** 55 3N 8 13W
Gweru, Zimbabwe .. **87 F2** 19 28 S 29 45 E
Gwi, Nigeria .... **83 D6** 9 0N 7 10 E
Gwinn, U.S.A. **114 B2** 46 19N 87 27W
Gwio Kura, Nigeria . **83 C7** 12 40N 11 2 E
Gwoza, Nigeria ..... **83 C7** 11 5N 13 40 E
Gwydir ➤, Australia . **95 D4** 29 27 S 149 48 E
Gwynedd □, U.K. ... **14 E3** 52 52N 4 10W
Gyandzha = Gäncä,
  Azerbaijan .... **35 K8** 40 45N 46 20 E
Gyaring Hu, China .. **60 C4** 34 50N 97 40 E
Gydanskiy Poluostrov,
  Russia .... **52 C8** 70 0N 78 0 E
Gympie, Australia ... **95 D5** 26 11 S 152 38 E
Gyomaendrőd, Hungary **28 D5** 46 56N 20 50 E
Gyöngyös, Hungary . **28 C4** 47 48N 19 56 E
Győr, Hungary ..... **28 C2** 47 41N 17 40 E
Győr-Moson-Sopron □,
  Hungary .... **28 C2** 47 40N 17 20 E
Gypsum Pt., Canada . **102 A6** 61 53N 114 35W
Gypsumville, Canada . **103 C9** 51 45N 98 40W
Gyueshevo, Bulgaria . **44 D6** 42 14N 22 28 E
Gyula, Hungary .... **28 D6** 46 38N 21 17 E
Gyumri, Armenia ... **35 K6** 40 47N 43 50 E
Gyzylarbat,
  Turkmenistan .... **52 F6** 39 4N 56 23 E
Gyzyletrek,
  Turkmenistan .... **71 B7** 37 36N 54 46 E
Gzhatsk = Gagarin,
  Russia .... **32 E8** 55 38N 35 0 E

H

Ha 'Arava ➤, Israel .. **74 E4** 30 50N 35 20 E
Ha Coi, Vietnam .... **58 G6** 21 26N 107 46 E
Ha Dong, Vietnam .. **58 G5** 20 58N 105 46 E
Ha Giang, Vietnam .. **58 F5** 22 50N 104 59 E
Ha Karmel □, Israel . **74 C4** 32 45N 35 5 E
Ha Tien, Vietnam ... **65 G5** 10 23N 104 29 E
Ha Tinh, Vietnam ... **64 C5** 18 20N 105 54 E
Ha Trung, Vietnam .. **64 C5** 19 58N 105 50 E
Ha Yaek Chalong,
  Thailand .... **65 a** 7 50N 98 22 E
Haaksbergen, Neths. . **17 B6** 52 9N 6 45 E
Haapsalu, Estonia ... **9 G20** 58 56N 23 30 E
Haarlem, Neths. .... **17 B4** 52 23N 4 39 E
Haast ➤, N.Z. ..... **91 K2** 43 50 S 169 2 E
Haast Bluff, Australia **92 D5** 23 22 S 132 0 E
Hab ➤, Pakistan .... **68 G2** 24 53N 66 41 E
Hab Nadi Chauki,
  Pakistan .... **68 G2** 25 0N 66 50 E
Habahe, China ..... **60 B3** 48 0N 86 30 E
Habaswein, Kenya .. **86 B4** 1 2N 39 30 E
Habay, Canada **102 B5** 58 50N 118 44W
Ḥabbānīyah, Iraq ... **70 C4** 33 17N 43 29 E
Ḥabbānīyah, Hawr al,
  Iraq .... **73 F10** 33 17N 43 29 E
Habichtswald △,
  Germany .... **24 D5** 51 15N 9 15 E
Habo, Sweden ...... **11 G8** 57 55N 14 6 E
Haboro, Japan ..... **54 B10** 44 22N 141 42 E
Ḥabshān, U.A.E. .... **71 F7** 23 50N 53 37 E
Hachenburg, Germany **24 E3** 50 40N 7 49 E
Hachijō-Jima, Japan . **55 H9** 33 5N 139 45 E
Hachinohe, Japan ... **54 D10** 40 30N 141 29 E
Hachiōji, Japan .... **55 G9** 35 40N 139 20 E
Hachōn, N. Korea ... **57 D15** 41 29N 129 2 E
Hacıbektaş, Turkey .. **72 C6** 38 56N 34 33 E
Hacılar, Turkey .... **72 C6** 38 38N 35 26 E
Hackås, Sweden .... **10 B8** 62 56N 14 30 E
Hackensack, U.S.A. . **117 F10** 40 53N 74 3W
Hackettstown, U.S.A. **117 F10** 40 51N 74 50W
Hadali, Pakistan .... **68 C5** 32 16N 72 11 E
Hadarba, Ras, Sudan **80 C4** 22 4N 36 51 E
Hadarom □, Israel .. **74 E3** 31 0N 35 0 E
Hadd, Ra's al, Oman **75 C6** 22 35N 59 50 E
Haddington, U.K. ... **13 F6** 55 57N 2 47W
Hadejia, Nigeria .... **83 C7** 12 30N 10 5 E
Hadejia ➤, Nigeria .. **83 C7** 12 30N 10 0 E
Hadera, Israel ..... **74 C3** 32 27N 34 55 E
Hadera, N. ➤, Israel **74 C3** 32 28N 34 52 E
Haderslev, Denmark . **11 J3** 55 15N 9 30 E
Hadhramaut =
  Ḥaḍramawt, Yemen **75 D4** 15 30N 49 30 E
Hadibou, Yemen ... **75 E5** 12 39N 54 2 E
Hadım, Turkey ..... **72 D5** 36 58N 32 26 E
Hadong, S. Korea ... **57 G14** 35 5N 127 44 E
Ḥaḍramawt, Yemen . **75 D4** 15 30N 49 30 E
Ḥadrānīyah, Iraq ... **70 C4** 35 38N 43 14 E
Hadrian's Wall, U.K. **14 B5** 55 0N 2 30W
Hadsten, Denmark .. **11 H4** 56 19N 10 3 E
Hadsund, Denmark .. **11 H4** 56 44N 10 11 E
Hadyach, Ukraine ... **33 G8** 50 21N 34 0 E
Haeju, N. Korea .... **57 E13** 38 3N 125 45 E
Haenam, S. Korea ... **57 G14** 34 34N 126 35 E
Haenertsburg, S. Africa **89 C4** 24 0 S 29 50 E
Haerhpin = Harbin,
  China .... **57 B14** 45 48N 126 40 E

Hafar al Bâţin,
  Si. Arabia .... **70 D5** 28 32N 45 52 E
Hafik, Turkey ...... **72 C7** 39 51N 37 23 E
Ḥafīrat al 'Aydā,
  Si. Arabia .... **70 E3** 26 26N 39 12 E
Ḥafīt, Oman .... **71 F7** 23 59N 55 49 E
Hafizabad, Pakistan . **68 C5** 32 5N 73 40 E
Haflong, India ..... **67 G18** 25 10N 93 5 E
Hafnarfjörður, Iceland **8 D3** 64 4N 21 57W
Haft Gel, Iran ...... **71 D6** 31 30N 49 32 E
Hafun, Ras, Somali Rep. **75 E5** 10 29N 51 30 E
Hagalil, Israel ..... **74 C4** 32 53N 35 18 E
Hagby, Sweden ..... **11 H10** 56 34N 16 11 E
Hagen, Germany .... **24 D3** 51 21N 7 27 E
Hagenow, Germany . **24 B7** 53 26N 11 12 E
Hagerman, U.S.A. .. **113 J2** 33 7N 104 20W
Hagerman Fossil
  Beds △, U.S.A. ... **108 E6** 42 48N 114 57W
Hagerstown, U.S.A. . **114 F7** 39 39N 77 43W
Hagersville, Canada . **116 D4** 42 58N 80 3W
Hagetmau, France .. **20 E3** 43 39N 0 37W
Hagfors, Sweden ... **10 D7** 60 3N 13 45 E
Hagi, Japan .... **55 G5** 34 30N 131 22 E
Hagolan, Syria ..... **74 C4** 33 0N 35 45 E
Hagondange, France **19 C13** 49 16N 6 11 E
Hags Hd., Ireland ... **12 D2** 52 57N 9 28W
Hague, C. de la, France **18 C5** 49 44N 1 56W
Hague, The = 's-
  Gravenhage, Neths. **17 B4** 52 7N 4 17 E
Haguenau, France ... **19 D14** 48 49N 7 47 E
Hai Duong, Vietnam **58 G6** 20 56N 106 19 E
Hai'an, Guangdong,
  China .... **59 G8** 20 18N 110 11 E
Hai'an, Jiangsu, China **59 A13** 32 37N 120 27 E
Haicheng, Fujian, China **59 E11** 24 23N 117 48 E
Haicheng, Liaoning,
  China .... **57 D12** 40 50N 122 45 E
Haidar Khel, Afghan. **68 C3** 33 58N 68 38 E
Haidarâbâd =
  Hyderabad, India . **66 L11** 17 22N 78 29 E
Haidargarh, India ... **69 F9** 26 37N 81 22 E
Haifa = Ḥefa, Israel . **74 C4** 32 46N 35 0 E
Haifeng, China ..... **59 F10** 22 58N 115 10 E
Haiger, Germany ... **24 E4** 50 43N 8 12 E
Haikou, China ..... **60 D6** 20 1N 110 16 E
Ḥā'il, Si. Arabia .... **70 E4** 27 28N 41 45 E
Hailar, China ...... **60 B6** 49 10N 119 38 E
Hailey, U.S.A. **108 E6** 43 31N 114 19W
Haileybury, Canada . **104 C4** 47 30N 79 38W
Hailin, China ...... **57 B15** 44 37N 129 30 E
Hailing Dao, China .. **59 G8** 21 35N 111 47 E
Hailong, China ..... **57 C13** 42 32N 125 40 E
Hailuoto, Finland ... **8 D21** 65 3N 24 45 E
Haimen, Guangdong,
  China .... **59 F11** 23 15N 116 38 E
Haimen, Jiangsu, China **59 B13** 31 52N 121 10 E
Hainan □, China .... **60 E5** 19 0N 109 30 E
Hainaut □, Belgium . **17 D4** 50 30N 4 0 E
Hainburg, Austria ... **27 C9** 48 9N 16 56 E
Haines, Alaska, U.S.A. **102 B1** 59 14N 135 26W
Haines, Oreg., U.S.A. **108 D5** 44 55N 117 56W
Haines City, U.S.A. . **115 L5** 28 7N 81 38W
Haines Junction, Canada **102 A1** 60 45N 137 30W
Hainfeld, Austria ... **26 C8** 48 3N 15 48 E
Haining, China ..... **59 B13** 30 28N 120 40 E
Haiphong, Vietnam . **58 G6** 20 47N 106 41 E
Haitan Dao, China .. **59 E12** 25 30N 119 45 E
Haiti ■, W. Indies ... **121 C5** 19 0N 72 30W
Haiya, Sudan ...... **80 D4** 18 20N 36 21 E
Haiyan, China ..... **59 B13** 30 28N 120 57 E
Haiyang, China .... **57 F11** 36 47N 121 9 E
Haiyuan,
  Guangxi Zhuangzu,
  China .... **58 F6** 22 8N 107 35 E
Haiyuan, Ningxia Huizu,
  China .... **56 F3** 36 35N 105 52 E
Haizhou, China .... **57 G10** 34 37N 119 7 E
Haizhou Wan, China **57 G10** 34 50N 119 20 E
Hajdú-Bihar □,
  Hungary .... **28 C6** 47 30N 21 30 E
Hajdúböszörmény,
  Hungary .... **28 C6** 47 40N 21 30 E
Hajdúdorog, Hungary **28 C6** 47 48N 21 30 E
Hajdúhadház, Hungary **28 C6** 47 40N 21 40 E
Hajdúnánás, Hungary **28 C6** 47 50N 21 26 E
Hajdúsámson, Hungary **28 C6** 47 37N 21 42 E
Hajdúszoboszló,
  Hungary .... **28 C6** 47 27N 21 22 E
Hajipur, India ..... **69 G11** 25 45N 85 13 E
Ḥājjī Muḥsin, Iraq .. **70 C5** 32 35N 45 29 E
Ḥājjīābād, Iran .... **71 D7** 28 19N 55 55 E
Ḥājjīābād-e Zarrīn, Iran **71 C7** 33 9N 54 51 E
Hajnówka, Poland .. **31 F10** 52 47N 23 35 E
Hakansson, Mts.,
  Dem. Rep. of
  the Congo .... **87 D2** 8 40 S 25 45 E
Hakkâri, Turkey .... **70 B4** 37 34N 43 44 E
Hakkâri Dağları, Turkey **73 C10** 37 30N 44 0 E
Hakken-Zan, Japan . **55 G7** 34 10N 135 54 E
Hakodate, Japan ... **54 D10** 41 45N 140 44 E
Hakos, Namibia .... **88 C2** 23 13 S 16 21 E
Håksberg, Sweden .. **10 D9** 60 11N 15 6 E
Haku-San, Japan ... **55 F8** 36 9N 136 46 E
Haku-San △, Japan .. **55 F8** 36 15N 136 45 E
Hakui, Japan ...... **55 F8** 36 53N 136 47 E
Hala, Pakistan ..... **66 G6** 25 43N 68 20 E
Ḥalab, Syria .... **70 B3** 36 10N 37 15 E
Ḥalabjah, Iraq ..... **70 C5** 35 10N 45 58 E
Halaib, Sudan ..... **80 C4** 22 12N 36 30 E
Halasa, Sudan ..... **81 E3** 14 26N 30 39 E
Ḥalat 'Ammār,
  Si. Arabia .... **70 D3** 29 10N 36 4 E
Halba, Lebanon .... **74 A5** 34 34N 36 6 E
Halberstadt, Germany **24 D7** 51 54N 11 3 E
Halcombe, N.Z. .... **91 J5** 40 8 S 175 30 E
Halcon, Phil. ...... **63 B6** 13 0N 121 12 E
Halde Fjäll =
  Haltiatunturi, Finland **8 B19** 69 17N 21 18 E
Halden, Norway .... **9 G14** 59 9N 11 23 E
Haldensleben, Germany **24 C7** 52 17N 11 30 E
Haldia, India ...... **67 H16** 22 5N 88 3 E
Haldimand, Canada . **116 D6** 42 57N 79 51W
Haldwani, India .... **69 E8** 29 31N 79 30 E
Hale ➤, Australia ... **94 C2** 24 56 S 135 53 E
Halesowen, U.K. ... **15 E5** 52 27N 2 3W
Halesworth, U.K. ... **15 E9** 52 21N 1 31 E
Haleyville, U.S.A. ... **115 H2** 34 14N 87 37W
Half Assini, Ghana .. **82 D4** 5 1N 2 50W
Halfmoon Bay, N.Z. . **91 M2** 46 50 S 168 5 E
Halfway ➤, Canada . **102 B4** 56 12N 121 32W
Halia, India .... **69 G10** 24 50N 82 19 E
Haliburton, Canada . **116 A6** 45 3N 78 30W
Halifax, Australia ... **94 B4** 18 32 S 146 22 E
Halifax, Canada **105 D7** 44 38N 63 35W
Halifax, U.K. **14 D6** 53 43N 1 52W
Halifax, U.S.A. **117 F8** 40 25N 76 55W
Halifax B., Australia . **94 B4** 18 50 S 147 0 E

Halifax I., Namibia .. **88 D2** 26 38 S 15 4 E
Halīl ➤, Iran ...... **71 E8** 27 40N 58 30 E
Halkirk, U.K. **13 C5** 58 30N 3 29W
Hall Beach = Sanirajak,
  Canada **101 B11** 68 46N 81 12W
Hall in Tirol, Austria . **26 D4** 47 17N 11 30 E
Hall Pen., Canada ... **101 B13** 63 30N 66 0W
Hall Pt., Australia .. **92 C3** 15 40 S 124 23 E
Hallabro, Sweden ... **11 H9** 56 22N 15 5 E
Halland, Sweden ... **9 H15** 57 8N 12 47 E
Hallands län, Sweden **11 H6** 57 0N 12 40 E
Hallands Väderö,
  Sweden .... **11 H6** 56 27N 12 34 E
Hallandsås, Sweden . **11 H7** 56 22N 13 0 E
Hällbybrunn, Sweden **10 E10** 59 24N 16 25 E
Halle, Belgium ..... **17 D4** 50 44N 4 13 E
Halle,
  Nordrhein-Westfalen,
  Germany .... **24 C4** 52 3N 8 22 E
Halle, Sachsen-Anhalt,
  Germany .... **24 D7** 51 30N 11 56 E
Hällefors, Sweden .. **10 E8** 59 47N 14 31 E
Hälleforsnäs, Sweden **10 E10** 59 10N 16 30 E
Hallein, Austria .... **26 D6** 47 40N 13 5 E
Hällekis, Sweden ... **11 F7** 58 38N 13 27 E
Hallen, Sweden .... **10 A8** 63 12N 14 0 E
Hallett, Australia ... **95 E2** 33 25 S 138 55 E
Hallettsville, U.S.A. . **113 L6** 29 27N 96 57W
Hallim, S. Korea .... **57 H14** 33 24N 126 15 E
Hallingdalselvi ➤,
  Norway .... **9 F13** 60 23N 9 35 E
Hallock, U.S.A. **112 A6** 48 47N 96 57W
Halls Creek, Australia **92 C4** 18 16 S 127 38 E
Hallsberg, Sweden .. **10 E9** 59 5N 15 7 E
Hallstahammar, Sweden **10 E10** 59 38N 16 15 E
Hallstatt, Austria ... **26 D6** 47 33N 13 38 E
Hallstavik, Sweden .. **10 D12** 60 5N 18 37 E
Hallstead, U.S.A. ... **117 E9** 41 58N 75 45W
Halmahera, Indonesia **63 D7** 0 40N 128 0 E
Halmeu, Romania .. **28 C8** 47 57N 23 2 E
Halmstad, Sweden .. **11 H6** 56 41N 12 52 E
Hals, Denmark ..... **11 H4** 57 0N 10 18 E
Hälsingborg =
  Helsingborg, Sweden **11 H6** 56 3N 12 42 E
Hälsingland, Sweden **10 C10** 61 40N 16 5 E
Halstad, U.S.A. **112 B6** 47 21N 96 50W
Haltern, Germany .. **24 D3** 51 44N 7 11 E
Haltiatunturi, Finland **8 B19** 69 17N 21 18 E
Haltwhistle, U.K. ... **14 C5** 54 58N 2 26W
Ḥālūl, Qatar ...... **71 E7** 25 40N 52 40 E
Halvad, India ...... **68 H4** 23 1N 71 11 E
Halvān, Iran ...... **71 C8** 33 57N 56 15 E
Ham, France ...... **19 C10** 49 45N 3 4 E
Ham Tan, Vietnam .. **65 G6** 10 40N 107 45 E
Ham Yen, Vietnam .. **64 A5** 22 4N 105 3 E
Hamab, Namibia ... **88 D2** 28 7 S 19 16 E
Hamada, Japan .... **55 G6** 34 56N 132 4 E
Hamadān, Iran ..... **71 C6** 34 52N 48 32 E
Hamadān □, Iran ... **71 C6** 35 0N 49 0 E
Hamāh, Syria ...... **70 C3** 35 5N 36 40 E
Hamamatsu, Japan . **55 G8** 34 45N 137 45 E
Hamar, Norway .... **9 F14** 60 48N 11 7 E
Ḥamāta, Gebel, Egypt **70 E2** 24 17N 35 0 E
Hambantota, Sri Lanka **66 R12** 6 10N 81 10 E
Hamber △, Canada . **102 C5** 52 20N 118 0W
Hamburg, Germany . **24 B5** 53 33N 9 59 E
Hamburg, Ark., U.S.A. **113 J9** 33 14N 91 48W
Hamburg, N.Y., U.S.A. **116 D6** 42 43N 78 50W
Hamburg, Pa., U.S.A. **117 F9** 40 33N 75 59W
Hamburg □, Germany **24 B5** 53 30N 10 0 E
Hamburg Fuhlsbüttel ✈
  (HAM), Germany . **24 B5** 53 38N 9 59 E
Ḥamḍ, W. al ➤,
  Si. Arabia .... **70 E3** 24 55N 36 20 E
Hamden, U.S.A. **117 E12** 41 23N 72 54W
Hamdibey, Turkey .. **47 B9** 39 50N 27 15 E
Häme, Finland ..... **9 F20** 61 30N 24 20 E
Hämeenlinna, Finland **9 F21** 61 0N 24 28 E
Hamélé, Ghana **82 C4** 10 56N 2 45W
Hamelin Pool, Australia **93 E1** 26 22 S 114 20 E
Hameln, Germany .. **24 C5** 52 6N 9 21 E
Hamerkaz □, Israel . **74 C3** 32 15N 34 55 E
Hamersley Ra.,
  Australia .... **92 D2** 22 0 S 117 45 E
Hamhung, N. Korea . **57 E14** 39 54N 127 30 E
Hami, China .... **60 B4** 42 55N 93 25 E
Hamilton, Australia . **95 F3** 37 45 S 142 2 E
Hamilton, Canada .. **116 C5** 43 15N 79 50W
Hamilton, N.Z. ..... **91 G5** 37 47 S 175 19 E
Hamilton, U.K. **13 F4** 55 46N 4 2W
Hamilton, Ala., U.S.A. **115 H1** 34 9N 87 59W
Hamilton, Mont., U.S.A. **108 C6** 46 15N 114 10W
Hamilton, N.Y., U.S.A. **117 D9** 42 50N 75 33W
Hamilton, Ohio, U.S.A. **114 F3** 39 24N 84 34W
Hamilton, Tex., U.S.A. **113 K5** 31 42N 98 7W
Hamilton, The ➤,
  Australia .... **95 D2** 26 40 S 135 19 E
Hamilton City, U.S.A. **110 F4** 39 45N 122 1W
Hamilton I., Australia **94 b** 20 21 S 148 56 E
Hamilton Inlet, Canada **105 B8** 54 0N 57 30W
Hamilton Mt., U.S.A. **117 C10** 43 25N 74 22W
Hamina, Finland ... **9 F22** 60 34N 27 12 E
Hamirpur, H.P., India **68 D7** 31 41N 76 31 E
Hamirpur, Ut. P., India **69 G9** 25 57N 80 9 E
Hamitabat, Turkey .. **45 E11** 41 30N 27 17 E
Hamlet, U.S.A. **115 H6** 34 53N 79 42W
Hamley Bridge,
  Australia .... **95 E2** 34 17 S 138 35 E
Hamlin = Hameln,
  Germany .... **24 C5** 52 6N 9 21 E
Hamlin, N.Y., U.S.A. **116 C7** 43 17N 77 55W
Hamlin, Tex., U.S.A. **113 J4** 32 53N 100 8W
Hamm, Germany ... **24 D3** 51 40N 7 50 E
Ḥammār, Hawr al, Iraq **70 D5** 30 50N 47 10 E
Hammarstrand, Sweden **10 A10** 63 7N 16 35 E
Hammerfest, Norway **8 A20** 70 39N 23 41 E
Hammerum, Denmark **11 H3** 56 9N 9 4 E
Hammond, Ind., U.S.A. **114 E2** 41 38N 87 30W
Hammond, La., U.S.A. **113 K9** 30 30N 90 28W
Hammond, N.Y., U.S.A. **117 B9** 44 27N 75 42W
Hammondsport, U.S.A. **116 D7** 42 25N 77 13W
Hammonton, U.S.A. **114 F8** 39 39N 74 48W
Hamneda, Sweden .. **11 H7** 56 41N 13 51 E
Hamoyet, Jebel, Sudan **80 D4** 17 33N 38 2 E
Hampden, N.Z. ..... **91 L3** 45 18 S 170 50 E
Hampshire □, U.K. . **15 F6** 51 7N 1 23W
Hampshire Downs, U.K. **15 F6** 51 15N 1 10W
Hampton, N.B., Canada **105 C6** 45 32N 65 51W
Hampton, Ont., Canada **116 C6** 43 58N 78 45W
Hampton, Ark., U.S.A. **113 J8** 33 32N 92 28W
Hampton, Iowa, U.S.A. **112 D8** 42 45N 93 13W

Hampton, N.H., U.S.A. **117 D14** 42 57N 70 50W
Hampton, S.C., U.S.A. **115 J5** 32 52N 81 7W
Hampton, Va., U.S.A. **114 G7** 37 2N 76 21W
Hampton Bays, U.S.A. **117 F12** 40 53N 72 30W
Hampton Tableland,
  Australia **93 F4** 32 0S 127 0 E
Hamra, Syria **10 C8** 34 59N 14 59 E
Hamrat esh Sheykh,
  Sudan **81 E2** 14 38N 27 55 E
Hamur, Turkey **73 C10** 39 37N 43 3 E
Hamyang, S. Korea **57 G14** 35 32N 127 42 E
Han Jiang →, China **59 F11** 23 25N 116 40 E
Han Shui, China **58 A7** 30 34N 114 17 E
Han Shui →, China **59 B10** 30 35N 114 18 E
Hanak, Si. Arabia **70 E3** 25 32N 37 0 E
Hanamaki, Japan **54 E10** 39 23N 141 7 E
Hanang, Tanzania **86 C4** 4 30 S 35 25 E
Hanau, Germany **25 E4** 50 7N 8 56 E
Hanbogd = Ihbulag,
  Mongolia **56 C4** 43 11N 107 10 E
Hançalar, Turkey **47 C11** 38 8N 29 24 E
Hâncești, Moldova **29 D13** 46 50N 28 36 E
Hancheng, China **56 G6** 35 31N 110 25 E
Hanchuan, China **59 B9** 30 40N 113 50 E
Hancock, Mich., U.S.A. **112 B10** 47 8N 88 35W
Hancock, N.Y., U.S.A. **117 E9** 41 57N 75 17W
Handa, Japan **55 G8** 34 53N 136 55 E
Handan, China **56 F8** 36 35N 114 28 E
Handeni, Tanzania **86 D4** 5 25 S 38 2 E
Handlová, Slovak Rep. **27 C11** 48 45N 18 35 E
Handub, Sudan **80 D4** 19 15N 37 16 E
Handwara, India **69 B6** 34 21N 74 20 E
Hanegev, Israel **74 E4** 30 50N 35 0 E
Hanford, U.S.A. **110 J7** 36 20N 119 39W
Hanford Reach △,
  U.S.A. **108 C4** 46 40N 119 28W
Hang Chat, Thailand **64 C2** 18 20N 99 21 E
Hang Dong, Thailand **64 C2** 18 41N 98 55 E
Hangang →, S. Korea **57 F14** 37 50N 126 30 E
Hangayn Nuruu,
  Mongolia **60 B4** 47 30N 99 0 E
Hangchou = Hangzhou,
  China **59 B13** 30 18N 120 11 E
Hanggin Houqi, China **56 D4** 40 58N 107 4 E
Hanggin Qi, China **56 E5** 39 52N 108 50 E
Hangu, China **57 E9** 39 18N 117 53 E
Hangzhou, China **59 B13** 30 18N 120 11 E
Hangzhou Wan, China **59 B13** 30 15N 120 45 E
Hanhongor, Mongolia **56 C3** 43 55N 104 28 E
Ḥanīdh, Si. Arabia **71 E6** 26 35N 48 38 E
Ḥanīsh, Yemen **75 E3** 13 45N 42 46 E
Haniska, Slovak Rep. **27 C14** 48 37N 21 15 E
Hanjiang, China **59 E12** 25 26N 119 6 E
Hankinson, U.S.A. **112 B6** 46 4N 96 54W
Hankö, Finland **9 G20** 59 50N 22 57 E
Hankou, China **59 B10** 30 35N 114 30 E
Hanksville, U.S.A. **109 G8** 38 22N 110 43W
Hanle, India **69 C8** 32 42N 79 4 E
Hanmer Springs, N.Z. **91 K4** 42 32 S 172 50 E
Hann →, Australia **92 C4** 17 26 S 126 17 E
Hann, Mt., Australia **92 C4** 15 45 S 126 0 E
Hanna, Canada **102 C6** 51 40N 111 54W
Hanna, U.S.A. **108 F10** 41 52N 106 34W
Hannah B., Canada **104 B4** 51 40N 80 0W
Hannibal, Mo., U.S.A. **112 F9** 39 42N 91 22W
Hannibal, N.Y., U.S.A. **117 C8** 43 19N 76 35W
Hannik, Sudan **80 D3** 18 12N 32 20 E
Hannover, Germany **24 C5** 52 22N 9 46 E
Hanö, Sweden **11 H8** 56 1N 14 50 E
Hanöbukten, Sweden **11 J8** 55 35N 14 30 E
Hanoi, Vietnam **58 G5** 21 5N 105 55 E
Hanover = Hannover,
  Germany **24 C5** 52 22N 9 46 E
Hanover, Canada **116 B3** 44 9N 81 2W
Hanover, S. Africa **88 E3** 31 4S 24 29 E
Hanover, N.H., U.S.A. **117 C12** 43 42N 72 17W
Hanover, Ohio, U.S.A. **116 F2** 40 4N 82 16W
Hanover, Pa., U.S.A. **114 F7** 39 48N 76 59W
Hanover, I., Chile **128 G2** 51 0 S 74 50W
Hans Lollik I.,
  U.S. Virgin Is. **121 e** 18 24N 64 53W
Hansdiha, India **69 G12** 24 36N 87 5 E
Hanshou, China **59 C8** 28 56N 111 50 E
Hansi, India **68 E6** 29 10N 75 57 E
Hanson, L., Australia **95 E2** 31 0 S 136 15 E
Hanstholm, Denmark **11 G2** 57 7N 8 36 E
Hantsavichy, Belarus **33 F4** 52 49N 26 30 E
Hanumangarh, India **68 E6** 29 35N 74 19 E
Hanyin, China **58 A7** 32 54N 108 28 E
Hanzhong, China **56 H4** 33 10N 107 1 E
Hanzhuang, China **57 G9** 34 33N 117 23 E
Haora, India **69 H13** 22 37N 88 20 E
Haoxue, China **59 B9** 30 1N 112 24 E
Haparanda, Sweden **8 D21** 65 52N 24 8 E
Happy, U.S.A. **113 H4** 34 45N 101 52W
Happy Camp, U.S.A. **108 F2** 41 48N 123 23W
Happy Valley-Goose
  Bay, Canada **105 B7** 53 15N 60 20W
Hapsu, N. Korea **57 D15** 41 13N 128 51 E
Hapur, India **68 E7** 28 45N 77 45 E
Ḥaql, Si. Arabia **74 F3** 29 10N 34 58 E
Har, Indonesia **63 F8** 5 16 S 133 14 E
Har-Ayrag, Mongolia **56 B5** 45 47N 109 16 E
Har Hu, China **60 C4** 38 20N 97 38 E
Har Us Nuur, Mongolia **60 B4** 48 0N 92 0 E
Har Yehuda, Israel **74 D3** 31 35N 34 57 E
Harad, Belarus **32 E6** 55 30N 30 3 E
Härädsbäck, Sweden **11 H8** 56 32N 14 26 E
Haranomachi, Japan **54 F10** 37 38N 140 58 E
Harare, Zimbabwe **87 F3** 17 43 S 31 2 E
Harat, Eritrea **81 D4** 16 5N 39 26 E
Harbin, China **57 B14** 45 48N 126 40 E
Harbiye, Turkey **72 D7** 36 10N 36 8 E
Harbo, Sweden **10 D11** 60 7N 17 12 E
Harboør, Denmark **11 H2** 56 38N 8 10 E
Harbour Beach, U.S.A. **116 C2** 43 51N 82 39W
Harbour Breton,
  Canada **105 C8** 47 29N 55 50W
Harbour Deep, Canada **105 B8** 50 25N 56 32W
Harburg, Germany **24 B5** 53 27N 9 58 E
Harburger Berge △,
  Germany **24 B5** 53 26N 9 51 E
Hårby, Denmark **11 J4** 55 13N 10 7 E
Harda, India **68 H7** 22 27N 77 5 E
Hardangerfjorden,
  Norway **9 F12** 60 5N 6 0 E
Hardangervidda,
  Norway **9 F12** 60 7N 7 20 E
Hardap □, Namibia **88 C2** 24 29 S 17 45 E
Hardap Dam, Namibia **88 C2** 24 32 S 17 50 E
Hardenberg, Neths. **17 B6** 52 34N 6 37 E
Harderwijk, Neths. **17 B5** 52 21N 5 38 E
Hardey →, Australia **92 D2** 22 45 S 116 8 E
Hardin, U.S.A. **108 D10** 45 44N 107 37W
Harding, S. Africa **89 E4** 30 35 S 29 55 E

Harding Ra., Australia **92 C3** 16 17 S 124 55 E
Hardisty, Canada **102 C6** 52 40N 111 18W
Hardoi, India **69 F9** 27 26N 80 6 E
Hardwar = Haridwar,
  India **68 E8** 29 58N 78 9 E
Hardwick, U.S.A. **117 B12** 44 30N 72 22W
Hardy, Pen., Chile **128 H3** 55 30 S 68 20W
Hardy, Pte., St. Lucia **121 f** 14 6N 60 56W
Hare B., Canada **105 B8** 51 15N 55 45W
Hareid, Norway **9 E12** 62 22N 6 1 E
Haren, Germany **24 C3** 52 47N 7 13 E
Harer, Ethiopia **81 F5** 9 20N 42 8 E
Harerge, Ethiopia **81 F5** 7 12N 42 0 E
Hareto, Ethiopia **81 F4** 9 23N 37 6 E
Harfleur, France **18 C7** 49 30N 0 10 E
Hargeisa, Somali Rep. **75 F3** 9 30N 44 2 E
Harghita □, Romania **29 D10** 46 30N 25 30 E
Harghita, Munții,
  Romania **29 D10** 46 25N 25 35 E
Hargshamn, Sweden **10 D12** 60 12N 18 30 E
Hari →, Indonesia **62 E2** 1 16 S 104 5 E
Haria, Canary Is. **48 E6** 29 8N 13 32W
Haridwar, India **68 E8** 29 58N 78 9 E
Harim, Jabal al, Oman **71 E8** 25 58N 56 14 E
Haringhata →, Bangla. **67 J16** 22 0N 89 58 E
Harīrūd →, Asia **66 A2** 37 24N 60 38 E
Härjedalen, Sweden **10 B7** 62 22N 13 5 E
Harlan, Iowa, U.S.A. **112 E7** 41 39N 95 19W
Harlan, Ky., U.S.A. **115 G4** 36 51N 83 19W
Hârlău, Romania **29 C11** 47 23N 26 55 E
Harlech, U.K. **14 E3** 52 52N 4 6W
Hårlev, Denmark **11 J6** 55 21N 12 14 E
Harlingen, Neths. **17 A5** 53 11N 5 25 E
Harlingen, U.S.A. **113 M6** 26 12N 97 42W
Harlow, U.K. **15 F8** 51 46N 0 8 E
Harlowton, U.S.A. **108 C9** 46 26N 109 50W
Harmancık, Turkey **47 B11** 39 41N 29 9 E
Harmånger, Sweden **10 C11** 61 55N 17 20 E
Harmil, Eritrea **81 D5** 16 30N 40 10 E
Harnai, Pakistan **68 D2** 30 6N 67 56 E
Harney Basin, U.S.A. **108 E4** 43 30N 119 0W
Harney L., U.S.A. **108 E4** 43 14N 119 8W
Harney Peak, U.S.A. **112 D3** 43 52N 103 32W
Härnön, Sweden **10 B12** 62 36N 18 0 E
Härnösand, Sweden **10 B11** 62 38N 17 55 E
Haro, Spain **38 C2** 42 35N 2 55W
Haroldswick, U.K. **13 A8** 60 48N 0 50W
Harp L., Canada **105 A7** 55 5N 61 50W
Harper, Liberia **82 E3** 4 25N 7 43W
Harplinge, Sweden **11 H6** 56 45N 12 45 E
Harr, Mauritania **82 B2** 15 20N 12 28W
Harrai, India **69 H8** 22 37N 79 13 E
Harrand, Pakistan **68 E4** 29 28N 70 3 E
Ḥarrat Khaybar,
  Si. Arabia **80 B5** 25 30N 39 45 E
Harricana →, Canada **104 B4** 50 56N 79 32W
Harriman, U.S.A. **115 H3** 35 56N 84 33W
Harrington Harbour,
  Canada **105 B8** 50 31N 59 30W
Harris, U.K. **13 D2** 57 50N 6 55W
Harris, L., Australia **95 E2** 31 10 S 135 10 E
Harris, Sd. of, U.K. **13 D1** 57 44N 7 6W
Harris, Pt., Canada **116 C2** 43 6N 82 9W
Harrisburg, Ill., U.S.A. **113 G10** 37 44N 88 32W
Harrisburg, Nebr.,
  U.S.A. **112 E3** 41 33N 103 44W
Harrisburg, Pa., U.S.A. **116 F8** 40 16N 76 53W
Harrismith, S. Africa **89 D4** 28 15 S 29 8 E
Harrison, Ark., U.S.A. **113 G8** 36 14N 93 7W
Harrison, Maine, U.S.A. **117 B14** 44 7N 70 39W
Harrison, Nebr., U.S.A. **112 D3** 42 41N 103 53W
Harrison, C., Canada **105 B8** 54 55N 57 55W
Harrison L., Canada **102 D4** 49 33N 121 50W
Harrisonburg, U.S.A. **114 F6** 38 27N 78 52W
Harrisonville, U.S.A. **112 F7** 38 39N 94 21W
Harriston, Canada **116 C4** 43 57N 80 53W
Harrisville, Mich.,
  U.S.A. **116 B1** 44 39N 83 17W
Harrisville, N.Y., U.S.A. **117 B9** 44 9N 75 19W
Harrisville, Pa., U.S.A. **116 E5** 41 8N 80 0W
Harrodsburg, U.S.A. **114 G3** 37 46N 84 51W
Harrogate, U.K. **14 C6** 54 0N 1 33W
Harrow □, U.K. **15 F7** 51 35N 0 21W
Harrowsmith, Canada **117 B8** 44 24N 76 40W
Harry S. Truman
  Reservoir, U.S.A. **112 F7** 38 16N 93 24W
Harsefeld, Germany **24 B5** 53 27N 9 30 E
Harsewinkel, Germany **24 D4** 51 56N 8 14 E
Harsīn, Iran **70 C5** 34 18N 47 33 E
Hârșova, Romania **29 F12** 44 40N 27 59 E
Harstad, Norway **8 B17** 68 48N 16 30 E
Harsud, India **68 H7** 22 6N 76 44 E
Hart, U.S.A. **114 D2** 43 42N 86 22W
Hart, L., Australia **95 E2** 31 10 S 136 25 E
Hartbees →, S. Africa **88 D3** 28 45 S 20 32 E
Hartberg, Austria **26 D8** 47 17N 15 58 E
Hartford, Conn., U.S.A. **117 E12** 41 46N 72 41W
Hartford, Ky., U.S.A. **114 G2** 37 27N 86 55W
Hartford, S. Dak.,
  U.S.A. **112 D6** 43 38N 96 57W
Hartford, Wis., U.S.A. **112 D10** 43 19N 88 22W
Hartford City, U.S.A. **114 E3** 40 27N 85 22W
Hartland, Canada **105 C6** 46 20N 67 32W
Hartland Pt., U.K. **15 F3** 51 1N 4 32W
Hartlepool, U.K. **14 C6** 54 42N 1 13W
Hartlepool □, U.K. **14 C6** 54 42N 1 17W
Hartley Bay, Canada **102 C3** 53 25N 129 15W
Hartmannberge,
  Namibia **88 B1** 17 0 S 13 0 E
Hartney, Canada **103 D8** 49 30N 100 35W
Hârtop, Moldova **29 D13** 46 39N 28 40 E
Harts →, S. Africa **88 D3** 28 24 S 24 17 E
Hartselle, U.S.A. **115 H2** 34 27N 86 56W
Hartshorne, U.S.A. **113 H7** 34 51N 95 34W
Hartstown, U.S.A. **116 E4** 41 33N 80 23W
Hartsville, U.S.A. **115 H5** 34 23N 80 4W
Hartswater, S. Africa **88 D3** 27 34 S 24 43 E
Hartwell, U.S.A. **115 H4** 34 21N 82 56W
Harunabad, Pakistan **68 E5** 29 35N 73 8 E
Harvand, Iran **71 D7** 28 25N 55 43 E
Harvey, Australia **93 F2** 33 5S 115 54 E
Harvey, Ill., U.S.A. **114 E2** 41 36N 87 50W
Harvey, N. Dak. U.S.A. **112 B5** 47 47N 99 56W
Harwich, U.K. **15 F9** 51 56N 1 17 E
Haryana □, India **68 E7** 29 0N 76 10 E
Haryn →, Belarus **33 F4** 52 7N 27 17 E
Harz, Germany **24 D6** 51 38N 10 44 E
Harz □, Germany **24 D6** 51 40N 10 18 E
Harzgerode, Germany **24 D7** 51 38N 11 8 E
Hasa □, Si. Arabia **71 E6** 25 50N 49 0 E
Hasaheisa, Sudan **81 E3** 14 44N 33 20 E
Ḥasanābād, Iran **71 C7** 32 8N 52 44 E
Hasb, W. →, Iraq **70 D5** 31 45N 44 17 E
Hasdo →, India **69 J10** 21 44N 82 44 E

Haselünne, Germany **24 C3** 52 40N 7 29 E
Hashimoto, Japan **55 G7** 34 19N 135 37 E
Hashtjerd, Iran **71 C6** 35 52N 50 40 E
Haskell, U.S.A. **113 J5** 33 10N 99 44W
Hasköy, Turkey **45 E10** 41 38N 26 52 E
Haslach, Germany **25 G4** 48 16N 8 5 E
Hasle, Denmark **11 J8** 55 11N 14 44 E
Haslemere, U.K. **15 F7** 51 5N 0 43W
Haslev, Denmark **11 J5** 55 18N 11 57 E
Hasparren, France **20 E2** 43 24N 1 18W
Hassa, Turkey **72 D7** 36 48N 36 29 E
Hassberge →, Germany **25 E6** 50 10N 10 45 E
Hassela, Sweden **10 B11** 62 7N 16 42 E
Hasselt, Belgium **17 D5** 50 56N 5 21 E
Hassfurt, Germany **25 E6** 50 2N 10 30 E
Hassi Messaoud, Algeria **78 B7** 31 51N 6 1 E
Hässleholm, Sweden **11 H7** 56 10N 13 46 E
Hassloch, Germany **25 F4** 49 22N 8 16 E
Hästholmen, Sweden **11 F8** 58 17N 14 38 E
Hastings, N.Z. **91 H6** 39 39 S 176 52 E
Hastings, U.K. **15 G8** 50 51N 0 35 E
Hastings, Mich., U.S.A. **114 D3** 42 39N 85 17W
Hastings, Minn., U.S.A. **112 C8** 44 44N 92 51W
Hastings, Nebr., U.S.A. **112 E5** 40 35N 98 23W
Hastings Ra., Australia **95 E5** 31 15 S 152 14 E
Hästveda, Sweden **11 H7** 56 17N 13 55 E
Hat Yai, Thailand **65 J3** 7 1N 100 27 E
Hatanbulag = Ergel,
  Mongolia **56 C5** 43 8N 109 5 E
Hatay = Antalya, Turkey **72 D5** 36 52N 30 45 E
Hatch, U.S.A. **109 K10** 32 40N 107 9W
Hatchet L., Canada **103 B8** 58 36N 103 40W
Haţeg, Romania **28 E7** 45 36N 22 55 E
Hateruma-Shima, Japan **55 M1** 24 3N 123 47 E
Hatfield P.O., Australia **95 E3** 33 54 S 143 49 E
Hatgal, Mongolia **60 A5** 50 26N 100 9 E
Hathras, India **68 F8** 27 36N 78 6 E
Hatia, Bangla. **67 H17** 22 30N 91 5 E
Hato Mayor, Dom. Rep. **121 C6** 18 46N 69 15W
Hatta, India **69 G8** 24 7N 79 36 E
Hattah, Australia **95 E3** 34 48 S 142 17 E
Hatteras, C., U.S.A. **115 H8** 35 14N 75 39W
Hattiesburg, U.S.A. **113 K10** 31 20N 89 17W
Hatvan, Hungary **28 C4** 47 40N 19 45 E
Hau Bon = Cheo Reo,
  Vietnam **62 B3** 13 25N 108 28 E
Hau Duc, Vietnam **64 E7** 15 20N 108 13 E
Haugesund, Norway **9 G11** 59 23N 5 13 E
Haukipudas, Finland **8 D21** 65 12N 25 20 E
Haultain →, Canada **103 B7** 55 51N 106 46W
Hauraki G., N.Z. **91 G5** 36 35 S 175 5 E
Hausruck, Austria **26 C6** 48 6N 13 30 E
Haut Atlas, Morocco **78 B4** 32 30N 5 0W
Haut-Jura △, France **19 F7** 46 23N 2 23 E
Haut-Languedoc △,
  France **20 E6** 43 30N 2 43 E
Haut Niger △, Guinea **82 C2** 10 20N 10 20W
Haut-Rhin □, France **19 E14** 48 0N 7 15 E
Haute-Corse □, France **21 F13** 42 30N 9 30 E
Haute-Garonne □,
  France **20 E5** 43 30N 1 30 E
Haute-Loire □, France **20 C7** 45 5N 3 50 E
Haute-Marne □, France **19 D12** 48 10N 5 20 E
Haute-Normandie □,
  France **18 C7** 49 20N 1 0 E
Haute-Saône □, France **19 E13** 47 45N 6 10 E
Haute-Savoie □, France **21 C10** 46 0N 6 20 E
Haute-Vienne □, France **20 C5** 45 50N 1 10 E
Hautes-Alpes □, France **21 D10** 44 42N 6 20 E
Hautes Fagnes = Hohe
  Venn, Belgium **17 D6** 50 30N 6 5 E
Hautes Fagnes = Hohes
  Venn-Eifel △, Europe **24 E2** 50 30N 6 10 E
Hautes-Pyrénées □,
  France **20 F4** 43 0N 0 10 E
Hauteville-Lompnès,
  France **21 C9** 45 58N 5 36 E
Hautmont, France **19 B10** 50 15N 3 55 E
Hauts-de-Seine □,
  France **19 D9** 48 52N 2 15 E
Hauts Plateaux, Algeria **76 C4** 35 0N 1 0 E
Hauzenberg, Germany **25 G9** 48 40N 13 37 E
Havana = La Habana,
  Cuba **120 B3** 23 8N 82 22W
Havana, U.S.A. **112 E9** 40 18N 90 4W
Havant, U.K. **15 G7** 50 51N 0 58W
Hävärna, Romania **29 B11** 48 4N 26 43 E
Havasor = Kıjzı, Turkey **70 B4** 38 18N 43 25 E
Havasu, L., U.S.A. **111 L12** 34 18N 114 28W
Havdhem, Sweden **11 G12** 57 10N 18 20 E
Havel →, Germany **24 C8** 52 50N 12 3 E
Havelian, Pakistan **68 B5** 34 2N 73 10 E
Havelock, Canada **116 B7** 44 26N 77 53W
Havelock, N.Z. **91 J4** 41 17 S 173 48 E
Havelock, U.S.A. **115 H7** 34 53N 76 54W
Haverfordwest, U.K. **15 F3** 51 48N 4 58W
Haverhill, U.S.A. **117 D13** 42 47N 71 5W
Haverstraw, U.S.A. **117 E11** 41 12N 73 58W
Håverud, Sweden **11 F6** 58 50N 12 28 E
Havirga, Mongolia **56 B7** 45 41N 113 5 E
Havířov, Czech Rep. **27 B11** 49 46N 18 20 E
Havlíčkův Brod,
  Czech Rep. **26 B8** 49 36N 15 33 E
Havneby, Denmark **11 J2** 55 5N 8 34 E
Havran, Turkey **47 B9** 39 33N 27 6 E
Havre, U.S.A. **108 B9** 48 33N 109 41W
Havre-Aubert, Canada **105 C7** 47 12N 61 56W
Havre-St.-Pierre,
  Canada **105 B7** 50 18N 63 33W
Havsa, Turkey **45 E10** 41 33N 26 48 E
Havza, Turkey **72 B6** 41 0N 35 35 E
Haw →, U.S.A. **115 H6** 35 36N 79 3W
Hawaii □, U.S.A. **106 H16** 19 30N 156 30W
Hawaii I., Pac. Oc. **106 J17** 20 30N 156 0W
Hawaiian Is., Pac. Oc. **106 H17** 20 30N 156 0W
Hawaiian Ridge,
  Pac. Oc. **97 E11** 24 0N 165 0W
Hawarden, U.S.A. **112 D6** 43 0N 96 29W
Hawea, L., N.Z. **91 L2** 44 28 S 169 19 E
Hawick, U.K. **13 F6** 55 26N 2 47W
Hawk Junction, Canada **104 C3** 48 5N 84 38W
Hawke B., N.Z. **91 H6** 39 25 S 177 20 E
Hawker, Australia **95 E2** 31 59 S 138 22 E
Hawke's Bay, Canada **105 B8** 50 36N 57 10W
Hawkesbury, Canada **104 C5** 45 37N 74 37W
Hawkesbury →,
  Australia **95 E5** 33 30 S 151 10 E
Hawkesbury I., Canada **102 C3** 53 37N 129 3W
Hawkesbury Pt.,
  Australia **94 A1** 11 55 S 134 5 E
Hawkinsville, U.S.A. **115 J4** 32 17N 83 28W
Hawley, Minn., U.S.A. **112 B6** 46 53N 96 19W
Hawley, Pa., U.S.A. **117 E9** 41 28N 75 11W
Hawrān, W. →, Iraq **70 C4** 33 58N 42 34 E
Hawsh Mūssá, Lebanon **74 B4** 33 45N 35 55 E
Hawthorne, U.S.A. **108 G4** 38 32N 118 38W

Hay, Australia **95 E3** 34 30 S 144 51 E
Hay →, Australia **94 C2** 24 50 S 138 0 E
Hay →, Canada **102 A5** 60 50N 116 26W
Hay, C., Australia **92 B4** 14 5 S 129 29 E
Hay L., Canada **116 B4** 44 53N 80 58W
Hay L., Canada **102 B5** 58 50N 118 50W
Hay-on-Wye, U.K. **15 E4** 52 5N 3 8W
Hay River, Canada **102 A5** 60 51N 115 44W
Hay Springs, U.S.A. **112 D3** 42 41N 102 41W
Haya = Tehoru,
  Indonesia **63 E7** 3 23 S 129 30 E
Hayachine-San, Japan **54 E10** 39 34N 141 29 E
Hayange, France **19 C13** 49 20N 6 2 E
Haydarlı, Turkey **47 C12** 38 16N 30 23 E
Hayden, U.S.A. **108 F10** 40 30N 107 16W
Haydon, Australia **94 B3** 18 0 S 141 30 E
Hayes, U.S.A. **112 C4** 44 23N 101 1W
Hayes →, Canada **104 A1** 57 3N 92 12W
Hayes Creek, Australia **92 B5** 13 43 S 131 22 E
Hayle, U.K. **15 G2** 50 11N 5 26W
Hayling I., U.K. **15 G7** 50 48N 0 59W
Haymana, Turkey **72 C5** 39 26N 32 31 E
Hayrabolu, Turkey **45 E11** 41 12N 27 5 E
Hays, Canada **102 C6** 50 6N 111 48W
Hays, U.S.A. **112 F5** 38 53N 99 20W
Haysyn, Ukraine **29 B14** 48 57N 29 25 E
Hayvoron, Ukraine **29 B14** 48 22N 29 52 E
Hayward, Calif., U.S.A. **110 H4** 37 40N 122 5W
Hayward, Wis., U.S.A. **112 B9** 46 1N 91 29W
Haywards Heath, U.K. **15 G7** 51 0N 0 5W
Hazafon □, Israel **74 C4** 32 40N 35 20 E
Hazārān, Kūh-e, Iran **71 D8** 29 35N 57 20 E
Hazard, U.S.A. **114 G4** 37 15N 83 12W
Hazaribag, India **69 H11** 23 58N 85 26 E
Hazaribag Road, India **69 G11** 24 12N 85 57 E
Hazebrouck, France **19 B9** 50 42N 2 31 E
Hazelton, Canada **102 B3** 55 20N 127 42W
Hazelton, U.S.A. **112 B4** 46 29N 100 17W
Hazen, U.S.A. **112 B4** 47 18N 101 38W
Hazlehurst, Ga., U.S.A. **115 K4** 31 52N 82 36W
Hazlehurst, Miss., U.S.A. **113 K9** 31 52N 90 24W
Hazlet, U.S.A. **117 F10** 40 25N 74 12W
Hazleton, U.S.A. **117 F9** 40 57N 75 59W
Hazro, Turkey **70 B4** 38 15N 40 47 E
He Xian, Anhui, China **59 B12** 31 45N 118 20 E
He Xian,
  Guangxi Zhuangzu,
  China **59 E8** 24 27N 111 30 E
Head of Bight, Australia **93 F5** 31 30 S 131 25 E
Headlands, Zimbabwe **87 F3** 18 15 S 32 2 E
Healdsburg, U.S.A. **110 G4** 38 37N 122 52W
Healdton, U.S.A. **113 H6** 34 14N 97 29W
Healesville, Australia **95 F4** 37 35 S 145 30 E
Heany Junction,
  Zimbabwe **87 G2** 20 6 S 28 54 E
Heard I., Ind. Oc. **3 G13** 53 0 S 74 0 E
Hearne, U.S.A. **113 K6** 30 53N 96 36W
Hearst, Canada **104 C3** 49 40N 83 41W
Heart →, U.S.A. **112 B4** 46 46N 100 50W
Heart's Content, Canada **105 C9** 47 54N 53 27W
Heath, Pte., Canada **105 C7** 49 8N 61 40W
Heathrow, London ✈
  (LHR), U.K. **15 F7** 51 28N 0 27W
Heavener, U.S.A. **113 H7** 34 53N 94 36W
Hebbronville, U.S.A. **113 M5** 27 18N 98 41W
Hebei □, China **56 E9** 39 0N 116 0 E
Hebel, Australia **95 D4** 28 58 S 147 47 E
Heber, U.S.A. **111 N11** 32 44N 115 32W
Heber City, U.S.A. **108 F8** 40 31N 111 25W
Heber Springs, U.S.A. **113 H9** 35 30N 92 2W
Hebert, Canada **103 C7** 50 30N 107 10W
Hebgen L., U.S.A. **108 D8** 44 52N 111 20W
Hebi, China **56 G8** 35 57N 114 7 E
Hebrides, U.K. **6 D4** 57 30N 7 0W
Hebrides, Sea of the,
  U.K. **13 D2** 57 5N 7 0W
Hebron = Al Khalīl,
  West Bank **74 D4** 31 32N 35 6 E
Hebron, Canada **101 C13** 58 5N 62 30W
Hebron, N. Dak., U.S.A. **112 B3** 46 54N 102 3W
Hebron, Nebr., U.S.A. **112 E6** 40 10N 97 35W
Heby, Sweden **10 E10** 59 56N 16 53 E
Hecate Str., Canada **102 C2** 53 10N 130 30W
Heceta I., U.S.A. **102 B2** 55 46N 133 40W
Hechi, China **58 E7** 24 40N 108 2 E
Hechingen, Germany **25 G4** 48 21N 8 57 E
Hechuan, China **58 B6** 30 2N 106 12 E
Hecla, U.S.A. **112 C5** 45 53N 98 9W
Hecla I., Canada **103 C9** 51 10N 96 43W
Hédé, France **18 D5** 48 18N 1 49W
Hede, Sweden **10 B7** 62 23N 13 30 E
Hedemora, Sweden **10 D9** 60 18N 15 58 E
Hedensted, Denmark **11 J3** 55 46N 9 42 E
Hedesunda, Sweden **10 D10** 60 24N 17 2 E
Heerde, Neths. **17 B6** 52 24N 6 2 E
Heerenveen, Neths. **17 B5** 52 57N 5 55 E
Heerhugowaard, Neths. **17 B4** 52 40N 4 51 E
Heerlen, Neths. **17 D5** 50 55N 5 58 E
Hefa, Israel **74 C4** 32 46N 35 0 E
Hefa □, Israel **74 C4** 32 40N 35 0 E
Hefei, China **59 B11** 31 52N 117 18 E
Hefeng, China **59 C8** 29 55N 109 52 E
Hegalig, Sudan **81 E3** 14 36N 31 54 E
Hegang, China **60 B8** 47 20N 130 19 E
Heiban, Sudan **81 E3** 11 13N 30 31 E
Heichengzhen, China **56 F4** 36 24N 106 3 E
Heide, Germany **24 A5** 54 10N 9 6 E
Heidelberg, Germany **25 F4** 49 24N 8 42 E
Heidelberg, S. Africa **88 E3** 34 6 S 20 59 E
Heidenau, Germany **24 E9** 50 59N 13 52 E
Heidenheim, Germany **25 G6** 48 41N 10 9 E
Heijing, China **58 E3** 25 22N 101 44 E
Heilbad Heiligenstadt,
  Germany **24 D6** 51 22N 10 8 E
Heilbron, S. Africa **89 D4** 27 16 S 27 59 E
Heilbronn, Germany **25 F5** 49 9N 9 13 E
Heilongjiang □, China **60 B7** 48 0N 126 0 E
Heilunkiang =
  Heilongjiang □, China **60 B7** 48 0N 126 0 E
Heimaey, Iceland **8 E3** 63 26N 20 17W
Heinola, Finland **9 F22** 61 13N 26 2 E
Heinze Kyun, Burma **64 E1** 14 25N 97 45 E
Heishan, China **57 D12** 41 40N 122 5 E
Heishui, Liaoning,
  China **57 C10** 42 8N 119 30 E
Heishui, Sichuan, China **58 A4** 32 4N 103 2 E
Hejaz = Ḥijāz □,
  Si. Arabia **70 E3** 24 0N 40 0 E
Hejian, China **56 E9** 38 25N 116 5 E
Hejiang, China **58 C5** 28 43N 105 46 E
Hejin, China **56 G6** 35 35N 110 42 E

Hekla, Iceland **8 E4** 63 56N 19 35W
Hekou, Guangdong,
  China **59 F9** 23 13N 112 45 E
Hekou, Yunnan, China **58 F4** 22 30N 103 59 E
Hel, Poland **30 D5** 54 37N 18 47 E
Helagsfjället, Sweden **10 B6** 62 54N 12 25 E
Helan Shan, China **56 E3** 38 30N 105 55 E
Helechosa, Spain **37 F6** 39 22N 4 53W
Helen Atoll, Pac. Oc. **63 D8** 2 40N 132 0 E
Helena, Ark., U.S.A. **113 H9** 34 32N 90 36W
Helena, Mont., U.S.A. **108 C7** 46 36N 112 2W
Helendale, U.S.A. **111 L9** 34 44N 117 19W
Helensburgh, U.K. **13 E4** 56 1N 4 43W
Helensville, N.Z. **91 G5** 36 41 S 174 29 E
Helenvale, Australia **94 B4** 15 43 S 145 14 E
Helgasjön, Sweden **11 H8** 56 55N 14 50 E
Helgeland, Norway **8 C15** 66 7N 13 29 E
Helgoland, Germany **24 A3** 54 10N 7 53 E
Heligoland = Helgoland,
  Germany **24 A3** 54 10N 7 53 E
Heligoland B. =
  Deutsche Bucht,
  Germany **24 A4** 54 15N 8 0 E
Heliopolis, Egypt **80 H7** 30 6N 31 17 E
Hella, Iceland **8 E3** 63 50N 20 24W
Hellertown, U.S.A. **117 F9** 40 35N 75 21W
Hellespont = Çanakkale
  Boğazı, Turkey **45 F10** 40 17N 26 32 E
Hellevoetsluis, Neths. **17 C4** 51 50N 4 8 E
Hellhole Gorge △,
  Australia **94 D3** 25 31 S 144 12 E
Hellín, Spain **39 G3** 38 31N 1 40W
Hells Canyon △, U.S.A. **108 D5** 45 30N 117 45W
Hell's Gate △, Kenya **86 C4** 0 54 S 36 19 E
Helmand □, Afghan. **66 D4** 31 20N 64 0 E
Helmand →, Afghan. **66 D2** 31 12N 61 34 E
Helme →, Germany **24 D7** 51 20N 11 21 E
Helmeringhausen,
  Namibia **88 D2** 25 54 S 16 57 E
Helmond, Neths. **17 C5** 51 29N 5 41 E
Helmsdale, U.K. **13 C5** 58 7N 3 39W
Helmsdale →, U.K. **13 C5** 58 7N 3 40W
Helmstedt, Germany **24 C7** 52 12N 11 0 E
Helong, China **57 C15** 42 40N 129 0 E
Helper, U.S.A. **108 G8** 39 41N 110 51W
Helsingborg, Sweden **11 H6** 56 3N 12 42 E
Helsinge, Denmark **11 H6** 56 2N 12 12 E
Helsingfors = Helsinki,
  Finland **9 F21** 60 15N 25 3 E
Helsingør, Denmark **11 H6** 56 2N 12 35 E
Helsinki, Finland **9 F21** 60 15N 25 3 E
Helska, Mierzeja,
  Poland **30 D5** 54 45N 18 40 E
Helston, U.K. **15 G2** 50 6N 5 17W
Helvellyn, U.K. **14 C4** 54 32N 3 1W
Helwân, Egypt **80 J7** 29 50N 31 20 E
Hemel Hempstead, U.K. **15 F7** 51 44N 0 28 E
Hemet, U.S.A. **111 M10** 33 45N 116 58W
Hemingford, U.S.A. **112 D3** 42 19N 103 4W
Hemmingford, Canada **117 A11** 45 3N 73 35W
Hempstead, U.S.A. **113 K6** 30 6N 96 5W
Hemse, Sweden **11 G12** 57 15N 18 22 E
Hemsön, Sweden **10 B12** 62 42N 18 5 E
Henan □, China **56 H8** 34 0N 114 0 E
Henares →, Spain **36 E7** 40 24N 3 30W
Henashi-Misaki, Japan **54 D9** 40 37N 139 51 E
Hendaye, France **20 E2** 43 23N 1 47W
Hendek, Turkey **72 B4** 40 48N 30 44 E
Henderson, Argentina **126 D3** 36 18 S 61 43W
Henderson, Ky., U.S.A. **114 G2** 37 50N 87 35W
Henderson, N.C., U.S.A. **115 G6** 36 20N 78 25W
Henderson, Nev., U.S.A. **111 J12** 36 2N 114 59W
Henderson, Tenn.,
  U.S.A. **115 H1** 35 26N 88 38W
Henderson, Tex., U.S.A. **113 J7** 32 9N 94 48W
Hendersonville, N.C.,
  U.S.A. **115 H4** 35 19N 82 28W
Hendersonville, Tenn.,
  U.S.A. **115 G2** 36 18N 86 37W
Hendijān, Iran **71 D6** 30 14N 49 43 E
Hendorābī, Iran **71 E7** 26 40N 53 37 E
Heng Jiang, China **58 C5** 28 40N 104 25 E
Heng Xian, China **58 F7** 22 40N 109 17 E
Hengcheng, China **56 E4** 38 18N 106 28 E
Hengchun, Taiwan **59 F13** 22 0N 120 44 E
Hengdaohezi, China **57 B15** 44 52N 129 0 E
Hengelo, Neths. **17 B6** 52 16N 6 48 E
Hengfeng, China **59 C10** 28 12N 115 48 E
Hengshan, Hunan,
  China **59 D9** 27 16N 112 45 E
Hengshan, Shaanxi,
  China **56 F5** 37 58N 109 5 E
Hengshui, China **56 F8** 37 41N 115 40 E
Hengyang, China **59 D9** 26 59N 112 22 E
Henichesk, Ukraine **33 J8** 46 12N 34 50 E
Hénin-Beaumont,
  France **19 B9** 50 25N 2 58 E
Henley-on-Thames,
  U.K. **15 F7** 51 32N 0 54W
Henlopen, C., U.S.A. **114 F8** 38 48N 75 6W
Hennan, Sweden **10 B9** 62 3N 15 54 E
Hennebont, France **18 E3** 47 49N 3 19W
Hennenman, S. Africa **88 D4** 27 59 S 27 1 E
Hennessey, U.S.A. **113 G6** 36 6N 97 54W
Hennigsdorf, Germany **24 C9** 52 38N 13 12 E
Henri Pittier △,
  Venezuela **121 D6** 10 26N 67 37W
Henrietta, U.S.A. **113 J5** 33 49N 98 12W
Henrietta, Ostrov =
  Genriyetty, Ostrov,
  Russia **53 B16** 77 6N 156 30 E
Henrietta Maria, C.,
  Canada **104 A3** 55 9N 82 20W
Henry, U.S.A. **112 E10** 41 7N 89 22W
Henryetta, U.S.A. **113 H7** 35 27N 95 59W
Henryville, Canada **117 A11** 45 8N 73 11W
Hensall, Canada **116 C3** 43 26N 81 30W
Henstedt-Ulzburg,
  Germany **24 B6** 53 47N 10 0 E
Hentiesbaai, Namibia **88 C1** 22 8 S 14 18 E
Hentiyn Nuruu,
  Mongolia **60 B5** 48 30N 108 30 E
Henty, Australia **95 F4** 35 30 S 147 0 E
Henzada, Burma **67 L19** 17 38N 95 26 E
Hephaestia, Greece **47 B7** 39 55N 25 14 E
Heping, China **59 E10** 24 29N 115 0 E
Heppner, U.S.A. **108 D4** 45 21N 119 33W
Hepu, China **58 G7** 21 40N 109 12 E
Hepworth, Canada **116 B3** 44 37N 81 9W
Hequ, China **56 E6** 39 20N 111 15 E
Héradsflói, Iceland **8 D6** 65 42N 14 12W
Héradsvötn →, Iceland **8 D4** 65 45N 19 25W
Heraklion = Iráklion,
  Greece **49 D7** 35 20N 25 12 E
Herald Cays, Australia **94 B4** 16 58 S 149 9 E

Herāt, *Afghan.* ..... **66 B3** 34 20N 62 7 E
Herāt □, *Afghan.* ..... **66 B3** 35 0N 62 0 E
Hérault □, *France* ... **20 E7** 43 34N 3 15 E
Hérault ➤, *France* ... **20 E7** 43 17N 3 26 E
Herbault, *France* ..... **18 E8** 47 36N 1 8 E
Herbert ➤, *Australia* . **94 B4** 18 31 S 146 17 E
Herbert River Falls △,
  Australia .... **94 B4** 18 15 S 145 32 E
Herberton, *Australia* .. **94 B4** 17 20 S 145 25 E
Herbertsdale, *S. Africa* **88 E3** 34 1 S 21 46 E
Herbignac, *France* **18 E4** 47 27N 2 18W
Herborn, *Germany* .... **24 E4** 50 40N 8 18 E
Herby, *Poland* .... **31 H5** 50 45N 18 50 E
Herceg-Novi,
  Serbia & M. ...... **44 D2** 42 30N 18 33 E
Herchmer, *Canada* ... **103 B10** 57 22N 94 10W
Herðubreið, *Iceland* .. **8 D5** 65 11N 16 21W
Hereford, *U.K.* **15 E5** 52 4N 2 43W
Hereford, *U.S.A.* **113 H3** 34 49N 102 24W
Herefordshire □, *U.K.* . **15 E5** 52 8N 2 40W
Hereke, *Turkey* ...... **45 F13** 40 47N 29 38 E
Herencia, *Spain* **37 F7** 39 21N 3 22W
Herentals, *Belgium* ... **17 C4** 51 12N 4 51 E
Herford, *Germany* .... **24 C4** 52 7N 8 39 E
Héricourt, *France* .... **19 E13** 47 32N 6 45 E
Herington, *U.S.A.* **112 F6** 38 40N 96 57W
Herisau, *Switz.* ...... **25 H5** 47 22N 9 17 E
Hérisson, *France* ..... **19 F9** 46 32N 2 42 E
Herkimer, *U.S.A.* **117 D10** 43 0N 74 59W
Herlong, *U.S.A.* **110 E6** 40 8N 120 8W
Herm, *U.K.* **15 H5** 49 30N 2 28W
Hermakivka, *Ukraine* . **29 B11** 48 42N 26 11 E
Hermann, *U.S.A.* **112 F9** 38 42N 91 27W
Hermannsburg,
  Australia .... **92 D5** 23 57 S 132 45 E
Hermannsburg,
  Germany .... **24 C6** 52 50N 10 5 E
Herment, *France* ..... **20 C6** 45 45N 2 24 E
Hermidale, *Australia* . **95 E4** 31 30 S 146 42 E
Hermiston, *U.S.A.* ... **108 D4** 45 51N 119 17W
Hermite, I., *Chile* .... **128 H3** 55 50 S 68 0W
Hermon, *U.S.A.* **117 B9** 44 28N 75 14W
Hermon, Mt. = Shaykh,
  J. ash, *Lebanon* ... **74 B4** 33 25N 35 50 E
Hermosillo, *Mexico* .. **118 B2** 29 10N 111 0W
Hernád ➤, *Hungary* . **28 C6** 47 56N 21 8 E
Hernandarias, *Paraguay* **127 B5** 25 20 S 54 40W
Hernandez, *U.S.A.* ... **110 J6** 36 24N 120 46W
Hernando, *Argentina* . **126 C3** 32 28 S 63 40W
Hernando, *U.S.A.* **113 H10** 34 50N 90 0W
Hernani, *Spain* **38 B3** 43 16N 1 58W
Herndon, *U.S.A.* **116 F8** 40 43N 76 51W
Herne, *Germany* ..... **17 C7** 51 32N 7 14 E
Herne Bay, *U.K.* ..... **15 F9** 51 21N 1 8 E
Herning, *Denmark* .... **11 H2** 56 8N 8 58 E
Heroica = Caborca,
  Mexico **118 A2** 30 40N 112 10W
Heroica Nogales =
  Nogales, *Mexico* ... **118 A2** 31 20N 110 56W
Heron Bay, *Canada* .. **104 C2** 48 40N 86 25W
Herradura, Pta. de la,
  Canary Is. **48 F5** 28 26N 14 8W
Herreid, *U.S.A.* **112 C4** 45 50N 100 4W
Herrenberg, *Germany* . **25 G4** 48 35N 8 52 E
Herrera, *Spain* **37 H6** 37 26N 4 55W
Herrera de Alcántara,
  Spain **37 F3** 39 39N 7 25W
Herrera de Pisuerga,
  Spain **36 C6** 42 35N 4 20W
Herrera del Duque,
  Spain **37 F5** 39 10N 5 3W
Herrestad, *Sweden* ... **11 F5** 58 21N 11 50 E
Herrin, *U.S.A.* **113 G10** 37 48N 89 2W
Herriot, *Canada* **103 B8** 56 22N 101 16W
Herrljunga, *Sweden* .. **11 F7** 58 5N 13 1 E
Hersbruck, *Germany* .. **25 F7** 49 30N 11 26 E
Herschel I., *Canada* .. **4 C1** 69 35N 139 5W
Hershey, *U.S.A.* **117 F8** 40 17N 76 39W
Hersonissos, *Greece* .. **49 D7** 35 18N 25 22 E
Herstal, *Belgium* ..... **17 D5** 50 40N 5 38 E
Hertford, *U.K.* **15 F7** 51 48N 0 4W
Hertfordshire □, *U.K.* . **15 F7** 51 51N 0 5W
's-Hertogenbosch, *Neths.* **17 C5** 51 42N 5 17 E
Hertsa, *Ukraine* ..... **29 B11** 48 9N 26 15 E
Hertzogville, *S. Africa* . **88 D4** 28 9 S 25 30 E
Hervás, *Spain* **36 E5** 40 16N 5 52W
Hervey B., *Australia* .. **94 C5** 25 0 S 152 52 E
Herzberg, *Brandenburg,
  Germany* .... **24 D9** 51 41N 13 14 E
Herzberg,
  *Niedersachsen,
  Germany* .... **24 D6** 51 38N 10 20 E
Herzliyya, *Israel* ..... **74 C3** 32 10N 34 50 E
Herzogenburg, *Austria* **26 C8** 48 17N 15 41 E
Heşar, *Fārs, Iran* .... **71 D6** 29 52N 50 16 E
Heşār, *Markazī, Iran* . **71 C6** 35 50N 49 12 E
Hesdin, *France* ...... **19 B9** 50 21N 2 2 E
Heshan, *China* ...... **58 F7** 23 50N 108 53 E
Heshui, *China* .... **56 G5** 35 48N 108 0 E
Heshun, *China* ...... **56 F7** 37 22N 113 32 E
Hesperia, *U.S.A.* **111 L9** 34 25N 117 18W
Hesse = Hessen □,
  Germany .... **24 E4** 50 30N 9 0 E
Hessen □, *Germany* .. **24 E4** 50 30N 9 0 E
Hessenreuther und
  Manteler Wald □,
  Germany .... **25 F8** 49 45N 12 1 E
Hestra, *Sweden* ..... **11 G7** 57 26N 13 35 E
Hetch Hetchy
  Aqueduct, *U.S.A.* .. **110 H5** 37 29N 122 19W
Hettinger, *U.S.A.* **112 C3** 46 0N 102 42W
Hettstedt, *Germany* .. **24 D7** 51 39N 11 31 E
Heuvelton, *U.S.A.* **117 B9** 44 37N 75 25W
Heves, *Hungary* ..... **28 C5** 47 36N 20 17 E
Heves □, *Hungary* ... **28 C5** 47 50N 20 0 E
Hewitt, *U.S.A.* **113 K6** 31 27N 97 11W
Hexham, *U.K.* **14 C5** 54 58N 2 4W
Hexi, *Yunnan, China* . **58 E4** 24 10N 102 42 E
Hexi, *Zhejiang, China* . **59 D12** 27 58N 119 38 E
Hexigten Qi, *China* ... **57 C9** 43 18N 117 30 E
Heydarābād, *Iran* .... **71 D7** 30 33N 55 38 E
Heysham, *U.K.* **14 C5** 54 3N 2 53W
Heyuan, *China* ...... **59 F10** 23 39N 114 40 E
Heywood, *Australia* .. **95 F3** 38 8 S 141 37 E
Heze, *China* .... **56 G8** 35 14N 115 20 E
Hezhang, *China* ..... **58 D5** 27 8N 104 41 E
Hi, Ko, *Thailand* .... **65 a** 7 44N 98 22 E
Hi Vista, *U.S.A.* **111 L9** 34 45N 117 46W
Hialeah, *U.S.A.* **115 N5** 25 50N 80 17W
Hiawatha, *U.S.A.* **112 F7** 39 51N 95 32W
Hibbing, *U.S.A.* **112 B8** 47 25N 92 56W
Hibernia Reef, *Australia* **92 B3** 12 0 S 123 23 E
Hickman, *U.S.A.* **113 G10** 36 34N 89 11W
Hickory, *U.S.A.* **115 H5** 35 44N 81 21W
Hicks, Pt., *Australia* .. **95 F4** 37 49 S 149 17 E

Hicks L., *Canada* **103 A9** 61 25N 100 0W
Hicksville, *U.S.A.* **117 F11** 40 46N 73 32W
Hida, *Romania* ...... **29 C8** 47 10N 23 19 E
Hida-Gawa ➤, *Japan* . **55 G8** 35 26N 137 3 E
Hida-Sammyaku, *Japan* **55 F8** 36 30N 137 40 E
Hidaka-Sammyaku,
  Japan .... **54 C11** 42 35N 142 45 E
Hidalgo, *Mexico* **119 C5** 24 15N 99 26W
Hidalgo □, *Mexico* .. **119 C5** 20 30N 99 10W
Hidalgo, Presa M.,
  Mexico **118 B3** 26 30N 108 35W
Hidalgo del Parral,
  Mexico **118 B3** 26 58N 105 40W
Hiddensee, *Germany* . **24 A9** 54 32N 13 6 E
Hieflau, *Austria* ..... **26 D7** 47 36N 14 46 E
Hiendelaencina, *Spain* . **38 D2** 41 5N 3 0W
Hierro, *Canary Is.* ... **48 G1** 27 44N 18 0W
Higashiajima-San, *Japan* **54 F10** 37 40N 140 10 E
Higashiōsaka, *Japan* . **55 G7** 34 40N 135 37 E
Higgins, *U.S.A.* **113 G4** 36 7N 100 2W
Higgins Corner, *U.S.A.* **110 F5** 39 2N 121 5W
High Bridge, *U.S.A.* .. **117 F10** 40 40N 74 54W
High Level, *Canada* .. **102 B5** 58 31N 117 8W
High Point, *U.S.A.* ... **115 H6** 35 57N 80 0W
High Prairie, *Canada* . **102 B5** 55 30N 116 30W
High River, *Canada* .. **102 C6** 50 30N 113 50W
High Tatra = Tatry,
  Slovak Rep. .... **27 B13** 49 20N 20 0 E
High Veld, *Africa* .... **76 J6** 27 0 S 27 0 E
High Wycombe, *U.K.* . **15 F7** 51 37N 0 45W
Highland □, *U.K.* **13 D4** 57 17N 4 21W
Highland Park, *U.S.A.* **114 D2** 42 11N 87 48W
Highmore, *U.S.A.* ... **112 C5** 44 31N 99 27W
Highrock L., *Man.,
  Canada* **103 B8** 55 45N 100 30W
Highrock L., *Sask.,
  Canada* **103 B7** 57 5N 105 32W
Higüey, *Dom. Rep.* .. **121 C6** 18 37N 68 42W
Hihya, *Egypt* .... **80 H7** 30 40N 31 36 E
Hiiumaa, *Estonia* .... **9 G20** 58 50N 22 45 E
Híjar, *Spain* **38 D4** 41 10N 0 27W
Hijāz □, *Si. Arabia* .. **70 E3** 24 0N 40 0 E
Hijo = Tagum, *Phil.* .. **61 H6** 7 33N 125 53 E
Hikari, *Japan* .... **55 H5** 33 58N 131 58 E
Hikmak, Ras el, *Egypt* **80 A2** 31 15N 27 51 E
Hiko, *U.S.A.* **110 H11** 37 32N 115 14W
Hikone, *Japan* ...... **55 G8** 35 15N 136 10 E
Hikurangi, *Gisborne,
  N.Z.* .... **91 H6** 37 55 S 178 4 E
Hikurangi, *Northland,
  N.Z.* .... **91 F5** 35 36 S 174 17 E
Hildburghausen,
  Germany .... **24 E6** 50 25N 10 42 E
Hildesheim, *Germany* . **24 C5** 52 9N 9 56 E
Hill ➤, *Australia* .... **93 F2** 30 23 S 115 3 E
Hill City, *Idaho, U.S.A.* **108 E6** 43 18N 115 3W
Hill City, *Kans., U.S.A.* **112 F5** 39 22N 99 51W
Hill City, *S. Dak., U.S.A.* **112 D3** 43 56N 103 35W
Hill Island L., *Canada* . **103 A7** 60 30N 109 50W
Hillaby, Mt., *Barbados* **121 g** 13 12N 59 35W
Hillared, *Sweden* ... **11 G7** 57 37N 13 10 E
Hillcrest, *Barbados* .. **121 g** 13 13N 59 31W
Hillcrest Center, *U.S.A.* **111 K8** 35 23N 118 57W
Hillegom, *Neths.* .... **17 B4** 52 18N 4 35 E
Hillerød, *Denmark* ... **11 J6** 55 56N 12 19 E
Hillerstorp, *Sweden* .. **11 G7** 57 20N 13 52 E
Hillsboro, *Kans., U.S.A.* **112 F6** 38 21N 97 12W
Hillsboro, *N. Dak.,
  U.S.A.* **112 B6** 47 26N 97 3W
Hillsboro, *Ohio, U.S.A.* **114 F4** 39 12N 83 37W
Hillsboro, *Oreg., U.S.A.* **110 E4** 45 31N 122 59W
Hillsboro, *Tex., U.S.A.* **113 J6** 32 1N 97 8W
Hillsborough, *Grenada* **121 D7** 12 28N 61 28W
Hillsborough, *U.S.A.* . **117 C13** 43 7N 71 54W
Hillsborough Channel,
  Australia .... **94 J7** 20 56 S 149 15 E
Hillsdale, *Mich., U.S.A.* **114 E3** 41 56N 84 38W
Hillsdale, *N.Y., U.S.A.* **117 D11** 42 11N 73 30W
Hillsport, *Canada* **104 C2** 49 27N 85 34W
Hillston, *Australia* ... **95 E4** 33 30 S 145 31 E
Hilo, *U.S.A.* **106 J17** 19 44N 155 5W
Hilton, *U.S.A.* **116 C7** 43 17N 77 48W
Hilton Head Island,
  U.S.A. **115 J5** 32 13N 80 45W
Hilvan, *Turkey* ...... **73 D8** 37 34N 38 58 E
Hilversum, *Neths.* ... **17 B5** 52 14N 5 10 E
Himachal Pradesh □,
  India .... **68 D7** 31 30N 77 0 E
Himalaya, *Asia* ..... **69 E11** 29 0N 84 0 E
Himamaylan, *Phil.* ... **61 F5** 10 6N 122 52 E
Himarë, *Albania* ..... **44 F3** 40 8N 19 43 E
Himatnagar, *India* ... **66 H8** 23 37N 72 57 E
Himeji, *Japan* ...... **55 G7** 34 50N 134 40 E
Himi, *Japan* .... **55 F8** 36 50N 136 55 E
Himmerland, *Denmark* **11 H3** 56 45N 9 30 E
Hims, *Syria* .... **74 A5** 34 40N 36 45 E
Hims □, *Syria* ...... **74 A6** 34 30N 37 0 E
Hinche, *Haiti* **121 C5** 19 9N 72 1W
Hinchinbrook I.,
  Australia .... **94 B4** 18 20 S 146 15 E
Hinchinbrook Island △,
  Australia .... **94 B4** 18 14 S 146 9 E
Hinckley, *U.K.* **15 E6** 52 33N 1 22W
Hinckley, *U.S.A.* **112 B8** 46 1N 92 56W
Hindaun, *India* ...... **68 F7** 26 44N 77 5 E
Hindmarsh, L., *Australia* **95 F3** 36 5 S 141 55 E
Hindsholm, *Denmark* . **11 J4** 55 30N 10 40 E
Hindu Bagh, *Pakistan* **68 D2** 30 56N 67 50 E
Hindu Kush, *Asia* ... **66 B7** 36 0N 71 0 E
Hindupur, *India* ..... **66 N10** 13 49N 77 32 E
Hines Creek, *Canada* . **102 B5** 56 20N 118 40W
Hinesville, *U.S.A.* ... **115 K5** 31 51N 81 36W
Hinganghat, *India* ... **66 J11** 20 30N 78 52 E
Hingham, *U.S.A.* **108 B8** 48 33N 110 25W
Hingir, *India* .... **69 J10** 21 57N 83 41 E
Hingoli, *India* ...... **66 K10** 19 41N 77 15 E
Hinigaran, *Phil.* .... **61 F5** 10 16N 122 50 E
Hinis, *Turkey* .... **73 C9** 39 22N 41 43 E
Hinna = Imi, *Ethiopia* **81 F5** 6 28N 42 10 E
Hinna, *Nigeria* ...... **83 C7** 10 25N 11 35 E
Hinnerup, *Denmark* .. **11 H4** 56 16N 10 4 E
Hinnøya, *Norway* .... **8 B16** 68 35N 15 50 E
Hinojosa del Duque,
  Spain **37 G5** 38 30N 5 9W
Hinsdale, *U.S.A.* **117 D12** 42 47N 72 29W
Hinterrhein ➤, *Switz.* **25 J5** 46 40N 9 25 E
Hinton, *Canada* **102 C5** 53 26N 117 34W
Hinton, *U.S.A.* **114 G5** 37 40N 80 54W
Hırızır Burnu, *Turkey* . **72 D6** 36 19N 35 46 E
Hirado, *Japan* ...... **55 H4** 33 22N 129 33 E
Hirakud Dam, *India* .. **67 J13** 21 32N 83 45 E
Hiran ➤, *India* ..... **69 H8** 23 6N 79 21 E
Hirapur, *India* ...... **69 G8** 24 22N 79 13 E
Hiratsuka, *Japan* .... **55 G9** 35 19N 139 21 E
Hirfanlı Barajı, *Turkey* **72 C5** 39 18N 33 31 E
Hiroo, *Japan* .... **54 C11** 42 17N 143 19 E
Hirosaki, *Japan* ..... **54 D10** 40 34N 140 28 E

Hiroshima, *Japan* .... **55 G6** 34 24N 132 30 E
Hiroshima □, *Japan* . **55 G6** 34 50N 133 0 E
Hirson, *France* ...... **19 C11** 49 55N 4 4 E
Hirtshals, *Denmark* .. **11 G3** 57 36N 9 57 E
Hisar, *India* .... **68 E6** 29 12N 75 45 E
Hisarcık, *Turkey* .... **47 B11** 39 15N 29 14 E
Hisaria, *Bulgaria* .... **45 D8** 42 30N 24 44 E
Hisb, Sha'ib ➤,
  W. ➤, *Iraq* ...... **70 D5** 31 45N 44 17 E
Hismá, *Si. Arabia* ... **70 D3** 28 30N 36 0 E
Hispaniola, *W. Indies* . **121 C5** 19 0N 71 0W
Hīt, *Iraq* .... **70 C4** 33 38N 42 49 E
Hita, *Japan* .... **55 H5** 33 20N 130 58 E
Hitachi, *Japan* ...... **55 F10** 36 36N 140 39 E
Hitchin, *U.K.* **15 F7** 51 58N 0 16W
Hitoyoshi, *Japan* .... **55 H5** 32 13N 130 45 E
Hitra, *Norway* ...... **8 E13** 63 30N 8 45 E
Hitzacker, *Germany* .. **24 B7** 53 9N 11 2 E
Hixon, *Canada* **102 C4** 53 25N 122 35W
Hiyyon, N. ➤, *Israel* . **74 E4** 30 25N 35 10 E
Hjalmar L., *Canada* .. **103 A7** 61 33N 109 25W
Hjälmaren, *Sweden* .. **10 E9** 59 18N 15 40 E
Hjältevad, *Sweden* ... **11 G9** 57 38N 15 20 E
Hjo, *Sweden* .... **11 F8** 58 22N 14 17 E
Hjørring, *Denmark* ... **11 G3** 57 29N 9 59 E
Hjortkvarn, *Sweden* .. **11 F9** 58 54N 15 26 E
Hkakabo Razi, *Burma* **67 E20** 28 25N 97 23 E
Hlinsko, *Czech Rep.* . **26 B8** 49 45N 15 54 E
Hlobane, *S. Africa* ... **89 D5** 27 42 S 31 0 E
Hlohovec, *Slovak Rep.* **27 C10** 48 26N 17 49 E
Hlučín, *Czech Rep.* .. **27 B11** 49 54N 18 11 E
Hluhluwe, *S. Africa* .. **89 D5** 28 1 S 32 15 E
Hluhluwe △, *S. Africa* **89 C5** 22 10 S 32 5 E
Hlukhiv, *Ukraine* .... **33 G7** 51 40N 33 58 E
Hlyboka, *Ukraine* .... **29 B10** 48 5N 25 56 E
Hlybokaye, *Belarus* .. **32 E4** 55 10N 27 45 E
Hnúšťa, *Slovak Rep.* . **27 C12** 48 35N 19 58 E
Ho, *Ghana* .... **83 D5** 6 37N 0 27 E
Ho Chi Minh City =
  Thanh Pho Ho Chi
  Minh, *Vietnam* .... **65 G6** 10 58N 106 40 E
Ho Thuong, *Vietnam* . **64 C5** 19 32N 105 48 E
Hoa Binh, *Vietnam* ... **58 G5** 20 50N 105 20 E
Hoa Da, *Vietnam* .... **65 G7** 11 16N 108 40 E
Hoa Hiep, *Vietnam* ... **65 G6** 11 34N 105 51 E
Hoai Nhon, *Vietnam* . **64 E7** 14 28N 109 1 E
Hoang Lien Son,
  Vietnam .... **58 F4** 22 0N 104 0 E
Hoanib ➤, *Namibia* . **88 B2** 19 27 S 12 46 E
Hoare B., *Canada* ... **101 B13** 65 17N 62 30W
Hoarusib ➤, *Namibia* . **88 B2** 19 3 S 12 36 E
Hobart, *Australia* .... **95 G4** 42 50 S 147 21 E
Hobart, *U.S.A.* **113 H5** 35 1N 99 6W
Hobbs, *U.S.A.* **113 J3** 32 42N 103 8W
Hobbs Coast, *Antarctica* **5 D14** 74 50 S 131 0W
Hobe Sound, *U.S.A.* . **115 M5** 27 4N 80 8W
Hoboken, *U.S.A.* **117 F10** 40 45N 74 4W
Hobro, *Denmark* ..... **11 H3** 56 39N 9 46 E
Hoburgen, *Sweden* .. **11 H12** 56 55N 18 7 E
Hocalar, *Turkey* ..... **47 C11** 38 36N 30 0 E
Hochfeld, *Namibia* ... **88 C2** 21 28 S 17 58 E
Hochharz △, *Germany* **24 D6** 51 48N 10 38 E
Hochschwab, *Austria* . **26 D8** 47 35N 15 0 E
Höchstadt, *Germany* . **25 F6** 49 42N 10 47 E
Hochtaunus △,
  Germany .... **25 E4** 50 20N 8 30 E
Hockenheim, *Germany* **25 F4** 49 18N 8 33 E
Hodaka-Dake, *Japan* . **55 F8** 36 17N 137 39 E
Hodeida = Al
  Ḩudaydah, *Yemen* . **75 E3** 14 50N 43 0 E
Hodgeville, *Canada* .. **103 C7** 50 7N 106 58W
Hodgson, *Canada* ... **103 C9** 51 13N 97 36W
Hódmezővásárhely,
  Hungary .... **28 D5** 46 28N 20 22 E
Hodna, Chott el, *Algeria* **78 A6** 35 26N 4 43 E
Hodonín, *Czech Rep.* . **27 C10** 48 50N 17 10 E
Hoeamdong, *N. Korea* **57 C16** 42 30N 130 16 E
Hœdic, Î. de, *France* . **18 E4** 47 20N 2 53W
Hoek van Holland,
  Neths. .... **17 C4** 52 0N 4 7 E
Hoengsŏng, *S. Korea* . **57 F14** 37 29N 127 59 E
Hoeryong, *N. Korea* .. **57 C15** 42 30N 129 45 E
Hoeyang, *N. Korea* ... **57 E14** 38 43N 127 36 E
Hof, *Germany* ...... **25 E7** 50 19N 11 55 E
Hofgeismar, *Germany* **24 D5** 51 29N 9 23 E
Hofheim, *Germany* ... **25 E6** 50 8N 8 26 E
Hofmeyr, *S. Africa* ... **88 E4** 31 39 S 25 50 E
Höfn, *Iceland* **8 D6** 64 15N 15 13W
Hofors, *Sweden* ..... **10 D10** 60 31N 16 15 E
Hofsjökull, *Iceland* ... **8 D4** 64 49N 18 48W
Hōfu, *Japan* .... **55 G5** 34 3N 131 34 E
Hogan Group, *Australia* **95 F4** 39 13 S 147 1 E
Höganäs, *Sweden* ... **11 H6** 56 12N 12 33 E
Hogarth, Mt., *Australia* **94 C2** 21 48 S 136 58 E
Hoggar = Ahaggar,
  Algeria .... **78 D7** 23 0N 6 30 E
Högsäter, *Sweden* ... **11 F6** 58 38N 12 5 E
Högsby, *Sweden* ..... **11 G10** 57 10N 16 1 E
Högsjö, *Sweden* ..... **10 E9** 59 4N 15 44 E
Hogsty Reef, *Bahamas* **121 B5** 21 41N 73 48W
Hoh ➤, *U.S.A.* **110 C2** 47 45N 124 29W
Hohe Acht, *Germany* . **25 E3** 50 22N 7 0 E
Hohe Tauern, *Austria* . **26 D5** 47 11N 12 40 E
Hohe Venn, *Belgium* . **17 D6** 50 30N 6 5 E
Hohenau, *Austria* .... **27 C10** 48 36N 16 55 E
Hohenems, *Austria* ... **26 D2** 47 22N 9 42 E
Hohenloher Ebene,
  Germany .... **25 F5** 49 14N 9 36 E
Hohenwald, *U.S.A.* .. **115 H2** 35 33N 87 33W
Hohenwestedt, *Germany* **24 A5** 54 5N 9 40 E
Hoher Rhön = Rhön,
  Germany .... **24 E5** 50 24N 9 58 E
Hoher Vogelsberg □,
  Germany .... **25 E5** 50 30N 9 15 E
Hohes Venn-Eifel △,
  Europe .... **24 E2** 50 30N 6 10 E
Hohhot, *China* ...... **56 D6** 40 52N 111 40 E
Hohlakas, *Greece* .... **49 D9** 35 57N 27 53 E
Hohoe, *Ghana* .... **83 D5** 7 8N 0 32 E
Hoi An, *Vietnam* ..... **64 E7** 15 30N 108 19 E
Hoi Xuan, *Vietnam* ... **58 G5** 20 25N 105 9 E
Hoisington, *U.S.A.* ... **112 F5** 38 31N 98 47W
Højer, *Denmark* ..... **11 K2** 54 58N 8 42 E
Hōjō, *Japan* .... **55 H6** 33 58N 132 46 E
Hok, *Sweden* .... **11 G8** 57 31N 14 16 E
Hökensås, *Sweden* ... **11 F8** 58 0N 14 5 E
Hökerum, *Sweden* ... **11 G7** 57 51N 13 16 E
Hokianga Harbour, *N.Z.* **91 F4** 35 31 S 173 22 E
Hokitika, *N.Z.* ...... **91 K3** 42 42 S 171 0 E
Hokkaidō □, *Japan* .. **54 C11** 43 30N 143 0 E
Hol-Hol, *Djibouti* .... **81 E5** 11 20N 42 50 E
Hola Pristan, *Ukraine* . **33 J7** 46 29N 32 32 E
Holbæk, *Denmark* ... **11 J5** 55 43N 11 43 E
Holbeach, *U.K.* ...... **15 E8** 52 48N 0 1 E
Holbrook, *Australia* .. **95 F4** 35 42 S 147 18 E
Holbrook, *U.S.A.* **109 J8** 34 54N 110 10W
Holden, *U.S.A.* **108 G7** 39 6N 112 16W

Holdenville, *U.S.A.* ... **113 H6** 35 5N 96 24W
Holdrege, *U.S.A.* **112 E5** 40 26N 99 23W
Holetown, *Barbados* . **121 g** 13 11N 59 38W
Holguín, *Cuba* **120 B4** 20 50N 76 20W
Holíč, *Slovak Rep.* ... **27 C10** 48 49N 17 10 E
Holice, *Czech Rep.* ... **26 A8** 50 5N 16 0 E
Höljes, *Sweden* ..... **10 D6** 60 50N 12 35 E
Hollabrunn, *Austria* .. **26 C9** 48 34N 16 5 E
Hollams Bird I.,
  Namibia .... **88 C1** 24 40 S 14 30 E
Holland, *Mich., U.S.A.* **114 D2** 42 47N 86 7W
Holland, *N.Y., U.S.A.* . **116 D6** 42 38N 78 32W
Hollandale, *U.S.A.* .. **113 J9** 33 10N 90 51W
Holley, *U.S.A.* **116 C6** 43 14N 78 2W
Hollfeld, *Germany* ... **25 F7** 49 56N 11 18 E
Hollidaysburg, *U.S.A.* **116 F6** 40 26N 78 24W
Hollis, *U.S.A.* **113 H5** 34 41N 99 55W
Hollister, *Calif., U.S.A.* **110 J5** 36 51N 121 24W
Hollister, *Idaho, U.S.A.* **108 E6** 42 21N 114 35W
Holly Hill, *U.S.A.* **115 L5** 29 16N 81 3W
Holly Springs, *U.S.A.* **113 H10** 34 46N 89 27W
Hollywood, *U.S.A.* ... **115 N5** 26 1N 80 9W
Holman, *Canada* **100 A8** 70 44N 117 44W
Hólmavík, *Iceland* ... **8 D3** 65 42N 21 40W
Holmen, *U.S.A.* **112 D9** 43 58N 91 15W
Holmes Reefs, *Australia* **94 B4** 16 27 S 148 0 E
Holmsjö, *Sweden* .... **11 H9** 56 25N 15 32 E
Holmsland Klit,
  Denmark .... **11 J2** 56 0N 8 5 E
Holmsund, *Sweden* .. **8 E19** 63 41N 20 20 E
Holod, *Romania* ..... **28 D7** 46 49N 22 8 E
Holovne, *Ukraine* .... **31 G11** 51 20N 24 5 E
Holoszbyntsi, *Ukraine* **29 B11** 48 50N 26 5 E
Holroyd ➤, *Australia* . **94 A3** 14 10 S 141 36 E
Holstebro, *Denmark* . **11 H2** 56 22N 8 37 E
Holsteinische
  Schweiz △, *Germany* **24 A6** 54 8N 10 30 E
Holsworthy, *U.K.* **15 G3** 50 48N 4 22W
Holton, *Canada* **105 B8** 54 31N 57 12W
Holton, *U.S.A.* **112 F7** 39 28N 95 44W
Holtville, *U.S.A.* **111 N11** 32 49N 115 23W
Holwerd, *Neths.* ..... **17 A5** 53 22N 5 54 E
Holy I., *Angl., U.K.* .. **14 D3** 53 17N 4 37W
Holy I.,
  Northumberland, U.K. **14 B6** 55 40N 1 47W
Holyhead, *U.K.* **14 D3** 53 18N 4 38W
Holyoke, *Colo., U.S.A.* **112 E3** 40 35N 102 18W
Holyoke, *Mass., U.S.A.* **117 D12** 42 12N 72 37W
Holyrood, *Canada* ... **105 C9** 47 27N 53 8W
Holzkirchen, *Germany* **25 H7** 47 52N 11 42 E
Holzminden, *Germany* **24 D5** 51 49N 9 31 E
Homa Bay, *Kenya* ... **86 C3** 0 36 S 34 30 E
Homalin, *Burma* ..... **67 G19** 24 55N 95 0 E
Homand, *Iran* .... **71 C8** 32 28N 59 37 E
Homathko ➤, *Canada* **102 C4** 51 0N 124 56W
Homberg, *Germany* .. **24 D5** 51 2N 9 25 E
Hombori, *Mali* **83 B4** 15 20N 1 38W
Homburg, *Germany* .. **25 F3** 49 28N 7 18 E
Home B., *Canada* **101 B13** 68 40N 67 10W
Home Hill, *Australia* .. **94 B4** 19 43 S 147 25 E
Homedale, *U.S.A.* ... **108 E5** 43 37N 116 56W
Homer, *Alaska, U.S.A.* **100 C4** 59 39N 151 33W
Homer, *La., U.S.A.* .. **113 J8** 32 48N 93 4W
Homer City, *U.S.A.* .. **116 F5** 40 32N 79 10W
Homestead, *Australia* **94 C4** 20 20 S 145 40 E
Homestead, *U.S.A.* .. **115 N5** 25 28N 80 29W
Homewood, *U.S.A.* .. **110 F6** 39 4N 120 8W
Homoine, *Mozam.* ... **89 C6** 23 55 S 35 8 E
Homoljske Planina,
  Serbia & M. ...... **44 B5** 44 10N 21 45 E
Homorod, *Romania* .. **29 D10** 46 5N 25 15 E
Homs = Ḩims, *Syria* . **74 A5** 34 40N 36 45 E
Homyel, *Belarus* ..... **33 F6** 52 28N 31 0 E
Hon Chong, *Vietnam* . **65 G5** 10 25N 104 30 E
Hon Me, *Vietnam* .... **64 C5** 19 23N 105 56 E
Honan = Henan □,
  China .... **56 H8** 34 0N 114 0 E
Honaz, *Turkey* ...... **47 D11** 37 46N 29 18 E
Honbetsu, *Japan* .... **54 C11** 43 7N 143 37 E
Honcut, *U.S.A.* **110 F5** 39 20N 121 32W
Honda Bay, *Phil.* .... **61 G3** 9 53N 118 49 E
Hondarribia, *Spain* ... **38 B3** 43 22N 1 47W
Hondeklipbaai, *S. Africa* **88 E2** 30 19 S 17 17 E
Hondo, *Japan* ...... **55 H5** 32 27N 130 12 E
Hondo, *U.S.A.* **113 L5** 29 21N 99 9W
Hondo, Rio ➤, *Belize* **119 D7** 18 25N 88 21W
Honduras ■,
  Cent. Amer. **120 D2** 14 40N 86 30W
Honduras, G. de,
  Caribbean **120 C2** 16 50N 87 0W
Hønefoss, *Norway* ... **9 F14** 60 10N 10 18 E
Honesdale, *U.S.A.* ... **117 E9** 41 34N 75 16W
Honey L., *U.S.A.* **110 E6** 40 15N 120 19W
Honfleur, *France* .... **18 C7** 49 25N 0 10 E
Høng, *Denmark* ..... **11 J5** 55 31N 11 18 E
Hong ➤, *Vietnam* ... **58 G5** 22 0N 104 0 E
Hong Gai, *Vietnam* .. **58 G6** 20 57N 107 5 E
Hong He ➤, *China* .. **56 H8** 32 25N 115 35 E
Hong Hu, *China* ..... **59 C9** 29 54N 113 24 E
Hong Kong □, *China* . **59 F10** 22 11N 114 14 E
Hong'an, *China* ..... **59 B10** 31 20N 114 40 E
Hongch'ŏn, *S. Korea* . **57 F14** 37 44N 127 53 E
Honghai Wan, *China* . **59 F10** 22 40N 115 0 E
Honghe, *China* ...... **58 F4** 23 0N 102 25 E
Hongjiang, *China* .... **59 D8** 27 7N 109 59 E
Hongliu He ➤, *China* **56 F5** 38 0N 109 50 E
Hongor, *Mongolia* ... **56 B7** 45 45N 112 50 E
Hongsa, *Laos* .... **64 C3** 19 43N 101 20 E
Hongshui He ➤, *China* **58 F7** 23 48N 109 30 E
Hongsŏng, *S. Korea* . **57 F14** 36 37N 126 38 E
Hongtong, *China* .... **56 F6** 36 16N 111 40 E
Honguedo, Détroit d',
  Canada **105 C7** 49 15N 64 0W
Hongwon, *N. Korea* . **57 E14** 40 0N 127 56 E
Hongya, *China* ...... **58 C4** 29 51N 103 2 E
Hongyuan, *China* .... **58 A4** 32 51N 102 40 E
Hongze Hu, *China* ... **57 H10** 33 15N 118 35 E
Honiara, *Solomon Is.* . **96 H7** 9 27 S 159 57 E
Honiton, *U.K.* **15 G4** 50 47N 3 11W
Honjō, *Japan* .... **54 E10** 39 23N 140 3 E
Honkorâb, Ras, *Egypt* **80 C4** 24 35N 35 10 E
Honningsvåg, *Norway* **8 A21** 70 59N 25 59 E
Honö, *Sweden* ...... **11 G5** 57 41N 11 39 E
Honolulu, *U.S.A.* **106 H16** 21 19N 157 52W

Hontoria del Pinar,
  Spain **38 D1** 41 50N 3 10W
Hood, Mt., *U.S.A.* ... **108 D3** 45 23N 121 42W
Hood, Pt., *Australia* .. **93 F2** 34 23 S 119 34 E
Hood River, *U.S.A.* .. **108 D3** 45 43N 121 31W
Hoodsport, *U.S.A.* ... **110 C3** 47 24N 123 9W
Hooge, *Germany* .... **24 A4** 54 34N 8 33 E
Hoogeveen, *Neths.* .. **17 B6** 52 44N 6 28 E
Hoogezand-Sappemeer,
  Neths. .... **17 A6** 53 9N 6 45 E
Hooghly = Hugli ➤,
  India .... **69 J13** 21 56N 88 4 E
Hooghly-Chinsura =
  Chunchura, *India* .. **69 H13** 22 53N 88 27 E
Hook Hd., *Ireland* ... **12 D5** 52 7N 6 56W
Hook I., *Australia* ... **94 J6** 20 4 S 149 0 E
Hook of Holland =
  Hoek van Holland,
  Neths. .... **17 C4** 52 0N 4 7 E
Hooker, *U.S.A.* **113 G4** 36 52N 101 13W
Hooker Creek, *Australia* **92 C5** 18 23 S 130 38 E
Hoonah, *U.S.A.* **102 B1** 58 7N 135 27W
Hooper Bay, *U.S.A.* . **100 B3** 61 32N 166 6W
Hoopeston, *U.S.A.* .. **114 E2** 40 28N 87 40W
Hoopstad, *S. Africa* .. **88 D4** 27 50 S 25 55 E
Höör, *Sweden* ...... **11 J7** 55 56N 13 33 E
Hoorn, *Neths.* ...... **17 B5** 52 38N 5 4 E
Hoover Dam, *U.S.A.* . **111 K12** 36 1N 114 44W
Hooversville, *U.S.A.* . **116 F6** 40 9N 78 55W
Hop Bottom, *U.S.A.* . **117 E9** 41 42N 75 46W
Hopa, *Turkey* .... **73 B9** 41 28N 41 30 E
Hope, *Canada* **102 D4** 49 25N 121 25W
Hope, *Ariz., U.S.A.* .. **111 M13** 33 43N 113 42W
Hope, *Ark., U.S.A.* ... **113 J8** 33 40N 93 36W
Hope, L., *S. Austral.,
  Australia* .... **95 D2** 28 24 S 139 18 E
Hope, L., *W. Austral.,
  Australia* .... **93 F3** 32 35 S 120 15 E
Hope, Pt., *U.S.A.* **4 C17** 68 20N 166 50W
Hope I., *Canada* **116 B4** 44 55N 80 11W
Hope Town, *Bahamas* **120 A4** 26 35N 76 57W
Hopedale, *Canada* ... **105 A7** 55 28N 60 13W
Hopedale, *U.S.A.* **117 D13** 42 8N 71 33W
Hopefield, *S. Africa* .. **88 E2** 33 3 S 18 22 E
Hopei = Hebei □, *China* **56 E9** 39 0N 116 0 E
Hopelchén, *Mexico* .. **119 D7** 19 46N 89 50W
Hopetoun, *Vic.,
  Australia* .... **95 F3** 35 42 S 142 22 E
Hopetoun, *W. Austral.,
  Australia* .... **93 F3** 33 57 S 120 7 E
Hopetown, *S. Africa* . **88 D3** 29 34 S 24 3 E
Hopevale, *Australia* .. **94 B4** 15 16 S 145 20 E
Hopewell, *U.S.A.* **114 G7** 37 18N 77 17W
Hopfgarten, *Austria* .. **26 D5** 47 27N 12 10 E
Hopkins, L., *Australia* **92 D4** 24 15 S 128 35 E
Hopkinsville, *U.S.A.* . **115 G2** 36 52N 87 29W
Hopland, *U.S.A.* **110 G3** 38 58N 123 7W
Hoquiam, *U.S.A.* **110 D3** 46 59N 123 53W
Hora Hoverla, *Ukraine* **29 B9** 48 7N 24 41 E
Horasan, *Turkey* .... **73 B10** 40 2N 42 10 E
Horažd'ovice,
  Czech Rep. .... **26 B6** 49 19N 13 42 E
Horb, *Germany* ..... **25 G4** 48 26N 8 47 E
Hörby, *Sweden* ..... **11 J7** 55 51N 13 40 E
Horcajo de Santiago,
  Spain **38 F1** 39 50N 3 1W
Horden Hills, *Australia* **92 D5** 20 15 S 130 0 E
Horezu, *Romania* .... **29 E8** 45 6N 24 0 E
Horgen, *Switz.* ...... **25 H4** 47 15N 8 35 E
Horgoš, *Serbia & M.* . **28 D4** 46 10N 20 0 E
Hořice, *Czech Rep.* .. **26 A8** 50 21N 15 39 E
Horinchove, *Ukraine* . **29 B8** 48 16N 23 26 E
Horinger, *China* ..... **56 D6** 40 28N 111 48 E
Horki, *Belarus* ...... **32 E6** 54 17N 30 59 E
Horlick Mts., *Antarctica* **5 E15** 84 0 S 102 0W
Horlivka, *Ukraine* ... **33 H10** 48 19N 38 5 E
Hormak, *Iran* .... **71 D9** 29 58N 60 51 E
Hormoz, *Iran* .... **71 E7** 27 35N 55 0 E
Hormoz, Jaz.-ye, *Iran* **71 E8** 27 8N 56 28 E
Hormozgān □, *Iran* . **71 E8** 27 30N 56 0 E
Hormuz, Kūh-e, *Iran* . **71 E7** 27 27N 55 10 E
Hormuz, Str. of,
  The Gulf .... **71 E8** 26 30N 56 30 E
Horn, *Austria* .... **26 C8** 48 39N 15 40 E
Horn, *Iceland* **8 C2** 66 28N 22 28W
Horn, *Sweden* ...... **11 G9** 57 54N 15 51 E
Horn ➤, *Canada* **102 A5** 61 30N 118 1W
Horn, Cape = Hornos,
  C. de, *Chile* .... **128 H3** 55 50 S 67 30W
Horn Head, *Ireland* .. **12 A3** 55 14N 8 0W
Horn I., *Australia* .... **94 A3** 10 37 S 142 17 E
Horn Plateau, *Canada* **102 A5** 62 15N 119 15W
Hornavan, *Sweden* .. **8 C17** 66 15N 17 30 E
Hornbeck, *U.S.A.* ... **113 K8** 31 20N 93 24W
Hornbrook, *U.S.A.* .. **108 F2** 41 55N 122 33W
Hornburg, *Germany* . **24 C6** 52 2N 10 37 E
Horncastle, *U.K.* **14 D7** 53 13N 0 7W
Horndal, *Sweden* .... **10 D10** 60 18N 16 23 E
Hornell, *U.S.A.* **116 D7** 42 20N 77 40W
Hornell L., *Canada* .. **102 A5** 62 20N 119 25W
Hornepayne, *Canada* **104 C3** 49 14N 84 48W
Horní Planá, *Czech Rep.* **26 C7** 48 46N 14 2 E
Hornings Mills, *Canada* **116 B4** 44 9N 80 12W
Hornitos, *U.S.A.* **110 H6** 37 30N 120 14W
Hornøya, *Norway* .... **8 A24** 70 23N 31 35 E
Hornos, C. de, *Chile* . **128 H3** 55 50 S 67 30W
Hornoy-le-Bourg,
  France .... **19 C8** 49 50N 1 54 E
Hornsea, *U.K.* **14 D7** 53 55N 0 11W
Hornslandet, *Sweden* . **10 C11** 61 35N 17 37 E
Hörnum, *Germany* ... **24 A4** 54 45N 8 17 E
Horobetsu =
  Noboribetsu, *Japan* **54 C10** 42 24N 141 6 E
Horodenka, *Ukraine* . **29 B9** 48 41N 25 29 E
Horodnya, *Ukraine* .. **33 G6** 51 55N 31 33 E
Horodok,
  *Khmelnytskyy,
  Ukraine* .... **33 H4** 49 10N 26 34 E
Horodok, *Lviv, Ukraine* **33 H2** 49 46N 23 32 E
Horodyshche, *Ukraine* **33 H6** 49 17N 31 27 E
Horokhiv, *Ukraine* ... **33 G3** 50 30N 24 45 E
Horovice, *Czech Rep.* **26 B6** 49 48N 13 53 E
Horqin Youyi Qianqi,
  China .... **57 A12** 46 5N 122 3 E
Horqueta, *Paraguay* . **126 A4** 23 15 S 56 55W
Horred, *Sweden* ..... **11 G6** 57 22N 12 28 E
Horse Creek, *U.S.A.* . **112 E2** 41 57N 105 10W
Horse I., *Canada* **103 C9** 53 20N 99 6W
Horse Is., *Canada* ... **105 B8** 50 15N 55 50W
Horsefly L., *Canada* . **102 C4** 52 25N 121 0W
Horseheads, *U.S.A.* . **116 D8** 42 10N 76 49W
Horsens, *Denmark* .. **11 J3** 55 52N 9 51 E
Horsham, *Australia* .. **95 F3** 36 44 S 142 13 E
Horsham, *U.K.* **15 F7** 51 4N 0 20W
Horšovský Týn,
  Czech Rep. .... **26 B5** 49 31N 12 58 E

Horten, Norway ...... 9 G14 59 25N 10 32 E
Hortobágy, Hungary .. 28 C6 47 30N 21 6 E
Hortobágyi △, Hungary 28 C6 47 36N 21 10 E
Horton, U.S.A. 112 F7 39 40N 95 32W
Horton →, Canada .. 100 B7 69 56N 126 52W
Hosaina, Ethiopia .... 81 F4 7 30N 37 47 E
Hose, Gunung-Gunung, Malaysia ...... 62 D4 2 5N 114 6 E
Hoseynābād, Khuzestān, Iran ...... 71 C6 32 45N 48 20 E
Hoseynābād, Kordestān, Iran ...... 70 C5 35 33N 47 8 E
Hoshangabad, India .. 68 H7 22 45N 77 45 E
Hoshiarpur, India .... 68 D6 31 30N 75 58 E
Hospet, India .... 66 M10 15 15N 76 20 E
Hoste, I., Chile 128 H3 55 0S 69 0W
Hostens, France 20 D3 44 30N 0 40W
Hot, Thailand .... 64 C2 18 8N 98 29 E
Hot Creek Range, U.S.A. 108 G6 38 40N 116 20W
Hot Springs, Ark., U.S.A. 113 H8 34 31N 93 3W
Hot Springs, S. Dak., U.S.A. 112 D3 43 26N 103 29W
Hot Springs △, U.S.A. 113 H8 34 32N 93 4W
Hotagen, Sweden .... 8 E16 63 59N 14 12 E
Hotan, China .... 60 C2 37 25N 79 55 E
Hotazel, S. Africa .... 88 D3 27 17S 22 58 E
Hotchkiss, U.S.A. 109 G10 38 48N 107 43W
Hotham, C., Australia 92 B5 12 2S 131 18 E
Hoting, Sweden ...... 8 D17 64 8N 16 15 E
Hotolisht, Albania .... 44 E4 41 10N 20 25 E
Hotte, Massif de la, Haiti 121 C5 18 30N 73 45W
Hottentotsbaai, Namibia 88 D1 26 8S 14 59 E
Houat, Î. de, France .. 18 E4 47 24N 2 58W
Houdan, France ...... 19 D8 48 48N 1 35 E
Houei Sai, Laos ...... 58 G3 20 18N 100 26 E
Houeillès, France .... 20 D4 44 12N 0 2 E
Houffalize, Belgium .. 17 D5 50 8N 5 48 E
Houghton, Mich., U.S.A. 112 B10 47 7N 88 34W
Houghton, N.Y., U.S.A. 116 D6 42 25N 78 10W
Houghton L., U.S.A. .. 114 C3 44 21N 84 44W
Houghton-le-Spring, U.K. 14 C6 54 51N 1 28W
Houhora Heads, N.Z. .. 91 F4 34 49S 173 9 E
Houlton, U.S.A. 115 B12 46 8N 67 51W
Houma, U.S.A. 113 L9 29 36N 90 43W
Houndé, Burkina Faso 82 C4 11 34N 3 31W
Hourtin, France 20 C2 45 11N 1 4W
Hourtin-Carcans, Étang d', France 20 C2 45 10N 1 6W
Housatonic →, U.S.A. 117 E11 41 10N 73 7W
Houston, Canada 102 C3 54 25N 126 39W
Houston, Mo., U.S.A. .. 113 G9 37 22N 91 58W
Houston, Tex., U.S.A. 113 L7 29 46N 95 22W
Hout →, S. Africa .... 89 C4 23 4S 29 36 E
Houtkraal, S. Africa .. 88 E3 30 23S 24 5 E
Houtman Abrolhos, Australia ...... 93 E1 28 43S 113 48 E
Hovd, Mongolia ...... 60 B4 48 2N 91 37 E
Hove, U.K. 15 G7 50 50N 0 10W
Hovenweep △, U.S.A. 109 H9 37 20N 109 0W
Hoveyzeh, Iran ...... 71 D6 31 27N 48 4 E
Hovmantorp, Sweden .. 11 H9 56 47N 15 7 E
Hövsgöl, Mongolia .... 56 C5 43 37N 109 39 E
Hövsgöl Nuur, Mongolia 60 A5 51 0N 100 30 E
Hovsta, Sweden ...... 10 E9 59 22N 15 15 E
Howakil, Eritrea ...... 81 D5 15 10N 40 16 E
Howar, Wadi →, Sudan 81 D2 17 30N 27 8 E
Howard, Australia .... 95 D5 25 16S 152 32 E
Howard, Pa., U.S.A. .. 116 F7 41 1N 77 40W
Howard, S. Dak., U.S.A. 112 C6 44 1N 97 32W
Howe, U.S.A. 108 E7 43 48N 113 0W
Howe, C., Australia .. 95 F5 37 30S 150 0 E
Howe I., Canada 117 B8 44 16N 76 17W
Howell, U.S.A. 114 D4 42 36N 83 56W
Howick, Canada 117 A11 45 11N 73 51W
Howick, S. Africa .... 89 D5 29 28S 30 14 E
Howick Group, Australia ...... 94 A4 14 20S 145 30 E
Howitt, L., Australia .. 95 D2 27 40S 138 40 E
Howland I., Pac. Oc. .. 96 G10 0 48N 176 38W
Howrah = Haora, India 69 H13 22 37N 88 20 E
Howth Hd., Ireland .. 12 C5 53 22N 6 3W
Höxter, Germany .... 24 D5 51 46N 9 22 E
Hoy, U.K. 13 C5 58 50N 3 15W
Hoya, Germany ...... 24 C5 52 49N 9 8 E
Høyanger, Norway .. 9 F12 61 13N 6 4 E
Hoyerswerda, Germany 24 D10 51 26N 14 14 E
Hoylake, U.K. 14 D4 53 24N 3 10W
Hoyos, Spain 36 E4 40 9N 6 45W
Hpa-an = Pa-an, Burma 67 L20 16 51N 97 40 E
Hpungan Pass, Burma 67 F20 27 30N 96 55 E
Hradec Králové, Czech Rep. ...... 26 A8 50 15N 15 50 E
Hrádek, Czech Rep. .. 27 C9 48 46N 16 16 E
Hranice, Czech Rep. .. 27 B10 49 34N 17 45 E
Hrazdan, Armenia .... 35 K7 40 30N 44 46 E
Hrebenka, Ukraine .. 33 G7 50 9N 33 10 E
Hrodna, Belarus ...... 30 E10 53 42N 23 52 E
Hrodzyanka, Belarus 32 F5 53 31N 28 42 E
Hron →, Slovak Rep. .. 27 D11 47 49N 18 45 E
Hrubieszów, Poland .. 31 H10 50 49N 23 51 E
Hrubý Jeseník, Czech Rep. ...... 27 A10 50 5N 17 10 E
Hrvatska = Croatia ■, Europe ...... 41 C13 45 20N 16 0 E
Hrymayliv, Ukraine .. 33 H4 49 20N 26 5 E
Hrynyava, Ukraine .. 29 C7 47 59N 24 53 E
Hsenwi, Burma ...... 67 H20 23 22N 97 55 E
Hsiamen = Xiamen, China ...... 59 E12 24 25N 118 4 E
Hsian = Xi'an, China 56 G5 34 15N 109 0 E
Hsinchu, Taiwan .... 59 E13 24 48N 120 58 E
Hsinhailien = Lianyungang, China 57 G10 34 40N 119 11 E
Hsinying, Taiwan .... 59 F13 23 18N 120 19 E
Hsopket, Burma .... 58 F2 23 11N 98 26 E
Hsüchou = Xuzhou, China ...... 57 G9 34 18N 117 10 E
Hu Xian, China ...... 56 G5 34 8N 108 42 E
Hua Hin, Thailand .. 64 F2 12 34N 99 58 E
Hua Xian, Henan, China 56 G8 35 30N 114 30 E
Hua Xian, Shaanxi, China ...... 56 G5 34 30N 109 48 E
Hua'an, China .... 59 E11 25 1N 117 32 E
Huab →, Namibia .... 88 B2 20 52S 13 25 E
Huachinera, Mexico .. 118 A3 30 9N 108 55W
Huacho, Peru 124 F3 11 10S 77 35W
Huade, China .... 56 D7 41 55N 113 59 E
Huadian, China ...... 57 C14 43 0N 126 40 E
Huai He →, China .... 59 F9 33 0N 118 30 E
Huai Had △, Thailand 64 D5 16 52N 104 17 E
Huai Nam Dang △, Thailand ...... 64 C2 19 30N 98 30 E

Huai Yot, Thailand ... 65 J2 7 45N 99 37 E
Huai'an, Hebei, China 56 D8 40 30N 114 20 E
Huai'an, Jiangsu, China 57 H10 33 30N 119 10 E
Huaibei, China ...... 56 G9 34 0N 116 48 E
Huaibin, China ...... 59 A10 32 32N 115 27 E
Huaide = Gongzhuling, China ...... 57 C13 43 30N 124 40 E
Huaidezhen, China .. 57 C13 43 48N 124 50 E
Huaihua, China ...... 58 D7 27 32N 109 57 E
Huaiji, China .... 59 F9 23 55N 112 12 E
Huainan, China ...... 59 A11 32 38N 116 58 E
Huaining, China ...... 59 B11 30 24N 116 40 E
Huairen, China ...... 56 E7 39 48N 113 20 E
Huairou, China ...... 56 D9 40 20N 116 35 E
Huaiyang, China .... 56 H8 33 40N 114 52 E
Huaiyin, China ...... 57 H10 33 30N 119 2 E
Huaiyuan, Anhui, China 57 H9 32 55N 117 10 E
Huaiyuan, Guangxi Zhuangzu, China ...... 58 E7 24 31N 108 22 E
Huajianzi, China .... 57 D13 41 23N 125 20 E
Huajuapan de Leon, Mexico 119 D5 17 50N 97 48W
Hualapai Peak, U.S.A. 109 J7 35 5N 113 54W
Hualien, Taiwan ...... 59 E13 24 0N 121 30 E
Huallaga →, Peru 124 E3 5 15S 75 30W
Huambo, Angola .... 85 G3 12 42S 15 54 E
Huan Jiang →, China 56 G5 34 28N 109 0 E
Huancabamba, Peru .. 124 E3 5 10S 79 15W
Huancane, Peru 124 G5 15 10S 69 44W
Huancavelica, Peru .. 124 F3 12 50S 75 5W
Huancayo, Peru 124 F3 12 5S 75 12W
Huanchaca, Bolivia .. 124 H5 20 15S 66 40W
Huang Hai = Yellow Sea, China ...... 57 G12 35 0N 123 0 E
Huang He →, China .. 57 F10 37 55N 118 50 E
Huang Xian, China .. 57 F11 37 38N 120 30 E
Huangchuan, China .. 59 A10 32 15N 115 10 E
Huanggang, China .. 59 B10 30 29N 114 52 E
Huangguoshu, China 58 E5 26 0N 105 40 E
Huanghua, China .... 56 E9 38 15N 117 18 E
Huangling, China .... 56 G5 35 34N 109 15 E
Huanglong, China .. 56 G5 35 30N 109 59 E
Huanglongtan, China 59 A8 32 40N 110 33 E
Huangmei, China .... 59 B10 30 5N 115 56 E
Huangpi, China ...... 59 B10 30 50N 114 22 E
Huangping, China .... 58 D6 26 52N 107 54 E
Huangshan, China .. 59 C12 29 42N 118 25 E
Huangshi, China .... 59 B10 30 10N 115 3 E
Huangsongdian, China 57 C14 43 45N 127 25 E
Huangyan, China .... 59 C13 28 38N 121 19 E
Huangyangsi, China 59 D8 26 33N 111 39 E
Huaning, China ...... 58 E4 24 17N 102 56 E
Huanjiang, China .... 58 E7 24 50N 108 18 E
Huantai, China ...... 57 F9 36 58N 118 0 E
Huánuco, Peru 124 E3 9 55S 76 15W
Huaping, China ...... 58 D3 26 46N 101 25 E
Huaraz, Peru 124 E3 9 30S 77 32W
Huarmey, Peru 124 F3 10 5S 78 5W
Huarong, China ...... 59 C9 29 29N 112 30 E
Huascarán, Peru 124 E3 9 8S 77 36W
Huasco, Chile 126 B1 28 30S 71 15W
Huasco →, Chile 126 B1 28 27S 71 13W
Huasna, U.S.A. 111 K6 35 6N 120 24W
Huatabampo, Mexico 118 B3 26 50N 109 50W
Huauchinango, Mexico 119 C5 20 11N 98 3W
Huautla de Jiménez, Mexico 119 D5 18 8N 96 51W
Huaxi, China .... 58 D6 26 26N 106 40 E
Huay Namota, Mexico 118 C4 21 56N 104 30W
Huayin, China ...... 56 G6 34 35N 110 5 E
Huayuan, China .... 58 C7 28 37N 109 29 E
Huayun, China ...... 58 B6 30 14N 106 41 E
Huazhou, China .... 59 G8 21 33N 110 33 E
Hubbard, Ohio, U.S.A. 116 E4 41 9N 80 34W
Hubbard, Tex., U.S.A. 113 K6 31 51N 96 48W
Hubbart Pt., Canada 103 B10 59 21N 94 41W
Hubei □, China ...... 59 B9 31 0N 112 0 E
Hubli, India .... 66 M9 15 22N 75 15 E
Huch'ang, N. Korea .. 57 D14 41 25N 127 2 E
Hucknall, U.K. 14 D6 53 3N 1 13W
Huddersfield, U.K. .. 14 D6 53 39N 1 47W
Hude, Germany ...... 24 B4 53 7N 8 26 E
Hudi, Sudan .... 80 D3 17 43N 34 18 E
Hudiksvall, Sweden .. 10 C11 61 43N 17 10 E
Hudson, Canada 104 B1 50 6N 92 9W
Hudson, Mass., U.S.A. 117 D13 42 23N 71 34W
Hudson, N.Y., U.S.A. 117 D11 42 15N 73 46W
Hudson, Wis., U.S.A. 112 C8 44 58N 92 45W
Hudson, Wyo., U.S.A. 108 E9 42 54N 108 35W
Hudson →, U.S.A. .. 117 F10 40 42N 74 2W
Hudson Bay, Nunavut, Canada 101 C11 60 0N 86 0W
Hudson Bay, Sask., Canada 103 C8 52 51N 102 23W
Hudson Falls, U.S.A. 117 C11 43 18N 73 35W
Hudson Mts., Antarctica 5 D16 74 32S 99 20W
Hudson Str., Canada 101 B13 62 0N 70 0W
Hudson's Hope, Canada 102 B4 56 0N 121 54W
Hue, Vietnam .... 64 D6 16 30N 107 35 E
Huebra →, Spain 36 D4 41 2N 6 48W
Huedin, Romania .... 28 D8 46 52N 23 2 E
Huehuetenango, Guatemala 120 C1 15 20N 91 28W
Huejúcar, Mexico 118 C4 22 21N 103 13W
Huélamo, Spain 38 E3 40 17N 1 48W
Huelgoat, France 18 D3 48 22N 3 46W
Huelma, Spain 37 H7 37 39N 3 28W
Huelva, Spain 37 H4 37 18N 6 57W
Huelva □, Spain 37 H4 37 40N 7 0W
Huelva →, Spain 37 H5 37 27N 6 0W
Huentelauquén, Chile 126 C1 31 38S 71 33W
Huércal-Overa, Spain 39 H3 37 23N 1 57W
Huerta, Sa. de la, Argentina 126 C2 31 10S 67 30W
Huertas, C. de las, Spain 39 G4 38 21N 0 24W
Huerva →, Spain 38 D4 41 39N 0 52W
Huesca, Spain 38 C4 42 8N 0 25W
Huesca □, Spain .... 38 C5 42 20N 0 1 E
Huéscar, Spain 39 H2 37 44N 2 35W
Huetamo, Mexico 118 D4 18 36N 100 54W
Huete, Spain 38 E2 40 10N 2 43W
Hugh →, Australia .. 94 D1 25 1S 134 1 E
Hughenden, Australia 94 C3 20 52S 144 10 E
Hughes, Australia .... 93 F4 30 42S 129 31 E
Hughesville, U.S.A. .. 117 E8 41 14N 76 44W
Hugli →, India ...... 69 J13 21 56N 88 4 E
Hugo, Colo., U.S.A. .. 112 F3 39 8N 103 28W
Hugo, Okla., U.S.A. .. 113 H7 34 1N 95 31W
Hugoton, U.S.A. 113 G4 37 11N 101 21W
Hui Xian = Huixian, China ...... 56 G7 35 27N 113 12 E
Hui Xian, China .... 56 H4 33 50N 106 4 E
Hui'an, China .... 59 E12 25 1N 118 43 E
Hui'anbu, China .... 56 F4 37 28N 106 38 E
Huichang, China .... 59 E10 25 32N 115 45 E
Huichapán, Mexico .. 119 C5 20 24N 99 40W

Huidong, Guangdong, China ...... 59 F10 22 58N 114 43 E
Huidong, Sichuan, China 58 D4 26 34N 102 35 E
Huifa He →, China .. 57 C14 43 0N 127 50 E
Huila, Nevado del, Colombia 124 C3 3 0N 76 0W
Huilai, China .... 59 F11 23 0N 116 18 E
Huili, China .... 58 D4 26 35N 102 17 E
Huimin, China ...... 57 F9 37 27N 117 28 E
Huinan, China ...... 57 C14 42 40N 126 2 E
Huinca Renancó, Argentina 126 C3 34 51S 64 22W
Huining, China ...... 56 G3 35 38N 105 0 E
Huinong, China ...... 56 E4 39 5N 106 35 E
Huisache, Mexico 118 C4 22 50N 100 25W
Huishui, China ...... 58 D6 26 7N 106 38 E
Huisne →, France .. 18 E7 47 59N 0 11 E
Huiting, China ...... 56 G9 34 5N 116 5 E
Huitong, China ...... 58 D7 26 51N 109 45 E
Huixian, China ...... 56 G7 35 27N 113 12 E
Huixtla, Mexico 119 D6 15 9N 92 28W
Huize, China .... 58 D4 26 24N 103 15 E
Huizhou, China ...... 59 F10 23 0N 114 23 E
Hukawng Valley, Burma 67 F20 26 30N 96 30 E
Hukou, China .... 59 C11 29 45N 116 21 E
Hūksan-chedo, S. Korea 57 G13 34 40N 125 30 E
Hukuntsi, Botswana 88 C3 23 58S 21 45 E
Hulayfā', Si. Arabia .. 70 E4 25 58N 40 45 E
Hulin He →, China .. 57 B12 45 0N 122 10 E
Hull = Kingston upon Hull, U.K. 14 D7 53 45N 0 21W
Hull, Canada 117 A9 45 25N 75 44W
Hull →, U.K. 14 D7 53 44N 0 20W
Hulst, Neths. .... 17 C4 51 17N 4 2 E
Hultsfred, Sweden .. 11 G9 57 30N 15 52 E
Hulun Nur, China .. 60 B6 49 0N 117 30 E
Huma, Tanjung, Malaysia ...... 65 c 5 29N 100 16 E
Humacao, Puerto Rico 121 d 18 9N 65 50W
Humahuaca, Argentina 126 A2 23 10S 65 25W
Humaitá, Brazil 124 E6 7 35S 63 1W
Humaitá, Paraguay .. 126 B4 27 2S 58 31W
Humansdorp, S. Africa 88 E3 34 2S 24 46 E
Humara, J., Sudan .. 81 D3 16 16N 30 59 E
Humbe, Angola ...... 88 B1 16 40S 14 55 E
Humber →, U.K. 14 D7 53 42N 0 27W
Humboldt, Canada .. 103 C7 52 15N 105 9W
Humboldt, Iowa, U.S.A. 112 D7 42 44N 94 13W
Humboldt, Tenn., U.S.A. 113 H10 35 49N 88 55W
Humboldt →, U.S.A. 108 F4 39 59N 118 36W
Humboldt Gletscher = Sermersuaq, Greenland 4 B4 79 30N 62 0W
Hume, U.S.A. 110 J8 36 48N 118 54W
Hume, L., Australia .. 95 F4 36 0S 147 5 E
Humenné, Slovak Rep. 27 C14 48 55N 21 50 E
Hummelsta, Sweden 10 E10 59 34N 16 58 E
Humphreys, Mt., U.S.A. 110 H8 37 17N 118 40W
Humphreys Peak, U.S.A. 109 J8 35 21N 111 41W
Humpolec, Czech Rep. 26 B8 49 31N 15 20 E
Humptulips, U.S.A. .. 110 C3 47 14N 123 57W
Hūn, Libya .... 79 C9 29 2N 16 0 E
Hun Jiang →, China 57 D13 40 50N 125 38 E
Húnaflói, Iceland 8 D3 65 50N 20 50W
Hunan □, China .... 59 D9 27 30N 112 0 E
Hunchun, China .... 57 C16 42 52N 130 28 E
Hundested, Denmark 11 J5 55 58N 11 52 E
Hundewali, Pakistan 68 D5 31 55N 72 38 E
Hundred Mile House, Canada 102 C4 51 38N 121 18W
Hunedoara, Romania 28 E7 45 40N 22 50 E
Hunedoara □, Romania 28 E7 45 50N 22 54 E
Hünfeld, Germany .. 24 E5 50 39N 9 46 E
Hung Yen, Vietnam .. 58 G6 20 39N 106 4 E
Hungary ■, Europe 27 D12 47 20N 19 20 E
Hungary, Plain of, Europe ...... 6 F10 47 0N 20 0 E
Hungerford, Australia 95 D3 28 58S 144 24 E
Hŭngnam, N. Korea 57 E14 39 49N 127 45 E
Huni Valley, Ghana .. 82 D4 5 33N 1 56W
Hunneberg, Sweden 11 F6 58 18N 12 30 E
Hunnebostrand, Sweden 11 F5 58 27N 11 18 E
Hunsberg, Namibia .. 88 D2 27 45S 17 12 E
Hunsrück, Germany 25 F3 49 56N 7 27 E
Hunstanton, U.K. .... 14 E8 52 56N 0 29 E
Hunte →, Germany .. 24 B4 53 14N 8 28 E
Hunter, U.S.A. 117 D10 42 13N 74 13W
Hunter I., Australia .. 95 G4 40 30S 144 45 E
Hunter I., Canada .. 102 C3 51 55N 131 0W
Hunter Ra., Australia 95 E5 32 45S 150 15 E
Hunters Road, Zimbabwe ...... 87 F2 19 9S 29 49 E
Hunterville, N.Z. .... 91 H5 39 56S 175 35 E
Huntingburg, U.S.A. 114 F2 38 18N 86 57W
Huntingdon, Canada 104 C5 45 6N 74 10W
Huntingdon, U.K. 15 E7 52 20N 0 11W
Huntington, Ind., U.S.A. 114 E3 40 53N 85 30W
Huntington, N.Y., U.S.A. 117 F11 40 52N 73 26W
Huntington, Oreg., U.S.A. 108 D5 44 21N 117 16W
Huntington, Utah, U.S.A. 108 G8 39 20N 110 58W
Huntington, W. Va., U.S.A. 114 F4 38 25N 82 27W
Huntington Beach, U.S.A. 111 M9 33 40N 118 5W
Huntly, N.Z. .... 91 G5 37 34S 175 11 E
Huntly, U.K. 13 D6 57 27N 2 47W
Huntsville, Canada .. 116 A5 45 20N 79 14W
Huntsville, Ala., U.S.A. 115 H2 34 44N 86 35W
Huntsville, Tex., U.S.A. 113 K7 30 43N 95 33W
Hunyani →, Zimbabwe 87 F3 15 57S 30 39 E
Hunyuan, China ...... 56 E7 39 42N 113 42 E
Hunza →, India ...... 69 B6 35 54N 74 20 E
Huo Xian = Huozhou, China ...... 56 F6 36 36N 111 42 E
Huong Khe, Vietnam 64 C5 18 13N 105 41 E
Huonville, Australia .. 95 G4 43 0S 147 5 E
Huoqiu, China ...... 59 A11 32 20N 116 12 E
Huoshan, Anhui, China 59 B11 31 25N 116 20 E
Huoshan, Anhui, China 59 B11 31 25N 116 20 E
Huoshao Dao = Lü-Tao, Taiwan ...... 59 F13 22 40N 121 30 E
Huozhou, China .... 56 F6 36 36N 111 42 E
Hupeh = Hubei □, China ...... 59 B9 31 0N 112 0 E
Hūr, Iran .... 71 D8 30 50N 57 7 E
Hurbanovo, Slovak Rep. 27 D11 47 51N 18 11 E
Hurd, C., Canada 116 A3 45 13N 81 44W
Hure Qi, China ...... 57 C11 42 45N 121 45 E
Hurghada, Egypt .... 80 B3 27 15N 33 50 E
Hurley, N. Mex., U.S.A. 109 K9 32 42N 108 8W

Hurley, Wis., U.S.A. 112 B9 46 27N 90 11W
Huron, Calif., U.S.A. 110 J6 36 12N 120 6W
Huron, Ohio, U.S.A. 116 E2 41 24N 82 33W
Huron, S. Dak., U.S.A. 112 C5 44 22N 98 13W
Huron, L., U.S.A. .. 116 B2 44 30N 82 40W
Huron East, Canada 116 C3 43 37N 81 18W
Hurricane, U.S.A. .. 109 H7 37 11N 113 17W
Hurso, Ethiopia .... 81 F5 9 35N 41 33 E
Hurungwe →, Zimbabwe 87 F2 16 7S 29 5 E
Hurunui →, N.Z. .. 91 K4 42 54S 173 18 E
Hurup, Denmark .... 11 H2 56 46N 8 25 E
Húsavík, Iceland 8 C5 66 3N 17 21W
Huși, Romania ...... 29 D13 46 41N 28 7 E
Huskvarna, Sweden 11 G8 57 47N 14 15 E
Hustadvika, Norway 8 E12 63 0N 7 0 E
Hustontown, U.S.A. 116 F6 40 3N 78 2W
Hustopeče, Czech Rep. 27 C9 48 57N 16 43 E
Husum, Germany .... 24 A5 54 28N 9 4 E
Husum, Sweden .... 10 A13 63 21N 19 12 E
Hutchinson, Kans., U.S.A. 113 F6 38 5N 97 56W
Hutchinson, Minn., U.S.A. 112 C7 44 54N 94 22W
Hutte Sauvage, L. de la, Canada 105 A7 56 15N 64 45W
Hüttenberg, Austria .. 26 E7 46 56N 14 33 E
Hüttener Berge △, Germany ...... 24 A5 54 24N 9 40 E
Hutton, Mt., Australia 95 D4 25 51S 148 20 E
Huwun, Ethiopia .... 81 G5 4 23N 40 6 E
Huy, Belgium .... 17 D5 50 31N 5 15 E
Huzhou, China ...... 59 B13 30 51N 120 8 E
Hvalpsund, Denmark 11 H3 56 42N 9 11 E
Hvammstangi, Iceland 8 D3 65 24N 20 57W
Hvar, Croatia .... 41 E13 43 11N 16 28 E
Hvarski Kanal, Croatia 41 E13 43 15N 16 35 E
Hvítá →, Iceland 8 D3 64 30N 21 58W
Hvízdets, Ukraine .. 29 B10 48 35N 25 17 E
Hwachon-chōsuji, S. Korea ...... 57 E14 38 5N 127 50 E
Hwang Ho = Huang He →, China ...... 57 F10 37 55N 118 50 E
Hwange, Zimbabwe 87 F2 18 18S 26 30 E
Hwange △, Zimbabwe 88 B4 19 0S 26 30 E
Hyannis, Mass., U.S.A. 114 E10 41 39N 70 17W
Hyannis, Nebr., U.S.A. 112 E4 42 0N 101 46W
Hyargas Nuur, Mongolia 60 B4 49 0N 93 0 E
Hybo, Sweden ...... 10 C10 61 49N 16 15 E
Hyde Park, U.S.A. .. 117 E11 41 47N 73 56W
Hyden, Australia .... 93 F2 32 24S 118 53 E
Hyder, U.S.A. 102 B2 55 55N 130 5W
Hyderabad, India .. 66 L11 17 22N 78 29 E
Hyderabad, Pakistan 68 G3 25 23N 68 24 E
Hyères, France ...... 21 E10 43 8N 6 9 E
Hyères, Îs. d', France 21 F10 43 0N 6 20 E
Hyesan, N. Korea .. 57 D15 41 20N 128 10 E
Hyland →, Canada 102 B3 59 52N 128 12W
Hyltebruk, Sweden .. 11 H7 56 59N 13 15 E
Hymia, India .... 69 C8 33 40N 78 2 E
Hyndman Peak, U.S.A. 108 C10 43 45N 114 8W
Hyōgo □, Japan .... 55 G7 35 15N 134 50 E
Hyrum, U.S.A. 108 F8 41 38N 111 51W
Hysham, U.S.A. 108 C10 46 18N 107 14W
Hythe, U.K. .... 15 F9 51 4N 1 5 E
Hyūga, Japan ...... 55 H5 32 25N 131 35 E
Hyvinge = Hyvinkää, Finland ...... 9 F21 60 38N 24 50 E
Hyvinkää, Finland .. 9 F21 60 38N 24 50 E

I

I-n-Gall, Niger ...... 83 B6 16 51N 7 1 E
I-n-Oudad, Algeria .. 83 A5 20 17N 4 38 E
I-n-Ouzzal, Algeria .. 83 A5 20 40N 2 35 E
I-n-Tadreft, Niger .. 83 B6 19 5N 18 4 E
Iablanița, Romania .. 28 E7 44 57N 22 19 E
Iaco →, Brazil 124 E5 9 3S 68 34W
Iacobeni, Romania .. 29 C10 47 25N 25 20 E
Iakora, Madag. ...... 89 C8 23 6S 46 40 E
Ialomița □, Romania 29 F12 44 30N 27 30 E
Ialomița →, Romania 29 F12 44 42N 27 51 E
Ialoveni, Moldova .. 29 D13 46 56N 28 47 E
Ialpug →, Moldova 29 E13 45 41N 28 35 E
Ianca, Romania ...... 29 F12 45 6N 27 29 E
Iara, Romania ...... 29 D8 46 31N 23 35 E
Iarda, Ethiopia ...... 81 E4 11 0N 35 30 E
Iargara, Moldova .. 29 D13 46 24N 28 23 E
Iași, Romania ...... 29 C12 47 10N 27 40 E
Iași □, Romania .... 29 C12 47 20N 27 0 E
Iasmos, Greece .... 45 E9 41 8N 25 12 E
Ib →, India .... 69 J10 21 34N 83 48 E
Iba, Phil. .... 61 D3 15 22N 120 0 E
Ibadan, Nigeria .... 83 D5 7 22N 3 58 E
Ibagué, Colombia .. 124 C3 4 20N 75 20W
Iballë, Albania ...... 44 D4 42 12N 20 0 E
Ibănești, Botoșani, Romania ...... 29 B11 48 4N 26 22 E
Ibănești, Mureș, Romania ...... 29 D9 46 45N 24 57 E
Ibar →, Serbia & M. 44 C4 43 43N 20 45 E
Ibaraki □, Japan .... 55 F10 36 10N 140 10 E
Ibarra, Ecuador 124 C3 0 21N 78 7W
Ibba, Sudan .... 81 G2 4 49N 29 2 E
Ibba, Bahr el →, Sudan 81 F2 5 30N 28 55 E
Ibbenbüren, Germany 24 C3 52 16N 7 43 E
Ibembo, Dem. Rep. of the Congo ...... 86 B1 2 35N 23 35 E
Ibera, L., Argentina 126 B4 28 30S 57 9W
Iberian Peninsula, Europe 6 H5 40 0N 5 0W
Iberville, Canada .. 117 A11 45 19N 73 17W
Iberville, Lac d', Canada 104 A5 55 55N 73 15W
Ibi, Nigeria .... 83 D6 8 15N 9 44 E
Ibiá, Brazil 125 G9 19 30S 46 30W
Ibiapaba, Sa. da, Brazil 125 D10 4 0S 41 30W
Ibicuí →, Brazil 127 B4 29 25S 56 47W
Ibicuy, Argentina .. 126 C4 33 55S 59 10W
Ibiza = Eivissa, Spain 48 C7 38 54N 1 26 E
Ibiza ✈ (IBZ), Spain 39 G8 38 53N 1 22 E
Iblei, Monti, Italy .. 43 E7 37 15N 14 45 E
Ibo, Mozam. .... 87 E5 12 22S 40 40 E
Ibonma, Indonesia .. 63 E8 3 29S 133 31 E
Ibotirama, Brazil 125 F10 12 13S 43 12W
Ibrāhīm →, Lebanon 74 A4 34 4N 35 38 E
'Ibrī, Oman .... 71 F8 23 14N 56 30 E
Ibshawāi, Egypt .... 80 J7 29 21N 30 40 E
Ibu, Indonesia ...... 63 D7 1 35N 127 33 E
Ibusuki, Japan ...... 55 J5 31 12N 130 40 E
Ica, Peru 124 F3 14 0S 75 48W
Ica →, Brazil 124 D5 2 55S 67 58W
Içana, Brazil 124 C5 0 21N 67 19W

Içana →, Brazil 124 C5 0 26N 67 19W
Icel = Mersin, Turkey 70 B2 36 51N 34 36 E
Iceland ■, Europe .. 8 D4 64 45N 19 0W
Iceland Plateau, Arctic 4 C7 64 0N 10 0W
Ich'ang = Yichang, China ...... 59 B8 30 40N 111 20 E
Ichchapuram, India 67 K14 19 10N 84 40 E
Ichhawar, India .... 68 H7 23 1N 77 1 E
Ichihara, Japan ...... 55 G10 35 28N 140 5 E
Ichikawa, Japan ...... 55 G9 35 44N 139 55 E
Ichilo →, Bolivia .. 124 G6 15 57S 64 50W
Ichinohe, Japan .... 54 D10 40 13N 141 17 E
Ichinomiya, Japan .. 55 G8 35 18N 136 48 E
Ichinoseki, Japan .. 54 E10 38 55N 141 8 E
Ichnya, Ukraine .... 33 G7 50 52N 32 24 E
Icod, Canary Is. 48 F3 28 22N 16 43W
Ida Grove, U.S.A. .. 112 D7 42 21N 95 28W
Idabel, U.S.A. 113 J7 33 54N 94 50W
Idaga Hamus, Ethiopia 81 E4 14 13N 39 48 E
Idah, Nigeria ...... 83 D6 7 5N 6 40 E
Idaho □, U.S.A. 108 D7 45 0N 115 0W
Idaho City, U.S.A. .. 108 E6 43 50N 115 50W
Idaho Falls, U.S.A. .. 108 E7 43 30N 112 2W
Idalia □, Australia .. 94 C3 24 49S 144 22 E
Idanha-a-Nova, Portugal 36 F3 39 50N 7 15W
Idar-Oberstein, Germany ...... 25 F3 49 43N 7 16 E
Idensalmi = Iisalmi, Finland ...... 8 E22 63 32N 27 10 E
Idfû, Egypt .... 80 C3 24 55N 32 49 E
Idhi Óros, Greece .. 49 D6 35 15N 24 45 E
Idhra, Greece ...... 46 D5 37 20N 23 28 E
Idi, Indonesia ...... 62 C1 5 2N 97 37 E
Idiofa, Dem. Rep. of the Congo ...... 84 E3 4 55S 19 42 E
Idkerberget, Sweden 10 D9 60 22N 15 15 E
Idku, Bahra el, Egypt 80 H7 31 18N 30 18 E
Idlib, Syria .... 70 C3 35 55N 36 36 E
Idre, Sweden ...... 10 C6 61 52N 12 42 E
Idria, U.S.A. 110 J6 36 25N 120 41W
Idrija, Slovenia .... 41 C11 46 0N 14 5 E
Idritsa, Russia ...... 32 C5 56 17N 28 53 E
Idutywa, S. Africa .. 89 E4 32 8S 28 18 E
Ieper, Belgium ...... 17 D2 50 51N 2 53 E
Ierápetra, Greece .. 49 E7 35 1N 25 44 E
Ierissós, Greece .... 44 F7 40 22N 23 52 E
Ierissoú Kólpos, Greece 44 F7 40 27N 23 57 E
Iernut, Romania .... 29 D9 46 27N 24 15 E
Iesi, Italy .... 41 E10 43 31N 13 14 E
Iésolo, Italy .... 41 C9 45 32N 12 38 E
Ifach, Penón de, Spain 39 G5 38 38N 0 5 E
Ifakara, Tanzania .. 84 F7 8 8S 36 41 E
'Ifâl, W. al →, Si. Arabia 70 D2 28 7N 35 3 E
Ifanadiana, Madag. 89 C8 21 19S 47 39 E
Ife, Nigeria .... 83 D5 7 30N 4 31 E
Iférouâne, Niger .... 83 B6 19 22N 8 24 E
Iffley, Australia .... 94 B3 18 53S 141 12 E
Ifon, Nigeria ...... 83 D6 6 58N 5 40 E
Iforas, Adrar des, Africa 83 B5 19 40N 1 40 E
Ifould, L., Australia 93 F5 30 52S 132 6 E
Iganga, Uganda .... 86 B3 0 37N 33 28 E
Igarapava, Brazil .. 125 H9 20 3S 47 47W
Igarka, Russia ...... 52 C9 67 30N 86 33 E
Igatimi, Paraguay .. 127 A4 24 5S 55 40W
Igbetti, Nigeria .... 83 D5 8 44N 4 8 E
Igbo-Ora, Nigeria .. 83 D5 7 29N 3 15 E
Igboho, Nigeria .... 83 D5 8 53N 3 50 E
Igbor, Nigeria ...... 83 D6 7 27N 8 34 E
Iğdır, Turkey ...... 73 C11 39 55N 44 2 E
Iggesund, Sweden .. 10 C11 61 39N 17 10 E
Iglésias, Italy ...... 42 C1 39 19N 8 32 E
Igloolik, Canada 101 B11 69 20N 81 49W
Igluligaarjuk = Chesterfield Inlet, Canada 100 B10 63 30N 90 45W
Iglulik = Igloolik, Canada 101 B11 69 20N 81 49W
'Igma, Gebel el, Egypt 80 B3 28 55N 34 0 E
Ignace, Canada 104 C1 49 30N 91 40W
Iğneada, Turkey .... 45 E11 41 50N 27 59 E
Iğneada Burnu, Turkey 45 E12 41 53N 28 2 E
Igoumenítsa, Greece 46 B2 39 32N 20 18 E
Igra, Russia .... 34 B11 57 33N 53 0 E
Iguaçu →, Brazil .. 127 B5 25 36S 54 36W
Iguaçu △, Brazil 127 B5 25 36S 54 26W
Iguaçu, Cat. del, Brazil 127 B5 25 41S 54 26W
Iguaçu Falls = Iguaçu, Cat. del, Brazil 127 B5 25 41S 54 26W
Iguala, Mexico 119 D5 18 20N 99 40W
Igualada, Spain .... 38 D6 41 37N 1 37 E
Iguassu = Iguaçu →, Brazil 127 B5 25 36S 54 36W
Iguatu, Brazil 125 E11 6 20S 39 18W
Iguazú △, Argentina 127 B5 25 42S 54 22W
Iguidi, Erg, Africa .. 78 C4 27 0N 7 0 E
Iharana, Madag. .... 89 A9 13 25S 50 0 E
Ihbulag, Mongolia .. 56 C4 43 11N 107 10 E
Iheya-Shima, Japan 55 L3 27 4N 127 58 E
Ihiala, Nigeria ...... 83 D6 5 51N 6 55 E
Ihosy, Madag. ...... 89 C8 22 24S 46 8 E
Ihotry, Farihy, Madag. 89 C7 21 56S 43 41 E
Ihugh, Nigeria ...... 83 D6 7 2N 9 4 E
Ii, Finland .... 8 D21 65 19N 25 22 E
Ii-Shima, Japan .... 55 L3 26 43N 127 47 E
Iida, Japan .... 55 G8 35 35N 137 50 E
Iijoki →, Finland .. 8 D21 65 20N 25 20 E
Iisalmi, Finland .... 8 E22 63 32N 27 10 E
Iiyama, Japan ...... 55 F9 36 51N 138 22 E
Iizuka, Japan ...... 55 H5 33 38N 130 42 E
Ijebu-Igbo, Nigeria 83 D5 6 56N 4 1 E
Ijebu-Ode, Nigeria .. 83 D5 6 47N 3 58 E
IJmuiden, Neths. .... 17 B4 52 28N 4 35 E
Ijo älv = Iijoki →, Finland ...... 8 D21 65 20N 25 20 E
IJssel →, Neths. .... 17 B5 52 35N 5 50 E
IJsselmeer, Neths. .. 17 B5 52 45N 5 20 E
Ijuí, Brazil 127 B5 28 23S 53 55W
Ijuí →, Brazil 127 B4 27 58S 55 20W
Ikalamavony, Madag. 89 C8 21 9S 46 35 E
Ikale, Nigeria ...... 83 D6 7 40N 5 37 E
Ikang, Nigeria ...... 83 E6 4 49N 8 30 E
Ikara, Nigeria ...... 83 C6 11 12N 8 15 E
Ikaría, Greece ...... 47 D8 37 35N 26 10 E
Ikast, Denmark .... 11 H3 56 8N 9 10 E
Ikeda, Japan .... 55 G7 34 1N 133 48 E
Ikeja, Nigeria ...... 83 D5 6 36N 3 23 E
Ikela, Dem. Rep. of the Congo ...... 84 E4 1 6S 23 6 E
Ikerre-Ekiti, Nigeria 83 D6 7 25N 5 19 E
Ikhtiman, Bulgaria .. 44 D7 42 27N 23 48 E
Iki, Japan .... 55 H4 33 45N 129 42 E
Ikire, Nigeria ...... 83 D5 7 23N 4 15 E
Ikizdere, Turkey ... 73 B9 40 46N 40 32 E

Ikom, *Nigeria* .... **83 D6**   6 0N   8 42 E
Ikongo, *Madag.* .... **89 C8** 21 52 S 47 27 E
Ikopa →, *Madag.* ...... **89 B8** 16 45 S 46 40 E
Ikorongo △, *Tanzania* . **86 C3**   1 50 S 34 53 E
Ikot Ekpene, *Nigeria* .. **83 D6**   5 12N   7 40 E
Ikparjuk = Arctic Bay,
  Canada **101 A11** 73 1N 85 7W
Ikungu, *Tanzania* ..... **86 C3**   1 33 S 33 42 E
Ikurun, *Nigeria* ...... **83 D5**   7 54N   4 40 E
Ila, *Nigeria* .... **83 D5**   8 0N   4 39 E
Ilagan, *Phil.* .... **61 C4** 17 7N 121 53 E
Ilaka, *Madag.* .... **89 B8** 19 33 S 48 52 E
Ilām, *Iran* .... **70 C5** 33 36N 46 36 E
Ilam, *Nepal* .... **69 F12** 26 58N 87 58 E
Ilam □, *Iran* .... **70 C5** 33 0N   47 0 E
Ilan, *Taiwan* .... **59 E13** 24 45N 121 44 E
Ilanskiy, *Russia* ..... **53 D10** 56 14N 96 3 E
Ilaro, *Nigeria* ...... **83 D5**   6 53N   3 3 E
Ilatane, *Niger* ...... **83 B5** 16 30N   4 45 E
Iława, *Poland* ...... **30 E6** 53 36N 19 34 E
Ile →, *Kazakhstan* ... **52 E8** 45 53N 77 10 E
Île-à-la-Crosse, *Canada* **103 B7** 55 27N 107 53W
Île-à-la-Crosse, Lac,
  Canada **103 B7** 55 40N 107 45W
Île-de-France □, *France* **19 D9** 49 0N   2 20 E
Ileanda, *Romania* .... **29 C8** 47 20N 23 38 E
Ilebo, *Dem. Rep. of
  the Congo* .... **84 E4**   4 17 S 20 55 E
Ilek, *Russia* .... **52 D6** 51 32N 53 21 E
Ilero, *Nigeria* ...... **83 D5**   8 0N   3 20 E
Ilesha, *Kwara, Nigeria* . **83 D5** 8 57N   3 28 E
Ilesha, *Oyo, Nigeria* .. **83 D5**   7 37N   4 40 E
Ilford, *Canada* **103 B9** 56 4N 95 35W
Ilfracombe, *Australia* . **94 C3** 23 30 S 144 30 E
Ilfracombe, *U.K.* **15 F3** 51 12N   4 8W
Ilgaz, *Turkey* .... **72 B5** 40 55N 33 37 E
Ilgaz Dağları, *Turkey* . **72 B5** 41 10N 33 50 E
Ilgın, *Turkey* .... **72 C4** 38 16N 31 55 E
Ilha de Moçambique,
  Mozam. .... **87 F5** 15 4 S 40 52 E
Ílhavo, *Portugal* **36 E2** 40 33N   8 43W
Ilhéus, *Brazil* ...... **125 F11** 14 49 S 39 2W
Ili = Ile →, *Kazakhstan* . **52 E8** 45 53N 77 10 E
Ilia, *Romania* .... **28 E7** 45 57N 22 40 E
Ilía □, *Greece* ...... **46 D3** 37 45N 21 35 E
Iliamna L., *U.S.A.* ... **100 C4** 59 30N 155 0W
Iliç, *Turkey* .... **73 C8** 39 27N 38 33 E
Ilıca, *Turkey* .... **47 B9** 39 52N 27 46 E
Ilichevsk, *Azerbaijan* . **73 C11** 39 22N 45 5 E
Iligan, *Phil.* .... **61 G6**   8 12N 124 13 E
Iligan Bay, *Phil.* .... **61 G6**   8 25N 124 5 E
Ilíki, L., *Greece* .... **46 C5** 38 24N 23 15 E
Ilin I., *Phil.* .... **61 E4** 12 14N 121 5 E
Iliodhrómia, *Greece* . **46 B5** 39 12N 23 50 E
Ilion, *U.S.A.* **117 D9** 43 1N 75 2W
Ilirska-Bistrica, *Slovenia* **41 C11** 45 34N 14 14 E
Ilkeston, *U.K.* **14 E6** 52 58N   1 19W
Ilkley, *U.K.* **14 D6** 53 56N   1 48W
Illampu = Ancohuma,
  Nevado, Bolivia ... **124 G5** 16 0 S 68 50W
Illana B., *Phil.* ..... **61 H5**   7 35N 123 45 E
Illapel, *Chile* ...... **126 C1** 32 0 S 71 10W
Ille-et-Vilaine □, *France* **18 D5** 48 10N   1 30W
Ille-sur-Têt, *France* . **20 F6** 42 40N   2 38 E
Illéla, *Niger* .... **83 C6** 14 32N   5 20 E
Iller →, *Germany* .... **25 G5** 48 23N   9 58 E
Illertissen, *Germany* . **25 G6** 48 12N 10 7 E
Illescas, *Spain* **36 E7** 40 8N   3 51W
Illetas, *Spain* ...... **48 B9** 39 32N   2 35 E
Illichivsk, *Ukraine* .. **33 J6** 46 20N 30 35 E
Illiers-Combray, *France* **18 D8** 48 18N   1 15 E
Illimani, Nevado, *Bolivia* **124 G5** 16 30 S 67 50W
Illinois □, *U.S.A.* **112 E10** 40 15N 89 30W
Illinois →, *U.S.A.* ... **112 F9** 38 58N 90 28W
Illizi, *Algeria* ...... **78 C7** 26 31N   8 32 E
Illkirch-Graffenstaden,
  France .... **19 D14** 48 34N   7 42 E
Íllora, *Spain* **37 H7** 37 17N   3 53W
Ilm →, *Germany* .... **24 D7** 51 6N   11 40 E
Ilmajoki, *Finland* ... **9 E20** 62 44N 22 34 E
Ilmen, Ozero, *Russia* . **32 C6** 58 15N 31 10 E
Ilmenau, *Germany* ... **24 E6** 50 41N 10 54 E
Ilnytsya, *Ukraine* ... **28 B8** 48 21N 23 5 E
Ilo, *Peru* .... **124 G4** 17 40 S 71 20W
Ilobu, *Nigeria* ...... **83 D5**   7 45N   4 25 E
Iloilo, *Phil.* .... **61 F5** 10 45N 122 33 E
Ilora, *Nigeria* ...... **83 D5**   7 45N   4 25 E
Ilorin, *Nigeria* ..... **83 D5**   8 30N   4 35 E
Ilovatka, *Russia* .... **34 E7** 50 30N 45 50 E
Ilovlya, *Russia* ..... **35 F7** 49 15N   4 2 E
Ilovlya →, *Russia* ... **35 F7** 49 14N 44 0 E
Iłowa, *Poland* ...... **31 G2** 51 30N 15 10 E
Iłubabor, *Ethiopia* .. **81 F4**   7 25N 35 0 E
Ilva Mică, *Romania* . **29 C9** 47 17N 24 40 E
Ilwaco, *U.S.A.* **110 D2** 46 19N 124 3W
Ilwaki, *Indonesia* ... **63 F7**   7 55 S 126 30 E
Ilyichevsk = Illichivsk,
  Ukraine .... **33 J6** 46 20N 30 35 E
Iłża, *Poland* .... **31 G8** 51 10N 21 15 E
Iłżanka →, *Poland* .. **31 G8** 51 14N 21 48 E
Imabari, *Japan* ..... **55 G6** 34 4N 133 0 E
Imaloto →, *Madag.* . **89 C8** 23 27 S 45 13 E
İmamoğlu, *Turkey* .. **72 D6** 37 15N 35 38 E
Imandra, Ozero, *Russia* **52 C4** 67 30N 33 0 E
Imanombo, *Madag.* .. **89 C8** 24 26 S 45 49 E
Imari, *Japan* .... **55 H4** 33 15N 129 52 E
Imasa, *Sudan* ...... **80 D4** 18 0N 36 12 E
Imathía □, *Greece* .. **44 F6** 40 30N 22 15 E
Imatra, *Finland* .... **32 B5** 61 12N 28 48 E
Iménas, *Mali* .... **83 B5** 16 20N   0 40 E
imeni 26 Bakinskikh
  Komissarov =
  Neftçala, *Azerbaijan* **71 B6** 39 19N 49 12 E
imeni 26 Bakinskikh
  Komissarov,
  Turkmenistan ..... **71 B7** 39 22N 54 10 E
Imeri, Serra, *Brazil* . **124 C5** 0 50N 65 25W
Imerimandroso, *Madag.* **89 B8** 17 26 S 48 35 E
Imi, *Ethiopia* ...... **81 F5**   6 28N 42 10 E
Imishly = İmişli,
  Azerbaijan .... **35 L9** 39 55N 48 4 E
İmişli, *Azerbaijan* .. **35 L9** 39 55N 48 4 E
Imlay, *U.S.A.* **108 F4** 40 40N 118 9W
Imlay City, *U.S.A.* .. **116 D1** 43 2N 83 5W
Immaseri, *Sudan* ... **81 D2** 5 46N 25 31 E
Immenstadt, *Germany* . **25 H6** 47 33N 10 13 E
Immingham, *U.K.* ... **14 D7** 53 37N   0 13W
Immokalee, *U.S.A.* .. **115 M5** 26 25N 81 25W
Imo □, *Nigeria* ..... **83 D6**   5 30N   7 10 E
Imo →, *Nigeria* ..... **83 E6**   4 36N   7 35 E
Imotski, *Croatia* .... **41 E14** 43 27N 17 12 E
Imperatriz, *Brazil* .. **125 E9**   5 30 S 47 29W
Impéria, *Italy* ...... **40 E5** 43 53N   8 3 E
Imperial, *Canada* ... **103 C7** 51 21N 105 28W
Imperial, *Calif., U.S.A.* **111 N11** 32 51N 115 34W
Imperial, *Nebr., U.S.A.* **112 E4** 40 31N 101 39W

Imperial Beach, *U.S.A.* **111 N9** 32 35N 117 8W
Imperial Dam, *U.S.A.* **111 N12** 32 55N 114 25W
Imperial Reservoir,
  U.S.A. **111 N12** 32 53N 114 28W
Imperial Valley, *U.S.A.* **111 N11** 33 0N 115 30W
Imperieuse Reef,
  Australia .... **92 C2** 17 36 S 118 50 E
Impfondo, *Congo* .... **84 D3**   1 40N 18 0 E
Imphal, *India* ...... **67 G18** 24 48N 93 56 E
Imphy, *France* ...... **19 F10** 46 55N   3 16 E
İmranlı, *Turkey* .... **73 C8** 39 54N 38 7 E
Imroz = Gökçeada,
  Turkey .... **45 F9** 40 10N 25 50 E
Imroz, *Turkey* ...... **45 F9** 40 10N 25 55 E
Imst, *Austria* ...... **26 D3** 47 15N 10 44 E
Imuris, *Mexico* **118 A2** 30 47N 110 52W
Imuruan B., *Phil.* ... **63 B5** 10 40N 119 10 E
In Akhmed, *Mali* ... **83 B4** 19 49N   0 56W
In Aleï, *Mali* **82 B4** 17 42N   2 30W
In Delimane, *Mali* ... **83 B5** 15 52N   1 31 E
In Guezzam, *Algeria* . **83 B6** 19 37N   5 52 E
In Koufi, *Mali* ..... **83 B5** 19 11N   1 25 E
In Salah, *Algeria* ... **78 C6** 27 10N   2 32 E
In Tallak, *Mali* ..... **83 B5** 16 19N   3 15 E
In Tebezas, *Mali* .... **83 B5** 17 49N   1 53 E
Ina, *Japan* .... **55 G8** 35 50N 137 55 E
Inagua △, *Bahamas* . **121 B5** 21 5N 73 24W
Inangahua, *N.Z.* .... **91 J3** 41 52 S 171 59 E
Inanwatan, *Indonesia* . **63 E8** 2 8 S 132 10 E
Iñapari, *Peru* ...... **124 F5** 11 0 S 69 40W
Inari, *Finland* ...... **8 B22** 68 54N 27 1 E
Inarijärvi, *Finland* .. **8 B22** 69 0N   28 0 E
Inawashiro-Ko, *Japan* . **54 F10** 37 29N 140 6 E
Inca, *Spain* .... **48 B9** 39 43N   2 54 E
Inca de Oro, *Chile* .. **126 B2** 26 45 S 69 54W
Incaguasi, *Chile* .... **126 B1** 29 12 S 71 5W
Ince Burun, *Turkey* . **72 A6** 42 7N 34 56 E
Incekum Burnu, *Turkey* **72 D5** 36 13N 33 57 E
İncesu, *Turkey* ..... **70 B2** 38 38N 35 11 E
Inch'ŏn, *S. Korea* ... **57 F14** 37 27N 126 40 E
Incio = Cruz de Incio,
  Spain **36 C3** 42 39N   7 21W
İncirliova, *Turkey* .. **47 D9** 37 50N 27 41 E
Incline Village, *U.S.A.* **110 F4** 39 10N 119 58W
Incomáti →, *Mozam.* . **89 D5** 25 46 S 32 43 E
Incudine, Mte., *France* **21 G13** 41 50N   9 12 E
Inda Silase, *Ethiopia* . **81 E4** 14 10N 38 15 E
Indal, *Sweden* ...... **10 B11** 62 35N 17 5 E
Indalsälven →, *Sweden* **10 B11** 62 36N 17 30 E
Indaw, *Burma* ...... **67 G20** 24 15N 96 5 E
Indbir, *Ethiopia* .... **81 F4**   8 7N 37 52 E
Independence, *Calif.,
  U.S.A.* **110 J8** 36 48N 118 12W
Independence, *Iowa,
  U.S.A.* **112 D9** 42 28N 91 54W
Independence, *Kans.,
  U.S.A.* **113 G7** 37 14N 95 42W
Independence, *Ky.,
  U.S.A.* **114 F3** 38 57N 84 33W
Independence, *Mo.,
  U.S.A.* **112 F7** 39 6N 94 25W
Independence Fjord,
  Greenland **4 A6** 82 10N 29 0W
Independence Mts.,
  U.S.A. **108 F5** 41 20N 116 0W
Independenţa, *Romania* **29 E12** 45 25N 27 42 E
Index, *U.S.A.* **110 C5** 47 50N 121 33W
India ■, *Asia* ...... **66 K11** 20 0N 78 0 E
Indian →, *U.S.A.* ... **115 M5** 27 59N 80 34W
Indian Cabins, *Canada* **102 B5** 59 52N 117 40W
Indian Harbour, *Canada* **105 B8** 54 27N 57 13W
Indian Head, *Canada* . **103 C8** 50 30N 103 41W
Indian Lake, *U.S.A.* . **117 C10** 43 47N 74 16W
Indian Ocean .... **50 K11** 5 0 S 75 0 E
Indian Springs, *U.S.A.* **111 J11** 36 35N 115 40W
Indiana, *U.S.A.* **116 F5** 40 37N 79 9W
Indiana □, *U.S.A.* .. **114 F3** 40 0N 86 0W
Indianapolis, *U.S.A.* . **114 F2** 39 46N 86 9W
Indianola, *Iowa, U.S.A.* **112 E8** 41 22N 93 34W
Indianola, *Miss., U.S.A.* **113 J9** 33 27N 90 39W
Indigirka →, *Russia* . **53 B15** 70 48N 148 54 E
Indija, *Serbia & M.* . **28 E5** 45 6N 20 7 E
Indio, *U.S.A.* **111 M10** 33 43N 116 13W
Indira Gandhi Canal,
  India .... **68 F5** 28 0N   72 0 E
Indo-China, *Asia* ... **50 H14** 15 0N 102 0 E
Indonesia ■, *Asia* .. **62 F5**   5 0 S 115 0 E
Indore, *India* ...... **68 H6** 22 42N 75 53 E
Indramayu, *Indonesia* . **63 G13** 6 20 S 108 19 E
Indravati →, *India* .. **67 K12** 19 20N 80 20 E
Indre □, *France* ..... **19 F8** 46 50N   1 39 E
Indre →, *France* .... **18 E7** 47 16N   0 11 E
Indre-et-Loire □, *France* **18 E7** 47 20N   0 40 E
Indulkana, *Australia* . **95 D1** 26 58 S 133 5 E
Indura, *Belarus* .... **30 E10** 53 26N 23 53 E
Indus →, *Pakistan* .. **68 G2** 24 20N 67 47 E
Indus, Mouths of the,
  Pakistan .... **68 H3** 24 0N   68 0 E
Inebolu, *Turkey* .... **72 B5** 41 55N 33 40 E
İnecik, *Turkey* ..... **45 F11** 40 56N 27 16 E
İnegöl, *Turkey* ..... **45 F13** 40 5N 29 31 E
Ineu, *Romania* ..... **28 D6** 46 26N 21 51 E
Infantes = Villanueva de
  los Infantes, *Spain* . **37 G7** 38 43N   1 1W
Infiernillo, Presa del,
  Mexico **118 D4** 18 9N 102 0W
Infiesto, *Spain* **36 B5** 43 21N   5 21W
Ingelstad, *Sweden* .. **11 H8** 56 45N 14 56 E
Ingenio, *Canary Is.* . **48 G4** 27 55N 15 26W
Ingenio Santa Ana,
  Argentina .... **126 B2** 27 25 S 65 40W
Ingersoll, *Canada* ... **116 C4** 43 4N 80 55W
Ingham, *Australia* .. **94 B4** 18 43 S 146 10 E
Ingleborough, *U.K.* . **14 C5** 54 10N   2 22W
Inglewood, *Queens.,
  Australia* .... **95 D5** 28 25 S 151 2 E
Inglewood, *Vic.,
  Australia* .... **95 F3** 36 29 S 143 53 E
Inglewood, *N.Z.* .... **91 H5** 39 9 S 174 14 E
Inglewood, *U.S.A.* .. **111 M8** 33 58N 118 21W
Ingólfshöfði, *Iceland* . **8 E5** 63 48N 16 39W
Ingolstadt, *Germany* . **25 G7** 48 46N 11 26 E
Ingomar, *U.S.A.* **108 C10** 46 35N 107 23W
Ingonish, *Canada* ... **105 C7** 46 42N 60 18W
Ingore, *Guinea-Biss.* . **82 C1** 12 24N 15 48W
Ingraj Bazar, *India* . **69 G13** 24 58N 88 10 E
Ingrid Christensen
  Coast, *Antarctica* . **5 C6** 69 30 S 76 0 E
Ingul = Inhul →,
  Ukraine .... **33 J7** 46 50N 32 0 E
Ingulec = Inhulec →,
  Ukraine .... **33 J7** 47 42N 33 14 E
Ingulets = Inhulets →,
  Ukraine .... **33 J7** 46 46N 32 47 E
Inguri = Enguri →,
  Georgia .... **35 J5** 42 38N 41 38 E
Ingushetia □, *Russia* . **35 J7** 43 20N 44 50 E

Ingwavuma, *S. Africa* . **89 D5** 27 9 S 31 59 E
Inhaca, *Mozam.* .... **89 D5** 26 1 S 32 57 E
Inhafenga, *Mozam.* . **89 C5** 20 36 S 33 53 E
Inhambane, *Mozam.* . **89 C6** 23 54 S 35 30 E
Inhambane □, *Mozam.* **89 C5** 22 30 S 34 20 E
Inhaminga, *Mozam.* . **87 F4** 18 26 S 35 0 E
Inharrime, *Mozam.* . **89 C6** 24 30 S 35 0 E
Inharrime →, *Mozam.* **89 C6** 24 30 S 35 0 E
Inhisar, *Turkey* .... **47 A12** 40 3N 30 23 E
Inhul →, *Ukraine* ... **33 J7** 46 50N 32 0 E
Inhulec →, *Ukraine* . **33 J7** 47 42N 33 14 E
Inhulets →, *Ukraine* . **33 J7** 46 46N 32 47 E
Iniesta, *Spain* **39 F3** 39 27N   1 21W
Ining = Yining, *China* **52 E9** 43 58N 81 10 E
Inírida →, *Colombia* . **124 C5** 3 55N 67 52W
Inishbofin, *Ireland* .. **12 C1** 53 37N 10 13W
Inisheer, *Ireland* ... **12 C2** 53 3N 9 32W
Inishfree B., *Ireland* . **12 A3** 55 4N 8 23W
Inishkea North, *Ireland* **12 B1** 54 9N 10 11W
Inishkea South, *Ireland* **12 B1** 54 7N 10 12W
Inishmaan, *Ireland* .. **12 C2** 53 5N 9 35W
Inishmore, *Ireland* .. **12 C2** 53 8N 9 45W
Inishowen Pen., *Ireland* **12 A4** 55 14N 7 15W
Inishshark, *Ireland* . **12 C1** 53 37N 10 16W
Inishturk, *Ireland* .. **12 C1** 53 42N 10 7W
Inishvickillane, *Ireland* **12 D1** 52 3N 10 37W
Injibara, *Ethiopia* .. **81 E4** 10 59N 37 0 E
Injune, *Australia* ... **95 D4** 25 53 S 148 32 E
Inklin →, *Canada* ... **102 B2** 58 50N 133 10W
Inland Kaikoura Ra.,
  N.Z. .... **91 J4** 41 59 S 173 41 E
Inland Sea = Setonaikai,
  Japan .... **55 G6** 34 20N 133 30 E
Inle L., *Burma* ..... **67 J20** 20 30N 96 58 E
Inlet, *U.S.A.* **117 C10** 43 45N 74 48W
Inn →, *Austria* ..... **26 C6** 48 35N 13 28 E
Innamincka, *Australia* **95 D3** 27 44 S 140 46 E
Inner Hebrides, *U.K.* . **13 E2** 57 0N 6 30W
Inner Mongolia = Nei
  Monggol Zizhiqu □,
  China .... **56 D7** 42 0N 112 0 E
Inner Sound, *U.K.* .. **13 D3** 57 30N 5 55W
Innerkip, *Canada* ... **116 C4** 43 13N 80 42W
Innetalling I., *Canada* **104 A4** 56 0N 79 0W
Innisfail, *Australia* .. **94 B4** 17 33 S 146 5 E
Innisfail, *Canada* ... **102 C6** 52 2N 113 57W
In'noshima, *Japan* .. **55 G6** 34 19N 133 10 E
Innsbruck, *Austria* .. **26 D4** 47 16N 11 23 E
Innviertel, *Austria* .. **26 C6** 48 15N 13 15 E
Inny →, *Ireland* **12 C4** 53 30N   7 50W
Inongo, *Dem. Rep. of
  the Congo* .... **84 E3**   1 55 S 18 30 E
Inönü, *Turkey* ...... **47 B12** 39 48N 30 9 E
Inoucdjouac = Inukjuak,
  Canada **101 C12** 58 25N 78 15W
Inowrocław, *Poland* . **31 F5** 52 50N 18 12 E
Inpundong, *N. Korea* . **57 D14** 41 25N 126 34 E
Inscription, Cr., *Australia* **93 E1** 25 29 S 112 59 E
Insein, *Burma* ...... **67 L20** 16 50N 96 5 E
Insjön, *Sweden* ..... **10 D9** 60 41N 15 6 E
Ińsko, *Poland* ...... **30 E2** 53 25N 15 32 E
Însurăţei, *Romania* . **29 F12** 44 50N 27 40 E
Inta, *Russia* .... **52 C6** 66 5N 60 8 E
Intendente Alvear,
  Argentina .... **126 D3** 35 12 S 63 32W
Intepe, *Turkey* ..... **47 A8** 40 1N 26 20 E
Interlaken, *Switz.* .. **25 J3** 46 41N   7 50 E
Interlaken, *U.S.A.* .. **117 D8** 42 37N 76 44W
International Falls,
  U.S.A. **112 A8** 48 36N 93 25W
Intiyaco, *Argentina* . **126 B3** 28 43 S 60 5W
Intorsura Buzăului,
  Romania .... **29 E11** 45 41N 26 2 E
Inukjuak, *Canada* .. **101 C12** 58 25N 78 15W
Inútil, B., *Chile* .... **128 G2** 53 30 S 70 15W
Inuvik, *Canada* **100 B6** 68 16N 133 40W
Inveraray, *U.K.* **13 E3** 56 14N   5 5W
Inverbervie, *U.K.* ... **13 E6** 56 51N   2 17W
Invercargill, *N.Z.* ... **91 M2** 46 24 S 168 24 E
Inverclyde □, *U.K.* . **13 F4** 55 55N   4 49W
Inverell, *Australia* .. **95 D5** 29 45 S 151 8 E
Invergordon, *U.K.* .. **13 D4** 57 41N   4 10W
Inverloch, *Australia* . **95 F4** 38 38 S 145 45 E
Invermere, *Canada* .. **102 C5** 50 30N 116 2W
Inverness, *Canada* .. **105 C7** 46 15N 61 19W
Inverness, *U.K.* **13 D4** 57 29N   4 13W
Inverness, *Calif., U.S.A.* **115 L4** 28 50N 82 20W
Inverness □, *U.K.* ... **13 D6** 57 17N 2 23W
Investigator Group,
  Australia .... **95 E1** 34 45 S 134 20 E
Investigator Str.,
  Australia .... **95 F2** 35 30 S 137 0 E
Inya, *Russia* .... **52 D9** 50 28N 86 37 E
Inyanga, *Zimbabwe* . **87 F3** 18 12 S 32 40 E
Inyangani, *Zimbabwe* **87 F3** 18 5 S 32 50 E
Inyantue, *Zimbabwe* . **88 B4** 18 33 S 26 39 E
Inyo Mts., *U.S.A.* .. **110 J9** 36 40N 118 0W
Inyokern, *U.S.A.* ... **111 K9** 35 39N 117 49W
Inza, *Russia* .... **34 D8** 53 55N 46 25 E
Inzhavino, *Russia* .. **34 D6** 52 22N 42 30 E
Iō-Jima, *Japan* ..... **55 J5** 30 48N 130 18 E
Ioánnina, *Greece* ... **46 B2** 39 42N 20 47 E
Ioánnina □, *Greece* . **46 B2** 39 39N 20 57 E
Iola, *U.S.A.* **113 G7** 37 55N 95 24W
Ion Corvin, *Romania* **29 F12** 44 7N 27 50 E
Iona, *U.K.* **13 E2** 56 20N   6 25W
Ione, *U.S.A.* **110 G6** 38 21N 120 56W
Ionia, *U.S.A.* **114 D3** 42 59N 85 4W
Ionian Is. = Iónioi Nísoi,
  Greece .... **46 C2** 38 40N 20 0 E
Ionian Sea, *Medit. S.* **6 H9** 37 30N 17 30 E
Iónioi Nísoi, *Greece* . **46 C2** 38 40N 20 0 E
Iónioi Nísoi □, *Greece* **46 C2** 38 40N 20 0 E
Ios, *Greece* .... **47 E7** 36 41N 25 20 E
Iowa □, *U.S.A.* **112 D8** 42 18N 93 30W
Iowa →, *U.S.A.* **112 E9** 41 10N 91 1W
Iowa City, *U.S.A.* .. **112 E9** 41 40N 91 32W
Iowa Falls, *U.S.A.* .. **112 D8** 42 31N 93 16W
Iowa Park, *U.S.A.* .. **113 J5** 33 57N 98 40W
Ipala, *Tanzania* .... **86 C3** 4 30 S 32 52 E
Ipameri, *Brazil* ..... **125 G9** 17 44 S 48 9W
Ipáti, *Greece* .... **46 C4** 38 52N 22 14 E
Ipatinga, *Brazil* .... **125 G10** 19 32 S 42 30W
Ipatovo, *Russia* .... **35 H6** 45 45N 42 50 E
Ipel' →, *Europe* .... **27 D11** 47 48N 18 53 E
Ipiales, *Colombia* ... **124 C3** 0 50N 77 37W
Ipin = Yibin, *China* . **58 C5** 28 45N 104 32 E
Ipixuna, *Brazil* ..... **124 E4** 7 0 S 71 40W
Ipoh, *Malaysia* ..... **65 K3** 4 35N 101 5 E
Ippy, *C.A.R.* .... **84 C4** 6 5N 21 7 E
Ipsala, *Turkey* ..... **45 F10** 40 55N 26 23 E
Ipsárion, Óros, *Greece* **45 F8** 40 40N 24 40 E
Ipswich, *Australia* .. **95 D5** 27 35 S 152 40 E
Ipswich, *U.K.* ...... **15 E9** 52 4N   1 10 E
Ipswich, *Mass., U.S.A.* **117 D14** 42 41N 70 50W
Ipswich, *S. Dak., U.S.A.* **112 C5** 45 27N 99 2W

Ipu, *Brazil* .... **125 D10** 4 23 S 40 44W
Iqaluit, *Canada* **101 B13** 63 44N 68 31W
Iquique, *Chile* ..... **124 H4** 20 19 S 70 5W
Iquitos, *Peru* ...... **124 D4** 3 45 S 73 10W
Irabu-Jima, *Japan* .. **55 M2** 24 50N 125 10 E
Iracoubo, *Fr. Guiana* **125 B8** 5 30N 53 10W
Irafshān, *Iran* ..... **71 E9** 26 42N 61 56 E
Iráklia, *Kikládhes,
  Greece* .... **47 E7** 36 50N 25 28 E
Iráklia, *Sérrai, Greece* **44 E7** 41 10N 23 16 E
Iráklion, *Greece* .... **49 D7** 35 20N 25 12 E
Iráklion □, *Greece* . **49 D7** 35 10N 25 10 E
Irala, *Paraguay* .... **127 B5** 25 55 S 54 35W
Iran ■, *Asia* .... **71 C7** 33 0N 53 0 E
Iran, Gunung-Gunung,
  Malaysia .... **62 D4** 2 20N 114 50 E
Iran, Plateau of, *Asia* **50 F9** 32 0N 55 0 E
Iran Ra. = Iran,
  Gunung-Gunung,
  Malaysia .... **62 D4** 2 20N 114 50 E
Īrānshahr, *Iran* .... **71 E9** 27 15N 60 40 E
Irapuato, *Mexico* ... **118 C4** 20 40N 101 30W
Iraq ■, *Asia* .... **70 C5** 33 0N 44 0 E
Irati, *Brazil* .... **127 B5** 25 25 S 50 38W
Irbes saurums, *Latvia* **30 A9** 57 45N 22 5 E
Irbid, *Jordan* ...... **74 C4** 32 35N 35 48 E
Irbid □, *Jordan* .... **74 C5** 32 15N 36 35 E
Iregua →, *Spain* .... **38 C2** 42 27N   2 24 E
Ireland ■, *Europe* .. **12 C4** 53 50N   7 52W
Irele, *Nigeria* ...... **83 D6** 7 40N   5 40 E
Irgiz, Bolshaya →,
  Russia .... **34 D9** 52 10N 49 10 E
Irhyangdong, *N. Korea* **57 D15** 41 15N 129 30 E
Iri, *S. Korea* .... **57 G14** 35 59N 127 0 E
Irian Jaya = Papua □,
  Indonesia .... **63 E9** 4 0 S 137 0 E
Irié, *Guinea* **82 D3** 8 15N   9 10W
Iriga, *Phil.* .... **61 E5** 13 25N 123 25 E
Iringa, *Tanzania* ... **86 D4** 7 48 S 35 43 E
Iringa □, *Tanzania* . **86 D4** 7 48 S 35 43 E
Iriomote, *Japan* .... **55 M1** 24 29N 123 53 E
Iriomote-Jima, *Japan* **55 M1** 24 19N 123 48 E
Iriona, *Honduras* ... **120 C2** 15 57N 85 11W
Iriri →, *Brazil* ..... **125 D8** 3 52 S 52 37W
Irish Republic ■,
  Europe **12 C4** 53 50N   7 52W
Irish Sea, *Europe* .. **14 D3** 53 38N   4 48W
Irkutsk, *Russia* .... **53 D11** 52 18N 104 20 E
Irligânli, *Turkey* ... **47 D11** 37 53N 29 12 E
Irma, *Canada* **103 C6** 52 55N 111 14W
Irô-Zaki, *Japan* .... **55 G9** 34 36N 138 51 E
Iroise, Mer d', *France* **18 D2** 48 15N 4 45W
Iron Baron, *Australia* **95 E2** 32 58 S 137 11 E
Iron Gate = Portile de
  Fier, *Europe* ...... **28 F7** 44 44N 22 30 E
Iron Knob, *Australia* **95 E2** 32 46 S 137 8 E
Iron Mountain, *U.S.A.* **114 C1** 45 49N 88 4W
Iron Range △, *Australia* **94 A3** 12 34 S 143 18 E
Iron River, *U.S.A.* .. **112 B10** 46 6N 88 39W
Irondequoit, *U.S.A.* . **116 C7** 43 13N 77 35W
Ironton, *Mo., U.S.A.* **113 G9** 37 36N 90 38W
Ironton, *Ohio, U.S.A.* **114 F4** 38 32N 82 41W
Ironwood, *U.S.A.* ... **112 B9** 46 27N 90 9W
Ironwood Forest △,
  U.S.A. **109 K8** 32 28N 111 36W
Iroquois, *Canada* ... **117 B9** 44 51N 75 19W
Iroquois Falls, *Canada* **104 C3** 48 46N 80 41W
Irosin, *Phil.* .... **61 E6** 12 42N 124 2 E
Irpin, *Ukraine* ..... **33 G6** 50 30N 30 15 E
Irrara Cr. →, *Australia* **95 D4** 29 35 S 145 31 E
Irrawaddy □, *Burma* **67 L19** 17 0N 95 0 E
Irrawaddy →, *Burma* **67 M19** 15 50N 95 6 E
Irrawaddy, Mouths of
  the, *Burma* .... **67 M19** 15 30N 95 0 E
Irricana, *Canada* ... **102 C6** 51 19N 113 37W
Irshava, *Ukraine* ... **28 B8** 48 19N 23 3 E
Irsina, *Italy* .... **43 B9** 40 45N 16 14 E
Irtysh →, *Russia* ... **52 C7** 61 4N 68 52 E
Irumu, *Dem. Rep. of
  the Congo* .... **86 B2** 1 32N 29 53 E
Irún, *Spain* **38 B3** 43 20N   1 52W
Irunea = Pamplona,
  Spain **38 C3** 42 48N   1 38W
Irurzun, *Spain* **38 C3** 42 55N   1 50W
Irvine, *U.K.* **13 F4** 55 37N   4 41W
Irvine, *Calif., U.S.A.* **111 M9** 33 41N 117 46W
Irvine, *Ky., U.S.A.* . **114 G4** 37 42N 83 58W
Irvinestown, *U.K.* .. **12 B4** 54 28N   7 39W
Irving, *U.S.A.* **113 J6** 32 49N 96 56W
Irvona, *U.S.A.* **116 F6** 40 46N 78 33W
Irwin →, *Australia* . **93 E1** 29 15 S 114 54 E
Irymple, *Australia* .. **95 E3** 34 14 S 142 8 E
Is, Jebel, *Sudan* .... **80 D4** 22 35N 36 55 E
Is-sur-Tille, *France* . **19 E12** 47 30N 5 8 E
Isa, *Nigeria* .... **83 C6** 13 14N   6 24 E
Isa Khel, *Pakistan* .. **68 C4** 32 41N 71 17 E
Isaac →, *Australia* . **94 C4** 22 55 S 149 20 E
Isabel, *U.S.A.* **112 C4** 45 24N 101 26W
Isabela, *Phil.* ...... **61 H5** 6 40N 121 59 E
Isabela, *Puerto Rico* **121 d** 18 30N 67 2W
Isabela, I., *Mexico* . **118 C3** 21 51N 105 55W
Isabela, Cord., *Nic.* . **120 D2** 13 30N 85 25W
Isabella, Ra., *Australia* **92 D3** 21 0 S 121 4 E
Isaccea, *Romania* ... **29 E13** 45 16N 28 27 E
Ísafjarðardjúp, *Iceland* **8 C2** 66 10N 23 0W
Ísafjörður, *Iceland* . **8 C2** 66 5N 23 9W
Isagarh, *India* ...... **68 G7** 24 48N 77 51 E
Isahaya, *Japan* ..... **55 H5** 32 52N 130 2 E
Isaka, *Tanzania* .... **86 C3** 3 56 S 32 59 E
Işalniţa, *Romania* .. **29 F8** 44 24N 23 44 E
Isan →, *India* ...... **69 F9** 26 51N 80 7 E
Isana = Içana →, *Brazil* **124 C5** 0 26N 67 19W
Isangi, *Dem. Rep. of
  the Congo* .... **84 D4** 0 52N 24 10 E
Isanlu Makutu, *Nigeria* **83 D6** 8 15N 5 36 E
Isar →, *Germany* ... **25 G8** 48 48N 12 57 E
Isarco →, *Italy* .... **41 B8** 46 57N 11 18 E
Ísari, *Greece* ...... **46 D3** 37 22N 22 0 E
Íscar, *Spain* **36 D6** 41 23N   4 32W
Ischia, *Italy* .... **42 B6** 40 44N 13 57 E
Isdell →, *Australia* . **92 C3** 16 27 S 124 51 E
Ise, *Japan* .... **55 G8** 34 25N 136 45 E
Ise-Shima △, *Japan* . **55 G8** 34 20N 136 48 E
Ise-Wan, *Japan* .... **55 G8** 34 43N 136 43 E
Isefjord, *Denmark* .. **11 J5** 55 52N 11 49 E
Isel →, *Austria* .... **26 E5** 46 54N 12 37 E
Íseo, *Italy* .... **40 C7** 45 40N 10 3 E
Íseo, L. d', *Italy* ... **40 C7** 45 43N 10 4 E
Iseramagazi, *Tanzania* **86 C3** 4 37 S 32 10 E
Isère □, *France* ..... **21 C9** 45 15N   5 40 E
Isère →, *France* .... **21 D8** 44 59N   4 51 E
Isernhagen, *Germany* **24 C5** 52 22N 9 51 E
Isérnia, *Italy* ...... **43 A7** 41 36N 14 14 E
Iseyin, *Nigeria* ..... **83 D5** 8 0N   3 36 E
Isfahan = Eşfahān, *Iran* **71 C6** 32 39N 51 43 E

Ishëm, *Albania* ..... **44 E3** 41 33N 19 34 E
Ishigaki-Shima, *Japan* **55 M2** 24 20N 124 10 E
Ishikari-Gawa →, *Japan* **54 C10** 43 15N 141 23 E
Ishikari-Sammyaku,
  Japan .... **54 C11** 43 30N 143 0 E
Ishikari-Wan, *Japan* . **54 C10** 43 25N 141 1 E
Ishim, *Russia* ...... **52 D7** 56 10N 69 30 E
Ishim →, *Russia* .... **52 D8** 57 45N 71 10 E
Ishinomaki, *Japan* .. **54 E10** 38 32N 141 20 E
Ishioka, *Japan* ..... **55 F10** 36 11N 140 16 E
Ishkuman, *Pakistan* . **69 A5** 36 30N 73 50 E
Ishpeming, *U.S.A.* .. **114 B2** 46 29N 87 40W
Isigny-sur-Mer, *France* **18 C5** 49 19N 1 6W
İsikli Dağı, *Turkey* . **45 F11** 40 45N 27 15 E
Işıklı, *Turkey* ...... **47 C11** 38 19N 29 51 E
Isil Kul, *Russia* .... **52 D8** 54 55N 71 16 E
Isili, *Italy* .... **42 C2** 39 44N 9 6 E
Isiolo, *Kenya* ...... **86 B4** 0 24N 37 33 E
Isiro, *Dem. Rep. of
  the Congo* .... **86 B2** 2 53N 27 40 E
Isisford, *Australia* .. **94 C3** 24 15 S 144 21 E
Iskenderun, *Turkey* . **70 B3** 36 32N 36 10 E
Iskenderun Körfezi,
  Turkey .... **72 D6** 36 40N 35 50 E
İskilip, *Turkey* ..... **72 B6** 40 45N 34 29 E
Iskůr →, *Bulgaria* .. **45 C8** 43 45N 24 25 E
Iskůr, Yazovir, *Bulgaria* **44 D7** 42 23N 23 30 E
Iskut →, *Canada* ... **102 B2** 56 45N 131 49W
Isla →, *U.K.* **13 E5** 56 32N   3 20W
Isla Coiba △, *Panama* **120 E3** 7 33N 81 36W
Isla Cristina, *Spain* . **37 H3** 37 13N   7 17W
Isla de Salamanca △,
  Colombia **121 D5** 10 59N 74 40W
Isla Gorge △, *Australia* **94 D4** 25 10 S 149 57 E
Isla Tiburón y San
  Esteban △, *Mexico* . **118 B2** 29 0N 112 27W
Isla Vista, *U.S.A.* .. **111 L7** 34 25N 119 53W
Islâhiye, *Turkey* .... **72 D7** 37 0N 36 35 E
Islam Headworks,
  Pakistan .... **68 E5** 29 49N 72 33 E
Islamabad, *Pakistan* . **68 C5** 33 40N 73 10 E
Islamgarh, *Pakistan* . **68 F4** 27 51N 70 48 E
Islamkot, *Pakistan* .. **68 G4** 24 42N 70 13 E
Islampur, *India* ..... **69 G11** 25 9N 85 12 E
Island L., *Canada* ... **103 C10** 53 47N 94 25W
Island Lagoon, *Australia* **95 E2** 31 30 S 136 40 E
Island Pond, *U.S.A.* . **117 B13** 44 49N 71 53W
Islands, B. of, *Canada* **105 C8** 49 11N 58 15W
Islands, B. of, *N.Z.* . **91 F5** 35 15 S 174 6 E
Islay, *U.K.* **13 F2** 55 46N   6 10W
Isle →, *France* **20 D3** 44 55N   0 15W
Isle aux Morts, *Canada* **105 C8** 47 35N 59 0W
Isle of Wight □, *U.K.* **15 G6** 50 41N   1 17W
Isle Royale △, *U.S.A.* **114 B1** 48 0N 88 54W
Isleton, *U.S.A.* **110 G5** 38 10N 121 37W
Ismail = Izmayil,
  Ukraine .... **29 E13** 45 22N 28 46 E
Ismâ'ilîya, *Egypt* ... **80 H8** 30 37N 32 18 E
Ismaning, *Germany* . **25 G7** 48 13N 11 40 E
Isna, *Egypt* .... **80 B3** 25 17N 32 30 E
Isoanala, *Madag.* ... **89 C8** 23 50 S 45 44 E
Isogstalo, *India* ..... **69 B8** 34 15N 78 46 E
Ísola del Liri, *Italy* . **41 G10** 41 41N 13 34 E
Ísola della Scala, *Italy* **40 C7** 45 16N 11 0 E
Ísola di Capo Rizzuto,
  Italy .... **43 D10** 38 58N 17 6 E
Isparta, *Turkey* .... **47 D12** 37 47N 30 30 E
İsperikh, *Bulgaria* .. **45 C10** 43 43N 26 50 E
Íspica, *Italy* .... **43 F7** 36 47N 14 55 E
Israel ■, *Asia* ...... **74 D3** 32 0N 34 50 E
Issatu, *Eritrea* ..... **81 D4** 16 20N 39 33 E
Issakly, *Russia* ..... **34 C10** 54 8N 51 32 E
Issia, *Ivory C.* **82 D3** 6 33N 6 33W
Issoire, *France* ..... **20 C7** 45 32N   3 15 E
Issoudun, *France* ... **19 F8** 46 57N   1 59 E
Issyk-Kul, Ozero =
  Ysyk-Köl, *Kyrgyzstan* **52 E8** 42 25N 77 15 E
Istállós-kő, *Hungary* . **28 B5** 48 4N 20 26 E
Istanbul, *Turkey* ... **45 E12** 41 0N 29 0 E
Istanbul □, *Turkey* . **45 E12** 41 0N 29 0 E
Istanbul ✈ (IST), *Turkey* **45 F12** 40 59N 28 49 E
İstanbul Boğazı, *Turkey* **45 E13** 41 10N 29 10 E
İstiaía, *Greece* ..... **46 C5** 38 57N 23 9 E
Istok, *Serbia & M.* . **44 D4** 42 45N 20 24 E
Istokpoga, L., *U.S.A.* **115 M5** 27 23N 81 17W
Istra, *Croatia* ...... **41 C10** 45 10N 14 0 E
Istres, *France* ...... **21 E8** 43 31N   4 59 E
Istria = Istra, *Croatia* **41 C10** 45 10N 14 0 E
Itá, *Paraguay* ...... **126 B4** 25 29 S 57 21W
Itaberaba, *Brazil* ... **125 F10** 12 32 S 40 18W
Itabira, *Brazil* ..... **125 G10** 19 37 S 43 13W
Itabirito, *Brazil* .... **127 A7** 20 15 S 43 48W
Itabuna, *Brazil* ..... **125 F11** 14 48 S 39 16W
Itacaunas →, *Brazil* . **125 E9** 5 21 S 49 8W
Itacoatiara, *Brazil* .. **124 D7** 3 8 S 58 25W
Itaipú, Reprêsa de,
  Brazil .... **127 B5** 25 30 S 54 30W
Itaituba, *Brazil* .... **125 D7** 4 10 S 55 50W
Itajaí, *Brazil* ...... **127 B6** 27 50 S 48 39W
Itajubá, *Brazil* ..... **127 A6** 22 24 S 45 30W
Itaka, *Tanzania* .... **87 D3** 8 50 S 32 49 E
Itala △, *S. Africa* ... **89 D5** 27 30 S 31 7 E
Italy ■, *Europe* .... **7 G8** 42 0N 13 0 E
Itamaraju, *Brazil* ... **125 G11** 17 5 S 39 31W
Itampolo, *Madag.* .. **89 C7** 24 41 S 43 57 E
Itandrano, *Madag.* . **89 C8** 21 47 S 45 17 E
Itapecuru-Mirim, *Brazil* **125 D10** 3 24 S 44 20W
Itaperuna, *Brazil* ... **127 A7** 21 10 S 41 54W
Itapetininga, *Brazil* . **127 A6** 23 36 S 48 7W
Itapeva, *Brazil* ..... **127 A6** 23 59 S 48 59W
Itapicuru →, *Bahia,
  Brazil* .... **125 F11** 11 47 S 37 32W
Itapicuru →, *Maranhão,
  Brazil* .... **125 D10** 2 52 S 44 12W
Itapipoca, *Brazil* ... **125 D11** 3 30 S 39 35W
Itapuá □, *Paraguay* . **127 B4** 26 40 S 55 40W
Itaquari, *Brazil* ..... **127 A7** 20 20 S 40 25W
Itaquí, *Brazil* ...... **126 B4** 29 8 S 56 30W
Itararé, *Brazil* ..... **127 A6** 24 6 S 49 23W
Itarsi, *India* .... **68 H7** 22 36N 77 51 E
Itatí, *Argentina* .... **126 B4** 27 16 S 58 15W
Itatiaia △, *Brazil* ... **127 A7** 22 24 S 44 38W
Itbayat, *Phil.* ...... **61 A4** 20 45N 121 50 E
Itchen →, *U.K.* **15 G6** 50 55N 1 22W
Itéa, *Greece* .... **46 C4** 38 25N 22 25 E
Itezhi Tezhi, L., *Zambia* **87 F2** 15 30 S 25 30 E
Ithaca = Itháki, *Greece* **46 C2** 38 25N 20 40 E
Ithaca, *U.S.A.* **117 D8** 42 27N 76 30W
Itháki, *Greece* ...... **46 C2** 38 25N 20 40 E
Iti △, *Greece* .... **46 C4** 38 50N 22 15 E
Itiquira →, *Brazil* .. **125 G7** 17 18 S 56 44W
Itiruçu, *Brazil* ..... **125 F10** 13 30 S 40 15 E
Itoigawa, *Japan* .... **55 F8** 37 2N 137 51 E
Iton →, *France* ..... **18 C8** 49 19N   1 8 E
Itonamas →, *Bolivia* **124 F6** 12 28 S 64 24W

Itri, Italy .... 42 A6 41 17N 13 32 E
Itsa, Egypt .... 80 J7 29 15N 30 47 E
Ittiri, Italy .... 42 B1 40 36N 8 34 E
Ittoqqortoormiit,
  Greenland 4 B6 70 20N 23 0W
Itu, Brazil .... 127 A6 23 17 S 47 15W
Itu, Nigeria .... 83 D6 5 10N 7 58 E
Itu Aba I., S. China Sea .... 62 B4 10 23N 114 21 E
Ituiutaba, Brazil .... 125 G9 19 0 S 49 25W
Itumbiara, Brazil .... 125 G9 18 20 S 49 10W
Ituna, Canada 103 C8 51 10N 103 24W
Itunge Port, Tanzania .... 87 D3 9 40 S 33 55 E
Iturbe, Argentina .... 126 A2 23 0 S 65 25W
Ituri →, Dem. Rep. of
  the Congo .... 86 B2 1 40N 27 1 E
Iturup, Ostrov, Russia .... 53 E15 45 0N 148 0 E
Ituxi →, Brazil .... 124 E6 7 18 S 64 51W
Ituyuro →, Argentina .... 126 A3 22 40 S 63 50W
Itzehoe, Germany .... 24 B5 53 55N 9 31 E
Ivahona, Madag. .... 89 C8 23 27 S 46 10 E
Ivaí →, Brazil .... 127 A5 23 18 S 53 42W
Ivalo, Finland .... 8 B22 68 38N 27 35 E
Ivalojoki →, Finland .... 8 B22 68 40N 27 40 E
Ivanava, Belarus .... 33 F3 52 7N 25 29 E
Ivančice, Czech Rep. .... 27 B9 49 6N 16 23 E
Ivane-Puste, Ukraine .... 29 B11 48 30N 26 10 E
Ivănești, Romania .... 29 D12 46 39N 27 27 E
Ivangorod, Russia .... 32 C5 59 27N 28 13 E
Ivanhoe, Australia .... 95 E3 32 56 S 144 20 E
Ivanhoe, Calif., U.S.A. 110 J7 36 23N 119 13W
Ivanhoe, Minn., U.S.A. 112 C6 44 28N 96 15W
Ivanhorod, Ukraine .... 29 B14 48 40N 29 50 E
Ivanić Grad, Croatia .... 41 C13 45 41N 16 25 E
Ivanjica, Serbia & M. .... 44 C4 43 35N 20 12 E
Ivanjska, Bos.-H. .... 28 F2 44 55N 17 4 E
Ivankoyskoye Vdkhr.,
  Russia .... 32 D9 56 37N 36 32 E
Ivano-Frankivsk,
  Ukraine .... 29 B9 48 40N 24 40 E
Ivano-Frankivska □,
  Ukraine .... 29 B9 48 45N 24 30 E
Ivanovo = Ivanava,
  Belarus .... 33 F3 52 7N 25 29 E
Ivanovo, Russia .... 32 D11 57 5N 41 0 E
Ivanščica, Croatia .... 41 B13 46 12N 16 13 E
Ivato, Madag. .... 89 C8 20 37 S 47 10 E
Ivatsevichy, Belarus .... 33 F3 52 43N 25 21 E
Ivaylovgrad, Bulgaria .... 45 E10 41 32N 26 8 E
Ivinheima →, Brazil .... 127 A5 23 14 S 53 42W
Ivinhema, Brazil .... 127 A5 22 10 S 53 37W
Ivohibe, Madag. .... 89 C8 22 31 S 46 57 E
Ivory Coast, W. Afr. 82 E4 4 20N 5 0W
Ivory Coast ■, Africa 82 D4 7 30N 5 0W
Ivösjön, Sweden .... 11 H8 56 8N 14 25 E
Ivrea, Italy .... 40 C4 45 28N 7 52 E
Ivrindi, Turkey .... 47 B9 39 34N 27 30 E
Ivujivik, Canada 101 B12 62 24N 77 55W
Ivybridge, U.K. 15 G4 50 23N 3 56W
Iwaizumi, Japan .... 54 E10 39 50N 141 45 E
Iwaki, Japan .... 55 F10 37 3N 140 55 E
Iwakuni, Japan .... 55 G6 34 15N 132 8 E
Iwamizawa, Japan .... 54 C10 43 12N 141 46 E
Iwanai, Japan .... 54 C10 42 58N 140 30 E
Iwata, Japan .... 55 G8 34 42N 137 51 E
Iwate, Japan .... 54 E10 39 30N 141 30 E
Iwate-San, Japan .... 54 E10 39 51N 141 0 E
Iwo, Japan .... 83 D5 7 39N 4 9 E
Iwonicz-Zdrój, Poland .... 31 J8 49 37N 21 47 E
Ixiamas, Bolivia .... 124 F5 13 50 S 68 5W
Ixopo, S. Africa .... 89 E5 30 11 S 30 5 E
Ixtepec, Mexico 119 D5 16 32N 95 10W
Ixtlán del Río, Mexico 118 C4 21 5N 104 21W
Iyal Bakhit, Sudan .... 81 E2 13 20N 28 39 E
Iyo, Japan .... 55 H6 33 45N 132 45 E
Izabal, L. de, Guatemala 120 C2 15 30N 89 10W
Izamal, Mexico 119 C7 20 56N 89 1W
Izberbash, Russia .... 35 J8 42 35N 47 52 E
Izbica, Poland .... 31 H10 50 53N 23 10 E
Izbica Kujawska, Poland .... 31 F5 52 25N 18 40 E
Izbiceni, Romania .... 29 G9 43 45N 24 40 E
Izena-Shima, Japan .... 55 L3 26 56N 127 56 E
Izgrev, Bulgaria .... 45 C10 43 36N 28 0 E
Izhevsk, Russia .... 52 D6 56 51N 53 14 E
Izmail, Ukraine .... 29 E13 45 22N 28 46 E
Izmir, Turkey .... 47 C9 38 25N 27 8 E
Izmir □, Turkey .... 47 C9 38 15N 27 40 E
Izmir Adnan
  Menderes ✈ (ADB),
  Turkey .... 47 C9 38 23N 27 6 E
Izmir Körfezi, Turkey .... 47 C8 38 30N 26 50 E
İzmit = Kocaeli, Turkey .... 45 F13 40 45N 29 50 E
Iznájar, Spain 37 H6 37 15N 4 19W
Iznalloz, Spain 37 H7 37 24N 3 30W
Iznik, Turkey .... 72 B3 40 27N 29 46 E
Iznik Gölü, Turkey .... 45 F13 40 27N 29 30 E
Izobil'nyy, Russia .... 35 H5 45 25N 41 44 E
Izola, Slovenia .... 41 C10 45 32N 13 39 E
Izra, Syria .... 74 C5 32 51N 36 15 E
Iztochni Rodopi,
  Bulgaria .... 45 E9 41 45N 25 30 E
Izu-Shotō, Japan .... 55 G10 34 30N 140 0 E
Izúcar de Matamoros,
  Mexico 119 D5 18 36N 98 28W
Izumi-Sano, Japan .... 55 G7 34 23N 135 18 E
Izumo, Japan .... 55 G6 35 20N 132 46 E
Izyaslav, Ukraine .... 33 G4 50 5N 26 50 E
Izyum, Ukraine .... 33 H9 49 12N 37 19 E

J

Jaba, Ethiopia .... 81 F4 6 20N 35 7 E
Jabal at Ta'ir, Red Sea .... 81 D5 15 35N 41 52 E
Jabalón →, Spain 37 G6 38 53N 4 5W
Jabalpur, India .... 69 H8 23 9N 79 58 E
Jabbūl, Syria .... 70 B3 36 4N 37 30 E
Jabiru, Australia .... 92 B5 12 40 S 132 53 E
Jablah, Syria .... 70 C3 35 20N 36 0 E
Jablanac, Croatia .... 41 D11 44 42N 14 56 E
Jablanica, Bos.-H. .... 28 G2 43 40N 17 45 E
Jablonec nad Nisou,
  Czech Rep. .... 26 A8 50 43N 15 10 E
Jablonica, Slovak Rep. .... 27 C10 48 37N 17 26 E
Jabłonowo Pomorskie,
  Poland .... 30 E6 53 23N 19 10 E
Jablunkov, Czech Rep. .... 27 B11 49 35N 18 46 E
Jaboatão, Brazil .... 125 E11 8 7 S 35 1W
Jaboticabal, Brazil .... 127 A6 21 15 S 48 17W
Jabukovac, Serbia & M. .... 44 B6 44 22N 22 21 E
Jaca, Spain 38 C4 42 35N 0 33W
Jacareí, Brazil .... 127 A6 23 20 S 46 0W
Jacarèzinho, Brazil .... 127 A6 23 5 S 49 58W
Jackman, U.S.A. 115 C10 45 35N 70 17W
Jacksboro, U.S.A. 113 J5 33 14N 98 9W
Jackson, Barbados .... 121 g 13 7N 59 36W
Jackson, Ala., U.S.A. 115 K2 31 31N 87 53W

Jackson, Calif., U.S.A. 110 G6 38 21N 120 46W
Jackson, Ky., U.S.A. 114 G4 37 33N 83 23W
Jackson, Mich., U.S.A. 114 D3 42 15N 84 24W
Jackson, Minn., U.S.A. 112 D7 43 37N 95 1W
Jackson, Miss., U.S.A. 113 J9 32 18N 90 12W
Jackson, Mo., U.S.A. 113 G10 37 23N 89 40W
Jackson, N.H., U.S.A. 117 B13 44 10N 71 11W
Jackson, Ohio, U.S.A. 114 F4 39 3N 82 39W
Jackson, Tenn., U.S.A. 115 H1 35 37N 88 49W
Jackson, Wyo., U.S.A. 108 E8 43 29N 110 46W
Jackson B., N.Z. .... 91 K2 43 58 S 168 42 E
Jackson L., U.S.A. 108 E8 43 52N 110 36W
Jacksons, N.Z. .... 91 K3 42 46 S 171 32 E
Jackson's Arm, Canada 105 C8 49 52N 56 47W
Jacksonville, Ala.,
  U.S.A. 115 J3 33 49N 85 46W
Jacksonville, Ark.,
  U.S.A. 113 H8 34 52N 92 7W
Jacksonville, Calif.,
  U.S.A. 110 H6 37 52N 120 24W
Jacksonville, Fla., U.S.A. 115 K5 30 20N 81 39W
Jacksonville, Ill., U.S.A. 112 F9 39 44N 90 14W
Jacksonville, N.C.,
  U.S.A. 115 H7 34 45N 77 26W
Jacksonville, Tex.,
  U.S.A. 113 K7 31 58N 95 17W
Jacksonville Beach,
  U.S.A. 115 K5 30 17N 81 24W
Jacmel, Haiti 121 C5 18 14N 72 32W
Jacob Lake, U.S.A. 109 H7 36 43N 112 13W
Jacobabad, Pakistan .... 68 E3 28 20N 68 29 E
Jacobina, Brazil .... 125 F10 11 11 S 40 30W
Jacques-Cartier □,
  Canada 105 C5 47 15N 71 33W
Jacques-Cartier, Dét. de,
  Canada 105 C7 50 0N 63 30W
Jacques-Cartier, Mt.,
  Canada 105 C6 48 57N 66 0W
Jacquet C., Ivory C. 82 D4 5 12N 4 25W
Jacuí →, Brazil .... 127 C5 30 2 S 51 15W
Jacumba, U.S.A. 111 N10 32 37N 116 11W
Jacundá →, Brazil .... 125 D8 1 57 S 50 26W
Jade, Germany .... 24 B4 53 20N 8 14 E
Jadebusen, Germany .... 24 B4 53 29N 8 12 E
Jadovnik, Serbia & M. .... 44 C3 43 20N 19 45 E
Jadraque, Spain 38 E2 40 55N 2 55W
Jaén, Peru .... 124 E3 5 25 S 78 40W
Jaén, Spain 37 H7 37 44N 3 43W
Jaén □, Spain 37 H7 37 50N 3 30W
Jafarabad, India .... 68 J4 20 52N 71 22 E
Jaffa = Tel Aviv-Yafo,
  Israel .... 74 C3 32 4N 34 48 E
Jaffa, C., Australia .... 95 F2 36 58 S 139 40 E
Jaffna, Sri Lanka .... 66 Q12 9 45N 80 2 E
Jaffray, Canada 103 D10 49 47N 94 26W
Jaffrey, U.S.A. 117 D12 42 49N 72 2W
Jagadhri, India .... 68 D7 30 10N 77 20 E
Jagadishpur, India .... 69 G11 25 30N 84 21 E
Jagdalpur, India .... 67 K13 19 3N 82 0 E
Jagersfontein, S. Africa .... 88 D4 29 44 S 25 27 E
Jaghin →, Iran .... 71 E8 27 17N 57 13 E
Jagodina, Serbia & M. .... 44 B5 44 5N 21 15 E
Jagraon, India .... 66 D9 30 50N 75 25 E
Jagst →, Germany .... 25 F5 49 14N 9 10 E
Jagtial, India .... 66 K11 18 50N 79 0 E
Jaguariaíva, Brazil .... 127 A6 24 10 S 49 50W
Jaguaribe →, Brazil .... 125 D11 4 25 S 37 45W
Jagüey Grande, Cuba 120 B3 22 35N 81 7W
Jahanabad, India .... 69 G11 25 13N 84 59 E
Jahazpur, India .... 68 G6 25 37N 75 17 E
Jahrom, Iran .... 71 D7 28 30N 53 31 E
Jaijon, India .... 68 D7 31 21N 76 9 E
Jailolo, Indonesia .... 63 D7 1 5N 127 30 E
Jailolo, Selat, Indonesia .... 63 D7 0 5N 129 5 E
Jaipur, India .... 68 F6 27 0N 75 50 E
Jais, India .... 69 F9 26 15N 81 32 E
Jaisalmer, India .... 68 F4 26 55N 70 54 E
Jaisinghnagar, India .... 69 H8 23 38N 78 34 E
Jaitaran, India .... 68 F5 26 12N 73 56 E
Jaithari, India .... 69 H8 23 14N 78 37 E
Jājarm, Iran .... 71 B8 36 58N 56 27 E
Jajce, Bos.-H. .... 28 F2 44 19N 17 17 E
Jakam →, India .... 68 H6 23 54N 74 13 E
Jakarta, Indonesia .... 63 G12 6 9 S 106 49 E
Jakhal, India .... 68 E6 29 48N 75 50 E
Jakhau, India .... 68 H3 23 13N 68 43 E
Jakobstad = Pietarsaari,
  Finland .... 8 E20 63 40N 22 43 E
Jakupica, Macedonia .... 44 E5 41 45N 21 22 E
Jal, U.S.A. 113 J3 32 7N 103 12W
Jalālābād, Afghan. .... 68 B4 34 30N 70 29 E
Jalalabad, India .... 69 F8 27 41N 79 42 E
Jalalpur Jattan, Pakistan .... 68 C6 32 38N 74 11 E
Jalama, U.S.A. 111 L6 34 29N 120 29W
Jalapa, Guatemala 120 D2 14 39N 89 59W
Jalapa Enríquez =
  Xalapa, Mexico 119 D5 19 32N 96 55W
Jalasjärvi, Finland .... 9 E20 62 29N 22 47 E
Jalaun, India .... 69 F8 26 8N 79 25 E
Jaldhaka →, Bangla. .... 69 F13 26 16N 89 16 E
Jalesar, India .... 68 F8 27 29N 78 19 E
Jaleswar, Nepal .... 69 F11 26 38N 85 48 E
Jalgaon, India .... 66 J9 21 0N 75 42 E
Jalībah, Iraq .... 70 D5 30 35N 46 32 E
Jalingo, Nigeria .... 83 D7 8 55N 11 25 E
Jalisco □, Mexico 118 D4 20 0N 104 0W
Jalkot, Pakistan .... 69 B5 35 14N 73 24 E
Jallas →, Spain 36 C1 42 54N 9 8W
Jalna, India .... 66 K9 19 48N 75 38 E
Jalón →, Spain 38 D3 41 47N 1 4W
Jalor, India .... 68 G5 25 21N 72 37 E
Jalpa, Mexico 118 C4 21 38N 102 58W
Jalpaiguri, India .... 67 F16 26 32N 88 46 E
Jaluit I., Marshall Is. .... 96 G8 6 0N 169 30 E
Jalūlā, Iraq .... 70 C5 34 16N 45 10 E
Jamaari, Nigeria .... 83 C6 11 44N 9 53 E
Jamaica ■, W. Indies .... 120 a 18 10N 77 30W
Jamalpur, Bangla. .... 67 G16 24 52N 89 56 E
Jamalpur, India .... 69 G12 25 18N 86 28 E
Jamalpurganj, India .... 69 H13 23 2N 87 59 E
Jamanxim →, Brazil .... 125 D7 4 43 S 56 18W
Jambewangi, Indonesia .... 63 J17 8 17 S 114 7 E
Jambi, Indonesia .... 62 E2 1 38 S 103 30 E
Jambi □, Indonesia .... 62 E2 1 30 S 102 30 E
Jambusar, India .... 68 H5 22 3N 72 51 E
James →, S. Dak.,
  U.S.A. 112 D6 42 52N 97 18W
James →, Va., U.S.A. 114 G7 36 56N 76 27W
James B., Canada 104 B3 54 0N 80 0W
James Ranges, Australia .... 92 D5 24 10 S 132 30 E
James Ross I., Antarctica .... 5 C18 63 58 S 57 50W
Jamesabad, Pakistan .... 68 G3 25 17N 69 15 E
Jamestown, Australia .... 95 E2 33 10 S 138 32 E
Jamestown, S. Africa .... 88 E4 31 6 S 26 45 E
Jamestown, N. Dak.,
  U.S.A. 112 B5 46 54N 98 42W
Jamestown, N.Y., U.S.A. 116 D5 42 6N 79 14W

Jamestown, Pa., U.S.A. 116 E4 41 29N 80 27W
Jamīlābād, Iran .... 71 C6 34 24N 48 28 E
Jamiltepec, Mexico 119 D5 16 17N 97 49W
Jamira →, India .... 69 J13 21 35N 88 28 E
Jamkhandi, India .... 66 L9 16 30N 75 15 E
Jammu, India .... 68 C6 32 43N 74 54 E
Jammu & Kashmir □,
  India .... 69 B7 34 25N 77 0 E
Jamnagar, India .... 68 H4 22 30N 70 6 E
Jamni →, India .... 69 G8 25 13N 78 35 E
Jampur, Pakistan .... 68 E4 29 39N 70 40 E
Jamrud, Pakistan .... 68 C4 33 59N 71 24 E
Jämsä, Finland .... 9 F21 61 53N 25 10 E
Jamshedpur, India .... 69 H12 22 44N 86 12 E
Jamtara, India .... 69 H12 23 59N 86 49 E
Jämtland, Sweden .... 8 E15 63 31N 14 0 E
Jämtlands län □, Sweden .... 10 B7 63 0N 14 40 E
Jan L., Canada 103 C8 54 56N 102 55W
Jan Mayen, Arctic 4 B7 71 0N 9 0W
Janakkala, Finland .... 9 F21 60 54N 24 36 E
Janaúba, Brazil .... 125 G10 15 48 S 43 19W
Jand, Pakistan .... 68 C5 33 30N 72 6 E
Jandaq, Iran .... 71 C7 34 3N 54 22 E
Jandía, Canary Is. 48 F5 28 6N 14 21W
Jandía, Pta. de,
  Canary Is. 48 F5 28 3N 14 31W
Jandola, Pakistan .... 68 C4 32 20N 70 9 E
Jandowae, Australia .... 95 D5 26 45 S 151 7 E
Jándula →, Spain 37 G6 38 3N 4 6W
Janesville, U.S.A. 112 D10 42 41N 89 1W
Janga, Ghana 83 C4 10 5N 1 0W
Jangamo, Mozam. .... 89 C6 24 6 S 35 21 E
Janghai, India .... 69 G10 25 33N 82 19 E
Janikowo, Poland .... 31 F5 52 45N 18 7 E
Janin = Ioánnina □,
  Greece .... 46 B2 39 39N 20 57 E
Janja, Bos.-H. .... 28 F4 44 40N 19 14 E
Janjanbureh, Gambia 82 C2 13 30N 14 47W
Janjgir, India .... 69 J10 22 1N 82 34 E
Janjina, Croatia .... 41 F14 42 58N 17 25 E
Janjina, Madag. .... 89 C8 20 14 S 45 18 E
Janos, Mexico 118 A3 30 45N 108 10W
Jánoshalma, Hungary .... 28 D4 46 18N 19 21 E
Jánosháza, Hungary .... 28 C2 47 8N 17 12 E
Jánossomorja, Hungary .... 28 C2 47 47N 17 11 E
Janów, Poland .... 31 H9 50 44N 19 27 E
Janów Lubelski, Poland .... 31 H9 50 48N 22 23 E
Janów Podlaski, Poland .... 31 F10 52 11N 23 11 E
Janowiec Wielkopolski,
  Poland .... 31 F4 52 45N 17 30 E
Januária, Brazil .... 125 G10 15 25 S 44 25W
Janub →, Sudan .... 81 F2 6 50N 28 45 E
Janub Dârfûr □, Sudan .... 81 E2 11 0N 25 0 E
Janub Kordofân □,
  Sudan .... 81 E3 12 0N 30 0 E
Janûb Sînî □, Egypt .... 74 F2 29 30N 33 50 E
Janubio, Canary Is. 48 F6 28 56N 13 50W
Janville, France .... 19 D8 48 10N 1 50 E
Janzé, France 18 E5 47 55N 1 28W
Jaora, India .... 68 H6 23 40N 75 10 E
Japan ■, Asia .... 55 G8 36 0N 136 0 E
Japan, Sea of, Asia .... 54 E7 40 0N 135 0 E
Japan Trench, Pac. Oc. .... 96 D6 32 0N 142 0 E
Japen = Yapen,
  Indonesia .... 63 E9 1 50 S 136 0 E
Japla, India .... 69 G11 24 33N 84 1 E
Japurá →, Brazil .... 124 D5 3 8 S 65 46W
Jaquarão, Brazil .... 127 C5 32 34 S 53 23W
Jaqué, Panama 120 E4 7 27N 78 8W
Jarābulus, Syria .... 70 B3 36 49N 38 1 E
Jaraicejo, Spain 37 F5 39 40N 5 49W
Jaraíz de la Vera, Spain 36 E5 40 4N 5 45W
Jarama →, Spain 36 E7 40 24N 3 32W
Jaramānah, Syria .... 72 F7 33 29N 36 21 E
Jarandilla, Spain 36 E5 40 8N 5 39W
Jaranwala, Pakistan .... 68 D5 31 15N 73 26 E
Jarash, Jordan .... 74 C4 32 17N 35 54 E
Jarash □, Jordan .... 74 C4 32 17N 35 54 E
Järbo, Sweden .... 10 D10 60 43N 16 36 E
Jardim, Brazil .... 126 A4 21 28 S 56 2W
Jardín →, Spain 39 G2 38 50N 2 10W
Jardine River △,
  Australia .... 94 A3 11 9 S 142 21 E
Jardines de la Reina,
  Arch. de los, Cuba 120 B4 20 50N 78 50W
Jargalang, China .... 57 C12 43 5N 122 55 E
Jargalant = Hovd,
  Mongolia .... 60 B4 48 2N 91 37 E
Jari →, Brazil .... 125 D8 1 9 S 51 54W
Jarīr, W. al →,
  Si. Arabia .... 70 E4 25 38N 42 30 E
Järlåsa, Sweden .... 10 E11 59 53N 17 12 E
Jarmen, Germany .... 24 B9 53 56N 13 20 E
Järna, Dalarna, Sweden .... 10 D8 60 33N 14 26 E
Järna, Stockholm,
  Sweden .... 10 E11 59 6N 17 34 E
Jarnac, France 20 C3 45 40N 0 11W
Jarny, France .... 19 C12 49 9N 5 53 E
Jarocin, Poland .... 31 G4 51 59N 17 29 E
Jaroměř, Czech Rep. .... 26 A8 50 22N 15 52 E
Jarosław, Poland .... 31 H9 50 2N 22 42 E
Järpás, Sweden .... 10 E6 58 23N 12 57 E
Järpen, Sweden .... 10 A7 63 21N 13 26 E
Jarrahdale, Australia .... 93 F2 32 24 S 116 5 E
Jarrahi →, Iran .... 71 D6 30 49N 48 48 E
Jarres, Plaine des, Laos .... 58 C4 19 27N 103 10 E
Jarso, Ethiopia .... 81 F4 5 15N 37 30 E
Jartai, China .... 56 E3 39 45N 105 48 E
Jarud Qi, China .... 57 B11 44 28N 120 50 E
Järvenpää, Finland .... 9 F21 60 29N 25 5 E
Jarvis, Canada 116 D4 42 53N 80 6W
Jarvis I., Pac. Oc. .... 97 H12 0 15 S 160 5W
Jarvorník, Czech Rep. .... 27 A10 50 23N 17 2 E
Järvsö, Sweden .... 10 C10 61 43N 16 10 E
Jarwa, India .... 69 F10 27 38N 82 30 E
Jaša Tomić, Serbia & M. .... 28 E5 45 26N 20 50 E
Jasdan, India .... 68 H4 22 2N 71 12 E
Jashpurnagar, India .... 69 H11 22 54N 84 9 E
Jasidih, India .... 69 G12 24 31N 86 39 E
Jasień, Poland .... 31 G2 51 46N 15 0 E
Jāsimīyah, Iraq .... 70 C5 33 45N 44 41 E
Jasin, Malaysia .... 65 L4 2 20N 102 26 E
Jāsk, Iran .... 71 E8 25 38N 57 45 E
Jasło, Poland .... 31 J8 49 45N 21 30 E
Jaso, India .... 69 G9 24 30N 80 29 E
Jasol, India .... 68 G4 25 57N 72 30 E
Jasper, Alta., Canada 102 C5 52 55N 118 5W
Jasper, Ont., Canada 117 B9 44 52N 75 57W
Jasper, Ala., U.S.A. 115 J2 33 50N 87 17W
Jasper, Fla., U.S.A. 115 K4 30 31N 82 57W
Jasper, Ind., U.S.A. 114 F2 38 24N 86 56W
Jasper, Tex., U.S.A. 113 K8 30 56N 94 1W
Jasper △, Canada 102 C5 52 50N 118 8W
Jasrasar, India .... 68 F5 27 43N 73 49 E

Jastarnia, Poland .... 30 D5 54 42N 18 40 E
Jastrebarsko, Croatia .... 41 C12 45 41N 15 39 E
Jastrowie, Poland .... 30 E3 53 26N 16 49 E
Jastrzębie Zdrój, Poland .... 31 J5 49 57N 18 35 E
Jász-Nagykun-
  Szolnok □, Hungary .... 28 C5 47 15N 20 30 E
Jászapáti, Hungary .... 28 C5 47 32N 20 10 E
Jászárokszállás, Hungary .... 28 C4 47 39N 19 58 E
Jászberény, Hungary .... 28 C4 47 30N 19 55 E
Jászkisér, Hungary .... 28 C5 47 27N 20 20 E
Jászladány, Hungary .... 28 C5 47 23N 20 10 E
Jataí, Brazil .... 125 G8 17 58 S 51 48W
Jati, Pakistan .... 68 G3 24 20N 68 19 E
Jatibarang, Indonesia .... 63 G13 6 28 S 108 18 E
Jatiluwih, Indonesia .... 63 J18 8 23 S 115 8 E
Jatinegara, Indonesia .... 63 G12 6 13 S 106 52 E
Játiva = Xàtiva, Spain 39 G4 38 59N 0 32W
Jättendal, Sweden .... 10 C11 61 58N 17 15 E
Jaú, Brazil .... 127 A6 22 10 S 48 30W
Jauja, Peru .... 124 F3 11 45 S 75 15W
Jaunpur, India .... 69 G10 25 46N 82 44 E
Java = Jawa, Indonesia .... 62 F3 7 0 S 110 0 E
Java Sea, Indonesia .... 62 E3 4 35 S 107 15 E
Java Trench, Ind. Oc. .... 62 F3 9 0 S 105 0 E
Javalambre, Sa. de,
  Spain 38 E4 40 6N 1 0W
Jávea, Spain .... 39 G5 38 48N 0 10 E
Jawa, Indonesia .... 62 F3 7 0 S 110 0 E
Jawad, India .... 68 G6 24 36N 74 51 E
Jawor, Poland .... 31 G3 51 4N 16 11 E
Jaworzno, Poland .... 31 H6 50 13N 19 11 E
Jaworzyna Śląska,
  Poland .... 31 H3 50 55N 16 28 E
Jay Peak, U.S.A. 117 B12 44 55N 72 32W
Jayanti, India .... 67 F16 26 45N 89 40 E
Jayapura, Indonesia .... 63 E10 2 28 S 140 38 E
Jayawijaya, Pegunungan,
  Indonesia .... 63 E9 5 0 S 139 0 E
Jaynagar, India .... 67 F15 26 43N 86 9 E
Jayrūd, Syria .... 70 C3 33 49N 36 44 E
Jayton, U.S.A. 113 J4 33 15N 100 34W
Jāz Mūrīān, Hāmūn-e,
  Iran .... 71 E8 27 20N 58 55 E
Jazīreh-ye Shīf, Iran .... 71 D6 29 4N 50 54 E
Jazminal, Mexico 118 C4 24 56N 101 25W
Jazzīn, Lebanon .... 74 B4 33 31N 35 14 E
Jean, U.S.A. 111 K11 35 47N 115 20W
Jean Marie River,
  Canada 102 A4 61 32N 120 38W
Jean-Rabel, Haiti 121 C5 19 50N 73 5W
Jeanerette, U.S.A. 113 L9 29 55N 91 40W
Jeanette, Ostrov =
  Zhannetty, Ostrov,
  Russia .... 53 B16 76 43N 158 0 E
Jeannette, U.S.A. 116 F5 40 20N 79 36W
Jebāl Bārez, Kūh-e, Iran .... 71 D8 28 30N 58 20 E
Jebba, Nigeria .... 83 D5 9 9N 4 48 E
Jebel, Bahr el →, Sudan .... 81 F3 9 30N 30 25 E
Jebel Dud, Sudan .... 81 E3 13 25N 33 9 E
Jebel Qerri, Sudan .... 81 D3 16 16N 32 50 E
Jedburgh, U.K. 13 F6 55 29N 2 33W
Jedda = Jiddah,
  Si. Arabia .... 75 C2 21 29N 39 10 E
Jeddore L., Canada 105 C8 48 3N 55 55W
Jedlicze, Poland .... 31 J8 49 43N 21 40 E
Jędrzejów, Poland .... 31 H7 50 35N 20 15 E
Jedwabne, Poland .... 31 E9 53 17N 22 18 E
Jeetzel →, Germany .... 24 B7 53 9N 11 3 E
Jefferson, Iowa, U.S.A. 112 D7 42 1N 94 23W
Jefferson, Ohio, U.S.A. 116 E4 41 44N 80 46W
Jefferson, Tex., U.S.A. 113 J7 32 46N 94 21W
Jefferson, Mt., Nev.,
  U.S.A. 108 G5 38 51N 117 0W
Jefferson, Mt., Oreg.,
  U.S.A. 108 D3 44 41N 121 48W
Jefferson City, Mo.,
  U.S.A. 112 F8 38 34N 92 10W
Jefferson City, Tenn.,
  U.S.A. 115 G4 36 7N 83 30W
Jeffersontown, U.S.A. 114 F3 38 12N 85 35W
Jeffersonville, U.S.A. 114 F3 38 17N 85 44W
Jeffrey City, U.S.A. 108 E10 42 30N 107 49W
Jega, Nigeria .... 83 C5 12 15N 4 23 E
Jeju = Cheju do,
  S. Korea .... 57 H14 33 29N 126 34 E
Jekyll I., U.S.A. 115 K5 31 4N 81 25W
Jelcz-Laskowice, Poland .... 31 G4 51 2N 17 19 E
Jelenia Góra, Poland .... 31 H2 50 50N 15 45 E
Jelgava, Latvia .... 9 H20 56 41N 23 49 E
Jelgava □, Latvia .... 9 H20 56 35N 23 45 E
Jelica, Serbia & M. .... 44 C4 43 50N 20 17 E
Jelli, Sudan .... 81 F3 5 25N 31 45 E
Jelšava, Slovak Rep. .... 27 C13 48 37N 20 15 E
Jemaja, Indonesia .... 65 L5 3 5N 105 45 E
Jemaluang, Malaysia .... 65 L4 2 16N 103 52 E
Jember, Indonesia .... 63 H15 8 11 S 113 41 E
Jembongan, Malaysia .... 62 C5 6 45N 117 20 E
Jena, Germany .... 24 E7 50 54N 11 35 E
Jena, U.S.A. 113 K8 31 41N 92 8W
Jenbach, Austria .... 26 D4 47 24N 11 47 E
Jenin, West Bank .... 74 C4 32 28N 35 18 E
Jenkins, U.S.A. 114 G4 37 10N 82 38W
Jenner, U.S.A. 110 G3 38 27N 123 7W
Jennings, U.S.A. 113 K8 30 13N 92 40W
Jepara, Indonesia .... 63 G14 7 40 S 109 14 E
Jeparit, Australia .... 95 F3 36 8 S 142 1 E
Jequié, Brazil .... 125 F10 13 51 S 40 5W
Jequitinhonha, Brazil .... 125 G11 16 30 S 41 0W
Jequitinhonha →, Brazil .... 125 G11 15 51 S 38 53W
Jerantut, Malaysia .... 65 L4 3 56N 102 22 E
Jerejak, Pulau, Malaysia .... 65 c 5 19N 100 19 E
Jérémie, Haiti 121 C5 18 40N 74 10W
Jerez, Punta, Mexico 119 C5 22 58N 97 40W
Jerez de García Salinas,
  Mexico 118 C4 22 39N 103 0W
Jerez de la Frontera,
  Spain 37 J4 36 41N 6 7W
Jerez de los Caballeros,
  Spain 37 G4 38 20N 6 45W
Jericho = El Arīḥā,
  West Bank .... 74 D4 31 52N 35 27 E
Jericho, Australia .... 94 C4 23 38 S 146 6 E
Jerichow, Germany .... 24 C8 52 30N 12 1 E
Jerid, Chott el = Djerid,
  Chott, Tunisia .... 78 B7 33 42N 8 30 E
Jerilderie, Australia .... 95 F4 35 20 S 145 41 E
Jermyn, U.S.A. 117 E9 41 31N 75 31W
Jerome, U.S.A. 108 E6 42 44N 114 31W
Jerramungup, Australia .... 93 F2 33 55 S 118 55 E
Jersey, U.K. 15 H5 49 11N 2 7W

Jersey City, U.S.A. 117 F10 40 44N 74 4W
Jersey Shore, U.S.A. 116 E7 41 12N 77 15W
Jerseyville, U.S.A. 112 F9 39 7N 90 20W
Jerusalem, Israel .... 74 D4 31 47N 35 10 E
Jervis B., Australia .... 95 F5 35 8 S 150 46 E
Jervis Inlet, Canada 102 C4 50 0N 123 57W
Jerzu, Italy .... 42 C2 39 47N 9 31 E
Jesenice, Slovenia .... 41 B11 46 28N 14 3 E
Jeseník, Czech Rep. .... 27 A10 50 14N 17 8 E
Jesenké, Slovak Rep. .... 27 C13 48 20N 20 10 E
Jesi = Iesi, Italy .... 41 E10 43 31N 13 14 E
Jessnitz, Germany .... 24 D8 51 40N 12 18 E
Jessore, Bangla. .... 67 H16 23 10N 89 10 E
Jesup, U.S.A. 115 K5 31 36N 81 53W
Jesús Carranza, Mexico 119 D5 17 26N 95 2W
Jesús María, Argentina .... 126 C3 30 59 S 64 5W
Jetmore, U.S.A. 113 F5 38 4N 99 54W
Jetpur, India .... 68 J4 21 45N 70 10 E
Jeumont, France .... 19 B11 50 18N 4 6 E
Jevnaker, Norway .... 9 F14 60 15N 10 26 E
Jewett, U.S.A. 116 F3 40 22N 81 2W
Jewett City, U.S.A. 117 E13 41 36N 71 59W
Jeyḥūnābād, Iran .... 71 C6 34 58N 48 59 E
Jeypore, India .... 67 K13 18 50N 82 38 E
Jeziorak, Jezioro,
  Poland .... 30 E6 53 40N 19 35 E
Jeziorany, Poland .... 30 E7 53 58N 20 46 E
Jeziorka →, Poland .... 31 F8 52 7N 21 15 E
Jha Jha, India .... 69 G12 24 46N 86 22 E
Jhaarkand =
  Jharkhand □, India .... 69 H11 24 0N 85 50 E
Jhabua, India .... 68 H6 22 46N 74 36 E
Jhajjar, India .... 68 E7 28 37N 76 42 E
Jhal, Pakistan .... 68 E2 28 17N 67 27 E
Jhal Jhao, Pakistan .... 66 F4 26 20N 65 35 E
Jhalawar, India .... 68 G7 24 40N 76 10 E
Jhalida, India .... 69 H11 23 22N 85 58 E
Jhalrapatan, India .... 68 G7 24 33N 76 10 E
Jhang Maghiana,
  Pakistan .... 68 D5 31 15N 72 22 E
Jhansi, India .... 69 G8 25 30N 78 36 E
Jhargram, India .... 69 H12 22 27N 86 59 E
Jharia, India .... 69 H12 23 45N 86 26 E
Jharkhand □, India .... 69 H11 24 0N 85 50 E
Jharsuguda, India .... 67 J14 21 56N 84 5 E
Jhelum, Pakistan .... 68 C5 33 0N 73 45 E
Jhelum →, Pakistan .... 68 D5 31 20N 72 10 E
Jhilmilli, India .... 69 H10 23 24N 82 51 E
Jhudo, Pakistan .... 68 G3 24 58N 69 18 E
Jhunjhunu, India .... 68 E6 28 10N 75 30 E
Ji-Paraná, Brazil .... 124 F6 10 52 S 62 57W
Ji Xian, Hebei, China .... 56 F8 37 35N 115 30 E
Ji Xian, Henan, China .... 56 G8 35 22N 114 5 E
Ji Xian, Shanxi, China .... 56 F6 36 7N 110 40 E
Jia Xian, Henan, China .... 56 H7 33 59N 113 12 E
Jia Xian, Shaanxi, China .... 56 E6 38 12N 110 28 E
Jiading, China .... 59 B13 31 22N 121 15 E
Jiahe, China .... 59 E9 25 38N 112 19 E
Jialing Jiang →, China .... 58 C6 29 30N 106 20 E
Jiamusi, China .... 60 B8 46 40N 130 26 E
Ji'an, Jiangxi, China .... 59 D10 27 6N 114 59 E
Ji'an, Jilin, China .... 57 D14 41 5N 126 10 E
Jianchang, China .... 57 D11 40 55N 120 35 E
Jianchangying, China .... 57 D10 40 10N 118 50 E
Jianchuan, China .... 58 D2 26 38N 99 55 E
Jiande, China .... 59 C12 29 21N 119 15 E
Jiang'an, China .... 58 C5 28 40N 105 3 E
Jiangbei, China .... 58 C6 29 40N 106 34 E
Jiangcheng, China .... 58 F3 22 36N 101 52 E
Jiangchuan, China .... 58 E4 24 28N 102 39 E
Jiangdu, China .... 59 A12 32 27N 119 36 E
Jiange, China .... 58 A5 32 4N 105 32 E
Jianghua, China .... 59 E8 25 0N 111 35 E
Jiangjin, China .... 58 C6 29 14N 106 14 E
Jiangkou, China .... 58 D7 27 40N 108 49 E
Jiangle, China .... 59 D11 26 42N 117 23 E
Jiangling, China .... 59 F9 22 32N 113 0 E
Jiangmen, China .... 59 F9 22 32N 113 0 E
Jiangshan, China .... 59 C12 28 40N 118 37 E
Jiangsu □, China .... 57 H11 33 0N 120 0 E
Jiangyan, China .... 59 B13 32 30N 120 7 E
Jiangyin, China .... 59 B13 31 54N 120 17 E
Jiangyong, China .... 59 E8 25 20N 111 22 E
Jiangyou, China .... 58 B5 31 44N 104 43 E
Jianhe, China .... 58 D7 26 37N 108 31 E
Jianli, China .... 59 C9 29 46N 112 56 E
Jianning, China .... 59 D11 26 50N 116 50 E
Jian'ou, China .... 59 D12 27 3N 118 17 E
Jianshi, China .... 58 B7 30 37N 109 38 E
Jianshui, China .... 58 F4 23 36N 102 43 E
Jianyang, Fujian, China .... 59 D12 27 20N 118 5 E
Jianyang, Sichuan, China .... 58 B5 30 24N 104 33 E
Jiao Xian = Jiaozhou,
  China .... 57 F11 36 18N 120 1 E
Jiaohe, Hebei, China .... 56 E9 38 2N 116 20 E
Jiaohe, Jilin, China .... 57 C14 43 40N 127 22 E
Jiaojiang, China .... 59 C13 28 40N 121 24 E
Jiaoling, China .... 59 E11 24 41N 116 12 E
Jiaozhou, China .... 57 F11 36 18N 120 1 E
Jiaozhou Wan, China .... 57 F11 36 5N 120 10 E
Jiaozuo, China .... 56 G7 35 16N 113 12 E
Jiashan, China .... 59 B13 30 55N 120 55 E
Jiawang, China .... 57 G9 34 28N 117 26 E
Jiaxiang, China .... 56 G9 35 25N 116 20 E
Jiaxing, China .... 59 B13 30 49N 120 45 E
Jiayi = Chiai, Taiwan .... 59 F13 23 29N 120 25 E
Jiayu, China .... 59 C9 29 49N 113 53 E
Jibiya, Nigeria .... 83 C6 13 5N 7 12 E
Jibou, Romania .... 29 C8 47 15N 23 17 E
Jibuti = Djibouti ■,
  Africa .... 81 E5 12 0N 43 0 E
Jicarón, I., Panama 120 E3 7 10N 81 50W
Jiddah, Si. Arabia .... 75 C2 21 29N 39 10 E
Jido, India .... 67 E19 29 2N 94 58 E
Jieshou, China .... 56 H8 33 18N 115 22 E
Jiexiu, China .... 56 F6 37 2N 111 55 E
Jieyang, China .... 59 F11 23 35N 116 12 E
Jigawa □, Nigeria .... 83 C6 12 0N 9 45 E
Jiggalong, Australia .... 92 D3 23 21 S 120 47 E
Jigni, India .... 69 G8 25 45N 79 25 E
Jihlava, Czech Rep. .... 27 C9 48 55N 15 35 E
Jihlava →, Czech Rep. .... 27 C9 48 55N 16 36 E
Jihlavský □, Czech Rep. .... 26 B8 49 30N 15 30 E
Jihočeský □, Czech Rep. .... 26 B7 49 8N 14 35 E
Jihomoravský □,
  Czech Rep. .... 27 B9 49 5N 16 30 E
Jijel, Algeria .... 78 A7 36 52N 5 50 E
Jijiga, Ethiopia .... 75 F3 9 20N 42 50 E
Jikamshi, Nigeria .... 83 C6 12 12N 7 45 E
Jikau, Sudan .... 81 F3 8 28N 33 47 E
Jilin, China .... 57 C14 43 44N 126 30 E
Jilin □, China .... 57 C14 44 0N 127 0 E
Jiloca →, Spain 38 D3 41 21N 1 39W
Jilong = Chilung, Taiwan .... 59 E13 25 3N 121 45 E

Jim Thorpe, *U.S.A.* 117 F9 40 52N 75 44W
Jima, *Ethiopia* 81 F4 7 40N 36 47 E
Jimbaran, Teluk, *Indonesia* 63 K18 8 46 S 115 9 E
Jimbolia, *Romania* 28 E5 45 47N 20 43 E
Jimena de la Frontera, *Spain* 37 J5 36 27N 5 24W
Jiménez, *Mexico* 118 B4 27 10N 104 54W
Jimo, *China* 57 F11 36 23N 120 30 E
Jin Jiang →, *China* 59 C10 28 24N 115 48 E
Jin Xian = Jinzhou, *China* 56 E8 38 2N 115 2 E
Jin Xian, *China* 57 E11 38 55N 121 42 E
Jinan, *China* 56 F9 36 38N 117 1 E
Jinchang, *China* 60 C5 38 30N 102 10 E
Jincheng, *China* 56 G7 35 29N 112 50 E
Jinchuan, *China* 58 B4 31 30N 102 3 E
Jind, *India* 68 E7 29 19N 76 22 E
Jindabyne, *Australia* 95 F4 36 25 S 148 35 E
Jindřichův Hradec, *Czech Rep.* 26 B8 49 10N 15 2 E
Jing He →, *China* 56 G5 34 27N 109 4 E
Jing Shan, *China* 59 B8 31 20N 111 35 E
Jing Xian, *China* 59 B12 30 38N 118 25 E
Jing'an, *China* 59 C10 28 50N 115 17 E
Jingbian, *China* 56 F5 37 20N 108 30 E
Jingchuan, *China* 56 G4 35 20N 107 20 E
Jingde, *China* 59 B12 30 15N 118 27 E
Jingdezhen, *China* 59 C11 29 20N 117 11 E
Jingdong, *China* 58 E3 24 23N 100 47 E
Jinggangshan, *China* 59 D10 26 58N 114 15 E
Jinggu, *China* 58 F3 23 35N 100 41 E
Jinghai, *China* 56 E9 38 55N 116 55 E
Jinghong, *China* 58 G3 22 0N 100 45 E
Jingjiang, *China* 59 A13 32 2N 120 16 E
Jingle, *China* 56 E6 38 20N 111 55 E
Jingmen, *China* 59 B9 31 0N 112 10 E
Jingning, *China* 56 G3 35 30N 105 43 E
Jingpo Hu, *China* 57 C15 43 55N 128 55 E
Jingshan, *China* 59 B9 31 1N 113 7 E
Jingtai, *China* 56 F3 37 10N 104 6 E
Jingxi, *China* 58 F6 23 8N 106 27 E
Jingxing, *China* 56 E8 38 2N 114 8 E
Jingyang, *China* 56 G5 34 30N 108 50 E
Jingyu, *China* 57 C14 42 25N 126 45 E
Jingyuan, *China* 56 F3 36 30N 104 40 E
Jingzhou, *China* 58 D7 26 33N 109 40 E
Jingziguan, *China* 56 H6 33 15N 111 0 E
Jinhua, *China* 59 C12 29 8N 119 38 E
Jining, *Nei Monggol Zizhiqu, China* 56 D7 41 5N 113 0 E
Jining, *Shandong, China* 56 G9 35 22N 116 34 E
Jinja, *Uganda* 86 B3 0 25N 33 12 E
Jinjang, *Malaysia* 65 L3 3 13N 101 39 E
Jinji, *China* 56 F4 37 58N 106 8 E
Jinjiang, *Fujian, China* 59 E12 24 43N 118 33 E
Jinjiang, *Yunnan, China* 58 D3 26 14N 100 34 E
Jinjini, *Ghana* 82 D4 7 26N 2 42W
Jinkou, *China* 59 B10 30 20N 114 8 E
Jinkouhe, *China* 58 C4 29 18N 103 4 E
Jinmen Dao, *China* 59 E12 24 25N 118 25 E
Jinnah Barrage, *Pakistan* 66 C7 32 58N 71 33 E
Jinning, *China* 58 E4 24 38N 102 38 E
Jinotega, *Nic.* 120 D2 13 6N 85 59W
Jinotepe, *Nic.* 120 D2 11 50N 86 10W
Jinping, *Guizhou, China* 58 D7 26 41N 109 10 E
Jinping, *Yunnan, China* 58 F4 22 45N 103 18 E
Jinsha, *China* 58 D6 27 29N 106 12 E
Jinsha Jiang →, *China* 58 C5 28 50N 104 36 E
Jinshan, *China* 59 B13 30 54N 121 10 E
Jinshi, *China* 59 C8 29 40N 111 50 E
Jintan, *China* 59 B12 31 42N 119 36 E
Jinxi, *Jiangxi, China* 59 D11 27 56N 116 45 E
Jinxi, *Liaoning, China* 57 D11 40 52N 120 50 E
Jinxian, *China* 59 C11 28 26N 116 17 E
Jinxiang, *China* 56 G9 35 5N 116 22 E
Jinyang, *China* 58 D4 27 28N 103 5 E
Jinyun, *China* 59 C13 28 35N 120 5 E
Jinzhai, *China* 59 B10 31 40N 115 53 E
Jinzhou, *Hebei, China* 56 E8 38 2N 115 2 E
Jinzhou, *Liaoning, China* 57 D11 41 5N 121 3 E
Jiparaná →, *Brazil* 124 E6 8 3 S 62 52W
Jipijapa, *Ecuador* 124 D2 1 0 S 80 40W
Jiquilpan, *Mexico* 118 D4 19 57N 102 42W
Jishan, *China* 56 G6 35 34N 110 58 E
Jishou, *China* 58 C7 28 21N 109 43 E
Jishui, *China* 59 D10 27 12N 115 8 E
Jisr ash Shughūr, *Syria* 70 C3 35 49N 36 18 E
Jitarning, *Australia* 93 F2 32 48 S 117 57 E
Jitra, *Malaysia* 65 J3 6 16N 100 25 E
Jiu →, *Romania* 29 G8 43 47N 23 48 E
Jiudengkou, *China* 56 E4 39 56N 106 40 E
Jiujiang, *Guangdong, China* 59 F9 22 50N 113 0 E
Jiujiang, *Jiangxi, China* 59 C10 29 42N 115 58 E
Jiuling Shan, *China* 59 C10 28 40N 114 40 E
Jiulong = Kowloon, *China* 59 F10 22 19N 114 11 E
Jiulong, *China* 58 C3 28 57N 101 31 E
Jiutai, *China* 57 B13 44 10N 125 50 E
Jiuxincheng, *China* 56 E8 39 17N 115 59 E
Jiuyuhang, *China* 59 B12 30 18N 119 56 E
Jixi, *Anhui, China* 59 B12 30 5N 118 34 E
Jixi, *Heilongjiang, China* 57 B16 45 20N 130 50 E
Jiyang, *China* 57 F9 37 0N 117 12 E
Jiyuan, *China* 56 G7 35 7N 112 57 E
Jīzān, *Si. Arabia* 75 D3 17 0N 42 20 E
Jize, *China* 56 F8 36 54N 114 56 E
Jizera →, *Czech Rep.* 26 A7 50 10N 14 43 E
Jizl, Wādī al →, *Si. Arabia* 70 E3 25 39N 38 25 E
Jizō-Zaki, *Japan* 55 G6 35 34N 133 20 E
Jizzakh, *Uzbekistan* 52 E7 40 6N 67 50 E
Joaçaba, *Brazil* 127 B5 27 5 S 51 31W
Joal Fadiout, *Senegal* 82 C1 14 9N 16 50W
João Pessoa, *Brazil* 125 E12 7 10 S 34 52W
Joaquín V. González, *Argentina* 126 B3 25 10 S 64 0W
Jobat, *India* 68 H6 22 25N 74 34 E
Jobourg, Nez de, *France* 18 C5 49 41N 1 57W
Jódar, *Spain* 37 H7 37 50N 3 21W
Jodhpur, *India* 68 F5 26 23N 73 8 E
Jodiya, *India* 68 H4 22 42N 70 18 E
Jōetsu, *Japan* 55 F9 37 12N 138 10 E
Jœuf, *France* 19 C12 49 12N 6 0 E
Jofane, *Mozam.* 89 C5 21 15 S 34 18 E
Jogbani, *India* 69 F12 26 25N 87 15 E
Jõgeva, *Estonia* 9 G22 58 45N 26 24 E
Jogjakarta = Yogyakarta, *Indonesia* 63 G14 7 49 S 110 22 E
Johannesburg, *S. Africa* 89 D4 26 10 S 28 2 E
Johannesburg, *U.S.A.* 111 K9 35 22N 117 38W
Johansfors, *Sweden* 11 H9 56 42N 15 32 E
Johilla →, *India* 69 H9 23 37N 81 14 E
John Crow Mts., *Jamaica* 120 a 18 5N 76 25W
John Day, *U.S.A.* 108 D4 44 25N 118 57W
John Day →, *U.S.A.* 108 D3 45 44N 120 39W
John Day Fossil Beds ⌂, *U.S.A.* 108 D4 44 33N 119 38W
John D'Or Prairie, *Canada* 102 B5 58 30N 115 8W
John F. Kennedy International, New York ✕ (JFK), *U.S.A.* 117 F11 40 38N 73 47W
John H. Kerr Reservoir, *U.S.A.* 115 G6 36 36N 78 18W
John o' Groats, *U.K.* 13 C5 58 38N 3 4W
Johnnie, *U.S.A.* 111 J10 36 25N 116 5W
John's Ra., *Australia* 94 C1 21 55 S 133 23 E
Johnson, *Kans., U.S.A.* 113 G4 37 34N 101 45W
Johnson, *Vt., U.S.A.* 117 B12 44 38N 72 41W
Johnson City, *N.Y., U.S.A.* 117 D9 42 7N 75 58W
Johnson City, *Tenn., U.S.A.* 115 G4 36 19N 82 21W
Johnson City, *Tex., U.S.A.* 113 K5 30 17N 98 25W
Johnsonburg, *U.S.A.* 116 E6 41 29N 78 41W
Johnsondale, *U.S.A.* 111 K8 35 58N 118 32W
Johnsons Crossing, *Canada* 102 A2 60 29N 133 18W
Johnston, L., *Australia* 93 F3 32 25 S 120 30 E
Johnston Falls = Mambilima Falls, *Zambia* 87 E2 10 31 S 28 45 E
Johnston I., *Pac. Oc.* 97 F11 17 10N 169 8W
Johnstone Str., *Canada* 102 C3 50 28N 126 0W
Johnstown, *N.Y., U.S.A.* 117 C10 43 0N 74 22W
Johnstown, *Ohio, U.S.A.* 116 F2 40 9N 82 41W
Johnstown, *Pa., U.S.A.* 116 F6 40 20N 78 55W
Johor, Selat, *Asia* 65 d 1 28N 103 47 E
Johor Bahru, *Malaysia* 65 d 1 28N 103 46 E
Jõhvi, *Estonia* 9 G22 59 22N 27 27 E
Joigny, *France* 19 E10 47 58N 3 20 E
Joinville, *Brazil* 127 B6 26 15 S 48 55W
Joinville, *France* 19 D12 48 27N 5 10 E
Joinville I., *Antarctica* 5 C18 65 0 S 55 30W
Jojutla, *Mexico* 119 D5 18 37N 99 11W
Jokkmokk, *Sweden* 8 C18 66 35N 19 50 E
Jökulsá á Bru →, *Iceland* 8 D6 65 40N 14 16W
Jökulsá á Fjöllum →, *Iceland* 8 C5 66 10N 16 30W
Jolfā, *Āzarbājān-e Sharqī, Iran* 70 B5 38 57N 45 38 E
Jolfā, *Eşfahan, Iran* 71 C6 32 58N 51 37 E
Joliet, *U.S.A.* 114 E1 41 32N 88 5W
Joliette, *Canada* 104 C5 46 3N 73 24W
Jolo, *Phil.* 61 J4 6 0N 121 0 E
Jolon, *U.S.A.* 110 K5 35 58N 121 9W
Jomalig I., *Phil.* 61 D5 14 42N 122 22 E
Jombang, *Indonesia* 63 G15 7 33 S 112 14 E
Jomda, *China* 58 B2 31 28N 98 12 E
Jonava, *Lithuania* 9 J21 55 8N 24 12 E
Jones Sound, *Canada* 4 B3 76 0N 85 0W
Jonesboro, *Ark., U.S.A.* 113 H9 35 50N 90 42W
Jonesboro, *La., U.S.A.* 113 J8 32 15N 92 43W
Jong →, *S. Leone* 82 D2 7 32N 12 23W
Jonglei, *Sudan* 81 F3 6 25N 30 50 E
Jonglei □, *Sudan* 81 F3 7 30N 32 30 E
Joniškis, *Lithuania* 9 H20 56 13N 23 35 E
Jönköping, *Sweden* 11 G8 57 45N 14 8 E
Jönköpings län □, *Sweden* 11 G8 57 30N 14 30 E
Jonquière, *Canada* 105 C5 48 27N 71 14W
Jonsered, *Sweden* 11 G6 57 45N 12 10 E
Jonzac, *France* 20 C3 45 27N 0 28W
Joplin, *U.S.A.* 113 G7 37 6N 94 31W
Jora, *India* 68 F6 26 20N 77 49 E
Jordan, *Mont., U.S.A.* 108 C10 47 19N 106 55W
Jordan, *N.Y., U.S.A.* 117 C8 43 4N 76 29W
Jordan ■, *Asia* 74 E5 31 0N 36 0 E
Jordan →, *Asia* 74 D4 31 48N 35 32 E
Jordan Valley, *U.S.A.* 108 E5 42 59N 117 3W
Jordanów, *Poland* 31 J6 49 41N 19 49 E
Jorhat, *India* 67 F19 26 45N 94 12 E
Jörn, *Sweden* 8 D19 65 4N 20 1 E
Jorong, *Indonesia* 62 E4 3 58 S 114 56 E
Jørpeland, *Norway* 9 G11 59 3N 6 1 E
Jorquera →, *Chile* 126 B2 28 3 S 69 58W
Jos, *Nigeria* 83 D6 9 53N 8 51 E
Jos Plateau, *Nigeria* 83 D6 9 55N 9 0 E
Jošanička Banja, *Serbia & M.* 44 C4 43 24N 20 47 E
José Batlle y Ordóñez, *Uruguay* 127 C4 33 20 S 55 10W
Joseni, *Romania* 29 D10 46 42N 25 29 E
Joseph, L., *Nfld. & L., Canada* 105 B6 52 45N 65 18W
Joseph, L., *Ont., Canada* 116 A5 45 10N 79 44W
Joseph Bonaparte G., *Australia* 92 B4 14 35 S 128 50 E
Joshinath, *India* 69 D8 30 34N 79 34 E
Joshinetsu-Kōgen △, *Japan* 55 F9 36 42N 138 32 E
Joshua Tree, *U.S.A.* 111 L10 34 8N 116 19W
Joshua Tree △, *U.S.A.* 111 M10 33 55N 116 0W
Josselin, *France* 18 E4 47 57N 2 33W
Jost Van Dyke, *Br. Virgin Is.* 121 e 18 29N 64 47W
Jostedalsbreen, *Norway* 9 F12 61 40N 6 59 E
Jotunheimen, *Norway* 9 F13 61 35N 8 25 E
Joubertberge, *Namibia* 88 B1 18 30 S 14 0 E
Joué-lès-Tours, *France* 18 E7 47 21N 0 40 E
Jourdanton, *U.S.A.* 113 L5 28 55N 98 33W
Joutseno, *Finland* 32 B5 61 7N 28 31 E
Jovellanos, *Cuba* 120 B3 22 40N 81 10W
Joyeuse, *France* 21 D8 44 29N 4 16 E
Józefów, *Lubelskie, Poland* 31 H10 50 28N 23 2 E
Józefów, *Mazowieckie, Poland* 31 F8 52 10N 21 11 E
Ju Xian, *China* 57 F10 36 35N 118 20 E
Juan Aldama, *Mexico* 118 C4 24 20N 103 23W
Juan Bautista Alberdi, *Argentina* 126 C3 34 26 S 61 48W
Juan de Fuca Str., *Canada* 110 B3 48 15N 124 0W
Juan de Nova, *Ind. Oc.* 89 B7 17 3 S 43 45 E
Juan Fernández, Arch. de, *Pac. Oc.* 97 L20 33 50 S 80 0W
Juan José Castelli, *Argentina* 126 B3 25 27 S 60 57W
Juan L. Lacaze, *Uruguay* 126 C4 34 26 S 57 25W
Juankoski, *Finland* 8 E23 63 3N 28 19 E
Juárez, *Argentina* 126 D4 37 40 S 59 43W
Juárez, *Mexico* 111 N11 32 20N 115 57W
Juárez, Sierra de, *Mexico* 118 A1 32 0N 116 0W
Juàzeiro, *Brazil* 125 E10 9 30 S 40 30W
Juàzeiro do Norte, *Brazil* 125 E11 7 10 S 39 18W
Juba = Giuba →, *Somali Rep.* 75 G3 1 30N 42 35 E
Juba, *Sudan* 81 G3 4 50N 31 35 E
Jubany, *Antarctica* 5 C18 62 30 S 58 0W
Jubayl, *Lebanon* 74 A4 34 5N 35 39 E
Jubbah, *Si. Arabia* 70 D4 28 2N 40 56 E
Jubbal, *India* 68 D7 31 5N 77 40 E
Jubbulpore = Jabalpur, *India* 69 H8 23 9N 79 58 E
Jübek, *Germany* 24 A5 54 33N 9 22 E
Jubga, *Russia* 35 H4 44 19N 38 48 E
Jubilee L., *Australia* 93 E4 29 0 S 126 50 E
Juby, C., *Morocco* 78 C3 28 0N 12 59W
Júcar = Xúquer →, *Spain* 39 F4 39 5N 0 10W
Júcaro, *Cuba* 120 B4 21 37N 78 51W
Juchitán, *Mexico* 119 D5 16 27N 95 5W
Judaea = Har Yehuda, *Israel* 74 D3 31 35N 34 57 E
Judenburg, *Austria* 26 D7 47 12N 14 38 E
Judith →, *U.S.A.* 108 C9 47 44N 109 39W
Judith, Pt., *U.S.A.* 117 E13 41 22N 71 29W
Judith Gap, *U.S.A.* 108 C9 46 41N 109 45W
Juelsminde, *Denmark* 11 J4 55 43N 10 1 E
Jugoslavia = Serbia & Montenegro ■, *Europe* 44 C4 43 20N 20 0 E
Juigalpa, *Nic.* 120 D2 12 6N 85 26W
Juillac, *France* 20 C5 45 20N 1 19 E
Juist, *Germany* 24 B2 53 40N 6 59 E
Juiz de Fora, *Brazil* 127 A7 21 43 S 43 19W
Jujuy □, *Argentina* 126 A2 23 20 S 65 40W
Julesburg, *U.S.A.* 112 E3 40 59N 102 16W
Juli, *Peru* 124 G5 16 10 S 69 25W
Julia Cr. →, *Australia* 94 C3 20 0 S 141 11 E
Julia Creek, *Australia* 94 C3 20 39 S 141 44 E
Juliaca, *Peru* 124 G4 15 25 S 70 10W
Julian, *U.S.A.* 111 M10 33 4N 116 38W
Julian, L., *Canada* 104 B4 54 25N 77 57W
Julian Alps = Julijske Alpe, *Slovenia* 41 B11 46 15N 14 1 E
Julianatop, *Suriname* 125 C7 3 40N 56 30W
Julianehåb = Qaqortoq, *Greenland* 101 B6 60 43N 46 0W
Jülich, *Germany* 24 E2 50 55N 6 22 E
Julijske Alpe, *Slovenia* 41 B11 46 15N 14 1 E
Julimes, *Mexico* 118 B3 28 25N 105 27W
Jullundur, *India* 68 D6 31 20N 75 40 E
Julu, *China* 56 F8 37 15N 115 2 E
Jumbo, *Zimbabwe* 87 F3 17 30 S 30 58 E
Jumbo Pk., *U.S.A.* 111 J12 36 12N 114 11W
Jumentos Cays, *Bahamas* 120 B4 23 0N 75 40W
Jumilla, *Spain* 39 G3 38 28N 1 19W
Jumla, *Nepal* 69 E10 29 15N 82 13 E
Jumna = Yamuna →, *India* 69 G9 25 30N 81 53 E
Junagadh, *India* 68 J4 21 30N 70 30 E
Junction, *Tex., U.S.A.* 113 K5 30 29N 99 46W
Junction, *Utah, U.S.A.* 109 G7 38 14N 112 13W
Junction B., *Australia* 94 A1 11 52 S 133 55 E
Junction City, *Kans., U.S.A.* 112 F6 39 2N 96 50W
Junction City, *Oreg., U.S.A.* 108 D2 44 13N 123 12W
Junction Pt., *Australia* 94 A1 11 45 S 133 50 E
Jundah, *Australia* 94 C3 24 46 S 143 2 E
Jundiaí, *Brazil* 127 A6 24 30 S 47 0W
Juneau, *U.S.A.* 102 B2 58 18N 134 25W
Junee, *Australia* 95 E4 34 53 S 147 35 E
Jungfrau, *Switz.* 25 J3 46 32N 7 58 E
Junggar Pendi, *China* 60 B3 44 30N 86 0 E
Jungshahi, *Pakistan* 68 G2 24 52N 67 44 E
Juniata →, *U.S.A.* 116 F7 40 30N 77 40W
Junín, *Argentina* 126 C3 34 33 S 60 57W
Junín de los Andes, *Argentina* 128 D2 39 45 S 71 0W
Jūniyah, *Lebanon* 74 B4 33 59N 35 38 E
Junlian, *China* 58 C5 28 8N 104 29 E
Juntas, *Chile* 126 B2 28 24 S 69 58W
Juntura, *U.S.A.* 108 E4 43 45N 118 5W
Jur, Nahr el →, *Sudan* 81 F2 8 45N 29 15 E
Jura = Jura, Mts. du, *Europe* 19 F13 46 40N 6 5 E
Jura = Schwäbische Alb, *Germany* 25 G5 48 20N 9 30 E
Jura, *U.K.* 13 F3 56 0N 5 50W
Jura □, *France* 19 F12 46 47N 5 45 E
Jura □, *Switz.* 25 H3 47 20N 7 20 E
Jūra →, *Lithuania* 30 C9 55 3N 22 9 E
Jura, Mts. du, *Europe* 19 F13 46 40N 6 5 E
Jura, Sd. of, *U.K.* 13 F3 55 57N 5 45W
Jurbarkas, *Lithuania* 9 J20 55 4N 22 46 E
Jurien, *Australia* 93 F2 30 18 S 115 2 E
Jurilovca, *Romania* 29 F13 44 46N 28 52 E
Jūrmala, *Latvia* 9 H20 56 58N 23 34 E
Jurong, *China* 59 B12 31 57N 119 9 E
Jurong, *Singapore* 65 d 1 19N 103 42 E
Juruá →, *Brazil* 124 D5 2 37 S 65 44W
Juruena, *Brazil* 124 F7 13 0 S 58 10W
Juruena →, *Brazil* 124 E7 7 20 S 58 3W
Juruti, *Brazil* 125 D7 2 9 S 56 4W
Jussey, *France* 19 E12 47 50N 5 55 E
Justo Daract, *Argentina* 126 C2 33 52 S 65 12W
Jutaí →, *Brazil* 124 D5 2 43 S 66 57W
Jüterbog, *Germany* 24 D9 51 59N 13 5 E
Juticalpa, *Honduras* 120 D2 14 40N 86 12W
Jutland = Jylland, *Denmark* 11 H3 56 25N 9 30 E
Juventud, I. de la, *Cuba* 120 B3 21 40N 82 40W
Juvigny-sous-Andaine, *France* 18 D6 48 32N 0 30W
Jüy Zar, *Iran* 70 C5 33 50N 46 18 E
Juye, *China* 56 G9 35 22N 116 5 E
Juzennecourt, *France* 19 D11 48 10N 4 58 E
Jvari, *Georgia* 35 J6 42 42N 42 4 E
Jwaneng, *Botswana* 85 J4 24 45 S 24 50 E
Jyderup, *Denmark* 11 J5 55 40N 11 26 E
Jylland, *Denmark* 11 H3 56 25N 9 30 E
Jyväskylä, *Finland* 9 E21 62 14N 25 50 E

K

K2, *Pakistan* 69 B7 35 58N 76 32 E
Ka →, *Nigeria* 83 C5 11 40N 4 10 E
Kaap Plateau, *S. Africa* 88 D3 28 30 S 24 0 E
Kaapkruis, *Namibia* 88 C1 21 55 S 13 57 E
Kaapstad = Cape Town, *S. Africa* 88 E2 33 55 S 18 22 E
Kaba, *Guinea* 82 C2 10 9N 11 40W
Kabaena, *Indonesia* 63 F6 5 15 S 122 0 E
Kabala, *S. Leone* 82 D2 9 38N 11 37W
Kabale, *Uganda* 86 C3 1 15 S 30 0 E
Kabalo, *Dem. Rep. of the Congo* 86 D2 6 0 S 27 0 E
Kabambare, *Dem. Rep. of the Congo* 86 C2 4 41 S 27 39 E
Kabango, *Dem. Rep. of the Congo* 87 D2 8 35 S 28 30 E
Kabanjahe, *Indonesia* 62 D1 3 6N 98 30 E
Kabankalan, *Phil.* 61 G5 9 59N 122 49 E
Kabara, *Mali* 82 B4 16 40N 2 50W
Kabardinka, *Russia* 33 K10 44 40N 37 57 E
Kabardino-Balkar Republic = Kabardino-Balkaria □, *Russia* 35 J6 43 30N 43 30 E
Kabardino-Balkaria □, *Russia* 35 J6 43 30N 43 30 E
Kabarega Falls = Murchison Falls, *Uganda* 86 B3 2 15N 31 30 E
Kabasalan, *Phil.* 61 H5 7 47N 122 44 E
Kabat, *Indonesia* 63 J17 8 16 S 114 19 E
Kabba, *Nigeria* 83 D6 7 50N 6 3 E
Kabetogama, *U.S.A.* 112 A8 48 28N 92 59W
Kabi, *Niger* 83 C7 13 30N 12 35 E
Kabin Buri, *Thailand* 64 F3 13 57N 101 43 E
Kabinakagami L., *Canada* 104 C3 48 54N 84 25W
Kabinda, *Dem. Rep. of the Congo* 84 F4 6 19 S 24 20 E
Kabna, *Sudan* 80 D3 19 6N 32 40 E
Kabompo, *Zambia* 87 E1 13 36 S 24 14 E
Kabompo →, *Zambia* 85 G4 14 10 S 23 11 E
Kabondo, *Dem. Rep. of the Congo* 87 D2 8 58 S 25 40 E
Kabongo, *Dem. Rep. of the Congo* 86 D2 7 22 S 25 33 E
Kabot, *Guinea* 82 C2 10 48N 14 57W
Kabou, *Togo* 83 D5 9 28N 0 55 E
Kabr, *Sudan* 81 E2 10 54N 26 50 E
Kabrousse, *Senegal* 82 C1 12 25N 16 45W
Kabūd Gonbad, *Iran* 71 B8 37 5N 59 45 E
Kabugao, *Phil.* 61 B4 18 2N 121 11 E
Kābul, *Afghan.* 68 B3 34 28N 69 11 E
Kābul □, *Afghan.* 66 B6 34 30N 69 0 E
Kābul →, *Pakistan* 68 C5 33 55N 72 14 E
Kabunga, *Dem. Rep. of the Congo* 86 C2 1 38 S 28 3 E
Kaburuang, *Indonesia* 63 D7 3 50N 126 30 E
Kabushiya, *Sudan* 81 D3 16 54N 33 41 E
Kabwe, *Zambia* 87 E2 14 30 S 28 29 E
Kačanik, *Serbia & M.* 44 D5 42 13N 21 12 E
Kačerginė, *Lithuania* 30 D10 54 56N 23 42 E
Kachchh, Gulf of, *India* 68 H3 22 50N 69 15 E
Kachchh, Rann of, *India* 68 H4 24 0N 70 0 E
Kachchhidhana, *India* 69 J8 21 44N 78 46 E
Kachebera, *Zambia* 87 E3 13 50 S 32 50 E
Kachia, *Nigeria* 83 D6 9 50N 7 55 E
Kachikau, *Botswana* 88 B3 18 8 S 24 26 E
Kachin □, *Burma* 58 D1 26 0N 97 30 E
Kachira, L., *Uganda* 86 C3 0 40 S 31 7 E
Kachiry, *Kazakhstan* 52 D8 53 10N 75 50 E
Kachisi, *Ethiopia* 81 F4 9 40N 37 50 E
Kachnara, *India* 68 H6 23 50N 75 6 E
Kachot, *Cambodia* 65 G4 11 30N 103 3 E
Kaçkar, *Turkey* 73 B9 40 45N 41 10 E
Kadan, *Czech Rep.* 26 A6 50 23N 13 16 E
Kadan Kyun, *Burma* 64 F2 12 30N 98 20 E
Kadanai →, *Afghan.* 68 D1 31 22N 65 45 E
Kadarkút, *Hungary* 28 D2 46 13N 17 39 E
Kadavu, *Fiji* 91 D8 19 0 S 178 15 E
Kade, *Ghana* 83 D4 6 7N 0 56W
Kadhimain = Al Kāzimīyah, *Iraq* 70 C5 33 22N 44 18 E
Kadi, *India* 68 H5 23 18N 72 23 E
Kadina, *Australia* 95 E2 33 55 S 137 43 E
Kadınhanı, *Turkey* 72 C5 38 14N 32 13 E
Kadiolo, *Mali* 82 C3 10 35N 7 41W
Kadipur, *India* 69 F10 26 10N 82 23 E
Kadirli, *Turkey* 70 B3 37 23N 36 5 E
Kadiyevka = Stakhanov, *Ukraine* 33 H10 48 35N 38 40 E
Kadodo, *Sudan* 81 E2 11 4N 29 31 E
Kadoka, *U.S.A.* 112 D4 43 50N 101 31W
Kadom, *Russia* 34 C6 54 37N 42 30 E
Kadoma, *Zimbabwe* 87 F2 18 20 S 29 52 E
Kâdugli, *Sudan* 81 E2 11 0N 29 45 E
Kaduna, *Nigeria* 83 C6 10 30N 7 21 E
Kaduna □, *Nigeria* 83 C6 11 0N 7 30 E
Kaduy, *Russia* 32 C9 59 12N 37 9 E
Kaédi, *Mauritania* 82 B2 16 9N 13 28W
Kaélé, *Cameroon* 83 C7 10 7N 14 27 E
Kaeng Khoĭ, *Thailand* 64 E3 14 35N 101 0 E
Kaeng Kra Chan △, *Thailand* 64 F2 12 57N 99 23 E
Kaeng Tana △, *Thailand* 64 E5 15 25N 105 32 E
Kaesŏng, *N. Korea* 57 F14 37 58N 126 35 E
Kāf, *Si. Arabia* 70 D3 31 25N 37 29 E
Kafan = Kapan, *Armenia* 70 B5 39 18N 46 27 E
Kafanchan, *Nigeria* 83 D6 9 40N 8 20 E
Kafareti, *Nigeria* 83 C7 10 25N 11 12 E
Kaffrine, *Senegal* 82 C1 14 8N 15 36W
Kafin, *Nigeria* 83 D6 9 30N 7 4 E
Kafin Madaki, *Nigeria* 83 C6 10 41N 9 46 E
Kafinda, *Zambia* 87 E3 12 32 S 30 20 E
Kafirévs, Ákra, *Greece* 46 C6 38 9N 24 38 E
Kafr el Battikh, *Egypt* 80 H7 31 25N 31 44 E
Kafr el Dauwâr, *Egypt* 80 H7 31 8N 30 8 E
Kafr el Sheikh, *Egypt* 80 H7 31 15N 30 50 E
Kafue, *Zambia* 87 F2 15 46 S 28 9 E
Kafue △, *Zambia* 87 F2 15 12 S 25 38 E
Kafue →, *Zambia* 85 H5 15 30 S 29 0 E
Kafue Flats, *Zambia* 87 F2 15 40 S 27 25 E
Kafulwe, *Zambia* 87 D2 9 0 S 29 1 E
Kaga, *Afghan.* 68 B4 34 14N 70 10 E
Kaga Bandoro, *C.A.R.* 84 C3 7 0N 19 10 E
Kagan, *Uzbekistan* 52 F7 39 43N 64 33 E
Kagarko, *Nigeria* 83 D6 9 28N 7 36 E
Kagawa □, *Japan* 55 G7 34 15N 134 0 E
Kagera □, *Tanzania* 86 C3 2 0 S 31 30 E
Kagera →, *Uganda* 86 C3 0 57 S 31 47 E
Kağızman, *Turkey* 70 B4 40 5N 43 10 E
Kagmar, *Sudan* 81 E3 14 24N 30 25 E
Kagoshima, *Japan* 55 J5 31 35N 130 33 E
Kagoshima □, *Japan* 55 J5 31 30N 130 30 E
Kagul = Cahul, *Moldova* 29 E13 45 50N 28 15 E
Kahak, *Iran* 71 B6 36 6N 49 46 E
Kahama, *Tanzania* 86 C3 4 8 S 32 30 E
Kahan, *Pakistan* 68 E3 29 18N 68 54 E
Kahang, *Malaysia* 65 L4 2 12N 103 32 E
Kahayan →, *Indonesia* 62 E4 3 40 S 114 0 E
Kahe, *Tanzania* 86 C4 3 30 S 37 25 E
Kahnūj, *Iran* 71 E8 27 55N 57 40 E
Kahoka, *U.S.A.* 112 E9 40 25N 91 44W
Kahoolawe, *U.S.A.* 106 H16 20 33N 156 37W
Kahramanmaraş, *Turkey* 70 B3 37 37N 36 53 E
Kâhta, *Turkey* 73 D8 37 46N 38 36 E
Kahul, Ozero, *Ukraine* 29 E13 45 24N 28 24 E
Kahurangi △, *N.Z.* 91 J4 41 10 S 172 32 E
Kahuta, *Pakistan* 68 C5 33 35N 73 24 E
Kahuzi-Biega △, *Dem. Rep. of the Congo* 86 C2 1 50 S 27 55 E
Kai, Kepulauan, *Indonesia* 63 F8 5 55 S 132 45 E
Kai Besar, *Indonesia* 63 F8 5 35 S 133 0 E
Kai Is. = Kai, Kepulauan, *Indonesia* 63 F8 5 55 S 132 45 E
Kai Kecil, *Indonesia* 63 F8 5 45 S 132 40 E
Kai Xian, *China* 58 B7 31 11N 108 21 E
Kaiama, *Nigeria* 83 D5 9 36N 4 1 E
Kaiapoi, *N.Z.* 91 K4 43 24 S 172 40 E
Kaieteur Falls, *Guyana* 124 B7 5 1N 59 10W
Kaifeng, *China* 56 G8 34 48N 114 21 E
Kaihua, *China* 59 C12 29 12N 118 20 E
Kaijiang, *China* 58 B6 31 7N 107 55 E
Kaikohe, *N.Z.* 91 F4 35 25 S 173 49 E
Kaikoura, *N.Z.* 91 K4 42 25 S 173 43 E
Kailahun, *S. Leone* 82 D2 8 18N 10 39W
Kailash = Kangrinboqe Feng, *China* 69 D9 31 0N 81 25 E
Kaili, *China* 58 D6 26 33N 107 59 E
Kailu, *China* 57 C11 43 38N 121 18 E
Kailua Kona, *U.S.A.* 106 J17 19 39N 155 59W
Kaimana, *Indonesia* 63 E8 3 39 S 133 45 E
Kaimanawa Mts., *N.Z.* 91 H5 39 15 S 175 56 E
Kaimganj, *India* 69 F8 27 33N 79 24 E
Kaimur Hills, *India* 69 G10 24 30N 82 0 E
Kainab →, *Namibia* 88 D2 28 32 S 19 34 E
Kainji Dam, *Nigeria* 83 D5 9 55N 4 35 E
Kainji Lake △, *Nigeria* 83 C5 10 5N 4 6 E
Kainji Res., *Nigeria* 83 C5 10 1N 4 40 E
Kainuu, *Finland* 8 D23 64 30N 29 7 E
Kaipara Harbour, *N.Z.* 91 G5 36 25 S 174 14 E
Kaiping, *China* 59 F9 22 23N 112 42 E
Kaipokok B., *Canada* 105 B8 54 54N 59 47W
Kaira, *India* 68 H5 22 45N 72 50 E
Kairana, *India* 68 E7 29 24N 77 15 E
Kaironi, *Indonesia* 63 E8 0 47 S 133 40 E
Kairouan, *Tunisia* 79 A8 35 45N 10 5 E
Kaiserslautern, *Germany* 25 F3 49 26N 7 45 E
Kaiserstuhl, *Germany* 25 G3 48 4N 7 40 E
Kaitaia, *N.Z.* 91 F4 35 8 S 173 17 E
Kaitangata, *N.Z.* 91 M2 46 17 S 169 51 E
Kaithal, *India* 68 E7 29 48N 76 26 E
Kaitu →, *Pakistan* 68 C4 33 10N 70 30 E
Kaiyang, *China* 58 D6 27 4N 106 59 E
Kaiyuan, *Liaoning, China* 57 C13 42 28N 124 1 E
Kaiyuan, *Yunnan, China* 58 F4 23 40N 103 12 E
Kajaani, *Finland* 8 D22 64 17N 27 46 E
Kajabbi, *Australia* 94 C3 20 0 S 140 1 E
Kajana = Kajaani, *Finland* 8 D22 64 17N 27 46 E
Kajang, *Malaysia* 65 L3 2 59N 101 48 E
Kajaran, *Armenia* 73 C12 39 10N 46 7 E
Kajiado, *Kenya* 86 C4 1 53 S 36 48 E
Kajo Kaji, *Sudan* 81 G3 3 58N 31 40 E
Kajuru, *Nigeria* 83 C6 10 15N 7 34 E
Kaka, *Sudan* 81 E3 10 38N 32 10 E
Kakabeka Falls, *Canada* 104 C2 48 24N 89 37W
Kakadu △, *Australia* 92 B5 12 0 S 132 3 E
Kakamas, *S. Africa* 88 D3 28 45 S 20 33 E
Kakamega, *Kenya* 86 B3 0 20N 34 46 E
Kakanj, *Bos.-H.* 28 F3 44 4N 18 4 E
Kakanui Mts., *N.Z.* 91 L3 45 10 S 170 30 E
Kakata, *Liberia* 82 D2 6 35N 10 20W
Kakdwip, *India* 69 J13 21 53N 88 11 E
Kake, *Japan* 55 G6 34 36N 132 19 E
Kake, *U.S.A.* 102 B2 56 59N 133 57W
Kakegawa, *Japan* 55 G9 34 45N 138 1 E
Kakeroma-Jima, *Japan* 55 K4 28 8N 129 14 E
Kakhib, *Russia* 35 J8 42 28N 46 34 E
Kakhovka, *Ukraine* 33 J7 46 45N 33 30 E
Kakhovske Vdskh., *Ukraine* 33 J7 47 5N 34 0 E
Kakinada, *India* 67 L13 16 57N 82 11 E
Kakisa →, *Canada* 102 A5 61 3N 118 10W
Kakisa L., *Canada* 102 A5 60 56N 117 43W
Kakogawa, *Japan* 55 G7 34 46N 134 51 E
Kakum △, *Ghana* 83 D4 5 24N 1 20W
Kakwa →, *Canada* 102 C5 54 37N 118 28W
Kāl Gūsheh, *Iran* 71 D8 30 59N 58 12 E
Kal Safīd, *Iran* 70 C5 34 52N 47 23 E
Kala, *Nigeria* 83 C7 12 2N 14 40 E
Kalaallit Nunaat = Greenland ☑, *N. Amer.* 4 C5 66 0N 45 0W
Kalabagh, *Pakistan* 68 C4 33 0N 71 28 E
Kalabahi, *Indonesia* 63 F6 8 13 S 124 31 E
Kalabáka, *Greece* 46 B3 39 42N 21 39 E
Kalabana, *Mali* 82 C3 14 10N 8 35W
Kalach, *Russia* 34 E5 50 22N 41 0 E
Kalach na Donu, *Russia* 35 F6 48 43N 43 32 E
Kaladan →, *Burma* 67 J18 20 20N 93 5 E
Kaladar, *Canada* 116 B7 44 37N 77 5W
Kalahari, *Africa* 88 C3 24 0 S 21 30 E
Kalahari Gemsbok △, *S. Africa* 88 D3 25 30 S 20 30 E
Kalajoki, *Finland* 8 D20 64 12N 24 10 E
Kalakamati, *Botswana* 89 C4 20 40 S 27 25 E
Kalakan, *Russia* 53 D12 55 15N 116 45 E
K'alak'unlun Shank'ou = Karakoram Pass, *Asia* 69 B7 35 33N 77 50 E
Kalam, *Pakistan* 69 B5 35 34N 72 30 E
Kalama, *Dem. Rep. of the Congo* 86 C2 2 52 S 28 35 E
Kalama, *U.S.A.* 110 E4 46 1N 122 51W
Kalámai, *Greece* 46 D4 37 3N 22 10 E
Kalamariá, *Greece* 44 F6 40 33N 22 55 E
Kalamazoo, *U.S.A.* 114 D3 42 17N 85 35W
Kalamazoo →, *U.S.A.* 114 D2 42 40N 86 10W
Kalambo Falls, *Tanzania* 87 D3 8 37 S 31 35 E
Kálamos, *Greece* 46 C5 38 17N 23 52 E
Kálamos Nisís, *Greece* 46 C2 38 37N 20 55 E
Kalan, *Turkey* 70 B3 39 7N 39 32 E
Kalankalan, *Guinea* 82 C3 10 7N 8 54W
Kalannie, *Australia* 93 F2 30 22 S 117 5 E
Kalāntarī, *Iran* 71 C7 32 10N 54 8 E
Kalao, *Indonesia* 63 F6 7 21 S 121 0 E
Kalaotoa, *Indonesia* 63 F6 7 20 S 121 50 E
Kälarne, *Sweden* 10 B10 62 59N 16 5 E
Kalasin, *Thailand* 64 D4 16 26N 103 30 E
Kalat, *Iran* 71 E8 25 29N 59 22 E
Kalat, *Pakistan* 66 E5 29 8N 66 31 E
Kalāteh, *Iran* 71 B7 36 33N 55 41 E
Kalāteh-ye Ganj, *Iran* 71 E8 27 31N 57 55 E
Kálathos, *Greece* 47 E10 36 9N 28 8 E
Kalaus →, *Russia* 35 H7 45 40N 44 7 E
Kalávrita, *Greece* 46 C4 38 3N 22 8 E
Kalbarri, *Australia* 93 E1 27 40 S 114 10 E
Kalbarri △, *Australia* 93 E1 27 51 S 114 30 E
Kale, *Antalya, Turkey* 47 E12 36 14N 30 0 E
Kale, *Denizli, Turkey* 47 D10 37 27N 28 49 E
Kalecik, *Turkey* 72 B5 40 4N 33 26 E
Kalegauk Kyun, *Burma* 67 M20 15 33N 97 35 E

Kalehe, *Dem. Rep. of the Congo* ..... 86 C2 2 6S 28 50 E
Kalema, *Tanzania* .... 86 C3 1 12 S 31 55 E
Kalemie, *Dem. Rep. of the Congo* ..... 86 D2 5 55 S 29 9 E
Kalety, *Poland* ...... 31 H5 50 35N 18 52 E
Kalewa, *Burma* ...... 67 H19 23 10N 94 15 E
Kaleybar, *Iran* ...... 70 B5 38 47N 47 2 E
Kalgoorlie-Boulder, *Australia* ...... 93 F3 30 40 S 121 22 E
Kali →, *India* ...... 69 F8 27 6N 79 55 E
Kali Sindh →, *India* . 68 G6 25 32N 76 17 E
Kaliakra, Nos, *Bulgaria* 45 C12 43 21N 28 30 E
Kalianda, *Indonesia* .. 62 F3 5 50 S 105 45 E
Kalibo, *Phil.* .... 61 F5 11 43N 122 22 E
Kalima, *Dem. Rep. of the Congo* ..... 86 C2 2 33 S 26 32 E
Kalimantan, *Indonesia* . 62 E4 0 0 114 0 E
Kalimantan Barat □, *Indonesia* ...... 62 E4 0 0 110 30 E
Kalimantan Selatan □, *Indonesia* ...... 62 E5 2 30 S 115 30 E
Kalimantan Tengah □, *Indonesia* ...... 62 E4 2 0 S 113 30 E
Kalimantan Timur □, *Indonesia* ...... 62 D5 1 30N 116 30 E
Kálimnos, *Greece* .... 47 D8 37 0N 27 0 E
Kalimpong, *India* .... 69 F13 27 4N 88 35 E
Kaliningrad, *Russia* ... 9 J19 54 42N 20 32 E
Kaliningrad ✈ (KGD), *Russia* .... 30 D7 54 45N 20 33 E
Kalininsk, *Russia* .... 34 E7 51 30N 44 40 E
Kalinkavichy, *Belarus* . 33 F5 52 12N 29 20 E
Kalinkovichi = Kalinkavichy, *Belarus* 33 F5 52 12N 29 20 E
Kalinovik, *Bos.-H.* ... 44 C2 43 31N 18 25 E
Kalipetrovo, *Bulgaria* . 45 B11 44 5N 27 14 E
Kaliro, *Uganda* ...... 86 B3 0 56N 33 30 E
Kalirrákhi, *Greece* .... 45 F8 40 40N 24 35 E
Kalispell, *U.S.A.* 108 B6 48 12N 114 19W
Kalisz, *Poland* ...... 31 G5 51 45N 18 8 E
Kalisz Pomorski, *Poland* 31 E2 53 17N 15 55 E
Kaliua, *Tanzania* .... 86 D3 5 5 S 31 48 E
Kalívia Thorikoú, *Greece* .... 46 D5 37 50N 23 55 E
Kalix = Kalixälven →, *Sweden* .... 8 D20 65 50N 23 11 E
Kalix, *Sweden* ...... 8 D20 65 53N 23 12 E
Kalixälven →, *Sweden* . 8 D20 65 50N 23 11 E
Kalka, *India* .... 68 D7 30 46N 76 57 E
Kalkan, *Turkey* ..... 47 E11 36 15N 29 23 E
Kalkarindji, *Australia* .. 92 C5 17 30 S 130 47 E
Kalkaska, *U.S.A.* 114 C3 44 44N 85 11W
Kalkfeld, *Namibia* .... 88 C2 20 57 S 16 14 E
Kalkfontein, *Botswana* . 88 C3 22 4 S 20 57 E
Kalkım, *Turkey* ..... 47 B9 39 48N 27 13 E
Kalkrand, *Namibia* ... 88 C2 24 1 S 17 35 E
Kallavesi, *Finland* .... 8 E22 62 58N 27 30 E
Källby, *Sweden* ..... 11 F7 58 30N 13 8 E
Kållered, *Sweden* .... 11 G6 57 32N 12 4 E
Kallimasiá, *Greece* ... 47 C8 38 18N 26 6 E
Kallinge, *Sweden* .... 11 H9 56 15N 15 18 E
Kallithéa, *Greece* .... 46 D5 37 55N 23 41 E
Kallmet, *Albania* .... 44 E3 41 51N 19 41 E
Kalloní, *Greece* ..... 47 B8 39 14N 26 12 E
Kallonís, Kólpos, *Greece* 47 B8 39 10N 26 10 E
Kallsjön, *Sweden* .... 8 E15 63 38N 13 0 E
Kalmar, *Sweden* .... 11 H10 56 40N 16 20 E
Kalmar län □, *Sweden* . 11 G10 57 25N 16 0 E
Kalmar sund, *Sweden* . 11 H10 56 40N 16 25 E
Kalmyk Republic = Kalmykia □, *Russia* . 35 G8 46 5N 46 1 E
Kalmykia □, *Russia* .. 35 G8 46 5N 46 1 E
Kalmykovo, *Kazakhstan* 52 E6 49 0N 51 47 E
Kalna, *India* .... 69 H13 23 13N 88 25 E
Kalnai, *India* .... 69 H10 22 46N 83 30 E
Kalocsa, *Hungary* .... 28 D4 46 32N 19 0 E
Kalofer, *Bulgaria* .... 45 D8 42 37N 24 59 E
Kalokhorio, *Cyprus* ... 49 E12 34 51N 33 2 E
Kaloko, *Dem. Rep. of the Congo* ..... 86 D2 6 47 S 25 48 E
Kalol, *Gujarat, India* .. 68 H5 23 15N 72 33 E
Kalol, *Gujarat, India* .. 68 H5 23 15N 72 33 E
Kalolímnos, *Greece* ... 47 D9 37 4N 27 5 E
Kalomo, *Zambia* ..... 87 F2 17 0 S 26 30 E
Kalonerón, *Greece* ... 46 D3 37 20N 21 38 E
Kalpi, *India* .... 69 F8 26 8N 79 47 E
Kaltern = Caldaro, *Italy* 22 A4 46 25N 11 14 E
Kaltungo, *Nigeria* .... 83 D7 9 48N 11 19 E
Kalu, *Pakistan* ...... 68 G2 25 5N 67 39 E
Kaluga, *Russia* ..... 32 E9 54 35N 36 10 E
Kalulushi, *Zambia* ... 87 E2 12 50 S 28 3 E
Kalundborg, *Denmark* . 11 J5 55 41N 11 5 E
Kalush, *Ukraine* ..... 33 H3 49 3N 24 23 E
Kalutara, *Sri Lanka* ... 66 R12 6 35N 80 0 E
Kalvarija, *Lithuania* ... 30 D10 54 24N 23 14 E
Kalyan, *India* ...... 66 K8 19 15N 73 9 E
Kalyazin, *Russia* .... 32 D9 57 15N 37 55 E
Kam, *Albania* ...... 44 D4 42 17N 20 18 E
Kam →, *Nigeria* .... 83 D7 8 15N 1 10 E
Kama, *Dem. Rep. of the Congo* ..... 86 C2 3 30 S 27 5 E
Kama →, *Russia* .... 6 D16 55 45N 52 0 E
Kamachumu, *Tanzania* . 54 E10 39 16N 141 53 E
Kamaishi, *Japan* .... 54 E10 39 16N 141 53 E
Kamalia, *Pakistan* ... 68 D5 30 44N 72 42 E
Kaman, *India* ...... 68 F6 27 39N 77 16 E
Kaman, *Turkey* ..... 72 C5 39 22N 33 44 E
Kamanjab, *Namibia* .. 88 B2 19 35 S 14 51 E
Kamapanda, *Zambia* .. 87 E1 12 5 S 24 0 E
Kamaran, *Yemen* .... 75 D3 15 21N 42 35 E
Kamativi, *Zimbabwe* .. 88 B4 18 20 S 27 6 E
Kamba, *Nigeria* ..... 83 C5 11 50N 3 45 E
Kambalda, *Australia* .. 93 F3 31 10 S 121 37 E
Kambar, *Pakistan* .... 68 F3 27 37N 68 1 E
Kambia, *S. Leone* 82 D2 9 3N 12 53W
Kambolé, *Togo* ...... 83 D5 8 43N 1 9 E
Kambolé, *Zambia* .... 87 D3 8 47 S 30 48 E
Kambos, *Cyprus* .... 49 D11 35 2N 32 44 E
Kambove, *Dem. Rep. of the Congo* ..... 87 E2 10 51 S 26 33 E
Kamchatka, Poluostrov, *Russia* .... 53 D16 57 0N 160 0 E
Kamchatka Pen. = Kamchatka, Poluostrov, *Russia* 53 D16 57 0N 160 0 E
Kamchiya →, *Bulgaria* 45 C11 43 4N 27 44 E
Kame Ruins, *Zimbabwe* 87 G2 20 7 S 28 25 E
Kamen, *Russia* ..... 52 D9 53 50N 81 30 E
Kamen-Rybolov, *Russia* 54 B6 44 46N 132 2 E
Kamenica, *Serbia & M.* 44 C6 43 27N 22 27 E
Kamenica, *Serbia & M.* 44 B3 44 25N 19 45 E
Kamenice nad Lipou, *Czech Rep.* ...... 26 B8 49 18N 15 2 E

Kamenjak, Rt, *Croatia* . 41 D10 44 47N 13 55 E
Kamenka = Kaminka, *Ukraine* .... 33 H7 49 3N 32 6 E
Kamenka, *Kazakhstan* . 34 E10 51 7N 50 19 E
Kamenka, *Penza, Russia* 34 D6 53 10N 44 5 E
Kamenka, *Voronezh, Russia* .... 33 G10 50 47N 39 20 E
Kamenka Bugskaya = Kamyanka-Buzka, *Ukraine* .... 33 G3 50 8N 24 16 E
Kamenka Dneprovskaya = Kamyanka-Dniprovska, *Ukraine* 33 J8 47 29N 34 28 E
Kamennomostskiy, *Russia* .... 35 H5 44 18N 40 13 E
Kameno, *Bulgaria* .... 45 D11 42 34N 27 18 E
Kamenolomni, *Russia* . 35 G5 47 40N 40 14 E
Kamensk-Shakhtinskiy, *Russia* .... 35 F5 48 23N 40 20 E
Kamensk Uralskiy, *Russia* .... 52 D7 56 25N 62 2 E
Kamenskiy, *Russia* ... 34 E7 50 48N 45 25 E
Kamenskoye, *Russia* .. 53 C17 62 45N 165 30 E
Kamenyak, *Bulgaria* .. 45 C10 43 24N 26 57 E
Kamenz, *Germany* .... 24 D10 51 15N 14 5 E
Kameoka, *Japan* .... 55 G7 35 0N 135 35 E
Kamiah, *U.S.A.* 108 C5 46 14N 116 2W
Kamień Krajeński, *Poland* .... 30 E4 53 32N 17 32 E
Kamień Pomorski, *Poland* .... 30 E1 53 57N 14 43 E
Kamienna →, *Poland* . 30 G8 51 6N 21 47 E
Kamienna Góra, *Poland* 31 H3 50 47N 16 2 E
Kamieńsk, *Poland* ... 31 G6 51 12N 19 29 E
Kamieskroon, *S. Africa* 88 E2 30 9 S 17 56 E
Kamilukuak L., *Canada* 103 A8 62 22N 101 40W
Kamin-Kashyrskyy, *Ukraine* .... 33 G3 51 39N 24 56 E
Kamina, *Dem. Rep. of the Congo* ..... 87 D2 8 45 S 25 0 E
Kaminak L., *Canada* .. 103 A10 62 10N 95 0W
Kaministiquia, *Canada* 104 C1 48 32N 89 35W
Kaminka, *Ukraine* .... 33 H7 49 3N 32 6 E
Kaminoyama, *Japan* .. 54 E10 38 9N 140 17 E
Kamiros, *Greece* .... 49 C9 36 20N 27 56 E
Kamituga, *Dem. Rep. of the Congo* ..... 86 C2 3 2 S 28 10 E
Kamla →, *India* ..... 69 G12 25 35N 86 36 E
Kamloops, *Canada* ... 102 C4 50 40N 120 20W
Kamnik, *Slovenia* .... 41 B11 46 14N 14 37 E
Kamo, *Armenia* ..... 35 K7 40 21N 45 7 E
Kamo, *Japan* .... 54 F9 37 39N 139 3 E
Kamoke, *Pakistan* ... 68 C6 32 4N 74 4 E
Kamp →, *Austria* .... 26 C8 48 23N 15 42 E
Kampala, *Uganda* .... 86 B3 0 20N 32 30 E
Kampar, *Malaysia* ... 65 K3 4 18N 101 9 E
Kampar →, *Indonesia* 62 D2 0 30N 103 8 E
Kampen, *Neths.* ..... 17 B5 52 33N 5 53 E
Kampene, *Dem. Rep. of the Congo* ..... 84 E5 3 36 S 26 40 E
Kamphaeng Phet, *Thailand* .... 64 D2 16 28N 99 30 E
Kampinoski △, *Poland* 31 F7 52 21N 20 40 E
Kampolombo, L., *Zambia* .... 87 E2 11 37 S 29 42 E
Kampong Chhnang, *Cambodia* ...... 65 F5 12 20N 104 35 E
Kampong Pengerang, *Malaysia* ...... 65 d 1 22N 104 7 E
Kampong Punggai, *Malaysia* ...... 65 d 1 27N 104 18 E
Kampong Saom, *Cambodia* ...... 65 G4 10 38N 103 30 E
Kampong Saom, Chaak, *Cambodia* ...... 65 G4 10 50N 103 32 E
Kampong Tanjong Langsat, *Malaysia* . 65 d 1 28N 104 1 E
Kampong Telok Ramunia, *Malaysia* . 65 d 1 22N 104 15 E
Kampong To, *Thailand* 65 J3 6 3N 101 13 E
Kampot, *Cambodia* ... 65 G5 10 36N 104 10 E
Kampti, *Burkina Faso* . 82 C4 10 7N 3 25W
Kampuchea = Cambodia ■, *Asia* .. 64 F5 12 15N 105 0 E
Kampung Air Putih, *Malaysia* ...... 65 K4 4 15N 103 10 E
Kampung Jerangau, *Malaysia* ...... 65 K4 4 50N 103 10 E
Kampung Raja, *Malaysia* ...... 65 K4 5 45N 102 35 E
Kampungbaru = Tolitoli, *Indonesia* ...... 63 D6 1 5N 120 50 E
Kamrau, Te uk, *Indonesia* ...... 63 E8 3 30 S 133 36 E
Kamsack, *Canada* 103 C8 51 34N 101 54W
Kamsai, *Guinea* 82 C2 10 40N 14 36W
Kamskoye Ustye, *Russia* 34 C9 55 10N 49 20 E
Kamuchawie L., *Canada* 103 B8 56 18N 101 59W
Kamui-Misaki, *Japan* .. 54 C10 43 20N 140 21 E
Kamyanets-Podilskyy, *Ukraine* .... 29 B11 48 45N 26 40 E
Kamyanka-Buzka, *Ukraine* .... 33 G3 50 8N 24 16 E
Kamyanka-Dniprovska, *Ukraine* .... 33 J8 47 29N 34 28 E
Kamyanyets, *Belarus* .. 31 F10 52 23N 23 49 E
Kamyanyuk →, *Belarus* 31 F10 52 23N 23 49 E
Kāmyārān, *Iran* ..... 70 C5 34 47N 46 56 E
Kamyshin, *Russia* ... 34 E8 50 10N 45 24 E
Kamyzyak, *Russia* ... 35 G9 46 4N 48 10 E
Kan, *Sudan* .... 81 F3 9 1N 31 47 E
Kanaaupscow, *Canada* 101 C12 53 39N 77 9W
Kanaaupscow →, *Canada* 104 B4 54 2N 76 30W
Kanab, *U.S.A.* 109 H7 37 3N 112 32W
Kanab →, *U.S.A.* 109 H7 36 24N 112 38W
Kanagi, *Japan* ...... 54 D10 40 54N 140 27 E
Kanairiktok →, *Canada* 105 A7 55 2N 60 18W
Kanália, *Greece* ..... 46 B4 39 30N 22 53 E
Kananga, *Dem. Rep. of the Congo* ..... 84 F4 5 55 S 22 18 E
Kanash, *Russia* ..... 34 C8 55 30N 47 32 E
Kanaskat, *U.S.A.* 110 C5 47 19N 121 54W
Kanastraíon Ákra = Palioúrion, Ákra, *Greece* .... 44 F7 39 57N 23 45 E
Kanawha →, *U.S.A.* .. 114 F4 38 50N 82 9W
Kanazawa, *Japan* .... 55 F8 36 30N 136 38 E
Kanchanaburi, *Thailand* 64 E2 14 2N 99 31 E
Kanchenjunga, *Nepal* . 69 F13 27 50N 88 10 E
Kanchipuram, *India* .. 66 N11 12 52N 79 45 E
Kańczuga, *Poland* ... 31 J9 49 59N 22 25 E
Kandaghat, *India* .... 68 D7 30 59N 77 7 E
Kandahar = Qandahār, *Afghan.* ...... 66 D4 31 32N 65 43 E
Kandalaksha, *Russia* .. 52 C4 67 9N 32 30 E

Kandangan, *Indonesia* . 62 E5 2 50 S 115 20 E
Kandanghaur, *Indonesia* 63 G13 6 21 S 108 6 E
Kandanos, *Greece* ... 49 D5 35 19N 23 44 E
Kandava, *Latvia* ..... 30 A9 57 2N 22 46 E
Kandavu = Kadavu, *Fiji* 91 D8 19 0 S 178 15 E
Kandhíla, *Greece* .... 46 D4 37 46N 22 22 E
Kandhkot, *Pakistan* .. 68 E3 28 16N 69 8 E
Kandhla, *India* ...... 68 E7 29 18N 77 19 E
Kandi, *Benin* .... 83 C5 11 7N 2 55 E
Kandi, *India* .... 69 H13 23 58N 88 5 E
Kandiaro, *Pakistan* ... 68 F3 27 4N 68 13 E
Kandıra, *Turkey* ..... 72 B4 41 4N 30 9 E
Kandla, *India* ...... 68 H4 23 0N 70 10 E
Kandreho, *Madag.* ... 89 B8 17 29 S 46 6 E
Kandy, *Sri Lanka* .... 66 R12 7 18N 80 43 E
Kane, *U.S.A.* 116 E6 41 40N 78 49W
Kane Basin, *Greenland* 4 B4 79 1N 70 0W
Kanel, *Senegal* 82 B2 15 30N 13 18W
Kaneohe, *U.S.A.* 106 H16 21 25N 157 48W
Kanevskaya, *Russia* .. 35 G4 46 3N 38 57 E
Kanfanar, *Croatia* .... 41 C10 45 7N 13 50 E
Kang, *Botswana* ..... 88 C3 23 41 S 22 50 E
Kang Krung △, *Thailand* 65 H2 9 30N 98 50 E
Kangaba, *Mali* 82 C3 11 56N 8 25W
Kangal, *Turkey* ..... 72 C7 39 14N 37 23 E
Kangān, *Fārs, Iran* ... 71 E7 27 50N 52 3 E
Kangān, *Hormozgān, Iran* .... 71 E8 25 48N 57 28 E
Kangar, *Malaysia* .... 65 J3 6 27N 100 12 E
Kangaré, *Mali* 82 C3 11 36N 8 4W
Kangaroo I., *Australia* . 95 F2 35 45 S 137 0 E
Kangaroo Mts., *Australia* .... 94 C3 23 29 S 141 51 E
Kangasala, *Finland* ... 9 F21 61 28N 24 4 E
Kangāvar, *Iran* ..... 71 C6 34 40N 48 0 E
Kangding, *China* ..... 58 B3 30 1N 101 57 E
Kangdong, *N. Korea* .. 57 E14 39 9N 126 5 E
Kangean, Kepulauan, *Indonesia* ...... 62 F5 6 55 S 115 23 E
Kangean Is. = Kangean, Kepulauan, *Indonesia* 62 F5 6 55 S 115 23 E
Kangen →, *Sudan* .... 81 F3 6 47N 33 9 E
Kanggye, *N. Korea* ... 57 D14 41 0N 126 35 E
Kanggyŏng, *S. Korea* . 57 F14 36 10N 127 0 E
Kanghwa, *S. Korea* .. 57 F14 37 45N 126 30 E
Kangikajik, *Greenland* . 4 B6 70 7N 22 0W
Kangiqliniq = Rankin Inlet, *Canada* 100 B10 62 30N 93 0W
Kangiqsualujjuaq, *Canada* 101 C13 58 30N 65 59W
Kangiqsujuaq, *Canada* 101 B12 61 30N 72 0W
Kangiqtugaapik = Clyde River, *Canada* ... 101 A13 70 30N 68 30W
Kangirsuk, *Canada* ... 101 B13 60 0N 70 0W
Kangkar Chemaran, *Malaysia* ...... 65 d 1 34N 104 12 E
Kangkar Sungai Tiram, *Malaysia* ...... 65 d 1 35N 103 55 E
Kangkar Teberau, *Malaysia* ...... 65 d 1 32N 103 51 E
Kangnŭng, *S. Korea* .. 57 F15 37 45N 128 54 E
Kangping, *China* .... 57 C12 42 43N 123 18 E
Kangra, *India* ...... 68 C7 32 6N 76 16 E
Kangrinboqê Feng, *China* .... 69 D9 31 0N 81 25 E
Kangto, *India* ...... 67 F18 27 50N 92 35 E
Kanhar →, *India* .... 69 G10 24 28N 83 8 E
Kani, *Ivory C.* 82 D3 8 29N 6 36W
Kaniama, *Dem. Rep. of the Congo* ..... 86 D1 7 30 S 24 12 E
Kaniapiskau = Caniapiscau →, *Canada* 105 A6 56 40N 69 30W
Kaniapiskau, L. = Caniapiscau, L. de, *Canada* 105 B6 54 10N 69 55W
Kanin, Poluostrov, *Russia* .... 52 C5 68 0N 45 0 E
Kanin Nos, Mys, *Russia* 52 C5 68 39N 43 32 E
Kanin Pen. = Kanin, Poluostrov, *Russia* . 52 C5 68 0N 45 0 E
Kaninë, *Albania* ..... 44 F3 40 23N 19 30 E
Kaniva, *Australia* .... 95 F3 36 22 S 141 18 E
Kanjiža, *Serbia & M.* .. 28 D5 46 3N 20 4 E
Kanjut Sar, *Pakistan* .. 69 A6 36 7N 75 25 E
Kankaanpää, *Finland* .. 9 F20 61 44N 22 50 E
Kankakee, *U.S.A.* 114 E2 41 7N 87 52W
Kankakee →, *U.S.A.* .. 114 E1 41 23N 88 15W
Kankan, *Guinea* 82 C3 10 23N 9 15W
Kankendy = Xankändi, *Azerbaijan* ...... 70 B5 39 52N 46 49 E
Kanker, *India* ...... 67 J12 20 10N 81 40 E
Kankossa, *Mauritania* . 82 B2 15 54N 11 31W
Kankroli, *India* ...... 68 G5 25 4N 73 53 E
Kannapolis, *U.S.A.* ... 115 H5 35 30N 80 37W
Kannauj, *India* ...... 69 F8 27 3N 79 56 E
Kannod, *India* ...... 66 H10 22 45N 76 40 E
Kano, *Nigeria* ...... 83 C6 12 2N 8 30 E
Kano □, *Nigeria* ..... 83 C6 11 30N 8 30 E
Kan'onji, *Japan* ..... 55 G6 34 7N 133 39 E
Kanoroba, *Ivory C.* ... 82 D3 9 7N 6 8W
Kanowit, *Malaysia* ... 62 D4 2 14N 112 20 E
Kanoya, *Japan* ..... 55 J5 31 25N 130 50 E
Kanpetlet, *Burma* ... 67 J18 21 10N 93 59 E
Kanpur, *India* ...... 69 F9 26 28N 80 20 E
Kansas □, *U.S.A.* 112 F6 38 30N 99 0W
Kansas →, *U.S.A.* 112 F7 39 7N 94 37W
Kansas City, *Kans., U.S.A.* 112 F7 39 7N 94 38W
Kansas City, *Mo., U.S.A.* 112 F7 39 6N 94 35W
Kansenia, *Dem. Rep. of the Congo* ..... 87 E2 10 20 S 26 0 E
Kansk, *Russia* ...... 53 D10 56 20N 95 37 E
Kansŏng, *S. Korea* ... 57 E15 38 24N 128 30 E
Kansu = Gansu □, *China* .... 56 G3 36 0N 104 0 E
Kantaphor, *India* .... 68 H7 22 35N 76 34 E
Kantang, *Thailand* ... 65 J2 7 25N 99 31 E
Kantemirovka, *Russia* . 33 H10 49 43N 39 55 E
Kantharalak, *Thailand* . 64 E5 14 39N 104 39 E
Kantli →, *India* ..... 68 E6 28 20N 75 30 E
Kanturk, *Ireland* 12 D3 52 11N 8 54W
Kanuma, *Japan* ..... 55 F9 36 34N 139 42 E
Kanus, *Namibia* ..... 88 D2 27 50 S 18 39 E
Kanye, *Botswana* .... 88 C4 24 55 S 25 28 E
Kanzenze, *Dem. Rep. of the Congo* ..... 87 E2 10 30 S 25 12 E
Kanzi, Ras, *Tanzania* .. 86 D4 7 1 S 39 33 E
Kao Phara, *Thailand* .. 65 a 8 3N 98 22 E
Kaohsiung, *Taiwan* ... 59 F13 22 35N 120 16 E
Kaokoveld, *Namibia* .. 88 B1 19 15 S 14 30 E
Kaolack, *Senegal* 82 C1 14 5N 16 8W

Kaoshan, *China* ..... 57 B13 44 38N 124 50 E
Kapaa, *U.S.A.* 106 G15 22 5N 159 19W
Kapadvanj, *India* .... 68 H5 23 5N 73 0 E
Kapaklı, *Turkey* ..... 45 E11 41 19N 27 59 E
Kapan, *Armenia* ..... 70 B5 39 18N 46 27 E
Kapanga, *Dem. Rep. of the Congo* ..... 84 F4 8 30 S 22 40 E
Kapchagai = Qapshaghay, *Kazakhstan* ...... 52 E8 43 51N 77 14 E
Kapela = Velika Kapela, *Croatia* ...... 41 C12 45 10N 15 5 E
Kapéllo, Ákra, *Greece* . 46 E5 36 9N 23 3 E
Kapema, *Dem. Rep. of the Congo* ..... 87 E2 10 45 S 28 22 E
Kapfenberg, *Austria* .. 26 D8 47 26N 15 18 E
Kapı Dağı, *Turkey* ... 45 F11 40 28N 27 52 E
Kapiri Mposhi, *Zambia* 87 E2 13 59 S 28 43 E
Kāpīsā □, *Afghan.* ... 66 B6 35 0N 69 20 E
Kapiskau →, *Canada* . 104 B3 52 47N 81 55W
Kapit, *Malaysia* ..... 62 D4 2 0N 112 55 E
Kapiti I., *N.Z.* ...... 91 J5 40 50 S 174 56 E
Kaplan, *U.S.A.* 113 K8 30 0N 92 17W
Kaplice, *Czech Rep.* .. 26 C7 48 42N 14 30 E
Kapoe, *Thailand* .... 65 H2 9 34N 98 32 E
Kapoeta, *Sudan* ..... 81 G3 4 50N 33 35 E
Kápolnásnyék, *Hungary* 28 C3 47 16N 18 41 E
Kapos →, *Hungary* ... 28 D3 46 44N 18 30 E
Kaposvár, *Hungary* ... 28 D2 46 25N 17 47 E
Kapowsin, *U.S.A.* 110 D4 46 59N 122 13W
Kappeln, *Germany* ... 24 A5 54 40N 9 55 E
Kappelshamn, *Sweden* 11 G12 57 52N 18 47 E
Kapps, *Namibia* ..... 88 C2 22 32 S 17 18 E
Kaprije, *Croatia* ..... 41 E12 43 42N 15 43 E
Kapsan, *N. Korea* .... 57 D15 41 4N 128 19 E
Kapsukas = Marijampolė, *Lithuania* ...... 9 J20 54 33N 23 19 E
Kaptai L., *Bangla.* .... 67 H18 22 40N 92 20 E
Kapuas →, *Indonesia* . 62 E3 0 25 S 109 20 E
Kapuas Hulu, Pegunungan, *Malaysia* 62 D4 1 30N 113 30 E
Kapuas Hulu Ra. = Kapuas Hulu, Pegunungan, *Malaysia* 62 D4 1 30N 113 30 E
Kapulo, *Dem. Rep. of the Congo* ..... 87 D2 8 18 S 29 15 E
Kapunda, *Australia* ... 95 E2 34 20 S 138 56 E
Kapuni, *N.Z.* .... 91 H5 39 29 S 174 8 E
Kapurthala, *India* .... 68 D6 31 23N 75 25 E
Kapuskasing, *Canada* . 104 C3 49 25N 82 30W
Kapuskasing →, *Canada* 104 C3 49 49N 82 0W
Kaputar, *Australia* ... 95 E5 30 15 S 150 10 E
Kaputir, *Kenya* ..... 86 B4 2 5N 35 28 E
Kapuvár, *Hungary* ... 28 C2 47 36N 17 1 E
Kara, *Russia* .... 52 C7 69 10N 65 0 E
Kara, W. →, *Si. Arabia* 80 C5 20 45N 41 42 E
Kara Ada, *Turkey* .... 47 E9 36 58N 27 28 E
Kara Bogaz Gol, Zaliv = Garabogazköl Aylagy, *Turkmenistan* ...... 52 E6 41 0N 53 30 E
Kara Burun, *Turkey* .. 47 E9 36 32N 27 58 E
Kara Kalpak Republic = Qoraqalpoghiston □, *Uzbekistan* ...... 52 E6 43 0N 58 0 E
Kara Kum, *Turkmenistan* 52 F6 39 30N 60 0 E
Kara Sea, *Russia* .... 52 B7 75 0N 70 0 E
Karaadilli, *Turkey* .... 47 C12 38 18N 30 37 E
Karabiğa, *Turkey* .... 45 F11 40 23N 27 17 E
Karabük, *Turkey* .... 72 B5 41 12N 32 37 E
Karaburun, *Albania* .. 44 F3 40 25N 19 20 E
Karaburun, *Turkey* ... 47 C8 38 41N 26 28 E
Karabutak = Qarabutaq, *Kazakhstan* ...... 52 E7 49 59N 60 14 E
Karacabey, *Turkey* ... 45 F12 40 12N 28 21 E
Karacakılavuz, *Turkey* 45 E11 41 8N 27 21 E
Karaca, *Turkey* ..... 45 E11 41 24N 28 22 E
Karacasu, *Turkey* .... 47 D10 37 43N 28 35 E
Karachala = Qaraçala, *Azerbaijan* ...... 35 L9 39 45N 48 53 E
Karachayevsk, *Russia* . 35 J5 43 50N 41 55 E
Karachev, *Russia* .... 33 F8 53 10N 35 5 E
Karachey-Cherkessia □, *Russia* .... 35 J5 43 40N 41 30 E
Karachi, *Pakistan* .... 68 G2 24 53N 67 0 E
Karad, *India* .... 66 L9 17 15N 74 10 E
Karadirek, *Turkey* .... 47 C12 38 34N 30 11 E
Karaga, *Ghana* 83 D4 9 58N 0 28W
Karaganda = Qaraghandy, *Kazakhstan* ...... 52 E8 49 50N 73 10 E
Karagayly = Qaraghayly, *Kazakhstan* ...... 52 E8 49 26N 76 0 E
Karaginskiy, Ostrov, *Russia* .... 53 D17 58 45N 164 0 E
Karagola Road, *India* . 69 G12 25 29N 87 23 E
Karahallı, *Turkey* .... 47 C11 38 21N 29 33 E
Karaikal, *India* ...... 66 P11 10 59N 79 50 E
Karaikkudi, *India* .... 66 P11 10 0N 78 45 E
Karaisali, *Turkey* .... 72 D6 37 16N 35 2 E
Karaj, *Iran* .... 71 C6 35 48N 51 0 E
Karak, *Malaysia* ..... 65 L4 3 25N 102 2 E
Karakalpakstan = Qoraqalpoghiston □, *Uzbekistan* ...... 52 E6 43 0N 58 0 E
Karakelong, *Indonesia* 63 D7 4 35N 126 50 E
Karakitang, *Indonesia* 63 D7 3 14N 125 28 E
Karakoçan, *Turkey* ... 73 C9 38 57N 40 2 E
Karakol, *Kyrgyzstan* .. 52 E8 42 30N 78 20 E
Karakoram Pass, *Asia* 69 B7 35 33N 77 50 E
Karakoram Ra., *Pakistan* .... 69 B7 35 30N 77 0 E
Karakurt, *Turkey* .... 73 B10 40 10N 42 37 E
Karakuwisa, *Namibia* . 88 B2 18 56 S 19 40 E
Karalon, *Russia* ..... 53 D12 57 5N 115 50 E
Karaman, *Jordan* ... 74 D4 31 57N 35 14 E
Karaman, *Balıkesir, Turkey* .... 47 B9 39 39N 28 0 E
Karaman, *Konya, Turkey* .... 70 B2 37 14N 33 13 E
Karamanlı, *Turkey* ... 47 E11 37 21N 29 47 E
Karamay, *China* ..... 60 B3 45 30N 84 58 E
Karambu, *Indonesia* .. 62 E5 3 53 S 116 6 E
Karamea Bight, *N.Z.* .. 91 J3 41 22 S 171 40 E
Karamnasa →, *India* .. 69 G10 25 31N 83 52 E
Karamürsel, *Turkey* .. 45 F13 40 41N 29 36 E
Karand, *Iran* .... 70 C5 34 16N 46 15 E
Karanganyar, *Indonesia* 63 G13 7 38 S 109 37 E
Karangasem, *Indonesia* 63 J18 8 27 S 115 37 E
Karanja, *India* ...... 66 J10 20 29N 77 31 E
Karanjia, *India* ...... 69 J11 21 47N 85 58 E
Karankasso, *Burkina Faso* 82 C4 10 50N 3 53W

Karaova, *Turkey* ..... 47 D9 37 5N 27 40 E
Karapınar, *Turkey* .... 72 D5 37 43N 33 6 E
Karasburg, *Namibia* .. 88 D2 28 0 S 18 44 E
Karasino, *Russia* .... 52 C9 66 50N 86 50 E
Karasjok, *Norway* .... 8 B21 69 27N 25 30 E
Karasu, *Turkey* ..... 72 B4 41 4N 30 46 E
Karasu →, *Turkey* ... 47 E12 36 38N 30 10 E
Karasuk, *Russia* ..... 52 D8 53 44N 78 2 E
Karasuyama, *Japan* .. 55 F9 36 39N 140 9 E
Karataş, *Adana, Turkey* 72 D6 36 36N 35 21 E
Karataş, *Manisa, Turkey* 47 C10 38 35N 28 16 E
Karataş Burnu, *Turkey* 72 D6 36 31N 35 24 E
Karatau, Khrebet = Qarataū, *Kazakhstan* 52 E7 43 30N 69 30 E
Karatoprak, *Turkey* .. 47 D9 37 2N 27 18 E
Karaul, *Russia* ...... 52 B9 70 6N 82 15 E
Karauli, *India* ...... 68 F7 26 30N 77 4 E
Karavastasë, L. e, *Albania* .... 44 F3 40 55N 19 30 E
Karávi, *Greece* ..... 46 E5 36 49N 23 37 E
Karavostasi, *Cyprus* .. 49 D11 35 8N 32 50 E
Karawang, *Indonesia* . 63 G12 6 30 S 107 15 E
Karawanken, *Europe* .. 26 C7 46 30N 14 40 E
Karayazı, *Turkey* .... 73 C10 39 41N 42 9 E
Karazhal, *Kazakhstan* . 52 E8 48 2N 70 49 E
Karbalā', *Iraq* ...... 70 C5 32 36N 44 3 E
Kårböle, *Sweden* .... 10 C9 61 59N 15 22 E
Karcag, *Hungary* .... 28 C5 47 19N 20 57 E
Karcha →, *Pakistan* .. 69 B7 34 45N 76 10 E
Karchana, *India* ..... 69 G9 25 17N 81 56 E
Karczew, *Poland* .... 31 F8 52 5N 21 15 E
Kardam, *Bulgaria* .... 45 C12 43 45N 28 6 E
Kardeljovo = Ploče, *Croatia* .... 41 E14 43 4N 17 26 E
Kardhámila, *Greece* .. 47 C8 38 35N 26 5 E
Kardhamílli, *Greece* .. 46 E4 36 53N 22 13 E
Kardhítsa, *Greece* ... 46 B3 39 23N 21 54 E
Kardhítsa □, *Greece* .. 46 B3 39 15N 21 50 E
Kärdla, *Estonia* ..... 9 G20 59 0N 22 45 E
Kareeberge, *S. Africa* . 88 E3 30 59 S 21 50 E
Kareha →, *India* .... 69 G12 25 44N 86 21 E
Kareima, *Sudan* ..... 80 D3 18 30N 31 49 E
Karelia □, *Russia* .... 52 C4 65 30N 32 30 E
Karelian Republic = Karelia □, *Russia* .. 52 C4 65 30N 32 30 E
Karera, *India* .... 68 G8 25 32N 78 9 E
Kārevāndar, *Iran* .... 71 E9 27 53N 60 44 E
Kargasok, *Russia* .... 52 D9 59 3N 80 53 E
Kargat, *Russia* ...... 52 D9 55 10N 80 15 E
Kargı, *Turkey* ...... 72 B6 41 11N 34 30 E
Kargil, *India* .... 69 B7 34 32N 76 12 E
Kargopol, *Russia* .... 52 B10 61 30N 38 58 E
Kargowa, *Poland* .... 31 F2 52 5N 15 51 E
Karguéri, *Niger* ..... 83 C7 13 27N 10 30 E
Karhal, *India* ...... 69 F8 27 1N 78 57 E
Karia ba Mohammed, *Morocco* 78 B4 34 22N 5 20W
Kariá, *Greece* ...... 46 C2 38 45N 20 39 E
Kariaí, *Greece* ...... 45 F8 40 14N 24 19 E
Kariān, *Iran* .... 71 E8 26 57N 57 14 E
Karianga, *Madag.* .... 89 C8 22 25 S 47 22 E
Kariba, *Zimbabwe* ... 87 F2 16 28 S 28 50 E
Kariba, L., *Zimbabwe* . 87 F2 16 40 S 28 25 E
Kariba Dam, *Zimbabwe* 87 F2 16 30 S 28 35 E
Kariba Gorge, *Zambia* 87 F2 16 30 S 28 50 E
Karibib, *Namibia* .... 88 C2 22 0 S 15 56 E
Karijini △, *Australia* ... 92 D2 23 8 S 118 15 E
Karimata, Kepulauan, *Indonesia* ...... 62 E3 1 25 S 109 0 E
Karimata, Selat, *Indonesia* ...... 62 E3 2 0 S 108 40 E
Karimata Is. = Karimata, Kepulauan, *Indonesia* 62 E3 1 25 S 109 0 E
Karimnagar, *India* ... 66 K11 18 26N 79 10 E
Karimun Kecil, Pulau, *Indonesia* ...... 65 d 1 8N 103 22 E
Karimunjawa, Kepulauan, *Indonesia* 62 F4 5 50 S 110 30 E
Karin, *Somali Rep.* ... 75 E4 10 50N 45 52 E
Káristos, *Greece* .... 46 C6 38 1N 24 29 E
Karīt, *Iran* .... 71 C8 33 29N 56 55 E
Kariya, *Japan* ...... 55 G8 34 58N 137 1 E
Kariyangwe, *Zimbabwe* 89 B4 17 58 S 27 38 E
Karjala, *Finland* ..... 32 A5 62 0N 30 25 E
Karkaralinsk = Qarqaraly, *Kazakhstan* ...... 52 E8 49 26N 75 30 E
Karkheh →, *Iran* .... 70 D5 31 2N 47 29 E
Karkinitska Zatoka, *Ukraine* .... 33 K7 45 56N 33 0 E
Karkinitskiy Zaliv = Karkinitska Zatoka, *Ukraine* .... 33 K7 45 56N 33 0 E
Karkuk = Kirkūk, *Iraq* 70 C5 35 30N 44 21 E
Karkur Tohl, *Egypt* ... 80 C2 22 5N 25 5 E
Karl Liebknecht, *Russia* 33 G8 51 40N 35 35 E
Karleby = Kokkola, *Finland* .... 8 E20 63 50N 23 8 E
Karlholmsbruk, *Sweden* 10 D11 60 31N 17 37 E
Karlino, *Poland* ..... 30 D2 54 3N 15 53 E
Karlivka, *Ukraine* .... 33 H8 49 29N 35 8 E
Karlobag, *Croatia* .... 41 D12 44 32N 15 5 E
Karlovac, *Croatia* .... 41 C12 45 31N 15 36 E
Karlovarský □, *Czech Rep.* ...... 26 A5 50 10N 12 50 E
Karlovka = Karlivka, *Ukraine* .... 33 H8 49 29N 35 8 E
Karlovo, *Bulgaria* .... 45 D8 42 38N 24 47 E
Karlovy Vary, *Czech Rep.* ...... 26 A5 50 13N 12 51 E
Karlsbad = Karlovy Vary, *Czech Rep.* .. 26 A5 50 13N 12 51 E
Karlsborg, *Sweden* ... 11 F8 58 33N 14 33 E
Karlshamn, *Sweden* .. 11 H8 56 10N 14 51 E
Karlskoga, *Sweden* ... 10 E8 59 28N 14 33 E
Karlskrona, *Sweden* .. 11 H9 56 10N 15 35 E
Karlsruhe, *Germany* .. 25 F4 49 0N 8 23 E
Karlstad, *Sweden* .... 10 E7 59 23N 13 30 E
Karlstad, *U.S.A.* 112 A6 48 35N 96 31W
Karlstadt, *Germany* .. 25 F5 49 57N 9 47 E
Karma, *Niger* ...... 83 C5 13 50N 1 34 E
Karmćla, *Lithuania* ... 30 D11 54 58N 24 4 E
Karmi'el, *Israel* ..... 74 C4 32 55N 35 18 E
Karnak, *Egypt* ...... 80 B3 25 43N 32 39 E
Karnal, *India* .... 68 E7 29 42N 77 2 E
Karnali →, *Nepal* .... 69 E9 28 45N 81 16 E
Karnaphuli Res. = Kaptai L., *Bangla.* .. 67 H18 22 40N 92 20 E
Karnaprayag, *India* .. 69 D8 30 16N 79 15 E
Karnataka □, *India* ... 66 N10 13 15N 77 0 E
Karnes City, *U.S.A.* .. 113 L6 28 53N 97 54W
Karnische Alpen, *Europe* .... 26 E6 46 36N 13 0 E
Karnobat, *Bulgaria* ... 45 D10 42 39N 26 59 E
Kärnten □, *Austria* ... 26 E6 46 52N 13 30 E
Karo, *Mali* 82 C4 12 16N 3 18W
Karoi, *Zimbabwe* .... 87 F2 16 48 S 29 45 E
Karon, Ao, *Thailand* .. 65 a 7 51N 98 17 E

Karonga, *Malawi* ..... **87 D3** 9 57 S 33 55 E
Karoo △, *S. Africa* .... **88 E3** 32 18 S 22 27 E
Karoonda, *Australia* ... **95 F2** 35 1 S 139 59 E
Karor, *Pakistan* ...... **68 D4** 31 15N 70 59 E
Karora, *Sudan* .... **80 D4** 17 44N 38 15 E
Káros, *Greece* .... **47 E7** 36 54N 25 40 E
Karounga, *Mali* **82 B3** 15 20N 7 35W
Karousádhes, *Greece* ... **46 B1** 39 47N 19 45 E
Karpacz, *Poland* ..... **31 H2** 50 46N 15 45 E
Karpasia, *Cyprus* .... **49 D13** 35 32N 34 15 E
Kárpathos, *Greece* .... **47 F9** 35 37N 27 10 E
Kárpathos, Stenón,
  Greece .... **47 F9** 36 0N 27 30 E
Karpatsky △, *Ukraine* . **29 B9** 48 20N 24 35 E
Karpenísion, *Greece* ... **46 C3** 38 55N 21 40 E
Karpuz Burnu =
  Apostolos Andreas,
  C., *Cyprus* .... **49 D13** 35 42N 34 35 E
Karpuzlu, *Turkey* .... **47 D9** 37 33N 27 51 E
Karratha, *Australia* ... **92 D2** 20 53 S 116 40 E
Kars, *Turkey* .... **73 B10** 40 40N 43 5 E
Karsakpay, *Kazakhstan* . **52 E7** 47 55N 66 40 E
Karsha, *Kazakhstan* ... **34 F10** 49 45N 51 35 E
Karshi = Qarshi,
  Uzbekistan .... **52 F7** 38 53N 65 48 E
Karsiyang, *India* ..... **69 F13** 26 56N 88 18 E
Karsog, *India* .... **68 D7** 31 23N 77 12 E
Karst = Kras, *Croatia* . **41 C10** 45 35N 14 0 E
Kartal, *Turkey* ...... **45 F13** 40 53N 29 11 E
Kartál Óros, *Greece* ... **45 E9** 41 15N 25 13 E
Kartaly, *Russia* ...... **52 D7** 53 3N 60 40 E
Kartapur, *India* ...... **68 D6** 31 27N 75 32 E
Karthaus, *U.S.A.* **116 E6** 41 8N 78 9W
Kartuzy, *Poland* ..... **30 D5** 54 22N 18 10 E
Karufa, *Indonesia* .... **63 E8** 3 50 S 133 20 E
Karuma △, *Uganda* ... **86 B3** 2 5N 32 15 E
Karumba, *Australia* ... **94 B3** 17 31 S 140 50 E
Karumo, *Tanzania* .... **86 C3** 2 25 S 32 50 E
Karumwa, *Tanzania* ... **86 C3** 3 12 S 32 38 E
Kārūn →, *Iran* ...... **71 D6** 30 26N 48 10 E
Karungu, *Kenya* ..... **86 C3** 0 50 S 34 10 E
Karup, *Denmark* ..... **11 H3** 56 19N 9 10 E
Karviná, *Czech Rep.* .. **27 B11** 49 53N 18 31 E
Karwar, *India* .... **66 M9** 14 55N 74 13 E
Karwar, *India* .... **68 F8** 27 26N 78 4 E
Karwendel △, *Austria* . **26 D4** 47 25N 11 30 E
Karwi, *India* .... **69 G9** 25 12N 80 57 E
Kaş, *Turkey* .... **47 E11** 36 11N 29 37 E
Kasaba, *Turkey* ...... **47 E11** 36 18N 29 44 E
Kasache, *Malawi* .... **87 E3** 13 25 S 34 20 E
Kasai →, *Dem. Rep. of
  the Congo* .... **84 E3** 3 30 S 16 10 E
Kasai-Oriental □,
  *Dem. Rep. of
  the Congo* .... **86 D1** 5 0 S 24 30 E
Kasaji, *Dem. Rep. of
  the Congo* .... **87 E1** 10 25 S 23 27 E
Kasama, *Zambia* ..... **87 E3** 10 16 S 31 9 E
Kasan-dong, *N. Korea* . **57 D14** 41 18N 126 55 E
Kasane, *Namibia* ..... **88 B3** 17 34 S 24 50 E
Kasanga, *Tanzania* .... **87 D3** 8 30 S 31 10 E
Kasanka △, *Zambia* .. **87 E3** 11 34 S 30 15 E
Kasar, Ras, *Sudan* .... **80 D4** 18 2N 38 36 E
Kasba L., *Canada* **103 A8** 60 20N 102 10W
Kāseh Garān, *Iran* ... **70 C5** 34 5N 46 2 E
Kasempa, *Zambia* .... **87 E2** 13 30 S 25 44 E
Kasenga, *Dem. Rep. of
  the Congo* .... **87 E2** 10 20 S 28 45 E
Kasese, *Uganda* ...... **86 B3** 0 13N 30 3 E
Kasewa, *Zambia* ..... **87 E2** 14 28 S 28 53 E
Kasganj, *India* ...... **69 F8** 27 48N 78 42 E
Kashabowie, *Canada* .. **104 C1** 48 40N 90 26W
Kashaf, *Iran* .... **71 C9** 35 58N 61 7 E
Kāshān, *Iran* .... **71 C6** 34 5N 51 30 E
Kashechewan, *Canada* . **104 B3** 52 18N 81 37W
Kashgar = Kashi, *China* **60 C2** 39 30N 76 2 E
Kashi, *China* .... **60 C2** 39 30N 76 2 E
Kashimbo, *Dem. Rep. of
  the Congo* .... **87 E2** 11 12 S 26 19 E
Kashin, *Russia* ...... **32 D9** 57 20N 37 36 E
Kashipur, *India* ..... **69 E8** 29 15N 79 0 E
Kashira, *Russia* ..... **32 E10** 54 45N 38 10 E
Kashiwazaki, *Japan* ... **55 F9** 37 22N 138 33 E
Kashk-e Kohneh,
  Afghan. .... **66 B3** 34 55N 62 30 E
Kashkū'īyeh, *Iran* ... **71 D7** 30 31N 55 40 E
Kāshmar, *Iran* ...... **71 C8** 35 16N 58 26 E
Kashmir, *Asia* ...... **69 C7** 34 0N 76 0 E
Kashmor, *Pakistan* ... **68 E3** 28 28N 69 32 E
Kashpirovka, *Russia* .. **34 D9** 53 0N 48 50 E
Kashun Noerh = Gaxun
  Nur, *China* .... **60 B5** 42 22N 100 30 E
Kasiari, *India* ...... **69 H12** 22 8N 87 14 E
Kasimov, *Russia* ..... **34 C5** 54 55N 41 20 E
Kasinge, *Dem. Rep. of
  the Congo* .... **86 D2** 6 15 S 26 58 E
Kasiruta, *Indonesia* ... **63 E7** 0 25 S 127 12 E
Kaskaskia →, *U.S.A.* . **112 G10** 37 58N 89 57W
Kaskattama →, *Canada* **103 B10** 57 3N 90 4W
Kaskinen, *Finland* ... **9 E19** 62 22N 21 15 E
Kaskö = Kaskinen,
  Finland .... **9 E19** 62 22N 21 15 E
Kaslo, *Canada* **102 D5** 49 55N 116 55W
Kasmere L., *Canada* .. **103 B8** 59 34N 101 10W
Kasongo, *Dem. Rep. of
  the Congo* .... **86 C2** 4 30 S 26 33 E
Kasongo Lunda,
  *Dem. Rep. of
  the Congo* .... **84 F3** 6 35 S 16 49 E
Kásos, *Greece* .... **47 F8** 35 20N 26 55 E
Kásos, Stenón, *Greece* . **47 F8** 35 30N 26 30 E
Kaspi, *Georgia* ...... **35 K7** 41 59N 44 26 E
Kaspichan, *Bulgaria* .. **45 C11** 43 18N 27 11 E
Kaspiysk, *Russia* .... **35 J8** 42 52N 47 40 E
Kaspiysky, *Russia* ... **35 H8** 45 22N 47 23 E
Kassab ed Doleib, *Sudan* **81 F3** 13 30N 33 35 E
Kassaba, *Egypt* ..... **80 C2** 22 40N 29 55 E
Kassalâ, *Sudan* ..... **81 D4** 15 30N 36 0 E
Kassalâ □, *Sudan* .... **81 D4** 15 20N 36 26 E
Kassándra, *Greece* ... **44 F7** 40 0N 23 30 E
Kassándrinon, *Greece* . **44 F7** 40 1N 23 27 E
Kassel, *Germany* .... **24 D5** 51 18N 9 26 E
Kassínge, *Angola* .... **80 D3** 18 46N 31 51 E
Kassiópi, *Greece* .... **49 A3** 39 48N 19 53 E
Kasson, *U.S.A.* **112 C8** 44 2N 92 45W
Kastamonu, *Turkey* .. **72 B5** 41 25N 33 43 E
Kastav, *Croatia* ..... **41 C11** 45 22N 14 20 E
Kastélli, *Greece* ..... **49 D5** 35 29N 23 38 E
Kastéllion, *Greece* ... **49 D7** 35 12N 25 20 E
Kastellórizon = Megiste,
  Greece .... **47 E11** 36 8N 29 34 E
Kastéllos, *Greece* .... **47 E9** 36 16N 27 49 E
Kasterlee, *Belgium* ... **17 C5** 51 15N 4 59 E
Kastlösa, *Sweden* .... **11 H10** 56 26N 16 25 E
Kastóri, *Greece* ..... **46 D4** 37 10N 22 17 E

Kastoría, *Greece* ..... **44 F5** 40 30N 21 19 E
Kastoría □, *Greece* ... **44 F5** 40 30N 21 15 E
Kastorías, Límni, *Greece* **44 F5** 40 30N 21 20 E
Kastornoye, *Russia* ... **33 G10** 51 55N 38 2 E
Kastós Nísis, *Greece* .. **46 C2** 38 35N 20 55 E
Kastrosikiá, *Greece* ... **46 B2** 39 6N 20 38 E
Kastrup, København ✈
  (CPH), *Denmark* ... **11 J6** 55 37N 12 39 E
Kastsyukovichy, *Belarus* **32 F7** 53 20N 32 4 E
Kasulu, *Tanzania* .... **86 C3** 4 37 S 30 5 E
Kasumi, *Japan* ...... **55 G7** 35 38N 134 38 E
Kasumkent, *Russia* ... **35 K9** 41 47N 48 15 E
Kasungu, *Malawi* .... **87 E3** 13 0 S 33 29 E
Kasungu △, *Malawi* .. **87 E3** 12 53 S 33 9 E
Kasur, *Pakistan* ..... **68 D6** 31 5N 74 25 E
Kata Tjuta = Olga, Mt.,
  Australia .... **93 E5** 25 20 S 130 50 E
Kataba, *Zambia* ..... **87 F2** 16 5 S 25 10 E
Katagum, *Nigeria* .... **83 C7** 12 18N 10 21 E
Katahdin, Mt., *U.S.A.* **115 C11** 45 54N 68 56W
Katako Kombe,
  *Dem. Rep. of
  the Congo* .... **86 C1** 3 25 S 24 20 E
Katákolon, *Greece* ... **46 D3** 37 38N 21 19 E
Katale, *Tanzania* ..... **86 C3** 4 52 S 31 7 E
Katanda, Katanga,
  *Dem. Rep. of
  the Congo* .... **86 D1** 7 52 S 24 13 E
Katanda, Nord-Kivu,
  *Dem. Rep. of
  the Congo* .... **86 C2** 0 55 S 29 21 E
Katanga □, *Dem. Rep.
  of the Congo* ...... **86 D2** 8 0 S 25 0 E
Katangi, *India* ...... **66 J11** 21 56N 79 50 E
Katanning, *Australia* .. **93 F2** 33 40 S 117 33 E
Katastári, *Greece* .... **46 D2** 37 50N 20 45 E
Katavi △, *Tanzania* .. **86 D3** 6 51 S 31 3 E
Katavi Swamp, *Tanzania* **86 D3** 6 50 S 31 10 E
Kateríni, *Greece* ..... **44 F6** 40 18N 22 37 E
Katha, *Burma* .... **67 G20** 24 10N 96 30 E
Katherîna, Gebel, *Egypt* **70 D2** 28 30N 33 57 E
Katherine, *Australia* .. **92 B5** 14 27 S 132 20 E
Katherine Gorge,
  Australia .... **92 B5** 14 18 S 132 28 E
Kathi, *India* .... **68 J6** 21 47N 74 3 E
Kathiawar, *India* .... **68 H4** 22 20N 71 0 E
Kathikas, *Cyprus* .... **49 E11** 34 55N 32 25 E
Kathmandu =
  Katmandu, *Nepal* .. **69 F11** 27 45N 85 20 E
Kathua, *India* .... **68 C6** 32 23N 75 34 E
Kati, *Mali* **82 C3** 12 41N 8 4W
Katihar, *India* ...... **69 G12** 25 34N 87 36 E
Katima Mulilo, *Zambia* **88 B3** 17 28 S 24 13 E
Katimbira, *Malawi* ... **87 E3** 12 40 S 34 0 E
Katingan =
  Mendawai →,
  Indonesia .... **62 E4** 3 30 S 113 0 E
Katiola, *Ivory C.* **82 D3** 8 10N 5 10W
Katlabukh, Ozero,
  Ukraine .... **29 E14** 45 28N 29 0 E
Katlanovo, *Macedonia* . **44 E5** 41 52N 21 40 E
Katmandu, *Nepal* .... **69 F11** 27 45N 85 20 E
Katni, *India* .... **69 H9** 23 51N 80 24 E
Káto Akhaḯa, *Greece* .. **46 C3** 38 8N 21 33 E
Káto Khorió, *Greece* .. **49 D7** 35 3N 25 47 E
Káto Pyrgos, *Cyprus* .. **49 D11** 35 11N 32 41 E
Káto Stavros, *Greece* .. **44 F7** 40 39N 23 43 E
Katokhí, *Greece* ..... **46 C3** 38 26N 21 15 E
Katompe, *Dem. Rep. of
  the Congo* .... **86 D2** 6 2 S 26 23 E
Katong, *Singapore* .... **65 d** 1 18N 103 53 E
Katonga →, *Uganda* . **86 B3** 0 34N 31 50 E
Katoomba, *Australia* .. **95 E5** 33 41 S 150 19 E
Katoúna, *Greece* ..... **46 C3** 38 47N 21 7 E
Katowice, *Poland* .... **31 H6** 50 17N 19 5 E
Katranci Daği, *Turkey* . **47 D12** 37 27N 30 25 E
Katrine, L., *U.K.* **13 E4** 56 15N 4 30W
Katrineholm, *Sweden* .. **10 F10** 59 9N 16 12 E
Katsepe, *Madag.* ..... **89 B8** 15 45 S 46 15 E
Katsina, *Nigeria* ..... **83 C6** 13 0N 7 32 E
Katsina □, *Nigeria* ... **83 C6** 12 50N 7 32 E
Katsina Ala, *Nigeria* .. **83 D6** 7 10N 9 30 E
Katsina Ala →, *Nigeria* **83 D6** 7 10N 9 20 E
Katsumoto, *Japan* .... **55 H4** 33 51N 129 42 E
Katsuura, *Japan* ..... **55 G10** 35 10N 140 20 E
Katsuyama, *Japan* .... **55 F8** 36 3N 136 30 E
Kattaviá, *Greece* ..... **49 D9** 35 57N 27 46 E
Kattegat, *Denmark* ... **11 H5** 56 40N 11 20 E
Katthammarsvik,
  Sweden .... **11 G12** 57 26N 18 51 E
Katul, J., *Sudan* ..... **81 E2** 14 12N 29 25 E
Katumba, *Dem. Rep. of
  the Congo* .... **86 D2** 7 40 S 25 17 E
Katwa, *India* .... **69 H13** 23 30N 88 5 E
Katwijk, *Neths.* ..... **17 B4** 52 12N 4 24 E
Kąty Wrocławskie,
  Poland .... **31 G3** 51 2N 16 45 E
Kauai, *U.S.A.* **106 H15** 22 3N 159 30W
Kauai Channel, *U.S.A.* **106 H15** 21 45N 158 50W
Kaub, *Germany* ..... **25 E3** 50 5N 7 46 E
Kaudom △, *Namibia* . **88 B3** 18 45 S 20 51 E
Kaufbeuren, *Germany* . **25 H6** 47 53N 10 37 E
Kaukauna, *U.S.A.* ... **114 C1** 44 17N 88 17W
Kaukauveld, *Namibia* . **88 C3** 20 0 S 20 15 E
Kaunakakai, *U.S.A.* .. **106 H16** 21 6N 157 1W
Kaunas, *Lithuania* ... **9 J20** 54 54N 23 54 E
Kaunas ✈ (KUN),
  Lithuania .... **30 D11** 54 57N 24 3 E
Kaunia, *Bangla.* ..... **69 G13** 25 46N 89 26 E
Kaunos, *Turkey* ..... **47 E10** 36 49N 28 39 E
Kaura Namoda, *Nigeria* **83 C6** 12 37N 6 33 E
Kauru, *Nigeria* ...... **83 C6** 10 33N 8 12 E
Kautokeino, *Norway* .. **8 B20** 69 0N 23 4 E
Kauwapur, *India* ..... **69 F10** 27 31N 82 18 E
Kavacha, *Russia* ..... **53 C17** 60 16N 169 51 E
Kavadarci, *Macedonia* . **44 E6** 41 11N 19 33 E
Kavajë, *Albania* ..... **44 E3** 41 11N 19 33 E
Kavak Daği, *Turkey* .. **47 D10** 37 10N 28 2 E
Kavaklı, *Turkey* ..... **45 E11** 41 39N 27 10 E
Kavaklıdere, *Turkey* .. **47 D10** 37 27N 28 21 E
Kavalerovo, *Russia* ... **54 B7** 44 15N 135 4 E
Kavali, *India* .... **66 M12** 14 55N 80 1 E
Kaválla, *Greece* ..... **45 F8** 40 57N 24 28 E
Kaválla □, *Greece* ... **45 E8** 41 5N 24 30 E
Kaválla Kólpos, *Greece* **45 F8** 40 50N 24 25 E
Kavār, *Iran* .... **71 D7** 29 11N 52 44 E
Kavarna, *Bulgaria* ... **45 C12** 43 26N 28 22 E
Kavi, *India* .... **68 H5** 22 12N 72 38 E
Kavīr, Dasht-e, *Iran* .. **71 C7** 34 30N 55 0 E
Kavkaz, *Russia* ...... **33 K9** 45 20N 36 40 E
Kävlinge, *Sweden* .... **11 J7** 55 47N 13 9 E

Kavos, *Greece* ...... **49 B4** 39 23N 20 3 E
Kavoúsi, *Greece* ..... **47 F7** 35 7N 25 51 E
Kaw, *Fr. Guiana* **125 C8** 4 30N 52 15W
Kawa, *Sudan* .... **81 E3** 13 42N 32 34 E
Kawagama L., *Canada* . **116 A6** 45 18N 78 45W
Kawagoe, *Japan* ..... **55 G9** 35 55N 139 29 E
Kawaguchi, *Japan* ... **55 G9** 35 52N 139 45 E
Kawambwa, *Zambia* .. **87 D2** 9 48 S 29 3 E
Kawanoe, *Japan* ..... **55 G6** 34 1N 133 34 E
Kawardha, *India* ..... **69 J9** 22 0N 81 17 E
Kawasaki, *Japan* ..... **55 G9** 35 31N 139 43 E
Kawasi, *Indonesia* ... **63 E7** 1 38 S 127 28 E
Kawerau, *N.Z.* ...... **91 H6** 38 7 S 176 42 E
Kawhia, *N.Z.* .... **91 H5** 38 5 S 174 49 E
Kawhia Harbour, *N.Z.* **91 H5** 38 5 S 174 51 E
Kawio, Kepulauan,
  Indonesia .... **63 D7** 4 30N 125 30 E
Kawnro, *Burma* ..... **67 H21** 22 48N 99 8 E
Kawthaung, *Burma* ... **65 H2** 10 5N 98 36 E
Kawthoolei = Kayin □,
  Burma .... **67 L20** 18 0N 97 30 E
Kawthule = Kayin □,
  Burma .... **67 L20** 18 0N 97 30 E
Kaxholmen, *Sweden* .. **11 G8** 57 51N 14 19 E
Kaya, *Burkina Faso* ... **83 C4** 13 4N 1 10W
Kayah □, *Burma* ..... **67 K20** 19 15N 97 15 E
Kayalıköy Baraji,
  Turkey .... **45 E11** 41 50N 27 5 E
Kayan →, *Indonesia* .. **62 D5** 2 55N 117 35 E
Kaycee, *U.S.A.* **108 E10** 43 43N 106 38W
Kayeli, *Indonesia* .... **63 E7** 3 20 S 127 10 E
Kayenta, *U.S.A.* **109 H8** 36 44N 110 15W
Kayes, *Mali* **82 C2** 14 25N 11 30W
Kayı, *Turkey* .... **47 B12** 39 12N 30 46 E
Kayima, S. *Leone* ... **82 D2** 8 54N 11 15W
Kayin □, *Burma* ..... **67 L20** 18 0N 97 30 E
Kaymakçı, *Turkey* ... **47 C10** 38 10N 28 8 E
Kayoa, *Indonesia* .... **63 D7** 0 1N 127 28 E
Kayomba, *Zambia* .... **87 E1** 13 11 S 24 2 E
Kaysatskoye, *Russia* .. **34 F8** 49 47N 46 49 E
Kayseri, *Turkey* ..... **70 B2** 38 45N 35 30 E
Kaysville, *U.S.A.* **108 F8** 41 2N 111 56W
Kaz Daği, *Turkey* .... **47 B9** 39 42N 26 55 E
Kazachye, *Russia* .... **53 B14** 70 52N 135 58 E
Kazakhstan ■, *Asia* .. **52 E7** 50 0N 70 0 E
Kazan, *Russia* .... **34 C9** 55 50N 49 10 E
Kazan →, *Canada* ... **103 A9** 64 2N 95 29W
Kazan-Rettō, *Pac. Oc.* . **96 E6** 25 0N 141 0 E
Kazanlŭk, *Bulgaria* ... **45 D9** 42 38N 25 20 E
Kazanskaya, *Russia* ... **34 F5** 49 50N 41 10 E
Kazatin = Kozyatyn,
  Ukraine .... **29 B9** 49 45N 28 50 E
Kazaure, *Nigeria* .... **83 C6** 12 42N 8 28 E
Kazbek, *Russia* ...... **35 J7** 42 42N 44 30 E
Kāzerūn, *Iran* ...... **71 D6** 29 38N 51 40 E
Kazi Magomed =
  Qazimämmäd,
  Azerbaijan .... **35 K9** 40 3N 49 0 E
Kazimierz Dolny,
  Poland .... **31 G8** 51 19N 21 57 E
Kazimierza Wielka,
  Poland .... **31 H7** 50 15N 20 30 E
Kazincbarcika, *Hungary* **28 B5** 48 17N 20 36 E
Kazlų Rūda, *Lithuania* . **30 D10** 54 46N 23 30 E
Kaztalovka, *Kazakhstan* **34 F9** 49 47N 48 43 E
Kazuma Pan △,
  Zimbabwe .... **87 F2** 18 20 S 25 48 E
Kazuno, *Japan* ...... **54 D10** 40 10N 140 45 E
Kazym →, *Russia* ... **52 C7** 63 54N 65 50 E
Kcynia, *Poland* ...... **31 F4** 53 0N 17 30 E
Ké-Macina, *Mali* **82 C3** 13 58N 5 22W
Kéa, *Greece* .... **46 D6** 37 35N 24 22 E
Keady, *U.K.* **12 B5** 54 15N 6 42W
Kearney, *U.S.A.* **112 E5** 40 42N 99 5W
Kearny, *U.S.A.* **109 K8** 33 3N 110 55W
Kearsarge, Mt., *U.S.A.* **117 C13** 43 22N 71 50W
Keban, *Turkey* ...... **73 C8** 38 50N 38 50 E
Keban Barajı, *Turkey* . **70 B3** 38 41N 38 33 E
Kebbi □, *Nigeria* .... **83 C5** 11 35N 4 0 E
Kébi, *Ivory C.* **82 D3** 9 18N 6 37W
Kebnekaise, *Sweden* .. **8 C18** 67 53N 18 33 E
Kebri Dehar, *Ethiopia* . **75 F3** 6 45N 44 17 E
Kebumen, *Indonesia* .. **63 G13** 7 42 S 109 40 E
Kecel, *Hungary* ...... **28 D4** 46 31N 19 16 E
Kechika →, *Canada* .. **102 B3** 59 41N 127 12W
Keçiborlu, *Turkey* .... **47 D12** 37 57N 30 18 E
Kecskemét, *Hungary* .. **28 D4** 46 57N 19 42 E
Kedada, *Ethiopia* .... **81 F4** 5 25N 35 58 E
Kėdainiai, *Lithuania* .. **9 J21** 55 15N 24 2 E
Kedarnath, *India* .... **69 D8** 30 44N 79 4 E
Kedgwick, *Canada* ... **105 C6** 47 40N 67 20W
Kédhros Óros, *Greece* . **49 D6** 35 11N 24 37 E
Kediri, *Indonesia* .... **63 G15** 7 51 S 112 1 E
Kedjebi, *Ghana* ..... **83 D5** 8 12N 0 25 E
Kédougou, *Senegal* ... **82 C2** 12 35N 12 10W
Keeler, *U.S.A.* **110 J9** 36 29N 117 52W
Keeley L., *Canada* ... **103 C7** 54 54N 108 8W
Keeling Is. = Cocos Is.,
  Ind. Oc. .... **96 J1** 12 10 S 96 55 E
Keelung = Chilung,
  Taiwan .... **59 E13** 25 3N 121 45 E
Keene, *Canada* **116 B6** 44 15N 78 10W
Keene, Calif., *U.S.A.* .. **111 K8** 35 13N 118 33W
Keene, N.H., *U.S.A.* .. **117 D12** 42 56N 72 17W
Keene, N.Y., *U.S.A.* .. **117 B11** 44 16N 73 46W
Keep River △, *Australia* **92 C4** 15 49 S 129 8 E
Keep Hill, *Ireland* **12 C3** 52 45N 8 16W
Keer-Weer, C., *Australia* **94 A3** 14 0 S 141 32 E
Keeseville, *U.S.A.* **117 B11** 44 29N 73 30W
Keetmanshoop, *Namibia* **88 D2** 26 35 S 18 8 E
Keewatin, *Canada* ... **103 D10** 49 46N 94 34W
Keewatin →, *Canada* . **103 B8** 56 29N 100 46W
Kefallinía, *Greece* .... **46 C2** 38 15N 20 30 E
Kefallinía □, *Greece* .. **46 C2** 38 15N 20 30 E
Kéfalos, *Greece* ..... **47 E8** 36 45N 26 57 E
Kefamenanu, *Indonesia* **63 F6** 9 28 S 124 29 E
Kefar Sava, *Israel* .... **74 C3** 32 11N 34 54 E
Keffi, *Nigeria* .... **83 D6** 8 55N 7 43 E
Kefken, *Turkey* ...... **72 B4** 41 4N 30 18 E
Keflavík, *Iceland* **8 D2** 64 2N 22 35W
Keftya, *Ethiopia* ..... **81 E4** 13 55N 37 25 E
Keg River, *Canada* ... **102 B5** 57 54N 117 55W
Kegaska, *Canada* **105 B7** 50 9N 61 18W
Keheili, *Sudan* ...... **80 D3** 17 12N 32 50 E
Kehl, *Germany* ...... **25 G3** 48 34N 7 50 E
Keighley, *U.K.* **14 D6** 53 52N 1 54W
Keila, *Estonia* ...... **9 G21** 59 18N 24 25 E
Keimoes, S. *Africa* ... **88 D3** 28 41 S 20 59 E
Keita, *Niger* .... **83 C6** 14 46N 5 56 E
Keitele, *Finland* ..... **8 E22** 63 10N 26 20 E
Keith, *Australia* ..... **95 F3** 36 6 S 140 20 E
Keith, *U.K.* **13 D6** 57 32N 2 57W
Kejimkujik △, *Canada* . **105 D6** 44 25N 65 25W

Kejserr Franz Joseph
  Fd., *Greenland* **4 B6** 73 30N 24 30W
Kekri, *India* .... **68 G6** 26 0N 75 10 E
Kelam, *Ethiopia* ..... **81 G4** 4 48N 35 58 E
Kelamet, *Eritrea* ..... **81 D4** 16 0N 38 30 E
Kelan, *China* .... **56 E6** 38 43N 111 31 E
Kelang = Klang,
  Malaysia .... **65 L3** 3 2N 101 26 E
Kelantan □, *Malaysia* . **65 J4** 6 13N 102 14 E
Kelantan →, *Malaysia* **65 J4** 6 13N 102 14 E
Kēlcyrē, *Albania* ..... **44 F4** 40 20N 20 12 E
Kelekçi, *Turkey* ..... **47 D11** 37 15N 29 20 E
Keles, *Turkey* .... **45 G13** 39 54N 29 14 E
Keleti-főcsatorna,
  Hungary .... **28 C6** 47 45N 21 20 E
Kelheim, *Germany* ... **25 G7** 48 54N 11 52 E
Kelkit, *Turkey* ...... **73 B8** 40 7N 39 16 E
Kelkit →, *Turkey* ... **72 B7** 40 45N 36 32 E
Kellerberrin, *Australia* . **93 F2** 31 36 S 117 38 E
Kellett, C., *Canada* ... **4 B1** 72 0N 126 0W
Kelleys I., *U.S.A.* **116 E2** 41 36N 82 42W
Kellogg, *U.S.A.* **108 C5** 47 32N 116 7W
Kells = Ceannanus Mor,
  Ireland **12 C5** 53 44N 6 53W
Kelmė, *Lithuania* .... **30 C9** 55 38N 22 56 E
Kelmentsi, *Ukraine* ... **29 B11** 48 28N 26 50 E
Kelokedhara, *Cyprus* .. **49 E11** 34 48N 32 39 E
Kelowna, *Canada* **102 D5** 49 50N 119 25W
Kelsey Creek, *Australia* **94 J6** 20 26 S 148 31 E
Kelseyville, *U.S.A.* ... **110 G4** 38 59N 122 50W
Kelso, *N.Z.* .... **91 L2** 45 54 S 169 15 E
Kelso, *U.K.* **13 F6** 55 36N 2 26W
Kelso, *U.S.A.* **110 D4** 46 9N 122 54W
Keluang, *Malaysia* ... **65 L4** 2 3N 103 18 E
Kelvington, *Canada* .. **103 C8** 52 10N 103 30W
Kem, *Russia* .... **52 C4** 65 0N 34 38 E
Kema, *Indonesia* ..... **63 D7** 1 22N 125 8 E
Kemah, *Turkey* ...... **70 B3** 39 32N 39 5 E
Kemaliye, Erzincan,
  Turkey .... **73 C8** 39 16N 38 29 E
Kemaliye, Manisa,
  Turkey .... **47 C10** 38 27N 28 25 E
Kemalpaşa, *Turkey* ... **47 C9** 38 25N 27 27 E
Kemaman, *Malaysia* .. **62 D2** 4 12N 103 18 E
Kemano, *Canada* **102 C3** 53 35N 128 0W
Kemasik, *Malaysia* ... **65 K4** 4 25N 103 27 E
Kembolcha, *Ethiopia* .. **81 E4** 11 2N 39 42 E
Kemer, Antalya, *Turkey* **47 E12** 36 36N 30 34 E
Kemer, Burdur, *Turkey* **47 D12** 37 21N 30 2 E
Kemer, Muğla, *Turkey* **47 E11** 36 40N 29 22 E
Kemer Baraji, *Turkey* . **47 D10** 37 15N 29 30 E
Kemerovo, *Russia* .... **52 D9** 55 20N 86 5 E
Kemi, *Finland* ...... **8 D21** 65 44N 24 34 E
Kemi älv = Kemijoki →,
  Finland .... **8 D21** 65 47N 24 32 E
Kemi träsk = Kemijärvi,
  Finland .... **8 C22** 66 43N 27 22 E
Kemijärvi, *Finland* ... **8 C22** 66 43N 27 22 E
Kemijoki →, *Finland* . **8 D21** 65 47N 24 32 E
Kemmerer, *U.S.A.* ... **108 F8** 41 48N 110 32W
Kemmuna = Comino,
  Malta .... **49 C1** 36 1N 14 20 E
Kemp, L., *U.S.A.* **113 J5** 33 46N 99 9W
Kemp Land, *Antarctica* **5 C5** 69 0 S 55 0 E
Kempas, *Malaysia* .... **65 d** 1 33N 103 42 E
Kempsey, *Australia* ... **95 E5** 31 1 S 152 50 E
Kempt, L., *Canada* ... **104 C5** 47 25N 74 22W
Kempten, *Germany* ... **25 H6** 47 45N 10 17 E
Kempton, *Australia* ... **95 G4** 42 31 S 147 12 E
Kemptville, *Canada* .. **117 B9** 45 0N 75 38W
Ken →, *India* .... **69 G9** 25 13N 80 27 E
Kenai, *U.S.A.* **100 B4** 60 33N 151 16W
Kendai, *India* .... **69 H10** 22 45N 82 37 E
Kendal, *Indonesia* .... **63 G14** 6 56 S 110 14 E
Kendal, *U.K.* **14 C5** 54 20N 2 44W
Kendall, *Australia* ... **95 E5** 31 35 S 152 44 E
Kendall →, *Australia* . **94 A3** 14 4 S 141 35 E
Kendallville, *U.S.A.* .. **114 E3** 41 27N 85 16W
Kendari, *Indonesia* ... **63 E6** 3 50 S 122 30 E
Kendawangan,
  Indonesia .... **62 E4** 2 32 S 110 17 E
Kende, *Nigeria* ...... **83 C5** 11 30N 4 12 E
Kendi, Pulau, *Malaysia* **65 c** 5 13N 100 11 E
Kendrapara, *India* .... **67 J15** 20 35N 86 30 E
Kendrevicës, Maja e,
  Albania .... **44 F3** 40 15N 19 52 E
Kendrew, S. *Africa* ... **88 E3** 32 32 S 24 30 E
Kene Thao, *Laos* ..... **64 D3** 17 44N 101 10 E
Kenedy, *U.S.A.* **113 L6** 28 49N 97 51W
Kenema, S. *Leone* ... **82 D2** 7 50N 11 14W
Keng Kok, *Laos* ..... **64 D5** 16 26N 105 12 E
Keng Tawng, *Burma* .. **67 J21** 20 45N 98 18 E
Keng Tung, *Burma* ... **58 G2** 21 0N 99 30 E
Kengeja, *Tanzania* .... **86 D4** 5 26 S 39 45 E
Kenhardt, S. *Africa* ... **88 D3** 29 19 S 21 12 E
Kéniéba, *Mali* **82 C2** 12 54N 11 17W
Kenitra, *Morocco* **78 B4** 34 15N 6 40W
Kenli, *China* .... **57 F10** 37 30N 118 20 E
Kenmare, *Ireland* **12 E2** 51 53N 9 36W
Kenmare, *U.S.A.* **112 A3** 48 41N 102 5W
Kenmare River, *Ireland* **12 E2** 51 48N 9 51W
Kennebago Lake, *U.S.A.* **117 A14** 45 4N 70 40W
Kennebec →, *U.S.A.* . **112 D5** 43 54N 99 52W
Kennebec →, *U.S.A.* . **115 D11** 43 45N 69 46W
Kennebunk, *U.S.A.* .. **117 C14** 43 23N 70 33W
Kennedy, *Zimbabwe* .. **88 B4** 18 52 S 27 10 E
Kennedy Ra., *Australia* **93 D2** 24 45 S 115 10 E
Kennedy Range △,
  Australia .... **93 D2** 24 34 S 115 2 E
Kenner, *U.S.A.* **113 L9** 29 59N 90 15W
Kennet →, *U.K.* **15 F7** 51 27N 0 57W
Kenneth Ra., *Australia* **93 D2** 23 50 S 117 8 E
Kennett, *U.S.A.* **113 G9** 36 14N 90 3W
Kennewick, *U.S.A.* .. **108 C4** 46 12N 119 7W
Kénogami →, *Canada* **104 B3** 51 6N 84 28W
Kenora, *Canada* **103 D10** 49 47N 94 29W
Kenosha, *U.S.A.* **114 D2** 42 35N 87 49W
Kensington, *Canada* .. **105 C7** 46 28N 63 34W
Kent, *Ohio, U.S.A.* .. **116 E3** 41 9N 81 22W
Kent, *Tex., U.S.A.* ... **113 K2** 31 4N 104 13W
Kent, *Wash., U.S.A.* .. **110 C4** 47 23N 122 14W
Kent □, *U.K.* .... **15 F8** 51 12N 0 40 E
Kent Group, *Australia* . **95 F4** 39 30 S 147 20 E
Kent Pen., *Canada* ... **100 B9** 68 30N 107 0W
Kentaū, *Kazakhstan* .. **52 E7** 43 32N 68 36 E
Kentland, *U.S.A.* **114 E2** 40 46N 87 27W
Kenton, *U.S.A.* **114 E4** 40 39N 83 37W
Kentucky □, *U.S.A.* .. **114 G3** 37 0N 84 0W
Kentucky →, *U.S.A.* . **114 F3** 38 41N 85 11W
Kentucky L., *U.S.A.* .. **115 G2** 37 1N 88 16W
Kentville, *Canada* **105 C7** 45 6N 64 29W
Kentwood, *U.S.A.* ... **113 K9** 30 56N 90 31W
Kenya ■, *Africa* ..... **86 B4** 1 0N 38 0 E
Kenya, Mt., *Kenya* ... **86 C4** 0 10 S 37 18 E
Keo Neua, Deo,
  Vietnam .... **64 C5** 18 23N 105 10 E

Keokuk, *U.S.A.* **112 E9** 40 24N 91 24W
Keonjhargarh, *India* .. **69 J11** 21 28N 85 35 E
Kep, *Cambodia* ...... **65 G5** 10 29N 104 19 E
Kep, *Vietnam* .... **64 B6** 21 24N 106 16 E
Kepala Batas, *Malaysia* **65 c** 5 31N 100 26 E
Kepez, *Turkey* ...... **45 F10** 40 5N 26 24 E
Kepi, *Indonesia* ..... **63 F9** 6 32 S 139 19 E
Kępice, *Poland* ...... **30 D3** 54 16N 16 51 E
Kępno, *Poland* ...... **31 G4** 51 18N 17 58 E
Kepsut, *Turkey* ..... **47 B10** 39 40N 28 9 E
Kerala □, *India* ..... **66 P10** 11 0N 76 15 E
Kerama-Rettō, *Japan* . **55 L3** 26 5N 127 15 E
Keran, *Pakistan* ..... **69 B5** 34 35N 73 59 E
Kerang, *Australia* .... **95 F3** 35 40 S 143 55 E
Keranyo, *Ethiopia* ... **81 F4** 7 30N 38 6 E
Kerao →, *Sudan* .... **81 E3** 11 0N 32 41 E
Keratéa, *Greece* ..... **46 D5** 37 48N 23 58 E
Keraudren, C., *Australia* **92 C2** 19 58 S 119 45 E
Kerava, *Finland* ..... **9 F21** 60 25N 25 5 E
Kerch, *Ukraine* ...... **33 K9** 45 20N 36 20 E
Kerchenskiy Proliv,
  Black Sea .... **33 K9** 45 10N 36 30 E
Kerchoual, *Mali* ..... **83 B5** 17 12N 0 20 E
Kerempe Burnu, *Turkey* **72 A5** 42 1N 33 20 E
Keren, *Eritrea* ...... **81 D4** 15 45N 38 28 E
Kerewan, *Gambia* **82 C1** 13 29N 16 10W
Kerguelen, *Ind. Oc.* .. **3 G13** 49 15 S 69 10 E
Keri, *Greece* .... **46 D2** 37 40N 20 49 E
Keri Kera, *Sudan* .... **81 E3** 12 21N 32 42 E
Kericho, *Kenya* ..... **86 C4** 0 22 S 35 15 E
Kerinci, *Indonesia* ... **62 E2** 1 40 S 101 15 E
Kerki, *Turkmenistan* .. **52 F7** 37 50N 65 12 E
Kerkinítis, Límni,
  Greece .... **44 E7** 41 12N 23 10 E
Kérkira, *Greece* ..... **49 A3** 39 38N 19 50 E
Kérkira □, *Greece* ... **46 B1** 39 37N 19 50 E
Kérkira ✈ (CFU),
  Greece .... **46 B1** 39 35N 19 54 E
Kerkouane, *Tunisia* ... **42 F4** 36 58N 11 2 E
Kerkrade, *Neths.* .... **17 D6** 50 53N 6 4 E
Kerma, *Sudan* .... **80 D3** 19 33N 30 32 E
Kermadec Is., *Pac. Oc.* **96 L10** 30 0 S 178 15W
Kermadec Trench,
  Pac. Oc. .... **96 L10** 30 30 S 176 0W
Kermān, *Iran* .... **71 D8** 30 15N 57 1 E
Kermān, *U.S.A.* **110 J6** 36 43N 120 4W
Kermān □, *Iran* ..... **71 D8** 30 0N 57 0 E
Kermān, Bābān-e, *Iran* **71 D8** 28 45N 59 45 E
Kermānshāh =
  Bākhtarān, *Iran* ... **70 C5** 34 23N 47 0 E
Kermen, *Bulgaria* .... **45 D10** 42 30N 26 16 E
Kermit, *U.S.A.* **113 K3** 31 52N 103 6W
Kern →, *U.S.A.* **111 K7** 35 16N 119 18W
Kernhof, *Austria* ..... **26 D8** 47 49N 15 32 E
Kernow = Cornwall □,
  U.K. **15 G3** 50 26N 4 40W
Kernville, *U.S.A.* **111 K8** 35 45N 118 26W
Keroh, *Malaysia* ..... **65 K3** 5 43N 101 1 E
Kérou, *Benin* .... **83 C5** 10 50N 2 5 E
Kérouane, *Guinea* **82 D3** 9 15N 9 0W
Kerpen, *Germany* .... **24 E2** 50 51N 6 41 E
Kerrera, *U.K.* **13 E3** 56 24N 5 33W
Kerrobert, *Canada* ... **103 C7** 51 56N 109 8W
Kerrville, *U.S.A.* **113 K5** 30 3N 99 8W
Kerry □, *Ireland* **12 D2** 52 7N 9 35W
Kerry Hd., *Ireland* ... **12 D2** 52 25N 9 56W
Kersa, *Ethiopia* ..... **81 F5** 9 28N 41 48 E
Kerulen →, *Asia* .... **60 B6** 48 48N 117 0 E
Kervo = Kerava, *Finland* **9 F21** 60 25N 25 5 E
Kerzaz, *Algeria* **78 C5** 29 29N 1 37W
Kesagami →, *Canada* . **104 B4** 51 40N 79 45W
Kesagami L., *Canada* . **104 B3** 50 23N 80 15W
Keşan, *Turkey* ...... **45 F10** 40 49N 26 38 E
Kesennuma, *Japan* ... **54 E10** 38 54N 141 35 E
Keshit, *Iran* .... **71 D8** 29 43N 58 17 E
Keşiş Dağ, *Turkey* ... **73 C8** 39 47N 39 46 E
Keskin, *Turkey* ..... **72 C5** 39 40N 33 36 E
Kestell, S. *Africa* .... **89 D4** 28 17 S 28 42 E
Kestenga, *Russia* .... **52 C5** 65 50N 31 45 E
Keswick, *U.K.* **14 C4** 54 36N 3 8W
Keszthely, *Hungary* ... **28 D2** 46 50N 17 15 E
Ket →, *Russia* ...... **52 D9** 58 55N 81 32 E
Keta, *Ghana* .... **83 D5** 5 49N 1 0 E
Keta Lagoon, *Ghana* .. **83 D5** 5 50N 0 55 E
Ketapang, Bali,
  Indonesia .... **63 J17** 8 9 S 114 23 E
Ketapang, Kalimantan,
  Indonesia .... **62 E4** 1 55 S 110 0 E
Ketchenery, *Russia* ... **35 G7** 47 18N 44 32 E
Ketchikan, *U.S.A.* ... **102 B2** 55 21N 131 39W
Ketchum, *U.S.A.* **108 E6** 43 41N 114 22W
Kete Krachi, *Ghana* .. **83 D4** 7 46N 0 1W
Ketef, Khalîg Umm el,
  Egypt .... **70 F2** 23 40N 35 35 E
Keti Bandar, *Pakistan* . **68 G2** 24 8N 67 27 E
Kétou, *Benin* .... **83 D5** 7 25N 2 45 E
Ketri, *India* .... **68 E6** 28 1N 75 50 E
Kętrzyn, *Poland* ..... **30 D8** 54 7N 21 22 E
Kettering, *U.K.* **15 E7** 52 24N 0 43W
Kettering, *U.S.A.* **114 F3** 39 41N 84 10W
Kettle →, *Canada* ... **103 B11** 56 40N 89 34W
Kettle Falls, *U.S.A.* .. **108 B4** 48 37N 118 3W
Kettle Pt., *Canada* ... **116 C2** 43 13N 82 1W
Kettleman City, *U.S.A.* **110 J7** 36 1N 119 58W
Kęty, *Poland* .... **31 J6** 49 51N 19 16 E
Keuka L., *U.S.A.* **116 D7** 42 30N 77 9W
Keuruu, *Finland* ..... **9 E21** 62 16N 24 41 E
Kevelaer, *Germany* ... **24 D2** 51 35N 6 15 E
Kewanee, *U.S.A.* **112 E10** 41 14N 89 56W
Kewaunee, *U.S.A.* ... **114 C2** 44 27N 87 31W
Keweenaw B., *U.S.A.* . **114 B1** 47 0N 88 15W
Keweenaw Pen., *U.S.A.* **114 B2** 47 30N 88 0W
Keweenaw Pt., *U.S.A.* . **114 B2** 47 25N 87 43W
Key Largo, *U.S.A.* ... **115 N5** 25 5N 80 27W
Key West, *U.S.A.* **107 F10** 24 33N 81 48W
Keyala, *Sudan* ...... **81 G3** 4 27N 32 52 E
Keynsham, *U.K.* **15 F5** 51 24N 2 29W
Keyser, *U.S.A.* **114 F6** 39 26N 78 59W
Kezhma, *Russia* ..... **53 D11** 58 59N 101 9 E
Kezi, *Zimbabwe* ..... **89 C4** 20 58 S 28 32 E
Kežmarok, Slovak Rep. **27 B13** 49 10N 20 28 E
Kgalagadi
  Transfrontier △,
  Africa .... **88 D3** 25 10 S 21 0 E
Khabarovsk, *Russia* .. **53 E14** 48 30N 135 5 E
Khabr, *Iran* .... **71 D8** 28 51N 56 22 E
Khābūr →, *Syria* .... **70 C4** 35 17N 40 35 E
Khachmas = Xaçmaz,
  Azerbaijan .... **35 K9** 41 31N 48 42 E
Khachrod, *India* ..... **68 H6** 23 25N 75 20 E
Khadari, W. el →,
  Sudan .... **81 E2** 10 29N 27 15 E
Khadro, *Pakistan* .... **68 F3** 26 11N 68 50 E
Khadyzhensk, *Russia* . **35 H4** 44 26N 39 32 E
Khadzhilyangar, *China* **69 B8** 35 45N 79 20 E
Khaga, *India* .... **69 G9** 25 47N 81 7 E

Khagaria, India 69 G12 25 30N 86 32 E
Khaipur, Pakistan 68 E5 29 34N 72 17 E
Khair, India 68 F7 27 57N 77 46 E
Khairabad, India 69 F8 27 33N 80 47 E
Khairagarh, India 69 J9 21 27N 81 2 E
Khairpur, Pakistan 68 F3 27 32N 68 49 E
Khairpur Nathan Shah, Pakistan 68 F2 27 6N 67 44 E
Khairwara, India 68 H5 23 58N 73 38 E
Khaisor →, Pakistan 68 D3 31 17N 68 59 E
Khajuri Kach, Pakistan 68 C3 32 4N 69 51 E
Khakassia □, Russia 52 D9 53 0N 90 0 E
Khakhea, Botswana 88 C3 24 48S 23 22 E
Khalafābād, Iran 71 D6 30 54N 49 24 E
Khalilabad, India 69 F10 26 48N 83 5 E
Khalīlī, Iran 71 E7 27 38N 53 17 E
Khalkhāl, Iran 71 B6 37 37N 48 32 E
Khálki, Dhodhekánisos, Greece 47 E9 36 17N 27 35 E
Khálki, Thessalía, Greece 46 B4 39 36N 22 30 E
Khalkidhikí □, Greece 44 F7 40 25N 23 20 E
Khalkís, Greece 46 C5 38 27N 23 42 E
Khalmer Yu, Russia 52 B7 67 58N 65 1 E
Kham Keut, Laos 64 C5 18 15N 104 43 E
Khamaria, India 69 H9 23 5N 80 48 E
Khambhaliya, India 68 H3 22 14N 69 41 E
Khambhat, India 68 H5 22 23N 72 33 E
Khambhat, G. of, India 66 J8 20 45N 72 30 E
Khamilonísíon, Greece 47 F8 35 50N 26 15 E
Khamīr, Iran 71 E7 26 57N 55 36 E
Khamir, Yemen 75 D3 16 2N 44 0 E
Khamsa, Egypt 74 E1 30 27N 32 23 E
Khān →, Namibia 88 C2 22 37S 14 56 E
Khān Abū Shāmat, Syria 74 B5 33 39N 36 53 E
Khān Āzād, Iraq 70 C5 33 7N 44 22 E
Khān Mujiddah, Iraq 70 C4 32 21N 43 48 E
Khān Shaykhūn, Syria 70 C3 35 26N 36 38 E
Khān Yūnis, Gaza Strip 74 D3 31 21N 34 18 E
Khanai, Pakistan 68 D2 30 30N 67 8 E
Khānaqīn, Iraq 70 C5 34 23N 45 25 E
Khānbāghī, Iran 71 B7 36 10N 55 25 E
Khandrá, Greece 47 E8 35 3N 26 8 E
Khandwa, India 66 J10 21 49N 76 22 E
Khandyga, Russia 53 C14 62 42N 135 35 E
Khāneh, Iran 70 B5 36 41N 45 8 E
Khanewal, Pakistan 68 D4 30 20N 71 55 E
Khangah Dogran, Pakistan 68 D5 31 50N 73 37 E
Khanh Duong, Vietnam 64 F7 12 44N 108 44 E
Khaniá, Greece 49 D6 35 30N 24 4 E
Khaniá □, Greece 49 D6 35 30N 24 0 E
Khaniadhana, India 68 G8 25 1N 78 8 E
Khaníon, Kólpos, Greece 49 D5 35 33N 23 55 E
Khanka, L., Asia 53 E14 45 0N 132 24 E
Khankendy = Xankändi, Azerbaijan 70 B5 39 52N 46 49 E
Khanna, India 68 D7 30 42N 76 16 E
Khanozai, Pakistan 68 D2 30 37N 67 19 E
Khanpur, Pakistan 68 E4 28 42N 70 35 E
Khanty-Mansiysk, Russia 52 C7 61 0N 69 0 E
Khao Laem △, Thailand 64 E2 14 56N 98 31 E
Khao Laem Res., Thailand 64 E2 14 50N 98 30 E
Khao Luang △, Thailand 65 H2 8 34N 99 42 E
Khao Phlu, Thailand 65 b 9 29N 99 59 E
Khao Pu-Khao Ya △, Thailand 65 J2 7 26N 99 57 E
Khao Sam Roi Yot △, Thailand 64 F2 12 13N 99 57 E
Khao Sok △, Thailand 65 H2 8 55N 98 38 E
Khao Yai △, Thailand 64 E3 14 21N 101 29 E
Khaoen Si Nakarin △, Thailand 64 E2 14 47N 99 0 E
Khapalu, Pakistan 69 B7 35 10N 76 20 E
Khapcheranga, Russia 53 E12 49 42N 112 24 E
Kharabali, Russia 35 G8 47 25N 47 15 E
Kharaghoda, India 68 H4 23 11N 71 46 E
Kharagpur, India 69 H12 22 20N 87 25 E
Khárakas, Greece 49 D7 35 1N 25 7 E
Kharan Kalat, Pakistan 66 E4 28 34N 65 21 E
Kharānaq, Iran 71 C7 32 20N 54 45 E
Kharda, India 66 K9 18 40N 75 34 E
Khardung La, India 69 B7 34 20N 77 43 E
Kharg = Khārk, Jazīreh-ye, Iran 71 D6 29 15N 50 28 E
Khârga, El Wâhât-el, Egypt 80 B3 25 10N 30 35 E
Khargon, India 66 J9 21 45N 75 40 E
Khari →, India 68 G6 25 54N 74 31 E
Kharian, Pakistan 68 C5 32 49N 73 52 E
Kharit, Wadi el →, Egypt 80 C3 24 26N 33 3 E
Khārk, Jazīreh-ye, Iran 71 D6 29 15N 50 28 E
Kharkiv, Ukraine 33 H9 49 58N 36 20 E
Kharkov = Kharkiv, Ukraine 33 H9 49 58N 36 20 E
Kharmanli, Bulgaria 45 E9 41 55N 25 55 E
Kharovsk, Russia 32 C11 59 56N 40 13 E
Kharsawangarh, India 69 H11 22 48N 85 50 E
Kharta, Turkey 72 B3 40 55N 29 7 E
Khartoum = Khartûm, Sudan 81 D3 15 31N 32 35 E
Khartûm, Sudan 81 D3 15 31N 32 35 E
Khasan, Russia 54 C5 42 25N 130 40 E
Khasavyurt, Russia 35 J8 43 16N 46 40 E
Khāsh, Iran 66 E2 28 15N 61 15 E
Khashm el Girba, Sudan 81 E4 14 59N 35 58 E
Khashum, Sudan 81 E1 14 29N 28 2 E
Khashuri, Georgia 35 J6 42 1N 43 6 E
Khaskovo, Bulgaria 45 E9 41 56N 25 30 E
Khaskovo □, Bulgaria 45 E9 41 56N 25 30 E
Khatanga, Russia 53 B11 72 0N 102 20 E
Khatanga →, Russia 53 B11 72 55N 106 0 E
Khatauli, India 68 E7 29 17N 77 43 E
Khatra, India 69 H12 22 59N 86 51 E
Khātūnābād, Iran 71 D7 30 1N 55 25 E
Khatyrka, Russia 53 C18 62 3N 175 15 E
Khavda, India 68 H3 23 51N 69 43 E
Khaybar, Harrat, Si. Arabia 70 E4 25 45N 40 0 E
Khayelitsha, S. Africa 85 L3 34 5S 18 42 E
Khāzimiyah, Iraq 70 C4 34 46N 43 37 E
Khazzān Jabal al Awliyā, Sudan 81 D3 15 24N 32 20 E
Khe Bo, Vietnam 64 C5 19 8N 104 41 E
Khe Long, Vietnam 64 B5 21 29N 104 46 E
Khe Sanh, Vietnam 64 D6 16 37N 106 45 E
Khed Brahma, India 68 G8 24 7N 73 5 E
Khekra, India 68 E7 28 52N 77 20 E
Khemarak Phouminville, Cambodia 65 G4 11 37N 102 59 E
Khemisset, Morocco 78 B4 33 50N 6 1W
Khemmarat, Thailand 64 D5 16 10N 105 15 E
Khenāmān, Iran 71 D8 30 27N 56 29 E
Khenchela, Algeria 78 A7 35 28N 7 11 E

Khersān →, Iran 71 D6 31 33N 50 22 E
Khérson, Greece 46 C4 38 1N 22 45 E
Kherson, Ukraine 33 J7 46 35N 32 35 E
Khersónisos Akrotíri, Greece 49 D6 35 30N 24 10 E
Kheta →, Russia 53 B11 71 54N 102 6 E
Khewari, Pakistan 68 G7 24 2N 76 34 E
Khilchipur, India 68 G7 24 2N 76 34 E
Khiliomódhion, Greece 46 D4 37 48N 22 51 E
Khilok, Russia 53 D12 51 30N 110 45 E
Khimki, Russia 32 E9 55 50N 37 20 E
Khíos, Greece 47 C8 38 27N 26 9 E
Khíos □, Greece 47 C8 38 27N 26 9 E
Khirsadoh, India 69 H8 22 11N 78 47 E
Khiuma = Hiiumaa, Estonia 9 G20 58 50N 22 45 E
Khiva, Uzbekistan 52 E7 41 30N 60 18 E
Khīyāv, Iran 70 B5 38 30N 47 45 E
Khlebarovo, Bulgaria 45 C10 43 37N 26 15 E
Khlong Khlung, Thailand 64 D2 16 12N 99 43 E
Khmelnik, Ukraine 33 H4 49 33N 27 58 E
Khmelnitskiy = Khmelnytskyy, Ukraine 33 H4 49 23N 27 0 E
Khmelnytskyy, Ukraine 33 H4 49 23N 27 0 E
Khmer Rep. = Cambodia ■, Asia 64 F5 12 15N 105 0 E
Khoai, Hon, Vietnam 65 H5 8 26N 104 50 E
Khodoriv, Ukraine 33 H3 49 24N 24 19 E
Khodzent = Khŭjand, Tajikistan 52 E7 40 17N 69 37 E
Khojak Pass, Afghan. 68 D2 30 51N 66 34 E
Khok Kloi, Thailand 65 a 8 17N 98 19 E
Khok Pho, Thailand 65 J3 6 43N 101 6 E
Kholm, Russia 32 D6 57 10N 31 15 E
Kholmsk, Russia 53 E15 47 40N 142 5 E
Khomas Hochland, Namibia 88 C2 22 40S 16 0 E
Khombole, Senegal 82 C1 14 43N 16 42W
Khomeyn, Iran 71 C6 33 40N 50 7 E
Khomeynī Shahr, Iran 71 C6 32 41N 51 31 E
Khomodino, Botswana 88 C3 22 46S 23 52 E
Khon Kaen, Thailand 64 D4 16 30N 102 47 E
Khong →, Cambodia 64 F5 13 32N 105 58 E
Khong Sedone, Laos 64 E5 15 34N 105 49 E
Khonuu, Russia 53 C15 66 30N 143 12 E
Khoper →, Russia 34 F6 49 30N 42 20 E
Khor el 'Atash, Sudan 81 E3 13 20N 34 15 E
Khóra, Greece 46 D3 37 3N 21 42 E
Khóra Sfakíon, Greece 49 D6 35 15N 24 9 E
Khorāsān □, Iran 71 C8 34 0N 58 0 E
Khorat = Nakhon Ratchasima, Thailand 64 E4 14 59N 102 12 E
Khorat, Cao Nguyen, Thailand 64 E4 15 30N 102 50 E
Khorixas, Namibia 88 C1 20 16S 14 59 E
Khorol, Ukraine 33 H7 49 48N 33 15 E
Khorramābād, Khorāsān Iran 71 C8 35 6N 57 57 E
Khorramābād, Lorestān, Iran 71 C6 33 30N 48 25 E
Khorrāmshahr, Iran 71 D6 30 29N 48 15 E
Khorugh, Tajikistan 52 F8 37 30N 71 36 E
Khosravī, Iran 71 D6 30 48N 51 28 E
Khosrowābād, Khuzestān, Iran 71 D6 30 10N 48 25 E
Khosrowābād, Kordestān, Iran 70 C5 35 31N 47 38 E
Khost, Pakistan 68 D2 30 13N 67 35 E
Khosüyeh, Iran 71 D7 28 32N 54 26 E
Khotyn, Ukraine 29 B11 48 31N 26 27 E
Khouribga, Morocco 78 B4 32 58N 6 57W
Khowst, Afghan. 68 C3 33 22N 69 58 E
Khowst □, Afghan. 66 C6 33 20N 70 0 E
Khoyniki, Belarus 33 G5 51 54N 29 55 E
Khrami →, Georgia 35 K7 41 25N 45 0 E
Khrenovoye, Russia 34 E5 51 4N 40 16 E
Khrisoúpolis, Greece 45 F8 40 58N 24 42 E
Khristianá, Greece 47 E7 36 14N 25 13 E
Khrysokhou B., Cyprus 49 D11 35 6N 32 25 E
Khtapodhiá, Greece 47 D7 37 24N 25 34 E
Khu Khan, Thailand 64 E5 14 42N 104 12 E
Khuan Wa, Thailand 65 a 7 53N 98 17 E
Khudzhand = Khŭjand, Tajikistan 52 E7 40 17N 69 37 E
Khuff, Si. Arabia 70 E5 24 55N 44 53 E
Khūgiāni, Afghan. 68 D1 31 34N 66 32 E
Khuis, Botswana 88 D3 26 40S 21 49 E
Khuiyala, India 68 F4 27 9N 70 25 E
Khŭjand, Tajikistan 52 E7 40 17N 69 37 E
Khujner, India 68 H7 23 47N 76 36 E
Khulna, Bangla. 67 H16 22 45N 89 34 E
Khulna □, Bangla. 67 H16 22 25N 89 35 E
Khulo, Georgia 35 K6 41 33N 42 19 E
Khumago, Botswana 88 C3 20 26S 24 32 E
Khŭnsorkh, Iran 71 E8 27 9N 56 7 E
Khunti, India 69 H11 23 5N 85 17 E
Khūr, Iran 71 C8 32 55N 58 18 E
Khurai, India 68 G8 24 3N 78 23 E
Khurays, Si. Arabia 71 E6 25 6N 48 2 E
Khureit, Sudan 81 E2 13 59N 26 3 E
Khurīyā Murīyā, Jazā'ir, Oman 75 D6 17 30N 55 58 E
Khurja, India 68 E7 28 15N 77 58 E
Khūrmāl, Iraq 70 C5 35 18N 46 2 E
Khurr, Wādī al, Iraq 70 C4 32 3N 43 52 E
Khūsf, Iran 71 C8 32 46N 58 53 E
Khush, Afghan. 66 C3 32 55N 62 10 E
Khushab, Pakistan 68 C5 32 20N 72 20 E
Khust, Ukraine 29 B8 48 10N 23 18 E
Khutse △, Botswana 88 C3 23 31S 24 12 E
Khuzdar, Pakistan 68 F2 27 52N 66 30 E
Khūzestān □, Iran 71 D6 31 0N 49 0 E
Khvāf, Iran 71 C9 34 33N 60 8 E
Khvājeh, Iran 70 B5 38 9N 46 35 E
Khvalynsk, Russia 34 D9 52 30N 48 2 E
Khvatovka, Russia 34 D8 52 24N 46 32 E
Khvor, Iran 71 C7 33 45N 55 0 E
Khvorgū, Iran 71 E8 27 34N 56 27 E
Khvormūj, Iran 71 D6 28 40N 51 30 E
Khvoy, Iran 70 B5 38 35N 45 0 E
Khvoynaya, Russia 32 C8 58 58N 34 28 E
Khyber Pass, Afghan. 68 B4 34 10N 71 8 E
Khyriv, Ukraine 28 49 32N 22 50 E
Kiabukwa, Dem. Rep. of the Congo 87 D1 8 40S 24 48 E
Kiama, Australia 95 E5 34 40S 150 50 E
Kiamba, Phil. 61 H6 6 2N 124 46 E
Kiambi, Dem. Rep. of the Congo 86 D2 7 15S 28 0 E
Kiambu, Kenya 86 C4 1 8S 36 50 E
Kiang West △, Gambia 82 C1 13 26N 15 50W
Kiangara, Madag. 89 B8 17 58S 47 2 E
Kiangsi = Jiangxi □, China 59 D11 27 30N 116 0 E

Kiangsu = Jiangsu □, China 57 H11 33 0N 120 0 E
Kiáton, Greece 46 C4 38 1N 22 45 E
Kibæk, Denmark 11 H2 56 2N 8 51 E
Kibale △, Uganda 86 B3 0 16N 30 18 E
Kibanga Port, Uganda 86 B3 0 10N 32 58 E
Kibara, Tanzania 86 C3 2 8S 33 30 E
Kibare, Mts., Dem. Rep. of the Congo 86 D2 8 25S 27 10 E
Kibira △, Burundi 86 C3 3 6S 30 24 E
Kibombo, Dem. Rep. of the Congo 86 C2 3 57S 25 53 E
Kibondo, Tanzania 86 C3 3 35S 30 45 E
Kibre Mengist, Ethiopia 81 F4 5 54N 38 59 E
Kibumbu, Burundi 86 C2 3 32S 29 45 E
Kibungo, Rwanda 86 C3 2 10S 30 32 E
Kibuye, Burundi 86 C2 3 39S 29 59 E
Kibuye, Rwanda 86 C2 2 3S 29 21 E
Kibwesa, Tanzania 86 D2 6 30S 29 58 E
Kibwezi, Kenya 86 C4 2 27S 37 57 E
Kicasalih, Turkey 45 E10 41 23N 26 48 E
Kičevo, Macedonia 44 E4 41 34N 20 59 E
Kichha, India 69 E8 28 53N 79 30 E
Kichha →, India 69 E8 28 41N 79 18 E
Kicking Horse Pass, Canada 102 C5 51 28N 116 16W
Kidal, Mali 83 B5 18 26N 1 22 E
Kidderminster, U.K. 15 E5 52 24N 2 15W
Kidepo Valley △, Uganda 86 B3 3 52N 33 50 E
Kidete, Tanzania 86 D4 6 25S 37 17 E
Kidira, Senegal 82 C2 14 28N 12 13W
Kidnappers, C., N.Z. 91 H6 39 38S 177 5 E
Kidsgrove, U.K. 14 D5 53 5N 2 14W
Kidston, Australia 94 B3 18 52S 144 8 E
Kidugallo, Tanzania 86 D4 6 49S 38 15 E
Kiel, Germany 24 A6 54 19N 10 8 E
Kiel Canal = Nord-Ostsee-Kanal, Germany 24 A5 54 12N 9 32 E
Kielce, Poland 31 H7 50 52N 20 42 E
Kielder Water, U.K. 14 B5 55 11N 2 31W
Kieler Bucht, Germany 24 A6 54 35N 10 25 E
Kiembara, Burkina Faso 82 C4 13 15N 2 44W
Kien Binh, Vietnam 65 H5 9 55N 105 19 E
Kien Tan, Vietnam 65 G5 10 7N 105 17 E
Kienge, Dem. Rep. of the Congo 87 E2 10 30S 27 30 E
Kiessé, Niger 83 C5 13 29N 4 1 E
Kiev = Kyyiv, Ukraine 33 G6 50 30N 30 28 E
Kifaya, Guinea 82 C2 12 10N 13 4W
Kiffa, Mauritania 82 B2 16 37N 11 24W
Kifisiá, Greece 46 C5 38 4N 23 49 E
Kifissós →, Greece 46 C5 38 35N 23 20 E
Kifrī, Iraq 70 C5 34 45N 45 0 E
Kigali, Rwanda 86 C3 1 59S 30 4 E
Kigarama, Tanzania 86 C3 1 1S 31 50 E
Kigelle, Sudan 81 F3 8 40N 34 2 E
Kigezi □, Uganda 86 C2 0 34S 29 55 E
Kigoma □, Tanzania 86 D3 5 0S 30 0 E
Kigoma-Ujiji, Tanzania 86 C2 4 55S 29 36 E
Kigomasha, Ras, Tanzania 86 C4 4 58S 38 58 E
Kiğı, Turkey 70 B4 39 18N 43 25 E
Kihei, U.S.A. 106 H16 20 47N 156 28W
Kihnu, Estonia 9 G21 58 9N 24 1 E
Kii-Sanchi, Japan 55 G8 34 20N 136 0 E
Kii-Suidō, Japan 55 H7 33 40N 134 45 E
Kikaiga-Shima, Japan 55 K4 28 19N 129 59 E
Kikinda, Serbia & M. 28 E5 45 50N 20 30 E
Kikládhes, Greece 46 E6 37 0N 24 30 E
Kikládhes □, Greece 46 E6 37 0N 25 0 E
Kikwit, Dem. Rep. of the Congo 84 E3 5 0S 18 45 E
Kil, Sweden 10 E7 59 30N 13 20 E
Kilafors, Sweden 10 C10 61 14N 16 36 E
Kilar, India 68 C7 33 6N 76 25 E
Kilauea Crater, U.S.A. 106 J17 19 25N 155 17W
Kilbrannan Sd., U.K. 13 F3 55 37N 5 26W
Kilchu, N. Korea 57 D15 40 57N 129 25 E
Kilcoy, Australia 95 D5 26 59S 152 30 E
Kildare, Ireland 12 C5 53 9N 6 55W
Kildare □, Ireland 12 C5 53 10N 6 50W
Kilfinnane, Ireland 12 D3 52 21N 8 28W
Kilgore, U.S.A. 113 J7 32 23N 94 53W
Kilibo, Benin 83 D5 8 32N 2 38 E
Kilifi, Kenya 86 C4 3 40S 39 48 E
Kilimanjaro, Tanzania 86 C4 3 7S 37 20 E
Kilimanjaro □, Tanzania 86 C4 4 0S 38 0 E
Kilimli, Turkey 72 B4 41 28N 31 50 E
Kilindini, Kenya 86 C4 4 4S 39 40 E
Kilis, Turkey 70 B3 36 42N 37 6 E
Kiliya, Ukraine 29 E14 45 28N 29 16 E
Kilkee, Ireland 12 D2 52 41N 9 39W
Kilkeel, U.K. 12 B5 54 4N 6 0W
Kilkenny, Ireland 12 D4 52 39N 7 15W
Kilkenny □, Ireland 12 D4 52 35N 7 15W
Kilkieran B., Ireland 12 C2 53 20N 9 41W
Kilkis, Greece 44 F6 40 58N 22 57 E
Kilkis □, Greece 44 F6 40 58N 22 57 E
Killala, Ireland 12 B2 54 13N 9 12W
Killala B., Ireland 12 B2 54 16N 9 8W
Killaloe, Canada 116 A7 45 33N 77 25W
Killaloe, Ireland 12 D3 52 48N 8 28W
Killarney, Australia 95 D5 28 20S 152 18 E
Killarney, Canada 103 D9 49 10N 99 40W
Killarney, Ireland 12 D2 52 4N 9 30W
Killary Harbour, Ireland 12 C2 53 38N 9 52W
Killdeer, U.S.A. 112 B3 47 26N 102 48W
Killeen, U.S.A. 113 K6 31 7N 97 44W
Killin, U.K. 13 E4 56 28N 4 19W
Killíni, Ilía, Greece 46 D3 37 55N 21 8 E
Killíni, Korinthía, Greece 46 D4 37 54N 22 25 E
Killorglin, Ireland 12 D2 52 6N 9 47W
Killybegs, Ireland 12 B3 54 38N 8 26W
Kilmarnock, U.K. 13 F4 55 37N 4 29W
Kilmez, Russia 34 B10 56 58N 51 0 E
Kilmez →, Russia 34 B10 56 58N 50 28 E
Kilmore, Australia 95 F3 37 25N 144 53 E
Kilondo, Tanzania 87 D3 9 45S 34 20 E
Kilosa, Tanzania 86 D4 6 48S 37 0 E
Kilrush, Ireland 12 D2 52 38N 9 29W
Kilwa Kisiwani, Tanzania 87 D4 8 58S 39 32 E
Kilwa Kivinje, Tanzania 87 D4 8 45S 39 25 E
Kilwa Masoko, Tanzania 87 D4 8 55S 39 30 E
Kilwinning, U.K. 13 F4 55 39N 4 43W
Kim →, Cameroon 83 D7 5 28N 11 7 E
Kimaam, Indonesia 63 F9 7 58S 138 53 E
Kimamba, Tanzania 86 D4 6 45S 37 10 E
Kimba, Australia 95 E2 33 8S 136 23 E
Kimball, Nebr., U.S.A. 112 E3 41 14N 103 40W
Kimball, S. Dak., U.S.A. 112 D5 43 45N 98 57W

Kimberley, Australia 92 C4 16 20S 127 0 E
Kimberley, Canada 102 D5 49 40N 115 59W
Kimberley, S. Africa 88 D3 28 43S 24 46 E
Kimberly, U.S.A. 108 E6 42 32N 114 22W
Kimch'aek, N. Korea 57 D15 40 40N 129 10 E
Kimch'ŏn, S. Korea 57 F15 36 11N 128 4 E
Kími, Greece 46 C6 38 38N 24 6 E
Kimje, S. Korea 57 G14 35 48N 126 45 E
Kimmirut, Canada 101 B13 62 50N 69 50W
Kímolos, Greece 46 E6 36 48N 24 37 E
Kimry, Russia 32 D9 56 55N 37 15 E
Kimstad, Sweden 11 F9 58 35N 15 58 E
Kinabalu, Gunung, Malaysia 62 C5 6 3N 116 14 E
Kínaros, Greece 47 E8 36 59N 26 15 E
Kinaskan L., Canada 102 B2 57 38N 130 8W
Kinbasket L., Canada 102 C5 52 0N 118 10W
Kincardine, Canada 116 B3 44 10N 81 40W
Kincolith, Canada 102 C3 55 0N 129 57W
Kinda, Dem. Rep. of the Congo 87 D2 9 18S 25 4 E
Kindberg, Austria 26 D8 47 30N 15 27 E
Kinde, U.S.A. 116 C2 43 56N 83 0W
Kinder Scout, U.K. 14 D6 53 24N 1 52W
Kindersley, Canada 103 C7 51 30N 109 10W
Kindia, Guinea 82 D2 10 0N 12 52W
Kindu, Dem. Rep. of the Congo 86 C2 2 55S 25 50 E
Kinel, Russia 34 D10 53 15N 50 40 E
Kineshma, Russia 34 B6 57 30N 42 5 E
Kinesi, Tanzania 86 C3 1 25S 33 50 E
King, L., Australia 93 F2 33 10S 119 35 E
King, Mt., Australia 94 D4 25 10S 147 30 E
King City, U.S.A. 110 J5 36 13N 121 8W
King Cr. →, Australia 94 C2 24 35S 139 30 E
King Edward →, Australia 92 B4 14 14S 126 35 E
King Frederick VI Land = Kong Frederik VI Kyst, Greenland 101 B15 63 0N 43 0W
King George B., Falk. Is. 128 G4 51 30S 60 30W
King George I., Antarctica 5 C18 60 0S 60 0W
King George Is., Canada 101 C11 57 20N 80 30W
King I. = Kadan Kyun, Burma 64 F2 12 30N 98 20 E
King I., Australia 95 F3 39 50S 144 0 E
King I., Canada 102 C3 52 10N 127 40W
King Leopold Ranges, Australia 92 C4 17 30S 125 45 E
King of Prussia, U.S.A. 117 F9 40 5N 75 23W
King Sd., Australia 92 C3 16 50S 123 20 E
King Sejong, Antarctica 5 C18 62 2S 58 0W
King William I., Canada 100 B10 69 10N 97 25W
King William's Town, S. Africa 88 E4 32 51S 27 22 E
Kingait = Cape Dorset, Canada 101 B12 64 14N 76 32W
Kingaok = Bathurst Inlet, Canada 100 B9 66 50N 108 1W
Kingaroy, Australia 95 D5 26 32S 151 51 E
Kingfisher, U.S.A. 113 H6 35 52N 97 56W
Kingirbān, Iraq 70 C5 34 40N 44 54 E
Kingisepp = Kuressaare, Estonia 9 G20 58 15N 22 30 E
Kingisepp, Russia 32 C5 59 25N 28 40 E
Kingman, Ariz., U.S.A. 111 K12 35 12N 114 4W
Kingman, Kans., U.S.A. 113 G5 37 39N 98 7W
Kingoonya, Australia 95 E2 30 55S 135 19 E
Kingri, Pakistan 68 D3 30 27N 69 49 E
Kings →, U.S.A. 110 J7 36 3N 119 50W
Kings Canyon △, U.S.A. 110 J8 36 50N 118 40W
King's Lynn, U.K. 14 E8 52 45N 0 24 E
Kings Mountain, U.S.A. 115 H5 35 15N 81 20W
Kings Park, U.S.A. 117 F11 40 53N 73 16W
King's Peak, U.S.A. 108 F8 40 46N 110 27W
Kingsbridge, U.K. 15 G4 50 17N 3 47W
Kingsburg, U.S.A. 110 J7 36 31N 119 33W
Kingscote, Australia 95 F2 35 40S 137 38 E
Kingscourt, Ireland 12 C5 53 55N 6 48W
Kingsland, U.S.A. 115 K5 30 48N 81 41W
Kingsley, U.S.A. 112 D7 42 35N 95 58W
Kingsport, U.S.A. 115 G4 36 33N 82 33W
Kingston, Canada 117 B8 44 14N 76 30W
Kingston, Jamaica 120 a 18 0N 76 50W
Kingston, N.Z. 91 L2 45 20S 168 43 E
Kingston, N.H., U.S.A. 117 D13 42 56N 71 3W
Kingston, N.Y., U.S.A. 117 E11 41 56N 73 59W
Kingston, Pa., U.S.A. 117 E9 41 16N 75 54W
Kingston, R.I., U.S.A. 117 E13 41 29N 71 30W
Kingston Pk., U.S.A. 111 K11 35 45N 115 54W
Kingston South East, Australia 95 F2 36 51S 139 55 E
Kingston upon Hull, U.K. 14 D7 53 45N 0 21W
Kingston upon Hull □, U.K. 14 D7 53 45N 0 21W
Kingston-upon-Thames □, U.K. 15 F7 51 24N 0 17W
Kingstown, St. Vincent 121 D7 13 10N 61 10W
Kingstree, U.S.A. 115 J6 33 40N 79 50W
Kingsville, Canada 116 D2 42 2N 82 45W
Kingsville, U.S.A. 113 M6 27 31N 97 52W
Kingussie, U.K. 13 D4 57 6N 4 2W
Kingwood, U.S.A. 113 K7 29 54N 95 11W
Kınık, Antalya, Turkey 47 E11 36 20N 29 20 E
Kınık, İzmir, Turkey 47 B9 39 6N 27 24 E
Kinistino, Canada 103 C7 52 57N 105 2W
Kinkala, Congo 84 E2 4 18S 14 49 E
Kinki □, Japan 55 H8 33 45N 136 0 E
Kinleith, N.Z. 91 H5 38 20S 175 56 E
Kinlochleven, U.K. 13 E4 56 43N 4 58W
Kinmount, Canada 116 B6 44 48N 78 45W
Kinna, Sweden 11 G6 57 32N 12 42 E
Kinnairds Hd., U.K. 13 D6 57 43N 2 1W
Kinnared, Sweden 11 G7 57 2N 13 7 E
Kinnarp, Sweden 11 F7 58 5N 13 32 E
Kinnekulle, Sweden 11 F7 58 35N 13 25 E
Kino, Mexico 118 B2 28 45N 111 59W
Kinoje →, Canada 104 B3 52 8N 81 25W
Kinomoto, Japan 55 G8 35 30N 136 13 E
Kinoni, Uganda 86 C3 0 41S 30 28 E
Kinoosao, Canada 103 B8 57 5N 102 1W
Kinross, U.K. 13 E5 56 13N 3 25W
Kinsale, Ireland 12 E3 51 42N 8 31W
Kinsale, Old Hd. of, Ireland 12 E3 51 37N 8 33W
Kinsha = Chang Jiang →, China 59 B13 31 48N 121 10 E
Kinshasa, Dem. Rep. of the Congo 84 E3 4 20S 15 15 E

Kinsley, U.S.A. 113 G5 37 55N 99 25W
Kinsman, U.S.A. 116 E4 41 26N 80 35W
Kinston, U.S.A. 115 H7 35 16N 77 35W
Kintamani, Indonesia 63 J18 8 5S 115 19 E
Kintampo, Ghana 83 D4 8 5N 1 41W
Kintore, U.K. 13 D6 57 14N 2 20W
Kintore Ra., Australia 92 D4 23 15S 128 47 E
Kintyre, U.K. 13 F3 55 30N 5 35W
Kintyre, Mull of, U.K. 13 F3 55 17N 5 47W
Kinushseo →, Canada 104 A3 55 15N 83 45W
Kinuso, Canada 102 B5 55 20N 115 25W
Kinyangiri, Tanzania 86 C3 4 25S 34 37 E
Kinyeti, Sudan 81 G3 3 57N 32 54 E
Kinzig →, Germany 25 G3 48 36N 7 49 E
Kinzua, U.S.A. 116 E6 41 52N 78 58W
Kinzua Dam, U.S.A. 116 E6 41 53N 79 0W
Kióni, Greece 46 C2 38 27N 20 41 E
Kiosk, Canada 104 C4 46 6N 78 53W
Kiowa, Kans., U.S.A. 113 G5 37 1N 98 29W
Kiowa, Okla., U.S.A. 113 H7 34 43N 95 54W
Kipahigan L., Canada 103 B8 55 20N 101 55W
Kipanga, Tanzania 86 D4 6 15S 35 20 E
Kiparissía, Greece 46 D3 37 15N 21 40 E
Kiparissiakós Kólpos, Greece 46 D3 37 25N 21 25 E
Kipawa, L., Canada 104 C4 46 50N 79 0W
Kipembawe, Tanzania 86 D3 7 38S 33 27 E
Kipengere Ra., Tanzania 87 D3 9 12S 34 15 E
Kipili, Tanzania 86 D3 7 28S 30 32 E
Kipini, Kenya 86 C5 2 30S 40 32 E
Kipling, Canada 103 C8 50 6N 102 38W
Kippure, Ireland 12 C5 53 11N 6 21W
Kipushi, Dem. Rep. of the Congo 87 E2 11 48S 27 12 E
Kirane, Mali 82 B2 15 20N 10 20W
Kiranomena, Madag. 89 B8 18 17S 46 2 E
Kiraz, Turkey 47 C10 38 14N 28 13 E
Kirazlı, Turkey 45 F10 40 2N 26 41 E
Kirchhain, Germany 24 E4 50 49N 8 56 E
Kirchheim, Germany 25 G5 48 39N 9 27 E
Kirchheimbolanden, Germany 25 F3 49 40N 8 0 E
Kirchschlag, Austria 27 D9 47 30N 16 19 E
Kireç, Turkey 47 B10 39 33N 28 22 E
Kirensk, Russia 53 D11 57 50N 107 55 E
Kirghizia = Kyrgyzstan ■, Asia 52 E8 42 0N 75 0 E
Kirghizstan = Kyrgyzstan ■, Asia 52 E8 42 0N 75 0 E
Kiribati ■, Pac. Oc. 96 H10 5 0S 180 0 E
Kırıkhan, Turkey 72 D7 36 31N 36 21 E
Kırıkkale, Turkey 72 C5 39 51N 33 32 E
Kirillov, Russia 32 C10 59 49N 38 24 E
Kirin = Jilin, China 57 C14 43 44N 126 30 E
Kirinyaga = Kenya, Mt., Kenya 86 C4 0 10S 37 18 E
Kirishi, Russia 32 C7 59 28N 32 0 E
Kirishima Yaku △, Japan 55 J5 31 24N 130 50 E
Kiritimati, Kiribati 97 G12 1 58N 157 27W
Kırka, Turkey 47 B12 39 7N 30 33 E
Kırkağaç, Turkey 47 B9 39 2N 27 40 E
Kirkby, U.K. 14 D5 53 30N 2 54W
Kirkby-in-Ashfield, U.K. 14 D6 53 6N 1 14W
Kirkby Lonsdale, U.K. 14 C5 54 12N 2 36W
Kirkby Stephen, U.K. 14 C5 54 29N 2 21W
Kirkcaldy, U.K. 13 E5 56 7N 3 9W
Kirkcudbright, U.K. 13 G4 54 50N 4 2W
Kirkee, India 66 K8 18 34N 73 56 E
Kirkenes, Norway 8 B23 69 40N 30 5 E
Kirkfield, Canada 116 B6 44 34N 78 59W
Kirkintilloch, U.K. 13 F4 55 56N 4 8W
Kirkjubæjarklaustur, Iceland 8 E4 63 47N 18 4W
Kirkkonummi, Finland 9 F21 60 8N 24 26 E
Kirkland Lake, Canada 104 C3 48 9N 80 2W
Kırklareli, Turkey 45 E11 41 44N 27 15 E
Kırklareli □, Turkey 45 E11 41 44N 27 15 E
Kirksville, U.S.A. 112 E8 40 12N 92 35W
Kirkük, Iraq 70 C5 35 30N 44 21 E
Kirkwall, U.K. 13 C6 58 59N 2 58W
Kirkwood, S. Africa 88 E4 33 22S 25 15 E
Kirn, Germany 25 F3 49 47N 7 26 E
Kirov, Kaluga, Russia 32 E8 54 3N 34 20 E
Kirov, Kirov, Russia 52 D5 58 35N 49 40 E
Kirovabad = Gäncä, Azerbaijan 35 K8 40 45N 46 20 E
Kirovograd = Kirovohrad, Ukraine 33 H7 48 35N 32 20 E
Kirovohrad, Ukraine 33 H7 48 35N 32 20 E
Kirovsk, Astrakhan, Russia 35 H9 45 51N 48 11 E
Kirovskiy, Kamchatka, Russia 53 D16 54 27N 155 42 E
Kirovskiy, Primorsk, Russia 54 B6 45 7N 133 30 E
Kirriemuir, U.K. 13 E5 56 41N 3 1W
Kirsanov, Russia 34 D6 52 35N 42 40 E
Kırşehir, Turkey 70 B2 39 14N 34 5 E
Kirtachi, Niger 83 C5 12 52N 2 30 E
Kirthar Range, Pakistan 68 F2 27 0N 67 0 E
Kirtland, U.S.A. 109 H9 36 44N 108 21W
Kiruna, Sweden 8 C19 67 52N 20 15 E
Kirundu, Dem. Rep. of the Congo 86 C2 0 50S 25 35 E
Kirya, Russia 34 C8 55 5N 46 55 E
Kiryū, Japan 55 F9 36 24N 139 20 E
Kisa, Sweden 11 G9 58 0N 15 39 E
Kisaga, Tanzania 86 D3 4 30S 34 23 E
Kisalaya, Nic. 120 D3 14 40N 84 3W
Kisalföld, Hungary 28 C2 47 30N 17 0 E
Kisámou, Kólpos, Greece 49 D5 35 30N 23 38 E
Kisanga, Dem. Rep. of the Congo 86 B2 2 30N 26 35 E
Kisangani, Dem. Rep. of the Congo 86 B2 0 35N 25 15 E
Kisar, Indonesia 63 F7 8 5S 127 10 E
Kisarawe, Tanzania 86 D4 6 53S 39 0 E
Kisarazu, Japan 55 G9 35 23N 139 55 E
Kisbér, Hungary 28 C3 47 30N 18 2 E
Kishanganga →, Pakistan 69 B5 34 18N 73 28 E
Kishanganj, India 69 F13 26 3N 88 14 E
Kishangarh, Raj., India 68 F6 26 34N 74 52 E
Kishangarh, Raj., India 68 F4 27 50N 70 30 E
Kishi, Nigeria 83 D5 9 1N 3 52 E
Kishinev = Chişinău, Moldova 29 C13 47 2N 28 50 E
Kishiwada, Japan 55 G7 34 28N 135 22 E
Kishtwar, India 69 C6 33 20N 75 48 E
Kisielice, Poland 30 E6 53 36N 19 16 E
Kisigo →, Tanzania 86 D3 6 35S 34 45 E
Kisii, Kenya 86 C3 0 40S 34 45 E
Kisiju, Tanzania 86 D4 7 23S 39 19 E
Kisir, Turkey 73 B10 41 0N 43 5 E
Kisizi, Uganda 86 C2 1 0S 29 58 E

Kiskomárom =
  Zalakomár, *Hungary*   **28 D2** 46 33N 17 10 E
Kiskörei-víztároló,
  Hungary   **28 C5** 47 31N 20 36 E
Kiskőrös, *Hungary*   **28 D4** 46 37N 19 20 E
Kiskundorozsma,
  Hungary   **28 D5** 46 16N 20 5 E
Kiskunfélegyháza,
  Hungary   **28 D4** 46 42N 19 53 E
Kiskunhalas, *Hungary*   **28 D4** 46 28N 19 37 E
Kiskunmajsa, *Hungary*   **28 D4** 46 30N 19 48 E
Kiskunsági △, *Hungary*   **28 D4** 46 39N 19 30 E
Kislovodsk, *Russia*   **35 J6** 43 50N 42 45 E
Kismayu = Chisimaio,
  Somali Rep.   **77 G8** 0 22 S 42 32 E
Kiso-Gawa ➤, *Japan*   **55 G8** 35 20N 136 45 E
Kiso-Sammyaku, *Japan*   **55 G8** 35 45N 137 45 E
Kisofukushima, *Japan*   **55 G8** 35 52N 137 43 E
Kisoro, *Uganda*   **86 C2** 1 17 S 29 48 E
Kissidougou, *Guinea*   **82 D2** 9 5N 10 5W
Kissimmee, *U.S.A.*   **115 L5** 28 18N 81 24W
Kissimmee ➤, *U.S.A.*   **115 M5** 27 9N 80 52W
Kississing L., *Canada*   **103 B8** 55 10N 101 20W
Kissónerga, *Cyprus*   **49 E11** 34 49N 32 34 E
Kissu, J., *Sudan*   **80 C2** 21 37N 25 10 E
Kistanje, *Croatia*   **41 E12** 43 58N 15 55 E
Kisújszállás, *Hungary*   **28 C5** 47 12N 20 50 E
Kisumu, *Kenya*   **86 C3** 0 3 S 34 45 E
Kisvárda, *Hungary*   **28 B7** 48 14N 22 4 E
Kiswani, *Tanzania*   **86 C4** 4 5 S 37 57 E
Kiswere, *Tanzania*   **87 E5** 9 27 S 39 30 E
Kit Carson, *U.S.A.*   **112 F3** 38 46N 102 –8W
Kita, *Mali*   **82 C3** 13 5N 9 25 W
Kitaibaraki, *Japan*   **55 F10** 36 50N 140 45 E
Kitakami, *Japan*   **54 E10** 39 20N 141 10 E
Kitakami-Gawa ➤,
  Japan   **54 E10** 38 25N 141 19 E
Kitakami-Sammyaku,
  Japan   **54 E10** 39 30N 141 30 E
Kitakata, *Japan*   **54 F9** 37 39N 139 52 E
Kitakyūshū, *Japan*   **55 H5** 33 50N 130 50 E
Kitale, *Kenya*   **86 B4** 1 0N 35 0 E
Kitami, *Japan*   **54 C11** 43 48N 143 54 E
Kitami-Sammyaku,
  Japan   **54 B11** 44 22N 142 43 E
Kitangiri, L., *Tanzania*   **86 C3** 4 5 S 34 20 E
Kitaya, *Tanzania*   **87 E5** 10 38 S 40 8 E
Kitchener, *Canada*   **116 C4** 43 27N 80 29W
Kitee, *Finland*   **32 A6** 62 5N 30 8 E
Kitega = Gitega,
  Burundi   **86 C2** 3 26 S 29 56 E
Kitengo, Dem. Rep. of
  the *Congo*   **86 D1** 7 26 S 24 8 E
Kitgum, *Uganda*   **86 B3** 3 17N 32 52 E
Kíthira, *Greece*   **46 E5** 36 8N 23 0 E
Kíthnos, *Greece*   **46 D6** 37 26N 24 27 E
Kiti, *Cyprus*   **49 E12** 34 50N 33 34 E
Kiti, C., *Cyprus*   **49 E12** 34 48N 33 36 E
Kitimat, *Canada*   **102 C3** 54 3N 128 38W
Kitinen ➤, *Finland*   **8 C22** 67 14N 27 27 E
Kitiyab, *Sudan*   **81 D3** 17 13N 33 35 E
Kítros, *Greece*   **44 F6** 40 22N 22 34 E
Kitsman, *Ukraine*   **29 B10** 48 26N 25 54 E
Kitsuki, *Japan*   **55 H5** 33 25N 131 37 E
Kittakittaooloo, L.,
  Australia   **95 D2** 28 3 S 138 14 E
Kittanning, *U.S.A.*   **116 F5** 40 49N 79 31W
Kittatinny Mts., *U.S.A.*   **117 F10** 41 0N 75 0W
Kittery, *U.S.A.*   **115 D10** 43 5N 70 45W
Kittilä, *Finland*   **8 C21** 67 40N 24 51 E
Kitui, *Kenya*   **86 C4** 1 17 S 38 0 E
Kitwanga, *Canada*   **102 B3** 55 6N 128 4W
Kitwe, *Zambia*   **87 E2** 12 54 S 28 13 E
Kitzbühel, *Austria*   **26 D5** 47 27N 12 24 E
Kitzbühler Alpen,
  Austria   **26 D5** 47 20N 12 20 E
Kitzingen, *Germany*   **25 F6** 49 44N 10 9 E
Kivarli, *India*   **68 G5** 24 33N 72 46 E
Kivertsi, *Ukraine*   **33 G3** 50 50N 25 28 E
Kividhes, *Cyprus*   **49 E11** 34 46N 32 51 E
Kivik, *Sweden*   **11 J8** 55 41N 14 13 E
Kivotós, *Greece*   **44 F5** 40 13N 21 26 E
Kivu, L., Dem. Rep. of
  the *Congo*   **86 C2** 1 48 S 29 0 E
Kiyev = Kyyiv, *Ukraine*   **33 G6** 50 30N 30 28 E
Kiyevskoye Vdkhr. =
  Kyyivske Vdskh.,
  Ukraine   **33 G6** 51 0N 30 25 E
Kıyıköy, *Turkey*   **45 E11** 41 38N 28 5 E
Kiziguru, *Rwanda*   **86 C3** 1 46 S 30 23 E
Kızıl Adalar, *Turkey*   **45 F13** 40 52N 29 5 E
Kızıl Irmak ➤, *Turkey*   **72 B6** 41 44N 35 58 E
Kızıl Jilga, *China*   **69 B8** 35 26N 78 50 E
Kizil Yurt, *Russia*   **35 J8** 43 13N 46 54 E
Kızılcabölük, *Turkey*   **47 D11** 37 37N 29 1 E
Kızılcadağ, *Turkey*   **47 D11** 37 1N 29 58 E
Kızılcahamam, *Turkey*   **72 B5** 40 30N 32 30 E
Kızılhisar, *Turkey*   **72 D3** 37 32N 29 17 E
Kızılırmak, *Turkey*   **72 B5** 40 21N 33 59 E
Kızılkaya, *Turkey*   **47 D12** 37 18N 30 27 E
Kızılören, *Turkey*   **47 C12** 38 15N 30 10 E
Kızıltepe, *Turkey*   **70 B4** 37 12N 40 35 E
Kizimkazi, *Tanzania*   **86 D4** 6 28 S 39 30 E
Kizlyar, *Russia*   **35 J8** 43 51N 46 40 E
Kizyl-Arvat =
  Gyzylarbat,
  Turkmenistan   **52 F6** 39 4N 56 23 E
Kjellerup, *Denmark*   **11 H3** 56 17N 9 25 E
Kjölur, *Iceland*   **8 D4** 64 50N 19 25 E
Kladanj, Bos.-H.   **42 C3** 44 14N 18 42 E
Kladnica, Serbia & M.   **44 C4** 43 23N 20 2 E
Kladno, *Czech Rep.*   **26 A7** 50 10N 14 7 E
Kladovo, Serbia & M.   **44 B6** 44 36N 22 33 E
Klaeng, *Thailand*   **64 F3** 12 47N 101 39 E
Klagenfurt, *Austria*   **26 E7** 46 38N 14 20 E
Klaipėda, *Lithuania*   **9 J19** 55 43N 21 10 E
Klaipėda □, *Lithuania*   **30 C8** 55 43N 21 7 E
Klaksvík, *Færoe Is.*   **8 E9** 62 14N 6 35W
Klamath ➤, *U.S.A.*   **108 F1** 41 33N 124 5W
Klamath Falls, *U.S.A.*   **108 E3** 42 13N 121 46W
Klamath Mts., *U.S.A.*   **108 F2** 41 20N 123 0W
Klamono, *Indonesia*   **63 E8** 1 8 S 131 30 E
Klang, *Malaysia*   **65 L3** 3 2N 101 26 E
Klanjec, *Croatia*   **41 B12** 46 3N 15 45 E
Klappan ➤, *Canada*   **102 B3** 58 0N 129 43 E
Klarälven ➤, *Sweden*   **10 E7** 59 23N 13 32 E
Klässbol, *Sweden*   **10 E6** 59 33N 12 45 E
Klatovy, *Czech Rep.*   **26 B6** 49 23N 13 18 E
Klawer, S. *Africa*   **88 E2** 31 44N 18 36 E
Klazienaveen, *Neths.*   **17 B6** 52 44N 7 0 E
Klé, *Mali*   **82 C3** 12 59N 6 38 W
Klecko, *Poland*   **31 F4** 52 38N 17 25 E
Kleczew, *Poland*   **31 F5** 52 22N 18 9 E
Kleena Kleene, *Canada*   **102 C4** 52 0N 124 59W
Klein-Karas, *Namibia*   **88 D2** 27 33 S 18 7 E
Klekovača, Bos.-H.   **41 D13** 44 25N 16 32 E
Klembivka, *Ukraine*   **29 B13** 48 23N 28 25 E

Klenoec, *Macedonia*   **44 E4** 41 32N 20 49 E
Klenovec, *Slovak Rep.*   **27 C12** 48 36N 19 54 E
Klerksdorp, S. *Africa*   **88 D4** 26 53 S 26 38 E
Kleszczele, *Poland*   **31 F10** 52 35N 23 19 E
Kletnya, *Russia*   **32 F7** 53 23N 33 12 E
Kletsk = Klyetsk,
  Belarus   **33 F4** 53 5N 26 45 E
Kletskiy, *Russia*   **35 F6** 49 16N 43 11 E
Kleve, *Germany*   **24 D2** 51 47N 6 7 E
Klickitat, *U.S.A.*   **108 D3** 45 49N 121 9W
Klickitat ➤, *U.S.A.*   **110 E5** 45 42N 121 17W
Klídhes, *Cyprus*   **49 D13** 35 42N 34 36 E
Klímovichi, *Belarus*   **32 F6** 53 36N 32 0 E
Klin, *Russia*   **32 D9** 56 20N 36 48 E
Klina, Serbia & M.   **44 D4** 42 37N 20 35 E
Klínaklini ➤, *Canada*   **102 C3** 51 21N 125 40W
Klintehamn, *Sweden*   **11 G12** 57 24N 18 12 E
Klíntsy, *Russia*   **33 F7** 52 50N 32 30 E
Klip ➤, S. *Africa*   **89 D4** 27 3 S 29 3 E
Klipdale, S. *Africa*   **88 E2** 34 19 S 19 57 E
Klippan, *Sweden*   **11 H7** 56 8N 13 10 E
Klipplaat, S. *Africa*   **88 E3** 33 1 S 24 22 E
Klishkivtsi, *Ukraine*   **29 B11** 48 26N 26 16 E
Klisura, *Bulgaria*   **45 D8** 42 40N 24 28 E
Kljajićevo, Serbia & M.   **28 E4** 45 45N 19 17 E
Ključ, Bos.-H.   **41 D13** 44 32N 16 48 E
Kłobuck, *Poland*   **31 H5** 50 55N 18 55 E
Klockestrand, *Sweden*   **10 B11** 62 53N 17 55 E
Kłodawa, *Poland*   **31 F5** 52 15N 18 55 E
Kłodzko, *Poland*   **31 H3** 50 28N 16 38 E
Klong Wang Chao △,
  Thailand   **64 D2** 16 20N 99 9 E
Klos, *Albania*   **44 E4** 41 28N 20 10 E
Klosterneuburg, *Austria*   **27 C9** 48 18N 16 19 E
Klosters, *Switz.*   **25 J5** 46 52N 9 52 E
Klötze, *Germany*   **24 C7** 52 37N 11 10 E
Klouto, *Togo*   **83 D5** 6 57N 0 44 E
Kluane △, *Canada*   **102 A1** 60 45N 139 30W
Kluane L., *Canada*   **100 B6** 61 15N 138 40W
Kluczbork, *Poland*   **31 H5** 50 58N 18 12 E
Klukwan, *U.S.A.*   **102 B1** 59 24N 135 54W
Klungkung, *Indonesia*   **63 K18** 8 32 S 115 24 E
Klyetsk, *Belarus*   **33 F4** 53 5N 26 45 E
Klyuchevskaya, Gora,
  Russia   **53 D17** 55 50N 160 30 E
Knäred, *Sweden*   **11 H7** 56 31N 13 19 E
Knaresborough, *U.K.*   **14 C6** 54 1N 1 28W
Knee L., Man., *Canada*   **104 A1** 55 3N 94 45W
Knee L., Sask., *Canada*   **103 B7** 55 51N 107 0W
Knezha, *Bulgaria*   **45 C8** 43 30N 24 5 E
Knight Inlet, *Canada*   **102 C3** 50 45N 125 40W
Knighton, *U.K.*   **15 E4** 52 21N 3 3W
Knights Ferry, *U.S.A.*   **110 H6** 37 50N 120 40W
Knights Landing, *U.S.A.*   **110 G5** 38 48N 121 43W
Knin, *Croatia*   **41 D13** 44 3N 16 17 E
Knislinge, *Sweden*   **11 H8** 56 12N 14 5 E
Knittelfeld, *Austria*   **26 D7** 47 13N 14 51 E
Knivsta, *Sweden*   **10 E11** 59 43N 17 48 E
Knjaževac, Serbia & M.   **44 C6** 43 35N 22 18 E
Knob, C., *Australia*   **93 F2** 34 32 S 119 16 E
Knock, *Ireland*   **12 C3** 53 48N 8 55W
Knockmealdown Mts.,
  Ireland   **12 D4** 52 14N 7 56W
Knokke-Heist, *Belgium*   **17 C3** 51 21N 3 17 E
Knossós, *Greece*   **49 D7** 35 16N 25 10 E
Knowlton, *Canada*   **117 A12** 45 13N 72 31W
Knox, *U.S.A.*   **114 E2** 41 18N 86 37W
Knox Coast, *Antarctica*   **5 C8** 66 30 S 108 0 E
Knoxville, Iowa, *U.S.A.*   **112 E8** 41 19N 93 6W
Knoxville, Pa., *U.S.A.*   **116 E7** 41 57N 77 27W
Knoxville, Tenn., *U.S.A.*   **115 H4** 35 58N 83 55W
Knud Rasmussen Land,
  Greenland   **4 A5** 79 0N 60 0W
Knysna, S. *Africa*   **88 E3** 34 2 S 23 2 E
Knyszyn, *Poland*   **30 E9** 53 20N 22 56 E
Ko Kha, *Thailand*   **64 C2** 18 11N 99 24 E
Ko Tarutao △, *Thailand*   **65 J2** 6 31N 99 26 E
Ko Yao, *Thailand*   **65 a** 8 7N 98 35 E
Koartac = Quaqtaq,
  Canada   **101 B13** 60 55N 69 40W
Koba, *Indonesia*   **63 F8** 6 37 S 134 37 E
Kobarid, *Slovenia*   **41 B10** 46 15N 13 30 E
Kobayashi, *Japan*   **55 J5** 31 56N 130 59 E
Kōbe, *Japan*   **55 G7** 34 45N 135 10 E
Kobelyaky, *Ukraine*   **33 H8** 49 11N 34 9 E
København, *Denmark*   **11 J6** 55 41N 12 34 E
København ✈ (CPH),
  Denmark   **11 J6** 55 37N 12 39 E
Københavns
  Amtskommune □,
  Denmark   **11 J6** 55 42N 12 21 E
Kobenni, *Mauritania*   **82 B3** 15 58N 9 24W
Kōbi-Sho, *Japan*   **55 M1** 25 56N 123 41 E
Koblenz, *Germany*   **25 E3** 50 21N 7 36 E
Kobo, *Ethiopia*   **81 E4** 12 2N 39 56 E
Kobryn, *Belarus*   **33 F3** 52 15N 24 22 E
Kobuleti, *Georgia*   **35 K5** 41 55N 41 45 E
Kobyletska Polyana,
  Ukraine   **29 B9** 48 3N 24 4 E
Kobylin, *Poland*   **31 G4** 51 43N 17 12 E
Kobyłka, *Poland*   **31 F8** 52 21N 21 10 E
Kobylkino, *Russia*   **34 C6** 54 8N 43 56 E
Koca ➤, *Turkey*   **45 F11** 40 8N 27 57 E
Kocabaş, *Turkey*   **47 D11** 37 49N 29 20 E
Kocaeli, *Turkey*   **45 F13** 40 45N 29 55 E
Kocaeli □, *Turkey*   **45 F13** 40 45N 29 55 E
Kočane, Serbia & M.   **44 C5** 43 12N 21 52 E
Kočani, *Macedonia*   **44 E6** 41 55N 22 25 E
Koçarlı, *Turkey*   **47 D9** 37 45N 27 43 E
Koceljevo, Serbia & M.   **44 B3** 44 28N 19 50 E
Kočevje, *Slovenia*   **41 C11** 45 30N 14 50 E
Koch Bihar, *India*   **67 F16** 26 22N 89 29 E
Kochang, S. *Korea*   **57 G14** 35 41N 127 55 E
Kochas, *India*   **69 G10** 25 15N 83 56 E
Kocher ➤, *Germany*   **25 F5** 49 13N 9 12 E
Kochi = Cochin, *India*   **66 Q10** 9 58N 76 20 E
Kōchi, *Japan*   **55 H6** 33 30N 133 35 E
Kōchi □, *Japan*   **55 H6** 33 40N 133 30 E
Kochiu = Gejiu, *China*   **58 F4** 23 20N 103 10 E
Kock, *Poland*   **31 G9** 51 38N 22 27 E
Kodarma, *India*   **69 G11** 24 28N 85 36 E
Kodiak, *U.S.A.*   **100 C4** 57 47N 152 24W
Kodiak I., *U.S.A.*   **100 C4** 57 30N 152 45W
Kodinar, *India*   **68 J4** 20 46N 70 46 E
Kodok, *Sudan*   **81 F3** 9 53N 32 7 E
Kodori ➤, *Georgia*   **35 J5** 42 47N 41 10 E
Koedoesberge, S. *Africa*   **88 E3** 32 40 S 20 11 E
Koes, *Namibia*   **88 D2** 26 0 S 19 15 E
Kofçaz, *Turkey*   **45 E11** 41 58N 27 12 E
Koffiefontein, S. *Africa*   **88 D4** 29 30 S 25 0 E
Kofiau, *Indonesia*   **63 E7** 1 11 S 129 50 E
Köflach, *Austria*   **26 D8** 47 4N 15 5 E
Koforidua, *Ghana*   **83 D4** 6 3N 0 17W
Kōfu, *Japan*   **55 G9** 35 40N 138 30 E
Koga, *Japan*   **55 F9** 36 11N 139 43 E

Kogaluc ➤, *Canada*   **105 A7** 56 12N 61 44W
Køge, *Denmark*   **11 J6** 55 27N 12 11 E
Køge Bugt, *Denmark*   **11 J6** 55 30N 12 20 E
Kogi □, *Nigeria*   **83 D6** 7 45N 6 45 E
Kogin Baba, *Nigeria*   **83 D7** 7 55N 11 35 E
Koh-i-Khurd, *Afghan.*   **68 C1** 33 30N 65 59 E
Koh-i-Maran, *Pakistan*   **68 E2** 29 18N 66 50 E
Kohat, *Pakistan*   **68 C4** 33 40N 71 29 E
Kohima, *India*   **67 G19** 25 35N 94 10 E
Kohkīlūyeh va Būyer
  Aḥmadi □, *Iran*   **71 D6** 31 30N 50 30 E
Kohler Ra., *Antarctica*   **5 D15** 77 0 S 110 0W
Kohlu, *Pakistan*   **68 E3** 29 54N 69 15 E
Kohtla-Järve, *Estonia*   **9 G22** 59 20N 27 20 E
Kohylnyk ➤, *Ukraine*   **29 E14** 45 49N 29 40 E
Koi Sanjaq, *Iraq*   **70 B5** 36 5N 44 38 E
Koillismaa, *Finland*   **8 D23** 65 44N 28 36 E
Koin-dong, N. *Korea*   **57 D14** 40 28N 126 18 E
Koinare, *Bulgaria*   **45 C8** 43 21N 24 8 E
Koindu, S. *Leone*   **82 D2** 8 26N 10 19W
Kojetín, *Czech Rep.*   **27 B10** 49 21N 17 20 E
Kojŏ, N. *Korea*   **57 E14** 38 58N 127 58 E
Kojonup, *Australia*   **93 F2** 33 48 S 117 10 E
Kojūr, *Iran*   **71 B6** 36 23N 51 43 E
Koka, *Sudan*   **80 C3** 20 5N 30 35 E
Kokand = Qŭqon,
  Uzbekistan   **52 E8** 40 30N 70 57 E
Kokas, *Indonesia*   **63 E8** 2 42 S 132 26 E
Kokava, *Slovak Rep.*   **27 C12** 48 35N 19 50 E
Kokchetav = Kökshetaū,
  Kazakhstan   **52 D7** 53 20N 69 25 E
Kokemäenjoki ➤,
  Finland   **9 F19** 61 32N 21 44 E
Kokhma, *Russia*   **34 B5** 56 57N 41 8 E
Koki, *Senegal*   **82 B1** 15 30N 15 59W
Kokkola, *Finland*   **8 E20** 63 50N 23 8 E
Koko, *Nigeria*   **83 C5** 11 28N 4 29 E
Koko Kyunzu, *Burma*   **67 M18** 14 10N 93 25 E
Kokolopozo, *Ivory C.*   **82 D3** 5 8N 6 5W
Kokomo, *U.S.A.*   **114 E2** 40 29N 86 8W
Kokoro, *Niger*   **83 C5** 14 12N 0 55 E
Koksan, N. *Korea*   **57 E14** 38 46N 126 40 E
Kökshetaū, *Kazakhstan*   **52 D7** 53 20N 69 25 E
Koksoak ➤, *Canada*   **101 C13** 58 30N 68 10W
Kokstad, S. *Africa*   **89 E4** 30 32 S 29 29 E
Kokubu, *Japan*   **55 J5** 31 44N 130 46 E
Kola, *Indonesia*   **63 F8** 5 35 S 134 30 E
Kola Pen. = Kolskiy
  Poluostrov, *Russia*   **52 C4** 67 30N 38 0 E
Kolachi ➤, *Pakistan*   **68 F2** 27 8N 67 2 E
Kolahoi, *India*   **69 B6** 34 12N 75 22 E
Kolahun, *Liberia*   **82 D2** 8 15N 10 4W
Kolaka, *Indonesia*   **63 E6** 4 3 S 121 46 E
Kolar, *India*   **66 N11** 13 12N 78 15 E
Kolar Gold Fields, *India*   **66 N11** 12 58N 78 16 E
Kolaras, *India*   **68 G6** 25 14N 77 36 E
Kolari, *Finland*   **8 C20** 67 20N 23 48 E
Kolárovo, *Slovak Rep.*   **27 D10** 47 54N 18 0 E
Kolašin, Serbia & M.   **44 D3** 42 50N 19 31 E
Kolayat, *India*   **68 F8** 27 50N 72 50 E
Kolbäck, *Sweden*   **10 E10** 59 34N 16 15 E
Kolbäcksån ➤, *Sweden*   **10 E10** 59 36N 16 16 E
Kolbermoor, *Germany*   **25 H8** 47 51N 12 4 E
Kolbuszowa, *Poland*   **31 H8** 50 15N 21 46 E
Kolchugino, *Russia*   **32 D9** 56 40N 39 22 E
Kolda, *Senegal*   **82 C2** 12 55N 14 57W
Koldegi, *Sudan*   **81 E3** 5 3N 30 16 E
Kolding, *Denmark*   **11 J3** 55 30N 9 29 E
Kolepom = Dolak,
  Pulau, *Indonesia*   **63 F9** 8 0 S 138 30 E
Kolguyev, Ostrov,
  Russia   **52 C5** 69 20N 48 30 E
Kolhapur, *India*   **66 L9** 16 43N 74 15 E
Kolia, *Ivory C.*   **82 D3** 9 46N 6 28W
Kolín, *Czech Rep.*   **26 A8** 50 2N 15 9 E
Kolind, *Denmark*   **11 H4** 56 21N 10 34 E
Kolkas rags, *Latvia*   **9 H20** 57 46N 22 37 E
Kolkata, *India*   **69 H13** 22 36N 88 24 E
Kollam = Quilon, *India*   **66 Q10** 8 50N 76 38 E
Kölleda, *Germany*   **24 D7** 51 11N 11 15 E
Kollum, *Neths.*   **17 A6** 53 17N 6 9 E
Kolmanskop, *Namibia*   **88 D2** 26 45 S 15 14 E
Köln, *Germany*   **24 E2** 50 56N 6 57 E
Kolno, *Poland*   **30 E8** 53 25N 21 56 E
Koło, *Poland*   **31 F5** 52 14N 18 40 E
Kołobrzeg, *Poland*   **30 D2** 54 10N 15 35 E
Kolochava, *Ukraine*   **29 B8** 48 26N 23 41 E
Kolokani, *Mali*   **82 C3** 13 35N 7 45W
Koloko, *Burkina Faso*   **82 C3** 11 5N 5 19W
Kolomna, *Russia*   **32 E10** 55 8N 38 45 E
Kolomyya, *Ukraine*   **29 B10** 48 31N 25 2 E
Kolondiéba, *Mali*   **82 C3** 11 5N 6 54W
Kolonodale, *Indonesia*   **63 E6** 2 0 S 121 19 E
Kolonowskie, *Poland*   **31 H5** 50 39N 18 22 E
Kolosib, *India*   **67 G18** 24 15N 92 45 E
Kolpashevo, *Russia*   **52 D9** 58 20N 83 5 E
Kolpino, *Russia*   **32 C6** 59 44N 30 39 E
Kolpny, *Russia*   **33 F9** 52 17N 37 1 E
Kolskiy Poluostrov,
  Russia   **52 C4** 67 30N 38 0 E
Kolsva, *Sweden*   **10 E9** 59 36N 15 51 E
Kolubara ➤,
  Serbia & M.   **44 B4** 44 35N 20 15 E
Koluszki, *Poland*   **31 G6** 51 45N 19 46 E
Kolwezi, Dem. Rep. of
  the *Congo*   **87 E2** 10 40 S 25 25 E
Kolyma ➤, *Russia*   **53 C17** 69 30N 161 0 E
Kolymskoye Nagorye,
  Russia   **53 C16** 63 0N 157 0 E
Kôm Hamâda, *Egypt*   **80 H7** 30 46N 30 41 E
Kôm Ombo, *Egypt*   **80 C3** 24 25N 32 52 E
Komadugu Gana ➤,
  Nigeria   **83 C7** 13 5N 12 24 E
Komandorskiye Is. =
  Komandorskiye
  Ostrova, *Russia*   **53 D17** 55 0N 167 0 E
Komandorskiye
  Ostrova, *Russia*   **53 D17** 55 0N 167 0 E
Komárno, *Slovak Rep.*   **27 D11** 47 49N 18 5 E
Komárom, *Hungary*   **28 C3** 47 43N 18 7 E
Komárom-Esztergom □,
  Hungary   **28 C3** 47 35N 18 20 E
Komatipoort, S. *Africa*   **89 D5** 25 25 S 31 55 E
Komatou Yialou,
  Cyprus   **49 D13** 35 25N 34 8 E
Komatsu, *Japan*   **55 F8** 36 25N 136 30 E
Komatsushima, *Japan*   **55 H7** 34 0N 134 35 E
Kombissiri,
  Burkina Faso   **83 C4** 12 4N 1 20W
Kombóti, *Greece*   **46 B3** 39 6N 21 5 E
Komen, *Slovenia*   **41 C10** 45 49N 13 45 E
Komenda, *Ghana*   **83 D4** 5 4N 1 28W
Komi □, *Russia*   **52 C6** 64 0N 55 0 E
Komiža, *Croatia*   **41 E13** 43 3N 16 11 E

Komló, *Hungary*   **28 D3** 46 15N 18 16 E
Kommunarsk =
  Alchevsk, *Ukraine*   **33 H10** 48 30N 38 45 E
Kommunizma, Pik,
  Tajikistan   **52 F8** 39 0N 72 2 E
Komodo, *Indonesia*   **63 F5** 8 37 S 119 20 E
Komoé ➤, *Ivory C.*   **82 D4** 5 12N 3 44W
Komoran, Pulau,
  Indonesia   **63 F9** 8 18 S 138 45 E
Komoro, *Japan*   **55 F9** 36 19N 138 26 E
Komotini, *Greece*   **45 E9** 41 9N 25 26 E
Komovi, Serbia & M.   **44 D3** 42 41N 19 39 E
Kompasberg, S. *Africa*   **88 E3** 31 45 S 24 32 E
Kompong Bang =
  Kampong Chhnang,
  Cambodia   **65 F5** 12 20N 104 35 E
Kompong Cham,
  Cambodia   **65 F5** 12 0N 105 30 E
Kompong Chhnang =
  Kampong Chhnang,
  Cambodia   **65 F5** 12 20N 104 35 E
Kompong Chikreng,
  Cambodia   **64 F5** 13 5N 104 18 E
Kompong Kleang,
  Cambodia   **64 F5** 13 6N 104 8 E
Kompong Luong,
  Cambodia   **65 G5** 11 49N 104 48 E
Kompong Pranak,
  Cambodia   **64 F5** 13 35N 104 55 E
Kompong Som =
  Kampong Saom,
  Cambodia   **65 G4** 10 38N 103 30 E
Kompong Som,
  Chhung = Kampong
  Saom, Chaak,
  Cambodia   **65 G4** 10 50N 103 32 E
Kompong Speu,
  Cambodia   **65 G5** 11 26N 104 32 E
Kompong Sralau,
  Cambodia   **64 E5** 14 5N 105 46 E
Kompong Thom,
  Cambodia   **64 F5** 12 35N 104 51 E
Kompong Trabeck,
  Cambodia   **64 F5** 13 6N 105 14 E
Kompong Trabeck,
  Cambodia   **65 G5** 11 9N 105 28 E
Kompong Trach,
  Cambodia   **65 G5** 11 25N 105 48 E
Kompong Tralach,
  Cambodia   **65 G5** 11 54N 104 47 E
Komrat = Comrat,
  Moldova   **29 D13** 46 18N 28 40 E
Komsberg, S. *Africa*   **88 E3** 32 40 S 20 45 E
Komsomolets, Ostrov,
  Russia   **53 A10** 80 30N 95 0 E
Komsomolsk, Amur,
  Russia   **53 D14** 50 30N 137 0 E
Komsomolsk, Ivanovo,
  Russia   **32 D11** 57 2N 40 20 E
Komsomolskiy, *Russia*   **34 C7** 54 37N 45 33 E
Kömür Burnu, *Turkey*   **47 C8** 38 39N 26 12 E
Kon Tum, *Vietnam*   **64 E7** 14 24N 108 0 E
Kon Tum, Plateau du,
  Vietnam   **64 E7** 14 30N 108 30 E
Kona, *Mali*   **82 C4** 14 57N 3 53W
Konakovo, *Russia*   **32 D9** 56 40N 36 51 E
Konarhā □, *Afghan.*   **66 B7** 34 30N 71 3 E
Konārī, *Iran*   **71 D6** 28 13N 51 36 E
Konch, *India*   **69 G8** 26 0N 79 10 E
Konde, *Tanzania*   **86 C4** 4 57 S 39 45 E
Kondiá, *Greece*   **47 B7** 39 49N 25 10 E
Kondinin, *Australia*   **93 F2** 32 34 S 118 8 E
Kondoa, *Tanzania*   **86 C4** 4 55 S 35 50 E
Kondókali, *Greece*   **49 A3** 39 38N 19 51 E
Kondopaga, *Russia*   **32 A8** 62 12N 34 17 E
Kondratyevo, *Russia*   **53 D10** 57 22N 98 15 E
Kondrovo, *Russia*   **32 E8** 54 48N 35 56 E
Konduga, *Nigeria*   **83 C7** 11 35N 13 26 E
Köneürgench,
  Turkmenistan   **52 E6** 42 19N 59 10 E
Konevo, *Russia*   **32 A10** 62 8N 39 20 E
Kong = Khong ➤,
  Cambodia   **64 F5** 13 32N 105 58 E
Kong, *Ivory C.*   **82 D4** 8 54N 4 36W
Kong, Koh, *Cambodia*   **65 G4** 11 20N 103 0 E
Kong Christian IX Land,
  Greenland   **4 C6** 68 0N 36 0W
Kong Christian X Land,
  Greenland   **4 B6** 74 0N 29 0W
Kong Frederik IX Land,
  Greenland   **4 C5** 67 0N 52 0W
Kong Frederik VI Kyst,
  Greenland   **101 B15** 63 0N 43 0W
Kong Frederik VIII
  Land, *Greenland*   **4 B6** 78 30N 26 0W
Kong Oscar Fjord,
  Greenland   **4 B6** 72 20N 24 0W
Kongeå ➤, *Denmark*   **11 J2** 55 23N 8 39 E
Kongerslev, *Denmark*   **11 H4** 56 54N 10 6 E
Kongju, S. *Korea*   **57 F14** 36 30N 127 0 E
Konglu, *Burma*   **67 F20** 27 13N 97 57 E
Kongola, *Namibia*   **88 B3** 17 45 S 23 20 E
Kongolo, Kasai-Or.,
  Dem. Rep. of
  the *Congo*   **86 D1** 5 26 S 24 49 E
Kongolo, Katanga,
  Dem. Rep. of
  the *Congo*   **86 D2** 5 22 S 27 0 E
Kongor, *Sudan*   **81 F3** 7 1N 31 27 E
Kongoussi,
  Burkina Faso   **83 C4** 13 19N 1 32W
Kongsberg, *Norway*   **9 G13** 59 39N 9 39 E
Kongsvinger, *Norway*   **9 F15** 60 12N 12 2 E
Kongwa, *Tanzania*   **86 D4** 6 11 S 36 26 E
Koni, Dem. Rep. of
  the *Congo*   **87 E2** 10 40 S 27 11 E
Koni, Mts., Dem. Rep. of
  the *Congo*   **87 E2** 10 36 S 27 10 E
Koniakari, *Mali*   **82 C2** 14 10N 10 20W
Koniecpol, *Poland*   **31 H6** 50 46N 19 40 E
Königs Wusterhausen,
  Germany   **24 C9** 52 19N 13 38 E
Königsbrunn, *Germany*   **24 C6** 52 15N 10 49 E
Königslutter, *Germany*   **24 C6** 52 15N 10 49 E
Konin, *Poland*   **31 F5** 52 12N 18 15 E
Konispol, *Albania*   **46 B2** 39 42N 20 10 E
Kónitsa, *Greece*   **46 A2** 40 5N 20 48 E
Konjic, Bos.-H.   **42 D2** 43 42N 17 58 E
Konkiep, *Namibia*   **88 D2** 26 49 S 17 15 E
Konkouré ➤, *Guinea*   **82 D2** 9 50N 13 42W
Könnern, *Germany*   **24 D7** 51 41N 11 47 E
Kono, S. *Leone*   **82 D2** 8 30N 11 5W
Konongo, *Ghana*   **83 D4** 6 40N 1 15W
Konosha, *Russia*   **32 B11** 61 0N 40 5 E
Kōnosu, *Japan*   **55 F9** 36 3N 139 31 E
Konotop, *Ukraine*   **33 G7** 51 12N 33 14 E
Konsankoro, *Guinea*   **82 D3** 9 28N 9 13W
Końskie, *Poland*   **31 G7** 51 15N 20 23 E

Konstancin-Jeziorna,
  Poland   **31 F8** 52 5N 21 7 E
Konstantinovka =
  Kostyantynivka,
  Ukraine   **33 H9** 48 32N 37 39 E
Konstantinovsk, *Russia*   **35 G5** 47 33N 41 10 E
Konstantynów Łódzki,
  Poland   **31 G6** 51 45N 19 20 E
Konstanz, *Germany*   **25 H5** 47 40N 9 10 E
Kont, *Iran*   **71 E9** 26 55N 61 50 E
Kontagora, *Nigeria*   **83 C6** 10 23N 5 27 E
Kontcha, *Cameroon*   **83 D7** 7 59N 12 15 E
Konya, *Turkey*   **70 D5** 37 52N 32 35 E
Konya Ovası, *Turkey*   **72 C5** 38 9N 33 5 E
Konz, *Germany*   **25 F2** 49 42N 6 34 E
Konza, *Kenya*   **86 C4** 1 45 S 37 7 E
Koocanusa, L., *Canada*   **108 B6** 49 20N 115 15W
Kookynie, *Australia*   **93 E3** 29 17 S 121 22 E
Koolyanobbing,
  Australia   **93 F2** 30 48 S 119 36 E
Koonibba, *Australia*   **95 E1** 31 54 S 133 25 E
Kooraawatha, *Australia*   **95 E4** 34 2 S 148 33 E
Koorda, *Australia*   **93 F2** 30 48 S 117 35 E
Kooskia, *U.S.A.*   **108 C6** 46 9N 115 59W
Kootenay △, *Canada*   **102 C5** 51 0N 116 0W
Kootenay ➤, *U.S.A.*   **102 D5** 49 19N 117 39W
Kootenay L., *Canada*   **102 D5** 49 45N 116 50W
Kootjieskolk, S. *Africa*   **88 E3** 31 15 S 20 21 E
Kopanovka, *Russia*   **35 G8** 47 28N 46 50 E
Kopaonik, Serbia & M.   **44 C4** 43 10N 20 50 E
Kopaonik △,
  Serbia & M.   **44 C4** 43 20N 20 50 E
Kópavogur, *Iceland*   **8 D3** 64 6N 21 55W
Kopayhorod, *Ukraine*   **29 B12** 48 52N 27 47 E
Koper, *Slovenia*   **41 C10** 45 31N 13 44 E
Kopervik, *Norway*   **9 G11** 59 17N 5 17 E
Kopet Dagh, *Asia*   **71 B8** 38 0N 58 0 E
Kopi, *Australia*   **95 E2** 33 24 S 135 40 E
Köping, *Sweden*   **10 E10** 59 31N 16 3 E
Köpingsvik, *Sweden*   **11 H10** 56 53N 16 43 E
Kopište, *Croatia*   **41 F13** 42 48N 16 42 E
Koplik, *Albania*   **44 D3** 42 15N 19 25 E
Köpmanholmen, *Sweden*   **10 A12** 63 10N 18 35 E
Kopparberg, *Sweden*   **10 E9** 59 52N 14 59 E
Koppeh Dāgh = Kopet
  Dagh, *Asia*   **71 B8** 38 0N 58 0 E
Koppies, S. *Africa*   **89 D4** 27 20 S 27 30 E
Koppom, *Sweden*   **10 E6** 59 43N 12 10 E
Koprivlen, *Bulgaria*   **44 E7** 41 31N 23 53 E
Koprivnica, *Croatia*   **41 B13** 46 12N 16 45 E
Kopřivnice, *Czech Rep.*   **27 B11** 49 36N 18 12 E
Koprivshtitsa, *Bulgaria*   **45 D8** 42 40N 24 19 E
Köprübaşı, *Turkey*   **47 C10** 38 43N 28 23 E
Kopychyntsi, *Ukraine*   **33 H3** 49 7N 25 58 E
Kora △, *Kenya*   **86 C4** 0 14 S 38 44 E
Korab, *Macedonia*   **44 E4** 41 44N 20 40 E
Korakiána, *Greece*   **49 A3** 39 42N 19 45 E
Koral, *India*   **68 J5** 21 50N 73 12 E
Korarou, L., *Mali*   **82 B4** 15 15N 3 55W
Korba, *India*   **69 H10** 22 20N 82 45 E
Korbach, *Germany*   **24 D4** 51 16N 8 52 E
Korbu, G., *Malaysia*   **65 K3** 4 41N 101 18 E
Korçë, *Albania*   **44 F4** 40 37N 20 50 E
Korčula, *Croatia*   **41 F13** 42 56N 16 57 E
Korčulanski Kanal,
  Croatia   **41 E13** 43 3N 16 40 E
Kord Kūy, *Iran*   **71 B7** 36 48N 54 7 E
Kord Sheykh, *Iran*   **71 D7** 28 31N 52 53 E
Kordestān = Kurdistān,
  Asia   **73 D10** 37 20N 43 30 E
Kordestān □, *Iran*   **70 C5** 36 0N 47 0 E
Kordofân, *Sudan*   **79 F11** 13 0N 29 0 E
Korea, North ■, *Asia*   **57 E14** 40 0N 127 0 E
Korea, South ■, *Asia*   **57 G15** 36 0N 128 0 E
Korea Bay, *Korea*   **57 E13** 39 0N 124 0 E
Korea Strait, *Asia*   **57 H15** 34 0N 129 30 E
Korem, *Ethiopia*   **81 E4** 12 30N 39 32 E
Korenevo, *Russia*   **33 G8** 51 27N 34 55 E
Korenovsk, *Russia*   **35 H4** 45 30N 39 22 E
Korets, *Ukraine*   **33 G4** 50 40N 27 5 E
Korfantów, *Poland*   **31 H4** 50 29N 17 34 E
Korgan, *Turkey*   **72 B7** 40 48N 37 6 E
Korgus, *Sudan*   **80 D3** 19 16N 33 29 E
Korhogo, *Ivory C.*   **82 D3** 9 29N 5 28W
Koribundu, S. *Leone*   **82 D2** 7 41N 11 46W
Korienzé, *Mali*   **82 B4** 15 23N 2 35W
Korinthía □, *Greece*   **46 D4** 37 50N 22 35 E
Korinthiakós Kólpos,
  Greece   **46 C4** 38 16N 22 30 E
Kórinthos, *Greece*   **46 D4** 37 56N 22 55 E
Kórinthos, *Greece*   **46 D4** 37 56N 22 55 E
Koríssa, Límni, *Greece*   **49 B3** 39 27N 19 53 E
Kōriyama, *Japan*   **54 F10** 37 24N 140 23 E
Korkuteli, *Turkey*   **47 D12** 37 4N 30 13 E
Kormakiti, C., *Cyprus*   **49 D11** 35 23N 32 56 E
Körmend, *Hungary*   **28 C1** 47 5N 16 35 E
Kornat, *Croatia*   **41 E12** 43 50N 15 20 E
Kornat △, *Croatia*   **41 E12** 43 50N 15 12 E
Kornešty = Cornești,
  Moldova   **29 C13** 47 21N 28 1 E
Korneuburg, *Austria*   **27 C9** 48 20N 16 20 E
Kórnik, *Poland*   **31 F4** 52 15N 17 6 E
Koro, *Fiji*   **91 C8** 17 19 S 179 23 E
Koro, *Ivory C.*   **82 D3** 8 32N 7 30W
Koro, *Mali*   **82 C4** 14 1N 2 58W
Koro Sea, *Fiji*   **91 C9** 17 30 S 179 45W
Korocha, *Russia*   **33 G9** 50 54N 37 19 E
Köroğlu Dağları, *Turkey*   **72 B5** 40 38N 33 0 E
Korogwe, *Tanzania*   **86 D4** 5 5 S 38 25 E
Koroleve, *Ukraine*   **29 B8** 48 12N 23 8 E
Koronadal, *Phil.*   **61 H6** 6 12N 125 1 E
Koróni, *Greece*   **46 E3** 36 48N 21 57 E
Korónia, Límni, *Greece*   **44 F7** 40 47N 23 10 E
Koronís, *Greece*   **47 D7** 37 12N 25 35 E
Koronowo, *Poland*   **31 E4** 53 19N 17 55 E
Körös ➤, *Hungary*   **28 D5** 46 43N 20 12 E
Körös Maros △,
  Hungary   **28 C5** 47 8N 20 52 E
Köröstarcsa, *Hungary*   **28 C5** 46 53N 21 3 E
Korosten, *Ukraine*   **33 G5** 50 54N 28 36 E
Korostyshev, *Ukraine*   **33 G5** 50 19N 29 4 E
Korotoyak, *Russia*   **33 G10** 51 11N 39 2 E
Korraraika, Helodranon'
  i, *Madag.*   **89 B7** 17 45 S 43 57 E
Korsakov, *Russia*   **53 E15** 46 36N 142 42 E
Korsberga, *Sweden*   **11 G9** 57 19N 15 1 E
Korshunovo, *Russia*   **53 D11** 58 37N 110 10 E
Korsør, *Denmark*   **11 J5** 55 20N 11 9 E
Korsun
  Shevchenkovskiy,
  Ukraine   **33 H6** 49 26N 31 16 E
Kortes, *Poland*   **30 D8** 54 11N 21 9 E
Korti, *Sudan*   **80 D3** 18 6N 31 33 E

Kortrijk, Belgium ..... 17 D3 50 50N 3 17 E
Korucu, Turkey ..... 47 B9 39 28N 27 22 E
Korwai, India ..... 68 G8 24 7N 78 5 E
Koryakskoye Nagorye, Russia ..... 53 C18 61 0N 171 0 E
Koryŏng, S. Korea ..... 57 G15 35 44N 128 15 E
Koryukovka, Ukraine ..... 33 G7 51 46N 32 16 E
Kosa, Ethiopia ..... 81 F4 7 50N 36 50 E
Kosaya Gora, Russia ..... 32 E9 54 10N 37 30 E
Kościan, Poland ..... 31 F3 52 5N 16 40 E
Kościerzyna, Poland ..... 30 D4 54 8N 17 59 E
Kosciusko, U.S.A. 113 J10 33 4N 89 35W
Kosciuszko, Mt., Australia ..... 95 F4 36 27S 148 16 E
Kösély →, Hungary ..... 28 C6 47 25N 21 5 E
Kosha, Sudan ..... 80 C3 20 50N 30 30 E
Koshava, Bulgaria ..... 44 B7 44 4N 23 2 E
K'oshih = Kashi, China ..... 60 C2 39 30N 76 2 E
Koshiki-Rettō, Japan ..... 55 J4 31 45N 129 49 E
Kosi, India ..... 68 F7 27 48N 77 29 E
Kosi →, India ..... 69 E8 28 41N 78 57 E
Košice, Slovak Rep. ..... 27 C14 48 42N 21 15 E
Košický □, Slovak Rep. ..... 27 C14 48 45N 21 15 E
Kosiv, Ukraine ..... 29 B10 48 19N 25 6 E
Kosjerić, Serbia & M. ..... 44 B3 44 0N 19 55 E
Kösk, Turkey ..... 47 D10 37 50N 28 3 E
Koskinoú, Greece ..... 49 C10 36 23N 28 13 E
Koslan, Russia ..... 52 C5 63 34N 49 14 E
Košong, N. Korea ..... 57 E15 38 40N 128 22 E
Kosovo □, Serbia & M. ..... 44 D4 42 30N 21 0 E
Kosovo Polje, Serbia & M. ..... 44 D5 42 40N 21 5 E
Kosovska Kamenica, Serbia & M. ..... 44 D5 42 35N 21 35 E
Kosovska Mitrovica, Serbia & M. ..... 44 D4 42 54N 20 52 E
Kossou, L. de, Ivory C. 82 D3 6 59N 5 31W
Kosta, Sweden ..... 11 H9 56 50N 15 24 E
Kostajnica, Croatia ..... 41 C13 45 17N 16 30 E
Kostanjevica, Slovenia ..... 41 C12 45 51N 15 27 E
Kostenets, Bulgaria ..... 44 D7 42 15N 23 52 E
Koster, S. Africa ..... 88 D4 25 52S 26 54 E
Kôstî, Sudan ..... 81 E3 13 8N 32 43 E
Kostinbrod, Bulgaria ..... 44 D7 42 49N 23 13 E
Kostolac, Serbia & M. ..... 44 B5 44 37N 21 15 E
Kostopil, Ukraine ..... 33 G4 50 51N 26 22 E
Kostroma, Russia ..... 32 D11 57 50N 40 58 E
Kostromskoye Vdkhr., Russia ..... 32 D11 57 52N 40 49 E
Kostryzhivka, Ukraine ..... 29 B10 48 39N 25 43 E
Kostrzyn, Lubuskie, Poland ..... 31 F1 52 35N 14 39 E
Kostrzyn, Wielkopolskie, Poland ..... 31 F4 52 24N 17 14 E
Kostyantynivka, Ukraine ..... 33 H9 48 32N 37 39 E
Kostyukovichi = Kastsyukovichy, Belarus ..... 32 F7 53 20N 32 4 E
Koszalin, Poland ..... 30 D3 54 11N 16 8 E
Kőszeg, Hungary ..... 28 C1 47 23N 16 33 E
Kot Addu, Pakistan ..... 68 D4 30 30N 71 0 E
Kot Kapura, India ..... 68 D6 30 35N 74 50 E
Kot Moman, Pakistan ..... 68 C5 32 13N 73 0 E
Kot Sultan, Pakistan ..... 68 D4 30 46N 70 56 E
Kota, India ..... 68 G6 25 14N 75 49 E
Kota Barrage, India ..... 68 G6 25 6N 75 51 E
Kota Belud, Malaysia ..... 62 C5 6 21N 116 26 E
Kota Bharu, Malaysia ..... 65 J4 6 7N 102 14 E
Kota Kinabalu, Malaysia ..... 62 C5 6 0N 116 4 E
Kota Kubu Bharu, Malaysia ..... 65 L3 3 34N 101 39 E
Kota Tinggi, Malaysia ..... 65 M4 1 44N 103 53 E
Kotaagung, Indonesia ..... 62 F2 5 38S 104 29 E
Kotabaru, Indonesia ..... 62 E5 3 20S 116 20 E
Kotabumi, Indonesia ..... 62 E2 4 49S 104 54 E
Kotamobagu, Indonesia ..... 63 D6 0 57N 124 31 E
Kotcho L., Canada 102 B4 59 7N 121 12W
Kotdwara, India ..... 69 E8 29 45N 78 32 E
Kotel, Bulgaria ..... 45 D10 42 52N 26 26 E
Kotelnich, Russia ..... 34 A9 58 22N 48 24 E
Kotelnikovo, Russia ..... 35 G6 47 38N 43 8 E
Kotelnyy, Ostrov, Russia ..... 53 B14 75 10N 139 0 E
Kothari →, India ..... 68 G6 25 20N 75 4 E
Köthen, Germany ..... 24 D7 51 45N 11 59 E
Kothi, Chhattisgarh, India ..... 69 H10 23 21N 82 3 E
Kothi, Mad. P., India ..... 69 G9 24 45N 80 40 E
Kotiro, Pakistan ..... 68 F2 26 17N 67 13 E
Kotka, Finland ..... 9 F22 60 28N 26 58 E
Kotlas, Russia ..... 52 C5 61 17N 46 43 E
Kotlenska Planina, Bulgaria ..... 45 D10 42 56N 26 30 E
Kotli, Pakistan ..... 68 C5 33 30N 73 55 E
Kotma, India ..... 69 H9 23 12N 81 58 E
Kotmul, Pakistan ..... 69 B6 35 32N 75 10 E
Koton-Karifi, Nigeria ..... 83 D6 8 3N 6 8 E
Kotonkoro, Nigeria ..... 83 C6 11 3N 5 58 E
Kotor, Serbia & M. ..... 44 D2 42 25N 18 47 E
Kotor Varoš, Bos.-H. ..... 42 F2 44 38N 17 22 E
Kotoriba, Croatia ..... 41 B13 46 23N 16 48 E
Kotovo, Russia ..... 34 E7 50 22N 44 45 E
Kotovsk, Russia ..... 34 D5 52 36N 41 32 E
Kotovsk, Ukraine ..... 33 J5 47 45N 29 35 E
Kotputli, India ..... 68 F7 27 43N 76 12 E
Kotri, Pakistan ..... 68 G3 25 22N 68 22 E
Kótronas, Greece ..... 46 E4 36 38N 22 29 E
Kötschach-Mauthen, Austria ..... 26 E6 46 41N 13 1 E
Kotturu, India ..... 66 M10 14 45N 76 10 E
Kotuy →, Russia ..... 53 B11 71 54N 102 6 E
Kotyuzhany, Ukraine ..... 29 B12 48 48N 27 42 E
Kouchibouguac △, Canada 105 C6 46 50N 65 0W
Koudougou, Burkina Faso 82 C4 12 10N 2 20W
Koufonísi, Greece ..... 49 E8 34 56N 26 8 E
Koufonísia, Greece ..... 47 E7 36 57N 25 35 E
Kougaberge, S. Africa ..... 88 E3 33 48S 23 50 E
Kouibli, Ivory C. 82 D3 7 15N 7 14W
Kouilou →, Congo ..... 84 E2 4 10S 12 5 E
Koula Moutou, Gabon ..... 84 E2 1 15S 12 25 E
Koulen = Kulen, Cambodia ..... 64 F5 13 50N 104 40 E
Koulikoro, Mali 82 C3 12 40N 7 50W
Kouloúra, Greece ..... 49 A3 39 42N 19 54 E
Koúm-bournoú, Ákra, Greece ..... 49 C10 36 15N 28 11 E
Koumala, Australia ..... 94 C4 21 38S 149 15 E
Koumankou, Mali 82 C3 11 58N 6 6W
Koumbia, Burkina Faso 82 C4 11 10N 3 50W
Koumbia, Guinea 82 C2 11 48N 13 29W
Koumboum, Guinea 82 C2 10 25N 13 0W
Koumpentoum, Senegal 82 C2 13 59N 14 34W

Koumra, Chad ..... 79 G9 8 50N 17 35 E
Koun-Fao, Ivory C. 82 D4 7 30N 3 15W
Koundara, Guinea 82 C2 12 29N 13 18W
Koundian, Guinea 82 C3 13 10N 10 35W
Koungheul, Senegal 82 C2 14 0N 14 50W
Kounradskiy = Kazakhstan ..... 52 E8 46 59N 75 0 E
Kountze, U.S.A. 113 K7 30 22N 94 19W
Koupéla, Burkina Faso 83 C4 12 11N 0 21W
Kourémalé, Mali 82 C3 11 59N 8 42W
Kouris →, Cyprus ..... 49 E11 34 38N 32 54 E
Kourou, Fr. Guiana 125 B8 5 9N 52 39W
Kourouba, Mali 82 C2 13 20N 10 57W
Kouroukoto, Mali 82 C2 12 35N 10 5W
Kourouma, Burkina Faso 82 C4 11 35N 4 50W
Kourounkcto, Mali 82 C3 13 52N 9 35W
Kouroussa, Guinea 82 C3 10 45N 9 45W
Koussanar, Senegal 82 C2 13 52N 14 5W
Koussané, Mali 82 C2 14 53N 11 14W
Koussane, Senegal 82 C2 14 10N 12 22W
Kousseri, Cameroon ..... 79 F8 12 0N 14 55 E
Koutiala, Mali 82 C3 12 25N 5 23W
Kouto, Ivory C. 82 D3 9 53N 6 25W
Kouvé, Togo ..... 83 D5 6 25N 1 25 E
Kouvola, Finland ..... 9 F22 60 52N 26 43 E
Kovačica, Serbia & M. ..... 28 E5 45 5N 20 38 E
Kovel, Ukraine ..... 33 G3 51 11N 24 38 E
Kovin, Serbia & M. ..... 28 F5 44 44N 20 59 E
Kovrov, Russia ..... 34 B5 56 25N 41 25 E
Kowal, Poland ..... 31 F6 52 32N 19 7 E
Kowalewo Pomorskie, Poland ..... 31 E5 53 10N 18 52 E
Kowanyama, Australia ..... 94 B3 15 29S 141 44 E
Kowloon, China ..... 59 F10 22 19N 114 11 E
Kowŏn, N. Korea ..... 57 E14 39 26N 127 14 E
Koyampattur = Coimbatore, India ..... 66 P10 11 2N 76 59 E
Köyceğiz, Turkey ..... 47 E10 36 57N 28 40 E
Köyceğiz Gölü, Turkey ..... 47 E10 36 56N 28 42 E
Koyulhisar, Turkey ..... 72 B7 40 20N 37 52 E
Koyunyeri, Turkey ..... 45 F10 40 50N 26 26 E
Koza, Japan ..... 55 L3 26 19N 127 46 E
Kozak, Turkey ..... 47 B9 39 15N 27 6 E
Kozan, Turkey ..... 70 B7 37 26N 35 50 E
Kozáni, Greece ..... 44 F5 40 19N 21 47 E
Kozáni □, Greece ..... 44 F5 40 18N 21 45 E
Kozara, Bos.-H. ..... 41 D14 45 0N 17 0 E
Kozara △, Bos.-H. ..... 28 F2 45 0N 17 0 E
Kozarac, Bos.-H. ..... 41 D13 44 58N 16 48 E
Kozelets, Ukraine ..... 33 G6 50 55N 31 7 E
Kozelsk, Russia ..... 32 E8 54 2N 35 48 E
Kozhikode = Calicut, India ..... 66 P9 11 15N 75 43 E
Kozięgłowy, Poland ..... 31 H6 50 37N 19 8 E
Kozienice, Poland ..... 31 G8 51 35N 21 34 E
Kozje, Slovenia ..... 41 B12 46 5N 15 35 E
Kozloduy, Bulgaria ..... 44 C7 43 45N 23 42 E
Kozlovets, Bulgaria ..... 45 C9 43 30N 25 20 E
Kozlovka, Russia ..... 34 C9 55 52N 48 14 E
Kozlu, Turkey ..... 72 B4 41 26N 31 45 E
Kozluk, Turkey ..... 73 C9 38 11N 41 31 E
Koźmin, Poland ..... 31 G4 51 48N 17 27 E
Kozmodemyansk, Russia ..... 34 B8 56 20N 46 36 E
Kożuchów, Poland ..... 31 G2 51 45N 15 31 E
Kozyatyn, Ukraine ..... 33 H5 49 45N 28 50 E
Kpabia, Ghana 83 D4 9 10N 0 20W
Kpalimé, Togo ..... 83 D5 6 57N 0 44 E
Kpandae, Ghana 83 D4 8 30N 0 2W
Kpessi, Togo ..... 83 D5 8 4N 1 16 E
Kra, Isthmus of = Kra, Kho Khot, Thailand ..... 65 G2 10 15N 99 30 E
Kra, Kho Khot, Thailand ..... 65 G2 10 15N 99 30 E
Kra Buri, Thailand ..... 65 G2 10 22N 98 46 E
Kraai →, S. Africa ..... 88 E4 30 40S 26 45 E
Krabi, Thailand ..... 65 H2 8 4N 98 55 E
Kracheh, Cambodia ..... 64 F6 12 32N 106 10 E
Kragan, Indonesia ..... 63 G14 6 43S 111 38 E
Kragerø, Norway ..... 9 G13 58 52N 9 25 E
Kragujevac, Serbia & M. ..... 44 B4 44 2N 20 56 E
Krajenka, Poland ..... 31 E3 53 18N 16 59 E
Krakatau = Rakata, Pulau, Indonesia ..... 62 F3 6 10S 105 20 E
Krakatoa = Rakata, Pulau, Indonesia ..... 62 F3 6 10S 105 20 E
Krakor, Cambodia ..... 64 F5 12 32N 104 12 E
Kraków, Poland ..... 31 H6 50 4N 19 57 E
Kraków ✈ (KRK), Poland ..... 31 H6 50 5N 19 52 E
Kralanh, Cambodia ..... 64 F4 13 35N 103 25 E
Králíky, Czech Rep. ..... 27 A9 50 6N 16 45 E
Kraljevo, Serbia & M. ..... 44 C4 43 44N 20 41 E
Kralovéhradecký □, Czech Rep. ..... 26 A8 50 25N 15 50 E
Královský Chlmec, Slovak Rep. ..... 27 C14 48 27N 22 0 E
Kralupy nad Vltavou, Czech Rep. ..... 26 A7 50 13N 14 20 E
Kramatorsk, Ukraine ..... 33 H9 48 50N 37 30 E
Kramfors, Sweden ..... 10 B11 62 55N 17 48 E
Kraniá, Greece ..... 44 G5 39 53N 21 18 E
Kraniá Elassónas, Greece ..... 46 B4 39 57N 22 2 E
Kranídhion, Greece ..... 46 D5 37 20N 23 10 E
Kranj, Slovenia ..... 41 B11 46 16N 14 22 E
Kranjska Gora, Slovenia ..... 41 B10 46 29N 13 48 E
Krankskop, S. Africa ..... 89 D5 28 0S 30 47 E
Krapina, Croatia ..... 41 B12 46 10N 15 52 E
Krapina →, Croatia ..... 41 C12 45 50N 15 50 E
Krapkowice, Poland ..... 31 H4 50 29N 17 56 E
Kras, Croatia ..... 41 C10 45 35N 14 0 E
Kraskino, Russia ..... 53 E14 42 44N 130 48 E
Kräslava, Latvia ..... 9 J22 55 52N 27 12 E
Kraslice, Czech Rep. ..... 26 A5 50 19N 12 31 E
Krasnaya Gorbatka, Russia ..... 34 C5 55 52N 41 45 E
Krasnaya Polyana, Russia ..... 35 J5 43 40N 40 13 E
Krasna, Ukraine ..... 29 C14 47 32N 29 27 E
Kraśnik, Poland ..... 31 H9 50 55N 22 15 E
Krasnoarmeisk, Ukraine ..... 33 H9 48 18N 37 11 E
Krasnoarmeysk, Russia ..... 34 E7 51 0N 45 42 E
Krasnoarmeyskiy, Russia ..... 35 G6 47 0N 42 12 E
Krasnobród, Poland ..... 31 H10 50 33N 23 12 E
Krasnodar, Russia ..... 35 H4 45 5N 39 0 E
Krasnogorskiy, Russia ..... 34 B9 56 10N 48 28 E
Krasnograd = Krasnohrad, Ukraine ..... 33 H8 49 27N 35 27 E
Krasnogvardeysk, Uzbekistan ..... 33 K8 45 32N 34 16 E
Krasnogvardeyskoye, Russia ..... 35 H5 45 5N 41 33 E
Krasnohrad, Ukraine ..... 33 H8 49 27N 35 27 E

Krasnokutsk, Ukraine ..... 33 G8 50 10N 34 50 E
Krasnolesnyy, Russia ..... 33 G10 51 53N 39 35 E
Krasnoperekopsk, Ukraine ..... 33 J7 46 0N 33 54 E
Krasnorechenskiy, Russia ..... 54 B7 44 41N 135 14 E
Krasnoselkup, Russia ..... 52 C9 65 20N 82 10 E
Krasnoslobodsk, Mordvinia, Russia ..... 34 C6 54 25N 43 45 E
Krasnoslobodsk, Volgograd, Russia ..... 35 F7 48 42N 44 33 E
Krasnoturinsk, Russia ..... 52 D7 59 46N 60 12 E
Krasnoyarsk, Russia ..... 53 D10 56 8N 93 0 E
Krasnoyarskoye, Russia ..... 30 D8 54 31N 21 56 E
Krasnoye = Krasnyy, Russia ..... 32 E6 54 25N 31 30 E
Krasnoyilsk, Ukraine ..... 29 C10 47 59N 25 38 E
Krasnozavodsk, Russia ..... 32 D10 56 27N 38 25 E
Krasny Sulin, Russia ..... 33 J11 47 52N 40 8 E
Krasnystaw, Poland ..... 31 H10 50 57N 23 5 E
Krasnyy, Russia ..... 32 E6 54 25N 31 30 E
Krasnyy Kholm, Russia ..... 32 C9 58 10N 37 10 E
Krasnyy Kut, Russia ..... 34 E8 50 50N 47 0 E
Krasnyy Liman, Ukraine ..... 33 H9 48 58N 37 50 E
Krasnyy Luch, Ukraine ..... 33 H10 48 13N 39 0 E
Krasnyy Profintern, Russia ..... 32 D11 57 45N 40 27 E
Krasnyy Yar, Astrakhan, Russia ..... 35 G9 46 43N 48 23 E
Krasnyy Yar, Samara, Russia ..... 34 D10 53 30N 50 22 E
Krasnyy Yar, Volgograd, Russia ..... 34 E7 50 42N 44 45 E
Krasnyye Baki, Russia ..... 34 B7 57 8N 45 10 E
Krasnyyoskolske Vdskh., Ukraine ..... 33 H9 49 27N 37 40 E
Kraszna →, Hungary ..... 28 B7 48 4N 22 20 E
Kratie = Kracheh, Cambodia ..... 64 F6 12 32N 106 10 E
Kratovo, Macedonia ..... 44 D6 42 6N 22 10 E
Krau, Indonesia ..... 63 E10 3 19S 140 5 E
Kravanh, Chuor Phnm, Cambodia ..... 65 G4 12 0N 103 32 E
Krefeld, Germany ..... 24 D2 51 20N 6 33 E
Krémaston, Límni, Greece ..... 46 C3 38 52N 21 30 E
Kremen, Croatia ..... 41 D12 44 28N 15 53 E
Kremenchuk, Ukraine ..... 33 H7 49 5N 33 25 E
Kremenchuksk Vdskh., Ukraine ..... 33 H7 49 20N 32 30 E
Kremenets, Ukraine ..... 33 G3 50 8N 25 43 E
Kremennaya, Ukraine ..... 33 H10 49 1N 38 10 E
Kremges = Svitlovodsk, Ukraine ..... 33 H7 49 2N 33 13 E
Kremmen, Germany ..... 24 C9 52 45N 13 1 E
Kremmling, U.S.A. 108 F10 40 4N 106 24W
Krems, Austria ..... 26 C8 48 25N 15 36 E
Kremsmünster, Austria ..... 26 C7 48 3N 14 8 E
Kretinga, Lithuania ..... 9 J19 55 53N 21 15 E
Krettsy, Russia ..... 32 C7 58 15N 32 30 E
Kreuzberg, Germany ..... 25 E5 50 22N 9 58 E
Kreuztal, Germany ..... 24 E4 50 57N 8 0 E
Kría Vrísi, Greece ..... 44 F6 40 41N 22 18 E
Kribi, Cameroon ..... 83 E6 2 57N 9 56 E
Krichem, Bulgaria ..... 45 D8 42 8N 24 28 E
Krichev = Krychaw, Belarus ..... 32 F6 53 40N 31 41 E
Krim, Slovenia ..... 41 C11 45 53N 14 30 E
Kriós, Ákra, Greece ..... 49 D5 35 13N 23 34 E
Krishna →, India ..... 67 M12 15 57N 80 59 E
Krishnanagar, India ..... 69 H13 23 24N 88 33 E
Kristdala, Sweden ..... 11 G10 57 24N 16 13 E
Kristiansand, Norway ..... 9 G13 58 8N 8 1 E
Kristianstad, Sweden ..... 11 H8 56 2N 14 9 E
Kristiansund, Norway ..... 8 E12 63 7N 7 45 E
Kristiinankaupunki, Finland ..... 9 E19 62 16N 21 21 E
Kristinehamn, Sweden ..... 10 E8 59 18N 14 7 E
Kristinestad = Kristiinankaupunki, Finland ..... 9 E19 62 16N 21 21 E
Kríti, Greece ..... 49 D7 35 15N 25 0 E
Kritsá, Greece ..... 49 D7 35 10N 25 41 E
Kriva →, Macedonia ..... 44 D5 42 5N 21 47 E
Kriva Palanka, Macedonia ..... 44 D6 42 11N 22 19 E
Krivaja →, Bos.-H. ..... 28 F3 44 27N 18 9 E
Krivelj, Serbia & M. ..... 44 B6 44 10N 22 5 E
Křivoklátsko △, Czech Rep. ..... 26 A6 50 1N 13 51 E
Krivoy Rog = Kryvyy Rih, Ukraine ..... 33 J7 47 51N 33 20 E
Križevci, Croatia ..... 41 B13 46 3N 16 32 E
Krk, Croatia ..... 41 C11 45 8N 14 40 E
Krka →, Croatia ..... 41 E12 43 5N 15 56 E
Krka △, Slovenia ..... 41 C12 45 50N 15 35 E
Krkonoše, Czech Rep. ..... 26 A8 50 50N 15 35 E
Krkonoše △, Czech Rep. ..... 26 A8 50 45N 15 40 E
Krnov, Czech Rep. ..... 27 A10 50 5N 17 40 E
Krobia, Poland ..... 31 G3 51 47N 16 59 E
Krokeaí, Greece ..... 46 D4 36 53N 22 32 E
Krokek, Sweden ..... 11 F10 58 40N 16 24 E
Krokodil →, Mozam. ..... 89 D5 25 14S 32 18 E
Krokom, Sweden ..... 10 A8 63 20N 14 30 E
Krokowa, Poland ..... 30 D5 54 47N 18 9 E
Krolevets, Ukraine ..... 33 G7 51 35N 33 20 E
Kroměříž, Czech Rep. ..... 27 B10 49 18N 17 21 E
Krompachy, Slovak Rep. ..... 27 C13 48 54N 20 52 E
Kromy, Russia ..... 33 F8 52 48N 35 47 E
Kronach, Germany ..... 25 E7 50 14N 11 19 E
Krong Kaoh Kong, Cambodia ..... 62 B2 11 35N 103 0 E
Kronobergs län □, Sweden ..... 11 H8 56 45N 14 30 E
Kronprins Olav Kyst, Antarctica ..... 5 C5 69 0S 42 0 E
Kronprinsesse Märtha Kyst, Antarctica 5 D2 73 30S 10 0W
Kronshtadt, Russia ..... 32 C5 59 57N 29 51 E
Kroonstad, S. Africa ..... 88 D4 27 43S 27 19 E
Kröpelin, Germany ..... 24 A7 54 4N 11 47 E
Kropotkin, Russia ..... 35 H5 45 28N 40 28 E
Kropp, Germany ..... 24 A5 54 24N 9 31 E
Krosna, Lithuania ..... 30 D10 54 23N 23 31 E
Krośniewice, Poland ..... 31 F6 51 11N 19 11 E
Krosno, Poland ..... 31 J8 49 42N 21 46 E
Krosno Odrzańskie, Poland ..... 31 F2 52 3N 15 7 E
Krotoszyn, Poland ..... 31 G4 51 42N 17 23 E
Krotovka, Russia ..... 34 D10 53 18N 51 13 E
Krraba, Albania ..... 44 E3 41 13N 20 0 E
Krrabë, Albania ..... 44 E3 41 13N 20 0 E
Krško, Slovenia ..... 41 C12 45 57N 15 30 E
Krstača, Serbia & M. ..... 44 D4 42 57N 20 8 E
Kruger △, S. Africa ..... 89 C5 24 0S 31 40 E

Krugersdorp, S. Africa ..... 89 D4 26 5S 27 46 E
Kruisfontein, S. Africa ..... 88 E3 33 59S 24 43 E
Krujë, Albania ..... 44 E3 41 32N 19 46 E
Krulevshchina = Krulyewshchyna, Belarus ..... 32 E4 55 5N 27 45 E
Krulyewshchyna, Belarus ..... 32 E4 55 5N 27 45 E
Krumbach, Germany ..... 25 G6 48 13N 10 22 E
Krumë, Albania ..... 44 D4 42 14N 20 28 E
Krumovgrad, Bulgaria ..... 45 E9 41 29N 25 38 E
Krung Thep = Bangkok, Thailand ..... 64 F3 13 45N 100 35 E
Krupanj, Serbia & M. ..... 44 B3 44 25N 19 22 E
Krupina, Slovak Rep. ..... 27 C12 48 22N 19 5 E
Krupinica →, Slovak Rep. ..... 27 C11 48 4N 18 55 E
Krupki, Belarus ..... 32 E5 54 19N 29 8 E
Kruševac, Serbia & M. ..... 44 C5 43 35N 21 28 E
Kruševo, Macedonia ..... 44 E5 41 23N 21 19 E
Krushelnyksya, Ukraine ..... 31 J10 49 7N 23 29 E
Kruszwica, Poland ..... 31 F5 52 40N 18 20 E
Krychaw, Belarus ..... 32 F6 53 40N 31 41 E
Krymsk, Russia ..... 35 K10 44 50N 38 0 E
Krymskiy Poluostrov = Krymskyy Pivostriv, Ukraine ..... 33 K8 45 0N 34 0 E
Krymskyy Pivostriv, Ukraine ..... 33 K8 45 0N 34 0 E
Krynica, Poland ..... 31 J7 49 25N 20 57 E
Krynica Morska, Poland ..... 30 D6 54 23N 19 28 E
Krynki, Poland ..... 31 E10 53 17N 23 43 E
Krynychne, Ukraine ..... 29 E13 45 28N 28 40 E
Kryvyy Rih, Ukraine ..... 33 J7 47 51N 33 20 E
Kryzhopil, Ukraine ..... 29 B13 48 23N 28 53 E
Krzepice, Poland ..... 31 H5 50 58N 18 50 E
Krzeszów, Poland ..... 31 H9 50 24N 22 21 E
Krzna →, Poland ..... 31 F10 52 8N 23 32 E
Krzywiń, Poland ..... 31 G3 51 58N 16 50 E
Krzyż Wielkopolski, Poland ..... 31 F2 52 52N 16 0 E
Ksar el Kebir, Morocco 78 B4 35 0N 6 0W
Ksar es Souk = Er Rachidia, Morocco 78 B5 31 58N 4 20W
Ksiąz Wielkopolski, Poland ..... 31 F5 52 4N 17 14 E
Kstovo, Russia ..... 34 B7 56 12N 44 13 E
Ku, W. el →, Sudan ..... 81 E2 13 37N 25 15 E
Kuah, Malaysia ..... 65 J2 6 19N 99 51 E
Kuala Belait, Malaysia ..... 62 D4 4 35N 114 11 E
Kuala Berang, Malaysia ..... 65 K4 5 5N 103 1 E
Kuala Dungun = Dungun, Malaysia ..... 65 K4 4 45N 103 25 E
Kuala Kangsar, Malaysia ..... 65 K3 4 46N 100 56 E
Kuala Kelawang, Malaysia ..... 65 L4 2 56N 102 5 E
Kuala Kerai, Malaysia ..... 65 K4 5 30N 102 12 E
Kuala Kerian, Malaysia ..... 65 c 5 10N 100 25 E
Kuala Lipis, Malaysia ..... 65 K4 4 10N 102 3 E
Kuala Lumpur, Malaysia ..... 65 L3 3 9N 101 41 E
Kuala Nerang, Malaysia ..... 65 J3 6 16N 100 37 E
Kuala Pilah, Malaysia ..... 65 L4 2 45N 102 15 E
Kuala Rompin, Malaysia ..... 65 L4 2 49N 103 29 E
Kuala Selangor, Malaysia ..... 65 L3 3 20N 101 15 E
Kuala Sepetang, Malaysia ..... 65 K3 4 49N 100 28 E
Kuala Terengganu, Malaysia ..... 65 K4 5 20N 103 8 E
Kualajelai, Indonesia ..... 62 E4 2 58S 110 46 E
Kualakapuas, Indonesia ..... 62 E4 2 55S 114 20 E
Kualakurun, Indonesia ..... 62 E4 1 10S 113 50 E
Kualapembuang, Indonesia ..... 62 E4 3 14S 112 38 E
Kualasimpang, Indonesia ..... 62 D1 4 17N 98 3 E
Kuancheng, China ..... 57 D10 40 37N 118 30 E
Kuandang, Indonesia ..... 63 D6 0 56N 123 1 E
Kuandian, China ..... 57 D13 40 45N 124 45 E
Kuangchou = Guangzhou, China ..... 59 F9 23 5N 113 10 E
Kuanshan, Taiwan ..... 59 F13 23 3N 121 9 E
Kuantan, Malaysia ..... 65 L4 3 49N 103 20 E
Kuba = Quba, Azerbaijan ..... 35 K9 41 21N 48 32 E
Kuban →, Russia ..... 35 K9 45 20N 37 30 E
Kuban Depression = Prikubanskaya Nizmennost, Russia ..... 35 H4 45 39N 38 0 E
Kubokawa, Japan ..... 55 H6 33 12N 133 8 E
Kubrat, Bulgaria ..... 45 C10 43 49N 26 31 E
Kubu, Indonesia ..... 63 J18 8 16S 115 10 E
Kubutambahan, Indonesia ..... 63 J18 8 5S 115 10 E
Kucar, Tanjung, Indonesia ..... 63 K18 8 53N 114 34 E
Kučevo, Serbia & M. ..... 44 B5 44 30N 21 40 E
Kucha Gompa, India ..... 69 B7 34 25N 76 56 E
Kuchaman, India ..... 68 F6 27 13N 74 47 E
Kuchinda, India ..... 69 J11 21 44N 84 21 E
Kuching, Malaysia ..... 62 D4 1 33N 110 25 E
Kuchino-eruba-Jima, Japan ..... 55 J5 30 28N 130 12 E
Kuchino-Shima, Japan ..... 55 K4 29 57N 129 55 E
Kuchman, India ..... 68 G7 24 22N 77 3 E
Kuchurhan →, Ukraine ..... 29 D14 46 33N 29 57 E
Kucing = Kuching, Malaysia ..... 62 D4 1 33N 110 25 E
Kçovë, Albania ..... 44 F3 40 47N 19 57 E
Küçükköy, Turkey ..... 47 B8 38 33N 26 24 E
Küçükmenderes →, Turkey ..... 47 D9 37 57N 27 14 E
Kud →, Pakistan ..... 68 F2 26 5N 66 20 E
Kuda, India ..... 66 H7 23 10N 71 15 E
Kudat, Malaysia ..... 62 C5 6 55N 116 55 E
Kudirkos Naumiestis, Lithuania ..... 30 D9 54 46N 22 53 E
Kudowa-Zdrój, Poland ..... 31 H3 50 27N 16 15 E
Kudus, Indonesia ..... 63 G14 6 48S 110 51 E
Kudymkar, Russia ..... 52 D6 59 1N 54 39 E
Kueiyang = Guiyang, China ..... 58 D6 26 32N 106 40 E
Kufra Oasis = Al Kufrah, Libya ..... 79 D10 24 17N 23 15 E
Kufstein, Austria ..... 26 D5 47 35N 12 11 E
Kugaaruk = Pelly Bay, Canada 101 B11 68 38N 89 50W
Kugluktuk, Canada 100 B8 67 50N 115 5W
Kühak, Iran ..... 66 F3 27 12N 63 10 E
Kühan, Iran ..... 66 B3 28 19N 61 14 E

Kühbonän, Iran ..... 71 D8 31 23N 56 19 E
Kühestak, Iran ..... 71 E8 26 47N 57 2 E
Kühin, Iran ..... 71 B6 36 22N 49 40 E
Kührī, Iran ..... 71 E9 26 55N 61 2 E
Kühnsdorf, Austria ..... 26 E7 46 37N 14 38 E
Kühpäyeh, Eşfahan, Iran ..... 71 C7 32 44N 52 20 E
Kühpäyeh, Kermän, Iran ..... 71 D8 30 35N 57 15 E
Kührän, Küh-e, Iran ..... 71 E8 26 46N 58 12 E
Kui Buri, Thailand ..... 65 F2 12 3N 99 52 E
Kuiseb →, Namibia ..... 88 C2 22 59S 14 31 E
Kuito, Angola ..... 85 G3 12 22S 16 55 E
Kuiu I., U.S.A. 102 B2 57 45N 134 10W
Kujang, N. Korea ..... 57 E14 39 57N 126 1 E
Kujawsko-Pomorskie □, Poland ..... 30 E5 53 0N 18 30 E
Kuji, Japan ..... 54 D10 40 11N 141 46 E
Kujū-San, Japan ..... 55 H5 33 5N 131 15 E
Kukava, Ukraine ..... 29 B12 48 37N 27 43 E
Kukavica, Serbia & M. ..... 44 D5 42 48N 21 57 E
Kukawa, Nigeria ..... 83 C7 12 58N 13 27 E
Kukës, Albania ..... 44 D4 42 5N 20 27 E
Kukmor, Russia ..... 34 B10 56 11N 50 54 E
Kukup, Malaysia ..... 65 d 1 20N 103 27 E
Kukup, Pulau, Malaysia ..... 65 d 1 18N 103 25 E
Kukvidze, Russia ..... 34 E6 50 40N 43 0 E
Kula, Bulgaria ..... 44 C6 43 52N 22 36 E
Kula, Serbia & M. ..... 28 E4 45 37N 19 32 E
Kula, Turkey ..... 47 C10 38 32N 28 40 E
Kulachi, Pakistan ..... 68 D4 31 56N 70 27 E
Kulai, Malaysia ..... 65 M4 1 44N 103 35 E
Kulaly, Ostrov, Kazakhstan ..... 35 H10 45 0N 50 0 E
Kulasekarappattinam, India ..... 66 Q11 8 20N 78 5 E
Kulautuva, Lithuania ..... 30 D10 54 56N 23 36 E
Kuldīga, Latvia ..... 9 H19 56 58N 21 59 E
Kuldja = Yining, China ..... 30 B8 56 55N 22 0 E
Kuldu, Sudan ..... 81 E2 12 50N 28 30 E
Kulebaki, Russia ..... 34 C6 55 22N 42 25 E
Kulen, Cambodia ..... 64 F5 13 50N 104 40 E
Kulen Vakuf, Bos.-H. ..... 41 D13 44 35N 16 2 E
Kulgam, India ..... 69 C6 33 36N 75 2 E
Kulgera, Australia ..... 94 D1 25 50S 133 18 E
Kulim, Malaysia ..... 65 K3 5 22N 100 34 E
Kulin, Australia ..... 93 F2 32 40S 118 2 E
Kulkayu = Hartley Bay, Canada 102 C3 53 25N 129 15W
Kullen, Sweden ..... 11 H6 56 18N 12 26 E
Kulmbach, Germany ..... 25 E7 50 6N 11 26 E
Külob, Tajikistan ..... 52 F7 37 55N 69 50 E
Kulp, Turkey ..... 73 C9 38 29N 41 2 E
Kulpawn →, Ghana 83 D4 10 20N 1 5W
Kulsary, Kazakhstan ..... 52 E6 46 59N 54 1 E
Kulti, India ..... 69 H12 23 43N 86 50 E
Kulu, India ..... 68 D7 31 58N 77 6 E
Kulu, Turkey ..... 72 C5 39 5N 33 4 E
Kulumbura, Australia ..... 92 B4 13 55S 126 35 E
Kulunda, Russia ..... 52 D8 52 35N 78 57 E
Kulungar, Afghan. ..... 68 C3 34 0N 69 2 E
Külvand, Iran ..... 71 D7 31 21N 54 35 E
Kulwin, Australia ..... 95 F3 35 0S 142 42 E
Kulyab = Külob, Tajikistan ..... 52 F7 37 55N 69 50 E
Kuma →, Russia ..... 35 H8 44 55N 47 0 E
Kumafşarı, Turkey ..... 47 D11 37 19N 29 32 E
Kumaganum, Nigeria ..... 83 C7 13 8N 10 38 E
Kumagaya, Japan ..... 55 F9 36 9N 139 22 E
Kumai, Indonesia ..... 62 E4 2 44N 111 43 E
Kumalar Dağı, Turkey ..... 47 C12 38 15N 30 20 E
Kumamba, Kepulauan, Indonesia ..... 63 E9 1 36S 138 45 E
Kumamoto, Japan ..... 55 H5 32 45N 130 45 E
Kumamoto □, Japan ..... 55 H5 32 55N 130 55 E
Kumanovo, Macedonia ..... 44 D5 42 9N 21 42 E
Kumara, N.Z. ..... 91 K3 42 37S 171 12 E
Kumarina, Australia ..... 93 D2 24 41S 119 32 E
Kumasi, Ghana 82 D4 6 41N 1 38W
Kumba, Cameroon ..... 83 E6 4 36N 9 24 E
Kumbağ, Turkey ..... 45 F11 40 51N 27 27 E
Kumbakonam, India ..... 66 P11 10 58N 79 25 E
Kumbarilla, Australia ..... 95 D5 27 15S 150 55 E
Kumbhraj, India ..... 68 G7 24 22N 77 3 E
Kumbia, Australia ..... 95 D5 26 41S 151 39 E
Kumbo, Cameroon ..... 83 D7 6 15N 10 36 E
Kümch'ŏn, N. Korea ..... 57 E14 38 10N 126 29 E
Kumdok, India ..... 69 C8 33 32N 78 10 E
Kume-Shima, Japan ..... 55 L3 26 20N 126 47 E
Kumeny, Russia ..... 34 A9 58 10N 49 47 E
Kumharsain, India ..... 68 D7 31 19N 77 27 E
Kumho →, S. Korea ..... 57 E14 35 48N 128 28 E
Kumi, Uganda ..... 86 B3 1 30N 33 58 E
Kumkale, Turkey ..... 45 G9 39 59N 26 11 E
Kumla, Sweden ..... 10 E9 59 8N 15 10 E
Kumluca, Turkey ..... 47 E12 36 22N 30 20 E
Kummerower See, Germany ..... 24 B8 53 49N 12 51 E
Kumo, Nigeria ..... 83 C7 10 1N 11 12 E
Kumo älv = Kokemäenjoki →, Finland ..... 9 F19 61 32N 21 44 E
Kumon Bum, Burma ..... 67 F20 26 30N 97 15 E
Kumylzhenskaya, Russia ..... 34 F6 49 51N 42 38 E
Kunágota, Hungary ..... 28 D6 46 26N 21 3 E
Kunashir, Ostrov, Russia ..... 53 E15 44 0N 146 0 E
Kunda, Estonia ..... 9 G22 59 30N 26 34 E
Kunda, India ..... 69 G9 25 43N 81 31 E
Kundar →, Pakistan ..... 68 D3 31 56N 69 19 E
Kundelungu △, Dem. Rep. of the Congo ..... 87 E2 10 30S 27 40 E
Kundelungu Ouest △, Dem. Rep. of the Congo ..... 87 D2 9 55S 27 17 E
Kundian, Pakistan ..... 68 C4 32 27N 71 28 E
Kundla, India ..... 68 J4 21 21N 71 25 E
Kung, Ao, Thailand ..... 65 a 8 5N 98 24 E
Kungala, Australia ..... 95 D5 29 58S 153 7 E
Kungälv, Sweden ..... 11 G6 57 53N 11 59 E
Kunghit I., Canada 102 C2 52 6N 131 3W
Kungrad = Qŭnghirot, Uzbekistan ..... 52 E6 43 6N 58 54 E
Kungsbacka, Sweden ..... 11 G6 57 30N 12 5 E
Kungsgården, Sweden ..... 10 D10 60 37N 16 35 E
Kungshamn, Sweden ..... 11 F5 58 22N 11 21 E
Kungsör, Sweden ..... 10 E10 59 25N 16 5 E
Kungu, Dem. Rep. of the Congo ..... 84 D3 2 47N 19 12 E
Kungur, Russia ..... 52 D6 57 25N 56 57 E
Kungurri, Australia ..... 94 K6 21 4S 148 45 E
Kunhar →, Pakistan ..... 69 B5 34 20N 73 30 E
Kunhegyes, Hungary ..... 28 C5 47 22N 20 36 E
Kunlong, Burma ..... 58 F2 23 20N 98 50 E
Kunlun Shan, Asia ..... 60 C3 36 0N 86 30 E
Kunmadaras, Hungary ..... 28 C5 47 28N 20 45 E
Kunming, China ..... 58 E4 25 1N 102 41 E
Kunovice, Czech Rep. ..... 27 B10 49 2N 17 21 E
Kunsan, S. Korea ..... 57 G14 35 59N 126 45 E

Kunshan, *China* ...... **59 B13** 31 22N 120 58 E
Kunszentmárton,
  Hungary .... **28 D5** 46 50N 20 20 E
Kunszentmiklós,
  Hungary .... **28 C4** 47 2N 19 8 E
Kuntaur, *Senegal* **82 C2** 13 40N 14 48W
Kununurra, *Australia* . **92 C4** 15 40 S 128 50 E
Kunwari →, *India* .... **69 F8** 26 26N 79 11 E
Kunya-Urgench =
  Köneürgench,
  Turkmenistan ..... **52 E6** 42 19N 59 10 E
Künzelsau, *Germany* . **25 F5** 49 17N 9 42 E
Kuopio, *Finland* ..... **8 E22** 62 53N 27 35 E
Kupa →, *Croatia* .... **41 C13** 45 28N 16 24 E
Kupang, *Indonesia* ... **63 F6** 10 19 S 123 39 E
Kupreanof I., *U.S.A.* . **102 B2** 56 50N 133 30W
Kupres, *Bos.-H.* ..... **28 G2** 43 59N 17 15 E
Kupyansk, *Ukraine* .. **33 H9** 49 52N 37 35 E
Kupyansk-Uzlovoi,
  Ukraine .... **33 H9** 49 40N 37 43 E
Kuqa, *China* .... **60 B3** 41 35N 82 30 E
Kür →, *Azerbaijan* .. **73 C13** 39 29N 49 15 E
Kür Dili, *Azerbaijan* . **71 B6** 39 3N 49 13 E
Kura = Kür →,
  Azerbaijan .... **73 C13** 39 29N 49 15 E
Kuranda, *Australia* ... **94 B4** 16 48 S 145 35 E
Kuranga, *India* ...... **68 H3** 22 4N 69 10 E
Kurashiki, *Japan* .... **55 G6** 34 40N 133 50 E
Kurayoshi, *Japan* .... **55 G6** 35 26N 133 50 E
Kürdämir, *Azerbaijan* . **35 K9** 40 25N 48 3 E
Kurdistan, *Asia* ..... **73 D10** 37 20N 43 30 E
Kürdzhali, *Bulgaria* .. **45 E9** 41 38N 25 21 E
Kure, *Japan* .... **55 G6** 34 14N 132 32 E
Küre, *Turkey* .... **72 B5** 41 48N 33 43 E
Küre Dağları, *Turkey* . **72 B5** 41 50N 34 10 E
Kuressaare, *Estonia* .. **9 G20** 58 15N 22 30 E
Kurgan, *Russia* ..... **52 D7** 55 26N 65 18 E
Kurganinsk, *Russia* .. **35 H5** 44 54N 40 34 E
Kurgannaya =
  Kurganinsk, *Russia* . **35 H5** 44 54N 40 34 E
Kuri, *India* .... **68 F4** 26 37N 70 43 E
Kuria Maria Is. =
  Khūrīyā Mūrīyā,
  Jazā'ir, *Oman* .... **75 D6** 17 30N 55 58 E
Kuridala, *Australia* ... **94 C3** 21 16 S 140 29 E
Kurigram, *Bangla.* ... **67 G16** 25 49N 89 39 E
Kurikka, *Finland* .... **9 E20** 62 36N 22 24 E
Kuril Is. = Kurilskiye
  Ostrova, *Russia* ... **53 E15** 45 0N 150 0 E
Kuril Trench, *Pac. Oc.* **96 C7** 44 0N 153 0 E
Kurilsk, *Russia* ..... **53 E15** 45 14N 147 53 E
Kurilskiye Ostrova,
  Russia .... **53 E15** 45 0N 150 0 E
Kurino, *Japan* ...... **55 J5** 31 57N 130 43 E
Kurinskaya Kosa = Kür
  Dili, *Azerbaijan* ... **71 B6** 39 3N 49 13 E
Kurkur, *Egypt* ...... **80 C3** 23 50N 32 0 E
Kurlovskiy, *Russia* ... **34 C5** 55 25N 40 40 E
Kurmuk, *Sudan* ..... **81 E3** 10 33N 34 21 E
Kurnool, *India* ...... **66 M11** 15 45N 78 0 E
Kuro-Shima,
  Kagoshima, Japan . **55 J4** 30 50N 129 57 E
Kuro-Shima, *Okinawa,*
  Japan .... **55 M2** 24 14N 124 1 E
Kuror, J., *Sudan* .... **80 C3** 20 27N 31 30 E
Kurow, *N.Z.* .... **91 L3** 44 44 S 170 29 E
Kurów, *Poland* ...... **31 G9** 51 23N 22 12 E
Kurram →, *Pakistan* . **68 C4** 32 36N 71 20 E
Kurri Kurri, *Australia* . **95 E5** 32 50 S 151 28 E
Kurrimine, *Australia* .. **94 B4** 17 47 S 146 6 E
Kursavka, *Russia* .... **35 H6** 44 29N 42 32 E
Kurshskaya Kosa △,
  Russia .... **30 C7** 55 7N 20 45 E
Kurshskiy Zaliv, *Russia* **9 J19** 55 9N 21 6 E
Kuršių Nerijos △,
  Lithuania .... **30 C8** 55 30N 21 6 E
Kursk, *Russia* ...... **33 G9** 51 42N 36 11 E
Kuršumlija, *Serbia & M.* **44 C5** 43 9N 21 19 E
Kuršumlijska Banja,
  Serbia & M. ...... **44 C5** 43 3N 21 11 E
Kurşunlu, *Bursa, Turkey* **45 F13** 40 3N 29 40 E
Kurşunlu, *Çankırı,*
  Turkey .... **72 B5** 40 51N 33 15 E
Kurtalan, *Turkey* .... **73 D9** 37 56N 41 44 E
Kurtbey, *Turkey* ..... **45 E10** 41 9N 26 35 E
Kuru, *Sudan* .... **81 F2** 7 43N 26 31 E
Kuru, Bahr el →, *Sudan* **81 F2** 8 10N 26 50 E
Kurucaşile, *Turkey* ... **72 B5** 41 49N 32 42 E
Kuruçay, *Turkey* .... **70 B3** 39 39N 38 29 E
Kuruktag, *China* .... **60 B3** 41 0N 89 0 E
Kuruman, *S. Africa* .. **88 D3** 27 28 S 23 28 E
Kuruman →, *S. Africa* . **88 D3** 26 56 S 20 39 E
Kurume, *Japan* ...... **55 H5** 33 15N 130 30 E
Kurun →, *Sudan* .... **81 F3** 5 30N 34 17 E
Kurunegala, *Sri Lanka* . **66 R12** 7 30N 80 23 E
Kurya, *Russia* ...... **52 C6** 61 42N 57 9 E
Kuş Gölü, *Turkey* .... **45 F11** 40 10N 27 55 E
Kuşadası, *Turkey* .... **72 D2** 37 52N 27 15 E
Kuşadası Körfezi,
  Turkey .... **47 D8** 37 56N 27 0 E
Kusamba, *Indonesia* .. **63 K18** 8 34 S 115 27 E
Kusatsu, *Japan* ...... **55 F9** 36 37N 138 36 E
Kusawa L., *Canada* ... **102 A1** 60 20N 136 13W
Kusel, *Germany* ..... **25 F3** 49 32N 7 24 E
Kushaka, *Nigeria* .... **83 C6** 10 32N 6 48 E
Kushalgarh, *India* ... **68 H6** 23 10N 74 27 E
Kushchevskaya, *Russia* . **35 G4** 46 33N 39 35 E
Kusheriki, *Nigeria* ... **83 C6** 10 33N 6 28 E
Kushima, *Japan* ..... **55 J5** 31 44N 131 16 E
Kushima, *Japan* ..... **55 H7** 33 28N 135 47 E
Kushimoto, *Japan* ... **55 J5** 31 29N 131 14 E
Kushiro, *Japan* ...... **54 C12** 43 0N 144 25 E
Kushiro-Gawa →, *Japan* **54 C12** 42 59N 144 23 E
Kushiro Shitsugen △,
  Japan .... **54 C12** 43 9N 144 26 E
Kūshk, *Iran* .... **71 D8** 28 46N 56 51 E
Kushka = Gushgy,
  Turkmenistan ..... **52 F7** 35 20N 62 18 E
Kūshkī, *Iran* .... **73 E11** 33 31N 47 13 E
Kushnytsya, *Ukraine* . **29 B8** 48 27N 23 15 E
Kushol, *India* .... **69 C8** 33 40N 76 36 E
Kushtia, *Bangla.* .... **67 H16** 23 55N 89 5 E
Kushum →, *Kazakhstan* **34 F10** 49 20N 50 45 E
Kuskokwim B., *U.S.A.* . **100 C3** 59 45N 162 25W
Kusmi, *India* .... **69 H10** 23 17N 83 55 E
Kussharo-Ko, *Japan* .. **54 C12** 43 38N 144 21 E
Kustanay = Qostanay,
  Kazakhstan ...... **52 D7** 53 10N 63 35 E
Kut, Ko, *Thailand* ... **65 G4** 11 40N 102 35 E
Kuta, *Indonesia* ..... **63 K18** 8 43 S 115 11 E
Kütahya, *Turkey* .... **47 B12** 39 30N 30 2 E
Kütahya □, *Turkey* .. **47 B11** 39 10N 29 30 E
Kutaisi, *Georgia* ..... **35 J6** 42 19N 42 40 E
Kutaraja = Banda Aceh,
  Indonesia .... **62 C1** 5 35N 95 20 E
Kutch, Gulf of =
  Kachchh, Gulf of,
  India .... **68 H3** 22 50N 69 15 E

Kutch, Rann of =
  Kachchh, Rann of,
  India .... **68 H4** 24 0N 70 0 E
Kutina, *Croatia* ..... **41 C13** 45 29N 16 48 E
Kutiyana, *India* ..... **68 J4** 21 36N 70 2 E
Kutjevo, *Croatia* .... **28 E2** 45 23N 17 55 E
Kutkashen, *Azerbaijan* . **35 K8** 40 58N 47 47 E
Kutná Hora, *Czech Rep.* **26 B8** 49 57N 15 16 E
Kutno, *Poland* ...... **31 F6** 52 15N 19 23 E
Kuttabul, *Australia* ... **94 K6** 21 5 S 148 54 E
Kutu, *Dem. Rep. of*
  the Congo .... **84 E3** 2 40 S 18 11 E
Kutum, *Sudan* ...... **81 E1** 14 10N 24 40 E
Kúty, *Slovak Rep.* .... **27 C10** 48 40N 17 3 E
Kuty, *Ukraine* ...... **29 B10** 48 16N 25 11 E
Kuujjuaq, *Canada* ... **101 C13** 58 6N 68 15W
Kuujjuarapik, *Canada* . **104 A4** 55 20N 77 35W
Kuusamo, *Finland* ... **8 D23** 65 57N 29 8 E
Kuusankoski, *Finland* . **9 F22** 60 55N 26 38 E
Kuvshinovo, *Russia* .. **32 D8** 57 2N 34 11 E
Kuwait = Al Kuwayt,
  Kuwait .... **70 D5** 29 30N 48 0 E
Kuwait ■, *Asia* ..... **70 D5** 29 30N 47 30 E
Kuwana, *Japan* ..... **55 G8** 35 5N 136 43 E
Kuwana →, *India* .... **69 F10** 26 25N 83 15 E
Kuybyshev = Samara,
  Russia .... **34 D10** 53 8N 50 6 E
Kuybyshev, *Russia* ... **52 D8** 55 27N 78 19 E
Kuybyshevo, *Ukraine* . **33 J9** 47 25N 36 40 E
Kuybyshevskoye
  Vdkhr., *Russia* .... **34 C9** 55 2N 49 30 E
Kuye He →, *China* .. **56 E6** 38 23N 110 46 E
Kūyeh, *Iran* .... **70 B5** 38 45N 47 57 E
Kuyucak, *Turkey* .... **47 D10** 37 55N 28 28 E
Kuyumba, *Russia* ... **53 C10** 60 58N 96 59 E
Kuzey Anadolu Dağları,
  Turkey .... **72 B7** 41 30N 35 0 E
Kuzmin, *Serbia & M.* . **28 E4** 45 2N 19 25 E
Kuznetsk, *Russia* .... **34 D8** 53 12N 46 40 E
Kuzomen, *Russia* .... **52 C4** 66 22N 36 50 E
Kvænangen, *Norway* . **8 A19** 70 5N 21 15 E
Kværndrup, *Denmark* . **11 J4** 55 10N 10 31 E
Kvaløy, *Norway* ..... **8 B18** 69 40N 18 30 E
Kvänum, *Sweden* ... **11 F7** 58 18N 13 11 E
Kvareli = Qvareli,
  Georgia .... **35 K7** 41 57N 45 47 E
Kvarner, *Croatia* .... **41 D11** 44 50N 14 10 E
Kvarnerič, *Croatia* ... **41 D11** 44 43N 14 37 E
Kvicksund, *Sweden* .. **10 E10** 59 27N 16 19 E
Kvillsfors, *Sweden* ... **11 G9** 57 24N 15 29 E
Kvismare kanal, *Sweden* **10 E9** 59 11N 15 35 E
Kvissleby, *Sweden* ... **10 B11** 62 18N 17 22 E
Kwa-Nobuhle, *S. Africa* **85 L5** 33 50 S 25 22 E
Kwabhaca, *S. Africa* .. **89 E4** 30 51 S 29 0 E
Kwakhanai, *Botswana* . **88 C3** 21 39 S 21 16 E
Kwakoegron, *Suriname* **125 B7** 5 12N 55 25W
Kwale, *Kenya* .... **86 C4** 4 15 S 39 31 E
Kwale, *Nigeria* ...... **83 D6** 5 46N 6 26 E
KwaMashu, *S. Africa* . **89 D5** 29 45 S 30 58 E
Kwando →, *Africa* ... **88 B3** 18 27 S 23 32 E
Kwangchow =
  Guangzhou, *China* . **59 F9** 23 5N 113 10 E
Kwangdaeri, *N. Korea* . **57 D14** 40 31N 127 32 E
Kwangju, *S. Korea* ... **57 G14** 35 9N 126 54 E
Kwango →, *Dem. Rep.*
  of the Congo ..... **84 E3** 3 14 S 17 22 E
Kwangsi-Chuang =
  Guangxi Zhuangzu
  Zizhiqu □, *China* .. **58 F7** 24 0N 109 0 E
Kwangtung =
  Guangdong □, *China* **59 F9** 23 0N 113 0 E
Kwara □, *Nigeria* .... **83 D6** 8 45N 4 30 E
Kwataboahegan →,
  Canada **104 B3** 51 9N 80 50W
Kwatisore, *Indonesia* .. **63 E8** 3 18 S 134 50 E
KwaZulu Natal □,
  S. Africa .... **89 D5** 29 0 S 30 0 E
Kweichow = Guizhou □,
  China .... **58 D6** 27 0N 107 0 E
Kwekwe, *Zimbabwe* .. **87 F2** 18 58 S 29 48 E
Kwidzyn, *Poland* .... **30 E5** 53 44N 18 55 E
Kwiha, *Ethiopia* ..... **81 E4** 13 29N 39 32 E
Kwinana New Town,
  Australia .... **93 F2** 32 15 S 115 47 E
Kwisa →, *Poland* .... **31 G2** 51 34N 15 24 E
Kwoka, *Indonesia* .... **63 E8** 0 31 S 132 27 E
Kwolla, *Nigeria* ..... **83 D6** 9 0N 9 15 E
Kyabra Cr. →, *Australia* **95 D3** 25 36 S 142 55 E
Kyabram, *Australia* ... **95 F4** 36 19 S 145 4 E
Kyaikto, *Burma* ..... **64 D1** 17 20N 97 3 E
Kyakhta, *Russia* ..... **53 D11** 50 30N 106 25 E
Kyambura □, *Uganda* . **86 C3** 0 7 S 30 9 E
Kyancutta, *Australia* .. **95 E2** 33 8 S 135 33 E
Kyaukpadaung, *Burma* **67 J19** 20 52N 95 8 E
Kyaukpyu, *Burma* ... **67 K18** 19 28N 93 30 E
Kyaukse, *Burma* ..... **67 J20** 21 36N 96 10 E
Kybartai, *Lithuania* ... **30 D9** 54 39N 22 45 E
Kyburz, *U.S.A.* **110 G6** 38 47N 120 18W
Kyelang, *India* ...... **68 C7** 32 35N 77 2 E
Kyenjojo, *Uganda* ... **86 B3** 0 40N 30 37 E
Kyjov, *Czech Rep.* ... **27 B10** 49 1N 17 7 E
Kyle, *Canada* **103 C7** 50 50N 108 2W
Kyle Dam, *Zimbabwe* . **87 G3** 20 15 S 31 0 E
Kyle of Lochalsh, *U.K.* **13 D3** 57 17N 5 44W
Kyll →, *Germany* .... **25 F2** 49 48N 6 41 E
Kyllburg, *Germany* ... **25 E2** 50 2N 6 34 E
Kymijoki →, *Finland* . **9 F22** 60 30N 26 55 E
Kymmene älv =
  Kymijoki →, *Finland* **9 F22** 60 30N 26 55 E
Kyneton, *Australia* ... **95 F3** 37 10 S 144 29 E
Kynuna, *Australia* .... **94 C3** 21 37 S 141 55 E
Kyō-ga-Saki, *Japan* .. **55 G7** 35 45N 135 15 E
Kyoga, L., *Uganda* ... **86 B3** 1 35N 33 0 E
Kyogle, *Australia* ..... **95 D5** 28 40 S 153 0 E
Kyom →, *Sudan* .... **81 F2** 8 58N 28 13 E
Kyongju, *S. Korea* ... **57 G15** 35 51N 129 14 E
Kyongpyaw, *Burma* .. **67 L19** 17 12N 95 10 E
Kyŏngsŏng, *N. Korea* . **57 D15** 41 35N 129 36 E
Kyōto, *Japan* .... **55 G7** 35 0N 135 45 E
Kyōto □, *Japan* ..... **55 G7** 35 15N 135 45 E
Kyparissovouno, *Cyprus* **49 D12** 35 19N 33 10 E
Kyperounda, *Cyprus* .. **49 E11** 34 56N 32 58 E
Kyrenia, *Cyprus* ..... **49 D12** 35 20N 33 20 E
Kyrgyzstan ■, *Asia* .. **52 E8** 42 0N 75 0 E
Kyritz, *Germany* ..... **24 C8** 52 56N 12 24 E
Kyrkhult, *Sweden* ... **11 H8** 56 21N 14 34 E
Kyrnasivka, *Ukraine* .. **29 B13** 48 35N 28 58 E
Kyrnychky, *Ukraine* .. **29 E14** 45 42N 29 4 E
Kyrönjoki →, *Finland* . **8 E19** 63 14N 21 45 E
Kyrönjoki →, *Finland* . **8 E19** 63 14N 21 45 E
Kystatyam, *Russia* ... **53 C13** 67 20N 123 10 E
Kytay, Ozero, *Ukraine* . **29 E14** 45 40N 29 13 E

Kythréa, *Cyprus* ..... **49 D12** 35 15N 33 29 E
Kyunhla, *Burma* ..... **67 H19** 23 25N 95 15 E
Kyuquot Sound, *Canada* **102 D3** 50 2N 127 22W
Kyurdamir = Kürdämir,
  Azerbaijan .... **35 K9** 40 25N 48 3 E
Kyūshū, *Japan* ...... **55 H5** 33 0N 131 0 E
Kyūshū □, *Japan* .... **55 H5** 33 0N 131 0 E
Kyūshū-Sanchi, *Japan* . **55 H5** 32 35N 131 17 E
Kyustendil, *Bulgaria* .. **44 D6** 42 16N 22 41 E
Kyusyur, *Russia* ..... **53 B13** 70 19N 127 30 E
Kyyiv, *Ukraine* ...... **33 G6** 50 30N 30 28 E
Kyyivske Vdskh.,
  Ukraine .... **33 G6** 51 0N 30 25 E
Kyzyl, *Russia* .... **53 D10** 51 50N 94 30 E
Kyzyl Kum, *Uzbekistan* **52 E7** 42 30N 65 0 E
Kyzyl-Kyya, *Kyrgyzstan* **52 E8** 40 16N 72 8 E
Kyzyl-Orda =
  Qyzylorda,
  Kazakhstan ...... **52 E7** 44 48N 65 28 E

L

La Albuera, *Spain* **37 G4** 38 45N 6 49W
La Alcarria, *Spain* **38 E2** 40 31N 2 45W
La Almarcha, *Spain* .. **38 F2** 39 41N 2 24W
La Almunia de Doña
  Godina, *Spain* **38 D3** 41 29N 1 23W
La Amistad △,
  Cent. Amer. **120 E3** 9 28N 83 18W
La Asunción, *Venezuela* **124 A6** 11 2N 63 53W
La Baie, *Canada* **105 C5** 48 19N 70 53W
La Banda, *Argentina* .. **126 B3** 27 45 S 64 10W
La Bañeza, *Spain* **36 C5** 42 17N 5 54W
La Barca, *Mexico* **118 C4** 20 20N 102 40W
La Barge, *U.S.A.* **108 E8** 42 16N 110 12W
La Bastide-Puylaurent,
  France .... **20 D7** 44 35N 3 55 E
La Baule, *France* **18 E4** 47 17N 2 24W
La Belle, *U.S.A.* **115 M5** 26 46N 81 26W
La Biche →, *Canada* . **102 B4** 59 57N 123 50W
La Biche, L., *Canada* . **102 C6** 54 50N 112 5W
La Bisbal d'Empordà,
  Spain .... **38 D8** 41 58N 3 2 E
La Blanquilla, *Venezuela* **124 A6** 11 51N 64 37W
La Bomba, *Mexico* ... **118 A1** 31 53N 115 2W
La Brea, *Trin. & Tob.* . **125 K15** 10 15N 61 37W
La Brède, *France* **20 D3** 44 41N 0 32W
La Bresse, *France* .... **19 D13** 48 2N 6 53 E
La Bureba, *Spain* **36 C7** 42 36N 3 24W
La Calera, *Chile* ..... **126 C1** 32 50 S 71 10W
La Campana △, *Chile* . **126 C1** 32 58 S 71 14W
La Campiña, *Spain* ... **37 H6** 37 45N 4 45W
La Canal = Sa Canal,
  Spain .... **48 C7** 38 51N 1 23 E
La Cañiza = A Cañiza,
  Spain **36 C2** 42 13N 8 16W
La Canourgue, *France* . **20 D7** 44 26N 3 13 E
La Capelle, *France* ... **19 C10** 49 59N 3 50 E
La Carlota, *Argentina* . **126 C3** 33 30 S 63 20W
La Carlota, *Phil.* ..... **61 F5** 10 25N 122 55 E
La Carlota, *Spain* **37 H6** 37 40N 4 56W
La Carolina, *Spain* ... **37 G7** 38 17N 3 38W
La Cavalerie, *France* .. **20 D7** 44 1N 3 10 E
La Ceiba, *Honduras* .. **120 C2** 15 40N 86 50W
La Chaise-Dieu, *France* **20 C7** 45 18N 3 42 E
La Chapelle d'Angillon,
  France .... **19 E9** 47 21N 2 25 E
La Chapelle-St-Luc,
  France .... **19 D11** 48 20N 4 3 E
La Chapelle-sur-Erdre,
  France **18 E5** 47 18N 1 34W
La Charité-sur-Loire,
  France .... **19 E10** 47 10N 3 1 E
La Chartre-sur-le-Loir,
  France .... **18 E7** 47 44N 0 34 E
La Châtaigneraie,
  France **20 B3** 46 39N 0 44W
La Châtre, *France* .... **19 F9** 46 35N 2 0 E
La Chaux-de-Fonds,
  Switz. .... **25 H2** 47 7N 6 50 E
La Chorrera, *Panama* . **120 E4** 8 53N 79 47W
La Ciotat, *France* .... **21 E9** 43 10N 5 37 E
La Clayette, *France* ... **19 F11** 46 17N 4 19 E
La Cocha, *Argentina* .. **126 B2** 27 50 S 65 40W
La Concepción, *Panama* **120 E3** 8 31N 82 37W
La Concordia, *Mexico* . **119 D6** 16 8N 92 38W
La Coruña = A Coruña,
  Spain **36 B2** 43 20N 8 25W
La Coruña □, *Spain* .. **36 B2** 43 10N 8 30W
La Côte-St-André,
  France .... **21 C9** 45 24N 5 15 E
La Crau, *France* ..... **20 C6** 45 41N 2 15 E
La Crau,
  Bouches-du-Rhône,
  France .... **21 E8** 43 32N 4 40 E
La Crau, *Var, France* . **21 E10** 43 9N 6 2 E
La Crescent, *U.S.A.* .. **112 D9** 43 50N 91 18W
La Crete, *Canada* **102 B5** 58 11N 116 24W
La Crosse, *Kans., U.S.A.* **112 F5** 38 32N 99 18W
La Crosse, *Wis., U.S.A.* **112 D9** 43 48N 91 15W
La Cruz, *Costa Rica* .. **120 D2** 11 4N 85 39W
La Cruz, *Mexico* **118 C3** 23 55N 106 54W
La Désirade,
  Guadeloupe ...... **120 b** 16 18N 61 3W
La Escondida, *Mexico* . **118 C5** 24 6N 99 55W
La Esmeralda, *Paraguay* **126 A3** 22 16 S 62 33W
La Esperanza, *Cuba* .. **120 B3** 22 46N 83 44W
La Esperanza, *Honduras* **120 D2** 14 15N 88 10W
La Estrada = A Estrada,
  Spain **36 C2** 42 43N 8 27W
La Faouët, *France* **18 D3** 48 2N 3 30W
La Fayette, *U.S.A.* ... **115 H3** 34 42N 85 17W
La Fé, *Cuba* **120 B3** 22 2N 84 15W
La Fère, *France* ..... **19 C10** 49 39N 3 21 E
La Ferté-Bernard,
  France .... **18 D7** 48 10N 0 40 E
La Ferté-Gaucher,
  France .... **19 D10** 48 47N 3 19 E
La Ferté-Macé, *France* **18 D6** 48 35N 0 22W
La Ferté-St-Aubin,
  France .... **19 E8** 47 42N 1 57 E
La Ferté-sous-Jouarre,
  France .... **19 D10** 48 56N 3 8 E
La Ferté-Vidame,
  France .... **18 D7** 48 37N 0 53 E
La Flèche, *France* **18 E6** 47 42N 0 4W
La Follette, *U.S.A.* ... **115 G3** 36 23N 84 7W
La Fregeneda, *Spain* .. **36 E4** 40 58N 6 54W
La Fuente de San
  Esteban, *Spain* ... **36 E4** 40 49N 6 15W
La Gacilly, *France* **18 E4** 47 45N 2 8W
La Gineta, *Spain* **39 F2** 39 8N 2 1W
La Grand'Combe,
  France .... **21 D8** 44 13N 4 2 E
La Grande, *U.S.A.* ... **108 D4** 45 20N 118 5W

La Grande →, *Canada* **104 B5** 53 50N 79 0W
La Grande Deux, Rés.,
  Canada **104 B4** 53 40N 76 55W
La Grande-Motte,
  France .... **21 E8** 43 23N 4 5 E
La Grande Quatre, Rés.,
  Canada **104 B5** 54 0N 73 15W
La Grande Trois, Rés.,
  Canada **104 B4** 53 40N 75 10W
La Grange, *Calif.,*
  U.S.A. **110 H6** 37 42N 120 27W
La Grange, *Ga., U.S.A.* **115 J3** 33 2N 85 2W
La Grange, *Ky., U.S.A.* **114 F3** 38 25N 85 23W
La Grange, *Tex., U.S.A.* **113 L6** 29 54N 96 52W
La Grave, *France* .... **21 C10** 45 3N 6 18 E
La Guaira, *Venezuela* . **124 A5** 10 36N 66 56W
La Guardia = A Guarda,
  Spain **36 D2** 41 56N 8 52W
La Gudiña = A Gudiña,
  Spain **36 C3** 42 4N 7 8W
La Guerche-de-
  Bretagne, *France* .. **18 E5** 47 57N 1 16W
La Guerche-sur-
  l'Aubois, *France* ... **19 F9** 46 58N 2 56 E
La Habana, *Cuba* **120 B3** 23 8N 82 22W
La Haute Vallée de
  Chevreuse △, *France* **19 D8** 48 35N 1 58 E
La Haye-du-Puits,
  France **18 C5** 49 17N 1 33W
La Horra, *Spain* **36 D7** 41 44N 3 53W
La Independencia,
  Mexico **119 D6** 16 31N 91 47W
La Isabela, *Dom. Rep.* **121 C5** 19 58N 71 2W
La Jonquera, *Spain* ... **38 C7** 42 25N 2 53 E
La Junta, *U.S.A.* **113 F3** 37 59N 103 33W
La Laguna, *Canary Is.* . **48 F3** 28 28N 16 18W
La Libertad, *Guatemala* **120 C1** 16 47N 90 7W
La Libertad, *Mexico* .. **118 B2** 29 55N 112 41W
La Ligua, *Chile* ...... **126 C1** 32 30 S 71 16W
La Línea de la
  Concepción, *Spain* . **37 J5** 36 15N 5 23W
La Loche, *Canada* ... **103 B7** 56 29N 109 26W
La Londe-les-Maures,
  France .... **21 E10** 43 8N 6 14 E
La Lora, *Spain* **36 C7** 42 45N 4 0W
La Loupe, *France* .... **18 D8** 48 29N 1 0 E
La Louvière, *Belgium* . **17 D4** 50 27N 4 10 E
La Lune, *Trin. & Tob.* . **125 K15** 10 3N 61 22W
La Machine, *France* ... **19 F10** 46 54N 3 27 E
La Maddalena, *Italy* .. **42 A2** 41 13N 9 24 E
La Malbaie, *Canada* .. **105 C5** 47 40N 70 10W
La Malinche △, *México* **119 D5** 19 15N 98 3W
La Mancha, *Spain* ... **39 F2** 39 10N 2 54W
La Mariña, *Spain* **36 B3** 43 30N 7 40W
La Martre, L., *Canada* . **102 A5** 63 15N 117 55W
La Mesa, *U.S.A.* **111 N9** 32 46N 117 3W
La Misión, *Mexico* ... **118 A1** 32 5N 116 50W
La Mothe-Achard,
  France **18 F5** 46 37N 1 40W
La Motte-Chalançon,
  France .... **21 D9** 44 30N 5 21 E
La Motte-du-Caire,
  France .... **21 D10** 44 20N 6 3 E
La Motte-Servolex,
  France .... **21 C9** 45 35N 5 53 E
La Moure, *U.S.A.* ... **112 B5** 46 21N 98 18W
La Muela, *Spain* **38 D3** 41 36N 1 7W
La Mure, *France* ..... **21 D9** 44 55N 5 48 E
La Negra, *Chile* ..... **126 A1** 23 46 S 70 18W
La Oliva, *Canary Is.* .. **48 F6** 28 36N 13 57W
La Orotava, *Canary Is.* . **48 F3** 28 22N 16 31W
La Oroya, *Peru* ...... **124 F3** 11 32 S 75 54W
La Pacaudière, *France* . **19 F10** 46 11N 3 52 E
La Palma, *Canary Is.* .. **48 F2** 28 40N 17 50W
La Palma, *Panama* ... **120 E4** 8 15N 78 0W
La Palma del Condado,
  Spain **37 H4** 37 21N 6 38W
La Paloma, *Chile* .... **126 C1** 30 35 S 71 0W
La Pampa □, *Argentina* **126 D2** 36 50 S 66 0W
La Paragua, *Venezuela* **124 B6** 6 50N 63 20W
La Paz, *Entre Ríos,*
  Argentina .... **126 C4** 30 50 S 59 45W
La Paz, *San Luis,*
  Argentina .... **126 C2** 33 30 S 67 20W
La Paz, *Bolivia* ...... **124 G5** 16 20 S 68 10W
La Paz, *Honduras* **120 D2** 14 20N 87 47W
La Paz, *Mexico* **118 C2** 24 10N 110 20W
La Paz, *Phil.* .... **61 D4** 15 26N 120 45 E
La Paz Centro, *Nic.* .. **120 D2** 12 20N 86 41W
La Pedrera, *Colombia* . **124 D5** 1 18 S 69 43W
La Pérade, *Canada* ... **105 C5** 46 35N 72 12W
La Perouse Str., *Asia* . **54 B11** 45 40N 142 0 E
La Pesca, *Mexico* **119 C5** 23 46N 97 47W
La Piedad, *Mexico* ... **118 C4** 20 20N 102 1W
La Pine, *U.S.A.* **108 E3** 43 40N 121 30W
La Plata, *Argentina* ... **126 D4** 35 0 S 57 55W
La Pobla de Lillet, *Spain* **38 C6** 42 16N 1 59 E
La Pocatière, *Canada* . **105 C5** 47 22N 70 2W
La Pola de Gordón,
  Spain **36 C5** 42 51N 5 41W
La Porta, *France* ..... **21 F13** 42 25N 9 21 E
La Porte, *Ind., U.S.A.* . **114 E2** 41 36N 86 43W
La Porte, *Tex., U.S.A.* . **113 L7** 29 39N 95 1W
La Presanella, *Italy* ... **40 B7** 46 13N 10 40 E
La Puebla = Sa Pobla,
  Spain .... **38 F8** 39 46N 3 1 E
La Puebla de Cazalla,
  Spain **37 H5** 37 10N 5 20W
La Puebla de los
  Infantes, *Spain* ... **37 H5** 37 47N 5 24W
La Puebla de
  Montalbán, *Spain* . **36 F6** 39 52N 4 22W
La Puebla del Río, *Spain* **37 H4** 37 16N 6 3W
La Puerta de Segura,
  Spain **37 G8** 38 22N 2 45W
La Purísima, *Mexico* .. **118 B2** 26 10N 112 4W
La Push, *U.S.A.* **110 C2** 47 55N 124 38W
La Quiaca, *Argentina* . **126 A2** 22 5 S 65 35W
La Réole, *France* ..... **20 D3** 44 35N 0 1 E
La Restinga, *Canary Is.* **48 G2** 27 38N 17 59W
La Rioja, *Argentina* ... **126 B2** 29 20 S 67 0W
La Rioja □, *Argentina* . **126 B2** 29 30 S 67 0W
La Rioja □, *Spain* **38 C2** 42 20N 2 20W
La Robla, *Spain* **36 C5** 42 50N 5 41W
La Roche-Bernard,
  France **18 E4** 47 31N 2 19W
La Roche-Canillac,
  France .... **20 C5** 45 12N 1 57 E
La Roche-en-Ardenne,
  Belgium .... **17 D5** 50 11N 5 35 E
La Roche-sur-Foron,
  France .... **19 F13** 46 4N 6 19 E
La Roche-sur-Yon,
  France **18 F5** 46 40N 1 25W
La Rochefoucauld,
  France .... **20 C4** 45 44N 0 24 E
La Rochelle, *France* ... **20 B2** 46 10N 1 9W

La Roda, *Spain* **39 F2** 39 13N 2 15W
La Roda de Andalucía,
  Spain **37 H6** 37 12N 4 46W
La Romana, *Dom. Rep.* **121 C6** 18 27N 68 57W
La Ronge, *Canada* ... **103 B7** 55 5N 105 20W
La Rumorosa, *Mexico* . **111 N10** 32 33N 116 4W
La Sabina = Sa Savina,
  Spain .... **48 C7** 38 44N 1 25 E
La Sagra, *Spain* **39 H2** 37 57N 2 35W
La Salle, *U.S.A.* **112 E10** 41 20N 89 6W
La Sanabria, *Spain* ... **36 C4** 42 0N 6 30W
La Sarre, *Canada* **104 C4** 48 45N 79 15W
La Scie, *Canada* **105 C8** 49 57N 55 36W
La Selva, *Spain* ..... **38 C6** 42 0N 2 45 E
La Selva Beach, *U.S.A.* **110 J5** 36 56N 121 51W
La Selva del Camp,
  Spain .... **38 D6** 41 13N 1 8 E
La Serena, *Chile* ..... **126 B1** 29 55 S 71 10W
La Serena, *Spain* **37 G5** 38 45N 5 40W
La Seu d'Urgell, *Spain* . **38 C6** 42 22N 1 23 E
La Seyne-sur-Mer,
  France .... **21 E9** 43 7N 5 52 E
La Sila, *Italy* .... **43 C9** 39 15N 16 35 E
La Solana, *Spain* **39 G7** 38 59N 3 14W
La Souterraine, *France* **19 F8** 46 15N 1 30 E
La Spézia, *Italy* ..... **40 D6** 44 7N 9 50 E
La Suze-sur-Sarthe,
  France .... **18 E7** 47 53N 0 2 E
La Tagua, *Colombia* .. **124 C4** 0 3N 74 40W
La Teste-de-Buch,
  France **20 D2** 44 37N 1 6W
La Tortuga, *Venezuela* **121 D6** 11 0N 65 22W
La Tour-du-Pin, *France* **21 C9** 45 33N 5 27 E
La Tranche-sur-Mer,
  France **18 F5** 46 20N 1 27W
La Tremblade, *France* . **20 C2** 45 46N 1 8W
La Trinité, *Martinique* . **120 c** 14 43N 60 58W
La Tuque, *Canada* ... **104 C5** 47 30N 72 50W
La Unión, *Chile* ..... **128 E2** 40 10 S 73 0W
La Unión, *El Salv.* ... **120 D2** 13 20N 87 50W
La Unión, *Spain* **39 H4** 37 38N 0 53W
La Urbana, *Venezuela* . **124 B5** 7 8N 66 56W
La Vache Pt.,
  Trin. & Tob. **125 K15** 10 47N 61 28W
La Vall d'Uixó, *Spain* . **38 F4** 39 49N 0 15W
La Vecilla de Curveño,
  Spain **36 C5** 42 51N 5 27W
La Vega, *Dom. Rep.* .. **121 C5** 19 20N 70 30W
La Vela de Coro,
  Venezuela **124 A5** 11 27N 69 34W
La Veleta, *Spain* **37 H7** 37 1N 3 22W
La Venta, *Mexico* **119 D6** 18 8N 94 3W
La Ventura, *Mexico* .. **118 C4** 24 38N 100 54W
La Voulte-sur-Rhône,
  France .... **21 D8** 44 48N 4 46 E
Laa an der Thaya,
  Austria .... **27 C9** 48 43N 16 23 E
Laaber, Grosse →,
  Germany .... **25 G8** 48 55N 12 30 E
Laage, *Germany* ..... **24 B8** 53 55N 12 21 E
Laas Caanood = Las
  Anod, *Somali Rep.* . **75 F4** 8 26N 47 19 E
Laatzen, *Germany* ... **24 C4** 52 19N 9 48 E
Laba →, *Russia* ..... **35 H4** 45 11N 39 42 E
Labasa, *Fiji* .... **91 C8** 16 30 S 179 27 E
Labason, *Phil.* ...... **61 G5** 8 4N 122 31 E
Labastide-Murat, *France* **20 D5** 44 39N 1 33 E
Labastide-Rouairoux,
  France .... **20 E6** 43 28N 2 39 E
Labbézanga, *Mali* .... **83 B5** 15 2N 0 48 E
Labe = Elbe →, *Europe* **24 B4** 53 50N 9 0 E
Labé, *Guinea* **82 C2** 11 24N 12 16W
Laberge, L., *Canada* .. **102 A1** 61 11N 135 12W
Labin, *Croatia* ...... **41 C11** 45 5N 14 8 E
Labinsk, *Russia* ..... **35 H5** 44 40N 40 48 E
Labis, *Malaysia* ..... **65 L4** 2 22N 103 2 E
Łabiszyn, *Poland* .... **31 F4** 52 57N 17 54 E
Labo, *Phil.* .... **61 D5** 14 9N 122 51 E
Laboe, *Germany* ..... **24 A6** 54 24N 10 13 E
Laborec →, *Slovak Rep.* **27 C14** 48 37N 21 58 E
Laborie, *St. Lucia* ... **121 f** 13 45N 61 2W
Labouheyre, *France* .. **20 D3** 44 13N 0 55W
Laboulaye, *Argentina* . **126 C3** 34 10 S 63 30W
Labrador, *Canada* ... **105 B6** 53 20N 61 0W
Labrador City, *Canada* **105 B6** 52 57N 66 55W
Labrador Sea, *Atl. Oc.* **101 C14** 57 0N 54 0W
Lábrea, *Brazil* ...... **124 E6** 7 15 S 64 51W
Labruguière, *France* .. **20 E6** 43 31N 2 16 E
Labuan, *Malaysia* ... **62 C5** 5 20N 115 14 E
Labuan, Pulau, *Malaysia* **62 C5** 5 21N 115 13 E
Labuha, *Indonesia* ... **63 E7** 0 30 S 127 30 E
Labuhan, *Indonesia* .. **63 G11** 6 22 S 105 50 E
Labuhanbajo, *Indonesia* **63 F6** 8 28 S 119 54 E
Labuk, Telok, *Malaysia* **62 C5** 6 10N 117 50 E
Labyrinth, L., *Australia* **95 E2** 30 40 S 135 11 E
Labytnangi, *Russia* ... **52 C7** 66 39N 66 21 E
Laç, *Albania* .... **44 E3** 41 38N 19 43 E
Lac-Bouchette, *Canada* **105 C5** 48 16N 72 11W
Lac Édouard, *Canada* . **104 C5** 47 40N 72 16W
Lac La Biche, *Canada* . **102 C6** 54 45N 111 58W
Lac la Martre = Wha Ti,
  Canada **100 B8** 63 8N 117 16W
Lac La Ronge △,
  Canada **103 B7** 55 9N 104 41W
Lac-Mégantic, *Canada* . **105 C5** 45 35N 70 53W
Lac Thien, *Vietnam* .. **64 F7** 12 25N 108 11 E
Lacanau, *France* **20 D2** 44 58N 1 5W
Lacanau, Étang de,
  France **20 D2** 44 58N 1 7W
Lacantúm →, *Mexico* . **119 D6** 16 36N 90 40W
Lacara →, *Spain* **37 G4** 38 55N 6 25W
Lacaune, *France* ..... **20 E6** 43 43N 2 40 E
Lacaune, Mts. de, *France* **20 E6** 43 43N 2 50 E
Laccadive Is. =
  Lakshadweep Is.,
  India .... **50 H11** 10 0N 72 30 E
Lacepede B., *Australia* . **95 F2** 36 40 S 139 40 E
Lacepede Is., *Australia* . **92 C3** 16 55 S 122 0 E
Lacerdónia, *Mozam.* .. **87 F4** 18 3 S 35 35 E
Lacey, *U.S.A.* **110 C4** 47 7N 122 49W
Lachhmangarh, *India* . **68 F6** 27 50N 75 4 E
Lachi, *Pakistan* ...... **68 C4** 33 25N 71 20 E
Lachine, *Canada* **104 C5** 45 30N 73 40W
Lachlan →, *Australia* . **95 E3** 34 22 S 143 55 E
Lachute, *Canada* **104 C5** 45 39N 74 21W
Lackawanna, *U.S.A.* .. **116 D6** 42 50N 78 50W
Lackawaxen, *U.S.A.* .. **117 E10** 41 29N 74 59W
Lacolle, *Canada* **117 A11** 45 5N 73 22W
Lacombe, *Canada* ... **102 C6** 52 30N 113 44W
Láconi, *Italy* .... **42 C2** 39 54N 9 4 E
Laconia, *U.S.A.* **117 C13** 43 32N 71 28W
Lacq, *France* **20 E3** 43 25N 0 35W
Ladakh Ra., *India* ... **69 C8** 34 0N 78 0 E

Lądek-Zdrój, Poland .. **31 H3** 50 21N 16 53 E
Ládhon →, Greece .... **46 D3** 37 40N 21 50 E
Ladik, Turkey .... **72 B6** 40 57N 35 58 E
Ladismith, S. Africa .. **88 E3** 33 28 S 21 15 E
Ladíspoli, Italy ...... **41 G9** 41 56N 12 5 E
Ladíz, Iran .... **71 D9** 28 55N 61 15 E
Ladnun, India .... **68 F6** 27 38N 74 25 E
Ladoga, L. =
Ladozhskoye Ozero,
Russia .... **32 B6** 61 15N 30 30 E
Ladozhskoye Ozero,
Russia .... **32 B6** 61 15N 30 30 E
Ladushkin, Russia .... **30 D7** 54 34N 20 10 E
Lady Elliott I., Australia **94 C5** 24 7 S 152 42 E
Lady Grey, S. Africa .. **88 E4** 30 43 S 27 13 E
Ladybrand, S. Africa .. **88 D4** 29 9 S 27 29 E
Ladybird, Canada **102 D4** 49 0N 123 49W
Ladysmith, S. Africa .. **89 D4** 28 32 S 29 46 E
Ladysmith, Canada ... **102 D4** 49 0N 123 49W
Ladysmith, U.S.A. **112 C9** 45 28N 91 12W
Ladyzhyn, Ukraine .... **29 B14** 48 40N 29 15 E
Lae, Papua N. G. ..... **96 H6** 6 40 S 147 2 E
Laem Khok Khom,
Thailand .... **65 b** 9 25N 99 56 E
Laem Khat, Thailand .. **65 a** 8 6N 98 26 E
Laem Nga, Thailand .. **65 a** 7 55N 98 27 E
Laem Ngop, Thailand . **65 F4** 12 10N 102 26 E
Laem Phan Wa,
Thailand .... **65 a** 7 47N 98 25 E
Laem Pho, Thailand ... **65 J3** 6 55N 101 19 E
Laem Phrom Thep,
Thailand .... **65 a** 7 45N 98 19 E
Laem Riang, Thailand . **65 a** 8 7N 98 27 E
Laem Sam Rong,
Thailand .... **65 b** 9 35N 100 4 E
Laem Son, Thailand ... **65 a** 7 59N 98 16 E
Laem Yamu, Thailand . **65 a** 7 59N 98 26 E
Læsø, Denmark .... **11 G5** 57 20N 11 5 E
Læsø Rende, Denmark . **11 G4** 57 20N 10 45 E
Lafayette, Colo., U.S.A. **112 F2** 39 58N 105 12W
Lafayette, Ind., U.S.A. **114 E2** 40 25N 86 54W
Lafayette, La., U.S.A. . **113 K9** 30 14N 92 1W
Lafayette, Tenn., U.S.A. **115 G2** 36 31N 86 2W
Laferte →, Canada **102 A5** 61 53N 117 44W
Lafia, Nigeria .... **83 D6** 8 30N 8 34 E
Lafiagi, Nigeria ...... **83 D6** 8 52N 5 20 E
Lafleche, Canada **103 D7** 49 45N 106 40W
Lafon, Sudan .... **81 F3** 5 5N 32 29 E
Lagan, Sweden .... **11 H7** 56 56N 13 58 E
Lagan →, Sweden ..... **11 H6** 56 30N 12 58 E
Lagan →, U.K. **12 B6** 54 36N 5 55W
Lagarfljót →, Iceland .. **8 D6** 65 40N 14 18W
Lage, Germany .... **24 D4** 51 59N 8 48 E
Lågen →, Oppland,
Norway .... **9 F14** 61 8N 10 25 E
Lågen →, Vestfold,
Norway .... **9 G14** 59 3N 10 3 E
Lägerdorf, Germany ... **24 B5** 53 53N 9 34 E
Laghouat, Algeria .... **78 B6** 33 50N 2 59 E
Lagnieu, France ...... **21 C9** 45 55N 5 20 E
Lagny-sur-Marne,
France .... **19 D9** 48 52N 2 44 E
Lago, Italy .... **43 C9** 39 10N 16 9 E
Lago de Sanabria y
Entorno △, Spain ... **36 C4** 42 9N 6 45W
Lagôa, Portugal **37 H2** 37 8N 8 27W
Lagoa do Peixe △,
Brazil .... **127 C5** 31 12 S 50 55W
Lagoa Vermelha, Brazil **127 B5** 28 13 S 51 32W
Lagoaça, Portugal **36 D4** 41 11N 6 44W
Lagodekhi, Georgia ... **35 K8** 41 50N 46 22 E
Lagónegro, Italy ..... **43 B8** 40 8N 15 45 E
Lagonoy G., Phil. ..... **61 E5** 13 35N 123 50 E
Lagos, Nigeria .... **83 D5** 6 25N 3 27 E
Lagos, Portugal **37 H2** 37 5N 8 41W
Lagos □, Nigeria ..... **83 D5** 6 28N 3 25 E
Lagos de Moreno,
Mexico **118 C4** 21 21N 101 55W
Lagrange, Australia ... **92 C3** 18 45 S 121 43 E
Lagrange B., Australia . **92 C3** 18 38 S 121 42 E
Laguardia, Spain **38 C2** 42 33N 2 35W
Laguépie, France ..... **20 D5** 44 8N 1 57 E
Laguna, Brazil .... **127 B6** 28 30 S 48 50W
Laguna, U.S.A. **109 J10** 35 2N 107 25W
Laguna Beach, U.S.A. . **111 M9** 33 33N 117 47W
Laguna de Duera, Spain **36 D6** 41 35N 4 43W
Laguna de la
Restinga △, Venezuela **121 D6** 10 58N 64 0W
Laguna del Laja △,
Chile .... **126 D1** 37 27 S 71 20W
Laguna del Tigre △,
Guatemala **120 C1** 17 32N 90 56W
Laguna Limpia,
Argentina .... **126 B4** 26 32 S 59 45W
Lagunas, Chile .... **126 A2** 21 0 S 69 45W
Lagunas, Peru .... **124 E3** 5 10 S 75 35W
Lagunas de Chacahua △,
Mexico **119 D5** 16 0N 97 43W
Lagunas de
Montebello △, Mexico **119 D6** 16 6N 91 41W
Lagunas de Ruidera △,
Spain **39 G2** 38 57N 2 52W
Lahad Datu, Malaysia . **63 C5** 5 0N 118 20 E
Lahad Datu, Teluk,
Malaysia .... **63 D5** 4 50N 118 20 E
Lahan Sai, Thailand .. **64 E4** 14 25N 102 52 E
Lahanam, Laos ...... **64 D5** 16 16N 105 16 E
Lahar, India .... **69 F8** 26 12N 78 57 E
Laharpur, India ...... **69 F9** 27 43N 80 56 E
Lahat, Indonesia ..... **62 D1** 1 22N 97 12 E
Lahewa, Indonesia .... **62 D1** 1 22N 97 12 E
Lähījān, Iran .... **71 B6** 37 10N 50 6 E
Lahn →, Germany .... **25 E3** 50 19N 7 37 E
Lahnstein, Germany .. **25 E3** 50 19N 7 37 E
Laholm, Sweden ..... **11 H6** 56 30N 13 2 E
Laholmsbukten, Sweden **11 H6** 56 30N 12 45 E
Lahore, Pakistan ..... **68 D6** 31 32N 74 22 E
Lahr, Germany ...... **25 G3** 48 20N 7 53 E
Lahti, Finland .... **9 F21** 60 58N 25 40 E
Lahtis = Lahti, Finland **9 F21** 60 58N 25 40 E
Lai, Chad .... **79 G9** 9 25N 16 18 E
Lai Chau, Vietnam ... **58 F4** 22 5N 103 3 E
Lai'an, China .... **59 A12** 32 28N 118 30 E
Laibin, China .... **58 F7** 23 42N 109 14 E
Laifeng, China .... **58 C7** 29 27N 109 20 E
L'Aigle, France ...... **18 D7** 48 46N 0 38 E
Laignes, France ...... **19 E11** 47 50N 4 20 E
L'Aiguillon-sur-Mer,
France **20 B2** 46 20N 1 18W
Laila = Layla, Si. Arabia **75 C4** 22 10N 46 40 E
Laingsburg, S. Africa .. **88 E3** 33 9 S 20 52 E
Lainio älven →, Sweden **8 C20** 67 35N 22 40 E
Lairg, U.K. **13 C4** 58 2N 4 24W
Laissac, France ...... **20 D6** 44 23N 2 50 E

Laixi, China .... **57 F11** 36 50N 120 31 E
Laiyang, China ...... **57 F11** 36 59N 120 45 E
Laiyuan, China ...... **56 E8** 39 20N 114 40 E
Laizhou, China ...... **57 F10** 37 8N 119 57 E
Laizhou Wan, China .. **57 F10** 37 30N 119 30 E
Laja →, Mexico **118 C4** 20 55N 100 46W
Lajere, Nigeria ...... **83 C7** 12 10N 11 25 E
Lajes, Brazil .... **127 B5** 27 48 S 50 20W
Lajkovac, Serbia & M. . **44 B4** 44 27N 20 14 E
Lajosmizse, Hungary .. **28 C4** 47 3N 19 32 E
Lak Sao, Laos .... **64 C5** 18 11N 104 59 E
Lakaband, Pakistan ... **68 D3** 31 2N 69 15 E
Lakamané, Mali **82 C3** 14 35N 9 44W
Lake Alpine, U.S.A. .. **110 G7** 38 29N 120 0W
Lake Andes, U.S.A. ... **112 D5** 43 9N 98 32W
Lake Arthur, U.S.A. .. **113 K8** 30 5N 92 41W
Lake Bindegolly △,
Australia .... **95 D3** 28 0 S 144 12 E
Lake Cargelligo,
Australia .... **95 E4** 33 15 S 146 22 E
Lake Charles, U.S.A. .. **113 K8** 30 14N 93 13W
Lake City, Colo., U.S.A. **109 G10** 38 2N 107 19W
Lake City, Fla., U.S.A. **115 K4** 30 11N 82 38W
Lake City, Mich., U.S.A. **114 C3** 44 20N 85 13W
Lake City, Minn., U.S.A. **112 C8** 44 27N 92 16W
Lake City, Pa., U.S.A. **116 D4** 42 1N 80 21W
Lake City, S.C., U.S.A. **115 J6** 33 52N 79 45W
Lake Cowichan, Canada **102 D4** 48 49N 124 3W
Lake District △, U.K. .. **14 C4** 54 30N 3 21W
Lake Elsinore, U.S.A. . **111 M9** 33 38N 117 20W
Lake Eyre △, Australia **95 D2** 28 40 S 137 31 E
Lake Gairdner △,
Australia .... **95 E2** 31 41 S 135 51 E
Lake George, U.S.A. .. **117 C11** 43 26N 73 43W
Lake Grace, Australia . **93 F2** 33 7 S 118 28 E
Lake Harbour =
Kimmirut, Canada .. **101 B13** 62 50N 69 50W
Lake Havasu City,
U.S.A. **111 L12** 34 27N 114 22W
Lake Hughes, U.S.A. .. **111 L8** 34 41N 118 26W
Lake Isabella, U.S.A. .. **111 K8** 35 38N 118 28W
Lake Jackson, U.S.A. .. **113 L7** 29 3N 95 27W
Lake Junction, U.S.A. . **108 D8** 44 35N 110 28W
Lake King, Australia .. **93 F2** 33 5 S 119 45 E
Lake Lenore, Canada .. **103 C8** 52 24N 104 59W
Lake Louise, Canada .. **102 C5** 51 30N 116 10W
Lake Malawi △, Malawi **87 E3** 14 2 S 34 53 E
Lake Mburo △, Uganda **86 C3** 0 33 S 30 56 E
Lake Mead △, U.S.A. . **111 K12** 36 15N 114 30W
Lake Meredith △,
U.S.A. **113 H4** 35 50N 101 50W
Lake Mills, U.S.A. **112 D8** 43 25N 93 32W
Lake Nakuru △, Kenya **86 C4** 0 21 S 36 8 E
Lake Placid, U.S.A. ... **117 B11** 44 17N 73 59W
Lake Pleasant, U.S.A. . **117 C10** 43 28N 74 25W
Lake Providence, U.S.A. **113 J9** 32 48N 91 10W
Lake Roosevelt △,
U.S.A. **108 C4** 47 57N 118 59W
Lake St. Peter, Canada **116 A6** 45 18N 78 2W
Lake Superior △,
Canada **104 C3** 47 45N 84 45W
Lake Torrens △,
Australia .... **95 E2** 30 55 S 137 40 E
Lake Village, U.S.A. .. **113 J9** 33 20N 91 17W
Lake Wales, U.S.A. ... **115 M5** 27 54N 81 35W
Lake Worth, U.S.A. ... **115 M5** 26 37N 80 3W
Lakeba, Fiji .... **91 D9** 18 13 S 178 47W
Lakefield, Canada **116 B6** 44 25N 78 16W
Lakefield △, Australia . **94 B3** 15 24 S 144 26 E
Lakehurst, U.S.A. **117 F10** 40 1N 74 19W
Lakeland, Australia ... **94 B3** 15 49 S 144 57 E
Lakeland, U.S.A. **115 M5** 28 3N 81 57W
Lakemba = Lakeba, Fiji **91 D9** 18 13 S 178 47W
Lakeport, Calif., U.S.A. **110 F4** 39 3N 122 55W
Lakeport, Mich., U.S.A. **116 D2** 43 7N 82 30W
Lakes Entrance,
Australia .... **95 F4** 37 50 S 148 0 E
Lakeside, Ariz., U.S.A. **109 J9** 34 9N 109 58W
Lakeside, Calif., U.S.A. **111 N10** 32 52N 116 55W
Lakeside, Nebr., U.S.A. **112 D3** 42 3N 102 26W
Lakeside, Ohio, U.S.A. **116 E2** 41 32N 82 46W
Lakeview, U.S.A. **108 E3** 42 11N 120 21W
Lakeville, U.S.A. **112 C8** 44 39N 93 14W
Lakewood, Colo., U.S.A. **112 F2** 39 44N 105 5W
Lakewood, N.J., U.S.A. **117 F10** 40 6N 74 13W
Lakewood, N.Y., U.S.A. **116 D5** 42 6N 79 19W
Lakewood, Ohio, U.S.A. **116 E3** 41 29N 81 48W
Lakewood, Wash.,
U.S.A. **110 C4** 47 11N 122 32W
Lakha, India .... **68 F4** 26 9N 70 54 E
Lakhaniá, Greece ..... **49 D9** 35 58N 27 54 E
Lakhimpur, India ..... **69 F9** 27 57N 80 46 E
Lakhnadon, India .... **69 H8** 22 36N 79 36 E
Lakhnau = Lucknow,
India .... **69 F9** 26 50N 81 0 E
Lakhonpheng, Laos ... **64 E5** 15 54N 105 34 E
Lakhpat, India .... **68 H3** 23 48N 68 47 E
Läki, Azerbaijan ..... **35 K8** 40 34N 47 22 E
Lakin, U.S.A. **113 G4** 37 57N 101 15W
Lakitusaki →, Canada . **104 B3** 54 21N 82 25W
Lakki, Pakistan ...... **68 C4** 32 36N 70 55 E
Lákkoi, Greece .... **49 D5** 35 24N 23 57 E
Lakonía □, Greece .... **46 E4** 36 55N 22 30 E
Lakonikós Kólpos,
Greece .... **46 E4** 36 40N 22 40 E
Lakor, Indonesia ..... **63 F7** 8 15 S 128 17 E
Lakota, Ivory C. **82 D3** 5 50N 5 30W
Lakota, U.S.A. **112 A5** 48 2N 98 21W
Laksar, India .... **68 E8** 29 46N 78 3 E
Laksefjorden, Norway . **8 A22** 70 45N 26 50 E
Lakselv, Norway ..... **8 A21** 70 2N 25 0 E
Lakshadweep Is., India **50 H11** 10 0N 72 30 E
Lakshmanpur, India .. **69 H10** 22 58N 83 3 E
Lakshmikantapur, India **69 H13** 22 5N 88 20 E
Lala Musa, Pakistan .. **68 C5** 32 40N 73 57 E
Lalago, Tanzania ..... **86 C3** 3 28 S 33 58 E
Lalapaşa, Turkey ..... **45 E10** 41 49N 26 44 E
Lalbenque, France .... **20 D5** 44 19N 1 34 E
L'Albufera, Spain **39 F4** 39 20N 0 27W
Lalganj, India .... **69 G11** 25 52N 85 13 E
Lalgola, India .... **69 G13** 24 25N 88 15 E
Lālī, Iran .... **71 C6** 32 21N 49 6 E
Lalibela, Ethiopia .... **81 E4** 12 3N 39 0 E
Lalín, China .... **57 B14** 45 12N 127 0 E
Lalín →, China .... **57 B13** 45 25N 125 40 E
Lalinde, France ...... **20 D4** 44 50N 0 44 E
Lalitapur, Nepal ..... **69 F11** 27 40N 85 20 E
Lalitpur, India .... **69 G8** 24 42N 78 28 E
Lalkua, India .... **69 E8** 29 5N 79 31 E
Lalsot, India .... **68 F7** 26 34N 76 20 E
Lam, Vietnam .... **64 B6** 21 21N 106 31 E
Lam Pao Res., Thailand **64 D4** 16 50N 103 15 E
Lamaing, Burma ...... **67 M20** 15 25N 97 53 E

Lamar, Colo., U.S.A. .. **112 F3** 38 5N 102 37W
Lamar, Mo., U.S.A. ... **113 G7** 37 30N 94 16W
Lamas, Peru .... **124 E3** 6 28 S 76 31W
Lamastre, France ..... **21 D8** 44 59N 4 35 E
Lambach, Austria ..... **26 C6** 48 6N 13 51 E
Lamballe, France **18 D4** 48 29N 2 31W
Lambaréné, Gabon ... **84 E2** 0 41 S 10 12 E
Lambasa = Labasa, Fiji **91 C8** 16 30 S 179 27 E
Lambay I., Ireland **12 C5** 53 29N 6 1W
Lambert Glacier,
Antarctica .... **5 D6** 71 0 S 70 0 E
Lambert's Bay, S. Africa **88 E2** 32 5 S 18 17 E
Lambesc, France ..... **21 E9** 43 39N 5 16 E
Lambeth, Canada **116 D3** 42 54N 81 18W
Lámbia, Greece ...... **46 D3** 37 52N 21 53 E
Lambomakondro,
Madag. .... **89 C7** 22 41 S 44 44 E
Lambro →, Italy ...... **40 C6** 45 8N 9 32 E
Lambton Shores,
Canada **116 C3** 43 10N 81 56W
Lame, Nigeria .... **83 C6** 10 30N 9 20 E
Lame Deer, U.S.A. ... **108 D10** 45 37N 106 40W
Lamego, Portugal **36 D3** 41 5N 7 52W
Lamèque, Canada **105 C7** 47 45N 64 38W
Lameroo, Australia ... **95 F3** 35 19 S 140 33 E
Lamesa, U.S.A. **113 J4** 32 44N 101 58W
Lamía, Greece .... **46 C4** 38 55N 22 26 E
Lamington △, Australia **95 D5** 28 13 S 153 12 E
Lamitan, Phil. .... **61 H5** 6 39N 122 8 E
Lammermuir Hills, U.K. **13 F6** 55 50N 2 40W
Lammhult, Sweden ... **11 G8** 57 10N 14 35 E
Lamoille →, U.S.A. ... **117 B11** 44 38N 73 13W
Lamon B., Phil. ...... **61 D5** 14 30N 122 20 E
Lamont, Canada **102 C6** 53 46N 112 50W
Lamont, Calif., U.S.A. . **111 K8** 35 15N 118 55W
Lamont, Wyo., U.S.A. **108 E10** 42 13N 107 29W
Lamotte-Beuvron,
France .... **19 E9** 47 36N 2 2 E
Lampa, Peru .... **124 G4** 15 22 S 70 22W
Lampang, Thailand ... **64 C2** 18 16N 99 32 E
Lampasas, U.S.A. **113 K5** 31 4N 98 11W
Lampazos de Naranjo,
Mexico **118 B4** 27 2N 100 32W
Lampertheim, Germany **25 F4** 49 35N 8 27 E
Lampeter, U.K. **15 E3** 52 7N 4 4W
Lampman, Canada ... **103 D8** 49 25N 102 50W
Lamprechtshausen,
Austria .... **26 D5** 48 0N 12 58 E
Lampung □, Indonesia **62 F2** 5 30 S 104 30 E
Lamta, India .... **69 H9** 22 8N 80 7 E
Lamu, Kenya .... **86 C5** 2 16 S 40 55 E
Lamy, U.S.A. **109 J11** 35 29N 105 53W
Lan Xian, China ..... **56 E6** 38 15N 111 35 E
Lan Yu = Hungt'ou Hsü,
Taiwan .... **59 G13** 22 0N 121 30 E
Lanak La, China ..... **69 B8** 34 27N 79 32 E
Lanak'o Shank'ou =
Lanak La, China ... **69 B8** 34 27N 79 32 E
Lanao, L., Phil. ...... **61 H6** 7 52N 124 15 E
Lanark, Canada **117 A8** 45 1N 76 22W
Lanark, U.K. **13 F5** 55 40N 3 47W
Lanbi Kyun, Burma ... **65 G2** 10 50N 98 20 E
Lancang, China ...... **58 F2** 22 36N 99 58 E
Lancang Jiang →, China **58 G3** 21 40N 101 10 E
Lancashire □, U.K. ... **14 D5** 53 50N 2 48W
Lancaster, Canada **117 A10** 45 10N 74 30W
Lancaster, U.K. **14 C5** 54 3N 2 48W
Lancaster, Calif., U.S.A. **111 L8** 34 42N 118 8W
Lancaster, Ky., U.S.A. **114 G3** 37 37N 84 35W
Lancaster, N.H., U.S.A. **117 B13** 44 29N 71 34W
Lancaster, N.Y., U.S.A. **116 D6** 42 54N 78 40W
Lancaster, Pa., U.S.A. **117 F8** 40 2N 76 19W
Lancaster, S.C., U.S.A. **115 H5** 34 43N 80 46W
Lancaster, Wis., U.S.A. **112 D9** 42 51N 90 43W
Lancaster Sd., Canada . **101 A11** 74 13N 84 0W
Lancelin, Australia ... **93 F2** 31 0 S 115 18 E
Lanchow = Lanzhou,
China .... **56 F2** 36 1N 103 52 E
Lanchyn, Ukraine .... **29 B9** 48 33N 24 45 E
Lanciano, Italy ...... **42 F11** 42 14N 14 23 E
Lancun, China .... **57 F11** 36 25N 120 10 E
Łańcut, Poland ...... **31 H9** 50 10N 22 13 E
Land Between the
Lakes △, U.S.A. **115 G1** 36 55N 88 7W
Landau, Bayern,
Germany .... **25 G8** 48 40N 12 41 E
Landau, Rhld-Pfz.,
Germany .... **25 F4** 49 12N 8 6 E
Landeck, Austria ..... **26 D3** 47 9N 10 34 E
Lander, U.S.A. **108 E9** 42 50N 108 44W
Lander →, Australia .. **92 D5** 22 0 S 132 0 E
Landerneau, France .. **18 D2** 48 28N 4 17W
Landeryd, Sweden ... **11 G7** 57 7N 13 15 E
Landes, France **20 D2** 44 0N 1 0W
Landes □, France **20 E3** 43 57N 0 48W
Landes de Gascogne △,
France **20 D3** 44 23N 0 50W
Landi Kotal, Pakistan . **68 B4** 34 7N 71 6 E
Landisburg, U.S.A. **116 F7** 40 21N 77 19W
Landivisiau, France ... **18 D2** 48 31N 4 6W
Landquart, Switz. .... **25 J5** 46 58N 9 32 E
Landrecies, France ... **19 B10** 50 7N 3 40 E
Land's End, U.K. **15 G2** 50 4N 5 44W
Landsberg, Germany .. **25 G6** 48 3N 10 53 E
Landsborough Cr. →,
Australia .... **94 C3** 22 28 S 144 35 E
Landshut, Germany ... **25 G8** 48 34N 12 8 E
Landskrona, Sweden .. **11 J6** 55 53N 12 50 E
Landstuhl, Germany .. **25 F3** 49 25N 7 34 E
Landvetter, Sweden .. **11 G6** 57 41N 12 17 E
Lanesboro, U.S.A. **117 E9** 41 57N 75 34W
Lanett, U.S.A. **115 E3** 32 52N 85 11W
Lang Qua, Vietnam ... **64 A5** 22 16N 104 27 E
Lang Shan, China .... **56 D4** 41 0N 106 30 E
Lang Son, Vietnam ... **58 G6** 21 52N 106 42 E
Lang Suan, Thailand .. **65 H2** 9 57N 99 4 E
Langå, Denmark ..... **11 H3** 56 23N 9 54 E
La'nga Co, China ..... **67 D12** 30 45N 81 15 E
Lángádhos, Greece ... **44 F7** 40 46N 23 6 E
Langádhia, Greece ... **46 D4** 37 43N 22 1 E
Lángao, China .... **10 A** 63 19N 114 4 E
Langano, L., Ethiopia .. **81 F4** 7 36N 38 43 E
Langar, Iran .... **71 C9** 35 23N 60 25 E
Langara I., Canada ... **102 C2** 54 14N 133 1W
Langas, Sweden ...... **11 G8** 57 23N 15 33 E
Langdai, China .... **58 D5** 26 6N 105 21 E
Langdon, U.S.A. **112 A5** 48 45N 98 22W
Länge Jan = Ölands
södra udde, Sweden . **11 H10** 56 12N 16 28 E
Langeac, France ..... **20 C7** 45 7N 3 29 E
Langeais, France ..... **18 E7** 47 20N 0 24 E
Langeb Baraka →,
Sudan .... **80 D4** 17 28N 36 50 E

Lardhos, Órmos, Greece **49 C10** 36 4N 28 2 E
Laredo, Spain **36 B7** 43 26N 3 28W
Laredo, U.S.A. **113 M5** 27 30N 99 30W
Laredo Sd., Canada .. **102 C3** 52 30N 128 53W
Largentière, France .. **21 D8** 44 34N 4 18 E
L'Argentière-la-Bessée,
France .... **21 D10** 44 47N 6 33 E
Largo, U.S.A. **115 M4** 27 55N 82 47W
Largs, U.K. **13 F4** 55 47N 4 52W
Lari, Italy .... **40 E7** 43 34N 10 35 E
Lariang, Indonesia ... **63 E5** 1 26 S 119 17 E
Larimore, U.S.A. **112 B6** 47 54N 97 38W
Larino, Italy .... **41 G11** 41 48N 14 54 E
Lárisa, Greece .... **46 B4** 39 36N 22 27 E
Lárisa □, Greece ..... **46 B4** 39 39N 22 24 E
Larkana, Pakistan .... **68 F3** 27 32N 68 18 E
Larnaca, Cyprus ..... **49 E12** 34 55N 33 38 E
Larnaca Bay, Cyprus . **49 E12** 34 53N 33 45 E
Larne, U.K. **12 B6** 54 51N 5 51W
Larned, U.S.A. **112 F5** 38 11N 99 6W
Laroquebrou, France . **20 D6** 44 58N 2 12 E
Larose, U.S.A. **113 L9** 29 34N 90 23W
Larrimah, Australia .. **92 C5** 15 35 S 133 12 E
Larsen Ice Shelf,
Antarctica .... **5 C17** 67 0 S 62 0W
Laruns, France **20 F3** 43 0N 0 26W
Larvik, Norway ...... **9 G14** 59 4N 10 2 E
Larzac, Causse du,
France .... **20 E7** 43 50N 3 17 E
Las Alpujarras, Spain . **39 J1** 36 55N 3 20W
Las Animas, U.S.A. .. **112 F3** 38 4N 103 13W
Las Anod, Somali Rep. **75 F4** 8 26N 47 19 E
Las Arenas, Spain **36 B6** 43 17N 4 50W
Las Batuecas △, Spain **36 E4** 40 32N 6 5W
Las Breñas, Argentina **126 B3** 27 5 S 61 7W
Las Cabezas de San
Juan, Spain **37 J5** 36 57N 5 58W
Las Cañadas del
Teide △, Canary Is. . **48 F3** 28 15N 16 37W
Las Cejas, Argentina . **128 B4** 26 53 S 64 44W
Las Chimeneas, Mexico **111 N10** 32 8N 116 5W
Las Cruces, U.S.A. ... **109 K10** 32 19N 106 47W
Las Flores, Argentina . **126 D4** 36 10 S 59 7W
Las Heras, Argentina . **126 C2** 32 51 S 68 49W
Las Lajas, Argentina .. **128 D2** 38 30 S 70 25W
Las Lomitas, Argentina **126 A3** 24 43 S 60 35W
Las Marismas, Spain . **37 H4** 37 5N 6 20W
Las Minas, Spain **39 G3** 38 20N 1 41W
Las Navas de la
Concepción, Spain .. **37 H5** 37 56N 5 30W
Las Navas del Marqués,
Spain **36 E6** 40 36N 4 20W
Las Palmas, Argentina **126 B4** 27 8 S 58 45W
Las Palmas, Canary Is. **48 F4** 28 7N 15 26W
Las Palmas →, Mexico **111 N10** 32 26N 116 54W
Las Palmas ✈ (LPA),
Canary Is. **48 G4** 27 55N 15 23W
Las Palmas de
Cocalán △, Chile ... **126 C1** 34 18 S 71 4W
Las Pedroñas, Spain . **39 F2** 39 26N 2 40W
Las Piedras, Uruguay . **127 C4** 34 44 S 56 14W
Las Pipinas, Argentina **126 D4** 35 30 S 57 19W
Las Plumas, Argentina **128 E3** 43 40 S 67 15W
Las Rosas, Argentina . **126 C3** 32 30 S 61 35W
Las Rozas, Spain **36 E7** 40 29N 3 52W
Las Tablas, Panama .. **120 E3** 7 49N 80 14W
Las Termas, Argentina **126 B3** 27 29 S 64 52W
Las Toscas, Argentina **126 B4** 28 21 S 59 18W
Las Truchas, Mexico . **118 D4** 17 57N 102 13W
Las Varillas, Argentina **126 C3** 31 50 S 62 50W
Las Vegas, N. Mex.,
U.S.A. **109 J11** 35 36N 105 13W
Las Vegas, Nev., U.S.A. **111 J11** 36 10N 115 9W
Las Vegas McCarran
International ✈
(LAS), U.S.A. **111 J11** 36 5N 115 9W
Lasarte, Spain **38 B2** 43 16N 2 1W
Lascano, Uruguay .... **127 C5** 33 35 S 54 12W
Lash-e Joveyn, Afghan. **66 D2** 31 45N 61 30 E
Lashburn, Canada **103 C7** 53 10N 109 40W
Lashio, Burma .... **67 H20** 22 56N 97 45 E
Lashkar, India .... **68 F8** 26 10N 78 10 E
Łasin, Poland .... **30 E6** 53 30N 19 2 E
Lasíthi, Greece ...... **49 D7** 35 11N 25 31 E
Lasíthi □, Greece .... **49 D7** 35 5N 25 50 E
Lásjerd, Iran .... **71 C7** 35 24N 53 4 E
Lask, Poland .... **31 G6** 51 34N 19 8 E
Łaskarzew, Poland ... **31 G8** 51 48N 21 36 E
Laško, Slovenia ...... **41 B12** 46 10N 15 16 E
Lassay-les-Châteaux,
France **18 D6** 48 27N 0 30W
Lassen Pk., U.S.A. ... **108 F3** 40 29N 121 31W
Lassen Volcanic △,
U.S.A. **108 F3** 40 30N 121 20W
Last Mountain L.,
Canada **103 C7** 51 5N 105 14W
Lastchance Cr. →,
U.S.A. **110 E5** 40 2N 121 15W
Lastoursville, Gabon . **84 E2** 0 55 S 12 38 E
Lastovo, Croatia ..... **41 F13** 42 46N 16 55 E
Lastovski Kanal, Croatia **41 F14** 42 50N 17 0 E
Lat Yao, Thailand .... **64 E2** 15 45N 99 48 E
Latacunga, Ecuador .. **124 D3** 0 50 S 78 35W
Latakia = Al
Lādhiqīyah, Syria ... **70 C2** 35 30N 35 45 E
Latchford, Canada ... **104 C4** 47 20N 79 50W
Latehar, India .... **69 H11** 23 45N 84 30 E
Laterza, Italy .... **43 B9** 40 37N 16 48 E
Latham, Australia .... **93 E2** 29 44 S 116 20 E
Lathen, Germany .... **24 C3** 52 52N 7 19 E
Lathi, India .... **68 F4** 27 43N 71 23 E
Lathrop Wells, U.S.A. . **111 J10** 36 39N 116 24W
Latiano, Italy .... **43 B10** 40 33N 17 43 E
Latina, Italy .... **42 A5** 41 28N 12 52 E
Latisana, Italy .... **41 C10** 45 47N 13 0 E
Latium = Lazio □, Italy **41 F9** 42 10N 12 30 E
Laton, U.S.A. **110 J7** 36 26N 119 41W
Latorytsya →,
Slovak Rep. .... **27 C14** 48 28N 21 50 E
Latouche Treville, C.,
Australia .... **92 C3** 18 27 S 121 49 E
Latrobe, Australia ... **95 G4** 41 14 S 146 30 E
Latrobe, U.S.A. **116 F5** 40 19N 79 23W
Latrónico, Italy ...... **43 B9** 40 5N 16 1 E
Latvia ■, Europe ..... **9 H20** 56 50N 24 0 E
Lau, Nigeria .... **83 D7** 9 11N 11 19 E
Lau Group, Fiji ...... **91 C9** 17 0 S 178 30W
Lauchhammer, Germany **24 D9** 51 29N 13 47 E
Lauda-Königshofen,
Germany .... **25 F5** 49 33N 9 42 E
Lauenburg, Germany . **24 B6** 53 22N 10 33 E
Lauenburgische Seen △,
Germany .... **24 B6** 53 38N 10 45 E
Lauf, Germany ...... **25 F7** 49 30N 11 16 E
Laughlin, U.S.A. **109 J6** 35 8N 114 35W
Laujar de Andarax,
Spain **39 H2** 37 0N 2 54W

Laukaa, *Finland* . . . . . . **9 E21** 62 24N 25 56 E
Launceston, *Australia* . . **95 G4** 41 24 S 147 8 E
Launceston, *U.K.* **15 G3** 50 38N 4 22W
Laune →, *Ireland* **12 D2** 52 7N 9 47W
Launglon Bok, *Burma* . . **64 F1** 13 50N 97 54 E
Laupheim, *Germany* . . . **25 G5** 48 14N 9 52 E
Laura, *Australia* . . . . . **94 B3** 15 32 S 144 32 E
Laureana di Borrello,
  Italy . . . . **43 D9** 38 30N 16 5 E
Laurel, *Miss., U.S.A.* . . **113 K10** 31 41N 89 8W
Laurel, *Mont., U.S.A.* . . **108 D9** 45 40N 108 46W
Laurencekirk, *U.K.* **13 E6** 56 50N 2 28W
Laurens, *U.S.A.* **115 H4** 34 30N 82 1W
Laurentian Plateau,
  Canada **105 B6** 52 0N 70 0W
Lauria, *Italy* . . . . **43 B8** 40 2N 15 50 E
Laurie L., *Canada* **103 B8** 56 35N 101 57W
Laurinburg, *U.S.A.* . . . **115 H6** 34 47N 79 28W
Laurium, *U.S.A.* **114 B1** 47 14N 88 27W
Lausanne, *Switz.* . . . . . **25 J2** 46 32N 6 38 E
Laut, *Indonesia* . . . . . . **62 D3** 4 45N 108 0 E
Laut, Pulau, *Indonesia* . **62 E5** 3 40 S 116 10 E
Laut Kecil, Kepulauan,
  Indonesia . . . . **62 E5** 4 45 S 115 40 E
Lauterbach, *Germany* . . **24 C5** 50 37N 9 24 E
Lauterecken, *Germany* . **25 F3** 49 38N 7 35 E
Lautoka, *Fiji* . . . . **91 C7** 17 37 S 177 27 E
Lauzès, *France* . . . . . . **20 D5** 44 34N 1 35 E
Lava →, *Russia* . . . . . . **30 D3** 54 37N 21 14 E
Lava Beds △, *U.S.A.* . . **108 F3** 41 40N 121 30W
Lavagh More, *Ireland* . . **12 B3** 54 46N 8 6W
Lavagna, *Italy* . . . . **40 D6** 44 18N 9 20 E
Laval, *France* **18 D6** 48 4N 0 48W
Lavalle, *Argentina* . . . . **126 B2** 28 15 S 65 15W
Lavant Station, *Canada* **117 A8** 45 3N 76 42W
Lāvar Meydān, *Iran* . . . **71 D7** 30 20N 54 30 E
Lávara, *Greece* . . . . . . **45 E10** 41 19N 26 22 E
Lavardac, *France* . . . . . **20 D4** 44 12N 0 20 E
Lavaur, *France* . . . . . . **20 E5** 43 40N 1 49 E
Lavelanet, *France* . . . . **20 F5** 42 57N 1 51 E
Lavello, *Italy* . . . . **43 A8** 41 3N 15 48 E
Laverton, *Australia* . . . **93 E3** 28 44 S 122 29 E
Lavis, *Italy* . . . . **40 B8** 46 8N 11 7 E
Lávkos, *Greece* . . . . . . **46 B5** 39 9N 23 14 E
Lavos, *Portugal* **36 E2** 40 6N 8 49W
Lavradio, *Portugal* **37 G1** 38 40N 9 3W
Lavras, *Brazil* . . . . **127 A7** 21 20 S 45 0W
Lavre, *Portugal* **37 G2** 38 46N 8 22W
Lávrion, *Greece* . . . . . . **46 D6** 37 40N 24 4 E
Lávris, *Greece* . . . . **49 D6** 35 25N 24 40 E
Lavumisa, *Swaziland* . . **89 D5** 27 20 S 31 55 E
Lavushi Manda △,
  Zambia . . . . **87 E3** 12 46 S 31 0 E
Lawas, *Malaysia* . . . . . **62 D5** 4 55N 115 40 E
Lawele, *Indonesia* . . . . **63 F6** 5 13 S 122 57 E
Lawn Hill △, *Australia* . **94 B2** 18 15 S 138 6 E
Lawng Pit, *Burma* . . . . **67 G20** 25 30N 97 25 E
Lawqah, Si. Arabia . . . . **70 D4** 29 49N 42 45 E
Lawra, *Ghana* **82 C4** 10 39N 2 51W
Lawrence, *N.Z.* . . . . . . **91 L2** 45 55 S 169 41 E
Lawrence, Kans., U.S.A. **112 F7** 38 58N 95 14W
Lawrence, Mass., U.S.A. **117 D13** 42 43N 71 10W
Lawrenceburg, Ind.,
  U.S.A. **114 F3** 39 6N 84 52W
Lawrenceburg, Tenn.,
  U.S.A. **115 H2** 35 14N 87 20W
Lawrenceville, Ga.,
  U.S.A. **115 J4** 33 57N 83 59W
Lawrenceville, Pa.,
  U.S.A. **116 E7** 41 59N 77 8W
Laws, *U.S.A.* **110 H8** 37 24N 118 20W
Lawton, *U.S.A.* **113 H5** 34 37N 98 25W
Lawu, *Indonesia* . . . . . **63 G14** 7 40 S 111 13 E
Lawz, J. al, Si. Arabia . . **80 B4** 28 39N 35 18 E
Laxå, *Sweden* . . . . **11 F8** 58 59N 14 37 E
Laxford, L., U.K. **13 C3** 58 24N 5 6W
Laxou, *France* . . . . **19 D13** 48 41N 5 8 E
Lay →, *France* **20 B2** 46 18N 1 17W
Layla, Si. Arabia . . . . . **75 C4** 22 10N 45 40 E
Laylān, *Iraq* . . . . **70 C5** 35 18N 44 31 E
Layon →, *France* **18 E6** 47 20N 0 45W
Layton, *U.S.A.* **108 F7** 41 4N 111 58W
Laytonville, *U.S.A.* . . . **108 G2** 39 41N 123 29W
Lazarevac, Serbia & M. . **44 B4** 44 23N 20 17 E
Lazarevskoye, *Russia* . **35 J4** 43 55N 39 21 E
Lazarivo, *Madag.* . . . . **89 C8** 23 54 S 44 59 E
Lazdijai, *Lithuania* . . . **30 D10** 54 14N 23 31 E
Lazio □, *Italy* . . . . **41 F9** 42 10N 12 30 E
Lazo, *Moldova* . . . . . . **29 C13** 47 33N 28 2 E
Lazo, *Russia* . . . . **54 C6** 43 25N 133 55 E
Le Beausset, *France* . . **21 E9** 43 12N 5 48 E
Le Bic, *Canada* **105 C6** 48 20N 68 41W
Le Blanc, *France* . . . . . **20 B5** 46 37N 1 3 E
Le Bleymard, *France* . . **20 D7** 44 30N 3 42 E
Le Bourgneuf-la-Fôret,
  France **18 D6** 48 10N 0 59W
Le Bugue, *France* . . . . **20 D4** 44 55N 0 56 E
Le Cateau Cambrésis,
  France . . . . **19 B10** 50 7N 3 32 E
Le Caylar, *France* . . . . **20 E7** 43 51N 3 19 E
Le Chambon-
  Feugerolles, *France* . **21 C8** 45 24N 4 19 E
Le Châtelet, *France* . . . **19 F9** 46 38N 2 16 E
Le Chesne, *France* . . . . **19 C11** 49 30N 4 45 E
Le Cheylard, *France* . . **21 D8** 44 55N 4 25 E
Le Conquet, *France* . . . **18 D2** 48 21N 4 46W
Le Creusot, *France* . . . **19 F11** 46 48N 4 24 E
Le Croisic, *France* **18 E4** 47 18N 2 30W
Le Donjon, *France* . . . . **19 F10** 46 22N 3 48 E
Le Dorat, *France* . . . . . **20 B5** 46 14N 1 5 E
Le François, *Martinique* **120 c** 14 38N 60 57W
Le Gosier, *Guadeloupe* **120 b** 16 14N 61 29W
Le Grand-Lucé, *France* **18 E7** 47 52N 0 28 E
Le Grand-Pressigny,
  France . . . . **18 F7** 46 55N 0 48 E
Le Grand-Quevilly,
  France . . . . **18 C8** 49 24N 1 3 E
Le Havre, *France* . . . . . **18 C7** 49 30N 0 5 E
Le Lamentin,
  Martinique . . . . . . **120 c** 14 35N 61 2W
Le Lavandou, *France* . . **21 E10** 43 8N 6 22 E
Le Lion-d'Angers,
  France **18 E6** 47 37N 0 43W
Le Louroux-Béconnais,
  France **18 E6** 47 30N 0 55W
Le Luc, *France* . . . . . . **21 E10** 43 23N 6 21 E
Le Lude, *France* . . . . . **18 E7** 47 39N 0 9 E
Le Mans, *France* . . . . . **18 E7** 48 0N 0 10 E
Le Marin, *Martinique* . . **120 c** 14 27N 60 55W
Le Mars, *U.S.A.* **112 D6** 42 47N 96 10W
Le Mayet-de-Montagne,
  France . . . . **19 F10** 46 4N 3 40 E
Le Mêle-sur-Sarthe,
  France . . . . **18 D7** 48 31N 0 22 E
Le Monastier-sur-
  Gazeille, *France* . . . **20 D7** 44 57N 3 59 E
Le Monêtier-les-Bains,
  France . . . . **21 D10** 44 58N 6 30 E

Le Mont-Dore, *France* . **20 C6** 45 35N 2 49 E
Le Mont-St-Michel,
  France **18 D5** 48 40N 1 30W
Le Moule, *Guadeloupe* **120 b** 16 20N 61 22W
Le Muy, *France* . . . . . . **21 E10** 43 28N 6 34 E
Le Palais, *France* **18 E3** 47 20N 3 10W
Le Perthus, *France* . . . . **20 F6** 42 30N 2 53 E
Le Prêcheur, *Martinique* **120 c** 14 50N 61 12W
Le Puy-en-Velay, *France* **20 C7** 45 3N 3 52 E
Le Robert, *Martinique* . **120 c** 14 40N 60 56W
Le St-Esprit, *Martinique* **120 c** 14 34N 60 56W
Le Sueur, *U.S.A.* **112 C8** 44 28N 93 55W
Le Teil, *France* . . . . . . **21 D8** 44 33N 4 40 E
Le Teilleul, *France* **18 D6** 48 32N 0 53W
Le Theil, *France* . . . . . **18 D7** 48 16N 0 42 E
Le Thillot, *France* . . . . **19 E13** 47 53N 6 46 E
Le Thuy, *Vietnam* . . . . **64 D6** 17 14N 106 49 E
Le Touquet-Paris-Plage,
  France . . . . **19 B8** 50 30N 1 36 E
Le Tréport, *France* . . . . **18 B8** 50 3N 1 20 E
Le Val-d'Ajol, *France* . . **19 E13** 47 55N 6 30 E
Le Verdon-sur-Mer,
  France **20 C2** 45 33N 1 4W
Le Vigan, *France* . . . . . **20 E7** 43 59N 3 36 E
Lea →, *U.K.* . . . . **15 F8** 51 31N 0 1 E
Leach, *Cambodia* . . . . . **65 F4** 12 21N 103 46 E
Lead, *U.S.A.* **112 C3** 44 21N 103 46W
Leader, *Canada* **103 C7** 50 50N 109 30W
Leadville, *U.S.A.* **109 G10** 39 15N 106 18W
Leaf →, *U.S.A.* **113 K10** 30 59N 88 44W
Leaf Rapids, *Canada* . . **103 B9** 56 30N 99 59W
Leamington, *Canada* . . **116 D2** 42 3N 82 36W
Leamington, *U.S.A.* . . . **108 G7** 39 32N 112 17W
Leamington Spa = Royal
  Leamington Spa, U.K. **15 E6** 52 18N 1 31W
Le'an, *China* . . . . **59 D10** 27 22N 115 48 E
Leandro Norte Alem,
  Argentina . . . . **127 B4** 27 34 S 55 15W
Leane, L., *Ireland* **12 D2** 52 2N 9 32W
Learmonth, *Australia* . . **92 D1** 22 13 S 114 10 E
Leask, *Canada* **103 C7** 53 5N 106 45W
Leatherhead, *U.K.* **15 F7** 51 18N 0 20W
Leavenworth, Kans.,
  U.S.A. **112 F7** 39 19N 94 55W
Leavenworth, Wash.,
  U.S.A. **108 C3** 47 36N 120 40W
Łeba, *Poland* . . . . **30 D4** 54 45N 17 32 E
Łeba →, *Poland* . . . . . **30 D4** 54 46N 17 33 E
Lebach, *Germany* . . . . **25 F2** 49 25N 6 54 E
Lebak, *Phil.* . . . . **61 H6** 6 32N 124 5 E
Lebam, *U.S.A.* **110 D3** 46 34N 123 33W
Lebane, Serbia & M. . . . **44 D5** 42 56N 21 44 E
Lebanon, Ind., U.S.A. . . **114 E2** 40 3N 86 28W
Lebanon, Kans., U.S.A. . **112 F5** 39 49N 98 33W
Lebanon, Ky., U.S.A. . . **114 G3** 37 34N 85 15W
Lebanon, Mo., U.S.A. . . **113 G8** 37 41N 92 40W
Lebanon, N.H., U.S.A. . . **117 C12** 43 39N 72 15W
Lebanon, Oreg., U.S.A. . **108 D2** 44 32N 122 55W
Lebanon, Pa., U.S.A. . . **117 F8** 40 20N 76 26W
Lebanon, Tenn., U.S.A. . **115 G2** 36 12N 86 18W
Lebanon ■, Asia . . . . . . **74 B5** 34 0N 36 0 E
Lebec, *U.S.A.* **111 L8** 34 50N 118 52W
Lebedyan, *Russia* . . . . **33 F10** 53 0N 39 10 E
Lebedyn, *Ukraine* . . . . **33 G8** 50 35N 34 30 E
Lebel-sur-Quévillon,
  Canada **104 C4** 49 3N 76 59W
Lebomboberge,
  S. Africa . . . . **89 C5** 24 30 S 32 0 E
Lębork, *Poland* . . . . . . **30 D4** 54 33N 17 46 E
Lebrija, *Spain* **37 J4** 36 53N 6 5W
Łebsko, Jezioro, *Poland* **30 D4** 54 40N 17 25 E
Lebu, *Chile* . . . . **126 D1** 37 40 S 73 47W
Leca da Palmeira,
  Portugal **36 D2** 41 12N 8 42W
Lecce, *Italy* . . . . **43 B11** 40 23N 18 11 E
Lecco, *Italy* . . . . **40 C6** 45 51N 9 23 E
Lecco, L. di, *Italy* . . . . **40 C6** 45 55N 9 19 E
Lécera, *Spain* **38 D4** 41 13N 0 43W
Lech, *Austria* . . . . **26 D3** 47 13N 10 9 E
Lech →, *Germany* . . . . **25 G6** 48 43N 10 56 E
Lechang, *China* . . . . . . **59 E9** 25 10N 113 20 E
Lechtaler Alpen, *Austria* **26 D3** 47 15N 10 30 E
Lecontes Mills, *U.S.A.* **116 E6** 41 5N 78 17W
Lectoure, *France* . . . . . **20 E4** 43 56N 0 38 E
Łęczna, *Poland* . . . . . . **31 G9** 51 18N 22 53 E
Łęczyca, *Poland* . . . . . **31 F6** 52 5N 19 15 E
Ledesma, *Spain* **36 D5** 41 6N 5 59W
Ledong, *China* . . . . **64 C7** 18 41N 109 5 E
Leduc, *Canada* **102 C6** 53 15N 113 30W
Lee, *U.S.A.* **117 D11** 42 19N 73 15W
Lee →, *Ireland* **12 E3** 51 53N 8 56W
Lee Vining, *U.S.A.* . . . **110 H7** 37 58N 119 7W
Leech L., *U.S.A.* **112 B7** 47 10N 94 24W
Leechburg, *U.S.A.* **116 F5** 40 37N 79 36W
Leeds, *U.K.* **14 D6** 53 48N 1 33W
Leeds, *U.S.A.* **115 J2** 33 33N 86 33W
Leek, *Neths.* . . . . **17 A6** 53 10N 6 24 E
Leek, *U.K.* **14 D5** 53 7N 2 1W
Leeman, *Australia* . . . . **93 E1** 29 57 S 114 58 E
Leeper, *U.S.A.* **116 E5** 41 22N 79 18W
Leer, *Germany* . . . . . . **24 B3** 53 13N 7 26 E
Leesburg, *U.S.A.* **115 L5** 28 49N 81 53W
Leesville, *U.S.A.* **113 K8** 31 9N 93 16W
Leeton, *Australia* . . . . . **95 E4** 34 33 S 146 23 E
Leetonia, *U.S.A.* **116 F4** 40 53N 80 45W
Leeu Gamka, S. Africa . **88 E3** 32 47 S 21 59 E
Leeuwarden, *Neths.* . . **17 A5** 53 15N 5 48 E
Leeuwin, C., *Australia* . **93 F2** 34 20 S 115 9 E
Leeuwin Naturaliste △,
  Australia . . . . **93 F2** 34 6 S 115 3 E
Leeward Is., Atl. Oc. . . . **121 C7** 16 30N 63 30W
Lefka, *Cyprus* . . . . **49 D11** 35 6N 32 51 E
Lefkonikó, *Cyprus* . . . . **49 D12** 35 18N 33 44 E
Lefroy, *Canada* **116 B5** 44 16N 79 34W
Lefroy, L., *Australia* . . . **93 F3** 31 21 S 121 40 E
Leg →, *Poland* . . . . . . **31 H8** 50 42N 21 50 E
Leganés, *Spain* **36 E7** 40 19N 3 45W
Legazpi, *Phil.* . . . . **61 E5** 13 10N 123 45 E
Lège-Cap-Ferret, *France* **20 D2** 44 48N 1 9W
Lege Hida, *Ethiopia* . . . **81 F5** 7 56N 41 4 E
Legendre I., *Australia* . . **92 D2** 20 22 S 116 55 E
Leghorn = Livorno, *Italy* **40 E7** 43 33N 10 19 E
Legionowo, *Poland* . . . . **31 F7** 52 25N 20 50 E
Legnago, *Italy* . . . . **41 C8** 45 11N 11 18 E
Legnano, *Italy* . . . . **40 C5** 45 36N 8 54 E
Legnica, *Poland* . . . . . . **31 G3** 51 12N 16 10 E
Legrad, *Croatia* . . . . . . **41 B13** 46 17N 16 51 E
Leh, *India* . . . . **69 B7** 34 9N 77 35 E
Lehigh Acres, *U.S.A.* . . **115 M5** 26 36N 81 39W
Leighton, *U.S.A.* **117 F9** 40 50N 75 43W
Lehliu, *Romania* . . . . . **29 F11** 44 29N 26 20 E
Leho, *Sudan* . . . . **81 F3** 7 7N 33 52 E
Lehre, *Germany* . . . . . . **24 C5** 52 22N 9 58 E
Lehututu, *Botswana* . . . **88 C3** 23 54 S 21 55 E
Lei Shui →, *China* . . . . **59 D9** 26 55N 112 35 E
Leiah, *Pakistan* . . . . . . **68 D4** 30 58N 70 58 E
Leibnitz, *Austria* . . . . . **26 E8** 46 47N 15 34 E

Leibo, *China* . . . . **58 C4** 28 11N 103 34 E
Leicester City □, U.K. . . **15 E6** 52 38N 1 9W
Leicester □, U.K. **15 E6** 52 38N 1 8W
Leicestershire □, U.K. . . **15 E6** 52 41N 1 17W
Leichhardt →, Australia **94 B2** 17 35 S 139 48 E
Leichhardt Ra.,
  Australia . . . . **94 C4** 20 46 S 147 40 E
Leiden, *Neths.* . . . . . . **17 B4** 52 9N 4 30 E
Leie →, *Belgium* . . . . . **17 C3** 51 2N 3 45 E
Leifers = Láives, *Italy* . **41 B8** 46 26N 11 18 E
Leimen, *Germany* . . . . **25 F4** 49 21N 8 41 E
Leine →, *Germany* . . . . **24 C5** 52 43N 9 36 E
Leinefelde, *Germany* . . **24 D6** 51 23N 10 19 E
Leinster, *Australia* . . . . **93 E3** 27 51 S 120 36 E
Leinster □, *Ireland* **12 C5** 53 3N 7 8W
Leinster, Mt., *Ireland* . . **12 D5** 52 37N 6 46W
Leipalingis, *Lithuania* . . **30 D10** 54 5N 23 51 E
Leipzig, *Germany* . . . . **24 D8** 51 18N 12 22 E
Leiria, *Portugal* **36 F2** 39 46N 8 53W
Leiria □, *Portugal* **36 F2** 39 46N 8 53W
Leirvik, *Norway* . . . . . . **9 G11** 59 47N 5 28 E
Leishan, *China* . . . . . . **58 D7** 26 15N 108 20 E
Leisler, Mt., *Australia* . **92 D4** 23 23 S 129 20 E
Leith, *U.K.* **13 F5** 55 59N 3 11W
Leith Hill, *U.K.* **15 F7** 51 11N 0 22W
Leitha →, *Europe* . . . . **27 D10** 47 50N 17 5 E
Leitrim, *Ireland* **12 B3** 54 0N 8 5W
Leitrim □, *Ireland* **12 B4** 54 8N 8 0W
Leitza, *Spain* **38 B3** 43 5N 1 55W
Leiyang, *China* . . . . . . **59 D9** 26 27N 112 45 E
Leizhou, *China* . . . . . . **59 G8** 20 52N 110 8 E
Leizhou Bandao, *China* **58 G7** 21 0N 110 0 E
Leizhou Wan, *China* . . **59 G8** 20 50N 110 20 E
Lek →, *Neths.* . . . . . . **17 C4** 51 54N 4 35 E
Leka, *Norway* . . . . **8 D14** 65 5N 11 35 E
Lekbibaj, *Albania* . . . . **44 D3** 42 17N 19 56 E
Lekeitio, *Spain* **38 B2** 43 20N 2 32W
Lekhainá, *Greece* . . . . **46 D3** 37 57N 21 16 E
Lekoui, Burkina Faso . . **82 C4** 12 37N 3 40W
Leksand, *Sweden* . . . . **10 D9** 60 44N 15 1 E
Lékva Óros, *Greece* . . . **49 D6** 35 18N 24 3 E
Leland, Mich., U.S.A. . . **114 C3** 45 1N 85 45W
Leland, Miss., U.S.A. . . **113 J9** 33 24N 90 54W
Leland, *Sweden* . . . . . . **10 E6** 59 10N 12 5 E
Leleque, *Argentina* . . . . **128 E2** 42 28 S 71 0W
Lelystad, *Neths.* . . . . . **17 B5** 52 30N 5 25 E
Lem, *Denmark* . . . . **11 H2** 56 1N 8 24 E
Lema, *Nigeria* . . . . **83 C5** 12 58N 4 13 E
Lema Shilindi, *Ethiopia* **81 G5** 4 50N 42 6 E
Léman, L., *Europe* . . . . **19 F13** 46 26N 6 30 E
Lembar, *Indonesia* . . . . **63 K19** 8 45 S 116 4 E
Lembuak, *Indonesia* . . . **63 K19** 8 36 S 116 11 E
Lemera, Dem. Rep. of
  the Congo . . . . **86 C2** 3 0 S 28 55 E
Lemery, *Phil.* . . . . **61 E4** 13 51N 120 56 E
Lemhi Ra., *U.S.A.* **108 D7** 44 30N 113 30W
Lemmer, *Neths.* . . . . . **17 B5** 52 51N 5 43 E
Lemmon, *U.S.A.* **112 C3** 45 57N 102 10W
Lemon Grove, *U.S.A.* . **111 N9** 32 45N 117 2W
Lemoore, *U.S.A.* **110 J7** 36 18N 119 46W
Lempdes, *France* . . . . . **20 C7** 45 22N 3 17 E
Lemvig, *Denmark* . . . . **11 H2** 56 33N 8 20 E
Lena →, *Russia* . . . . . . **53 B13** 72 52N 126 40 E
Lenart, *Slovenia* . . . . . **41 B13** 46 36N 15 48 E
Lenartovce, Slovak Rep. **27 C13** 48 18N 20 19 E
Lencloître, *France* . . . . **18 F7** 46 50N 0 20 E
Léndas, *Greece* . . . . . . **49 E6** 34 56N 24 56 E
Lendava, *Slovenia* . . . . **41 B13** 46 35N 16 25 E
Lendeh, *Iran* . . . . **71 D6** 30 58N 50 25 E
Lendinara, *Italy* . . . . . . **41 C8** 45 5N 11 36 E
Lengerich, *Germany* . . . **24 C3** 52 11N 7 52 E
Lenggong, *Malaysia* . . **65 K3** 5 6N 100 58 E
Lenggries, *Germany* . . . **25 H7** 47 41N 11 35 E
Lengshuijiang, *China* . . **59 D8** 27 40N 111 26 E
Lengshuitan, *China* . . . **59 D8** 26 27N 111 35 E
Lengua de Vaca, Pta.,
  Chile . . . . **126 C1** 30 14 S 71 38W
Lengwe △, *Malawi* . . . **87 F3** 16 14 S 34 45 E
Lengyeltóti, *Hungary* . . **28 D2** 46 40N 17 40 E
Lenhovda, *Sweden* . . . **11 G9** 57 0N 15 16 E
Lenina, Kanal →,
  Russia . . . . **35 J7** 43 44N 45 17 E
Lenino, *Ukraine* . . . . . . **33 K8** 45 17N 35 46 E
Leninogorsk,
  Kazakhstan . . . . . . **52 D9** 50 20N 83 30 E
Leninsk, *Russia* . . . . . . **35 F7** 48 40N 45 15 E
Leninsk-Kuznetskiy,
  Russia . . . . **52 D9** 54 44N 86 10 E
Leninskoye, *Russia* . . . **34 A8** 58 23N 47 3 E
Lenk, *Switz.* . . . . **25 J3** 46 27N 7 28 E
Lenkoran = Länkäran,
  Azerbaijan . . . . **71 B6** 38 48N 48 52 E
Lenmalu, *Indonesia* . . . **63 E8** 1 45 S 130 15 E
Lenne →, *Germany* . . . **24 D3** 51 25N 7 29 E
Lennestadt, *Germany* . . **24 D4** 51 8N 8 4 E
Lennox, *U.S.A.* **112 D6** 43 21N 96 53W
Lennoxville, *Canada* . . **117 A13** 45 22N 71 51W
Leno, *Italy* . . . . **40 C7** 45 22N 10 13 E
Lenoir, *U.S.A.* **115 H5** 35 55N 81 32W
Lenoir City, *U.S.A.* . . . **115 H3** 35 48N 84 16W
Lenore L., *Canada* **103 C8** 52 30N 104 59W
Lenox, *U.S.A.* **117 D11** 42 22N 73 17W
Lens, *France* . . . . **19 B9** 50 26N 2 50 E
Lensahn, *Germany* . . . . **24 A6** 54 13N 10 53 E
Lensk, *Russia* . . . . **53 C12** 60 48N 114 55 E
Lentekhi, *Georgia* . . . . **35 J6** 42 47N 42 45 E
Lenti, *Hungary* . . . . . . **28 D1** 46 37N 16 33 E
Lentini, *Italy* . . . . **43 E7** 37 17N 15 0 E
Lenwood, *U.S.A.* **111 L9** 34 53N 117 7W
Lenya, *Burma* . . . . **62 B1** 11 33N 98 57 E
Lenzen, *Germany* . . . . **24 B7** 53 5N 11 29 E
Léo, Burkina Faso **82 C4** 11 3N 2 2W
Leoben, *Austria* . . . . . . **26 D8** 47 22N 15 5 E
Leodhas = Lewis, U.K. . **13 C2** 58 9N 6 40W
Leola, *U.S.A.* **112 C5** 45 43N 98 56W
Leominster, *U.K.* **15 E5** 52 14N 2 43W
Leominster, *U.S.A.* . . . **117 D13** 42 32N 71 46W
Léon, *France* **20 E2** 43 53N 1 18W
León, *Mexico* **118 C4** 21 7N 101 40W
León, Nic. **120 D2** 12 20N 86 51W
León, *Spain* **36 C5** 42 38N 5 34W
León □, *Spain* **36 C5** 42 40N 5 55W
León →, *U.S.A.* **113 K6** 31 14N 97 28W
León, Montes de, *Spain* **36 C4** 42 30N 6 18W
Leonardo da Vinci,
  Roma ✈ (FCO), *Italy* **41 G9** 41 48N 12 15 E
Leonardtown, *U.S.A.* . . **114 F7** 38 17N 76 38W
Leonardville, Namibia . . **88 C2** 23 29 S 18 49 E
Leonberg, *Germany* . . . **25 G5** 48 48N 9 1 E
Leonding, *Austria* . . . . **26 C7** 48 16N 14 15 E
Leonessa, *Italy* . . . . . . **41 F9** 42 33N 12 58 E
Leonforte, *Italy* . . . . . . **43 E7** 37 38N 14 23 E
Leongatha, *Australia* . . **95 F4** 38 30 S 145 58 E
Leonídhion, *Greece* . . . **46 D4** 37 9N 22 52 E
Leonora, *Australia* . . . . **93 E3** 28 49 S 121 19 E

Leopoldina, *Brazil* . . . . **127 A7** 21 28 S 42 40W
Leopoldsburg, *Belgium* **17 C5** 51 7N 5 13 E
Leoti, *U.S.A.* **112 F4** 38 29N 101 21W
Leova, *Moldova* . . . . . . **29 D13** 46 28N 28 15 E
Leoville, *Canada* **103 C7** 53 39N 107 33W
Lepe, *Spain* **37 H3** 37 15N 7 12W
Lepel = Lyepyel, Belarus **32 E5** 54 50N 28 40 E
Lepenoú, *Greece* . . . . . **46 C3** 38 42N 21 17 E
Leping, *China* . . . . **59 C11** 28 47N 117 7 E
Lépo, L. do, Angola . . . **88 B2** 17 0 S 19 0 E
Lepontine, Alpi, *Italy* . . **40 B5** 46 22N 8 27 E
Leppävirta, *Finland* . . . **9 E22** 62 29N 27 46 E
Lepsény, *Hungary* . . . . **28 D3** 47 0N 18 15 E
Lequeitio = Lekeitio,
  Spain **38 B2** 43 20N 2 32W
Lercara Friddi, *Italy* . . . **42 E6** 37 45N 13 36 E
Lerdo, *Mexico* **118 B4** 25 32N 103 32W
Léré, *Chad* . . . . **83 D7** 9 39N 14 13 E
Léré, Mali **82 B4** 15 45N 4 55W
Lere, Bauchi, Nigeria . . **83 D6** 9 43N 9 18 E
Lere, Kaduna, Nigeria . . **83 C6** 10 23N 8 35 E
Leribe, Lesotho . . . . . . **89 D4** 28 51 S 28 3 E
Lérici, *Italy* . . . . **40 D6** 44 4N 9 55 E
Lérida = Lleida, *Spain* . **38 D5** 41 37N 0 39 E
Lérins, Îs. de, *France* . . **21 E11** 43 31N 7 3 E
Lerma, *Spain* **36 C7** 42 0N 3 47W
Léros, *Greece* . . . . **47 D8** 37 10N 26 50 E
Lérouville, *France* . . . . **19 D12** 48 44N 5 30 E
Lerum, *Sweden* . . . . . . **11 G6** 57 46N 12 16 E
Lerwick, *U.K.* **13 A7** 60 9N 1 9W
Leş, *Romania* . . . . **28 D6** 46 58N 21 50 E
Les Abrets, *France* . . . **21 C9** 45 32N 5 35 E
Les Andelys, *France* . . **18 C8** 49 15N 1 25 E
Les Borges Blanques,
  Spain . . . . **38 D5** 41 31N 0 52 E
Les Cayes, *Haiti* **121 C5** 18 15N 73 46W
Les Coteaux, *Canada* . . **117 A10** 45 15N 74 13W
Les Essarts, *France* . . . **18 F5** 46 47N 1 12W
Les Herbiers, *France* . . **18 F5** 46 52N 1 1W
Les Minquiers, Plateau
  des, Chan. Is. **18 D4** 48 58N 2 8W
Les Pieux, *France* **18 C5** 49 30N 1 48W
Les Ponts-de-Cé, *France* **18 E6** 47 25N 0 30W
Les Riceys, *France* . . . . **19 E11** 47 59N 4 22 E
Les Sables-d'Olonne,
  France **20 B2** 46 30N 1 45W
Les Vans, *France* . . . . . **21 D8** 44 25N 4 7 E
Lesbos = Lésvos, *Greece* **47 B8** 39 10N 26 20 E
L'Escala, *Spain* . . . . . . **38 C8** 42 7N 3 8 E
Leshan, *China* . . . . **58 C4** 29 33N 103 41 E
Leshwe △, Dem. Rep. of
  the Congo . . . . **87 E2** 12 45 S 29 30 E
Lésina, *Italy* . . . . **41 G12** 41 52N 15 21 E
Lésina, L. di, *Italy* . . . . **41 G12** 41 53N 15 26 E
Lesjöfors, *Sweden* . . . . **10 E8** 59 58N 14 11 E
Lesko, *Poland* . . . . **31 J9** 49 30N 22 23 E
Leskov I., Antarctica . . . **5 B1** 56 0 S 28 0W
Leskovac, Serbia & M. . **44 C5** 43 0N 21 58 E
Leskovik, *Albania* . . . . **44 F4** 40 10N 20 34 E
Leśna, *Poland* . . . . **31 G2** 51 1N 15 15 E
Lesnoven, *France* **18 D2** 48 35N 4 20W
Leśnica, *Poland* . . . . . . **31 H5** 50 26N 18 11 E
Leśnica, Serbia & M. . . **44 B3** 44 39N 19 20 E
Lesnoye, *Russia* . . . . . **32 C8** 58 15N 35 18 E
Lesopilnoye, *Russia* . . **54 A7** 46 44N 134 20 E
Lesotho ■, Africa . . . . . **89 D4** 29 40 S 28 0 E
Lesozavodsk, *Russia* . . **53 E14** 45 30N 133 29 E
Lesparre-Médoc, *France* **20 C3** 45 18N 0 57W
Lessay, *France* **18 C5** 49 14N 1 30W
Lesse →, Belgium . . . . **17 D4** 50 15N 4 54 E
Lesse et Lomme △,
  Belgium . . . . **17 D5** 50 8N 5 9 E
Lessebo, *Sweden* . . . . . **11 H9** 56 45N 15 16 E
Lesser Antilles,
  W. Indies **121 D7** 15 0N 61 0W
Lesser Slave L., *Canada* **102 B5** 55 30N 115 25W
Lesser Sunda Is.,
  Indonesia . . . . **63 F6** 8 0 S 120 0 E
Lessines, *Belgium* . . . . **17 D3** 50 42N 3 50 E
Lester, *U.S.A.* **110 C5** 47 12N 121 29W
Lester B. Pearson
  International,
  Toronto ✈ (YYZ),
  Canada **116 C5** 43 40N 79 34W
Lestock, *Canada* **103 C8** 51 19N 103 59W
Lesuer I., *Australia* . . . **92 B4** 13 50 S 127 17 E
Lesueur △, *Australia* . . **93 F2** 30 11 S 115 10 E
Lésvos, *Greece* . . . . . . **47 B8** 39 10N 26 20 E
Leszno, *Poland* . . . . . . **31 G3** 51 50N 16 30 E
Letaba, S. Africa . . . . . **89 C5** 23 59 S 31 50 E
Letälven, *Sweden* . . . . **10 E8** 59 5N 14 20 E
Létavértes, *Hungary* . . . **28 C6** 47 23N 21 55 E
Letchworth, *U.K.* **15 F7** 51 59N 0 13W
Letea, Ostrov, *Romania* **29 E14** 45 18N 29 20 E
Lethbridge, *Canada* . . . **102 D6** 49 45N 112 45W
Lethem, Guyana **124 C7** 3 20N 59 50W
Leti, Kepulauan,
  Indonesia . . . . **63 F7** 8 10 S 128 0 E
Leti Is. = Leti,
  Kepulauan, *Indonesia* **63 F7** 8 10 S 128 0 E
Letiahau →, Botswana . **88 C3** 21 16 S 24 0 E
Leticia, Colombia . . . . . **124 D5** 4 9 S 70 0W
Leting, *China* . . . . **57 E10** 39 23N 118 55 E
Letjiesbos, S. Africa . . . **88 E3** 32 34 S 22 16 E
Letlhakane, Botswana . . **88 C4** 21 27 S 25 30 E
Letlhakeng, Botswana . . **88 C3** 24 0 S 24 59 E
Letong, *Indonesia* . . . . **62 D3** 2 58N 105 42 E
Letpadan, Burma . . . . . **67 L19** 17 45N 95 45 E
Letpan, Burma . . . . **67 K19** 19 28N 94 10 E
Letsôk-aw Kyun, Burma **65 G2** 11 30N 98 25 E
Letterkenny, Ireland . . . **12 B4** 54 57N 7 45W
Leu, Romania . . . . **29 F9** 44 10N 24 0 E
Leucadia, *U.S.A.* **111 M9** 33 4N 117 18W
Leucate, *France* . . . . . . **20 F7** 42 56N 3 3 E
Leucate, Étang de,
  France . . . . **20 F7** 42 50N 3 0 E
Leuchars, *U.K.* **13 E6** 56 24N 2 53W
Leuk, *Switz.* . . . . **25 J3** 46 19N 7 37 E
Leuser, G., Indonesia . . **62 D1** 3 46N 97 12 E
Leutkirch, *Germany* . . . **25 H6** 47 49N 10 1 E
Leuven, *Belgium* . . . . . **17 D4** 50 52N 4 42 E
Leuze-en-Hainaut,
  Belgium . . . . **17 D3** 50 36N 3 37 E
Lev Tolstoy, *Russia* . . . **32 F10** 53 13N 39 29 E
Levádhia, *Greece* . . . . . **46 C4** 38 27N 22 54 E
Levan, *Albania* . . . . . . **44 F3** 40 40N 19 28 E
Levanger, *Norway* . . . . **8 E14** 63 45N 11 19 E
Levant, Î. du, *France* . . **21 E10** 43 3N 6 28 E
Lévanto, *Italy* . . . . **40 D6** 44 10N 9 38 E
Levanzo, *Italy* . . . . **42 E5** 38 0N 12 20 E
Levelland, *U.S.A.* **113 J3** 33 35N 102 23W
Leven, *U.K.* **13 E6** 56 12N 3 0W
Leven, L., *U.K.* **13 E5** 56 12N 3 22W
Leven, Toraka, Madag. . **89 A8** 12 30 S 47 45 E
Leveque C., *Australia* . . **92 C3** 16 20 S 123 0 E
Leverano, *Italy* . . . . . . **43 B10** 40 17N 18 0 E

Leverkusen, Germany . . **24 D3** 51 1N 7 1 E
Levice, Slovak Rep. . . . **27 C11** 48 13N 18 35 E
Lévico Terme, *Italy* . . . **41 C8** 46 0N 11 18 E
Levie, *France* . . . . **21 G13** 41 40N 9 7 E
Levier, *France* . . . . **19 F13** 46 58N 6 8 E
Levin, *N.Z.* . . . . **91 J5** 40 37 S 175 18 E
Lévis, *Canada* **105 C5** 46 48N 71 9W
Levis, L., *Canada* **102 A5** 62 37N 117 58W
Lévítha, *Greece* . . . . . . **47 D8** 37 0N 26 28 E
Levittown, N.Y., U.S.A. **117 F11** 40 44N 73 31W
Levittown, Pa., U.S.A. . **117 F10** 40 9N 74 51W
Levka, *Bulgaria* . . . . . . **45 E10** 41 52N 26 15 E
Levkás, *Greece* . . . . . . **46 C2** 38 40N 20 43 E
Levkás □, *Greece* . . . . **46 C2** 38 45N 20 40 E
Levkímmi, *Greece* . . . . **49 B4** 39 25N 20 3 E
Levkímmi, Ákra, Greece **49 B4** 39 29N 20 4 E
Levkôsia = Nicosia,
  Cyprus . . . . **49 D12** 35 10N 33 25 E
Levoča, Slovak Rep. . . . **27 B13** 49 2N 20 35 E
Levroux, *France* . . . . . . **19 F8** 46 59N 1 38 E
Levski, *Bulgaria* . . . . . **45 C9** 43 21N 25 10 E
Levskigrad = Karlovo,
  Bulgaria . . . . **45 D8** 42 38N 24 47 E
Lewes, *U.K.* . . . . **15 G8** 50 52N 0 1 E
Lewes, *U.S.A.* **114 F8** 38 46N 75 9W
Lewin Brzeski, *Poland* . **31 H4** 50 45N 17 37 E
Lewis →, *U.S.A.* **110 E4** 45 51N 122 48W
Lewis, Butt of, *U.K.* . . . **13 C2** 58 31N 6 16W
Lewis Ra., *Australia* . . . **92 D4** 20 3 S 128 50 E
Lewis Range, *U.S.A.* . . **108 C7** 48 5N 113 5W
Lewis Run, *U.S.A.* **116 E6** 41 52N 78 40W
Lewisburg, Pa., U.S.A. . **116 F8** 40 58N 76 54W
Lewisburg, Tenn., U.S.A. **115 H2** 35 27N 86 48W
Lewisburg, W. Va.,
  U.S.A. **114 G5** 37 48N 80 27W
Lewisporte, *Canada* . . . **105 C8** 49 15N 55 3W
Lewiston, Idaho, U.S.A. **108 C5** 46 25N 117 1W
Lewiston, Maine, U.S.A. **115 C11** 44 6N 70 13W
Lewiston, N.Y., U.S.A. . **116 C5** 43 11N 79 3W
Lewistown, Mont.,
  U.S.A. **108 C9** 47 4N 109 26W
Lewistown, Pa., U.S.A. . **116 F7** 40 36N 77 34W
Lexington, Ill., U.S.A. . . **112 E10** 40 39N 88 47W
Lexington, Ky., U.S.A. . **114 F3** 38 3N 84 30W
Lexington, Mich., U.S.A. **116 C2** 43 16N 82 32W
Lexington, Mo., U.S.A. . **112 F8** 39 11N 93 52W
Lexington, N.C., U.S.A. **115 H5** 35 49N 80 15W
Lexington, N.Y., U.S.A. **117 D10** 42 15N 74 22W
Lexington, Nebr., U.S.A. **112 E5** 40 47N 99 45W
Lexington, Ohio, U.S.A. **116 F2** 40 41N 82 35W
Lexington, Va., U.S.A. . **115 H1** 35 39N 88 24W
Lexington Park, U.S.A. . **114 F7** 38 16N 76 27W
Leyburn, *U.K.* **14 C6** 54 19N 1 48W
Leye, *China* . . . . **58 E6** 24 48N 106 29 E
Leyland, *U.K.* **14 D5** 53 42N 2 43W
Leyre →, *France* **20 D2** 44 39N 1 1W
Leyte □, *Phil.* . . . . **61 F6** 11 0N 125 0 E
Leyte Gulf, *Phil.* . . . . . **61 F6** 10 50N 125 25 E
Leżajsk, *Poland* . . . . . . **31 H9** 50 16N 22 25 E
Lezay, *France* **20 B3** 46 15N 0 1W
Lezhë, *Albania* . . . . . . **44 E3** 41 47N 19 39 E
Lezhi, *China* . . . . **58 B5** 30 19N 104 58 E
Lézignan-Corbières,
  France . . . . **20 E6** 43 13N 2 43 E
Lezoux, *France* . . . . . . **20 C7** 45 49N 3 21 E
Lgov, *Russia* . . . . **33 G8** 51 42N 35 16 E
Lhasa, *China* . . . . **60 D4** 29 25N 90 58 E
Lhazê, *China* . . . . **60 D3** 29 5N 87 38 E
Lhokkruet, *Indonesia* . . **62 D1** 4 55N 95 24 E
Lhokseumawe,
  Indonesia . . . . **62 C1** 5 10N 97 10 E
L'Hospitalet de
  Llobregat, *Spain* . . . **38 D7** 41 21N 2 6 E
Li, *Thailand* . . . . **64 D2** 17 48N 98 57 E
Li Shui →, China . . . . . **59 C9** 29 24N 112 1 E
Li Xian, Gansu, China . **56 G3** 34 10N 105 5 E
Li Xian, Hebei, China . **56 E8** 38 30N 115 35 E
Li Xian, Hunan, China . **59 C8** 29 36N 111 42 E
Liádhoi, *Greece* . . . . . . **47 E8** 36 50N 26 11 E
Liancheng, *China* . . . . **59 E11** 25 42N 116 40 E
Liancourt Rocks = Tok-
  do, Asia . . . . **55 F5** 37 15N 131 52 E
Lianga, *Phil.* . . . . **61 G7** 8 38N 126 6 E
Liangcheng,
  Nei Monggol Zizhiqu,
  China . . . . **56 D7** 40 28N 112 25 E
Liangcheng, Shandong,
  China . . . . **57 G10** 35 32N 119 37 E
Liangdang, *China* . . . . **56 H4** 33 56N 106 18 E
Lianghe, *China* . . . . . . **58 E2** 24 50N 98 20 E
Lianghekou, *China* . . . . **58 C7** 29 11N 108 44 E
Liangping, *China* . . . . . **58 B6** 30 38N 107 47 E
Liangpran, *Indonesia* . . **62 D4** 1 14N 114 23 E
Lianhua, *China* . . . . . . **59 D9** 27 3N 113 54 E
Lianjiang, Fujian, China **59 D12** 26 12N 119 27 E
Lianjiang, Guangdong,
  China . . . . **59 G8** 21 40N 110 20 E
Lianping, *China* . . . . . . **59 E10** 24 26N 114 30 E
Lianshan, *China* . . . . . **59 E9** 24 38N 112 8 E
Lianshanguan, *China* . . **57 D12** 40 53N 123 43 E
Lianshui, *China* . . . . . . **57 H10** 33 42N 119 20 E
Lianshui, *China* . . . . . . **57 H10** 33 42N 119 20 E
Lianyungang, *China* . . . **57 G10** 34 40N 119 11 E
Lianzhou, *China* . . . . . **59 E9** 24 51N 112 22 E
Liao He →, China . . . . . **57 D11** 41 0N 121 50 E
Liaocheng, *China* . . . . . **56 F8** 36 28N 115 58 E
Liaodong Bandao,
  China . . . . **57 E12** 40 0N 122 30 E
Liaodong Wan, China . . **57 D11** 40 20N 121 10 E
Liaoning □, China . . . . **57 D12** 41 40N 122 30 E
Liaotung, G. of =
  Liaodong Wan, China **57 D11** 40 20N 121 10 E
Liaoyang, *China* . . . . . **57 D12** 41 15N 122 58 E
Liaoyuan, *China* . . . . . **57 C13** 42 58N 125 2 E
Liaozhong, *China* . . . . **57 D12** 41 23N 122 50 E
Liapádhes, *Greece* . . . . **46 B1** 39 42N 19 40 E
Liard →, Canada **102 A4** 61 51N 121 18W
Liard River, Canada . . . **102 B3** 59 38N 126 10W
Liari, *Pakistan* . . . . **68 G2** 25 37N 66 30 E
Libau = Liepāja, Latvia . **9 H19** 56 30N 21 0 E
Libby, *U.S.A.* **108 B6** 48 23N 115 33W
Libenge, Dem. Rep. of
  the Congo . . . . **84 D3** 3 40N 18 55 E
Liberal, *U.S.A.* **113 G4** 37 3N 100 55W
Liberec, Czech Rep. . . . **26 A8** 50 47N 15 7 E
Liberecký □, Czech Rep. **26 A8** 50 45N 15 0 E
Liberia, Costa Rica . . . **120 D2** 10 40N 85 30W
Liberia ■, W. Afr. **82 D3** 6 30N 9 30W
Liberty, Mo., U.S.A. . . . **112 F7** 39 15N 94 25W
Liberty, N.Y., U.S.A. . . **117 E10** 41 48N 74 45W
Liberty, Pa., U.S.A. . . . **116 E7** 41 34N 77 6W
Liberty, Tex., U.S.A. . . **113 K7** 30 3N 94 48W
Libin, *Belgium* . . . . . . **17 E5** 49 59N 5 15 E
Líbiya, Sahrā', Africa . . **79 C10** 25 0N 25 0 E
Libo, *China* . . . . **58 E6** 25 22N 107 53 E

Libobo, Tanjung,
  Indonesia ...... **63 E7**   0 54 S 128 28 E
Libode, S. Africa ...... **89 E4** 31 33 S   29 2 E
Libohově, Albania ...... **44 F4** 40 3N 20 10 E
Libourne, France **20 D3** 44 55N   0 14W
Libramont, Belgium .... **17 E5** 49 55N   5 23 E
Librazhd, Albania ...... **44 E4** 41 12N 20 22 E
Libreville, Gabon ...... **84 D1**   0 25N   9 26 E
Libya ■, N. Afr. ...... **79 C9** 27 0N 17 0 E
Libyan Desert = Lîbiya,
  Sahrâ', Africa ...... **79 C10** 25 0N 25 0 E
Libyan Plateau = Ed-
  Déffa, Egypt ...... **80 A2** 30 40N 26 30 E
Licantén, Chile ...... **126 D1** 35 55 S 72 0W
Licata, Italy ...... **42 E6** 37 6N 13 56 E
Lice, Turkey ...... **73 C9** 38 27N 40 39 E
Licheng, China ...... **56 F7** 36 28N 113 20 E
Lichfield, U.K. **15 E6** 52 41N   1 49W
Lichinga, Mozam. ...... **87 E4** 13 13 S 35 11 E
Lichtenburg, S. Africa .... **88 D4** 26 8 S 26 8 E
Lichtenfels, Germany .... **25 E7** 50 8N 11 4 E
Lichuan, Hubei, China .... **58 B7** 30 18N 108 57 E
Lichuan, Jiangxi, China .. **59 D11** 27 18N 116 55 E
Licking ➤, U.S.A. **114 F3** 39 6N 84 30W
Licosa, Punta, Italy ...... **43 B7** 40 15N 14 54 E
Licungo ➤, Mozam. .... **87 F4** 17 40 S 37 15 E
Lida, Belarus ...... **9 K21** 53 53N 25 15 E
Liden, Sweden ...... **10 B10** 62 42N 16 48 E
Lidhorkíon, Greece ...... **46 C4** 38 32N 22 12 E
Lidhult, Sweden ...... **11 H7** 56 50N 13 27 E
Lidköping, Sweden ...... **11 F7** 58 31N 13 7 E
Lido, Italy ...... **41 C9** 45 25N 12 22 E
Lido, Niger ...... **83 C5** 12 54N   3 44 E
Lido di Roma = Óstia,
  Lido di, Italy ...... **41 G9** 41 43N 12 17 E
Lidzbark, Poland ...... **31 E6** 53 15N 19 49 E
Lidzbark Warmiński,
  Poland ...... **30 D7** 54 7N 20 34 E
Liebenwalde, Germany .. **24 C9** 52 52N 13 24 E
Lieberose, Germany ...... **24 D10** 51 59N 14 17 E
Liebig, Mt., Australia .... **92 D5** 23 18 S 131 22 E
Liebling, Romania ...... **28 E6** 45 36N 21 20 E
Liechtenstein ■, Europe .. **25 H5** 47 8N   9 35 E
Liège, Belgium ...... **17 D5** 50 38N   5 35 E
Liège □, Belgium ...... **17 D5** 50 32N   5 35 E
Liegnitz = Legnica,
  Poland ...... **31 G3** 51 12N 16 10 E
Lienart, Dem. Rep. of
  the Congo ...... **86 B2**   3 3N 25 31 E
Lienyünchiangshih =
  Lianyungang, China .. **57 G10** 34 40N 119 11 E
Lienz, Austria ...... **26 E5** 46 50N 12 46 E
Liepāja, Latvia ...... **9 H19** 56 30N 21 0 E
Liepāja □, Latvia ...... **30 B8** 56 30N 21 30 E
Liepājas ezers, Latvia .. **30 B8** 56 27N 21 3 E
Lier, Belgium ...... **17 C4** 51 7N   4 34 E
Liernais, France ...... **19 E11** 47 13N   4 16 E
Lieşti, Romania ...... **29 E12** 45 38N 27 34 E
Liévin, France ...... **19 B9** 50 24N   2 47 E
Lièvre ➤, Canada **104 C4** 45 31N 75 26W
Liezen, Austria ...... **26 D7** 47 34N 14 15 E
Liffey ➤, Ireland **12 C5** 53 21N   6 13W
Lifford, Ireland **12 B4** 54 51N   7 29W
Liffré, France **18 D5** 48 12N   1 30W
Lifudzin, Russia ...... **54 B7** 44 21N 134 58 E
Ligao, Phil. ...... **61 E5** 13 14N 123 32 E
Lightning Ridge,
  Australia ...... **95 D4** 29 22 S 148 0 E
Lignano Sabbiadoro,
  Italy ...... **41 C10** 45 42N 13 9 E
Ligny-en-Barrois, France **19 D12** 48 36N   5 20 E
Ligonha ➤, Mozam. .... **87 F4** 16 54 S 39 9 E
Ligonier, U.S.A. **116 F5** 40 15N 79 14W
Ligoúrion, Greece ...... **46 D5** 37 37N 23 4 E
Ligueil, France ...... **18 E7** 47 2N   0 49 E
Liguria □, Italy ...... **40 D5** 44 30N   8 50 E
Ligurian Sea, Medit. S. .. **6 G7** 43 20N   9 0 E
Lihou Reefs and Cays,
  Australia ...... **94 B5** 17 25 S 151 40 E
Lihue, U.S.A. **106 H15** 21 59N 159 23W
Lihue Calel △,
  Argentina ...... **126 D2** 38 0 S 65 10W
Lijiang, China ...... **58 D3** 26 55N 100 20 E
Likasi, Dem. Rep. of
  the Congo ...... **87 E2** 10 55 S 26 48 E
Likenäs, Sweden ...... **10 D7** 60 37N 13 3 E
Likhoslavl, Russia ...... **32 D8** 57 12N 35 30 E
Likhovskoy, Russia ...... **33 H11** 48 10N 40 10 E
Likoma I., Malawi ...... **87 E3** 12 3 S 34 45 E
Likumburu, Tanzania .. **87 D4**   9 43 S 35 8 E
L'Île-Bouchard, France .. **18 E7** 47 7N   0 26 E
L'Île-Rousse, France .... **21 F12** 42 38N   8 57 E
Liling, China ...... **59 D9** 27 42N 113 29 E
Lilla Edet, Sweden ...... **11 F6** 58 9N 12 8 E
Lille, France ...... **19 B10** 50 38N   3 3 E
Lille Bælt, Denmark .... **11 J3** 55 20N   9 45 E
Lillebonne, France ...... **18 C7** 49 30N   0 32 E
Lillehammer, Norway .... **9 F14** 61 8N 10 30 E
Lillesand, Norway ...... **9 G13** 58 15N   8 23 E
Lillhärdal, Sweden ...... **10 C8** 61 51N 14 5 E
Lillian Pt., Australia .... **93 E4** 27 40 S 126 6 E
Lillo, Spain **36 F7** 39 45N   3 20W
Lillooet, Canada **102 C4** 50 44N 121 57W
Lillooet ➤, Canada **102 D4** 49 15N 121 57W
Lilongwe, Malawi ...... **87 E3** 14 0 S 33 48 E
Liloy, Phil. ...... **63 C6**   8 4N 122 39 E
Lim ➤, Bos.-H. ...... **44 C3** 43 45N 19 15 E
Lim Chu Kang,
  Singapore ...... **65 d**   1 26N 103 43 E
Lima, Indonesia ...... **63 E7**   3 39 S 127 58 E
Lima, Peru ...... **124 F3** 12 0 S 77 0W
Lima, Mont., U.S.A. **108 D7** 44 38N 112 36W
Lima, Ohio, U.S.A. **114 E3** 40 44N 84 6W
Lima ➤, Portugal **36 D2** 41 41N   8 50W
Liman, Indonesia ...... **63 G14**   7 48 S 111 45 E
Liman, Russia ...... **35 H8** 45 45N 47 12 E
Limanowa, Poland ...... **31 J7** 49 42N 20 22 E
Limassol, Cyprus ...... **49 E12** 34 42N 33 1 E
Limavady, U.K. **12 A5** 55 3N   6 56W
Limay ➤, Argentina .... **128 D3** 39 0 S 68 0W
Limay Mahuida,
  Argentina ...... **126 D2** 37 10 S 66 45W
Limbach-Oberfrohna,
  Germany ...... **24 E8** 50 52N 12 43 E
Limbang, Brunei ...... **62 D5**   4 42N 115 6 E
Limbara, Mte., Italy .... **42 B2** 40 51N   9 10 E
Limbaži, Latvia ...... **9 H21** 57 31N 24 42 E
Limbdi, India ...... **68 H4** 22 34N 71 51 E
Limbe, Cameroon ...... **83 E6**   4 1N   9 10 E
Limburg, Germany ...... **25 E4** 50 22N   8 4 E
Limburg □, Belgium .... **17 C5** 51 2N   5 25 E
Limburg □, Neths. ...... **17 C5** 51 20N   5 55 E
Limedsforsen, Sweden .. **10 D7** 60 52N 13 25 E
Limeira, Brazil ...... **127 A6** 22 35 S 47 28W
Limenária, Greece ...... **45 F8** 40 38N 24 32 E
Limerick, Ireland **12 D3** 52 40N   8 37W
Limerick, U.S.A. **117 C14** 43 41N 70 48W
Limerick □, Ireland **12 D3** 52 30N   8 50W
Limestone, U.S.A. **116 D6** 42 2N 78 38W
Limestone ➤, Canada .. **103 B10** 56 31N 94 7W
Limfjorden, Denmark .. **11 H3** 56 55N   9 0 E
Limia = Lima ➤,
  Portugal **36 D2** 41 41N   8 50W
Limín Khersónisou,
  Greece ...... **47 F7** 35 18N 25 21 E
Limingen, Norway ...... **8 D15** 64 48N 13 35 E
Limmared, Sweden ...... **11 G7** 57 34N 13 20 E
Limmen Bight, Australia **94 A2** 14 40 S 135 35 E
Limmen Bight ➤,
  Australia ...... **94 B2** 15 7 S 135 44 E
Límni, Greece ...... **46 C5** 38 43N 23 18 E
Límnos, Greece ...... **47 B7** 39 50N 25 5 E
Limoges, Canada **117 A9** 45 20N 75 16W
Limoges, France ...... **20 C5** 45 50N   1 15 E
Limón, Costa Rica **120 E3** 10 0N 83 2W
Limon, U.S.A. **112 F3** 39 16N 103 41W
Limone Piemonte, Italy .. **40 D4** 44 12N   7 34 E
Limousin □, France .... **20 C5** 45 30N   1 30 E
Limousin, Plateaux du,
  France ...... **20 C5** 45 45N   1 15 E
Limoux, France ...... **20 E6** 43 4N   2 12 E
Limpopo □, S. Africa .. **89 C4** 24 5 S 29 0 E
Limpopo ➤, Africa .... **89 D5** 25 5 S 33 30 E
Limuru, Kenya ...... **86 C4**   1 2 S 36 35 E
Lin Xian, China ...... **56 F6** 37 57N 110 58 E
Lin'an, China ...... **59 B12** 30 15N 119 42 E
Linapacan I. Phil. ...... **61 F3** 11 27N 119 49 E
Linapacan Str., Phil. .... **61 F3** 11 37N 119 56 E
Linares, Chile ...... **126 D1** 35 50 S 71 40W
Linares, Mexico **119 C5** 24 50N 99 40W
Linares, Spain **37 G7** 38 10N   3 40W
Linaro, Capo, Italy ...... **41 F8** 42 2N 11 50 E
Línas Mte., Italy ...... **42 C1** 39 25N   8 38 E
Linate, Milano ✈ (LIN),
  Italy ...... **40 C6** 45 27N   9 16 E
Lincang, China ...... **58 F3** 23 58N 100 1 E
Lincheng, China ...... **56 F8** 37 25N 114 30 E
Linchuan, China ...... **59 D11** 27 57N 116 15 E
Lincoln = Beamsville,
  Canada **116 C5** 43 12N 79 28W
Lincoln, Argentina ...... **126 C3** 34 55 S 61 30W
Lincoln, N.Z. ...... **91 K4** 43 38 S 172 30 E
Lincoln, U.K. **14 D7** 53 14N   0 32W
Lincoln, Calif., U.S.A. .. **110 G5** 38 54N 121 17W
Lincoln, Ill., U.S.A. **112 E10** 40 9N 89 22W
Lincoln, Kans., U.S.A. .. **112 F5** 39 3N 98 9W
Lincoln, Maine, U.S.A. .. **115 C11** 45 22N 68 30W
Lincoln, N.H., U.S.A. .. **117 B13** 44 3N 71 40W
Lincoln, N. Mex., U.S.A. **109 K11** 33 30N 105 23W
Lincoln, Nebr., U.S.A. .. **112 E6** 40 49N 96 41W
Lincoln City, U.S.A. **108 D1** 44 57N 124 1W
Lincoln Hav = Lincoln
  Sea, Arctic **4 A5** 84 0N 55 0W
Lincoln Sea, Arctic **4 A5** 84 0N 55 0W
Lincolnshire □, U.K. **14 D7** 53 14N   0 32W
Lincolnshire Wolds,
  U.K. **14 D7** 53 26N   0 13W
Lincolnton, U.S.A. **115 H5** 35 29N 81 16W
Lind, U.S.A. **108 C4** 46 58N 118 37W
Linda, U.S.A. **110 F5** 39 8N 121 34W
Lindau, Germany ...... **25 H5** 47 33N   9 41 E
Linden, Guyana **124 B7**   6 0N 58 10W
Linden, Ala., U.S.A. **115 J2** 32 18N 87 48W
Linden, Calif., U.S.A. .. **110 G5** 38 1N 121 5W
Linden, Tex., U.S.A. **113 J7** 33 1N 94 22W
Lindenhurst, U.S.A. **117 F11** 40 41N 73 23W
Lindesberg, Sweden .... **10 E9** 59 36N 15 15 E
Lindesnes, Norway ...... **9 H12** 57 58N   7 3 E
Líndhos, Greece ...... **49 C10** 36 6N 28 4 E
Líndhos, Ákra, Greece .. **49 C10** 36 4N 28 10 E
Lindi, Tanzania ...... **87 D4**   9 58 S 39 38 E
Lindi □, Tanzania ...... **87 D4**   9 40 S 38 30 E
Lindi ➤, Dem. Rep. of
  the Congo ...... **86 B2**   0 33N 25 5 E
Lindö, Sweden ...... **11 F10** 58 37N 16 15 E
Lindome, Sweden ...... **11 G6** 57 35N 12 5 E
Lindoso, Portugal **36 D2** 41 52N   8 11W
Lindow, Germany ...... **24 C8** 52 58N 12 59 E
Lindsay, Canada **116 B6** 44 22N 78 43W
Lindsay, Calif., U.S.A. .. **110 J7** 36 12N 119 5W
Lindsay, Okla., U.S.A. .. **113 H6** 34 50N 97 38W
Lindsborg, U.S.A. **112 F6** 38 35N 97 40W
Lindsdal, Sweden ...... **11 H10** 56 44N 16 18 E
Line Islands, Pac. Oc. .. **97 H12**   7 0N 160 0W
Linesville, U.S.A. **116 E4** 41 39N 80 26W
Linfen, China ...... **56 F6** 36 3N 111 30 E
Ling Xian, Hunan,
  China ...... **59 D9** 26 29N 113 48 E
Ling Xian, Shandong,
  China ...... **56 F9** 37 22N 116 30 E
Lingao, China ...... **64 C7** 19 56N 109 42 E
Lingayen, Phil. ...... **63 A6** 16 1N 120 14 E
Lingayen G., Phil. ...... **61 C4** 16 10N 120 15 E
Lingbi, China ...... **57 H9** 33 33N 117 33 E
Lingbo, Sweden ...... **10 C10**   6 3N 16 41 E
Lingchuan,
  Guangxi Zhuangzu,
  China ...... **59 E8** 25 26N 110 21 E
Lingchuan, Shanxi,
  China ...... **56 G7** 35 45N 113 12 E
Lingen, Germany ...... **24 C3** 52 31N   7 19 E
Lingga, Indonesia ...... **62 E2**   0 12 S 104 37 E
Lingga, Kepulauan,
  Indonesia ...... **62 E2**   0 10 S 104 30 E
Lingga Arch. = Lingga,
  Kepulauan, Indonesia **62 E2**   0 10 S 104 30 E
Linghed, Sweden ...... **11 F9** 58 26N 15 47 E
Lingle, U.S.A. **112 D2** 42 8N 104 21W
Lingqiu, China ...... **56 E8** 39 28N 114 22 E
Lingshan, China ...... **58 F7** 22 25N 109 18 E
Lingshi, China ...... **56 F6** 36 48N 111 48 E
Lingshou, China ...... **56 E8** 38 20N 114 5 E
Lingshui, China ...... **64 C8** 18 27N 110 0 E
Lingtai, China ...... **56 G4** 35 0N 107 40 E
Linguère, Senegal **82 B1** 15 25N 15 5W
Lingui, China ...... **59 E8** 25 12N 110 8 E
Lingwu, China ...... **56 E4** 38 6N 106 20 E
Lingyuan, China ...... **57 D10** 41 10N 119 15 E
Lingyun, China ...... **58 E6** 24 20N 106 35 E
Linhai, China ...... **59 C13** 28 50N 121 8 E
Linhares, Brazil ...... **125 G10** 19 25 S 40 4W
Linhe, China ...... **56 D4** 40 48N 107 20 E
Linjiang, China ...... **57 D14** 41 50N 127 0 E
Linköping, Sweden ...... **11 F9** 58 28N 15 36 E
Linkou, China ...... **57 B16** 45 15N 130 18 E
Linli, China ...... **59 C8** 29 27N 111 30 E
Linnhe, L., U.K. **13 E3** 56 36N   5 25W
Linqi, China ...... **56 G7** 35 45N 113 52 E
Linqing, China ...... **56 F8** 36 50N 115 42 E
Linqu, China ...... **57 F10** 36 25N 118 30 E
Linru, China ...... **56 G7** 34 11N 112 52 E
Lins, Brazil ...... **127 A6** 21 40 S 49 44W
Linshui, China ...... **58 B6** 30 21N 106 57 E

Linstead, Jamaica ...... **120 a**   18 8N 77 2W
Linta ➤, Madag. ...... **89 D7** 25 2 S 44 5 E
Linth ➤, Switz. ...... **25 H5** 47 7N   9 7 E
Linthal, Switz. ...... **25 J5** 46 54N   9 0 E
Linton, Ind., U.S.A. **114 F2** 39 2N 87 10W
Linton, N. Dak., U.S.A. **112 B4** 46 16N 100 14W
Lintong, China ...... **56 G5** 34 20N 109 10 E
Linwood, Canada **116 C4** 43 35N 80 43W
Linwu, China ...... **59 E9** 25 19N 112 31 E
Linxi, China ...... **57 C10** 43 36N 118 2 E
Linxia, China ...... **60 C5** 35 36N 103 10 E
Linxiang, China ...... **59 C9** 29 28N 113 23 E
Linyanti ➤, Africa ...... **88 B4** 17 50 S 25 5 E
Linyi, China ...... **57 G10** 35 5N 118 21 E
Linz, Austria ...... **26 C7** 48 18N 14 18 E
Linzhenzhen, China .... **56 F5** 36 30N 109 59 E
Linzi, China ...... **57 F10** 36 50N 118 20 E
Lion, G. du, France .... **20 E7** 43 10N   4 0 E
Lionárisso, Cyprus ...... **49 D13** 35 28N 34 8 E
Lioni, Italy ...... **43 B8** 40 52N 15 11 E
Lions, G. of = Lion, G.
  du, France ...... **20 E7** 43 10N   4 0 E
Lion's Den, Zimbabwe .. **87 F3** 17 15 S 30 5 E
Lion's Head, Canada .. **116 B3** 44 58N 81 15W
Liozno = Lyozna,
  Belarus ...... **32 E6** 55 0N 30 50 E
Lipa, Phil. ...... **61 E4** 13 57N 121 10 E
Lipali, Mozam. ...... **87 F4** 15 50 S 35 50 E
Lipany, Slovak Rep. .... **27 B13** 49 9N 20 58 E
Lipari, Italy ...... **43 D7** 38 26N 14 58 E
Lipari, I., Italy ...... **43 D7** 38 29N 14 56 E
Lipari, Is. = Eólie, Ís.,
  Italy ...... **43 D7** 38 30N 14 57 E
Lipcani, Moldova ...... **29 B11** 48 14N 26 48 E
Lipetsk, Russia ...... **33 F10** 52 37N 39 35 E
Lipiany, Poland ...... **31 E1** 53 2N 14 58 E
Liping, China ...... **58 D7** 26 15N 109 7 E
Lipkany = Lipcani,
  Moldova ...... **29 B11** 48 14N 26 48 E
Lipnik nad Bečvou,
  Czech Rep. ...... **27 B10** 49 32N 17 36 E
Lipno, Poland ...... **31 F6** 52 49N 19 15 E
Lipova, Romania ...... **28 D6** 46 8N 21 42 E
Lipovcy Manzovka,
  Russia ...... **54 B5** 44 12N 132 26 E
Lipovets, Ukraine ...... **33 H5** 49 12N 29 1 E
Lippe ➤, Germany ...... **24 D2** 51 39N   6 36 E
Lippstadt, Germany .... **24 D4** 51 41N   8 22 E
Lipscomb, U.S.A. **113 G4** 36 14N 100 16W
Lipsk, Poland ...... **30 E10** 53 44N 23 24 E
Lipsko, Poland ...... **31 G8** 51 9N 21 40 E
Lipsói, Greece ...... **47 D8** 37 19N 26 50 E
Liptovský Hrádok,
  Slovak Rep. ...... **27 B12** 49 2N 19 44 E
Liptovský Milkuláš,
  Slovak Rep. ...... **27 B12** 49 6N 19 35 E
Liptrap, C., Australia .. **95 F4** 38 50 S 145 55 E
Lipu, China ...... **59 E8** 24 30N 110 22 E
Liquillo, Sierra de,
  Puerto Rico ...... **121 d** 18 20N 65 47W
Lira, Uganda ...... **86 B3**   2 17N 32 57 E
Liri ➤, Italy ...... **42 A6** 41 25N 13 52 E
Liria = Lliria, Spain .. **39 F4** 39 37N   0 35W
Lisala, Dem. Rep. of
  the Congo ...... **84 D4**   2 12N 21 38 E
Lisboa, Portugal ...... **37 G1** 38 42N   9 10 E
Lisboa □, Portugal **37 F1** 39 0N   9 12W
Lisboa ✈ (LIS), Portugal **37 G1** 38 46N   9 8W
Lisbon = Lisboa,
  Portugal ...... **37 G1** 38 42N   9 10 E
Lisbon, N. Dak., U.S.A. **112 B6** 46 27N 97 41W
Lisbon, N.H., U.S.A. .. **117 B13** 44 13N 71 55W
Lisbon, Ohio, U.S.A. .. **116 F4** 40 46N 80 46W
Lisbon Falls, U.S.A. **115 D10** 44 0N 70 4W
Lisburn, U.K. **12 B5** 54 31N   6 3W
Lisburne, C., U.S.A. **4 C17** 68 53N 166 13W
Liscannor B., Ireland .. **12 D2** 52 55N   9 24W
Liscia ➤, Italy ...... **42 A2** 41 11N   9 9 E
Lishe Jiang ➤, China .. **58 E3** 24 15N 101 35 E
Lishi, China ...... **56 F6** 37 31N 111 8 E
Lishu, China ...... **57 C13** 43 20N 124 18 E
Lishui, Jiangsu, China .. **59 B12** 31 38N 119 2 E
Lishui, Zhejiang, China **59 C12** 28 28N 119 54 E
Lisianski I., Pac. Oc. .. **96 E10** 26 2N 174 0W
Lisichansk =
  Lysychansk, Ukraine **33 H10** 48 55N 38 30 E
Lisieux, France ...... **18 C7** 49 10N   0 12 E
Liski, Russia ...... **33 G10** 51 3N 39 30 E
L'Isle-Jourdain, Gers,
  France ...... **20 E5** 43 36N   1 5 E
L'Isle-Jourdain, Vienne,
  France ...... **20 B4** 46 13N   0 31 E
L'Isle-sur-la-Sorgue,
  France ...... **21 E9** 43 54N   5 2 E
Lisle-sur-Tarn, France .. **20 E5** 43 52N   1 49 E
Lismore, Australia ...... **95 D5** 28 44 S 153 21 E
Lismore, Ireland **12 D4** 52 8N   7 55W
Lista, Norway ...... **9 G12** 58 7N   6 39 E
Lister, Mt., Antarctica .. **5 D11** 78 0 S 162 0 E
Liston, Australia ...... **95 D5** 28 39 S 152 6 E
Listowel, Canada **116 C4** 43 44N 80 58W
Listowel, Ireland **12 D2** 52 27N   9 29W
Lit, U.S.A. ...... **48 B3** 63 19N 14 51 E
Lit-et-Mixe, France **20 D2** 44 2N   1 15W
Litang,
  Guangxi Zhuangzu,
  China ...... **58 F7** 23 12N 109 8 E
Litang, Sichuan, China .. **58 B3** 30 1N 100 17 E
Litang Qu ➤, China .... **58 C3** 28 4N 101 32 E
Litani ➤, Lebanon ...... **74 B4** 33 20N 35 15 E
Litchfield, Calif., U.S.A. **110 E6** 40 24N 120 23W
Litchfield, Conn., U.S.A. **117 E11** 41 45N 73 11W
Litchfield, Ill., U.S.A. .. **112 F10** 39 11N 89 39W
Litchfield, Minn., U.S.A. **112 C7** 45 8N 94 32W
Litchfield △, Australia .. **92 B5** 13 14 S 131 1 E
Liteni, Romania ...... **29 C11** 47 32N 26 32 E
Lithgow, Australia ...... **95 E5** 33 25 S 150 8 E
Lithínon, Ákra, Greece **49 E6** 34 55N 24 44 E
Lithuania ■, Europe .... **9 J20** 55 30N 24 0 E
Litija, Slovenia ...... **41 B11** 46 3N 14 50 E
Lititz, U.S.A. **117 F8** 40 9N 76 18W
Litókhoron, Greece ...... **44 F6** 40 8N 22 34 E
Litoměřice, Czech Rep. .. **26 A7** 50 33N 14 10 E
Litomyšl, Czech Rep. .. **27 B9** 49 52N 16 20 E
Litschau, Austria ...... **26 C8** 48 58N 15 4 E
Little Abaco, Bahamas .. **120 A4** 26 50N 77 30W
Little Barrier I., N.Z. .. **91 G5** 36 12 S 175 8 E
Little Belt Mts., U.S.A. **108 C8** 46 40N 110 45W
Little Bighorn
  Battlefield △, U.S.A. **108 D10** 45 34N 107 26W
Little Blue ➤, U.S.A. .. **112 F6** 39 42N 96 41W
Little Buffalo ➤,
  Canada **102 A6** 61 0N 113 46W
Little Cayman,
  Cayman Is. **120 C3** 19 41N 80 3W

Little Churchill ➤,
  Canada **103 B9** 57 30N 95 22W
Little Colorado ➤,
  U.S.A. **109 H8** 36 12N 111 48W
Little Current, Canada .. **104 C3** 45 55N 82 0W
Little Current ➤,
  Canada **104 B3** 50 57N 84 36W
Little Falls, Minn.,
  U.S.A. **112 C7** 45 59N 94 22W
Little Falls, N.Y., U.S.A. **117 C10** 43 3N 74 51W
Little Fork ➤, U.S.A. .. **112 A8** 48 31N 93 35W
Little Grand Rapids,
  Canada **103 C9** 52 0N 95 29W
Little Humboldt ➤,
  U.S.A. **108 F5** 41 1N 117 43W
Little Inagua I.,
  Bahamas **121 B5** 21 40N 73 50W
Little Karoo, S. Africa .. **88 E3** 33 45 S 21 0 E
Little Khingan Mts. =
  Xiao Hinggan Ling,
  China ...... **60 B7** 49 0N 127 0 E
Little Lake, U.S.A. **111 K9** 35 56N 117 55W
Little Laut Is. = Laut
  Kecil, Kepulauan,
  Indonesia ...... **62 E5**   4 45 S 115 40 E
Little Mecatina = Petit-
  Mécatina ➤, Canada **105 B8** 50 40N 59 30W
Little Minch, U.K. **13 D2** 57 35N   6 45W
Little Missouri ➤,
  U.S.A. **112 B3** 47 36N 102 25W
Little Ouse ➤, U.K. .... **15 E9** 52 22N   1 12 E
Little Rann, India ...... **68 H4** 23 25N 71 25 E
Little Red ➤, U.S.A. .. **113 H9** 35 11N 91 27W
Little River, N.Z. ...... **91 K4** 43 45 S 172 49 E
Little Rock, U.S.A. **113 H8** 34 45N 92 17W
Little Ruaha ➤,
  Tanzania ...... **86 D4**   7 57 S 37 53 E
Little Sable Pt., U.S.A. **114 D2** 43 38N 86 33W
Little Scarcies ➤,
  S. Leone **82 D2**   8 50N 13 10W
Little Sioux ➤, U.S.A. **112 E6** 41 48N 96 4W
Little Smoky ➤,
  Canada **102 C5** 54 44N 117 11W
Little Snake ➤, U.S.A. **108 F9** 40 27N 108 26W
Little Tobago,
  Trin. & Tob. **125 J16** 11 18N 60 30W
Little Valley, U.S.A. **116 D6** 42 15N 78 48W
Little Wabash ➤,
  U.S.A. **114 G1** 37 55N 88 5W
Little White ➤, U.S.A. **112 D4** 43 40N 100 40W
Little Zab = Zāb aş
  Şağhīr ➤, Iraq ...... **70 C4** 35 17N 43 29 E
Littlefield, U.S.A. **113 J3** 33 55N 102 20W
Littlehampton, U.K. **15 G7** 50 49N   0 32W
Littleton, U.S.A. **117 B13** 44 18N 71 46W
Litvínov, Czech Rep. .. **26 A6** 50 36N 13 37 E
Liu He ➤, China ...... **57 D11** 40 55N 121 35 E
Liu Jiang ➤, China .... **58 F7** 23 55N 109 30 E
Liuba, China ...... **56 H4** 33 38N 106 55 E
Liucheng, China ...... **58 E7** 24 38N 109 14 E
Liugou, China ...... **57 D10** 40 57N 118 15 E
Liuhe, China ...... **57 C13** 42 17N 125 43 E
Liuheng Dao, China .... **59 C14** 29 40N 122 5 E
Liujiang, China ...... **58 E7** 24 26N 109 11 E
Liukang Tenggaja =
  Sabalana, Kepulauan,
  Indonesia ...... **63 F5**   6 45 S 118 50 E
Liuli, Tanzania ...... **87 E3** 11 3 S 34 38 E
Liuwa Plain, Zambia .. **85 G4** 14 20 S 22 30 E
Liuyang, China ...... **59 C9** 28 10N 113 37 E
Liuzhou, China ...... **58 E7** 24 22N 109 22 E
Liuzhuang, China ...... **57 H11** 33 12N 120 18 E
Livada, Romania ...... **28 C8** 47 52N 23 5 E
Livadherón, Greece .... **44 F5** 40 2N 21 57 E
Livadhia, Cyprus ...... **49 E12** 34 57N 33 38 E
Livádhion, Greece ...... **46 A4** 40 8N 22 9 E
Livarot, France ...... **18 D7** 48 58N   0 9 E
Live Oak, Calif., U.S.A. **110 F5** 39 17N 121 40W
Live Oak, Fla., U.S.A. .. **115 K4** 30 18N 82 59W
Liveras, Cyprus ...... **49 D11** 35 23N 32 57 E
Livermore, U.S.A. **110 H5** 37 41N 121 47W
Livermore, Mt., U.S.A. **113 K2** 30 38N 104 11W
Livermore Falls, U.S.A. **115 C11** 44 29N 70 11W
Liverpool, Canada **105 D7** 44 5N 64 41W
Liverpool, U.K. **14 D4** 53 25N   3 0W
Liverpool, U.S.A. **117 C8** 43 6N 76 13W
Liverpool Bay, U.K. **14 D4** 53 30N   3 20W
Liverpool Ra., Australia **95 E5** 31 50 S 150 30 E
Livingston, Guatemala .. **120 C2** 15 50N 88 50W
Livingston, U.K. **13 F5** 55 54N   3 30W
Livingston, Ala., U.S.A. **115 J1** 32 35N 88 11W
Livingston, Calif., U.S.A. **110 H6** 37 23N 120 43W
Livingston, Mont.,
  U.S.A. **108 D8** 45 40N 110 34W
Livingston, S.C., U.S.A. **115 J5** 33 32N 80 53W
Livingston, Tenn.,
  U.S.A. **115 G3** 36 23N 85 19W
Livingston, Tex., U.S.A. **113 K7** 30 43N 94 56W
Livingston, L., U.S.A. .. **113 K7** 30 50N 95 10W
Livingston Manor,
  U.S.A. **117 E10** 41 54N 74 50W
Livingstone, Zambia .... **87 F2** 17 46 S 25 52 E
Livingstonia, Malawi .. **87 E3** 10 38 S 34 5 E
Livingstone Mts.,
  Tanzania ...... **87 D3**   9 40 S 34 20 E
Livingstone Mts., N.Z. **91 L2** 45 15 S 167 40 E
Livno, Bos.-H. ...... **28 G2** 43 50N 17 1 E
Livny, Russia ...... **33 F9** 52 30N 37 30 E
Livonia, Mich., U.S.A. .. **114 D4** 42 23N 83 23W
Livonia, N.Y., U.S.A. .. **116 D7** 42 49N 77 40W
Livorno, Italy ...... **40 E7** 43 33N 10 19 E
Livradois-Forez △,
  France ...... **20 E7** 44 0N   3 2 E
Livramento, Brazil ...... **127 C4** 30 55 S 55 30W
Livron-sur-Drôme,
  France ...... **21 D8** 44 46N   4 51 E
Liwale, Tanzania ...... **87 D4**   9 48 S 37 58 E
Liwiec ➤, Poland ...... **31 F8** 52 36N 21 34 E
Liwonde △, Malawi .... **87 E4** 14 48 S 35 20 E
Lixi, China ...... **58 D3** 26 20N 102 4 E
Lixian, China ...... **58 B4** 31 23N 103 13 E
Lixouríon, Greece ...... **46 C1** 38 14N 20 37 E
Liyang, China ...... **59 B12** 31 26N 119 28 E
Lizard I., Australia ...... **94 A4** 14 42 S 145 30 E
Lizard Pt., U.K. **15 H2** 49 57N   5 13W
Lizzano, Italy ...... **43 B10** 40 23N 17 27 E
Ljig, Serbia & M. ...... **44 B4** 44 13N 20 18 E
Ljubija, Bos.-H. ...... **41 D13** 44 55N 16 35 E
Ljubinje, Bos.-H. ...... **44 D2** 42 58N 18 5 E
Ljubljana, Slovenia .... **41 B11** 46 4N 14 33 E
Ljubljana ✈ (LJU),
  Slovenia ...... **41 B11** 46 14N 14 33 E
Ljubno, Slovenia ...... **41 B11** 46 25N 14 46 E
Ljubovija, Serbia & M. **44 B3** 44 11N 19 22 E
Ljugarn, Sweden ...... **11 G12** 57 20N 18 43 E
Ljung, Sweden ...... **11 G7** 57 59N 13 3 E

Ljungan ➤, Sweden .... **10 B11** 62 18N 17 23 E
Ljungaverk, Sweden .... **10 B10** 62 30N 16 5 E
Ljungby, Sweden ...... **11 H7** 56 49N 13 55 E
Ljungbyholm, Sweden .. **11 H10** 56 39N 16 5 E
Ljungdalen, Sweden .... **10 B6** 62 51N 12 47 E
Ljungsbro, Sweden ...... **11 F9** 58 31N 15 30 E
Ljungskile, Sweden ...... **11 F5** 58 14N 11 55 E
Ljusdal, Sweden ...... **10 C10** 61 46N 16 3 E
Ljusfallshammar,
  Sweden ...... **11 F9** 58 48N 15 30 E
Ljusnan ➤, Sweden .... **10 C11** 61 12N 17 8 E
Ljusne, Sweden ...... **10 C11** 61 13N 17 7 E
Ljutomer, Slovenia ...... **41 B13** 46 31N 16 11 E
Llagostera, Spain ...... **38 D7** 41 50N   2 54 E
Llancanelo, Salina,
  Argentina ...... **126 D2** 35 40 S 69 8W
Llandeilo, U.K. **15 F4** 51 53N   3 59W
Llandovery, U.K. **15 F4** 51 59N   3 48W
Llandrindod Wells, U.K. **15 E4** 52 14N   3 22W
Llandudno, U.K. **14 D4** 53 19N   3 50W
Llanelli, U.K. **15 F3** 51 41N   4 10W
Llanes, Spain **36 B6** 43 25N   4 50W
Llangollen, U.K. **14 E4** 52 58N   3 11W
Llanidloes, U.K. **15 E4** 52 27N   3 31W
Llano, U.S.A. **113 K5** 30 45N 98 41W
Llano ➤, U.S.A. **113 K5** 30 39N 98 26W
Llano Estacado, U.S.A. **113 J3** 33 30N 103 0W
Llanos, S. Amer. **124 C4**   5 0N 71 35W
Llanos de Challe △,
  Chile ...... **126 B1** 28 8 S 71 1W
Llanquihue, L., Chile .. **128 E1** 41 10 S 72 50W
Llanwrtyd Wells, U.K. .. **15 E4** 52 7N   3 38W
Llebeig, C. des, Spain .. **48 B9** 39 33N   2 18 E
Lleida, Spain ...... **38 D5** 41 37N   0 39 E
Lleida □, Spain ...... **38 C6** 42 6N   1 0 E
Llentrisca, C., Spain .... **48 C7** 38 52N   1 15 E
Llera, Mexico **119 C5** 23 19N 99 1W
Llerena, Spain **37 G5** 38 17N   6 0W
Lleyn Peninsula, U.K. .. **14 E3** 52 51N   4 36W
Llico, Chile ...... **126 C1** 34 46 S 72 5W
Lliria, Spain **39 F4** 39 37N   0 35W
Llobregat ➤, Spain .... **38 D7** 41 19N   2 9 E
Llodio, Spain **38 B2** 43 9N   2 58W
Lloret de Mar, Spain .. **38 D7** 41 41N   2 53 E
Lloyd B., Australia ...... **94 A3** 12 45 S 143 27 E
Lloyd L., Canada **103 B7** 57 22N 108 57W
Lloydminster, Canada .. **103 C7** 53 17N 110 0W
Llucena del Cid, Spain . **38 E4** 40 9N   0 7W
Llucmajor, Spain ...... **48 B9** 39 29N   2 53 E
Llullaillaco △, Chile .... **126 A2** 24 50 S 68 51W
Llullaillaco, Volcán,
  S. Amer. ...... **126 A2** 24 43 S 68 30W
Lo ➤, Vietnam ...... **64 B5** 21 18N 105 25 E
Loa, U.S.A. **109 G8** 38 24N 111 39W
Loa ➤, Chile ...... **126 A1** 21 26 S 70 41W
Loaita I., S. China Sea .. **62 B4** 10 41N 114 25 E
Loange ➤, Dem. Rep.
  of the Congo ...... **84 E4**   4 17 S 20 2 E
Loano, Italy ...... **40 D5** 44 8N   8 15 E
Lobatse, Botswana ...... **88 D4** 25 12 S 25 40 E
Löbau, Germany ...... **24 D10** 51 5N 14 40 E
Lobenstein, Germany .. **24 E7** 50 25N 11 39 E
Lobería, Argentina ...... **126 D4** 38 10 S 58 40W
Löberöd, Sweden ...... **11 J7** 55 47N 13 31 E
Lobez, Poland ...... **30 E2** 53 38N 15 39 E
Lobito, Angola ...... **85 G2** 12 18 S 13 35 E
Lobo ➤, Ivory C. **82 D3**   6 2N   6 45W
Lobos, Argentina ...... **126 D4** 35 10 S 59 0W
Lobos, I., Mexico **118 B2** 27 15N 110 30W
Lobos, I. de, Canary Is. **48 F6** 28 45N 13 50W
Łobżenica, Poland ...... **31 E4** 53 18N 17 15 E
Loc Binh, Vietnam ...... **64 B6** 21 46N 106 54 E
Loc Ninh, Vietnam ...... **65 G6** 11 50N 106 34 E
Locarno, Switz. ...... **25 J4** 46 10N   8 47 E
Loch Baghasdail =
  Lochboisdale, U.K. .. **13 D1** 57 9N   7 20W
Loch Garman =
  Wexford, Ireland .. **12 D5** 52 20N   6 28W
Loch Lomond and the
  Trossachs △, U.K. .. **13 E4** 56 10N   4 40W
Loch Nam Madadh =
  Lochmaddy, U.K. .. **13 D1** 57 36N   7 10W
Lochaber, U.K. **13 E3** 56 59N   5 1W
Locharbriggs, U.K. **13 F5** 55 7N   3 35W
Lochboisdale, U.K. **13 D1** 57 9N   7 20W
Loche, L. La, Canada .. **103 B7** 56 30N 109 30W
Lochem, Neths. ...... **17 B6** 52 9N   6 26 E
Loches, France ...... **18 E7** 47 7N   1 0 E
Lochgilphead, U.K. **13 E3** 56 2N   5 26W
Lochinvar △, Zambia .. **87 F2** 15 55 S 27 15 E
Lochinver, U.K. **13 C3** 58 9N   5 14W
Lochnagar, Australia .. **94 C4** 23 33 S 145 38 E
Lochnagar, U.K. **13 E5** 56 57N   3 15W
Łochów, Poland ...... **31 F8** 52 33N 21 42 E
Lochy, L., U.K. **13 E4** 57 0N   4 53W
Lock, Australia ...... **95 E2** 33 34 S 135 46 E
Lock Haven, U.S.A. **116 E7** 41 8N 77 28W
Lockeford, U.S.A. **110 G5** 38 10N 121 9W
Lockeport, Canada **105 D6** 43 47N 65 4W
Lockerbie, U.K. **13 F5** 55 7N   3 21W
Lockhart, U.S.A. **113 L6** 29 53N 97 40W
Lockhart, L., Australia **93 F2** 33 15 S 119 3 E
Lockhart River,
  Australia ...... **94 A3** 12 58 S 143 30 E
Lockney, U.S.A. **113 H4** 34 7N 101 27W
Lockport, U.S.A. **116 C6** 43 10N 78 42W
Locle, Le, Switz. ...... **25 H3** 47 3N   6 44 E
Locronan, France **18 D2** 48 7N   4 5W
Locri, Italy ...... **43 D9** 38 14N 16 16 E
Locronan, France **18 D2** 48 7N   4 13W
Lod, Israel ...... **74 D3** 31 57N 34 54 E
Lodeinoye Pole, Russia .. **32 B7** 60 44N 33 33 E
Lodève, France ...... **20 E7** 43 44N   3 19 E
Lodge Bay, Canada **105 B8** 52 8N 55 50W
Lodge Grass, U.S.A. **108 D10** 45 19N 107 22W
Lodgepole Cr. ➤,
  U.S.A. **112 E2** 41 20N 104 30W
Lodhran, Pakistan ...... **68 E4** 29 32N 71 30 E
Lodi, Italy ...... **40 C6** 45 9N   9 30 E
Lodi, Calif., U.S.A. **110 G5** 38 8N 121 16W
Lodi, Ohio, U.S.A. **116 E3** 41 2N 82 0W
Lodja, Dem. Rep. of
  the Congo ...... **86 C1**   3 30 S 23 23 E
Lodosa, Spain **38 C2** 42 25N   2 4W
Lödöse, Sweden ...... **11 F6** 58 2N 12 9 E
Lodwar, Kenya ...... **86 B4**   3 10N 35 40 E
Łódź, Poland ...... **31 G6** 51 45N 19 27 E
Łódzkie □, Poland ...... **31 G6** 51 30N 19 30 E
Loei, Thailand ...... **64 D3** 17 29N 101 35 E
Loengo, Dem. Rep. of
  the Congo ...... **86 C2**   4 48 S 26 30 E
Loeriesfontein, S. Africa **88 E2** 31 0 S 19 26 E
Lofa ➤, Liberia **83 D2**   6 35N 11 8W
Lofa Man △, Liberia .. **82 D2**   7 55N 12 41 E
Lofer, Austria ...... **26 D5** 47 35N 12 41 E
Lofoten, Norway ...... **8 B15** 68 30N 14 0 E
Lofsdalen, Sweden ...... **10 B7** 62 10N 13 20 E

Lofsen →, Sweden .... 10 B7 62 7N 13 57 E
Loftahammar, Sweden .. 11 G10 57 54N 16 41 E
Loga, Niger .... 83 C5 13 40N 3 15 E
Logan, Iowa, U.S.A. .. 112 E7 41 39N 95 47W
Logan, Ohio, U.S.A. ... 114 F4 39 32N 82 25W
Logan, Utah, U.S.A. .. 108 F8 41 44N 111 50W
Logan, W. Va., U.S.A. .. 114 G5 37 51N 81 59W
Logan, Mt., Canada .. 100 B5 60 34N 140 23W
Logandale, U.S.A. 111 J12 36 36N 114 29W
Logansport, Ind., U.S.A. 114 E2 40 45N 86 22W
Logansport, La., U.S.A. 113 K8 31 58N 94 0W
Logirim, Sudan .... 81 G3 4 43N 33 14 E
Logo, Sudan .... 81 F3 5 20N 30 18 E
Logone →, Chad ..... 79 F9 12 6N 15 2 E
Logroño, Spain 38 C2 42 28N 2 27W
Logrosán, Spain 37 F5 39 20N 5 32W
Løgstør, Denmark .... 11 H3 56 58N 9 14 E
Løgumkloster, Denmark 11 J2 55 4N 8 57 E
Lohals, Denmark ..... 11 J4 55 8N 10 55 E
Lohardaga, India .... 69 H11 23 27N 84 45 E
Loharia, India .... 68 H6 23 45N 74 14 E
Loharu, India .... 68 E6 28 27N 75 49 E
Lohja, Finland .... 9 F21 60 12N 24 5 E
Löhne, Germany ..... 24 C4 52 11N 8 40 E
Lohr, Germany .... 25 F5 49 59N 9 35 E
Lohri Wah →, Pakistan 68 F2 27 27N 67 37 E
Loi-kaw, Burma ..... 67 K20 19 40N 97 17 E
Loimaa, Finland ..... 9 F20 60 50N 23 3 E
Loir →, France 18 E6 47 33N 0 32W
Loir-et-Cher □, France 18 E8 47 40N 1 20 E
Loire □, France ...... 21 C8 45 40N 4 5 E
Loire →, France 18 E4 47 16N 2 10W
Loire Anjou
  Touraine △, France . 18 E6 47 14N 0 5W
Loire-Atlantique □,
  France 18 E5 47 25N 1 40W
Loiret □, France ...... 19 E9 47 55N 2 30 E
Loitz, Germany ...... 24 B9 53 58N 13 8 E
Loja, Ecuador .... 124 D3 3 59 S 79 16W
Loja, Spain 37 H6 37 10N 4 10W
Loji = Kawasi, Indonesia 63 E7 1 38 S 127 28 E
Lojo = Lohja, Finland . 9 F21 60 12N 24 5 E
Løjt Kirkeby, Denmark 11 J3 55 7N 9 26 E
Lojung, China .... 58 E7 24 27N 109 36 E
Loka, Sudan .... 81 G3 4 13N 31 0 E
Lokandu, Dem. Rep. of
  the Congo .... 86 C2 2 30 S 25 45 E
Lokeren, Belgium .... 17 C3 51 6N 3 59 E
Lokgwabe, Botswana .. 88 C3 24 10 S 21 50 E
Lokhvitsa, Ukraine ... 33 G7 50 25N 33 18 E
Lokichokio, Kenya ... 86 B3 4 19N 34 13 E
Lokitaung, Kenya .... 86 B4 4 12N 35 48 E
Lokkan tekojärvi,
  Finland .... 8 C22 67 55N 27 35 E
Løkken, Denmark .... 11 G3 57 22N 9 41 E
Loknya, Russia ...... 32 D6 56 49N 30 4 E
Loko, Nigeria .... 83 D6 8 1N 7 53 E
Lokoja, Nigeria ...... 83 D6 7 47N 6 45 E
Lokot, Russia .... 33 F8 52 34N 34 36 E
Lol →, Sudan .... 81 F2 9 13N 26 30 E
Lola, Guinea 82 D3 7 52N 8 29W
Lola, Mt., U.S.A. 110 F6 39 26N 120 22W
Lolibai, Gebel, Sudan . 81 G3 3 50N 33 0 E
Lolimi, Sudan .... 81 G3 4 35N 34 0 E
Loliondo, Tanzania ... 86 C4 2 2 S 35 39 E
Lolland, Denmark .... 11 K5 54 45N 11 30 E
Lollar, Germany ..... 24 E4 50 37N 8 43 E
Lolo, U.S.A. 108 C6 46 45N 114 5W
Lolodorf, Cameroon .. 83 E7 3 16N 10 49 E
Lom, Bulgaria .... 44 C7 43 48N 23 12 E
Lom →, Bulgaria ..... 44 C7 43 45N 23 15 E
Lom Kao, Thailand ... 64 D3 16 53N 101 14 E
Lom Sak, Thailand ... 64 D3 16 47N 101 15 E
Loma, U.S.A. 108 C8 47 56N 110 30W
Loma Linda, U.S.A. .. 111 L9 34 3N 117 16W
Lomami →, Dem. Rep.
  of the Congo ...... 86 B1 0 46N 24 16 E
Lomas de Zamóra,
  Argentina .... 126 C4 34 45 S 58 25W
Lombadina, Australia . 92 C3 16 31 S 122 54 E
Lombárdia □, Italy ... 40 C6 45 40N 9 30 E
Lombardy =
  Lombárdia □, Italy .. 40 C6 45 40N 9 30 E
Lombez, France ...... 20 E4 43 29N 0 55 E
Lomblen, Indonesia .. 63 F6 8 30 S 123 32 E
Lombok, Indonesia ... 62 F5 8 45 S 116 30 E
Lombok, Selat,
  Indonesia .... 63 K18 8 30 S 115 50 E
Lomé, Togo .... 83 D5 6 9N 1 20 E
Lomela, Dem. Rep. of
  the Congo .... 84 E4 2 19 S 23 15 E
Lomela →, Dem. Rep.
  of the Congo ...... 84 E4 0 15 S 20 40 E
Lomianki, Poland .... 31 F7 52 21N 20 54 E
Lomma, Sweden ..... 11 J7 55 43N 13 6 E
Lommel, Belgium .... 17 C5 51 14N 5 19 E
Lomond, Canada 102 C6 50 24N 112 36W
Lomond, L., U.K. 13 E4 56 8N 4 38W
Lomonosov Ridge,
  Arctic .... 4 A 88 0N 140 0 E
Lomphat, Cambodia .. 64 F6 13 30N 106 59 E
Lompobatang, Indonesia 63 F5 5 24 S 119 56 E
Lompoc, U.S.A. 111 L6 34 38N 120 28W
Łomża, Poland ...... 31 E9 53 10N 22 2 E
Lon, Ko, Thailand ... 65 a 7 47N 98 23 E
Loncoche, Chile ..... 128 D2 39 20 S 72 50W
Londa, India .... 66 M9 15 30N 74 30 E
Londiani, Kenya ..... 86 C4 0 10 S 35 33 E
Londinières, France .. 18 C8 49 50N 1 25 E
London, Canada 116 D3 42 59N 81 15W
London, U.K. 15 F7 51 30N 0 3W
London, Ky., U.S.A. .. 114 G3 37 8N 84 5W
London, Ohio, U.S.A. 114 F4 39 53N 83 27W
London, Greater □,
  U.K. 15 F7 51 36N 0 5W
London Gatwick ✈
  (LGW), U.K. 15 F7 51 10N 0 11W
London Heathrow ✈
  (LHR), U.K. 15 F7 51 28N 0 27W
London Stansted ✈
  (STN), U.K. ...... 15 F8 51 54N 0 14 E
Londonderry, U.K. ... 12 B4 55 0N 7 20W
Londonderry □, U.K. . 12 B4 55 0N 7 20W
Londonderry, C.,
  Australia .... 92 B4 13 45 S 126 55 E
Londonderry, I., Chile 128 H2 55 0 S 71 0W
Londres, Argentina .. 128 B3 27 43 S 67 7W
Londrina, Brazil ..... 127 A5 23 18 S 51 10W
Lone Pine, U.S.A. ... 110 J8 36 36N 118 4W
Lonely Mine, Zimbabwe 89 B4 19 30 S 28 49 E
Long B., U.S.A. 115 J6 33 35N 78 45W
Long Beach, Calif.,
  U.S.A. 111 M8 33 47N 118 11W
Long Beach, N.Y.,
  U.S.A. 117 F11 40 35N 73 39W
Long Beach, Wash.,
  U.S.A. 110 D2 46 21N 124 3W

Long Branch, U.S.A. .. 117 F11 40 18N 74 0W
Long Creek, U.S.A. .. 108 D4 44 43N 119 6W
Long Eaton, U.K. 14 E6 52 53N 1 15W
Long I., Australia ... 94 J6 20 22 S 148 51 E
Long I., Bahamas 121 B4 23 20N 75 10W
Long I., Canada 104 B4 54 50N 79 20W
Long I., Ireland 12 E2 51 30N 9 34W
Long I., U.S.A. 117 F11 40 45N 73 30W
Long Island Sd., U.S.A. 117 E12 41 10N 73 0W
Long L., Canada 104 C2 49 30N 86 50W
Long Lake, U.S.A. ... 117 C10 43 58N 74 25W
Long Point B., Canada 116 D4 42 40N 80 10W
Long Prairie →, U.S.A. 112 C7 46 20N 94 36W
Long Pt., Canada 116 D4 42 35N 80 2W
Long Range Mts.,
  Canada 105 C8 49 30N 57 30W
Long Reef, Australia . 92 B4 14 1 S 125 48 E
Long Spruce, Canada . 103 B10 56 24N 94 21W
Long Str. = Longa,
  Proliv, Russia ..... 4 C16 70 0N 175 0 E
Long Thanh, Vietnam . 65 G6 10 47N 106 57 E
Long Xian, China .... 56 G4 34 55N 106 55 E
Long Xuyen, Vietnam . 65 G5 10 19N 105 28 E
Longá, Greece .... 46 E3 36 53N 21 55 E
Longa, Proliv, Russia . 4 C16 70 0N 175 0 E
Long'an, China ...... 58 F6 23 10N 107 40 E
Longarone, Italy ..... 41 B9 46 16N 12 18 E
Longbenton, U.K. 14 B6 55 1N 1 31W
Longboat Key, U.S.A. . 115 M4 27 23N 82 39W
Longchang, China ... 58 C5 29 18N 105 15 E
Longchi, China ...... 58 C4 29 25N 103 24 E
Longchuan, Guangdong,
  China .... 59 E10 24 5N 115 17 E
Longchuan, Yunnan,
  China .... 58 E1 24 23N 97 58 E
Longde, China ...... 56 G4 35 30N 106 20 E
Longeau, France .... 19 E12 47 47N 5 20 E
Longford, Australia .. 95 G4 41 32 S 147 3 E
Longford, Ireland ... 12 C4 53 43N 7 49W
Longford □, Ireland .. 12 C4 53 42N 7 45W
Longhai, China ..... 59 E11 24 25N 117 46 E
Longhua, China ..... 57 D9 41 18N 117 45 E
Longhui, China ..... 59 D8 27 7N 111 2 E
Longido, Tanzania ... 86 C4 2 43 S 36 42 E
Longiram, Indonesia . 62 E5 0 5 S 115 45 E
Longkou, Jiangxi, China 59 D10 26 8N 115 10 E
Longkou, Shandong,
  China .... 57 F11 37 40N 120 18 E
Longlac, Canada 104 C2 49 45N 86 25W
Longli, China .... 58 D6 26 25N 106 58 E
Longlin, China ...... 58 E5 24 47N 105 20 E
Longling, China ..... 58 E2 24 37N 98 39 E
Longmeadow, U.S.A. . 117 D12 42 3N 72 34W
Longmen, China .... 59 F10 23 40N 114 18 E
Longming, China .... 58 F6 22 59N 107 18 E
Longmont, U.S.A. ... 112 E2 40 10N 105 6W
Longnan, China ..... 59 E10 24 55N 114 47 E
Longnawan, Indonesia 62 D4 1 51N 114 55 E
Longobucco, Italy .... 43 C9 39 27N 16 37 E
Longquan, China .... 59 C12 28 7N 119 10 E
Longreach, Australia . 94 C3 23 28 S 144 14 E
Longshan, China .... 58 C7 29 29N 109 25 E
Longsheng, China ... 59 E8 25 48N 110 0 E
Longué-Jumelles, France 18 E6 47 22N 0 8W
Longueau, France ... 19 C9 49 52N 2 21 E
Longueuil, Canada ... 117 A11 45 32N 73 28W
Longuyon, France ... 19 C12 49 27N 5 35 E
Longvic, France ..... 19 E12 47 17N 5 4 E
Longview, Tex., U.S.A. 113 J7 32 30N 94 44W
Longview, Wash., U.S.A. 110 D4 46 8N 122 57W
Longwy, France ..... 19 C12 49 30N 5 46 E
Longxi, China ...... 56 G3 34 53N 104 40 E
Longyan, China ..... 59 E11 25 10N 117 0 E
Longyearbyen, Svalbard 4 B8 78 13N 15 40 E
Longyou, China ..... 59 C12 29 1N 119 8 E
Longzhou, China .... 58 F6 22 22N 106 50 E
Lonigo, Italy .... 41 C8 45 23N 11 23 E
Löningen, Germany .. 24 C3 52 44N 7 46 E
Lonja →, Croatia .... 41 C13 45 22N 16 40 E
Lonoke, U.S.A. 113 H9 34 47N 91 54W
Lonquimay, Chile ... 128 D2 38 26 S 71 14W
Lons-le-Saunier, France 19 F12 46 40N 5 31 E
Lönsboda, Sweden ... 11 H8 56 24N 14 20 E
Looe, U.K. 15 G3 50 22N 4 28W
Lookout, C., Canada . 104 A3 55 18N 83 56W
Lookout, C., U.S.A. .. 115 H7 34 35N 76 32W
Loolmalasin, Tanzania 86 C4 3 0 S 35 53 E
Loon →, Alta., Canada 102 B5 57 8N 115 3W
Loon →, Man., Canada 103 B8 55 53N 101 59W
Loon Lake, Canada .. 103 C7 54 2N 109 10W
Loongana, Australia .. 93 F4 30 52 S 127 5 E
Loop Hd., Ireland ... 12 D2 52 34N 9 56W
Lop Buri, Thailand ... 64 E3 14 48N 100 37 E
Lop Nor = Lop Nur,
  China .... 60 B4 40 20N 90 10 E
Lop Nur, China ..... 60 B4 40 20N 90 10 E
Lopare, Bos.-H. ..... 28 F3 44 39N 18 46 E
Lopatin, Russia ..... 35 J8 43 50N 47 35 E
Lopatina, Gora, Russia 53 D15 50 47N 143 10 E
Lopaye, Sudan ...... 81 F3 6 37N 33 40 E
Lopez, Phil. .... 61 E5 13 53N 122 15 E
Lopez, U.S.A. 117 E8 41 27N 76 20W
Lopez, C., Gabon .... 84 E1 0 47 S 8 40 E
Lopphavet, Norway .. 8 A19 70 27N 21 15 E
Lora →, Afghan. .... 66 D4 31 35N 66 32 E
Lora, Hämūn-i-,
  Pakistan .... 66 E4 29 38N 64 58 E
Lora Cr. →, Australia 95 D2 28 10 S 135 22 E
Lora del Río, Spain .. 37 H5 37 39N 5 33W
Lorain, U.S.A. 116 E2 41 28N 82 11W
Loralai, Pakistan .... 68 D3 30 20N 68 41 E
Lorca, Spain 39 H3 37 41N 1 42W
Lord Howe I., Pac. Oc. 96 L7 31 33 S 159 6 E
Lord Howe Ridge,
  Pac. Oc. .... 96 L8 30 0 S 162 30 E
Lordsburg, U.S.A. ... 109 K9 32 21N 108 43W
Lorestan □, Iran .... 71 C6 33 30N 48 40 E
Loreto, Brazil ...... 125 E9 7 5 S 45 10W
Loreto, Italy .... 41 E10 43 26N 13 36 E
Loreto, Mexico 118 B2 26 1N 111 21W
Lorgues, France .... 21 E10 43 28N 6 22 E
Lorhosso, Burkina Faso 82 C4 10 17N 3 38W
Lorient, France 18 E3 47 45N 3 23W
Lőrinci, Hungary .... 28 C4 47 44N 19 41 E
Lormi, India .... 69 H9 22 17N 81 41 E
Lorn, U.K. 13 E3 56 26N 5 10W
Lorn, Firth of, U.K. .. 13 E3 56 20N 5 40W
Lorne, Australia .... 95 F3 38 33 S 143 59 E
Loronyo, Sudan ..... 81 G3 4 38N 32 38 E
Lorovouno, Cyprus .. 49 D11 35 8N 32 36 E
Lörrach, Germany ... 25 H3 47 36N 7 38 E
Lorraine △, France .. 19 D12 48 55N 5 50 E
Lorraine □, France .. 19 D13 48 53N 6 0 E
Los, Iles de, Guinea .. 82 D2 9 30N 13 50W
Los Alamos, Calif.,
  U.S.A. 111 L6 34 44N 120 17W

Los Alamos, N. Mex.,
  U.S.A. 109 J10 35 53N 106 19W
Los Alcornocales △,
  Spain 37 J5 36 21N 5 32W
Los Altos, U.S.A. 110 H4 37 23N 122 7W
Los Andes, Chile .... 126 C1 32 50 S 70 40W
Los Angeles, Chile ... 126 D1 37 28 S 72 23W
Los Angeles, U.S.A. .. 111 M8 34 4N 118 15W
Los Angeles, Bahia de,
  Mexico 118 B2 28 56N 113 34W
Los Angeles Aqueduct,
  U.S.A. 111 K9 35 22N 118 5W
Los Angeles
  International ✈
  (LAX), U.S.A. 111 M8 33 57N 118 25W
Los Banos, U.S.A. ... 110 H6 37 4N 120 51W
Los Barrios, Spain ... 37 J5 36 11N 5 30W
Los Blancos, Argentina 126 A3 23 40 S 62 30W
Los Cardones △,
  Argentina .... 126 B2 25 8 S 65 55W
Los Chiles, Costa Rica 120 D3 11 2N 84 43W
Los Corrales de Buelna,
  Spain 36 B6 43 16N 4 4W
Los Cristianos,
  Canary Is. 48 F3 28 3N 16 42W
Los Gallardos, Spain .. 39 H3 37 10N 1 57W
Los Gatos, U.S.A. ... 110 H5 37 14N 121 59W
Los Haïtises △,
  Dom. Rep. 121 C6 19 4N 69 36W
Los Hermanos Is.,
  Venezuela 121 D7 11 45N 64 25W
Los Islotes, Canary Is. . 48 E6 29 4N 13 44W
Los Llanos de Aridane,
  Canary Is. 48 F2 28 38N 17 54W
Los Loros, Chile ..... 126 B1 27 50 S 70 6W
Los Lunas, U.S.A. ... 109 J10 34 48N 106 44W
Los Mochis, Mexico .. 118 B3 25 45N 108 57W
Los Monegros, Spain . 38 D4 41 29N 0 13W
Los Nietos, Spain 39 H4 37 39N 0 47W
Los Olivos, U.S.A. ... 111 L6 34 40N 120 7W
Los Palacios, Cuba ... 120 B3 22 35N 83 15W
Los Palacios y
  Villafranca, Spain .. 37 H5 37 10N 5 55W
Los Reyes, Mexico ... 118 D4 19 34N 102 30W
Los Roques Is.,
  Venezuela 121 D6 11 50N 66 45W
Los Santos de Maimona,
  Spain 37 G4 38 27N 6 22W
Los Teques, Venezuela 124 A5 10 21N 67 2W
Los Testigos, Is.,
  Venezuela 124 A6 11 23N 63 6W
Los Vilos, Chile ..... 126 C1 32 10 S 71 30W
Los Yébenes, Spain .. 37 F7 39 36N 3 55W
Łosice, Poland ...... 31 F9 52 13N 22 43 E
Loskop Dam, S. Africa 89 D4 25 23 S 29 20 E
Løsning, Denmark ... 11 J3 55 48N 9 42 E
Lossiemouth, U.K. ... 13 D5 57 42N 3 17W
Lossen △, Sweden ... 10 B6 62 26N 12 45 E
Lostwithiel, U.K. 15 G3 50 24N 4 41W
Lot □, France .... 20 D5 44 39N 1 40 E
Lot →, France .... 20 D4 44 18N 0 20 E
Lot-et-Garonne □,
  France .... 20 D4 44 22N 0 30 E
Lota, Chile .... 126 D1 37 5 S 73 10W
Lotagipi Swamp, Sudan 81 G3 4 36N 34 55 E
Lotfābād, Iran ...... 71 B8 37 32N 59 20 E
Lothair, S. Africa .... 89 D5 26 22 S 30 27 E
Lotorp, Sweden ..... 11 F9 58 44N 15 50 E
Lötschbergtunnel, Switz. 25 J3 46 26N 7 43 E
Löttorp, Sweden .... 11 G11 57 10N 17 0 E
Lotung, Taiwan ..... 59 E13 24 41N 121 46 E
Loubomo, Congo .... 84 E2 4 9 S 12 47 E
Loudéac, France 18 D4 48 11N 2 47W
Loudi, China .... 59 D8 27 42N 111 59 E
Loudonville, U.S.A. .. 116 F2 40 38N 82 14W
Loudun, France ..... 18 E7 47 3N 0 5 E
Louga, Senegal 82 B1 15 45N 16 5W
Loughborough, U.K. .. 14 E6 52 47N 1 11W
Loughrea, Ireland ... 12 C3 53 12N 8 33W
Loughros More B.,
  Ireland 12 B3 54 48N 8 32W
Louhans, France .... 19 F12 46 38N 5 12 E
Louis Trichardt,
  S. Africa .... 89 C4 23 1 S 29 43 E
Louis XIV, Pte., Canada 104 B4 54 37N 79 45W
Louisa, U.S.A. 114 F4 38 7N 82 36W
Louisbourg, Canada .. 105 C8 45 55N 60 0W
Louise I., Canada ... 102 C2 52 55N 131 50W
Louiseville, Canada .. 104 C5 46 20N 72 56W
Louisiade Arch.,
  Papua N.G. .... 96 J7 11 10 S 153 0 E
Louisiana, U.S.A. ... 112 F9 39 27N 91 3W
Louisiana □, U.S.A. .. 113 K9 30 50N 92 0W
Louisville, Ky., U.S.A. 114 F3 38 15N 85 46W
Louisville, Miss., U.S.A. 113 J10 33 7N 89 3W
Louisville, Ohio, U.S.A. 116 F3 40 50N 81 16W
Loulay, France 20 B3 46 3N 0 30W
Loulé, Portugal 37 H3 37 9N 8 0W
Louny, Czech Rep. ... 26 A6 50 20N 13 48 E
Loup City, U.S.A. ... 112 E5 41 17N 98 58W
Loups Marins, Lacs des,
  Canada 104 A5 56 30N 73 45W
Lourdes, France 20 E3 43 6N 0 3W
Lourinhã, Portugal .. 37 F1 39 14N 9 17W
Lousã, Portugal 36 E2 40 7N 8 14W
Louta, Burkina Faso .. 82 C4 13 30N 3 10W
Louth, Australia .... 95 E4 30 30 S 145 8 E
Louth, Ireland 12 C5 53 58N 6 32W
Louth, U.K. 14 D7 53 22N 0 1W
Louth □, Ireland 12 C5 53 56N 6 34W
Loutrá Aidhipsoú,
  Greece .... 46 C5 38 54N 23 2 E
Loutráki, Greece .... 46 D4 37 58N 22 57 E
Louvain = Leuven,
  Belgium .... 17 D4 50 52N 4 42 E
Louviers, France .... 18 C8 49 12N 1 10 E
Louwsburg, S. Africa . 89 D5 27 37 S 31 7 E
Lovat →, Russia .... 32 C6 58 14N 31 28 E
Lovćen, Serbia & M. . 44 D2 42 23N 18 51 E
Lovćen, Serbia & M. . 44 D2 42 20N 18 50 E
Lovech, Bulgaria .... 45 C8 43 8N 24 42 E
Lovech □, Bulgaria .. 45 C8 43 15N 24 45 E
Loveland, U.S.A. 112 E2 40 24N 105 5W
Lovell, U.S.A. 108 D9 44 50N 108 24W
Lovelock, U.S.A. 108 F4 40 11N 118 28W
Lóvere, Italy .... 40 C7 45 49N 10 4 E
Lövestad, Sweden ... 11 J7 55 40N 13 54 E
Loviisa, Finland .... 9 F22 60 28N 26 12 E
Loving, U.S.A. 113 J2 32 17N 104 6W
Lovington, U.S.A. ... 113 J3 32 57N 103 21W
Loviisa = Loviisa,
  Finland .... 9 F22 60 28N 26 12 E
Lovosice, Czech Rep. . 26 A7 50 30N 14 2 E
Lovran, Croatia ..... 41 C11 45 18N 14 15 E
Lovrin, Romania .... 28 E5 45 58N 20 48 E
Lövstabruk, Sweden .. 10 D11 60 59N 17 53 E

Lövstabukten, Sweden . 10 D11 60 35N 17 45 E
Low, L., Canada 104 B4 52 29N 76 17W
Low Pt., Australia ... 93 F4 32 25 S 127 25 E
Low Tatra = Nízké
  Tatry, Slovak Rep. .. 27 C12 48 55N 19 30 E
Lowa, Dem. Rep. of
  the Congo .... 86 C2 1 25 S 25 47 E
Lowa →, Dem. Rep. of
  the Congo .... 86 C2 1 24 S 25 51 E
Lowell, U.S.A. 117 D13 42 38N 71 19W
Lowellville, U.S.A. ... 116 E4 41 2N 80 32W
Löwen →, Namibia .. 88 D2 26 51 S 18 17 E
Lower Alkali L., U.S.A. 108 F3 41 16N 120 2W
Lower Arrow L.,
  Canada 102 D5 49 40N 118 5W
Lower Austria =
  Niederösterreich □,
  Austria .... 26 C8 48 25N 15 40 E
Lower California = Baja
  California, Mexico .. 118 A1 31 10N 115 12W
Lower Hutt, N.Z. .... 91 J5 41 10 S 174 55 E
Lower Lake, U.S.A. .. 110 G4 38 55N 122 37W
Lower Manitou L.,
  Canada 103 D10 49 15N 93 0W
Lower Post, Canada .. 102 B3 59 58N 128 30W
Lower Red L., U.S.A. 112 B7 47 58N 95 0W
Lower Saxony =
  Niedersachsen □,
  Germany .... 24 C4 52 50N 9 0 E
Lower Tunguska =
  Tunguska,
  Nizhnyaya →, Russia 53 C9 65 48N 88 4 E
Lower Zambezi △,
  Zambia .... 87 F2 15 25 S 29 40 E
Lowestoft, U.K. ..... 15 E9 52 29N 1 45 E
Lowgar □, Afghan. .. 66 B6 34 0N 69 0 E
Łowicz, Poland ..... 31 F6 52 6N 19 55 E
Lowville, U.S.A. 117 C9 43 47N 75 29W
Loxton, Australia .... 95 E3 34 28 S 140 31 E
Loxton, S. Africa .... 88 E3 31 30 S 22 22 E
Loyalton, U.S.A. 110 F6 39 41N 120 14W
Loyalty Is. = Loyauté,
  Îs., N. Cal. .... 96 K8 20 50 S 166 30 E
Loyang = Luoyang,
  China .... 56 G7 34 40N 112 26 E
Loyauté, Îs., N. Cal. .. 96 K8 20 50 S 166 30 E
Loyev = Loyew, Belarus 33 G6 51 56N 30 46 E
Loyew, Belarus ..... 33 G6 51 56N 30 46 E
Loyoro, Uganda ..... 86 B3 3 22N 34 14 E
Lož, Slovenia .... 41 C11 45 43N 14 30 E
Lozère □, France .... 20 D7 44 35N 3 30 E
Loznica, Serbia & M. . 44 B8 44 32N 19 12 E
Lozova, Ukraine .... 33 H9 49 0N 36 20 E
Lü Shan, China ..... 59 C11 29 30N 115 55 E
Lü-Tao, Taiwan ..... 59 F13 22 40N 121 30 E
Luachimo, Angola ... 84 F4 7 23 S 20 48 E
Luajan →, India .... 69 G11 24 44N 85 1 E
Lualaba →, Dem. Rep.
  of the Congo ...... 86 B2 0 26N 25 20 E
Luampa, Zambia .... 87 F1 15 4 S 24 20 E
Lu'an, China .... 59 B11 31 45N 116 29 E
Luan Chau, Vietnam . 58 G4 21 38N 103 24 E
Luan He →, China .. 57 E10 39 20N 119 5 E
Luan Xian, China ... 57 E10 39 40N 118 40 E
Luancheng,
  Guangxi Zhuangzu,
  China .... 58 F7 22 48N 108 55 E
Luancheng, Hebei,
  China .... 56 F8 37 53N 114 40 E
Luanco, Spain 36 B5 43 37N 5 48W
Luanda, Angola ..... 84 F2 8 50 S 13 15 E
Luang, Thale, Thailand 65 J3 7 30N 100 15 E
Luang Prabang, Laos . 58 H4 19 52N 102 10 E
Luangwa, Zambia ... 87 F3 15 35 S 30 16 E
Luangwa →, Zambia . 87 E3 14 25 S 30 25 E
Luangwa Valley,
  Zambia .... 87 E3 13 30 S 31 30 E
Luanne, China ...... 57 D9 40 55N 117 40 E
Luanping, China .... 57 D9 40 53N 117 23 E
Luanshya, Zambia ... 87 E2 13 3 S 28 28 E
Luapula □, Zambia .. 87 E2 11 0 S 29 0 E
Luapula →, Africa ... 87 D2 9 26 S 28 33 E
Luarca, Spain 36 B4 43 32N 6 32W
Luashi, Dem. Rep. of
  the Congo .... 87 E1 10 50 S 23 36 E
Luau, Angola .... 84 G4 10 40 S 22 10 E
Lubaczów, Poland ... 31 H10 50 10N 23 8 E
Lubań, Poland ...... 31 G2 51 5N 15 15 E
Lubana, Ozero =
  Lubānas Ezers, Latvia 9 H22 56 45N 27 0 E
Lubānas Ezers, Latvia . 9 H22 56 45N 27 0 E
Lubang, Phil. .... 61 E4 13 52N 120 7 E
Lubang Is., Phil. .... 63 B6 13 50N 120 12 E
Lubango, Angola .... 85 G2 14 55 S 13 30 E
Lubao, Dem. Rep. of
  the Congo .... 86 D2 5 17 S 25 42 E
Lubartów, Poland ... 31 G9 51 28N 22 42 E
Lubawa, Poland .... 30 E6 53 30N 19 48 E
Lübbecke, Germany .. 24 C4 52 18N 8 37 E
Lübben, Germany ... 24 D9 51 56N 13 54 E
Lübbenau, Germany . 24 D9 51 52N 13 57 E
Lubbock, U.S.A. 113 J4 33 35N 101 51W
Lübeck, Germany ... 24 B6 53 52N 10 40 E
Lübecker Bucht,
  Germany .... 24 A6 54 3N 10 54 E
Lubefu, Dem. Rep. of
  the Congo .... 86 C1 4 47 S 24 27 E
Lubefu →, Dem. Rep.
  of the Congo ...... 86 C1 4 10 S 23 0 E
Lubelskie □, Poland .. 31 G9 51 20N 22 50 E
Lubero = Luofu,
  Dem. Rep. of
  the Congo .... 86 C2 0 10 S 29 15 E
Lubersac, France .... 20 C5 45 26N 1 23 E
Lubicon L., Canada .. 102 B5 56 23N 115 56W
Lubień Kujawski,
  Poland .... 31 F6 52 23N 19 9 E
Lubilash →, Dem. Rep.
  of the Congo ...... 84 F4 7 40 S 22 30 E
Lubin, Poland ...... 31 G3 51 24N 16 11 E
Lublin, Poland ...... 31 G9 51 12N 22 38 E
Lubliniec, Poland ... 31 H5 50 43N 18 45 E
Lubnān, Jabal, Lebanon 74 B4 33 45N 35 40 E
Lubniewice, Poland .. 31 F2 52 31N 15 16 E
Lubny, Ukraine ..... 33 G7 50 3N 32 58 E
Lubongola, Dem. Rep.
  of the Congo ...... 86 C2 2 35 S 27 50 E
L'ubochňa, Slovak Rep. 27 B13 49 7N 19 20 E
Luboń, Poland ...... 31 F3 52 21N 16 51 E
Lubsko, Poland ..... 31 G1 51 45N 14 57 E
Lubsza →, Poland ... 31 G9 51 45N 15 15 E
Lübtheen, Germany .. 24 B7 53 18N 11 5 E
Lubuagan, Phil. ..... 61 C4 17 21N 121 10 E
Lubudi →, Dem. Rep. of
  the Congo .... 87 D2 9 0 S 25 35 E
Lubuklinggau, Indonesia 62 E2 3 15 S 102 55 E
Lubuksikaping,
  Indonesia .... 62 D2 0 10N 100 15 E
Lubumbashi, Dem. Rep.
  of the Congo ...... 87 E2 11 40 S 27 28 E
Lubunda, Dem. Rep. of
  the Congo .... 86 D2 5 12 S 26 41 E
Lubungu, Zambia ... 87 E2 14 35 S 26 24 E
Lubuskie □, Poland .. 31 F2 52 10N 15 20 E
Lubutu, Dem. Rep. of
  the Congo .... 86 C2 0 45 S 26 30 E
Luc An Chau, Vietnam 64 A5 22 6N 104 43 E
Luc-en-Diois, France . 21 D9 44 36N 5 28 E
Lucan, Canada 116 C3 43 11N 81 24W
Lucania, Mt., Canada . 100 B5 61 1N 140 27W
Lucas Channel, Canada 116 A3 45 21N 81 45W
Lucban, Phil. .... 61 D4 14 6N 121 33 E
Lucca, Italy .... 40 E7 43 50N 10 29 E
Lucé, France .... 18 D8 48 26N 1 27 E
Luce Bay, U.K. 13 G4 54 45N 4 48W
Lucea, Jamaica ..... 120 a 18 27N 78 10W
Lucedale, U.S.A. 115 K1 30 56N 88 35W
Lucena, Phil. .... 61 E4 13 56N 121 37 E
Lucena, Spain 37 H6 37 27N 4 31W
Lučenec, Slovak Rep. . 27 C12 48 18N 19 42 E
Lucera, Italy .... 43 A8 41 30N 15 20 E
Lucerne = Luzern,
  Switz. .... 25 H4 47 3N 8 18 E
Lucerne, U.S.A. 110 F4 39 6N 122 48W
Lucerne Valley, U.S.A. 111 L10 34 27N 116 57W
Lucero, Mexico 118 A3 30 49N 106 30W
Luchena →, Spain .. 39 H3 37 44N 1 50W
Lucheng, China ..... 56 F7 36 20N 113 11 E
Lucheringo →, Mozam. 87 E4 11 43 S 36 17 E
Lüchow, Germany ... 24 C7 52 58N 11 8 E
Luchuan, China ..... 59 F8 22 21N 110 12 E
Lucia, U.S.A. 110 J5 36 2N 121 33W
Lucinda, Australia ... 94 B4 18 32 S 146 20 E
Luckau, Germany ... 24 D9 51 50N 13 42 E
Luckenwalde, Germany 24 C9 52 5N 13 10 E
Luckhoff, S. Africa ... 88 D3 29 44 S 24 43 E
Lucknow, Canada ... 116 C3 43 57N 81 31W
Lucknow, India ..... 69 F9 26 50N 81 0 E
Luçon, France 20 B2 46 28N 1 10W
Lüda = Dalian, China 57 E11 38 50N 121 40 E
Luda Kamchiya →,
  Bulgaria .... 45 C11 43 3N 27 29 E
Ludbreg, Croatia .... 41 B13 46 15N 16 38 E
Lüdenscheid, Germany 24 D3 51 13N 7 37 E
Lüderitz, Namibia ... 88 D2 26 41 S 15 8 E
Lüderitzbaai, Namibia 88 D2 26 36 S 15 8 E
Ludhiana, India ..... 68 D6 30 57N 75 56 E
Ludian, China ...... 58 D4 27 10N 103 33 E
Luding Qiao, China .. 58 C4 29 53N 102 12 E
Lüdinghausen, Germany 24 D3 51 46N 7 27 E
Ludington, U.S.A. ... 114 D2 43 57N 86 27W
Ludlow, U.K. 15 E5 52 22N 2 42W
Ludlow, Calif., U.S.A. 111 L10 34 43N 116 10W
Ludlow, Pa., U.S.A. .. 116 E6 41 43N 78 56W
Ludlow, Vt., U.S.A. .. 117 C12 43 24N 72 42W
Ludus, Romania .... 29 D9 46 29N 24 5 E
Ludvika, Sweden .... 10 D9 60 8N 15 14 E
Ludwigsburg, Germany 25 G5 48 53N 9 11 E
Ludwigsfelde, Germany 24 C9 52 17N 13 17 E
Ludwigshafen, Germany 25 F4 49 29N 8 26 E
Ludwigslust, Germany . 24 B7 53 19N 11 30 E
Ludza, Latvia .... 32 D4 56 32N 27 43 E
Lueki, Dem. Rep. of
  the Congo .... 86 C2 3 20 S 25 48 E
Luena, Dem. Rep. of
  the Congo .... 87 D2 9 28 S 25 43 E
Luena, Zambia ...... 87 E3 10 40 S 30 25 E
Luenha = Ruenya →,
  Africa .... 87 F3 16 24 S 33 48 E
Lüeyang, China ..... 56 H4 33 22N 106 10 E
Lufeng, Guangdong,
  China .... 59 F10 22 57N 115 38 E
Lufeng, Yunnan, China 58 E4 25 0N 102 5 E
Lufira →, Dem. Rep. of
  the Congo .... 87 D2 9 30 S 27 0 E
Lufkin, U.S.A. 113 K7 31 21N 94 44W
Lufupa, Dem. Rep. of
  the Congo .... 87 E1 10 37 S 24 56 E
Luga, Russia .... 32 C5 58 40N 29 55 E
Luga →, Russia ..... 32 C5 59 40N 28 18 E
Lugano, Switz. ...... 25 J4 46 1N 8 57 E
Lugano, L. di, Switz. . 40 C6 46 0N 9 0 E
Lugansk = Luhansk,
  Ukraine .... 33 H10 48 38N 39 15 E
Lugard's Falls, Kenya . 86 C4 3 6 S 38 41 E
Lugela, Mozam. ..... 87 F4 16 25 S 36 43 E
Lugenda →, Mozam. . 87 E4 11 25 S 38 33 E
Lugh Ganana =
  Somali Rep. ...... 75 G3 3 48N 42 34 E
Lugnaquillia, Ireland . 12 D5 52 58N 6 28W
Lugo, Italy .... 41 D8 44 25N 11 54 E
Lugo, Spain 36 B3 43 2N 7 35W
Lugo □, Spain 36 C3 43 0N 7 30W
Lugoj, Romania ..... 28 E6 45 42N 21 57 E
Lugovoy = Qulan,
  Kazakhstan .... 52 E8 42 55N 72 43 E
Luhansk, Ukraine ... 33 H10 48 38N 39 15 E
Luhe →, Germany ... 24 B6 53 18N 10 11 E
Luhe, China .... 59 A12 32 19N 118 50 E
Luho →, Germany .. 24 B6 53 23N 10 13 E
Luhuo, China .... 58 B3 31 21N 100 48 E
Luiana, Angola ..... 88 B3 17 25 S 22 59 E
Luichow Pen. = Leizhou
  Bandao, China .... 58 G7 21 0N 110 0 E
Luimneach = Limerick,
  Ireland 12 D3 52 40N 8 37W
Luing, U.K. 13 E3 56 14N 5 39W
Luino, Italy .... 40 C5 45 59N 8 44 E
Luís Correia, Brazil .. 125 D10 3 0 S 41 35W
Luitpold Coast,
  Antarctica .... 5 D1 78 30 S 32 0W
Luiza, Dem. Rep. of
  the Congo .... 84 F4 7 40 S 22 30 E
Luizi, Dem. Rep. of
  the Congo .... 86 D2 6 0 S 27 25 E
Luján, Argentina .... 126 C4 34 45 S 59 5W
Lujiang, China ...... 59 B11 31 20N 117 15 E
Lukanga Swamp,
  Zambia .... 87 E2 14 30 S 27 40 E
Lukavac, Bos.-H. .... 28 F3 44 33N 18 32 E
Lukenie →, Dem. Rep.
  of the Congo ...... 84 E3 3 0 S 18 50 E
Lukhisaral, India .... 69 G12 25 11N 86 5 E
Lŭki, Bulgaria ...... 45 E8 41 50N 24 43 E
Lukolela, Dem. Rep. of
  the Congo .... 86 D1 5 23 S 24 32 E
Lukosi, Zimbabwe ... 87 F2 18 30 S 26 30 E
Lukovit, Bulgaria .... 45 C8 43 13N 24 11 E
Łuków, Poland ...... 31 G9 51 55N 22 23 E

Lukoyanov, Russia .... **34 C7** 55 2N 44 29 E
Lukusuzi △, Zambia .. **87 E3** 12 43 S 32 36 E
Luleå, Sweden ...... **8 D20** 65 35N 22 10 E
Luleälven →, Sweden . **8 D19** 65 35N 22 10 E
Lüleburgaz, Turkey .. **45 E11** 41 23N 27 22 E
Luliang, China ...... **58 E4** 25 0N 103 40 E
Luling, U.S.A. **113 L6** 29 41N 97 39W
Lulong, China ...... **57 E10** 39 53N 118 51 E
Lulonga →, Dem. Rep.
of the Congo ...... **84 D3** 1 0N 18 10 E
Lulua →, Dem. Rep. of
the Congo .... **84 E4** 4 30 S 20 30 E
Lumajang, Indonesia .. **63 H15** 8 8 S 113 13 E
Lumbala N'guimbo,
Angola .... **85 G4** 14 18 S 21 18 E
Lumberton, U.S.A. ... **115 H6** 34 37N 79 0W
Lumsden, Canada **103 C8** 50 39N 104 52W
Lumsden, N.Z. ...... **91 L2** 45 44 S 168 27 E
Lumut, Malaysia .... **65 K3** 4 13N 100 37 E
Lumut, Tanjung,
Indonesia .... **62 E3** 3 50 S 105 58 E
Luna, India .... **68 H3** 23 43N 69 16 E
Lunan, China ...... **58 E4** 24 40N 103 18 E
Lunavada, India .... **68 H5** 23 8N 73 37 E
Lunca, Romania .... **29 C10** 47 22N 25 1 E
Lunca Corbului,
Romania .... **29 F9** 44 42N 24 45 E
Lund, Sweden ...... **11 J7** 55 44N 13 12 E
Lundazi, Zambia .... **87 E3** 12 20 S 33 7 E
Lunderskov, Denmark . **11 J3** 55 29N 9 19 E
Lundi →, Zimbabwe .. **87 G3** 21 43 S 32 34 E
Lundu, Malaysia .... **62 D3** 1 40N 109 50 E
Lundy, U.K. **15 F3** 51 10N 4 41W
Lune →, U.K. **14 C5** 54 0N 2 51W
Lüneburg, Germany .. **24 B6** 53 15N 10 24 E
Lüneburg Heath =
Lüneburger Heide,
Germany .... **24 B6** 53 10N 10 12 E
Lüneburger Heide,
Germany .... **24 B6** 53 10N 10 12 E
Lunel, France ...... **21 E8** 43 39N 4 9 E
Lünen, Germany .... **24 D3** 51 37N 7 31 E
Lunenburg, Canada .. **105 D7** 44 22N 64 18W
Lunéville, France ... **19 D13** 48 36N 6 30 E
Lunga →, Zambia ... **87 E2** 14 34 S 26 25 E
Lungi Airport, S. Leone **82 D2** 8 40N 13 17W
Lunglei, India ...... **67 H18** 22 55N 92 45 E
Luni, India .... **68 G5** 26 0N 73 6 E
Luni →, India ...... **68 G4** 24 41N 71 14 E
Luninets = Luninyets,
Belarus .... **33 F4** 52 15N 26 50 E
Luning, U.S.A. **108 G4** 38 30N 118 11W
Lunino, Russia ..... **34 D7** 53 38N 45 18 E
Luninyets, Belarus ... **33 F4** 52 15N 26 50 E
Lunkaransar, India .. **68 E5** 28 29N 73 44 E
Lunsemfwa →, Zambia **87 E3** 14 54 S 30 12 E
Lunsemfwa Falls,
Zambia .... **87 E2** 14 30 S 29 6 E
Luo →, China ...... **56 G6** 34 35N 110 20 E
Luocheng, China .... **58 E7** 24 48N 108 53 E
Luochuan, China .... **56 G5** 35 45N 109 26 E
Luoci, China .... **58 E4** 25 19N 102 18 E
Luoding, China ..... **58 E6** 25 24N 106 43 E
Luoding, China ..... **59 F8** 22 45N 111 40 E
Luofu, Dem. Rep. of
the Congo .... **86 C2** 0 10 S 29 15 E
Luohe, China ...... **56 H8** 33 32N 114 2 E
Luojiang, China .... **58 B5** 31 18N 104 33 E
Luonan, China ..... **56 G6** 34 5N 110 10 E
Luoning, China .... **56 G6** 34 35N 111 40 E
Luoshan, China .... **59 A10** 32 13N 114 30 E
Luotian, China ..... **59 B10** 30 46N 115 22 E
Luoxiao Shan, China . **59 D10** 26 30N 114 1 E
Luoyang, China .... **56 G7** 34 40N 112 26 E
Luoyuan, China .... **59 D12** 26 28N 119 30 E
Luozigou, China .... **57 C16** 43 42N 130 18 E
Lupanshui, China ... **58 D5** 26 38N 104 48 E
Lupeni, Romania ... **29 E8** 45 21N 23 13 E
Lupilichi, Mozam. ... **87 E4** 11 47 S 35 13 E
Łupków, Poland .... **31 J9** 49 15N 22 4 E
Lupoing, China .... **58 E5** 24 53N 104 21 E
Luquan, China ..... **58 E4** 25 35N 102 25 E
Luque, Paraguay .... **126 B4** 25 19 S 57 25W
Lúras, Italy .... **42 B2** 40 56N 9 10 E
Luray, U.S.A. **114 F6** 38 40N 78 28W
Lure, France .... **19 E13** 47 40N 6 30 E
Lurgan, U.K. **12 B5** 54 28N 6 19W
Lusaka, Zambia .... **87 F2** 15 28 S 28 16 E
Lusaka □, Zambia ... **87 F2** 15 30 S 29 0 E
Lusambo, Dem. Rep. of
the Congo .... **86 C1** 4 58 S 23 28 E
Lusangaye, Dem. Rep. of
the Congo .... **86 C2** 4 54 S 26 0 E
Luseland, Canada ... **103 C7** 52 5N 109 24W
Lusenga Plain △,
Zambia .... **87 D2** 9 22 S 29 14 E
Lushan, Henan, China **56 H7** 33 45N 112 55 E
Lushan, Sichuan, China **58 B4** 30 12N 102 52 E
Lushi, China ...... **56 G6** 34 3N 111 3 E
Lushnjë, Albania ... **44 F3** 40 55N 19 41 E
Lushoto, Tanzania .. **86 C4** 4 47 S 38 20 E
Lushui, China ..... **58 E2** 25 58N 98 44 E
Lüshun, China ..... **57 E11** 38 45N 121 15 E
Lusignan, France ... **20 B4** 46 26N 0 8 E
Lusigny-sur-Barse,
France .... **19 D11** 48 16N 4 15 E
Lusk, U.S.A. **112 D2** 42 46N 104 27W
Lussac-les-Châteaux,
France .... **20 B4** 46 24N 0 43 E
Lustenau, Austria ... **26 D2** 47 26N 9 39 E
Lūt, Dasht-e, Iran .. **71 D8** 31 30N 58 0 E
Luta = Dalian, China . **57 E11** 38 50N 121 40 E
Lutherstadt Wittenberg,
Germany .... **24 D8** 51 53N 12 39 E
Luton, U.K. **15 F7** 51 53N 0 24W
Luton □, U.K. **15 F7** 51 53N 0 24W
Łutselk'e, Canada ... **103 A6** 62 24N 110 44W
Lutsk, Ukraine ..... **33 G3** 50 50N 25 15 E
Lützow Holmbukta,
Antarctica ...... **5 C4** 69 10 S 37 30 E
Lutzputs, S. Africa .. **88 D3** 28 3 S 20 40 E
Luuq = Lugh Ganana,
Somali Rep. ..... **75 G3** 3 48N 42 34 E
Luverne, Ala., U.S.A. **115 K2** 31 43N 86 16W
Luverne, Minn., U.S.A. **112 D6** 43 39N 96 13W
Luvua, Dem. Rep. of
the Congo .... **87 D2** 8 48 S 25 17 E
Luvua →, Dem. Rep. of
the Congo .... **86 D2** 6 50 S 27 30 E
Luvuvhu →, S. Africa **89 C5** 22 25 S 31 18 E
Luwegu →, Tanzania . **87 D4** 8 31 S 37 23 E
Luwuk, Indonesia ... **63 E6** 0 56 S 122 47 E
Luxembourg, Lux. ... **17 E6** 49 37N 6 9 E
Luxembourg □, Belgium **17 E5** 49 58N 5 30 E
Luxembourg ■, Europe **7 F7** 49 45N 6 0 E
Luxembourg ✈ (LUX),
Lux. .... **17 E6** 49 37N 6 10 E

Luxeuil-les-Bains,
France .... **19 E13** 47 49N 6 24 E
Luxi, Hunan, China .. **59 C8** 28 20N 110 7 E
Luxi, Yunnan, China . **58 E4** 24 40N 103 55 E
Luxi, Yunnan, China . **58 E2** 24 27N 98 36 E
Luxor = El Uqsur, Egypt **80 B3** 25 41N 32 38 E
Luy-de-Béarn →,
France **20 E3** 43 39N 0 48W
Luy-de-France →,
France **20 E3** 43 39N 0 48W
Luyi, China .... **56 H8** 33 50N 115 35 E
Luz-St-Sauveur, France **20 F4** 42 53N 0 0W
Luzern, Switz. ..... **25 H4** 47 3N 8 18 E
Luzern □, Switz. .... **25 H3** 47 2N 7 55 E
Luzhai, China ...... **58 E7** 24 29N 109 42 E
Luzhany, Ukraine ... **29 B10** 48 22N 25 47 E
Luzhi, China ...... **58 D5** 26 21N 105 16 E
Luzhou, China ..... **58 C5** 28 52N 105 20 E
Luziânia, Brazil .... **125 G9** 16 20 S 48 0W
Lužnice →, Czech Rep. **26 B7** 49 14N 14 23 E
Luzon, Phil. ...... **61 D4** 16 0N 121 0 E
Luzon Strait, Asia .. **59 G13** 21 0N 120 40 E
Luzy, France ...... **19 F10** 46 47N 3 58 E
Luzzi, Italy .... **43 C9** 39 27N 16 17 E
Lviv, Ukraine ..... **33 H3** 49 50N 24 0 E
Lvov = Lviv, Ukraine . **33 H3** 49 50N 24 0 E
Lwówek, Poland .... **31 F3** 52 28N 16 10 E
Lwówek Śląski, Poland **31 G2** 51 7N 15 38 E
Lyakhavichy, Belarus . **33 F4** 53 2N 26 32 E
Lyakhovskiye, Ostrova,
Russia .... **53 B15** 73 40N 141 0 E
Lyaki = Läki, Azerbaijan **35 K8** 40 34N 47 22 E
Lyal I., Canada **116 B3** 44 57N 81 24W
Lyaskovets, Bulgaria . **45 C9** 43 6N 25 44 E
Lyasnaya, Belarus ... **31 F10** 52 9N 23 31 E
Lybster, U.K. **13 C5** 58 18N 3 15W
Lycaonia, Turkey ... **72 D5** 38 0N 33 0 E
Lychen, Germany ... **24 B9** 53 12N 13 18 E
Lychkova, Russia ... **32 D7** 57 55N 32 24 E
Lycia, Turkey ..... **47 E11** 36 30N 29 30 E
Lyckeby →, Sweden .. **11 H9** 56 12N 15 39 E
Lycksele, Sweden ... **8 D18** 64 38N 18 40 E
Lycosura, Greece ... **46 D4** 37 20N 22 3 E
Lydda = Lod, Israel .. **74 D3** 31 57N 34 54 E
Lydenburg, S. Africa . **89 D5** 25 10 S 30 29 E
Lydia, Turkey ..... **47 C10** 38 48N 28 19 E
Łydynia →, Poland .. **31 F7** 52 43N 20 26 E
Lyell, N.Z. .... **91 J4** 41 48 S 172 4 E
Lyell I., Canada **102 C2** 52 40N 131 35W
Lyepyel, Belarus .... **32 E5** 54 50N 28 40 E
Lygnern, Sweden ... **11 G6** 57 30N 12 15 E
Lykens, U.S.A. **117 F8** 40 34N 76 42W
Lyman, Ukraine .... **29 E14** 45 41N 29 45 E
Lyman, U.S.A. **108 F8** 41 20N 110 18W
Lymanske, Ukraine .. **29 D14** 46 40N 29 58 E
Lyme B., U.K. **15 G4** 50 42N 2 53W
Lyme Regis, U.K. ... **15 G5** 50 43N 2 57W
Lymington, U.K. **15 G6** 50 45N 1 32W
Łyna →, Poland .... **9 J19** 54 37N 21 14 E
Lynchburg, U.S.A. .. **114 G6** 37 25N 79 9W
Lynd →, Australia .. **94 B3** 16 28 S 143 18 E
Lynd Ra., Australia .. **95 D4** 25 30 S 149 20 E
Lynden, Canada **116 C4** 43 14N 80 9W
Lynden, U.S.A. **110 B4** 48 57N 122 27W
Lyndhurst, Australia . **95 E2** 30 15 S 138 18 E
Lyndon →, Australia . **93 D1** 23 29 S 114 6 E
Lyndonville, N.Y.,
U.S.A. **116 C6** 43 20N 78 23W
Lyndonville, Vt., U.S.A. **117 B12** 44 31N 72 1W
Lyngen, Norway .... **8 B19** 69 45N 20 30 E
Lynher Reef, Australia **92 C3** 15 27 S 121 55 E
Lynn, U.S.A. **117 D14** 42 28N 70 57W
Lynn Lake, Canada .. **103 B8** 56 51N 101 3W
Lynnwood, U.S.A. .. **110 C4** 47 49N 122 19W
Lynton, U.K. **15 F4** 51 13N 3 50W
Lyntupy, Belarus ... **9 J22** 55 4N 26 23 E
Lynx L., Canada **103 A7** 62 25N 106 15W
Lyon, France ...... **21 C8** 45 46N 4 50 E
Lyon St-Exupéry ✈
(LYS), France ... **21 C9** 45 44N 5 2 E
Lyonnais, France ... **21 C8** 45 45N 4 15 E
Lyonnais, Mts. du,
France .... **21 C8** 45 45N 4 15 E
Lyons = Lyon, France . **21 C8** 45 46N 4 50 E
Lyons, Ga., U.S.A. .. **115 J4** 32 12N 82 19W
Lyons, Kans., U.S.A. . **112 F5** 38 21N 98 12W
Lyons, N.Y., U.S.A. . **116 C8** 43 5N 77 0W
Lyons →, Australia .. **93 E2** 25 2 S 115 9 E
Lyons Falls, U.S.A. .. **117 C9** 43 37N 75 22W
Lyozna, Belarus .... **32 E6** 55 0N 30 50 E
Lys = Leie →, Belgium **17 C3** 51 2N 3 45 E
Lysá nad Labem,
Czech Rep. ...... **26 A7** 50 11N 14 51 E
Lysekil, Sweden .... **11 F5** 58 17N 11 26 E
Lyskovo, Russia .... **34 B7** 56 0N 45 3 E
Lystrup, Denmark .. **11 H4** 56 14N 10 14 E
Lysva, Sweden ..... **10 D7** 60 1N 13 9 E
Lysychansk, Ukraine . **33 H10** 48 55N 38 30 E
Lytham St. Anne's, U.K. **14 D4** 53 45N 3 0W
Lyttelton, N.Z. ..... **91 K4** 43 35 S 172 44 E
Lytton, Canada **102 C4** 50 13N 121 31W
Lyuban, Russia .... **32 C6** 59 16N 31 18 E
Lyubertsy, Russia .. **32 C9** 55 39N 37 50 E
Lyubim, Russia .... **32 C11** 58 20N 40 39 E
Lyubimets, Bulgaria . **45 E10** 41 50N 26 5 E
Lyuboml, Ukraine .. **31 G11** 51 11N 24 4 E
Lyubotyn, Ukraine .. **33 H8** 50 0N 36 0 E
Lyubytino, Russia .. **32 C7** 58 50N 33 16 E
Lyudinovo, Russia .. **32 F8** 53 52N 34 28 E

M

M.R. Gomez, Presa,
Mexico **119 B5** 26 10N 99 0W
M.R. Stefanik,
Bratislava ✈ (BTS),
Slovak Rep. ..... **27 C10** 48 11N 17 9 E
Ma →, Vietnam .... **58 H5** 19 47N 105 56 E
Ma'adaba, Jordan ... **74 E4** 30 43N 35 47 E
Maamba, Zambia ... **88 B4** 17 17 S 26 28 E
Ma'ān, Jordan .... **74 E4** 30 12N 35 44 E
Ma'ān □, Jordan ... **74 F5** 30 0N 36 0 E
Maanselkä, Finland . **8 C23** 63 52N 28 32 E
Ma'anshan, China .. **59 B12** 31 44N 118 29 E
Maarianhamina, Finland **9 F18** 60 5N 19 55 E
Ma'arrat an Nu'mān,
Syria .... **70 C3** 35 43N 36 43 E
Maas →, Neths. .... **17 C4** 51 45N 4 32 E
Maaseik, Belgium ... **17 C5** 51 6N 5 45 E
Maasin, Phil. ...... **63 B6** 10 8N 124 50 E
Maastricht, Neths. .. **17 D5** 50 50N 5 40 E
Maave, Mozam. .... **89 C5** 21 4 S 34 47 E
Mababe Depression,
Botswana .... **88 B3** 18 50 S 24 15 E
Mabalane, Mozam. .. **89 C5** 23 37 S 32 31 E
Mabel L., Canada ... **102 C5** 50 35N 118 43W
Mabenge, Dem. Rep. of
the Congo .... **86 B1** 4 15N 24 12 E

Maberly, Canada **117 B8** 44 50N 76 32W
Mabian, China ..... **58 C4** 28 47N 103 37 E
Mabil, Ethiopia .... **81 E4** 10 26N 36 52 E
Mablethorpe, U.K. .. **14 D8** 53 20N 0 15 E
Mably, France ..... **19 F11** 46 5N 4 4 E
Maboma, Dem. Rep. of
the Congo .... **86 B2** 2 30N 28 10 E
Mabonto, S. Leone .. **82 D2** 8 53N 11 50W
Mabrouk, Mali **83 B4** 19 29N 1 15W
Mabuasehube △,
Botswana .... **88 D3** 25 5 S 21 10 E
Mac Bac, Vietnam .. **65 H6** 9 46N 106 7 E
Macachín, Argentina . **126 D3** 37 10 S 63 43W
Macaé, Brazil ..... **127 A7** 22 20 S 41 43W
Macael, Spain **39 H2** 37 20N 2 18W
McAlester, U.S.A. .. **113 H7** 34 56N 95 46W
McAllen, U.S.A. ... **113 M5** 26 12N 98 14W
MacAlpine L., Canada **100 B9** 66 32N 102 45W
Macamic, Canada ... **104 C4** 48 45N 79 0W
Macao = Macau, China **59 F9** 22 12N 113 33 E
Macão, Portugal ... **37 F3** 39 35N 7 59W
Macapá, Brazil **125 C8** 0 5N 51 4W
Macarao △, Venezuela **121 D6** 10 22N 67 7W
McArthur →, Australia **94 B2** 15 54 S 136 40 E
McArthur, Port,
Australia ...... **94 B2** 16 4 S 136 23 E
Macau, Brazil ..... **125 E11** 5 15 S 36 40W
Macau, China ..... **59 F9** 22 12N 113 33 E
McBride, Canada ... **102 C4** 53 20N 120 19W
McCall, U.S.A. **108 D5** 44 55N 116 6W
McCamey, U.S.A. ... **113 K3** 31 8N 102 14W
McCammon, U.S.A. . **108 E7** 42 39N 112 12W
McCauley I., Canada . **102 C2** 53 40N 130 15W
McCleary, U.S.A. ... **110 C3** 47 3N 123 16W
Macclenny, U.S.A. .. **115 K4** 30 17N 82 7W
Macclesfield, U.K. .. **14 D5** 53 15N 2 8W
M'Clintock Chan.,
Canada **100 A9** 72 0N 102 0W
McClintock Ra.,
Australia ...... **92 C4** 18 44 S 127 38 E
McCloud, U.S.A. ... **108 F2** 41 15N 122 8W
McCluer I., Australia . **92 B5** 11 5 S 133 0 E
McClure, U.S.A. ... **116 F7** 40 42N 77 19W
McClure, L., U.S.A. . **110 H6** 37 35N 120 16W
M'Clure Str., Canada . **98 B7** 75 0N 119 0W
McClusky, U.S.A. ... **112 B4** 47 29N 100 27W
McComb, U.S.A. ... **113 K9** 31 15N 90 27W
McConaughy, L., U.S.A. **112 E4** 41 14N 101 40W
McCook, U.S.A. **112 E4** 40 12N 100 38W
McCreary, Canada .. **103 C9** 50 47N 99 29W
McCullough Mt., U.S.A. **111 K11** 35 35N 115 13W
McCusker →, Canada . **103 B7** 55 32N 108 39W
McDame, Canada ... **102 B3** 59 44N 129 57W
McDermitt, U.S.A. .. **108 F5** 41 59N 117 43W
McDonald, U.S.A. .. **116 F4** 40 22N 80 14W
Macdonald, L., Australia **92 D4** 23 30 S 129 0 E
McDonald Is., Ind. Oc. **3 G13** 53 0 S 73 0 E
MacDonnell Ranges,
Australia ...... **92 D5** 23 40 S 133 0 E
MacDowell L., Canada **104 B1** 52 15 S 92 45W
Macduff, U.K. **13 D6** 57 40N 2 31W
Maceda, Spain **36 C3** 42 16N 7 39W
Macedonia, U.S.A. .. **116 E3** 41 19N 81 31W
Macedonia ■, Europe . **44 E5** 41 53N 21 40 E
Maceió, Brazil ..... **125 E11** 9 40 S 35 41W
Maceira, Portugal .. **36 F2** 39 41N 8 55W
Macenta, Guinea ... **82 D3** 8 35N 9 32W
Macerata, Italy .... **41 E10** 43 18N 13 27 E
McFarland, U.S.A. .. **111 K7** 35 41N 119 14W
McFarlane →, Canada **103 B7** 59 12N 107 58W
Macfarlane, L., Australia **95 E2** 32 0 S 136 40 E
McGehee, U.S.A. ... **113 J9** 33 38N 91 24W
McGill, U.S.A. **108 G6** 39 23N 114 47W
Macgillycuddy's Reeks,
Ireland **12 E2** 51 58N 9 45W
McGraw, U.S.A. ... **117 D8** 42 36N 76 8W
McGregor, U.S.A. .. **112 D9** 43 1N 91 11W
McGregor Ra., Australia **95 D3** 27 0 S 142 45 E
MacGuire, Mt., Australia **94 J6** 20 18 S 148 23 E
Mach, Pakistan .... **66 E5** 29 50N 67 20 E
Māch Kowr, Iran ... **71 E9** 25 48N 61 28 E
Machado = Jiparaná →,
Brazil .... **124 E6** 8 3 S 62 52W
Machagai, Argentina . **126 B3** 26 56 S 60 2W
Machakos, Kenya ... **86 C4** 1 30 S 37 15 E
Machala, Ecuador .. **124 D3** 3 20 S 79 57W
Machanga, Mozam. .. **89 C6** 20 59 S 35 0 E
Machattie, L., Australia **94 C2** 24 50 S 139 48 E
Machault, France ... **19 C11** 49 21N 4 29 E
Machava, Mozam. .. **89 D5** 25 54 S 32 28 E
Machece, Mozam. .. **87 F4** 19 15 S 35 32 E
Machecoul, France . **18 F5** 47 0N 1 49W
Macheke, Zimbabwe . **89 B5** 18 5 S 31 51 E
Macheng, China ... **59 B10** 31 12N 115 2 E
Machero, Spain **37 F6** 39 21N 4 20W
Machhu →, India ... **68 H4** 23 6N 70 46 E
Machias, Maine, U.S.A. **115 C12** 44 43N 67 28W
Machias, N.Y., U.S.A. **116 D6** 42 25N 78 30W
Machichi →, Canada . **103 B10** 57 3N 92 6W
Machico, Madeira .. **48 D3** 32 43N 16 44W
Machilipatnam, India **67 L12** 16 12N 81 8 E
Machiques, Venezuela **124 A4** 10 4N 72 34W
Machupicchu, Peru .. **124 F4** 13 8 S 72 30W
Machynlleth, U.K. .. **15 E4** 52 35N 3 50W
Macia, Mozam. .... **89 D5** 25 2 S 33 8 E
Maciejowice, Poland . **31 G8** 51 36N 21 26 E
McIlwraith Ra.,
Australia ...... **94 A3** 13 50 S 143 20 E
Măcin, Romania ... **29 E13** 45 16N 28 8 E
Macina, Mali **82 C4** 14 50N 5 0W
McInnes L., Canada . **103 C10** 52 13N 93 45W
McIntosh, U.S.A. ... **112 C4** 45 55N 101 21W
McIntosh L., Canada . **103 B8** 55 45N 105 0W
Macintosh Ra., Australia **93 E4** 27 39 S 125 32 E
Macintyre →, Australia **95 D5** 28 37 S 150 47 E
Macizo Galaico, Spain **36 C3** 42 30N 7 30W
Mackay, Australia .. **94 K7** 21 8 S 149 11 E
Mackay, U.S.A. **108 E7** 43 55N 113 37W
MacKay →, Canada . **102 B6** 57 10N 111 38W
McKay Ra., Australia **92 D3** 23 0 S 122 30 E
McKeesport, U.S.A. . **116 F5** 40 21N 79 52W
McKellar, Canada .. **116 A5** 45 30N 79 55W
McKenna, U.S.A. ... **110 D4** 46 56N 122 33W
McKenzie, U.S.A. .. **115 G1** 36 8N 88 31W
Mackenzie, Canada . **102 B4** 55 20N 123 5W
Mackenzie →, Canada **100 B6** 69 10N 134 20W
Mackenzie →, Australia **94 C4** 23 38 S 149 46 E
Mackenzie Bay, Canada **4 B1** 69 0N 137 30W
Mackenzie City =
Linden, Guyana .. **124 B7** 6 0N 58 10W
Mackenzie Mts., Canada **100 B6** 64 0N 130 0W
Mackinaw City, U.S.A. **114 C3** 45 47N 84 44W
McKinlay, Australia . **94 C3** 21 16 S 141 18 E
McKinlay →, Australia **94 C3** 20 50 S 141 28 E
McKinley, Mt., U.S.A. **100 B4** 63 4N 151 0W

McKinley Sea, Arctic . **4 A7** 82 0N 0 0W
McKinney, U.S.A. ... **113 J6** 33 12N 96 37W
Mackinnon Road, Kenya **86 C4** 3 40 S 39 1 E
McKittrick, U.S.A. .. **111 K7** 35 18N 119 37W
Macklin, Canada ... **103 C7** 52 20N 109 56W
Macksville, Australia . **95 E5** 30 40 S 152 56 E
McLaughlin, U.S.A. . **112 C4** 45 49N 100 49W
Maclean, Australia .. **95 D5** 29 26 S 153 16 E
McLean, U.S.A. ... **113 H4** 35 14N 100 36W
McLeansboro, U.S.A. **112 F10** 38 6N 88 32W
Maclear, S. Africa .. **89 E4** 31 2 S 28 23 E
Maclear, C., Malawi . **87 E3** 13 58 S 34 49 E
Macleay →, Australia **95 E5** 30 56 S 153 0 E
McLennan, Canada .. **102 B5** 55 42N 116 50W
MacLeod →, Canada . **102 C5** 54 9N 115 44W
MacLeod, B., Canada **103 A7** 62 53N 110 0W
MacLeod, L., Australia **93 D1** 24 9 S 113 47 E
MacLeod Lake, Canada **102 C4** 54 58N 123 0W
McLoughlin, Mt., U.S.A. **108 E2** 42 27N 122 19W
McMechen, U.S.A. .. **116 G4** 39 57N 80 44W
McMinnville, Oreg.,
U.S.A. **108 D2** 45 13N 123 12W
McMinnville, Tenn.,
U.S.A. **115 H3** 35 41N 85 46W
McMurdo Sd.,
Antarctica ...... **5 D11** 77 0 S 170 0 E
McMurray = Fort
McMurray, Canada . **102 B6** 56 44N 111 7W
McMurray, U.S.A. .. **110 B4** 48 19N 122 14W
Macodoene, Mozam. . **89 C6** 23 32 S 35 5 E
Macomb, U.S.A. ... **112 E9** 40 27N 90 40W
Macomer, Italy .... **42 B1** 40 16N 8 47 E
Mâcon, France .... **19 F11** 46 19N 4 50 E
Macon, Ga., U.S.A. . **115 J4** 32 51N 83 38W
Macon, Miss., U.S.A. **115 J1** 33 6N 88 34W
Macon, Mo., U.S.A. . **112 F8** 39 44N 92 28W
Macossa, Mozam. .. **87 F3** 17 55 S 33 56 E
Macoun L., Canada . **103 B8** 56 32N 103 40W
Macovane, Mozam. .. **89 C6** 21 30 S 35 2 E
McPherson, U.S.A. .. **112 F6** 38 22N 97 40W
McPherson Pk., U.S.A. **111 L7** 34 53N 119 53W
McPherson Ra.,
Australia ...... **95 D5** 28 15 S 153 15 E
Macquarie →, Australia **95 E4** 30 7 S 147 24 E
Macquarie Harbour,
Australia ...... **95 D5** 42 15 S 145 23 E
Macquarie Is., Pac. Oc. **96 N7** 54 36 S 158 55 E
MacRobertson Land,
Antarctica ...... **5 D6** 71 0 S 64 0 E
Macroom, Ireland .. **12 E3** 51 54N 8 57W
MacTier, Canada ... **116 A5** 45 9N 79 46W
Macubela, Mozam. .. **87 F4** 16 53 S 37 49 E
Macugnaga, Italy ... **40 C5** 45 58N 7 58 E
Macuira △, Colombia **121 D5** 12 9N 71 21W
Macuiza, Mozam. ... **87 F3** 18 7 S 34 29 E
Macumba, The →,
Australia ...... **95 D2** 27 52 S 137 12 E
Macuro, Venezuela .. **125 K15** 10 42N 61 55W
Macusani, Peru .... **124 F4** 14 4 S 70 29W
Macuse, Mozam. ... **87 F4** 17 45 S 37 10 E
Macuspana, Mexico . **119 D6** 17 46N 92 36W
Macusse, Angola ... **88 B3** 17 48 S 20 23 E
Mada →, Nigeria ... **83 D6** 7 59N 7 55 E
Ma'dabā □, Jordan .. **74 D4** 31 43N 35 47 E
Madadeni, S. Africa . **89 D5** 27 43 S 30 3 E
Madagali, Nigeria .. **83 C7** 10 56N 13 33 E
Madagascar ■, Africa **89 C8** 20 0 S 47 0 E
Madā'in Sālih, Si. Arabia **70 E3** 26 46N 37 57 E
Madama, Niger .... **79 D8** 22 0N 13 40 E
Madame, I., Canada . **105 C7** 45 30N 60 58W
Madan, Bulgaria ... **45 E8** 41 30N 24 57 E
Madaoua, Niger ... **83 C6** 14 5N 6 27 E
Madara, Nigeria ... **83 C7** 11 45N 10 35 E
Madaripur, Bangla. . **67 H17** 23 19N 90 15 E
Madauk, Burma .... **67 L20** 17 56N 96 52 E
Madawaska, Canada . **116 A7** 45 30N 78 0W
Madawaska →, Canada **116 A8** 45 27N 76 21W
Madaya, Burma .... **67 H20** 22 12N 96 10 E
Madbar, Sudan .... **81 F3** 6 17N 30 45 E
Maddalena, Italy ... **42 A2** 41 16N 9 23 E
Maddaloni, Italy ... **43 A7** 41 2N 14 23 E
Madeira, Atl. Oc. ... **48 D3** 32 50N 17 0W
Madeira →, Brazil .. **124 D7** 3 22 S 58 45W
Madeleine, Îs. de la,
Canada **105 C7** 47 30N 61 40W
Maden, Turkey .... **73 C8** 38 23N 39 40 E
Madera, Mexico ... **118 B3** 29 12N 108 7W
Madera, Calif., U.S.A. **110 J6** 36 57N 120 3W
Madera, Pa., U.S.A. . **116 F6** 40 49N 78 26W
Madha, India ..... **66 F9** 18 0N 75 55 E
Madhavpur, India .. **68 J3** 21 15N 69 58 E
Madhepura, India .. **69 F12** 26 11N 86 23 E
Madhubani, India .. **69 F12** 26 21N 86 7 E
Madhupur, India ... **69 G12** 24 16N 86 39 E
Madhya Pradesh □,
India .... **68 H8** 22 50N 78 0 E
Madidi →, Bolivia .. **124 F5** 12 32 S 66 52W
Madikeri, India .... **66 N9** 12 30N 75 45 E
Madikwe △, S. Africa **89 D5** 27 38 S 32 15 E
Madill, U.S.A. **113 H6** 34 6N 96 46W
Madimba, Dem. Rep. of
the Congo .... **84 E3** 4 58 S 15 5 E
Ma'din, Syria ..... **70 C3** 35 45N 39 36 E
Madina, Mali **82 C3** 13 8N 8 50W
Madinani, Ivory C. .. **82 D3** 9 37N 6 57W
Madingou, Congo .. **84 E2** 4 10 S 13 33 E
Madirovalo, Madag. . **89 B8** 16 26 S 46 32 E
Madison, Calif., U.S.A. **110 G5** 38 41N 121 59W
Madison, Fla., U.S.A. **115 K4** 30 28N 83 25W
Madison, Ind., U.S.A. **114 F3** 38 44N 85 23W
Madison, Nebr., U.S.A. **112 E6** 41 50N 97 27W
Madison, Ohio, U.S.A. **116 E3** 41 46N 81 3W
Madison, S. Dak., U.S.A. **112 D6** 44 0N 97 7W
Madison, Wis., U.S.A. **112 D10** 43 4N 89 24W
Madison →, U.S.A. . **108 D8** 45 56N 111 31W
Madison Heights, U.S.A. **114 G6** 37 25N 79 8W
Madisonville, Ky.,
U.S.A. **114 G2** 37 20N 87 30W
Madisonville, Tex.,
U.S.A. **113 K7** 30 57N 95 55W
Madista, Botswana .. **88 C4** 21 15 S 25 6 E
Madiun, Indonesia .. **63 G14** 7 38 S 111 32 E
Madoc, Canada **116 B7** 44 30N 77 28W
Madol, Sudan ..... **81 F2** 9 3N 27 45 E
Madon →, France .. **19 D13** 48 36N 6 6 E
Madona, Latvia .... **9 H22** 56 53N 26 5 E
Madonie, Italy ..... **42 E6** 37 50N 13 50 E
Madonna di Campíglio,
Italy .... **40 B7** 46 14N 10 49 E
Madra Dağı, Turkey . **47 B9** 39 23N 27 12 E
Madrakah, Ra's al,
Oman .... **75 D6** 19 0N 57 50 E
Madras = Chennai, India **66 N12** 13 8N 80 19 E
Madras = Tamil
Nadu □, India ... **66 P10** 11 0N 77 0 E
Madras, U.S.A. **108 D3** 44 38N 121 8W
Madre, Laguna, U.S.A. **113 M6** 27 0N 97 30W

Madre, Sierra, Phil. . **61 C5** 17 0N 122 0 E
Madre de Dios →,
Bolivia .... **124 F5** 10 59 S 66 8W
Madre de Dios, I., Chile **128 G1** 50 20 S 75 10W
Madre del Sur, Sierra,
Mexico **119 D5** 17 30N 100 0W
Madre Occidental,
Sierra, Mexico ... **118 B3** 27 0N 107 0W
Madre Oriental, Sierra,
Mexico **118 C5** 25 0N 100 0W
Madri, India ...... **68 G5** 24 16N 73 32 E
Madrid, Spain **36 E7** 40 25N 3 45W
Madrid □, Spain ... **117 B9** 44 45N 75 8W
Madrid □, Spain ... **36 E7** 40 30N 3 45W
Madrid Barajas ✈
(MAD), Spain ... **36 E7** 40 26N 3 34W
Madridejos, Spain .. **37 F7** 39 28N 3 33W
Madrigal de las Altas
Torres, Spain ... **36 D6** 41 5N 5 0W
Madrona, Sierra, Spain **37 G6** 38 27N 4 16W
Madroñera, Spain .. **37 F5** 39 26N 5 42W
Madu, Sudan ..... **81 E2** 14 37N 26 4 E
Madura, Australia .. **93 F4** 31 55 S 127 0 E
Madura, Indonesia .. **63 G15** 7 30 S 114 0 E
Madura, Selat, Indonesia **63 G15** 7 30 S 113 20 E
Madurai, India .... **66 Q11** 9 55N 78 10 E
Madurantakam, India **66 N11** 12 30N 79 50 E
Madzhalis, Russia .. **35 J8** 42 9N 47 47 E
Mae Chan, Thailand . **64 B2** 20 9N 99 52 E
Mae Hong Son,
Thailand .... **64 C2** 19 16N 97 56 E
Mae Khlong →,
Thailand .... **64 F3** 13 24N 100 0 E
Mae Phrik, Thailand . **64 D2** 17 27N 99 7 E
Mae Ping △, Thailand **64 D2** 17 37N 98 51 E
Mae Ramat, Thailand **64 D2** 16 58N 98 31 E
Mae Rim, Thailand . **64 C2** 18 54N 98 57 E
Mae Sot, Thailand .. **64 D2** 16 43N 98 34 E
Mae Suai, Thailand . **58 H2** 19 39N 99 33 E
Mae Tha, Thailand . **64 C2** 18 28N 99 8 E
Mae Wong △, Thailand **64 E2** 15 54N 99 12 E
Mae Yom △, Thailand **58 H3** 18 43N 100 15 E
Maebashi, Japan ... **55 F9** 36 24N 139 4 E
Maella, Spain ..... **38 D5** 41 8N 0 7 E
Maesteg, U.K. **15 F4** 51 36N 3 40W
Maestra, Sierra, Cuba **120 B4** 20 15N 77 0W
Maevatanana, Madag. **89 B8** 16 56 S 46 49 E
Mafeking = Mafikeng,
S. Africa .... **88 D4** 25 50 S 25 38 E
Mafeking, Canada .. **103 C8** 52 40N 101 10W
Maféré, Ivory C. ... **82 D4** 5 30N 3 2W
Mafeteng, Lesotho .. **88 D4** 29 51 S 27 15 E
Maffra, Australia ... **95 F4** 37 53 S 146 58 E
Mafia I., Tanzania .. **86 D4** 7 45 S 39 50 E
Mafikeng, S. Africa . **88 D4** 25 50 S 25 38 E
Mafra, Brazil ..... **127 B6** 26 10 S 49 55W
Mafra, Portugal ... **37 G1** 38 55N 9 20W
Mafungabusi Plateau,
Zimbabwe ...... **87 F2** 18 30 S 29 8 E
Magadan, Russia ... **53 D16** 59 38N 150 50 E
Magadi, Kenya .... **86 C4** 1 54 S 36 19 E
Magadi, L., Kenya .. **86 C4** 1 54 S 36 19 E
Magaliesburg, S. Africa **89 D4** 26 0 S 27 32 E
Magallanes, Estrecho de,
Chile .... **128 G2** 52 30 S 75 0W
Magaluf, Spain .... **38 B9** 39 29N 2 32 E
Maganguè, Colombia **124 B4** 9 14N 74 45W
Magaria, Niger .... **83 C6** 13 4N 9 5 E
Magburaka, S. Leone **82 D2** 8 47N 12 0W
Magdalen Is. =
Madeleine, Îs. de la,
Canada **105 C7** 47 30N 61 40W
Magdalena, Argentina **126 D4** 35 5 S 57 30W
Magdalena, Bolivia . **124 F6** 13 13 S 63 57W
Magdalena, Mexico . **118 A2** 30 50N 112 0W
Magdalena, U.S.A. . **109 J10** 34 7N 107 15W
Magdalena □,
Colombia **124 A4** 11 6N 74 51W
Magdalena →, Mexico **118 A2** 30 40N 112 25W
Magdalena, B., Mexico **118 C2** 24 30N 112 10W
Magdalena, Llano de la,
Mexico **118 C2** 25 0N 111 30W
Magdeburg, Germany **24 C7** 52 7N 11 38 E
Magdelaine Cays,
Australia ...... **94 B5** 16 33 S 150 18 E
Magdub, Sudan ... **81 E3** 13 42N 25 5 E
Magee, U.S.A. **113 K10** 31 52N 89 44W
Magelang, Indonesia **63 G14** 7 29 S 110 13 E
Magellan's Str. =
Magallanes, Estrecho
de, Chile ...... **128 G2** 52 30 S 75 0W
Magenta, Italy .... **40 C5** 45 28N 8 53 E
Magenta, L., Australia **93 F2** 33 30 S 119 2 E
Magerøya, Norway . **8 A21** 71 3N 25 40 E
Maggia →, Switz. .. **25 J4** 46 18N 8 36 E
Maggiorasca, Mte., Italy **40 D6** 44 33N 9 29 E
Maggiore, Lago, Italy **40 D5** 45 57N 8 39 E
Maggotty, Jamaica .. **120 a** 18 9N 77 46W
Maghâgha, Egypt .. **80 J7** 28 38N 30 50 E
Maghama, Mauritania **82 B2** 15 32N 12 57W
Magherafelt, U.K. .. **12 B5** 54 45N 6 37W
Maghreb, N. Afr. ... **78 B5** 32 0N 4 0 E
Magione, Italy .... **41 E9** 43 10N 12 12 E
Magistralnyy, Russia **53 D11** 56 16N 107 36 E
Maglaj, Bos.-H. .... **28 F3** 44 33N 18 7 E
Magliano in Toscana,
Italy .... **41 F8** 42 36N 11 17 E
Máglie, Italy ...... **43 B11** 40 7N 18 18 E
Magnac-Laval, France **20 B5** 46 13N 1 11 E
Magnetic Pole (North),
Canada **4 A2** 88 30N 107 0W
Magnetic Pole (South),
Antarctica ...... **5 C9** 64 8 S 138 8 E
Magnísia □, Greece . **46 B4** 39 15N 23 0 E
Magnitogorsk, Russia **52 D6** 53 27N 59 4 E
Magnolia, Ark., U.S.A. **113 J8** 33 16N 93 14W
Magnolia, Miss., U.S.A. **113 K9** 31 9N 90 28W
Magny-en-Vexin, France **19 C8** 49 9N 1 47 E
Mago △, Ethiopia .. **81 F4** 5 40N 36 18 E
Magog, Canada **117 A12** 45 18N 72 9W
Magoro, Uganda ... **86 B3** 1 45N 34 12 E
Magosa = Famagusta,
Cyprus .... **49 D12** 35 8N 33 55 E
Magoúladhes, Greece **49 A3** 39 45N 19 42 E
Magoye, Zambia ... **87 F2** 16 1 S 27 30 E
Magozal, Mexico ... **119 C5** 21 34N 97 59W
Magpie, L., Canada . **105 B7** 51 0N 64 41W
Magrath, Canada ... **102 D6** 49 25N 112 50W
Magre →, Spain ... **39 F4** 39 11N 0 25W
Magrur, Sudan .... **81 E3** 14 1N 30 27 E
Magrur, Wadi →, Sudan **81 D2** 16 5N 26 30 E
Magta Lahjar,
Mauritania **82 B2** 17 28N 13 17W
Maguan, China .... **58 F5** 23 0N 104 21 E
Maguarinho, C., Brazil **125 D9** 0 15 S 48 30W
Magude, Mozam. ... **89 D5** 25 2 S 32 40 E
Magurski △, Poland . **31 J8** 49 30N 21 30 E

Mağusa = Famagusta, Cyprus 49 D12 35 8N 33 55 E
Maguse L., Canada 103 A9 61 37N 95 10W
Maguse Pt., Canada 103 A10 61 20N 93 50W
Magvana, Nigeria 68 H3 23 13N 69 22 E
Magwe, Burma 67 J19 20 10N 95 0 E
Magwe, Sudan 81 G3 4 8N 32 17 E
Maha Sarakham, Thailand 64 D4 16 12N 103 16 E
Mahābād, Iran 70 B5 36 50N 45 45 E
Mahabharat Lekh, Nepal 69 E10 28 30N 82 0 E
Mahabo, Madag. 89 C7 20 23 S 44 40 E
Mahadeo Hills, India 69 H8 22 20N 78 30 E
Mahaffey, U.S.A. 116 F6 40 53N 78 44W
Mahagi, Dem. Rep. of the Congo 86 B3 2 20N 31 0 E
Mahajamba →, Madag. 89 B8 15 33 S 47 8 E
Mahajamba, Helodranon' i, Madag. 89 B8 15 24 S 47 5 E
Mahajan, India 68 E5 28 48N 73 56 E
Mahajanga, Madag. 89 B8 15 40 S 46 25 E
Mahajanga □, Madag. 89 B8 17 0 S 47 0 E
Mahajilo →, Madag. 89 B8 19 42 S 45 22 E
Mahakam →, Indonesia 62 E5 0 35 S 117 17 E
Mahalapye, Botswana 88 C4 23 1 S 26 51 E
Mahale Mts., Tanzania 86 D3 6 20 S 30 0 E
Mahale Mts. △, Tanzania 86 D2 6 10 S 29 50 E
Mahallāt, Iran 71 C6 33 55N 50 30 E
Māhān, Iran 71 D8 30 5N 57 18 E
Mahan →, India 69 H10 23 30N 82 50 E
Mahanadi →, India 67 J15 20 20N 86 25 E
Mahananda →, India 69 G12 25 12N 87 52 E
Mahanoro, Madag. 89 B8 19 54 S 48 48 E
Mahanoy City, U.S.A. 117 F8 40 49N 76 9W
Maharashtra □, India 66 J9 20 30N 75 30 E
Mahasham, W. →, Egypt 74 E3 30 15N 34 10 E
Mahasoa, Madag. 89 C8 22 12 S 46 6 E
Mahasolo, Madag. 89 B8 19 7 S 46 22 E
Mahattat ash Shīdīyah, Jordan 74 F4 29 55N 35 55 E
Mahattat 'Unayzah, Jordan 74 E4 30 30N 35 47 E
Mahavavy →, Madag. 89 B8 15 57 S 45 54 E
Mahaxay, Laos 64 D5 17 22N 105 12 E
Mahbubnagar, India 66 L10 16 45N 77 59 E
Mahdah, Oman 71 E7 24 24N 55 59 E
Mahdia, Tunisia 79 A8 35 28N 11 0 E
Mahe, India 69 C8 33 10N 78 32 E
Mahendragarh, India 68 E7 28 17N 76 14 E
Mahenge, Tanzania 87 D4 8 45 S 36 41 E
Maheno, N.Z. 91 L3 45 10 S 170 50 E
Mahesana, India 68 H5 23 39N 72 26 E
Maheshwar, India 68 H6 22 11N 75 35 E
Mahgawan, India 69 F8 26 29N 78 37 E
Mahi →, India 68 H5 22 15N 72 55 E
Mahia Pen., N.Z. 91 H6 39 9 S 177 55 E
Mahilyow, Belarus 32 F6 53 55N 30 18 E
Mahinerangi, L., N.Z. 91 L2 45 50 S 169 56 E
Mahmiya, Sudan 81 D3 17 12N 33 43 E
Mahmud Kot, Pakistan 68 D4 30 16N 71 0 E
Mahmudia, Romania 29 E14 45 5N 29 5 E
Mahmudiye, Turkey 47 B12 39 48N 30 15 E
Mahmutbey, Turkey 45 E12 41 3N 28 49 E
Mahnomen, U.S.A. 112 B7 47 19N 95 58W
Mahoba, India 69 G8 25 15N 79 55 E
Mahón = Maó, Spain 48 B11 39 53N 4 16 E
Mahon, Menorca ✕ (MAH), Spain 38 F9 39 50N 4 16 E
Mahone Bay, Canada 105 D7 44 30N 64 20W
Mahopac, U.S.A. 117 E11 41 22N 73 45W
Mahuta, Nigeria 83 C5 11 32N 4 58 E
Mahuva, India 68 J4 21 5N 71 48 E
Mahya Dağı, Turkey 45 E11 41 47N 27 36 E
Mai-Ndombe, L., Dem. Rep. of the Congo 84 E3 2 0 S 18 20 E
Mai-Sai, Thailand 58 G2 20 20N 99 55 E
Mai Thon, Ko, Thailand 65 a 7 40N 98 28 E
Maia, Portugal 36 D2 41 14N 8 37W
Maia, Spain 38 B3 43 12N 1 29W
Maials, Spain 38 D5 41 22N 0 30 E
Maîche, France 19 E13 47 16N 6 48 E
Maicurú →, Brazil 125 D8 2 14 S 54 17W
Máida, Italy 43 D9 38 51N 16 22 E
Maidan Khula, Afghan. 68 C3 33 36N 69 50 E
Maidenhead, U.K. 15 F7 51 31N 0 42W
Maidstone, Canada 103 C7 53 5N 109 20W
Maidstone, U.K. 15 F8 51 16N 0 32 E
Maiduguri, Nigeria 83 C7 12 0N 13 20 E
Maiella △, Italy 41 F11 42 5N 14 5 E
Măieruş, Romania 29 E10 45 53N 25 31 E
Maigatari, Nigeria 83 C6 12 46N 9 27 E
Maignelay Montigny, France 19 C9 49 32N 2 30 E
Maigo, Phil. 61 G5 8 10N 123 57 E
Maigudo, Ethiopia 81 F4 7 30N 37 8 E
Maihar, India 69 G9 24 16N 80 45 E
Maijdi, Bangla. 67 H17 22 48N 91 10 E
Maikala Ra., India 67 J12 22 0N 81 0 E
Maiko △, Dem. Rep. of the Congo 86 C2 0 30 S 27 50 E
Mailani, India 69 E9 28 17N 80 21 E
Maillezais, France 20 B3 46 22N 0 45W
Mailsi, Pakistan 68 E5 29 48N 72 15 E
Main →, Germany 25 F4 50 0N 8 18 E
Main →, U.K. 12 B5 54 48N 6 18W
Main Range △, Australia 95 D5 28 11 S 152 27 E
Main Ridge, Trin. & Tob. 125 J16 11 16N 60 40W
Mainburg, Germany 25 G7 48 38N 11 47 E
Maine, France 18 D6 48 20N 0 15 E
Maine □, U.S.A. 115 C11 45 20N 69 0W
Maine →, Ireland 12 D2 52 9N 9 45W
Maine-et-Loire □, France 18 E6 47 31N 0 30W
Maïne-Soroa, Niger 83 C7 13 13N 12 2 E
Maingkwan, Burma 67 F20 26 15N 96 37 E
Mainit, L., Phil. 61 G6 9 31N 125 30 E
Mainland, Orkney, U.K. 13 C5 58 59N 3 8W
Mainland, Shet., U.K. 13 A7 60 15N 1 22W
Mainoru, Australia 94 A1 14 0 S 134 6 E
Mainpuri, India 69 F8 27 18N 79 4 E
Maintal, Germany 25 E4 50 1N 8 52 E
Maintenon, France 19 D8 48 35N 1 35 E
Maintirano, Madag. 89 B7 18 3 S 44 1 E
Mainz, Germany 25 E4 50 1N 8 14 E
Maipú, Argentina 126 D4 36 52 S 57 50W
Maiquetía, Venezuela 124 A5 10 36N 66 57W
Máira →, Italy 40 D4 44 49N 7 38 E
Mairabari, India 67 F18 26 30N 92 22 E
Maisí, Cuba 121 B5 20 17N 74 9W
Maisí, Pta. de, Cuba 121 B5 20 10N 74 10W
Maitland, N.S.W., Australia 95 E5 32 33 S 151 36 E

Maitland, S. Austral., Australia 95 E2 34 23 S 137 40 E
Maitland →, Canada 116 C3 43 45N 81 43W
Maitri, Antarctica 5 D3 70 0 S 3 0W
Maiyema, Nigeria 83 C5 12 5N 4 25 E
Maiyuan, China 59 E11 25 34N 117 28 E
Maíz, Is. del, Nic. 120 D3 12 15N 83 4W
Maizuru, Japan 55 G7 35 25N 135 22 E
Majalengka, Indonesia 63 G13 6 50 S 108 13 E
Majene, Indonesia 63 E5 3 38 S 118 57 E
Majete △, Malawi 87 F3 15 54 S 34 34 E
Majevica, Bos.-H. 28 F3 44 45N 18 50 E
Maji, Ethiopia 81 F4 6 12N 35 30 E
Majiang, China 58 D6 26 28N 107 32 E
Majorca = Mallorca, Spain 48 B10 39 30N 3 0 E
Maka, Senegal 82 C2 13 40N 14 10W
Makaha, Zimbabwe 89 B5 17 20 S 32 39 E
Makak, Cameroon 83 E7 3 36N 11 0 E
Makalamabedi, Botswana 88 C3 20 19 S 23 51 E
Makale, Indonesia 63 E5 3 6 S 119 51 E
Makamba, Burundi 86 C2 4 8 S 29 49 E
Makari, Cameroon 83 C7 12 35N 10 27 E
Makarikari = Makgadikgadi Salt Pans, Botswana 88 C4 20 40 S 25 45 E
Makarov Basin, Arctic 4 A 87 0N 150 0W
Makarovo, Russia 53 D11 57 40N 107 45 E
Makarska, Croatia 41 E14 43 20N 17 2 E
Makaryev, Russia 34 B6 57 52N 43 50 E
Makasar = Ujung Pandang, Indonesia 63 F5 5 10 S 119 20 E
Makasar, Selat, Indonesia 63 E5 1 0 S 118 20 E
Makasar, Str. of = Makasar, Selat, Indonesia 63 E5 0 5 S 118 20 E
Makat, Kazakhstan 52 E6 47 39N 53 19 E
Makedonija = Macedonia ■, Europe 44 E5 41 53N 21 40 E
Makeni, S. Leone 82 D2 8 55N 12 5W
Makeyevka = Makiyivka, Ukraine 33 H9 48 0N 38 0 E
Makgadikgadi △, Botswana 88 C3 20 27 S 24 47 E
Makgadikgadi Salt Pans, Botswana 88 C4 20 40 S 25 45 E
Makhachkala, Russia 35 J8 43 0N 47 30 E
Makhado = Louis Trichardt, S. Africa 89 C4 23 1 S 29 43 E
Makharadze = Ozurgeti, Georgia 35 K5 41 55N 42 2 E
Makhfar al Buṣayyah, Iraq 70 D5 30 0N 46 10 E
Makhmūr, Iraq 70 C4 35 46N 43 35 E
Makian, Indonesia 63 D7 0 20N 127 20 E
Makindu, Kenya 86 C4 2 18 S 37 50 E
Makinsk, Kazakhstan 52 D8 52 37N 70 26 E
Makiv, Ukraine 29 B11 48 48N 26 43 E
Makiyivka, Ukraine 33 H9 48 0N 38 0 E
Makkah, Si. Arabia 75 C2 21 30N 39 54 E
Makkovik, Canada 105 A8 55 10N 59 10W
Makó, Hungary 28 D5 46 14N 20 33 E
Mako, Senegal 82 C2 12 52N 12 20W
Makokou, Gabon 84 D2 0 40N 12 50 E
Makongo, Dem. Rep. of the Congo 86 B2 3 25N 26 17 E
Makoro, Dem. Rep. of the Congo 86 B2 3 10N 29 59 E
Maków Mazowiecki, Poland 31 F8 52 52N 21 6 E
Maków Podhalański, Poland 31 J6 49 43N 19 45 E
Makrá, Greece 47 E7 36 15N 25 54 E
Makrai, India 66 H10 22 2N 77 0 E
Makran Coast Range, Pakistan 66 G4 25 40N 64 0 E
Makrana, India 68 F6 27 2N 74 46 E
Makrany, Belarus 31 G11 51 48N 24 7 E
Mákri, Greece 45 F9 40 52N 25 40 E
Makriyialos, Greece 49 D7 35 2N 25 59 E
Makū, Iran 70 B5 39 15N 44 31 E
Makunda, Botswana 88 C3 22 30 S 20 7 E
Makung, Taiwan 59 F12 23 34N 119 34 E
Makurazaki, Japan 55 J5 31 15N 130 20 E
Makurdi, Nigeria 83 D6 7 43N 8 35 E
Makūyeh, Iran 71 D7 29 7N 53 9 E
Makwassie, S. Africa 88 D4 27 17 S 26 0 E
Makwiro, Zimbabwe 89 B5 17 58 S 30 25 E
Mâl, Mauritania 82 B2 16 58N 13 23W
Mal B., Ireland 12 D2 52 50N 9 30W
Mala, Pta., Panama 120 E3 7 28N 80 2W
Mala Belozërka, Ukraine 33 J8 47 12N 34 56 E
Malá Fatra △, Slovak Rep. 27 B12 49 10N 19 0 E
Mala Kapela, Croatia 41 D12 44 45N 15 30 E
Mała Panew →, Poland 31 H4 50 43N 17 54 E
Mala Vyska, Ukraine 33 H6 48 39N 31 36 E
Malabang, Phil. 61 H6 7 36N 124 3 E
Malabar Coast, India 66 P9 11 0N 75 0 E
Malabon, Phil. 61 D4 14 21N 121 0 E
Malabu, Nigeria 83 D7 9 32N 12 48 E
Malacca, Straits of, Indonesia 65 L3 3 0N 101 0 E
Malacky, Slovak Rep. 27 C10 48 27N 17 0 E
Malad City, U.S.A. 108 E7 42 12N 112 15W
Maladzyechna, Belarus 32 E4 54 20N 26 50 E
Málaga, Spain 37 J6 36 43N 4 23W
Málaga □, Spain 37 J6 36 38N 4 58W
Malagarasi, Tanzania 86 D3 5 5 S 30 50 E
Malagarasi →, Tanzania 86 D2 5 12 S 29 47 E
Malagasy Rep. = Madagascar ■, Africa 89 C8 20 0 S 47 0 E
Malagón, Spain 37 F7 39 11N 3 52W
Malagón →, Spain 37 H3 37 35N 7 29W
Malahide, Ireland 12 C5 53 26N 6 9W
Malaimbandy, Madag. 89 C8 20 20 S 45 36 E
Malakal, Sudan 81 F3 9 33N 31 40 E
Malakand, Pakistan 68 B4 34 40N 71 55 E
Malakwal, Pakistan 68 C5 32 34N 73 13 E
Malamala, Indonesia 63 E6 3 21 S 120 55 E
Malanda, Australia 94 B4 17 22 S 145 35 E
Malang, Indonesia 63 G15 7 59 S 112 45 E
Malangen, Norway 8 B18 69 24N 18 37 E
Malanje, Angola 84 F3 9 36 S 16 17 E
Mälaren, Sweden 10 E11 59 30N 17 10 E
Malargüe, Argentina 126 D2 35 32 S 69 30W
Malartic, Canada 104 C4 48 9N 78 9W
Malaryta, Belarus 31 G11 51 50N 24 3 E
Malatya, Turkey 70 B3 38 25N 38 0 E
Malawi ■, Africa 87 E3 11 55 S 34 0 E
Malawi, L. = Nyasa, L., Africa 87 E3 12 30 S 34 30 E
Malay Pen., Asia 65 J3 7 25N 100 0 E

Malaya Belozërka = Mala Belozërka, Ukraine 33 J8 47 12N 34 56 E
Malaya Vishera, Russia 32 C7 58 55N 32 25 E
Malaya Viska = Mala Vyska, Ukraine 33 H6 48 39N 31 36 E
Malaybalay, Phil. 61 G6 8 5N 125 7 E
Malāyer, Iran 71 C6 34 19N 48 51 E
Malaysia ■, Asia 65 K4 5 0N 110 0 E
Malazgirt, Turkey 70 B4 39 10N 42 33 E
Malbaza, Niger 83 C6 13 59N 5 38 E
Malbon, Australia 94 C3 21 5 S 140 17 E
Malbooma, Australia 95 E1 30 41 S 134 11 E
Malbork, Poland 30 D6 54 3N 19 1 E
Malcésine, Italy 40 C7 45 46N 10 48 E
Malchin, Germany 24 B8 53 44N 12 44 E
Malcolm, Australia 93 E3 28 51 S 121 25 E
Malcolm, Pt., Australia 93 F3 33 48 S 123 45 E
Malczyce, Poland 31 G3 51 14N 16 29 E
Maldah, India 69 G13 25 2N 88 9 E
Maldegem, Belgium 17 C3 51 14N 3 26 E
Malden, Mass., U.S.A. 117 D13 42 26N 71 4W
Malden, Mo., U.S.A. 113 G10 36 34N 89 57W
Malden I., Kiribati 97 H12 4 3 S 155 1W
Maldives ■, Ind. Oc. 50 J11 5 0N 73 0 E
Maldon, U.K. 15 F8 51 44N 0 42 E
Maldonado, Uruguay 127 C5 34 59 S 55 0W
Maldonado, Punta, Mexico 119 D5 16 19N 98 35W
Malè, Italy 40 B7 46 21N 10 55 E
Male, Maldives 51 J11 4 0N 73 28 E
Malé Karpaty, Slovak Rep. 27 C10 48 30N 17 20 E
Maléa, Ákra, Greece 46 E5 36 28N 23 7 E
Malegaon, India 66 J9 20 30N 74 38 E
Malei, Mozam. 87 F4 17 12 S 36 58 E
Malek, Sudan 81 F3 6 4N 31 36 E
Malek Kandī, Iran 70 B5 37 9N 46 6 E
Malela, Dem. Rep. of the Congo 86 C2 4 22 S 26 8 E
Malema, Mozam. 87 E4 14 57 S 37 20 E
Máleme, Greece 49 D5 35 31N 23 49 E
Målerås, Sweden 11 H9 56 54N 15 34 E
Malerkotla, India 68 D6 30 32N 75 58 E
Máles, Greece 49 D7 35 6N 25 35 E
Malesherbes, France 19 D9 48 15N 2 24 E
Maleshevska Planina, Europe 44 E7 41 38N 23 7 E
Malesina, Greece 46 C5 38 37N 23 14 E
Malestroit, France 18 E4 47 49N 2 25W
Malfa, Italy 43 D7 38 35N 14 50 E
Malgobek, Russia 35 J7 43 30N 44 34 E
Malgomaj, Sweden 8 D17 64 40N 16 30 E
Malgrat de Mar, Spain 38 D7 41 39N 2 46 E
Malha, Sudan 81 D2 15 8N 25 10 E
Malhargarh, India 68 G6 24 17N 74 59 E
Malheur →, U.S.A. 108 D5 44 4N 116 59W
Malheur L., U.S.A. 108 E4 43 20N 118 48W
Mali, Guinea 82 C2 12 10N 12 20W
Mali ■, Africa 82 B4 17 0N 3 0W
Mali →, Burma 67 G20 25 40N 97 40 E
Mali Kanal, Serbia & M. 28 E4 45 36N 19 24 E
Mali Kyun, Burma 64 F2 13 0N 98 20 E
Malibu, U.S.A. 111 L8 34 2N 118 41W
Maliku, Indonesia 63 E6 0 39 S 123 16 E
Malili, Indonesia 63 E6 2 42 S 121 6 E
Mälilla, Sweden 11 G9 57 23N 15 48 E
Malimba, Mts., Dem. Rep. of the Congo 86 D2 7 30 S 29 30 E
Malin Hd., Ireland 12 A4 55 23N 7 23W
Malin Pen., Ireland 12 A4 55 20N 7 17W
Malindi, Kenya 86 C5 3 12 S 40 5 E
Malines = Mechelen, Belgium 17 C4 51 2N 4 29 E
Malino, Indonesia 63 D6 1 0N 121 0 E
Malinyi, Tanzania 87 D4 8 56 S 36 0 E
Malipo, China 58 F5 23 7N 104 42 E
Maliq, Albania 44 F4 40 45N 20 48 E
Malita, Phil. 63 C7 6 19N 125 39 E
Maliwun, Burma 64 F2 10 17N 98 40 E
Maliya, India 68 H4 23 5N 70 46 E
Maljenik, Serbia & M. 44 C5 43 54N 21 43 E
Malka Mari △, Kenya 86 B5 4 11N 40 46 E
Malkara, Turkey 45 F10 40 53N 26 53 E
Malkinia Górna, Poland 31 F9 52 42N 22 5 E
Malko Tŭrnovo, Bulgaria 45 E11 41 59N 27 31 E
Mallacoota Inlet, Australia 95 F4 37 34 S 149 40 E
Mallaig, U.K. 13 D3 57 0N 5 50W
Mallaoua, Niger 83 C6 13 9N 9 36 E
Mallawan, India 69 F9 27 4N 80 12 E
Mallawi, Egypt 80 B3 27 44N 30 44 E
Mallemort, France 21 E9 43 43N 5 11 E
Málles Venosta, Italy 40 B7 46 41N 10 32 E
Mállia, Greece 49 D7 35 17N 25 32 E
Mallion, Kólpos, Greece 49 D7 35 19N 25 27 E
Mallorca, Spain 48 B10 39 30N 3 0 E
Mallorytown, Canada 115 B9 44 29N 75 53W
Mallow, Ireland 12 D3 52 8N 8 39W
Malmbäck, Sweden 11 G8 57 34N 14 28 E
Malmberget, Sweden 8 C19 67 11N 20 40 E
Malmédy, Belgium 17 D6 50 25N 6 2 E
Malmesbury, S. Africa 88 E2 33 28 S 18 41 E
Malmivaara = Malmberget, Sweden 8 C19 67 11N 20 40 E
Malmköping, Sweden 10 E10 59 8N 16 44 E
Malmö, Sweden 11 J7 55 36N 12 59 E
Malmslätt, Sweden 11 F9 58 27N 15 33 E
Malmyzh, Russia 34 B10 56 31N 50 41 E
Malnaş, Romania 29 D10 46 2N 25 49 E
Malo Konare, Bulgaria 45 D8 42 12N 24 24 E
Maloarkhangelsk, Russia 33 F9 52 28N 36 30 E
Malolos, Phil. 61 D4 14 50N 120 49 E
Malolotja △, Swaziland 89 D5 26 5 S 31 6 E
Malombe L., Malawi 87 E4 14 40 S 35 15 E
Małomice, Poland 31 G2 51 34N 15 2 E
Malomir, Bulgaria 45 D10 42 16N 26 32 E
Malone, U.S.A. 117 B10 44 51N 74 18W
Małopolskie □, Poland 31 J7 49 50N 20 0 E
Malorad, Bulgaria 44 C7 43 28N 23 41 E
Måløy, Norway 9 F11 61 57N 5 6 E
Maloyaroslovets, Russia 32 E9 55 2N 36 20 E
Malpartida, Spain 37 F4 39 26N 6 30W
Malpaso, Canary Is. 48 G1 27 43N 18 3W
Malpelo, I. de, Colombia 124 C2 4 3N 81 35W
Malpica de Bergantiños, Spain 36 B2 43 19N 8 50W
Malpur, India 68 H5 23 21N 73 27 E
Malpura, India 68 F6 26 17N 75 23 E
Mals = Málles Venosta, Italy 40 B7 46 41N 10 32 E
Malta, Idaho, U.S.A. 108 E7 42 18N 113 22W
Malta, Mont., U.S.A. 108 B10 48 21N 107 52W

Malta ■, Europe 49 D2 35 55N 14 26 E
Maltahöhe, Namibia 88 C2 24 55 S 17 0 E
Maltepe, Turkey 45 F13 40 55N 29 8 E
Malton, Canada 116 C5 43 42N 79 38W
Malton, U.K. 14 C7 54 8N 0 49W
Maluku, Indonesia 63 E7 1 0 S 127 0 E
Maluku □, Indonesia 63 E7 3 0 S 128 0 E
Maluku Sea = Molucca Sea, Indonesia 63 E6 0 0 125 0 E
Maluku Utara □, Indonesia 63 D7 1 0N 129 0 E
Malumfashi, Nigeria 83 C6 11 48N 7 39 E
Malung, Sweden 10 D7 60 42N 13 44 E
Malungsfors, Sweden 10 D7 60 44N 13 33 E
Maluwe, Ghana 82 D4 8 40N 2 17W
Malvan, India 66 L8 16 2N 73 30 E
Malvern, U.S.A. 113 H8 34 22N 92 49W
Malvern Hills, U.K. 15 E5 52 0N 2 19W
Malvinas, Is. = Falkland Is. □, Atl. Oc. 128 G5 51 30 S 59 0W
Malý Dunaj →, Slovak Rep. 27 D11 47 45N 18 9 E
Malya, Tanzania 86 C3 3 5 S 33 38 E
Malye Derbety, Russia 35 G8 47 57N 44 42 E
Malyn, Ukraine 33 G5 50 46N 29 3 E
Malyy Lyakhovskiy, Ostrov, Russia 53 B15 74 7N 140 36 E
Mama, Russia 53 D12 58 18N 112 54 E
Mamadysh, Russia 34 C10 55 44N 51 23 E
Mamaguape, Brazil 125 E11 6 50 S 35 4W
Mamarr Mitlā, Egypt 74 E1 30 2N 32 54 E
Mamasa, Indonesia 63 E5 2 55 S 119 20 E
Mambasa, Dem. Rep. of the Congo 86 B2 1 22N 29 3 E
Mamberamo →, Indonesia 63 E9 2 0 S 137 50 E
Mambilima Falls, Zambia 87 E2 10 31 S 28 45 E
Mambirima, Dem. Rep. of the Congo 87 E2 11 25 S 27 33 E
Mambo, Tanzania 86 C4 4 52 S 38 22 E
Mambrui, Kenya 86 C5 3 5 S 40 5 E
Mamburao, Phil. 61 E4 13 13N 120 39 E
Mameigwess L., Canada 104 B2 52 35N 87 50W
Mamers, France 18 D7 48 21N 0 22 E
Mamfé, Cameroon 83 D6 5 50N 9 15 E
Mammoth, U.S.A. 109 K8 32 43N 110 39W
Mammoth Cave △, U.S.A. 114 G3 37 8N 86 13W
Mamonovo, Russia 30 D6 54 28N 19 55 E
Mamoré →, Bolivia 124 F5 10 23 S 65 53W
Mamou, Guinea 82 C2 10 15N 12 0W
Mamoudzou, Mayotte 77 H8 12 48 S 45 14 E
Mampatá, Guinea-Biss. 82 C2 11 54N 14 53W
Mampikony, Madag. 89 B8 16 6 S 47 38 E
Mampong, Ghana 83 D4 7 6N 1 26W
Mamry, Jezioro, Poland 30 D8 54 5N 21 50 E
Mamuju, Indonesia 63 E5 2 41 S 118 50 E
Mamuno, Botswana 88 C3 22 16 S 20 1 E
Mamuras, Albania 44 E3 41 34N 19 41 E
Man, Ivory C. 82 D3 7 30N 7 40W
Man, I. of, U.K. 14 C3 54 15N 4 30W
Man-Bazar, India 69 H12 23 4N 86 39 E
Man Na, Burma 67 H20 23 27N 97 19 E
Mana →, Fr. Guiana 125 B8 5 45N 53 55W
Mana Pools △, Zimbabwe 87 F2 15 56 S 29 25 E
Manaar, G. of = Mannar, G. of, Asia 66 Q11 8 30N 79 0 E
Manacapuru, Brazil 124 D6 3 16 S 60 37W
Manacor, Spain 48 B10 39 34N 3 13 E
Manado, Indonesia 63 D6 1 29N 124 51 E
Managua, Nic. 120 D2 12 6N 86 20W
Managua, L. de, Nic. 120 D2 12 20N 86 30W
Manakara, Madag. 89 C8 22 8 S 48 1 E
Manali, India 68 C7 32 16N 77 10 E
Manama = Al Manāmah, Bahrain 71 E6 26 10N 50 30 E
Manambao →, Madag. 89 B7 17 35 S 44 0 E
Manambato →, Madag. 89 B7 19 18 S 44 22 E
Manambolo →, Madag. 89 B7 19 18 S 44 23 E
Manambolosy, Madag. 89 B8 16 2 S 49 40 E
Mananara →, Madag. 89 C8 23 21 S 47 42 E
Mananara Avaratra, Madag. 89 B8 16 10 S 49 46 E
Mananara △, Madag. 89 B8 16 14 S 49 45 E
Mananjary, Madag. 89 C8 21 13 S 48 20 E
Manankoro, Mali 82 C3 10 28N 7 25W
Manantenina, Madag. 89 C8 24 17 S 47 19 E
Manaos = Manaus, Brazil 124 D7 3 0 S 60 0W
Manapire →, Venezuela 124 B5 7 42N 66 7W
Manapouri, N.Z. 91 L1 45 34 S 167 39 E
Manapouri, L., N.Z. 91 L1 45 32 S 167 32 E
Manaqil, Sudan 81 E3 14 15N 32 59 E
Manār, Jabal, Yemen 75 E3 14 2N 44 17 E
Manaravolo, Madag. 89 C8 24 17 S 44 27 E
Manas, China 60 B3 44 17N 85 56 E
Manas →, India 67 F17 26 12N 90 40 E
Manaslu, Nepal 69 E11 28 33N 84 33 E
Manasquan, U.S.A. 117 F10 40 8N 74 3W
Manassa, U.S.A. 109 H11 37 11N 105 56W
Manatí, Puerto Rico 121 d 18 26N 66 29W
Manaung, Burma 67 K18 18 45N 93 40 E
Manaus, Brazil 124 D7 3 0 S 60 0W
Manavgat, Turkey 72 D4 36 47N 31 28 E
Manawan L., Canada 103 B8 55 24N 103 14W
Manay, Phil. 61 H7 7 17N 126 33 E
Manbij, Syria 70 B3 36 31N 37 57 E
Mancha Real, Spain 37 H7 37 48N 3 39W
Manche □, France 18 C5 49 10N 1 20W
Manchegorsk, Russia 52 C4 67 54N 32 58 E
Manchester, U.K. 14 D5 53 29N 2 12W
Manchester, Calif., U.S.A. 110 G3 38 58N 123 41W
Manchester, Conn., U.S.A. 117 E12 41 47N 72 31W
Manchester, Ga., U.S.A. 115 J3 32 51N 84 37W
Manchester, Iowa, U.S.A. 112 D9 42 29N 91 27W
Manchester, Ky., U.S.A. 114 G4 37 9N 83 46W
Manchester, N.H., U.S.A. 117 D13 42 59N 71 28W
Manchester, N.Y., U.S.A. 116 D7 42 56N 77 16W
Manchester, Pa., U.S.A. 117 F8 40 4N 76 43W
Manchester, Tenn., U.S.A. 115 H2 35 29N 86 5W
Manchester, Vt., U.S.A. 117 C11 43 10N 73 5W
Manchester International ✕ (MAN), U.K. 14 D5 53 21N 2 17W
Manchester L., Canada 103 A7 61 28N 107 29W
Manchhar L., Pakistan 68 F2 26 25N 67 39 E
Manchuria = Dongbei, China 53 E13 45 0N 125 0 E
Manchurian Plain, China 50 E16 47 0N 124 0 E
Manciano, Italy 41 F8 42 35N 11 31 E

Mancifa, Ethiopia 81 F5 6 53N 41 50 E
Mand →, India 69 J10 21 42N 83 15 E
Mand →, Iran 71 D7 28 20N 52 30 E
Manda, Ludewe, Tanzania 87 E3 10 30 S 34 40 E
Manda, Mbeya, Tanzania 86 D3 7 58 S 32 29 E
Manda, Mbeya, Tanzania 87 D3 8 30 S 32 49 E
Mandabé, Madag. 89 C7 21 0 S 44 55 E
Mandaguari, Brazil 127 A5 23 32 S 51 42W
Mandah = Töhöm, Mongolia 56 B5 44 27N 108 2 E
Mandal, Norway 9 G12 58 2N 7 25 E
Mandala, Puncak, Indonesia 63 E10 4 44 S 140 20 E
Mandalay, Burma 67 J20 22 0N 96 4 E
Mandale = Mandalay, Burma 67 J20 22 0N 96 4 E
Mandalgarh, India 68 G6 25 12N 75 6 E
Mandalgovi, Mongolia 56 B4 45 45N 106 10 E
Mandalī, Iraq 70 C5 33 43N 45 28 E
Mandan, U.S.A. 112 B4 46 50N 100 54W
Mandaon, Phil. 61 E5 12 13N 123 17 E
Mandar, Teluk, Indonesia 63 E5 3 35 S 119 15 E
Mándas, Italy 42 C2 39 40N 9 8 E
Mandaue, Phil. 61 F5 10 20N 123 56 E
Mandelieu-la-Napoule, France 21 E10 43 34N 6 57 E
Mandera, Kenya 86 B5 3 55N 41 53 E
Mandeville, Jamaica 120 a 18 2N 77 31W
Mandi, India 68 D7 31 39N 76 58 E
Mandi Dabwali, India 68 E6 29 58N 74 42 E
Mandiana, Guinea 82 C3 10 37N 8 39W
Mandimba, Mozam. 87 E4 14 20 S 35 40 E
Mandioli, Indonesia 63 E7 0 40 S 127 20 E
Mandla, India 69 H9 22 39N 80 30 E
Mandø, Denmark 11 J2 55 18N 8 33 E
Mandorah, Australia 92 B5 12 32 S 130 42 E
Mandoto, Madag. 89 B8 19 34 S 46 17 E
Mandoúdhion, Greece 46 C5 38 48N 23 29 E
Mándra, Greece 46 C5 38 4N 23 30 E
Mandra, Pakistan 68 C5 33 23N 73 12 E
Mandráki, Greece 47 E9 36 36N 27 11 E
Mandrare →, Madag. 89 D8 25 10 S 46 30 E
Mandritsara, Madag. 89 B8 15 50 S 48 49 E
Mandronarivo, Madag. 89 C8 21 7 S 45 38 E
Mandsaur, India 68 G6 24 3N 75 8 E
Mandurah, Australia 93 F2 32 36 S 115 48 E
Mandúria, Italy 43 B10 40 24N 17 38 E
Mandvi, India 68 H3 22 51N 69 22 E
Mandya, India 66 N10 12 30N 77 0 E
Mandzai, Pakistan 68 D2 30 55N 67 6 E
Mané, Burkina Faso 83 C4 12 59N 1 21W
Maneh, Iran 71 B8 37 39N 57 7 E
Manengouba, Mts., Cameroon 83 E6 5 0N 9 50 E
Manera, Madag. 89 C8 5 0N 9 50 E
Manérbio, Italy 40 C7 45 21N 10 8 E
Maneroo Cr. →, Australia 94 C3 23 21 S 143 53 E
Manfalût, Egypt 80 B3 27 20N 30 52 E
Manfredónia, Italy 41 G12 41 38N 15 55 E
Manfredónia, G. di, Italy 41 G13 41 35N 16 5 E
Manga, Burkina Faso 83 C4 11 40N 1 4W
Manga, Niger 83 C7 15 0N 14 0 E
Mangabeiras, Chapada das, Brazil 125 F9 10 0 S 46 30W
Mangalia, Romania 29 G13 43 50N 28 35 E
Mangalore, India 66 N9 12 55N 74 47 E
Mangan, India 69 F13 27 31N 88 32 E
Mangaung, S. Africa 85 K5 29 10 S 26 25 E
Mangawan, India 69 G9 24 41N 81 33 E
Mangaweka, N.Z. 91 H5 39 48 S 175 47 E
Manggar, Indonesia 62 E3 2 50 S 108 10 E
Manggawitu, Indonesia 63 E8 4 8 S 133 32 E
Manggis, Indonesia 63 J18 8 29 S 115 31 E
Mangindrano, Madag. 89 A8 14 17 S 48 58 E
Mangkalihat, Tanjung, Indonesia 63 D5 1 2N 118 59 E
Mangla, Pakistan 68 C5 33 7N 73 39 E
Mangla Dam, Pakistan 69 C5 33 9N 73 44 E
Manglaur, India 68 E7 29 44N 77 49 E
Mangnai, China 60 C4 37 52N 91 43 E
Mango, Togo 83 C5 10 20N 0 30 E
Mangoche, Malawi 87 E4 14 25 S 35 16 E
Mangoky →, Madag. 89 C7 21 29 S 43 41 E
Mangole, Indonesia 63 E6 1 50 S 125 55 E
Mangombe, Dem. Rep. of the Congo 86 C2 1 20 S 26 48 E
Mangonui, N.Z. 91 F4 35 1 S 173 32 E
Mangoro →, Madag. 89 B8 20 0 S 48 45 E
Mangrol, Mad. P., India 68 J4 21 7N 70 7 E
Mangrol, Raj., India 68 G6 25 20N 76 31 E
Manguéigne, Chad 81 G4 10 30N 21 15 E
Mangueira, L. da, Brazil 127 C5 33 0 S 52 50W
Mangum, U.S.A. 113 H5 34 53N 99 30W
Mangystau, Poluostrov, Kazakhstan 52 E6 44 30N 52 30 E
Manhattan, U.S.A. 112 F6 39 11N 96 35W
Manhiça, Mozam. 89 D5 25 23 S 32 49 E
Mani, Madag. 89 C8
Maniago, Italy 41 B9 46 10N 12 43 E
Manica, Mozam. 89 B5 18 58 S 32 59 E
Manica □, Mozam. 89 B5 19 10 S 33 45 E
Manicaland □, Zimbabwe 87 F3 19 10 S 32 30 E
Manicoré, Brazil 124 E6 5 48 S 61 16W
Manicouagan →, Canada 105 C6 49 30N 68 30W
Manicouagan, Rés., Canada 105 B6 51 5N 68 40W
Maniema □, Dem. Rep. of the Congo 86 C2 3 0 S 26 0 E
Manifah, Si. Arabia 71 E6 27 44N 49 0 E
Manifold, C., Australia 94 C5 22 41 S 150 50 E
Maniganggo, China 58 B2 31 56N 99 10 E
Manigotagan, Canada 103 C9 51 6N 96 18W
Manigotagan →, Canada 103 C9 51 7N 96 20W
Manihari, India 69 G12 25 21N 87 38 E
Manihiki, Cook Is. 97 J11 10 24 S 161 1W
Manika, Plateau de la, Dem. Rep. of the Congo 87 E2 10 0 S 25 5 E
Manikpur, India 69 G9 25 4N 81 7 E
Manila, Phil. 61 D4 14 40N 121 3 E
Manila, U.S.A. 108 F9 40 59N 109 43W
Manila B., Phil. 61 D4 14 40N 120 35 E
Manilla, Australia 95 E5 30 45 S 150 43 E
Maningrida, Australia 94 A1 12 3 S 134 13 E
Maninian, Ivory C. 82 C3 9 31N 7 52W
Manipur □, India 67 G19 25 0N 94 0 E
Manipur →, Burma 67 H19 23 45N 94 20 E
Manisa, Turkey 47 C9 38 38N 27 30 E

Manisa □, Turkey ..... 47 C9 38 40N 28 0 E
Manistee, U.S.A. 114 C2 44 15N 86 19W
Manistee →, U.S.A. ... 114 C2 44 15N 86 21W
Manistique, U.S.A. ... 114 C2 45 57N 86 15W
Manito, L., Canada ... 103 C9 51 0N 98 45W
Manitoba □, Canada ... 103 B9 53 30N 97 0W
Manitou, Canada 103 D9 49 15N 98 32W
Manitou, L., Canada ... 105 B6 50 55N 65 17W
Manitou Is., Canada ... 114 C3 45 8N 86 0W
Manitou L., Canada ... 103 C7 52 43N 109 43W
Manitou Springs, U.S.A. 112 F2 38 52N 104 55W
Manitoulin I., Canada .. 104 C3 45 40N 82 30W
Manitouwadge, Canada . 104 C2 49 8N 85 48W
Manitowoc, U.S.A. 114 C2 44 5N 87 40W
Manizales, Colombia .. 124 B3 5 5N 75 32W
Manja, Madag. .... 89 C7 21 26 S 44 20 E
Manjacaze, Mozam. ... 89 C5 24 45 S 34 0 E
Manjakandriana,
  Madag. .... 89 B8 18 55 S 47 47 E
Manjhand, Pakistan ... 68 G3 25 50N 68 10 E
Manjil, Iran .... 71 B6 36 46N 49 30 E
Manjimup, Australia .. 93 F2 34 15 S 116 6 E
Manjra →, India ..... 66 K10 18 49N 77 52 E
Mankato, Kans., U.S.A. 112 F5 39 47N 98 13W
Mankato, Minn., U.S.A. 112 C8 44 10N 94 0W
Mankayane, Swaziland . 89 D5 26 40 S 31 4 E
Mankera, Pakistan ... 68 D4 31 23N 71 26 E
Mankim, Cameroon ... 83 D7 5 6N 12 3 E
Mankono, Ivory C. ... 82 D3 8 1N 6 10W
Mankota, Canada 103 D7 49 25N 107 5W
Manlay = Üydzin,
  Mongolia .... 56 B4 44 9N 107 0 E
Manlleu, Spain ...... 38 C7 42 2N 2 17 E
Manmad, India ...... 66 J9 20 18N 74 28 E
Mann Ranges, Australia 93 E5 26 6 S 130 5 E
Manna, Indonesia .... 62 E2 4 25 S 102 55 E
Mannahill, Australia .. 95 E3 32 25 S 140 0 E
Mannar, Sri Lanka ... 66 Q11 9 1N 79 54 E
Mannar, G. of, Asia .. 66 Q11 8 30N 79 0 E
Mannar I., Sri Lanka .. 66 Q11 9 5N 79 45 E
Mannheim, Germany .. 25 F4 49 29N 8 29 E
Manning, Canada 102 B5 56 53N 117 39W
Manning, Oreg., U.S.A. 116 E3 45 45N 123 13W
Manning, S.C., U.S.A. . 115 J5 33 42N 80 13W
Mannu →, Italy ..... 42 C2 39 16N 9 0 E
Mannu, C., Italy ..... 42 B1 40 3N 8 21 E
Mannum, Australia ... 95 E2 34 50 S 139 20 E
Mano, S. Leone 82 D2 8 3N 12 2W
Mano →, Liberia 82 D2 6 56N 11 30W
Mano River, Liberia .. 82 D2 7 20N 11 6W
Manoharpur, India ... 69 H11 22 23N 85 12 E
Manokwari, Indonesia . 63 E8 0 54 S 134 0 E
Manolás, Greece ..... 46 C3 38 4N 21 21 E
Manombo, Madag. ... 89 C7 22 57 S 43 28 E
Manono, Dem. Rep. of
  the Congo .... 86 D2 7 15 S 27 25 E
Manoppello, Italy .... 41 F11 42 15N 14 3 E
Manosque, France .... 21 E9 43 49N 5 47 E
Manotick, Canada 117 A9 45 13N 75 41W
Manouane →, Canada . 105 B5 50 45N 70 45W
Manouane, L., Canada . 105 B5 50 45N 70 45W
Manp'o, N. Korea .... 57 D14 41 6N 126 24 E
Manpojin = Manp'o,
  N. Korea .... 57 D14 41 6N 126 24 E
Manpur, Chhattisgarh,
  India .... 69 H10 23 17N 83 35 E
Manpur, Mad. P., India 69 H10 22 26N 75 37 E
Manresa, Spain ...... 38 D6 41 48N 1 50 E
Mansa, Gujarat, India . 68 H5 23 27N 72 45 E
Mansa, Punjab, India . 68 E6 30 0N 75 27 E
Mansa, Zambia ...... 87 E2 11 13 S 28 55 E
Mânsâsen, Sweden ... 10 A8 63 5N 14 18 E
Mansehra, Pakistan .. 68 B5 34 20N 73 15 E
Mansel I., Canada 101 B11 62 0N 80 0W
Mansfield, Australia .. 95 F4 37 4 S 146 6 E
Mansfield, U.K. 14 D6 53 9N 1 11W
Mansfield, La., U.S.A. . 113 J8 32 2N 93 43W
Mansfield, Mass., U.S.A. 117 D13 42 2N 71 13W
Mansfield, Ohio, U.S.A. 116 F2 40 45N 82 31W
Mansfield, Pa., U.S.A. . 116 E7 41 48N 77 5W
Mansfield, Mt., U.S.A. . 117 B12 44 33N 72 49W
Mansilla de las Mulas,
  Spain 36 C5 42 30N 5 25W
Mansle, France ...... 20 C4 45 52N 0 12 E
Mansoa, Guinea-Biss. . 82 C1 12 0N 15 20W
Manson Creek, Canada 102 B5 55 37N 124 32W
Manta, Ecuador ..... 124 D2 1 0 S 80 40W
Mantadia △, Madag. . 89 B8 18 54 S 48 21 E
Mantalingajan, Mt., Phil. 61 G2 8 55N 117 45 E
Mantare, Tanzania ... 86 C3 2 42 S 33 13 E
Manteca, U.S.A. 110 H5 37 48N 121 13W
Manteo, U.S.A. 115 H8 35 55N 75 40W
Mantes-la-Jolie, France 19 D8 48 58N 1 41 E
Manthani, India ..... 66 K11 18 40N 79 35 E
Manti, U.S.A. 108 G8 39 16N 111 38W
Mantiqueira, Serra da,
  Brazil .... 127 A7 22 0 S 44 0W
Manton, U.S.A. 114 C3 44 25N 85 24W
Mantorp, Sweden .... 11 F9 58 21N 15 20 E
Mántova, Italy ...... 40 C7 45 9N 10 48 E
Mänttä, Finland ..... 9 E21 62 3N 24 40 E
Mantua = Mántova, Italy 40 C7 45 9N 10 48 E
Manturovo, Russia ... 34 A7 58 23N 44 45 E
Manu, Peru .... 124 F4 12 10 S 70 51W
Manu →, Peru ...... 124 F4 12 16 S 70 55W
Manu'a Is.,
  Amer. Samoa ...... 91 B14 14 13 S 169 35W
Manuel Alves →, Brazil 125 F9 11 19 S 48 28W
Manui, Indonesia .... 63 E6 3 35 S 123 5 E
Manukau, N.Z. ...... 91 G5 37 0 S 174 52 E
Manuripi →, Bolivia . 124 F5 11 6 S 67 36W
Many, U.S.A. 113 K8 31 34N 93 29W
Manyara, L., Tanzania . 86 C4 3 40 S 35 50 E
Manyas, Turkey ..... 45 F11 40 2N 27 59 E
Manych →, Ukraine .. 29 B9 48 39N 24 21 E
Manych →, Russia ... 35 G5 47 13N 40 40 E
Manych-Gudilo, Ozero,
  Russia .... 35 G6 46 24N 42 38 E
Manyonga →, Tanzania 86 C3 4 10 S 34 15 E
Manyoni, Tanzania ... 86 D3 5 45 S 34 55 E
Manzai, Pakistan .... 68 C4 32 12N 70 15 E
Manzala, Bahra el,
  Egypt .... 80 H7 31 10N 31 56 E
Manzanar ○, U.S.A. . 110 J7 36 44N 119 5W
Manzanares, Spain ... 37 F7 39 2N 3 22W
Manzaneda, Spain ... 36 C3 42 12N 7 15W
Manzanillo, Cuba 120 B4 20 20N 77 31W
Manzanillo, Mexico .. 118 D4 19 0N 104 20W
Manzanillo, Pta.,
  .... 120 E4 9 30N 79 40W
Manzano Mts., U.S.A. . 109 J10 34 40N 106 20W
Manzariyeh, Iran .... 71 C6 34 53N 50 50 E
Manzhouli, China .... 60 B6 49 35N 117 25 E
Manzini, Swaziland .. 89 D5 26 30 S 31 25 E
Mao, Chad .... 79 F9 14 4N 15 19 E
Mao, Spain .... 48 B11 39 53N 4 16 E
Maoke, Pegunungan,
  Indonesia .... 63 E9 3 40 S 137 30 E

Maolin, China .... 57 C12 43 58N 123 30 E
Maoming, China ..... 59 G8 21 50N 110 54 E
Maopi T'ou, China ... 59 G13 21 56N 120 43 E
Maouri, Dallol →, Niger 83 C5 12 5N 3 8 E
Maoxing, China ..... 58 B4 31 41N 103 49 E
Mapam Yumco, China . 60 C3 30 45N 81 28 E
Mapastepec, Mexico .. 119 D6 15 26N 92 54W
Maphrao, Ko, Thailand 65 a 7 56N 98 26 E
Mapia, Kepulauan,
  Indonesia .... 63 D8 0 50N 134 20 E
Mapimí, Mexico 118 B4 25 50N 103 50W
Mapimí, Bolsón de,
  Mexico 118 B4 27 30N 104 15W
Maping, China ...... 59 B9 31 34N 113 32 E
Mapinga, Tanzania ... 86 D4 6 40 S 39 12 E
Mapinhane, Mozam. .. 89 C6 22 20 S 35 0 E
Maple Creek, Canada . 103 D7 49 55N 109 29W
Maple Valley, U.S.A. . 110 C4 47 25N 122 3W
Mapleton, U.S.A. 108 D2 44 2N 123 52W
Mapuera →, Brazil .. 124 D7 1 5 S 57 2W
Mapulanguene, Mozam. 89 C5 24 29 S 32 6 E
Maputo, Mozam. .... 89 D5 25 58 S 32 32 E
Maputo →, Mozam. .. 89 D5 26 23 S 32 48 E
Maputo □, Mozam. .. 89 D5 26 0 S 32 25 E
Maputo, B. de, Mozam. 89 D5 25 50 S 32 45 E
Maqiaohe, China .... 57 B16 44 40N 130 30 E
Maqnā, Si. Arabia ... 70 D2 28 25N 34 50 E
Maquan He =
  Brahmaputra →, Asia 69 H13 23 40N 90 35 E
Maqueda, Spain 36 E6 40 4N 4 22W
Maquela do Zombo,
  Angola .... 84 F3 6 0 S 15 15 E
Maquinchao, Argentina 128 E3 41 15 S 68 50W
Maquoketa, U.S.A. ... 112 D9 42 4N 90 40W
Mar, Serra co, Brazil . 127 B6 25 30 S 49 0W
Mar Chiquita, L.,
  Argentina .... 126 C3 30 40 S 62 50W
Mar del Plata, Argentina 126 D4 38 0 S 57 30W
Mar Menor, Spain ... 39 H4 37 40N 0 45W
Mara, Tanzania ..... 86 C3 1 30 S 34 32 E
Mara □, Tanzania ... 86 C3 1 45 S 34 20 E
Maraã, Brazil .... 124 D5 1 52 S 65 25W
Maracá, I. de, Brazil .. 125 C8 2 10N 50 30W
Maracaibo, Venezuela . 124 A4 10 40N 71 37W
Maracaibo, L. de,
  Venezuela 124 B4 9 40N 71 30W
Maracaju, Brazil ..... 127 A4 21 38 S 55 9W
Maracas Bay Village,
  Trin. & Tob. 125 K15 10 46N 61 28W
Maracay, Venezuela .. 124 A5 10 15N 67 28W
Maracena, Spain 37 H7 37 12N 3 38W
Maradi, Niger .... 83 C6 13 29N 7 20 E
Marägheh, Iran ..... 70 B5 37 30N 46 12 E
Marāh, Si. Arabia ... 70 E5 25 0N 45 35 E
Marahoue △, Ivory C. . 82 D3 8 0N 7 8W
Marais du Cotentin et du
  Bessin △, France ... 18 C5 49 10N 1 30W
Marais Poitevin, Val de
  Sèvre et Vendée △,
  France 20 B3 46 18N 0 35W
Marajó, I. de, Brazil .. 125 D9 1 0 S 49 30W
Marākand, Iran ..... 70 B5 38 51N 45 16 E
Marakele △, S. Africa . 89 K4 24 14 S 27 52 E
Maralal, Kenya ...... 86 B4 1 0N 36 38 E
Maralinga, Australia .. 93 F5 30 13 S 131 32 E
Maramaraereğlisi,
  Turkey .... 45 F11 40 57N 27 57 E
Marambio, Antarctica . 5 C18 64 0 S 56 0W
Marampa, S. Leone ... 82 D2 8 45N 12 28W
Maramureş □, Romania 29 C7 47 45N 24 0 E
Maran, Malaysia ..... 65 L4 3 35N 102 45 E
Marana, U.S.A. 109 K8 32 27N 111 13W
Maranboy, Australia .. 92 B5 14 40 S 132 39 E
Maranchón, Spain ... 38 D2 41 6N 2 15W
Marand, Iran .... 70 B5 38 30N 45 45 E
Marang, Malaysia .... 65 K4 5 12N 103 13 E
Maranguape, Brazil .. 125 D11 3 55 S 38 50W
Maranhão = São Luís,
  Brazil .... 125 D10 2 39 S 44 15W
Maranhão □, Brazil .. 125 E9 5 0 S 46 0W
Marano, L., Italy ..... 41 C5 45 44N 13 10 E
Maranoa →, Australia . 95 D4 27 50 S 148 37 E
Marañón →, Peru ... 124 D4 4 30 S 73 35W
Marão, Mozam. ..... 89 C5 24 18 S 34 2 E
Maras =
  Kahramanmaraş,
  Turkey .... 70 B3 37 37N 36 53 E
Mărăşeşti, Romania ... 29 E12 45 52N 27 14 E
Maratea, Italy .... 43 C8 39 59N 15 43 E
Marateca, Portugal ... 37 G2 38 34N 8 40W
Marathasa, Cyprus ... 49 E11 34 59N 32 51 E
Marathókambos, Greece 47 D8 37 43N 26 42 E
Marathon, Australia .. 94 C3 20 51 S 143 32 E
Marathon, Canada ... 104 C2 48 44N 86 23W
Marathón, Greece .... 46 C5 38 11N 23 58 E
Marathon, N.Y., U.S.A. 117 D8 42 27N 76 2W
Marathon, Tex., U.S.A. 113 K3 30 12N 103 15W
Marathóvouno, Cyprus 49 D12 35 13N 33 37 E
Maratua, Indonesia ... 63 D5 2 10N 118 35 E
Maraval, Trin. & Tob. . 125 K15 10 42N 61 31W
Marawi City, Phil. .... 61 G6 8 0N 124 21 E
Marāwih, U.A.E. ..... 71 E7 24 18N 53 18 E
Marazliyivka, Ukraine 29 D15 46 8N 30 3 E
Marbella, Spain 37 J6 36 30N 4 57W
Marble Bar, Australia . 92 D2 21 9 S 119 44 E
Marble Falls, U.S.A. .. 113 K5 30 35N 98 16W
Marblehead, U.S.A. .. 117 D14 42 30N 70 51W
Marburg, Germany ... 24 E4 50 47N 8 46 E
Marcal →, Hungary .. 28 C2 47 41N 17 40 E
Marcali, Hungary .... 28 C2 46 35N 17 25 E
Marcaria, Italy ...... 40 C7 45 7N 10 32 E
Mărculeşti, Moldova .. 29 C13 47 52N 28 14 E
March, U.K. .... 15 E8 52 33N 0 5 E
Marche, France ...... 20 B5 46 5N 1 20 E
Marche □, Italy ...... 41 E10 43 30N 13 0 E
Marche-en-Famenne,
  Belgium .... 17 D5 50 14N 5 19 E
Marchena, Spain 37 H5 37 18N 5 23W
Marches = Marche □,
  Italy .... 41 E10 43 30N 13 15 E
Marchesale △, Italy .. 43 D9 38 32N 16 13 E
Marciana Marina, Italy 40 F7 42 48N 10 12 E
Marcianise, Italy ..... 43 A7 41 2N 14 17 E
Marcigny, France .... 19 F11 46 17N 4 2 E
Marcillat-en-Combraille,
  France .... 19 F9 46 12N 2 38 E
Marck, France .... 19 B8 50 57N 1 57 E
Marckolsheim, France . 19 D14 48 10N 7 30 E
Marco, U.S.A. 115 N5 25 58N 81 44W
Marcos Juárez,
  Argentina .... 126 C3 32 42 S 62 5W
Marcus I. = Minami-
  Tori-Shima, Pac. Oc. . 96 E7 24 20N 153 58 E

Marcus Necker Ridge,
  Pac. Oc. .... 96 F9 20 0N 175 0 E
Marcy, Mt., U.S.A. ... 117 B11 44 7N 73 56W
Mardan, Pakistan .... 68 B5 34 20N 72 0 E
Mardarivka, Ukraine . 29 C14 47 32N 29 44 E
Mardin, Turkey ..... 70 B4 37 20N 40 43 E
Mårdsjö, Sweden .... 10 A9 63 18N 15 35 E
Marécchia →, Italy .. 41 D9 44 4N 12 34 E
Maree →, U.K. 13 D3 57 40N 5 26W
Mareeba, Australia ... 94 B4 16 59 S 145 28 E
Mareetsane, S. Africa . 88 D4 26 9 S 25 25 E
Maremma, Italy ..... 41 F8 42 45N 11 30 E
Maremma →, Italy ... 40 F8 42 35N 11 8 E
Maréna, Kayes, Mali .. 82 C2 14 36N 10 45W
Maréna, Koulikouro,
  Mali 82 C3 13 55N 7 20W
Marengo, U.S.A. 112 E8 41 48N 92 4W
Marennes, France 20 C2 45 49N 1 7W
Marerano, Madag. ... 89 C7 21 23 S 44 52 E
Marettimo, Italy ..... 42 E5 37 58N 12 4 E
Mareuil, France ..... 20 C4 45 26N 0 29 E
Marfa, U.S.A. 113 K2 30 19N 104 1W
Marfa Pt., Malta ..... 49 D1 35 59N 14 19 E
Marganets = Marhanets,
  Ukraine .... 33 J8 47 40N 34 40 E
Margaret →, Australia 92 C4 18 9 S 125 41 E
Margaret Bay, Canada . 102 C3 51 20N 127 35W
Margaret L., Canada .. 102 B5 58 56N 115 25W
Margaret River,
  Australia .... 93 F2 33 57 S 115 4 E
Margarita, I. de,
  Venezuela 124 A6 11 0N 64 0W
Margarítion, Greece .. 46 B2 39 22N 20 26 E
Margaritovo, Russia .. 54 C7 43 25N 134 45 E
Margate, S. Africa .... 89 E5 30 50 S 30 20 E
Margate, U.K. .... 15 F9 51 23N 1 23 E
Margeride, Mts. de la,
  France .... 20 D7 44 43N 3 38 E
Margherita di Savóia,
  Italy .... 43 A9 41 22N 16 9 E
Margherita Pk., Uganda 86 B3 0 22N 29 51 E
Marghita, Romania ... 28 C7 47 22N 22 22 E
Margonin, Poland .... 31 F4 52 58N 17 5 E
Margosatubig, Phil. .. 61 H5 7 34N 123 10 E
Mărgow, Dasht-e,
  Afghan. .... 66 D3 30 40N 62 30 E
Marguerite, Canada .. 102 C4 52 30N 122 25W
Marhanets, Ukraine .. 33 J8 47 40N 34 40 E
Mari El □, Russia .... 34 B8 56 30N 48 0 E
Mari Indus, Pakistan .. 68 C4 32 57N 71 34 E
Mari Republic = Mari
  El □, Russia ...... 34 B8 56 30N 48 0 E
María, Sa. de, Spain .. 39 H2 37 39N 2 14W
María Elena, Chile ... 126 A2 22 18 S 69 40W
María Grande,
  Argentina .... 126 C4 31 45 S 59 55W
Maria I., N. Terr.,
  Australia .... 94 A2 14 52 S 135 45 E
Maria I., Tas., Australia 95 G4 42 35 S 148 0 E
Maria Island △,
  Australia .... 95 G4 42 38 S 148 5 E
Maria van Diemen, C.,
  N.Z. .... 91 F4 34 29 S 172 40 E
Mariager, Denmark ... 11 H3 56 40N 9 59 E
Mariager Fjord,
  Denmark .... 11 H4 56 42N 10 19 E
Mariakani, Kenya .... 86 C4 3 50 S 39 27 E
Mariala △, Australia .. 95 D4 25 57 S 145 2 E
Marian, Australia .... 94 K6 21 9 S 148 57 E
Marian L., Canada ... 102 A5 63 0N 116 15W
Mariana Trench,
  Pac. Oc. .... 96 F6 13 0N 145 0 E
Marianao, Cuba 120 B3 23 8N 82 24W
Marianna, Ark., U.S.A. 113 H9 34 46N 90 46W
Marianna, Fla., U.S.A. 115 K3 30 46N 85 14W
Mariannelund, Sweden 11 G9 57 37N 15 35 E
Mariánské Lázně,
  Czech Rep. .... 26 B5 49 58N 12 41 E
Marias →, U.S.A. ... 108 C8 47 56N 110 30W
Mariato, Punta, Panama 120 E3 7 12N 80 52W
Mariazell, Austria .... 26 D8 47 47N 15 19 E
Maribo, Denmark .... 11 K5 54 48N 11 30 E
Maribor, Slovenia .... 41 B12 46 36N 15 40 E
Marico →, Africa .... 88 C4 23 35 S 26 57 E
Maricopa, Ariz., U.S.A. 109 K7 33 4N 112 3W
Maricopa, Calif., U.S.A. 111 K7 35 4N 119 24W
Marīdī, Sudan ...... 81 G2 4 55N 29 25 E
Marīdī, Wadi →, Sudan 81 F2 6 15N 29 21 E
Marié →, Brazil ..... 124 D5 0 27 S 66 26W
Marie Byrd Land,
  Antarctica .... 5 D14 79 30 S 125 0W
Marie-Galante,
  Guadeloupe .... 120 b 15 56N 61 16W
Maricourt =
  Kangiqsujuaq, Canada 101 B12 61 30N 72 0W
Mariefred, Sweden ... 10 E11 59 15N 17 12 E
Mariehamn =
  Maarianhamina,
  Finland .... 9 F18 60 5N 19 55 E
Marieholm, Sweden .. 11 J7 55 53N 13 10 E
Mariembourg, Belgium 17 D4 50 6N 4 31 E
Marienbad =
  Mariánské
  Lázně, Czech Rep. .. 26 B5 49 58N 12 41 E
Marienberg, Germany . 24 E9 50 39N 13 9 E
Mariental, Namibia .. 88 C2 24 36 S 18 0 E
Marienville, U.S.A. ... 116 E5 41 28N 79 8W
Mariestad, Sweden ... 11 F7 58 43N 13 50 E
Marietta, Ga., U.S.A. . 115 J3 33 57N 84 33W
Marietta, Ohio, U.S.A. 114 F5 39 25N 81 27W
Marieville, Canada ... 117 A11 45 26N 73 10W
Mariga →, Nigeria ... 83 C6 9 40N 5 55 E
Marignane, France ... 21 E9 43 25N 5 13 E
Marihatag, Phil. ..... 61 G7 8 48N 126 18 E
Mariinsk, Russia ..... 52 D9 56 10N 87 20 E
Mariinskiy Posad, Russia 34 B8 56 10N 47 45 E
Marijampolė, Lithuania 9 J20 54 33N 23 19 E
Marijampolės □,
  Lithuania .... 30 D10 54 34N 23 21 E
Marília, Brazil ...... 127 A6 22 13 S 50 0W
Marín, Spain 36 C2 42 23N 8 42W
Marine, U.S.A. 110 J5 36 41N 121 48W
Marine City, U.S.A. .. 116 D2 42 43N 82 30W
Marineo, Italy ...... 42 E6 37 57N 13 25 E
Marinette, U.S.A. 114 C2 45 6N 87 38W
Maringá, Brazil ..... 127 A5 23 26 S 52 2W
Marinha Grande,
  Portugal 36 F2 39 45N 8 56W
Marion, Ala., U.S.A. .. 115 J2 32 38N 87 19W
Marion, Ill., U.S.A. ... 113 G10 37 44N 88 56W
Marion, Ind., U.S.A. .. 114 E3 40 32N 85 40W
Marion, Iowa, U.S.A. . 112 D9 42 2N 91 36W
Marion, Kans., U.S.A. 112 F6 38 21N 97 1W
Marion, N.C., U.S.A. . 115 H5 35 41N 82 1W
Marion, Ohio, U.S.A. . 114 E4 40 35N 83 8W
Marion, S.C., U.S.A. . 115 H6 34 11N 79 24W

Marion, Va., U.S.A. .. 115 G5 36 50N 81 31W
Mariposa, U.S.A. 110 H7 37 29N 119 58W
Mariscal Estigarribia,
  Paraguay .... 126 A3 22 3 S 60 40W
Maritime Alps =
  Maritimes, Alpes,
  Europe .... 21 D11 44 10N 7 10 E
Maritimes, Alpes,
  Europe .... 21 D11 44 10N 7 10 E
Maritsa = Évros →,
  Greece .... 72 B2 41 40N 26 34 E
Maritsá, Greece ..... 49 C10 36 22N 28 8 E
Mariupol, Ukraine ... 33 J9 47 5N 37 31 E
Mariusa △, Venezuela . 121 E7 9 24N 61 27W
Marīvān, Iran .... 70 C5 35 30N 46 25 E
Marj 'Uyūn, Lebanon . 74 B4 33 20N 35 35 E
Marka = Merca,
  Somali Rep. .... 75 G3 1 48N 44 50 E
Marka, Si. Arabia .... 80 D5 18 14N 41 19 E
Markam, China ...... 58 C2 29 42N 98 38 E
Markaryd, Sweden ... 11 H7 56 28N 13 35 E
Markdale, Canada ... 116 B4 44 19N 80 39W
Marked Tree, U.S.A. .. 113 H9 35 32N 90 25W
Markelsdorfer Huk,
  Germany .... 24 A7 54 33N 11 4 E
Market Drayton, U.K. . 14 E5 52 54N 2 29W
Market Harborough,
  U.K. 15 E7 52 29N 0 55W
Market Rasen, U.K. .. 14 D7 53 24N 0 20W
Markham, Canada ... 116 C5 43 52N 79 16W
Markham, Mt.,
  Antarctica .... 5 E11 83 0 S 164 0 E
Marki, Poland .... 31 F8 52 20N 21 2 E
Märkische Schweiz △,
  Germany .... 24 C10 52 34N 14 2 E
Markkleeberg, Germany 24 D8 51 16N 12 23 E
Markleeville, U.S.A. .. 110 G7 38 42N 119 47W
Markoupoulon, Greece 46 D5 37 53N 23 57 E
Markovac, Serbia & M. 44 B5 44 14N 21 7 E
Markovo, Russia ..... 53 C17 64 40N 170 24 E
Markoye, Burkina Faso 83 C5 14 39N 0 2 E
Marks, Russia .... 34 E8 51 45N 46 50 E
Marksville, U.S.A. ... 113 K8 31 8N 92 4W
Markt Schwaben,
  Germany .... 25 G7 48 11N 11 52 E
Marktoberdorf,
  Germany .... 25 H6 47 45N 10 37 E
Marktredwitz, Germany 25 E8 50 1N 12 6 E
Marl, Germany ...... 24 D3 51 39N 7 4 E
Marla, Australia ..... 95 D1 27 19 S 133 33 E
Marlbank, Canada ... 116 B7 44 26N 77 6W
Marlboro, Mass., U.S.A. 117 D13 42 19N 71 33W
Marlboro, N.Y., U.S.A. 117 E11 41 36N 73 59W
Marlborough, Australia 94 C4 22 46 S 149 52 E
Marlborough, U.K. ... 15 F6 51 25N 1 43W
Marlborough Downs,
  U.K. 15 F6 51 27N 1 53W
Marle, France .... 19 C10 49 43N 3 47 E
Marlin, U.S.A. 113 K6 31 18N 96 54W
Marlow, Germany .... 24 A8 54 9N 12 33 E
Marlow, U.S.A. 113 H6 34 39N 97 58W
Marlow, U.K. 15 F7 51 34N 0 46W
Marmagao, India .... 66 M8 15 25N 73 56 E
Marmande, France ... 20 D4 44 30N 0 10 E
Marmara, Turkey .... 45 F11 40 35N 27 34 E
Marmara, Sea of =
  Marmara Denizi,
  Turkey .... 45 F12 40 45N 28 15 E
Marmara Denizi, Turkey 45 F12 40 45N 28 15 E
Marmara Gölü, Turkey 47 C10 38 37N 28 2 E
Marmaris, Turkey .... 47 E10 36 50N 28 14 E
Marmaris Limanı,
  Turkey .... 47 E10 36 50N 28 19 E
Marmion, Mt., Australia 93 E2 29 16 S 119 50 E
Marmion L., Canada .. 104 C1 48 55N 91 20W
Marmolada, Mte., Italy 41 B8 46 26N 11 51 E
Marmolejo, Spain 37 G6 38 3N 4 13W
Marmora, Canada ... 116 B7 44 28N 77 41W
Mármora, La, Italy ... 42 C2 39 59N 9 20 E
Marnay, France ..... 19 E12 47 16N 5 48 E
Marne, Germany .... 24 B5 53 56N 9 2 E
Marne □, France .... 19 D11 48 50N 4 10 E
Marne →, France ... 19 D9 48 48N 2 24 E
Marneuli, Georgia ... 35 K7 41 30N 44 48 E
Maroala, Madag. .... 89 B8 15 23 S 47 59 E
Maroantsetra, Madag. 89 B8 15 26 S 49 44 E
Maroelaboom, Namibia 88 B2 19 15 S 18 53 E
Marofandilia, Madag. . 89 C7 20 7 S 44 34 E
Marojejy △, Madag. .. 89 A8 14 26 S 49 21 E
Marolambo, Madag. .. 89 C8 20 2 S 48 7 E
Maromandia, Madag. . 89 A8 14 13 S 48 5 E
Maromokotro, Madag. 89 A8 14 0 S 49 0 E
Marondera, Zimbabwe 87 F3 18 5 S 31 42 E
Maroni →, Fr. Guiana 125 B8 5 30N 54 0W
Marónia, Greece .... 45 F9 40 53N 25 30 E
Maronne →, France . 20 C5 45 5N 1 56 E
Maroochydore, Australia 95 D5 26 29 S 153 5 E
Maroona, Australia .. 95 F3 37 27 S 142 54 E
Maros →, Hungary .. 28 D5 46 15N 20 13 E
Marosakoa, Madag. .. 89 B8 15 26 S 46 38 E
Maroseranana, Madag. 89 B8 18 32 S 48 51 E
Maróstica, Italy ..... 41 C8 45 44N 11 40 E
Marotandrano, Madag. 89 B8 16 10 S 48 50 E
Marotaolano, Madag. . 89 A8 12 47 S 49 15 E
Maroua, Cameroon .. 83 C7 10 40N 14 20 E
Marovato, Madag. ... 89 B8 15 48 S 48 5 E
Marovoay, Madag. ... 89 B8 16 6 S 46 39 E
Marquard, S. Africa .. 88 D4 28 40 S 27 28 E
Marquesas Is. =
  Marquises, Is.,
  French Polynesia ... 97 H14 9 30 S 140 0W
Marquette, U.S.A. ... 114 B2 46 33N 87 24W
Marquise, France .... 19 B8 50 50N 1 40 E
Marquises, Îs.,
  French Polynesia ... 97 H14 9 30 S 140 0W
Marra, Djebel, Sudan . 79 F10 13 10N 24 22 E
Marra, Gebel, Sudan . 81 F2 7 20N 27 35 E
Marracuene, Mozam. . 89 D5 25 45 S 32 35 E
Marradi, Italy .... 41 D8 44 4N 11 37 E
Marrakech, Morocco .. 78 B4 31 9N 8 0W
Marrawah, Australia . 95 G3 40 55 S 144 42 E
Marree, Australia .... 95 D2 29 39 S 138 1 E
Marrero, U.S.A. 113 L9 29 54N 90 6W
Marrimane, Mozam. . 89 C5 22 58 S 33 0 E
Marromeu, Mozam. .. 89 B6 18 15 S 36 25 E
Marroví, Mozam. .... 89 B6 19 0 S 36 0 E
Marrúbiu, Italy ...... 42 C1 39 44N 8 35 E
Marrupa, Mozam. ... 87 E4 13 8 S 37 30 E
Mars Hill, U.S.A. 115 B12 46 31N 67 52W
Marsá 'Alam, Egypt .. 80 B3 25 5N 34 54 E

Marsá Matrûh, Egypt . 80 A2 31 19N 27 9 E
Marsá Sha'b, Sudan .. 80 C4 22 52N 35 47 E
Marsabit, Kenya ..... 86 B4 2 18N 38 0 E
Marsabit △, Kenya ... 86 B4 2 23N 37 56 E
Marsala, Italy .... 42 E5 37 48N 12 26 E
Marsalforn, Malta .... 49 C1 36 4N 14 16 E
Mârşani, Romania ... 29 F9 44 1N 24 1 E
Marsberg, Germany .. 24 D4 51 28N 8 52 E
Marsciano, Italy ..... 41 F9 42 54N 12 20 E
Marsden, Australia .. 95 E4 33 47 S 147 32 E
Marseillan, France ... 20 E7 43 23N 3 31 E
Marseille, France .... 21 E9 43 18N 5 23 E
Marseille ✈ (MRS),
  France .... 21 E9 43 26N 5 14 E
Marseilles = Marseille,
  France .... 21 E9 43 18N 5 23 E
Marsh I., U.S.A. 113 L9 29 34N 91 53W
Marshall, Liberia 82 D2 6 8N 10 22W
Marshall, Ark., U.S.A. 113 H8 35 55N 92 38W
Marshall, Mich., U.S.A. 114 D3 42 16N 84 58W
Marshall, Minn., U.S.A. 112 C7 44 25N 95 45W
Marshall, Mo., U.S.A. 112 F8 39 7N 93 12W
Marshall, Tex., U.S.A. 113 J7 32 33N 94 23W
Marshall →, Australia 94 C2 22 59 S 136 59 E
Marshall Is. ■, Pac. Oc. 96 G9 9 0N 171 0 E
Marshalltown, U.S.A. . 112 D8 42 3N 92 55W
Marshbrook, Zimbabwe 89 B5 18 33 S 31 9 E
Marshfield, Mo., U.S.A. 113 G8 37 15N 92 54W
Marshfield, Vt., U.S.A. 117 B12 44 20N 72 20W
Marshfield, Wis., U.S.A. 112 C9 44 40N 90 10W
Marshūn, Iran .... 71 B6 36 19N 49 23 E
Mársico Nuovo, Italy . 43 B8 40 25N 15 44 E
Märsta, Sweden ..... 10 E11 59 37N 17 52 E
Marstal, Denmark ... 11 K4 54 51N 10 30 E
Marstrand, Sweden .. 11 G5 57 53N 11 35 E
Mart, U.S.A. 113 K6 31 33N 96 50W
Marta →, Italy ...... 41 F8 42 14N 11 42 E
Martaban, Burma .... 67 L20 16 30N 97 35 E
Martaban, G. of, Burma 67 L20 16 5N 96 30 E
Martano, Italy .... 43 B11 40 12N 18 18 E
Martapura, Kalimantan,
  Indonesia .... 62 E4 3 22 S 114 47 E
Martapura, Sumatera,
  Indonesia .... 62 E2 4 19 S 104 22 E
Marte, Nigeria ...... 83 C7 12 23N 13 46 E
Martel, France ...... 20 D5 44 57N 1 37 E
Martelange, Belgium . 17 E5 49 49N 5 43 E
Martellago, Italy ..... 41 C9 45 33N 12 9 E
Martés, Sierra, Spain . 39 F4 39 20N 1 0W
Martfű, Hungary .... 28 C5 47 1N 20 17 E
Martha's Vineyard,
  U.S.A. 117 E14 41 25N 70 38W
Martigné-Ferchaud,
  France 18 E5 47 50N 1 20W
Martigny, Switz. ..... 25 J3 46 6N 7 3 E
Martigues, France .... 21 E9 43 24N 5 4 E
Martin, Slovak Rep. .. 27 B11 49 6N 18 58 E
Martin, S. Dak., U.S.A. 112 D4 43 11N 101 44W
Martin, Tenn., U.S.A. . 113 G10 36 21N 88 51W
Martín →, Spain 38 D4 41 18N 0 19W
Martin, L., U.S.A. 115 J3 32 45N 85 55W
Martina Franca, Italy . 43 B10 40 42N 17 20 E
Martinborough, N.Z. . 91 J5 41 14 S 175 29 E
Martínez, Calif., U.S.A. 110 G4 38 1N 122 8W
Martínez, Ga., U.S.A. 115 J4 33 31N 82 4W
Martinique Ø, W. Indies 120 c 14 40N 61 0W
Martinique Passage,
  W. Indies 121 C7 15 15N 61 0W
Martínon, Greece .... 46 C5 38 35N 23 12 E
Martinópolis, Brazil .. 127 A5 22 11 S 51 12W
Martin's Bay, Barbados 121 g 13 12N 59 29W
Martins Ferry, U.S.A. . 116 F4 40 6N 80 44W
Martinsberg, Austria . 26 C8 48 22N 15 9 E
Martinsburg, Pa., U.S.A. 116 F6 40 19N 78 20W
Martinsburg, W. Va.,
  U.S.A. 114 F7 39 27N 77 58W
Martinsicuro, Italy ... 41 F10 42 54N 13 54 E
Martinsville, Ind., U.S.A. 114 F2 39 26N 86 25W
Martinsville, Va., U.S.A. 115 G6 36 41N 79 52W
Marton, N.Z. .... 91 J5 40 4 S 175 23 E
Martorell, Spain ..... 38 D6 41 28N 1 56 E
Martos, Spain 37 H7 37 44N 3 58W
Martuni, Armenia .... 35 K7 40 8N 45 20 E
Maru, Nigeria .... 83 C6 12 22N 6 22 E
Marudi, Malaysia .... 62 D4 4 11N 114 19 E
Maruf, Afghan. ...... 66 D5 31 30N 67 6 E
Marugame, Japan .... 55 G6 34 15N 133 40 E
Marunga, Angola .... 88 B3 17 28 S 20 2 E
Marungu, Mts.,
  Dem. Rep. of
  the Congo .... 86 D3 7 30 S 30 0 E
Marv Dasht, Iran .... 71 D7 29 50N 52 40 E
Marvast, Iran .... 71 D7 30 30N 54 15 E
Marvejols, France .... 20 D7 44 33N 3 19 E
Marvel Loch, Australia 93 F2 31 28 S 119 29 E
Marwar, India .... 68 G5 25 43N 73 45 E
Mary, Turkmenistan .. 52 F7 37 40N 61 50 E
Maryborough = Port
  Laoise, Ireland ... 12 C4 53 2N 7 18W
Maryborough, Queens.,
  Australia .... 95 D5 25 31 S 152 37 E
Maryborough, Vic.,
  Australia .... 95 F3 37 0 S 143 44 E
Maryfield, Canada ... 103 D8 49 50N 101 35W
Maryland □, U.S.A. .. 114 F7 39 0N 76 30W
Maryland Junction,
  Zimbabwe .... 87 F3 17 45 S 30 31 E
Maryport, U.K. 14 C4 54 44N 3 28W
Mary's Harbour, Canada 105 B8 52 18N 55 51W
Marystown, Canada .. 105 C8 47 10N 55 10W
Marysville, Canada .. 102 D5 49 35N 116 0W
Marysville, Calif., U.S.A. 110 F5 39 9N 121 35W
Marysville, Kans., U.S.A. 112 F6 39 51N 96 39W
Marysville, Mich., U.S.A. 116 D2 42 54N 82 29W
Marysville, Ohio, U.S.A. 114 E4 40 14N 83 22W
Marysville, Wash.,
  U.S.A. 110 B4 48 3N 122 11W
Maryvale, Australia .. 95 D5 28 4 S 152 12 E
Maryville, Mo., U.S.A. 112 E7 40 21N 94 52W
Maryville, Tenn., U.S.A. 115 H4 35 46N 83 58W
Marzûq, Libya ...... 79 C8 25 53N 13 57 E
Masahunga, Tanzania 86 C3 2 6 S 33 18 E
Masai, Malaysia ..... 65 d 1 29N 103 53 E
Masai Mara △, Kenya 86 C4 1 25 S 35 5 E
Masai Steppe, Tanzania 86 C4 4 30 S 36 30 E
Masaka, Uganda ..... 86 C3 0 21 S 31 45 E
Masalembo, Kepulauan,
  Indonesia .... 62 F4 5 35 S 114 30 E
Masalima, Kepulauan,
  Indonesia .... 62 F5 5 4 S 117 5 E
Masalli, Azerbaijan .. 73 C13 39 3N 48 40 E
Masamba, Indonesia . 63 E6 2 30 S 120 15 E
Masan, S. Korea ..... 57 G15 35 11N 128 32 E
Masandam, Ra's, Oman 71 E8 26 30N 56 30 E
Masasi, Tanzania .... 87 E4 10 45 S 38 52 E
Masaya, Nic. 120 D2 12 0N 86 7W
Masba, Nigeria ...... 83 C7 11 35N 13 1 E
Masbate, Phil. ...... 61 E5 12 21N 123 36 E

Máscali, Italy .... 43 E8 37 45N 15 12 E
Mascara, Algeria ...... 78 A6 35 26N 0 6 E
Mascota, Mexico 118 C4 20 30N 104 50W
Masela, Indonesia ..... 63 F7 8 9 S 129 51 E
Maseru, Lesotho ...... 88 D4 29 18 S 27 30 E
Mashaba, Zimbabwe ... 87 G3 20 2 S 30 29 E
Mashābih, Si. Arabia .. 70 E3 25 35N 36 30 E
Mashan, China .... 58 F7 23 40N 108 11 E
Mashar, Sudan .... 81 F2 9 16N 26 51 E
Mashatu = Botswana .. 89 C4 22 5 S 29 5 E
Mashegu, Nigeria ..... 83 D6 10 0N 5 35 E
Masherbrum, Pakistan . 69 B7 35 38N 76 18 E
Mashhad, Iran .... 71 B8 36 20N 59 35 E
Mashi, Nigeria .... 83 C6 13 0N 7 54 E
Mashīz, Iran .... 71 D8 29 56N 56 37 E
Māshkel, Hāmūn-i-,
  Pakistan .... 66 E3 28 20N 62 56 E
Mashki Chāh, Pakistan 66 E3 29 5N 62 30 E
Mashonaland,
  Zimbabwe .... 85 H6 16 30 S 31 0 E
Mashonaland Central □,
  Zimbabwe .... 89 B5 17 30 S 31 0 E
Mashonaland East □,
  Zimbabwe .... 89 B5 18 0 S 32 0 E
Mashonaland West □,
  Zimbabwe .... 89 B4 17 30 S 29 30 E
Mashrakh, India ...... 69 F11 26 7N 84 48 E
Mashtaga = Maştağa,
  Azerbaijan .... 35 K10 40 35N 49 57 E
Masindi, Uganda ...... 86 B3 1 40N 31 43 E
Masindi Port, Uganda . 86 B3 1 43N 32 2 E
Maşīrah, Oman .... 75 C6 21 0N 58 50 E
Maşīrah, Khalīj, Oman 75 C6 20 10N 58 10 E
Masisi, Dem. Rep. of
  the Congo .... 86 C2 1 23 S 28 49 E
Masjed Soleyman, Iran 71 D6 31 55N 49 18 E
Mask, L., Ireland 12 C2 53 36N 9 22W
Maskin, Oman .... 71 F8 23 36N 56 50 E
Maslen Nos, Bulgaria . 45 D11 42 18N 27 48 E
Maslinica, Croatia .... 41 E13 43 24N 16 13 E
Masnou = El Masnou,
  Spain .... 38 D7 41 28N 2 20 E
Masoala △, Madag. ... 89 B9 15 30 S 50 12 E
Masoala, Tanjon' i,
  Madag. .... 89 B9 15 59 S 50 13 E
Masoarivo, Madag. .... 89 B7 19 3 S 44 19 E
Masohi = Amahai,
  Indonesia .... 63 E7 3 20 S 128 55 E
Masomeloka, Madag. .. 89 C8 20 17 S 48 37 E
Mason, Nev., U.S.A. ... 110 G7 38 56N 119 8W
Mason, Tex., U.S.A. ... 113 K5 30 45N 99 14W
Mason City, U.S.A. ... 112 D8 43 9N 93 12W
Maspalomas, Canary Is. 48 G4 27 46N 15 35W
Maspalomas, Pta.,
  Canary Is. 48 G4 27 43N 15 36W
Masqat, Oman .... 75 C6 23 37N 58 36 E
Massa, Italy .... 40 D7 44 1N 10 9 E
Massa Maríttima, Italy 40 E7 43 1N 10 52 E
Massachusetts □, U.S.A. 117 D13 42 30N 72 0W
Massachusetts B., U.S.A. 117 D14 42 20N 70 50W
Massafra, Italy .... 43 B10 40 35N 17 7 E
Massakory, Chad ..... 79 F9 13 0N 15 49 E
Massanella, Spain ..... 48 B9 39 48N 2 51 E
Massangena, Mozam. .. 89 C5 21 34 S 33 0 E
Massango, Angola ..... 84 F3 8 2 S 16 21 E
Massat, France .... 20 F5 42 53N 1 21 E
Massawa = Mitsiwa,
  Eritrea .... 81 D4 15 35N 39 25 E
Massénya, Chad ...... 79 F9 11 21N 16 9 E
Masset, Canada 102 C2 54 2N 132 10W
Masseube, France ..... 20 E4 43 25N 0 34 E
Massiac, France ...... 20 C7 45 15N 3 11 E
Massiah Street,
  Barbados .... 121 g 13 9N 59 29W
Massif Central, France . 20 D7 44 55N 3 0 E
Massif des Bauges △,
  France .... 19 G13 45 40N 6 10 E
Massigui, Mali 82 C3 11 48N 6 50W
Massillon, U.S.A. 116 F3 40 48N 81 32W
Massinga, Mozam. .... 89 C6 23 15 S 35 22 E
Massingir, Mozam. .... 89 C5 23 51 S 32 4 E
Masson-Angers, Canada 117 A9 45 32N 75 25W
Masson I., Antarctica . 5 C7 66 10 S 93 20 E
Maştağa, Azerbaijan .. 35 K10 40 35N 49 57 E
Mastanli =
  Momchilgrad,
  Bulgaria .... 45 E9 41 33N 25 23 E
Masterton, N.Z. ...... 91 J5 40 56 S 175 39 E
Mastic, U.S.A. 117 F12 40 47N 72 54W
Mástikho, Ákra, Greece 47 C8 38 10N 26 2 E
Mastuj, Pakistan ..... 69 A5 36 20N 72 36 E
Mastung, Pakistan .... 66 E5 29 50N 66 56 E
Mastūrah, Si. Arabia .. 80 C4 23 7N 38 52 E
Masty, Belarus .... 32 F3 53 27N 24 38 E
Masuda, Japan .... 55 G5 34 40N 131 51 E
Masvingo, Zimbabwe .. 87 G3 20 8 S 30 49 E
Masvingo □, Zimbabwe 87 G3 21 0 S 31 30 E
Maswa □, Tanzania ... 86 C3 2 58 S 34 19 E
Maşyāf, Syria .... 70 C3 35 4N 36 20 E
Maszewo, Poland ..... 30 E2 53 29N 15 3 E
Mat →, Albania ...... 44 E3 41 40N 19 35 E
Matabeleland,
  Zimbabwe .... 85 H5 18 0 S 27 0 E
Matabeleland North □,
  Zimbabwe .... 87 F2 19 0 S 28 0 E
Matabeleland South □,
  Zimbabwe .... 87 G2 21 0 S 29 0 E
Matachel →, Spain ... 37 G4 38 50N 6 17W
Matachewan, Canada .. 104 C3 47 56N 80 39W
Matadi, Dem. Rep. of
  the Congo .... 84 F2 5 52 S 13 31 E
Matagalpa, Nic. 120 D2 13 0N 85 58W
Matagami, Canada 104 C4 49 45N 77 34W
Matagami, L., Canada . 104 C4 49 50N 77 40W
Matagorda B., U.S.A. . 113 L6 28 15N 96 30W
Matagorda I., U.S.A. . 113 L6 28 15N 95 30W
Matak, Indonesia ..... 65 b 3 18N 106 16 E
Mátala, Greece .... 49 E6 34 59N 24 45 E
Matam, Senegal 82 B2 15 34N 13 17W
Matameye, Niger ..... 83 C6 13 26N 8 28 E
Matamoros, Campeche,
  Mexico 119 D6 18 50N 90 50W
Matamoros, Coahuila,
  Mexico 118 B4 25 33N 103 15W
Matamoros, Tamaulipas,
  Mexico 119 B5 25 50N 97 30W
Ma'ţan as Sarra, Libya . 79 D10 21 45N 22 0 E
Matandu →, Tanzania . 87 D3 8 45 S 34 19 E
Matane, Canada 105 C6 48 50N 67 33W
Matang, China .... 58 F5 23 30N 104 7 E
Matankari, Niger ..... 83 C5 13 46N 4 1 E
Matanomadh, India ... 68 H3 23 33N 68 57 E
Matanzas, Cuba 120 B3 23 0N 81 40W
Matapa, Botswana .... 88 C3 23 11 S 24 39 E
Matapan, C. = Taínaron,
  Ákra, Greece .... 46 E4 36 22N 22 27 E

Matapédia, Canada 105 C6 48 0N 66 59W
Matapo △, Zimbabwe . 87 G2 20 36 S 29 40 E
Matara, Sri Lanka .... 66 S12 5 58N 80 30 E
Mataram, Indonesia ... 63 K19 8 35 S 116 7 E
Matarani, Peru .... 124 G4 17 0 S 72 10W
Mataranka, Australia .. 92 B5 14 55 S 133 4 E
Matarma, Râs, Egypt .. 74 E1 30 27N 32 44 E
Mataró, Spain .... 38 D7 41 32N 2 29 E
Matarraña →, Spain .. 38 D5 41 14N 0 22 E
Mataruška Banja,
  Serbia & M. .... 44 C4 43 40N 20 40 E
Matatiele, S. Africa ... 89 E4 30 20 S 28 49 E
Mataura, N.Z. .... 91 M2 46 11 S 168 51 E
Matehuala, Mexico 118 C4 23 40N 100 40W
Mateke Hills, Zimbabwe 87 G3 21 48 S 31 0 E
Matelot, Trin. & Tob. . 125 K15 10 50N 61 7W
Matera, Italy .... 43 B9 40 40N 16 36 E
Matese △, Italy .... 43 A7 41 24N 14 23 E
Matese, Monti del, Italy 43 A7 41 24N 14 22 E
Mátészalka, Hungary .. 28 C7 47 58N 22 20 E
Matfors, Sweden ...... 10 B11 62 21N 17 2 E
Matha, France 20 C3 45 52N 0 20W
Mathenīko △, Uganda . 86 B3 2 49N 34 27 E
Mathis, U.S.A. 113 L6 28 6N 97 50W
Mathráki, Greece ..... 49 A3 39 48N 19 31 E
Mathura, India .... 68 F7 27 30N 77 40 E
Mati, Phil. .... 61 H7 6 55N 126 15 E
Matiakoali,
  Burkina Faso .... 83 C5 12 28N 1 2 E
Matiali, India .... 69 F13 26 56N 88 49 E
Matías Romero, Mexico 119 D5 16 53N 95 2W
Matibane, Mozam. .... 87 E5 14 49 S 40 45 E
Matiri Ra., N.Z. ...... 91 J4 41 38 S 172 20 E
Matjiesfontein, S. Africa 88 E3 33 14 S 20 35 E
Matla →, India .... 69 J13 21 40N 88 40 E
Matlamanyane,
  Botswana .... 88 B4 19 33 S 25 57 E
Matli, Pakistan .... 68 G3 25 2N 68 39 E
Matlock, U.K. 14 D6 53 9N 1 33W
Matna, Sudan .... 81 E4 13 49N 35 10 E
Mato Grosso □, Brazil 125 F8 14 0 S 55 0W
Mato Grosso, Planalto
  do, Brazil .... 125 G8 15 0 S 55 0W
Mato Grosso do Sul □,
  Brazil .... 125 G8 18 0 S 55 0W
Matobo = Matopo △,
  Zimbabwe .... 87 G2 20 36 S 28 20 E
Matopo △, Zimbabwe . 87 G2 20 36 S 28 20 E
Matopos, Zimbabwe ... 87 G2 20 20 S 28 29 E
Matosinhos, Portugal .. 36 D2 41 11N 8 42W
Matour, France .... 19 F11 46 19N 4 29 E
Matroosberg, S. Africa . 88 E2 33 23 S 19 40 E
Maţruḥ, Oman .... 75 C6 23 37N 58 30 E
Matsena, Nigeria ..... 83 C7 13 5N 10 5 E
Matsesta, Russia ...... 35 J4 43 34N 39 51 E
Matsu Tao, Taiwan ... 59 E13 26 9N 119 56 E
Matsue, Japan .... 55 G6 35 25N 133 10 E
Matsumae, Japan ..... 54 D10 41 26N 140 7 E
Matsumoto, Japan .... 55 F9 36 15N 138 0 E
Matsusaka, Japan ..... 55 G8 34 34N 136 32 E
Matsuura, Japan ...... 55 H4 33 20N 129 49 E
Matsuyama, Japan .... 55 H6 33 45N 132 45 E
Mattagami →, Canada 104 B3 50 43N 81 29W
Mattancheri, India .... 66 Q10 9 50N 76 15 E
Mattawa, Canada 104 C4 46 20N 78 45W
Matterhorn, Switz. .... 25 K3 45 58N 7 39 E
Mattersburg, Austria .. 27 D9 47 44N 16 24 E
Matthew Town,
  Bahamas 121 B5 20 57N 73 40W
Matthews Ridge,
  Guyana 124 B6 7 37N 60 10W
Mattice, Canada 104 C3 49 40N 83 20W
Mattituck, U.S.A. 117 F12 40 59N 72 32W
Mattō, Japan .... 55 F8 36 31N 136 34 E
Mattoon, U.S.A. 114 F1 39 29N 88 23W
Matuba, Mozam. ..... 89 C5 24 28 S 32 49 E
Matucana, Peru .... 124 F3 11 55 S 76 25W
Matún = Khowst,
  Afghan. .... 68 C3 33 22N 69 58 E
Matura B., Trin. & Tob. 125 K15 10 39N 61 1W
Maturín, Venezuela ... 124 B6 9 45N 63 11W
Matusadona △,
  Zimbabwe .... 87 F2 16 58 S 28 42 E
Matveyev Kurgan,
  Russia .... 33 J10 47 35N 38 57 E
Matxitxako, C., Spain . 38 B2 43 28N 2 47W
Mau, Mad. P., India .. 69 F8 26 17N 78 41 E
Mau, Ut. P., India .... 69 G10 25 56N 83 33 E
Mau, Ut. P., India .... 69 G9 25 17N 81 23 E
Mau Escarpment, Kenya 86 C4 0 40 S 36 0 E
Mau Ranipur, India ... 69 G8 25 16N 79 8 E
Maubeuge, France .... 19 B10 50 17N 3 57 E
Maud, Pt., Australia .. 92 D1 23 6 S 113 45 E
Maude, Australia ..... 95 E3 34 29 S 144 18 E
Maués, Brazil .... 124 D7 3 20 S 57 45W
Mauganj, India .... 67 G12 24 50N 81 55 E
Maughold Hd., I. of Man 14 C3 54 18N 4 18W
Mauguio, France ..... 20 E7 43 37N 4 1 E
Maui, U.S.A. 106 H16 20 48N 156 20W
Maulamyaing =
  Moulmein, Burma .. 67 L20 16 30N 97 40 E
Maule □, Chile .... 126 D1 36 5 S 72 30W
Mauléon-Licharre,
  France 20 E3 43 14N 0 54W
Maumee, U.S.A. 114 E4 41 34N 83 39W
Maumee →, U.S.A. ... 114 E4 41 42N 83 28W
Maumere, Indonesia .. 63 F6 8 38 S 122 13 E
Maumusson, Pertuis de,
  France 20 C2 45 48N 1 14W
Maun, Botswana ...... 88 C3 20 0 S 23 26 E
Mauna Kea, U.S.A. ... 106 J17 19 50N 155 28W
Mauna Loa, U.S.A. ... 106 J17 19 30N 155 35W
Maungmagan Kyunzu,
  Burma .... 64 E1 14 0N 97 48 E
Maupin, U.S.A. 108 D3 45 11N 121 5W
Maure-de-Bretagne,
  France 18 E5 47 59N 1 58W
Maurepas, L., U.S.A. .. 113 K9 30 15N 90 30W
Maures, France .... 21 E10 43 15N 6 15 E
Mauriac, France ...... 20 C6 45 13N 2 19 E
Maurice, L., Australia . 93 E5 29 30 S 131 0 E
Mauricie △, Canada ... 104 C5 46 45N 73 0W
Maurienne, France .... 21 C10 45 13N 6 30 E
Mauritania ■, Africa .. 78 E3 20 50N 10 0W
Mauritius ■, Ind. Oc. . 77 J9 20 0 S 57 0 E
Mauron, France 18 D4 48 9N 2 18W
Mauston, U.S.A. 112 D9 43 48N 90 5W
Mauterndorf, Austria .. 26 D6 47 9N 13 40 E
Mauthen, Austria ..... 26 E6 46 40N 13 0 E
Mauvezin, France ..... 20 E4 43 44N 0 53 E
Mauzé-sur-le-Mignon,
  France 20 B3 46 12N 0 41W

Mavli, India .... 68 G5 24 45N 73 55 E
Mavrovë, Albania .... 44 F3 40 26N 19 32 E
Mavrovo △, Macedonia 44 E4 41 36N 20 45 E
Mavuradonha Mts.,
  Zimbabwe .... 87 F3 16 30 S 31 30 E
Mawa, Dem. Rep. of
  the Congo .... 86 B2 2 45N 26 40 E
Mawai, India .... 69 H9 22 30N 81 4 E
Mawana, India .... 68 E7 29 6N 77 58 E
Mawand, Pakistan .... 68 E3 29 33N 68 38 E
Mawk Mai, Burma ... 67 J20 20 14N 97 37 E
Mawlaik, Burma ...... 67 H19 23 40N 94 26 E
Mawlamyine =
  Moulmein, Burma .. 67 L20 16 30N 97 40 E
Mawqaq, Si. Arabia .. 70 E4 27 25N 41 8 E
Mawson Base,
  Antarctica .... 5 C6 67 30 S 62 53 E
Mawson Coast,
  Antarctica .... 5 C6 68 30 S 63 0 E
Max, U.S.A. 112 B4 47 49N 101 18W
Maxcanú, Mexico 119 C6 20 40N 92 0W
Maxesibeni, S. Africa .. 89 E4 30 49 S 29 23 E
Maxhamish L., Canada 102 B4 59 50N 123 17W
Maxixe, Mozam. ...... 89 C6 23 54 S 35 17 E
Maxville, Canada 117 A10 45 17N 74 51W
Maxwell, U.S.A. 110 F4 39 17N 122 11W
Maxwelton, Australia . 94 C3 20 43 S 142 41 E
May, C., U.S.A. 114 F8 38 56N 74 58W
May Pen, Jamaica .... 120 a 17 58N 77 15W
Maya →, Russia ...... 53 D14 60 28N 134 28 E
Maya Mts., Belize 119 D7 16 30N 89 0W
Mayaguana, Bahamas . 121 B5 22 30N 72 44W
Mayagüez, Puerto Rico 121 d 18 12N 67 9W
Mayahi, Niger .... 83 C6 13 58N 7 40 E
Mayaky, Ukraine ..... 29 C14 47 26N 29 33 E
Mayāmey, Iran .... 71 B7 36 24N 55 42 E
Mayang, China .... 58 D7 27 53N 109 49 E
Mayanup, Australia ... 93 F2 33 57 S 116 27 E
Mayapán, Mexico 119 C7 20 28N 89 11W
Mayapan, Yucatán,
  Mexico 119 C7 20 30N 89 25W
Mayari, Cuba 121 B4 20 40N 75 41W
Mayarō, B., Trin. & Tob. 125 K16 10 14N 61 0W
Maybell, U.S.A. 108 F9 40 31N 108 5W
Maybole, U.K. 13 F4 55 21N 4 42W
Maychew, Ethiopia ... 81 E4 12 50N 39 31 E
Maydān, Iraq .... 70 C5 34 55N 45 37 E
Maydena, Australia ... 95 G4 42 45 S 146 30 E
Mayen, Germany ..... 25 E3 50 19N 7 13 E
Mayenne, France 18 D6 48 20N 0 38W
Mayenne □, France ... 18 D6 48 10N 0 40W
Mayenne →, France ... 18 E6 47 30N 0 32W
Mayer, U.S.A. 109 J7 34 24N 112 14W
Mayerthorpe, Canada . 102 C5 53 57N 115 8W
Mayfield, Ky., U.S.A. . 115 G1 36 44N 88 38W
Mayfield, N.Y., U.S.A. . 117 C10 43 6N 74 16W
Mayhill, U.S.A. 109 K11 32 53N 105 29W
Maykop, Russia ...... 35 H5 44 35N 40 10 E
Maymyo, Burma ..... 64 A1 22 2N 96 28 E
Maynard, Mass., U.S.A. 117 D13 42 26N 71 27W
Maynard, Wash., U.S.A. 110 C4 47 59N 122 55W
Maynard Hills, Australia 93 E2 28 28 S 119 49 E
Mayne →, Australia .. 94 C3 23 40 S 141 55 E
Maynooth, Ireland ... 12 C5 53 23N 6 34W
Mayo, Canada 100 B6 63 38N 135 57W
Mayo □, Ireland 12 C2 53 53N 9 3W
Mayo Daga, Nigeria .. 83 D7 6 59N 11 25 E
Mayo Faran, Nigeria . 83 D7 8 57N 12 4 E
Mayon Volcano, Phil. . 61 E5 13 15N 123 41 E
Mayor I., N.Z. .... 91 G6 37 16 S 176 17 E
Mayorga, Spain 36 C5 42 10N 5 16W
Mayotte ☑, Ind. Oc. . 85 G9 12 50 S 45 10 E
Mayraira Pt., Phil. ... 61 B4 18 39N 120 51 E
Maysān □, Iraq ...... 70 D5 31 55N 47 15 E
Mayskiy, Russia ...... 35 J7 43 47N 44 2 E
Maysville, U.S.A. 114 F4 38 39N 83 46W
Mayu, Indonesia ..... 63 D7 1 30N 126 30 E
Mayville, N. Dak.,
  U.S.A. 112 B6 47 30N 97 20W
Mayville, N.Y., U.S.A. 116 D5 42 15N 79 30W
Mayya, Russia .... 53 C14 61 44N 130 18 E
Mazabuka, Zambia ... 87 F2 15 52 S 27 44 E
Mazagán = El Jadida,
  Morocco 78 B4 33 11N 8 17W
Mazagão, Brazil ...... 125 D8 0 7 S 51 16W
Mazamet, France ..... 20 E6 43 30N 2 20 E
Mazán, Peru .... 124 D4 3 30 S 73 0W
Māzandarān □, Iran .. 71 B7 36 30N 52 0 E
Mazapil, Mexico 118 C4 24 38N 101 34W
Mazara del Vallo, Italy 42 F5 37 39N 12 35 E
Mazarrón, Spain 39 H3 37 38N 1 19W
Mazarrón, G. de, Spain 39 H3 37 27N 1 19W
Mazaruni →, Guyana . 124 B7 6 25N 58 35W
Mazatán, Mexico 118 B2 29 0N 110 8W
Mazatenango,
  Guatemala 120 D1 14 35N 91 30W
Mazatlán, Mexico 118 C3 23 13N 106 25W
Mažeikiai, Lithuania . 9 H20 56 20N 22 20 E
Māzhān, Iran .... 71 C8 32 30N 59 0 E
Mazīnān, Iran .... 71 B8 36 19N 56 56 E
Mazoe, Mozam. ...... 87 F3 16 42 S 33 7 E
Mazoe →, Mozam. ... 87 F3 16 20 S 33 30 E
Mazowe, Zimbabwe .. 87 F3 17 28 S 30 58 E
Mazowieckie □, Poland 31 F8 52 40N 21 0 E
Mazrūb, Sudan ...... 81 E2 14 0N 29 20 E
Mazu Dao, China .... 59 D12 26 10N 119 55 E
Mazurian Lakes =
  Mazurski, Pojezierze,
  Poland .... 30 E7 53 50N 21 0 E
Mazurski, Pojezierze,
  Poland .... 30 E7 53 50N 21 0 E
Mazyr, Belarus .... 33 F5 51 59N 29 15 E
Mbaba, Senegal 82 C1 14 59N 16 44W
Mbabane, Swaziland .. 89 D5 26 18 S 31 6 E
Mbagne, Mauritania .. 82 B2 16 6N 14 47W
M'bahiakro, Ivory C. . 82 D4 7 33N 4 19W
Mbaïki, C.A.R. ...... 84 D3 3 53N 18 1 E
Mbala, Zambia .... 87 D3 8 46 S 31 24 E
Mbalabala, Zimbabwe 89 C4 20 27 S 29 3 E
Mbale, Uganda .... 86 B3 1 8N 34 12 E
Mbalmayo, Cameroon 83 E7 3 33N 11 33 E
Mbam →, Cameroon . 83 E7 4 24N 11 17 E
Mbamba Bay, Tanzania 87 E3 11 13 S 34 49 E
Mbandaka, Dem. Rep. of
  the Congo .... 84 D3 0 1N 18 18 E
Mbanga, Cameroon ... 83 E6 4 30N 9 33 E
Mbanza Congo, Angola 84 F2 6 18 S 14 16 E
Mbanza Ngungu,
  Dem. Rep. of
  the Congo .... 84 F2 5 12 S 14 53 E
Mbarangandu, Tanzania 87 D4 10 11 S 36 48 E
Mbarara, Uganda .... 86 C3 0 35 S 30 40 E
Mbashe →, S. Africa .. 89 E4 32 15 S 28 54 E
Mbatto, Ivory C. 82 D4 6 28N 4 22W
Mbenkuru →, Tanzania 87 D4 9 25 S 39 50 E

Mberengwa, Zimbabwe 87 G2 20 29 S 29 57 E
Mberengwa, Mt.,
  Zimbabwe .... 87 G2 20 37 S 29 55 E
Mberubu, Nigeria .... 83 D6 6 10N 7 38 E
Mbesuma, Zambia .... 87 E3 10 0 S 32 2 E
Mbeya, Tanzania ..... 87 D3 8 54 S 33 29 E
Mbeya □, Tanzania ... 86 D3 8 15 S 33 30 E
M'bili, Sudan .... 81 F2 7 35N 28 15 E
Mbinga, Tanzania .... 87 E4 10 50 S 35 0 E
Mbini = Río Muni □,
  Eq. Guin. .... 84 D2 1 30N 10 0 E
Mboki, C.A.R. .... 81 F2 5 19N 25 58 E
M'bonge, Cameroon .. 83 E6 4 33N 9 5 E
Mboro, Senegal 82 B1 15 9N 16 54W
M'boukou, Rés. de,
  Cameroon .... 83 D7 6 23N 12 50 E
Mboune, Senegal 82 C2 14 42N 13 34W
Mbour, Senegal 82 C1 14 22N 16 54W
Mbout, Mauritania ... 82 B2 16 1N 12 38W
Mbuji-Mayi, Dem. Rep.
  of the Congo .... 86 D1 6 9 S 23 40 E
Mbulu, Tanzania ..... 86 C4 3 45 S 35 30 E
Mburucuyá, Argentina . 126 B4 28 1 S 58 14W
McCarran International,
  Las Vegas ✈ (LAS),
  U.S.A. 111 J11 36 5N 115 9W
Mchinja, Tanzania .... 87 D4 9 44 S 39 45 E
Mchinji, Malawi ...... 87 E3 13 47 S 32 58 E
McMurdo, Antarctica . 5 D11 77 0 S 140 0 E
Mdantsane, S. Africa . 85 L5 32 56 S 27 46 E
Mead, L., U.S.A. 111 J12 36 1N 114 44W
Meade, U.S.A. 113 G4 37 17N 100 20W
Meadow Lake, Canada 103 C7 54 10N 108 26W
Meadow Lake △,
  Canada 103 C7 54 27N 109 0W
Meadow Valley
  Wash →, U.S.A. ... 111 J12 36 40N 114 34W
Meadville, U.S.A. 116 E4 41 39N 80 9W
Meaford, Canada 116 B4 44 36N 80 35W
Mealhada, Portugal ... 36 E2 40 22N 8 27W
Mealy Mts., Canada .. 105 B8 53 10N 58 0W
Meander River, Canada 102 B5 59 2N 117 42W
Meares, C., U.S.A. ... 108 D2 45 37N 124 0W
Mearim →, Brazil .... 125 D10 3 4 S 44 35W
Meath □, Ireland 12 C5 53 40N 6 57W
Meath Park, Canada .. 103 C7 53 27N 105 22W
Meaulne, France ..... 19 F9 46 36N 2 36 E
Meaux, France .... 19 D9 48 58N 2 50 E
Mebechi-Gawa →,
  Japan .... 54 D10 40 31N 141 31 E
Mebulu, Tanjung,
  Indonesia .... 63 K18 8 50 S 115 5 E
Mecanhelas, Mozam. . 87 F4 15 12 S 35 54 E
Mecca = Makkah,
  Si. Arabia .... 75 C2 21 30N 39 54 E
Mecca, U.S.A. 111 M10 33 34N 116 5W
Mechanicsburg, U.S.A. 116 F8 40 13N 77 1W
Mechanicville, U.S.A. . 117 D11 42 54N 73 41W
Mechara, Ethiopia .... 81 F5 8 36N 40 20 E
Mechelen, Belgium ... 17 C4 51 2N 4 29 E
Mecheria, Algeria 78 B5 33 35N 0 18W
Mechernich, Germany . 24 E2 50 35N 6 39 E
Mechetinskaya, Russia 35 G5 46 45N 40 32 E
Mecidiye, Turkey .... 45 F10 40 38N 26 32 E
Mecitözü, Turkey .... 72 B6 40 32N 35 17 E
Mecklenburg-
  Vorpommern □,
  Germany .... 24 B8 53 45N 12 15 E
Mecklenburger Bucht,
  Germany .... 24 A7 54 20N 11 40 E
Meconta, Mozam. .... 87 E4 14 59 S 39 50 E
Mecsek, Hungary .... 28 D3 46 10N 18 18 E
Meda, Portugal 36 E3 40 57N 7 18W
Medan, Indonesia .... 62 D1 3 40N 98 38 E
Médanos de Coro △,
  Venezuela 121 D6 11 35N 69 44W
Medanosa, Pta.,
  Argentina .... 128 F3 48 8 S 66 0W
Mede, Italy .... 40 C5 45 6N 8 44 E
Medea, Algeria .... 78 A6 36 12N 2 50 E
Medebach, Germany .. 24 D4 51 12N 8 42 E
Medellín, Colombia ... 124 B3 6 15N 75 35W
Medelpad, Sweden .... 10 B10 62 33N 16 30 E
Medemblik, Neths. ... 17 B5 52 46N 5 8 E
Mederdra, Mauritania 82 B1 17 0N 15 38W
Medford, Mass., U.S.A. 117 D13 42 25N 71 7W
Medford, Oreg., U.S.A. 108 E2 42 19N 122 52W
Medford, Wis., U.S.A. 112 C9 45 9N 90 20W
Medgidia, Romania ... 29 F13 44 15N 28 19 E
Medi, Sudan .... 81 F3 5 4N 30 42 E
Media Agua, Argentina 126 C2 31 58 S 68 25W
Media Luna, Argentina 126 C2 34 45 S 66 44W
Medianeira, Brazil ... 127 B5 25 17 S 54 5W
Mediaş, Romania ..... 29 D9 46 9N 24 22 E
Medicina, Italy .... 41 D8 44 28N 11 38 E
Medicine Bow, U.S.A. . 108 F10 41 54N 106 12W
Medicine Bow Pk.,
  U.S.A. 108 F10 41 21N 106 19W
Medicine Bow Ra.,
  U.S.A. 108 F10 41 10N 106 25W
Medicine Hat, Canada 103 D6 50 0N 110 45W
Medicine Lake, U.S.A. 112 A2 48 30N 104 30W
Medicine Lodge, U.S.A. 113 G5 37 17N 98 35W
Medina = Al Madīnah,
  Si. Arabia .... 70 E3 24 35N 39 52 E
Medina, N. Dak., U.S.A. 112 B5 46 54N 99 18W
Medina, N.Y., U.S.A. . 116 C6 43 13N 78 23W
Medina, Ohio, U.S.A. . 116 E3 41 8N 81 52W
Medina →, U.S.A. ... 113 L5 29 16N 98 29W
Medina de Pomar, Spain 36 C7 42 56N 3 29W
Medina de Ríoseco,
  Spain 36 D5 41 53N 5 3W
Medina del Campo,
  Spain 36 D6 41 18N 4 55W
Medina L., U.S.A. 113 L5 29 32N 98 56W
Medina Sidonia, Spain 37 J5 36 28N 5 57W
Medinaceli, Spain 38 D2 41 12N 2 30W
Medinipur, India ..... 69 H12 22 25N 87 21 E
Mediterranean Sea,
  Europe .... 6 H7 35 0N 15 0 E
Médoc, France 20 C3 45 10N 0 50W
Medulin, Croatia ..... 41 D10 44 49N 13 55 E
Medveda, Serbia & M. . 44 D5 42 50N 21 32 E
Medvedevo, Russia ... 34 B8 56 37N 47 47 E
Medveditsa →, Tver,
  Russia .... 32 D9 57 5N 37 30 E
Medveditsa →,
  Volgograd, Russia .. 34 F6 49 35N 42 41 E
Medvedok, Russia .... 34 B10 57 30N 50 10 E
Medvezhi, Ostrava,
  Russia .... 53 B17 71 0N 161 0 E
Medvezhyegorsk, Russia 52 C4 63 0N 34 25 E
Medway □, U.K. ..... 15 F8 51 25N 0 32 E
Medway →, U.K. .... 15 F8 51 27N 0 46 E
Medzev, Slovak Rep. . 27 C13 48 43N 20 55 E
Medzilaborce,
  Slovak Rep. .... 27 B14 49 17N 21 52 E

Medžitlija, Macedonia . 44 F5 40 56N 21 26 E
Meekatharra, Australia 93 E2 26 32 S 118 29 E
Meeker, U.S.A. 108 F10 40 2N 107 55W
Meelpaeg Res., Canada 105 C8 48 15N 56 33W
Meersburg, Germany .. 25 H5 47 41N 9 16 E
Meerut, India .... 68 E7 29 1N 77 42 E
Meeteetse, U.S.A. 108 D9 44 9N 108 52W
Mega, Ethiopia .... 81 G4 3 57N 38 19 E
Megálo Khorío, Greece 47 E11 36 27N 27 24 E
Megálo Petalí, Greece . 46 D6 38 0N 24 15 E
Megalópolis, Greece .. 46 D4 37 25N 22 7 E
Meganísi Nísis, Greece 46 C2 38 39 S 20 46 E
Mégara, Greece ...... 46 D5 37 58N 23 22 E
Megasini, India ...... 69 J12 21 38N 86 21 E
Megdhova →, Greece . 46 B3 39 10N 21 45 E
Mégève, France ...... 21 C10 45 51N 6 37 E
Meghalaya □, India .. 67 G17 25 50N 91 0 E
Meghezez, Ethiopia .. 81 F4 9 18N 39 26 E
Meghna →, Bangla. .. 67 H17 22 50N 90 50 E
Mégiscane, L., Canada 104 C4 48 35N 75 55W
Megiste, Greece ...... 47 E11 36 8N 29 34 E
Megra, Russia .... 32 B9 60 5N 37 40 E
Mehadia, Romania ... 28 F7 44 56N 22 23 E
Meharry, Mt., Australia 92 D2 22 59 S 118 35 E
Mehedeby, Sweden ... 10 D11 60 27N 17 25 E
Mehedinţi □, Romania 28 F7 44 40N 22 45 E
Mehekar, India .... 66 J10 20 9N 76 34 E
Mehndawal, India .... 69 F10 26 58N 83 5 E
Mehr Jān, Iran .... 71 C7 33 50N 55 6 E
Mehrābād, Iran ...... 70 B5 36 53N 47 55 E
Mehrān, Iran .... 70 C5 33 7N 46 10 E
Mehrīz, Iran .... 71 D7 31 35N 54 28 E
Mehun-sur-Yèvre,
  France .... 19 E9 47 10N 2 13 E
Mei Jiang →, China .. 59 E11 24 25N 116 35 E
Mei Xian, China ...... 56 G4 34 18N 107 55 E
Meicheng, China ..... 59 C12 29 29N 119 16 E
Meichengzhen, China . 59 C8 28 9N 111 40 E
Meichuan, China ..... 59 B10 30 18N 115 31 E
Meigu, China .... 58 C4 28 16N 103 20 E
Meiktila, Burma ..... 67 J19 20 53N 95 54 E
Meinerzhagen, Germany 24 D3 51 6N 7 38 E
Meiningen, Germany .. 24 E6 50 34N 10 25 E
Meira, Serra de, Spain 36 B3 43 15N 7 15W
Meiringen, Switz. .... 25 J4 46 43N 8 12 E
Meishan, China ...... 58 B4 30 3N 103 23 E
Meissen, Germany .... 24 D9 51 9N 13 29 E
Meissner-Kaufunger
  Wald △, Germany .. 24 D5 51 16N 9 45 E
Meitan, China .... 58 D6 27 45N 107 29 E
Meizhou, China ...... 59 E11 24 16N 116 6 E
Meja, India .... 69 G10 25 9N 82 7 E
Mejillones, Chile ..... 126 A1 23 10 S 70 30W
Mekdela, Ethiopia ... 81 E4 11 24N 39 10 E
Mekele, Ethiopia ..... 81 E4 13 33N 39 30 E
Mekhtar, Pakistan ... 66 D6 30 30N 69 15 E
Meknès, Morocco 78 B4 33 57N 5 33W
Meko, Nigeria .... 83 D5 7 27N 2 52 E
Mekong →, Asia ..... 65 H6 9 30N 106 15 E
Mekongga, Indonesia . 63 E6 3 39 S 121 15 E
Mekrou →, Benin .... 83 C5 12 25N 2 50 E
Mekvari = Kür →,
  Azerbaijan .... 73 C13 39 29N 49 15 E
Mel, Italy .... 41 B9 46 4N 12 5 E
Melagiri Hills, India .. 66 N10 12 20N 77 30 E
Melaka, Malaysia .... 65 L4 2 15N 102 15 E
Melalap, Malaysia .... 62 C5 5 10N 116 5 E
Melambes, Greece .... 49 D6 35 8N 24 40 E
Melanesia, Pac. Oc. .. 96 H7 4 0 S 155 0 E
Melaya, Indonesia .... 63 J17 8 17 S 114 30 E
Melbourne, Australia . 95 F4 37 50 S 145 0 E
Melbourne, U.S.A. ... 115 L5 28 5N 80 37W
Melchor Múzquiz,
  Mexico 118 B4 27 50N 101 30W
Melchor Ocampo,
  Mexico 118 C4 24 52N 101 40W
Méldola, Italy .... 41 D9 44 7N 12 5 E
Meldorf, Germany .... 24 A5 54 5N 9 5 E
Melegnano, Italy ..... 40 C6 45 21N 9 19 E
Melenci, Serbia & M. . 28 E5 45 32N 20 20 E
Melenki, Russia ...... 34 C5 55 20N 41 37 E
Mélèzes →, Canada .. 104 A5 57 40N 69 29W
Melfi, Italy .... 43 B8 41 0N 15 39 E
Melfort, Canada 103 C8 52 50N 104 37W
Melfort, Zimbabwe ... 87 F3 18 0 S 31 25 E
Melgaço, Portugal 36 C2 42 7N 8 15W
Melgar de Fernamental,
  Spain 36 C6 42 27N 4 17W
Melhus, Norway ...... 8 E14 63 17N 10 18 E
Melide, Spain 36 C2 42 55N 8 1W
Meligalá, Greece ..... 46 D3 37 15N 21 59 E
Melilla, N. Afr. 78 A5 35 21N 2 57W
Melíli, Italy .... 43 E8 37 11N 15 7 E
Melipilla, Chile ...... 126 C1 33 42 S 71 15W
Mélissa, Ákra, Greece 49 D6 35 6N 24 33 E
Melissa Óros, Greece . 47 D8 37 32N 26 4 E
Melita, Canada 103 D8 49 15N 101 0W
Mélito di Porto Salvo,
  Italy .... 43 E8 37 55N 15 47 E
Melitopol, Ukraine ... 33 J8 46 50N 35 22 E
Melk, Austria .... 26 C8 48 13N 15 20 E
Mellan Fryken, Sweden 10 E7 59 45N 13 10 E
Mellansel, Sweden ... 8 E18 63 26N 18 19 E
Mellbystrand, Sweden 11 H6 56 30N 12 56 E
Melle, France 20 B3 46 14N 0 10W
Melle, Germany ...... 24 C4 52 12N 8 20 E
Mellen, U.S.A. 112 B9 46 20N 90 40W
Mellerud, Sweden .... 11 F6 58 41N 12 28 E
Mellette, U.S.A. 112 C5 45 9N 98 30W
Mellid = Melide, Spain 36 C2 42 55N 8 1W
Mellieha, Malta ...... 49 D1 35 57N 14 22 E
Mellish Reef, Australia 94 B5 17 25 S 155 50 E
Mellit, Sudan .... 81 E2 14 7N 25 34 E
Mellrichstadt, Germany 24 E6 50 25N 10 17 E
Melnik, Bulgaria ..... 44 E7 41 30N 23 25 E
Mělník, Czech Rep. ... 26 A7 50 22N 14 23 E
Melnytsya-Podilska,
  Ukraine .... 29 B11 48 37N 26 10 E
Melo, Uruguay .... 127 C5 32 20 S 54 10W
Melolo, Indonesia .... 63 F6 9 53 S 120 40 E
Melouprey, Cambodia 64 F5 13 48N 105 16 E
Melrose, Australia .... 95 E4 32 42 S 146 57 E
Melrose, U.K. 13 F6 55 36N 2 43W
Melrose, Minn., U.S.A. 112 C7 45 40N 94 49W
Melrose, N. Mex., U.S.A. 113 H3 34 26N 103 38W
Melstone, U.S.A. 108 C10 46 36N 107 52W
Melsungen, Germany . 24 D5 51 7N 9 32 E
Melton Mowbray, U.K. 14 E7 52 47N 0 54W
Melun, France .... 19 D9 48 32N 2 39 E
Melur, India .... 66 P11 10 2N 78 23 E
Melut, Sudan .... 81 E3 10 27N 32 13 E
Melville, Canada 103 C8 50 55N 102 50W
Melville, U.S.A. 113 K9 30 42N 91 45W
Melville, C., Australia 94 A3 14 11 S 144 30 E
Melville, L., Canada .. 105 B8 53 30N 60 0W
Melville B., Australia . 94 A2 12 0 S 136 45 E
Melville I., Australia . 92 B5 11 30 S 131 0 E
Melville I., Canada ... 98 B8 75 30N 112 0W

Melville Pen., Canada . 101 B11 68 0N 84 0W
Mélykút, Hungary .... 28 D4 46 11N 19 25 E
Memaliaj, Albania .... 44 F3 40 25N 19 56 E
Memba, Mozam. ..... 87 E5 14 11S 40 30 E
Memboro, Indonesia .. 63 F5 9 30S 119 30 E
Membrilla, Spain 37 G7 38 59N 3 21W
Memel = Klaipėda,
  Lithuania .... 9 J19 55 43N 21 10 E
Memel, S. Africa ..... 89 D4 27 38S 29 36 E
Memmingen, Germany . 25 H6 47 58N 10 10 E
Mempawah, Indonesia . 62 D3 0 30N 109 5 E
Memphis, Egypt ..... 80 J7 29 52N 31 12 E
Memphis, Mich., U.S.A. 116 D2 42 54N 82 46W
Memphis, Tenn., U.S.A. 113 H10 35 8N 90 3W
Memphis, Tex., U.S.A. 113 H4 34 44N 100 33W
Memphremagog, L.,
  U.S.A. 117 B12 45 0N 72 12W
Mena, Ukraine ...... 33 G7 51 31N 32 13 E
Mena, U.S.A. 113 H7 34 35N 94 15W
Mena →, Ethiopia .... 81 F5 5 40N 40 50 E
Menai Strait, U.K. ... 14 D3 53 11N 4 13W
Ménaka, Mali .... 83 B5 15 59N 2 18 E
Menan = Chao
  Phraya →, Thailand . 64 F3 13 32N 100 36 E
Menarandra →, Madag. 89 D7 25 17S 44 30 E
Menard, U.S.A. 113 K5 30 55N 99 47W
Menawashei, Sudan ... 81 E1 12 41N 24 59 E
Mendawai →, Indonesia 62 E4 3 30S 113 0 E
Mende, France ...... 20 D7 44 31N 3 30 E
Mendebo Mts., Ethiopia 81 F4 7 0N 39 22 E
Mendeleyev Ridge,
  Arctic 4 B17 80 0N 178 0W
Menden, Germany .... 24 D3 51 26N 7 47 E
Menderes, Turkey .... 47 C9 38 14N 27 8 E
Mendez, Mexico 119 B5 25 7N 98 34W
Mendhar, India ..... 69 C6 33 35N 74 10 E
Mendi, Ethiopia ..... 81 F4 9 47N 35 4 E
Mendip Hills, U.K. ... 15 F5 51 17N 2 40W
Mendocino, U.S.A. ... 108 G2 39 19N 123 48W
Mendocino, C., U.S.A. 108 F1 40 26N 124 25W
Mendota, Calif., U.S.A. 110 J6 36 45N 120 23W
Mendota, Ill., U.S.A. . 112 E10 41 33N 89 7W
Mendoyo, Indonesia .. 63 J17 8 23S 114 42 E
Mendoza, Argentina .. 126 C2 32 50S 68 52W
Mendoza □, Argentina 126 C2 33 0S 69 0W
Mene Grande,
  Venezuela 124 B4 9 49N 70 56W
Menemen, Turkey .... 47 C9 38 34N 27 3 E
Menen, Belgium ..... 17 D3 50 47N 3 7 E
Menfi, Italy .... 42 E5 37 36N 12 58 E
Mengdingjie, China .. 58 F2 23 31N 98 58 E
Mengeš, Slovenia .... 41 B11 46 10N 14 35 E
Menggala, Indonesia .. 62 E3 4 30S 105 15 E
Mengíbar, Spain 37 H7 37 58N 3 48W
Mengjin, China ..... 56 G7 34 55N 112 45 E
Mengla, China ...... 58 G3 21 20N 101 25 E
Menglian, China ..... 58 F2 22 21N 99 27 E
Mengshan, China .... 59 E8 24 14N 110 55 E
Mengyin, China ..... 57 G9 35 40N 117 58 E
Mengzhe, China ..... 58 F3 22 0N 100 15 E
Mengzi, China ...... 58 F4 23 20N 103 22 E
Menihek, Canada 105 B6 54 28N 56 36W
Menihek L., Canada .. 105 B6 54 0N 67 0W
Menin = Menen,
  Belgium .... 17 D3 50 47N 3 7 E
Menindee, Australia .. 95 E3 32 20S 142 25 E
Menindee L., Australia 95 E3 32 20S 142 25 E
Meningie, Australia ... 95 F2 35 50S 139 18 E
Menjangan, Pulau,
  Indonesia .... 63 J17 8 7S 114 31 E
Menlo Park, U.S.A. .. 110 H4 37 27N 122 12W
Menominee, U.S.A. .. 114 C2 45 6N 87 37W
Menominee →, U.S.A. 114 C2 45 6N 87 36W
Menomonie, U.S.A. .. 112 C9 44 53N 91 55W
Menongue, Angola ... 85 G3 14 48S 17 52 E
Menorca, Spain ..... 48 B11 40 0N 4 0 E
Menorca ✈ (MAH),
  Spain .... 38 F9 39 50N 4 16 E
Mentakab, Malaysia .. 65 L4 3 29N 102 21 E
Mentawai, Kepulauan,
  Indonesia .... 62 E1 2 0S 99 0 E
Menton, France ..... 21 E11 43 50N 7 29 E
Mentor, U.S.A. 116 E3 41 40N 81 21W
Menzies, Australia ... 93 E3 29 40S 121 2 E
Meob B., Namibia ... 88 C1 24 25S 14 34 E
Me'ona, Israel ...... 74 B4 33 1N 35 15 E
Meoqui, Mexico 118 B3 28 17N 105 29W
Mepaco, Mozam. .... 87 F3 15 57S 30 48 E
Meppel, Neths. ...... 17 B6 52 42N 6 12 E
Meppen, Germany ... 24 C3 52 42N 7 17 E
Mequinenza, Spain .. 38 D5 41 22N 0 17 E
Mequinenza, Embalse
  de, Spain .... 38 D5 41 25N 0 15 E
Mer, France .... 18 E8 47 42N 1 30 E
Merabéllou, Kólpos,
  Greece .... 49 D7 35 10N 25 50 E
Merak, Indonesia .... 63 F12 6 10N 106 26 E
Meramangye, L.,
  Australia .... 93 E5 28 25S 132 13 E
Meran = Merano, Italy 41 B8 46 40N 11 9 E
Merano, Italy .... 41 B8 46 40N 11 9 E
Merate, Italy .... 40 C6 45 42N 9 25 E
Merauke, Indonesia .. 63 F10 8 29S 140 24 E
Merbein, Australia ... 95 E3 34 10S 142 2 E
Merbuk, Gunung,
  Indonesia .... 63 J17 8 13S 114 39 E
Merca = Marka,
  Somali Rep. ...... 75 G3 1 48N 44 50 E
Mercantour →, France 21 D10 44 16N 6 43 E
Mercato Saraceno, Italy 41 E9 43 57N 12 12 E
Merced, U.S.A. 110 H6 37 18N 120 29W
Merced →, U.S.A. ... 110 H6 37 21N 120 59W
Merced Pk., U.S.A. .. 110 H7 37 36N 119 24W
Mercedes, Buenos Aires,
  Argentina 126 C4 34 40S 59 30W
Mercedes, Corrientes,
  Argentina 126 B4 29 10S 58 5W
Mercedes, San Luis,
  Argentina 126 C2 33 40S 65 21W
Mercedes, Uruguay ... 126 C4 33 12S 58 0W
Mercedes, U.S.A. 113 M6 26 9N 97 55W
Merceditas, Chile 126 B1 28 20S 70 35W
Mercer, N.Z. .... 91 G5 37 16S 175 5 E
Mercer, U.S.A. 116 E4 41 14N 80 15W
Mercer Island, U.S.A. 110 C4 47 35N 122 15W
Mercury, U.S.A. 111 J11 36 40N 115 58W
Mercy, C., Canada ... 101 B13 65 0N 63 30W
Merdrignac, France .. 18 D4 48 11N 2 27W
Mere, U.K. 15 F5 51 6N 2 16W
Meredith, C., Falk. Is. 122 J4 52 15S 60 40W
Meredith, L., U.S.A. . 113 H4 35 43N 101 33W
Merefa, Ukraine ..... 33 H9 49 48N 36 3 E
Merei, Romania ..... 29 E11 45 7N 26 43 E
Merga = Nukheila,
  Sudan .... 80 D2 19 1N 26 21 E
Mergui, Burma ...... 64 F2 12 26N 98 34 E
Mergui Arch. = Myeik
  Kyunzu, Burma ... 65 G1 11 30N 97 30 E

Méribel-les-Allues,
  France .... 21 C10 45 25N 6 34 E
Meriç, Turkey ...... 45 E10 41 11N 26 25 E
Meriç →, Turkey .... 45 F10 40 52N 26 12 E
Mérida, Mexico 119 C7 20 58N 89 37W
Mérida, Spain 37 G4 38 55N 6 25W
Mérida, Venezuela ... 124 B4 8 24N 71 8W
Mérida, Cord. de,
  Venezuela 124 B4 9 0N 71 0W
Meriden, U.K. 15 E6 52 26N 1 38W
Meriden, U.S.A. 117 E12 41 32N 72 48W
Meridian, Calif., U.S.A. 110 F5 39 9N 121 55W
Meridian, Idaho, U.S.A. 108 E5 43 37N 116 24W
Meridian, Miss., U.S.A. 115 J1 32 22N 88 42W
Mérignac, France 20 D3 44 51N 0 39W
Mérinaghène, Senegal . 82 B1 15 57N 15 55W
Merinda, Australia ... 94 C4 20 2S 148 11 E
Mering, Germany .... 25 G6 48 16N 10 59 E
Meringa, Nigeria .... 83 C7 10 44N 12 9 E
Merir, Pac. Oc. ..... 63 D8 4 10N 132 30 E
Merirumã, Brazil 125 C8 1 15N 54 50W
Merkel, U.S.A. 113 J5 32 28N 100 1W
Mermaid Reef, Australia 92 C2 17 6S 119 36 E
Merowe, Sudan ...... 80 D3 18 29N 31 46 E
Merredin, Australia .. 93 F2 31 28S 118 18 E
Merrick, U.K. 13 F4 55 8N 4 28W
Merrickville, Canada .. 117 B9 44 55N 75 50W
Merrill, Oreg., U.S.A. 108 E3 42 1N 121 36W
Merrill, Wis., U.S.A. . 112 C10 45 11N 89 41W
Merrimack →, U.S.A. 117 D14 42 49N 70 49W
Merriman, U.S.A. ... 112 D4 42 55N 101 42W
Merritt, Canada 102 C4 50 10N 120 45W
Merritt Island, U.S.A. 115 L5 28 21N 80 42W
Merriwa, Australia ... 95 E5 32 6S 150 22 E
Merry I., Canada 104 A4 55 29N 77 31W
Merryville, U.S.A. ... 113 K8 30 45N 93 33W
Mersa Fatma, Eritrea . 81 E5 14 57N 40 17 E
Mersch, Lux. .... 17 E6 49 44N 6 7 E
Merse →, Italy ..... 41 E8 43 5N 11 22 E
Mersea I., U.K. ..... 15 F8 51 47N 0 58 E
Merseburg, Germany . 24 D7 51 22N 11 59 E
Mersey →, U.K. 14 D4 53 25N 3 1W
Merseyside □, U.K. .. 14 D4 53 31N 3 2W
Mersin, Turkey ...... 70 B2 36 51N 34 36 E
Mersing, Malaysia ... 65 L4 2 25N 103 50 E
Merta, India .... 68 F6 26 39N 74 4 E
Merta Road, India ... 68 F5 26 43N 73 55 E
Merthyr Tydfil, U.K. . 15 F4 51 45N 3 22W
Merthyr Tydfil □, U.K. 15 F4 51 46N 3 21W
Mértola, Portugal 37 H3 37 40N 7 40W
Mertzon, U.S.A. 113 K4 31 16N 100 49W
Méru, France .... 19 C9 49 13N 2 8 E
Meru, Kenya .... 86 B4 0 3N 37 40 E
Meru, Tanzania ..... 86 C4 3 15S 36 46 E
Meru △, Kenya ..... 86 B4 0 5N 38 10 E
Merville, France ..... 19 B9 50 38N 2 38 E
Méry-sur-Seine, France 19 D10 48 31N 3 54 E
Merzifon, Turkey .... 72 B6 40 53N 35 32 E
Merzig, Germany .... 25 F2 49 26N 6 37 E
Mesa, U.S.A. 109 K8 33 25N 111 50W
Mesa Verde △, U.S.A. 109 H9 37 11N 108 29W
Mesagne, Italy ...... 43 B10 40 34N 17 48 E
Mesanagrós, Greece .. 49 C9 36 1N 27 49 E
Mesaoría, Cyprus .... 49 D12 35 12N 33 14 E
Mesarás, Kólpos, Greece 49 D6 35 6N 24 47 E
Meschede, Germany .. 24 D4 51 20N 8 18 E
Mescit, Turkey ...... 73 B9 40 21N 41 11 E
Mesfinto, Ethiopia ... 81 E4 13 20N 37 22 E
Mesgouez, L., Canada 104 B5 51 20N 75 0W
Meshchovsk, Russia .. 32 E8 54 22N 35 17 E
Meshed = Mashhad, Iran 71 B8 36 20N 59 35 E
Meshoppen, U.S.A. .. 117 E8 41 36N 76 3W
Meshra er Req, Sudan 81 F2 8 25N 29 18 E
Mesilinka →, Canada 102 B4 56 6N 124 30W
Mesilla, U.S.A. 109 K10 32 16N 106 48W
Meslay-du-Maine,
  France 18 E6 47 58N 0 33W
Mesocco, Switz. ..... 25 J5 46 23N 9 12 E
Mesolóngion, Greece . 46 C3 38 21N 21 28 E
Mesopotamia = Al
  Jazirah, Iraq ...... 70 C5 33 30N 44 0 E
Mesopotamia, U.S.A. . 116 E4 41 27N 80 57W
Mesopotamon, Greece . 46 B2 39 14N 20 32 E
Mesoraca, Italy ..... 43 C9 39 5N 16 48 E
Mésou Volímais =
  Volímais, Greece ... 46 D2 37 52N 20 39 E
Mesquite, U.S.A. 109 H6 36 47N 114 6W
Messaad, Algeria .... 78 B6 34 8N 3 30 E
Messac, France 18 E5 47 49N 1 50W
Messalo →, Mozam. .. 87 E4 11 25S 39 15 E
Messaména, Cameroon 83 E7 3 48N 12 49 E
Messeue →, Mozam. .. 85 D3 37 12N 21 58 E
Messina = Musina,
  S. Africa .... 89 C5 22 20S 30 5 E
Messina, Italy .... 43 D8 38 11N 15 34 E
Messina, Str. di, Italy 43 D8 38 15N 15 35 E
Messíni, Greece ..... 46 D4 37 4N 22 1 E
Messínia □, Greece ... 46 D3 37 10N 22 0 E
Messiniakós Kólpos,
  Greece .... 46 E4 36 45N 22 5 E
Messkirch, Germany . 25 H5 47 59N 9 7 E
Messlingen, Sweden .. 10 B6 62 40N 12 50 E
Messonghi, Greece ... 49 B3 39 29N 19 56 E
Mesta →, Bulgaria ... 44 E7 40 54N 24 49 E
Mestá, Ákra, Greece .. 47 C7 38 16N 25 53 E
Mestanza, Spain 37 G6 38 35N 4 4W
Mestre, Italy .... 41 C9 45 29N 12 15 E
Mesudiye, Turkey .... 72 B7 40 28N 37 46 E
Meta →, S. Amer. ... 124 B5 6 12N 67 28W
Meta Incognita Pen.,
  Canada 101 B13 62 45N 68 30W
Metabetchouan, Canada 105 C5 48 26N 71 52W
Metairie, U.S.A. 113 L9 29 58N 90 10W
Metalici, Munții,
  Romania .... 28 D7 46 15N 22 50 E
Metaline Falls, U.S.A. 108 A5 48 52N 117 22W
Metallifere, Colline,
  Italy .... 40 E8 43 10N 10 55 E
Metán, Argentina 126 B3 25 30S 65 0W
Metangula, Mozam. .. 87 E3 12 40S 34 50 E
Metauro →, Italy .... 41 E10 43 50N 13 3 E
Metema, Ethiopia .... 81 E4 12 56N 36 13 E
Metengobalame,
  Mozam. .... 87 E3 14 49S 34 30 E
Méthana, Greece .... 46 D5 37 35N 23 23 E
Methóni, Greece ..... 46 E3 36 49N 21 42 E
Methven, N.Z. ...... 91 K3 43 38S 171 40 E
Metil, Mozam. ...... 87 F4 16 24S 39 0 E
Metkovets, Bulgaria .. 44 C7 43 37N 23 10 E
Metković, Croatia ... 41 E14 43 6N 17 39 E
Metlakatla, U.S.A. ... 100 C6 55 8N 131 35W
Metlika, Slovenia .... 41 C12 45 40N 15 20 E
Metropolis, U.S.A. ... 113 G10 37 9N 88 44W
Métsovon, Greece .... 46 B3 39 48N 21 12 E
Metu, Ethiopia ...... 81 F4 8 18N 35 35 E
Metz, France .... 19 C13 49 8N 6 10 E
Metzingen, Germany . 25 G5 48 31N 9 17 E

Meulaboh, Indonesia . 62 D1 4 11N 96 3 E
Meung-sur-Loire, France 19 E8 47 50N 1 40 E
Meureudu, Indonesia . 62 C1 5 19N 96 10 E
Meurthe →, France .. 19 D13 48 47N 6 9 E
Meurthe-et-Moselle □,
  France .... 19 D13 48 52N 6 0 E
Meuse □, France .... 19 C12 49 8N 5 25 E
Meuse →, Europe ... 17 D5 50 45N 5 41 E
Meuselwitz, Germany . 24 D8 51 2N 12 17 E
Mexia, U.S.A. 113 K6 31 41N 96 29W
Mexiana, I., Brazil ... 125 D9 0 0 49 30W
Mexicali, Mexico 111 N11 32 40N 115 30W
Mexican Plateau,
  Mexico 98 G9 25 0N 104 0W
Mexican Water, U.S.A. 109 H9 36 57N 109 32W
México, Mexico 119 D5 19 20N 99 10W
Mexico, Maine, U.S.A. 117 B14 44 34N 70 33W
Mexico, Mo., U.S.A. . 112 F9 39 10N 91 53W
Mexico, N.Y., U.S.A. . 117 C8 43 28N 76 18W
México □, Mexico ... 119 D5 19 20N 99 10W
Mexico ■, Cent. Amer. 118 C4 25 0N 105 0W
Mexico, G. of,
  Cent. Amer. 119 C7 25 0N 90 0W
Mexico B., U.S.A. ... 117 C8 43 35N 76 20W
Meydän-e Naftün, Iran 71 D6 31 56N 49 18 E
Meydani, Ra's-e, Iran 71 E8 25 24N 59 6 E
Meyenburg, Germany . 24 B8 53 18N 12 14 E
Meymac, France ..... 20 C6 45 32N 2 10 E
Meymaneh, Afghan. .. 66 B4 35 53N 64 38 E
Meyrueis, France .... 20 D7 44 12N 3 27 E
Meyssac, France ..... 20 C5 45 3N 1 40 E
Meyzieu, France ..... 21 C6 45 46N 4 59 E
Mezdra, Bulgaria .... 44 C7 43 12N 23 42 E
Mèze, France .... 20 E7 43 27N 3 36 E
Mezen, Russia ...... 52 C5 65 50N 44 20 E
Mezen →, Russia .... 52 C5 65 44N 44 22 E
Mézenc, Mt., France . 21 D8 44 54N 4 11 E
Mezeş, Munții, Romania 28 C8 47 5N 23 5 E
Mezha →, Russia .... 32 E6 55 44N 31 33 E
Mézidon-Canon, France 18 C6 49 5N 0 1W
Mézières-en-Brenne,
  France .... 20 B5 46 49N 1 13 E
Mézilhac, France .... 21 D8 44 49N 4 21 E
Mézin, France ...... 20 D4 44 4N 0 16 E
Mezőberény, Hungary 28 D6 46 49N 21 3 E
Mezőfalva, Hungary .. 28 D3 46 55N 18 49 E
Mezőhegyes, Hungary 28 D5 46 19N 20 49 E
Mezőkövácsháza,
  Hungary .... 28 D5 46 25N 20 57 E
Mezőkövesd, Hungary 28 C5 47 49N 20 35 E
Mézos, France 20 D2 44 5N 1 10W
Mezőtúr, Hungary ... 28 C5 47 1N 20 41 E
Mezquital, Mexico ... 118 C4 23 29N 104 23W
Mezzolombardo, Italy 40 B8 46 13N 11 5 E
Mfolozi →, S. Africa . 89 D5 28 25S 32 26 E
Mgeta, Tanzania .... 87 D4 8 22S 36 6 E
Mglin, Russia .... 33 F7 53 2N 32 50 E
Mhlaba Hills, Zimbabwe 87 F3 18 30S 30 30 E
Mhow, India .... 68 H6 22 33N 75 50 E
Miahuatlán, Mexico .. 119 D5 16 21N 96 36W
Miajadas, Spain 37 F5 39 9N 5 54W
Miami, Fla., U.S.A. .. 115 N5 25 47N 80 11W
Miami, Okla., U.S.A. . 113 G7 36 53N 94 53W
Miami, Tex., U.S.A. .. 113 H4 35 42N 100 38W
Miami Beach, U.S.A. . 115 N5 25 47N 80 8W
Mian Xian, China .... 56 H4 33 10N 106 32 E
Mianchi, China ..... 56 G6 34 48N 111 48 E
Miändarreh, Iran .... 71 C7 35 37N 53 39 E
Miändowāb, Iran .... 70 B5 37 0N 46 5 E
Miandrivazo, Madag. . 89 B8 19 31S 45 29 E
Miāneh, Iran .... 70 B5 37 30N 47 40 E
Mianning, China .... 58 C4 28 32N 102 9 E
Mianwali, Pakistan ... 68 C4 32 38N 71 28 E
Mianyang, China .... 58 B5 31 22N 104 47 E
Mianzhu, China ..... 58 B5 31 22N 104 8 E
Miaoli, Taiwan ...... 59 E13 24 37N 120 49 E
Miarinarivo,
  Antananarivo, Madag. 89 B8 18 57S 46 55 E
Miarinarivo, Toamasina,
  Madag. .... 89 B8 16 38S 48 15 E
Miariravaratra, Madag. 89 C8 20 13S 47 31 E
Miass, Russia .... 52 D7 54 59N 60 6 E
Miasteczko Krajeńskie,
  Poland .... 31 E4 53 7N 17 1 E
Miastko, Poland ..... 30 E3 54 0N 16 58 E
Mica, S. Africa ...... 89 C5 24 10S 30 48 E
Micăsasa, Romania .. 29 D9 46 7N 24 7 E
Michalovce, Slovak Rep. 27 C14 48 47N 21 58 E
Michigan □, U.S.A. .. 114 C3 44 0N 85 0W
Michigan, L., U.S.A. . 114 D2 44 0N 87 0W
Michigan City, U.S.A. 114 E2 41 43N 86 54W
Michika, Nigeria .... 83 C7 10 36N 13 23 E
Michipicoten I., Canada 104 C2 47 40N 85 40W
Michoacán □, Mexico 118 D4 19 0N 102 0W
Michurin, Bulgaria .. 45 D11 42 9N 27 51 E
Michurinsk, Russia .. 34 D5 52 58N 40 27 E
Mico, Pta., Nic. 120 D3 12 0N 83 30W
Micoud, St. Lucia ... 121 f 13 49N 60 54W
Micronesia, Pac. Oc. . 96 G7 11 0N 160 0 E
Micronesia, Federated
  States of ■, Pac. Oc. 96 G7 9 0N 150 0 E
Mid-Oceanic Ridge,
  Ind. Oc. .... 96 M1 42 0S 90 0 E
Midai, Indonesia .... 62 D3 3 0N 107 47 E
Midale, Canada 103 D8 49 25N 103 20W
Middelburg, Neths. .. 17 C3 51 30N 3 36 E
Middelburg,
  Eastern Cape,
  S. Africa .... 88 E4 31 30S 25 0 E
Middelburg,
  Mpumalanga,
  S. Africa .... 89 D4 25 49S 29 28 E
Middelfart, Denmark . 11 J3 55 30N 9 43 E
Middelpos, S. Africa . 88 E3 31 55S 20 13 E
Middelwit, S. Africa . 88 C4 24 51S 27 3 E
Middle Alkali L., U.S.A. 108 F3 41 27N 120 5W
Middle Bass I., U.S.A. 116 E2 41 41N 82 49W
Middle East, Asia .... 50 F7 38 0N 40 0 E
Middle Fork Feather →,
  U.S.A. 110 F5 38 33N 121 30W
Middle I., Australia .. 93 F3 34 6S 123 11 E
Middle Loup →, U.S.A. 112 E5 41 17N 98 24W
Middle Sackville,
  Canada 105 D7 44 47N 63 42W
Middleboro, U.S.A. .. 117 E14 41 54N 70 55W
Middleburg, Fla., U.S.A. 115 K5 30 4N 81 52W
Middleburg, N.Y., U.S.A. 117 D10 42 36N 74 20W
Middleburg, Pa., U.S.A. 116 F7 40 47N 77 3W
Middlebury, U.S.A. .. 117 B11 44 1N 73 10W
Middlemount, Australia 94 C4 22 50S 148 40 E
Middleport, N.Y., U.S.A. 116 C6 43 13N 78 29W
Middleport, Ohio,
  U.S.A. 114 F4 39 0N 82 3W
Middlesbrough, U.K. . 14 C6 54 35N 1 13W

Middlesbrough □, U.K. 14 C6 54 28N 1 13W
Middlesex, Belize 120 C2 17 2N 88 31W
Middlesex, N.J., U.S.A. 117 F10 40 36N 74 30W
Middlesex, N.Y., U.S.A. 116 D7 42 42N 77 16W
Middleton, Australia . 94 C3 22 22S 141 32 E
Middleton, Canada .. 105 D6 44 57N 65 4W
Middleton Cr. →,
  Australia .... 94 C3 22 35S 141 51 E
Middletown, U.K. ... 12 B5 54 17N 6 51W
Middletown, Calif.,
  U.S.A. 110 G4 38 45N 122 37W
Middletown, Conn.,
  U.S.A. 117 E12 41 34N 72 39W
Middletown, N.Y.,
  U.S.A. 117 E10 41 27N 74 25W
Middletown, Ohio,
  U.S.A. 114 F3 39 31N 84 24W
Middletown, Pa., U.S.A. 116 F8 40 12N 76 44W
Midge Point, Australia 94 J6 20 39S 148 43 E
Midhurst, U.K. 15 G7 50 59N 0 44W
Mīdī, Yemen .... 81 D5 16 20N 42 45 E
Midi, Canal du →,
  France .... 20 E5 43 45N 1 21 E
Midi-d'Ossau, Pic du,
  France 20 F3 42 50N 0 26W
Midi-Pyrénées □, France 20 E5 43 55N 1 45 E
Midland, Australia ... 93 F2 31 54S 116 1 E
Midland, Canada 116 B5 44 45N 79 50W
Midland, Calif., U.S.A. 111 M12 33 52N 114 48W
Midland, Mich., U.S.A. 114 D3 43 37N 84 14W
Midland, Pa., U.S.A. . 116 F4 40 39N 80 27W
Midland, Tex., U.S.A. 113 K3 32 0N 102 3W
Midlands □, Zimbabwe 87 F2 19 40S 29 0 E
Midleton, Ireland 12 E3 51 55N 8 10W
Midlothian, U.S.A. .. 113 J6 32 30N 97 0W
Midlothian □, U.K. .. 13 F5 55 51N 3 5W
Midongy,
  Tangorombohitr' i,
  Madag. .... 89 C8 23 30S 47 0 E
Midongy Atsimo,
  Madag. .... 89 C8 23 35S 47 1 E
Midou →, France ... 20 E3 43 54N 0 30W
Midouze →, France .. 20 E3 43 48N 0 51W
Midsayap, Phil. ..... 61 H6 7 12N 124 32 E
Midu, China .... 58 E3 25 18N 100 30 E
Midway Is., Pac. Oc. . 96 E10 28 13N 177 22W
Midway Wells, U.S.A. 111 N11 32 41N 115 7W
Midwest, U.S.A. 107 B9 42 0N 90 0W
Midwest, Wyo., U.S.A. 108 E10 43 25N 106 16W
Midwest City, U.S.A. 113 H6 35 27N 97 14W
Midyat, Turkey ..... 70 B4 37 25N 41 23 E
Midzŏr, Bulgaria .... 44 C6 43 24N 22 40 E
Mie □, Japan .... 55 G8 34 30N 136 10 E
Miechów, Poland .... 31 H7 50 21N 20 5 E
Miedwie, Jezioro,
  Poland .... 31 E1 53 17N 14 54 E
Międzybórz, Poland .. 31 G4 51 25N 17 34 E
Międzychód, Poland .. 31 F2 52 35N 15 53 E
Międzylesie, Poland .. 31 H3 50 8N 16 40 E
Międzyrzec Podlaski,
  Poland .... 31 G9 51 58N 22 45 E
Międzyrzecz, Poland . 31 F2 52 26N 15 35 E
Międzyzdroje, Poland . 30 E1 53 56N 14 26 E
Miejska Górka, Poland 31 G3 51 39N 16 58 E
Miélan, France ..... 20 E4 43 27N 0 19 E
Mielec, Poland ..... 31 H8 50 15N 21 25 E
Mienga, Angola ..... 88 B2 17 12S 19 48 E
Miercurea-Ciuc,
  Romania .... 29 D10 46 21N 25 48 E
Miercurea Sibiului,
  Romania .... 29 E8 45 53N 23 48 E
Mieres, Spain 36 B5 43 18N 5 48W
Mieroszów, Poland .. 31 H3 50 40N 16 11 E
Mieso, Ethiopia ..... 81 F5 9 15N 40 43 E
Mieszkowice, Poland . 31 F1 52 47N 14 30 E
Mifflintown, U.S.A. .. 116 F7 40 34N 77 24W
Mifraz Ḥefa, Israel .. 74 C4 32 52N 35 0 E
Migennes, France ... 19 E10 47 58N 3 31 E
Migliarino, Italy .... 41 D8 44 46N 11 56 E
Migliarino-San Rossore-
  Massaciuccoli △, Italy 40 E7 43 44N 10 20 E
Miguel Alemán, Presa,
  Mexico 119 D5 18 15N 96 40W
Miguelturra, Spain ... 37 G7 38 58N 3 53W
Mihăileni, Romania .. 29 C11 47 58N 26 9 E
Mihăilești, Romania .. 29 F10 44 20N 25 54 E
Mihailovca, Moldova . 29 D13 46 33N 28 56 E
Mihalgazi, Turkey .. 47 A12 40 2N 30 34 E
Mihalıççık, Turkey .. 72 C4 39 53N 31 30 E
Mihara, Japan ...... 55 G6 34 24N 133 5 E
Miheşu de Cîmpie,
  Romania .... 29 D9 46 41N 24 9 E
Mijas, Spain 37 J6 36 36N 4 40W
Mikese, Tanzania .... 86 D4 6 48S 37 55 E
Mikha-Tskhakaya =
  Senaki, Georgia ... 35 J6 42 15N 42 7 E
Mikhailovka,
  Montana, Bulgaria 44 C7 43 27N 23 16 E
Mikhaylovka,
  Bulgaria .... 34 E6 50 3N 43 5 E
Mikhaylovo, Russia .. 32 E9 55 4N 37 59 E
Mikhnevo, Russia ... 32 E9 55 4N 37 59 E
Míkinai, Greece ..... 46 D4 37 43N 22 46 E
Mikkeli, Finland .... 9 F22 61 43N 27 15 E
Mikkwa →, Canada .. 102 B6 58 25N 114 46W
Mikniya, Sudan ..... 81 D3 17 0N 33 45 E
Mikołajki, Poland ... 30 E8 53 49N 21 37 E
Mikónos, Greece .... 47 D7 37 30N 25 25 E
Míkrí Préspa, Límni,
  Greece .... 44 F5 40 47N 21 3 E
Míkrón Dhérion, Greece 45 E10 41 19N 26 6 E
Mikstat, Poland ..... 31 G4 51 32N 17 59 E
Mikulov, Czech Rep. . 27 C9 48 48N 16 39 E
Mikumi, Tanzania ... 86 D4 7 26S 37 0 E
Mikun, Tanzania .... 86 D4 7 35S 37 15 E
Milaca, U.S.A. 112 C8 45 45N 93 39W
Milagro, Ecuador 124 D3 2 11S 79 36W
Milagros, Phil. ..... 61 E5 12 13N 123 30 E
Milan = Milano, Italy 40 C6 45 28N 9 10 E
Milan, Mo., U.S.A. .. 112 E8 40 12N 93 7W
Milan, Tenn., U.S.A. 115 H1 35 55N 88 46W
Milang, Australia .... 95 F2 35 24S 138 58 E
Milange, Mozam. .... 87 F4 16 3S 35 45 E
Milano, Italy .... 40 C6 45 28N 9 12 E
Milano, Madag. ..... 89 A8 13 37S 49 34 E
Milâs, Turkey ...... 47 D9 37 20N 27 50 E
Milazzo, Italy ...... 43 D8 38 13N 15 15 E
Milbank, U.S.A. 112 C6 45 13N 96 38W
Milden, Canada 103 C7 51 29N 107 32W
Mildenhall, U.K. .... 15 E8 52 21N 0 32 E
Mildmay, Canada ... 116 B3 44 3N 81 7W
Mildura, Australia ... 95 E3 34 13S 142 9 E
Mile, China .... 58 E4 24 28N 103 20 E

Miléai, Greece ...... 46 B5 39 20N 23 9 E
Miles, Australia ..... 95 D5 26 40S 150 9 E
Miles City, U.S.A. ... 108 B2 46 25N 105 51W
Milești, Moldova .... 29 C13 47 13N 28 3 E
Milestone, Canada ... 103 D8 49 59N 104 31W
Mileto, Italy .... 43 D9 38 36N 16 4 E
Miletto, Mte., Italy .. 43 A7 41 27N 14 22 E
Miletus, Turkey ..... 47 D9 37 30N 27 18 E
Milevsko, Czech Rep. 26 B7 49 27N 14 21 E
Milford, Calif., U.S.A. 110 E6 40 10N 120 22W
Milford, Conn., U.S.A. 117 E11 41 14N 73 3W
Milford, Del., U.S.A. 114 F8 38 55N 75 26W
Milford, Mass., U.S.A. 117 D13 42 8N 71 31W
Milford, N.H., U.S.A. 117 D13 42 50N 71 39W
Milford, Pa., U.S.A. . 117 E10 41 19N 74 48W
Milford, Utah, U.S.A. 109 G7 38 24N 113 1W
Milford Haven, U.K. . 15 F2 51 42N 5 7W
Milford Sd., N.Z. .... 91 L1 44 41S 167 47 E
Milford Sound, N.Z. . 91 L1 44 41S 167 55 E
Milh, Baḥr al =
  Buḥayrat ar, Iraq .. 70 C4 32 40N 43 35 E
Milicz, Poland ...... 31 G4 51 31N 17 19 E
Milikapiti, Australia .. 92 B5 11 26S 130 40 E
Miling, Australia .... 93 F2 30 30S 116 17 E
Militello in Val di
  Catánia, Italy ..... 43 E7 37 16N 14 48 E
Milk →, U.S.A. 108 B10 48 4N 106 19W
Milk, Wadi el →, Sudan 80 D3 17 55N 30 20 E
Milk River, Canada .. 102 D6 49 10N 112 5W
Mill I., Antarctica ... 5 C8 66 0S 101 30 E
Mill Valley, U.S.A. .. 110 H4 37 54N 122 32W
Millárs →, Spain 38 F4 39 55N 0 1W
Millau, France ...... 20 D7 44 8N 3 4 E
Millbridge, Canada .. 116 B7 44 41N 77 36W
Millbrook, Canada ... 116 B6 44 10N 78 29W
Millbrook, U.S.A. ... 117 E11 41 47N 73 42W
Mille Lacs, L. des,
  Canada 104 C1 48 45N 90 35W
Mille Lacs L., U.S.A. 112 B8 46 15N 93 39W
Milledgeville, U.S.A. . 115 J4 33 5N 83 14W
Millen, U.S.A. 115 J5 32 48N 81 57W
Millennium I. = Caroline
  I., Kiribati 97 H12 9 58S 150 13W
Miller, U.S.A. 112 C5 44 31N 98 59W
Millerovo, Russia .... 35 F5 48 57N 40 28 E
Millersburg, Ohio,
  U.S.A. 116 F3 40 33N 81 55W
Millersburg, Pa., U.S.A. 116 F8 40 32N 76 58W
Millerton, U.S.A. ... 117 E11 41 57N 73 31W
Millerton L., U.S.A. . 110 J7 37 1N 119 41W
Millet, St. Lucia .... 121 f 13 55N 60 59W
Millevaches, Plateau de,
  France .... 20 C6 45 45N 2 0 E
Millheim, U.S.A. 116 F7 40 54N 77 29W
Millicent, Australia .. 95 F3 37 34S 140 21 E
Millington, U.S.A. .. 113 H10 35 20N 89 53W
Millinocket, U.S.A. .. 115 C11 45 39N 68 43W
Millmerran, Australia 95 D5 27 53S 151 16 E
Millom, U.K. 14 C4 54 13N 3 16W
Mills L., Canada 102 A5 61 30N 118 20W
Millsboro, U.S.A. ... 116 G5 40 0N 80 0W
Millstream-
  Chichester △,
  Australia .... 92 D2 21 35S 117 6 E
Milltown Malbay,
  Ireland 12 D2 52 52N 9 24W
Millville, N.J., U.S.A. 114 F8 39 24N 75 2W
Millville, Pa., U.S.A. 117 E8 41 7N 76 32W
Millwood L., U.S.A. . 113 J8 33 42N 93 58W
Milna, Croatia ...... 41 E13 43 20N 16 28 E
Milne →, Australia .. 94 C2 21 10S 137 33 E
Milo, U.S.A. 115 C11 45 15N 68 59W
Mílos, Greece ...... 46 E6 36 44N 24 25 E
Miłosław, Poland ... 31 F4 52 12N 17 32 E
Milot, Albania ...... 44 E3 41 41N 19 43 E
Milparinka, Australia 95 D3 29 46S 141 57 E
Miltenberg, Germany 25 F5 49 41N 9 16 E
Milton, N.S., Canada 105 D7 44 4N 64 45W
Milton, Ont., Canada 116 C5 43 31N 79 53W
Milton, N.Z. .... 91 M2 46 7S 169 59 E
Milton, Calif., U.S.A. 110 G6 38 3N 120 51W
Milton, Fla., U.S.A. . 115 K2 30 38N 87 3W
Milton, Pa., U.S.A. .. 116 F7 41 1N 76 51W
Milton, Vt., U.S.A. .. 117 B11 44 38N 73 7W
Milton-Freewater,
  U.S.A. 108 D4 45 56N 118 23W
Milton Keynes, U.K. . 15 E7 52 1N 0 44W
Milton Keynes □, U.K. 15 E7 52 1N 0 44W
Miluo, China .... 59 C9 29 0N 112 59 E
Milverton, Canada ... 116 C4 43 34N 80 55W
Milwaukee, U.S.A. .. 114 D2 43 2N 87 55W
Milwaukee Deep,
  Atl. Oc. 121 C6 19 50N 68 0W
Milwaukie, U.S.A. .. 110 E4 45 27N 122 38W
Mim, Ghana 82 D4 6 57N 2 33W
Mimizan, France 20 D2 44 12S 1 13W
Mimoň, Czech Rep. .. 26 A7 50 38N 14 43 E
Min Jiang →, Fujian,
  China .... 59 E12 26 0N 119 35 E
Min Jiang →, Sichuan,
  China .... 58 C5 28 45N 104 40 E
Min Xian, China .... 56 G3 34 25N 104 5 E
Mina Pirquitas,
  Argentina 126 A2 22 40S 66 30W
Mină Su'ud, Si. Arabia 71 D6 28 45N 48 28 E
Mina'al Aḥmadī, Kuwait 71 D6 29 5N 48 10 E
Minago →, Canada .. 103 C9 54 33N 98 59W
Minaki, Canada 103 D10 49 59N 94 40W
Minamata, Japan .... 55 H5 32 10N 130 30 E
Minami-Arapusa △,
  Japan .... 55 G9 35 30N 138 14 E
Minami-Tori-Shima,
  Pac. Oc. .... 96 E7 24 20N 153 58 E
Minas, Uruguay 127 C4 34 20S 55 10W
Minas, Sierra de las,
  Guatemala 120 C2 15 9N 89 31W
Minas Basin, Canada 105 C7 45 20N 64 12W
Minas de Riotinto, Spain 37 H4 37 42N 6 35W
Minas Gerais □, Brazil 125 G9 18 50S 46 0W
Minatitlán, Mexico .. 119 D6 17 59N 94 31W
Minbu, Burma ...... 67 J19 20 10N 94 52 E
Minchinabad, Pakistan 68 D5 30 10N 73 34 E
Mincio →, Italy ..... 40 C7 45 4N 10 59 E
Minčol, Slovak Rep. . 27 B13 49 15N 20 58 E
Mindanao, Phil. .... 61 H6 8 0N 125 0 E
Mindanao Sea = Bohol
  Sea, Phil. .... 63 C6 9 0N 124 0 E
Mindanao Trench,
  Pac. Oc. .... 61 E7 12 0N 126 6 E
Mindel →, Germany . 25 G6 48 31N 10 23 E
Mindelheim, Germany 25 G6 48 3N 10 29 E
Minden, Canada 116 B6 44 55N 78 43W
Minden, Germany ... 24 C4 52 17N 8 55 E
Minden, La., U.S.A. . 113 J8 32 37N 93 17W
Minden, Nev., U.S.A. 110 G7 38 57N 119 46W
Mindiptana, Indonesia 63 F10 5 55S 140 22 E
Mindoro, Phil. ..... 61 E4 13 0N 121 0 E

Mindoro Str., *Phil.* .... **61 E4** 12 30N 120 30 E
Mine, *Japan* .... **55 G5** 34 12N 131 7 E
Minehead, *U.K.* **15 F4** 51 12N 3 29W
Mineola, *N.Y., U.S.A.* **117 F11** 40 45N 73 39W
Mineola, *Tex., U.S.A.* **113 J7** 32 40N 95 29W
Mineral King, *U.S.A.* .. **110 J8** 36 27N 118 36W
Mineral Wells, *U.S.A.* .. **113 J5** 32 48N 98 7W
Mineralnyye Vody,
  Russia .... **35 H6** 44 15N 43 8 E
Minersville, *U.S.A.* .. **117 F8** 40 41N 76 16W
Minerva, *U.S.A.* **116 F3** 40 44N 81 6W
Minervino Murge, *Italy* **43 A9** 41 5N 16 5 E
Minetto, *U.S.A.* **117 C8** 43 24N 76 28W
Mingäçevir, *Azerbaijan* **35 K8** 40 45N 47 0 E
Mingäçevir Su Anbarı,
  Azerbaijan .... **35 K8** 40 57N 46 50 E
Mingan, *Canada* **105 B7** 50 20N 64 0W
Mingechaur =
  Mingäçevir,
  Azerbaijan .... **35 K8** 40 45N 47 0 E
Mingechaurskoye
  Vdkhr. = Mingäçevir
  Su Anbarı, *Azerbaijan* **35 K8** 40 57N 46 50 E
Mingela, *Australia* .... **94 B4** 19 52 S 146 38 E
Mingenew, *Australia* .. **93 E2** 29 12 S 115 21 E
Mingera Cr. →,
  Australia .... **94 C2** 20 38 S 137 45 E
Minggang, *China* ...... **59 A10** 32 24N 114 3 E
Mingguang, *China* .... **59 A11** 32 46N 117 59 E
Mingin, *Burma* ...... **67 H19** 22 50N 94 30 E
Mingir, *Moldova* .... **29 D13** 46 40N 28 20 E
Minglanilla, *Spain* **39 F3** 39 34N 1 38W
Minglun, *China* ...... **58 E7** 25 10N 108 21 E
Mingo Junction, *U.S.A.* **116 F4** 40 19N 80 37W
Mingorria, *Spain* **36 E6** 40 45N 4 40W
Mingshan, *China* ...... **58 B4** 30 6N 103 10 E
Mingteke Daban =
  Mintaka Pass,
  Pakistan .... **69 A6** 37 0N 74 58 E
Mingxi, *China* ...... **59 D11** 26 18N 117 12 E
Mingyuegue, *China* .. **57 C15** 43 2N 128 50 E
Minho = Miño →, *Spain* **36 D2** 41 52N 8 40W
Minhou, *China* ...... **59 E12** 26 0N 119 15 E
Minićevo, *Serbia & M.* **28 G7** 43 42N 22 18 E
Minidoka, *U.S.A.* **108 E7** 42 45N 113 29W
Minigwal, L., *Australia* **93 E3** 29 31 S 123 14 E
Minilya →, *Australia* .. **93 D1** 23 45 S 114 0 E
Minilya Roadhouse,
  Australia .... **93 D1** 23 55 S 114 0 E
Minipi L., *Canada* **105 B7** 52 25N 60 45W
Mink L., *Canada* **102 A5** 61 54N 117 40W
Minkammen, *Sudan* .. **81 F3** 6 3N 31 32 E
Minna, *Nigeria* ...... **83 D6** 9 37N 6 30 E
Minneapolis, *Kans.,*
  U.S.A. **112 F6** 39 8N 97 42W
Minneapolis, *Minn.,*
  U.S.A. **112 C8** 44 59N 93 16W
Minnedosa, *Canada* .. **103 C9** 50 14N 99 50W
Minnesota □, *U.S.A.* .. **112 B8** 46 0N 94 15W
Minnesota →, *U.S.A.* .. **112 C8** 44 54N 93 9W
Minnewaukan, *U.S.A.* **112 A5** 48 4N 99 15W
Minnipa, *Australia* .... **95 E2** 32 51 S 135 9 E
Minnitaki L., *Canada* .. **104 C1** 49 57N 92 10W
Mino, *Japan* .... **55 G8** 35 32N 136 55 E
Miño, *Spain* **36 B2** 43 21N 8 12W
Miño →, *Spain* **36 D2** 41 52N 8 40W
Minoa, *Greece* ...... **47 F7** 35 6N 25 45 E
Minorca = Menorca,
  Spain .... **48 B11** 40 0N 4 0 E
Minot, *U.S.A.* **112 A4** 48 14N 101 18W
Minqin, *China* ...... **56 E2** 38 38N 103 20 E
Minqing, *China* ...... **59 D12** 26 15N 118 50 E
Minsen, *Germany* .... **24 B3** 53 41N 7 58 E
Minsk, *Belarus* ...... **32 F4** 53 52N 27 30 E
Mińsk Mazowiecki,
  Poland .... **31 F8** 52 10N 21 33 E
Mintabie, *Australia* .. **95 D1** 27 15 S 133 7 E
Mintaka Pass, *Pakistan* **69 A6** 37 0N 74 58 E
Minto, *Canada* **105 C6** 46 5N 66 5W
Minto, L., *Canada* **104 A5** 57 13N 75 0W
Minton, *Canada* **103 D8** 49 10N 104 35W
Minturn, *U.S.A.* **108 G10** 39 35N 106 26W
Minturno, *Italy* ...... **42 A6** 41 15N 13 45 E
Minûf, *Egypt* .... **80 H7** 30 26N 30 52 E
Minusinsk, *Russia* .... **53 D10** 53 43N 91 20 E
Minutang, *India* ...... **67 E20** 28 15N 96 30 E
Minya el Qamh, *Egypt* **80 H7** 30 31N 31 21 E
Minya Konka = Gongga
  Shan, *China* ...... **58 C3** 29 40N 101 55 E
Mionica, *Bos.-H.* .... **44 B4** 44 51N 18 29 E
Mionica, *Serbia & M.* .. **44 B4** 44 14N 20 6 E
Miquelon, *Canada* **104 C4** 49 25N 76 27W
Miquelon, *St.-P. & M.* .. **105 C8** 47 8N 56 22W
Mir, *Niger* .... **83 C7** 14 5N 11 59 E
Mīr Kūh, *Iran* ...... **71 E8** 26 22N 58 55 E
Mīr Shahdād, *Iran* .... **71 E8** 26 15N 58 29 E
Mira, *Italy* .... **41 C9** 45 26N 12 8 E
Mira, *Portugal* **36 E2** 40 26N 8 44W
Mira →, *Portugal* **37 H2** 37 43N 8 47W
Mira por vos Cay,
  Bahamas **121 B5** 22 9N 74 30W
Mirabella Eclano, *Italy* **43 A7** 41 2N 14 59 E
Mirador-Río Azul △,
  Guatemala **120 C2** 17 45N 89 50W
Miraj, *India* .... **66 L9** 16 50N 74 45 E
Miram Shah, *Pakistan* **68 C4** 33 0N 70 2 E
Miramar, *Argentina* .. **126 D4** 38 15 S 57 50W
Miramar, *Mozam.* .... **89 C6** 23 50 S 35 35 E
Miramas, *France* ...... **21 E8** 43 33N 4 59 E
Mirambeau, *France* .. **20 C3** 45 23N 0 35W
Miramichi, *Canada* .. **105 C6** 47 2N 65 28W
Miramichi B., *Canada* .. **105 C7** 47 15N 65 0W
Miramont-de-Guyenne,
  France .... **20 D4** 44 37N 0 21 E
Miranda, *Brazil* ...... **125 H7** 20 10 S 56 15W
Miranda →, *Brazil* .... **125 G7** 19 25 S 57 20W
Miranda de Ebro, *Spain* **38 C2** 42 41N 2 57W
Miranda do Corvo,
  Portugal **36 E2** 40 6N 8 20W
Miranda do Douro,
  Portugal **36 D4** 41 30N 6 16W
Mirande, *France* ...... **20 E4** 43 31N 0 25 E
Mirandela, *Portugal* .. **36 D3** 41 32N 7 20W
Mirándola, *Italy* ...... **40 D8** 44 53N 11 4 E
Mirandópolis, *Brazil* .. **127 A5** 21 9 S 51 6W
Mirango, *Malawi* .... **87 E3** 13 32 S 34 58 E
Mirani, *Australia* .... **94 K6** 21 8 S 148 53 E
Mirano, *Italy* ...... **41 C9** 45 30N 12 7 E
Miras, *Albania* ...... **44 F4** 40 35N 20 45 E
Mirassol, *Brazil* ...... **127 A6** 20 46 S 49 28W
Mīrbāt, *Oman* ...... **75 D5** 17 0N 54 45 E
Mirear, *Egypt* ...... **80 C4** 23 15N 35 41 E
Mirebeau, *France* .... **18 F7** 46 49N 0 10 E
Mirebeau-sur-Bèze,
  France .... **19 E12** 47 25N 5 20 E
Mirecourt, *France* .... **19 D13** 48 20N 6 10 E
Mirgorod = Myrhorod,
  Ukraine .... **33 H7** 49 58N 33 37 E

Miri, *Malaysia* .... **62 D4** 4 23N 113 59 E
Miriam Vale, *Australia* **94 C5** 24 20 S 151 33 E
Miribel, *France* ...... **19 G11** 45 50N 4 57 E
Mirim, L., *S. Amer.* .... **127 C5** 32 45 S 52 50W
Mirnyy, *Russia* ...... **53 C12** 62 33N 113 53 E
Miroč, *Serbia & M.* .... **44 B6** 44 32N 22 16 E
Mirokhan, *Pakistan* .. **68 F3** 27 46N 68 6 E
Mirond L., *Canada* **103 B8** 55 6N 102 47W
Mirosławiec, *Poland* .. **30 E3** 53 20N 16 5 E
Mirpur, *Pakistan* .... **69 C5** 33 32N 73 56 E
Mirpur Batoro, *Pakistan* **68 G3** 24 44N 68 16 E
Mirpur Bibiwari,
  Pakistan .... **68 E2** 28 33N 67 44 E
Mirpur Khas, *Pakistan* **68 G3** 25 30N 69 0 E
Mirpur Sakro, *Pakistan* **68 G2** 24 33N 67 41 E
Mirria, *Niger* .... **83 C6** 13 43N 9 7 E
Mirsk, *Poland* ...... **31 H2** 50 58N 15 23 E
Mirtağ, *Turkey* ...... **70 B4** 38 23N 41 56 E
Miryang, *S. Korea* .... **57 G15** 35 31N 128 44 E
Mirzaani, *Georgia* .... **35 K8** 41 24N 46 5 E
Mirzapur, *India* ...... **69 G10** 25 10N 82 34 E
Mirzapur-cum-
  Vindhyachal =
  Mirzapur, *India* .... **69 G10** 25 10N 82 34 E
Misantla, *Mexico* **119 D5** 19 56N 96 50W
Misawa, *Japan* ...... **54 D10** 40 41N 141 24 E
Miscou I., *Canada* **105 C7** 47 57N 64 31W
Mish'āb, Ra's al,
  Si. Arabia .... **71 D6** 28 15N 48 43 E
Mishan, *China* ...... **60 B8** 45 37N 131 48 E
Mishawaka, *U.S.A.* .. **114 E2** 41 40N 86 11W
Mishbih, Gebel, *Egypt* **80 C3** 22 38N 34 44 E
Mishima, *Japan* ...... **55 G9** 35 10N 138 52 E
Misión, *Mexico* **111 N10** 32 6N 116 53W
Misiones □, *Argentina* **127 B5** 27 0 S 55 0W
Misiones □, *Paraguay* **126 B4** 27 0 S 56 0W
Miskah, *Si. Arabia* .... **70 E4** 24 49N 42 56 E
Miskitos, Cayos, *Nic.* .. **120 D3** 14 26N 82 50W
Miskolc, *Hungary* .... **28 B5** 48 7N 20 50 E
Misoke, *Dem. Rep. of*
  the Congo .... **86 C2** 0 42 S 28 2 E
Misool, *Indonesia* .... **63 E8** 1 52 S 130 10 E
Misrātah, *Libya* ...... **79 B9** 32 24N 15 3 E
Misrātah, *Libya* ...... **79 B9** 32 24N 15 3 E
Missanabie, *Canada* .. **104 C3** 48 20N 84 6W
Missinaibi →, *Canada* .. **104 B3** 50 43N 81 29W
Missinaibi L., *Canada* .. **104 C3** 48 23N 83 40W
Mission, *Canada* **102 D4** 49 10N 122 15W
Mission, *S. Dak., U.S.A.* **112 D4** 43 18N 100 39W
Mission, *Tex., U.S.A.* .. **113 M5** 26 13N 98 20W
Mission Beach, *Australia* **94 B4** 17 53 S 146 5 E
Mission Viejo, *U.S.A.* .. **111 M9** 33 36N 117 40W
Missirah, *Senegal* **82 C1** 13 40N 16 30W
Missisa L., *Canada* **104 B2** 52 20N 85 7W
Missisicabi →, *Canada* **104 B4** 51 14N 79 31W
Mississagi →, *Canada* .. **104 C3** 46 15N 83 9W
Mississauga, *Canada* .. **116 C5** 43 32N 79 35W
Mississippi □, *U.S.A.* .. **113 J10** 33 0N 90 0W
Mississippi →, *U.S.A.* .. **113 L10** 29 9N 89 15W
Mississippi L., *Canada* **117 A8** 45 5N 76 10W
Mississippi River Delta,
  U.S.A. **113 L9** 29 10N 89 15W
Mississippi Sd., *U.S.A.* **113 K10** 30 20N 89 0W
Missoula, *U.S.A.* **108 C7** 46 52N 114 1W
Missouri □, *U.S.A.* **112 F8** 38 25N 92 30W
Missouri →, *U.S.A.* **112 F9** 38 49N 90 7W
Missouri City, *U.S.A.* .. **113 L7** 29 37N 95 32W
Missouri Valley, *U.S.A.* **112 E7** 41 34N 95 53W
Mist, *U.S.A.* **110 E3** 45 59N 123 15W
Mistassini →, *Canada* .. **105 B5** 48 53N 72 13W
Mistassini L., *Canada* .. **105 C5** 48 42N 72 20W
Mistassini L., *Canada* .. **104 B5** 51 0N 73 30W
Mistastin L., *Canada* .. **105 A7** 55 57N 63 20W
Mistelbach, *Austria* .. **27 C9** 48 34N 16 34 E
Misterbianco, *Italy* .. **43 E8** 37 31N 15 1 E
Mistinibi, L., *Canada* .. **105 A7** 55 56N 64 17W
Mistissini, *Canada* **105 C5** 48 53N 72 12W
Mistretta, *Italy* ...... **43 E7** 37 56N 14 22 E
Misty L., *Canada* **103 B8** 58 53N 101 40W
Misurata = Mişrātah,
  Libya .... **79 B9** 32 24N 15 3 E
Mît Ghamr, *Egypt* .... **80 H7** 30 42N 31 12 E
Mitatitá, *Sudan* ...... **81 D4** 15 59N 36 12 E
Mitchell, *Australia* .... **95 D4** 26 29 S 147 58 E
Mitchell, *Canada* **116 C3** 43 28N 81 12W
Mitchell, *Nebr., U.S.A.* **112 E3** 41 57N 103 49W
Mitchell, *Oreg., U.S.A.* **108 D3** 44 34N 120 9W
Mitchell, *S. Dak., U.S.A.* **112 D6** 43 43N 98 2W
Mitchell →, *Australia* .. **94 B3** 15 12 S 141 35 E
Mitchell, Mt., *U.S.A.* .. **115 H4** 35 46N 82 16W
Mitchell and Alice
  Rivers △, *Australia* .. **94 B3** 15 28 S 142 5 E
Mitchell Ranges,
  Australia .... **94 A2** 12 49 S 135 36 E
Mitchelstown, *Ireland* **12 D3** 52 15N 8 16W
Mitha Tiwana, *Pakistan* **68 C5** 32 13N 72 6 E
Mithi, *Pakistan* ...... **68 G3** 24 44N 69 48 E
Míthimna, *Greece* .... **47 B8** 39 20N 26 12 E
Mithrao, *Pakistan* .... **68 F3** 27 28N 69 40 E
Mitilíni, *Greece* ...... **47 B8** 39 6N 26 35 E
Mitilinoí, *Greece* .... **47 D8** 37 42N 26 56 E
Mito, *Japan* .... **55 F10** 36 20N 140 30 E
Mitrofanovka, *Russia* .. **33 H10** 49 58N 39 42 E
Mitrovica = Kosovska
  Mitrovica,
  Serbia & M. ...... **44 D4** 42 54N 20 52 E
Mitsinjo, *Madag.* ...... **89 B8** 16 1 S 45 52 E
Mitsiwa, *Eritrea* ...... **81 D4** 15 35N 39 25 E
Mitsiwa Channel, *Eritrea* **81 D5** 15 30N 40 0 E
Mitsukaidō, *Japan* .... **55 F9** 36 1N 139 59 E
Mittagong, *Australia* .. **95 E5** 34 28 S 150 29 E
Mittelberg, *Austria* .. **26 D3** 47 20N 10 10 E
Mittelfranken □,
  Germany .... **25 F6** 49 25N 10 40 E
Mittellandkanal →,
  Germany .... **24 C9** 52 20N 8 2 E
Mittenwalde, *Germany* **24 C9** 52 15N 13 31 E
Mittersill, *Austria* .... **26 D5** 47 16N 12 29 E
Mitterteich, *Germany* **25 F8** 49 57N 12 14 E
Mittimatalik = Pond
  Inlet, *Canada* **101 A12** 72 40N 77 0W
Mittweida, *Germany* .. **24 E8** 50 59N 12 59 E
Mitú, *Colombia* **124 C4** 1 15N 70 13W
Mitumba, Mts.,
  Dem. Rep. of
  the Congo .... **86 D2** 7 0 S 27 30 E
Mitumba, *Tanzania* .. **86 D3** 7 8 S 31 2 E
Mitwaba, *Dem. Rep. of*
  the Congo .... **87 D2** 8 2 S 27 17 E
Mityana, *Uganda* .... **86 B3** 0 23N 32 2 E
Mixteco →, *Mexico* .. **119 D5** 18 11N 98 30W
Miyagi □, *Japan* ...... **54 E10** 38 15N 140 45 E
Miyāh, W. el →, *Egypt* **80 C3** 25 0N 33 23 E
Miyāh, W. el →, *Syria* **70 C3** 34 44N 39 57 E
Miyake-Jima, *Japan* .. **55 G9** 34 5N 139 30 E
Miyako, *Japan* ...... **54 E10** 39 40N 141 59 E
Miyako-Jima, *Japan* .. **55 M2** 24 45N 125 20 E
Miyako-Rettō, *Japan* .. **55 M2** 24 24N 125 0 E

Miyakonojō, *Japan* .... **55 J5** 31 40N 131 5 E
Miyani, *India* .... **68 J3** 21 50N 69 26 E
Miyanoura-Dake, *Japan* **55 J5** 30 20N 130 31 E
Miyazaki, *Japan* ...... **55 J5** 31 56N 131 30 E
Miyazaki □, *Japan* .... **55 H5** 32 30N 131 30 E
Miyazu, *Japan* ...... **55 G7** 35 35N 135 10 E
Miyet, Bahr el = Dead
  Sea, *Asia* .... **74 D4** 31 30N 35 30 E
Miyi, *China* .... **58 D4** 26 47N 102 9 E
Miyoshi, *Japan* ...... **55 G6** 34 48N 132 51 E
Miyun, *China* ...... **56 D9** 40 28N 116 50 E
Miyun Shuiku, *China* .. **57 D9** 40 30N 117 0 E
Mizan Teferi, *Ethiopia* **81 F4** 6 59N 35 30 E
Mizdah, *Libya* ...... **79 B8** 31 30N 13 0 E
Mizen Hd., Cork,
  Ireland **12 E2** 51 27N 9 50W
Mizen Hd., Wicklow,
  Ireland **12 D5** 52 51N 6 4W
Mizhhirya, *Ukraine* .. **29 B8** 48 32N 23 30 E
Mizhi, *China* .... **56 F6** 37 47N 110 12 E
Mizil, *Romania* ...... **29 F11** 44 59N 26 29 E
Mizoram □, *India* .... **67 H18** 23 30N 92 40 E
Mizpe Ramon, *Israel* .. **74 E3** 30 34N 34 49 E
Mizuho, *Antarctica* .. **5 D5** 70 30 S 41 0 E
Mizusawa, *Japan* .... **54 E10** 39 8N 141 8 E
Mjällby, *Sweden* ...... **11 H8** 56 3N 14 40 E
Mjöbäck, *Sweden* .... **11 G6** 57 28N 12 53 E
Mjölby, *Sweden* ...... **11 F9** 58 20N 15 10 E
Mjörn, *Sweden* ...... **11 G6** 57 55N 12 25 E
Mjøsa, *Norway* ...... **9 F14** 60 40N 11 0 E
Mkata, *Tanzania* .... **86 D4** 5 45 S 38 20 E
Mkhaya △, *Swaziland* **89 D5** 26 34 S 31 45 E
Mkokotoni, *Tanzania* .. **86 D4** 5 55 S 39 15 E
Mkomazi, *Tanzania* .. **86 C4** 4 40 S 38 7 E
Mkomazi △, *Tanzania* **86 C4** 4 45 S 38 2 E
Mkomazi →, *S. Africa* **89 E5** 30 12 S 30 50 E
Mkulwe, *Tanzania* .... **87 D3** 8 37 S 32 20 E
Mkumbi, Ras, *Tanzania* **86 D4** 7 38 S 39 55 E
Mkushi, *Zambia* ...... **87 E2** 14 25 S 29 15 E
Mkushi River, *Zambia* **87 E2** 13 32 S 29 45 E
Mkuze, *S. Africa* ...... **89 D5** 27 10 S 32 0 E
Mkuze →, *S. Africa* .. **89 D4** 29 27 S 29 30 E
Mladá Boleslav,
  Czech Republic .... **26 A7** 50 27N 14 53 E
Mladenovac,
  Serbia & M. ...... **44 B4** 44 28N 20 44 E
Mlala Hills, *Tanzania* .. **86 D3** 6 50 S 31 40 E
Mlange = Mulanje,
  Malawi .... **87 F4** 16 2 S 35 33 E
Mlanje, Pic, *Malawi* .. **85 H7** 15 57 S 35 38 E
Mlava →, *Serbia & M.* **44 B5** 44 45N 21 13 E
Mława, *Poland* ...... **31 E7** 53 9N 20 25 E
Mlawula △, *Swaziland* **89 D5** 26 12 S 32 2 E
Mlinište, *Bos.-H.* ...... **41 D13** 44 15N 16 50 E
Mljet, *Croatia* .... **41 F14** 42 43N 17 30 E
Mljet △, *Croatia* ...... **41 F14** 42 48N 17 25 E
Mljetski Kanal, *Croatia* **41 F14** 42 48N 17 35 E
Młynary, *Poland* ...... **30 D6** 54 12N 19 46 E
Mmabatho, *S. Africa* .. **88 D4** 25 49 S 25 30 E
Mme, *Cameroon* ...... **83 D7** 6 18N 10 14 E
Mnichovo Hradiště,
  Czech Republic .... **26 A7** 50 32N 14 59 E
Mo i Rana, *Norway* .. **8 C16** 66 20N 14 7 E
Moa, *Cuba* **121 B4** 20 40N 74 56W
Moa, *Indonesia* ...... **63 F7** 8 0 S 128 0 E
Moa →, *S. Leone* **82 D2** 6 59N 11 36W
Moab, *U.S.A.* **109 G9** 38 35N 109 33W
Moala, *Fiji* .... **91 D8** 18 36 S 179 53 E
Moama, *Australia* .... **95 F3** 36 7 S 144 46 E
Moamba, *Mozam.* .... **89 D5** 25 36 S 32 15 E
Moapa, *U.S.A.* **111 J12** 36 40N 114 37W
Moate, *Ireland* **12 C4** 53 24N 7 44W
Moba, *Dem. Rep. of*
  the Congo .... **86 D2** 7 0 S 29 48 E
Mobārakābād, *Iran* .. **71 D7** 28 24N 53 20 E
Mobaye, *C.A.R.* ...... **84 D4** 4 25N 21 5 E
Mobayi, *Dem. Rep. of*
  the Congo .... **84 D4** 4 15N 21 8 E
Moberley Lake, *Canada* **102 B4** 55 50N 121 44W
Moberly, *U.S.A.* **112 F8** 39 25N 92 26W
Mobile, *U.S.A.* **115 K1** 30 41N 88 3W
Mobile B., *U.S.A.* **115 K2** 30 30N 88 0W
Mobridge, *U.S.A.* **112 C4** 45 32N 100 26W
Moc Chau, *Vietnam* .. **64 B5** 20 50N 104 38 E
Moc Hoa, *Vietnam* .. **65 G5** 10 46N 105 56 E
Mocabe Kasari,
  Dem. Rep. of
  the Congo .... **87 D2** 9 58 S 26 12 E
Moçambique, *Mozam.* **87 F5** 15 3 S 40 42 E
Mocanaqua, *U.S.A.* .. **117 E8** 41 9N 76 8W
Mochima △, *Venezuela* **121 D7** 10 30N 64 5W
Mochudi, *Botswana* .. **88 C4** 24 27 S 26 7 E
Mocimboa da Praia,
  Mozam. .... **87 E5** 11 25 S 40 20 E
Mociu, *Romania* ...... **29 D9** 46 46N 24 3 E
Möckeln, *Sweden* .... **11 H8** 56 40N 14 15 E
Mockfjärd, *Sweden* .. **10 D8** 60 30N 14 57 E
Moclips, *U.S.A.* **110 C2** 47 14N 124 13W
Mocoa, *Colombia* **124 C3** 1 7N 76 35W
Mococa, *Brazil* ...... **127 A6** 21 28 S 47 0W
Mocorito, *Mexico* **118 B3** 25 30N 107 53W
Moctezuma, *Mexico* .. **118 B3** 29 50N 109 0W
Moctezuma →, *Mexico* **119 C5** 21 59N 98 34W
Mocuba, *Mozam.* .... **87 F4** 16 54 S 36 57 E
Mocúzari, Presa, *Mexico* **118 B3** 27 10N 109 10W
Modane, *France* ...... **21 C10** 45 12N 6 40 E
Modasa, *India* .... **68 H5** 23 30N 73 21 E
Modder →, *S. Africa* .. **88 D3** 29 2 S 24 37 E
Modderrivier, *S. Africa* **88 D3** 29 2 S 24 38 E
Módena, *Italy* ...... **40 D7** 44 40N 10 55 E
Modena, *U.S.A.* **109 H7** 37 48N 113 56W
Modesto, *U.S.A.* **110 H6** 37 39N 121 0W
Módica, *Italy* .... **43 F7** 36 52N 14 46 E
Modimolle, *S. Africa* .. **89 C4** 24 42 S 28 22 E
Mödling, *Austria* ...... **27 C9** 48 5N 16 17 E
Modo, *Sudan* .... **81 F3** 5 31N 30 33 E
Modra, *Slovak Rep.* .. **27 C10** 48 19N 17 20 E
Modriča, *Bos.-H.* .... **28 F3** 44 57N 18 17 E
Moe, *Australia* ...... **95 F4** 38 12 S 146 19 E
Moebase, *Mozam.* .... **87 F4** 17 3 S 38 41 E
Moëlan-sur-Mer, *France* **18 E3** 47 49N 3 38W
Moengo, *Suriname* .. **125 B8** 5 45N 54 20W
Moffat, *U.K.* **13 F5** 55 21N 3 27W
Moga, *India* .... **68 D6** 30 48N 75 8 E
Mogadishu = Muqdisho,
  Somali Rep. ...... **75 G4** 2 2N 45 25 E
Mogador = Essaouira,
  Morocco **78 B4** 31 32N 9 42W
Mogadouro, *Portugal* **36 D4** 41 22N 6 47W
Mogalakwena →,
  S. Africa .... **89 C4** 22 38 S 28 40 E

Mogho, *Ethiopia* ...... **81 G5** 4 54N 40 16 E
Mogi das Cruzes, *Brazil* **127 A6** 23 31 S 46 11W
Mogi-Guaçu →, *Brazil* **127 A6** 20 53 S 48 10W
Mogi-Mirim, *Brazil* .. **127 A6** 22 29 S 47 0W
Mogielnica, *Poland* .. **31 G7** 51 42N 20 41 E
Mogige, *Ethiopia* .... **81 F4** 5 24N 36 14 E
Mogilev = Mahilyow,
  Belarus .... **32 F6** 53 55N 30 18 E
Mogilev-Podolskiy =
  Mohyliv-Podilskyy,
  Ukraine .... **29 B12** 48 26N 27 48 E
Mogilno, *Poland* ...... **31 F4** 52 39N 17 55 E
Mogincual, *Mozam.* .. **87 F5** 15 35 S 40 25 E
Mogliano Véneto, *Italy* **41 C9** 45 33N 12 14 E
Mogocha, *Russia* .... **53 D12** 53 40N 119 50 E
Mogollon Rim, *U.S.A.* **109 J8** 34 10N 110 50W
Mogok, *Burma* ...... **67 H20** 23 0N 96 40 E
Mógoro, *Italy* .... **42 C1** 39 41N 8 47 E
Moguer, *Spain* **37 H4** 37 15N 6 52W
Mogumber, *Australia* **93 F2** 31 2 S 116 3 E
Mohács, *Hungary* .... **28 E3** 45 58N 18 41 E
Mohales Hoek, *Lesotho* **88 E4** 30 7 S 27 26 E
Mohall, *U.S.A.* **112 A4** 48 46N 101 31W
Moḩammadābād, *Iran* **71 B8** 37 52N 59 5 E
Mohammedia, *Morocco* **78 B4** 33 44N 7 21W
Mohana →, *India* .... **69 G11** 24 43N 85 0 E
Mohanlalganj, *India* .. **69 F9** 26 41N 80 58 E
Mohave, L., *U.S.A.* .. **111 K12** 35 12N 114 34W
Mohawk →, *U.S.A.* .. **117 D11** 42 47N 73 41W
Moheda, *Sweden* .... **11 G8** 57 1N 14 35 E
Mohenjodaro, *Pakistan* **68 F3** 27 19N 68 7 E
Moher, Cliffs of, *Ireland* **12 D2** 52 58N 9 27W
Mohicanville Reservoir,
  U.S.A. **116 F3** 40 45N 82 0W
Möhne →, *Germany* .. **24 D3** 51 29N 7 57 E
Mohoro, *Tanzania* .... **86 D4** 8 6 S 39 8 E
Mohyliv-Podilskyy,
  Ukraine .... **29 B12** 48 26N 27 48 E
Moia, *Sudan* .... **81 F2** 5 3N 28 2 E
Moidart, L., *U.K.* **13 E3** 56 47N 5 52W
Moineşti, *Romania* .. **29 D11** 46 28N 26 31 E
Moira →, *Canada* **116 B7** 44 21N 77 24W
Moirans, *France* ...... **21 C9** 45 20N 5 33 E
Moirans-en-Montagne,
  France .... **19 F12** 46 26N 5 43 E
Moires, *Greece* ...... **49 D6** 35 4N 24 56 E
Moisaküla, *Estonia* .. **9 G21** 58 3N 25 12 E
Moisie, *Canada* **105 B6** 50 12N 66 1W
Moisie →, *Canada* **105 B6** 50 14N 66 5W
Moissac, *France* ...... **20 D5** 44 7N 1 5 E
Moïssala, *Chad* ...... **79 G9** 8 21N 17 46 E
Moitaco, *Venezuela* .. **124 B6** 8 12N 62 42W
Mojácar, *Spain* **39 H3** 37 6N 1 55W
Mojados, *Spain* **36 D6** 41 26N 4 40W
Mojave, *U.S.A.* **111 K8** 35 3N 118 10W
Mojave △, *U.S.A.* **111 K11** 35 7N 115 30W
Mojave Desert, *U.S.A.* **111 L10** 35 0N 116 30W
Mojiang, *China* ...... **58 F3** 23 37N 101 35 E
Mojo, *Bolivia* .... **126 A2** 21 48 S 65 33W
Mojo, *Ethiopia* ...... **81 F4** 8 35N 39 5 E
Mojokerto, *Indonesia* **63 G15** 7 28 S 112 26 E
Mokai, *N.Z.* .... **91 H5** 38 32 S 175 56 E
Mokambo, *Dem. Rep. of*
  the Congo .... **87 E2** 12 25 S 28 20 E
Mokameh, *India* ...... **69 G11** 25 24N 85 55 E
Mokau, *N.Z.* .... **91 H5** 38 42 S 174 39 E
Mokelumne →, *U.S.A.* **110 G5** 38 13N 121 28W
Mokelumne Hill, *U.S.A.* **110 G6** 38 18N 120 43W
Mokhós, *Greece* ...... **49 D7** 35 16N 25 27 E
Mokhotlong, *Lesotho* **89 D4** 29 22 S 29 2 E
Möklinta, *Sweden* .... **10 D10** 60 4N 16 33 E
Mokokchung, *India* .. **67 F19** 26 15N 94 30 E
Mokolo, *Cameroon* .. **83 C7** 10 50N 13 55 E
Mokolo →, *S. Africa* .. **89 C4** 23 14 S 27 43 E
Mokopane, *S. Africa* .. **89 C4** 24 10 S 28 55 E
Mokp'o, *S. Korea* .... **57 G14** 34 50N 126 25 E
Mokra Gora,
  Serbia & M. ...... **44 D4** 42 50N 20 30 E
Mokronog, *Slovenia* .. **41 C12** 45 57N 15 9 E
Moksha →, *Russia* .... **34 C6** 54 45N 41 53 E
Mokshan, *Russia* .... **34 D7** 53 25N 44 35 E
Mokwa, *Nigeria* ...... **83 D6** 9 19N 5 0 E
Mol, *Belgium* .... **17 C5** 51 11N 5 5 E
Mola di Bari, *Italy* .... **43 A10** 41 4N 17 5 E
Molale, *Ethiopia* ...... **81 E4** 10 10N 39 41 E
Moláoi, *Greece* ...... **46 E4** 36 49N 22 56 E
Molara, *Italy* .... **42 B2** 40 52N 9 43 E
Molat, *Croatia* ...... **41 D11** 44 15N 14 50 E
Molchanovo, *Russia* .. **52 D9** 57 40N 83 50 E
Mold, *U.K.* **14 D4** 53 9N 3 8W
Moldavia = Moldova ■,
  Europe .... **29 C13** 47 0N 28 0 E
Moldavia, *Romania* .. **29 D12** 46 30N 27 0 E
Molde, *Norway* ...... **8 E12** 62 45N 7 9 E
Moldova ■, *Europe* .. **29 C13** 47 0N 28 0 E
Moldova Nouă,
  Romania .... **28 F6** 44 45N 21 41 E
Moldoveanu, Vf.,
  Romania .... **29 E9** 45 36N 24 45 E
Moldoviţa, *Romania* .. **29 C9** 47 41N 25 32 E
Mole △, *Ghana* **83 D4** 9 43N 1 44W
Mole →, *U.K.* **15 F7** 51 24N 0 21W
Mole Creek, *Australia* **95 G4** 41 34 S 146 24 E
Molepolole, *Botswana* **88 C4** 24 28 S 25 28 E
Molfetta, *Italy* ...... **43 A9** 41 12N 16 36 E
Molina de Aragón,
  Spain **38 E3** 40 46N 1 52W
Molina de Segura, *Spain* **39 G3** 38 3N 1 12W
Moline, *U.S.A.* **112 E9** 41 30N 90 31W
Molinella, *Italy* ...... **41 D8** 44 37N 11 40 E
Molinos, *Argentina* .. **126 B2** 25 28 S 66 15W
Moliro, *Dem. Rep. of*
  the Congo .... **86 D3** 8 12 S 30 30 E
Moliterno, *Italy* ...... **43 B8** 40 14N 15 52 E
Molkom, *Sweden* .... **10 E7** 59 37N 13 44 E
Mölle, *Sweden* ...... **11 H6** 56 17N 12 31 E
Molledo, *Spain* **36 B6** 43 8N 4 6W
Molleno, *Peru* ...... **124 G4** 17 0 S 72 0W
Mollerin, L., *Australia* **93 F2** 30 30 S 117 35 E
Mollerussa, *Spain* .... **38 D5** 41 37N 0 54 E
Mollina, *Spain* **37 H6** 37 8N 4 38W
Mölln, *Germany* ...... **24 B6** 53 37N 10 41 E
Mölltorp, *Sweden* .... **11 F8** 58 30N 14 26 E
Mölndal, *Sweden* .... **11 G6** 57 40N 12 3 E
Mölnlycke, *Sweden* .. **11 G6** 57 40N 12 8 E
Molochansk, *Ukraine* **33 J8** 47 15N 35 35 E
Molochnaya →,
  Ukraine .... **33 J8** 46 30N 35 20 E
Molodechno =
  Maladzyechna,
  Belarus .... **32 E4** 54 20N 26 50 E
Molodove, *Ukraine* .. **29 D14** 46 13N 29 39 E

Molokai, *U.S.A.* **106 H16** 21 8N 157 0W
Molong, *Australia* .... **95 E4** 33 5 S 148 54 E
Molopo →, *Africa* .... **88 D3** 28 30 S 20 12 E
Mólos, *Greece* ...... **46 C4** 38 47N 22 37 E
Molsheim, *France* .... **19 D14** 48 33N 7 29 E
Molson L., *Canada* .. **103 C9** 54 22N 96 40W
Molteno, *S. Africa* .... **88 E4** 31 22 S 26 22 E
Molu, *Indonesia* ...... **63 F8** 6 45 S 131 40 E
Molucca Sea, *Indonesia* **63 E6** 0 0 125 0 E
Moluccas = Maluku,
  Indonesia .... **63 E7** 1 0 S 127 0 E
Moma, *Dem. Rep. of*
  the Congo .... **86 C1** 1 35 S 23 52 E
Moma, *Mozam.* ...... **87 F4** 16 47 S 39 4 E
Mombasa, *Kenya* .... **86 C4** 4 2 S 39 43 E
Mombetsu, *Japan* .... **54 B11** 44 21N 143 22 E
Mombuey, *Spain* **36 C4** 42 3N 6 20W
Momchilgrad, *Bulgaria* **45 E9** 41 33N 25 23 E
Momi, *Dem. Rep. of*
  the Congo .... **86 C2** 1 42 S 27 0 E
Mompós, *Colombia* .. **124 B4** 9 14N 74 26W
Møn, *Denmark* ...... **11 K6** 54 57N 12 20 E
Mon □, *Burma* ...... **67 L20** 16 0N 97 30 E
Mona, Canal de la =
  Mona Passage,
  W. Indies **121 C6** 18 30N 67 45W
Mona, Isla, *Puerto Rico* **121 C6** 18 5N 67 54W
Mona, Pta., *Costa Rica* **120 E3** 9 37N 82 36W
Mona Passage, *W. Indies* **121 C6** 18 30N 67 45W
Monaca, *U.S.A.* **116 F4** 40 41N 80 17W
Monaco ■, *Europe* .. **21 E11** 43 46N 7 23 E
Monadhliath Mts., *U.K.* **13 D4** 57 10N 4 4W
Monadnock, Mt., *U.S.A.* **117 D12** 42 52N 72 7W
Monaghan, *Ireland* .. **12 B5** 54 15N 6 57W
Monaghan □, *Ireland* .. **12 B5** 54 11N 6 56W
Monahans, *U.S.A.* .. **113 K3** 31 36N 102 54W
Monapo, *Mozam.* .... **87 E5** 14 56 S 40 19 E
Monar, L., *U.K.* **13 D3** 57 26N 5 8W
Monarch Mt., *Canada* **102 C3** 51 55N 125 57W
Monashee Mts., *Canada* **102 C5** 51 0N 118 43W
Monasterevin, *Ireland* **12 C4** 53 8N 7 4W
Monastir = Bitola,
  Macedonia ...... **44 E5** 41 1N 21 20 E
Moncada, *Phil.* ...... **61 D4** 15 44N 120 34 E
Moncalieri, *Italy* .... **40 D4** 45 0N 7 41 E
Moncalvo, *Italy* ...... **40 C5** 45 3N 8 16 E
Moncão, *Portugal* **36 C2** 42 4N 8 27W
Moncarapacho, *Portugal* **37 H3** 37 5N 7 46W
Moncayo, Sierra del,
  Spain **38 D3** 41 48N 1 50W
Mönchengladbach,
  Germany .... **24 D2** 51 11N 6 27 E
Monchique, *Portugal* **37 H2** 37 19N 8 38W
Moncks Corner, *U.S.A.* **115 J5** 33 12N 80 1W
Monclova, *Mexico* **118 B4** 26 50N 101 30W
Moncontour, *France* .. **18 D4** 48 22N 2 38W
Moncton, *Canada* **105 C7** 46 7N 64 51W
Mondariz, *Spain* **36 C2** 42 14N 8 27W
Mondego →, *Portugal* **36 E2** 40 9N 8 52W
Mondego, C., *Portugal* **36 E2** 40 11N 8 54W
Mondeodo, *Indonesia* **63 E6** 3 34 S 122 9 E
Mondeville, *France* .. **18 C6** 49 10N 0 18W
Mondolfo, *Italy* ...... **41 E10** 43 45N 13 6 E
Mondoñedo, *Spain* .. **36 B3** 43 25N 7 23W
Mondovì, *Italy* ...... **40 D4** 44 23N 7 49 E
Mondragon, *Phil.* .... **61 E6** 12 31N 124 45 E
Mondragone, *Italy* .. **42 A6** 41 7N 13 53 E
Mondrain I., *Australia* **93 F3** 34 9 S 122 14 E
Moneague, *Jamaica* .. **120 a** 18 16N 77 7W
Monemvasía, *Greece* **46 E5** 36 41N 23 3 E
Monessen, *U.S.A.* **116 F5** 40 9N 79 54W
Monesterio, *Spain* .. **37 G4** 38 6N 6 15W
Monestier-de-Clermont,
  France .... **21 D9** 44 55N 5 38 E
Monett, *U.S.A.* **113 G8** 36 55N 93 55W
Moneymore, *U.K.* .. **12 B5** 54 41N 6 40W
Monfalcone, *Italy* .... **41 C10** 45 49N 13 32 E
Monflanquin, *France* **20 D4** 44 32N 0 47 E
Monforte, *Portugal* .. **37 F3** 39 6N 7 25W
Monforte de Lemos,
  Spain **36 C3** 42 31N 7 33W
Mong Cai, *Vietnam* .. **64 B6** 21 27N 107 54 E
Mong Hsu, *Burma* .. **58 G2** 21 54N 98 30 E
Mong Kung, *Burma* .. **67 J20** 21 35N 97 35 E
Mong Nai, *Burma* .. **67 J20** 20 32N 97 46 E
Mong Pawk, *Burma* .. **67 H21** 22 4N 99 16 E
Mong Ping, *Burma* .. **58 G2** 21 22N 99 2 E
Mong Ton, *Burma* .. **67 J21** 20 17N 98 45 E
Mong Wa, *Burma* .. **67 J22** 21 26N 100 27 E
Mong Yai, *Burma* .. **67 H21** 22 21N 98 3 E
Mongalla, *Sudan* .... **81 F3** 5 8N 31 42 E
Mongers, L., *Australia* **93 E2** 29 25 S 117 5 E
Monghyr = Munger,
  India .... **69 G12** 25 23N 86 30 E
Mongibello = Etna, *Italy* **43 E7** 37 50N 14 55 E
Mongo, *Chad* .... **79 F9** 12 14N 18 43 E
Mongo →, *S. Leone* .. **82 D2** 9 35N 12 10W
Mongolia ■, *Asia* .... **53 E10** 47 0N 103 0 E
Mongolia, Plateau of,
  Asia .... **50 E14** 45 0N 105 0 E
Mongonu, *Nigeria* .... **83 C7** 12 40N 13 32 E
Mongu, *Zambia* ...... **85 H4** 15 16 S 23 12 E
Môngua, *Angola* ...... **88 B2** 16 43 S 15 20 E
Monifieth, *U.K.* **13 E6** 56 30N 2 48W
Monistrol-sur-Loire,
  France .... **21 C8** 45 17N 4 11 E
Monkey Bay, *Malawi* **87 E4** 14 7 S 35 1 E
Monkey Mia, *Australia* **93 E1** 25 48 S 113 43 E
Monkey River Town,
  Belize **119 D7** 16 22N 88 29W
Mońki, *Poland* ...... **30 E9** 53 23N 22 48 E
Monkoto, *Dem. Rep. of*
  the Congo .... **84 E4** 1 38 S 20 35 E
Monkton, *Canada* **116 C3** 43 35N 81 5W
Monmouth, *Ill., U.S.A.* **112 E9** 40 55N 90 39W
Monmouth, *Oreg.,*
  U.S.A. **108 D2** 44 51N 123 14W
Monmouthshire □, *U.K.* **15 F5** 51 48N 2 54W
Mono, L., *U.S.A.* **110 H7** 38 1N 119 1W
Monolith, *U.S.A.* **111 K8** 35 7N 118 22W
Monólithos, *Greece* .. **49 C9** 36 7N 27 45 E
Monópoli, *Italy* ...... **43 B10** 40 57N 17 18 E
Monor, *Hungary* ...... **28 C4** 47 21N 19 27 E
Monos I., *Trin. & Tob.* **125 K15** 10 42N 61 44W
Monóvar, *Spain* **39 G4** 38 28N 0 53W
Monreal del Campo,
  Spain **38 E3** 40 47N 1 20W
Monreale, *Italy* ...... **42 D6** 38 5N 13 17 E
Monroe, *Ga., U.S.A.* .. **115 J4** 33 47N 83 43W
Monroe, *La., U.S.A.* .. **113 J8** 32 30N 92 7W
Monroe, *Mich., U.S.A.* **114 E4** 41 55N 83 24W
Monroe, *N.C., U.S.A.* **115 H5** 34 59N 80 33W
Monroe, *N.Y., U.S.A.* **117 E10** 41 19N 74 11W
Monroe, *Utah, U.S.A.* **109 G7** 38 38N 112 7W
Monroe, *Wash., U.S.A.* **110 C5** 47 51N 121 58W

Monroe, Wis., U.S.A. 112 D10 42 36N 89 38W
Monroe City, U.S.A. 112 F9 39 39N 91 44W
Monroeton, U.S.A. 117 E8 41 43N 76 29W
Monroeville, Ala., U.S.A. 115 K2 31 31N 87 20W
Monroeville, Pa., U.S.A. 116 F5 40 26N 79 45W
Monrovia, Liberia 82 D2 6 18N 10 47W
Mons, Belgium 17 D3 50 27N 3 58 E
Møns Klint, Denmark 11 K6 54 57N 12 33 E
Monsaraz, Portugal 37 G3 38 28N 7 22W
Monse, Indonesia 63 E6 4 7 S 123 15 E
Monségur, France 20 D4 44 38N 0 4 E
Monsélice, Italy 41 C8 45 14N 11 45 E
Mönsterås, Sweden 11 G10 57 3N 16 26 E
Mont Cenis, Col du, France 21 C10 45 15N 6 55 E
Mont-de-Marsan, France 20 E3 43 54N 0 31W
Mont-Joli, Canada 105 C6 48 37N 68 10W
Mont-Laurier, Canada 104 C4 46 35N 75 30W
Mont-Louis, Canada 105 C6 49 15N 65 44W
Mont Peko △, Ivory C. 82 D3 9 5N 7 15W
Mont-roig del Camp, Spain 38 D5 41 5N 0 58 E
Mont-St-Michel, Le, France 18 D5 48 40N 1 30W
Mont Sangbe △, Ivory C. 82 D3 8 0N 7 10W
Mont-Tremblant ⌓, Canada 104 C5 46 30N 74 30W
Montabaur, Germany 24 E3 50 25N 7 50 E
Montagnac, France 20 E7 43 29N 3 28 E
Montagnana, Italy 41 C8 45 14N 11 28 E
Montagne d'Ambre △, Madag. 89 A8 12 37 S 49 8 E
Montagne de Reims ⌓, France 19 C11 49 8N 4 0 E
Montagu, S. Africa 88 E3 33 45 S 20 8 E
Montagu I., Antarctica 5 B1 58 25 S 26 20W
Montague, Canada 105 C7 46 10N 62 39W
Montague, I., Mexico 118 A2 31 40N 114 56W
Montague Ra., Australia 93 E2 27 15 S 119 30 E
Montague Sd., Australia 92 B4 14 28 S 125 20 E
Montaigu, France 18 F5 46 59N 1 18W
Montalbán, Spain 38 E4 40 50N 0 45W
Montalbano Iónico, Italy 43 B9 40 17N 16 34 E
Montalbo, Spain 38 F2 39 53N 2 42W
Montalcino, Italy 41 E8 43 3N 11 29 E
Montalegre, Portugal 36 D3 41 49N 7 47W
Montalto, Italy 43 D8 38 10N 15 55 E
Montalto di Castro, Italy 41 F8 42 21N 11 37 E
Montalto Uffugo, Italy 43 C9 39 24N 16 9 E
Montalvo, U.S.A. 111 L7 34 15N 119 12W
Montamarta, Spain 36 D5 41 39N 5 49W
Montana, Bulgaria 44 C7 43 27N 23 16 E
Montaña, Peru 124 E4 6 0 S 73 0W
Montana □, Bulgaria 44 C7 43 30N 23 20 E
Montana □, U.S.A. 108 C9 47 0N 110 0W
Montaña Clara, I., Canary Is. 48 E6 29 17N 13 33W
Montañas de Malaga ⌓, Spain 37 J6 36 48N 4 32W
Montánchez, Spain 37 F4 39 15N 6 8W
Montargil, Portugal 37 F2 39 5N 8 10W
Montargis, France 19 E9 47 59N 2 43 E
Montauban, France 20 D5 44 2N 1 21 E
Montauk, U.S.A. 117 E13 41 3N 71 57W
Montauk Pt., U.S.A. 117 E13 41 4N 71 52W
Montbard, France 19 E11 47 38N 4 20 E
Montbarrey, France 19 E12 47 1N 5 39 E
Montbéliard, France 19 E13 47 31N 6 48 E
Montblanc, Spain 38 D6 41 23N 1 4 E
Montbrison, France 21 C8 45 36N 4 3 E
Montcalm, Pic de, France 20 F5 42 40N 1 25 E
Montceau-les-Mines, France 19 F11 46 40N 4 23 E
Montcenis, France 21 B8 46 47N 4 23 E
Montclair, U.S.A. 117 F10 40 49N 74 13W
Montcornet, France 19 C11 49 40N 4 1 E
Montcuq, France 20 D5 44 21N 1 13 E
Montdidier, France 19 C9 49 38N 2 35 E
Monte Albán, Mexico 119 D5 17 2N 96 45W
Monte Alegre, Brazil 125 D8 2 0 S 54 0W
Monte Azul, Brazil 125 G10 15 9 S 42 53W
Monte-Carlo, Monaco 21 E11 43 44N 7 25 E
Monte Caseros, Argentina 126 C4 30 10 S 57 50W
Monte Comán, Argentina 126 C2 34 40 S 67 53W
Monte Cristi, Dom. Rep. 121 C5 19 52N 71 39W
Monte Cucco ⌓, Italy 41 E9 43 22N 12 43 E
Monte Lindo →, Paraguay 126 A4 23 56 S 57 12W
Monte Patria, Chile 126 C1 30 42 S 70 58W
Monte Quemado, Argentina 126 B3 25 53 S 62 41W
Monte Redondo, Portugal 36 F2 39 53N 8 50W
Monte Rio, U.S.A. 110 G4 38 28N 123 0W
Monte San Giovanni Campano, Italy 42 A6 41 38N 13 31 E
Monte San Savino, Italy 41 E8 43 20N 11 43 E
Monte Sant' Ángelo, Italy 41 G12 41 42N 15 59 E
Monte Santu, C. di, Italy 42 B2 40 5N 9 44 E
Monte Sibillini △, Italy 41 F10 42 55N 13 15 E
Monte Subasio ⌓, Italy 41 E9 43 5N 12 40 E
Monte Vista, U.S.A. 109 H10 37 35N 106 9W
Monteagudo, Argentina 127 B5 27 14 S 54 8W
Montealegre del Castillo, Spain 39 G3 38 48N 1 17W
Montebello, Canada 104 C5 45 40N 74 55W
Montebello Iónico, Italy 43 E8 37 59N 15 45 E
Montebello Is., Australia 92 D2 20 30 S 115 45 E
Montebelluna, Italy 41 C9 45 47N 12 3 E
Montebourg, France 18 C5 49 30N 1 20W
Montecastrilli, Italy 41 F9 42 39N 12 29 E
Montecatini Terme, Italy 40 E7 43 53N 10 46 E
Montecito, U.S.A. 111 L7 34 26N 119 40W
Montecristo, Italy 40 F7 42 20N 10 19 E
Montefalco, Italy 41 F9 42 54N 12 39 E
Montefiascone, Italy 41 F9 42 32N 12 2 E
Montefrío, Spain 37 H7 37 20N 4 0W
Montegiórgio, Italy 41 E10 43 6N 13 33 E
Montego Bay, Jamaica 120 a 18 28N 77 55W
Montehermoso, Spain 36 E4 40 5N 6 21W
Montejicar, Spain 37 H7 37 33N 3 30W
Montélimar, France 21 D8 44 33N 4 45 E
Montella, Italy 43 B8 40 51N 15 1 E
Montellano, Spain 37 J5 36 59N 5 29W
Montello, U.S.A. 112 D10 43 48N 89 20W
Montemor-o-Novo, Portugal 37 G2 38 40N 8 12W
Montemor-o-Velho, Portugal 36 E2 40 11N 8 40W
Montemorelos, Mexico 119 B5 25 11N 99 42W
Montendre, France 20 C3 45 16N 0 26W
Montenegro, Brazil 127 B5 29 39 S 51 29W
Montenegro □, Serbia & M. 44 D3 42 40N 19 20 E
Montenero di Bisáccia, Italy 41 G11 41 57N 14 47 E
Montepuez, Mozam. 87 E4 13 8 S 38 59 E
Montepuez →, Mozam. 87 E5 12 32 S 40 27 E
Montepulciano, Italy 41 E8 43 5N 11 47 E
Montereale, Italy 41 F10 42 31N 13 15 E
Montereau-Faut-Yonne, France 19 D9 48 22N 2 57 E
Monterey, U.S.A. 110 J5 36 37N 121 55W
Monterey B., U.S.A. 110 J5 36 45N 122 0W
Montería, Colombia 124 B3 8 46N 75 53W
Monteros, Argentina 126 B2 27 11 S 65 30W
Monterotondo, Italy 41 F9 42 3N 12 37 E
Monterrey, Mexico 118 B4 25 40N 100 30W
Montes Azules ⌓, Mexico 119 D6 16 21N 91 3W
Montes Claros, Brazil 125 G10 16 30 S 43 50W
Montesano, U.S.A. 110 D3 46 59N 123 36W
Montesano sulla Marcellana, Italy 43 B8 40 16N 15 42 E
Montesárchio, Italy 43 A7 41 4N 14 38 E
Montescaglioso, Italy 43 B9 40 33N 16 40 E
Montesilvano, Italy 41 F11 42 29N 14 8 E
Montesinho ⌓, Portugal 36 D4 41 54N 6 52W
Montevarchi, Italy 41 E8 43 31N 11 34 E
Montevideo, Uruguay 127 C4 34 50 S 56 11W
Montevideo, U.S.A. 112 C7 44 57N 95 43W
Montezuma, U.S.A. 112 E8 41 35N 92 32W
Montezuma Castle ⌓, U.S.A. 109 J8 34 34N 111 45W
Montfaucon, France 18 E5 47 6N 1 7W
Montfaucon-d'Argonne, France 19 C12 49 16N 5 8 E
Montfaucon-en-Velay, France 21 C8 45 11N 4 20 E
Montfort-le-Gesnois, France 18 D7 48 3N 0 25 E
Montfort-sur-Meu, France 18 D5 48 9N 1 58W
Montfragüe ⌓, Spain 36 F5 39 48N 5 52W
Montgenèvre, France 21 D10 44 56N 6 43 E
Montgomery, U.K. 15 E4 52 34N 3 8W
Montgomery Ala., U.S.A. 115 J2 32 23N 86 19W
Montgomery Pa., U.S.A. 116 E8 41 10N 76 53W
Montgomery W. Va., U.S.A. 114 F5 38 11N 81 19W
Montgomery City, U.S.A. 112 F9 38 59N 91 30W
Montguyon, France 20 C3 45 12N 0 12W
Monthermé, France 19 C11 49 52N 4 42 E
Monthey, Switz. 25 J2 46 15N 6 56 E
Monthois, France 19 C11 49 19N 4 43 E
Monti, Italy 42 B2 40 49N 9 19 E
Monti Lucretili ⌓, Italy 41 F9 42 5N 12 50 E
Monti Picentini ⌓, Italy 43 B8 40 45N 15 2 E
Monti Simbruini ⌓, Italy 41 G10 41 55N 13 13 E
Monticelli d'Ongina, Italy 40 C6 45 5N 9 56 E
Monticello, Ark., U.S.A. 113 J9 33 38N 91 47W
Monticello, Fla., U.S.A. 115 K4 30 33N 83 52W
Monticello, Ind., U.S.A. 114 E2 40 45N 86 46W
Monticello, Iowa, U.S.A. 112 D9 42 15N 91 12W
Monticello, Ky., U.S.A. 115 G3 36 50N 84 51W
Monticello, Minn., U.S.A. 112 C8 45 18N 93 48W
Monticello, Miss., U.S.A. 113 K9 31 33N 90 7W
Monticello, N.Y., U.S.A. 117 E10 41 39N 74 42W
Monticello, Utah, U.S.A. 109 H9 37 52N 109 21W
Montichiari, Italy 40 C7 45 25N 10 23 E
Montier-en-Der, France 19 D11 48 30N 4 45 E
Montignac, France 20 C5 45 4N 1 10 E
Montigny-les-Metz, France 19 C13 49 7N 6 10 E
Montigny-sur-Aube, France 19 E11 47 57N 4 45 E
Montijo, Portugal 37 G2 38 41N 8 54W
Montijo, Spain 37 G4 38 52N 6 39W
Montilla, Spain 37 H6 37 36N 4 40W
Montivilliers, France 18 C7 49 33N 0 12 E
Montluçon, France 19 F9 46 22N 2 36 E
Montmagny, Canada 105 C5 46 58N 70 34W
Montmarault, France 19 F9 46 19N 2 57 E
Montmartre, Canada 103 C8 50 14N 103 27W
Montmédy, France 19 C12 49 30N 5 20 E
Montmélian, France 21 C10 45 30N 6 4 E
Montmirail, France 19 D10 48 51N 3 30 E
Montmoreau-St-Cybard, France 20 C4 45 23N 0 8 E
Montmorillon, France 20 B4 46 26N 0 50 E
Montmort-Lucy, France 19 D10 48 55N 3 49 E
Monto, Australia 94 C5 24 52 S 151 6 E
Montoire-sur-le-Loir, France 18 E7 47 45N 0 52 E
Montongbuwoh, Indonesia 63 K19 8 33 S 116 4 E
Montório al Vomano, Italy 41 F10 42 35N 13 38 E
Montoro, Spain 37 G6 38 1N 4 27W
Montour Falls, U.S.A. 116 D8 42 21N 76 51W
Montoursville, U.S.A. 116 E8 41 15N 76 55W
Montpelier, Idaho, U.S.A. 108 E8 42 19N 111 18W
Montpelier, Vt., U.S.A. 117 B12 44 16N 72 35W
Montpellier, France 20 E7 43 37N 3 52 E
Montpezat-de-Quercy, France 20 D5 44 15N 1 30 E
Montpon-Ménestérol, France 20 D4 45 0N 0 11 E
Montréal, Canada 117 A11 45 31N 73 34W
Montréal, Aude, France 20 E6 43 13N 2 8 E
Montréal, Gers, France 20 E4 43 56N 0 11 E
Montreal →, Canada 104 C3 47 14N 84 39W
Montreal L., Canada 103 C7 54 20N 105 45W
Montreal Lake, Canada 103 C7 54 3N 105 46W
Montredon-Labessonnié, France 20 E6 43 45N 2 18 E
Montrésor, France 18 E8 47 10N 1 10 E
Montret, France 19 F12 46 40N 5 7 E
Montreuil, Pas-de-Calais, France 19 B8 50 27N 1 45 E
Montreuil, Seine-St-Denis, France 19 D9 48 51N 2 27 E
Montreuil-Bellay, France 18 E6 47 8N 0 9W
Montreux, Switz. 25 J2 46 26N 6 55 E
Montrevel-en-Bresse, France 19 F12 46 21N 5 8 E
Montrichard, France 18 E8 47 20N 1 10 E
Montrose, U.K. 13 E6 56 44N 2 27W
Montrose, Colo., U.S.A. 109 G10 38 29N 107 53W
Montrose, Pa., U.S.A. 117 E9 41 50N 75 53W
Monts, Pte. des, Canada 105 C6 49 20N 67 12W
Montsalvy, France 20 D6 44 41N 2 30 E
Montsant, Serra de, Spain 38 D6 41 17N 1 0 E
Montsauche-les-Settons, France 19 E11 47 13N 4 2 E
Montsec, Serra del, Spain 38 C5 42 5N 0 45 E
Montseny ⌓, Spain 38 D7 41 43N 2 22W
Montserrat, Spain 38 D6 41 36N 1 49 E
Montserrat ⊠, W. Indies 121 C7 16 40N 62 10W
Montuenga, Spain 36 D6 41 3N 4 38W
Montuiri, Spain 48 B9 39 34N 2 59 E
Monywa, Burma 67 H19 22 7N 95 11 E
Monza, Italy 40 C6 45 35N 9 16 E
Monze, Zambia 87 F2 16 17 S 27 29 E
Monze, C., Pakistan 68 G2 24 47N 66 37 E
Monzón, Spain 38 D5 41 52N 0 10 E
Mooers, U.S.A. 117 B11 44 58N 73 35W
Mooi →, S. Africa 89 D5 28 45 S 30 34 E
Mooi River, S. Africa 89 D4 29 13 S 29 50 E
Moonah →, Australia 94 C2 22 3 S 138 33 E
Moonda, L., Australia 94 D3 25 52 S 140 25 E
Moonie, Australia 95 D5 27 46 S 150 20 E
Moonie →, Australia 95 D4 29 19 S 148 43 E
Moonta, Australia 95 E2 34 6 S 137 32 E
Moora, Australia 93 F2 30 37 S 115 58 E
Moorcroft, U.S.A. 112 C2 44 16N 104 57W
Moore →, Australia 93 F2 31 22 S 115 30 E
Moore, L., Australia 93 E2 29 50 S 117 35 E
Moore Park, Australia 94 C5 24 43 S 152 17 E
Moore River △, Australia 93 F2 31 7 S 115 39 E
Moorefield, U.S.A. 114 F6 39 5N 78 59W
Moores Res., U.S.A. 117 B13 44 45N 71 50W
Moorfoot Hills, U.K. 13 F5 55 44N 3 8W
Moorhead, U.S.A. 112 B6 46 53N 96 45W
Moormerland, Germany 24 B3 53 20N 7 20 E
Moorpark, U.S.A. 111 L8 34 17N 118 53W
Moorreesburg, S. Africa 88 E2 33 6 S 18 38 E
Moorrinya △, Australia 94 C3 21 42 S 144 58 E
Moosburg, Germany 25 G7 48 27N 11 56 E
Moose →, Canada 104 B3 51 20N 80 25W
Moose →, U.S.A. 117 C9 43 38N 75 24W
Moose Creek, Canada 117 A10 45 15N 74 58W
Moose Factory, Canada 104 B3 51 16N 80 32W
Moose Jaw, Canada 103 C7 50 24N 105 30W
Moose Jaw →, Canada 103 C7 50 34N 105 18W
Moose Lake, U.S.A. 112 B8 46 27N 92 46W
Moose Mountain ⌓, Canada 103 D8 49 48N 102 25W
Moosehead L., U.S.A. 115 C11 45 38N 69 40W
Mooselookmeguntic L., U.S.A. 115 C10 44 55N 70 49W
Moosilauke, Mt., U.S.A. 117 B13 44 3N 71 40W
Moosomin, Canada 103 C8 50 9N 101 40W
Moosonee, Canada 104 B3 51 17N 80 39W
Moosup, U.S.A. 117 E13 41 43N 71 53W
Mopane, S. Africa 89 C4 22 37 S 29 52 E
Mopeia Velha, Mozam. 87 F4 17 30 S 35 40 E
Mopipi, Botswana 88 C3 21 6 S 24 55 E
Mopoi, C.A.R. 86 A2 5 6N 26 54 E
Mopti, Mali 82 C4 14 30N 4 0W
Moqatta, Sudan 81 E4 14 38N 35 50 E
Moqor, Afghan. 68 C2 32 50N 67 42 E
Moquegua, Peru 124 G4 17 15 S 70 46W
Mór, Hungary 28 C3 47 25N 18 12 E
Mora, Cameroon 83 C7 11 2N 14 7 E
Móra, Portugal 37 G2 38 55N 8 10W
Mora, Spain 37 F7 39 41N 3 46W
Mora, Sweden 10 C8 61 2N 14 38 E
Mora, Minn., U.S.A. 112 C8 45 53N 93 18W
Mora, N. Mex., U.S.A. 109 J11 35 58N 105 20W
Mora →, U.S.A. 113 H2 35 35N 104 25W
Mora de Rubielos, Spain 38 E4 40 15N 0 45W
Móra d'Ebre, Spain 38 D5 41 6N 0 38 E
Mòra la Nova, Spain 38 D5 41 7N 0 39 E
Morača →, Serbia & M. 44 D3 42 20N 19 9 E
Moradabad, India 69 E8 28 50N 78 50 E
Morafenobe, Madag. 89 B7 17 50 S 44 53 E
Morąg, Poland 30 E6 53 55N 19 56 E
Moral de Calatrava, Spain 37 G7 38 51N 3 33W
Moraleja, Spain 36 E4 40 6N 6 43W
Moramanga, Madag. 89 B8 18 56 S 48 12 E
Moran, Kans., U.S.A. 113 G7 37 55N 95 10W
Moran, Wyo., U.S.A. 108 E8 43 53N 110 37W
Moranbah, Australia 94 C4 22 1 S 148 6 E
Morano Cálabro, Italy 43 C9 39 50N 16 8 E
Morant Bay, Jamaica 120 a 17 53N 76 25W
Morant Cays, Jamaica 120 C4 17 22N 76 0W
Morant Pt., Jamaica 120 a 17 55N 76 12W
Morar, India 68 F8 26 14N 78 14 E
Morar, L., U.K. 13 E3 56 57N 5 40W
Moratalla, Spain 39 G3 38 14N 1 49W
Moratuwa, Sri Lanka 66 R11 6 45N 79 55 E
Morava →, Slovak Rep. 27 C9 48 10N 16 59 E
Moravia, U.S.A. 117 D8 42 43N 76 25W
Moravian Hts. = Českomoravská Vrchovina, Czech Rep. 26 B8 49 30N 15 40 E
Moravica →, Serbia & M. 44 C4 43 52N 20 8 E
Moravița, Romania 28 E6 45 17N 21 14 E
Moravská Třebová, Czech Rep. 27 B9 49 45N 16 40 E
Moravské Budějovice, Czech Rep. 26 B8 49 4N 15 49 E
Morawa, Australia 93 E2 29 13 S 116 0 E
Morawhanna, Guyana 124 B7 8 30N 59 40W
Moray □, U.K. 13 D5 57 31N 3 18W
Moray Firth, U.K. 13 D5 57 40N 3 52W
Morbach, Germany 25 F3 49 48N 7 6 E
Morbegno, Italy 40 B6 46 8N 9 34 E
Morbi, India 68 H4 22 50N 70 42 E
Morbihan □, France 18 E4 47 55N 2 50W
Mörbylånga, Sweden 11 H10 56 32N 16 22 E
Morcenx, France 20 D3 44 3N 0 55W
Morcone, Italy 43 A7 41 20N 14 40 E
Mordelles, France 18 D5 48 5N 1 52W
Morden, Canada 103 D9 49 15N 98 10W
Mordoğan, Turkey 47 C8 38 30N 26 37 E
Mordovian Republic = Mordvinia □, Russia 34 C7 54 20N 44 30 E
Mordovo, Russia 34 D5 52 6N 40 50 E
Mordvinia □, Russia 34 C7 54 20N 44 30 E
Mordy, Poland 31 F9 52 13N 22 31 E
Morea, Greece 6 H10 37 45N 22 10 E
Moreau →, U.S.A. 112 C4 45 18N 100 43W
Morecambe, U.K. 14 C5 54 5N 2 52W
Morecambe B., U.K. 14 C5 54 7N 3 0W
Moree, Australia 95 D4 29 28 S 149 54 E
Morehead, U.S.A. 114 F4 38 11N 83 26W
Morehead City, U.S.A. 115 H7 34 43N 76 43W
Morel →, India 68 F7 26 13N 76 36 E
Morelia, Mexico 118 D4 19 42N 101 7W
Morella, Australia 94 C3 23 0 S 143 52 E
Morella, Spain 38 E4 40 35N 0 5W
Morelos, Mexico 118 B3 26 42N 107 40W
Morelos □, Mexico 119 D5 18 40N 99 10W
Moremi ⌓, Botswana 88 B3 19 18 S 23 10 E
Morena, India 68 F8 26 30N 78 4 E
Morena, Sierra, Spain 37 G7 38 20N 4 0W
Moreni, Romania 29 F10 44 59N 25 36 E
Moreno Valley, U.S.A. 111 M10 33 56N 117 15W
Moresby I., Canada 102 C2 52 30N 131 40W
Morestel, France 21 C9 45 40N 5 28 E
Moreton I., Australia 95 D5 27 10 S 153 25 E
Moreton Island △, Australia 95 D5 27 2 S 153 24 E
Moreuil, France 19 C9 49 46N 2 30 E
Morey, Spain 48 B10 39 44N 3 20 E
Morez, France 19 F13 46 31N 6 2 E
Morgan, U.S.A. 108 F8 41 2N 111 41W
Morgan City, U.S.A. 113 L9 29 42N 91 12W
Morgan Hill, U.S.A. 110 H5 37 8N 121 39W
Morganfield, U.S.A. 114 G2 37 41N 87 55W
Morganton, U.S.A. 115 H5 35 45N 81 41W
Morgantown, U.S.A. 114 F6 39 38N 79 57W
Morgenzon, S. Africa 89 D4 26 45 S 29 36 E
Morges, Switz. 25 J2 46 31N 6 29 E
Morghak, Iran 71 D8 29 7N 57 54 E
Morgongåva, Sweden 10 E10 59 57N 16 58 E
Morhange, France 19 D13 48 55N 6 38 E
Morhar →, India 69 G11 25 29N 85 11 E
Mori, Italy 40 C7 45 51N 10 59 E
Mori, Japan 54 C10 42 6N 140 35 E
Moriarty, U.S.A. 109 J10 34 59N 106 3W
Moribaya, Guinea 82 D3 9 53N 9 32W
Morice L., Canada 102 C3 53 50N 127 40W
Moriki, Nigeria 83 C6 12 52N 6 30 E
Morinville, Canada 102 C6 53 49N 113 41W
Morioka, Japan 54 E10 39 45N 141 8 E
Moris, Mexico 118 B3 28 8N 108 32W
Morlaàs, France 20 E3 43 21N 0 18W
Morlaix, France 18 D3 48 36N 3 52W
Mörlunda, Sweden 11 G9 57 19N 15 52 E
Mormanno, Italy 43 C8 39 53N 15 59 E
Mormant, France 19 D9 48 37N 2 52 E
Mornington, Australia 95 F4 38 15 S 145 5 E
Mornington, I., Chile 128 F1 49 50 S 75 30W
Mornington I., Australia 94 B2 16 30 S 139 30 E
Mórnos →, Greece 46 C3 38 25N 21 50 E
Moro, Pakistan 68 F2 26 40N 68 0 E
Moro, Sudan 81 E3 10 50N 30 9 E
Moro →, Pakistan 68 E2 29 42N 67 22 E
Moro G., Phil. 61 H5 6 30N 123 0 E
Morocco ■, N. Afr. 78 B4 32 0N 5 50W
Morogoro, Tanzania 86 D4 6 50 S 37 40 E
Morogoro □, Tanzania 86 D4 8 0 S 37 0 E
Moroleón, Mexico 118 C4 20 8N 101 32W
Morombe, Madag. 89 C7 21 45 S 43 22 E
Moron, Argentina 126 C4 34 39 S 58 37W
Morón, Cuba 120 B4 22 8N 78 39W
Morón de Almazán, Spain 38 D2 41 29N 2 27W
Morón de la Frontera, Spain 37 H5 37 6N 5 28W
Morona →, Peru 124 D3 4 40 S 77 10W
Morondava, Madag. 89 C7 20 17 S 44 17 E
Morondo, Ivory C. 82 D3 8 57N 6 47W
Morongo Valley, U.S.A. 111 L10 34 3N 116 37W
Moroni, Comoros Is. 77 H8 11 40 S 43 16 E
Moroni, U.S.A. 108 G8 39 32N 111 35W
Moronou, Ivory C. 82 D4 6 16N 4 59W
Morotai, Indonesia 63 D7 2 10N 128 30 E
Moroto, Uganda 86 B3 2 28N 34 42 E
Moroto, Mt., Uganda 86 B3 2 30N 34 43 E
Morozov, Bulgaria 45 D9 42 30N 25 10 E
Morozovsk, Russia 35 F5 48 25N 41 50 E
Morpeth, U.K. 14 B6 55 10N 1 41W
Morphou, Cyprus 49 D11 35 12N 32 59 E
Morphou Bay, Cyprus 49 D11 35 15N 32 50 E
Morrilton, U.S.A. 113 H8 35 9N 92 44W
Morrinhos, Brazil 125 G9 17 45 S 49 10W
Morrinsville, N.Z. 91 G5 37 40 S 175 32 E
Morris, Canada 103 D9 49 25N 97 22W
Morris, Ill., U.S.A. 112 E10 41 22N 88 26W
Morris, Minn., U.S.A. 112 C7 45 35N 95 55W
Morris, N.Y., U.S.A. 117 D9 42 33N 75 15W
Morris, Pa., U.S.A. 116 E7 41 35N 77 17W
Morris, Mt., Australia 93 E5 26 9 S 131 4 E
Morris Jesup, Kap, Greenland 4 A5 83 40N 34 0W
Morrisburg, Canada 117 B9 44 55N 75 7W
Morristown, Ariz., U.S.A. 109 K7 33 51N 112 37W
Morristown, N.J., U.S.A. 117 F10 40 48N 74 29W
Morristown, N.Y., U.S.A. 117 B9 44 35N 75 39W
Morristown, Tenn., U.S.A. 115 G4 36 13N 83 18W
Morrisville, N.Y., U.S.A. 117 D9 42 53N 75 35W
Morrisville, Pa., U.S.A. 117 F10 40 13N 74 47W
Morrisville, Vt., U.S.A. 117 B12 44 34N 72 36W
Morro, Pta., Chile 126 B1 27 6 S 71 0W
Morro Bay, U.S.A. 110 K6 35 22N 120 51W
Morro del Jable, Canary Is. 48 F5 28 3N 14 23W
Morro Jable, Pta. de, Canary Is. 48 F5 28 2N 14 20W
Morrocoy △, Venezuela 121 D6 10 48N 68 13W
Morrosquillo, G. de, Colombia 120 E4 9 35N 75 40W
Mörrum, Sweden 11 H8 56 12N 14 45 E
Morrumbene, Mozam. 89 C6 23 31 S 35 16 E
Mörrumsån →, Sweden 11 H8 56 10N 14 45 E
Mors, Denmark 11 H2 56 50N 8 45 E
Morshansk, Russia 34 D5 53 28N 41 50 E
Mörsil, Sweden 10 A7 63 19N 13 40 E
Mortagne →, France 19 D13 48 33N 6 27 E
Mortagne-au-Perche, France 18 D7 48 31N 0 33 E
Mortagne-sur-Gironde, France 20 C3 45 28N 0 47W
Mortagne-sur-Sèvre, France 18 F6 47 0N 0 59W
Mortain, France 18 D6 48 40N 0 57W
Mortara, Italy 40 C5 45 15N 8 44 E
Morteau, France 19 E13 47 3N 6 35 E
Morteros, Argentina 126 C3 30 50 S 62 0W
Mortlach, Canada 103 C7 50 27N 106 4W
Mortlake, Australia 95 F3 38 5 S 142 50 E
Morton, Tex., U.S.A. 113 J3 33 44N 102 46W
Morton, Wash., U.S.A. 110 D4 46 34N 122 17W
Moruga, Trin. & Tob. 125 K15 10 4N 61 16W
Morundah, Australia 95 E4 34 57 S 146 19 E
Moruya, Australia 95 F5 35 58 S 150 3 E
Morvan, France 19 E11 47 5N 4 3 E
Morvan ⌓, France 19 E11 47 12N 4 3 E
Morven, Australia 95 D4 26 22 S 147 5 E
Morvern, U.K. 13 E3 56 38N 5 44W
Morwell, Australia 95 F4 38 10 S 146 22 E
Moryń, Poland 31 F1 52 51N 14 22 E
Morzine, France 19 F13 46 11N 6 42 E
Mosalsk, Russia 32 E8 54 30N 34 55 E
Mosbach, Germany 25 F5 49 21N 9 9 E
Moščenice, Croatia 41 C11 45 17N 14 16 E
Mosciano Sant' Ángelo, Italy 41 F10 42 42N 13 52 E
Moscos Is., Burma 64 E1 14 0N 97 30 E
Moscow = Moskva, Russia 32 E9 55 45N 37 35 E
Moscow, Idaho, U.S.A. 108 C5 46 44N 117 0W
Moscow, Pa., U.S.A. 117 E9 41 20N 75 31W
Mosel →, Europe 19 B14 50 22N 7 36 E
Moselle = Mosel →, Europe 19 B14 50 22N 7 36 E
Moselle □, France 19 D13 48 59N 6 33 E
Moses Lake, U.S.A. 108 C4 47 8N 119 17W
Mosgiel, N.Z. 91 L3 45 53 S 170 21 E
Moshaweng →, S. Africa 88 D3 26 35 S 22 50 E
Moshi, Tanzania 86 C4 3 22 S 37 18 E
Moshupa, Botswana 88 C4 24 46 S 25 29 E
Mosina, Poland 31 F3 52 15N 16 50 E
Mosjøen, Norway 8 D15 65 51N 13 12 E
Moskenesøya, Norway 8 C15 67 58N 13 0 E
Moskenstraumen, Norway 8 C15 67 47N 12 45 E
Moskva, Russia 32 E9 55 45N 37 35 E
Moskva →, Russia 32 E10 55 5N 38 51 E
Moslavačka Gora, Croatia 41 C13 45 40N 16 37 E
Mosomane, Botswana 88 C4 24 2 S 26 19 E
Mosonmagyaróvár, Hungary 28 C2 47 52N 17 18 E
Mošorin, Serbia & M. 28 E5 45 19N 20 4 E
Mospino, Ukraine 33 J9 47 52N 38 0 E
Mosquera, Colombia 124 C3 2 35N 78 24W
Mosquero, U.S.A. 113 H3 35 47N 103 58W
Mosqueruela, Spain 38 E4 40 21N 0 27W
Mosquitia, Honduras 120 C3 15 20N 84 10W
Mosquito Coast = Mosquitia, Honduras 120 C3 15 20N 84 10W
Mosquito Creek L., U.S.A. 116 E4 41 18N 80 46W
Mosquito L., Canada 103 A8 62 35N 103 20W
Mosquitos, G. de los, Panama 120 E3 9 15N 81 10W
Moss, Norway 9 G14 59 27N 10 40 E
Moss Vale, Australia 95 E5 34 32 S 150 25 E
Mossbank, Canada 103 D7 49 56N 105 56W
Mossburn, N.Z. 91 L2 45 41 S 168 15 E
Mosselbaai, S. Africa 88 E3 34 11 S 22 8 E
Mossendjo, Congo 84 E2 2 55 S 12 42 E
Mossgiel, Australia 95 E3 33 15 S 144 5 E
Mössingen, Germany 25 G5 48 24N 9 4 E
Mossman, Australia 94 B4 16 21 S 145 15 E
Mossoró, Brazil 125 E11 5 10 S 37 15W
Mossuril, Mozam. 87 E5 14 58 S 40 42 E
Most, Czech Rep. 26 A6 50 31N 13 38 E
Mosta, Malta 49 D1 35 55N 14 26 E
Mostaganem, Algeria 78 A6 35 54N 0 5 E
Mostar, Bos.-H. 28 G2 43 22N 17 50 E
Mostardas, Brazil 127 C5 31 2 S 50 51W
Mostiska = Mostyska, Ukraine 31 J10 49 48N 23 4 E
Móstoles, Spain 36 E7 40 19N 3 53W
Mosty = Masty, Belarus 32 F3 53 27N 24 38 E
Mostyska, Ukraine 31 J10 49 48N 23 4 E
Mosul = Al Mawşil, Iraq 70 B4 36 15N 43 5 E
Mosŭlpo, S. Korea 57 H14 33 20N 126 17 E
Mota, Ethiopia 81 E4 11 5N 37 52 E
Mota del Cuervo, Spain 39 F2 39 30N 2 52W
Mota del Marqués, Spain 36 D5 41 38N 5 11W
Motagua →, Guatemala 120 C2 15 44N 88 14W
Motala, Sweden 11 F9 58 32N 15 1 E
Motaze, Mozam. 89 C5 24 48 S 32 52 E
Moțca, Romania 29 C11 47 15N 26 37 E
Moth, India 69 G8 25 43N 78 57 E
Motherwell, U.K. 13 F5 55 47N 3 58W
Motihari, India 69 F11 26 30N 84 55 E
Motilla del Palancar, Spain 39 F3 39 34N 1 55W
Motnik, Slovenia 41 B11 46 14N 14 54 E
Motovun, Croatia 41 C10 45 20N 13 50 E
Motozintla de Mendoza, Mexico 119 D6 15 21N 92 14W
Motril, Spain 37 J7 36 31N 3 37W
Motru, Romania 28 F7 44 48N 22 59 E
Motru →, Romania 29 F8 44 32N 23 31 E
Mott, U.S.A. 112 B3 46 23N 102 20W
Móttola, Italy 43 B10 40 38N 17 2 E
Motueka, N.Z. 91 J4 41 7 S 173 1 E
Motueka →, N.Z. 91 J4 41 5 S 173 1 E
Motul, Mexico 119 C7 21 0N 89 20W
Mouchalagane →, Canada 105 B6 50 56N 68 41W
Moúdhros, Greece 47 B7 39 50N 25 18 E
Mouding, China 58 E3 25 20N 101 28 E
Moudjeria, Mauritania 82 B2 17 50N 12 28W
Moudon, Switz. 25 J2 46 40N 6 49 E
Mouila, Gabon 84 E2 1 50 S 11 0 E
Moulamein, Australia 95 F3 35 3 S 144 1 E
Moule à Chique, C., St. Lucia 121 f 13 43N 60 57W
Moulianá, Greece 49 D7 35 10N 25 59 E
Moulins, France 19 F10 46 35N 3 19 E
Moulmein, Burma 67 L20 16 30N 97 40 E
Moulouya, O. →, Morocco 78 B5 35 5N 2 25W
Moultrie, U.S.A. 115 K4 31 11N 83 47W
Moultrie, L., U.S.A. 115 J5 33 20N 80 5W
Mound City, Mo., U.S.A. 112 E7 40 7N 95 14W
Mound City, S. Dak., U.S.A. 112 C4 45 44N 100 4W
Moúnda, Ákra, Greece 46 C2 38 3N 20 47 E
Moundou, Chad 79 G9 8 40N 16 10 E
Moundsville, U.S.A. 116 G4 39 55N 80 44W
Moung, Cambodia 64 F4 12 46N 103 27 E
Mount Airy, U.S.A. 115 G5 36 31N 80 37W
Mount Albert, Canada 116 B5 44 8N 79 19W
Mount Aspiring △, N.Z. 91 L2 44 19 S 168 47 E
Mount Barker, S. Austral., Australia 95 F2 35 5 S 138 52 E
Mount Barker, W. Austral., Australia 93 F2 34 38 S 117 40 E
Mount Brydges, Canada 116 D3 42 54N 81 29W
Mount Burr, Australia 95 F3 37 34 S 140 26 E
Mount Carmel = Ha Karmel △, Israel 74 C4 32 45N 35 5 E
Mount Carmel, Ill., U.S.A. 114 F2 38 25N 87 46W
Mount Carmel, Pa., U.S.A. 117 F8 40 47N 76 24W
Mount Charleston, U.S.A. 111 J11 36 16N 115 37W
Mount Clemens, U.S.A. 116 D2 42 35N 82 53W
Mount Coolon, Australia 94 C4 21 25 S 147 25 E

Mount Darwin, Zimbabwe 87 F3 16 47 S 31 38 E
Mount Desert I., U.S.A. 115 C11 44 21N 68 20W
Mount Dora, U.S.A. 115 L5 28 48N 81 38W
Mount Edziza ⌂, Canada 102 B2 57 30N 130 45W
Mount Elgon △, E. Afr. 86 B3 1 4N 34 42 E
Mount Field △, Australia 95 G4 42 39 S 146 35 E
Mount Fletcher, S. Africa 89 E4 30 40 S 28 30 E
Mount Forest, Canada 116 C4 43 59N 80 43W
Mount Gambier, Australia 95 F3 37 50 S 140 46 E
Mount Garnet, Australia 94 B4 17 37 S 145 6 E
Mount Holly, U.S.A. 117 G10 39 59N 74 47W
Mount Holly Springs, U.S.A. 116 F7 40 7N 77 12W
Mount Hope, N.S.W., Australia 95 E4 32 51 S 145 51 E
Mount Hope, S. Austral., Australia 95 E2 34 7 S 135 23 E
Mount Isa, Australia 94 C2 20 42 S 139 26 E
Mount Jewett, U.S.A. 116 E6 41 44N 78 39W
Mount Kaputar △, Australia 95 E5 30 16 S 150 10 E
Mount Kenya △, Kenya 86 C4 0 7 S 37 21 E
Mount Kilimanjaro △, Tanzania 86 C4 3 2 S 37 19 E
Mount Kisco, U.S.A. 117 E11 41 12N 73 44W
Mount Laguna, U.S.A. 111 N10 32 52N 116 25W
Mount Larcom, Australia 94 C5 23 48 S 150 59 E
Mount Lofty Ra., Australia 95 E2 34 35 S 139 5 E
Mount Magnet, Australia 93 E2 28 2 S 117 47 E
Mount Maunganui, N.Z. 91 G6 37 40 S 176 14 E
Mount Molloy, Australia 94 B4 16 42 S 145 20 E
Mount Morgan, Australia 94 C5 23 40 S 150 25 E
Mount Morris, U.S.A. 116 D7 42 44N 77 52W
Mount Pearl, Canada 105 C9 47 31N 52 47W
Mount Penn, U.S.A. 117 F9 40 20N 75 54W
Mount Perry, Australia 95 D5 25 13 S 151 42 E
Mount Pleasant, Iowa, U.S.A. 112 E9 40 58N 91 33W
Mount Pleasant, Mich., U.S.A. 114 D3 43 36N 84 46W
Mount Pleasant, Pa., U.S.A. 116 F5 40 9N 79 33W
Mount Pleasant, S.C., U.S.A. 115 J6 32 47N 79 52W
Mount Pleasant, Tenn., U.S.A. 115 H2 35 32N 87 12W
Mount Pleasant, Tex., U.S.A. 113 J7 33 9N 94 58W
Mount Pleasant, Utah, U.S.A. 108 G8 39 33N 111 27W
Mount Pocono, U.S.A. 117 E9 41 7N 75 22W
Mount Rainier △, U.S.A. 110 D5 46 55N 121 50W
Mount Revelstoke △, Canada 102 C5 51 5N 118 30W
Mount Robson ⌂, Canada 102 C5 53 0N 119 0W
Mount St. Helens ⌂, U.S.A. 110 D4 46 14N 122 11W
Mount Selinda, Zimbabwe 89 C5 20 24 S 32 43 E
Mount Shasta, U.S.A. 108 F2 41 19N 122 19W
Mount Signal, U.S.A. 111 N11 32 39N 115 37W
Mount Sterling, Ill., U.S.A. 112 F9 39 59N 90 45W
Mount Sterling, Ky., U.S.A. 114 F4 38 4N 83 56W
Mount Surprise, Australia 94 B3 18 10 S 144 17 E
Mount Union, U.S.A. 116 F7 40 23N 77 53W
Mount Upton, U.S.A. 117 D9 42 26N 75 23W
Mount Vernon, Ill., U.S.A. 114 F1 38 19N 88 55W
Mount Vernon, Ind., U.S.A. 112 F10 38 17N 88 57W
Mount Vernon, N.Y., U.S.A. 117 F11 40 55N 73 50W
Mount Vernon, Ohio, U.S.A. 116 F2 40 23N 82 29W
Mount Vernon, Wash., U.S.A. 110 B4 48 25N 122 20W
Mount William △, Australia 95 G4 40 56 S 148 14 E
Mountain Ash, U.K. 15 F4 51 40N 3 23W
Mountain Center, U.S.A. 111 M10 33 42N 116 44W
Mountain City, Nev., U.S.A. 108 F6 41 50N 115 58W
Mountain City, Tenn., U.S.A. 115 G5 36 29N 81 48W
Mountain Dale, U.S.A. 117 E10 41 41N 74 32W
Mountain Grove, U.S.A. 113 G8 37 8N 92 16W
Mountain Home, Ark., U.S.A. 113 G8 36 20N 92 23W
Mountain Home, Idaho, U.S.A. 108 E6 43 8N 115 41W
Mountain Iron, U.S.A. 112 B8 47 32N 92 37W
Mountain Pass, U.S.A. 111 K11 35 29N 115 35W
Mountain View, Ark., U.S.A. 113 H8 35 52N 92 7W
Mountain View, Calif., U.S.A. 110 H4 37 23N 122 5W
Mountain View, Hawaii, U.S.A. 106 J17 19 33N 155 7W
Mountain Zebra △, S. Africa 88 E4 32 14 S 25 27 E
Mountainair, U.S.A. 109 J10 34 31N 106 15W
Mountlake Terrace, U.S.A. 110 C4 47 47N 122 19W
Mountmellick, Ireland 12 C4 53 7N 7 20W
Mountrath, Ireland 12 D4 53 0N 7 28W
Moura, Australia 94 C4 24 35 S 149 58 E
Moura, Brazil 124 D6 1 32 S 61 38W
Moura, Portugal 37 G3 38 7N 7 30W
Mourão, Portugal 37 G3 38 22N 7 22W
Mourdi, Dépression du, Chad 79 E10 18 10N 23 0 E
Mourdiah, Mali 82 C3 14 35N 7 25W
Mourenx, France 20 E3 43 22N 0 38W
Mouri, Ghana 83 D4 5 6N 1 14W
Mourilyan, Australia 94 B4 17 35 S 146 3 E
Mourmelon-le-Grand, France 19 C11 49 8N 4 22 E
Mourne →, U.K. 12 B4 54 52N 7 26W
Mourne Mts., U.K. 12 B5 54 10N 6 0W
Mourniaí, Greece 49 D6 35 29N 24 1 E
Mournies = Mourniaí, Greece 49 D6 35 29N 24 1 E
Mouscron, Belgium 17 D3 50 45N 3 12 E
Moussoro, Chad 79 F9 13 41N 16 35 E
Mouthe, France 19 F13 46 44N 6 12 E
Moutier, Switz. 25 H3 47 16N 7 21 E
Moûtiers, France 21 C10 45 29N 6 32 E
Moutong, Indonesia 63 D6 0 28N 121 13 E
Mouy, France 19 C9 49 18N 2 20 E
Mouzáki, Greece 46 B3 39 25N 21 37 E
Mouzon, France 19 C12 49 36N 5 3 E
Movas, Mexico 118 B3 28 10N 109 25W
Moville, Ireland 12 A4 55 11N 7 3W
Mowandjum, Australia 92 C3 17 22 S 123 40 E
Moy →, Ireland 12 B2 54 8N 9 8W
Moyale, Kenya 81 G4 3 30N 39 0 E
Moyamba, S. Leone 82 D2 8 4N 12 30W
Moyen Atlas, Morocco 78 B4 33 0N 5 0W
Moyne, L. le, Canada 105 A6 56 45N 68 47W
Moyo, Indonesia 62 F5 8 10 S 117 40 E
Moyobamba, Peru 124 E3 6 0 S 77 0W
Moyyero →, Russia 53 C11 68 44N 103 42 E
Moyynty, Kazakhstan 52 E8 47 10N 73 18 E
Mozambique = Moçambique, Mozam. 87 F5 15 3 S 40 42 E
Mozambique ■, Africa 87 F4 19 0 S 35 0 E
Mozambique Chan., Africa 89 B7 17 30 S 42 30 E
Mozdok, Russia 35 J7 43 45N 44 48 E
Mozdūrān, Iran 71 B9 36 9N 60 35 E
Mozhaysk, Russia 32 E9 55 30N 36 2 E
Mozhga, Russia 34 B11 56 26N 52 15 E
Mozhnābād, Iran 71 C9 34 7N 60 6 E
Mozirje, Slovenia 41 B11 46 22N 14 58 E
Mozyr = Mazyr, Belarus 33 F5 51 59N 29 15 E
Mpanda, Tanzania 86 D3 6 23 S 31 1 E
Mpésoba, Mali 82 C3 12 31N 5 39W
Mphoengs, Zimbabwe 89 C4 21 10 S 27 51 E
Mpika, Zambia 87 E3 11 51 S 31 25 E
Mpulungu, Zambia 87 D3 8 51 S 31 5 E
Mpumalanga, S. Africa 89 D5 29 50 S 30 33 E
Mpumalanga □, S. Africa 89 D5 26 0 S 30 0 E
Mpwapwa, Tanzania 86 D4 6 23 S 36 30 E
Mqanduli, S. Africa 89 E4 31 49 S 28 45 E
Mqinvartsveri = Kazbek, Russia 35 J7 42 42N 44 30 E
Mrągowo, Poland 30 E8 53 52N 21 18 E
Mramor, Serbia & M. 44 C5 43 20N 21 45 E
Mrkonjić Grad, Bos.-H. 28 F2 44 26N 17 4 E
Mrkopalj, Croatia 41 C11 45 21N 14 52 E
Mrocza, Poland 31 E4 53 16N 17 35 E
Msambansovu, Zimbabwe 87 F3 15 50 S 30 3 E
M'sila →, Algeria 78 A6 35 30N 4 29 E
Msoro, Zambia 87 E3 13 35 S 31 50 E
Msta →, Russia 32 C6 58 25N 31 20 E
Mstislavl = Mstsislaw, Belarus 32 E6 54 0N 31 50 E
Mstsislaw, Belarus 32 E6 54 0N 31 50 E
Mszana Dolna, Poland 31 J7 49 41N 20 5 E
Mszczonów, Poland 31 G7 51 58N 20 33 E
Mtama, Tanzania 87 E4 10 17 S 39 21 E
Mtamvuna →, S. Africa 89 E5 31 6 S 30 12 E
Mtilikwe →, Zimbabwe 87 G3 21 9 S 31 30 E
Mtsensk, Russia 32 F9 53 17N 36 36 E
Mtskheta, Georgia 35 K7 41 52N 44 45 E
Mtubatuba, S. Africa 89 D5 28 30 S 32 8 E
Mtwalume, S. Africa 89 E5 30 30 S 30 38 E
Mtwara-Mikindani, Tanzania 87 E5 10 20 S 40 20 E
Mu Gia, Deo, Vietnam 64 D5 17 40N 105 47 E
Mu Ko Chang △, Thailand 65 G4 11 59N 102 22 E
Mu Us Shamo, China 56 E5 39 0N 109 0 E
Muang Chiang Rai = Chiang Rai, Thailand 58 H2 19 52N 99 50 E
Muang Khong, Laos 64 E5 14 7N 105 51 E
Muang Lamphun, Thailand 64 C2 18 40N 99 2 E
Muang Mai, Thailand 65 a 8 5N 98 21 E
Muang Pak Beng, Laos 58 H3 19 54N 101 8 E
Muar, Malaysia 65 L4 2 3N 102 34 E
Muarabungo, Indonesia 62 E2 1 28 S 102 52 E
Muaraenim, Indonesia 62 E2 3 40 S 103 50 E
Muarajuloi, Indonesia 62 E4 0 12 S 114 3 E
Muarakaman, Indonesia 62 E5 0 2 S 116 45 E
Muaratebo, Indonesia 62 E2 1 30 S 102 26 E
Muaratembesi, Indonesia 62 E2 1 42 S 103 8 E
Muaratewe, Indonesia 62 E4 0 58 S 114 52 E
Mubarakpur, India 69 F10 26 6N 83 18 E
Mubarraz = Al Mubarraz, Si. Arabia 71 E6 25 30N 49 40 E
Mubende, Uganda 86 B3 0 33N 31 22 E
Mubi, Nigeria 83 C7 10 18N 13 16 E
Mucajaí →, Brazil 124 C6 2 25N 60 52W
Muchachos, Roque de los, Canary Is. 48 F2 28 44N 17 52W
Mücheln, Germany 24 D7 51 17N 11 47 E
Muchinga Mts., Zambia 87 E3 11 30 S 31 30 E
Muchkapskiy, Russia 34 E6 51 52N 42 28 E
Muchuan, China 58 C5 28 57N 103 55 E
Muck, U.K. 13 E2 56 50N 6 15W
Muckadilla, Australia 95 D4 26 35 S 148 23 E
Muckle Flugga, U.K. 13 A8 60 51N 0 54W
Mucur, Turkey 72 C6 39 3N 34 22 E
Mucuri, Brazil 125 G11 18 0 S 39 36W
Mucusso, Angola 88 B3 18 1 S 21 25 E
Muda, Canary Is. 48 F6 28 34N 13 57W
Mudanjiang, China 57 B15 44 38N 129 30 E
Mudanya, Turkey 45 F12 40 25N 28 50 E
Muddy Cr. →, U.S.A. 109 H8 38 24N 110 42W
Mudgee, Australia 95 E4 32 32 S 149 31 E
Mudjatik →, Canada 103 B7 56 1N 107 36W
Mudurnu, Turkey 72 B4 40 27N 31 12 E
Muecate, Mozam. 87 E4 14 55 S 39 40 E
Mueda, Mozam. 87 E4 11 36 S 39 28 E
Mueller Ra., Australia 92 C4 18 18 S 126 46 E
Muende, Mozam. 87 E3 14 28 S 33 0 E
Muerto, Mar, Mexico 119 D6 16 10N 94 10W
Mufu Shan, China 59 C10 29 20N 114 30 E
Mufulira, Zambia 87 E2 12 32 S 28 15 E
Mufumbiro Range, Africa 86 C2 1 25 S 29 30 E
Mugardos, Spain 36 B2 43 27N 8 15W
Muge →, Portugal 37 F2 39 8N 8 44W
Múggia, Italy 41 C10 45 36N 13 46 E
Mughal Sarai, India 69 G10 25 18N 83 7 E
Mughayrā', Si. Arabia 70 D3 29 17N 37 41 E
Mugi, Japan 55 H7 33 40N 134 25 E
Mugia = Muxía, Spain 36 B1 43 3N 9 10W
Mugila, Mts., Dem. Rep. of the Congo 86 D2 7 0 S 28 50 E
Muğla, Turkey 47 D10 37 15N 28 22 E
Muğla □, Turkey 47 D10 37 15N 28 0 E
Muglad, Sudan 81 E2 11 2N 27 50 E
Müglizh, Bulgaria 45 D9 42 37N 25 32 E
Mugu, Nepal 69 E10 29 45N 82 30 E
Muhammad, Râs, Egypt 70 E2 27 44N 34 16 E
Muhammad Qol, Sudan 80 C4 20 53N 37 9 E
Muhammadabad, India 69 F10 26 4N 83 25 E
Muhesi →, Tanzania 86 D4 7 0 S 35 20 E
Mühlacker, Germany 25 G4 48 57N 8 51 E
Mühldorf, Germany 25 G8 48 14N 12 32 E
Mühlhausen, Germany 24 D6 51 12N 10 27 E
Mühlig Hofmann fjell, Antarctica 5 D3 72 30 S 5 0 E
Mühlviertel, Austria 26 C7 48 30N 14 10 E
Muhos, Finland 8 D22 64 47N 25 59 E
Muhu, Estonia 9 G20 58 36N 23 11 E
Muhutwe, Tanzania 86 C3 1 35 S 31 45 E
Muine Bheag, Ireland 12 D5 52 42N 6 58W
Muir, L., Australia 93 F2 34 30 S 116 40 E
Muir of Ord, U.K. 13 D4 57 32N 4 28W
Mujnak = Muynak, Uzbekistan 52 E6 43 44N 59 10 E
Muka, Tanjung, Malaysia 65 c 5 28N 100 11 E
Mukacheve, Ukraine 28 B7 48 27N 22 45 E
Mukachevo = Mukacheve, Ukraine 28 B7 48 27N 22 45 E
Mukah, Malaysia 62 D4 2 55N 112 5 E
Mukandwara, India 68 G6 24 49N 75 59 E
Mukawwa, Geziret, Egypt 80 C4 23 55N 35 53 E
Mukawwar, Sudan 80 C4 20 50N 37 17 E
Mukdahan, Thailand 64 D5 16 32N 104 43 E
Mukden = Shenyang, China 57 D12 41 48N 123 27 E
Mukerian, India 68 D6 31 57N 75 37 E
Mukhavyets, Belarus 31 F10 52 5N 23 39 E
Mukhtolovo, Russia 34 C6 55 29N 43 15 E
Mukinbudin, Australia 93 F2 30 55 S 118 5 E
Mukishi, Dem. Rep. of the Congo 87 D1 8 30 S 24 44 E
Mukomuko, Indonesia 62 E2 2 30 S 101 10 E
Mukomwenze, Dem. Rep. of the Congo 86 D2 6 49 S 27 15 E
Muktsar, India 68 D6 30 30N 74 30 E
Mukur = Moqor, Afghan. 68 C2 32 50N 67 42 E
Mukutawa →, Canada 103 C9 53 10N 97 24W
Mukwela, Zambia 87 F2 17 0 S 26 40 E
Mula, Spain 39 G3 38 3N 1 33W
Mula →, Pakistan 68 F2 27 57N 67 36 E
Mulange, Dem. Rep. of the Congo 86 C2 3 40 S 27 10 E
Mulanje, Malawi 87 F4 16 2 S 35 33 E
Mulanje, Mt., Malawi 87 F4 16 0 S 35 30 E
Mulchén, Chile 126 D1 37 45 S 72 20W
Mulde →, Germany 24 D8 51 53N 12 15 E
Mule Creek Junction, U.S.A. 112 D2 43 19N 104 8W
Muleba, Tanzania 86 C3 1 50 S 31 37 E
Mulejé, Mexico 118 B2 26 53N 112 1W
Muleshoe, U.S.A. 113 H3 34 13N 102 43W
Muletta, Gara, Ethiopia 81 F5 9 15N 41 44 E
Mulgrave, Canada 105 C7 45 38N 61 31W
Mulhacén, Spain 37 H7 37 4N 3 20W
Mülheim, Germany 24 D2 51 25N 6 54 E
Mulhouse, France 19 E14 47 40N 7 20 E
Muli, China 58 D3 27 52N 101 8 E
Muling, China 57 B16 44 35N 130 10 E
Mull, U.K. 13 E3 56 25N 5 56W
Mull, Sound of, U.K. 13 E3 56 30N 5 50W
Mullaittivu, Sri Lanka 66 Q12 9 15N 80 49 E
Mullen, U.S.A. 112 D4 42 3N 101 1W
Mullens, U.S.A. 114 G5 37 35N 81 23W
Muller, Pegunungan, Indonesia 62 D4 0 30N 113 30 E
Mullet Pen., Ireland 12 B1 54 13N 10 2W
Mullewa, Australia 93 E2 28 29 S 115 30 E
Müllheim, Germany 25 H3 47 47N 7 36 E
Mulligan →, Australia 94 D2 25 0 S 139 0 E
Mullingar, Ireland 12 C4 53 31N 7 21W
Mullins, U.S.A. 115 H6 34 12N 79 15W
Mullsjö, Sweden 11 G7 57 56N 13 55 E
Mullumbimby, Australia 95 D5 28 30 S 153 30 E
Mulobezi, Zambia 87 F2 16 45 S 25 7 E
Mulroy B., Ireland 12 A4 55 15N 7 46W
Multan, Pakistan 68 D4 30 15N 71 36 E
Mulumbe, Mts., Dem. Rep. of the Congo 87 D2 8 40 S 27 30 E
Mulungushi Dam, Zambia 87 E2 14 48 S 28 48 E
Mulvane, U.S.A. 113 G6 37 29N 97 15W
Mulwad, Sudan 80 D3 18 45N 30 39 E
Mumbai, India 66 K8 18 55N 72 50 E
Mumbwa, Zambia 87 F2 15 0 S 27 0 E
Mumra, Russia 35 H8 45 45N 47 41 E
Mun →, Thailand 64 E5 15 19N 105 30 E
Muna, Indonesia 63 F6 5 0 S 122 30 E
Munabao, India 68 G4 25 45N 70 17 E
Munamagi, Estonia 9 H22 57 43N 27 4 E
Muncan, Indonesia 63 K18 8 34 S 115 11 E
Muncar, Indonesia 63 J17 8 26 S 114 20 E
Münchberg, Germany 25 E7 50 11N 11 47 E
Müncheberg, Germany 24 C10 52 30N 14 9 E
München, Germany 25 G7 48 8N 11 34 E
Munchen-Gladbach = Mönchengladbach, Germany 24 D2 51 11N 6 27 E
München International ✕ (MUC), Germany 25 G7 48 20N 11 50 E
Muncho Lake, Canada 102 B3 59 0N 125 50W
Munch'ŏn, N. Korea 57 E14 39 14N 127 19 E
Muncie, U.S.A. 114 E3 40 12N 85 23W
Muncoonie, L., Australia 94 D2 25 12 S 138 40 E
Mundabbera, Australia 95 D5 25 36 S 151 18 E
Munday, U.S.A. 113 J5 33 27N 99 38W
Münden, Germany 24 D5 51 25N 9 38 E
Münden ⌂, Germany 24 D5 51 28N 9 42 E
Mundiwindi, Australia 92 D3 23 47 S 120 9 E
Mundo →, Spain 39 G2 38 30N 2 15W
Mundo Novo, Brazil 125 F10 11 50 S 40 29W
Mundra, India 68 H3 22 54N 69 48 E
Mundrabilla, Australia 93 F4 31 52 S 127 51 E
Munera, Spain 39 F2 39 2N 2 29W
Mungallala, Australia 95 D4 26 28 S 147 34 E
Mungallala Cr. →, Australia 95 D4 28 53 S 147 5 E
Mungana, Australia 94 B3 17 8 S 144 27 E
Mungaoli, India 68 G8 24 24N 78 7 E
Mungari, Mozam. 87 F3 17 12 S 33 30 E
Mungbere, Dem. Rep. of the Congo 86 B2 2 36N 28 28 E
Mungeli, India 69 H9 22 4N 81 41 E
Munger, India 69 G12 25 23N 86 30 E
Mungkan Kandju △, Australia 94 A3 13 35 S 142 52 E
Munich = München, Germany 25 G7 48 8N 11 34 E
Munising, U.S.A. 114 B2 46 25N 86 40W
Munka-Ljungby, Sweden 11 H6 56 16N 12 58 E
Munkebo, Denmark 11 J4 55 27N 10 34 E
Munkedal, Sweden 11 F5 58 28N 11 40 E
Munkfors, Sweden 10 E7 59 47N 13 30 E
Munku-Sardyk, Russia 53 D11 51 45N 100 20 E
Münnerstadt, Germany 25 E6 50 14N 10 12 E
Muñoz Gamero, Pen., Chile 128 G2 52 30 S 73 5W
Munroe L., Canada 103 B9 59 13N 98 35W
Munsan, S. Korea 57 F14 37 51N 126 48 E
Munster, France 19 D14 48 2N 7 8 E
Münster, Niedersachsen, Germany 24 C6 52 58N 10 5 E
Münster, Nordrhein-Westfalen, Germany 24 D3 51 58N 7 37 E
Munster □, Ireland 12 D3 52 18N 8 44W
Muntadgin, Australia 93 F2 31 45 S 118 33 E
Muntele Mare, Vf., Romania 29 D8 46 30N 23 12 E
Muntok, Indonesia 62 E3 2 5 S 105 10 E
Munyama, Zambia 87 F2 16 5 S 28 31 E
Munzur Dağları, Turkey 73 C8 39 30N 39 10 E
Muong Beng, Laos 58 G3 20 23N 101 46 E
Muong Boum, Vietnam 58 F4 22 24N 102 49 E
Muong Et, Laos 64 B5 20 49N 104 1 E
Muong Hai, Laos 58 G3 21 3N 101 49 E
Muong Hiem, Laos 64 B4 20 5N 103 22 E
Muong Houn, Laos 58 G3 20 8N 101 23 E
Muong Hung, Vietnam 58 G4 20 56N 103 53 E
Muong Kau, Laos 64 E5 15 6N 105 47 E
Muong Khao, Laos 64 C4 19 38N 103 32 E
Muong Khoua, Laos 58 G4 21 5N 102 31 E
Muong Liep, Laos 64 C3 18 29N 101 40 E
Muong May, Laos 64 E6 14 49N 106 56 E
Muong Ngeun, Laos 58 G3 20 36N 101 3 E
Muong Ngoi, Laos 58 G4 20 43N 102 41 E
Muong Nhie, Vietnam 58 F4 22 12N 102 28 E
Muong Nong, Laos 64 D6 16 22N 106 30 E
Muong Ou Tay, Laos 58 F3 22 7N 101 48 E
Muong Oua, Laos 64 C3 18 18N 101 20 E
Muong Peun, Laos 58 G4 20 13N 103 52 E
Muong Phalane, Laos 64 D5 16 39N 105 34 E
Muong Phieng, Laos 64 C3 19 6N 101 32 E
Muong Phine, Laos 64 D6 16 32N 106 2 E
Muong Sai, Laos 58 G3 20 42N 101 59 E
Muong Saiapoun, Laos 64 C3 18 24N 101 31 E
Muong Sen, Vietnam 64 C5 19 24N 104 8 E
Muong Sing, Laos 58 G3 21 11N 101 9 E
Muong Son, Laos 58 G4 20 27N 103 19 E
Muong Soui, Laos 64 C4 19 33N 102 52 E
Muong Va, Laos 58 G4 21 53N 102 19 E
Muong Xia, Vietnam 64 B5 20 19N 104 50 E
Muonio, Finland 8 C20 67 57N 23 40 E
Muonio älv = Muonionjoki →, Finland 8 C20 67 11N 23 34 E
Muonioälven = Muonionjoki →, Finland 8 C20 67 11N 23 34 E
Muonionjoki →, Finland 8 C20 67 11N 23 34 E
Muping, China 57 F11 37 22N 121 36 E
Mupoi, Sudan 81 F2 5 28N 27 40 E
Muqaddam, Wadi →, Sudan 80 D3 18 4N 31 30 E
Muqdisho, Somali Rep. 75 G4 2 2N 45 25 E
Mur →, Austria 27 E9 46 18N 16 52 E
Mûr-de-Bretagne, France 18 D4 48 12N 3 0W
Muradiye, Manisa, Turkey 47 C9 38 39N 27 21 E
Muradiye, Van, Turkey 73 C10 39 0N 43 44 E
Murakami, Japan 54 E9 38 14N 139 29 E
Murallón, Cerro, Chile 128 F2 49 48 S 73 30W
Muranda, Rwanda 86 C2 1 52 S 29 20 E
Murang'a, Kenya 86 C4 0 45 S 37 9 E
Murashi, Russia 52 D5 59 30N 49 0 E
Murat, France 20 C6 45 7N 2 53 E
Murat →, Turkey 73 C9 38 46N 40 0 E
Murat Dağı, Turkey 47 C11 38 55N 29 43 E
Muratlı, Turkey 45 E11 41 10N 27 29 E
Murato, France 21 F13 42 35N 9 20 E
Murau, Austria 26 D7 47 6N 14 10 E
Murava, Belarus 31 F11 52 39N 24 15 E
Muravera, Italy 42 C2 39 25N 9 34 E
Murayama, Japan 54 E10 38 30N 140 25 E
Murça, Portugal 36 D3 41 24N 7 28W
Murchison →, Australia 93 E1 27 45 S 114 0 E
Murchison, Mt., Antarctica 5 D11 73 0 S 168 0 E
Murchison Falls, Uganda 86 B3 2 15N 31 30 E
Murchison Falls △, Uganda 86 B3 2 17N 31 48 E
Murchison Ra., Australia 94 C1 20 0 S 134 10 E
Murchison Rapids, Malawi 87 F3 15 55 S 34 35 E
Murcia, Spain 39 G3 38 5N 1 10W
Murcia □, Spain 39 H3 37 50N 1 30W
Murdo, U.S.A. 112 D4 43 53N 100 43W
Murdoch Pt., Australia 94 A3 14 37 S 144 55 E
Mürefte, Turkey 45 F11 40 40N 27 14 E
Mureş □, Romania 29 D9 46 45N 24 40 E
Mureş →, Romania 28 D5 46 15N 20 13 E
Mureşul = Mureş →, Romania 28 D5 46 15N 20 13 E
Muret, France 20 E5 43 30N 1 20 E
Murewa, Zimbabwe 89 B5 17 39 S 31 47 E
Murfreesboro, N.C., U.S.A. 115 G7 36 27N 77 6W
Murfreesboro, Tenn., U.S.A. 115 H2 35 51N 86 24W
Murgab = Murghob, Tajikistan 52 F8 38 10N 74 2 E
Murgab →, Turkmenistan 71 B9 38 18N 61 12 E
Murgenella, Australia 92 B5 11 34 S 132 56 E
Murgeni, Romania 29 D13 46 12N 28 1 E
Murgha Kibzai, Pakistan 68 D3 30 44N 69 25 E
Murghob, Tajikistan 52 F8 38 10N 74 2 E
Murgon, Australia 95 D5 26 15 S 151 54 E
Muri, India 69 H11 23 22N 85 52 E
Muria, Indonesia 63 G14 6 36 S 110 53 E
Muriaé, Brazil 127 A7 21 8 S 42 23W
Murias de Paredes, Spain 36 C4 42 52N 6 11W
Muriel Mine, Zimbabwe 87 F3 17 14 S 30 40 E
Müritz, Germany 24 B8 53 25N 12 42 E
Müritz △, Germany 24 B8 53 25N 12 51 E
Murliganj, India 69 G12 25 54N 86 59 E
Murmansk, Russia 52 C4 68 57N 33 10 E
Murnau, Germany 25 H7 47 40N 11 12 E
Muro, France 21 F12 42 34N 8 54 E
Muro, Spain 48 B10 39 44N 3 3 E
Muro, C. de, France 21 G12 41 44N 8 37 E
Muro de Alcoy, Spain 39 G4 38 46N 0 26W
Muro Lucano, Italy 43 B8 40 45N 15 29 E
Murom, Russia 34 C6 55 35N 42 3 E
Muroran, Japan 54 C10 42 25N 141 0 E
Muros, Spain 36 C1 42 45N 9 5W
Muros y de Noya, Ría de, Spain 36 C1 42 45N 9 0W
Muroto, Japan 55 H7 33 18N 134 9 E
Muroto-Misaki, Japan 55 H7 33 15N 134 10 E
Murovani Kurylivtsi, Ukraine 29 B12 48 44N 27 31 E
Murowana Goślina, Poland 31 F3 52 35N 17 0 E
Murphy, U.S.A. 108 E5 43 13N 116 33W
Murphys, U.S.A. 110 G6 38 8N 120 28W
Murrat, Sudan 80 D2 18 51N 29 33 E
Murrat Wells, Sudan 80 C3 21 3N 32 55 E
Murray, Ky., U.S.A. 115 G1 36 37N 88 19W
Murray, Utah, U.S.A. 108 F8 40 40N 111 53W
Murray →, Australia 95 F2 35 20 S 139 22 E
Murray, L., U.S.A. 115 H5 34 3N 81 13W
Murray Bridge, Australia 95 F2 35 6 S 139 14 E
Murray Harbour, Canada 105 C7 46 0N 62 28W
Murray River △, Australia 95 E3 34 23 S 140 32 E
Murraysburg, S. Africa 88 E3 31 58 S 23 47 E
Murree, Pakistan 68 C5 33 56N 73 28 E
Murrieta, U.S.A. 111 M9 33 33N 117 13W
Murro di Porco, Capo, Italy 43 F8 37 0N 15 20 E
Murrumbidgee →, Australia 95 E3 34 43 S 143 12 E
Murrumburrah, Australia 95 E4 34 32 S 148 22 E
Murrurundi, Australia 95 E5 31 42 S 150 51 E
Murshid, Sudan 80 C3 21 40N 31 10 E
Murshidabad, India 69 G13 24 11N 88 19 E
Murska Sobota, Slovenia 41 B13 46 39N 16 12 E
Murtle L., Canada 102 C5 52 8N 119 38W
Murtoa, Australia 95 F3 36 35 S 142 28 E
Murtosa, Portugal 36 E2 40 44N 8 40W
Murungu, Tanzania 86 C3 4 12 S 31 10 E
Mururoa, French Polynesia 97 K14 21 52 S 138 55W
Murwara, India 69 H9 23 46N 80 28 E
Murwillumbah, Australia 95 D5 28 18 S 153 27 E
Mürz →, Austria 26 D8 47 30N 15 25 E
Mürzzuschlag, Austria 26 D8 47 36N 15 41 E
Muş, Turkey 70 B4 38 45N 41 30 E
Mûsa, Gebel, Egypt 70 D2 28 33N 33 59 E
Musa Khel, Pakistan 68 D3 30 59N 69 52 E
Mūsa Qal'eh, Afghan. 66 C4 32 20N 64 50 E
Musafirkhana, India 69 F9 26 22N 81 48 E
Musala, Bulgaria 44 D7 42 13N 23 37 E
Musala, Indonesia 62 D1 1 41N 98 28 E
Musan, N. Korea 57 C15 42 12N 129 12 E
Musangu, Dem. Rep. of the Congo 87 E1 10 28 S 23 55 E
Musasa, Tanzania 86 C3 3 25 S 31 30 E
Musay'īd, Qatar 71 E6 25 0N 51 33 E
Muscat = Masqat, Oman 75 C6 23 37N 58 36 E
Muscatine, U.S.A. 112 E9 41 25N 91 3W
Musengezi = Unsengedsi →, Zimbabwe 87 F3 15 43 S 31 14 E
Musgrave Harbour, Canada 105 C9 49 27N 53 58W
Musgrave Ranges, Australia 93 E5 26 0 S 132 0 E
Mushie, Dem. Rep. of the Congo 84 E3 2 56 S 16 55 E
Mushin, Nigeria 83 D5 6 32N 3 21 E
Musi →, Indonesia 62 E2 2 20 S 104 56 E
Musina, S. Africa 89 C5 22 20 S 30 5 E
Muskeg →, Canada 102 A4 60 20N 123 20W
Muskegon, U.S.A. 114 D2 43 14N 86 16W
Muskegon →, U.S.A. 114 D2 43 14N 86 21W
Muskegon Heights, U.S.A. 114 D2 43 12N 86 16W
Muskogee, U.S.A. 113 H7 35 45N 95 22W
Muskoka, L., Canada 116 B5 45 0N 79 25W
Muskwa →, Canada 102 B4 58 47N 122 48W
Muslīmiyah, Syria 70 B3 36 19N 37 12 E
Musmar, Sudan 80 D4 18 13N 35 40 E
Musofu, Zambia 87 E2 13 30 S 29 0 E
Musoma, Tanzania 86 C3 1 30 S 33 48 E
Musquaro, L., Canada 105 B7 50 38N 61 5W
Musquodoboit Harbour, Canada 105 D7 44 50N 63 9W
Musselburgh, U.K. 13 F5 55 57N 3 2W
Musselshell →, U.S.A. 108 C10 47 21N 107 57W
Mussidan, France 20 C4 45 2N 0 22 E
Mussomeli, Italy 42 E6 37 35N 13 45 E
Mussoorie, India 68 D8 30 27N 78 6 E
Mussuco, Angola 88 B2 17 2 S 19 3 E
Mustafakemalpaşa, Turkey 45 F12 40 2N 28 24 E
Mustang, Nepal 69 E10 29 10N 83 55 E
Musters, L., Argentina 128 F3 45 20 S 69 25W
Musudan, N. Korea 57 D15 40 50N 129 43 E
Muswellbrook, Australia 95 E5 32 16 S 150 56 E
Muszyna, Poland 31 J7 49 22N 20 55 E
Mût, Egypt 80 B2 25 28N 28 58 E
Mut, Turkey 70 B2 36 40N 33 28 E
Mutanda, Mozam. 89 C5 21 0 S 33 34 E
Mutanda, Zambia 87 E2 12 24 S 26 13 E
Mutare, Zimbabwe 87 F3 18 58 S 32 38 E
Muting, Indonesia 63 F10 7 23 S 140 20 E
Mutki = Mirtağ, Turkey 70 B4 38 23N 41 56 E
Mutoko, Zimbabwe 89 B5 17 24 S 32 13 E
Mutoray, Russia 53 C11 60 56N 101 0 E
Mutshatsha, Dem. Rep. of the Congo 87 E1 10 35 S 24 20 E
Mutsu, Japan 54 D10 41 5N 140 55 E
Mutsu-Wan, Japan 54 D10 41 5N 140 55 E
Muttaburra, Australia 94 C3 22 38 S 144 29 E
Muttalip, Turkey 47 B12 39 50N 30 32 E
Mutton I., Ireland 12 D2 52 49N 9 32W
Mutuáli, Mozam. 87 E4 14 55 S 37 0 E
Mutum Biyu, Nigeria 83 D7 8 40N 10 50 E
Muweilih, Egypt 74 E3 30 42N 34 19 E
Muxía, Spain 36 B1 43 3N 9 10W
Muy Muy, Nic. 120 D2 12 39N 85 36W
Muyinga, Burundi 86 C3 3 14 S 30 33 E
Muynak, Uzbekistan 52 E6 43 44N 59 10 E
Muzaffarabad, Pakistan 69 B5 34 25N 73 30 E
Muzaffargarh, Pakistan 68 D4 30 5N 71 14 E
Muzaffarnagar, India 68 E7 29 26N 77 40 E
Muzaffarpur, India 69 F11 26 7N 85 23 E
Muzafirpur, Pakistan 68 D3 30 58N 69 9 E
Muzhi, Russia 52 C7 65 25N 64 40 E
Muzillac, France 18 E4 47 35N 2 30W
Muzūra, Egypt 80 J7 28 53N 30 48 E
Mvôlô, Sudan 81 F2 6 2N 29 53 E
Mvuma, Zimbabwe 87 F3 19 16 S 30 30 E
Mvurwi, Zimbabwe 87 F3 17 0 S 30 57 E
Mwabvi ⌂, Malawi 87 F3 16 42 S 35 0 E

Mwadui, Tanzania .... 86 C3 3 26 S 33 32 E
Mwambo, Tanzania ... 87 E5 10 30 S 40 22 E
Mwandi, Zambia ...... 87 F1 17 30 S 24 51 E
Mwanza, Dem. Rep. of
  the Congo .... 86 D2 7 55 S 26 43 E
Mwanza, Tanzania .... 86 C3 2 30 S 32 58 E
Mwanza, Tanzania .... 87 F1 16 58 S 24 28 E
Mwanza □, Tanzania .. 86 C3 2 0 S 33 0 E
Mwaya, Tanzania ..... 87 D3 9 32 S 33 55 E
Mweelrea, Ireland 12 C2 53 39N 9 49W
Mweka, Dem. Rep. of
  the Congo .... 84 E4 4 50 S 21 34 E
Mwenezi, Zimbabwe ... 87 G3 21 15 S 30 48 E
Mwenezi →, Mozam. ... 87 G3 22 40 S 31 50 E
Mwenga, Dem. Rep. of
  the Congo .... 86 C2 3 1 S 28 28 E
Mweru, L., Zambia .... 87 D2 9 0 S 28 40 E
Mweru Wantipa △,
  Zambia .... 87 D2 8 39 S 29 25 E
Mweza Range,
  Zimbabwe .... 87 G3 21 0 S 30 0 E
Mwilambwe, Dem. Rep.
  of the Congo ...... 86 D2 8 7 S 25 5 E
Mwimbi, Tanzania .... 87 D3 8 38 S 31 39 E
Mwinilunga, Zambia .. 87 E1 11 43 S 24 25 E
My Tho, Vietnam ..... 65 G6 10 29N 106 23 E
Myajlar, India .... 68 F4 26 15N 70 20 E
Myanaung, Burma .... 67 K19 18 18N 95 22 E
Myanmar = Burma ■,
  Asia .... 67 J20 21 0N 96 30 E
Myaungmya, Burma ... 67 L19 16 30N 94 40 E
Myedna, Belarus ..... 31 G10 51 52N 23 42 E
Myeik Kyunzu, Burma 65 G1 11 30N 97 30 E
Myers Chuck, U.S.A. .. 102 B2 55 44N 132 11W
Myerstown, U.S.A. 117 F8 40 22N 76 19W
Myingyan, Burma ..... 67 J19 21 30N 95 20 E
Myitkyina, Burma .... 67 G20 25 24N 97 26 E
Myjava, Slovak Rep. .. 27 C10 48 41N 17 37 E
Mykines, Føroe Is. 8 E9 62 7N 7 35W
Mykolayiv, Ukraine ... 33 J7 46 58N 32 0 E
Mymensingh, Bangla. . 67 G17 24 45N 90 24 E
Mynydd Du, U.K. 15 F4 51 52N 3 50W
Mýrdalsjökull, Iceland 8 E4 63 40N 19 6W
Myrhorod, Ukraine ... 33 H7 49 58N 33 37 E
Myrtle Beach, U.S.A. . 115 J6 33 42N 78 53W
Myrtle Creek, U.S.A. . 108 E2 43 1N 123 17W
Myrtle Point, U.S.A. . 108 E1 43 4N 124 8W
Myrtou, Cyprus ..... 49 D12 35 18N 33 4 E
Mysia, Turkey .... 45 G11 39 50N 27 0 E
Myślenice, Poland .... 31 J6 49 51N 19 57 E
Myślibórz, Poland .... 31 F1 52 55N 14 50 E
Mysłowice, Poland ... 31 H6 50 15N 19 12 E
Mysore = Karnataka □,
  India .... 66 N10 13 15N 77 0 E
Mysore, India .... 66 N10 12 17N 76 41 E
Mystic, U.S.A. 117 E13 41 21N 71 58W
Myszków, Poland .... 31 H6 50 45N 19 22 E
Myszyniec, Poland ... 30 E8 53 23N 21 21 E
Mytishchi, Russia .... 32 E9 55 50N 37 50 E
Mývatn, Iceland 8 D5 65 36N 17 0W
Mže →, Czech Rep. .. 26 B6 49 46N 13 24 E
Mzimba, Malawi ..... 87 E3 11 55 S 33 39 E
Mzimkulu →, S. Africa 89 E4 30 44 S 30 28 E
Mzimvubu →, S. Africa 89 E4 31 38 S 29 33 E
Mzuzu, Malawi ...... 87 E3 11 30 S 33 55 E

N

Na Hearadh = Harris,
  U.K. 13 D2 57 50N 6 55W
Na Noi, Thailand .... 64 C3 18 19N 100 43 E
Na Phao, Laos ...... 64 D5 17 35N 105 44 E
Na Sam, Vietnam .... 58 F6 22 3N 106 37 E
Na San, Vietnam .... 64 B5 21 12N 104 2 E
Na Thon, Thailand ... 65 b 9 32N 99 56 E
Naab →, Germany ... 25 F8 49 1N 12 2 E
Na'am, Sudan .... 81 F2 9 42N 28 27 E
Na'am →, Sudan .... 81 F2 6 48N 29 57 E
Naantali, Finland .... 9 F19 60 29N 22 2 E
Naas, Ireland 12 C5 53 12N 6 40W
Nababeep, S. Africa .. 88 D2 29 36 S 17 46 E
Nabadwip = Navadwip,
  India .... 69 H13 23 34N 88 20 E
Nabawa, Australia ... 93 E1 28 30 S 114 48 E
Nabberu, L., Australia 93 E3 25 50 S 120 30 E
Nabburg, Germany ... 25 F8 49 27N 12 11 E
Naberezhnyye Chelny,
  Russia .... 34 C11 55 42N 52 19 E
Nabeul, Tunisia ..... 79 A8 36 30N 10 44 E
Nabha, India .... 68 D7 30 26N 76 14 E
Nabid, Iran .... 71 D8 29 40N 57 38 E
Nabire, Indonesia ... 63 E9 3 15 S 135 26 E
Nabisar, Pakistan ... 68 G3 25 8N 69 40 E
Nabisipi →, Canada .. 105 B7 50 14N 62 13W
Nabiswera, Uganda .. 86 B3 1 27N 32 15 E
Nāblus = Nābulus,
  West Bank .... 74 C4 32 14N 35 15 E
Naboomspruit, S. Africa 89 C4 24 32 S 28 40 E
Nabou, Burkina Faso . 82 C4 11 25N 2 50W
Nabua, Phil. .... 61 E5 13 24N 123 22 E
Nābulus, West Bank .. 74 C4 32 14N 35 15 E
Nacala, Mozam. .... 87 E5 14 31 S 40 34 E
Nacala-Velha, Mozam. 87 E5 14 32 S 40 34 E
Nacaome, Honduras .. 120 D2 13 31N 87 30W
Nacaroa, Mozam. .... 87 E4 14 22 S 39 56 E
Naches, U.S.A. 108 C3 46 44N 120 42W
Naches →, U.S.A. ... 110 D5 46 38N 120 31W
Nachicapau, L., Canada 105 A6 56 40N 68 5W
Nachingwea, Tanzania 87 E4 10 23 S 38 49 E
Nachna, India ...... 68 F4 27 34N 71 41 E
Nacimiento →, U.S.A. 110 K6 35 46N 120 53W
Naco, Mexico 118 A3 31 20N 109 56W
Nacogdoches, U.S.A. .. 113 K7 31 36N 94 39W
Nácori Chico, Mexico . 118 B3 29 39N 109 1W
Nacozari, Mexico 118 A3 30 24N 109 39W
Nådendal = Naantali,
  Finland .... 9 F19 60 29N 22 2 E
Nadi, Fiji .... 91 C7 17 42 S 177 20 E
Nadi, Sudan .... 80 D3 18 40N 33 41 E
Nadiad, India ...... 68 H5 22 41N 72 56 E
Nădlac, Romania .... 28 D5 46 10N 20 50 E
Nador, Morocco 78 B5 35 14N 2 58W
Nadur, Malta .... 49 C1 36 2N 14 18 E
Nadūshan, Iran ..... 71 C7 32 2N 53 35 E
Nadvirna, Ukraine ... 29 B9 48 37N 24 30 E
Nadvornaya = Nadvirna,
  Ukraine .... 29 B9 48 37N 24 30 E
Nadym, Russia ...... 52 C8 65 35N 72 42 E
Nadym →, Russia ... 52 C8 66 12N 72 0 E
Næstved, Denmark ... 9 G11 55 13N 11 44 E
Nafada, Nigeria ..... 83 C7 11 8N 11 20 E
Naft-e Safīd, Iran ... 71 D6 31 40N 49 17 E

Naftshahr, Iran ...... 70 C5 34 0N 45 30 E
Nafud Desert = An
  Nafūd, Si. Arabia .. 70 D4 28 15N 41 0 E
Nag Hammādi, Egypt . 80 B3 26 2N 32 18 E
Naga, Phil. .... 61 E5 13 38N 123 15 E
Nagahama, Japan .... 55 G8 35 23N 136 16 E
Nagai, Japan .... 54 E10 38 6N 140 2 E
Nagaland □, India ... 67 G19 26 0N 94 30 E
Nagano, Japan ...... 55 F9 36 40N 138 10 E
Nagano □, Japan .... 55 F9 36 15N 138 0 E
Nagaoka, Japan ..... 55 F9 37 27N 138 51 E
Nagappattinam, India 66 P11 10 46N 79 51 E
Nagar →, Bangla. ... 69 G13 24 27N 89 12 E
Nagar Parkar, Pakistan 68 G4 24 28N 70 46 E
Nagasaki, Japan ..... 55 H4 32 47N 129 50 E
Nagasaki □, Japan ... 55 H4 32 50N 129 40 E
Nagato, Japan ...... 55 G5 34 19N 131 5 E
Nagaur, India ...... 68 F5 27 15N 73 45 E
Nagda, India .... 68 H6 23 27N 75 25 E
Nagercoil, India .... 66 Q10 8 12N 77 26 E
Nagina, India ...... 69 E8 29 30N 78 30 E
Nagīneh, Iran ...... 71 C8 34 20N 57 15 E
Nagir, Pakistan ..... 69 A6 36 12N 74 42 E
Nagod, India .... 69 G9 24 34N 80 36 E
Nagold, Germany ... 25 G4 48 32N 8 43 E
Nagold →, Germany . 25 G4 48 52N 8 42 E
Nagoorin, Australia .. 94 C5 24 17 S 151 15 E
Nagorno-Karabakh □,
  Azerbaijan .... 70 B5 39 55N 46 45 E
Nagornyy, Russia .... 53 D13 55 58N 124 57 E
Nagoya, Japan ...... 55 G8 35 10N 136 50 E
Nagpur, India ...... 66 J11 21 8N 79 10 E
Nagua, Dom. Rep. ... 121 C6 19 23N 69 50W
Naguabo, Puerto Rico 121 d 18 13N 65 44W
Nagyatád, Hungary .. 28 D2 46 14N 17 22 E
Nagyecsed, Hungary .. 28 C7 47 53N 22 24 E
Nagykálló, Hungary .. 28 C6 47 53N 21 51 E
Nagykanizsa, Hungary 28 D2 46 28N 17 0 E
Nagykáta, Hungary .. 28 C4 47 25N 19 45 E
Nagykőrös, Hungary .. 28 C4 47 5N 19 48 E
Naha, Japan .... 55 L3 26 13N 127 42 E
Nahan, India .... 68 D7 30 33N 77 18 E
Nahanni →, Canada .. 102 A4 61 36N 125 41W
Nahanni Butte, Canada 102 A4 61 2N 123 31W
Nahargarh, Mad. P.,
  India .... 68 G6 24 10N 75 14 E
Nahargarh, Raj., India 68 G7 24 55N 76 50 E
Nahariyya, Israel .... 70 C2 33 1N 35 5 E
Nahāvand, Iran ..... 71 C6 34 10N 48 22 E
Nahe →, Germany ... 25 F3 49 58N 7 57 E
Nahîrne, Ukraine .... 29 E13 45 26N 28 27 E
Nahîya, W. →, Egypt . 80 B3 28 55N 31 0 E
Nahuelbuta △, Chile . 126 D1 37 44 S 72 57W
Nai Yong, Thailand .. 65 a 14 8N 98 22 E
Naicá, Mexico 118 B3 27 53N 105 31W
Naicam, Canada 103 C8 52 30N 104 30W
Naikoon △, Canada .. 102 C2 53 55N 131 55W
Naila, Germany ..... 25 E7 50 19N 11 42 E
Naimisharanya, India 69 F9 27 21N 80 30 E
Nain, Canada 105 A7 56 34N 61 40W
Nā'īn, Iran .... 71 C7 32 54N 53 0 E
Naini Tal, India .... 69 E8 29 30N 79 30 E
Nainpur, India ..... 66 H12 22 30N 80 10 E
Naintré, France ..... 18 F7 46 46N 0 29 E
Nainwa, India ...... 68 G6 25 46N 75 51 E
Naipu, Romania .... 29 F10 44 12N 25 47 E
Nairn, U.K. 13 D5 57 35N 3 53W
Nairobi, Kenya ..... 86 C4 1 17 S 36 48 E
Nairobi △, Kenya ... 86 C4 1 22 S 36 50 E
Naissaar, Estonia ... 9 G21 59 34N 24 29 E
Naita, Mt., Ethiopia . 81 F4 5 30N 35 18 E
Naivasha, Kenya .... 86 C4 0 40 S 36 30 E
Naivasha, L., Kenya .. 86 C4 0 48 S 36 20 E
Najac, France ...... 20 D5 44 14N 1 58 E
Najaf = An Najaf, Iraq 70 C5 32 3N 44 15 E
Najafābād, Iran ..... 71 C6 32 40N 51 15 E
Najd, Si. Arabia .... 75 B3 26 30N 42 0 E
Nájera, Spain 38 C2 42 26N 2 48W
Najerilla →, Spain .. 38 C2 42 32N 2 48W
Najibabad, India .... 68 E8 29 40N 78 20 E
Najin, N. Korea ..... 57 C16 42 12N 130 15 E
Najmah, Si. Arabia .. 71 E6 26 42N 50 6 E
Najrān, Si. Arabia .. 75 D3 17 34N 44 18 E
Naju, S. Korea ...... 57 G14 35 3N 126 43 E
Nakadōri-Shima, Japan 55 H4 32 57N 129 4 E
Nakalagba, Dem. Rep. of
  the Congo .... 86 B2 2 50N 27 58 E
Nakaminato, Japan .. 55 F10 36 21N 140 36 E
Nakamura, Japan ... 55 H6 32 59N 132 56 E
Nakano, Japan ...... 55 F9 36 45N 138 22 E
Nakano-Shima, Japan 55 K4 29 51N 129 52 E
Nakashibetsu, Japan . 54 C12 43 33N 144 59 E
Nakfa, Eritrea ...... 81 D4 16 40N 38 32 E
Nakfa △, Eritrea .... 81 D4 17 28N 38 55 E
Nakha Yai, Thailand . 65 a 8 3N 98 28 E
Nakhichevan =
  Naxçıvan, Azerbaijan 70 B5 39 12N 45 15 E
Nakhichevan Rep. =
  Naxçıvan □,
  Azerbaijan .... 52 F5 39 25N 45 26 E
Nakhl, Egypt .... 74 F2 29 55N 33 43 E
Nakhl-e Taqī, Iran .. 71 E7 27 28N 52 36 E
Nakhodka, Russia ... 53 E14 42 53N 132 54 E
Nakhon Nayok,
  Thailand .... 64 E3 14 12N 101 13 E
Nakhon Pathom,
  Thailand .... 64 F3 13 49N 100 3 E
Nakhon Phanom,
  Thailand .... 64 D5 17 23N 104 43 E
Nakhon Ratchasima,
  Thailand .... 64 E4 14 59N 102 12 E
Nakhon Sawan,
  Thailand .... 64 E3 15 35N 100 10 E
Nakhon Si Thammarat,
  Thailand .... 65 H3 8 29N 100 0 E
Nakhon Thai, Thailand 64 D3 17 5N 100 44 E
Nakhtarana, India .. 68 H3 23 20N 69 15 E
Nakina, Canada 104 B2 50 10N 86 40W
Nakło nad Notecią,
  Poland .... 31 E4 53 9N 17 38 E
Nako, Burkina Faso . 82 C4 10 40N 3 4W
Nakodar, India ..... 68 D6 31 8N 75 31 E
Nakskov, Denmark .. 11 K5 54 50N 11 8 E
Naktong →, S. Korea 57 G15 35 7N 128 57 E
Nakuru, Kenya ...... 86 C4 0 15 S 36 4 E
Nakuru, L., Kenya ... 86 C4 0 23 S 36 5 E
Nakusp, Canada 102 C5 50 20N 117 45W
Nal, Pakistan .... 68 G1 25 20N 65 30 E
Nalázi, Mozam. ..... 89 C5 24 3 S 33 20 E
Nalchik, Russia ..... 35 J6 43 30N 43 33 E
Nalerigu, Ghana 83 C4 10 35N 0 25W
Nalgonda, India .... 66 L11 17 6N 79 15 E
Nalhati, India ...... 69 G12 24 17N 87 52 E

Naliya, India .... 68 H3 23 16N 68 50 E
Nallamalai Hills, India 66 M11 15 30N 78 50 E
Nallhan, Turkey ..... 72 B4 40 11N 31 20 E
Nalón →, Spain 36 B4 43 32N 6 4W
Nam Can, Vietnam ... 65 H5 8 46N 104 59 E
Nam Co, China ...... 60 C4 30 30N 90 45 E
Nam Dinh, Vietnam .. 58 G6 20 25N 106 5 E
Nam Du, Hon, Vietnam 65 H5 9 41N 104 21 E
Nam Nao △, Thailand 64 D3 16 44N 101 32 E
Nam Ngum Dam, Laos 64 C4 18 35N 102 34 E
Nam-Phan, Vietnam . 65 G6 10 30N 106 0 E
Nam Phong, Thailand 64 D4 16 42N 102 52 E
Nam Tha, Laos ...... 58 G3 20 58N 101 30 E
Nam Tok, Thailand .. 64 E2 14 21N 99 4 E
Namacunde, Angola .. 88 B2 17 18 S 15 50 E
Namacurra, Mozam. . 89 B6 17 30 S 36 50 E
Namak, Daryācheh-ye,
  Iran .... 71 C7 34 30N 52 0 E
Namak, Kavir-e, Iran . 71 C8 34 30N 57 30 E
Namakzār, Daryācheh-
  ye, Iran .... 71 C9 34 0N 60 30 E
Namaland, Namibia . 88 C2 26 0 S 17 0 E
Namangan, Uzbekistan 52 E8 41 0N 71 40 E
Namapa, Mozam. .... 87 E4 13 43 S 39 50 E
Namaqualand, S. Africa 88 E2 30 0 S 17 25 E
Namasagali, Uganda . 86 B3 1 2N 33 0 E
Namber, Indonesia ... 63 E8 1 2 S 134 49 E
Nambour, Australia .. 95 D5 26 32 S 152 58 E
Nambucca Heads,
  Australia .... 95 E5 30 37 S 153 0 E
Nambung △, Australia 93 F2 30 30 S 115 5 E
Namche Bazar, Nepal 69 F12 27 51N 86 47 E
Namchonjŏm = Nam-
  ch'on, N. Korea .... 57 E14 38 15N 126 26 E
Namecunda, Mozam. . 87 E4 14 54 S 37 37 E
Nameponda, Mozam. . 87 F4 15 50 S 39 50 E
Náměšť nad Oslavou,
  Czech Rep. .... 27 B9 49 12N 16 10 E
Námestovo, Slovak Rep. 27 B12 49 24N 19 25 E
Nametil, Mozam. .... 87 F4 15 40 S 39 21 E
Namew L., Canada ... 103 C8 54 14N 101 56W
Namgia, India ...... 69 D8 31 48N 78 40 E
Namhkam, Burma ... 58 E1 23 50N 97 41 E
Namib Desert, Namibia 88 C2 22 30 S 15 0 E
Namib-Naukluft △,
  Namibia .... 88 C2 24 40 S 15 16 E
Namibe, Angola ..... 85 H2 15 7 S 12 11 E
Namibe □, Angola ... 88 B1 16 35 S 12 30 E
Namibia ■, Africa ... 88 C2 22 0 S 18 9 E
Namibwoestyn = Namib
  Desert, Namibia ... 88 C2 22 30 S 15 0 E
Namīn, Iran .... 73 C13 38 25N 48 30 E
Namlea, Indonesia ... 63 E7 3 18 S 127 5 E
Namoi →, Australia .. 95 E4 30 12 S 149 30 E
Nampa, U.S.A. 108 E5 43 34N 116 34W
Nampala, Mali 82 B3 15 20N 5 30W
Namp'o, N. Korea ... 57 E13 38 52N 125 10 E
Nampō-Shotō, Japan . 55 J10 32 0N 140 0 E
Nampula, Mozam. ... 87 F4 15 6 S 39 15 E
Namrole, Indonesia .. 63 E7 3 46 S 126 46 E
Namse Shankou, China 58 D3 30 0N 82 25 E
Namsen →, Norway .. 8 D14 64 28N 11 37 E
Namsos, Norway .... 8 D14 64 29N 11 30 E
Namtok Chat Trakan △,
  Thailand .... 64 D3 17 17N 100 40 E
Namtok Mae Surin △,
  Thailand .... 64 C2 18 55N 98 2 E
Namtsy, Russia ...... 53 C13 62 43N 129 37 E
Namtu, Burma ...... 67 H20 23 5N 97 28 E
Namtumbo, Tanzania 87 E4 10 30 S 36 4 E
Namu, Canada 102 C3 51 52N 127 50W
Namur, Belgium .... 17 D4 50 27N 4 52 E
Namur □, Belgium ... 17 D4 50 17N 5 0 E
Namutoni, Namibia . 88 B2 18 49 S 16 55 E
Namwala, Zambia ... 87 F2 15 44 S 26 30 E
Namwŏn, S. Korea .. 57 G14 35 23N 127 23 E
Namysłów, Poland ... 31 G4 51 6N 17 42 E
Nan, Thailand ...... 64 C3 18 48N 100 46 E
Nan →, Thailand .... 64 E3 15 42N 100 9 E
Nan-ch'ang = Nanchang,
  China .... 59 C10 28 42N 115 55 E
Nan Ling, China ..... 59 E8 25 0N 112 30 E
Nan Xian, China .... 59 C9 29 20N 112 22 E
Nana, Romania ..... 29 F11 44 17N 26 34 E
Nana Kru, Liberia ... 82 B2 4 55N 8 45W
Nanaimo, Canada ... 102 D4 49 10N 124 0W
Nanam, N. Korea ... 57 D15 41 44N 129 40 E
Nanan, China .... 59 E12 24 59N 118 21 E
Nanango, Australia .. 95 D5 26 40 S 152 0 E
Nan'ao, China ...... 59 F11 23 28N 117 5 E
Nanao, Japan .... 55 F8 37 0N 137 0 E
Nanbu, China .... 58 B6 31 18N 106 3 E
Nanchang, Jiangxi,
  China .... 59 C10 28 42N 115 55 E
Nanchang, Kiangsi,
  China .... 59 C10 28 34N 115 48 E
Nancheng, China .... 59 D11 27 33N 116 35 E
Nanching = Nanjing,
  China .... 59 A12 32 2N 118 47 E
Nanchong, China .... 58 B6 30 43N 106 2 E
Nanchuan, China ... 58 C6 29 9N 107 6 E
Nancy, France ...... 19 D13 48 42N 6 12 E
Nanda Devi, India ... 69 D8 30 23N 79 59 E
Nanda Kot, India ... 69 D9 30 17N 80 5 E
Nandan, China ..... 58 E6 24 58N 107 29 E
Nandan, Japan ..... 55 G7 34 10N 134 42 E
Nanded, India ...... 66 K10 19 10N 77 20 E
Nandewar Ra., Australia 95 E5 30 15 S 150 35 E
Nandi = Nadi, Fiji ... 91 C7 17 42 S 177 20 E
Nandigram, India ... 69 H12 22 1N 87 58 E
Nandurbar, India ... 66 J9 21 20N 74 15 E
Nandyal, India ..... 66 M11 15 30N 78 30 E
Nanfeng, Guangdong,
  China .... 59 F8 23 45N 111 47 E
Nanfeng, Jiangxi, China 59 D11 27 12N 116 28 E
Nanga-Eboko,
  Cameroon .... 83 E7 4 41N 12 22 E
Nanga Parbat, Pakistan 69 B6 35 10N 74 35 E
Nangade, Mozam. ... 87 E4 11 5 S 39 36 E
Nangapinoh, Indonesia 62 E4 0 20 S 111 44 E
Nangarhār □, Afghan. 66 B7 34 20N 70 0 E
Nangeya Mts., Uganda 86 B3 3 30N 33 30 E
Nangis, France ...... 19 D10 48 33N 3 1 E
Nanhua, China ..... 58 E3 25 10N 101 21 E
Nanhuang, China ... 57 F11 36 58N 120 48 E
Nanhui, China ...... 59 B13 31 5N 121 44 E
Nanjeko, Zambia .... 87 F1 15 31 S 23 30 E
Nanji Shan, China ... 59 D13 27 27N 121 4 E
Nanjiang, China .... 58 A6 32 35N 106 51 E
Nanjing, China ..... 59 A12 32 2N 118 47 E
Nanjing, Jiangsu, China 59 A12 32 2N 118 47 E
Nanjirinji, Tanzania . 87 D4 9 41 S 39 5 E
Nankana Sahib, Pakistan 68 D5 31 27N 73 38 E

Nankang, China ..... 59 E10 25 40N 114 45 E
Nanking = Nanjing,
  China .... 59 A12 32 2N 118 47 E
Nankoku, Japan .... 55 H6 33 39N 133 44 E
Nanling, China ..... 59 B12 30 55N 118 20 E
Nanning, China ..... 58 F7 22 48N 108 20 E
Nannup, Australia ... 93 F2 33 59 S 115 48 E
Nanpara, India ..... 69 F9 27 52N 81 33 E
Nanpi, China .... 56 E9 38 2N 116 45 E
Nanping, Fujian, China 59 D12 26 38N 118 10 E
Nanping, Henan, China 59 C9 29 55N 112 3 E
Nanri Dao, China ... 59 E12 25 15N 119 25 E
Nanripe, Mozam. ... 87 E4 13 52 S 38 52 E
Nansei-Shotō = Ryūkyū-
  rettō, Japan ...... 55 M3 26 0N 126 0 E
Nansen Basin, Arctic . 4 A10 84 0N 50 0 E
Nansen Cordillera,
  Arctic .... 4 A 87 0N 90 0 E
Nansen Sd., Canada .. 4 B3 81 0N 91 0W
Nanshan I., S. China Sea 62 B5 10 45N 115 49 E
Nansio, Tanzania .... 86 C3 2 3 S 33 4 E
Nant, France .... 20 D7 44 1N 3 18 E
Nanterre, France .... 19 D9 48 53N 2 13 E
Nantes, France 18 E5 47 12N 1 33W
Nanticoke, U.S.A. ... 117 E8 41 12N 76 0W
Nanton, Canada 102 C6 50 21N 113 46W
Nantong, China ..... 59 A13 32 1N 120 52 E
Nantou, Taiwan ..... 59 F13 23 57N 120 35 E
Nantua, France ..... 19 F12 46 10N 5 35 E
Nantucket I., U.S.A. . 114 E10 41 16N 70 5W
Nantwich, U.K. 14 D5 53 4N 2 31W
Nanty Glo, U.S.A. ... 116 F6 40 28N 78 50W
Nanuque, Brazil .... 125 G10 17 50 S 40 21W
Nanusa, Kepulauan,
  Indonesia .... 63 D7 4 45N 127 1 E
Nanutarra Roadhouse,
  Australia .... 92 D2 22 32 S 115 30 E
Nanxi, China .... 58 C5 28 54N 104 59 E
Nanxiong, China .... 59 E10 25 6N 114 15 E
Nanyang, China .... 56 H7 33 11N 112 30 E
Nanyi Hu, China .... 59 B12 31 5N 119 0 E
Nanyuki, Kenya .... 86 B4 0 2N 37 4 E
Nanzhang, China ... 59 B8 31 45N 111 50 E
Nao, C. de la, Spain . 39 G5 38 44N 0 14 E
Naococane, L., Canada 105 B5 52 50N 70 45W
Naoussa, Imathia, Greece 44 F6 40 42N 22 9 E
Naoussa, Kikládhes,
  Greece .... 47 D7 37 7N 25 14 E
Naozhou Dao, China . 59 G8 20 55N 110 20 E
Napa, U.S.A. 110 G4 38 18N 122 17W
Napa →, U.S.A. 110 G4 38 10N 122 19W
Napanee, Canada 116 B8 44 15N 77 0W
Napanoch, U.S.A. ... 117 E10 41 44N 74 22W
Nape, Laos .... 58 E6 18 18N 105 6 E
Nape Pass = Keo Neua,
  Deo, Vietnam ..... 64 C5 18 23N 105 10 E
Napier, N.Z. .... 91 H6 39 30 S 176 56 E
Napier Broome B.,
  Australia .... 92 B4 14 2 S 126 37 E
Napier Pen., Australia 94 A2 12 4 S 135 43 E
Napierville, Canada .. 117 A11 45 11N 73 25W
Naples = Nápoli, Italy 43 B7 40 50N 14 15 E
Naples, U.S.A. 115 M5 26 8N 81 48W
Napo, China .... 58 F5 23 22N 105 50 E
Napo →, Peru ...... 124 D4 3 20 S 72 40W
Napoleon, N. Dak.,
  U.S.A. 112 B5 46 30N 99 46W
Napoleon, Ohio, U.S.A. 114 E3 41 23N 84 8W
Nápoli, Italy .... 43 B7 40 50N 14 15 E
Nápoli, G. di, Italy .. 43 B7 40 43N 14 10 E
Nápoli Capodichino ✈
  (NAP), Italy ...... 43 B7 40 53N 14 16 E
Napopo, Dem. Rep. of
  the Congo .... 86 B2 4 15N 28 0 E
Naqâda, Egypt ...... 80 B3 25 53N 32 42 E
Naqadeh, Iran ...... 73 D11 36 57N 45 23 E
Naqb, Ra's an, Jordan 74 F4 30 0N 35 29 E
Naqqāsh, Iran ...... 71 C6 35 40N 49 6 E
Nara, Japan .... 55 G7 34 40N 135 49 E
Nara, Mali 82 B3 15 10N 7 20W
Nara □, Japan ...... 55 G8 34 30N 136 0 E
Nara Canal, Pakistan 68 G3 24 30N 69 20 E
Nara Visa, U.S.A. ... 113 H3 35 37N 103 6W
Naracoorte, Australia 95 F3 36 58 S 140 45 E
Naradhan, Australia . 95 E4 33 34 S 146 17 E
Naraini, India ...... 69 G9 25 11N 80 29 E
Narasapur, India .... 67 L12 16 26N 81 40 E
Narathiwat, Thailand 65 J3 6 30N 101 48 E
Narayanganj, Bangla. 67 H17 23 40N 90 33 E
Narayanpet, India ... 66 L10 16 45N 77 30 E
Narberth, U.K. 15 F3 51 47N 4 44W
Narbonne, France ... 20 E7 43 11N 3 0 E
Narca →, Spain 36 B4 43 33N 6 44W
Nardín, Iran .... 71 B7 37 3N 55 59 E
Nardò, Italy .... 43 B11 40 11N 18 2 E
Narembeen, Australia 93 F2 32 7 S 118 24 E
Narendranagar, India 68 D8 30 10N 78 18 E
Nares Str., Arctic ... 98 A13 80 0N 70 0W
Naretha, Australia .. 93 F3 31 0 S 124 45 E
Narew →, Poland ... 31 F7 52 26N 20 41 E
Nari →, Pakistan ... 68 F2 28 0N 67 40 E
Narin, Afghan. ..... 66 A6 36 5N 69 0 E
Narindra, Helodrano' i,
  Madag. .... 89 A8 14 55 S 47 30 E
Narita, Japan ...... 55 G10 35 47N 140 19 E
Nariva Swamp,
  Trin. & Tob. 125 K15 10 26N 61 4W
Närke, Sweden ..... 10 E8 59 10N 15 0 E
Narmada →, India .. 68 J5 21 38N 72 36 E
Narman, Turkey .... 73 B9 40 20N 41 57 E
Narmland, Sweden .. 9 F15 60 0N 13 30 E
Narnaul, India ..... 68 E7 28 5N 76 11 E
Narni, Italy .... 41 F9 42 30N 12 31 E
Naro, Ghana 82 C4 10 22N 2 27W
Naro Fominsk, Russia 32 E9 55 23N 36 43 E
Narok, Kenya ...... 86 C4 1 55 S 35 52 E
Narón, Spain 36 B2 43 32N 8 9W
Narooma, Australia . 95 F5 36 14 S 150 4 E
Narrabri, Australia .. 95 E4 30 19 S 149 46 E
Narrandera, Australia 95 E4 34 42 S 146 31 E
Narrogin, Australia .. 93 F2 32 58 S 117 14 E
Narromine, Australia 95 E4 32 12 S 148 12 E
Narrows, The, Canada 103 C8 54 0N 101 54W
Narsimhapur, India . 69 H8 22 54N 79 14 E
Narsinghgarh, India . 68 H7 23 45N 76 40 E
Nartkala, Russia .... 35 J6 43 33N 43 51 E
Naruto, Japan ...... 55 G7 34 11N 134 37 E
Narva, Estonia ..... 32 C5 59 23N 28 12 E
Narva →, Russia .... 9 G22 59 27N 28 2 E
Narva Bay = Narva
  Laht, Estonia ..... 9 G19 59 35N 27 35 E

Narva Laht, Estonia .. 9 G19 59 35N 27 35 E
Narvik, Norway ..... 8 B17 68 28N 17 26 E
Narvskoye Vdkhr.,
  Russia .... 32 C5 59 18N 28 14 E
Narwana, India ..... 68 E7 29 39N 76 6 E
Narwiański △, Poland 31 F9 52 5N 22 53 E
Naryan-Mar, Russia . 52 C6 67 42N 53 12 E
Narym, Russia ...... 52 D9 59 0N 81 30 E
Naryn, Kyrgyzstan .. 52 E8 41 26N 75 58 E
Nasa, Norway .... 8 C16 66 29N 15 23 E
Năsăud, Romania ... 29 C9 47 19N 24 29 E
Naseby, N.Z. .... 91 L3 45 1 S 170 10 E
Naselle, U.S.A. 110 D3 46 22N 123 49W
Naser, Buheirat en,
  Egypt .... 80 C3 23 0N 32 30 E
Nashua, Mont., U.S.A. 108 B10 48 8N 106 22W
Nashua, N.H., U.S.A. 117 D13 42 45N 71 28W
Nashville, Ark., U.S.A. 113 J8 33 57N 93 51W
Nashville, Ga., U.S.A. 115 K4 31 12N 83 15W
Nashville, Tenn., U.S.A. 115 G2 36 10N 86 47W
Našice, Croatia ..... 28 E3 45 32N 18 4 E
Nasielsk, Poland .... 31 F7 52 35N 20 50 E
Nasik, India .... 66 K8 19 58N 73 50 E
Nasipit, Phil. ...... 61 G6 8 57N 125 19 E
Nasir, Sudan .... 81 F3 8 36N 33 4 E
Nasirabad, India .... 68 F6 26 15N 74 45 E
Nasirabad, Pakistan . 68 E3 28 23N 68 24 E
Nasiriyah = An
  Nāşirīyah, Iraq .... 70 D5 31 0N 46 15 E
Naskaupi →, Canada . 105 B7 53 47N 60 51W
Naso, Italy .... 43 D7 38 7N 14 47 E
Naşrābād, Iran ..... 71 C6 34 8N 51 26 E
Naşriān-e Pa'īn, Iran 70 C5 32 52N 46 52 E
Nass →, Canada 102 C3 55 0N 129 40W
Nassarawa, Nigeria .. 83 D6 8 32N 7 41 E
Nassarawa □, Nigeria 83 D6 8 30N 8 20 E
Nassau, Bahamas 120 A4 25 5N 77 20W
Nassau, U.S.A. 117 D11 42 31N 73 37W
Nassau, B., Chile .... 128 H3 55 20 S 68 0W
Nasser, L. = Naser,
  Buheirat en, Egypt . 80 C3 23 0N 32 30 E
Nassian, Ivory C. 82 D4 8 28N 3 28W
Nässjö, Sweden ..... 11 G8 57 39N 14 42 E
Nastapoka →, Canada 104 A4 56 55N 76 33W
Nastapoka, Is., Canada 104 A4 56 55N 76 50W
Nasugbu, Phil. ..... 61 D4 14 5N 120 38 E
Näsum, Sweden ..... 11 H8 56 10N 14 29 E
Näsviken, Sweden ... 10 C10 61 46N 16 52 E
Nata, Botswana ..... 88 C4 20 12 S 26 12 E
Nata →, Botswana .. 88 C4 20 14 S 26 10 E
Natal, Brazil .... 125 E11 5 47 S 35 13W
Natal, Indonesia .... 62 D1 0 35N 99 7 E
Natal, S. Africa ..... 85 K6 28 30 S 30 30 E
Natal Drakensberg △,
  S. Africa .... 89 D4 29 27 S 29 30 E
Natalinci, Serbia & M. 28 F5 44 15N 20 49 E
Natanz, Iran .... 71 C6 33 30N 51 55 E
Natashquan, Canada . 105 B7 50 14N 61 46W
Natashquan →, Canada 105 B7 50 7N 61 50W
Natchez, U.S.A. 113 K9 31 34N 91 24W
Natchitoches, U.S.A. . 113 K8 31 46N 93 5W
Nathalia, Australia .. 95 F4 36 1 S 145 13 E
Nathdwara, India ... 68 G5 24 55N 73 50 E
Nati, Pta., Spain .... 48 A10 40 3N 3 50 E
Natimuk, Australia .. 95 F3 36 42 S 142 0 E
Nation →, Canada ... 102 B4 55 30N 123 32W
National City, U.S.A. . 111 N9 32 41N 117 6W
Natitingou, Benin ... 83 C5 10 20N 1 26 E
Natividad, I., Mexico . 118 B1 27 50N 115 10W
Natkyizin, Burma ... 64 E1 14 57N 97 59 E
Natron, L., Tanzania . 86 C4 2 20 S 36 0 E
Natrona Heights, U.S.A. 116 F5 40 37N 79 44W
Natrūn, W. el →, Egypt 80 H7 30 25N 30 13 E
Nättraby, Sweden ... 11 H9 56 13N 15 31 E
Natukanaoka Pan,
  Namibia .... 88 B2 18 40 S 15 45 E
Natuna Besar,
  Kepulauan, Indonesia 62 D3 4 0N 108 15 E
Natuna Is. = Natuna
  Besar, Kepulauan,
  Indonesia .... 62 D3 4 0N 108 15 E
Natuna Selatan,
  Kepulauan, Indonesia 62 D3 2 45N 109 0 E
Natural Bridge, U.S.A. 117 B9 44 5N 75 30W
Natural Bridges △,
  U.S.A. 109 H8 37 36N 110 1W
Naturaliste, C., Australia 95 G4 40 50 S 148 15 E
Nau Qala, Afghan. .. 68 B3 34 5N 68 5 E
Naucelle, France .... 20 D6 44 13N 2 20 E
Nauders, Austria .... 26 E3 46 54N 10 30 E
Nauen, Germany .... 24 C8 52 36N 12 52 E
Naugatuck, U.S.A. .. 117 E11 41 30N 73 3W
Naujaat = Repulse Bay,
  Canada 101 B11 66 30N 86 30W
Naujoji Akmenė,
  Lithuania .... 30 B9 56 19N 22 54 E
Naumburg, Germany 24 D7 51 9N 11 47 E
Nä'ūr at Tunayb, Jordan 74 D4 31 48N 35 57 E
Nauru ■, Pac. Oc. ... 96 H8 1 0 S 166 0 E
Naushahra = Nowshera,
  Pakistan .... 66 C8 34 0N 72 0 E
Naushahro, Pakistan . 68 F3 26 50N 68 7 E
Naushon I., U.S.A. .. 117 E14 41 29N 70 45W
Nauta, Peru .... 124 D4 4 31 S 73 35W
Nautanwa, India .... 67 F13 27 20N 83 25 E
Naute △, Namibia ... 88 D2 26 55 S 17 57 E
Nautla, Mexico 119 C5 20 20N 96 50W
Nava, Mexico 118 B4 28 25N 100 46W
Nava, Spain 36 B5 43 21N 5 31W
Nava del Rey, Spain . 36 D5 41 22N 5 6W
Navadwip, India .... 69 H13 23 34N 88 20 E
Navahermosa, Spain . 37 F6 39 41N 4 28W
Navahrudak, Belarus 32 F3 53 40N 25 50 E
Navajo Reservoir,
  U.S.A. 109 H10 36 48N 107 36W
Navalcarnero, Spain . 36 E6 40 17N 4 5W
Navalmoral de la Mata,
  Spain 36 F5 39 52N 5 33W
Navalvillar de Pela,
  Spain 37 F5 39 9N 5 24W
Navan = An Uaimh,
  Ireland 12 C5 53 39N 6 41W
Navapolatsk, Belarus 32 E5 55 32N 28 37 E
Navarin, Mys, Russia 4 C16 62 15N 179 5 E
Navarino, I., Chile ... 128 H3 55 0 S 67 40W
Navarra □, Spain ... 38 C3 42 40N 1 40W
Navarre, U.S.A. 116 F3 40 43N 81 31W
Navarro →, U.S.A. .. 110 F3 39 11N 123 45W
Navas de San Juan,
  Spain 37 G7 38 10N 3 19W
Navasota, U.S.A. ... 113 K6 30 23N 96 5W
Navassa I., W. Indies 121 C5 18 30N 75 0W
Nävekvarn, Sweden . 11 F10 58 38N 16 49 E
Naver →, U.K. 13 C4 58 32N 4 14W
Navia, Spain 36 B4 43 35N 6 42W
Navia →, Spain 36 B4 43 15N 6 50W
Navia de Suarna, Spain 36 C3 42 58N 7 3W

Navibandar, India ..... 68 J3 21 26N 69 48 E
Navidad, Chile ...... 126 C1 33 57 S 71 50W
Naviraí, Brazil ...... 127 A5 23 8 S 54 13W
Navlakhi, India ..... 68 H4 22 58N 70 28 E
Navlya, Russia ...... 33 F8 52 53N 34 30 E
Năvodari, Romania .. 29 F13 44 19N 28 36 E
Navoi = Nawoiy,
  Uzbekistan .... 52 E7 40 9N 65 22 E
Navojoa, Mexico 118 B3 27 0N 109 30W
Navolato, Mexico 118 C3 24 47N 107 42W
Návpaktos, Greece ... 46 C3 38 24N 21 50 E
Návplion, Greece .... 46 D4 37 33N 22 50 E
Navrongo, Ghana 83 C4 10 51N 1 3W
Navsari, India ...... 66 J8 20 57N 72 59 E
Nawa Kot, Pakistan .. 68 E4 28 21N 71 24 E
Nawab Khan, Pakistan 68 D3 30 17N 69 12 E
Nawabganj, Ut. P., India 69 F9 26 56N 81 14 E
Nawabganj, Ut. P., India 69 E8 28 32N 79 40 E
Nawabshah, Pakistan . 68 F3 26 15N 68 25 E
Nawada, India ...... 69 G11 24 50N 85 33 E
Nawakot, Nepal ..... 69 F11 27 55N 85 10 E
Nawalgarh, India .... 68 F6 27 50N 75 15 E
Nawanshahr, India ... 69 C6 32 33N 74 48 E
Nawar, Dasht-i-,
  Afghan. .... 68 C3 33 52N 68 0 E
Nawi, Sudan .... 80 D3 18 32N 30 50 E
Nawoiy, Uzbekistan .. 52 E7 40 9N 65 22 E
Naxçivan, Azerbaijan . 70 B5 39 12N 45 15 E
Naxçivan □, Azerbaijan 52 F5 39 25N 45 26 E
Náxos, Greece ...... 47 D7 37 8N 25 25 E
Nay, France 20 E3 43 10N 0 18W
Nay, Mui, Vietnam .. 62 B3 12 55N 109 23 E
Nãy Band, Büshehr, Iran 71 E7 27 20N 52 40 E
Nãy Band, Khorãsãn,
  Iran .... 71 C8 32 20N 57 34 E
Nayakhan, Russia .... 53 C16 61 56N 159 0 E
Nayarit □, Mexico ... 118 C4 22 0N 105 0W
Nayé, Senegal 82 C2 14 28N 12 12W
Nayong, China ...... 58 D5 26 50N 105 20 E
Nayoro, Japan ...... 54 B11 44 21N 142 28 E
Nayyäl, W. →,
  Si. Arabia .... 70 D3 28 35N 39 4 E
Nazaré, Brazil ...... 125 F11 13 2 S 39 0W
Nazaré, Portugal 37 F1 39 36N 9 4W
Nazareth = Nazerat,
  Israel .... 74 C4 32 42N 35 17 E
Nazareth, U.S.A. 117 F9 40 44N 75 19W
Nazas, Mexico 118 B4 25 10N 104 6W
Nazas →, Mexico 118 B4 25 35N 103 25W
Nazca, Peru .... 124 F4 14 50 S 74 57W
Naze, The, U.K. ..... 15 F9 51 53N 1 18 E
Nazerat, Israel ..... 74 C4 32 42N 35 17 E
Nazük, Iran .... 70 B5 39 1N 45 4 E
Nazilli, Turkey ...... 47 D10 37 55N 28 15 E
Nazko, Canada 102 C4 53 1N 123 37W
Nazko →, Canada ... 102 C4 53 7N 123 34W
Nazret, Ethiopia .... 81 F4 8 32N 39 22 E
Nazwa, Oman .... 75 C6 22 56N 57 32 E
Nchanga, Zambia .... 87 E2 12 30 S 27 49 E
Ncheu, Malawi ...... 87 E3 14 50 S 34 47 E
Ndala, Tanzania ..... 86 C3 4 45 S 33 15 E
Ndalatando, Angola .. 84 F2 9 12 S 14 48 E
Ndali, Benin .... 83 D5 9 50N 2 46 E
Ndareda, Tanzania ... 86 C4 4 12 S 35 30 E
Ndélé, C.A.R. ...... 84 C4 8 25N 20 36 E
Ndiael →, Senegal ... 82 B1 16 15N 16 0W
Ndikinimeki, Cameroon 83 E7 4 46N 10 50 E
N'Dioum, Senegal ... 82 B2 16 31N 14 39W
Ndjamena, Chad ..... 79 F8 12 10N 14 59 E
Ndola, Zambia ...... 87 E2 13 0 S 28 34 E
Ndoto Mts., Kenya ... 86 B4 2 0N 37 0 E
Nduguti, Tanzania ... 86 C3 4 18 S 34 41 E
Ndumu △, S. Africa .. 89 D5 26 52 S 32 15 E
Néa Alikarnassós,
  Greece .... 47 F7 35 18N 25 13 E
Néa Ankhíalos, Greece 46 B4 39 16N 22 49 E
Néa Epídhavros, Greece 46 D5 37 40N 23 7 E
Néa Flippiás, Greece . 46 B2 39 12N 20 53 E
Néa Ionia, Greece .... 46 B4 39 15N 22 56 E
Néa Kallikrátia, Greece 44 F7 40 21N 23 3 E
Néa Mákri, Greece ... 46 C5 38 5N 23 59 E
Néa Moudhaniá, Greece 44 F7 40 15N 23 17 E
Néa Péramos, Attikí,
  Greece .... 46 C5 38 0N 23 26 E
Néa Péramos, Kaválla,
  Greece .... 45 F8 40 50N 24 18 E
Néa Víssi, Greece .... 45 E10 41 34N 26 33 E
Néa Zíkhna, Greece .. 44 E7 41 2N 23 49 E
Neagh, Lough, U.K. .. 12 B5 54 37N 6 25W
Neah Bay, U.S.A. 110 B2 48 22N 124 37W
Neale, L., Australia .. 92 D5 24 15 S 130 0 E
Neales, The →,
  Australia .... 95 D2 28 8 S 136 47 E
Neamţ □, Romania .. 29 C11 47 0N 26 20 E
Neápolis, Kozáni,
  Greece .... 44 F5 40 20N 21 24 E
Neápolis, Kríti, Greece 49 D7 35 15N 25 37 E
Neápolis, Lakonía,
  Greece .... 46 E5 36 27N 23 8 E
Near Is., U.S.A. ..... 100 C1 52 30N 174 0 E
Neath, U.K. 15 F4 51 39N 3 48W
Neath Port Talbot □,
  U.K. 15 F4 51 42N 3 45W
Nebbou, Burkina Faso 83 C4 11 9N 1 51W
Nebelat el Hagana,
  Sudan .... 81 E2 13 13N 29 2 E
Nebine Cr. →, Australia 95 D4 29 27 S 146 56 E
Nebitdag, Turkmenistan 52 F6 39 30N 54 22 E
Nebo, Australia ..... 94 C4 21 42 S 148 42 E
Nebolchy, Russia .... 32 C7 59 8N 33 18 E
Nebraska □, U.S.A. .. 112 E5 41 30N 99 30W
Nebraska City, U.S.A. 112 E7 40 41N 95 52W
Nébrodi, Monti, Italy 43 E7 37 54N 14 35 E
Necedah, U.S.A. 112 C9 44 2N 90 4W
Nechako →, Canada . 102 C4 53 55N 122 42W
Neches →, U.S.A. ... 113 L8 29 58N 93 51W
Nechisar △, Ethiopia 81 F4 5 58N 37 55 E
Neckar →, Germany .. 25 F4 49 27N 8 29 E
Neckartal-Odenwald △,
  Germany .... 25 F4 49 28N 9 7 E
Necochea, Argentina . 126 D4 38 30 S 58 50W
Neda, Spain 36 B2 43 30N 8 9W
Nedelino, Bulgaria ... 45 E9 41 27N 25 2 E
Nedelišće, Croatia ... 41 B13 46 23N 16 22 E
Nédha →, Greece .... 46 D3 37 25N 21 45 E
Nedoboyivtsi, Ukraine 29 B11 48 26N 26 21 E
Needles, Canada 102 D5 49 53N 118 7W
Needles, U.S.A. 111 L12 34 51N 114 37W
Needles, The, U.K. .. 15 G6 50 39N 1 35W
Neembucú □, Paraguay 126 B4 27 0 S 58 0W
Neemuch = Nimach,
  India .... 68 G6 24 30N 74 56 E
Neenah, U.S.A. 114 C1 44 11N 88 28W
Neepawa, Canada ... 103 C9 50 15N 99 30W
Neftçala, Azerbaijan . 71 B6 39 19N 49 12 E
Neftegorsk, Russia .. 35 H4 44 25N 39 45 E
Neftekumsk, Russia .. 35 H7 44 46N 44 50 E

Nefyn, U.K. 14 E3 52 56N 4 31W
Négala, Mali 82 C3 12 52N 8 30W
Negapatam =
  Nagappattinam, India 66 P11 10 46N 79 51 E
Negara, Indonesia ... 63 J17 8 22 S 114 37 E
Negaunee, U.S.A. ... 114 B2 46 30N 87 36W
Negele, Ethiopia .... 81 F4 5 20N 39 36 E
Negev Desert =
  Hanegev, Israel .... 74 E4 30 50N 35 0 E
Negoiul, Vf., Romania 29 E9 45 38N 24 35 E
Negombo, Sri Lanka . 66 R11 7 12N 79 50 E
Negotin, Serbia & M. . 44 B6 44 16N 22 37 E
Negotino, Macedonia . 44 E6 41 29N 22 7 E
Negra, Peña, Spain .. 36 C4 42 11N 6 30W
Negra, Pta., Peru .... 124 E2 6 6 S 81 10W
Negrais, C. = Maudin
  Sun, Burma ...... 67 M19 16 0N 94 30 E
Negreşti, Romania ... 29 D12 46 50N 27 30 E
Negreşti-Oaş, Romania 29 C8 47 52N 23 26 E
Negril, Jamaica ..... 120 a 18 22N 78 20W
Negro →, Argentina .. 128 E4 41 2 S 62 47W
Negro →, Brazil ..... 124 D7 3 0 S 60 0W
Negro →, Uruguay ... 127 C4 33 24 S 58 22W
Negros, Phil. ...... 61 G5 9 30N 122 40 E
Negru Vodă, Romania 29 G13 43 47N 28 21 E
Neguac, Canada 105 C6 47 15N 65 5W
Nehalem →, U.S.A. .. 110 E3 45 40N 123 56W
Nehãvand, Iran ..... 71 C6 35 56N 49 31 E
Nehbandãn, Iran .... 71 D9 31 35N 60 5 E
Nehoiu, Romania ... 29 E11 45 24N 26 20 E
Nei Monggol Zizhiqu □,
  China .... 56 D7 42 0N 112 0 E
Neijiang, China ..... 58 C5 29 35N 104 55 E
Neillsville, U.S.A. ... 112 C9 44 34N 90 36W
Neilton, U.S.A. 108 C2 47 25N 123 53W
Neiqiu, China ...... 56 F8 37 15N 114 30 E
Neiva, Colombia 124 C3 2 56N 75 18W
Neixiang, China ..... 56 H6 33 10N 111 52 E
Nejanilini L., Canada 103 B9 59 33N 97 48W
Nejd = Najd, Si. Arabia 75 B3 26 30N 42 0 E
Nejo, Ethiopia ...... 81 F4 9 30N 35 28 E
Nekã, Iran .... 71 B7 36 39N 53 19 E
Nekemte, Ethiopia ... 81 F4 9 4N 36 30 E
Nekheb, Egypt ...... 80 B3 25 10N 32 48 E
Neksø, Denmark .... 11 J9 55 4N 15 8 E
Nelas, Portugal 36 E3 40 32N 7 52W
Nelia, Australia ..... 94 C3 20 39 S 142 12 E
Nelidovo, Russia .... 32 D7 56 13N 32 49 E
Neligh, U.S.A. 112 D5 42 8N 98 2W
Nelkan, Russia ..... 53 D14 57 40N 136 4 E
Nellore, India ...... 66 M11 14 27N 79 59 E
Nelson, Canada 102 D5 49 30N 117 20W
Nelson, N.Z. .... 91 J4 41 18 S 173 16 E
Nelson, U.K. 14 D5 53 50N 2 13W
Nelson, Ariz., U.S.A. 109 J7 35 31N 113 19W
Nelson, Nev., U.S.A. 111 K12 35 42N 114 50W
Nelson →, Canada ... 103 C9 54 33N 98 2W
Nelson, C., Australia . 95 F3 38 26 S 141 32 E
Nelson, Estrecho, Chile 128 G2 51 30 S 75 0W
Nelson Forks, Canada 102 B4 59 30N 124 0W
Nelson House, Canada 103 B9 55 47N 98 51W
Nelson L., Canada ... 103 B8 55 48N 100 7W
Nelson Lakes △, N.Z. 91 J4 41 55 S 172 44 E
Nelspoort, S. Africa .. 88 E3 32 7 S 23 0 E
Nelspruit, S. Africa .. 89 D5 25 29 S 30 59 E
Néma, Mauritania ... 82 B3 16 40N 7 15W
Neman = Nemunas →,
  Lithuania .... 9 J19 55 25N 21 10 E
Neman, Russia ...... 9 J20 55 2N 22 2 E
Neméa, Greece ..... 46 D4 37 49N 22 40 E
Nemeiben L., Canada 103 B7 55 20N 105 20W
Nemerçkë, Mal., Albania 44 F4 40 15N 20 15 E
Nemira, Vf., Romania 29 D11 46 17N 26 19 E
Nemiscau, Canada .. 104 B4 51 18N 76 54W
Nemiscau, L., Canada 104 B4 51 25N 76 40W
Nemours, France .... 19 D9 48 16N 2 40 E
Nemšová, Slovak Rep. 27 C11 48 58N 18 7 E
Nemunas →, Lithuania 9 J19 55 25N 21 10 E
Nemuro, Japan ...... 54 C12 43 20N 145 35 E
Nemuro-Kaikyō, Japan 54 C12 43 30N 145 30 E
Nemyriv, Ukraine ... 31 H10 50 7N 23 27 E
Nen Jiang →, China . 57 B13 45 28N 124 30 E
Nenagh, Ireland 12 D3 52 52N 8 11W
Nenasi, Malaysia .... 65 L4 3 9N 103 23 E
Nene →, U.K. ...... 15 E8 52 49N 0 11 E
Nénita, Greece ..... 47 C8 38 14N 26 6 E
Nenjiang, China .... 60 B7 49 10N 125 10 E
Neno, Malawi ...... 87 F3 15 25 S 34 40 E
Neodesha, U.S.A. ... 113 G7 37 25N 95 41W
Neokhórion,
  Aitolía kai Akarnanía,
  Greece .... 46 C3 38 25N 21 17 E
Neokhórion, Árta,
  Greece .... 46 B2 39 4N 21 0 E
Néon Karlovásion,
  Greece .... 47 D8 37 45N 26 42 E
Néon Petrítsi, Greece 44 E7 41 16N 23 15 E
Neosho, U.S.A. 113 G7 36 52N 94 22W
Neosho →, U.S.A. ... 113 H7 36 48N 95 18W
Nepal ■, Asia ...... 69 F11 28 0N 84 30 E
Nepalganj, Nepal .... 69 E9 28 5N 81 40 E
Nepalganj Road, India 69 E9 28 1N 81 41 E
Nephi, U.S.A. 108 G8 39 43N 111 50W
Nephin, Ireland 12 B2 54 1N 9 22W
Nepi, Italy .... 41 F9 42 14N 12 21 E
Nepomuk, Czech Rep. 26 B6 49 29N 13 35 E
Neptune, U.S.A. 117 F10 40 13N 74 2W
Nera →, Italy ...... 41 F9 42 26N 12 24 E
Nera →, Romania ... 28 F6 44 48N 21 25 E
Nérac, France ...... 20 D4 44 8N 0 21 E
Nerang, Australia ... 95 D5 27 58 S 153 20 E
Neratovice, Czech Rep. 26 A7 50 16N 14 31 E
Nerchinsk, Russia ... 53 D12 52 0N 116 39 E
Nereju, Romania .... 29 E11 45 43N 26 43 E
Nerekhta, Russia ... 32 D11 57 26N 40 38 E
Neretsytsa, Ukraine . 29 B8 48 7N 23 46 E
Néret, L., Canada ... 105 B5 54 45N 70 44W
Neretvanski Kanal,
  Croatia .... 41 E14 43 7N 17 10 E
Neringa, Lithuania .. 9 J19 55 20N 21 5 E
Neris →, Lithuania .. 9 J21 55 8N 24 16 E
Nerja, Spain 37 J7 36 43N 3 55W
Nerl →, Russia ..... 32 D11 56 11N 40 34 E
Nerpio, Spain 39 G2 38 11N 2 16W
Nerva, Spain 37 H4 37 42N 6 30W
Nervi, Italy .... 40 D6 44 23N 9 2 E
Neryungri, Russia ... 53 D13 57 38N 124 28 E
Nescopeck, U.S.A. .. 117 E8 41 3N 76 12W
Nesebŭr, Bulgaria ... 45 D11 42 41N 27 46 E
Ness, L., U.K. 13 D4 57 15N 4 32W
Ness City, U.S.A. ... 112 F5 38 27N 99 54W
Nesterov, Russia .... 30 D9 54 38N 22 41 E
Nesterov, Ukraine ... 33 G2 50 4N 23 58 E
Nestórion, Greece ... 44 F5 40 24N 21 5 E
Néstos →, Greece ... 45 E8 41 20N 24 35 E
Nesvady, Slovak Rep. 27 D11 47 56N 18 7 E
Nesvizh = Nyasvizh,
  Belarus .... 33 F4 53 14N 26 38 E

Netanya, Israel ..... 74 C3 32 20N 34 51 E
Netarhat, India ..... 69 H11 23 29N 84 16 E
Nete →, Belgium .... 17 C4 51 7N 4 14 E
Netherdale, Australia 94 K6 21 10 S 148 33 E
Netherlands ■, Europe 17 C5 52 0N 5 30 E
Netherlands Antilles ☑,
  W. Indies 124 A5 12 15N 69 0W
Neto →, Italy ...... 43 C10 39 12N 17 9 E
Netrang, India ...... 68 J5 21 39N 73 21 E
Nettancourt, France . 19 D11 48 51N 4 57 E
Nettetal, Germany .. 24 D2 51 19N 6 12 E
Nettilling L., Canada 101 B12 66 30N 71 0W
Nettuno, Italy ..... 42 A5 41 27N 12 39 E
Netzahualcoyotl, Presa,
  Mexico 119 D6 17 10N 93 30W
Neu-Isenburg, Germany 25 E4 50 3N 8 42 E
Neu-Ulm, Germany .. 25 G6 48 22N 10 0 E
Neubrandenburg,
  Germany .... 24 B9 53 33N 13 15 E
Neubukow, Germany 24 A8 54 2N 11 39 E
Neuburg, Germany .. 25 G7 48 44N 11 11 E
Neuchâtel, Switz. ... 25 J2 47 0N 6 55 E
Neuchâtel □, Switz. . 25 J2 47 0N 6 55 E
Neuchâtel, Lac de,
  Switz. .... 25 J2 46 53N 6 50 E
Neudau, Austria .... 26 D9 47 11N 16 6 E
Neuenhagen, Germany 24 C9 52 30N 13 38 E
Neuenhaus, Germany 24 C2 52 30N 6 58 E
Neuf-Brisach, France 19 D14 48 1N 7 30 E
Neufahrn, Bayern,
  Germany .... 25 G8 48 41N 12 11 E
Neufahrn, Bayern,
  Germany .... 25 G7 48 18N 11 40 E
Neufchâteau, Belgium 17 E5 49 50N 5 25 E
Neufchâteau, France . 19 D12 48 21N 5 40 E
Neufchâtel-en-Bray,
  France .... 18 C8 49 44N 1 26 E
Neufchâtel-sur-Aisne,
  France .... 19 C11 49 26N 4 1 E
Neuhaus, Germany .. 24 B6 53 17N 10 56 E
Neuillé-Pont-Pierre,
  France .... 18 E7 47 33N 0 33 E
Neuilly-St-Front, France 19 C10 49 10N 3 15 E
Neukalen, Germany . 24 B8 53 49N 12 46 E
Neumarkt, Germany . 25 F7 49 16N 11 27 E
Neumünster, Germany 24 A5 54 4N 9 58 E
Neung-sur-Beuvron,
  France .... 19 E8 47 30N 1 50 E
Neunkirchen, Austria 26 D9 47 43N 16 4 E
Neunkirchen, Germany 25 F3 49 20N 7 9 E
Neuquén, Argentina . 128 D3 38 55 S 68 0W
Neuquén □, Argentina 126 D2 38 0 S 69 50W
Neuruppin, Germany 24 C8 52 55N 12 48 E
Neusäss, Germany .. 25 G6 48 24N 10 50 E
Neuse →, U.S.A. ... 115 H7 35 6N 76 29W
Neusiedl, Austria ... 27 D9 47 57N 16 50 E
Neusiedler See, Austria 27 D9 47 50N 16 47 E
Neusiedler See-
  Seewinkel △, Austria 27 D9 47 50N 16 45 E
Neuss, Germany .... 24 D2 51 11N 6 42 E
Neussargues-Moissac,
  France .... 20 C7 45 9N 3 0 E
Neustadt, Bayern,
  Germany .... 25 F8 49 44N 12 10 E
Neustadt, Bayern,
  Germany .... 25 G7 48 48N 11 46 E
Neustadt, Bayern,
  Germany .... 25 F6 49 34N 10 37 E
Neustadt, Bayern,
  Germany .... 25 F5 50 19N 11 7 E
Neustadt, Brandenburg,
  Germany .... 24 C8 52 50N 12 27 E
Neustadt, Hessen,
  Germany .... 24 E5 50 51N 9 9 E
Neustadt, Niedersachsen,
  Germany .... 24 C5 52 30N 9 30 E
Neustadt, Rhld-Pfz.,
  Germany .... 25 F4 49 21N 8 10 E
Neustadt, Sachsen,
  Germany .... 24 D10 51 2N 14 12 E
Neustadt,
  Schleswig-Holstein,
  Germany .... 24 A6 54 6N 10 49 E
Neustadt, Thüringen,
  Germany .... 24 E7 50 45N 11 43 E
Neustrelitz, Germany 24 B9 53 21N 13 4 E
Neuvic, France ..... 20 C6 45 23N 2 16 E
Neuville-sur-Saône,
  France .... 21 C8 45 52N 4 51 E
Neuvy-le-Roi, France 18 E7 47 36N 0 36 E
Neuvy-St-Sépulchre,
  France .... 19 F8 46 35N 1 48 E
Neuvy-sur-Barangeon,
  France .... 19 E9 47 20N 2 15 E
Neuwerk, Germany .. 24 B4 53 55N 8 30 E
Neuwied, Germany .. 24 E3 50 26N 7 29 E
Neva →, Russia ..... 32 C6 59 50N 30 30 E
Nevada, Iowa, U.S.A. 112 D8 42 1N 93 27W
Nevada, Mo., U.S.A. 113 G7 37 51N 94 22W
Nevada □, U.S.A. ... 108 G5 39 0N 117 0W
Nevada City, U.S.A. 110 F6 39 16N 121 1W
Nevado, Cerro,
  Argentina .... 126 D2 35 30 S 68 32W
Nevado de Colima =
  Volcán de Colima △,
  Mexico 118 D4 19 30N 103 40W
Nevado de Tres
  Cruces △, Chile ... 126 B2 27 13 S 69 5W
Nevel, Russia ...... 32 D5 56 0N 29 55 E
Nevers, France ..... 19 F10 47 0N 3 9 E
Nevertire, Australia . 95 E4 31 50 S 147 44 E
Nevesinje, Bos.-H. .. 44 C2 43 14N 18 6 E
Neville, Canada 103 D7 49 58N 107 39W
Nevinnomyssk, Russia 35 H6 44 40N 42 0 E
Nevis, St. Kitts & Nevis 121 C7 17 0N 62 30W
Nevrokop = Gotse
  Delchev, Bulgaria .. 44 E7 41 36N 23 46 E
Nevşehir, Turkey ... 70 B2 38 33N 34 40 E
Nevskoye, Russia ... 30 D9 54 32N 22 39 E
New →, U.S.A. 114 F5 38 10N 81 12W
New Aiyansh, Canada 102 B3 55 12N 129 4W
New Albany, Ind.,
  U.S.A. 114 F3 38 18N 85 49W
New Albany, Miss.,
  U.S.A. 113 H10 34 29N 89 0W
New Albany, Pa., U.S.A. 117 E8 41 36N 76 27W
New Amsterdam,
  Guyana 124 B7 6 15N 57 36W
New Angledool,
  Australia .... 95 D4 29 5 S 147 55 E
New Baltimore, U.S.A. 116 D2 42 41N 82 44W
New Bedford, U.S.A. 117 E14 41 38N 70 56W
New Berlin, N.Y., U.S.A. 117 D9 42 37N 75 20W
New Berlin, Pa., U.S.A. 116 F8 40 50N 76 57W
New Bern, U.S.A. ... 115 H7 35 7N 77 3W
New Bethlehem, U.S.A. 116 F5 41 0N 79 20W
New Bloomfield, U.S.A. 116 F7 40 25N 77 11W

New Boston, U.S.A. .. 113 J7 33 28N 94 25W
New Braunfels, U.S.A. 113 L5 29 42N 98 8W
New Brighton, N.Z. .. 91 K4 43 29 S 172 43 E
New Brighton, U.S.A. 116 F4 40 42N 80 19W
New Britain,
  Papua N. G. ...... 96 H7 5 50 S 150 20 E
New Britain, U.S.A. . 117 E12 41 40N 72 47W
New Brunswick, U.S.A. 117 F10 40 30N 74 27W
New Brunswick □,
  Canada 105 C6 46 50N 66 30W
New Bussa, Nigeria .. 83 D5 9 53N 4 31 E
New Caledonia ☑,
  Pac. Oc. .... 96 K8 21 0 S 165 0 E
New Castile = Castilla-
  La Mancha □, Spain 6 H5 39 30N 3 30W
New Castle, Ind., U.S.A. 114 F3 39 55N 85 22W
New Castle, Pa., U.S.A. 116 F4 41 0N 80 21W
New City, U.S.A. ... 117 E11 41 9N 73 59W
New Concord, U.S.A. 116 G3 39 59N 81 54W
New Cumberland,
  U.S.A. 116 F4 40 30N 80 36W
New Cuyama, U.S.A. 111 L7 34 57N 119 38W
New Delhi, India ... 68 E7 28 37N 77 13 E
New Denver, Canada 102 D5 50 0N 117 25W
New Don Pedro
  Reservoir, U.S.A. .. 110 H6 37 43N 120 24W
New England, U.S.A. 107 B12 43 0N 71 0W
New England, N. Dak.,
  U.S.A. 112 B3 46 32N 102 52W
New England Ra.,
  Australia .... 95 E5 30 20 S 151 45 E
New Forest, U.K. ... 15 G6 50 53N 1 34W
New Galloway, U.K. . 13 F4 55 5N 4 9W
New Glasgow, Canada 105 C7 45 35N 62 36W
New Guinea, Oceania 96 H5 4 0 S 136 0 E
New Hamburg, Canada 116 C4 43 23N 80 42W
New Hampshire □,
  U.S.A. 117 C13 44 0N 71 30W
New Hampton, U.S.A. 112 D8 43 3N 92 19W
New Hanover, S. Africa 89 D5 29 22 S 30 31 E
New Hartford, U.S.A. 117 C9 43 4N 75 18W
New Haven, Conn.,
  U.S.A. 117 E12 41 18N 72 55W
New Haven, Mich.,
  U.S.A. 116 D2 42 44N 82 48W
New Hazelton, Canada 102 B3 55 20N 127 30W
New Hebrides =
  Vanuatu ■, Pac. Oc. 96 J8 15 0 S 168 0 E
New Holland, U.S.A. 117 F8 40 6N 76 5W
New Iberia, U.S.A. .. 113 K9 30 1N 91 49W
New Ireland,
  Papua N. G. ...... 96 H7 3 20 S 151 50 E
New Jersey □, U.S.A. 114 E8 40 0N 74 30W
New Kensington, U.S.A. 116 F5 40 34N 79 46W
New Lexington, U.S.A. 114 G4 39 43N 82 13W
New Liskeard, Canada 104 C4 47 31N 79 41W
New London, Conn.,
  U.S.A. 117 E12 41 22N 72 6W
New London, Ohio,
  U.S.A. 116 E2 41 5N 82 24W
New London, Wis.,
  U.S.A. 112 C10 44 23N 88 45W
New Madrid, U.S.A. 113 G10 36 36N 89 32W
New Martinsville, U.S.A. 114 F5 39 39N 80 52W
New Meadows, U.S.A. 108 D5 44 58N 116 18W
New Melones L., U.S.A. 110 H6 37 57N 120 31W
New Mexico □, U.S.A. 109 J10 34 30N 106 0W
New Milford, Conn.,
  U.S.A. 117 E11 41 35N 73 25W
New Milford, Pa., U.S.A. 117 E9 41 52N 75 44W
New Norcia, Australia 93 F2 30 57 S 116 13 E
New Norfolk, Australia 94 G4 42 46 S 147 2 E
New Orleans, U.S.A. 113 L9 29 58N 90 4W
New Philadelphia,
  U.S.A. 116 F3 40 30N 81 27W
New Plymouth, N.Z. 91 H5 39 4 S 174 5 E
New Plymouth, U.S.A. 108 E5 43 58N 116 49W
New Port Richey, U.S.A. 115 L4 28 16N 82 43W
New Providence,
  Bahamas 120 A4 25 25N 78 35W
New Quay, U.K. 15 E3 52 13N 4 21W
New Radnor, U.K. .. 15 E4 52 15N 3 9W
New Richmond, Canada 105 C6 48 15N 65 45W
New Richmond, U.S.A. 112 C8 45 7N 92 32W
New River Gorge △,
  U.S.A. 114 G5 37 53N 81 5W
New Roads, U.S.A. . 113 K9 30 42N 91 26W
New Rochelle, U.S.A. 117 F11 40 55N 73 47W
New Rockford, U.S.A. 112 B5 47 41N 99 8W
New Romney, U.K. . 15 G8 50 59N 0 57 E
New Ross, Ireland .. 12 D5 52 23N 6 57W
New Salem, U.S.A. .. 112 B4 46 51N 101 25W
New Scone = Scone,
  U.K. 13 E5 56 25N 3 24W
New Siberian I. =
  Novaya Sibir, Ostrov,
  Russia .... 53 B16 75 10N 150 0 E
New Siberian Is. =
  Novosibirskiye
  Ostrova, Russia .... 53 B15 75 0N 142 0 E
New Smyrna Beach,
  U.S.A. 115 L5 29 1N 80 56W
New South Wales □,
  Australia .... 95 E4 33 0 S 146 0 E
New Tecumseth, Canada 116 B5 44 9N 79 52W
New Town, U.S.A. ... 112 B3 47 59N 102 30W
New Tredegar, U.K. . 15 F4 51 44N 3 16W
New Ulm, U.S.A. ... 112 C7 44 19N 94 28W
New Waterford, Canada 105 C7 46 13N 60 4W
New-Wes-Valley,
  Canada 105 C9 49 8N 53 36W
New Westminster,
  Canada 110 A4 49 13N 122 55W
New York, U.S.A. ... 117 F11 40 45N 74 0W
New York □, U.S.A. 117 D9 43 0N 75 0W
New York J.F. Kennedy
  International ✈ (JFK), 117 F11 40 38N 73 47W
New York Mts., U.S.A. 109 J6 35 0N 115 20W
New Zealand ■,
  Oceania .... 91 J6 40 0 S 176 0 E
Newaj →, India ..... 68 G7 24 24N 76 49 E
Newala, Tanzania ... 87 E4 10 58 S 39 18 E
Newark, Del., U.S.A. 114 F8 39 41N 75 46W
Newark, N.J., U.S.A. 117 F10 40 44N 74 10W
Newark, N.Y., U.S.A. 116 C7 43 3N 77 6W
Newark, Ohio, U.S.A. 116 F2 40 3N 82 24W
Newark International ✈
  (EWR), U.S.A. 117 F10 40 42N 74 10W
Newark-on-Trent, U.K. 14 D7 53 5N 0 48W
Newark Valley, U.S.A. 117 D8 42 14N 76 11W
Newberg, U.S.A. 108 D2 45 18N 122 58W
Newberry, Mich., U.S.A. 113 B3 46 21N 85 30W
Newberry, S.C., U.S.A. 115 H5 34 17N 81 37W
Newberry Springs,
  U.S.A. 111 L10 34 50N 116 41W

Newboro L., Canada 117 B8 44 38N 76 20W
Newbridge = Droichead
  Nua, Ireland 12 C5 53 11N 6 48W
Newburgh, Canada .. 117 B8 44 19N 76 52W
Newburgh, U.S.A. ... 117 E10 41 30N 74 1W
Newbury, U.K. 15 F6 51 24N 1 20W
Newbury, N.H., U.S.A. 117 C12 43 19N 72 3W
Newbury, Vt., U.S.A. 117 B12 44 5N 72 4W
Newburyport, U.S.A. 117 D14 42 49N 70 53W
Newcastle, Australia . 95 E5 33 0 S 151 46 E
Newcastle, Canada .. 105 C6 47 1N 65 38W
Newcastle, Ont., Canada 104 D4 43 55N 78 35W
Newcastle, S. Africa . 89 D4 27 45 S 29 58 E
Newcastle, U.K. 12 B6 54 13N 5 54W
Newcastle, Calif., U.S.A. 110 G5 38 53N 121 8W
Newcastle, Wyo., U.S.A. 112 D2 43 50N 104 11W
Newcastle Emlyn, U.K. 15 E3 52 2N 4 28W
Newcastle Ra., Australia 92 C5 15 45 S 130 15 E
Newcastle-under-Lyme,
  U.K. 14 D5 53 1N 2 14W
Newcastle-upon-Tyne,
  U.K. 14 C6 54 58N 1 36W
Newcastle Waters,
  Australia .... 94 B1 17 30 S 133 28 E
Newcastle West, Ireland 12 D2 52 27N 9 3W
Newcomb, U.S.A. ... 117 C10 43 58N 74 10W
Newcomerstown, U.S.A. 116 F3 40 16N 81 36W
Newdegate, Australia 93 F2 33 6 S 119 0 E
Newell, Australia ... 94 B4 16 20 S 145 16 E
Newell, U.S.A. 112 C3 44 43N 103 25W
Newfane, U.S.A. 116 C6 43 17N 78 43W
Newfield, U.S.A. 117 D8 42 18N 76 33W
Newfound L., U.S.A. 117 C13 43 40N 71 47W
Newfoundland, Canada 105 C8 49 0N 55 0W
Newfoundland &
  Labrador □, Canada 105 B8 53 0N 58 0W
Newhall, U.S.A. 111 L8 34 23N 118 32W
Newhaven, U.K. .... 15 G8 50 47N 0 3 E
Newkirk, U.S.A. 113 G6 36 53N 97 3W
Newlyn, U.K. 15 G2 50 6N 5 34W
Newman, Australia .. 92 D2 23 18 S 119 45 E
Newman, U.S.A. 110 H5 37 19N 121 1W
Newmarket, Ireland . 12 D2 52 13N 9 0W
Newmarket, Canada . 116 B5 44 3N 79 28W
Newmarket, U.K. ... 15 E8 52 15N 0 25 E
Newmarket, U.S.A. . 117 C14 43 4N 70 56W
Newnan, U.S.A. 115 J3 33 23N 84 48W
Newport, Ireland ... 12 C2 53 53N 9 33W
Newport, Newp., U.K. 15 F5 51 35N 3 0W
Newport, Ark., U.S.A. 113 H9 35 37N 91 16W
Newport, Ky., U.S.A. 114 F3 39 5N 84 30W
Newport, N.H., U.S.A. 117 C12 43 22N 72 10W
Newport, N.Y., U.S.A. 117 C9 43 11N 75 1W
Newport, Oreg., U.S.A. 108 D1 44 39N 124 3W
Newport, Pa., U.S.A. 116 F7 40 29N 77 8W
Newport, R.I., U.S.A. 117 E13 41 29N 71 19W
Newport, Tenn., U.S.A. 115 H4 35 58N 83 11W
Newport, Vt., U.S.A. 117 B12 44 56N 72 13W
Newport, Wash., U.S.A. 108 B5 48 11N 117 3W
Newport □, U.K. ... 15 F4 51 33N 3 1W
Newport Beach, U.S.A. 111 M9 33 37N 117 56W
Newport News, U.S.A. 114 G7 36 59N 76 25W
Newport Pagnell, U.K. 15 E7 52 5N 0 43W
Newquay, U.K. 15 G2 50 25N 5 6W
Newry, U.K. 12 B5 54 11N 6 21W
Newton, Ill., U.S.A. . 112 F10 38 59N 88 10W
Newton, Iowa, U.S.A. 112 E8 41 42N 93 3W
Newton, Kans., U.S.A. 113 F6 38 3N 97 21W
Newton, Mass., U.S.A. 117 D13 42 21N 71 12W
Newton, Miss., U.S.A. 113 J10 32 19N 89 10W
Newton, N.C., U.S.A. 115 H5 35 40N 81 13W
Newton, N.J., U.S.A. 117 E10 41 3N 74 45W
Newton, Tex., U.S.A. 113 K8 30 51N 93 46W
Newton Abbot, U.K. 15 G4 50 32N 3 37W
Newton Aycliffe, U.K. 14 C6 54 37N 1 34W
Newton Falls, U.S.A. 116 E4 41 11N 80 59W
Newton Stewart, U.K. 13 G4 54 57N 4 30W
Newtonmore, U.K. .. 13 D4 57 4N 4 8W
Newtown, U.K. 15 E4 52 31N 3 19W
Newtownabbey, U.K. 12 B6 54 40N 5 56W
Newtownards, U.K. .. 12 B6 54 36N 5 42W
Newtownbarry =
  Bunclody, Ireland .. 12 D5 52 39N 6 40W
Newtownstewart, U.K. 12 B4 54 43N 7 23W
Newville, U.S.A. 116 F7 40 10N 77 24W
Nexon, France ...... 20 C5 45 41N 1 11 E
Neya, Russia ...... 34 A6 58 21N 43 49 E
Neyrīz, Iran .... 71 D7 29 15N 54 19 E
Neyshābūr, Iran .... 71 B8 36 10N 58 50 E
Nezhin = Nizhyn,
  Ukraine .... 33 G6 51 5N 31 55 E
Nezperce, U.S.A. ... 108 C5 46 14N 116 14W
Nezvysko, Ukraine .. 29 B10 48 46N 25 15 E
Ngabang, Indonesia . 62 D3 0 23N 109 55 E
Ngabordamlu, Tanjung,
  Indonesia .... 63 F8 6 56 S 134 11 E
N'Gage, Angola .... 84 F3 7 46 S 15 16 E
Ngala, Nigeria ..... 83 C7 12 20N 14 11 E
Ngambé, Centre,
  Cameroon .... 83 D7 5 48N 11 29 E
Ngambé, Littoral,
  Cameroon .... 83 E7 4 21N 10 40 E
Ngami Depression,
  Botswana .... 88 C3 20 30 S 22 46 E
Ngamo, Zimbabwe .. 87 F2 19 3 S 27 32 E
Ngangala, Sudan ... 81 G3 4 42N 31 55 E
Nganglong Kangri,
  China .... 67 C12 33 0N 81 0 E
Ngao, Thailand ..... 64 C2 18 46N 99 59 E
Ngaoundéré, Cameroon 84 C2 7 15N 13 35 E
Ngapara, N.Z. ...... 91 L3 44 57 S 170 46 E
Ngara, Tanzania .... 86 C3 2 29 S 30 40 E
Ngawi, Indonesia ... 63 G14 7 24 S 111 26 E
Nghia Lo, Vietnam .. 58 G5 21 33N 104 28 E
Ngoboli, Sudan ..... 81 G3 4 57N 32 37 E
Ngoma, Malawi ..... 87 E3 13 8 S 33 45 E
Ngomahura, Zimbabwe 87 G3 20 26 S 30 43 E
Ngomba, Tanzania .. 87 D3 8 20 S 32 53 E
Ngoring Hu, China .. 60 C4 34 55N 97 5 E
Ngorkou, Mali 82 B4 15 40N 3 41W
Ngorongoro, Tanzania 86 C4 3 11 S 35 32 E
Ngorongoro △,
  Tanzania .... 86 C4 3 40 S 35 30 E
Ngozi, Burundi ..... 86 C2 2 54 S 29 50 E
Ngudu, Tanzania ... 86 C3 2 58 S 33 25 E
Nguigmi, Niger ..... 79 F8 14 20N 13 20 E
Nguila, Cameroon ... 83 E7 4 41N 11 43 E
Nguiu, Australia .... 92 B5 11 46 S 130 38 E
Ngukurr, Australia .. 94 A1 14 44 S 134 44 E
Ngunga, Tanzania ... 86 D3 3 37 S 33 37 E
Nguru, Nigeria ..... 83 C7 12 56N 10 29 E
Nguru Mts., Tanzania 86 D4 6 0 S 37 30 E
Ngusi, Malawi ...... 87 E3 14 0 S 34 50 E
Nguyen Binh, Vietnam 58 F5 22 39N 105 56 E

Nha Trang, *Vietnam* ... **65 F7** 12 16N 109 10 E
Nhacoongo, *Mozam.* .... **89 C6** 24 18 S 35 14 E
Nhamaabué, *Mozam.* ... **87 F4** 17 25 S 35 5 E
Nhangulaze, L., *Mozam.* **89 C5** 24 0 S 34 30 E
Nhill, *Australia* .... **95 F3** 36 18 S 141 40 E
Nho Quan, *Vietnam* ... **58 G5** 20 18N 105 45 E
Nhulunbuy, *Australia* .. **94 A2** 12 10 S 137 20 E
Nia-nia, *Dem. Rep. of*
  the Congo .... **86 B2** 1 30N 27 40 E
Niafounké, *Mali* **82 B4** 16 0N 4 5W
Niagara Falls, *Canada* . **116 C5** 43 7N 79 5W
Niagara Falls, *U.S.A.* .. **116 C6** 43 5N 79 4W
Niagara-on-the-Lake,
  Canada **116 C5** 43 15N 79 4W
Niah, *Malaysia* .... **62 D4** 3 58N 113 46 E
Niamey, *Niger* .... **83 C5** 13 27N 2 6 E
Niandan-Koro, *Guinea* . **82 C3** 11 5N 9 15W
Nianforando, *Guinea* .. **82 D2** 9 37N 10 36W
Niangara, *Dem. Rep. of*
  the Congo .... **86 B2** 3 42N 27 50 E
Niangbo, *Ivory C.* **82 D3** 8 49N 5 10W
Niangoloko,
  Burkina Faso **82 C4** 10 15N 4 55W
Niantic, *U.S.A.* **117 E12** 41 20N 72 11W
Niaro, *Sudan* .... **81 E3** 10 38N 31 31 E
Nias, *Indonesia* ...... **62 D1** 1 0N 97 30 E
Niassa △, *Mozam.* .... **87 E4** 12 4S 36 57 E
Niassa □, *Mozam.* .... **87 E4** 13 30 S 36 0 E
Nibāk, *Si. Arabia* .... **71 E7** 24 25N 50 50 E
Nibe, *Denmark* .... **11 H3** 56 59N 9 38 E
Nicaragua ■,
  Cent. Amer. **120 D2** 11 40N 85 30W
Nicaragua, L. de, *Nic.* . **120 D2** 12 0N 85 30W
Nicastro, *Italy* .... **43 D9** 38 59N 16 19 E
Nice, *France* .... **21 E11** 43 42N 7 14 E
Nice ✈ (NCE), *France* . **21 E11** 43 41N 7 12 E
Niceville, *U.S.A.* **115 K2** 30 31N 86 30W
Nichicun, L., *Canada* . **105 B5** 53 5N 71 0W
Nichinan, *Japan* ..... **55 J5** 31 38N 131 23 E
Nicholas Channel,
  W. Indies **120 B3** 23 30N 80 5W
Nicholasville, *U.S.A.* .. **114 G3** 37 53N 84 34W
Nichols, *U.S.A.* **117 D8** 42 1N 76 22W
Nicholson, *Australia* .. **92 C4** 18 2S 128 54 E
Nicholson, *U.S.A.* **117 E9** 41 37N 75 47W
Nicholson →, *Australia* **94 B2** 17 31 S 139 36 E
Nicholson L., *Canada* . **103 A8** 62 40N 102 40W
Nicholson Ra., *Australia* **93 E2** 27 15 S 116 45 E
Nicholville, *U.S.A.* ... **117 B10** 44 41N 74 39W
Nicobar Is., *Ind. Oc.* .. **50 J13** 8 0N 93 30 E
Nicola, *Canada* **102 C4** 50 12N 120 40W
Nicolls Town, *Bahamas* **120 A4** 25 8N 78 0W
Nicopolis, *Greece* .... **46 B2** 39 5N 20 43 E
Nicosia, *Cyprus* ..... **49 D12** 35 10N 33 25 E
Nicosia, *Italy* .... **43 E7** 37 45N 14 24 E
Nicótera, *Italy* ...... **43 D8** 38 33N 15 56 E
Nicoya, *Costa Rica* ... **120 D2** 10 9N 85 27W
Nicoya, G. de,
  Costa Rica **120 E3** 10 0N 85 0W
Nicoya, Pen. de,
  Costa Rica **120 E2** 9 45N 85 40W
Nida, *Lithuania* ...... **30 C8** 55 20N 21 4 E
Nidd →, *U.K.* **14 D6** 53 59N 1 23W
Nidda, *Germany* ..... **25 E5** 50 23N 9 1 E
Nidda →, *Germany* ... **25 E4** 50 17N 8 48 E
Nidwalden □, *Switz.* .. **25 J4** 46 50N 8 25 E
Nidzica, *Poland* ...... **31 E7** 53 25N 20 28 E
Niebüll, *Germany* .... **24 A4** 54 46N 8 48 E
Nied →, *Germany* .... **19 C13** 49 23N 6 40 E
Niederaula, *Germany* . **24 E5** 50 47N 9 36 E
Niederbayern □,
  Germany .... **25 G8** 48 40N 12 50 E
Niederbronn-les-Bains,
  France .... **19 D14** 48 57N 7 39 E
Niedere Tauern, *Austria* **26 D7** 47 20N 14 0 E
Niederlausitz, *Germany* **24 D9** 51 42N 13 59 E
Niederösterreich □,
  Austria .... **26 C8** 48 25N 15 40 E
Niedersachsen □,
  Germany .... **24 C4** 52 50N 9 0 E
Niedersächsisches
  Wattenmeer △,
  Germany .... **24 B3** 53 45N 7 30 E
Niekerkshoop, *S. Africa* **88 D3** 29 19 S 22 51 E
Niellé, *Ivory C.* **82 C3** 10 5N 5 38W
Niemba, *Dem. Rep. of*
  the Congo .... **86 D2** 5 58 S 28 24 E
Niemen = Nemunas →,
  Lithuania .... **9 J19** 55 25N 21 10 E
Niemodlin, *Poland* ... **31 H4** 50 38N 17 38 E
Nienburg, *Germany* ... **24 C5** 52 39N 9 13 E
Niepołomice, *Poland* .. **31 H7** 50 3N 20 13 E
Niers →, *Germany* ... **24 D1** 51 43N 5 57 E
Niesky, *Germany* ..... **24 D10** 51 17N 14 49 E
Nieszawa, *Poland* .... **31 F5** 52 52N 18 50 E
Nieu Bethesda, *S. Africa* **88 E3** 31 51 S 24 34 E
Nieuw Amsterdam,
  Suriname **125 B7** 5 53N 55 5W
Nieuw Nickerie,
  Suriname **125 B7** 6 0N 56 59W
Nieuwoudtville,
  S. Africa .... **88 E2** 31 23 S 19 7 E
Nieuwpoort, *Belgium* . **17 C2** 51 8N 2 45 E
Nieves, Pico de las,
  Canary Is. **48 G4** 27 57N 15 35W
Nièvre □, *France* ..... **19 E10** 47 10N 3 40 E
Niga, *Mali* **82 C3** 13 38N 5 27W
Niğde, *Turkey* .... **70 B2** 37 58N 34 40 E
Nigel, *S. Africa* ...... **89 D4** 26 27 S 28 25 E
Niger □, *Nigeria* ..... **83 D6** 10 0N 5 30 E
Niger ■, *W. Afr.* ..... **83 B7** 17 30N 10 0 E
Niger →, *W. Afr.* .... **83 D6** 5 33N 6 33 E
Niger Delta, *Nigeria* .. **83 E6** 4 25N 6 0 E
Nigeria ■, *W. Afr.* ... **83 D6** 8 30N 8 0 E
Nighasin, *India* ...... **69 E9** 28 14N 80 52 E
Nightcaps, *N.Z.* ..... **91 L2** 45 57 S 168 2 E
Nigríta, *Greece* ...... **44 F7** 40 56N 23 29 E
Nii-Jima, *Japan* ..... **55 G9** 34 20N 139 15 E
Niigata, *Japan* ...... **54 F9** 37 58N 139 0 E
Niigata □, *Japan* .... **55 F9** 37 15N 138 45 E
Niihama, *Japan* ..... **55 H6** 33 55N 133 16 E
Niihau, *U.S.A.* **106 H14** 21 54N 160 9W
Niimi, *Japan* .... **55 G6** 34 59N 133 28 E
Niitsu, *Japan* .... **54 F9** 37 48N 139 7 E
Nijar, *Spain* **39 J2** 36 53N 2 15W
Nijil, *Jordan* .... **74 E4** 30 32N 35 33 E
Nijkerk, *Neths.* ...... **17 B5** 52 13N 5 30 E
Nijmegen, *Neths.* .... **17 C5** 51 50N 5 52 E
Nijverdal, *Neths.* .... **17 B6** 52 22N 6 28 E
Nik Pey, *Iran* .... **71 B6** 36 50N 48 10 E
Nike, *Nigeria* .... **83 D6** 6 26N 7 29 E
Nikiniki, *Indonesia* .. **63 F6** 9 49 S 124 30 E
Nikiski, *U.S.A.* **100 B4** 60 41N 151 18W
Nikki, *Benin* .... **83 D5** 9 58N 3 12 E
Nikkō △, *Japan* ..... **55 F9** 36 45N 139 35 E

Nikkō △, *Japan* ...... **55 F9** 36 56N 139 37 E
Nikolayev = Mykolayiv,
  Ukraine .... **33 J7** 46 58N 32 0 E
Nikolayevsk, *Russia* .. **34 E7** 50 0N 45 35 E
Nikolayevsk-na-Amur,
  Russia .... **53 D15** 53 8N 140 44 E
Nikolsk, *Russia* ...... **34 D8** 53 49N 46 4 E
Nikolskoye, *Russia* ... **53 D17** 55 12N 166 0 E
Nikopol, *Bulgaria* .... **45 C8** 43 43N 24 54 E
Nikopol, *Ukraine* .... **33 J8** 47 35N 34 25 E
Niksar, *Turkey* ...... **72 B7** 40 31N 37 2 E
Nīkshahr, *Iran* ...... **71 E9** 26 15N 60 10 E
Nikšić, *Serbia & M.* .. **44 D2** 42 50N 18 57 E
Nîl, Nahr en →, *Africa* **80 H7** 30 10N 31 6 E
Nîl el Abyad →, *Sudan* **81 D3** 15 38N 32 31 E
Nîl el Azraq →, *Sudan* **81 D3** 15 38N 32 31 E
Niland, *U.S.A.* **111 M11** 33 14N 115 31W
Nile = Nîl, Nahr en →,
  Africa .... **80 H7** 30 10N 31 6 E
Nile Delta, *Egypt* .... **80 H7** 31 40N 31 0 E
Niles, *Mich., U.S.A.* .. **114 E2** 41 50N 86 15W
Niles, *Ohio, U.S.A.* ... **116 E4** 41 11N 80 46W
Nilüfer →, *Turkey* ... **45 F12** 40 18N 28 27 E
Nim Ka Thana, *India* . **68 F6** 27 44N 75 48 E
Nimach, *India* .... **68 G6** 24 30N 74 56 E
Nimbahera, *India* .... **68 G6** 24 37N 74 45 E
Nîmes, *France* .... **21 E8** 43 50N 4 23 E
Nimfaíon, Ákra =
  Pínnes, Ákra, *Greece* **45 F8** 40 5N 24 20 E
Nimmitabel, *Australia* . **95 F4** 36 29 S 149 15 E
Nimule, *Sudan* ...... **81 G3** 3 32N 32 3 E
Nimule □, *Sudan* .... **81 G3** 3 38N 32 2 E
Nin, *Croatia* .... **41 D12** 44 16N 15 12 E
Nīnawá, *Iraq* .... **70 B4** 36 25N 43 10 E
Nīnawá □, *Iraq* ..... **70 B4** 36 15N 43 0 E
Nindigully, *Australia* .. **95 D4** 28 21 S 148 50 E
Nineveh = Nīnawá, *Iraq* **70 B4** 36 25N 43 10 E
Ning Xian, *China* .... **56 G4** 35 30N 107 58 E
Ningaloo △, *Australia* . **92 D1** 22 23 S 113 32 E
Ning'an, *China* ...... **57 B15** 44 22N 129 20 E
Ningbo, *China* .... **59 C13** 29 51N 121 28 E
Ningcheng, *China* .... **57 D10** 41 32N 119 53 E
Ningde, *China* .... **59 D12** 26 38N 119 23 E
Ningdu, *China* .... **59 D10** 26 25N 115 59 E
Ninggang, *China* ..... **59 D9** 26 42N 113 55 E
Ningguo, *China* ...... **59 B12** 30 35N 119 0 E
Ninghai, *China* ...... **59 C13** 29 15N 121 27 E
Ninghua, *China* ...... **59 D11** 26 14N 116 45 E
Ningjin, *China* .... **56 F8** 37 35N 114 57 E
Ningjing Shan *China* .. **58 C2** 30 0N 98 20 E
Ninglang, *China* ..... **58 D3** 27 20N 100 55 E
Ningling, *China* ...... **56 G8** 34 25N 115 22 E
Ningming, *China* ..... **58 F6** 22 8N 107 4 E
Ningnan, *China* ...... **58 D4** 27 5N 102 36 E
Ningpo = Ningbo, *China* **59 C13** 29 51N 121 28 E
Ningqiang, *China* .... **56 H4** 32 47N 106 15 E
Ningshan, *China* ..... **56 H5** 33 21N 108 21 E
Ningsia Hui A.R. =
  Ningxia Huizu
  Zizhiqu □, *China* .. **56 F4** 38 0N 106 0 E
Ningwu, *China* ...... **56 E7** 39 0N 112 18 E
Ningxia Huizu
  Zizhiqu □, *China* .. **56 F4** 38 0N 106 0 E
Ningxiang, *China* .... **59 C9** 28 15N 112 30 E
Ningyang, *China* ..... **56 G9** 35 47N 116 45 E
Ningyuan, *China* ..... **59 E8** 25 37N 111 57 E
Ninh Binh, *Vietnam* .. **58 G5** 20 15N 105 55 E
Ninh Giang, *Vietnam* . **64 B6** 20 44N 106 24 E
Ninh Hoa, *Vietnam* .. **64 F7** 12 30N 109 7 E
Ninh Ma, *Vietnam* ... **64 F7** 12 48N 109 21 E
Nini-Suihien △, *Ghana* **82 D4** 5 20N 2 34W
Ninove, *Belgium* ..... **17 D4** 50 51N 4 2 E
Nioaque, *Brazil* **127 A4** 21 5S 55 50W
Niobrara, *U.S.A.* **112 D6** 42 45N 98 2W
Niobrara →, *U.S.A.* . **112 D6** 42 46N 98 3W
Niokolo-Koba △,
  Senegal **82 C2** 13 3N 13 2W
Niono, *Mali* **82 C3** 14 15N 6 0W
Nionsamoridougou,
  Guinea **82 D3** 8 45N 8 50W
Nioro du Rip, *Senegal* . **82 C1** 13 40N 15 50W
Nioro du Sahel, *Mali* . **82 B3** 15 15N 9 30W
Niort, *France* **20 B3** 46 19N 0 29W
Nipawin, *Canada* **103 C8** 53 20N 104 0W
Nipigon, *Canada* **104 C2** 49 0N 88 17W
Nipigon, L., *Canada* .. **104 C2** 49 50N 88 30W
Nipishish L., *Canada* .. **105 B7** 54 12N 60 45W
Nipissing, L., *Canada* . **104 C4** 46 20N 80 0W
Nipomo, *U.S.A.* **111 K6** 35 3N 120 29W
Nipton, *U.S.A.* **111 K11** 35 28N 115 16W
Niquelândia, *Brazil* ... **125 F9** 14 33 S 48 23W
Nīr, *Iran* .... **70 B5** 38 2N 47 59 E
Nirasaki, *Japan* ..... **55 G9** 35 42N 138 27 E
Nirmal, *India* .... **66 K11** 19 3N 78 20 E
Nirmali, *India* .... **69 F12** 26 20N 86 35 E
Niš, *Serbia & M.* .... **44 C5** 43 19N 21 58 E
Nisa, *Portugal* **37 F3** 39 30N 7 41W
Nişāb, *Si. Arabia* .... **70 D5** 29 11N 44 43 E
Nişāb, *Yemen* .... **75 E4** 14 25N 46 29 E
Nišava →, *Serbia & M.* **44 C6** 43 20N 21 46 E
Niscemi, *Italy* .... **43 E7** 37 9N 14 23 E
Nishinomiya, *Japan* .. **55 G7** 34 45N 135 20 E
Nishino'omote, *Japan* . **55 J5** 30 43N 130 59 E
Nishiwaki, *Japan* .... **55 G7** 34 59N 134 58 E
Nísiros, *Greece* ...... **47 E9** 36 35N 27 12 E
Niška Banja,
  Serbia & M. ...... **44 C6** 43 18N 22 1 E
Niskibi →, *Canada* ... **104 A2** 56 29N 88 9W
Nisko, *Poland* .... **31 H9** 50 35N 22 7 E
Nisporeni, *Moldova* .. **29 C13** 47 4N 28 10 E
Nisqually →, *U.S.A.* . **110 C4** 47 6N 122 42W
Nissáki, *Greece* ...... **49 A3** 39 43N 19 52 E
Nissan →, *Sweden* ... **11 H6** 56 40N 12 51 E
Nissum Bredning,
  Denmark .... **11 H2** 56 40N 8 20 E
Nissum Fjord, *Denmark* **11 H2** 56 20N 8 11 E
Nistru = Dnister →,
  Europe .... **33 J6** 46 18N 30 17 E
Nisutlin →, *Canada* .. **102 A2** 60 14N 132 34W
Nitchequon, *Canada* .. **105 B5** 53 10N 70 58W
Niterói, *Brazil* ...... **127 A7** 22 52 S 43 0W
Nith →, *Canada* **116 C4** 43 12N 80 23W
Nith →, *U.K.* **13 F5** 55 14N 3 33W
Nitmiluk △, *Australia* . **92 B5** 14 6S 132 15 E
Nitra, *Slovak Rep.* .... **27 C11** 48 19N 18 4 E
Nitra →, *Slovak Rep.* . **27 D11** 47 46N 18 10 E
Nitriansky □,
  Slovak Rep. ...... **27 C11** 48 10N 18 30 E
Nittedal, *Norway* .... **11 F5** 60 1N 10 58 E
Nittenau, *Germany* ... **25 F8** 49 12N 12 16 E
Niuafo'ou, *Tonga* .... **91 B11** 15 30 S 175 58W
Niue, *Cook Is.* .... **97 J11** 19 2 S 169 54W
Niulan Jiang →, *China* **58 D4** 27 30N 103 5 E

Niuzhuang, *China* ... **57 D12** 40 58N 122 28 E
Nivala, *Finland* ...... **8 E21** 63 56N 24 57 E
Nivelles, *Belgium* .... **17 D4** 50 35N 4 20 E
Nivernais, *France* .... **19 E10** 47 15N 3 30 E
Niwas, *India* .... **69 H9** 23 3N 80 26 E
Nixon, *U.S.A.* **113 L6** 29 16N 97 46W
Nizamabad, *India* .... **66 K11** 18 45N 78 7 E
Nizamghat, *India* .... **67 E19** 28 20N 95 45 E
Nizhne Kolymsk, *Russia* **53 C17** 68 34N 160 55 E
Nizhneangarsk, *Russia* . **53 D11** 55 47N 109 30 E
Nizhnegorskiy =
  Nyzhnohirskyy,
  Ukraine .... **33 K8** 45 27N 34 38 E
Nizhnekamsk, *Russia* . **34 C10** 55 38N 51 49 E
Nizhneudinsk, *Russia* . **53 D10** 54 54N 99 3 E
Nizhnevartovsk, *Russia* **52 C8** 60 56N 76 38 E
Nizhniy Chir, *Russia* . **35 F6** 48 22N 43 0 E
Nizhniy Lomov, *Russia* **34 D7** 53 34N 43 38 E
Nizhniy Novgorod,
  Russia .... **34 B7** 56 20N 44 0 E
Nizhniy Tagil, *Russia* . **52 D6** 57 55N 59 57 E
Nizhyn, *Ukraine* ..... **33 G6** 51 5N 31 55 E
Nizina Mazowiecka,
  Poland .... **31 F8** 52 30N 21 0 E
Nizip, *Turkey* .... **70 B3** 37 5N 37 50 E
Nízké Tatry, *Slovak Rep.* **27 C12** 48 55N 19 30 E
Nízké Tatry △,
  Slovak Rep. ...... **27 C12** 48 55N 19 37 E
Nízký Jeseník,
  Czech Rep. .... **27 B10** 49 50N 17 30 E
Nizza Monferrato, *Italy* **40 D7** 44 46N 8 21 E
Njakwa, *Malawi* ..... **87 E3** 11 1S 33 56 E
Njanji, *Zambia* ...... **87 E3** 14 25 S 31 46 E
Njegoš, *Serbia & M.* .. **44 D2** 42 53N 18 45 E
Njinjo, *Tanzania* ..... **87 D4** 8 48 S 38 54 E
Njombe, *Tanzania* .... **87 D3** 9 20 S 34 50 E
Njombe →, *Tanzania* . **86 D4** 6 56 S 35 6 E
Njurundabommen,
  Sweden .... **10 B11** 62 15N 17 25 E
Nkambe, *Cameroon* .. **83 D7** 6 35N 10 40 E
Nkana, *Zambia* ...... **87 E2** 12 50 S 28 8 E
Nkandla, *S. Africa* ... **89 D5** 28 37 S 31 5 E
Nkawkaw, *Ghana* **83 D4** 6 36N 0 49W
Nkayi, *Zimbabwe* .... **87 F2** 19 41 S 29 20 E
Nkhotakota, *Malawi* .. **87 E3** 12 56 S 34 15 E
Nkhotakota □, *Malawi* **87 E3** 12 50 S 34 0 E
Nkongsamba, *Cameroon* **83 E6** 4 55N 9 55 E
Nkurenkuru, *Namibia* . **88 B2** 17 42 S 18 32 E
Nkwanta, *Ghana* **82 D4** 6 10N 2 10W
Nmai →, *Burma* ..... **58 F2** 25 30N 97 25 E
Noakhali = Maijdi,
  Bangla. .... **67 H17** 22 48N 91 10 E
Nobel, *Canada* **116 A4** 45 25N 80 6W
Nobeoka, *Japan* ..... **55 H5** 32 36N 131 41 E
Noblejas, *Spain* **36 F7** 39 58N 3 26W
Noblesville, *U.S.A.* ... **114 E3** 40 3N 86 1W
Noboribetsu, *Japan* ... **54 C10** 42 24N 141 6 E
Noce →, *Italy* .... **40 B8** 46 9N 11 4 E
Nocera Inferiore, *Italy* . **43 B7** 40 44N 14 38 E
Nocera Umbra, *Italy* .. **41 E9** 43 8N 12 47 E
Noci, *Italy* .... **43 B10** 40 48N 17 7 E
Nocona, *U.S.A.* **113 J6** 33 47N 97 44W
Nocrich, *Romania* .... **29 E9** 45 55N 24 26 E
Noda, *Japan* .... **55 G9** 35 56N 139 52 E
Nogales, *Mexico* **118 A2** 31 20N 110 56W
Nogales, *U.S.A.* **109 L8** 31 20N 110 56W
Nogaro, *France* **20 E3** 43 45N 0 2W
Nogat →, *Poland* .... **30 D6** 54 17N 19 17 E
Nōgata, *Japan* .... **55 H5** 33 48N 130 44 E
Nogent, *France* ...... **19 D11** 48 1N 5 20 E
Nogent-le-Rotrou,
  France .... **18 D7** 48 20N 0 50 E
Nogent-sur-Seine,
  France .... **19 D10** 48 30N 3 30 E
Noggerup, *Australia* .. **93 F2** 33 32 S 116 5 E
Noginsk, *Moskva, Russia* **32 E10** 55 50N 38 25 E
Noginsk, *Tunguska,*
  Russia .... **53 C10** 64 30N 90 50 E
Nogoa →, *Australia* .. **94 C4** 23 40 S 147 55 E
Nogoyá, *Argentina* ... **126 C4** 32 24 S 59 48W
Nógrád □, *Hungary* .. **28 C4** 48 0N 19 30 E
Noguera Pallaresa →,
  Spain .... **38 D5** 41 55N 0 55 E
Noguera
  Ribagorzana →,
  Spain .... **38 D5** 41 40N 0 43 E
Nohar, *India* .... **68 E6** 29 11N 74 49 E
Nohfelden, *Germany* .. **25 F3** 49 35N 7 7 E
Nohta, *India* .... **69 H8** 23 40N 79 34 E
Noia, *Spain* **36 C2** 42 48N 8 53W
Noire, Montagne, *France* **20 E6** 43 28N 2 18 E
Noires, Mts., *France* .. **18 D3** 48 11N 3 40W
Noirétable, *France* .... **20 C7** 45 48N 3 46 E
Noirmoutier, Î. de,
  France **18 F4** 46 58N 2 10W
Noirmoutier-en-l'Île,
  France **18 F4** 47 0N 2 14W
Nojane, *Botswana* .... **88 C3** 23 15 S 20 14 E
Nojima-Zaki, *Japan* .. **55 G9** 34 54N 139 53 E
Nok Kundi, *Pakistan* .. **66 E3** 28 50N 62 45 E
Nok Ta Phao, Ko,
  Thailand .... **65 b** 9 23N 99 40 E
Nokaneng, *Botswana* . **88 B3** 19 40 S 22 17 E
Nokia, *Finland* ...... **9 F20** 61 30N 23 30 E
Nokomis, *Canada* **103 C8** 51 35N 105 0W
Nokomis L., *Canada* .. **103 B8** 57 0N 103 0W
Nola, *C.A.R.* .... **84 D3** 3 35N 16 4 E
Nola, *Italy* .... **43 B7** 40 55N 14 38 E
Nolay, *France* .... **19 F11** 46 58N 4 35 E
Noli, C. di, *Italy* ..... **40 D5** 44 12N 8 25 E
Nolinsk, *Russia* ...... **34 B9** 57 28N 49 57 E
Noma Omuramba →,
  Namibia .... **88 B3** 18 52 S 20 53 E
Nombre de Dios,
  Panama **120 E4** 9 34N 79 28W
Nome, *U.S.A.* **100 B3** 64 30N 165 25W
Nomo-Zaki, *Japan* ... **55 H4** 32 35N 129 44 E
Nonacho L., *Canada* .. **103 A7** 61 42N 109 40W
Nonda, *Australia* ..... **94 C3** 20 40 S 142 28 E
None, *Italy* .... **40 D4** 44 56N 7 32 E
Nong Chang, *Thailand* **64 E2** 15 23N 99 51 E
Nong Het, *Laos* ...... **64 C4** 19 29N 103 59 E
Nong Khai, *Thailand* . **64 D4** 17 50N 102 46 E
Nong'an, *China* ...... **57 B13** 44 25N 125 5 E
Nongoma, *S. Africa* .. **89 D5** 27 58 S 31 35 E
Nongsa, *Indonesia* ... **65 d** 1 11N 104 8 E
Nonoava, *Mexico* **118 B3** 27 28N 106 44W
Nonoava →, *Mexico* . **118 B3** 27 29N 106 45W
Nonthaburi, *Thailand* . **64 F3** 13 51N 100 34 E
Nontron, *France* ..... **20 C4** 45 31N 0 40 E
Nonza, *France* .... **21 F13** 42 47N 9 21 E
Noonamah, *Australia* . **92 B5** 12 40 S 131 4 E
Noondie, L., *Australia* . **93 E2** 28 30 S 119 30 E
Noord Brabant □,
  Neths. .... **17 C5** 51 40N 5 0 E
Noord Holland □,
  Neths. .... **17 B4** 52 30N 4 45 E

Noordbeveland, *Neths.* . **17 C3** 51 35N 3 50 E
Noordoostpolder, *Neths.* **17 B5** 52 45N 5 45 E
Noordwijk, *Neths.* .... **17 B4** 52 14N 4 26 E
Noosa Heads, *Australia* **95 D5** 26 25 S 153 6 E
Nootka I., *Canada* **102 D3** 49 38N 126 42W
Nopiming △, *Canada* . **103 C9** 50 30N 95 37W
Nora, *Eritrea* .... **81 D5** 16 6N 40 4 E
Nora, *Sweden* .... **10 E9** 59 32N 15 2 E
Noralee, *Canada* **102 C3** 53 59N 126 26W
Noranda = Rouyn-
  Noranda, *Canada* .. **104 C4** 48 20N 79 0W
Norberg, *Sweden* .... **10 D9** 60 4N 15 56 E
Nórcia, *Italy* .... **41 F10** 42 48N 13 5 E
Norco, *U.S.A.* **111 M9** 33 56N 117 33W
Nord □, *France* ...... **19 B10** 50 15N 3 30 E
Nord-Kivu □, *Dem. Rep.*
  of the Congo ...... **86 C2** 1 0 S 29 0 E
Nord-Ostsee-Kanal,
  Germany .... **24 A5** 54 12N 9 32 E
Nord-Pas-de-Calais □,
  France .... **19 B9** 50 30N 2 50 E
Nordaustlandet,
  Svalbard .... **4 B9** 79 14N 23 0 E
Nordborg, *Denmark* .. **11 J3** 55 5N 9 50 E
Nordby, *Denmark* .... **11 J2** 55 27N 8 24 E
Norddeich, *Germany* .. **24 B3** 53 37N 7 10 E
Nordegg, *Canada* **102 C5** 52 29N 116 5W
Norden, *Germany* .... **24 B3** 53 35N 7 12 E
Nordenham, *Germany* . **24 B4** 53 30N 8 30 E
Norderney, *Germany* .. **24 B3** 53 42N 7 9 E
Norderstedt, *Germany* . **24 B5** 53 42N 10 1 E
Nordfjord, *Norway* ... **9 F11** 61 55N 5 30 E
Nordfriesische Inseln,
  Germany .... **24 A4** 54 40N 8 20 E
Nordhausen, *Germany* . **24 D6** 51 30N 10 47 E
Nordhorn, *Germany* .. **24 C3** 52 26N 7 4 E
Nordøyar, *Færøe Is.* .. **8 E9** 62 17N 6 35W
Nördinge-Nol, *Sweden* **11 G6** 57 56N 12 5 E
Nordingrå, *Sweden* ... **10 B12** 62 56N 18 17 E
Nordjylland
  Amtskommune □,
  Denmark .... **11 G4** 57 20N 10 0 E
Nordkapp, *Norway* ... **8 A21** 71 10N 25 50 E
Nordkapp, *Svalbard* .. **4 A9** 80 31N 20 0 E
Nordkinnhalvøya,
  Norway .... **8 A22** 70 55N 27 40 E
Nödlicher Teutoburger
  Wald-
  Wiehengebirge △,
  Germany .... **24 C4** 52 15N 8 10 E
Nördlingen, *Germany* . **25 G6** 48 51N 10 30 E
Nordrhein-Westfalen □,
  Germany .... **24 D3** 51 45N 7 30 E
Nordstrand, *Germany* . **24 A4** 54 30N 8 52 E
Nordvik, *Russia* ..... **53 B12** 74 2N 111 32 E
Nore →, *Ireland* **12 D4** 52 25N 6 58W
Norfolk, *Canada* **116 D4** 42 50N 80 23W
Norfolk, *Nebr., U.S.A.* **112 D6** 42 2N 97 25W
Norfolk, *Va., U.S.A.* .. **114 G7** 36 51N 76 17W
Norfolk □, *U.K.* ...... **15 E8** 52 39N 0 54 E
Norfolk I., *Pac. Oc.* ... **96 K8** 28 58 S 168 3 E
Norfork L., *U.S.A.* **113 G8** 36 15N 92 14W
Norilsk, *Russia* ...... **53 C9** 69 20N 88 6 E
Norma, Mt., *Australia* . **94 C3** 20 55 S 140 42 E
Normal, *U.S.A.* **112 E10** 40 31N 88 59W
Norman, *U.S.A.* **113 H6** 35 13N 97 26W
Norman →, *Australia* . **94 B3** 19 18 S 141 51 E
Norman Wells, *Canada* **100 B7** 65 17N 126 51W
Normanby →, *Australia* **94 A3** 14 23 S 144 10 E
Normandie-Maine △,
  France **18 D6** 48 30N 0 20W
Normandin, *Canada* .. **104 C5** 48 49N 72 31W
Normanhurst, Mt.,
  Australia .... **93 E3** 25 4 S 122 30 E
Normanton, *Australia* . **94 B3** 17 40 S 141 10 E
Normétal, *Canada* **104 C4** 49 0N 79 22W
Norquay, *Canada* **103 C8** 51 53N 102 5W
Norquinco, *Argentina* . **128 E2** 41 51 S 70 55W
Norra Dellen, *Sweden* . **10 C10** 61 55N 16 43 E
Norra Kvill △, *Sweden* **11 G9** 57 46N 15 35 E
Norra Ulvön, *Sweden* . **10 A12** 63 3N 18 40 E
Norrahammar, *Sweden* **11 G8** 57 43N 14 7 E
Norrbottens län □,
  Sweden .... **8 C19** 66 50N 20 0 E
Nørre Åby, *Denmark* . **11 J3** 55 27N 9 52 E
Nørre Alslev, *Denmark* **11 K5** 54 54N 11 52 E
Nørresundby, *Denmark* **11 G3** 57 5N 9 52 E
Norrhult-Klavreström,
  Sweden .... **11 G9** 57 1N 15 33 E
Norris Point, *Canada* . **105 C8** 49 31N 57 53W
Norristown, *U.S.A.* ... **117 F9** 40 7N 75 21W
Norrköping, *Sweden* .. **11 F10** 58 37N 16 11 E
Norrland, *Sweden* .... **8 E16** 62 15N 15 45 E
Norrsundet, *Sweden* .. **10 D11** 60 56N 17 8 E
Norrtälje, *Sweden* .... **10 E12** 59 46N 18 42 E
Norseman, *Australia* .. **93 F3** 32 8 S 121 43 E
Norsk, *Russia* .... **53 D14** 52 30N 130 5 E
Norte, Pta. del,
  Canary Is. **48 G2** 27 51N 17 57W
Norte, Serra do, *Brazil* **125 C7** 11 20 S 59 0W
North, C., *Canada* **105 C7** 47 2N 60 20W
North Adams, *U.S.A.* . **117 D11** 42 42N 73 7W
North America, *Pac. Oc.* **98 F10** 40 0N 100 0W
North Arm, *Canada* ... **102 A5** 62 0N 114 30W
North Atlantic Ocean,
  Atl. Oc. **2 C7** 30 0N 50 0W
North Augusta, *U.S.A.* **115 J5** 33 30N 81 59W
North Ayrshire □, *U.K.* **13 F4** 55 45N 4 44W
North Bass I., *U.S.A.* . **116 E2** 41 44N 82 53W
North Battleford,
  Canada **103 C7** 52 50N 108 17W
North Bay, *Canada* ... **104 C4** 46 20N 79 30W
North Belcher Is.,
  Canada **104 A4** 56 50N 79 50W
North Bend, *Oreg.,*
  U.S.A. **108 E1** 43 24N 124 14W
North Bend, *Wash.,*
  U.S.A. **110 C5** 47 30N 121 47W
North Bennington,
  U.S.A. **117 D11** 42 56N 73 15W
North Berwick, *U.K.* .. **13 E6** 56 4N 2 42W
North Berwick, *U.S.A.* **117 C14** 43 18N 70 44W
North C., *Canada* **105 C7** 47 5N 64 0W
North C., *N.Z.* .... **91 F4** 34 23 S 173 4 E
North Canadian →,
  U.S.A. **113 H7** 35 16N 95 31W
North Canton, *U.S.A.* . **116 F3** 40 53N 81 24W
North Cape =
  Nordkapp, *Norway* . **8 A21** 71 10N 25 50 E
North Cape =
  Nordkapp, *Svalbard* **4 A9** 80 31N 20 0 E
North Caribou L.,
  Canada **104 B1** 52 50N 90 40W
North Carolina □,
  U.S.A. **115 H6** 35 30N 80 0W
North Cascades △,
  U.S.A. **108 B3** 48 45N 121 10W

North Channel, *Canada* **104 C3** 46 0N 83 0W
North Channel, *U.K.* .. **13 F3** 55 13N 5 52W
North Charleston,
  U.S.A. **115 J6** 32 53N 79 58W
North Chicago, *U.S.A.* **114 D2** 42 19N 87 51W
North Creek, *U.S.A.* .. **117 C11** 43 41N 73 59W
North Dakota □, *U.S.A.* **112 B5** 47 30N 100 15W
North Downs, *U.K.* ... **15 F8** 51 19N 0 21 E
North East, *U.S.A.* ... **116 D5** 42 13N 79 50W
North East Frontier
  Agency = Arunachal
  Pradesh □, *India* .. **67 F19** 28 0N 95 0 E
North East
  Lincolnshire □, *U.K.* **14 D7** 53 34N 0 2W
North Eastern □, *Kenya* **86 B5** 1 30N 40 0 E
North Esk →, *U.K.* ... **13 E6** 56 46N 2 24W
North European Plain,
  Europe .... **6 E10** 55 0N 25 0 E
North Foreland, *U.K.* . **15 F9** 51 22N 1 28 E
North Fork, *U.S.A.* ... **110 H7** 37 14N 119 21W
North Fork
  American →, *U.S.A.* **110 G5** 38 57N 120 59W
North Fork Feather →,
  U.S.A. **110 F5** 38 33N 121 30W
North Fork Grand →,
  U.S.A. **112 C3** 45 47N 102 16W
North Fork Red →,
  U.S.A. **113 H5** 34 24N 99 14W
North Frisian Is. =
  Nordfriesische Inseln,
  Germany .... **24 A4** 54 40N 8 20 E
North Gower, *Canada* . **117 A9** 45 8N 75 43W
North Hd., *Australia* .. **93 F1** 30 14 S 114 59 E
North Henik L., *Canada* **103 A9** 61 45N 97 40W
North Highlands, *U.S.A.* **110 G5** 38 40N 121 23W
North Horr, *Kenya* ... **86 B4** 3 20N 37 8 E
North I., *Kenya* ...... **86 B4** 4 5N 36 5 E
North I., *N.Z.* .... **91 H5** 38 0 S 175 0 E
North Kingsville, *U.S.A.* **116 E4** 41 54N 80 42W
North Kitui △, *Kenya* . **86 C4** 0 15 S 38 29 E
North Knife →, *Canada* **103 B10** 58 53N 94 45W
North Koel →, *India* . **69 G10** 24 45N 83 50 E
North Korea ■, *Asia* .. **57 E14** 40 0N 127 0 E
North Lakhimpur, *India* **67 F19** 27 14N 94 7 E
North Lanarkshire □,
  U.K. **13 F5** 55 52N 3 56W
North Las Vegas, *U.S.A.* **111 J11** 36 12N 115 7W
North Lincolnshire □,
  U.K. **14 D7** 53 36N 0 30W
North Little Rock,
  U.S.A. **113 H8** 34 45N 92 16W
North Loup →, *U.S.A.* **112 E5** 41 17N 98 24W
North Luangwa △,
  Zambia .... **87 E3** 11 49 S 32 9 E
North Magnetic Pole,
  Canada **4 A2** 88 30N 107 0W
North Minch, *U.K.* ... **13 C3** 58 5N 5 55W
North Moose L., *Canada* **103 C8** 54 11N 100 6W
North Moose L., *Man.,*
  Canada **103 C8** 54 4N 100 12W
North Myrtle Beach,
  U.S.A. **115 J6** 33 48N 78 42W
North Nahanni →,
  Canada **102 A4** 62 15N 123 20W
North Olmsted, *U.S.A.* **116 E3** 41 25N 81 56W
North Ossetia □, *Russia* **35 J7** 43 30N 44 30 E
North Pagai, I. = Pagai
  Utara, Pulau,
  Indonesia .... **62 E2** 2 35 S 100 0 E
North Palisade, *U.S.A.* **110 H8** 37 6N 118 31W
North Platte, *U.S.A.* .. **112 E4** 41 8N 100 46W
North Platte →, *U.S.A.* **112 E4** 41 7N 100 42W
North Pole, *Arctic* .... **4 A** 90 0N 0 0W
North Portal, *Canada* . **103 D8** 49 0N 102 33W
North Powder, *U.S.A.* . **108 D5** 45 2N 117 55W
North Pt., *Barbados* ... **121 g** 13 20N 59 37W
North Pt., *Trin. & Tob.* **125 J16** 11 21N 60 31W
North Pt., *U.S.A.* **116 A1** 45 2N 83 16W
North Rhine
  Westphalia =
  Nordrhein-
  Westfalen □,
  Germany .... **24 D3** 51 45N 7 30 E
North River, *Canada* .. **105 B8** 53 49N 57 6W
North Ronaldsay, *U.K.* **13 B6** 59 22N 2 26W
North Saskatchewan →,
  Canada **103 C7** 53 15N 105 5W
North Sea, *Europe* .... **16** 56 0N 4 0 E
North Seal →, *Canada* **103 B9** 58 50N 98 7W
North Somerset □, *U.K.* **15 F5** 51 24N 2 45W
North Sporades = Vórai
  Sporádhes, *Greece* . **46 B5** 39 15N 23 30 E
North Sydney, *Canada* **105 C7** 46 12N 60 15W
North Syracuse, *U.S.A.* **117 C8** 43 8N 76 7W
North Taranaki Bight,
  N.Z. .... **91 H5** 38 50 S 174 15 E
North Thompson →,
  Canada **102 C4** 50 40N 120 20W
North Tonawanda,
  U.S.A. **116 C6** 43 2N 78 53W
North Troy, *U.S.A.* ... **117 B12** 45 0N 72 24W
North Truchas Pk.,
  U.S.A. **109 J11** 36 0N 105 30W
North Twin I., *Canada* **104 B4** 53 20N 80 0W
North Tyne →, *U.K.* .. **14 B5** 55 0N 2 8W
North Uist, *U.K.* **13 D1** 57 40N 7 15W
North Vancouver,
  Canada **102 D4** 49 19N 123 4W
North Vernon, *U.S.A.* . **114 F3** 39 0N 85 38W
North Wabasca L.,
  Canada **102 B6** 56 0N 113 55W
North Walsham, *U.K.* . **14 E9** 52 50N 1 22 E
North West = Severo-
  Zapadnyy □, *Russia* **52 C4** 65 0N 40 0 E
North-West □, *S. Africa* **88 D4** 24 56 S 27 18 E
North West C., *Australia* **92 D1** 21 45 S 114 9 E
North West Christmas I.
  Ridge, *Pac. Oc.* **97 G11** 6 30N 165 0W
North West Frontier □,
  Pakistan .... **68 C4** 34 0N 72 0 E
North West Highlands,
  U.K. **13 D4** 57 33N 4 58W
North West River,
  Canada **105 B7** 53 30N 60 10W
North Western □,
  Zambia .... **87 E2** 13 30 S 25 30 E
North Wildwood, *U.S.A.* **114 F8** 39 0N 74 48W
North York Moors, *U.K.* **14 C7** 54 23N 0 53W
North York Moors △,
  U.K. **14 C7** 54 27N 0 51W
North Yorkshire □, *U.K.* **14 C6** 54 15N 1 25W
Northallerton, *U.K.* ... **14 C6** 54 20N 1 26W
Northam, *Australia* ... **93 F2** 31 35 S 116 42 E
Northam, *S. Africa* ... **88 C4** 24 56 S 27 18 E
Northampton, *Australia* **93 E1** 28 27 S 114 33 E
Northampton, *U.K.* ... **15 E7** 52 15N 0 53W
Northampton, *Mass.,*
  U.S.A. **117 D12** 42 19N 72 38W

Northampton, Pa.,
U.S.A. **117 F9** 40 41N 75 30W
Northamptonshire □,
U.K. **15 E7** 52 16N 0 55W
Northbridge, U.S.A. .. **117 D13** 42 9N 71 39W
Northcliffe, Australia .. **93 F2** 34 39 S 116 7 E
Northeast Providence
Chan., W. Indies **120 A4** 26 0N 76 0W
Northeim, Germany .... **24 D6** 51 42N 10 0 E
Northern = Limpopo □,
S. Africa .... **89 C4** 24 5 S 29 0 E
Northern □, Ghana **83 D4** 9 30N 1 0W
Northern □, Malawi .. **87 E3** 11 0 S 34 0 E
Northern □, S. Leone .. **82 D2** 9 15N 11 30W
Northern □, Zambia .. **87 E3** 10 30 S 31 0 E
Northern Areas □,
Pakistan .... **69 A5** 36 30N 73 0 E
Northern Cape □,
S. Africa .... **88 D3** 30 0 S 20 0 E
Northern Circars, India **67 L13** 17 30N 82 30 E
Northern Indian L.,
Canada **103 B9** 57 20N 97 20W
Northern Ireland □,
U.K. **12 B5** 54 45N 7 0W
Northern Light L.,
Canada **104 C1** 48 15N 90 39W
Northern Marianas ☑,
Pac. Oc. .... **96 F6** 17 0N 145 0 E
Northern Mid-Atlantic
Ridge, Atl. Oc. **4 D6** 35 0N 35 0W
Northern Province □,
S. Africa .... **89 C4** 24 0 S 29 0 E
Northern Range,
Trin. & Tob. **125 K15** 10 46N 61 15W
Northern Territory □,
Australia .... **92 D5** 20 0 S 133 0 E
Northfield, Minn.,
U.S.A. **112 C8** 44 27N 93 9W
Northfield, Vt., U.S.A. **117 B12** 44 9N 72 40W
Northland □, N.Z. .... **91 F4** 35 30 S 173 30 E
Northome, U.S.A. **112 B7** 47 52N 94 17W
Northport, Ala., U.S.A. **115 J2** 33 14N 87 35W
Northport, Wash.,
U.S.A. **108 B5** 48 55N 117 48W
Northumberland □,
U.K. **14 B6** 55 12N 2 0W
Northumberland, C.,
Australia .... **95 F3** 38 5 S 140 40 E
Northumberland Is.,
Australia .... **94 C4** 21 30 S 149 50 E
Northumberland Str.,
Canada **105 C7** 46 20N 64 0W
Northville, U.S.A. **117 C10** 43 13N 74 11W
Northwest Providence
Channel, W. Indies .. **120 A4** 26 0N 78 0W
Northwest Territories □,
Canada **100 B9** 63 0N 118 0W
Northwich, U.K. **14 D5** 53 15N 2 31W
Northwich, Iowa,
U.S.A. **112 D8** 43 27N 93 13W
Northwood, N. Dak.,
U.S.A. **112 B6** 47 44N 97 34W
Norton, U.S.A. **112 F5** 39 50N 99 53W
Norton, Zimbabwe .... **87 F3** 17 52 S 30 40 E
Norton Sd., U.S.A. **100 B3** 63 50N 164 0W
Nortorf, Germany .... **24 A5** 54 10N 9 50 E
Norwalk, Calif., U.S.A. **111 M8** 33 54N 118 5W
Norwalk, Conn., U.S.A. **117 E11** 41 7N 73 22W
Norwalk, Iowa, U.S.A. **112 C8** 41 29N 93 41W
Norwalk, Ohio, U.S.A. **116 E2** 41 15N 82 37W
Norway, Maine, U.S.A. **115 C10** 44 13N 70 32W
Norway, Mich., U.S.A. **114 C2** 45 47N 87 55W
Norway ■, Europe .... **8 E14** 63 0N 11 0 E
Norway House, Canada **103 C9** 53 59N 97 50W
Norwegian Sea, Atl. Oc. **7 B6** 66 0N 1 0 E
Norwich, Canada **116 D4** 42 59N 80 36W
Norwich, U.K. .... **15 E9** 52 38N 1 18 E
Norwich, Conn., U.S.A. **117 E12** 41 31N 72 5W
Norwich, N.Y., U.S.A. **117 D9** 42 32N 75 32W
Norwood, Canada **116 B7** 44 23N 77 59W
Norwood, U.S.A. **117 B10** 44 45N 75 0W
Noshiro, Japan ...... **54 D10** 40 12N 140 0 E
Nosivka, Ukraine .... **33 G6** 50 54N 31 37 E
Nosovka = Nosivka,
Ukraine .... **33 G6** 50 54N 31 37 E
Noşratābād, Iran .... **71 D8** 29 55N 60 0 E
Noss Hd., U.K. **13 C5** 58 28N 3 3W
Nossebro, Sweden .... **11 F6** 58 12N 12 43 E
Nossob →, S. Africa .. **88 D3** 26 55 S 20 45 E
Nossombougou, Mali .. **82 C3** 13 5N 7 55W
Nosy Barren, Madag. .. **85 H8** 18 25 S 43 40 E
Nosy Be, Madag. ...... **85 G9** 13 25 S 48 15 E
Nosy Boraha, Madag. .. **89 B8** 16 50 S 49 55 E
Nosy Lava, Madag. .... **85 A8** 14 33 S 47 36 E
Nosy Varika, Madag. .. **85 C8** 20 35 S 48 32 E
Noteć →, Poland .... **31 F2** 52 44N 15 26 E
Notikewin →, Canada .. **102 B5** 57 2N 117 38W
Notio Aigaio = Notios
Aiyaíon □ .... **47 E7** 36 52N 25 34 E
Notios Aiyaíon □ .... **47 E7** 36 52N 25 34 E
Notios Evvoïkos Kólpos,
Greece .... **46 C5** 38 20N 24 0 E
Noto, Italy .... **43 F8** 36 53N 15 4 E
Noto, G. di, Italy .... **43 F8** 36 50N 15 12 E
Notodden, Norway .... **9 G13** 59 35N 9 17 E
Notre Dame B., Canada **105 C8** 49 45N 55 30W
Notre-Dame-de-
Koartac = Quaqtaq,
Canada **101 B13** 60 55N 69 40W
Notre-Dame-des-Bois,
Canada **117 A13** 45 24N 71 4W
Notre-Dame-
d'Ivugivic = Ivujivik,
Canada **101 B12** 62 24N 77 55W
Notre-Dame-du-Nord,
Canada **104 C4** 47 36N 79 30W
Notsé, Togo .... **83 D5** 7 0N 1 17 E
Nottawasaga B., Canada **116 B4** 44 35N 80 15W
Nottaway →, Canada .. **104 B4** 51 22N 78 55W
Nottingham, U.K. **14 E6** 52 58N 1 10W
Nottingham, City of □,
U.K. **14 E6** 52 58N 1 10W
Nottingham I., Canada **101 B12** 63 20N 77 55W
Nottinghamshire □,
U.K. **14 D6** 53 10N 1 3W
Nottoway →, U.S.A. .. **114 G7** 36 33N 76 55W
Notwane →, Botswana **88 C4** 23 35 S 26 58 E
Nouâdhibou, Mauritania **78 D2** 20 54N 17 0W
Nouâdhibou, Ras,
Mauritania **78 D2** 20 50N 17 0W
Nouakchott, Mauritania **82 B1** 18 9N 15 58W
Nouâmghâr, Mauritania **82 B1** 19 20N 16 20W
Nouméa, N. Cal. ...... **96 K8** 22 17 S 166 30 E
Nouna, Burkina Faso .. **82 C4** 12 45N 3 52W
Noupoort, S. Africa .. **88 E3** 31 10 S 24 57 E
Nouveau Comptoir =
Wemindji, Canada .. **104 B4** 53 0N 78 49W

Nouvelle-Amsterdam, Î.,
Ind. Oc. .... **3 F13** 38 30 S 77 30 E
Nouvelle-Calédonie =
New Caledonia ☑,
Pac. Oc. .... **96 K8** 21 0 S 165 0 E
Nouzonville, France .. **19 C11** 49 48N 4 44 E
Nová Baňa, Slovak Rep. **27 C11** 48 28N 18 39 E
Nová Bystřice,
Czech Rep. .... **26 B8** 49 2N 15 8 E
Nova Casa Nova, Brazil **125 E10** 9 25 S 41 5W
Nova Esperança, Brazil **127 A5** 23 8 S 52 24W
Nova Friburgo, Brazil .. **127 A7** 22 16 S 42 30W
Nova Gorica, Slovenia **41 C10** 45 47N 13 39 E
Nova Gradiška, Croatia **28 E2** 45 17N 17 28 E
Nova Iguaçu, Brazil .. **127 A7** 22 45 S 43 28W
Nova Iorque, Brazil .. **125 E10** 7 0 S 44 5W
Nova Kakhovka,
Ukraine .... **33 J7** 46 42N 33 27 E
Nova Lamego,
Guinea-Biss. **82 C2** 12 19N 14 11W
Nova Lima, Brazil .... **127 A7** 19 59 S 43 51W
Nova Lusitânia, Mozam. **87 F3** 19 50 S 34 34 E
Nova Mambone,
Mozam. .... **89 C6** 21 0 S 35 3 E
Nova Odesa, Ukraine .. **33 J6** 47 19N 31 47 E
Nová Paka, Czech Rep. **26 A8** 50 29N 15 30 E
Nova Pavova,
Serbia & M. .... **28 F5** 44 56N 20 14 E
Nova Scotia □, Canada **105 C7** 45 10N 63 0W
Nova Siri, Italy ...... **43 B9** 40 10N 16 35 E
Nova Sofala, Mozam. .. **89 C5** 20 7 S 34 42 E
Nova Ushytsya, Ukraine **29 B12** 48 50N 27 17 E
Nova Varoš,
Serbia & M. .... **44 C3** 43 29N 19 48 E
Nova Venécia, Brazil .. **125 G10** 18 45 S 40 24W
Nova Zagora, Bulgaria **45 D10** 42 32N 26 1 E
Novaci, Macedonia .... **44 E5** 41 5N 21 29 E
Novaci, Romania ...... **29 E8** 45 10N 23 42 E
Novaféltria, Italy .... **41 E9** 43 53N 12 17 E
Novannenskiy =
Novoannenskiy,
Russia .... **34 E6** 50 32N 42 39 E
Novar, Canada **116 A5** 45 27N 79 15W
Novara, Italy .... **40 C5** 45 28N 8 38 E
Novato, U.S.A. **110 G4** 38 6N 122 35W
Novaya Kakhovka =
Nova Kakhovka,
Ukraine .... **33 J7** 46 42N 33 27 E
Novaya Kazanka,
Kazakhstan .... **35 F9** 48 56N 49 36 E
Novaya Ladoga, Russia **32 B7** 60 7N 32 16 E
Novaya Lyalya, Russia **52 D7** 59 4N 60 45 E
Novaya Sibir, Ostrov,
Russia .... **53 B16** 75 10N 150 0 E
Novaya Zemlya, Russia **52 B6** 75 0N 56 0 E
Nové Město,
Slovak Rep. .... **27 C10** 48 45N 17 50 E
Nové Město na Moravě,
Czech Rep. .... **26 B9** 49 34N 16 5 E
Nové Město nad Metují,
Czech Rep. .... **27 A9** 50 20N 16 10 E
Nové Zámky,
Slovak Rep. .... **27 C11** 48 2N 18 8 E
Novelda, Spain **39 G4** 38 24N 0 45W
Novellara, Italy ...... **40 D7** 44 51N 10 44 E
Noventa Vicentina, Italy **41 C8** 45 17N 11 32 E
Novgorod, Russia .... **32 C6** 58 30N 31 25 E
Novgorod-Severskiy =
Novhorod-Siverskyy,
Ukraine .... **33 G7** 52 2N 33 10 E
Novhorod-Siverskyy,
Ukraine .... **33 G7** 52 2N 33 10 E
Novi Bečej, Serbia & M. **28 E5** 45 36N 20 10 E
Novi Iskar, Bulgaria .. **44 D7** 42 48N 23 21 E
Novi Kneževac,
Serbia & M. .... **28 D5** 46 4N 20 8 E
Novi Lígure, Italy .... **40 D5** 44 46N 8 47 E
Novi Pazar, Bulgaria .. **45 C11** 43 25N 27 15 E
Novi Pazar, Serbia & M. **44 C4** 43 12N 20 28 E
Novi Sad, Serbia & M. **28 E4** 45 18N 19 52 E
Novi Slankamen,
Serbia & M. .... **28 E5** 45 8N 20 15 E
Novi Travnik, Bos.-H. **28 F2** 44 10N 17 40 E
Novi Vinodolski, Croatia **41 C11** 45 10N 14 48 E
Novigrad, Istra, Croatia **41 C10** 45 19N 13 33 E
Novigrad, Zadar,
Croatia .... **41 D12** 44 10N 15 32 E
Novigradsko More,
Croatia .... **41 D12** 44 12N 15 33 E
Novo Hamburgo, Brazil **127 B5** 29 37 S 51 7W
Novo Ivanivka, Ukraine **29 E14** 45 55N 29 35 E
Novo Mesto, Slovenia **41 C12** 45 47N 15 12 E
Novo Miloševo,
Serbia & M. .... **28 E5** 45 42N 20 20 E
Novo Remanso, Brazil **125 E10** 9 41 S 42 4W
Novoaleksandrovsk,
Russia .... **35 H5** 45 29N 41 17 E
Novoaleksandrovskaya =
Novoaleksandrovsk,
Russia .... **35 H5** 45 29N 41 17 E
Novoaltaysk, Russia .. **52 D9** 53 30N 84 0 E
Novoannenskiy, Russia **34 E6** 50 32N 42 39 E
Novoazovsk, Ukraine .. **33 J10** 47 15N 38 4 E
Novocheboksarsk,
Russia .... **34 B8** 56 5N 47 27 E
Novocherkassk, Russia **35 G5** 47 27N 40 15 E
Novodevichye, Russia **34 D9** 53 37N 48 50 E
Novogrudok =
Navahrudak, Belarus **32 F3** 53 40N 25 50 E
Novohrad-Volynskyy,
Ukraine .... **33 G4** 50 34N 27 35 E
Novokachalinsk, Russia **54 B6** 45 5N 132 0 E
Novokhopersk, Russia **34 E5** 51 5N 41 39 E
Novokuybyshevsk,
Russia .... **34 D9** 53 7N 49 58 E
Novokuznetsk, Russia **52 D9** 53 45N 87 10 E
Novomirgorod, Ukraine **33 H6** 48 45N 31 33 E
Novomoskovsk, Russia **32 E10** 54 5N 38 15 E
Novomoskovsk, Ukraine **33 H8** 48 33N 35 17 E
Novopolotsk =
Navapolatsk, Belarus **32 E5** 55 32N 28 37 E
Novorossiysk, Russia **33 K9** 44 43N 37 46 E
Novorybnoye, Russia **53 B11** 72 50N 105 50 E
Novorzhev, Russia .... **32 D5** 57 3N 29 25 E
Novoselytsya, Ukraine **29 B11** 48 14N 26 15 E
Novoshakhtinsk, Russia **33 J10** 47 46N 39 58 E
Novosibirsk, Russia .. **52 D9** 55 0N 83 5 E
Novosibirskiye Ostrova,
Russia .... **53 B15** 75 0N 142 0 E
Novosil, Russia ...... **33 F9** 52 59N 37 2 E
Novosokolniki, Russia **32 D6** 56 20N 30 2 E
Novotitarovskaya,
Russia .... **35 H4** 45 17N 39 2 E
Novotroitsk, Russia .. **52 D6** 51 10N 58 15 E
Novoukrayinka, Ukraine **33 H6** 48 25N 31 30 E
Novouljanovsk, Russia **34 C9** 54 9N 48 24 E

Novouzensk, Russia .. **34 E9** 50 32N 48 17 E
Novovolynsk, Ukraine **31 H11** 50 45N 24 4 E
Novovoronezhskiy,
Russia .... **33 G10** 51 19N 39 13 E
Novoyavoriske, Ukraine **31 J10** 49 53N 23 33 E
Novozybkov, Russia .. **33 F6** 52 30N 32 0 E
Novska, Croatia ...... **41 C14** 45 19N 17 0 E
Novvy Urengoy, Russia **52 C8** 65 48N 76 52 E
Nový Bor, Czech Rep. .. **26 A7** 50 46N 14 35 E
Novy Bug = Novyy Buh,
Ukraine .... **33 J7** 47 34N 32 29 E
Nový Bydžov,
Czech Rep. .... **26 A8** 50 14N 15 29 E
Novy Dvor, Belarus .. **32 E2** 52 50N 24 21 E
Novy Dwór Mazowiecki,
Poland .... **31 F7** 52 26N 20 44 E
Nový Jičín, Czech Rep. **27 B11** 49 30N 18 2 E
Novyy Afon, Georgia .. **35 J5** 43 7N 40 50 E
Novyy Buh, Ukraine .. **33 J7** 47 34N 32 29 E
Novyy Oskol, Russia .. **33 G9** 50 44N 37 55 E
Novyy Port, Russia .. **52 C8** 67 40N 72 30 E
Now Shahr, Iran ...... **71 B6** 36 40N 51 30 E
Nowa Deba, Poland .. **31 H8** 50 26N 21 41 E
Nowa Ruda, Poland .. **31 H3** 50 35N 16 30 E
Nowa Sarzyna, Poland **31 H9** 50 21N 22 21 E
Nowa Sól, Poland .... **31 G2** 51 48N 15 44 E
Nowata, U.S.A. **113 G7** 36 42N 95 38W
Nowbarān, Iran ...... **71 C6** 35 8N 49 42 E
Nowe, Poland .... **30 E5** 53 41N 18 44 E
Nowe Miasteczko,
Poland .... **31 G2** 51 42N 15 42 E
Nowe Miasto, Poland **31 G7** 51 38N 20 34 E
Nowe Miasto
Lubawskie, Poland .. **30 E6** 53 27N 19 33 E
Nowe Skalmierzyce,
Poland .... **31 G4** 51 43N 18 0 E
Nowe Warpno, Poland **30 E1** 53 42N 14 18 E
Nowgong, Assam, India **67 F18** 26 20N 92 50 E
Nowgong, Mad. P., India **69 G8** 25 4N 79 27 E
Nowogard, Poland .... **30 E2** 53 41N 15 10 E
Nowogród, Poland .... **31 E8** 53 14N 21 53 E
Nowogród Bobrzanski,
Poland .... **31 G2** 51 48N 15 15 E
Nowogrodziec, Poland **31 G2** 51 12N 15 24 E
Nowra, Australia .... **95 E5** 34 53 S 150 35 E
Nowshera, Pakistan .. **66 C8** 34 0N 72 0 E
Nowy Dwór Gdański,
Poland .... **30 D6** 54 13N 19 7 E
Nowy Sącz, Poland .. **31 J7** 49 40N 20 41 E
Nowy Staw, Poland .. **30 D6** 54 13N 19 2 E
Nowy Targ, Poland .. **31 J7** 49 29N 20 2 E
Nowy Tomyśl, Poland **31 F3** 52 19N 16 10 E
Nowy Wiśnicz, Poland **31 J7** 49 55N 20 28 E
Noxen, U.S.A. **117 E8** 41 25N 76 4W
Noxon, U.S.A. **108 C6** 48 0N 115 43W
Noyabr'sk, Russia .... **52 C8** 64 34N 76 21 E
Noyant, France ...... **18 E7** 47 30N 0 6 E
Noyers, France ...... **19 E10** 47 40N 4 0 E
Noyon, France ...... **19 C9** 49 34N 2 59 E
Noyon, Mongolia .... **56 C2** 43 2N 102 4 E
Nozay, France **18 E5** 47 34N 1 38W
Nqutu, S. Africa .... **89 D5** 28 13 S 30 32 E
Nsanje, Malawi ...... **87 F4** 16 55 S 35 12 E
Nsawam, Ghana **83 D4** 5 50N 0 24W
Nsomba, Zambia .... **87 E2** 10 45 S 29 51 E
Nsukka, Nigeria ...... **83 D6** 6 51N 7 29 E
Ntui, Cameroon ...... **83 E7** 4 27N 11 38 E
Nu Jiang →, China .. **58 E2** 29 58N 97 25 E
Nu Shan, China ...... **58 E2** 26 0N 99 20 E
Nuba Mts. = Nubah,
Jibalan, Sudan .... **81 E3** 12 0N 31 0 E
Nubah, Jibalan, Sudan **81 E3** 12 0N 31 0 E
Nubia, Africa .... **76 D7** 21 0N 32 0 E
Nubian Desert =
Nûbîya, Es Sahrâ en,
Sudan .... **80 C3** 21 30N 33 30 E
Nûbîya, Es Sahrâ en,
Sudan .... **80 C3** 21 30N 33 30 E
Nubledo, Spain **36 B5** 43 31N 5 52W
Nuboai, Indonesia .... **63 E9** 2 10 S 136 30 E
Nubra →, India ...... **69 B7** 34 35N 77 35 E
Nucet, Romania ...... **28 D7** 46 28N 22 35 E
Nueces →, U.S.A. **113 M6** 27 51N 97 30W
Nueltin L., Canada .. **103 A9** 60 30N 99 30W
Nueva Carteya, Spain **37 H6** 37 35N 4 28W
Nueva Gerona, Cuba .. **120 B3** 21 53N 82 49W
Nueva Palmira, Uruguay **126 C4** 33 52 S 58 20W
Nueva Rosita, Mexico **118 B4** 28 0N 101 11W
Nueva San Salvador,
El Salv. **120 D2** 13 40N 89 18W
Nuéve de Julio,
Argentina .... **126 D3** 35 30 S 61 0W
Nuevitas, Cuba **120 B4** 21 30N 77 20W
Nuevo, G., Argentina **128 E4** 43 0 S 64 30W
Nuevo Casas Grandes,
Mexico **118 A3** 30 22N 108 0W
Nuevo Guerrero,
Mexico **119 B5** 26 34N 99 15W
Nuevo Laredo, Mexico **119 B5** 27 30N 99 30W
Nuevo León □, Mexico **118 C5** 25 0N 100 0W
Nuevo Rocafuerte,
Ecuador .... **124 D3** 0 55 S 75 27W
Nugget Pt., N.Z. .... **91 M2** 46 27 S 169 50 E
Nugrus, Gebel, Egypt **80 C3** 24 47N 34 35 E
Nuhaka, N.Z. .... **91 H6** 39 3 S 177 45 E
Nuits-St-Georges,
France .... **19 E11** 47 10N 4 56 E
Nukey Bluff, Australia **95 E2** 32 26 S 135 29 E
Nukhayb, Iraq ...... **70 C4** 32 4N 42 3 E
Nukheila, Sudan .... **80 D2** 19 1N 26 21 E
Nuku'alofa, Tonga .. **91 E12** 21 10 S 174 0W
Nukus, Uzbekistan .. **52 E6** 42 27N 59 41 E
Nules, Spain **38 F4** 39 51N 0 9W
Nullagine, Australia .. **92 D3** 21 53 S 120 7 E
Nullagine →, Australia **92 D3** 21 20 S 120 20 E
Nullarbor, Australia .. **93 F5** 31 28 S 130 55 E
Nullarbor →, Australia **93 F5** 32 39 S 115 37 E
Nullarbor Plain,
Australia .... **93 F4** 31 10 S 129 0 E
Numalla, L., Australia **95 D3** 28 43 S 144 20 E
Numan, Nigeria ...... **83 D7** 9 29N 12 3 E
Numata, Japan ...... **55 F9** 36 45N 139 4 E
Numatinna →, Sudan **81 F2** 7 38N 27 20 E
Numazu, Japan ...... **55 G9** 35 7N 138 51 E
Numbulwar, Australia **94 A2** 14 15 S 135 45 E
Numfoor, Indonesia .. **63 E8** 1 0 S 134 50 E
Numurkah, Australia **95 F4** 36 5 S 145 26 E
Nunaksaluk I., Canada **105 A7** 55 49N 60 20W
Nunap Isua, Greenland **101 C15** 59 48N 43 55W
Nunavut □, Canada .. **101 D8** 66 0N 85 0W
Nunda, U.S.A. **116 D7** 42 35N 77 56W
Nuneaton, U.K. **15 E6** 52 32N 1 27W
Nungarin, Australia .. **93 F2** 31 12 S 118 6 E

Nungo, Mozam. ...... **87 E4** 13 23 S 37 43 E
Nungwe, Tanzania .. **86 C3** 2 48 S 32 2 E
Nunivak I., U.S.A. .. **100 B3** 60 10N 166 30W
Nunkun, India ...... **69 C7** 33 57N 76 2 E
Núoro, Italy .... **42 B2** 40 20N 9 20 E
Nūrābād, Iran ...... **71 E8** 27 47N 57 12 E
Nure →, Italy ...... **40 C6** 45 3N 9 49 E
Nuremberg = Nürnberg,
Germany .... **25 F7** 49 27N 11 3 E
Nuri, Mexico **118 B3** 28 2N 109 22W
Nuri, Sudan .... **80 D3** 18 29N 31 59 E
Nuriootpa, Australia .. **95 E2** 34 27 S 139 0 E
Nurlat, Russia ...... **34 C10** 54 39N 50 45 E
Nurmes, Finland .... **8 E23** 63 33N 29 10 E
Nürnberg, Germany .. **25 F7** 49 27N 11 3 E
Nurpur, Pakistan .... **68 D4** 31 53N 71 54 E
Nurra, La, Italy ...... **42 B1** 40 45N 8 15 E
Nurran, L. = Terewah,
L., Australia ...... **95 D4** 29 52 S 147 35 E
Nurrari Lakes, Australia **93 E5** 29 1 S 130 5 E
Nurri, Italy .... **42 C2** 39 43N 9 14 E
Nürtingen, Germany .. **25 G5** 48 37N 9 19 E
Nus, Italy .... **40 C4** 45 43N 7 28 E
Nusa Barung, Indonesia **63 H15** 8 30 S 113 30 E
Nusa Dua, Indonesia **63 K18** 8 48 S 115 14 E
Nusa Kambangan,
Indonesia .... **63 G13** 7 40 S 108 10 E
Nusa Tenggara Barat □,
Indonesia .... **62 F5** 8 50 S 117 30 E
Nusa Tenggara Timur □,
Indonesia .... **63 F6** 9 30 S 122 0 E
Nusaybin, Turkey .... **73 D9** 37 3N 41 10 E
Nushki, Pakistan .... **68 E2** 29 35N 66 0 E
Nuuk, Greenland **101 B14** 64 10N 51 35W
Nuwakot, Nepal ...... **69 E10** 28 10N 83 55 E
Nuweiba', Egypt .... **70 D2** 28 59N 34 39 E
Nuwerus, S. Africa .. **88 E2** 31 8 S 18 24 E
Nuweveldberge,
S. Africa .... **88 E3** 32 10 S 21 45 E
Nuyts, C., Australia .. **93 F5** 32 2 S 132 21 E
Nuyts, Pt., Australia .. **93 G2** 35 4 S 116 38 E
Nuyts Arch., Australia **95 E1** 32 35 S 133 20 E
Nxai Pan △, Botswana **88 B3** 19 50 S 24 46 E
Nxau-Nxau, Botswana **88 B3** 18 57 S 21 4 E
Nyaake, Liberia **82 E3** 4 52N 7 37W
Nyabing, Australia .. **93 F2** 33 33 S 118 9 E
Nyack, U.S.A. **117 E11** 41 5N 73 55W
Nyagan, Russia ...... **52 C7** 62 30N 65 38 E
Nyahanga, Tanzania **86 C3** 2 20 S 33 37 E
Nyahua, Tanzania .... **86 D3** 5 25 S 33 23 E
Nyahururu, Kenya .. **86 B4** 0 2N 36 27 E
Nyainqentanglha Shan,
China .... **60 C4** 30 0N 90 0 E
Nyakanazi, Tanzania **86 C3** 3 2 S 31 10 E
Nyakrom, Ghana **83 D4** 5 40N 0 50W
Nyâlâ, Sudan .... **81 E1** 12 2N 24 58 E
Nyamandhlovu,
Zimbabwe .... **87 F2** 19 55 S 28 16 E
Nyambiti, Tanzania .. **86 C3** 2 48 S 33 27 E
Nyamlell, Sudan .... **81 F2** 9 7N 26 52 E
Nyamwaga, Tanzania **86 C3** 1 27 S 34 33 E
Nyandekwa, Tanzania **86 C3** 3 57 S 32 32 E
Nyanding →, Sudan **81 F3** 8 40N 32 41 E
Nyandoma, Russia .. **32 B11** 61 40N 40 12 E
Nyanga △, Zimbabwe **87 F3** 18 17 S 32 46 E
Nyangana, Namibia .. **88 B3** 18 0 S 20 40 E
Nyanguge, Tanzania **86 C3** 2 30 S 33 12 E
Nyankpala, Ghana .. **83 D4** 9 21N 0 58W
Nyanza, Rwanda .... **86 C2** 2 20 S 29 42 E
Nyanza □, Kenya .... **86 C3** 0 10 S 34 15 E
Nyanza-Lac, Burundi **86 C2** 4 21 S 29 36 E
Nyaponges, Sudan .. **81 F3** 5 10N 33 45 E
Nyasa, L., Africa .... **87 E3** 12 30 S 34 30 E
Nyasvizh, Belarus .. **33 F4** 53 14N 26 38 E
Nyazura, Zimbabwe **87 F3** 18 40 S 32 16 E
Nyazwidzi →,
Zimbabwe .... **87 G3** 20 0 S 31 17 E
Nyborg, Denmark .. **11 J4** 55 18N 10 47 E
Nybro, Sweden ...... **11 H9** 56 44N 15 55 E
Nyda, Russia .... **52 C8** 66 40N 72 58 E
Nyeri, Kenya .... **86 C4** 0 23 S 36 56 E
Nyerol, Sudan ...... **81 F3** 8 41N 32 1 E
Nyhammar, Sweden **10 D8** 60 17N 14 58 E
Nyíka △, Malawi .... **87 E3** 10 30 S 33 57 E
Nyinahin, Ghana **82 D4** 6 43N 2 3W
Nyíradony, Hungary **28 C6** 47 41N 21 55 E
Nyírbátor, Hungary **28 C7** 47 49N 22 9 E
Nyíregyháza, Hungary **28 C6** 47 58N 21 47 E
Nykarleby =
Uusikaarlepyy,
Finland .... **8 E20** 63 32N 22 31 E
Nykøbing, Storstrøm,
Denmark .... **11 K5** 54 56N 11 52 E
Nykøbing, Vestsjælland,
Denmark .... **11 J5** 55 55N 11 40 E
Nykøbing, Viborg,
Denmark .... **11 H2** 56 48N 8 51 E
Nyköping, Sweden .. **11 F11** 58 45N 17 1 E
Nykroppa, Sweden .. **10 E8** 59 37N 14 18 E
Nykvarn, Sweden .... **10 E11** 59 11N 17 25 E
Nyland, Sweden ...... **10 A11** 63 1N 17 45 E
Nylstroom = Modimolle,
S. Africa .... **89 C4** 24 42 S 28 22 E
Nymagee, Australia .. **95 E4** 32 7 S 146 20 E
Nymboida →, Australia **95 D5** 29 38 S 152 26 E
Nymburk, Czech Rep. **26 A8** 50 10N 15 1 E
Nynäshamn, Sweden **11 F11** 58 54N 17 57 E
Nyngan, Australia .... **95 E4** 31 30 S 147 8 E
Nyoma Rap, India .... **69 C8** 33 10N 78 40 E
Nyoman = Nemunas →,
Lithuania .... **9 J19** 55 25N 21 10 E
Nyon, Switz. .... **25 J2** 46 23N 6 14 E
Nyong →, Cameroon **83 E6** 3 17N 9 54 E
Nyons, France ...... **21 D9** 44 22N 5 10 E
Nýřany, Czech Rep. **26 B6** 49 43N 13 9 E
Nýrsko, Czech Rep. **26 B6** 49 18N 13 9 E
Nysa, Poland .... **31 H4** 50 30N 17 22 E
Nysa →, Europe .... **24 C10** 52 4N 14 46 E
Nysa Kłodzka →,
Poland .... **31 H4** 50 49N 17 40 E
Nysäter, Sweden .... **10 E6** 59 17N 12 47 E
Nyslott = Savonlinna,
Finland .... **32 B5** 61 52N 28 53 E
Nyssa, U.S.A. **108 E5** 43 53N 117 0W
Nystad = Uusikaupunki,
Finland .... **9 F19** 60 47N 21 25 E
Nysted, Denmark .... **11 K5** 54 40N 11 44 E
Nyunzu, Dem. Rep. of
the Congo .... **86 D2** 5 57 S 27 58 E
Nyurba, Russia ...... **53 C12** 63 17N 118 28 E
Nyzhankovychi, Ukraine **31 J9** 49 40N 22 49 E
Nzhnohirskyy, Ukraine **33 K8** 45 44N 34 56 E
Nzhnohirskyy, Ukraine **33 K8** 48 46N 34 56 E
Nzébéla, Guinea **82 D3** 8 9N 9 57W

Nzérékoré, Guinea **82 D3** 7 49N 8 48W
Nzeto, Angola ...... **84 F2** 7 10 S 12 52 E
Nzilo, Chutes de,
Dem. Rep. of
the Congo .... **87 E2** 10 18 S 25 27 E
N'zo →, Ivory C. **82 D3** 6 15N 7 15W
N'zo →, Ivory C. **82 D3** 6 15N 7 3W
Nzubuka, Tanzania .. **86 C3** 4 45 S 32 50 E

O

O Barco, Spain **36 C4** 42 23N 6 58W
O Carballiño, Spain .. **36 C2** 42 26N 8 5W
O Corgo, Spain **36 C3** 42 56N 7 25W
O Pino, Spain **36 C2** 42 56N 8 20W
O Porriño, Spain **36 C2** 42 56N 8 37W
Ō-Shima, Japan ...... **55 G9** 34 44N 139 24 E
Oa, Mull of, U.K. **13 F2** 55 35N 6 20W
Oacoma, U.S.A. **112 D5** 43 48N 99 24W
Oahe, L., U.S.A. **112 C4** 44 27N 100 24W
Oahe Dam, U.S.A. .. **112 C4** 44 27N 100 24W
Oahu, U.S.A. **106 H16** 21 28N 157 58W
Oak Harbor, U.S.A. **114 B4** 48 18N 122 39W
Oak Hill, U.S.A. **114 G5** 37 59N 81 9W
Oak Ridge, U.S.A. .. **115 G3** 36 1N 84 16W
Oak View, U.S.A. .. **111 L7** 34 24N 119 18W
Oakan-Dake, Japan .. **54 C12** 43 27N 144 10 E
Oakdale, Calif., U.S.A. **110 H6** 37 46N 120 51W
Oakdale, La., U.S.A. **113 K8** 30 49N 92 40W
Oakes, U.S.A. **112 B5** 46 8N 98 6W
Oakesdale, U.S.A. .. **108 C5** 47 8N 117 15W
Oakey, Australia .... **95 D5** 27 25 S 151 43 E
Oakfield, U.S.A. **116 C6** 43 4N 78 16W
Oakham, U.K. **15 E7** 52 40N 0 43W
Oakhurst, U.S.A. .. **110 H7** 37 19N 119 40W
Oakland, U.S.A. **110 H4** 37 49N 122 16W
Oakley, Idaho, U.S.A. **108 E7** 42 15N 113 53W
Oakley, Kans., U.S.A. **112 F4** 39 8N 100 51W
Oakover →, Australia **92 D3** 21 0 S 120 40 E
Oakridge, U.S.A. **108 E2** 43 45N 122 28W
Oakville, Canada **116 C5** 43 27N 79 41W
Oakville, U.S.A. **110 D3** 46 51N 123 14W
Oamaru, N.Z. ...... **91 L3** 45 5 S 170 59 E
Oancea, Romania .. **29 E12** 45 21N 27 42 E
Oasi Faunistica di
Vendicari △, Italy .. **43 F8** 36 49N 15 6 E
Oasis, Calif., U.S.A. **111 M10** 33 28N 116 6W
Oasis, Nev., U.S.A. .. **110 H9** 37 29N 117 55W
Oates Land, Antarctica **5 C11** 69 0 S 160 0 E
Oatlands, Australia .. **95 G4** 42 17 S 147 21 E
Oatman, U.S.A. **111 K12** 35 1N 114 19W
Oaxaca, Mexico **119 D5** 17 2N 96 40W
Oaxaca □, Mexico .. **119 D5** 17 0N 97 0W
Ob →, Russia ...... **52 C7** 66 45N 69 30 E
Oba, Canada **104 C3** 49 4N 84 7W
Obala, Cameroon .. **83 E7** 4 9N 11 32 E
Obama, Japan ...... **55 G7** 35 30N 135 45 E
Oban, Nigeria ...... **83 D6** 5 17N 8 33 E
Oban, U.K. **13 E3** 56 25N 5 29W
Obbia, Somali Rep. .. **75 F4** 5 25N 48 30 E
Obera, Argentina .. **127 B4** 27 21 S 55 2W
Oberammergau,
Germany .... **25 H7** 47 36N 11 4 E
Oberasbach, Germany **25 F6** 49 25N 10 57 E
Oberbayern □,
Germany .... **25 G7** 48 5N 11 50 E
Oberdrauburg, Austria **26 E5** 46 44N 12 58 E
Obere Donau △,
Germany .... **25 G5** 48 5N 9 0 E
Oberer Bayerischer
Wald △, Germany .. **25 F8** 49 15N 12 40 E
Oberfranken □,
Germany .... **25 E7** 50 10N 11 20 E
Oberhausen, Germany **24 D2** 51 28N 6 51 E
Oberkirch, Germany **25 G4** 48 31N 8 4 E
Oberlausitz, Germany **24 D10** 51 16N 14 18 E
Oberlin, Kans., U.S.A. **112 F4** 39 49N 100 32W
Oberlin, La., U.S.A. **113 K8** 30 37N 92 46W
Oberlin, Ohio, U.S.A. **116 E2** 41 18N 82 13W
Obernai, France .... **19 D14** 48 28N 7 30 E
Oberndorf, Germany **25 G4** 48 17N 8 34 E
Oberon, Australia .. **95 E4** 33 45 S 149 52 E
Oberösterreich □,
Austria .... **26 C7** 48 10N 14 0 E
Oberpfalz □, Germany **25 F8** 49 20N 12 10 E
Oberpfälzer Wald △,
Germany .... **25 F8** 49 30N 12 30 E
Oberpfälzer Wald □
Germany .... **25 F8** 49 40N 12 20 E
Oberstdorf, Germany **25 H6** 47 24N 10 15 E
Obertyn, Ukraine .. **29 B10** 48 42N 25 10 E
Oberursel, Germany **25 E4** 50 11N 8 35 E
Oberwart, Austria .. **27 D9** 47 17N 16 12 E
Obi, Indonesia ...... **63 E7** 1 23 S 127 45 E
Obiaruku, Nigeria .. **83 D6** 5 51N 6 9 E
Óbidos, Brazil ...... **125 D7** 1 50 S 55 30W
Óbidos, Portugal **37 F1** 39 19N 9 10W
Obihiro, Japan ...... **54 C11** 42 56N 143 12 E
Obilatu, Indonesia .. **63 E7** 1 25 S 127 20 E
Obilnoye, Russia .. **35 G7** 47 32N 44 30 E
Obing, Germany .... **25 G8** 48 0N 12 24 E
Objat, France ...... **20 C5** 45 16N 1 24 E
Obluchye, Russia .. **53 E14** 49 1N 131 4 E
Obninsk, Russia .... **32 D9** 55 8N 36 37 E
Oboa, Mt., Uganda **86 B3** 1 45N 34 45 E
Obonga, U.S.A. **116 E2** 41 18N 82 13W
Oborniki, Poland .... **31 F3** 52 39N 16 50 E
Oborniki Śląskie,
Poland .... **31 G3** 51 17N 16 53 E
Oboyan, Russia .... **33 G9** 51 15N 36 21 E
Obozerskiy, Russia .. **52 C5** 63 34N 40 21 E
Obshchi Syrt, Russia **6 E16** 52 0N 53 0 E
Obskaya Guba, Russia **52 C8** 69 0N 73 0 E
Obuasi, Ghana **83 D4** 6 17N 1 40W
Obubra, Nigeria .... **83 D6** 6 8N 8 20 E
Obudu, Nigeria .... **83 D6** 6 38N 9 5 E
Obwalden □, Switz. **25 J4** 46 55N 8 15 E
Ocala, U.S.A. **115 L4** 29 11N 82 8W
Ocampo, Chihuahua,
Mexico **118 B3** 28 9N 108 24W
Ocampo, Tamaulipas,
Mexico **119 C5** 22 50N 99 20W
Ocaña, Spain **36 F7** 39 55N 3 30W
Ocanomowoc, U.S.A. **112 D10** 43 7N 88 30W

Occidental, Cordillera,
Colombia **124 C3** 5 0N 76 0W
Occidental, Grand Erg,
Algeria .... **78 B6** 30 20N 1 0 E
Ocean City, Md., U.S.A. **114 F8** 38 20N 75 5W
Ocean City, N.J., U.S.A. **114 F8** 39 17N 74 35W
Ocean City, Wash.,
U.S.A. **110 C2** 47 4N 124 10W
Ocean Falls, Canada . **102 C3** 52 18N 127 48W
Ocean I. = Banaba,
Kiribati .... **96 H8** 0 45 S 169 50 E
Ocean Park, U.S.A. .. **110 D2** 46 30N 124 3W
Oceano, U.S.A. **111 K6** 35 6N 120 37W
Oceanport, U.S.A. ... **117 F10** 40 19N 74 3W
Oceanside, U.S.A. ... **111 M9** 33 12N 117 23W
Ochagavía, Spain **38 C3** 42 55N 1 5W
Ochakiv, Ukraine .... **33 J6** 46 37N 31 33 E
Ochil Hills, U.K. **13 E5** 56 14N 3 40W
Ocho Rios, Jamaica . **120 a** 18 24N 77 6W
Ochsenfurt, Germany . **25 F6** 49 40N 10 4 E
Ochsenhausen, Germany **25 G5** 48 4N 9 57 E
Ocilla, U.S.A. **115 K4** 31 36N 83 15W
Ockelbo, Sweden .... **10 D10** 60 54N 16 45 E
Ocmulgee ➤, U.S.A. . **115 K4** 31 58N 82 33W
Ocna Mureş, Romania . **29 D8** 46 23N 23 55 E
Ocna Sibiului, Romania **29 E9** 45 52N 24 2 E
Ocnele Mari, Romania **29 E8** 45 8N 24 18 E
Ocniţa, Moldova .... **29 B12** 48 25N 27 30 E
Oconee ➤, U.S.A. ... **115 K4** 31 58N 82 33W
Oconto, U.S.A. **114 C2** 44 53N 87 52W
Oconto Falls, U.S.A. . **114 C1** 44 52N 88 9W
Ocosingo, Mexico ... **119 D6** 17 10N 92 15W
Ocotal, Nic. **120 D2** 13 41N 86 31W
Ocotlán, Mexico **118 C4** 20 21N 102 42W
Ocotlán de Morelos,
Mexico **119 D5** 16 48N 96 40W
Ocreza ➤, Portugal .. **37 F3** 39 32N 7 50W
Ócsa, Hungary ..... **28 C4** 47 17N 19 15 E
Octeville, France **18 C5** 49 38N 1 40W
Oda, Ghana **83 D4** 5 50N 0 51W
Oda, Japan .... **55 G6** 35 11N 132 30 E
Oda, J., Sudan ..... **80 C4** 20 21N 36 39 E
Ódáðahraun, Iceland . **8 D5** 65 5N 17 0W
Ódákra, Sweden .... **11 H6** 56 7N 12 45 E
Odate, Japan ...... **54 D10** 40 16N 140 34 E
Odawara, Japan .... **55 G9** 35 20N 139 6 E
Odda, Norway ...... **9 F12** 60 3N 6 35 E
Odder, Denmark .... **11 J4** 55 58N 10 10 E
Odei ➤, Canada **103 B9** 56 6N 96 54W
Odemira, Portugal ... **37 H2** 37 35N 8 40W
Ödemiş, Turkey .... **47 C10** 38 15N 28 0 E
Odendaalsrus, S. Africa **88 D4** 27 48 S 26 45 E
Odensbacken, Sweden . **10 E9** 59 10N 15 32 E
Odense, Denmark ... **11 J4** 55 22N 10 23 E
Odenwald = Neckartal-
Odenwald △,
Germany .... **25 F5** 49 30N 9 5 E
Odenwald, Germany .. **25 F5** 49 35N 9 0 E
Oder ➤, Europe .... **24 B10** 53 33N 14 38 E
Oder-Havel Kanal,
Germany .... **24 C10** 52 52N 14 2 E
Oderzo, Italy ...... **41 C9** 45 47N 12 29 E
Odesa, Ukraine ..... **33 J6** 46 30N 30 45 E
Ödeshög, Sweden ... **11 F8** 58 14N 14 39 E
Odessa = Odesa,
Ukraine .... **33 J6** 46 30N 30 45 E
Odessa, Canada **117 B8** 44 17N 76 43W
Odessa, Tex., U.S.A. . **113 K3** 31 52N 102 23W
Odessa, Wash., U.S.A. **108 C4** 47 20N 118 41W
Odiakwe, Botswana .. **88 C4** 20 12 S 25 17 E
Odiel ➤, Spain **37 H4** 37 10N 6 55W
Odienné, Ivory C. ... **82 D3** 9 30N 7 34W
Odintsovo, Russia ... **32 E9** 55 39N 37 15 E
Odiongan, Phil. ..... **61 E4** 12 24N 121 59 E
Odobeşti, Romania .. **29 E12** 45 43N 27 4 E
Odolanów, Poland ... **31 G4** 51 34N 17 40 E
O'Donnell, U.S.A. ... **113 J4** 32 58N 101 50W
Odorheiu Secuiesc,
Romania .... **29 D10** 46 21N 25 21 E
Odoyevo, Russia .... **32 F9** 53 56N 36 42 E
Odra = Oder ➤, Europe **24 B10** 53 33N 14 38 E
Odra ➤, Spain **36 C7** 42 14N 4 17W
Odžaci, Serbia & M. . **28 E4** 45 30N 19 17 E
Odžak, Bos.-H. ..... **28 E3** 45 3N 18 18 E
Odzi, Zimbabwe .... **89 B5** 19 0 S 32 20 E
Odzi ➤, Zimbabwe .. **89 B5** 19 45 S 32 23 E
Oebisfelde, Germany . **24 C6** 52 27N 10 57 E
Oeiras, Brazil ...... **125 E10** 7 0 S 42 8W
Oeiras, Portugal **37 G1** 38 41N 9 18W
Oelrichs, U.S.A. **112 D3** 43 11N 103 14W
Oelsnitz, Germany ... **25 E8** 50 24N 12 10 E
Oelwein, U.S.A. **112 D9** 42 41N 91 55W
Oenpelli, Australia .. **92 B5** 12 20 S 133 4 E
Oetz, Austria ...... **26 D3** 47 13N 10 53 E
Of, Turkey .... **73 B9** 40 59N 40 23 E
Ofanto ➤, Italy .... **43 A9** 41 22N 16 13 E
Offa, Nigeria ...... **83 D5** 8 13N 4 42 E
Offaly □, Ireland ... **12 C4** 53 15N 7 30W
Offenbach, Germany . **25 E4** 50 6N 8 44 E
Offenburg, Germany . **25 G3** 48 28N 7 56 E
Officer, The ➤,
Australia .... **93 E5** 27 46 S 132 30 E
Offida, Italy .... **41 F10** 42 56N 13 41 E
Ofidhoussa, Greece .. **47 E8** 36 33N 26 8 E
Ofotfjorden, Norway . **8 B17** 68 27N 17 0 E
Ofunato, Japan ..... **54 E10** 39 4N 141 43 E
Oga, Japan .... **54 E9** 39 55N 139 50 E
Oga-Hantō, Japan ... **54 E9** 39 58N 139 47 E
Ogaki, Japan .... **55 G8** 35 21N 136 37 E
Ogallala, U.S.A. **112 E4** 41 8N 101 43W
Ogasawara Gunto,
Pac. Oc. .... **96 E6** 27 0N 142 0 E
Ogbomosho, Nigeria . **83 D5** 8 1N 4 11 E
Ogden, U.S.A. **108 F7** 41 13N 111 58W
Ogdensburg, U.S.A. . **117 B9** 44 42N 75 30W
Ogeechee ➤, U.S.A. . **115 K5** 31 50N 81 3W
Ogilby, U.S.A. **111 N12** 32 49N 114 50W
Oglio ➤, Italy ..... **40 C7** 45 2N 10 39 E
Oglio Nord △, Italy . **40 C6** 45 22N 9 54 E
Oglio Sud △, Italy .. **40 C6** 45 7N 10 27 E
Ogmore, Australia ... **94 C4** 22 37 S 149 35 E
Ognon ➤, France ... **19 E12** 47 16N 5 28 E
Ogoja, Nigeria ..... **83 D6** 6 38N 8 39 E
Ogoki, Canada **104 B2** 51 38N 85 58W
Ogoki ➤, Canada ... **104 B2** 51 38N 85 57W
Ogoki L., Canada ... **104 B2** 50 50N 87 10W
Ogoki Res., Canada .. **104 B2** 50 45N 88 15W
Ogooué ➤, Gabon .. **84 E1** 1 0 S 9 0 E
Ogosta ➤, Bulgaria . **44 C7** 43 48N 23 55 E
Ogowe = Ogooué ➤,
Gabon .... **84 E1** 1 0 S 9 0 E
Ogowe, Nigeria **83 D6** 5 0N 7 30E
Ogr = Sharafa, Sudan **81 E2** 11 59N 27 7 E
Ogražden, Macedonia **44 E6** 41 30N 22 50 E
Ogre, Latvia .... **9 H21** 56 49N 24 36 E
Ogrein, Sudan ...... **80 D3** 17 55N 34 50 E

Ogulin, Croatia ..... **41 C12** 45 16N 15 16 E
Ogun □, Nigeria .... **83 D5** 7 0N 3 0 E
Ogurchinskiy, Ostrov,
Turkmenistan .... **71 B7** 38 55N 53 2 E
Oguta, Nigeria ..... **83 D6** 5 44N 6 44 E
Ogwashi-Uku, Nigeria **83 D6** 6 15N 6 30 E
Ogwe, Nigeria ...... **83 E6** 5 0N 7 14 E
Ohai, N.Z. .... **91 L2** 45 55 S 168 0 E
Ohakune, N.Z. ..... **91 H5** 39 24 S 175 24 E
Ohata, Japan ...... **54 D10** 41 24N 141 10 E
Ohau, L., N.Z. ..... **91 L2** 44 15 S 169 53 E
Ohio □, U.S.A. **116 F2** 40 15N 82 45W
Ohio ➤, U.S.A. **114 G1** 36 59N 89 8W
Ohře ➤, Czech Rep. . **26 A7** 50 30N 14 10 E
Ohre ➤, Germany ... **24 C7** 52 18N 11 46 E
Ohrid, Macedonia ... **44 E4** 41 8N 20 52 E
Ohridsko Jezero,
Macedonia ...... **44 E4** 41 8N 20 52 E
Öhringen, Germany .. **25 F5** 49 12N 9 31 E
Oi Qu, China ...... **58 C2** 28 37N 98 16 E
Oiapoque, Brazil **125** 3 50N 51 50W
Oikou, China ...... **57 E9** 38 35N 117 42 E
Oil City, U.S.A. **116 E5** 41 26N 79 42W
Oil Springs, Canada . **116 D2** 42 47N 82 7W
Oildale, U.S.A. **111 K7** 35 25N 119 1W
Oinousa, Greece .... **47 C8** 38 33N 26 14 E
Oise □, France ..... **19 C9** 49 28N 2 30 E
Oise ➤, France ..... **19 C9** 49 0N 2 4 E
Oiseaux du Djoudj △,
Senegal **82 B1** 16 24N 16 14W
Oistins, Barbados ... **121 g** 13 4N 59 33W
Oistins B., Barbados . **121 g** 13 4N 59 33W
Öita, Japan .... **55 H5** 33 14N 131 36 E
Ōita □, Japan ...... **55 H5** 33 15N 131 30 E
Oiticica, Brazil ..... **125 E10** 5 3 S 41 5W
Ojacaliente, Mexico . **118 C4** 22 34N 102 15W
Ojai, U.S.A. **111 L7** 34 27N 119 15W
Ojcowski △, Poland . **31 H6** 50 15N 19 50 E
Ojiya, Japan .... **55 F9** 37 18N 138 48 E
Ojo de Liebre △, Mexico **118 B2** 27 50N 114 0W
Ojos del Salado, Cerro,
Argentina .... **126 B2** 27 0 S 68 40W
Oka ➤, Russia ..... **34 B7** 56 20N 43 59 E
Okaba, Indonesia ... **63 F9** 8 6 S 139 42 E
Okahandja, Namibia . **88 C2** 22 0 S 16 59 E
Okanagan L., Canada **102 C5** 50 0N 119 30W
Okanogan, U.S.A. ... **108 B4** 48 22N 119 35W
Okanogan ➤, U.S.A. **108 B4** 48 6N 119 44W
Okány, Hungary .... **28 D6** 46 52N 21 21 E
Okapi △, Dem. Rep. of
the Congo .... **86 B2** 2 30N 27 20 E
Okaputa, Namibia ... **88 C2** 20 5 S 17 0 E
Okara, Pakistan .... **68 D5** 30 50N 73 31 E
Okaukuejo, Namibia . **88 B2** 19 10 S 16 0 E
Okavango Delta,
Botswana .... **88 B3** 18 45 S 22 45 E
Okavango Swamp =
Okavango Delta,
Botswana .... **88 B3** 18 45 S 22 45 E
Okaya, Japan ...... **55 F9** 36 5N 138 10 E
Okayama, Japan .... **55 G6** 34 40N 133 54 E
Okayama □, Japan .. **55 G6** 35 0N 133 50 E
Okazaki, Japan ..... **55 G8** 34 57N 137 10 E
Oke-Iho, Nigeria ... **83 D5** 8 1N 3 18 E
Okęcie, Warszawa ✈
(WAW), Poland .. **31 F7** 52 9N 20 59 E
Okeechobee, U.S.A. . **115 M5** 27 15N 80 50W
Okeechobee L., U.S.A. **115 M5** 27 0N 80 50W
Okefenokee ⌣, U.S.A. **115 K4** 30 44N 82 7W
Okefenokee Swamp,
U.S.A. **115 K4** 30 40N 82 20W
Okehampton, U.K. .. **15 G4** 50 44N 4 0W
Okene, Nigeria ..... **83 D6** 7 32N 6 11 E
Oker ➤, Germany ... **24 C6** 52 32N 9 34 E
Okha, India .... **68 H3** 22 27N 69 4 E
Okha, Russia ...... **53 D15** 53 40N 143 0 E
Ōkhi Óros, Greece .. **46 C6** 38 5N 24 5 E
Okhotsk, Russia .... **53 D15** 59 20N 143 10 E
Okhotsk, Sea of, Asia **53 D15** 55 0N 145 0 E
Okhotskiy Perevoz,
Russia .... **53 C14** 61 52N 135 35 E
Okhtyrka, Ukraine .. **33 G8** 50 25N 35 0 E
Oki-Shotō, Japan ... **55 F6** 36 5N 133 15 E
Okiep, S. Africa .... **88 D2** 29 39 S 17 53 E
Okigwi, Nigeria .... **83 D6** 5 52N 7 20 E
Okija, Nigeria ..... **83 D6** 5 54N 6 55 E
Okinawa □, Japan .. **55 L4** 26 40N 128 0 E
Okinawa-Guntō, Japan **55 L4** 26 40N 128 0 E
Okinawa-Jima, Japan **55 L4** 26 32N 128 0 E
Okino-erabu-Shima,
Japan .... **55 L4** 27 21N 128 33 E
Okitipupa, Nigeria .. **83 D5** 6 31N 4 50 E
Oklahoma □, U.S.A. **113 H6** 35 20N 97 30W
Oklahoma City, U.S.A. **113 H6** 35 30N 97 30W
Okmulgee, U.S.A. ... **113 H7** 35 37N 95 58W
Oknitsa = Ocniţa,
Moldova .... **29 B12** 48 25N 27 30 E
Oko, W. ➤, Sudan .. **80 C4** 21 15N 35 56 E
Okolo, Uganda ..... **86 B3** 2 37N 31 8 E
Okolona, U.S.A. **113 J10** 34 0N 88 45W
Okombahe, Namibia . **88 C2** 21 23 S 15 22 E
Okonek, Poland .... **30 E3** 53 32N 16 51 E
Okotoks, Canada ... **102 C6** 50 43N 113 58W
Okrika, Nigeria .... **83 E6** 4 40N 7 10 E
Oksibil, Indonesia .. **63 E10** 4 59 S 140 35 E
Oktabrsk = Oktyabrsk,
Kazakhstan ..... **52 E6** 49 28N 57 25 E
Oktyabrsk, Kazakhstan **52 E6** 49 28N 57 25 E
Oktyabrsk, Russia ... **34 D9** 53 11N 48 40 E
Oktyabrskiy =
Aktsyabrski, Belarus **33 F5** 52 38N 28 53 E
Oktyabrskiy, Russia . **35 G5** 47 30N 40 4 E
Oktyabrskoy
Revolyutsi, Ostrov,
Russia .... **53 B10** 79 30N 97 0 E
Oktyabrskoye =
Zhovtneve Ukraine . **33 J7** 46 54N 32 3 E
Okulovka, Russia ... **32 C7** 58 25N 33 18 E
Okuru, N.Z. .... **91 K2** 43 55 S 168 55 E
Okushiri-Tō, Japan . **54 C9** 42 15N 139 30 E
Okuta, Nigeria ..... **83 D5** 9 14N 3 12 E
Okwa ➤, Botswana . **88 C3** 22 30 S 20 13 E
Ola, U.S.A. **113 H8** 35 2N 93 13W
Ólafsfjörður, Iceland . **8 C4** 66 4N 18 39W
Ólafsvík, Iceland ... **8 D2** 64 53N 23 43W
Olaine, Latvia ..... **30 B10** 56 48N 23 59 E
Olancha, U.S.A. **111 J8** 36 17N 118 1W
Olancha Pk., U.S.A. . **111 J8** 36 15N 118 7W
Olanchito, Honduras **120 C2** 15 30N 86 30W
Öland, Sweden ..... **11 H10** 56 45N 16 38 E
Ölands norra udde,
Sweden .... **11 G11** 57 22N 17 5 E
Ölands södra udde,
Sweden .... **11 H10** 56 12N 16 23 E
Olargues, France ... **20 E6** 43 34N 2 53 E

Olary, Australia ..... **95 E3** 32 18 S 140 19 E
Olascoaga, Argentina **126 D3** 35 15 S 60 39W
Olathe, U.S.A. **112 F7** 38 53N 94 49W
Olavarría, Argentina . **126 D3** 36 55 S 60 20W
Oława, Poland ...... **31 H4** 50 57N 17 20 E
Olbernhau, Germany **25 E9** 50 40N 13 19 E
Ólbia, Italy .... **42 B2** 40 55N 9 31 E
Ólbia, G. di, Italy ... **42 B2** 40 55N 9 39 E
Olching, Germany ... **25 G7** 48 12N 11 21 E
Olcott, U.S.A. **116 C6** 43 20N 78 42W
Old Bahama Chan. =
Bahama, Canal Viejo
de, W. Indies **120 B4** 22 10N 77 30W
Old Baldy Pk. = San
Antonio, Mt., U.S.A. **111 L9** 34 17N 117 38W
Old Castile = Castilla y
Leon □, Spain ... **36 D6** 42 0N 5 0W
Old Crow, Canada .. **100 B6** 67 30N 139 55W
Old Dale, U.S.A. ... **111 L11** 34 8N 115 47W
Old Forge, N.Y., U.S.A. **117 C10** 43 43N 74 58W
Old Forge, Pa., U.S.A. **117 E9** 41 22N 75 45W
Old Perlican, Canada **105 C9** 48 5N 53 1W
Old Shinyanga,
Tanzania .... **86 C3** 3 33 S 33 27 E
Old Speck Mt., U.S.A. **117 B14** 44 34N 70 57W
Old Town, U.S.A. ... **115 C11** 44 56N 68 39W
Old Washington, U.S.A. **116 F3** 40 2N 81 27W
Old Wives L., Canada **103 C7** 50 5N 106 0W
Oldbury, U.K. **15 F5** 51 38N 2 33W
Oldcastle, Ireland .. **12 C4** 53 46N 7 10W
Oldeani, Tanzania .. **86 C4** 3 22 S 35 35 E
Oldenburg,
Niedersachsen,
Germany .... **24 B4** 53 9N 8 13 E
Oldenburg,
Schleswig-Holstein,
Germany .... **24 A6** 54 17N 10 52 E
Oldenzaal, Neths. ... **17 B6** 52 19N 6 53 E
Oldham, U.K. **14 D5** 53 33N 2 7W
Oldman ➤, Canada . **102 D6** 49 57N 111 42W
Oldmeldrum, U.K. .. **13 D6** 57 20N 2 19W
Olds, Canada **102 C6** 51 50N 114 10W
Olduvai Gorge,
Tanzania .... **86 C4** 2 57 S 35 23 E
Oldziyt, Mongolia ... **56 B5** 44 40N 109 1 E
Olean, U.S.A. **116 D6** 42 5N 78 26W
Olecko, Poland ..... **30 D9** 54 2N 22 31 E
Oléggio, Italy ...... **40 C5** 45 36N 8 38 E
Oleiros, Portugal ... **36 F3** 39 56N 7 56W
Oleiros, Spain **36 B2** 43 20N 8 19W
Olekma ➤, Russia .. **53 C13** 60 22N 120 42 E
Olekminsk, Russia .. **53 C13** 60 25N 120 30 E
Oleksandriya,
Kirovohrad, Ukraine **33 H7** 48 42N 33 3 E
Oleksandriya, Rivne,
Ukraine .... **33 G4** 50 37N 26 19 E
Oleksandrovka, Ukraine **33 H7** 48 55N 32 20 E
Olema, U.S.A. **110 G4** 38 3N 122 47W
Olenek, Russia ..... **53 B13** 73 0N 120 10 E
Olenek ➤, Russia ... **53 B13** 73 0N 120 10 E
Olenino, Russia .... **32 D7** 56 15N 33 30 E
Oléron, Î. d', France . **20 C2** 45 55N 1 15W
Olesk, Ukraine ..... **31 G11** 51 6N 24 11 E
Oleśnica, Poland ... **31 G4** 51 13N 17 22 E
Olesno, Poland ..... **31 H5** 50 51N 18 26 E
Olevsk, Ukraine .... **33 G5** 51 12N 27 39 E
Olga, Russia .... **53 E14** 43 50N 135 14 E
Olga, L., Canada ... **104 C4** 49 47N 77 15W
Olga, Mt., Australia . **93 E5** 25 20 S 130 50 E
Ølgod, Denmark ... **11 J2** 55 49N 8 36 E
Olhão, Portugal **37 H3** 37 3N 7 48W
Olhopil, Ukraine ... **29 B14** 48 12N 29 30 E
Olhovatka, Russia .. **30 D9** 54 30N 22 18 E
Olib, Croatia ...... **41 D11** 44 23N 14 44 E
Oliena, Italy ...... **42 B2** 40 16N 9 24 E
Oliete, Spain **38 D4** 41 1N 0 41W
Olifants = Elefantes ➤,
Africa .... **89 C5** 24 10 S 32 40 E
Olifants ➤, Namibia **88 B2** 25 30 S 19 30 E
Olifantshoek, S. Africa **88 D3** 27 57 S 22 42 E
Ólimbos, Greece .... **47 F9** 35 44N 27 11 E
Ólimbos, Óros, Greece **44 F6** 40 6N 22 23 E
Olímpia, Brazil ..... **127 A6** 20 44 S 48 54W
Olimpos-Beydaglari △,
Turkey .... **47 E12** 36 36N 30 30 E
Olinda, Brazil ...... **125 E12** 8 1 S 34 51W
Olite, Spain **38 C3** 42 29N 1 40W
Oliva, Argentina .... **126 C3** 32 0 S 63 38W
Oliva, Spain **39 G4** 38 58N 0 9W
Oliva, Punta del, Spain **36 B5** 43 37N 5 28W
Oliva de la Frontera,
Spain **37 G4** 38 17N 6 54W
Olivares, Spain **38 F2** 39 46N 2 20W
Olivehurst, U.S.A. .. **110 F5** 39 6N 121 34W
Oliveira de Azeméis,
Portugal **36 E2** 40 49N 8 29W
Oliveira do Douro,
Portugal **36 D2** 41 8N 8 12W
Olivenza, Spain **37 G3** 38 41N 7 9W
Oliver, Canada **102 D5** 49 13N 119 37W
Oliver L., Canada ... **103 B8** 56 56N 103 22W
Olivet, France ..... **19 E8** 47 51N 1 55 E
Olkhovka, Russia ... **34 F7** 49 48N 44 32 E
Olkusz, Poland ..... **31 H6** 50 18N 19 33 E
Ollagüe, Chile ..... **126 A2** 21 15 S 68 10W
Olmedo, Spain **36 D6** 41 20N 4 43W
Olmeto, France .... **21 G12** 41 43N 8 55 E
Olney, Ill., U.S.A. .. **114 F1** 38 44N 88 5W
Olney, Tex., U.S.A. . **113 J5** 33 22N 98 45W
Olofström, Sweden .. **11 H8** 56 17N 14 32 E
Oloma, Cameroon .. **83 E7** 3 29N 11 19 E
Olomane ➤, Canada **105 B7** 50 14N 60 37W
Olomouc, Czech Rep. **27 B10** 49 38N 17 12 E
Olomoucký □,
Czech Rep. ..... **27 B10** 49 45N 17 5 E
Olonets, Russia .... **32 B7** 61 0N 32 54 E
Olongapo, Phil. .... **61 D4** 14 50N 120 18 E
Olonne-sur-Mer, France **20 B2** 46 32N 1 47W
Oloron, Gave d' ➤,
France **20 E3** 43 33N 1 5W
Oloron-Ste-Marie,
France **20 E3** 43 11N 0 38W
Olot, Spain .... **38 C7** 42 11N 2 30 E
Olovo, Bos.-H. ..... **28 F3** 44 8N 18 35 E
Olovyannaya, Russia **53 D12** 50 58N 115 35 E
Oloy ➤, Russia .... **53 C16** 66 29N 159 29 E
Olpe, Germany .... **24 D3** 51 2N 7 51 E
Olsene, Italy .... **55 G5** 33 59N 33 11 E
Olszanica, Ukraine . **33 H6** 48 16N 36 8 E
Olshany, Ukraine ... **33 G8** 50 3N 35 53 E
Olsztyn, Poland .... **30 E7** 53 48N 20 29 E
Olsztynek, Poland .. **30 E7** 53 34N 20 19 E
Olt □, Romania .... **29 F9** 44 20N 24 30 E
Olt ➤, Romania .... **29 G9** 43 43N 24 51 E
Oltedal, Norway .... **9 G11** 58 37N 6 10 E
Olten, Switz. ...... **25 H3** 47 21N 7 53 E
Olteniţa, Romania .. **29 F11** 44 7N 26 42 E
Olton, U.S.A. **113 H3** 34 11N 102 8W

Oltu, Turkey ...... **73 B9** 40 35N 41 58 E
Oluanpi, Taiwan .... **59 G13** 21 54N 120 51 E
Olula del Río, Spain . **39 H2** 37 21N 2 18W
Olur, Turkey ...... **73 B10** 40 49N 42 8 E
Olutanga, Phil. .... **61 H5** 7 26N 122 54 E
Olvega, Spain **38 D2** 41 47N 2 0W
Olvera, Spain **37 J5** 36 55N 5 18W
Olymbos, Cyprus ... **49 D12** 35 21N 33 45 E
Olympia, Greece ... **46 D3** 37 39N 21 39 E
Olympia, U.S.A. **110 D4** 47 3N 122 53W
Olympic Dam, Australia **95 E2** 30 30 S 136 55 E
Olympic Mts., U.S.A. **110 C3** 47 55N 123 45W
Olympus, Cyprus ... **49 E11** 34 56N 32 52 E
Olympus, Mt. =
Ólimbos, Óros, Greece **44 F6** 40 6N 22 23 E
Olympus, Mt. = Uludağ,
Turkey .... **45 F13** 40 4N 29 13 E
Olympus, Mt., U.S.A. **110 C3** 47 48N 123 43W
Olyphant, U.S.A. ... **117 E9** 41 27N 75 36W
Om ➤, Russia ..... **52 D8** 54 59N 73 22 E
Om Hajer, Eritrea .. **81 E4** 14 20N 36 41 E
Om Koi, Thailand .. **64 D2** 17 48N 98 22 E
Ōmachi, Japan .... **54 D10** 41 45N 141 5 E
Ōmae-Zaki, Japan .. **55 F8** 36 30N 137 50 E
Omagari, Japan .... **55 G9** 34 36N 138 14 E
Ōmagari, Japan .... **54 E10** 39 27N 140 29 E
Omagh, U.K. **12 B4** 54 36N 7 19W
Omagh □, U.K. **12 B4** 54 35N 7 15W
Omaha, U.S.A. **112 E7** 41 17N 95 58W
Omak, U.S.A. **108 B4** 48 25N 119 31W
Omalos, Greece .... **49 D5** 35 19N 23 55 E
Oman ■, Asia ..... **75 C6** 23 0N 58 0 E
Oman, G. of, Asia .. **71 E8** 24 30N 58 30 E
Omaruru, Namibia .. **88 C2** 21 26 S 16 0 E
Omaruru ➤, Namibia **88 C1** 22 7 S 14 15 E
Omate, Peru ...... **124 G4** 16 45 S 71 0W
Ombai, Selat, Indonesia **63 F6** 8 30 S 124 50 E
Omboué, Gabon ... **84 E1** 1 35 S 9 15 E
Ombrone ➤, Italy .. **40 F8** 42 42N 11 5 E
Omdurmân, Sudan .. **81 D3** 15 40N 32 28 E
Omegna, Italy ..... **40 C5** 45 53N 8 24 E
Omemee, Canada ... **116 B6** 44 18N 78 33W
Ometepe, I. de, Nic. . **120 D2** 11 32N 85 35W
Ometepec, Mexico .. **119 D5** 16 39N 98 23W
Ominato, Japan .... **54 D10** 41 17N 141 10 E
Omineca ➤, Canada **102 B4** 56 3N 124 16W
Omiš, Croatia ..... **41 E13** 43 28N 16 40 E
Omišalj, Croatia ... **41 C11** 45 13N 14 32 E
Ōmiya, Japan ..... **55 G9** 35 54N 139 38 E
Ommen, Neths. .... **17 B6** 52 31N 6 26 E
Omnögovĭ □, Mongolia **56 C3** 43 15N 104 0 E
Omo ➤, Ethiopia ... **81 F4** 5 54N 35 5 E
Omo ➤, Ethiopia ... **81 F4** 6 25N 36 10 E
Omo Valley, Ethiopia **81 F4** 5 7N 36 0 E
Omodeo, L., Italy .. **42 B1** 40 9N 8 56 E
Omodhos, Cyprus .. **49 E11** 34 51N 32 48 E
Omoko, Nigeria .... **83 D6** 5 19N 6 40 E
Omolon ➤, Russia . **53 C16** 68 42N 158 36 E
Omono-Gawa ➤, Japan **54 E10** 39 46N 140 3 E
Omsk, Russia ..... **52 D8** 55 0N 73 12 E
Omsukchan, Russia . **53 C16** 62 32N 155 48 E
Ōmu, Japan ...... **54 B11** 44 34N 142 58 E
Omul, Vf., Romania . **29 E10** 45 27N 25 29 E
Omulew ➤, Poland . **31 E8** 53 5N 21 33 E
Ōmura, Japan ..... **55 H4** 32 56N 129 57 E
Omuramba ➤, Namibia **88 B2** 17 45 S 20 25 E
Omuramba Ovambo ➤,
Namibia .... **88 B2** 18 45 S 16 59 E
Omurtag, Bulgaria .. **45 C10** 43 8N 26 26 E
Ōmuta, Japan ..... **55 H5** 33 5N 130 26 E
Oña, Spain **36 C7** 42 43N 3 25W
Onaga, U.S.A. **112 F6** 39 29N 96 10W
Onalaska, U.S.A. ... **112 D9** 43 53N 91 14W
Onancock, U.S.A. .. **114 G8** 37 42N 75 45W
Onang, Indonesia .. **63 E5** 3 2 S 118 49 E
Onaping L., Canada **104 C3** 47 3N 81 30W
Oñati, Spain **38 B2** 43 3N 2 25W
Onavas, Mexico **118 B3** 28 28N 109 30W
Onawa, U.S.A. **112 D6** 42 2N 96 6W
Oncócua, Angola ... **88 B1** 16 30 S 13 25 E
Onda, Spain **38 F4** 39 55N 0 17W
Ondaejin, N. Korea . **57 D15** 41 34N 129 40 E
Ondangwa, Namibia **88 B2** 17 57 S 16 4 E
Ondarroa, Spain ... **38 B2** 43 19N 2 25W
Ondjiva, Angola ... **88 B2** 16 48 S 15 50 E
Ondo, Nigeria ..... **83 D5** 7 4N 4 47 E
Ondo □, Nigeria ... **83 D6** 6 45N 5 0 E
Öndörshil, Mongolia **56 B5** 45 13N 108 5 E
Öndverðarnes, Iceland **8 D1** 64 52N 24 0W
One Tree, Australia .. **95 E3** 34 11 S 144 43 E
Onega, Russia ..... **52 C4** 64 0N 38 10 E
Onega ➤, Russia ... **6 C13** 63 58N 38 2 E
Onega, L. =
Onezhskoye
Ozero, Russia ... **32 B8** 61 44N 35 22 E
Oneida, U.S.A. **117 C9** 43 6N 75 39W
Oneida L., U.S.A. .. **117 C9** 43 12N 75 54W
O'Neill, U.S.A. **112 D5** 42 27N 98 39W
Onekotan, Ostrov,
Russia .... **53 E16** 49 25N 154 45 E
Onema, Dem. Rep. of
the Congo .... **86 C1** 4 35 S 24 30 E
Oneonta, U.S.A. ... **117 D9** 42 27N 75 4W
Oneşti, Romania ... **29 D11** 46 17N 26 47 E
Onezhskoye Ozero,
Russia .... **32 B8** 61 44N 35 22 E
Ongarue, N.Z. ..... **91 H5** 38 42 S 175 19 E
Ongers ➤, S. Africa **88 E3** 31 4 S 23 13 E
Ongerup, Australia .. **93 F2** 33 58 S 118 28 E
Ongjin, N. Korea ... **57 F13** 37 56N 125 21 E
Ongkharak, Thailand **64 E3** 14 8N 101 1 E
Ongniud Qi, China .. **57 C10** 43 0N 118 38 E
Ongole, India ..... **66 M12** 15 33N 80 2 E
Ongon = Havirga,
Mongolia .... **56 B7** 45 41N 113 5 E
Oni, Georgia ...... **35 J6** 42 33N 43 26 E
Onida, U.S.A. **112 C4** 44 42N 100 4W
Onilahy ➤, Madag. . **89 C7** 23 34 S 43 45 E
Onitsha, Nigeria ... **83 D6** 6 6N 6 42 E
Onoda, Japan ..... **55 G5** 33 59N 131 11 E
Onpyŏng-ni, S. Korea **57 H14** 33 25N 126 55 E
Ons, I. de, Spain ... **36 C2** 42 23N 8 55W
Onsala, Sweden .... **11 G6** 57 26N 12 0 E
Onslow, Australia ... **92 D2** 21 40 S 115 12 E
Onslow B., U.S.A. .. **115 H7** 34 20N 77 15W
Ontake-San, Japan .. **55 G8** 35 53N 137 29 E
Ontario, Calif., U.S.A. **111 L9** 34 4N 117 39W
Ontario, Oreg., U.S.A. **108 D5** 44 2N 116 58W
Ontario □, Canada .. **104 B2** 48 0N 83 0W

Ontario, L., N. Amer. . **116 C7** 43 20N 78 0W
Ontinyent, Spain ... **39 G4** 38 50N 0 35W
Ontonagon, U.S.A. . **112 B10** 46 52N 89 19W
Ontur, Spain **39 G3** 38 38N 1 29W
Onyx, U.S.A. **111 K8** 35 41N 118 14W
Oodnadatta, Australia **95 D2** 27 33 S 135 30 E
Oombulgurri, Australia **92 C4** 15 15 S 127 45 E
Oorindi, Australia .. **94 C3** 20 40 S 141 1 E
Oost-Vlaanderen □,
Belgium .... **17 C3** 51 5N 3 50 E
Oostende, Belgium .. **17 C2** 51 15N 2 54 E
Oosterhout, Neths. .. **17 C4** 51 39N 4 47 E
Oosterschelde ➤, Neths. **17 C4** 51 33N 4 0 E
Oosterwolde, Neths. . **17 B6** 53 0N 6 17 E
Ootacamund =
Udagamandalam,
India .... **66 P10** 11 30N 76 44 E
Ootsa L., Canada ... **102 C3** 53 50N 126 2W
Op Luang △, Thailand **64 C2** 18 12N 98 32 E
Opaka, Bulgaria .... **45 C10** 43 28N 26 10 E
Opala, Dem. Rep. of
the Congo .... **86 C1** 0 40 S 24 20 E
Opalenica, Poland .. **31 F3** 52 18N 16 24 E
Opan, Bulgaria ..... **45 D9** 42 13N 25 41 E
Opanake, Sri Lanka . **66 R12** 6 35N 80 40 E
Opasatika, Canada .. **104 C3** 49 30N 82 50W
Opasquia □, Canada **104 B1** 53 33N 93 5W
Opatija, Croatia .... **41 C11** 45 21N 14 17 E
Opatów, Poland .... **31 H8** 50 50N 21 27 E
Opava, Czech Rep. . **27 B10** 49 57N 17 58 E
Opelika, U.S.A. **115 J3** 32 39N 85 23W
Opelousas, U.S.A. .. **113 K8** 30 32N 92 5W
Opémisca L., Canada **104 C5** 49 56N 74 52W
Opheim, U.S.A. **108 B10** 48 51N 106 24W
Ophthalmia Ra.,
Australia .... **92 D2** 23 15 S 119 30 E
Opi, Nigeria ...... **83 D6** 6 36N 7 28 E
Opinaca ➤, Canada **104 B4** 52 15N 78 2W
Opinaca, Rés., Canada **104 B4** 52 39N 76 20W
Opinnagau ➤, Canada **104 B3** 54 12N 82 25W
Opiscotéo, L., Canada **105 B6** 53 10N 68 10W
Opobo, Nigeria .... **83 E6** 4 35N 7 34 E
Opochka, Russia ... **32 D5** 56 42N 28 45 E
Opoczno, Poland ... **31 G7** 51 22N 20 18 E
Opol, Phil. .... **61 G6** 8 31N 124 34 E
Opole, Poland ..... **31 H4** 50 42N 17 58 E
Opole Lubelskie, Poland **31 G8** 51 9N 21 58 E
Opolskie □, Poland . **31 H5** 50 30N 18 0 E
Oponono L., Namibia **88 B2** 18 8 S 15 45 E
Oporto = Porto,
Portugal **36 D2** 41 8N 8 40W
Opotiki, N.Z. ...... **91 H6** 38 1 S 177 19 E
Opp, U.S.A. **115 K2** 31 17N 86 16W
Oppdal, Norway ... **9 E13** 62 35N 9 41 E
Óppido Mamertina, Italy **43 D8** 38 16N 15 59 E
Opportunity, U.S.A. . **108 C5** 47 39N 117 15W
Oprişor, Romania .. **28 F8** 44 17N 23 5 E
Oprtalj, Croatia .... **41 C10** 45 23N 13 50 E
Opua, N.Z. .... **91 F5** 35 19 S 174 9 E
Opunake, N.Z. ..... **91 H4** 39 26 S 173 52 E
Opuwo, Namibia ... **88 B1** 18 3 S 13 45 E
Opuzen, Croatia ... **41 E14** 43 1N 17 34 E
Ora, Cyprus .... **49 E12** 34 51N 33 12 E
Oracle, U.S.A. **109 K8** 32 37N 110 46W
Oradea, Romania ... **28 C6** 47 2N 21 58 E
Öræfajökull, Iceland . **8 D5** 64 2N 16 39W
Orahovac, Serbia & M. **44 D4** 42 24N 20 40 E
Orahovica, Croatia . **28 E3** 45 35N 17 52 E
Orai, India .... **69 G8** 25 58N 79 30 E
Oraison, France .... **21 E9** 43 55N 5 55 E
Oral = Zhayyq ➤,
Kazakhstan ..... **52 E6** 47 0N 51 48 E
Oral, Kazakhstan ... **34 E10** 51 20N 51 20 E
Oran, Algeria **95 E4** 33 45N 0 39W
Orange, Australia ... **95 E4** 33 15 S 149 7 E
Orange, France .... **21 D8** 44 8N 4 47 E
Orange, Calif., U.S.A. **111 M9** 33 47N 117 51W
Orange, Mass., U.S.A. **117 D12** 42 35N 72 19W
Orange, Tex., U.S.A. **113 K8** 30 6N 93 44W
Orange, Va., U.S.A. . **114 F6** 38 15N 78 7W
Orange ➤, S. Africa **88 D2** 28 41 S 16 28 E
Orange, C., Brazil ... **125 C8** 4 20N 51 30W
Orange Cove, U.S.A. **110 J7** 36 38N 119 19W
Orange Free State =
Free State □, S. Africa **88 D3** 28 30 S 27 0 E
Orange Grove, U.S.A. **113 M6** 27 58N 97 56W
Orange Walk, Belize **119 D7** 18 6N 88 33W
Orangeburg, U.S.A. . **115 J5** 33 30N 80 52W
Orangeville, Canada **116 C4** 43 55N 80 5W
Orango, Guinea-Biss. **82 C1** 11 5N 16 0W
Orani, Phil. .... **61 D4** 14 49N 120 32 E
Oranienburg, Germany **24 C9** 52 45N 13 14 E
Oranje = Orange ➤,
S. Africa .... **88 D2** 28 41 S 16 28 E
Oranjemund, Namibia **88 D2** 28 38 S 16 29 E
Oranjerivier, S. Africa **88 D3** 29 40 S 24 12 E
Oranjestad, Aruba .. **121 D5** 12 32N 70 2W
Orapa, Botswana ... **85 J5** 21 15 S 25 30 E
Orarak, Sudan ..... **81 F3** 6 15N 32 23 E
Oras, Phil. .... **61 E6** 12 9N 125 28 E
Orašje, Bos.-H. .... **28 E3** 45 3N 18 42 E
Orăştie, Romania ... **29 E8** 45 50N 23 10 E
Orava ➤, Slovak Rep. **27 B12** 49 9N 19 8 E
Orava, Vodna nádrž,
Slovak Rep. ..... **27 B12** 49 25N 19 35 E
Oraviţa, Romania ... **28 E6** 45 6N 21 43 E
Orb ➤, France ..... **20 E7** 43 15N 3 18 E
Orba ➤, Italy ...... **40 D5** 44 53N 8 37 E
Ørbæk, Denmark ... **11 J4** 55 17N 10 39 E
Orbe, Switz. ...... **25 J2** 46 43N 6 32 E
Orbec, France ..... **18 C7** 49 1N 0 23 E
Orbetello, Italy .... **41 F8** 42 27N 11 13 E
Órbigo ➤, Spain ... **36 C5** 42 5N 5 42W
Orbisonia, U.S.A. .. **116 F7** 40 15N 77 54W
Orbost, Australia ... **95 F4** 37 40 S 148 29 E
Ørbyhus, Sweden ... **10 D11** 60 15N 17 43 E
Orcadas, Antarctica **5 C18** 60 44 S 44 37W
Orcas I., U.S.A. **110 B4** 48 42N 122 56W
Orce, Spain **39 H2** 37 44N 2 28W
Orce ➤, Spain **39 H2** 37 44N 2 28W
Orchard City, U.S.A. **109 G10** 38 50N 107 58W
Orchies, France .... **19 B10** 50 28N 3 14 E
Orchila, I., Venezuela **121 D6** 11 48N 66 10W
Orchilla, Pta., Canary Is. **48 G1** 27 42N 18 10W
Orcia ➤, Italy ..... **41 F8** 43 0N 11 30 E
Orco ➤, Italy ...... **40 C4** 45 10N 7 52 E
Ord ➤, Australia ... **111 L6** 15 33N 120 52W
Ord, U.S.A. **112 E5** 41 36N 98 56W
Ord, Mt., Australia . **92 C4** 17 20 S 125 34 E
Ordenes = Ordes, Spain **36 B2** 43 5N 8 29W
Orderville, U.S.A. .. **109 H7** 37 17N 112 38W
Ordes, Spain **36 B2** 43 5N 8 29W
Ordesa y Monte
Perido △, Spain .. **38 C4** 42 40N 0 10W
Ording = St-Peter-
Ording, Germany . **24 A4** 54 20N 8 36 E

Ordos = Mu Us Shamo,
China .... **56 E5** 39 0N 109 0 E
Ordu, Turkey .... **72 B7** 40 55N 37 53 E
Ordubad, Azerbaijan .. **73 C12** 38 54N 46 1 E
Orduña, Álava, Spain .. **38 C2** 42 58N 2 58W
Orduña, Granada, Spain **37 H7** 37 20N 3 30W
Ordway, U.S.A. **112 F3** 38 13N 103 46W
Ordzhonikidze, Ukraine **33 J8** 47 39N 34 3 E
Ore, Dem. Rep. of
the Congo .... **86 B2** 3 17N 29 30 E
Ore Mts. = Erzgebirge,
Germany .... **24 E8** 50 27N 12 55 E
Orebić, Croatia ...... **41 F14** 43 0N 17 11 E
Örebro, Sweden ...... **10 E9** 59 20N 15 18 E
Örebro län □, Sweden .. **10 E8** 59 27N 15 0 E
Orecchiella △, Italy ... **40 D7** 44 16N 10 22 E
Oregon, U.S.A. **112 D10** 42 1N 89 20W
Oregon □, U.S.A. **108 E3** 44 0N 121 0W
Oregon City, U.S.A. ... **110 E4** 45 21N 122 36W
Oregon Dunes △, U.S.A. **108 E1** 42 3N 123 26W
Öregrund, Sweden .... **10 D12** 60 21N 18 30 E
Öregrundsgrepen,
Sweden .... **10 D12** 60 25N 18 15 E
Orekhov = Orikhiv,
Ukraine .... **33 J8** 47 30N 35 48 E
Orekhovo-Zuyevo,
Russia .... **32 E10** 55 50N 38 55 E
Orel, Russia .... **33 F9** 52 57N 36 3 E
Orel →, Ukraine ..... **33 H8** 48 40N 34 39 E
Orellana, Spain **37 F5** 39 1N 5 32W
Orellana, Canal de,
Spain **37 F5** 39 2N 6 0W
Orellana, Embalse de,
Spain **37 F5** 39 5N 5 10W
Orem, U.S.A. **108 F8** 40 19N 111 42W
Ören, Turkey .... **47 D9** 37 3N 27 57 E
Orenburg, Russia ..... **52 D6** 51 45N 55 6 E
Örencik, Turkey ...... **47 B11** 39 16N 29 33 E
Orense = Ourense,
Spain **36 C3** 42 19N 7 55W
Orense □, Spain **36 C3** 42 15N 7 51W
Orepuki, N.Z. .... **91 M1** 46 19 S 167 46 E
Orestías, Greece ...... **45 E10** 41 30N 26 33 E
Orestos Pereyra, Mexico **118 B3** 26 31N 105 40W
Øresund, Europe ..... **11 J6** 55 45N 12 45 E
Orford Ness, U.K. .... **15 E9** 52 5N 1 35 E
Organ Pipe Cactus △,
U.S.A. **109 K7** 32 0N 113 10W
Organos, Pta. de los,
Canary Is. **48 F2** 28 12N 17 17W
Organyà, Spain ...... **38 C6** 42 13N 1 20 E
Orgaz, Spain **37 F7** 39 39N 3 53W
Orgeyev = Orhei,
Moldova .... **29 C13** 47 24N 28 50 E
Orhaneli, Turkey ..... **45 G12** 39 54N 28 59 E
Orhaneli →, Turkey ... **45 G12** 39 50N 28 55 E
Orhangazi, Turkey .... **45 F13** 40 29N 29 18 E
Orhei, Moldova ...... **29 C13** 47 24N 28 50 E
Orhon Gol →,
Mongolia .... **60 A5** 50 21N 105 0 E
Óriá, Italy .... **43 B10** 40 30N 17 38 E
Oriental, Cordillera,
Colombia **124 B4** 6 0N 73 0W
Oriental, Grand Erg,
Algeria .... **78 B7** 30 0N 5 30 E
Orientale □, Dem. Rep.
of the Congo ...... **86 B2** 2 20N 25 0 E
Oriente, Argentina .... **126 D3** 38 44 S 63 37W
Orihuela, Spain **39 G4** 38 7N 0 55W
Orihuela del Tremedal,
Spain **38 E3** 40 33N 1 39W
Orikhiv, Ukraine ..... **33 J8** 47 30N 35 48 E
Orikum, Albania ..... **44 F3** 40 20N 19 26 E
Orillia, Canada **116 B5** 44 40N 79 24W
Orinoco →, Venezuela **124 B6** 9 15N 61 30W
Orion, Canada **103 D6** 49 27N 110 49W
Oriskany, U.S.A. **117 C9** 43 10N 75 20W
Orissa □, India ...... **67 K14** 20 0N 84 0 E
Orissaare, Estonia .... **9 G20** 58 34N 23 5 E
Oristano, Italy .... **42 C1** 39 54N 8 36 E
Oristano, G. di, Italy .. **42 C1** 39 50N 8 29 E
Orizaba, Mexico **119 D5** 18 51N 97 6W
Orizaba, Pico de, Mexico **119 D5** 19 0N 97 20W
Orizare, Bulgaria ..... **45 D11** 42 44N 27 39 E
Orjen, Bos.-H. .... **44 D2** 42 35N 18 34 E
Orjiva, Spain **37 J7** 36 53N 3 24W
Orkanger, Norway .... **8 E13** 63 18N 9 52 E
Örkelljunga, Sweden .. **11 H7** 56 17N 13 17 E
Örken, Sweden ...... **11 G9** 57 6N 15 1 E
Örkény, Hungary .... **28 C4** 47 9N 19 26 E
Orkla →, Norway .... **8 E13** 63 18N 9 51 E
Orkney, S. Africa .... **88 D4** 26 58 S 26 40 E
Orkney □, U.K. **13 B5** 59 2N 3 13W
Orkney Is., U.K. **13 B6** 59 0N 3 0W
Orland, U.S.A. **110 F4** 39 45N 122 12W
Orlando, U.S.A. **115 L5** 28 33N 81 23W
Orlando, C. d', Italy .. **43 D7** 38 10N 14 43 E
Orléanais, France .... **19 E9** 48 0N 2 0 E
Orléans, France ...... **19 E8** 47 54N 1 52 E
Orleans, U.S.A. **117 B12** 44 49N 72 12W
Orléans, Î. d', Canada . **105 C5** 46 54N 70 58W
Orlice →, Czech Rep. . **26 A8** 50 13N 15 50 E
Orlivka, Ukraine ..... **29 E13** 45 19N 28 27 E
Orlov, Slovak Rep. ... **27 B13** 49 17N 20 51 E
Orlov Gay, Russia .... **34 E9** 50 56N 48 19 E
Orlová, Czech Rep. ... **27 B11** 49 51N 18 26 E
Orlovat, Serbia & M. .. **28 E5** 45 14N 20 33 E
Orly, Paris ✈ (ORY),
France .... **19 D9** 48 44N 2 23 E
Ormara, Pakistan .... **66 G4** 25 16N 64 33 E
Ormea, Italy .... **40 D4** 44 9N 7 54 E
Ormília, Greece ...... **44 F7** 40 16N 23 39 E
Ormoc, Phil. .... **61 F6** 11 0N 124 37 E
Ormond, N.Z. .... **91 H6** 38 33 S 177 56 E
Ormond Beach, U.S.A. **115 L5** 29 17N 81 3W
Ormož, Slovenia ..... **41 B13** 46 25N 16 10 E
Ormskirk, U.K. **14 D5** 53 35N 2 54W
Ormstown, Canada ... **117 A11** 45 8N 74 0W
Ornans, France ...... **19 E13** 47 7N 6 10 E
Orne □, France ...... **18 D7** 48 40N 0 5 E
Orne →, France **18 C6** 49 18N 0 15W
Orneta, Poland ...... **30 D7** 54 8N 20 9 E
Ornö, Sweden .... **10 E12** 59 4N 18 24 E
Örnsköldsvik, Sweden . **10 A12** 63 17N 18 40 E
Oro, N. Korea .... **57 D14** 40 1N 127 27 E
Oro →, Mexico **118 B3** 25 35N 105 2W
Oro Grande, U.S.A. .. **111 L9** 34 36N 117 20W
Oro Valley, U.S.A. ... **109 K8** 32 26N 110 58W
Orobie, Alpi, Italy .... **40 B6** 46 7N 10 0 E
Orobie Bergamasche △,
Italy .... **40 C6** 46 0N 9 45 E
Orobie Valtellinesi △,
Italy .... **40 B6** 46 5N 9 45 E
Orocué, Colombia **124 C4** 4 48N 71 20W
Orodara, Burkina Faso **82 C4** 11 0N 4 55W
Orodo, Nigeria ...... **83 D6** 5 34N 7 4 E
Orofino, U.S.A. **108 C5** 46 29N 116 15W

Orol Dengizi = Aral Sea,
Asia .... **52 E7** 44 30N 60 0 E
Oromiya □, Ethiopia .. **81 F5** 7 0N 40 0 E
Oromocto, Canada ... **105 C6** 45 54N 66 29W
Oron, Nigeria .... **83 E6** 4 48N 8 14 E
Orono, Canada **116 C6** 43 59N 78 37W
Orono, U.S.A. **115 C11** 44 53N 68 40W
Oronsay, U.K. **13 E2** 56 1N 6 15W
Oropesa, Spain **36 F5** 39 57N 5 10W
Oroquieta, Phil. ..... **61 G5** 8 32N 123 44 E
Orosei, Italy .... **42 B2** 40 23N 9 42 E
Orosei, G. di, Italy ... **42 B2** 40 15N 9 44 E
Orosháza, Hungary ... **28 D5** 46 32N 20 42 E
Oroszlány, Hungary .. **28 C3** 47 29N 18 19 E
Orotukan, Russia ..... **53 C16** 62 16N 151 42 E
Oroville, Calif., U.S.A. . **110 F5** 39 31N 121 33W
Oroville, Wash., U.S.A. **108 B4** 48 56N 119 26W
Oroville, L., U.S.A. ... **110 F5** 39 33N 121 29W
Orrefors, Sweden .... **11 H9** 56 50N 15 45 E
Orroroo, Australia .... **95 E2** 32 43 S 138 38 E
Orrviken, Sweden .... **10 A8** 63 6N 14 26 E
Orrville, U.S.A. **116 F3** 40 50N 81 46W
Orsa, Sweden .... **10 C8** 61 7N 14 37 E
Orsara di Púglia, Italy . **43 A8** 41 17N 15 16 E
Orsasjön, Sweden .... **10 C8** 61 7N 14 37 E
Orsha, Belarus ...... **32 E6** 54 30N 30 25 E
Örsjö, Sweden .... **11 H9** 56 42N 15 45 E
Orsk, Russia .... **52 D6** 51 12N 58 34 E
Orşova, Romania .... **28 F7** 44 41N 22 25 E
Ørsted, Denmark .... **11 H4** 56 30N 10 20 E
Örsundsbro, Sweden .. **10 E11** 59 44N 17 18 E
Orta, L. d', Italy ..... **40 C5** 45 49N 8 24 E
Orta Nova, Italy ..... **43 A8** 41 19N 15 42 E
Ortaca, Turkey ...... **47 E10** 36 49N 28 45 E
Ortakent, Turkey .... **47 D9** 37 5N 27 21 E
Ortaklar, Turkey ..... **47 D9** 37 53N 27 30 E
Ortaköy, Çorum, Turkey **72 C6** 40 16N 35 15 E
Ortaköy, Niğde, Turkey **72 C6** 38 44N 34 3 E
Orte, Italy .... **41 F9** 42 27N 12 23 E
Ortegal, C., Spain ... **36 B3** 43 43N 7 52W
Orthez, France **20 E3** 43 29N 0 48W
Ortigueira, Spain **36 B3** 43 40N 7 50W
Orting, U.S.A. **110 C4** 47 6N 122 12W
Ortisei, Italy .... **41 B8** 46 34N 11 40 E
Ortles, Italy .... **40 B7** 46 31N 10 33 E
Ortón →, Bolivia .... **124 F5** 10 50 S 67 0W
Ortona, Italy .... **41 F11** 42 21N 14 24 E
Ortonville, U.S.A. **112 C6** 45 19N 96 27W
Orūmīyeh, Iran ...... **70 B5** 37 40N 45 0 E
Orūmīyeh, Daryācheh-
ye, Iran .... **70 B5** 37 50N 45 30 E
Orune, Italy .... **42 B2** 40 25N 9 20 E
Oruro, Bolivia ...... **124 G5** 18 0 S 67 9W
Orust, Sweden ...... **11 F5** 58 10N 11 40 E
Oruzgān □, Afghan. .. **66 C5** 33 30N 66 0 E
Orvault, France **18 E5** 47 17N 1 38W
Orvieto, Italy .... **41 F9** 42 43N 12 7 E
Orwell, N.Y., U.S.A. .. **117 C9** 43 35N 75 50W
Orwell, Ohio, U.S.A. .. **116 E4** 41 32N 80 52W
Orwell →, U.K. ...... **15 F9** 51 59N 1 18 E
Orwigsburg, U.S.A. ... **117 F8** 40 38N 76 6W
Oryakhovo, Bulgaria .. **44 C7** 43 40N 23 57 E
Orynyn, Ukraine ..... **29 B11** 48 46N 26 24 E
Orzinuovi, Italy ...... **40 C6** 45 24N 9 55 E
Orzyc →, Poland .... **31 F8** 52 46N 21 14 E
Orzysz, Poland ...... **30 E8** 53 50N 21 58 E
Osa, →, Poland ...... **31 B3** 53 33N 18 46 E
Osa, Pen. de, Costa Rica **120 E3** 8 0N 84 0W
Osage, U.S.A. **112 D8** 43 17N 92 49W
Osage →, U.S.A. **112 F9** 38 35N 91 57W
Osage City, U.S.A. ... **112 F7** 38 38N 95 50W
Ōsaka, Japan .... **55 G7** 34 40N 135 30 E
Osawatomie, U.S.A. .. **112 F7** 38 31N 94 57W
Osborne, U.S.A. **112 F5** 39 26N 98 42W
Osby, Sweden .... **11 H7** 56 23N 13 59 E
Osceola, Ark., U.S.A. . **113 H10** 35 42N 89 58W
Osceola, Iowa, U.S.A. . **112 E8** 41 2N 93 46W
Oschatz, Germany ... **24 D9** 51 17N 13 6 E
Oschersleben, Germany **24 C7** 52 1N 11 14 E
Óschiri, Italy .... **42 B2** 40 43N 9 6 E
Oscoda, U.S.A. **116 B1** 44 26N 83 20W
Osečina, Serbia & M. . **44 B3** 44 23N 19 34 E
Osel = Saaremaa,
Estonia .... **9 G20** 58 30N 22 30 E
Osery, Russia .... **32 E10** 54 52N 38 28 E
Osgoode, Canada **117 A9** 45 8N 75 36W
Osh, Kyrgyzstan ..... **52 E8** 40 37N 72 49 E
Oshakati, Namibia ... **85 H3** 17 45 S 15 40 E
Oshawa, Canada **116 C6** 43 50N 78 50W
Oshigambo, Namibia . **88 B2** 17 45 S 16 5 E
Oshkosh, Nebr., U.S.A. **112 E3** 41 24N 102 21W
Oshkosh, Wis., U.S.A. **112 C10** 44 1N 88 33W
Oshmyany = Ashmyany,
Belarus .... **9 J21** 54 26N 25 52 E
Oshnovīyeh, Iran .... **70 B5** 37 2N 45 6 E
Oshogbo, Nigeria .... **83 D5** 7 48N 4 37 E
Oshtorīnān, Iran ..... **71 C6** 34 1N 48 38 E
Oshwe, Dem. Rep. of
the Congo .... **84 E3** 3 25 S 19 28 E
Osi, Nigeria .... **83 D6** 8 8N 5 14 E
Osieczna, Poland .... **31 G3** 51 55N 16 40 E
Osijek, Croatia ...... **28 E3** 45 34N 18 41 E
Ósilo, Italy .... **42 B1** 40 45N 8 40 E
Ósimo, Italy .... **41 E10** 43 28N 13 30 E
Osintorf, Belarus .... **32 E6** 54 40N 30 39 E
Osipovichi =
Asipovichy, Belarus . **32 F5** 53 19N 28 33 E
Osiyan, India .... **68 F5** 26 43N 72 55 E
Osizweni, S. Africa ... **89 D5** 27 49 S 30 7 E
Oskaloosa, U.S.A. ... **112 E8** 41 18N 92 39W
Oskarshamn, Sweden . **11 G10** 57 15N 16 27 E
Oskarström, Sweden .. **11 H6** 56 48N 12 58 E
Oskélanéo, Canada .. **104 C4** 48 5N 75 15W
Öskemen, Kazakhstan **52 E9** 50 0N 82 36 E
Oskol →, Ukraine .... **33 H9** 49 6N 37 25 E
Oslo, Norway .... **9 G14** 59 55N 10 45 E
Oslob, Phil. .... **61 G5** 9 31N 123 26 E
Oslofjorden, Norway . **9 G14** 59 20N 10 35 E
Osmanabad, India ... **66 K10** 18 5N 76 10 E
Osmancık, Turkey ... **72 B6** 40 58N 34 47 E
Osmaniye, Turkey ... **70 B3** 37 5N 36 10 E
Ösmo, Sweden ...... **10 F11** 58 58N 17 55 E
Osnabrück, Germany . **24 C4** 52 17N 8 3 E
Ošno Lubuskie, Poland **31 F1** 52 28N 14 51 E
Osoblaha, Czech Rep. . **27 A10** 50 17N 17 44 E
Osogovska Planina,
Macedonia .... **44 D6** 42 10N 22 30 E
Osor, Italy .... **41 D11** 44 42N 14 24 E
Osório, Brazil .... **127 B5** 29 53 S 50 17W
Osorno, Chile .... **128 E2** 40 25 S 73 0W
Osorno, Spain **36 C6** 42 24N 4 22W
Osoyoos, Canada **102 D5** 49 0N 119 30W
Osøyra, Norway ..... **9 F11** 60 9N 5 30 E
Óspika →, Canada ... **102 B4** 56 20N 124 0 E
Osprey Reef, Australia **94 A4** 13 52 S 146 36 E

Oss, Neths. .... **17 C5** 51 46N 5 32 E
Ossa, Mt., Australia .. **95 G4** 41 52 S 146 3 E
Óssa, Óros, Greece ... **46 B4** 39 47N 22 42 E
Ossa de Montiel, Spain **39 G2** 38 58N 2 45W
Ossabaw I., U.S.A. ... **115 K5** 31 50N 81 5W
Osse →, France ...... **20 D4** 44 7N 0 17 E
Osse →, Nigeria ..... **83 D6** 6 10N 5 20 E
Ossi, Italy .... **42 B1** 40 40N 8 35 E
Ossining, U.S.A. **117 E11** 41 10N 73 55W
Ossipee, U.S.A. **117 C13** 43 41N 71 7W
Ossokmanuan L.,
Canada **105 B7** 53 25N 65 0W
Ossora, Russia ...... **53 D17** 59 20N 163 13 E
Ostashkov, Russia .... **32 D7** 57 4N 33 2 E
Ostavall, Sweden .... **10 B9** 62 26N 15 29 E
Oste →, Germany .... **24 B5** 53 49N 9 2 E
Ostend = Oostende,
Belgium .... **17 C2** 51 15N 2 54 E
Oster, Ukraine ...... **33 G6** 50 57N 30 53 E
Österbotten =
Pohjanmaa, Finland . **8 E20** 62 58N 22 50 E
Osterburg, Germany .. **24 C7** 52 47N 11 45 E
Osterburg, U.S.A. **116 F6** 40 16N 78 31W
Osterburken, Germany **25 F5** 49 25N 9 26 E
Österbybruk, Sweden . **10 D11** 60 13N 17 55 E
Österbymo, Sweden .. **11 G9** 57 49N 15 15 E
Österdalälven, Sweden **10 C7** 61 30N 13 45 E
Østerdalen, Norway .. **9 F14** 61 40N 10 50 E
Österfärnebo, Sweden **10 D10** 60 19N 16 48 E
Österforse, Sweden ... **10 A11** 63 9N 17 3 E
Östergötlands län □,
Sweden .... **11 F9** 58 35N 15 45 E
Osterholz-Scharmbeck,
Germany .... **24 B4** 53 13N 8 47 E
Østerild, Denmark ... **11 G2** 57 2N 8 51 E
Östermyra = Seinäjoki,
Finland .... **9 E20** 62 40N 22 51 E
Osterode, Germany ... **24 D6** 51 43N 10 15 E
Östersund, Sweden ... **10 A8** 63 10N 14 38 E
Östervåla, Sweden ... **10 D11** 60 11N 17 11 E
Ostfriesische Inseln,
Germany .... **24 B3** 53 42N 7 0 E
Ostfriesland, Germany **24 B3** 53 20N 7 30 E
Östhammar, Sweden . **10 D12** 60 16N 18 22 E
Óstia, Lido di, Italy ... **41 G9** 41 43N 12 17 E
Ostíglia, Italy .... **41 C8** 45 4N 11 8 E
Ostmark, Sweden .... **10 D6** 60 17N 12 45 E
Östra Husby, Sweden . **11 F10** 58 35N 16 33 E
Ostrava, Czech Rep. . **27 B11** 49 51N 18 18 E
Ostravský □, Czech Rep. **27 B11** 49 40N 18 10 E
Ostróda, Poland ..... **30 E6** 53 42N 19 58 E
Ostrogozhsk, Russia .. **33 G9** 50 55N 39 7 E
Ostroh, Ukraine ..... **33 G4** 50 20N 26 30 E
Ostrołęka, Poland .... **31 E8** 53 4N 21 32 E
Ostrołęka □, Poland .. **31 E8** 53 4N 21 32 E
Ostrov, Bulgaria ..... **45 C8** 43 40N 24 9 E
Ostrov, Czech Rep. .. **26 A5** 50 18N 12 57 E
Ostrov, Romania ..... **29 F12** 44 6N 27 24 E
Ostrov, Russia ...... **32 D5** 57 25N 28 20 E
Ostrów Lubelski, Poland **31 G9** 51 29N 22 51 E
Ostrów Mazowiecka,
Poland .... **31 F8** 52 50N 21 51 E
Ostrów Wielkopolski,
Poland .... **31 G4** 51 36N 17 44 E
Ostrowiec-
Świętokrzyski, Poland **31 H8** 50 55N 21 22 E
Ostrožac, Bos.-H. .... **28 G2** 43 43N 17 49 E
Ostrzeszów, Poland .. **31 G4** 51 25N 17 52 E
Ostseebad
Kühlungsborn,
Germany .... **24 A7** 54 8N 11 44 E
Osttirol □, Austria ... **26 E5** 46 50N 12 30 E
Ostuni, Italy .... **43 B10** 40 44N 17 35 E
Osum →, Albania .... **44 F4** 40 40N 20 10 E
Osŭm →, Bulgaria ... **45 C8** 43 40N 24 50 E
Ōsumi-Kaikyō, Japan . **55 J5** 30 55N 131 0 E
Ōsumi-Shotō, Japan .. **55 J5** 30 30N 130 0 E
Osun □, Nigeria ..... **83 D5** 7 30N 4 30 E
Osuna, Spain **37 H5** 37 14N 5 8W
Oswegatchie →, U.S.A. **117 B9** 44 42N 75 30W
Oswego, U.S.A. **117 C8** 43 27N 76 31W
Oswego →, U.S.A. ... **117 C8** 43 27N 76 30W
Oswestry, U.K. **14 E4** 52 52N 3 3W
Oświęcim, Poland ... **31 H6** 50 2N 19 11 E
Otaci, Moldova ..... **29 B12** 48 27N 27 47 E
Otago □, N.Z. ...... **91 L2** 45 15 S 170 0 E
Otago Harbour, N.Z. . **91 L3** 45 47 S 170 42 E
Otaheite B.,
Trin. & Tob. **125 K15** 10 15N 61 30W
Otake, Japan .... **55 G6** 34 12 S 132 13 E
Otaki, N.Z. .... **91 J5** 40 45 S 175 10 E
Otaru, Japan .... **54 C10** 43 10N 141 0 E
Otaru-Wan = Ishikari-
Wan, Japan .... **54 C10** 43 25N 141 1 E
Otava →, Czech Rep. . **26 B7** 49 26N 14 12 E
Otavalo, Ecuador **124 C3** 0 13N 78 20W
Otavi, Namibia ...... **88 B2** 19 40 S 17 24 E
Otchinjau, Angola ... **88 B1** 16 30 S 13 56 E
Otelec, Romania ..... **28 E5** 45 36N 20 50 E
Otelnuk, L., Canada .. **105 A6** 56 9N 68 12W
Oṭelu Roşu, Romania . **28 E7** 45 30N 22 20 E
Otero de Rey = Outeiro
de Rei, Spain **36 B3** 43 6N 7 36W
Othello, U.S.A. **108 C4** 46 50N 119 10W
Othonoí, Greece ..... **46 B1** 39 52N 19 22 E
Óthris, Óros, Greece . **46 B4** 39 2N 22 37 E
Oti →, Togo .... **83 C5** 10 40N 0 35 E
Otjiwarongo, Namibia **88 C2** 20 30 S 16 33 E
Otmuchów, Poland .. **31 H4** 50 28N 17 10 E
Otočac, Croatia ..... **41 D12** 44 53N 15 12 E
Otoineppu, Japan ... **54 B11** 44 44N 142 16 E
Otok, Croatia .... **28 E3** 45 13N 18 52 E
Otopeni, Bucureşti ✈
(OTP), Romania ... **45 B10** 44 30N 26 11 E
Otorohanga, N.Z. ... **91 H5** 38 12 S 175 14 E
Otoskwin →, Canada . **104 B2** 52 13N 88 6W
Otra →, Norway .... **9 G13** 58 9N 8 1 E
Otradnyy, Russia .... **34 D10** 53 20N 51 21 E
Otranto, Italy .... **43 B11** 40 9N 18 28 E
Otranto, C. d', Italy .. **43 B11** 40 7N 18 30 E
Otranto, Str. of, Italy . **43 B11** 40 15N 18 40 E
Otrokovice, Czech Rep. **27 B10** 49 12N 17 32 E
Otse, S. Africa ...... **88 D4** 25 2 S 25 45 E
Ōtsu, Japan .... **55 G7** 35 0N 135 50 E
Ōtsuki, Japan .... **55 G9** 35 36N 138 57 E
Ottawa = Outaouais →,
Canada **104 C5** 45 27N 74 8W
Ottawa, Canada **117 A9** 45 27N 75 42W
Ottawa, Ill., U.S.A. ... **112 E10** 41 21N 88 51W
Ottawa, Kans., U.S.A. **112 F7** 38 37N 95 16W
Ottawa Is., Canada ... **101 C11** 59 35N 80 10W
Ottélé, Cameroon .... **83 E7** 3 38N 11 19 E
Ottensheim, Austria .. **26 C7** 48 21N 14 12 E
Otter Cr. →, U.S.A. .. **117 B11** 44 13N 73 17W
Otter L., Canada **103 B8** 55 35N 104 39W
Otterndorf, Germany . **24 B4** 53 48N 8 53 E
Otterup, Denmark ... **11 J4** 55 30N 10 22 E
Otterville, Canada ... **116 D4** 42 55N 80 36W

Ottery St. Mary, U.K. . **15 G4** 50 44N 3 17W
Otto Beit Bridge,
Zimbabwe .... **87 F2** 15 59 S 28 56 E
Ottosdal, S. Africa ... **88 D4** 26 46 S 25 59 E
Ottumwa, U.S.A. **112 E8** 41 1N 92 25W
Otu, Nigeria .... **83 D5** 8 14N 3 22 E
Otukpa, Nigeria ..... **83 D6** 7 9N 7 41 E
Oturkpo, Nigeria .... **83 D6** 7 16N 8 8 E
Otway, B., Chile ..... **128 G2** 53 30 S 74 0W
Otway, C., Australia .. **95 F3** 38 52 S 143 30 E
Otwock, Poland ..... **31 F8** 52 5N 21 20 E
Otyniya, Ukraine .... **29 B9** 48 44N 24 51 E
Ou →, Canada **103 B10** 57 51N 92 44W
Ou, Nigeria .... **83 D5** 7 10N 5 39 E
Ou →, Laos .... **64 B4** 20 4N 102 13 E
Ou Neua, Laos ...... **64 A3** 22 18N 101 48 E
Ou-Sammyaku, Japan **54 E10** 39 20N 140 35 E
Ouachita →, U.S.A. .. **113 K9** 31 38N 91 49W
Ouachita, L., U.S.A. .. **113 H8** 34 34N 93 12W
Ouachita Mts., U.S.A. **113 H7** 34 40N 94 25W
Ouagadougou,
Burkina Faso **83 C4** 12 25N 1 30W
Ouahigouya,
Burkina Faso **82 C4** 13 31N 2 25W
Ouahran = Oran,
Algeria **78 A5** 35 45N 0 39W
Ouallâta, Mauritania . **82 B3** 17 20N 6 55W
Ouallam, Niger ...... **83 C5** 14 23N 2 10 E
Ouallene, Algeria .... **78 D6** 24 41N 1 11 E
Ouargaye, Burkina Faso **83 C5** 11 40N 0 5 E
Ouargla, Algeria ..... **78 B7** 31 59N 5 16 E
Ouarkoye, Burkina Faso **82 C4** 12 5N 3 40W
Ouarzazate, Morocco . **78 B4** 30 55N 6 50W
Ouassouas, Mali ..... **83 B5** 16 10N 1 23 E
Ouatagouna, Mali ... **83 B5** 15 11N 0 43 E
Oubangi →, Dem. Rep.
of the Congo ...... **84 E3** 0 30 S 17 50 E
Ouche →, France .... **19 E12** 47 6N 5 16 E
Ouddorp, Neths. .... **17 C3** 51 50N 3 57 E
Oude Rijn →, Neths. . **17 B4** 52 12N 4 24 E
Oudeïka, Mali **83 B4** 17 30N 1 40W
Oudenaarde, Belgium **17 D3** 50 50N 3 37 E
Oudon →, France **18 E6** 47 41N 0 53W
Oudtshoorn, S. Africa **88 E3** 33 35 S 22 14 E
Ouéllé, Ivory C. **82 D4** 7 26N 4 1W
Ouémé →, Benin .... **83 D5** 6 30N 2 30 E
Ouessa, Burkina Faso **82 C4** 11 4N 2 47W
Ouessant, Î. d', France **18 D1** 48 28N 5 6W
Ouesso, Congo ...... **84 D3** 1 37N 16 5 E
Ouest, Pte. de l', Canada **105 C7** 49 52N 64 40W
Ouezzane, Morocco .. **78 B4** 34 51N 5 35W
Ougarou, Burkina Faso **83 C5** 12 10N 0 58 E
Oughterard, Ireland .. **12 C2** 53 26N 9 18W
Ouidi, Benin .... **83 D5** 6 25N 2 0 E
Ouidi, Niger .... **83 C7** 14 10N 13 0 E
Ouistreham, France .. **18 C6** 49 17N 0 18W
Oujda, Morocco **78 B5** 34 41N 1 55W
Oujeft, Mauritania ... **82 A2** 20 2N 13 0W
Oulainen, Finland ... **8 D21** 64 17N 24 47 E
Ould Yenjé, Mauritania **82 B2** 15 38N 12 16W
Oullins, France ...... **21 C8** 45 43N 4 49 E
Oulu, Finland .... **8 D21** 65 1N 25 29 E
Oulujärvi, Finland .... **8 D22** 64 25N 27 15 E
Oulujoki →, Finland .. **8 D21** 65 1N 25 30 E
Oulx, Italy .... **40 C3** 45 2N 6 50 E
Oum Chalouba, Chad **79 E10** 15 48N 20 46 E
Oum Hadjer, Chad ... **79 F9** 13 18N 19 41 E
Oumé, Ivory C. **82 D3** 6 21N 5 27W
Ounasjoki →, Finland **8 C21** 66 31N 25 40 E
Ounguati, Namibia .. **88 C2** 22 0 S 15 46 E
Ounianga Sérir, Chad **79 E10** 18 54N 20 51 E
Our →, Lux. .... **17 E6** 49 55N 6 5 E
Ouranópolis, Greece . **44 F7** 40 20N 23 58 E
Ouray, U.S.A. **109 G10** 38 1N 107 40W
Ourcq →, France .... **19 C10** 49 1N 3 1 E
Ourense, Spain **36 C3** 42 19N 7 55W
Ouricuri, Brazil ..... **125 E10** 7 53 S 40 5W
Ourinhos, Brazil .... **127 A6** 23 0 S 49 54W
Ouro Fino, Brazil .... **127 A6** 22 16 S 46 25W
Ouro-Ndia, Mali **82 B4** 15 8N 4 35W
Ouro Prêto, Brazil ... **127 A7** 20 20 S 43 30W
Ouro Sogui, Senegal . **82 B2** 15 36N 13 19W
Oursi, Burkina Faso .. **83 C4** 14 41N 0 27W
Ourthe →, Belgium .. **17 D5** 50 29N 5 35 E
Ouse →, E. Susx., U.K. **15 G8** 50 47N 0 4 E
Ouse →, N. Yorks.,
U.K. **14 D7** 53 44N 0 55W
Oust, France .... **20 F5** 42 52N 1 13 E
Oust →, France **18 E4** 47 35N 2 6W
Outamba-Kilimi △,
S. Leone **82 D2** 9 50N 12 40W
Outaouais →, Canada **104 C5** 45 27N 74 8W
Outardes →, Canada . **105 C6** 49 24N 69 30W
Outeiro de Rei, Spain **36 B3** 43 6N 7 36W
Outer Hebrides, U.K. . **13 D1** 57 30N 7 40W
Outes = Serra de Outes,
Spain **36 C2** 42 55N 8 55W
Outjo, Namibia ..... **88 C2** 20 5 S 16 7 E
Outlook, Canada **103 C7** 51 30N 107 0W
Outokumpu, Finland **8 E23** 62 43N 29 1 E
Outreau, France .... **19 B8** 50 40N 1 36 E
Ouvèze →, France ... **21 E8** 43 59N 4 51 E
Ouyen, Australia .... **95 F3** 35 1 S 142 22 E
Ouzouer-le-Marché,
France .... **19 E8** 47 54N 1 32 E
Ovada, Italy .... **40 D5** 44 38N 8 38 E
Ovalau, Fiji .... **91 C8** 17 40 S 178 48 E
Ovalle, Chile .... **126 C1** 30 33 S 71 18W
Ovamboland, Namibia **88 B2** 18 30 S 16 0 E
Ovar, Portugal **36 E2** 40 51N 8 40W
Overath, Germany ... **24 E3** 50 56N 7 17 E
Overflakkee, Neths. .. **17 C4** 51 44N 4 10 E
Overijssel □, Neths. .. **17 B6** 52 25N 6 35 E
Overland Park, U.S.A. **112 F7** 38 55N 94 50W
Overton, U.S.A. **111 J12** 36 33N 114 27W
Övertorneå, Sweden . **8 C20** 66 23N 23 38 E
Overum, Sweden .... **11 F10** 58 0N 16 20 E
Ovid, U.S.A. **117 D8** 42 41N 76 49W
Ovidiopol, Ukraine .. **33 J6** 46 15N 30 30 E
Oviedo, Romania ... **29 F12** 44 16N 28 34 E
Oviedo, Spain **36 B5** 43 25N 5 50W
Oviksfjällen, Sweden . **10 A7** 63 0N 13 49 E
Oviši, Latvia .... **9 H19** 57 33N 21 44 E
Ovoot, Mongolia .... **56 B7** 45 21N 113 45 E
Övör Hangay □,
Mongolia .... **56 B2** 45 0N 102 30 E
Øvre Ardal, Norway . **9 F12** 61 19N 7 48 E
Øvre Fryken, Sweden **10 E7** 60 0N 13 17 E
Ovruch, Ukraine .... **33 G5** 51 25N 28 45 E
Owaka, N.Z. .... **91 M2** 46 27 S 169 40 E

Owase, Japan .... **55 G8** 34 7N 136 12 E
Owatonna, U.S.A. ... **112 C8** 44 5N 93 14W
Owbeh, Afghan. ..... **66 B3** 34 28N 63 10 E
Owego, U.S.A. **117 D8** 42 6N 76 16W
Owen Falls Dam,
Uganda .... **86 B3** 0 30N 33 5 E
Owen Sound, Canada **116 B4** 44 35N 80 55W
Owens →, U.S.A. **110 J9** 36 32N 117 59W
Owens L., U.S.A. **111 J9** 36 26N 117 57W
Owensboro, U.S.A. .. **114 G2** 37 46N 87 7W
Owerri, Nigeria ..... **83 D6** 5 29N 7 0 E
Owl →, Canada **103 B10** 57 51N 92 44W
Owo, Nigeria .... **83 D6** 7 10N 5 39 E
Owosso, U.S.A. **114 D3** 43 0N 84 10W
Owyhee, U.S.A. **108 F5** 41 57N 116 6W
Owyhee →, U.S.A. ... **108 E5** 43 49N 117 2W
Owyhee, L., U.S.A. ... **108 E5** 43 38N 117 14W
Ox Mts. = Slieve
Gamph, Ireland ... **12 B3** 54 6N 9 0W
Öxarfjörður, Iceland . **8 C5** 66 15N 16 45W
Oxbow, Canada **103 D8** 49 14N 102 10W
Oxelösund, Sweden . **11 F11** 58 43N 17 5 E
Oxford, N.Z. .... **91 K4** 43 18 S 172 11 E
Oxford, U.K. **15 F6** 51 46N 1 15W
Oxford, Mass., U.S.A. **117 D13** 42 7N 71 52W
Oxford, Miss., U.S.A. **113 H10** 34 22N 89 31W
Oxford, N.C., U.S.A. . **115 G6** 36 19N 78 35W
Oxford, N.Y., U.S.A. . **117 D9** 42 27N 75 36W
Oxford, Ohio, U.S.A. **114 F3** 39 31N 84 45W
Oxford, L., Canada .. **103 C9** 54 51N 95 37W
Oxfordshire □, U.K. .. **15 F6** 51 48N 1 16W
Oxía Nísís, Greece .. **46 C3** 38 18N 21 6 E
Oxie, Sweden .... **11 J7** 55 33N 13 6 E
Oxílithos, Greece .... **46 C6** 38 35N 24 7 E
Oxnard, U.S.A. **111 L7** 34 12N 119 11W
Oxsjövålen, Sweden . **10 B7** 62 34N 13 57 E
Oxus = Amudarya →,
Uzbekistan .... **52 E6** 43 58N 59 34 E
Oya, Malaysia ...... **62 D4** 2 55N 111 55 E
Oyama, Japan ...... **55 F9** 36 18N 139 48 E
Oyambre △, Spain ... **36 B6** 43 22N 4 21W
Oyem, Gabon .... **84 D2** 1 34N 11 31 E
Oyen, Canada **103 C6** 51 22N 110 28W
Øyer, Norway ...... **9 F14** 61 10N 10 22 E
Øygarden, Norway .. **9 F11** 60 23N 4 50 E
Oykel →, U.K. **13 D4** 57 56N 4 26W
Oymyakon, Russia ... **53 C15** 63 25N 142 44 E
Oyo, Nigeria .... **83 D5** 7 46N 3 56 E
Oyo □, Nigeria ...... **83 D5** 8 15N 3 30 E
Oyonnax, France .... **19 F12** 46 16N 5 40 E
Oyster Bay, U.S.A. ... **117 F11** 40 52N 73 32W
Öyübari, Japan ..... **54 C11** 43 1N 142 5 E
Özalp, Turkey ...... **73 C10** 38 39N 43 59 E
Ozamiz, Phil. .... **61 G5** 8 15N 123 50 E
Ozark, Ala., U.S.A. .. **115 K3** 31 28N 85 39W
Ozark, Ark., U.S.A. .. **113 H8** 35 29N 93 50W
Ozark, Mo., U.S.A. .. **113 G8** 37 1N 93 12W
Ozark Plateau, U.S.A. **113 G9** 37 20N 91 40W
Ozarks, L. of the, U.S.A. **112 F8** 38 12N 92 38W
Ožarów, Poland ..... **31 H8** 50 53N 21 40 E
Ozd, Hungary .... **28 B5** 48 14N 20 15 E
Ozernoye, Russia ... **34 E10** 51 46N 51 28 E
Ozersk, Russia ...... **30 D8** 54 25N 22 0 E
Ozette L., U.S.A. **110 B2** 48 6N 124 38W
Ozieri, Italy .... **42 B2** 40 35N 9 0 E
Ozimek, Poland ..... **31 H5** 50 41N 18 11 E
Ozinki, Russia ...... **34 E9** 51 12N 49 44 E
Ozona, U.S.A. **113 K4** 30 43N 101 12W
Ozorków, Poland .... **31 G6** 51 57N 19 16 E
Ozren, Bos.-H. ...... **28 B3** 43 55N 18 29 E
Ozuluama, Mexico .. **119 C5** 21 40N 97 50W
Ozun, Romania ..... **29 E10** 45 47N 25 50 E
Ozurgeti, Georgia ... **35 K5** 41 55N 42 17 E

P

Pa, Burkina Faso **82 C4** 11 33N 3 19W
Pa-an, Burma .... **67 L20** 16 51N 97 40 E
Pa Mong Dam, Thailand **64 D4** 18 0N 102 22 E
Pa Sak →, Thailand .. **64 B2** 15 30N 101 0 E
Paamiut, Greenland .. **101 B15** 62 0N 49 43W
Paar →, Germany ... **25 G7** 48 46N 11 36 E
Paarl, S. Africa ..... **88 E2** 33 45 S 18 56 E
Pab Hills, Pakistan .. **68 F2** 26 30N 66 45 E
Pabbay, U.K. **13 D1** 57 46N 7 14W
Pabianice, Poland ... **31 G6** 51 40N 19 20 E
Pabna, Bangla. ...... **67 G16** 24 1N 89 18 E
Pabo, Uganda .... **86 B3** 3 1N 32 10 E
Pacaja →, Brazil .... **125 D8** 1 56 S 50 50W
Pacaraima, Sa., S. Amer. **124 C6** 4 0N 62 30W
Pacasmayo, Peru .... **124 E3** 7 20 S 79 35W
Paceco, Italy .... **42 E5** 37 59N 12 33 E
Pachhar, India ...... **68 G7** 24 40N 77 42 E
Pachino, Italy .... **43 F8** 36 43N 15 5 E
Pachitea →, Peru ... **124 E4** 8 46 S 74 33W
Pachmarhi, India .... **69 H8** 22 28N 78 26 E
Pachpadra, India .... **66 G8** 25 58N 72 10 E
Pachuca, Mexico **119 C5** 20 7N 98 44W
Pacific, Canada **102 C3** 54 48N 128 28W
Pacific-Antarctic Ridge,
Pac. Oc. .... **97 M16** 43 0 S 115 0W
Pacific Grove, U.S.A. **110 J5** 36 38N 121 56W
Pacific Ocean **97 G14** 10 0N 140 0W
Pacific Rim △, Canada **102 D4** 48 40N 124 45W
Pacifica, U.S.A. **110 H4** 37 36N 122 30W
Pacitan, Indonesia .. **63 H14** 8 12 S 111 7 E
Packwood, U.S.A. ... **110 D5** 46 36N 121 40W
Pacov, Czech Rep. ... **26 B8** 49 27N 15 0 E
Pacy-sur-Eure, France **18 C8** 49 1N 1 23 E
Padaido, Kepulauan,
Indonesia .... **63 E9** 1 15 S 136 30 E
Padang, Indonesia ... **62 E2** 1 0 S 100 20 E
Padang Endau, Malaysia **65 L4** 2 40N 103 38 E
Padangpanjang,
Indonesia .... **62 E2** 0 40 S 100 20 E
Padangsidempuan,
Indonesia .... **62 D1** 1 30N 99 15 E
Padborg, Denmark .. **11 K3** 54 49N 9 21 E
Paddle Prairie, Canada **102 B5** 57 57N 117 29W
Paddockwood, Canada **103 C7** 53 30N 105 30W
Paderborn, Germany **24 D4** 51 42N 8 45 E
Padeş, Vf., Romania . **28 E7** 45 40N 22 52 E
Padina, Romania .... **29 F12** 44 50N 27 8 E
Padma, India .... **69 G11** 24 12N 85 22 E
Pádova, Italy .... **41 C8** 45 25N 11 53 E
Padra, India .... **68 H5** 22 15N 73 7 E
Padrauna, India .... **69 F10** 26 54N 83 59 E
Padre I. △, U.S.A. ... **113 M6** 27 10N 97 25W
Padre Island △, U.S.A. **113 M6** 27 0N 97 17W
Padrón, Spain **36 C2** 42 41N 8 39W
Padstow, U.K. **15 G3** 50 33N 4 58W
Padua = Pádova, Italy **41 C8** 45 25N 11 53 E
Paducah, Ky., U.S.A. **114 G1** 37 5N 88 37W
Paducah, Tex., U.S.A. **113 H4** 34 1N 100 18W
Padul, Spain **37 H7** 37 2N 3 37W
Paengnyŏng-do,
S. Korea .... **57 F13** 37 57N 124 40 E

Paeroa, N.Z. .... **91 G5** 37 23 S 175 41 E
Paesana, Italy .... **40 D4** 44 41N 7 16 E
Pafúri, Mozam. ...... **89 C5** 22 28 S 31 17 E
Pag, Croatia .... **41 D12** 44 25N 15 3 E
Paga, Ghana **83 C4** 11 1N 1 8W
Pagadian, Phil. ...... **61 H5** 7 55N 123 30 E
Pagai Selatan, Pulau,
 Indonesia .... **62 E2** 3 0 S 100 15 E
Pagai Utara, Pulau,
 Indonesia .... **62 E2** 2 35 S 100 0 E
Pagalu = Annobón,
 Atl. Oc. .... **77 G4** 1 25 S 5 36 E
Pagara, India .... **69 G9** 24 22N 80 1 E
Pagastikós Kólpos,
 Greece .... **46 B5** 39 15N 23 0 E
Pagatan, Indonesia .. **62 E5** 3 33 S 115 59 E
Page, U.S.A. **109 H8** 36 57N 111 27W
Pagégiai, Lithuania .. **30 C8** 55 9N 21 54 E
Pago Pago,
 Amer. Samoa ...... **91 B13** 14 16 S 170 43W
Pagosa Springs, U.S.A. **109 H10** 37 16N 107 1W
Pagwa River, Canada . **104 B2** 50 2N 85 14W
Pahala, U.S.A. **106 J17** 19 12N 155 29W
Pahang □, Malaysia .. **65 L4** 3 30N 102 30 E
Pahiatua, N.Z. ...... **91 J5** 40 27 S 175 50 E
Pahokee, U.S.A. **115 M5** 26 50N 80 40W
Pahrump, U.S.A. **111 J11** 36 12N 115 59W
Pahute Mesa, U.S.A. . **110 H10** 37 20N 116 45W
Pai, Thailand ...... **64 C2** 19 19N 98 27 E
Paicines, U.S.A. **110 J5** 36 44N 121 17W
Paide, Estonia ...... **9 G21** 58 53N 25 33 E
Paignton, U.K. **15 G4** 50 26N 3 35W
Paihō, Taiwan ...... **59 F13** 23 21N 120 25 E
Päijänne, Finland .... **9 F21** 61 30N 25 30 E
Pailani, India ...... **69 G9** 25 45N 80 26 E
Pailin, Cambodia .... **64 F4** 12 46N 102 36 E
Paimpol, France **18 D3** 48 48N 3 4W
Painan, Indonesia .... **62 E2** 1 21 S 100 34 E
Painesville, U.S.A. .. **116 E3** 41 43N 81 15W
Paint Hills = Wemindji,
 Canada **104 B4** 53 0N 78 49W
Paint L., Canada **103 B9** 55 28N 97 57W
Painted Desert, U.S.A. **109 J8** 36 0N 111 0W
Paintsville, U.S.A. .. **114 G4** 37 49N 82 48W
País Vasco □, Spain .. **38 C2** 42 50N 2 45W
Paisley, Canada **116 B3** 44 18N 81 16W
Paisley, U.K. **13 F4** 55 50N 4 25W
Paisley, U.S.A. **108 E3** 42 42N 120 32W
Paita, Peru .... **124 E2** 5 11 S 81 9W
Paiva →, Portugal **36 D2** 41 4N 8 16W
Paizhou, China ...... **59 B9** 30 12N 113 55 E
Pajares, Spain **36 B5** 43 1N 5 46W
Pajares, Puerto de, Spain **36 C5** 42 58N 5 46W
Pajęczno, Poland .... **31 G5** 51 10N 19 0 E
Pak Lay, Laos ...... **64 C3** 18 15N 101 27 E
Pak Phanang, Thailand **65 H3** 8 21N 100 12 E
Pak Sane, Laos ...... **64 C4** 18 22N 103 39 E
Pak Song, Laos ...... **64 E6** 15 11N 106 14 E
Pak Suong, Laos .... **58 H4** 19 58N 102 15 E
Pakaur, India ...... **69 G12** 24 38N 87 51 E
Pakenham, Canada .. **117 A8** 45 18N 76 18W
Pákhnes, Greece .... **49 D6** 35 16N 24 4 E
Pakhuis, S. Africa .. **88 E2** 32 9 S 19 5 E
Pakistan ■, Asia .... **68 E4** 30 0N 70 0 E
Pakkading, Laos .... **64 C4** 18 19N 103 59 E
Paklenica △, Croatia . **41 D12** 44 20N 15 39 E
Pakokku, Burma .... **67 J19** 21 20N 95 0 E
Pakość, Poland ...... **31 F5** 52 48N 18 6 E
Pakowki L., Canada .. **103 D6** 49 20N 111 0W
Pakpattan, Pakistan .. **68 D5** 30 25N 73 27 E
Pakrac, Croatia ...... **28 E2** 45 27N 17 12 E
Pakruojis, Lithuania . **30 C10** 55 58N 23 52 E
Paks, Hungary ...... **28 D3** 46 38N 18 55 E
Paktīā □, Afghan. .... **66 C6** 33 30N 69 15 E
Paktīkā □, Afghan. .. **66 C6** 32 30N 69 0 E
Pakwach, Uganda .... **86 B3** 2 28N 31 27 E
Pakxe, Laos .... **64 E5** 15 5N 105 52 E
Pal Lahara, India .. **69 J11** 21 27N 85 11 E
Pala, Chad .... **79 G9** 9 25N 15 5 E
Pala, Dem. Rep. of
 the Congo .... **86 D2** 6 45 S 29 30 E
Pala, U.S.A. **111 M9** 33 22N 117 5W
Palabek, Uganda .... **86 B3** 3 22N 32 33 E
Palacios, U.S.A. **113 L6** 28 42N 96 13W
Palafrugell, Spain .. **38 D8** 41 55N 3 10 E
Palagiano, Italy ...... **43 B10** 40 35N 17 2 E
Palagonía, Italy ...... **43 E7** 37 19N 14 45 E
Palagruža, Croatia .. **41 F13** 42 24N 16 15 E
Palaiokastron, Greece **49 D8** 35 12N 26 15 E
Palaiokhóra, Greece .. **49 D5** 35 16N 23 39 E
Paláiros, Greece ...... **46 C2** 38 47N 20 53 E
Palaiseau, France .... **19 D9** 48 43N 2 15 E
Palam, India .... **66 K10** 19 0N 77 0 E
Palamás, Greece .... **46 B4** 39 26N 22 4 E
Palamós, Spain ...... **38 D8** 41 50N 3 10 E
Palampur, India .... **68 C7** 32 10N 76 30 E
Palamut, Turkey .... **47 C9** 38 59N 27 41 E
Palana, Australia .... **95 F4** 39 45 S 147 55 E
Palana, Russia ...... **53 D16** 59 10N 159 59 E
Palanan, Phil. ...... **61 C5** 17 8N 122 29 E
Palanan Pt., Phil. .... **61 C5** 17 17N 122 30 E
Palandri, Pakistan .. **69 C5** 33 42N 73 40 E
Palanga, Lithuania .. **9 J19** 55 58N 21 3 E
Palangkaraya, Indonesia **62 E4** 2 16 S 113 56 E
Palani Hills, India .. **66 P10** 10 14N 77 33 E
Palanpur, India .... **68 G5** 24 10N 72 25 E
Palapye, Botswana .. **88 C4** 22 30 S 27 7 E
Palas, Pakistan ...... **69 B5** 35 4N 73 14 E
Palas de Rei, Spain .. **36 C3** 42 52N 7 52W
Palashi, India ...... **69 H13** 23 47N 88 15 E
Palasponga, India .. **69 J11** 21 47N 85 34 E
Palatka, Russia ...... **53 C16** 60 6N 150 54 E
Palatka, U.S.A. **115 L5** 29 39N 81 38W
Palau, Italy .... **42 A2** 41 11N 9 23 E
Palau ■, Pac. Oc. .... **96 G5** 7 30N 134 30 E
Palauk, Burma ...... **64 F2** 13 10N 98 40 E
Palawan, Phil. ...... **66 Q10** 8 45N 77 45 E
Palayankottai, India . **66 Q10** 8 45N 77 45 E
Palazzo, Pte., France . **21 F12** 42 28N 8 30 E
Palazzo San Gervásio,
 Italy .... **43 B8** 40 56N 15 59 E
Palazzolo Acréide, Italy **43 E7** 37 4N 14 54 E
Paldiski, Estonia .... **9 G21** 59 23N 24 9 E
Pale, Bos.-H. .... **28 G3** 43 50N 18 38 E
Paleleh, Indonesia .. **63 D6** 1 10N 121 50 E
Palembang, Indonesia **62 E2** 3 0 S 104 50 E
Palencia, Spain **36 C6** 42 1N 4 34W
Palencia □, Spain **36 C6** 42 31N 4 33W
Palenque, Mexico **119 D6** 17 31N 91 58W
Paleokastrítsa, Greece **49 A3** 39 40N 19 41 E
Paleometokho, Cyprus **49 D12** 35 7N 33 11 E
Palermo, Italy ...... **42 D6** 38 7N 13 22 E
Palermo, U.S.A. **110 G3** 39 26N 121 33W
Palermo ✗ (PMO), Italy **42 D6** 38 11N 13 5 E
Palestine, Chile ...... **128 A3** 32 50 S 69 47W
Palestine, Asia ...... **74 D4** 32 0N 35 0 E
Palestine, U.S.A. **113 K7** 31 46N 95 38W

Palestrina, Italy .... **41 G9** 41 50N 12 53 E
Paletwa, Burma .... **67 J18** 21 10N 92 50 E
Palghat, India ...... **66 P10** 10 46N 76 42 E
Palgrave, Mt., Australia **92 D2** 23 22 S 115 58 E
Pali, India .... **68 G5** 25 50N 73 20 E
Palikir, Micronesia .. **96 G7** 6 55N 158 9 E
Palinuro, Italy ...... **43 B8** 40 2N 15 17 E
Palinuro, C., Italy .. **43 B8** 40 2N 15 16 E
Paliouri, Ákra, Greece **44 G7** 39 57N 23 45 E
Palisades Reservoir,
 U.S.A. **108 E8** 43 20N 111 12W
Paliseul, Belgium .... **17 E5** 49 54N 5 8 E
Palitana, India ...... **68 J4** 21 32N 71 49 E
Palizada, Mexico **119 D6** 18 18N 92 8W
Palk Bay, Asia ...... **66 Q11** 9 30N 79 15 E
Palk Strait, Asia .... **66 Q11** 10 0N 79 45 E
Palkānah, Iraq ...... **70 C5** 35 49N 44 26 E
Palkot, India .... **69 H11** 22 53N 84 39 E
Pallanza = Verbánia,
 Italy .... **40 C5** 45 56N 8 33 E
Pallarenda, Australia . **94 B4** 19 12 S 146 46 E
Pallasovka, Russia .. **34 E8** 50 4N 47 0 E
Pallès, Bishti i, Albania **44 E3** 41 24N 19 24 E
Pallinup →, Australia . **93 F2** 34 27 S 118 50 E
Pallu, India .... **68 E6** 28 59N 74 14 E
Palm Bay, U.S.A. **115 L5** 28 2N 80 35W
Palm Beach, U.S.A. .. **115 M6** 26 43N 80 2W
Palm Coast, U.S.A. .. **115 L5** 29 32N 81 10W
Palm Desert, U.S.A. . **111 M10** 33 43N 116 22W
Palm Is., Australia .. **94 B4** 18 40 S 146 35 E
Palm Springs, U.S.A. **111 M10** 33 50N 116 33W
Palma, Mozam. ...... **87 E5** 10 46 S 40 29 E
Palma, B. de, Spain .. **48 B9** 39 30N 2 39 E
Palma de Mallorca,
 Spain .... **48 B9** 39 35N 2 39 E
Palma de Mallorca ✗
 (PMI), Spain ...... **39 F7** 39 34N 2 43 E
Palma del Río, Spain . **37 H5** 37 43N 5 17W
Palma di Montechiaro,
 Italy .... **42 E6** 37 11N 13 46 E
Palma Soriano, Cuba . **120 B4** 20 15N 76 0W
Palmares, Brazil .... **125 E11** 8 41 S 35 28W
Palmarola, Italy .... **42 B5** 40 56N 12 51 E
Palmas, Brazil ...... **127 B5** 26 29 S 52 0W
Palmas, C., Liberia .. **82 E3** 4 27N 7 46W
Pálmas, G. di, Italy .. **42 D1** 39 0N 8 30 E
Palmdale, U.S.A. **111 L8** 34 35N 118 7W
Palmeira das Missões,
 Brazil .... **127 B5** 27 55 S 53 17W
Palmeira dos Índios,
 Brazil .... **125 E11** 9 25 S 36 37W
Palmela, Portugal .. **37 G2** 38 32N 8 57W
Palmer, Antarctica .. **5 C17** 64 35 S 60 0W
Palmer, U.S.A. **100 B5** 61 36N 149 7W
Palmer →, Australia . **94 B3** 16 0 S 142 26 E
Palmer Arch., Antarctica **5 C17** 64 15 S 65 0W
Palmer Lake, U.S.A. . **112 F2** 39 7N 104 55W
Palmer Land, Antarctica **5 D18** 73 0 S 63 0W
Palmerston, Australia **92 B5** 12 31 S 130 59 E
Palmerston, Canada .. **116 C4** 43 50N 80 51W
Palmerston, N.Z. .... **91 L3** 45 29 S 170 43 E
Palmerston North, N.Z. **91 J5** 40 21 S 175 39 E
Palmetto, U.S.A. **117 F9** 40 48N 75 37W
Palmetto, U.S.A. **115 M4** 27 31N 82 34W
Palmi, Italy .... **43 D8** 38 21N 15 51 E
Palmira, Argentina .. **126 C2** 32 59 S 68 34W
Palmira, Colombia .. **124 C3** 3 32N 76 16W
Palmyra = Tudmur,
 Syria .... **70 C3** 34 36N 38 15 E
Palmyra, Mo., U.S.A. **112 F9** 39 48N 91 32W
Palmyra, N.J., U.S.A. **117 F9** 40 1N 75 1W
Palmyra, N.Y., U.S.A. **116 C7** 43 5N 77 18W
Palmyra, Pa., U.S.A. . **117 F8** 40 18N 76 36W
Palmyra Is., Pac. Oc. **97 G11** 5 52N 162 5W
Palo Alto, U.S.A. **110 H4** 37 27N 122 10W
Palo Seco, Trin. & Tob. **125 K15** 10 4N 61 36W
Palo Verde, U.S.A. .. **111 M12** 33 26N 114 44W
Palo Verde △,
 Costa Rica **120 D2** 10 21N 85 21W
Paloich, Sudan ...... **81 E3** 10 28N 32 32 E
Palomar Mt., U.S.A. . **111 M10** 33 22N 116 50W
Palompon, Phil. .... **61 F6** 11 3N 124 23 E
Palopo, Indonesia .. **63 E6** 3 0 S 120 16 E
Palos, C. de, Spain .. **39 H4** 37 38N 0 40W
Palos de la Frontera,
 Spain **37 H4** 37 14N 6 53W
Palos Verdes, U.S.A. . **111 M8** 33 48N 118 23W
Palos Verdes, Pt., U.S.A. **111 M8** 33 43N 118 26W
Pålsboda, Sweden .. **10 E9** 59 3N 15 22 E
Palu, Indonesia ...... **63 E5** 1 0 S 119 52 E
Palu, Turkey .... **70 B3** 38 45N 40 0 E
Paluke, Liberia **82 D3** 5 2N 8 5W
Paluzza, Italy ...... **41 B10** 46 32N 13 1 E
Palwal, India .... **68 E7** 28 8N 77 19 E
Pama, Burkina Faso .. **83 C5** 11 19N 0 44 E
Pama →, Burkina Faso **83 C5** 11 27N 0 40 E
Pamanukan, Indonesia **63 G13** 6 16 S 107 49 E
Pamekasan, Indonesia **63 G15** 7 10 S 113 28 E
Pamenang, Indonesia **63 J19** 8 24 S 116 6 E
Pamiers, France .... **20 E5** 43 7N 1 39 E
Pamir, Tajikistan .... **52 F8** 37 40N 73 0 E
Pamlico →, U.S.A. .. **115 H7** 35 20N 76 28W
Pamlico Sd., U.S.A. .. **115 H8** 35 20N 76 0W
Pampa, U.S.A. **113 H4** 35 32N 100 58W
Pampa de las Salinas,
 Argentina .... **126 C2** 32 1 S 66 58W
Pampanua, Indonesia **63 E6** 4 16 S 120 8 E
Pampas, Argentina .. **126 D3** 35 0 S 63 0W
Pampas, Peru .... **124 F4** 12 20 S 74 50W
Pamphylia, Turkey .. **72 D4** 37 0N 31 20 E
Pamplona, Colombia **124 B4** 7 23N 72 39W
Pamplona, Spain **38 C3** 42 48N 1 38W
Pampoenpoort, S. Africa **88 E3** 31 3 S 22 40 E
Pamukçu, Turkey .... **47 B9** 39 30N 27 54 E
Pamukkale, Turkey .. **47 D11** 37 55N 29 8 E
Pan de Azúcar △, Chile **126 B1** 26 0 S 70 40W
Pan Xian, China .... **58 E5** 25 46N 104 38 E
Pana, U.S.A. **112 F10** 39 23N 89 5W
Panabo, Phil. ...... **61 H6** 7 19N 125 40 E
Panaca, U.S.A. **109 H6** 37 47N 114 23W
Panagyurishte, Bulgaria **45 C8** 42 30N 24 15 E
Panaitan, Indonesia . **63 G11** 6 36 S 105 12 E
Panaji, India .... **66 M8** 15 25N 73 50 E
Panamá, Panama **120 E4** 9 0N 79 25W
Panama ■, Cent. Amer. **120 E4** 8 48N 79 55W
Panamá, G. de, Panama **120 E4** 8 4N 79 20W
Panama Canal, Panama **120 E4** 9 10N 79 37W
Panama City, U.S.A. **115 K3** 30 10N 85 40W
Panamint Range, U.S.A. **111 J9** 36 20N 117 20W
Panamint Springs,
 U.S.A. **111 J9** 36 20N 117 28W
Panão, Peru .... **124 E3** 9 55 S 75 55W
Panaon I., Phil. .... **61 F6** 10 3N 125 13 E
Panare, Thailand .... **65 J3** 6 51N 101 30 E
Panarea, Italy ...... **43 D8** 38 38N 15 4 E
Panaro →, Italy .... **41 D8** 44 55N 11 25 E

Panay, Phil. .... **61 F5** 11 10N 122 30 E
Panay, G., Phil. .... **61 F5** 11 0N 122 30 E
Pančevo, Serbia & M. **28 F5** 44 52N 20 41 E
Panch'iao, Taiwan .. **59 E13** 25 1N 121 27 E
Panciu, Romania .... **29 E12** 45 54N 27 8 E
Pancorbo, Desfiladero,
 Spain **36 C7** 42 32N 3 5W
Pâncota, Romania .. **28 D6** 46 20N 21 45 E
Panda, Mozam. ...... **89 C5** 24 2 S 34 45 E
Pandan, Malaysia .. **65 d** 1 32N 103 46 E
Pandan, Antique, Phil. **61 F5** 11 45N 122 10 E
Pandan, Catanduanes,
 Phil. .... **61 D6** 14 3N 124 10 E
Pandan, Selat, Singapore **65 d** 1 15N 103 44 E
Pandan Tampoi =
 Tampoi, Malaysia . **65 d** 1 30N 103 39 E
Pandegelang, Indonesia **63 G12** 6 25 S 106 5 E
Pandhana, India .... **68 J7** 21 42N 76 13 E
Pandharpur, India .. **66 L9** 17 41N 75 20 E
Pando, Uruguay .... **127 C4** 34 44 S 56 0W
Pando, L. = Hope, L.,
 Australia .... **95 D2** 28 24 S 139 18 E
Pandokrátor, Greece . **49 A3** 39 45N 19 50 E
Pandora, Costa Rica . **120 E3** 9 43N 83 3W
Pandrup, Denmark .. **11 G3** 57 14N 9 40 E
Panevéggio-Pale di San
 Martino △, Italy .. **41 B8** 46 14N 11 46 E
Panevėžys, Lithuania **9 J21** 55 42N 24 25 E
Panfilov, Kazakhstan . **52 E8** 44 10N 80 0 E
Panfilovo, Russia .... **34 E6** 50 25N 42 46 E
Pang-Long, Burma .. **67 H21** 23 11N 98 45 E
Pang Sida △, Thailand **64 E4** 14 5N 102 17 E
Pang-Yang, Burma .. **67 H21** 22 7N 98 48 E
Panga, Dem. Rep. of
 the Congo .... **86 B2** 1 52N 26 18 E
Pangaíon Óros, Greece **45 F8** 40 50N 24 0 E
Pangalanes, Canal des =
 Ampangalana,
 Lakandranon',
 Madag. .... **89 C8** 22 48 S 47 50 E
Pangani, Tanzania .. **86 D4** 5 25 S 38 58 E
Pangani →, Tanzania **86 D4** 5 26 S 38 58 E
Pangfou = Bengbu,
 China .... **57 H9** 32 58N 117 20 E
Pangil, Dem. Rep. of
 the Congo .... **86 C2** 3 10 S 26 35 E
Pangkah, Tanjung,
 Indonesia .... **63 G15** 6 51 S 112 33 E
Pangkajene, Indonesia **63 E5** 4 46 S 119 34 E
Pangkalanbrandan,
 Indonesia .... **62 D1** 4 1N 98 20 E
Pangkalanbuun,
 Indonesia .... **62 E4** 2 41 S 111 37 E
Pangkalpinang,
 Indonesia .... **62 E3** 2 0 S 106 0 E
Pangnirtung, Canada . **101 B13** 66 8N 65 43W
Pangong Tso, India .. **69 C8** 34 40N 78 40 E
Panguitch, U.S.A. .. **109 H7** 37 50N 112 26W
Pangutaran Group, Phil. **61 H4** 6 18N 120 34 E
Panhandle, U.S.A. .. **113 H4** 35 21N 101 23W
Pani Mines, India .. **68 H5** 22 29N 73 50 E
Pania-Mutombo,
 Dem. Rep. of
 the Congo .... **86 D1** 5 11 S 23 51 E
Panikota I., India .. **68 J4** 20 46N 71 21 E
Panipat, India ...... **68 E7** 29 25N 77 2 E
Panjal Range = Pir
 Panjal Range, India **68 C7** 32 30N 76 50 E
Panjang, Hon, Vietnam **65 H4** 9 20N 103 28 E
Panjgur, Pakistan .. **66 F4** 27 0N 64 5 E
Panjim = Panaji, India **66 M8** 15 25N 73 50 E
Panjin, China ...... **57 D12** 41 3N 122 2 E
Panjinad Barrage,
 Pakistan .... **68 E4** 29 22N 71 15 E
Panjnad →, Pakistan **68 E4** 28 57N 70 30 E
Panjwai, Afghan. .... **68 D1** 31 26N 65 27 E
Pankshin, Nigeria .. **83 D6** 9 16N 9 25 E
Panmunjŏm, N. Korea **57 F14** 37 59N 126 38 E
Panna, India .... **69 G9** 24 40N 80 15 E
Panna Hills, India .. **69 G9** 24 40N 81 15 E
Pannawonica, Australia **92 D2** 21 39 S 116 19 E
Panngga, Tanjung,
 Indonesia .... **63 K19** 8 54 S 116 2 E
Pannirtuuq =
 Pangnirtung, Canada **101 B13** 66 8N 65 43W
Pano Akil, Pakistan . **68 F3** 27 51N 69 7 E
Pano Lefkara, Cyprus **49 E12** 34 53N 33 20 E
Pano Panayia, Cyprus **49 E11** 34 55N 32 38 E
Panorama, Brazil .. **127 A5** 21 21 S 51 51W
Pánormon, Greece .. **49 D6** 35 25N 24 41 E
Pansemal, India .... **68 J6** 21 39N 74 42 E
Panshan = Panjin, China **57 D12** 41 3N 122 2 E
Panshi, China ...... **57 C14** 42 58N 126 5 E
Pantanal, Brazil .... **124 H7** 17 30 S 57 40W
Pantanos de Centla △,
 Mexico **119 D6** 18 25N 92 25W
Pantar, Indonesia .. **63 F6** 8 28 S 124 10 E
Pante Macassar,
 E. Timor .... **63 F6** 9 30 S 123 58 E
Pante Makasar = Pante
 Macassar, E. Timor . **63 F6** 9 30 S 123 58 E
Pantelleria, Italy .... **42 F4** 36 50N 11 57 E
Pantón, Spain **36 C3** 42 31N 7 37W
Pánuco, Mexico **119 C5** 22 0N 98 15W
Panyam, Nigeria .... **83 D6** 9 27N 9 8 E
Panyu, China .... **59 F9** 22 51N 113 20 E
Panzhihua, China .. **58 D3** 26 33N 101 44 E
Páola, Italy .... **43 C9** 39 21N 16 2 E
Paola, Malta .... **49 D2** 35 52N 14 30 E
Paola, U.S.A. **112 F7** 38 35N 94 53W
Paonia, U.S.A. **109 G10** 38 52N 107 36W
Paoting = Baoding,
 China .... **56 E8** 38 50N 115 28 E
Paot'ou = Baotou, China **56 D6** 40 32N 110 2 E
Paoua, C.A.R. ...... **84 C3** 7 9N 16 20 E
Pápa, Hungary ...... **28 C2** 47 22N 17 30 E
Papa Stour, U.K. **13 A7** 60 20N 1 42W
Papa Westray, U.K. .. **13 B6** 59 20N 2 55W
Papagayo →, Mexico . **119 D5** 16 36N 99 43W
Papagayo, G. de,
 Costa Rica **120 D2** 10 30N 85 50W
Papakura, N.Z. ...... **91 G5** 37 4 S 174 59 E
Papantla, Mexico .. **119 C5** 20 30N 97 30W
Papar, Malaysia .... **62 C5** 5 45N 116 0 E
Paparoa, N.Z. ...... **91 K3** 42 5 S 171 26 E
Pápas, Ákra, Greece . **46 C3** 38 13N 21 6 E
Papeete, Tahiti ...... **97 J13** 17 32 S 149 34W
Papenburg, Germany . **24 B3** 53 5N 7 23 E
Paphlagonia, Turkey . **72 B5** 41 30N 33 0 E
Paphos, Cyprus .... **49 E11** 34 46N 32 25 E
Papigochic →, Mexico **118 B3** 29 9N 109 40W
Papiki, Guyana **124 B7** 5 55N 59 10W
Papoutsa, Cyprus .. **49 E12** 34 54N 33 4 E
Papua □, Indonesia . **63 E9** 4 0 S 137 0 E
Papua New Guinea ■,
 Oceania .... **96 H6** 8 0 S 145 0 E
Papudo, Chile ...... **126 C1** 32 29 S 71 27W

Papuk, Croatia ...... **28 E2** 45 30N 17 30 E
Papun, Burma ...... **67 K20** 18 2N 97 30 E
Papunya, Australia . **92 D5** 23 15 S 131 54 E
Pará = Belém, Brazil **125 D9** 1 20 S 48 30W
Pará □, Brazil ...... **125 D8** 3 20 S 52 0W
Paraburdoo, Australia **92 D2** 23 14 S 117 32 E
Paracale, Phil. ...... **61 D5** 14 17N 122 48 E
Paracatu, Brazil .... **125 G9** 17 10 S 46 50W
Paracel Is., S. China Sea **62 A4** 15 50N 112 0 E
Parachilna, Australia . **95 E2** 31 10 S 138 21 E
Parachinar, Pakistan **68 C4** 33 55N 70 5 E
Paraćin, Serbia & M. **44 C5** 43 54N 21 27 E
Paradas, Spain **37 H5** 37 18N 5 29W
Paradela, Spain **36 C3** 42 44N 7 37W
Paradhísi, Greece .. **49 C10** 36 18N 28 7 E
Paradip, India ...... **67 J15** 20 15N 86 35 E
Paradise, Calif., U.S.A. **111 J11** 36 9N 115 10W
Paradise, Nev., U.S.A. **111 J11** 36 9N 115 10W
Paradise →, Canada . **105 B8** 53 27N 57 17W
Paradise Hill, Canada **103 C7** 53 32N 109 28W
Paradise River, Canada **105 B8** 53 27N 57 17W
Paradise Valley, U.S.A. **108 F5** 41 30N 117 32W
Parado, Indonesia .. **63 F5** 8 42 S 118 30 E
Paragould, U.S.A. .. **113 G9** 36 3N 90 29W
Paragua →, Venezuela **124 B6** 6 55N 62 55W
Paraguaçu →, Brazil **125 F11** 12 45 S 38 54W
Paraguaçu Paulista,
 Brazil .... **127 A5** 22 22 S 50 35W
Paraguaná, Pen. de,
 Venezuela **124 A5** 12 0N 70 0W
Paraguarí, Paraguay . **126 B4** 25 36 S 57 0W
Paraguarí □, Paraguay **126 B4** 26 0 S 57 10W
Paraguay ■, S. Amer. **126 A4** 23 0 S 57 0W
Paraguay →, Paraguay **126 B4** 27 18 S 58 38W
Paraíba = João Pessoa,
 Brazil .... **125 E12** 7 10 S 34 52W
Paraíba □, Brazil .... **125 E11** 7 0 S 36 0W
Paraíba do Sul →,
 Brazil .... **127 A7** 21 37 S 41 3W
Parainen, Finland .. **9 F20** 60 18N 22 18 E
Paraíso, Mexico **119 D6** 18 24N 93 14W
Parak, Iran .... **71 E7** 27 38N 52 25 E
Parakhino Paddubye,
 Russia .... **32 C7** 58 26N 33 10 E
Parakou, Benin .... **83 D5** 9 25N 2 40 E
Paralimni, Cyprus .. **49 D12** 35 2N 33 58 E
Parálion-Ástrous,
 Greece .... **46 D4** 37 25N 22 45 E
Paramaribo, Suriname **125 B7** 5 50N 55 10W
Paramithiá, Greece .. **46 B2** 39 30N 20 35 E
Páramos del Batallón y
 La Negra △,
 Venezuela **121 E5** 8 2N 71 55W
Paramushir, Ostrov,
 Russia .... **53 D16** 50 24N 156 0 E
Paran →, Israel .... **74 E4** 30 20N 35 10 E
Paraná, Argentina .. **126 C3** 31 45 S 60 30W
Paraná, Brazil ...... **125 F9** 12 30 S 47 48W
Paraná □, Brazil .... **127 A5** 24 30 S 51 0W
Paraná →, Argentina **126 C4** 33 43 S 59 15W
Paranaguá, Brazil .. **127 B6** 25 30 S 48 30W
Paranaíba, Brazil .. **125 G8** 19 40 S 51 11W
Paranaíba →, Brazil **125 H8** 20 6 S 51 4W
Paranapanema →,
 Brazil .... **127 A5** 22 40 S 53 9W
Paranapiacaba, Serra do,
 Brazil .... **127 A6** 24 31 S 48 35W
Paranas, Phil. ...... **61 F6** 11 42N 125 2 E
Paranavaí, Brazil .. **127 A5** 23 4 S 52 56W
Parang, Maguindanao,
 Phil. .... **63 C6** 7 23N 124 16 E
Parang, Sulu, Phil. .. **61 J4** 5 55N 120 54 E
Parângul Mare, Vf.,
 Romania .... **29 E11** 45 20N 23 37 E
Parapara, Papua New Guinea,
 N.Z. .... **91 J5** 40 57 S 175 3 E
Parápola, Greece .. **46 E5** 36 55N 23 27 E
Parras, Cerro de, Peru **124 F3** 10 45 S 76 10W
Parauapebas, Brazil **125 E9** 6 20 S 50 37W
Parbati →, Mad. P.,
 India .... **68 G7** 25 50N 76 30 E
Parbati →, Raj., India **68 F7** 26 54N 77 53 E
Parbhani, India .... **66 K10** 19 8N 76 52 E
Parchim, Germany .. **24 B7** 53 26N 11 52 E
Parczew, Poland .... **31 G9** 51 40N 22 52 E
Pardes Hanna-Karkur,
 Israel .... **74 C3** 32 28N 34 57 E
Pardilla, Spain **36 D7** 41 33N 3 43W
Pardo →, Bahia, Brazil **125 G11** 15 40 S 39 0W
Pardo →, Mato Grosso,
 Brazil .... **127 A5** 21 46 S 52 9W
Pardubice, Czech Rep. **26 A8** 50 3N 15 45 E
Pardubický □,
 Czech Rep. ...... **26 B8** 49 50N 16 0 E
Pare, Indonesia ...... **63 G15** 7 43 S 112 12 E
Pare Mts., Tanzania . **86 C4** 4 0 S 37 45 E
Parecis, Serra dos, Brazil **124 F7** 13 0 S 60 0W
Paredes de Nava, Spain **36 C6** 42 9N 4 42W
Paren, Russia .... **53 C17** 62 30N 163 15 E
Parent, Canada **104 C5** 47 55N 74 35W
Parent, L., Canada .. **104 C4** 48 31N 77 1W
Parentis-en-Born,
 France **20 D2** 44 21N 1 4W
Parepare, Indonesia . **63 E5** 4 0 S 119 40 E
Parfino, Russia ...... **32 C6** 57 59N 31 34 E
Párga, Greece ...... **46 B2** 39 15N 20 29 E
Pargas = Parainen,
 Finland .... **9 F20** 60 18N 22 18 E
Pargo, Pta. do, Madeira **48 D2** 32 49N 17 17W
Paria, G. de, Venezuela **125 K14** 10 20N 62 0W
Pariaguán, Venezuela **124 B6** 8 51N 64 34W
Paricutín, Cerro, Mexico **118 D4** 19 28N 102 15W
Parigi, Indonesia .... **63 E6** 0 50 S 120 5 E
Parika, Guyana **124 B7** 6 50N 58 20W
Parikkala, Finland .. **32 B5** 61 33N 29 31 E
Parima, Serra, Brazil **124 C6** 2 30N 64 0W
Parinari, Peru ...... **124 D4** 4 35 S 74 25W
Pariñas, Pta., S. Amer. **122 D2** 4 30 S 82 0W
Parintins, Brazil .... **125 D7** 2 40 S 56 50W
Pariparit Kyun, Burma **67 M18** 14 55N 93 45 E
Paris, Canada **116 C4** 43 12N 80 25W
Paris, France .... **19 D9** 48 50N 2 20 E
Paris, Idaho, U.S.A. . **108 E8** 42 14N 111 24W
Paris, Ky., U.S.A. .. **114 F3** 38 13N 84 15W
Paris, Tenn., U.S.A. **115 G1** 36 18N 88 19W
Paris, Tex., U.S.A. .. **113 J7** 33 40N 95 33W
Paris, Ville de □, France **19 D9** 48 50N 2 20 E
Paris Charles de
 Gaulle ✗ (CDG),
 France .... **19 D9** 49 0N 2 32 E
Paris Orly ✗ (ORY),
 France .... **19 D9** 48 44N 2 23 E
Parish, U.S.A. **117 C8** 43 25N 76 8W
Parishville, U.S.A. .. **117 B10** 44 38N 74 49W
Park, U.S.A. **110 B4** 48 45N 122 18W
Park City, U.S.A. .. **113 G6** 37 48N 97 20W
Park Falls, U.S.A. .. **112 C9** 45 56N 90 27W

Park Head, Canada .. **116 B3** 44 36N 81 9W
Park Hills, U.S.A. .. **113 G9** 37 53N 90 28W
Park Range, U.S.A. . **108 G10** 40 0N 106 30W
Park Rapids, U.S.A. . **112 B7** 46 55N 95 4W
Park River, U.S.A. .. **112 A6** 48 24N 97 45W
Park Rynie, S. Africa **89 E5** 30 25 S 30 45 E
Parkā Bandar, Iran .. **71 E8** 25 55N 59 35 E
Parkano, Finland .... **9 E20** 62 1N 23 0 E
Parker, Ariz., U.S.A. **111 L12** 34 9N 114 17W
Parker, Pa., U.S.A. . **116 E5** 41 5N 79 41W
Parker Dam, U.S.A. **111 L12** 34 18N 114 8W
Parkersburg, U.S.A. **114 F5** 39 16N 81 34W
Parkes, Australia .... **95 E4** 33 9 S 148 11 E
Parkfield, U.S.A. **110 K6** 35 54N 120 26W
Parkhill, Canada **116 C3** 43 15N 81 38W
Parkland, U.S.A. **110 C4** 47 9N 122 26W
Parkston, U.S.A. **112 D5** 43 24N 97 59W
Parksville, Canada .. **102 D4** 49 20N 124 21W
Parla, Spain **36 E7** 40 14N 3 46W
Pârlița, Moldova .... **29 C12** 47 19N 27 52 E
Parma, Italy .... **40 D7** 44 48N 10 20 E
Parma, Idaho, U.S.A. **108 E5** 43 47N 116 57W
Parma, Ohio, U.S.A. **116 E3** 41 23N 81 43W
Parma →, Italy ...... **40 D7** 44 56N 10 26 E
Parnaguá, Brazil .... **125 F10** 10 10 S 44 38W
Parnaíba, Brazil .... **125 D10** 2 54 S 41 47W
Parnaíba →, Brazil .. **125 D10** 3 0 S 41 50W
Parnassós, Greece .. **46 C4** 38 35N 22 30 E
Párnis, Greece ...... **46 C5** 38 14N 23 45 E
Párnitha, Greece .... **46 C5** 38 10N 23 44 E
Párnon Óros, Greece **46 D4** 37 15N 22 45 E
Pärnu, Estonia ...... **9 G21** 58 28N 24 33 E
Paroo →, Australia .. **95 E3** 31 28 S 143 32 E
Páros, Greece ...... **47 D7** 37 5N 25 12 E
Parowan, U.S.A. **109 H7** 37 51N 112 50W
Parpaillon, France .. **21 D10** 44 30N 6 40 E
Parral, Chile .... **126 D1** 36 10 S 71 52W
Parras, Mexico **118 B4** 25 30N 102 20W
Parrett →, U.K. **15 F4** 51 12N 3 1W
Parris I., U.S.A. **115 J5** 32 20N 80 41W
Parrsboro, Canada .. **105 C7** 45 30N 64 25W
Parry I., Canada **116 A4** 45 18N 80 10W
Parry Sound, Canada **116 A5** 45 20N 80 0W
Parsberg, Germany .. **25 F7** 49 10N 11 43 E
Parsęta →, Poland .. **30 D2** 54 11N 15 34 E
Parsnip →, Canada .. **102 B4** 55 10N 123 2W
Parsons, U.S.A. **113 G7** 37 20N 95 16W
Parsons Ra., Australia **94 A2** 13 30 S 135 15 E
Partanna, Italy ...... **42 E5** 37 43N 12 53 E
Partinico, Italy ...... **42 D6** 38 3N 13 7 E
Partizánske, Slovak Rep. **27 C11** 48 38N 18 23 E
Partridge I., Canada **104 A2** 55 59N 87 37W
Paru →, Brazil ...... **125 D8** 1 33 S 52 38W
Parvān □, Afghan. .. **66 B6** 35 0N 69 0 E
Parvatipuram, India **67 K13** 18 50N 83 25 E
Parvatsar, India .... **68 F6** 26 52N 74 49 E
Pårył, Sweden ...... **11 H9** 56 13N 15 55 E
Parys, S. Africa .... **88 D4** 26 52 S 27 46 E
Pas, Pta. des, Spain . **48 C7** 38 46N 1 26 E
Pas-de-Calais □, France **19 B9** 50 30N 2 30 E
Pasada, Spain **36 B5** 43 23N 5 40W
Pasadena, Canada .. **105 C8** 49 1N 57 36W
Pasadena, Calif., U.S.A. **111 L8** 34 9N 118 9W
Pasadena, Tex., U.S.A. **113 L7** 29 43N 95 13W
Pasaje →, Argentina **126 B3** 25 39 S 63 56W
Pasalimani, Turkey . **45 F11** 40 29N 27 36 E
Pasar, Indonesia .... **63 J17** 8 27 S 115 37 E
Pașcani, Romania .. **29 C11** 47 14N 26 45 E
Pascagoula, U.S.A. . **113 K10** 30 21N 88 33W
Pascagoula →, U.S.A. **113 K10** 30 23N 88 37W
Pasco, U.S.A. **108 C4** 46 14N 119 6W
Pasco, Cerro de, Peru **124 F3** 10 45 S 76 10W
Pasco I., Australia .. **92 D2** 20 57 S 115 20 E
Pascoag, U.S.A. **117 E13** 41 57N 71 42W
Pascua, I. de, Chile . **97 K17** 27 7 S 109 23W
Pasewalk, Germany . **24 B9** 53 30N 13 58 E
Pasfield L., Canada . **103 B7** 58 24N 105 20W
Pasha →, Russia .... **32 B7** 60 29N 32 55 E
Pasinler, Turkey .... **73 C9** 39 59N 41 41 E
Pasir Mas, Malaysia **65 J4** 6 2N 102 8 E
Pasir Panjang, Singapore **65 d** 1 18N 103 46 E
Pasir Putih, Malaysia **65 K4** 5 50N 102 24 E
Pasirian, Indonesia . **63 H15** 8 13 S 113 8 E
Pasirkuning, Indonesia **62 E2** 0 30 S 104 33 E
Påskallavik, Sweden **11 G10** 57 10N 16 27 E
Paskūh, Iran .... **71 E9** 27 34N 61 39 E
Pasłęk, Poland ...... **30 D6** 54 3N 19 41 E
Pasłęka →, Poland .. **30 D6** 54 26N 19 46 E
Pasley, C., Australia **93 F3** 33 52 S 123 35 E
Pašman, Croatia .... **41 E12** 43 58N 15 20 E
Pasni, Pakistan ...... **66 G3** 25 15N 63 27 E
Paso Cantinela, Mexico **111 N11** 32 33N 115 47W
Paso de Indios,
 Argentina .... **128 E3** 43 55 S 69 0W
Paso de los Libres,
 Argentina .... **126 B4** 29 44 S 57 10W
Paso de los Toros,
 Uruguay .... **127 C4** 32 45 S 56 30W
Paso Robles, U.S.A. **109 J3** 35 38N 120 41W
Paspébiac, Canada .. **105 C6** 48 3N 65 17W
Pasrur, Pakistan .... **68 C6** 32 16N 74 43 E
Passage West, Ireland **12 E3** 51 52N 8 21W
Passaic, U.S.A. **117 F10** 40 51N 74 7W
Passau, Germany .... **25 G9** 48 34N 13 28 E
Passero, C., Italy .... **43 F8** 36 41N 15 10 E
Passo Fundo, Brazil **127 B5** 28 10 S 52 20W
Passos, Brazil ...... **125 H9** 20 45 S 46 37W
Passow, Germany .. **24 B10** 53 8N 14 6 E
Passy, France ...... **21 C10** 45 55N 6 41 E
Pastavy, Belarus .... **9 J22** 55 4N 26 50 E
Pastaza →, Peru .... **124 D3** 4 50 S 76 52W
Pasto, Colombia **124 C3** 1 13N 77 17W
Pastrana, Spain **38 E2** 40 27N 2 53W
Pasuruan, Indonesia **63 G15** 7 40 S 112 44 E
Pasym, Poland ...... **30 E7** 53 48N 20 49 E
Pásztó, Hungary .... **28 C4** 47 52N 19 43 E
Patagonia, Argentina **128 F3** 45 0 S 69 0W
Patagonia, U.S.A. .. **109 L8** 31 33N 110 45W
Patambar, Iran ...... **71 D9** 29 45N 60 17 E
Patan = Lalitapur, Nepal **69 F11** 27 40N 85 20 E
Patan, Gujarat, India **66 H8** 23 54N 72 14 E
Patan, Maharashtra,
 India .... **68 H5** 23 54N 72 14 E
Patani, Indonesia .. **63 D7** 0 20N 128 50 E
Pātārlagele, Romania **29 E11** 45 19N 26 21 E
Pataudi, India ...... **68 E7** 28 18N 76 48 E
Patchewollock, Australia **95 F3** 35 22 S 142 12 E
Patchogue, U.S.A. .. **117 F11** 40 46N 73 1W
Patea, N.Z. .... **91 H5** 39 45 S 174 30 E
Pategi, Nigeria ...... **83 D6** 8 50N 5 45 E
Patensie, S. Africa .. **88 E3** 33 46 S 24 49 E
Paternò, Italy ...... **43 E7** 37 34N 14 54 E
Paterna, Spain **39 F4** 39 30N 0 26W

Paternion, Austria .... 26 E6 46 43N 13 38 E
Paternò, Italy .... 43 E7 37 34N 14 54 E
Pateros, U.S.A. 108 B4 48 3N 119 54W
Paterson, U.S.A. 117 F10 40 55N 74 11W
Paterson Ra., Australia 92 D3 21 45 S 122 10 E
Pathankot, India ...... 68 C6 32 18N 75 45 E
Pathein = Bassein,
  Burma .... 67 L19 16 45N 94 30 E
Pathfinder Reservoir,
  U.S.A. 108 E10 42 28N 106 51W
Pathiu, Thailand ...... 65 G2 10 42N 99 19 E
Pathum Thani, Thailand 64 E3 14 1N 100 32 E
Pati, Indonesia .... 63 G14 6 45 S 111 1 E
Patía →, Colombia 124 C3   2 13N 78 40W
Patiala, Punjab, India 68 D7 30 23N 76 26 E
Patiala, Ut. P., India 69 F8 27 43N 79 1 E
Patine Kouka, Senegal 82 C2 12 45N 13 45W
Patitírion, Greece .... 46 B5 39 8N 23 50 E
Pátmos, Greece .... 47 D8 37 21N 26 36 E
Patna, India .... 69 G11 25 35N 85 12 E
Patnos, Turkey .... 73 C10 39 13N 42 45 E
Pato Branco, Brazil .. 127 B5 26 13 S 52 40W
Patong, Ao, Thailand .. 65 a   7 54N 98 17 E
Patonga, Uganda ..... 86 B3   2 45N 33 15 E
Patos, Albania .... 44 F3 40 42N 19 38 E
Patos, Brazil .... 125 E11 6 55 S 37 16W
Patos, L. dos, Brazil . 127 C5 31 20 S 51 0W
Patos, Río de los →,
  Argentina .... 126 C2 31 18 S 69 25W
Patos de Minas, Brazil 125 G9 18 35 S 46 32W
Patquía, Argentina ... 126 C2 30 2 S 66 55W
Pátrai, Greece .... 46 C3 38 14N 21 47 E
Pátraikós Kólpos,
  Greece .... 46 C3 38 17N 21 30 E
Patras = Pátrai, Greece 46 C3 38 14N 21 47 E
Patrocínio, Brazil ... 125 G9 18 57 S 47 0W
Pattada, Italy .... 42 B2 40 35N   9 6 E
Pattani, Thailand ..... 65 J3   6 48N 101 15 E
Pattaya, Thailand .... 62 B2 12 52N 100 55 E
Patten, U.S.A. 115 C11 46 0N 68 38W
Patterson, Calif., U.S.A. 110 H5 37 28N 121 8W
Patterson, La., U.S.A. 113 L9 29 42N 91 18W
Patterson, Mt., U.S.A. 110 G7 38 29N 119 20W
Patti, Punjab, India .. 68 D6 31 17N 74 54 E
Patti, Ut. P., India ... 69 G10 25 55N 82 12 E
Patti, Italy .... 43 D7 38 8N 14 58 E
Pattoki, Pakistan .... 68 D5 31 5N 73 52 E
Patton, U.S.A. 116 F6 40 38N 78 39W
Patuakhali, Bangla. .. 67 H17 22 20N 90 25 E
Patuanak, Canada 103 B7 55 55N 107 43W
Patuca →, Honduras .. 120 C2 15 50N 84 18W
Patuca →, Honduras .. 120 C3 15 50N 84 18W
Patuca, Punta, Honduras 120 C3 15 49N 84 14W
Pătulele, Romania .... 28 F7 44 21N 22 47 E
Pátzcuaro, Mexico 118 D4 19 30N 101 40W
Pau, France 20 E3 43 19N   0 25W
Pau, Gave de →, France 20 E2 43 33N   1 12W
Pauillac, France 20 C3 45 11N   0 46W
Pauk, Burma .... 67 J19 21 27N 94 30 E
Paul I., Canada 105 A7 56 30N 61 20W
Paul Smiths, U.S.A. .. 117 B10 44 26N 74 15W
Paulatuk, Canada 100 B7 69 25N 124 0W
Paulhan, France ...... 20 E7 43 33N   3 28 E
Paulistana, Brazil ... 125 E10 8 9 S 41 9W
Paulo Afonso, Brazil . 125 E11 9 21 S 38 5W
Paulpietersburg,
  S. Africa .... 89 D5 27 23 S 30 50 E
Pauls Valley, U.S.A. .. 113 H6 34 44N 97 13W
Pauma Valley, U.S.A. . 111 M10 33 16N 116 58W
Pauri, India .... 69 D8 30 9N 78 47 E
Pāveh, Iran .... 70 C5 35 3N 46 22 E
Pavelets, Russia ..... 32 F10 53 49N 39 14 E
Pavia, Italy .... 40 C6 45 7N   9 8 E
Pavilion, U.S.A. 116 D6 42 52N 78 1W
Pavilly, France ...... 18 C7 49 34N   0 57 E
Pävilosta, Latvia .... 9 H19 56 53N 21 14 E
Pavlikeni, Bulgaria .. 45 C9 43 14N 25 20 E
Pavlodar, Kazakhstan 52 D8 52 33N 77 0 E
Pavlograd = Pavlohrad,
  Ukraine .... 33 H8 48 30N 35 52 E
Pavlohrad, Ukraine ... 33 H8 48 30N 35 52 E
Pavlovo, Russia ...... 34 C6 55 58N 43 5 E
Pavlovsk, Russia ..... 34 E5 50 26N 40 5 E
Pavlovskaya, Russia .. 35 G4 46 17N 39 47 E
Pavlovskiy-Posad,
  Russia .... 32 E10 55 47N 38 42 E
Pavullo nel Frignano,
  Italy .... 40 D7 44 20N 10 50 E
Pawai, Pulau, Singapore 65 d   1 11N 103 44 E
Pawayan, India .... 69 E9 28 4N 80 6 E
Pawhuska, U.S.A. 113 G6 36 40N 96 20W
Pawling, U.S.A. 117 E11 41 34N 73 36W
Pawnee, U.S.A. 113 G6 36 20N 96 48W
Pawnee City, U.S.A. .. 112 E6 40 7N 96 9W
Pawtucket, U.S.A. 117 E13 41 53N 71 23W
Paximádhia, Greece .. 49 E6 35 0N 24 35 E
Paxoí, Greece .... 46 B2 39 14N 20 12 E
Paxton, Ill., U.S.A. .. 114 E1 40 27N 88 6W
Paxton, Nebr., U.S.A. . 112 E4 41 7N 101 21W
Payakumbuh, Indonesia 62 E2 0 20 S 100 35 E
Payerne, Switz. ...... 25 J2 46 49N   6 56 E
Payette, U.S.A. 108 D5 44 5N 116 56W
Paymogo, Spain 37 H3 37 44N   7 21W
Payne Bay = Kangirsuk,
  Canada 101 B13 60 0N 70 0W
Payne L., Canada 101 C12 59 30N 74 30W
Paynes Find, Australia 93 E2 29 15 S 117 42 E
Paynesville, Liberia .. 82 D2   6 20N 10 45W
Paynesville, U.S.A. .. 112 C7 45 23N 94 43W
Pays de la Loire □,
  France 18 E6 47 45N   0 25W
Paysandú, Uruguay .. 126 C4 32 19 S 58 8W
Payson, U.S.A. 109 J8 34 14N 111 20W
Paz →, Guatemala ... 120 D1 13 44N 90 10W
Paz, B. de la, Mexico . 118 C2 24 15N 110 25W
Pāzanān, Iran .... 71 D6 30 35N 49 59 E
Pazar, Turkey .... 73 B9 41 10N 40 50 E
Pazarcık, Turkey .... 72 D7 37 30N 37 17 E
Pazardzhik, Bulgaria . 45 D8 42 12N 24 20 E
Pazarköy, Turkey .... 47 B9 39 51N 27 24 E
Pazaryeri, Turkey .... 47 C11 39 0N 29 56 E
Pazaryolu, Turkey .... 73 B9 40 21N 40 47 E
Pazin, Croatia .... 41 C10 45 14N 13 56 E
Pčinja →, Macedonia . 44 E5 41 50N 21 45 E
Pe Ell, U.S.A. 110 D3 46 34N 123 18W
Peabody, U.S.A. 117 D14 42 31N 70 56W
Peace →, Canada 102 B6 59 0N 111 25W
Peace Point, Canada . 102 B6 59 7N 112 27W
Peace River, Canada . 102 B5 56 15N 117 18W
Peach Springs, U.S.A. 109 J7 35 32N 113 25W
Peachland, Canada ... 102 D5 49 47N 119 45W
Peachtree City, U.S.A. 115 J3 33 25N 84 35W
Peak, The = Kinder
  Scout □, U.K. 14 D6 53 24N   1 52W
Peak Charles △,
  Australia .... 93 F3 32 42 S 121 10 E

Peak District △, U.K. .. 14 D6 53 24N   1 46W
Peak Hill, N.S.W.,
  Australia .... 95 E4 32 47 S 148 11 E
Peak Hill, W. Austral.,
  Australia .... 93 E2 25 35 S 118 43 E
Peak Ra., Australia ... 94 C4 22 50 S 148 20 E
Peake Cr. →, Australia 95 D2 28 2 S 136 7 E
Peal de Becerro, Spain 37 H7 37 55N   3 7W
Peale, Mt., U.S.A. 109 G9 38 26N 109 14W
Pearblossom, U.S.A. . 111 L9 34 30N 117 55W
Pearl →, U.S.A. 113 K10 30 11N 89 32W
Pearl City, U.S.A. 106 H16 21 24N 157 59W
Pearl Harbor, U.S.A. . 106 H16 21 21N 157 57W
Pearl River = Zhu
  Jiang →, China .... 59 F9 22 45N 113 37 E
Pearl River, U.S.A. .. 117 E10 41 4N 74 2W
Pearsall, U.S.A. 113 L5 28 54N 99 6W
Peary Land, Greenland 4 A6 82 40N 33 0W
Pease →, U.S.A. 113 H5 34 12N 99 2W
Peawanuck, Canada .. 101 C11 55 5N 85 12W
Pebane, Mozam. ..... 87 F4 17 10 S 38 8 E
Pebas, Peru .... 124 D4   3 15 S 71 46W
Pebble Beach, U.S.A. . 110 J5 36 34N 121 57W
Peć, Serbia & M. ..... 44 D4 42 40N 20 17 E
Péccioli, Italy .... 40 E7 43 33N 10 43 E
Pechea, Romania ..... 29 E12 45 36N 27 49 E
Pechenga, Russia .... 52 C4 69 29N 31 4 E
Pechenizhyn, Ukraine . 29 B9 48 30N 24 48 E
Pechiguera, Pta.,
  Canary Is. 48 F6 28 51N 13 53W
Pechnezhskoye Vdkhr.,
  Ukraine .... 33 G9 50 5N 36 54 E
Pechora, Russia ..... 52 C6 65 10N 57 11 E
Pechora →, Russia ... 52 C6 68 13N 54 15 E
Pechorskaya Guba,
  Russia .... 52 C6 68 40N 54 0 E
Pechory, Russia ...... 9 H22 57 48N 27 40 E
Pecica, Romania ..... 28 D6 46 10N 21 3 E
Pecka, Serbia & M. .. 44 B3 44 18N 19 33 E
Pécora, C., Italy ..... 42 C1 39 27N   8 23 E
Pecos, U.S.A. 113 K3 31 26N 103 30W
Pecos →, U.S.A. 113 L3 29 42N 101 22W
Pécs, Hungary .... 28 D3 46 5N 18 15 E
Pedder, L., Australia . 95 G4 42 55 S 146 10 E
Peddie, S. Africa ..... 89 E4 33 14 S 27 7 E
Pedernales, Dom. Rep. 121 C5 18 2N 71 44W
Pedernales →, Cyprus 49 D12 35 10N 33 54 E
Pedirka, Australia .... 95 D2 26 40 S 135 14 E
Pedra Azul, Brazil ... 125 G10 16 2 S 41 17W
Pedreguer, Spain .... 39 G5 38 48N   0 3 E
Pedreiras, Brazil .... 125 D10 4 32 S 44 40W
Pedro Afonso, Brazil . 125 E9   9 0 S 48 10W
Pedro Cays, Jamaica . 120 C4 17 5N 77 48W
Pedro de Valdivia, Chile 126 A2 22 55 S 69 38W
Pedro Juan Caballero,
  Paraguay .... 127 A4 22 30 S 55 40W
Pedro Muñoz, Spain . 37 F8 39 25N   2 56W
Pedrógão Grande,
  Portugal 36 F2 39 55N   8 9W
Pee Dee →, U.S.A. .. 115 J6 33 22N 79 16W
Peebinga, Australia .. 95 E3 34 52 S 140 57 E
Peebles, U.K. 13 F5 55 40N   3 11W
Peekskill, U.S.A. 117 E11 41 17N 73 55W
Peel, I. of Man 14 C3 54 13N   4 40W
Peel →, Australia .... 95 E5 30 50 S 150 29 E
Peel →, Canada 100 B6 67 0N 135 0W
Peel Sd., Canada 100 A10 73 0N 96 0W
Peene →, Germany .. 24 A9 54 9N 13 46 E

Peera Peera Poolanna
  L., Australia .... 95 D2 26 30 S 138 0 E
Peerless Lake, Canada 102 B6 56 37N 114 40W
Peers, Canada 102 C5 53 40N 116 0W
Pegasus Bay, N.Z. ... 91 K4 43 20 S 173 10 E
Peggau, Austria ..... 26 D8 47 12N 15 21 E
Pegnitz, Germany .... 25 F7 49 44N 11 31 E
Pegnitz →, Germany . 25 F6 49 30N 10 59 E
Pego, Spain 39 G4 38 51N   0 8W
Pegu, Burma .... 67 L20 17 20N 96 29 E
Pegu Yoma, Burma ... 67 K20 19 0N 96 0 E
Pehčevo, Macedonia . 44 E6 41 41N 22 55 E
Pehlivanköy, Turkey . 45 E10 41 21N 26 54 E
Pehuajó, Argentina .. 126 D3 35 45 S 62 0W
Pei Xian = Pizhou,
  China .... 56 G9 34 44N 116 55 E
Peine, Chile .... 126 A2 23 45 S 68 8W
Peine, Germany ...... 24 C6 52 19N 10 14 E
Pei'ping = Beijing, China 56 E9 39 55N 116 20 E
Peipus, L. = Chudskoye,
  Ozero, Russia ..... 9 G22 58 13N 27 30 E
Peissenberg, Germany 25 H7 47 48N 11 4 E
Peitz, Germany ...... 24 D10 51 51N 14 24 E
Peixe, Brazil .... 125 F9 12 0 S 48 40W
Peixe →, Brazil ..... 125 H8 21 31 S 51 58W
Pek →, Serbia & M. .. 44 B5 44 45N 21 29 E
Pekalongan, Indonesia 63 G13 6 53 S 109 40 E
Pekan, Malaysia ..... 65 L4   3 30N 103 25 E
Pekan Nenas, Malaysia 65 d   1 31N 103 31 E
Pekanbaru, Indonesia 62 D2   0 30N 101 15 E
Pekang, Taiwan ...... 59 F13 23 34N 120 18 E
Pekin, U.S.A. 112 E10 40 35N 89 40W
Peking = Beijing, China 56 E9 39 55N 116 20 E
Pekutatan, Indonesia 63 J17 8 25 S 114 49 E
Péla, Guinea 82 D3   7 37N   9 7W
Pelabuhan Klang,
  Malaysia .... 65 L3   3 0N 101 23 E
Pelabuhan Ratu, Teluk,
  Indonesia .... 63 G12 7 5 S 106 30 E
Pelabuhanratu,
  Indonesia .... 63 G12 7 0 S 106 32 E
Pélagos, Greece ..... 46 B6 39 17N 24 4 E
Pelaihari, Indonesia . 62 E4   3 55 S 114 45 E
Pelat, Mt., France ... 21 D10 44 16N   6 42 E
Pełczyce, Poland .... 31 E2 53 3N 15 16 E
Peleaga, Vf., Romania 28 E7 45 22N 22 55 E
Pelée, Mt., Martinique 120 c 14 48N 61 10W
Pelee, Pt., Canada ... 104 D3 41 54N 82 31W
Pelee I., Canada 116 E2 41 47N 82 40W
Pelekech, Kenya ..... 86 B4   3 52N 35 8 E
Peleng, Indonesia .... 63 E6   1 20 S 123 30 E
Pelentong, Malaysia .. 65 d   1 32N 103 49 E
Pélézi, Ivory C. 82 D3   7 24N   6 54W
Pelhřimov, Czech Rep. 26 B8 49 24N 15 12 E
Pelican, U.S.A. 102 B1 57 58N 136 14W
Pelican L., Canada ... 103 C8 52 28N 100 20W
Pelican Narrows,
  Canada 103 B8 55 10N 102 56W
Pelister △, Macedonia 44 F5 41 0N 21 10 E
Pelješac, Croatia ..... 41 F14 42 55N 17 25 E
Pelkosenniemi, Finland 8 C22 67 6N 27 28 E
Pella, S. Africa ...... 88 D2 29 1 S 19 6 E
Pella, U.S.A. 112 E8 41 25N 92 55W
Pélla □, Greece ...... 44 F6 40 52N 22 0 E
Pello, Finland .... 8 C21 66 47N 23 59 E
Pellworm, Germany .. 24 A4 54 31N   8 39 E
Pelly →, Canada 100 B6 62 47N 137 19W
Pelly Bay, Canada ... 101 B11 68 38N 89 50W

Peloponnese =
  Pelopónnisos □,
  Greece .... 46 D4 37 10N 22 0 E
Pelopónnisos □, Greece 46 D4 37 10N 22 0 E
Peloritani, Monti, Italy 43 D8 38 3N 15 20 E
Pelorus Sd., N.Z. .... 91 J4 40 59 S 173 59 E
Pelotas, Brazil ...... 127 C5 31 42 S 52 23W
Pelotas →, Brazil ... 127 B5 27 28 S 51 55W
Pelovo, Bulgaria ..... 45 C8 43 26N 24 17 E
Pelplin, Poland ...... 30 E5 53 55N 18 42 E
Pelvoux, Massif du,
  France .... 21 D10 44 52N   6 20 E
Pemalang, Indonesia . 63 G13 6 53 S 109 23 E
Pemangkat, Pulau,
  Malaysia .... 65 L5   2 37N 104 21 E
Pematangsiantar,
  Indonesia .... 62 D1   2 57N 99 5 E
Pemba, Mozam. ..... 87 E5 12 58 S 40 30 E
Pemba, Zambia ...... 87 F2 16 30 S 27 28 E
Pemba Channel,
  Tanzania .... 86 D4   5 0 S 39 37 E
Pemba I., Tanzania ... 86 D4   5 0 S 39 45 E
Pemberton, Australia . 93 F2 34 30 S 116 0 E
Pemberton, Canada .. 102 C4 50 25N 122 50W
Pembina, U.S.A. 112 A6 48 58N 97 15W
Pembroke, Canada ... 104 C4 45 50N 77 7W
Pembroke, U.K. 15 F3 51 41N   4 55W
Pembrokeshire □, U.K. 15 F3 51 52N   4 56W
Pembrokeshire Coast △,
  U.K. 15 F2 51 50N   5 2W
Pen-y-Ghent, U.K. ... 14 C5 54 10N   2 14W
Peña, Sierra de la, Spain 38 C4 42 32N   0 45W
Peña de Francia, Sierra
  de la, Spain 36 E4 40 32N   6 10W
Penafiel, Portugal ... 36 D2 41 12N   8 17W
Peñafiel, Spain 36 D6 41 35N   4 7W
Peñaflor, Spain 37 H5 37 43N   5 21W
Penal, Trin. & Tob. .. 125 K15 10 9N 61 29W
Penalara, Spain 36 E7 40 51N   3 57W
Penamacôr, Portugal . 36 E3 40 10N   7 10W
Penang = Pinang,
  Malaysia .... 65 c   5 25N 100 15 E
Penápolis, Brazil .... 127 A6 21 30 S 50 0W
Peñaranda de
  Bracamonte, Spain . 36 E5 40 53N   5 13W
Peñarroya, Spain 38 E4 40 25N   0 40W
Peñarroya-Pueblonuevo,
  Spain 37 G5 38 19N   5 16W
Penarth, U.K. 15 F4 51 26N   3 11W
Peñas, C. de, Spain .. 36 B5 43 42N   5 52W
Penas, G. de, Chile .. 128 F2 47 0 S 75 0W
Peñas de San Pedro,
  Spain 39 G3 38 44N   2 0W
Peñas del Chache,
  Canary Is. 48 E6 29 6N 13 33W
Peñausende, Spain ... 36 D5 41 17N   5 52W
Pench'i = Benxi, China 57 D12 41 20N 123 48 E
Pend Oreille →, U.S.A. 108 B5 49 4N 117 37W
Pend Oreille, L., U.S.A. 108 B5 48 10N 116 21W
Pendálofon, Greece .. 44 F5 40 14N 21 12 E
Pendembu, Eastern,
  S. Leone 82 D2   8 10N 10 42W
Pendembu, Northern,
  S. Leone 82 D2   9 7N 11 14W
Pender B., Australia . 92 C3 16 45 S 122 42 E
Pendik, Turkey ...... 45 F13 40 53N 29 13 E
Pendjari →, Benin ... 83 C5 11 15N   1 32 E
Pendjari □, Benin ... 83 C5 10 55N   0 50 E
Pendleton, U.S.A. ... 108 D4 45 40N 118 47W
Pendra, India .... 69 H9 22 46N 81 57 E
Peneda-Gerês △,
  Portugal 36 D2 41 57N   8 15W
Penedo, Brazil ...... 125 F11 10 15 S 36 36W
Penelokan, Indonesia . 63 J18 8 17 S 115 22 E
Penetanguishene,
  Canada 116 B5 44 50N 79 55W
Penfield, U.S.A. 116 E6 41 13N 78 35W
Pengalengan, Indonesia 63 G12 7 9 S 107 30 E
Penge, Kasai-Or.,
  Dem. Rep. of
  the Congo .... 86 D1   5 30 S 24 33 E
Penge, Sud-Kivu,
  Dem. Rep. of
  the Congo .... 86 C2   4 27 S 28 25 E
P'enghu Ch'üntou,
  Taiwan .... 59 F12 23 34N 119 30 E
Penglai, China .... 57 F11 37 48N 120 42 E
Pengshan, China ..... 58 B4 30 14N 103 58 E
Pengshui, China ..... 58 C7 29 17N 108 12 E
Penguin, Australia ... 95 G4 41 8 S 146 6 E
Pengxi, China .... 58 B5 30 44N 105 45 E
Pengze, China .... 59 C11 29 52N 116 32 E
Penhalonga, Zimbabwe 87 F3 18 52 S 32 40 E
Peniche, Portugal ... 37 F1 39 19N   9 22W
Penicuik, U.K. 13 F5 55 50N   3 13W
Penida, Nusa, Indonesia 63 K18 8 45 S 115 30 E
Peninsular Malaysia □,
  Malaysia .... 65 L4   4 0N 102 0 E
Peñíscola, Spain ..... 38 E5 40 22N   0 24 E
Penitente, Serra do,
  Brazil .... 125 E9   8 45 S 46 20W
Penkridge, U.K. 14 E5 52 44N   2 6W
Penmarch, France ... 18 E2 47 49N   4 21W
Penmarch, Pte. de,
  France 18 E2 47 48N   4 22W
Penn Hills, U.S.A. ... 116 F5 40 28N 79 52W
Penn Yan, U.S.A. 116 D7 42 40N 77 3W
Penna, Punta della, Italy 41 F11 42 10N 14 43 E
Pennant, Canada 103 C7 50 32N 108 14W
Penne, Italy .... 41 F10 42 27N 13 49 E
Penner →, India .... 66 M12 14 35N 80 10 E
Pennine, Alpi, Alps .. 25 J3 46 4N   7 30 E
Pennines, U.K. 14 C5 54 45N   2 27W
Pennington →, Nigeria 83 E6   4 45N   5 35 E
Pennington, Mte., Italy 40 E8 44 6N 12 53 E
Pennsburg, U.S.A. ... 117 F9 40 23N 75 29W
Pennsylvania □, U.S.A. 114 E7 40 45N 77 30W
Penny, Canada 102 C4 53 51N 121 20W
Peno, Russia .... 32 D7 57 2N 32 49 E
Penobscot →, U.S.A. 115 C11 44 30N 68 48W
Penobscot B., U.S.A. . 115 C11 44 35N 68 50W
Penola, Australia .... 95 F3 37 25 S 140 48 E
Penong, Australia .... 93 F5 31 56 S 133 1 E
Penonomé, Panama .. 120 E3   8 31N 80 21W
Penrith, Australia .... 95 E5 33 43 S 150 38 E
Penrith, U.K. 14 C5 54 40N   2 45W
Penryn, U.K. 15 G2 50 9N   5 7W
Pensacola, U.S.A. ... 115 K2 30 25N 87 13W
Pensacola Mts.,
  Antarctica .... 5 E1 84 0 S 40 0W
Pense, Canada 103 C8 50 25N 104 59W
Penshurst, Australia . 95 F3 37 49 S 142 20 E
Penticton, Canada ... 102 D5 49 30N 119 38W
Pentland, Australia .. 94 C4 20 32 S 145 25 E

Pentland Firth, U.K. .. 13 C5 58 43N   3 10W
Pentland Hills △, U.K. 13 F5 55 50N   3 20W
Pentland Hills △, U.K. 13 F5 55 48N   3 25W
Penza, Russia .... 34 D7 53 15N 45 5 E
Penzance, U.K. 15 G2 50 7N   5 33W
Penzberg, Germany .. 25 H7 47 45N 11 23 E
Penzhino, Russia .... 53 C17 63 30N 167 55 E
Penzhinskaya Guba,
  Russia .... 53 C17 61 30N 163 0 E
Penzhou, China ...... 58 B4 31 4N 103 32 E
Penzlin, Germany .... 24 B9 53 30N 13 5 E
Peoria, Ariz., U.S.A. . 109 K7 33 35N 112 14W
Peoria, Ill., U.S.A. ... 112 E10 40 42N 89 36W
Pepacton Reservoir,
  U.S.A. 117 D10 42 5N 74 58W
Pepani →, S. Africa . 88 D3 25 49 S 22 47 E
Pepel, S. Leone 82 D2   8 43N 13 3W
Peqin, Albania .... 44 E3 41 3N 19 44 E
Perabumulih, Indonesia 62 E2   3 27 S 104 15 E
Perak →, Malaysia .. 65 K3   4 0N 100 50 E
Perakhóra, Greece ... 46 C4 38 2N 22 56 E
Perales de Alfambra,
  Spain 38 E4 40 38N   1 0W
Perales del Puerto, Spain 36 E4 40 10N   6 40W
Pérama, Kérkira, Greece 49 A3 39 34N 19 54 E
Pérama, Kríti, Greece . 49 D6 35 20N 24 40 E
Perancak, Indonesia . 63 J17 8 24 S 114 37 E
Peräpohjola, Finland . 8 C22 66 16N 26 10 E
Perast, Serbia & M. .. 44 D2 42 31N 18 47 E
Percé, Canada 105 C7 48 31N 64 13W
Perche, France ...... 18 D8 48 7N 16 16 E
Perche →, France ... 18 D5 48 55N   1 11W
Percy, France 18 D5 48 55N   1 11W
Percy Is., Australia .. 94 C5 21 39 S 150 16 E
Perdido, Mte., Spain . 38 C5 42 40N   0 5 E
Perdu, Mt. = Perdido,
  Mte., Spain .... 38 C5 42 40N   0 5 E
Perechyn, Ukraine ... 28 B7 48 44N 22 28 E
Perehinske, Ukraine .. 29 B9 48 49N 24 11 E
Pereira, Colombia 124 C3   4 49N 75 43W
Perelazovskiy, Russia 35 F6 49 38N 42 35 E
Perenjori, Australia .. 93 E2 29 26 S 116 16 E
Perescena, Moldova .. 29 C13 47 16N 28 46 E
Pereslavl-Zalesskiy,
  Russia .... 32 D10 56 45N 38 50 E
Peretu, Romania ..... 29 F10 44 3N 25 5 E
Pereyaslav-
  Khmelnytskyy,
  Ukraine .... 33 G6 50 3N 31 28 E
Pereyma, Ukraine .... 29 B14 48 4N 29 30 E
Pérez, I., Mexico 119 C7 22 24N 89 42W
Perg, Austria .... 26 C7 48 15N 14 38 E
Pergamino, Argentina 126 C3 33 52 S 60 30W
Pergau →, Malaysia . 65 K3   5 23N 102 2 E
Pérgine Valsugana, Italy 41 B8 46 4N 11 14 E
Pérgola, Italy .... 41 E9 43 34N 12 50 E
Perham, U.S.A. 112 B7 46 36N 95 34W
Perhentian, Kepulauan,
  Malaysia .... 65 K4   5 54N 102 42 E
Periam, Romania .... 28 D5 46 2N 20 52 E
Péribonka →, Canada 105 C5 48 45N 72 5W
Péribonka, L., Canada 105 B5 50 1N 71 10W
Perico, Argentina .... 126 A2 24 20 S 65 5W
Pericos, Mexico 118 B3 25 3N 107 42W
Périers, France 18 C5 49 11N   1 25W
Périgord, France .... 20 D4 45 0N   0 40 E
Périgord-Limousin,
  France .... 20 C4 45 40N   0 50 E
Périgueux, France ... 20 C4 45 10N   0 42 E
Perijá △, Venezuela . 121 E5   9 30N 72 55W
Perijá, Sierra de,
  Colombia 124 B4   9 30N 73 3W
Peristéra, Greece .... 46 B5 39 15N 23 58 E
Peristerona →, Cyprus 49 D12 35 8N 33 5 E
Perito Moreno,
  Argentina .... 128 F2 46 36 S 70 56W
Perivol = Dragovishtitsa,
  Bulgaria .... 44 D6 42 22N 22 39 E
Perkasie, U.S.A. 117 F9 40 22N 75 18W
Perković, Croatia .... 41 E13 43 41N 16 10 E
Perlas, Arch. de las,
  Panama 120 E4   8 41N 79 7W
Perlas, Punta de, Nic. 120 D3 12 30N 83 30W
Perleberg, Germany . 24 B7 53 5N 11 52 E
Perlez, Serbia & M. .. 44 E5 45 11N 20 22 E
Perm, Russia .... 52 D6 58 0N 56 10 E
Pérmet, Albania ..... 44 F4 40 15N 20 21 E
Pernambuco = Recife,
  Brazil .... 125 E12 8 0 S 35 0W
Pernambuco □, Brazil 125 E11 8 0 S 37 0W
Pernatty Lagoon,
  Australia .... 95 E2 31 30 S 137 12 E
Pernik, Bulgaria ..... 44 D7 42 35N 23 2 E
Peron Is., Australia .. 92 B5   13 9 S 130 4 E
Peron Pen., Australia . 93 E1 26 0 S 113 10 E
Perosa Argentina, Italy 40 D4 44 58N   7 10 E
Perow, Canada 102 C3 54 35N 126 10W
Perpignan, France ... 20 F6 42 42N   2 53 E
Perris, U.S.A. 111 M9 33 47N 117 14W
Perros-Guirec, France 18 D3 48 49N   3 28W
Perry, Fla., U.S.A. ... 115 K4 30 7N 83 35W
Perry, Ga., U.S.A. ... 115 J4 32 28N 83 44W
Perry, Iowa, U.S.A. . 112 E7 41 51N 94 6W
Perry, Okla., U.S.A. . 113 G6 36 17N 97 14W
Perryton, U.S.A. 113 G4 36 24N 100 48W
Perryville, U.S.A. 113 G10 37 43N 89 52W
Persan, France ...... 19 C9 49 9N   2 16 E
Persberg, Sweden ... 10 E8 59 47N 14 15 E
Perşembe, Turkey ... 72 B7 41 5N 37 4 E
Persepolis, Iran ..... 71 D7 29 55N 52 50 E
Pershotravensk, Ukraine 33 G4 50 13N 27 40 E
Persia = Iran ■, Asia 71 E6 27 0N 53 0 E
Persian Gulf, Asia ... 71 E6 27 0N 50 0 E
Pertek, Turkey ...... 73 C8 39 1N 39 19 E
Perth, Australia ...... 93 F2 31 57 S 115 52 E
Perth, Canada 115 B9 44 55N 76 15W
Perth, U.K. 13 E5 56 24N   3 26W
Perth & Kinross □, U.K. 13 E5 56 45N   3 55W
Perth Amboy, U.S.A. 117 F10 40 31N 74 16W
Perth-Andover, Canada 105 C6 46 44N 67 42W
Pertré, France 18 D5 48 2N   0 30W
Pertuisato, C., France 21 G13 41 21N   9 11 E
Peru, Ind., U.S.A. ... 114 E2 40 45N 86 4W
Peru, N.Y., U.S.A. ... 117 B11 44 35N 73 32W
Peru ■, S. Amer. .... 124 D4   4 0 S 75 0W
Peru Basin, Pac. Oc. . 97 J18 20 0 S 95 0W
Peru-Chile Trench,
  Pac. Oc. .... 124 G3 20 0 S 72 0W
Perúgia, Italy .... 41 E9 43 7N 12 23 E
Perušić, Croatia ..... 41 D12 44 40N 15 22 E
Pervomaysk, Russia . 34 C6 54 56N 43 58 E
Pervomaysk, Ukraine 33 H6 48 10N 30 46 E

Pervouralsk, Russia .. 52 D6 56 59N 59 59 E
Pésaro, Italy .... 41 E9 43 54N 12 55 E
Pescadores = P'enghu
  Ch'üntou, Taiwan .. 59 F12 23 34N 119 30 E
Pescara, Italy .... 41 F11 42 28N 14 13 E
Pescara →, Italy .... 41 F11 42 28N 14 13 E
Peschanokopskoye,
  Russia .... 35 G5 46 14N 41 4 E
Péscia, Italy .... 40 E7 43 54N 10 41 E
Pescina, Italy .... 41 F10 42 2N 13 39 E
Peshawar, Pakistan .. 68 B4 34 2N 71 37 E
Peshkopi, Albania ... 44 E4 41 41N 20 25 E
Peshtera, Bulgaria ... 45 D8 42 2N 24 18 E
Peshtigo, U.S.A. 114 C2 45 4N 87 46W
Peski, Russia .... 34 E6 51 14N 42 29 E
Pêso da Régua, Portugal 36 D3 41 10N   7 47W
Pesqueira, Brazil .... 125 E11 8 20 S 36 42W
Pessac, France 20 D3 44 48N   0 37W
Pest □, Hungary ..... 28 C5 47 29N 19 5 E
Pestovo, Russia ..... 32 C8 58 33N 35 42 E
Pestravka, Russia ... 34 D9 52 28N 49 57 E
Péta, Greece .... 46 B3 39 10N 21 2 E
Petah Tiqwa, Israel .. 74 C3 32 6N 34 53 E
Petalídhion, Greece .. 46 E3 36 57N 21 55 E
Petaling Jaya, Malaysia 65 L3   3 4N 101 42 E
Petaloudhes, Greece . 49 C10 36 18N 28 5 E
Petaluma, U.S.A. 110 G4 38 14N 122 39W
Pétange, Lux. .... 17 E5 49 33N   5 55 E
Petaro, Pakistan ..... 68 G3 25 31N 68 18 E
Petatlán, Mexico 118 D4 17 31N 101 16W
Petauke, Zambia ..... 87 E3 14 14 S 31 20 E
Petawawa, Canada ... 104 C4 45 54N 77 17W
Petén Itzá, L.,
  Guatemala 120 C2 16 58N 89 50W
Peter I., Br. Virgin Is. 121 e 18 22N 64 35W
Peter I.s Øy, Antarctica 5 C16 69 0 S 91 0W
Peter Pond L., Canada 103 B7 55 55N 108 44W
Peterbell, Canada 104 C3 48 36N 83 21W
Peterborough, Australia 95 E2 32 58 S 138 51 E
Peterborough, Canada 104 B6 44 20N 78 20W
Peterborough, U.K. .. 15 E7 52 35N   0 15W
Peterborough, U.S.A. 117 D13 42 53N 71 57W
Peterborough □, U.K. 15 E7 52 35N   0 15W
Peterculter, U.K. 13 D6 57 6N   2 16W
Peterhead, U.K. 13 D7 57 31N   1 48W
Peterlee, U.K. 14 C6 54 47N   1 20W
Petermann Ranges,
  Australia .... 92 E5 26 0 S 130 30 E
Petersburg, Alaska,
  U.S.A. 100 C6 56 48N 132 58W
Petersburg, Pa., U.S.A. 116 F6 40 34N 78 3W
Petersburg, Va., U.S.A. 114 G7 37 14N 77 24W
Petersburg, W. Va.,
  U.S.A. 114 F6 39 1N 79 5W
Petersfield, U.K. 15 F7 51 1N   0 56W
Petershagen, Germany 24 C4 52 23N   8 58 E
Petília Policastro, Italy 43 C9 39 7N 16 48 E
Petit-Canal, Guadeloupe 120 b 16 25N 61 31W
Petit Goâve, Haiti ... 121 C5 18 27N 72 51W
Petit Jardin, Canada . 105 C8 48 28N 59 14W
Petit Lac Manicouagan,
  Canada 105 B6 51 25N 67 40W
Petit-Mécatina →,
  Canada 105 B8 50 40N 59 30W
Petit-Mécatina, Î. du,
  Canada 105 B8 50 30N 59 25W
Petit Piton, St. Lucia . 121 f 13 51N 61 5W
Petit-Saguenay, Canada 105 C5 48 15N 70 4W
Petit Saint Bernard, Col
  du, Italy .... 21 C10 45 40N   6 52 E
Petitcodiac, Canada . 105 C6 45 57N 65 11W
Petite Terre, Îles de la,
  Guadeloupe .... 120 b 16 13N 61 9W
Petitot →, Canada .. 102 A4 60 14N 123 29W
Petitsikapau L., Canada 105 B6 54 37N 66 25W
Petlad, India .... 68 H5 22 30N 72 45 E
Peto, Mexico 119 C7 20 10N 88 53W
Petone, N.Z. .... 91 J5 41 13 S 174 53 E
Petorca, Chile .... 126 C1 32 15 S 70 56W
Petoskey, U.S.A. 114 C3 45 22N 84 57W
Petra, Jordan .... 74 E4 30 20N 35 22 E
Petra, Spain .... 38 B10 39 37N   3 6 E
Petra, Ostrova, Russia 4 B13 76 15N 118 30 E
Petra Velikogo, Zaliv,
  Russia .... 54 C6 42 40N 132 0 E
Petrel = Petrer, Spain 39 G4 38 30N   0 46W
Petrella, Monte, Italy . 42 A6 41 18N 13 40 E
Petrer, Spain 39 G4 38 30N   0 46W
Petreto-Bicchisano,
  France .... 21 G12 41 47N   8 58 E
Petrich, Bulgaria .... 44 E7 41 24N 23 13 E
Petrified Forest △,
  U.S.A. 109 J9 35 0N 109 30W
Petrijanec, Croatia .. 41 B13 46 23N 16 17 E
Petrikov = Pyetrikaw,
  Belarus .... 33 F5 52 11N 28 29 E
Petrila, Romania .... 28 E8 45 29N 23 29 E
Petrinja, Croatia ..... 41 C13 45 28N 16 18 E
Petrodvorets, Russia . 32 C5 59 52N 29 54 E
Petrolândia, Brazil .. 125 E11 9 5 S 38 20W
Petrólia, Canada 116 D2 42 54N 82 9W
Petrolina, Brazil ..... 125 E10 9 24 S 40 30W
Petropavl, Kazakhstan 52 D7 54 53N 69 13 E
Petropavlovsk =
  Petropavl, Kazakhstan 52 D7 54 53N 69 13 E
Petropavlovsk-
  Kamchatskiy, Russia 53 D16 53 3N 158 43 E
Petropavlovskiy =
  Akhtubinsk, Russia . 35 F8 48 13N 46 7 E
Petrópolis, Brazil .... 127 A7 22 33 S 43 9W
Petroşani, Romania .. 29 E8 45 28N 23 20 E
Petrova Gora, Croatia 41 C12 45 15N 15 45 E
Petrovac, Serbia & M. 44 B5 44 22N 21 26 E
Petrovac, Serbia & M. 44 E3 44 13N 18 57 E
Petrovaradin,
  Serbia & M. .... 28 E4 45 16N 19 55 E
Petrovsk, Russia .... 34 D7 52 22N 45 19 E
Petrovsk-Zabaykalskiy,
  Russia .... 53 D11 51 20N 108 55 E
Petrovskaya, Russia . 33 K9 45 25N 38 30 E
Petrozavodsk, Russia 8 B10 61 41N 34 20 E
Petrus Steyn, S. Africa 89 D4 27 38 S 28 8 E
Petrusburg, S. Africa . 88 D4 29 4 S 25 26 E
Peumo, Chile .... 126 C1 34 21 S 71 12W
Peureulak, Indonesia 62 D1   4 48N 97 45 E
Pevek, Russia .... 53 C18 69 41N 171 19 E
Peveragno, Italy ..... 40 D4 44 20N   7 37 E
Peyrehorade, France 20 E2 43 34N   1 7W
Peyruis, France ...... 21 D9 44 1N   5 56 E
Pézenas, France ..... 20 E7 43 28N   3 26 E
Pezinok, Slovak Rep. 27 C10 48 17N 17 17 E
Pfaffenhofen, Germany 25 G7 48 31N 11 31 E
Pfälzerwald △, Germany 25 F3 49 8N   7 52 E
Pfarrkirchen, Germany 25 G8 48 25N 12 57 E
Pfeffenhausen, Germany 25 G7 48 40N 11 58 E
Pforzheim, Germany . 25 G4 48 52N   8 41 E

Pfullendorf, Germany . 25 H5 47 55N 9 15 E
Pfungstadt, Germany . 25 F4 49 48N 8 35 E
Pha Taem △, Thailand . 64 E5 15 32N 105 30 E
Phagwara, India . . . . 66 D9 31 10N 75 40 E
Phaistós, Greece . . . . 49 D6 35 2N 25 6 E
Phala, Botswana . . . . 88 C4 23 45 S 26 50 E
Phalera = Phulera, India 68 F6 26 52N 75 16 E
Phalodi, India . . . . 68 F5 27 12N 72 24 E
Phalsbourg, France . . 19 D14 48 46N 7 15 E
Phaluai, Ko, Thailand . 65 b 9 32N 99 41 E
Phan, Thailand . . . . 64 C2 19 28N 99 43 E
Phan Rang, Vietnam . . 65 G7 11 34N 109 0 E
Phan Ri = Hoa Da,
  Vietnam . . . . . . 65 G7 11 16N 108 40 E
Phan Thiet, Vietnam . . 65 G7 11 1N 108 9 E
Phanae, Greece . . . . 47 C7 38 8N 25 57 E
Phanat Nikhom,
  Thailand . . . . . . 64 F3 13 27N 101 11 E
Phangan, Ko, Thailand . 65 H3 9 45N 100 0 E
Phangnga, Thailand . . 65 H2 8 28N 98 30 E
Phangnga, Ao, Thailand 65 a 8 16N 98 33 E
Phanom Sarakham,
  Thailand . . . . . . 64 F3 13 45N 101 21 E
Phaphund, India . . . . 69 F8 26 36N 79 28 E
Pharenda, India . . . . 69 F10 27 5N 83 17 E
Pharr, U.S.A. 113 M5 26 12N 98 11W
Phatthalung, Thailand . 65 J3 7 39N 100 6 E
Phayao, Thailand . . . 64 C2 19 11N 99 55 E
Phelps, U.S.A. 116 D7 42 58N 77 3W
Phelps L., Canada . . . 103 B8 59 15N 103 15W
Phenix City, U.S.A. . . 115 J3 32 28N 85 0W
Phet Buri, Thailand . . 64 F2 13 1N 99 55 E
Phetchabun, Thailand . 64 D3 16 25N 101 8 E
Phetchabun, Thiu Khao,
  Thailand . . . . . . 64 E3 16 0N 101 20 E
Phetchaburi = Phet Buri,
  Thailand . . . . . . 64 F2 13 1N 99 55 E
Phi Phi, Ko, Thailand . 65 J2 7 45N 98 46 E
Phibun Mangsahan,
  Thailand . . . . . . 64 E5 15 14N 105 14 E
Phichai, Thailand . . . 64 D3 17 22N 100 10 E
Phichit, Thailand . . . 64 D3 16 26N 100 22 E
Philadelphia, Miss.,
  U.S.A. 113 J10 32 46N 89 7W
Philadelphia, N.Y.,
  U.S.A. 117 B9 44 9N 75 43W
Philadelphia, Pa., U.S.A. 117 G9 39 57N 75 10W
Philip, U.S.A. 112 C4 44 2N 101 40W
Philippeville, Belgium . 17 D4 50 12N 4 33 E
Philippi, Greece . . . . 45 E8 41 1N 24 16 E
Philippi, U.S.A. 114 F5 39 9N 80 3W
Philippi L., Australia . 94 C2 24 20 S 138 55 E
Philippine Sea, Pac. Oc. 50 H16 18 0N 125 0 E
Philippines ■, Asia . . 61 F5 12 0N 123 0 E
Philippolis, S. Africa . 88 E4 30 15 S 25 16 E
Philippopolis = Plovdiv,
  Bulgaria . . . . . . 45 D8 42 8N 24 44 E
Philipsburg, Canada . . 117 A11 45 2N 73 5W
Philipsburg, Mont.,
  U.S.A. 108 C7 46 20N 113 18W
Philipsburg, Pa., U.S.A. 116 F6 40 54N 78 13W
Philipstown = Daingean,
  Ireland 12 C4 53 18N 7 17W
Philipstown, S. Africa . 88 E3 30 28 S 24 30 E
Phillip I., Australia . . 95 F4 38 30 S 145 12 E
Phillips, U.S.A. 112 C9 45 42N 90 24W
Phillipsburg, Kans.,
  U.S.A. 112 F5 39 45N 99 19W
Phillipsburg, N.J., U.S.A. 117 F9 40 42N 75 12W
Philmont, U.S.A. . . . 117 D11 42 15N 73 39W
Philomath, U.S.A. . . . 108 D2 44 32N 123 22W
Phimai, Thailand . . . 64 E4 15 13N 102 30 E
Phitsanulok, Thailand . 64 D3 16 50N 100 12 E
Phnom Dangrek,
  Thailand . . . . . . 62 B2 14 20N 104 0 E
Phnom Penh, Cambodia 65 G5 11 33N 104 55 E
Phnum Penh = Phnom
  Penh, Cambodia . . 65 G5 11 33N 104 55 E
Phoenicia, U.S.A. . . . 117 D10 42 5N 74 14W
Phoenix, Ariz., U.S.A. . 109 K7 33 27N 112 4W
Phoenix, N.Y., U.S.A. . 117 C8 43 14N 76 18W
Phoenix Is., Kiribati . . 96 H10 3 30 S 172 0W
Phoenixville, U.S.A. . . 117 F9 40 8N 75 31W
Phon, Thailand . . . . 64 E4 15 49N 102 36 E
Phon Tiou, Laos . . . 64 D5 17 53N 104 37 E
Phong →, Thailand . . 64 D4 16 23N 102 56 E
Phong Saly, Laos . . . 58 G4 21 42N 102 9 E
Phong Tho, Vietnam . . 64 A4 22 32N 103 21 E
Phonhong, Laos . . . . 64 C4 18 30N 102 25 E
Phonum, Thailand . . . 65 H2 8 49N 98 48 E
Phosphate Hill,
  Australia . . . . . . 94 C2 21 53 S 139 58 E
Photharam, Thailand . . 64 F2 13 41N 99 51 E
Phra Nakhon Si
  Ayutthaya, Thailand . 64 E3 14 25N 100 30 E
Phra Thong, Ko,
  Thailand . . . . . . 65 H2 9 5N 98 17 E
Phrae, Thailand . . . . 64 C3 18 7N 100 9 E
Phrom Phiram, Thailand 64 D3 17 2N 100 12 E
Phrygia, Turkey . . . . 72 C4 38 40N 30 0 E
Phu Chong-Na Yoi △,
  Thailand . . . . . . 64 E5 14 25N 105 30 E
Phu Dien, Vietnam . . . 64 C5 18 58N 105 31 E
Phu Hin Rang Kla △,
  Thailand . . . . . . 64 D3 17 0N 100 59 E
Phu Kradung △,
  Thailand . . . . . . 64 D3 17 0N 101 44 E
Phu Loi, Laos . . . . . 64 B4 20 14N 103 14 E
Phu Luang △, Thailand . 64 D3 17 15N 101 29 E
Phu Ly, Vietnam . . . . 58 G5 20 35N 105 50 E
Phu Phan △, Thailand . 64 D4 17 0N 103 56 E
Phu Quoc, Dao, Vietnam 65 G4 10 20N 104 0 E
Phu Tho, Vietnam . . . 58 G5 21 24N 105 13 E
Phuc Yen, Vietnam . . . 58 G5 21 16N 105 45 E
Phuket, Thailand . . . 65 a 7 53N 98 24 E
Phuket, Ko, Thailand . 65 a 8 0N 98 22 E
Phul, India . . . . . . 68 D6 30 19N 75 14 E
Phulad, India . . . . . 68 G5 25 38N 73 49 E
Phulchari, Bangla. . . . 69 G13 25 11N 89 37 E
Phulera, India . . . . . 68 F6 26 52N 75 16 E
Phulpur, India . . . . . 69 G10 25 31N 82 49 E
Phun Phin, Thailand . . 65 H2 9 7N 99 12 E
Piacenza, Italy . . . . 40 C6 45 1N 9 40 E
Piai, Tanjung, Malaysia 65 d 1 17N 103 30 E
Pian Cr. →, Australia . 95 E4 30 2 S 148 12 E
Pian-Upe →, Uganda . 86 B3 1 44N 34 20 E
Piana, France . . . . . 21 F12 42 15N 8 34 E
Pianella, Italy . . . . 41 F11 42 24N 14 2 E
Pianosa, Puglia, Italy . 41 A9 42 12N 15 44 E
Pianosa, Toscana, Italy 40 F7 42 35N 10 5 E
Piapot, Canada 103 D7 49 59N 109 8W
Piatra, Romania . . . . 29 G10 43 51N 25 9 E

Piatra Craiului △,
  Romania . . . . . . 29 E10 45 30N 25 12 E
Piatra Neamț, Romania 29 D11 46 56N 26 21 E
Piatra Olt, Romania . . 29 F9 44 22N 24 16 E
Piauí □, Brazil . . . . . 125 E10 7 0 S 43 0W
Piauí →, Brazil . . . . 125 E10 6 38 S 42 42W
Piave →, Italy . . . . . 41 C9 45 32N 12 44 E
Piazza Ármerina, Italy . 43 E7 37 21N 14 20 E
Pibor →, Sudan . . . . 81 F3 7 35N 33 0 E
Pibor Post, Sudan . . . 81 F3 6 47N 33 3 E
Picardie □, France . . . 19 C10 49 50N 3 0 E
Picardie, Plaine de,
  France . . . . . . 19 C9 50 0N 2 0 E
Picardy = Picardie □,
  France . . . . . . 19 C10 49 50N 3 0 E
Picayune, U.S.A. . . . 113 K10 30 32N 89 41W
Picerno, Italy . . . . . 43 B8 40 38N 15 38 E
Pichhor, India . . . . . 69 G8 25 58N 78 20 E
Pichilemu, Chile . . . . 126 C1 34 22 S 72 0W
Pichor, India . . . . . 68 G8 25 11N 78 11 E
Pickerel L., Canada . . 104 C1 48 40N 91 25W
Pickering, U.K. 14 C7 54 15N 0 46W
Pickering, Vale of, U.K. 14 C7 54 14N 0 45W
Pickle Lake, Canada . . 104 B1 51 30N 90 12W
Pickwick L., U.S.A. . . 115 H1 35 4N 88 15W
Pico Bonito △,
  Honduras 120 C2 15 34N 86 48W
Pico Truncado,
  Argentina . . . . . . 128 F3 46 40 S 68 0W
Picos, Brazil . . . . . . 125 E10 7 5 S 41 28W
Picos de Europa △,
  Spain 36 B6 43 14N 4 59W
Picton, Australia . . . . 95 E5 34 12 S 150 34 E
Picton, Canada 116 B7 44 1N 77 9W
Picton, N.Z. . . . . . . 91 J5 41 18 S 174 3 E
Pictou, Canada 105 C7 45 41N 62 42W
Picture Butte, Canada . 102 D6 49 55N 112 45W
Pictured Rocks △,
  U.S.A. 114 B2 46 30N 86 30W
Picún Leufú, Argentina 128 D3 39 30 S 69 5W
Pidbuzh, Ukraine . . . 31 J10 49 19N 23 14 E
Pidurutalagala,
  Sri Lanka . . . . . . 66 R12 7 10N 80 50 E
Piechowice, Poland . . 31 H5 50 51N 15 36 E
Piedimonte Matese, Italy 43 A7 41 22N 14 22 E
Piedmont = Piemonte □,
  Italy . . . . . . 40 D5 45 0N 8 0 E
Piedmont, Ala., U.S.A. 115 J3 33 55N 85 37W
Piedmont, S.C., U.S.A. 107 D10 34 0N 81 30W
Piedra →, Spain 38 D3 41 18N 1 47W
Piedrabuena, Spain . . 37 G6 39 0N 4 10W
Piedrahita, Spain . . . 36 E5 40 28N 5 23W
Piedralaves, Spain . . . 36 E6 40 19N 4 42W
Piedras Blancas, Spain . 36 B5 43 33N 5 58W
Piedras Negras, Mexico 118 B4 28 42N 100 31W
Piekary Śląskie, Poland 31 H5 50 24N 18 57 E
Pieksämäki, Finland . . 9 E22 62 18N 27 10 E
Piemonte □, Italy . . . 40 D5 45 0N 8 0 E
Pienaarsrivier, S. Africa 89 D4 25 15 S 28 18 E
Pieniężno, Poland . . . 30 D7 54 14N 20 8 E
Pieniński △, Europe . . 27 B13 49 25N 20 28 E
Pieńsk, Poland . . . . . 31 G2 51 16N 15 2 E
Piercefield, U.S.A. . . . 117 B10 44 13N 74 35W
Pierceland, Canada . . 103 C7 54 20N 109 46W
Piería □, Greece . . . . 44 F6 40 13N 22 25 E
Pierpont, U.S.A. 116 E4 41 45N 80 34W
Pierre, U.S.A. 112 C4 44 22N 100 21W
Pierre-Buffière, France 20 C5 45 41N 1 22 E
Pierre-de-Bresse, France 19 F12 46 54N 5 13 E
Pierrefontaine-les-
  Varans, France . . . 19 E13 47 14N 6 32 E
Pierrefort, France . . . 20 D6 44 55N 2 50 E
Pierrelatte, France . . . 21 D8 44 23N 4 43 E
Pierreville, Trin. & Tob. 125 K16 10 16N 61 0W
Pieštany, Slovak Rep. . 27 C10 48 38N 17 55 E
Piesting →, Austria . . 27 C9 48 6N 16 40 E
Pieszyce, Poland . . . . 31 H3 50 43N 16 33 E
Piet Retief, S. Africa . . 89 D5 27 1 S 30 50 E
Pietarsaari, Finland . . 8 E20 63 40N 22 43 E
Pietermaritzburg,
  S. Africa . . . . . . 89 D5 29 35 S 30 25 E
Pietersburg =
  Polokwane, S. Africa 89 C4 23 54 S 29 25 E
Pietragalla, Italy . . . . 43 B8 40 45N 15 53 E
Pietrasanta, Italy . . . 40 E7 43 57N 10 14 E
Pietroșița, Romania . . 29 E10 45 11N 25 26 E
Pietrosul, Vf.,
  Maramureș, Romania 29 C9 47 35N 24 43 E
Pietrosul, Vf., Suceava,
  Romania . . . . . . 29 C10 47 12N 25 18 E
Pieve di Cadore, Italy . 41 B9 46 26N 12 22 E
Pieve di Teco, Italy . . 40 D4 44 3N 7 56 E
Pievepélago, Italy . . . 40 D7 44 12N 10 37 E
Pigadhítsa, Greece . . . 44 G5 39 59N 21 23 E
Pigeon L., Canada . . . 116 B6 44 27N 78 30W
Piggott, U.S.A. 113 G9 36 23N 90 11W
Pigna, Italy . . . . . . 40 E4 43 56N 7 40 E
Pigüe, Argentina . . . . 126 D3 37 36 S 62 25W
Pihani, India . . . . . . 69 F9 27 36N 80 15 E
Pihlajavesi, Finland . . 9 F23 61 45N 28 45 E
Pijijiapan, Mexico . . . 119 D6 15 42N 93 14W
Pikalevo, Russia . . . . 32 C8 59 37N 34 9 E
Pikangikum Berens,
  Canada 103 C10 51 49N 94 0W
Pikes Peak, U.S.A. . . . 112 F2 38 50N 105 3W
Piketberg, S. Africa . . 88 E2 32 55 S 18 40 E
Pikeville, U.S.A. 114 G4 37 29N 82 31W
Pikou, China . . . . . . 57 E12 39 18N 122 22 E
Pikwitonei, Canada . . 103 B9 55 35N 97 9W
Piła, Poland . . . . . . 31 E3 53 10N 16 48 E
Pila, Spain 39 G3 38 16N 1 11W
Pilaía, Greece . . . . . 44 F6 40 32N 22 59 E
Pilanesberg △, S. Africa 88 D4 25 15 S 27 4 E
Pilani, India . . . . . . 68 E6 28 22N 75 33 E
Pilar, Paraguay . . . . 126 B4 26 50 S 58 20W
Pilar da Horadada,
  Spain 39 H4 37 52N 0 47W
Pilat △, France . . . . 21 C8 45 20N 4 30 E
Pilawa, Poland . . . . . 31 G8 51 57N 21 32 E
Pilaya →, Bolivia . . . 124 H6 20 55 S 64 4W
Pilbara, Australia . . . 92 D2 23 35 S 117 25 E
Pilcomayo →, Paraguay 126 B4 25 21 S 57 42W
Pilgrim's Rest, S. Africa 89 C5 24 55 S 30 44 E
Pilgrimstad, Sweden . . 10 B9 62 57N 15 2 E
Pili, Greece . . . . . . 47 E9 36 50N 27 15 E
Pilibhit, India . . . . . 69 E8 28 40N 79 50 E
Pilica →, Poland . . . . 31 G8 51 52N 21 17 E
Pilion, Greece . . . . . 46 B5 39 27N 23 6 E
Pilis, Hungary . . . . . 28 C4 47 17N 19 35 E
Pilisvörösvár, Hungary 28 C4 47 38N 18 54 E
Pilkhawa, India . . . . 68 E7 28 43N 77 42 E
Pilliga, Australia . . . . 95 E4 30 21 S 148 54 E
Pílos, Greece . . . . . . 46 E3 36 55N 21 42 E
Pilot Mound, Canada . 103 D9 49 15N 98 54W
Pilot Point, U.S.A. . . 113 J6 33 24N 96 58W
Pilot Rock, U.S.A. . . . 108 D4 45 29N 118 50W
Pilsen = Plzeň,
  Czech Rep. . . . . . 26 B6 49 45N 13 22 E
Pilštanj, Slovenia . . . 41 B12 46 8N 15 39 E

Piltene, Latvia . . . . . 30 A8 57 13N 21 40 E
Pilzno, Poland . . . . . 31 J8 49 58N 21 16 E
Pima, U.S.A. 109 K9 32 54N 109 50W
Pimba, Australia . . . . 95 E2 31 18 S 136 46 E
Pimenta Bueno, Brazil 124 F6 11 35 S 61 10W
Pimentel, Peru . . . . . 124 E3 6 45 S 79 55W
Pina de Ebro, Spain . . 38 D4 41 29N 0 33W
Pinamalayan, Phil. . . . 61 E4 13 2N 121 29 E
Pinang, Malaysia . . . . 65 c 5 25N 100 15 E
Pinar, C. des, Spain . . 48 B10 39 53N 3 12 E
Pinar del Río, Cuba . . 120 B3 22 26N 83 40W
Pınarbaşı, Çanakkale,
  Turkey . . . . . . 47 B8 39 53N 26 15 E
Pınarbaşı, Kayseri,
  Turkey . . . . . . 72 C7 38 43N 36 23 E
Pınarhisar, Turkey . . . 45 E11 41 37N 27 30 E
Pinatubo, Mt., Phil. . . 61 D3 15 8N 120 21 E
Pincehely, Hungary . . 28 D3 46 41N 18 27 E
Pinchang, China . . . . 58 B6 31 36N 107 3 E
Pincher Creek, Canada 102 D6 49 30N 113 57W
Pinchi L., Canada . . . 102 C4 54 38N 124 30W
Pinckneyville, U.S.A. . 112 F10 38 5N 89 23W
Pińczów, Poland . . . . 31 H7 50 32N 20 32 E
Pindar, Australia . . . . 93 E2 28 30 S 115 47 E
Pindi Gheb, Pakistan . 68 C5 33 14N 72 21 E
Pindiga, Nigeria . . . . 83 D7 9 58N 10 53 E
Pindos △, Greece . . . 46 B3 39 52N 21 11 E
Pindos Óros, Greece . . 46 B3 40 0N 21 0 E
Pindus Mts. = Pindos
  Óros, Greece . . . . 46 B3 40 0N 21 0 E
Pine →, B.C., Canada . 102 B4 56 8N 120 43W
Pine →, Sask., Canada 103 B7 58 50N 105 38W
Pine, C., Canada 105 C9 46 37N 53 32W
Pine Bluff, U.S.A. . . . 113 H9 34 13N 92 1W
Pine Bluffs, U.S.A. . . . 112 E2 41 11N 104 4W
Pine City, U.S.A. . . . 112 C8 45 50N 92 59W
Pine Cr. →, U.S.A. . . 116 E7 41 10N 77 16W
Pine Creek, U.S.A. . . . 92 B5 13 50 S 131 50 E
Pine Falls, Canada . . . 103 C9 50 34N 96 11W
Pine Flat Res., U.S.A. . 110 J7 36 50N 119 20W
Pine Grove, U.S.A. . . 117 F8 40 33N 76 23W
Pine Pass, Canada . . . 102 B4 55 25N 122 42W
Pine Point, Canada . . 102 A6 60 50N 114 28W
Pine Ridge, U.S.A. . . . 112 D3 43 2N 102 33W
Pine River, Canada . . 103 C8 51 45N 100 30W
Pine River, U.S.A. . . . 112 B7 46 43N 94 24W
Pine Valley, U.S.A. . . 111 N10 32 50N 116 32W
Pinecrest, U.S.A. 110 G6 38 12N 120 1W
Pineda de Mar, Spain . 38 D7 41 37N 2 42 E
Pinedale, Calif., U.S.A. 110 J7 36 50N 119 48W
Pinedale, Wyo., U.S.A. 108 E9 42 52N 109 52W
Pinega →, Russia . . . 52 C5 64 30N 44 19 E
Pinehill, Australia . . . 94 C4 23 38 S 146 57 E
Pinehouse L., Canada . 103 B7 55 32N 106 35W
Pineimuta →, Canada . 104 B1 52 8N 88 33W
Pinerolo, Italy . . . . . 40 D4 44 53N 7 21 E
Pineto, Italy . . . . . . 41 F11 42 36N 14 4 E
Pinetop, U.S.A. 109 J9 34 8N 109 56W
Pinetown, S. Africa . . 89 D5 29 48 S 30 54 E
Pineville, U.S.A. 113 K8 31 19N 92 26W
Piney, France . . . . . 19 D11 48 22N 4 21 E
Ping →, Thailand . . . 64 E3 15 42N 100 9 E
Pingba, China . . . . . 58 D6 26 23N 106 12 E
Pingbian, China . . . . 58 F4 23 0N 103 45 E
Pingchuan, China . . . 58 D3 27 35N 101 55 E
Pingding, China . . . . 56 F7 37 47N 113 38 E
Pingdingshan, China . . 56 H7 33 43N 113 27 E
Pingdong, Taiwan . . . 59 F13 22 39N 120 30 E
Pingdu, China . . . . . 57 F10 36 42N 119 59 E
Pingelly, Australia . . . 93 F2 32 32 S 117 5 E
Pingguo, China . . . . 58 F6 23 19N 107 36 E
Pinghe, China . . . . . 59 E11 24 17N 117 21 E
Pinghu, China . . . . . 59 B13 30 40N 121 2 E
Pingjiang, China . . . . 59 C9 28 45N 113 36 E
Pingle, China . . . . . 59 E8 24 40N 110 40 E
Pingli, China . . . . . . 58 A7 32 27N 109 28 E
Pingliang, China . . . . 56 G4 35 35N 106 31 E
Pinglu, China . . . . . 56 E7 39 31N 112 30 E
Pingluo, China . . . . . 56 E4 38 52N 106 30 E
Pingnan, Fujian, China 59 D12 26 55N 119 0 E
Pingnan,
  Guangxi Zhuangzu,
  China . . . . . . 59 F8 23 33N 110 22 E
Pingquan, China . . . . 57 D10 41 1N 118 37 E
Pingrup, Australia . . . 93 F2 33 32 S 118 29 E
Pingshan, China . . . . 58 C5 28 39N 104 3 E
Pingtang, China . . . . 58 E6 25 31N 107 17 E
Pingtang, China . . . . 58 E6 25 49N 107 17 E
P'ingtung, Taiwan . . . 59 F13 22 38N 120 30 E
Pingwu, China . . . . . 56 H3 32 25N 104 30 E
Pingxiang,
  Guangxi Zhuangzu,
  China . . . . . . 58 F6 22 6N 106 46 E
Pingxiang, Jiangxi,
  China . . . . . . 59 D9 27 43N 113 48 E
Pingyao, China . . . . . 56 F7 37 12N 112 10 E
Pingyi, China . . . . . . 57 G9 35 30N 117 35 E
Pingyin, China . . . . . 56 F9 36 20N 116 25 E
Pingyuan, Guangdong,
  China . . . . . . 59 E10 24 37N 115 57 E
Pingyuan, Shandong,
  China . . . . . . 56 F9 37 10N 116 22 E
Pingyuanjie, China . . . 58 F4 23 45N 103 48 E
Pinhal, Brazil . . . . . 127 A6 22 10 S 46 46W
Pinhal Novo, Portugal . 37 G2 38 38N 8 55W
Pinheiro, Brazil . . . . 125 D9 2 31 S 45 5W
Pinheiro Machado,
  Brazil . . . . . . 127 C5 31 34 S 53 23W
Pinhel, Portugal 36 E3 40 50N 7 1W
Pini, Indonesia . . . . . 62 D1 0 10N 98 40 E
Piniós →, Ilía, Greece . 46 D3 37 48N 21 20 E
Piniós →, Tríkkala,
  Greece . . . . . . 46 B4 39 55N 22 41 E
Pinjarra, Australia . . . 93 F2 32 37 S 115 52 E
Pink Mountain, Canada 102 B4 57 3N 122 52W
Pinnacles, Austria . . . 26 D7 47 22N 16 9 E
Pinnacles △, U.S.A. . . 110 J5 36 33N 121 19W
Pinnaroo, Australia . . 95 F3 35 17 S 140 53 E
Pinneberg, Germany . . 24 B5 53 40N 9 48 E
Pínnes, Ákra, Greece . 45 F8 40 5N 24 20 E
Pinon Hills, U.S.A. . . 111 L9 34 26N 117 39W
Pinos, Mexico 118 C4 22 20N 101 40W
Pinos, Mt., U.S.A. . . . 111 L7 34 49N 119 8W
Pinos Puente, Spain . . 37 H7 37 15N 3 45W
Pinotepa Nacional,
  Mexico 119 D5 16 19N 98 3W
Pinrang, Indonesia . . . 63 E5 3 46 S 119 41 E
Pins, Pte. aux, Canada 116 D3 42 15N 81 51W
Pinsk, Belarus . . . . . 32 B4 52 10N 26 1 E
Pintados, Chile . . . . 124 H5 20 35 S 69 40W
Pinyang, China . . . . 59 D13 27 42N 120 31 E
Pinyug, Russia . . . . . 52 C5 60 5N 48 0 E
Pioche, U.S.A. 109 H6 37 56N 114 27W
Piombino, Italy . . . . 40 F7 42 55N 10 32 E

Piombino, Canale di,
  Italy . . . . . . 40 F7 42 53N 10 30 E
Pioner, Ostrov, Russia . 53 B10 79 50N 92 0 E
Pionerskiy, Russia . . . 30 D7 54 56N 20 14 E
Pionki, Poland . . . . . 31 G8 51 29N 21 28 E
Piorini, L., Brazil . . . 124 D6 3 15 S 62 35W
Piotrków Trybunalski,
  Poland . . . . . . 31 G6 51 23N 19 43 E
Piove di Sacco, Italy . . 41 C9 45 18N 12 2 E
Pip, Iran . . . . 71 E9 26 45N 60 10 E
Pipar, India . . . . . . 68 F5 26 25N 73 31 E
Pipar Road, India . . . 68 F5 26 27N 73 27 E
Pīparia, Mad. P., India 68 H8 22 45N 78 23 E
Pīparia, Mad. P., India 68 J7 21 49N 77 14 E
Pipéri, Greece . . . . . 46 B6 39 20N 24 19 E
Pipestone, U.S.A. . . . 112 D6 44 0N 96 19W
Pipestone →, Canada . 104 B2 52 53N 89 23W
Pipestone Cr. →,
  Canada 103 D8 49 38N 100 15W
Piplan, Pakistan . . . . 68 C4 32 17N 71 21 E
Piploda, India . . . . . 68 H6 23 37N 74 56 E
Pipmuacan, Rés.,
  Canada 105 C5 49 45N 70 30W
Pippingarra, Australia . 92 D2 20 27 S 118 42 E
Pipriac, France 18 E5 47 59N 1 58W
Piqua, U.S.A. 114 E3 40 9N 84 15W
Piquiri →, Brazil . . . 127 A5 24 3 S 54 14W
Pir Panjal Range, India 68 C7 32 30N 76 50 E
Pir Sohrāb, Iran . . . . 71 E9 25 44N 60 54 E
Pira, Benin . . . . 83 D5 8 28N 1 48 E
Piracicaba, Brazil . . . 127 A6 22 45 S 47 40W
Piracuruca, Brazil . . . 125 D10 3 50 S 41 50W
Piraeus = Piraiévs,
  Greece . . . . . . 46 D5 37 57N 23 42 E
Piraiévs, Greece . . . . 46 D5 37 57N 23 42 E
Pirajuí, Brazil . . . . . 127 A6 21 59 S 49 29W
Piram I., India . . . . . 68 J5 21 36N 72 21 E
Piran, Slovenia . . . . . 41 C10 45 31N 13 33 E
Pirané, Argentina . . . 126 B4 25 42 S 59 6W
Pirano = Piran, Slovenia 41 C10 45 31N 13 33 E
Pirapora, Brazil . . . . 125 G10 17 20 S 44 56W
Pirawa, India . . . . . . 68 G7 24 10N 76 2 E
Pirdop, Bulgaria . . . . 45 D8 42 40N 24 10 E
Pírgos, Ilía, Greece . . 46 D3 37 40N 21 27 E
Pírgos, Kríti, Greece . . 47 F7 35 0N 25 9 E
Pirgovo, Bulgaria . . . 45 C9 43 44N 25 43 E
Piribebuy, Paraguay . . 126 B4 25 26 S 57 2W
Pirimapun, Indonesia . 63 F9 6 20 S 138 24 E
Pirin △, Bulgaria . . . . 44 E7 41 48N 23 22 E
Pirin Planina, Bulgaria 44 E7 41 40N 23 30 E
Pírineos = Pyrénées,
  Europe . . . . . . 20 F4 42 45N 0 18 E
Piripiri, Brazil . . . . . 125 D10 4 15 S 41 46W
Pirmasens, Germany . . 25 F3 49 12N 7 36 E
Pirna, Germany . . . . 24 E9 50 57N 13 56 E
Pirot, Serbia & M. . . . 44 C6 43 9N 22 33 E
Piru, Indonesia . . . . . 63 E7 3 4 S 128 12 E
Piru, U.S.A. 111 L8 34 25N 118 48W
Piryatin = Pyryatyn,
  Ukraine . . . . . . 33 G7 50 15N 32 25 E
Piryí, Greece . . . . . . 47 C8 38 13N 25 59 E
Pisa, Italy . . . . 40 E7 43 43N 10 23 E
Pisa →, Poland . . . . 31 E8 53 14N 21 52 E
Pisa, Firenze ✈ (PSA),
  Italy . . . . . . 40 E7 43 40N 10 22 E
Pisagne, Italy . . . . . 40 D7 45 49N 10 10 E
Pisagua, Chile . . . . . 124 G4 19 40 S 70 15W
Pisarovina, Croatia . . 41 C12 45 35N 15 50 E
Pisco, Peru . . . . 124 F3 13 50 S 76 12W
Piscu, Romania . . . . 29 E12 45 30N 27 43 E
Písek, Czech Rep. . . . 26 B7 49 19N 14 10 E
Pishan, China . . . . . 60 C2 37 30N 78 33 E
Pishchanka, Ukraine . . 31 G10 51 35N 23 50 E
Pishchanka, Ukraine . . 29 B13 48 12N 28 54 E
Pīshīn, Iran . . . . . . 71 E9 26 6N 61 47 E
Pishin, Pakistan . . . . 68 D2 30 35N 67 0 E
Pishin Lora →, Pakistan 68 E1 29 9N 64 5 E
Pis·dia, Turkey . . . . 72 D4 37 30N 31 40 E
Pising, Indonesia . . . . 63 F6 5 8 S 121 53 E
Pismo Beach, U.S.A. . 111 K6 35 9N 120 38W
Piso, L., Liberia 82 D2 6 50N 11 15W
Pissila, Burkina Faso . 83 C4 13 7N 0 50W
Pissis, Cerro, Argentina 126 B2 27 45 S 68 48W
Pissos, France 20 D3 44 19N 0 49W
Pissouri, Cyprus . . . . 49 E11 34 40N 32 42 E
Pisticci, Italy . . . . . . 43 B9 40 23N 16 33 E
Pistóia, Italy . . . . . . 40 E7 43 55N 10 54 E
Pistol B., Canada . . . 103 A10 62 25N 92 37W
Pisuerga →, Spain . . . 36 D6 41 33N 4 52W
Piszy, Poland . . . . . . 30 E8 53 38N 21 49 E
Pit →, U.S.A. 108 F2 40 47N 122 6W
Pita, Guinea 82 C2 11 5N 12 15W
Pitarpunga, L.,
  Australia . . . . . . 95 E3 34 24 S 143 30 E
Pitcairn I., Pac. Oc. . 97 K14 25 5 S 130 5W
Pitch L., Trin. & Tob. 125 K15 10 12N 61 39W
Piteå, Sweden . . . . . 8 D19 65 20N 21 25 E
Piteälven →, Sweden . 8 D19 65 20N 21 25 E
Piterka, Russia . . . . 34 E8 50 41N 47 29 E
Pitești, Romania . . . . 29 F9 44 52N 24 54 E
Pithapuram, India . . . 67 L13 17 10N 82 15 E
Pithara, Australia . . . 93 F2 30 20 S 116 35 E
Píthion, Greece . . . . 45 E10 41 24N 26 40 E
Pithiviers, France . . . 19 D9 48 10N 2 13 E
Pithoragarh, India . . . 69 E9 29 35N 80 13 E
Pithoro, Pakistan . . . 68 G3 25 31N 69 23 E
Pitigliano, Italy . . . . 41 F8 42 38N 11 40 E
Pitkyaranta, Russia . . 32 B6 61 34N 31 37 E
Pitlochry, U.K. 13 E5 56 42N 3 44W
Pitsilia, Cyprus . . . . 49 E12 34 55N 33 0 E
Pitt I., Canada 102 C3 53 30N 129 50W
Pittsburg, Calif., U.S.A. 110 G5 38 2N 121 53W
Pittsburg, Kans., U.S.A. 113 G7 37 25N 94 42W
Pittsburg, Tex., U.S.A. 113 J7 33 0N 94 59W
Pittsburgh, U.S.A. . . . 116 F5 40 26N 80 1W
Pittsfield, Ill., U.S.A. . 112 F9 39 36N 90 49W
Pittsfield, Maine, U.S.A. 115 C11 44 47N 69 23W
Pittsfield, Mass., U.S.A. 117 D11 42 27N 73 15W
Pittsfield, N.H., U.S.A. 117 C13 43 18N 71 20W
Pittston, U.S.A. 117 E9 41 19N 75 47W
Pittsworth, Australia . 95 D5 27 41 S 151 37 E
Pituri →, Australia . . 94 C2 22 35 S 138 30 E
Piura, Peru . . . . . . 124 E2 5 15 S 80 38W
Piva →, Serbia & M. . 44 C2 43 20N 18 50 E
Piwniczna, Poland . . . 31 J7 49 26N 20 42 E
Pixley, U.S.A. 110 K7 35 58N 119 18W
Piyai, Greece . . . . . 46 B3 39 17N 21 25 E
Pizarra, Spain 37 J6 36 50N 4 42W
Pizhou, China . . . . . 56 G9 34 44N 116 10 E
Pizzo, Italy . . . . . . 43 D9 38 44N 16 10 E
Placentia, Canada . . . 105 C9 47 20N 54 0W
Placentia B., Canada . 105 C9 47 0N 54 40W
Placer, Masbate, Phil. . 61 F5 11 52N 123 55 E
Placer, Surigao N., Phil. 61 G6 9 36N 125 35 E
Placerville, U.S.A. . . . 110 G6 38 44N 120 48W
Placetas, Cuba 120 B4 22 15N 79 44W
Plačkovica, Macedonia 44 E6 41 45N 22 30 E
Plain, U.S.A. 110 C5 47 46N 120 39W
Plainfield, N.J., U.S.A. 117 F10 40 37N 74 25W

Plainfield, Ohio, U.S.A. 116 F3 40 13N 81 43W
Plainfield, Vt., U.S.A. . 117 B12 44 17N 72 26W
Plains, Mont., U.S.A. . 108 C6 47 28N 114 53W
Plains, Tex., U.S.A. . . 113 J3 33 11N 102 50W
Plainview, Nebr., U.S.A. 112 D6 42 21N 97 47W
Plainview, Tex., U.S.A. 113 H4 34 11N 101 43W
Plainwell, U.S.A. 114 D3 42 27N 85 38W
Plaisance, France . . . 20 E4 43 36N 0 3 E
Plaistow, U.S.A. 117 D13 42 50N 71 6W
Pláka, Greece . . . . . 47 B7 40 0N 25 24 E
Pláka, Ákra, Greece . . 49 D8 35 11N 26 19 E
Plakenska Planina,
  Macedonia . . . . . 44 E5 41 14N 21 2 E
Planá, Czech Rep. . . . 26 B5 49 50N 12 44 E
Plana Cays, Bahamas . 121 B5 22 38N 73 30W
Planada, U.S.A. 110 H6 37 16N 120 19W
Plancoët, France 18 D4 48 32N 2 13W
Plandište, Serbia & M. . 28 E6 45 16N 21 10 E
Plano, U.S.A. 113 J6 33 1N 96 42W
Plant City, U.S.A. . . . 115 M4 28 1N 82 7W
Plaquemine, U.S.A. . . 113 K9 30 17N 91 14W
Plasencia, Spain 36 E4 40 3N 6 8W
Plaški, Croatia . . . . . 41 C12 45 4N 15 22 E
Plaster City, U.S.A. . . 111 N11 32 47N 115 51W
Plaster Rock, Canada . 105 C6 46 53N 67 22W
Plastun, Russia . . . . 54 B8 44 45N 136 19 E
Plata, Río de la,
  S. Amer. . . . . . . 126 C4 34 45 S 57 30W
Plátani →, Italy . . . . 42 E6 37 23N 13 16 E
Plátanos, Greece . . . . 49 D5 35 28N 23 33 E
Plateau □, Nigeria . . . 83 D6 8 30N 9 0 E
Platí, Ákra, Greece . . . 45 F8 40 27N 24 0 E
Platte, U.S.A. 112 D5 43 23N 98 51W
Platte →, Mo., U.S.A. 112 F7 39 16N 94 50W
Platte →, Nebr., U.S.A. 112 E7 41 4N 95 53W
Platteville, U.S.A. . . . 112 D9 42 44N 90 29W
Plattling, Germany . . . 25 G8 48 46N 12 53 E
Plattsburgh, U.S.A. . . 117 B11 44 42N 73 28W
Plattsmouth, U.S.A. . . 112 E7 41 1N 95 53W
Plau, Germany . . . . . 24 B8 53 27N 12 15 E
Plauen, Germany . . . 24 E8 50 30N 12 8 E
Plauer See, Germany . 24 B8 53 28N 12 17 E
Plav, Serbia & M. . . . 44 D3 42 38N 19 57 E
Plavinas, Latvia . . . . 9 H21 56 35N 25 46 E
Plavnica, Serbia & M. . 44 D3 42 20N 19 13 E
Plavno, Croatia . . . . 41 D13 44 9N 16 18 E
Plavsk, Russia . . . . . 32 F9 53 40N 37 18 E
Playa Blanca, Canary Is. 48 F6 28 55N 13 37W
Playa Blanca Sur,
  Canary Is. 48 F6 28 51N 13 50W
Playa de las Americas,
  Canary Is. 48 F3 28 5N 16 43W
Playa de Mogán,
  Canary Is. 48 G4 27 48N 15 47W
Playa del Inglés,
  Canary Is. 48 G4 27 45N 15 33W
Playa Esmeralda,
  Canary Is. 48 F5 28 8N 14 16W
Playgreen L., Canada . 103 C9 54 0N 98 15W
Pleasant Bay, Canada . 105 C7 46 51N 60 48W
Pleasant Hill, U.S.A. . 110 H4 37 57N 122 4W
Pleasant Mount, U.S.A. 117 E9 41 44N 75 26W
Pleasanton, Calif.,
  U.S.A. 110 H5 37 39N 121 52W
Pleasanton, Tex., U.S.A. 113 L5 28 58N 98 29W
Pleasantville, N.J.,
  U.S.A. 114 F8 39 24N 74 32W
Pleasantville, Pa., U.S.A. 116 E5 41 35N 79 34W
Pléaux, France . . . . . 20 C6 45 8N 2 13 E
Plei Ku, Vietnam . . . . 64 F7 13 57N 108 0 E
Plélan-le-Grand, France 18 D4 48 0N 2 7W
Pléneuf-Val-André,
  France 18 D4 48 35N 2 32W
Plenița, Romania . . . . 29 F8 44 14N 23 10 E
Plenty →, Australia . . 94 C2 23 25 S 136 31 E
Plenty, B. of, N.Z. . . . 91 G6 37 45 S 177 0 E
Plentywood, U.S.A. . . 112 A2 48 47N 104 34W
Plérin, France 18 D4 48 32N 2 46W
Plessisville, Canada . . 105 C5 46 14N 71 47W
Plestin-les-Grèves,
  France 18 D3 48 40N 3 39W
Pleszew, Poland . . . . 31 G4 51 53N 17 47 E
Pleternica, Croatia . . . 28 E2 45 17N 17 48 E
Plétipi, L., Canada . . . 105 B5 51 44N 70 6W
Pleven, Bulgaria . . . . 45 C8 43 26N 24 37 E
Plevlja, Serbia & M. . . 44 C3 43 21N 19 21 E
Plevna, Canada 116 B8 44 58N 76 59W
Plitvička Jezera △,
  Croatia . . . . . . 41 D12 44 54N 15 35 E
Plješevica, Croatia . . 41 D12 44 45N 15 45 E
Ploaghe, Italy . . . . . 42 B1 40 40N 8 45 E
Ploče, Croatia . . . . . 41 E14 43 4N 17 26 E
Płock, Poland . . . . . 31 F6 52 32N 19 40 E
Plöckenpass, Italy . . . 41 B9 46 37N 12 57 E
Plöckenstein, Germany 25 G9 48 46N 13 51 E
Ploemeur, France . . . 18 E3 47 44N 3 26W
Ploërmel, France . . . 18 E4 47 55N 2 26W
Ploiești, Romania . . . 29 F11 44 57N 26 5 E
Plomárion, Greece . . . 47 C8 38 59N 26 24 E
Plombières-les-Bains,
  France . . . . . . 19 E13 47 58N 6 27 E
Plomin, Croatia . . . . 41 C11 45 8N 14 10 E
Plön, Germany . . . . 24 A6 54 10N 10 25 E
Plonge, Lac la, Canada 103 B7 55 8N 107 20W
Płońsk, Poland . . . . 31 F7 52 37N 20 21 E
Plopeni, Romania . . . 29 E10 45 4N 25 59 E
Plopișului, Munții,
  Romania . . . . . . 28 C7 47 5N 22 30 E
Ploty, Poland . . . . . 30 E2 53 48N 15 18 E
Plouaret, France 18 D3 48 37N 3 28W
Plouay, France 18 E3 47 55N 3 21W
Ploučnice →,
  Czech Rep. . . . . . 26 A7 50 46N 14 13 E
Ploudalmézeau, France 18 D2 48 34N 4 41W
Plouescat, France . . . 18 D2 48 39N 4 10W
Plougasnou, France . . 18 D3 48 42N 3 49W
Plougastel-Daoulas,
  France 18 D2 48 22N 4 17W
Plouguerneau, France . 18 D2 48 36N 4 30W
Plouha, France 18 D4 48 41N 2 57W
Plouhinec, France . . . 18 E2 48 1N 4 29W
Plovdiv, Bulgaria . . . 45 D8 42 8N 24 44 E
Plum, U.S.A. 116 F5 40 29N 79 47W
Plum I., U.S.A. 117 E12 41 11N 72 12W
Plummer, U.S.A. . . . 108 C5 47 20N 116 53W
Plumtree, Zimbabwe . 87 G2 20 27 S 27 55 E
Plunge, Lithuania . . . 9 J19 55 53N 21 59 E
Pluvigner, France . . . 18 E3 47 46N 3 1W
Plymouth, Trin. & Tob. 125 J16 11 54N 60 47W
Plymouth, U.K. 15 G3 50 22N 4 10W
Plymouth, Calif., U.S.A. 110 G6 38 29N 120 51W
Plymouth, Ind., U.S.A. 114 E2 41 21N 86 19W
Plymouth, Mass., U.S.A. 117 E14 41 57N 70 40W
Plymouth, N.C., U.S.A. 115 H7 35 52N 76 43W

Plymouth, *N.H., U.S.A.* 117 C13 43 46N 71 41W
Plymouth, *Pa., U.S.A.* 117 E9 41 14N 75 57W
Plymouth, *Wis., U.S.A.* 114 D2 43 45N 87 59W
Plympton-Wyoming,
  Canada 116 D2 42 57N 82 7W
Plynlimon = Pumlumon
  Fawr, *U.K.* 15 E4 52 28N 3 46W
Plyusa, *Russia* 32 C5 58 28N 29 27 E
Plyusa →, *Russia* 32 C5 59 4N 28 6 E
Plzeň, *Czech Rep.* 26 B6 49 45N 13 22 E
Plzeňská □, *Czech Rep.* 26 B6 49 35N 13 0 E
Pniewy, *Poland* 31 F3 52 31N 16 16 E
Pô, *Burkina Faso* 83 C4 11 14N 1 5W
Pô →, *Burkina Faso* 83 C4 11 25N 1 5W
Po →, *Italy* 41 D9 44 57N 12 4 E
Po, Foci del, *Italy* 41 D9 44 55N 12 30 E
Po Hai = Bo Hai, *China* 57 E10 39 0N 119 0 E
Pobé, *Benin* 83 D5 7 0N 2 56 E
Pobé, *Burkina Faso* 83 C4 13 53N 1 42W
Pobeda, *Russia* 53 C15 65 12N 146 12 E
Pobedy, Pik, *Kyrgyzstan* 52 E8 42 0N 79 58 E
Pobiedziska, *Poland* 31 F4 52 29N 17 11 E
Pobla de Segur, *Spain* 38 C5 42 15N 0 58 E
Pobladura del Valle,
  Spain 36 C5 42 6N 5 44W
Pobra de Trives, *Spain* 36 C3 42 20N 7 15W
Pocahontas, *Ark., U.S.A.* 113 G9 36 16N 90 58W
Pocahontas, Iowa,
  U.S.A. 112 D7 42 44N 94 40W
Pocatello, *U.S.A.* 108 E7 42 52N 112 27W
Počátky, *Czech Rep.* 26 B8 49 15N 15 14 E
Pochep, *Russia* 33 F7 52 58N 33 29 E
Pochinki, *Russia* 34 C7 54 41N 44 59 E
Pochinok, *Russia* 32 E7 54 28N 32 29 E
Pöchlarn, *Austria* 26 C8 48 12N 15 12 E
Pochutla, *Mexico* 119 D5 15 50N 96 31W
Pocito Casas, *Mexico* 118 B2 28 32N 111 6W
Pocomoke City, *U.S.A.* 114 F8 38 5N 75 34W
Poços de Caldas, *Brazil* 127 A6 21 50 S 46 33W
Podbořany, *Czech Rep.* 26 A6 50 14N 13 25 E
Podděbice, *Poland* 31 G5 51 54N 18 58 E
Poděbrady, *Czech Rep.* 26 A8 50 9N 15 8 E
Podensac, *France* 20 D3 44 40N 0 22W
Podenzano, *Italy* 40 D6 44 57N 9 41 E
Podgorač, *Croatia* 28 E3 45 27N 18 13 E
Podgorica, *Serbia & M.* 44 D3 42 30N 19 19 E
Podgorie, *Albania* 44 F4 40 49N 20 48 E
Podilska Vysochyna,
  Ukraine 29 B13 49 0N 28 0 E
Podkarpackie □, *Poland* 31 H9 50 0N 22 0 E
Podkova, *Bulgaria* 45 E9 41 24N 25 24 E
Podlapača, *Croatia* 41 D12 44 37N 15 47 E
Podlaskie □, *Poland* 31 E10 53 10N 23 0 E
Podoleni, *Romania* 29 D11 46 46N 26 39 E
Podolínec, *Slovak Rep.* 27 B13 49 16N 20 31 E
Podolsk, *Russia* 32 E9 55 25N 37 30 E
Podor, *Senegal* 82 B1 16 40N 15 2W
Podporozhye, *Russia* 32 B8 60 55N 34 2 E
Podu Iloaiei, *Romania* 29 C12 47 13N 27 16 E
Podu Turcului, *Romania* 29 D12 46 11N 27 25 E
Podujevo, *Serbia & M.* 44 D5 42 54N 21 10 E
Podyji □, *Czech Rep.* 26 C8 48 51N 15 57 E
Poel, *Germany* 24 B6 54 0N 11 25 E
Pofadder, *S. Africa* 88 D2 29 10 S 19 22 E
Poggiardo, *Italy* 43 B11 40 3N 18 21 E
Poggibonsi, *Italy* 40 E8 43 28N 11 9 E
Póggio Mirteto, *Italy* 41 F9 42 16N 12 41 E
Pogoanele, *Romania* 29 F12 44 55N 27 0 E
Pogorzela, *Poland* 31 G4 51 50N 17 12 E
Pogradec, *Albania* 44 F4 40 54N 20 37 E
Pogranichnyy, *Russia* 54 B5 44 25N 131 24 E
Poh, *Indonesia* 63 E6 0 46 S 122 51 E
P'ohang, *S. Korea* 57 F15 36 1N 129 23 E
Pohjanmaa, *Finland* 8 E20 62 58N 22 50 E
Pohnpei, *Micronesia* 96 G7 6 55N 158 10 E
Pohorelá, *Slovak Rep.* 27 C13 48 50N 20 2 E
Pohořelice, *Czech Rep.* 27 C9 48 59N 16 31 E
Pohorje, *Slovenia* 41 B12 46 30N 15 20 E
Pohri, *India* 68 G6 25 32N 77 22 E
Poiana Mare, *Romania* 28 G8 43 57N 23 5 E
Poiana Ruscăi, Munţii,
  Romania 28 E7 45 45N 22 25 E
Poiana Stampei,
  Romania 29 C10 47 19N 25 8 E
Poinsett, C., *Antarctica* 5 C8 65 42 S 113 18 E
Point Arena, *U.S.A.* 110 G3 38 55N 123 41W
Point Baker, *U.S.A.* 102 B2 56 21N 133 37W
Point Edward, *Canada* 104 D3 43 0N 82 30W
Point Fortin,
  Trin. & Tob. 125 K15 10 10N 61 42W
Point Hope, *U.S.A.* 100 B3 68 21N 166 47W
Point L., *Canada* 100 B8 65 15N 113 4W
Point Lisas, *Trin. & Tob.* 125 K15 10 32N 61 30W
Point Pelee △, *Canada* 116 E2 41 57N 82 31W
Point Pleasant, *N.J.,*
  U.S.A. 117 F10 40 5N 74 4W
Point Pleasant, *W. Va.,*
  U.S.A. 114 F4 38 51N 82 8W
Point Reyes △, *U.S.A.* 110 G2 38 10N 122 55W
Pointe-à-Pitre,
  Guadeloupe 120 b 16 10N 61 32W
Pointe-au-Pic = La
  Malbaie, *Canada* 105 C5 47 40N 70 10W
Pointe-Claire, *Canada* 117 A11 45 26N 73 50W
Pointe-Gatineau,
  Canada 117 A9 45 28N 75 42W
Pointe-Noire, *Congo* 84 E2 4 48 S 11 53 E
Pointe Noire,
  Guadeloupe 120 b 16 14N 61 47W
Poio, *Spain* 36 C2 42 28N 8 41W
Poirino, *Italy* 40 D4 44 56N 7 48 E
Poisonbush Ra.,
  Australia 92 D3 22 30 S 121 30 E
Poissonnier Pt.,
  Australia 92 C2 19 57 S 119 10 E
Poitiers, *France* 18 F7 46 35N 0 20 E
Poitou, *France* 20 B3 46 40N 0 10W
Poitou-Charentes □,
  France 20 B4 46 10N 0 15 E
Poix-de-Picardie, *France* 19 C8 49 47N 1 58 E
Poix-Terron, *France* 19 C11 49 38N 4 38 E
Pojoaque, *U.S.A.* 109 J11 35 54N 106 1W
Pokaran, *India* 66 F7 27 0N 71 50 E
Pokataroo, *Australia* 95 D4 29 30 S 148 36 E
Pokhara, *Nepal* 69 E10 28 14N 83 58 E
Pokhvistnevo, *Russia* 34 D11 53 36N 52 0 E
Poko, Dem. Rep. of
  the Congo 86 B2 3 7N 26 52 E
Poko, *Sudan* 81 F3 5 41N 31 55 E
Pokrov, *Russia* 32 E10 55 55N 39 7 E
Pokrovskoye, *Russia* 33 J10 47 25N 38 54 E
Pola = Pula, *Croatia* 41 D10 44 54N 13 57 E
Pola, *Russia* 32 D7 57 55N 32 0 E
Pola de Allande, *Spain* 36 B4 43 16N 6 37W
Pola de Lena, *Spain* 36 B5 43 10N 5 49W
Pola de Siero, *Spain* 36 B5 43 24N 5 39W
Pola de Somiedo, *Spain* 36 B4 43 5N 6 15W
Folacca, *U.S.A.* 109 J8 35 50N 110 23W
Polan, *Iran* 71 E9 25 30N 61 10 E
Pol'ana, *Slovak Rep.* 27 C12 48 38N 19 29 E
Poland ■, *Europe* 31 G3 52 0N 20 0 E
Polanica-Zdrój, *Poland* 31 H3 50 24N 16 32 E
Połaniec, *Poland* 31 H8 50 26N 21 17 E
Polanów, *Poland* 30 D3 54 7N 16 41 E
Polar Bear △, *Canada* 104 A2 55 0N 83 45W
Polatlı, *Turkey* 72 C5 39 36N 32 9 E
Polatsk, *Belarus* 32 E5 55 30N 28 50 E
Polcura, *Chile* 126 D1 37 17 S 71 43W
Połczyn-Zdrój, *Poland* 30 E3 53 47N 16 5 E
Poleski □, *Poland* 31 G10 51 29N 23 5 E
Polessk, *Russia* 9 J19 54 50N 21 8 E
Polesye = Pripet
  Marshes, *Europe* 33 F5 52 10N 28 10 E
Polgar, *Hungary* 28 C6 47 54N 21 6 E
Pólgyo-ri, *S. Korea* 57 G14 34 51N 127 21 E
Poli, *Cameroon* 83 C7 8 34N 13 15 E
Políaigos, *Greece* 46 E6 36 45N 24 38 E
Policastro, G. di, *Italy* 43 C8 40 0N 15 35 E
Polička, *Czech Rep.* 27 B9 49 43N 16 15 E
Policoro, *Italy* 43 B9 40 13N 16 41 E
Polignano a Mare, *Italy* 43 A9 41 0N 17 13 E
Poligny, *France* 19 F12 46 50N 5 42 E
Políkhnitas, *Greece* 47 B8 39 6N 26 10 E
Polillo Is., *Phil.* 61 D4 14 56N 122 0 E
Polillo Strait, *Phil.* 61 D4 14 44N 121 51 E
Polis, *Cyprus* 49 D11 35 2N 32 26 E
Polístena, *Italy* 43 D9 38 24N 16 4 E
Políyiros, *Greece* 44 F7 40 23N 23 25 E
Polk, *U.S.A.* 116 E5 41 22N 79 56W
Polkowice, *Poland* 31 G3 51 29N 16 3 E
Polla, *Italy* 43 B8 40 31N 15 29 E
Pollachi, *India* 66 P10 10 35N 77 0 E
Pollença, *Spain* 48 B10 39 54N 3 1 E
Pollença, B. de, *Spain* 48 B10 39 53N 3 8 E
Póllica, *Italy* 43 B8 40 11N 15 3 E
Pollino △, *Italy* 43 C9 40 0N 16 12 E
Pollino, Mte., *Italy* 43 C9 39 55N 16 11 E
Polna, *Russia* 32 C5 58 31N 28 5 E
Polnovat, *Russia* 52 C7 63 50N 65 54 E
Pology, *Ukraine* 33 J9 47 29N 36 15 E
Polokwane, *S. Africa* 89 C4 23 54 S 29 25 E
Polonne, *Ukraine* 33 G4 50 6N 27 30 E
Polonnoye = Polonne,
  Ukraine 33 G4 50 6N 27 30 E
Polski Trŭmbesh,
  Bulgaria 45 C9 43 20N 25 38 E
Polsko Kosovo, *Bulgaria* 45 C9 43 23N 25 38 E
Polson, *U.S.A.* 108 C6 47 41N 114 9W
Poltár, *Slovak Rep.* 27 C12 48 26N 19 48 E
Poltava, *Ukraine* 33 H8 49 35N 34 35 E
Põltsamaa, *Estonia* 9 G21 58 39N 25 58 E
Polunochnoye, *Russia* 52 C7 60 52N 60 25 E
Põlva, *Estonia* 9 G22 58 3N 27 3 E
Polyana, *Ukraine* 28 B7 48 38N 22 58 E
Polynesia, *Pac. Oc.* 97 F11 10 0 S 162 0W
Polynésie française =
  French Polynesia ☑,
  Pac. Oc. 97 K13 20 0 S 145 0W
Pomarance, *Italy* 40 E7 43 18N 10 52 E
Pomaro, *Mexico* 118 D4 18 20N 103 18W
Pombal, *Portugal* 36 F2 39 55N 8 40W
Pómbia, *Greece* 49 E6 35 0N 24 51 E
Pomene, *Mozam.* 89 C6 22 53 S 35 33 E
Pomeroy, Ohio, *U.S.A.* 114 F4 39 2N 82 2W
Pomeroy, Wash., *U.S.A.* 108 C5 46 28N 117 36W
Pomézia, *Italy* 42 A5 41 40N 12 30 E
Pomichna, *Ukraine* 33 H6 48 13N 31 36 E
Pomona, *Australia* 95 D5 26 22 S 152 52 E
Pomona, *U.S.A.* 111 L9 34 4N 117 45W
Pomorie, *Bulgaria* 45 D11 42 32N 27 41 E
Pomorskie □, *Poland* 30 D5 54 30N 18 0 E
Pomorskie, Pojezierze,
  Poland 30 E3 53 40N 16 37 E
Pomos, *Cyprus* 49 D11 35 9N 32 33 E
Pomos, C., *Cyprus* 49 D11 35 10N 32 33 E
Pompano Beach, *U.S.A.* 115 M5 26 14N 80 8W
Pompei, *Italy* 43 B7 40 45N 14 30 E
Pompey, *France* 19 D13 48 46N 6 6 E
Pompeys Pillar, *U.S.A.* 108 D10 45 59N 107 57W
Pompeys Pillar △,
  U.S.A. 108 D10 46 0N 108 0W
Ponape = Pohnpei,
  Micronesia 96 G7 6 55N 158 10 E
Ponask L., *Canada* 104 B1 54 0N 92 41W
Ponca, *U.S.A.* 112 D6 42 34N 96 43W
Ponca City, *U.S.A.* 113 G6 36 42N 97 5W
Ponce, *Puerto Rico* 121 d 18 1N 66 37W
Ponchatoula, *U.S.A.* 113 K9 30 26N 90 26W
Poncheville, L., *Canada* 104 B4 50 10N 76 55W
Pond, *U.S.A.* 111 K7 35 43N 119 20W
Pond Inlet, *Canada* 101 A12 72 40N 77 0W
Ponds, I. of, *Canada* 105 B8 53 27N 55 52W
Ponferrada, *Spain* 36 C4 42 32N 6 35W
Pongo, Wadi →, *Sudan* 81 F2 8 42N 27 40 E
Poniatowa, *Poland* 31 G9 51 11N 22 3 E
Poniec, *Poland* 31 G3 51 48N 16 50 E
Ponnani, *India* 66 P9 10 45N 75 59 E
Ponoka, *Canada* 102 C6 52 42N 113 40W
Ponorogo, *Indonesia* 63 G14 7 52 S 111 27 E
Pons = Ponts, *Spain* 38 D6 41 55N 1 12 E
Pons, *France* 20 C3 45 35N 0 34W
Ponsul →, *Portugal* 36 F3 39 40N 7 31W
Pont-à-Mousson, *France* 19 D13 48 54N 6 1 E
Pont-Audemer, *France* 18 C7 49 21N 0 30 E
Pont-Aven, *France* 18 E3 47 51N 3 47W
Pont Canavese, *Italy* 40 C4 45 25N 7 36 E
Pont-de-Roide, *France* 19 E13 47 23N 6 45 E
Pont-de-Salars, *France* 20 D6 44 18N 2 44 E
Pont-de-Vaux, *France* 19 F11 46 26N 4 56 E
Pont-de-Veyle, *France* 19 F11 46 17N 4 53 E
Pont-du-Château,
  France 19 G10 45 47N 3 15 E
Pont-l'Abbé, *France* 18 E2 47 52N 4 15W
Pont-l'Évêque, *France* 18 C7 49 18N 0 11 E
Pont-St-Esprit, *France* 21 D8 44 16N 4 40 E
Pont-St-Martin, *Italy* 40 C4 45 36N 7 48 E
Pont-Ste-Maxence,
  France 19 C9 49 18N 2 35 E
Pont-sur-Yonne, *France* 19 D10 48 18N 3 10 E
Ponta do Sol, *Madeira* 48 D2 32 41N 17 6W
Ponta Grossa, *Brazil* 127 B5 25 7 S 50 10W
Ponta Pora, *Brazil* 127 A4 22 20 S 55 35W
Pontacq, *France* 20 E3 43 11N 0 8W
Pontailler-sur-Saône,
  France 19 E12 47 13N 5 25 E
Pontarlier, *France* 19 F13 46 54N 6 20 E

Pontassieve, *Italy* 41 E8 43 46N 11 26 E
Pontaumur, *France* 20 C6 45 52N 2 40 E
Pontcharra, *France* 21 C10 45 26N 6 1 E
Pontchartrain L., *U.S.A.* 113 K10 30 5N 90 5W
Pontchâteau, *France* 18 E4 47 25N 2 5W
Ponte da Barca, *Portugal* 36 D2 41 48N 8 25W
Ponte de Sor, *Portugal* 37 F3 39 17N 8 1W
Ponte di Legno, *Italy* 40 B7 46 16N 10 31 E
Ponte do Lima, *Portugal* 36 D2 41 46N 8 35W
Ponte do Pungué,
  Mozam. 87 F3 19 30 S 34 33 E
Ponte-Leccia, *France* 21 F13 42 28N 9 13 E
Ponte nelle Alpi, *Italy* 41 B9 46 11N 12 16 E
Ponte Nova, *Brazil* 127 A7 20 25 S 42 54W
Pontearas, *Spain* 36 C2 42 11N 8 28W
Pontedeume, *Spain* 36 B2 43 24N 8 10W
Pontecorvo, *Italy* 42 A6 41 27N 13 40 E
Pontevedra, *Spain* 36 C2 42 26N 8 40W
Pontevedra □, *Spain* 36 C2 42 25N 8 39W
Pontevedra, R. de →,
  Spain 36 C2 42 22N 8 45W
Pontevico, *Italy* 40 C7 45 16N 10 5 E
Pontiac, *Ill., U.S.A.* 112 E10 40 53N 88 38W
Pontiac, *Mich., U.S.A.* 114 D4 42 38N 83 18W
Pontian Kechil, *Malaysia* 65 d 1 29N 103 23 E
Pontianak, *Indonesia* 62 E3 0 3 S 109 15 E
Pontine Is. = Ponziane,
  Ísole, *Italy* 42 B5 40 55N 12 57 E
Pontine Mts. = Kuzey
  Anadolu Dağları,
  Turkey 72 B7 41 30N 35 0 E
Pontínia, *Italy* 42 A6 41 25N 13 2 E
Pontivy, *France* 18 D4 48 5N 2 58W
Pontoise, *France* 19 C9 49 3N 2 5 E
Ponton →, *Canada* 102 B5 58 27N 116 11W
Pontorson, *France* 18 D5 48 34N 1 30W
Pontrémoli, *Italy* 40 D6 44 22N 9 53 E
Pontrieux, *France* 18 D3 48 42N 3 10W
Ponts, *Spain* 38 D6 41 55N 1 12 E
Pontypool, *Canada* 116 B6 44 6N 78 38W
Pontypool, *U.K.* 15 F4 51 42N 3 2W
Ponza, *Italy* 42 B5 40 55N 12 58 E
Ponziane, Ísole, *Italy* 42 B5 40 55N 12 57 E
Poochera, *Australia* 95 E1 32 43 S 134 51 E
Poole, *U.K.* 15 G6 50 43N 1 59W
Poole □, *U.K.* 15 G6 50 43N 1 59W
Poona = Pune, *India* 66 K8 18 29N 73 57 E
Pooncarie, *Australia* 95 E3 33 22 S 142 31 E
Poopelloe L., *Australia* 95 E3 31 40 S 144 0 E
Poopó, L. de, *Bolivia* 124 G5 18 30 S 67 35W
Popayán, *Colombia* 124 C3 2 27N 76 36W
Poperinge, *Belgium* 17 D2 50 51N 2 42 E
Popilta L., *Australia* 95 E3 33 10 S 141 42 E
Popina, *Bulgaria* 45 B10 44 7N 26 57 E
Popio L., *Australia* 95 E3 33 10 S 141 42 E
Poplar, *U.S.A.* 112 A2 48 7N 105 12W
Poplar →, *Canada* 103 C9 53 0N 97 19W
Poplar Bluff, *U.S.A.* 113 G9 36 46N 90 24W
Poplarville, *U.S.A.* 113 K10 30 51N 89 32W
Popocatépetl, Volcán,
  Mexico 119 D5 19 2N 98 38W
Popokabaka, *Dem. Rep.
  of the Congo* 84 F3 5 41 S 16 40 E
Pópoli, *Italy* 41 F10 42 10N 13 50 E
Popovača, *Croatia* 41 C13 45 30N 16 41 E
Popovo, *Bulgaria* 45 C10 43 21N 26 18 E
Poppberg, *Germany* 25 F7 49 26N 11 37 E
Poppi, *Italy* 41 E8 43 43N 11 46 E
Poprad, *Slovak Rep.* 27 B13 49 3N 20 18 E
Poprad →, *Slovak Rep.* 27 B13 49 38N 20 42 E
Porali →, *Pakistan* 68 G2 25 58N 66 26 E
Porbandar, *India* 68 J3 21 44N 69 43 E
Porcher I., *Canada* 102 C2 53 50N 130 30W
Porcuna, *Spain* 37 H6 37 52N 4 11W
Porcupine →, *Canada* 103 B8 59 11N 104 46W
Porcupine →, *U.S.A.* 100 B5 66 34N 145 19W
Porcupine Gorge △,
  Australia 94 C3 20 22 S 144 26 E
Pordenone, *Italy* 41 C9 45 57N 12 39 E
Pordim, *Bulgaria* 45 C8 43 23N 24 51 E
Poreč, *Croatia* 41 C10 45 14N 13 36 E
Poretskoye, *Russia* 34 C8 55 9N 46 21 E
Pori, *Finland* 9 F19 61 29N 21 48 E
Porí, *Greece* 46 F5 35 58N 23 13 E
Porkhov, *Russia* 32 D5 57 45N 29 38 E
Porlamar, *Venezuela* 124 A6 10 57N 63 51W
Porlezza, *Italy* 40 B6 46 2N 9 7 E
Porma →, *Spain* 36 C5 42 49N 5 28W
Pornic, *France* 18 E4 47 7N 2 5W
Poronaysk, *Russia* 53 E15 49 13N 143 0 E
Póros, *Greece* 46 D5 37 30N 23 30 E
Poroshiri-Dake, *Japan* 54 C11 42 41N 142 52 E
Poroszló, *Hungary* 28 C5 47 39N 20 40 E
Poroto Mts., *Tanzania* 87 D3 9 0 S 33 30 E
Porpoise B., *Antarctica* 5 C9 66 0 S 127 0 E
Porquerolles, Î. de,
  France 21 F10 43 0N 6 13 E
Porrentruy, *Switz.* 25 H3 47 25N 7 6 E
Porreres, *Spain* 48 B10 39 31N 3 2 E
Porsangen, *Norway* 8 A21 70 40N 25 40 E
Porsgrunn, *Norway* 9 G13 59 10N 9 40 E
Port Alberni, *Canada* 102 D4 49 14N 124 50W
Port Alfred, *S. Africa* 88 E4 33 36 S 26 55 E
Port Alice, *Canada* 102 C3 50 20N 127 25W
Port Allegany, *U.S.A.* 116 E6 41 48N 78 17W
Port Allen, *U.S.A.* 113 K9 30 27N 91 12W
Port Alma, *Australia* 94 C5 23 38 S 150 53 E
Port Angeles, *U.S.A.* 110 B3 48 7N 123 27W
Port Antonio, *Jamaica* 120 a 18 10N 76 26W
Port Aransas, *U.S.A.* 113 M6 27 50N 97 4W
Port Arthur, *Australia* 95 G4 43 7 S 147 50 E
Port Arthur, *U.S.A.* 113 L8 29 54N 93 56W
Port au Choix, *Canada* 105 B8 50 43N 57 22W
Port au Port B., *Canada* 105 C8 48 40N 58 50W
Port-au-Prince, *Haiti* 121 C5 18 40N 72 20W
Port Augusta, *Australia* 95 E2 32 30 S 137 50 E
Port Austin, *U.S.A.* 116 B2 44 3N 83 1W
Port Bell, *Uganda* 86 B3 0 18N 32 35 E
Port Bergé Vaovao,
  Madag. 89 B8 15 33 S 47 40 E
Port Blandford, *Canada* 105 C9 48 20N 54 10W
Port-Bouët, *Ivory C.* 82 D4 5 16N 3 57W
Port Bradshaw,
  Australia 94 A2 12 30 S 137 20 E
Port Broughton,
  Australia 95 E2 33 37 S 137 56 E
Port Burwell, *Canada* 116 D4 42 40N 80 48W
Port Canning, *India* 69 H13 22 23N 88 40 E
Port-Cartier, *Canada* 105 B6 50 2N 66 50W
Port Chalmers, *N.Z.* 91 L3 45 49 S 170 30 E
Port Charlotte, *U.S.A.* 115 M4 26 59N 82 6W
Port Chester, *U.S.A.* 117 F11 41 0N 73 40W
Port Clements, *Canada* 102 C2 53 40N 132 10W

Port Clinton, *U.S.A.* 114 E4 41 31N 82 56W
Port Colborne, *Canada* 116 D5 42 50N 79 10W
Port Coquitlam, *Canada* 102 D4 49 15N 122 45W
Port Credit, *Canada* 116 C5 43 33N 79 35W
Port-Cros △, *France* 21 F10 43 0N 6 24 E
Port Curtis, *Australia* 94 C5 23 57 S 151 20 E
Port d'Alcúdia, *Spain* 48 B10 39 50N 3 7 E
Port Dalhousie, *Canada* 116 C5 43 13N 79 16W
Port d'Andratx, *Spain* 48 B9 39 32N 2 23 E
Port Darwin, *Australia* 92 B5 12 24 S 130 45 E
Port Darwin, *Falk. Is.* 128 G5 51 50 S 59 0W
Port Davey, *Australia* 95 G4 43 16 S 145 55 E
Port-de-Bouc, *France* 21 E8 43 24N 4 59 E
Port-de-Paix, *Haiti* 121 C5 19 50N 72 50W
Port de Pollença, *Spain* 48 B10 39 54N 3 4 E
Port de Sóller, *Spain* 48 B9 39 48N 2 42 E
Port Dickson, *Malaysia* 65 L3 2 30N 101 49 E
Port Douglas, *Australia* 94 B4 16 30 S 145 30 E
Port Dover, *Canada* 116 D4 42 47N 80 12W
Port Edward, *Canada* 102 C2 54 12N 130 10W
Port Elgin, *Canada* 116 B3 44 25N 81 25W
Port Elizabeth, *S. Africa* 88 E4 33 58 S 25 40 E
Port Ellen, *U.K.* 13 F2 55 38N 6 11W
Port-en-Bessin-Huppain,
  France 18 C6 49 21N 0 45W
Port Erin, *I. of Man* 14 C3 54 5N 4 45W
Port Essington, *Australia* 92 B5 11 15 S 132 10 E
Port Ewen, *U.S.A.* 117 E11 41 54N 73 59W
Port Fairy, *Australia* 95 F3 38 22 S 142 12 E
Port Fouâd = Bûr Fuad,
  Egypt 80 H8 31 15N 32 20 E
Port Gamble, *U.S.A.* 110 C4 47 51N 122 35W
Port-Gentil, *Gabon* 84 E1 0 40 S 8 50 E
Port Germein, *Australia* 95 E2 33 1 S 138 1 E
Port Gibson, *U.S.A.* 113 K9 31 58N 90 59W
Port Glasgow, *U.K.* 13 F4 55 56N 4 41W
Port Harcourt, *Nigeria* 83 E6 4 40N 7 10 E
Port Hardy, *Canada* 102 C3 50 41N 127 30W
Port Harrison =
  Inukjuak, *Canada* 101 C12 58 25N 78 15W
Port Hawkesbury,
  Canada 105 C7 45 36N 61 22W
Port Hedland, *Australia* 92 D2 20 25 S 118 35 E
Port Henry, *U.S.A.* 117 B11 44 3N 73 28W
Port Hood, *Canada* 105 C7 46 0N 61 32W
Port Hope, *Canada* 116 C6 43 56N 78 20W
Port Hope, *U.S.A.* 116 C2 43 57N 82 43W
Port Hope Simpson,
  Canada 105 B8 52 33N 56 18W
Port Hueneme, *U.S.A.* 111 L7 34 7N 119 12W
Port Huron, *U.S.A.* 116 D2 42 58N 82 26W
Port Iliç, *Azerbaijan* 73 C13 38 53N 48 47 E
Port Jefferson, *U.S.A.* 117 F11 40 57N 73 3W
Port Jervis, *U.S.A.* 117 E10 41 22N 74 41W
Port-Joinville, *France* 18 F4 46 45N 2 23W
Port Katon, *Russia* 33 J10 46 52N 38 46 E
Port Kelang =
  Pelabuhan Klang,
  Malaysia 65 L3 3 0N 101 23 E
Port Kenny, *Australia* 95 E1 33 10 S 134 41 E
Port Laoise, *Ireland* 12 C4 53 2N 7 18W
Port Lavaca, *U.S.A.* 113 L6 28 37N 96 38W
Port Leyden, *U.S.A.* 117 C9 43 35N 75 21W
Port Lincoln, *Australia* 95 E2 34 42 S 135 52 E
Port Loko, *S. Leone* 82 D2 8 48N 12 46W
Port Louis, *France* 18 E3 47 42N 3 22W
Port-Louis, *Guadeloupe* 120 b 16 28N 61 32W
Port Louis, *Mauritius* 77 H9 20 10 S 57 30 E
Port MacDonnell,
  Australia 95 F3 38 5 S 140 48 E
Port McNeill, *Canada* 102 C3 50 35N 127 6W
Port Macquarie,
  Australia 95 E5 31 25 S 152 25 E
Port Maria, *Jamaica* 120 a 18 22N 76 54W
Port Matilda, *U.S.A.* 116 F6 40 48N 78 3W
Port Mellon, *Canada* 102 D4 49 32N 123 31W
Port-Menier, *Canada* 105 C7 49 51N 64 15W
Port Moody, *Canada* 110 A4 49 17N 122 51W
Port Morant, *Jamaica* 120 a 17 54N 76 19W
Port Moresby,
  Papua N. G. 96 H6 9 24 S 147 8 E
Port Musgrave, *Australia* 94 A3 11 55 S 141 50 E
Port-Navalo, *France* 18 E4 47 34N 2 54W
Port Neches, *U.S.A.* 113 L8 30 0N 93 59W
Port Nolloth, *S. Africa* 88 D2 29 17 S 16 52 E
Port Nouveau-Québec =
  Kangiqsualujjuaq,
  Canada 101 C13 58 30N 65 59W
Port of Spain,
  Trin. & Tob. 121 D7 10 40N 61 31W
Port Orange, *U.S.A.* 115 L5 29 9N 80 59W
Port Orchard, *U.S.A.* 110 C4 47 32N 122 38W
Port Orford, *U.S.A.* 108 E1 42 45N 124 30W
Port Pegasus, *N.Z.* 91 M1 47 12 S 167 41 E
Port Perry, *Canada* 116 B6 44 6N 78 56W
Port Phillip B., *Australia* 95 F3 38 10 S 144 50 E
Port Pirie, *Australia* 95 E2 33 10 S 138 1 E
Port Renfrew, *Canada* 102 D4 48 30N 124 20W
Port Roper, *Australia* 94 A2 14 45 S 135 25 E
Port Rowan, *Canada* 116 D4 42 40N 80 30W
Port Safaga = Bûr
  Safâga, *Egypt* 70 E2 26 43N 33 57 E
Port Said = Bûr Sa'îd,
  Egypt 80 H8 31 16N 32 18 E
Port St. Joe, *U.S.A.* 115 L3 29 49N 85 18W
Port St. Johns =
  Umzimvubu, *S. Africa* 89 E4 31 38 S 29 33 E
Port-St-Louis-du-Rhône,
  France 21 E8 43 23N 4 49 E
Port St. Lucie, *U.S.A.* 115 M5 27 20N 80 20W
Port Ste-Marie, *France* 20 D4 44 15N 0 25 E
Port Sanilac, *U.S.A.* 116 C2 43 26N 82 33W
Port Severn, *Canada* 116 B5 44 48N 79 43W
Port Shepstone,
  S. Africa 89 E5 30 44 S 30 28 E
Port Simpson, *Canada* 102 C2 54 30N 130 20W
Port Stanley = Stanley,
  Falk. Is. 128 G5 51 40 S 59 51W
Port Stanley, *Canada* 116 D3 42 40N 81 10W
Port Sudan = Bûr Sûdân,
  Sudan 80 D4 19 32N 37 9 E
Port Sulphur, *U.S.A.* 113 L10 29 29N 89 42W
Port-sur-Saône, *France* 19 E13 47 42N 6 8 E
Port Talbot, *U.K.* 15 F4 51 35N 3 47W
Port Taufiq = Bûr
  Taufîq, *Egypt* 80 J8 29 54N 32 32 E
Port Townsend, *U.S.A.* 110 B4 48 7N 122 45W
Port-Vendres, *France* 20 F7 42 32N 3 8 E
Port Vila, *Vanuatu* 96 J8 17 45 S 168 18 E
Port Washington, *U.S.A.* 114 D2 43 23N 87 53W
Port Wakefield,
  Australia 95 E2 34 12 S 138 10 E
Port Washington, *U.S.A.* 114 D2 43 23N 87 53W
Portadown, *U.K.* 12 B5 54 25N 6 27W
Portaferry, *U.K.* 12 B6 54 23N 5 33W

Portage, *Pa., U.S.A.* 116 F6 40 23N 78 41W
Portage, *Wis., U.S.A.* 112 D10 43 33N 89 28W
Portage la Prairie,
  Canada 103 D9 49 58N 98 18W
Portageville, *U.S.A.* 113 G10 36 26N 89 42W
Portalegre, *Portugal* 37 F3 39 19N 7 25W
Portalegre □, *Portugal* 37 F3 39 20N 7 40W
Portales, *U.S.A.* 113 H3 34 11N 103 20W
Portarlington, *Ireland* 12 C4 53 9N 7 14W
Portbou, *Spain* 38 C8 42 25N 3 9 E
Portel, *Portugal* 37 G3 38 19N 7 41W
Portela, Lisboa ✈ (LIS),
  Portugal 37 G1 38 46N 9 8W
Porter L., *N.W.T.,*
  Canada 103 A7 61 41N 108 5W
Porter L., *Sask., Canada* 103 B7 56 20N 107 20W
Porterville, *S. Africa* 88 E2 33 0 S 19 0 E
Porterville, *U.S.A.* 110 J8 36 4N 119 1W
Portes-lès-Valence,
  France 21 D8 44 52N 4 54 E
Porthcawl, *U.K.* 15 F4 51 29N 3 42W
Porthill, *U.S.A.* 108 B5 48 59N 116 30W
Porthmadog, *U.K.* 14 E3 52 55N 4 8W
Portile de Fier, *Europe* 28 F7 44 44N 22 30 E
Portimão, *Portugal* 37 H2 37 8N 8 32W
Portishead, *U.K.* 15 F5 51 29N 2 46W
Portiţei, Gura, *Romania* 29 F14 44 41N 29 2 E
Portknockie, *U.K.* 13 D6 57 42N 2 51W
Portland, *N.S.W.,*
  Australia 95 E5 33 20 S 150 0 E
Portland, *Vic., Australia* 95 F3 38 20 S 141 35 E
Portland, *Conn., U.S.A.* 117 B8 44 42N 76 12W
Portland, *Conn., U.S.A.* 117 E12 41 34N 72 38W
Portland, *Maine, U.S.A.* 101 D12 43 39N 70 16W
Portland, *Mich., U.S.A.* 114 D3 42 52N 84 54W
Portland, *Oreg., U.S.A.* 110 E4 45 32N 122 37W
Portland, *Pa., U.S.A.* 117 F9 40 55N 75 6W
Portland, *Tex., U.S.A.* 113 M6 27 53N 97 20W
Portland ✈ (PDX),
  U.S.A. 110 E4 45 35N 122 36W
Portland, I. of, *U.K.* 15 G5 50 33N 2 26W
Portland B., *Australia* 95 F3 38 15 S 141 45 E
Portland Bight, *Jamaica* 120 a 17 52N 77 5W
Portland Bill, *U.K.* 15 G5 50 31N 2 28W
Portland Canal, *U.S.A.* 102 B2 55 56N 130 0W
Portland Pt., *Jamaica* 120 a 17 42N 77 11W
Portmadoc =
  Porthmadog, *U.K.* 14 E3 52 55N 4 8W
Portmore, *Jamaica* 120 a 17 53N 77 53W
Porto, *France* 21 F12 42 16N 8 42 E
Porto, *Portugal* 36 D2 41 8N 8 40W
Porto □, *Portugal* 36 D2 41 8N 8 20W
Porto, G. de, *France* 21 F12 42 17N 8 34 E
Pôrto Alegre, *Brazil* 127 C5 30 5 S 51 10W
Porto Azzurro, *Italy* 40 F7 42 46N 10 24 E
Pôrto Cristo, *Spain* 48 B10 39 33N 3 20 E
Pôrto de Móz, *Brazil* 125 D8 1 41 S 52 13W
Porto Empédocle, *Italy* 42 E6 37 17N 13 32 E
Pôrto Esperança, *Brazil* 124 G7 19 37 S 57 29W
Pôrto Franco, *Brazil* 125 E9 6 20 S 47 24W
Pôrto Lágos, *Greece* 45 F8 41 1N 25 6 E
Pôrto Mendes, *Brazil* 127 A5 24 30 S 54 15W
Pôrto Moniz, *Madeira* 48 D2 32 52N 17 11W
Pôrto Murtinho, *Brazil* 124 H7 21 45 S 57 55W
Pôrto Nacional, *Brazil* 125 F9 10 40 S 48 30W
Porto-Novo, *Benin* 83 D5 6 23N 2 42 E
Porto Petro, *Spain* 48 B10 39 22N 3 13 E
Porto San Giórgio, *Italy* 41 E10 43 11N 13 49 E
Porto Sant' Elpídio, *Italy* 41 E10 43 15N 13 45 E
Porto Santo, I. de,
  Madeira 78 B2 33 45N 16 25W
Porto Santo Stéfano,
  Italy 40 F8 42 26N 11 7 E
Pôrto São José, *Brazil* 127 A5 22 43 S 53 10W
Pôrto Seguro, *Brazil* 125 G11 16 26 S 39 5W
Porto Tolle, *Italy* 41 D9 44 56N 12 22 E
Pôrto Tórres, *Italy* 42 B1 40 50N 8 24 E
Pôrto União, *Brazil* 127 B5 26 10 S 51 10W
Pôrto Válter, *Brazil* 124 E4 8 15 S 72 40W
Porto-Vecchio, *France* 21 G13 41 35N 9 16 E
Pôrto Velho, *Brazil* 124 E6 8 46 S 63 54W
Portobelo, *Panama* 120 E4 9 35N 79 42W
Portoferráio, *Italy* 40 F7 42 48N 10 20 E
Portogruaro, *Italy* 41 C9 45 47N 12 50 E
Portola, *U.S.A.* 110 F6 39 49N 120 28W
Portomaggiore, *Italy* 41 D8 44 42N 11 48 E
Portoscuso, *Italy* 42 C1 39 12N 8 24 E
Portovénere, *Italy* 40 D6 44 3N 9 51 E
Portoviejo, *Ecuador* 124 D2 1 7 S 80 28W
Portpatrick, *U.K.* 13 G3 54 51N 5 7W
Portree, *U.K.* 13 D2 57 25N 6 12W
Portrush, *U.K.* 12 A5 55 12N 6 40W
Portsmouth, *Dominica* 121 C7 15 34N 61 27W
Portsmouth, *U.K.* 15 G6 50 48N 1 6W
Portsmouth, *N.H.,*
  U.S.A. 115 D10 43 5N 70 45W
Portsmouth, *Ohio,*
  U.S.A. 114 F4 38 44N 82 57W
Portsmouth, *R.I., U.S.A.* 117 E13 41 36N 71 15W
Portsmouth, *Va., U.S.A.* 115 G7 36 50N 76 18W
Portsmouth □, *U.K.* 15 G6 50 48N 1 6W
Portsoy, *U.K.* 13 D6 57 41N 2 41W
Portstewart, *U.K.* 12 A5 55 11N 6 43W
Porttipahdan tekojärvi,
  Finland 8 B22 68 5N 26 40 E
Portugal ■, *Europe* 36 F3 40 0N 8 0W
Portugalete, *Spain* 38 B1 43 19N 3 4W
Portumna, *Ireland* 12 C3 53 6N 8 14W
Portville, *U.S.A.* 116 D6 42 3N 78 20W
Porvenir, *Chile* 128 G2 53 10 S 70 16W
Porvoo, *Finland* 9 F21 60 24N 25 40 E
Porzuna, *Spain* 37 F6 39 9N 4 9W
Posada, *Italy* 42 B2 40 38N 9 43 E
Posada →, *Italy* 42 B2 40 40N 9 45 E
Posadas, *Argentina* 127 B4 27 30 S 55 50W
Posadas, *Spain* 37 H5 37 47N 5 11W
Poschiavo, *Switz.* 25 J6 46 19N 10 4 E
Posets, *Spain* 38 C5 42 39N 0 25 E
Posht-e Badam, *Iran* 71 C7 33 2N 55 23 E
Posídhion, Ákra, *Greece* 44 F7 39 57N 23 30 E
Posidónia, *Greece* 47 F9 35 30N 27 10 E
Poso, *Indonesia* 63 E6 1 20 S 120 55 E
Posse, *Brazil* 125 F9 14 4 S 46 18W
Possession I., *Antarctica* 5 D11 72 4 S 172 0 E
Pössneck, *Germany* 24 E7 50 42N 11 35 E
Possum Kingdom L.,
  U.S.A. 113 J5 32 52N 98 26W
Post, *U.S.A.* 113 J4 33 12N 101 23W
Post Falls, *U.S.A.* 108 C5 47 43N 116 57W
Postavy = Pastavy,
  Belarus 9 J22 55 4N 26 50 E
Poste-de-la-Baleine =
  Kuujjuarapik, *Canada* 104 A4 55 20N 77 35W
Postmasburg, *S. Africa* 88 D3 28 18 S 23 5 E
Postojna, *Slovenia* 41 C11 45 46N 14 12 E
Poston, *U.S.A.* 111 M12 34 0N 114 24W

Postville, *Canada* ... **105 B8** 54 54N 59 47W
Potamós, *Andikíthira,*
　Greece .... **46 F5** 35 52N 23 15 E
Potamós, *Kíthira, Greece* **46 E4** 36 15N 22 58 E
Potchefstroom, *S. Africa* **88 D4** 26 41 S 27 7 E
Potcoava, *Romania* ... **29 F9** 44 30N 24 39 E
Poteau, *U.S.A.* **113 H7** 35 3N 94 37W
Poteet, *U.S.A.* **113 L5** 29 2N 98 35W
Potenza, *Italy* .... **43 B8** 40 38N 15 48 E
Potenza →, *Italy* .... **41 E10** 43 25N 13 40 E
Potenza Picena, *Italy* . **41 E10** 43 22N 13 37 E
Poteriteri, L., *N.Z.* .. **91 M1** 46 5 S 167 10 E
Potgietersrus =
　Mokopane, *S. Africa* **89 C4** 24 10 S 28 55 E
Poti, *Georgia* .... **35 J5** 42 10N 41 38 E
Potiskum, *Nigeria* ... **83 C7** 11 39N 11 2 E
Potlogi, *Romania* .... **29 F10** 44 34N 25 34 E
Potomac →, *U.S.A.* .. **114 G7** 38 0N 76 23W
Potosí, *Bolivia* ...... **124 G5** 19 38 S 65 50W
Potosi Mt., *U.S.A.* ... **111 K11** 35 57N 115 29W
Pototan, *Phil.* .... **61 F5** 10 54N 122 38 E
Potrerillos, *Chile* ... **126 B2** 26 30 S 69 30W
Potsdam, *Germany* ... **24 C9** 52 25N 13 4 E
Potsdam, *U.S.A.* **117 B10** 44 40N 74 59W
Pottenstein, *Germany* . **25 F7** 49 46N 11 24 E
Potters Bar, *U.K.* **15 F7** 51 42N 0 11W
Pottstown, *U.S.A.* **117 C11** 43 43N 73 50W
Pottstown, *U.S.A.* **117 F9** 40 15N 75 39W
Pottsville, *U.S.A.* **117 F8** 40 41N 76 12W
Pottuvil, *Sri Lanka* .. **66 R12** 6 55N 81 50 E
P'otzu, *Taiwan* ...... **59 F13** 23 30N 120 25 E
Pouancé, *France* **18 E5** 47 44N 1 10W
Pouce Coupé, *Canada* . **102 B4** 55 40N 120 10W
Poughkeepsie, *U.S.A.* . **117 E11** 41 42N 73 56W
Pouilly-sur-Loire, *France* **19 E9** 47 17N 2 57 E
Poulaphouca Res.,
　Ireland **12 C5** 53 8N 6 30W
Poulsbo, *U.S.A.* **110 C4** 47 44N 122 39W
Poultney, *U.S.A.* **117 C11** 43 31N 73 14W
Poulton-le-Fylde, *U.K.* **14 D5** 53 51N 2 58W
Pouso Alegre, *Brazil* . **127 A6** 22 14 S 45 57W
Pout, *Senegal* **82 C1** 14 45N 17 0W
Pouthisat, *Cambodia* . **64 F4** 12 34N 103 50 E
Pouzauges, *France* ... **18 F6** 46 47N 0 50W
Pova de Santa Iria,
　Portugal **37 G1** 38 51N 9 4W
Povážská Bystrica,
　Slovak Rep. ..... **27 B11** 49 8N 18 27 E
Poverty B., *N.Z.* ..... **91 H7** 38 43 S 178 2 E
Povlen, *Serbia & M.* .. **44 B3** 44 9N 19 44 E
Póvoa de Lanhoso,
　Portugal **36 D2** 41 33N 8 15W
Póvoa de Varzim,
　Portugal **36 D2** 41 25N 8 46W
Povorino, *Russia* .... **34 E6** 51 12N 42 5 E
Powassan, *Canada* ... **104 C4** 46 5N 79 25W
Poway, *U.S.A.* **111 N9** 32 58N 117 2W
Powder →, *U.S.A.* ... **112 B2** 46 45N 105 26W
Powder River, *U.S.A.* . **108 E10** 43 2N 106 59W
Powell, *U.S.A.* **108 D9** 44 45N 108 46W
Powell, L., *U.S.A.* ... **109 H8** 36 57N 111 29W
Powell River, *Canada* . **102 D4** 49 50N 124 35W
Powers, *U.S.A.* **114 C2** 45 41N 87 32W
Powys □, *U.K.* **15 E4** 52 20N 3 20W
Poyang Hu, *China* ... **59 C11** 29 5N 116 20 E
Poyarkovo, *Russia* ... **53 E13** 49 36N 128 41 E
Poysdorf, *Austria* .... **27 C9** 48 40N 16 37 E
Poza de la Sal, *Spain* . **36 C7** 42 35N 3 31W
Poza Rica, *Mexico* ... **119 C5** 20 33N 97 27W
Požarevac, *Serbia & M.* **44 B5** 44 35N 21 18 E
Pozanti, *Turkey* ..... **72 D6** 37 25N 34 50 E
Pozazal, Puerto, *Spain* **36 C6** 42 56N 4 10W
Požega, *Croatia* ..... **28 E2** 45 20N 17 40 E
Požega, *Serbia & M.* .. **44 C4** 43 53N 20 2 E
Poznań, *Poland* ...... **31 F3** 52 25N 16 55 E
Poznań ✈ (POZ),
　Poland .... **31 F3** 52 26N 16 45 E
Pozo, *U.S.A.* **111 K6** 35 20N 120 24W
Pozo Alcón, *Spain* ... **37 H8** 37 42N 2 56W
Pozo Almonte, *Chile* . **124 H5** 20 10 S 69 50W
Pozo Colorado,
　Paraguay .... **126 A4** 23 30 S 58 45W
Pozoblanco, *Spain* ... **37 G6** 38 23N 4 51W
Pozzomaggiore, *Italy* . **42 B1** 40 24N 8 39 E
Pozzuoli, *Italy* ...... **43 B7** 40 49N 14 7 E
Pra →, *Ghana* **83 D4** 5 1N 1 37W
Prabuty, *Poland* ..... **30 E6** 53 47N 19 15 E
Prača, *Bos.-H.* ...... **28 G3** 43 47N 18 43 E
Prachatice, *Czech Rep.* **26 B6** 49 1N 14 0 E
Prachin Buri, *Thailand* **64 E3** 14 0N 101 25 E
Prachuap Khiri Khan,
　Thailand .... **65 G2** 11 49N 99 48 E
Pradelles, *France* .... **20 D7** 44 46N 3 52 E
Prades, *France* ...... **20 F6** 42 38N 2 23 E
Prado, *Brazil* .... **125 G11** 17 20 S 39 13W
Prado del Rey, *Spain* . **37 J5** 36 48N 5 33W
Præstø, *Denmark* .... **11 J6** 55 8N 12 2 E
Pragersko, *Slovenia* .. **41 B12** 46 27N 15 42 E
Prague = Praha,
　Czech Rep. ...... **26 A7** 50 5N 14 22 E
Praha, *Czech Rep.* ... **26 A7** 50 5N 14 22 E
Praha ✈ (PRG),
　Czech Rep. ...... **26 A7** 50 7N 14 15 E
Prahecq, *France* **20 B3** 46 19N 0 26W
Prahova □, *Romania* . **29 E10** 45 10N 26 0 E
Prahova →, *Romania* . **29 F10** 44 50N 25 50 E
Prahovo, *Serbia & M.* **44 B6** 44 18N 22 39 E
Praia, *C. Verde Is.* ... **77 E1** 15 2N 23 34W
Práia a Mare, *Italy* .. **43 C8** 39 50N 15 45 E
Praid, *Romania* ...... **29 D10** 46 32N 25 10 E
Prainha, *Amazonas,*
　Brazil .... **124 E6** 7 10 S 60 30W
Prainha, *Pará, Brazil* . **125 D8** 1 45 S 53 30W
Prairie, *Australia* .... **94 C3** 20 50 S 144 35 E
Prairie City, *U.S.A.* .. **108 D4** 44 28N 118 43W
Prairie Dog Town
　Fork →, *U.S.A.* .. **113 H5** 34 30N 99 23W
Prairie du Chien, *U.S.A.* **112 D9** 43 3N 91 9W
Prairies, L. of the,
　Canada **103 C8** 51 16N 101 32W
Pramánda, *Greece* ... **46 B3** 39 32N 21 8 E
Prampram, *Ghana* ... **83 D5** 5 43N 0 8 E
Pran Buri, *Thailand* .. **64 F2** 12 23N 99 55 E
Prang, *Ghana* **83 D4** 8 1N 0 56W
Prapat, *Indonesia* .... **62 D1** 2 41N 98 58 E
Prasonísi, Ákra, *Greece* **49 D9** 35 42N 27 46 E
Prästmon, *Sweden* ... **10 A11** 63 5N 17 45 E
Praszka, *Poland* ..... **31 G5** 51 5N 18 31 E
Prata, *Brazil* .... **125 G9** 19 25 S 48 54W
Pratabpur, *India* .... **69 H10** 23 28N 83 15 E
Pratapgarh, *Raj., India* **68 G6** 24 2N 74 40 E
Pratapgarh, *Ut.P., India* **69 G9** 25 56N 81 59 E
Prato, *Italy* .... **40 E8** 43 53N 11 6 E

Prátola Peligna, *Italy* . **41 F10** 42 6N 13 52 E
Prats-de-Mollo-la-
　Preste, *France* .... **20 F6** 42 25N 2 27 E
Pratt, *U.S.A.* **113 G5** 37 39N 98 44W
Prattville, *U.S.A.* **115 J2** 32 28N 86 29W
Pravdinsk, *Russia* ... **30 D8** 54 27N 21 1 E
Pravdinsk, *Russia* ... **34 B6** 56 29N 43 10 E
Pravets, *Bulgaria* .... **44 D7** 42 53N 23 55 E
Pravia, *Spain* **36 B4** 43 30N 6 12W
Praya, *Indonesia* .... **62 F5** 8 39 S 116 17 E
Pré-en-Pail, *France* .. **18 D6** 48 28N 0 12W
Precipice △, *Australia* **95 D5** 25 18 S 150 5 E
Precordillera, *Argentina* **126 C2** 30 0 S 69 1W
Predáppio, *Italy* ..... **41 D8** 44 6N 11 59 E
Predazzo, *Italy* ...... **41 B8** 46 19N 11 36 E
Predeal, *Romania* .... **29 E10** 45 30N 25 34 E
Preeceville, *Canada* .. **103 C8** 51 57N 102 40W
Pregolya →, *Russia* .. **30 D7** 54 41N 20 22 E
Pregrada, *Croatia* ... **41 B12** 46 11N 15 45 E
Preiļi, *Latvia* .... **9 H22** 56 18N 26 43 E
Preko, *Croatia* ...... **41 D12** 44 7N 15 10 E
Prelog, *Croatia* ...... **41 B13** 46 18N 16 32 E
Prémery, *France* ..... **19 E10** 47 10N 3 18 E
Premià de Mar, *Spain* **38 D7** 41 29N 2 22 E
Premuda, *Croatia* ... **41 D11** 44 20N 14 36 E
Prentice, *U.S.A.* **112 C9** 45 33N 90 17W
Prenzlau, *Germany* .. **24 B9** 53 19N 13 50 E
Preobrazhen'ye, *Russia* **54 C6** 42 54N 133 54 E
Preparis North Channel,
　Ind. Oc. .... **67 M18** 15 12N 93 40 E
Preparis South Channel,
　Ind. Oc. .... **67 M18** 14 36N 93 40 E
Přerov, *Czech Rep.* .. **27 B10** 49 28N 17 27 E
Prescott, *Canada* **117 B9** 44 45N 75 30W
Prescott, *Ariz., U.S.A.* **109 J7** 34 33N 112 28W
Prescott, *Ark., U.S.A.* **113 J8** 33 48N 93 23W
Prescott Valley, *U.S.A.* **109 J7** 34 40N 112 18W
Preservation Inlet, *N.Z.* **91 M1** 46 8 S 166 35 E
Preševo, *Serbia & M.* . **44 D5** 42 19N 21 39 E
Presho, *U.S.A.* **112 D4** 43 54N 100 3W
Presicce, *Italy* .... **43 C11** 39 54N 18 16 E
Presidencia de la Plaza,
　Argentina .... **126 B4** 27 0 S 59 50W
Presidencia Roque
　Saenz Peña, *Argentina* **126 B3** 26 45 S 60 30W
Presidente Epitácio,
　Brazil .... **125 H8** 21 56 S 52 6W
Presidente Hayes □,
　Paraguay .... **126 A4** 24 0 S 59 0W
Presidente Prudente,
　Brazil .... **127 A5** 22 5 S 51 25W
Presidio, *Mexico* **118 B4** 29 29N 104 23W
Presidio, *U.S.A.* **113 L2** 29 34N 104 22W
Preslav, *Bulgaria* .... **45 C10** 43 10N 26 52 E
Preslavska Planina,
　Bulgaria .... **45 C10** 43 10N 26 45 E
Prešov, *Slovak Rep.* .. **27 B14** 49 0N 21 15 E
Prešovský □,
　Slovak Rep. ..... **27 B13** 49 10N 21 0 E
Prespa, *Bulgaria* ..... **45 E8** 41 44N 24 55 E
Préspa, L., *Greece* ... **44 F5** 40 48N 21 4 E
Prespa, L. = Frespansko
　Jezero, *Macedonia* **44 F5** 40 55N 21 0 E
Prespansko Jezero,
　Macedonia ...... **44 F5** 40 55N 21 0 E
Presque I., *U.S.A.* ... **116 D4** 42 9N 80 6W
Presque Isle, *U.S.A.* . **115 B12** 46 41N 68 1W
Prestatyn, *U.K.* **14 D4** 53 20N 3 24W
Prestea, *Ghana* **82 D4** 5 22N 2 7W
Presteigne, *U.K.* **15 E5** 52 17N 3 0W
Přeštice, *Czech Rep.* . **26 B6** 49 34N 13 20 E
Preston, *Canada* **116 C4** 43 23N 80 21W
Preston, *U.K.* **14 D5** 53 46N 2 42W
Preston, *Idaho, U.S.A.* **108 E8** 42 6N 111 53W
Preston, *Minn., U.S.A.* **112 D8** 43 40N 92 5W
Preston, C., *Australia* . **92 D2** 20 51 S 116 12 E
Prestonburg, *U.S.A.* .. **114 G4** 37 39N 82 46W
Prestwick, *U.K.* **13 F4** 55 29N 4 37W
Pretoria, *S. Africa* ... **89 D4** 25 44 S 28 12 E
Preuilly-sur-Claise,
　France .... **18 F7** 46 51N 0 56 E
Préveza, *Greece* ..... **46 C2** 38 57N 20 45 E
Préveza □, *Greece* ... **46 B2** 39 10N 20 40 E
Prey Veng, *Cambodia* **65 G5** 11 35N 105 29 E
Priazovskoye, *Ukraine* **33 J8** 46 44N 35 40 E
Pribilof Is., *U.S.A.* ... **100 C2** 57 0N 170 0W
Priboj, *Serbia & M.* .. **44 C3** 43 35N 19 32 E
Příbram, *Czech Rep.* . **26 B7** 49 41N 14 2 E
Price, *U.S.A.* **108 G8** 39 36N 110 49W
Price I., *Canada* **102 C3** 52 23N 128 41W
Prichard, *U.S.A.* **115 K1** 30 44N 88 5W
Priego, *Spain* **38 E2** 40 26N 2 21W
Priego de Córdoba,
　Spain **37 H6** 37 27N 4 12W
Priekule, *Latvia* ..... **9 H19** 56 26N 21 35 E
Priekule, *Lithuania* .. **30 C8** 55 33N 21 19 E
Prien, *Germany* ..... **25 H8** 47 51N 12 20 E
Prienai, *Lithuania* ... **9 J20** 54 38N 23 57 E
Prieska, *S. Africa* .... **88 D3** 29 40 S 22 42 E
Priest L., *U.S.A.* **108 B5** 48 35N 116 52W
Priest River, *U.S.A.* .. **108 B5** 48 10N 116 54W
Priest Valley, *U.S.A.* . **110 J6** 36 10N 120 39W
Prievidza, *Slovak Rep.* **27 C11** 48 46N 18 36 E
Prignitz, *Germany* ... **24 B8** 52 56N 11 45 E
Prijedor, *Bos.-H.* .... **41 D13** 44 58N 16 41 E
Prijepolje, *Serbia & M.* **44 C3** 43 27N 19 40 E
Prikaspiyskaya
　Nizmennost = Caspian
　Depression, *Eurasia* **35 G9** 47 0N 48 0 E
Prikro, *Ivory C.* **82 D4** 7 40N 3 59W
Prikubanskaya
　Nizmennost, *Russia* **35 H4** 45 39N 38 33 E
Prilep, *Macedonia* ... **44 E5** 41 21N 21 32 E
Priluki = Pryluky,
　Ukraine .... **33 G7** 50 30N 32 24 E
Prime Seal I., *Australia* **95 G4** 40 3 S 147 43 E
Primorsk, *Russia* .... **30 D4** 54 44N 20 0 E
Primorsk, *Russia* .... **32 B5** 60 2N 28 37 E
Primorsko, *Bulgaria* . **45 D11** 42 15N 27 44 E
Primorsko-Akhtarsk,
　Russia .... **33 J10** 46 2N 38 10 E
Primorskoye, *Ukraine* **33 J9** 46 58N 36 20 E
Primrose L., *Canada* . **103 C7** 54 55N 109 45W
Prince Albert, *Canada* **103 C7** 53 15N 105 50W
Prince Albert, *S. Africa* **88 E3** 33 12 S 22 2 E
Prince Albert △, *Canada* **103 C7** 54 0N 106 25W
Prince Albert Mts.,
　Antarctica .... **5 D11** 76 0 S 161 30 E
Prince Albert Pen.,
　Canada **100 A8** 72 30N 116 0W
Prince Albert Sd.,
　Canada **100 A8** 70 25N 115 0W
Prince Alfred, C.,
　Canada **4 B1** 74 20N 124 40W

Prince Charles I.,
　Canada **101 B12** 67 47N 76 12W
Prince Charles Mts.,
　Antarctica .... **5 D6** 72 0 S 67 0 E
Prince Edward I. □,
　Canada **105 C7** 46 20N 63 20W
Prince Edward Is.,
　Ind. Oc. .... **3 G11** 46 35 S 38 0 E
Prince Edward Pt.,
　Canada **116 C8** 43 56N 76 52W
Prince George, *Canada* **102 C4** 53 55N 122 50W
Prince of Wales, C.,
　U.S.A. **98 C3** 65 36N 168 5W
Prince of Wales I.,
　Australia .... **94 A3** 10 40 S 142 10 E
Prince of Wales I.,
　Canada **100 A10** 73 0N 99 0W
Prince of Wales I.,
　U.S.A. **100 C6** 55 47N 132 50W
Prince Patrick I., *Canada* **4 B2** 77 0N 120 0W
Prince Regent Inlet,
　Canada **4 B3** 73 0N 90 0W
Prince Rupert, *Canada* **102 C2** 54 20N 130 20W
Princes Town,
　Trin. & Tob. **125 K15** 10 16N 61 23W
Princess Charlotte B.,
　Australia .... **94 A3** 14 25 S 144 0 E
Princess May Ranges,
　Australia .... **92 C4** 15 30 S 125 30 E
Princess Royal I.,
　Canada **102 C3** 53 0N 128 40W
Princeton, *Canada* ... **102 D4** 49 27N 120 30W
Princeton, *Calif., U.S.A.* **110 F4** 39 24N 122 1W
Princeton, *Ill., U.S.A.* . **112 E10** 41 23N 89 28W
Princeton, *Ind., U.S.A.* **114 F2** 38 21N 87 34W
Princeton, *Ky., U.S.A.* **114 G2** 37 7N 87 53W
Princeton, *Mo., U.S.A.* **112 E8** 40 24N 93 35W
Princeton, *W. Va.,
　U.S.A.* **114 G5** 37 22N 81 6W
Principe, I. de, *Atl. Oc.* **76 F4** 1 37N 7 27 E
Principe da Beira, *Brazil* **124 F6** 12 20 S 64 30W
Prineville, *U.S.A.* **108 D3** 44 18N 120 51W
Prins Harald Kyst,
　Antarctica .... **5 D4** 70 0 S 35 1 E
Prinsesse Astrid Kyst,
　Antarctica .... **5 D3** 70 45 S 12 30 E
Prinsesse Ragnhild Kyst,
　Antarctica .... **5 D4** 70 15 S 27 30 E
Prinzapolca, *Nic.* **120 D3** 13 20N 83 35W
Prior, C., *Spain* **36 B2** 43 34N 8 17W
Priozersk, *Russia* .... **32 B6** 61 2N 30 7 E
Pripet = Prypyat →,
　Europe .... **33 G6** 51 20N 30 15 E
Pripet Marshes, *Europe* **33 F5** 52 10N 28 10 E
Pripyat Marshes = Pripet
　Marshes, *Europe* . **33 F5** 52 10N 28 10 E
Pripyats = Prypyat →,
　Europe .... **33 G6** 51 20N 30 15 E
Prislop, Pasul, *Romania* **29 C9** 47 37N 24 48 E
Pristen, *Russia* ...... **33 G9** 51 15N 36 44 E
Priština, *Serbia & M.* . **44 D5** 42 40N 21 13 E
Pritzwalk, *Germany* .. **24 B8** 53 9N 12 10 E
Privas, *France* .... **21 D8** 44 45N 4 37 E
Priverno, *Italy* ...... **42 A6** 41 29N 13 11 E
Privolzhsk, *Russia* ... **34 B5** 57 23N 41 16 E
Privolzhskaya
　Vozvyshennost,
　Russia .... **34 E7** 51 0N 46 0 E
Privolzhskiy, *Russia* . **34 E8** 51 25N 46 3 E
Privolzhskiy □, *Russia* **34 B10** 56 0N 50 0 E
Privolzhye, *Russia* ... **34 D9** 52 52N 48 33 E
Priyutnoye, *Russia* .. **35 G6** 46 12N 43 40 E
Prizren, *Serbia & M.* . **44 D4** 42 13N 20 45 E
Prizzi, *Italy* .... **42 E6** 37 43N 13 26 E
Prnjavor, *Bos.-H.* .... **28 F2** 44 52N 17 43 E
Probolinggo, *Indonesia* **63 G15** 7 46 S 113 13 E
Prochowice, *Poland* .. **31 G3** 51 17N 16 20 E
Proctor, *U.S.A.* **117 C11** 43 40N 73 2W
Proddatur, *India* ..... **66 M11** 14 45N 78 30 E
Prodhromos, *Cyprus* . **49 E11** 34 57N 32 50 E
Proença-a-Nova,
　Portugal **36 F3** 39 45N 7 54W
Profítis Ilías, *Greece* . **49 C9** 36 17N 27 56 E
Profondeville, *Belgium* **17 D4** 50 23N 4 52 E
Progreso, Coahuila,
　Mexico **118 B4** 27 28N 101 4W
Progreso, Yucatán,
　Mexico **119 C7** 21 20N 89 40W
Prokhladnyy, *Russia* . **35 J7** 43 50N 44 2 E
Prokletije, *Albania* ... **44 D3** 42 30N 19 45 E
Prokopyevsk, *Russia* . **52 D9** 54 0N 86 45 E
Prokuplje, *Serbia & M.* **44 C5** 43 16N 21 36 E
Proletarsk, *Russia* ... **35 G5** 46 42N 41 50 E
Proletarskaya =
　Proletarsk, *Russia* . **35 G5** 46 42N 41 50 E
Prome, *Burma* .... **67 K19** 18 49N 95 13 E
Prophet →, *Canada* .. **102 B4** 58 48N 122 40W
Prophet River, *Canada* **102 B4** 58 6N 122 43W
Propriá, *Brazil* ...... **125 F11** 10 13 S 36 51W
Propriano, *France* ... **21 G12** 41 40N 8 52 E
Proserpine, *Australia* . **94 J6** 20 21 S 148 36 E
Prosna →, *Poland* ... **31 F4** 52 6N 17 44 E
Prospect, *U.S.A.* **117 C9** 43 18N 75 9W
Prosser, *U.S.A.* **108 C4** 46 12N 119 46W
Prostějov, *Czech Rep.* **27 B10** 49 30N 17 9 E
Prostki, *Poland* ...... **30 E9** 53 42N 22 25 E
Proston, *Australia* ... **95 D5** 26 8 S 151 32 E
Proszowice, *Poland* .. **31 H7** 50 13N 20 16 E
Próti, *Greece* .... **46 D2** 37 5N 21 32 E
Provadiya, *Bulgaria* .. **45 C11** 43 12N 27 30 E
Provence, *France* .... **21 E9** 43 40N 5 46 E
Provence-Alpes-Côte
　d'Azur □, *France* . **21 D10** 44 0N 6 15 E
Providence, *Ky., U.S.A.* **114 G2** 37 24N 87 46W
Providence, *R.I., U.S.A.* **117 E13** 41 49N 71 24W
Providence Bay, *Canada* **104 C3** 45 41N 82 15W
Providence Mts., *U.S.A.* **111 K11** 35 10N 115 15W
Providencia, I. de,
　Colombia **120 D3** 13 25N 81 26W
Provideniya, *Russia* .. **53 C19** 64 23N 173 18W
Provins, *France* ...... **19 D10** 48 33N 3 15 E
Provo, *U.S.A.* **108 F8** 40 14N 111 39W
Provost, *Canada* **103 C6** 52 25N 110 20W
Prozor, *Bos.-H.* ...... **28 G2** 43 50N 17 34 E
Prrenjas, *Albania* .... **44 E4** 41 4N 20 32 E
Prudhoe Bay, *U.S.A.* . **100 A5** 70 18N 148 22W
Prudhoe I., *Australia* . **94 C4** 21 19 S 149 41 E
Prud'homme, *Canada* **103 C7** 52 20N 105 54W
Prudnik, *Poland* ..... **31 H4** 50 20N 17 38 E
Prüm, *Germany* ..... **25 E2** 50 12N 6 25 E
Prundu, *Romania* .... **29 F11** 44 10N 26 22 E
Pruszcz Gdański, *Poland* **30 D5** 54 17N 18 40 E
Pruszków, *Poland* .... **31 F7** 52 9N 20 49 E
Prut →, *Romania* .... **29 E13** 45 28N 28 10 E
Pruzhany, *Belarus* ... **33 F3** 52 33N 24 28 E
Prvić, *Croatia* .... **41 D11** 44 55N 14 45 E

Prydz B., *Antarctica* .. **5 C6** 69 0 S 74 0 E
Pryluky, *Ukraine* .... **33 G7** 50 30N 32 24 E
Pryor, *U.S.A.* **113 G7** 36 19N 95 19W
Prypyat →, *Europe* .. **33 G6** 51 20N 30 15 E
Przasnysz, *Poland* ... **31 E7** 53 2N 20 54 E
Przedbórz, *Poland* ... **31 G6** 51 6N 19 53 E
Przedecz, *Poland* .... **31 F5** 52 20N 18 53 E
Przemków, *Poland* ... **31 G2** 51 31N 15 48 E
Przemyśl, *Poland* .... **31 J9** 49 50N 22 45 E
Przeworsk, *Poland* ... **31 H9** 50 6N 22 32 E
Przevalsk = Karakol,
　Kyrgyzstan ...... **52 E8** 42 30N 78 20 E
Przhevalsk = Karakol,
　Kyrgyzstan ...... **52 E8** 42 30N 78 20 E
Przysucha, *Poland* ... **31 G7** 51 22N 20 38 E
Psakhná, *Greece* ..... **46 C5** 38 34N 23 35 E
Psará, *Greece* .... **47 C7** 38 37N 25 38 E
Psathoúra, *Greece* ... **46 B6** 39 30N 24 12 E
Psel →, *Ukraine* ..... **33 H7** 49 10N 33 37 E
Pserimos, *Greece* .... **47 E9** 36 56N 27 8 E
Psíra, *Greece* .... **49 D7** 35 12N 25 52 E
Pskov, *Russia* .... **32 D5** 57 50N 28 25 E
Pskovskoye, Ozero,
　Russia .... **32 D5** 58 0N 27 58 E
Psunj, *Croatia* .... **28 E2** 45 25N 17 19 E
Pteleón, *Greece* ..... **46 B4** 39 3N 22 57 E
Ptich = Ptsich →,
　Belarus .... **33 F5** 52 9N 28 52 E
Ptolemaís, *Greece* ... **44 F5** 40 30N 21 43 E
Ptsich →, *Belarus* ... **33 F5** 52 9N 28 52 E
Ptuj, *Slovenia* .... **41 B12** 46 28N 15 50 E
Ptujska Gora, *Slovenia* **41 B12** 46 23N 15 47 E
Pu Xian, *China* ...... **56 F6** 36 24N 111 6 E
Pua, *Thailand* .... **64 C3** 19 11N 100 55 E
Puán, *Argentina* ..... **126 D3** 37 30 S 62 45W
Pu'an, *China* .... **58 E5** 25 50N 104 57 E
Puan, *S. Korea* ...... **57 G14** 35 44N 126 44 E
Pubei, *China* .... **58 F7** 22 16N 109 31 E
Pucallpa, *Peru* ...... **124 E4** 8 25 S 74 30W
Pucheng, *China* ...... **59 D12** 27 59N 118 31 E
Pucheni, *Romania* ... **29 E10** 45 12N 25 17 E
Pučheng, *Germany* ... **25 G7** 48 9N 11 21 E
Púchov, *Slovak Rep.* . **27 B11** 49 3N 18 20 E
Pucioasa, *Romania* .. **29 E10** 45 5N 25 25 E
Pučišća, *Croatia* ..... **41 E13** 43 22N 16 43 E
Puck, *Poland* .... **30 D5** 54 45N 18 23 E
Pucka, Zatoka, *Poland* **30 D5** 54 30N 18 40 E
Pudasjärvi, *Finland* .. **8 D22** 65 23N 26 53 E
Puding, *China* .... **58 D5** 26 18N 105 44 E
Pudozh, *Russia* ...... **32 B9** 61 48N 36 32 E
Puducherry =
　Pondicherry, *India* **66 P11** 11 59N 79 50 E
Pudukkottai, *India* ... **66 P11** 10 28N 78 47 E
Puebla, *Mexico* **119 D5** 19 3N 98 12W
Puebla □, *Mexico* ... **119 D5** 18 30N 98 0W
Puebla de Alcocer,
　Spain **37 G5** 38 59N 5 14W
Puebla de Don
　Fadrique, *Spain* .. **39 H2** 37 58N 2 25W
Puebla de Don Rodrigo,
　Spain **37 F6** 39 5N 4 37W
Puebla de Guzmán,
　Spain **37 H3** 37 37N 7 15W
Puebla de la Calzada,
　Spain **37 G4** 38 54N 6 37W
Puebla de Sanabria,
　Spain **36 C4** 42 4N 6 38W
Puebla de Trives =
　Pobra de Trives, *Spain* **36 C3** 42 20N 7 10W
Pueblo, *U.S.A.* **108 F2** 38 16N 104 37W
Pueblo Hundido, *Chile* **126 B1** 26 20 S 70 5W
Puelches, *Argentina* .. **126 D2** 38 5 S 65 51W
Puelén, *Argentina* ... **126 D2** 37 32 S 67 38W
Puente Alto, *Chile* ... **126 C1** 33 32 S 70 35W
Puente-Genil, *Spain* . **37 H6** 37 22N 4 47W
Puente la Reina, *Spain* **38 C2** 42 40N 1 49W
Puenteareas =
　Ponteareas, *Spain* . **36 C2** 42 10N 8 28W
Puentedeume =
　Pontedeume, *Spain* **36 B2** 43 24N 8 10W
Puentes de Garcia
　Rodriguez = As
　Pontes de García
　Rodríguez, *Spain* . **36 B3** 43 27N 7 50W
Pu'er, *China* .... **58 F3** 23 0N 101 15 E
Puerca, Pta., *Puerto Rico* **121 d** 18 13N 65 36W
Puerco →, *U.S.A.* ... **109 J10** 34 22N 107 50W
Puerto Aisén, *Chile* .. **128 F2** 45 27 S 73 0W
Puerto Ángel, *Mexico* **119 D5** 15 40N 96 29W
Puerto Arista, *Mexico* **119 D6** 15 56N 93 48W
Puerto Armuelles,
　Panama **120 E3** 8 20N 82 51W
Puerto Ayacucho,
　Venezuela **124 B5** 5 40N 67 35W
Puerto Barrios,
　Guatemala **120 C2** 15 40N 88 32W
Puerto Bermejo,
　Argentina .... **126 B4** 26 55 S 58 34W
Puerto Bermúdez, *Peru* **124 F4** 10 20 S 74 58W
Puerto Bolívar, *Ecuador* **124 D3** 3 19 S 79 55W
Puerto Cabello,
　Venezuela **124 A5** 10 28N 68 1W
Puerto Cabezas, *Nic.* . **120 D3** 14 0N 83 30W
Puerto Cabo Gracias á
　Dios, *Nic.* **120 D3** 15 0N 83 10W
Puerto Carreño,
　Colombia **124 B5** 6 12N 67 22W
Puerto Castilla,
　Honduras **120 C2** 16 0N 86 0W
Puerto Chicama, *Peru* **124 E3** 7 45 S 79 20W
Puerto Coig, *Argentina* **128 G3** 50 54 S 69 15W
Puerto Cortés,
　Costa Rica **120 E3** 8 55N 84 0W
Puerto Cortés,
　Honduras **120 C2** 15 51N 88 0W
Puerto Cumarebo,
　Venezuela **124 A5** 11 29N 69 30W
Puerto de Alcudia =
　Port d'Alcúdia, *Spain* **48 B10** 39 50N 3 7 E
Puerto de Cabrera,
　Spain .... **48 B9** 39 8N 2 56 E
Puerto de Gran Tarajal,
　Canary Is. **48 F5** 28 13N 14 1W
Puerto de la Cruz,
　Canary Is. **48 F3** 28 24N 16 32W
Puerto de los Ángeles △,
　Mexico **118 C3** 23 20N 105 45W
Puerto de Mazarrón,
　Spain **39 H3** 37 34N 1 15W
Puerto de Pozo Negro,
　Canary Is. **48 F6** 28 19N 13 55W
Puerto de Sóller = Port
　de Sóller, *Spain* .. **48 B9** 39 48N 2 42 E
Puerto de Somosierra,
　Spain **36 D7** 41 9N 3 35W
Puerto del Carmen,
　Canary Is. **48 F6** 28 55N 13 38W

Puerto del Rosario,
　Canary Is. **48 F6** 28 30N 13 52W
Puerto Deseado,
　Argentina .... **128 F3** 47 55 S 66 0W
Puerto Escondido,
　Mexico **119 D5** 15 50N 97 3W
Puerto Heath, *Bolivia* **124 F5** 12 34 S 68 39W
Puerto Inírida,
　Colombia **124 C5** 3 53N 67 52W
Puerto Juárez, *Mexico* **119 C7** 21 11N 86 49W
Puerto La Cruz,
　Venezuela **124 A6** 10 13N 64 38W
Puerto Leguízamo,
　Colombia .... **124 D4** 0 12 S 74 46W
Puerto Limón, *Colombia* **124 C4** 3 23N 73 30W
Puerto Lobos, *Argentina* **128 E3** 42 0 S 65 3W
Puerto Lumbreras,
　Spain **39 H3** 37 34N 1 48W
Puerto Madryn,
　Argentina .... **128 E3** 42 48 S 65 4W
Puerto Maldonado, *Peru* **124 F5** 12 30 S 69 10W
Puerto Manatí, *Cuba* . **120 B4** 21 22N 76 50W
Puerto Montt, *Chile* .. **128 E2** 41 28 S 73 0W
Puerto Morazán, *Nic.* **120 D2** 12 51N 87 11W
Puerto Morelos, *Mexico* **119 C7** 20 49N 86 52W
Puerto Natales, *Chile* . **128 G2** 51 45 S 72 15W
Puerto Padre, *Cuba* .. **120 B4** 21 13N 76 35W
Puerto Páez, *Venezuela* **124 B5** 6 13N 67 28W
Puerto Peñasco, *Mexico* **118 A2** 31 20N 113 33W
Puerto Pinasco,
　Paraguay .... **126 A4** 22 36 S 57 50W
Puerto Plata, *Dom. Rep.* **121 C5** 19 48N 70 45W
Puerto Pollensa = Port
　de Pollença, *Spain* **48 B10** 39 54N 3 4 E
Puerto Princesa, *Phil.* **61 G3** 9 46N 118 45 E
Puerto Quepos,
　Costa Rica **120 E3** 9 29N 84 6W
Puerto Real, *Spain* ... **37 J4** 36 33N 6 12W
Puerto Rico, *Canary Is.* **48 G4** 27 47N 15 42W
Puerto Rico ☒, *W. Indies* **121 d** 18 15N 66 45W
Puerto Rico Trench,
　Atl. Oc. **121 C6** 19 50N 66 0W
Puerto San Julián,
　Argentina .... **128 F3** 49 18 S 67 43W
Puerto Sastre, *Paraguay* **126 A4** 22 2 S 57 55W
Puerto Serrano, *Spain* **37 J5** 36 56N 5 33W
Puerto Suárez, *Bolivia* **124 G7** 18 58 S 57 52W
Puerto Vallarta, *Mexico* **118 C3** 20 36N 105 15W
Puerto Wilches,
　Colombia **124 B4** 7 21N 73 54W
Puertollano, *Spain* ... **37 G6** 38 43N 4 7W
Pueyrredón, L.,
　Argentina .... **128 F2** 47 20 S 72 0W
Púez Odle △, *Italy* ... **41 B8** 46 37N 11 48 E
Puffin I., *Ireland* **12 E1** 51 50N 10 24W
Pugachev, *Russia* .... **34 D9** 52 0N 48 49 E
Pugal, *India* .... **68 E5** 28 30N 72 48 E
Puge, *China* .... **58 D4** 27 20N 102 31 E
Puge, *Tanzania* ...... **86 C3** 4 45 S 33 11 E
Puget Sound, *U.S.A.* . **108 C2** 47 50N 122 30W
Puget-Théniers, *France* **21 E10** 43 58N 6 53 E
Púglia □, *Italy* ...... **43 A9** 41 15N 16 15 E
Pugödong, *N. Korea* . **57 C16** 42 5N 130 0 E
Pugu, *Tanzania* ...... **86 D4** 6 55 S 39 4 E
Pügünzī, *Iran* .... **71 E8** 25 49N 59 10 E
Pui, *Romania* .... **28 E8** 45 30N 23 4 E
Puiești, *Romania* .... **29 D12** 46 25N 27 33 E
Puig Major, *Spain* ... **48 B9** 39 48N 2 47 E
Puigcerdà, *Spain* ..... **38 C6** 42 24N 1 50 E
Puigmal, *Spain* ...... **38 C7** 42 23N 2 7 E
Puigpunyent, *Spain* .. **48 B9** 39 38N 2 32 E
Puijiang, *China* ...... **58 B4** 30 14N 103 30 E
Puisaye, Collines de la,
　France .... **19 E10** 47 37N 3 20 E
Puiseaux, *France* .... **19 D9** 48 11N 2 30 E
Pujehun, *S. Leone* ... **82 D2** 7 23N 11 45W
Pujiang, *China* ...... **59 C12** 29 59N 119 54 E
Pujols, *France* **20 D3** 44 48N 0 2W
Pujon-chŏsuji, *N. Korea* **57 D14** 40 35N 127 35 E
Pukaki, L., *N.Z.* ..... **91 L3** 44 4 S 170 1 E
Pukapuka, *Cook Is.* .. **97 J11** 10 53 S 165 49W
Pukaskwa △, *Canada* **104 C2** 48 20N 86 0W
Pukatawagan, *Canada* **103 B8** 55 45N 101 20W
Pukchin, *N. Korea* ... **57 D13** 40 12N 125 45 E
Pukch'ŏng, *N. Korea* . **57 D15** 40 14N 128 10 E
Pukë, *Albania* .... **44 D3** 42 2N 19 53 E
Pukekohe, *N.Z.* ...... **91 G5** 37 12 S 174 55 E
Pukhrayan, *India* .... **69 F8** 26 14N 79 51 E
Pukou, *China* .... **59 A12** 32 7N 118 38 E
Pula, *Croatia* .... **41 D10** 44 54N 13 57 E
Pula, *Italy* .... **42 C1** 39 1N 9 0 E
Pulacayo, *Bolivia* .... **124 H5** 20 25 S 66 41W
Pulandian, *China* .... **57 E11** 39 25N 121 58 E
Pularumpi, *Australia* . **92 B5** 11 24 S 130 26 E
Pulaski, *N.Y., U.S.A.* . **117 C8** 43 34N 76 8W
Pulaski, *Tenn., U.S.A.* **115 H2** 35 12N 87 2W
Pulaski, *Va., U.S.A.* .. **114 G5** 37 3N 80 47W
Pulau →, *Indonesia* .. **63 F9** 5 50 S 138 15 E
Puławy, *Poland* ...... **31 G8** 51 23N 21 59 E
Pulga, *U.S.A.* **110 F5** 39 48N 121 29W
Pulicat L., *India* ..... **66 N12** 13 40N 80 15 E
Pullman, *U.S.A.* **108 C5** 46 44N 117 10W
Pulog, Mt., *Phil.* ..... **61 C4** 16 40N 120 50 E
Pułtusk, *Poland* ..... **31 F8** 52 43N 21 6 E
Pülümür, *Turkey* ..... **73 C8** 39 30N 39 51 E
Pumlumon Fawr, *U.K.* **15 E4** 52 28N 3 46W
Puná, I., *Ecuador* .... **124 D2** 2 55 S 80 5W
Punakaiki, *N.Z.* ...... **91 K3** 42 7 S 171 20 E
Punakha, *Bhutan* .... **67 F16** 27 42N 89 52 E
Punasar, *India* ...... **68 F5** 27 6N 73 6 E
Punata, *Bolivia* ...... **124 G5** 17 32 S 65 50W
Punch, *India* .... **69 C6** 33 48N 74 4 E
Punch →, *Pakistan* .. **68 C5** 33 12N 73 40 E
Punda Maria, *S. Africa* **89 C5** 22 40 S 31 5 E
P'ungsan, *N. Korea* .. **57 D15** 40 50N 128 9 E
Pungue, Ponte de,
　Mozam. .... **87 F3** 19 0 S 34 0 E
Puning, *China* .... **59 F11** 23 20N 116 12 E
Punjab □, *India* ...... **68 D7** 31 0N 76 0 E
Punjab □, *Pakistan* .. **68 E6** 32 0N 72 30 E
Puno, *Peru* .... **124 G4** 15 55 S 70 3W
Punpun →, *India* .... **69 G11** 25 31N 85 18 E
Punta, Cerro de,
　Puerto Rico ...... **121 d** 18 10N 66 37W
Punta Alta, *Argentina* **128 D4** 38 53 S 62 4W
Punta Arenas, *Chile* . **128 G2** 53 10 S 71 0W
Punta de Díaz, *Chile* . **126 B1** 28 0 S 70 45W
Punta del Hidalgo,
　Canary Is. **48 F3** 28 33N 16 19W
Punta Gorda, *Belize* . **119 D7** 16 10N 88 45W
Punta Gorda, *U.S.A.* . **115 M5** 26 56N 82 3W
Punta Prieta, *Mexico* . **118 B2** 28 58N 114 17W
Punta Prima, *Spain* .. **48 B11** 39 48N 4 16 E
Punta Umbria, *Spain* **37 H4** 37 10N 6 56W
Puntarenas, *Costa Rica* **120 E3** 10 0N 84 50W

Punto Fijo, *Venezuela* . 124 A4 11 50N 70 13W
Punxsatawney, *U.S.A.* . 116 F6 40 57N 78 59W
Pupuan, *Indonesia* . . . 63 J18 8 19 S 115 0 E
Puqi, *China* . . . . 59 C9 29 40N 113 50 E
Puquio, *Peru* . . . . 124 F4 14 45 S 74 10W
Pur →, *Russia* . . . . 52 C8 67 31N 77 55 E
Puracé, Vol., *Colombia* 124 C3 2 21N 76 23W
Puracić, *Bos.-H.* . . . . . 28 F3 44 33N 18 28 E
Puralia = Puruliya, *India* 69 H12 23 17N 86 24 E
Puranpur, *India* . . . . . 69 E9 28 31N 80 9 E
Purbeck, Isle of, *U.K.* . 15 G5 50 39N 1 59W
Purcell, *U.S.A.* 113 H6 35 1N 97 22W
Purcell Mts., *Canada* . 102 D5 49 55N 116 15W
Puri, *India* . . . . 67 K14 19 50N 85 58 E
Purmerend, *Neths.* . . . 17 B4 52 32N 4 58 E
Purnia, *India* . . . . 69 G12 25 45N 87 31 E
Purnululu △, *Australia* . 92 C4 17 20 S 128 20 E
Pursat = Pouthisat,
  Cambodia . . . . 64 F4 12 34N 103 50 E
Purukcahu, *Indonesia* . 62 E4 0 35 S 114 35 E
Puruliya, *India* . . . . . . 69 H12 23 17N 86 24 E
Purus →, *Brazil* . . . . . 124 D6 3 42 S 61 28W
Puruvesi, *Finland* . . . . 32 B5 61 50N 29 30 E
Purvis, *U.S.A.* 113 K10 31 9N 89 25W
Pûrvomay, *Bulgaria* . . 45 D9 42 8N 25 17 E
Purwa, *India* . . . . 69 F9 26 28N 80 47 E
Purwakarta, *Indonesia* 63 G12 6 35 S 107 29 E
Purwo, Tanjung,
  Indonesia . . . . 63 K18 8 44 S 114 21 E
Purwodadi, *Indonesia* . 63 G14 7 51 S 110 0 E
Purwokerto, *Indonesia* 63 G13 7 25 S 109 14 E
Puryŏng, *N. Korea* . . . 57 C15 42 5N 129 43 E
Pusa, *India* . . . . 69 G11 25 59N 85 41 E
Pusan, *S. Korea* . . . . . 57 G15 35 5N 129 0 E
Pushchino, *Russia* . . . 32 C6 59 45N 30 25 E
Pushkin, *Russia* . . . . . 32 C6 59 45N 30 25 E
Pushkino, *Moskva,*
  Russia . . . . 32 D7 56 2N 37 49 E
Pushkino, *Saratov,*
  Russia . . . . 34 E8 51 16N 47 0 E
Püspökladány, *Hungary* 28 C6 47 19N 21 6 E
Pustoshka, *Russia* . . . 32 D5 56 20N 29 30 E
Puszczykowo, *Poland* . 31 F3 52 18N 16 49 E
Putahow L., *Canada* . . 103 B8 59 54N 100 40W
Putao, *Burma* . . . . 67 F20 27 28N 97 30 E
Putaruru, *N.Z.* . . . . . . 91 H5 38 2 S 175 50 E
Putbus, *Germany* . . . . 24 A9 54 22N 13 28 E
Putian, *China* . . . . . . 59 E12 25 23N 119 0 E
Putignano, *Italy* . . . . . 43 B10 40 51N 17 7 E
Puting, Tanjung,
  Indonesia . . . . 62 E4 3 31 S 111 46 E
Putlitz, *Germany* . . . . 24 B8 53 15N 12 2 E
Putna, *Romania* . . . . . 29 C10 47 50N 25 33 E
Putna →, *Romania* . . . 29 E12 45 42N 27 26 E
Putnam, *U.S.A.* 117 E13 41 55N 71 55W
Putnok, *Hungary* . . . . 28 B5 48 18N 20 26 E
Putorana, Gory, *Russia* 53 C10 69 0N 95 0 E
Putrajaya, *Malaysia* . . 65 L3 2 55N 101 40 E
Puttalam, *Sri Lanka* . . 66 Q11 8 1N 79 55 E
Puttgarden, *Germany* . 24 A7 54 30N 11 10 E
Püttlingen, *Germany* . 25 F2 49 17N 6 53 E
Putumayo →, *S. Amer.* 124 D5 3 7 S 67 58W
Putuo, *China* . . . . 59 C14 29 58N 122 20 E
Putussibau, *Indonesia* . 62 D4 0 50N 112 56 E
Putyla, *Ukraine* . . . . . 29 B10 48 0N 25 5 E
Puvirnituq, *Canada* . . 101 B12 60 2N 77 10W
Puy-de-Dôme, *France* . 20 C6 45 46N 2 57 E
Puy-de-Dôme □, *France* 20 C7 45 40N 2 50 E
Puy-l'Évêque, *France* . 20 D5 44 31N 1 9 E
Puyallup, *U.S.A.* 110 C4 47 12N 122 18W
Puyang, *China* . . . . . . 56 G8 35 40N 115 1 E
Puylaurens, *France* . . . 20 E6 43 35N 2 0 E
Pûzeh Rîg, *Iran* . . . . . 71 E8 27 20N 58 40 E
Puzhaykove, *Ukraine* . 29 B14 48 7N 29 50 E
Pwani □, *Tanzania* . . . 86 D4 7 0 S 39 0 E
Pweto, *Dem. Rep. of*
  the Congo . . . . 87 D2 8 25 S 28 51 E
Pwllheli, *U.K.* 14 E3 52 53N 4 25W
Pyana →, *Russia* . . . . . 34 C8 55 43N 46 1 E
Pyapon, *Burma* . . . . . 67 L19 16 20N 95 40 E
Pyasina →, *Russia* . . . 53 B9 73 30N 87 0 E
Pyatigorsk, *Russia* . . . 35 H6 44 2N 43 6 E
Pyatykhatky, *Ukraine* . 33 H7 48 28N 33 38 E
Pydna, *Greece* . . . . . . 44 F6 40 20N 22 34 E
Pye = Prome, *Burma* . . 67 K19 18 49N 95 13 E
Pyetrikaw, *Belarus* . . . 33 F5 52 11N 28 29 E
Pyhäjoki, *Finland* . . . . 8 D21 64 28N 24 14 E
Pyinmana, *Burma* . . . . 67 K20 19 45N 96 12 E
Pyla, C., *Cyprus* . . . . . 49 E12 34 56N 33 51 E
Pymatuning Reservoir,
  U.S.A. 116 E4 41 30N 80 28W
Pyŏktong, *N. Korea* . . 57 D13 40 50N 125 50 E
Pyŏnggang, *N. Korea* . 57 E14 38 24N 127 17 E
P'yŏngt'aek, *S. Korea* . 57 F14 37 1N 127 4 E
P'yŏngyang, *N. Korea* . 57 E13 39 0N 125 30 E
Pyote, *U.S.A.* 113 K3 31 32N 103 8W
Pyramid L., *U.S.A.* . . . 108 G4 40 1N 119 35W
Pyramid Pk., *U.S.A.* . . 111 J10 36 25N 116 37W
Pyramids, *Egypt* . . . . . 80 J7 29 58N 31 9 E
Pyrénées, *Europe* . . . . 20 F4 42 45N 0 18 E
Pyrénées △, *France* . . 20 F3 42 52N 0 10W
Pyrénées-Atlantiques □,
  France 20 E3 43 10N 0 50W
Pyrénées-Orientales □,
  France . . . . 20 F6 42 35N 2 26 E
Pyryatyn, *Ukraine* . . . 33 G7 50 15N 32 25 E
Pyrzyce, *Poland* . . . . . 31 E1 53 10N 14 55 E
Pyskowice, *Poland* . . . 31 H5 50 24N 18 38 E
Pytalovo, *Russia* . . . . 32 D4 57 5N 27 55 E
Pyu, *Burma* . . . . 67 K20 18 30N 96 28 E
Pyzdry, *Poland* . . . . . . 31 F4 52 11N 17 42 E

Q

Qaanaaq, *Greenland* . . 4 B4 77 40N 69 0W
Qabirri →, *Azerbaijan* . 35 K8 41 3N 46 17 E
Qachasnek, *S. Africa* . 89 E4 30 6 S 28 42 E
Qa'el Jafr, *Jordan* . . . . 74 E5 30 20N 36 25 E
Qa'emābād, *Iran* . . . . 71 D9 31 44N 60 2 E
Qā'emshahr, *Iran* . . . . 71 B7 36 30N 52 53 E
Qagan Nur, *China* . . . 56 C8 43 30N 114 55 E
Qahremānshahr =
  Bākhtarān, *Iran* . . . . 70 C5 34 23N 47 0 E
Qaidam Pendi, *China* . 60 C4 37 0N 95 0 E
Qajarīyeh, *Iran* . . . . . 71 D6 31 1N 48 22 E
Qala, Ras il, *Malta* . . . 49 C1 36 2N 14 20 E
Qala Point = Qala, Ras
  il, *Malta* . . . . 49 C1 36 2N 14 20 E
Qala Viala, *Pakistan* . . 68 D2 30 49N 67 17 E
Qala Yangi, *Afghan.* . . 68 B2 34 20N 66 30 E
Qal'at al Akhdar,
  Si. Arabia . . . . 70 E3 28 0N 37 10 E

Qal'at Dīzah, *Iraq* . . . . 70 B5 36 11N 45 7 E
Qal'at Şālih, *Iraq* . . . . 70 D5 31 31N 47 16 E
Qal'at Sukkar, *Iraq* . . . 70 D5 31 51N 46 5 E
Qalyûb, *Egypt* . . . . 80 H7 30 12N 31 11 E
Qamani'tuaq = Baker
  Lake, *Canada* 100 B10 64 20N 96 3W
Qamdo, *China* . . . . 58 B1 31 15N 97 6 E
Qamruddin Karez,
  Pakistan . . . . 68 D3 31 45N 68 20 E
Qandahār, *Afghan.* . . . 66 D4 31 32N 65 43 E
Qandahār □, *Afghan.* . . 66 D4 31 0N 65 0 E
Qapān, *Iran* . . . . 71 B7 37 40N 55 47 E
Qapshaghay,
  Kazakhstan . . . . . . 52 E8 43 51N 77 14 E
Qaqortoq, *Greenland* . 101 B6 60 43N 46 0W
Qâra, *Egypt* . . . . 80 B2 29 38N 26 30 E
Qara Qash →, *China* . . 69 B8 35 0N 78 30 E
Qarabutaq, *Kazakhstan* 52 E7 49 59N 60 14 E
Qaraçala, *Azerbaijan* . 35 L9 39 45N 48 53 E
Qaraghandy,
  Kazakhstan . . . . . . 52 E8 49 50N 73 10 E
Qaraghayly, *Kazakhstan* 52 E8 49 26N 76 0 E
Qārah, *Si. Arabia* . . . . 70 D4 29 55N 40 3 E
Qarataū, *Kazakhstan* . 52 E8 43 10N 70 28 E
Qarataū, *Kazakhstan* . 52 E7 43 30N 69 30 E
Qardho = Gardo,
  Somali Rep. . . . . . . 75 F4 9 30N 49 6 E
Qardud, *Sudan* . . . . . . 81 E2 10 20N 29 56 E
Qareh →, *Iran* . . . . 70 B5 39 25N 47 22 E
Qareh Tekān, *Iran* . . . 71 B6 36 38N 49 29 E
Qarqan He →, *China* . . 60 C3 39 30N 88 30 E
Qarqaraly, *Kazakhstan* 52 E8 49 26N 75 30 E
Qarrasa, *Sudan* . . . . . 81 E3 14 38N 32 5 E
Qarshi, *Uzbekistan* . . . 52 F7 38 53N 65 48 E
Qartabā, *Lebanon* . . . 74 A4 34 4N 35 50 E
Qaryat al Gharab, *Iraq* 70 D5 31 27N 44 48 E
Qaryat al 'Ulyā,
  Si. Arabia . . . . 70 E5 27 33N 47 42 E
Qasr 'Amra, *Jordan* . . 70 D3 31 48N 36 35 E
Qaşr-e Qand, *Iran* . . . 71 E9 26 15N 60 45 E
Qasr Farâfra, *Egypt* . . 80 B2 27 0N 28 1 E
Qatanā, *Syria* . . . . 74 B5 33 26N 36 4 E
Qatar ■, *Asia* . . . . 71 E6 25 30N 51 15 E
Qatlīsh, *Iran* . . . . 71 B8 37 50N 57 19 E
Qattâra, *Egypt* . . . . . . 80 A2 30 12N 27 3 E
Qattâra, Munkhafed el,
  Egypt . . . . 80 B2 29 30N 27 30 E
Qattâra Depression =
  Qattâra, Munkhafed
  el, *Egypt* . . . . 80 B2 29 30N 27 30 E
Qawām al Ḥamzah = Al
  Ḥamzah, *Iraq* . . . . . 70 D5 31 43N 44 58 E
Qāyen, *Iran* . . . . 71 C8 33 40N 59 10 E
Qazaqstan =
  Kazakhstan ■, *Asia* . 52 E7 50 0N 70 0 E
Qazımämmäd,
  Azerbaijan . . . . 35 K9 40 3N 49 0 E
Qazvin, *Iran* . . . . 71 B6 36 15N 50 0 E
Qazvin □, *Iran* . . . . . . 71 B6 36 20N 50 0 E
Qeissan, *Sudan* . . . . . 81 E3 11 4N 34 40 E
Qena, *Egypt* . . . . 80 B3 26 10N 32 43 E
Qena, W. →, *Egypt* . . . 80 B3 26 12N 32 44 E
Qeqertarsuaq,
  Greenland 101 B5 69 45N 53 0W
Qeqertarsuaq,
  Greenland 101 B14 69 15N 53 38W
Qeshlāq, *Iran* . . . . 70 C5 34 55N 46 28 E
Qeshm, *Iran* . . . . 71 E8 26 55N 56 10 E
Qeys, *Iran* . . . . 71 E7 26 32N 53 58 E
Qezel Owzen →, *Iran* . 71 B6 36 45N 49 22 E
Qezi'ot, *Israel* . . . . . . 74 E3 30 52N 34 26 E
Qi Xian, *China* . . . . . . 56 G8 34 40N 114 48 E
Qian Gorlos, *China* . . . 57 B13 45 5N 124 42 E
Qian Xian, *China* . . . . 56 G5 34 31N 108 15 E
Qiancheng, *China* . . . . 58 D7 27 12N 109 50 E
Qianjiang,
  Guangxi Zhuangzu,
  China . . . . 58 F7 23 38N 108 58 E
Qianjiang, *Hubei, China* 59 B9 30 24N 112 55 E
Qianjiang, *Sichuan,*
  China . . . . 58 C7 29 33N 108 47 E
Qianshan, *China* . . . . . 59 B11 30 37N 116 35 E
Qianwei, *China* . . . . . 58 C4 29 13N 103 56 E
Qianxi, *China* . . . . 58 D6 27 3N 106 3 E
Qianyang, *Hunan, China* 59 D8 27 18N 110 10 E
Qianyang, *Shaanxi,*
  China . . . . 56 G4 34 40N 107 8 E
Qianyang, *Zhejiang,*
  China . . . . 59 B12 30 11N 119 25 E
Qiaojia, *China* . . . . . . 58 D4 26 56N 102 58 E
Qichun, *China* . . . . . . 59 B10 30 18N 115 25 E
Qidong, *Hunan, China* 59 D9 26 49N 112 7 E
Qidong, *Jiangsu, China* 59 B13 31 48N 121 38 E
Qijiang, *China* . . . . . . 58 C6 28 57N 106 35 E
Qikiqtarjuaq, *Canada* . 101 B13 67 33N 63 0W
Qila Safed, *Pakistan* . . 66 E2 29 0N 61 30 E
Qila Saifullāh, *Pakistan* 68 D3 30 45N 68 17 E
Qilian Shan, *China* . . . 60 C4 38 30N 96 0 E
Qimen, *China* . . . . 59 C11 29 50N 117 42 E
Qin He →, *China* . . . . 56 G7 35 1N 113 22 E
Qin Jiang →,
  Guangxi Zhuangzu,
  China . . . . 58 F7 21 53N 108 35 E
Qin Jiang →, *Jiangxi,*
  China . . . . 59 D10 26 15N 115 55 E
Qin Ling = Qinling
  Shandi, *China* . . . . . 56 H5 33 50N 108 10 E
Qin'an, *China* . . . . 56 G3 34 48N 105 40 E
Qing Xian, *China* . . . . 56 E9 38 35N 116 45 E
Qingcheng, *China* . . . . 57 F9 37 15N 117 40 E
Qingdao, *China* . . . . . 57 F11 36 5N 120 20 E
Qingfeng, *China* . . . . . 56 G8 35 52N 115 8 E
Qinghai □, *China* . . . . 60 C4 36 0N 98 0 E
Qinghai Hu, *China* . . . 60 C5 36 40N 100 10 E
Qinghecheng, *China* . . 57 D13 41 28N 124 15 E
Qinghemen, *China* . . . 57 D11 41 48N 121 25 E
Qingjian, *China* . . . . . 56 F6 37 8N 110 8 E
Qingjiang = Huaiyin,
  China . . . . 57 H10 33 30N 119 2 E
Qingliu, *China* . . . . . . 59 D11 26 11N 116 48 E
Qinglong, *China* . . . . . 58 E5 25 49N 105 12 E
Qingping, *China* . . . . . 58 D6 26 11N 107 47 E
Qingpu, *China* . . . . . . 59 B13 31 10N 121 6 E
Qingshui, *China* . . . . . 56 G4 34 48N 106 8 E
Qingshuihe, *China* . . . 56 E6 39 55N 111 35 E
Qingtian, *China* . . . . . 59 C13 28 12N 120 15 E
Qingtongxia Shuiku,
  China . . . . 56 F3 37 50N 105 58 E
Qingxi, *China* . . . . 58 D7 26 51N 108 43 E
Qingxu, *China* . . . . . . 56 F7 37 34N 112 22 E
Qingyang, *Anhui, China* 59 B11 30 38N 117 50 E
Qingyang, *Gansu, China* 56 F4 36 2N 107 55 E
Qingyi Jiang →, *China* . 58 C4 29 32N 103 44 E
Qingyuan, *Guangdong,*
  China . . . . 59 F9 23 40N 112 59 E
Qingyuan, *Liaoning,*
  China . . . . 57 C13 42 10N 124 55 E

Qingyuan, *Zhejiang,*
  China . . . . 59 D12 27 36N 119 3 E
Qingyun, *China* . . . . . . 57 F9 37 45N 117 20 E
Qingzhen, *China* . . . . . 58 D6 26 31N 106 25 E
Qinhuangdao, *China* . . 57 E10 39 56N 119 30 E
Qinling Shandi, *China* . 56 H5 33 50N 108 10 E
Qinshui, *China* . . . . . . 56 G7 35 40N 112 8 E
Qinyang = Jiyuan, *China* 56 G7 35 7N 112 57 E
Qinyuan, *China* . . . . . . 56 F7 36 29N 112 20 E
Qinzhou, *China* . . . . . . 58 G7 21 58N 108 38 E
Qionghai, *China* . . . . . 64 C8 19 15N 110 26 E
Qionglai, *China* . . . . . 58 B4 30 25N 103 31 E
Qionglai Shan, *China* . 58 B4 30 0N 102 30 E
Qiongzhou Haixia,
  China . . . . 64 B8 20 10N 110 15 E
Qiqihar, *China* . . . . . . 53 E13 47 26N 124 0 E
Qiraîya, W. →, *Egypt* . 74 E3 30 27N 34 0 E
Qiryat Ata, *Israel* . . . . 74 C4 32 47N 35 6 E
Qiryat Gat, *Israel* . . . . 74 D3 31 32N 34 46 E
Qiryat Mal'akhi, *Israel* 74 D3 31 44N 34 44 E
Qiryat Shemona, *Israel* 74 B4 33 13N 35 35 E
Qiryat Yam, *Israel* . . . 74 C4 32 51N 35 4 E
Qishan, *China* . . . . . . 56 G4 34 25N 107 38 E
Qitai, *China* . . . . 60 B3 44 2N 89 35 E
Qiubei, *China* . . . . 58 E5 24 2N 104 12 E
Qixia, *China* . . . . 57 F11 37 17N 120 52 E
Qiyang, *China* . . . . 59 D8 26 35N 111 50 E
Qizilağac Körfäzi,
  Azerbaijan . . . . 71 B6 39 9N 49 0 E
Qojūr, *Iran* . . . . 70 B5 36 12N 47 55 E
Qom, *Iran* . . . . 71 C6 34 40N 51 0 E
Qom □, *Iran* . . . . 71 C6 34 40N 51 0 E
Qomolangma Feng =
  Everest, Mt., *Nepal* . 69 E12 28 5N 86 58 E
Qomsheh, *Iran* . . . . . . 71 D6 32 0N 51 55 E
Qoraqalpoghistan □,
  Uzbekistan . . . . 52 E6 43 0N 58 0 E
Qorveh, *Iran* . . . . 73 E12 35 10N 47 48 E
Qostanay, *Kazakhstan* 52 D7 53 10N 63 35 E
Qotūr, *Iran* . . . . 73 C11 38 28N 44 25 E
Qu Jiang →, *China* . . . 58 C6 30 1N 106 24 E
Qu Xian, *China* . . . . . . 58 B6 30 48N 106 58 E
Quabbin Reservoir,
  U.S.A. 117 D12 42 20N 72 20W
Quairading, *Australia* . 93 F2 32 0 S 117 21 E
Quakenbrück, *Germany* 24 C3 52 41N 7 57 E
Quakertown, *U.S.A.* . . 117 F9 40 26N 75 21W
Qualicum Beach,
  Canada 102 D4 49 22N 124 26W
Quambatook, *Australia* 95 F3 35 49 S 143 34 E
Quambone, *Australia* . 95 E4 30 57 S 147 53 E
Quamby, *Australia* . . . 94 C3 20 22 S 140 17 E
Quan Long = Ca Mau,
  Vietnam . . . . 65 H5 9 7N 105 8 E
Quanah, *U.S.A.* 113 H5 34 18N 99 44W
Quang Ngai, *Vietnam* . 64 E7 15 13N 108 58 E
Quang Tri, *Vietnam* . . 64 D6 16 45N 107 13 E
Quang Yen, *Vietnam* . 58 G6 20 56N 106 52 E
Quannan, *China* . . . . . 59 E10 24 55N 114 33 E
Quantock Hills, *U.K.* . . 15 F4 51 8N 3 10W
Quanzhou, *Fujian,*
  China . . . . 59 E12 24 55N 118 34 E
Quanzhou,
  Guangxi Zhuangzu,
  China . . . . 59 E8 25 57N 111 5 E
Qu'Appelle, *Canada* . . 103 C8 50 33N 103 53W
Quaqtaq, *Canada* 101 B13 60 55N 69 40W
Quaraí, *Brazil* . . . . 126 C4 30 15 S 56 20W
Quarré-les-Tombes,
  France . . . . 19 E11 47 21N 4 0 E
Quarteira, *Portugal* . . 37 H2 37 4N 8 6W
Quartu Sant'Elena, *Italy* 42 C2 39 15N 9 10 E
Quartzsite, *U.S.A.* . . . 111 M12 33 40N 114 13W
Quatsino Sd., *Canada* . 102 C3 50 25N 127 58W
Quba, *Azerbaijan* . . . . 35 K9 41 21N 48 32 E
Qūchān, *Iran* . . . . 71 B8 37 10N 58 27 E
Queanbeyan, *Australia* 95 F4 35 17 S 149 14 E
Québec, *Canada* 105 C5 46 52N 71 13W
Québec □, *Canada* . . . 105 C6 48 0N 74 0W
Quebrada del
  Condorito △,
  Argentina . . . . 126 C3 31 49 S 64 40W
Quedlinburg, *Germany* 24 D7 51 47N 11 8 E
Queen Alexandra Ra.,
  Antarctica . . . . 5 E11 85 0 S 170 0 E
Queen Charlotte City,
  Canada 102 C2 53 15N 132 2W
Queen Charlotte Is.,
  Canada 102 C2 53 20N 132 10W
Queen Charlotte Sd.,
  Canada 102 C3 51 0N 128 0W
Queen Charlotte Strait,
  Canada 102 C3 50 45N 127 10W
Queen Elizabeth △,
  U.K. 13 E4 56 7N 4 30W
Queen Elizabeth △,
  Uganda . . . . 86 C3 0 0 30 0 E
Queen Elizabeth Is.,
  Canada 98 B10 76 0N 95 0W
Queen Mary Land,
  Antarctica . . . . 5 D7 70 0 S 95 0 E
Queen Maud G.,
  Canada 100 B9 68 15N 102 30W
Queen Maud Land =
  Dronning Maud Land,
  Antarctica . . . . 5 D3 72 30 S 12 0 E
Queen Maud Mts.,
  Antarctica . . . . 5 E13 86 0 S 160 0W
Queens Chan., *Australia* 92 B4 15 0 S 129 30 E
Queenscliff, *Australia* . 95 F3 38 16 S 144 39 E
Queensland □, *Australia* 94 C3 22 0 S 142 0 E
Queenstown, *Australia* 95 G4 42 4 S 145 35 E
Queenstown, *N.Z.* . . . 91 L2 45 1 S 168 40 E
Queenstown, *Singapore* 65 d 1 18N 103 48 E
Queenstown, *S. Africa* 88 E4 31 52 S 26 52 E
Queets, *U.S.A.* 110 C2 47 32N 124 20W
Queguay Grande →,
  Uruguay . . . . 126 C4 32 9 S 58 9W
Queimadas, *Brazil* . . . 125 F11 11 0 S 39 38W
Quelimane, *Mozam.* . . 87 F4 17 53 S 36 58 E
Quellón, *Chile* . . . . . . 128 E2 43 7 S 73 37W
Quelpart = Cheju do,
  S. Korea . . . . 57 H14 33 29N 126 34 E
Queluz, *Portugal* 37 G1 38 43N 9 15W
Quemado, *N. Mex.,*
  U.S.A. 109 J9 34 20N 108 30W
Quemado, *Tex., U.S.A.* 113 L4 28 58N 100 35W
Quemoy = Chinmen,
  Taiwan . . . . 59 E13 24 26N 118 19 E
Quemú-Quemú,
  Argentina . . . . 126 D3 36 3 S 63 36W
Quequén, *Argentina* . . 126 D4 38 30 S 58 30W
Querétaro, *Mexico* . . . 118 C4 20 36N 100 23W
Querétaro □, *Mexico* . 118 C5 20 30N 100 0W
Querfurt, *Germany* . . . 24 D7 51 22N 11 35 E
Quérigut, *France* . . . . 20 F6 42 42N 2 6 E
Querqueville, *France* . 18 C5 49 40N 1 42W

Quesada, *Spain* 37 H7 37 51N 3 4W
Queshan, *China* . . . . . 56 H8 32 55N 114 2 E
Quesnel, *Canada* 102 C4 53 0N 122 30W
Quesnel →, *Canada* . . 102 C4 52 58N 122 29W
Quesnel L., *Canada* . . 102 C4 52 30N 121 20W
Questa, *U.S.A.* 109 H11 36 42N 105 36W
Questembert, *France* . 18 E4 47 40N 2 28W
Quetico △, *Canada* . . . 104 C1 48 30N 91 45W
Quetta, *Pakistan* . . . . 68 D2 30 15N 66 55 E
Queyras →, *France* . . 21 D10 44 45N 6 50 E
Quezaltenango,
  Guatemala 120 D1 14 50N 91 30W
Quezon City, *Phil.* . . . 61 D4 14 38N 121 0 E
Qufār, *Si. Arabia* . . . . 70 E4 27 26N 41 37 E
Qui Nhon, *Vietnam* . . 64 F7 13 40N 109 13 E
Quibaxe, *Angola* . . . . 84 F2 8 24 S 14 27 E
Quibdo, *Colombia* . . . 124 B3 5 42N 76 40W
Quiberon, *France* 18 E3 47 29N 3 9W
Quiberon, Presqu'île de,
  France 18 E3 47 30N 3 8W
Quickborn, *Germany* . 24 B5 53 42N 9 52 E
Quiet L., *Canada* 102 A2 61 5N 133 5W
Quiindy, *Paraguay* . . . 126 B4 25 58 S 57 14W
Quila, *Mexico* 118 C3 24 23N 107 13W
Quilán, C., *Chile* . . . . 128 E2 43 15 S 74 30W
Quilcene, *U.S.A.* 110 C4 47 49N 122 53W
Quilimarí, *Chile* . . . . . 126 C1 32 5 S 71 30W
Quilino, *Argentina* . . . 126 C3 30 14 S 64 29W
Quill Lakes, *Canada* . . 103 C8 51 55N 104 13W
Quillabamba, *Peru* . . . 124 F4 12 50 S 72 50W
Quillagua, *Chile* . . . . . 126 A2 21 40 S 69 40W
Quillaicillo, *Chile* . . . . 126 C1 31 17 S 71 40W
Quillan, *France* . . . . . 20 F6 42 53N 2 10 E
Quillota, *Chile* . . . . . . 126 C1 32 54 S 71 16W
Quilmes, *Argentina* . . 126 C4 34 43 S 58 15W
Quilon, *India* . . . . 66 Q10 8 50N 76 38 E
Quilpie, *Australia* . . . . 95 D3 26 35 S 144 11 E
Quilpué, *Chile* . . . . . . 126 C1 33 5 S 71 33W
Quilua, *Mozam.* . . . . . 87 F4 16 17 S 39 54 E
Quimilí, *Argentina* . . . 126 B3 27 40 S 62 30W
Quimper, *France* 18 E2 48 0N 4 9W
Quimperlé, *France* . . . 18 E3 47 53N 3 33W
Quinault →, *U.S.A.* . . . 110 C2 47 21N 124 18W
Quincy, *Calif., U.S.A.* . 110 F6 39 56N 120 57W
Quincy, *Fla., U.S.A.* . . 115 K3 30 35N 84 34W
Quincy, *Ill., U.S.A.* . . . 112 F9 39 56N 91 23W
Quincy, *Mass., U.S.A.* . 117 D14 42 15N 71 0W
Quincy, *Wash., U.S.A.* 108 C4 47 22N 119 56W
Quines, *Argentina* . . . 126 C2 32 13 S 65 48W
Quinga, *Mozam.* . . . . 87 F5 15 49 S 40 15 E
Quingey, *France* . . . . 19 E12 47 7N 5 52 E
Quintana de la Serena,
  Spain 37 G5 38 45N 5 40W
Quintana Roo □,
  Mexico 119 D7 19 0N 88 0W
Quintanar de la Orden,
  Spain 37 F7 39 36N 3 5W
Quintanar de la Sierra,
  Spain 38 D2 41 57N 2 55W
Quintanar del Rey,
  Spain 39 F3 39 21N 1 56W
Quinte West, *Canada* . 116 B7 44 10N 77 34W
Quintero, *Chile* . . . . . 126 C1 32 45 S 71 30W
Quintin, *France* 18 D4 48 26N 2 56W
Quinto, *Spain* 38 D4 41 25N 0 32W
Quípar →, *Spain* 39 G3 38 15N 1 40W
Quirihue, *Chile* . . . . . 126 D1 36 15 S 72 35W
Quirindi, *Australia* . . . 95 E5 31 28 S 150 40 E
Quirinópolis, *Brazil* . . 125 G8 18 32 S 50 30W
Quiroga, *Spain* 36 C3 42 28N 7 18W
Quissac, *France* . . . . 21 E8 43 55N 4 0 E
Quissanga, *Mozam.* . . 87 E5 12 24 S 40 28 E
Quissico, *Mozam.* . . . 89 C5 24 42 S 34 44 E
Quitilipi, *Argentina* . . 126 B3 26 50 S 60 13W
Quitman, *U.S.A.* 115 K4 30 47N 83 34W
Quito, *Ecuador* . . . . . 124 D3 0 15 S 78 35W
Quixadá, *Brazil* . . . . . 125 D11 4 55 S 39 0W
Quixaxe, *Mozam.* . . . 87 F5 15 17 S 40 4 E
Qujing, *China* . . . . . . 58 E4 25 32N 103 41 E
Qulan, *Kazakhstan* . . 52 E8 42 55N 72 43 E
Qul'ān, Jazā'ir, *Egypt* . 70 E2 24 22N 35 31 E
Qumbu, *S. Africa* . . . . 89 E4 31 10 S 28 48 E
Quneitra, *Syria* . . . . . 74 B4 33 7N 35 48 E
Qünghirot, *Uzbekistan* 52 E6 43 6N 58 54 E
Qu'nyido, *China* . . . . 58 B2 31 15N 98 6 E
Quoin I., *Australia* . . . 92 B4 14 54 S 129 32 E
Quoin Pt., *S. Africa* . . 88 E2 34 46 S 19 37 E
Quorn, *Australia* . . . . 95 E2 32 25 S 138 5 E
Qŭqon, *Uzbekistan* . . 52 E8 40 30N 70 57 E
Qurein, *Sudan* . . . . . . 81 E3 13 30N 34 50 E
Qurnat as Sawdā',
  Lebanon . . . . 74 A5 34 18N 36 6 E
Qûs, *Egypt* . . . . 80 B3 25 55N 32 50 E
Qusar, *Azerbaijan* . . . 35 K9 41 25N 48 26 E
Quşaybā', *Si. Arabia* . 70 E4 26 53N 43 35 E
Quşaybah, *Iraq* . . . . . 70 C4 34 24N 40 59 E
Quseir, *Egypt* . . . . . . 70 E2 26 7N 34 16 E
Qûshchī, *Iran* . . . . . . 70 B5 37 59N 45 3 E
Quthing, *Lesotho* . . . . 89 E4 30 25 S 27 36 E
Qūṭīābād, *Iran* . . . . . . 71 C6 35 47N 48 30 E
Quwo, *China* . . . . 56 G6 35 38N 111 25 E
Quyang, *China* . . . . . . 56 E8 38 35N 114 40 E
Quynh Nhai, *Vietnam* . 64 B4 21 49N 103 33 E
Quyon, *Canada* 117 A8 45 31N 76 14W
Quzhou, *China* . . . . . 59 C12 28 57N 118 54 E
Quzi, *China* . . . . 56 F4 36 20N 107 20 E
Qvareli, *Georgia* . . . . 35 K7 41 57N 45 47 E
Qyzylorda, *Kazakhstan* 52 E7 44 48N 65 28 E

R

Ra, Ko, *Thailand* . . . . 65 H2 9 13N 98 16 E
Raab, *Austria* . . . . . . 26 C6 48 21N 13 39 E
Raahe, *Finland* . . . . . 8 D21 64 40N 24 28 E
Raalte, *Neths.* . . . . . . 17 B6 52 23N 6 16 E
Raasay, *U.K.* 13 D2 57 25N 6 4W
Raasay, Sd. of, *U.K.* . . 13 D2 57 30N 6 8W
Rab, *Croatia* . . . . 41 D11 44 45N 14 45 E
Raba, *Indonesia* . . . . 63 F5 8 36 S 118 55 E
Rába →, *Hungary* . . . 28 C2 47 38N 17 38 E
Rabā →, *Poland* . . . . . 31 H7 50 8N 20 30 E
Rabaçal →, *Portugal* . 36 D3 41 30N 7 12W
Rabah, *Nigeria* . . . . . 83 C6 13 5N 5 30 E
Rabai, *Kenya* . . . . 86 C4 3 50 S 39 31 E
Rabak, *Sudan* . . . . . . 81 E3 13 10N 32 44 E
Rabastens, *France* . . 20 E5 43 50N 1 43 E
Rabastens-de-Bigorre,
  France . . . . 20 E4 43 23N 0 9 E
Rabat = Victoria, *Malta* 49 C1 36 3N 14 14 E
Rabat, *Malta* . . . . 49 D1 35 53N 14 24 E
Rabat, *Morocco* 78 B4 34 2N 6 48W
Rabaul, *Papua N. G.* . 96 H7 4 24 S 152 18 E
Rābigh, *Si. Arabia* . . . 75 C2 22 50N 39 5 E
Rabka, *Poland* . . . . . . 31 J6 49 37N 19 59 E
Râbniţa, *Moldova* . . . 29 C14 47 45N 29 0 E

Rābor, *Iran* . . . . 71 D8 29 17N 56 55 E
Rača, *Serbia & M.* . . . 44 B4 44 14N 21 0 E
Răcăciuni, *Romania* . . 29 D11 46 20N 26 59 E
Răcăşdia, *Romania* . . 28 F6 45 7N 21 38 E
Racconigi, *Italy* . . . . . 40 D4 44 46N 7 46 E
Race, C., *Canada* 105 C9 46 40N 53 5W
Rach Gia, *Vietnam* . . 65 G5 10 5N 105 5 E
Rachid, *Mauritania* . . 82 B2 18 45N 11 35W
Raciąż, *Poland* . . . . . . 31 F7 52 46N 20 10 E
Racibórz, *Poland* . . . . 31 H5 50 7N 18 18 E
Racichy, *Belarus* . . . . 30 E10 53 54N 23 42 E
Racine, *U.S.A.* 114 D2 42 41N 87 51W
Rackerby, *U.S.A.* 110 F5 39 26N 121 22W
Radama, Nosy, *Madag.* 89 A8 14 0 S 47 47 E
Radama, Saikanosy,
  Madag. . . . . 89 A8 14 16 S 47 53 E
Radan, *Serbia & M.* . . 44 D5 42 59N 21 29 E
Rădăuţi, *Romania* . . . 29 C10 47 50N 25 59 E
Rădăuţi-Prut, *Romania* 29 B11 48 14N 26 5 E
Radbuza →, *Czech Rep.* 26 B6 49 45N 13 22 E
Radcliff, *U.S.A.* 114 G3 37 51N 85 57W
Radeberg, *Germany* . . 24 D9 51 7N 13 55 E
Radebeul, *Germany* . . 24 D9 51 6N 13 39 E
Radeče, *Slovenia* . . . . 41 B12 46 5N 15 14 E
Radekhiv, *Ukraine* . . . 33 G3 50 25N 24 32 E
Radekhov = Radekhiv,
  Ukraine . . . . 33 G3 50 25N 24 32 E
Radenthein, *Austria* . . 26 E6 46 48N 13 43 E
Radew →, *Poland* . . . 30 D2 54 2N 15 52 E
Radford, *U.S.A.* 114 G5 37 8N 80 34W
Radhanpur, *India* . . . 68 H4 23 50N 71 38 E
Radhwa, Jabal,
  Si. Arabia . . . . 70 E3 24 34N 38 18 E
Radika →, *Macedonia* . 44 E4 41 38N 20 37 E
Radisson, *Qué., Canada* 104 B4 53 47N 77 37W
Radisson, *Sask., Canada* 103 C7 52 30N 107 20W
Radium Hot Springs,
  Canada 102 C5 50 35N 116 2W
Radlje ob Dravi,
  Slovenia . . . . 41 B12 46 38N 15 13 E
Radnevo, *Bulgaria* . . . 45 D9 42 17N 25 58 E
Radnice, *Czech Rep.* . 26 B6 49 51N 13 35 E
Radnor Forest, *U.K.* . . 15 E4 52 17N 3 10W
Radolfzell, *Germany* . 25 H4 47 39N 8 59 E
Radom, *Poland* . . . . . 31 G8 51 23N 21 12 E
Radomir, *Bulgaria* . . . 44 D7 42 37N 22 59 E
Radomka →, *Poland* . 31 G8 51 43N 21 28 E
Radomsko, *Poland* . . 31 G6 51 5N 19 28 E
Radomyshl, *Ukraine* . 33 G5 50 30N 29 12 E
Radomyśl Wielki,
  Poland . . . . 31 H8 50 14N 21 15 E
Radoszyce, *Poland* . . 31 G7 51 4N 20 15 E
Radoviš, *Macedonia* . 44 E6 41 38N 22 28 E
Radovljica, *Slovenia* . 41 B11 46 22N 14 12 E
Radstadt, *Austria* . . . 26 D6 47 24N 13 28 E
Radstock, C., *Australia* 95 E1 33 12 S 134 20 E
Răducăneni, *Romania* 29 D12 46 58N 27 54 E
Raduša, *Macedonia* . . 44 E5 42 7N 21 15 E
Radvanichy, *Belarus* . 31 F11 52 1N 24 0 E
Radviliškis, *Lithuania* . 9 J20 55 49N 23 33 E
Radville, *Canada* 103 D8 49 30N 104 15W
Radwá, J., *Si. Arabia* . 80 C4 24 34N 38 18 E
Radymno, *Poland* . . . 31 J9 49 59N 22 52 E
Radzanów, *Poland* . . 31 F7 52 56N 20 8 E
Radziejów, *Poland* . . 31 F5 52 40N 18 30 E
Radzyń Chełmiński,
  Poland . . . . 30 E5 53 28N 18 55 E
Radzyń Podlaski,
  Poland . . . . 31 G9 51 47N 22 37 E
Rae, *Canada* 102 A5 62 50N 116 3W
Rae Bareli, *India* . . . . 69 F9 26 18N 81 20 E
Rae Isthmus, *Canada* . 101 B11 66 40N 87 30W
Raeren, *Belgium* . . . . 17 D6 50 41N 6 7 E
Raeside, L., *Australia* . 93 E3 29 20 S 122 0 E
Raetihi, *N.Z.* . . . . 91 H5 39 25 S 175 17 E
Rafaela, *Argentina* . . 126 C3 31 10 S 61 30W
Rafah, *Gaza Strip* . . . 74 D3 31 18N 34 14 E
Rafai, *C.A.R.* . . . . 86 B1 4 59N 23 58 E
Raffadali, *Italy* . . . . . 42 E6 37 24N 13 32 E
Raffili, *Sudan* . . . . . . 81 F2 6 50N 28 0 E
Rafḥā, *Si. Arabia* . . . 70 D4 29 35N 43 35 E
Rafsanjān, *Iran* . . . . . 71 D8 30 30N 56 5 E
Raft Pt., *Australia* . . . 92 C3 16 4 S 124 26 E
Rāgā, *Sudan* . . . . 81 F2 8 28N 25 41 E
Ragachow, *Belarus* . . 33 F6 53 8N 30 5 E
Ragag, *Sudan* . . . . . . 81 E1 10 59N 24 40 E
Ragama, *Sri Lanka* . . 66 R11 7 0N 79 50 E
Ragged, Mt., *Australia* 93 F3 33 27 S 123 25 E
Ragged Pt., *Barbados* . 121 g 13 10N 59 26W
Raghunathpalli, *India* . 69 H11 22 14N 84 48 E
Raghunathpur, *India* . 69 H12 23 33N 86 40 E
Raglan, *N.Z.* . . . . 91 G5 37 55 S 174 55 E
Ragusa, *Italy* . . . . 43 F7 36 55N 14 44 E
Raha, *Indonesia* . . . . 63 E6 4 55 S 123 0 E
Rahad, Nahr ed →,
  Sudan . . . . 81 E3 14 28N 33 31 E
Rahaeng = Tak,
  Thailand . . . . 64 D2 16 52N 99 8 E
Rahatgarh, *India* . . . . 69 H8 23 47N 78 22 E
Rahden, *Germany* . . . 24 C4 52 26N 8 36 E
Raheita, *Eritrea* . . . . 81 E5 12 46N 43 4 E
Rahimyar Khan,
  Pakistan . . . . 68 E4 28 30N 70 25 E
Rāhjerd, *Iran* . . . . . . 71 C6 34 22N 50 22 E
Rahole △, *Kenya* . . . . 86 B4 0 5N 38 57 E
Rahon, *India* . . . . 68 D7 31 3N 76 7 E
Raichur, *India* . . . . . . 66 L10 16 10N 77 20 E
Raiganj, *India* . . . . . . 69 G13 25 37N 88 10 E
Raigarh, *India* . . . . . . 67 J13 21 56N 83 25 E
Raijua, *Indonesia* . . . 63 F6 10 37 S 121 36 E
Raikot, *India* . . . . 68 D7 30 41N 75 42 E
Railton, *Australia* . . . 95 G4 41 25 S 146 28 E
Rainbow Bridge △,
  U.S.A. 109 H8 37 5N 110 58W
Rainbow Lake, *Canada* 102 B5 58 30N 119 23W
Rainier, *U.S.A.* 110 D4 46 53N 122 41W
Rainier, Mt., *U.S.A.* . . 110 D5 46 52N 121 46W
Rainy L., *Canada* 103 D10 48 42N 93 10W
Rainy River, *Canada* . 103 D10 48 43N 94 29W
Raippaluoto, *Finland* . 8 E19 63 13N 21 14 E
Raipur, *India* . . . . 67 J12 21 17N 81 45 E
Ra'is, *Si. Arabia* . . . . 80 C4 23 33N 38 43 E
Raisen, *India* . . . . . . 68 H8 23 20N 77 48 E
Raisio, *Finland* . . . . . 9 F20 60 28N 22 11 E
Raj Nandgaon, *India* . 67 J12 21 5N 81 5 E
Raj Nilgiri, *India* . . . . 69 J12 21 28N 86 46 E
Raja, Ujung, *Indonesia* 62 D1 3 40N 96 25 E
Raja Ampat, Kepulauan,
  Indonesia . . . . 63 E8 0 30 S 130 0 E
Rajahmundry, *India* . . 67 L12 17 1N 81 48 E
Rajang →, *Malaysia* . . 62 D4 2 30N 112 0 E
Rajanpur, *Pakistan* . . 68 E4 29 6N 70 19 E
Rajapalaiyam, *India* . . 66 Q10 9 25N 77 35 E
Rajasthan □, *India* . . . 68 F5 26 45N 73 30 E
Rajasthan Canal =
  Indira Gandhi Canal,
  India . . . . 68 F5 28 0N 72 0 E

Rajauri, *India* .... 69 C6 33 25N 74 21 E
Rajgarh, *Mad. P., India* 68 G7 24 2N 76 45 E
Rajgarh, *Raj., India* ... 68 E7 27 14N 76 38 E
Rajgarh, *Raj., India* ... 68 E6 28 40N 75 25 E
Rajgir, *India* .... 69 G11 25 2N 85 25 E
Rajgród, *Poland* .... 30 E9 53 42N 22 42 E
Rajkot, *India* .... 68 H4 22 15N 70 56 E
Rajmahal Hills, *India* .. 69 G12 24 30N 87 30 E
Rajpipla, *India* .... 66 J8 21 50N 73 30 E
Rajpur, *India* .... 68 H6 22 18N 74 21 E
Rajpura, *India* .... 68 D7 30 25N 76 32 E
Rajshahi, *Bangla.* ...... 67 G16 24 22N 88 39 E
Rajshahi □, *Bangla.* .... 69 G13 25 0N 89 0 E
Rajula, *India* .... 68 J4 21 3N 71 26 E
Rakaia, *N.Z.* .... 91 K4 43 45 S 172 1 E
Rakaia →, *N.Z.* .... 91 K4 43 36 S 172 15 E
Rakan, Ra's, *Qatar* ..... 71 E6 26 10N 51 20 E
Rakaposhi, *Pakistan* .... 69 A6 36 10N 74 25 E
Rakata, Pulau, *Indonesia* 62 F3 6 10 S 105 20 E
Rakhiv, *Ukraine* .... 29 B9 48 3N 24 12 E
Rakhni, *Pakistan* .... 68 D3 30 4N 69 56 E
Rakhni →, *Pakistan* ..... 68 E3 29 31N 69 36 E
Rakhny-Lisovi, *Ukraine* . 29 B13 48 47N 28 29 E
Rakitnoye, *Russia* ...... 54 B7 45 36N 134 17 E
Rakitovo, *Bulgaria* ..... 45 E8 41 59N 24 5 E
Rakiura △, *N.Z.* .... 91 M1 47 0 S 167 50 E
Rakoniewice, *Poland* .... 31 F3 52 10N 16 16 E
Rakops, *Botswana* .... 88 C3 21 1 S 24 28 E
Rakovica, *Croatia* ...... 41 D12 44 59N 15 38 E
Rakovník, *Czech Rep.* ... 26 A6 50 6N 13 42 E
Rakovski, *Bulgaria* ..... 45 D8 42 21N 24 57 E
Rakvere, *Estonia* .... 9 G22 59 20N 26 25 E
Raleigh, *U.S.A.* 115 H6 35 47N 78 39W
Ralja, *Serbia & M.* ..... 44 B4 44 33N 20 34 E
Ralls, *U.S.A.* 113 J4 33 41N 101 24W
Ralston, *U.S.A.* 116 E8 41 30N 76 57W
Ram →, *Canada* 102 A4 62 1N 123 41W
Rām Allāh, *West Bank* ... 74 D4 31 55N 35 10 E
Rama, *Nic.* 120 D3 12 9N 84 15W
Ramacca, *Italy* .... 43 E7 37 23N 14 42 E
Ramakona, *India* .... 69 J8 21 43N 78 50 E
Ramales de la Victoria,
  Spain 36 B7 43 15N 3 28W
Rāmallāh = Rām Allāh,
  West Bank .... 74 D4 31 55N 35 10 E
Raman, *Thailand* .... 65 J3 6 29N 101 18 E
Ramanathapuram, *India* .. 66 Q11 9 25N 78 55 E
Ramanetaka, B. de,
  Madag. .... 89 A8 14 13 S 47 52 E
Ramanujganj, *India* ..... 69 H10 23 48N 83 42 E
Ramat Gan, *Israel* ...... 74 C3 32 4N 34 48 E
Ramatlhabama,
  S. Africa .... 88 D4 25 37 S 25 33 E
Ramban, *India* .... 69 C6 33 14N 75 12 E
Rambervillers, *France* .. 19 D13 48 20N 6 38 E
Rambipuji, *Indonesia* ... 63 H15 8 12 S 113 37 E
Rambouillet, *France* .... 19 D8 48 39N 1 50 E
Rame Hd., *Australia* .... 95 F4 37 47 S 149 30 E
Ramechhap, *Nepal* .... 69 F12 27 25N 86 10 E
Ramenskoye, *Russia* ..... 32 E10 55 32N 38 15 E
Ramganga →, *India* ...... 69 F8 27 5N 79 58 E
Ramgarh, *Jharkhand,*
  India .... 69 H11 23 40N 85 35 E
Ramgarh, *Raj., India* ... 68 F6 27 16N 75 14 E
Ramgarh, *Raj., India* ... 68 F4 27 30N 70 36 E
Rāmhormoz, *Iran* .... 71 D6 31 15N 49 35 E
Ramīān, *Iran* .... 71 B7 37 3N 55 16 E
Ramingining, *Australia* . 94 A2 12 19 S 135 3 E
Ramla, *Israel* .... 74 D3 31 55N 34 52 E
Ramlu, *Eritrea* .... 81 E5 13 32N 41 40 E
Ramm = Rum, *Jordan* ..... 74 F4 29 39N 35 26 E
Ramm, *Jabal, Jordan* .... 74 F4 29 35N 35 24 E
Râmna →, *Romania* .... 29 E12 45 36N 27 3 E
Ramnad =
  Ramanathapuram,
  India .... 66 Q11 9 25N 78 55 E
Ramnagar,
  Jammu & Kashmir,
  India .... 69 C6 32 47N 75 18 E
Ramnagar, *Uttaranchal,*
  India .... 69 E8 29 24N 79 7 E
Ramnäs, *Sweden* .... 10 E10 59 46N 16 12 E
Râmnicu Sărat,
  Romania .... 29 E12 45 26N 27 3 E
Râmnicu Vâlcea,
  Romania .... 29 E9 45 9N 24 21 E
Ramon, *Russia* .... 33 G10 51 55N 39 21 E
Ramona, *U.S.A.* 111 M10 33 2N 116 52W
Ramonville-St-Agne,
  France .... 20 E5 43 33N 1 28 E
Ramore, *Canada* 104 C3 48 30N 80 25W
Ramos →, *Nigeria* .... 83 D6 5 8N 5 22 E
Ramotswa, *Botswana* ..... 88 C4 24 50 S 25 52 E
Rampur, *H.P., India* .... 68 D7 31 26N 77 43 E
Rampur, *Mad. P., India* . 68 H5 23 25N 73 53 E
Rampur, *Ut. P., India* .. 69 E8 28 50N 79 5 E
Rampur Hat, *India* ...... 69 G12 24 10N 87 50 E
Rampura, *India* .... 68 G6 24 30N 75 27 E
Ramrama Tola, *India* .... 69 J8 21 52N 78 55 E
Ramree I., *Burma* .... 67 K19 19 0N 93 40 E
Rāmsar, *Iran* .... 71 B6 36 53N 50 41 E
Ramsey, *I. of Man* 14 C3 54 20N 4 22W
Ramsey, *U.S.A.* 117 E10 41 4N 74 9W
Ramsey L., *Canada* 104 C3 47 13N 82 15W
Ramsgate, *U.K.* .... 15 F9 51 20N 1 25 E
Ramsjö, *Sweden* .... 10 B9 62 11N 15 37 E
Ramstein, *Germany* ...... 25 F3 49 27N 7 32 E
Ramtek, *India* .... 66 J11 21 20N 79 15 E
Ramvik, *Sweden* .... 10 B11 62 49N 17 51 E
Rana Pratap Sagar Dam,
  India .... 68 G6 24 58N 75 38 E
Ranaghat, *India* .... 69 H13 23 15N 88 35 E
Ranahu, *Pakistan* .... 68 G3 25 55N 69 45 E
Rancagua, *Chile* .... 126 C1 34 10 S 70 50W
Rancharia, *Brazil* ...... 127 A5 22 15 S 50 55W
Ranchester, *U.S.A.* 108 D10 44 54N 107 10W
Ranchi, *India* .... 69 H11 23 19N 85 27 E
Rancho Cucamonga,
  U.S.A. 111 L9 34 10N 117 30W
Randalstown, *U.K.* 12 B5 54 45N 6 19W
Randan, *France* .... 19 F10 46 2N 3 21 E
Randazzo, *Italy* .... 43 E7 37 53N 14 57 E
Randers, *Denmark* .... 11 H4 56 29N 10 1 E
Randers Fjord,
  Denmark .... 11 H4 56 37N 10 20 E
Randfontein, *S. Africa* . 89 D4 26 8 S 27 45 E
Randle, *U.S.A.* 110 D5 46 32N 121 57W
Randolph, *Mass., U.S.A.* 117 D13 42 10N 71 2W
Randolph, *N.Y., U.S.A.* . 116 D6 42 10N 78 59W
Randolph, *Utah, U.S.A.* . 108 F8 41 40N 111 11W
Randolph, *Vt., U.S.A.* .. 117 C12 43 55N 72 40W
Råneälven →, *Sweden* .... 8 D20 65 50N 22 20 E
Rångea, *Thailand* .... 65 J3 6 19N 101 44 E
Rangaunu B., *N.Z.* ...... 91 F4 34 51 S 173 15 E

Rangeley, *U.S.A.* 117 B14 44 58N 70 39W
Rangeley L., *U.S.A.* 117 B14 44 55N 70 43W
Rangely, *U.S.A.* 108 F9 40 5N 108 48W
Ranger, *U.S.A.* 113 J5 32 28N 98 41W
Rangia, *India* .... 67 F17 26 28N 91 38 E
Rangiora, *N.Z.* .... 91 K4 43 19 S 172 36 E
Rangitaiki →, *N.Z.* ..... 91 G6 37 54 S 176 49 E
Rangitata →, *N.Z.* ...... 91 K3 43 45 S 171 15 E
Rangitoto ke te tonga =
  D'Urville I., *N.Z.* .. 91 J4 40 50 S 173 55 E
Rangkasbitung,
  Indonesia .... 63 G12 6 21 S 106 15 E
Rangon →, *Burma* .... 67 L20 16 28N 96 40 E
Rangoon, *Burma* .... 67 L20 16 45N 96 20 E
Rangpur, *Bangla.* .... 67 G16 25 42N 89 22 E
Rangsit, *Thailand* ...... 64 F3 13 59N 100 37 E
Ranibennur, *India* ...... 66 M9 14 35N 75 30 E
Raniganj, *Ut P., India* . 69 F9 27 3N 82 13 E
Raniganj, *W. Bengal,*
  India .... 67 H15 23 40N 87 5 E
Ranikhet, *India* .... 69 E8 29 39N 79 25 E
Raniwara, *India* .... 66 G8 24 50N 72 10 E
Rāniyah, *Iraq* .... 70 B5 36 15N 44 53 E
Ranka, *India* .... 69 H10 23 59N 83 47 E
Ranken →, *Australia* .... 94 C2 20 31 S 137 36 E
Rankin, *U.S.A.* 113 K4 31 13N 101 56W
Rankin Inlet, *Canada* ... 100 B10 62 30N 93 0W
Rankins Springs,
  Australia .... 95 E4 33 49 S 146 14 E
Rankweil, *Austria* ...... 26 D2 47 17N 9 39 E
Rannoch, L., *U.K.* 13 E4 56 41N 4 20W
Rannoch Moor, *U.K.* 13 E4 56 38N 4 48W
Ranobe, Helodranon' i,
  Madag. .... 89 C7 23 3 S 43 33 E
Ranohira, *Madag.* .... 89 C8 22 29 S 45 24 E
Ranomafana,
  Toamasina, *Madag.* .. 89 B8 18 57 S 48 50 E
Ranomafana, Toliara,
  Madag. .... 89 C8 24 34 S 47 0 E
Ranomafana △, *Madag.* ... 89 C8 21 16 S 47 25 E
Ranomena, *Madag.* .... 89 C8 23 25 S 47 17 E
Ranong, *Thailand* .... 65 H2 9 56N 98 40 E
Ranotsara Nord, *Madag.* . 89 C8 22 48 S 46 36 E
Rānsa, *Iran* .... 71 C6 33 39N 48 18 E
Ransiki, *Indonesia* ..... 63 E8 1 30 S 134 10 E
Rantabe, *Madag.* .... 89 B8 15 42 S 49 39 E
Rantauprapat, *Indonesia* 62 D1 2 15N 99 50 E
Rantemario, *Indonesia* .. 63 E5 3 15 S 119 57 E
Rantoul, *U.S.A.* 114 E1 40 19N 88 9W
Ranum, *Denmark* .... 11 H3 56 54N 9 14 E
Ranyah, W. →,
  Si. Arabia .... 80 C5 21 18N 43 20 E
Raon l'Étape, *France* ... 19 D13 48 24N 6 50 E
Raoping, *China* .... 59 F11 23 42N 117 1 E
Raoyang, *China* .... 56 E8 38 15N 115 45 E
Rap, Ko, *Thailand* ...... 65 b 9 19N 99 58 E
Rapa, *French Polynesia* . 97 K13 27 35 S 144 20W
Rapa Nui = Pascua, I.
  de, *Chile* .... 97 K17 27 7 S 109 23W
Rapallo, *Italy* .... 40 D6 44 21N 9 14 E
Rapar, *India* .... 68 H4 23 34N 70 38 E
Râpch, *Iran* .... 71 E8 25 40N 59 15 E
Raper, C., *Canada* 101 B13 69 44N 67 6W
Rapid City, *U.S.A.* 112 D3 44 5N 103 14W
Rapid River, *U.S.A.* 114 C2 45 55N 86 58W
Rapla, *Estonia* .... 9 G21 59 1N 24 52 E
Rapti →, *India* .... 69 F10 26 18N 83 41 E
Rapu Rapu L., *Phil.* .... 61 E6 13 12N 124 9 E
Raqaba ez Zarqa →,
  Sudan .... 81 F2 9 14N 29 44 E
Raquette →, *U.S.A.* 117 B10 45 0N 74 42W
Raquette Lake, *U.S.A.* .. 117 C10 43 49N 74 40W
Rarotonga, *Cook Is.* .... 97 K12 21 30 S 160 0W
Ra's al 'Ayn, *Syria* .... 70 B4 36 45N 40 12 E
Ra's al Khaymah,
  U.A.E. .... 71 E7 25 50N 55 59 E
Râs el Mâ, *Mali* 82 B4 16 35N 4 30W
Râs Ghârib, *Egypt* ...... 80 B3 28 6N 33 18 E
Râs Mallap, *Egypt* ...... 80 B3 29 18N 32 50 E
Râs Muhammad △,
  Egypt .... 80 B3 27 45N 34 16 E
Rasca, Pta. de la,
  Canary Is. 48 G3 27 59N 16 41W
Rășcani, *Moldova* .... 29 C12 47 58N 27 33 E
Raseiniai, *Lithuania* ... 9 J20 55 25N 23 5 E
Rashad, *Sudan* .... 81 E3 11 55N 31 0 E
Rashîd, *Egypt* .... 80 H7 31 21N 30 22 E
Rashîd, Masab, *Egypt* ... 80 H7 31 22N 30 17 E
Rashmi, *India* .... 68 G6 25 4N 74 22 E
Rasht, *Iran* .... 71 B6 37 20N 49 40 E
Rasi Salai, *Thailand* ... 64 E5 15 20N 104 9 E
Rașka, *Serbia & M.* ..... 44 C4 43 19N 20 39 E
Râsnov, *Romania* .... 29 E10 45 35N 25 27 E
Rason L., *Australia* .... 93 E3 28 45 S 124 25 E
Rașova, *Romania* .... 29 F12 44 15N 27 55 E
Rasovo, *Bulgaria* .... 44 C7 43 42N 23 17 E
Rasra, *India* .... 69 G10 25 50N 83 50 E
Rasskazovo, *Russia* ..... 34 D5 52 35N 41 50 E
Rast, *Romania* .... 29 G8 43 53N 23 16 E
Rastatt, *Germany* .... 25 G4 48 50N 8 11 E
Rastede, *Germany* .... 24 B4 53 15N 8 12 E
Râstolița, *Romania* ..... 29 D9 46 59N 24 58 E
Rasul, *Pakistan* .... 68 C5 32 42N 73 34 E
Raszków, *Poland* .... 31 G4 51 43N 17 40 E
Rat Buri, *Thailand* ..... 64 F2 13 30N 99 54 E
Rat Islands, *U.S.A.* .... 100 C1 52 0N 178 0 E
Rat L., *Canada* 103 B9 56 10N 99 40W
Rătan, *Sweden* .... 10 B8 62 29N 14 33 E
Ratangarh, *India* .... 68 E6 28 5N 74 35 E
Raţāwī, *Iraq* .... 70 D5 30 38N 47 13 E
Rath, *India* .... 69 G8 25 36N 79 37 E
Rath Luirc, *Ireland* 12 D3 52 21N 8 40W
Rathdrum, *Ireland* 12 D5 52 56N 6 14W
Rathenow, *Germany* ...... 24 C8 52 37N 12 19 E
Rathkeale, *Ireland* 12 D3 52 32N 8 56W
Rathlin I., *U.K.* 12 A5 55 18N 6 14W
Rathmelton, *Ireland* 12 A4 55 2N 7 38W
Ratibor = Racibórz,
  Poland .... 31 H5 50 7N 18 18 E
Rätikon, *Austria* .... 26 D2 47 0N 9 55 E
Ratingen, *Germany* ...... 24 D2 51 18N 6 52 E
Ratlam, *India* .... 68 H6 23 20N 75 0 E
Ratnagiri, *India* .... 66 L8 16 57N 73 18 E
Ratodero, *Pakistan* ..... 68 F3 27 48N 68 18 E
Raton, *U.S.A.* 113 G2 36 54N 104 24W
Rattaphum, *Thailand* .... 65 J3 7 8N 100 16 E
Rattray Hd., *U.K.* 13 D7 57 38N 1 50W
Rättvik, *Sweden* .... 10 D9 60 52N 15 7 E
Ratz, Mt., *Canada* 102 B2 57 23N 132 12W
Ratzeburg, *Germany* ..... 24 B6 53 40N 10 46 E
Raub, *Malaysia* .... 65 L3 3 47N 101 52 E
Rauch, *Argentina* .... 126 D4 36 45 S 59 5W
Raudales de Malpaso,
  Mexico 119 D6 17 30N 93 30W
Raufarhöfn, *Iceland* 8 C6 66 27N 15 57W
Raufoss, *Norway* .... 9 F14 60 44N 10 37 E

Raukumara Ra., *N.Z.* .... 91 H6 38 5 S 177 55 E
Rauma, *Finland* .... 9 F19 61 10N 21 30 E
Raumo = Rauma,
  Finland .... 9 F19 61 10N 21 30 E
Raung, Gunung,
  Indonesia .... 63 J17 8 8 S 114 3 E
Raurkela, *India* .... 69 H11 22 14N 84 50 E
Rausu-Dake, *Japan* ...... 54 B12 44 4N 145 7 E
Rāut →, *Moldova* .... 29 C14 47 15N 29 9 E
Rava-Ruska, *Ukraine* .... 31 H10 50 15N 23 42 E
Rava Russkaya = Rava-
  Ruska, *Ukraine* ...... 31 H10 50 15N 23 42 E
Ravalli, *U.S.A.* 108 C6 47 17N 114 11W
Ravānsar, *Iran* .... 70 C5 34 43N 46 40 E
Ravanusa, *Italy* .... 42 E6 37 16N 13 58 E
Rāvar, *Iran* .... 71 D8 31 20N 56 51 E
Ravena, *U.S.A.* 117 D11 42 28N 73 49W
Ravenna, *Italy* .... 41 D9 44 25N 12 12 E
Ravenna, *Nebr., U.S.A.* . 112 E5 41 1N 98 55W
Ravenna, *Ohio, U.S.A.* .. 116 E3 41 9N 81 15W
Ravensburg, *Germany* .... 25 H5 47 46N 9 36 E
Ravenshoe, *Australia* ... 94 B4 17 37 S 145 29 E
Ravensthorpe, *Australia* 93 F3 33 35 S 120 2 E
Ravenswood, *Australia* .. 94 C4 20 6 S 146 54 E
Ravenswood, *U.S.A.* 114 F5 38 57N 81 46W
Ravi →, *Pakistan* .... 68 D4 30 35N 71 49 E
Ravna Gora, *Croatia* .... 41 C11 45 24N 14 50 E
Ravna Reka,
  Serbia & M. .... 44 B5 44 1N 21 35 E
Ravne na Koroškem,
  Slovenia .... 41 B11 46 36N 14 59 E
Rawa Mazowiecka,
  Poland .... 31 G7 51 46N 20 12 E
Rawalpindi, *Pakistan* ... 68 C5 33 38N 73 8 E
Rawāndūz, *Iraq* .... 70 B5 36 40N 44 30 E
Rawang, *Malaysia* .... 65 L3 3 20N 101 35 E
Rawene, *N.Z.* .... 91 F4 35 25 S 173 32 E
Rawicz, *Poland* .... 31 G3 51 36N 16 52 E
Rawka →, *Poland* .... 31 F7 52 9N 20 8 E
Rawlinna, *Australia* .... 93 F4 30 58 S 125 28 E
Rawlins, *U.S.A.* 108 F10 41 47N 107 14W
Rawlinson Ra., *Australia* 93 D4 24 40 S 128 30 E
Rawson, *Argentina* ...... 128 E3 43 15 S 65 5W
Raxaul, *India* .... 69 F11 26 59N 84 51 E
Ray, *U.S.A.* 112 A3 48 21N 103 10W
Ray, C., *Canada* 105 C8 47 33N 59 15W
Raya Ring, Ko, *Thailand* 65 a 8 18N 98 29 E
Rayadurg, *India* .... 66 M10 14 40N 76 50 E
Rayagada, *India* .... 67 K13 19 15N 83 20 E
Rāyen, *Iran* .... 71 D8 29 34N 57 26 E
Rayleigh, *U.K.* .... 15 F8 51 36N 0 37 E
Raymond, *Canada* 102 D6 49 30N 112 35W
Raymond, *Calif., U.S.A.* 110 H7 37 13N 119 54W
Raymond, *N.H., U.S.A.* .. 117 C13 43 2N 71 11W
Raymond, *Wash., U.S.A.* . 110 D3 46 41N 123 44W
Raymondville, *U.S.A.* ... 113 M6 26 29N 97 47W
Raymore, *Canada* 103 C8 51 25N 104 31W
Rayón, *Mexico* 118 B2 29 43N 110 35W
Rayong, *Thailand* .... 64 F3 12 40N 101 20 E
Rayville, *U.S.A.* 113 J9 32 29N 91 46W
Raz, Pte. du, *France* ... 18 D2 48 2N 4 47W
Razan, *Iran* .... 71 C6 35 23N 49 2 E
Ražana, *Serbia & M.* .... 44 B3 44 6N 19 55 E
Ražanj, *Serbia & M.* .... 44 C5 43 40N 21 31 E
Razāzah, Buhayrat ar,
  Iraq .... 70 C4 32 40N 43 35 E
Razazah, L. = Razāzah,
  Buhayrat ar, *Iraq* ... 70 C4 32 40N 43 35 E
Razdelna, *Bulgaria* ..... 45 C11 43 13N 27 41 E
Razdel'naya = Rozdilna,
  Ukraine .... 29 D15 46 50N 30 2 E
Razdolnoye, *Russia* ..... 54 C5 43 30N 131 52 E
Razdolnoye, *Ukraine* .... 33 K7 45 46N 33 29 E
Razeh, *Iran* .... 71 C6 32 47N 48 9 E
Razgrad, *Bulgaria* ...... 45 C10 43 33N 26 34 E
Razim, Lacul, *Romania* .. 29 F14 44 50N 29 0 E
Razlog, *Bulgaria* .... 44 E7 41 53N 23 28 E
Razmak, *Pakistan* .... 68 C3 32 45N 69 50 E
Ré, Î. de, *France* 20 B2 46 12N 1 30W
Reading, *U.K.* 15 F7 51 27N 0 58W
Reading, *U.S.A.* 117 F9 40 20N 75 56W
Reading □, *U.K.* 15 F7 51 27N 0 58W
Realicó, *Argentina* ..... 126 D3 35 0 S 64 15W
Réalmont, *France* .... 20 E6 43 48N 2 10 E
Ream, *Cambodia* .... 65 G4 10 34N 103 39 E
Reata, *Mexico* 118 B4 26 8N 101 5W
Reay Forest, *U.K.* 13 C4 58 22N 4 55W
Rebais, *France* .... 19 D10 48 50N 3 10 E
Rebi, *Indonesia* .... 63 F8 6 23 S 134 7 E
Rebiana, *Libya* .... 79 D10 24 12N 22 10 E
Rebiana, Sahrâ', *Libya* . 79 D10 24 30N 21 0 E
Rebun-Tō, *Japan* .... 54 B10 45 23N 141 2 E
Recanati, *Italy* .... 41 E10 43 24N 13 32 E
Recaș, *Romania* .... 28 E6 45 46N 21 30 E
Recco, *Italy* .... 40 D6 44 22N 9 9 E
Recherche, Arch. of the,
  Australia .... 93 F3 34 15 S 122 50 E
Rechna Doab, *Pakistan* .. 68 D5 31 35N 73 30 E
Rechytsa, *Belarus* ...... 33 F6 52 21N 30 24 E
Recife, *Brazil* .... 125 E12 8 0 S 35 0W
Recklinghausen,
  Germany .... 17 C7 51 37N 7 12 E
Reconquista, *Argentina* . 126 B4 29 10 S 59 45W
Recreo, *Argentina* ...... 126 B2 29 25 S 65 10W
Recz, *Poland* .... 31 E2 53 16N 15 31 E
Red →, *La., U.S.A.* 113 K9 31 1N 91 45W
Red →, *N. Dak., U.S.A.* . 100 C10 49 0N 97 15W
Red Bank, *U.S.A.* 117 F10 40 21N 74 5W
Red Bay, *Canada* 105 B8 51 44N 56 25W
Red Bluff, *U.S.A.* 110 F2 40 11N 122 15W
Red Bluff L., *U.S.A.* ... 113 K3 31 54N 103 55W
Red Cliffs, *Australia* .. 95 E3 34 19 S 142 11 E
Red Cloud, *U.S.A.* 112 E5 40 5N 98 32W
Red Creek, *U.S.A.* 117 C8 43 14N 76 45W
Red Deer, *Canada* 102 C6 52 20N 113 50W
Red Deer →, *Alta.,*
  Canada 103 C7 50 58N 110 0W
Red Deer →, *Man.,*
  Canada 103 C8 52 53N 101 1W
Red Deer L., *Canada* 103 C8 52 55N 101 20W
Red Hook, *U.S.A.* 117 E11 41 55N 73 53W
Red Indian L., *Canada* .. 105 C8 48 35N 57 0W
Red L., *Canada* 103 C10 51 3N 93 49W
Red Lake, *Canada* 103 C10 51 3N 93 49W
Red Lake Falls, *U.S.A.* . 112 B6 47 53N 96 16W
Red Lake Road, *Canada* .. 103 C10 49 59N 93 25W
Red Lodge, *U.S.A.* 108 D9 45 11N 109 15W
Red Mountain, *U.S.A.* ... 111 K9 35 37N 117 38W
Red Oak, *U.S.A.* 112 E7 41 1N 95 14W
Red Rock, *Canada* 104 C2 48 55N 88 15W
Red Rock, *U.S.A.* 112 E8 41 22N 92 59W
Red Rocks Pt., *Australia* 93 F4 32 13 S 127 32 E
Red Sea, *Asia* .... 75 C2 25 0N 36 0 E
Red Slate Mt., *U.S.A.* .. 110 H8 37 31N 118 52W
Red Sucker L., *Canada* .. 104 B1 54 9N 93 40W
Red Tower Pass = Turnu
  Roșu, P., *Romania* ... 29 E9 45 33N 24 17 E

Red Wing, *U.S.A.* 112 C8 44 34N 92 31W
Reda, *Poland* .... 30 D5 54 40N 18 19 E
Redang, *Malaysia* .... 65 K4 5 49N 103 2 E
Redange, *Lux.* .... 17 E5 49 46N 5 52 E
Redcar, *U.K.* 14 C6 54 37N 1 4W
Redcar & Cleveland □,
  U.K. 14 C7 54 29N 1 0W
Redcliff, *Canada* 103 C6 50 10N 110 50W
Redcliffe, *Australia* ... 95 D5 27 12 S 153 0 E
Redcliffe, Mt., *Australia* 93 E3 28 30 S 121 30 E
Redding, *U.S.A.* 108 F2 40 35N 122 24W
Redditch, *U.K.* 15 E6 52 18N 1 55W
Redfield, *U.S.A.* 112 C5 44 53N 98 31W
Redford, *U.S.A.* 117 B11 44 38N 73 48W
Redhead, *Trin. & Tob.* .. 125 K16 10 44N 60 58W
Redkino, *Russia* .... 32 D9 56 39N 36 16 E
Redlands, *U.S.A.* 111 M9 34 4N 117 11W
Redmond, *Oreg., U.S.A.* . 108 D3 44 17N 121 11W
Redmond, *Wash., U.S.A.* . 110 C4 47 41N 122 7W
Redon, *France* 18 E4 47 40N 2 6W
Redonda, *Antigua & B.* .. 121 C7 16 58N 62 19W
Redondela, *Spain* 36 C2 42 15N 8 38W
Redondo, *Portugal* 37 G3 38 39N 7 37W
Redondo Beach, *U.S.A.* .. 111 M8 33 50N 118 23W
Redruth, *U.K.* 15 G2 50 14N 5 14W
Redvers, *Canada* 103 D8 49 35N 101 40W
Redwater, *Canada* 102 C6 53 55N 113 6W
Redwood, *U.S.A.* 117 B9 44 18N 75 48W
Redwood △, *U.S.A.* 108 F1 41 40N 124 5W
Redwood City, *U.S.A.* ... 110 H4 37 30N 122 15W
Redwood Falls, *U.S.A.* .. 112 C7 44 32N 95 7W
Ree, L., *Ireland* 12 C3 53 35N 8 0W
Reed, L., *Canada* 103 C8 54 38N 100 30W
Reed City, *U.S.A.* 114 D3 43 53N 85 31W
Reedley, *U.S.A.* 110 J7 36 36N 119 27W
Reedsburg, *U.S.A.* 112 D9 43 32N 90 0W
Reedsport, *U.S.A.* 108 E1 43 42N 124 6W
Reedsville, *U.S.A.* 116 F7 40 39N 77 35W
Reefton, *N.Z.* .... 91 K3 42 6 S 171 51 E
Rees, *Germany* .... 24 D2 51 46N 6 24 E
Reese →, *U.S.A.* 108 F5 40 48N 117 4W
Refahiye, *Turkey* .... 73 C8 39 54N 38 47 E
Reftele, *Sweden* .... 11 G7 57 11N 13 35 E
Refugio, *U.S.A.* 113 L6 28 18N 97 17W
Rega →, *Poland* .... 30 D2 54 10N 15 18 E
Regalbuto, *Italy* .... 43 E7 37 39N 14 38 E
Regen, *Germany* .... 25 F9 48 58N 13 9 E
Regen →, *Germany* .... 25 F8 49 1N 12 6 E
Regensburg, *Germany* .... 25 F8 49 1N 12 6 E
Regenstauf, *Germany* .... 25 F8 49 7N 12 6 E
Reggâne = Zaouiet
  Reggâne, *Algeria* .... 78 C6 26 32N 0 3 E
Réggio di Calábria, *Italy* 43 D8 38 6N 15 39 E
Réggio nell'Emília, *Italy* 40 D7 44 43N 10 36 E
Reghin, *Romania* .... 29 D9 46 46N 24 42 E
Regina, *Canada* 103 C8 50 27N 104 35W
Regina Beach, *Canada* ... 103 C8 50 47N 105 0W
Registro, *Brazil* .... 127 A6 24 29 S 47 49W
Reguengos de
  Monsaraz, *Portugal* .. 37 G3 38 25N 7 32W
Rehar →, *India* .... 69 H10 23 55N 82 40 E
Rehli, *India* .... 69 H8 23 38N 79 5 E
Rehoboth, *Namibia* ...... 88 C2 23 15 S 17 4 E
Rehovot, *Israel* .... 74 D3 31 54N 34 48 E
Reichenbach, *Germany* ... 24 E8 50 37N 12 17 E
Reid, *Australia* .... 93 F4 30 49 S 128 26 E
Reidsville, *U.S.A.* 115 G6 36 21N 79 40W
Reigate, *U.K.* 15 F7 51 14N 0 12W
Reillo, *Spain* 38 F3 39 54N 1 53W
Reims, *France* .... 19 C11 49 15N 4 1 E
Reina Adelaida, Arch.,
  Chile .... 128 G2 52 20 S 74 0W
Reina Sofía, Tenerife ✈
  (TFS), *Canary Is.* ... 48 F3 28 3N 16 33W
Reinbek, *Germany* .... 24 B6 53 30N 10 16 E
Reindeer →, *Canada* 103 B8 55 36N 103 11W
Reindeer I., *Canada* 103 C9 52 30N 98 0W
Reindeer L., *Canada* 103 B8 57 15N 102 15W
Reinga, C., *N.Z.* .... 91 F4 34 25 S 172 43 E
Reinosa, *Spain* 36 B6 43 2N 4 15W
Reitz, *S. Africa* .... 89 D4 27 48 S 28 29 E
Reivilo, *S. Africa* ..... 88 D3 27 36 S 24 8 E
Rejaf, *Sudan* .... 81 G3 4 45N 31 32 E
Rejmyre, *Sweden* .... 11 F9 58 50N 15 55 E
Rejowiec Fabryczny,
  Poland .... 31 G10 51 5N 23 17 E
Reka →, *Slovenia* .... 41 C11 45 40N 14 0 E
Rekovac, *Serbia & M.* ... 44 C5 43 51N 21 3 E
Reliance, *Canada* 103 A7 63 0N 109 20W
Remagen, *Germany* .... 24 E3 50 34N 7 11 E
Rémalard, *France* .... 18 D7 48 26N 0 47 E
Remanso, *Brazil* .... 125 E10 9 41 S 42 4W
Remarkable, Mt.,
  Australia .... 95 E2 32 48 S 138 10 E
Rembang, *Indonesia* ..... 63 G14 6 42 S 111 21 E
Remedios, *Panama* 120 E3 8 15N 81 50W
Remeshk, *Iran* .... 71 E8 26 55N 58 50 E
Remetea, *Romania* .... 29 D10 46 45N 25 29 E
Remich, *Lux.* .... 17 E6 49 32N 6 22 E
Remiremont, *France* ..... 19 D13 48 9N 6 36 E
Remo, *Ethiopia* .... 81 F5 6 48N 41 20 E
Remontnoye, *Russia* ..... 35 G6 46 34N 43 37 E
Remscheid, *Germany* ..... 21 E8 43 55N 4 35 E
Ren Xian, *China* .... 56 F8 37 8N 114 40 E
Rende, *Italy* .... 43 C9 39 20N 16 11 E
Rendína, *Greece* .... 46 B3 39 4N 21 58 E
Rendsburg, *Germany* ..... 24 A5 54 17N 9 39 E
Renfrew, *Canada* 117 A8 45 30N 76 40W
Renfrewshire □, *U.K.* ... 13 F4 55 49N 4 38W
Rengat, *Indonesia* ...... 62 E2 0 30 S 102 45 E
Rengo, *Chile* .... 126 C1 34 24 S 70 50W
Renhua, *China* .... 59 E9 25 5N 113 40 E
Renhuai, *China* .... 58 D6 27 48N 106 24 E
Reni, *Ukraine* .... 29 E13 45 28N 28 15 E
Renk, *Sudan* .... 81 E3 11 50N 32 50 E
Renmark, *Australia* ..... 95 E3 34 11 S 140 43 E
Rennell Sd., *Canada* 102 C2 53 23N 132 35W
Renner Springs,
  Australia .... 94 B1 18 20 S 133 47 E
Rennes, *France* 18 D5 48 7N 1 41W
Rennie L., *Canada* 103 A7 61 32N 105 35W
Reno, *U.S.A.* 110 F7 39 31N 119 48W
Reno →, *Italy* .... 41 D9 44 38N 12 16 E
Renovo, *U.S.A.* 116 E7 41 20N 77 45W
Renqiu, *China* .... 56 E9 38 43N 116 5 E
Rens, *Denmark* .... 11 K3 54 54N 9 5 E
Renshou, *China* .... 58 C5 30 3N 104 9 E
Rensselaer, *Ind., U.S.A.* 114 E2 40 57N 87 9W
Rensselaer, *N.Y., U.S.A.* 117 D11 42 38N 73 45W
Rentería, *Spain* 38 B3 43 19N 1 54W
Renton, *U.S.A.* 110 C4 47 29N 122 12W
Réo, *Burkina Faso* 82 C4 12 28N 2 35W
Reotipur, *India* .... 69 G10 25 33N 83 45 E
Répcelak, *Hungary* ...... 28 C2 47 24N 17 1 E

Republic, *Mo., U.S.A.* .. 113 G8 37 7N 93 29W
Republic, *Wash., U.S.A.* 108 B4 48 39N 118 44W
Republican →, *U.S.A.* ... 112 F6 39 4N 96 48W
Repulse B., *Australia* .. 94 J6 20 35 S 148 46 E
Repulse Bay, *Canada* 101 B11 66 30N 86 30W
Requena, *Peru* .... 124 E4 5 5 S 73 52W
Requena, *Spain* 39 F3 39 30N 1 4W
Réquista, *France* .... 20 D6 44 1N 2 32 E
Resadiye = Datça,
  Turkey .... 47 E9 36 46N 27 40 E
Reşadiye, *Turkey* .... 72 B7 40 23N 37 20 E
Reşadiye Yarımadası,
  Turkey .... 47 E9 36 40N 27 45 E
Resavica, *Serbia & M.* .. 44 B5 44 4N 21 31 E
Resen, *Macedonia* .... 44 E5 41 5N 21 0 E
Reserve, *U.S.A.* 109 K9 33 43N 108 45W
Resht = Rasht, *Iran* .... 71 B6 37 20N 49 40 E
Resistencia, *Argentina* . 126 B4 27 30 S 59 0W
Reșița, *Romania* .... 28 E6 45 18N 21 53 E
Resko, *Poland* .... 30 E2 53 47N 15 25 E
Resolution I., *Canada* .. 101 B13 61 30N 65 0W
Resolution I., *N.Z.* .... 91 L1 45 40 S 166 40 E
Ressano Garcia,
  Mozam. .... 89 D5 25 25 S 32 0 E
Reston, *Canada* 103 D8 49 33N 101 6W
Reszel, *Poland* .... 30 D8 54 4N 21 10 E
Retalhuleu, *Guatemala* .. 120 D1 14 33N 91 46W
Retenue, L. de,
  Dem. Rep. of
  the Congo .... 87 E2 11 0 S 27 0 E
Retezat △, *Romania* ..... 28 E7 45 23N 22 56 E
Retezat, Munţii,
  Romania .... 28 E8 45 25N 23 0 E
Retford, *U.K.* 14 D7 53 19N 0 56W
Rethel, *France* .... 19 C11 49 30N 4 20 E
Rethem, *Germany* .... 24 C5 52 47N 9 22 E
Réthímnon, *Greece* ...... 49 D6 35 18N 24 30 E
Réthímnon □, *Greece* .... 49 D6 35 23N 24 28 E
Reti, *Pakistan* .... 68 E3 28 5N 69 48 E
Retiche, Alpi, *Switz.* .. 25 J6 46 30N 10 0 E
Retiers, *France* 18 E5 47 55N 1 23W
Retortillo, *Spain* 36 E4 40 48N 6 21W
Retournac, *France* ...... 21 C8 45 12N 4 2 E
Rétság, *Hungary* .... 28 C4 47 58N 19 10 E
Réunion ☒, *Ind. Oc.* .... 77 J9 21 0 S 56 0 E
Reus, *Spain* .... 38 D6 41 10N 1 5 E
Reuterstadt
  Stavenhagen,
  Germany .... 24 B8 53 42N 12 54 E
Reutlingen, *Germany* .... 25 G5 48 29N 9 12 E
Reutte, *Austria* .... 26 D3 47 29N 10 42 E
Reval = Tallinn, *Estonia* 9 G21 59 22N 24 48 E
Revel, *France* .... 20 E5 43 28N 2 1 E
Revelganj, *India* .... 69 G11 25 50N 84 40 E
Revelstoke, *Canada* 102 C5 51 0N 118 10W
Reventazón, *Peru* .... 124 E2 6 10 S 80 58W
Revigny-sur-Ornain,
  France .... 19 D11 48 49N 4 59 E
Revillagigedo, Is. de,
  Pac. Oc. 118 D2 18 40N 112 0W
Revin, *France* .... 19 C11 49 55N 4 39 E
Revúca, *Slovak Rep.* .... 27 C13 48 41N 20 7 E
Revuè →, *Mozam.* .... 87 F3 19 50 S 34 0 E
Rewa, *India* .... 69 G9 24 33N 81 25 E
Rewari, *India* .... 68 E7 28 15N 76 40 E
Rexburg, *U.S.A.* 108 E8 43 49N 111 47W
Rey, *Iran* .... 71 C6 35 35N 51 25 E
Rey, I. del, *Panama* 120 E4 8 20N 78 30W
Rey Malabo, *Eq. Guin.* .. 83 E6 3 45N 8 50 E
Reyðarfjörður, *Iceland* . 8 D6 65 2N 14 13W
Reyes, Pt., *U.S.A.* 110 H3 38 0N 123 0W
Reyhanlı, *Turkey* .... 72 D7 36 16N 36 35 E
Reykjahlíð, *Iceland* 8 D5 65 40N 16 55W
Reykjanes, *Iceland* 8 E2 63 48N 22 40W
Reykjavík, *Iceland* 8 D3 64 10N 21 57W
Reynolds Ra., *Australia* 92 D5 22 30 S 133 0 E
Reynoldsville, *U.S.A.* .. 116 E6 41 5N 78 58W
Reynosa, *Mexico* 119 B5 26 5N 98 18W
Rēzekne, *Latvia* .... 9 H22 56 30N 27 17 E
Rezina, *Moldova* .... 29 C13 47 45N 28 58 E
Rezovo, *Bulgaria* .... 45 D12 42 0N 28 0 E
Rezvān, *Iran* .... 71 E8 27 34N 56 6 E
Rgotina, *Serbia & M.* ... 44 B6 44 1N 22 17 E
Rhamnus, *Greece* .... 46 C6 38 12N 24 3 E
Rhayader, *U.K.* 15 E4 52 18N 3 29W
Rheda-Wiedenbrück,
  Germany .... 24 D4 51 51N 8 20 E
Rhede, *Germany* .... 24 D2 51 50N 6 42 E
Rhein →, *Europe* .... 17 C6 51 52N 6 2 E
Rhein-Main-Donau-
  Kanal, *Germany* ...... 25 F7 49 1N 11 27 E
Rhein-Ruhr,
  Düsseldorf ✈ (DUS),
  Germany .... 24 D2 51 17N 6 46 E
Rhein-Taunus △,
  Germany .... 25 E4 50 10N 8 10 E
Rhein-Westerwald △,
  Germany .... 24 E3 50 32N 7 20 E
Rheinbach, *Germany* ..... 24 E2 50 38N 6 57 E
Rheine, *Germany* .... 24 C3 52 17N 7 26 E
Rheinfelden, *Germany* ... 25 H3 47 33N 7 47 E
Rheinhessen-Pfalz □,
  Germany .... 25 F3 49 20N 8 0 E
Rheinland-Pfalz □,
  Germany .... 25 E2 50 0N 7 0 E
Rhinelander, *U.S.A.* 112 C10 45 38N 89 25W
Rhinns Pt., *U.K.* 13 F2 55 40N 6 29W
Rhino Camp, *Uganda* ..... 86 B3 3 0N 31 22 E
Rhir, Cap, *Morocco* 78 B4 30 38N 9 54W
Rho, *Italy* .... 40 C6 45 32N 9 2 E
Rhode Island □, *U.S.A.* . 117 E13 41 40N 71 30W
Rhodes = Ródhos,
  Greece .... 49 C10 36 15N 28 10 E
Rhodope Mts. =
  Rhodopi Planina,
  Bulgaria .... 45 E8 41 40N 24 20 E
Rhodopi Planina,
  Bulgaria .... 45 E8 41 40N 24 20 E
Rhön, *Germany* .... 24 E5 50 24N 9 58 E
Rhondda, *U.K.* 15 F4 51 39N 3 31W
Rhondda Cynon Taff □,
  U.K. 15 F4 51 42N 3 27W
Rhône □, *France* .... 21 C8 45 54N 4 35 E
Rhône →, *France* .... 21 E8 43 28N 4 42 E
Rhône-Alpes □, *France* .. 21 C9 45 40N 5 20 E
Rhum, *U.K.* 13 E2 57 0N 6 20W
Rhyl, *U.K.* 14 D4 53 20N 3 29W

Ri-Aba, Eq. Guin. 83 E6 3 28N 8 40 E
Ria Formosa ⌓, Portugal 37 H3 37 1N 7 48W
Riachão, Brazil 125 E9 7 20 S 46 37W
Riangnom, Sudan 81 F3 9 55N 30 1 E
Riaño, Spain 36 C6 42 59N 4 59W
Rians, France 21 E9 43 37N 5 44 E
Riansáres →, Spain 37 F7 39 32N 3 18W
Riasi, India 69 C6 33 10N 74 50 E
Riau □, Indonesia 62 D2 0 0 102 35 E
Riau, Kepulauan, Indonesia 62 D2 0 30N 104 20 E
Riau Arch. = Riau, Kepulauan, Indonesia 62 D2 0 30N 104 20 E
Riaza, Spain 36 D7 41 18N 3 30W
Riaza →, Spain 36 D7 41 42N 3 55W
Riba de Saelices, Spain 38 E2 40 55N 2 17W
Riba-Roja de Turia, Spain 39 F4 39 33N 0 34W
Ribadavia, Spain 36 C2 42 17N 8 8W
Ribadeo, Spain 36 B3 43 35N 7 5W
Ribadesella, Spain 36 B5 43 30N 5 7W
Ribado, Nigeria 83 D7 9 16N 12 47 E
Ribao, Cameroon 83 D7 6 32N 11 30 E
Ribas = Ribes de Freser, Spain 38 C7 42 19N 2 15 E
Ribas do Rio Pardo, Brazil 125 H8 20 27 S 53 46W
Ribauè, Mozam. 87 E4 14 57 S 38 17 E
Ribble →, U.K. 14 D5 53 52N 2 25W
Ribe, Denmark 11 J2 55 19N 8 44 E
Ribe Amtskommune □, Denmark 11 J2 55 35N 8 45 E
Ribeauvillé, France 19 D14 48 10N 7 20 E
Ribécourt-Dreslincourt, France 19 C9 49 30N 2 55 E
Ribeira = Santa Uxía, Spain 36 C2 42 36N 8 58W
Ribeira Brava, Madeira 48 D2 32 41N 17 4W
Ribeirão Prêto, Brazil 127 A6 21 10 S 47 50W
Ribemont, France 19 C10 49 47N 3 27 E
Ribera, Italy 42 E6 37 30N 13 16 E
Ribérac, France 20 C4 45 15N 0 20 E
Riberalta, Bolivia 124 F5 11 0 S 66 0W
Ribes de Freser, Spain 38 C7 42 19N 2 15 E
Ribnica, Slovenia 41 C11 45 45N 14 45 E
Ribnitz-Damgarten, Germany 24 A8 54 15N 12 27 E
Ričany, Czech Rep. 26 B7 50 0N 14 40 E
Riccarton, N.Z. 91 K4 43 32 S 172 37 E
Ríccia, Italy 43 A7 41 30N 14 50 E
Riccione, Italy 41 E9 43 59N 12 39 E
Rice, U.S.A. 111 L12 34 5N 114 51W
Rice L., Canada 116 B6 44 12N 78 10W
Rice Lake, U.S.A. 112 C9 45 30N 91 44W
Rich, C., Canada 116 B4 44 43N 80 38W
Richard Toll, Senegal 82 B1 16 25N 15 42W
Richards Bay, S. Africa 89 D5 28 48 S 32 6 E
Richardson →, Canada 103 B6 58 25N 111 14W
Richardson Lakes, U.S.A. 114 C10 44 46N 70 58W
Richardson Springs, U.S.A. 110 F5 39 51N 121 46W
Riche, C., Australia 93 F2 34 36 S 118 47 E
Richelieu, France 18 E7 47 1N 0 20 E
Richey, U.S.A. 112 B2 47 39N 105 4W
Richfield, U.S.A. 109 G8 38 46N 112 5W
Richfield Springs, U.S.A. 117 D10 42 51N 74 59W
Richford, U.S.A. 117 B12 45 0N 72 40W
Richibucto, Canada 105 C7 46 42N 64 54W
Richland, Ga., U.S.A. 115 J3 32 5N 84 40W
Richland, Wash., U.S.A. 108 C4 46 17N 119 18W
Richland Center, U.S.A. 112 D9 43 21N 90 23W
Richlands, U.S.A. 114 G5 37 6N 81 48W
Richmond, Australia 94 C3 20 43 S 143 8 E
Richmond, N.Z. 91 J4 41 20 S 173 12 E
Richmond, U.K. 14 C6 54 25N 1 43W
Richmond, Calif., U.S.A. 110 H4 37 56N 122 21W
Richmond, Ind., U.S.A. 114 F3 39 50N 84 53W
Richmond, Ky., U.S.A. 114 G3 37 45N 84 18W
Richmond, Mich., U.S.A. 116 D2 42 49N 82 45W
Richmond, Mo., U.S.A. 112 F8 39 17N 93 58W
Richmond, Tex., U.S.A. 113 L7 29 35N 95 46W
Richmond, Utah, U.S.A. 108 F8 41 56N 111 48W
Richmond, Va., U.S.A. 114 G7 37 33N 77 27W
Richmond, Vt., U.S.A. 117 B12 44 24N 72 59W
Richmond Hill, Canada 116 C5 43 52N 79 27W
Richmond Ra., Australia 95 D5 29 0 S 152 45 E
Richtersveld Δ, S. Africa 88 D2 28 15 S 17 10 E
Richwood, U.S.A. 114 F5 38 14N 80 32W
Ricla, Spain 38 D3 41 31N 1 24W
Ridder = Leninogorsk, Kazakhstan 52 D9 50 20N 83 30 E
Riddlesburg, U.S.A. 116 F6 40 9N 78 15W
Ridgecrest, U.S.A. 111 K9 35 38N 117 40W
Ridgefield, Conn., U.S.A. 117 E11 41 17N 73 30W
Ridgefield, Wash., U.S.A. 110 E4 45 49N 122 45W
Ridgeland, U.S.A. 115 J5 32 29N 80 59W
Ridgetown, Canada 116 D3 42 26N 81 52W
Ridgewood, U.S.A. 117 F10 40 59N 74 7W
Ridgway, U.S.A. 116 E6 41 25N 78 44W
Riding Mountain Δ, Canada 103 C9 50 50N 100 0W
Ridley, Mt., Australia 93 F3 33 12 S 122 7 E
Riebeek-Oos, S. Africa 88 E4 33 10 S 26 10 E
Ried, Austria 26 C6 48 14N 13 30 E
Riedlingen, Germany 25 G5 48 9N 9 28 E
Riedstadt, Germany 25 F4 49 45N 8 30 E
Rienza →, Italy 41 B8 46 49N 11 47 E
Riesa, Germany 24 D9 51 17N 13 17 E
Riesi, Italy 43 E7 37 17N 14 5 E
Riet →, S. Africa 88 D3 29 0 S 23 54 E
Rietavas, Lithuania 30 C8 55 44N 21 56 E
Rietbron, S. Africa 88 E3 32 54 S 23 10 E
Rietfontein, Namibia 88 C3 21 58 S 20 58 E
Rieti, Italy 41 F9 42 24N 12 51 E
Rieupeyroux, France 20 D6 44 19N 2 12 E
Riez, France 21 E10 43 49N 6 6 E
Rif = Er Rif, Morocco 78 A5 35 1N 4 1W
Riffe L., U.S.A. 110 D4 46 32N 122 26W
Rifle, U.S.A. 108 G10 39 32N 107 47W
Rift Valley, Africa 76 G7 7 0N 30 0 E
Rift Valley □, Kenya 86 B4 0 20N 36 0 E
Rīga, Latvia 9 H21 56 53N 24 8 E
Rīga ✈ (RIX), Latvia 30 B10 56 54N 23 59 E
Riga, G. of, Latvia 9 H20 57 40N 23 45 E
Rigacikun, Nigeria 83 C6 10 40N 7 28 E
Rīgān, Iran 71 D8 28 37N 58 58 E
Rīgas Jūras Līcis = Riga, G. of, Latvia 9 H20 57 40N 23 45 E
Rigaud, Canada 117 A10 45 29N 74 18W
Rigby, U.S.A. 108 E8 43 40N 111 55W
Rīgestān, Afghan. 66 D4 30 15N 65 0 E
Riggins, U.S.A. 108 D5 45 25N 116 19W
Rignac, France 20 D6 44 25N 2 16 E
Rigolet, Canada 105 B8 54 10N 58 23W
Rihand Dam, India 69 G10 24 9N 83 2 E
Riihimäki, Finland 9 F21 60 45N 24 48 E
Riiser-Larsen-halvøya, Antarctica 5 C4 68 0 S 35 0 E
Rijau, Nigeria 83 C6 11 8N 5 17 E
Rijeka, Croatia 41 C11 45 20N 14 21 E
Rijeka Crnojevića, Serbia & M. 44 D3 42 24N 19 1 E
Rijssen, Neths. 17 B6 52 19N 6 31 E
Rika →, Ukraine 29 B8 48 11N 23 16 E
Rike, Ethiopia 81 E4 10 50N 39 53 E
Rikuchū-Kaigan Δ, Japan 54 E11 39 20N 142 0 E
Rikuzentakada, Japan 54 E10 39 0N 141 40 E
Rila, Bulgaria 44 D7 42 7N 23 7 E
Rila Planina, Bulgaria 44 D7 42 10N 23 20 E
Riley, U.S.A. 108 E4 43 32N 119 28W
Rima →, Nigeria 83 C6 13 4N 5 10 E
Rimah, Wadi ar →, Si. Arabia 70 E4 26 5N 41 30 E
Rimau, Pulau, Malaysia 65 c 5 15N 100 16 E
Rimavská Sobota, Slovak Rep. 27 C13 48 22N 20 2 E
Rimbey, Canada 102 C6 52 35N 114 15W
Rimbo, Sweden 10 E12 59 44N 18 21 E
Rimersburg, U.S.A. 116 E5 41 3N 79 30W
Rimforsa, Sweden 11 F9 58 6N 15 43 E
Rimi, Nigeria 83 C6 12 58N 7 43 E
Rímini, Italy 41 D9 44 3N 12 33 E
Rimouski, Canada 105 C6 48 27N 68 30W
Rimrock, U.S.A. 110 D5 46 38N 121 10W
Rinca, Indonesia 63 F5 8 45 S 119 35 E
Rincón de la Victoria, Spain 37 J6 36 43N 4 18W
Rincón de Romos, Mexico 118 C4 22 14N 102 18W
Rinconada, Argentina 126 A2 22 26 S 66 10W
Rind →, India 69 G9 25 53N 80 33 E
Ringarum, Sweden 11 F10 58 21N 16 26 E
Ringas, India 68 F6 27 21N 75 34 E
Ringe, Denmark 11 J4 55 13N 10 28 E
Ringim, Nigeria 83 C6 12 13N 9 10 E
Ringkøbing, Denmark 11 H2 56 5N 8 15 E
Ringkøbing Amtskommune □, Denmark 11 H2 56 10N 8 45 E
Ringkøbing Fjord, Denmark 11 H2 56 0N 8 15 E
Ringsjön, Sweden 11 J7 55 55N 13 30 E
Ringsted, Denmark 11 J5 55 25N 11 46 E
Ringvassøy, Norway 8 B18 69 56N 19 15 E
Ringwood, U.S.A. 117 E10 41 7N 74 15W
Rinía, Greece 47 D7 37 23N 25 13 E
Rinjani, Indonesia 62 F5 8 24 S 116 28 E
Rinteln, Germany 24 C5 52 10N 9 8 E
Río, Punta del, Spain 39 J2 36 49N 2 24W
Rio Branco, Brazil 124 E5 9 58 S 67 49W
Río Branco, Uruguay 127 C5 32 40 S 53 40W
Río Bravo ⌓, N. Amer. 118 B4 29 2N 102 45W
Río Bravo del Norte →, Mexico 119 B5 25 57N 97 9W
Rio Brilhante, Brazil 127 A5 21 48 S 54 33W
Rio Claro, Brazil 127 A6 22 19 S 47 35W
Rio Claro, Trin. & Tob. 121 D7 10 20N 61 25W
Río Colorado, Argentina 128 D4 39 0 S 64 0W
Río Cuarto, Argentina 126 C3 33 10 S 64 25W
Rio das Pedras, Mozam. 89 C6 23 8 S 35 28 E
Rio de Janeiro, Brazil 127 A7 23 0 S 43 12W
Rio de Janeiro □, Brazil 127 A7 22 50 S 43 0W
Rio do Sul, Brazil 127 B6 27 13 S 49 37W
Río Dulce Δ, Guatemala 120 C2 15 43N 88 50W
Río Gallegos, Argentina 128 G3 51 35 S 69 15W
Río Grande, Argentina 128 G3 53 50 S 67 45W
Rio Grande, Brazil 127 C5 32 0 S 52 20W
Río Grande, Mexico 118 C4 23 50N 103 2W
Río Grande, Nic. 120 D3 12 54N 83 33W
Río Grande, Puerto Rico 121 d 18 23N 65 50W
Rio Grande, U.S.A. 113 N6 25 58N 97 9W
Rio Grande City, U.S.A. 113 M5 26 23N 98 49W
Río Grande de Santiago →, Mexico 118 C3 21 36N 105 26W
Rio Grande do Norte □, Brazil 125 E11 5 40 S 36 0W
Rio Grande do Sul □, Brazil 127 C5 30 0 S 53 0W
Río Hato, Panama 120 E3 8 22N 80 10W
Río Lagartos, Mexico 119 C7 21 36N 88 10W
Rio Largo, Brazil 125 E11 9 28 S 35 50W
Rio Maior, Portugal 37 F2 39 19N 8 57W
Rio Marina, Italy 40 F7 42 49N 10 25 E
Río Mulatos, Bolivia 124 G5 19 40 S 66 50W
Río Muni □, Eq. Guin. 84 D2 1 30N 10 0 E
Rio Negro, Brazil 127 B6 26 0 S 49 55W
Rio Pardo, Brazil 127 C5 30 0 S 52 30W
Río Pilcomayo Δ, Argentina 126 B4 25 5 S 58 5W
Río Platano ⌓, Honduras 120 C3 15 45N 85 0W
Rio Rancho, U.S.A. 109 J10 35 14N 106 38W
Río Segundo, Argentina 126 C3 31 40 S 63 59W
Río Tercero, Argentina 126 C3 32 15 S 64 8W
Rio Tinto, Portugal 36 D2 41 11N 8 34W
Rio Verde, Brazil 125 G8 17 50 S 51 0W
Río Verde, Mexico 119 C5 21 56N 99 59W
Rio Vista, U.S.A. 110 G5 38 10N 121 42W
Ríobamba, Ecuador 124 D3 1 50 S 78 45W
Ríohacha, Colombia 124 A4 11 33N 72 55W
Riom, France 20 C7 45 54N 3 7 E
Riom-ès-Montagnes, France 20 C6 45 17N 2 39 E
Rion-des-Landes, France 20 E3 43 55N 0 56W
Rionero in Vúlture, Italy 43 B8 40 55N 15 40 E
Rioni →, Georgia 35 J5 42 14N 41 44 E
Riós, Spain 36 D3 41 58N 7 16W
Riosucio, Colombia 124 B3 7 27N 77 7W
Riou L., Canada 103 B7 59 7N 106 25W
Rioz, France 19 E13 47 26N 6 5 E
Ripatransone, Italy 41 F10 42 59N 13 46 E
Ripley, Canada 116 B3 44 4N 81 35W
Ripley, Calif., U.S.A. 111 M12 33 32N 114 39W
Ripley, N.Y., U.S.A. 116 D5 42 16N 79 43W
Ripley, Tenn., U.S.A. 113 H10 35 45N 89 32W
Ripley, W. Va., U.S.A. 114 F5 38 49N 81 43W
Ripoll, Spain 38 C7 42 15N 2 13 E
Ripon, U.K. 14 C6 54 9N 1 31W
Ripon, Calif., U.S.A. 110 H5 37 44N 121 7W
Ripon, Wis., U.S.A. 114 D1 43 51N 88 50W
Riposto, Italy 43 E8 37 44N 15 12 E
Risan, Serbia & M. 44 D2 42 32N 18 42 E
Riscle, France 20 E3 43 39N 0 5W
Rishā', W. ar →, Si. Arabia 70 E5 25 33N 44 5 E
Rishiri-Rebun-Sarobetsu Δ, Japan 54 B10 45 26N 141 30 E
Rishiri-Tō, Japan 54 B10 45 11N 141 15 E
Rishon le Ẕiyyon, Israel 74 D3 31 58N 34 48 E
Risle →, France 18 C7 49 26N 0 23 E
Risnjak Δ, Croatia 41 C11 45 25N 14 36 E
Rison, U.S.A. 113 J8 33 58N 92 11W
Risør, Norway 9 G13 58 43N 9 13 E
Rita Blanca Cr. →, U.S.A. 113 H3 35 40N 102 29W
Riti, Nigeria 83 D6 7 57N 9 41 E
Ritter, Mt., U.S.A. 110 H7 37 41N 119 12W
Rittman, U.S.A. 116 F3 40 58N 81 47W
Ritzville, U.S.A. 108 C4 47 8N 118 23W
Riva del Garda, Italy 40 C7 45 53N 10 50 E
Riva Lígure, Italy 40 E4 43 50N 7 50 E
Rivadavia, Buenos Aires, Argentina 126 D3 35 29 S 62 59W
Rivadavia, Mendoza, Argentina 126 C2 33 13 S 68 30W
Rivadavia, Salta, Argentina 126 A3 24 5 S 62 54W
Rivadavia, Chile 126 B1 29 57 S 70 35W
Rivarolo Canavese, Italy 40 C4 45 19N 7 43 E
Rivas, Nic. 120 D2 11 30N 85 50W
Rive-de-Gier, France 21 C8 45 32N 4 37 E
River Cess, Liberia 82 D3 5 30N 9 32W
River Jordan, Canada 110 B2 48 26N 124 3W
Rivera, Argentina 126 D3 37 12 S 63 14W
Rivera, Uruguay 127 C4 31 0 S 55 50W
Riverbank, U.S.A. 110 H6 37 44N 120 56W
Riverdale, U.S.A. 110 J7 36 26N 119 52W
Riverhead, U.S.A. 117 F12 40 55N 72 40W
Riverhurst, Canada 103 C7 50 55N 106 50W
Rivers, Canada 103 C8 50 2N 100 14W
Rivers □, Nigeria 83 E6 4 30N 7 10 E
Rivers Inlet, Canada 102 C3 51 42N 127 15W
Riversdale, S. Africa 88 E3 34 7 S 21 15 E
Riverside, U.S.A. 111 M9 33 59N 117 22W
Riverton, Australia 95 E2 34 10 S 138 46 E
Riverton, Canada 103 C9 51 1N 97 0W
Riverton, N.Z. 91 M2 46 21 S 168 0 E
Riverton, U.S.A. 108 E9 43 2N 108 23W
Riverton Heights, U.S.A. 110 C4 47 28N 122 17W
Rives, France 21 C9 45 21N 5 31 E
Rivesaltes, France 20 F6 42 47N 2 50 E
Riviera, U.S.A. 111 K12 35 4N 114 35W
Riviera di Levante, Italy 40 D6 44 15N 9 30 E
Riviera di Ponente, Italy 40 D5 44 10N 8 20 E
Rivière-au-Renard, Canada 105 C7 48 59N 64 23W
Rivière-du-Loup, Canada 105 C6 47 50N 69 30W
Rivière-Pentecôte, Canada 105 C6 49 57N 67 1W
Rivière-Pilote, Martinique 120 c 14 26N 60 53W
Rivière St-Paul, Canada 105 B8 51 28N 57 45W
Rivière-Salée, Martinique 120 c 14 31N 61 0W
Rivne, Ukraine 29 D14 46 1N 29 10 E
Rivne, Ukraine 33 G4 50 40N 26 10 E
Rívoli, Italy 40 C4 45 3N 7 31 E
Rivoli B., Australia 95 F3 37 32 S 140 3 E
Rixheim, France 19 E14 47 40N 7 24 E
Riyadh = Ar Riyāḑ, Si. Arabia 70 E5 24 41N 46 42 E
Rize, Turkey 73 B9 41 0N 40 30 E
Rizhao, China 57 G10 35 25N 119 30 E
Rizokarpaso, Cyprus 49 D13 35 36N 34 23 E
Rizzuto, C., Italy 43 D10 38 53N 17 5 E
Rjukan, Norway 9 G13 59 54N 8 33 E
Ro, Greece 47 E11 36 9N 29 33 E
Roa, Spain 36 D7 41 41N 3 56W
Road Town, Br. Virgin Is. 121 e 18 27N 64 37W
Roan Plateau, U.S.A. 108 G9 39 20N 109 20W
Roanne, France 19 F11 46 3N 4 4 E
Roanoke, Ala., U.S.A. 115 J3 33 9N 85 22W
Roanoke, Va., U.S.A. 114 G6 37 16N 79 56W
Roanoke →, U.S.A. 115 H7 35 57N 76 42W
Roanoke I., U.S.A. 115 H8 35 55N 75 40W
Roanoke Rapids, U.S.A. 115 G7 36 28N 77 40W
Roatán, Honduras 120 C2 16 18N 86 35W
Robāt Sang, Iran 71 C8 35 35N 59 10 E
Robāţkarīm, Iran 71 C6 35 25N 50 59 E
Robāţkarīm □, Iran 71 B6 35 26N 50 59 E
Robbins I., Australia 95 G4 40 42 S 145 0 E
Róbbio, Italy 40 C5 45 17N 8 35 E
Robe →, Australia 92 D2 21 42 S 116 15 E
Röbel, Germany 24 B8 53 22N 12 35 E
Robert Lee, U.S.A. 113 K4 31 54N 100 29W
Robertsdale, U.S.A. 116 F6 40 11N 78 6W
Robertsganj, India 69 G10 24 44N 83 4 E
Robertson, S. Africa 88 E2 33 46 S 19 50 E
Robertson I., Antarctica 5 C18 65 15 S 59 30W
Robertson Ra., Australia 92 D3 23 15 S 121 0 E
Robertsport, Liberia 82 D2 6 45N 11 26W
Robertstown, Australia 95 E2 33 58 S 139 5 E
Roberval, Canada 105 C5 48 32N 72 15W
Robeson Chan., N. Amer. 4 A4 82 0N 61 30W
Robesonia, U.S.A. 117 F8 40 21N 76 8W
Robi, Ethiopia 81 F4 7 52N 39 38 E
Robinson, U.S.A. 114 F2 39 0N 87 44W
Robinson →, Australia 94 B2 16 3 S 137 16 E
Robinson Ra., Australia 93 E2 25 40 S 119 0 E
Robinvale, Australia 95 E3 34 40 S 142 45 E
Robledo, Spain 39 G2 38 46N 2 26W
Roblin, Canada 103 C8 51 14N 101 21W
Roboré, Bolivia 124 G7 18 10 S 59 45W
Robson, Canada 102 D5 49 20N 117 41W
Robson, Mt., Canada 102 C5 53 10N 119 10W
Robstown, U.S.A. 113 M6 27 47N 97 40W
Roca, C. da, Portugal 37 G1 38 40N 9 31W
Roca Partida, I., Mexico 118 D2 19 1N 112 2W
Rocamadour, France 20 D5 44 48N 1 37 E
Rocas, I., Brazil 125 D12 4 0 S 34 1W
Rocca San Casciano, Italy 41 D8 44 3N 11 50 E
Roccadáspide, Italy 43 B8 40 27N 15 10 E
Roccastrada, Italy 41 F8 43 0N 11 10 E
Roccella Iónica, Italy 43 D9 38 19N 16 24 E
Rocha, Uruguay 127 C5 34 30 S 54 25W
Rochdale, U.K. 14 D5 53 38N 2 9W
Rochechouart, France 20 C4 45 50N 0 49 E
Rochefort, Belgium 17 D5 50 9N 5 12 E
Rochefort, France 20 C3 45 56N 0 57W
Rochefort-en-Terre, France 18 E4 47 42N 2 22W
Rochelle, U.S.A. 112 E10 41 56N 89 4W
Rocher River, Canada 102 A6 61 23N 112 44W
Rocheservière, France 18 F5 46 57N 1 30W
Rochester, U.K. 15 F8 51 23N 0 31 E
Rochester, Ind., U.S.A. 114 E2 41 4N 86 13W
Rochester, Minn., U.S.A. 112 C8 44 1N 92 28W
Rochester, N.H., U.S.A. 117 C14 43 18N 70 59W
Rochester, N.Y., U.S.A. 116 C7 43 10N 77 37W
Rociu, Romania 29 F10 44 43N 25 2 E
Rock →, Canada 102 A3 60 7N 127 7W
Rock Creek, U.S.A. 116 E4 41 40N 80 52W
Rock Falls, U.S.A. 112 E10 41 47N 89 41W
Rock Hill, U.S.A. 115 H5 34 56N 81 1W
Rock Island, U.S.A. 112 E9 41 30N 90 34W
Rock Rapids, U.S.A. 112 D6 43 26N 96 10W
Rock Sound, Bahamas 120 B4 24 54N 76 12W
Rock Springs, Mont., U.S.A. 108 C10 46 49N 106 15W
Rock Springs, Wyo., U.S.A. 108 F9 41 35N 109 14W
Rock Valley, U.S.A. 112 D6 43 12N 96 18W
Rockall, Atl. Oc. 6 D3 57 37N 13 42W
Rockdale, Tex., U.S.A. 113 K6 30 39N 97 0W
Rockdale, Wash., U.S.A. 110 C5 47 22N 121 28W
Rockeby = Mungkan Kandju Δ, Australia 94 A3 13 35 S 142 52 E
Rockefeller Plateau, Antarctica 5 E14 80 0 S 140 0W
Rockford, U.S.A. 112 D10 42 16N 89 6W
Rockglen, Canada 103 D7 49 11N 105 57W
Rockhampton, Australia 94 C5 23 22 S 150 32 E
Rockingham, Australia 93 F2 32 15 S 115 38 E
Rockingham, U.S.A. 115 H6 34 57N 79 46W
Rockingham B., Australia 94 B4 18 5 S 146 10 E
Rocklake, U.S.A. 112 A5 48 47N 99 15W
Rockland, Canada 117 A9 45 33N 75 17W
Rockland, Idaho, U.S.A. 108 E7 42 34N 112 53W
Rockland, Maine, U.S.A. 115 C11 44 6N 69 7W
Rockland, Mich., U.S.A. 112 B10 46 44N 89 11W
Rocklin, U.S.A. 110 G5 38 48N 121 14W
Rockly B., Trin. & Tob. 125 J16 11 9N 60 46W
Rockmart, U.S.A. 115 H3 34 0N 85 3W
Rockport, Mass., U.S.A. 117 D14 42 39N 70 37W
Rockport, Mo., U.S.A. 112 E7 40 25N 95 31W
Rockport, Tex., U.S.A. 113 L6 28 2N 97 3W
Rocksprings, U.S.A. 113 K4 30 1N 100 13W
Rockville, Conn., U.S.A. 117 E12 41 52N 72 28W
Rockville, Md., U.S.A. 114 F7 39 5N 77 9W
Rockwall, U.S.A. 113 J6 32 56N 96 28W
Rockwell City, U.S.A. 112 D7 42 24N 94 38W
Rockwood, Canada 116 C4 43 37N 80 8W
Rockwood, Maine, U.S.A. 115 C11 45 41N 69 45W
Rockwood, Tenn., U.S.A. 115 H3 35 52N 84 41W
Rocky Ford, U.S.A. 112 F3 38 3N 103 43W
Rocky Gully, Australia 93 F2 34 30 S 116 57 E
Rocky Harbour, Canada 105 C8 49 36N 57 55W
Rocky Island L., Canada 104 C3 46 55N 83 0W
Rocky Lane, Canada 102 B5 58 31N 116 22W
Rocky Mount, U.S.A. 115 H7 35 57N 77 48W
Rocky Mountain Δ, U.S.A. 108 F11 40 25N 105 45W
Rocky Mountain House, Canada 102 C6 52 22N 114 55W
Rocky Mts., N. Amer. 108 G10 49 0N 115 0W
Rocky Point, Namibia 88 B2 19 3 S 12 30 E
Rocroi, France 19 C11 49 55N 4 30 E
Rod, Pakistan 66 E3 28 10N 63 5 E
Rødby, Denmark 11 K5 54 41N 11 23 E
Rødbyhavn, Denmark 11 K5 54 39N 11 22 E
Roddickton, Canada 105 B8 50 51N 56 8W
Rødding, Denmark 11 J3 55 23N 9 3 E
Rödeby, Sweden 11 H9 56 15N 15 37 E
Rødekro, Denmark 11 J3 55 4N 9 20 E
Rodenkirchen, Germany 24 B4 53 23N 8 26 E
Rodez, France 20 D6 44 21N 2 33 E
Rodholívas, Greece 44 F7 40 55N 24 0 E
Rodhópi □, Greece 45 E9 41 5N 25 30 E
Rodhopoú, Greece 49 D5 35 34N 23 45 E
Ródhos, Greece 49 C10 36 15N 28 10 E
Ródhos ✈ (RHO), Greece 47 E10 36 23N 28 12 E
Rodi Gargánico, Italy 41 G12 41 55N 15 53 E
Rodna, Romania 29 C9 47 25N 24 50 E
Rodnei, Munţii, Romania 29 C9 47 35N 24 35 E
Rodney, Canada 116 D3 42 34N 81 41W
Rodney, C., N.Z. 91 G5 36 17 S 174 50 E
Rodniki, Russia 34 B5 57 7N 41 47 E
Rodonit, Kepi i, Albania 44 E3 41 35N 19 27 E
Rodriguez, Ind. Oc. 3 E13 19 45 S 63 20 E
Roe →, U.K. 12 A5 55 6N 6 59W
Roebling, U.S.A. 117 F10 40 7N 74 47W
Roebourne, Australia 92 D2 20 44 S 117 9 E
Roebuck B., Australia 92 C3 18 5 S 122 20 E
Roermond, Neths. 17 C6 51 12N 6 0 E
Roes Welcome Sd., Canada 101 B11 65 0N 87 0W
Roeselare, Belgium 17 D3 50 57N 3 7 E
Rogachev = Ragachow, Belarus 33 F6 53 8N 30 5 E
Rogačica, Serbia & M. 44 B3 44 4N 19 40 E
Rogagua, L., Bolivia 124 F5 13 43 S 66 50W
Rogaška Slatina, Slovenia 41 B12 46 15N 15 42 E
Rogatec, Slovenia 41 B12 46 15N 15 46 E
Rogatica, Bos.-H. 28 G4 43 47N 19 0 E
Rogatyn, Ukraine 33 H3 49 24N 24 36 E
Rogdhia, Greece 49 D7 35 22N 25 1 E
Rogers, U.S.A. 113 G7 36 20N 94 7W
Rogers City, U.S.A. 114 C4 45 25N 83 49W
Rogersville, Canada 105 C6 46 44N 65 26W
Roggan →, Canada 104 B4 54 24N 79 25W
Roggan L., Canada 104 B4 54 8N 77 50W
Roggeveldberge, S. Africa 88 E3 32 10 S 20 10 E
Roggiano Gravina, Italy 43 C9 39 37N 16 9 E
Rogliano, France 21 F13 42 57N 9 30 E
Rogliano, Italy 43 C9 39 10N 16 19 E
Rogoaguado, L., Bolivia 124 F5 13 0 S 65 30W
Rogojampi, Indonesia 63 J17 8 19 S 114 17 E
Rogoźno, Poland 31 F3 52 45N 16 59 E
Rogue →, U.S.A. 108 E1 42 26N 124 26W
Rohan, France 18 D4 48 4N 2 45W
Róhda, Greece 49 A3 39 48N 19 46 E
Rohnert Park, U.S.A. 110 G4 38 16N 122 40W
Rohri, Pakistan 68 F3 27 45N 68 51 E
Rohri Canal, Pakistan 68 F3 26 15N 68 27 E
Rohtak, India 68 E7 28 55N 76 43 E
Roi Et, Thailand 64 D4 16 4N 103 40 E
Roja, Latvia 9 H20 57 29N 22 43 E
Rojas, Argentina 126 C3 34 10 S 60 45W
Rojişte, Romania 29 F8 44 4N 23 56 E
Rojo, C., Mexico 119 C5 21 33N 97 20W
Rokan →, Indonesia 62 D2 2 0N 100 50 E
Rokel →, S. Leone 82 D2 8 30N 12 48W
Rokiškis, Lithuania 9 J21 55 55N 25 35 E
Rokitno, Russia 33 G8 50 57N 35 56 E
Rokycany, Czech Rep. 26 B6 49 43N 13 35 E
Rolândia, Brazil 127 A5 23 18 S 51 23W
Rolla, U.S.A. 113 G9 37 57N 91 46W
Rolleston, Australia 94 C4 24 28 S 148 35 E
Rollingstone, Australia 94 B4 19 2 S 146 24 E
Rom, Sudan 81 F3 9 54N 32 16 E
Roma, Australia 95 D4 26 32 S 148 49 E
Roma, Italy 41 G9 41 54N 12 29 E
Roma, Sweden 11 G12 57 32N 18 26 E
Roma, U.S.A. 113 M5 26 25N 99 1W
Roma Fiumicino ✈ (FCO), Italy 41 G9 41 48N 12 15 E
Romain C., U.S.A. 115 J6 33 0N 79 22W
Romaine, Canada 105 B7 50 13N 60 40W
Romaine →, Canada 105 B7 50 18N 63 47W
Roman, Bulgaria 44 C7 43 8N 23 57 E
Roman, Romania 29 D11 46 57N 26 55 E
Roman-Kosh, Gora, Ukraine 33 K8 44 37N 34 15 E
Romanche →, France 21 C9 45 5N 5 43 E
Romang, Indonesia 63 F7 7 30 S 127 20 E
Români, Egypt 74 E1 30 59N 32 38 E
Romania ■, Europe 29 D10 46 0N 25 0 E
Romanija, Bos.-H. 28 G3 43 50N 18 45 E
Romano, Cayo, Cuba 120 B4 22 0N 77 30W
Romans-sur-Isère, France 21 C9 45 3N 5 3 E
Romanshorn, Switz. 25 H5 47 33N 9 22 E
Rombari, Sudan 81 G3 4 33N 31 2 E
Romblon, Phil. 61 E5 12 33N 122 17 E
Rome = Roma, Italy 41 G9 41 54N 12 29 E
Rome, Ga., U.S.A. 115 H3 34 15N 85 10W
Rome, N.Y., U.S.A. 117 C9 43 13N 75 27W
Rome, Pa., U.S.A. 117 E8 41 51N 76 21W
Rometta, Italy 43 D8 38 10N 15 25 E
Romilly-sur-Seine, France 19 D10 48 31N 3 44 E
Romney, U.S.A. 114 F6 39 21N 78 45W
Romney Marsh, U.K. 15 F8 51 2N 0 54 E
Romny, Ukraine 33 G7 50 48N 33 28 E
Rømø, Denmark 11 J2 55 10N 8 30 E
Romodan, Ukraine 33 G7 49 55N 33 15 E
Romodanovo, Russia 34 C7 54 26N 45 23 E
Romont, Switz. 25 J2 46 42N 6 54 E
Romorantin-Lanthenay, France 19 E8 47 21N 1 45 E
Romsdalen, Norway 9 E12 62 25N 7 52 E
Romsey, U.K. 15 G6 51 0N 1 29W
Ron, Vietnam 64 D6 17 53N 106 27 E
Rona, U.K. 13 D3 57 34N 5 59W
Ronan, U.S.A. 108 C6 47 32N 114 6W
Roncador, Cayos, Colombia 120 D3 13 32N 80 4W
Roncador, Serra do, Brazil 125 F8 12 30 S 52 30W
Ronciglione, Italy 41 F9 42 17N 12 13 E
Ronco →, Italy 41 D9 44 24N 12 12 E
Ronda, Spain 37 J5 36 46N 5 12W
Ronda, Serranía de, Spain 37 J5 36 44N 5 3W
Rondane, Norway 9 F13 61 57N 9 50 E
Rondônia □, Brazil 124 F6 11 0 S 63 0W
Rondonópolis, Brazil 125 G8 16 28 S 54 38W
Rong, Koh, Cambodia 65 G4 10 45N 103 15 E
Rong Jiang →, China 58 E7 24 35N 109 20 E
Rong Xian, Guangxi Zhuangzu, China 59 F8 22 50N 110 31 E
Rong Xian, Sichuan, China 58 C5 29 23N 104 22 E
Rong'an, China 58 E7 25 14N 109 22 E
Rongchang, China 58 C5 29 20N 105 32 E
Ronge, L. la, Canada 103 B7 55 6N 105 17W
Rongjiang, China 58 E7 25 57N 108 28 E
Rongshui, China 58 E7 25 5N 109 12 E
Rønne, Denmark 11 J8 55 6N 14 43 E
Ronne Ice Shelf, Antarctica 5 D18 78 0 S 60 0W
Ronneby, Sweden 11 H9 56 12N 15 17 E
Ronnebyån →, Sweden 11 H9 56 11N 15 18 E
Rönneshytta, Sweden 11 F9 58 56N 15 2 E
Ronsard, C., Australia 93 D1 24 46 S 113 10 E
Ronse, Belgium 17 D3 50 45N 3 35 E
Roodepoort, S. Africa 89 D4 26 11 S 27 54 E
Roof Butte, U.S.A. 109 H9 36 28N 109 5W
Rooiboklaagte →, Namibia 88 C3 20 50 S 21 0 E
Roorkee, India 68 E7 29 52N 77 59 E
Roosendaal, Neths. 17 C4 51 32N 4 29 E
Roosevelt, U.S.A. 108 F8 40 18N 109 59W
Roosevelt →, Brazil 124 E6 7 35 S 60 20W
Roosevelt, Mt., Canada 102 B3 58 26N 125 20W
Roosevelt I., Antarctica 5 D12 79 30 S 162 0W
Ropczyce, Poland 31 H8 50 4N 21 38 E
Roper →, Australia 94 A2 14 43 S 135 27 E
Roper Bar, Australia 94 A1 14 44 S 134 44 E
Roque Pérez, Argentina 126 D4 35 25 S 59 24W
Roquefort, France 20 D3 44 2N 0 20W
Roquemaure, France 21 D8 44 3N 4 48 E
Roquetas de Mar, Spain 39 J2 36 46N 2 36W
Roquetes, Spain 38 E5 40 50N 0 30 E
Roquevaire, France 21 E9 43 20N 5 36 E
Roraima □, Brazil 124 C6 2 0N 61 30W
Roraima, Mt., Venezuela 124 B6 5 10N 60 40W
Røros, Norway 9 E14 62 35N 11 23 E
Rorschach, Switz. 25 H5 47 28N 9 28 E
Rosa, Zambia 87 D3 9 33 S 31 15 E
Rosa, L., Bahamas 121 B5 21 0N 73 30W
Rosa, Monte, Europe 40 C4 45 57N 7 53 E
Rosal de la Frontera, Spain 37 H3 37 59N 7 13W
Rosalia, U.S.A. 108 C5 47 14N 117 22W
Rosamond, U.S.A. 111 L8 34 52N 118 10W
Rosans, France 21 D9 44 24N 5 29 E
Rosario, Argentina 126 C3 33 0 S 60 40W
Rosário, Brazil 125 D10 3 0 S 44 15W
Rosario, Baja Calif., Mexico 118 B1 30 0N 115 50W
Rosario, Sinaloa, Mexico 118 C3 23 0N 105 52W
Rosario, Paraguay 126 A4 24 30 S 57 35W
Rosario de la Frontera, Argentina 126 B3 25 50 S 65 0W
Rosario de Lerma, Argentina 126 A2 24 59 S 65 35W
Rosario del Tala, Argentina 126 C4 32 20 S 59 10W
Rosário do Sul, Brazil 127 C5 30 15 S 54 55W
Rosarito, Mexico 111 N9 32 18N 117 4W
Rosarno, Italy 43 D8 38 29N 15 58 E
Rosas = Roses, Spain 38 C8 42 19N 3 10 E
Roscoe, U.S.A. 117 E10 41 56N 74 55W
Roscoff, France 18 D3 48 44N 3 58W
Roscommon, Ireland 12 C3 53 38N 8 11W
Roscommon □, Ireland 12 C3 53 49N 8 23W
Roscrea, Ireland 12 D4 52 57N 7 49W
Rose →, Australia 94 A2 14 16 S 135 45 E
Rose Blanche-Harbour Le Cou, Canada 105 C8 47 38N 58 45W
Rose Pt., Canada 102 C2 54 11N 131 39W
Rose Valley, Canada 103 C8 52 19N 103 49W
Roseau, Dominica 121 C7 15 17N 61 24W
Roseau, U.S.A. 112 A7 48 51N 95 46W
Rosebery, Australia 95 G4 41 46 S 145 33 E
Rosebud, S. Dak., U.S.A. 112 D4 43 14N 100 51W

Rosebud, Tex., U.S.A. . 113 K6 31 4N 96 59W
Roseburg, U.S.A. 108 E2 43 13N 123 20W
Rosedale, U.S.A. 113 J9 33 51N 91 2W
Rosehearty, U.K. 13 D6 57 42N 2 7W
Roseland, U.S.A. 110 G4 38 45N 121 17W
Rosemary, Canada .. 102 C6 50 46N 112 5W
Rosenberg, U.S.A. ... 113 L7 29 34N 95 49W
Rosendaël, France ... 19 A9 51 3N 2 24 E
Rosenheim, Germany . 25 H8 47 51N 12 7 E
Roses, Spain .... 38 C8 42 19N 3 10 E
Roses, G. de, Spain .. 38 C8 42 10N 3 15 E
Roseto degli Abruzzi,
Italy .... 41 F11 42 41N 14 1 E
Rosetown, Canada ... 103 C7 51 35N 107 59W
Rosetta = Rashîd, Egypt 80 H7 31 21N 30 22 E
Roseville, Calif., U.S.A. 110 G5 38 45N 121 17W
Roseville, Mich., U.S.A. 116 D2 42 30N 82 56W
Rosewood, Australia . 95 D5 27 38 S 152 36 E
Roshkhvâr, Iran .... 71 C8 34 58N 59 37 E
Rosières-en-Santerre,
France .... 19 C9 49 49N 2 42 E
Rosignano Maríttimo,
Italy .... 40 E7 43 24N 10 28 E
Rosignol, Guyana ... 124 B7 6 15N 57 30W
Roşiori de Vede,
Romania .... 29 F10 44 9N 25 0 E
Rositsa, Bulgaria ... 45 C11 43 57N 27 57 E
Rositsa →, Bulgaria . 45 C9 43 10N 25 30 E
Roskilde, Denmark .. 11 J6 55 38N 12 3 E
Roskilde
Amtskommune □,
Denmark .... 11 J6 55 35N 12 5 E
Roskovec, Albania .. 44 F3 40 44N 19 43 E
Roslavl, Russia ..... 32 F7 53 57N 32 55 E
Rosmaninhal, Portugal 36 F3 39 44N 7 5W
Rosmead, S. Africa .. 88 E4 31 29 S 25 8 E
Rosolini, Italy ...... 43 F7 36 49N 14 57 E
Rosporden, France .. 18 E3 47 57N 3 50W
Ross, Australia ..... 95 G4 42 2 S 147 30 E
Ross, N.Z. .... 91 K3 42 53 S 170 49 E
Ross Béthio, Mauritania 82 B1 16 15N 16 8W
Ross Dependency,
Antarctica ...... 5 D12 76 0 S 170 0W
Ross I., Antarctica .. 5 D11 77 30 S 168 0 E
Ross Ice Shelf,
Antarctica ...... 5 E12 80 0 S 180 0 E
Ross L., U.S.A. 108 B3 48 44N 121 4W
Ross-on-Wye, U.K. .. 15 F5 51 54N 2 34W
Ross River, Australia . 94 C1 23 44 S 134 30 E
Ross River, Canada .. 102 A2 62 30N 131 30W
Ross Sea, Antarctica . 5 D11 74 0 S 178 0 E
Rossall Pt., U.K. ... 14 D4 53 55N 3 3W
Rossan Pt., Ireland .. 12 B3 54 42N 8 47W
Rossano, Italy ...... 43 C9 39 36N 16 39 E
Rossburn, Canada ... 103 C8 50 40N 100 49W
Rosseau, Canada ... 116 A5 45 16N 79 39W
Rosseau L., Canada .. 116 A5 45 10N 79 35W
Rosses, The, Ireland . 12 A3 55 2N 8 20W
Rossignol, L., Canada 104 B5 52 43N 73 40W
Rossignol L., Canada . 105 D6 44 12N 65 10W
Rossland, Canada ... 102 D5 49 6N 117 50W
Rosslare, Ireland 12 D5 52 17N 6 24W
Rosslare Harbour,
Ireland 12 D5 52 15N 6 20W
Rosslau, Germany ... 24 D8 51 52N 12 15 E
Rosso, Mauritania .. 82 B1 16 40N 15 45W
Rosso, C., France ... 21 F12 42 13N 8 32 E
Rossosh, Russia .... 33 G10 50 15N 39 28 E
Røssvatnet, Norway . 8 D16 65 45N 14 5 E
Røst, Norway ...... 8 C15 67 32N 12 0 E
Rosthern, Canada ... 103 C7 52 40N 106 20W
Rostock, Germany ... 24 A8 54 5N 12 8 E
Rostov, Don, Russia . 33 J10 47 15N 39 45 E
Rostov, Yaroslavl,
Russia .... 32 D10 57 14N 39 25 E
Rostrenen, France ... 18 D3 48 14N 3 21W
Roswell, Ga., U.S.A. . 115 H3 34 2N 84 22W
Roswell, N. Mex., U.S.A. 115 H3 33 24N 104 32W
Rota, Spain 37 J4 36 37N 6 20W
Rotan, U.S.A. 113 J4 32 51N 100 28W
Rotenburg, Hessen,
Germany .... 24 E5 50 59N 9 44 E
Rotenburg,
Niedersachsen,
Germany .... 24 B5 53 6N 9 25 E
Roth, Germany ..... 25 F7 49 15N 11 5 E
Rothaargebirge,
Germany .... 24 D4 51 2N 8 13 E
Rothaargebirge △,
Germany .... 24 E4 51 0N 8 15 E
Rothenburg ob der
Tauber, Germany . 25 F6 49 23N 10 11 E
Rother →, U.K. ..... 15 G8 50 59N 0 45 E
Rothera, Antarctica . 5 C17 67 25 S 63 0W
Rotherham, U.K. ... 14 D6 53 26N 1 20W
Rothes, U.K. 13 D5 57 32N 3 13W
Rothesay, Canada ... 105 C6 45 23N 66 0W
Rothesay, U.K. 13 F3 55 50N 5 3W
Roti, Indonesia .... 63 F6 10 50 S 123 0 E
Rotja, Pta., Spain ... 39 G6 38 38N 1 35 E
Roto, Australia ..... 95 E4 33 0 S 145 30 E
Rotondo, Mte., France 21 F13 42 14N 9 8 E
Rotorua, L., N.Z. ... 91 J4 41 55 S 172 39 E
Rotorua, N.Z. ...... 91 H6 38 9 S 176 16 E
Rotorua, L., N.Z. ... 91 H6 38 5 S 176 18 E
Rott →, Germany ... 25 G9 48 27N 13 25 E
Rottenburg, Germany 25 G4 48 28N 8 56 E
Rottenmann, Austria . 26 D7 47 31N 14 22 E
Rotterdam, Neths. .. 17 C4 51 55N 4 30 E
Rotterdam, U.S.A. .. 117 D10 42 48N 74 1W
Rottne, Sweden .... 11 G8 57 1N 14 54 E
Rottnest I., Australia . 93 F2 32 0 S 115 27 E
Rottumeroog, Neths. . 17 A6 53 33N 6 34 E
Rottweil, Germany .. 25 G4 48 9N 8 37 E
Rotuma, Fiji .... 96 J9 12 25 S 177 5 E
Roubaix, France .... 19 B10 50 40N 3 10 E
Roudnice nad Labem,
Czech Rep. ..... 26 A7 50 25N 14 15 E
Rouen, France ..... 18 C8 49 27N 1 4 E
Rouergue, France ... 20 D5 44 15N 2 0 E
Rouillac, France 20 C3 45 47N 0 4W
Rouleau, Canada ... 103 C8 50 10N 104 56W
Round Mountain, U.S.A. 108 G5 38 43N 117 4W
Round Mt., Australia . 95 E5 30 26 S 152 16 E
Round Rock, U.S.A. . 113 K6 30 31N 97 41W
Roundup, U.S.A. ... 108 C9 46 27N 108 33W
Rousay, U.K. 13 B5 59 10N 3 2W
Rouses Point, U.S.A. . 117 B11 44 59N 73 22W
Rouseville, U.S.A. .. 116 E5 41 28N 79 42W
Roussillon, Isère, France 21 C8 45 24N 4 49 E
Roussillon,
Pyrénées-Or., France 20 F6 42 30N 2 35 E
Rouxville, S. Africa . 88 E4 30 25 S 26 50 E
Rouyn-Noranda,
Canada 104 C4 48 20N 79 0W
Rovaniemi, Finland . 8 C21 66 29N 25 41 E

Rovato, Italy .... 40 C7 45 34N 10 0 E
Rovenki, Ukraine ... 33 H10 48 5N 39 21 E
Rovereto, Italy ..... 40 C8 45 53N 11 3 E
Rovigo, Italy .... 41 C8 45 4N 11 47 E
Rovinj, Croatia ..... 41 C10 45 5N 13 40 E
Rovno = Rivne, Ukraine 33 G4 50 40N 26 10 E
Rovnoye, Russia .... 34 E8 50 52N 46 3 E
Rovuma = Ruvuma →,
Tanzania .... 87 E5 10 29 S 40 28 E
Row'ān, Iran .... 71 C6 35 8N 48 51 E
Rowena, Australia .. 95 D4 29 48 S 148 55 E
Rowley Shoals, Australia 92 C2 17 30 S 119 0 E
Roxa, Guinea-Biss. .. 82 C1 11 15N 15 45W
Roxas, Capiz, Phil. .. 61 F5 11 36N 122 49 E
Roxas, Isabela, Phil. . 61 C4 17 8N 121 36 E
Roxas, Mind. Or., Phil. 61 B4 12 35N 121 31 E
Roxborough,
Trin. & Tob. 125 J16 11 15N 60 35W
Roxburgh, N.Z. .... 91 L2 45 33 S 169 19 E
Roxbury, U.S.A. ... 116 F7 40 6N 77 39W
Roxen, Sweden ..... 11 F9 58 30N 15 40 E
Roy, Mont., U.S.A. . 108 C9 47 20N 108 58W
Roy, N. Mex., U.S.A. 113 H2 35 57N 104 12W
Roy, Utah, U.S.A. .. 108 F7 41 10N 112 2W
Royal Canal, Ireland . 12 C4 53 30N 7 13W
Royal Leamington Spa,
U.K. 15 E6 52 18N 1 31W
Royal Natal △, S. Africa 89 D4 28 43 S 28 51 E
Royal Tunbridge Wells,
U.K. .... 15 F8 51 7N 0 16 E
Royale, Isle, U.S.A. . 112 B10 48 0N 88 54W
Royan, France 20 C2 45 37N 1 2W
Roye, France .... 19 C9 49 42N 2 48 E
Royston, U.K. 15 E7 52 3N 0 0W
Rožaj, Serbia & M. .. 44 D4 42 50N 20 11 E
Różan, Poland ...... 31 F8 52 52N 21 25 E
Rozay-en-Brie, France 19 D9 48 41N 2 58 E
Rozdilna, Ukraine .. 29 D15 46 50N 30 2 E
Rozhnyativ, Ukraine . 29 B9 48 38N 24 2 E
Rozhyshche, Ukraine . 33 G3 50 54N 25 15 E
Rožmitál pod
Třemšínem,
Czech Rep. ..... 26 B6 49 36N 13 53 E
Rožňava, Slovak Rep. 27 C13 48 37N 20 35 E
Rozogi, Poland ..... 30 E8 53 28N 21 19 E
Rozoy-sur-Serre, France 19 C11 49 40N 4 8 E
Rozzano, Italy ...... 40 C6 45 22N 9 10 E
Rrëshen, Albania ... 44 E3 41 47N 19 49 E
Rrogozhinë, Albania . 44 E3 41 2N 19 50 E
Rtanj, Serbia & M. .. 44 C5 43 45N 21 50 E
Rtishchevo, Russia .. 34 D6 52 18N 43 46 E
Rúa = A Rúa, Spain . 36 C3 42 24N 7 6W
Ruacaná, Namibia .. 88 B1 17 27 S 14 21 E
Ruaha △, Tanzania . 86 D3 7 41 S 34 30 E
Ruahine Ra., N.Z. .. 91 H6 39 55 S 176 2 E
Ruapehu, N.Z. ..... 91 H5 39 17 S 175 35 E
Ruapuke I., N.Z. ... 91 M2 46 46 S 168 31 E
Ruâq, W. →, Egypt . 74 F2 30 0N 33 49 E
Rub' al Khālī, Si. Arabia 75 D4 19 0N 48 0 E
Rubeho Mts., Tanzania 86 D4 6 50 S 36 25 E
Rubezhnoye =
Rubizhne, Ukraine . 33 H10 49 6N 38 25 E
Rubh a' Mhail, U.K. . 13 F2 55 56N 6 8W
Rubha Hunish, U.K. . 13 D2 57 42N 6 20W
Rubha Robhanais =
Lewis, But. of, U.K. . 13 C2 58 31N 6 16W
Rubi, Spain .... 38 D7 41 29N 2 2 E
Rubicon →, U.S.A. . 110 G5 38 53N 121 4W
Rubicone →, Italy .. 41 D9 44 8N 12 28 E
Rubik, Albania ..... 44 E3 41 46N 19 47 E
Rubino, Ivory C. 82 D4 6 4N 4 18W
Rubizhne, Ukraine .. 33 H10 49 6N 38 25 E
Rubondo △, Tanzania 86 C3 2 18 S 31 58 E
Rubtsovsk, Russia ... 52 D9 51 30N 81 10 E
Ruby L., U.S.A. 108 F6 40 10N 115 28W
Ruby Mts., U.S.A. .. 108 F6 40 30N 115 20W
Rubyvale, Australia . 94 C4 23 25 S 147 42 E
Rucheng, China .... 59 E9 25 33N 113 38 E
Ruciane-Nida, Poland 30 E8 53 40N 21 32 E
Rüd Sar, Iran ...... 71 B6 37 8N 50 18 E
Ruda, Sweden ...... 11 G10 57 6N 16 7 E
Ruda Śląska, Poland . 31 H5 50 16N 18 50 E
Rudall, Australia ... 95 E2 33 43 S 136 17 E
Rudall River △,
Australia .... 92 D3 22 34 S 122 13 E
Rüdersdorf, Germany 24 C9 52 27N 13 47 E
Rudewa, Tanzania .. 87 E3 10 7 S 34 40 E
Rudkøbing, Denmark 11 K4 54 56N 10 41 E
Rudky, Ukraine .... 31 J10 49 35N 23 29 E
Rudna, Poland ..... 31 G3 51 30N 16 17 E
Rudnik, Bulgaria ... 45 D11 42 36N 27 30 E
Rudnik, Poland ..... 31 H9 50 26N 22 15 E
Rudnik, Serbia & M. . 44 B4 44 7N 20 35 E
Rudnya, Russia .... 32 E6 54 55N 31 7 E
Rudnytsa, Ukraine .. 29 B13 48 16N 28 54 E
Rudnyy, Kazakhstan . 52 D7 52 57N 63 7 E
Rudo, Bos.-H. ...... 44 C4 43 41N 19 23 E
Rudolf, Ostrov, Russia 52 A6 81 45N 58 30 E
Rudolstadt, Germany . 24 E7 50 44N 11 19 E
Rudong, China ..... 59 A13 32 20N 121 12 E
Rudozem, Bulgaria .. 45 E8 41 29N 24 51 E
Rudyard, U.S.A. ... 114 B3 46 14N 84 36W
Rue, France .... 19 B8 50 15N 1 40 E
Ruenya →, Africa .. 87 F3 16 24 S 33 48 E
Rufa'a, Sudan ...... 81 E3 14 44N 33 22 E
Rufiji →, Tanzania .. 86 D4 7 50 S 39 15 E
Rufino, Argentina ... 126 C3 34 20 S 62 50W
Rufisque, Senegal ... 82 C1 14 40N 17 15W
Rufunsa, Zambia ... 87 F2 15 4 S 29 34 E
Rugao, China .... 59 A13 32 23N 120 31 E
Rugby, U.K. 15 E6 52 23N 1 16W
Rugby, U.S.A. 112 A5 48 22N 100 0W
Rügen, Germany .... 24 A9 54 22N 13 24 E
Rügen □, Germany .. 24 A9 54 25N 13 25 E
Rugles, France ..... 18 D7 48 50N 0 40 E
Ruhengeri, Rwanda . 86 C2 1 30 S 29 36 E
Ruhland, Germany .. 24 D9 51 27N 13 52 E
Ruhnu, Estonia .... 9 H20 57 48N 23 15 E
Ruhr →, Germany .. 24 D2 51 27N 6 43 E
Ruhuhu →, Tanzania 87 E3 10 31 S 34 34 E
Rui'an, China ...... 59 D13 27 47N 120 40 E
Ruichang, China .... 59 C10 29 40N 115 40 E
Ruidoso, U.S.A. 109 K11 33 20N 105 41W
Ruijin, China .... 59 E10 25 48N 116 0 E
Ruili, China .... 58 E1 24 0N 97 43 E
Ruivo, Pico, Madeira . 48 D3 32 45N 16 56W
Ruj, Bulgaria .... 44 D6 42 52N 22 34 E
Rujen, Macedonia ... 44 D6 42 9N 22 30 E
Rujm Tal'at a Jamā'ah,
Jordan .... 74 E4 30 24N 35 30 E
Ruk, Pakistan ...... 68 F3 27 50N 68 42 E

Rukhla, Pakistan .... 68 C4 32 27N 71 57 E
Ruki →, Dem. Rep. of
the Congo ...... 84 E3 0 5N 18 17 E
Rukwa □, Tanzania . 86 D3 7 0 S 31 30 E
Rukwa, L., Tanzania . 86 D3 8 0 S 32 20 E
Rulhieres, C., Australia 92 B4 13 56 S 127 22 E
Rum = Rhum, U.K. . 13 E2 57 0N 6 20W
Rum, Jordan .... 74 F4 29 39N 35 26 E
Rum Cay, Bahamas . 121 B5 23 40N 74 58W
Rum Jungle, Australia 92 B5 13 0 S 130 59 E
Ruma, Serbia & M. .. 28 E4 45 0N 19 50 E
Rumāḥ, Si. Arabia .. 70 E5 25 29N 47 10 E
Rumania = Romania ■,
Europe .... 29 D10 46 0N 25 0 E
Rumaylah, Iraq ..... 70 D5 30 47N 47 37 E
Rumbêk, Sudan .... 81 F2 6 54N 29 37 E
Rumburk, Czech Rep. 26 A7 50 57N 14 32 E
Rumford, U.S.A. 115 C10 44 33N 70 33W
Rumia, Poland ..... 30 D5 54 37N 18 25 E
Rumilly, France ..... 21 C9 45 53N 5 56 E
Rumoi, Japan ...... 54 C10 43 56N 141 39 E
Rumonge, Burundi .. 86 C2 3 59 S 29 26 E
Rumson, U.S.A. 117 F11 40 23N 74 0W
Rumuruti, Kenya ... 86 B4 0 17N 36 32 E
Runan, China ...... 56 H8 33 0N 114 30 E
Runanga, N.Z. ..... 91 K3 42 25 S 171 15 E
Runaway, C., N.Z. .. 91 G6 37 32 S 177 59 E
Runaway Bay, Jamaica 120 a 18 27N 77 20W
Runcorn, U.K. 14 D5 53 21N 2 44W
Rundu, Namibia .... 88 B2 17 52 S 19 43 E
Rungwa, Tanzania .. 86 D3 6 55 S 33 32 E
Rungwa →, Tanzania 86 D3 7 36 S 31 50 E
Rungwe, Tanzania .. 87 D3 9 11 S 33 32 E
Rungwe, Mt., Tanzania 87 D3 9 8 S 33 40 E
Runka, Nigeria ..... 83 C6 12 28N 7 20 E
Runn, Sweden ...... 10 D9 60 30N 15 40 E
Runton Ra., Australia . 92 D3 23 31 S 123 6 E
Ruokolahti, Finland . 32 B5 61 17N 28 50 E
Ruoqiang, China .... 60 C3 38 55N 88 10 E
Rupa, India .... 67 F18 27 15N 92 21 E
Rupar, India .... 68 D7 31 2N 76 38 E
Rupat, India .... 62 D2 1 45N 101 40 E
Rupea, Romania .... 29 D10 46 2N 25 22 E
Rupen →, India .... 68 H4 23 28N 71 31 E
Rupert, U.S.A. 108 E7 42 37N 113 41W
Rupert →, Canada .. 104 B4 51 29N 78 45W
Rupert B., Canada .. 104 B4 51 35N 79 0W
Rupert House =
Waskaganish, Canada 104 B4 51 30N 78 40W
Rupsa, India .... 69 J12 21 37N 87 1 E
Rur →, Germany .... 24 D2 51 11N 5 59 E
Rurrenabaque, Bolivia 124 F5 14 30 S 67 32W
Rus →, Spain 39 F2 39 30N 2 30W
Rusambo, Zimbabwe 87 F3 16 30 S 32 4 E
Rusape, Zimbabwe .. 87 F3 18 35 S 32 8 E
Ruschuk = Ruse,
Bulgaria .... 45 C9 43 48N 25 59 E
Ruse, Bulgaria ...... 45 C9 43 48N 25 59 E
Ruse □, Bulgaria .... 45 C10 43 35N 26 20 E
Rusenski Lom △,
Bulgaria .... 44 C7 43 40N 26 10 E
Rușețu, Romania ... 29 F12 44 57N 27 14 E
Rush, Ireland 12 C5 53 31N 6 6W
Rushan, China ..... 57 F11 36 56N 121 30 E
Rushden, U.K. 15 E7 52 18N 0 35W
Rushmore, Mt., U.S.A. 112 D3 43 53N 103 28W
Rushville, Ill., U.S.A. 112 E9 40 7N 90 34W
Rushville, Ind., U.S.A. 114 F3 39 37N 85 27W
Rushville, Nebr., U.S.A. 112 D3 42 43N 102 28W
Russas, Brazil ...... 125 D11 4 55 S 37 50W
Russell, Canada 103 C8 50 50N 101 20W
Russell, Kans., U.S.A. 112 F5 38 54N 98 52W
Russell, N.Y., U.S.A. . 117 B9 44 27N 75 9W
Russell, Pa., U.S.A. . 116 E5 41 56N 79 8W
Russell Cave △, U.S.A. 115 H3 34 59N 85 49W
Russell L., Man.,
Canada 103 B8 56 15N 101 30W
Russell L., N.W.T.,
Canada 102 A5 63 5N 115 44W
Russellkonda, India . 67 K14 19 57N 84 42 E
Russellville, Ala., U.S.A. 115 H2 34 30N 87 44W
Russellville, Ark., U.S.A. 113 H8 35 17N 93 8W
Russellville, Ky., U.S.A. 115 G2 36 51N 86 53W
Rüsselsheim, Germany 25 F4 49 59N 8 25 E
Russi, Italy .... 41 D9 44 22N 12 2 E
Russia ■, Eurasia ... 53 C11 62 0N 105 0 E
Russian →, U.S.A. . 110 G3 38 27N 123 8W
Russkoye Ustie, Russia 4 B15 71 0N 149 0 E
Rust, Austria .... 27 D9 47 49N 16 42 E
Rustam, Pakistan ... 68 B5 34 25N 72 13 E
Rustam Shahr, Pakistan 68 F2 26 58N 66 6 E
Rustavi, Georgia ... 35 K7 41 30N 45 0 E
Rustenburg, S. Africa 88 D4 25 41 S 27 14 E
Ruston, U.S.A. 113 J8 32 32N 92 38W
Rutana, Burundi ... 86 C3 3 55 S 30 0 E
Rute, Spain 37 H6 37 19N 4 23W
Ruteng, Indonesia .. 63 F6 8 35 S 120 30 E
Ruth, U.S.A. 116 C2 43 42N 82 45W
Rutherford, U.S.A. .. 110 G4 38 26N 122 24W
Rutland, U.S.A. 117 C12 43 37N 72 58W
Rutland □, U.K. 15 E7 52 38N 0 40W
Rutland Water, U.K. . 15 E7 52 39N 0 38W
Rutledge →, Canada 103 A6 61 4N 112 0W
Rutledge L., Canada . 103 A6 61 33N 110 47W
Rutqa, W. →, Syria . 73 E9 34 30N 41 3 E
Rutshuru, Dem. Rep. of
the Congo ...... 86 C2 1 13 S 29 25 E
Ruvo di Púglia, Italy . 43 A9 41 7N 16 29 E
Ruvu, Tanzania .... 86 D4 6 49 S 38 43 E
Ruvu →, Tanzania .. 86 D4 6 23 S 38 52 E
Ruvuba △, Burundi . 86 C2 3 5 S 29 33 E
Ruvuma □, Tanzania 87 E4 10 20 S 40 28 E
Ruvuma →, Tanzania 87 E5 10 29 S 40 28 E
Ruwais, U.A.E. ..... 71 E7 24 5N 52 50 E
Ruwenzori □, Uganda 86 B2 0 30 S 29 55 E
Ruya →, Zimbabwe . 89 B5 16 27 S 32 5 E
Ruyigi, Burundi .... 86 C3 3 29 S 30 15 E
Ruyuan, China ..... 59 E9 24 46N 113 16 E
Ruzayevka, Russia .. 34 C7 54 4N 45 0 E
Růzhevo Konare,
Bulgaria .... 45 D8 42 23N 24 46 E
Ružomberok,
Slovak Rep. ..... 27 B12 49 3N 19 17 E
Ruzyne, Praha ✈
(PRG), Czech Rep. . 26 A7 50 7N 14 15 E
Rwanda ■, Africa .. 86 C3 2 0 S 30 0 E
Ryakhovo, Bulgaria . 45 C10 43 58N 26 18 E
Ryan, L., U.K. 13 G3 55 0N 5 2W
Ryazan, Russia ..... 32 E10 54 40N 39 40 E
Ryazhsk, Russia .... 32 F11 53 45N 40 3 E

Rybachiy, Russia .... 30 C7 55 10N 20 50 E
Rybache = Rybachye,
Kazakhstan ..... 52 E9 46 40N 81 20 E

Rybinsk, Russia .... 32 C10 58 5N 38 50 E
Rybinskoye Vdkhr.,
Russia .... 32 C10 58 30N 38 25 E
Rybnik, Poland ..... 31 H5 50 6N 18 32 E
Rybnitsa = Râbniţa,
Moldova .... 29 C14 47 45N 29 0 E
Rybnoye, Russia .... 32 E10 54 45N 39 30 E
Rychnov nad Kněžnou,
Czech Rep. ..... 27 A9 50 10N 16 17 E
Rychwał, Poland .... 31 F5 52 4N 18 10 E
Rycroft, Canada 102 B5 55 45N 118 40W
Ryd, Sweden .... 11 H8 56 27N 14 42 E
Rydaholm, Sweden . 11 H8 56 59N 14 18 E
Ryde, U.K. 15 G6 50 43N 1 9W
Ryderwood, U.S.A. . 110 D3 46 23N 123 3W
Rydzyna, Poland ... 31 G3 51 47N 16 39 E
Rye, U.K. .... 15 G8 50 57N 0 45 E
Rye →, U.K. 14 C7 54 11N 0 44W
Rye Bay, U.K. ..... 15 G8 50 52N 0 49 E
Rye Patch Reservoir,
U.S.A. 108 F4 40 28N 118 19W
Ryegate, U.S.A. 108 C9 46 18N 109 15W
Ryki, Poland .... 31 G8 51 38N 21 56 E
Ryley, Canada 102 C6 53 17N 112 26W
Rylsk, Russia .... 33 G8 51 36N 34 43 E
Rylstone, Australia .. 95 E4 32 46 S 149 58 E
Rymanów, Poland .. 31 J8 49 35N 21 51 E
Ryn, Poland .... 30 E8 53 57N 21 34 E
Ryn Peski, Kazakhstan 35 G9 47 30N 49 0 E
Ryōtsu, Japan ...... 54 E9 38 5N 138 26 E
Rypin, Poland ...... 31 E6 53 3N 19 25 E
Ryssby, Sweden .... 11 H8 56 52N 14 10 E
Rysy, Europe .... 27 B13 49 10N 20 9 E
Ryūgasaki, Japan ... 55 G10 35 54N 140 11 E
Ryūkyū Is. = Ryūkyū-
rettō, Japan ..... 55 M3 26 0N 126 0 E
Ryūkyū-rettō, Japan . 55 M3 26 0N 126 0 E
Rzepin, Poland ..... 31 F1 52 20N 14 49 E
Rzeszów, Poland ... 31 H8 50 5N 21 58 E
Rzhev, Russia ...... 32 D8 56 20N 34 20 E

S

Sa, Thailand .... 64 C3 18 34N 100 45 E
Sa Canal, Spain ..... 48 C7 38 51N 1 23 E
Sa Conillera, Spain .. 48 C7 38 59N 1 13 E
Sa Dec, Vietnam .... 65 G5 10 20N 105 46 E
Sa Dragonera, Spain 48 B9 39 35N 2 19 E
Sa Mesquida, Spain . 48 B11 39 55N 4 16 E
Sa Savina, Spain .... 48 C7 38 44N 1 25 E
Sa'ādatābād, Fārs, Iran 71 D7 30 10N 53 5 E
Sa'ādatābād,
Hormozgān, Iran . 71 D7 28 3N 55 53 E
Sa'ādatābād, Kermān,
Iran .... 71 D7 29 40N 55 51 E
Saale →, Germany .. 24 D7 51 56N 11 54 E
Saaler Bodden,
Germany .... 24 A8 54 20N 12 27 E
Saalfeld, Germany .. 24 E7 50 38N 11 21 E
Saalfelden, Austria .. 26 D5 47 25N 12 51 E
Saanich, Canada 110 B3 48 29N 123 26W
Saar →, Europe .... 17 E6 49 41N 6 32 E
Saar-Hunsrück △,
Germany .... 25 F2 49 30N 6 59 E
Saarbrücken, Germany 25 F2 49 14N 6 59 E
Saarburg, Germany . 25 F2 49 36N 6 32 E
Saaremaa, Estonia .. 9 G20 58 30N 22 30 E
Saarijärvi, Finland .. 9 E21 62 43N 25 16 E
Saariselkä, Finland . 8 B23 68 16N 28 15 E
Saarland □, Germany 25 F2 49 20N 6 45 E
Saarlouis, Germany . 25 F2 49 19N 6 45 E
Sab 'Ābar, Syria .... 70 C3 33 46N 37 41 E
Saba, W. Indies 121 C7 17 38N 63 14W
Šabac, Serbia & M. . 44 B3 44 48N 19 42 E
Sabadell, Spain ..... 38 D7 41 28N 2 7 E
Sabah □, Malaysia .. 62 C5 6 0N 117 0 E
Sabak Bernam, Malaysia 65 L3 3 46N 100 58 E
Sabalān, Kūhhā-ye, Iran 70 B5 38 15N 47 45 E
Sabalana, Kepulauan,
Indonesia .... 63 F5 6 45 S 118 50 E
Sábana de la Mar,
Dom. Rep. 121 C6 19 7N 69 24W
Sábanalarga, Colombia 124 A4 10 38N 74 55W
Sabang, Indonesia .. 62 C1 5 50N 95 15 E
Săbăoani, Romania . 29 C11 47 1N 26 51 E
Sabará, Brazil ...... 125 G10 19 55 S 43 46W
Sabattis, U.S.A. 117 B10 44 6N 74 40W
Saberania, Indonesia 63 E9 2 5 S 138 18 E
Sabhah, Libya ...... 79 C8 27 9N 14 29 E
Sabi →, India ...... 68 E7 28 29N 76 44 E
Sabidana, J., Sudan . 80 D4 18 4N 36 50 E
Sabie, S. Africa ..... 89 D5 25 10 S 30 48 E
Sabinal, Mexico 118 A3 30 58N 107 25W
Sabinal, U.S.A. 113 L5 29 19N 99 28W
Sabiñánigo, Spain ... 38 C4 42 31N 0 22W
Sabinar, Punta del,
Spain 39 J2 36 43N 2 44W
Sabinas, Mexico 118 B4 27 50N 101 10W
Sabinas →, Mexico . 118 B4 27 37N 100 42W
Sabinas Hidalgo, Mexico 118 B4 26 30N 100 10W
Sabine →, U.S.A. .. 113 L8 29 59N 93 47W
Sabine L., U.S.A. ... 113 L8 29 53N 93 51W
Sabine Pass, U.S.A. . 113 L8 29 44N 93 54W
Sabinov, Slovak Rep. 27 B14 49 6N 21 5 E
Sabinsville, U.S.A. .. 116 E7 41 52N 77 31W
Sabirabad, Azerbaijan 35 K9 40 5N 48 30 E
Sablayan, Phil. ..... 61 E4 12 50N 120 50 E
Sable, Canada 105 A6 55 30N 68 21W
Sable, C., Canada ... 105 D6 43 29N 65 38W
Sable, C., U.S.A. ... 121 B7 25 9N 81 8W
Sable I., Canada 105 D8 44 0N 60 0W
Sable-sur-Sarthe, France 18 E6 47 50N 0 20W
Sabôr →, Portugal .. 36 D3 41 10N 7 7W
Sabou, Burkina Faso 82 C4 12 1N 2 15W
Sabrina Coast,
Antarctica ...... 5 C9 68 0 S 120 0 E
Sabugal, Portugal .. 36 E3 40 20N 7 5W
Sabulubbek, Indonesia 62 E1 1 36 S 98 40 E
Sabuncu, Turkey ... 47 B12 39 13N 30 14 E
Sabzevār, Iran ...... 71 B8 36 15N 57 40 E
Sabzvārān, Iran .... 71 D8 28 45N 57 50 E
Sac City, U.S.A. 112 D7 42 25N 95 0W
Sacedón, Spain 38 E2 40 29N 2 41W
Săcele, Romania .... 29 E11 45 37N 25 41 E
Sachigo →, Canada . 104 A2 55 6N 88 58W
Sachigo, L., Canada . 104 B1 53 50N 92 12W
Sachkhere, Georgia . 35 J6 42 5N 43 15 E
Sachsen □, Germany 24 E9 50 55N 13 10 E
Sachsen-Anhalt □,
Germany .... 24 D7 52 0N 12 0 E
St. Abb's Head, U.K. . 13 F6 55 55N 2 8W

Sächsische Schweiz △,
Germany .... 24 E10 50 55N 14 10 E
Sacile, Italy .... 41 C9 45 57N 12 30 E
Sackets Harbor, U.S.A. 117 C8 43 57N 76 7W
Sackville, Canada ... 105 C7 45 54N 64 22W
Saco, Maine, U.S.A. . 115 D10 43 30N 70 27W
Saco, Mont., U.S.A. . 108 B10 48 28N 107 21W
Sacramento, U.S.A. . 110 G5 38 35N 121 29W
Sacramento →, U.S.A. 110 G5 38 3N 121 56W
Sacramento Mts., U.S.A. 109 K11 32 30N 105 30W
Sacramento Valley,
U.S.A. 110 G5 39 30N 122 0W
Sacratif, C., Spain ... 37 J7 36 42N 3 28W
Săcueni, Romania ... 28 C7 47 20N 22 5 E
Sada, Spain 36 B2 43 22N 8 15W
Sada-Misaki, Japan .. 55 H6 33 20N 132 1 E
Sádaba, Spain 38 C3 42 19N 1 12W
Sadabad, India ..... 68 F8 27 27N 78 3 E
Sadani, Tanzania ... 86 D4 5 58 S 38 35 E
Sadao, Thailand .... 65 J3 6 38N 100 26 E
Sadd el Aali, Egypt .. 80 C3 23 54N 32 54 E
Saddle Mt., U.S.A. . 110 E3 45 58N 123 41W
Sade, Nigeria ...... 83 C7 11 22N 10 45 E
Sadimi, Dem. Rep. of
the Congo ...... 87 D1 9 25 S 23 32 E
Sadiola, Mali 82 C2 13 50N 11 40W
Sa'dīyah, Hawr as, Iraq 70 C5 32 55N 46 30 E
Sado, Japan .... 54 F9 38 0N 138 25 E
Sado →, Portugal .. 37 G2 38 29N 8 55W
Sadon, Burma ...... 67 G20 25 28N 97 55 E
Sadon, Russia ...... 35 J6 42 52N 43 58 E
Sadovoye, Russia ... 35 G7 47 47N 44 31 E
Sadra, India .... 68 H5 23 21N 72 43 E
Sadri, India .... 68 G5 25 11N 73 26 E
Sæby, Denmark .... 11 G4 57 21N 10 30 E
Saegertown, U.S.A. . 116 E4 41 43N 80 9W
Saelices, Spain 38 F2 39 55N 2 49W
Safaalan, Turkey ... 45 E12 41 26N 28 6 E
Safaga, Egypt ...... 80 B3 26 42N 34 0 E
Şafājah, Si. Arabia .. 70 E3 26 25N 39 0 E
Šafárikovo = Tornal'a,
Slovak Rep. ..... 27 C13 48 25N 20 20 E
Säffle, Sweden ..... 10 E6 59 8N 12 55 E
Safford, U.S.A. 109 K9 32 50N 109 43W
Saffron Walden, U.K. 15 E8 52 1N 0 16 E
Safi, Morocco 78 B4 32 18N 9 20W
Şafiâbâd, Iran ...... 71 B8 36 45N 57 58 E
Safid Dasht, Iran ... 71 C6 33 27N 48 11 E
Safid Kūh, Afghan. .. 66 B3 34 45N 63 0 E
Safid Rūd →, Iran .. 71 B6 37 23N 50 11 E
Safipur, India ...... 69 F9 26 44N 80 21 E
Safonovo, Russia ... 32 E7 55 4N 33 16 E
Safranbolu, Turkey . 72 B5 41 15N 32 41 E
Saft Rashīn, Egypt .. 80 J7 28 58N 30 55 E
Şafwān, Iraq .... 70 D5 30 7N 47 43 E
Sag Harbor, U.S.A. . 117 F12 41 0N 72 18W
Saga, Japan .... 55 H5 33 15N 130 16 E
Saga □, Japan ...... 55 H5 33 15N 130 20 E
Sagae, Japan .... 54 E10 38 22N 140 17 E
Sagala, Mali 82 C3 14 9N 6 38W
Sagamore, U.S.A. .. 116 F5 40 46N 79 14W
Sagar, Karnataka, India 66 M9 14 14N 75 6 E
Sagar, Mad. P., India 69 H8 23 50N 78 44 E
Sagara, L., Tanzania 86 D3 5 20 S 31 0 E
Sagay, Phil. .... 61 F5 10 57N 123 25 E
Saginaw, U.S.A. 114 D4 43 26N 83 56W
Saginaw →, U.S.A. . 114 D4 43 39N 83 51W
Saginaw B., U.S.A. . 114 D4 43 50N 83 40W
Sagleipie, Liberia ... 82 D3 7 0N 8 52W
Saglouc = Salluit,
Canada 101 B12 62 14N 75 38W
Sagŏ-ri, S. Korea ... 57 G14 35 25N 126 49 E
Sagone, France ..... 21 F12 42 7N 8 42 E
Sagone, G. de, France 21 F12 42 4N 8 40 E
Sagres, Portugal ... 37 J2 37 0N 8 58W
Sagua la Grande, Cuba 120 B3 22 50N 80 10W
Saguache, U.S.A. ... 109 G10 38 5N 106 8W
Saguaro △, U.S.A. .. 109 K8 32 12N 110 38W
Saguenay →, Canada 105 C5 48 22N 71 0W
Sagunt, Spain 38 F4 39 42N 0 18W
Sagunto = Sagunt, Spain 38 F4 39 42N 0 18W
Sagwara, India ..... 68 H6 23 41N 74 1 E
Sahaba, Sudan ..... 80 D3 18 57N 30 25 E
Sahagún, Spain 36 C5 42 18N 5 2W
Saham al Jawlān, Syria 74 C4 32 45N 35 55 E
Sahamandrevo, Madag. 89 C8 23 15 S 45 35 E
Sahand, Kūh-e, Iran . 70 B5 37 44N 46 27 E
Sahara, Africa ...... 78 D6 23 0N 5 0 E
Saharan Atlas =
Saharien, Atlas,
Algeria .... 78 B6 33 30N 1 0 E
Saharanpur, India .. 68 E7 29 58N 77 33 E
Saharien, Atlas, Algeria 78 B6 33 30N 1 0 E
Saharsa, India ...... 69 G12 25 53N 86 36 E
Sahasinaka, Madag. . 89 C8 21 49 S 47 49 E
Sahaswan, India .... 69 E8 28 5N 78 45 E
Sahel, Africa .... 78 E5 16 0N 5 0 E
Sahel, Canal du, Mali 82 C3 14 20N 6 0W
Sahibganj, India .... 69 G12 25 12N 87 40 E
Şāhilīyah, Iraq ..... 70 C4 33 43N 42 42 E
Sahiwal, Pakistan ... 68 D5 30 45N 73 8 E
Şahneh, Iran .... 70 C5 34 29N 47 41 E
Sahrawi = Western
Sahara ■, Africa . 78 D3 25 0N 13 0W
Sahuaripa, Mexico .. 118 B3 29 0N 109 13W
Sahuarita, U.S.A. ... 109 L8 31 57N 110 58W
Sahuayo, Mexico ... 118 C4 20 4N 102 43W
Şahy, Slovak Rep. .. 27 C11 48 4N 18 55 E
Sai →, India .... 69 G10 25 39N 82 47 E
Sai Buri, Thailand .. 65 J3 6 43N 101 45 E
Sa'id Bundas, Sudan 79 G10 8 24N 24 48 E
Sa'īdābād = Sīrjān, Iran 71 D7 29 30N 55 45 E
Sa'īdābād, Iran ..... 71 B7 36 8N 54 11 E
Sa'īdīyeh, Iran ...... 71 B6 36 20N 48 55 E
Saïdpur, Bangla. .... 67 G16 25 48N 89 0 E
Saidpur, India ...... 69 G10 25 33N 83 11 E
Saidu Sharif, Pakistan 69 B5 34 43N 72 24 E
Saignes, France .... 20 C6 45 20N 2 31 E
Saigon = Thanh Pho Ho
Chi Minh, Vietnam 65 G6 10 58N 106 40 E
Saijō, Japan .... 55 H6 33 55N 133 11 E
Saikai △, Japan .... 55 H4 33 12N 129 36 E
Saikanosy Masoala,
Madag. .... 89 B9 15 45 S 50 10 E
Saikhoa Ghat, India . 67 F19 27 50N 95 40 E
Saiki, Japan .... 55 H5 32 58N 131 51 E
Sailana, India ...... 68 H6 23 28N 74 55 E
Saillans, France .... 21 D9 44 42N 5 12 E
Sailolof, Indonesia .. 63 E8 1 15 S 130 46 E
Saimaa, Finland .... 9 F23 61 15N 28 15 E
Saimaa, canal =
Saimaan, Finland . 9 F23 61 15N 28 15 E
Sä'in Dezh, Iran .... 70 B5 36 40N 46 25 E
St. Abb's Head, U.K. . 13 F6 55 55N 2 8W

St-Affrique, *France* .... **20 E6** 43 57N 2 53 E
St-Agrève, *France* .... **21 C8** 45 0N 4 23 E
St-Aignan, *France* .... **18 E8** 47 16N 1 22 E
St. Alban's, *Canada* ... **105 C8** 47 51N 55 50W
St. Albans, *U.K.* **15 F7** 51 45N 0 19W
St. Albans, *Vt., U.S.A.* **117 B11** 44 49N 73 5W
St. Albans, *W. Va.,*
  U.S.A. **114 F5** 38 23N 81 50W
St. Alban's Head, *U.K.* **15 G5** 50 34N 2 4W
St. Albert, *Canada* ... **102 C6** 53 37N 113 32W
St-Amand-en-Puisaye,
  France .... **19 E10** 47 32N 3 5 E
St-Amand-les-Eaux,
  France .... **19 B10** 50 27N 3 25 E
St-Amand-Montrond,
  France .... **19 F9** 46 43N 2 30 E
St-Amarin, *France* .... **19 E14** 47 54N 7 2 E
St-Amour, *France* .... **19 F12** 46 26N 5 21 E
St-André-de-Cubzac,
  France **20 D3** 44 59N 0 26W
St-André-les-Alpes,
  France .... **21 E10** 43 58N 6 30 E
St. Andrew's, *Canada* . **105 C8** 47 45N 59 15W
St. Andrews, *U.K.* **13 E6** 56 20N 2 47W
St-Anicet, *Canada* ... **117 A10** 45 8N 74 22W
St. Anns B., *Canada* .. **105 C7** 46 22N 60 25W
St. Ann's Bay, *Jamaica* **120 a** 18 26N 77 12W
St. Anthony, *Canada* .. **105 B8** 51 22N 55 35W
St. Anthony, *U.S.A.* .. **108 E8** 43 58N 111 41W
St-Antoine, *Canada* ... **105 C7** 46 22N 64 45W
St-Antonin-Noble-Val,
  France .... **20 D5** 44 10N 1 45 E
St. Arnaud, *Australia* . **95 F3** 36 40 S 143 16 E
St-Astier, *France* .... **20 C4** 45 8N 0 31 E
St-Aubin-du-Cormier,
  France **18 D5** 48 15N 1 26W
St-Augustin, *Canada* .. **105 B8** 51 13N 58 38W
St-Augustin ➤, *Canada* **105 B8** 51 16N 58 40W
St. Augustine, *U.S.A.* . **115 L5** 29 54N 81 19W
St-Aulaye, *France* .... **20 C4** 45 12N 0 1 E
St. Austell, *U.K.* **15 G3** 50 20N 4 47W
St-Avold, *France* ..... **19 C13** 49 6N 6 43 E
St. Barbe, *Canada* **105 B8** 51 12N 56 46W
St-Barthélemy, *W. Indies* **121 C7** 17 50N 62 50W
St-Béat, *France* ...... **20 F4** 42 55N 0 41 E
St. Bees Hd., *U.K.* ... **14 C4** 54 31N 3 38W
St. Bees I., *Australia* . **94 J7** 20 56 S 149 26 E
St-Benoît-du-Sault,
  France .... **20 B5** 46 26N 1 24 E
St-Bonnet-en-
  Champsaur, *France* . **21 D10** 44 40N 6 5 E
St-Brevin-les-Pins,
  France **18 E4** 47 14N 2 10W
St-Brice-en-Coglès,
  France **18 D5** 48 25N 1 22W
St. Bride's, *Canada* ... **105 C9** 46 56N 54 10W
St. Brides B., *U.K.* ... **15 F2** 51 49N 5 9W
St-Brieuc, *France* **18 D4** 48 30N 2 46W
St-Calais, *France* .... **18 E7** 47 55N 0 45 E
St-Cast-le-Guildo,
  France **18 D4** 48 37N 2 18W
St. Catharines, *Canada* **116 C5** 43 10N 79 15W
St. Catherines I., *U.S.A.* **115 K5** 31 40N 81 10W
St. Catherine's Pt., *U.K.* **15 G6** 50 34N 1 18W
St-Céré, *France* ...... **20 D5** 44 51N 1 54 E
St-Cergue, *Switz.* .... **25 J2** 46 27N 6 10 E
St-Cernin, *France* .... **20 C6** 45 5N 2 25 E
St-Chamond, *France* .. **21 C8** 45 28N 4 31 E
St. Charles, *Ill., U.S.A.* **114 E1** 41 54N 88 19W
St. Charles, *Mo., U.S.A.* **112 F9** 38 47N 90 29W
St. Charles, *Va., U.S.A.* **114 F7** 36 48N 83 4W
St-Chély-d'Apcher,
  France .... **20 D7** 44 48N 3 17 E
St-Chinian, *France* ... **20 E6** 43 25N 2 56 E
St. Christopher-Nevis =
  St. Kitts & Nevis ■,
  W. Indies **121 C7** 17 20N 62 40W
St-Ciers-sur-Gironde,
  France **20 C3** 45 17N 0 37W
St. Clair, *Mich., U.S.A.* **116 D2** 42 50N 82 30W
St. Clair, *Pa., U.S.A.* . **117 F8** 40 43N 76 12W
St. Clair ➤, *U.S.A.* .. **116 D2** 42 38N 82 31W
St. Clair, L., *Canada* . **104 D3** 42 30N 82 45W
St. Clair, L., *U.S.A.* .. **116 D2** 42 27N 82 39W
St. Clairsville, *U.S.A.* . **116 F4** 40 5N 80 54W
St-Claud, *France* ..... **20 C4** 45 54N 0 28 E
St. Claude, *Canada* ... **103 D9** 49 40N 98 20W
St. Claude, *France* ... **19 F12** 46 22N 5 52 E
St. Clears, *U.K.* **15 F3** 51 49N 4 31W
St-Clet, *Canada* **117 A10** 45 21N 74 13W
St. Cloud, *Fla., U.S.A.* **115 L5** 28 15N 81 17W
St. Cloud, *Minn., U.S.A.* **112 C7** 45 34N 94 10W
St. Cricq, C., *Australia* **93 E1** 25 17 S 113 6 E
St. Croix, *U.S. Virgin Is.* **121 C7** 17 45N 64 45W
St. Croix ➤, *U.S.A.* .. **112 C8** 44 45N 92 48W
St. Croix Falls, *U.S.A.* **112 C8** 45 24N 92 38W
St-Cyprien, *France* ... **20 F7** 42 37N 3 2 E
St-Cyr-sur-Mer, *France* **21 E9** 43 11N 5 43 E
St. David's, *Canada* .. **105 C8** 48 12N 58 52W
St. David's, *U.K.* **15 F2** 51 53N 5 16W
St. David's Head, *U.K.* **15 F2** 51 54N 5 19W
St-Denis, *France* ..... **19 D9** 48 56N 2 22 E
St-Dié, *France* .... **19 D13** 48 17N 6 56 E
St-Dizier, *France* ..... **19 D11** 48 38N 4 56 E
St-Égrève, *France* .... **21 C9** 45 14N 5 41 E
St. Elias, Mt., *U.S.A.* . **100 B5** 60 18N 140 56W
St. Elias Mts., *N. Amer.* **102 A1** 60 33N 139 28W
St-Eloy-les-Mines,
  France .... **19 F9** 46 10N 2 51 E
St-Émilion, *France* ... **20 D3** 44 53N 0 9W
St-Étienne, *France* ... **21 C8** 45 27N 4 22 E
St-Étienne-de-Tinée,
  France .... **21 D10** 44 16N 6 56 E
St-Étienne-du-Rouvray,
  France .... **18 C8** 49 23N 1 6 E
St. Eugène, *Canada* .. **117 A10** 45 30N 74 28W
St. Eustatius, *W. Indies* **121 C7** 17 20N 63 0W
St-Exupery, Lyon ✈
  (LYS), *France* ...... **21 C9** 45 44N 5 2 E
St-Fargeau, *France* ... **19 E10** 47 39N 3 4 E
St-Félicien, *Canada* .. **104 C5** 48 40N 72 25W
St-Florent, *France* .... **21 F13** 42 41N 9 18 E
St-Florent, G. de, *France* **21 F13** 42 47N 9 12 E
St-Florent-sur-Cher,
  France .... **19 F9** 46 59N 2 15 E
St-Florentin, *France* .. **19 E10** 48 0N 3 45 E
St-Flour, *France* ..... **20 C7** 45 2N 3 6 E
St. Francis, *U.S.A.* ... **112 F4** 39 47N 101 48W
St. Francis ➤, *U.S.A.* . **113 D9** 34 38N 90 36W
St. Francis, C., *S. Africa* **88 E3** 34 14 S 24 49 E
St. Francisville, *U.S.A.* **113 K9** 30 47N 91 23W
St-François, L., *Canada* **117 A10** 45 10N 74 22W
St-Fulgent, *France* ... **18 F5** 46 50N 1 10W
St-Gabriel, *Canada* ... **104 C5** 46 17N 73 24W
St. Gallen = Sankt
  Gallen, *Switz.* ..... **25 H5** 47 26N 9 22 E
St-Galmier, *France* ... **19 G11** 45 35N 4 19 E

St-Gaudens, *France* ... **20 E4** 43 6N 0 44 E
St-Gaultier, *France* ... **18 F8** 46 39N 1 26 E
St-Gengoux-le-National,
  France .... **19 F11** 46 37N 4 40 E
St-Geniez-d'Olt, *France* **20 D6** 44 27N 2 58 E
St. George, *Australia* . **95 D4** 28 1 S 148 30 E
St. George, *Canada* ... **105 C6** 45 11N 66 50W
St. George, *S.C., U.S.A.* **115 J5** 33 11N 80 35W
St. George, *Utah, U.S.A.* **109 H7** 37 6N 113 35W
St. George, C., *Canada* **105 C8** 48 30N 59 16W
St. George, C., *U.S.A.* **115 L3** 29 40N 85 5W
St. George Ra., *Australia* **92 C4** 18 40 S 125 0 E
St-Georges, *Canada* .. **105 C8** 48 26N 58 31W
St.-Georges, *Canada* .. **105 C5** 46 8N 70 40W
St-George's, *Grenada* . **121 D7** 12 5N 61 43W
St. George's B., *Canada* **105 C8** 48 24N 58 53W
St. Georges Basin,
  N.S.W., Australia .. **95 F5** 35 7 S 150 36 E
St. George's Basin,
  W. Austral., Australia **92 C4** 15 23 S 125 2 E
St. George's Channel,
  Europe **12 E6** 52 0N 6 0W
St. Georges Hd.,
  Australia .... **95 F5** 35 12 S 150 42 E
St-Georges-lès-
  Baillargeaux, *France* **20 B4** 46 41N 0 22 E
St-Germain-de-Calberte,
  France .... **20 D7** 44 13N 3 48 E
St-Germain-en-Laye,
  France .... **19 D9** 48 54N 2 6 E
St-Germain-Lembron,
  France .... **20 C7** 45 27N 3 14 E
St-Gervais-d'Auvergne,
  France .... **19 F9** 46 4N 2 50 E
St-Gervais-les-Bains,
  France .... **21 C10** 45 53N 6 42 E
St-Gildas, Pte. de,
  France **18 E4** 47 8N 2 14W
St-Gilles, *France* ..... **21 E8** 43 40N 4 26 E
St-Girons, *Ariège,*
  France .... **20 F5** 42 59N 1 8 E
St-Girons, *Landes,*
  France **20 E2** 43 56N 1 18W
St. Gotthard P. = San
  Gottardo, P. del,
  Switz. .... **25 J4** 46 33N 8 33 E
St. Helena, *Atl. Oc.* ... **76 H3** 15 58 S 5 42W
St. Helena, *U.S.A.* **108 G2** 38 30N 122 28W
St. Helena, Mt., *U.S.A.* **110 G4** 38 40N 122 36W
St. Helena B., *S. Africa* **88 E2** 32 40 S 18 10 E
St. Helens, *Australia* .. **95 G4** 41 20 S 148 15 E
St. Helens, *U.K.* **14 D5** 53 27N 2 44W
St. Helens, *U.S.A.* **110 E4** 45 52N 122 48W
St. Helens, Mt., *U.S.A.* **110 D4** 46 12N 122 12W
St. Helier, *U.K.* **15 H5** 49 10N 2 7W
St-Herblain, *France* ... **18 E5** 47 13N 1 40W
St-Hilaire-du-Harcouët,
  France **18 D5** 48 35N 1 5W
St-Hippolyte, *France* .. **19 E13** 47 19N 6 50 E
St-Hippolyte-du-Fort,
  France .... **20 E7** 43 58N 3 52 E
St-Honoré-les-Bains,
  France .... **19 F10** 46 54N 3 50 E
St-Hubert, *Belgium* ... **17 D5** 50 2N 5 23 E
St-Hyacinthe, *Canada* **104 C5** 45 40N 72 58W
St. Ignace, *U.S.A.* **114 C3** 45 52N 84 44W
St. Ignace I., *Canada* . **104 C2** 48 45N 88 0W
St. Ignatius, *U.S.A.* ... **108 C6** 47 19N 114 6W
St-Imier, *Switz.* ...... **25 H7** 47 9N 6 58 E
St. Ives, *Cambs., U.K.* **15 E7** 52 20N 0 4W
St. Ives, *Corn., U.K.* .. **15 G2** 50 12N 5 30W
St-James, *France* **18 D5** 48 31N 1 20W
St. James, *U.S.A.* **112 D7** 43 59N 94 38W
St-Jean ➤, *Canada* ... **105 B7** 50 17N 64 20W
St-Jean, L., *Canada* ... **105 C5** 48 40N 72 0W
St-Jean-d'Angély,
  France **20 C3** 45 57N 0 31W
St-Jean-de-Braye,
  France .... **19 E8** 47 53N 1 58 E
St-Jean-de-Luz, *France* **20 E2** 43 23N 1 39W
St-Jean-de-Maurienne,
  France .... **21 C10** 45 16N 6 21 E
St-Jean-de-Monts,
  France **18 F4** 46 47N 2 4W
St-Jean-du-Gard, *France* **20 D7** 44 7N 3 52 E
St-Jean-en-Royans,
  France .... **21 C9** 45 1N 5 18 E
St-Jean-Pied-de-Port,
  France **20 E2** 43 10N 1 14W
St-Jean-Port-Joli,
  Canada **105 C5** 47 15N 70 13W
St-Jean-sur-Richelieu,
  Canada **117 A11** 45 20N 73 20W
St-Jérôme, *Canada* ... **104 C5** 45 47N 74 0W
St. John, *Canada* **105 C6** 45 20N 66 8W
St. John, *U.S.A.* **113 G5** 38 0N 98 46W
St. John ➤, *U.S.A.* ... **105 C6** 45 12N 66 5W
St. John, C., *Canada* . **105 C8** 50 0N 55 32W
St. John I.,
  U.S. Virgin Is. ..... **121 e** 18 20N 64 42W
St. John's, *Antigua & B.* **121 C7** 17 6N 61 51W
St. John's, *Canada* ... **105 C9** 47 35N 52 40W
St. Johns, *Ariz., U.S.A.* **109 J9** 34 30N 109 22W
St. Johns, *Mich., U.S.A.* **114 D3** 43 0N 84 33W
St. Johns ➤, *U.S.A.* .. **115 K5** 30 24N 81 24W
St. John's Pt., *Ireland* **12 B3** 54 34N 8 27W
St. Johnsbury, *U.S.A.* . **117 B12** 44 25N 72 1W
St. Johnsville, *U.S.A.* . **117 D10** 43 0N 74 43W
St-Joseph, *Martinique* **120 c** 14 39N 61 4W
St. Joseph, *La., U.S.A.* **113 K9** 31 55N 91 14W
St. Joseph, *Mo., U.S.A.* **112 F7** 39 46N 94 50W
St. Joseph ➤, *U.S.A.* . **114 D2** 42 7N 86 29W
St. Joseph, I., *Canada* **104 C3** 46 12N 83 58W
St. Joseph, L., *Canada* **104 B1** 51 10N 90 35W
St-Jovite, *Canada* **104 C5** 46 8N 74 38W
St-Juéry, *France* ..... **20 E6** 43 57N 2 12 E
St-Julien-Chapteuil,
  France .... **21 C8** 45 2N 4 4 E
St-Julien-de-Vouvantes,
  France **18 E5** 47 38N 1 13W
St-Julien-en-Genevois,
  France .... **19 F13** 46 9N 6 5 E
St-Junien, *France* .... **20 C4** 45 53N 0 55 E
St-Just-en-Chaussée,
  France .... **19 C9** 49 30N 2 25 E
St-Just-en-Chevalet,
  France .... **20 C7** 45 55N 3 50 E
St. Kitts & Nevis ■,
  W. Indies **121 C7** 17 20N 62 40W
St. Laurent, *Canada* .. **103 C9** 50 25N 97 58W
St-Laurent-de-la-
  Salanque, *France* .. **20 F6** 42 46N 2 59 E
St-Laurent-du-Pont,
  France .... **21 C9** 45 23N 5 45 E
St-Laurent-en-
  Grandvaux, *France* **19 F12** 46 35N 5 58 E

St-Laurent-Médoc,
  France **20 C3** 45 8N 0 49W
St. Lawrence, *Australia* **94 C4** 22 16 S 149 31 E
St. Lawrence, *Canada* . **105 C8** 46 54N 55 23W
St. Lawrence ➤,
  Canada **105 C6** 49 30N 66 0W
St. Lawrence, Gulf of,
  Canada **105 C7** 48 25N 62 0W
St. Lawrence I., *U.S.A.* **100 B3** 63 30N 170 30W
St. Lawrence Islands △,
  Canada **117 B9** 44 27N 75 52W
St. Leonard, *Canada* .. **105 C6** 47 12N 67 58W
St-Léonard-de-Noblat,
  France .... **20 C5** 45 49N 1 29 E
St. Lewis ➤, *Canada* . **105 B8** 52 26N 56 11W
St-Lô, *France* **18 C5** 49 7N 1 5W
St-Louis, *France* ..... **19 E14** 47 35N 7 34 E
St-Louis, *Guadeloupe* . **120 b** 15 56N 61 19W
St. Louis, *Senegal* **82 B1** 16 8N 16 27W
St. Louis, *U.S.A.* **112 F9** 38 37N 90 12W
St. Louis ➤, *U.S.A.* .. **112 B8** 47 15N 92 45W
St-Loup-sur-Semouse,
  France .... **19 E13** 47 53N 6 16 E
St. Lucia ■, *W. Indies* . **121 f** 14 0N 60 57W
St. Lucia, L., *S. Africa* **89 D5** 28 5 S 32 30 E
St. Lucia Channel,
  W. Indies **121 D7** 14 15N 61 0W
St-Maarten ⊘, *W. Indies* **121 C7** 18 0N 63 5W
St. Magnus B., *U.K.* .. **13 A7** 60 25N 1 35W
St-Maixent-l'École,
  France **20 B3** 46 24N 0 12W
St-Malo, *France* **18 D4** 48 39N 2 1W
St-Malo, G. de, *France* **18 D4** 48 50N 2 30W
St-Mandrier-sur-Mer,
  France .... **21 E9** 43 4N 5 57 E
St-Marc, *Haiti* **121 C5** 19 10N 72 41W
St-Marcellin, *France* .. **21 C9** 45 9N 5 20 E
St-Marcouf, Îs., *France* **18 C5** 49 30N 1 10W
St. Maries, *U.S.A.* **108 C5** 47 19N 116 35W
St-Martin ⊘, *W. Indies* **121 C7** 18 0N 63 0W
St. Martin, C.,
  Martinique .... **120 c** 14 52N 61 14W
St. Martin, L., *Canada* **103 C9** 51 40N 98 30W
St-Martin-de-Crau,
  France .... **21 E8** 43 38N 4 48 E
St-Martin-de-Ré, *France* **20 B2** 46 12N 1 21W
St-Martin-d'Hères,
  France .... **21 C9** 45 9N 5 45 E
St-Martin-Vésubie,
  France .... **21 D11** 44 4N 7 15 E
St. Martins, *Barbados* . **121 g** 13 5N 59 28W
St-Martory, *France* ... **20 E4** 43 9N 0 56 E
St. Mary Pk., *Australia* **95 E2** 31 32 S 138 34 E
St. Marys, *Australia* ... **95 G4** 41 35 S 148 11 E
St. Marys, *Canada* **116 C3** 43 20N 81 10W
St. Mary's, *Corn., U.K.* **15 H1** 49 55N 6 18W
St. Mary's, *Orkney, U.K.* **13 C6** 58 54N 2 54W
St. Marys, *Ga., U.S.A.* **115 K5** 30 44N 81 33W
St. Marys, *Pa., U.S.A.* . **116 E6** 41 26N 78 34W
St. Mary's, C., *Canada* **105 C9** 46 50N 54 12W
St. Mary's B., *Canada* **105 C9** 46 50N 53 50W
St. Marys Bay, *Canada* **105 D6** 44 25N 66 10W
St-Mathieu, Pte., *France* **18 D2** 48 20N 4 46W
St. Matthew I., *U.S.A.* **100 B2** 60 24N 172 42W
St-Maurice ➤, *Canada* **104 C5** 46 21N 72 31W
St. Mawes, *U.K.* **15 G2** 50 10N 5 2W
St-Maximin-la-Ste-
  Baume, *France* ..... **21 E9** 43 27N 5 52 E
St-Médard-en-Jalles,
  France **20 D3** 44 53N 0 43W
St-Méen-le-Grand,
  France **18 D4** 48 11N 2 12W
St-Mihiel, *France* ..... **19 D12** 48 54N 5 32 E
St. Moritz, *Switz.* ..... **25 J5** 46 30N 9 51 E
St-Nazaire, *France* **18 E4** 47 17N 2 12W
St-Nicolas-de-Port,
  France .... **19 D13** 48 38N 6 18 E
St-Niklaas, *Belgium* ... **17 C4** 51 10N 4 8 E
St-Omer, *France* ..... **19 B9** 50 45N 2 15 E
St-Palais-sur-Mer,
  France **20 C2** 45 38N 1 8W
St-Pamphile, *Canada* .. **105 C6** 46 58N 69 48W
St-Pardoux-la-Rivière,
  France .... **20 C4** 45 29N 0 45 E
St. Pascal, *Canada* **105 C6** 47 32N 69 48W
St. Paul, *Canada* **102 C6** 54 0N 111 17W
St. Paul, *France* ...... **21 D10** 44 31N 6 45 E
St. Paul, *Minn., U.S.A.* **112 C8** 44 57N 93 6W
St. Paul, *Nebr., U.S.A.* **112 E5** 41 13N 98 27W
St. Paul ➤, *Canada* ... **105 B8** 51 27N 57 42W
St. Paul ➤, *Liberia* .. **82 D2** 6 25N 10 48W
St. Paul, I., *Ind. Oc.* .. **3 F13** 38 55 S 77 34 E
St-Paul-de-Fenouillet,
  France .... **20 F6** 42 48N 2 30 E
St. Paul I., *Canada* ... **105 C7** 47 12N 60 9W
St-Paul-lès-Dax, *France* **20 E2** 43 44N 1 3W
St-Péray, *France* ..... **21 D8** 44 57N 4 50 E
St. Peter, *U.S.A.* **112 C8** 44 20N 93 57W
St-Peter-Ording,
  Germany .... **24 A4** 54 20N 8 36 E
St. Peter Port, *U.K.* ... **15 H5** 49 26N 2 33W
St. Peters, *N.S., Canada* **105 C7** 45 40N 60 53W
St. Peters, *P.E.I.,*
  Canada **105 C7** 46 25N 62 35W
St. Petersburg = Sankt-
  Peterburg, *Russia* .. **32 C6** 59 55N 30 20 E
St. Petersburg, *U.S.A.* **115 M4** 27 46N 82 39W
St-Philbert-de-Grand-
  Lieu, *France* **18 E5** 47 2N 1 39W
St-Pie, *Canada* **117 A12** 45 30N 72 54W
St-Pierre, *Martinique* . **120 c** 14 45N 61 10W
St-Pierre, *St-P. & M.* .. **105 C8** 46 46N 56 12W
St-Pierre, L., *Canada* .. **104 C5** 46 12N 72 52W
St-Pierre-d'Oléron,
  France **20 C2** 45 57N 1 19W
St-Pierre-en-Port,
  France .... **18 C7** 49 48N 0 30 E
St-Pierre-et-
  Miquelon ⊘, *N. Amer.* **105 C8** 46 55N 56 10W
St-Pierre-le-Moûtier,
  France .... **19 F10** 46 47N 3 7 E
St-Pierre-sur-Dives,
  France **18 C6** 49 2N 0 1W
St-Pol-de-Léon, *France* **18 D3** 48 41N 4 0W
St-Pol-sur-Mer, *France* **19 A9** 51 1N 2 20 E
St-Pol-sur-Ternoise,
  France .... **19 B9** 50 23N 2 20 E
St-Pons, *France* ...... **20 E6** 43 30N 2 45 E
St-Pourçain-sur-Sioule,
  France .... **19 F10** 46 18N 3 18 E
St-Priest, *France* ..... **21 C8** 45 42N 4 57 E
St-Quay-Portrieux,
  France **18 D4** 48 39N 2 51W
St-Quentin, *Canada* ... **105 C6** 47 30N 67 23W
St-Quentin, *France* ... **19 C10** 49 50N 3 16 E
St-Rambert-d'Albon,
  France .... **21 C8** 45 17N 4 49 E

St-Raphaël, *France* .... **21 E10** 43 25N 6 46 E
St. Regis, *U.S.A.* **108 C6** 47 18N 115 6W
St-Renan, *France* **18 D2** 48 26N 4 37W
St-Saëns, *France* ..... **18 C8** 49 41N 1 16 E
St-Savin, *France* ..... **20 B4** 46 34N 0 53 E
St-Savinien, *France* ... **20 C3** 45 53N 0 42W
St. Sebastien, Tanjon' i,
  Madag. .... **89 A8** 12 26 S 48 44 E
St-Seine-l'Abbaye,
  France .... **19 E11** 47 26N 4 47 E
St-Sernin-sur-Rance,
  France .... **20 E6** 43 54N 2 35 E
St-Sever, *France* **20 E3** 43 45N 0 35W
St-Siméon, *Canada* ... **105 C5** 47 51N 69 54W
St. Simons I., *U.S.A.* .. **115 K5** 31 12N 81 15W
St. Simons Island, *U.S.A.* **115 K5** 31 9N 81 22W
St. Stephen, *Canada* .. **105 C6** 45 16N 67 17W
St-Sulpice, *France* .... **20 E5** 43 46N 1 41 E
St-Sulpice-Laurière,
  France .... **20 B5** 46 3N 1 29 E
St-Sulpice-les-Feuilles,
  France .... **20 B5** 46 19N 1 21 E
St-Syprien = St-Cyprien,
  France .... **20 F7** 42 37N 3 2 E
St-Thégonnec, *France* . **18 D3** 48 31N 3 57W
St. Thomas, *Canada* .. **116 D3** 42 45N 81 10W
St. Thomas I.,
  U.S. Virgin Is. ..... **121 e** 18 20N 64 55W
St-Tite, *Canada* **104 C5** 46 45N 72 34W
St-Tropez, *France* .... **21 E10** 43 17N 6 38 E
St-Troud = St. Truiden,
  Belgium .... **17 D5** 50 48N 5 10 E
St. Truiden, *Belgium* .. **17 D5** 50 48N 5 10 E
St-Vaast-la-Hougue,
  France **18 C5** 49 35N 1 17W
St-Valery-en-Caux,
  France .... **18 C7** 49 52N 0 43 E
St-Valéry-sur-Somme,
  France .... **19 B8** 50 11N 1 38 E
St-Vallier, *France* ..... **19 F11** 46 38N 4 22 E
St-Vallier-de-Thiey,
  France .... **21 E10** 43 42N 6 51 E
St-Varent, *France* **18 F6** 46 53N 0 13W
St-Vaury, *France* ..... **20 B5** 46 12N 1 46 E
St-Vincent, *Italy* ..... **40 C4** 45 45N 7 39 E
St. Vincent, G., *Australia* **95 F2** 35 0 S 138 0 E
St. Vincent & the
  Grenadines ■,
  W. Indies **121 D7** 13 0N 61 10W
St-Vincent-de-Tyrosse,
  France **20 E2** 43 39N 1 19W
St. Vincent Passage,
  W. Indies **121 D7** 13 30N 61 0W
St-Vith, *Belgium* ..... **17 D6** 50 17N 6 9 E
St-Vivien-de-Médoc,
  France **20 C2** 45 25N 1 2W
St. Walburg, *Canada* .. **103 C7** 53 39N 109 12W
St-Yrieix-la-Perche,
  France .... **20 C5** 45 31N 1 12 E
Ste-Adresse, *France* .. **18 C7** 49 31N 0 5 E
Ste-Agathe-des-Monts,
  Canada **104 C5** 46 3N 74 17W
Ste-Anne, *Guadeloupe* **120 b** 16 13N 61 24W
Ste-Anne, L., *Canada* . **105 B6** 50 0N 67 42W
Ste-Anne-des-Monts-
  Tourelle, *Canada* ... **105 C6** 49 8N 66 30W
Ste-Croix, *Switz.* ..... **25 J2** 46 49N 6 34 E
Ste-Enimie, *France* ... **20 D7** 44 22N 3 26 E
Ste-Foy-la-Grande,
  France .... **20 D4** 44 50N 0 13 E
Ste. Genevieve, *U.S.A.* **112 G9** 37 59N 90 2W
Ste-Hermine, *France* .. **20 B2** 46 32N 1 4W
Ste-Livrade-sur-Lot,
  France .... **20 D4** 44 24N 0 36 E
Ste-Marguerite ➤,
  Canada **105 B6** 50 9N 66 36W
Ste-Marie, *Canada* ... **105 C5** 46 26N 71 0W
Ste-Marie, *Martinique* **120 c** 14 48N 61 1W
Ste-Marie-aux-Mines,
  France .... **19 D14** 48 15N 7 12 E
Ste-Maure-de-Touraine,
  France .... **18 E7** 47 7N 0 37 E
Ste-Maxime, *France* .. **21 E10** 43 19N 6 39 E
Ste-Menehould, *France* **19 C11** 49 5N 4 54 E
Ste-Mère-Église, *France* **18 C5** 49 24N 1 19W
Ste. Rose, *Guadeloupe* **120 b** 16 20N 61 45W
Ste. Rose du Lac,
  Canada **103 C9** 51 4N 99 30W
Ste-Savine, *France* .... **19 D11** 48 18N 4 3 E
Ste-Sigolène, *France* .. **21 C8** 45 15N 4 14 E
Saintes, *France* **20 C3** 45 45N 0 37W
Saintes, Îs. des,
  Guadeloupe .... **120 b** 15 50N 61 35W
Stes-Maries-de-la-Mer,
  France .... **21 E8** 43 26N 4 26 E
Saintfield, *U.K.* **12 B6** 54 28N 5 49W
Saintonge, *France* **20 C3** 45 40N 0 50W
Saipan, *Pac. Oc.* ..... **96 F6** 15 12N 145 45 E
Sairang, *India* .... **67 H18** 23 50N 92 45 E
Sairecábur, Cerro,
  Bolivia .... **126 A2** 22 43 S 67 54W
Saitama □, *Japan* ..... **55 F9** 36 25N 139 30 E
Saitei = Kadınhanı,
  Turkey .... **72 C5** 38 14N 32 13 E
Saiti, *Moldova* .... **29 D14** 46 30N 29 24 E
Saiyid, *Pakistan* ...... **68 C5** 33 7N 73 2 E
Saja-Besaya ➤, *Spain* . **36 B6** 43 10N 4 0W
Sajama, *Bolivia* **124 D5** 18 7S 69 0W
Sajan, *Serbia & M.* ... **28 B5** 45 50N 20 20 E
Sajó ➤, *Hungary* ..... **28 C5** 47 56N 21 7 E
Sajószentpéter, *Hungary* **28 B5** 48 12N 20 44 E
Sajum, *India* .... **69 C8** 33 20N 79 0 E
Sak ➤, *S. Africa* ..... **88 E3** 30 52 S 20 25 E
Sakaba, *Nigeria* ...... **83 C6** 11 4N 5 35 E
Sakai, *Japan* .... **55 G6** 34 30N 135 30 E
Sakaide, *Japan* ...... **55 G6** 34 19N 133 50 E
Sakaiminato, *Japan* ... **55 G6** 35 38N 133 11 E
Sakākah, *Si. Arabia* ... **70 D4** 30 0N 40 8 E
Sakami ➤, *Canada* ... **104 B4** 53 40N 76 40W
Sakami, L., *Canada* ... **104 B4** 53 15N 77 0W
Sâkâne, 'Erg i-n, *Mali* . **83 A4** 20 30N 1 30W
Sakania, *Dem. Rep. of*
  the Congo .... **87 E2** 12 43 S 28 30 E
Sakaraha, *Madag.* .... **89 C7** 22 55 S 44 32 E
Sakarya, *Turkey* ...... **72 B4** 40 48N 30 25 E
Sakarya ➤, *Turkey* ... **72 B4** 41 7N 30 39 E
Sakashima-Guntō, *Japan* **55 M2** 24 46N 124 0 E
Sakassou, *Ivory C.* **82 D3** 7 58N 5 19W
Sakata, *Japan* .... **54 E9** 38 55N 139 50 E
Sakchu, *N. Korea* ..... **57 D13** 40 23N 125 2 E
Sakeny ➤, *Madag.* .... **89 C8** 20 0 S 45 25 E
Sakété, *Benin* .... **83 D5** 6 40N 2 45 E
Sakha □, *Russia* ...... **53 C13** 66 0N 130 0 E
Sakhalin, *Russia* ...... **53 D15** 51 0N 143 0 E
Sakhalinskiy Zaliv,
  Russia .... **53 D15** 54 0N 141 0 E

Şaki, *Azerbaijan* ...... **35 K8** 41 10N 47 5 E
Sakai, *Lithuania* ...... **9 J20** 54 59N 23 2 E
Sakon Nakhon, *Thailand* **64 D5** 17 10N 104 9 E
Sakrand, *Pakistan* .... **68 F3** 26 10N 68 15 E
Sakri, *India* .... **69 F12** 26 13N 86 5 E
Sakrivier, *S. Africa* .... **88 E3** 30 54 S 20 28 E
Sakskøbing, *Denmark* .. **11 J14** 54 49N 11 39 E
Sakti, *India* .... **69 H10** 22 2N 82 58 E
Sakuma, *Japan* .... **55 G8** 35 3N 137 49 E
Sakurai, *Japan* .... **55 G7** 34 30N 135 51 E
Saky, *Ukraine* .... **33 K7** 45 9N 33 34 E
Sal ➤, *Russia* .... **35 G5** 47 31N 40 45 E
Sala, *Eritrea* .... **81 D4** 16 53N 37 36 E
Sala, *Sweden* .... **10 E10** 59 58N 16 35 E
Sala, *Eritrea* .... **81 D4** 16 53N 37 36 E
Sala Consilina, *Italy* .. **43 B8** 40 23N 15 36 E
Sala-y-Gómez, *Pac. Oc.* **97 K17** 26 28 S 105 28W
Salaberry-de-
  Valleyfield, *Canada* . **117 A10** 45 15N 74 8W
Salacgrīva, *Latvia* .... **30 A11** 57 45N 24 21 E
Salada, L., *Mexico* **109 K6** 32 20N 115 40W
Saladas, *Argentina* ... **126 B4** 28 15 S 58 40W
Saladillo, *Argentina* ... **126 D4** 35 40 S 59 55W
Salado ➤, *Buenos Aires,*
  Argentina .... **126 D4** 35 44 S 57 22W
Salado ➤, *La Pampa,*
  Argentina .... **128 D3** 37 30 S 67 0W
Salado ➤, *Santa Fe,*
  Argentina .... **126 C3** 31 40 S 60 41W
Salado ➤, *Mexico* **113 M5** 26 52N 99 19W
Salaga, *Ghana* **83 D4** 8 31N 0 31W
Sālah, *Syria* .... **74 C5** 32 40N 36 45 E
Ṣalāḥ ad Dīn □, *Iraq* . **70 C4** 34 35N 43 35 E
Sālaj □, *Romania* ..... **28 C8** 47 15N 23 0 E
Sálakhos, *Greece* .... **49 C9** 36 17N 27 57 E
Salala, *Liberia* **82 D2** 6 42N 10 7W
Salala, *Sudan* .... **80 C4** 21 17N 36 16 E
Salālah, *Oman* .... **75 D5** 16 56N 53 59 E
Salamanca, *Chile* .... **126 C1** 31 46 S 70 59W
Salamanca, *Spain* **36 E5** 40 58N 5 39W
Salamanca, *U.S.A.* ... **116 D6** 42 10N 78 43W
Salamanca □, *Spain* .. **36 E5** 40 57N 5 40W
Salāmatābād, *Iran* .... **70 C5** 35 39N 47 50 E
Salamís, *Cyprus* ..... **49 D12** 35 11N 33 54 E
Salamís, *Greece* ...... **46 D5** 37 56N 23 30 E
Salar de Atacama, *Chile* **126 A2** 23 30 S 68 25W
Salar de Uyuni, *Bolivia* **124 H5** 20 30 S 67 45W
Sălard, *Romania* ..... **28 C7** 47 12N 22 3 E
Salas, *Spain* **36 B4** 43 25N 6 15W
Salas de los Infantes,
  Spain **36 C7** 42 2N 3 17W
Salatiga, *Indonesia* ... **63 G14** 7 19 S 110 30 E
Salaverry, *Peru* ...... **124 E3** 8 15 S 79 0W
Salawati, *Indonesia* ... **63 E8** 1 7 S 130 52 E
Salaya, *India* .... **68 H3** 22 19N 69 35 E
Salayar, *Indonesia* ... **63 F6** 6 7 S 120 30 E
Salazar ➤, *Spain* **38 C3** 42 40N 1 20W
Salbris, *France* ...... **19 E9** 47 25N 2 3 E
Salcia, *Romania* ...... **29 G9** 43 56N 24 55 E
Sălciua, *Romania* ..... **29 D8** 46 24N 23 26 E
Salcombe, *U.K.* **15 G4** 50 14N 3 47W
Saldaña, *Spain* **36 C6** 42 32N 4 48W
Saldanha, *S. Africa* ... **88 E2** 33 0 S 17 58 E
Saldanha B., *S. Africa* . **88 E2** 33 6 S 18 0 E
Saldus, *Latvia* .... **9 H20** 56 38N 22 30 E
Saldus □, *Latvia* ..... **30 B9** 56 35N 22 30 E
Sale, *Australia* .... **95 F4** 38 6 S 147 6 E
Salé, *Morocco* .... **78 B4** 34 3N 6 48 E
Sale, *Italy* .... **40 D5** 44 59N 8 48 E
Sale, *U.K.* **14 D5** 53 26N 2 19W
Salekhard, *Russia* ..... **52 C7** 66 30N 66 35 E
Salem, *India* .... **66 P11** 11 40N 78 11 E
Salem, *Ill., U.S.A.* **114 F1** 38 38N 88 57W
Salem, *Ind., U.S.A.* ... **114 F2** 38 36N 86 6W
Salem, *Mass., U.S.A.* .. **117 D14** 42 31N 70 53W
Salem, *Mo., U.S.A.* ... **113 G9** 37 39N 91 32W
Salem, *N.H., U.S.A.* .. **117 D13** 42 45N 71 12W
Salem, *N.J., U.S.A.* ... **114 F8** 39 34N 75 28W
Salem, *N.Y., U.S.A.* .. **117 C11** 43 10N 73 20W
Salem, *Ohio, U.S.A.* .. **116 F4** 40 54N 80 52W
Salem, *Oreg., U.S.A.* . **108 D2** 44 56N 123 2W
Salem, *S. Dak., U.S.A.* **112 D6** 43 44N 97 23W
Salem, *Va., U.S.A.* ... **114 G5** 37 18N 80 3W
Salemi, *Italy* .... **42 E5** 37 49N 12 48 E
Sälen, *Sweden* .... **10 C7** 61 15N 13 22 E
Salernes, *France* ..... **21 E10** 43 34N 6 15 E
Salerno, *Italy* .... **43 B7** 40 41N 14 47 E
Salerno, G. di, *Italy* ... **43 B7** 40 35N 14 40 E
Salford, *U.K.* **14 D5** 53 30N 2 18W
Salgir ➤, *Ukraine* ..... **33 K8** 45 38N 35 1 E
Salgótarján, *Hungary* .. **28 B4** 48 5N 19 47 E
Salgueiro, *Brazil* ..... **125 E11** 8 4 S 39 6W
Salibabu, *Indonesia* ... **63 D7** 3 51N 126 40 E
Salibea = Salybia,
  Trin. & Tob. **125 K15** 10 43N 61 2W
Salida, *U.S.A.* **106 C5** 38 32N 106 0W
Salies-de-Béarn, *France* **20 E3** 43 28N 0 56W
Salihli, *Turkey* .... **72 C3** 38 28N 28 8 E
Salihorsk, *Belarus* .... **33 F4** 52 51N 27 27 E
Salima, *Malawi* .... **85 G6** 13 47 S 34 28 E
Salina, *Italy* .... **43 D7** 38 34N 14 50 E
Salina, *Kans., U.S.A.* .. **112 F6** 38 50N 97 37W
Salina, *Utah, U.S.A.* ... **109 G8** 38 58N 111 51W
Salina Cruz, *Mexico* ... **119 D5** 16 10N 95 10W
Salina di Margherita di
  Savoia, *Italy* .... **43 A9** 41 23N 16 4 E
Salinas, *Brazil* .... **125 G10** 16 10 S 42 10W
Salinas, *Chile* .... **126 A2** 23 31 S 69 29W
Salinas, *Ecuador* ..... **124 D2** 2 10 S 80 58W
Salinas, *U.S.A.* **110 J5** 36 40N 121 39W
Salinas ➤, *Guatemala* . **119 D6** 16 28N 90 31W
Salinas ➤, *U.S.A.* **110 J5** 36 45N 121 48W
Salinas, B. de, *Nic.* **120 D2** 11 4N 85 45W
Salinas, Pampa de las,
  Argentina .... **126 C2** 31 58 S 66 42W
Salinas Ambargasta,
  Argentina .... **126 B3** 29 0 S 65 0W
Salinas Grandes,
  Argentina .... **126 C3** 30 0 S 65 0W
Salinas Pueblo
  Missions, *U.S.A.* **109 J10** 34 16N 106 5W
Saline ➤, *Ark., U.S.A.* **113 J8** 33 10N 92 8W
Saline ➤, *Kans., U.S.A.* **112 F6** 38 52N 97 30W
Saline di Trapani e
  Paceco, *Italy* .... **42 E5** 37 59N 12 28 E
Salines, C. de, *Spain* .. **48 B10** 39 16N 3 4 E
Salinópolis, *Brazil* ..... **125 D9** 0 40 S 47 20W
Salins-les-Bains, *France* **19 F13** 46 58N 5 52 E
Salir, *Portugal* **37 H2** 37 14N 8 2W
Salisbury, *U.K.* **15 F6** 51 4N 1 47W
Salisbury, *Md., U.S.A.* **114 F8** 38 22N 75 36W
Salisbury, *N.C., U.S.A.* **115 H5** 35 40N 80 29W
Salisbury I., *Canada* ... **101 B12** 63 30N 77 0W
Salisbury Plain, *U.K.* .. **15 F6** 51 14N 1 55W

Săliște, Romania	29 E8	45 45N	23 56 E
Salka, Nigeria	83 C5	10 20N	4 58 E
Şalkhad, Syria	74 C5	32 29N	36 43 E
Salkove, Ukraine	29 B14	48 15N	29 59 E
Salla, Finland	8 C23	66 50N	28 49 E
Sallanches, France	21 C10	45 55N	6 38 E
Sallent, Spain	38 D6	41 49N	1 54 E
Salles, France	20 D3	44 33N	0 52W
Salles-Curan, France	20 D6	44 11N	2 48 E
Salling, Denmark	11 H2	56 40N	8 55 E
Salliq = Coral Harbour, Canada	101 B11	64 8N	83 10W
Sallisaw, U.S.A.	113 H7	35 28N	94 47W
Salluit, Canada	101 B12	62 14N	75 38W
Sallom Junction, Sudan	80 D4	19 17N	37 6 E
Salmās, Iran	70 B5	38 11N	44 47 E
Salmerón, Spain	38 E2	40 33N	2 29W
Salmo, Canada	102 D5	49 10N	117 20W
Salmon, U.S.A.	108 D7	45 11N	113 54W
Salmon →, Canada	102 C4	54 3N	122 40W
Salmon →, U.S.A.	108 D5	45 51N	116 47W
Salmon Arm, Canada	102 C5	50 40N	119 15W
Salmon Gums, Australia	93 F3	32 59 S	121 38 E
Salmon River Mts., U.S.A.	108 D6	45 0N	114 30W
Salo, Finland	9 F20	60 22N	23 10 E
Salò, Italy	40 C7	45 36N	10 31 E
Salobreña, Spain	37 J7	36 44N	3 35W
Salome, U.S.A.	111 M13	33 47N	113 37W
Salon, India	69 F9	26 2N	81 27 E
Salon-de-Provence, France	21 E9	43 39N	5 6 E
Salonica = Thessaloníki, Greece	44 F6	40 38N	22 58 E
Salonta, Romania	28 D6	46 49N	21 42 E
Salor →, Spain	37 F3	39 39N	7 3W
Salou, Spain	38 D6	41 4N	1 8 E
Salou, C. de, Spain	38 D6	41 3N	1 10 E
Saloum →, Senegal	82 C1	13 50N	16 45W
Salpausselkä, Finland	9 F22	61 3N	26 15 E
Salsacate, Argentina	126 C2	31 20 S	65 5W
Salses, France	20 F6	42 50N	2 55 E
Salsk, Russia	35 G5	46 28N	41 30 E
Salso →, Italy	42 E6	37 6N	13 57 E
Salsomaggiore Terme, Italy	40 D6	44 49N	9 59 E
Salt, Spain	38 D7	41 59N	2 47 E
Salt →, Canada	102 B6	60 0N	112 25W
Salt →, U.S.A.	109 K7	33 23N	112 19W
Salt L., The, Australia	95 E3	30 6 S	142 8 E
Salt Lake City, U.S.A.	108 F8	40 45N	111 53W
Salt Range, Pakistan	68 C5	32 30N	72 25 E
Salta, Argentina	126 A2	24 57 S	65 25W
Salta □, Argentina	126 A2	24 48 S	65 30W
Saltaira, Italy	41 E9	43 45N	12 50 E
Saltash, U.K.	15 G3	50 24N	4 14W
Saltburn by the Sea, U.K.	14 C7	54 35N	0 58W
Saltcoats, U.K.	13 F4	55 38N	4 47W
Saltee Is., Ireland	12 D5	52 7N	6 37W
Saltfjellet, Norway	8 C16	66 40N	15 15 E
Saltfjorden, Norway	8 C16	67 15N	14 10 E
Saltholm, Denmark	11 J6	55 38N	12 43 E
Saltillo, Mexico	118 B4	25 25N	101 0W
Salto, Argentina	126 C3	34 20 S	60 15W
Salto, Uruguay	126 C4	31 27 S	57 50W
Salto del Guaíra, Paraguay	127 A5	24 3 S	54 17W
Salton City, U.S.A.	111 M11	33 29N	115 51W
Salton Sea, U.S.A.	111 M11	33 15N	115 45W
Saltpond, Ghana	83 D4	5 15N	1 3W
Saltsburg, U.S.A.	116 F5	40 29N	79 27W
Saltsjöbaden, Sweden	10 E12	59 15N	18 20 E
Saluda →, U.S.A.	115 J5	34 1N	81 4W
Salûm, Egypt	80 A2	31 31N	25 7 E
Salûm, Khâlig el, Egypt	80 A2	31 30N	25 24 E
Salur, India	67 K13	18 27N	83 18 E
Saluzzo, Italy	40 D4	44 39N	7 29 E
Salvador, Brazil	125 F11	13 0 S	38 30W
Salvador, Canada	103 C7	52 10N	109 32W
Salvador, El ■, Cent. Amer.	120 D2	13 50N	89 0W
Salvador, L., U.S.A.	113 L9	29 43N	90 15W
Salvaterra de Magos, Portugal	37 F2	39 1N	8 47W
Sálvora, I. de, Spain	36 C2	42 30N	8 58W
Salween →, Burma	67 L20	16 31N	97 37 E
Salyan, Azerbaijan	52 F5	39 33N	48 59 E
Salybia, Trin. & Tob.	125 K15	10 43N	61 2W
Salza →, Austria	26 D7	47 40N	14 43 E
Salzach →, Austria	26 C5	48 12N	12 56 E
Salzburg, Austria	26 D6	47 48N	13 2 E
Salzburg □, Austria	26 D6	47 15N	13 0 E
Salzgitter, Germany	24 C6	52 9N	10 19 E
Salzkotten, Germany	24 D4	51 40N	8 37 E
Salzwedel, Germany	24 C7	52 52N	11 10 E
Sam, India	68 F4	26 50N	70 31 E
Sam Neua, Laos	58 G5	20 29N	104 5 E
Sam Ngao, Thailand	64 D2	17 18N	99 0 E
Sam Rayburn Reservoir, U.S.A.	113 K7	31 4N	94 5W
Sam Son, Vietnam	64 C5	19 44N	105 54 E
Sam Teu, Laos	64 C5	19 59N	104 38 E
Sama de Langreo = Langreo, Spain	36 B5	43 18N	5 40W
Samagaltay, Russia	53 D10	50 36N	95 3 E
Samales Group, Phil.	61 J4	6 0N	122 0 E
Samâlût, Egypt	80 B3	28 20N	30 42 E
Samana, India	68 D7	30 10N	76 13 E
Samana Cay, Bahamas	121 B5	23 3N	73 45W
Samandağı, Turkey	72 D6	36 5N	35 59 E
Samandıra, Turkey	45 F13	40 59N	29 13 E
Samanga, Tanzania	87 D4	8 20 S	39 13 E
Samangān □, Afghan.	66 B5	36 15N	68 3 E
Samangwa, Dem. Rep. of the Congo	86 C1	4 23 S	24 10 E
Samani, Japan	54 C11	42 7N	142 56 E
Samanli Dağları, Turkey	45 F13	40 32N	29 10 E
Samar, Phil.	61 F6	12 0N	125 0 E
Samara, Russia	34 D10	53 8N	50 6 E
Samara →, Russia	34 D10	53 10N	50 4 E
Samara →, Ukraine	33 H8	48 28N	35 7 E
Samaria = Shōmrōn, West Bank	74 C4	32 15N	35 13 E
Samariá, Greece	49 D5	35 17N	23 58 E
Samariá △, Greece	46 F5	35 18N	23 57 E
Samarinda, Indonesia	62 E5	0 30 S	117 9 E
Samarkand = Samarqand, Uzbekistan	52 F7	39 40N	66 55 E
Samarqand, Uzbekistan	52 F7	39 40N	66 55 E
Sāmarrā', Iraq	70 C4	34 12N	43 52 E
Samastipur, India	69 G11	25 50N	85 50 E
Samaxı, Azerbaijan	35 K9	40 38N	48 37 E
Samba, Dem. Rep. of the Congo	86 C2	4 38 S	26 22 E
Samba, India	69 C6	32 32N	75 10 E
Sambalpur, India	67 J14	21 28N	84 4 E
Sambar, Tanjung, Indonesia	62 E4	2 59 S	110 19 E
Sambas, Indonesia	62 D3	1 20N	109 20 E
Sambava, Madag.	89 A9	14 16 S	50 10 E
Sambawizi, Zimbabwe	87 F2	18 24 S	26 13 E
Sambhal, India	69 E8	28 35N	78 37 E
Sambhar, India	68 F6	26 52N	75 6 E
Sambhar L., India	68 F6	26 55N	75 12 E
Sambiase, Italy	43 D9	38 58N	16 17 E
Sambir, Ukraine	31 J10	49 30N	23 10 E
Sambor, Cambodia	64 F6	12 46N	106 0 E
Samborombón, B., Argentina	126 D4	36 5 S	57 20W
Sambuca di Sicília, Italy	42 E6	37 39N	13 7 E
Samburu □, Kenya	86 B4	0 37N	37 31 E
Samch'ŏk, S. Korea	57 F15	37 30N	129 10 E
Samch'onp'o, S. Korea	57 G15	35 0N	128 6 E
Same, Tanzania	86 C4	4 2 S	37 38 E
Samer, France	19 B8	50 38N	1 44 E
Samfya, Zambia	87 E2	11 22 S	29 31 E
Sámi, Greece	46 C2	38 15N	20 39 E
Sämkir, Azerbaijan	35 K8	40 50N	46 0 E
Şamlı, Turkey	47 B9	39 48N	27 51 E
Samnah, Si. Arabia	70 E3	25 10N	37 15 E
Samo Alto, Chile	126 C1	30 22 S	71 0W
Samoa ■, Pac. Oc.	91 B13	14 0 S	172 0W
Samoan Is., Pac. Oc.	91 B13	14 0 S	171 0W
Samobor, Croatia	41 C12	45 47N	15 44 E
Samoëns, France	19 F13	46 5N	6 45 E
Samokov, Bulgaria	44 D7	42 18N	23 35 E
Samorogouan, Burkina Faso	82 C4	11 21N	4 57W
Sámos, Greece	47 D8	37 45N	26 50 E
Samoš, Serbia & M.	28 E5	45 13N	20 46 E
Samos, Spain	36 C3	42 44N	7 20W
Sámos □, Greece	47 D8	37 45N	26 50 E
Samothráki = Mathráki, Greece	49 A3	39 48N	19 31 E
Samothráki, Greece	45 F9	40 28N	25 28 E
Samoylovka, Russia	34 E6	51 12N	43 43 E
Sampa, Ghana	82 D4	8 0N	2 36 E
Sampacho, Argentina	126 C3	33 20 S	64 50W
Sampalan, Indonesia	63 K18	8 41 S	115 34 E
Sampang, Indonesia	63 G15	7 11 S	113 13 E
Samper de Calanda, Spain	38 D4	41 11N	0 28W
Sampéyre, Italy	40 D4	44 34N	7 11 E
Sampit, Indonesia	62 E4	2 34 S	113 0 E
Sampit, Teluk, Indonesia	62 E4	3 5 S	113 3 E
Samrong, Cambodia	64 E4	14 15N	103 30 E
Samrong, Thailand	64 E3	15 10N	100 40 E
Samsø, Denmark	11 J4	55 50N	10 35 E
Samsø Bælt, Denmark	11 J4	55 45N	10 45 E
Samsun, Turkey	72 B7	41 15N	36 22 E
Samtredia, Georgia	35 J6	42 7N	42 24 E
Samui, Ko, Thailand	65 b	9 30N	100 0 E
Samur →, Russia	35 K8	41 53N	48 32 E
Samurskiy Khrebet, Russia	35 K8	41 55N	47 11 E
Samusole, Dem. Rep. of the Congo	87 E1	10 2 S	24 0 E
Samut Prakan, Thailand	64 F3	13 32N	100 40 E
Samut Songkhram →, Thailand	62 B1	13 24N	100 1 E
Samwari, Pakistan	68 E2	28 30N	66 46 E
San, Mali	82 C4	13 15N	4 57W
San →, Cambodia	64 F5	13 32N	105 57 E
San →, Poland	31 H8	50 45N	21 51 E
San Adrián, Spain	38 C3	42 20N	1 56W
San Adrián, C. de, Spain	36 B2	43 21N	8 50W
San Agustín, □, Phil.	61 H7	6 20N	126 13 E
San Agustín de Valle Fértil, Argentina	126 C2	30 35 S	67 30W
San Ambrosio, Pac. Oc.	97 K20	26 28 S	79 53W
San Andreas, U.S.A.	110 G6	38 12N	120 41W
San Andres, Phil.	61 E6	13 36N	124 6 E
San Andrés, I. de, Caribbean	120 D3	12 42N	81 46W
San Andrés del Rabanedo, Spain	36 C5	42 37N	5 36W
San Andres Mts., U.S.A.	109 K10	33 0N	106 30W
San Andrés Tuxtla, Mexico	119 D5	18 30N	95 20W
San Angelo, U.S.A.	113 K4	31 28N	100 26W
San Anselmo, U.S.A.	110 H4	37 59N	122 34W
San Antonio, Belize	119 D7	16 15N	89 2W
San Antonio, Chile	126 C1	33 40 S	71 40W
San Antonio, Phil.	61 D4	14 57N	120 5 E
San Antonio, N. Mex., U.S.A.	109 K10	33 55N	106 52W
San Antonio, Tex., U.S.A.	113 L5	29 25N	98 30W
San Antonio →, U.S.A.	113 L6	28 30N	96 54W
San Antonio, C., Argentina	126 D4	36 15 S	56 40W
San Antonio, C. de, Cuba	120 B3	21 50N	84 57W
San Antonio, C. de, Spain	39 G5	38 48N	0 12 E
San Antonio, Mt., U.S.A.	111 L9	34 17N	117 38W
San Antonio de los Baños, Cuba	120 B3	22 54N	82 31W
San Antonio de los Cobres, Argentina	126 A2	24 10 S	66 17W
San Antonio Oeste, Argentina	128 E4	40 40 S	65 0W
San Arcángelo, Italy	43 B9	40 14N	16 14 E
San Ardo, U.S.A.	110 J6	36 1N	120 54W
San Agustín, Canary Is.	48 G4	27 47N	15 32W
San Augustine, U.S.A.	113 K7	31 30N	94 7W
San Bartolome, Canary Is.	48 F6	28 59N	13 37W
San Bartolome de Tirajana, Canary Is.	48 G4	27 54N	15 34W
San Bartolomeo in Galdo, Italy	43 A8	41 24N	15 1 E
San Benedetto del Tronto, Italy	41 F10	42 57N	13 53 E
San Benedetto Po, Italy	40 C7	45 2N	10 55 E
San Benedicto, I., Mexico	118 D2	19 18N	110 49W
San Benito, U.S.A.	113 M6	26 8N	97 38W
San Benito →, U.S.A.	110 J5	36 53N	121 34W
San Benito Mt., U.S.A.	110 J6	36 22N	120 37W
San Bernardino, U.S.A.	111 L9	34 7N	117 19W
San Bernardino Mts., U.S.A.	111 L10	34 10N	116 45W
San Bernardino Str., Phil.	61 E6	13 0N	125 0 E
San Bernardo, Chile	126 C1	33 40 S	70 50W
San Bernardo, I. de, Colombia	124 B3	9 45N	75 50W
San Blas, Mexico	118 B3	26 4N	108 46W
San Blas, Arch. de, Panama	120 E4	9 50N	78 31W
San Blas, C., U.S.A.	115 L3	29 40N	85 21W
San Bonifacio, Italy	41 C8	45 24N	11 16 E
San Borja, Bolivia	124 F5	14 50 S	66 52W
San Buenaventura = Ventura, U.S.A.	111 L7	34 17N	119 18W
San Buenaventura, Mexico	118 B4	27 5N	101 32W
San Carlos = Sant Carles, Spain	48 B8	39 3N	1 34 E
San Carlos, Argentina	126 C2	33 50 S	69 0W
San Carlos, Chile	126 D1	36 10 S	72 0W
San Carlos, Baja Calif. S., Mexico	118 C2	24 47N	112 6W
San Carlos, Coahuila, Mexico	119 B5	29 0N	100 54W
San Carlos, Nic.	120 D3	11 12N	84 50W
San Carlos, Neg. Occ., Phil.	61 F5	10 29N	123 25 E
San Carlos, Pangasinan, Phil.	61 D4	15 55N	120 20 E
San Carlos, Uruguay	127 C5	34 46 S	54 58W
San Carlos, U.S.A.	109 K8	33 21N	110 27W
San Carlos, Venezuela	124 B5	9 40N	68 36W
San Carlos de Bariloche, Argentina	128 E2	41 10 S	71 25W
San Carlos de Bolívar, Argentina	128 D4	36 15 S	61 6W
San Carlos de la Rápita = Sant Carles de la Ràpita, Spain	38 E5	40 37N	0 35 E
San Carlos del Zulia, Venezuela	124 B4	9 1N	71 55W
San Carlos L., U.S.A.	109 K8	33 11N	110 32W
San Cataldo, Italy	42 E6	37 29N	13 59 E
San Celoni = Sant Celoni, Spain	38 D7	41 42N	2 30 E
San Clemente, Chile	126 D1	35 30 S	71 29W
San Clemente, Spain	39 F2	39 24N	2 25W
San Clemente, U.S.A.	111 M9	33 26N	117 37W
San Clemente I., U.S.A.	111 N8	32 53N	118 29W
San Cristóbal = Es Migjorn Gran, Spain	48 B11	39 57N	4 3 E
San Cristóbal, Argentina	126 C3	30 20 S	61 10W
San Cristóbal, Dom. Rep.	121 C5	18 25N	70 6W
San Cristóbal, Guatemala	120 D1	14 0N	90 50W
San Cristóbal, Venezuela	124 B4	7 46N	72 14W
San Cristóbal de la Casas, Mexico	119 D6	16 50N	92 33W
San Damiano d'Asti, Italy	40 D5	44 50N	8 4 E
San Daniele del Friuli, Italy	41 B10	46 9N	13 1 E
San Diego, Calif., U.S.A.	111 N9	32 43N	117 9W
San Diego, Tex., U.S.A.	113 M5	27 46N	98 14W
San Diego, C., Argentina	128 G3	54 40 S	65 10W
San Diego de la Unión, Mexico	118 C4	21 28N	100 52W
San Diego International ✈ (SAN), U.S.A.	111 N9	32 44N	117 11W
San Dimitri, Ras, Malta	49 C1	36 4N	14 11 E
San Dimitri Point = Dimitri, Ras, Malta	49 C1	36 4N	14 11 E
San Donà di Piave, Italy	41 C9	45 38N	12 34 E
San Estanislao, Paraguay	126 A4	24 39 S	56 26W
San Esteban de Gormaz, Spain	38 D1	41 34N	3 13W
San Felice Circeo, Italy	42 A6	41 14N	13 5 E
San Felice sul Panaro, Italy	41 D8	44 50N	11 8 E
San Felipe, Chile	126 C1	32 43 S	70 42W
San Felipe, Mexico	118 A2	31 0N	114 52W
San Felipe, Venezuela	124 A5	10 20N	68 44W
San Felipe →, U.S.A.	111 M11	33 12N	115 49W
San Félix, Chile	126 B1	28 56 S	70 28W
San Félix, Pac. Oc.	97 K20	26 23 S	80 0W
San Fernando = Sant Ferran, Spain	48 C7	38 42N	1 28 E
San Fernando, Chile	126 C1	34 30 S	71 0W
San Fernando, Baja Calif., Mexico	118 B1	29 55N	115 10W
San Fernando, Tamaulipas, Mexico	119 C5	24 51N	98 10W
San Fernando, La Union, Phil.	61 C4	16 40N	120 23 E
San Fernando, Pampanga, Phil.	61 D4	15 5N	120 37 E
San Fernando, Spain	37 J4	36 28N	6 17W
San Fernando, Trin. & Tob.	121 D7	10 16N	61 28W
San Fernando, U.S.A.	111 L8	34 17N	118 26W
San Fernando de Apure, Venezuela	124 B5	7 54N	67 15W
San Fernando de Atabapo, Venezuela	124 C5	4 3N	67 42W
San Fernando di Púglia, Italy	43 A9	41 18N	16 5 E
San Francisco, Argentina	126 C3	31 30 S	62 5W
San Francisco, U.S.A.	110 H4	37 47N	122 25W
San Francisco →, U.S.A.	109 K9	32 59N	109 22W
San Francisco, C. de, Colombia	122 C3	6 18N	77 29W
San Francisco, Paso de, S. Amer.	126 B2	27 0 S	68 0W
San Francisco de Macorís, Dom. Rep.	121 C5	19 19N	70 15W
San Francisco del Monte de Oro, Argentina	126 C2	32 36 S	66 8W
San Francisco del Oro, Mexico	118 B3	26 52N	105 50W
San Francisco International ✈ (SFO), U.S.A.	110 H4	37 37N	122 22W
San Francisco Javier = Sant Francesc de Formentera, Spain	48 C7	38 42N	1 26 E
San Fratello, Italy	43 D7	38 1N	14 36 E
San Gabriel, Chile	126 C1	33 47 S	70 15W
San Gabriel Mts., U.S.A.	111 L9	34 20N	118 0W
San Gavino Monreale, Italy	42 C1	39 33N	8 47 E
San German, Puerto Rico	121 d	18 4N	67 4W
San Gimignano, Italy	40 E8	43 28N	11 2 E
San Giórgio di Nogaro, Italy	41 C10	45 50N	13 13 E
San Giórgio Iónico, Italy	43 B10	40 27N	17 23 E
San Giovanni Bianco, Italy	40 C6	45 52N	9 39 E
San Giovanni in Fiore, Italy	43 C9	39 15N	16 42 E
San Giovanni in Persiceto, Italy	41 D8	44 38N	11 11 E
San Giovanni Rotondo, Italy	41 G12	41 42N	15 44 E
San Giovanni Valdarno, Italy	41 E8	43 34N	11 32 E
San Giuliano Terme, Italy	40 E7	43 46N	10 26 E
San Gorgonio Mt., U.S.A.	111 L10	34 7N	116 51W
San Gottardo, P. del, Switz.	25 J4	46 33N	8 33 E
San Gregorio, Uruguay	127 C4	32 37 S	55 40W
San Gregorio, U.S.A.	110 H4	37 20N	122 23W
San Guiseppe Jato, Italy	42 E6	37 57N	13 11 E
San Ignacio, Belize	119 D7	17 10N	89 5W
San Ignacio, Bolivia	124 G6	16 20 S	60 55W
San Ignacio, Mexico	118 B2	27 27N	113 0W
San Ignacio, Paraguay	120 C2	26 52 S	57 3W
San Ignacio, L., Mexico	118 B2	27 0N	113 10W
San Ignacio, L., Mexico	118 B2	26 50N	113 11W
San Ildefonso, C., Phil.	61 C5	16 0N	122 1 E
San Isidro, Argentina	126 C4	34 29 S	58 31W
San Isidro, Phil.	61 H7	6 50N	126 5 E
San Jacinto, U.S.A.	111 M10	33 47N	116 57W
San Jaime = Sant Jaume, Spain	48 B11	39 54N	4 4 E
San Javier, Misiones, Argentina	127 B4	27 55 S	55 5W
San Javier, Santa Fe, Argentina	126 C4	30 40 S	59 55W
San Javier, Bolivia	124 G6	16 18 S	62 30W
San Javier, Chile	126 D1	35 40 S	71 45W
San Javier, Spain	39 H4	37 49N	0 50W
San Jerónimo Taviche, Mexico	119 D5	16 38N	96 32W
San Joaquín, U.S.A.	110 J6	36 36N	120 11W
San Joaquín →, U.S.A.	110 G5	38 4N	121 51W
San Joaquin Valley, U.S.A.	110 J6	37 20N	121 0W
San Jon, U.S.A.	113 H3	35 6N	103 20W
San Jordi = Sant Jordi, Spain	48 B9	39 33N	2 46 E
San Jorge, Argentina	126 C4	31 54 S	61 50W
San Jorge, B. de, Mexico	118 A2	31 20N	113 20W
San Jorge, G., Argentina	128 F3	46 0 S	66 0W
San José = San Josep, Spain	48 C7	38 55N	1 18 E
San José, Costa Rica	120 E3	9 55N	84 2W
San José, Guatemala	120 D1	14 0N	90 50W
San José, Mexico	118 C2	25 0N	110 50W
San Jose, Mind. Occ., Phil.	61 E4	12 27N	121 4 E
San Jose, Nueva Ecija, Phil.	61 D4	15 45N	120 55 E
San Jose, U.S.A.	110 H5	37 20N	121 53W
San Jose →, U.S.A.	109 J10	34 25N	106 45W
San Jose de Buenavista, Phil.	63 B6	10 45N	121 56 E
San José de Chiquitos, Bolivia	124 G6	17 53 S	60 50W
San José de Feliciano, Argentina	126 C4	30 26 S	58 46W
San José de Jáchal, Argentina	126 C2	30 15 S	68 46W
San José de Mayo, Uruguay	126 C4	34 27 S	56 40W
San José del Cabo, Mexico	118 C3	23 0N	109 40W
San José del Guaviare, Colombia	124 C4	2 35N	72 38W
San Josep, Spain	48 C7	38 55N	1 18 E
San Juan, Argentina	126 C2	31 30 S	68 30W
San Juan, Mexico	118 C4	21 20N	102 50W
San Juan, Phil.	61 F6	10 16N	125 10 E
San Juan, Puerto Rico	121 d	18 28N	66 7W
San Juan □, Argentina	126 C2	31 9 S	69 0W
San Juan →, Argentina	126 C2	32 20 S	67 25W
San Juan →, Nic.	120 D3	10 56N	83 42W
San Juan →, U.S.A.	109 H8	37 16N	110 26W
San Juan Bautista = Sant Joan Baptista, Spain	48 B8	39 5N	1 31 E
San Juan Bautista, Paraguay	126 B4	26 37 S	57 6W
San Juan Bautista, U.S.A.	110 J5	36 51N	121 32W
San Juan Bautista Valle Nacional, Mexico	119 D5	17 47N	96 19W
San Juan Capistrano, U.S.A.	111 M9	33 30N	117 40W
San Juan Cr. →, U.S.A.	110 J5	35 40N	120 22W
San Juan de Alicante, Spain	39 G4	38 24N	0 26W
San Juan de Guadalupe, Mexico	118 C4	24 38N	102 44W
San Juan de la Costa, Mexico	118 C2	24 23N	110 45W
San Juan de los Morros, Venezuela	124 B5	9 55N	67 21W
San Juan del Norte, Nic.	120 D3	10 58N	83 40W
San Juan del Norte, B. de, Nic.	120 D3	11 0N	83 40W
San Juan del Río, Mexico	119 C5	20 25N	100 0W
San Juan del Sur, Nic.	120 D2	11 20N	85 51W
San Juan I., U.S.A.	110 B3	48 32N	123 5W
San Juan Island △, U.S.A.	110 B4	48 27N	123 0W
San Juan Mts., U.S.A.	109 H10	37 30N	107 0W
San Just, Sierra de, Spain	38 E4	40 45N	0 49W
San Justo, Argentina	126 C3	30 47 S	60 30W
San Kamphaeng, Thailand	64 C2	18 45N	99 8 E
San Lázaro, C., Mexico	118 C2	24 50N	112 18W
San Lázaro, Sa., Mexico	118 C3	23 25N	110 0W
San Leandro, U.S.A.	110 H4	37 44N	122 9W
San Leonardo de Yagüe, Spain	38 D1	41 51N	3 5W
San Lorenzo = Sant Llorenç des Cardassar, Spain	48 B10	39 37N	3 17 E
San Lorenzo, Argentina	126 C3	32 45 S	60 45W
San Lorenzo, Ecuador	124 C3	1 15N	78 50W
San Lorenzo, Paraguay	126 B4	25 20 S	57 32W
San Lorenzo →, Mexico	118 C3	24 15N	107 24W
San Lorenzo, Mte., Argentina	128 F2	47 40 S	72 20W
San Lorenzo de la Parrilla, Spain	38 F2	39 51N	2 22W
San Lorenzo de Morunys = Sant Llorenç de Morunys, Spain	38 C6	42 8N	1 35 E
San Lucas, Bolivia	124 H5	20 5 S	65 7W
San Lucas, Baja Calif. S., Mexico	118 C3	22 53N	109 54W
San Lucas, Baja Calif. S., Mexico	118 C2	27 10N	112 14W
San Lucas, U.S.A.	110 J5	36 8N	121 1W
San Lucas, C., Mexico	118 C3	22 50N	110 0W
San Lúcido, Italy	43 C9	39 18N	16 3 E
San Luis, Argentina	126 C2	33 20 S	66 20W
San Luis, Cuba	120 B3	22 17N	83 46W
San Luis, Guatemala	120 C2	16 14N	89 27W
San Luis, Ariz., U.S.A.	109 K6	32 29N	114 47W
San Luis, Colo., U.S.A.	109 H11	37 12N	105 25W
San Luis □, Argentina	126 C2	34 0 S	66 0W
San Luis, I., Mexico	118 B2	29 58N	114 26W
San Luis, Sierra de, Argentina	126 C2	32 30 S	66 10W
San Luis de la Paz, Mexico	118 C4	21 19N	100 32W
San Luis Obispo, U.S.A.	111 K6	35 17N	120 40W
San Luis Potosí, Mexico	118 C4	22 9N	100 59W
San Luis Potosí □, Mexico	118 C4	22 10N	101 0W
San Luis Reservoir, U.S.A.	110 H5	37 4N	121 5W
San Luis Río Colorado, Mexico	118 A2	32 29N	114 58W
San Manuel, U.S.A.	109 K8	32 36N	110 38W
San Marco, C., Italy	42 C1	39 51N	8 26 E
San Marco Argentano, Italy	43 C9	39 33N	16 7 E
San Marco in Lámis, Italy	41 G12	41 43N	15 38 E
San Marcos, Guatemala	120 D1	14 59N	91 52W
San Marcos, Mexico	118 B2	27 13N	112 6W
San Marcos, Calif., U.S.A.	111 M9	33 9N	117 10W
San Marcos, Tex., U.S.A.	113 L6	29 53N	97 56W
San Marino, San Marino	41 E9	43 55N	12 30 E
San Marino ■, Europe	41 E9	43 56N	12 25 E
San Martín, Antarctica	5 C17	68 11 S	67 0W
San Martín, Argentina	126 C2	33 5 S	68 28W
San Martín →, Bolivia	124 F6	13 8 S	63 43W
San Martín, L., Argentina	128 F2	48 50 S	72 50W
San Martín de la Vega, Spain	36 E7	40 13N	3 34W
San Martín de los Andes, Argentina	128 E2	40 10 S	71 20W
San Martín de Valdeiglesias, Spain	36 E6	40 21N	4 24W
San Mateo = Sant Mateu, Baleares, Spain	48 B7	39 3N	1 23 E
San Mateo = Sant Mateu, Valencia, Spain	38 E5	40 28N	0 10 E
San Mateo, Phil.	61 C4	16 54N	121 33 E
San Mateo, U.S.A.	110 H4	37 34N	122 19W
San Matías, Bolivia	124 G7	16 25 S	58 20W
San Matías, G., Argentina	128 E4	41 30 S	64 0W
San Miguel = Sant Miguel, Spain	48 B7	39 3N	1 26 E
San Miguel, El Salv.	120 D2	13 30N	88 12W
San Miguel, Panama	120 E4	8 27N	78 55W
San Miguel, U.S.A.	110 K6	35 45N	120 42W
San Miguel →, Bolivia	124 F6	13 52 S	63 56W
San Miguel de Tucumán, Argentina	126 B2	26 50 S	65 20W
San Miguel del Monte, Argentina	126 D4	35 23 S	58 50W
San Miguel I., U.S.A.	111 L6	34 2N	120 23W
San Miniato, Italy	40 E7	43 41N	10 51 E
San Nicolás, Canary Is.	48 G4	27 58N	15 47W
San Nicolás, Phil.	61 B4	18 10N	120 36 E
San Nicolás de los Arroyas, Argentina	126 C3	33 25 S	60 10W
San Nicolas I., U.S.A.	111 M7	33 15N	119 30W
San Onofre, U.S.A.	111 M9	33 22N	117 34W
San Pablo, Bolivia	126 A2	21 43 S	66 38W
San Pablo, Phil.	61 D4	14 11N	121 31 E
San Pablo, U.S.A.	110 H4	37 58N	122 21W
San Páolo di Civitate, Italy	41 G12	41 44N	15 15 E
San Pedro, Buenos Aires, Argentina	126 C4	33 40 S	59 40W
San Pedro, Misiones, Argentina	127 B5	26 30 S	54 10W
San Pedro, Chile	126 C1	33 54 S	71 28W
San Pédro, Ivory C.	82 E3	4 50N	6 33W
San Pedro, Mexico	118 C2	23 55N	110 17W
San Pedro □, Paraguay	126 A4	24 0 S	57 0W
San Pedro →, Chihuahua, Mexico	118 B3	28 20N	106 10W
San Pedro →, Nayarit, Mexico	118 C3	21 45N	105 30W
San Pedro →, U.S.A.	109 K8	32 59N	110 47W
San Pedro, Pta., Chile	126 B1	25 30 S	70 38W
San Pedro, Sierra de, Spain	37 F4	39 18N	6 40W
San Pedro Channel, U.S.A.	111 M8	33 30N	118 25W
San Pedro de Atacama, Chile	126 A2	22 55 S	68 15W
San Pedro de Jujuy, Argentina	126 A3	24 12 S	64 55W
San Pedro de las Colonias, Mexico	118 B4	25 50N	102 59W
San Pedro de Macorís, Dom. Rep.	121 C6	18 30N	69 18W
San Pedro del Norte, Nic.	120 D3	13 4N	84 33W
San Pedro del Paraná, Paraguay	126 B4	26 43 S	56 13W
San Pedro del Pinatar, Spain	39 H4	37 50N	0 50W
San Pedro Mártir △, Mexico	118 A1	31 0N	115 21W
San Pedro Mártir, Sierra, Mexico	118 A1	31 0N	115 30W
San Pedro Mixtepec, Mexico	119 D5	16 2N	97 7W
San Pedro Ocampo = Melchor Ocampo, Mexico	118 C4	24 52N	101 40W
San Pedro Sula, Honduras	120 C2	15 30N	88 0W
San Pietro, Italy	42 C1	39 8N	8 17 E
San Pietro Vernótico, Italy	43 B11	40 29N	18 0 E
San Quintín, Mexico	118 A1	30 29N	115 57W
San Rafael, Argentina	126 C2	34 40 S	68 21W
San Rafael, Calif., U.S.A.	110 H4	37 58N	122 32W
San Rafael, N. Mex., U.S.A.	109 J10	35 7N	107 53W
San Rafael Mt., U.S.A.	111 L7	34 41N	119 52W
San Rafael Mts., U.S.A.	111 L7	34 40N	119 50W
San Ramón de la Nueva Orán, Argentina	126 A3	23 10 S	64 20W
San Remo, Italy	40 E4	43 49N	7 46 E
San Roque, Argentina	126 B4	28 25 S	58 45W

San Roque, Spain **37 J5** 36 17N 5 21W
San Rosendo, Chile .. **126 D1** 37 16 S 72 43W
San Saba, U.S.A. **113 K5** 31 12N 98 43W
San Salvador, El Salv. . **120 D2** 13 40N 89 10W
San Salvador, El Salv. . **48 B10** 39 27N 3 11 E
San Salvador de Jujuy,
  Argentina .... **126 A3** 24 10 S 64 48W
San Salvador I.,
  Bahamas **121 B5** 24 0N 74 40W
San Salvo, Italy ..... **41 F11** 42 3N 14 44 E
San Sebastián =
  Donostia-San
  Sebastián, Spain ... **38 B3** 43 17N 1 58W
San Sebastián, Argentina **128 G3** 53 10 S 68 30W
San Sebastian,
  Puerto Rico .... **121 d** 18 20N 66 59W
San Sebastián de la
  Gomera, Canary Is. . **48 F2** 28 5N 17 7W
San Serra = Son Serra,
  Spain .... **48 B10** 39 43N 3 13 E
San Serverino Marche,
  Italy .... **41 E10** 43 13N 13 10 E
San Severo, Italy ..... **41 G12** 41 41N 15 23 E
San Simeon, U.S.A. ... **110 K5** 35 39N 121 11W
San Simon, U.S.A. **109 K9** 32 16N 109 14W
San Stéfano di Cadore,
  Italy .... **41 B9** 46 34N 12 33 E
San Stino di Livenza,
  Italy .... **41 C9** 45 44N 12 41 E
San Telmo = Sant Telm,
  Spain .... **48 B9** 39 35N 2 21 E
San Telmo, Mexico ... **118 A1** 30 58N 116 6W
San Turbucio, Mexico .. **118 C4** 24 8N 101 32W
San Valentin, Mte.,
  Chile .... **128 F2** 46 30 S 73 30W
San Vicente de
  Alcántara, Spain ... **37 F3** 39 22N 7 8W
San Vicente de la
  Barquera, Spain ... **36 B6** 43 23N 4 29W
San Vincente del
  Raspeig, Spain **39 G4** 38 24N 0 31W
San Vincenzo, Italy ... **40 E7** 43 6N 10 32 E
San Vito, Costa Rica .. **120 E3** 8 50N 82 58W
San Vito, Italy ...... **42 C2** 39 26N 9 32 E
San Vito, C., Italy .... **42 D5** 38 11N 12 41 E
San Vito al Tagliamento,
  Italy .... **41 C9** 45 54N 12 52 E
San Vito Chietino, Italy **41 F11** 42 18N 14 27 E
San Vito dei Normanni,
  Italy .... **41 B10** 40 39N 17 42 E
Sana', Yemen .... **75 D3** 15 27N 44 12 E
Sana →, Bos.-H. ..... **41 C13** 45 3N 16 23 E
Sanaba, Burkina Faso . **82 C4** 12 25N 3 47W
Sanafīr, Si. Arabia ... **80 B3** 27 56N 34 42 E
Sanaga →, Cameroon . **83 E6** 3 35N 9 38 E
Sanaloa, Presa, Mexico **118 C3** 24 50N 107 20W
Sanana, Indonesia ... **63 E7** 2 4 S 125 58 E
Sanand, India .... **68 H5** 22 59N 72 25 E
Sanandaj, Iran ...... **70 C5** 35 18N 47 1 E
Sanandita, Bolivia ... **126 A3** 21 40 S 63 45W
Sanary-sur-Mer, France **21 E9** 43 7N 5 49 E
Sanawad, India ...... **68 H7** 22 11N 76 5 E
Sancellas = Sencelles,
  Spain .... **48 B9** 39 39N 2 54 E
Sancergues, France ... **19 E9** 47 10N 2 54 E
Sancerre, France .... **19 E9** 47 20N 2 50 E
Sancerrois, Collines du,
  France .... **19 E9** 47 20N 2 40 E
Sancha He →, China .. **58 D6** 26 48N 106 7 E
Sanchahe, China ..... **57 B14** 44 50N 126 2 E
Sánchez, Dom. Rep. .. **121 C6** 19 15N 69 36W
Sanchor, India ...... **68 G4** 24 45N 71 55 E
Sancoins, France .... **19 F9** 46 47N 2 55 E
Sancti Spíritus, Cuba . **120 B4** 21 52N 79 33W
Sancy, Puy de, France . **20 C6** 45 32N 2 50 E
Sand →, S. Africa ... **89 C5** 22 25 S 30 5 E
Sand Hills, U.S.A. ... **112 D4** 42 10N 101 30W
Sand Lakes △, Canada **103 B9** 57 51N 98 32W
Sand Springs, U.S.A. . **113 G6** 36 9N 96 7W
Sanda, Japan .... **55 G7** 34 53N 135 14 E
Sandakan, Malaysia .. **62 C5** 5 53N 118 4 E
Sandan = Sambor,
  Cambodia .... **64 F6** 12 46N 106 0 E
Sandanski, Bulgaria .. **44 E7** 41 35N 23 16 E
Sandaré, Mali **82 C2** 14 40N 10 15W
Sandared, Sweden ... **11 G6** 57 43N 12 47 E
Sandarne, Sweden ... **10 C11** 61 16N 17 9 E
Sanday, U.K. **13 B6** 59 16N 2 31W
Sandefjord, Norway .. **9 G14** 59 10N 10 15 E
Sanders, U.S.A. **109 J9** 35 13N 109 20W
Sanderson, U.S.A. ... **113 K3** 30 9N 102 24W
Sandersville, U.S.A. .. **115 J4** 32 59N 82 48W
Sandfire Roadhouse,
  Australia .... **93 C3** 19 45 S 121 15 E
Sandfly L., Canada ... **103 B7** 55 43N 106 6W
Sandfontein, Namibia . **88 C2** 23 48 S 29 1 E
Sandhammaren, C.,
  Sweden .... **11 J8** 55 23N 14 14 E
Sandheads, The, India . **69 J13** 21 10N 88 20 E
Sandía, Peru .... **124 F5** 14 10 S 69 30W
Sandikli, Turkey ..... **47 C12** 38 28N 30 17 E
Sandila, India .... **69 F9** 27 5N 80 31 E
Sandnes, Norway .... **9 G11** 58 50N 5 45 E
Sandnessjøen, Norway . **8 C15** 66 2N 12 38 E
Sandoa, Dem. Rep. of
  the Congo .... **84 F4** 9 41 S 23 0 E
Sandomierz, Poland .. **31 H8** 50 40N 21 43 E
Sândominic, Romania . **29 D10** 46 35N 25 47 E
Sandover →, Australia **94 C2** 21 43 S 136 32 E
Sandoway, Burma .... **67 K19** 18 20N 94 30 E
Sandoy, Færoe Is. **8 F9** 61 52N 6 46W
Sandpoint, U.S.A. ... **108 B5** 48 17N 116 33W
Sandray, U.K. **13 E1** 56 53N 7 31W
Sandringham, U.K. ... **14 E8** 52 51N 0 31 E
Sandstone, Australia . **93 E2** 27 59 S 119 16 E
Sandu, China .... **58 E6** 26 0N 107 52 E
Sandusky, Mich., U.S.A. **116 C2** 43 25N 82 50W
Sandusky, Ohio, U.S.A. **116 E2** 41 27N 82 42W
Sandvig, Sweden .... **11 J8** 55 18N 14 47 E
Sandviken, Sweden ... **10 D10** 60 38N 16 46 E
Sandwich, C., Australia **94 B4** 18 14 S 146 18 E
Sandwich B., Canada . **105 B8** 53 40N 57 15W
Sandwich B., Namibia . **88 C1** 23 25 S 14 20 E
Sandy, Oreg., U.S.A. .. **110 E4** 45 24N 122 16W
Sandy, Pa., U.S.A. ... **116 E6** 41 6N 78 46W
Sandy, Utah, U.S.A. .. **108 F8** 40 35N 111 50W
Sandy Bay, Canada .. **103 B8** 55 31N 102 19W
Sandy Bight, Australia . **93 F3** 33 50 S 123 20 E
Sandy C., Queens.,
  Australia .... **94 C5** 24 42 S 153 15 E
Sandy C., Tas., Australia **95 G3** 41 25 S 144 45 E
Sandy Cay, Bahamas . **121 B4** 23 13N 75 18W
Sandy Cr. →, U.S.A. . **108 F9** 41 51N 109 47W
Sandy L., Canada **104 B1** 53 2N 93 0W
Sandy Lake, Canada .. **104 B1** 53 0N 93 15W
Sandy Valley, U.S.A. .. **111 K11** 35 49N 115 36W
Sânfjällets △, Sweden . **10 B7** 62 11N 13 35 E

Sanford, Fla., U.S.A. .. **115 L5** 28 48N 81 16W
Sanford, Maine, U.S.A. **115 D10** 43 27N 70 47W
Sanford, N.C., U.S.A. . **115 H6** 35 29N 79 10W
Sanford →, Australia . **93 E2** 27 22 S 115 53 E
Sanford, Mt., U.S.A. .. **100 B5** 62 13N 144 8W
Sang-i-Masha, Afghan. . **68 C2** 33 8N 67 27 E
Sanga, Mozam. ...... **87 E4** 12 22 S 35 21 E
Sanga →, Congo .... **84 E3** 1 5 S 17 0 E
Sangamner, India .... **66 K9** 19 37N 74 15 E
Sanganeb Atoll △,
  Sudan .... **80 D4** 19 33N 37 13 E
Sangar, Afghan. ..... **68 C1** 32 56N 65 30 E
Sangar, Russia ...... **53 C13** 64 2N 127 31 E
Sangar Sarai, Afghan. . **68 B4** 34 27N 70 35 E
Sangareddi, Guinea ... **82 C2** 11 7N 13 52W
Sangarh →, Pakistan . **68 D4** 30 43N 70 44 E
Sangasso, Mali **82 C3** 12 5N 5 35W
Sangatte, France .... **19 B8** 50 56N 1 44 E
Sangay, Ecuador ..... **124 D3** 2 0 S 78 20W
Sange, Dem. Rep. of
  the Congo .... **86 D2** 6 58 S 28 21 E
Sangeang, Indonesia .. **63 F5** 8 12 S 119 6 E
Sângeorz-Băi, Romania **29 C9** 47 22N 24 41 E
Sanger, U.S.A. **110 J7** 36 42N 119 33W
Sangerhausen, Germany **24 D7** 51 28N 11 18 E
Sanggan He →, China **56 E9** 38 12N 117 15 E
Sanggau, Indonesia ... **62 D4** 0 5N 110 30 E
Sanghar, Pakistan .... **68 F3** 26 2N 68 57 E
Sangihe, Kepulauan,
  Indonesia .... **63 D7** 3 0N 125 30 E
Sangihe, Pulau,
  Indonesia .... **63 D7** 3 35N 125 30 E
Sangju, S. Korea ..... **57 F15** 36 25N 128 10 E
Sangkapura, Indonesia **62 F4** 5 52 S 112 40 E
Sangkhla, Thailand ... **64 E2** 14 57N 98 28 E
Sangkulirang, Indonesia **62 D5** 0 59N 117 58 E
Sangla, Pakistan .... **68 D5** 31 43N 73 23 E
Sangli, India .... **66 L9** 16 55N 74 33 E
Sangmélima, Cameroon **83 E7** 2 57N 12 1 E
Sangod, India .... **68 G7** 24 55N 76 17 E
Sangre de Cristo Mts.,
  U.S.A. **113 G2** 37 30N 105 20W
Sangre Grande,
  Trin. & Tob. **125 K15** 10 35N 61 8W
Sangro →, Italy ..... **41 F11** 42 14N 14 32 E
Sangrur, India ...... **68 D6** 30 14N 75 50 E
Sangudo, Canada **102 C6** 53 50N 114 54W
Sangue →, Brazil .... **124 F7** 11 1 S 58 39W
Sangüesa, Spain **38 C3** 42 37N 1 17W
Sanguinaires, Îs., France **21 G12** 41 51N 8 36 E
Sangzhi, China ...... **59 C8** 29 25N 110 12 E
Sanhala, Ivory C. **82 C3** 10 3N 6 51W
Sanibel, U.S.A. **115 M4** 26 26N 82 1W
Sanikiluaq, Canada ... **101 C12** 56 32N 79 14W
Sanin-Kaigan △, Japan **55 G7** 35 39N 134 37 E
Sanirajak, Canada ... **101 B11** 68 46N 81 12W
Sanjawi, Pakistan .... **68 D3** 30 17N 68 21 E
Sanje, Uganda .... **86 C3** 0 49 S 31 30 E
Sanjiang, China ..... **58 E7** 25 48N 109 37 E
Sanjo, Japan .... **54 F9** 37 37N 138 57 E
Sankh →, India ..... **69 H11** 22 15N 84 48 E
Sankt Andrä, Austria .. **26 E7** 46 46N 14 50 E
Sankt Augustin,
  Germany .... **24 E3** 50 45N 7 10 E
Sankt Blasien, Germany **25 H4** 47 47N 8 7 E
Sankt Gallen, Switz. .. **25 H5** 47 26N 9 22 E
Sankt Gallen □, Switz. . **25 H5** 47 25N 9 22 E
Sankt Goar, Germany . **25 E3** 50 12N 7 43 E
Sankt Ingbert, Germany **25 F3** 49 16N 7 6 E
Sankt Johann im
  Pongau, Austria .... **26 D7** 47 22N 13 12 E
Sankt Johann in Tirol,
  Austria .... **26 D5** 47 30N 12 25 E
Sankt Michel = Mikkeli,
  Finland .... **9 F22** 61 43N 27 15 E
Sankt-Peterburg, Russia **32 C6** 59 55N 30 20 E
Sankt Pölten, Austria .. **26 C8** 48 12N 15 38 E
Sankt Ulrich = Ortisei,
  Italy .... **41 B8** 46 34N 11 40 E
Sankt Valentin, Austria **26 C7** 48 11N 14 33 E
Sankt Veit an der Glan,
  Austria .... **26 E7** 46 47N 14 22 E
Sankt Wendel, Germany **25 F3** 49 27N 7 9 E
Sankt Wolfgang, Austria **26 D6** 47 43N 13 27 E
Sankuru →, Dem. Rep.
  of the Congo ...... **84 E4** 4 17 S 20 25 E
Sanliurfa, Turkey .... **70 B3** 37 12N 38 50 E
Sanlúcar de Barrameda,
  Spain **37 J4** 36 46N 6 21W
Sanluri, Italy .... **42 C1** 39 34N 8 54 E
Sânmartin, Romania .. **29 D10** 46 19N 25 58 E
Sanmen, China ...... **59 C13** 29 5N 121 35 E
Sanmenxia, China .... **56 G6** 34 47N 111 12 E
Sanming, China ...... **59 D11** 26 15N 117 40 E
Sannaspos, S. Africa .. **88 D4** 29 6 S 26 34 E
Sannicandro Gargánico,
  Italy .... **41 G12** 41 50N 15 34 E
Sânnicolau Mare,
  Romania .... **28 D5** 46 5N 20 39 E
Sannieshof, S. Africa .. **88 D4** 26 30 S 25 47 E
Sannīn, J., Lebanon ... **74 B4** 33 57N 35 52 E
Sannūr, W. →, Egypt . **80 B3** 28 59N 31 3 E
Sanok, Poland ...... **31 J9** 49 35N 22 10 E
Sanquhar, U.K. **13 F5** 55 22N 3 54W
Sans Souci, Trin. & Tob. **125 K16** 10 50N 61 0W
Sansanding, Mali **82 C3** 13 48N 6 0W
Sansepolcro, Italy .... **41 E9** 43 34N 12 8 E
Sansha, China ...... **59 D13** 26 58N 120 12 E
Sanshui, China ...... **59 F9** 23 10N 112 56 E
Sanski Most, Bos.-H. .. **41 D13** 44 46N 16 40 E
Sansui, China .... **58 D7** 26 58N 108 39 E
Sant Antoni Abat, Spain **48 C7** 38 59N 1 19 E
Sant Boi de Llobregat,
  Spain .... **38 D7** 41 21N 2 2 E
Sant Carles, Spain ... **48 B8** 39 3N 1 34 E
Sant Carles de la Ràpita,
  Spain .... **38 E5** 40 37N 0 35 E
Sant Celoni, Spain ... **38 D7** 41 42N 2 30 E
Sant Feliu de Guíxols,
  Spain .... **38 D8** 41 45N 3 1 E
Sant Feliu de Llobregat,
  Spain .... **38 D7** 41 23N 2 2 E
Sant Ferran, Spain ... **48 C7** 38 42N 1 28 E
Sant Francesc de
  Formentera, Spain .. **48 C7** 38 42N 1 26 E
Sant Jaume, Spain ... **48 B11** 39 54N 4 4 E
Sant Joan Baptista,
  Spain .... **48 B8** 39 5N 1 31 E
Sant Jordi, Ibiza, Spain **48 C7** 38 53N 1 24 E
Sant Jordi, Mallorca,
  Spain .... **48 B9** 39 33N 2 46 E
Sant Jordi, G. de, Spain **38 E6** 40 53N 1 2 E
Sant Llorenç de
  Morunys, Spain .... **38 C6** 42 8N 1 35 E

Sant Llorenç del Munt y
  l'Obac △, Spain **38 D3** 41 39N 1 55W
Sant Llorenç des
  Cardassar, Spain ... **48 B10** 39 37N 3 17 E
Sant Mateu, Baleares,
  Spain .... **48 B7** 39 3N 1 23 E
Sant Mateu, Valencia,
  Spain .... **38 E5** 40 28N 0 10 E
Sant Miguel, Spain ... **48 B7** 39 3N 1 26 E
Sant Telm, Spain .... **48 B9** 39 35N 2 21 E
Sant' Ágata Militello,
  Italy .... **43 D7** 38 2N 14 8 E
Santa Agnés, Spain ... **48 B7** 39 3N 1 21 E
Santa Ana, Bolivia ... **124 F5** 13 50 S 65 40W
Santa Ana, El Salv. ... **120 D2** 14 0N 89 31W
Santa Ana, Mexico ... **118 A2** 30 31N 111 8W
Santa Ana, U.S.A. ... **111 M9** 33 46N 117 52W
Santa' Ángelo Lodigiano,
  Italy .... **40 C6** 45 14N 9 25 E
Santa' Antíoco, Italy .. **42 C1** 39 4N 8 27 E
Santa Bárbara, Chile .. **126 D1** 37 40 S 72 1W
Santa Barbara,
  Honduras **120 D2** 14 53N 88 14W
Santa Bárbara, Mexico **118 B3** 26 48N 105 50W
Santa Bárbara, Spain . **38 E5** 40 42N 0 29 E
Santa Barbara, U.S.A. . **111 L7** 34 25N 119 42W
Santa Bárbara, Mt.,
  Spain **39 H2** 37 23N 2 50W
Santa Barbara Channel,
  U.S.A. **111 L7** 34 15N 120 0W
Santa Bárbara I., U.S.A. **111 M7** 33 29N 119 2W
Santa Catalina, Gulf of,
  U.S.A. **111 N9** 33 10N 117 50W
Santa Catalina I.,
  Mexico **118 B2** 25 40N 110 50W
Santa Catalina I., U.S.A. **111 M8** 33 23N 118 25W
Santa Catarina □, Brazil **127 B6** 27 25 S 48 30W
Santa Catarina, I. de,
  Brazil .... **127 B6** 27 30 S 48 40W
Santa Caterina di
  Pittinuri, Italy ..... **42 B1** 40 6N 8 27 E
Santa Caterina
  Villarmosa, Italy ... **43 E7** 37 35N 14 2 E
Santa Cecília, Brazil .. **127 B5** 26 56 S 50 18W
Santa Clara, Cuba **120 B4** 22 20N 80 0W
Santa Clara, Calif.,
  U.S.A. **110 H5** 37 21N 121 57W
Santa Clara, Utah,
  U.S.A. **109 H7** 37 8N 113 39W
Santa Clara, El Golfo
  de, Mexico **118 A2** 31 42N 114 30W
Santa Clara de Olimar,
  Uruguay .... **127 C5** 32 50 S 54 54W
Santa Clarita, U.S.A. .. **111 L8** 34 24N 118 30W
Santa Clotilde, Peru .. **124 D4** 2 33 S 73 45W
Santa Coloma de
  Farners, Spain .... **38 D7** 41 50N 2 39 E
Santa Coloma de
  Gramenet, Spain ... **38 D7** 41 27N 2 13 E
Santa Comba, Spain .. **36 B2** 43 2N 8 49W
Santa Croce Camerina,
  Italy .... **43 F7** 36 50N 14 31 E
Santa Croce di
  Magliano, Italy .... **41 G11** 41 42N 14 59 E
Santa Cruz, Argentina . **128 G3** 50 0 S 68 32W
Santa Cruz, Bolivia ... **124 G6** 17 43 S 63 10W
Santa Cruz, Chile .... **126 C1** 34 38 S 71 27W
Santa Cruz, Costa Rica **120 D2** 10 15N 85 35W
Santa Cruz, Madeira .. **48 D3** 32 42N 16 46W
Santa Cruz, Phil. .... **61 D4** 14 20N 121 24 E
Santa Cruz, U.S.A. ... **110 J4** 36 58N 122 1W
Santa Cruz →,
  Argentina .... **128 G3** 50 10 S 68 20W
Santa Cruz de la Palma,
  Canary Is. **48 F2** 28 41N 17 46W
Santa Cruz de la
  Palma ✈ (SPC),
  Canary Is. **48 F2** 28 40N 17 45W
Santa Cruz de Mudela,
  Spain **37 G7** 38 39N 3 28W
Santa Cruz de Tenerife,
  Canary Is. **48 F3** 28 28N 16 15W
Santa Cruz del Norte,
  Cuba **120 B3** 23 9N 81 55W
Santa Cruz del Retamar,
  Spain **36 E6** 40 8N 4 14W
Santa Cruz del Sur,
  Cuba **120 B4** 20 44N 78 0W
Santa Cruz do Rio
  Pardo, Brazil ..... **127 A6** 22 54 S 49 37W
Santa Cruz do Sul,
  Brazil .... **127 B5** 29 42 S 52 25W
Santa Cruz I., U.S.A. .. **111 M7** 34 1N 119 43W
Santa Cruz Is.,
  Solomon Is. ...... **96 J8** 10 30 S 166 0 E
Santa Cruz Mts.,
  Jamaica .... **120 a** 17 58N 77 43W
Santa Domingo, Cay,
  Bahamas **120 B4** 21 25N 75 15W
Sant' Egídio alla
  Vibrata, Italy ..... **41 F10** 42 49N 13 42 E
Santa Elena, Argentina **126 C4** 30 58 S 59 47W
Santa Elena, C.,
  Costa Rica **120 D2** 10 54N 85 56W
Sant' Eufémia, G. di,
  Italy .... **43 D9** 38 51N 16 4 E
Santa Eulàlia des Riu,
  Spain .... **48 C8** 38 59N 1 32 E
Santa Fe, Argentina .. **126 C3** 31 35 S 60 41W
Santa Fe, Spain **37 H7** 37 11N 3 43W
Santa Fe, U.S.A. **109 J11** 35 41N 105 57W
Santa Fé □, Argentina **126 C3** 31 50 S 60 55W
Santa Fé do Sul, Brazil **125 H8** 20 13 S 50 56W
Santa Filomena, Brazil **125 E9** 9 6 S 45 50W
Santa Fiora, Italy .... **41 F8** 42 50N 11 35 E
Santa Gertrudis, Spain **48 C7** 39 0N 1 26 E
Santa Giustina, Italy .. **41 B9** 46 10N 12 5 E
Santa Inês, Brazil .... **125 F11** 13 17 S 39 48W
Santa Inés, Spain **37 G5** 38 32N 5 37W
Santa Inés, I., Chile ... **128 G2** 54 0 S 73 0W
Santa Isabel, Argentina **126 D2** 36 10 S 66 54W
Santa Isabel, Pico,
  Eq. Guin. .... **83 E6** 3 36N 8 49 E
Santa Isabel do Morro,
  Brazil .... **125 F8** 11 34 S 50 40W
Santa Lucía, Corrientes,
  Argentina .... **126 B4** 28 58 S 59 5W
Santa Lucía, San Juan,
  Argentina .... **126 C2** 31 30 S 68 30W
Santa Lucía, Spain ... **39 H4** 37 35N 0 58W
Santa Lucia, Uruguay . **126 C4** 34 27 S 56 24W
Santa Lucia Range,
  U.S.A. **110 K5** 36 0N 121 20W
Santa Magdalena, I.,
  Mexico **118 C2** 24 40N 112 15W
Santa Margarita,
  Argentina .... **126 D3** 38 28 S 61 35W

Santa Margarita, Spain **48 B10** 39 42N 3 6 E
Santa Margarita, U.S.A. **110 K6** 35 23N 120 37W
Santa Margarita →,
  U.S.A. **111 M9** 33 13N 117 23W
Santa Margarita, I.,
  Mexico **118 C2** 24 30N 111 50W
Santa Margherita, Italy **42 D1** 38 58N 8 58 E
Santa Margherita
  Lígure, Italy ...... **40 D6** 44 20N 9 11 E
Santa María, Argentina **126 B2** 26 40 S 66 0W
Santa Maria, Brazil ... **127 B5** 29 40 S 53 48W
Santa María, Phil. .... **61 C4** 17 22N 120 29 E
Santa Maria, U.S.A. .. **111 L6** 34 57N 120 26W
Santa María →, Mexico **118 A3** 31 0N 107 14W
Santa María, B. de,
  Mexico **118 B3** 25 10N 108 40W
Santa Maria, C. de,
  Portugal **37 J3** 36 58N 7 53W
Santa Maria Cápua
  Vétere, Italy ...... **43 A7** 41 5N 14 15 E
Santa Maria da Feira,
  Portugal **36 E2** 40 55N 8 35W
Santa Maria da Vitória,
  Brazil .... **125 F10** 13 24 S 44 12W
Santa Maria del Camí,
  Spain .... **48 B9** 39 38N 2 47 E
Santa Maria di Léuca,
  C., Italy .... **43 C11** 39 47N 18 22 E
Santa María la Real de
  Nieva, Spain **36 D6** 41 4N 4 24W
Santa Marinella, Italy . **41 F8** 42 2N 11 52 E
Santa Marta, Colombia **124 A4** 11 15N 74 13W
Santa Marta, Sierra
  Nevada de, Colombia **124 A4** 10 55N 73 50W
Santa Marta de Tormes,
  Spain **36 E5** 40 57N 5 38W
Santa Marta Grande, C.,
  Brazil .... **127 B6** 28 43 S 48 50W
Santa Marta Ortigueira,
  Ría de, Spain **36 B3** 43 44N 7 45W
Santa Maura = Levkás,
  Greece .... **46 C2** 38 40N 20 43 E
Santa Monica, U.S.A. . **111 M8** 34 1N 118 29W
Santa Monica Mts. △,
  U.S.A. **111 L8** 34 4N 118 44W
Santa Olalla, Huelva,
  Spain **37 H4** 37 54N 6 14W
Santa Olalla, Toledo,
  Spain **36 E6** 40 2N 4 25W
Santa Paula, U.S.A. .. **111 L7** 34 21N 119 4W
Santa Pola, Spain **39 G4** 38 13N 0 35W
Santa Ponça, Spain .. **48 B9** 39 30N 2 28 E
Santa Rita, U.S.A. ... **109 K10** 32 48N 108 4W
Santa Rosa, La Pampa,
  Argentina .... **126 D3** 36 40 S 64 17W
Santa Rosa, San Luis,
  Argentina .... **126 C2** 32 21 S 65 10W
Santa Rosa, Brazil ... **127 B5** 27 52 S 54 29W
Santa Rosa, Calif.,
  U.S.A. **110 G4** 38 26N 122 43W
Santa Rosa, N. Mex.,
  U.S.A. **113 H2** 34 57N 104 41W
Santa Rosa I., Calif.,
  U.S.A. **111 M6** 33 58N 120 6W
Santa Rosa I., Fla.,
  U.S.A. **115 K2** 30 20N 86 50W
Santa Rosa Range,
  U.S.A. **108 F5** 41 45N 117 40W
Santa Rosalía, Mexico **118 B2** 27 20N 112 20W
Santa Sylvina, Argentina **126 B3** 27 50 S 61 10W
Santa Tecla = Nueva San
  Salvador, El Salv. .. **120 D2** 13 40N 89 18W
Santa Teresa, Argentina **126 C3** 33 25 S 60 47W
Santa Teresa, Australia **94 C1** 24 8 S 134 22 E
Santa Teresa, Mexico . **119 B5** 25 17N 97 51W
Santa Teresa △,
  Uruguay .... **127 C5** 33 57 S 53 31W
Santa Teresa di Riva,
  Italy .... **43 E8** 37 57N 15 22 E
Santa Teresa Gallura,
  Italy .... **42 A2** 41 14N 9 11 E
Santa Uxía, Spain ... **36 C2** 42 36N 8 58W
Santa Vitória do Palmar,
  Brazil .... **127 C5** 33 32 S 53 25W
Santa Ynez →, U.S.A. **111 L6** 35 41N 120 36W
Santa Ynez Mts., U.S.A. **111 L6** 34 30N 120 0W
Santa Ysabel, U.S.A. . **111 M10** 33 7N 116 40W
Santadi, Italy .... **42 C1** 39 5N 8 43 E
Santaella, Spain **37 H6** 37 34N 4 51W
Santai, China .... **58 B5** 31 5N 104 58 E
Santana, Madeira **48 D3** 32 48N 16 52W
Sântana, Romania ... **28 D6** 46 20N 21 30 E
Santana, Coxilha de,
  Brazil .... **127 C4** 30 50 S 55 35W
Santana do Livramento,
  Brazil .... **127 C4** 30 55 S 55 30W
Santander, Spain **36 B7** 43 27N 3 51W
Santander Jiménez,
  Mexico **119 C5** 24 11N 98 29W
Santanilla, Is., Honduras **120 C3** 17 22N 83 57W
Santanyí, Spain ..... **48 B10** 39 20N 3 5 E
Santaquin, U.S.A. ... **108 G8** 39 59N 111 47W
Santarcángelo di
  Romagna, Italy .... **41 D9** 44 4N 12 26 E
Santarém, Brazil .... **125 D8** 2 25 S 54 42W
Santarém, Portugal .. **37 F2** 39 12N 8 42W
Santarém □, Portugal . **37 F2** 39 10N 8 40W
Santaren Channel,
  W. Indies **120 B4** 24 0N 79 30W
Santee, U.S.A. **111 N10** 32 50N 116 58W
Santee →, U.S.A. ... **115 J6** 33 7N 79 17W
Santéramo in Colle, Italy **43 A9** 40 49N 16 45 E
Santerno →, Italy ... **41 D8** 44 34N 11 58 E
Santhià, Italy .... **40 C5** 45 22N 8 10 E
Santi-Quaranta =
  Sarandë, Albania .. **44 G3** 39 52N 19 55 E
Santiago, Brazil ..... **127 B5** 29 11 S 54 52W
Santiago, Canary Is. .. **48 F2** 28 1N 17 12W
Santiago, Chile ...... **126 C1** 33 24 S 70 40W
Santiago, Panama **120 E3** 8 0N 81 0W
Santiago, Phil. ...... **61 C4** 16 41N 121 33 E
Santiago □, Chile .... **126 C1** 33 30 S 70 50W
Santiago →, Mexico .. **98 G9** 25 11N 105 26W
Santiago →, Peru .... **124 D3** 4 27 S 77 38W
Santiago, Punta de,
  Eq. Guin. .... **83 E6** 3 12N 8 40 E
Santiago de Compostela,
  Spain **36 C2** 42 52N 8 37W
Santiago de Cuba, Cuba **120 C4** 20 0N 75 49W

Santiago de los
  Cabelleros, Dom. Rep. **121 C5** 19 30N 70 40W
Santiago del Estero,
  Argentina .... **126 B3** 27 50 S 64 15W
Santiago del Estero □,
  Argentina .... **126 B3** 27 40 S 63 15W
Santiago del Teide,
  Canary Is. **48 F3** 28 17N 16 48W
Santiago do Cacém,
  Portugal **37 G2** 38 1N 8 42W
Santiago Ixcuintla,
  Mexico **118 C3** 21 50N 105 11W
Santiago Papasquiaro,
  Mexico **118 C3** 25 0N 105 20W
Santiaguillo, L. de,
  Mexico **118 C4** 24 50N 104 50W
Santiguila, Mali **82 C3** 12 42N 7 25W
Santillana, Spain **36 B6** 43 24N 4 6W
Santisteban del Puerto,
  Spain **37 G7** 38 17N 3 15W
Santo Amaro, Brazil .. **125 F11** 12 30 S 38 43W
Santo André, Brazil .. **127 A6** 23 39 S 46 29W
Santo Ângelo, Brazil .. **127 B5** 28 15 S 54 15W
Santo Antônio do Içá,
  Brazil .... **124 D5** 3 5 S 67 57W
Santo Antônio do
  Leverger, Brazil .... **125 G7** 15 52 S 56 5W
Santo Domingo,
  Dom. Rep. **121 C6** 18 30N 69 59W
Santo Domingo,
  Baja Calif., Mexico . **118 A1** 30 43N 116 2W
Santo Domingo,
  Baja Calif. S., Mexico **118 B2** 25 32N 112 2W
Santo Domingo, Nic. . **120 D3** 12 14N 84 59W
Santo Domingo de la
  Calzada, Spain **38 C2** 42 26N 2 57W
Santo Domingo de los
  Colorados, Ecuador . **124 D3** 0 15 S 79 9W
Santo Domingo Pueblo,
  U.S.A. **109 J10** 35 31N 106 22W
Santo Stéfano di
  Cămastro, Italy .... **43 D7** 38 1N 14 22 E
Santo Tirso, Portugal . **36 D2** 41 21N 8 28W
Santo Tomás, Mexico . **118 A1** 31 33N 116 24W
Santo Tomás →, Peru . **124 F4** 12 59 S 72 8W
Santo Tomé, Argentina **127 B4** 28 40 S 56 5W
Santo Tomé de
  Guayana = Ciudad
  Guayana, Venezuela . **124 B6** 8 0N 62 30W
Santomera, Spain **39 G3** 38 4N 1 3W
Santoña, Spain **36 B7** 43 29N 3 27W
Santorini = Thíra,
  Greece .... **47 E7** 36 23N 25 27 E
Santos, Brazil ...... **127 A6** 24 0 S 46 20W
Santos, Sierra de los,
  Spain **37 G5** 38 7N 5 12W
Santos Dumont, Brazil **127 A7** 22 55 S 43 10W
Sanur, Indonesia .... **63 K18** 8 41 S 115 15 E
Sanwer, India .... **68 H6** 22 59N 75 50 E
Sanxenxo, Spain **36 C2** 42 24N 8 48W
Sanyuan, China ..... **56 G5** 34 35N 108 58 E
São Bartolomeu de
  Messines, Portugal . **37 H2** 37 15N 8 17W
São Bernardo do
  Campo, Brazil .... **127 A6** 23 45 S 46 34W
São Borja, Brazil .... **127 B4** 28 39 S 56 0W
São Brás d'Alportel,
  Portugal **37 H3** 37 8N 7 37W
São Carlos, Brazil ... **127 A6** 22 0 S 47 50W
São Cristóvão, Brazil . **125 F11** 11 1 S 37 15W
São Domingos, Brazil . **125 F9** 13 25 S 46 19W
São Domingos,
  Guine-Biss. ...... **82 C1** 12 19N 16 13 E
São Francisco, Brazil . **125 G10** 16 0 S 44 50W
São Francisco →, Brazil **125 F11** 10 30 S 36 24W
São Francisco do Sul,
  Brazil .... **127 B6** 26 15 S 48 36W
São Gabriel, Brazil ... **127 C5** 30 20 S 54 20W
São Gonçalo, Brazil .. **127 A7** 22 48 S 43 5W
Sao Hill, Tanzania ... **87 D4** 8 20 S 35 12 E
São João, Guinea-Biss. **82 C1** 11 32N 15 25W
São João da Boa Vista,
  Brazil .... **127 A6** 22 0 S 46 52W
São João da Madeira,
  Portugal **36 E2** 40 54N 8 30W
São João da Pesqueira,
  Portugal **36 D3** 41 8N 7 24W
São João del Rei, Brazil **127 A7** 21 8 S 44 15W
São João do Araguaia,
  Brazil .... **125 E9** 5 23 S 48 46W
São João do Piauí,
  Brazil .... **125 E10** 8 21 S 42 15W
São Joaquim, Brazil .. **127 B6** 28 18 S 49 56W
São Joaquim △, Brazil **127 B6** 28 12 S 49 37W
São Jorge, Pta. de,
  Madeira **48 D3** 32 50N 16 53W
São José, Brazil ..... **127 B5** 27 38 S 48 39W
São José do Norte,
  Brazil .... **127 C5** 32 1 S 52 3W
São José do Rio Prêto,
  Brazil .... **127 A6** 20 50 S 49 20W
São José dos Campos,
  Brazil .... **127 A6** 23 7 S 45 52W
São Leopoldo, Brazil . **127 A6** 29 50 S 51 10W
São Lourenço, Brazil . **127 A6** 22 7 S 45 3W
São Lourenço →, Brazil **125 G7** 17 53 S 57 27W
São Lourenço, Pta. de,
  Madeira **48 D3** 32 44N 16 39W
São Lourenço do Sul,
  Brazil .... **127 C5** 31 22 S 51 58W
São Luís, Brazil ..... **125 D10** 2 39 S 44 15W
São Luís Gonzaga,
  Brazil .... **127 B5** 28 25 S 55 0W
São Marcos →, Brazil **125 G9** 18 15 S 47 37W
São Marcos, B. de,
  Brazil .... **125 D10** 2 0 S 44 0W
São Martinho da
  Cortiça, Portugal .. **36 E2** 40 18N 8 8W
São Mateus, Brazil ... **125 G11** 18 44 S 39 50W
São Mateus →, Brazil **125 G11** 18 44 S 39 50W
São Mateus do Sul,
  Brazil .... **127 B5** 25 52 S 50 23W
São Miguel do Oeste,
  Brazil .... **127 B5** 26 45 S 53 34W
São Paulo, Brazil .... **127 A6** 23 32 S 46 37W
São Paulo □, Brazil .. **127 A6** 22 0 S 49 0W
São Paulo, I., Atl. Oc. . **2 D8** 0 50N 31 40W
São Paulo de Olivença,
  Brazil .... **124 D5** 3 27 S 68 48W
São Pedro do Sul,
  Portugal **36 E2** 40 46N 8 4W
São Roque, Madeira .. **48 D3** 32 46N 16 48W
São Roque, C. de, Brazil **125 E11** 5 30 S 35 16W
São Sebastião do
  Paraíso, Brazil .... **127 A6** 20 54 S 46 59W

São Teotónio, Portugal 37 H2 37 30N 8 42W
São Tomé,
　São Tomé & Príncipe 76 F4 0 10N 6 39 E
São Tomé, C. de, Brazil 127 A7 22 0 S 40 59W
São Tomé & Príncipe ■,
　Africa 77 F4 0 12N 6 39 E
São Vicente, Brazil 127 A6 23 57 S 46 23W
São Vicente, Madeira 48 D2 32 48N 17 3W
São Vicente, C. de,
　Portugal 37 H1 37 0N 9 0W
Saona, I., Dom. Rep. 121 C6 18 10N 68 40W
Saône →, France 19 G11 45 44N 4 50 E
Saône-et-Loire □,
　France 19 F11 46 30N 4 50 E
Saonek, Indonesia 63 E8 0 22 S 130 55 E
Sápai, Greece 45 E9 41 2N 25 43 E
Sapam, Ao, Thailand 65 a 8 0N 98 26 E
Sapanca, Turkey 72 B4 40 41N 30 16 E
Saparua, Indonesia 63 E7 3 33 S 128 40 E
Sapele, Nigeria 83 D6 5 50N 5 40 E
Sapelo I., U.S.A. 115 K5 31 25N 81 12W
Saphane, Turkey 47 B11 39 1N 29 13 E
Sapi △, Zimbabwe 87 F2 15 48 S 29 42 E
Sapiéntza, Greece 46 E3 36 45N 21 43 E
Sapo △, Liberia 82 D3 5 15N 8 30W
Sapone, Burkina Faso 83 C4 12 3N 1 35W
Saposoa, Peru 124 E3 6 55 S 76 45W
Sapouy, Burkina Faso 83 C4 11 34N 1 44W
Sapozhok, Russia 34 D5 53 59N 40 41 E
Sapphire, Australia 94 C4 23 28 S 147 43 E
Sapporo, Japan 54 C10 43 0N 141 21 E
Sapri, Italy 43 B8 40 4N 15 38 E
Sapulpa, U.S.A. 113 H6 35 59N 96 5W
Saqqez, Iran 70 B5 36 15N 46 20 E
Sar Dasht,
　Āzarbāyjān-e Gharbī,
　Iran 73 D11 36 9N 45 28 E
Sar Dasht, Khuzestān,
　Iran 71 C6 32 32N 48 52 E
Sar-e Pol □, Afghan. 66 B4 36 20N 65 50 E
Sar Gachīneh = Yāsūj,
　Iran 71 D6 30 31N 51 31 E
Sar Planina, Macedonia 44 E4 42 0N 21 0 E
Sara, Burkina Faso 82 C4 11 40N 3 53W
Sara, Phil. 61 F5 11 16N 123 1 E
Šara △, Serbia & M. 44 D5 42 12N 21 0 E
Sara Buri = Saraburi,
　Thailand 64 E3 14 30N 100 55 E
Sarāb, Iran 70 B5 37 55N 47 40 E
Sarabadi, Iraq 70 C5 33 1N 44 48 E
Saraburi, Thailand 64 E3 14 30N 100 55 E
Saradiya, India 68 J4 21 34N 70 2 E
Saraféré, Mali 82 B4 15 50N 3 40W
Saragossa = Zaragoza,
　Spain 38 D4 41 39N 0 53W
Saraguro, Ecuador 124 D3 3 35 S 79 16W
Sarai Naurang, Pakistan 68 C4 32 50N 70 47 E
Saraikela, India 69 H11 22 42N 85 56 E
Saraiu, Romania 29 F13 44 43N 28 10 E
Sarajevo, Bos.-H. 28 G3 43 52N 18 26 E
Sarakhs, Turkmenistan 71 B9 36 32N 61 13 E
Saran, Gunung,
　Indonesia 62 E4 0 30 S 111 25 E
Saranac L., U.S.A. 117 B10 44 20N 74 10W
Saranac Lake, U.S.A. 117 B10 44 20N 74 8W
Saranda, Tanzania 86 D3 5 45 S 34 59 E
Sarandë, Albania 44 G3 39 52N 19 55 E
Sarandí del Yí, Uruguay 127 C4 33 18 S 55 38W
Sarandí Grande,
　Uruguay 126 C4 33 44 S 56 20W
Sarangani B., Phil. 61 J6 6 0N 125 13 E
Sarangani Is., Phil. 61 J6 5 25N 125 25 E
Sarangarh, India 67 J13 21 30N 83 5 E
Saransk, Russia 34 C7 54 10N 45 10 E
Sarapul, Russia 52 D6 56 28N 53 48 E
Sarasota, U.S.A. 115 M4 27 20N 82 32W
Sarata, India 29 D14 46 1N 29 40 E
Sarata →, Ukraine 29 E14 45 51N 29 41 E
Saratoga, Calif., U.S.A. 110 H4 37 16N 122 2W
Saratoga, Wyo., U.S.A. 108 F10 41 27N 106 49W
Saratoga △, U.S.A. 117 D11 43 0N 73 37W
Saratoga Springs, U.S.A. 117 C11 43 5N 73 47W
Saratok, Malaysia 62 D4 1 55N 111 17 E
Saratov, Russia 34 E7 51 30N 46 2 E
Sarāvān, Iran 71 E9 27 25N 62 15 E
Saravane, Laos 64 E6 15 43N 106 25 E
Sarawak □, Malaysia 62 D4 2 0N 113 0 E
Saray, Tekirdağ, Turkey 45 E11 41 26N 27 55 E
Saray, Van, Turkey 73 C11 38 38N 44 9 E
Saraya, Guinea 82 C2 12 50N 11 45W
Saraya, Senegal 82 C2 12 50N 11 45W
Sarayçık, Turkey 47 B11 39 1N 29 49 E
Sarayköy, Turkey 47 D10 37 55N 28 54 E
Saraylar, Turkey 45 F11 40 39N 27 40 E
Sarayönü, Turkey 72 C5 38 16N 32 24 E
Sarbāz, Iran 71 E9 26 38N 61 19 E
Sarbīsheh, Iran 71 C8 32 30N 59 40 E
Sárbogárd, Hungary 28 D3 46 50N 18 40 E
Sarca →, Italy 40 C7 45 52N 10 52 E
Sarcelles, France 19 D9 49 1N 2 23 E
Sarda →, India 67 F12 27 21N 81 23 E
Sardarshahr, India 68 E6 28 30N 74 29 E
Sardhana, India 68 E7 29 9N 77 39 E
Sardina, Pta., Canary Is. 48 F4 28 9N 15 44W
Sardinia = Sardegna □,
　Italy 42 B1 40 0N 9 0 E
Sardis, Turkey 47 C10 38 28N 28 2 E
Sārdūīyeh = Dar Mazār,
　Iran 71 D8 29 14N 57 20 E

Sariyer, Turkey 45 E13 41 10N 29 3 E
Sarju →, India 69 F9 27 21N 81 23 E
Sark, U.K. 15 H5 49 25N 2 22W
Sarkad, Hungary 28 D6 46 47N 21 23 E
Sarkari Tala, India 68 F4 27 39N 70 52 E
Şarkışla, Turkey 72 C7 39 21N 36 25 E
Şarköy, Turkey 45 F11 40 36N 27 6 E
Sarlat-la-Canéda, France 20 D5 44 54N 1 13 E
Sărmăşag, Romania 28 C7 47 21N 22 50 E
Sărmaşu, Romania 29 D9 46 45N 24 13 E
Sarmi, Indonesia 63 E9 1 49 S 138 44 E
Sarmiento, Argentina 128 F3 45 35 S 69 5W
Sarmizegetusa, Romania 28 E7 45 31N 22 47 E
Särna, Sweden 10 C7 61 41N 13 8 E
Sarnano, Italy 41 E10 43 2N 13 18 E
Sarnen, Switz. 25 J4 46 53N 8 13 E
Sarnia, Canada 116 D2 42 58N 82 23W
Sarno, Italy 43 B7 40 49N 14 37 E
Sarnthein = Sarentino,
　Italy 41 B8 46 38N 11 21 E
Särö, Sweden 11 G5 57 31N 11 57 E
Sarolangun, Indonesia 62 E2 2 19 S 102 42 E
Saronikós Kólpos,
　Greece 46 D5 37 45N 23 45 E
Saronno, Italy 40 C6 45 38N 9 2 E
Saros Körfezi, Turkey 45 F10 40 30N 26 15 E
Sárospatak, Hungary 28 B6 48 18N 21 33 E
Sarpsborg, Norway 9 G14 59 16N 11 7 E
Sarracín, Spain 36 C7 42 15N 3 45W
Sarralbe, France 19 D14 49 0N 7 1 E
Sarre = Saar →, Europe 19 D14 49 41N 6 32 E
Sarre, Italy 40 C4 45 40N 7 15 E
Sarre-Union, France 19 D14 48 57N 7 4 E
Sarrebourg, France 19 D14 48 43N 7 3 E
Sarreguemines, France 19 C14 49 5N 7 4 E
Sarria, Spain 36 C3 42 49N 7 29W
Sarrión, Spain 38 E4 40 9N 0 49W
Sarro, Mali 82 C3 13 40N 5 15W
Sarstedt, Germany 24 C5 52 14N 9 52 E
Sartène, France 21 G12 41 38N 8 58 E
Sarthe □, France 18 D7 48 10N 0 10 E
Sarthe →, France 18 E6 47 33N 0 31W
Sartilly, France 18 D5 48 45N 1 28W
Saruhanlı, Turkey 47 C9 38 44N 27 36 E
Sărulești, Romania 29 F11 44 25N 26 39 E
Saruna →, Pakistan 68 F2 26 31N 67 7 E
Sárvár, Hungary 28 C1 47 15N 16 56 E
Sarvar, India 68 F6 26 4N 75 0 E
Sarvestān, Iran 71 D7 29 20N 53 10 E
Särvfjället, Sweden 10 B7 62 42N 13 30 E
Sárviz →, Hungary 28 D3 46 24N 18 41 E
Sary-Tash, Kyrgyzstan 52 F8 39 44N 73 15 E
Sarych, Mys, Ukraine 33 K7 44 25N 33 45 E
Saryshagan, Kazakhstan 52 E8 46 12N 73 38 E
Sarzana, Italy 40 D6 44 7N 9 58 E
Sarzeau, France 18 E4 47 31N 2 48W
Sasan Gir, India 68 J4 21 10N 70 36 E
Sasaram, India 69 G11 24 57N 84 5 E
Sasebo, Japan 55 H4 33 10N 129 43 E
Saser, India 69 B7 34 50N 77 50 E
Saskatchewan □,
　Canada 103 C7 54 40N 106 0W
Saskatchewan →,
　Canada 103 C8 53 37N 100 40W
Saskatoon, Canada 103 C7 52 10N 106 38W
Saskylakh, Russia 53 B12 71 55N 114 1 E
Saslaya △, Nic. 120 D2 13 45N 85 4W
Sasolburg, S. Africa 89 D4 26 46 S 27 49 E
Sasovo, Russia 34 C5 54 25N 41 55 E
Sassandra, Ivory C. 82 E3 4 55N 6 8W
Sassandra →, Ivory C. 82 E3 4 58N 6 5W
Sássari, Italy 42 B1 40 43N 8 34 E
Sassnitz, Germany 24 A9 54 29N 13 39 E
Sasso Marconi, Italy 41 D8 44 24N 11 15 E
Sassocorvaro, Italy 41 E9 43 47N 12 30 E
Sassoferrato, Italy 41 E9 43 26N 12 51 E
Sasstown, Liberia 82 E3 4 45N 8 27W
Sassuolo, Italy 40 D7 44 33N 10 47 E
Sástago, Spain 38 D4 41 19N 0 21W
Sasyk, Ozero, Ukraine 29 E14 45 45N 29 20 E
Sata-Misaki, Japan 55 J5 31 0N 130 40 E
Satadougou, Mali 82 C2 12 25N 11 25W
Satakunda = Satakunta,
　Finland 9 F20 61 45N 23 0 E
Satakunta, Finland 9 F20 61 45N 23 0 E
Satama-Soukoura,
　Ivory C. 82 D4 7 55N 4 27W
Satara, India 66 L8 17 44N 73 58 E
Satara, S. Africa 89 C5 24 29 S 31 47 E
Satbarwa, India 69 H11 23 55N 84 16 E
Sätenäs, Sweden 11 F6 58 27N 12 41 E
Säter, Sweden 10 D9 60 21N 15 45 E
Satevó, Mexico 118 B3 27 57N 106 7W
Satilla →, U.S.A. 115 K5 30 59N 81 29W
Satmala Hills, India 66 J9 20 15N 74 40 E
Satna, India 69 G9 24 35N 80 50 E
Šator, Bos.-H. 41 D13 44 11N 16 37 E
Sátoraljaújhely, Hungary 28 B6 48 25N 21 41 E
Satpura Ra., India 66 J10 21 25N 76 10 E
Satrup, Germany 24 A5 54 41N 9 36 E
Satsuna-Shotō, Japan 55 K5 30 0N 130 0 E
Sattahip, Thailand 64 F3 12 41N 100 54 E
Satu Mare, Romania 28 C7 47 46N 22 55 E
Satu Mare □, Romania 28 C7 47 45N 23 0 E
Satui, Indonesia 62 E5 3 50 S 115 27 E
Satun, Thailand 65 J3 6 43N 100 2 E
Saturnina →, Brazil 124 F7 12 15 S 58 10W
Sauce, Argentina 126 C4 30 5 S 58 46W
Sauceda, Mexico 118 B4 25 55N 101 18W
Saucillo, Mexico 118 B3 28 1N 105 17W
Sauda, Norway 9 G12 59 40N 6 20 E
Sauðárkrókur, Iceland 8 D4 65 45N 19 40W
Saudi Arabia ■, Asia 70 B3 26 0N 44 0 E
Saugeen →, Canada 116 B3 44 30N 81 22W
Saugerties, U.S.A. 117 D11 42 5N 73 57W
Saugues, France 20 D7 44 58N 3 32 E
Saugus, U.S.A. 111 L8 34 35N 118 32W
Saujon, France 20 C3 45 41N 0 55W
Sauk Centre, U.S.A. 112 C7 45 44N 94 57W
Sauk Rapids, U.S.A. 112 C7 45 35N 94 10W
Saulgau, Germany 25 G8 48 1N 9 29 E
Saulieu, France 19 E11 47 17N 4 14 E
Sault, France 21 D9 44 6N 5 24 E
Sault Ste. Marie, Canada 104 C3 46 30N 84 20W
Sault Ste. Marie, U.S.A. 101 D11 46 30N 84 21W
Saumlaki, Indonesia 63 F8 7 55 S 131 20 E
Saumur, France 18 E6 47 15N 0 5W
Saunders, C., N.Z. 91 L3 45 53 S 170 45 E
Saunders I., Antarctica 5 B1 57 48 S 26 28W
Saunders Point,
　Australia 93 E4 27 52 S 125 38 E
Sauri, Nigeria 83 C6 11 42N 6 44 E
Saurimo, Angola 84 F4 9 40 S 20 12 E
Sausalito, U.S.A. 110 H4 37 51N 122 29W
Sauveterre-de-Béarn,
　France 20 E3 43 24N 0 57W
Sauzé-Vaussais, France 20 B4 46 8N 0 8 E

Savá, Honduras 120 C2 15 32N 86 15W
Sava, Italy 43 B10 40 24N 17 33 E
Sava →, Serbia & M. 28 B5 44 50N 20 26 E
Savage, U.S.A. 112 B2 47 27N 104 21W
Savage I. = Niue,
　Cook Is. 97 J11 19 2 S 169 54W
Savage River, Australia 95 G4 41 31 S 145 14 E
Savai'i, Samoa 91 A12 13 28 S 172 24W
Savalou, Benin 83 D5 7 57N 1 58 E
Savane, Mozam. 87 F4 19 37 S 35 8 E
Savanna, U.S.A. 112 D9 42 5N 90 8W
Savanna-la-Mar,
　Jamaica 120 a 18 10N 78 10W
Savannah, Ga., U.S.A. 115 J5 32 5N 81 6W
Savannah, Mo., U.S.A. 112 F7 39 56N 94 50W
Savannah, Tenn., U.S.A. 115 H1 35 14N 88 15W
Savannah →, U.S.A. 115 J5 32 2N 80 53W
Savannakhet, Laos 64 D5 16 30N 104 49 E
Savant L., Canada 104 B1 50 16N 90 44W
Savant Lake, Canada 104 B1 50 14N 90 40W
Sāvārsin, Romania 28 D7 46 1N 22 14 E
Savaştepe, Turkey 47 B9 39 22N 27 42 E
Savé, Benin 83 D5 8 2N 2 29 E
Save →, France 20 E5 43 47N 1 17 E
Save →, Mozam. 89 C5 21 16 S 34 0 E
Sāveh, Iran 71 C6 35 2N 50 20 E
Savelugu, Ghana 83 D4 9 38N 0 54W
Savenay, France 18 E5 47 20N 1 55W
Săveni, Romania 29 C11 47 57N 26 52 E
Saverne, France 19 D14 48 43N 7 25 E
Savigliano, Italy 40 D4 44 38N 7 40 E
Savigny-sur-Braye,
　France 18 E7 47 53N 0 49 E
Sávio →, Italy 41 D9 44 19N 12 20 E
Šavnik, Serbia & M. 44 D3 42 59N 19 10 E
Savoie □, France 21 C10 45 26N 6 25 E
Savolax = Savo, Finland 8 E22 62 45N 27 30 E
Savona, Italy 40 D6 44 17N 8 30 E
Savona, U.S.A. 116 D7 42 17N 77 13W
Savonlinna, Finland 32 B5 61 52N 28 53 E
Savoy = Savoie □,
　France 21 C10 45 26N 6 25 E
Şavşat, Turkey 73 B10 41 15N 42 20 E
Sävsjö, Sweden 11 G8 57 20N 14 40 E
Savur, Turkey 70 B4 37 34N 40 53 E
Sawahlunto, Indonesia 62 E2 0 40 S 100 52 E
Sawai, Indonesia 63 E7 3 0 S 129 5 E
Sawai Madhopur, India 68 G7 26 0N 76 25 E
Sawang Daen Din,
　Thailand 64 D4 17 28N 103 28 E
Sawankhalok, Thailand 64 D2 17 19N 99 50 E
Sawara, Japan 55 G10 35 55N 140 30 E
Sawatch Range, U.S.A. 109 G10 38 30N 106 30W
Sawel Mt., U.K. 12 B4 54 50N 7 2W
Sawi, Thailand 65 G2 10 14N 99 5 E
Sawla, Ghana 82 D4 9 17N 2 25W
Sawmills, Zimbabwe 87 F2 19 30 S 28 2 E
Sawtooth, U.S.A. 108 D6 44 0N 114 50W
Sawtooth Range, U.S.A. 108 E6 44 3N 114 58W
Sawu, Indonesia 63 F6 10 35 S 121 50 E
Sawu Sea, Indonesia 63 F6 9 30 S 121 50 E
Saxby →, Australia 94 B3 18 25 S 140 53 E
Saxmundham, U.K. 15 E9 52 13N 1 30 E
Saxony = Sachsen □,
　Germany 24 E9 50 55N 13 10 E
Saxony, Lower =
　Niedersachsen □,
　Germany 24 C4 52 50N 9 0 E
Saxton, U.S.A. 116 F6 40 13N 78 15W
Say, Mali 82 C4 13 50N 4 57W
Say, Niger 83 C5 13 8N 2 22 E
Saya, Nigeria 83 D5 9 30N 3 18 E
Sayabec, Canada 105 C6 48 35N 67 41W
Sayaboury, Laos 64 C3 19 15N 101 45 E
Sayán, Peru 124 F3 11 8 S 77 12W
Sayan, Vostochnyy,
　Russia 53 D10 54 0N 96 0 E
Sayan, Zapadnyy, Russia 53 D10 52 30N 94 0 E
Saydā, Lebanon 74 B4 33 35N 35 25 E
Sayhandulaan = Oldziyt,
　Mongolia 56 B5 44 40N 109 1 E
Sayhūt, Yemen 75 D5 15 12N 51 10 E
Saykhin, Kazakhstan 35 F8 48 50N 46 47 E
Saylac = Zeila,
　Somali Rep. 75 E3 11 21N 43 30 E
Saynshand, Mongolia 56 B5 44 55N 110 11 E
Sayre, Okla., U.S.A. 113 H5 35 18N 99 38W
Sayre, Pa., U.S.A. 117 E8 41 59N 76 32W
Sayreville, U.S.A. 117 F10 40 28N 74 22W
Sayula, Mexico 118 D4 19 50N 103 40W
Sayward, Canada 102 C3 50 21N 125 55W
Sazanit, Albania 44 F3 40 30N 19 20 E
Sázava →, Czech Rep. 26 B7 49 53N 14 24 E
Sazin, Pakistan 69 B5 35 35N 73 30 E
Sazlika →, Bulgaria 45 E9 41 59N 25 50 E
Scaër, France 18 D3 48 2N 3 42W
Scafell Pike, U.K. 14 C4 54 27N 3 14W
Scalea, Italy 43 C8 39 49N 15 47 E
Scalloway, U.K. 13 A7 60 9N 1 17W
Scalpay, U.K. 13 D3 57 18N 6 0W
Scandia, Canada 102 C6 50 20N 112 2W
Scandiano, Italy 40 D7 44 36N 10 43 E
Scandicci, Italy 41 E8 43 45N 11 11 E
Scandinavia, Europe 8 E16 64 0N 12 0 E
Scansano, Italy 41 F8 42 41N 11 20 E
Scapa Flow, U.K. 13 C5 58 53N 3 3W
Scappoose, U.S.A. 110 E4 45 45N 122 53W
Scarámia, Capo, Italy 43 F7 36 47N 14 29 E
Scarba, U.K. 13 E3 56 11N 5 43W
Scarborough,
　Trin. & Tob. 121 D7 11 11N 60 42W
Scarborough, U.K. 14 C7 54 17N 0 24W
Scariff I., Ireland 12 E1 51 44N 10 15W
Scarp, U.K. 13 C1 58 1N 7 8W
Scarpe →, France 19 B10 50 26N 3 23 E
Scebeli, Wabi →,
　Somali Rep. 75 G3 2 0N 44 0 E
Scedro, Croatia 41 E13 43 6N 16 43 E
Schaal See, Germany 24 B6 53 40N 10 59 E
Schaalsee △, Germany 24 B6 53 40N 10 59 E
Schaffhausen, Switz. 25 H4 47 42N 8 39 E
Schagen, Neths. 17 B4 52 49N 4 48 E
Schaghticoke, U.S.A. 117 D11 42 54N 73 35W
Schärding, Austria 26 C6 48 27N 13 27 E
Scharhörn, Germany 24 B4 53 57N 8 24 E
Scheessel, Germany 24 B5 53 10N 9 34 E
Schefferville, Canada 105 B6 54 48N 66 50W
Scheibbs, Austria 26 D8 48 1N 15 9 E
Schelde →, Belgium 17 C4 51 15N 4 16 E
Schell Creek Ra., U.S.A. 108 G6 39 15N 114 30W
Schenectady, U.S.A. 117 D11 42 49N 73 57W
Schenevus, U.S.A. 117 D10 42 33N 74 50W
Scherfede, Germany 24 D5 51 32N 9 2 E
Schesslitz, Germany 25 F7 49 58N 11 1 E

Schiedam, Neths. 17 C4 51 55N 4 25 E
Schiermonnikoog, Neths. 17 A6 53 30N 6 15 E
Schiltigheim, France 19 D14 48 35N 7 45 E
Schio, Italy 41 C8 45 43N 11 21 E
Schiphol, Amsterdam ✈
　(AMS), Neths. 17 B4 52 18N 4 45 E
Schladming, Austria 26 D6 47 23N 13 41 E
Schlanders = Silandro,
　Italy 40 B7 46 38N 10 46 E
Schlei →, Germany 24 A5 54 40N 10 0 E
Schleiden, Germany 24 E2 50 31N 6 28 E
Schleiz, Germany 24 E7 50 35N 11 49 E
Schleswig, Germany 24 A5 54 31N 9 34 E
Schleswig-Holstein □,
　Germany 24 A5 54 30N 9 30 E
Schlüchtern, Germany 25 E5 50 20N 9 32 E
Schmalkalden, Germany 24 E6 50 44N 10 26 E
Schmölln, Germany 24 E8 50 54N 12 19 E
Schneeberg, Austria 26 D8 47 47N 15 48 E
Schneeberg, Germany 24 E8 50 35N 12 38 E
Schneverdingen,
　Germany 24 B5 53 7N 9 48 E
Schœlcher, Martinique 120 c 14 36N 61 7W
Schoharie, U.S.A. 117 D10 42 40N 74 19W
Schoharie Cr. →, U.S.A. 117 D10 42 57N 74 18W
Scholls, U.S.A. 110 E4 45 24N 122 56W
Schönberg,
　Mecklenburg-Vorpommern,
　Germany 24 B6 53 52N 10 56 E
Schönberg,
　Schleswig-Holstein,
　Germany 24 A6 54 23N 10 21 E
Schönebeck, Germany 24 C7 52 1N 11 44 E
Schöningen, Germany 24 C6 52 8N 10 56 E
Schopfheim, Germany 25 H3 47 38N 7 50 E
Schorndorf, Germany 25 G5 48 47N 9 32 E
Schortens, Germany 24 B3 53 31N 7 56 E
Schouten I., Australia 95 G4 42 20 S 148 20 E
Schouten Is. = Supiori,
　Indonesia 63 E9 1 0 S 136 0 E
Schouwen, Neths. 17 C3 51 43N 3 45 E
Schramberg, Germany 25 G4 48 13N 8 22 E
Schrankogel, Austria 26 D4 47 3N 11 7 E
Schreiber, Canada 104 C2 48 45N 87 20W
Schrems, Austria 26 C8 48 47N 15 4 E
Schrobenhausen,
　Germany 25 G7 48 34N 11 16 E
Schroon Lake, U.S.A. 117 C11 43 50N 73 46W
Schruns, Austria 26 D2 47 5N 9 56 E
Schuler, Canada 103 C6 50 20N 110 6W
Schumacher, Canada 104 C3 48 30N 81 16W
Schurz, U.S.A. 108 G4 38 57N 118 49W
Schuyler, U.S.A. 112 E6 41 27N 97 4W
Schuylerville, U.S.A. 117 C11 43 6N 73 35W
Schuylkill →, U.S.A. 117 G9 39 53N 75 12W
Schuylkill Haven, U.S.A. 117 F8 40 37N 76 11W
Schwabach, Germany 25 F7 49 19N 11 2 E
Schwaben □, Germany 25 G6 48 15N 10 30 E
Schwäbisch-Fränkischer
　Wald △, Germany 25 G5 49 0N 9 30 E
Schwäbisch Gmünd,
　Germany 25 G5 48 48N 9 47 E
Schwäbisch Hall,
　Germany 25 F5 49 6N 9 44 E
Schwäbische Alb,
　Germany 25 G5 48 20N 9 30 E
Schwabmünchen,
　Germany 25 G6 48 10N 10 46 E
Schwalmstadt, Germany 24 E5 50 55N 9 10 E
Schwandorf, Germany 25 F8 49 20N 12 7 E
Schwaner, Pegunungan,
　Indonesia 62 E4 1 0 S 112 30 E
Schwanewede, Germany 24 B4 53 14N 8 36 E
Schwarmstedt, Germany 24 C5 52 39N 9 38 E
Schwarze Elster →,
　Germany 24 D8 51 48N 12 50 E
Schwarzenberg,
　Germany 24 E8 50 32N 12 47 E
Schwarzrand, Namibia 88 D2 25 37 S 16 50 E
Schwaz, Austria 26 D4 47 20N 11 44 E
Schwechat, Austria 27 C9 48 9N 16 28 E
Schwechat, Wien ✈
　(VIA), Austria 27 C9 48 7N 16 35 E
Schwedt, Germany 24 B10 53 3N 14 16 E
Schweinfurt, Germany 25 E6 50 3N 10 14 E
Schweizer-Reneke,
　S. Africa 88 D4 27 11 S 25 18 E
Schwenningen =
　Villingen-
　Schwenningen,
　Germany 25 G4 48 3N 8 26 E
Schwerin, Germany 24 B7 53 36N 11 22 E
Schweriner See,
　Germany 24 B7 53 43N 11 28 E
Schwetzingen, Germany 25 F4 49 23N 8 35 E
Schwyz, Switz. 25 H4 47 2N 8 39 E
Schwyz □, Switz. 25 H4 47 2N 8 39 E
Sciacca, Italy 42 E6 37 31N 13 3 E
Scicli, Italy 43 F7 36 47N 14 42 E
Sciliar △, Italy 41 B8 46 28N 11 35 E
Scilla, Italy 43 D8 38 15N 15 43 E
Scilly, Isles of, U.K. 15 H1 49 56N 6 22W
Ścinawa, Poland 31 G3 51 25N 16 26 E
Scione, Greece 44 F7 39 57N 23 36 E
Scioto →, U.S.A. 114 F4 38 44N 83 1W
Scituate, U.S.A. 117 D14 42 12N 70 44W
Scobey, U.S.A. 112 A2 48 47N 105 25W
Scone, Australia 95 E5 32 5 S 150 52 E
Scone, U.K. 13 E5 56 25N 3 24W
Scordia, Italy 43 E7 37 18N 14 51 E
Scoresbysund =
　Ittoqqortoormiit,
　Greenland 4 B6 70 20N 23 0W
Scornicești, Romania 29 F9 44 34N 24 33 E
Scotia, Calif., U.S.A. 108 F1 40 29N 124 6W
Scotia, N.Y., U.S.A. 117 D11 42 50N 73 58W
Scotia Sea, Antarctica 5 B18 56 5 S 56 0W
Scotland, Canada 116 C4 43 1N 80 22W
Scotland □, U.K. 13 E5 57 0N 4 0W
Scott, Antarctica 5 D11 77 0 S 165 0 E
Scott, C., Australia 92 B4 13 30 S 129 49 E
Scott City, U.S.A. 112 F4 38 29N 100 54W
Scott I., Antarctica 5 C11 67 0 S 179 0 E
Scott Inlet, Canada 101 A12 71 0N 71 0W
Scott Is., Canada 102 C3 50 48N 128 40W
Scott L., Canada 103 B7 59 55N 106 18W
Scott Reef, Australia 92 B3 14 0 S 121 50 E
Scottburgh, S. Africa 89 E5 30 15 S 30 47 E
Scottdale, U.S.A. 116 F5 40 6N 79 35W
Scottish Borders □, U.K. 13 F6 55 35N 2 50W
Scottsbluff, U.S.A. 112 E2 41 52N 103 40W
Scottsboro, U.S.A. 115 H3 34 40N 86 2W
Scottsburg, U.S.A. 114 F3 38 41N 85 47W

Scottsdale, Australia 95 G4 41 9 S 147 31 E
Scottsdale, U.S.A. 109 K7 33 29N 111 56W
Scottsville, Ky., U.S.A. 115 G2 36 45N 86 11W
Scottsville, N.Y., U.S.A. 116 C7 43 2N 77 47W
Scottville, U.S.A. 114 D2 43 58N 86 17W
Scranton, U.S.A. 117 E9 41 25N 75 40W
Scugog, L., Canada 116 B6 44 10N 78 55W
Sculeni, Moldova 29 C12 47 20N 27 37 E
Scunthorpe, U.K. 14 D7 53 36N 0 39W
Scuol Schuls, Switz. 25 J6 46 48N 10 17 E
Scutari = Shkodër,
　Albania 44 D3 42 4N 19 32 E
Scutari = Üsküdar,
　Turkey 45 F13 41 0N 29 5 E
Seabrook, L., Australia 93 F2 30 55 S 119 40 E
Seaford, U.K. 15 G8 50 47N 0 7 E
Seaford, U.S.A. 114 F8 38 39N 75 37W
Seaforth, Australia 94 J6 20 55 S 148 57 E
Seaforth, Canada 116 C3 43 35N 81 25W
Seaforth, L., U.K. 13 D2 57 52N 6 36W
Seagraves, U.S.A. 113 J3 32 57N 102 34W
Seaham, U.K. 14 C6 54 50N 1 20W
Seal →, Canada 103 B10 59 4N 94 48W
Seal L., Canada 105 B7 54 20N 61 30W
Sealy, U.S.A. 113 L6 29 47N 96 9W
Searchlight, U.S.A. 111 K12 35 28N 114 55W
Searcy, U.S.A. 113 H9 35 15N 91 44W
Searles L., U.S.A. 111 K9 35 44N 117 21W
Seascale, U.K. 14 C4 54 24N 3 29W
Seaside, Calif., U.S.A. 110 J5 36 37N 121 50W
Seaside, Oreg., U.S.A. 110 E3 46 0N 123 56W
Seaspray, Australia 95 F4 38 25 S 147 15 E
Seattle, U.S.A. 110 C4 47 36N 122 20W
Seattle-Tacoma
　International ✈
　(SEA), U.S.A. 110 C4 47 27N 122 18W
Seaview Ra., Australia 94 B4 18 40 S 145 45 E
Sebago, L., U.S.A. 117 C14 43 52N 70 34W
Sebago Lake, U.S.A. 117 C14 43 51N 70 34W
Sebastián Vizcaíno, B.,
　Mexico 118 B2 28 0N 114 30W
Sebastopol = Sevastopol,
　Ukraine 33 K7 44 35N 33 30 E
Sebastopol, U.S.A. 110 G4 38 24N 122 49W
Sebba, Burkina Faso 83 C5 13 35N 0 32 E
Sebderat, Eritrea 81 D4 15 26N 36 42 E
Sébékoro, Mali 82 C3 12 58N 9 0W
Seben, Turkey 72 B4 40 24N 31 34 E
Sebeş, Romania 29 E8 45 58N 23 34 E
Sebeşului, Munţii,
　Romania 29 E8 45 36N 23 40 E
Sebewaing, U.S.A. 114 D4 43 44N 83 27W
Sebezh, Russia 32 D5 56 14N 28 22 E
Sebha = Sabhah, Libya 79 C8 27 9N 14 29 E
Sébi, Mali 82 B4 15 50N 4 12W
Şebinkarahisar, Turkey 73 B8 40 22N 38 28 E
Sebiş, Romania 28 D7 46 23N 22 13 E
Sebnitz, Germany 24 E10 50 58N 14 15 E
Sebring, Fla., U.S.A. 115 M5 27 30N 81 27W
Sebring, Ohio, U.S.A. 116 F3 40 55N 81 2W
Sebringville, Canada 116 C3 43 24N 81 4W
Sebta = Ceuta, N. Afr. 78 A4 35 52N 5 18W
Sebuku, Indonesia 62 E5 3 30 S 116 25 E
Sebuku, Teluk, Malaysia 62 D5 4 0N 118 10 E
Sečanj, Serbia & M. 28 E5 45 25N 20 47 E
Secchia →, Italy 40 C8 45 4N 11 0 E
Sechelt, Canada 102 D4 49 25N 123 42W
Sechura, Desierto de,
　Peru 124 E2 6 0 S 80 30W
Seclin, France 19 B10 50 33N 3 2 E
Secondigny, France 18 F6 46 37N 0 26W
Sečovce, Slovak Rep. 27 C14 48 42N 21 40 E
Secretary I., N.Z. 91 L1 45 15 S 166 56 E
Secunderabad, India 66 L11 17 28N 78 30 E
Security-Widefield,
　U.S.A. 112 F2 38 45N 104 45W
Sedalia, U.S.A. 112 F8 38 42N 93 14W
Sedan, France 19 C11 49 43N 4 57 E
Sedan, U.S.A. 113 G6 37 8N 96 11W
Sedano, Spain 36 C7 42 43N 3 49W
Sedbergh, U.K. 14 C5 54 20N 2 31W
Seddon, N.Z. 91 J5 41 40 S 174 7 E
Seddonville, N.Z. 91 J4 41 33 S 172 1 E
Sedé Boqér, Israel 74 E3 30 52N 34 47 E
Sedeh, Fārs, Iran 71 D7 30 45N 52 11 E
Sedeh, Khorāsān, Iran 71 C8 33 20N 59 14 E
Séderon, France 21 D9 44 12N 5 32 E
Sederot, Israel 74 D3 31 32N 34 37 E
Sédhiou, Senegal 82 C1 12 44N 15 30W
Sedico, Italy 41 B9 46 8N 12 6 E
Sedlčany, Czech Rep. 26 B7 49 40N 14 25 E
Sedley, Canada 103 C8 50 10N 104 0W
Sedona, U.S.A. 109 J8 34 52N 111 46W
Sedova, Pik, Russia 52 B6 73 29N 54 58 E
Sedro Woolley, U.S.A. 110 B4 48 30N 122 14W
Seduva, Lithuania 30 C10 55 45N 23 45 E
Sędziszów Małopolski,
　Poland 31 H8 50 5N 21 45 E
Seebad Ahlbeck,
　Germany 24 B10 53 56N 14 10 E
Seefeld in Tirol, Austria 26 D4 47 19N 11 13 E
Seehausen, Germany 24 C7 52 54N 11 45 E
Seeheim, Namibia 88 D2 26 50 S 17 45 E
Seeheim-Jugenheim,
　Germany 25 F4 49 49N 8 40 E
Seeis, Namibia 88 C2 22 9 S 17 39 E
Seekoei →, S. Africa 88 E4 30 18 S 25 1 E
Seeley's Bay, Canada 117 B8 44 29N 76 14W
Seelow, Germany 24 C10 52 32N 14 23 E
Sées, France 18 D7 48 38N 0 10 E
Seesen, Germany 24 D6 51 54N 10 10 E
Seevetal, Germany 24 B6 53 26N 10 1 E
Seewinkel = Neusiedler
　See-Seewinkel △,
　Austria 27 D9 47 50N 16 45 E
Sefadu, S. Leone 82 D2 8 35N 10 58W
Seferihisar, Turkey 47 C8 38 10N 26 50 E
Séfeto, Mali 82 C3 14 8N 9 49W
Sefwi Bekwai, Ghana 82 D4 6 10N 2 25W
Segamat, Malaysia 65 L4 2 30N 102 50 E
Segezha, Russia 52 C4 63 44N 34 19 E
Ségou, Mali 82 C3 13 30N 6 16W
Segovia = Coco →,
　Cent. Amer. 120 D3 15 0N 83 8W
Segovia, Spain 36 E6 40 57N 4 10W
Segovia □, Spain 36 E6 40 55N 4 10W
Segré, France 18 E6 47 40N 0 52W
Segre →, Spain 38 D5 41 40N 0 43 E
Séguéla, Ivory C. 82 D3 7 55N 6 40W
Séguénéga,
　Burkina Faso 83 C4 13 25N 1 58W

Seguin, U.S.A. 113 L6 29 34N 97 58W
Segundo →, Argentina 126 C3 30 53 S 62 44W
Segura →, Spain 39 G4 38 3N 0 44W
Segura, Sierra de, Spain 39 G2 38 5N 2 45W
Seh Konj, Kūh-e, Iran 71 D8 30 6N 57 30 E
Seh Qal'eh, Iran ..... 71 C8 33 40N 58 24 E
Sehitwa, Botswana .... 88 C3 20 30 S 22 30 E
Sehlabathebe △,
Lesotho .... 89 D4 29 53 S 29 7 E
Sehore, India .... 68 H7 23 10N 77 5 E
Sehwan, Pakistan .... 68 F2 26 28N 67 53 E
Şeica Mare, Romania . 29 D9 46 1N 24 7 E
Seil, U.K. 13 E3 56 18N 5 38W
Seiland, Norway ...... 8 A20 70 25N 23 15 E
Seilhac, France ...... 20 C5 45 22N 1 43 E
Seiling, U.S.A. 113 G5 36 9N 98 56W
Seille →, Moselle,
France .... 19 C13 49 7N 6 11 E
Seille →,
Saône-et-Loire, France 19 F11 46 31N 4 57 E
Sein, Î. de, France ... 18 D2 48 2N 4 52W
Seinäjoki, Finland ... 9 E20 62 40N 22 51 E
Seine →, France ..... 18 C7 49 26N 0 26 E
Seine, B. de la, France . 18 C6 49 40N 0 40W
Seine-et-Marne □,
France .... 19 D10 48 45N 3 0 E
Seine-Maritime □,
France .... 18 C7 49 40N 1 0 E
Seine-St-Denis □,
France .... 19 D9 48 58N 2 24 E
Seini, Romania ...... 29 C8 47 44N 23 21 E
Seirijai, Lithuania ... 30 D10 54 14N 23 49 E
Seistan = Sīstān, Asia . 71 D9 30 50N 61 0 E
Seistan, Daryācheh-ye =
Sīstān, Daryācheh-ye,
Iran .... 71 D9 31 0N 61 0 E
Sejerø, Denmark ..... 11 J5 55 54N 11 9 E
Sejerø Bugt, Denmark . 11 J5 55 53N 11 15 E
Sejny, Poland .... 30 D10 54 6N 23 21 E
Seka, Ethiopia .... 81 F4 8 10N 36 52 E
Sekayu, Indonesia .... 62 E2 2 51 S 103 51 E
Seke, Tanzania .... 86 C3 3 20 S 33 31 E
Sekenke, Tanzania .... 86 C3 4 18 S 34 11 E
Seki, Turkey .... 47 E11 36 48N 29 33 E
Sekondi-Takoradi,
Ghana 82 E4 4 58N 1 45W
Sekota, Ethiopia ..... 81 E4 12 40N 39 2 E
Seksna, Russia .... 32 C10 59 13N 38 30 E
Sekudai, Malaysia .... 65 d 1 32N 103 39 E
Sekuma, Botswana .... 88 C3 24 36 S 23 50 E
Selah, U.S.A. 108 C3 46 39N 120 32W
Selama, Malaysia ..... 65 K3 5 12N 100 42 E
Selárgius, Italy ...... 42 C2 39 16N 9 10 E
Selaru, Indonesia .... 63 F8 8 9 S 131 0 E
Selatan, Selat, Malaysia 65 c 5 15N 100 20 E
Selb, Germany .... 25 E8 50 10N 12 7 E
Selby, U.K. 14 D6 53 47N 1 5W
Selby, U.S.A. 112 C4 45 31N 100 2W
Selca, Croatia .... 41 E13 43 20N 16 50 E
Selden, U.S.A. 112 F4 39 33N 100 34W
Sele →, Italy .... 43 B7 40 29N 14 56 E
Selebi-Pikwe, Botswana 89 C4 21 58 S 27 48 E
Selemdzha →, Russia . 53 D13 51 42N 128 53 E
Selendi, Manisa, Turkey 47 C10 38 43N 28 50 E
Selendi, Manisa, Turkey 47 C9 38 46N 27 53 E
Selenga = Selenge
Mörön →, Asia .... 60 A5 52 16N 106 16 E
Selenge Mörön →, Asia 60 A5 52 16N 106 16 E
Selenicë, Albania .... 44 F3 40 33N 19 39 E
Selenter See, Germany . 24 A6 54 18N 10 26 E
Sélestat, France ..... 19 D14 48 16N 7 26 E
Seletan, Tanjung,
Indonesia .... 62 E4 4 10 S 114 40 E
Selevac, Serbia & M. .. 44 B4 44 28N 20 52 E
Sélibabi, Mauritania .. 82 B2 15 10N 12 15W
Seliger, Ozero, Russia . 32 D7 57 15N 33 0 E
Seligman, U.S.A. 109 J7 35 20N 112 53W
Şelim, Turkey .... 73 B10 40 30N 42 46 E
Selima, El Wâhât el,
Sudan .... 80 C2 21 22N 29 19 E
Selimiye, Turkey ..... 47 D9 37 24N 27 40 E
Selinda Spillway →,
Botswana .... 88 B3 18 35 S 23 10 E
Selinous, Greece ..... 46 D3 37 35N 21 37 E
Selinsgrove, U.S.A. ... 116 F8 40 48N 76 52W
Selizharovo, Russia ... 32 D7 56 51N 33 27 E
Selkirk, Canada 103 C9 50 10N 96 55W
Selkirk, U.K. 13 F6 55 33N 2 50W
Selkirk I. = Horse I.,
Canada 103 C9 53 20N 99 6W
Selkirk Mts., Canada .. 100 C8 51 15N 117 40W
Sellafield, U.K. 14 C4 54 25N 3 29W
Sellama, Sudan ...... 81 E2 12 51N 29 46 E
Sellía, Greece .... 49 D6 35 12N 24 23 E
Sellières, France ..... 19 F12 46 50N 5 32 E
Sells, U.S.A. 109 L8 31 55N 111 53W
Sellye, Hungary ...... 28 E2 45 52N 17 51 E
Selma, Ala., U.S.A. ... 115 J2 32 25N 87 1W
Selma, Calif., U.S.A. . 110 J7 36 34N 119 37W
Selma, N.C., U.S.A. .. 115 H6 35 32N 78 17W
Selmer, U.S.A. 115 H1 35 10N 88 36W
Selongey, France ..... 19 E12 47 36N 5 11 E
Selous △, Tanzania ... 87 D4 8 37 S 37 42 E
Selowandoma Falls,
Zimbabwe .... 87 G3 21 15 S 31 50 E
Selpele, Indonesia .... 63 E8 0 1 S 130 5 E
Selsey Bill, U.K. 15 G7 50 43N 0 47W
Seltso, Russia .... 32 F8 53 22N 34 4 E
Seltz, France .... 19 D15 48 54N 8 4 E
Selu, Indonesia ...... 63 F8 7 32 S 130 55 E
Sélune →, France 18 D5 48 38N 1 22W
Selva = La Selva del
Camp, Spain ...... 38 D6 41 13N 1 8 E
Selva, Argentina ..... 126 B3 29 50 S 62 0W
Selva Lancandona =
Montes Azules △,
Mexico 119 D6 16 21N 91 3W
Selvas, Brazil .... 124 E5 6 30 S 67 0W
Selwyn L., Canada 103 B8 60 0N 104 30W
Selwyn Mts., Canada .. 100 B6 63 0N 130 0W
Selwyn Ra., Australia .. 94 C3 21 10 S 140 0 E
Selyatyn, Ukraine .... 29 C10 47 50N 25 12 E
Seman →, Albania ... 44 F3 40 47N 19 30 E
Semarang, Indonesia .. 63 G14 7 0 S 110 26 E
Sembabule, Uganda ... 86 C3 0 4 S 31 25 E
Sembawang, Singapore . 65 d 1 27N 103 50 E
Sembung, Indonesia ... 63 J18 8 28 S 115 11 E
Şemdinli, Turkey ..... 73 D11 37 18N 44 31 E
Sémé, Senegal 82 B2 15 4N 13 41W
Semeih, Sudan .... 81 E3 12 43N 30 53 E
Semenanjung
Blambangan,
Indonesia .... 63 K17 8 42 S 114 29 E
Semenov, Russia ..... 34 B7 56 43N 44 30 E
Semenovka, Chernihiv,
Ukraine .... 33 F7 52 8N 32 36 E

Semenovka,
Kremenchuk, Ukraine 33 H7 49 37N 33 10 E
Semeru, Indonesia .... 63 H15 8 4 S 112 55 E
Semey, Kazakhstan ... 52 D9 50 30N 80 10 E
Semikarakorskiy, Russia 35 G5 47 31N 40 48 E
Semiluki, Russia ..... 33 G10 51 41N 39 2 E
Seminoe Reservoir,
U.S.A. 108 F10 42 9N 106 55W
Seminole, Okla., U.S.A. 113 H6 35 14N 96 41W
Seminole, Tex., U.S.A. 113 J3 32 43N 102 39W
Seminole Draw →,
U.S.A. 113 J3 32 27N 102 20W
Semipalatinsk = Semey,
Kazakhstan .... 52 D9 50 30N 80 10 E
Semirara Is., Phil. .... 61 F4 12 0N 121 20 E
Semitau, Indonesia ... 62 D4 0 29N 111 57 E
Semiyarka, Kazakhstan 52 D8 50 55N 78 23 E
Semiyarskoye =
Semiyarka,
Kazakhstan .... 52 D8 50 55N 78 23 E
Semmering P., Austria . 26 D8 47 41N 15 45 E
Semnān, Iran .... 71 C7 35 40N 53 23 E
Semnān □, Iran ...... 71 C7 36 0N 54 0 E
Semporna, Malaysia .. 63 D5 4 30N 118 33 E
Semuda, Indonesia ... 62 E4 2 51 S 112 58 E
Semur-en-Auxois,
France .... 19 E11 47 30N 4 20 E
Sen →, Cambodia .... 62 B3 13 45N 105 12 E
Sena, Iran .... 71 D6 28 27N 51 36 E
Sena, Mozam. .... 87 F4 17 25 S 35 0 E
Sena Madureira, Brazil 124 E5 9 5 S 68 45W
Senador Pompeu, Brazil 125 E11 5 40 S 39 20W
Senaki, Georgia ...... 35 J6 42 15N 42 7 E
Senang, Pulau,
Singapore .... 65 d 1 10N 103 44 E
Senanga, Zambia ..... 85 H4 16 7 S 23 16 E
Senatobia, U.S.A. 113 H10 34 37N 89 58W
Sencelles, Spain ..... 48 B9 39 39N 2 54 E
Sendafa, Ethiopia .... 81 F4 9 11N 39 3 E
Sendai, Kagoshima,
Japan .... 55 J5 31 50N 130 20 E
Sendai, Miyagi, Japan . 54 E10 38 15N 140 53 E
Sendai-Wan, Japan ... 54 E10 38 15N 141 0 E
Senden, Bayern,
Germany .... 25 G6 48 19N 10 4 E
Senden,
Nordrhein-Westfalen,
Germany .... 24 D3 51 52N 7 22 E
Sendhwa, India ...... 68 J6 21 41N 75 6 E
Sene →, Ghana 83 D4 7 30N 0 33W
Senec, Slovak Rep. ... 27 C10 48 12N 17 15 E
Seneca, U.S.A. 115 H4 34 41N 82 57W
Seneca Falls, U.S.A. .. 117 D8 42 55N 76 48W
Seneca L., U.S.A. 116 D8 42 40N 76 54W
Senecaville L., U.S.A. . 116 G3 39 55N 81 25W
Senegal ■, W. Afr. ... 82 C2 14 30N 14 30W
Sénégal →, W. Afr. .. 82 B1 15 48N 16 32W
Senegambia, Africa ... 76 E2 12 45N 12 0W
Senekal, S. Africa .... 89 D4 28 20 S 27 36 E
Senftenberg, Germany . 24 D10 51 32N 14 0 E
Senga Hill, Zambia ... 87 D3 9 19 S 31 11 E
Senge Khambab =
Indus →, Pakistan . 68 G2 24 20N 67 47 E
Sengiley, Russia ..... 34 D9 53 58N 48 46 E
Sengua →, Zimbabwe . 87 F2 17 7 S 28 5 E
Senhor-do-Bonfim,
Brazil .... 125 F10 10 30 S 40 10W
Senica, Slovak Rep. ... 27 C10 48 41N 17 25 E
Senigállia, Italy ...... 41 E10 43 43N 13 13 E
Senio →, Italy .... 41 D9 44 35N 12 15 E
Senirkent, Turkey .... 47 C12 38 6N 30 33 E
Senise, Italy .... 43 B9 40 9N 16 17 E
Senj, Croatia .... 41 D11 45 0N 14 58 E
Senja, Norway .... 8 B17 69 25N 17 30 E
Senkaku-Shotō, Japan . 55 L1 25 45N 124 0 E
Senkuang, Indonesia .. 65 d 1 11N 104 2 E
Senlis, France .... 19 C9 49 13N 2 35 E
Senmonorom, Cambodia 64 F6 12 27N 107 12 E
Sennâr, Sudan .... 81 E3 13 30N 33 35 E
Sennar □, Sudan ..... 81 E3 13 0N 34 0 E
Senneterre, Canada ... 104 C4 48 25N 77 15W
Senno, Belarus ...... 32 E5 54 45N 29 43 E
Sénnori, Italy .... 42 B1 40 47N 8 35 E
Seno, Laos .... 64 D5 16 35N 104 50 E
Senonches, France .... 18 D8 48 34N 1 2 E
Senorbì, Italy .... 42 C2 39 32N 9 8 E
Senožeče, Slovenia ... 41 C11 45 43N 14 3 E
Sens, France .... 19 D10 48 11N 3 15 E
Senta, Serbia & M. ... 28 E5 45 55N 20 3 E
Sentani, Indonesia ... 63 E10 2 36 S 140 37 E
Sentery = Lubao,
Dem. Rep. of
the Congo .... 86 D2 5 17 S 25 42 E
Sentinel, U.S.A. 109 K7 32 52N 113 13W
Šentjur, Slovenia .... 41 B12 46 14N 15 24 E
Sentosa, Singapore ... 65 d 1 15N 103 50 E
Senya Beraku, Ghana . 83 D4 5 28N 0 31W
Seo de Urgel = La Seu
d'Urgell, Spain .... 38 C6 42 22N 1 23 E
Seohara, India ...... 69 E8 29 15N 78 33 E
Seonath →, India .... 69 J10 21 44N 82 28 E
Seondha, India ...... 69 F8 26 9N 78 48 E
Seoni, India .... 69 H8 22 5N 79 30 E
Seoni Malwa, India ... 68 H8 22 27N 77 28 E
Seoul = Sŏul, S. Korea 57 F14 37 31N 126 58 E
Sepīdān, Iran .... 71 D7 30 20N 52 5 E
Sepo-ri, N. Korea .... 57 E14 38 57N 127 25 E
Sépôlno Krajeńskie,
Poland .... 30 E4 53 26N 17 30 E
Sepone, Laos .... 64 D6 16 45N 106 13 E
Sepopol, Poland ..... 30 D8 54 16N 21 2 E
Sept-Îles, Canada 105 B6 50 13N 66 22W
Septemvri, Bulgaria .. 45 D8 42 13N 24 6 E
Sepúlveda, Spain 36 D7 41 18N 3 45W
Sequeros, Spain 36 E4 40 31N 6 2W
Sequoia △, U.S.A. 110 J8 36 30N 118 30W
Serafimovich, Russia .. 34 F6 49 36N 42 43 E
Seraing, Belgium ..... 17 D5 50 35N 5 32 E
Serakhis →, Cyprus .. 49 D11 35 13N 32 55 E
Seram, Indonesia ..... 63 E7 3 10 S 129 0 E
Seram Sea, Indonesia . 63 E7 2 30 S 128 30 E
Serampore = Serampur,
India .... 69 H13 22 44N 88 30 E
Serang, Indonesia .... 63 G12 6 8 S 106 10 E
Serangoon, Singapore . 65 d 1 23N 103 54 E
Serasan, Indonesia ... 62 D3 2 29N 109 4 E
Şerbettar, Turkey .... 45 E10 41 27N 26 46 E
Serbia □, Serbia & M. . 44 C5 43 30N 21 0 E
Serbia & Montenegro ■,
Europe .... 44 C4 43 0N 21 0 E
Şercaia, Romania .... 29 E10 45 49N 25 9 E
Serdo, Ethiopia ...... 81 E5 11 56N 41 14 E
Serdobsk, Russia ..... 34 D7 52 28N 44 10 E
Sered', Slovak Rep. ... 27 C10 48 17N 17 44 E
Seredka, Russia ...... 32 C5 58 12N 28 8 E
Serednye, Ukraine .... 29 48 32N 22 30 E

Şereflikoçhisar, Turkey 72 C5 38 56N 33 32 E
Seregno, Italy .... 40 C6 45 39N 9 12 E
Seremban, Malaysia .. 65 L3 2 43N 101 53 E
Serengeti △, Tanzania . 86 C3 2 11 S 35 0 E
Serengeti Plain,
Tanzania .... 86 C4 2 40 S 35 0 E
Serenje, Zambia ..... 87 E3 13 14 S 30 15 E
Seret →, Ukraine .... 29 B10 48 37N 25 52 E
Sereth = Siret →,
Romania .... 29 E12 45 24N 28 1 E
Sergach, Russia ...... 34 C7 55 30N 45 30 E
Sergen, Turkey ...... 45 E11 41 41N 27 42 E
Sergino, Russia ...... 52 C7 62 25N 65 12 E
Sergipe □, Brazil .... 125 F11 10 30 S 37 30W
Sergiyev Posad, Russia 32 D10 56 20N 38 10 E
Seria, Brunei .... 62 D4 4 37N 114 23 E
Serian, Malaysia ..... 62 D4 1 10N 110 31 E
Seriate, Italy .... 40 C6 45 41N 9 43 E
Sérifontaine, France .. 19 C8 49 20N 1 45 E
Sérifos, Greece ...... 46 D6 37 9N 24 30 E
Sérignan, France ..... 20 E7 43 17N 3 17 E
Sérigny →, Canada ... 105 A6 56 47N 66 0W
Serik, Turkey .... 72 D4 36 55N 31 7 E
Seringapatam Reef,
Australia .... 92 B3 13 38 S 122 5 E
Serinhisar, Turkey ... 47 D11 37 36N 29 18 E
Seririt, Indonesia .... 63 J17 8 13 S 114 56 E
Sermaize-les-Bains,
France .... 19 D11 48 47N 4 54 E
Sermata, Indonesia ... 63 F7 8 15 S 128 50 E
Sermersuaq, Greenland 4 B4 79 30N 62 0W
Sérmide, Italy .... 41 D8 45 0N 11 18 E
Sernovodsk, Russia ... 34 D10 53 54N 51 16 E
Serock, Poland ...... 31 F8 52 31N 21 4 E
Serón, Spain 39 H2 37 20N 2 29W
Seròs, Spain .... 38 D5 41 27N 0 24 E
Serov, Russia .... 52 D7 59 29N 60 35 E
Serowe, Botswana .... 88 C4 22 25 S 26 43 E
Serpa, Portugal 37 H3 37 57N 7 38W
Serpeddì, Punta, Italy . 42 C2 39 19N 9 18 E
Serpentara, Italy ..... 42 C2 39 8N 9 36 E
Serpentine Lakes,
Australia .... 93 E4 28 30 S 129 10 E
Serpent's Mouth =
Sierpe, Bocas de la,
Venezuela 125 L15 10 0N 61 30W
Serpis →, Spain 39 G4 38 59N 0 9W
Serpneve, Ukraine .... 29 D14 46 18N 29 1 E
Serpukhov, Russia .... 32 E9 54 55N 37 28 E
Serra da Estrela △,
Portugal 36 E3 40 27N 7 33W
Serra de Outes, Spain . 36 C2 42 52N 8 55W
Serra do Navio, Brazil . 125 C8 0 59N 52 3W
Serra San Bruno, Italy . 43 D9 38 35N 16 20 E
Serradilla, Spain 36 F4 39 50N 6 9W
Sérrai, Greece .... 44 E7 41 5N 23 31 E
Sérrai □, Greece ..... 44 E7 41 5N 23 37 E
Serramanna, Italy .... 42 C1 39 25N 8 55 E
Serranía San Luís △,
Paraguay .... 126 A4 22 35 S 57 22W
Serras d'Aire e
Candeeiros △,
Portugal 37 F2 39 31N 8 48W
Serravalle Scrívia, Italy 40 D5 44 43N 8 51 E
Serre-Ponçon, L. de,
France .... 21 D10 44 22N 6 20 E
Serres, France .... 21 D9 44 26N 5 43 E
Serrezuela, Argentina . 126 C2 30 40 S 65 20W
Serrinha, Brazil ..... 125 F11 11 39 S 39 0W
Sersale, Italy .... 43 C9 39 1N 16 43 E
Sertã, Portugal 36 F2 39 48N 8 6W
Sertanópolis, Brazil .. 127 A5 23 4 S 51 2W
Sêrtar, China .... 58 A3 32 20N 100 41 E
Serua, Indonesia ..... 63 F8 6 18 S 130 1 E
Serui, Indonesia ..... 63 E9 1 53 S 136 10 E
Serule, Botswana .... 88 C4 21 57 S 27 20 E
Sérvia, Greece .... 44 F6 40 11N 22 0 E
Serzedelo, Portugal ... 36 D2 41 24N 8 18W
Ses Salines, Spain .... 48 B10 39 21N 3 3 E
Sese Is., Uganda ..... 86 C3 0 20 S 32 20 E
Sesepe, Indonesia .... 63 E7 1 30 S 127 59 E
Sesfontein, Namibia .. 88 B1 19 7 S 13 39 E
Sesheke, Zambia ..... 88 B3 17 29 S 24 13 E
Sésia →, Italy .... 40 C5 45 5N 8 37 E
Sesimbra, Portugal ... 37 G1 38 28N 9 6W
Sessa Aurunca, Italy .. 42 A6 41 14N 13 56 E
S'Espalmador, Spain .. 48 C7 38 47N 1 26 E
S'Espardell, Spain .... 48 C7 38 48N 1 29 E
S'Estanyol, Spain .... 48 B9 39 22N 2 54 E
Sestao, Spain 38 B2 43 18N 3 0W
Sesto Calende, Italy ... 40 C5 45 43N 8 37 E
Sesto San Giovanni,
Italy .... 40 C6 45 32N 9 14 E
Sestri Levante, Italy ... 40 D6 44 16N 9 24 E
Sestriere, Italy ...... 40 D3 44 57N 6 53 E
Sestroretsk, Russia ... 32 B6 60 5N 29 58 E
Sestrunj, Croatia ..... 41 D11 44 10N 15 0 E
Sestu, Italy .... 42 C2 39 18N 9 5 E
Setana, Japan .... 54 C9 42 26N 139 51 E
Sète, France .... 20 E7 43 25N 3 42 E
Sete Lagôas, Brazil ... 125 G10 19 27 S 44 16W
Sétif, Algeria .... 78 A7 36 9N 5 26 E
Seto, Japan .... 55 G8 35 14N 137 6 E
Setonaikai, Japan .... 55 G6 34 20N 133 30 E
Setonaikai △, Japan .. 55 G6 34 15N 133 15 E
Settat, Morocco 78 B4 33 0N 7 40W
Séttimo Torinese, Italy 40 C4 45 9N 7 46 E
Setting L., Canada 103 C9 55 0N 98 38W
Settle, U.K. 14 C5 54 5N 2 16W
Settlement Pt., Bahamas 115 M6 26 40N 79 0W
Settlers, S. Africa .... 89 C4 25 2 S 28 30 E
Setúbal, Portugal 37 G2 38 30N 8 58W
Setúbal □, Portugal .. 37 G2 38 25N 8 35W
Setúbal, B. de, Portugal 37 G2 38 40N 8 56W
Seugne →, France ... 20 C3 45 42N 0 32W
Seul, Lac, Canada 104 B1 50 20N 92 30W
Seur, France .... 19 F12 47 6N 5 4 E
Seurre, France .... 19 F12 47 1N 5 8 E
Sevan, Armenia ...... 35 K7 40 33N 44 56 E
Sevan, Ozero = Sevana
Lich, Armenia ..... 35 K7 40 30N 45 20 E
Sevana Lich, Armenia . 35 K7 40 30N 45 20 E
Sevastopol, Ukraine .. 33 K7 44 35N 33 30 E
Seven Sisters, Canada . 102 C3 54 56N 128 10W
Sever →, Portugal ... 37 F3 39 40N 7 32W
Sévérac-le-Château,
France .... 20 D7 44 20N 3 5 E
Şevketiye, Turkey .... 45 F10 40 12N 26 29 E
Severn →, Canada ... 104 A2 56 2N 87 36W
Severn →, U.K. 15 F5 51 35N 2 40W
Severn L., Canada 104 B1 53 54N 90 48W
Severnaya Zemlya,
Russia .... 53 B10 79 0N 100 0 E
Severo-Kurilsk, Russia 53 D16 50 40N 156 8 E
Severo-Yeniseyskiy,
Russia .... 53 C10 60 22N 93 1 E

Severo-Zapadnyy □,
Russia .... 52 C4 65 0N 40 0 E
Severočeský □,
Czech Rep. .... 26 A7 50 30N 14 0 E
Severodonetsk =
Syeverodonetsk,
Ukraine .... 33 H10 48 58N 38 35 E
Severodvinsk, Russia .. 52 C4 64 27N 39 58 E
Severomorský □,
Czech Rep. .... 27 B10 49 38N 17 40 E
Severomorsk, Russia .. 52 A5 69 5N 33 27 E
Sevier, U.S.A. 109 G7 38 39N 112 11W
Sevier →, U.S.A. 109 G7 39 4N 113 6W
Sevier Desert, U.S.A. . 108 G7 39 40N 112 45W
Sevier L., U.S.A. 108 G7 38 54N 113 9W
Sevilla, Spain 37 H5 37 23N 5 58W
Sevilla □, Spain 37 H5 37 25N 5 30W
Seville = Sevilla, Spain 37 H5 37 23N 5 58W
Sevlievo, Bulgaria .... 45 C9 43 2N 25 6 E
Sevnica, Slovenia .... 41 B12 46 15N 15 19 E
Sèvre-Nantaise →,
France 18 E5 47 12N 1 33W
Sèvre-Niortaise →,
France 20 B3 46 28N 0 50W
Sevsk, Russia .... 33 F8 52 10N 34 30 E
Sewa →, S. Leone ... 82 D2 7 20N 12 10W
Sewani, India .... 68 E6 28 58N 75 39 E
Seward, Alaska, U.S.A. 100 B5 60 7N 149 27W
Seward, Nebr., U.S.A. 112 E6 40 55N 97 6W
Seward, Pa., U.S.A. .. 116 F5 40 25N 79 1W
Seward Peninsula,
U.S.A. 100 B3 65 30N 166 0W
Sewell, Chile .... 126 C1 34 10 S 70 23W
Sewer, Indonesia ..... 63 F8 5 53 S 134 40 E
Sewickley, U.S.A. 116 F4 40 32N 80 12W
Sexsmith, Canada 102 B5 55 21N 118 47W
Seychelles ■, Ind. Oc. . 50 K9 5 0 S 56 0 E
Seyðisfjörður, Iceland . 8 D6 65 16N 13 57W
Seydişehir, Turkey ... 72 D4 37 25N 31 51 E
Seydvān, Iran .... 70 B5 38 34N 45 2 E
Seyhan →, Turkey ... 70 D6 36 43N 34 53 E
Seyhan Barajı, Turkey . 72 D6 37 2N 35 18 E
Seyitgazi, Turkey .... 47 B12 39 27N 30 42 E
Seyitömer, Turkey ... 47 B11 39 34N 29 52 E
Seym →, Ukraine .... 33 G7 51 27N 32 34 E
Seymen, Turkey ..... 45 E11 41 6N 27 57 E
Seymour, Australia ... 95 F4 37 0 S 145 10 E
Seymour, S. Africa ... 89 E4 32 33 S 26 46 E
Seymour, Conn., U.S.A. 117 E11 41 24N 73 4W
Seymour, Ind., U.S.A. 114 F3 38 58N 85 53W
Seymour, Tex., U.S.A. 113 J5 33 35N 99 16W
Seyne, France .... 21 D10 44 21N 6 22 E
Seyssel, France ...... 21 C9 45 57N 5 50 E
Sezana, Slovenia ..... 41 C10 45 43N 13 41 E
Sézanne, France ..... 19 D10 48 40N 3 40 E
Sezze, Italy .... 42 A6 41 30N 13 3 E
Sfântu Gheorghe,
Covasna, Romania . 29 E10 45 52N 25 48 E
Sfântu Gheorghe,
Tulcea, Romania ... 29 F14 44 53N 29 36 E
Sfântu Gheorghe,
Brațul →, Romania 29 F14 44 51N 29 36 E
Sfax, Tunisia .... 79 B8 34 49N 10 48 E
Sha Xia →, China .... 59 D12 26 35N 114 30 E
Sha Xian, China ..... 59 D11 26 23N 117 45 E
Shaanxi □, China .... 56 G5 35 0N 109 0 E
Shaba = Katanga □,
Dem. Rep. of
the Congo .... 86 D2 8 0 S 25 0 E
Shaba △, Kenya ...... 86 B4 0 38N 37 48 E
Shaballe = Scebeli,
Wabi →, Somali Rep. 75 G3 2 0N 44 0 E
Shabla, Bulgaria ..... 45 C12 43 31N 28 32 E
Shabogamo L., Canada 105 B6 53 15N 66 30W
Shabunda, Dem. Rep. of
the Congo .... 86 C2 2 40 S 27 16 E
Shache, China .... 60 C2 38 20N 77 10 E
Shackleton Ice Shelf,
Antarctica .... 5 C8 66 0 S 100 0 E
Shackleton Inlet,
Antarctica .... 5 E11 83 0 S 160 0 E
Shādegān, Iran ...... 71 D6 30 40N 48 38 E
Shadi, China .... 59 D10 26 7N 114 47 E
Shadi, India .... 69 C7 33 24N 77 14 E
Shadrinsk, Russia .... 52 D7 56 5N 63 32 E
Shadyside, U.S.A. 116 G4 39 58N 80 45W
Shaffa, Nigeria ...... 83 C7 10 30N 12 6 E
Shafter, U.S.A. 111 K7 35 30N 119 16W
Shaftesbury, U.K. 15 F5 51 0N 2 11W
Shagamu, Nigeria .... 83 D5 6 51N 3 39 E
Shagram, Pakistan ... 69 A5 36 24N 72 20 E
Shah Alizai, Pakistan . 68 E2 29 25N 66 33 E
Shah Bunder, Pakistan 68 G2 24 13N 67 56 E
Shahabad, Punjab, India 68 D7 30 10N 76 55 E
Shahabad, Raj., India . 68 G7 25 15N 77 11 E
Shahabad, Ut. P., India 69 F8 27 36N 79 56 E
Shahadpur, Pakistan .. 68 G3 25 55N 68 35 E
Shahba, Syria .... 74 C5 32 52N 36 38 E
Shahdād, Iran .... 71 D8 30 30N 57 40 E
Shahdād, Namakzār-e,
Iran .... 71 D8 30 20N 58 20 E
Shahdadkot, Pakistan . 68 F2 27 50N 67 55 E
Shahdol, India ...... 69 H9 23 19N 81 26 E
Shahe, China .... 56 F8 37 0N 114 32 E
Shahganj, India ..... 69 F10 26 3N 82 44 E
Shahgarh, India ..... 66 F6 27 15N 69 50 E
Shahjahanpur, India .. 69 F8 27 54N 79 57 E
Shahpur, India ...... 68 H7 22 12N 77 58 E
Shahpur, Baluchistan,
Pakistan .... 68 E3 28 46N 68 27 E
Shahpur, Punjab,
Pakistan .... 68 C5 32 17N 72 26 E
Shahpur Chakar,
Pakistan .... 68 F3 26 9N 68 39 E
Shahpura, Mad. P., India 69 H9 23 10N 80 45 E
Shahpura, Raj., India . 68 G6 25 38N 74 56 E
Shahr-e Bābak, Iran .. 71 D7 30 7N 55 9 E
Shahr-e Kord, Iran ... 71 C6 32 15N 50 55 E
Shāhrakht, Iran ..... 71 C9 33 38N 60 16 E
Shahrig, Pakistan .... 68 D2 30 15N 67 40 E
Shahukou, China .... 56 D7 40 20N 112 18 E
Shaikhabad, Afghan. . 68 B3 34 2N 68 45 E
Shajapur, India ...... 68 H7 23 27N 76 21 E
Shakargarh, Pakistan . 68 C6 32 17N 75 10 E
Shakawe, Botswana .. 88 B3 18 28 S 21 49 E
Shaker Heights, U.S.A. 116 E3 41 29N 81 32W
Shakhty, Russia ..... 35 G5 47 40N 40 16 E
Shakhunya, Russia ... 34 B8 57 40N 46 46 E
Shaki, Nigeria .... 83 D5 8 41N 3 21 E
Shakskyi Valley, Asia . 69 A7 36 7N 76 20 E
Shala, L., Ethiopia ... 81 F4 7 30N 38 30 E
Shali, Russia .... 35 J7 43 9N 45 55 E
Shallow Lake, Canada . 116 B3 44 36N 81 5W
Shalqar, Kazakhstan .. 52 E6 47 48N 59 39 E
Shalskiy, Russia ..... 32 B8 61 45N 36 20 E
Shaluli Shan, China .. 58 B2 30 40N 99 55 E
Shām, Iran .... 71 E8 26 39N 57 21 E

Shām, Bādiyat ash, Asia 70 C3 32 0N 40 0 E
Shamâl Bahr el
Ghazal □, Sudan .. 81 F2 8 0N 27 30 E
Shamâl Dârfûr □, Sudan 81 E2 15 0N 25 0 E
Shamâl Kordofân □,
Sudan .... 81 E3 15 0N 30 0 E
Shamâl Sînî □, Egypt . 80 B3 30 0N 33 30 E
Shamattawa, Canada .. 104 A1 55 51N 92 5W
Shamattawa →, Canada 104 A2 55 1N 85 23W
Shambe, Sudan ...... 81 F3 7 8N 30 46 E
Shambu, Ethiopia .... 81 F4 9 32N 37 3 E
Shamīl, Iran .... 71 E8 27 30N 56 55 E
Shamkhor = Şämkir,
Azerbaijan .... 35 K8 40 50N 46 0 E
Shāmkūh, Iran ...... 71 C8 35 47N 57 50 E
Shamli, India .... 68 E7 29 32N 77 18 E
Shammar, Jabal,
Si. Arabia .... 70 E4 27 40N 41 0 E
Shamo = Gobi, Asia .. 56 C6 44 0N 110 0 E
Shamo, L., Ethiopia .. 81 F4 5 45N 37 30 E
Shamokin, U.S.A. 117 F8 40 47N 76 34W
Shamrock, U.S.A. 113 H4 35 13N 100 15W
Shamva, Zimbabwe ... 87 F3 17 20 S 31 32 E
Shan □, Burma ...... 67 J21 21 30N 98 30 E
Shan Xian, China .... 56 G9 34 50N 116 5 E
Shanan →, Ethiopia .. 81 F5 8 0N 40 20 E
Shanchengzhen, China 57 C13 42 20N 125 20 E
Shāndak, Iran .... 71 D9 28 28N 60 27 E
Shandon, U.S.A. 110 K6 35 39N 120 23W
Shandong □, China ... 57 F10 36 0N 118 0 E
Shandong Bandao,
China .... 57 F11 37 0N 121 0 E
Shang Xian =
Shangzhou, China .. 56 H5 33 50N 109 58 E
Shanga, Nigeria ..... 78 F6 11 12N 4 33 E
Shangalowe, Dem. Rep.
of the Congo ...... 87 E2 10 50 S 26 30 E
Shangani, Zimbabwe .. 89 B4 19 41 S 29 20 E
Shangani →, Zimbabwe 87 F2 18 41 S 27 10 E
Shangbancheng, China 57 D10 40 50N 118 1 E
Shangcheng, China ... 59 B10 31 47N 115 26 E
Shangchuan Dao, China 59 G9 21 40N 112 50 E
Shangdu, China ...... 56 D7 41 30N 113 30 E
Shanggao, China ..... 59 C10 28 17N 114 55 E
Shanghai, China ..... 59 B13 31 15N 121 26 E
Shanghai Shi □, China 59 B13 31 10N 121 30 E
Shanghang, China .... 59 E11 25 2N 116 23 E
Shanglin, China ..... 58 F7 23 27N 108 33 E
Shangnan, China ..... 56 H6 33 32N 110 50 E
Shangqiu, China ..... 56 G8 34 26N 115 36 E
Shangrao, China ..... 59 C11 28 25N 117 59 E
Shangshui, China .... 56 H8 33 42N 114 35 E
Shangsi, China ...... 58 F6 22 8N 107 58 E
Shangyou, China ..... 59 E10 25 48N 114 32 E
Shangzhi, China ..... 57 B14 45 22N 127 56 E
Shangzhou, China .... 56 H5 33 50N 109 58 E
Shanhetun, China .... 57 B14 44 33N 127 15 E
Shani, Nigeria .... 83 C7 10 14N 12 2 E
Shanklin, U.K. 15 G6 50 38N 1 11W
Shannon, N.Z. ...... 91 J5 40 33 S 175 25 E
Shannon △, Australia . 93 F2 31 55 S 117 51 E
Shannon →, Ireland . 12 D2 52 35N 9 30W
Shannon, Mouth of the,
Ireland 12 D2 52 30N 9 55W
Shannon Airport,
Ireland 12 D3 52 42N 8 57W
Shansi = Shanxi □,
China .... 56 F7 37 0N 112 0 E
Shantar, Ostrov
Bolshoy, Russia .... 53 D14 55 9N 137 40 E
Shantipur, India ..... 69 H13 23 17N 88 25 E
Shantou, China ...... 59 F11 23 18N 116 40 E
Shantung = Shandong □,
China .... 57 G10 36 0N 118 0 E
Shanwei, China ...... 59 F10 22 48N 115 22 E
Shanxi □, China ..... 56 F7 37 0N 112 0 E
Shanyang, China ..... 56 H5 33 31N 109 55 E
Shanyin, China ...... 56 E7 39 25N 112 56 E
Shaodong, China ..... 59 D8 27 15N 111 43 E
Shaoguan, China ..... 59 E9 24 48N 113 35 E
Shaoshan, China ..... 59 D9 27 55N 112 33 E
Shaowu, China ...... 59 D11 27 22N 117 28 E
Shaoxing, China ..... 59 C13 30 0N 120 35 E
Shaoyang, Hunan, China 59 D8 27 14N 111 25 E
Shaoyang, Hunan, China 59 D8 26 59N 111 20 E
Shap, U.K. 14 C5 54 32N 2 40W
Shapinsay, U.K. 13 B6 59 3N 2 51W
Shaqq el Gi'eifer,
Sudan .... 81 D2 15 16N 26 0 E
Shaqra', Si. Arabia ... 70 E5 25 15N 45 16 E
Shaqrā', Yemen ...... 75 E4 13 22N 45 44 E
Sharafa, Sudan ...... 81 E2 11 59N 27 7 E
Sharafkhāneh, Iran ... 70 B5 38 11N 45 29 E
Sharbot Lake, Canada . 117 B8 44 46N 76 41W
Sharhorod, Ukraine .. 29 B13 48 45N 28 5 E
Shari, Japan .... 54 C12 43 55N 144 40 E
Sharjah = Ash Shāriqah,
U.A.E. .... 71 E7 25 23N 55 26 E
Shark B., Australia ... 93 E1 25 30 S 113 32 E
Shark Bay △, Australia 93 F2 32 49 S 118 49 E
Sharm el Sheikh, Egypt 80 B3 27 53N 34 18 E
Sharon, Mass., U.S.A. 117 D13 42 7N 71 11W
Sharon, Pa., U.S.A. .. 116 E4 41 14N 80 31W
Sharon Springs, Kans.,
U.S.A. 112 F4 38 54N 101 45W
Sharon Springs, N.Y.,
U.S.A. 117 D10 42 48N 74 37W
Sharp Pt., Australia .. 94 A3 10 58 S 142 43 E
Sharpe L., Canada 104 B1 54 24N 93 40W
Sharpsville, U.S.A. ... 116 E4 41 15N 80 29W
Sharq el Istiwa'iya □,
Sudan .... 81 G3 5 0N 33 0 E
Sharya, Russia ...... 34 A7 58 22N 45 20 E
Shasha, Ethiopia .... 81 F4 6 29N 35 59 E
Shashemene, Ethiopia 81 F4 7 13N 38 33 E
Shashi, Botswana .... 89 C4 21 15 S 27 27 E
Shashi →, Africa .... 87 G2 21 14 S 29 20 E
Shashi, China .... 59 B9 30 25N 112 14 E
Shasta, Mt., U.S.A. .. 108 F2 41 25N 122 12W
Shasta L., U.S.A. 108 F2 40 43N 122 25W
Shatawi, Sudan ...... 81 E3 14 39N 32 6 E
Shatsk, Russia ...... 34 C5 54 0N 41 45 E
Shatskyi △, Ukraine .. 31 G10 51 30N 23 52 E
Shatt al'Arab →, Iran 71 E6 30 0N 48 31 E
Shatura, Russia ..... 32 E10 55 33N 39 21 E
Shaumyani = Shulaveri,
Georgia .... 35 K7 41 22N 44 45 E
Shaunavon, Canada .. 103 D7 49 35N 108 25W
Shaver L., U.S.A. 110 H7 37 9N 119 18W
Shaw →, Australia ... 92 D2 20 21 S 119 17 E
Shaw L., Australia ... 94 J7 20 30 S 149 2 E
Shawanaga, Canada .. 116 A4 45 31N 80 17W

Shawangunk Mts.,
   U.S.A. **117 E10** 41 35N 74 30W
Shawano, *U.S.A.* **114 C1** 44 47N 88 36W
Shawinigan, *Canada* ... **104 C5** 46 35N 72 50W
Shawnee, *U.S.A.* **113 H6** 35 20N 96 55W
Shay Gap, *Australia* ... **92 D3** 20 30 S 120 10 E
Shayang, *China* ...... **59 B9** 30 42N 112 29 E
Shaybārā, *Si. Arabia* ... **70 E3** 25 26N 36 47 E
Shayib el Banat, Gebel,
   Egypt .... **80 B3** 26 59N 33 29 E
Shaykh, J. ash, *Lebanon* **74 B4** 33 25N 35 50 E
Shaykh Miskīn, *Syria* ... **74 C5** 32 49N 36 9 E
Shaykh Sa'īd, *Iraq* .... **70 C5** 32 34N 46 17 E
Shchekino, *Russia* ..... **32 E9** 54 1N 37 34 E
Shchigry, *Russia* ...... **33 G9** 51 55N 36 58 E
Shchors, *Ukraine* ..... **33 G6** 51 48N 31 56 E
Shchuchinsk,
   Kazakhstan .... **52 D8** 52 56N 70 12 E
She Xian, *Anhui, China* **59 C12** 29 50N 118 25 E
She Xian, *Hebei, China* **56 F8** 36 30N 113 40 E
Shebekino, *Russia* .... **33 G9** 50 28N 36 54 E
Shebele = Scebeli,
   Wabi →, *Somali Rep.* **75 G3** 2 0N 44 0 E
Sheboygan, *U.S.A.* **114 D2** 43 46N 87 45W
Shebshi Mts., *Nigeria* .. **83 D7** 8 30N 12 0 E
Shediac, *Canada* **105 C7** 46 14N 64 32W
Sheelin, L., *Ireland* ... **12 C4** 53 48N 7 20W
Sheep Haven, *Ireland* .. **12 A4** 55 11N 7 52W
Sheerness, *U.K.* ...... **15 F8** 51 26N 0 47 E
Sheet Harbour, *Canada* **105 D7** 44 56N 62 31W
Sheffield, *U.K.* **14 D6** 53 23N 1 28W
Sheffield, *Ala., U.S.A.* **115 H2** 34 46N 87 41W
Sheffield, *Mass., U.S.A.* **117 D11** 42 5N 73 21W
Sheffield, *Pa., U.S.A.* .. **116 E5** 41 42N 79 3W
Shehojele, *Ethiopia* .... **81 E4** 10 40N 35 9 E
Shehong, *China* ...... **58 B5** 30 54N 105 18 E
Sheikh Idris, *Sudan* ... **81 E3** 11 43N 33 30 E
Sheikhpura, *India* .... **69 G11** 25 9N 85 53 E
Shek Hasan, *Ethiopia* .. **81 E4** 12 5N 35 58 E
Shekhupura, *Pakistan* .. **68 D5** 31 42N 73 58 E
Sheki = Şaki, *Azerbaijan* **35 K8** 41 10N 47 5 E
Shelburne, *N.S., Canada* **105 D6** 43 47N 65 20W
Shelburne, *Ont., Canada* **116 B4** 44 4N 80 15W
Shelburne, *U.S.A.* **117 B11** 44 23N 73 14W
Shelburne B., *Australia* **94 A3** 11 50 S 142 50 E
Shelburne Falls, *U.S.A.* **117 D12** 42 36N 72 45W
Shelby, *Mich., U.S.A.* .. **114 D2** 43 37N 86 22W
Shelby, *Miss., U.S.A.* .. **113 J9** 33 57N 90 46W
Shelby, *Mont., U.S.A.* **108 B8** 48 30N 111 51W
Shelby, *N.C., U.S.A.* .. **115 H5** 35 17N 81 32W
Shelby, *Ohio, U.S.A.* .. **116 F2** 40 53N 82 40W
Shelbyville, *Ill., U.S.A.* **112 F10** 39 24N 88 48W
Shelbyville, *Ind., U.S.A.* **114 F3** 39 31N 85 47W
Shelbyville, *Ky., U.S.A.* **114 F3** 38 13N 85 14W
Shelbyville, *Tenn.,
   U.S.A.* **115 H2** 35 29N 86 28W
Sheldon, *U.S.A.* **112 D7** 43 11N 95 51W
Sheldrake, *Canada* **105 B7** 50 20N 64 51W
Shelengu, Khawr →,
   Sudan .... **81 E2** 10 33N 28 40 E
Shelikhova, Zaliv,
   Russia .... **53 D16** 59 30N 157 0 E
Shell Lakes, *Australia* .. **93 E4** 29 20 S 127 30 E
Shellbrook, *Canada* ... **103 C7** 53 13N 106 24W
Shellharbour, *Australia* **95 E5** 34 31 S 150 51 E
Shelon →, *Russia* ..... **32 C6** 58 13N 30 47 E
Shelter I., *U.S.A.* **117 E12** 41 5N 72 21W
Shelton, *Conn., U.S.A.* **117 E11** 41 19N 73 5W
Shelton, *Wash., U.S.A.* **110 C3** 47 13N 123 6W
Shemakha = Şamaxi,
   Azerbaijan .... **35 K9** 40 38N 48 37 E
Shēmi, *Albania* .... **44 D4** 42 7N 20 13 E
Shemsi, *Sudan* .... **80 D2** 19 2N 29 57 E
Shen Xian, *China* .... **56 F8** 36 15N 115 40 E
Shenandoah, *Iowa,
   U.S.A.* **112 E7** 40 46N 95 22W
Shenandoah, *Pa., U.S.A.* **117 F8** 40 49N 76 12W
Shenandoah, *Va., U.S.A.* **114 F6** 38 29N 78 37W
Shenandoah △, *U.S.A.* **114 F6** 38 35N 78 22W
Shenandoah →, *U.S.A.* **114 F7** 39 19N 77 44W
Shenchi, *China* ...... **56 E7** 39 8N 112 10 E
Shendam, *Nigeria* .... **83 D6** 8 49N 9 30 E
Shendî, *Sudan* .... **81 D3** 16 46N 33 22 E
Shenge, *S. Leone* **82 D2** 7 54N 12 55W
Shengfang, *China* ..... **56 E9** 39 3N 116 42 E
Shēngjergj, *Albania* ... **44 E4** 41 17N 20 10 E
Shēngjin, *Albania* .... **44 E3** 41 50N 19 35 E
Shengzhou, *China* .... **59 C13** 29 35N 120 50 E
Shenjingzi, *China* .... **57 B13** 44 40N 124 30 E
Shenmu, *China* ...... **56 E6** 38 50N 110 29 E
Shenqiu, *China* ...... **56 H8** 33 25N 115 5 E
Shensi = Shaanxi □,
   China .... **56 G5** 35 0N 109 0 E
Shenyang, *China* ..... **57 D12** 41 48N 123 27 E
Shenzhen, *China* ..... **59 F10** 22 32N 114 5 E
Sheo, *India* .... **68 F4** 26 11N 71 15 E
Sheopur Kalan, *India* .. **66 G10** 25 40N 76 40 E
Shepetivka, *Ukraine* .. **33 G4** 50 10N 27 10 E
Shepetovka =
   Shepetivka, *Ukraine* **33 G4** 50 10N 27 10 E
Shepparton, *Australia* . **95 F4** 36 23 S 145 26 E
Sheppey, I. of, *U.K.* .. **15 F8** 51 25N 0 48 E
Shepton Mallet, *U.K.* .. **15 F5** 51 11N 2 33W
Sheqi, *China* .... **56 H7** 33 12N 112 57 E
Sher Qila, *Pakistan* ... **69 A6** 36 7N 74 2 E
Sherab, *Sudan* .... **81 E1** 10 44N 24 41 E
Sherborne, *U.K.* **15 G5** 50 57N 2 31W
Sherbro I., *S. Leone* ... **82 D2** 7 30N 12 40W
Sherbrooke, *N.S.,
   Canada* **105 C7** 45 8N 61 59W
Sherbrooke, *Qué.,
   Canada* **117 A13** 45 28N 71 57W
Sherburne, *U.S.A.* **117 D9** 42 41N 75 30W
Shereik, *Sudan* ...... **80 D3** 18 44N 33 47 E
Shergarh, *India* ...... **68 F5** 26 20N 72 18 E
Sherghati, *India* ..... **69 G11** 24 34N 84 47 E
Sheridan, *Ark., U.S.A.* **113 H8** 34 19N 92 24W
Sheridan, *Wyo., U.S.A.* **108 D10** 44 48N 106 58W
Sheringham, *U.K.* .... **14 E9** 52 56N 1 13 E
Sherkin I., *Ireland* **12 E2** 51 28N 9 26W
Sherkot, *India* .... **69 E8** 29 22N 78 35 E
Sherman, *U.S.A.* **113 J6** 33 40N 96 35W
Sherpur, *India* .... **69 G10** 25 34N 83 30 E
Sherridon, *Canada* **103 B8** 55 8N 101 5W
Sherwood Forest, *U.K.* **14 D6** 53 6N 1 7W
Sherwood Park, *Canada* **102 C6** 53 31N 113 19W
Sheslay →, *Canada* ... **102 B2** 58 48N 132 5W
Shethanei L., *Canada* .. **103 B9** 58 48N 97 50W
Shetland □, *U.K.* **13 A7** 60 30N 1 30W
Shetland Is., *U.K.* **13 A7** 60 30N 1 30W
Shetrunji →, *India* ... **68 J5** 21 19N 72 7 E
Shevchenkovo, *Ukraine* **29 E14** 45 33N 29 20 E
Shewa Gimira, *Ethiopia* **81 F4** 7 4N 35 51 E
Sheyenne →, *U.S.A.* .. **112 B6** 47 2N 96 50W

Shibām, *Yemen* ...... **75 D4** 15 59N 48 36 E
Shibata, *Japan* ...... **54 F9** 37 57N 139 20 E
Shibecha, *Japan* ..... **54 C12** 43 17N 144 36 E
Shibetsu, *Japan* ..... **54 B11** 44 10N 142 23 E
Shibīn el Kōm, *Egypt* **80 H7** 30 31N 30 55 E
Shibīn el Qanâtir, *Egypt* **80 H7** 30 19N 31 19 E
Shibing, *China* ...... **58 D7** 27 2N 108 7 E
Shibogama L., *Canada* **104 B2** 53 35N 88 15W
Shibushi, *Japan* ..... **55 J5** 31 25N 131 8 E
Shicheng, *China* ..... **59 D11** 26 22N 116 20 E
Shickshinny, *U.S.A.* .. **117 E8** 41 9N 76 9W
Shickshock Mts. = Chic-
   Chocs, Mts., *Canada* **105 C6** 48 55N 66 0W
Shidao, *China* .... **57 F12** 36 50N 122 25 E
Shidian, *China* ...... **58 E2** 24 40N 99 5 E
Shido, *Japan* .... **55 G7** 34 19N 134 10 E
Shiel, L., *U.K.* **13 E3** 56 48N 5 34W
Shield, C., *Australia* .. **94 A2** 13 20 S 136 20 E
Shieli, *Kazakhstan* ... **52 E7** 44 20N 66 15 E
Shifang, *China* ...... **58 B5** 31 8N 104 10 E
Shiga □, *Japan* ...... **55 G8** 35 20N 136 0 E
Shigu, *China* .... **58 D2** 26 51N 99 56 E
Shiguaigou, *China* ... **56 D6** 40 52N 110 15 E
Shihchiachuang =
   Shijiazhuang, *China* **56 E8** 38 2N 114 28 E
Shihezi, *China* ...... **60 B3** 44 15N 86 2 E
Shijak, *Albania* ..... **44 E3** 41 21N 19 33 E
Shijiazhuang, *China* .. **56 E8** 38 2N 114 28 E
Shijiu Hu, *China* .... **59 B12** 31 25N 118 50 E
Shikabe, *Japan* ...... **54 C10** 42 0N 140 52 E
Shikarpur, *India* ..... **68 E8** 28 17N 78 7 E
Shikarpur, *Pakistan* .. **68 F3** 27 57N 68 39 E
Shikohabad, *India* ... **69 F8** 27 6N 78 36 E
Shikoku □, *Japan* .... **55 H6** 33 30N 133 30 E
Shikoku-Sanchi, *Japan* **55 H6** 33 30N 133 30 E
Shikotsu-Ko, *Japan* .. **54 C10** 42 45N 141 25 E
Shikotsu-Tōya △, *Japan* **54 C10** 44 4N 145 8 E
Shiliguri, *India* ..... **67 F16** 26 45N 88 25 E
Shilka, *Russia* ...... **53 D12** 52 0N 115 55 E
Shilka →, *Russia* .... **53 D13** 53 20N 121 26 E
Shillelagh, *Ireland* ... **12 D5** 52 45N 6 32W
Shillington, *U.S.A.* ... **117 F9** 40 18N 75 58W
Shillong, *India* ...... **67 G17** 25 35N 91 53 E
Shilo, *West Bank* .... **74 C4** 32 4N 35 18 E
Shilong, *China* ...... **59 F9** 23 5N 113 52 E
Shilou, *China* .... **56 F6** 37 0N 110 48 E
Shilovo, *Russia* ..... **34 C5** 54 25N 40 57 E
Shimabara, *Japan* .... **55 H5** 32 48N 130 20 E
Shimada, *Japan* ..... **55 G9** 34 49N 138 10 E
Shimane □, *Japan* ... **55 G6** 35 0N 132 30 E
Shimanovsk, *Russia* .. **53 D13** 52 15N 127 30 E
Shimba Hills △, *Kenya* **86 C4** 4 14 S 39 25 E
Shimen, *China* ...... **59 C8** 29 35N 111 20 E
Shimenjie, *China* .... **59 C11** 29 29N 116 48 E
Shimian, *China* ...... **58 C4** 29 17N 102 23 E
Shimizu, *Japan* ...... **55 G9** 35 0N 138 30 E
Shimodate, *Japan* .... **55 F9** 36 20N 139 55 E
Shimoga, *India* ...... **66 N9** 13 57N 75 32 E
Shimoni, *Kenya* ..... **86 C4** 4 38 S 39 20 E
Shimonoseki, *Japan* .. **55 H5** 33 58N 130 55 E
Shimpuru Rapids,
   Namibia .... **88 B2** 17 45 S 19 55 E
Shimsk, *Russia* ...... **32 C6** 58 15N 30 50 E
Shin, L., *U.K.* **13 C4** 58 5N 4 30W
Shinan, *China* .... **58 F7** 22 44N 109 53 E
Shinano-Gawa →,
   Japan .... **55 F9** 36 50N 138 30 E
Shināş, *Oman* .... **71 E8** 24 46N 56 28 E
Shīndand, *Afghan.* ... **66 C3** 33 12N 62 8 E
Shinglehouse, *U.S.A.* . **116 E6** 41 58N 78 12W
Shingū, *Japan* .... **55 H7** 33 40N 135 55 E
Shingwidzi, *S. Africa* . **89 C5** 23 5 S 31 25 E
Shinjō, *Japan* .... **54 E10** 38 46N 140 18 E
Shinkafe, *Nigeria* .... **83 C6** 13 8N 6 29 E
Shinshār, *Syria* ...... **74 A5** 34 36N 36 43 E
Shinyanga, *Tanzania* . **86 C3** 3 45 S 33 27 E
Shinyanga □, *Tanzania* **86 C3** 3 50 S 34 0 E
Shio-no-Misaki, *Japan* **55 H7** 33 25N 135 45 E
Shiogama, *Japan* ..... **54 E10** 38 19N 141 1 E
Shiojiri, *Japan* ...... **55 F9** 36 6N 137 58 E
Shipchenski Prokhod,
   Bulgaria .... **45 D9** 42 45N 25 15 E
Shiping, *China* ...... **58 F4** 23 45N 102 23 E
Shippagan, *Canada* ... **105 C7** 47 45N 64 45W
Shippensburg, *U.S.A.* **116 F7** 40 3N 77 31W
Shippenville, *U.S.A.* .. **116 E5** 41 15N 79 28W
Shiprock, *U.S.A.* **109 H9** 36 47N 108 41W
Shiqian, *China* ...... **58 D7** 27 32N 108 13 E
Shiqma, N. →, *Israel* **74 D3** 31 37N 34 30 E
Shiquan, *China* ...... **56 H5** 33 5N 108 15 E
Shiquan He = Indus →,
   Pakistan .... **68 G2** 24 20N 67 47 E
Shīr Kūh, *Iran* ...... **71 D7** 31 39N 54 3 E
Shiragami-Misaki, *Japan* **54 D10** 41 24N 140 12 E
Shirakawa, *Fukushima,
   Japan* .... **55 F10** 37 7N 140 13 E
Shirakawa, *Gifu, Japan* **55 F8** 36 17N 136 56 E
Shirane-San, *Gumma,
   Japan* .... **55 F9** 36 48N 139 22 E
Shirane-San, *Yamanashi,
   Japan* .... **55 G9** 35 42N 138 9 E
Shiraoi, *Japan* ...... **54 C10** 42 33N 141 21 E
Shīrāz, *Iran* .... **71 D7** 29 42N 52 30 E
Shirbīn, *Egypt* ...... **80 H7** 31 11N 31 32 E
Shire →, *Africa* ..... **87 F4** 17 42 S 35 19 E
Shiretoko-Misaki, *Japan* **54 B12** 44 21N 145 20 E
Shirinab →, *Pakistan* **68 D2** 30 15N 66 28 E
Shiriya-Zaki, *Japan* .. **54 D10** 41 25N 141 30 E
Shiroishi, *Japan* ..... **54 F10** 38 0N 140 37 E
Shīrvān, *Iran* .... **71 B8** 37 30N 57 50 E
Shirwa, L. = Chilwa, L.,
   Malawi .... **87 F4** 15 15 S 35 40 E
Shishi, *China* .... **59 E12** 24 44N 118 37 E
Shishou, *China* ...... **59 C9** 29 38N 112 22 E
Shitai, *China* .... **59 B11** 30 12N 117 25 E
Shivpuri, *India* ...... **68 G7** 25 26N 77 42 E
Shixing, *China* ...... **59 E10** 24 46N 114 5 E
Shiyan, *China* .... **59 A8** 32 35N 110 5 E
Shiyata, *Egypt* ...... **80 B2** 29 25N 25 7 E
Shizhu, *China* .... **58 C7** 30 0N 108 0 E
Shizong, *China* ...... **58 E5** 24 50N 104 0 E
Shizuishan, *China* .... **56 E4** 39 15N 106 50 E
Shizuoka, *Japan* ..... **55 G9** 34 57N 138 24 E
Shizuoka □, *Japan* ... **55 G9** 35 15N 138 40 E
Shklov = Shklow,
   Belarus .... **32 E6** 54 16N 30 15 E
Shklow, *Belarus* ..... **32 E6** 54 16N 30 15 E
Shkodër, *Albania* .... **44 D3** 42 4N 19 32 E
Shkumbini →, *Albania* **44 E3** 41 2N 19 31 E
Shmidta, Ostrov, *Russia* **53 A10** 81 0N 91 0 E
Shō-Gawa →, *Japan* .. **55 F8** 36 47N 137 4 E
Shoal L., *Canada* **103 D9** 49 33N 95 1W
Shoal Lake, *Canada* .. **103 C8** 50 30N 100 35W
Shōdo-Shima, *Japan* .. **55 G7** 34 30N 134 15 E
Sholapur = Solapur,
   India .... **66 L9** 17 43N 75 56 E
Shōmrōn, *West Bank* . **74 C4** 32 15N 35 13 E

Shoreham by Sea, *U.K.* **15 G7** 50 50N 0 16W
Shori →, *Pakistan* ... **68 E3** 28 29N 69 44 E
Shorkot Road, *Pakistan* **68 D5** 30 47N 72 15 E
Shoshone, *Calif., U.S.A.* **111 K10** 35 58N 116 16W
Shoshone, *Idaho, U.S.A.* **108 E6** 42 56N 114 25W
Shoshone L., *U.S.A.* .. **108 D8** 44 22N 110 43W
Shoshone Mts., *U.S.A.* **108 G5** 39 20N 117 25W
Shoshong, *Botswana* .. **88 C4** 22 56 S 26 31 E
Shoshoni, *U.S.A.* **108 E9** 43 14N 108 7W
Shostka, *Ukraine* .... **33 G7** 51 57N 33 32 E
Shouchang, *China* .... **59 C12** 29 18N 119 12 E
Shouguang, *China* .... **57 F10** 37 52N 118 45 E
Shouyang, *China* ..... **56 F7** 37 54N 113 8 E
Show Low, *U.S.A.* ... **109 J9** 34 15N 110 2W
Shpola, *Ukraine* ..... **33 H6** 49 1N 31 30 E
Shpykiv, *Ukraine* .... **29 B13** 48 47N 28 34 E
Shreveport, *U.S.A.* ... **113 J8** 32 31N 93 45W
Shrewsbury, *U.K.* **15 E5** 52 43N 2 45W
Shri Mohangarh, *India* **68 F4** 27 17N 71 18 E
Shrirampur, *India* ... **69 H13** 22 44N 88 21 E
Shropshire □, *U.K.* .. **15 E5** 52 36N 2 45W
Shū, *Kazakhstan* ..... **52 E8** 43 36N 73 42 E
Shū →, *Kazakhstan* .. **50 E10** 45 0N 67 44 E
Shuangbai, *China* .... **58 E3** 24 42N 101 38 E
Shuangcheng, *China* .. **57 B14** 45 20N 126 15 E
Shuangfeng, *China* ... **59 D9** 27 29N 112 11 E
Shuanggou, *China* .... **57 G9** 34 2N 117 30 E
Shuangjiang, *China* ... **58 F2** 23 26N 99 58 E
Shuangliao, *China* ... **57 C12** 43 29N 123 30 E
Shuangshanzi, *China* . **57 D10** 40 20N 119 8 E
Shuangyang, *China* ... **57 C13** 43 28N 125 40 E
Shuangyashan, *China* . **60 B8** 46 28N 131 5 E
Shubra el Kheima, *Egypt* **80 H7** 30 6N 31 15 E
Shubra Khit, *Egypt* .. **80 H7** 31 2N 30 42 E
Shucheng, *China* ..... **59 B11** 31 28N 116 57 E
Shugozero, *Russia* ... **32 C8** 59 54N 34 10 E
Shuguri Falls, *Tanzania* **87 D4** 8 33 S 37 22 E
Shuiji, *China* .... **59 D12** 27 13N 118 20 E
Shuiye, *China* .... **56 F8** 36 7N 114 8 E
Shujalpur, *India* ..... **68 H7** 23 18N 76 46 E
Shukpa Kunzang, *India* **69 B8** 34 22N 78 22 E
Shulan, *China* .... **57 B14** 44 28N 127 0 E
Shulaveri, *Georgia* ... **35 K7** 41 22N 44 45 E
Shule, *China* .... **60 C2** 39 25N 76 3 E
Shumagin Is., *U.S.A.* . **100 C4** 55 7N 160 30W
Shumen, *Bulgaria* .... **45 C10** 43 18N 26 55 E
Shumerlya, *Russia* ... **34 C8** 55 30N 46 25 E
Shumikha, *Russia* .... **52 D7** 55 10N 63 15 E
Shunchang, *China* .... **59 D11** 26 54N 117 48 E
Shunde, *China* .... **59 F9** 22 42N 113 14 E
Shungay, *Kazakhstan* . **35 F8** 48 30N 46 45 E
Shuo Xian = Shuozhou,
   China .... **56 E7** 39 20N 112 33 E
Shuozhou, *China* ..... **56 E7** 39 20N 112 33 E
Shūr →, *Fārs, Iran* .. **71 D7** 28 30N 55 0 E
Shūr →, *Kermān, Iran* **71 D8** 30 52N 57 37 E
Shūr →, *Yazd, Iran* .. **71 D7** 31 45N 55 15 E
Shūr Āb, *Iran* .... **71 C6** 34 23N 51 11 E
Shūr Gaz, *Iran* ...... **71 D8** 29 10N 59 20 E
Shūrāb, *Iran* .... **71 C8** 33 43N 56 29 E
Shūrjestān, *Iran* ..... **71 D7** 31 24N 52 25 E
Shurugwi, *Zimbabwe* . **87 F3** 19 40 S 30 0 E
Shūsf, *Iran* .... **71 D9** 31 50N 60 5 E
Shūsh, *Iran* .... **73 F13** 32 11N 48 15 E
Shūshtar, *Iran* ...... **71 D6** 32 0N 48 50 E
Shuswap L., *Canada* .. **102 C5** 50 55N 119 3W
Shuya, *Russia* .... **34 B5** 56 50N 41 28 E
Shuyang, *China* ...... **57 G10** 34 10N 118 42 E
Shūzū, *Iran* .... **71 D7** 29 52N 54 30 E
Shwebo, *Burma* ...... **67 H19** 22 30N 95 45 E
Shwegu, *Burma* ...... **67 G20** 24 15N 96 26 E
Shweli →, *Burma* .... **67 H20** 23 45N 96 45 E
Shymkent, *Kazakhstan* **52 E7** 42 18N 69 36 E
Shyok, *India* .... **69 B8** 34 13N 78 12 E
Shyok →, *India* ..... **69 B6** 35 13N 75 53 E
Shyroke, *Ukraine* .... **28 B8** 43 15N 23 6 E
Shyroke, *Ukraine* .... **33 J7** 47 40N 33 25 E
Si Chon, *Thailand* ... **65 H2** 9 0N 99 54 E
Si Kiang = Xi Jiang →,
   China .... **59 F9** 22 5N 113 20 E
Si Lanna △, *Thailand* . **64 C2** 19 17N 99 12 E
Si-ngan = Xi'an, *China* **56 G5** 34 15N 109 0 E
Si Prachan, *Thailand* . **64 E3** 14 37N 100 9 E
Si Racha, *Thailand* ... **64 F3** 13 10N 100 48 E
Si Xian, *China* ...... **57 H9** 33 30N 117 50 E
Siachen Glacier, *Asia* . **69 B7** 35 20N 77 30 E
Siahaf →, *Pakistan* .. **68 E3** 29 3N 68 57 E
Siahan Range, *Pakistan* **66 F4** 27 30N 64 40 E
Siaksriindrapura,
   Indonesia .... **62 D2** 0 51N 102 0 E
Sialkot, *Pakistan* .... **68 C6** 32 32N 74 30 E
Siam = Thailand ■, *Asia* **64 E4** 16 0N 102 0 E
Sian = Xi'an, *China* .. **56 G5** 34 15N 109 0 E
Sian Ka'an, *Mexico* .. **119 D7** 19 35N 87 40W
Sianow, *Poland* ...... **30 D3** 54 13N 16 18 E
Siantan, *Indonesia* ... **62 D3** 3 10N 106 15 E
Siāreh, *Iran* .... **71 D9** 28 5N 60 14 E
Siargao I., *Phil.* ..... **61 G7** 9 52N 126 3 E
Siari, *Pakistan* ...... **69 B7** 34 55N 76 40 E
Siasi, *Phil.* .... **63 C6** 5 34N 120 50 E
Siasi I., *Phil.* .... **61 J4** 5 33N 120 51 E
Siátista, *Greece* ..... **44 F5** 40 15N 21 33 E
Siau, *Indonesia* ...... **63 D7** 2 50N 125 25 E
Šiauliai, *Lithuania* ... **9 J20** 55 56N 23 15 E
Šiauliai □, *Lithuania* . **30 C10** 55 56N 23 19 E
Siazan = Siyäzän,
   Azerbaijan .... **35 K9** 41 3N 49 10 E
Sibâi, Gebel el, *Egypt* **80 B3** 25 45N 34 10 E
Sibang, *Indonesia* .... **63 K18** 8 34 S 115 13 E
Sibayi, L., *S. Africa* .. **89 D5** 27 20 S 32 45 E
Sibdu, *Sudan* .... **81 E1** 10 57N 26 17 E
Šibenik, *Croatia* ..... **41 E12** 43 48N 15 54 E
Siberia = Sibirskiy □,
   Russia .... **53 D10** 58 0N 90 0 E
Siberia, *Russia* ...... **50 C13** 60 0N 100 0 E
Siberut, *Indonesia* ... **62 E1** 1 30 S 99 0 E
Sibi, *Pakistan* .... **68 E2** 29 30N 67 54 E
Sibil = Oksibil,
   Indonesia .... **63 E10** 4 59 S 140 35 E
Sibiloi △, *Kenya* ..... **86 B4** 4 0N 36 20 E
Sibirskiy □, *Russia* ... **53 D10** 58 0N 90 0 E
Sibiti, *Congo* .... **84 E2** 3 38 S 13 19 E
Sibiu, *Romania* ...... **29 E9** 45 45N 24 9 E
Sibiu □, *Romania* .... **29 E9** 45 50N 24 15 E
Sibley, *U.S.A.* **112 D7** 43 24N 95 45W
Sibolga, *Indonesia* ... **62 D1** 1 42N 98 45 E
Sibsagar, *India* ...... **67 F19** 27 0N 94 36 E
Sibu, *Malaysia* ...... **62 D4** 2 18N 111 49 E
Sibuco, *Phil.* .... **61 H5** 7 20N 122 10 E
Sibuguey B., *Phil.* ... **61 H5** 7 50N 122 45 E
Sibutu, *Phil.* .... **63 D5** 4 45N 119 30 E
Sibutu Group, *Phil.* .. **61 J3** 4 45N 119 20 E
Sibutu Passage, *E. Indies* **63 D5** 4 50N 120 0 E
Sibuyan I., *Phil.* ..... **61 E5** 12 25N 122 40 E

Sibuyan Sea, *Phil.* ... **61 E5** 12 30N 122 20 E
Sic, *Romania* .... **29 D8** 46 56N 23 53 E
Sicamous, *Canada* **102 C5** 50 49N 119 0W
Siccus →, *Australia* .. **95 E2** 31 55 S 139 17 E
Sichuan □, *China* .... **58 B5** 30 30N 103 0 E
Sichuan Pendi, *China* . **58 B5** 31 0N 105 0 E
Sicilia, *Italy* .... **43 E7** 37 30N 14 30 E
Sicily = Sicilia, *Italy* .. **43 E7** 37 30N 14 30 E
Sicily, Str. of .... **42 E6** 37 35N 11 56 E
Sicuani, *Peru* .... **124 F4** 14 21 S 71 10W
Šid, *Serbia & M.* .... **28 E4** 45 8N 19 14 E
Sidamo, *Ethiopia* .... **81 G4** 5 0N 37 50 E
Sidaoueт, *Niger* ..... **83 B6** 18 34N 8 3 E
Sidári, *Greece* ...... **49 A3** 39 47N 19 41 E
Siddhapur, *India* .... **68 H5** 23 56N 72 45 E
Siddipet, *India* ...... **66 K11** 18 5N 78 51 E
Sidensjö, *Sweden* .... **10 A12** 63 18N 18 17 E
Sidéradougou,
   Burkina Faso **82 C4** 10 42N 4 12W
Siderno, *Italy* .... **43 D9** 38 16N 16 18 E
Sidheros, Ákra, *Greece* **49 D8** 35 19N 26 19 E
Sidhi, *India* .... **69 G9** 24 25N 81 53 E
Sidhirókastron, *Greece* **44 E7** 41 13N 23 24 E
Sîdi Abd el Rahmân,
   Egypt .... **80 A2** 30 55N 29 44 E
Sîdi Barrâni, *Egypt* .. **80 A2** 31 38N 25 58 E
Sidi-bel-Abbès, *Algeria* **78 A5** 35 13N 0 39W
Sîdi Haneish, *Egypt* .. **80 A2** 31 10N 27 35 E
Sidi Ifni, *Morocco* ... **78 C3** 29 29N 10 12W
Sîdi Omar, *Egypt* .... **80 A1** 31 24N 24 57 E
Sidlaw Hills, *U.K.* ... **13 E5** 56 32N 3 2W
Sidley, Mt., *Antarctica* **5 D14** 77 2 S 126 2W
Sidmouth, *U.K.* **15 G4** 50 40N 3 15W
Sidmouth, C., *Australia* **94 A3** 13 25 S 143 36 E
Sidney, *Canada* **102 D4** 48 39N 123 24W
Sidney, *Mont., U.S.A.* **112 B2** 47 43N 104 9W
Sidney, *N.Y., U.S.A.* .. **117 D9** 42 19N 75 24W
Sidney, *Nebr., U.S.A.* **112 E3** 41 8N 102 59W
Sidney, *Ohio, U.S.A.* . **114 E3** 40 17N 84 9W
Sidney Lanier, L., *U.S.A.* **115 H4** 34 10N 84 4W
Sīdo, *Mali* **82 C3** 11 7N 7 20W
Sidoarjo, *Indonesia* .. **63 G15** 7 27 S 112 43 E
Sidon = Saydā, *Lebanon* **74 B4** 33 35N 35 25 E
Sidra, G. of = Surt,
   Khalīj, *Libya* ...... **79 B9** 31 40N 18 30 E
Siedlce, *Poland* ...... **31 F9** 52 10N 22 20 E
Sieg →, *Germany* .... **24 E3** 50 46N 7 6 E
Siegburg, *Germany* ... **24 E3** 50 47N 7 12 E
Siegen, *Germany* ..... **24 E4** 50 51N 8 0 E
Siem Pang, *Cambodia* **64 E6** 14 7N 106 23 E
Siem Reap = Siemreab,
   Cambodia .... **64 F4** 13 20N 103 52 E
Siemiatycze, *Poland* .. **31 F9** 52 27N 22 53 E
Siemreab, *Cambodia* . **64 F4** 13 20N 103 52 E
Siena, *Italy* .... **41 E8** 43 19N 11 21 E
Sieniawa, *Poland* .... **31 H9** 50 11N 22 38 E
Sieradz, *Poland* ..... **31 G5** 51 37N 18 41 E
Sieraków, *Poland* .... **31 F3** 52 39N 16 0 E
Sierck-les-Bains, *France* **19 C13** 49 26N 6 20 E
Sierning, *Austria* .... **26 C7** 48 2N 14 18 E
Sierpc, *Poland* .... **31 F6** 52 55N 19 43 E
Sierpe, Bocas de la,
   Venezuela **125 L15** 10 0N 61 30W
Sierra Blanca, *U.S.A.* . **109 L11** 31 11N 105 22W
Sierra Blanca Peak,
   U.S.A. **109 K11** 33 23N 105 49W
Sierra City, *U.S.A.* ... **110 F6** 39 34N 120 38W
Sierra Colorada,
   Argentina .... **128 E3** 40 35 S 67 50W
Sierra de Aracena y
   Picas de Aroche △,
   Spain **37 H4** 37 53N 6 41W
Sierra de Bahoruco △,
   Dom. Rep. **121 C5** 18 10N 71 25W
Sierra de Baza △, *Spain* **39 H2** 37 20N 2 48W
Sierra de Castril △,
   Spain **39 H2** 37 54N 2 50W
Sierra de España △,
   Spain **39 H3** 37 55N 1 31W
Sierra de Gredos △,
   Spain **36 E5** 40 17N 5 17W
Sierra de Grazalema △,
   Spain **37 J5** 36 31N 5 28W
Sierra de
   Hornachuelos △,
   Spain **37 H5** 37 56N 5 14W
Sierra de Huétor △,
   Spain **37 H7** 37 14N 3 30W
Sierra de La Culata △,
   Venezuela **121 E5** 8 45N 71 10W
Sierra de Lancandón △,
   Guatemala **120 C1** 16 59N 90 23W
Sierra de las Nieves △,
   Spain **37 J6** 36 35N 4 58W
Sierra de las Quijadas △,
   Argentina .... **126 C2** 32 29 S 67 5W
Sierra de María-Los
   Vélez △, *Spain* **39 H2** 37 41N 2 10W
Sierra de San Luis △,
   Venezuela **121 D6** 11 20N 69 43W
Sierra de Yeguas, *Spain* **37 H6** 37 7N 4 52W
Sierra do São
   Mamede △, *Portugal* **37 F3** 39 17N 7 18W
Sierra Gorda, *Chile* .. **126 A2** 22 50 S 69 15W
Sierra Leone ■, *W. Afr.* **82 D2** 9 0N 12 0W
Sierra Madre, *Mexico* **119 D6** 16 0N 93 0W
Sierra Mágina △, *Spain* **37 H7** 37 44N 3 28W
Sierra Mojada, *Mexico* **118 B4** 27 19N 103 42W
Sierra Nevada, *Spain* . **37 H7** 37 3N 3 15W
Sierra Nevada, *U.S.A.* **110 H8** 39 0N 120 30W
Sierra Nevada △, *Spain* **37 H7** 37 4N 3 7W
Sierra Nevada △,
   Venezuela **121 E5** 8 35N 70 45W
Sierra Nevada de Santa
   Marta △, *Colombia* **121 D5** 10 56N 73 30W
Sierra Norte de
   Seville △, *Spain* ... **37 H5** 37 56N 5 45W
Sierra Subbéticas,
   Spain **37 H6** 37 30N 4 31W
Sierra Vista, *U.S.A.* .. **109 L8** 31 33N 110 18W
Sierraville, *U.S.A.* ... **110 F6** 39 36N 120 22W
Sierre, *Switz.* .... **25 J3** 46 17N 7 31 E
Sīfanī, *Ethiopia* ..... **81 E5** 12 18N 40 19 E
Sifié, *Ivory C.* **82 D3** 8 0N 7 9W
Sífnos, *Greece* ...... **49 E6** 37 0N 24 45 E
Sifton, *Canada* **103 C8** 51 21N 100 8W
Sifton Pass, *Canada* .. **102 B3** 57 52N 126 15W
Sighetu-Marmației,
   Romania .... **29 C8** 47 57N 23 52 E
Sighişoara, *Romania* .. **29 D9** 46 12N 24 50 E

Sigli, *Indonesia* ..... **62 C1** 5 25N 96 0 E
Siglufjörður, *Iceland* . **8 C4** 66 12N 18 55W
Sigmaringen, *Germany* **25 G5** 48 5N 9 12 E
Signa, *Italy* .... **40 E8** 43 45N 11 10 E
Signakhi = Tsnori,
   Georgia .... **35 K7** 41 40N 45 57 E
Signal, *U.S.A.* **111 L13** 34 30N 113 38W
Signal de Botrange,
   Belgium .... **17 D6** 50 29N 6 4 E
Signal Pk., *U.S.A.* ... **111 M12** 33 20N 114 2W
Signy l, *Antarctica* ... **5 C18** 60 45 S 45 56W
Signy-l'Abbaye, *France* **19 C11** 49 40N 4 25 E
Sigsig, *Ecuador* ..... **124 D3** 3 0 S 78 50W
Sigüenza, *Spain* **38 D2** 41 3N 2 40W
Siguiri, *Guinea* **82 C3** 11 31N 9 10W
Sigulda, *Latvia* ...... **9 H21** 57 10N 24 55 E
Sihora, *India* .... **69 H9** 23 29N 80 6 E
Sihui, *China* .... **59 F9** 23 20N 112 40 E
Siikajoki →, *Finland* . **8 D21** 64 50N 24 43 E
Siilinjärvi, *Finland* ... **8 E22** 63 4N 27 39 E
Siirt, *Turkey* .... **73 D9** 37 57N 41 55 E
Sijarira Ra. = Chizarira,
   Zimbabwe .... **87 F2** 17 36 S 27 45 E
Sika, *India* .... **68 H3** 22 26N 69 47 E
Sikani Chief →, *Canada* **102 B4** 57 47N 122 15W
Sikao, *Thailand* ..... **65 J2** 7 34N 99 21 E
Sikar, *India* .... **68 F6** 27 33N 75 10 E
Sikasso, *Mali* **82 C3** 11 18N 5 35W
Sikeston, *U.S.A.* **113 G10** 36 53N 89 35W
Sikhote Alin, Khrebet,
   Russia .... **53 E14** 45 0N 136 0 E
Sikhote Alin Ra. =
   Sikhote Alin, Khrebet,
   Russia .... **53 E14** 45 0N 136 0 E
Sikiá, *Greece* .... **44 F7** 40 2N 23 56 E
Síkinos, *Greece* ..... **47 E7** 36 40N 25 8 E
Sikkim □, *India* ..... **67 F16** 27 50N 88 30 E
Siklós, *Hungary* ..... **28 E3** 45 50N 18 19 E
Sil →, *Spain* **36 C3** 42 27N 7 43W
Silacayoapan, *Mexico* **119 D5** 17 30N 98 9W
Šilalė, *Lithuania* .... **30 C9** 55 28N 22 12 E
Silandro, *Italy* ...... **40 B7** 46 38N 10 46 E
Silawad, *India* ...... **68 J6** 21 54N 74 54 E
Silay, *Phil.* .... **61 F5** 10 47N 122 58 E
Silba, *Croatia* .... **41 D11** 44 24N 14 41 E
Silchar, *India* .... **67 G18** 24 49N 92 48 E
Şile, *Turkey* .... **45 E13** 41 10N 29 37 E
Siler City, *U.S.A.* ... **115 H6** 35 44N 79 28W
Silesia = Śląsk, *Poland* **31 C9** 51 0N 16 30 E
Silgarhi Doti, *Nepal* . **69 E9** 29 15N 81 0 E
Silghat, *India* .... **67 F18** 26 35N 93 0 E
Sili, *Burkina Faso* ... **82 C4** 11 37N 2 30W
Silifke, *Turkey* ...... **70 B2** 36 22N 33 58 E
Siliguri = Shiliguri, *India* **67 F16** 26 45N 88 25 E
Siling Co, *China* ..... **60 C3** 31 50N 89 20 E
Silistea Nouă, *Romania* **29 F10** 44 23N 25 1 E
Silistra, *Bulgaria* .... **45 B11** 44 6N 27 19 E
Silivri, *Turkey* ...... **45 E12** 41 4N 28 14 E
Siljan, *Sweden* ...... **10 D8** 60 55N 14 45 E
Siljansnäs, *Sweden* ... **10 D8** 60 47N 14 52 E
Silkeborg, *Denmark* .. **11 H3** 56 10N 9 32 E
Silkwood, *Australia* .. **94 B4** 17 45 S 146 2 E
Silla, *Spain* **39 F4** 39 22N 0 25W
Sillajhuay, Cordillera,
   Chile .... **124 G5** 19 46 S 68 40W
Sillamäe, *Estonia* .... **9 G22** 59 24N 27 45 E
Sillé-le-Guillaume,
   France **18 D6** 48 10N 0 8W
Silleda, *Spain* **36 C2** 42 42N 8 14W
Silloth, *U.K.* **14 C4** 54 52N 3 23W
Šilo, *Croatia* .... **45 E9** 41 10N 22 53 E
Siloam Springs, *U.S.A.* **113 G7** 36 11N 94 32W
Silopi, *Turkey* ...... **73 D10** 37 15N 42 2 E
Silsbee, *U.S.A.* **113 K7** 30 21N 94 11W
Siluko, *Nigeria* ...... **83 D6** 6 35N 5 10 E
Šilutė, *Lithuania* .... **9 J19** 55 21N 21 33 E
Silvan, *Turkey* ...... **73 C9** 38 7N 41 2 E
Silvani, *India* .... **69 H8** 23 18N 78 25 E
Silver City, *U.S.A.* .. **109 K9** 32 46N 108 17W
Silver Cr. →, *U.S.A.* **108 E4** 43 16N 119 13W
Silver Creek, *U.S.A.* . **116 D5** 42 33N 79 10W
Silver L., *U.S.A.* **110 G6** 38 39N 120 6W
Silver Lake, *Calif.,
   U.S.A.* **111 K10** 35 21N 116 7W
Silver Lake, *Oreg.,
   U.S.A.* **108 E3** 43 8N 121 3W
Silverdalen, *Sweden* . **11 G9** 57 32N 15 45 E
Silverton, *Colo., U.S.A.* **109 H10** 37 49N 107 40W
Silverton, *Tex., U.S.A.* **113 H4** 34 28N 101 19W
Silves, *Portugal* **37 H2** 37 11N 8 26W
Silvi Marina, *Italy* ... **41 F11** 42 34N 14 5 E
Silvies →, *U.S.A.* ... **108 E4** 43 34N 119 2 E
Silvrettahorn, *Switz.* . **40 B7** 46 50N 10 6 E
Silwa Bahari, *Egypt* .. **80 C3** 24 45N 32 55 E
Silz, *Austria* .... **26 D3** 47 16N 10 56 E
Simaltala, *India* ..... **69 G12** 24 43N 86 33 E
Simanggang = Bandar
   Sri Aman, *Malaysia* **62 D4** 1 15N 111 32 E
Simao, *China* .... **58 F3** 22 47N 101 5 E
Simard, L., *Canada* .. **104 C4** 47 40N 78 40W
Şīmareh →, *Iran* .... **73 F12** 33 9N 47 41 E
Simav, *Turkey* ...... **47 B10** 39 4N 28 58 E
Simav →, *Turkey* ... **45 F12** 40 23N 28 31 E
Simav Dağları, *Turkey* **47 B10** 39 30N 29 15 E
Simba, *Tanzania* .... **86 C4** 2 10 S 37 36 E
Simbach, *Germany* ... **25 G9** 48 16N 13 2 E
Simbirsk, *Russia* .... **34 C9** 54 20N 48 25 E
Simbo, *Tanzania* .... **86 C2** 4 51 S 29 41 E
Simcoe, *Canada* **116 D4** 42 50N 80 20W
Simcoe, L., *Canada* .. **116 B5** 44 25N 79 20W
Simdega, *India* ...... **69 H11** 22 37N 84 31 E
Simenovgrad, *Bulgaria* **45 D9** 42 1N 25 59 E
Simeria, *Romania* .... **28 E8** 45 51N 23 1 E
Simeto →, *Italy* ..... **43 E8** 37 24N 15 6 E
Simeulue, *Indonesia* . **62 D1** 2 45N 95 45 E
Simferopol, *Ukraine* . **33 K8** 44 55N 34 3 E
Sími, *Greece* .... **47 E9** 36 35N 27 50 E
Simi Valley, *U.S.A.* .. **111 L8** 34 16N 118 47W
Simien Mts., *Ethiopia* **81 E4** 13 19N 38 0 E
Simikot, *Nepal* ...... **69 E9** 30 0N 81 50 E
Simitli, *Bulgaria* ..... **44 E7** 41 52N 23 7 E
Simla, *India* .... **68 D7** 31 2N 77 9 E
Simlângsdalen, *Sweden* **11 H7** 56 43N 13 6 E
Şimleu-Silvaniei,
   Romania .... **28 C7** 47 17N 22 50 E
Simmern, *Germany* ... **25 F3** 49 59N 7 32 E
Simmie, *Canada* **103 D7** 49 56N 108 6W
Simmler, *U.S.A.* **111 K7** 35 21N 119 59W
Simnas, *Lithuania* ... **30 D10** 54 24N 23 39 E
Simo älv = Simojoki →,
   Finland .... **8 D21** 65 35N 25 1 E
Simojoki →, *Finland* . **8 D21** 65 35N 25 1 E
Simojovel, *Mexico* ... **119 D6** 17 12N 92 38W
Simonette →, *Canada* **102 B5** 55 9N 118 15W
Simonstown, *S. Africa* **88 E2** 34 14 S 18 26 E
Simontornya, *Hungary* **28 D3** 46 45N 18 33 E
Simpang Empat,
   Malaysia .... **65 c** 5 27N 100 29 E

Simplonpass, Switz. ... 25 J4 46 15N 8 3 E
Simplontunnel, Switz. .. 25 J4 46 15N 8 7 E
Simpson Desert, Australia . 94 D2 25 0 S 137 0 E
Simpson Desert △, Australia . 94 C2 24 59 S 138 21 E
Simpson Pen., Canada . 101 B11 68 34N 88 45W
Simpungdong, N. Korea 57 D15 40 56N 129 29 E
Simrishamn, Sweden .. 11 J8 55 33N 14 22 E
Simsbury, U.S.A. ... 117 E12 41 53N 72 48W
Simushir, Ostrov, Russia 53 E16 46 50N 152 30 E
Sin Cowe I., S. China Sea .... 62 C4 9 53N 114 19 E
Sinabang, Indonesia .. 62 D1 2 30N 96 24 E
Sinadogo, Somali Rep. . 75 F4 5 50N 47 0 E
Sinai = Es Sînâ', Egypt 74 F3 29 0N 34 0 E
Sinai, Mt. = Mûsa, Gebel, Egypt .... 70 D2 28 33N 33 59 E
Sinai Peninsula, Egypt . 50 G7 29 30N 34 0 E
Sinaia, Romania .... 29 E10 45 21N 25 38 E
Sinaloa □, Mexico ... 118 C3 25 0N 107 30W
Sinaloa de Leyva, Mexico 118 B3 25 50N 108 20W
Sinalunga, Italy .... 41 E8 43 12N 11 4 E
Sinan, China ...... 58 D7 27 56N 108 13 E
Sinandrei, Romania .. 28 E6 45 52N 21 13 E
Sinarádhes, Greece ... 49 A3 39 34N 19 51 E
Sincan, Turkey ..... 72 B5 39 58N 32 36 E
Sincanlı, Turkey .... 47 C12 38 45N 30 15 E
Sincelejo, Colombia .. 124 B3 9 18N 75 24W
Sinch'ang, N. Korea .. 57 D15 40 7N 128 28 E
Sinchang-ni, N. Korea . 57 E14 39 24N 126 8 E
Sinclair, U.S.A. 108 F10 41 47N 107 7W
Sinclair Mills, Canada . 102 C4 54 5N 121 40W
Sinclair's B., U.K. ... 13 C5 58 31N 3 5W
Sinclairville, U.S.A. .. 116 D5 42 16N 79 16W
Sincorá, Serra do, Brazil 125 F10 13 30 S 41 0W
Sind, Pakistan ..... 68 G3 26 0N 68 30 E
Sind □, Pakistan .... 68 G3 26 0N 69 0 E
Sind →, Jammu & Kashmir, India ...... 69 B6 34 18N 74 45 E
Sind →, Mad. P., India 69 F8 26 26N 79 13 E
Sind Sagar Doab, Pakistan ...... 68 D4 32 0N 71 30 E
Sindal, Denmark .... 11 G4 57 28N 10 10 E
Sindangan, Phil. .... 61 G5 8 10N 123 5 E
Sindangbarang, Indonesia ...... 63 G12 7 27 S 107 1 E
Sinde, Zambia ..... 87 F2 17 28 S 25 51 E
Sindelfingen, Germany . 25 G4 48 42N 9 0 E
Sindh = Sind □, Pakistan 68 G3 26 0N 69 0 E
Sindri, India ...... 69 H12 23 45N 86 42 E
Sine →, Senegal 82 C1 14 10N 16 28W
Sinegorskiy, Russia .. 35 G5 47 55N 40 52 E
Sinekli, Turkey ..... 45 E12 41 14N 28 12 E
Sinelnikovo = Synelnykove, Ukraine 33 H8 48 25N 35 30 E
Sinendé, Benin ..... 83 C5 10 20N 2 22 E
Sines, Portugal 37 H2 37 56N 8 51W
Sines, C. de, Portugal . 37 H2 37 58N 8 53W
Sineu, Spain ...... 48 B10 39 38N 3 1 E
Sinfra, Ivory C. 82 D3 6 35N 5 56W
Sing Buri, Thailand .. 64 E3 14 53N 100 25 E
Singa, Sudan ...... 81 E3 13 10N 33 57 E
Singapore ■, Asia ... 65 d 1 17N 103 51 E
Singapore, Straits of, Asia .... 65 d 1 15N 104 0 E
Singapore Changi ✈ (SIN), Singapore .. 65 M4 1 23N 103 59 E
Singaraja, Indonesia .. 63 J18 8 7 S 115 6 E
Singen, Germany .... 25 H4 47 45N 8 50 E
Singida, Tanzania ... 86 C3 4 49 S 34 48 E
Singida □, Tanzania .. 86 D3 6 0 S 34 30 E
Singitikós Kólpos, Greece .... 44 F7 40 6N 24 0 E
Singkaling Hkamti, Burma .... 67 G19 26 0N 95 39 E
Singkang, Indonesia .. 63 E6 4 8 S 120 1 E
Singkawang, Indonesia 62 D3 1 0N 108 57 E
Singkep, Indonesia .. 62 E2 0 30 S 104 25 E
Singleton, Australia .. 95 E5 32 33 S 151 0 E
Singleton, Mt., N. Terr., Australia ...... 92 D5 22 0 S 130 46 E
Singleton, Mt., W. Austral., Australia 93 E2 29 27 S 117 15 E
Singö, Sweden ..... 10 D12 60 12N 18 45 E
Singoli, India ..... 68 G6 25 0N 75 22 E
Singora = Songkhla, Thailand ...... 65 J3 7 13N 100 37 E
Singosan, N. Korea .. 57 E14 38 52N 127 25 E
Sinhung, N. Korea ... 57 D14 40 11N 127 34 E
Siniátsikon, Óros, Greece .... 44 F5 40 25N 21 35 E
Siniscóla, Italy .... 42 B2 40 34N 9 41 E
Sinj, Croatia ...... 41 E13 43 42N 16 39 E
Sinjai, Indonesia .... 63 F6 5 7 S 120 20 E
Sinjajevina, Serbia & M. 44 D3 42 57N 19 22 E
Sinjär, Iraq .... 70 B4 36 19N 41 52 E
Sinkat, Sudan ..... 80 D4 18 55N 36 49 E
Sinkiang Uighur = Xinjiang Uygur Zizhiqu □, China .. 60 B3 42 0N 86 0 E
Sinmak, N. Korea ... 57 E14 38 25N 126 14 E
Sinnamary, Fr. Guiana . 125 B8 5 25N 53 0W
Sinni →, Italy ..... 43 B9 40 8N 16 41 E
Sinnuris, Egypt .... 80 J7 29 26N 30 31 E
Sinoie, Lacul, Romania 29 F13 44 35N 28 50 E
Sinop, Turkey ..... 72 A6 42 1N 35 11 E
Sinor, India ...... 68 J5 21 55N 73 20 E
Sinp'o, N. Korea .... 57 E15 40 0N 128 13 E
Sinsheim, Germany .. 25 F4 49 15N 8 52 E
Sinsk, Russia ...... 53 C13 61 8N 126 48 E
Sintang, Indonesia .. 62 D4 0 5N 111 35 E
Sinton, U.S.A. 113 L6 28 2N 97 31W
Sintra, Portugal 37 G1 38 47N 9 25W
Sintra-Cascais △, Portugal 37 G1 38 50N 9 25W
Sinŭiju, N. Korea ... 57 D13 40 5N 124 24 E
Sinyukha →, Ukraine . 33 H6 48 3N 30 51 E
Sinzig, Germany .... 24 E3 50 32N 7 4 E
Sio →, Hungary .... 28 D3 46 20N 18 53 E
Siocon, Phil. ...... 61 H5 7 40N 122 10 E
Siófok, Hungary .... 28 D3 46 54N 18 3 E
Sion, Switz. ...... 25 J3 46 14N 7 20 E
Sion Mills, U.K. 12 B4 54 48N 7 29W
Sioux City, U.S.A. .. 112 D6 42 30N 96 24W
Sioux Falls, U.S.A. .. 112 D6 43 33N 96 44W
Sioux Lookout, Canada 104 B1 50 10N 91 50W
Sioux Narrows, Canada 103 D10 49 25N 94 10W
Sipalay, Phil. ..... 61 G5 9 45N 122 24 E
Sipan, Croatia ..... 44 D1 42 45N 17 52 E
Siparia, Trin. & Tob. .. 125 K15 10 8N 61 31W
Sipil Daği △, Turkey .. 47 C9 38 35N 27 30 E

Siping, China .... 57 C13 43 8N 124 21 E
Sipiwesk L., Canada .. 103 B9 55 5N 97 35W
Siple, Antarctica .... 5 D7 75 0 S 74 0 E
Sipovo, Bos.-H. .... 28 F2 44 16N 17 6 E
Sipra →, India ..... 68 H6 23 55N 75 28 E
Sipura, Indonesia ... 62 E1 2 18 S 99 40 E
Siquia →, Nic. 120 D3 12 10N 84 20W
Siquijor, Phil. ..... 61 G5 9 12N 123 35 E
Siquirres, Costa Rica . 120 D3 10 6N 83 30W
Şîr Abu Nu'ayr, U.A.E. 71 E7 25 20N 54 20 E
Şîr Banî Yâs, U.A.E. . 71 E7 24 19N 52 37 E
Sir Edward Pellew Group, Australia .. 94 B2 15 40 S 137 10 E
Sir Graham Moore Is., Australia ...... 92 B4 13 53 S 126 34 E
Sir James MacBrien, Mt., Canada 100 B7 62 7N 127 41W
Sira →, Norway .... 9 G12 58 23N 6 34 E
Siracusa, Italy ..... 43 E8 37 4N 15 17 E
Sirajganj, Bangla. ... 69 G13 24 25N 89 47 E
Sirakoro, Mali 82 C3 12 41N 9 14W
Sirasso, Ivory C. 82 D3 9 16N 6 6W
Sirathu, India ..... 69 G9 25 39N 81 19 E
Siret, Romania ..... 29 C11 47 55N 26 5 E
Siret →, Romania ... 29 E12 45 24N 28 1 E
Sirghâyâ, Syria .... 74 B5 33 51N 36 8 E
Siria, Romania ..... 28 D6 46 16N 21 38 E
Sirino, Mte., Italy ... 43 B8 40 7N 15 50 E
Sîrjân, Iran .... 71 D7 29 30N 55 45 E
Sirmaur, India ..... 69 G9 24 51N 81 23 E
Sírna, Greece ...... 47 E8 36 22N 26 42 E
Şırnak, Turkey ..... 73 D10 37 31N 42 46 E
Sirohi, India ...... 68 G5 24 52N 72 53 E
Sironj, India ...... 68 G7 24 5N 77 39 E
Síros, Greece ...... 46 D6 37 28N 24 57 E
Sirretta Pk., U.S.A. .. 111 K8 35 56N 118 19W
Sîrrî, Iran .... 71 E7 25 55N 54 32 E
Sirsa, India ...... 68 E6 29 33N 75 4 E
Sirsa →, India ..... 69 F8 26 51N 79 4 E
Siruela, Spain 37 G5 38 58N 5 3W
Sisak, Croatia ..... 41 C13 45 30N 16 21 E
Sisaket, Thailand ... 64 E5 15 8N 104 23 E
Sisante, Spain 39 F2 39 25N 2 12W
Sisargas, Is., Spain .. 36 B2 43 21N 8 50W
Sishen, S. Africa .... 88 D3 27 47 S 22 59 E
Sishui, Henan, China . 56 G7 34 48N 113 15 E
Sishui, Shandong, China 57 G9 35 42N 117 18 E
Sisipuk L., Canada ... 103 B8 55 45N 101 50W
Sisophon, Cambodia .. 64 F4 13 38N 102 59 E
Sisseton, U.S.A. 112 C6 45 40N 97 3W
Sissonne, France .... 19 C10 49 34N 3 51 E
Sīstān, Asia ...... 71 D9 30 50N 61 0 E
Sīstān, Daryâcheh-ye, Iran .... 71 D9 31 0N 61 0 E
Sīstān va Balūchestān □, Iran .... 71 E9 27 0N 62 0 E
Sisteron, France .... 21 D9 44 12N 5 57 E
Sisters, U.S.A. 108 D3 44 18N 121 33W
Siswa Bazar, India .. 69 F10 27 9N 83 46 E
Sitakili, Mali 82 C2 13 7N 11 14W
Sitamarhi, India .... 69 F11 26 37N 85 30 E
Sitampiky, Madag. ... 89 B8 16 41 S 46 6 E
Sitapur, India ..... 69 F9 27 38N 80 45 E
Siteki, Swaziland ... 89 D5 26 32 S 31 58 E
Sitges, Spain ..... 38 D6 41 17N 1 47 E
Sithonía, Greece .... 44 F7 40 0N 23 45 E
Sitía, Greece ...... 49 D8 35 13N 26 6 E
Sitka, U.S.A. 102 B1 57 3N 135 20W
Sitoti, Botswana .... 88 C3 23 15 S 23 40 E
Sitra, Egypt ...... 80 B2 28 40N 26 53 E
Sittang Myit →, Burma 67 L20 17 20N 96 45 E
Sittard, Neths. ..... 17 C5 51 0N 5 52 E
Sittensen, Germany .. 24 B5 53 17N 9 32 E
Sittingbourne, U.K. .. 15 F8 51 21N 0 45 E
Sittona, Eritrea .... 81 E4 14 25N 37 23 E
Sittoung = Sittang Myit →, Burma .. 67 L20 17 20N 96 45 E
Sittwe, Burma ..... 67 J18 20 18N 92 45 E
Situbondo, Indonesia . 63 G16 7 42 S 114 0 E
Siuna, Nic. 120 D3 13 37N 84 45W
Siuri, India ...... 69 H12 23 50N 87 34 E
Siutghiol, Lacul, Romania .... 29 F13 44 15N 28 35 E
Sīvand, Iran ...... 71 D7 30 5N 52 55 E
Sivas, Turkey ..... 70 B3 39 43N 36 58 E
Sivaslı, Turkey ..... 47 C11 38 31N 29 42 E
Siverek, Turkey .... 70 B3 37 50N 39 19 E
Sivrihisar, Turkey ... 72 C4 39 30N 31 35 E
Sîwa, Egypt ...... 80 B2 29 11N 25 31 E
Sîwa, El Wâhât es, Egypt 80 B2 29 10N 25 30 E
Siwa Oasis = Sîwa, El Wâhât es, Egypt, El 80 B2 29 10N 25 30 E
Siwalik Range, Nepal . 69 F10 28 0N 83 0 E
Siwan, India ...... 69 F11 26 13N 84 21 E
Siwana, India ..... 68 G5 25 38N 72 25 E
Six Cross Roads, Barbados .... 121 g 13 7N 59 28W
Sixmilebridge, Ireland . 12 D3 52 44N 8 46W
Sixth Cataract, Sudan . 81 D3 16 20N 32 42 E
Siyäl, Jazâ'ir, Egypt . 80 C4 22 49N 36 12 E
Siyäzän, Azerbaijan .. 35 K9 41 3N 49 10 E
Siziwang Qi, China .. 56 D6 41 25N 111 40 E
Sjælland, Denmark .. 11 J5 55 30N 11 30 E
Sjællands Odde, Denmark .... 11 J5 55 58N 11 24 E
Sjenica, Serbia & M. . 44 C3 43 16N 20 0 E
Sjöbo, Sweden ..... 11 J7 55 37N 13 45 E
Sjötorp, Sweden .... 11 F7 58 22N 13 17 E
Sjötorp, Sweden .... 11 F8 58 50N 14 0 E
Sjumen = Shumen, Bulgaria .... 45 C10 43 18N 26 55 E
Sjuntorp, Sweden ... 11 F6 58 12N 12 13 E
Skadarsko Jezero, Serbia & M. .... 44 D3 42 10N 19 20 E
Skadovsk, Ukraine .. 33 J7 46 17N 32 52 E
Skælskør, Denmark .. 11 J5 55 15N 11 18 E
Skærbæk, Denmark .. 11 J2 55 9N 8 45 E
Skaftafell, Iceland ... 8 D5 64 1N 17 0W
Skagaförður, Iceland . 8 D4 65 54N 19 35W
Skagastølstindane, Norway .... 9 F12 61 28N 7 52 E
Skagaströnd, Iceland . 8 D3 65 50N 20 19W
Skagen, Denmark ... 11 G4 57 43N 10 35 E
Skagern, Sweden ... 10 E8 59 0N 14 20 E
Skagerrak, Denmark . 11 G2 57 30N 9 0 E
Skagit →, U.S.A. ... 110 B4 48 23N 122 22W
Skagway, U.S.A. 100 C6 59 28N 135 19W
Skala-Podilska, Ukraine 29 B11 48 50N 26 15 E

Skala Podolskaya = Skala-Podilska, Ukraine ...... 29 B11 48 50N 26 15 E
Skalat, Ukraine .... 33 H3 49 23N 25 55 E
Skalbmierz, Poland .. 31 H7 50 20N 20 25 E
Skälderviken, Sweden . 11 H6 56 22N 12 30 E
Skalica, Slovak Rep. .. 27 C10 48 50N 17 15 E
Skallingen, Denmark . 11 J2 55 32N 8 13 E
Skalni Dol = Kamenyak, Bulgaria .... 45 C10 43 24N 26 57 E
Skanderborg, Denmark 11 H3 56 2N 9 55 E
Skaneateles, U.S.A. .. 117 D8 42 57N 76 26W
Skaneateles L., U.S.A. 117 D8 42 51N 76 22W
Skänninge, Sweden .. 11 F9 58 24N 15 5 E
Skanör med Falsterbo, Sweden .... 11 J6 55 24N 12 50 E
Skantzoúra, Greece .. 46 B6 39 5N 24 6 E
Skara, Sweden ..... 11 F7 58 25N 13 30 E
Skärblacka, Sweden .. 11 F9 58 33N 15 54 E
Skardu, Pakistan ... 69 B6 35 20N 75 44 E
Skåre, Sweden ..... 10 E7 59 26N 13 26 E
Skärhamn, Sweden .. 11 G5 57 59N 11 34 E
Skarszewy, Poland .. 30 D5 54 4N 18 25 E
Skaryszew, Poland .. 31 G8 51 19N 21 15 E
Skarżysko-Kamienna, Poland .... 31 G7 51 7N 20 52 E
Skattkärr, Sweden .. 10 E7 59 25N 13 40 E
Skattungbyn, Sweden . 10 C8 61 10N 14 56 E
Skawina, Poland .... 31 J6 49 59N 19 50 E
Skebokvarn, Sweden . 10 E12 59 58N 18 36 E
Skeena →, Canada .. 102 C2 54 9N 130 5 E
Skeena Mts., Canada . 102 B3 56 40N 128 30W
Skegness, U.K. .... 14 D8 53 9N 0 20 E
Skeldon, Guyana ... 124 B7 5 55N 57 20W
Skeleton Coast, Namibia 85 H2 20 0 S 13 0 E
Skeleton Coast △, Namibia .... 88 C1 20 0 S 13 0 E
Skellefteå, Sweden .. 8 D19 64 45N 20 50 E
Skellefteälven →, Sweden .... 8 D19 64 45N 21 10 E
Skelleftehamn, Sweden 8 D19 64 40N 21 9 E
Skender Vakuf, Bos.-H. 28 F2 44 29N 17 22 E
Skerries, The, U.K. .. 14 D3 53 25N 4 36W
Skhidnytsya, Ukraine . 31 J10 49 13N 23 20 E
Skhíza, Greece ..... 46 E3 36 41N 21 40 E
Skhoinoúsa, Greece .. 47 E7 36 53N 25 31 E
Ski, Norway ...... 9 G14 59 43N 10 52 E
Skíathos, Greece .... 46 B5 39 12N 23 30 E
Skibbereen, Ireland .. 12 E2 51 33N 9 16W
Skiddaw, U.K. 14 C4 54 39N 3 9W
Skidegate, Canada .. 102 C2 53 15N 132 1W
Skídhra, Greece .... 44 F6 40 46N 22 10 E
Skien, Norway ..... 9 G13 59 12N 9 35 E
Skierniewice, Poland . 31 G7 51 58N 20 10 E
Skikda, Algeria .... 78 A7 36 50N 6 58 E
Skillingaryd, Sweden . 11 G8 57 27N 14 5 E
Skillinge, Sweden ... 11 J8 55 30N 14 16 E
Skilloura, Cyprus ... 49 D12 35 14N 33 10 E
Skinári, Ákra, Greece . 46 D2 37 56N 20 42 E
Skinnskatteberg, Sweden 10 E9 59 50N 15 42 E
Skipton, U.K. 14 D5 53 58N 2 3W
Skiring, C., Senegal .. 82 C1 12 26N 16 46W
Skirmish Pt., Australia . 94 A1 11 59 S 134 17 E
Skiropoúla, Greece .. 46 C6 38 50N 24 21 E
Skíros, Greece ..... 46 B6 38 55N 24 34 E
Skivarp, Sweden ... 11 J7 55 26N 13 34 E
Skive, Denmark .... 11 H3 56 33N 9 2 E
Skjálfandafljót →, Iceland 8 D5 65 59N 17 25W
Skjálfandi, Iceland ... 8 C5 66 5N 17 30W
Skjern, Denmark .... 11 J2 55 57N 8 30 E
Skoczów, Poland ... 31 J5 49 49N 18 45 E
Škofja Loka, Slovenia . 41 B11 46 9N 14 19 E
Skoghall, Sweden ... 10 E7 59 20N 13 30 E
Skogstorp, Sweden .. 10 E10 59 19N 16 29 E
Skoki, Poland ..... 31 F4 52 40N 17 11 E
Skole, Ukraine ..... 33 H2 49 3N 23 30 E
Skópelos, Greece ... 46 B5 39 9N 23 47 E
Skopí, Greece ..... 49 D8 35 11N 26 2 E
Skopin, Russia ..... 34 D4 53 55N 39 32 E
Skopje, Macedonia .. 44 D5 42 1N 21 26 E
Skopje ✈ (SKP), Macedonia ...... 44 E5 41 59N 21 24 E
Skórcz, Poland ..... 30 E5 53 47N 18 30 E
Skørping, Denmark .. 11 H3 56 50N 9 53 E
Skövde, Sweden .... 11 F7 58 24N 13 50 E
Skovorodino, Russia . 53 D13 54 0N 124 0 E
Skowhegan, U.S.A. .. 115 C11 44 46N 69 43W
Skradin, Croatia .... 41 E12 43 52N 15 53 E
Skrea, Sweden ..... 11 H6 56 53N 12 34 E
Skrunda, Latvia .... 30 B9 56 41N 22 1 E
Skrwa →, Poland ... 31 F6 52 35N 19 32 E
Skukuza, S. Africa .. 89 D5 24 59 S 31 35 E
Skull, Ireland 12 E2 51 32N 9 34W
Skultorp, Sweden ... 11 F7 58 24N 13 51 E
Skultuna, Sweden ... 10 E10 59 43N 16 25 E
Skunk →, U.S.A. ... 112 E9 40 42N 91 7W
Skuodas, Lithuania .. 9 H19 56 16N 21 33 E
Skurup, Sweden .... 11 J7 55 28N 13 30 E
Skutskär, Sweden ... 10 D11 60 37N 17 25 E
Skvyra, Ukraine .... 33 H5 49 44N 29 40 E
Skwierzyna, Poland .. 31 F2 52 33N 15 30 E
Skye, U.K. 13 D2 57 15N 6 10W
Skykomish, U.S.A. .. 108 C3 47 42N 121 22W
Skyros = Skíros, Greece 46 C6 38 55N 24 34 E
Skyttorp, Sweden ... 10 D11 60 5N 17 44 E
Slade Pt., Australia .. 94 K7 21 5 S 149 13 E
Slættaratindur, Færoe Is. 8 E9 62 18N 7 1W
Slagelse, Denmark .. 11 J5 55 23N 11 19 E
Slamet, Indonesia ... 63 G13 7 16 S 109 8 E
Slaney →, Ireland .. 12 D5 52 26N 6 33W
Slangberge, S. Africa . 88 E3 31 32 S 20 48 E
Slănic, Romania .... 29 E10 45 14N 25 58 E
Slano, Croatia ..... 44 D1 42 48N 17 53 E
Slantsy, Russia .... 32 C5 59 7N 28 5 E
Slaný, Czech Rep. ... 26 A7 50 13N 14 6 E
Śląskie □, Poland ... 31 H6 50 20N 19 0 E
Slätbaken, Sweden .. 11 F10 58 25N 16 45 E
Slate Is., Canada 104 C2 48 40N 87 0W
Slatina, Croatia .... 28 E2 45 42N 17 45 E
Slatina, Romania ... 29 F9 44 28N 24 22 E
Slatina Timiş, Romania 28 E7 45 15N 22 16 E
Slatington, U.S.A. .. 117 F9 40 45N 75 37W
Slaton, U.S.A. 113 J4 33 26N 101 39W
Slave →, Canada ... 102 A6 61 18N 113 39W
Slave Coast, W. Afr. . 83 D5 6 0N 2 30 E
Slave Lake, Canada .. 102 B6 55 17N 114 43W
Slave Pt., Canada ... 102 A5 61 11N 115 56W
Slavgorod, Russia ... 52 D8 53 1N 78 37 E
Slavinja, Serbia & M. . 44 C6 43 8N 22 50 E

Slavonski Brod, Croatia 28 E3 45 11N 18 1 E
Slavsk, Russia ..... 30 C8 55 3N 21 30 E
Slavska, Ukraine .... 29 B8 48 51N 23 27 E
Slavskoye, Russia ... 30 D7 54 30N 20 27 E
Slavuta, Ukraine .... 33 G4 50 15N 27 2 E
Slavyanka, Russia ... 54 C5 42 53N 131 21 E
Slavyanovo, Bulgaria . 45 C8 43 28N 24 52 E
Slavyansk = Slovyansk, Ukraine ...... 33 H9 48 55N 37 36 E
Slavyansk-na-Kubani, Russia .... 33 K10 45 15N 38 11 E
Sława, Poland ..... 31 G3 51 52N 16 2 E
Slawharad, Belarus .. 32 F6 53 27N 31 0 E
Sławno, Poland .... 30 D3 54 20N 16 41 E
Sławoborze, Poland .. 30 E2 53 55N 15 42 E
Sleaford, U.K. 14 D7 53 0N 0 24W
Sleaford B., Australia . 95 E2 34 55 S 135 45 E
Sleeper Is., Canada .. 101 C11 58 30N 81 0W
Sleeping Bear Dunes △, U.S.A. 114 C2 44 50N 86 5W
Sleepy Eye, U.S.A. .. 112 C7 44 18N 94 43W
Slemon L., Canada .. 102 A5 63 13N 116 4W
Slesin, Poland ..... 31 F5 52 22N 18 14 E
Slide Mt., U.S.A. ... 117 E10 42 0N 74 25W
Slidell, U.S.A. 113 K10 30 17N 89 47W
Sliema, Malta ..... 49 D2 35 55N 14 30 E
Slieve Aughty, Ireland . 12 C3 53 4N 8 30W
Slieve Bloom, Ireland . 12 C4 53 4N 7 40W
Slieve Donard, Ireland 12 B6 54 11N 5 55W
Slieve Gamph, Ireland 12 B3 54 6N 9 0W
Slieve Gullion, Ireland 12 B5 54 7N 6 26W
Slieve League, Ireland 12 B3 54 40N 8 42W
Slieve Mish, Ireland .. 12 D2 52 12N 9 50W
Slievenamon, Ireland . 12 D4 52 25N 7 34W
Sligeach = Sligo, Ireland 12 B3 54 16N 8 28W
Sligo, Ireland 12 B3 54 16N 8 28W
Sligo, U.S.A. 116 E5 41 6N 79 29W
Sligo □, Ireland 12 B3 54 8N 8 42W
Sligo B., Ireland 12 B3 54 18N 8 40W
Slippery Rock, U.S.A. . 116 E4 41 3N 80 3W
Slite, Sweden ..... 11 G12 57 42N 18 48 E
Sliven, Bulgaria .... 45 D10 42 42N 26 19 E
Slivnitsa, Bulgaria .. 44 D7 42 50N 23 0 E
Sljeme, Croatia .... 41 C12 45 57N 15 58 E
Sloan, U.S.A. 111 K11 35 57N 115 13W
Sloansville, U.S.A. .. 117 D10 42 45N 74 22W
Slobidka, Ukraine ... 29 C14 47 54N 29 21 E
Slobozia, Moldova .. 29 D14 46 45N 29 42 E
Slobozia, Argeş, Romania .... 29 F10 44 30N 25 14 E
Slobozia, Ialomiţa, Romania .... 29 F12 44 34N 27 23 E
Slocan, Canada 102 D5 49 48N 117 28W
Słomniki, Poland ... 31 H7 50 16N 20 4 E
Slonim, Belarus .... 33 F3 53 4N 25 19 E
Slough, U.K. 15 F7 51 30N 0 36W
Slough □, U.K. 15 F7 51 30N 0 36W
Sloughhouse, U.S.A. . 110 G5 38 26N 121 12W
Slovak Rep. ■, Europe 27 C13 48 30N 20 0 E
Slovakia = Slovak Rep. ■, Europe .. 27 C13 48 30N 20 0 E
Slovakian Ore Mts. = Slovenské Rudohorie, Slovak Rep. ..... 27 C12 48 45N 20 0 E
Slovenia ■, Europe .. 41 C11 45 58N 14 30 E
Slovenija = Slovenia ■, Europe .... 41 C11 45 58N 14 30 E
Slovenj Gradec, Slovenia 41 B12 46 31N 15 5 E
Slovenska Bistrica, Slovenia .... 41 B12 46 24N 15 35 E
Slovenské Konjice, Slovenia .... 41 B12 46 20N 15 28 E
Slovenské Rudohorie, Slovak Rep. .... 27 C12 48 45N 20 0 E
Slovenský Raj △, Slovak Rep. .... 27 C13 48 53N 20 25 E
Slovyansk, Ukraine .. 33 H9 48 55N 37 36 E
Słowiński □, Poland .. 30 D3 54 35N 17 20 E
Słubice, Poland .... 31 F1 52 22N 14 35 E
Sluch →, Ukraine ... 33 G4 51 37N 26 38 E
Sluis, Neths. ...... 17 C3 51 18N 3 23 E
Slünchev Bryag, Bulgaria .... 45 D11 42 40N 27 41 E
Slunj, Croatia ..... 41 C12 45 6N 15 33 E
Słupca, Poland ..... 31 F4 52 15N 17 52 E
Słupia →, Poland ... 30 D3 54 35N 16 51 E
Słupsk, Poland .... 30 D3 54 30N 17 3 E
Slurry, S. Africa .... 88 D4 25 49 S 25 42 E
Slutsk, Belarus .... 33 F4 53 2N 27 31 E
Slyne Hd., Ireland ... 12 C1 53 25N 10 10W
Slyudyanka, Russia .. 53 D11 51 40N 103 40 E
Småland, Sweden ... 11 G9 57 15N 15 25 E
Smålandsfarvandet, Denmark .... 11 J5 55 10N 11 20 E
Smålandsstenar, Sweden 11 G7 57 10N 13 25 E
Smalltree L., Canada . 103 A8 61 0N 105 0W
Smallwood Res., Canada 105 B7 54 5N 64 30W
Smarhon, Belarus ... 32 E4 54 20N 26 24 E
Smarje, Slovenia ... 41 B12 46 15N 15 34 E
Smartt Syndicate Dam, S. Africa ...... 88 E3 30 45 S 23 10 E
Smartville, U.S.A. .. 110 F5 39 13N 121 18W
Smeaton, Canada ... 103 C8 53 30N 104 49W
Smederevo, Serbia & M. 44 B4 44 40N 20 57 E
Smederevska Palanka, Serbia & M. .... 44 B4 44 22N 20 58 E
Smedjebacken, Sweden 10 D9 60 8N 15 25 E
Smela = Smila, Ukraine 33 H6 49 15N 31 58 E
Smerwick Harbour, Ireland 12 D1 52 12N 10 23W
Smethport, U.S.A. .. 116 E6 41 49N 78 27W
Smidovich, Russia ... 53 E14 48 36N 133 49 E
Śmigiel, Poland .... 31 F3 52 1N 16 32 E
Smila, Ukraine ..... 33 H6 49 15N 31 58 E
Smilyan, Bulgaria ... 45 E8 41 29N 24 46 E
Smith, Canada 102 B6 55 10N 114 0W
Smith Center, U.S.A. . 112 F5 39 47N 98 47W
Smith River △, U.S.A. 108 F2 41 55N 124 0W
Smith Sd., N. Amer. . 4 B4 78 25N 74 0W
Smithburne →, Australia .... 94 B3 17 3 S 140 57 E
Smithers, Canada ... 102 C3 54 45N 127 10W
Smithfield, S. Africa . 89 E4 30 9 S 26 30 E
Smithfield, N.C., U.S.A. 115 H6 35 31N 78 21W
Smithfield, Utah, U.S.A. 108 F8 41 50N 111 50W
Smiths Falls, Canada . 117 B9 44 55N 76 0W
Smithton, Australia .. 95 G4 40 53 S 145 6 E
Smithville, Canada .. 116 C5 43 6N 79 33W
Smithville, U.S.A. ... 113 K6 30 1N 97 10W
Smoky →, Canada .. 102 B5 56 10N 117 21W
Smoky Bay, Australia . 95 E1 32 22 S 134 13 E
Smoky Hill →, U.S.A. 112 F6 39 4N 96 48W
Smoky Hills, U.S.A. . 112 F5 39 15N 99 30W
Smoky Lake, Canada . 102 C6 54 10N 112 30W

Smøla, Norway .... 8 E13 63 23N 8 3 E
Smolensk, Russia ... 32 E7 54 45N 32 5 E
Smolikas, Óros, Greece 44 F4 40 9N 20 58 E
Smolník, Slovak Rep. . 27 C14 48 43N 20 44 E
Smooth Rock Falls, Canada 104 C3 49 17N 81 37W
Smoothstone L., Canada 103 C7 54 40N 106 50W
Smorgon = Smarhon, Belarus .... 32 E4 54 20N 26 24 E
Smotrich, Ukraine ... 29 B11 48 50N 26 33 E
Smotrych →, Ukraine 29 B11 48 34N 26 39 E
Smulţi, Romania .... 29 E12 45 57N 27 44 E
Smyadovo, Bulgaria . 45 C11 43 2N 27 1 E
Smygehamn, Sweden . 11 J7 55 21N 13 22 E
Smyrna = İzmir, Turkey 47 C9 38 25N 27 8 E
Smyrna, U.S.A. 114 F8 39 18N 75 36W
Snæfell, Iceland 8 D6 64 48N 15 34W
Snaefell, I. of Man .. 14 C3 54 16N 4 27W
Snæfellsjökull, Iceland 8 D2 64 49N 23 46W
Snake →, U.S.A. ... 108 C4 46 12N 119 2W
Snake I., Australia ... 95 F4 38 47 S 146 33 E
Snake Range, U.S.A. . 108 G6 39 0N 114 20W
Snake River Plain, U.S.A. 108 E7 42 50N 114 0W
Snasahögarna, Sweden 10 A6 63 13N 12 21 E
Snåsavatnet, Norway . 8 D14 64 12N 12 0 E
Snedsted, Denmark .. 11 H2 56 55N 8 32 E
Sneek, Neths. ..... 17 A5 53 2N 5 40 E
Sneeuberge, S. Africa 88 E3 31 46 S 24 20 E
Snejbjerg, Denmark .. 11 H2 56 8N 8 54 E
Snelling, U.S.A. 110 H6 37 31N 120 26W
Snezhnoye, Ukraine . 33 J10 48 0N 38 58 E
Snežnik, Slovenia ... 41 C11 45 36N 14 35 E
Śniadowo, Poland ... 31 E8 53 2N 22 0 E
Sniardwy, Jezioro, Poland .... 30 E8 53 48N 21 50 E
Śnieżka, Europe .... 26 A8 50 44N 15 44 E
Snigirevka = Snihurivka, Ukraine ...... 33 J7 47 2N 32 49 E
Snihurivka, Ukraine . 33 J7 47 2N 32 49 E
Snina, Slovak Rep. .. 27 C15 48 58N 22 9 E
Snizort, L., U.K. 13 D2 57 33N 6 28W
Snøhetta, Norway ... 9 E13 62 19N 9 16 E
Snohomish, U.S.A. .. 110 C4 47 55N 122 6W
Snoul, Cambodia ... 65 F6 12 4N 106 26 E
Snow Hill, U.S.A. ... 114 F8 38 11N 75 24W
Snow Lake, Canada .. 103 C8 54 52N 100 3W
Snow Mt., Calif., U.S.A. 110 F4 39 23N 122 45W
Snow Mt., Maine, U.S.A. 117 A14 45 18N 70 48W
Snow Shoe, U.S.A. .. 116 E7 41 2N 77 57W
Snowbird L., Canada . 103 A8 60 45N 103 0W
Snowdon, U.K. 14 D3 53 4N 4 5W
Snowdonia □, U.K. .. 14 D4 53 7N 3 59W
Snowdrift = Łutselk'e, Canada 103 A6 62 24N 110 44W
Snowdrift →, Canada 103 A6 62 24N 110 44W
Snowflake, U.S.A. .. 109 J8 34 30N 110 5W
Snowshoe Pk., U.S.A. 108 B6 48 13N 115 41W
Snowtown, Australia . 95 E2 33 46 S 138 14 E
Snowville, U.S.A. ... 108 F7 41 58N 112 43W
Snowy →, Australia . 95 F4 37 46 S 148 30 E
Snowy Mt., U.S.A. .. 117 C10 43 42N 74 23W
Snowy Mts., Australia 95 F4 36 30 S 148 20 E
Snug Corner, Bahamas 121 B5 22 33N 73 52W
Snyatyn, Ukraine ... 29 B10 48 27N 25 38 E
Snyder, Okla., U.S.A. . 113 H5 34 40N 98 57W
Snyder, Tex., U.S.A. . 113 J4 32 44N 100 55W
Soahanina, Madag. .. 89 B7 18 42 S 44 13 E
Soalala, Madag. .... 89 B8 16 6 S 45 20 E
Soaloka, Madag. .... 89 B8 18 32 S 45 15 E
Soamanonga, Madag. . 89 C7 23 52 S 44 47 E
Soan →, Pakistan .. 68 C4 33 1N 71 44 E
Soanierana-Ivongo, Madag. .... 89 B8 16 55 S 49 35 E
Soars, Romania .... 29 E9 45 56N 24 55 E
Soavina, Madag. ... 89 C8 20 23 S 46 56 E
Soavinandriana, Madag. 89 B8 19 9 S 46 45 E
Sob →, Ukraine .... 29 B14 48 40N 29 15 E
Soba, Nigeria ..... 83 C6 10 58N 8 4 E
Sobat →, Sudan ... 81 F3 9 22N 31 33 E
Sobhapur, India .... 68 H8 22 47N 78 17 E
Sobinka, Russia .... 32 E11 56 0N 40 0 E
Sobótka, Poland ... 31 H3 50 54N 16 44 E
Sobra, Croatia ..... 41 F14 42 44N 17 34 E
Sobradinho, Reprêsa de, Brazil .... 125 E10 9 30 S 42 0W
Sobral, Brazil ..... 125 D10 3 50 S 40 20W
Sobrance, Slovak Rep. 27 C15 48 45N 22 11 E
Sobreira Formosa, Portugal 36 F3 39 46N 7 51W
Soc Giang, Vietnam .. 58 F6 22 54N 106 1 E
Soc Trang, Vietnam .. 65 H5 9 37N 105 50 E
Soča →, Europe .... 26 E6 46 20N 13 40 E
Socastee, U.S.A. ... 115 J6 33 41N 79 1W
Soch'e = Shache, China 60 C2 38 20N 77 10 E
Sochi, Russia ..... 35 J4 43 35N 39 40 E
Société, Is. de la, French Polynesia . 97 J12 17 0 S 151 0W
Society Is. = Société, Is. de la, French Polynesia . 97 J12 17 0 S 151 0W
Socompa, Portezuelo de, Chile .... 126 A2 24 27 S 68 18W
Socorro, N. Mex., U.S.A. 109 J10 34 4N 106 54W
Socorro, Tex., U.S.A. . 109 L10 31 39N 106 18W
Socorro, I., Mexico .. 118 D2 18 45N 110 58W
Socotra, Yemen .... 75 E5 12 30N 54 0 E
Socovos, Spain 39 G3 38 20N 1 58W
Socuéllamos, Spain .. 39 F2 39 16N 2 47W
Soda L., U.S.A. 109 J5 35 10N 116 4W
Soda Plains, India ... 69 B8 35 30N 79 0 E
Soda Springs, U.S.A. . 108 E8 42 39N 111 36W
Sodankylä, Finland .. 8 C22 67 29N 26 40 E
Soddy-Daisy, U.S.A. . 115 H3 35 17N 85 10W
Söderåkra, Sweden .. 11 H10 56 1N 16 55 E
Söderbärke, Sweden . 10 D9 60 8N 15 18 E
Söderfors, Sweden .. 10 D11 60 23N 17 25 E
Söderhamn, Sweden . 10 C11 61 18N 17 10 E
Söderköping, Sweden . 11 F10 58 31N 16 35 E
Södermanland, Sweden 9 G17 58 56N 16 55 E
Södermanlands län □, Sweden .... 10 E10 59 10N 16 30 E
Södertälje, Sweden .. 10 E11 59 12N 17 39 E
Sodiri, Sudan ..... 81 E2 14 27N 29 0 E
Sodo, Ethiopia ..... 81 F4 7 0N 37 41 E
Södra Dellen, Sweden 10 C10 61 48N 16 43 E
Södra Finnskoga, Sweden .... 10 D6 60 42N 12 34 E
Södra Sandby, Sweden 11 J7 55 43N 13 21 E
Södra Ulvön, Sweden 10 A13 63 0N 18 40 E
Södra Vi, Sweden ... 11 G9 57 45N 15 45 E
Sodražica, Slovenia .. 41 C11 45 45N 14 39 E

Sodus, U.S.A. **116 C7** 43 14N 77 4W
Sodwana Bay △,
S. Africa ...... **89 D5** 27 35 S 32 43 E
Soekmekaar, S. Africa **89 C4** 23 30 S 29 55 E
Soest, Germany ..... **24 D4** 51 34N 8 7 E
Soest, Neths. ...... **17 B5** 52 9N 5 19 E
Sofádhes, Greece .... **46 B4** 39 20N 22 4 E
Sofara, Mali **82 C4** 13 59N 4 9W
Sofia = Sofiya, Bulgaria **44 D7** 42 45N 23 20 E
Sofia →, Madag. .... **89 B8** 15 27 S 47 23 E
Sofikón, Greece ..... **46 D5** 37 47N 23 3 E
Sofiya, Bulgaria .... **44 D7** 42 45N 23 20 E
Sofiya □, Bulgaria ... **44 D7** 42 15N 23 0 E
Sofiya ✈ (SOF),
Bulgaria ...... **44 D7** 42 46N 23 28 E
Sōfu-Gan, Japan .... **55 K10** 29 49N 140 21 E
Sogakofe, Ghana .... **83 D5** 6 2N 0 39 E
Sogamoso, Colombia . **124 B4** 5 43N 72 56W
Sogār, Iran .... **71 E8** 25 53N 58 6 E
Sögel, Germany .... **24 C3** 52 50N 7 31 E
Sogndalsfjøra, Norway **9 F12** 61 14N 7 5 E
Søgne, Norway ..... **9 G12** 58 5N 7 48 E
Sognefjorden, Norway **9 F11** 61 10N 5 50 E
Söğüt, Bilecik, Turkey **47 A12** 40 2N 30 11 E
Söğüt, Burdur, Turkey . **47 D11** 37 2N 29 50 E
Söğüt Dağı, Turkey .. **47 D11** 37 50N 29 55 E
Söğütköy, Turkey ... **47 E10** 36 40N 28 45 E
Sögwipo, S. Korea ... **57 H14** 33 13N 126 34 E
Soh, Iran .... **71 C6** 33 26N 51 27 E
Sohâg, Egypt ...... **80 B3** 26 33N 31 43 E
Sohagpur, India .... **68 H8** 22 42N 78 12 E
Sŏhori, N. Korea .... **57 D15** 40 7N 128 23 E
Soignies, Belgium ... **17 D4** 50 35N 4 5 E
Soin, Burkina Faso .. **82 C4** 12 47N 3 50W
Soira, Eritrea ..... **81 E4** 14 45N 39 30 E
Soissons, France .... **19 C10** 49 25N 3 19 E
Sojat, India ...... **68 G5** 25 55N 73 45 E
Sok →, Russia ..... **34 D10** 53 24N 50 8 E
Sokal, Ukraine ..... **33 G3** 50 31N 24 15 E
Söke, Turkey ...... **47 D9** 37 48N 27 28 E
Sokelo, Dem. Rep. of
the Congo ...... **87 D1** 9 55 S 24 36 E
Sokhós, Greece ..... **44 F7** 40 48N 23 22 E
Sokhumi, Georgia ... **35 J5** 43 0N 41 0 E
Soko Banja, Serbia & M. **44 C5** 43 40N 21 51 E
Sokodé, Togo ..... **83 D5** 9 0N 1 11 E
Sokol, Russia ..... **32 C11** 59 30N 40 5 E
Sokolac, Bos.-H. ... **28 G3** 43 56N 18 48 E
Sokółka, Poland .... **30 E10** 53 25N 23 30 E
Sokolo, Ségou, Mali .. **82 C3** 14 53N 6 8W
Sokolo, Sikasso, Mali . **82 C3** 10 52N 6 59W
Sokolov, Czech Rep. . **26 A5** 50 12N 12 40 E
Sokołów Małopolski,
Poland .... **31 H9** 50 12N 22 7 E
Sokołów Podlaski,
Poland .... **31 F9** 52 25N 22 15 E
Sokoły, Poland .... **31 F9** 52 59N 22 42 E
Sokoto, Nigeria .... **83 C6** 13 2N 5 16 E
Sokoto □, Nigeria ... **83 C6** 12 30N 6 0 E
Sokoto →, Nigeria .. **83 C5** 11 20N 4 10 E
Sokyrnytsya, Ukraine . **29 B8** 48 7N 23 23 E
Sokyryany, Ukraine .. **29 B12** 48 27N 27 25 E
Sol Iletsk, Russia ... **52 D6** 51 10N 55 0 E
Sola →, Poland .... **31 H6** 50 4N 19 15 E
Solai, Kenya ...... **86 B4** 0 2N 36 12 E
Solander I., N.Z. ... **91 M1** 46 34 S 166 54 E
Solano, Phil. ...... **61 C4** 16 31N 121 15 E
Solapur, India ..... **66 L9** 17 43N 75 56 E
Solca, Romania .... **29 C10** 47 40N 25 50 E
Solda Gölü, Turkey .. **47 D11** 37 33N 29 42 E
Soldăneşti, Moldova . **29 C13** 47 49N 28 48 E
Soldeu, Andorra .... **38 C6** 42 35N 1 40 E
Soldotna, U.S.A. ... **100 B4** 60 29N 151 3W
Soléa, Cyprus ..... **49 D12** 35 5N 33 4 E
Solec Kujawski, Poland **31 E5** 53 5N 18 14 E
Soledad, Colombia .. **124 A4** 10 55N 74 46W
Soledad, U.S.A. **110 J5** 36 26N 121 20W
Soledad, Venezuela .. **124 B6** 8 10N 63 34W
Solent, The, U.K. .. **15 G6** 50 45N 1 25W
Solenzara, France ... **21 G13** 41 53N 9 23 E
Solesmes, France ... **19 B10** 50 10N 3 30 E
Solfonn, Norway ... **9 F12** 60 2N 6 57 E
Solhan, Turkey .... **70 B4** 38 57N 41 3 E
Soligorsk = Salihorsk,
Belarus ...... **33 F4** 52 51N 27 27 E
Solihull, U.K. **15 E6** 52 26N 1 47W
Solikamsk, Russia ... **52 D6** 59 38N 56 50 E
Solila, Madag. .... **89 C8** 21 25 S 46 37 E
Solimões =
Amazonas →,
S. Amer. ...... **125 D9** 0 5 S 50 0W
Solin, Croatia ..... **41 E13** 43 33N 16 30 E
Solingen, Germany .. **24 D3** 51 10N 7 5 E
Sollebrunn, Sweden . **11 F6** 58 8N 12 32 E
Sollefteå, Sweden ... **10 A11** 63 12N 17 20 E
Sollentuna, Sweden . **10 E11** 59 26N 17 56 E
Sóller, Spain ..... **48 B9** 39 46N 2 43 E
Sollerön, Sweden ... **10 D8** 60 55N 14 37 E
Solling, Germany ... **24 D5** 51 45N 9 32 E
Solling-Vogler △,
Germany ...... **24 D5** 51 45N 9 32 E
Solnechnogorsk, Russia **32 D9** 56 10N 36 57 E
Solo →, Indonesia .. **63 G15** 6 47 S 112 22 E
Solofra, Italy ..... **43 B7** 40 50N 14 51 E
Sologne, France .... **19 E8** 47 40N 1 45 E
Solok, Indonesia ... **62 E2** 0 45 S 100 40 E
Sololá, Guatemala .. **120 D1** 14 49N 91 10W
Solomon, N. Fork →,
U.S.A. **112 F5** 39 29N 98 26W
Solomon, S. Fork →,
U.S.A. **112 F5** 39 25N 99 12W
Solomon Is. ■, Pac. Oc. **96 H7** 6 0 S 155 0 E
Solon, China ..... **60 B7** 46 32N 121 10 E
Solon Springs, U.S.A. **112 B9** 46 22N 91 49W
Solor, Indonesia ... **63 F6** 8 27 S 123 0 E
Solotcha, Russia ... **32 E10** 54 48N 39 53 E
Solothurn, Switz. ... **25 H3** 47 13N 7 32 E
Solothurn □, Switz. . **25 H3** 47 18N 7 40 E
Solotvyn, Ukraine ... **29 B9** 48 42N 24 25 E
Solsona, Spain .... **38 C6** 42 0N 1 31 E
Solt, Hungary ..... **28 D4** 46 45N 19 1 E
Šolta, Croatia ..... **41 E13** 43 24N 16 15 E
Solţānābād, Khorāsān,
Iran .... **71 C8** 34 13N 59 58 E
Solţānābād, Khorāsān,
Iran .... **71 B8** 36 29N 58 5 E
Soltau, Germany ... **24 C5** 52 59N 9 50 E
Solţy, Russia ..... **32 C6** 58 10N 30 30 E
Solunska Glava,
Macedonia ..... **44 E5** 41 44N 21 31 E
Solvang, U.S.A. ... **111 L6** 34 36N 120 8W
Solvay, U.S.A. **117 C8** 43 3N 76 13W
Sölvesborg, Sweden . **11 H8** 56 5N 14 35 E

Solway Firth, U.K. ... **14 C4** 54 49N 3 35W
Solwezi, Zambia .... **87 E2** 12 11 S 26 21 E
Sōma, Japan ...... **54 F10** 37 40N 140 50 E
Soma, Turkey ..... **47 B9** 39 10N 27 35 E
Somabhula, Zimbabwe **89 B4** 19 42 S 29 40 E
Somali Pen., Africa .. **76 F8** 7 0N 46 0 E
Somali Rep. ■, Africa **75 F4** 7 0N 47 0 E
Somalia = Somali
Rep. ■, Africa .. **75 F4** 7 0N 47 0 E
Sombernon, France .. **19 E11** 47 20N 4 40 E
Sombor, Serbia & M. . **28 E4** 45 46N 19 9 E
Sombra, Canada **116 D2** 42 43N 82 29W
Sombrerete, Mexico . **118 C4** 23 40N 103 40W
Sombrero, Anguilla .. **121 C7** 18 37N 63 30W
Somcuta Mare, Romania **29 C8** 47 31N 23 28 E
Somdari, India .... **68 G5** 25 47N 72 38 E
Someiedo △, Spain .. **36 B4** 43 5N 6 11W
Somers, U.S.A. **108 B6** 48 5N 114 13W
Somerset, Ky., U.S.A. **114 G3** 37 5N 84 36W
Somerset, Mass., U.S.A. **117 E13** 41 47N 71 8W
Somerset, Pa., U.S.A. **116 F5** 40 1N 79 5W
Somerset □, U.K. ... **15 F5** 51 9N 3 0W
Somerset East, S. Africa **88 E4** 32 42 S 25 35 E
Somerset I., Canada . **100 A10** 73 30N 93 0W
Somerset West, S. Africa **88 E2** 34 8 S 18 50 E
Somersworth, U.S.A. **117 C14** 43 16N 70 52W
Somerton, U.S.A. ... **109 K6** 32 36N 114 43W
Somerville, U.S.A. .. **117 F10** 40 35N 74 38W
Someş →, Romania . **28 C7** 47 49N 22 43 E
Someşul Mare →,
Romania ...... **29 C8** 47 9N 23 55 E
Somme □, France ... **19 C9** 49 57N 2 20 E
Somme →, France .. **19 B8** 50 11N 1 38 E
Somme, B. de la, France **18 B8** 50 14N 1 33 E
Sommen, Jönköping,
Sweden ...... **11 F8** 58 12N 14 58 E
Sommen, Östergötland,
Sweden ...... **11 F9** 58 0N 15 15 E
Sommepy-Tahure,
France .... **19 C11** 49 15N 4 31 E
Sömmerda, Germany . **24 D7** 51 9N 11 7 E
Sommesous, France . **19 D11** 48 44N 4 12 E
Sommières, France .. **21 E8** 43 47N 4 6 E
Somnath, India .... **68 J4** 20 53N 70 22 E
Somogy □, Hungary . **28 D2** 46 19N 17 30 E
Somogyszob, Hungary **28 D2** 46 18N 17 20 E
Somoto, Nic. **120 D2** 13 28N 86 37W
Sompolno, Poland .. **31 F5** 52 26N 18 30 E
Somport, Puerto de,
Spain **38 C4** 42 48N 0 31W
Son →, India ..... **69 G11** 25 42N 84 52 E
Son Ha, Vietnam ... **64 E7** 15 3N 108 34 E
Son Hoa, Vietnam .. **64 F7** 13 2N 108 58 E
Son La, Vietnam ... **58 G4** 21 20N 103 50 E
Son Serra, Spain ... **48 B10** 39 43N 3 13 E
Son Servera, Spain .. **48 B10** 39 37N 3 21 E
Son Tay, Vietnam ... **58 G5** 21 8N 105 30 E
Soná, Panama **120 E3** 8 0N 81 20W
Sonamarg, India ... **69 B6** 34 18N 75 21 E
Sonamukhi, India .. **69 H12** 23 18N 87 27 E
Sonar →, India .... **69 G8** 24 24N 79 56 E
Sŏnch'ŏn, N. Korea .. **57 E13** 39 48N 124 55 E
Sondags →, S. Africa **88 E4** 33 44 S 25 51 E
Sóndalo, Italy ..... **40 B7** 46 20N 10 19 E
Sondar, India ..... **69 C6** 33 28N 75 56 E
Sønder Feldir g,
Denmark ...... **11 J2** 55 57N 8 47 E
Sønder Omme,
Denmark ...... **11 J2** 55 50N 8 54 E
Sønderborg, Denmark **11 K3** 54 55N 9 49 E
Sønderjyllands
Amtskommune □,
Denmark ...... **11 J3** 55 10N 9 10 E
Sondershausen,
Germany ...... **24 D6** 51 22N 10 51 E
Sóndrio, Italy ..... **40 B6** 46 10N 9 52 E
Sone, Mozam. ..... **87 F3** 17 23 S 34 55 E
Sonepur, India .... **67 J13** 20 55N 83 50 E
Song, Nigeria ..... **83 D7** 9 49N 12 39 E
Song, Thailand .... **64 C3** 18 28N 100 11 E
Song Cau, Vietnam . **64 F7** 13 27N 109 18 E
Song Xian, China .. **56 G7** 34 12N 112 8 E
Songan, Indonesia .. **63 J18** 8 13 S 115 24 E
Sŏngch'ŏn, N. Korea **57 E14** 39 12N 126 15 E
Songea, Tanzania ... **87 E4** 10 40 S 35 40 E
Songeons, France ... **19 C8** 49 32N 1 50 E
Songhua Hu, China . **57 C14** 43 35N 126 50 E
Songhua Jiang →, China **60 B8** 47 45N 132 30 E
Songimvelo △, S. Africa **89 D5** 25 50 S 31 2 E
Songjiang, China ... **59 B13** 31 1N 121 12 E
Songjin, N. Korea .. **57 D15** 40 40N 129 10 E
Songjŏng-ni, S. Korea **57 G14** 35 8N 126 47 E
Songkan, China .... **58 C6** 28 35N 106 52 E
Songkhla, Thailand . **65 J3** 7 13N 100 37 E
Songming, China ... **58 E4** 25 12N 103 2 E
Songnim, N. Korea . **57 E13** 38 45N 125 39 E
Songo, Mozam. .... **85 H6** 15 34 S 32 38 E
Songo, Sudan ..... **79 G10** 9 47N 24 21 E
Songpan, China ... **58 A4** 32 40N 103 30 E
Songtao, China .... **58 C7** 28 11N 109 10 E
Songwe, Dem. Rep. of
the Congo ...... **86 C2** 3 20 S 20 16 E
Songwe →, Africa .. **87 D3** 9 44 S 33 58 E
Songxi, China ..... **59 D12** 27 31N 118 44 E
Songzi, China ..... **59 B8** 30 12N 111 45 E
Sonhat, India ..... **69 H10** 23 29N 82 31 E
Sonid Youqi, China . **56 C7** 42 45N 112 48 E
Sonipat, India .... **68 E7** 29 0N 77 5 E
Sonkach, India .... **68 H7** 22 59N 76 21 E
Sonkovo, Russia ... **32 D9** 57 50N 37 5 E
Sonmiani, Pakistan .. **68 G2** 25 25N 66 40 E
Sonmiani B., Pakistan **68 G2** 25 15N 66 30 E
Sonnino, Italy ..... **42 A6** 41 25N 13 14 E
Sono →, Brazil ..... **125 E9** 9 58 S 48 11W
Sonoma, U.S.A. ... **110 G4** 38 18N 122 28W
Sonora, Calif., U.S.A. **110 H6** 37 59N 120 23W
Sonora, Tex., U.S.A. **113 K4** 30 34N 100 39W
Sonora □, Mexico .. **118 B2** 29 0N 111 0W
Sonora →, Mexico . **118 B2** 28 50N 111 33W
Sonoran Desert, U.S.A. **111 L12** 33 40N 114 15W
Sonoyta, Mexico ... **118 A2** 31 51N 112 50W
Sonqor, Iran ...... **73 E12** 34 47N 47 36 E
Sŏnsan, S. Korea ... **57 F15** 36 14N 128 17 E
Sonseca, Spain **37 F7** 39 42N 3 57W
Sonsonate, El Salv. . **120 D2** 13 43N 89 44W
Sonstorp, Sweden .. **11 F9** 58 44N 15 38 E
Sonthofen, Germany . **25 H6** 47 30N 10 16 E
Soochow = Suzhou,
China .... **59 B13** 31 19N 120 38 E
Sooke, Canada **110 B3** 48 13N 123 43W
Sop Hao, Laos .... **58 G5** 20 33N 104 27 E
Sop Prap, Thailand . **64 D2** 17 53N 99 20 E
Sopelana, Spain ... **38 B2** 43 23N 2 58W
Sopi, Indonesia .... **63 D7** 2 34N 128 28 E
Sopo, Nahr →, Sudan **81 F2** 8 40N 26 30 E
Sopot, Bulgaria .... **45 D8** 42 39N 24 45 E
Sopot, Poland ..... **30 D5** 54 27N 18 31 E

Sopot, Serbia & M. .. **44 B4** 44 29N 20 36 E
Sopotnica, Macedonia **44 E5** 41 23N 21 13 E
Sopron, Hungary ... **28 C1** 47 45N 16 32 E
Sopur, India ...... **69 B6** 34 18N 74 27 E
Sør-Rondane, Antarctica **5 D4** 72 0 S 25 0 E
Sora, Italy ...... **41 G10** 41 43N 13 37 E
Sorah, Pakistan ... **68 F3** 27 13N 68 56 E
Sŏrak-san, S. Korea . **57 E15** 38 5N 128 28 E
Sorano, Italy ..... **41 F8** 42 41N 11 43 E
Soraon, India ..... **69 G9** 25 37N 81 51 E
Sorbas, Spain **39 H2** 37 6N 2 7W
Sore, France ...... **20 D3** 44 18N 0 35 E
Sorel-Tracy, Canada . **104 C5** 46 0N 73 10W
Soresina, Italy .... **40 C6** 45 17N 9 51 E
Sörforsa, Sweden ... **10 C10** 61 43N 16 58 E
Soria, Spain **38 D2** 41 43N 2 32W
Soria □, Spain **38 D2** 41 46N 2 28W
Soriano, Uruguay ... **126 C4** 33 24 S 58 19W
Soriano nel Cimino, Italy **41 F9** 42 25N 12 14 E
Sorkh, Kuh-e, Iran .. **71 C8** 35 40N 58 30 E
Sorø, Denmark .... **11 J5** 55 26N 11 32 E
Soro, Guinea **82 C3** 10 9N 9 48W
Soroca, Moldova ... **29 B13** 48 8N 28 12 E
Sorocaba, Brazil ... **127 A6** 23 31 S 47 27W
Soroki = Soroca,
Moldova ...... **29 B13** 48 8N 28 12 E
Sorong, Indonesia .. **63 E8** 0 55 S 131 15 E
Soroní, Greece .... **49 C10** 36 21N 28 1 E
Soroti, Uganda .... **86 B3** 1 43N 33 35 E
Sørøya, Norway ... **8 A20** 70 40N 22 30 E
Sørøysundet, Norway **8 A20** 70 25N 23 0 E
Sorraia →, Portugal **37 G2** 38 55N 8 53W
Sorrell, Australia ... **95 G4** 42 47 S 147 34 E
Sorrento, Italy .... **43 B7** 40 37N 14 22 E
Sorsele, Sweden ... **8 D17** 65 31N 17 30 E
Sörsjön, Sweden ... **10 C7** 61 24N 13 5 E
Sorso, Italy ...... **42 B1** 40 48N 8 34 E
Sorsogon, Phil. .... **61 E6** 13 0N 124 0 E
Sortavala, Russia ... **32 B6** 61 42N 30 41 E
Sortino, Italy ..... **43 E8** 37 9N 15 2 E
Sorvizhi, Russia ... **34 B9** 57 52N 48 32 E
Sos del Rey Católico,
Spain **38 C3** 42 30N 1 13W
Sŏsan, S. Korea ... **57 F14** 36 47N 126 27 E
Soscumica, L., Canada **104 B4** 50 15N 77 27W
Sösdala, Sweden ... **11 H7** 56 2N 13 41 E
Sosna →, Russia ... **33 F10** 52 42N 38 55 E
Sosnovka, Kirov, Russia **34 B10** 56 17N 51 17 E
Sosnovka, Tambov,
Russia .... **34 D5** 53 13N 41 24 E
Sosnovyy Bor, Russia . **32 C5** 59 55N 29 6 E
Sosnowiec, Poland .. **31 H6** 50 20N 19 10 E
Sospel, France .... **21 E11** 43 52N 7 27 E
Sossus Vlei, Namibia . **88 C2** 24 40 S 15 23 E
Šoštanj, Slovenia ... **41 B12** 46 23N 15 4 E
Sot →, India ..... **69 F8** 27 27N 79 37 E
Sotkamo, Finland .. **8 D23** 64 8N 28 23 E
Soto del Barco, Spain **36 B4** 43 32N 6 4W
Soto la Marina →,
Mexico **119 C5** 23 40N 97 40W
Soto y Amío, Spain . **36 C5** 42 46N 5 53W
Sotrondio, Spain ... **36 B5** 43 17N 5 36W
Sotuta, Mexico **119 C7** 20 29N 89 43W
Souanké, Congo ... **84 D2** 2 10N 14 3 E
Soubré, Ivory C. ... **82 D3** 5 50N 6 35W
Souderton, U.S.A. .. **117 F9** 40 19N 75 19W
Soúdha, Greece .... **49 D6** 35 29N 24 4 E
Soúdhas, Kólpos, Greece **49 D6** 35 25N 24 10 E
Souflion, Greece ... **45 E10** 41 12N 26 18 E
Soufrière, Guadeloupe **120 b** 16 5N 61 40W
Soufrière, St. Lucia .. **121 f** 13 51N 61 3W
Soufrière Bay, Dominica **121 f** 13 53N 61 6W
Souillac, France ... **20 D5** 44 53N 1 29 E
Souilly, France .... **19 C12** 49 3N 5 17 E
Soukhouma, Laos .. **64 E5** 14 38N 105 48 E
Sŏul, S. Korea .... **57 F14** 37 31N 126 58 E
Soulac-sur-Mer, France **20 C2** 45 30N 1 7W
Soulougou,
Burkina Faso ... **83 C5** 13 1N 0 25 E
Soultz-sous-Forêts,
France .... **19 D14** 48 57N 7 52 E
Sound, The = Øresund,
Europe .... **11 J6** 55 45N 12 45 E
Sound, The, U.K. ... **15 G3** 50 20N 4 10W
Soúnion, Ákra, Greece **46 D6** 37 37N 24 1 E
Sources, Mt. aux,
Lesotho ...... **89 D4** 28 45 S 28 50 E
Soure, Brazil ..... **125 D9** 0 35 S 48 30W
Soure, Portugal ... **36 E2** 40 4N 8 38W
Souris, Man., Canada **103 D8** 49 40N 100 20W
Souris, P.E.I., Canada **105 C7** 46 21N 62 15W
Souris →, Canada .. **112 A5** 49 40N 99 34W
Sourou →, Africa .. **82 C4** 12 45N 3 25 E
Soúrpi, Greece .... **46 B4** 39 6N 22 54 E
Sousa, Brazil ..... **125 E11** 6 45 S 38 10W
Sousel, Portugal ... **37 G3** 38 57N 7 40W
Sousse, Tunisia .... **79 A8** 35 50N 10 38 E
Soustons, France ... **20 E2** 43 45N 1 19W
Sout →, S. Africa .. **88 E2** 31 35 S 18 24 E
South Africa ■, Africa **88 E3** 32 0 S 23 0 E
South America ... **122 E5** 10 0 S 60 0W
South Atlantic Ocean **2 F8** 20 0 S 10 0W
South Aulatsivik I.,
Canada **105 A7** 56 45N 61 30W
South Australia □,
Australia ...... **95 E2** 32 0 S 139 0 E
South Ayrshire □, U.K. **13 F4** 55 18N 4 41W
South Baldy, U.S.A. . **109 J10** 33 59N 107 11W
South Bass I., U.S.A. **116 E2** 41 38N 82 53W
South Bend, Ind., U.S.A. **114 E2** 41 41N 86 15W
South Bend, Wash.,
U.S.A. **110 D3** 46 40N 123 48W
South Boston, U.S.A. **115 G6** 36 42N 78 54W
South Branch, Canada **105 C8** 47 55N 59 2W
South Brook, Canada **105 C8** 49 26N 56 5W
South Carolina □,
U.S.A. **115 J5** 34 0N 81 0W
South Charleston,
U.S.A. **114 F5** 38 22N 81 44W
South China Sea, Asia **62 C4** 10 0N 113 0 E
South Dakota □, U.S.A. **112 C5** 44 15N 100 0W
South Deerfield, U.S.A. **117 D12** 42 29N 72 37W
South Downs, U.K. . **15 G7** 50 52N 0 25W
South-East Indian Rise,
Ind. Oc. ...... **5 B10** 43 0 S 80 0 E
South East Is., Australia **93 F3** 34 17 S 123 30 E
South Esk →, U.K. . **13 E6** 56 43N 2 31W
South Foreland, U.K. **15 F9** 51 8N 1 24 E

South Fork
American →, U.S.A. **110 G5** 38 45N 121 5W
South Fork Feather →,
U.S.A. **110 F5** 39 17N 121 36W
South Fork Grand →,
U.S.A. **112 C3** 45 43N 102 17W
South Fork
Republican →, U.S.A. **112 E4** 40 3N 101 31W
South Georgia,
Antarctica ..... **128 G9** 54 30 S 37 0W
South
Gloucestershire □,
U.K. **15 F5** 51 32N 2 28W
South Hadley, U.S.A. **117 D12** 42 16N 72 35W
South Haven, U.S.A. **114 D2** 42 24N 86 16W
South Henik L., Canada **103 A9** 61 30N 97 20W
South Honshu Ridge,
Pac. Oc. ...... **96 E6** 23 0N 143 0 E
South Horr, Kenya .. **86 B4** 2 12N 36 56 E
South I., Kenya .... **86 B4** 2 35N 36 35 E
South I., N.Z. ..... **91 L3** 44 0 S 170 0 E
South Indian Lake,
Canada **103 B9** 56 47N 98 56W
South Invercargill, N.Z. **91 M2** 46 26 S 168 23 E
South Island △, Kenya **86 B4** 2 39N 36 35 E
South Kitui △, Kenya **86 C4** 1 48 S 38 46 E
South Knife →, Canada **103 B10** 58 55N 94 37W
South Koel →, India **69 H11** 22 32N 85 14 E
South Korea ■, Asia **57 G15** 36 0N 128 0 E
South Lake Tahoe,
U.S.A. **110 G6** 38 57N 119 59W
South Lanarkshire □,
U.K. **13 F5** 55 37N 3 53W
South Loup →, U.S.A. **112 E5** 41 4N 98 39W
South Luangwa △,
Zambia ...... **87 E3** 13 0 S 31 20 E
South Magnetic Pole,
Antarctica ..... **5 C9** 64 8 S 138 8 E
South Milwaukee,
U.S.A. **114 D2** 42 55N 87 52W
South Molton, U.K. . **15 F4** 51 1N 3 51W
South Moose L., Canada **103 C8** 53 46N 100 8W
South Nahanni →,
Canada **102 A4** 61 3N 123 21W
South Nation →,
Canada **117 A9** 45 34N 75 6W
South Natuna Is. =
Natuna Selatan,
Kepulauan, Indonesia **62 D3** 2 45N 109 0 E
South Negril Pt.,
Jamaica ...... **120 a** 18 16N 78 22W
South Orkney Is.,
Antarctica ..... **5 C18** 63 0 S 45 0W
South Ossetia □,
Georgia ...... **35 J7** 42 21N 44 2 E
South Pagai, I. = Pagai
Selatan, Pulau,
Indonesia ..... **62 E2** 3 0 S 100 15 E
South Paris, U.S.A. . **117 B14** 44 14N 70 31W
South Pittsburg, U.S.A. **115 H3** 35 1N 85 42W
South Platte →, U.S.A. **112 E4** 41 7N 100 42W
South Pole, Antarctica **5 E** 90 0 S 0 W
South Porcupine,
Canada **104 C3** 48 30N 81 12W
South Portland, U.S.A. **115 D10** 43 38N 70 15W
South Pt., Barbados . **121 g** 13 2N 59 32W
South River, Canada . **116 A5** 45 52N 79 23W
South River, U.S.A. . **117 F10** 40 27N 74 23W
South Ronaldsay, U.K. **13 C6** 58 48N 2 58W
South Sandwich Is.,
Antarctica ..... **5 B1** 57 0 S 27 0W
South Saskatchewan →,
Canada **103 C7** 53 15N 105 5W
South Seal →, Canada **103 B9** 58 48N 98 8W
South Shetland Is.,
Antarctica ..... **5 C18** 62 0 S 59 0W
South Shields, U.K. . **14 C6** 55 0N 1 25W
South Sioux City, U.S.A. **112 D6** 42 28N 96 24W
South Taranaki Bight,
N.Z. .... **91 H5** 39 40 S 174 5 E
South Thompson →,
Canada **102 C4** 50 40N 120 20W
South Twin I., Canada **104 B4** 53 7N 79 52W
South Tyne →, U.K. **14 C5** 54 59N 2 8W
South Uist, U.K. ... **13 D1** 57 20N 7 15W
South West C., Australia **95 G4** 43 34 S 146 3 E
South West C., N.Z. . **91 M1** 47 15 S 167 28 E
South Williamsport,
U.S.A. **116 E8** 41 13N 77 0W
Southampton, Canada **116 B3** 44 30N 81 25W
Southampton, U.K. . **15 G6** 50 54N 1 23W
Southampton □, U.K. **15 G6** 50 54N 1 23W
Southampton I., Canada **101 B11** 64 30N 84 0W
Southaven, U.S.A. .. **113 H9** 34 59N 90 2W
Southbank, Canada . **102 C3** 54 2N 125 46W
Southbridge, N.Z. .. **91 K4** 43 48 S 172 16 E
Southbridge, U.S.A. **117 D12** 42 5N 72 2W
Southeast Pacific Basin,
Pac. Oc. ...... **5 C15** 16 30 S 92 0W
Southend, Canada .. **103 B8** 56 19N 103 22W
Southend-on-Sea, U.K. **15 F8** 51 32N 0 44 E
Southend-on-Sea □,
U.K. .... **15 F8** 51 32N 0 44 E
Southern □, Malawi . **87 F4** 15 0 S 35 0 E
Southern □, S. Leone **82 D2** 8 0N 12 30W
Southern □, Zambia . **87 F2** 16 20 S 26 20 E
Southern Alps, N.Z. . **91 K3** 43 41 S 170 11 E
Southern Cross,
Australia ...... **93 F2** 31 12 S 119 15 E
Southern Indian L.,
Canada **103 B9** 57 10N 98 30W
Southern Ocean,
Antarctica ..... **5 C6** 62 0 S 60 0 E
Southern Pines, U.S.A. **115 H6** 35 11N 79 24W
Southern Uplands, U.K. **13 F5** 55 28N 3 52W
Southland □, N.Z. .. **91 L1** 45 30 S 168 0 E
Southold, U.S.A. ... **117 E12** 41 4N 72 26W
Southport, Australia . **95 D5** 27 58 S 153 25 E
Southport, U.K. ... **14 D4** 53 39N 3 0W
Southport, Fla., U.S.A. **115 K3** 30 17N 85 38W
Southport, N.Y., U.S.A. **116 D8** 42 3N 76 49W
Southwest Pacific
Basin, Pac. Oc. .. **5 A12** 42 0 S 170 0W
Southwold, U.K. ... **15 E9** 52 20N 1 41 E

Southwood △, Australia **95 D5** 27 48 S 150 8 E
Soutpansberg, S. Africa **89 C4** 23 0 S 29 30 E
Souvigny, France ... **19 F10** 46 33N 3 10 E
Soverato, Italy .... **43 D9** 38 41N 16 33 E
Sovetsk, Kaliningrad,
Russia .... **9 J19** 55 6N 21 50 E
Sovetsk, Kirov, Russia **34 B9** 57 38N 48 53 E
Sovetskaya Gavan =
Vanino, Russia .. **53 E15** 48 50N 140 5 E
Soviceille, Italy .... **41 E8** 43 17N 11 13 E
Soweto, S. Africa .. **89 D4** 26 14 S 27 54 E
Sōya-Kaikyō = La
Perouse Str., Asia . **54 B11** 45 40N 142 0 E
Sōya-Misaki, Japan . **54 B10** 45 30N 141 55 E
Soyaux, France .... **20 C4** 45 39N 0 12 E
Sozopol, Bulgaria .. **45 D11** 42 23N 27 42 E
Sozh →, Belarus ... **33 F6** 51 57N 30 48 E
Spa, Belgium ..... **17 D5** 50 29N 5 53 E
Spain ■, Europe ... **7 H5** 39 0N 4 0W
Spalding, Australia . **95 E2** 33 30 S 138 37 E
Spalding, U.K. **14 E7** 52 48N 0 9W
Spangler, U.S.A. ... **116 F6** 40 39N 78 48W
Spanish, Canada ... **104 C3** 46 12N 82 20W
Spanish Fork, U.S.A. **108 F8** 40 7N 111 39W
Spanish Town,
Br. Virgin Is. ... **121 e** 17 43N 64 26W
Spanish Town, Jamaica **120 a** 18 0N 76 57W
Sparks, U.S.A. **110 F7** 39 32N 119 45W
Sparreholm, Sweden **10 E10** 59 4N 16 49 E
Sparta = Spárti, Greece **46 D4** 37 5N 22 25 E
Sparta, Mich., U.S.A. **114 D3** 43 10N 85 42W
Sparta, N.J., U.S.A. . **117 E10** 41 2N 74 38W
Sparta, Wis., U.S.A. **112 D9** 43 56N 90 49W
Spartanburg, U.S.A. **115 H5** 34 56N 81 57W
Spartansburg, U.S.A. **116 E5** 41 49N 79 41W
Spárti, Greece .... **46 D4** 37 5N 22 25 E
Spartivento, C.,
Calabria, Italy ... **43 E9** 37 55N 16 4 E
Spartivento, C., Sard.,
Italy .... **42 D1** 38 53N 8 50 E
Sparwood, Canada . **102 D6** 49 44N 114 53W
Spas-Demensk, Russia **32 E7** 54 20N 34 0 E
Spas-Klepiki, Russia . **32 E11** 55 10N 40 10 E
Spassk Dalniy, Russia **53 E14** 44 40N 132 48 E
Spassk-Ryazanskiy,
Russia .... **32 E11** 54 24N 40 25 E
Spátha, Ákra, Greece **49 D5** 35 42N 23 43 E
Spatsizi →, Canada . **102 B3** 57 42N 128 7W
Spatsizi Plateau
Wilderness △, Canada **102 B3** 57 40N 128 0W
Spean →, U.K. **13 E4** 56 55N 4 59W
Spearfish, U.S.A. ... **112 C3** 44 30N 103 52W
Spearman, U.S.A. .. **113 G4** 36 12N 101 12W
Speculator, U.S.A. . **117 C10** 43 30N 74 25W
Speia, Moldova ... **29 D14** 46 59N 29 19 E
Speightstown, Barbados **121 g** 13 15N 59 39W
Spello, Italy ..... **41 F9** 42 59N 12 40 E
Spence Bay = Taloyoak,
Canada **100 B10** 69 32N 93 32W
Spencer, Idaho, U.S.A. **108 D7** 44 22N 112 11W
Spencer, Iowa, U.S.A. **112 D7** 43 9N 95 9W
Spencer, N.Y., U.S.A. **117 D8** 42 13N 76 30W
Spencer, Nebr., U.S.A. **112 D5** 42 53N 98 42W
Spencer, C., Australia **95 F2** 35 20 S 136 53 E
Spencer B., Namibia . **88 D1** 25 30 S 14 47 E
Spencer G., Australia **95 E2** 34 0 S 137 20 E
Spencerville, Canada **117 B9** 44 51N 75 33W
Spences Bridge, Canada **102 C4** 50 25N 121 20W
Spennymoor, U.K. . **14 C6** 54 42N 1 36W
Spenser Mts., N.Z. . **91 K4** 42 15 S 172 45 E
Spentrup, Denmark . **11 H4** 56 33N 10 2 E
Sperkhiós →, Greece **46 C4** 38 57N 22 3 E
Sperrin Mts., U.K. . **12 B5** 54 50N 7 0W
Spessart, Germany .. **25 F5** 49 56N 9 18 E
Spétsai, Greece .... **46 D5** 37 15N 23 10 E
Spey →, U.K. **13 D5** 57 40N 3 6W
Speyer, Germany .. **25 F4** 49 29N 8 25 E
Spezand, Pakistan .. **68 E2** 29 59N 67 0 E
Spezzano Albanese,
Italy .... **43 C9** 39 40N 16 19 E
Spiekeroog, Germany **24 B3** 53 46N 7 42 E
Spiez, Switz. ..... **25 J3** 46 40N 7 40 E
Spíli, Greece ..... **49 D6** 35 13N 24 31 E
Spilimbergo, Italy .. **41 B9** 46 7N 12 54 E
Spin Búldak, Afghan. **68 D2** 31 1N 66 25 E
Spinalónga, Greece . **49 D7** 35 18N 25 44 E
Spinazzola, Italy ... **43 B9** 40 58N 16 5 E
Spineni, Romania .. **29 F9** 44 43N 24 37 E
Spirit Lake, U.S.A. . **110 D4** 46 15N 122 9W
Spirit River, Canada **102 B5** 55 45N 118 50W
Spiritwood, Canada . **103 C7** 53 24N 107 33W
Spišská Nová Ves,
Slovak Rep. ... **27 C13** 48 58N 20 34 E
Spišské Podhradie,
Slovak Rep. ... **27 B13** 49 0N 20 48 E
Spital, Austria .... **26 D7** 47 42N 14 18 E
Spithead, U.K. **15 G6** 50 45N 1 10W
Spittal an der Drau,
Austria ...... **26 E6** 46 48N 13 31 E
Spitzbergen = Svalbard,
Arctic .... **51 B5** 78 0N 17 0 E
Spjelkavik, Norway . **9 E12** 62 28N 6 22 E
Split, Croatia ..... **41 E13** 43 31N 16 26 E
Split ✈ (SPU), Croatia **41 E13** 43 33N 16 15 E
Split L., Canada ... **103 B9** 56 8N 96 15W
Split Lake, Canada . **103 B9** 56 8N 96 15W
Splitski Kanal, Croatia **41 E13** 43 31N 16 20 E
Splügenpass, Switz. . **25 J5** 46 30N 9 20 E
Spofford, U.S.A. ... **113 L4** 29 10N 100 25W
Spokane, U.S.A. ... **108 C5** 47 40N 117 24W
Spoleto, Italy ..... **41 F9** 42 44N 12 44 E
Spooner, U.S.A. ... **112 C9** 45 50N 91 53W
Sporyy Navolok, Mys,
Russia .... **52 B7** 75 50N 68 40 E
Sprague, U.S.A. ... **108 C5** 47 18N 117 59W
Spratly I., S. China Sea **62 C4** 8 20N 111 55 E
Spratly Is., S. China Sea **62 C4** 8 20N 112 0 E
Spray, U.S.A. **108 D4** 44 50N 119 48W
Spree →, Germany . **24 C9** 52 32N 13 13 E
Spreewald, Germany **24 D9** 51 55N 13 52 E
Spremberg, Germany **24 D10** 51 34N 14 22 E
Sprengisandur, Iceland **8 D5** 64 52N 18 7W
Spring City, U.S.A. . **117 F9** 40 11N 75 33W
Spring Creek, U.S.A. **108 F6** 40 45N 115 38W
Spring Garden, U.S.A. **110 F6** 39 52N 120 47W
Spring Hall, Barbados **121 g** 13 18N 59 36W
Spring Hill, U.S.A. . **115 L4** 28 27N 82 41W
Spring Mts., U.S.A. **109 H6** 36 0N 115 45W
Spring Valley, U.S.A. **111 N10** 32 45N 117 5W
Springbok, S. Africa **88 D2** 29 42 S 17 54 E
Springdale, Canada . **105 C8** 49 30N 56 6W
Springdale, U.S.A. . **113 G7** 36 11N 94 8W
Springe, Germany .. **24 C5** 52 13N 9 33 E

Springer, *U.S.A.* **113 G2** 36 22N 104 36W
Springerville, *U.S.A.* .. **109 J9** 34 8N 109 17W
Springfield, *Canada* .. **116 D4** 42 50N 80 56W
Springfield, *N.Z.* ...... **91 K3** 43 19 S 171 56 E
Springfield, *Colo.,*
  U.S.A. **113 G3** 37 24N 102 37W
Springfield, *Ill., U.S.A.* .. **112 F10** 39 48N 89 39W
Springfield, *Mass.,*
  U.S.A. **117 D12** 42 6N 72 35W
Springfield, *Mo., U.S.A.* .. **113 G8** 37 13N 93 17W
Springfield, *Ohio, U.S.A.* **114 F4** 39 55N 83 49W
Springfield, *Oreg.,*
  U.S.A. **108 D2** 44 3N 123 1W
Springfield, *Tenn.,*
  U.S.A. **115 G2** 36 31N 86 53W
Springfield, *Vt., U.S.A.* .. **117 C12** 43 18N 72 29W
Springfontein, *S. Africa* **88 E4** 30 15 S 25 40 E
Springhill, *Canada* **105 C7** 45 40N 64 4W
Springhill, *U.S.A.* **113 J8** 33 0N 93 28W
Springhouse, *Canada* .. **102 C4** 51 56N 122 7W
Springs, *S. Africa* ...... **89 D4** 26 13 S 28 25 E
Springsure, *Australia* .. **94 C4** 24 8 S 148 6 E
Springvale, *U.S.A.* **117 C14** 43 28N 70 48W
Springville, *Calif, U.S.A.* **110 J8** 36 8N 118 49W
Springville, *N.Y., U.S.A.* **116 D6** 42 31N 78 40W
Springville, *Utah, U.S.A.* **108 F8** 40 10N 111 37W
Springwater, *Canada* .. **116 D7** 42 38N 77 35W
Spruce-Creek, *U.S.A.* .. **116 F6** 40 36N 78 9W
Spruce Knob-Seneca
  Rocks △, *U.S.A.* **114 F6** 38 50N 79 30W
Spruce Mt., *U.S.A.* **117 B12** 44 12N 72 19W
Spur, *U.S.A.* **113 J4** 33 28N 100 52W
Spurn Hd., *U.K.* ...... **14 D8** 53 35N 0 8 E
Spuž, *Serbia & M.* .... **44 D3** 42 32N 19 10 E
Spuzzum, *Canada* **102 D4** 49 37N 121 23W
Squam L., *U.S.A.* **117 C13** 43 45N 71 32W
Squamish, *Canada* **102 D4** 49 45N 123 10W
Square Islands, *Canada* **105 B8** 52 47N 55 47W
Squillace, G. di, *Italy* .. **43 D9** 38 45N 16 50 E
Squinzano, *Italy* ...... **43 B11** 40 26N 18 2 E
Squires, Mt., *Australia* .. **93 E4** 26 14 S 127 28 E
Srbac, *Bos.-H.* .... **28 E2** 45 7N 17 30 E
Srbica, *Serbia & M.* .... **44 D4** 42 45N 20 47 E
Srbija = Serbia □,
  Serbia & M. .... **44 C5** 43 30N 21 0 E
Srbobran, *Serbia & M.* .. **28 E4** 45 32N 19 48 E
Sre Ambel, *Cambodia* .. **65 G4** 11 8N 103 46 E
Sre Khtum, *Cambodia* .. **65 F6** 12 10N 106 52 E
Sre Umbell = Sre
  Ambel, *Cambodia* .. **65 G4** 11 8N 103 46 E
Srebrenica, *Bos.-H.* .... **28 F4** 44 6N 19 18 E
Sredinny Ra. =
  Sredinnyy Khrebet,
  Russia .... **53 D16** 57 0N 160 0 E
Sredinnyy Khrebet,
  Russia .... **53 D16** 57 0N 160 0 E
Središče, *Slovenia* .... **41 B13** 46 24N 16 17 E
Sredna Gora, *Bulgaria* .. **45 D8** 42 40N 24 20 E
Srednekolymsk, *Russia* **53 C16** 67 27N 153 40 E
Sredni Rodopi, *Bulgaria* **45 E8** 41 40N 24 45 E
Srednogorie, *Bulgaria* .. **45 D8** 42 43N 24 10 E
Śrem, *Poland* .... **31 F4** 52 6N 17 2 E
Sremska Mitrovica,
  Serbia & M. .... **28 F4** 44 59N 19 38 E
Sremski Karlovci,
  Serbia & M. .... **28 E4** 45 12N 19 56 E
Srepok →, *Cambodia* .. **64 F6** 13 33N 106 16 E
Sretensk, *Russia* ...... **53 D12** 52 10N 117 40 E
Sri Lanka ■, *Asia* .... **66 R12** 7 30N 80 50 E
Srikakulam, *India* .... **67 K13** 18 14N 83 58 E
Srinagar, *India* .... **69 B6** 34 5N 74 50 E
Srinagarind Res.,
  Thailand .... **64 E2** 14 35N 99 0 E
Środa Śląska, *Poland* .. **31 G3** 51 10N 16 36 E
Środa Wielkopolski,
  Poland .... **31 F4** 52 15N 17 19 E
Srono, *Indonesia* ...... **63 J17** 8 24 S 114 16 E
Srpska Crnja,
  Serbia & M. .... **28 E5** 45 38N 20 44 E
Srpski Itebej,
  Serbia & M. .... **28 E5** 45 35N 20 44 E
Staaten →, *Australia* .. **94 B3** 16 24 S 141 17 E
Staaten River △,
  Australia .... **94 B3** 16 15 S 142 40 E
Staberhuk, *Germany* .. **24 A7** 54 23N 11 18 E
Stade, *Germany* ...... **24 B5** 53 35N 9 29 E
Stadskanaal, *Neths.* .... **17 A6** 53 4N 6 55 E
Stadtallendorf, *Germany* **24 C5** 50 48N 9 1 E
Stadthagen, *Germany* .. **24 C5** 52 19N 9 13 E
Stadtlohn, *Germany* .. **24 D2** 51 59N 6 55 E
Stadtroda, *Germany* .. **24 E7** 50 52N 11 44 E
Staffa, *U.K.* **13 E2** 56 27N 6 21W
Staffanstorp, *Sweden* .. **11 J7** 55 39N 13 13 E
Stafford, *U.K.* **14 E5** 52 49N 2 7W
Stafford, *U.S.A.* **113 G5** 37 58N 98 36W
Stafford Springs, *U.S.A.* **117 E12** 41 57N 72 18W
Staffordshire □, *U.K.* .. **14 E5** 52 53N 2 10W
Stagnone, *Italy* .... **42 E5** 37 53N 12 26 E
Stagnone di Marsala □,
  Italy .... **42 E5** 37 52N 12 26 E
Staines, *U.K.* **15 F7** 51 26N 0 29W
Stainz, *Austria* .... **26 E8** 46 53N 15 17 E
Stakhanov, *Ukraine* .... **33 H10** 48 35N 38 40 E
Stalać, *Serbia & M.* .... **44 C5** 43 43N 21 28 E
Stalis, *Greece* .... **49 D7** 35 17N 25 25 E
Stallarholmen, *Sweden* **10 E11** 59 22N 17 12 E
Ställdalen, *Sweden* .... **10 E8** 59 56N 14 56 E
Stalowa Wola, *Poland* .. **31 H9** 50 34N 22 3 E
Stalybridge, *U.K.* **14 D5** 53 28N 2 3W
Stamford, *Australia* .... **94 C3** 21 15 S 143 46 E
Stamford, *U.K.* **15 E7** 52 39N 0 29W
Stamford, *Conn., U.S.A.* **117 E11** 41 3N 73 32W
Stamford, *N.Y., U.S.A.* .. **117 D10** 42 25N 74 38W
Stamford, *Tex., U.S.A.* .. **113 J5** 32 57N 99 48W
Stampriet, *Namibia* .... **88 C2** 24 20 S 18 28 E
Stamps, *U.S.A.* **113 J8** 33 22N 93 30W
Stančevo = Kalipetrovo,
  Bulgaria .... **45 B11** 44 5N 27 14 E
Standerton, *S. Africa* .. **89 D4** 26 55 S 29 7 E
Standish, *U.S.A.* **114 D4** 43 59N 83 57W
Stanford, *S. Africa* .... **88 E2** 34 26 S 19 29 E
Stanford, *U.S.A.* **108 C8** 47 9N 110 13W
Stånga, *Sweden* .... **11 G12** 57 17N 18 29 E
Stanger, *S. Africa* ...... **89 D5** 29 27 S 31 14 E
Stängselåsen =
  Salpausselkä, *Finland* **9 F22** 61 3N 26 15 E
Stanišić, *Serbia & M.* .. **28 E4** 45 56N 19 10 E
Stanislaus →, *U.S.A.* .. **110 H5** 37 40N 121 14W
Stanisławów, *Poland* .. **31 F8** 52 18N 21 33 E
Stanley, *Australia* ...... **95 G4** 40 46 S 145 19 E
Stanley, *Falk. Is.* ...... **128 G5** 51 40 S 59 51W
Stanley, *U.K.* **14 C6** 54 53N 1 41W
Stanley, *Idaho, U.S.A.* .. **108 D6** 44 13N 114 56W
Stanley, *N. Dak., U.S.A.* **112 A3** 48 19N 102 23W
Stanley, *N.Y., U.S.A.* .. **116 D7** 42 48N 77 6W
Stanley Mission, *Canada* **103 B8** 55 25N 104 33W
Stanovoy Khrebet,
  Russia .... **53 D13** 55 0N 130 0 E

Stanovoy Ra. =
  Stanovoy Khrebet,
  Russia .... **53 D13** 55 0N 130 0 E
Stansmore Ra., *Australia* **92 D4** 21 23 S 128 33 E
Stansted, London ✈
  (STN), *U.K.* .... **15 F8** 51 54N 0 14 E
Stanthorpe, *Australia* .. **95 D5** 28 36 S 151 59 E
Stanton, *U.S.A.* **113 J4** 32 8N 101 48W
Stanwood, *U.S.A.* **110 B4** 48 15N 122 23W
Staples, *U.S.A.* **112 B7** 46 21N 94 48W
Stąporków, *Poland* .... **31 G7** 51 9N 20 31 E
Star City, *Canada* **103 C8** 52 50N 104 20W
Star Lake, *U.S.A.* **117 B9** 44 10N 75 2W
Stará L'ubovña,
  Slovak Rep. .... **27 B13** 49 18N 20 42 E
Stara Moravica,
  Serbia & M. .... **28 E4** 45 50N 19 30 E
Stara Pazova,
  Serbia & M. .... **28 F5** 44 58N 20 10 E
Stara Planina, *Bulgaria* **44 C7** 43 15N 23 0 E
Stara Sil, *Ukraine* ...... **31 J9** 49 29N 22 58 E
Stará Turá, *Slovak Rep.* **27 C10** 48 47N 17 42 E
Stara Ushytsya, *Ukraine* **29 B12** 48 35N 27 8 E
Stara Zagora, *Bulgaria* .. **45 D9** 42 26N 25 39 E
Starachowice, *Poland* .. **31 G8** 51 3N 21 2 E
Staraya Russa, *Russia* .. **32 D6** 57 58N 31 23 E
Staraya Ukrainka,
  Ukraine .... **29 E11** 46 19N 26 11 E
Starbuck I., *Kiribati* .... **97 H12** 5 37 S 155 55W
Starcke △, *Australia* .. **94 A4** 14 56 S 145 2 E
Stargard Szczeciński,
  Poland .... **30 E2** 53 20N 15 0 E
Stari Bar, *Serbia & M.* .. **44 D3** 42 7N 19 10 E
Stari Trg, *Slovenia* .... **41 C12** 45 29N 15 7 E
Staritsa, *Russia* .... **32 D8** 56 33N 34 55 E
Starke, *U.S.A.* **115 L4** 29 57N 82 7W
Starnberg, *Germany* .. **25 H7** 48 0N 11 21 E
Starnberger See,
  Germany .... **25 H7** 47 54N 11 19 E
Starobilsk, *Ukraine* .... **33 H10** 49 16N 39 0 E
Starodub, *Russia* ...... **33 F7** 52 30N 32 50 E
Starogard Gdański,
  Poland .... **30 E5** 53 59N 18 30 E
Starokonstantinov =
  Starokonstyantyniv,
  Ukraine .... **33 H4** 49 48N 27 10 E
Starokonstyantyniv,
  Ukraine .... **33 H4** 49 48N 27 10 E
Starokozache, *Ukraine* **29 D14** 46 20N 29 59 E
Starominskaya, *Russia* **33 J10** 46 33N 39 0 E
Staroshcherbinovskaya,
  Russia .... **33 J10** 46 40N 38 53 E
Start Pt., *U.K.* **15 G4** 50 13N 3 39W
Stary Sącz, *Poland* .... **31 J7** 49 33N 20 35 E
Stary Biryuzyak, *Russia* **35 H8** 44 46N 46 50 E
Staryy Chartoriysk,
  Ukraine .... **33 G3** 51 15N 25 54 E
Staryy Krym, *Ukraine* .. **33 K8** 45 3N 35 8 E
Staryy Oskol, *Russia* .. **33 G9** 51 19N 37 55 E
Staryy Sambir, *Ukraine* **31 J9** 49 27N 22 59 E
Stassfurt, *Germany* .... **24 D7** 51 51N 11 35 E
Staszów, *Poland* ...... **31 H8** 50 33N 21 10 E
State College, *U.S.A.* .. **116 F7** 40 48N 77 52W
Stateline, *U.S.A.* **110 G7** 38 57N 119 56W
Staten, I. = Estados, I.
  de Los, *Argentina* .. **128 G4** 54 40 S 64 30W
Staten I., *U.S.A.* **117 F10** 40 35N 74 9W
Statesboro, *U.S.A.* **115 J5** 32 27N 81 47W
Statesville, *U.S.A.* **115 H5** 35 47N 80 53W
Statia = St. Eustatius,
  W. Indies **121 C7** 17 20N 63 0W
Stauffer, *U.S.A.* **111 L7** 34 45N 119 3W
Staunton, *Ill., U.S.A.* .. **112 F10** 39 1N 89 47W
Staunton, *Va., U.S.A.* .. **114 F6** 38 9N 79 4W
Stavanger, *Norway* .... **9 G11** 58 57N 5 40 E
Staveley, *N.Z.* .... **91 K3** 43 40 S 171 32 E
Stavelot, *Belgium* ...... **17 D5** 50 23N 5 55 E
Stavern, *Norway* ...... **9 G14** 59 0N 10 1 E
Stavoren, *Neths.* ...... **17 B5** 52 53N 5 22 E
Stavropol, *Russia* ...... **35 H6** 45 5N 42 0 E
Stavros, *Cyprus* ...... **49 D11** 35 1N 32 38 E
Stavrós, *Greece* ...... **49 D6** 35 12N 24 45 E
Stavrós, Ákra, *Greece* .. **49 D6** 35 26N 24 58 E
Stavroúpolis, *Greece* .. **45 E8** 41 12N 24 45 E
Stawell, *Australia* ...... **95 F3** 37 5 S 142 47 E
Stawell →, *Australia* .. **94 C3** 20 20 S 142 55 E
Stawiski, *Poland* ...... **30 E9** 53 22N 22 9 E
Stawiszyn, *Poland* .... **31 G5** 51 56N 18 4 E
Stayner, *Canada* **116 B4** 44 25N 80 5W
Stayton, *U.S.A.* **108 D2** 44 48N 122 48W
Steamboat Springs,
  U.S.A. **108 F10** 40 29N 106 50W
Steblevë, *Albania* ...... **44 E4** 41 23N 20 33 E
Steele, *U.S.A.* **112 B5** 46 51N 99 55W
Steelton, *U.S.A.* **116 F8** 40 14N 76 50W
Steen River, *Canada* .. **102 B5** 59 40N 117 12W
Steens Mt., *U.S.A.* **108 E4** 42 35N 118 40W
Steenwijk, *Neths.* ...... **17 B6** 52 47N 6 7 E
Steep Pt., *Australia* .... **93 E1** 26 8 S 113 8 E
Steep Rock, *Canada* .. **103 C9** 51 30N 98 48W
Ştefăneşti, *Moldova* .. **29 D14** 46 27N 29 42 E
Ştefăneşti, *Romania* .. **29 C12** 47 44N 27 15 E
Stefanie L. = Chew
  Bahir, *Ethiopia* .... **81 G4** 4 40N 36 50 E
Stefansson Bay,
  Antarctica .... **5 C5** 67 20 S 59 8 E
Stege, *Denmark* ...... **11 K6** 54 59N 12 18 E
Ştei, *Romania* .... **28 D7** 46 32N 22 27 E
Steiermark □, *Austria* .. **26 D8** 47 26N 15 0 E
Steigerwald, *Germany* .. **25 F6** 49 44N 10 26 E
Steigerwald △, *Germany* **25 F6** 49 50N 10 26 E
Steilacoom, *U.S.A.* **110 C4** 47 10N 122 36W
Steilrandberge, *Namibia* **88 B1** 17 45 S 13 20 E
Steinbach, *Canada* .. **103 D9** 49 32N 96 40W
Steinfort, *Germany* .... **24 C3** 52 9N 7 20 E
Steinhausen, *Namibia* .. **88 C2** 21 49 S 18 20 E
Steinheim, *Germany* .. **24 D5** 51 51N 9 5 E
Steinhuder Meer,
  Germany .... **24 C5** 52 29N 9 21 E
Steinhuder Meer △,
  Germany .... **24 C5** 52 30N 9 16 E
Steinkjer, *Norway* ...... **8 D14** 64 1N 11 31 E
Steinkopf, *S. Africa* .... **88 D2** 29 18 S 17 43 E
Steinwald △, *Germany* **25 F8** 49 55N 12 3 E
Stellarton, *Canada* **105 C7** 45 32N 62 30W
Stellenbosch, *S. Africa* **88 E2** 33 58 S 18 50 E
Stelvio, Paso dello, *Italy* **40 B7** 46 32N 10 27 E
Stenay, *France* .... **19 C12** 49 29N 5 12 E
Stendal, *Germany* .... **24 C7** 52 36N 11 53 E
Stende, *Latvia* .... **30 A9** 57 11N 22 33 E
Stenhamra, *Sweden* .. **10 E11** 59 20N 17 41 E
Stenstorp, *Sweden* .... **11 F7** 58 17N 13 45 E
Stenungsund, *Sweden* **11 F5** 58 6N 11 50 E
Steornabhaigh =
  Stornoway, *U.K.* **13 C2** 58 13N 6 23W
Stepanakert =
  Xankändi, *Azerbaijan* **70 B5** 39 52N 46 49 E

Stepanavan, *Armenia* .. **35 K7** 41 1N 44 23 E
Stephens Creek,
  Australia .... **95 E3** 31 50 S 141 30 E
Stephens I., *Canada* .. **102 C2** 54 10N 130 45W
Stephens L., *Canada* .. **103 B9** 56 32N 95 0W
Stephenville, *Canada* .. **105 C8** 48 31N 58 35W
Stephenville, *U.S.A.* .. **113 J5** 32 13N 98 12W
Stepnica, *Poland* ...... **30 E1** 53 38N 14 36 E
Steppe, *Asia* .... **50 D9** 50 0N 50 0 E
Stereá Ellas □, *Greece* **46 C4** 38 50N 23 0 E
Sterkstroom, *S. Africa* **88 E4** 31 32 S 26 32 E
Sterling, *Colo., U.S.A.* .. **112 E3** 40 37N 103 13W
Sterling, *Ill., U.S.A.* .. **112 E10** 41 48N 89 42W
Sterling, *Kans., U.S.A.* **113 F5** 38 13N 98 12W
Sterling City, *U.S.A.* .. **113 K4** 31 51N 101 0W
Sterling Heights, *U.S.A.* **114 D4** 42 35N 83 0W
Sterling Run, *U.S.A.* .. **116 E6** 41 25N 78 12W
Sterlitamak, *Russia* .. **52 D6** 53 40N 56 0 E
Sternberg, *Germany* .. **24 B7** 53 42N 11 50 E
Šternberk, *Czech Rep.* **27 B10** 49 45N 17 15 E
Stérnes, *Greece* ...... **49 D6** 35 30N 24 9 E
Storozhinets =
  Storozhynets, *Ukraine* **29 B10** 48 14N 25 45 E
Storozhynets, *Ukraine* **29 B10** 48 14N 25 45 E
Storrs, *U.S.A.* **117 E12** 41 49N 72 15W
Storsjön, *Gävleborg,*
  Sweden .... **10 D10** 60 35N 16 45 E
Storsjön, *Jämtland,*
  Sweden .... **10 B7** 62 48N 13 7 E
Storsjön, *Jämtland,*
  Sweden .... **10 A8** 63 9N 14 30 E
Storstrøms
  Amtskommune □,
  Denmark .... **11 J5** 54 50N 11 45 E
Storuman, *Sweden* .... **8 D17** 65 5N 17 10 E
Storuman, *Sweden* .... **8 D17** 65 13N 16 50 E
Storvätteshågna, *Sweden* **10 B6** 62 6N 12 30 E
Storvik, *Sweden* ...... **10 D10** 60 35N 16 33 E
Storvreta, *Sweden* .... **10 E11** 59 58N 17 44 E
Stouffville, *Canada* **116 C5** 43 58N 79 15W
Stoughton, *Canada* .. **103 D8** 49 40N 103 0W
Stour →, *Dorset, U.K.* **15 G6** 50 43N 1 47W
Stour →, *Kent, U.K.* .. **15 F9** 51 18N 1 22 E
Stour →, *Suffolk, U.K.* **15 F9** 51 57N 1 4 E
Stourbridge, *U.K.* **15 E5** 52 28N 2 8W
Stout L., *Canada* **103 C10** 52 0N 94 40W
Stove Pipe Wells
  Village, *U.S.A.* **111 J9** 36 35N 117 11W
Støvring, *Denmark* .... **11 H3** 56 54N 9 50 E
Stow, *U.S.A.* **116 E3** 41 10N 81 27W
Stowbtsy, *Belarus* .... **32 F4** 53 30N 26 43 E
Stowmarket, *U.K.* .... **15 E9** 52 12N 1 0 E
Stowbtsy, *Belarus* .... **32 F4** 53 30N 26 43 E
Strabane, *U.K.* **12 B4** 54 50N 7 27W
Stracin, *Macedonia* .. **44 D6** 42 13N 22 2 E
Stradella, *Italy* .... **40 C6** 45 5N 9 18 E
Strahan, *Australia* .... **95 G4** 42 9 S 145 20 E
Strajitsa, *Bulgaria* .... **45 D9** 43 14N 25 58 E
Strakonice, *Czech Rep.* **26 B6** 49 15N 13 53 E
Straldzha, *Bulgaria* .. **45 D10** 42 35N 26 40 E
Stralsund, *Germany* .. **24 A9** 54 18N 13 4 E
Strand, *S. Africa* ...... **88 E2** 34 9 S 18 48 E
Stranda,
  Møre og Romsdal,
  Norway .... **9 E12** 62 19N 6 58 E
Stranda,
  Nord-Trøndelag,
  Norway .... **8 E14** 63 33N 10 14 E
Strandby, *Denmark* .. **11 G4** 57 30N 10 29 E
Strangford L., *U.K.* .. **12 B6** 54 30N 5 37W
Strängnäs, *Sweden* .. **10 E11** 59 23N 17 2 E
Stranraer, *U.K.* **13 G3** 54 54N 5 1W
Strasbourg, *Canada* .. **103 C8** 51 4N 104 55W
Strasbourg, *France* .. **19 D14** 48 35N 7 42 E
Strasburg, *Germany* .. **24 B9** 53 30N 13 43 E
Strǎşeni, *Moldova* .. **29 C13** 47 8N 28 36 E
Stratford, *N.Z.* ...... **91 H5** 39 20 S 174 19 E
Stratford, *Calif., U.S.A.* **110 J7** 36 11N 119 49W
Stratford, *Conn., U.S.A.* **117 E11** 41 12N 73 8W
Stratford, *Tex., U.S.A.* **113 G3** 36 20N 102 4W
Stratford-upon-Avon,
  U.K. **15 E6** 52 12N 1 42W
Strath Spey, *U.K.* **13 D5** 57 9N 3 49W
Strathalbyn, *Australia* .. **95 F2** 35 13 S 138 53 E
Strathaven, *U.K.* **13 F4** 55 40N 4 5W
Strathcona △, *Canada* **102 D3** 49 38N 125 40W
Strathmore, *Canada* .. **102 C6** 51 5N 113 18W
Strathmore, *U.K.* **13 E5** 56 37N 3 7W
Strathmore, *U.S.A.* .. **110 J7** 36 9N 119 4W
Strathnaver, *Canada* .. **102 C4** 53 20N 122 33W
Strathpeffer, *U.K.* **13 D4** 57 35N 4 32W
Strathroy, *Canada* **116 D3** 42 58N 81 38W
Strathy Pt., *U.K.* **13 C4** 58 36N 4 1W
Strattanville, *U.S.A.* .. **116 E5** 41 12N 79 19W
Stratton, *U.S.A.* **112 F3** 39 19N 102 36W
Stratton Mt., *U.S.A.* .. **117 C12** 43 4N 72 55W
Straubing, *Germany* .. **25 G8** 48 52N 12 34 E
Straumnes, *Iceland* .. **8 C2** 66 26N 23 8W
Strausberg, *Germany* .. **24 C9** 52 35N 13 54 E
Strawberry →, *U.S.A.* **108 F8** 40 10N 110 24W
Strawberry Res., *U.S.A.* **108 F8** 40 8N 111 9W
Streaky B., *Australia* .. **95 E1** 32 48 S 134 13 E
Streaky Bay, *Australia* **95 E1** 32 51 S 134 18 E
Streator, *U.S.A.* **112 E10** 41 8N 88 50W
Středočeský □,
  Czech Rep. .... **26 B7** 49 55N 14 30 E
Streetsboro, *U.S.A.* .. **116 E3** 41 14N 81 21W
Streetsville, *Canada* .. **116 C5** 43 35N 79 42W
Strehaia, *Romania* .. **29 F8** 44 37N 23 10 E
Strelcha, *Bulgaria* .... **45 D8** 42 25N 24 19 E
Strelka, *Russia* ...... **53 D10** 58 5N 93 3 E
Streng →, *Cambodia* **64 F4** 13 12N 103 37 E
Stresa, *Italy* .... **40 C5** 45 52N 8 38 E
Streymoy, *Færoe Is.* .. **8 E9** 62 8N 7 5W
Strezhevoy, *Russia* .. **52 C8** 60 42N 77 34 E
Stříbro, *Czech Rep.* .. **26 A6** 49 44N 13 0 E
Strilky, *Ukraine* ...... **31 J9** 49 23N 23 18 E
Strimón →, *Greece* .. **44 F7** 40 46N 23 51 E
Strimonikós Kólpos,
  Greece .... **44 F7** 40 33N 24 0 E
Strofádhes, *Greece* .. **46 D3** 37 15N 21 0 E
Stroma, *U.K.* **13 C5** 58 41N 3 7W
Strómboli, *Italy* ...... **43 D8** 38 47N 15 13 E
Stromeferry, *U.K.* **13 D3** 57 21N 5 33W
Stromness, *U.K.* **13 C5** 58 58N 3 17W
Strömstad, *Sweden* .. **11 F5** 58 56N 11 10 E
Strömsund, *Sweden* .. **8 E16** 63 51N 15 33 E
Strongili, *Greece* ...... **47 E11** 36 6N 29 42 E
Stróngoli, *Italy* .... **43 C10** 39 16N 17 5 E
Strongsville, *U.S.A.* .. **116 E3** 41 19N 81 50W

Stronie Śląskie, *Poland* **31 H3** 50 18N 16 53 E
Stronsay, *U.K.* **13 B6** 59 7N 2 35W
Stropkov, *Slovak Rep.* **27 B14** 49 13N 21 39 E
Stroud, *U.K.* **15 F5** 51 45N 2 13W
Stroud Road, *Australia* **95 E5** 32 18 S 151 57 E
Stroudsburg, *U.S.A.* .. **117 F9** 40 59N 75 12W
Stroumbi, *Cyprus* .... **49 E11** 34 53N 32 29 E
Struer, *Denmark* ...... **11 H2** 56 30N 8 35 E
Struga, *Macedonia* .. **44 E4** 41 11N 20 44 E
Strugi Krasnyye, *Russia* **32 C5** 58 21N 29 1 E
Strumica, *Macedonia* **44 E6** 41 28N 22 41 E
Strumica →, *Europe* .. **44 E7** 41 20N 23 22 E
Strumok, *Ukraine* .... **29 E14** 45 43N 29 27 E
Struthers, *Canada* **104 C2** 48 41N 85 51W
Struthers, *U.S.A.* **116 E4** 41 4N 80 39W
Stryama, *Bulgaria* .... **45 D8** 42 16N 24 54 E
Stryker, *U.S.A.* **108 B6** 48 41N 114 46W
Stryków, *Poland* ...... **31 G6** 51 55N 19 33 E
Stryy, *Ukraine* .... **33 H2** 49 16N 23 48 E
Strzegom, *Poland* .... **31 H3** 50 58N 16 20 E
Strzelce Krajeńskie,
  Poland .... **31 F2** 52 52N 15 33 E
Strzelce Opolskie,
  Poland .... **31 H5** 50 31N 18 18 E
Strzelecki Cr. →,
  Australia .... **95 D2** 29 37 S 139 59 E
Strzelin, *Poland* ...... **31 H4** 50 46N 17 2 E
Strzelno, *Poland* ...... **31 F5** 52 35N 18 9 E
Strzybnica, *Poland* .... **31 H5** 50 28N 18 48 E
Strzyżów, *Poland* ...... **31 J8** 49 52N 21 47 E
Stuart, *Fla., U.S.A.* .. **115 M5** 27 12N 80 15W
Stuart, *Nebr., U.S.A.* .. **112 D5** 42 36N 99 8W
Stuart →, *Canada* **102 C4** 54 0N 123 35W
Stuart Bluff Ra.,
  Australia .... **92 D5** 22 50 S 131 52 E
Stuart L., *Canada* **102 C4** 54 30N 124 30W
Stuart Ra., *Australia* .. **95 D1** 29 10 S 134 56 E
Stubbekøbing, *Denmark* **11 K6** 54 53N 12 9 E
Stuben, *Austria* ...... **26 D3** 47 10N 10 8 E
Studen Kladenets,
  Yazovir, *Bulgaria* .. **45 E9** 41 37N 25 30 E
Studenka, *Czech Rep.* **27 B11** 49 44N 18 5 E
Stugun, *Sweden* ...... **10 A9** 63 10N 15 40 E
Stuhr, *Germany* ...... **24 B4** 53 5N 8 44 E
Stull L., *Canada* **104 B1** 54 24N 92 34W
Stung Treng = Stoeng
  Treng, *Cambodia* .. **64 F5** 13 31N 105 58 E
Stupart →, *Canada* .. **104 B1** 56 0N 93 25W
Stupava, *Slovak Rep.* **27 C10** 48 17N 17 2 E
Stupino, *Russia* ...... **32 E10** 54 57N 38 2 E
Sturgeon B., *Canada* .. **103 C9** 52 0N 97 50W
Sturgeon Bay, *U.S.A.* **114 C2** 44 50N 87 23W
Sturgeon Falls, *Canada* **104 C4** 46 25N 79 57W
Sturgeon L., *Alta.,*
  Canada **102 B5** 55 6N 117 32W
Sturgeon L., *Ont.,*
  Canada **104 C1** 50 0N 90 45W
Sturgeon L., *Ont.,*
  Canada **116 B6** 44 28N 78 43W
Sturgis, *Canada* **103 C8** 51 56N 102 36W
Sturgis, *Mich., U.S.A.* **114 E3** 41 48N 85 25W
Sturgis, *S. Dak., U.S.A.* **112 C3** 44 25N 103 31W
Sturkö, *Sweden* ...... **11 H9** 56 5N 15 42 E
Štúrovo, *Slovak Rep.* .. **27 D11** 47 48N 18 41 E
Sturt △, *Australia* .... **95 D3** 27 17 S 141 37 E
Sturt Cr. →, *Australia* **92 C4** 19 8 S 127 50 E
Sturt Stony Desert,
  Australia .... **95 D3** 28 30 S 141 0 E
Stutterheim, *S. Africa* **88 E4** 32 33 S 27 28 E
Stuttgart, *Germany* .. **25 G5** 48 48N 9 11 E
Stuttgart, *U.S.A.* **113 H9** 34 30N 91 33W
Stuttgart
  Echterdingen ✈
  (STR), *Germany* .. **25 G5** 48 42N 9 11 E
Stuyvesant, *U.S.A.* .. **117 D11** 42 23N 73 45W
Stykkishólmur, *Iceland* **8 D2** 65 2N 22 40W
Styria = Steiermark □,
  Austria .... **26 D8** 47 26N 15 0 E
Styrsö, *Sweden* ...... **11 G5** 57 37N 11 46 E
Su Xian = Suzhou,
  China .... **56 H9** 33 41N 116 59 E
Suakin, *Sudan* .... **80 D4** 19 8N 37 20 E
Suan, *N. Korea* ...... **57 E14** 38 42N 126 22 E
Suaqui, *Mexico* **118 B3** 29 12N 109 41W
Subang, *Indonesia* .... **63 G12** 6 34 S 107 45 E
Subansiri →, *India* .. **67 F18** 26 48N 93 50 E
Subarnarekha →, *India* **69 H12** 22 34N 87 24 E
Subayhah, *Si. Arabia* .. **70 D3** 30 2N 38 50 E
Subcetate, *Romania* .. **29 E8** 45 51N 22 41 E
Subi, *Indonesia* ...... **62 D3** 2 58N 108 50 E
Subiaco, *Italy* .... **41 G10** 41 56N 13 5 E
Subotica, *Serbia & M.* **28 D4** 46 6N 19 39 E
Suca, *Ethiopia* .... **81 F4** 6 31N 39 14 E
Suceava, *Romania* .. **29 C11** 47 38N 26 16 E
Suceava □, *Romania* .. **29 C11** 47 37N 25 40 E
Suceava →, *Romania* **29 C11** 47 32N 26 32 E
Sucha-Beskidzka,
  Poland .... **31 J6** 49 44N 19 35 E
Suchań, *Poland* ...... **31 E2** 53 18N 15 18 E
Suchou = Suzhou,
  China .... **54 C6** 43 8N 133 9 E
Suchitoto, *El Salv.* .. **120 D2** 13 56N 89 0W
Suchou = Suzhou, *China* **59 B13** 31 19N 120 38 E
Suchou = Xuzhou,
  China .... **57 G9** 34 18N 117 10 E
Suchowola, *Poland* .. **30 E10** 53 33N 23 3 E
Suck →, *Ireland* **12 C3** 53 17N 8 3W
Sucre, *Bolivia* .... **124 G5** 19 0 S 65 15W
Sućuraj, *Croatia* ...... **41 E14** 43 10N 17 8 E
Sucuriú →, *Brazil* .. **125 H8** 20 47 S 51 38W
Sud, Pte. du, *Canada* **105 C7** 49 3N 62 14W
Sud-Kivu □, *Dem. Rep.*
  of the Congo ...... **86 C2** 3 0 S 28 30 E
Sud-Ouest, Pte., *Canada* **105 C7** 49 23 S 63 36W
Sudak, *Ukraine* ...... **33 K8** 44 51N 34 57 E
Sudan ■, *Africa* ...... **81 E3** 15 0N 30 0 E
Sudbury, *Canada* **104 C3** 46 30N 81 0W
Sudbury, *U.K.* .... **15 E8** 52 2N 0 45 E
Sudd, *Sudan* .... **81 F3** 8 20N 30 0 E
Sudeifel = Deutsch-
  Luxemburgischer-
  Germany .... **25 F2** 49 58N 6 12 E
Süderbrarup, *Germany* **24 A5** 54 38N 9 45 E
Süderlügum, *Germany* **24 A4** 54 50N 8 55 E
Süderoogsand, *Germany* **24 A4** 54 27N 8 28 E
Sudeten Mts. = Sudety,
  Europe .... **27 A9** 50 20N 16 45 E
Sudety, *Europe* ...... **27 A9** 50 20N 16 45 E
Südheide △, *Germany* **24 C6** 52 46N 10 0 E
Suðuroy, *Færoe Is.* .. **8 F9** 61 32N 6 50W
Sudi, *Tanzania* ...... **87 E4** 10 11 S 39 57 E
Sudirman, Pegunungan,
  Indonesia .... **63 E9** 4 30 S 137 0 E
Sudiți, *Romania* ...... **29 F12** 44 35N 27 38 E

Sudogda, *Russia* ...... **34 C5** 55 55N 40 50 E
Sudong, Pulau,
  Singapore ...... **65 d** 1 12N 103 43 E
Sudova Vyshnya,
  Ukraine ...... **31 J10** 49 46N 23 22 E
Sudr, *Egypt* ...... **80 B3** 29 40N 32 42 E
Sudzha, *Russia* ...... **33 G8** 51 14N 35 17 E
Sue ➤, *Sudan* ...... **81 F2** 7 41N 28 3 E
Sueca, *Spain* **39 F4** 39 12N 0 21W
Sŭedinenie, *Bulgaria* ...... **45 D8** 42 16N 24 33 E
Suemez I., *U.S.A.* **102 B2** 55 15N 133 20W
Suez = El Suweis, *Egypt* ...... **80 J8** 29 58N 32 31 E
Suez, G. of = Suweis,
  Khalîg el, *Egypt* ...... **80 J8** 28 40N 33 0 E
Suez Canal = Suweis,
  Qanâ es, *Egypt* ...... **80 H8** 31 0N 32 20 E
Suffield, *Canada* **102 C6** 50 12N 111 10W
Suffolk, *U.S.A.* **114 G7** 36 44N 76 35W
Suffolk □, *U.K.* ...... **15 E9** 52 16N 1 0 E
Şugag, *Romania* ...... **29 E8** 45 47N 23 37 E
Sugargrove, *U.S.A.* **116 E5** 41 59N 79 21W
Sugarive ➤, *India* ...... **69 F12** 26 16N 86 24 E
Suğla Gölü, *Turkey* ...... **72 D5** 37 20N 32 0 E
Sugluk = Salluit, *Canada* **101 B12** 62 14N 75 38W
Suhaia, Lacul, *Romania* **29 G10** 43 45N 25 15 E
Şuḩār, *Oman* ...... **71 E8** 24 20N 56 40 E
Sühbaatar, *Mongolia* ...... **56 B8** 50 30N 114 0 E
Suhl, *Germany* ...... **24 E6** 50 36N 10 42 E
Suhut, *Turkey* ...... **47 C12** 38 31N 30 32 E
Sui, *Pakistan* ...... **68 E3** 28 37N 69 19 E
Sui Xian, *China* ...... **56 G8** 34 25N 115 2 E
Šuica, *Bos.-H.* ...... **28 G2** 43 52N 17 11 E
Suichang, *China* ...... **59 C12** 28 29N 119 15 E
Suichuan, *China* ...... **59 D10** 26 20N 114 32 E
Suide, *China* ...... **56 F6** 37 30N 110 12 E
Suifenhe, *China* ...... **57 B16** 44 25N 131 10 E
Suihua, *China* ...... **60 B7** 46 32N 126 55 E
Suijiang, *China* ...... **58 C4** 28 40N 103 59 E
Suining, *Hunan, China* ...... **59 D8** 26 35N 110 10 E
Suining, *Jiangsu, China* **57 H9** 33 56N 117 58 E
Suining, *Sichuan, China* **58 B5** 30 26N 105 35 E
Suiping, *China* ...... **56 H7** 33 10N 113 59 E
Suippes, *France* ...... **19 C11** 49 8N 4 30 E
Suir ➤, *Ireland* **12 D4** 52 16N 7 9W
Suisun City, *U.S.A.* **110 G4** 38 15N 122 2W
Suixi, *China* ...... **59 F8** 21 18N 110 5 E
Suiyang, *Guizhou, China* **58 D6** 27 58N 107 18 E
Suiyang, *Heilongjiang,
  China* ...... **57 B16** 44 30N 130 56 E
Suizhong, *China* ...... **57 D11** 40 21N 120 20 E
Suizhou, *China* ...... **59 B9** 31 42N 113 24 E
Sujangarh, *India* ...... **68 F6** 27 42N 74 31 E
Sukabumi, *Indonesia* ...... **63 G12** 6 56 S 106 50 E
Sukadana, *Indonesia* ...... **62 E3** 1 10 S 110 0 E
Sukagawa, *Japan* ...... **55 F10** 37 17N 140 23 E
Sukaraja, *Indonesia* ...... **62 E4** 2 28 S 110 25 E
Sukawati, *Indonesia* ...... **63 K18** 8 35 S 115 17 E
Sukch'ŏn, *N. Korea* ...... **57 E13** 39 22N 125 35 E
Sukhindol, *Bulgaria* ...... **45 C9** 43 11N 25 10 E
Sukhinichi, *Russia* ...... **32 E8** 54 8N 35 10 E
Sukhona ➤, *Russia* ...... **52 D4** 61 15N 46 39 E
Sukhothai, *Thailand* ...... **64 D2** 17 1N 99 49 E
Sukhumi = Sokhumi,
  Georgia ...... **35 J5** 43 0N 41 0 E
Sukkur, *Pakistan* ...... **68 F3** 27 42N 68 54 E
Sukkur Barrage,
  Pakistan ...... **68 F3** 27 40N 68 50 E
Sukovo, *Serbia & M.* ...... **44 C6** 43 4N 22 37 E
Sukri ➤, *India* ...... **68 G4** 25 4N 71 43 E
Sukumo, *Japan* ...... **55 H6** 32 56N 132 44 E
Sukunka ➤, *Canada* **102 B4** 55 45N 121 15W
Sula ➤, *Ukraine* ...... **33 H7** 49 40N 32 41 E
Sula, Kepulauan,
  Indonesia ...... **63 E7** 1 45 S 125 0 E
Sulaco ➤, *Honduras* **120 C2** 15 2N 87 44W
Sulaiman Range,
  Pakistan ...... **68 D3** 30 30N 69 50 E
Sulak ➤, *Russia* ...... **35 J8** 43 20N 47 34 E
Sülār, *Iran* ...... **71 D6** 31 53N 51 54 E
Sulawesi, *Indonesia* ...... **63 E6** 2 0 S 120 0 E
Sulawesi Sea = Celebes
  Sea, *Indonesia* ...... **63 D6** 3 0N 123 0 E
Sulawesi Selatan □,
  Indonesia ...... **63 E6** 2 30 S 120 0 E
Sulawesi Tengah □,
  Indonesia ...... **63 E6** 1 30 S 121 0 E
Sulawesi Tenggara □,
  Indonesia ...... **63 E6** 3 50 S 122 0 E
Sulawesi Utara □,
  Indonesia ...... **63 D6** 1 0N 124 0 E
Sulechów, *Poland* ...... **31 F2** 52 5N 15 40 E
Sulęcin, *Poland* ...... **31 F2** 52 26N 15 10 E
Sulejów, *Poland* ...... **31 G6** 51 26N 19 53 E
Sulejówek, *Poland* ...... **31 F8** 52 13N 21 17 E
Süleymanlı, *Turkey* ...... **47 C9** 38 58N 27 47 E
Sulima, *S. Leone* **82 D2** 6 58N 11 32W
Sulina, *Romania* ...... **29 E14** 45 10N 29 40 E
Sulina, Braţul ➤,
  Romania ...... **29 E14** 45 10N 29 40 E
Sulingen, *Germany* ...... **24 C4** 52 41N 8 48 E
Suliţa, *Romania* ...... **29 C11** 47 39N 26 59 E
Sulitjelma, *Norway* ...... **8 C17** 67 9N 16 3 E
Sułkowice, *Poland* ...... **31 J6** 49 50N 19 49 E
Sullana, *Peru* ...... **124 D2** 4 52 S 80 39W
Süller, *Turkey* ...... **47 C11** 38 9N 29 29 E
Sullivan, *Ill., U.S.A.* **112 F10** 39 36N 88 37W
Sullivan, *Ind., U.S.A.* **114 F2** 39 6N 87 24W
Sullivan, *Mo., U.S.A.* **112 F9** 38 13N 91 10W
Sullivan Bay, *Canada* **102 C3** 50 55N 126 50W
Sullivan I. = Lanbi
  Kyun, *Burma* ...... **65 G2** 10 50N 98 20 E
Sullom Voe, *U.K.* **13 A7** 60 27N 1 20W
Sully-sur-Loire, *France* ...... **19 E9** 47 45N 2 20 E
Sulmierzyce, *Poland* ...... **31 G4** 51 37N 17 32 E
Sulmona, *Italy* ...... **41 F10** 42 3N 13 55 E
Süloğlu, *Turkey* ...... **45 E10** 41 44N 26 53 E
Sulphur, *La., U.S.A.* **113 K8** 30 14N 93 23W
Sulphur, *Okla., U.S.A.* **113 H6** 34 31N 96 58W
Sulphur Pt., *Canada* **102 A6** 60 56N 114 48W
Sulphur Springs, *U.S.A.* **113 J7** 33 8N 95 36W
Sultan, *Canada* **104 C3** 47 36N 82 47W
Sultan, *U.S.A.* **110 C5** 47 52N 121 49W
Sultan Dağları, *Turkey* **72 C4** 38 20N 31 20 E
Sultanhisar, *Turkey* ...... **47 D10** 37 53N 28 9 E
Sultaniye, *Turkey* ...... **45 F10** 40 37N 26 8 E
Sultanpur, *Mad. P.,
  India* ...... **68 H8** 23 9N 77 56 E
Sultanpur, *Punjab, India* **68 D6** 31 13N 75 11 E
Sultanpur, *Ut. P., India* **69 F10** 26 18N 82 4 E
Sulu Arch., *Phil.* ...... **61 J4** 6 0N 121 0 E
Sulu Sea, *E. Indies* ...... **61 G4** 8 0N 120 0 E
Sülüklü, *Turkey* ...... **72 C5** 38 53N 32 20 E
Sululta, *Ethiopia* ...... **81 F4** 9 10N 38 43 E
Suluova, *Turkey* ...... **72 B6** 40 46N 35 32 E
Suluq, *Libya* ...... **79 B10** 31 44N 20 14 E
Sulzbach, *Germany* ...... **25 F3** 49 18N 7 3 E

Sulzbach-Rosenberg,
  Germany ...... **25 F7** 49 30N 11 44 E
Sulzberger Ice Shelf,
  Antarctica ...... **5 E13** 78 0 S 150 0W
Sumalata, *Indonesia* ...... **63 D6** 1 0N 122 31 E
Sumampa, *Argentina* ...... **126 B3** 29 25 S 63 29W
Sumatera, *Indonesia* ...... **62 D2** 0 40N 100 20 E
Sumatera Barat □,
  Indonesia ...... **62 E2** 1 0 S 101 0 E
Sumatera Utara □,
  Indonesia ...... **62 D1** 2 30N 98 0 E
Sumatra = Sumatera,
  Indonesia ...... **62 D2** 0 40N 100 20 E
Šumava △, *Czech Rep.* ...... **26 C6** 49 0N 13 49 E
Sumba, *Indonesia* ...... **63 F5** 9 45 S 119 35 E
Sumba, Selat, *Indonesia* **63 F5** 9 0 S 118 40 E
Sumbawa, *Indonesia* ...... **62 F5** 8 26 S 117 30 E
Sumbawa Besar,
  Indonesia ...... **62 F5** 8 30 S 117 26 E
Sumbawanga □,
  Tanzania ...... **84 F6** 8 0 S 31 30 E
Sumbe, *Angola* ...... **84 G2** 11 10 S 13 48 E
Sumbu △, *Zambia* ...... **87 D3** 8 43 S 30 22 E
Sumburgh Hd., *U.K.* **13 B7** 59 52N 1 17W
Sumdeo, *India* ...... **69 D8** 31 26N 78 44 E
Sumdo, *China* ...... **69 B8** 35 6N 78 41 E
Sumedang, *Indonesia* ...... **63 G12** 6 52 S 107 55 E
Sümeg, *Hungary* ...... **28 D2** 46 59N 17 20 E
Sumeih, *Sudan* ...... **81 F2** 9 50N 27 39 E
Sumen = Shumen,
  Bulgaria ...... **45 C10** 43 18N 26 55 E
Sumenep, *Indonesia* ...... **63 G15** 7 1 S 113 52 E
Sumgait = Sumqayıt,
  Azerbaijan ...... **35 K9** 40 34N 49 38 E
Summer L., *U.S.A.* **108 E3** 42 50N 120 45W
Summerland, *Canada* **102 D5** 49 32N 119 41W
Summerside, *Canada* **105 C7** 46 24N 63 47W
Summersville, *U.S.A.* **114 F5** 38 17N 80 51W
Summerville, *Ga.,
  U.S.A.* **115 H3** 34 29N 85 21W
Summerville, *S.C.,
  U.S.A.* **115 J5** 33 1N 80 11W
Summit Lake, *Canada* **102 C4** 54 20N 122 40W
Summit Peak, *U.S.A.* **109 H10** 37 21N 106 42W
Sumner, *Iowa, U.S.A.* **112 D8** 42 51N 92 6W
Sumner, *Wash., U.S.A.* **110 C4** 47 12N 122 14W
Sumoto, *Japan* ...... **55 G7** 34 21N 134 54 E
Šumperk, *Czech Rep.* ...... **27 B9** 49 59N 16 59 E
Sumqayıt, *Azerbaijan* ...... **35 K9** 40 34N 49 38 E
Sumter, *U.S.A.* **115 J5** 33 55N 80 21W
Sumy, *Ukraine* ...... **33 G8** 50 57N 34 50 E
Sun City, *S. Africa* ...... **88 D4** 25 17 S 27 3 E
Sun City, *Ariz., U.S.A.* **109 K7** 33 36N 112 17W
Sun City, *Calif., U.S.A.* **111 M9** 33 42N 117 11W
Sun City Center, *U.S.A.* **115 M4** 27 43N 82 18W
Sun Lakes, *U.S.A.* **109 K8** 33 10N 111 52W
Sun Valley, *U.S.A.* **108 E6** 43 42N 114 21W
Sunagawa, *Japan* ...... **54 C10** 43 29N 141 55 E
Sunan, *N. Korea* ...... **57 E13** 39 15N 125 40 E
Sunart, L., *U.K.* **13 E3** 56 42N 5 43W
Sunburst, *U.S.A.* **108 B8** 48 53N 111 55W
Sunbury, *Australia* ...... **95 F3** 37 35 S 144 44 E
Sunbury, *U.S.A.* **117 F8** 40 52N 76 48W
Sunchales, *Argentina* ...... **126 C3** 30 58 S 61 35W
Suncho Corral,
  Argentina ...... **126 B3** 27 55 S 63 27W
Sunch'ŏn, *S. Korea* ...... **57 G14** 34 52N 127 31 E
Suncook, *U.S.A.* **117 C13** 43 8N 71 27W
Sunda, Selat, *Indonesia* **62 F3** 6 20 S 105 30 E
Sunda Is., *Indonesia* ...... **96 H2** 5 0 S 105 0 E
Sunda Str. = Sunda,
  Selat, *Indonesia* ...... **62 F3** 6 20 S 105 30 E
Sundance, *Canada* **103 B10** 56 32N 94 4W
Sundance, *U.S.A.* **112 C2** 44 24N 104 23W
Sundar Nagar, *India* ...... **68 D7** 31 32N 76 53 E
Sundarbans, *Asia* ...... **67 J16** 22 0N 89 0 E
Sundargarh, *India* ...... **67 H14** 22 4N 84 5 E
Sundays = Sondags ➤,
  S. Africa ...... **88 E4** 33 44 S 25 51 E
Sunderland, *Canada* **116 B5** 44 16N 79 4W
Sunderland, *U.K.* **14 C6** 54 55N 1 23W
Sundown △, *Australia* ...... **95 D5** 28 49 S 151 38 E
Sundre, *Canada* **102 C6** 51 49N 114 38W
Sunds, *Denmark* ...... **11 H3** 56 13N 9 1 E
Sundsvall, *Sweden* ...... **10 B11** 62 23N 17 17 E
Sundsvallsbukten,
  Sweden ...... **10 B11** 62 21N 17 25 E
Sung Hei, *Vietnam* ...... **65 G6** 10 20N 106 2 E
Sungai Acheh, *Malaysia* **65 c** 5 8N 100 30 E
Sungai Kolok, *Thailand* **65 J3** 6 2N 101 58 E
Sungai Lembing,
  Malaysia ...... **65 L4** 3 55N 103 3 E
Sungai Petani, *Malaysia* **65 K3** 5 37N 100 30 E
Sungaigerong, *Indonesia* **62 E2** 2 59 S 104 52 E
Sungailiat, *Indonesia* ...... **62 E3** 1 51 S 106 8 E
Sungaipenuh, *Indonesia* **62 E2** 2 1 S 101 20 E
Sungari = Songhua
  Jiang ➤, *China* ...... **60 B8** 47 45N 132 30 E
Sunghua Chiang =
  Songhua Jiang ➤,
  China ...... **60 B8** 47 45N 132 30 E
Sungikai, *Sudan* ...... **81 E2** 12 20N 29 51 E
Sungurlu, *Turkey* ...... **72 B6** 40 12N 34 21 E
Sunja, *Croatia* ...... **41 C13** 45 21N 16 35 E
Sunland Park, *U.S.A.* **109 L10** 31 50N 106 40W
Sunnansjö, *Sweden* ...... **10 D8** 60 13N 14 58 E
Sunndalsøra, *Norway* ...... **9 E13** 62 40N 8 33 E
Sunne, *Sweden* ...... **10 E7** 59 52N 13 5 E
Sunnemo, *Sweden* ...... **10 E7** 59 53N 13 44 E
Sunnyside, *U.S.A.* **108 C3** 46 20N 120 0W
Sunnyvale, *U.S.A.* **110 H4** 37 23N 122 2W
Suntar, *Russia* ...... **53 C12** 62 15N 117 30 E
Sunyani, *Ghana* **82 D4** 7 21N 2 22W
Suomenselkä, *Finland* ...... **8 E21** 62 52N 24 0 E
Suomussalmi, *Finland* ...... **8 D23** 64 54N 29 10 E
Suoyarvi, *Russia* ...... **32 A7** 62 3N 32 20 E
Supai, *U.S.A.* **109 H7** 36 15N 112 41W
Supaul, *India* ...... **69 F12** 26 10N 86 40 E
Superior, *Ariz., U.S.A.* **109 K8** 33 18N 111 6W
Superior, *Mont., U.S.A.* **108 C6** 47 12N 114 53W
Superior, *Nebr., U.S.A.* **112 E5** 40 1N 98 4W
Superior, *Wis., U.S.A.* **112 B8** 46 44N 92 6W
Superior, *L., N. Amer.* **104 C2** 47 0N 87 0W
Supetar, *Croatia* ...... **41 E13** 43 25N 16 32 E
Suphan Buri, *Thailand* **64 E3** 14 14N 100 10 E
Suphan Dağı, *Turkey* ...... **70 B4** 38 54N 42 48 E
Supiori, *Indonesia* ...... **63 E9** 1 0 S 136 0 E
Suprasl, *Poland* ...... **31 E10** 53 13N 23 19 E
Supraśl ➤, *Poland* ...... **31 E9** 53 7N 22 58 E
Supung Shuiku, *China* **57 D13** 40 35N 124 50 E
Suqian, *China* ...... **57 H10** 33 54N 118 8 E
Suquṭra = Socotra,
  Yemen ...... **75 E5** 12 30N 54 0 E
Şūr, *Lebanon* ...... **74 B4** 33 19N 35 16 E
Şūr, *Oman* ...... **75 C6** 22 34N 59 32 E
Sur, Pt., *U.S.A.* **110 J5** 36 18N 121 54W

Sura ➤, *Russia* ...... **34 C8** 56 6N 46 0 E
Surab, *Pakistan* ...... **68 E2** 28 25N 66 15 E
Surabaja = Surabaya,
  Indonesia ...... **63 G15** 7 17 S 112 45 E
Surabaya, *Indonesia* ...... **63 G15** 7 17 S 112 45 E
Surahammar, *Sweden* ...... **10 E10** 59 43N 16 13 E
Suraia, *Romania* ...... **29 E12** 45 40N 27 25 E
Surakarta, *Indonesia* ...... **63 G14** 7 35 S 110 48 E
Surakhany, *Azerbaijan* **35 K10** 40 25N 50 1 E
Şūran, *Syria* ...... **70 C3** 35 15N 36 45 E
Şūrān, *Syria* ...... **72 D5** 35 28N 32 0 E
Şuranji, *Slovak Rep.* ...... **27 C11** 48 6N 18 10 E
Surat, *Australia* ...... **95 D4** 27 10 S 149 6 E
Surat, *India* ...... **66 J8** 21 12N 72 55 E
Surat Thani, *Thailand* ...... **65 H2** 9 6N 99 20 E
Suratgarh, *India* ...... **68 E5** 29 18N 73 55 E
Suraż, *Poland* ...... **31 F9** 52 57N 22 57 E
Surazh, *Belarus* ...... **32 E6** 55 25N 30 44 E
Surazh, *Russia* ...... **33 F7** 53 5N 32 27 E
Surduc, *Romania* ...... **29 C8** 47 15N 23 23 E
Surduc Pasul, *Romania* **29 E8** 45 21N 23 23 E
Surdulica, *Serbia & M.* ...... **44 D6** 42 41N 22 11 E
Surendranagar, *India* ...... **68 H4** 22 45N 71 40 E
Surf, *U.S.A.* **111 L6** 34 41N 120 36W
Surfers Paradise,
  Australia ...... **95 D5** 28 0 S 153 25 E
Surgères, *France* **20 B3** 46 7N 0 47W
Surgut, *Russia* ...... **52 C8** 61 14N 73 20 E
Suri, *India* ...... **69 H12** 23 50N 87 34 E
Suriapet, *India* ...... **66 L11** 17 10N 79 40 E
Surigao, *Phil.* ...... **61 G6** 9 47N 125 29 E
Surigao Strait, *Phil.* ...... **61 F6** 10 15N 125 23 E
Surin, *Thailand* ...... **64 E4** 14 50N 103 34 E
Surin Nua, Ko, *Thailand* **65 H1** 9 30N 97 55 E
Surinam = Suriname ■,
  S. Amer. **125 C7** 4 0N 56 0W
Suriname ■, *S. Amer.* **125 C7** 4 0N 56 0W
Suriname ➤, *Suriname* **125 B7** 5 50N 55 15W
Sürmaq, *Iran* ...... **71 D7** 31 3N 52 48 E
Sürmene, *Turkey* ...... **73 B9** 41 0N 40 1 E
Surovikino, *Russia* ...... **35 F6** 48 32N 42 55 E
Surrey, *Canada* **110 A4** 49 10N 122 54W
Surrey □, *U.K.* **15 F7** 51 15N 0 31W
Sursand, *India* ...... **69 F11** 26 39N 85 43 E
Sursar ➤, *India* ...... **69 F12** 26 14N 87 3 E
Sursee, *Switz.* ...... **25 H4** 47 11N 8 6 E
Sursk, *Russia* ...... **34 D7** 53 3N 45 40 E
Surskoye, *Russia* ...... **34 C8** 54 30N 46 44 E
Surt, *Libya* ...... **79 B9** 31 11N 16 39 E
Surt, Khalīj, *Libya* ...... **79 B9** 31 40N 18 30 E
Surtanahu, *Pakistan* ...... **68 F4** 26 22N 70 0 E
Surte, *Sweden* ...... **11 G6** 57 50N 12 1 E
Surtsey, *Iceland* **8 E3** 63 20N 20 30W
Sürüç, *Turkey* ...... **73 D8** 36 58N 38 25 E
Suruga-Wan, *Japan* ...... **55 G9** 34 45N 138 30 E
Susa, *Italy* ...... **40 C4** 45 8N 7 3 E
Suså ➤, *Denmark* ...... **11 J5** 55 12N 11 42 E
Sušac, *Croatia* ...... **41 F13** 42 46N 16 30 E
Susak, *Croatia* ...... **41 D11** 44 30N 14 18 E
Susaki, *Japan* ...... **55 H6** 33 22N 133 17 E
Süsangerd, *Iran* ...... **71 D6** 31 35N 48 6 E
Susanville, *U.S.A.* **108 F3** 40 25N 120 39W
Susch, *Switz.* ...... **25 J6** 46 46N 10 5 E
Suşehri, *Turkey* ...... **73 B8** 40 10N 38 6 E
Sušice, *Czech Rep.* ...... **26 B6** 49 17N 13 30 E
Susleni, *Moldova* ...... **29 C13** 47 25N 28 59 E
Susner, *India* ...... **68 H7** 23 57N 76 5 E
Susong, *China* ...... **59 B11** 30 10N 116 5 E
Susquehanna, *U.S.A.* **117 E9** 41 57N 75 36W
Susquehanna ➤, *U.S.A.* **117 G8** 39 33N 76 5W
Susques, *Argentina* ...... **126 A2** 23 35 S 66 25W
Sussex, *Canada* **105 C6** 45 45N 65 37W
Sussex, *U.S.A.* **117 E10** 41 13N 74 37W
Sussex, E. □, *U.K.* ...... **15 G8** 51 0N 0 20 E
Sussex, W. □, *U.K.* **15 G7** 51 0N 0 30W
Sustut ➤, *Canada* **102 B3** 56 20N 127 30W
Susuman, *Russia* ...... **53 C15** 62 47N 148 10 E
Susunu, *Indonesia* ...... **63 E8** 3 7 S 133 39 E
Susurluk, *Turkey* ...... **47 B10** 39 54N 28 8 E
Susuz, *Turkey* ...... **73 B10** 40 46N 43 8 E
Susz, *Poland* ...... **30 E6** 53 44N 19 20 E
Sütçüler, *Turkey* ...... **72 D4** 37 29N 30 57 E
Şuţeşti, *Romania* ...... **29 E12** 45 13N 27 27 E
Sutherland, *S. Africa* ...... **88 E3** 32 24 S 20 40 E
Sutherland, *U.K.* **13 C4** 58 12N 4 50W
Sutherland, *U.S.A.* **112 E4** 41 10N 101 8W
Sutherland Falls, *N.Z.* **91 L1** 44 48 S 167 46 E
Sutherlin, *U.S.A.* **108 E2** 43 23N 123 19W
Suthri, *India* ...... **68 H3** 23 3N 68 55 E
Sutjeska △, *Bos.-H.* ...... **28 G3** 43 50N 18 32 E
Sutlej ➤, *Pakistan* ...... **68 E4** 29 23N 71 3 E
Sutter, *U.S.A.* **110 F5** 39 10N 121 45W
Sutter Creek, *U.S.A.* **110 G6** 38 24N 120 48W
Sutton, *Canada* **117 A12** 45 6N 72 37W
Sutton, *Nebr., U.S.A.* **112 E6** 40 36N 97 52W
Sutton, *W. Va., U.S.A.* **114 F5** 38 40N 80 43W
Sutton ➤, *Canada* **104 A3** 55 15N 83 45W
Sutton Coldfield, *U.K.* **15 E6** 52 35N 1 49W
Sutton in Ashfield, *U.K.* **14 D6** 53 8N 1 16W
Sutton L., *Canada* **104 B3** 54 15N 84 42W
Suttor ➤, *Australia* ...... **94 C4** 21 36 S 147 2 E
Suttsu, *Japan* ...... **54 C10** 42 48N 140 14 E
Suva, *Fiji* ...... **91 D8** 18 6 S 178 30 E
Suva Gora, *Macedonia* **44 E5** 41 45N 21 3 E
Suva Planina,
  Serbia & M. ...... **44 C6** 43 10N 22 5 E
Suva Reka, *Serbia & M.* **44 D5** 42 21N 20 50 E
Suvorov, *Russia* ...... **32 E9** 54 7N 36 30 E
Suvorov Is. = Suwarrow
  Is., *Cook Is.* ...... **97 J11** 15 0 S 163 0W
Suvorove, *Ukraine* ...... **29 E14** 45 35N 28 59 E
Suvorovo, *Bulgaria* ...... **45 C11** 43 20N 27 35 E
Suwałki, *Poland* ...... **30 D9** 54 8N 22 59 E
Suwana, *Indonesia* ...... **63 K18** 8 44 S 115 36 E
Suwannaphum, *Thailand* **64 E4** 15 33N 103 47 E
Suwannee ➤, *U.S.A.* **115 L4** 29 17N 83 10W
Suwanose-Jima, *Japan* ...... **55 K4** 29 38N 129 43 E
Suwarrow Is., *Cook Is.* **97 J11** 15 0 S 163 0W
Suwayq aş Şuqban, *Iraq* **70 D5** 31 32N 46 7 E
Suweis, Khalîg el, *Egypt* **80 J8** 28 40N 33 0 E
Suweis, Qanâ es, *Egypt* **80 H8** 31 0N 32 20 E
Suwŏn, *S. Korea* ...... **57 F14** 37 17N 127 1 E
Suzdal, *Russia* ...... **32 D11** 56 29N 40 26 E
Suzhou, *Anhui, China* **56 H9** 33 41N 116 59 E
Suzhou, *Jiangsu, China* **59 B13** 31 19N 120 38 E
Suzu, *Japan* ...... **55 F8** 37 25N 137 17 E
Suzu-Misaki, *Japan* ...... **55 F8** 37 31N 137 21 E
Suzuka, *Japan* ...... **55 G8** 34 55N 136 36 E
Suzzara, *Italy* ...... **40 D7** 44 59N 10 45 E
Svalbard, *Arctic* ...... **51 B5** 78 0N 17 0 E
Svalbard Radio =
  Longyearbyen,
  Svalbard ...... **4 B8** 78 13N 15 40 E
Svalöv, *Sweden* ...... **11 J7** 55 57N 13 8 E
Svalyava, *Ukraine* ...... **28 B8** 48 33N 22 59 E
Svaneke, *Denmark* ...... **11 J9** 55 8N 15 5 E
Svängsta, *Sweden* ...... **11 H8** 56 16N 14 47 E
Svappavaara, *Sweden* ...... **8 C19** 67 40N 21 3 E

Svärdsjö, *Sweden* ...... **10 D9** 60 45N 15 54 E
Svartå, *Sweden* ...... **10 E8** 59 8N 14 32 E
Svartisen, *Norway* ...... **8 C15** 66 40N 13 59 E
Svartvik, *Sweden* ...... **10 B11** 62 19N 17 24 E
Svatove, *Ukraine* ...... **33 H10** 49 35N 38 15 E
Svatovo = Svatove,
  Ukraine ...... **33 H10** 49 35N 38 15 E
Svay Chek, *Cambodia* ...... **64 F4** 13 48N 102 58 E
Svay Rieng, *Cambodia* **65 G5** 11 9N 105 45 E
Svealand □, *Sweden* ...... **10 D9** 60 20N 15 0 E
Svedala, *Sweden* ...... **11 J7** 55 30N 13 15 E
Sveg, *Sweden* ...... **10 B8** 62 2N 14 21 E
Svendborg, *Denmark* ...... **11 J4** 55 4N 10 35 E
Svenljunga, *Sweden* ...... **11 G7** 57 29N 13 5 E
Svenstavik, *Sweden* ...... **10 B8** 62 45N 14 26 E
Svenstrup, *Denmark* ...... **11 H3** 56 58N 9 50 E
Sverdlovsk, *Ukraine* ...... **33 H10** 48 5N 39 47 E
Sverdrup Is., *Canada* **98 B10** 79 0N 97 0W
Svetac, *Croatia* ...... **41 E12** 43 3N 15 43 E
Sveti Nikola, Prokhad,
  Europe ...... **44 C6** 43 27N 22 6 E
Sveti Nikole, *Macedonia* **44 E5** 41 51N 21 56 E
Sveti Rok, *Croatia* ...... **41 D12** 44 22N 15 39 E
Svetlaya, *Russia* ...... **54 A9** 46 33N 138 18 E
Svetlogorsk, *Belarus* ...... **33 F5** 52 38N 29 46 E
Svetlogorsk, *Russia* ...... **30 D7** 54 56N 20 10 E
Svetlograd, *Russia* ...... **35 H6** 45 25N 42 58 E
Svetlovodsk =
  Svitlovodsk, *Ukraine* **33 H7** 49 2N 33 13 E
Svetlyy, *Russia* ...... **30 D7** 54 41N 20 8 E
Svilaja Planina, *Croatia* **41 E13** 43 49N 16 31 E
Svilajnac, *Serbia & M.* **44 B5** 44 15N 21 11 E
Svilengrad, *Bulgaria* ...... **45 F10** 41 49N 26 12 E
Svir ➤, *Russia* ...... **32 B7** 60 30N 32 48 E
Sviritsa, *Russia* ...... **32 B7** 60 29N 32 51 E
Svishtov, *Bulgaria* ...... **45 C9** 43 36N 25 23 E
Svislach, *Belarus* ...... **31 E11** 53 3N 24 2 E
Svitava ➤, *Czech Rep.* **27 B9** 49 11N 16 37 E
Svitavy, *Czech Rep.* ...... **27 B9** 49 47N 16 28 E
Svitlovodsk, *Ukraine* ...... **33 H7** 49 2N 33 13 E
Svobodnyy, *Russia* ...... **53 D13** 51 20N 128 0 E
Svoge, *Bulgaria* ...... **44 D7** 42 59N 23 23 E
Svolvær, *Norway* ...... **8 B16** 68 15N 14 34 E
Svratka ➤, *Czech Rep.* **27 B9** 49 11N 16 38 E
Svrljig, *Serbia & M.* ...... **44 C6** 43 25N 22 6 E
Svyetlahorsk, *Belarus* ...... **33 F5** 52 38N 29 46 E
Swabian Alps =
  Schwäbische Alb,
  Germany ...... **25 G5** 48 20N 9 30 E
Swaffham, *U.K.* ...... **15 E8** 52 39N 0 42 E
Swainsboro, *U.S.A.* **115 J4** 32 36N 82 20W
Swakop ➤, *Namibia* ...... **88 C2** 22 38 S 14 36 E
Swakopmund, *Namibia* **88 C1** 22 37 S 14 30 E
Swale ➤, *U.K.* **14 C6** 54 5N 1 20W
Swan ➤, *Australia* ...... **93 F2** 32 3 S 115 45 E
Swan ➤, *Canada* **103 C8** 52 30N 100 45W
Swan Hill, *Australia* ...... **95 F3** 35 20 S 143 33 E
Swan Hills, *Canada* **102 C5** 54 43N 115 24W
Swan Is. = Santanilla, Is.,
  Honduras **120 C3** 17 22N 83 57W
Swan L., *Canada* **103 C8** 52 30N 100 40W
Swan Peak, *U.S.A.* **108 C7** 47 43N 113 38W
Swan Ra., *U.S.A.* **108 C7** 48 0N 113 45W
Swan River, *Canada* **103 C8** 52 10N 101 16W
Swanage, *U.K.* **15 G6** 50 36N 1 58W
Swansea, *Australia* ...... **95 G4** 42 8 S 148 4 E
Swansea, *Canada* **116 C5** 43 38N 79 28W
Swansea, *U.K.* **15 F4** 51 37N 3 57W
Swansea □, *U.K.* **15 F3** 51 38N 4 3W
Swar ➤, *Pakistan* ...... **69 B5** 34 40N 72 5 E
Swartberge, *S. Africa* ...... **88 E3** 33 20 S 22 0 E
Swartmodder, *S. Africa* **88 D3** 28 1 S 20 32 E
Swartnossob ➤,
  Namibia ...... **88 C2** 23 8 S 18 42 E
Swartruggens, *S. Africa* **88 D4** 25 39 S 26 42 E
Swarzędz, *Poland* ...... **31 F4** 52 25N 17 4 E
Swastika, *Canada* **104 C3** 48 7N 80 6W
Swatow = Shantou,
  China ...... **59 F11** 23 18N 116 40 E
Swaziland ■, *Africa* ...... **89 D5** 26 30 S 31 30 E
Sweden ■, *Europe* ...... **9 G16** 57 0N 15 0 E
Swedru, *Ghana* **83 D4** 5 32N 0 41W
Sweet Home, *U.S.A.* **108 D2** 44 24N 122 44W
Sweetgrass, *U.S.A.* **108 B8** 48 59N 111 58W
Sweetwater, *Nev., U.S.A.* **110 G7** 38 27N 119 9W
Sweetwater, *Tenn.,
  U.S.A.* **115 H3** 35 36N 84 28W
Sweetwater, *Tex., U.S.A.* **113 J4** 32 28N 100 25W
Sweetwater ➤, *U.S.A.* **108 E10** 42 31N 107 2W
Swellendam, *S. Africa* ...... **88 E3** 34 1 S 20 26 E
Świdnica, *Poland* ...... **31 H3** 50 50N 16 30 E
Świdnik, *Poland* ...... **31 G9** 51 13N 22 39 E
Świdwin, *Poland* ...... **30 E2** 53 47N 15 49 E
Świebodzice, *Poland* ...... **31 H3** 50 51N 16 20 E
Świebodzin, *Poland* ...... **31 F2** 52 15N 15 31 E
Świecie, *Poland* ...... **30 E5** 53 25N 18 30 E
Świerzawa, *Poland* ...... **31 G2** 51 1N 15 54 E
Świętokrzyski △,
  Poland ...... **31 H7** 50 53N 20 59 E
Świętokrzyskie □,
  Poland ...... **31 H7** 51 0N 20 0 E
Świętokrzyskie, Góry,
  Poland ...... **31 H7** 51 0N 20 30 E
Swift Current, *Canada* **103 C7** 50 20N 107 45W
Swift Current ➤,
  Canada **103 C7** 50 38N 107 44W
Swilly, L., *Ireland* **12 A4** 55 12N 7 33W
Swindon, *U.K.* **15 F6** 51 34N 1 46W
Swindon □, *U.K.* **15 F6** 51 34N 1 46W
Swinemünde =
  Świnoujście, *Poland* **30 E1** 53 54N 14 16 E
Swinford, *Ireland* **12 C3** 53 57N 8 58W
Świnoujście, *Poland* ...... **30 E1** 53 54N 14 16 E
Switzerland ■, *Europe* ...... **25 J4** 46 30N 8 0 E
Swords, *Ireland* **12 C5** 53 28N 6 13W
Swoyerville, *U.S.A.* **117 E9** 41 18N 75 53W
Syasstroy, *Russia* ...... **32 B7** 60 9N 73 33 E
Sychevka, *Russia* ...... **32 D8** 55 59N 34 16 E
Syców, *Poland* ...... **31 G4** 51 19N 17 40 E
Sydenham ➤, *Canada* **116 D2** 42 33N 82 25W
Sydney, *Australia* ...... **95 E5** 33 53 S 151 10 E
Sydney, *Canada* **105 C7** 46 7N 60 7W
Sydney L., *Canada* **103 C10** 50 41N 94 25W
Sydney Mines, *Canada* **105 C7** 46 18N 60 15W
Sydprøven = Alluitsup
  Paa, *Greenland* **101 B15** 60 30N 45 35W
Sydra, G. of = Surt,
  Khalīj, *Libya* ...... **79 B9** 31 40N 18 30 E
Syeverodonetsk,
  Ukraine ...... **33 H10** 48 58N 38 35 E
Syke, *Germany* ...... **24 C4** 52 55N 8 50 E
Sykesville, *U.S.A.* **116 E6** 41 3N 78 50W
Syktyvkar, *Russia* ...... **52 C6** 61 45N 50 40 E
Sylacauga, *U.S.A.* **115 J2** 33 10N 86 15W
Sylarna, *Sweden* ...... **8 E15** 63 2N 12 13 E

Sylhet, *Bangla.* ...... **67 G17** 24 54N 91 52 E
Sylhet □, *Bangla.* ...... **67 G17** 24 50N 91 50 E
Sylt, *Germany* ...... **24 A4** 54 54N 8 22 E
Sylvan Beach, *U.S.A.* **117 C9** 43 12N 75 44W
Sylvan Lake, *Canada* **102 C6** 52 20N 114 3W
Sylvania, *U.S.A.* **115 J5** 32 45N 81 38W
Sylvester, *U.S.A.* **115 K4** 31 32N 83 50W
Sym, *Russia* ...... **52 C9** 60 20N 88 18 E
Symón, *Mexico* **118 C4** 24 42N 102 35W
Synelnykove, *Ukraine* ...... **33 H8** 48 25N 35 30 E
Synevyr △, *Ukraine* ...... **29 B8** 48 30N 23 40 E
Synevyrska Polyana,
  Ukraine ...... **29 B8** 48 35N 23 41 E
Synnott Ra., *Australia* ...... **92 C4** 16 30 S 125 20 E
Synyak, *Ukraine* ...... **28 B7** 48 35N 22 51 E
Syowa, *Antarctica* ...... **5 C5** 68 50 S 12 0 E
Syracuse, *Kans., U.S.A.* **113 G4** 37 59N 101 45W
Syracuse, *N.Y., U.S.A.* **117 C8** 43 3N 76 9W
Syracuse, *Nebr., U.S.A.* **112 E6** 40 39N 96 11W
Syrdarya ➤,
  Kazakhstan ...... **52 E7** 46 3N 61 0 E
Syria ■, *Asia* ...... **70 C3** 35 0N 38 0 E
Syrian Desert = Shām,
  Bādiyat ash, *Asia* ...... **70 C3** 32 0N 40 0 E
Syssleback, *Sweden* ...... **10 D6** 60 44N 12 52 E
Syzran, *Russia* ...... **34 D9** 53 12N 48 30 E
Szabolcs-Szatmár-
  Bereg □, *Hungary* ...... **28 B6** 48 2N 21 45 E
Szadek, *Poland* ...... **31 G5** 51 41N 18 59 E
Szamocin, *Poland* ...... **31 E4** 53 2N 17 7 E
Szamos ➤, *Hungary* ...... **28 B7** 48 7N 22 20 E
Szamotuły, *Poland* ...... **31 F3** 52 37N 16 33 E
Szarvas ➤, *Hungary* ...... **28 D6** 46 10N 21 15 E
Szarvas, *Hungary* ...... **28 D5** 46 50N 20 38 E
Százhalombatta,
  Hungary ...... **28 C3** 47 20N 18 58 E
Szczebrzeszyn, *Poland* **31 H9** 50 42N 22 59 E
Szczecin, *Poland* ...... **30 E1** 53 27N 14 27 E
Szczecinek, *Poland* ...... **30 E3** 53 43N 16 41 E
Szczeciński, Zalew =
  Stettiner Haff,
  Germany ...... **24 B10** 53 47N 14 15 E
Szczekociny, *Poland* ...... **31 H6** 50 38N 19 48 E
Szczucin, *Poland* ...... **31 H8** 50 18N 21 4 E
Szczuczyn, *Poland* ...... **30 E9** 53 36N 22 19 E
Szczyrk, *Poland* ...... **31 J6** 49 43N 19 2 E
Szczytna, *Poland* ...... **31 H3** 50 25N 16 28 E
Szczytno, *Poland* ...... **30 E7** 53 33N 21 0 E
Szechuan Basin =
  Sichuan Pendi, *China* **58 B5** 31 0N 105 0 E
Szechwan = Sichuan □,
  China ...... **58 B5** 30 30N 103 0 E
Szécsény, *Hungary* ...... **28 B4** 48 7N 19 30 E
Szeged, *Hungary* ...... **28 D5** 46 16N 20 10 E
Szeghalom, *Hungary* ...... **28 C6** 47 1N 21 10 E
Székesfehérvár,
  Hungary ...... **28 C3** 47 15N 18 25 E
Szekszárd, *Hungary* ...... **28 D3** 46 22N 18 42 E
Szendrő, *Hungary* ...... **28 B5** 48 24N 20 41 E
Szentendre, *Hungary* ...... **28 C4** 47 39N 19 4 E
Szentes, *Hungary* ...... **28 D5** 46 39N 20 21 E
Szentgotthárd, *Hungary* **28 D1** 46 58N 16 19 E
Szentlőrinc, *Hungary* ...... **28 D3** 46 3N 18 1 E
Szerencs, *Hungary* ...... **28 B6** 48 10N 21 12 E
Szigetszentmiklós,
  Hungary ...... **28 C4** 47 21N 19 3 E
Szigetvár, *Hungary* ...... **28 D2** 46 3N 17 46 E
Szikszó, *Hungary* ...... **28 B5** 48 12N 20 56 E
Szklarska Poreba,
  Poland ...... **31 H2** 50 50N 15 33 E
Szlichtyngowa, *Poland* **31 G3** 51 42N 16 15 E
Szob, *Hungary* ...... **28 C3** 47 48N 18 53 E
Szolnok, *Hungary* ...... **28 C5** 47 10N 20 15 E
Szombathely, *Hungary* **28 C1** 47 14N 16 38 E
Szprotawa, *Poland* ...... **31 G2** 51 33N 15 35 E
Sztum, *Poland* ...... **30 E6** 53 55N 19 1 E
Sztutowo, *Poland* ...... **30 D6** 54 20N 19 15 E
Szubin, *Poland* ...... **31 E4** 53 2N 17 45 E
Szydłowiec, *Poland* ...... **31 G7** 51 15N 20 51 E
Szypliszki, *Poland* ...... **30 D10** 54 17N 23 2 E

T

Ta Khli Khok, *Thailand* **64 E3** 15 18N 100 20 E
Ta Lai, *Vietnam* ...... **65 G6** 11 24N 107 23 E
Tab, *Hungary* ...... **28 D3** 46 44N 18 2 E
Tabacal, *Argentina* ...... **126 A3** 23 15 S 64 15W
Tabaco, *Phil.* ...... **61 E5** 13 22N 123 44 E
Tabagné, *Ivory C.* **82 D4** 7 59N 3 4W
Ţābah, *Si. Arabia* ...... **70 E4** 26 55N 42 38 E
Tabanan, *Indonesia* ...... **63 K18** 8 32 S 115 8 E
Tabankort, *Niger* ...... **83 B5** 17 44N 0 20 E
Tabas, *Khorāsān, Iran* **71 C9** 32 48N 60 12 E
Tabas, *Khorāsān, Iran* **71 C8** 33 35N 56 55 E
Tabasará, Serranía de,
  Panama **120 E3** 8 35N 81 40W
Tabasco □, *Mexico* **119 D6** 17 45N 93 30W
Tabāsīn, *Iran* ...... **71 D8** 31 12N 57 54 E
Tabatinga, Serra da,
  Brazil ...... **125 F10** 10 30 S 44 0W
Taber, *Canada* **102 D6** 49 47N 112 8W
Taberg, *Sweden* ...... **11 G8** 57 40N 14 6 E
Taberg, *U.S.A.* **117 C9** 43 18N 75 37W
Tabla, *Niger* ...... **83 C5** 13 46N 3 1 E
Tablas de Daimiel △,
  Spain **37 F7** 39 9N 3 40W
Tablas I., *Phil.* ...... **61 E5** 12 25N 122 2 E
Tablas Strait, *Phil.* ...... **61 E4** 12 40N 121 48 E
Table B., *Canada* **105 B8** 53 40N 56 25W
Table B., *S. Africa* ...... **88 E2** 33 35 S 18 25 E
Table Mt., *S. Africa* ...... **88 E2** 34 0 S 18 22 E
Table Rock L., *U.S.A.* **113 G8** 36 36N 93 19W
Tabletop, Mt., *Australia* **94 C4** 23 24 S 147 11 E
Tábor, *Czech Rep.* ...... **26 B7** 49 25N 14 39 E
Tabora, *Tanzania* ...... **86 D3** 5 2 S 32 50 E
Tabora □, *Tanzania* ...... **86 D3** 5 0 S 33 0 E
Tabou, *Ivory C.* **82 E3** 4 30N 7 20W
Tabrīz, *Iran* ...... **70 B5** 38 7N 46 20 E
Tabuaeran, *Kiribati* **97 G12** 3 51N 159 22W
Tabuenca, *Spain* **38 D3** 41 42N 1 33W
Tabūk, *Si. Arabia* ...... **70 D3** 28 23N 36 15 E
Taburno-
  Camposauro △, *Italy* **41 A7** 41 8N 14 37 E
Täby, *Sweden* ...... **10 E12** 59 28N 18 4 E
Tacámbaro de Codallos,
  Mexico **118 D4** 19 14N 101 28W
Tacheng, *China* ...... **60 B3** 46 40N 82 58 E
Tach'i, *Taiwan* ...... **59 E13** 24 46N 121 0 E
Tachia, *Taiwan* ...... **59 E13** 24 25N 120 28 E
Tach'ing Shan = Daqing
  Shan, *China* ...... **56 D6** 40 40N 111 0 E
Tachov, *Czech Rep.* ...... **26 B5** 49 47N 12 39 E
Tácina ➤, *Italy* ...... **43 D9** 38 57N 16 55 E

Tacloban, *Phil.* ... **61 F6** 11 15N 124 58 E
Tacna, *Peru* ... **124 G4** 18 0 S 70 20W
Tacoma, *U.S.A.* ... **110 C4** 47 14N 122 26W
Tacuarembó, *Uruguay* ... **127 C4** 31 45 S 56 0W
Tademaït, Plateau du, *Algeria* ... **78 C6** 28 30N 2 30 E
Tadio, L., *Ivory C.* ... **82 D3** 5 10N 5 15W
Tadjoura, *Djibouti* ... **81 E5** 11 50N 42 55 E
Tadjoura, Golfe de, *Djibouti* ... **81 E5** 11 50N 43 0 E
Tadmor, *N.Z.* ... **91 J4** 41 27 S 172 45 E
Tadoule L., *Canada* ... **103 B9** 58 36N 98 20W
Tadoussac, *Canada* ... **105 C6** 48 11N 69 42W
Tadrés △, *Niger* ... **83 B6** 16 0N 7 10 E
Tadzhikistan ■ = Tajikistan ■, *Asia* ... **52 F8** 38 30N 70 0 E
Taechŏn-ni, *S. Korea* ... **57 F14** 36 21N 126 36 E
Taegu, *S. Korea* ... **57 G15** 35 50N 128 37 E
Taegwan, *N. Korea* ... **57 D13** 40 13N 125 12 E
Taejŏn, *S. Korea* ... **57 F14** 36 20N 127 28 E
Taen, Ko, *Thailand* ... **65 b** 9 22N 99 57 E
Tafalla, *Spain* ... **38 C3** 42 30N 1 41W
Tafar, *Sudan* ... **81 F2** 6 52N 28 15 E
Tafelbaai = Table B., *S. Africa* ... **88 E2** 33 35 S 18 25 E
Tafermaar, *Indonesia* ... **63 F8** 6 47 S 134 10 E
Tafí Viejo, *Argentina* ... **126 B2** 26 43 S 65 17W
Tafihãn, *Iran* ... **71 D7** 29 25N 52 39 E
Tafiré, *Ivory C.* ... **82 D3** 9 4N 5 4W
Tafresh, *Iran* ... **71 C6** 34 45N 49 57 E
Taft, *Iran* ... **71 D7** 31 45N 54 14 E
Taft, *Phil.* ... **61 F6** 11 57N 125 30 E
Taft, *U.S.A.* ... **111 K7** 35 8N 119 28W
Taftãn, Küh-e, *Iran* ... **71 D9** 28 40N 61 0 E
Taga Dzong, *Bhutan* ... **67 F16** 27 5N 89 55 E
Taganrog, *Russia* ... **33 J10** 47 12N 38 50 E
Taganrogskiy Zaliv, *Russia* ... **33 J10** 47 0N 38 30 E
Tagânt, *Mauritania* ... **82 B2** 18 20N 11 0W
Tagatay, *Phil.* ... **61 D4** 14 6N 120 56 E
Tagbilaran, *Phil.* ... **61 G5** 9 39N 123 51 E
Tággia, *Italy* ... **40 E4** 43 52N 7 51 E
Tagish, *Canada* ... **102 A2** 60 19N 134 16W
Tagish L., *Canada* ... **102 A2** 60 10N 134 20W
Tagliacozzo, *Italy* ... **41 F10** 42 4N 13 14 E
Tagliamento →, *Italy* ... **41 C10** 45 38N 13 6 E
Táglio di Po, *Italy* ... **41 D9** 45 0N 12 12 E
Tago, *Phil.* ... **61 G7** 9 2N 126 13 E
Tagomago, *Spain* ... **48 B8** 39 2N 1 39 E
Tagourâret, *Mauritania* ... **82 B3** 17 45N 7 45W
Taguatinga, *Brazil* ... **125 F10** 12 16 S 42 26W
Tagudin, *Phil.* ... **61 C4** 16 56N 120 27 E
Tagum, *Phil.* ... **61 H6** 7 33N 125 53 E
Tagus = Tejo →, *Europe* ... **37 F2** 38 40N 9 24W
Tahakopa, *N.Z.* ... **91 M2** 46 30 S 169 23 E
Tahan, Gunung, *Malaysia* ... **65 K4** 4 34N 102 17 E
Tahat, *Algeria* ... **78 D7** 23 18N 5 33 E
Tãherĩ, *Iran* ... **71 E7** 27 43N 52 20 E
Tahiti, *French Polynesia* ... **97 J13** 17 37 S 149 27W
Tahlequah, *U.S.A.* ... **113 H7** 35 55N 94 58W
Tahoe, L., *U.S.A.* ... **110 G6** 39 6N 120 2W
Tahoe City, *U.S.A.* ... **110 F6** 39 10N 120 9W
Tahoka, *U.S.A.* ... **113 J4** 33 10N 101 48W
Taholah, *U.S.A.* ... **110 C2** 47 21N 124 17W
Tahoua, *Niger* ... **83 C6** 14 57N 5 16 E
Tahrüd, *Iran* ... **71 D8** 29 26N 57 49 E
Tahsis, *Canada* ... **102 D3** 49 55N 126 40W
Tahta, *Egypt* ... **80 B3** 26 44N 31 32 E
Tahtaköprü, *Turkey* ... **45 G13** 39 57N 29 39 E
Tahtalı Dağları, *Turkey* ... **72 C7** 38 20N 36 0 E
Tahulandang, *Indonesia* ... **63 D7** 2 27N 125 23 E
Tahuna, *Indonesia* ... **63 D7** 3 38N 125 30 E
Taï, *Ivory C.* ... **82 D3** 5 55N 7 30W
Taï △, *Ivory C.* ... **82 D3** 5 25N 7 5W
Tai Hu, *China* ... **59 B12** 31 5N 120 10 E
Tai Rom Yen △, *Thailand* ... **65 H2** 8 45N 99 30 E
Tai Shan, *China* ... **57 F9** 36 25N 117 20 E
Tai'an, *China* ... **57 F9** 36 12N 117 8 E
Taibei = T'aipei, *Taiwan* ... **59 E13** 25 2N 121 30 E
Taibique, *Canary Is.* ... **48 G2** 27 42N 17 58W
Taibus Qi, *China* ... **56 D8** 41 54N 115 22 E
Taicang, *China* ... **59 B13** 31 30N 121 5 E
T'aichung, *Taiwan* ... **59 E13** 24 9N 120 37 E
Taieri →, *N.Z.* ... **91 M3** 46 3 S 170 12 E
Taigu, *China* ... **56 F7** 37 28N 112 30 E
Taihang Shan, *China* ... **56 G7** 36 0N 113 30 E
Taihape, *N.Z.* ... **91 H5** 39 41 S 175 48 E
Taihe, *Anhui, China* ... **56 H8** 33 20N 115 42 E
Taihe, *Jiangxi, China* ... **59 D10** 26 47N 114 52 E
Taihu, *China* ... **59 B11** 30 22N 116 20 E
Taijiang, *China* ... **58 D7** 26 39N 108 21 E
Taikang, *China* ... **56 G8** 34 5N 114 50 E
Tailem Bend, *Australia* ... **95 F2** 35 12 S 139 29 E
Tailfingen, *Germany* ... **25 G5** 48 15N 9 1 E
Tailuko, *Taiwan* ... **59 E13** 24 9N 121 37 E
Taimyr Peninsula = Taymyr, Poluostrov, *Russia* ... **53 B11** 75 0N 100 0 E
Tain, *U.K.* ... **13 D4** 57 49N 4 4W
T'ainan, *Taiwan* ... **59 F13** 23 0N 120 10 E
Taínaron, Ákra, *Greece* ... **46 E4** 36 22N 22 27 E
Taining, *China* ... **59 D11** 26 54N 117 9 E
T'aipei, *Taiwan* ... **59 E13** 25 2N 121 30 E
Taiping, *China* ... **59 B12** 30 15N 118 6 E
Taiping, *Malaysia* ... **65 K3** 4 51N 100 44 E
Taipingchen, *China* ... **56 H6** 33 35N 111 42 E
Tairbeart = Tarbert, *U.K.* ... **13 D2** 57 54N 6 49W
Taishan, *China* ... **59 F9** 22 14N 112 41 E
Taishun, *China* ... **59 D12** 27 30N 119 42 E
Taita Hills, *Kenya* ... **86 C4** 3 25 S 38 15 E
Taitao, Pen. de, *Chile* ... **128 F2** 46 30 S 75 0W
T'aitung, *Taiwan* ... **59 F13** 22 43 S 121 4 E
Taivalkoski, *Finland* ... **8 D23** 65 33N 28 12 E
Taiwan ■, *Asia* ... **59 F13** 23 30N 121 0 E
Taiwan Strait, *Asia* ... **59 E12** 24 40N 120 0 E
Taixing, *China* ... **59 A13** 32 11N 120 0 E
Taiyara, *Sudan* ... **81 E3** 13 12N 30 47 E
Taïyetos Óros, *Greece* ... **46 D4** 37 0N 22 23 E
Taiyiba, *Israel* ... **74 C4** 32 36N 35 27 E
Taiyuan, *China* ... **56 F7** 37 52N 112 33 E
Taizhong = T'aichung, *Taiwan* ... **59 E13** 24 9N 120 37 E
Taizhou, *China* ... **59 A12** 32 28N 119 55 E
Taizhou Liedao, *China* ... **59 C13** 28 30N 121 55 E
Ta'izz, *Yemen* ... **75 E3** 13 35N 44 2 E
Tãjãbãd, *Iran* ... **71 D7** 30 2N 54 24 E
Tajikistan ■, *Asia* ... **52 F8** 38 30N 70 0 E
Tajima, *Japan* ... **55 F9** 37 12N 139 46 E
Tajo = Tejo →, *Europe* ... **37 F2** 38 40N 9 24W
Tajrīsh, *Iran* ... **71 C6** 35 48N 51 25 E
Tak, *Thailand* ... **64 D2** 16 52N 99 8 E
Takāb, *Iran* ... **70 B5** 36 24N 47 7 E
Takachiho, *Japan* ... **55 H5** 32 42N 131 18 E

Takachu, *Botswana* ... **88 C3** 22 37 S 21 58 E
Takada, *Japan* ... **55 F9** 37 7N 138 15 E
Takahagi, *Japan* ... **55 F10** 36 43N 140 45 E
Takaka, *N.Z.* ... **91 J4** 40 51 S 172 50 E
Takamatsu, *Japan* ... **55 G7** 34 20N 134 5 E
Takaoka, *Japan* ... **55 F8** 36 47N 137 0 E
Takapuna, *N.Z.* ... **91 G5** 36 47 S 174 47 E
Takasaki, *Japan* ... **55 F9** 36 20N 139 0 E
Takatsuki, *Japan* ... **55 G7** 34 51N 135 37 E
Takaungu, *Kenya* ... **86 C4** 3 38 S 39 52 E
Takayama, *Japan* ... **55 F8** 36 18N 137 11 E
Take-Shima, *Japan* ... **55 J5** 30 49N 130 26 E
Takefu, *Japan* ... **55 G8** 35 50N 136 10 E
Takengon, *Indonesia* ... **62 D1** 4 45N 96 50 E
Takeo, *Japan* ... **55 H5** 33 12N 130 1 E
Takeshima = Tok-do, *Asia* ... **55 F5** 37 15N 131 52 E
Tãkestãn, *Iran* ... **71 C6** 36 0N 49 40 E
Taketa, *Japan* ... **55 H5** 32 58N 131 24 E
Takev, *Cambodia* ... **65 G5** 10 59N 104 47 E
Takh, *India* ... **69 C7** 33 6N 77 32 E
Takht-Sulaiman, *Pakistan* ... **68 D3** 31 40N 69 58 E
Takikawa, *Japan* ... **54 C10** 43 33N 141 54 E
Takla L., *Canada* ... **102 B3** 55 15N 125 45W
Takla Landing, *Canada* ... **102 B3** 55 30N 125 50W
Takla Makan = Taklamakan Shamo, *China* ... **60 C3** 38 0N 83 0 E
Taklamakan Shamo, *China* ... **60 C3** 38 0N 83 0 E
Taku →, *Canada* ... **102 B2** 58 30N 133 50W
Takua Thung, *Thailand* ... **65 a** 8 24N 98 27 E
Takum, *Nigeria* ... **83 D6** 7 18N 9 36 E
Tal Halãl, *Iran* ... **71 D7** 28 54N 55 1 E
Tala, *Uruguay* ... **127 C4** 34 21 S 55 46W
Talachyn, *Belarus* ... **32 E5** 54 25N 29 42 E
Talacogan, *Phil.* ... **61 G6** 8 32N 125 39 E
Talagang, *Pakistan* ... **68 C5** 32 55N 72 25 E
Talagante, *Chile* ... **126 C1** 33 40 S 70 50W
Talak, *Niger* ... **83 B6** 18 0N 5 0 E
Talamanca, Cordillera de, *Cent. Amer.* ... **120 E3** 9 20N 83 20W
Talant, *France* ... **19 E11** 47 19N 4 58 E
Talara, *Peru* ... **124 D2** 4 38 S 81 18W
Talas, *Kyrgyzstan* ... **52 E8** 42 30N 72 13 E
Talas, *Turkey* ... **72 C6** 38 41N 35 33 E
Talâta, *Egypt* ... **74 E1** 30 36N 32 20 E
Talata Mafara, *Nigeria* ... **83 C6** 12 38N 6 4 E
Talaud, Kepulauan, *Indonesia* ... **63 D7** 4 30N 126 50 E
Talaud Is. = Talaud, Kepulauan, *Indonesia* ... **63 D7** 4 30N 126 50 E
Talavera de la Reina, *Spain* ... **36 F6** 39 55N 4 46W
Talavera la Real, *Spain* ... **37 G4** 38 53N 6 46W
Talayan, *Phil.* ... **61 H6** 6 52N 124 24 E
Talayuela, *Spain* ... **36 F5** 39 59N 5 36W
Talbandh, *India* ... **69 H12** 22 3N 86 20 E
Talbert, Sillon de, *France* ... **18 D3** 48 53N 3 5W
Talbot, C., *Australia* ... **92 B4** 13 48 S 126 43 E
Talbragar →, *Australia* ... **95 E4** 32 12 S 148 37 E
Talca, *Chile* ... **126 D1** 35 28 S 71 40W
Talcahuano, *Chile* ... **126 D1** 36 40 S 73 10W
Talcher, *India* ... **67 J14** 21 0N 85 18 E
Talcho, *Niger* ... **83 C5** 14 44N 3 28 E
Taldy Kurgan = Taldyqorghan, *Kazakhstan* ... **52 E8** 45 10N 78 45 E
Taldyqorghan, *Kazakhstan* ... **52 E8** 45 10N 78 45 E
Tälesh, *Iran* ... **71 B6** 37 58N 48 58 E
Tälesh, Kühhä-ye, *Iran* ... **71 B6** 37 42N 48 55 E
Talguharai, *Sudan* ... **80 D4** 18 19N 35 56 E
Tali Post, *Sudan* ... **81 F3** 5 55N 30 44 E
Taliabu, *Indonesia* ... **63 E6** 1 50 S 125 0 E
Talibon, *Phil.* ... **63 B6** 10 9N 124 20 E
Talibong, Ko, *Thailand* ... **65 J2** 7 15N 99 23 E
Talihina, *U.S.A.* ... **113 H7** 34 45N 95 3W
Talisayan, *Phil.* ... **61 G6** 9 5N 124 40 E
Taliwang, *Indonesia* ... **62 F5** 8 50 S 116 55 E
Tall 'Afar, *Iraq* ... **70 B4** 36 22N 42 27 E
Tall Kalakh, *Syria* ... **74 A5** 34 41N 36 15 E
Talla, *Egypt* ... **80 B3** 28 5N 30 43 E
Talladega, *U.S.A.* ... **115 J2** 33 26N 86 6W
Tallahassee, *U.S.A.* ... **115 K3** 30 27N 84 17W
Tallangatta, *Australia* ... **95 F4** 36 15 S 147 19 E
Tallard, *France* ... **21 D10** 44 28N 6 3 E
Tällberg, *Sweden* ... **10 D9** 60 51N 15 2 E
Tallering Pk., *Australia* ... **93 E2** 28 6 S 115 37 E
Talli, *Pakistan* ... **68 E3** 29 32N 68 8 E
Tallinn, *Estonia* ... **9 G21** 59 22N 24 48 E
Tallmadge, *U.S.A.* ... **116 E3** 41 6N 81 27W
Tallulah, *U.S.A.* ... **113 J9** 32 25N 91 11W
Tălmaciu, *Romania* ... **29 E9** 45 38N 24 19 E
Talmont-St-Hilaire, *France* ... **20 B2** 46 27N 1 37W
Talne, *Ukraine* ... **33 H6** 48 50N 30 44 E
Talnoye = Talne, *Ukraine* ... **33 H6** 48 50N 30 44 E
Talodi, *Sudan* ... **81 E3** 10 35N 30 22 E
Talovaya, *Russia* ... **34 E5** 51 6N 40 45 E
Taloyoak, *Canada* ... **100 B10** 69 32N 93 32W
Talpa de Allende, *Mexico* ... **118 C4** 20 23N 104 51W
Talparo, *Trin. & Tob.* ... **125 K15** 10 30N 61 17W
Talsi, *Latvia* ... **9 H20** 57 10N 22 30 E
Talsi □, *Latvia* ... **30 A9** 57 22N 22 40 E
Taltal, *Chile* ... **126 B1** 25 23 S 70 33W
Taltson →, *Canada* ... **102 A6** 61 24N 112 46W
Talwood, *Australia* ... **95 D4** 28 29 S 149 29 E
Talyawalka Cr. →, *Australia* ... **95 E3** 32 28 S 142 22 E
Tam Ky, *Vietnam* ... **64 E7** 15 34N 108 29 E
Tam Quan, *Vietnam* ... **64 E7** 14 35N 109 3 E
Tama, *U.S.A.* ... **112 E8** 41 58N 92 35W
Tama △, *Ethiopia* ... **81 F4** 5 58N 36 5 E
Tamale, *Ghana* ... **83 D4** 9 22N 0 50W
Taman, *Russia* ... **33 K9** 45 14N 36 41 E
Taman Negara △, *Malaysia* ... **65 K4** 4 38N 102 26 E
Tamani, *Mali* ... **82 C3** 13 20N 6 50W
Tamano, *Japan* ... **55 G6** 34 29N 133 59 E
Tamanrasset, *Algeria* ... **78 D7** 22 50N 5 30 E
Tamaqua, *U.S.A.* ... **117 F9** 40 48N 75 58W
Tamar →, *U.K.* ... **15 G3** 50 27N 4 15W
Tamarinda, *Spain* ... **48 B10** 39 55N 3 49 E
Tamarite de Litera, *Spain* ... **38 D5** 41 52N 0 25 E
Tamási, *Hungary* ... **28 D3** 46 40N 18 18 E
Tamaské, *Niger* ... **83 C6** 14 49N 5 43 E
Tamaulipas □, *Mexico* ... **119 C5** 24 0N 99 0W
Tamaulipas, Sierra de, *Mexico* ... **119 C5** 23 30N 98 20W

Tamazula, *Mexico* ... **118 C3** 24 55N 106 58W
Tamazunchale, *Mexico* ... **119 C5** 21 16N 98 47W
Tamba-Dabatou, *Guinea* ... **82 C2** 11 50N 10 40W
Tambacounda, *Senegal* ... **82 C2** 13 45N 13 40W
Tambelan, Kepulauan, *Indonesia* ... **62 D3** 1 0N 107 30 E
Tambellup, *Australia* ... **93 F2** 34 4 S 117 37 E
Tambo, *Australia* ... **94 C4** 24 54 S 146 14 E
Tambo de Mora, *Peru* ... **124 F3** 13 30 S 76 8W
Tambohorano, *Madag.* ... **89 B7** 17 30 S 43 58 E
Tambora, *Indonesia* ... **62 F5** 8 12 S 118 5 E
Tambov, *Russia* ... **34 D5** 52 45N 41 28 E
Tambre →, *Spain* ... **36 C2** 42 49N 8 53W
Tambuku, *Indonesia* ... **63 G15** 7 8 S 113 40 E
Tamburâ, *Sudan* ... **81 F2** 5 40N 27 25 E
Tãmchekket, *Mauritania* ... **82 B2** 17 25N 10 40W
Tâmega →, *Portugal* ... **36 D2** 41 5N 8 21W
Tamenglong, *India* ... **67 G18** 25 0N 93 35 E
Tamgué, Massif du, *Guinea* ... **82 C2** 12 0N 12 18W
Tamiahua, L. de, *Mexico* ... **119 C5** 21 30N 97 30W
Tamil Nadu □, *India* ... **66 P10** 11 0N 77 0 E
Tamis →, *Serbia & M.* ... **28 B5** 44 51N 20 39 E
Tamluk, *India* ... **69 H12** 22 18N 87 58 E
Tammerfors = Tampere, *Finland* ... **9 F20** 61 30N 23 50 E
Tammisaari, *Finland* ... **9 F20** 60 0N 23 26 E
Tämnaren, *Sweden* ... **10 D11** 60 10N 17 25 E
Tamo Abu, Pegunungan, *Malaysia* ... **62 D5** 3 10N 115 5 E
Tampa, *U.S.A.* ... **115 M4** 27 57N 82 27W
Tampa, Tanjung, *Indonesia* ... **63 K19** 8 55 S 116 12 E
Tampa B., *U.S.A.* ... **115 M4** 27 50N 82 30W
Tampere, *Finland* ... **9 F20** 61 30N 23 50 E
Tampico, *Mexico* ... **119 C5** 22 20N 97 50W
Tampin, *Malaysia* ... **65 L4** 2 28N 102 13 E
Tampoi, *Malaysia* ... **65 d** 1 30N 103 39 E
Tamsweg, *Austria* ... **26 D6** 47 7N 13 49 E
Tamu, *Burma* ... **67 G19** 24 13N 94 12 E
Tamuja →, *Spain* ... **37 F4** 39 38N 6 29W
Tamworth, *Australia* ... **95 E5** 31 7 S 150 58 E
Tamworth, *Canada* ... **116 B8** 44 29N 77 0W
Tamworth, *U.K.* ... **15 E6** 52 39N 1 41W
Tamyang, *S. Korea* ... **57 G14** 35 19N 126 59 E
Tan An, *Vietnam* ... **65 G6** 10 32N 106 25 E
Tan Chau, *Vietnam* ... **65 G5** 10 48N 105 12 E
Tan-Tan, *Morocco* ... **78 C3** 28 29N 11 1W
Tana →, *Kenya* ... **86 C5** 2 32 S 40 31 E
Tana →, *Norway* ... **8 A23** 70 30N 28 14 E
Tana, L., *Ethiopia* ... **81 E4** 13 5N 37 30 E
Tana River Primate △, *Kenya* ... **86 C5** 1 55 S 40 7 E
Tanabe, *Japan* ... **55 H7** 33 44N 135 22 E
Tanafjorden, *Norway* ... **8 A23** 70 45N 28 25 E
Tanahbala, *Indonesia* ... **62 E1** 0 30 S 98 30 E
Tanahgrogot, *Indonesia* ... **62 E5** 1 55 S 116 15 E
Tanahjampea, *Indonesia* ... **63 F6** 7 10 S 120 35 E
Tanahmasa, *Indonesia* ... **62 E1** 0 12 S 98 39 E
Tanahmerah, *Indonesia* ... **63 F10** 6 5 S 140 16 E
Tanakpur, *India* ... **69 E9** 29 5N 80 7 E
Tanakura, *Japan* ... **55 F10** 37 10N 140 20 E
Tanami, *Australia* ... **92 C4** 19 59 S 129 43 E
Tanami Desert, *Australia* ... **92 C5** 18 50 S 132 0 E
Tanana →, *U.S.A.* ... **100 B4** 65 10N 151 58W
Tananarive = Antananarivo, *Madag.* ... **89 B8** 18 55 S 47 31 E
Tánaro →, *Italy* ... **40 D5** 44 55N 8 40 E
Tancheng, *China* ... **57 G10** 34 25N 118 20 E
Tanch'ŏn, *N. Korea* ... **57 D15** 40 27N 128 54 E
Tanda, *Ut. P., India* ... **69 F10** 26 33N 82 35 E
Tanda, *Ut. P., India* ... **69 E8** 28 57N 78 56 E
Tanda, *Ivory C.* ... **82 D4** 7 48N 3 10W
Tandag, *Phil.* ... **61 G7** 9 4N 126 9 E
Tandaia, *Tanzania* ... **87 D3** 9 25 S 34 15 E
Tãndãrei, *Romania* ... **29 F12** 44 39N 27 40 E
Tandaué, *Angola* ... **88 B2** 16 58 S 18 5 E
Tandil, *Argentina* ... **126 D4** 37 15 S 59 6W
Tandil, Sa. del, *Argentina* ... **126 D4** 37 30 S 59 0W
Tandlianwala, *Pakistan* ... **68 D5** 31 3N 73 9 E
Tando Adam, *Pakistan* ... **68 G3** 25 45N 68 40 E
Tando Allahyar, *Pakistan* ... **68 G3** 25 28N 68 43 E
Tando Bago, *Pakistan* ... **68 G3** 24 47N 68 58 E
Tando Mohommed Khan, *Pakistan* ... **68 G3** 25 8N 68 32 E
Tandou L., *Australia* ... **95 E3** 32 40 S 142 5 E
Tandragee, *U.K.* ... **12 B5** 54 21N 6 24W
Tandsjöborg, *Sweden* ... **10 C8** 61 42N 14 43 E
Tane-ga-Shima, *Japan* ... **55 J5** 30 30N 131 0 E
Taneatua, *N.Z.* ... **91 H6** 38 4 S 177 1 E
Tanen Tong Dan = Dawna Ra., *Burma* ... **64 D2** 16 30N 98 30 E
Tanew →, *Poland* ... **31 H9** 50 29N 22 16 E
Tanezrouft, *Algeria* ... **78 D6** 23 9N 0 11 E
Tang, Koh, *Cambodia* ... **65 G4** 10 16N 103 7 E
Tang, Ra's-e, *Iran* ... **71 E8** 25 21N 59 52 E
Tang Krasang, *Cambodia* ... **64 F5** 12 34N 105 3 E
Tanga, *Tanzania* ... **86 D4** 5 5 S 39 2 E
Tanga □, *Tanzania* ... **86 D4** 5 20 S 38 0 E
Tanganyika, L., *Africa* ... **86 D3** 6 40 S 30 0 E
Tangaza, *Nigeria* ... **83 C5** 13 19N 4 55 E
Tanger, *Morocco* ... **78 A4** 35 50N 5 49W
Tangerang, *Indonesia* ... **63 G12** 6 11 S 106 37 E
Tangerhütte, *Germany* ... **24 C7** 52 26N 11 48 E
Tangermünde, *Germany* ... **24 C7** 52 33N 11 58 E
Tanggu, *China* ... **57 E9** 39 2N 117 40 E
Tanggula Shan, *China* ... **60 C4** 32 40N 92 10 E
Tanghe, *China* ... **56 H7** 32 47N 112 50 E
Tanghla Range = Tanggula Shan, *China* ... **60 C4** 32 40N 92 10 E
Tangier = Tanger, *Morocco* ... **78 A4** 35 50N 5 49W
Tangorin, *Australia* ... **94 C3** 21 47 S 144 12 E
Tangorombohitr'i Makay, *Madag.* ... **89 C8** 21 0 S 45 15 E
Tangshan, *China* ... **57 E10** 39 38N 118 10 E
Tangtou, *China* ... **57 G10** 35 28N 118 30 E
Tanguiéta, *Benin* ... **83 C5** 10 35N 1 21 E
Tangxi, *China* ... **59 C12** 29 3N 119 25 E
Tangyan He →, *China* ... **58 C7** 28 54N 108 19 E
Tanimbar, Kepulauan, *Indonesia* ... **63 F8** 7 30 S 131 30 E
Tanimbar Is. = Tanimbar, Kepulauan, *Indonesia* ... **63 F8** 7 30 S 131 30 E
Taninthari = Tenasserim, *Burma* ... **65 F2** 12 6N 99 3 E
Tanjay, *Phil.* ... **61 G5** 9 30N 123 5 E
Tanjong Malim, *Malaysia* ... **65 L3** 3 42N 101 31 E
Tanjong Pelepas, *Malaysia* ... **65 d** 1 21N 103 33 E
Tanjore = Thanjavur, *India* ... **66 P11** 10 48N 79 12 E

Tanjung, *Indonesia* ... **63 J19** 8 21 S 116 9 E
Tanjung, *Phil.* ... **62 E5** 2 10 S 115 25 E
Tanjung Tokong, *Malaysia* ... **65 c** 5 28N 100 18 E
Tanjungbalai, *Indonesia* ... **62 D1** 2 55N 99 44 E
Tanjungbatu, *Indonesia* ... **62 D5** 2 23N 118 3 E
Tanjungkarang Telukbetung, *Indonesia* ... **62 F3** 5 20 S 105 10 E
Tanjungpandan, *Indonesia* ... **62 E3** 2 43 S 107 38 E
Tanjungpinang, *Indonesia* ... **62 D2** 1 5N 104 30 E
Tanjungredeb, *Indonesia* ... **62 D5** 2 9N 117 29 E
Tanjungselor, *Indonesia* ... **62 D5** 2 55N 117 25 E
Tank, *Pakistan* ... **68 C4** 32 14N 70 25 E
Tankhala, *India* ... **68 J5** 21 58N 73 47 E
Tankwa-Karoo △, *S. Africa* ... **88 E2** 32 14 S 19 50 E
Tännäs, *Sweden* ... **10 B6** 62 25N 12 40 E
Tannersville, *U.S.A.* ... **117 E9** 41 3N 75 18W
Tannis Bugt, *Denmark* ... **11 G4** 57 40N 10 15 E
Tannu-Ola, *Russia* ... **53 D10** 51 0N 94 0 E
Tannum Sands, *Australia* ... **94 C5** 23 57 S 151 22 E
Tano →, *Ghana* ... **82 D4** 5 7N 2 56W
Tanon Str., *Phil.* ... **61 F5** 10 20N 123 30 E
Tanout, *Niger* ... **83 C6** 14 50N 8 55 E
Tanshui, *Taiwan* ... **59 E13** 25 10N 121 28 E
Tansilla, *Burkina Faso* ... **82 C4** 12 25N 4 23W
Tanta, *Egypt* ... **80 H7** 30 45N 30 57 E
Tantoyuca, *Mexico* ... **119 C5** 21 21N 98 10W
Tantung = Dandong, *China* ... **57 D13** 40 10N 124 20 E
Tanumshede, *Sweden* ... **11 F5** 58 42N 11 20 E
Tanunda, *Australia* ... **95 E2** 34 30 S 139 0 E
Tanus, *France* ... **20 D6** 44 8N 2 19 E
Tanzania ■, *Africa* ... **86 D3** 6 0 S 34 0 E
Tanzilla →, *Canada* ... **102 B2** 58 8N 130 43W
Tao, Ko, *Thailand* ... **65 G2** 10 5N 99 52 E
Tao'an = Taonan, *China* ... **57 B12** 45 22N 122 40 E
Tao'er He →, *China* ... **57 B13** 45 45N 124 5 E
Taohua Dao, *China* ... **59 C14** 29 50N 122 20 E
Taolanaro, *Madag.* ... **89 D8** 25 2 S 47 0 E
Taole, *China* ... **56 E4** 38 48N 106 40 E
Taonan, *China* ... **57 B12** 45 22N 122 40 E
Taormina, *Italy* ... **43 E8** 37 51N 15 17 E
Taos, *U.S.A.* ... **109 H11** 36 24N 105 35W
Taoudenni, *Mali* ... **78 D5** 22 40N 3 55W
Taoyuan, *China* ... **59 C8** 28 55N 111 16 E
T'aoyüan, *Taiwan* ... **59 E13** 25 0N 121 4 E
Tapa, *Estonia* ... **9 G21** 59 15N 25 50 E
Tapa Shan = Daba Shan, *China* ... **58 B7** 32 0N 109 0 E
Tapachula, *Mexico* ... **119 E6** 14 54N 92 17W
Tapah, *Malaysia* ... **65 K3** 4 12N 101 15 E
Tapajós →, *Brazil* ... **125 D8** 2 24 S 54 41W
Tapaktuan, *Indonesia* ... **62 D1** 3 15N 97 10 E
Tapanahoni →, *Suriname* ... **125 C8** 4 20N 54 25W
Tapanui, *N.Z.* ... **91 L2** 45 56 S 169 18 E
Tapauá →, *Brazil* ... **124 E6** 5 40 S 64 21W
Tapes, *Brazil* ... **127 C5** 30 40 S 51 23W
Tapeta, *Liberia* ... **82 D3** 6 29N 8 52W
Taphan Hin, *Thailand* ... **64 D3** 16 13N 100 26 E
Tapi →, *India* ... **66 J8** 21 8N 72 41 E
Tapia de Casariego, *Spain* ... **36 B4** 43 34N 6 56W
Tapirapecó, Serra, *Venezuela* ... **124 C6** 1 10N 65 0W
Tapo-Capara △, *Venezuela* ... **121 E5** 7 55N 71 15W
Tapolca, *Hungary* ... **28 D2** 46 53N 17 29 E
Tapuae-o-Uenuku, *N.Z.* ... **91 K4** 42 0 S 173 39 E
Tapul Group, *Phil.* ... **61 J4** 5 35N 120 50 E
Tapurucuará, *Brazil* ... **124 D5** 0 24 S 65 2W
Taqtaq, *Iraq* ... **70 C5** 35 53N 44 35 E
Taquara, *Brazil* ... **127 B5** 29 36 S 50 46W
Taquari →, *Brazil* ... **124 G7** 19 15 S 57 17W
Tara, *Australia* ... **95 D5** 27 17 S 150 31 E
Tara, *Canada* ... **116 B3** 44 28N 81 9W
Tara, *Russia* ... **52 D8** 56 55N 74 24 E
Tara, *Zambia* ... **87 F2** 16 58 S 26 45 E
Tara △, *Serbia & M.* ... **44 C3** 43 55N 19 30 E
Tara →, *Serbia & M.* ... **44 C3** 43 21N 18 51 E
Taraba □, *Nigeria* ... **83 D7** 8 0N 10 30 E
Taraba →, *Nigeria* ... **83 D7** 8 30N 10 15 E
Tarābulus, *Lebanon* ... **74 A4** 34 31N 35 50 E
Tarābulus, *Libya* ... **79 B8** 32 49N 13 7 E
Taraclia, *Taraclia, Moldova* ... **29 E13** 45 54N 28 40 E
Taraclia, *Tighina, Moldova* ... **29 D14** 46 34N 29 7 E
Taradehi, *India* ... **69 H8** 23 18N 79 21 E
Tarajalejo, *Canary Is.* ... **48 F5** 28 12N 14 7W
Tarakan, *Indonesia* ... **62 D5** 3 20N 117 35 E
Tarakit, Mt., *Kenya* ... **86 B4** 2 2N 35 10 E
Tarama-Jima, *Japan* ... **55 M2** 24 39N 124 42 E
Taran, Mys, *Russia* ... **9 J18** 54 56N 19 59 E
Taranagar, *India* ... **68 E6** 28 43N 74 50 E
Taranaki □, *N.Z.* ... **91 H5** 39 25 S 174 30 E
Taranaki, Mt., *N.Z.* ... **91 H5** 39 17 S 174 5 E
Tarancón, *Spain* ... **38 E1** 40 1N 3 1W
Tarangire △, *Tanzania* ... **86 C4** 4 21 S 36 7 E
Taransay, *U.K.* ... **13 D1** 57 54N 7 0W
Táranto, *Italy* ... **43 B10** 40 28N 17 14 E
Táranto, G. di, *Italy* ... **43 C10** 40 8N 17 20 E
Tarapacá, *Colombia* ... **124 D5** 2 56 S 69 46W
Tarapacá □, *Chile* ... **126 A2** 20 45 S 69 30W
Tarapoto, *Peru* ... **124 E3** 6 30 S 76 20W
Tarare, *France* ... **21 C8** 45 54N 4 26 E
Tararua Ra., *N.Z.* ... **91 J5** 40 45 S 175 25 E
Tarascon, *France* ... **21 E8** 43 48N 4 39 E
Tarascon-sur-Ariège, *France* ... **20 F5** 42 50N 1 36 E
Tarashcha, *Ukraine* ... **33 H6** 49 30N 30 31 E
Tarauacá, *Brazil* ... **124 E4** 8 6 S 70 48W
Tarauacá →, *Brazil* ... **124 E5** 6 42 S 69 48W
Taravo →, *France* ... **21 G12** 41 42N 8 49 E
Tarawa, *Kiribati* ... **96 G9** 1 30N 173 0 E
Tarawera, L., *N.Z.* ... **91 H6** 38 13 S 176 27 E
Taraz, *Kazakhstan* ... **52 E8** 42 54N 71 22 E
Tarazona, *Spain* ... **38 D3** 41 55N 1 43W
Tarazona de la Mancha, *Spain* ... **39 F3** 39 16N 1 55W
Tarbagatay, Khrebet, *Kazakhstan* ... **52 E9** 48 0N 83 0 E
Tarbat Ness, *U.K.* ... **13 D5** 57 52N 3 47W
Tarbela Dam, *Pakistan* ... **68 B5** 34 8N 72 52 E
Tarbert, *Arg. & Bute, U.K.* ... **13 F3** 55 52N 5 25W
Tarbert, *W. Isles, U.K.* ... **13 D2** 57 54N 6 49W
Tarbes, *France* ... **20 E4** 43 15N 0 3 E
Tarboro, *U.S.A.* ... **115 H7** 35 54N 77 32W

Tarcento, *Italy* ... **41 B10** 46 13N 13 13 E
Tarcoola, *Australia* ... **95 E1** 30 44 S 134 36 E
Tarcoon, *Australia* ... **95 E4** 30 15 S 146 43 E
Tardets-Sorholus, *France* ... **20 E3** 43 8N 0 52W
Tardoire →, *France* ... **20 C4** 45 52N 0 14 E
Taree, *Australia* ... **95 E5** 31 50 S 152 30 E
Tarfa, W. el →, *Egypt* ... **80 B3** 28 25N 30 50 E
Tarfaya, *Morocco* ... **78 C3** 27 55N 12 55W
Târgovişte, *Romania* ... **29 F10** 44 57N 25 27 E
Târgu Bujor, *Romania* ... **29 E12** 45 52N 27 55 E
Târgu Cărbuneşti, *Romania* ... **29 F8** 44 57N 23 31 E
Târgu Frumos, *Romania* ... **29 C12** 47 12N 27 2 E
Târgu-Jiu, *Romania* ... **29 E8** 45 5N 23 19 E
Târgu Lăpuş, *Romania* ... **29 C8** 47 27N 23 54 E
Târgu Mureş, *Romania* ... **29 D9** 46 31N 24 38 E
Târgu Neamţ, *Romania* ... **29 C11** 47 12N 26 25 E
Târgu Ocna, *Romania* ... **29 D11** 46 16N 26 39 E
Târgu Secuiesc, *Romania* ... **29 E11** 46 0N 26 10 E
Târguşor, *Romania* ... **29 F4** 44 27N 28 25 E
Tărhăus, Vf., *Romania* ... **29 D11** 46 40N 26 8 E
Tarif, *U.A.E.* ... **71 E7** 24 3N 53 46 E
Tarifa, *Spain* ... **37 J5** 36 1N 5 36W
Tarija, *Bolivia* ... **126 A3** 21 30 S 64 40W
Tarija □, *Bolivia* ... **126 A3** 21 30 S 63 30W
Tariku →, *Indonesia* ... **63 E9** 2 55 S 138 26 E
Tarim Basin = Tarim Pendi, *China* ... **60 C3** 40 0N 84 0 E
Tarim He →, *China* ... **60 C3** 39 30N 88 30 E
Tarim Pendi, *China* ... **60 C3** 40 0N 84 0 E
Taritatu →, *Indonesia* ... **63 E9** 2 54 S 138 27 E
Tarka →, *S. Africa* ... **88 E4** 32 10 S 26 0 E
Tarkastad, *S. Africa* ... **88 E4** 32 0 S 26 16 E
Tarkhankut, Mys, *Ukraine* ... **33 K7** 45 25N 32 30 E
Tarko Sale, *Russia* ... **52 C8** 64 55N 77 50 E
Tarkwa, *Ghana* ... **82 D4** 5 20N 2 0W
Tarlac, *Phil.* ... **61 D4** 15 29N 120 35 E
Tarm, *Denmark* ... **11 J2** 55 56N 8 31 E
Tarma, *Peru* ... **124 F3** 11 25 S 75 45W
Tarn □, *France* ... **20 E6** 43 49N 2 8 E
Tarn →, *France* ... **20 D5** 44 5N 1 6 E
Tarn-et-Garonne □, *France* ... **20 D5** 44 8N 1 20 E
Tarna →, *Hungary* ... **28 C4** 47 31N 19 59 E
Tárnaveni, *Romania* ... **29 D9** 46 19N 24 13 E
Tárnava Mare →, *Romania* ... **29 D8** 46 10N 23 43 E
Tárnava Mică →, *Romania* ... **29 D8** 46 9N 23 55 E
Târnăveni, *Romania* ... **29 D9** 46 19N 24 13 E
Tarnica, *Poland* ... **31 J9** 49 4N 22 44 E
Tarnobrzeg, *Poland* ... **31 H8** 50 35N 21 41 E
Tarnogród, *Poland* ... **31 H9** 50 22N 22 45 E
Tarnos, *France* ... **20 E2** 43 32N 1 28W
Tárnova, *Moldova* ... **28 B12** 48 10N 27 40 E
Tárnova, *Romania* ... **28 D6** 46 23N 21 59 E
Tarnów, *Poland* ... **31 H8** 50 3N 21 0 E
Tarnowskie Góry, *Poland* ... **31 H5** 50 27N 18 54 E
Tärnsjö, *Sweden* ... **10 D10** 60 9N 16 56 E
Táro →, *Italy* ... **40 C7** 45 2N 10 15 E
Tãrom, *Iran* ... **71 D7** 28 11N 55 46 E
Taroom, *Australia* ... **95 D4** 25 36 S 149 48 E
Taroudannt, *Morocco* ... **78 B4** 30 30N 8 52W
Tarp, *Germany* ... **24 A5** 54 39N 9 24 E
Tarpon Springs, *U.S.A.* ... **115 L4** 28 9N 82 45W
Tarquínia, *Italy* ... **41 F8** 42 15N 11 45 E
Tarragona, *Spain* ... **38 D6** 41 5N 1 17 E
Tarragona □, *Spain* ... **38 D6** 41 5N 1 0 E
Tarraleah, *Australia* ... **95 G4** 42 17 S 146 26 E
Tarrasa = Terrassa, *Spain* ... **38 D7** 41 34N 2 1 E
Tàrrega, *Spain* ... **38 D6** 41 39N 1 9 E
Tarrytown, *U.S.A.* ... **117 E11** 41 4N 73 52W
Tars, *Denmark* ... **11 G4** 57 23N 10 7 E
Tarshiha = Me'ona, *Israel* ... **74 B4** 33 1N 35 15 E
Tarsus, *Turkey* ... **72 D6** 36 58N 34 55 E
Tartagal, *Argentina* ... **126 A3** 22 30 S 63 50W
Tärtär, *Azerbaijan* ... **35 K8** 40 20N 46 58 E
Tärtär →, *Azerbaijan* ... **35 K8** 40 26N 47 20 E
Tartas, *France* ... **20 E3** 43 50N 0 49W
Tartu, *Estonia* ... **9 G22** 58 20N 26 44 E
Tartūs, *Syria* ... **70 C2** 34 55N 35 55 E
Tarumizu, *Japan* ... **55 J5** 31 29N 130 42 E
Tarussa, *Russia* ... **32 E9** 54 44N 37 10 E
Tarutao = Ko Tarutao △, *Thailand* ... **65 J2** 6 31N 99 26 E
Tarutao, Ko, *Thailand* ... **65 J2** 6 33N 99 40 E
Tarutung, *Indonesia* ... **62 D1** 2 0N 98 54 E
Tarutyne, *Ukraine* ... **29 D14** 46 12N 29 9 E
Tarvísio, *Italy* ... **41 B10** 46 30N 13 35 E
Tasek, *Canada* ... **102 C4** 52 8N 123 45W
Tash-Kömür = Tash-Kumyr, *Kyrgyzstan* ... **52 E8** 41 40N 72 10 E
Tash-Kumyr = Tash-Kömür, *Kyrgyzstan* ... **52 E8** 41 40N 72 10 E
Tashauz = Dashhowuz, *Turkmenistan* ... **52 E6** 41 49N 59 58 E
Tashi Chho Dzong = Thimphu, *Bhutan* ... **67 F16** 27 31N 89 45 E
Tashk, Daryācheh-ye, *Iran* ... **71 D7** 29 45N 53 35 E
Tashkent = Toshkent, *Uzbekistan* ... **52 E7** 41 20N 69 10 E
Tashtagol, *Russia* ... **52 D9** 52 47N 87 53 E
Tasiilaq, *Greenland* ... **4 C6** 65 40N 37 20W
Tasikmalaya, *Indonesia* ... **63 G13** 7 18 S 108 12 E
Tåsinge, *Denmark* ... **11 J4** 55 0N 10 35 E
Tãsjön, *Sweden* ... **8 D16** 64 15N 15 40 E
Taskan, *Russia* ... **53 C16** 62 59N 150 20 E
Tasker, *Niger* ... **83 C7** 15 8N 10 40 E
Taşköprü, *Turkey* ... **72 B6** 41 30N 34 15 E
Taşlâc, *Moldova* ... **29 D14** 46 53N 29 8 E
Tasman △, *N.Z.* ... **91 J4** 40 59 S 173 25 E
Tasman B., *N.Z.* ... **91 J4** 40 59 S 173 18 E
Tasman Mts., *N.Z.* ... **91 J4** 41 3 S 172 25 E
Tasman Pen., *Australia* ... **95 G4** 43 10 S 148 0 E
Tasman Plateau, *S. Ocean* ... **5 A10** 48 0 S 146 0 E
Tasman Sea, *Pac. Oc.* ... **96 L8** 36 0 S 160 0 E
Tasmania □, *Australia* ... **95 G4** 42 0 S 146 30 E
Tassili n'Ajjer, *Algeria* ... **78 C7** 25 47N 8 1 E
Tassili Tin-Rerhoh, *Algeria* ... **83 A5** 20 5N 3 55 E
Tata, *Hungary* ... **28 C3** 47 37N 18 19 E
Tatabánya, *Hungary* ... **28 C3** 47 32N 18 25 E
Tataouine, *Tunisia* ... **79 B8** 32 56N 10 27 E
Tatar Republic = Tatarstan □, *Russia* ... **34 C10** 55 30N 51 30 E
Tatarbunary, *Ukraine* ... **29 E14** 45 50N 29 39 E
Tatarsk, *Russia* ... **52 D8** 55 14N 76 0 E
Tatarstan □, *Russia* ... **34 C10** 55 30N 51 30 E
Tateyama, *Japan* ... **55 G9** 35 0N 139 50 E

Tathlina L., *Canada* **102 A5** 60 33N 117 39W
Tathra, *Australia* ...... **95 F4** 36 44 S 149 59 E
Tatinnai L., *Canada* **103 A9** 60 55N 97 40W
Tatla L., *Canada* **102 C4** 52 0N 124 20W
Tatshsu, *Turkey* .... **45 F11** 40 24N 27 55 E
Tatnam, C., *Canada* **103 B10** 57 16N 91 0W
Tatra = Tatry,
  Slovak Rep. .... **27 B13** 49 20N 20 0 E
Tatranský △,
  Slovak Rep. .... **27 B13** 49 10N 20 0 E
Tatry, *Slovak Rep.* ..... **27 B13** 49 20N 20 0 E
Tatshenshini ➤, *Canada* **102 B1** 59 28N 137 45W
Tatsuno, *Japan* .... **55 G7** 34 52N 134 33 E
Tatta, *Pakistan* .... **68 G2** 24 42N 67 55 E
Tatuí, *Brazil* .... **127 A6** 23 25 S 47 53W
Tatum, *U.S.A.* **113 J3** 33 16N 103 19W
Tat'ung = Datong, *China* **56 D7** 40 6N 113 18 E
Taubaté, *Brazil* .... **127 A6** 23 0 S 45 36W
Tauberbischofsheim,
  Germany .... **25 F5** 49 37N   9 39 E
Taucha, *Germany* ..... **24 D8** 51 23N 12 29 E
Tauern-tunnel, *Austria* . **26 D6** 47 0N 13 12 E
Taufikia, *Sudan* .... **81 F3** 9 24N 31 37 E
Taulé, *France* **18 D3** 48 37N   3 55W
Taumarunui, *N.Z.* ..... **91 H5** 38 53 S 175 15 E
Taumaturgo, *Brazil* .... **124 E4** 8 54 S 72 51W
Taung, *S. Africa* ..... **88 D3** 27 33 S 24 47 E
Taungdwingyi, *Burma* .. **67 J19** 20 1N 95 40 E
Taunggyi, *Burma* ..... **67 J20** 20 50N 97 0 E
Taungup, *Burma* ..... **67 K19** 18 51N 94 14 E
Taungup Taunggya,
  Burma .... **67 K18** 18 20N 93 40 E
Taunsa, *Pakistan* ..... **68 D4** 30 42N 70 39 E
Taunsa Barrage,
  Pakistan .... **68 D4** 30 42N 70 50 E
Taunton, *U.K.* **15 F4** 51 1N   3 5W
Taunton, *U.S.A.* **117 E13** 41 54N 71 6W
Taunus, *Germany* ..... **25 E4** 50 13N   8 34 E
Taupo, *N.Z.* .... **91 H6** 38 41 S 176 7 E
Taupo, L., *N.Z.* .... **91 H5** 38 46 S 175 55 E
Tauragė, *Lithuania* .... **9 J20** 55 14N 22 16 E
Tauragė □, *Lithuania* .. **30 C9** 55 15N 22 17 E
Tauranga, *N.Z.* .... **91 G6** 37 42 S 176 11 E
Tauranga Harb., *N.Z.* .. **91 G6** 37 30 S 176 5 E
Taureau, Rés., *Canada* . **104 C5** 46 46N 73 50W
Taurianova, *Italy* ..... **43 D9** 38 21N 16 1 E
Taurus Mts. = Toros
  Dağları, *Turkey* .... **70 B2** 37 0N 32 30 E
Tauste, *Spain* **38 D3** 41 58N   1 18W
Tauz = Tovuz,
  Azerbaijan .... **35 K7** 40 59N 45 40 E
Tavas, *Turkey* .... **47 D11** 37 34N 29 4 E
Tavastehus =
  Hämeenlinna, *Finland* **9 F21** 61 0N 24 28 E
Tavda, *Russia* .... **52 D7** 58 7N 65 8 E
Tavda ➤, *Russia* ..... **52 D7** 57 47N 67 18 E
Tavernes de la
  Valldigna, *Spain* **39 F4** 39 5N   0 13W
Taveta, *Tanzania* ..... **86 C4** 3 23 S 37 37 E
Taveuni, *Fiji* .... **91 C9** 16 51 S 179 58W
Taviano, *Italy* .... **43 C11** 39 59N 18 1 E
Tavignano ➤, *France* .. **21 F13** 42 7N   9 33 E
Tavira, *Portugal* **37 H3** 37 8N   7 40W
Tavistock, *Canada* **116 C4** 43 19N 80 50W
Tavistock, *U.K.* **15 G3** 50 33N   4 9W
Tavolara, *Italy* .... **42 B2** 40 54N   9 42 E
Távora ➤, *Portugal* ... **36 D3** 41 8N   7 35W
Tavoy, *Burma* .... **64 E2** 14 2N 98 12 E
Tavşanlı, *Turkey* ..... **47 B11** 39 32N 29 30 E
Taw ➤, *U.K.* **15 F3** 51 4N   4 4W
Tawa ➤, *India* .... **68 H8** 22 48N 77 48 E
Tawas City, *U.S.A.* **114 C4** 44 16N 83 31W
Tawau, *Malaysia* ..... **62 D5** 4 20N 117 55 E
Taweisha, *Sudan* ..... **81 E2** 12 19N 26 40 E
Tawitawi, *Phil.* .... **63 B6** 5 10N 120 0 E
Tawu, *Taiwan* .... **59 F13** 22 30N 120 50 E
Taxco de Alarcón,
  Mexico **119 D5** 18 33N 99 36W
Taxila, *Pakistan* ..... **68 C5** 33 42N 72 52 E
Tay △, *U.K.* **13 E5** 56 43N   3 59W
Tay ➤, *U.K.* **13 E5** 56 37N   3 38W
Tay, Firth of, *U.K.* **13 E5** 56 25N   3 8W
Tay, L., *Australia* ..... **93 F3** 32 55 S 120 48 E
Tay, L., *U.K.* **13 E4** 56 32N   4 8W
Tay Ninh, *Vietnam* .... **65 G6** 11 20N 106 5 E
Tayabamba, *Peru* ..... **124 E3** 8 15 S 77 16W
Tayabas Bay, *Phil.* .... **61 E4** 13 45N 121 45 E
Taylakova, *Russia* .... **52 D8** 59 13N 74 0 E
Taylakovy = Taylakova,
  Russia .... **52 D8** 59 13N 74 0 E
Taylor, *Canada* **102 B4** 56 13N 120 40W
Taylor, *Nebr., U.S.A.* .. **112 E5** 41 46N 99 23W
Taylor, *Pa., U.S.A.* **117 E9** 41 23N 75 43W
Taylor, *Tex., U.S.A.* ... **113 K6** 30 34N 97 25W
Taylor, Mt., *U.S.A.* **109 J10** 35 14N 107 37W
Taylorville, *U.S.A.* **112 F10** 39 33N 89 18W
Taymā, *Si. Arabia* .... **70 E3** 27 35N 38 45 E
Taymyr, Oz., *Russia* ... **53 B11** 74 20N 102 0 E
Taymyr, Poluostrov,
  Russia .... **53 B11** 75 0N 100 0 E
Tayport, *U.K.* **13 E6** 56 27N   2 52W
Tayrona △, *Colombia* .. **121 D5** 11 17N 74 2W
Tayshet, *Russia* ..... **53 D10** 55 58N 98 1 E
Taytay, *Phil.* .... **61 F3** 10 45N 119 30 E
Tayshir △, *N.Z.* .... **91 L1** 45 15 S 167 45 E
Te Aroha, *N.Z.* .... **91 G5** 37 32 S 175 44 E
Te Awamutu, *N.Z.* .... **91 H5** 38 1 S 175 20 E
Te Ika a Maui = North
  I., *N.Z.* .... **91 H5** 38 0 S 175 0 E
Te Kuiti, *N.Z.* .... **91 H5** 38 20 S 175 11 E
Te-n-Dghâmcha,
  Sebkhet, *Mauritania* . **82 B1** 18 30N 15 55W
Te Puke, *N.Z.* .... **91 G6** 37 46 S 176 22 E

Te Waewae B., *N.Z.* ... **91 M1** 46 13 S 167 33 E
Te Wai Pounamu =
  South I., *N.Z.* .... **91 L3** 44 0 S 170 0 E
Teaca, *Romania* ..... **29 D9** 46 55N 24 30 E
Teague, *U.S.A.* **113 K6** 31 38N 96 17W
Teapa, *Mexico* **119 D6** 18 35N 92 56W
Teba, *Spain* **37 J6** 36 59N   4 55W
Tebakang, *Malaysia* ... **62 D4** 1 6N 110 30 E
Teberda, *Russia* ..... **35 J5** 43 30N 41 46 E
Teberu, *Malaysia* ..... **65 d** 1 30N 103 42 E
Tébessa, *Algeria* ..... **78 A7** 35 22N   8 8 E
Tebicuary ➤, *Paraguay* **126 B4** 26 36 S 58 16W
Tebingtinggi, *Riau,*
  Indonesia .... **62 E2** 1 0N 102 45 E
Tebingtinggi,
  Sumatera Utara,
  Indonesia .... **62 D1** 3 20N 99 9 E
Tebulos, *Georgia* ..... **35 J7** 42 36N 45 17 E
Tecate, *Mexico* **111 N10** 32 34N 116 38W
Tecer Dağları, *Turkey* . **72 C7** 39 27N 37 27 E
Tech ➤, *France* .... **20 F7** 42 36N   3 3 E
Techiman, *Ghana* **82 D4** 7 35N   1 58W
Techirghiol, *Romania* .. **29 F13** 44 4N 28 32 E
Tecka, *Argentina* ..... **128 E2** 43 29 S 70 48W
Tecomán, *Mexico* **118 D4** 18 55N 103 53W
Tecopa, *U.S.A.* **111 K10** 35 51N 116 13W
Tecoripa, *Mexico* **118 B3** 28 37N 109 57W
Tecuala, *Mexico* **118 C3** 22 23N 105 27W
Tecumseh, *Canada* **116 D2** 42 19N 82 54W
Tecumseh, *Mich., U.S.A.* **114 D4** 42 0N 83 57W
Tecumseh, *Okla., U.S.A.* **113 H6** 35 15N 96 56W
Tedzhen = Tejen,
  Turkmenistan .... **52 F7** 37 23N 60 31 E
Tees ➤, *U.K.* **14 C6** 54 37N   1 10W
Tees B., *U.K.* **14 C6** 54 40N   1 9W
Teeswater, *Canada* ... **116 C3** 43 59N 81 17W
Tefé, *Brazil* .... **124 D6** 3 25 S 64 50W
Tefenni, *Turkey* ..... **47 D11** 37 18N 29 45 E
Tegal, *Indonesia* ..... **63 G13** 6 52 S 109 8 E
Tegallalang, *Indonesia* . **63 J18** 8 27 S 115 17 E
Tegalsari, *Indonesia* ... **63 J17** 8 25 S 114 8 E
Tegel, Berlin ✈ (TXL),
  Germany .... **24 C9** 52 35N 13 14 E
Tegernsee, *Germany* ... **25 H7** 47 43N 11 46 E
Teggiano, *Italy* .... **43 B8** 40 23N 15 32 E
Tegid, L. = Bala, L.,
  U.K. **14 E4** 52 53N   3 37W
Tegina, *Nigeria* .... **83 D6** 10 5N   6 11 E
Tegucigalpa, *Honduras* . **120 D2** 14 5N 87 14W
Teguidda i-n-Tessoumt,
  Niger .... **83 B6** 17 25N   6 37 E
Tehachapi, *U.S.A.* **111 K8** 35 8N 118 27W
Tehachapi Mts., *U.S.A.* **111 L8** 35 0N 118 30W
Tehamiyam, *Sudan* ... **80 D4** 18 20N 36 32 E
Teheran = Tehrān, *Iran* **71 C6** 35 41N 51 25 E
Tehilla, *Sudan* .... **80 D4** 17 42N 36 6 E
Téhini, *Ivory C.* **82 D4** 9 39N   3 40W
Tehoru, *Indonesia* ..... **63 E7** 3 23 S 129 30 E
Tehrān, *Iran* .... **71 C6** 35 44N 51 30 E
Tehrān □, *Iran* .... **71 C6** 35 30N 51 30 E
Tehri, *India* .... **69 D8** 30 23N 78 29 E
Tehuacán, *Mexico* **119 D5** 18 30N 97 30W
Tehuantepec, *Mexico* .. **119 D5** 16 21N 95 13W
Tehuantepec, G. de,
  Mexico **119 D5** 15 50N 95 12W
Tehuantepec, Istmo de,
  Mexico **119 D6** 17 0N 94 30W
Teide, Pico de,
  Canary Is. **48 F3** 28 15N 16 38W
Teifi ➤, *U.K.* **15 E3** 52 5N   4 41W
Teign ➤, *U.K.* **15 G4** 50 32N   3 32W
Teignmouth, *U.K.* **15 G4** 50 33N   3 31W
Teiuș, *Romania* .... **29 D8** 46 12N 23 40 E
Teixeira Pinto,
  Guinea-Biss. **82 C1** 12 3N 16 0W
Tejakula, *Indonesia* ... **63 J18** 8 8 S 115 20 E
Tejam, *India* .... **69 E9** 29 57N 80 11 E
Tejen, *Turkmenistan* ... **52 F7** 37 23N 60 31 E
Tejen ➤, *Turkmenistan* . **71 B9** 37 24N 60 38 E
Tejo ➤, *Europe* **37 F2** 38 40N   9 24W
Tejon Pass, *U.S.A.* **111 L8** 34 49N 118 53W
Tekamah, *U.S.A.* **112 E6** 41 47N 96 13W
Tekapo, L., *N.Z.* ..... **91 K3** 43 53 S 170 33 E
Tekax, *Mexico* **119 C7** 20 11N 89 18W
Teke, *Turkey* .... **45 E13** 41 4N 29 39 E
Tekeli, *Kazakhstan* .... **52 E8** 44 50N 79 0 E
Tekeze ➤, *Ethiopia* ... **81 E4** 14 20N 35 50 E
Tekija, *Serbia & M.* ... **44 B6** 44 42N 22 26 E
Tekirdağ, *Turkey* ..... **45 F11** 40 58N 27 30 E
Tekirdağ □, *Turkey* ... **45 E11** 41 0N 27 0 E
Tekirova, *Turkey* ..... **47 E12** 36 30N 30 32 E
Tekkali, *India* .... **67 K14** 18 37N 84 15 E
Tekke, *Turkey* .... **72 B7** 40 42N 36 12 E
Tekman, *Turkey* ..... **73 C9** 39 38N 41 0 E
Tekoa, *U.S.A.* **108 C5** 47 14N 117 4W
Tekong Besar Pulau,
  Singapore .... **65 d** 1 25N 104 3 E
Tel Aviv ✈ (TLV), *Israel* **74 C3** 32 5N 34 49 E
Tel Aviv-Yafo, *Israel* ... **74 C3** 32 4N 34 48 E
Tel Lakhish, *Israel* ... **74 D3** 31 34N 34 51 E
Tel Megiddo, *Israel* ... **74 C4** 32 35N 35 11 E
Tela, *Honduras* **120 C2** 15 40N 87 28W
Telanaipura = Jambi,
  Indonesia .... **62 E2** 1 38 S 103 30 E
Telaščica △, *Croatia* ... **41 E12** 43 55N 15 10 E
Telavi, *Georgia* .... **35 J7** 42 0N 45 30 E
Telč, *Czech Rep.* ..... **26 B8** 49 11N 15 28 E
Telciu, *Romania* ..... **29 C9** 47 25N 24 24 E
Telde, *Canary Is.* **48 G4** 27 59N 15 25W
Telegraph Creek,
  Canada **102 B2** 58 0N 131 10W
Telekhany =
  Tsyelyakhany, *Belarus* **33 F3** 52 30N 25 46 E
Telemark, *Norway* .... **9 G12** 59 15N   7 40 E
Telén, *Argentina* ..... **126 D2** 36 15 S 65 31W
Teleneşti, *Moldova* .... **29 C13** 47 30N 28 23 E
Teleng, *Iran* .... **71 E9** 25 47N 61 3 E
Teleño, *Spain* **36 C4** 42 23N   6 22W
Teleorman □, *Romania* . **29 G10** 44 0N 25 0 E
Teleorman ➤, *Romania* **29 G10** 44 15N 25 20 E
Teles Pires ➤, *Brazil* .. **124 E7** 7 21 S 58 3W
Telescope Pk., *U.S.A.* . **111 J9** 36 10N 117 50W
Teletaye, *Mali* .... **83 B5** 16 31N   1 30 E
Telfer Mine, *Australia* . **92 C3** 21 40 S 122 12 E
Telford, *U.K.* **15 E5** 52 40N   2 27W
Telford and Wrekin □,
  U.K. **15 E5** 52 45N   2 27W
Telfs, *Austria* .... **26 D4** 47 19N 11 4 E
Télimélé, *Guinea* **82 C2** 10 54N 13 2W
Teljo, J., *Sudan* .... **81 E2** 14 42N 25 26 E
Telkwa, *Canada* **102 C3** 54 41N 127 5W
Tell City, *U.S.A.* **114 G2** 37 57N 86 46W
Tellicherry, *India* ..... **66 P9** 11 45N 75 30 E
Telluride, *U.S.A.* **109 H10** 37 56N 107 49W
Teloloapán, *Mexico* ... **119 D5** 18 21N 99 51W

Telpos Iz, *Russia* ..... **6 C17** 63 16N 59 13 E
Telsen, *Argentina* ..... **128 E3** 42 30 S 66 50W
Telšiai, *Lithuania* ..... **9 H20** 55 59N 22 14 E
Telšiai □, *Lithuania* ... **30 C9** 55 55N 22 15 E
Teltow, *Germany* ..... **24 C9** 52 24N 13 15 E
Teluk Anson = Teluk
  Intan, *Malaysia* ..... **65 K3** 4 3N 101 0 E
Teluk Bahang, *Malaysia* **65 c** 5 28N 100 13 E
Teluk Betung =
  Tanjungkarang
  Telukbetung,
  Indonesia .... **62 F3** 5 20 S 105 10 E
Teluk Intan, *Malaysia* .. **65 K3** 4 3N 101 0 E
Teluk Kumbar, *Malaysia* **65 c** 5 18N 100 14 E
Telukbutun, *Indonesia* . **62 D3** 4 13N 108 12 E
Telukdalem, *Indonesia* . **62 D1** 0 33N 97 50 E
Tema, *Ghana* **83 D5** 5 41N   0 0W
Temax, *Mexico* **119 C7** 21 10N 88 50W
Temba, *S. Africa* ..... **89 D4** 25 20 S 28 17 E
Tembagapura, *Indonesia* **63 E9** 4 20 S 137 0 E
Tembe, *Dem. Rep. of*
  the Congo .... **86 C2** 0 16 S 28 14 E
Tembe △, *S. Africa* .... **89 D5** 26 51 S 32 24 E
Tembleque, *Spain* **36 F7** 39 41N   3 30W
Temblor Range, *U.S.A.* **111 K7** 35 20N 119 50W
Teme ➤, *U.K.* **15 E5** 52 11N   2 13W
Temecula, *U.S.A.* **111 M9** 33 30N 117 9W
Temerloh, *Malaysia* ... **62 D2** 3 27N 102 25 E
Teminabuan, *Indonesia* . **63 E8** 1 26 S 132 1 E
Temir, *Kazakhstan* .... **52 E6** 49 1N 57 14 E
Temirtau, *Kazakhstan* . **52 D8** 50 5N 72 56 E
Temirtau, *Russia* ..... **52 D9** 53 10N 87 30 E
Temiscamie ➤, *Canada* **105 B5** 50 59N 73 5W
Témiscaming, *Canada* . **104 C4** 46 44N 79 5W
Témiscamingue, L.,
  Canada **104 C4** 47 10N 79 25W
Temnikov, *Russia* .... **34 C6** 54 40N 43 11 E
Temo ➤, *Italy* .... **42 B1** 40 17N   8 28 E
Temosachic, *Mexico* ... **118 B3** 28 58N 107 50W
Tempe, *U.S.A.* **109 K8** 33 25N 111 56W
Témpio Pausánia, *Italy* **42 B2** 40 54N   9 6 E
Tempiute, *U.S.A.* **110 H11** 37 39N 115 38W
Temple, *U.S.A.* **113 K6** 31 6N 97 21W
Temple B., *Australia* ... **94 A3** 12 15 S 143 3 E
Templemore, *Ireland* .. **12 D4** 52 47N   7 51W
Templeton, *U.S.A.* ... **110 K6** 35 33N 120 42W
Templeton ➤, *Australia* **94 C2** 21 0 S 138 40 E
Templin, *Germany* ... **24 B9** 53 7N 13 28 E
Tempoal, *Mexico* **119 C5** 21 31N 98 23W
Temryuk, *Russia* ..... **33 K9** 45 15N 37 24 E
Temska ➤, *Serbia & M.* **44 C6** 43 17N 22 33 E
Temuco, *Chile* .... **128 D2** 38 45 S 72 40W
Temuka, *N.Z.* .... **91 L3** 44 14 S 171 17 E
Tenabo, *Mexico* **119 C6** 20 2N 90 12W
Tenaha, *U.S.A.* **113 K7** 31 57N 94 15W
Tenakee Springs, *U.S.A.* **102 B1** 57 47N 135 13W
Tenali, *India* .... **67 L12** 16 15N 80 35 E
Tenancingo, *Mexico* ... **119 D5** 19 0N 99 33W
Tenango, *Mexico* **119 D5** 19 7N 99 33W
Tenasserim, *Burma* ... **65 F2** 12 6N 99 3 E
Tenasserim □, *Burma* . **64 F2** 14 0N 98 30 E
Tenby, *U.K.* **15 F3** 51 40N   4 42W
Tenda, Colle di, *France* **21 D11** 44 7N   7 36 E
Tendaho, *Ethiopia* .... **81 E5** 11 48N 40 54 E
Tende, *France* .... **21 D11** 44 5N   7 35 E
Tendelti, *Sudan* ..... **81 E3** 13 1N 31 55 E
Tendrovskaya Kosa,
  Ukraine .... **33 J6** 46 16N 31 35 E
Tendukhera, *India* .... **69 H8** 23 24N 79 33 E
Teneguía, Volcanes de,
  Canary Is. **48 F2** 28 28N 17 51W
Teneida, *Egypt* .... **80 B2** 25 30N 29 19 E
Tenenkou, *Mali* **82 C4** 14 28N   4 55W
Ténéré, *Niger* .... **83 B7** 19 0N 10 30 E
Tenerife, *Canary Is.* ... **48 F3** 28 15N 16 35W
Tenerife, Pico,
  Canary Is. **48 G1** 27 43N 18 1W
Tenerife Norte ✈
  (TFN), *Canary Is.* **48 F3** 28 28N 16 17W
Tenerife Sur ✈ (TFS),
  Canary Is. **48 F3** 28 3N 16 33W
Teng Xian,
  Guangxi Zhuangzu,
  China .... **59 F8** 23 21N 110 56 E
Teng Xian, *Shandong,*
  China .... **57 G9** 35 5N 117 10 E
Tengah, Kepulauan,
  Indonesia .... **62 F5** 7 5 S 118 15 E
Tengchong, *China* .... **58 E2** 25 0N 98 28 E
Tengchowfu = Penglai,
  China .... **57 F11** 37 48N 120 42 E
Tenggarong, *Indonesia* . **62 E5** 0 24 S 116 58 E
Tenggol, Pulau,
  Malaysia .... **65 K4** 4 48N 103 41 E
Tengiz, Ozero,
  Kazakhstan .... **52 D7** 50 30N 69 0 E
Tenhult, *Sweden* ..... **11 G8** 57 41N 14 20 E
Teniente Enciso △,
  Paraguay .... **126 A3** 21 5 S 61 8W
Teniente Rodolfo
  Marsh, *Antarctica* ... **5 C18** 62 30 S 58 0W
Tenino, *U.S.A.* **110 D4** 46 51N 122 51W
Tenkasi, *India* .... **66 Q10** 8 55N 77 20 E
Tenke, *Katanga,*
  Dem. Rep. of
  the Congo .... **87 E2** 11 22 S 26 40 E
Tenke, *Katanga,*
  Dem. Rep. of
  the Congo .... **87 E2** 10 32 S 26 7 E
Tenkodogo,
  Burkina Faso **83 C4** 11 54N   0 19W
Tenna ➤, *Italy* .... **41 E10** 43 14N 13 47 E
Tennant Creek,
  Australia .... **94 B1** 19 30 S 134 15 E
Tennessee □, *U.S.A.* .. **115 H2** 36 0N 86 30W
Tennessee ➤, *U.S.A.* .. **114 G1** 37 4N 88 34W
Teno, Pta. de, *Canary Is.* **48 F3** 28 21N 16 55W
Tenom, *Malaysia* ..... **62 C5** 5 4N 115 57 E
Tenosique, *Mexico* **119 D6** 17 30N 91 24W
Tenryū-Gawa ➤, *Japan* **55 G8** 35 39N 137 48 E
Tenterden, *U.K.* ..... **15 F8** 51 4N   0 42 E
Tenterfield, *Australia* .. **95 D5** 29 0 S 152 0 E
Teo, *Spain* **36 C2** 42 45N   8 30W
Teófilo Otoni, *Brazil* ... **125 G10** 17 50 S 41 30W
Tepa, *Indonesia* ..... **63 F7** 7 52 S 129 31 E
Tepalcatepec ➤, *Mexico* **118 D4** 18 35N 101 59W
Tepecik, *Bursa, Turkey* . **45 F12** 40 7N 28 25 E
Tepecik, *Kütahya,*
  Turkey .... **47 B11** 39 32N 29 28 E
Tepehuanes, *Mexico* ... **118 B3** 25 21N 105 44W
Tepelenë, *Albania* .... **44 F4** 40 17N 20 2 E
Tepetongo, *Mexico* ... **118 C4** 22 28N 103 9W
Tepic, *Mexico* **118 C4** 21 30N 104 54W
Teplá, *Czech Rep.* .... **26 B5** 49 59N 12 52 E
Teplice, *Czech Rep.* ... **26 A6** 50 40N 13 48 E
Teplyk, *Ukraine* ..... **29 B14** 48 40N 29 44 E
Tepoca, C., *Mexico* ... **118 A2** 30 20N 112 25W

Tequila, *Mexico* **118 C4** 20 54N 103 47W
Ter ➤, *Spain* .... **38 C8** 42 2N   3 12 E
Ter Apel, *Neths.* ..... **17 B7** 52 53N   7 5 E
Téra, *Niger* .... **83 C5** 14 0N   0 45 E
Tera ➤, *Spain* **36 D5** 41 54N   5 44W
Teraina, *Kiribati* **97 G11** 4 43N 160 25W
Terakeka, *Sudan* ..... **81 F3** 5 26N 31 45 E
Téramo, *Italy* .... **41 F10** 42 39N 13 42 E
Terang, *Australia* ..... **95 F3** 38 15 S 142 55 E
Terazit, Massif de, *Niger* **83 A6** 20 0N   8 30 E
Tercan, *Turkey* ..... **73 C9** 39 47N 40 23 E
Tercero ➤, *Argentina* .. **126 C3** 32 58 S 61 47W
Terceira, *Azores* **50 D3** 38 43N 27 13W
Terebovlya, *Ukraine* ... **33 H3** 49 18N 25 44 E
Teregova, *Romania* ... **28 E7** 45 10N 22 16 E
Tereida, *Sudan* .... **81 E3** 10 35N 31 17 E
Terek ➤, *Russia* ..... **35 J8** 44 0N 47 30 E
Terepaima △, *Venezuela* **121 E6** 9 58N 69 17W
Tereshka ➤, *Russia* ... **34 E8** 51 48N 46 26 E
Teresina, *Brazil* ..... **125 E10** 5 9 S 42 45W
Teresópolis, *Brazil* .... **127 A7** 22 25 S 42 59W
Terespol, *Poland* ..... **31 F10** 52 5N 23 37 E
Teresva ➤, *Ukraine* ... **29 B8** 48 0N 23 22 E
Terewah, L., *Australia* . **95 D4** 29 52 S 147 35 E
Terges ➤, *Portugal* ... **37 H3** 37 49N   7 41W
Tergnier, *France* ..... **19 C10** 49 40N   3 17 E
Teridgerie Cr. ➤,
  Australia .... **95 E4** 30 25 S 148 50 E
Terlizzi, *Italy* .... **43 A9** 41 8N 16 32 E
Terme, *Turkey* .... **72 B7** 41 11N 37 0 E
Términi Imerese, *Italy* .. **42 E6** 37 59N 13 42 E
Términos, L. de, *Mexico* **119 D6** 18 35N 91 30W
Termiz, *Uzbekistan* ... **52 F7** 37 15N 67 15 E
Térmoli, *Italy* .... **41 F12** 42 0N 15 0 E
Ternate, *Indonesia* ... **63 D7** 0 45N 127 25 E
Terneuzen, *Neths.* .... **17 C3** 51 20N   3 50 E
Terney, *Russia* ..... **53 E14** 45 3N 136 37 E
Terni, *Italy* .... **41 F9** 42 34N 12 37 E
Ternitz, *Austria* ..... **26 D9** 47 43N 16 2 E
Ternivka, *Ukraine* .... **29 B14** 48 32N 29 58 E
Ternopil, *Ukraine* ..... **33 H3** 49 30N 25 40 E
Ternopol = Ternopil,
  Ukraine .... **33 H3** 49 30N 25 40 E
Terowie, *Australia* .... **95 E2** 33 8 S 138 55 E
Terpní, *Greece* .... **44 F7** 40 55N 23 26 E
Terra Bella, *U.S.A.* ... **111 K7** 35 58N 119 3W
Terra Nova △, *Canada* . **105 C9** 48 33N 53 55W
Terrace, *Canada* **102 C3** 54 30N 128 35W
Terrace Bay, *Canada* .. **104 C2** 48 47N 87 5W
Terracina, *Italy* .... **42 A6** 41 17N 13 15 E
Terralba, *Italy* .... **42 C1** 39 43N   8 39 E
Terrasini, *Italy* .... **42 D6** 38 10N 13 4 E
Terrassa, *Spain* ..... **38 D7** 41 34N   2 1 E
Terrasson-la-Villedieu,
  France .... **20 C5** 45 8N   1 18 E
Terre Haute, *U.S.A.* ... **114 F2** 39 28N 87 25W
Terrebonne B., *U.S.A.* . **113 L9** 29 5N 90 35W
Terrell, *U.S.A.* **113 J6** 32 44N 96 17W
Terrenceville, *Canada* . **105 C9** 47 40N 54 44W
Terry, *U.S.A.* **112 B2** 46 47N 105 19W
Terschelling, *Neths.* ... **17 A5** 53 25N   5 20 E
Tersko-Kumskiy Kanal,
  Russia .... **35 H7** 44 32N 44 38 E
Terter = Tärtär ➤,
  Azerbaijan .... **35 K8** 40 26N 47 20 E
Teruel, *Spain* **38 E3** 40 22N   1 8W
Teruel □, *Spain* **38 E4** 40 48N   1 0W
Tervel, *Bulgaria* ..... **45 C11** 43 45N 27 28 E
Tervola, *Finland* ..... **8 C21** 66 6N 24 49 E
Teryaweyna L.,
  Australia .... **95 E3** 32 18 S 143 22 E
Tešanj, *Bos.-H.* .... **28 F8** 44 38N 18 1 E
Teseney, *Eritrea* ..... **81 D4** 15 5N 36 42 E
Tesha ➤, *Russia* ..... **34 C6** 55 38N 42 9 E
Teshio, *Japan* .... **54 B10** 44 53N 141 44 E
Teshio-Gawa ➤, *Japan* **54 B10** 44 53N 141 45 E
Tešica, *Serbia & M.* ... **44 C5** 43 27N 21 45 E
Tesiyn Gol ➤,
  Mongolia .... **60 A4** 50 40N 93 20 E
Teslić, *Bos.-H.* .... **28 F8** 44 37N 17 54 E
Teslin, *Canada* **102 A2** 60 10N 132 43W
Teslin ➤, *Canada* **102 A2** 61 34N 134 35W
Teslin L., *Canada* **102 A2** 60 15N 132 57W
Tessalit, *Mali* .... **83 A5** 20 12N   1 0 E
Tessaoua, *Niger* ..... **83 C6** 13 47N   7 56 E
Tessin, *Germany* ..... **24 A8** 54 2N 12 26 E
Tessit, *Mali* .... **83 B5** 15 13N   0 18 E
Test ➤, *U.K.* **15 G6** 50 56N   1 29W
Testa del Gargano, *Italy* **41 G13** 41 50N 16 10 E
Testigos, Is. Las,
  Venezuela **121 D7** 11 23N 63 7W
Tét, *Hungary* .... **28 C2** 47 30N 17 33 E
Têt ➤, *France* .... **20 F7** 42 44N   3 2 E
Tetachuck L., *Canada* . **102 C3** 53 18N 125 55W
Tetas, Pta., *Chile* ..... **126 A1** 23 31 S 70 38W
Tete, *Mozam.* .... **87 F3** 16 13 S 33 33 E
Tete □, *Mozam.* ..... **87 F3** 15 15 S 32 40 E
Teterev ➤, *Ukraine* ... **33 G6** 51 1N 30 5 E
Teterow, *Germany* .... **24 B8** 53 46N 12 34 E
Teteven, *Bulgaria* .... **45 D8** 42 58N 24 17 E
Tethul ➤, *Canada* **102 A6** 60 35N 112 12W
Tetiyev, *Ukraine* ..... **33 H5** 49 22N 29 38 E
Teton ➤, *U.S.A.* **108 C8** 47 56N 110 31W
Tétouan, *Morocco* **78 A4** 35 35N   5 21W
Tetovo, *Macedonia* ... **44 D4** 42 1N 20 59 E
Tetyushi, *Russia* ..... **34 C9** 54 55N 48 49 E
Teuco ➤, *Argentina* ... **126 B3** 25 35 S 60 11W
Teulada, *Italy* .... **42 D1** 38 58N   8 46 E
Teulon, *Canada* **103 C9** 50 23N 97 16W
Teun, *Indonesia* ..... **63 F7** 6 59 S 129 8 E
Teutoburger Wald,
  Germany .... **24 C4** 52 5N   8 22 E
Tevere ➤, *Italy* .... **41 G9** 41 44N 12 14 E
Teverya, *Israel* .... **74 C4** 32 47N 35 32 E
Teviot ➤, *U.K.* **13 F6** 55 29N   2 38W
Tewantin, *Australia* ... **95 D5** 26 27 S 153 3 E
Tewkesbury, *U.K.* **15 F5** 51 59N   2 9W
Texada I., *Canada* **102 D4** 49 40N 124 25W
Texarkana, *Ark., U.S.A.* **113 J8** 33 26N 94 2W
Texarkana, *Tex., U.S.A.* **113 J7** 33 26N 94 3W
Texas, *Australia* ..... **95 D5** 28 49 S 151 9 E
Texas □, *U.S.A.* **113 K5** 31 40N 98 30W
Texas City, *U.S.A.* **113 L7** 29 24N 94 54W
Texel, *Neths.* .... **17 A4** 53 5N   4 50 E
Texhoma, *U.S.A.* **113 G4** 36 30N 101 47W
Texline, *U.S.A.* **113 G3** 36 23N 103 2W
Texoma, L., *U.S.A.* ... **113 J6** 33 50N 96 34W
Teykovo, *Russia* ..... **34 B5** 56 55N 40 50 E
Teza ➤, *Russia* ..... **34 B6** 56 32N 41 55 E
Tezin, *Afghan.* .... **68 B3** 34 24N 69 30 E
Teziutlán, *Mexico* ... **119 D5** 19 50N 97 22W
Tezpur, *India* .... **67 F18** 26 40N 92 45 E
Tezzeron L., *Canada* .. **102 C4** 54 43N 124 30W
Tha-anne ➤, *Canada* .. **103 A10** 60 31N 94 37W

Tha Deua, *Laos* .... **64 D4** 17 57N 102 53 E
Tha Deua, *Laos* .... **64 C3** 19 26N 101 50 E
Tha Pla, *Thailand* ..... **64 D3** 17 48N 100 32 E
Tha Rua, *Thailand* .... **64 E3** 14 34N 100 44 E
Tha Sala, *Thailand* .... **65 H2** 8 40N 99 56 E
Tha Song Yang,
  Thailand .... **64 D1** 17 34N 97 55 E
Thaba Putsoa, *Lesotho* **89 D4** 29 45 S 28 0 E
Thabana Ntlenyana,
  Lesotho .... **89 D4** 29 30 S 29 16 E
Thabazimbi, *S. Africa* . **89 C4** 24 40 S 27 21 E
Thādiq, *Si. Arabia* ... **70 E5** 25 18N 45 52 E
Thai Binh, *Vietnam* ... **58 G6** 20 35N 106 1 E
Thai Muang, *Thailand* . **65 H2** 8 24N 98 16 E
Thai Nguyen, *Vietnam* . **58 G5** 21 35N 105 55 E
Thailand ■, *Asia* .... **64 E4** 16 0N 102 0 E
Thailand, G. of, *Asia* . **65 G3** 11 30N 101 0 E
Thakhek, *Laos* .... **64 D5** 17 25N 104 45 E
Thal, *Pakistan* .... **68 C4** 33 28N 70 33 E
Thal Desert, *Pakistan* . **68 D4** 31 10N 71 30 E
Thala La = Hkakabo
  Razi, *Burma* .... **67 E20** 28 25N 97 23 E
Thalabarivat, *Cambodia* **64 F5** 13 33N 105 57 E
Thallon, *Australia* .... **95 D4** 28 39 S 148 49 E
Thalu, Ko, *Thailand* ... **65 b** 9 26N 99 54 E
Thalwil, *Switz.* .... **25 H4** 47 17N   8 35 E
Thames, *N.Z.* .... **91 G5** 37 7 S 175 34 E
Thames ➤, *Canada* ... **116 D2** 42 20N 82 25W
Thames ➤, *U.K.* ..... **15 F8** 51 29N   0 34 E
Thames ➤, *U.S.A.* ... **117 E12** 41 18N 72 5W
Thames Estuary, *U.K.* . **15 F8** 51 29N   0 52 E
Thamesford, *Canada* .. **116 C4** 43 4N 81 0W
Thamesville, *Canada* .. **116 D3** 42 33N 81 59W
Than, *India* .... **68 H4** 22 34N 71 11 E
Than Uyen, *Vietnam* .. **64 B4** 22 0N 103 54 E
Thana Gazi, *India* .... **68 F7** 27 5N 76 19 E
Thandla, *India* .... **68 H6** 23 0N 74 34 E
Thane, *India* .... **66 K8** 19 12N 72 59 E
Thanesar, *India* ..... **68 D7** 30 1N 76 52 E
Thanet, I. of, *U.K.* ... **15 F9** 51 21N   1 20 E
Thangool, *Australia* ... **94 C5** 24 38 S 150 42 E
Thanh Hoa, *Vietnam* .. **64 C5** 19 48N 105 46 E
Thanh Hung, *Vietnam* . **65 H5** 9 55N 105 43 E
Thanh Pho Ho Chi
  Minh, *Vietnam* ..... **65 G6** 10 58N 106 40 E
Thanjavur, *India* ..... **66 P11** 10 48N 79 12 E
Thann, *France* .... **19 E14** 47 48N   7 5 E
Thano Bula Khan,
  Pakistan .... **68 G2** 25 22N 67 50 E
Thaolinta L., *Canada* . **103 A9** 61 30N 96 25W
Thaon-les-Vosges,
  France .... **19 D13** 48 15N   6 24 E
Thap Lan △, *Thailand* . **64 E4** 14 15N 102 16 E
Thap Sakae, *Thailand* . **65 G2** 11 30N 99 37 E
Thap Than, *Thailand* .. **64 E2** 15 27N 99 54 E
Thar Desert, *India* .... **68 F5** 28 0N 72 0 E
Tharad, *India* .... **68 G4** 24 30N 71 44 E
Thargomindah, *Australia* **95 D3** 27 58 S 143 46 E
Tharrawaddy, *Burma* .. **67 L19** 17 38N 95 48 E
Tharthār, Buḩayrat ath,
  Iraq .... **70 C4** 34 0N 43 15 E
Tharthar, L. = Tharthār,
  Buḩayrat ath, *Iraq* ... **70 C4** 34 0N 43 15 E
Tharthār, W. ath ➤,
  Iraq .... **70 C4** 33 59N 43 12 E
Thasopoúla, *Greece* ... **45 F8** 40 49N 24 45 E
Thásos, *Greece* .... **45 F8** 40 40N 24 40 E
That Khe, *Vietnam* ... **58 F6** 22 16N 106 28 E
Thatcher, *Ariz., U.S.A.* . **109 K9** 32 51N 109 46W
Thatcher, *Colo., U.S.A.* **113 G2** 37 33N 104 7W
Thaton, *Burma* .... **67 L20** 16 55N 97 22 E
Thau, Bassin de, *France* **20 E7** 43 23N   3 36 E
Thaungdut, *Burma* ... **67 G19** 24 30N 94 40 E
Thayer, *U.S.A.* **113 G9** 36 31N 91 33W
Thayetmyo, *Burma* ... **67 K19** 19 20N 95 10 E
Thazi, *Burma* .... **67 J20** 21 0N 96 5 E
The Bight, *Bahamas* .. **121 B4** 24 19N 75 24W
The Crane, *Barbados* .. **121 g** 13 6N 59 27W
The Dalles, *U.S.A.* **108 D3** 45 36N 121 10W
The Great Divide =
  Great Dividing Ra.,
  Australia .... **94 C4** 23 0 S 146 0 E
The Hague = 's-
  Gravenhage, *Neths.* .. **17 B4** 52 7N   4 17 E
The Pas, *Canada* **103 C8** 53 45N 101 15W
The Range, *Zimbabwe* . **87 F3** 19 2 S 31 2 E
The Rock, *Australia* ... **95 F4** 35 15 S 147 2 E
The Settlement,
  Br. Virgin Is. .... **121 e** 18 43N 64 22W
The Woodlands, *U.S.A.* **113 K7** 30 9N 95 27W
Thebes = Thívai, *Greece* **46 C5** 38 19N 23 19 E
Thebes, *Egypt* .... **80 B3** 25 40N 32 35 E
Thedford, *U.S.A.* **112 E4** 41 59N 100 35W
Theebine, *Australia* ... **95 D5** 25 57 S 152 34 E
Thekulthili L., *Canada* . **103 A7** 61 3N 110 0W
Thelon ➤, *Canada* **103 A8** 64 16N 96 4W
Thénezay, *France* **18 F6** 46 44N   0 2W
Thenon, *France* .... **20 C5** 45 9N   1 4 E
Theodore, *Australia* ... **94 C5** 24 55 S 150 3 E
Theodore, *Canada* **103 C8** 51 26N 102 55W
Theodore, *U.S.A.* **115 K1** 30 33N 88 10W
Theodore Roosevelt △,
  U.S.A. **112 B3** 47 0N 103 25W
Theodore Roosevelt L.,
  U.S.A. **109 K8** 33 40N 111 10W
Thepha, *Thailand* ..... **65 J3** 6 52N 100 58 E
Thérain ➤, *France* ... **19 C9** 49 15N   2 27 E
Theresa, *U.S.A.* **117 B9** 44 13N 75 48W
Thermaïkós Kólpos,
  Greece .... **44 F6** 40 15N 22 45 E
Thermí, *Greece* .... **44 F7** 38 11N 26 29 E
Thermopolis, *U.S.A.* .. **108 E9** 43 39N 108 13W
Thermopylae P., *Greece* **46 C4** 38 48N 22 35 E
Thesprotía □, *Greece* .. **46 B2** 39 27N 20 22 E
Thessalía □, *Greece* .. **46 B3** 39 30N 22 0 E
Thessalon, *Canada* ... **104 C3** 46 20N 83 30W
Thessaloníki, *Greece* .. **44 F6** 40 38N 22 58 E
Thessaloníki □, *Greece* **44 F7** 40 45N 23 0 E
Thessaloníki ✈ (SKG),
  Greece .... **44 F7** 40 30N 23 0 E
Thessalonikis, Gulf of =
  Thermaïkós Kólpos,
  Greece .... **44 F6** 40 15N 22 45 E
Thessaly = Thessalía □,
  Greece .... **46 B4** 39 25N 22 0 E
Thetford, *U.K.* .... **15 E8** 52 25N   0 45 E
Thetford Mines, *Canada* **105 C5** 46 8N 71 18W
Theun ➤, *Laos* .... **64 C5** 18 19N 104 0 E
Theunissen, *S. Africa* . **88 D4** 28 26 S 26 43 E
Thevenard, *Australia* .. **95 E1** 32 9 S 133 38 E
Thiámis ➤, *Greece* ... **46 B2** 39 15N 20 6 E
Thibodaux, *U.S.A.* **113 L9** 29 48N 90 49W
Thicket Portage, *Canada* **103 B9** 55 19N 97 42W
Thief River Falls, *U.S.A.* **112 A6** 48 7N 96 10W
Thiel Mts., *Antarctica* . **5 E16** 85 15 S 91 0W

Thiene, *Italy* .... **41 C8** 45 42N 11 29 E
Thiérache, *France* ..... **19 C10** 49 51N 3 45 E
Thiers, *France* .... **20 C7** 45 52N 3 33 E
Thiès, *Senegal* **82 C1** 14 50N 16 51W
Thiesi, *Italy* .... **42 B1** 40 31N 8 43 E
Thiet, *Sudan* .... **81 F2** 7 37N 28 49 E
Thika, *Kenya* .... **86 C4** 1 1S 37 5 E
Thikombia, *Fiji* .... **91 B9** 15 44 S 179 55W
Thille-Boubacar, *Senegal* **82 B1** 16 31N 15 5W
Thimphu, *Bhutan* ..... **67 F16** 27 31N 89 45 E
Pingvallavatn, *Iceland* ... **8 D3** 64 11N 21 9W
Thionville, *France* ..... **19 C13** 49 20N 6 10 E
Thíra, *Greece* .... **47 E7** 36 23N 25 27 E
Thirasía, *Greece* ..... **47 E7** 36 26N 25 21 E
Third Cataract, *Sudan* .. **80 D3** 19 42N 30 20 E
Thirsk, *U.K.* **14 C6** 54 14N 1 19W
Thiruvananthapuram =
  Trivandrum, *India* ... **66 Q10** 8 41N 77 0 E
Thisted, *Denmark* ..... **11 H2** 56 58N 8 40 E
Thistle I., *Australia* ... **95 F2** 35 0 S 136 8 E
Thívai, *Greece* ...... **46 C5** 38 19N 23 19 E
Thiviers, *France* ..... **20 C4** 45 25N 0 54 E
Thizy, *France* .... **19 F11** 46 2N 4 18 E
Þjórsá →, *Iceland* **8 E3** 63 47N 20 48W
Thlewiaza →, *Canada* .. **103 A10** 60 29N 94 40W
Thmar Puok, *Cambodia* . **64 F4** 13 57N 103 4 E
Tho Vinh, *Vietnam* .... **64 C5** 19 16N 105 42 E
Thoa →, *Canada* **103 A7** 60 31N 109 47W
Thoen, *Thailand* ..... **64 D2** 17 43N 99 12 E
Thoeng, *Thailand* .... **64 C3** 19 41N 100 12 E
Thohoyandou, *S. Africa* . **85 J6** 22 58 S 30 29 E
Tholdi, *Pakistan* ..... **69 B7** 35 5N 76 6 E
Thomas, *U.S.A.* **113 H5** 35 45N 98 45W
Thomas, L., *Australia* .. **95 D2** 26 4 S 137 58 E
Thomaston, *U.S.A.* ... **115 J3** 32 53N 84 20W
Thomasville, *Ala.*,
  U.S.A. **115 K2** 31 55N 87 44W
Thomasville, *Ga., U.S.A.* **115 K4** 30 50N 83 59W
Thomasville, *N.C.*,
  U.S.A. **115 H5** 35 53N 80 5W
Thompson, *Canada* **103 B9** 55 45N 97 52W
Thompson, *U.S.A.* **117 E9** 41 52N 75 31W
Thompson →, *Canada* .. **102 C4** 50 15N 121 24W
Thompson →, *U.S.A.* .. **112 F8** 39 46N 93 37W
Thompson Falls, *U.S.A.* . **108 C6** 47 36N 115 21W
Thompson Pk., *U.S.A.* . **108 F2** 41 0N 123 0W
Thompson Springs,
  U.S.A. **109 G9** 38 58N 109 43W
Thompsontown, *U.S.A.* . **116 F7** 40 33N 77 14W
Thomson, *U.S.A.* **115 J4** 33 28N 82 30W
Thomson →, *Australia* . **94 C3** 25 11 S 142 53 E
Thônes, *France* ...... **21 C10** 45 54N 6 18 E
Thong Yang, *Thailand* .. **65 b** 9 28N 99 56 E
Thonon-les-Bains,
  France .... **19 F13** 46 22N 6 29 E
Thorez, *Ukraine* ..... **33 H10** 48 4N 38 34 E
Þórisvatn, *Iceland* **8 D4** 64 20N 18 55W
Thornaby on Tees, *U.K.* . **14 C6** 54 33N 1 18W
Thornbury, *Canada* ... **116 B4** 44 34N 80 26W
Thorne, *U.K.* **14 D7** 53 37N 0 57W
Thornhill, *Canada* **102 C3** 54 31N 128 32W
Thorold, *Canada* **116 C5** 43 7N 79 12W
Þórshöfn, *Iceland* **8 C6** 66 12N 15 20W
Thouarcé, *France* **18 E6** 47 17N 0 30W
Thouars, *France* **18 F6** 47 0N 0 15W
Thouet →, *France* **18 E6** 47 17N 0 15W
Thouin, C., *Australia* .. **92 D2** 20 20 S 118 10 E
Thousand Oaks, *U.S.A.* . **111 L8** 34 10N 118 50W
Thrace, *Turkey* ...... **45 F10** 41 0N 27 0 E
Thrakikón Pélagos,
  Greece .... **45 F8** 40 30N 25 0 E
Three Forks, *U.S.A.* ... **108 D8** 45 54N 111 33W
Three Gorges Dam,
  China .... **59 B8** 30 45N 111 15 E
Three Hills, *Canada* ... **102 C6** 51 43N 113 15W
Three Hummock I.,
  Australia .... **95 G3** 40 25 S 144 55 E
Three Pagodas Pass,
  Asia .... **64 E2** 15 20N 98 30 E
Three Points, C., *Ghana* . **82 E4** 4 42N 2 6W
Three Rivers, *Calif.*,
  U.S.A. **110 J8** 36 26N 118 54W
Three Rivers, *Tex.*,
  U.S.A. **113 L5** 28 28N 98 11W
Three Sisters, *U.S.A.* .. **108 D3** 44 4N 121 51W
Three Springs, *Australia* **93 E2** 29 32 S 115 45 E
Throssell, L., *Australia* . **93 E3** 27 33 S 124 10 E
Throssell Ra., *Australia* . **92 D3** 22 3 S 121 43 E
Thrushton △, *Australia* . **95 D4** 27 47 S 147 40 E
Thuan Hoa, *Vietnam* .. **65 H5** 8 58N 105 30 E
Thubun Lakes, *Canada* . **103 A6** 61 30N 112 0W
Thueyts, *France* ..... **21 D8** 44 41N 4 9 E
Thuin, *Belgium* ...... **17 D4** 50 20N 4 17 E
Thuir, *France* .... **20 F6** 42 38N 2 45 E
Thule = Qaanaaq,
  Greenland **4 B4** 77 40N 69 0W
Thule Air Base =
  Uummannaq,
  Greenland **4 B5** 70 58N 52 0W
Thun, *Switz.* .... **25 J3** 46 45N 7 38 E
Thunder B., *U.S.A.* ... **116 B1** 45 0N 83 20W
Thunder Bay, *Canada* . **104 C2** 48 20N 89 15W
Thunersee, *Switz.* .... **25 J3** 46 43N 7 39 E
Thung Salaeng Luang △,
  Thailand .... **64 D3** 16 43N 100 50 E
Thung Song, *Thailand* . **65 H2** 8 10N 99 40 E
Thunkar, *Bhutan* ..... **67 F17** 27 55N 91 0 E
Thuong Tra, *Vietnam* .. **64 D6** 16 2N 107 42 E
Thur →, *Switz.* ...... **25 H5** 47 32N 9 10 E
Thurgau □, *Switz.* .... **25 H5** 47 34N 9 10 E
Thüringen □, *Germany* . **24 D6** 51 0N 11 0 E
Thüringer Wald,
  Germany .... **24 E6** 50 35N 11 0 E
Thurles, *Ireland* **12 D4** 52 41N 7 49W
Thurn P., *Austria* .... **26 D5** 47 20N 12 25 E
Thurrock □, *U.K.* .... **15 F8** 51 31N 0 23 E
Thursday I., *Australia* .. **94 A3** 10 30 S 142 3 E
Thurso, *Canada* **104 C4** 45 36N 75 15W
Thurso, *U.K.* **13 C5** 58 36N 3 32W
Thurso →, *U.K.* **13 C5** 58 36N 3 32W
Thurston I., *Antarctica* . **5 D16** 72 0 S 100 0W
Thury-Harcourt, *France* . **18 D6** 48 59N 0 30W
Thutade L., *Canada* ... **102 B3** 57 0N 126 55W
Thy, *Denmark* .... **11 H2** 56 55N 8 20 E
Thyborøn, *Denmark* ... **11 H2** 56 42N 8 12 E
Thyolo, *Malawi* ...... **87 F4** 16 7 S 35 5 E
Ti-n-Amzi →, *Niger* .. **83 B5** 18 20N 4 32 E
Ti-n-Barraouene, O. →,
  Africa .... **83 B5** 18 40N 4 5 E
Ti-n-Zaouatene, *Algeria* **83 B5** 19 55N 2 55 E
Ti Tree, *Australia* .... **94 C1** 22 5 S 133 22 E
Tiadiaye, *Senegal* **82 C1** 14 25N 16 40W
Tian Shan, *Asia* ..... **60 B3** 40 30N 76 0 E
Tianchang, *China* .... **59 A12** 32 40N 119 0 E
Tiandong, *China* ..... **58 F6** 23 35N 107 7 E
Tiandong, *China* ..... **58 F6** 23 36N 107 8 E
Tian'e, *China* .... **58 E6** 25 1N 107 9 E

Tianhe, *China* .... **58 E7** 24 48N 108 40 E
Tianjin, *China* ...... **57 E9** 39 8N 117 10 E
Tiankoura,
  Burkina Faso **82 C4** 10 47N 3 17W
Tianlin, *China* ...... **58 E6** 24 21N 106 12 E
Tianmen, *China* ..... **59 B9** 30 39N 113 9 E
Tianquan, *China* ..... **58 B4** 30 7N 102 43 E
Tiantai, *China* ...... **59 C13** 29 10N 121 2 E
Tianyang, *China* ..... **58 F6** 23 42N 106 53 E
Tianyar, *Indonesia* ... **63 J18** 8 12 S 115 30 E
Tianzhen, *China* ..... **56 D8** 40 24N 114 5 E
Tianzhu, *China* ...... **58 D7** 26 54N 109 11 E
Tianzhuangtai, *China* .. **57 D12** 40 43N 122 5 E
Tiaret, *Algeria* ...... **78 A6** 35 20N 1 21 E
Tiassalé, *Ivory C.* **82 D4** 5 58N 4 57W
Tibagi, *Brazil* .... **127 A5** 24 30 S 50 24W
Tibagi →, *Brazil* .... **127 A5** 22 47 S 51 1W
Tibati, *Cameroon* .... **83 D7** 6 22N 12 30 E
Tibe, *Ethiopia* ...... **81 F4** 9 2N 37 12 E
Tiber = Tevere →, *Italy* **41 G9** 41 44N 12 14 E
Tiberias = Teverya,
  Israel .... **74 C4** 32 47N 35 32 E
Tiberias, L. = Yam
  Kinneret, *Israel* .... **74 C4** 32 45N 35 35 E
Tibesti, *Chad* .... **79 D9** 21 0N 17 30 E
Tibet = Xizang
  Zizhiqu □, *China* ... **60 C3** 32 0N 88 0 E
Tibet, Plateau of, *Asia* . **50 F12** 32 0N 86 0 E
Tibiao, *Phil.* .... **61 F5** 11 17N 122 2 E
Tibiri, *Niger* .... **83 C6** 13 34N 7 4 E
Tibleş, Vf., *Romania* .. **29 C9** 47 32N 24 15 E
Tiblleşului, Munţii,
  Romania .... **29 C9** 47 38N 24 5 E
Tibnī, *Syria* .... **70 C3** 35 36N 39 50 E
Tibooburra, *Australia* .. **95 D3** 29 26 S 142 1 E
Tibro, *Sweden* ...... **11 F8** 58 28N 14 10 E
Tiburón, I., *Mexico* ... **118 B2** 29 0N 112 30W
Ticao I., *Phil.* ...... **61 E5** 12 31N 123 42 E
Tichît, *Mauritania* ... **82 B3** 18 21N 9 29W
Ticho, *Ethiopia* ..... **81 F4** 7 50N 39 32 E
Ticino □, *Switz.* .... **25 J4** 46 20N 8 45 E
Ticino →, *Italy* ..... **25 K5** 45 9N 9 14 E
Ticleni, *Romania* .... **29 F8** 44 53N 23 24 E
Ticonderoga, *U.S.A.* .. **117 C11** 43 51N 73 26W
Ticul, *Mexico* **119 C7** 20 20N 89 31W
Tidaholm, *Sweden* ... **11 F7** 58 12N 13 58 E
Tidan, *Sweden* ...... **11 F8** 58 34N 14 0 E
Tiddim, *Burma* ...... **67 H18** 23 28N 93 45 E
Tidioute, *U.S.A.* **116 E5** 41 41N 79 24W
Tidjikja, *Mauritania* .. **82 B2** 18 29N 11 35W
Tidore, *Indonesia* ... **63 D7** 0 40N 127 25 E
Tiébissou, *Ivory C.* ... **82 D3** 7 9N 5 10W
Tiel, *Neths.* .... **17 C5** 51 53N 5 26 E
Tiel, *Senegal* **82 C1** 14 55N 15 5W
Tieling, *China* ...... **57 C12** 42 20N 123 55 E
Tielt, *Belgium* ...... **17 C3** 51 0N 3 20 E
Tien Shan = Tian Shan,
  Asia .... **60 B3** 40 30N 76 0 E
Tien-tsin = Tianjin,
  China .... **57 E9** 39 8N 117 10 E
Tien Yen, *Vietnam* ... **64 B6** 21 20N 107 24 E
T'ienching = Tianjin,
  China .... **57 E9** 39 8N 117 10 E
Tienen, *Belgium* .... **17 D4** 50 48N 4 57 E
Tiénigbé, *Ivory C.* ... **82 D3** 8 11N 5 43W
Tientsin = Tianjin, *China* **57 E9** 39 8N 117 10 E
Tieri, *Australia* ..... **94 C4** 23 2 S 148 21 E
Tierp, *Sweden* ...... **10 D11** 60 20N 17 30 E
Tierra Amarilla, *Chile* . **126 B1** 27 28 S 70 18W
Tierra Amarilla, *U.S.A.* **109 H10** 36 42N 106 33W
Tierra Colorada, *Mexico* **119 D5** 17 10N 99 35W
Tierra de Barros, *Spain* . **37 G4** 38 40N 6 30W
Tierra de Campos, *Spain* **36 C6** 42 10N 4 50W
Tierra del Fuego, I. Gr.
  de, *Argentina* ...... **128 G3** 54 0 S 69 0W
Tiétar →, *Spain* **36 F4** 39 50N 6 1W
Tieté →, *Brazil* ..... **127 A5** 20 40 S 51 35W
Tiffin, *U.S.A.* **114 E4** 41 7N 83 11W
Tifton, *U.S.A.* **115 K4** 31 27N 83 31W
Tifu, *Indonesia* ..... **63 E7** 3 39 S 126 24 E
Tighina, *Moldova* .... **29 D14** 46 50N 29 30 E
Tigil, *Russia* .... **53 D16** 57 49N 158 40 E
Tignish, *Canada* **105 C7** 46 58N 64 2W
Tigray □, *Ethiopia* ... **81 E4** 13 35N 39 15 E
Tigre →, *Peru* ...... **124 D4** 4 30 S 74 10W
Tigre →, *Venezuela* .. **124 B6** 9 20N 62 30W
Tigris = Dijlah, Nahr →,
  Asia .... **70 D5** 31 0N 47 25 E
Tigveni, *Romania* .... **29 E9** 45 10N 24 31 E
Tigyaing, *Burma* ..... **67 H20** 23 45N 96 10 E
Tîh, Gebel el, *Egypt* .. **80 B3** 29 32N 33 26 E
Tijara, *India* .... **68 F7** 27 56N 76 31 E
Tijuana, *Mexico* **111 N9** 32 30N 117 10W
Tikal, *Guatemala* **120 C2** 17 13N 89 24W
Tikal △, *Guatemala* .. **120 C2** 17 23N 89 34W
Tikamgarh, *India* .... **69 G8** 24 44N 78 50 E
Tikaré, *Burkina Faso* .. **83 C4** 13 15N 1 43W
Tikhoretsk, *Russia* ... **35 H5** 45 56N 40 5 E
Tikhvin, *Russia* ..... **32 C7** 59 35N 33 30 E
Tikiraqjuaq = Whale
  Cove, *Canada* **103 A10** 62 10N 92 34W
Tiko, *Cameroon* ..... **83 E6** 4 4N 9 20 E
Tikrīt, *Iraq* .... **70 C4** 34 35N 43 37 E
Tiksi, *Russia* .... **53 B13** 71 40N 128 45 E
Tilamuta, *Indonesia* .. **63 D6** 0 32N 122 23 E
Tilburg, *Neths.* ..... **17 C5** 51 31N 5 6 E
Tilbury, *Canada* **116 D2** 42 17N 82 23W
Tilbury, *U.K.* .... **15 F8** 51 27N 0 22 E
Tilcara, *Argentina* ... **126 A2** 23 36 S 65 23W
Tilden, *U.S.A.* **113 L5** 28 27N 98 33W
Tilemses, *Niger* ..... **83 B5** 15 37N 4 44 E
Tilemsi, Vallée du, *Mali* **83 B5** 17 42N 0 15 E
Tilhar, *India* .... **69 F8** 28 0N 79 45 E
Tilichiki, *Russia* .... **53 C17** 60 27N 166 5 E
Tilissos, *Greece* ..... **49 D7** 35 20N 25 1 E
Till →, *U.K.* **14 B5** 55 41N 2 13W
Tillabéri, *Niger* ..... **83 C5** 14 28N 1 28 E
Tillamook, *U.S.A.* ... **108 D2** 45 27N 123 51W
Tillberga, *Sweden* ... **10 E10** 59 40N 16 39 E
Tillia, *Niger* .... **83 B5** 16 8N 4 47 E
Tillsonburg, *Canada* .. **116 D4** 42 53N 80 44W
Tillyeria, *Cyprus* .... **49 D11** 35 6N 32 40 E
Tilogne, *Senegal* **82 B2** 16 0N 13 40W
Tílos, *Greece* .... **47 E9** 36 27N 27 27 E
Tilpa, *Australia* ..... **95 E3** 30 57 S 144 24 E
Tilt →, *U.K.* **13 E5** 56 46N 3 51W
Tilton, *U.S.A.* **117 C13** 43 27N 71 36W
Tiltonsville, *U.S.A.* .. **116 F4** 40 10N 80 41W
Tim, *Denmark* .... **11 H2** 56 12N 8 19 E
Timagami, *Canada* ... **104 C3** 47 0N 80 10W
Timanfaya △, *Canary Is.* **48 F6** 29 0N 13 46W
Timaru, *N.Z.* .... **91 L3** 44 23 S 171 14 E
Timashevo, *Russia* ... **34 D10** 53 22N 51 9 E
Timashevsk, *Russia* .. **35 H4** 45 35N 39 0 E
Timau, *Kenya* .... **86 B4** 0 4N 37 15 E
Timbákion, *Greece* ... **49 D6** 35 4N 24 45 E

Timbedgha, *Mauritania* **82 B3** 16 17N 8 16W
Timber Creek, *Australia* **92 C5** 15 40 S 130 29 E
Timber Lake, *U.S.A.* .. **112 C4** 45 26N 101 5W
Timber Mt., *U.S.A.* .. **110 H10** 37 6N 116 28W
Timbo, *Guinea* **82 C2** 10 35N 11 50W
Timbo, *Liberia* **82 D3** 5 35N 9 45W
Timbuktu =
  Tombouctou, *Mali* .. **82 B4** 16 50N 3 0W
Timeiaouîne, *Algeria* . **83 A5** 20 27N 1 50 E
Timétrine, Mts., *Mali* . **83 B4** 19 25N 1 0W
Timfi Óros, *Greece* ... **46 B2** 39 59N 20 45 E
Timfristós, Óros, *Greece* **46 C3** 38 57N 21 50 E
Timi, *Cyprus* .... **49 E11** 34 44N 32 31 E
Timimoun, *Algeria* ... **78 C6** 29 14N 0 16 E
Timirist, Râs, *Mauritania* **82 B1** 19 21N 16 30W
Timiskaming, L. =
  Témiscamingue, L.,
  Canada **104 C4** 47 10N 79 25W
Timişoara, *Romania* .. **28 E6** 45 43N 21 15 E
Timmersdala, *Sweden* . **11 F7** 58 32N 13 46 E
Timmins, *Canada* **104 C3** 48 28N 81 25W
Timok →, *Serbia & M.* . **28 B6** 44 10N 22 40 E
Timor, *Asia* .... **63 F7** 9 0 S 125 0 E
Timor Leste = East
  Timor ■, *Asia* ..... **63 F7** 8 50 S 126 0 E
Timor Sea, *Ind. Oc.* .. **92 B4** 12 0 S 127 0 E
Timrå, *Sweden* ...... **10 B11** 62 29N 17 18 E
Tin Can Bay, *Australia* . **95 D5** 25 56 S 153 0 E
Tin Ethisane, *Mali* ... **83 B4** 19 3N 0 52W
Tin Gornai, *Mali* **83 B4** 16 38N 0 38W
Tin Mt., *U.S.A.* **110 J9** 36 50N 117 10W
Tina →, *S. Africa* .... **89 E4** 31 18 S 29 13 E
Tîna, Khalîg el, *Egypt* . **80 H8** 31 20N 32 42 E
Tinaca Pt., *Phil.* .... **61 J6** 5 30N 125 25 E
Tinajo, *Canary Is.* ... **48 E6** 29 4N 13 42W
Tinca, *Romania* ..... **28 D6** 46 46N 21 58 E
Tindal, *Australia* .... **92 B5** 14 31 S 132 22 E
Tindouf, *Algeria* **78 C4** 27 42N 8 10W
Tinée →, *France* ..... **21 E11** 43 55N 7 11 E
Tineo, *Spain* **36 B4** 43 21N 6 19W
Tinfunque △, *Paraguay* **126 A3** 23 55 S 60 17W
Ting Jiang →, *China* .. **59 E11** 24 56N 116 35 E
Tinggi, Pulau, *Malaysia* **65 L5** 2 18N 104 7 E
Tinglev, *Denmark* .... **11 K3** 54 57N 9 13 E
Tingo Maria, *Peru* ... **124 E3** 9 10 S 75 54W
Tingrela, *Ivory C.* **82 C3** 10 27N 6 25W
Tingsryd, *Sweden* .... **11 H9** 56 31N 15 0 E
Tingstäde, *Sweden* ... **11 G12** 57 44N 18 37 E
Tinh Bien, *Vietnam* ... **65 G5** 10 36N 104 57 E
Tinnevelly = Tirunelveli,
  India .... **66 Q10** 8 45N 77 45 E
Tinogasta, *Argentina* .. **126 B2** 28 5 S 67 32W
Tínos, *Greece* ...... **47 D7** 37 33N 25 8 E
Tiñoso, C., *Spain* **39 H3** 37 32N 1 6W
Tinpahar, *India* ..... **69 G12** 24 59N 87 44 E
Tintina, *Argentina* ... **126 B3** 27 2 S 62 45W
Tintinara, *Australia* .. **95 F3** 35 48 S 140 2 E
Tintioulé, *Guinea* **82 C3** 10 13N 9 12W
Tinto →, *Spain* **37 H4** 37 12N 6 55W
Tioga, *N. Dak., U.S.A.* . **112 A3** 48 23N 102 56W
Tioga, *Pa., U.S.A.* ... **116 E7** 41 55N 77 8W
Tioman, Pulau, *Malaysia* **65 L5** 2 50N 104 10 E
Tione di Trento, *Italy* . **40 B7** 46 2N 10 43 E
Tionesta, *U.S.A.* **116 E5** 41 30N 79 28W
Tior, *Sudan* .... **81 F3** 6 26N 31 11 E
Tipongpani, *India* .... **67 F19** 27 20N 95 55 E
Tipperary, *Ireland* ... **12 D3** 52 28N 8 10W
Tipperary □, *Ireland* .. **12 D4** 52 37N 7 55W
Tipton, *Calif., U.S.A.* . **110 J7** 36 4N 119 19W
Tipton, *Iowa, U.S.A.* .. **112 E9** 41 46N 91 8W
Tipton Mt., *U.S.A.* ... **111 K12** 35 32N 114 12W
Tiptonville, *U.S.A.* ... **113 G10** 36 23N 89 29W
Tīrān, *Iran* .... **71 C6** 32 45N 51 8 E
Tīrān, *Si. Arabia* .... **80 B3** 27 57N 34 32 E
Tiranë, *Albania* ..... **44 E3** 41 18N 19 49 E
Tiranë ✈ (TIA), *Albania* **43 A12** 41 57N 19 42 E
Tirano, *Italy* .... **40 B7** 46 13N 10 10 E
Tiraspol, *Moldova* ... **29 D14** 46 55N 29 35 E
Tirdout, *Mali* **83 B4** 16 7N 1 5W
Tire, *Turkey* .... **47 C9** 38 5N 27 45 E
Tirebolu, *Turkey* .... **73 B8** 40 58N 38 45 E
Tiree, *U.K.* **13 E2** 56 31N 6 55W
Tiree, Passage of, *U.K.* **13 E2** 56 30N 6 30W
Tîrgovişte = Târgovişte,
  Romania .... **29 F10** 44 55N 25 27 E
Tîrgu-Jiu = Târgu-Jiu,
  Romania .... **29 E8** 45 5N 23 19 E
Tîrgu Mureş = Târgu
  Mureş, *Romania* ... **29 D9** 46 31N 24 38 E
Tirich Mir, *Pakistan* .. **66 A7** 36 15N 71 55 E
Tiriolo, *Italy* .... **43 D9** 38 57N 16 30 E
Tiriro, *Guinea* **82 C3** 10 27N 8 40W
Tiritiri o te Moana =
  Southern Alps, *N.Z.* . **91 K3** 43 41 S 170 11 E
Tírnavos, *Greece* .... **46 B4** 39 45N 22 18 E
Tirodi, *India* .... **66 J11** 21 40N 79 44 E
Tirol □, *Austria* ..... **26 D3** 47 3N 10 43 E
Tirschenreuth, *Germany* **25 F8** 49 53N 12 19 E
Tirso →, *Italy* ...... **42 C1** 39 53N 8 32 E
Tirstrup, *Denmark* ... **11 H4** 56 18N 10 42 E
Tiruchchirappalli, *India* **66 P11** 10 45N 78 45 E
Tirunelveli, *India* .... **66 Q10** 8 45N 77 45 E
Tirupati, *India* ...... **66 N11** 13 39N 79 25 E
Tiruppur, *India* ..... **66 P10** 11 5N 77 22 E
Tiruvannamalai, *India* . **66 N11** 12 15N 79 5 E
Tisa, *India* .... **68 C7** 32 50N 76 9 E
Tisa →, *Serbia & M.* .. **28 E5** 45 15N 20 17 E
Tisdale, *Canada* **103 C8** 52 50N 104 0W
Tishomingo, *U.S.A.* .. **113 H6** 34 14N 96 41W
Tisjön, *Sweden* ...... **10 D7** 60 56N 13 0 E
Tisnaren, *Sweden* .... **11 F9** 58 58N 15 56 E
Tišnov, *Czech Rep.* ... **27 B9** 49 21N 16 25 E
Tisovec, *Slovak Rep.* . **27 C12** 48 41N 19 56 E
Tisza = Tisa →,
  Serbia & M. .... **28 E5** 45 15N 20 17 E
Tiszaföldvár, *Hungary* . **28 D5** 46 58N 20 14 E
Tiszafüred, *Hungary* .. **28 C5** 47 38N 20 50 E
Tiszalök, *Hungary* ... **28 B6** 48 1N 21 20 E
Tiszavasvári, *Hungary* . **28 C6** 47 58N 21 18 E
Tit-Ary, *Russia* ..... **53 B13** 71 55N 127 2 E
Titagarh, *Spain* **38 F3** 39 53N 1 9W
Titao, *Burkina Faso* .. **83 C4** 13 45N 2 5W
Titel, *Serbia & M.* ... **28 E5** 45 10N 20 18 E
Tithwal, *Pakistan* .... **69 B5** 34 21N 73 50 E
Titicaca, L., *S. Amer.* . **124 G5** 15 30 S 69 30W
Titisee, *Germany* .... **25 H4** 47 54N 8 10 E
Titiwa, *Nigeria* ..... **83 C7** 12 14N 12 53 E
Tito, *Italy* .... **43 B8** 40 35N 15 40 E
Titova Korenica, *Croatia* **41 D12** 44 45N 15 41 E
Titu, *Romania* ...... **29 F10** 44 39N 25 32 E
Titule, *Dem. Rep. of*
  the Congo .... **86 B2** 3 15N 25 31 E
Titusville, *Fla., U.S.A.* **115 L5** 28 37N 80 49W

Titusville, *Pa., U.S.A.* **116 E5** 41 38N 79 41W
Tivaouane, *Senegal* ... **82 C1** 14 56N 16 45W
Tivat, *Serbia & M.* ... **44 D2** 42 28N 18 43 E
Tivedens △, *Sweden* .. **11 F8** 58 45N 14 35 E
Tiverton, *U.K.* **15 G4** 50 54N 3 29W
Tívoli, *Italy* .... **41 G9** 41 58N 12 45 E
Tiyo, *Eritrea* .... **81 E5** 14 41N 40 15 E
Tizi-Ouzou, *Algeria* .. **78 A6** 36 42N 4 3 E
Tizimín, *Mexico* **119 C7** 21 0N 88 1W
Tiznit, *Morocco* **78 C4** 29 48N 9 45W
Tjæreborg, *Denmark* .. **11 J2** 55 28N 8 36 E
Tjällmo, *Sweden* ..... **11 F9** 58 43N 15 27 E
Tjeggelvas, *Sweden* .. **8 C17** 66 37N 17 45 E
Tjeggelvas = Tjeggelvas,
  Sweden .... **8 C17** 66 37N 17 45 E
Tjirebon = Cirebon,
  Indonesia .... **63 G13** 6 45 S 108 32 E
Tjluring, *Indonesia* ... **63 J17** 8 25 S 114 13 E
Tjörn, *Sweden* ...... **11 F5** 58 0N 11 35 E
Tkibuli = Tqibuli,
  Georgia .... **35 J6** 42 26N 43 0 E
Tkvarcheli = Tqvarcheli,
  Georgia .... **35 J5** 42 47N 41 42 E
Tlacotalpan, *Mexico* .. **119 D5** 18 37N 95 40W
Tlahualilo, *Mexico* ... **118 B4** 26 20N 103 30W
Tlaquepaque, *Mexico* . **118 C4** 20 39N 103 19W
Tlaxcala, *Mexico* **119 D5** 19 20N 98 14W
Tlaxcala □, *Mexico* ... **119 D5** 19 30N 98 20W
Tlaxiaco, *Mexico* **119 D5** 17 18N 97 40W
Tlemcen, *Algeria* **78 B5** 34 52N 1 21W
Tlumach, *Ukraine* ... **29 B10** 48 51N 25 0 E
Tłuszcz, *Poland* ..... **31 F8** 52 25N 21 25 E
Tlyarata, *Russia* .... **35 J8** 42 9N 46 26 E
To Bong, *Vietnam* ... **64 F7** 12 45N 109 16 E
Toa Payoh, *Singapore* . **65 d** 1 20N 103 51 E
Toad →, *Canada* **102 B4** 59 25N 124 57W
Toad River, *Canada* .. **102 B3** 58 51N 125 14W
Toamasina, *Madag.* ... **89 B8** 18 10 S 49 25 E
Toamasina □, *Madag.* . **89 B8** 18 0 S 49 0 E
Toay, *Argentina* ..... **126 D3** 36 43 S 64 38W
Toba, *China* .... **58 B1** 31 19N 97 42 E
Toba, *Japan* .... **55 G8** 34 30N 136 51 E
Toba, Danau, *Indonesia* **62 D1** 2 30N 97 30 E
Toba Kakar, *Pakistan* . **68 D3** 31 30N 69 0 E
Toba Tek Singh,
  Pakistan .... **68 D5** 30 55N 72 25 E
Tobago, *Trin. & Tob.* . **121 D7** 11 10N 60 30W
Tobarra, *Spain* **39 G3** 38 37N 1 44W
Tobelo, *Indonesia* ... **63 D7** 1 45N 127 56 E
Tobermory, *Canada* .. **116 A3** 45 12N 81 40W
Tobermory, *U.K.* **13 E2** 56 38N 6 5W
Tobi, *Pac. Oc.* ...... **63 D8** 2 40N 131 10 E
Tobin, *U.S.A.* **110 F5** 39 55N 121 19W
Tobin, L., *Australia* ... **92 D4** 21 45 S 125 49 E
Tobin L., *Canada* **103 C8** 53 35N 103 30W
Toblach = Dobbiaco,
  Italy .... **41 B9** 46 44N 12 14 E
Tobol, *Indonesia* ..... **62 E3** 3 0 S 106 25 E
Tobol →, *Russia* ..... **52 D7** 58 10N 68 12 E
Toboli, *Indonesia* .... **63 E6** 0 38 S 120 5 E
Tobolsk, *Russia* ..... **52 D7** 58 15N 68 10 E
Tobor, *Senegal* **82 C1** 12 40N 16 15W
Tobruk = Tubruq, *Libya* **79 B10** 32 7N 23 55 E
Tobyhanna, *U.S.A.* .. **117 E9** 41 11N 75 25W
Tobyl = Tobol →,
  Russia .... **52 D7** 58 10N 68 12 E
Tocantinópolis, *Brazil* . **125 E9** 6 20 S 47 25W
Tocantins □, *Brazil* .. **125 F9** 10 0 S 48 0W
Tocantins →, *Brazil* .. **125 D9** 1 45 S 49 10W
Toccoa, *U.S.A.* **115 H4** 34 35N 83 19W
Toce →, *Italy* .... **40 C5** 45 56N 8 29 E
Tochi →, *Pakistan* ... **68 C4** 32 49N 70 41 E
Tochigi, *Japan* ...... **55 F9** 36 25N 139 45 E
Tochigi □, *Japan* .... **55 F9** 36 45N 139 45 E
Tocina, *Spain* **37 H5** 37 37N 5 44W
Töcksfors, *Sweden* ... **10 E5** 59 31N 11 52 E
Toco, *Trin. & Tob.* ... **125 K16** 10 49N 60 57W
Toconao, *Chile* ..... **126 A2** 23 11 S 68 1W
Tocopilla, *Chile* ..... **126 A1** 22 5 S 70 10W
Tocumwal, *Australia* .. **95 F4** 35 51 S 145 31 E
Tocuyo →, *Venezuela* . **124 A5** 11 3N 68 23W
Todd →, *Australia* .... **94 C2** 24 52 S 135 48 E
Todeli, *Indonesia* .... **63 E6** 1 40 S 124 29 E
Todenyang, *Kenya* ... **86 B4** 4 35N 35 56 E
Todgarh, *India* ...... **68 G5** 25 42N 73 58 E
Todi, *Italy* .... **41 F9** 42 47N 12 24 E
Todos os Santos, B. de,
  Brazil .... **125 F11** 12 48 S 38 38W
Todos Santos, *Mexico* . **118 C2** 23 27N 110 13W
Todtnau, *Germany* ... **25 H4** 47 49N 7 56 E
Toe Hd., *U.K.* **13 D1** 57 50N 7 8W
Toécé, *Burkina Faso* .. **83 C4** 11 50N 1 16W
Tofield, *Canada* **102 C6** 53 25N 112 40W
Tofino, *Canada* **102 D3** 49 11N 125 55W
Töfsingdalens △,
  Sweden .... **10 B6** 62 10N 12 28 E
Tofua, *Tonga* .... **91 D11** 19 45 S 175 5W
Tōgane, *Japan* ...... **55 G10** 35 33N 140 22 E
Togba, *Mauritania* ... **82 B2** 17 26N 10 12W
Togian, Kepulauan,
  Indonesia .... **63 E6** 0 20 S 121 50 E
Togliatti, *Russia* .... **34 D9** 53 32N 49 24 E
Togo ■, *W. Afr.* ..... **83 D5** 8 30N 1 35 E
Togtoh, *China* ...... **56 D6** 40 15N 111 10 E
Tohma →, *Turkey* .... **72 C7** 38 29N 38 23 E
Tōhoku □, *Japan* .... **54 E10** 39 50N 141 45 E
Tōhöm, *Mongolia* .... **56 B5** 44 27N 108 2 E
Toinya, *Sudan* ...... **81 F2** 6 17N 29 46 E
Toiyabe Range, *U.S.A.* **108 G5** 39 30N 117 0W
Tojikiston =
  Tajikistan ■, *Asia* .. **52 F8** 38 30N 70 0 E
Tojo, *Indonesia* ..... **63 E6** 1 20 S 121 15 E
Tōjō, *Japan* .... **55 G6** 34 53N 133 16 E
Tok, *U.S.A.* **100 B5** 63 20N 142 59W
Tok-do, *Asia* .... **55 F5** 37 15N 131 52 E
Tokachi-Dake, *Japan* . **54 C11** 43 17N 142 5 E
Tokachi-Gawa →,
  Japan .... **54 C11** 42 44N 143 42 E
Tokaj, *Hungary* ..... **28 B6** 48 8N 21 27 E
Tokala, *Indonesia* .... **63 E6** 1 30 S 121 40 E
Tōkamachi, *Japan* ... **55 F9** 37 8N 138 43 E
Tokanui, *N.Z.* ...... **91 M2** 46 34 S 168 56 E
Tokar, *Sudan* .... **80 D4** 18 27N 37 56 E
Tokara-Rettō, *Japan* . **55 K4** 29 37N 129 43 E
Tokarahi, *N.Z.* ..... **91 L3** 44 56 S 170 39 E
Tokashiki-Shima, *Japan* **55 L3** 26 11N 127 21 E
Tokat, *Turkey* ...... **72 B7** 40 22N 36 35 E
Tōkch'ŏn, *N. Korea* .. **57 E14** 39 45N 126 18 E
Tokeland, *U.S.A.* **110 D3** 46 42N 123 59W
Tokelau Is., *Pac. Oc.* . **96 H10** 9 0 S 171 45W
Tokmak, *Kyrgyzstan* .. **52 E8** 42 49N 75 15 E
Tokmak, *Ukraine* .... **33 J8** 47 16N 35 42 E
Toko Ra., *Australia* ... **94 C2** 23 5 S 138 20 E
Tokoro →, *Japan* ..... **54 B12** 44 7N 144 5 E
Tokuno-Shima, *Japan* . **55 L4** 27 56N 128 55 E
Tokushima, *Japan* ... **55 H7** 34 4N 134 34 E
Tokushima □, *Japan* .. **55 H7** 33 55N 134 0 E
Tokuyama, *Japan* ... **55 G5** 34 3N 131 50 E

Tōkyō, *Japan* .... **55 G9** 35 45N 139 45 E
Tolaga Bay, *N.Z.* .... **91 H7** 38 21 S 178 20 E
Tolbukhin = Dobrich,
  Bulgaria .... **45 C11** 43 37N 27 49 E
Toledo, *Brazil* ...... **127 A5** 24 44 S 53 45W
Toledo, *Spain* **36 F6** 39 50N 4 2W
Toledo, *Ohio, U.S.A.* . **114 E4** 41 39N 83 33W
Toledo, *Oreg., U.S.A.* . **108 D2** 44 37N 123 56W
Toledo, *Wash., U.S.A.* **108 C2** 46 26N 122 51W
Toledo, Montes de,
  Spain **37 F6** 39 33N 4 20W
Toledo Bend Reservoir,
  U.S.A. **113 K8** 31 11N 93 34W
Tolentino, *Italy* ..... **41 E10** 43 12N 13 17 E
Tolfa, *Italy* .... **41 F8** 42 9N 11 56 E
Tolga, *Australia* ..... **94 B4** 17 15 S 145 29 E
Toliara, *Madag.* ..... **89 C7** 23 21 S 43 40 E
Toliara □, *Madag.* ... **89 C8** 21 0 S 45 0 E
Tolima, *Colombia* **124 C3** 4 40N 75 19W
Tolitoli, *Indonesia* ... **63 D6** 1 5N 120 50 E
Tolkmicko, *Poland* ... **30 D6** 54 19N 19 31 E
Tollarp, *Sweden* ..... **11 J7** 55 55N 13 58 E
Tollensee, *Germany* .. **24 B9** 53 30N 13 13 E
Tollhouse, *U.S.A.* ... **110 H7** 37 1N 119 24W
Tolmezzo, *Italy* ..... **41 B10** 46 24N 13 1 E
Tolmin, *Slovenia* .... **41 B10** 46 11N 13 45 E
Tolna, *Hungary* ..... **28 D3** 46 25N 18 48 E
Tolna □, *Hungary* .... **28 D3** 46 30N 18 30 E
Tolo, Teluk, *Indonesia* . **63 E6** 2 20 S 122 10 E
Tolochin = Talachyn,
  Belarus .... **32 E5** 54 25N 29 42 E
Tolosa, *Spain* **38 B2** 43 8N 2 5W
Tolox, *Spain* **37 J6** 36 41N 4 54W
Toluca, *Mexico* **119 D5** 19 20N 99 40W
Tom Burke, *S. Africa* . **89 C4** 23 5 S 28 0 E
Tom Price, *Australia* .. **92 D2** 22 40 S 117 48 E
Toma, *Burkina Faso* .. **82 C4** 12 45N 2 53W
Tomah, *U.S.A.* **112 D9** 43 59N 90 30W
Tomahawk, *U.S.A.* .. **112 C10** 45 28N 89 44W
Tomakomai, *Japan* ... **54 C10** 42 38N 141 36 E
Tomales, *U.S.A.* **110 G4** 38 15N 122 53W
Tomales B., *U.S.A.* .. **110 G3** 38 15N 123 58W
Tomar, *Portugal* **37 F2** 39 36N 8 25W
Tómaros, Óros, *Greece* **46 B2** 39 29N 20 48 E
Tomarza, *Turkey* .... **72 C6** 38 27N 35 48 E
Tomashevka, *Belarus* . **31 G10** 51 33N 23 36 E
Tomashpil, *Ukraine* .. **29 B13** 48 35N 28 31 E
Tomaszów Lubelski,
  Poland .... **31 H10** 50 27N 23 25 E
Tomaszów Mazowiecki,
  Poland .... **31 G7** 51 30N 20 2 E
Tomatlán, *Mexico* **118 D3** 19 56N 105 15W
Tombadonkéa, *Guinea* **82 C2** 11 0N 14 25W
Tombador, Serra do,
  Brazil .... **124 F7** 12 0 S 58 0W
Tombe, *Sudan* ...... **81 F3** 5 53N 31 40 E
Tombigbee →, *U.S.A.* . **115 K2** 31 8N 87 57W
Tombouctou, *Mali* ... **82 B4** 16 50N 3 0W
Tombstone, *U.S.A.* .. **109 L8** 31 43N 110 4W
Tombua, *Angola* ..... **88 B1** 15 55 S 11 55 E
Tomé, *Chile* .... **126 D1** 36 36 S 72 57W
Tomelilla, *Sweden* ... **11 J7** 55 33N 13 58 E
Tomelloso, *Spain* **37 F7** 39 10N 3 2W
Tomini, *Indonesia* ... **63 D6** 0 30N 120 30 E
Tomini, Teluk,
  Indonesia .... **63 E6** 0 10 S 121 0 E
Tominian, *Mali* **82 C4** 13 17N 4 35W
Tomiño, *Spain* **36 D2** 41 59N 8 46W
Tomintoul, *U.K.* **13 D5** 57 15N 3 23W
Tomislavgrad, *Bos.-H.* **28 G2** 43 42N 17 13 E
Tomkinson Ranges,
  Australia .... **93 E4** 26 11 S 129 5 E
Tommot, *Russia* ..... **53 D13** 59 4N 126 20 E
Tomnop Ta Suos,
  Cambodia .... **65 G5** 11 20N 104 15 E
Tomo →, *Colombia* ... **124 B5** 5 20N 67 48W
Toms Place, *U.S.A.* .. **110 H8** 37 34N 118 41W
Toms River, *U.S.A.* .. **117 G10** 39 58N 74 12W
Tomsk, *Russia* ...... **52 D9** 56 30N 85 5 E
Tomtabacken, *Sweden* **11 G8** 57 30N 14 30 E
Tona, *Spain* .... **38 D7** 41 51N 2 14 E
Tonalá, *Mexico* **119 D6** 16 8N 93 41W
Tonale, Passo del, *Italy* **40 B7** 46 16N 10 35 E
Tonantins, *Brazil* .... **124 D5** 2 45 S 67 45W
Tonasket, *U.S.A.* **108 B4** 48 42N 119 26W
Tonawanda, *U.S.A.* .. **116 D6** 43 1N 78 53W
Tonb, *Iran* .... **71 E7** 26 15N 55 5 E
Tonbridge, *U.K.* ..... **15 F8** 51 11N 0 17 E
Tondano, *Indonesia* .. **63 D6** 1 35N 124 54 E
Tondela, *Portugal* ... **36 E2** 40 31N 8 5W
Tønder, *Denmark* .... **11 K2** 54 58N 8 50 E
Tondi Kiwindi, *Niger* . **83 C5** 14 28N 2 2 E
Tondibi, *Mali* **83 B4** 16 39N 0 14W
Tonekābon, *Iran* ..... **71 B6** 36 45N 51 12 E
Tong Xian, *China* .... **56 E9** 39 55N 116 35 E
Tonga ■, *Pac. Oc.* ... **91 D11** 19 50 S 174 30W
Tonga Trench, *Pac. Oc.* **96 J10** 18 0 S 173 0W
Tongaat, *S. Africa* ... **89 D5** 29 33 S 31 9 E
Tong'an, *China* ..... **59 E12** 24 37N 118 8 E
Tongareva, *Cook Is.* .. **97 H12** 9 0 S 158 0W
Tongariro △, *N.Z.* ... **91 H5** 39 5 S 175 33 E
Tongatapu Group,
  Tonga .... **91 E12** 21 0 S 175 0W
Tongbai, *China* ..... **59 A9** 32 20N 113 23 E
Tongcheng, *Anhui*,
  China .... **59 B11** 31 4N 116 56 E
Tongcheng, *Hubei*,
  China .... **59 C9** 29 15N 113 50 E
Tongchŏn-ni, *N. Korea* **57 E14** 39 50N 127 25 E
Tongdao, *China* ..... **58 D7** 26 10N 109 42 E
Tongeren, *Belgium* ... **17 D5** 50 47N 5 28 E
Tonghai, *China* ..... **58 E4** 24 40N 102 55 E
Tonghua, *China* ..... **57 D13** 41 42N 125 58 E
Tongjosŏn Man,
  N. Korea .... **57 E15** 39 30N 128 0 E
Tongking, G. of = Tonkin, G. of, *Asia* .. **60 E5** 20 0N 108 0 E
Tongliang, *China* .... **58 C6** 29 50N 106 3 E
Tongliao, *China* ..... **57 C12** 43 38N 122 18 E
Tongling, *China* ..... **59 B11** 30 55N 117 48 E
Tonglu, *China* ...... **59 C12** 29 45N 119 37 E
Tongnan = Anyue,
  China .... **58 B5** 30 9N 105 50 E
Tongobory, *Madag.* .. **89 C7** 23 32 S 44 20 E
Tongoy, *Chile* ...... **126 C1** 30 16 S 71 31W

Tongren, China ...... 58 D7 27 43N 109 11 E
Tongres = Tongeren,
  Belgium .... 17 D5 50 47N 5 28 E
Tongsa Dzong, Bhutan 67 F17 27 31N 90 31 E
Tongue, U.K. 13 C4 58 29N 4 25W
Tongue →, U.S.A. .. 112 B2 46 25N 105 52W
Tongwei, China ..... 56 G3 35 0N 105 5 E
Tongxiang, China ... 59 B13 30 39N 120 34 E
Tongxin, China ..... 56 F3 36 59N 105 58 E
Tongyang, N. Korea . 57 E14 39 9N 126 53 E
Tongyu, China ...... 57 B12 44 45N 123 4 E
Tongzi, China ...... 58 C6 28 9N 106 49 E
Tonj, Sudan .... 81 F2 7 20N 28 44 E
Tonj →, Sudan ...... 81 F2 7 31N 28 55 E
Tonk, India .... 68 F6 26 6N 75 54 E
Tonkawa, U.S.A. 113 G6 36 41N 97 18W
Tonkin = Bac Phan,
  Vietnam .... 64 B5 22 0N 105 0 E
Tonkin, G. of, Asia .. 60 E5 20 0N 108 0 E
Tonle Sap, Cambodia . 64 F4 13 0N 104 0 E
Tonnay-Charente,
  France 20 C3 45 56N 0 55W
Tonneins, France ... 20 D4 44 23N 0 19 E
Tonnerre, France ... 19 E10 47 51N 3 59 E
Tönning, Germany .. 24 A4 54 19N 8 56 E
Tono, Japan .... 54 E10 39 19N 141 32 E
Tonopah, U.S.A. ... 109 G5 38 4N 117 14W
Tonosí, Panama ... 120 E3 7 20N 80 20W
Tons →, Haryana, India 68 D7 30 30N 77 39 E
Tons →, Ut. P., India 69 F10 26 1N 83 33 E
Tønsberg, Norway .. 9 G14 59 19N 10 25 E
Tonto ◠, U.S.A. ... 109 K8 33 39N 111 7W
Tonya, Turkey ..... 73 B8 40 53N 40 6 E
Toobanna, Australia . 94 B4 18 42 S 146 9 E
Toodyay, Australia .. 93 F2 31 34 S 116 28 E
Tooele, U.S.A. 108 F7 40 32N 112 18W
Toompine, Australia . 95 D3 27 15 S 144 19 E
Toora, Australia .... 95 F4 38 39 S 146 23 E
Toora-Khem, Russia . 53 D10 52 28N 96 17 E
Toowoomba, Australia 95 D5 27 32 S 151 56 E
Top Springs, Australia . 92 C5 16 37 S 131 51 E
Topalu, Romania ... 29 F13 44 31N 28 3 E
Topaz, U.S.A. 110 G7 38 41N 119 30W
Topeka, U.S.A. 112 F7 39 3N 95 40W
Top'al'a →, Slovak Rep. 27 C14 48 45N 21 45 E
Topley, Canada 102 C3 54 49N 126 18W
Toplița →, Serbia & M. 44 C5 43 15N 21 49 E
Toplița, Romania ... 29 D10 46 55N 25 20 E
Topocalma, Pta., Chile 126 C1 34 10 S 72 2W
Topock, U.S.A. 111 L12 34 46N 114 29W
Topola, Serbia & M. . 44 B4 44 17N 20 41 E
Topolčani, Macedonia . 44 E5 41 14N 21 25 E
Topol'čany, Slovak Rep. 27 C11 48 35N 18 12 E
Topolnitsa →, Bulgaria 45 D8 42 11N 24 18 E
Topolobampo, Mexico . 118 B3 25 40N 109 4W
Topoloveni, Romania . 29 F10 44 49N 25 5 E
Topolovgrad, Bulgaria . 45 D10 42 5N 26 20 E
Topolvățu Mare,
  Romania .... 28 E6 45 46N 21 41 E
Toppenish, U.S.A. ... 108 C3 46 23N 120 19W
Topraisar, Romania . 29 F13 44 1N 28 27 E
Topusko, Croatia ... 41 C12 45 18N 15 59 E
Torà, Spain .... 38 D6 41 49N 1 25 E
Tora Kit, Sudan .... 81 E3 11 2N 32 36 E
Toraka Vestale, Madag. 89 B7 16 20 S 43 58 E
Torata, Peru ...... 124 G4 17 23 S 70 1W
Torbalı, Turkey .... 47 C9 38 10N 27 21 E
Torbat-e Ḥeydārīyeh,
  Iran .... 71 C8 35 15N 59 12 E
Torbat-e Jām, Iran .. 71 C9 35 16N 60 35 E
Torbay, Canada 105 C9 47 40N 52 42W
Torbay □, U.K. 15 G4 50 26N 3 31W
Torbjörntorp, Sweden . 11 F7 58 12N 13 36 E
Tordesillas, Spain .. 36 D6 41 30N 5 0W
Töreboda, Sweden .. 11 F8 58 41N 14 7 E
Torekov, Sweden ... 11 H6 56 26N 12 37 E
Torelló, Spain ..... 38 C7 42 3N 2 16 E
Toreno, Spain 36 C4 42 42N 6 30W
Torfaen □, U.K. ... 15 F4 51 43N 3 3W
Torgau, Germany ... 24 D8 51 34N 13 0 E
Torgelow, Germany .. 24 B10 53 37N 14 1 E
Torhamn, Sweden ... 11 H9 56 5N 15 50 E
Torhout, Belgium ... 17 C3 51 5N 3 7 E
Torhovytsya, Ukraine . 29 B10 48 36N 25 26 E
Tori, Ethiopia ..... 81 F3 7 53N 33 35 E
Tori-Shima, Japan .. 55 J10 30 29N 140 19 E
Torigni-sur-Vire, France 18 C6 49 3N 0 58W
Torija, Spain 38 E1 40 44N 3 2W
Torin, Mexico 118 B2 27 33N 110 15W
Torino, Italy ...... 40 C4 45 3N 7 40 E
Torit, Sudan ...... 81 G3 4 27N 32 31 E
Torkamān, Iran .... 70 B5 37 35N 47 23 E
Torkovichi, Russia .. 32 C6 58 51N 30 21 E
Tormac, Romania ... 28 E6 45 30N 21 30 E
Tormes →, Spain ... 36 D4 41 18N 6 29W
Tornado Mt., Canada . 102 D6 49 55N 114 40W
Tornal'a, Slovak Rep. . 27 C13 48 25N 20 20 E
Torneå = Tornio,
  Finland .... 8 D21 65 50N 24 12 E
Torneälven →, Europe 8 D21 65 50N 24 12 E
Torneträsk, Sweden .. 8 B18 68 24N 19 15 E
Tornio, Finland .... 8 D21 65 50N 24 12 E
Tornionjoki =
  Torneälven →,
  Europe .... 8 D21 65 50N 24 12 E
Tornquist, Argentina . 126 D3 38 8 S 62 15W
Toro, Baleares, Spain . 48 B11 39 59N 4 8 E
Toro, Zamora, Spain . 36 D5 41 35N 5 24W
Torö, Sweden ..... 11 F11 58 48N 17 50 E
Toro ◠, Uganda ... 86 C3 0 5 S 30 22 E
Toro, Cerro del, Chile . 126 B2 29 10 S 69 50W
Toro Pk., U.S.A. ... 111 M10 33 34N 116 24W
Törökszentmiklós,
  Hungary .... 28 C5 47 11N 20 27 E
Toróníios Kólpos,
  Greece .... 44 F7 40 5N 23 30 E
Toronto, Canada ... 116 C5 43 39N 79 20W
Toronto, U.S.A. ... 116 F4 40 28N 80 36W
Toronto Lester B.
  Pearson
  International ✈
  (YYZ), Canada ... 116 C5 43 40N 79 34W
Toropets, Russia ... 32 D6 56 30N 31 40 E
Tororo, Uganda .... 86 B3 0 45N 34 12 E
Toros Dağları, Turkey . 70 B2 37 0N 32 30 E
Torpa, India ...... 69 H11 22 57N 85 6 E
Torquay, U.K. 15 G4 50 27N 3 32W
Torquemada, Spain . 36 C6 42 2N 4 19W
Torrance, U.S.A. ... 111 M8 33 50N 118 19W
Torrão, Portugal ... 37 G2 38 16N 8 11W
Torre de Moncorvo,
  Portugal 36 D3 41 12N 7 8W
Torre del Campo, Spain 37 H7 37 46N 3 53W
Torre del Greco, Italy . 43 B7 40 47N 14 22 E
Torre del Mar, Spain . 37 J6 36 44N 4 6W
Torre-Pacheco, Spain . 39 H4 37 44N 0 57W

Torre Péllice, Italy .... 40 D4 44 49N 7 13 E
Torreblanca, Spain ... 38 E5 40 14N 0 12 E
Torrecampo, Spain ... 37 G6 38 29N 4 41W
Torrecilla en Cameros,
  Spain 38 C2 42 15N 2 38W
Torredembarra, Spain . 38 D6 41 9N 1 24 E
Torredonjimeno, Spain 37 H7 37 46N 3 57W
Torrejón de Ardoz,
  Spain 36 E7 40 27N 3 29W
Torrejoncillo, Spain . 36 F4 39 54N 6 28W
Torrelaguna, Spain .. 36 E7 40 50N 3 38W
Torrelavega, Spain .. 36 B6 43 20N 4 5W
Torremaggiore, Italy . 41 G12 41 41N 15 17 E
Torremolinos, Spain . 37 J6 36 38N 4 30W
Torrens, L., Australia . 95 E2 31 0 S 137 50 E
Torrens Cr. →,
  Australia .... 94 C4 22 23 S 145 9 E
Torrens Creek, Australia 94 C4 20 48 S 145 3 E
Torrent, Spain 39 F4 39 27N 0 28W
Torrenueva, Spain .. 37 G7 38 38N 3 22W
Torreón, Mexico 118 B4 25 33N 103 26W
Torreperogil, Spain .. 37 G7 38 2N 3 17W
Torres, Brazil ...... 127 B5 29 21 S 49 44W
Torres, Mexico 118 B2 28 46N 110 47W
Torres Novas, Portugal 37 F2 39 27N 8 33W
Torres Strait, Australia 96 H6 9 50 S 142 20 E
Torres Vedras, Portugal 37 F1 39 5N 9 15W
Torrevieja, Spain ... 39 H4 37 59N 0 42W
Torrey, U.S.A. 109 G8 38 18N 111 25W
Torridge →, U.K. .. 15 G3 51 0N 4 13W
Torridon, L., U.K. .. 13 D3 57 35N 5 50W
Torrijos, Spain 36 F6 39 59N 4 18W
Tørring, Denmark ... 11 J3 55 52N 9 29 E
Torrington, Conn.,
  U.S.A. 117 E11 41 48N 73 7W
Torrington, Wyo., U.S.A. 112 D2 42 4N 104 11W
Torroella de Montgrí,
  Spain .... 38 C8 42 2N 3 8 E
Torrox, Spain 37 J7 36 46N 3 57W
Torsås, Sweden ..... 11 H9 56 24N 16 0 E
Torsby, Sweden .... 10 D6 60 7N 13 0 E
Torshälla, Sweden ... 10 E10 59 25N 16 28 E
Tórshavn, Færoe Is. .. 8 E9 62 5N 6 56W
Torslanda, Sweden .. 11 G5 57 44N 11 45 E
Torsö, Sweden ..... 11 F7 58 48N 13 45 E
Tortola, Br. Virgin Is. . 121 e 18 19N 64 45W
Tórtoles de Esgueva,
  Spain 36 D6 41 49N 4 2W
Tortolì, Italy ...... 42 C2 39 55N 9 39 E
Tortona, Italy ...... 40 D5 44 54N 8 52 E
Tortorici, Italy ..... 43 D7 38 2N 14 49 E
Tortosa, Spain ..... 38 E5 40 49N 0 31 E
Tortosa, C., Spain ... 38 E5 40 41N 0 52 E
Tortosendo, Portugal . 36 E3 40 15N 7 31W
Tortue, I. de la, Haiti . 121 B5 20 5N 72 57W
Tortuguero ◠,
  Costa Rica 120 D3 10 31N 83 29W
Tortum, Turkey ..... 73 B9 40 19N 41 35 E
Ţorūd, Iran .... 71 C7 35 25N 55 5 E
Torul, Turkey ...... 73 B8 40 34N 39 18 E
Toruń, Poland ..... 31 E5 53 2N 18 39 E
Torun, Ukraine ..... 29 B8 48 40N 23 34 E
Tory I., Ireland 12 A3 55 16N 8 14W
Torysa →, Slovak Rep. 27 C14 48 39N 21 21 E
Torzhok, Russia .... 32 D8 57 5N 34 55 E
Torzym, Poland .... 31 F2 52 19N 15 5 E
Tosa, Japan .... 55 H6 33 24N 133 23 E
Tosa-Shimizu, Japan . 55 H6 32 52N 132 58 E
Tosa-Wan, Japan ... 55 H6 33 15N 133 30 E
Toscana □, Italy ... 40 E8 43 25N 11 0 E
Toscano, Arcipelago,
  Italy .... 40 F7 42 30N 10 30 E
Toshkent, Uzbekistan . 52 E7 41 20N 69 10 E
Tosno, Russia ...... 32 C6 59 38N 30 46 E
Tossa de Mar, Spain . 38 D7 41 43N 2 56 E
Tösse, Sweden ..... 11 F6 58 58N 12 39 E
Tostado, Argentina .. 126 B3 29 15 S 61 50W
Tostedt, Germany ... 24 B5 53 17N 9 42 E
Tostón, Pta. de,
  Canary Is. 48 F5 28 42N 14 2W
Tosu, Japan .... 55 H5 33 22N 130 31 E
Tosya, Turkey ..... 72 B6 41 1N 34 2 E
Toszek, Poland ..... 31 H5 50 27N 18 32 E
Totana, Spain 39 H3 37 45N 1 30W
Totebo, Sweden .... 11 G10 57 38N 16 12 E
Toteng, Botswana ... 88 C3 20 22 S 22 58 E
Tôtes, France ...... 18 C8 49 41N 1 2 E
Tótkomlós, Hungary . 28 D5 46 24N 20 45 E
Totma, Russia ...... 52 C5 60 0N 42 40 E
Totnes, U.K. 15 G4 50 26N 3 42W
Totness, Suriname ... 125 B7 5 53N 56 19W
Toto, Nigeria ...... 83 D6 8 35N 7 5 E
Totonicapán, Guatemala 120 D1 14 58N 91 12W
Totten Glacier,
  Antarctica .... 5 C8 66 45 S 116 10 E
Tottenham, Australia . 95 E4 32 14 S 147 21 E
Tottenham, Canada .. 116 B5 44 1N 79 49W
Tottori, Japan ..... 55 G7 35 30N 134 15 E
Tottori □, Japan ... 55 G7 35 30N 134 12 E
Touaret, Niger ..... 83 A6 20 17N 7 8 E
Touba, Ivory C. 82 D3 8 22N 7 40W
Touba, Senegal 82 C1 14 50N 15 55W
Toubkal, Djebel,
  Morocco 78 B4 31 0N 8 0W
Toucy, France ..... 19 E10 47 44N 3 15 E
Tougan, Burkina Faso . 82 C4 13 11N 2 58W
Touggourt, Algeria .. 78 B7 33 6N 6 4 E
Tougouri, Burkina Faso 83 C4 13 20N 0 30W
Tougué, Guinea 82 C2 11 25N 11 50W
Toukoto, Mali 82 C3 13 27N 9 52W
Toul, France ...... 19 D12 48 40N 5 53 E
Touleppleu, Ivory C. . 82 D3 6 32N 8 24W
Toulon, France ..... 21 E9 43 10N 5 55 E
Toulouse, France ... 20 E5 43 37N 1 27 E
Toulouse Blagnac ✈
  (TLS), France .... 20 E5 43 37N 1 22 E
Toummo, Niger ..... 79 D8 22 45N 14 8 E
Toumodi, Ivory C. .. 82 D3 6 32 S 5 4W
Tounan, Taiwan .... 59 F13 23 41N 120 28 E
Toungo, Nigeria .... 83 D7 8 0N 12 3 E
Toungoo, Burma .... 67 K20 19 0N 96 30 E
Touques →, France .. 18 C7 49 22N 0 8 E
Touraine, France ... 18 E7 47 20N 0 30 E
Tourcoing, France .. 19 B10 50 42N 3 10 E
Touriñán, C., Spain .. 36 B1 43 3N 9 17W
Tournai, Belgium ... 17 D3 50 35N 3 25 E
Tournan-en-Brie, France 19 D9 48 44N 2 46 E
Tournay, France .... 20 E4 43 13N 0 13 E
Tournon-St-Martin,
  France .... 18 F7 46 45N 0 58 E
Tournon-sur-Rhône,
  France .... 21 C8 45 4N 4 50 E
Tournus, France .... 19 F11 46 35N 4 54 E
Tours, France ...... 18 E7 47 22N 0 40 E
Toussora, Mt., C.A.R. . 84 C4 9 7N 23 14 E
Touws →, S. Africa .. 88 E3 33 45 S 21 11 E
Touwsrivier, S. Africa . 88 E3 33 20 S 20 2 E

Tovarkovskiy, Russia . 32 F10 53 40N 38 14 E
Tovste, Ukraine .... 29 B10 48 50N 25 44 E
Tovuz, Azerbaijan .. 35 K7 41 0N 45 40 E
Towada, Japan ..... 54 D10 40 37N 141 13 E
Towada-Hachimantai △,
  Japan .... 54 D10 40 20N 140 55 E
Towada-Ko, Japan .. 54 D10 40 28N 140 55 E
Towanda, U.S.A. ... 117 E8 41 46N 76 27W
Towang, India ..... 67 F17 27 37N 91 50 E
Tower, U.S.A. 112 B8 47 48N 92 17W
Towerhill Cr. →,
  Australia .... 94 C3 22 28 S 144 35 E
Towner, U.S.A. 112 A4 48 21N 100 25W
Townsend, U.S.A. .. 108 C8 46 19N 111 31W
Townshend I., Australia 94 C5 22 10 S 150 31 E
Townsville, Australia . 94 B4 19 15 S 146 45 E
Towraghondi, Afghan. . 66 B3 35 13N 62 16 E
Towson, U.S.A. 114 F7 39 24N 76 36W
Towuti, Danau,
  Indonesia .... 63 E6 2 45 S 121 32 E
Toya-Ko, Japan .... 54 C10 42 35N 140 51 E
Toyama, Japan ..... 55 F8 36 40N 137 15 E
Toyama □, Japan ... 55 F8 36 45N 137 30 E
Toyama-Wan, Japan . 55 F8 37 0N 137 30 E
Toyapakeh, Indonesia . 63 K18 8 41 S 115 29 E
Toyohashi, Japan ... 55 G8 34 45N 137 25 E
Toyokawa, Japan ... 55 G8 34 48N 137 27 E
Toyonaka, Japan ... 55 G7 34 50N 135 28 E
Toyooka, Japan .... 55 G7 35 35N 134 48 E
Toyota, Japan ..... 55 G8 35 3N 137 7 E
Tozeur, Tunisia .... 78 B7 33 56N 8 0 E
Tozkhurmato, Iraq .. 70 C5 34 56N 44 38 E
Tqibuli, Georgia .... 35 J6 42 26N 43 0 E
Tqvarcheli, Georgia .. 35 J5 42 47N 41 42 E
Trá Li = Tralee, Ireland 12 D2 52 16N 9 42W
Tra On, Vietnam ... 65 H5 9 58N 105 55 E
Trabancos →, Spain . 36 D5 41 36N 5 15W
Traben-Trarbach,
  Germany .... 25 F3 49 57N 7 7 E
Trabzon, Turkey .... 73 B8 41 0N 39 45 E
Tracadie-Sheila, Canada 105 C7 47 30N 64 55W
Tracy, Calif., U.S.A. .. 110 H5 37 44N 121 26W
Tracy, Minn., U.S.A. . 112 C7 44 14N 95 37W
Tradate, Italy ...... 40 C5 45 43N 8 54 E
Trade Town, Liberia . 82 D3 5 40N 9 50W
Trafalgar, C., Spain .. 37 J4 36 10N 6 2W
Traian, Brăila, Romania 29 E12 45 11N 27 44 E
Traian, Tulcea, Romania 29 E13 45 2N 28 15 E
Trail, Canada 102 D5 49 5N 117 40W
Trainor L., Canada .. 102 A4 60 24N 120 17W
Trákhonas, Cyprus .. 49 D12 35 12N 33 21 E
Tralee, Ireland 12 D2 52 16N 9 42W
Tralee B., Ireland ... 12 D2 52 17N 9 55W
Tramore, Ireland ... 12 D4 52 10N 7 10W
Tramore B., Ireland .. 12 D4 52 9N 7 10W
Tran Ninh, Cao Nguyen,
  Laos .... 64 C4 19 30N 103 10 E
Tranås, Sweden .... 11 F8 58 3N 14 59 E
Tranbjerg, Denmark . 11 H4 56 6N 10 9 E
Trancas, Argentina .. 126 B2 26 11 S 65 20W
Trancoso, Portugal .. 36 E3 40 49N 7 21W
Tranebjerg, Denmark . 11 J4 55 51N 10 36 E
Tranemo, Sweden ... 11 G7 57 30N 13 20 E
Trang, Thailand .... 65 J2 7 33N 99 38 E
Trangahy, Madag. ... 89 B7 19 7 S 44 31 E
Trangan, Indonesia .. 63 F8 6 40 S 134 20 E
Trangie, Australia ... 95 E4 32 4 S 148 0 E
Trångsviken, Sweden . 10 A7 63 19N 13 59 E
Trani, Italy .... 43 A9 41 17N 16 25 E
Tranoroa, Madag. ... 89 C8 24 42 S 45 4 E
Tranqueras, Uruguay . 127 C4 31 13 S 55 45W
Transantarctic Mts.,
  Antarctica .... 5 E12 85 0 S 170 0W
Transilvania, Romania . 29 D9 46 30N 24 0 E
Transilvanian Alps =
  Carpații Meridionali,
  Romania .... 29 E9 45 30N 25 0 E
Transnistria = Stînga
  Nistrului □, Moldova 29 C14 47 20N 29 15 E
Transtrand, Sweden .. 10 C7 61 6N 13 20 E
Transtrandsfjällen,
  Sweden .... 10 C6 61 8N 13 0 E
Transylvania =
  Transilvania, Romania 29 D9 46 30N 24 0 E
Trápani, Italy ...... 42 D5 38 1N 12 29 E
Trapper Pk., U.S.A. .. 108 D6 45 54N 114 18W
Traralgon, Australia .. 95 F4 38 12 S 146 34 E
Trarza, Mauritania .. 82 B2 17 30N 15 0W
Trasacco, Italy ..... 41 G10 41 57N 13 32 E
Trăscău, Munţii,
  Romania .... 29 D8 46 14N 23 14 E
Trasimeno, L., Italy .. 41 E9 43 8N 12 6 E
Träslövsläge, Sweden . 11 G6 57 4N 12 16 E
Trasvase Tajo-Segura,
  Canal de, Spain ... 38 E2 40 15N 2 55W
Trat, Thailand ..... 65 F4 12 14N 102 33 E
Tratani →, Pakistan .. 68 E3 29 19N 68 20 E
Traun, Austria ..... 26 C7 48 14N 14 15 E
Traunreut, Germany . 25 H8 47 58N 12 36 E
Traunsee, Austria ... 26 D7 47 55N 13 50 E
Traunstein, Germany . 25 H8 47 52N 12 37 E
Traveller's L., Australia 95 E3 33 20 S 142 0 E
Travemünde, Germany . 24 B6 53 57N 10 52 E
Travers, Mt., N.Z. ... 91 K4 42 1 S 172 45 E
Traverse City, U.S.A. . 114 C3 44 46N 85 38W
Travis, L., U.S.A. ... 113 K5 30 24N 97 55W
Travnik, Bos.-H. .... 44 B2 44 17N 17 39 E
Trbovlje, Slovenia ... 41 B12 46 12N 15 5 E
Trébbia →, Italy .... 40 C6 45 4N 9 41 E
Trebel →, Germany .. 24 B9 53 54N 13 2 E
Trébeurden, France .. 18 D3 48 46N 3 35W
Trebević △, Bos.-H. .. 28 G3 43 20N 18 45 E
Trébič, Czech Rep. .. 26 B8 49 14N 15 55 E
Trebinje, Bos.-H. ... 44 D2 42 44N 18 22 E
Trebisacce, Italy .... 43 C9 39 52N 16 32 E
Trebišnjica →, Bos.-H. 44 D2 42 47N 18 8 E
Trebišov, Slovak Rep. . 27 C14 48 38N 21 41 E
Trebižat →, Bos.-H. .. 41 F8 43 20N 17 35 E
Trebnje, Slovenia ... 41 C12 45 54N 15 1 E
Trěboň, Czech Rep. .. 26 B8 49 1N 14 48 E
Trebonne, Australia .. 94 B4 18 37 S 146 5 E
Trebujena, Spain 37 J4 36 52N 6 11W
Trecate, Italy ...... 40 C5 45 26N 8 44 E
Tregaron, U.K. 15 E4 52 14N 3 56W
Tregnago, Italy ..... 41 C8 45 31N 11 10 E
Tregrosse Is., Australia 94 B5 17 41 S 150 43 E
Tréguier, France 18 D3 48 47N 3 16W
Trégunc, France 18 E3 47 51N 3 51W
Treherne, Canada ... 103 D9 49 38N 98 42W
Tréia, Italy .... 41 E10 43 19N 13 19 E
Treignac, France ... 20 C5 45 32N 1 48 E
Treinta y Tres, Uruguay 127 C5 33 16 S 54 17W
Treis-karden, Germany 25 E3 50 10N 7 18 E
Treklyano, Bulgaria .. 44 D6 42 33N 22 36 E
Trelawney, Zimbabwe . 89 B5 17 30 S 30 30 E

Trélazé, France 18 E6 47 26N 0 30W
Trelew, Argentina ... 128 E3 43 10 S 65 20W
Trélissac, France ... 20 C4 45 11N 0 47 E
Trelleborg, Sweden .. 11 J7 55 20N 13 10 E
Tremadog Bay, U.K. . 14 E3 52 51N 4 18W
Trémiti, Italy ...... 41 F12 42 8N 15 30 E
Tremonton, U.S.A. .. 108 F7 41 43N 112 10W
Tremp, Spain ...... 38 C5 42 10N 0 52 E
Trenche →, Canada .. 104 C5 47 46N 72 53W
Trenčiansky □,
  Slovak Rep. ...... 27 C11 48 45N 18 20 E
Trenčín, Slovak Rep. . 27 C11 48 52N 18 4 E
Trenggalek, Indonesia . 63 H14 8 3 S 111 43 E
Trenque Lauquen,
  Argentina .... 126 D3 36 5 S 62 45W
Trent →, Canada ... 116 B7 44 6N 77 34W
Trent →, U.K. 14 D7 53 41N 0 42W
Trentino-Alto Adige □,
  Italy .... 41 B8 46 30N 11 0 E
Trento, Italy ...... 41 B8 46 4N 11 8 E
Trenton = Quinte West,
  Canada 116 B7 44 10N 77 34W
Trenton, Mo., U.S.A. . 112 E8 40 5N 93 37W
Trenton, N.J., U.S.A. . 117 F10 40 14N 74 46W
Trenton, Nebr., U.S.A. 112 E4 40 11N 101 1W
Trepassey, Canada .. 105 C9 46 43N 53 25W
Trepuzzi, Italy ..... 43 B11 40 24N 18 4 E
Tres Arroyos, Argentina 126 D3 38 26 S 60 20W
Três Corações, Brazil . 127 A6 21 44 S 45 15W
Três Lagoas, Brazil .. 125 H8 20 50 S 51 43W
Tres Lomas, Argentina 126 D3 36 27 S 62 51W
Tres Marías, Islas,
  Mexico 118 C3 21 25N 106 28W
Tres Montes, C., Chile . 128 F1 46 50 S 75 30W
Tres Pinos, U.S.A. .. 110 J5 36 48N 121 19W
Três Pontas, Brazil .. 127 A6 21 23 S 45 29W
Tres Puentes, Chile .. 126 B1 27 50 S 70 15W
Tres Puntas, C.,
  Argentina .... 128 F3 47 0 S 66 0W
Três Rios, Brazil .... 127 A7 22 6 S 43 15W
Tres Valles, Mexico .. 119 D5 18 15N 96 8W
Tresco, U.K. 15 H1 49 57N 6 20W
Treska →, Macedonia . 44 E5 42 0N 21 20 E
Treskavica, Bos.-H. .. 28 G3 43 40N 18 20 E
Trespaderne, Spain .. 36 C7 42 47N 3 24W
Tresticklan △, Sweden . 11 F5 59 0N 11 42 E
Trets, France ...... 21 E9 43 27N 5 41 E
Treuchtlingen, Germany 25 G6 48 58N 10 54 E
Treuenbrietzen,
  Germany .... 24 C8 52 5N 12 52 E
Trevi, Italy .... 41 F9 42 53N 12 45 E
Treviglio, Italy ..... 40 C6 45 31N 9 35 E
Trevínca, Peña, Spain . 36 C4 42 15N 6 46W
Treviso, Italy ...... 41 C9 45 40N 12 15 E
Trévoux, France .... 21 C8 45 57N 4 47 E
Trgovište, Serbia & M. 44 D6 42 20N 22 10 E
Triabunna, Australia . 95 G4 42 30 S 147 55 E
Triánda, Greece .... 49 C10 36 25N 28 10 E
Triangle, Zimbabwe .. 89 C5 21 2 S 31 28 E
Triaucourt-en-Argonne,
  France .... 19 D12 48 59N 5 2 E
Tribal Areas □, Pakistan 68 C4 33 0N 70 0 E
Tribsees, Germany ... 24 A8 54 5N 12 44 E
Tribulation, C., Australia 94 B4 16 5 S 145 29 E
Tribune, U.S.A. 112 F4 38 28N 101 45W
Tricárico, Italy ..... 43 B9 40 37N 16 9 E
Tricase, Italy ...... 43 C11 39 56N 18 22 E
Trichinopoly =
  Tiruchchirappalli,
  India .... 66 P11 10 45N 78 45 E
Trichur, India ..... 66 P10 10 30N 76 18 E
Trida, Australia .... 95 E4 33 1 S 145 1 E
Trier, Germany ..... 25 F2 49 45N 6 38 E
Trieste, Italy ...... 41 C10 45 40N 13 46 E
Trieste, G. di, Italy ... 41 C10 45 40N 13 35 E
Trieux →, France ... 18 D3 48 43N 3 9W
Triggiano, Italy ..... 43 A9 41 4N 16 55 E
Triglav, Slovenia .... 41 B10 46 21N 13 50 E
Triglavski △, Slovenia . 41 B10 46 20N 13 50 E
Trigno →, Italy ..... 41 F11 42 4N 14 48 E
Trigueros, Spain 37 H4 37 24N 6 50W
Tríkeri, Greece ..... 46 B5 39 6N 23 5 E
Trikhonis, Límni, Greece 46 C3 38 34N 21 30 E
Tríkkala, Greece .... 46 B3 39 34N 21 47 E
Tríkkala □, Greece .. 46 B3 39 41N 21 30 E
Trikomo, Cyprus .... 49 D12 35 17N 33 52 E
Trikora, Puncak,
  Indonesia .... 63 E9 4 15 S 138 45 E
Trilj, Croatia ...... 41 E13 43 38N 16 42 E
Trillo, Spain 38 E2 40 42N 2 35W
Trim, Ireland 12 C5 53 33N 6 48W
Trincomalee, Sri Lanka 66 Q12 8 38N 81 15 E
Trindade, Brazil .... 125 G9 16 40 S 49 30W
Trindade, I., Atl. Oc. . 2 F8 20 20 S 29 50W
Trinidad, Bolivia ... 124 F6 14 46 S 64 50W
Trinidad, Cuba 120 B4 21 48N 80 0W
Trinidad, Trin. & Tob. . 121 D7 10 30N 61 15W
Trinidad, Uruguay ... 126 C4 33 30 S 56 50W
Trinidad, U.S.A. 113 G2 37 10N 104 31W
Trinidad →, Mexico . 119 D5 17 49N 95 9W
Trinidad & Tobago ■,
  W. Indies 121 D7 10 30N 61 20W
Trinitápoli, Italy .... 43 A9 41 21N 16 5 E
Trinity, Canada 105 C9 48 59N 53 55W
Trinity, U.S.A. 113 K7 30 57N 95 22W
Trinity →, Calif., U.S.A. 108 F2 41 11N 123 42W
Trinity →, Tex., U.S.A. 113 L7 29 45N 94 43W
Trinity B., Canada .. 105 C9 48 20N 53 10W
Trinity Hills,
  Trin. & Tob. 125 K15 10 7N 61 7W
Trinity Is., U.S.A. ... 100 C4 56 33N 154 25W
Trinity Range, U.S.A. . 108 F4 40 15N 118 45W
Trinkitat, Sudan .... 80 D4 18 45N 37 51 E
Trino, Italy .... 40 C5 45 12N 8 18 E
Trion, U.S.A. 117 H3 34 33N 85 19W
Trionto, C., Italy .... 43 C9 39 37N 16 43 E
Triora, Italy .... 40 D4 44 1N 7 46 E
Tripoli = Tarābulus,
  Lebanon .... 74 A4 34 31N 35 50 E
Tripoli = Tarābulus,
  Libya .... 79 B8 32 49N 13 7 E
Trípolis, Greece .... 46 D4 37 31N 22 25 E
Tripolitania, N. Afr. .. 79 B8 31 0N 13 0 E
Tripura □, India .... 67 H18 24 0N 92 0 E
Tripylos, Cyprus .... 49 E11 34 59N 32 41 E
Trischen, Germany ... 24 A4 54 5N 8 40 E
Tristan da Cunha,
  Atl. Oc. .... 77 K2 37 6 S 12 20W
Trisul, India ...... 69 D8 30 19N 79 47 E
Trivandrum, India .. 66 Q10 8 41N 77 0 E
Trivento, Italy ..... 41 G11 41 47N 14 33 E
Trnava, Slovak Rep. . 27 C10 48 23N 17 35 E
Trnavský □, Slovak Rep. 27 C10 48 20N 17 45 E
Trochu, Canada 102 C6 51 50N 113 13W

Troezen, Greece .... 46 D5 37 25N 23 15 E
Trogir, Croatia ..... 41 E13 43 32N 16 15 E
Troglav, Croatia .... 41 E13 43 56N 16 36 E
Tróia, Italy .... 43 A8 41 22N 15 18 E
Troilus, L., Canada .. 104 B5 50 50N 74 35W
Troina, Italy ...... 43 E7 37 47N 14 36 E
Trois-Pistoles, Canada 105 C6 48 5N 69 10W
Trois-Rivières, Canada 104 C5 46 25N 72 34W
Trois-Rivières,
  Guadeloupe ...... 120 b 15 57N 61 40W
Troisdorf, Germany .. 24 E3 50 49N 7 11 E
Troitsk, Russia ..... 52 D7 54 10N 61 35 E
Troitsko Pechorsk,
  Russia .... 52 C6 62 40N 56 10 E
Troitskoye, Russia ... 35 G7 46 26N 44 15 E
Trölladyngja, Iceland . 8 D5 64 54N 17 16W
Trollhättan, Sweden . 11 F6 58 17N 12 20 E
Trollheimen, Norway . 8 E13 62 46N 9 1 E
Trombetas →, Brazil . 125 D7 1 55 S 55 35W
Tromsø, Norway .... 8 B18 69 40N 18 56 E
Trona, U.S.A. 111 K9 35 46N 117 23W
Tronador, Mte.,
  Argentina .... 128 E2 41 10 S 71 50W
Trøndelag, Norway .. 8 D14 64 17N 11 50 E
Trondheim, Norway . 8 E14 63 36N 10 25 E
Trondheimsfjorden,
  Norway .... 8 E14 63 35N 10 30 E
Trönninge, Sweden .. 11 H6 56 37N 12 51 E
Tronto →, Italy .... 41 F10 42 54N 13 55 E
Troodos, Cyprus .... 49 E11 34 55N 32 52 E
Troon, U.K. 13 F4 55 33N 4 39W
Tropea, Italy ...... 43 D8 38 41N 15 54 E
Tropic, U.S.A. 109 H7 37 37N 112 5W
Tropojë, Albania .... 44 D4 42 23N 20 10 E
Trosa, Sweden ..... 11 F11 58 54N 17 23 E
Trostan, U.K. 12 A5 55 3N 6 10W
Trostberg, Germany . 25 G8 48 1N 12 33 E
Trostyanets, Ukraine . 29 B14 48 31N 29 11 E
Trostyanets, Ukraine . 33 G8 50 33N 34 59 E
Trou Gras Pt., St. Lucia 121 f 13 51N 60 53W
Trout →, Canada ... 102 A5 61 19N 119 51W
Trout L., N.W.T.,
  Canada 102 A4 60 40N 121 14W
Trout L., Ont., Canada 103 C10 51 20N 93 15W
Trout Lake, Canada .. 102 B6 56 30N 114 32W
Trout Lake, U.S.A. .. 110 E5 46 0N 121 32W
Trout River, Canada .. 105 C8 49 29N 58 8W
Trout Run, U.S.A. .. 116 E7 41 23N 77 3W
Trouville-sur-Mer,
  France .... 18 C7 49 21N 0 5 E
Trowbridge, U.K. ... 15 F5 51 18N 2 12W
Troy, Turkey ...... 47 B8 39 57N 26 12 E
Troy, Ala., U.S.A. ... 115 K3 31 48N 85 58W
Troy, Kans., U.S.A. .. 112 F7 39 47N 95 5W
Troy, Mo., U.S.A. .. 112 F9 38 59N 90 59W
Troy, Mont., U.S.A. . 108 B6 48 28N 115 53W
Troy, N.Y., U.S.A. .. 117 D11 42 44N 73 41W
Troy, Ohio, U.S.A. .. 114 E3 40 2N 84 12W
Troy, Pa., U.S.A. ... 117 E8 41 47N 76 47W
Troyan, Bulgaria ... 45 D8 42 57N 24 43 E
Troyes, France ..... 19 D11 48 19N 4 3 E
Trpanj, Croatia .... 41 E14 43 1N 17 15 E
Trstenik, Serbia & M. . 44 C5 43 36N 21 0 E
Trubchevsk, Russia .. 33 F7 52 33N 33 47 E
Truchas Peak, U.S.A. . 113 H2 35 58N 105 39W
Trucial States = United
  Arab Emirates ■,
  Asia .... 71 F7 23 50N 54 0 E
Truckee, U.S.A. 110 F6 39 20N 120 11W
Trudfront, Russia ... 35 H8 45 56N 47 40 E
Trudovoye, Russia ... 54 C6 43 17N 132 5 E
Trujillo, Honduras .. 120 C2 16 0N 86 0W
Trujillo, Peru ...... 124 E3 8 6 S 79 0W
Trujillo, Spain 37 F5 39 28N 5 55W
Trujillo, U.S.A. 113 H2 35 32N 104 42W
Trujillo, Venezuela .. 124 B4 9 22N 70 38W
Truk, Micronesia ... 96 G7 7 25N 151 46 E
Trumann, U.S.A. ... 113 H9 35 41N 90 31W
Trumansburg, U.S.A. 117 D8 42 33N 76 40W
Trumbull, Mt., U.S.A. 109 H7 36 25N 113 8W
Trün, Bulgaria ..... 44 D6 42 51N 22 38 E
Trun, France ...... 18 D7 48 50N 0 2 E
Trundle, Australia ... 95 E4 32 53 S 147 35 E
Trung-Phan = Annam,
  Vietnam .... 64 E7 16 0N 108 0 E
Truro, Canada 105 C7 45 21N 63 14W
Truro, U.K. 15 G2 50 16N 5 4W
Truskavets, Ukraine . 33 H2 49 17N 23 30 E
Trüstenik, Bulgaria .. 45 C8 43 31N 24 28 E
Trustrup, Denmark .. 11 H4 56 20N 10 46 E
Trutch, Canada 102 B4 57 44N 122 57W
Truth or Consequences,
  U.S.A. 109 K10 33 8N 107 15W
Trutnov, Czech Rep. . 26 A8 50 37N 15 54 E
Truxton, U.S.A. 117 D8 42 45N 76 2W
Truyère →, France .. 20 D6 44 38N 2 34 E
Tryavna, Bulgaria ... 45 D9 42 54N 25 25 E
Tryonville, U.S.A. .. 116 E5 41 42N 79 48W
Trzcianka, Poland ... 31 E3 53 3N 16 25 E
Trzciel, Poland ..... 31 F2 52 23N 15 50 E
Trzcińsko Zdrój, Poland 31 F1 52 58N 14 35 E
Trzebiatów, Poland .. 30 D2 54 3N 15 18 E
Trzebiez, Poland .... 30 E1 53 38N 14 31 E
Trzebnica, Poland ... 31 G4 51 20N 17 1 E
Trzemeszno, Poland . 31 F4 52 33N 17 48 E
Tržič, Slovenia ..... 41 B11 46 22N 14 18 E
Tsagaan Aman, Russia 35 G8 47 34N 46 43 E
Tsamandás, Greece .. 46 B2 39 46N 20 21 E
Tsandi, Namibia .... 88 B1 17 42 S 14 50 E
Tsaratanana, Madag. . 89 B8 16 47 S 47 39 E
Tsaratanana, Mt. de =
  Maromokotro,
  Madag. .... 89 A8 14 0 S 49 0 E
Tsarevo, Bulgaria ... 45 D9 42 28N 25 52 E
Tsaritsáni, Greece ... 46 B4 39 53N 22 14 E
Tsau, Botswana .... 88 C3 20 8 S 22 22 E
Tsavo East △, Kenya . 86 C4 2 44 S 38 47 E
Tsavo West △, Kenya . 86 C4 3 19 S 37 57 E
Tsebrykove, Ukraine . 33 J6 47 9N 30 10 E
Tsentralnyy □, Russia . 34 D4 52 0N 40 0 E
Tsetserleg, Mongolia . 60 B5 47 36N 101 32 E
Tsévié, Togo ...... 83 D5 6 25N 1 20 E
Tshabong, Botswana . 88 D3 26 2 S 22 29 E
Tshane, Botswana ... 88 C3 24 5 S 21 54 E
Tshela, Dem. Rep. of
  the Congo .... 84 E2 4 57 S 13 4 E
Tshesebe, Botswana . 89 C4 21 51 S 27 32 E
Tshibeke, Dem. Rep. of
  the Congo .... 86 C2 2 40 S 28 35 E
Tshibinda, Dem. Rep. of
  the Congo .... 86 C2 2 23 S 28 43 E
Tshikapa, Dem. Rep. of
  the Congo .... 84 F4 6 28 S 20 48 E
Tshilenge, Dem. Rep. of
  the Congo .... 86 D1 6 17 S 23 48 E

Tshinsenda, *Dem. Rep.*
of the Congo ...... **87 E2** 12 20 S 28 0 E
Tshofa, *Dem. Rep. of*
the Congo .... **86 D2** 5 13 S 25 16 E
Tshwane, *Botswana* .. **88 C3** 22 24 S 22 1 E
Tsigara, *Botswana* ... **88 C4** 20 22 S 25 54 E
Tsihombe, *Madag.* .... **89 D8** 25 10 S 45 41 E
Tsiigehtchic, *Canada* .. **100 B6** 67 15N 134 0W
Tsimlyansk, *Russia* ... **35 G6** 47 40N 42 6 E
Tsimlyansk Res. =
Tsimlyanskoye
Vdkhr., *Russia* .... **35 F6** 48 0N 43 0 E
Tsimlyanskoye Vdkhr.,
Russia .... **35 F6** 48 0N 43 0 E
Tsinan = Jinan, *China* .. **56 F9** 36 38N 117 1 E
Tsineng, *S. Africa* .... **88 D3** 27 5 S 23 5 E
Tsínga, *Greece* .... **45 E8** 41 23N 24 44 E
Tsinghai = Qinghai □,
China .... **60 C4** 36 0N 98 0 E
Tsingtao = Qingdao,
China .... **57 F11** 36 5N 120 20 E
Tsingy de Bemaraha △,
Madag. .... **89 B8** 18 35 S 45 25 E
Tsingy de Namoroka △,
Madag. .... **89 B8** 16 29 S 45 25 E
Tsinjoarivo, *Madag.* ... **89 B8** 19 37 S 47 40 E
Tsinjomitondraka,
Madag. .... **89 B8** 15 40 S 47 8 E
Tsiroanomandidy,
Madag. .... **89 B8** 18 46 S 46 2 E
Tsiteli-Tsqaro, *Georgia* .. **35 K8** 41 33N 46 0 E
Tsitondroina, *Madag.* .. **89 C8** 21 19 S 46 0 E
Tsitsikamma △,
S. Africa .... **88 E3** 34 3 S 23 40 E
Tsivilsk, *Russia* ...... **34 C5** 55 50N 47 25 E
Tsivory, *Madag.* ...... **89 C8** 24 4 S 46 5 E
Tskhinvali, *Georgia* ... **35 J7** 42 14N 44 1 E
Tsna →, *Russia* ...... **34 C6** 54 55N 41 58 E
Tsnori, *Georgia* ...... **35 K7** 41 40N 45 57 E
Tso Moriri, L., *India* ... **69 C8** 32 50N 78 20 E
Tsobis, *Namibia* ...... **88 B2** 19 27 S 17 30 E
Tsodilo Hill, *Botswana* .. **88 B3** 18 49 S 21 43 E
Tsogttsetsiy =
Baruunsuu, *Mongolia* .. **56 C3** 43 43N 105 35 E
Tsolo, *S. Africa* ...... **89 E4** 31 18 S 28 37 E
Tsomo, *S. Africa* ..... **89 E4** 32 0 S 27 42 E
Tsu, *Japan* .... **55 G8** 34 45N 136 25 E
Tsu L., *Canada* **102 A6** 60 40N 111 52W
Tsuchiura, *Japan* ..... **55 F10** 36 5N 140 15 E
Tsuen Wan, *China* .... **59 F10** 22 22N 114 6 E
Tsugaru-Kaikyō, *Japan* .. **54 D10** 41 35N 141 0 E
Tsumeb, *Namibia* ..... **88 B2** 19 9 S 17 44 E
Tsumis, *Namibia* ..... **88 C2** 23 39 S 17 29 E
Tsuruga, *Japan* ...... **55 G8** 35 45N 136 2 E
Tsurugi-San, *Japan* ... **55 H7** 33 51N 134 6 E
Tsuruoka, *Japan* ..... **54 E9** 38 44N 139 50 E
Tsushima, *Gifu, Japan* . **55 G8** 35 10N 136 43 E
Tsushima, *Nagasaki,*
Japan .... **55 G4** 34 20N 129 20 E
Tsuyama, *Japan* ...... **55 G7** 35 3N 134 0 E
Tsvetkovo, *Ukraine* ... **33 H6** 49 8N 31 33 E
Tsyelyakhany, *Belarus* .. **33 F3** 52 30N 25 46 E
Tua →, *Portugal* **36 D3** 41 13N 7 26W
Tual, *Indonesia* ...... **63 F8** 5 38 S 132 44 E
Tuam, *Ireland* **12 C3** 53 31N 8 51W
Tuamotu Arch. =
Tuamotu Is.,
French Polynesia ... **97 J13** 17 0 S 144 0W
Tuamotu Is.,
French Polynesia ... **97 J13** 17 0 S 144 0W
Tuamotu Ridge,
Pac. Oc. .... **97 K14** 20 0 S 138 0W
Tuanfeng, *China* ..... **59 B10** 30 38N 114 52 E
Tuanxi, *China* .... **58 D6** 27 28N 107 8 E
Tuao, *Phil.* .... **61 C4** 17 55N 121 22 E
Tuapse, *Russia* ...... **35 H4** 44 5N 39 10 E
Tuas, *Singapore* ...... **65 d** 1 19N 103 39 E
Tuatapere, *N.Z.* ...... **91 M1** 46 8 S 167 41 E
Tuba City, *U.S.A.* **109 H8** 36 8N 111 14W
Tuban, *Indonesia* ..... **63 G15** 6 54 S 112 3 E
Tubarão, *Brazil* ...... **127 B6** 28 30 S 49 0W
Tūbās, *West Bank* .... **74 C4** 32 20N 35 22 E
Tubas →, *Namibia* ... **88 C2** 22 54 S 14 35 E
Tübingen, *Germany* ... **25 G5** 48 31N 9 4 E
Tubruq, *Libya* .... **79 B10** 32 7N 23 55 E
Tubuai Is.,
French Polynesia ... **97 K13** 25 0 S 150 0W
Tuc Trung, *Vietnam* ... **65 G6** 11 1N 107 12 E
Tucacas, *Venezuela* ... **124 A5** 10 48N 68 19W
Tuch'ang, *Taiwan* .... **59 E13** 24 42N 121 25 E
Tuchodi →, *Canada* .. **102 B4** 58 17N 123 42W
Tuchów, *Poland* ...... **31 J8** 49 54N 21 1 E
Tuckanarra, *Australia* . **93 E2** 27 7 S 118 5 E
Tucson, *U.S.A.* **109 K8** 32 13N 110 58W
Tucumán □, *Argentina* .. **126 B2** 26 48 S 65 2W
Tucumcari, *U.S.A.* ... **113 H3** 35 10N 103 44W
Tucupita, *Venezuela* .. **124 B6** 9 2N 62 3W
Tucuruí, *Brazil* ...... **125 D9** 3 42 S 49 44W
Tucuruí, Reprêsa de,
Brazil .... **125 D9** 4 0 S 49 30W
Tuczno, *Poland* ...... **31 E3** 53 13N 15 10 E
Tudela, *Spain* **38 C3** 42 4N 1 39W
Tudmur, *Syria* .... **70 C3** 34 36N 38 15 E
Tudor, L., *Canada* **105 A6** 55 50N 65 25W
Tudora, *Romania* ..... **29 C11** 47 31N 26 45 E
Tuela →, *Portugal* ... **36 D3** 41 30N 7 12W
Tugela →, *S. Africa* .. **89 D5** 29 14 S 31 30 E
Tuguegarao, *Phil.* .... **61 C4** 17 35N 121 42 E
Tugur, *Russia* .... **53 D14** 53 44N 136 45 E
Tui, *Spain* **36 C2** 42 3N 8 39W
Tuineje, *Canary Is.* ... **48 F5** 28 19N 14 3W
Tukangbesi, Kepulauan,
Indonesia .... **63 F6** 6 0 S 124 0 E
Tukarak I., *Canada* ... **104 A4** 56 15N 78 45W
Tukayyid, *Iraq* .... **70 D5** 29 47N 45 36 E
Tūkh, *Egypt* .... **80 H7** 30 21N 31 12 E
Tukhlya, *Ukraine* ..... **29 B8** 48 55N 23 28 E
Tukkae, Ao, *Thailand* .. **65 a** 7 51N 98 25 E
Tukobo, *Ghana* **82 D4** 5 1N 2 47W
Tuktoyaktuk, *Canada* .. **100 B6** 69 27N 133 2W
Tukums, *Latvia* ...... **9 H20** 56 58N 23 10 E
Tukums □, *Latvia* .... **30 B10** 56 55N 23 0 E
Tukuyu, *Tanzania* .... **87 D3** 9 17 S 33 35 E
Tula, *Hidalgo, Mexico* . **119 C5** 20 5N 99 20W
Tula, *Tamaulipas,*
Mexico **119 C5** 23 0N 99 40W
Tula, *Nigeria* .... **83 D7** 9 51N 11 27 E
Tula, *Russia* .... **32 E9** 54 13N 37 38 E
Tulancingo, *Mexico* ... **119 C5** 20 5N 98 22W
Tulare, *Serbia & M.* ... **44 D5** 42 48N 21 28 E
Tulare, *U.S.A.* **110 J7** 36 13N 119 21W
Tulare Lake Bed, *U.S.A.* .. **110 K7** 36 0N 119 48W
Tularosa, *U.S.A.* **109 K10** 33 5N 106 1W
Tulbagh, *S. Africa* .... **88 E2** 33 16 S 19 6 E
Tulcán, *Ecuador* **124 C3** 0 48N 77 43W

Tulcea, *Romania* ..... **29 E13** 45 13N 28 46 E
Tulcea □, *Romania* ... **29 E13** 45 0N 28 30 E
Tulchyn, *Ukraine* ..... **29 B13** 48 41N 28 49 E
Tūleh, *Iran* .... **71 C7** 34 35N 52 33 E
Tulemalu L., *Canada* .. **103 A9** 62 58N 99 25W
Tulghes, *Romania* .... **29 D10** 46 58N 25 45 E
Tuli, *Zimbabwe* ...... **87 G2** 21 58 S 29 13 E
Tulia, *U.S.A.* **113 H4** 34 32N 101 46W
Tuliszków, *Poland* .... **31 F5** 52 5N 18 18 E
Tulita, *Canada* **100 B7** 64 57N 125 30W
Tülkarm, *West Bank* .. **74 C4** 32 19N 35 2 E
Tulla, *Ireland* **12 D3** 52 53N 8 46W
Tullahoma, *U.S.A.* ... **115 H2** 35 22N 86 13W
Tullamore, *Australia* .. **95 E4** 32 39 S 147 36 E
Tullamore, *Ireland* ... **12 C4** 53 16N 7 31W
Tulle, *France* .... **20 C5** 45 16N 1 46 E
Tulln, *Austria* .... **26 C9** 48 20N 16 4 E
Tullow, *Ireland* **12 D5** 52 49N 6 45W
Tully, *Australia* ...... **94 B4** 17 56 S 145 55 E
Tully, *U.S.A.* **117 D8** 42 48N 76 7W
Tulnici, *Romania* ..... **29 E11** 45 51N 26 38 E
Tulovo, *Bulgaria* ..... **45 D9** 42 33N 25 32 E
Tulsa, *U.S.A.* **113 G7** 36 10N 95 55W
Tulsequah, *Canada* ... **102 B2** 58 39N 133 35W
Tulu Milki, *Ethiopia* ... **81 F4** 9 55N 38 20 E
Tulu Welel, *Ethiopia* .. **81 F3** 8 56N 34 47 E
Tulua, *Colombia* **124 C3** 4 6N 76 11W
Tulucești, *Romania* ... **29 E13** 45 34N 28 2 E
Tulun, *Russia* .... **53 D11** 54 32N 100 35 E
Tulungagung, *Indonesia* . **63 H14** 8 5 S 111 54 E
Tuma →, *Nic.* **120 D3** 13 6N 84 35W
Tuma, *Russia* .... **32 E11** 55 10N 40 30 E
Tumacacori △, *U.S.A.* . **109 L8** 31 34N 111 3W
Tumaco, *Colombia* ... **124 C3** 1 50N 78 45W
Tumatumari, *Guyana* .. **124 B7** 5 20N 58 55W
Tumba, *Sweden* ...... **10 E11** 59 12N 17 48 E
Tumba, L., *Dem. Rep. of*
the Congo .... **84 E3** 0 50 S 18 0 E
Tumbarumba, *Australia* . **95 F4** 35 44 S 148 0 E
Tumbaya, *Argentina* ... **126 A2** 23 50 S 65 26W
Tumbes, *Peru* .... **124 D2** 3 37 S 80 27W
Tumbur, *Sudan* ...... **81 G3** 4 20N 31 34 E
Tumbwe, *Dem. Rep. of*
the Congo .... **87 E2** 11 25 S 27 15 E
Tumby Bay, *Australia* .. **95 E2** 34 21 S 136 8 E
Tumd Youqi, *China* ... **56 D6** 40 30N 110 30 E
Tumen, *China* .... **57 C15** 43 0N 129 50 E
Tumen Jiang →, *China* . **57 C16** 42 20N 130 35 E
Tumeremo, *Venezuela* .. **124 B6** 7 18N 61 30W
Tumkur, *India* .... **66 N10** 13 18N 77 6 E
Tump, *Pakistan* ...... **66 F3** 26 7N 62 16 E
Tumpat, *Malaysia* .... **65 J4** 6 11N 102 10 E
Tumu, *Ghana* **82 C4** 10 56N 1 56W
Tumucumaque, Serra,
Brazil **125 C8** 2 0N 55 0W
Tumut, *Australia* ..... **95 F4** 35 16 S 148 13 E
Tumwater, *U.S.A.* **110 C4** 47 1N 122 54W
Tuna, *India* .... **68 H4** 22 59N 70 5 E
Tunadal, *Sweden* ..... **10 B11** 62 26N 17 22 E
Tunapuna, *Trin. & Tob.* . **125 K15** 10 38N 61 24W
Tunas de Zaza, *Cuba* .. **120 B4** 21 39N 79 34W
Tunbridge Wells =
Royal Tunbridge
Wells, *U.K.* .... **15 F8** 51 7N 0 16 E
Tunçbilek, *Turkey* .... **47 B11** 39 37N 29 29 E
Tunceli, *Turkey* ...... **73 C8** 39 6N 39 31 E
Tuncurry, *Australia* ... **95 E5** 32 17 S 152 29 E
Tundla, *India* .... **68 F8** 27 12N 78 17 E
Tundubai, *Sudan* ..... **80 D2** 18 36N 28 35 E
Tunduru, *Tanzania* ... **87 E4** 11 8 S 37 25 E
Tundzha →, *Bulgaria* .. **45 E10** 41 40N 26 35 E
Tungabhadra →, *India* . **66 M11** 15 57N 78 15 E
Tungaru, *Sudan* ..... **81 E3** 10 9N 30 52 E
Tungla, *Nic.* **120 D3** 13 24N 84 21W
Tungsha Tao = Dongsha
Dao, *China* .... **59 G11** 20 45N 116 43 E
Tungshih, *Taiwan* .... **59 E13** 24 12N 120 43 E
Tungsten, *Canada* **102 A3** 61 57N 128 16W
Tunguska,
Nizhnyaya →, *Russia* . **53 C9** 65 48N 88 4 E
Tunguska,
Podkamennaya →,
Russia .... **53 C10** 61 50N 90 13 E
Tunica, *U.S.A.* **113 H9** 34 41N 90 23W
Tunis, *Tunisia* .... **78 A7** 36 50N 10 11 E
Tunis ✕ (TUN), *Tunisia* . **42 F3** 36 52N 10 14 E
Tunisia ■, *Africa* .... **78 B6** 33 30N 9 10 E
Tunja, *Colombia* **124 B4** 5 33N 73 25W
Tunkhannock, *U.S.A.* .. **117 E9** 41 32N 75 57W
Tunliu, *China* .... **56 F7** 36 13N 112 52 E
Tunnel Creek △,
Australia .... **92 C4** 17 41 S 125 18 E
Tunnsjøen, *Norway* ... **8 D15** 64 45N 13 25 E
Tunø, *Denmark* ...... **11 J4** 55 57N 10 27 E
Tunungayualok I.,
Canada **105 A7** 56 0N 61 0W
Tunuyán, *Argentina* ... **126 C2** 33 35 S 69 0W
Tunuyán →, *Argentina* . **126 C2** 33 33 S 67 30W
Tuo Jiang →, *China* ... **58 C5** 28 50N 105 35 E
Tuolumne, *U.S.A.* **110 H6** 37 58N 120 15W
Tuolumne →, *U.S.A.* .. **110 H5** 37 36N 121 13W
Tūp Āghāj, *Iran* ..... **70 B5** 36 3N 47 50 E
Tupã, *Brazil* .... **127 A5** 21 57 S 50 28W
Tupelo, *U.S.A.* **115 H1** 34 16N 88 43W
Tupik, *Russia* .... **32 E7** 55 42N 33 22 E
Tupinambaranas, *Brazil* . **124 D7** 3 0 S 58 0W
Tupiza, *Bolivia* ...... **126 A2** 21 30 S 65 40W
Tupižnica, *Serbia & M.* . **44 C6** 43 43N 22 10 E
Tupman, *U.S.A.* **111 K7** 35 18N 119 21W
Tupper, *Canada* **102 B4** 55 32N 120 1W
Tupper Lake, *U.S.A.* .. **117 B10** 44 14N 74 28W
Tupungato, Cerro,
S. Amer. .... **126 C2** 33 15 S 69 50W
Tuquan, *China* .... **57 B11** 45 18N 121 38 E
Túquerres, *Colombia* .. **124 C3** 1 5N 77 37W
Tura, *Russia* .... **53 C11** 64 20N 100 17 E
Turabah, Ḥa'il,
Si. Arabia .... **70 D4** 28 20N 43 15 E
Turabah, *Makkah,*
Si. Arabia .... **80 C5** 21 15N 41 34 E
Turan, *Iran* .... **71 C8** 35 39N 56 42 E
Turan, *Russia* .... **53 D10** 51 55N 95 0 E
Ţurayf, *Si. Arabia* .... **70 D3** 31 41N 38 39 E
Turbacz, *Poland* ..... **31 J7** 49 30N 20 8 E
Turbe, *Bos.-H.* ...... **28 F2** 44 15N 17 35 E
Turčianske Teplice,
Slovak Rep. ...... **27 C11** 48 52N 18 52 E
Turcoaia, *Romania* ... **29 E13** 45 7N 28 11 E
Turda, *Romania* ..... **29 D8** 46 34N 23 47 E
Turek, *Poland* .... **31 F5** 52 3N 18 30 E
Turen, *Venezuela* **124 B5** 9 17N 69 6W
Turfan = Turpan, *China* . **60 B3** 43 58N 89 10 E
Turfan Basin = Turpan
Hami, *China* ...... **50 E12** 42 40N 89 25 E
Turfan Depression =
Turpan Hami, *China* . **50 E12** 42 40N 89 25 E

Turgeon →, *Canada* .. **104 C4** 50 0N 78 56W
Türgovishte, *Bulgaria* .. **45 C10** 43 17N 26 38 E
Turgut, *Turkey* ...... **47 D10** 37 22N 28 4 E
Turgutlu, *Turkey* ..... **47 C9** 38 30N 27 43 E
Turgwe →, *Zimbabwe* . **89 C5** 21 31 S 32 15 E
Turhal, *Turkey* .... **72 B7** 40 24N 36 5 E
Turia →, *Spain* **39 F4** 39 27N 0 19W
Turiaçu, *Brazil* ...... **125 D9** 1 40 S 45 19W
Turiaçu →, *Brazil* .... **125 D9** 1 36 S 45 19W
Turiec →, *Slovak Rep.* . **27 B11** 49 7N 18 55 E
Turin = Torino, *Italy* .. **40 C4** 45 3N 7 40 E
Turka, *Ukraine* ...... **31 J10** 49 10N 23 2 E
Turkana, L., *Africa* ... **86 B4** 3 30N 36 5 E
Türkeli, *Turkey* ...... **45 F11** 40 30N 27 30 E
Turkestan = Türkistan,
Kazakhstan .... **52 E7** 43 17N 68 16 E
Türkeve, *Hungary* .... **28 C5** 47 6N 20 44 E
Turkey ■, *Eurasia* ... **72 C7** 39 0N 36 0 E
Turkey Creek, *Australia* . **92 C4** 17 2 S 128 12 E
Turki, *Russia* .... **34 D6** 52 0N 43 15 E
Türkistan, *Kazakhstan* . **52 E7** 43 17N 68 16 E
Türkmenbashi,
Turkmenistan ...... **52 E6** 40 5N 53 5 E
Turkmenistan ■, *Asia* . **52 F6** 39 0N 59 0 E
Türkmenli, *Turkey* .... **47 B8** 39 45N 26 30 E
Türkoğlu, *Turkey* .... **72 D7** 37 23N 36 50 E
Turks & Caicos Is. ☑,
W. Indies **121 B5** 21 20N 71 20W
Turks Island Passage,
W. Indies **121 B5** 21 30N 71 30W
Turku, *Finland* ...... **9 F20** 60 30N 22 19 E
Turkwel →, *Kenya* ... **86 B4** 3 6N 36 6 E
Turlock, *U.S.A.* **110 H6** 37 30N 120 51W
Turnagain →, *Canada* . **102 B3** 59 12N 127 35W
Turnagain, C., *N.Z.* ... **91 J6** 40 28 S 176 38 E
Turneffe Is., *Belize* ... **119 D7** 17 20N 87 50W
Turner, *U.S.A.* **108 B9** 48 51N 108 24W
Turner Pt., *Australia* .. **94 A1** 11 47 S 133 32 E
Turner Valley, *Canada* . **102 C6** 50 40N 114 17W
Turners Falls, *U.S.A.* .. **117 D12** 42 36N 72 33W
Turnhout, *Belgium* ... **17 C4** 51 19N 4 57 E
Türnitz, *Austria* ...... **26 D8** 47 55N 15 29 E
Turnor L., *Canada* **103 B7** 56 35N 108 35W
Turnov, *Czech Rep.* ... **26 A8** 50 34N 15 10 E
Turnovo = Veliko
Tŭrnovo, *Bulgaria* .. **45 C9** 43 5N 25 41 E
Turnu Măgurele,
Romania .... **29 G9** 43 46N 24 56 E
Turnu Roșu, P.,
Romania .... **29 E9** 45 33N 24 17 E
Turobin, *Poland* ..... **31 H9** 50 50N 22 44 E
Turpan, *China* .... **60 B3** 43 58N 89 10 E
Turpan Hami, *China* .. **50 E12** 42 40N 89 25 E
Turrës, Kala e, *Albania* . **44 E3** 41 10N 19 28 E
Turriff, *U.K.* **13 D6** 57 32N 2 27W
Tursāq, *Iraq* .... **70 C5** 33 27N 45 47 E
Tursi, *Italy* .... **43 B9** 40 15N 16 15 E
Turtle Head I., *Australia* . **94 A3** 10 56 S 142 37 E
Turtle Is., *S. Leone* ... **82 D2** 7 40N 13 50W
Turtle L., *Canada* **103 C7** 53 36N 108 38W
Turtle Lake, *U.S.A.* ... **112 B4** 47 31N 100 53W
Turtleford, *Canada* ... **103 C7** 53 23N 108 57W
Turuépano △, *Venezuela* . **121 D7** 10 34N 62 43W
Turukhansk, *Russia* ... **53 C9** 65 21N 88 5 E
Turzovka, *Slovak Rep.* . **27 B11** 49 25N 18 35 E
Tuscaloosa, *U.S.A.* ... **115 J2** 33 12N 87 34W
Tuscánia, *Italy* ...... **41 F8** 42 25N 11 52 E
Tuscany = Toscana □,
Italy .... **40 E8** 43 25N 11 0 E
Tuscarawas →, *U.S.A.* . **116 F3** 40 24N 81 25W
Tuscarora Mt., *U.S.A.* . **116 F7** 40 55N 77 55W
Tuscola, *Ill., U.S.A.* ... **114 F1** 39 48N 88 17W
Tuscola, *Tex., U.S.A.* .. **113 J5** 32 12N 99 48W
Tuscumbia, *U.S.A.* ... **115 H2** 34 44N 87 42W
Tuskegee, *U.S.A.* **115 J3** 32 25N 85 42W
Tustin, *U.S.A.* **111 M9** 33 44N 117 49W
Tuszyn, *Poland* ...... **31 G6** 51 36N 19 33 E
Tutak, *Turkey* .... **73 C10** 39 31N 42 46 E
Tutayev, *Russia* ...... **32 D10** 57 53N 39 32 E
Tuticorin, *India* ...... **66 Q11** 8 50N 78 12 E
Tutin, *Serbia & M.* .... **44 D4** 42 58N 20 20 E
Tutóia, *Brazil* .... **125 D10** 2 45 S 42 20W
Tutong, *Brunei* ...... **62 D4** 4 47N 114 40 E
Tutova →, *Romania* .. **29 D12** 46 17N 27 30 E
Tutrakan, *Bulgaria* ... **45 B10** 44 2N 26 40 E
Tuttle Creek L., *U.S.A.* . **112 F6** 39 22N 96 40W
Tuttlingen, *Germany* .. **25 H4** 47 58N 8 48 E
Tutuala, *E. Timor* .... **63 F7** 8 25 S 127 15 E
Tutuila, *Amer. Samoa* . **91 B13** 14 19 S 170 50W
Tutume, *Botswana* ... **85 J5** 20 30 S 27 5 E
Tutun, *Egypt* .... **80 J7** 29 9N 30 46 E
Tututepec, *Mexico* ... **119 D5** 16 9N 97 38W
Tuva □, *Russia* ...... **53 D10** 51 30N 95 0 E
Tuvalu ■, *Pac. Oc.* ... **96 H9** 8 0 S 178 0 E
Tuxer Alpen, *Austria* .. **26 D4** 47 10N 11 45 E
Tuxpan, *Mexico* **119 C5** 20 58N 97 23W
Tuxtla Gutiérrez,
Mexico **119 D6** 16 50N 93 10W
Tuy = Tui, *Spain* **36 C2** 42 3N 8 39W
Tuy An, *Vietnam* ..... **64 F7** 13 17N 109 16 E
Tuy Duc, *Vietnam* .... **65 F6** 12 15N 107 27 E
Tuy Hoa, *Vietnam* ... **64 F7** 13 5N 109 10 E
Tuy Phong, *Vietnam* .. **65 G7** 11 14N 108 43 E
Tuya L., *Canada* **102 B2** 59 7N 130 35W
Tuyen Hoa, *Vietnam* .. **64 D6** 17 50N 106 10 E
Tuyen Quang, *Vietnam* . **58 G5** 21 50N 105 10 E
Tüysarkān, *Iran* ..... **71 C6** 34 33N 48 27 E
Tuz Gölü, *Turkey* .... **72 C5** 38 42N 33 18 E
Ţūz Khurmātū =
Tozkhurmato, *Iraq* .. **70 C5** 34 56N 44 38 E
Tuzi, *Serbia & M.* .... **44 D3** 42 22N 19 20 E
Tuzigoot △, *U.S.A.* ... **109 J7** 34 46N 112 2W
Tuzla, *Bos.-H.* .... **28 F3** 44 34N 18 41 E
Tuzlov →, *Russia* .... **35 J10** 47 17N 39 57 E
Tuzluca, *Turkey* ...... **73 B10** 40 3N 43 39 E
Tuzly, ... **29 E16** 45 54N 30 5 E
Tvååker, *Sweden* ..... **11 G6** 57 4N 12 25 E
Tvardița, *Moldova* ... **29 D13** 46 11N 28 27 E
Tver, *Russia* .... **32 D8** 56 55N 35 55 E
Tvrdošovce, *Slovak Rep.* . **27 C11** 48 6N 18 4 E
Tvrditsa, *Bulgaria* .... **45 D10** 42 42N 25 55 E
Twain, *U.S.A.* **110 E5** 40 1N 121 3W
Twain Harte, *U.S.A.* .. **110 G6** 38 2N 120 14W
Twardogóra, *Poland* .. **31 G4** 51 23N 17 28 E
Tweed →, *U.K.* ..... **14 B7** 55 42N 2 10 E
Tweed, *Canada* **114 B7** 44 29N 77 19W
Tweed →, *U.K.* **13 F6** 55 45N 2 0W
Tweed Heads, *Australia* . **95 D5** 28 10 S 153 31 E
Tweedsmuir △, *Canada* . **102 C3** 53 0N 126 20W
Twentynine Palms,
U.S.A. **111 L10** 34 8N 116 3W
Twillingate, *Canada* ... **105 C9** 49 42N 54 45W
Twin Bridges, *U.S.A.* .. **108 D7** 45 33N 112 20W
Twin Falls, *Canada* ... **105 B7** 53 30N 64 32W
Twin Falls, *U.S.A.* **108 E6** 42 34N 114 28W
Twin Valley, *U.S.A.* .. **112 B6** 47 16N 96 16W
Twinsburg, *U.S.A.* ... **116 E3** 41 18N 81 26W

Twistringen, *Germany* . **24 C4** 52 48N 8 37 E
Twitchell Reservoir,
U.S.A. **111 L6** 34 59N 120 19W
Two Harbors, *U.S.A.* .. **112 B9** 47 2N 91 40W
Two Hills, *Canada* **102 C6** 53 43N 111 52W
Two Rivers, *U.S.A.* ... **114 C2** 44 9N 87 34W
Two Rocks, *Australia* . **93 F2** 31 30 S 115 35 E
Twofold B., *Australia* .. **95 F4** 37 8 S 149 59 E
Tyachiv, *Ukraine* ..... **33 H2** 48 1N 23 35 E
Tychy, *Poland* .... **31 H5** 50 9N 18 59 E
Tyczyn, *Poland* ...... **31 J9** 49 58N 22 2 E
Tykocin, *Poland* ..... **31 E9** 53 13N 22 46 E
Tyler, *Minn., U.S.A.* .. **112 C6** 44 18N 96 8W
Tyler, *Tex., U.S.A.* ... **113 J7** 32 21N 95 18W
Tyligul →, *Ukraine* ... **33 J6** 46 34N 30 57 E
Tymanivka, *Ukraine* .. **29 B13** 48 34N 28 52 E
Tŷn nad Vltavou,
Czech Rep. .... **26 B7** 49 13N 14 26 E
Tynda, *Russia* .... **53 D13** 55 10N 124 43 E
Tyndall, *U.S.A.* **112 D6** 43 0N 97 50W
Tyne →, *U.K.* **14 C6** 54 59N 1 32W
Tyne & Wear □, *U.K.* . **14 B6** 55 6N 1 17W
Tynemouth, *U.K.* **14 B6** 55 1N 1 26W
Tyre = Sūr, *Lebanon* .. **74 B4** 33 19N 35 16 E
Tyresta △, *Sweden* ... **10 E12** 59 12N 18 14 E
Tyrifjorden, *Norway* .. **9 F14** 60 2N 10 8 E
Tyringe, *Sweden* ..... **11 H7** 56 9N 13 35 E
Tyrnyauz, *Russia* ..... **35 J6** 43 21N 42 45 E
Tyrol = Tirol □, *Austria* . **26 D3** 47 3N 10 43 E
Tyrone, *U.S.A.* **116 F6** 40 40N 78 14W
Tyrone □, *U.K.* **12 B4** 54 38N 7 11W
Tyrrell →, *Australia* .. **95 F3** 35 26 S 142 51 E
Tyrrell, L., *Australia* ... **95 F3** 35 20 S 142 50 E
Tyrrell L., *Canada* **103 A7** 63 7N 105 27W
Tyrrhenian Sea,
Medit. Sea .... **6 G8** 40 0N 12 30 E
Tysfjorden, *Norway* ... **8 B17** 68 7N 16 25 E
Tysmenytsya, *Ukraine* . **29 B9** 48 54N 24 51 E
Tystberga, *Sweden* ... **11 F11** 58 51N 17 15 E
Tytuvėnai, *Lithuania* .. **30 C10** 55 36N 23 12 E
Tyub Karagan, Mys,
Kazakhstan .... **35 H10** 44 40N 50 19 E
Tyuleni, Ostrova,
Kazakhstan .... **35 H10** 45 2N 50 16 E
Tyuleniy, *Russia* ..... **35 H8** 44 28N 47 30 E
Tyuleniy, Mys,
Azerbaijan .... **35 K10** 40 12N 50 22 E
Tyumen, *Russia* ..... **52 D7** 57 11N 65 29 E
Tywi →, *U.K.* **15 F3** 51 48N 4 21W
Tywyn, *U.K.* **15 E3** 52 35N 4 5W
Tzaneen, *S. Africa* ... **89 C5** 23 47 S 30 9 E
Tzermiádhes, *Greece* . **49 D7** 35 12N 25 29 E
Tzoumérka, Óros,
Greece .... **46 B3** 39 30N 21 26 E
Tzukong = Zigong,
China .... **58 C5** 29 15N 104 48 E

U

U Taphao, *Thailand* ... **64 F3** 12 35N 101 0 E
U.S.A. = United States
of America ■,
N. Amer. **106 C7** 37 0N 96 0W
U.S. Virgin Is. ☑,
W. Indies .... **121 e** 18 20N 65 0W
Uatumã →, *Brazil* ... **124 D7** 2 26 S 57 37W
Uaupés, *Brazil* ...... **124 D5** 0 8 S 67 5W
Uaupés →, *Brazil* **124 C5** 0 2N 67 16W
Uaxactún, *Guatemala* . **120 C2** 17 25N 89 29W
Ub, *Serbia & M.* ..... **44 B4** 44 28N 20 6 E
Ubá, *Brazil* .... **127 A7** 21 8 S 43 0W
Ubaitaba, *Nigeria* .... **83 C7** 10 29N 13 13 E
Ubaitaba, *Brazil* ..... **125 F11** 14 18 S 39 20W
Ubangi = Oubangi →,
Dem. Rep. of
the Congo .... **84 E3** 0 30 S 17 50 E
Ubauro, *Pakistan* .... **68 E3** 28 15N 69 45 E
Ubaye →, *France* .... **21 D10** 44 28N 6 18 E
Ubayyiḍ, W. al →, *Iraq* . **70 C4** 32 34N 43 48 E
Ube, *Japan* .... **55 H5** 33 56N 131 15 E
Úbeda, *Spain* **37 G7** 38 3N 3 23W
Uberaba, *Brazil* ..... **125 G9** 19 50 S 47 55W
Uberlândia, *Brazil* .... **125 G9** 19 0 S 48 20W
Überlingen, *Germany* . **25 H5** 47 46N 9 10 E
Ubiaja, *Nigeria* ...... **83 D6** 6 41N 6 22 E
Ubin, Pulau, *Singapore* . **65 d** 1 25N 103 56 E
Ubolratna Res.,
Thailand .... **64 D4** 16 45N 102 30 E
Ubon Ratchathani,
Thailand .... **64 E5** 15 15N 104 50 E
Ubondo, *Dem. Rep. of*
the Congo .... **86 C2** 0 55 S 25 42 E
Ubort →, *Belarus* .... **33 F5** 52 6N 28 30 E
Ubrique, *Spain* **37 J5** 36 41N 5 27W
Ubud, *Indonesia* ..... **63 J18** 8 30 S 115 16 E
Ubundu, *Dem. Rep. of*
the Congo .... **86 C2** 0 22 S 25 30 E
Ucayali →, *Peru* ..... **124 D4** 4 30 S 73 30W
Uchab, *Namibia* ..... **88 B2** 19 47 S 17 42 E
Uchiura-Wan, *Japan* .. **54 C10** 42 25N 140 40 E
Uchquduq, *Uzbekistan* . **52 E7** 41 50N 62 50 E
Uchte, *Germany* ..... **24 C4** 52 29N 8 52 E
Uchur →, *Russia* ..... **53 D14** 58 48N 130 35 E
Uckermark, *Germany* .. **24 B9** 53 15N 13 50 E
Ucluelet, *Canada* **102 D3** 48 57N 125 32W
Uda →, *Russia* ...... **53 D14** 54 42N 135 14 E
Udagamandalam, *India* . **66 P10** 11 30N 76 44 E
Udainagar, *India* ..... **68 H7** 22 33N 76 13 E
Udaipur, *India* .... **68 G5** 24 36N 73 44 E
Udaipur Garhi, *Nepal* . **69 F12** 27 0N 86 35 E
Udala, *India* .... **69 J12** 21 35N 86 34 E
Udbina, *Croatia* ..... **41 D12** 44 31N 15 47 E
Uddeholm, *Sweden* ... **10 D7** 60 1N 13 38 E
Uddevalla, *Sweden* ... **11 F5** 58 21N 11 55 E
Uddjaure, *Sweden* ... **8 D17** 65 25N 21 15 E
Uden, *Neths.* .... **17 C5** 51 40N 5 37 E
Udgir, *India* .... **66 K10** 18 25N 77 5 E
Udhampur, *India* ..... **69 C6** 33 0N 75 5 E
Údine, *Italy* .... **41 B10** 46 3N 13 14 E
Udmurtia □, *Russia* ... **34 C9** 57 30N 52 30 E
Udon Thani, *Thailand* . **64 D4** 17 29N 102 46 E
Udupi, *India* .... **66 N9** 13 25N 74 42 E
Udvoy Balkan, *Bulgaria* . **45 D11** 42 50N 26 50 E
Udzungwa △, *Tanzania* . **86 D4** 7 52 S 36 35 E
Udzungwa Range,
Tanzania .... **87 D4** 9 30 S 35 10 E
Ueckermünde, *Germany* . **24 B10** 53 44N 14 3 E
Ueda, *Japan* .... **55 F9** 36 24N 138 16 E
Uedineniya, Ostrov,
Russia .... **4 B12** 78 0N 85 0 E
Uele →, *Dem. Rep. of*
the Congo .... **84 D4** 3 45N 24 45 E

Uelen, *Russia* **53 C19** 66 10N 170 0W
Uelzen, *Germany* .... **24 C6** 52 57N 10 32 E
Uetersen, *Germany* ... **24 B5** 53 40N 9 40 E
Uetze, *Germany* ..... **24 C6** 52 28N 10 11 E
Ufa, *Russia* .... **52 D6** 54 45N 55 55 E
Uffenheim, *Germany* .. **25 F6** 49 33N 10 14 E
Ugab →, *Namibia* .... **88 C1** 20 55 S 13 30 E
Ugalla →, *Tanzania* .. **86 D3** 5 8 S 30 42 E
Ugalla River △,
Tanzania .... **86 D3** 5 50 S 31 54 E
Uganda ■, *Africa* .... **86 B3** 2 0N 32 0 E
Ugento, *Italy* .... **43 C11** 39 56N 18 10 E
Ugep, *Nigeria* .... **83 D6** 5 53N 8 2 E
Ughelli, *Nigeria* ...... **83 D6** 5 33N 6 0 E
Ugie, *S. Africa* .... **89 E4** 31 10 S 28 13 E
Uğijar, *Spain* **37 J7** 36 58N 3 7W
Ugine, *France* .... **21 C10** 45 45N 6 25 E
Uglegorsk, *Russia* .... **53 E15** 49 5N 142 2 E
Uglich, *Russia* .... **32 D10** 57 33N 38 20 E
Ugljan, *Croatia* ...... **41 D12** 44 12N 15 10 E
Ugljane, *Croatia* ..... **41 E13** 43 35N 16 46 E
Ugra →, *Russia* ..... **32 E9** 54 30N 36 7 E
Uğurlu, *Bulgaria* ..... **45 C8** 43 6N 24 26 E
Uh →, *Slovak Rep.* .. **27 C15** 48 37N 22 0 E
Uherské Hradiště,
Czech Rep. .... **27 B10** 49 4N 17 30 E
Uherský Brod,
Czech Rep. .... **27 B10** 49 1N 17 40 E
Úhlava →, *Czech Rep.* . **26 B6** 49 45N 13 24 E
Uhlenhorst, *Namibia* .. **88 C2** 23 45 S 17 55 E
Uhniv, *Ukraine* ...... **31 H10** 50 22N 23 45 E
Uhrichsville, *U.S.A.* ... **116 F3** 40 24N 81 21W
Uíbhist a Deas = South
Uist, *U.K.* **13 D1** 57 20N 7 15W
Uíbhist a Tuath = North
Uist, *U.K.* **13 D1** 57 40N 7 15W
Uig, *U.K.* **13 D2** 57 35N 6 21W
Uíge, *Angola* .... **84 F2** 7 30 S 14 40 E
Uijŏngbu, *S. Korea* ... **57 F14** 37 48N 127 0 E
Ŭiju, *N. Korea* .... **57 D13** 40 15N 124 35 E
Uinta Mts., *U.S.A.* **108 F8** 40 45N 110 30W
Uis, *Namibia* .... **88 C1** 21 8 S 14 49 E
Uitenhage, *S. Africa* .. **88 E4** 33 40 S 25 28 E
Uithuizen, *Neths.* .... **17 A6** 53 24N 6 41 E
Ujazd, *Poland* .... **31 H5** 50 23N 18 21 E
Újfehértó, *Hungary* ... **28 C6** 47 49N 21 41 E
Ujh →, *India* .... **68 C6** 32 10N 75 18 E
Ujhani, *India* .... **69 F8** 28 0N 79 6 E
Uji-guntō, *Japan* ..... **55 J4** 31 15N 129 25 E
Ujjain, *India* .... **68 H6** 23 9N 75 43 E
Ujście, *Poland* .... **31 E3** 53 3N 16 45 E
Újszász, *Hungary* .... **28 C5** 47 19N 20 7 E
Ujung Pandang,
Indonesia .... **63 F5** 5 10 S 119 20 E
Uka, *Russia* .... **53 D17** 57 50N 162 0 E
Ukara I., *Tanzania* .... **86 C3** 1 50 S 33 0 E
Uke-Shima, *Japan* .... **55 K4** 28 2N 129 14 E
Ukerewe I., *Tanzania* .. **86 C3** 2 0 S 33 0 E
Ukholovo, *Russia* .... **34 D5** 53 47N 40 30 E
Ukhrul, *India* .... **67 G19** 25 10N 94 25 E
Ukhta, *Russia* .... **52 C6** 63 34N 53 41 E
Ukiah, *U.S.A.* **110 F3** 39 9N 123 13W
Ukmergė, *Lithuania* ... **9 J21** 55 15N 24 45 E
Ukraine ■, *Europe* ... **33 H7** 49 0N 32 0 E
Ukwi, *Botswana* ..... **88 C3** 23 29 S 20 30 E
Ulaan-Uul, *Mongolia* .. **56 B6** 44 13N 111 10 E
Ulaanbaatar, *Mongolia* . **53 E11** 47 55N 106 53 E
Ulaangom, *Mongolia* .. **60 A4** 50 5N 92 10 E
Ulaanjirem, *Mongolia* . **56 B3** 45 5N 105 30 E
Ulamba, *Dem. Rep. of*
the Congo .... **87 D1** 9 3 S 23 38 E
Ulan Bator =
Ulaanbaatar,
Mongolia .... **53 E11** 47 55N 106 53 E
Ulan Erge, *Russia* .... **35 G7** 46 19N 44 53 E
Ulan Khol, *Russia* .... **35 H8** 45 18N 47 4 E
Ulan Ude, *Russia* .... **53 D11** 51 45N 107 40 E
Ulanów, *Poland* ...... **31 H9** 50 30N 22 16 E
Ulaş, *Sivas, Turkey* ... **72 C7** 39 26N 37 2 E
Ulaş, *Tekirdağ, Turkey* . **45 E11** 41 14N 27 42 E
Ulaya, *Morogoro,*
Tanzania .... **86 D4** 7 3 S 36 55 E
Ulaya, *Tabora, Tanzania* . **86 C3** 4 25 S 33 30 E
Ulcinj, *Serbia & M.* ... **44 E3** 41 58N 19 10 E
Ulco, *S. Africa* .... **88 D3** 28 21 S 24 15 E
Ule älv = Oulujoki →,
Finland .... **8 D21** 65 1N 25 30 E
Ule träsk = Oulujärvi,
Finland .... **8 D22** 64 25N 27 15 E
Uleåborg = Oulu,
Finland .... **8 D21** 65 1N 25 29 E
Ulefoss, *Norway* ..... **9 G13** 59 17N 9 16 E
Ulëz, *Albania* .... **44 E3** 41 46N 19 54 E
Ulfborg, *Denmark* .... **11 H2** 56 16N 8 20 E
Ulhasnagar, *India* .... **66 K8** 19 15N 73 10 E
Uliastay, *Mongolia* ... **60 B4** 47 56N 97 28 E
Uljma, *Serbia & M.* ... **28 E6** 45 2N 21 10 E
Ulla →, *Spain* **36 C2** 42 39N 8 44W
Ulladulla, *Australia* ... **95 F5** 35 21 S 150 29 E
Ullapool, *U.K.* **13 D3** 57 54N 5 9W
Ullared, *Sweden* ..... **11 G6** 57 8N 12 42 E
Ulldecona, *Spain* .... **38 E5** 40 36N 0 20 E
Ullswater, *U.K.* **14 C5** 54 34N 2 52W
Ullŭng-do, *S. Korea* .. **55 F5** 37 30N 130 30 E
Ulmarra, *Australia* ... **95 E5** 29 37 S 153 4 E
Ulmeni, *Buzău,*
Romania .... **29 E11** 45 4N 26 40 E
Ulmeni, *Maramureș,*
Romania .... **29 C8** 47 28N 23 18 E
Ulongué, *Mozam.* .... **87 E3** 14 37 S 34 19 E
Ulricehamn, *Sweden* .. **11 G7** 57 46N 13 26 E
Ulsan, *S. Korea* ...... **57 G15** 35 20N 129 15 E
Ulsberg, *Norway* ..... **10 B3** 62 45N 9 59 E
Ulster □, *U.K.* **12 B5** 54 35N 6 30W
Ulstrem, *Bulgaria* .... **45 D10** 42 1N 26 27 E
Ulubat Gölü, *Turkey* .. **45 F12** 40 9N 28 35 E
Ulubey, *Turkey* ...... **47 C11** 38 5N 29 18 E
Uluborlu, *Turkey* ..... **47 C12** 38 4N 30 28 E
Uluçınar, *Turkey* ..... **72 D6** 36 37N 35 55 E
Uludağ, *Turkey* ...... **45 F13** 40 4N 29 13 E
Uludağ △, *Turkey* .... **45 F13** 40 9N 29 12 E
Uluguru Mts., *Tanzania* . **86 D4** 7 15 S 37 40 E
Ulukışla, *Turkey* ..... **72 D6** 37 33N 34 28 E
Ulungur He →, *China* . **60 B3** 47 1N 87 24 E
Uluru = Ayers Rock,
Australia .... **93 E5** 25 23 S 131 5 E
Uluru-Kata Tjuta △,
Australia .... **93 E5** 25 19 S 131 1 E
Ulutau, *Kazakhstan* ... **52 E7** 48 39N 67 1 E
Uluwatu, *Indonesia* ... **63 K18** 8 50 S 115 5 E
Ulva, *U.K.* **13 E2** 56 29N 6 13W
Ulverston, *U.K.* **14 C4** 54 13N 3 5W
Ulverstone, *Australia* .. **95 G4** 41 11 S 146 11 E
Ulya, *Russia* .... **53 D15** 59 10N 142 0 E

Ulyanovo, Russia 30 D9 54 50N 22 6 E
Ulyanovsk = Simbirsk, Russia 34 C9 54 20N 48 25 E
Ulyasutay = Uliastay, Mongolia 60 B4 47 56N 97 28 E
Ulysses, U.S.A. 113 G4 37 35N 101 22W
Umag, Croatia 41 C10 45 26N 13 31 E
Umala, Bolivia 124 G5 17 25 S 68 5W
Uman, Ukraine 33 H6 48 40N 30 12 E
Umaria, India 67 H12 23 35N 80 50 E
Umarkot, Pakistan 68 G6 25 15N 69 40 E
Umarpada, India 68 J5 21 27N 73 30 E
Umatilla, U.S.A. 108 D4 45 55N 119 21W
Umbagog L., U.S.A. 117 B13 44 46N 71 3W
Umbakumba, Australia 94 A2 13 47 S 136 50 E
Umbértide, Italy 41 E9 43 18N 12 20 E
Umbrella Mts., N.Z. 91 L2 45 35 S 169 5 E
Umbria □, Italy 41 F9 42 53N 12 30 E
Umeå, Sweden 8 E19 63 45N 20 20 E
Umeälven →, Sweden 8 E19 63 45N 20 20 E
Umera, Indonesia 63 E7 0 12 S 129 37 E
Umfolozi ⌓, S. Africa 89 D5 28 18 S 31 50 E
Umfuli →, Zimbabwe 87 F2 17 30 S 29 23 E
Umfurudzi ⌓, Zimbabwe 87 F3 17 6 S 31 40 E
Umgusa, Zimbabwe 87 F2 19 29 S 27 52 E
Umim Urūmah, Si. Arabia 80 B4 25 43N 36 35 E
Umka, Serbia & M. 44 B4 44 40N 20 19 E
Umkomaas, S. Africa 89 E5 30 13 S 30 48 E
Umlazi, S. Africa 85 L6 29 59 S 30 54 E
Umm ad Daraj, J., Jordan 74 C4 32 18N 35 48 E
Umm al Qaywayn, U.A.E. 71 E7 25 30N 55 35 E
Umm al Qittayn, Jordan 74 C5 32 18N 36 40 E
Umm Arda, Sudan 81 D3 15 17N 32 31 E
Umm Bāb, Qatar 71 E6 25 12N 50 48 E
Umm Badr, Sudan 81 E2 14 13N 27 58 E
Umm Baiyud, Sudan 81 E3 12 5N 31 40 E
Umm Bel, Sudan 81 E2 13 35N 28 0 E
Umm Birkah, Si. Arabia 80 B4 27 44N 36 31 E
Umm Boim, Sudan 81 E2 11 43N 25 27 E
Umm Dam, Sudan 81 E3 13 45N 30 59 E
Umm Debi, Sudan 81 E3 14 37N 30 23 E
Umm Dubban, Sudan 81 D3 15 23N 32 52 E
Umm Durman = Omdurmân, Sudan 81 D3 15 40N 32 28 E
Umm el Fahm, Israel 74 C4 32 31N 35 9 E
Umm Gafala, Sudan 81 E2 13 22N 27 15 E
Umm Gimala, Sudan 81 E2 11 27N 28 12 E
Umm Inderaba, Sudan 80 D3 15 58N 30 41 E
Umm Keddada, Sudan 81 E2 13 33N 26 35 E
Umm Koweika, Sudan 81 E3 13 10N 32 16 E
Umm Lajj, Si. Arabia 70 E3 25 0N 37 23 E
Umm Merwa, Sudan 80 D3 18 4N 32 30 E
Umm Qantur, Sudan 81 E3 14 17N 31 22 E
Umm Qurein, Sudan 81 F2 9 58N 28 55 E
Umm Ruwaba, Sudan 81 E3 12 50N 31 20 E
Umm Saiyala, Sudan 81 E3 14 25N 31 10 E
Umm Shanqa, Sudan 81 E2 13 14N 27 14 E
Umm Shutur, Sudan 81 F3 7 17N 33 14 E
Umm Sidr, Sudan 81 E2 14 29N 25 10 E
Umm Zehetir, Egypt 80 J8 28 48N 32 31 E
Umnak I., U.S.A. 100 C3 53 15N 168 20W
Umniati →, Zimbabwe 87 F2 16 49 S 28 45 E
Umpqua →, U.S.A. 108 E1 43 40N 124 12W
Umreth, India 68 H5 22 41N 73 4 E
Umtata, S. Africa 89 E4 31 36 S 28 49 E
Umuahia, Nigeria 83 D6 5 31N 7 26 E
Umuarama, Brazil 127 A5 23 45 S 53 20W
Umurbey, Turkey 45 F10 40 13N 26 36 E
Umvukwe Ra., Zimbabwe 87 F3 16 45 S 30 45 E
Umzimvubu, S. Africa 89 E4 31 38 S 29 33 E
Umzingwane →, Zimbabwe 87 G2 22 12 S 29 56 E
Umzinto, S. Africa 89 E5 30 15 S 30 45 E
Una, India 68 J4 20 46N 71 8 E
Una →, Bos.-H. 41 D13 45 0N 16 20 E
Unac →, Bos.-H. 41 D13 44 30N 16 9 E
Unadilla, U.S.A. 117 D9 42 20N 75 19W
Unalakleet, U.S.A. 100 B3 63 52N 160 47W
Unalaska, U.S.A. 100 C3 53 53N 166 32W
Unalaska I., U.S.A. 100 C3 53 35N 166 50W
'Unayzah, Si. Arabia 70 E4 26 6N 43 58 E
'Unayzah, J., Asia 70 C3 32 12N 39 18 E
Uncastillo, Spain 38 C3 42 21N 1 8W
Uncía, Bolivia 124 G5 18 25 S 66 40W
Uncompahgre Peak, U.S.A. 109 G10 38 4N 107 28W
Uncompahgre Plateau, U.S.A. 109 G9 38 20N 108 15W
Undara Volcanic △, Australia 94 B3 18 14 S 144 41 E
Unden, Sweden 11 F8 58 45N 14 25 E
Underbool, Australia 95 F3 35 10 S 141 51 E
Undersaker, Sweden 10 A7 63 19N 13 21 E
Unecha, Russia 33 F7 52 50N 32 37 E
Ungarie, Australia 95 E4 33 38 S 146 56 E
Ungarra, Australia 95 E2 34 12 S 136 2 E
Ungava, Pén. d', Canada 101 C12 60 0N 74 0W
Ungava B., Canada 101 C13 59 30N 67 30W
Ungeny = Ungheni, Moldova 29 C12 47 11N 27 51 E
Unggi, N. Korea 57 C16 42 16N 130 28 E
Ungheni, Moldova 29 C12 47 11N 27 51 E
Unguala →, Ethiopia 81 F5 6 6N 41 9 E
Ungwana B., Kenya 86 C5 2 40 S 40 20 E
Ungwatiri, Sudan 81 D4 16 52N 36 10 E
Uni, Russia 34 B10 57 46N 51 31 E
União da Vitória, Brazil 127 B5 26 13 S 51 5W
Uničov, Czech Rep. 27 B10 49 46N 17 8 E
Uniejów, Poland 31 G5 51 59N 18 46 E
Unije, Croatia 41 D11 44 40N 14 15 E
Unimak I., U.S.A. 100 C3 54 45N 164 0W
Union, Miss., U.S.A. 113 J10 32 34N 89 7W
Union, Mo., U.S.A. 112 F9 38 27N 91 0W
Union, S.C., U.S.A. 115 H5 34 43N 81 37W
Union City, Calif., U.S.A. 110 H4 37 36N 122 1W
Union City, N.J., U.S.A. 117 F10 40 45N 74 2W
Union City, Pa., U.S.A. 116 E5 41 54N 79 51W
Union City, Tenn., U.S.A. 113 G10 36 26N 89 3W
Union Gap, U.S.A. 108 C3 46 33N 120 28W
Union Springs, U.S.A. 115 J3 32 9N 85 43W
Uniondale, S. Africa 88 E3 33 39 S 23 7 E
Uniontown, U.S.A. 114 F6 39 54N 79 44W
Unionville, U.S.A. 112 E8 40 29N 93 1W
Unirea, Romania 29 F12 44 15N 27 35 E
United Arab Emirates ■, Asia 71 F7 23 50N 54 0 E
United Kingdom ■, Europe 7 E5 53 0N 2 0W
United States of America ■, N. Amer. 106 C7 37 0N 96 0W
Unity, Canada 103 C7 52 30N 109 5W
Universales, Mtes., Spain 38 E3 40 18N 1 33W
University Park, U.S.A. 109 K10 32 17N 106 45W
Unjha, India 68 H5 23 46N 72 24 E
Unna, Germany 24 D3 51 32N 7 42 E
Unnao, India 69 F9 26 35N 80 30 E
Uno, Ilha, Guinea-Biss. 82 C1 11 15N 16 13W
Unsengedsi →, Zimbabwe 87 F3 15 43 S 31 14 E
Unst, U.K. 13 A8 60 44N 0 53W
Unstrut →, Germany 24 D7 51 10N 11 48 E
Unterfranken □, Germany 25 F5 50 0N 10 0 E
Unterschleissheim, Germany 25 G7 48 17N 11 34 E
Unuk →, Canada 102 B2 56 5N 131 3W
Ünye, Turkey 72 B7 41 5N 37 15 E
Unzen-Amakusa △, Japan 55 H5 32 15N 130 10 E
Unzha, Russia 34 A7 58 0N 44 0 E
Unzha →, Russia 34 B6 57 49N 43 47 E
Uozu, Japan 55 F8 36 48N 137 24 E
Upata, Venezuela 124 B6 8 1N 62 24W
Upemba △, Dem. Rep. of the Congo 87 D2 9 0 S 26 35 E
Upemba, L., Dem. Rep. of the Congo 87 D2 8 30 S 26 20 E
Upernavik, Greenland 4 B5 72 49N 56 20W
Upington, S. Africa 88 D3 28 25 S 21 15 E
Upleta, India 68 J4 21 46N 70 16 E
'Upolu, Samoa 91 A13 13 58 S 172 0W
Upper □, Ghana 83 C4 10 30N 1 30W
Upper Alkali L., U.S.A. 108 F3 41 47N 120 8W
Upper Arrow L., Canada 102 C5 50 30N 117 50W
Upper Foster L., Canada 103 B7 56 47N 105 20W
Upper Hutt, N.Z. 91 J5 41 8 S 175 5 E
Upper Klamath L., U.S.A. 108 E3 42 25N 121 55W
Upper Lake, U.S.A. 110 F4 39 10N 122 54W
Upper Manzanilla, Trin. & Tob. 125 K15 10 31N 61 4W
Upper Missouri River Breaks ⌓, U.S.A. 108 C9 47 50N 108 55W
Upper Musquodoboit, Canada 105 C7 45 10N 62 58W
Upper Red L., U.S.A. 112 A7 48 8N 94 45W
Upper Sandusky, U.S.A. 114 E4 40 50N 83 17W
Upper Volta = Burkina Faso ■, Africa 82 C4 12 0N 1 0W
Upphärad, Sweden 11 F6 58 9N 12 19 E
Uppland, Sweden 10 D12 59 59N 17 48 E
Upplands-Väsby, Sweden 10 E11 59 31N 17 54 E
Uppsala, Sweden 10 E11 59 53N 17 38 E
Uppsala län □, Sweden 10 D11 60 0N 17 30 E
Upshi, India 69 C7 33 48N 77 52 E
Upstart, C., Australia 94 B4 19 41 S 147 45 E
Upton, U.S.A. 112 C2 44 6N 104 38W
Uqsuqtuuq = Gjoa Haven, Canada 100 B10 68 38N 95 53W
Ur, Iraq 70 D5 30 55N 46 25 E
Urad Qianqi, China 56 D5 40 40N 108 30 E
Urakawa, Japan 54 C11 42 9N 142 47 E
Ural = Uralskiy □, Russia 52 C7 64 0N 70 0 E
Ural = Zhayyq →, Kazakhstan 52 E6 47 0N 51 48 E
Ural, Australia 95 E4 33 21 S 146 12 E
Ural Mts. = Uralskie Gory, Eurasia 52 D6 60 0N 59 0 E
Uralla, Australia 95 E5 30 37 S 151 29 E
Uralsk = Oral, Kazakhstan 34 E10 51 20N 51 20 E
Uralskie Gory, Eurasia 52 D6 60 0N 59 0 E
Uralskiy □, Russia 52 C7 64 0N 70 0 E
Urambo, Tanzania 86 D3 5 4 S 32 0 E
Urandangi, Australia 94 C2 21 32 S 138 14 E
Uranium City, Canada 103 B7 59 34N 108 37W
Uraricoera →, Brazil 124 C6 3 2N 60 30W
Urawa, Japan 55 G9 35 50N 139 40 E
Uray, Russia 52 C7 60 5N 65 15 E
'Uray'irah, Si. Arabia 71 E6 25 57N 48 53 E
Urbana, Ill., U.S.A. 114 E1 40 7N 88 12W
Urbana, Ohio, U.S.A. 114 E4 40 7N 83 45W
Urbánia, Italy 41 E9 43 40N 12 31 E
Urbel →, Spain 36 C7 42 21N 3 40W
Urbino, Italy 41 E9 43 43N 12 38 E
Urbión, Picos de, Spain 38 C2 42 1N 2 52W
Urcos, Peru 124 F4 13 40 S 71 38W
Urdinarrain, Argentina 126 C4 32 37 S 58 52W
Urdos, France 20 F3 42 51N 0 35W
Urdzhar, Kazakhstan 52 E9 47 5N 81 38 E
Ure →, U.K. 14 C6 54 5N 1 20W
Uren, Russia 34 B7 57 35N 45 55 E
Ures, Mexico 118 B2 29 30N 110 30W
Urewera △, N.Z. 91 H6 38 29 S 177 7 E
Urfa = Sanliurfa, Turkey 70 B3 37 12N 38 50 E
Urganch, Uzbekistan 52 E7 41 40N 60 41 E
Urgench = Urganch, Uzbekistan 52 E7 41 40N 60 41 E
Ürgüp, Turkey 70 B2 38 38N 34 56 E
Uri, India 69 B6 34 8N 74 2 E
Uri □, Switz. 25 J4 46 43N 8 35 E
Uribia, Colombia 124 A4 11 43N 72 16W
Uricani, Romania 28 E8 45 20N 23 9 E
Uriondo, Bolivia 126 A3 21 41 S 64 41W
Urique, Mexico 118 B3 27 13N 107 55W
Urique →, Mexico 118 B3 26 29N 107 58W
Urk, Neths. 17 B5 52 39N 5 36 E
Urkiola △, Spain 38 B3 43 6N 1 2W
Urla, Turkey 47 C8 38 20N 26 47 E
Urlați, Romania 29 F11 44 59N 26 15 E
Urmia = Orūmīyeh, Iran 70 B5 37 40N 45 0 E
Uroševac, Serbia & M. 44 D5 42 23N 21 10 E
Uroyan, Montanas de, Puerto Rico 121 d 18 12N 67 0W
Urshult, Sweden 11 H8 56 31N 14 50 E
Uruaçu, Brazil 125 F9 14 30 S 49 10W
Uruapan, Mexico 118 D4 19 30N 102 0W
Urubamba →, Peru 124 F4 10 43 S 73 48W
Uruçara, Brazil 124 D7 2 32 S 57 45W
Uruçuí, Brazil 125 E10 7 20 S 44 28W
Uruguai →, Brazil 127 B5 26 0 S 53 30W
Uruguaiana, Brazil 126 B4 29 50 S 57 0W
Uruguay ■, S. Amer. 126 C4 32 30 S 56 30W
Uruguay →, S. Amer. 126 C4 34 12 S 58 18W
Urumchi = Ürümqi, China 52 E9 43 45N 87 45 E
Ürümqi, China 52 E9 43 45N 87 45 E
Urup →, Russia 35 H5 45 0N 41 10 E
Urup, Ostrov, Russia 53 E16 46 0N 151 0 E
Uryupinsk, Russia 34 E5 50 45N 41 58 E
Urzhum, Russia 34 B9 57 10N 49 56 E
Urziceni, Romania 29 F11 44 46N 26 42 E
Usa →, Russia 52 C6 66 16N 59 49 E
Uşak, Turkey 47 C11 38 43N 29 28 E
Uşak □, Turkey 47 C11 38 30N 29 0 E
Usakos, Namibia 88 C2 21 54 S 15 31 E
Ušće, Serbia & M. 44 C4 43 30N 20 39 E
Usedom, Germany 24 B10 53 55N 14 2 E
Usedom ⌓, Germany 24 B10 53 55N 14 0 E
Useless Loop, Australia 93 E1 26 8 S 113 23 E
'Usfān, Si. Arabia 80 C4 21 58N 39 27 E
Ush-Tobe, Kazakhstan 52 E8 45 16N 78 0 E
Ushakova, Ostrov, Russia 4 A12 82 0N 80 0 E
Ushakovo, Russia 30 D7 54 37N 20 16 E
Ushant = Ouessant, Î. d', France 18 D1 48 28N 5 6W
Ushashi, Tanzania 86 C3 1 59 S 33 57 E
Ushat, Sudan 81 F2 7 59N 29 28 E
'Ushayrah, Si. Arabia 80 C5 21 46N 40 42 E
Ushibuka, Japan 55 H5 32 11N 130 1 E
Ushuaia, Argentina 128 G3 54 50 S 68 23W
Ushumun, Russia 53 D13 52 47N 126 32 E
Ushytsya →, Ukraine 29 B12 48 35N 27 8 E
Usk, Canada 102 C3 54 38N 128 26W
Usk →, U.K. 15 F5 51 33N 2 58W
Uska, India 69 F10 27 12N 83 7 E
Üsküdar, Turkey 45 F13 41 0N 29 5 E
Uslar, Germany 24 D5 51 39N 9 38 E
Usman, Russia 33 F10 52 5N 39 48 E
Usoke, Tanzania 86 D3 5 8 S 32 24 E
Usolye Sibirskoye, Russia 53 D11 52 48N 103 40 E
Usoro, Nigeria 83 D6 5 33N 6 11 E
Uspallata, P. de, Argentina 126 C2 32 37 S 69 22W
Uspenskiy, Kazakhstan 52 E8 48 41N 72 43 E
Ussel, France 20 C6 45 32N 2 18 E
Usson-du-Poitou, France 20 B4 46 16N 0 31 E
Ussuri →, Asia 54 A7 48 27N 135 0 E
Ussuriysk, Russia 53 E14 43 48N 131 59 E
Ussurka, Russia 54 B6 45 12N 133 31 E
Ust-Bolsheretsk, Russia 53 D16 52 50N 156 15 E
Ust-Buzulukskaya, Russia 34 E6 50 8N 42 11 E
Ust-Chaun, Russia 53 C18 68 47N 170 30 E
Ust-Chorna, Ukraine 29 B8 48 19N 23 56 E
Ust-Donetskiy, Russia 35 G5 47 35N 40 55 E
Ust-Ilimsk, Russia 53 D11 58 3N 102 39 E
Ust-Ishim, Russia 52 D8 57 45N 71 10 E
Ust-Kamchatsk, Russia 53 D17 56 10N 162 28 E
Ust-Kamenogorsk = Öskemen, Kazakhstan 52 E9 50 0N 82 36 E
Ust-Khayryuzovo, Russia 53 D16 57 15N 156 45 E
Ust-Kut, Russia 53 D11 56 50N 105 42 E
Ust-Kuyga, Russia 53 B14 70 1N 135 43 E
Ust-Labinsk, Russia 35 H4 45 15N 39 41 E
Ust-Luga, Russia 32 C5 59 35N 28 20 E
Ust-Maya, Russia 53 C14 60 30N 134 28 E
Ust-Mil, Russia 53 D14 59 40N 133 11 E
Ust-Nera, Russia 53 C15 64 35N 143 15 E
Ust-Nyukzha, Russia 53 D13 56 34N 121 37 E
Ust-Olenek, Russia 53 B12 73 0N 120 5 E
Ust-Omchug, Russia 53 C15 61 9N 149 38 E
Ust-Port, Russia 52 C9 69 40N 84 26 E
Ust-Tsilma, Russia 52 C6 65 28N 52 11 E
Ust Urt = Ustyurt Plateau, Asia 52 E6 44 0N 55 0 E
Ustaritz, France 20 E2 43 24N 1 27W
Ustecký □, Czech Rep. 26 A7 50 30N 14 0 E
Uster, Switz. 25 H4 47 22N 8 43 E
Ústí nad Labem, Czech Rep. 26 A7 50 41N 14 3 E
Ústí nad Orlicí, Czech Rep. 27 B9 49 58N 16 24 E
Ústica, Italy 42 D6 38 42N 13 11 E
Ustinov = Izhevsk, Russia 52 D6 56 51N 53 14 E
Ustka, Poland 30 D3 54 35N 16 55 E
Ustroń, Poland 31 J5 49 43N 18 48 E
Ustrzyki Dolne, Poland 31 J9 49 27N 22 40 E
Ustyluh, Ukraine 31 H11 50 51N 24 10 E
Ustyurt Plateau, Asia 52 E6 44 0N 55 0 E
Ustyuzhna, Russia 32 C9 58 50N 36 32 E
Usu, China 60 B3 44 27N 84 40 E
Usuki, Japan 55 H5 33 8N 131 49 E
Usulután, El Salv. 120 D2 13 25N 88 28W
Usumacinta →, Mexico 119 D6 17 0N 91 0W
Usumbura = Bujumbura, Burundi 86 C2 3 16 S 29 18 E
Usure, Tanzania 86 C3 4 40 S 34 22 E
Usutuo →, Mozam. 89 D5 26 48 S 32 7 E
Uta, Indonesia 63 E9 4 33 S 136 0 E
Utah □, U.S.A. 108 G8 39 20N 111 30W
Utah L., U.S.A. 108 F8 40 10N 111 58W
Utansjö, Sweden 10 B11 62 46N 17 55 E
Utara, Selat, Malaysia 65 c 5 28N 100 20 E
Utarni, India 68 F4 26 5N 71 58 E
Utatlan, Guatemala 120 C1 15 2N 91 11W
Ute Creek →, U.S.A. 113 H3 35 21N 103 50W
Utebo, Spain 38 D3 41 43N 1 0W
Utena, Lithuania 9 J21 55 27N 25 40 E
Utete, Tanzania 86 D4 8 0 S 38 45 E
Uthai Thani, Thailand 64 E3 15 22N 100 3 E
Uthal, Pakistan 68 G2 25 44N 66 40 E
Utiariti, Brazil 124 F7 13 0 S 58 10W
Utica, N.Y., U.S.A. 117 C9 43 6N 75 14W
Utica, Ohio, U.S.A. 116 F2 40 14N 82 27W
Utiel, Spain 39 F3 39 37N 1 11W
Utikuma L., Canada 102 B5 55 50N 115 30W
Utö, Sweden 10 F12 58 56N 18 16 E
Utopia, Australia 94 C1 22 14 S 134 33 E
Utraula, India 69 F10 27 19N 82 25 E
Utrecht, Neths. 17 B5 52 5N 5 8 E
Utrecht, S. Africa 89 D5 27 38 S 30 20 E
Utrecht □, Neths. 17 B5 52 6N 5 7 E
Utrera, Spain 37 H5 37 12N 5 48W
Utsjoki →, Finland 8 B22 69 51N 26 59 E
Utsunomiya, Japan 55 F9 36 30N 139 50 E
Uttar Pradesh □, India 69 F9 27 0N 80 0 E
Uttaradit, Thailand 64 D3 17 36N 100 5 E
Uttaranchal □, India 69 D8 30 0N 79 30 E
Uttoxeter, U.K. 14 E6 52 54N 1 52W
Utuado, Puerto Rico 121 d 18 16N 66 42W
Uummannaq, Greenland 4 B4 77 0N 69 0W
Uummannaq, Greenland 4 B5 70 58N 52 0W
Uummannarsuaq = Nunap Isua, Greenland 101 C15 59 48N 43 55W
Uusikaarlepyy, Finland 8 E20 63 32N 22 31 E
Uusikaupunki, Finland 9 F19 60 47N 21 25 E
Uva, Russia 34 B11 56 59N 52 13 E
Uvac →, Serbia & M. 44 C3 43 35N 19 30 E
Uvalde, U.S.A. 113 L5 29 13N 99 47W
Uvarovo, Russia 34 E6 51 59N 42 14 E
Uvat, Russia 52 D7 59 5N 68 50 E
Uvinza, Tanzania 86 D3 5 5 S 30 24 E
Uvira, Dem. Rep. of the Congo 86 C2 3 22 S 29 3 E
Uvs Nuur, Mongolia 60 A4 50 20N 92 30 E
'Uwairidh, Ḥarrat al, Si. Arabia 70 E3 26 50N 38 0 E
Uwajima, Japan 55 H6 33 10N 132 35 E
Uwanda ⌓, Tanzania 86 D3 7 46 S 32 0 E
Uweinat, Jebel, Sudan 80 C1 21 54N 24 58 E
Uxbridge, Canada 116 B5 44 6N 79 7W
Uxin Qi, China 56 E5 38 50N 109 5 E
Uxmal, Mexico 119 C7 20 22N 89 46W
Üydzin, Mongolia 56 B4 44 9N 107 0 E
Uyo, Nigeria 83 D6 5 1N 7 53 E
Üyüklü Tepe, Turkey 47 D9 37 5N 27 21 E
Uyûn Mûsa, Egypt 74 F1 29 53N 32 40 E
Uyuni, Bolivia 124 H5 20 28 S 66 47W
Uzbekistan ■, Asia 52 E7 41 30N 65 0 E
Uzen, Bolshoi →, Kazakhstan 35 F9 49 6N 49 56 E
Uzen, Mal →, Kazakhstan 35 F9 49 4N 49 44 E
Uzerche, France 20 C5 45 25N 1 34 E
Uzès, France 21 D8 44 1N 4 26 E
Uzh →, Ukraine 33 G6 51 15N 30 12 E
Uzhgorod = Uzhhorod, Ukraine 28 B7 48 36N 22 18 E
Uzhhorod, Ukraine 28 B7 48 36N 22 18 E
Uzhok, Ukraine 28 B7 48 59N 22 52 E
Užice, Serbia & M. 44 C3 43 55N 19 50 E
Uzlovaya, Russia 32 F10 54 0N 38 5 E
Üzümlü, Turkey 47 E11 36 44N 29 14 E
Uzunköprü, Turkey 45 E10 41 16N 26 43 E
Uzunkuyu, Turkey 47 C8 38 17N 26 33 E

V

Vaal →, S. Africa 88 D3 29 4 S 23 38 E
Vaal Dam, S. Africa 89 D4 27 0 S 28 14 E
Vaalbos △, S. Africa 88 D3 28 22 S 24 20 E
Vaalwater, S. Africa 89 C4 24 15 S 28 8 E
Vaasa, Finland 8 E19 63 6N 21 38 E
Vabre, France 20 E6 43 42N 2 24 E
Vác, Hungary 28 C4 47 49N 19 10 E
Vacaria, Brazil 127 B5 28 31 S 50 52W
Vacaville, U.S.A. 110 G5 38 21N 121 59W
Vaccarès, Étang de, France 21 E8 43 32N 4 34 E
Vach = Vakh →, Russia 52 C8 60 45N 76 45 E
Vache, Î. à, Haiti 121 C5 18 2N 73 35W
Väckelsång, Sweden 11 H8 56 37N 14 58 E
Väddö, Sweden 10 D12 60 0N 18 50 E
Väderstad, Sweden 11 F8 58 19N 14 55 E
Vadnagar, India 68 H5 23 47N 72 40 E
Vado Ligure, Italy 40 D5 44 17N 8 26 E
Vadodara, India 68 H5 22 20N 73 10 E
Vadsø, Norway 8 A23 70 3N 29 50 E
Vadstena, Sweden 11 F8 58 28N 14 54 E
Vaduz, Liech. 25 H5 47 8N 9 31 E
Værøy, Norway 8 C15 67 40N 12 40 E
Vágar, Færoe Is. 8 E9 62 5N 7 15W
Vaggeryd, Sweden 11 G8 57 30N 14 10 E
Vagney, France 19 D13 48 1N 6 43 E
Vagnhärad, Sweden 11 F11 58 57N 17 33 E
Vagos, Portugal 36 E2 40 33N 8 42W
Vågsfjorden, Norway 8 B17 68 50N 16 50 E
Váh →, Slovak Rep. 27 D11 47 43N 18 7 E
Vahsel B., Antarctica 5 D1 75 0 S 35 0W
Váhtjer = Gällivare, Sweden 8 C19 67 9N 20 40 E
Vái, Greece 49 D8 35 15N 26 18 E
Vaigach, Russia 52 B6 70 10N 59 0 E
Vaiges, France 18 D6 48 2N 0 30W
Vaihingen, Germany 25 G4 48 54N 8 57 E
Vail, U.S.A. 106 C5 39 40N 106 20W
Vailly-sur-Aisne, France 19 C10 49 24N 3 31 E
Vaisali →, India 69 F8 26 28N 78 53 E
Vaison-la-Romaine, France 21 D9 44 14N 5 4 E
Vakarel, Bulgaria 44 D7 42 35N 23 40 E
Vakfıkebir, Turkey 73 B8 41 2N 39 17 E
Vakh →, Russia 52 C8 60 45N 76 45 E
Vakhtan, Russia 34 B8 57 53N 46 47 E
Vál, Hungary 28 C3 47 22N 18 40 E
Val-de-Marne □, France 19 D9 48 45N 2 28 E
Val-d'Isère, France 21 C10 45 27N 6 59 E
Val-d'Oise □, France 19 C9 49 5N 2 10 E
Val-d'Or, Canada 104 C4 48 7N 77 47W
Val Grande △, Italy 40 B5 46 3N 8 25 E
Val Marie, Canada 103 D7 49 15N 107 45W
Val Thorens, France 21 C10 45 20N 6 33 E
Valaam, Russia 32 B6 61 22N 30 57 E
Valadares, Portugal 36 D2 41 5N 8 38W
Valahia, Romania 29 F9 44 35N 25 0 E
Valais □, Switz. 25 J3 46 12N 7 45 E
Valais, Alpes du, Switz. 25 J3 46 5N 7 35 E
Valandovo, Macedonia 44 E6 41 19N 22 34 E
Valašské Meziříčí, Czech Rep. 27 B10 49 29N 17 59 E
Valáxa, Greece 46 C6 38 50N 24 29 E
Vålberg, Sweden 10 E7 59 23N 13 11 E
Valbo, Sweden 10 D10 60 40N 17 0 E
Valbondione, Italy 40 B7 46 2N 10 1 E
Vălcani, Romania 28 D5 46 0N 20 26 E
Vâlcea □, Romania 29 F9 45 0N 24 10 E
Valcheta, Argentina 128 E3 40 40 S 66 8W
Valdagno, Italy 41 C8 45 39N 11 18 E
Valdahon, France 19 E13 47 8N 6 21 E
Valdai Hills = Valdayskaya Vozvyshennost, Russia 32 D7 57 0N 33 30 E
Valday, Russia 32 D7 57 58N 33 9 E
Valdayskaya Vozvyshennost, Russia 32 D7 57 0N 33 30 E
Valdeazogues →, Spain 37 G6 38 45N 4 55W
Valdecañas, Embalse de, Spain 36 F5 39 45N 5 25W
Valdemarsvik, Sweden 11 F10 58 14N 16 40 E
Valdemoro, Spain 36 E7 40 12N 3 40W
Valdepeñas, Spain 37 G7 38 43N 3 25W
Valderaduey →, Spain 36 D5 41 31N 5 42W
Valdérice, Italy 42 D5 38 4N 12 37 E
Valderrobres, Spain 38 E5 40 53N 0 9 E
Valdés, Pen., Argentina 128 E4 42 30 S 63 45W
Valdez, U.S.A. 100 B5 61 7N 146 16W
Valdivia, Chile 128 D2 39 50 S 73 14W
Valdobbiádene, Italy 41 C8 45 54N 12 0 E
Valdosta, U.S.A. 115 K4 30 50N 83 17W
Valdoviño, Spain 36 B2 43 36N 8 8W
Valdres, Norway 9 F13 61 5N 9 5 E
Vale, Georgia 35 K6 41 30N 42 58 E
Vale, U.S.A. 108 E5 43 59N 117 15W
Vale of Glamorgan □, U.K. 15 F4 51 28N 3 25W
Valea lui Mihai, Romania 28 C7 47 32N 22 11 E
Valea Mărului, Romania 29 E12 45 49N 27 42 E
Valemount, Canada 102 C5 52 50N 119 15W
Valença, Brazil 125 F11 13 20 S 39 5W
Valença, Portugal 36 C2 42 1N 8 34W
Valença do Piauí, Brazil 125 E10 6 20 S 41 45W
Valençay, France 19 E8 47 9N 1 34 E
Valence, France 21 D8 44 57N 4 54 E
Valence d'Agen, France 20 D4 44 6N 0 53 E
Valencia, Spain 39 F4 39 27N 0 23W
Valencia, Trin. & Tob. 125 K15 10 39N 61 11W
Valencia, U.S.A. 109 J10 34 48N 106 43W
Valencia, Venezuela 124 A5 10 11N 68 0W
Valencia □, Spain 39 F4 39 20N 0 40W
Valencia ✕ (VLC), Spain 39 F4 39 20N 0 26W
Valencia, G. de, Spain 39 F5 39 30N 0 20 E
Valencia de Alcántara, Spain 37 F3 39 25N 7 14W
Valencia de Don Juan, Spain 36 C5 42 17N 5 31W
Valencia I., Ireland 12 E1 51 54N 10 22W
Valenciennes, France 19 B10 50 20N 3 34 E
Văleni, Romania 29 F9 44 15N 24 45 E
Vălenii de Munte, Romania 29 E11 45 11N 26 2 E
Valensole, France 21 E9 43 50N 5 59 E
Valentigney, France 19 E13 47 27N 6 51 E
Valentim, Sa. do, Brazil 125 E10 6 0 S 43 30W
Valentin, Russia 54 C7 43 8N 134 17 E
Valentine, U.S.A. 113 K2 30 35N 104 30W
Valenza, Italy 40 C5 45 1N 8 38 E
Valera, Venezuela 124 B4 9 19N 70 37W
Valga, Estonia 9 H22 57 47N 26 2 E
Valguarnera Caropepe, Italy 43 E7 37 30N 14 23 E
Valier, U.S.A. 108 B7 48 18N 112 16W
Valinco, G. de, France 21 G12 41 40N 8 52 E
Valjevo, Serbia & M. 44 B3 44 18N 19 53 E
Valka, Latvia 9 H21 57 46N 26 3 E
Valkeakoski, Finland 9 F20 61 16N 24 2 E
Valkenswaard, Neths. 17 C5 51 21N 5 29 E
Vall de Uxó = La Vall d'Uixó, Spain 38 F4 39 49N 0 15W
Valla, Sweden 10 E10 59 2N 16 20 E
Valladolid, Mexico 119 C7 20 40N 88 11W
Valladolid, Spain 36 D6 41 38N 4 43W
Valladolid □, Spain 36 D6 41 38N 4 43W
Vallata, Italy 43 A8 41 2N 15 15 E
Valldemossa, Spain 48 B9 39 43N 2 37 E
Valle d'Aosta □, Italy 40 C4 45 45N 7 15 E
Valle de Arán, Spain 38 C5 42 50N 0 55 E
Valle de la Pascua, Venezuela 124 B5 9 13N 66 0W
Valle de las Palmas, Mexico 111 N10 32 20N 116 43W
Valle de Santiago, Mexico 118 C4 20 25N 101 15W
Valle de Suchil, Mexico 118 C4 23 38N 103 55W
Valle de Zaragoza, Mexico 118 B3 27 28N 105 49W
Valle del Ticino ⌓, Italy 40 C6 45 22N 9 0 E
Valle Fértil, Sierra del, Argentina 126 C2 30 20 S 68 0W
Valle Gran Rey, Canary Is. 48 F2 28 5N 17 20W
Valle Hermoso, Mexico 119 B5 25 35N 97 40W
Valledupar, Colombia 124 A4 10 29N 73 15W
Vallehermoso, Canary Is. 48 F2 28 10N 17 15W
Vallejo, U.S.A. 110 G4 38 7N 122 14W
Vallenar, Chile 126 B1 28 30 S 70 50W
Vallentuna, Sweden 10 E12 59 32N 18 5 E
Valleraugue, France 20 D7 44 6N 3 39 E
Vallet, France 18 E5 47 10N 1 15W
Valletta, Malta 49 D2 35 54N 14 31 E
Valley Center, U.S.A. 111 M9 33 13N 117 2W
Valley City, U.S.A. 112 B6 46 55N 98 0W
Valley Falls, Oreg., U.S.A. 108 E3 42 29N 120 17W
Valley Falls, R.I., U.S.A. 117 E13 41 54N 71 24W
Valley of the Kings, Egypt 80 B3 25 41N 32 34 E
Valley Springs, U.S.A. 110 G6 38 12N 120 50W
Valley View, U.S.A. 117 F8 40 39N 76 33W
Valley Wells, U.S.A. 111 K11 35 27N 115 46W
Valleyview, Canada 102 B5 55 5N 117 17W
Valli di Comácchio, Italy 41 D9 44 40N 12 15 E
Vallimanca, Arroyo, Argentina 126 D4 35 40 S 59 10W
Vallo della Lucánia, Italy 43 B8 40 14N 15 16 E
Vallon-Pont-d'Arc, France 21 D8 44 24N 4 24 E
Vallorbe, Switz. 25 J2 46 42N 6 20 E
Valls, Spain 38 D6 41 18N 1 15 E
Valmaseda = Balmaseda, Spain 38 B1 43 11N 3 12W
Valmiera, Latvia 9 H21 57 37N 25 29 E
Valnera, Spain 36 B7 43 9N 3 40W
Valognes, France 18 C5 49 30N 1 28W
Valona = Vlorë, Albania 44 F3 40 32N 19 28 E
Valongo, Portugal 36 D2 41 8N 8 30W
Valozhyn, Belarus 32 E4 54 3N 26 30 E
Valpaços, Portugal 36 D3 41 36N 7 17W
Valparaíso, Chile 126 C1 33 2 S 71 40W
Valparaíso, Mexico 118 C4 22 50N 103 32W
Valparaiso, U.S.A. 114 E2 41 28N 87 4W
Valparaíso □, Chile 126 C1 33 2 S 71 40W
Valpovo, Croatia 28 E3 45 39N 18 25 E
Valréas, France 21 D9 44 24N 5 0 E
Vals, Switz. 25 J5 46 39N 9 11 E
Vals →, S. Africa 88 D4 27 23 S 26 30 E
Vals, Tanjung, Indonesia 63 F9 8 26 S 137 25 E
Vals-les-Bains, France 21 D8 44 42N 4 24 E
Valsad, India 66 J8 20 40N 72 58 E
Valtellina, Italy 40 B6 46 11N 9 55 E
Valuyki, Russia 33 G10 50 10N 38 5 E
Valverde, Canary Is. 48 G2 27 48N 17 55W
Valverde del Camino, Spain 37 H4 37 35N 6 47W
Valverde del Fresno, Spain 36 E4 40 15N 6 51W
Vama, Romania 29 C10 47 34N 25 42 E
Vamdrup, Denmark 11 J3 55 25N 9 17 E
Våmhus, Sweden 10 C8 61 7N 14 29 E
Vammala, Finland 9 F20 61 20N 22 54 E
Vámos, Greece 49 D6 35 24N 24 13 E
Van, Turkey 70 B4 38 30N 43 20 E
Van, L. = Van Gölü, Turkey 70 B4 38 30N 43 0 E
Van Alstyne, U.S.A. 113 J6 33 25N 96 35W
Van Blommestein Meer, Suriname 125 C7 4 45N 55 5W
Van Buren, Canada 105 C6 47 10N 67 55W
Van Buren, Ark., U.S.A. 113 H7 35 26N 94 21W
Van Buren, Maine, U.S.A. 115 B11 47 10N 67 58W

Van Buren, Mo., U.S.A. 113 G9 37 0N 91 1W
Van Canh, Vietnam ... 64 F7 13 37N 109 0 E
Van Diemen, C.,
N. Terr., Australia .. 92 B5 11 9 S 130 24 E
Van Diemen, C.,
Queens., Australia .. 94 B2 16 30 S 139 46 E
Van Diemen G.,
Australia .... 92 B5 11 45 S 132 0 E
Van Gölü, Turkey ... 70 B4 38 30N 43 0 E
Van Horn, U.S.A. 113 K2 31 3N 104 50W
Van Ninh, Vietnam ... 64 F7 12 42N 109 14 E
Van Rees, Pegunungan,
Indonesia .... 63 E9 2 35 S 138 15 E
Van Wert, U.S.A. 114 E3 40 52N 84 35W
Van Yen, Vietnam ... 58 G5 21 4N 104 42 E
Vanadzor, Armenia ... 35 K7 40 48N 44 30 E
Vanavara, Russia .... 53 C11 60 22N 102 16 E
Vancouver, Canada ... 102 D4 49 15N 123 10W
Vancouver, U.S.A. ... 110 E4 45 38N 122 40W
Vancouver, Australia . 93 G2 35 2 S 118 11 E
Vancouver I., Canada . 102 D3 49 50N 126 0W
Vancouver
International ✈
(YVR) 110 A3 49 10N 123 10W
Vanda = Vantaa,
Finland .... 9 F21 60 18N 24 58 E
Vandalia, Ill., U.S.A. . 112 F10 38 58N 89 6W
Vandalia, Mo., U.S.A. 112 F9 39 19N 91 29W
Vandenburg, U.S.A. .. 111 L6 34 35N 120 33W
Vanderbijlpark,
S. Africa .... 89 D4 26 42 S 27 54 E
Vandergrift, U.S.A. .. 116 F5 40 36N 79 34W
Vanderhoof, Canada .. 102 C4 54 0N 124 0W
Vanderkloof Dam,
S. Africa .... 88 E3 30 4 S 24 40 E
Vanderlin I., Australia . 94 B2 15 44 S 137 2 E
Vänern, Sweden .... 11 F7 58 47N 13 30 E
Vänersborg, Sweden .. 11 F6 58 26N 12 19 E
Vang Vieng, Laos ... 58 C4 18 58N 102 32 E
Vanga, Kenya ...... 86 C4 4 35 S 39 12 E
Vangaindrano, Madag. 89 C8 23 21 S 47 36 E
Vanguard, Canada ... 103 D7 49 55N 107 20W
Vanino, Russia ..... 53 E15 48 50N 140 5 E
Vânju Mare, Romania . 28 F7 44 25N 22 52 E
Vanna, Norway .... 8 A18 70 6N 19 50 E
Vännäs, Sweden .... 8 E18 63 58N 19 48 E
Vannes, France 18 E4 47 40N 2 47W
Vanoise, Massif de la,
France .... 21 C10 45 25N 6 40 E
Vanrhynsdorp, S. Africa 88 E2 31 36 S 18 44 E
Vansbro, Sweden .... 10 D8 60 32N 14 15 E
Vansittart B., Australia 92 B4 14 3 S 126 17 E
Vantaa, Finland .... 9 F21 60 18N 24 58 E
Vanua Balavu, Fiji .. 91 C9 17 40 S 178 57W
Vanua Levu, Fiji .... 91 C8 16 33 S 179 15 E
Vanuatu ■, Pac. Oc. .. 96 J8 15 0 S 168 0 E
Vanwyksvlei, S. Africa 88 E3 30 18 S 21 49 E
Vanzylsrus, S. Africa . 88 D3 26 52 S 22 4 E
Vapnyarka, Ukraine .. 29 B13 48 32N 28 45 E
Var □, France ..... 21 E10 43 27N 6 18 E
Var →, France ..... 21 E11 43 39N 7 12 E
Vara, Sweden ..... 11 F6 58 16N 12 55 E
Varades, France 18 E5 47 25N 1 1W
Varáita →, Italy .... 40 D4 44 9N 7 53 E
Varallo, Italy ..... 40 C5 45 49N 8 15 E
Varāmīn, Iran ..... 71 C6 35 20N 51 39 E
Varāmīn □, Iran .... 71 B6 35 18N 51 35 E
Varanasi, India .... 69 G10 25 22N 83 0 E
Varangerfjorden,
Norway .... 8 A23 70 3N 29 25 E
Varangerhalvøya,
Norway .... 8 A23 70 25N 29 30 E
Varano, Lago di, Italy . 41 G12 41 53N 15 45 E
Varaždin, Croatia ... 41 B13 46 20N 16 20 E
Varazze, Italy ..... 40 D5 44 22N 8 34 E
Varberg, Sweden ... 11 G6 57 6N 12 20 E
Vardak □, Afghan. ... 66 B6 34 0N 68 0 E
Vardar = Axiós →,
Greece .... 44 F6 40 57N 22 35 E
Varde, Denmark .... 11 J2 55 38N 8 29 E
Varde Å →, Denmark . 11 J2 55 35N 8 19 E
Vardø, Norway .... 8 A24 70 23N 31 5 E
Varel, Germany .... 24 B4 53 24N 8 9 E
Varella, Mui, Vietnam . 64 F7 12 54N 109 26 E
Varéna, Lithuania ... 9 J21 54 12N 24 30 E
Varennes-sur-Allier,
France .... 19 F10 46 19N 3 24 E
Varennes-Vauzelles,
France .... 19 E10 47 3N 3 9 E
Vareš, Bos.-H. ..... 28 F3 44 12N 18 23 E
Varese, Italy ...... 40 C5 45 48N 8 50 E
Vârfurile, Romania .. 28 D7 46 19N 22 31 E
Vårgårda, Sweden ... 11 F6 58 2N 12 49 E
Varginha, Brazil .... 127 A6 21 33 S 45 25W
Vargön, Sweden .... 11 F6 58 22N 12 20 E
Varillas, Chile ..... 126 A1 24 0 S 70 10W
Varkaus, Finland ... 9 E22 62 19N 27 50 E
Värmdölandet, Sweden 10 E12 59 20N 18 33 E
Värmeln, Sweden ... 10 E6 59 35N 12 54 E
Värmlands län □,
Sweden .... 10 E6 60 0N 13 20 E
Värmlandsbro, Sweden 10 E7 59 11N 13 0 E
Varna, Bulgaria .... 45 C11 43 13N 27 56 E
Varna →, Bulgaria ... 45 C11 43 20N 27 31 E
Värnamo, Sweden ... 11 G8 57 10N 14 3 E
Varnsdorf, Czech Rep. 26 A7 50 55N 14 35 E
Várpalota, Hungary .. 28 C3 47 12N 18 8 E
Vars, Canada 117 A9 45 21N 75 21W
Vars, France ...... 21 D10 44 37N 6 42 E
Varto, Turkey ...... 73 C9 39 10N 41 27 E
Varvarin, Serbia & M. . 44 C5 43 43N 21 20 E
Varysburg, U.S.A. ... 116 D6 42 46N 78 19W
Varzaneh, Iran ..... 71 C7 32 25N 52 40 E
Varzi, Italy .... 40 D6 44 49N 9 12 E
Varzo, Italy .... 40 C5 46 12N 8 15 E
Varzy, France ..... 19 E10 47 22N 3 20 E
Vas □, Hungary .... 28 C1 47 10N 16 55 E
Vasa = Vaasa, Finland . 8 E19 63 6N 21 38 E
Vasa Barris →, Brazil . 125 F11 11 10 S 37 10W
Vásárosnamény,
Hungary .... 28 B7 48 9N 22 19 E
Vascão →, Portugal .. 37 H3 37 31N 7 31W
Vașcău, Romania ... 28 D7 46 28N 22 30 E
Vascongadas = País
Vasco □, Spain ... 38 C2 42 50N 2 45W
Vashkivtsi, Ukraine .. 29 B10 48 23N 25 31 E
Vasht = Khāsh, Iran .. 66 E2 28 15N 61 15 E
Vasilevichi, Belarus .. 33 F5 52 15N 29 50 E
Vasilikón, Greece ... 46 C5 38 25N 23 40 E
Vasilkov = Vasylkiv,
Ukraine .... 33 G6 50 7N 30 15 E
Vaslui, Romania ... 29 D12 46 38N 27 42 E
Vaslui □, Romania .. 29 D12 46 30N 27 45 E
Väsman, Sweden ... 10 D9 60 9N 15 5 E
Vassar, Canada 103 D9 49 10N 95 55W
Vassar, U.S.A. 114 D4 43 22N 83 35W
Västerás, Sweden ... 10 E10 59 37N 16 38 E
Västerbotten, Sweden . 8 D18 64 36N 20 4 E

Västerdalälven →,
Sweden .... 10 D8 60 30N 14 7 E
Västergötland, Sweden 11 F7 58 0N 13 10 E
Västerhaninge, Sweden 10 E12 59 7N 18 6 E
Västervik, Sweden ... 11 G10 57 43N 16 33 E
Västmanland, Sweden . 9 G16 59 45N 16 20 E
Västmanlands län □,
Sweden .... 10 E10 59 45N 16 20 E
Vasto, Italy .... 41 F11 42 8N 14 40 E
Västra Götalands
Län □, Sweden ... 11 F6 58 0N 13 0 E
Vasvár, Hungary ... 28 C1 47 3N 16 47 E
Vasylivka, Ukraine .. 33 J8 47 27N 35 0 E
Vasylkiv, Ukraine ... 33 G6 50 7N 30 15 E
Vatan, France ..... 19 E8 47 4N 1 50 E
Vatersay, U.K. 13 E1 56 55N 7 32W
Váthia, Greece ..... 46 E4 36 29N 22 29 E
Vatican City ■, Europe 41 G9 41 54N 12 27 E
Vaticano, C., Italy ... 43 D8 38 37N 15 50 E
Vatili, Cyprus ..... 49 D12 35 6N 33 40 E
Vatin, Serbia & M. ... 28 E6 45 12N 21 20 E
Vatnajökull, Iceland .. 8 D5 64 30N 16 48W
Vatoa, Fiji .... 91 D9 19 50 S 178 13W
Vatólakkos, Greece .. 49 D5 35 27N 23 53 E
Vatoloha, Madag. ... 89 B8 17 52 S 47 48 E
Vatomandry, Madag. . 89 B8 19 20 S 48 59 E
Vatra-Dornei, Romania 29 C10 47 22N 25 22 E
Vatrak →, India .... 68 H5 23 9N 73 2 E
Vättern, Sweden .... 11 F8 58 25N 14 30 E
Vaucluse □, France .. 21 E9 43 50N 5 20 E
Vaucouleurs, France . 19 D12 48 37N 5 40 E
Vaud □, Switz. ..... 25 J2 46 35N 6 30 E
Vaudreuil-Dorion,
Canada 117 A10 45 23N 74 3W
Vaughn, Mont., U.S.A. 108 C8 47 33N 111 33W
Vaughn, N. Mex., U.S.A. 109 J11 34 36N 105 13W
Vaujours L., Canada .. 104 A5 55 27N 74 15W
Vaupés = Uaupés →,
Brazil 124 C5 0 2N 67 16W
Vaupés □, Colombia . 124 C4 1 0N 71 0W
Vauvert, France .... 21 E8 43 42N 4 17 E
Vauxhall, Canada ... 102 C6 50 5N 112 9W
Vav, India .... 68 G4 24 22N 71 31 E
Vavatenina, Madag. . 89 B8 17 28 S 49 12 E
Vava'u, Tonga ..... 91 D12 18 36 S 174 0W
Vavoua, Ivory C. ... 82 D3 7 23N 6 29W
Vawkavysk, Belarus .. 33 F3 53 9N 24 30 E
Vaxholm, Sweden ... 10 E12 59 25N 18 20 E
Växjö, Sweden ..... 11 H8 56 52N 14 50 E
Våxtorp, Sweden ... 11 H7 56 25N 13 8 E
Vaygach, Ostrov, Russia 52 C6 70 0N 60 0 E
Váyia, Greece ..... 46 C5 38 19N 23 11 E
Váyia, Ákra, Greece .. 49 C10 36 15N 28 11 E
Veaikevárri =
Svappavaara, Sweden 8 C19 67 40N 21 3 E
Vechelde, Germany .. 24 C6 52 16N 10 22 E
Vechta, Germany ... 24 C4 52 44N 8 17 E
Vechte →, Neths. ... 17 B6 52 34N 6 6 E
Vecsés, Hungary ... 28 C4 47 26N 19 19 E
Veddige, Sweden ... 11 G6 57 17N 12 20 E
Vedea →, Romania .. 29 G10 43 42N 25 41 E
Vedia, Argentina ... 126 C3 34 30 S 61 31W
Vedrette di Ries-
Aurina △, Italy ... 41 B9 46 54N 12 5 E
Vedum, Sweden ... 11 F7 58 11N 13 0 E
Veendam, Neths. ... 17 A6 53 5N 6 52 E
Veenendaal, Neths. . 17 B5 52 2N 5 34 E
Vefsna →, Norway .. 8 D15 65 48N 13 10 E
Vega, Norway ..... 8 D14 65 40N 11 55 E
Vega, U.S.A. 113 H3 35 15N 102 26W
Vega Baja, Puerto Rico 121 d 18 27N 66 23W
Vegadeo, Spain 36 B3 43 27N 7 4W
Vegorrítis, Límni,
Greece .... 44 F5 40 45N 21 45 E
Vegreville, Canada .. 102 C6 53 30N 112 5W
Veinge, Sweden .... 11 H7 56 33N 13 6 E
Veisiejai, Lithuania .. 30 D10 54 6N 23 42 E
Vejbystrand, Sweden . 11 H6 56 19N 12 45 E
Vejen, Denmark .... 11 J3 55 30N 9 9 E
Vejer de la Frontera,
Spain 37 J5 36 15N 5 59W
Vejle, Denmark .... 11 J3 55 43N 9 30 E
Vejle Amtskommune □,
Denmark .... 11 J3 55 45N 9 20 E
Vejle Fjord, Denmark . 11 J3 55 40N 9 50 E
Vela Luka, Croatia ... 41 F13 42 59N 16 44 E
Velas, C., Costa Rica . 120 D2 10 21N 85 52W
Velasco, Sierra de,
Argentina ...... 126 B2 29 20 S 67 10W
Velay, Mts. du, France . 20 D7 45 0N 3 40 E
Velbert, Germany ... 24 D3 51 20N 7 3 E
Velddrif, S. Africa ... 88 E2 32 42 S 18 11 E
Velebit △, Croatia ... 41 D12 44 50N 15 15 E
Velebit Planina, Croatia 41 D12 44 50N 15 20 E
Velebitski Kanal,
Croatia .... 41 D11 44 45N 14 55 E
Veleka →, Bulgaria .. 45 D11 42 4N 27 58 E
Velenci-tó, Hungary . 28 C3 47 13N 18 36 E
Velenje, Slovenia ... 41 B12 46 23N 15 8 E
Veles, Macedonia ... 44 E5 41 46N 21 47 E
Velestínon, Greece .. 46 B4 39 23N 22 43 E
Vélez-Málaga, Spain . 37 J6 36 48N 4 5W
Vélez Rubio, Spain .. 39 H2 37 41N 2 5W
Velhas →, Brazil .... 125 G10 17 13 S 44 49W
Velika, Croatia ..... 28 E2 45 27N 17 40 E
Velika Gorica, Croatia . 41 C13 45 44N 16 5 E
Velika Kapela, Croatia 41 C12 45 10N 15 5 E
Velika Kladuša, Bos.-H. 41 C12 45 11N 15 48 E
Velika Kruša,
Serbia & M. ..... 44 D4 42 19N 20 39 E
Velika Morava →,
Serbia & M. ..... 44 B5 44 43N 21 3 E
Velika Plana,
Serbia & M. ..... 44 B5 44 20N 21 4 E
Velikaya →, Russia .. 32 C5 57 48N 28 10 E
Velikaya Kema, Russia 54 B8 45 30N 137 12 E
Velikaya Lepetikha,
Ukraine .... 33 J7 47 2N 33 58 E
Veliké Kapušany,
Slovak Rep. ..... 27 C15 48 34N 22 5 E
Velike Lašče, Slovenia . 41 C11 45 49N 14 45 E
Veliki Jastrebac,
Serbia & M. ..... 44 C5 43 25N 21 30 E
Veliki Kanal,
Serbia & M. ..... 28 E4 45 45N 19 15 E
Veliki Popović,
Serbia & M. ..... 44 B5 44 8N 21 18 E
Velikiye Luki, Russia . 32 D6 56 25N 30 32 E
Veliko Gradište,
Serbia & M. ..... 44 B5 44 46N 21 29 E
Veliko Tŭrnovo,
Bulgaria .... 45 C9 43 5N 25 41 E
Velikonda Range, India 66 M11 14 45N 79 10 E
Vélingara, Kolda,
Senegal 82 C2 13 12N 14 5W
Vélingara, Louga,
Senegal 82 B2 15 0N 14 40W
Velingrad, Bulgaria .. 44 D7 42 4N 23 58 E

Velino, Mte., Italy ... 41 F10 42 9N 13 23 E
Velizh, Russia ..... 32 E6 55 36N 31 11 E
Velké Karlovice,
Czech Rep. ..... 27 B11 49 20N 18 17 E
Velké Meziříčí,
Czech Rep. ..... 26 B9 49 21N 16 1 E
Vel'ký Javorník,
Slovak Rep. ..... 27 B11 49 19N 18 22 E
Vel'ký Krtíš,
Slovak Rep. ..... 27 C12 48 12N 19 21 E
Vel'ký Meder,
Slovak Rep. ..... 27 D10 47 52N 17 46 E
Vel'ký Tribeč,
Slovak Rep. ..... 27 C11 48 28N 18 15 E
Velletri, Italy ...... 42 A5 41 41N 12 47 E
Vellinge, Sweden ... 11 J6 55 29N 13 0 E
Vellmar, Germany ... 24 D5 51 22N 9 28 E
Vellore, India ..... 66 N11 12 57N 79 10 E
Velsk, Russia ..... 32 B11 61 10N 42 5 E
Velten, Germany ... 24 C9 52 42N 13 10 E
Veluwezoom △, Neths. 17 B6 52 5N 6 0 E
Velva, U.S.A. 112 A4 48 4N 100 56W
Velvendós, Greece .. 44 F6 40 15N 22 6 E
Velyka Mykhaylivka,
Ukraine .... 29 C14 47 4N 29 52 E
Velyki Luchky, Ukraine 28 B7 48 25N 22 34 E
Velykyy Bereznyy,
Ukraine .... 28 B7 48 54N 22 28 E
Velykyy Bychkiv,
Ukraine .... 29 C9 47 58N 24 1 E
Vemb, Denmark .... 11 H2 56 21N 8 21 E
Vemdalen, Sweden .. 10 B7 62 27N 13 51 E
Ven, Sweden ...... 11 J6 55 55N 12 45 E
Venaco, France .... 21 F13 42 14N 9 11 E
Venado Tuerto,
Argentina ...... 126 C3 33 50 S 62 0W
Venafro, Italy ..... 43 A7 41 29N 14 2 E
Venarey-les-Laumes,
France .... 19 E11 47 32N 4 26 E
Venaría, Italy ..... 40 C4 45 8N 7 38 E
Venčane, Serbia & M. . 44 B4 44 24N 20 28 E
Vence, France ..... 21 E11 43 43N 7 6 E
Vendas Novas, Portugal 37 G2 38 39N 8 27W
Vendée □, France ... 18 F5 46 50N 1 35W
Vendée →, France ... 18 F5 46 20N 1 10W
Vendéen, Bocage,
France 20 B2 46 40N 1 20W
Vendeuvre-sur-Barse,
France .... 19 D11 48 14N 4 28 E
Vendôme, France ... 18 E8 47 47N 1 3 E
Vendrell = El Vendrell,
Spain .... 38 D6 41 10N 1 30 E
Vendsyssel, Denmark . 11 G4 57 22N 10 0 E
Vendychany, Ukraine . 29 B12 48 38N 27 48 E
Venelles, France ... 21 E9 43 35N 5 28 E
Véneta, L., Italy .... 41 C9 45 23N 12 25 E
Véneto □, Italy .... 41 C9 45 30N 12 0 E
Venev, Russia ..... 32 E10 54 22N 38 17 E
Venézia, Italy ..... 41 C9 45 27N 12 21 E
Venézia, G. di, Italy .. 41 C10 45 15N 13 0 E
Venezuela ■, S. Amer. 124 B5 8 0N 66 0W
Venezuela, G. de,
Venezuela 124 A4 11 30N 71 0W
Vengurla, India .... 66 M8 15 53N 73 45 E
Venice = Venézia, Italy 41 C9 45 27N 12 21 E
Venice, U.S.A. 115 M4 27 6N 82 27W
Vénissieux, France .. 21 C8 45 42N 4 53 E
Venjansjön, Sweden . 10 D8 60 54N 14 0 E
Venkatapuram, India . 67 K12 18 20N 80 30 E
Venlo, Neths. ..... 17 C6 51 22N 6 11 E
Vennesla, Norway .. 9 G12 58 15N 7 59 E
Venosa, Italy ..... 43 B8 40 58N 15 49 E
Venray, Neths. .... 17 C6 51 31N 6 0 E
Venta, Lithuania ... 30 B9 56 12N 22 42 E
Venta →, Latvia .... 30 A8 57 24N 21 33 E
Venta de Baños, Spain 36 D6 41 55N 4 30W
Venta de Cardeña =
Cardeña, Spain ... 37 G6 38 16N 4 20W
Ventana, Punta de la,
Mexico 118 C3 24 4N 109 48W
Ventana, Sa. de la,
Argentina ...... 126 D3 38 0 S 62 30W
Ventersburg, S. Africa . 88 D4 28 7 S 27 9 E
Venterstad, S. Africa . 88 E4 30 47 S 25 48 E
Ventimíglia, Italy ... 40 E4 43 47N 7 36 E
Ventnor, U.K. 15 G6 50 36N 1 12W
Ventoténe, Italy .... 42 B6 40 47N 13 25 E
Ventoux, Mt., France . 21 D9 44 10N 5 17 E
Ventspils, Latvia .... 9 H19 57 25N 21 32 E
Ventspils □, Latvia .. 30 A8 57 20N 21 50 E
Ventuarí →, Venezuela 124 C5 3 58N 67 2W
Ventucopa, U.S.A. .. 111 L7 34 50N 119 29W
Ventura, U.S.A. 111 L7 34 17N 119 18W
Venus B., Australia .. 95 F4 38 40 S 145 42 E
Vera, Argentina .... 126 B3 29 30 S 60 20W
Vera, Spain 39 H3 37 15N 1 51W
Veracruz, Mexico ... 119 D5 19 10N 96 10W
Veracruz □, Mexico . 119 D5 19 0N 96 15W
Veraval, India ..... 68 J4 20 53N 70 27 E
Verbánia, Italy ..... 40 C5 45 56N 8 33 E
Verbicaro, Italy .... 43 C8 39 45N 15 55 E
Verbier, Switz. ..... 25 J3 46 6N 7 13 E
Vercelli, Italy ..... 40 C5 45 19N 8 25 E
Verchovchyna, Ukraine 33 H8 48 32N 34 10 E
Vercors △, France .. 21 D9 45 0N 5 25 E
Verdalsøra, Norway . 8 E14 63 48N 11 30 E
Verde →, Argentina . 128 E3 41 56 S 65 5W
Verde →, Goiás, Brazil 125 G8 1 1 S 50 14W
Verde →,
Mato Grosso do Sul,
Brazil .... 125 H8 21 25 S 52 20W
Verde →, Chihuahua,
Mexico 118 B3 26 29N 107 58W
Verde →, Oaxaca,
Mexico 119 D5 15 59N 97 50W
Verde →, Veracruz,
Mexico 118 C4 21 10N 102 50W
Verde →, Paraguay .. 126 A4 23 9 S 57 37W
Verde →, U.S.A. ... 109 K8 33 33N 111 40W
Verde, Cay, Bahamas . 120 B4 23 0N 75 5W
Verde Island Pass, Phil. 61 E4 13 34N 120 51 E
Verden, Germany ... 24 C5 52 55N 9 14 E
Verdhikoúsa, Greece . 46 B3 39 47N 21 59 E
Verdi, U.S.A. 110 F7 39 31N 119 59W
Verdon →, France .. 21 E10 43 50N 6 5 E
Verdon-sur-Mer, Le,
France 20 C2 45 33N 1 4W
Verdun, France .... 19 C12 49 9N 5 24 E
Verdun-sur-le-Doubs,
France .... 19 F12 46 54N 5 1 E
Vereeniging, S. Africa . 89 D4 26 38 S 27 57 E
Verga, C., Guinea ... 82 C2 10 30N 14 10W
Vergara, Uruguay ... 127 C5 32 56 S 53 57W
Vergato, Italy ..... 40 D8 44 17N 11 7 E

Verkhnedvinsk =
Vyerkhnyadzvinsk,
Belarus .... 32 E4 55 45N 27 58 E
Verkhnevilyuysk, Russia 53 C13 63 27N 120 18 E
Verkhniy Baskunchak,
Russia .... 35 F8 48 14N 46 44 E
Verkhovye, Russia .. 33 F9 52 55N 37 15 E
Verkhovyna, Ukraine . 29 B9 48 9N 24 47 E
Verkhoyansk, Russia . 53 C14 67 35N 133 25 E
Verkhoyansk Ra. =
Verkhoyanskiy
Khrebet, Russia ... 53 C13 66 0N 129 0 E
Verkhoyanskiy Khrebet,
Russia .... 53 C13 66 0N 129 0 E
Vermenton, France .. 19 E10 47 40N 3 42 E
Vermilion, Canada .. 103 C6 53 20N 110 50W
Vermilion, U.S.A. ... 116 E2 41 25N 82 22W
Vermilion →, Canada 103 C6 53 22N 110 51W
Vermilion, B., U.S.A. . 113 L9 29 45N 91 55W
Vermilion Bay, Canada 103 D10 49 51N 93 34W
Vermilion L., U.S.A. .. 112 B8 47 53N 92 26W
Vermilion →, U.S.A. . 112 B8 47 38N 96 56W
Vermillion, U.S.A. ... 112 D6 42 47N 96 56W
Vermillion →, Canada 104 C5 47 38N 72 56W
Vermont □, U.S.A. .. 117 C12 44 0N 73 0W
Vermosh, Albania ... 44 D3 42 35N 19 42 E
Vernadsky, Antarctica 5 C17 65 0 S 64 0W
Vernal, U.S.A. 108 F9 40 27N 109 32W
Vernalis, U.S.A. 110 H5 37 36N 121 17W
Vernazza, Italy .... 40 D6 44 8N 9 45 E
Verner, Canada 104 C3 46 25N 80 8W
Verneuil-sur-Avre,
France .... 18 D7 48 45N 0 55 E
Vernier, Switz. ..... 25 J2 46 11N 6 12 E
Vérnio, Italy ...... 40 D8 44 3N 11 9 E
Vernon, Canada 102 C5 50 20N 119 15W
Vernon, France .... 18 C8 49 5N 1 30 E
Vernon, U.S.A. 113 H5 34 9N 99 17W
Vernonia, U.S.A. ... 110 E3 45 52N 123 11W
Vernouillet, France .. 18 D8 48 58N 1 58 E
Vero Beach, U.S.A. .. 115 M5 27 38N 80 24W
Véroia, Greece .... 44 F6 40 34N 22 12 E
Véroli, Italy ...... 41 G10 41 41N 13 25 E
Verona, Canada 117 B8 44 29N 76 42W
Verona, Italy ...... 40 C7 45 27N 10 59 E
Verona, U.S.A. 112 D10 42 59N 89 32W
Verrès, Italy ...... 40 C4 45 40N 7 42 E
Versailles, France ... 19 D9 48 48N 2 8 E
Versmold, Germany . 24 C4 52 2N 8 9 E
Vert, C., Senegal ... 82 C1 14 45N 17 30W
Vertou, France 18 E5 47 10N 1 28W
Vertus, France ..... 19 D11 48 54N 4 0 E
Verulam, S. Africa .. 89 D5 29 38 S 31 2 E
Verviers, Belgium ... 17 D5 50 37N 5 52 E
Vervins, France .... 19 C10 49 50N 3 53 E
Verzej, Slovenia .... 41 B13 46 34N 16 13 E
Verzy, France ..... 19 C11 49 9N 4 10 E
Vescovato, France .. 21 F13 42 30N 9 27 E
Veselí nad Lužnicí,
Czech Rep. ..... 26 B7 49 12N 14 43 E
Veselie, Bulgaria ... 45 D11 42 18N 27 38 E
Veselovskoye Vdkhr.,
Russia .... 35 G5 46 58N 41 25 E
Veshenskaya, Russia . 34 F5 49 35N 41 44 E
Vesle →, France ... 19 C10 49 23N 3 28 E
Vesoul, France ..... 19 E13 47 40N 6 11 E
Vessigebro, Sweden . 11 H6 56 58N 12 40 E
Vesterålen, Norway . 8 B16 68 45N 15 0 E
Vestfjorden, Norway . 8 C15 67 55N 14 0 E
Vestmannaeyjar, Iceland 8 E3 63 27N 20 15W
Vestsjællands
Amtskommune □,
Denmark .... 11 J5 55 30N 11 20 E
Vestspitsbergen,
Svalbard .... 4 B8 78 40N 17 0 E
Vestvågøy, Norway .. 8 B15 68 18N 13 50 E
Vesuvio, Italy ..... 43 B7 40 49N 14 26 E
Vesuvius, Mt. = Vesuvio,
Italy .... 43 B7 40 49N 14 26 E
Veszprém, Hungary .. 28 C2 47 8N 17 57 E
Veszprém □, Hungary 28 C2 47 5N 17 55 E
Vésztő, Hungary ... 28 D6 46 55N 21 16 E
Vetlanda, Sweden ... 11 G9 57 24N 15 3 E
Vetluga, Russia .... 34 B7 57 53N 45 45 E
Vetlugu →, Russia .. 34 B8 56 36N 46 4 E
Vetluzhskiy, Kostroma,
Russia .... 34 A7 58 23N 45 26 E
Vetluzhskiy,
Nizhniy Novgorod,
Russia .... 34 B7 57 17N 45 12 E
Vetovo, Bulgaria ... 45 C10 43 42N 26 16 E
Vetralla, Italy ..... 41 F9 42 20N 12 2 E
Vetren, Bulgaria ... 45 D8 42 15N 24 3 E
Vettore, Mte., Italy .. 41 F10 42 49N 13 16 E
Veurne, Belgium ... 17 C2 51 5N 2 40 E
Veveno →, Sudan .. 81 F3 6 40N 32 58 E
Vevey, Switz. ...... 25 J2 46 28N 6 51 E
Vévi, Greece ...... 44 F5 40 47N 21 38 E
Veynes, France .... 21 D9 44 32N 5 49 E
Veys, Iran .... 71 D6 31 30N 49 0 E
Vézelay, France .... 19 E10 47 27N 3 45 E
Vézelise, France ... 19 D13 48 30N 6 5 E
Vézère →, France .. 20 D4 44 53N 0 53 E
Vezhen, Bulgaria ... 45 D8 42 50N 24 20 E
Vezirköprü, Turkey .. 72 B6 41 8N 35 10 E
Vezzani, France .... 21 F13 42 10N 9 15 E
Vi Thanh, Vietnam .. 65 H5 9 42N 105 26 E
Viacha, Bolivia ..... 124 G5 16 39 S 68 18W
Viadana, Italy ..... 40 D7 44 56N 10 31 E
Viamão, Brazil ..... 127 C5 30 5 S 51 0W
Viana, Brazil ...... 125 D10 3 13 S 44 55W
Viana, Spain 38 C2 42 31N 2 22W
Viana do Alentejo,
Portugal 37 G3 38 17N 7 59W
Viana do Bolo, Spain . 36 C3 42 11N 7 6W
Viana do Castelo,
Portugal 36 D2 41 42N 8 50W
Viana do Castelo □,
Portugal 36 D2 41 50N 8 30W
Vianden, Lux. ..... 17 E6 49 56N 6 12 E
Viangchan = Vientiane,
Laos .... 64 D4 17 58N 102 36 E
Vianópolis, Brazil ... 125 G9 16 40 S 48 35W
Viar →, Spain 37 H5 37 36N 5 50W
Viaréggio, Italy .... 40 E7 43 52N 10 14 E
Viaur →, France ... 20 D5 44 8N 1 58 E
Vibble, Sweden .... 11 G12 57 37N 18 16 E
Vibo Valéntia, Italy .. 43 D9 38 40N 16 6 E
Viborg, Denmark ... 11 H3 56 27N 9 23 E
Viborg
Amtskommune □,
Denmark .... 11 H3 56 30N 9 30 E
Vibraye, France .... 18 D7 48 3N 0 44 E
Vic, Spain .... 38 D7 41 58N 2 19 E
Vic, Étang de, France . 20 E7 43 25N 3 50 E
Vic-en-Bigorre, France 20 E4 43 24N 0 5 E
Vic-Fezensac, France . 20 E4 43 47N 0 19 E

Vic-le-Comte, France . 19 G10 45 39N 3 14 E
Vic-sur-Cère, France . 20 D6 44 59N 2 38 E
Vícar, Spain 39 J2 36 50N 2 38W
Vicenza, Italy ..... 41 C8 45 33N 11 33 E
Vichada →, Colombia 124 C5 4 55N 67 50W
Vichuga, Russia .... 34 B5 57 12N 41 55 E
Vichy, France ..... 19 F10 46 9N 3 26 E
Vicksburg, Ariz., U.S.A. 111 M13 33 45N 113 45W
Vicksburg, Miss., U.S.A. 113 J9 32 21N 90 53W
Vico, France ...... 21 F12 42 10N 8 49 E
Vico, L. di, Italy .... 41 F9 42 19N 12 10 E
Vico del Gargano, Italy 41 G12 41 54N 15 57 E
Vicovu de Sus, Romania 29 C10 47 56N 25 41 E
Victor, India ...... 68 J4 21 0N 71 30 E
Victor, U.S.A. 116 D7 42 58N 77 24W
Victor Harbor, Australia 95 F2 35 30 S 138 37 E
Victoria, Argentina .. 126 C3 32 40 S 60 10W
Victoria, Chile ..... 128 D2 38 13 S 72 20W
Victoria, Guinea 82 C2 10 50N 14 32W
Victoria, Malta .... 49 C1 36 3N 14 14 E
Victoria, Phil. ..... 61 D4 15 35N 120 41 E
Victoria, Romania .. 29 E9 45 44N 24 41 E
Victoria, Kans., U.S.A. 112 F5 38 52N 99 9W
Victoria, Tex., U.S.A. . 113 L6 28 48N 97 0W
Victoria □, Australia . 95 F3 37 0 S 144 0 E
Victoria →, Australia 92 C4 15 10 S 129 40 E
Victoria, Grand L.,
Canada 104 C4 47 31N 77 30W
Victoria, L., Africa .. 86 C3 1 0 S 33 0 E
Victoria, L., Australia . 95 E3 33 57 S 141 15 E
Victoria Beach, Canada 103 C9 50 40N 96 35W
Victoria de Durango =
Durango, Mexico .. 118 C4 24 3N 104 39W
Victoria de las Tunas =
Cuba 120 B4 20 58N 76 59W
Victoria Falls,
Zimbabwe ...... 87 F2 17 58 S 25 52 E
Victoria Harbour,
Canada 116 B5 44 45N 79 45W
Victoria I., Canada .. 100 A8 71 0N 111 0W
Victoria L., Canada .. 105 C8 48 20N 57 27W
Victoria Ld., Antarctica 5 D11 75 0 S 160 0 E
Victoria Nile →,
Uganda .... 86 B3 2 14N 31 26 E
Victoria River, Australia 92 C5 16 25 S 131 0 E
Victoria Str., Canada . 100 B9 69 31N 100 30W
Victoria West, S. Africa 88 E3 31 25 S 23 4 E
Victorias, Phil. .... 61 F5 10 54N 123 5 E
Victoriaville, Canada . 105 C5 46 4N 71 56W
Victorica, Argentina . 126 D2 36 20 S 65 30W
Victorville, U.S.A. ... 111 L9 34 32N 117 18W
Vicuña, Chile ..... 126 C1 30 0 S 70 50W
Vicuña Mackenna,
Argentina ...... 126 C3 33 53 S 64 25W
Vidal, U.S.A. 111 L12 34 7N 114 31W
Vidal Junction, U.S.A. 111 L12 34 11N 114 34W
Vidalia, U.S.A. 115 J4 32 13N 82 25W
Vidamlya, Belarus .. 31 F10 52 19N 23 47 E
Vidauban, France .. 21 E10 43 25N 6 27 E
Videbæk, Denmark . 11 H2 56 6N 8 38 E
Videle, Romania ... 29 F10 44 17N 25 31 E
Vídho, Greece ..... 49 A3 39 38N 19 55 E
Vidigueira, Portugal . 37 G3 38 12N 7 48W
Vidin, Bulgaria .... 44 C6 43 59N 22 50 E
Vidio, C., Spain 36 B4 43 35N 6 14W
Vidisha, India ..... 68 H7 23 28N 77 53 E
Vidra, Romania ... 29 E11 45 56N 26 55 E
Viduša, Bos.-H. .... 44 D2 42 55N 18 21 E
Vidzy, Belarus ..... 9 J22 55 23N 26 37 E
Viechtach, Germany . 25 F8 49 4N 12 53 E
Viedma, Argentina .. 128 E4 40 50 S 63 0W
Viedma, L., Argentina 128 F2 49 30 S 72 30W
Vieira do Minho,
Portugal 36 D2 41 38N 8 8W
Vielha, Spain ..... 38 C5 42 43N 0 44 E
Viella = Vielha, Spain . 38 C5 42 43N 0 44 E
Vielsalm, Belgium .. 17 D5 50 17N 5 54 E
Vienenburg, Germany 24 D6 51 57N 10 34 E
Vieng Pou Kha, Laos . 58 G3 20 41N 101 4 E
Vienna = Wien, Austria 27 C9 48 12N 16 22 E
Vienna, Ill., U.S.A. .. 113 G10 37 25N 88 54W
Vienna, Mo., U.S.A. . 112 F9 38 11N 91 57W
Vienne, France .... 21 C8 45 31N 4 53 E
Vienne □, France ... 20 B4 46 30N 0 42 E
Vienne →, France .. 18 E7 47 13N 0 5 E
Vientiane, Laos .... 64 D4 17 58N 102 36 E
Vientos, Paso de los,
Caribbean 121 C5 20 0N 74 0W
Vieques, Isla de,
Puerto Rico ..... 121 d 18 8N 65 25W
Vierge Pt., St. Lucia .. 121 f 13 49N 60 53W
Vierheim, Germany . 25 F4 49 31N 8 35 E
Viersen, Germany .. 24 D2 51 15N 6 23 E
Vierwaldstättersee,
Switz. .... 25 J4 47 0N 8 30 E
Vierzon, France .... 19 E9 47 13N 2 5 E
Vieste, Italy ...... 41 G13 41 53N 16 10 E
Vietnam ■, Asia ... 64 C6 19 0N 106 0 E
Vieux-Boucau-les-Bains,
France 20 E2 43 48N 1 23W
Vieux Fort, St. Lucia . 121 f 13 46N 60 58W
Vif, France .... 21 C9 45 5N 5 41 E
Vigan, Phil. ...... 61 C4 17 35N 120 28 E
Vigévano, Italy .... 40 C5 45 19N 8 51 E
Vigia, Brazil ...... 125 D9 0 50 S 48 5W
Vigía Chico, Mexico . 119 D7 19 46N 87 35W
Víglas, Ákra, Greece . 49 D9 35 54N 27 51 E
Vignemale, France .. 20 F3 42 47N 0 10W
Vignelles-lès-
Hattonchâtel, France 19 D12 48 59N 5 43 E
Vignola, Italy ..... 40 D8 44 29N 11 1 E
Vigo, Spain 36 C2 42 12N 8 41W
Vigo, Ría de, Spain .. 36 C2 42 15N 8 47 E
Vigso Bugt, Denmark 11 G2 57 8N 8 47 E
Vihiers, France 18 E6 47 10N 0 30W
Vihowa, Pakistan ... 68 D4 31 8N 70 30 E
Vihowa →, Pakistan . 68 D4 31 8N 70 41 E
Vijayawada, India .. 67 L12 16 31N 80 39 E
Víjosë →, Albania .. 44 F3 40 37N 19 24 E
Vík, Iceland 8 E4 63 25N 19 1W
Vika, Sweden ..... 10 D8 60 57N 14 28 E
Vikarbyn, Sweden .. 10 D9 60 55N 15 1 E
Vikeke = Viqueque,
E. Timor .... 63 F7 8 52 S 126 23 E
Viken, Skåne, Sweden 11 H6 56 9N 12 34 E
Viken, Västra Götaland,
Sweden .... 11 F8 58 39N 14 20 E
Viking, Canada 102 C6 53 7N 111 50W
Vikmanshyttan, Sweden 10 D9 60 17N 15 49 E
Vikna, Norway .... 8 D14 64 55N 10 58 E
Vikos-Aoos △, Greece 46 B2 40 5N 20 45 E

Vila do Conde, *Portugal* **36 D2** 41 21N 8 45W
Vila Franca de Xira,
  Portugal **37 G2** 38 57N 8 59W
Vila Gamito, *Mozam.* . **87 E3** 14 12 S 33 0 E
Vila Gomes da Costa,
  Mozam. **89 C5** 24 20 S 33 37 E
Vila Machado, *Mozam.* **87 F3** 19 15 S 34 14 E
Vila Mouzinho, *Mozam.* **87 E3** 14 48 S 34 25 E
Vila Nova de Famalicão,
  Portugal **36 D2** 41 25N 8 32W
Vila Nova de Fos Côa,
  Portugal **36 D3** 41 5N 7 9W
Vila Nova de Gaia,
  Portugal **36 D2** 41 4N 8 40W
Vila Nova de Ourém,
  Portugal **36 F2** 39 40N 8 35W
Vila Pouca de Aguiar,
  Portugal **36 D3** 41 30N 7 38W
Vila Real, *Portugal* **36 D3** 41 17N 7 48W
Vila Real □, *Portugal* . **36 D3** 41 36N 7 35W
Vila-real de los Infantes,
  Spain **38 F4** 39 55N 0 3W
Vila Real de Santo
  António, *Portugal* ... **37 H3** 37 10N 7 28W
Vila Vasco da Gama,
  Mozam. **87 E3** 14 54 S 32 14 E
Vila Velha, *Brazil* . **127 A7** 20 20 S 40 17W
Vila Viçosa, *Portugal* . **37 G3** 38 45N 7 27W
Vilafranca del Maestrat,
  Spain **38 E4** 40 26N 0 16E
Vilafranca del Penedès,
  Spain **38 D6** 41 21N 1 40 E
Vilagarcía de Arousa,
  Spain **36 C2** 42 34N 8 46W
Vilaine →, *France* **18 E4** 47 30N 2 27W
Vilanandro, Tanjona,
  Madag. **89 B7** 16 11 S 44 27 E
Vilanculos, *Mozam.* . **89 C6** 22 1 S 35 17 E
Vilanova de Castelló,
  Spain **39 F4** 39 5N 0 31W
Vilanova i la Geltrú,
  Spain **38 D6** 41 13N 1 40 E
Vilar Formoso, *Portugal* **36 E4** 40 38N 6 45W
Vilaseca, *Spain* ..... **38 D6** 41 7N 1 9 E
Vilaseca-Salou =
  Vilaseca, *Spain* .... **38 D6** 41 7N 1 9 E
Viljberg, *Denmark* .... **11 H2** 56 12N 8 46 E
Vilcheka, Zemlya,
  Russia **4 A11** 80 30N 60 30 E
Vilches, *Spain* **37 G7** 38 12N 3 30W
Vileyka, *Belarus* .... **32 E4** 54 30N 26 53 E
Vilhelmina, *Sweden* .. **8 D17** 64 35N 16 39 E
Vilhena, *Brazil* .... **124 F6** 12 40 S 60 5W
Viliya = Neris →,
  Lithuania **9 J21** 55 8N 24 16 E
Viljandi, *Estonia* .... **9 G21** 58 28N 25 30 E
Vilkaviškis, *Lithuania* . **30 D10** 54 39N 23 2 E
Vilkija, *Lithuania* .... **30 C10** 55 3N 23 35 E
Vilkitskogo, Proliv,
  Russia **53 B11** 78 0N 103 0 E
Vilkovo = Vylkove,
  Ukraine **29 E14** 45 28N 29 32 E
Villa Abecia, *Bolivia* . **126 A2** 21 0 S 68 18W
Villa Ahumada, *Mexico* **118 A3** 30 38N 106 30W
Villa Ana, *Argentina* . **126 B4** 28 28 S 59 40W
Villa Ángela, *Argentina* **126 B3** 27 34 S 60 45W
Villa Bella, *Bolivia* ... **124 F5** 10 25 S 65 22W
Villa Cañás, *Argentina* . **126 C3** 34 0 S 61 35W
Villa Colón, *Argentina* . **126 C2** 31 38 S 68 20W
Villa Constitución,
  Argentina **126 C3** 33 15 S 60 20W
Villa de María,
  Argentina **126 B3** 29 55 S 63 43W
Villa del Rio, *Spain* . **37 H6** 37 59N 4 17W
Villa Dolores, *Argentina* **126 C2** 31 58 S 65 15W
Villa Frontera, *Mexico* . **118 B4** 26 56N 101 27W
Villa Guillermina,
  Argentina **126 B4** 28 15 S 59 29W
Villa Hayes, *Paraguay* . **126 B4** 25 5 S 57 20W
Villa Iris, *Argentina* .. **126 D3** 38 12 S 63 12W
Villa Juárez, *Mexico* . **118 B4** 27 37N 100 44W
Villa María, *Argentina* . **126 C3** 32 20 S 63 10W
Villa Mazán, *Argentina* **126 B2** 28 40 S 66 30W
Villa Minozzo, *Italy* ... **40 D7** 44 22N 10 28 E
Villa Montes, *Bolivia* . **126 A3** 21 10 S 63 30W
Villa Ocampo, *Argentina* **126 B4** 28 30 S 59 20W
Villa Ocampo, *Mexico* . **118 B3** 26 29N 105 30W
Villa Ojo de Agua,
  Argentina **126 B3** 29 30 S 63 44W
Villa San Giovanni, *Italy* **43 D8** 38 13N 15 38 E
Villa San José, *Argentina* **126 C4** 32 12 S 58 15W
Villa San Martín,
  Argentina **126 B3** 28 15 S 64 9W
Villa Santina, *Italy* ... **41 B9** 46 24N 12 55 E
Villa Unión, *Mexico* . **118 C3** 23 12N 106 14W
Villablino, *Spain* **36 C4** 42 57N 6 19W
Villacarlos, *Spain* .... **48 B11** 39 53N 4 17 E
Villacarriedo, *Spain* .. **36 B7** 43 14N 3 48W
Villacarrillo, *Spain* ... **37 G7** 38 7N 3 3W
Villacastín, *Spain* **36 E6** 40 46N 4 25W
Villach, *Austria* ..... **26 E6** 46 37N 13 51 E
Villacidro, *Italy* ..... **42 C1** 39 27N 8 44 E
Villada, *Spain* **36 C6** 42 15N 4 59W
Villadiego, *Spain* **36 C6** 42 31N 4 1W
Villadóssola, *Italy* ... **40 B5** 46 4N 8 16 E
Villafeliche, *Spain* ... **38 D3** 41 10N 1 30W
Villafranca, *Spain* ... **38 C5** 42 17N 1 46W
Villafranca de los
  Barros, *Spain* **37 G4** 38 35N 6 18W
Villafranca de los
  Caballeros, *Baleares*,
  Spain **48 B10** 39 34N 3 25 E
Villafranca de los
  Caballeros, *Toledo*,
  Spain **37 F7** 39 26N 3 21W
Villafranca del Cid =
  Vilafranca del
  Maestrat, *Spain* ... **38 E4** 40 26N 0 16E
Villafranca del
  Panadés = Vilafranca
  del Penedès, *Spain* . **38 D6** 41 21N 1 40 E
Villafranca di Verona,
  Italy **40 C7** 45 21N 10 50 E
Villafranca Tirrena, *Italy* **43 D8** 38 20N 15 25 E
Villagrán, *Mexico* **119 C5** 24 29N 99 29W
Villaguay, *Argentina* . **126 C4** 32 0 S 59 0W
Villaharta, *Spain* **37 G6** 38 9N 4 54W
Villahermosa, *Mexico* . **119 D6** 17 59N 92 55W
Villahermosa, *Spain* . **39 G2** 38 46N 2 52W
Villaines-la-Juhel,
  France **18 D6** 48 21N 0 20W
Villajoyosa, *Spain* **39 G4** 38 30N 0 12W
Villalba, *Spain* **36 B3** 43 26N 7 40W
Villalba de Guardo,
  Spain **36 C6** 42 42N 4 49W
Villalón de Campos,
  Spain **36 C5** 42 5N 5 4W
Villalpando, *Spain* ... **36 D5** 41 51N 5 25W

Villaluenga, *Spain* **36 E7** 40 2N 3 54W
Villamanán, *Spain* ... **36 C5** 42 19N 5 35W
Villamartín, *Spain* ... **37 J5** 36 52N 5 38W
Villamayor de Santiago,
  Spain **38 F2** 39 50N 2 59W
Villamblard, *France* .. **20 C4** 45 2N 0 32 E
Villanova Monteleone,
  Italy **42 B1** 40 30N 8 28 E
Villanueva, *U.S.A.* ... **113 H2** 35 16N 105 22W
Villanueva de
  Castellón = Vilanova
  de Castelló, *Spain* . **39 F4** 39 5N 0 31W
Villanueva de Córdoba,
  Spain **37 G6** 38 20N 4 38W
Villanueva de la Fuente,
  Spain **39 G2** 38 42N 2 42W
Villanueva de la Serena,
  Spain **37 G5** 38 59N 5 50W
Villanueva de la Sierra,
  Spain **36 E4** 40 12N 6 24W
Villanueva de los
  Castillejos, *Spain* .. **37 H3** 37 30N 7 15W
Villanueva de los
  Infantes, *Spain* ... **37 G7** 38 43N 3 1W
Villanueva del
  Arzobispo, *Spain* .. **39 G2** 38 10N 3 0W
Villanueva del Fresno,
  Spain **37 G3** 38 23N 7 10W
Villanueva y Geltrú =
  Vilanova i la Geltrú,
  Spain **38 D6** 41 13N 1 40 E
Villaputzu, *Italy* .... **42 C2** 39 26N 9 34 E
Villaquilambre, *Spain* . **36 C5** 42 39N 5 33W
Villar del Arzobispo,
  Spain **38 F4** 39 44N 0 50W
Villar del Rey, *Spain* . **37 F4** 39 7N 6 50W
Villard-de-Lans, *France* **21 C9** 45 3N 5 33 E
Villarramiel. *Spain* ... **36 C6** 42 2N 4 55W
Villarreal = Vila-real de
  los Infantes, *Spain* . **38 F4** 39 55N 0 3W
Villarrica, *Chile* .... **128 D2** 39 15 S 72 15W
Villarrica, *Paraguay* .. **126 B4** 25 40 S 56 30W
Villarrobledo, *Spain* .. **39 F2** 39 18N 2 36W
Villarroya de la Sierra,
  Spain **38 D3** 41 27N 1 46W
Villarrubia de los Ojos,
  Spain **37 F7** 39 14N 3 36W
Villars-les-Dombes,
  France **19 F12** 46 0N 5 3 E
Villasayas, *Spain* ... **38 D2** 41 24N 2 39W
Villaseca de los
  Gamitos = Villaseco
  de los Gamitos, *Spain* **36 D4** 41 2N 6 7W
Villaseco de los
  Gamitos, *Spain* **36 D4** 41 2N 6 7W
Villasimíus, *Italy* .... **42 C2** 39 8N 9 31 E
Villastar, *Spain* **38 E3** 40 17N 1 9W
Villatobas, *Spain* **36 F7** 39 54N 3 20W
Villavicencio, *Argentina* **126 C2** 32 28 S 69 0W
Villavicencio, *Colombia* **124 C4** 4 9N 73 37W
Villaviciosa, *Spain* ... **36 B5** 43 32N 5 27W
Villazón, *Bolivia* .... **126 A2** 22 0 S 65 35W
Ville-Marie, *Canada* .. **104 C4** 47 20N 79 30W
Ville Platte, *U.S.A.* .. **113 K8** 30 41N 92 17W
Villedieu-les-Poêles,
  France **18 D5** 48 50N 1 13W
Villefort, *France* .... **20 D7** 44 28N 3 56 E
Villefranche-de-
  Lauragais, *France* . **20 E5** 43 25N 1 44 E
Villefranche-de-
  Rouergue, *France* .. **20 D6** 44 21N 2 2 E
Villefranche-du-
  Périgord, *France* .. **20 D5** 44 38N 1 5 E
Villefranche-sur-Saône,
  France **21 C8** 45 59N 4 43 E
Villel, *Spain* **38 E3** 40 14N 1 12W
Villemur-sur-Tarn,
  France **20 E5** 43 51N 1 31 E
Villena, *Spain* **39 G4** 38 39N 0 52W
Villenauxe-la-Grande,
  France **19 D10** 48 35N 3 33 E
Villeneuve-d'Ornon,
  France **20 D3** 44 46N 0 33W
Villeneuve-d'Ascq,
  France **19 B10** 50 38N 3 9 E
Villeneuve-
  l'Archevêque, *France* **19 D10** 48 14N 3 32 E
Villeneuve-lès-Avignon,
  France **21 E8** 43 58N 4 49 E
Villeneuve-sur-Allier,
  France **19 F10** 46 40N 3 13 E
Villeneuve-sur-Lot,
  France **20 D4** 44 24N 0 42 E
Villeneuve-sur-Yonne,
  France **19 D10** 48 5N 3 18 E
Villeréal, *France* .... **20 D4** 44 38N 0 45 E
Villers-Bocage, *France* . **18 C6** 49 3N 0 40W
Villers-Cotterêts, *France* **19 C10** 49 15N 3 4 E
Villers-sur-Mer, *France* **18 C6** 49 21N 0 2W
Villersexel, *France* ... **19 E13** 47 33N 6 26 E
Villerupt, *France* .... **19 C12** 49 28N 5 55 E
Villeurbanne, *France* . **21 C8** 45 50N 4 55 E
Villiers, *S. Africa* .... **89 D4** 27 2 S 28 36 E
Villingen-Schwenningen,
  Germany **25 G4** 48 3N 8 26 E
Villmanstrand =
  Lappeenranta,
  Finland **9 F23** 61 3N 28 12 E
Vilna, *Canada* **102 C6** 54 7N 111 55W
Vilnius, *Lithuania* .... **9 J21** 54 38N 25 19 E
Vils, *Austria* .... **26 D3** 47 33N 10 38 E
Vils →, *Bayern*,
  Germany **25 G9** 48 37N 13 11 E
Vils →, *Bayern*,
  Germany **25 F7** 49 10N 11 57 E
Vilsbiburg, *Germany* . **25 G8** 48 26N 12 22 E
Vilshofen, *Germany* .. **25 G9** 48 37N 13 11 E
Vilusi, *Serbia & M.* .. **44 D2** 42 44N 18 34 E
Vilvoorde, *Belgium* ... **17 D4** 50 56N 4 26 E
Vilyuy →, *Russia* .... **53 C13** 64 24N 126 26 E
Vilyuysk, *Russia* .... **53 C13** 63 40N 121 35 E
Vimianzo, *Spain* **36 B1** 43 7N 9 2W
Vimioso, *Portugal* ... **36 D4** 41 35N 6 31W
Vimmerby, *Sweden* .. **11 G9** 57 40N 15 55 E
Vimoutiers, *France* ... **18 D7** 48 57N 0 10 E
Vimperk, *Czech Rep.* . **26 B6** 49 3N 13 46 E
Viña del Mar, *Chile* . **126 C1** 33 0 S 71 30W
Vinarós, *Spain* ..... **38 E5** 40 30N 0 27 E
Vinchina, *Argentina* . **126 B2** 28 45 S 68 15W
Vindelälven →, *Sweden* **8 E18** 63 55N 19 50 E
Vindeln, *Sweden* .... **8 D18** 64 12N 19 43 E
Vinderup, *Denmark* .. **11 H2** 56 29N 8 45 E
Vindhya Ra., *India* ... **68 H7** 22 50N 77 0 E
Vineland, *U.S.A.* **114 F8** 39 29N 75 2W
Vineuil, *France* ..... **18** 47 35N 1 22 E
Vinga, *Romania* .... **28 D6** 46 1N 21 14 E

Vingåker, *Sweden* ... **10 E9** 59 2N 15 52 E
Vinh, *Vietnam* ...... **64 C5** 18 45N 105 38 E
Vinh Linh, *Vietnam* .. **64 D6** 17 4N 107 2 E
Vinh Long, *Vietnam* . **65 G5** 10 16N 105 57 E
Vinh Yen, *Vietnam* .. **58 G5** 21 21N 105 33 E
Vinica, *Croatia* **26 D3** 41 50N 7 5W
Vinica, *Macedonia* ... **44 E6** 41 53N 22 30 E
Vinica, *Slovenia* .... **41 C12** 45 28N 15 15 E
Vinica, *U.S.A.* **113 G7** 36 39N 95 9W
Vinkovci, *Croatia* .... **28 E3** 45 19N 18 48 E
Vinnitsa = Vinnytsya,
  Ukraine **33 H5** 49 15N 28 30 E
Vinnytsya, *Ukraine* .. **33 H5** 49 15N 28 30 E
Vinslöv, *Sweden* .... **11 H7** 56 7N 13 55 E
Vinson Massif,
  Antarctica **5 D16** 78 35 S 85 25W
Vintјärn, *Sweden* ... **10 D9** 60 22N 16 0 E
Vinton, Calif., *U.S.A.* . **110 F6** 39 48N 120 10W
Vinton, Iowa, *U.S.A.* . **112 D8** 42 10N 92 1W
Vinton, La., *U.S.A.* .. **113 K8** 30 11N 93 35W
Vințu de Jos, *Romania* **29 D8** 46 0N 23 30 E
Viöl, *Germany* ...... **24 A5** 54 34N 9 11 E
Vipava, *Slovenia* .... **41 C10** 45 51N 13 58 E
Vipiteno, *Italy* ...... **41 B8** 46 54N 11 26 E
Viqueque, *E. Timor* .. **63 F7** 8 52 S 126 23 E
Vir, *Croatia* .... **41 D12** 44 17N 15 3 E
Virac, *Phil.* .... **61 E6** 13 30N 124 20 E
Virachey, *Cambodia* . **64 F6** 13 59N 106 49 E
Virachey Δ, *Cambodia* **64 E6** 14 14N 106 55 E
Virago Sd., *Canada* .. **102 C2** 54 0N 132 30W
Viramgam, *India* .... **68 H5** 23 5N 72 0 E
Viranşehir, *Turkey* ... **70 B3** 37 13N 39 45 E
Virawah, *Pakistan* ... **68 G4** 24 31N 70 46 E
Virbalis, *Lithuania* ... **30 D10** 54 39N 22 49 E
Virden, *Canada* **103 D8** 49 50N 100 56W
Vire, *France* **18 D6** 48 50N 0 53W
Vire →, *France* **18 C5** 49 20N 1 7W
Vírgenes, C., *Argentina* **128 G3** 52 19 S 68 21W
Virgin →, *U.S.A.* **109 H6** 36 28N 114 21W
Virgin Gorda,
  Br. Virgin Is. .... **121 e** 18 30N 64 26W
Virgin Is. (British) ∅,
  W. Indies .... **121 e** 18 30N 64 30W
Virgin Is. (U.S.) ∅,
  W. Indies .... **121 e** 18 20N 65 0W
Virgin Islands Δ,
  U.S. Virgin Is. **121 C7** 18 21N 64 43W
Virginia, *S. Africa* ... **88 D4** 28 8 S 26 55 E
Virginia, *U.S.A.* **112 B8** 47 31N 92 32W
Virginia □, *U.S.A.* ... **114 G7** 37 30N 78 45W
Virginia Beach, *U.S.A.* **114 G8** 36 51N 75 59W
Virginia City, Mont.,
  U.S.A. **108 D8** 45 18N 111 56W
Virginia City, Nev.,
  U.S.A. **110 F7** 39 19N 119 39W
Virginia Falls, *Canada* **102 A3** 61 38N 125 42W
Virginiatown, *Canada* . **104 C4** 48 9N 79 36W
Virje, *Croatia* .... **41 B13** 46 4N 16 59 E
Viroqua, *U.S.A.* **112 D9** 43 34N 90 53W
Virovitica, *Croatia* ... **28 E2** 45 51N 17 21 E
Virpazar, *Serbia & M.* **44 D3** 42 14N 19 6 E
Virpur, *India* .... **68 J4** 21 51N 70 42 E
Virserum, *Sweden* ... **11 G9** 57 20N 15 35 E
Virton, *Belgium* ..... **17 E5** 49 35N 5 32 E
Virudunagar, *India* ... **66 Q10** 9 30N 77 58 E
Virunga Δ, *Dem. Rep. of
  the Congo* **86 B2** 0 5N 29 38 E
Vis, *Croatia* .... **41 E13** 43 4N 16 10 E
Visalia, *U.S.A.* **110 J7** 36 20N 119 18W
Visayan Sea, *Phil.* ... **61 F5** 11 30N 123 30 E
Visby, *Sweden* ...... **11 G12** 57 37N 18 18 E
Viscount Melville Sd.,
  Canada **98 B9** 74 10N 108 0W
Visé, *Belgium* ...... **17 D5** 50 44N 5 41 E
Višegrad, *Bos.-H.* ... **28 G3** 43 47N 19 17 E
Viseu, *Brazil* .... **125 D9** 1 10 S 46 5W
Viseu, *Portugal* **36 E3** 40 40N 7 55W
Viseu □, *Portugal* ... **36 E3** 40 40N 7 55W
Vișeu de Sus, *Romania* **29 C9** 47 45N 24 25 E
Vishakhapatnam, *India* **67 L13** 17 45N 83 20 E
Vișina, *Romania* .... **29 F9** 44 20N 24 27 E
Vișinești, *Moldova* ... **29 D13** 46 20N 28 27 E
Visingsö, *Sweden* ... **11 F8** 58 2N 14 20 E
Viskafors, *Sweden* ... **11 G6** 57 37N 12 50 E
Viskan →, *Sweden* .. **11 G6** 57 14N 12 12 E
Viški Kanal, *Croatia* . **41 E13** 43 4N 16 5 E
Vislanda, *Sweden* ... **11 H8** 56 46N 14 30 E
Visnagar, *India* ..... **68 H5** 23 45N 72 32 E
Višnja Gora, *Slovenia* . **41 C11** 45 58N 14 45 E
Viso, Mte., *Italy* .... **40 D4** 44 38N 7 5 E
Viso del Marqués, *Spain* **37 G7** 38 32N 3 34W
Visoko, *Bos.-H.* ..... **28 G3** 43 58N 18 10 E
Visokoi I., *Antarctica* . **5 B1** 56 43 S 27 15W
Visp, *Switz.* .... **25 J3** 46 17N 7 52 E
Visselfjärda, *Sweden* . **11 H9** 56 33N 15 35 E
Vissenbjerg, *Germany* **24 C5** 52 59N 9 34 E
Vissenbjerg, *Denmark* **11 J4** 55 23N 10 7 E
Vista, *U.S.A.* **111 M9** 33 12N 117 14W
Vistonís, Ormos =
  Vistonís, Límni,
  Greece **45 E9** 41 0N 25 7 E
Vistonís, Límni, *Greece* **45 E9** 41 0N 25 7 E
Vistula = Wisła →,
  Poland **30 D5** 54 22N 18 55 E
Vit →, *Bulgaria* ..... **35 C8** 43 30N 24 30 E
Vitanje, *Slovenia* .... **41 B12** 46 25N 15 18 E
Vitebsk = Vitsyebsk,
  Belarus **32 E6** 55 10N 30 15 E
Viterbo, *Italy* .... **41 F9** 42 25N 12 6 E
Vitez, *Bos.-H.* ...... **28 F2** 44 10N 17 48 E
Viti Levu, *Fiji* ...... **91 C7** 17 30 S 177 30 E
Vitigudino, *Spain* **36 D4** 41 1N 6 26W
Vitim, *Russia* .... **53 D12** 59 28N 112 35 E
Vitim →, *Russia* .... **53 D12** 59 26N 112 34 E
Vitina, *Bos.-H.* ...... **41 E14** 43 17N 17 29 E
Vítina, *Greece* ...... **46 D4** 37 40N 22 10 E
Vítkov, *Czech Rep.* .. **27 B10** 49 46N 17 45 E
Vitória, *Brazil* ...... **125 H10** 20 20 S 40 22W
Vitória da Conquista,
  Brazil **125 F10** 14 51 S 40 51W
Vitória de São Antão,
  Brazil **125 E11** 8 10 S 35 20W
Vitoria-Gasteiz, *Spain* . **38 C2** 42 50N 2 41W
Vitosha Δ, *Bulgaria* .. **44 D7** 42 30N 23 10 E
Vitré, *France* **18 D5** 48 8N 1 12W
Vitry-le-François, *France* **19 D11** 48 43N 4 33 E
Vitry-sur-Seine, *France* **19 D9** 48 47N 2 24 E
Vitsand, *Sweden* .... **10 D7** 60 20N 13 0 E
Vitsi, Óros, *Greece* .. **44 F5** 40 40N 21 25 E
Vitsyebsk, *Belarus* ... **32 E6** 55 10N 30 15 E
Vittangi, *Sweden* .... **8 C18** 67 40N 21 25 E
Vittaurt, *Sweden* .... **11 H7** 56 58N 13 57 E
Vittel, *France* .... **19 D12** 48 12N 5 57 E
Vittória, *Italy* .... **43 F7** 36 57N 14 32 E
Vittório Véneto, *Italy* . **41 C9** 45 59N 12 18 E
Vittsjö, *Sweden* ..... **11 H7** 56 20N 13 40 E
Viveiro, *Spain* **36 B3** 43 39N 7 38W

Vivian, *U.S.A.* **113 J8** 32 53N 93 59W
Viviers, *France* ..... **21 D8** 44 30N 4 40 E
Vivonne, *France* .... **20 B4** 46 25N 0 15 E
Vizcaíno, Desierto de,
  Mexico **118 B2** 27 40N 113 50W
Vizcaíno, Sierra, *Mexico* **118 B2** 27 30N 114 0W
Vizcaya □, *Spain* **38 B2** 43 15N 2 45W
Vizianagaram, *India* .. **67 K13** 18 6N 83 30 E
Vizille, *France* ...... **21 C9** 45 5N 5 46 E
Viziñada, *Croatia* .... **41 C10** 45 20N 13 46 E
Viziru, *Romania* ..... **29 E12** 45 0N 27 43 E
Vizzini, *Italy* .... **43 E7** 37 10N 14 45 E
Vlaardingen, *Neths.* .. **17 C4** 51 55N 4 21 E
Vladeasa, Vf., *Romania* **28 D7** 46 47N 22 50 E
Vladičin Han,
  Serbia & M. **44 D6** 42 42N 22 1 E
Vladikavkaz, *Russia* .. **35 J7** 43 0N 44 35 E
Vladimir, *Russia* .... **32 D11** 56 15N 40 30 E
Vladimir Volynskiy =
  Volodymyr-
  Volynskyy, *Ukraine* **33 G3** 50 50N 24 18 E
Vladimirci, *Serbia & M.* **44 B3** 44 36N 19 50 E
Vladimirovac,
  Serbia & M. **28 E5** 45 1N 20 53 E
Vladimirovka, *Russia* . **35 F8** 48 27N 46 10 E
Vladimirovo, *Bulgaria* **44 C7** 43 32N 23 22 E
Vladimorvka,
  Kazakhstan **34 E10** 50 51N 51 8 E
Vladislavovka, *Ukraine* **33 K8** 45 12N 35 29 E
Vladivostok, *Russia* .. **53 E14** 43 10N 131 53 E
Vlǎhița, *Romania* .... **29 D10** 46 21N 25 31 E
Vlakhiótis, *Greece* ... **46 E4** 36 52N 22 42 E
Vlasenica, *Bos.-H.* ... **28 F3** 44 11N 18 59 E
Vlašić, *Bos.-H.* ...... **28 F2** 44 19N 17 37 E
Vlašim, *Czech Rep.* .. **26 B7** 49 40N 14 53 E
Vlasinsko Jezero,
  Serbia & M. **44 D6** 42 44N 22 22 E
Vlasotince, *Serbia & M.* **44 D6** 42 59N 22 7 E
Vlieland, *Neths.* ..... **17 A4** 53 16N 4 55 E
Vlissingen, *Neths.* ... **17 C3** 51 26N 3 34 E
Vlorë, *Albania* ...... **44 F3** 40 32N 19 28 E
Vlorë, Gjiri i, *Albania* **44 F3** 40 29N 19 27 E
Vltava →, *Czech Rep.* **26 A7** 50 21N 14 30 E
Vo Dat, *Vietnam* .... **65 G6** 11 9N 107 31 E
Vobarno, *Italy* ...... **40 C7** 45 39N 10 30 E
Voćin, *Croatia* ...... **28 E2** 45 37N 17 33 E
Vöcklabruck, *Austria* . **26 C6** 48 1N 13 39 E
Vodice, *Croatia* ..... **41 E12** 43 47N 15 47 E
Vodňany, *Czech Rep.* **26 B7** 49 9N 14 11 E
Vodnjan, *Croatia* .... **41 D10** 44 59N 13 52 E
Voe, *U.K.* **13 A7** 60 21N 1 16W
Vogel Pk., *Nigeria* ... **83 D7** 8 24N 11 47 E
Vogelkop = Doberai,
  Jazirah, *Indonesia* . **63 E8** 1 25 S 133 0 E
Vogelsberg, *Germany* . **24 E5** 50 31N 9 12 E
Voghera, *Italy* ...... **40 D6** 44 59N 9 1 E
Vohibinany, *Madag.* . **89 B8** 18 49 S 49 4 E
Vohilava, *Madag.* .... **89 C8** 21 4 S 48 0 E
Vohimarina = Iharana,
  Madag. **89 A9** 13 25 S 50 0 E
Vohimena, Tanjon' i,
  Madag. **89 D8** 25 36 S 45 8 E
Vohipeno, *Madag.* ... **89 C8** 22 22 S 47 51 E
Voi, *Kenya* .... **86 C4** 3 25 S 38 32 E
Void-Vacon, *France* .. **19 D12** 48 40N 5 36 E
Voineşti, Iaşi, *Romania* **29 C12** 47 5N 27 27 E
Voineşti, Prahova,
  Romania **29 E10** 45 5N 25 14 E
Voiotía □, *Greece* ... **46 C5** 38 20N 23 0 E
Voiron, *France* ...... **21 C9** 45 22N 5 35 E
Voisey B., *Canada* ... **105 A7** 56 15N 61 50W
Voitsberg, *Austria* ... **26 D8** 47 3N 15 9 E
Vojens, *Denmark* .... **11 J3** 55 16N 9 18 E
Vojmsjön, *Sweden* ... **8 D17** 65 0N 16 24 E
Vojnic, *Croatia* ...... **41 C12** 45 19N 15 43 E
Vojnik, *Italy* .... **41 B12** 46 18N 15 19 E
Vojvodina □,
  Serbia & M. **28 E5** 45 20N 20 0 E
Vokhtoga, *Russia* .... **32 C11** 58 46N 41 8 E
Volary, *Czech Rep.* .. **26 C6** 48 54N 13 52 E
Volborg, *U.S.A.* **112 C2** 45 51N 105 41W
Volcán de Colima Δ,
  Mexico **118 D4** 19 30N 103 40W
Volcano Is. = Kazan-
  Rettō, Pac. Oc. .... **96 E6** 25 0N 141 0 E
Volcans Δ, Rwanda .. **86 C2** 1 30 S 29 26 E
Volcans d'Auvergne Δ,
  France **20 C6** 45 20N 2 40 E
Volchansk = Vovchansk,
  Ukraine **33 G9** 50 17N 36 58 E
Volchya →, *Ukraine* .. **33 H8** 48 32N 36 0 E
Volda, *Norway* ...... **9 E12** 62 9N 6 5 E
Volga = Privolzhskiy □,
  Russia **34 B10** 56 0N 50 0 E
Volga, *Russia* .... **32 C10** 57 58N 38 16 E
Volga →, *Russia* .... **35 F8** 46 0N 48 30 E
Volga Hts. =
  Privolzhskaya
  Vozvyshennost,
  Russia **34 E7** 51 0N 46 0 E
Volgo-Baltiyskiy Kanal,
  Russia **32 B9** 60 0N 38 0 E
Volgo-Donskoy Kanal,
  Russia **35 F7** 48 40N 43 37 E
Volgodonsk, *Russia* .. **35 G6** 47 33N 42 5 E
Volgograd, *Russia* ... **35 F7** 48 40N 44 25 E
Volgogradskoye Vdkhr.,
  Russia **34 E8** 50 0N 45 20 E
Volgorechensk, *Russia* **34 B5** 57 28N 41 14 E
Volímai, *Greece* ..... **46 D2** 37 52N 20 59 E
Volíntiri, *Moldova* ... **29 D14** 46 26N 29 37 E
Volissós, *Greece* .... **47 C7** 38 29N 25 54 E
Volkach, *Germany* ... **25 F6** 49 52N 10 14 E
Völkermarkt, *Austria* . **26 E7** 46 39N 14 39 E
Volkhov, *Russia* ..... **32 C7** 59 55N 32 15 E
Volkhov →, *Russia* .. **32 B7** 60 8N 32 20 E
Völklingen, *Germany* . **25 F2** 49 15N 6 50 E
Volkovysk =
  Vawkavysk, *Belarus* **33 F3** 53 9N 24 30 E
Volksrust, *S. Africa* .. **89 D4** 27 24 S 29 53 E
Volochanka, *Russia* .. **53 B10** 71 0N 94 28 E
Volodarsk, *Russia* ... **34 B6** 56 12N 43 15 E
Volodymyr-Volynskyy,
  Ukraine **33 G3** 50 50N 24 18 E
Vologda, *Russia* ..... **32 C10** 59 10N 39 45 E
Volokolamsk, *Russia* . **32 D8** 56 5N 35 57 E
Volokonovka, *Russia* . **33 G9** 50 33N 37 52 E
Vólos, *Greece* ...... **46 B4** 39 24N 22 59 E
Volosovo, *Russia* .... **32 C5** 59 27N 29 32 E
Volovets, *Ukraine* ... **29 B8** 48 43N 23 11 E
Volovo, *Russia* ...... **32 F10** 53 35N 38 1 E
Volsk, *Russia* .... **34 D8** 52 5N 47 22 E
Volta □, *Ghana* ..... **83 D5** 7 0N 0 30 E

Volta →, *Ghana* ..... **83 D5** 5 46N 0 41 E
Volta, L., *Ghana* **83 D5** 7 30N 0 0W
Volta Blanche = White
  Volta →, *Ghana* ... **83 D4** 9 10N 1 15W
Volta Redonda, *Brazil* **127 A7** 22 31 S 44 5W
Voltaire, C., *Australia* . **92 B4** 14 16 S 125 35 E
Volterra, *Italy* ...... **40 E7** 43 24N 10 51 E
Voltri, *Italy* .... **40 D5** 44 26N 8 45 E
Volturno →, *Italy* ... **42 A6** 41 1N 13 55 E
Vólvi, L., *Greece* .... **44 F7** 40 40N 23 34 E
Volyně, *Czech Rep.* .. **26 B6** 49 10N 13 53 E
Volzhsk, *Russia* ..... **34 C9** 55 57N 48 23 E
Volzhskiy, *Russia* .... **35 F7** 48 56N 44 46 E
Vondrozo, *Madag.* ... **89 C8** 22 49 S 47 20 E
Vónitsa, *Greece* ..... **46 C2** 38 55N 20 53 E
Vopnafjörður, *Iceland* . **8 D6** 65 45N 14 50W
Vorarlberg □, *Austria* . **26 D2** 47 20N 10 0 E
Vóras Óros, *Greece* .. **44 F5** 40 57N 21 45 E
Vorbasse, *Denmark* .. **11 J3** 55 39N 9 6 E
Vorchdorf, *Austria* ... **26 D6** 48 0N 13 55 E
Vorderrhein →, *Switz.* **25 J5** 46 49N 9 25 E
Vordingborg, *Denmark* **11 J5** 55 0N 11 54 E
Vorë, *Albania* .... **44 E3** 41 23N 19 40 E
Voreio Aigaio = Vórios
  Aiyaíon □, *Greece* . **47 C7** 38 50N 25 30 E
Voreppe, *France* ..... **21 C9** 45 18N 5 39 E
Vóriai Sporádhes,
  Greece **46 B5** 39 15N 23 30 E
Vórios Aiyaíon □,
  Greece **47 C7** 38 50N 25 30 E
Vórios Evvoïkos Kólpos,
  Greece **46 C5** 38 45N 23 15 E
Vorkuta, *Russia* ..... **52 C7** 67 48N 64 20 E
Vormsi, *Estonia* ..... **9 G20** 59 1N 23 13 E
Vóroi, *Greece* ...... **49 F6** 35 4N 24 49 E
Vorona →, *Russia* ... **34 E6** 51 22N 42 3 E
Voronezh, *Russia* .... **33 G10** 51 40N 39 10 E
Voronezh, *Ukraine* .. **33 G7** 51 47N 33 28 E
Voronezh →, *Russia* . **33 G10** 51 32N 39 10 E
Vorontsovo-
  Aleksandrovskoye =
  Zelenokumsk, *Russia* **35 H6** 44 24N 44 0 E
Vorpommersche
  Boddenlandschaft □,
  Germany **24 A8** 54 25N 12 32 E
Vorskla →, *Ukraine* .. **33 H8** 48 50N 34 10 E
Võrts Järv, *Estonia* ... **9 G22** 58 16N 26 3 E
Võru, *Estonia* .... **9 H22** 57 48N 26 54 E
Vosges, *France* ..... **19 D14** 48 20N 7 10 E
Vosges □, *France* ... **19 D13** 48 12N 6 20 E
Vosges du Nord Δ,
  France **19 D14** 49 0N 7 30 E
Voskopojë, *Albania* .. **44 F4** 40 35N 20 33 E
Voskresensk, *Russia* . **32 E10** 55 19N 38 43 E
Voskresenskoye, *Russia* **34 B7** 56 51N 45 30 E
Voss, *Norway* .... **9 F12** 60 38N 6 26 E
Vostok, *Antarctica* ... **5 D8** 78 30 S 106 50 E
Vostok I., *Kiribati* ... **97 J12** 10 5 S 152 23W
Votice, *Czech Rep.* ... **26 B7** 49 38N 14 39 E
Votsuri-Shima, *Japan* . **55 M1** 25 45N 123 29 E
Vouga →, *Portugal* .. **36 E2** 40 41N 8 40W
Vouillé, *France* ...... **18 F7** 46 38N 0 10 E
Voúxa, Ákra, *Greece* . **49 D5** 35 37N 23 32 E
Vouzela, *Portugal* ... **36 E2** 40 43N 8 7W
Vouziers, *France* .... **19 C11** 49 22N 4 40 E
Vovchansk, *Ukraine* . **33 G9** 50 17N 36 58 E
Vowchyn, *Belarus* ... **31 F10** 52 18N 23 18 E
Voyageurs □, *U.S.A.* . **112 A8** 48 32N 93 0W
Vozhe, Ozero, *Russia* **32 B10** 60 45N 39 0 E
Vozhega, *Russia* .... **32 B11** 60 29N 40 12 E
Voznesensk, *Ukraine* . **33 J6** 47 35N 31 21 E
Voznesenye, *Russia* . **32 B8** 61 0N 35 28 E
Vrå, *Denmark* .... **11 G3** 57 21N 9 56 E
Vráble, *Slovak Rep.* . **27 C11** 48 15N 18 16 E
Vraćevšnica,
  Serbia & M. **44 B4** 44 2N 20 34 E
Vrakhnéika, *Greece* .. **46 C3** 38 10N 21 40 E
Vrancea □, *Romania* . **29 E11** 45 50N 26 45 E
Vrancei, Munții,
  Romania **29 E11** 46 0N 26 30 E
Vrangelya, Ostrov,
  Russia **53 B19** 71 0N 180 0 E
Vranica, *Bos.-H.* .... **28 G2** 43 55N 17 50 E
Vranje, *Serbia & M.* . **44 D5** 42 34N 21 54 E
Vranjska Banja,
  Serbia & M. **44 D6** 42 34N 22 1 E
Vranov nad Topľou,
  Slovak Rep. **27 C14** 48 53N 21 40 E
Vransko, *Slovenia* ... **41 B11** 46 17N 14 58 E
Vransko Jezero, *Croatia* **41 E12** 43 53N 15 34 E
Vrapčište, *Macedonia* **44 E4** 41 50N 20 53 E
Vratsa, *Bulgaria* ..... **44 C7** 43 15N 23 30 E
Vrbas, *Serbia & M.* .. **28 E4** 45 40N 19 40 E
Vrbas →, *Bos.-H.* ... **28 E2** 45 8N 17 13 E
Vrbnik, *Croatia* ..... **41 C11** 45 4N 14 40 E
Vrbovec, *Croatia* .... **41 C13** 45 53N 16 28 E
Vrbovsko, *Croatia* ... **41 C12** 45 24N 15 5 E
Vrchlabí, *Czech Rep.* . **26 A8** 50 38N 15 37 E
Vrede, *S. Africa* ..... **89 D4** 27 24 S 29 6 E
Vredefort, *S. Africa* .. **88 D4** 27 0 S 27 12 E
Vreden, *Germany* ... **24 C2** 52 2N 6 50 E
Vredenburg, *S. Africa* **88 E2** 32 56 S 18 0 E
Vredendal, *S. Africa* . **88 E2** 31 41 S 18 35 E
Vretstorp, *Sweden* ... **10 E8** 59 1N 14 53 E
Vrgorac, *Croatia* .... **41 E14** 43 12N 17 20 E
Vrhnika, *Slovenia* ... **41 C11** 45 58N 14 15 E
Vridi, *Ivory C.* **82 D4** 5 15N 4 3W
Vrigstad, *Sweden* .... **11 G8** 57 21N 14 28 E
Vrindavan, *India* .... **68 F7** 27 37N 77 40 E
Vríses, *Greece* ...... **49 D6** 35 23N 24 13 E
Vrnograč, *Bos.-H.* ... **41 C12** 45 10N 15 57 E
Vrondádhes, *Greece* . **47 C8** 38 25N 26 7 E
Vršac, *Serbia & M.* .. **28 E6** 45 8N 21 20 E
Vrsar, *Croatia* ...... **41 D10** 45 9N 13 36 E
Vrsi, *Croatia* .... **41 D11** 44 20N 15 5 E
Vrútky, *Slovak Rep.* . **27 B11** 49 7N 18 55 E
Vryburg, *S. Africa* ... **88 D3** 26 55 S 24 45 E
Vryheid, *S. Africa* ... **89 D5** 27 45 S 30 47 E
Vsetín, *Czech Rep.* .. **27 B11** 49 20N 18 0 E
Vu Liet, *Vietnam* .... **64 C5** 18 43N 105 23 E
Vůcha →, *Bulgaria* .. **45 C8** 42 10N 24 26 E
Vučitrn, *Serbia & M.* . **44 D4** 42 49N 20 59 E
Vukovar, *Croatia* .... **28 E4** 45 21N 18 59 E
Vulcan, *Canada* **102 C6** 50 25N 113 15W
Vulcan, *Romania* .... **29 E8** 45 23N 23 17 E
Vulcanești, *Moldova* . **29 E13** 45 41N 28 18 E
Vulcano, *Italy* ...... **43 D7** 38 24N 14 58 E
Vülchedrum, *Bulgaria* **44 C7** 43 42N 23 27 E
Vulkaneshty =
  Vulcanești, *Moldova* **29 E13** 45 41N 28 18 E
Vunduzi →, *Mozam.* . **87 F3** 18 56 S 34 1 E
Vung Tau, *Vietnam* .. **65 G6** 10 21N 107 4 E
Vutcani, *Romania* ... **29 D12** 46 26N 27 59 E
Vuya, *Sudan* .... **81 F2** 5 21N 29 40 E
Vuzlove, *Ukraine* .... **28 B7** 48 22N 22 24 E

Vwaza △, Malawi	87 E3	10 58 S	33 25 E
Vyartsilya, Russia	32 A6	62 8N	30 45 E
Vyatka = Kirov, Russia	52 D5	58 35N	49 40 E
Vyatka →, Russia	34 C10	55 37N	51 28 E
Vyatskiye Polyany, Russia	34 B10	56 14N	51 5 E
Vyazemskiy, Russia	53 E14	47 32N	134 45 E
Vyazma, Russia	32 E8	55 10N	34 15 E
Vyazniki, Russia	34 B6	56 10N	42 10 E
Vyborg, Russia	32 B5	60 43N	28 47 E
Vychegda →, Russia	52 C5	61 18N	46 36 E
Vychodné Beskydy, Europe	27 B15	49 20N	22 0 E
Vyerkhnyadzvinsk, Belarus	32 E4	55 45N	27 58 E
Vyhoda, Ukraine	29 B8	48 56N	23 55 E
Vyksa, Russia	34 C6	55 19N	42 11 E
Vylkove, Ukraine	29 E14	45 28N	29 32 E
Vylok, Ukraine	28 B7	48 8N	22 50 E
Vynohradiv, Ukraine	28 B7	48 9N	23 2 E
Vyrnwy, L., U.K.	14 E4	52 48N	3 31W
Vyshhorod, Ukraine	29 B8	48 44N	23 39 E
Vyshkove, Ukraine	28 B7	48 3N	23 25 E
Vyshniy Volochek, Russia	32 D8	57 30N	34 30 E
Vyshzha = imeni 26 Bakinskikh Komissarov, Turkmenistan	71 B7	39 22N	54 10 E
Vyškov, Czech Rep.	27 B9	49 17N	17 0 E
Vysokaye, Belarus	31 F10	52 22N	23 22 E
Vysoké Mýto, Czech Rep.	27 B9	49 58N	16 10 E
Vysokovsk, Russia	32 D9	56 22N	36 30 E
Vyšší Brod, Czech Rep.	26 C7	48 37N	14 19 E
Vytegra, Russia	32 B9	61 0N	36 27 E
Vyzhnytsya, Ukraine	29 B10	48 15N	25 11 E
Vyzhnytsya △, Ukraine	29 B10	48 7N	25 15 E

W

W du Benin △, Benin	83 C5	11 57N	2 43 E
W du Burkina Faso △, Burkina Faso	83 C4	11 52N	2 50W
W du Niger △, Niger	83 C5	13 31N	2 28 E
W.A.C. Bennett Dam, Canada	102 B4	56 2N	122 6W
Wa, Ghana	82 C4	10 7N	2 25W
Waal →, Neths.	17 C5	51 37N	5 0 E
Waalwijk, Neths.	17 C5	51 42N	5 4 E
Waat, Sudan	81 F3	8 10N	32 7 E
Wabakimi △, Canada	104 B2	50 43N	89 29W
Wabana, Canada	105 C9	47 40N	53 0W
Wabasca →, Canada	102 B5	58 22N	115 20W
Wabasca-Desmarais, Canada	102 B6	55 57N	113 56W
Wabash, U.S.A.	114 E3	40 48N	85 49W
Wabash →, U.S.A.	114 G1	37 48N	88 2W
Wabi →, Ethiopia	81 F5	7 45N	40 50 E
Wabigoon L., Canada	103 D10	49 44N	92 44W
Wabowden, Canada	103 C9	54 55N	98 38W
Wabu Hu, China	59 A11	32 20N	116 50 E
Wabuk Pt., Canada	104 A2	55 20N	85 5W
Wabush, Canada	105 B6	52 55N	66 52W
Wąchock, Poland	31 G8	51 4N	21 1 E
Waco, U.S.A.	113 K6	31 33N	97 9W
Waconichi, L., Canada	104 B5	50 8N	74 0W
Wad Ban Naqa, Sudan	81 D3	16 32N	33 9 E
Wad Banda, Sudan	81 E2	13 10N	27 56 E
Wad el Haddad, Sudan	81 E3	13 50N	33 30 E
Wad en Nau, Sudan	81 E3	14 10N	33 34 E
Wad Hamid, Sudan	81 D3	16 30N	32 45 E
Wad Medani, Sudan	81 E3	14 28N	33 30 E
Wad Thana, Pakistan	68 F2	27 22N	66 23 E
Wadai, Africa	76 E5	12 0N	19 0 E
Wadayama, Japan	55 G7	35 19N	134 52 E
Waddeneilanden, Neths.	17 A5	53 25N	5 10 E
Waddenzee, Neths.	17 A5	53 6N	5 10 E
Waddi, Chappal, Nigeria	83 D7	7 2N	11 43W
Waddington, Canada	117 B9	44 52N	75 12W
Waddington, Mt., Canada	102 C3	51 23N	125 15W
Waddy Pt., Australia	95 C5	24 58 S	153 21 E
Wadebridge, U.K.	15 G3	50 31N	4 51W
Wadena, Canada	103 C8	51 57N	103 47W
Wadena, U.S.A.	112 B7	46 26N	95 8W
Wädenswil, Switz.	25 H4	47 14N	8 40 E
Wadern, Germany	25 F2	49 32N	6 53 E
Wadeye, Australia	92 B4	14 28 S	129 52 E
Wadhams, Canada	102 C3	51 30N	127 30W
Wadi as Sir, Jordan	74 D4	31 56N	35 49 E
Wadi Gemâl, Egypt	80 C4	24 35N	35 10 E
Wadi Halfa, Sudan	80 C3	21 53N	31 19 E
Wadi Rum △, Jordan	74 F4	29 30N	35 20 E
Wadian, China	59 A9	32 42N	112 29 E
Wadlew, Poland	31 G6	51 31N	19 23 E
Wadowice, Poland	31 J6	49 52N	19 30 E
Wadsworth, Nev., U.S.A.	108 G4	39 38N	119 17W
Wadsworth, Ohio, U.S.A.	116 E3	41 2N	81 44W
Waegwan, S. Korea	57 G15	35 59N	128 23 E
Wafangdian, China	57 E11	39 38N	121 58 E
Wafrah, Si. Arabia	70 D5	28 33N	47 56 E
Wageningen, Neths.	17 C5	51 58N	5 40 E
Wager B., Canada	101 B11	65 26N	88 40W
Waghete, Indonesia	63 E9	4 10 S	135 50 E
Wagin, Australia	93 F2	33 17S	117 25 E
Wagner, U.S.A.	112 D5	43 5N	98 18W
Wagon Mound, U.S.A.	113 G2	36 1N	104 42W
Wagoner, U.S.A.	113 H7	35 58N	95 22W
Wągrowiec, Poland	31 F4	52 48N	17 11 E
Wah, Pakistan	68 C5	33 45N	72 40 E
Wahai, Indonesia	63 E7	2 48 S	129 35 E
Wahiawa, U.S.A.	106 H15	21 30N	158 2W
Wâhid, Egypt	74 E1	30 48N	32 21 E
Wahnai, Afghan.	68 C1	32 40N	65 50 E
Wahni, Ethiopia	81 E4	12 45N	37 10 E
Wahoo, U.S.A.	112 E6	41 13N	96 37W
Wahpeton, U.S.A.	112 B6	46 16N	96 36W
Waiau →, N.Z.	91 K4	42 47 S	173 22 E
Waibeem, Indonesia	63 E8	0 30 S	132 59 E
Waiblingen, Germany	25 G5	48 49N	9 18 E
Waidhofen an der Thaya, Austria	26 C8	48 49N	15 17 E
Waidhofen an der Ybbs, Austria	26 D7	47 57N	14 46 E
Waigeo, Indonesia	63 E8	0 20 S	130 40 E
Waihi, N.Z.	91 G5	37 23 S	175 52 E
Waihou →, N.Z.	91 G5	37 15 S	175 40 E
Waika, Dem. Rep. of the Congo	86 C2	2 22 S	25 42 E
Waikabubak, Indonesia	63 F5	9 45 S	119 25 E
Waikaremoana, L., N.Z.	91 H6	38 49 S	177 9 E
Waikari, N.Z.	91 K4	42 58 S	172 41 E
Waikato →, N.Z.	91 G5	37 23 S	174 43 E
Waikerie, Australia	95 E3	34 9 S	140 0 E
Waikokopu, N.Z.	91 H6	39 3 S	177 52 E
Waikouaiti, N.Z.	91 L3	45 36 S	170 41 E
Wailuku, U.S.A.	106 H16	20 53N	156 30W
Waimakariri →, N.Z.	91 K4	43 24 S	172 42 E
Waimate, N.Z.	91 L3	44 45 S	171 3 E
Wainganga →, India	66 K11	18 50N	79 55 E
Waingapu, Indonesia	63 F6	9 35 S	120 11 E
Waini →, Guyana	124 B7	8 20N	59 50W
Wainwright, Canada	103 C6	52 50N	110 50W
Waiouru, N.Z.	91 H5	39 28 S	175 41 E
Waipara, N.Z.	91 K4	43 3 S	172 46 E
Waipawa, N.Z.	91 H6	39 56 S	176 38 E
Waipiro, N.Z.	91 H7	38 2 S	178 22 E
Waipoua Forest, N.Z.	91 F4	35 39 S	173 33 E
Waipu, N.Z.	91 F5	35 59 S	174 29 E
Waipukurau, N.Z.	91 J6	40 1 S	176 33 E
Wairakei, N.Z.	91 H6	38 37 S	176 6 E
Wairarapa, L., N.Z.	91 J5	41 14 S	175 15 E
Wairoa, N.Z.	91 G5	37 25 S	177 25 E
Wairoa →, N.Z.	91 L3	44 56 S	171 7 E
Waitangi, N.Z.	91 F5	35 16 S	174 5 E
Waitara, N.Z.	91 H5	38 59 S	174 15 E
Waitomo Caves, N.Z.	91 H5	38 16 S	175 7 E
Waitsburg, U.S.A.	108 C5	46 16N	118 9W
Waiuku, N.Z.	91 G5	37 15 S	174 45 E
Wajima, Japan	55 F8	37 30N	137 0 E
Wajir, Kenya	86 B5	1 42N	40 5 E
Waka, Ethiopia	81 F4	7 2N	37 20 E
Wakasa, Japan	55 G7	35 20N	134 24 E
Wakasa-Wan, Japan	55 G7	35 40N	135 30 E
Wakatipu, L., N.Z.	91 L2	45 5 S	168 33 E
Wakaw, Canada	103 C7	52 39N	105 44W
Wakayama, Japan	55 G7	34 15N	135 15 E
Wakayama □, Japan	55 H7	33 50N	135 30 E
Wake Forest, U.S.A.	115 H6	35 59N	78 30W
Wake I., Pac. Oc.	96 F8	19 18N	166 36 E
WaKeeney, U.S.A.	112 F5	39 1N	99 53W
Wakefield, Jamaica	120 a	18 26N	77 42W
Wakefield, N.Z.	91 J4	41 24 S	173 5 E
Wakefield, U.K.	14 D6	53 41N	1 29W
Wakefield, Mass., U.S.A.	117 D13	42 30N	71 4W
Wakefield, Mich., U.S.A.	112 B10	46 29N	89 56W
Wakkanai, Japan	54 B10	45 28N	141 35 E
Wakkerstroom, S. Africa	89 D5	27 24 S	30 10 E
Wakool, Australia	95 F3	35 28 S	144 23 E
Wakool →, Australia	95 F3	35 5 S	143 33 E
Wakre, Indonesia	63 E8	0 19 S	131 5 E
Wakuach, L., Canada	105 A6	55 34N	67 32W
Walamba, Zambia	87 E2	13 30 S	28 42 E
Wałbrzych, Poland	31 H3	50 45N	16 18 E
Walbury Hill, U.K.	15 F6	51 21N	1 28W
Walcha, Australia	95 E5	30 55 S	151 31 E
Walcheren, Neths.	17 C3	51 30N	3 35 E
Walcott, U.S.A.	108 F10	41 46N	106 51W
Wałcz, Poland	31 E3	53 17N	16 27 E
Waldbröl, Germany	24 E3	50 52N	7 37 E
Waldburg Ra., Australia	93 D2	24 40 S	117 35 E
Waldeck, Germany	24 D5	51 12N	9 4 E
Walden, Colo., U.S.A.	108 F10	40 44N	106 17W
Walden, N.Y., U.S.A.	117 E10	41 34N	74 11W
Waldkirch, Germany	25 G3	48 5N	7 58 E
Waldkirchen, Germany	25 G9	48 43N	13 36 E
Waldkraiburg, Germany	25 G8	48 11N	12 24 E
Waldport, U.S.A.	108 D1	44 26N	124 4W
Waldron, U.S.A.	113 H7	34 54N	94 5W
Waldviertel, Austria	26 C8	48 30N	15 30 E
Walebing, Australia	93 F2	30 41 S	116 13 E
Walembele, Ghana	82 C4	10 30N	1 58W
Walensee, Switz.	25 H5	47 7N	9 13 E
Wales □, U.K.	15 E3	52 19N	4 43W
Walewale, Ghana	83 C4	10 21N	0 50W
Walgett, Australia	95 E4	30 0 S	148 5 E
Walgreen Coast, Antarctica	5 D15	75 15 S	105 0W
Walker, U.S.A.	112 B7	47 6N	94 35W
Walker, L., Canada	105 B6	50 20N	67 11W
Walker L., Canada	103 C9	54 42N	95 57W
Walker L., U.S.A.	108 G4	38 42N	118 43W
Walkerston, Australia	94 K7	21 11 S	149 8 E
Walkerton, Canada	116 B3	44 10N	81 10W
Wall, U.S.A.	112 D3	44 0N	102 8W
Walla Walla, U.S.A.	108 C4	46 4N	118 20W
Wallace, Idaho, U.S.A.	108 C6	47 28N	115 56W
Wallace, N.C., U.S.A.	115 H7	34 44N	77 59W
Wallaceburg, Canada	116 D2	42 34N	82 23W
Wallachia = Valahia, Romania	29 F9	44 35N	25 0 E
Wallal, Australia	95 D4	26 32 S	146 7 E
Wallal Downs, Australia	94 C3	19 47 S	120 0 E
Wallambin, L., Australia	93 F2	30 57 S	117 35 E
Wallangarra, Australia	95 D5	28 56 S	151 58 E
Wallaroo, Australia	95 E2	33 56 S	137 39 E
Walldürn, Germany	25 F5	49 34N	9 22 E
Wallenhorst, Germany	24 C4	52 21N	8 1 E
Wallenpaupack, L., U.S.A.	117 E9	41 25N	75 15W
Wallingford, U.S.A.	117 E12	41 27N	72 50W
Wallis & Futuna, Is., Pac. Oc.	96 J10	13 18 S	176 10W
Wallowa, U.S.A.	108 D5	45 34N	117 32W
Wallowa Mts., U.S.A.	108 D5	45 20N	117 30W
Walls, U.K.	13 A7	60 14N	1 33W
Walls of Jerusalem △, Australia	95 G4	41 56 S	146 15 E
Wallula, U.S.A.	108 C4	46 5N	118 54W
Wallumbilla, Australia	95 D4	26 33 S	149 9 E
Walmsley, L., Canada	103 A7	63 25N	108 36W
Walney, I. of, U.K.	14 C4	54 6N	3 15W
Walnut Canyon △, U.S.A.	109 J8	35 15N	111 20W
Walnut Creek, U.S.A.	110 H4	37 54N	122 4W
Walnut Ridge, U.S.A.	113 G9	36 4N	90 57W
Walpole, Australia	93 F2	34 58 S	116 44 E
Walpole, U.S.A.	117 D13	42 9N	71 15W
Wals, Austria	26 D5	47 47N	12 58 E
Walsall, U.K.	15 E6	52 35N	1 58W
Walsenburg, U.S.A.	113 G2	37 38N	104 47W
Walsh, U.S.A.	113 G3	37 23N	102 17W
Walsh →, Australia	94 B3	16 31 S	143 42 E
Walsrode, Germany	24 C5	52 51N	9 35 E
Walterboro, U.S.A.	115 J5	32 55N	80 40W
Walters, U.S.A.	113 H5	34 22N	98 19W
Waltershausen, Germany	24 E6	50 54N	10 33 E
Waltham, U.S.A.	117 D13	42 23N	71 14W
Waltman, U.S.A.	108 E10	43 4N	107 12W
Walton, U.S.A.	117 D9	42 10N	75 8W
Walton-on-the-Naze, U.K.	15 F9	51 51N	1 17 E
Walvis Bay, Namibia	88 C1	23 0 S	14 28 E
Walvisbaai = Walvis Bay, Namibia	88 C1	23 0 S	14 28 E
Wamba, Dem. Rep. of the Congo	86 B2	2 10N	27 57 E
Wamba, Kenya	86 B4	0 58N	37 19 E
Wamba, Nigeria	83 D6	8 57N	8 42 E
Wamego, U.S.A.	112 F6	39 12N	96 18W
Wamena, Indonesia	63 E9	4 4 S	138 57 E
Wamsutter, U.S.A.	108 F9	41 40N	107 58W
Wamulan, Indonesia	63 E7	3 27 S	126 7 E
Wan Xian, China	56 E8	38 47N	115 7 E
Wana, Pakistan	68 C3	32 20N	69 32 E
Wanaaring, Australia	95 D3	29 38 S	144 9 E
Wanaka, N.Z.	91 L2	44 42 S	169 9 E
Wanaka, L., N.Z.	91 L2	44 33 S	169 7 E
Wan'an, China	59 D10	26 26 S	114 49 E
Wanapitei L., Canada	104 C3	46 45N	80 40W
Wandel Sea = McKinley Sea, Arctic	4 A7	82 0N	0 0W
Wandérama, Ivory C.	82 D4	8 37N	4 25W
Wanderer, Zimbabwe	87 F3	19 36 S	30 1 E
Wandhari, Pakistan	68 F2	27 42N	66 48 E
Wanding, China	58 E2	24 9N	98 1 E
Wandoan, Australia	95 D4	26 5 S	149 55 E
Wanfu, China	57 D12	40 8N	122 38 E
Wang →, Thailand	64 D2	17 8N	99 2 E
Wang Kai, Sudan	81 F2	9 3N	29 23 E
Wang Noi, Thailand	64 E3	14 13N	100 44 E
Wang Saphung, Thailand	64 D3	17 18N	101 46 E
Wang Thong, Thailand	64 D3	16 50N	100 26 E
Wanga, Dem. Rep. of the Congo	86 B2	2 58N	29 12 E
Wangal, Indonesia	63 F8	6 8 S	134 9 E
Wanganella, Australia	95 F3	35 6 S	144 49 E
Wanganui, N.Z.	91 H5	39 56 S	175 3 E
Wangaratta, Australia	95 F4	36 21 S	146 19 E
Wangary, Australia	95 E2	34 35 S	135 29 E
Wangcang, China	58 A6	32 18N	106 20 E
Wangcheng, China	59 C9	28 22N	112 49 E
Wangdu, China	56 E8	38 40N	115 7 E
Wangen, Germany	25 H5	47 41N	9 50 E
Wangerooge, Germany	24 B3	53 47N	7 54 E
Wangiwangi, Indonesia	63 F6	5 22 S	123 37 E
Wangjiang, China	59 B11	30 10N	116 42 E
Wangmo, China	58 E6	25 11N	106 5 E
Wangolodougou, Ivory C.	82 D3	9 55N	5 10W
Wanging, China	57 C15	43 12N	129 42 E
Wankaner, India	68 H4	22 35N	71 0 E
Wanless, Canada	103 C8	54 11N	101 21W
Wanneroo, Australia	93 F2	31 42 S	115 46 E
Wannian, China	59 C11	28 42N	117 4 E
Wanning, China	64 C8	18 48N	110 22 E
Wanon Niwat, Thailand	64 D4	17 38N	103 46 E
Wanquan, China	56 D8	40 50N	114 40 E
Wanrong, China	56 G6	35 25N	110 50 E
Wanshan, China	58 D7	27 30N	109 12 E
Wanshengchang, China	58 C6	28 57N	106 53 E
Wantage, U.K.	15 F6	51 35N	1 25W
Wanxian, China	58 B7	30 42N	108 20 E
Wanyuan, China	58 A7	32 4N	108 3 E
Wanzai, China	59 C10	28 7N	114 30 E
Wapakoneta, U.S.A.	114 E3	40 34N	84 12W
Wapato, U.S.A.	108 C3	46 27N	120 25W
Wapawekka L., Canada	103 C8	54 55N	104 40W
Wapikopa L., Canada	104 B2	52 56N	87 53W
Wapiti →, Canada	102 B5	55 5N	118 18W
Wappingers Falls, U.S.A.	117 E11	41 36N	73 55W
Wapsipinicon →, U.S.A.	112 E9	41 44N	90 19W
Wapusk △, Canada	103 B10	57 46N	93 22W
Warab □, Sudan	81 F2	7 30N	28 30 E
Warangal, India	66 L11	17 58N	79 35 E
Waraseoni, India	69 J9	21 45N	80 2 E
Waratah, Australia	95 G4	41 30 S	145 30 E
Waratah B., Australia	95 F4	38 54 S	146 5 E
Warburg, Germany	24 D5	51 29N	9 11 E
Warburton, Vic., Australia	95 F4	37 47 S	145 42 E
Warburton, W. Austral., Australia	93 E4	26 8 S	126 35 E
Warburton, The →, Australia	95 D2	28 4 S	137 28 E
Warburton Ra., Australia	93 E4	25 55 S	126 28 E
Ward, N.Z.	91 J5	41 49 S	174 11 E
Ward →, Australia	95 D4	26 28 S	146 6 E
Ward Mt., U.S.A.	110 H8	37 12N	118 54W
Warden, S. Africa	89 D4	27 50 S	29 0 E
Wardha, India	66 J11	20 45N	78 39 E
Wardha →, India	66 K11	19 57N	79 11 E
Ware, Canada	102 B3	57 26N	125 41W
Ware, U.S.A.	117 D12	42 16N	72 14W
Waregem, Belgium	17 D3	50 53N	3 27 E
Wareham, U.S.A.	117 E14	41 46N	70 43W
Waremme, Belgium	17 D5	50 43N	5 15 E
Waren, Germany	24 B8	53 31N	12 40 E
Warendorf, Germany	24 D4	51 57N	8 1 E
Warialda, Australia	95 D5	29 29 S	150 33 E
Wariap, Indonesia	63 E8	1 30 S	134 5 E
Warin Chamrap, Thailand	64 E5	15 12N	104 53 E
Warka, Poland	31 G8	51 47N	21 12 E
Warkopi, Indonesia	63 E8	1 12 S	134 9 E
Warm Springs, U.S.A.	109 G5	38 10N	116 20W
Warman, Canada	103 C7	52 19N	106 30W
Warmbad = Bela Bela, S. Africa	89 C4	24 51 S	28 19 E
Warmbad, Namibia	88 D2	28 25 S	18 42 E
Warmińsko-Mazurskie □, Poland	30 D8	54 0N	21 0 E
Warminster, U.K.	15 F5	51 12N	2 10W
Warminster, U.S.A.	117 F9	40 12N	75 6W
Warner Mts., U.S.A.	108 F3	41 40N	120 15W
Warner Robins, U.S.A.	115 J4	32 37N	83 36W
Warnow →, Germany	24 A8	54 10N	12 4 E
Waroona, Australia	93 F2	32 50 S	115 58 E
Warracknabeal, Australia	95 F3	36 9 S	142 26 E
Warragul, Australia	95 F4	38 10 S	145 58 E
Warrego →, Australia	95 E4	30 24 S	145 21 E
Warrego Ra., Australia	94 C4	24 58 S	146 0 E
Warren, Australia	95 E4	31 42 S	147 51 E
Warren, Ark., U.S.A.	113 J8	33 37N	92 4W
Warren, Mich., U.S.A.	114 D4	42 30N	83 0W
Warren, Minn., U.S.A.	112 A6	48 12N	96 46W
Warren, Ohio, U.S.A.	116 E4	41 14N	80 49W
Warren, Pa., U.S.A.	116 E5	41 51N	79 9W
Warrenpoint, U.K.	12 B5	54 6N	6 15W
Warrensburg, Mo., U.S.A.	112 F8	38 46N	93 44W
Warrensburg, N.Y., U.S.A.	117 C11	43 29N	73 46W
Warrenton, S. Africa	88 D3	28 9 S	24 47 E
Warrenton, U.S.A.	110 D3	46 10N	123 56W
Warri, Nigeria	83 D6	5 30N	5 41 E
Warrina, Australia	95 D2	28 12 S	135 50 E
Warrington, U.K.	14 D5	53 24N	2 35W
Warrington, U.S.A.	115 K2	30 23N	87 17W
Warrnambool, Australia	95 F3	38 25 S	142 30 E
Warroad, U.S.A.	112 A7	48 54N	95 19W
Warruwi, Australia	94 A1	11 36 S	133 10 E
Warsa, Indonesia	63 E9	0 47 S	135 55 E
Warsak Dam, Pakistan	68 B4	34 11N	71 19 E
Warsaw = Warszawa, Poland	31 F8	52 13N	21 0 E
Warsaw, Ind., U.S.A.	114 E3	41 14N	85 51W
Warsaw, N.Y., U.S.A.	116 D6	42 45N	78 8W
Warsaw, Ohio, U.S.A.	116 F3	40 20N	82 0W
Warstein, Germany	24 D4	51 26N	8 22 E
Warszawa, Poland	31 F8	52 13N	21 0 E
Warszawa ✈ (WAW), Poland	31 F7	52 9N	20 59 E
Warta, Poland	31 G5	51 43N	18 38 E
Warta →, Poland	31 F1	52 35N	14 39 E
Warthe = Warta →, Poland	31 F1	52 35N	14 39 E
Waru, Indonesia	63 E8	3 30 S	130 36 E
Warwick, Australia	95 D5	28 10 S	152 1 E
Warwick, U.K.	15 E6	52 18N	1 35W
Warwick, N.Y., U.S.A.	117 E10	41 16N	74 22W
Warwick, R.I., U.S.A.	117 E13	41 42N	71 28W
Warwickshire □, U.K.	15 E6	52 14N	1 38W
Wasaga Beach, Canada	116 B4	44 31N	80 1W
Wasagaming, Canada	103 C9	50 39N	99 58W
Wasatch Ra., U.S.A.	108 F8	40 30N	111 15W
Wasbank, S. Africa	89 D5	28 15 S	30 9 E
Wasco, Calif., U.S.A.	111 K7	35 36N	119 20W
Wasco, Oreg., U.S.A.	108 D3	45 36N	120 42W
Wase, Nigeria	83 D6	9 3N	9 54 E
Waseca, U.S.A.	112 C8	44 5N	93 30W
Wasekamio L., Canada	103 B7	56 45N	108 45W
Wash, The, U.K.	14 E8	52 58N	0 20 E
Washago, Canada	116 B5	44 45N	79 20W
Washburn, N. Dak., U.S.A.	112 B4	47 17N	101 2W
Washburn, Wis., U.S.A.	112 B9	46 40N	90 54W
Washim, India	66 J10	20 3N	77 0 E
Washington, U.K.	14 C6	54 55N	1 30W
Washington, D.C., U.S.A.	114 F7	38 54N	77 2W
Washington, Ga., U.S.A.	115 J4	33 44N	82 44W
Washington, Ind., U.S.A.	114 F2	38 40N	87 10W
Washington, Iowa, U.S.A.	112 E9	41 18N	91 42W
Washington, Mo., U.S.A.	112 F9	38 33N	91 1W
Washington, N.C., U.S.A.	115 H7	35 33N	77 3W
Washington, N.J., U.S.A.	117 F10	40 46N	74 59W
Washington, Pa., U.S.A.	116 F4	40 7N	80 15W
Washington, Utah, U.S.A.	109 H7	37 8N	113 31W
Washington □, U.S.A.	108 C3	47 30N	120 30W
Washington, Mt., U.S.A.	117 B13	44 16N	71 18W
Washington Court House, U.S.A.	114 F4	39 32N	83 26W
Washington I., U.S.A.	114 C2	45 23N	86 54W
Washougal, U.S.A.	110 E4	45 35N	122 21W
Washpool △, Australia	95 D5	29 22 S	152 20 E
Wasian, Indonesia	63 E8	1 47 S	133 19 E
Wasilków, Poland	31 E10	53 12N	23 13 E
Wasilla, U.S.A.	100 B5	61 35N	149 26W
Wasior, Indonesia	63 E8	2 43 S	134 30 E
Waskaganish, Canada	104 B4	51 30N	78 40W
Waskaiowaka, L., Canada	103 B9	56 33N	96 23W
Waskesiu Lake, Canada	103 C7	53 55N	106 5W
Wasserburg, Germany	25 G8	48 3N	12 14 E
Wasserkuppe, Germany	24 E5	50 29N	9 55 E
Wassy, France	19 D11	48 30N	4 58 E
Waswanipi, Canada	104 C4	49 40N	76 29W
Waswanipi, L., Canada	104 C4	49 35N	76 40W
Watampone, Indonesia	63 E6	4 29 S	120 25 E
Watamu, Kenya	86 C5	3 23 S	40 0 E
Watarrka △, Australia	92 D5	24 20 S	131 30 E
Water Park Pt., Australia	94 C5	22 56 S	150 47 E
Water Valley, U.S.A.	113 H10	34 10N	89 38W
Waterberg Plateau △, Namibia	88 C2	20 25 S	17 18 E
Waterberge, S. Africa	89 C4	24 10 S	28 0 E
Waterbury, Conn., U.S.A.	117 E11	41 33N	73 3W
Waterbury, Vt., U.S.A.	117 B12	44 20N	72 46W
Waterbury L., Canada	103 B8	58 10N	104 22W
Waterdown, Canada	116 C5	43 20N	79 53W
Waterford, Canada	116 D4	42 56N	80 17W
Waterford, Ireland	12 D4	52 15N	7 8W
Waterford, Calif., U.S.A.	110 H6	37 38N	120 46W
Waterford, Pa., U.S.A.	116 E5	41 57N	79 59W
Waterford □, Ireland	12 D4	52 10N	7 40W
Waterford Harbour, Ireland	12 D5	52 8N	6 58W
Waterhen L., Canada	103 C9	52 10N	99 40W
Waterloo, Belgium	17 D4	50 43N	4 25 E
Waterloo, Ont., Canada	116 C4	43 30N	80 32W
Waterloo, Qué., Canada	117 A12	45 22N	72 32W
Waterloo, S. Leone	82 D2	8 26N	13 8W
Waterloo, Ill., U.S.A.	112 F9	38 20N	90 9W
Waterloo, Iowa, U.S.A.	112 D8	42 30N	92 21W
Waterloo, N.Y., U.S.A.	116 D8	42 54N	76 52W
Watersmeet, U.S.A.	112 B10	46 16N	89 11W
Waterton Lakes △, Canada	102 D6	48 45N	115 0W
Watertown, Conn., U.S.A.	117 E11	41 36N	73 7W
Watertown, N.Y., U.S.A.	117 C9	43 59N	75 55W
Watertown, S. Dak., U.S.A.	112 C6	44 54N	97 7W
Watertown, Wis., U.S.A.	112 D10	43 12N	88 43W
Waterval-Boven, S. Africa	89 D5	25 40 S	30 18 E
Waterville, Canada	117 A13	45 16N	71 54W
Waterville, Maine, U.S.A.	115 C11	44 33N	69 38W
Waterville, N.Y., U.S.A.	117 D9	42 56N	75 23W
Waterville, Pa., U.S.A.	116 E7	41 19N	77 21W
Waterville, Wash., U.S.A.	108 C3	47 39N	120 4W
Watervliet, U.S.A.	117 D11	42 44N	73 42W
Wates, Indonesia	63 G14	7 51 S	110 10 E
Watford, Canada	116 D3	42 57N	81 53W
Watford, U.K.	15 F7	51 40N	0 24W
Watford City, U.S.A.	112 B3	47 48N	103 17W
Wathaman →, Canada	103 B8	57 16N	102 59W
Wathaman L., Canada	103 B8	56 58N	103 44W
Watheroo, Australia	93 F2	30 19 S	115 48 E
Watheroo △, Australia	93 F2	30 15 S	115 54 E
Wating, China	56 G4	35 40N	106 38 E
Watkins Glen, U.S.A.	116 D8	42 23N	76 52W
Watling I. = San Salvador I., Bahamas	121 B5	24 0N	74 40W
Watonga, U.S.A.	113 H5	35 51N	98 25W
Watrous, Canada	103 C7	51 40N	105 25W
Watrous, U.S.A.	113 H2	35 48N	104 59W
Watsa, Dem. Rep. of the Congo	86 B2	3 4N	29 30 E
Watseka, U.S.A.	114 E2	40 47N	87 44W
Watson, Australia	93 F5	30 29 S	131 31 E
Watson, Canada	103 C8	52 10N	104 30W
Watson Lake, Canada	102 A3	60 6N	128 49W
Watsontown, U.S.A.	116 E8	41 5N	76 52W
Watsonville, U.S.A.	110 J5	36 55N	121 45W
Wattiwarriganna Cr. →, Australia	95 D2	28 57 S	136 10 E
Wattwil, Switz.	25 H5	47 18N	9 6 E
Watuata = Batuata, Indonesia	63 F6	6 12 S	122 42 E
Watubela, Kepulauan, Indonesia	63 E8	4 28 S	131 35 E
Watubela Is. = Watubela, Kepulauan, Indonesia	63 E8	4 28 S	131 35 E
Wau = Wâw, Sudan	81 F2	7 45N	28 1 E
Waubamik, Canada	116 A4	45 27N	80 1W
Waubay, U.S.A.	112 C6	45 20N	97 18W
Wauchope, N.S.W., Australia	95 E5	31 28 S	152 45 E
Wauchope, N. Terr., Australia	94 C1	20 36 S	134 15 E
Wauchula, U.S.A.	115 M5	27 33N	81 49W
Waukarlycarly, L., Australia	92 D3	21 18 S	121 56 E
Waukegan, U.S.A.	114 D2	42 22N	87 50W
Waukesha, U.S.A.	114 D1	43 1N	88 14W
Waukon, U.S.A.	112 D9	43 16N	91 29W
Waupaca, U.S.A.	112 C10	44 21N	89 5W
Waupun, U.S.A.	112 D10	43 38N	88 44W
Waurika, U.S.A.	113 H6	34 10N	98 0W
Wausau, U.S.A.	112 C10	44 49N	89 38W
Wautoma, U.S.A.	112 C10	44 4N	89 18W
Wauwatosa, U.S.A.	114 D2	43 3N	88 0W
Waveney →, U.K.	15 E9	52 35N	1 39 E
Waverley, N.Z.	91 H5	39 46 S	174 37 E
Waverly, Iowa, U.S.A.	112 D8	42 44N	92 29W
Waverly, N.Y., U.S.A.	117 E8	42 1N	76 32W
Wavre, Belgium	17 D4	50 43N	4 38 E
Wâw, Sudan	81 F2	7 45N	28 1 E
Wâw al Kabîr, Libya	79 C9	25 16N	16 43 E
Wawa, Canada	104 C3	47 59N	84 47W
Wawa, Nigeria	83 D5	9 54N	4 27 E
Wawa, Sudan	80 C3	20 30N	30 22 E
Wawanesa, Canada	103 D9	49 36N	99 40W
Wawona, U.S.A.	110 H7	37 32N	119 39W
Waxahachie, U.S.A.	113 J6	32 24N	96 51W
Way, L., Australia	93 E3	26 45 S	120 16 E
Waycross, U.S.A.	115 K4	31 13N	82 21W
Wayi, Sudan	81 F3	8 3N	30 10 E
Wayland, U.S.A.	116 D7	42 34N	77 35W
Wayne, Nebr., U.S.A.	112 D6	42 14N	97 1W
Wayne, W. Va., U.S.A.	114 F4	38 13N	82 27W
Waynesboro, Ga., U.S.A.	115 J4	33 6N	82 1W
Waynesboro, Miss., U.S.A.	115 K1	31 40N	88 39W
Waynesboro, Pa., U.S.A.	114 F7	39 45N	77 35W
Waynesboro, Va., U.S.A.	114 F6	38 4N	78 53W
Waynesburg, U.S.A.	114 F5	39 54N	80 11W
Waynesville, U.S.A.	115 H4	35 28N	82 58W
Waynoka, U.S.A.	113 G5	36 35N	98 53W
Wazirabad, Pakistan	68 C6	32 30N	74 8 E
Wda →, Poland	30 E5	53 25N	18 29 E
We, Indonesia	62 C1	5 51N	95 18 E
Weald, The, U.K.	15 F8	51 4N	0 20 E
Wear →, U.K.	14 C6	54 55N	1 23W
Weatherford, Okla., U.S.A.	113 H5	35 32N	98 43W
Weatherford, Tex., U.S.A.	113 J6	32 46N	97 48W
Weaverville, U.S.A.	108 F2	40 44N	122 56W
Webb City, U.S.A.	113 G7	37 9N	94 28W
Webequie, Canada	104 B2	52 59N	87 21W
Webo = Nyaake, Liberia	82 E3	4 52N	7 37W
Webster, Mass., U.S.A.	117 D13	42 3N	71 53W
Webster, N.Y., U.S.A.	116 C7	43 13N	77 26W
Webster, S. Dak., U.S.A.	112 C6	45 20N	97 31W
Webster City, U.S.A.	112 D8	42 28N	93 49W
Webster Springs, U.S.A.	114 F5	38 29N	80 25W
Weda, Indonesia	63 E7	0 21N	127 50 E
Weda, Teluk, Indonesia	63 E7	0 20N	128 0 E
Weddell I., Falk. Is.	128 G4	51 50 S	61 0W
Weddell Sea, Antarctica	5 D1	72 30 S	40 0W
Wedderburn, Australia	95 F3	36 26 S	143 33 E
Wedel, Germany	24 B5	53 34N	9 42 E
Wedgeport, Canada	105 D6	43 44N	65 59W
Wedza, Zimbabwe	87 F3	18 40 S	31 33 E
Wee Waa, Australia	95 E4	30 11 S	149 26 E
Weed, U.S.A.	108 F2	41 25N	122 23W
Weed Heights, U.S.A.	110 G7	38 59N	119 13W
Weedsport, U.S.A.	117 C8	43 3N	76 35W
Weedville, U.S.A.	116 E6	41 17N	78 30W
Weenen, S. Africa	89 D5	28 48 S	30 7 E
Weener, Germany	24 B3	53 9N	7 20 E
Weert, Neths.	17 C5	51 15N	5 43 E
Węgierska-Górka, Poland	31 J6	49 36N	19 7 E
Węgliniec, Poland	31 G2	51 18N	15 10 E
Węgorzewo, Poland	30 D8	54 13N	21 43 E
Węgorzyno, Poland	30 E2	53 32N	15 33 E
Węgrów, Poland	31 F9	52 24N	22 0 E
Wehda □, Sudan	81 F3	8 30N	30 0 E
Wei He →, Hebei, China	56 F8	36 10N	115 45 E
Wei He →, Shaanxi, China	56 G6	34 38N	110 15 E
Weichang, China	57 D9	41 58N	117 49 E
Weichuan, China	56 G7	34 20N	113 59 E
Weida, Germany	24 E8	50 46N	12 2 E
Weiden, Germany	25 F8	49 41N	12 10 E
Weifang, China	57 F10	36 44N	119 7 E
Weihai, China	57 F12	37 30N	122 6 E
Weil, Germany	25 H3	47 35N	7 37 E
Weilburg, Germany	24 E4	50 29N	8 17 E
Weilheim, Germany	25 H7	47 50N	11 9 E
Weimar, Germany	24 E7	50 58N	11 19 E
Weinan, China	56 G5	34 31N	109 29 E
Weingarten, Germany	25 H5	47 49N	9 38 E
Weinheim, Germany	25 F4	49 32N	8 39 E
Weining, China	58 D5	26 50N	104 17 E
Weipa, Australia	94 A3	12 40 S	141 50 E
Weir →, Australia	95 D4	28 20 S	149 50 E
Weir →, Canada	103 B10	56 54N	93 21W
Weir River, Canada	103 B10	56 49N	94 6W
Weirton, U.S.A.	116 F4	40 24N	80 35W
Weiser, U.S.A.	108 D5	44 10N	117 0W
Weishan, Shandong, China	57 G9	34 47N	117 5 E
Weishan, Yunnan, China	58 E3	25 12N	100 20 E
Weissenburg, Germany	25 F6	49 2N	10 58 E
Weissenfels, Germany	24 D7	51 11N	12 4 E
Weisswasser, Germany	24 D10	51 30N	14 36 E
Weitra, Austria	26 C8	48 43N	14 54 E
Weixi, China	58 D2	27 10N	99 10 E
Weixin, China	58 D5	27 48N	105 3 E

Weiyuan, China 56 G3 35 7N 104 10 E
Weiz, Austria 26 D8 47 13N 15 39 E
Weizhou Dao, China 58 G7 21 0N 109 5 E
Wejherowo, Poland 30 D5 54 35N 18 12 E
Wekusko L., Canada 103 C9 54 40N 99 50W
Welch, U.S.A. 114 G5 37 26N 81 35W
Weldya, Ethiopia 81 E4 11 50N 39 34 E
Welega, Ethiopia 81 F3 9 25N 34 20 E
Welford △, Australia 94 D3 25 5 S 143 16 E
Welkite, Ethiopia 81 F4 8 15N 37 42 E
Welkom, S. Africa 88 D4 28 0 S 26 46 E
Welland, Canada 116 D5 43 0N 79 15W
Welland →, U.K. 15 E7 52 51N 0 5W
Wellesley Is., Australia 94 B2 16 42 S 139 30 E
Wellingborough, U.K. 15 E7 52 19N 0 41W
Wellington, Australia 95 E4 32 35 S 148 59 E
Wellington, Canada 116 C7 43 57N 77 20W
Wellington, N.Z. 91 J5 41 19 S 174 46 E
Wellington, S. Africa 88 E2 33 38 S 19 1 E
Wellington, Somst., U.K. 15 G4 50 58N 3 13W
Wellington, Telford & Wrekin, U.K. 15 E5 52 42N 2 30W
Wellington, Colo., U.S.A. 112 E2 40 42N 105 0W
Wellington, Kans., U.S.A. 113 G6 37 16N 97 24W
Wellington, Nev., U.S.A. 110 G7 38 45N 119 23W
Wellington, Ohio, U.S.A. 116 E2 41 10N 82 13W
Wellington, Tex., U.S.A. 113 H4 34 51N 100 13W
Wellington, I., Chile 128 F2 49 30 S 75 0W
Wellington, L., Australia 95 F4 38 6 S 147 20 E
Wells, U.K. 15 F5 51 13N 2 39W
Wells, Maine, U.S.A. 117 C14 43 20N 70 35W
Wells, N.Y., U.S.A. 117 C10 43 24N 74 17W
Wells, Nev., U.S.A. 108 F6 41 7N 114 58W
Wells, L., Australia 93 E3 26 44 S 123 15 E
Wells, Mt., Australia 92 C4 17 25 S 127 8 E
Wells Gray ⌂, Canada 102 C4 52 30N 120 15W
Wells-next-the-Sea, U.K. 14 E8 52 57N 0 51 E
Wells River, U.S.A. 117 B12 44 9N 72 4W
Wellsboro, U.S.A. 116 E7 41 45N 77 18W
Wellsburg, U.S.A. 116 F4 40 16N 80 37W
Wellsville, N.Y., U.S.A. 116 D7 42 7N 77 57W
Wellsville, Ohio, U.S.A. 116 F4 40 36N 80 39W
Wellsville, Utah, U.S.A. 108 F8 41 38N 111 56W
Wellton, U.S.A. 109 K6 32 40N 114 8W
Welmel, Wabi →, Ethiopia 81 F5 5 38N 40 47 E
Welo, Ethiopia 81 E4 11 50N 39 48 E
Wels, Austria 26 C7 48 9N 14 1 E
Welshpool, U.K. 15 E4 52 39N 3 8W
Welwyn Garden City, U.K. 15 F7 51 48N 0 12W
Wem, U.K. 14 E5 52 52N 2 44W
Wembere →, Tanzania 86 C3 4 10 S 34 15 E
Wemindji, Canada 104 B4 53 0N 78 49W
Wen Xian, China 56 G7 34 55N 113 5 E
Wenatchee, U.S.A. 108 C3 47 25N 120 19W
Wenchang, China 64 C8 19 38N 110 42 E
Wencheng, China 59 D13 27 46N 120 4 E
Wenchi, Ghana 82 D4 7 46N 2 8W
Wenchow = Wenzhou, China 59 D13 28 0N 120 38 E
Wenchuan, China 58 B4 31 22N 103 35 E
Wenden, U.S.A. 111 M13 33 49N 113 33W
Wendeng, China 57 F12 37 15N 122 5 E
Wendesi, Indonesia 63 E8 2 30 S 134 17 E
Wendo, Ethiopia 81 F4 6 40N 38 27 E
Wendover, U.S.A. 108 F6 40 44N 114 2W
Weng'an, China 58 D6 27 5N 107 25 E
Wengcheng, China 59 E9 24 22N 113 50 E
Wengyuan, China 59 E10 24 20N 114 9 E
Wenjiang, China 58 B4 30 44N 103 55 E
Wenling, China 59 C13 28 21N 121 20 E
Wenlock →, Australia 94 A3 12 2 S 141 55 E
Wenshan, China 58 F5 23 20N 104 18 E
Wenshang, China 56 G9 35 45N 116 30 E
Wenshui, China 56 F7 37 26N 112 1 E
Wensleydale, U.K. 14 C6 54 17N 2 0W
Wensu, China 60 B3 41 15N 80 10 E
Wensum →, U.K. 14 E8 52 40N 1 15 E
Wentworth, Australia 95 E3 34 2 S 141 54 E
Wentzel L., Canada 102 B6 59 2N 114 28W
Wenut, Indonesia 63 E8 3 11 S 133 19 E
Wenxi, China 56 G6 35 20N 111 10 E
Wenxian, China 56 H3 32 43N 104 36 E
Wenzhou, China 59 D13 28 0N 120 38 E
Weott, U.S.A. 108 F2 40 20N 123 55W
Wepener, S. Africa 88 D4 29 42 S 27 3 E
Werda, Botswana 88 D3 25 24 S 23 15 E
Werdau, Germany 24 E8 50 44N 12 22 E
Werder, Germany 24 C8 52 23N 12 55 E
Werdohl, Germany 24 D3 51 15N 7 46 E
Wereilu, Ethiopia 81 E4 10 40N 39 28 E
Weri, Indonesia 63 E8 3 10 S 132 38 E
Werneck, Germany 25 F6 49 58N 10 5 E
Wernigerode, Germany 24 D6 51 50N 10 47 E
Werra →, Germany 24 D5 51 24N 9 39 E
Werrimull, Australia 95 E3 34 25 S 141 38 E
Werris Creek, Australia 95 E5 31 18 S 150 38 E
Wertach →, Germany 25 G6 48 22N 10 54 E
Wertheim, Germany 25 F5 49 45N 9 32 E
Wertingen, Germany 25 G6 48 33N 10 41 E
Wesel, Germany 24 D2 51 39N 6 37 E
Weser →, Germany 24 B4 53 36N 8 28 E
Weser-Ems □, Germany 24 C3 53 0N 7 30 E
Weserbergland, Germany 24 C5 52 12N 9 7 E
Weserbergland Schaumburg Hameln ⌂, Germany 24 C5 52 8N 9 20 E
Wesiri, Indonesia 63 F7 7 30 S 126 30 E
Weslemkoon L., Canada 116 A7 45 2N 77 25W
Wesleyville, U.S.A. 116 D4 42 9N 80 0W
Wessel, C., Australia 94 A2 10 59 S 136 46 E
Wessel Is., Australia 94 A2 11 10 S 136 45 E
Wesselburen, Germany 24 A4 54 13N 8 54 E
Wessington Springs, U.S.A. 112 C5 44 5N 98 34W
West, U.S.A. 113 K6 31 48N 97 6W
West →, U.S.A. 117 D12 42 52N 72 33W
West Antarctica, Antarctica 5 D15 80 0 S 90 0W
West Baines →, Australia 92 C4 15 38 S 129 59 E
West Bank ☒, Asia 74 C4 32 6N 35 13 E
West Bend, U.S.A. 114 D1 43 25N 88 11W
West Bengal □, India 69 H13 23 0N 88 0 E
West Berkshire □, U.K. 15 F6 51 25N 1 17W
West Beskids = Západné Beskydy, Europe 27 B12 49 30N 19 0 E
West Branch, U.S.A. 114 C3 44 17N 84 14W
West Branch Susquehanna →, U.S.A. 117 F8 40 53N 76 48W
West Bromwich, U.K. 15 E6 52 32N 1 59W
West Burra, U.K. 13 A7 60 5N 1 21W
West Canada Cr. →, U.S.A. 117 C10 43 1N 74 58W
West Cape Howe, Australia 93 G2 35 8 S 117 36 E
West Chazy, U.S.A. 117 B11 44 49N 73 28W
West Chester, U.S.A. 117 G9 39 58N 75 36W
West Coast ⌂, Namibia 88 C1 21 53 S 14 14 E
West Coast ⌂, S. Africa 88 E2 33 13 S 18 0 E
West Columbia, U.S.A. 113 L7 29 9N 95 39W
West Covina, U.S.A. 111 L9 34 4N 117 54W
West Des Moines, U.S.A. 112 E8 41 35N 93 43W
West Dunbartonshire □, U.K. 13 F4 55 59N 4 30W
West End, Bahamas 120 A4 26 41N 78 58W
West Falkland, Falk. Is. 128 G5 51 40 S 60 0W
West Fargo, U.S.A. 112 B6 46 52N 96 54W
West Farmington, U.S.A. 116 E4 41 23N 80 58W
West Fjord = Vestfjorden, Norway 8 C15 67 55N 14 0 E
West Fork Trinity →, U.S.A. 113 J6 32 48N 96 54W
West Frankfort, U.S.A. 112 G10 37 54N 88 55W
West Hartford, U.S.A. 117 E12 41 45N 72 44W
West Haven, U.S.A. 117 E12 41 17N 72 57W
West Hazleton, U.S.A. 117 F9 40 58N 76 0W
West Helena, U.S.A. 113 H9 34 33N 90 38W
West Hurley, U.S.A. 117 E10 41 59N 74 7W
West Ice Shelf, Antarctica 5 C7 67 0 S 85 0 E
West Indies, Cent. Amer. 121 D7 15 0N 65 0W
West Jordan, U.S.A. 108 F8 40 36N 111 56W
West Lorne, Canada 116 D3 42 36N 81 36W
West Lothian □, U.K. 13 F5 55 54N 3 36W
West Lunga →, Zambia 87 E1 13 6 S 24 39 E
West MacDonnell △, Australia 92 D5 23 38 S 132 59 E
West Memphis, U.S.A. 113 H9 35 9N 90 11W
West Midlands □, U.K. 15 E6 52 26N 2 0W
West Mifflin, U.S.A. 116 F5 40 22N 79 52W
West Milton, U.S.A. 116 E8 41 1N 76 50W
West Monroe, U.S.A. 113 J8 32 31N 92 9W
West Newton, U.S.A. 116 F5 40 14N 79 46W
West Nicholson, Zimbabwe 87 G2 21 2 S 29 20 E
West Palm Beach, U.S.A. 115 M5 26 43N 80 3W
West Plains, U.S.A. 113 G9 36 44N 91 51W
West Point, N.Y., U.S.A. 117 E11 41 24N 73 58W
West Point, Nebr., U.S.A. 112 E6 41 51N 96 43W
West Point, Va., U.S.A. 114 G7 37 32N 76 48W
West Pt. = Ouest, Pte. de l', Canada 105 C7 49 52N 64 40W
West Pt., Australia 95 F2 35 1 S 135 56 E
West Road →, Canada 102 C4 53 18N 122 53W
West Rutland, U.S.A. 117 C11 43 38N 73 5W
West Schelde = Westerschelde →, Neths. 17 C3 51 25N 3 25 E
West Seneca, U.S.A. 116 D6 42 51N 78 48W
West Siberian Plain, Russia 50 C11 62 0N 75 0 E
West Sussex □, U.K. 15 G7 50 55N 0 30W
West-Terschelling, Neths. 17 A5 53 22N 5 13 E
West Valley City, U.S.A. 108 F8 40 42N 111 57W
West Virginia □, U.S.A. 114 F5 38 45N 80 30W
West-Vlaanderen □, Belgium 17 D2 51 0N 3 0 E
West Walker →, U.S.A. 110 G7 38 54N 119 9W
West Wyalong, Australia 95 E4 33 56 S 147 10 E
West Yellowstone, U.S.A. 108 D8 44 40N 111 6W
West Yorkshire □, U.K. 14 D6 53 45N 1 40W
Westall, Pt., Australia 95 E1 32 55 S 134 4 E
Westbrook, U.S.A. 115 D10 43 41N 70 22W
Westbury, Australia 95 G4 41 30 S 146 51 E
Westby, U.S.A. 112 A2 48 52N 104 3W
Westend, U.S.A. 111 K9 35 42N 117 24W
Westerland, Germany 9 J13 54 54N 8 17 E
Westerly, U.S.A. 117 E13 41 22N 71 50W
Western □, Ghana 82 D4 5 30N 2 30W
Western □, Kenya 86 B3 0 30N 34 30 E
Western □, S. Leone 82 D2 8 30N 13 20W
Western □, Zambia 87 F1 15 0 S 24 4 E
Western Australia □, Australia 93 E2 25 0 S 118 0 E
Western Cape □, S. Africa 88 E3 34 0 S 20 0 E
Western Dvina = Daugava →, Latvia 9 H21 57 4N 24 3 E
Western Ghats, India 66 N9 14 0N 75 0 E
Western Isles □, U.K. 13 D1 57 30N 7 10W
Western Sahara ■, Africa 78 D3 25 0N 13 0W
Western Samoa = Samoa ■, Pac. Oc. 91 B13 14 0 S 172 0W
Westernport, U.S.A. 114 F6 39 29N 79 3W
Westerschelde →, Neths. 17 C3 51 25N 3 25 E
Westerstede, Germany 24 B3 53 15N 7 55 E
Westerwald, Germany 24 E3 50 38N 7 56 E
Westfield, Mass., U.S.A. 117 D12 42 7N 72 45W
Westfield, N.Y., U.S.A. 116 D5 42 20N 79 35W
Westfield, Pa., U.S.A. 116 E7 41 55N 77 32W
Westhill, U.K. 13 D6 57 9N 2 19W
Westhope, U.S.A. 112 A4 48 55N 101 1W
Westland △, N.Z. 91 K2 43 16 S 170 16 E
Westland Bight, N.Z. 91 K3 42 55 S 170 5 E
Westlock, Canada 102 C6 54 9N 113 55W
Westmar, Australia 95 D4 27 55 S 149 44 E
Westmeath □, Ireland 12 C4 53 33N 7 34W
Westminster, U.S.A. 114 F7 39 34N 76 59W
Westmont, U.S.A. 116 F6 40 19N 78 58W
Westmoreland, Barbados 121 g 13 13N 59 37W
Westmorland, U.S.A. 111 M11 33 2N 115 37W
Weston, Oreg., U.S.A. 108 D4 45 49N 118 26W
Weston, W. Va., U.S.A. 114 F5 39 2N 80 28W
Weston I., Canada 104 B4 52 33N 79 36W
Weston-super-Mare, U.K. 15 F5 51 21N 2 58W
Westover, U.S.A. 116 F6 40 45N 78 40W
Westport, Canada 117 B8 44 40N 76 25W
Westport, Ireland 12 C2 53 48N 9 31W
Westport, N.Z. 91 J3 41 46 S 171 37 E
Westport, N.Y., U.S.A. 117 B11 44 11N 73 26W
Westport, Oreg., U.S.A. 110 D3 46 8N 123 23W
Westport, Wash., U.S.A. 110 D2 46 53N 124 6W
Westray, Canada 103 C8 53 36N 101 24W
Westray, U.K. 13 B5 59 18N 3 0W
Westree, Canada 104 C3 47 26N 81 34W
Westville, U.S.A. 110 F6 39 8N 120 42W
Westwood, U.S.A. 108 F3 40 18N 121 0W
Wetar, Indonesia 63 F7 7 48 S 126 30 E
Wetaskiwin, Canada 102 C6 52 55N 113 24W
Wete, Tanzania 84 F7 5 4 S 39 43 E
Wetherby, U.K. 14 D6 53 56N 1 23W
Wethersfield, U.S.A. 117 E12 41 42N 72 40W
Wetteren, Belgium 17 D3 51 0N 3 53 E
Wetzlar, Germany 24 E4 50 32N 8 31 E
Wewoka, U.S.A. 113 H6 35 9N 96 30W
Wexford, Ireland 12 D5 52 20N 6 28W
Wexford □, Ireland 12 D5 52 20N 6 25W
Wexford Harbour, Ireland 12 D5 52 20N 6 25W
Weyburn, Canada 103 D8 49 40N 103 50W
Weyer Markt, Austria 26 D7 47 51N 14 40 E
Weyhe, Germany 24 C4 52 58N 8 49 E
Weyib →, Ethiopia 81 F5 7 15N 40 15 E
Weymouth, Canada 105 D6 44 30N 66 1W
Weymouth, U.K. 15 G5 50 37N 2 28W
Weymouth, U.S.A. 117 D14 42 13N 70 58W
Weymouth, C., Australia 94 A3 12 37 S 143 27 E
Wha Ti, Canada 100 B8 63 8N 117 16W
Whakaari = White I., N.Z. 91 G6 37 30 S 177 13 E
Whakatane, N.Z. 91 G6 37 57 S 177 1 E
Whale →, Canada 105 A6 58 15N 67 40W
Whale Cove, Canada 103 A10 62 10N 92 34W
Whales, B. of, Antarctica 5 D12 78 0 S 165 0W
Whalsay, U.K. 13 A8 60 22N 0 59W
Whangamata, N.Z. 91 G5 37 12 S 175 53 E
Whangamomona, N.Z. 91 H5 39 8 S 174 44 E
Whanganui △, N.Z. 91 H5 39 17 S 174 53 E
Whangarei, N.Z. 91 F5 35 43 S 174 21 E
Whangarei Harb., N.Z. 91 F5 35 45 S 174 28 E
Wharfe →, U.K. 14 D6 53 51N 1 9W
Wharfedale, U.K. 14 C5 54 6N 2 1W
Wharton, N.J., U.S.A. 117 F10 40 54N 74 35W
Wharton, Pa., U.S.A. 116 E6 41 31N 78 1W
Wharton, Tex., U.S.A. 113 L6 29 19N 96 6W
Wheatland, Calif., U.S.A. 110 F5 39 1N 121 25W
Wheatland, Wyo., U.S.A. 112 D2 42 3N 104 58W
Wheatley, Canada 116 D2 42 6N 82 27W
Wheaton, Md., U.S.A. 114 F7 39 3N 77 3W
Wheaton, Minn., U.S.A. 112 C6 45 48N 96 30W
Wheelbarrow Pk., U.S.A. 110 H10 37 26N 116 5W
Wheeler, Oreg., U.S.A. 108 D2 45 41N 123 53W
Wheeler, Tex., U.S.A. 113 H4 35 27N 100 16W
Wheeler →, Canada 105 A6 57 2N 67 13W
Wheeler L., U.S.A. 115 H2 34 48N 87 23W
Wheeler Pk., N. Mex., U.S.A. 109 H11 36 34N 105 25W
Wheeler Pk., Nev., U.S.A. 109 G6 38 57N 114 15W
Wheeler Ridge, U.S.A. 111 L8 35 0N 118 57W
Wheeling, U.S.A. 116 F4 40 4N 80 43W
Whernside, U.K. 14 C5 54 14N 2 24W
Whiskey Jack L., Canada 103 B8 58 23N 101 55W
Whiskeytown-Shasta-Trinity ⌂, U.S.A. 108 F2 40 45N 122 15W
Whistleduck Cr. →, Australia 94 C2 20 15 S 135 18 E
Whistler, Canada 102 C4 50 7N 122 58W
Whitby, Canada 116 C6 43 52N 78 56W
Whitby, U.K. 14 C7 54 29N 0 37W
White →, Ark., U.S.A. 113 J9 33 57N 91 5W
White →, Ind., U.S.A. 114 F2 38 25N 87 45W
White →, S. Dak., U.S.A. 112 D5 43 42N 99 27W
White →, Tex., U.S.A. 113 J4 33 14N 100 56W
White →, Utah, U.S.A. 108 F9 40 4N 109 41W
White →, Vt., U.S.A. 117 C12 43 37N 72 20W
White →, Wash., U.S.A. 110 C4 47 12N 122 15W
White, L., Australia 92 D4 21 9 S 128 56 E
White B., Canada 105 C8 50 0N 56 35W
White Bird, U.S.A. 108 D5 45 46N 116 18W
White Butte, U.S.A. 112 B3 46 23N 103 18W
White City, U.S.A. 108 E2 42 26N 122 51W
White Cliffs, Australia 95 E3 30 50 S 143 10 E
White Hall, U.S.A. 112 F9 39 26N 90 24W
White Haven, U.S.A. 117 E9 41 4N 75 47W
White Horse, Vale of, U.K. 15 F6 51 37N 1 30W
White I., N.Z. 91 G6 37 30 S 177 13 E
White L., Canada 117 A8 45 18N 76 31W
White L., U.S.A. 113 L8 29 44N 92 30W
White Mountain Peak, U.S.A. 109 G4 37 38N 118 15W
White Mts., Calif., U.S.A. 110 H8 37 30N 118 15W
White Mts., N.H., U.S.A. 117 B13 44 15N 71 15W
White Mts. △, Australia 94 C4 20 43 S 145 12 E
White Nile = Nîl el Abyad →, Sudan 81 D3 15 38N 32 31 E
White Nile Dam = Khazzān Jabal al Awliyā, Sudan 81 D3 15 24N 32 20 E
White Otter L., Canada 104 C1 49 5N 91 55W
White Pass, U.S.A. 110 D5 46 38N 121 24W
White Plains, U.S.A. 117 E11 41 2N 73 46W
White River, Canada 104 C2 48 35N 85 20W
White River, S. Africa 89 D5 25 20 S 31 0 E
White River, U.S.A. 112 D4 43 34N 100 45W
White Rock, Canada 110 A4 49 2N 122 48W
White Russia = Belarus ■, Europe 32 F4 53 30N 27 0 E
White Sands ⌂, U.S.A. 109 K10 32 46N 106 20W
White Sea = Beloye More, Russia 52 C4 66 30N 38 0 E
White Sulphur Springs, Mont., U.S.A. 108 C8 46 33N 110 54W
White Sulphur Springs, W. Va., U.S.A. 114 G5 37 48N 80 18W
White Swan, U.S.A. 110 D6 46 23N 120 44W
White Volta →, Ghana 83 D4 9 10N 1 15W
Whitecliffs, N.Z. 91 K3 43 26 S 171 55 E
Whitecourt, Canada 102 C5 54 10N 115 45W
Whiteface Mt., U.S.A. 117 B11 44 22N 73 54W
Whitefield, U.S.A. 117 B13 44 23N 71 37W
Whitefish, U.S.A. 108 B6 48 25N 114 20W
Whitefish L., Canada 103 A7 62 41N 106 48W
Whitefish Point, U.S.A. 114 B3 46 45N 84 59W
Whitegull, L. = Goélands, L. aux, Canada 105 A7 55 27N 64 17W
Whitehall, Mich., U.S.A. 114 D2 43 24N 86 21W
Whitehall, Mont., U.S.A. 108 D7 45 52N 112 6W
Whitehall, N.Y., U.S.A. 117 C11 43 33N 73 24W
Whitehall, Wis., U.S.A. 112 C9 44 22N 91 19W
Whitehaven, U.K. 14 C4 54 33N 3 35W
Whitehorse, Canada 102 A1 60 43N 135 3W
Whitemark, Australia 95 G4 40 7 S 148 3 E
Whiteplains, Liberia 82 D2 6 28N 10 40W
Whiteriver, U.S.A. 109 K9 33 50N 109 58W
Whitesand →, Canada 102 A5 60 9N 115 45W
Whitesands, S. Africa 88 E3 34 23 S 20 50 E
Whitesboro, N.Y., U.S.A. 117 C9 43 7N 75 18W
Whitesboro, Tex., U.S.A. 113 J6 33 39N 96 54W
Whiteshell ⌂, Canada 103 D9 50 0N 95 40W
Whitesville, U.S.A. 116 D7 42 2N 77 46W
Whiteville, U.S.A. 115 H6 34 20N 78 42W
Whitewater, U.S.A. 114 D1 42 50N 88 44W
Whitewater Baldy, U.S.A. 109 K9 33 20N 108 39W
Whitewater L., Canada 104 B2 50 50N 89 10W
Whitewood, Australia 94 C3 21 28 S 143 30 E
Whitewood, Canada 103 C8 50 20N 102 20W
Whithorn, U.K. 13 G4 54 44N 4 26W
Whitianga, N.Z. 91 G5 36 47 S 175 41 E
Whitman, U.S.A. 117 D14 42 5N 70 56W
Whitney, Canada 116 A6 45 31N 78 14W
Whitney, Mt., U.S.A. 110 J8 36 35N 118 18W
Whitney Point, U.S.A. 117 D9 42 20N 75 58W
Whitstable, U.K. 15 F9 51 21N 1 3 E
Whitsunday I., Australia 94 J7 20 15 S 149 4 E
Whitsunday Islands △, Australia 94 J7 20 15 S 149 0 E
Whitsunday Passage, Australia 94 J6 20 16 S 148 51 E
Whittier, U.S.A. 111 M8 33 58N 118 3W
Whittlesea, Australia 95 F4 37 27 S 145 9 E
Wholdaia L., Canada 103 A8 60 43N 104 20W
Whyalla, Australia 95 E2 33 2 S 137 30 E
Wiang Kosai △, Thailand 64 D2 17 54N 99 29 E
Wiarton, Canada 116 B3 44 40N 81 10W
Wiawso, Ghana 82 D4 6 10N 2 25W
Wiay, U.K. 13 D1 57 24N 7 13W
Wiązów, Poland 31 H4 50 50N 17 10 E
Wibaux, U.S.A. 112 B2 46 59N 104 11W
Wichian Buri, Thailand 64 E3 15 39N 101 7 E
Wichita, U.S.A. 113 G6 37 42N 97 20W
Wichita Falls, U.S.A. 113 J5 33 54N 98 30W
Wick, U.K. 13 C5 58 26N 3 5W
Wicked Pt., Canada 116 C7 43 52N 77 15W
Wickenburg, U.S.A. 109 K7 33 58N 112 44W
Wickepin, Australia 93 F2 32 50 S 117 30 E
Wickham, Australia 92 D2 20 42 S 117 11 E
Wickham, C., Australia 95 F3 39 35 S 143 57 E
Wickliffe, U.S.A. 116 E3 41 36N 81 28W
Wicklow, Ireland 12 D5 52 59N 6 3W
Wicklow □, Ireland 12 D5 52 57N 6 25W
Wicklow Hd., Ireland 12 D6 52 58N 6 0W
Wicklow Mts., Ireland 12 C5 52 58N 6 26W
Wicklow Mts. △, Ireland 12 C5 53 6N 6 21W
Widawa, Poland 31 G5 51 27N 18 51 E
Widawka →, Poland 31 G5 51 27N 18 52 E
Widgeegoara Cr. →, Australia 95 D4 28 51 S 146 34 E
Widgiemooltha, Australia 93 F3 31 30 S 121 34 E
Widnes, U.K. 14 D5 53 23N 2 45W
Więcbork, Poland 31 E4 53 21N 17 30 E
Wiehengebirge = Nördlicher Teutoburger Wald-Wiehengebirge ⌂, Germany 24 C4 52 18N 8 10 E
Wiehl, Germany 24 E3 50 56N 7 34 E
Wiek, Germany 24 A9 54 37N 13 17 E
Wielbark, Poland 30 E7 53 24N 20 55 E
Wieleń, Poland 31 F3 52 53N 16 9 E
Wielichowo, Poland 31 F3 52 7N 16 22 E
Wieliczka, Poland 31 J7 50 0N 20 5 E
Wielkopolski △, Poland 31 F3 52 18N 16 45 E
Wielkopolskie □, Poland 31 F4 52 10N 17 30 E
Wieluń, Poland 31 G5 51 15N 18 34 E
Wien, Austria 27 C9 48 12N 16 22 E
Wien ✕ (VIA), Austria 27 C9 48 7N 16 35 E
Wiener Neustadt, Austria 27 D9 47 49N 16 16 E
Wieprz →, Poland 31 G8 51 34N 21 49 E
Wieprza →, Poland 30 D3 54 26N 16 25 E
Wieruszów, Poland 31 G5 51 19N 18 9 E
Wiesbaden, Germany 25 E4 50 4N 8 14 E
Wiesental, Germany 25 F4 49 13N 8 31 E
Wiesloch, Germany 25 F4 49 18N 8 41 E
Wiesmoor, Germany 24 B3 53 24N 7 47 E
Wieżyca, Poland 30 D5 54 14N 18 8 E
Wigan, U.K. 14 D5 53 33N 2 38W
Wiggins, Colo., U.S.A. 112 E2 40 14N 104 4W
Wiggins, Miss., U.S.A. 113 K10 30 51N 89 8W
Wight, I. of □, U.K. 15 G6 50 40N 1 20W
Wigierski △, Poland 30 D10 54 5N 23 5 E
Wigry, Jezioro, Poland 30 D10 54 2N 23 8 E
Wigston, U.K. 15 E6 52 35N 1 6W
Wigton, U.K. 14 C4 54 50N 3 10W
Wigtown, U.K. 13 G4 54 53N 4 27W
Wigtown B., U.K. 13 G4 54 46N 4 15W
Wil, Switz. 25 H5 47 28N 9 3 E
Wilamowice, Poland 31 J6 49 55N 19 9 E
Wilber, U.S.A. 112 E6 40 29N 96 58W
Wilberforce, Canada 116 A6 45 2N 78 13W
Wilberforce, C., Australia 94 A2 11 54 S 136 35 E
Wilburton, U.S.A. 113 H7 34 55N 95 19W
Wilcannia, Australia 95 E3 31 30 S 143 26 E
Wilcox, U.S.A. 116 E6 41 35N 78 41W
Wildbad, Germany 25 G4 48 44N 8 33 E
Wildeshausen, Germany 24 C4 52 54N 8 27 E
Wildeshauser Geest ⌂, Germany 24 C4 52 54N 8 30 E
Wildon, Austria 26 E8 46 52N 15 31 E
Wildrose, U.S.A. 111 J9 36 14N 117 11W
Wildspitze, Austria 26 E3 46 53N 10 53 E
Wilga →, Poland 31 G8 51 52N 21 18 E
Wilge →, S. Africa 89 D4 27 3 S 28 20 E
Wilhelm II Coast, Antarctica 5 C7 68 0 S 90 0 E
Wilhelmsburg, Austria 26 C8 48 6N 15 36 E
Wilhelmshaven, Germany 24 B4 53 31N 8 7 E
Wilhelmstal, Namibia 88 C2 21 58 S 16 21 E
Wilkes-Barre, U.S.A. 117 E9 41 15N 75 53W
Wilkes Land, Antarctica 5 D9 69 0 S 120 0 E
Wilkie, Canada 103 C7 52 27N 108 42W
Wilkinsburg, U.S.A. 116 F5 40 26N 79 53W
Wilkinson Lakes, Australia 93 E5 29 40 S 132 39 E
Willandra Creek →, Australia 95 E4 33 22 S 145 52 E
Willapa B., U.S.A. 108 C2 46 40N 124 0W
Willapa Hills, U.S.A. 110 D3 46 35N 123 25W
Willard, N.Y., U.S.A. 116 D8 42 40N 76 50W
Willard, Ohio, U.S.A. 116 E2 41 3N 82 44W
Willcox, U.S.A. 109 K9 32 15N 109 50W
Willemstad, Neth. Ant. 121 D6 12 5N 69 0W
Willet, U.S.A. 117 D9 42 28N 75 55W
William →, Canada 103 B7 59 8N 109 19W
William 'Bill' Dannely Res., U.S.A. 115 J2 32 10N 87 10W
William Creek, Australia 95 D2 28 58 S 136 22 E
Williams, Australia 93 F2 33 2 S 116 52 E
Williams, Ariz., U.S.A. 109 J7 35 15N 112 11W
Williams, Calif., U.S.A. 110 F4 39 9N 122 9W
Williams Harbour, Canada 105 B8 52 33N 55 47W
Williams Lake, Canada 102 C4 52 10N 122 10W
Williamsburg, Ky., U.S.A. 115 G3 36 44N 84 10W
Williamsburg, Pa., U.S.A. 116 F6 40 28N 78 12W
Williamsburg, Va., U.S.A. 114 G7 37 17N 76 44W
Williamson, N.Y., U.S.A. 116 C7 43 14N 77 11W
Williamson, W. Va., U.S.A. 114 G4 37 41N 82 17W
Williamsport, U.S.A. 116 E7 41 15N 77 0W
Williamston, U.S.A. 115 H7 35 51N 77 4W
Williamstown, Australia 95 F3 37 51 S 144 52 E
Williamstown, Ky., U.S.A. 114 F3 38 38N 84 34W
Williamstown, Mass., U.S.A. 117 D11 42 41N 73 12W
Williamstown, N.Y., U.S.A. 117 C9 43 26N 75 53W
Willimantic, U.S.A. 117 E12 41 43N 72 13W
Willingboro, U.S.A. 114 E8 40 3N 74 54W
Williston, S. Africa 88 E3 31 20 S 20 53 E
Williston, Fla., U.S.A. 115 L4 29 23N 82 27W
Williston, N. Dak., U.S.A. 112 A3 48 9N 103 37W
Williston L., Canada 102 B4 56 0N 124 0W
Willits, U.S.A. 108 G2 39 25N 123 21W
Willmar, U.S.A. 112 C7 45 7N 95 3W
Willmore Wilderness ⌂, Canada 102 C5 53 45N 119 30W
Willoughby, U.S.A. 116 E3 41 39N 81 24W
Willow Bunch, Canada 103 D7 49 20N 105 35W
Willow L., Canada 102 A5 62 10N 119 8W
Willow Wall, The, China 57 C12 42 10N 122 0 E
Willowick, U.S.A. 116 E3 41 38N 81 28W
Willowlake →, Canada 102 A4 62 42N 123 8W
Willowmore, S. Africa 88 E3 33 15 S 23 30 E
Willows, U.S.A. 110 F4 39 31N 122 12W
Willowvale = Gatyana, S. Africa 89 E4 32 16 S 28 31 E
Wills, L., Australia 92 D4 21 25 S 128 51 E
Wills Cr. →, Australia 94 C3 22 43 S 140 2 E
Willsboro, U.S.A. 117 B11 44 21N 73 24W
Willunga, Australia 95 F2 35 15 S 138 30 E
Wilmette, U.S.A. 114 D2 42 5N 87 42W
Wilmington, Australia 95 E2 32 39 S 138 7 E
Wilmington, Del., U.S.A. 114 F8 39 45N 75 33W
Wilmington, N.C., U.S.A. 115 H7 34 14N 77 55W
Wilmington, Ohio, U.S.A. 114 F4 39 27N 83 50W
Wilmington, Vt., U.S.A. 117 D12 42 52N 72 52W
Wilmslow, U.K. 14 D5 53 19N 2 13W
Wilpena Cr. →, Australia 95 E2 31 25 S 139 29 E
Wilsall, U.S.A. 108 D8 45 59N 110 38W
Wilson, N.C., U.S.A. 115 H7 35 44N 77 55W
Wilson, N.Y., U.S.A. 116 C6 43 19N 78 50W
Wilson, Pa., U.S.A. 117 F9 40 41N 75 15W
Wilson →, Australia 92 C4 16 48 S 128 16 E
Wilson Bluff, Australia 93 F4 31 41 S 129 0 E
Wilson Inlet, Australia 93 G2 35 0 S 117 22 E
Wilsons Promontory, Australia 95 F4 38 55 S 146 25 E
Wilster, Germany 24 B5 53 55N 9 23 E
Wilton, U.S.A. 112 B4 47 10N 100 47W
Wilton →, Australia 94 A1 14 45 S 134 33 E
Wiltshire □, U.K. 15 F6 51 18N 1 53W
Wiltz, Lux. 17 E5 49 57N 5 55 E
Wiluna, Australia 93 E3 26 36 S 120 14 E
Wimborne Minster, U.K. 15 G6 50 48N 1 59W
Wimereux, France 19 B8 50 45N 1 37 E
Wimmera →, Australia 95 F3 36 8 S 141 56 E
Winam G., Kenya 86 C3 0 20 S 34 15 E
Winburg, S. Africa 88 D4 28 30 S 27 2 E
Winchendon, U.S.A. 117 D12 42 41N 72 3W
Winchester, U.K. 15 F6 51 4N 1 18W
Winchester, Conn., U.S.A. 117 E11 41 53N 73 9W
Winchester, Idaho, U.S.A. 108 C5 46 14N 116 38W
Winchester, Ind., U.S.A. 114 E3 40 10N 84 59W
Winchester, Ky., U.S.A. 114 G3 38 0N 84 11W
Winchester, N.H., U.S.A. 117 D12 42 46N 72 23W
Winchester, Nev., U.S.A. 111 J11 36 6N 115 10W
Winchester, Tenn., U.S.A. 115 H2 35 11N 86 7W
Winchester, Va., U.S.A. 114 F6 39 11N 78 10W
Wind →, U.S.A. 108 E9 43 12N 108 12W
Wind Cave △, U.S.A. 112 D3 43 32N 103 17W
Wind River Range, U.S.A. 108 E9 43 0N 109 30W
Windau = Ventspils, Latvia 9 H19 57 25N 21 32 E
Windber, U.S.A. 116 F6 40 14N 78 50W
Winder, U.S.A. 115 J4 34 0N 83 45W
Windermere, U.K. 14 C5 54 23N 2 55W
Windhoek, Namibia 88 C2 22 35 S 17 4 E
Windischgarsten, Austria 26 D7 47 42N 14 21 E
Windom, U.S.A. 112 D7 43 52N 95 7W
Windorah, Australia 94 D3 25 24 S 142 36 E
Window Rock, U.S.A. 109 J9 35 41N 109 3W
Windrush →, U.K. 15 F6 51 43N 1 24W
Windsor, Australia 95 E5 33 37 S 150 50 E
Windsor, N.S., Canada 105 D7 44 59N 64 5W
Windsor, Ont., Canada 116 D2 42 18N 83 0W
Windsor, U.K. 15 F7 51 29N 0 36W
Windsor, Colo., U.S.A. 112 E2 40 29N 104 54W
Windsor, Conn., U.S.A. 117 E12 41 50N 72 39W
Windsor, Mo., U.S.A. 112 F8 38 32N 93 31W
Windsor, N.Y., U.S.A. 117 D9 42 5N 75 37W
Windsor, Vt., U.S.A. 117 C12 43 29N 72 24W
Windsor & Maidenhead □, U.K. 15 F7 51 29N 0 40W
Windsorton, S. Africa 88 D3 28 16 S 24 44 E
Windward Is., W. Indies 121 D7 13 0N 61 0W
Windward Passage = Vientos, Paso de los, Caribbean 121 C5 20 0N 74 0W
Winefred L., Canada 103 B6 55 30N 110 30W
Winejok, Sudan 81 F2 9 1N 27 30 E
Winfield, U.S.A. 113 G6 37 15N 96 59W
Wingate Mts., Australia 92 B5 14 25 S 130 40 E
Wingham, Australia 95 E5 31 48 S 152 22 E
Wingham, Canada 116 C3 43 55N 81 20W
Winisk, Canada 104 A2 55 20N 85 15W
Winisk →, Canada 104 A2 55 17N 85 5W
Winisk L., Canada 104 B2 52 55N 87 22W
Wink, U.S.A. 113 K3 31 45N 103 9W
Winkler, Canada 103 D9 49 10N 97 56W
Winklern, Austria 26 E5 46 52N 12 52 E
Winlock, U.S.A. 110 D4 46 30N 122 56W
Winneba, Ghana 83 D4 5 25N 0 36W
Winnebago, L., U.S.A. 114 D1 44 0N 88 26W

Winnecke Cr. →,
　Australia .... 92 C5 18 35 S 131 34 E
Winnemucca, U.S.A. .. 108 F5 40 58N 117 44W
Winnemucca L., U.S.A. 108 F4 40 7N 119 21W
Winnett, U.S.A. 108 C9 47 0N 108 21W
Winnfield, U.S.A. 113 K8 31 56N 92 38W
Winnibigoshish, L.,
　U.S.A. 112 B7 47 27N 94 13W
Winnipeg, Canada 103 D9 49 54N 97 9W
Winnipeg, L., Canada . 103 C9 52 0N 97 0W
Winnipeg, L., Canada . 103 C9 52 0N 97 0W
Winnipeg Beach,
　Canada 103 C9 50 30N 96 58W
Winnipegosis, Canada . 103 C9 51 39N 99 55W
Winnipegosis L., Canada 103 C9 52 30N 100 0W
Winnipesaukee, L.,
　U.S.A. 117 C13 43 38N 71 21W
Winnisquam L., U.S.A. 117 C13 43 33N 71 31W
Winnsboro, La., U.S.A. 113 J9 32 10N 91 43W
Winnsboro, S.C., U.S.A. 115 H5 34 23N 81 5W
Winnsboro, Tex., U.S.A. 113 J7 32 58N 95 17W
Winokapau, L., Canada 105 B7 53 15N 62 50W
Winona, Minn., U.S.A. 112 C9 44 3N 91 39W
Winona, Miss., U.S.A. 113 J10 33 29N 89 44W
Winooski, U.S.A. 117 B11 44 29N 73 11W
Winooski →, U.S.A. .. 117 B11 44 32N 73 17W
Winschoten, Neths. ... 17 A7 53 9N 7 3 E
Winsen, Germany ..... 24 B6 53 22N 10 13 E
Winsford, U.K. 14 D5 53 12N 2 31W
Winslow, Ariz., U.S.A. 109 J8 35 2N 110 42W
Winslow, Wash., U.S.A. 110 C4 47 38N 122 31W
Winsted, U.S.A. 117 E11 41 55N 73 4W
Winston-Salem, U.S.A. 115 G5 36 6N 80 15W
Winter Garden, U.S.A. 115 L5 28 34N 81 35W
Winter Haven, U.S.A. 115 M5 28 1N 81 44W
Winter Park, U.S.A. .. 115 L5 28 36N 81 20W
Winterberg, Germany . 24 D4 51 11N 8 33 E
Winterhaven, U.S.A. . 111 N12 32 47N 114 39W
Winters, U.S.A. 110 G5 38 32N 121 58W
Wintersville, U.S.A. .. 116 F4 40 23N 80 42W
Winterswijk, Neths. .. 17 C6 51 58N 6 43 E
Winterthur, Switz. ... 25 H4 47 30N 8 44 E
Winthrop, U.S.A. 108 B3 48 28N 120 10W
Winton, Australia .... 94 C3 22 24 S 143 3 E
Winton, N.Z. .... 91 M2 46 8 S 168 20 E
Wipper →, Germany .. 24 D7 51 16N 11 12 E
Wirrulla, Australia ... 95 E1 32 24 S 134 31 E
Wisbech, U.K. .... 15 E8 52 41N 0 9 E
Wisconsin □, U.S.A. .. 112 C10 44 45N 89 30W
Wisconsin →, U.S.A. . 112 D9 43 0N 91 15W
Wisconsin Rapids,
　U.S.A. 112 C10 44 23N 89 49W
Wisdom, U.S.A. 108 D7 45 37N 113 27W
Wishaw, U.K. 13 F5 55 46N 3 54W
Wishek, U.S.A. 112 B5 46 16N 99 33W
Wisła, Poland .... 31 J5 49 38N 18 53 E
Wisła →, Poland ..... 30 D5 54 22N 18 55 E
Wisłok →, Poland .... 31 H9 50 13N 22 32 E
Wisłoka →, Poland ... 31 H8 50 27N 21 23 E
Wismar, Germany .... 24 B7 53 54N 11 29 E
Wisner, U.S.A. 112 E6 41 59N 96 55W
Wissant, France ..... 19 B8 50 52N 1 40 E
Wissembourg, France . 19 C14 49 2N 7 57 E
Wisznice, Poland .... 31 G10 51 48N 23 13 E
Witbank, S. Africa ... 89 D4 25 51 S 29 14 E
Witdraai, S. Africa ... 88 D3 26 58 S 20 48 E
Witham, U.K. .... 15 F8 51 48N 0 40 E
Witham →, U.K. 14 E7 52 59N 0 2W
Withernsea, U.K. .... 14 D8 53 44N 0 1 E
Witjira △, Australia ... 95 D2 26 22 S 135 37 E
Witkowo, Poland .... 31 F4 52 26N 17 45 E
Witney, U.K. 15 F6 51 48N 1 28W
Witnica, Poland ..... 31 F1 52 40N 14 54 E
Witnossob →, Namibia 88 D3 23 55 S 18 45 E
Wittdün, Germany ... 24 A4 54 38N 8 23 E
Witten, Germany .... 24 D3 51 26N 7 20 E
Wittenberge, Germany 24 B7 53 0N 11 45 E
Wittenburg, Germany . 24 B7 53 31N 11 4 E
Wittenheim, France .. 19 E14 47 44N 7 20 E
Wittenoom, Australia . 92 D2 22 15 S 118 20 E
Wittingen, Germany .. 24 C6 52 44N 10 44 E
Wittlich, Germany ... 25 F2 49 59N 6 53 E
Wittmund, Germany .. 24 B3 53 34N 7 46 E
Wittow, Germany .... 24 A9 54 38N 13 20 E
Wittstock, Germany .. 24 B8 53 10N 12 28 E
Witvlei, Namibia .... 88 C2 22 23 S 18 32 E
Witzenhausen, Germany 24 D5 51 20N 9 51 E
Wkra →, Poland ..... 31 F7 52 27N 20 44 E
Władysławowo, Poland 30 D5 54 48N 18 25 E
Wleń, Poland .... 31 G2 51 2N 15 39 E
Wlingi, Indonesia .... 63 H15 8 5 S 112 25 E
Włocławek, Poland ... 31 F6 52 40N 19 3 E
Włodawa, Poland .... 31 G10 51 33N 23 31 E
Włoszczowa, Poland .. 31 H6 50 50N 19 55 E
Woburn, U.S.A. 117 D13 42 29N 71 9W
Wodian, China ...... 56 H7 32 50N 112 35 E
Wodonga = Albury-
　Wodonga, Australia . 95 F4 36 3 S 145 56 E
Wodzisław Śląski,
　Poland .... 31 H5 50 1N 18 26 E
Wœrth, France ...... 19 D14 48 57N 7 45 E
Woinbogoin, China ... 58 A2 32 51N 98 39 E
Woippy, France ..... 19 C13 49 10N 6 8 E
Wojcieszow, Poland .. 31 H2 50 58N 15 55 E
Wokam, Indonesia ... 63 F8 5 45 S 134 28 E
Woking, U.K. 15 F7 51 19N 0 34W
Wokingham, U.K. 15 F7 51 24N 0 49W
Wokingham □, U.K. .. 15 F7 51 25N 0 51W
Wolbrom, Poland .... 31 H6 50 24N 19 45 E
Wołczyn, Poland ..... 31 G5 51 1N 18 3 E
Woldegk, Germany ... 24 B9 53 27N 13 34 E
Wolf →, Canada 102 A2 60 17N 132 33W
Wolf Creek, U.S.A. .. 108 C7 47 0N 112 4W
Wolf L., Canada 102 A2 60 24N 131 40W
Wolf Point, U.S.A. ... 108 A2 48 5N 105 39W
Wolfe I., Canada 117 B8 44 7N 76 20W
Wolfeboro, U.S.A. ... 117 C13 43 35N 71 13W
Wolfen, Germany .... 24 D8 51 39N 12 15 E
Wolfenbüttel, Germany 24 C6 52 10N 10 33 E
Wolfratshausen,
　Germany .... 25 H7 47 54N 11 24 E
Wolfsberg, Austria ... 26 E7 46 50N 14 52 E
Wolfsburg, Germany . 24 C6 52 25N 10 48 E
Wolgast, Germany ... 24 A9 54 3N 13 46 E
Wolhusen, Switz. .... 25 H4 47 4N 8 4 E
Wolin, Poland .... 30 E1 53 50N 14 37 E
Wollaston, Is., Chile . 128 H3 55 40 S 67 30W
Wollaston L., Canada . 103 B8 58 7N 103 10W
Wollaston Lake, Canada 103 B8 58 3N 103 33W
Wollaston Pen., Canada 100 B8 69 30N 115 0W
Wollongong, Australia 95 E5 34 25 S 150 54 E
Wolmaransstad,
　S. Africa .... 88 D4 27 12 S 25 59 E
Wolmirstedt, Germany 24 C7 52 14N 11 37 E
Wołomin, Poland .... 31 F8 52 19N 21 15 E
Wołów, Poland ...... 31 G3 51 20N 16 38 E
Wolseley, S. Africa ... 88 E2 33 26 S 19 7 E

Wolsey, U.S.A. 112 C5 44 24N 98 28W
Wolstenholme, C.,
　Canada 98 C12 62 35N 77 30W
Wolsztyn, Poland .... 31 F3 52 8N 16 5 E
Wolvega, Neths. ..... 17 B6 52 52N 6 0 E
Wolverhampton, U.K. 15 E5 52 35N 2 7W
Wondai, Australia .... 95 D5 26 20 S 151 49 E
Wongalarroo L.,
　Australia .... 95 E3 31 32 S 144 0 E
Wongan Hills, Australia 93 F2 30 51 S 116 37 E
Wŏnju, S. Korea ..... 57 F14 37 22N 127 58 E
Wonosari, Indonesia . 63 G14 7 58 S 110 36 E
Wonosobo, Indonesia . 63 G13 7 22 S 109 54 E
Wonowon, Canada ... 102 B4 56 44N 121 48W
Wŏnsan, N. Korea .... 57 E14 39 11N 127 27 E
Wonthaggi, Australia . 95 F4 38 37 S 145 37 E
Wood Buffalo △,
　Canada 102 B6 59 0N 113 41W
Wood Is., Australia ... 92 C3 16 24 S 123 19 E
Wood L., Canada 103 B8 55 17N 103 17W
Woodah I., Australia .. 94 A2 13 27 S 136 10 E
Woodbourne, U.S.A. . 117 E10 41 46N 74 36W
Woodbridge, Canada . 116 C5 43 47N 79 36W
Woodbridge, U.K. ... 15 E9 52 6N 1 20 E
Woodburn, U.S.A. ... 108 D2 45 9N 122 51W
Woodenbong, Australia 95 D5 28 24 S 152 39 E
Woodend, Australia .. 95 F3 37 20 S 144 33 E
Woodford, Australia .. 95 D5 26 58 S 152 47 E
Woodfords, U.S.A. ... 110 G7 38 47N 119 50W
Woodlake, U.S.A. ... 110 J7 36 25N 119 6W
Woodland, Calif., U.S.A. 110 G5 38 41N 121 46W
Woodland, Maine,
　U.S.A. 115 C12 45 9N 67 25W
Woodland, Pa., U.S.A. 116 F6 40 59N 78 21W
Woodland, Wash.,
　U.S.A. 110 E4 45 54N 122 45W
Woodland Caribou △,
　Canada 103 C10 51 0N 94 45W
Woodlands, Singapore 65 d 1 27N 103 47 E
Woodridge, Canada .. 103 D9 49 20N 96 9W
Woodroffe, Mt.,
　Australia .... 93 E5 26 20 S 131 45 E
Woods, L., Australia .. 94 B1 17 50 S 133 30 E
Woods, L. of the,
　Canada 103 D10 49 15N 94 45W
Woodstock, Australia . 94 B4 19 35 S 146 50 E
Woodstock, N.B.,
　Canada 105 C6 46 11N 67 37W
Woodstock, Ont.,
　Canada 116 C4 43 10N 80 45W
Woodstock, U.K. 15 F6 51 51N 1 20W
Woodstock, Ill., U.S.A. 112 D10 42 19N 88 27W
Woodstock, Vt., U.S.A. 117 C12 43 37N 72 31W
Woodsville, U.S.A. ... 117 B13 44 9N 72 2W
Woodville, N.Z. ..... 91 J5 40 20 S 175 53 E
Woodville, Miss., U.S.A. 113 K9 31 6N 91 18W
Woodville, Tex., U.S.A. 113 K7 30 47N 94 25W
Woodward, U.S.A. ... 113 G5 36 26N 99 24W
Woody, U.S.A. 111 K8 35 42N 118 50W
Woody →, Canada ... 103 C8 52 31N 100 51W
Woolacombe, U.K. ... 15 F3 51 10N 4 13W
Woolamai, C., Australia 95 F4 38 30 S 145 23 E
Wooler, U.K. 14 B5 55 33N 2 1W
Woolgoolga, Australia 95 E5 30 6 S 153 11 E
Woomera, Australia .. 95 E2 31 5 S 136 50 E
Woonsocket, R.I.,
　U.S.A. 117 E13 42 0N 71 31W
Woonsocket, S. Dak.,
　U.S.A. 112 C5 44 3N 98 17W
Wooramel →, Australia 93 E1 25 45 S 114 17 E
Wooramel Roadhouse,
　Australia .... 93 E1 25 45 S 114 17 E
Wooster, U.S.A. 116 F3 40 48N 81 56W
Worcester, S. Africa .. 88 E2 33 39 S 19 27 E
Worcester, U.K. 15 E5 52 11N 2 12W
Worcester, Mass., U.S.A. 117 D13 42 16N 71 48W
Worcester, N.Y., U.S.A. 117 D10 42 36N 74 45W
Worcestershire □, U.K. 15 E5 52 13N 2 10W
Wörgl, Austria ...... 26 D5 47 29N 12 3 E
Workington, U.K. ... 14 C4 54 39N 3 33W
Worksop, U.K. 14 D6 53 18N 1 7W
Workum, Neths. ..... 17 B5 52 59N 5 26 E
Wormhout, France ... 19 B9 50 52N 2 28 E
Worms, Germany .... 25 F4 49 37N 8 21 E
Worsley, Canada 102 B5 56 31N 119 8W
Wörth, Germany ..... 25 F8 49 1N 12 24 E
Wortham, U.S.A. 113 K6 31 47N 96 28W
Wörther See, Austria . 26 E7 46 37N 14 10 E
Worthing, Barbados .. 121 g 13 5N 59 35W
Worthing, U.K. 15 G7 50 49N 0 21W
Worthington, Minn.,
　U.S.A. 112 D7 43 37N 95 36W
Worthington, Pa., U.S.A. 116 F5 40 50N 79 38W
Wosi, Indonesia ..... 63 E7 0 15 S 128 0 E
Wou-han = Wuhan,
　China .... 59 B10 30 31N 114 18 E
Wousi = Wuxi, China . 59 B13 31 33N 120 18 E
Wowoni, Indonesia .. 63 E6 4 5 S 123 5 E
Wrangel I. = Vrangelya,
　Ostrov, Russia ..... 53 B19 71 0N 180 0 E
Wrangell, U.S.A. 102 B2 56 28N 132 23W
Wrangell Mts., U.S.A. 100 B5 61 30N 142 0W
Wrath, C., U.K. 13 C3 58 38N 5 1W
Wray, U.S.A. 112 E3 40 5N 102 13W
Wrekin, The, U.K. ... 15 E5 52 41N 2 32W
Wrens, U.S.A. 115 J4 33 12N 82 23W
Wrexham, U.K. 14 D4 53 3N 3 0W
Wrexham □, U.K. 14 D5 53 1N 2 58W
Wriezen, Germany ... 24 C10 52 42N 14 7 E
Wright = Paranas, Phil. 61 F6 11 42N 125 2 E
Wright Pt., Canada ... 112 D2 43 47N 105 30W
Wrightson, Mt., U.S.A. 109 L8 31 42N 110 51W
Wrightwood, U.S.A. . 111 L9 34 21N 117 38W
Wrigley, Canada 100 B7 63 16N 123 37W
Wrocław, Poland .... 31 G4 51 5N 17 5 E
Wronki, Poland ..... 31 F3 52 41N 16 21 E
Września, Poland .... 31 F4 52 21N 17 36 E
Wschowa, Poland ... 31 G3 51 48N 16 20 E
Wu Jiang →, China .. 58 C6 29 40N 107 20 E
Wu'an, China .... 56 F8 36 40N 114 15 E
Wubin, Australia .... 93 F2 30 6 S 116 37 E
Wubu, China .... 56 F6 37 28N 110 42 E
Wuchang, China ..... 57 B14 44 55N 127 5 E
Wucheng, China ..... 56 F9 37 12N 116 20 E
Wuchuan, Guangdong,
　China .... 59 G8 21 33N 110 43 E
Wuchuan, Guizhou,
　China .... 58 C7 28 25N 108 3 E
Wuchuan,
　Nei Monggol Zizhiqu,
　China .... 56 D6 41 5N 111 28 E
Wudi, China .... 57 F9 37 40N 117 35 E
Wuding, China ...... 58 E4 25 24N 102 21 E
Wuding He →, China . 56 F6 37 2N 110 23 E
Wudinna, Australia .. 95 E2 33 0 S 135 22 E
Wudu, China .... 56 H3 33 22N 104 54 E

Wufeng, China ...... 59 B8 30 12N 110 42 E
Wugang, China ...... 59 D8 26 44N 110 35 E
Wugong Shan, China . 59 D9 27 30N 114 0 E
Wuhan, China .... 59 B10 30 31N 114 18 E
Wuhe, China .... 57 H9 33 10N 117 50 E
Wuhsi = Wuxi, China . 59 B13 31 33N 120 18 E
Wuhu, China .... 59 B12 31 22N 118 21 E
Wujiang, China ...... 59 B13 31 10N 120 38 E
Wukari, Nigeria ..... 83 D6 7 51N 9 42 E
Wulajie, China ...... 57 B14 44 6N 126 33 E
Wulanbulang, China . 56 D6 41 5N 110 55 E
Wular L., India ...... 69 B6 34 20N 74 30 E
Wulehe, Ghana 83 D5 8 39N 0 0W
Wulian, China .... 57 G10 35 40N 119 12 E
Wuliang Shan, China . 58 E3 24 30N 100 40 E
Wuliaru, Indonesia .. 63 F8 7 27 S 131 0 E
Wuling Shan, China .. 58 C7 28 30N 110 0 E
Wulong, China ...... 58 C6 29 22N 107 43 E
Wulumuchi = Ürümqi,
　China .... 52 E9 43 45N 87 45 E
Wum, Cameroon ..... 83 D7 6 24N 10 2 E
Wuming, China ...... 58 F7 23 12N 108 18 E
Wun Rog, Sudan .... 81 F2 9 0N 28 20 E
Wuning, China ...... 59 C10 29 17N 115 5 E
Wunnummin L., Canada 104 B2 52 55N 89 10W
Wunsiedel, Germany . 25 E8 50 2N 12 0 E
Wunstorf, Germany .. 24 C5 52 25N 9 26 E
Wuntho, Burma ..... 67 H19 23 55N 95 45 E
Wupatki △, U.S.A. ... 109 J8 35 35N 111 20W
Wuping, China ...... 59 E11 25 5N 116 5 E
Wuppertal, Germany . 24 D3 51 16N 7 12 E
Wuppertal, S. Africa . 88 E2 32 13 S 19 12 E
Wuqing, China ...... 57 E9 39 23N 117 4 E
Wurtsboro, U.S.A. ... 117 E10 41 35N 74 29W
Würzburg, Germany . 25 F5 49 46N 9 55 E
Wurzen, Germany ... 24 D8 51 22N 12 44 E
Wushan, China ...... 56 G3 34 43N 104 53 E
Wushishi, Nigeria ... 83 D6 9 46N 6 7 E
Wusuli Jiang =
　Ussuri →, Asia .... 54 A7 48 27N 135 0 E
Wutach →, Germany . 25 H4 47 37N 8 15 E
Wutai, China .... 56 E7 38 40N 113 12 E
Wuting = Huimin, China 57 F9 37 27N 117 28 E
Wutong, China ...... 59 E8 25 24N 110 4 E
Wutonghaolai, China . 57 C11 42 50N 120 5 E
Wutongqiao, China .. 58 C4 29 22N 103 50 E
Wuwei, Anhui, China . 59 B11 31 18N 117 54 E
Wuwei, Gansu, China 60 C5 37 57N 102 34 E
Wuxi, Jiangsu, China . 59 B13 31 33N 120 18 E
Wuxi, Sichuan, China 58 B7 31 23N 109 35 E
Wuxiang, China ..... 56 F7 36 49N 112 50 E
Wuxuan, China ...... 58 F7 23 34N 109 38 E
Wuxue, China .... 59 C10 29 51N 115 30 E
Wuyang, China ...... 56 H7 33 25N 113 35 E
Wuyi, Hebei, China .. 56 F8 37 46N 115 56 E
Wuyi, Zhejiang, China 59 C12 28 52N 119 50 E
Wuyi Shan, China ... 59 D11 27 0N 117 0 E
Wuyishan, China .... 59 D12 27 45N 118 0 E
Wuyo, Nigeria ...... 83 C7 10 23N 11 50 E
Wuyuan, Jiangxi, China 59 C11 29 15N 117 50 E
Wuyuan,
　Nei Monggol Zizhiqu,
　China .... 56 D5 41 2N 108 20 E
Wuzhai, China ...... 56 E6 38 54N 111 48 E
Wuzhi Shan, China .. 64 C7 18 45N 109 45 E
Wuzhong, China ..... 56 E4 38 2N 106 12 E
Wuzhou, China ...... 59 F8 23 30N 111 18 E
Wyaaba Cr. →,
　Australia .... 94 B3 16 27 S 141 35 E
Wyalkatchem, Australia 93 F2 31 8 S 117 22 E
Wyalusing, U.S.A. ... 117 E8 41 40N 76 16W
Wyandotte, U.S.A. .. 114 D4 42 12N 83 9W
Wyandra, Australia .. 95 D4 27 12 S 145 56 E
Wyangala, L., Australia 95 E4 33 54 S 149 0 E
Wyara, L., Australia .. 95 D3 28 42 S 144 14 E
Wycheproof, Australia 95 F3 36 5 S 143 17 E
Wye →, U.K. 15 F5 51 38N 2 40W
Wyemandoo, Australia 93 E2 28 28 S 118 29 E
Wyk, Germany ...... 24 A4 54 41N 8 33 E
Wymondham, U.K. .. 15 E9 52 35N 1 7 E
Wymore, U.S.A. 112 E6 40 7N 96 40W
Wyndham, Australia . 92 C4 15 33 S 128 3 E
Wyndham, N.Z. ..... 91 M2 46 20 S 168 51 E
Wynne, U.S.A. 113 H9 35 14N 90 47W
Wynyard, Australia .. 95 G4 41 5 S 145 44 E
Wynyard, Canada ... 103 C8 51 45N 104 10W
Wyola L., Australia .. 93 E5 29 8 S 130 17 E
Wyoming = Plympton-
　Wyoming, Canada .. 116 D2 42 57N 82 7W
Wyoming □, U.S.A. .. 108 E10 43 0N 107 30W
Wyomissing, U.S.A. . 117 F9 40 20N 75 59W
Wyong, Australia .... 95 E5 33 14 S 151 24 E
Wyrzysk, Poland .... 31 E4 53 10N 17 17 E
Wyśmierzyce, Poland 31 G7 51 37N 20 50 E
Wysoka, Poland ..... 31 E4 53 13N 17 2 E
Wysokie Mazowieckie,
　Poland .... 31 F9 52 55N 22 30 E
Wyszków, Poland .... 31 F8 52 36N 21 25 E
Wyszogród, Poland .. 31 F7 52 23N 20 9 E
Wytheville, U.S.A. ... 114 G5 36 57N 81 5W
Wyżyna Małopolska,
　Poland .... 31 H7 50 45N 20 0 E

X

Xaafuun, Somali Rep. . 75 E5 10 25N 51 16 E
Xaçmaz, Azerbaijan .. 35 K9 41 31N 48 42 E
Xai-Xai, Mozam. .... 89 D5 25 6 S 33 31 E
Xainza, China .... 60 C3 30 58N 88 35 E
Xalapa, Mexico 119 D5 19 32N 96 55W
Xangongo, Angola ... 88 B2 16 45 S 15 5 E
Xankändi, Azerbaijan . 70 B5 39 52N 46 49 E
Xanlar, Azerbaijan ... 35 K8 40 37N 46 12 E
Xanten, Germany .... 24 D2 51 39N 6 26 E
Xánthi, Greece ...... 45 E8 41 10N 24 58 E
Xánthi □, Greece .... 45 E8 41 10N 24 58 E
Xanthos, Turkey .... 47 E11 36 19N 29 18 E
Xanxerê, Brazil ..... 127 B5 26 53 S 52 23W
Xapuri, Brazil .... 124 F5 10 35 S 68 35W
Xar Moron He →,
　China .... 57 C11 43 25N 120 35 E
Xarrë, Albania ...... 44 G4 39 44N 20 3 E
Xátiva, Spain 39 G4 38 59N 0 32W
Xau, L., Botswana ... 88 C3 21 15 S 24 44 E
Xavantina, Brazil .... 127 A5 21 15 S 52 48W
Xenia, U.S.A. 114 F4 39 41N 83 56W
Xeropotamos →,
　Cyprus .... 49 E11 34 42N 32 33 E
Xertigny, France .... 19 D13 48 3N 6 24 E
Xhora, S. Africa ..... 89 E4 31 55 S 28 38 E
Xhumo, Botswana ... 88 C3 21 7 S 24 35 E
Xi Jiang →, China ... 59 F9 22 5N 113 20 E
Xi Xian, Henan, China 56 H8 32 20N 114 42 E
Xi Xian, Shanxi, China 56 F6 36 41N 110 58 E
Xia Xian, China ..... 56 G6 35 8N 111 12 E

Xiachengzi, China ... 57 B16 44 40N 130 18 E
Xiachuan Dao, China 59 G9 21 40N 112 40 E
Xiaguan, China ..... 60 D5 25 32N 100 16 E
Xiajiang, China ..... 59 D10 27 30N 115 10 E
Xiajin, China .... 56 F9 36 56N 116 0 E
Xiamen, China ...... 59 E12 24 25N 118 4 E
Xi'an, China .... 56 G5 34 15N 109 0 E
Xian Xian, China .... 56 E9 38 12N 116 6 E
Xianfeng, China ..... 58 C7 29 40N 109 8 E
Xiang Jiang →, China 59 C9 28 55N 112 50 E
Xiangcheng, Henan,
　China .... 56 H8 33 29N 114 52 E
Xiangcheng, Henan,
　China .... 56 H7 33 50N 113 27 E
Xiangcheng, Sichuan,
　China .... 58 C2 28 53N 99 47 E
Xiangdu, China ..... 58 F6 23 13N 106 58 E
Xiangfan, China ..... 59 A9 32 2N 112 8 E
Xianggang = Hong
　Kong □, China ..... 59 F10 22 11N 114 14 E
Xianghuang Qi, China 56 C7 42 2N 113 50 E
Xiangning, China .... 56 G6 35 58N 110 50 E
Xiangquan, China ... 56 F7 36 30N 113 1 E
Xiangquan He =
　Sutlej →, Pakistan . 68 E4 29 23N 71 3 E
Xiangshan, China .... 59 C13 29 29N 121 51 E
Xiangshui, China .... 57 G10 34 12N 119 33 E
Xiangtan, China ..... 59 D7 27 51N 112 54 E
Xiangxiang, China ... 59 D7 27 43N 112 28 E
Xiangyin, China ..... 59 C9 28 38N 112 54 E
Xiangyun, China .... 58 E3 25 34N 100 35 E
Xiangzhou, China ... 58 F7 23 58N 109 40 E
Xianju, China .... 59 C13 28 51N 120 44 E
Xianning, China ..... 59 C10 29 51N 114 16 E
Xianshui He →, China 58 B3 30 10N 100 59 E
Xiantao, China ...... 59 B9 30 25N 113 25 E
Xianyang, China .... 56 G5 34 20N 108 40 E
Xianyou, China ..... 59 E12 25 28N 118 38 E
Xiao Hinggan Ling,
　China .... 60 B7 49 0N 127 0 E
Xiao Xian, China .... 56 G9 34 15N 116 55 E
Xiaofeng, China ..... 59 B12 30 35N 119 32 E
Xiaogan, China ..... 59 B9 30 55N 113 50 E
Xiaojin, China ...... 58 B4 30 59N 102 21 E
Xiaolan, China ...... 59 F9 22 38N 113 13 E
Xiaoshan, China .... 59 B13 30 12N 120 18 E
Xiaoyi, China .... 56 F6 37 8N 111 48 E
Xiapu, China .... 59 D12 26 54N 119 59 E
Xiawa, China .... 57 C11 42 35N 120 38 E
Xiayi, China .... 56 G9 34 15N 116 10 E
Xichang, China ...... 58 D4 27 51N 102 19 E
Xichou, China .... 58 F5 23 25N 104 42 E
Xichuan, China ..... 56 H6 33 0N 111 30 E
Xide, China .... 58 C4 28 6N 102 19 E
Xiemahe, China ..... 59 B8 31 38N 111 12 E
Xieng Khouang, Laos 64 C4 19 17N 103 25 E
Xifei He →, China ... 56 H9 32 45N 116 40 E
Xifeng, Gansu, China 56 G4 35 40N 107 40 E
Xifeng, Guizhou, China 58 D6 27 7N 106 42 E
Xifeng, Liaoning, China 57 C13 42 42N 124 50 E
Xifengzhen = Xifeng,
　China .... 56 G4 35 40N 107 40 E
Xigazê, China .... 60 D3 29 5N 88 45 E
Xihe, China .... 56 G3 34 2N 105 20 E
Xihua, China .... 56 H8 33 45N 114 30 E
Xilaganí, Greece .... 45 F9 40 58N 25 28 E
Xiliao He →, China .. 57 C12 43 32N 123 35 E
Xilin, China .... 58 E5 24 30N 105 6 E
Xilókastron, Greece .. 46 C4 38 5N 22 38 E
Ximana, Mozam. .... 87 F3 19 24 S 33 58 E
Xime, Guinea-Biss. .. 82 C2 11 59N 14 57W
Ximeng, China ...... 58 F2 22 50N 99 27 E
Xin Jiang →, China .. 59 C11 28 45N 116 35 E
Xin Xian = Xinzhou,
　China .... 56 E7 38 22N 112 46 E
Xinavane, Mozam. ... 89 D5 25 2 S 32 47 E
Xinbin, China .... 57 D13 41 40N 125 2 E
Xincai, China .... 59 A10 32 43N 114 58 E
Xinchang, China .... 59 C13 29 28N 120 52 E
Xincheng,
　Guangxi Zhuangzu,
　China .... 58 E7 24 5N 108 39 E
Xincheng, Jiangxi, China 59 D10 26 48N 114 4 E
Xindu, China .... 58 B5 30 50N 104 10 E
Xinfeng, Guangdong,
　China .... 59 E10 24 5N 114 16 E
Xinfeng, Jiangxi, China 59 D11 27 7N 116 11 E
Xinfeng, Jiangxi, China 59 E10 25 3N 114 30 E
Xinfengjiang Skuiku,
　China .... 59 F10 23 52N 114 30 E
Xing Xian, China .... 56 E6 38 27N 111 7 E
Xing'an,
　Guangxi Zhuangzu,
　China .... 59 E8 25 38N 110 40 E
Xingan, Jiangxi, China 59 D10 27 46N 115 20 E
Xingcheng, China ... 57 D11 40 40N 120 45 E
Xingguo, China ..... 59 D10 26 21N 115 21 E
Xinghe, China .... 56 D7 40 55N 113 55 E
Xinghua, China ..... 57 H10 32 58N 119 48 E
Xinghua Wan, China 59 E12 25 15N 119 20 E
Xinglong, China .... 57 D9 40 25N 117 30 E
Xingning, China .... 59 E10 24 3N 115 42 E
Xingping, China .... 56 G5 34 20N 108 28 E
Xingren, China ...... 58 E5 25 24N 105 11 E
Xingshan, China .... 59 B8 31 15N 110 45 E
Xingtai, China ...... 56 F8 37 3N 114 32 E
Xingu →, Brazil ..... 125 D8 1 30 S 51 53W
Xingwen, China ..... 58 C5 28 22N 105 12 E
Xingyang, China .... 56 G7 34 45N 112 52 E
Xinhe, China .... 56 E8 37 30N 115 15 E
Xinhua, China .... 59 D8 27 42N 111 13 E
Xinhuang, China .... 58 D7 27 21N 109 12 E
Xinhui, China .... 59 F9 22 25N 113 0 E
Xining, China .... 60 C5 36 34N 101 40 E
Xinjiang, China ..... 56 G6 35 34N 111 11 E
Xinjiang Uygur
　Zizhiqu □, China .. 60 B3 42 0N 86 0 E
Xinjie, China .... 58 D3 26 48N 101 15 E
Xinjin = Pulandian,
　China .... 57 E11 39 25N 121 58 E
Xinjin, China .... 58 B4 30 24N 103 47 E
Xinkai He →, China .. 57 C12 43 32N 123 35 E
Xinle, China .... 56 E8 38 25N 114 40 E
Xinlitun, China ...... 57 D12 42 0N 122 8 E
Xinlong, China ...... 58 B3 30 57N 100 12 E
Xinmin, China ...... 57 D12 41 59N 122 50 E
Xinning, China ...... 59 D8 26 28N 110 50 E
Xinping, China ...... 58 E3 24 5N 101 59 E
Xinshao, China ...... 59 D8 27 21N 111 26 E
Xintai, China .... 57 G9 35 55N 117 45 E
Xintian, China ...... 59 E9 25 55N 112 15 E
Xinxian, China ...... 59 B10 31 36N 113 51 E
Xinxiang, China ..... 56 G7 35 18N 113 50 E
Xinxing, China ...... 59 F9 22 28N 112 15 E
Xinyang, China ..... 59 A10 32 6N 114 3 E
Xinye, China .... 59 A9 32 28N 112 21 E

Xinyi, China .... 59 F8 22 25N 111 0 E
Xinyu, China .... 59 D10 27 49N 114 58 E
Xinzhan, China ...... 57 C14 43 50N 127 18 E
Xinzheng, China .... 56 G7 34 20N 113 45 E
Xinzhou, Hubei, China 59 B10 30 50N 114 48 E
Xinzhou, Shanxi, China 56 E7 38 22N 112 46 E
Xinzo de Limia, Spain 36 C3 42 3N 7 47W
Xiongyuecheng, China 57 D12 40 12N 122 5 E
Xiping, Henan, China 56 H8 33 22N 114 5 E
Xiping, Henan, China 56 H6 33 25N 111 8 E
Xiping, Zhejiang, China 59 C12 28 16N 119 29 E
Xique-Xique, Brazil .. 125 F10 10 50 S 42 40W
Xisha Qundao = Paracel
　Is., S. China Sea ... 62 A4 15 50N 112 0 E
Xishui, Guizhou, China 58 C6 28 19N 106 9 E
Xishui, Hubei, China . 59 B10 30 30N 115 15 E
Xitole, Guinea-Biss. .. 82 C2 11 43N 14 50W
Xiu Shui →, China ... 59 C10 29 25N 115 58 E
Xiuning, China ...... 59 C12 29 45N 118 10 E
Xiuren, China .... 59 E8 24 33N 110 12 E
Xiushan, China ...... 58 C7 28 25N 108 57 E
Xiushui, China ...... 59 C10 29 2N 114 15 E
Xiuwen, China ...... 58 D6 26 49N 106 32 E
Xiuyan, China .... 57 D12 40 18N 123 11 E
Xixabangma Feng,
　China .... 67 E14 28 20N 85 40 E
Xixia, China .... 56 H6 33 25N 111 29 E
Xixiang, China ...... 56 H4 33 0N 107 44 E
Xiyang, China .... 56 F7 37 38N 113 38 E
Xizang Zizhiqu □, China 60 C3 32 0N 88 0 E
Xlendi, Malta .... 49 C1 36 1N 14 12 E
Xochob, Mexico 119 D7 19 28N 89 45W
Xu Jiang →, China ... 59 D11 28 0N 116 25 E
Xuan Loc, Vietnam .. 65 G6 10 56N 107 14 E
Xuan'en, China ...... 58 C7 30 0N 109 30 E
Xuanhua, China ..... 56 D8 40 40N 115 2 E
Xuanhua, China ..... 58 B6 31 18N 107 38 E
Xuanwei, China ..... 58 C5 26 5N 103 59 E
Xuanzhou, China .... 59 B12 30 56N 118 43 E
Xuchang, China ..... 56 G7 34 2N 113 48 E
Xudat, Azerbaijan ... 35 K9 41 38N 48 41 E
Xuefeng Shan, China 59 D8 27 5N 110 35 E
Xuejiaping, China ... 59 B8 31 39N 110 16 E
Xun Jiang →, China .. 59 F8 23 35N 111 30 E
Xun Xian, China .... 56 G8 35 42N 114 33 E
Xundian, China ...... 58 E4 25 36N 103 15 E
Xunwu, China .... 59 E10 24 54N 115 37 E
Xunyang, China ..... 56 H5 32 48N 109 22 E
Xunyi, China .... 56 G5 35 8N 108 20 E
Xupu, China .... 59 D8 27 53N 110 32 E
Xúquer →, Spain 39 F4 39 5N 0 10W
Xushui, China .... 56 E8 39 2N 115 40 E
Xuwen, China .... 59 G8 20 20N 110 10 E
Xuyen Moc, Vietnam 65 G6 10 34N 107 25 E
Xuyong, China ...... 58 C5 28 10N 105 22 E
Xuzhou, China ...... 57 G9 34 18N 117 10 E
Xylophagou, Cyprus . 49 E12 34 54N 33 51 E

Y

Ya Xian, China ...... 64 C7 18 14N 109 29 E
Yaamba, Australia ... 94 C5 23 8 S 150 22 E
Ya'an, China .... 58 C4 29 58N 103 5 E
Yaapeet, Australia ... 95 F3 35 45 S 142 3 E
Yabassi, Cameroon .. 83 E6 4 30N 9 57 E
Yabelo, Ethiopia .... 81 F4 4 50N 38 8 E
Yabelo △, Ethiopia .. 81 F4 6 0N 37 50 E
Yablanitsa, Bulgaria . 45 C8 43 2N 24 5 E
Yablonovy Ra. =
　Yablonovyy Khrebet,
　Russia .... 53 D12 53 0N 114 0 E
Yablonovyy Khrebet,
　Russia .... 53 D12 53 0N 114 0 E
Yabluniv, Ukraine ... 29 B9 48 24N 24 57 E
Yabrai Shan, China .. 56 E2 39 40N 103 0 E
Yabrūd, Syria .... 74 B5 33 58N 36 39 E
Yabucoa, Puerto Rico 121 d 18 3N 65 53W
Yacambú △, Venezuela 121 E6 9 42N 69 27W
Yacheng, China ..... 64 C7 18 22N 109 6 E
Yacuiba, Bolivia ..... 126 A3 22 0 S 63 43W
Yacuma →, Bolivia .. 124 F5 13 38 S 65 23W
Yadgir, India .... 66 L10 16 45N 77 5 E
Yadkin →, U.S.A. ... 115 H5 35 29N 80 9W
Yadrin, Russia ...... 34 C8 55 57N 46 12 E
Yaeyama-Rettō, Japan 55 M1 24 30N 123 40 E
Yagaba, Ghana 83 C4 10 14N 1 20W
Yağcılar, Turkey .... 47 B10 39 25N 28 23 E
Yagodnoye, Russia .. 53 C15 62 33N 149 40 E
Yahila,
　Dem. Rep. of
　the Congo .... 86 B1 0 13N 24 28 E
Yahk, Canada 102 D5 49 6N 116 10W
Yahotyn, Ukraine ... 33 G6 50 17N 31 46 E
Yahuma, Dem. Rep. of
　the Congo .... 84 D4 1 0N 23 10 E
Yahyalı, Turkey ..... 72 C6 38 5N 35 18 E
Yaita, Japan .... 55 F9 36 48N 139 56 E
Yaiza, Canary Is. 48 F6 28 57N 13 46W
Yajiang, China ...... 58 B3 30 2N 100 57 E
Yajua, Nigeria ...... 83 C7 11 27N 12 49 E
Yakima, U.S.A. 108 C3 46 36N 120 31W
Yakima →, U.S.A. ... 108 C3 47 0N 120 30W
Yako, Burkina Faso .. 82 C4 12 59N 2 15W
Yakobi I., U.S.A. 102 B1 58 0N 136 30W
Yakoruda, Bulgaria .. 44 D7 42 1N 23 39 E
Yaku-Shima, Japan .. 55 J5 30 20N 130 30 E
Yakumo, Japan ..... 54 C10 42 15N 140 16 E
Yakutat, U.S.A. 100 C6 59 33N 139 44W
Yakutia = Sakha □,
　Russia .... 53 C13 66 0N 130 0 E
Yakutsk, Russia ..... 53 C13 62 5N 129 50 E
Yala, Thailand ...... 65 J3 6 33N 101 18 E
Yalaboro, Australia .. 94 J6 20 50 S 148 40 E
Yale, U.S.A. 116 C2 43 8N 82 48W
Yalgoo, Australia .... 93 E2 28 16 S 116 39 E
Yalgorup △, Australia 93 D2 24 34 S 115 2 E
Yalinga, C.A.R. ..... 84 C4 6 33N 23 10 E
Yalkubul, Punta, Mexico 119 C7 21 32N 88 37W
Yalleroi, Australia ... 94 C4 24 3 S 145 42 E
Yalobusha →, U.S.A. 113 J9 33 33N 90 10W
Yalong Jiang →, China 58 D3 26 40N 101 55 E
Yalova, Turkey ...... 45 F13 40 41N 29 15 E
Yalpuh, Ozero, Ukraine 29 E13 45 30N 28 41 E
Yalu Jiang →, China . 57 E13 40 0N 124 22 E
Yalvaç, Turkey ...... 72 C4 38 17N 31 10 E
Yam Ha Melah = Dead
　Sea, Asia .... 74 D4 31 30N 35 30 E
Yam Kinneret, Israel . 74 C4 32 45N 35 35 E
Yamada, Japan ...... 55 H5 33 33N 130 49 E
Yamagata, Japan .... 54 E10 38 15N 140 15 E
Yamagata □, Japan .. 54 E10 38 30N 140 0 E
Yamaguchi, Japan ... 55 G5 34 10N 131 32 E
Yamaguchi □, Japan . 55 G5 34 20N 131 40 E

Yamal, Poluostrov, Russia ..... 52 B8 71 0N 70 0 E
Yamal Pen. = Yamal, Poluostrov, Russia .. 52 B8 71 0N 70 0 E
Yamanashi □, Japan .. 55 G9 35 40N 138 40 E
Yamanie Falls △, Australia ... 94 B4 18 29 S 146 9 E
Yamba, Australia .... 95 D5 29 26 S 153 23 E
Yambarran Ra., Australia ... 92 C5 15 10 S 130 25 E
Yambéring, Guinea .. 82 C2 11 50N 12 18 E
Yâmbiô, Sudan ...... 81 G2 4 35N 28 16 E
Yambol, Bulgaria .... 45 D10 42 30N 26 30 E
Yamdena, Indonesia .. 63 F8 7 45 S 131 20 E
Yame, Japan .... 55 H5 33 13N 130 35 E
Yamethin, Burma .... 67 J20 20 29N 96 18 E
Yamma-Yamma, L., Australia ... 95 D3 26 16 S 141 20 E
Yamoussoukro, Ivory C. 82 D3 6 49N 5 17W
Yampa →, U.S.A. 108 F9 40 32N 108 59W
Yampi Sd., Australia .. 92 C3 16 8 S 123 38 E
Yampil, Moldova .... 33 H5 48 15N 28 15 E
Yampol = Yampil, Moldova ... 33 H5 48 15N 28 15 E
Yamrat, Nigeria ..... 83 C6 10 11N 9 55 E
Yamrukchal = Botev, Bulgaria ... 45 D8 42 44N 24 52 E
Yamuna →, India .... 69 G9 25 30N 81 53 E
Yamunanagar, India .. 68 D7 30 7N 77 17 E
Yamzho Yumco, China 60 D4 28 48N 90 35 E
Yan, Nigeria .... 83 C7 10 5N 12 11 E
Yana →, Russia ..... 53 B14 71 30N 136 0 E
Yanagawa, Japan .... 55 H5 33 10N 130 24 E
Yanai, Japan .... 55 H6 33 58N 132 7 E
Yan'an, China .... 56 F5 36 35N 109 26 E
Yanbian, China ...... 58 D3 26 47N 101 31 E
Yanbu 'al Baḥr, Si. Arabia ... 70 F3 24 0N 38 5 E
Yanchang, China .... 56 F6 36 43N 110 1 E
Yancheng, Henan, China 56 H8 33 35N 114 0 E
Yancheng, Jiangsu, China ... 57 H11 33 23N 120 8 E
Yanchep Beach, Australia ... 93 F2 31 33 S 115 37 E
Yanchi, China .... 56 F4 37 48N 107 20 E
Yanchuan, China .... 56 F6 36 51N 110 10 E
Yanco Cr. →, Australia 95 F4 35 14 S 145 35 E
Yandicoogina, Australia 92 D2 22 49 S 119 12 E
Yandoon, Burma .... 67 L19 17 0N 95 40 E
Yanfeng, China ...... 58 E3 25 52N 101 8 E
Yanfolila, Mali 82 C3 11 11N 8 9W
Yang Xian, China .... 56 H4 33 15N 107 30 E
Yang-Yang, Senegal .. 82 B1 15 30N 15 20W
Yangambi, Dem. Rep. of the Congo ... 86 B1 0 47N 24 24 E
Yangbi, China .... 58 E2 25 41N 99 58 E
Yangcheng, China ... 56 G7 35 28N 112 22 E
Yangch'ü = Taiyuan, China ... 56 F7 37 52N 112 33 E
Yangchun, China .... 59 F8 22 11N 111 48 E
Yanggao, China ..... 56 D7 40 21N 113 55 E
Yanggu, China ...... 56 F8 36 8N 115 43 E
Yangjiang, China .... 59 G8 21 50N 111 59 E
Yangliuqing, China .. 57 E9 39 17N 117 0 E
Yangon = Rangoon, Burma ... 67 L20 16 45N 96 20 E
Yangping, China ..... 59 B8 31 12N 111 25 E
Yangpingguan, China 56 H4 32 58N 106 5 E
Yangquan, China .... 56 F7 37 58N 113 31 E
Yangshan, China .... 59 E9 24 30N 112 40 E
Yangshuo, China .... 59 E8 24 48N 110 29 E
Yangtse = Chang Jiang →, China ... 59 B13 31 48N 121 10 E
Yangtze Kiang = Chang Jiang →, China ... 59 B13 31 48N 121 10 E
Yangudi Rassa △, Ethiopia ... 81 E5 10 50N 40 42 E
Yangxin, China ...... 59 C10 29 50N 115 12 E
Yangyang, S. Korea .. 57 E15 38 4N 128 38 E
Yangyuan, China .... 56 D8 40 1N 114 10 E
Yangzhong, China ... 59 A12 32 2N 119 35 E
Yangzhou, China .... 59 A12 32 21N 119 26 E
Yanhe, China .... 58 C7 28 18N 108 29 E
Yanji, China .... 57 C15 42 59N 129 30 E
Yanjin, China .... 58 C5 28 4N 104 18 E
Yanjing, China ...... 58 C2 29 7N 98 33 E
Yankari △, Nigeria .. 83 D7 9 50N 10 28 E
Yankton, U.S.A. 112 D6 42 53N 97 23W
Yanonge, Dem. Rep. of the Congo ... 86 B1 0 35N 24 38 E
Yanqi, China .... 60 B3 42 5N 86 35 E
Yanqing, China ...... 56 D8 40 30N 115 58 E
Yanshan, Hebei, China 57 E9 38 4N 117 22 E
Yanshan, Jiangxi, China 59 C11 28 15N 117 41 E
Yanshan, Yunnan, China 58 F5 23 35N 104 20 E
Yanshou, China ..... 57 B15 45 28N 128 22 E
Yantabulla, Australia 95 D4 29 21 S 145 0 E
Yantai, China .... 57 F11 37 34N 121 22 E
Yantarnyy, Russia ... 30 D6 54 52N 19 57 E
Yanting, China ...... 58 B5 31 11N 105 24 E
Yantra →, Bulgaria .. 45 C9 43 40N 25 37 E
Yanwa, China .... 58 D2 27 35N 98 55 E
Yanyuan, China ..... 58 D3 27 25N 101 30 E
Yanzhou, China ..... 56 G9 35 35N 116 49 E
Yao Noi, Ko, Thailand 65 a 8 7N 98 37 E
Yao Xian, China ..... 56 G5 34 55N 108 59 E
Yao Yai, Ko, Thailand 65 a 8 0N 98 35 E
Yao'an, China .... 58 E3 25 31N 101 18 E
Yaodu, China .... 58 A5 32 45N 105 22 E
Yaoundé, Cameroon . 83 E7 3 50N 11 35 E
Yaowan, China ...... 57 G10 34 15N 118 3 E
Yap, Pac. Oc. .... 96 G5 9 30N 138 10 E
Yapen, Indonesia .... 63 E9 1 50 S 136 0 E
Yapen, Selat, Indonesia 63 E9 1 20 S 136 10 E
Yapero, Indonesia ... 63 E9 4 59 S 137 11 E
Yappar →, Australia . 94 B3 18 22 S 141 16 E
Yaqui →, Mexico 118 B2 27 37N 110 39W
Yar-Sale, Russia ..... 52 C8 66 50N 70 50 E
Yaraka, Australia .... 94 C3 24 53 S 144 3 E
Yaransk, Russia ..... 34 B8 57 22N 47 49 E
Yarbasan, Turkey .... 47 C10 38 59N 28 49 E
Yardımcı Burnu, Turkey 47 E12 36 13N 30 25 E
Yare →, U.K. .... 15 E9 52 35N 1 38 E
Yaremcha, Ukraine .. 29 B9 48 27N 24 33 E
Yarensk, Russia ..... 52 C5 62 11N 49 15 E
Yarfa, Si. Arabia .... 80 C4 24 37N 38 35 E
Yarí →, Colombia ... 124 D4 0 20 S 72 20W
Yarkand = Shache, China ... 60 C2 38 20N 77 10 E
Yarker, Canada 117 B8 44 23N 76 46W
Yarkhun →, Pakistan 69 A5 36 17N 72 30 E
Yarlung Zangbo Jiang = Brahmaputra →, Asia 69 H13 23 40N 90 35 E
Yarmouth, Canada .. 105 D6 43 50N 66 7W
Yarmūk →, Syria ... 74 C4 32 42N 35 40 E
Yaroslavl, Russia .... 32 D10 57 35N 39 55 E
Yarqa, W. →, Egypt . 74 F2 30 0N 33 49 E

Yarra Yarra Lakes, Australia ... 93 E2 29 40 S 115 45 E
Yarram, Australia .... 95 F4 38 29 S 146 39 E
Yarraman, Australia .. 95 D5 26 50 S 152 0 E
Yarras, Australia .... 95 E5 31 25 S 152 20 E
Yartsevo, Sib., Russia 53 C10 60 20N 90 0 E
Yartsevo, Smolensk, Russia ... 32 E7 55 6N 32 43 E
Yarumal, Colombia .. 124 B3 6 58N 75 24W
Yasawa Group, Fiji .. 91 C7 17 0 S 177 23 E
Yaselda, Belarus .... 33 F4 52 7N 26 28 E
Yasen, Ukraine ...... 29 B9 48 45N 24 10 E
Yashi, Nigeria .... 83 C6 12 23N 7 54 E
Yashikera, Nigeria ... 83 D5 9 44N 3 9 E
Yashkul, Russia ..... 35 G7 46 11N 45 21 E
Yasin, Pakistan ...... 69 A5 36 24N 73 23 E
Yasinovataya, Ukraine 33 H9 48 7N 37 57 E
Yasinski, L., Canada . 104 B4 53 16N 77 35W
Yasinya, Ukraine .... 29 B9 48 16N 24 21 E
Yasothon, Thailand .. 64 E5 15 50N 104 10 E
Yass, Australia ...... 95 E4 34 49 S 148 54 E
Yásuj, Iran .... 71 D6 30 31N 51 31 E
Yatağan, Turkey ..... 47 D10 37 20N 28 10 E
Yatakala, Niger ...... 83 C5 14 50N 0 22 E
Yates Center, U.S.A. . 113 G7 37 53N 95 44W
Yathkyed L., Canada . 103 A9 62 40N 98 0W
Yatsushiro, Japan ... 55 H5 32 30N 130 40 E
Yatta Plateau, Kenya 86 C4 2 0 S 38 0 E
Yauco, Puerto Rico .. 121 d 18 2N 66 51W
Yavari →, Peru ..... 124 D4 4 21 S 70 2W
Yávaros, Mexico 118 B3 26 42N 109 31W
Yavatmal, India ..... 66 J11 20 20N 78 15 E
Yavne, Israel .... 74 D3 31 52N 34 45 E
Yavoriv, Ukraine .... 31 J10 49 55N 23 20 E
Yavorov = Yavoriv, Ukraine ... 31 J10 49 55N 23 20 E
Yavuzeli, Turkey .... 72 D7 37 18N 37 24 E
Yawatahama, Japan .. 55 H6 33 27N 132 24 E
Yawri B., S. Leone ... 82 D2 8 22N 13 0W
Yaxi, China .... 58 D6 27 33N 106 41 E
Yazd, Iran .... 71 D7 31 55N 54 27 E
Yazd □, Iran .... 71 D7 32 0N 55 0 E
Yazd-e Khvāst, Iran .. 71 D7 31 31N 52 7 E
Yazıköy, Turkey ..... 47 E9 36 40N 27 20 E
Yazman, Pakistan ... 68 E4 29 8N 71 45 E
Yazoo →, U.S.A. 113 J9 32 22N 90 54W
Yazoo City, U.S.A. .. 113 J9 32 51N 90 25W
Ybbs, Austria .... 26 C8 48 12N 15 4 E
Ybycuí □, Paraguay .. 126 B4 26 5 S 56 46W
Ybytyruzú △, Paraguay 127 B4 25 51 S 56 11W
Yding Skovhøj, Denmark ... 11 J3 55 59N 9 46 E
Ye, Burma .... 64 E1 15 15N 97 15 E
Ye Xian, China ...... 56 H7 33 35N 113 25 E
Yebyu, Burma ...... 64 E2 14 15N 98 13 E
Yechŏn, S. Korea .... 57 F15 36 39N 128 27 E
Yecla, Spain 39 G3 38 35N 1 5W
Yécora, Mexico 118 B3 28 20N 108 58W
Yedebub Biheroch Bihereseboch na Hizboch □, Ethiopia 81 F4 12 0N 36 0 E
Yedintsy = Ecineţ, Moldova ... 29 B12 48 9N 27 18 E
Yedseram →, Nigeria 83 C7 12 30N 14 5 E
Yeghegnadzor, Armenia 73 C11 39 44N 45 19 E
Yegorlyk →, Russia . 35 G5 46 35N 41 57 E
Yegorlykskaya, Russia 35 G5 46 35N 40 35 E
Yegoryevsk, Russia .. 32 E10 55 27N 38 55 E
Yegros, Paraguay .... 126 B4 26 20 S 56 25W
Yehbuah, Indonesia . 63 J17 8 23 S 114 45 E
Yehuda, Midbar, Israel 74 D4 31 35N 35 15 E
Yei, Sudan .... 81 G3 4 9N 30 40 E
Yei, Nahr →, Sudan . 81 F3 6 15N 30 13 E
Yejmiadzin, Armenia 35 K7 40 12N 44 19 E
Yekaterinburg, Russia 52 D7 56 50N 60 30 E
Yelabuga, Russia .... 34 C11 55 45N 52 4 E
Yelarbon, Australia .. 95 D5 28 33 S 150 38 E
Yelatma, Russia ..... 34 C5 55 0N 41 45 E
Yelets, Russia .... 33 F10 52 40N 38 30 E
Yélimané, Mali 82 B2 15 9N 10 34W
Yelizavetgrad = Kirovohrad, Ukraine 33 H7 48 35N 32 20 E
Yell, U.K. 13 A7 60 35N 1 5W
Yell Sd., U.K. 13 A7 60 33N 1 15W
Yellow Sea, China ... 57 G12 35 0N 123 0 E
Yellowhead Pass, Canada ... 102 C5 52 53N 118 25W
Yellowknife, Canada . 102 A6 62 27N 114 29W
Yellowknife →, Canada 102 A6 62 31N 114 19W
Yellowstone △, U.S.A. 108 D8 44 40N 110 30W
Yellowstone →, U.S.A. 112 B3 47 59N 103 59W
Yellowstone L., U.S.A. 108 D8 44 27N 110 22W
Yelnya, Russia ...... 32 E7 54 35N 33 15 E
Yelsk, Belarus ...... 33 G5 51 50N 29 10 E
Yelwa, Nigeria ...... 83 C5 10 49N 4 41 E
Yemen ■, Asia ...... 75 E3 15 0N 44 0 E
Yen Bai, Vietnam ... 58 G5 21 42N 104 52 E
Yenagoa, Nigeria ... 83 E6 4 58N 6 16 E
Yenakiyeve, Ukraine 33 H10 48 15N 38 15 E
Yenakiyevo = Yenakiyeve, Ukraine 33 H10 48 15N 38 15 E
Yenangyaung, Burma 67 J19 20 30N 95 0 E
Yenbo = Yanbu 'al Baḥr, Si. Arabia ... 70 F3 24 0N 38 5 E
Yenda, Australia .... 95 E4 34 13 S 146 14 E
Yende Millimou, Guinea 82 D2 8 55N 10 10W
Yendéré, Burkina Faso 82 C4 10 12N 4 59W
Yendi, Ghana 83 D4 9 29N 0 1W
Yéni, Niger .... 83 C5 13 30N 1 1 E
Yenice, Ankara, Turkey 72 C5 39 14N 32 42 E
Yenice, Aydın, Turkey 47 D10 37 49N 28 35 E
Yenice, Çanakkale, Turkey ... 47 B9 39 55N 27 17 E
Yenice, Edirne, Turkey 45 F10 40 42N 26 9 E
Yenice, Turkey ..... 72 D6 37 37N 35 33 E
Yenifoça, Turkey .... 47 C8 38 44N 26 51 E
Yenihisar, Turkey ... 47 D9 37 22N 27 16 E
Yeniköy, Bursa, Turkey 45 F13 40 31N 29 22 E
Yeniköy, Çanakkale, Turkey ... 47 B8 39 55N 26 10 E
Yeniköy, Kütahya, Turkey ... 47 C11 38 52N 29 17 E
Yenipazar, Turkey ... 47 D10 37 49N 28 11 E
Yenisaía, Greece .... 45 E8 41 1N 24 57 E
Yenişehir, Turkey ... 45 F13 40 16N 29 37 E
Yenisey →, Russia .. 52 B9 71 50N 82 40 E
Yeniseysk, Russia ... 53 D10 58 27N 92 13 E
Yeniseyskiy Zaliv, Russia ... 52 B9 72 20N 81 0 E
Yennádhi, Greece ... 49 C9 36 2N 27 56 E
Yenne, France ...... 21 C9 45 43N 5 44 E
Yenotayevka, Russia 35 G8 47 15N 47 0 E
Yenyuka, Russia .... 53 D13 57 57N 121 15 E
Yeo →, U.K. 15 G5 51 2N 2 49W
Yeo, L., Australia .... 93 E3 28 0 S 124 30 E

Yeo I., Canada 116 A3 45 24N 81 48W
Yeola, India .... 66 J9 20 2N 74 30 E
Yeoryioúpolis, Greece 49 D6 35 20N 24 15 E
Yeovil, U.K. 15 G5 50 57N 2 38W
Yeppoon, Australia .. 94 C5 23 5 S 150 47 E
Yepes, Spain 36 F7 39 55N 3 39W
Yeráki, Greece ...... 46 D4 37 0N 22 42 E
Yerbent, Turkmenistan 52 F6 39 30N 58 50 E
Yerbogachen, Russia 53 C11 61 16N 108 0 E
Yerevan, Armenia ... 35 K7 40 10N 44 31 E
Yerington, U.S.A. ... 108 G4 38 59N 119 10W
Yerkesik, Turkey .... 47 D10 37 7N 28 19 E
Yerköy, Turkey ..... 72 C6 39 38N 34 28 E
Yermak, Kazakhstan . 52 D8 52 2N 76 55 E
Yermo, U.S.A. 111 L10 34 54N 116 50W
Yerólakkos, Cyprus . 49 D12 35 11N 33 15 E
Yeropol, Russia ..... 53 C17 65 15N 168 40 E
Yeropótamos →, Greece 49 D6 35 3N 24 50 E
Yeroskipos, Cyprus .. 49 E11 34 46N 32 28 E
Yershov, Russia ..... 34 E9 51 23N 48 27 E
Yerushalayim = Jerusalem, Israel ... 74 D4 31 47N 35 10 E
Yerville, France ..... 18 C7 49 40N 0 53 E
Yes Tor, U.K. 15 G4 50 41N 4 0W
Yesan, S. Korea ..... 57 F14 36 41N 126 51 E
Yeşilhisar, Turkey ... 72 C6 38 20N 35 5 E
Yeşilırmak →, Turkey 72 B7 41 22N 36 0 E
Yeşilkent, Turkey ... 72 D7 36 57N 36 12 E
Yeşilköy, Turkey .... 45 F12 40 58N 28 49 E
Yeşilova, Turkey .... 47 D11 37 31N 29 46 E
Yeşilyurt, Manisa, Turkey ... 47 C10 38 22N 28 40 E
Yeşilyurt, Muğla, Turkey 47 D10 37 10N 28 20 E
Yesnogorsk, Russia .. 32 E9 54 32N 37 38 E
Yeso, U.S.A. 113 H2 34 26N 104 37W
Yessentuki, Russia .. 35 H6 44 5N 42 53 E
Yessey, Russia ...... 53 C11 68 29N 102 10 E
Yeste, Spain 39 G2 38 22N 2 19W
Yetman, Australia ... 95 D5 28 56 S 150 48 E
Yeu, Î. d', France 18 F4 46 42N 2 20W
Yevlakh = Yevlax, Azerbaijan ... 35 K8 40 39N 47 7 E
Yevlax, Azerbaijan .. 35 K8 40 39N 47 7 E
Yevpatoriya, Ukraine 33 K7 45 15N 33 20 E
Yeya →, Russia ..... 33 J10 46 40N 38 40 E
Yeysk, Russia .... 33 J10 46 40N 38 12 E
Yezd = Yazd, Iran ... 71 D7 31 55N 54 27 E
Yezerishche, Belarus 32 E5 55 50N 29 59 E
Yhati, Paraguay ..... 126 B4 25 45 S 56 35W
Yhú, Paraguay ...... 127 B4 25 0 S 56 0W
Yi →, Uruguay ...... 126 C4 33 7 S 57 8W
Yi 'Allaq, G., Egypt .. 74 E2 30 22N 33 32 E
Yi He →, China ..... 57 G10 34 10N 118 8 E
Yi Xian, Anhui, China 59 C11 29 55N 117 57 E
Yi Xian, Hebei, China 56 E8 39 20N 115 30 E
Yi Xian, Liaoning, China 57 D11 41 30N 121 22 E
Yialí, Greece .... 47 E9 36 41N 27 11 E
Yialiás →, Cyprus ... 49 D12 35 9N 33 44 E
Yi'allaq, G., Egypt ... 80 A3 30 21N 33 31 E
Yialousa, Cyprus .... 49 D13 35 32N 34 10 E
Yiáltra, Greece ..... 46 C4 38 51N 22 59 E
Yianisádhes, Greece . 49 D8 35 20N 26 10 E
Yiannitsa, Greece ... 44 F6 40 46N 22 24 E
Yibin, China .... 58 C5 28 45N 104 32 E
Yichang, China ...... 59 B9 30 40N 111 20 E
Yicheng, Henan, China 59 B9 31 41N 112 12 E
Yicheng, Shanxi, China 56 G6 35 42N 111 40 E
Yichuan, China ...... 56 F6 36 2N 110 10 E
Yichun, Heilongjiang, China ... 60 B7 47 44N 128 52 E
Yichun, Jiangxi, China 59 D10 27 48N 114 22 E
Yidu, China .... 57 F10 36 43N 118 28 E
Yidun, China .... 58 B2 30 22N 99 21 E
Yifag, Ethiopia ..... 81 E4 12 4N 37 46 E
Yifeng, China .... 59 C10 28 12N 114 45 E
Yihuang, China ..... 59 D11 27 30N 116 12 E
Yijun, China .... 56 G5 35 28N 109 8 E
Yıldız Dağları, Turkey 45 E11 41 48N 27 36 E
Yıldızeli, Turkey .... 72 C7 39 51N 36 36 E
Yiliang, Yunnan, China 58 D5 28 38N 104 2 E
Yiliang, Yunnan, China 58 E4 24 56N 103 11 E
Yilong, China .... 58 B6 31 34N 106 23 E
Yimen, China .... 58 E4 24 40N 102 10 E
Yimianpo, China .... 57 B15 45 7N 128 2 E
Yinchuan, China .... 56 E4 38 30N 106 15 E
Yindarlgooda, L., Australia ... 93 F3 30 40 S 121 52 E
Ying He →, China ... 56 H9 32 30N 116 30 E
Ying Xian, China .... 56 E7 39 32N 113 10 E
Yingcheng, China ... 59 B9 30 56N 113 35 E
Yingde, China ...... 59 E9 24 10N 113 25 E
Yingjiang, China .... 58 E1 24 41N 97 55 E
Yingjing, China ..... 58 C4 29 41N 102 52 E
Yingkou, China ..... 57 D12 40 37N 122 18 E
Yingshan, Henan, China 59 B9 31 35N 113 50 E
Yingshan, Hubei, China 59 B10 31 11N 115 32 E
Yingshan, Sichuan, China ... 58 B6 31 4N 106 35 E
Yingshang, China ... 59 A11 32 38N 116 12 E
Yingtan, China ..... 59 C11 28 12N 117 0 E
Yining, China .... 52 E9 43 58N 81 10 E
Yinjiang, China ..... 58 C7 28 1N 108 21 E
Yinmabin, Burma ... 67 H19 22 10N 94 55 E
Yiofiros →, Greece .. 49 D7 35 20N 25 6 E
Yioúra, Nótios Aiyaíon, Greece ... 46 D6 37 32N 24 40 E
Yioúra, Thessalía, Greece ... 46 B6 39 23N 24 10 E
Yipinglang, China ... 58 E3 25 10N 101 52 E
Yirba Muda, Ethiopia 81 F4 6 12N 38 42 E
Yirga Alem, Ethiopia 81 F4 6 48N 38 22 E
Yirol, Sudan .... 81 F3 6 33N 30 30 E
Yirrkala, Australia ... 94 A2 12 14 S 136 56 E
Yishan, China ...... 58 E7 24 28N 108 38 E
Yishui, China .... 57 G10 35 47N 118 30 E
Yishun, Singapore ... 65 d 1 26N 103 50 E
Yíthion, Greece ..... 46 D4 36 46N 22 34 E
Yitong, China .... 57 C13 43 13N 125 20 E
Yiwu, China .... 59 C13 29 20N 120 3 E
Yixing, China .... 59 B12 31 21N 119 48 E
Yiyang, Henan, China 56 G7 34 27N 112 10 E
Yiyang, Hunan, China 59 C9 28 35N 112 18 E
Yiyang, Jiangxi, China 59 C11 28 27N 117 22 E
Yizhang, China ..... 59 E9 25 27N 112 57 E
Yizheng, China ..... 59 A12 32 30N 119 19 E
Yli-Kitka, Finland ... 8 C23 66 8N 28 30 E
Ylitornio, Finland ... 8 C20 66 19N 23 39 E
Ylivieska, Finland ... 8 D21 64 4N 24 28 E
Yngaren, Sweden ... 11 F10 58 50N 16 35 E
Yoakum, U.S.A. 113 L6 29 17N 97 9W
Yob →, Eritrea ...... 81 D4 17 15N 37 50 E
Yobe □, Nigeria ..... 83 C7 12 0N 11 30 E
Yog Pt., Phil. .... 63 B6 14 6N 124 12 E
Yogan, Togo .... 83 D5 6 23N 1 30 E
Yoğuntaş, Turkey ... 45 E11 41 50N 27 4 E
Yogyakarta, Indonesia 63 G14 7 49 S 110 22 E

Yogyakarta □, Indonesia ... 63 G14 7 48 S 110 22 E
Yoho △, Canada 102 C5 51 25N 116 30W
Yojoa, L. de, Honduras 120 D2 14 53N 88 0W
Yōju, S. Korea ...... 57 F14 37 20N 127 35 E
Yok Don △, Vietnam 64 F6 12 50N 107 40 E
Yokadouma, Cameroon 84 D2 3 26N 14 55 E
Yokkaichi, Japan .... 55 G8 34 55N 136 38 E
Yoko, Cameroon .... 83 D7 5 32N 12 20 E
Yokohama, Japan ... 55 G9 35 27N 139 28 E
Yokosuka, Japan .... 55 G9 35 20N 139 40 E
Yokote, Japan ...... 54 E10 39 20N 140 30 E
Yola, Nigeria .... 83 D7 9 10N 12 29 E
Yolaina, Cordillera de, Nic. ... 120 D3 11 30N 84 0W
Yoloten, Turkmenistan 71 B9 37 18N 62 21 E
Yom →, Thailand ... 62 A2 15 35N 100 1 E
Yonago, Japan ...... 55 G6 35 25N 133 19 E
Yonaguni-Jima, Japan 55 M1 24 27N 123 0 E
Yonan, N. Korea .... 57 F14 37 55N 126 11 E
Yonezawa, Japan .... 54 F10 37 57N 140 4 E
Yong Peng, Malaysia 65 L4 2 0N 103 3 E
Yong'an, China ..... 59 E11 25 59N 117 25 E
Yongcheng, China ... 56 H9 33 55N 116 20 E
Yŏngch'ŏn, S. Korea 57 G15 35 58N 128 56 E
Yongchuan, China .. 58 C5 29 17N 105 55 E
Yongchun, China ... 59 E12 25 16N 118 20 E
Yongde, China ...... 58 E2 24 5N 99 25 E
Yongdeng, China ... 56 F2 36 38N 103 25 E
Yongding, China .... 59 E11 24 43N 116 45 E
Yŏngdŏk, S. Korea .. 57 F15 36 24N 129 22 E
Yŏngdŭngpo, S. Korea 57 F14 37 31N 126 54 E
Yongfeng, China .... 59 D10 27 20N 115 22 E
Yongfu, China ...... 58 E7 24 59N 109 59 E
Yonghe, China ...... 56 F6 36 46N 110 38 E
Yŏnghŭng, N. Korea 57 E14 39 31N 127 18 E
Yongji, China .... 56 G6 34 52N 110 28 E
Yongjia, China ...... 59 C13 28 10N 120 45 E
Yŏngju, S. Korea .... 57 F15 36 50N 128 40 E
Yongkang, Yunnan, China ... 58 E2 24 9N 99 20 E
Yongkang, Zhejiang, China ... 59 C13 28 55N 120 2 E
Yongnian, China .... 56 F8 36 47N 114 29 E
Yongning, Guangxi Zhuangzu, China .. 58 F7 22 44N 108 28 E
Yongning, Ningxia Huizu, China 56 E4 38 15N 106 14 E
Yongqing, China .... 56 E9 39 25N 116 28 E
Yongren, China ..... 58 D3 26 7N 101 40 E
Yongshan, China .... 58 C5 28 11N 103 35 E
Yongsheng, China .. 58 D3 26 38N 100 46 E
Yongshun, China ... 58 C7 29 2N 109 51 E
Yongtai, China ..... 59 E12 25 49N 118 58 E
Yŏngwŏl, S. Korea .. 57 F15 37 11N 128 28 E
Yongxin = Jinggangshan, China 59 D10 26 58N 114 15 E
Yongxing, China .... 59 D9 26 9N 113 8 E
Yongxiu, China ..... 59 C10 29 2N 115 42 E
Yongzhou, China ... 59 D8 26 17N 111 37 E
Yonibana, S. Leone . 82 D2 8 30N 12 19W
Yonkers, U.S.A. 117 F11 40 56N 73 54W
Yonne □, France .... 19 E10 47 50N 3 40 E
Yonne →, France ... 19 D9 48 23N 2 58 E
York, Australia ..... 93 F2 31 52 S 116 47 E
York, U.K. 14 D6 53 58N 1 6W
York, Ala., U.S.A. ... 113 J10 32 29N 88 18W
York, Nebr., U.S.A. . 112 E6 40 52N 97 36W
York, Pa., U.S.A. ... 114 F7 39 58N 76 44W
York, C., Australia .. 94 A3 10 42 S 142 31 E
York, City of □, U.K. 14 D6 53 58N 1 6W
York, Kap, Greenland 4 B4 75 55N 66 25W
York, Vale of, U.K. .. 14 C6 54 15N 1 25W
York Haven, U.S.A. . 116 F8 40 7N 76 46W
York Sd., Australia .. 92 C4 15 0 S 125 5 E
Yorke Pen., Australia 95 E2 34 50 S 137 40 E
Yorkshire Dales △, U.K. 14 C5 54 12N 2 10W
Yorkshire Wolds, U.K. 14 C7 54 8N 0 31W
Yorkton, Canada 103 C8 51 11N 102 28W
Yorkville, U.S.A. 110 G3 38 52N 123 13W
Yoro, Honduras 120 C2 15 9N 87 7W
Yoron-Jima, Japan .. 55 L4 27 2N 128 26 E
Yorosso, Mali 82 C4 12 17N 4 55W
Yos Sudarso, Pulau = Dolak, Pulau, Indonesia 63 F9 8 0 S 138 30 E
Yosemite △, U.S.A. . 110 H7 37 45N 119 40W
Yosemite Village, U.S.A. 110 H7 37 45N 119 35W
Yoshino-Kumano △, Japan ... 55 H8 34 12N 135 55 E
Yoshkar Ola, Russia 34 B8 56 38N 47 55 E
Yŏsu, S. Korea ..... 57 G14 34 47N 127 45 E
Yotvata, Israel ..... 74 F4 29 55N 35 2 E
You Jiang →, China . 58 F6 22 50N 108 6 E
You Xian, China .... 59 D9 27 1N 113 17 E
Youbou, Canada 110 B2 48 53N 124 13W
Youghal, Ireland 12 E4 51 56N 7 52W
Youghal B., Ireland . 12 E4 51 55N 7 49W
Youkounkoun, Guinea 82 C2 12 35N 13 11W
Young, Australia .... 95 E4 34 19 S 148 18 E
Young, Canada 103 C7 51 47N 105 45W
Young, Uruguay .... 126 C4 32 44 S 57 36W
Younghusband, L., Australia ... 95 E2 30 50 S 136 5 E
Younghusband Pen., Australia ... 95 F2 36 0 S 139 25 E
Youngstown, Canada 103 C6 51 35N 111 10W
Youngstown, N.Y., U.S.A. ... 116 C5 43 15N 79 3W
Youngstown, Ohio, U.S.A. ... 116 E4 41 6N 80 39W
Youngsville, U.S.A. . 116 E5 41 51N 79 19W
Youngwood, U.S.A. 116 F5 40 14N 79 34W
Youxi, China .... 59 D12 26 17N 118 12 E
Youyang, China ..... 58 C7 28 47N 108 42 E
Youyu, China .... 56 D7 40 10N 112 20 E
Yozgat, Turkey ..... 72 C6 39 51N 34 47 E
Ypacaraí △, Paraguay 126 B4 25 18 S 57 19W
Ypané →, Paraguay . 126 A4 23 29 S 57 19W
Yport, France ...... 18 C7 49 45N 0 15 E
Ypres = Ieper, Belgium 17 D2 50 51N 2 53 E
Yreka, U.S.A. 108 F2 41 44N 122 38W
Yssingeaux, France . 21 C8 45 9N 4 8 E
Ystad, Sweden ..... 11 J7 55 26N 13 50 E
Ysyk-Köl, Kyrgyzstan 52 E8 42 25N 77 15 E
Ythan →, U.K. 13 D7 57 19N 1 59W
Ytterhogdal, Sweden 10 B8 62 12N 14 56 E
Ytyk-Kyuyel, Russia 53 C14 62 30N 133 45 E
Yu Jiang →, China .. 58 F7 23 22N 110 3 E
Yu Xian = Yuzhou, China ... 56 G7 34 10N 113 28 E
Yu Xian, Hebei, China 56 E8 39 50N 114 35 E

Yu Xian, Shanxi, China 56 E7 38 5N 113 20 E
Yuan Jiang →, Hunan, China 59 C8 28 55N 111 50 E
Yuan Jiang →, Yunnan, China 58 F4 22 20N 103 59 E
Yuan'an, China ..... 59 B8 31 3N 111 34 E
Yuanjiang, Hunan, China 59 C9 28 47N 112 21 E
Yuanjiang, Yunnan, China 58 F4 23 32N 102 0 E
Yüanli, Taiwan ..... 59 E13 24 27N 120 39 E
Yüanlin, Taiwan .... 59 F13 23 58N 120 30 E
Yuanling, China .... 59 C8 28 29N 110 22 E
Yuanmou, China ... 58 E3 25 42N 101 53 E
Yuanyang, Henan, China 56 G6 35 18N 113 40 E
Yuanyang, Yunnan, China 58 F4 23 12N 102 43 E
Yuba →, U.S.A. 110 F5 39 8N 121 36W
Yuba City, U.S.A. .. 110 F5 39 8N 121 37W
Yūbari, Japan ...... 54 C10 43 4N 141 59 E
Yubdo, Ethiopia .... 81 F4 8 58N 35 24 E
Yübetsu, Japan ..... 54 B11 44 13N 143 50 E
Yubo, Sudan .... 81 F2 5 23N 27 30 E
Yucatán □, Mexico . 119 C7 21 30N 86 30W
Yucatán, Canal de, Caribbean ... 120 B2 22 0N 86 30W
Yucatán, Península de, Mexico ... 98 H11 19 30N 89 0W
Yucatan Basin, Cent. Amer. ... 98 H11 19 0N 86 0W
Yucatan Channel = Yucatán, Canal de, Caribbean ... 120 B2 22 0N 86 30W
Yucca, U.S.A. 111 L12 34 52N 114 9W
Yucca Valley, U.S.A. 111 L10 34 8N 116 27W
Yucheng, China .... 56 F9 36 55N 116 32 E
Yuci, China .... 56 F7 37 42N 112 46 E
Yudu, China .... 59 E10 25 59N 115 30 E
Yuechi, China ...... 58 B6 30 34N 106 25 E
Yuendumu, Australia 92 D5 22 16 S 131 49 E
Yueqing, China ..... 59 C13 28 9N 120 59 E
Yueqing Wan, China 59 D13 28 5N 121 22 E
Yuexi, Anhui, China 59 B11 30 50N 116 20 E
Yuexi, Sichuan, China 58 C4 28 37N 102 26 E
Yueyang, China ..... 59 C9 29 21N 113 5 E
Yugan, China .... 59 C11 28 43N 116 37 E
Yugoslavia = Serbia & Montenegro ■, Europe 44 C4 43 20N 20 0 E
Yuhuan, China ..... 59 C13 28 9N 121 12 E
Yühuan Dao, China 59 C13 28 5N 121 15 E
Yujiang, China ..... 59 C11 28 10N 116 43 E
Yukhnov, Russia ... 32 E8 54 44N 35 15 E
Yukon →, U.S.A. ... 100 B3 62 32N 163 54W
Yukon Territory □, Canada ... 100 B6 63 0N 135 0W
Yüksekova, Turkey . 73 D11 37 34N 44 16 E
Yukta, Russia ...... 53 C11 63 26N 105 42 E
Yukuhashi, Japan ... 55 H5 33 44N 130 59 E
Yulara, Australia ... 93 E5 25 10 S 130 55 E
Yule →, Australia ... 92 D2 20 41 S 118 17 E
Yuleba, Australia ... 95 D4 26 37 S 149 24 E
Yuli, Nigeria .... 83 D7 9 44N 10 12 E
Yuli, Taiwan .... 59 F13 23 20N 121 18 E
Yulin, Guangxi Zhuangzu, China 59 F8 22 40N 110 8 E
Yülin, Hainan, China 65 C7 18 10N 109 31 E
Yulin, Shaanxi, China 56 E5 38 20N 109 30 E
Yuma, Ariz., U.S.A. 111 N12 32 43N 114 37W
Yuma, Colo., U.S.A. 112 E3 40 8N 102 43W
Yuma, B. de, Dom. Rep. 121 C6 18 20N 68 35W
Yumbe, Uganda .... 86 B3 3 28N 31 15 E
Yumbi, Dem. Rep. of the Congo ... 86 C2 1 12 S 26 15 E
Yumen, China ...... 60 C4 39 50N 97 30 E
Yumurtalık, Turkey . 72 D6 36 45N 35 43 E
Yun Gui Gaoyuan, China ... 58 E3 26 0N 104 0 E
Yun Ho →, China ... 57 E9 39 10N 117 10 E
Yun Ling, China .... 58 D2 27 0N 99 20 E
Yun Xian, Hubei, China 59 A8 32 50N 110 46 E
Yun Xian, Yunnan, China 58 E3 24 27N 100 8 E
Yuna, Australia ..... 93 E2 28 20 S 115 0 E
Yunak, Turkey ..... 72 C4 38 49N 31 43 E
Yunan, China .... 59 F8 23 12N 111 32 E
Yuncheng, Henan, China 56 G8 35 36N 115 57 E
Yuncheng, Shanxi, China 56 G6 35 2N 111 0 E
Yunfu, China .... 59 F9 22 50N 112 5 E
Yungas, Bolivia .... 124 G5 17 0 S 66 0W
Yungay, Chile ...... 126 D1 37 10 S 72 5W
Yunhe, China .... 59 C12 28 8N 119 33 E
Yunkai Dashan, China 59 F8 22 20N 111 0 E
Yunlin, Taiwan ..... 59 F13 23 42N 120 30 E
Yunlong, China ..... 58 E2 25 57N 99 13 E
Yunmeng, China ... 59 B9 31 20N 113 43 E
Yunnan □, China ... 58 E4 25 0N 102 0 E
Yunquera de Henares, Spain ... 38 E1 40 47N 3 11W
Yunt Dağı, Turkey .. 47 C9 38 56N 27 13 E
Yunta, Australia .... 95 E3 32 34 S 139 36 E
Yunxi, China .... 56 H6 33 0N 110 22 E
Yunxiao, China ..... 59 F11 23 59N 117 18 E
Yuping, China ...... 58 D7 27 13N 108 56 E
Yupyongdong, N. Korea 57 D15 41 49N 128 53 E
Yuqing, China ...... 58 D6 27 13N 107 53 E
Yuraygir △, Australia 95 D5 29 45 S 153 15 E
Yurga, Russia ...... 52 D9 55 42N 84 51 E
Yurimaguas, Peru .. 124 E3 5 55 S 76 7W
Yurkivka, Ukraine .. 29 B13 48 42N 28 35 E
Yuryev-Polskiy, Russia 32 D10 56 30N 39 40 E
Yuryevets, Russia ... 34 B6 57 25N 43 2 E
Yuscarán, Honduras 120 D2 13 58N 86 45W
Yûsef, Bahr →, Egypt 80 B3 28 55N 30 35 E
Yushanzhen, China . 58 C7 29 28N 108 22 E
Yushe, China .... 56 F7 37 4N 112 58 E
Yushu, Jilin, China .. 57 B14 44 43N 126 38 E
Yushu, Qinghai, China 58 A1 33 5N 96 55 E
Yüsufeli, Turkey .... 73 B9 40 50N 41 33 E
Yutai, China .... 56 G9 35 0N 116 45 E
Yutian, China ...... 56 E9 39 53N 117 45 E
Yuxarı Qarabağ = Nagorno-Karabakh □, Azerbaijan ... 70 B5 39 55N 46 45 E
Yuxi, China .... 58 E4 24 30N 102 35 E
Yuyao, China .... 59 B13 30 3N 121 10 E
Yuzawa, Japan ..... 54 E10 39 10N 140 30 E
Yuzha, Russia ...... 34 B6 56 34N 42 1 E
Yuzhno-Sakhalinsk, Russia ... 53 E15 46 58N 142 45 E

Yuzhnyy □, Russia ...... 35 H5 44 0N 40 0 E
Yuzhou, China ...... 56 G7 34 10N 113 28 E
Yvelines □, France .... 19 D8 48 40N 1 45 E
Yverdon-les-Bains,
  Switz. .... 25 J2 46 47N 6 39 E
Yvetot, France .... 18 C7 49 37N 0 44 E
Yzeure, France .... 19 F10 46 33N 3 22 E

Z

Zaandam, Neths. ...... 17 B4 52 27N 4 50 E
Záb al Kabīr ➤, Iraq .. 70 C4 36 1N 43 24 E
Záb aş Şaghīr ➤, Iraq .. 70 C4 35 17N 43 29 E
Žabalj, Serbia & M. .... 28 E5 45 21N 20 5 E
Žabari, Serbia & M. .... 44 B5 44 22N 21 15 E
Zabarjad, Egypt ...... 80 C4 23 40N 36 12 E
Zabaykalsk, Russia .... 53 E12 49 40N 117 25 E
Żabki, Poland .... 31 F8 52 17N 21 7 E
Ząbkowice Śląskie,
  Poland .... 31 H3 50 35N 16 50 E
Žabljak, Serbia & M. ... 44 C3 43 18N 19 5 E
Żabików, Poland ...... 31 F9 53 0N 23 19 E
Żabno, Poland .... 31 H7 50 9N 20 53 E
Zābol, Iran .... 71 D9 31 0N 61 32 E
Zābol □, Afghan. ...... 66 D5 32 0N 67 0 E
Zābolī, Iran .... 71 E9 27 10N 61 35 E
Zabolotiv, Ukraine .... 29 B10 48 28N 25 18 E
Zabolottya, Ukraine ... 31 G11 51 38N 24 16 E
Zabré, Burkina Faso ... 83 C4 11 12N 0 36W
Zábřeh, Czech Rep. .... 27 B9 49 53N 16 52 E
Zabrze, Poland .... 31 H5 50 18N 18 50 E
Zabuzhzhya, Ukraine .. 31 G10 51 21N 23 42 E
Zabzuga, Ghana ...... 83 D5 9 20N 0 30 E
Zacapa, Guatemala ... 120 D2 14 59N 89 31W
Zacapu, Mexico 118 D4 19 50N 101 43W
Zacatecas, Mexico 118 C4 22 49N 102 34W
Zacatecas □, Mexico ... 118 C4 23 30N 103 0W
Zacatecoluca, El Salv. . 120 D2 13 29N 88 51W
Zachary, U.S.A. 113 K9 30 39N 91 9W
Zachodnio-
  Pomorskie □, Poland 30 E2 53 40N 15 50 E
Zacoalco, Mexico 118 C4 20 14N 103 33W
Zacualtipán, Mexico ... 119 C5 20 39N 98 36W
Zadar, Croatia .... 41 D12 44 8N 15 14 E
Zadawa, Nigeria ...... 83 C7 11 33N 10 19 E
Zadetkyi Kyun, Burma . 65 G2 10 0N 98 25 E
Zadonsk, Russia ...... 33 F10 52 25N 38 56 E
Zafarqand, Iran ...... 71 C7 33 11N 52 29 E
Zafora, Greece .... 47 E8 36 5N 26 24 E
Zafra, Spain 37 G4 38 26N 6 30W
Zagań, Poland .... 31 G2 51 39N 15 22 E
Zagarė, Lithuania .... 30 B10 56 21N 23 15 E
Zagazig, Egypt .... 80 H7 30 40N 31 30 E
Zağheh, Iran .... 71 C6 33 30N 48 42 E
Zaglivérion, Greece ... 44 F7 40 36N 23 15 E
Zagnanado, Benin .... 83 D5 7 18N 2 28 E
Zagorá, Greece ...... 46 B5 39 27N 23 6 E
Zagorje, Slovenia .... 41 B11 46 8N 15 0 E
Zagórów, Poland ..... 31 F4 52 10N 17 54 E
Zagórz, Poland ...... 31 J9 49 30N 22 14 E
Zagreb, Croatia ..... 41 C12 45 50N 15 58 E
Zagreb ✈ (ZAG),
  Croatia .... 41 C13 45 45N 16 4 E
Zāgros, Kūhhā-ye, Iran 71 C6 33 45N 48 5 E
Zagros Mts. = Zāgros,
  Kūhhā-ye, Iran .... 71 C6 33 45N 48 5 E
Žagubica, Serbia & M. . 44 B5 44 15N 21 47 E
Zaguinaso, Ivory C. ... 82 C3 10 1N 6 14W
Zagyva ➤, Hungary ... 28 C5 47 5N 20 4 E
Zahamena △, Madag. .. 89 B8 17 37 S 48 49 E
Zāhedān, Fārs, Iran ... 71 D7 28 46N 53 52 E
Zāhedān,
  Sīstān va Balūchestān,
  Iran .... 71 D9 29 30N 60 50 E
Zahlah, Lebanon ..... 74 B4 33 52N 35 50 E
Zahna, Germany ..... 24 D8 51 55N 12 49 E
Zainsk, Russia .... 34 C11 55 18N 52 4 E
Zaïre = Congo ➤,
  Africa .... 84 F2 6 4S 12 24 E
Zaječar, Serbia & M. .. 44 C6 43 53N 22 18 E
Zaka, Zimbabwe ..... 89 C5 20 20 S 31 29 E
Zakamensk, Russia ... 53 D11 50 23N 103 17 E
Zakarpatska □, Ukraine 29 B8 48 20N 23 20 E
Zakataly = Zaqatala,
  Azerbaijan .... 35 K8 41 38N 46 35 E
Zakháro, Greece ..... 46 D3 37 30N 21 39 E
Zakhodnaya Dzvina =
  Daugava ➤, Latvia . 9 H21 57 4N 24 3 E
Zákhū, Iraq .... 70 B4 37 10N 42 50 E
Zákinthos, Greece .... 46 D2 37 47N 20 54 E
Zákinthos □, Greece .. 46 D2 37 47N 20 57 E
Zakopane, Poland .... 31 J6 49 18N 19 57 E
Zakroczym, Poland ... 31 F7 52 26N 20 38 E
Zákros, Greece ...... 49 D8 35 6N 26 10 E
Zala □, Hungary ..... 28 D1 46 42N 16 50 E
Zala ➤, Hungary ..... 28 D1 46 43N 17 16 E
Zalaegerszeg, Hungary 28 D1 46 53N 16 47 E
Zalakomár, Hungary .. 28 D2 46 33N 17 10 E
Zalalövő, Hungary ... 28 D1 46 51N 16 35 E
Zalamea de la Serena,
  Spain 37 G5 38 40N 5 38W
Zalamea la Real, Spain 37 H4 37 41N 6 38W
Zalău, Romania ...... 28 C8 47 12N 23 3 E
Žalec, Slovenia ...... 41 B12 46 16N 15 10 E
Zaleshchiki =
  Zalishchyky, Ukraine 29 B10 48 45N 25 45 E
Zalesye, Russia ...... 30 D8 54 50N 21 31 E
Zalew Wiślany, Poland 30 D6 54 20N 19 50 E
Zalewo, Poland ...... 30 E6 53 50N 19 41 E
Zalingei, Sudan ...... 79 F10 12 51N 23 29 E
Zalishchyky, Ukraine . 29 B10 48 45N 25 45 E
Zama L., Canada 102 B5 58 45N 119 5W
Zambeke, Dem. Rep. of
  the Congo .... 86 B2 2 8N 25 17 E
Zambeze ➤, Africa ... 87 F4 18 35 S 36 20 E
Zambezi = Zambeze ➤,
  Africa .... 87 F4 18 35 S 36 20 E
Zambezi, Zambia ..... 85 G4 13 30 S 23 15 E
Zambezi △, Zimbabwe . 87 F2 17 54 S 25 41 E
Zambézia □, Mozam. .. 87 F2 16 15 S 37 30 E
Zambia ■, Africa ..... 87 F2 15 0 S 28 0 E
Zamboanga, Phil. .... 61 H5 6 59N 122 3 E
Zambrów, Poland .... 31 F9 52 59N 22 14 E
Zametchino, Russia ... 34 D6 53 30N 42 30 E
Zamfara □, Nigeria ... 83 C6 12 10N 6 0 E
Zamfara ➤, Nigeria ... 83 C5 12 5N 4 2 E
Zamora, Mexico 118 D4 20 0N 102 21W
Zamora, Spain 36 D5 41 30N 5 45W
Zamora □, Spain 36 D5 41 30N 5 46W
Zamość, Poland ...... 31 H10 50 43N 23 15 E
Zamtang, China ...... 58 A3 32 26N 101 6 E
Zan, Ghana 83 D4 9 26N 0 17W
Záncara ➤, Spain 39 F1 39 18N 3 18W

Zandvoort, Neths. .... 17 B4 52 22N 4 32 E
Zanesville, U.S.A. 116 G2 39 56N 82 1W
Zangābād, Iran ...... 70 B5 38 26N 46 44 E
Zangue ➤, Mozam. ... 87 F4 17 50 S 35 21 E
Zanjān, Iran .... 71 B6 36 40N 48 35 E
Zanjān □, Iran .... 71 B6 37 20N 49 30 E
Zanjān ➤, Iran .... 71 B6 37 8N 47 47 E
Zannone, Italy ...... 42 B6 40 58N 13 3 E
Zante = Zákinthos,
  Greece .... 46 D2 37 47N 20 54 E
Zanthus, Australia ... 93 F3 31 2 S 123 34 E
Zanzibar, Tanzania ... 86 D4 6 12 S 39 12 E
Zaouiet El-Kala = Bordj
  Omar Driss, Algeria . 78 C7 28 10N 6 40 E
Zaouiet Reggâne,
  Algeria .... 78 C6 26 32N 0 3 E
Zaoyang, China ...... 59 A9 32 10N 112 45 E
Zaozhuang, China .... 57 G9 34 50N 117 35 E
Zap Suyu = Zāb al
  Kabīr ➤, Iraq ..... 70 C4 36 1N 43 24 E
Zapadna Morava ➤,
  Serbia & M. .... 44 C5 43 38N 21 30 E
Zapadnaya Dvina =
  Daugava ➤, Latvia . 9 H21 57 4N 24 3 E
Zapadnaya Dvina,
  Russia .... 32 D7 56 15N 32 3 E
Západné Beskydy,
  Europe .... 27 B12 49 30N 19 0 E
Zapadni Rodopi,
  Bulgaria .... 44 E7 41 50N 24 0 E
Západočeský □,
  Czech Rep. .... 26 B6 49 35N 13 0 E
Zapala, Argentina .... 128 D2 39 0 S 70 5W
Zapaleri, Cerro, Bolivia 126 A2 22 49 S 67 11W
Zapata, U.S.A. 113 M5 26 55N 99 16W
Zapatón ➤, Spain 37 F4 39 0N 6 49W
Zaporizhzhya, Ukraine 33 J8 47 50N 35 10 E
Zaporozhye =
  Zaporizhzhya,
  Ukraine .... 33 J8 47 50N 35 10 E
Zaqatala, Azerbaijan .. 35 K8 41 38N 46 35 E
Zara, Turkey .... 70 B3 39 58N 37 43 E
Zaragoza, Coahuila,
  Mexico 118 B4 28 30N 101 0W
Zaragoza, Nuevo León,
  Mexico 119 C5 24 0N 99 46W
Zaragoza, Spain 38 D4 41 39N 0 53W
Zaragoza □, Spain ... 38 D4 41 35N 1 0W
Zarand, Kermān, Iran . 71 D8 30 46N 56 34 E
Zarand, Markazī, Iran . 71 C6 35 18N 50 25 E
Zărandului, Munţii,
  Romania .... 28 D7 46 14N 22 7 E
Zaranj, Afghan. ...... 66 D2 30 55N 61 55 E
Zarasai, Lithuania ... 9 J22 55 40N 26 20 E
Zárate, Argentina .... 126 C4 34 7 S 59 0W
Zarautz, Spain 38 B2 43 17N 2 10W
Zaraysk, Russia ..... 32 E10 54 48N 38 53 E
Zard, Kūh-e, Iran .... 71 C6 32 22N 50 4 E
Zāreh, Iran .... 71 C6 35 7N 49 9 E
Zari, Nigeria .... 83 C7 13 4N 12 45 E
Zaria, Nigeria .... 83 C6 11 0N 7 40 E
Zarki, Poland .... 31 H6 50 38N 19 23 E
Zárkon, Greece ...... 46 B4 39 38N 22 6 E
Zarneh, Iran .... 70 C5 33 55N 46 10 E
Zărneşti, Romania ... 29 E10 45 33N 25 18 E
Zarós, Greece .... 49 D6 35 8N 24 54 E
Żarów, Poland ...... 31 H3 50 56N 16 29 E
Zarqā', Nahr az ➤,
  Jordan .... 74 C4 32 10N 35 37 E
Zarrīn, Iran .... 71 C7 32 46N 54 37 E
Zaruma, Ecuador .... 124 D3 3 40 S 79 38W
Żary, Poland .... 31 G2 51 37N 15 10 E
Zarza de Granadilla,
  Spain 36 E4 40 14N 6 3W
Zarzis, Tunisia ...... 79 B8 33 31N 11 2 E
Zas, Spain 36 B2 43 4N 8 53W
Zaskar ➤, India ..... 69 B7 34 13N 77 20 E
Zaskar Mts., India ... 69 C7 33 15N 77 30 E
Zastavna, Ukraine ... 29 B10 48 31N 25 51 E
Zastron, S. Africa .... 88 E4 30 18 S 27 7 E
Žatec, Czech Rep. .... 26 A6 50 20N 13 32 E
Zator, Poland .... 31 J6 49 59N 19 28 E
Zatyshshya, Ukraine .. 29 C14 47 20N 29 51 E
Zavala, Bos.-H. ...... 44 D1 42 50N 17 59 E
Zāvāreh, Iran .... 71 C7 33 29N 52 28 E
Zave, Zimbabwe ..... 89 B5 17 6 S 30 1 E
Zavetnoye, Russia ... 35 G6 47 13N 43 50 E
Zavidovići, Bos.-H. ... 28 F3 44 27N 18 10 E
Zavitinsk, Russia .... 53 D13 50 10N 129 20 E
Zavodovski, I.,
  Antarctica .... 5 B1 56 0 S 27 45W
Zavolzhsk, Russia .... 34 B6 57 30N 42 0 E
Zavolzhye, Russia .... 34 B6 56 37N 43 26 E
Zawadzkie, Poland ... 31 H5 50 37N 18 28 E
Zawichost, Poland ... 31 H8 50 48N 21 51 E
Zawidów, Poland .... 31 G2 51 1N 15 1 E
Zawiercie, Poland ... 31 H6 50 30N 19 24 E
Zāwiyat al Baydā = Al
  Baydā, Libya ..... 79 B10 32 50N 21 44 E
Zāwyet Shammas, Egypt 80 A2 31 30N 26 37 E
Zāwyet Um el Rakham,
  Egypt .... 80 A2 31 18N 27 1 E
Zāwyet Ungeîla, Egypt 80 A2 31 23N 26 42 E
Zāyā, Iraq .... 70 C5 33 33N 44 13 E
Zāyandeh ➤, Iran .... 71 C7 32 35N 52 0 E
Zaysan, Kazakhstan .. 52 E9 47 28N 84 52 E
Zaysan, Oz., Kazakhstan 52 E9 48 0N 83 0 E
Zayü, China .... 58 C1 28 48N 97 27 E
Zazafotsy, Madag. ... 89 C8 21 11 S 46 21 E
Zázrivá, Slovak Rep. .. 27 B12 49 16N 19 7 E
Zbarazh, Ukraine .... 33 H3 49 43N 25 44 E
Zbąszyń, Poland ..... 31 F2 52 14N 15 56 E
Zbąszynek, Poland ... 31 F2 52 16N 15 51 E
Zblewo, Poland ..... 30 E5 53 56N 18 19 E
Zbruch ➤, Ukraine ... 29 B11 48 32N 26 27 E
Žďár nad Sázavou,
  Czech Rep. .... 26 B8 49 34N 15 57 E
Zdolbuniv, Ukraine ... 33 G4 50 30N 26 15 E
Ždrelo, Serbia & M. ... 44 B5 44 16N 21 28 E
Zduńska Wola, Poland 31 G5 51 37N 18 59 E
Zduny, Poland ...... 31 G4 51 39N 17 21 E
Zeballos, Canada 102 D3 49 59N 126 50W
Zebediela, S. Africa .. 89 C4 24 20 S 29 17 E
Zebila, Ghana 83 C4 10 55N 0 30W
Zeebrugge, Belgium .. 17 C3 51 19N 3 12 E
Zeehan, Australia .... 95 G4 41 52 S 145 25 E
Zeeland □, Neths. .... 17 C3 51 30N 3 50 E
Zeerust, S. Africa .... 88 D4 25 31 S 26 4 E
Zefat, Israel .... 74 C4 32 58N 35 29 E
Zege, Ethiopia ...... 81 E4 11 43N 37 18 E
Zeggerene, Iracher, Mali 83 B5 16 49N 2 16 E
Zégoua, Mali 82 C3 10 32N 5 35W
Zehdenick, Germany .. 24 C9 52 58N 13 20 E
Zeil, Mt., Australia ... 92 D5 23 30 S 132 23 E
Zeila, Somali Rep. .... 75 E3 11 21N 43 30 E
Zeist, Neths. .... 17 B5 52 5N 5 15 E
Zeitz, Germany ...... 24 D8 51 2N 12 7 E

Zelechów, Poland .... 31 G8 51 49N 21 54 E
Zelena, Ukraine ..... 29 B9 48 3N 24 45 E
Zelengora, Bos.-H. ... 44 C2 43 22N 18 30 E
Zelenodolsk, Russia .. 34 C9 55 55N 48 30 E
Zelenogorsk, Russia .. 32 B5 60 12N 29 43 E
Zelenograd, Russia ... 32 D9 56 1N 37 12 E
Zelenogradsk, Russia . 9 J19 54 53N 20 29 E
Zelenokumsk, Russia . 35 H6 44 24N 44 0 E
Železná Ruda,
  Czech Rep. .... 26 B6 49 8N 13 15 E
Železnik, Serbia & M. . 44 B4 44 43N 20 23 E
Zelienople, U.S.A. 116 F4 40 48N 80 8W
Żeliezovce, Slovak Rep. 27 C11 48 3N 18 40 E
Zelina, Croatia ...... 41 C13 45 57N 16 16 E
Zell, Baden-W.,
  Germany .... 25 H3 47 42N 7 52 E
Zell, Rhld-Pfz.,
  Germany .... 25 E3 50 1N 7 10 E
Zell am See, Austria .. 26 D5 47 19N 12 47 E
Zella-Mehlis, Germany 24 E6 50 39N 10 40 E
Zelów, Poland ...... 31 G6 51 28N 19 14 E
Zeltweg, Austria ..... 26 D7 47 11N 14 45 E
Žemaitijos △, Lithuania 30 B8 56 2N 21 55 E
Zémio, C.A.R. .... 86 A2 5 2N 25 5 E
Zempléni-hegység,
  Hungary .... 28 B6 48 25N 21 25 E
Zemplínska Šírava,
  Slovak Rep. .... 27 C15 48 48N 22 0 E
Zempoala, Mexico 119 D5 19 27N 96 24W
Zemun, Serbia & M. .. 44 B4 44 51N 20 25 E
Zengbé, Cameroon ... 83 D7 5 46N 13 4 E
Zengcheng, China .... 59 F9 23 13N 113 52 E
Zenica, Bos.-H. ...... 28 F2 44 10N 17 57 E
Žepče, Bos.-H. ...... 28 F3 44 28N 18 2 E
Zeraf, Bahr ez ➤,
  Sudan .... 81 F3 9 42N 30 52 E
Zerbst, Germany ..... 24 D8 51 58N 12 5 E
Zerków, Poland ..... 31 F4 52 4N 17 32 E
Zermatt, Switz. ...... 25 J3 46 2N 7 46 E
Zernez, Switz. .... 25 J6 46 42N 10 7 E
Zernograd, Russia ... 35 G5 46 52N 40 19 E
Zerqan, Albania ..... 44 E4 41 27N 20 20 E
Zestaponi, Georgia ... 35 J6 42 6N 43 0 E
Zetel, Germany ...... 24 B3 53 25N 7 58 E
Zeulenroda, Germany . 24 E7 50 39N 11 59 E
Zeven, Germany ..... 24 B5 53 17N 9 16 E
Zevenaar, Neths. .... 17 C6 51 56N 6 5 E
Zévio, Italy .... 40 C8 45 22N 11 8 E
Zeya, Russia .... 53 D13 53 48N 127 14 E
Zeya ➤, Russia ...... 53 D13 51 42N 128 53 E
Zeytinbağı, Turkey ... 45 F12 40 24N 28 47 E
Zeytindağ, Turkey ... 47 C9 38 58N 27 4 E
Zgharta, Lebanon .... 74 A4 34 21N 35 53 E
Zgierz, Poland ...... 31 G6 51 50N 19 27 E
Zgorzelec, Poland .... 31 G2 51 10N 15 0 E
Zgurița, Moldova .... 29 B13 48 8N 28 1 E
Zhabinka, Belarus ... 31 F11 52 13N 24 2 E
Zhabokrych, Ukraine . 29 B13 48 23N 28 59 E
Zhailma, Kazakhstan . 52 D7 51 37N 61 33 E
Zhambyl = Taraz,
  Kazakhstan .... 52 E8 42 54N 71 22 E
Zhangaly, Kazakhstan . 35 G10 47 1N 50 37 E
Zhangaqazaly,
  Kazakhstan .... 52 E7 45 48N 62 6 E
Zhangbei, China ..... 56 D8 41 10N 114 45 E
Zhangguangcai Ling,
  China .... 57 B15 45 0N 129 0 E
Zhangjiakou, China .. 56 D8 40 48N 114 55 E
Zhangping, China .... 59 E11 25 17N 117 23 E
Zhangpu, China ..... 59 E11 24 8N 117 35 E
Zhangshu, China .... 59 C10 28 4N 115 29 E
Zhangwu, China ..... 57 C12 42 43N 122 52 E
Zhangye, China ..... 60 C5 38 50N 100 23 E
Zhangzhou, China ... 59 E11 24 30N 117 35 E
Zhanhua, China ..... 57 F10 37 40N 118 8 E
Zhanjiang, China .... 59 G8 21 15N 110 20 E
Zhannetty, Ostrov,
  Russia .... 53 B16 76 43N 158 0 E
Zhanyi, China .... 58 E4 25 38N 103 48 E
Zhanyu, China ...... 57 B12 44 30N 122 30 E
Zhao Xian, China .... 56 F8 37 43N 114 45 E
Zhao'an, China ...... 59 F11 23 41N 117 10 E
Zhaocheng, China ... 56 F6 36 22N 111 38 E
Zhaojue, China ...... 58 C4 28 1N 102 49 E
Zhaoping, China ..... 59 E8 24 11N 110 48 E
Zhaoqing, China ..... 59 F9 23 0N 112 20 E
Zhaotong, China .... 58 D4 27 20N 103 44 E
Zhaoyuan, Heilongjiang,
  China .... 57 B13 45 27N 125 0 E
Zhaoyuan, Shandong,
  China .... 57 F11 37 20N 120 23 E
Zharkovskiy, Russia .. 32 E7 55 56N 32 19 E
Zhashkiv, Ukraine ... 33 H6 49 15N 30 5 E
Zhashui, China ...... 56 H5 33 40N 109 8 E
Zhayyq ➤, Kazakhstan 52 E6 47 0N 51 48 E
Zhdanov = Mariupol,
  Ukraine .... 33 J9 47 5N 37 31 E
Zhecheng, China .... 56 G8 34 7N 115 20 E
Zhegao, China ...... 59 B11 31 46N 117 45 E
Zhejiang □, China ... 59 C13 29 0N 120 0 E
Zheleznodorozhnyy,
  Russia .... 30 D8 54 22N 21 19 E
Zheleznogorsk, Russia 33 F8 52 22N 35 23 E
Zheleznogorsk-Ilimskiy,
  Russia .... 53 D11 56 34N 104 8 E
Zheltye Vody = Zhovti
  Vody, Ukraine .... 33 H7 48 21N 33 31 E
Zhen'an, China ...... 56 H5 33 27N 109 9 E
Zhenba, China ...... 58 A6 32 34N 107 58 E
Zhenfeng, China ..... 58 E5 25 22N 105 40 E
Zheng'an, China ..... 58 C6 28 32N 107 27 E
Zhengding, China ... 56 E8 38 8N 114 32 E
Zhenghe, China ..... 59 D12 27 20N 118 50 E
Zhengyang, China ... 59 A10 32 37N 114 22 E
Zhengyangguan, China 59 A11 32 30N 116 29 E
Zhengzhou, China ... 56 G7 34 45N 113 34 E
Zhenhai, China ..... 59 C13 29 59N 121 42 E
Zhenkang, China .... 58 F2 23 58N 99 0 E
Zhenlai, China ...... 57 B12 45 50N 123 5 E
Zhenning, China .... 58 D5 26 4N 105 45 E
Zhenping, Henan, China 56 H7 33 10N 112 16 E
Zhenping, Shaanxi,
  China .... 58 B7 31 59N 109 31 E
Zhenxiong, China .... 58 D5 27 27N 104 50 E
Zhenyuan, Gansu, China 56 G4 35 35N 107 30 E
Zhenyuan, Guizhou,
  China .... 58 D7 27 4N 108 21 E
Zherdevka, Russia ... 34 E5 51 56N 41 10 E
Zherebkove, Ukraine . 29 C14 47 50N 29 52 E
Zherong, China ..... 59 D12 27 15N 119 52 E
Zhetiqara, Kazakhstan 52 D7 52 11N 61 12 E
Zhezqazghan,
  Kazakhstan .... 52 E7 47 44N 67 40 E
Zhicheng, China ..... 59 B8 30 25N 111 27 E
Zhidan, China ...... 56 F5 36 48N 108 48 E
Zhigansk, Russia .... 53 C13 66 48N 123 27 E
Zhigulevsk, Russia ... 34 D9 53 28N 49 30 E

Zhijiang, Hubei, China 59 B8 30 28N 111 45 E
Zhijiang, Hunan, China 58 D7 27 27N 109 42 E
Zhijin, China .... 58 D5 26 37N 105 45 E
Zhilinda, Russia ..... 53 C12 70 0N 114 20 E
Zhilino, Russia ...... 30 D8 54 54N 21 54 E
Zhirnovsk, Russia ... 34 E7 50 57N 44 49 E
Zhitomir = Zhytomyr,
  Ukraine .... 33 G5 50 20N 28 40 E
Zhizdra, Russia ..... 32 F8 53 45N 34 40 E
Zhlobin, Belarus .... 33 F6 52 55N 30 0 E
Zhmerinka =
  Zhmerynka, Ukraine 33 H5 49 2N 28 2 E
Zhmerynka, Ukraine . 33 H5 49 2N 28 2 E
Zhob, Pakistan ...... 68 D3 31 20N 69 31 E
Zhob ➤, Pakistan .... 68 C3 32 4N 69 50 E
Zhodino = Zhodzina,
  Belarus .... 32 E5 54 5N 28 17 E
Zhodzina, Belarus ... 32 E5 54 5N 28 17 E
Zhokhova, Ostrov,
  Russia .... 53 B16 76 4N 152 40 E
Zhongdian, China ... 58 D2 27 48N 99 42 E
Zhongdong, China ... 58 F6 24 40N 109 40 E
Zhongdu, China ..... 58 E7 24 40N 109 40 E
Zhongning, China ... 56 F3 37 29N 105 40 E
Zhongshan, Antarctica 5 C6 69 0 S 39 50 E
Zhongshan, Guangdong,
  China .... 59 F9 22 26N 113 20 E
Zhongshan,
  Guangxi Zhuangzu,
  China .... 59 E8 24 29N 111 18 E
Zhongtiao Shan, China 56 G6 35 0N 111 10 E
Zhongwei, China .... 56 F3 37 30N 105 12 E
Zhongxiang, China ... 59 B9 31 12N 112 34 E
Zhongyang, China ... 56 F6 37 20N 111 11 E
Zhorany, Ukraine ... 31 G10 51 19N 23 52 E
Zhoucun, China ..... 57 F9 36 47N 117 48 E
Zhouning, China .... 59 D12 27 12N 119 20 E
Zhoushan, China .... 59 B14 30 1N 122 6 E
Zhoushan Dao, China . 59 C14 30 5N 122 10 E
Zhouzhi, China ..... 56 G5 34 10N 108 12 E
Zhovti Vody, Ukraine . 33 H7 48 21N 33 31 E
Zhovtneve, Ukraine .. 31 H11 50 42N 24 12 E
Zhovtneve, Ukraine .. 33 J7 46 54N 32 3 E
Zhovtnevoye =
  Zhovtneve, Ukraine . 33 J7 46 54N 32 3 E
Zhu Jiang ➤, China .. 59 F9 22 45N 113 30 E
Zhuanghe, China .... 57 E12 39 40N 123 0 E
Zhucheng, China .... 57 G10 36 0N 119 27 E
Zhugqu, China ...... 56 H3 33 40N 104 30 E
Zhuhai, China ...... 59 F9 22 17N 113 34 E
Zhuji, China .... 59 C13 29 40N 120 10 E
Zhukovka, Russia ... 32 F7 53 35N 33 50 E
Zhumadian, China ... 56 H8 32 59N 114 2 E
Zhuo Xian = Zhuozhou,
  China .... 56 E8 39 28N 115 58 E
Zhuolu, China ...... 56 D8 40 20N 115 12 E
Zhuozhou, China .... 56 E8 39 28N 115 58 E
Zhuozi, China ...... 56 D7 41 0N 112 25 E
Zhushan, China ..... 58 A7 32 15N 110 13 E
Zhuxi, China .... 58 A7 32 25N 109 40 E
Zhuzhou, China ..... 59 D9 27 49N 113 12 E
Zhvanets, Ukraine ... 29 B11 48 33N 26 30 E
Zhytomyr, Ukraine .. 33 G5 50 20N 28 40 E
Zi Shui ➤, China .... 59 C9 28 40N 112 40 E
Žiar nad Hronom,
  Slovak Rep. ...... 27 C11 48 35N 18 53 E
Ziārān, Iran .... 71 B6 36 7N 50 32 E
Ziarat, Pakistan ..... 68 D2 30 25N 67 49 E
Zibo, China .... 57 F10 36 47N 118 3 E
Zichang, China ..... 56 F5 37 18N 109 40 E
Zidarovo, Bulgaria .. 45 D11 42 20N 27 24 E
Zidi = Wandhari,
  Pakistan .... 68 F2 27 42N 66 48 E
Ziębice, Poland ..... 31 H4 50 37N 17 2 E
Zielona Góra, Poland . 31 G2 51 57N 15 31 E
Zierikzee, Neths. .... 17 C3 51 40N 3 55 E
Ziesar, Germany .... 24 C8 52 16N 12 17 E
Zifta, Egypt .... 80 H7 30 43N 31 14 E
Zigey, Chad .... 79 F9 14 43N 15 50 E
Zigong, China ...... 58 C5 29 15N 104 48 E
Ziguinchor, Senegal . 82 C1 12 35N 16 20W
Zihuatanejo, Mexico . 118 D4 17 38N 101 33W
Zijin, China .... 59 F10 23 33N 115 8 E
Zile, Turkey .... 72 B6 40 15N 35 52 E
Žilina, Slovak Rep. ... 27 B11 49 12N 18 42 E
Žilinský □, Slovak Rep. 27 B12 49 10N 19 0 E
Zillah, Libya .... 79 C9 28 30N 17 33 E
Zillertaler Alpen,
  Austria .... 26 E6 47 6N 11 45 E
Zima, Russia .... 53 D11 54 0N 102 5 E
Zimapán, Mexico ... 119 C5 20 54N 99 20W
Zimba, Zambia ..... 87 F2 17 20 S 26 11 E
Zimbabwe, Zimbabwe 87 G3 20 16 S 30 54 E
Zimbabwe ■, Africa .. 87 F3 19 0 S 30 0 E
Zimi, S. Leone 82 D2 7 20N 11 20W
Zimnicea, Romania .. 29 G10 43 40N 25 22 E
Zimovniki, Russia ... 35 G6 47 10N 42 25 E
Zinave △, Mozam. ... 89 C5 21 35 S 33 40 E
Zinder, Niger .... 83 C6 13 48N 9 0 E
Zinga, Tanzania ..... 87 D4 9 16 S 38 49 E
Zingaro △, Italy ..... 42 D5 38 6N 12 53 E
Zingst, Germany .... 24 A8 54 26N 12 39 E
Ziniaré, Burkina Faso . 83 C4 12 35N 1 18W
Zinnowitz, Germany . 24 A9 54 4N 13 54 E
Zion, U.S.A. 114 D2 42 27N 87 50W
Zion △, U.S.A. 109 H7 37 15N 113 5W
Zirbitzkogel, Austria . 26 D7 47 4N 14 34 E
Zirc, Hungary ...... 28 C2 47 17N 17 52 E
Žiri, Slovenia ...... 41 B11 46 5N 14 5 E
Zirje, Croatia ...... 41 E12 43 39N 15 42 E
Zirl, Austria .... 26 D4 47 17N 11 14 E
Zirndorf, Germany .. 25 F6 49 26N 10 57 E
Ziros, Greece ...... 49 D8 35 5N 26 8 E
Zirreh, Gowd-e, Afghan. 66 E3 29 45N 62 0 E
Zisterdorf, Austria .. 27 C9 48 33N 16 45 E
Zitava ➤, Slovak Rep. 27 C11 48 14N 18 21 E
Zítsa, Greece ...... 46 B2 39 47N 20 40 E
Zittau, Germany .... 24 E10 50 53N 14 48 E
Zitundo, Mozam. ... 89 D5 26 48 S 32 47 E
Zivinice, Bos.-H. .... 28 F3 44 27N 18 39 E
Ziwa Magharibi =
  Kagera □, Tanzania . 86 C3 2 0 S 31 30 E
Ziway, L., Ethiopia ... 81 F4 8 0N 38 50 E
Zixi, China .... 59 D11 27 45N 117 4 E
Zixing, China .... 59 E9 25 59N 113 21 E
Ziyang, Shaanxi, China 56 H5 32 32N 108 31 E
Ziyang, Sichuan, China 58 B5 30 6N 104 40 E
Ziyuan, China ...... 59 D8 26 25N 110 6 E
Zizhong, China ..... 58 C5 29 48N 104 47 E
Zlarin, Croatia ..... 41 E12 43 42N 15 49 E
Zlatar, Croatia ...... 41 B13 46 5N 16 3 E
Zlataritsa, Bulgaria .. 45 C9 43 2N 25 55 E

Zlatibor, Serbia & M. . 44 C3 43 45N 19 43 E
Zlatitsa, Bulgaria .... 45 D8 42 41N 24 7 E
Zlatna, Romania .... 29 D8 46 8N 23 11 E
Zlatna Panega, Bulgaria 45 C8 43 5N 24 9 E
Zlatni Pyasŭti, Bulgaria 45 C12 43 17N 28 3 E
Zlatograd, Bulgaria .. 45 E9 41 22N 25 7 E
Zlatoust, Russia .... 52 D6 55 10N 59 40 E
Zletovo, Macedonia .. 44 E6 41 59N 22 17 E
Zlín, Czech Rep. .... 27 B10 49 14N 17 40 E
Zlínský □, Czech Rep. 27 B10 49 14N 17 40 E
Złocieniec, Poland ... 30 E3 53 30N 16 1 E
Złoczew, Poland .... 31 G5 51 24N 18 35 E
Zlot, Serbia & M. .... 44 B5 44 1N 21 58 E
Złotoryja, Poland ... 31 G2 51 8N 15 55 E
Złotów, Poland ..... 30 E4 53 22N 17 2 E
Zmeinogorsk,
  Kazakhstan .... 52 D9 51 10N 82 13 E
Żmigród, Poland .... 31 G3 51 28N 16 53 E
Zmiyev, Ukraine .... 33 H9 49 39N 36 27 E
Znamenka =
  Znamyanka, Ukraine 33 H7 48 45N 32 30 E
Znamensk, Russia ... 30 D8 54 36N 21 16 E
Znamyanka, Ukraine . 33 H7 48 45N 32 30 E
Znin, Poland .... 31 F4 52 51N 17 44 E
Znojmo, Czech Rep. . 26 C9 48 50N 16 2 E
Zobeyrī, Iran .... 70 C5 34 10N 46 40 E
Zobia, Dem. Rep. of
  the Congo .... 86 B2 3 0N 25 59 E
Zoetermeer, Neths. .. 17 B4 52 3N 4 30 E
Zogang, China ...... 58 C1 29 55N 97 42 E
Zogno, Italy .... 40 C7 45 48N 9 40 E
Zogqên, China ...... 58 A2 32 13N 98 47 E
Zolochev = Zolochiv,
  Ukraine .... 33 H3 49 45N 24 51 E
Zolochiv, Ukraine ... 33 H3 49 45N 24 51 E
Zolotonosha, Ukraine 33 H7 49 39N 32 5 E
Zolotyy Potik, Ukraine 29 B10 48 54N 25 20 E
Zomba, Malawi ..... 87 F4 15 22 S 35 19 E
Zongo, Dem. Rep. of
  the Congo .... 84 D3 4 20N 18 35 E
Zonguldak, Turkey .. 72 B4 41 28N 31 50 E
Zongyang, China .... 59 B11 30 42N 117 12 E
Zonqor Pt., Malta ... 49 D2 35 52N 14 34 E
Zonza, France ...... 21 G13 41 45N 9 11 E
Zorgo, Burkina Faso . 83 C4 12 15N 0 35W
Zorita, Spain 37 F5 39 17N 5 39W
Zorleni, Romania ... 29 D12 46 14N 27 44 E
Zornitsa, Bulgaria ... 45 D10 42 23N 26 58 E
Zorritos, Peru ...... 124 D2 3 43 S 80 40W
Zory, Poland .... 31 H5 50 3N 18 44 E
Zossen, Germany ... 24 C9 52 13N 13 27 E
Zou Xiang, China ... 56 G9 35 30N 116 58 E
Zouan-Hounien,
  Ivory C. .... 82 D3 6 55N 8 9 E
Zouar, Chad .... 79 D9 20 30N 16 32 E
Zouérate = Zouîrât,
  Mauritania 78 D3 22 44N 12 21W
Zouîrât, Mauritania .. 78 D3 22 44N 12 21W
Zourika, Niger ...... 83 B6 19 16N 7 52 E
Zourma, Burkina Faso 83 C4 11 20N 0 50W
Zoutkamp, Neths. ... 17 A6 53 20N 6 18 E
Zrenjanin, Serbia & M. 28 E5 45 22N 20 23 E
Zuarungu, Ghana ... 83 C4 10 49N 0 46W
Zuba, Nigeria ...... 83 D6 9 11N 7 12 E
Zubayr, Yemen ..... 81 D5 15 3N 42 10 E
Zubtsov, Russia .... 32 D8 56 10N 34 34 E
Zuénoula, Ivory C. .. 82 D3 7 34N 6 3W
Zuera, Spain 38 D4 41 51N 0 49W
Zufar, Oman .... 75 D5 17 40N 54 0 E
Zug □, Switz. .... 25 H4 47 9N 8 35 E
Zugdidi, Georgia .... 35 J5 42 30N 41 55 E
Zugersee, Switz. .... 25 H4 47 25N 10 59 E
Zugspitze, Germany . 25 H6 47 25N 10 59 E
Zuid-Holland □, Neths. 17 C4 52 0N 4 35 E
Zuidbeveland, Neths. . 17 C3 51 30N 3 50 E
Zuidhorn, Neths. .... 17 A6 53 15N 6 23 E
Zújar, Spain 37 H8 37 34N 2 50W
Zújar ➤, Spain 37 G5 39 1N 5 47W
Zukowo, Poland .... 30 D5 54 23N 18 22 E
Zula, Eritrea .... 81 D4 15 17N 39 40 E
Zülpich, Germany ... 24 E2 50 41N 6 39 E
Zumaia, Spain 38 B2 43 19N 2 15W
Zumárraga, Spain ... 38 B2 43 5N 2 19W
Zumbo, Mozam. .... 87 F3 15 35 S 30 26 E
Zummo, Nigeria .... 83 D7 9 51N 12 59 E
Zumpango, Mexico .. 119 D5 19 48N 99 6W
Zungeru, Nigeria .... 83 D6 9 48N 6 8 E
Zunhua, China ...... 57 D9 40 18N 117 58 E
Zuni, U.S.A. 109 J9 35 4N 108 51W
Zunyi, China .... 58 D6 27 42N 106 53 E
Zuo Jiang ➤, China .. 58 F6 22 50N 108 6 E
Zuozhou, China ..... 58 F6 22 42N 107 27 E
Županja, Croatia .... 28 E3 45 4N 18 48 E
Žur, Serbia & M. .... 44 D4 42 13N 20 34 E
Zurbāţīyah, Iraq .... 70 C5 33 9N 45 33 E
Zürich, Switz. ...... 25 H4 47 22N 8 32 E
Zürich □, Switz. ..... 25 H4 47 26N 8 40 E
Zürichsee, Switz. .... 25 H4 47 26N 8 40 E
Zuromin, Poland .... 31 E6 53 4N 19 45 E
Žut, Croatia .... 41 E12 43 52N 15 17 E
Zutphen, Neths. .... 17 B6 52 9N 6 12 E
Zuurberg △, S. Africa . 88 E4 33 12 S 25 42 E
Zuwārah, Libya ..... 79 B8 32 58N 12 1 E
Zūzan, Iran .... 71 C8 34 22N 59 53 E
Zužemberk, Slovenia . 41 C11 45 52N 14 56 E
Zvenigorodka =
  Zvenyhorodka,
  Ukraine .... 33 H6 49 4N 30 56 E
Zvenyhorodka, Ukraine 33 H6 49 4N 30 56 E
Zverinogolovskoye,
  Russia .... 52 D7 54 26N 64 50 E
Zvezdets, Bulgaria ... 45 D11 42 6N 27 26 E
Zvishavane, Zimbabwe 87 G3 20 17 S 30 2 E
Zvolen, Slovak Rep. .. 27 C12 48 33N 19 10 E
Zvonce, Serbia & M. .. 44 D6 42 57N 22 34 E
Zvornik, Bos.-H. .... 28 F4 44 26N 19 5 E
Zwedru = Tchien,
  Liberia 82 D3 5 59N 8 15W
Zweibrücken, Germany 25 F3 49 15N 7 21 E
Zwelitsha, S. Africa .. 85 L5 32 55 S 27 22 E
Zwenkau, Germany .. 24 D8 51 13N 12 20 E
Zwettl, Austria ..... 26 C8 48 35N 15 9 E
Zwickau, Germany .. 24 E8 50 44N 12 30 E
Zwierzyniec, Poland . 31 H9 50 36N 22 58 E
Zwiesel, Germany ... 25 F9 49 1N 13 14 E
Zwoleń, Poland ..... 31 G8 51 21N 21 28 E
Zwolle, Neths. ...... 17 B6 52 31N 6 6 E
Zwolle, U.S.A. 113 K8 31 38N 93 39W
Zychlin, Poland ..... 31 F6 52 15N 19 37 E
Żyrardów, Poland ... 31 F7 52 3N 20 28 E
Zyryan, Kazakhstan .. 52 E9 49 43N 84 20 E
Zyryanka, Russia .... 53 C16 65 45N 150 51 E
Zyryanovsk = Zyryan,
  Kazakhstan .... 52 E9 49 43N 84 20 E
Żywiec, Poland ..... 31 J6 49 42N 19 10 E
Zyyi, Cyprus .... 49 E12 34 43N 33 20 E

AFGHANISTAN	ALBANIA	ALGERIA	ANDORRA	ANGOLA	ANTIGUA & BARBUDA	ARGENTINA
BARBADOS	BELARUS	BELGIUM	BELIZE	BENIN	BHUTAN	BOLIVIA
BURUNDI	CAMBODIA	CAMEROON	CANADA	CAPE VERDE	CENTRAL AFRICAN REP.	CHAD
CROATIA	CUBA	CYPRUS	CZECH REPUBLIC	DENMARK	DJIBOUTI	DOMINICA
ESTONIA	ETHIOPIA	FIJI ISLANDS	FINLAND	FRANCE	GABON	GAMBIA
GUINEA	GUINEA-BISSAU	GUYANA	HAITI	HONDURAS	HUNGARY	ICELAND
IVORY COAST	JAMAICA	JAPAN	JORDAN	KAZAKHSTAN	KENYA	KIRIBATI
LESOTHO	LIBERIA	LIBYA	LIECHTENSTEIN	LITHUANIA	LUXEMBOURG	MACEDONIA
MARSHALL ISLANDS	MAURITANIA	MAURITIUS	MEXICO	MICRONESIA	MOLDOVA	MONACO
NEW ZEALAND	NICARAGUA	NIGER	NIGERIA	NORTHERN MARIANAS	NORWAY	OMAN
PORTUGAL	PUERTO RICO	QATAR	ROMANIA	RUSSIA	RWANDA	SAMOA
SINGAPORE	SLOVAK REPUBLIC	SLOVENIA	SOLOMON ISLANDS	SOMALIA	SOUTH AFRICA	SPAIN
SWEDEN	SWITZERLAND	SYRIA	TAIWAN	TAJIKISTAN	TANZANIA	THAILAND
UGANDA	UKRAINE	UNITED ARAB EMIRATES	UNITED KINGDOM	UNITED STATES	URUGUAY	UZBEKISTAN